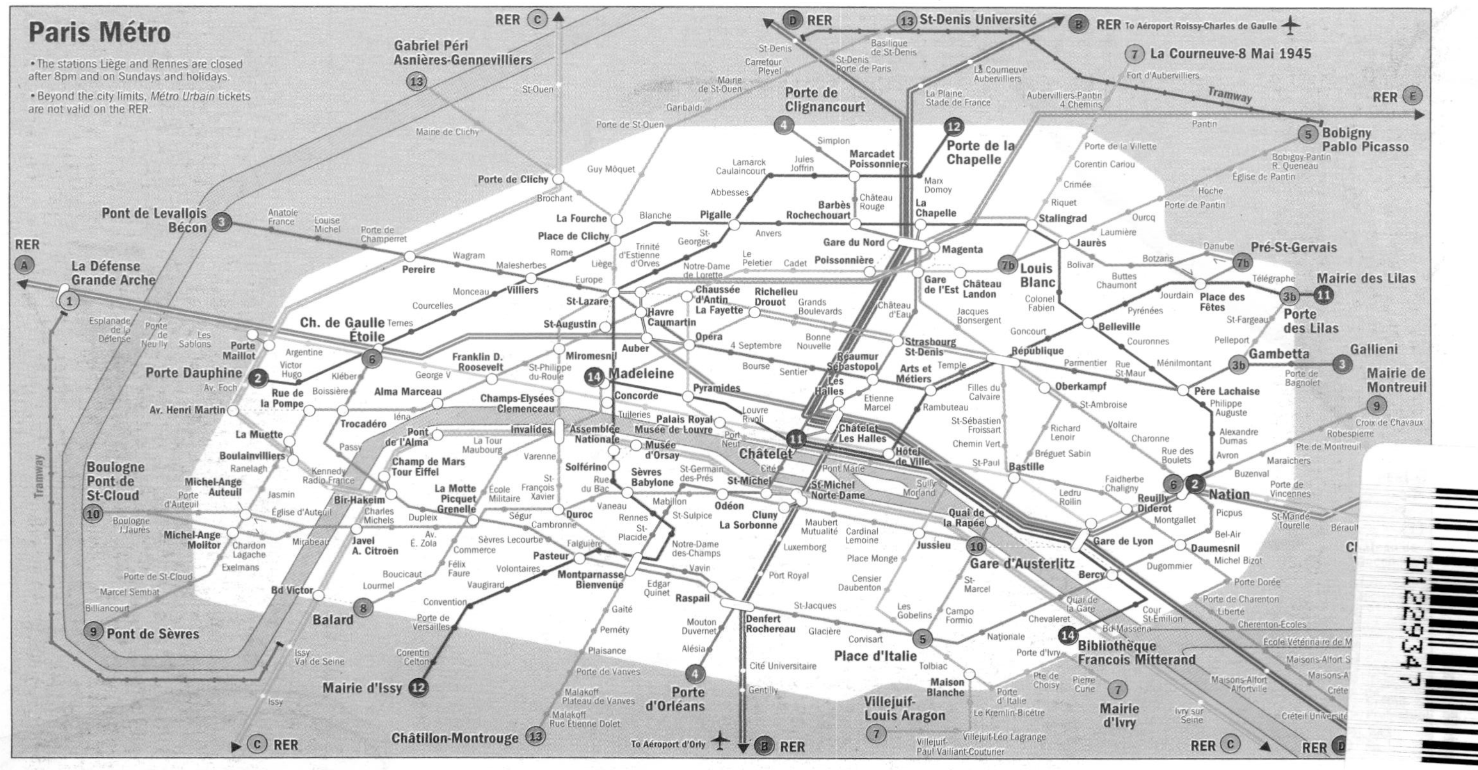

Paris Métro
• The stations Liège and Rennes are closed after 8pm and on Sundays and holidays.
• Beyond the city limits, Métro Urbain tickets are not valid on the RER.
RER C
Gabriel Péri Asnières-Gennevilliers
13
St-Ouen
D RER
St-Denis
Carrefour Pleyel
Mairie de St-Ouen
Garibaldi
13 St-Denis Université
Basilique de St-Denis
St-Denis Porte de Paris
La Courneuve Aubervilliers
La Plaine Stade de France
B RER To Aéroport Roissy-Charles de Gaulle
7 La Courneuve-8 Mai 1945
Fort d'Aubervilliers
Aubervilliers-Pantin 4 Chemins
Tramway
RER E
Pantin
5 Bobigny Pablo Picasso
Bobigny-Pantin R. Queneau
Église de Pantin
Hoche
Porte de Pantin
Ourcq
Laumière
Porte de la Villette
Corentin Cariou
Crimée
Riquet
Stalingrad
Jaurès
Porte de Clignancourt
4
Simplon
Marcadet Poissonniers
12 Porte de la Chapelle
Marx Dormoy
La Chapelle
Jules Joffrin
Lamarck Caulaincourt
Abbesses
Château Rouge
Barbès Rochechouart
Pigalle
Anvers
Blanche
Maine de Clichy
Porte de St-Ouen
Guy Môquet
Porte de Clichy
Brochant
La Fourche
Place de Clichy
Pont de Levallois Bécon
3
Anatole France
Louise Michel
Porte de Champerret
Pereire
Wagram
Malesherbes
Rome
Liège
Trinité d'Estienne d'Orves
St-Georges
Notre-Dame de Lorette
Le Peletier
Cadet
Poissonnière
Gare du Nord
Magenta
RER A
La Défense Grande Arche
1
Esplanade de la Défense
Pont de Neuilly
Les Sablons
Porte Maillot
Argentine
Ch. de Gaulle Étoile
6
Ternes
Courcelles
Monceau
Villiers
Europe
St-Lazare
St-Augustin
Havre Caumartin
Chaussée d'Antin La Fayette
Richelieu Drouot
Grands Boulevards
Bonne Nouvelle
Opéra
Auber
4 Septembre
Bourse
Sentier
Miromesnil
14 Madeleine
Concorde
Tuileries
Pyramides
Palais Royal Musée du Louvre
Louvre Rivoli
Réaumur Sébastopol
Les Halles
Étienne Marcel
Arts et Métiers
Strasbourg St-Denis
Château d'Eau
Gare de l'Est
Château Landon
Jacques Bonsergent
7b Louis Blanc
Colonel Fabien
Bolivar
Buttes Chaumont
Botzaris
Danube
7b Pré-St-Gervais
Télégraphe
Place des Fêtes
Jourdain
Pyrénées
Belleville
Goncourt
République
Temple
Filles du Calvaire
Parmentier
Rue St-Maur
Couronnes
Ménilmontant
Oberkampf
St-Ambroise
Voltaire
Charonne
Rue des Boulets
Père Lachaise
Philippe Auguste
Alexandre Dumas
Avron
3b 11 Mairie des Lilas
Porte des Lilas
St-Fargeau
Pelleport
3b Gambetta
3 Gallieni
Porte de Bagnolet
Mairie de Montreuil
9
Croix de Chavaux
Robespierre
Pte de Montreuil
Maraichers
Buzenval
Porte de Vincennes
6 2 Nation
St-Mandé Tourelle
Bérault
Picpus
Bel-Air
Montgallet
Daumesnil
Michel Bizot
Porte Dorée
Porte de Charenton
Liberté
Charenton-Écoles
École Vétérinaire de Maisons-Alfort
Maisons-Alfort Stade
Maisons-Alfort Les Juilliottes
Créteil
Créteil Université
RER D
Porte Dauphine
2
Victor Hugo
Av. Foch
Kléber
Boissière
Rue de la Pompe
Av. Henri Martin
Trocadéro
Iéna
Alma Marceau
George V
Franklin D. Roosevelt
St-Philippe du-Roule
Champs-Elysées Clemenceau
Invalides
Assemblée Nationale
Musée d'Orsay
Pont Neuf
11 Châtelet
Châtelet Les Halles
Hôtel de Ville
Cité
Pont Marie
St-Michel
St-Michel Notre-Dame
Sully Morland
Rambuteau
St-Sébastien Froissart
Chemin Vert
St-Paul
Richard Lenoir
Bréguet Sabin
Bastille
Ledru Rollin
Faidherbe Chaligny
Reuilly Diderot
Gare de Lyon
Quai de la Rapée
10 Gare d'Austerlitz
Bercy
Dugommier
La Muette
Passy
Pont de l'Alma
La Tour Maubourg
Varenne
Solférino
Rue du Bac
Sèvres Babylone
St-Germain des-Prés
Mabillon
Odéon
Cluny La Sorbonne
Boulainvilliers
Ranelagh
Kennedy Radio France
Champ de Mars Tour Eiffel
Bir-Hakeim
La Motte Picquet Grenelle
École Militaire
St-François Xavier
Vaneau
Duroc
Rennes
St-Placide
St-Sulpice
Maubert Mutualité
Cardinal Lemoine
Jussieu
Place Monge
Censier Daubenton
Luxembourg
Boulogne Pont de St-Cloud
10
Boulogne J.Jaurès
Porte d'Auteuil
Michel-Ange Auteuil
Michel-Ange Molitor
Jasmin
Église d'Auteuil
Chardon Lagache
Mirabeau
Exelmans
Charles Michels
Dupleix
Javel A. Citroën
Av. É. Zola
Ségur
Cambronne
Sèvres Lecourbe
Commerce
Félix Faure
Pasteur
Falguière
Notre-Dame des-Champs
Vavin
Montparnasse Bienvenüe
Edgar Quinet
Raspail
Port Royal
Porte de St-Cloud
Marcel Sembat
Billiancourt
9 Pont de Sèvres
Tramway
Bd Victor
Boucicaut
Lourmel
8 Balard
Volontaires
Vaugirard
Convention
Porte de Versailles
Corentin Celton
Mairie d'Issy 12
Issy Val de Seine
Issy
C RER
Gaîté
Pernéty
Plaisance
Porte de Vanves
Malakoff Plateau de Vanves
Malakoff Rue Étienne Dolet
Châtillon-Montrouge 13
Mouton Duvernet
Alésia
4 Porte d'Orléans
To Aéroport d'Orly
B RER
Denfert Rochereau
Glacière
Cité Universitaire
Gentilly
St-Jacques
Corvisart
5 Place d'Italie
Les Gobelins
Campo Formio
St-Marcel
Nationale
Chevaleret
Quai de la Gare
Tolbiac
Maison Blanche
Porte d'Italie
Le Kremlin-Bicêtre
Villejuif-Léo Lagrange
Villejuif-Paul Vaillant-Couturier
Villejuif-Louis Aragon
7
Porte d'Ivry
Pte de Choisy
Pierre Curie
7 Mairie d'Ivry
14 Bibliothèque François Mitterand
Bd Masséna
Cour St-Émilion
Maisons-Alfort Alfortville
Ivry sur Seine
RER C
RER D

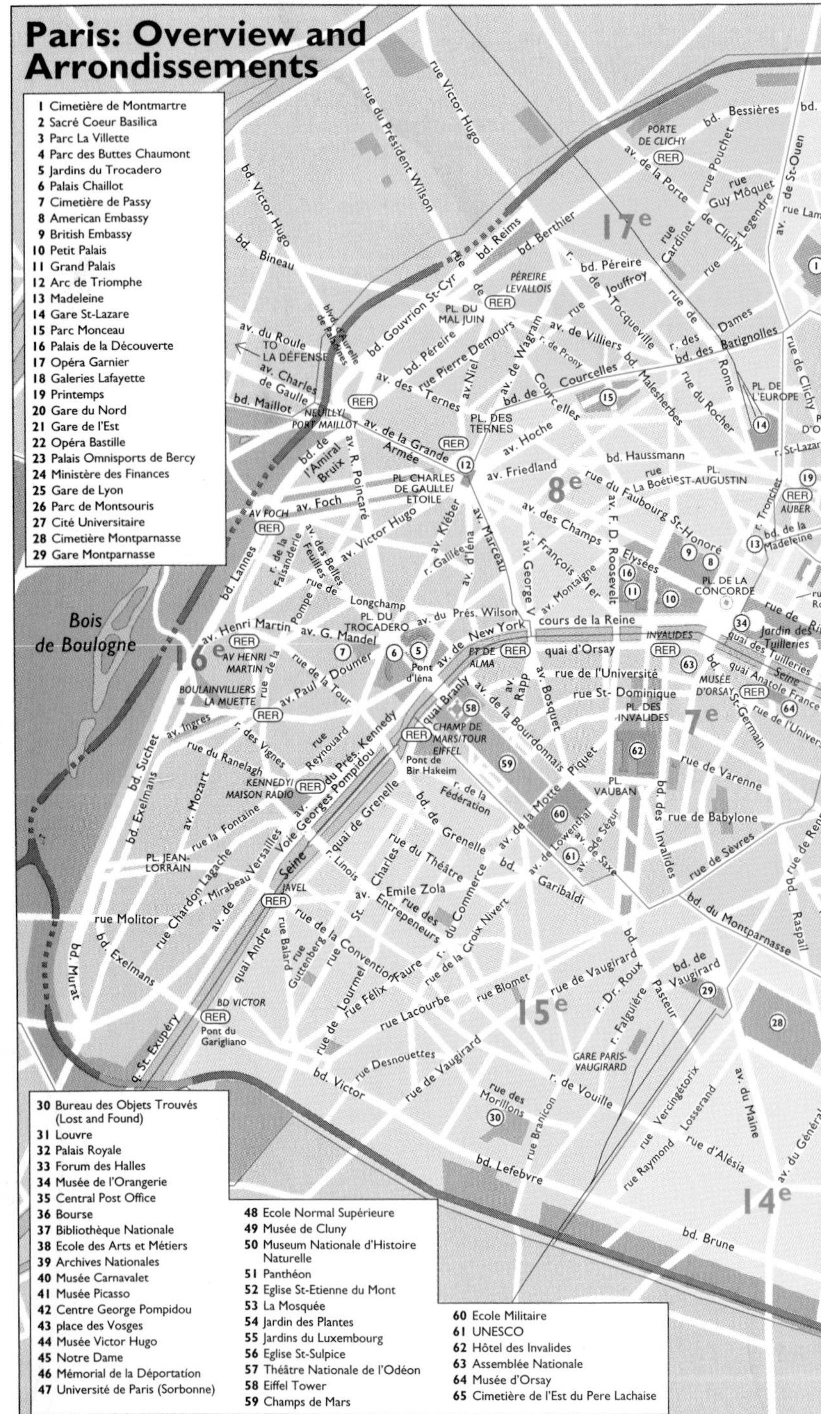
Paris: Overview and Arrondissements
1 Cimetière de Montmartre
2 Sacré Coeur Basilica
3 Parc La Villette
4 Parc des Buttes Chaumont
5 Jardins du Trocadero
6 Palais Chaillot
7 Cimetière de Passy
8 American Embassy
9 British Embassy
10 Petit Palais
11 Grand Palais
12 Arc de Triomphe
13 Madeleine
14 Gare St-Lazare
15 Parc Monceau
16 Palais de la Découverte
17 Opéra Garnier
18 Galeries Lafayette
19 Printemps
20 Gare du Nord
21 Gare de l'Est
22 Opéra Bastille
23 Palais Omnisports de Bercy
24 Ministère des Finances
25 Gare de Lyon
26 Parc de Montsouris
27 Cité Universitaire
28 Cimetière Montparnasse
29 Gare Montparnasse
Bois de Boulogne
16e
17e
8e
7e
15e
14e
TO LA DÉFENSE
Seine
30 Bureau des Objets Trouvés (Lost and Found)
31 Louvre
32 Palais Royale
33 Forum des Halles
34 Musée de l'Orangerie
35 Central Post Office
36 Bourse
37 Bibliothèque Nationale
38 Ecole des Arts et Métiers
39 Archives Nationales
40 Musée Carnavalet
41 Musée Picasso
42 Centre George Pompidou
43 place des Vosges
44 Musée Victor Hugo
45 Notre Dame
46 Mémorial de la Déportation
47 Université de Paris (Sorbonne)
48 Ecole Normal Supérieure
49 Musée de Cluny
50 Museum Nationale d'Histoire Naturelle
51 Panthéon
52 Eglise St-Etienne du Mont
53 La Mosquée
54 Jardin des Plantes
55 Jardins du Luxembourg
56 Eglise St-Sulpice
57 Théâtre Nationale de l'Odéon
58 Eiffel Tower
59 Champs de Mars
60 Ecole Militaire
61 UNESCO
62 Hôtel des Invalides
63 Assemblée Nationale
64 Musée d'Orsay
65 Cimetière de l'Est du Pere Lachaise

18e
19e
10e
2e
3e
11e
20e
4e
5e
6e
12e
13e
N
bd. Ney
bd. Macdonald
Canal de l'Ourcq
Championnet
bd. Ornano
rue Duhesme
Ordener
Custine
rue de Clignancourt
bd. Barbès
rue des Poissonniers
rue de la Chapelle
rue Marx Dormoy
r. l'Evangile
rue Riquet
rue d'Aubervilliers
rue Archereau
rue de l'Ourcq
av. Corentin Cariou
rue de Flandre
rue de Crimée
Bassin de la Villette
av. Jean Jaurès
bd. Sérurier
bd. Indochine
bd. d'Algérie
av. Jean Lolive
rue Manin
r. David d'Angiers
bd. de Rochechouart
bd. de la Chapelle
PL. PIGALLE
av. Trudaine
RER
PL. DE STALINGRAD
r. Armand Carel
av. Secrétan
PL. DU COLONEL FABIEN
Canal St-Martin
rue La Fayette
rue Poissonnière
Châteaudun
r. Paradis
r. d'Hauteville
rue du Fg. Poissonnière
r. de Fg. St-Denis
bd. de Strasbourg
bd. de Magenta
r. Château d'Eau
bd. de la Villette
du Temple
rue du Faubourg
rue des Pyrénées
PL. GAMBETTA
bd. Mortier
av. Gambetta
bd. Montmartre
bd. Poissonnière
bd. St-Denis
blvd. St-Martin
PL. DE LA REPUBLIQUE
av. Parmentier
rue St-Maur
bd. de Belleville
rue Réaumur
rue Montmartre
r. Etienne Marcel
bd. de Sébastopol
rue St-Martin
rue de Turbigo
rue Beaubourg
rue du Temple
av. de la République
rue Oberkampf
av. Gambetta
rue du Louvre
rue St-Honoré
r. des Halles
rue de Rivoli
rue des Archives
rue Vieille du Temple
bd. Beaumarchais
bd. R. Lenoir
bd. Voltaire
rue du Chemin Vert
bd. de Ménilmontant
Louvre
Pont Neuf
rue de Rivoli
rue St-Antoine
rue de la Roquette
rue de Charonne
av. Philippe Auguste
bd. de Charonne
bd. Davout
quai St-Michel
Ile de la Cité
r. de Seine
ST-MICHEL
St-Germain
quai de la Tournelle
Ile St-Louis
bd. Henri IV
rue de Lyon
rue du Faubourg St-Antoine
rue Ledru Rollin
rue de Montreuil
NATION
PL. MAUBERT
r. des Ecoles
bd. St-Michel
LUXEMBOURG
rue Monge
quai St-Bernard
Cours de Vincennes
PL. DE LA NATION
bd. Picpus
av. Ledru
bd. Diderot
Pont de Sully
PL. DE LA CONTRE-SCARPE
rue d'Ulm
rue Mouffetard
Seine
av. Daumesnil
rue de Picpus
av. du Dr. Arnold Netter
rue Guy Lussac
r. G. St-Hilaire
rue Buffon
rue Censier
PL. FÉLIX ÉBOUÉ
PORT ROYAL
r. C. Bernard
GARE D'AUSTERLITZ
Pont de Bercy
bd. de Bercy
bd. St-Marcel
av. des Gobelins
bd. de Port Royal
rue de Charenton
av. Daumesnil
bd. Mi. Bizot
bd. Soult
bd. Arago
bd. de l'Hôpital
quai de Bercy
rue de Bercy
rue de la Gare
rue du Chevaleret
Pont de Tolbiac
av. du Gén
bd. Poniatowski
Parc Zoologique
bd. St-Jacques
PL. D'ALESIA
bd. A. Blanqui
rue Jeanne d'Arc
rue de Tolbiac
Bois de Vincennes
Alésia
av. de Choisy
rue National
Pont National
rue de Tolbiac
rue de Paris
av. d'Ivry
rue Regnault
BD. MASSÉNA
bd. de Masséna
av. d'Italie
bd. Kellerman
CITÉ UNIVERSITAIRE
0
1 mile
0
1 km

Paris: 1er and 2e

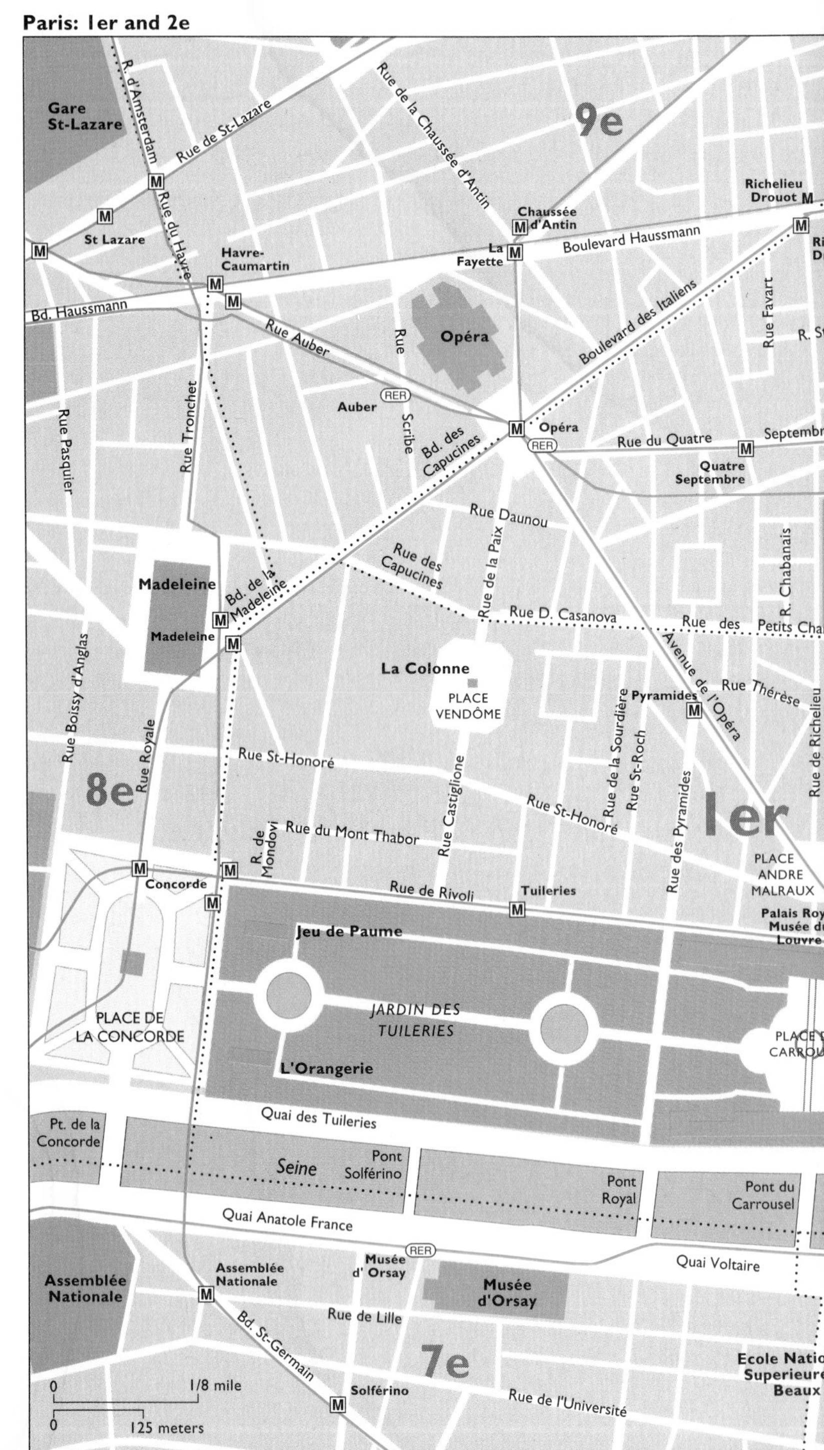

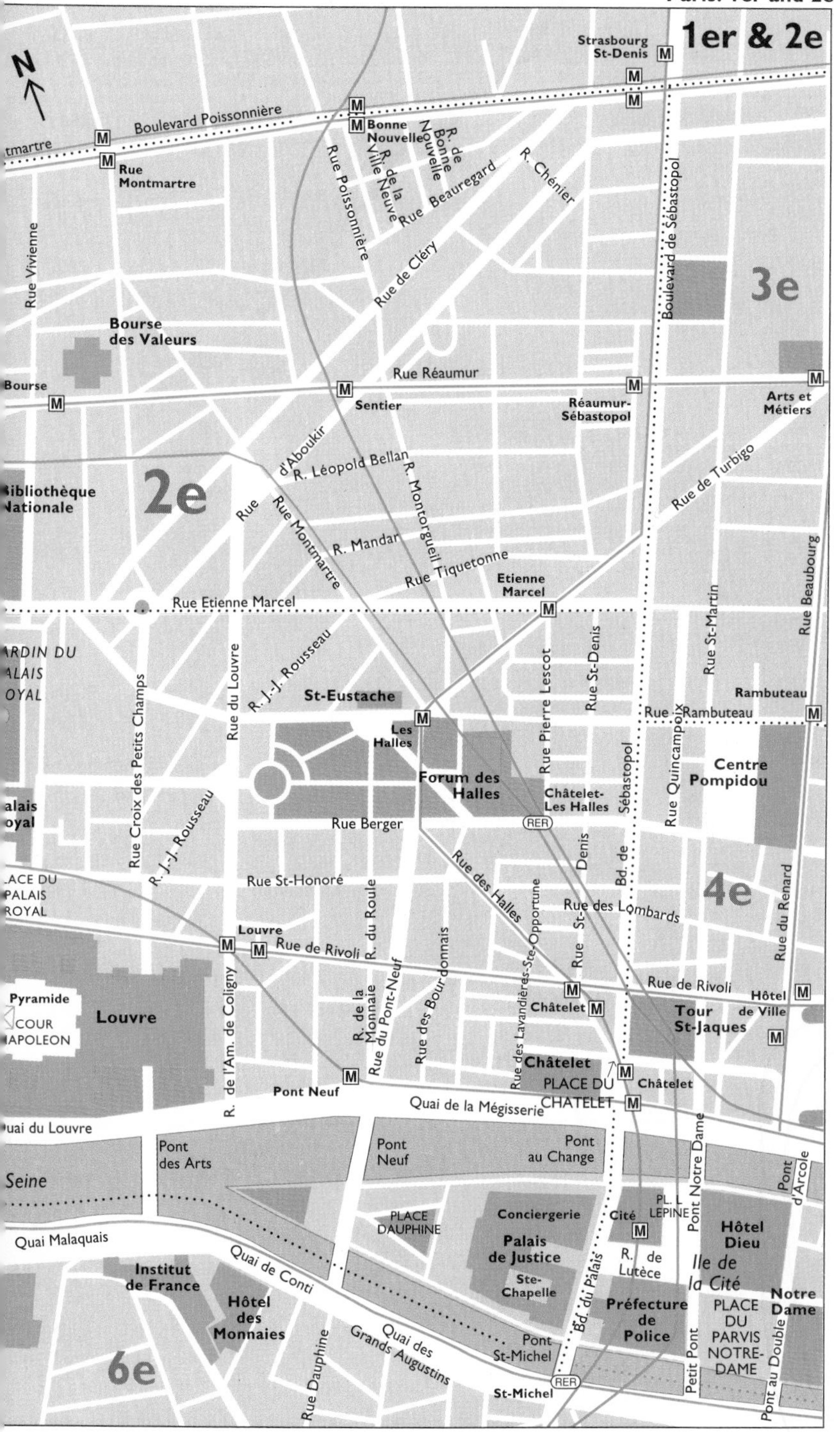

1er & 2e
N
Strasbourg St-Denis
Boulevard Poissonnière
Bonne Nouvelle
R. de Bonne Nouvelle
R. de la Ville Neuve
Rue Beauregard
R. Chénier
Rue Montmartre
Rue Poissonnière
Rue de Cléry
Boulevard de Sébastopol
3e
Rue Vivienne
Bourse des Valeurs
Bourse
Rue Réaumur
Sentier
Réaumur-Sébastopol
Arts et Métiers
Bibliothèque Nationale
2e
Rue d'Aboukir
R. Léopold Bellan
R. Montorgueil
Rue de Turbigo
Rue Montmartre
R. Mandar
Rue Tiquetonne
Etienne Marcel
Rue Etienne Marcel
Rue Beaubourg
Jardin du Palais Royal
R. J.-J. Rousseau
Rue du Louvre
Rue Pierre Lescot
Rue St-Denis
Rue St-Martin
St-Eustache
Les Halles
Rambuteau
Rue Rambuteau
Rue Quincampoix
Centre Pompidou
Forum des Halles
Châtelet-Les Halles
Bd. de Sébastopol
RER
Rue Croix des Petits Champs
Palais Royal
Rue Berger
Rue des Halles
Place du Palais Royal
Rue St-Honoré
Rue Ste-Opportune
Rue des Lombards
4e
Rue du Renard
Louvre
Rue de Rivoli
R. du Roule
Rue des Bourdonnais
Rue des Lavandières-Ste-Opportune
Rue de Rivoli
Hôtel de Ville
Pyramide
Cour Napoleon
Louvre
R. de l'Am. de Coligny
R. de la Monnaie
Rue du Pont-Neuf
Châtelet
Tour St-Jaques
Châtelet
Place du Chatelet
Pont Neuf
Quai de la Mégisserie
Quai du Louvre
Pont des Arts
Pont Neuf
Pont au Change
Rue Notre Dame
Pont d'Arcole
Seine
Place Dauphine
Conciergerie
Cité
Pl. L. Lepine
Hôtel Dieu
Quai Malaquais
Palais de Justice
R. de Lutèce
Ile de la Cité
Institut de France
Quai de Conti
Ste-Chapelle
Bd. du Palais
Préfecture de Police
Place du Parvis Notre-Dame
Notre Dame
Hôtel des Monnaies
Quai des Grands Augustins
Pont St-Michel
Petit Pont
Pont au Double
6e
Rue Dauphine
St-Michel

Paris: 5e and 6e

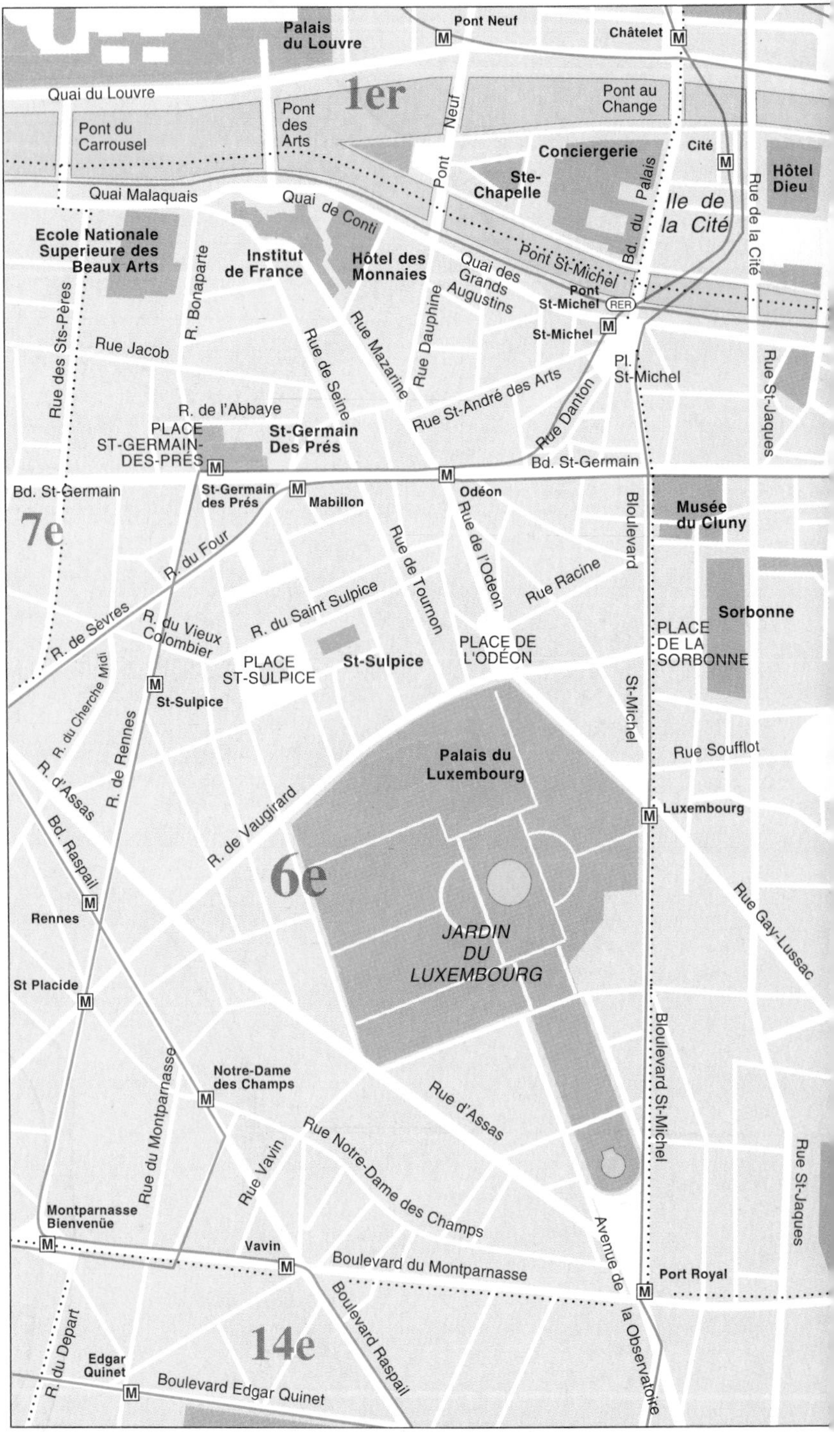

Palais du Louvre
Pont Neuf
Châtelet
1er
Quai du Louvre
Pont du Carrousel
Pont des Arts
Pont Neuf
Pont au Change
Cité
Hôtel Dieu
Conciergerie
Ste-Chapelle
Bd. du Palais
Ile de la Cité
Rue de la Cité
Quai Malaquais
Quai de Conti
Ecole Nationale Superieure des Beaux Arts
Institut de France
Hôtel des Monnaies
Quai des Grands Augustins
Pont St-Michel
Pont St-Michel
RER
St-Michel
R. Bonaparte
Rue des Sts-Pères
Rue Jacob
Rue de Seine
Rue Mazarine
Rue Dauphine
Rue St-André des Arts
Pl. St-Michel
Rue St-Jaques
R. de l'Abbaye
PLACE ST-GERMAIN-DES-PRÉS
St-Germain Des Prés
Rue Danton
Bd. St-Germain
Bd. St-Germain
St-Germain des Prés
Mabillon
Odéon
Boulevard St-Michel
Musée du Cluny
7e
R. du Four
Rue de Tournon
Rue de l'Odeon
Rue Racine
Sorbonne
R. de Sevres
R. du Vieux Colombier
R. du Saint Sulpice
PLACE DE L'ODÉON
PLACE DE LA SORBONNE
PLACE ST-SULPICE
St-Sulpice
St-Sulpice
R. du Cherche Midi
R. de Rennes
Palais du Luxembourg
Rue Soufflot
R. d'Assas
Luxembourg
R. de Vaugirard
Bd. Raspail
6e
Rue Gay-Lussac
Rennes
JARDIN DU LUXEMBOURG
St Placide
Notre-Dame des Champs
Rue d'Assas
Rue du Montparnasse
Rue Vavin
Rue Notre-Dame des Champs
Boulevard St-Michel
Rue St-Jaques
Montparnasse Bienvenüe
Vavin
Boulevard du Montparnasse
Avenue de la Observatoire
Port Royal
R. du Depart
Boulevard Raspail
14e
Edgar Quinet
Boulevard Edgar Quinet

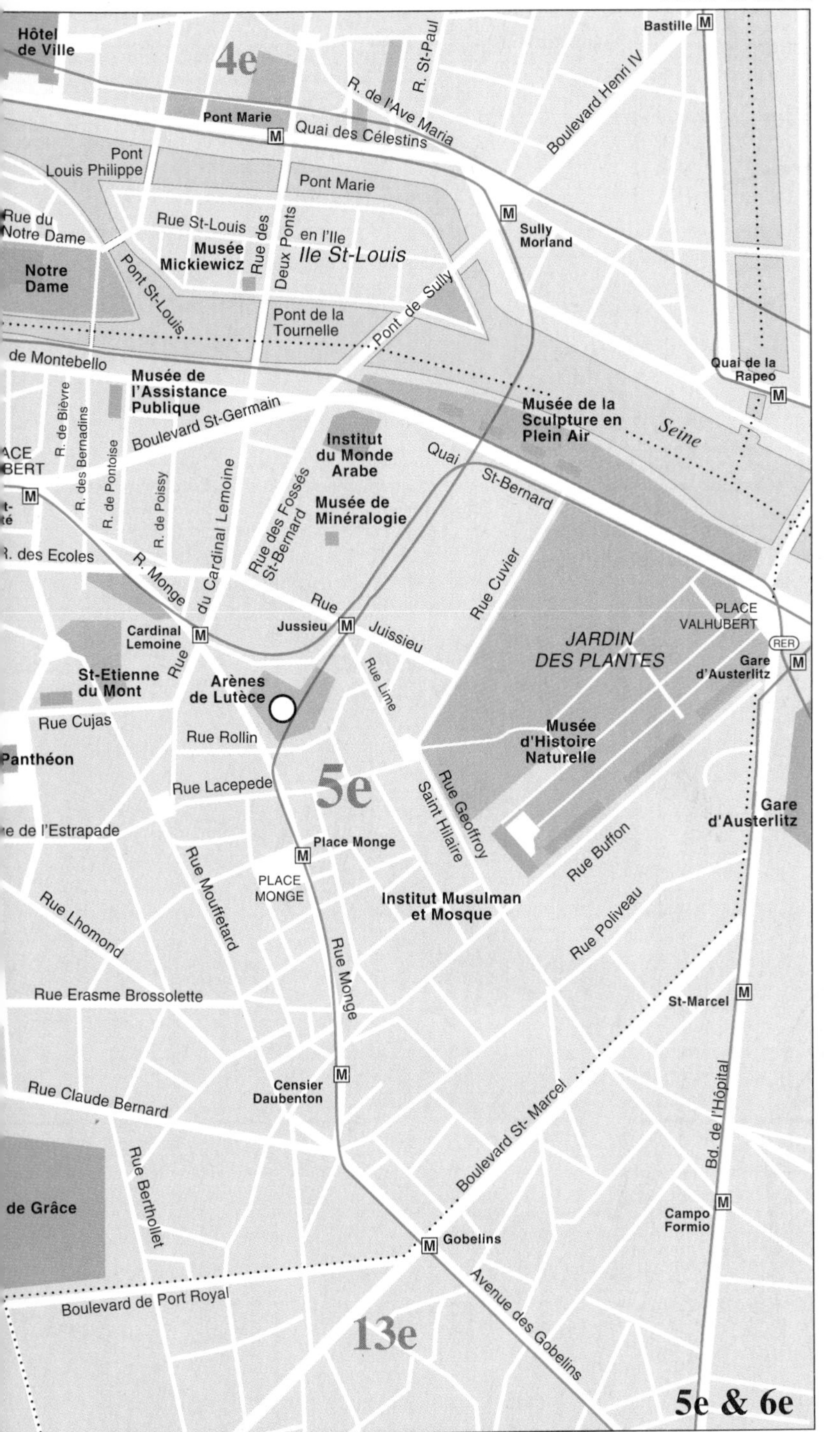
Hôtel de Ville
4e
Pont Marie
Quai des Célestins
R. de l'Ave Maria
R. St-Paul
Bastille
Boulevard Henri IV
Pont Louis Philippe
Pont Marie
Rue St-Louis en l'Ile
Rue des Deux Ponts
Ile St-Louis
Musée Mickiewicz
Sully Morland
Rue du Notre Dame
Notre Dame
Pont St-Louis
Pont de Sully
Pont de la Tournelle
de Montebello
Musée de l'Assistance Publique
Boulevard St-Germain
Quai de la Rapeo
Musée de la Sculpture en Plein Air
Seine
R. de Bièvre
R. des Bernadins
R. de Pontoise
R. de Poissy
Rue du Cardinal Lemoine
Rue des Fossés St-Bernard
Institut du Monde Arabe
Musée de Minéralogie
Quai St-Bernard
R. des Ecoles
R. Monge
Rue Cuvier
Rue Juissieu
Jussieu
PLACE VALHUBERT
JARDIN DES PLANTES
RER
Gare d'Austerlitz
Cardinal Lemoine
St-Etienne du Mont
Arènes de Lutèce
Rue Lime
Rue Cujas
Rue Rollin
Panthéon
Musée d'Histoire Naturelle
Rue Lacepede
5e
Rue Geoffroy Saint Hilaire
Gare d'Austerlitz
de l'Estrapade
Place Monge
PLACE MONGE
Rue Mouffetard
Rue Buffon
Institut Musulman et Mosque
Rue Lhomond
Rue Poliveau
Rue Monge
Rue Erasme Brossolette
St-Marcel
Censier Daubenton
Rue Claude Bernard
Boulevard St-Marcel
Bd. de l'Hôpital
Rue Berthollet
de Grâce
Campo Formio
Gobelins
Boulevard de Port Royal
Avenue des Gobelins
13e
5e & 6e

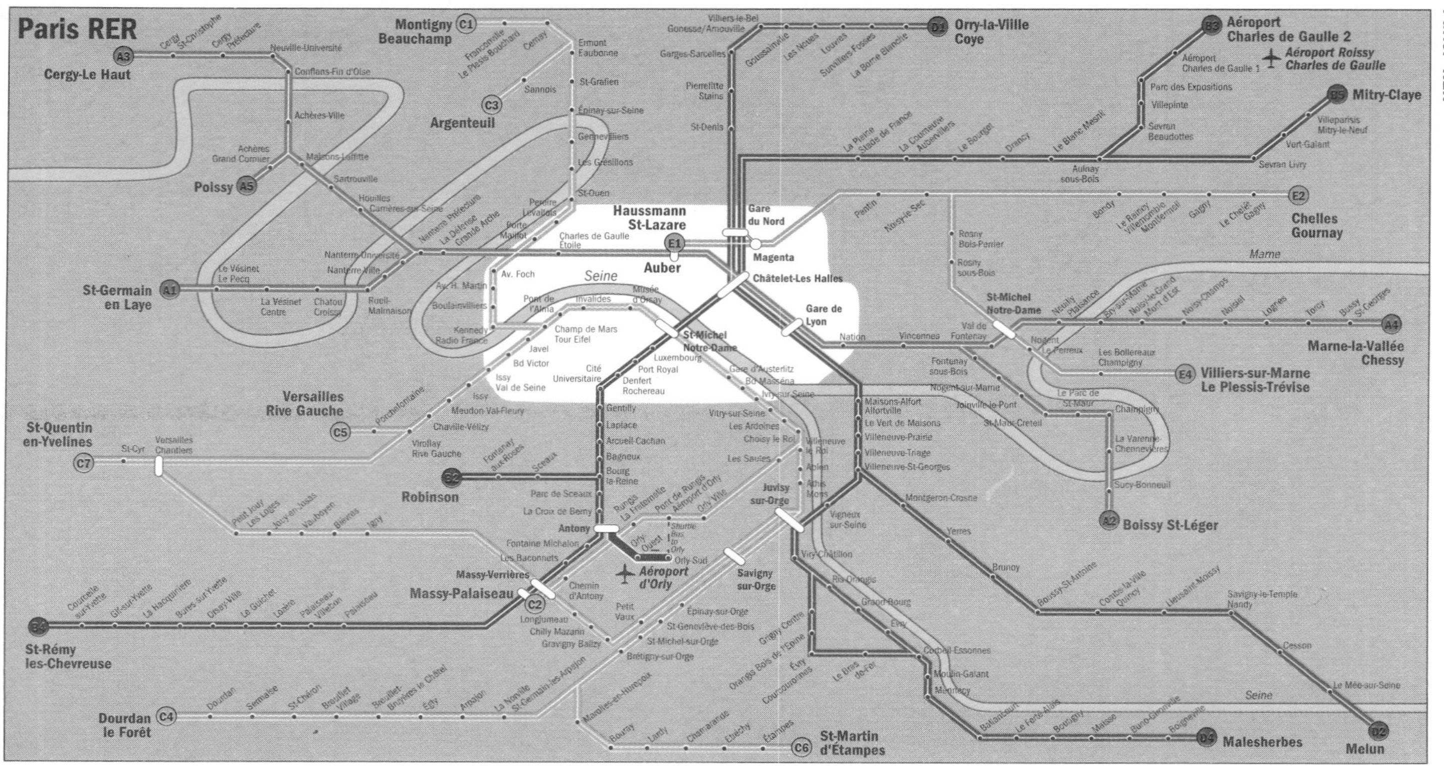
Paris RER
Cergy-Le Haut
A3
Poissy
A5
St-Germain en Laye
A1
Montigny Beauchamp
C1
Argenteuil
C3
Versailles Rive Gauche
C5
St-Quentin en-Yvelines
C7
Robinson
B2
Massy-Palaiseau
C2
St-Rémy les-Chevreuse
B4
Dourdan le Forêt
C4
St-Martin d'Étampes
C6
Malesherbes
D4
Melun
D2
Boissy St-Léger
A2
Villiers-sur-Marne Le Plessis-Trévise
E4
Marne-la-Vallée Chessy
A4
Chelles Gournay
E2
Mitry-Claye
B5
Aéroport Charles de Gaulle 2
B3
Aéroport Roissy Charles de Gaulle
Orry-la-Ville Coye
D1
Haussmann St-Lazare
E1
Auber
Gare du Nord
Magenta
Châtelet-Les Halles
Gare de Lyon
St-Michel Notre-Dame
Aéroport d'Orly
Juvisy sur-Orge
Savigny sur-Orge
Massy-Verrières
Antony
Seine
Marne

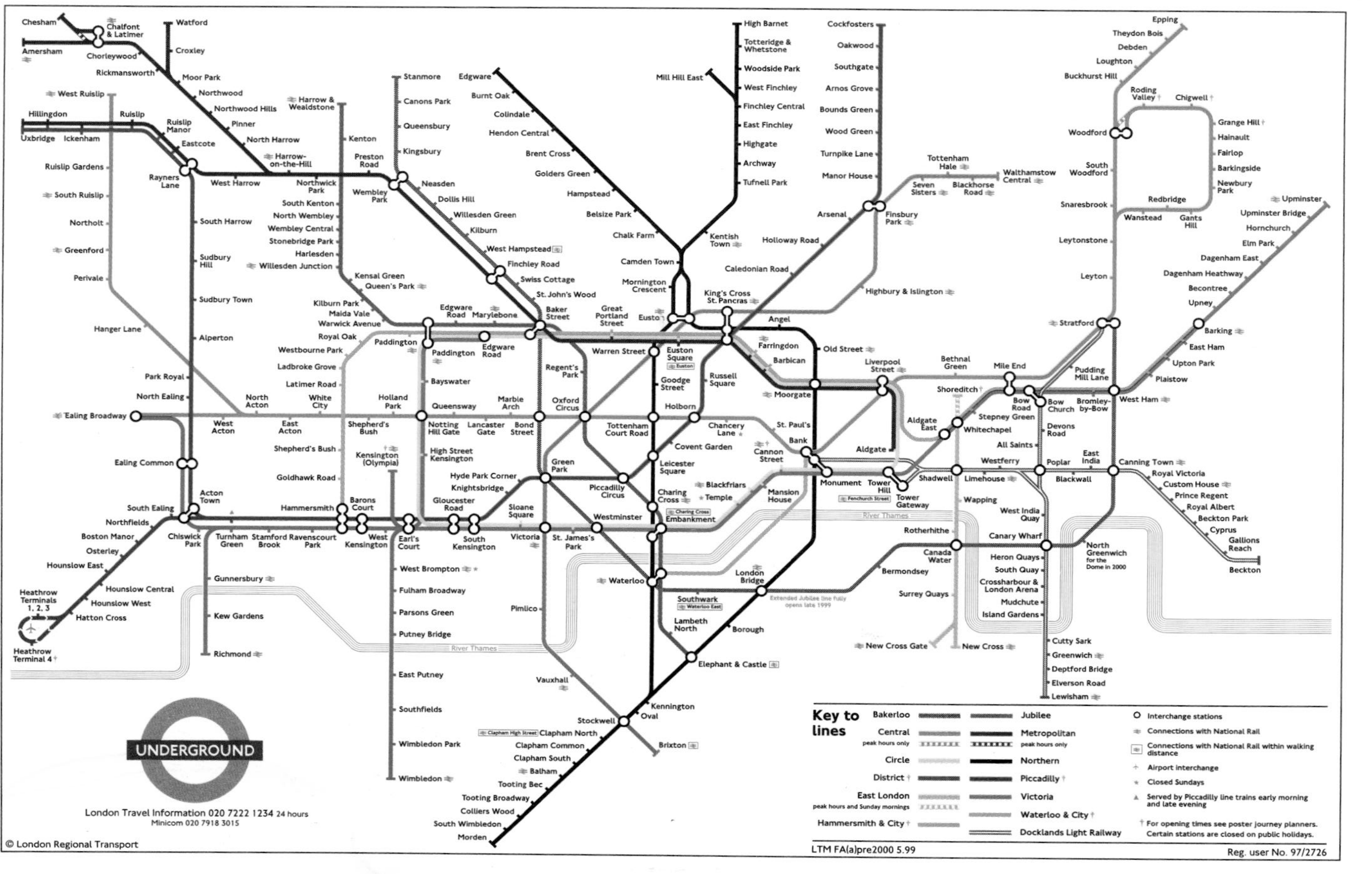

Chesham
Chalfont & Latimer
Amersham
Chorleywood
Rickmansworth
Watford
Croxley
Moor Park
Northwood
Northwood Hills
Pinner
North Harrow
Harrow-on-the-Hill
West Harrow
West Ruislip
Hillingdon
Uxbridge
Ickenham
Ruislip
Ruislip Manor
Eastcote
Rayners Lane
Ruislip Gardens
South Ruislip
Northolt
Greenford
Perivale
Hanger Lane
South Harrow
Sudbury Hill
Sudbury Town
Alperton
Park Royal
North Ealing
Ealing Broadway
Ealing Common
Acton Town
South Ealing
Northfields
Boston Manor
Osterley
Hounslow East
Hounslow Central
Hounslow West
Hatton Cross
Heathrow Terminals 1, 2, 3
Heathrow Terminal 4
Harrow & Wealdstone
Kenton
Preston Road
Northwick Park
South Kenton
North Wembley
Wembley Central
Stonebridge Park
Harlesden
Willesden Junction
Kensal Green
Queen's Park
Kilburn Park
Maida Vale
Warwick Avenue
Royal Oak
Westbourne Park
Ladbroke Grove
Latimer Road
Stanmore
Canons Park
Queensbury
Kingsbury
Wembley Park
Neasden
Dollis Hill
Willesden Green
Kilburn
West Hampstead
Finchley Road
Swiss Cottage
St. John's Wood
Edgware
Burnt Oak
Colindale
Hendon Central
Brent Cross
Golders Green
Hampstead
Belsize Park
Chalk Farm
Camden Town
Mornington Crescent
High Barnet
Totteridge & Whetstone
Woodside Park
West Finchley
Mill Hill East
Finchley Central
East Finchley
Highgate
Archway
Tufnell Park
Kentish Town
Cockfosters
Oakwood
Southgate
Arnos Grove
Bounds Green
Wood Green
Turnpike Lane
Manor House
Arsenal
Finsbury Park
Holloway Road
Caledonian Road
Tottenham Hale
Seven Sisters
Blackhorse Road
Walthamstow Central
Highbury & Islington
King's Cross St. Pancras
Euston
Angel
Old Street
Great Portland Street
Edgware Road
Marylebone
Baker Street
Paddington
Warren Street
Euston Square
Euston
Farringdon
Barbican
Moorgate
Liverpool Street
North Acton
West Acton
East Acton
White City
Holland Park
Shepherd's Bush
Notting Hill Gate
Bayswater
Queensway
Lancaster Gate
Marble Arch
Bond Street
Oxford Circus
Regent's Park
Goodge Street
Tottenham Court Road
Holborn
Russell Square
Chancery Lane
St. Paul's
Bank
Kensington (Olympia)
High Street Kensington
Hyde Park Corner
Knightsbridge
Green Park
Piccadilly Circus
Leicester Square
Covent Garden
Charing Cross
Embankment
Charing Cross
Blackfriars
Temple
Mansion House
Cannon Street
Monument
Tower Hill
Fenchurch Street
Tower Gateway
Aldgate
Aldgate East
Goldhawk Road
Hammersmith
Barons Court
West Kensington
Earl's Court
Gloucester Road
South Kensington
Sloane Square
Victoria
St. James's Park
Westminster
Chiswick Park
Turnham Green
Stamford Brook
Ravenscourt Park
Gunnersbury
Kew Gardens
Richmond
West Brompton
Fulham Broadway
Parsons Green
Putney Bridge
East Putney
Southfields
Wimbledon Park
Wimbledon
Pimlico
Vauxhall
Stockwell
Brixton
Waterloo
Southwark
Waterloo East
Lambeth North
London Bridge
Borough
Elephant & Castle
Kennington
Oval
Clapham High Street
Clapham North
Clapham Common
Clapham South
Balham
Tooting Bec
Tooting Broadway
Colliers Wood
South Wimbledon
Morden
Extended Jubilee line fully opens late 1999
River Thames
River Thames
Bethnal Green
Shoreditch
Whitechapel
Mile End
Stepney Green
Bow Road
Bow Church
Pudding Mill Lane
Bromley-by-Bow
Devons Road
All Saints
Westferry
Shadwell
Limehouse
Wapping
Rotherhithe
Canada Water
Surrey Quays
Bermondsey
New Cross Gate
New Cross
Poplar
East India
Blackwall
West India Quay
Canary Wharf
Heron Quays
South Quay
Crossharbour & London Arena
Mudchute
Island Gardens
North Greenwich for the Dome in 2000
Cutty Sark
Greenwich
Deptford Bridge
Elverson Road
Lewisham
Canning Town
Royal Victoria
Custom House
Prince Regent
Royal Albert
Beckton Park
Cyprus
Gallions Reach
Beckton
Stratford
West Ham
Plaistow
Upton Park
East Ham
Barking
Upney
Becontree
Dagenham Heathway
Dagenham East
Elm Park
Hornchurch
Upminster Bridge
Upminster
Leyton
Leytonstone
Snaresbrook
South Woodford
Woodford
Wanstead
Redbridge
Gants Hill
Newbury Park
Barkingside
Fairlop
Hainault
Grange Hill
Chigwell
Roding Valley
Buckhurst Hill
Loughton
Debden
Theydon Bois
Epping
UNDERGROUND
London Travel Information 020 7222 1234 24 hours
Minicom 020 7918 3015
© London Regional Transport
Key to lines
Bakerloo
Central
peak hours only
Circle
District †
East London
peak hours and Sunday mornings
Hammersmith & City †
Jubilee
Metropolitan
peak hours only
Northern
Piccadilly †
Victoria
Waterloo & City †
Docklands Light Railway
Interchange stations
Connections with National Rail
Connections with National Rail within walking distance
Airport interchange
Closed Sundays
Served by Piccadilly line trains early morning and late evening
† For opening times see poster journey planners. Certain stations are closed on public holidays.
LTM FA(a)pre2000 5.99
Reg. user No. 97/2726

London
Regent's Park
Outer Circle
Inner Circle
Chester Rd.
Albany St.
Eversholt St.
Euston Station
Hampstead Rd.
Euston Rd.
Gower St.
Tottenham Court
Cleveland St.
Maida Vale
Abbey Rd.
Abercorn Pl.
Grove End Rd.
Circus Rd.
Wellington Rd.
Prince Albert Rd.
Hall Rd.
St. John's Wood Rd.
Lisson Grove
Park Rd.
Clifton Rd.
Bloomfield Rd.
Edgware Rd.
Marylebone Rd.
Devonshire St.
Portland Pl.
Gt. Portland St.
Harrow Rd.
Marylebone Flyover
Crawford St.
Upper Montague St.
Gloucester Pl.
Baker St.
Marylebone High St.
Harley St.
Seymour Pl.
Berners St.
Bishop's Bridge Rd.
Paddington Station
Praed St.
Sussex Gdns.
Manchester Square
Wigmore St.
Oxford Circus
Oxford St.
Dean St.
Marble Arch
Oxford St.
Duke St.
Bond St.
Regent St.
Queensway
Craven Hill
Bayswater Rd.
N. Carriage Dr.
Speaker's Corner
Grosvenor Square
Brook St.
Grosvenor St.
Brewer St.
U.S. Embassy
Berkeley Square
Piccadilly Circus
Bayswater Rd.
Sth. Audley St.
Park Lane
Kensington Gardens
Hyde Park
Curzon St.
Jermyn St.
The Serpentine
Piccadilly
St. James's Palace
Pall Mall
Kensington Palace
W. Carriage Dr.
Hyde Park Corner
Green Park
St. James's Park
S. Carriage Rd.
Constitution Hill
Kensington Rd.
Kensington Gore
Knightsbridge
Kensington Rd.
Grosvenor Pl.
Birdcage Walk
Royal Albert Hall
Sloane St.
Palace Gate
Prince Consort Rd.
Exhibition Rd.
Basil St.
Belgrave Square
Victoria & Albert Museum
Brompton Rd.
Pavilion Rd.
Cadogan Pl.
Victoria
Gloucester Rd.
Queen's Gate
Walton St.
Pont St.
Eaton Square
Buckingham Palace Rd.
Victoria Station
Natural History Museum
Cromwell Rd.
Wilton Rd.
Draycott Ave.
Sloane Sq.
Coach Station
Vauxhall
Sloane Ave.
Ixworth Pl.
Warwick Way
Old Brompton Rd.
Pimlico Rd.
Belgrave Rd.
Cale St.
Royal Hospital Rd.
Chelsea Br. Rd.
Ebury Br. Rd.
Sutherland St.
Lupus St.
Sydney St.
King's Rd.
Old Church St.
Flood St.
Royal Hospital
Grosvenor Rd.
Redcliffe Gdns.
Fulham Rd.
Oakley St.
Finborough Rd.
Carlyle's House
Chelsea Embankment
Chelsea Br.
Beaufort St.
Cheyne Walk
River Thames
Albert Br.
Battersea Park

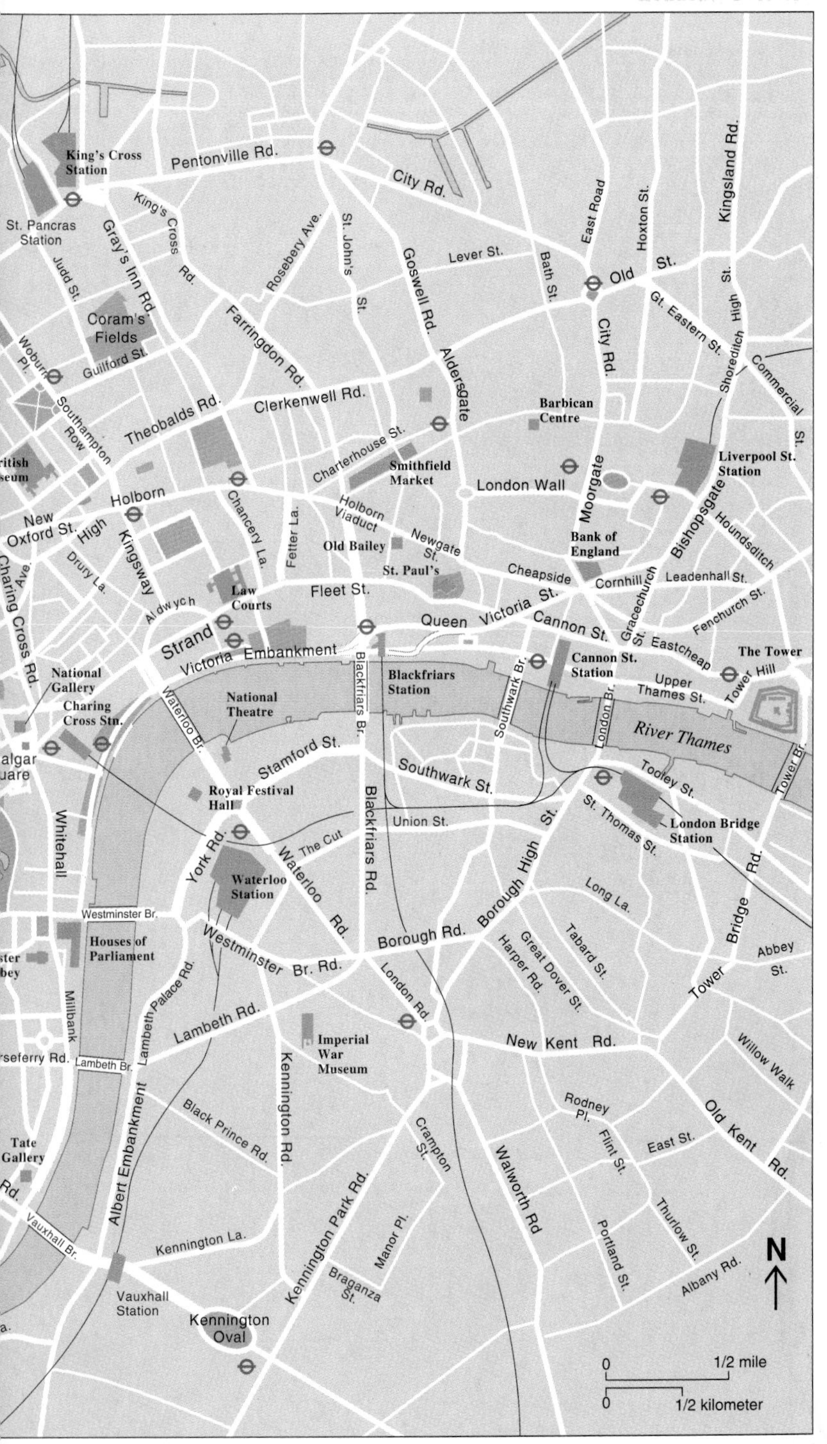
King's Cross Station
Pentonville Rd.
City Rd.
St. Pancras Station
King's Cross Rd.
Gray's Inn Rd.
Judd St.
Rosebery Ave.
St. John's St.
Goswell Rd.
Lever St.
Bath St.
East Road
Hoxton St.
Kingsland Rd.
Old St.
Coram's Fields
Guilford St.
Farringdon Rd.
Aldersgate
City Rd.
Gt. Eastern St.
Shoreditch High St.
Commercial St.
Woburn Pl.
Southampton Row
Theobalds Rd.
Clerkenwell Rd.
Barbican Centre
Charterhouse St.
Smithfield Market
London Wall
Liverpool St. Station
British Museum
Holborn
Chancery La.
Holborn Viaduct
Moorgate
Bishopsgate
Houndsditch
New Oxford St.
High
Kingsway
Drury La.
Fetter La.
Old Bailey
Newgate St.
Bank of England
St. Paul's
Cheapside
Cornhill
Gracechurch St.
Leadenhall St.
Fenchurch St.
Charing Cross Rd.
Ave.
Aldwych
Law Courts
Fleet St.
Queen Victoria St.
Cannon St.
Eastcheap
The Tower
Strand
Victoria Embankment
Cannon St. Station
Tower Hill
National Gallery
Charing Cross Stn.
Waterloo Br.
National Theatre
Blackfriars Br.
Blackfriars Station
Southwark Br.
London Br.
Upper Thames St.
River Thames
Tower Br.
Trafalgar Square
Stamford St.
Southwark St.
Tooley St.
Royal Festival Hall
Whitehall
Blackfriars Rd.
Union St.
St. Thomas St.
London Bridge Station
York Rd.
The Cut
Waterloo Rd.
Borough High St.
Waterloo Station
Long La.
Westminster Br.
Borough Rd.
Tower Bridge Rd.
Houses of Parliament
Westminster Br. Rd.
Tabard St.
Great Dover St.
Harper Rd.
Abbey St.
Westminster Abbey
Lambeth Palace Rd.
London Rd.
Millbank
Lambeth Rd.
Imperial War Museum
New Kent Rd.
Willow Walk
Horseferry Rd.
Lambeth Br.
Kennington Rd.
Albert Embankment
Black Prince Rd.
Rodney Pl.
Flint St.
East St.
Old Kent Rd.
Tate Gallery
Crampton St.
Walworth Rd
Kennington Park Rd.
Manor Pl.
Thurlow St.
Portland St.
Vauxhall Br.
Kennington La.
Albany Rd.
Braganza St.
Vauxhall Station
Kennington Oval
N
0
1/2 mile
0
1/2 kilometer

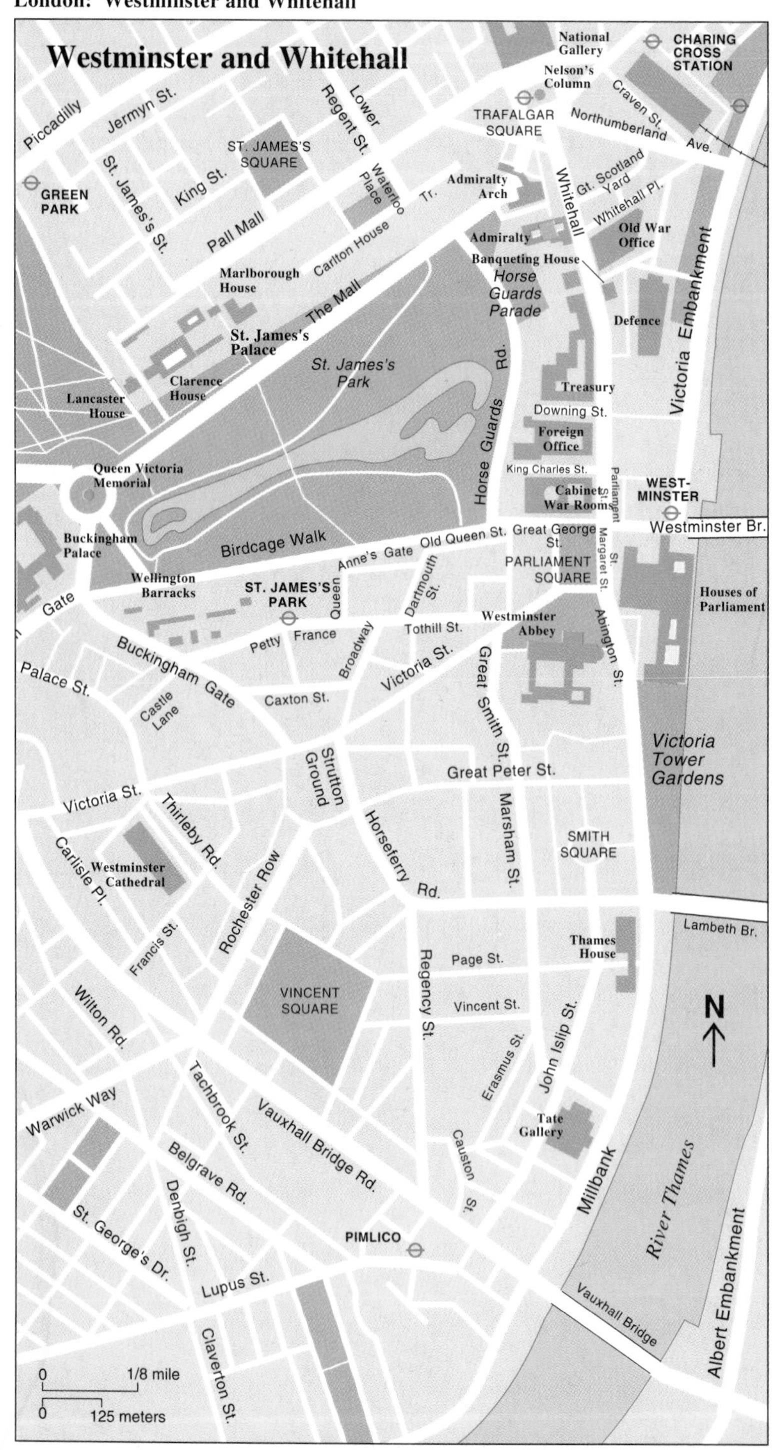
Westminster and Whitehall
National Gallery
CHARING CROSS STATION
Nelson's Column
Craven St.
TRAFALGAR SQUARE
Northumberland Ave.
Piccadilly
Jermyn St.
Lower Regent St.
ST. JAMES'S SQUARE
GREEN PARK
St. James's St.
King St.
Waterloo Place
Tr.
Admiralty Arch
Whitehall
Gt. Scotland Yard
Whitehall Pl.
Pall Mall
Carlton House
Admiralty
Old War Office
Banqueting House
Horse Guards Parade
Marlborough House
The Mall
Defence
Victoria Embankment
St. James's Palace
St. James's Park
Horse Guards Rd.
Treasury
Clarence House
Lancaster House
Downing St.
Foreign Office
Queen Victoria Memorial
King Charles St.
Cabinet War Rooms
Parliament St.
WEST-MINSTER
Westminster Br.
Buckingham Palace
Birdcage Walk
Old Queen St.
Great George St.
Anne's Gate
PARLIAMENT SQUARE
Margaret St.
Wellington Barracks
ST. JAMES'S PARK
Queen
Dartmouth St.
Houses of Parliament
Gate
Westminster Abbey
Tothill St.
Petty France
Broadway
Abingdon St.
Buckingham Gate
Palace St.
Victoria St.
Great Smith St.
Castle Lane
Caxton St.
Victoria Tower Gardens
Strutton Ground
Great Peter St.
Victoria St.
Thirleby Rd.
Horseferry Rd.
Marsham St.
SMITH SQUARE
Carlisle Pl.
Westminster Cathedral
Rochester Row
Lambeth Br.
Francis St.
Thames House
Page St.
Regency St.
VINCENT SQUARE
Vincent St.
Wilton Rd.
N
Erasmus St.
John Islip St.
Tachbrook St.
Warwick Way
Vauxhall Bridge Rd.
Tate Gallery
Causton St.
Belgrave Rd.
Millbank
River Thames
Denbigh St.
St. George's Dr.
PIMLICO
Albert Embankment
Lupus St.
Vauxhall Bridge
Claverton St.
0
1/8 mile
0
125 meters

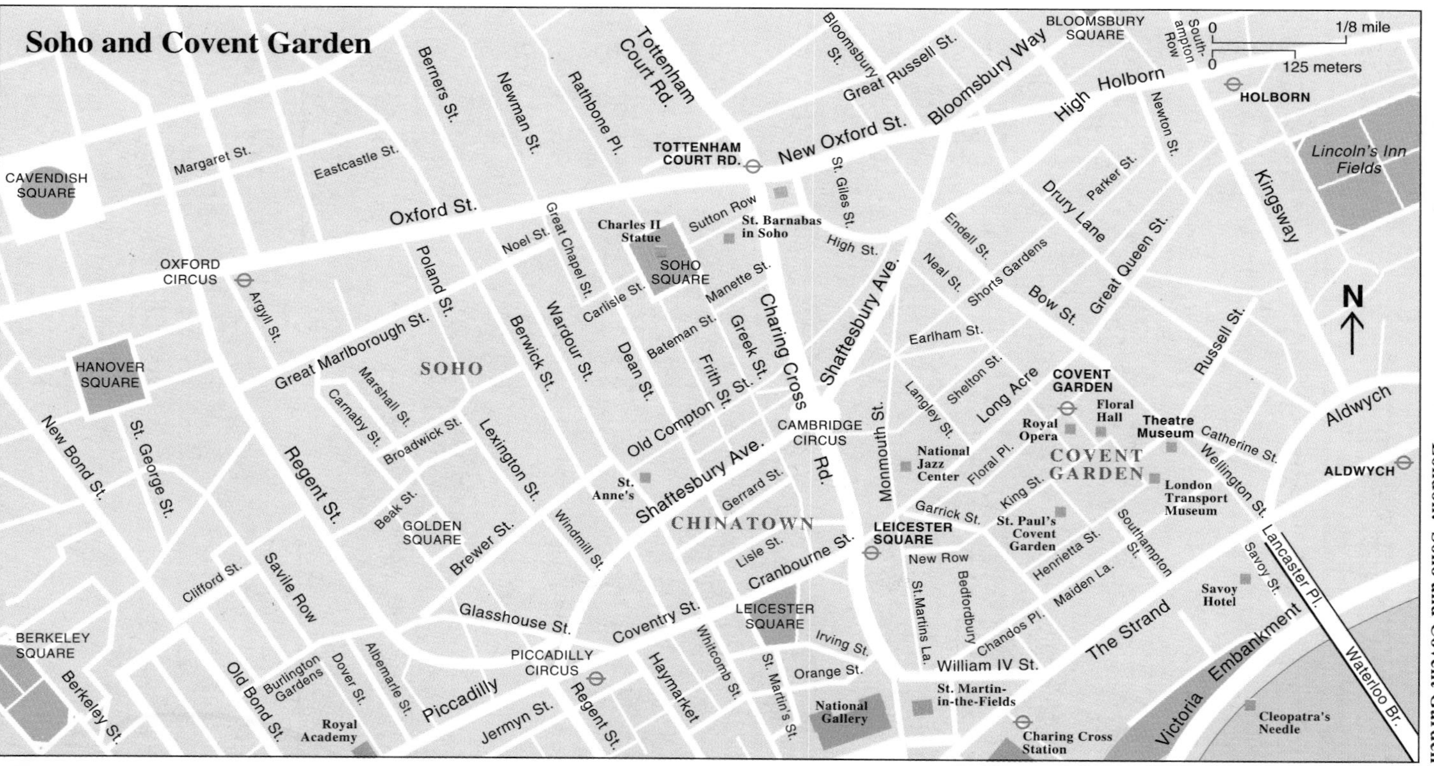
Soho and Covent Garden
1/8 mile
125 meters
N
HOLBORN
Lincoln's Inn Fields
Kingsway
Aldwych
ALDWYCH
Waterloo Br.
Lancaster Pl.
Victoria Embankment
Cleopatra's Needle
Savoy St.
Savoy Hotel
Wellington St.
Catherine St.
Russell St.
Theatre Museum
London Transport Museum
South-ampton Row
Newton St.
High Holborn
BLOOMSBURY SQUARE
Great Queen St.
Parker St.
Drury Lane
Bow St.
COVENT GARDEN
Floral Hall
Royal Opera
COVENT GARDEN
Southampton St.
The Strand
Maiden La.
Henrietta St.
St. Paul's Covent Garden
King St.
Floral Pl.
Long Acre
Shorts Gardens
Endell St.
Neal St.
Earlham St.
Shelton St.
Langley St.
National Jazz Center
Garrick St.
LEICESTER SQUARE
New Row
Bedfordbury
Chandos Pl.
William IV St.
St. Martin-in-the-Fields
Charing Cross Station
St.Martins La.
Bloomsbury Way
Great Russell St.
Bloomsbury St.
New Oxford St.
St. Giles St.
High St.
Shaftesbury Ave.
Monmouth St.
CAMBRIDGE CIRCUS
Charing Cross Rd.
National Gallery
Irving St.
Orange St.
St. Barnabas in Soho
Sutton Row
TOTTENHAM COURT RD.
Tottenham Court Rd.
Manette St.
Greek St.
Frith St.
Gerrard St.
Lisle St.
Cranbourne St.
LEICESTER SQUARE
St. Martin's St.
CHINATOWN
SOHO SQUARE
Charles II Statue
Bateman St.
Old Compton St.
Shaftesbury Ave.
Whitcomb St.
Coventry St.
Haymarket
Rathbone Pl.
Carlisle St.
Dean St.
St. Anne's
Great Chapel St.
Wardour St.
Windmill St.
PICCADILLY CIRCUS
Regent St.
Newman St.
Noel St.
Berwick St.
Lexington St.
Brewer St.
Glasshouse St.
Jermyn St.
Piccadilly
SOHO
Berners St.
Oxford St.
Poland St.
Broadwick St.
GOLDEN SQUARE
Beak St.
Eastcastle St.
Great Marlborough St.
Marshall St.
Carnaby St.
Albemarle St.
Dover St.
Royal Academy
Regent St.
Savile Row
Burlington Gardens
Margaret St.
Argyll St.
OXFORD CIRCUS
Old Bond St.
Clifford St.
St. George St.
HANOVER SQUARE
CAVENDISH SQUARE
New Bond St.
BERKELEY SQUARE
Berkeley St.

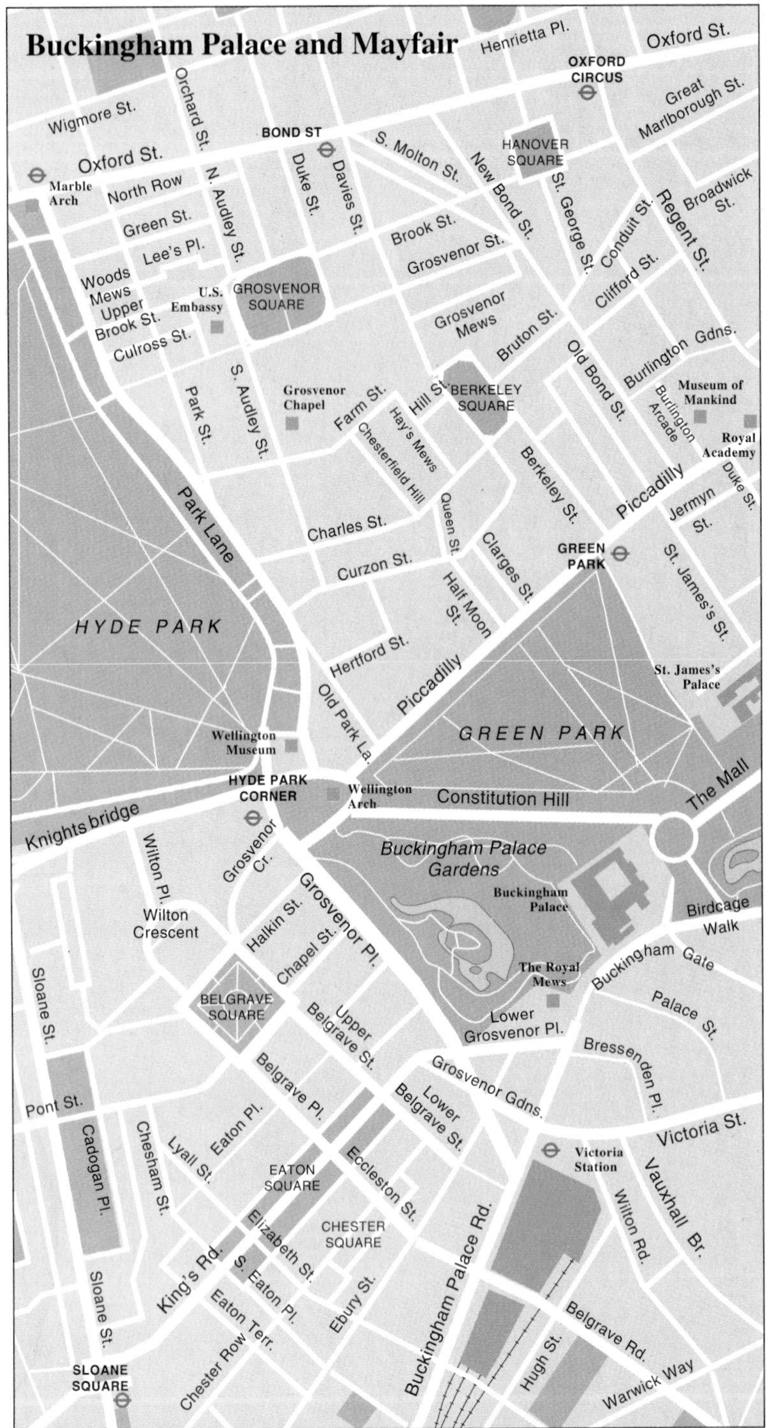
Buckingham Palace and Mayfair
Henrietta Pl.
Oxford St.
OXFORD CIRCUS
Great Marlborough St.
Wigmore St.
Orchard St.
BOND ST
S. Molton St.
HANOVER SQUARE
Oxford St.
Marble Arch
North Row
N. Audley St.
Duke St.
Davies St.
New Bond St.
St. George St.
Regent St.
Broadwick St.
Green St.
Brook St.
Conduit St.
Lee's Pl.
Grosvenor St.
Woods Mews
Upper Brook St.
U.S. Embassy
GROSVENOR SQUARE
Clifford St.
Culross St.
Grosvenor Mews
Bruton St.
Old Bond St.
Burlington Gdns.
Park St.
S. Audley St.
Grosvenor Chapel
Farm St.
Hill St.
BERKELEY SQUARE
Hay's Mews
Chesterfield Hill
Burlington Arcade
Museum of Mankind
Royal Academy
Berkeley St.
Piccadilly
Duke St.
Jermyn St.
Park Lane
Charles St.
Queen St.
Clarges St.
GREEN PARK
St. James's St.
Curzon St.
Half Moon St.
HYDE PARK
Hertford St.
Piccadilly
St. James's Palace
Old Park La.
GREEN PARK
Wellington Museum
HYDE PARK CORNER
Wellington Arch
Constitution Hill
The Mall
Knights bridge
Wilton Pl.
Grosvenor Cr.
Buckingham Palace Gardens
Grosvenor Pl.
Buckingham Palace
Wilton Crescent
Halkin St.
Birdcage Walk
Chapel St.
Buckingham Gate
Sloane St.
The Royal Mews
BELGRAVE SQUARE
Upper Belgrave St.
Lower Grosvenor Pl.
Palace St.
Bressenden Pl.
Belgrave Pl.
Grosvenor Gdns.
Lower Belgrave St.
Pont St.
Victoria St.
Cadogan Pl.
Chesham St.
Eaton Pl.
Lyall St.
EATON SQUARE
Eccleston St.
Victoria Station
Vauxhall Br.
Wilton Rd.
CHESTER SQUARE
Elizabeth St.
Buckingham Palace Rd.
King's Rd.
S. Eaton Pl.
Ebury St.
Sloane St.
Eaton Terr.
Belgrave Rd.
Hugh St.
Chester Row
Warwick Way
SLOANE SQUARE

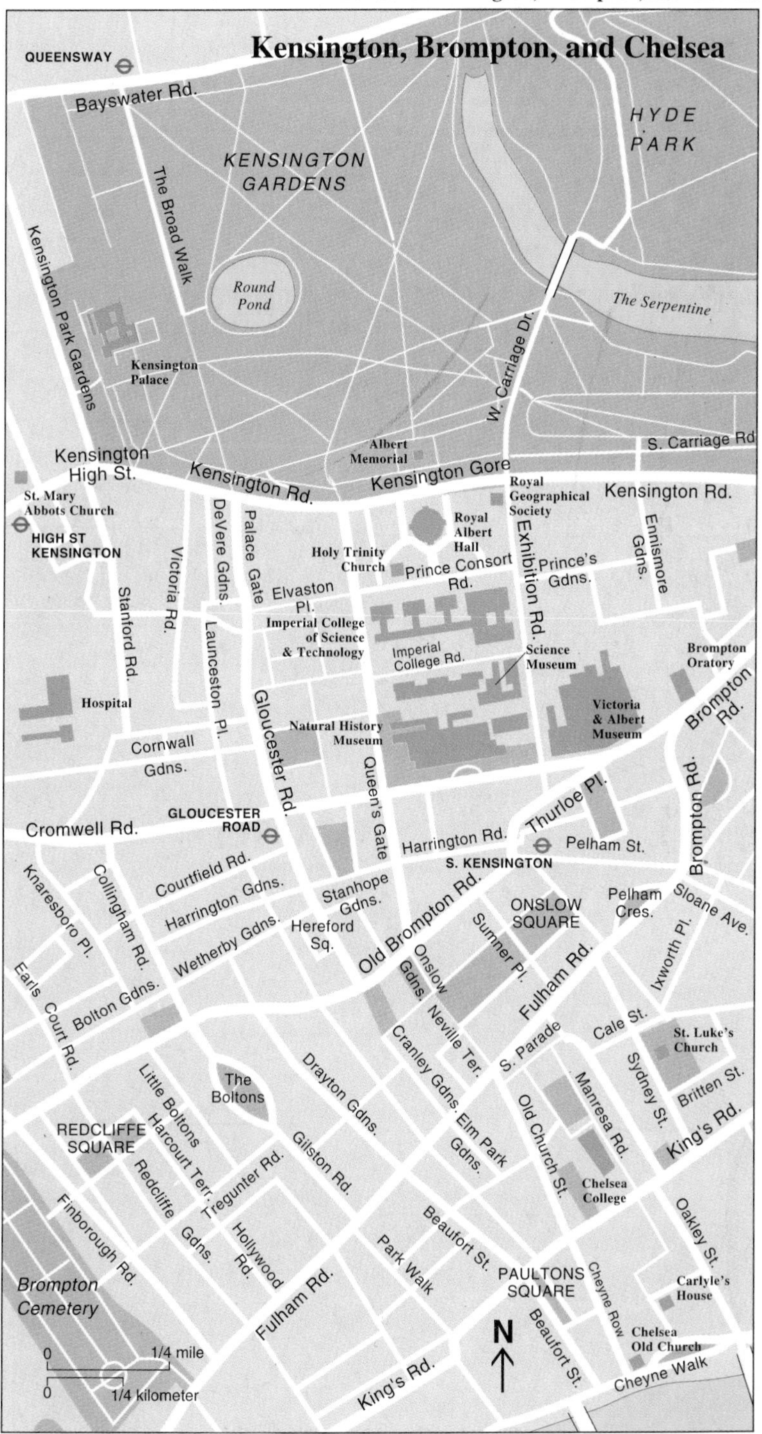
Kensington, Brompton, and Chelsea
QUEENSWAY
Bayswater Rd.
HYDE PARK
KENSINGTON GARDENS
The Broad Walk
Kensington Park Gardens
Round Pond
The Serpentine
Kensington Palace
W. Carriage Dr.
Albert Memorial
S. Carriage Rd.
Kensington High St.
Kensington Rd.
Kensington Gore
Royal Geographical Society
Kensington Rd.
St. Mary Abbots Church
HIGH ST KENSINGTON
Victoria Rd.
DeVere Gdns.
Palace Gate
Royal Albert Hall
Exhibition Rd.
Ennismore Gdns.
Holy Trinity Church
Prince Consort Rd.
Prince's Gdns.
Stanford Rd.
Elvaston Pl.
Launceston Pl.
Imperial College of Science & Technology
Imperial College Rd.
Science Museum
Brompton Oratory
Hospital
Gloucester Rd.
Natural History Museum
Victoria & Albert Museum
Brompton Rd.
Cornwall Gdns.
Queen's Gate
Brompton Rd.
GLOUCESTER ROAD
Cromwell Rd.
Thurloe Pl.
Harrington Rd.
Pelham St.
S. KENSINGTON
Knaresboro Pl.
Collingham Rd.
Courtfield Rd.
Harrington Gdns.
Stanhope Gdns.
Old Brompton Rd.
ONSLOW SQUARE
Pelham Cres.
Sloane Ave.
Wetherby Gdns.
Hereford Sq.
Sumner Pl.
Ixworth Pl.
Earls Court Rd.
Bolton Gdns.
Onslow Gdns.
Fulham Rd.
Neville Ter.
Cale St.
S. Parade
St. Luke's Church
The Boltons
Drayton Gdns.
Cranley Gdns.
Sydney St.
Britten St.
Little Boltons
Manresa Rd.
King's Rd.
REDCLIFFE SQUARE
Harcourt Terr.
Elm Park Gdns.
Old Church St.
Redcliffe Gdns.
Tregunter Rd.
Gilston Rd.
Chelsea College
Oakley St.
Finborough Rd.
Hollywood Rd.
Beaufort St.
Park Walk
PAULTONS SQUARE
Cheyne Row
Carlyle's House
Brompton Cemetery
Fulham Rd.
N
Beaufort St.
Chelsea Old Church
0
1/4 mile
0
1/4 kilometer
King's Rd.
Cheyne Walk

London: City of London

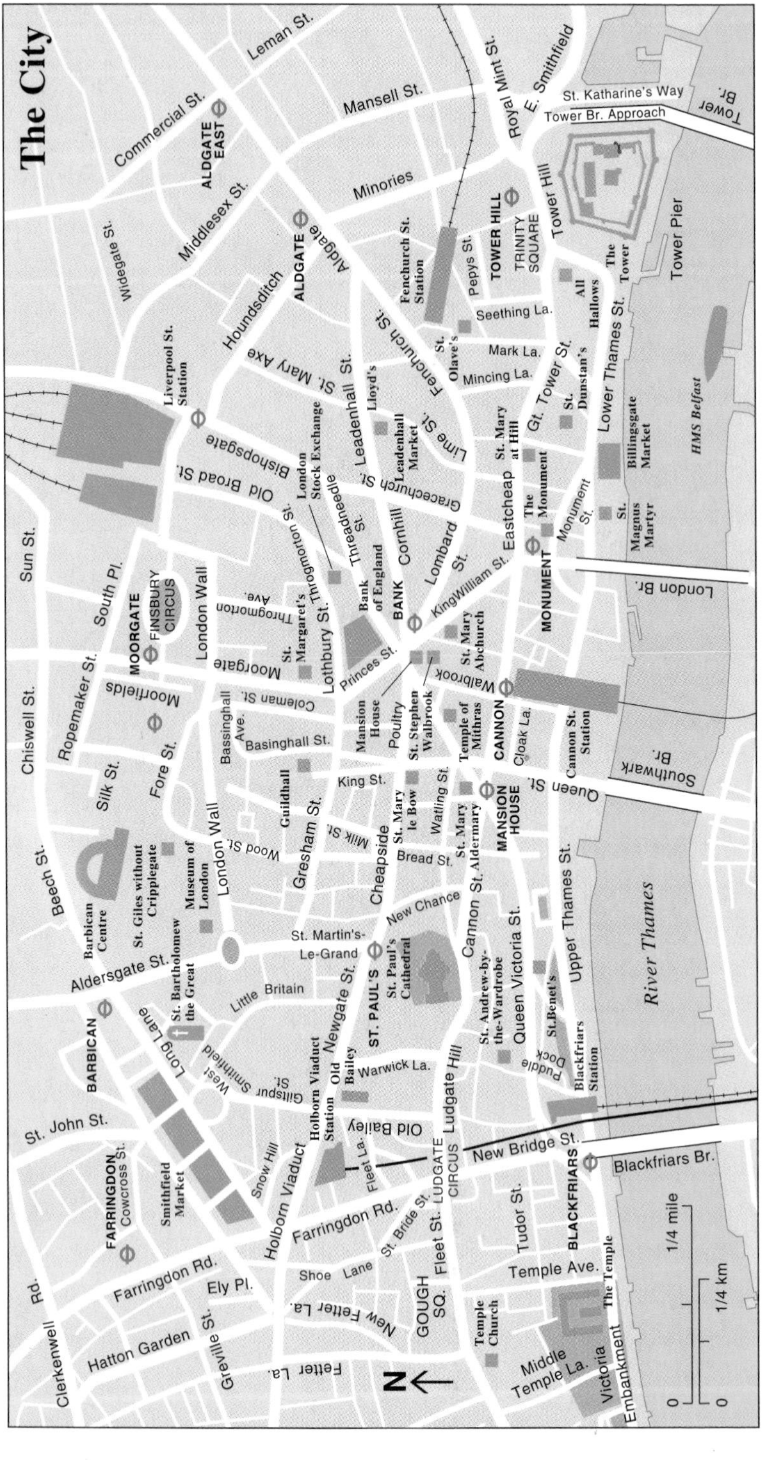

The City

Leman St.
Commercial St.
Mansell St.
ALDGATE EAST
Middlesex St.
Widegate St.
Minories
ALDGATE
Aldgate
Houndsditch
Royal Mint St.
E. Smithfield
St. Katharine's Way
Tower Br. Approach
Tower Br.
TOWER HILL
TRINITY SQUARE
Tower Hill
Pepys St.
Fenchurch St. Station
Seething La.
The Tower
Tower Pier
All Hallows
St. Olave's
Mark La.
Mincing La.
Fenchurch St.
Liverpool St. Station
St. Mary Axe
Leadenhall St.
Lloyd's
Lime St.
Gt. Tower St.
St. Dunstan's
Lower Thames St.
HMS Belfast
Bishopsgate
Old Broad St.
London Stock Exchange
Leadenhall Market
St. Mary at Hill
Billingsgate Market
Gracechurch St.
Threadneedle St.
Cornhill
Eastcheap
The Monument
Monument St.
St. Magnus Martyr
Sun St.
South Pl.
MOORGATE
FINSBURY CIRCUS
London Wall
Throgmorton St.
Throgmorton Ave.
Bank of England
BANK
Lombard St.
King William St.
MONUMENT
London Br.
Chiswell St.
Ropemaker St.
Moorfields
Moorgate
St. Margaret's
Lothbury St.
Princes St.
St. Mary Abchurch
Walbrook
Coleman St.
Mansion House
Poultry
St. Stephen Walbrook
Temple of Mithras
CANNON
Cloak La.
Cannon St. Station
Southwark Br.
Fore St.
Silk St.
Bassinghall Ave.
Basinghall St.
Guildhall
King St.
Watling St.
MANSION HOUSE
Queen St.
Beech St.
Barbican Centre
St. Giles without Cripplegate
Museum of London
Wood St.
Milk St.
Gresham St.
Cheapside
St. Mary le Bow
Bread St.
St. Mary Aldermary
Upper Thames St.
River Thames
Aldersgate St.
St. Bartholomew the Great
St. Martin's-Le-Grand
New Change
St. Paul's Cathedral
ST. PAUL'S
Cannon St.
St. Andrew-by-the-Wardrobe
Queen Victoria St.
St. Benet's
Little Britain
Newgate St.
BARBICAN
Long Lane
West Smithfield
Giltspur St.
Holborn Viaduct Station
Old Bailey
Warwick La.
Ludgate Hill
Puddle Dock
Blackfriars Station
St. John St.
Old Bailey
Fleet La.
LUDGATE CIRCUS
New Bridge St.
BLACKFRIARS
Blackfriars Br.
FARRINGDON
Cowcross St.
Smithfield Market
Snow Hill
Holborn Viaduct
Farringdon Rd.
St. Bride St.
Fleet St.
Tudor St.
Clerkenwell Rd.
Farringdon Rd.
Ely Pl.
Shoe Lane
Temple Ave.
The Temple
Hatton Garden
Greville St.
New Fetter La.
GOUGH SQ.
Temple Church
Middle Temple La.
Victoria Embankment
Fetter La.
N
1/4 mile
1/4 km
0
0

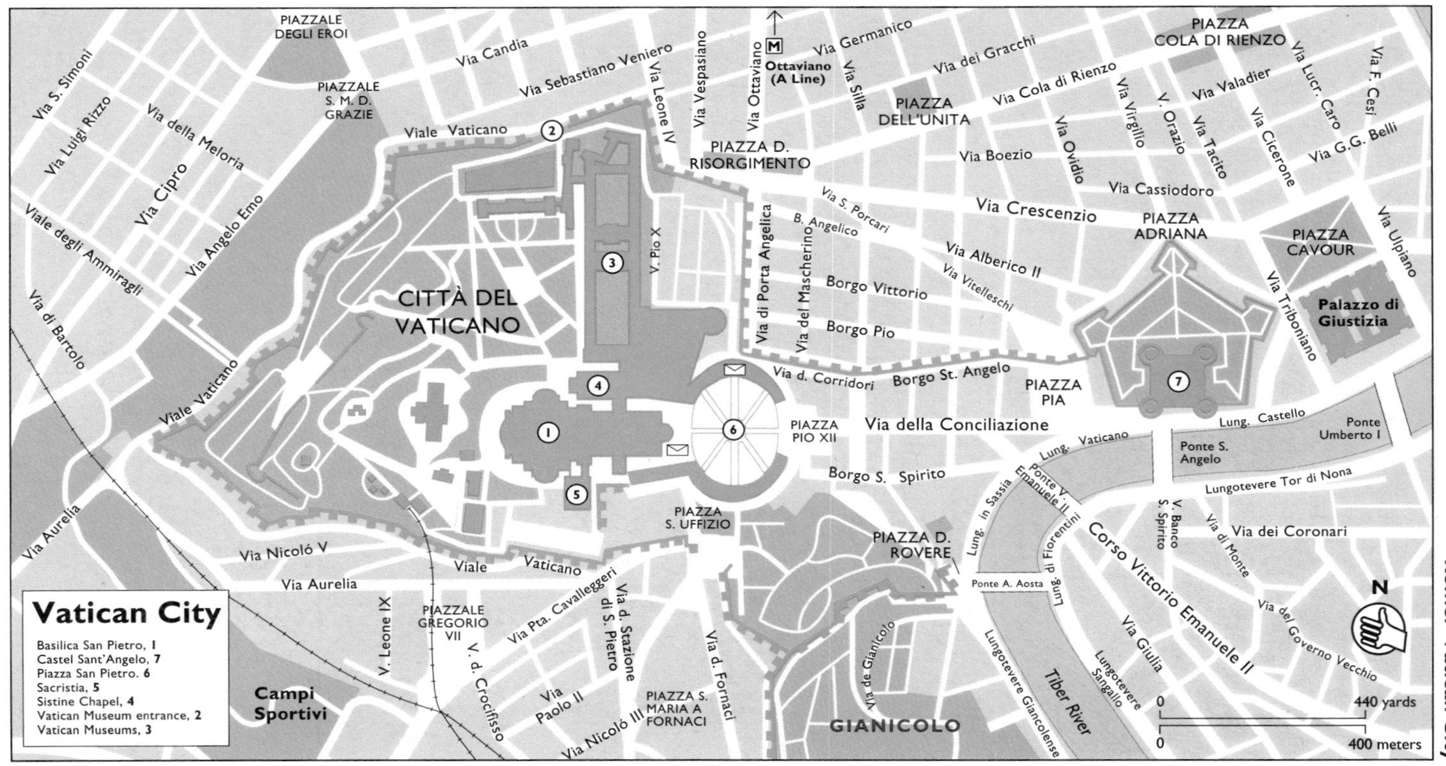
Vatican City
Basilica San Pietro, 1
Castel Sant'Angelo, 7
Piazza San Pietro. 6
Sacristia, 5
Sistine Chapel, 4
Vatican Museum entrance, 2
Vatican Museums, 3
CITTÀ DEL VATICANO
PIAZZA PIO XII
Via della Conciliazione
PIAZZA PIA
PIAZZA D. RISORGIMENTO
PIAZZA CAVOUR
Palazzo di Giustizia
PIAZZA ADRIANA
Via Crescenzio
PIAZZA COLA DI RIENZO
Via Cola di Rienzo
PIAZZA DELL'UNITA
Ottaviano (A Line)
Via Ottaviano
Via Vespasiano
Via Leone IV
Via Germanico
Via Silla
Via dei Gracchi
Via Valadier
Via Lucr. Caro
Via F. Cesi
Via G.G. Belli
Via Cicerone
Via Tacito
V. Orazio
Via Virgilio
Via Ovidio
Via Boezio
Via Cassiodoro
Via Ulpiano
Via Triboniano
Via S. Porcari
B. Angelico
Via Alberico II
Via Vitelleschi
Borgo Vittorio
Borgo Pio
Via di Porta Angelica
Via del Mascherino
V. Pio X
Via d. Corridori
Borgo St. Angelo
Borgo S. Spirito
PIAZZA S. UFFIZIO
PIAZZA D. ROVERE
Viale Vaticano
Via Candia
Via Sebastiano Veniero
PIAZZALE DEGLI EROI
PIAZZALE S. M. D. GRAZIE
Via S. Simoni
Via Luigi Rizzo
Via della Meloria
Via Cipro
Via Angelo Emo
Viale degli Ammiragli
Via di Bartolo
Via Aurelia
Via Nicoló V
V. Leone IX
PIAZZALE GREGORIO VII
V. d. Crocifisso
Via Pta. Cavalleggeri
Via d. Stazione di S. Pietro
Via Paolo II
Via Nicoló III
PIAZZA S. MARIA A FORNACI
Via d. Fornaci
Via de Gianicolo
GIANICOLO
Campi Sportivi
Lung. Castello
Ponte Umberto I
Ponte S. Angelo
Lung. Vaticano
Ponte V. Emanuele II
Lung. in Sassia
Lung. di Fiorentini
Ponte A. Aosta
Lungotevere Gianicolense
Tiber River
Lungotevere Sangallo
Lungotevere Tor di Nona
V. Banco S. Spirito
Via di Monte
Via dei Coronari
Corso Vittorio Emanuele II
Via Giulia
Via del Governo Vecchio
N
0
440 yards
0
400 meters

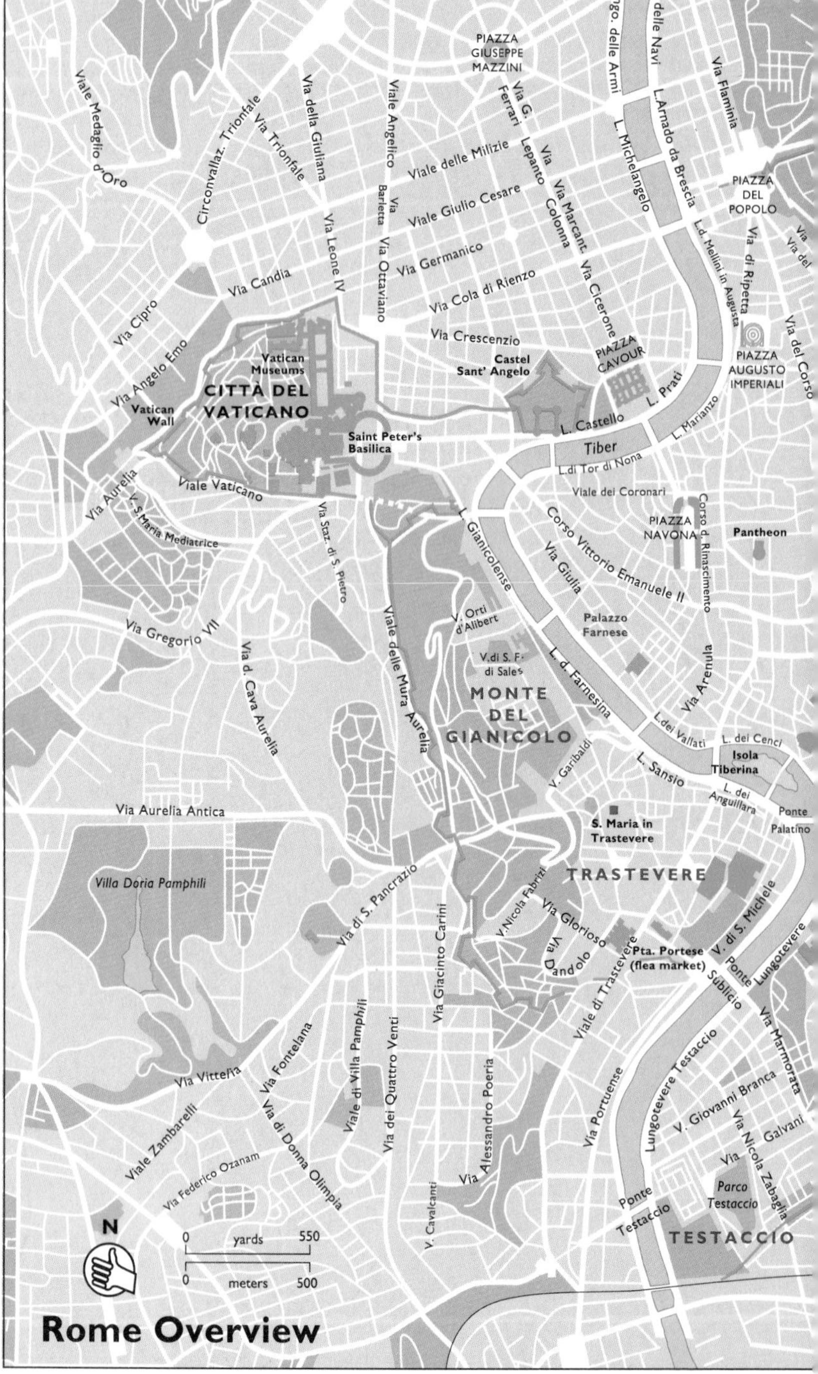
Rome Overview
PIAZZA GIUSEPPE MAZZINI
Lungo. delle Armi
L. delle Navi
Via Flaminia
Viale Medaglio d'Oro
Circonvallaz. Trionfale
Via Trionfale
Via della Giuliana
Viale Angelico
Via G. Ferrari
Via Lepanto
L. Michelangelo
L.Arnado da Brescia
Viale delle Milizie
Via Barletta
Viale Giulio Cesare
Via Colonna
Via Marcant.
PIAZZA DEL POPOLO
Via Leone IV
Via Ottaviano
Via Germanico
Via Cicerone
L.d. Mellini in Augusta
Via di Ripetta
Via Candia
Via Cola di Rienzo
Via Cipro
Via Crescenzio
PIAZZA AUGUSTO IMPERIALI
Via del Corso
Vatican Museums
PIAZZA CAVOUR
Castel Sant' Angelo
Via Angelo Emo
CITTÀ DEL VATICANO
Vatican Wall
L. Prati
L. Castello
L. Marianzo
Saint Peter's Basilica
Tiber
L.di Tor di Nona
Via Aurelia
Viale Vaticano
V.S.Maria Mediatrice
Viale dei Coronari
Via Staz. di S. Pietro
L. Gianicolense
Corso Vittorio Emanuele II
PIAZZA NAVONA
Corso d. Rinascimento
Pantheon
Via Giulia
V. Orti d'Alibert
Palazzo Farnese
Via Gregorio VII
V.di S. F. di Sales
Viale delle Mura Aurelia
L. d. Farnesina
Via Arenula
Via d. Cava Aurelia
MONTE DEL GIANICOLO
L.dei Vallati
L. dei Cenci
Isola Tiberina
V. Garibaldi
L. Sansio
L. dei Anguillara
Ponte Palatino
Via Aurelia Antica
S. Maria in Trastevere
Villa Doria Pamphili
TRASTEVERE
Via di S. Pancrazio
V.Nicola Fabrizi
Via Glorioso
Via Dandolo
Viale di Trastevere
Pta. Portese (flea market)
V. di S. Michele
Ponte Sublicio
Lungotevere
Via Giacinto Carini
Via Marmorata
Via Fontelana
Viale di Villa Pamphili
Via dei Quattro Venti
Via Vitteria
Lungotevere Testaccio
V. Giovanni Branca
Via Alessandro Poeria
Via Portuense
Viale Zambarelli
Via di Donna Olimpia
Via Nicola Zabaglia
Via Galvani
Via Federico Ozanam
Via Cavalcanti
Ponte Testaccio
Parco Testaccio
TESTACCIO
N
0 yards 550
0 meters 500

Villa Borghese
Via Po
V. Isonzo
Via Salaria
Viale Regina Margherita
V. Dalmazia
Via Nizza
Via Nomentana
Corso d'Italia
Via Piave
Via Boncompagni
Via V. Veneto
V. Ludovisi
Spanish Steps
Via Sistina
V. dei due Macelli
Via Barberini
Via XX Settembre
Biblioteca Nazionale
SALARIO
Museo Nazionale Romano
PIAZZA DEL CINQUECENTO
PIAZZA DELLA REPUBBLICA
Via del Tritone
V. d. Quattro Fontane
Policlinico Universita
Viale Regina Elena
Via dell'Università
Via del Policlinico
Via Palestro
Via Castro Pretorio
Stazione Termini
Trevi Fountain
Palazzo dei Quirinale
Via Nazionale
Via Marsala
Via Giovanni Giolitti
Via Tiburtina
Via Panisperna
Via Cavour
Via Merulana
Via Giovanni Lanza
PIAZZA VITTORIO EMANUELE
V. dei Fori Imperiali
Forum
PIAZZA DEL COLOSSEO
Colosseum
Via Labicana
Viale Manzoni
V. S. Croce in Gerusalemme
V. Statilia
PIAZZA DI PTA. MAGGIORE
Via Emanuele Filiberto
MONTE PALATINO
Via di S. Gregorio
Via Claudia
Parco del Celio
CELIO
Via dei Cerchi
Circo Massimo (Circus Maximus)
Via del Circo Massimo
Via di S. Prisca
Via di S. Stefano Rotondo
P. DI SAN GIOVANNI IN LATERANO
San Giovanni in Laterano
Via dell'Amba Aradam
Via d. Laterani
Via della Navicella
Via Appia
P. DEI RE DI ROMA
Nuova
Via Cerveteri
Viale Aventino
Via Aventina
Via delle Terme
Via Druso
Via Gallia
Viale Metronio
Via Etruria
Terme di Caracalla
Viale di Terme di Caracalla
Via di Porta Latina
Via di Porta Sebastiano
Via Satrico
Via Concordia
Viale d. Piramide Cestia
Viale Giotto
Viale Guido Baccelli
Via Vetulonia
Via Siria

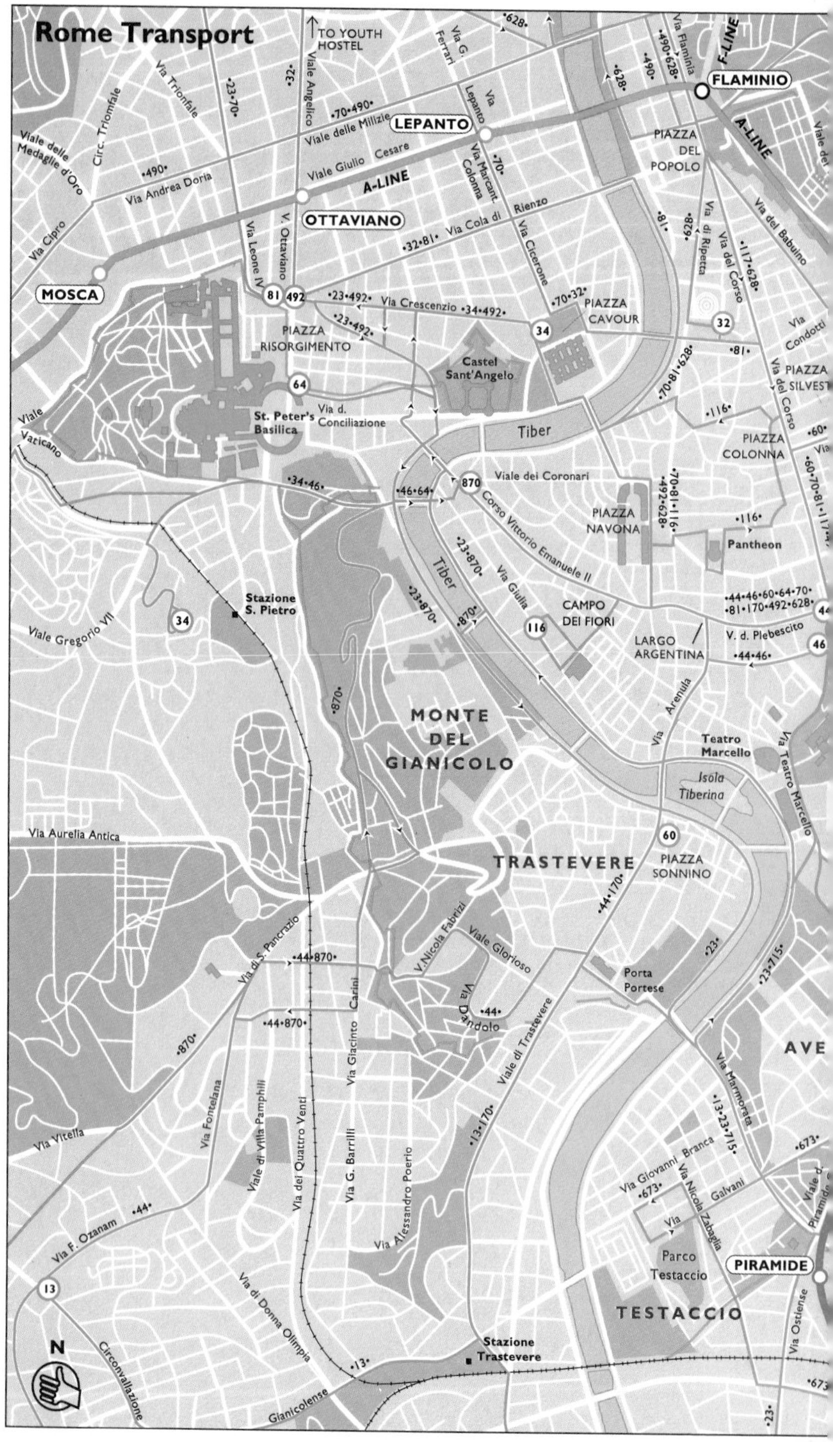

Rome Transport
TO YOUTH HOSTEL
FLAMINIO
LEPANTO
OTTAVIANO
MOSCA
PIRAMIDE
A-LINE
F-LINE
PIAZZA DEL POPOLO
PIAZZA CAVOUR
PIAZZA RISORGIMENTO
Castel Sant'Angelo
St. Peter's Basilica
Tiber
PIAZZA NAVONA
PIAZZA COLONNA
Pantheon
CAMPO DEI FIORI
LARGO ARGENTINA
Stazione S. Pietro
MONTE DEL GIANICOLO
Teatro Marcello
Isola Tiberina
TRASTEVERE
PIAZZA SONNINO
Porta Portese
Parco Testaccio
TESTACCIO
Stazione Trastevere
AVE
N
Via Trionfale
Circ. Trionfale
Viale delle Medaglie d'Oro
Via Andrea Doria
Via Cipro
Viale Angelico
Viale delle Milizie
Viale Giulio Cesare
Via Leone IV
V. Ottaviano
Via Cola di Rienzo
Via Cicerone
Via Marcant. Colonna
Via Lepanto
Via G. Ferrari
Via Flaminia
Via di Ripetta
Via del Corso
Via del Babuino
Via Condotti
Via Crescenzio
Via d. Conciliazione
Viale Vaticano
Viale dei Coronari
Corso Vittorio Emanuele II
Via Giulia
V. d. Plebescito
Via Arenula
Via Teatro Marcello
Viale Gregorio VII
Via Aurelia Antica
Via di S. Pancrazio
V. Nicola Fabrizi
Viale Glorioso
Via Dandolo
Viale di Trastevere
Via Giacinto Carini
Via Marmorata
Via Vitella
Via Fontelana
Viale di Villa Pamphili
Via dei Quattro Venti
Via G. Barrilli
Via Alessandro Poerio
Via Giovanni Branca
Via Nicola Zabaglia
Via Galvani
Via F. Ozanam
Via di Donna Olimpia
Circonvallazione Gianicolense
Via Ostiense
PIAZZA SILVEST

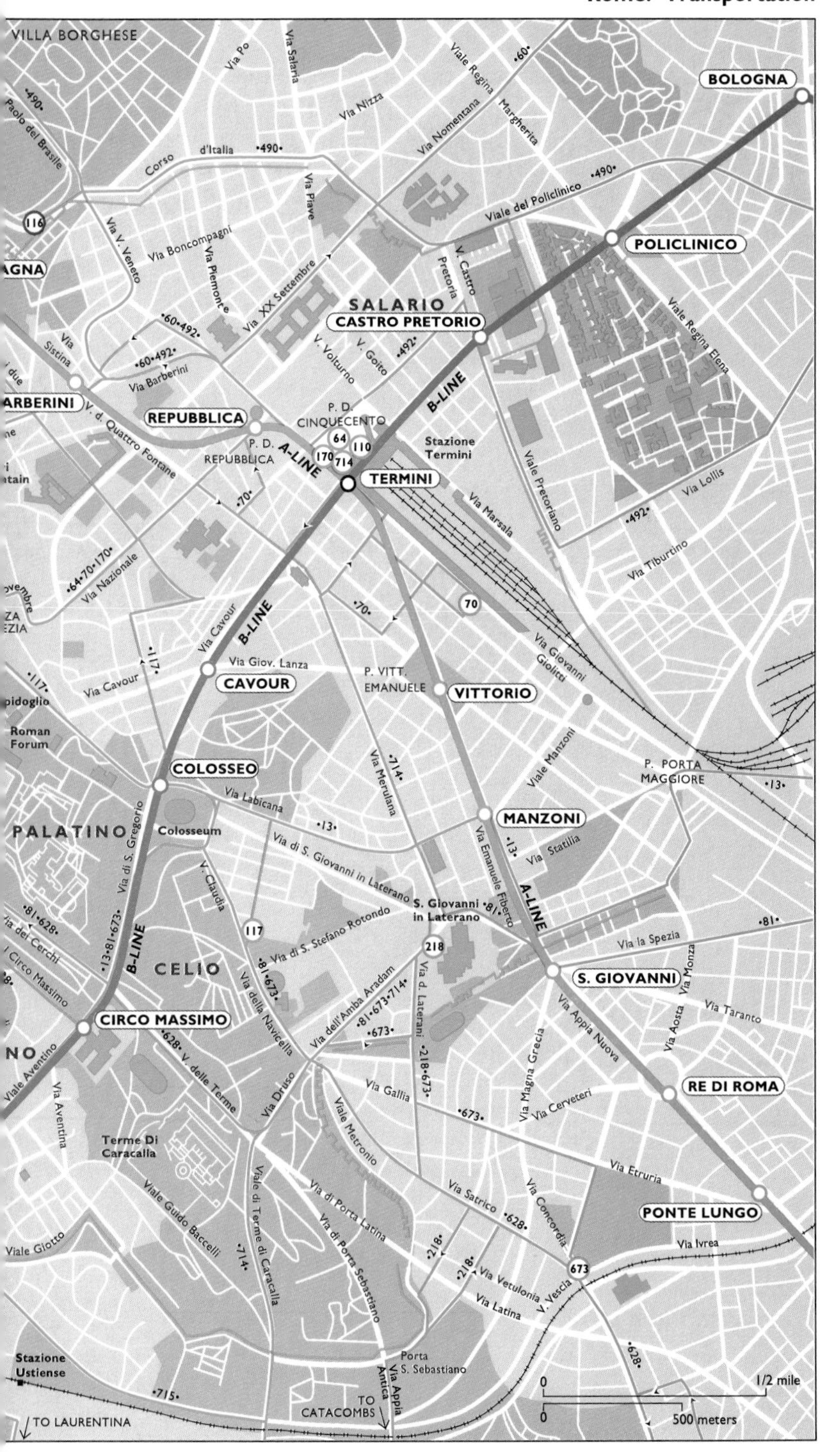

VILLA BORGHESE
BOLOGNA
POLICLINICO
SALARIO
CASTRO PRETORIO
BARBERINI
REPUBBLICA
P. D. CINQUECENTO
Stazione Termini
TERMINI
P. D. REPUBBLICA
A-LINE
B-LINE
CAVOUR
P. VITT. EMANUELE
VITTORIO
Roman Forum
COLOSSEO
Colosseum
PALATINO
MANZONI
P. PORTA MAGGIORE
S. Giovanni in Laterano
S. GIOVANNI
CELIO
CIRCO MASSIMO
RE DI ROMA
Terme Di Caracalla
PONTE LUNGO
Porta S. Sebastiano
Stazione Ustiense
TO CATACOMBS
TO LAURENTINA
Via Po
Via Salaria
Viale Regina Margherita
Via Nizza
Via Nomentana
Corso d'Italia
Paolo del Brasile
Via Piave
Viale del Policlinico
Via V. Veneto
Via Boncompagni
Via Piemonte
Via XX Settembre
V. Castro Pretoria
Viale Regina Elena
Via Sistina
Via Barberini
V. Volturno
V. Goito
V. d. Quattro Fontane
Viale Pretoriano
Via Lollis
Via Marsala
Via Tiburtino
Via Nazionale
Via Cavour
Via Giov. Lanza
Via Giovanni Giolitti
Viale Manzoni
Via Merulana
Via Labicana
Via di S. Gregorio
Via di S. Giovanni in Laterano
Via Emanuele Filiberto
Via Statilia
V. Claudia
Via di S. Stefano Rotondo
Via la Spezia
Via dei Cerchi
Circo Massimo
Via della Navicella
Via dell'Amba Aradam
Via d. Laterani
Via Appia Nuova
Via Monza
Via Taranto
Via Aosta
Via Magna Grecia
Viale Aventino
V. delle Terme
Via Druso
Via Gallia
Via Cerveteri
Via Aventina
Viale Metronio
Via Etruria
Viale Guido Baccelli
Viale di Terme di Caracalla
Via di Porta Latina
Via di Porta Sebastiano
Via Satrico
Via Concordia
Via Ivrea
Viale Giotto
Via Vetulonia
V. Vescia
Via Latina
Via Appia Antica
0
1/2 mile
500 meters

Central Rome

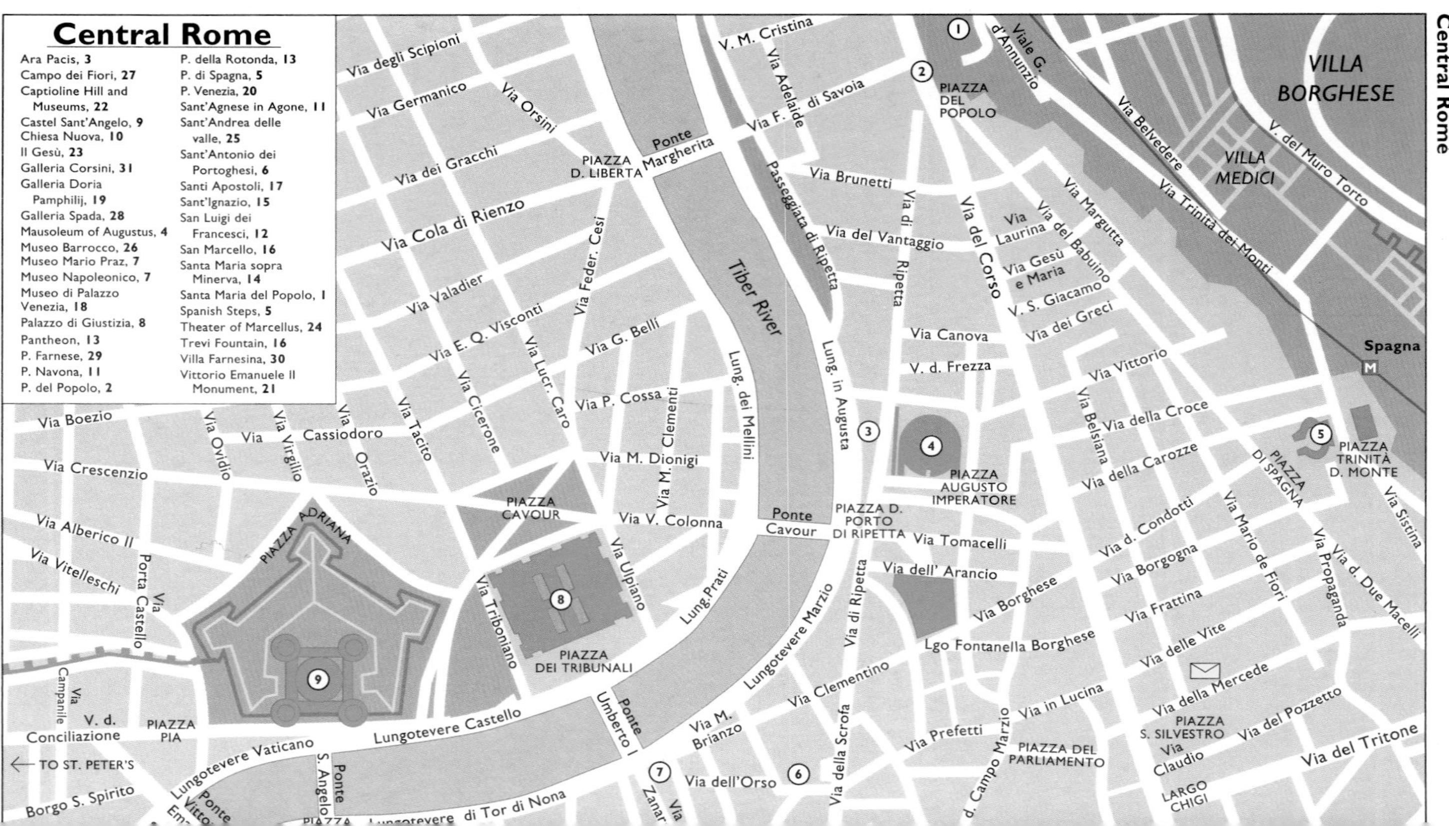

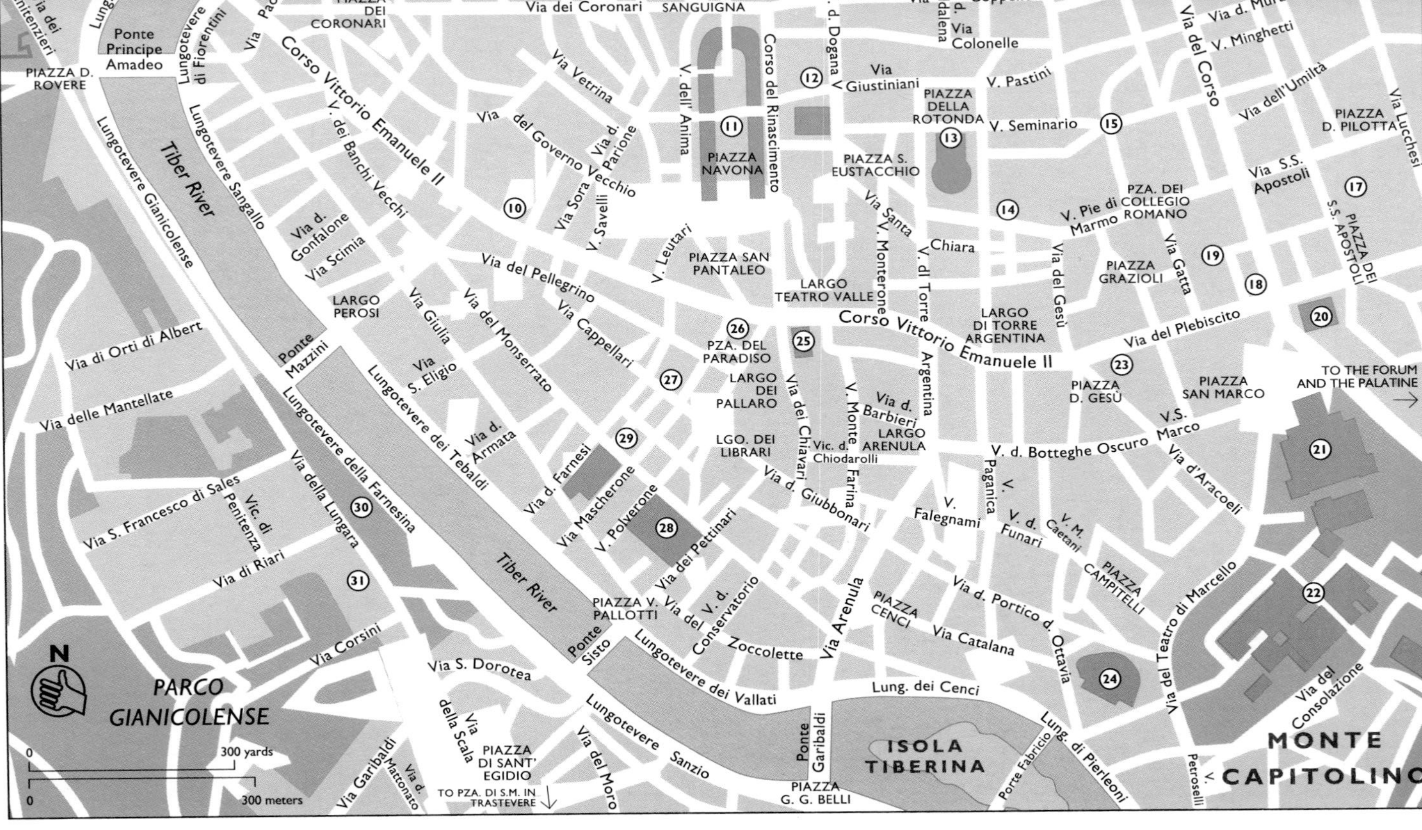

Via dei Penitenzieri
Lung.
Ponte Principe Amadeo
Lungotevere di Fiorentini
PIAZZA D. ROVERE
Via Pao
PIAZZA DEI CORONARI
Via dei Coronari
SANGUIGNA
V. d. Dogana V
Via Colonelle
Via d. Muratte
V. Minghetti
Via del Corso
Corso Vittorio Emanuele II
V. dei Banchi Vecchi
Via Vetrina
Via del Governo Vecchio
Via d. Parione
V. dell' Anima
PIAZZA NAVONA
Corso del Rinascimento
Via Giustiniani
PIAZZA DELLA ROTONDA
V. Pastini
V. Seminario
Via dell'Umiltà
PIAZZA D. PILOTTA
Via Lucchesi
Tiber River
Lungotevere Gianicolense
Lungotevere Sangallo
Via d. Gonfalone
Via Scimia
Via Sora
V. Savelli
PIAZZA S. EUSTACCHIO
Via Santa
V. Monterone
Chiara
V. dl Torre Argentina
V. Pie di Marmo
PZA. DEI COLLEGIO ROMANO
Via S.S. Apostoli
PIAZZA DEI S.S. APOSTOLI
V. Leutari
PIAZZA SAN PANTALEO
Via del Pellegrino
Via Cappellari
LARGO TEATRO VALLE
Via del Gesù
PIAZZA GRAZIOLI
Via Gatta
LARGO PEROSI
Via Giulia
Via del Monserrato
PZA. DEL PARADISO
Corso Vittorio Emanuele II
LARGO DI TORRE ARGENTINA
Via del Plebiscito
Via di Orti di Albert
Ponte Mazzini
Via S. Eligio
LARGO DEI PALLARO
Via dei Chiavari
V. Monte Farina
Via d. Barbieri
LARGO ARENULA
PIAZZA D. GESÙ
PIAZZA SAN MARCO
TO THE FORUM AND THE PALATINE
Via delle Mantellate
Lungotevere dei Tebaldi
Via d. Armata
LGO. DEI LIBRARI
Vic. d. Chiodarolli
V. d. Botteghe Oscuro
V.S. Marco
Via d'Aracoeli
Lungotevere della Farnesina
Via della Lungara
Via S. Francesco di Sales
Vic. di Penitenza
Via d. Farnesi
Via Mascherone
V. Polverone
Via d. Giubbonari
V. Paganica
V. Falegnami
V. d. Funari
V. M. Caetani
PIAZZA CAMPITELLI
Via di Riari
Via dei Pettinari
PIAZZA V. PALLOTTI
Via del
V. d. Conservatorio
Via Arenula
PIAZZA CENCI
Via d. Portico d. Ottavia
Via Catalana
Via del Teatro di Marcello
Via Corsini
Ponte Sisto
Zoccolette
Lungotevere dei Vallati
Lung. dei Cenci
Via S. Dorotea
Via del Consolazione
N
PARCO GIANICOLENSE
Via della Scala
PIAZZA DI SANT' EGIDIO
Lungotevere Sanzio
Via del Moro
Ponte Garibaldi
ISOLA TIBERINA
Lung. di Pierleoni
Ponte Fabricio
MONTE CAPITOLINO
V. Petroselli
0
300 yards
300 meters
Via Garibaldi
Via d. Mattonato
TO PZA. DI S.M. IN TRASTEVERE
PIAZZA G. G. BELLI
10
11
12
13
14
15
17
18
19
20
21
22
23
24
25
26
27
28
29
30
31

Rome: Villa Borghese

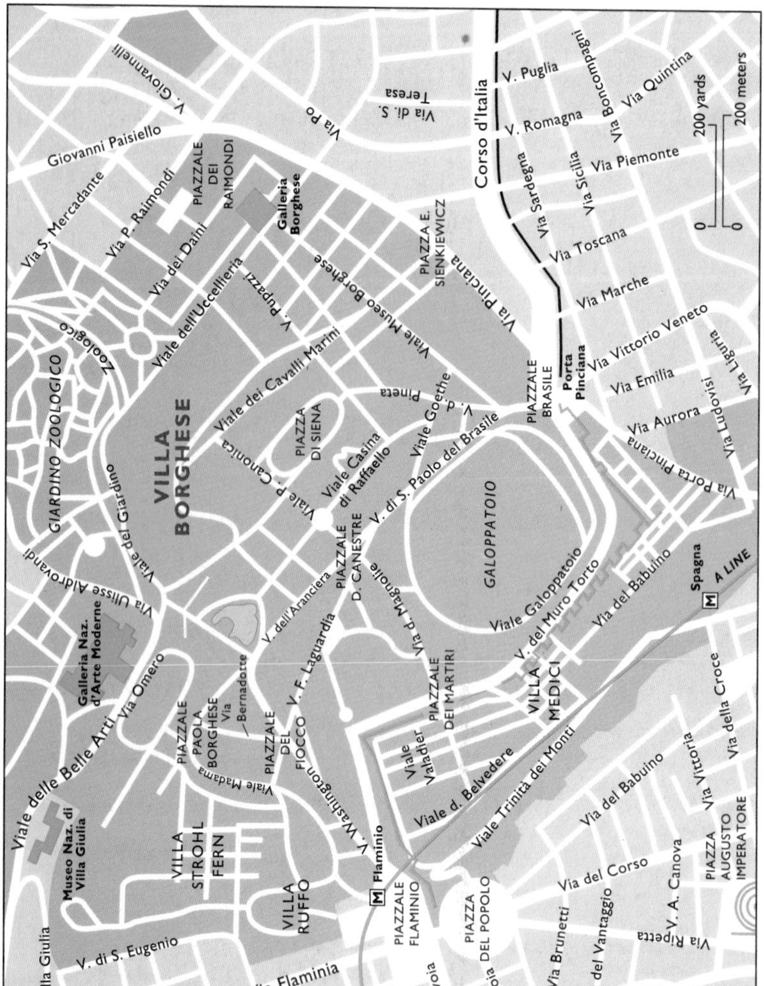

Villa Borghese
N
Corso d'Italia
V. Puglia
V. Romagna
Via Boncompagni
Via Quintina
Via Piemonte
Via Sicilia
Via Sardegna
Via Toscana
Via Marche
Via Vittorio Veneto
Via Liguria
Via Emilia
Via Aurora
Via Porta Pinciana
Via Ludovisi
Porta Pinciana
PIAZZALE BRASILE
Via Pinciana
PIAZZA E. SIENKIEWICZ
Via di S. Teresa
Via Po
V. Giovannelli
Giovanni Paisiello
Via S. Mercadante
Via P. Raimondi
PIAZZALE DEI RAIMONDI
Galleria Borghese
Viale Museo Borghese
Via dei Daini
Viale dell'Uccelleria
V. Pupazzi
Zoologico
GIARDINO ZOOLOGICO
VILLA BORGHESE
Viale dei Cavalli Marini
V. d. Pineta
PIAZZA DI SIENA
Viale P. Canonica
Viale Casina di Raffaello
Viale Goethe
V. di S. Paolo del Brasile
PIAZZALE D. CANESTRE
GALOPPATOIO
Viale Galoppatoio
V. del Muro Torto
Via del Babuino
Spagna
A LINE
Viale del Giardino
Via Ulisse Aldrovandi
Galleria Naz. d'Arte Moderne
V. dell'Aranciera
Via d. Magnolie
V. F. Laguardia
PIAZZALE DEI MARTIRI
VILLA MEDICI
Via Omero
PIAZZALE PAOLA BORGHESE
Via Bernadotte
PIAZZALE DEL FIOCCO
Viale Madama
V. Washington
Viale Valadier
Viale d. Belvedere
Viale Trinità dei Monti
Viale delle Belle Arti
Museo Naz. di Villa Giulia
VILLA STROHL FERN
VILLA RUFFO
Flaminio
PIAZZALE FLAMINIO
PIAZZA DEL POPOLO
Via del Corso
Via della Croce
Via Vittoria
PIAZZA AUGUSTO IMPERATORE
V. A. Canova
Via Ripetta
Via Brunetti
Via del Vantaggio
Via di Villa Giulia
V. di S. Eugenio
Via Flaminia
PIAZZA DELLA MARINA
V. D. A. Azuni
V. G. Pisanelli
V. Romanosi
V. Disavoia
Via Savoia
Lungo. in Augusta
Ponte Margherita
Lungo. d. Mellini
Lungo. Arnaldo da Brescia
Lungotevere delle Navi
Ponte Nenni
Ponte d. Risorg
Fiume Tevere
Ponte G. Matteotti
Lungo. Michelangelo
Lungotevere delle Armi
PIAZZA MONTE GRAPPA
PIAZZA DELLE CINQUE GIORNATE
PIAZZA D. LIBERTA
Via Fed. Cesi
Via G. Belli
Via Giulio Cesare
A LINE
Via degli Scipioni
Via Pompeo Magno
Via dei Gracchi
Via Valadier
PIAZZA COLA DI RIENZO
Via E. Q. Visconte
Viale Giuseppe Mazzini
Via Settembrini
Viale della Milizie
Lepanto
Via Marc. Colonna
Via Ezio
Via Boezio
0 200 yards
0 200 meters

■ Let's Go writers travel on your budget.

"Guides that penetrate the veneer of the holiday brochures and mine the grit of real life."

—The Economist

"The writers seem to have experienced every rooster-packed bus and lunar-surfaced mattress about which they write."

—The New York Times

"All the dirt, dirt cheap."

—People

■ Great for independent travelers.

"The guides are aimed not only at young budget travelers but at the independent traveler; a sort of streetwise cookbook for traveling alone."

—The New York Times

"Flush with candor and irreverence, chock full of budget travel advice."

—The Des Moines Register

"An indispensible resource, *Let's Go*'s practical information can be used by every traveler."

—The Chattanooga Free Press

■ Let's Go is completely revised each year.

"Only *Let's Go* has the zeal to annually update every title on its list."

—The Boston Globe

"Unbeatable: good sightseeing advice; up-to-date info on restaurants, hotels, and inns; a commitment to money-saving travel; and a wry style that brightens nearly every page."

—The Washington Post

■ All the important information you need.

"*Let's Go* authors provide a comedic element while still providing concise information and thorough coverage of the country. Anything you need to know about budget traveling is detailed in this book."

—The Chicago Sun-Times

"Value-packed, unbeatable, accurate, and comprehensive."

—Los Angeles Times

Let's Go Publications

Let's Go: Alaska & the Pacific Northwest 2001
Let's Go: Australia 2001
Let's Go: Austria & Switzerland 2001
Let's Go: Boston 2001 **New Title!**
Let's Go: Britain & Ireland 2001
Let's Go: California 2001
Let's Go: Central America 2001
Let's Go: China 2001
Let's Go: Eastern Europe 2001
Let's Go: Europe 2001
Let's Go: France 2001
Let's Go: Germany 2001
Let's Go: Greece 2001
Let's Go: India & Nepal 2001
Let's Go: Ireland 2001
Let's Go: Israel 2001
Let's Go: Italy 2001
Let's Go: London 2001
Let's Go: Mexico 2001
Let's Go: Middle East 2001
Let's Go: New York City 2001
Let's Go: New Zealand 2001
Let's Go: Paris 2001
Let's Go: Peru, Bolivia & Ecuador 2001 **New Title!**
Let's Go: Rome 2001
Let's Go: San Francisco 2001 **New Title!**
Let's Go: South Africa 2001
Let's Go: Southeast Asia 2001
Let's Go: Spain & Portugal 2001
Let's Go: Turkey 2001
Let's Go: USA 2001
Let's Go: Washington, D.C. 2001
Let's Go: Western Europe 2001 **New Title!**

Let's Go *Map Guides*

Amsterdam
Berlin
Boston
Chicago
Florence
Hong Kong
London
Los Angeles
Madrid
New Orleans
New York City
Paris
Prague
Rome
San Francisco
Seattle
Sydney
Washington, D.C.

Coming Soon: *Dublin* and *Venice*

EUROPE

2001

Rebecca S. Tinio editor
Amy M. Cain associate editor
Craig Chosiad associate editor
Victoria C. Hallett associate editor

researcher-writers
Katie Heikkinen
Jamie L. Jones
Rochelle Lundy

John Fiore map editor

St. Martin's Press New York

HELPING LET'S GO If you want to share your discoveries, suggestions, or corrections, please drop us a line. We read every piece of correspondence, whether a postcard, a 10-page email, or a coconut. Please note that mail received after May 2001 may be too late for the 2002 book, but will be kept for future editions. **Address mail to:**

Let's Go: Europe
67 Mount Auburn Street
Cambridge, MA 02138
USA

Visit Let's Go at **http://www.letsgo.com,** or send email to:

feedback@letsgo.com
Subject: "Let's Go: Europe"

In addition to the invaluable travel advice our readers share with us, many are kind enough to offer their services as researchers or editors. Unfortunately, our charter enables us to employ only currently enrolled Harvard students.

Distributed outside the USA and Canada by Macmillan.

ISBN: 0-312-24673-0

First edition
10 9 8 7 6 5 4 3 2 1

Let's Go: Europe is written by Let's Go Publications, 67 Mount Auburn Street, Cambridge, MA 02138, USA.

Printed in the USA on recycled paper with biodegradable soy ink.

ADVERTISING DISCLAIMER All advertisements appearing in Let's Go publications are sold by an independent agency not affiliated with the editorial production of the guides. Advertisers are never given preferential treatment, and the guides are researched, written, and published independent of advertising. Advertisements do not imply endorsement of products or services by Let's Go, and Let's Go does not vouch for the accuracy of information provided in advertisements.

If you are interested in purchasing advertising space in a Let's Go publication, contact: Let's Go Advertising Sales, 67 Mount Auburn St., Cambridge, MA 02138, USA.

HOW TO USE THIS BOOK

Welcome to *Let's Go: Europe 2001!* Whether your upcoming European adventure is akin to that thrilling first date, dinner with an old flame, or a golden anniversary, we can help you plan the perfect outing. We'll arm you with places to go, suave conversation topics, and all of the practical details to ensure that your excursion goes off without a hitch. Tongue-tied over coffee? Forget your wallet? Need a room? Fear not—*Let's Go* in hand, you'll dive into a love affair with Europe, new or renewed, like the savvy, swingin' romantic you know you are.

THE ORGANIZATION OF THIS BOOK

PLANNING AND PRIMPING. Get ready for your date with the first chapter of this book, **Discover Europe,** our recommendations for travel in Europe. **Suggested Itineraries** list what you shouldn't miss and how long it will take to see it. For those awkward silences over the appetizer, memorize (or, if necessary, jot down on a notecard) a few urbane references to Socrates and Surrealism, gleaned from the **European Culture from Athens to ABBA** chapter, our general introduction to the art, music, and literature of Europe. Meanwhile, the **Essentials** section outlines the practical information you will need to plan and carry out the date flawlessly (hint: bring a breath mint).

THE BIG NIGHT. The reservations are made and you look great—now head out on your date! We've organized your potential destinations alphabetically by country; look here for the perfect places to stay, dine, sightsee, party, or just relax. The **black tabs** in the margins will help you navigate between chapters quickly and easily.

PICK-UP LINES. *"Na Schatz, diese Nacht sollte nie zu Ende kommen...lass' uns nach Nordfinland im Winter."* (Translation: "Hey baby, I don't want this night to end...let's head to northern Finland in the winter.") To find other places where the sun never rises, consult the **time zone map** in our **appendix;** our **phrasebook** and **glossary** of foreign words supply the words of love in 24 European languages.

A FEW NOTES ABOUT LET'S GO FORMAT

RANKING ESTABLISHMENTS. In each section (accommodations, food, sights, etc.), we list establishments in order from best to worst. Our absolute favorites are denoted by the highest honor given out by Let's Go, the Let's Go thumbs-up (☒).

PHONE CODES AND TELEPHONE NUMBERS. Okay, tiger, the date went well, and you've got the digits—now get 'em right. The **phone code** for each region, city, or town appears opposite the name of that region, city, or town, and is denoted by the ☎ icon. **Phone numbers** in text are also preceded by the ☎ icon.

GRAYBOXES AND WHITEBOXES. Grayboxes at times provide wonderful cultural insight, at times simply crude humor. In any case, they're usually amusing, so enjoy. **Whiteboxes,** on the other hand, provide important practical information, such as warnings (☒) and helpful hints and further resources (☒).

BORDER CROSSINGS AND EXCURSIONS. For additional outings (perhaps a weekend fling?), we include helpful **border crossing** information in many chapters (look for the ☒ symbol), as well as **excursions** from major destinations (denoted by the ☒). Because you're *money*, baby, and you and Europe are a match made in heaven.

HOW NOT TO USE THIS BOOK: As part of a complete breakfast, a hat, an aid in hitchhiking (which *Let's Go* does not recommend), a weapon, a ☒Prince William homing device, an MSG substitute, or a doorstop (wait, we do that).

A NOTE TO OUR READERS The information for this book was gathered by *Let's Go* researchers from May through August of 2000. Each listing is based on one researcher's opinion, formed during his or her visit at a particular time. Those traveling at other times may have different experiences since prices, dates, hours, and conditions are always subject to change. You are urged to check the facts presented in this book beforehand to avoid inconvenience and surprises.

CONTENTS

MAPS

RESEARCHER-WRITERS

Katie Heikkinen *Finland*

She never did get to wear her capri pants, but Katie sure had style. Transforming the land of Moomins, saunas, and cell phones into her personal playground, Katie dazzled like the midnight sun 24-7. Mrs. Claus is probably still jealous. Her inner compass perfected directions as her discerning palate honed in on the finest lunch specials (especially the filling ones). Before the office's "it girl" moved on to Estonia for *Let's Go: Eastern Europe 2001*, everyone back home had become a proponent of Åland independence and developed a penchant for the way Swedes say "Åbo." Aaah-boh. So sexy.

Jamie L. Jones *Sweden and Denmark*

After landing in Stockholm, Jamie received the key to the city—and never looked back. A vet of *Let's Go: Germany 1999*, Jamie fell in love with her route, and we fell in love with her sophisticated, clean-as-a-whistle copy. Armed with exceptional technological skill, Jamie sent us memos, newsletters, and a restructured Sweden chapter sure to win everyone over to botels and reindeer. Stale sea biscuits? Questionable Danish fashion trends? This tourist office darling covered it all, sailing (on a shrimp cruise with inebriated locals, perhaps?) straight into *Let's Go* lore.

Rochelle Lundy *Iceland and Norway*

Forget what you see on TV—Rochelle was the ultimate Survivor as she conquered her 3D itinerary. Cool and composed in the face of stomach-churning ferries, nights at the airport, indefinite bus strikes, and an earthquake, Rochelle still found the time and energy to befriend elves in Iceland, trolls in Norway, polar bears in the Arctic Circle, and the occasional high school chum. After getting to know the gas station in Stykkishólmur *very* well, Rochelle worked her magic all over Norway. Our coverage—and the numerous fish she rescued—is incredibly grateful.

REGIONAL EDITORS AND RESEARCHER-WRITERS

LET'S GO: AUSTRIA AND SWITZERLAND 2001

Nathaniel V. Popper *Editor*
Rebecca L. Schoff *Associate Editor*
Emily Griffin *Lake Geneva, Lake Neuchâtel, Northeastern, Northwestern and Central Switzerland*
Glenn Kinen *Tyrol, Vorarlberg, Salzkammergut, Hohe Tauern National Park, and Stryria*
Kristin E. Meyer *The Jungfrau Region, Wallis, Italian Switzerland, Graubünden, Appenzell*
Diana P. Moreno *Vienna, Burgenland, Lower Austria, Linz, Salzburg, Carinthia, Graz*

LET'S GO: BRITAIN AND IRELAND 2001

Johs Pierce *Editor*
Lisa M. Herman *Associate Editor*
Teresa Crockett *Midlands, Northwest England, Southern and Central Scotland*
Emily A. Harrison *Wales, Midlands, Northwest England*
Winnie Li *Edinburgh, Central Scotland, Highlands and Islands*
Kate D. Nesin *East Anglia, Midlands, Northeast and Northwest England*
Jason Schwartz *South and Southwest England*

LET'S GO: EASTERN EUROPE 2001

Andrea Volfová *Editor*
Matthew DeTar Gibson, Xunhua Wong *Associate Editors*
Taryn Arthur *Moscow, St. Petersburg*
Jessica Lucy Berenbeim *Hungary*
Kate Damon *Bulgaria, Macedonia*
Michal Engelman *Southeastern Poland, Ukraine*
Kieran Fitzgerald *Bosnia-Herzegovina, Croatia*
Katie Heikkinen *Estonia*
Kit Hodge *Romania*
Katharine Holt *Poland*
Maxfield Morange *The Carpathians, Slovakia, Slovenia*

Jennifer O'Brien *Belarus, Kaliningrad, Latvia, Lithuania*
Nicholas Topjian *Czech Republic, Silesia*

LET'S GO: FRANCE 2001
Alexander F. Mindlin *Editor*
Jeffrey Dubner, Fiona McKinnon *Associate Editors*
David I. L. Beecher *Southwest France*
Sarah A. Dolgonos *Berry Limousin, Poitou-Charentes, and the Loire Valley*
Chloe Taylor Evans *Eastern Normandy and the Northeast*
Catherine Gowl *Brittany and western Normandy*
Jérôme Luc Martin *Provence, Lyon, Burgundy, and the Auvergne*
Matthew Sussman *Côte d'Azur, Corsica, and the Alps*

LET'S GO: GERMANY 2001
Paul C. Dilley *Editor*
Megan M. Anderson *Associate Editor*
David A. Boyajian *Bavaria*
Margaret Coe *Berlin, Sachsen, and Thüringen*
Karoun Demirjian *Niedersachsen, Nordrhein-Westfalia, and Rheinland-Pfalz*
Liz Glynn *Berlin, Hessen, Niedersachsen, Sachsen and Sachsen-Anhalt*
Dan Koski-Karell *Brandenburg, Hamburg, Mecklenburg-Vorpommern, and Schleswig-Holstein*
Aram Yang *Bavaria, Baden-Württemberg, and Hessen*

LET'S GO: GREECE 2001
Nora Brennan Morrison *Editor*
Jen Taylor *Associate Editor*
Erzulie Coquillon *Sterea Ellada, Saronic Gulf, Sporades, Evia, and Northeast Aegean Islands*
Ben Davis *Thessaly, Epirus, Macedonia, Thrace, and Northeast Aegean Islands*
Eric Green *Athens and Cyclades*
Deirdre Aoife O'Dwyer *Crete, Cyclades, and Northeast Aegean Islands*
Kristi Schaeffer *Peloponnese and Ionian Islands*
Rianna Stefanakis *Cyprus and Dodecanese*

LET'S GO: IRELAND 2001
Maja Groff *Editor*
Derek (Teddy) Wayne *Associate Editor*
Mandy Davis *Counties Armagh, Cavan, Clare, Fermanagh, Galway, Leitrim,*
Sarah C. Haskins *Counties Carlow, Dublin, Kildare, Kilkenny, Longford, Meath, Waterford, Westmeath, Wexford, Wicklow*
Kalen Ingram *Counties Cork, Kerry, Limerick, Tipperary, Waterford*
Ian T. McClure *Counties Antrim, Derry, Donegal, Down, Louth*

LET'S GO: ITALY 2001
Marc A. Wallenstein *Editor*
Fiona McKinnon, Matthew S. Ryan *Associate Editors*
Charles DeSimone *Southern Italy*
Shanya Dingle *Northeast Italy*
Amber Lavicka *Liguria*
Sarah Jessop *Sicily*
Marko Soldo *Lombardy and Piedmont*
Sam Spital *Central Italy*

LET'S GO: LONDON 2001
John T. Reuland *Editor*
Whitney K. Bryant, Daryl Sng, Tobie E. Whitman *London*

LET'S GO: PARIS 2001
Lucy Ives *Editor*
Alexander Reed Clark, Anna Kate Fishko, Alexandra Haggiag *Paris*

LET'S GO: ROME 2001
Brady R. Dewar *Editor*
Adriane Noel Giebel, Charles R. Scott, Jeff Zinsmeister *Rome*

LET'S GO: SPAIN AND PORTUGAL 2001

Meredith Petrin	*Editor*
Tova Carlin, Marla Kaplan	*Associate Editors*
Iciar Garcia	*Northwestern Spain and Northern Portugal*
Jennifer Hyman	*Barcelona, Balearic Islands, East Coast*
David Modigliani	*Extremadura, Madrid*
Alexandra Price	*Northeastern Spain*
Marcella Prieto	*Andalucía*
Luis Rego	*Portugal*

LET'S GO: TURKEY 2001

Elizabeth S. Daniel	*Editor*
Siobhan K. Quinlan	*Associate Editor*
Caitlin Aiko Harrington	*Western Mediterranean, Konya*
Peter Henninger	*İstanbul and Northwestern Turkey*
Inga Hunter	*Northwestern Turkey, Aegean Coast*
Alexander D. Schrank	*North Central Anatolia, Ankara, Black Sea Coast*
Selin Tüysüzoğlu	*Cappadocia, Northern Cyprus, Eastern Mediterranean*

LET'S GO: WESTERN EUROPE 2001

Katharine F. Douglas	*Editor*
Dan Barnes, Karen Kiang, Carla Mastraccio	*Associate Editors*
Cristin Hodgens	*Belgium, The Netherlands, Luxembourg*

ACKNOWLEDGMENTS

EUROPE THANKS: Our superb RW's, for conquering Scandinavia in style; Sarah and Melissa G., for all the lovin'; John for the maps, and Durcak for the whale; Molooshka, for making it all work; the Europod, for putting up with the cages and hanging on with us to the end; the regional researchers, for writing the book, and their editors, for helping us perfect it; our special place, the playground; and Sebastian, for never leaving us.

BECKY THANKS: My chickadees, who were just so good: Amy, for keeping me honest, Vicky, for teaching me to dance, and Craig, for always asking. Kate, for inspiring me to make beautiful spreadsheets. Sunny, Matt, Andrea, Dan, Karen, Carla, and Bede, for putting the "fun" in "funk." Everyone else at the *Go,* for smiling. Paul, for always being a gentleman. My roomies (school, summer, and temporary) for tolerating my vagrancy. Maria, Alex, Kim, Sarah, and everyone else who dragged me out of the office, and the Aments, for giving me a place to go. The Orchestra of the Holden Consort, for keeping me in tune. My family, for all of their support—nutritional, postal, and otherwise. And Seth, for always being on the other end of the line and making everything—eight months of everything, and more—so absolutely worth it.

AMY THANKS: Beckylia, the mama of all chickadees, for her turtle jokes and generosity. Vicky, for the giggly happiness, SSY apparel, and for introducing me to the world of Polly-o. Craig, for leprechaun humor and loving format. The ladies of EEUR and WEUR (and sometimes Matt), for dancing; and the guys, for tolerating the girliness. 7 Story St., for fulfilling the summer of stain, especially Blaz-dog, Chenaily-o, and McMurray. The playground, for the fireman's pole and fountains. Brandon, for his delivery service and help moving furniture. Bethesda, for having so many DJBs. William, my prince, for waiting for me. Shreena, Merran, Grace, Gita, Charlie, and Brian, for keeping in touch all summer. And Mom, Dad, James, and Michael, for loving their silly Moof.

CRAIG THANKS: (Beck/Vick/Am)y for humbling me with editorial prowess, making this book real, and somewhere along the way becoming friends; EEUR and GRE (esp. Nora) for help above and beyond the call; the ladies for dance and enthusiasm; the men for silent solidarity; all the Euro Pod and D.S. for putting up with me; Ankur for format fanaticism; Matt, Graeme, and Alex for talking; and Taryn for eXile. Also, Will, Akiva, and Richard for *Hamlet;* Tom for law; Nat and Helixcode for movies; Hans and Charlie, my hosts West; *The Onion* for my mug; Sam Sloan for everything; Sinatra for music; Grandma for longevity and generosity; Mom, Dad, and Lynn for love; and Costin.

VICKY THANKS: Becky, for Scooby snacks. Aimée, my long-lost Bethesda siamese twin—I feel like you're ready for SSY. Craig, for knowing that William wants a doll. My Eurotrashy pals: Sunny, for but, but but, but, but; Kate, for "Lucky;" Carla, for trips (and falls); DeTar, for blushing; Dan, for the window sill; and mini-Karen, for being mini. Super stain Blaz, guitar wonder Chenaily-o, decor master Murray, dragon slayer CT; Scooter, and my evil Viking for Good Times, cheese wars, bum baby bum, bye bye bye and bye bye cocktail. Georgia, for the keys to the Peab. SEAS, for Mather slumming. My fam, Cara, Rob (and the rest of the Brown house), Becca, Kirsten, Robby, my blockmates, the beautiful people of FM, THC, and another publication, for keeping me amused.

Editor
Rebecca S. Tinio
Associate Editors
Amy M. Cain, Craig Chosiad, Victoria C. Hallett
Managing Editors
Melissa Gibson, Sarah Jacoby
Map Editors
Mike Durcak, John Fiore

Publishing Director
Kaya Stone
Editor-in-Chief
Kate McCarthy
Production Manager
Melissa Rudolph
Cartography Manager
John Fiore
Editorial Managers
Alice Farmer, Ankur Ghosh, Aarup Kubal, Anup Kubal
Financial Manager
Bede Sheppard
Low-Season Manager
Melissa Gibson
Marketing & Publicity Managers
Olivia L. Cowley, Esti Iturralde
New Media Manager
Daryush Jonathan Dawid
Personnel Manager
Nicholas Grossman
Photo Editor
Dara Cho
Production Associates
Sanjay Mavinkurve, Nicholas Murphy, Rosalinda Rosalez, Matthew Daniels, Rachel Mason, Daniel Visel
Some Design
Matthew Daniels
Office Coordinators
Sarah Jacoby, Chris Russell

Director of Advertising Sales
Cindy Rodriguez
Senior Advertising Associates
Adam Grant, Rebecca Rendell
Advertising Artwork Editor
Palmer Truelson

President
Andrew M. Murphy
General Manager
Robert B. Rombauer
Assistant General Manager
Anne E. Chisholm

N
Reykjavík
ICELAND
Norwegian Sea
0
400 miles
0
400 kilometers
Faroe Islands
Trondheim
Shetland Islands
ATLANTIC OCEAN
NORWAY
Bergen
Oslo
Orkney Islands
NORTHERN IRELAND
SCOTLAND
North Sea
SWEDEN
Glasgow
Edinburgh
Göteborg
Belfast
IRELAND
DENMARK
GREAT BRITAIN
Dublin
Copenhagen
Hamburg
WALES
ENGLAND
Cardiff
NETHERLANDS
Amsterdam
Berlin
London
Brussels
GERMANY
Bonn
Frankfurt
BELGIUM
Prague
LUXEMBOURG
CZECH REPUBLIC
Paris
LIECHTENSTEIN
Munich
Nantes
Zurich
Vienna
Bay of Biscay
SWITZERLAND
Bern
AUSTRIA
Geneva
Ljubljana
Bordeaux
Lyon
SLOVENIA
Santiago de Campostela
Milan
Venice
FRANCE
Zagreb
CROATIA
Marseille
Nice
Florence
BOSNIA-HERZEGOVINA
PORTUGAL
ANDORRA
MONACO
SAN MARINO
Dubrovnik
Madrid
Corsica (Fr.)
Adriatic
Lisbon
Barcelona
Rome
SPAIN
ITALY
Valencia
Naples
Seville
Sardinia (It.)
Tyrrhenian Sea
Granada
Balearic Islands (Sp.)
Tangier
GIBRALTAR
Mediterranean
Algiers
Sicily
Rabat
Sea
MOROCCO
ALGERIA
TUNISIA
MALTA

Europe
Honnigsvåg
Rovaniemi
meå
Gulf of Bothnia
FINLAND
L. Onega
L. Ladoga
Helsinki
Tallinn
St. Petersburg
Stockholm
ESTONIA
Volga R.
Nizhny Novgorod
Rīga
LATVIA
Moscow
Baltic Sea
LITHUANIA
Vilnius
RUSSIA
RUSSIA
Gdańsk
Minsk
Warsaw
BELARUS
KAZAKHSTAN
Volgograd
POLAND
Kiev
Kharkiv
Dnieper River
Kraków
Lviv
UKRAINE
SLOVAKIA
ratislava
Caspian Sea
Budapest
MOLDOVA
Sea of Azov
Chișinău
HUNGARY
Odessa
Rostov-na-Donu
ROMANIA
Yalta
GEORGIA
Belgrade
Bucharest
YUGOSLAVIA
Black Sea
ARMENIA
Sarajevo
BULGARIA
MONTENEGRO
Sofia
AZERBAIJAN
FYR MACEDONIA
Istanbul
Tiranë
Ankara
IRAN
Thessaloniki
ALBANIA
Aegean Sea
TURKEY
Izmir
onian Sea
Athens
SYRIA
IRAQ
GREECE
Nicosia
Sea of Crete
Crete
LEBANON
CYPRUS

DISCOVER EUROPE

The days of the Romans, Huns, Byzantines, Franks, Vikings, and Ottomans are over, but Europe continues to be conquered—by droves of visitors after cultural treasures, reckless nightlife, deeply tanned languor, and pulse-quickening outdoor adventure. Although its paths are well-worn, Europe is never clichéd or yesterday's news. Certainly, the continent wears its history on its sleeve, from its glorious museums and extravagant monuments to the rubble of war-damaged sites. But Europe pushes inevitably forward, with a spirit of alliance in the west and new independence in the east. Indulge liberally in the offerings that have delighted visitors for centuries—yes, the usual Western European suspects really are that amazing, and will inspire superlatives in any language. Europe's true splendor, however, is in the cacophonous symphony of identities that resonates throughout the *entire* continent. Relish Europe's dissonances as well as its harmonies, sample its more exotic flavors, and pick up some phrases in a language you never knew existed; discover a continent as new as it is old and forge your own journey.

FACTS AND FIGURES

POPULATION: 727,000,000 (1995).

LANGUAGES: Over 60 native tongues in three major language families: **Romance, Germanic,** and **Slavic.**

Europe's most multilingual citizens are the **Danes**–almost half of them speak **3.4** languages.

RELIGIONS: Catholic (36.97%), Eastern Orthodox (23.59%), Protestant (10.93%), Jewish (0.33%).

ALCOHOL: In 1995, Europeans consumed **7L of pure alcohol per person.** It would take **3.8 billion** half-liters of beer to fill London's Millennium Dome.

LAND MASS: 4 million sq. mi.

MOUNTAIN RANGES: Sierra Nevada, Pyrenees, Alps, Apennines, Carpathians, Balkans, and Urals.

RIVERS: Danube, Dnieper, Don, Rhine, Volga, Vistula, Elbe, Rhône, and Oder.

THE CONTINENT THAT COULD: Europe is traversed by 147,760km of **electrified rail lines.**

SWITCHED ON: Although Europe has one-fifteenth of the world's landmass and one-seventh its population, it generates **one-fourth** of the world's electricity.

THINGS TO DO

Europe is a cacophony, yada yada yada, which means it can be as overwhelming as it is exciting. Here we humbly suggest ways to make sense of it all. Museum hoppers, ruins lovers, hikers, partyers, and sun-worshipers, check out the **themed highlights** that follow. Peruse our **Let's Go Picks** for quirky gems, and follow along on our **Suggested Itineraries.** For more country-specific attractions, see the **Discover** sections at the beginning of each chapter, and for advice on when to go, consult the **Essentials** section (p. 9). But don't let us cramp your style—mix and match, choose your own adventure, and make Europe *yours*.

THE OLD AND THE BEAUTIFUL

Museum lovers, look no further—these cultural wonders are the best Europe has to offer. **London** is one of Europe's finest museum cities (p. 152): ogle the Rosetta Stone and other imperialist booty at the **British Museum;** saunter through the histories of art, design, and style at the **Victoria and Albert Museum;** and don't miss the spectacular modern art at the **Tate Gallery.** On the other side of the Chunnel, **Paris** is just as impressive (p. 319)—the *Venus de Milo* and *Mona Lisa* at the **Louvre** will stop you in your tracks; the **Musée d'Orsay** will impress with all that is Impressionist; and the pipes and modern art of the **Centre National d'Art et de Culture Georges-Pompidou** will wriggle their way into your heart. Drop down to Spain for **Bilbao's** striking **Museo Guggenheim** (p. 887) and **Madrid's** stunning museums (p. 832): the **Prado** shelters the world's largest collection of paintings; the **Museo Thyssen-Bornemizsa** is practically the *Cliffs Notes* of major artistic trends in painting; and the **Museo Nacional Centro de Arte Reina Sofía** harbors Picasso's *Guernica.* Delight in **Barcelona's** fanciful *Modernista* buildings and its museums devoted to Picasso and Miró (p. 867).

Want more art? Try **Italy.** First stop: **Venice** (p. 602), whose winding waterways embrace the Venetian offerings of the **Accademia** and the modern art of the **Collezione Guggenheim.** Next up: **Florence** (p. 629), home of the Renaissance; you could lounge for an entire day at the splendid **Uffizi,** then drool for another at the image of human perfection, Michelangelo's *David,* in the **Accademia.** The **Sistine Chapel,** in the **Vatican Museums** in Rome (p. 577), will knock off your stinky socks. In Central Europe, **Vienna** hosts the renowned **Kunsthistoriches Museum** and the Klimt-rich **Austrian Gallery** (p. 99). Across the German border, wander through **Munich's Deutsches Museum** and twin **Pinakotheks** (p. 454) before continuing north to **Weimar,** birthplace of the **Bauhaus** architectural movement (p. 424). **Berlin**'s excellent museums will make you feel at home in a black turtleneck (p. 402), while Hamburg's **Erotic Art Museum** could make you feel at home without it, too. Believe it or not, the biggest sin you could commit in **Amsterdam** (p. 684) would be to miss the **Rijksmuseum;** note also the **van Gogh Museum** and the why-the-heck-not **Hash Marijuana Hemp Museum.**

In Russia, **Moscow's Kremlin** once contained the secrets to an empire; it still holds the legendary Fabergé eggs (p. 791). The **Hermitage,** in **St. Petersburg,** holds the world's largest art collection (p. 802). Budapest's **Museum of Fine Arts** houses little-seen but nonetheless spectacular works by Raphael, Rembrandt, and the rest of the usual suspects (p. 520). Finally, Rīga's **Occupation Museum,** depicting the Soviet occupation, may be the finest museum in the Baltics (p. 656).

RAMPARTS, RUINS, AND RELICS

For those who prefer their history in the wild instead of a museum case, Europe's castles, churches, and ruins are a dream come true. In London, royals do the waving thing around **Buckingham Palace** and **St. James's Palace** (p. 165), while choirboys croon at **Westminster Abbey** (p. 164) and **St. Paul's Cathedral** (p. 167). Venture away from the city to ponder the mysteries of **Stonehenge** (p. 184) and scale the towers of magnificent **Warwick Castle** (p. 191). Across the water, don't miss Paris's breathtaking **Cathédrale de Notre-Dame** (p. 334). Elsewhere in France, the *châteaux* of the **Loire Valley** (p. 354) and Normandy's fortified abbey of **Mont-St-Michel** (p. 350) are must-sees, or follow in the footsteps of pilgrims to **Lourdes** (p. 363). To the south, Spain houses the largest Gothic cathedral in the world, in **Seville** (p. 853), as well as Madrid's amazingly luxurious **Palacio Real** (p. 839). Muslim-infused southern Spain also awaits, offering the **mosque** in **Córdoba** (p. 849) and the **Alhambra** in **Granada** (p. 864). In **Italy, Rome** almost invented architecture as we know it (p. 577); can we say **Pantheon, Colosseum,** and **Forum?** Oh yeah, and Michelangelo's *Pietà* in **St. Peter's Basilica.** Dive off the heel of the boot into **Greece,** where the crumbling **Acropolis,** the very foundation of Western civilization, still towers above **Athens** (p. 477). After visiting one of the foremost collections of classical art at Athens' **National Archaeological Museum,** journey to the navel of the ancient world to learn your fate from the **oracle** at **Delphi** (p. 484) or visit *the* **temple of Apollo** on **Delos** (p. 499). Across the

Aegean, discover İstanbul's Byzantine **Hagia Sophia** and Ottoman **Blue Mosque** (p. 945), not neglecting the nerve center of the Ottoman Empire, **Topkapi Palace** (p. 952), or the Classical finds at **Ephesus** (p. 961).

In Switzerland, Lord Byron once scratched his name into a pillar in Montreux's chilling **Chateau de Chillon** (p. 925), not far from Lausanne and its spectacular Gothic **cathedral** (p. 924). Go a little crazy in **Mad King Ludwig's castles,** in the Bavarian Alps (p. 468) of Germany, and marvel at the optical illusion that makes Denmark's **Egeskov Slot** appear to float on water (p. 283). The kaleidoscopic onion domes of **St. Basil's Cathedral** are Moscow's emblem (p. 797), and **Prague Castle** has been the seat of the Bohemian government for 1000 years (p. 259).

THE GREAT OUTDOORS

Enough urban warrior—you're ready to commune with the streams, hug a few trees, and heed the call of the wild. Britain brims with national parks; our favorite is the **Lake District National Park** (p. 198). For more dramatic scenery, head north to the **Scottish Highlands;** the **Isle of Skye** (p. 218) and the **Outer Hebrides** (p. 218) are particularly breathtaking. Ireland's **Ring of Kerry** provides wee Irish towns (p. 559), while **Killarney National Park** features spectacular mountains (p. 558). In the French Alps, **Chamonix** tempts skiers with some of the world's steepest slopes (p. 383), while **Grenoble** brims with hiking opportunities (p. 382). In Spain, the **Parque Nacional de Ordesa** is set among the breath-taking Pyrenees (p. 881). Across the Mediterranean, the **Aeolian Islands** north of Sicily boast pristine beaches, belching volcanoes, and bubbling thermal springs (p. 650). Drop down to Greece and hike up **Mt. Olympus,** where the gods used to sip ambrosia; a two-day hike will bring you to the summit (p. 490). In **Crete,** get in touch with your inner mountain goat with a trek down the **Samaria Gorge** (p. 504). Turkey's **Butterfly Valley,** near **Fethiye,** will enchant and astound (p. 964). The dramatic **Tatra** mountain range stretches across Eastern Europe; lace up your hiking boots in Slovakia's **Starý Smokovec** (p. 818) or Poland's **Zakopane** (p. 752). Austria's **Kitzbühel** (p. 124) and **Innsbruck** (p. 120) quench every hiking and skiing desire. For fresh Swiss Alpine air, head to the glaciers of **Grindelwald** (p. 937), make the pilgrimage to the **Matterhorn,** near **Zermatt** (p. 938), or dive into the adventure sports of **Interlaken** (p. 935). From there, disappear into Germany's buckling **Bavarian Alps** (p. 468), then take to the hiking trails of the **Black Forest** (p. 451). If you dare, tackle the **fjords** and **glaciers** of western Norway (p. 721).

FÊTES! FESTAS! ¡FIESTAS! FESTIVALS!

The Europeans, they throw a damn good party. In the second half of February, **Cadíz** (p. 858) and **Nice** (p. 373) go crazy for **Carnaval,** when people start dancing in the streets. Right on its toes, the Spanish city of **Valencia** sets effigies on fire and prances around wildly for **Las Fallas** (Mar. 12-19; p. 866). Next up, **Seville** steals the scene during **Semana Santa** (Palm Sunday to Good Friday; p. 853), parading around town venerating sacred icons, then shakes loose with the **Feria de Abril** (late Apr. to early May; p. 853). Enjoy the outdoor concerts and pale, glowing night skies of St. Petersburg's **White Nights Festival** (end of May to end of June; p. 808). **Dublin** celebrates James Joyce during **Bloomsday** with a week of celebration around June 16 (p. 546). Make a date in Scandinavia for **Midsummer** (June 22-23), when you get to dance around bonfires and midsummer poles. Horse races take **Siena** by storm during **Il Palio** (July 2 and Aug. 16; p. 639). Drink your wine and have the time of your life when the bulls run for **San Fermines** in **Pamplona** (July 6-14; p. 882). During the concurrent **Love Parade** in **Berlin,** yes is the word (2nd weekend in July; p. 402). The **Festival d'Avignon** brings in a crazy range of events from early July to early August (p. 366). Cross the Channel for the **Edinburgh International Festival,** which entertains with all things artsy (Aug. 12-Sept. 1; p. 206). The efficient Germans even party well; head to **Munich** for the world-famous **Oktoberfest,** which (strangely enough) starts September 22 and then goes strong until October 7 (p. 454). Rest from October to March, then begin the madness all over again.

LET'S GO SPRING BREAK

So you've seen all the sights and climbed all the mountains—now soak up the rays. And when the sun goes down, nightlife wakes up. Check out the scene in **London** (p. 152) and **Edinburgh,** with the highest concentration of pubs in Europe (p. 206); when it's not raining, even England hosts a tempting beach culture. The old artists' enclave of **St. Ives** offers sparkling beaches and blue blue water (p. 185), while **Newquay** is a surfing capital (p. 185). **Malin Head,** at Ireland's northernmost point on the **Inishowen Peninsula,** offers a beach covered with semi-precious stones (p. 566). Dublin's hearty pub scene knocks back a few at **Temple Bar, Grafton St.,** and the **Guinness Brewery** (p. 551). France's **St-Malo** combines the beauty and history of Normandy (p. 352). Skip down to Portugal, where you can party all night and sun all day along the **Algarve, Lagos** in particular (p. 768). Along Spain's **Costa del Sol, Marbella's** beaches are lined with hip, happening clubs (p. 860), while **Tossa de Mar** along the **Costa Blanca** boasts beaches, red cliffs, small bays, and medieval alleys (p. 879). Spain's **Balearic Islands** are a must for party kids; **Ibiza** (p. 888) is manic by night. Dance your way through the mad nightlife of **Madrid** (p. 842), **Barcelona** (p. 876), and the **French Riviera** (p. 369) before moving along to Italy and the fishing villages of **Cinque Terre,** which cling to cliffs over the bright blue sea (p. 625). Farther north in Italy, Europe's deepest lake, **Lake Como,** is peaceful perfection (p. 613), and **Milan**'s night scene is chic and dynamic (p. 615). Most visitors to Italy don't venture south of Rome—a huge mistake, given the breathtaking, almost unspeakable, beauty of the **Amalfi Coast,** where the bikini was invented (p. 647). The **Blue Grotto** glows nearby on the island of **Capri** (p. 649). Bop down to the Greek islands: **Corfu** harbors the beautiful beach of **Agios Gordios** (p. 495); as the sun sets over volcanic beaches in **Santorini,** the bars salute Helios with classical music (p. 501). **Ios,** a frat party run amok, has more places to get drunk than anywhere else in Greece (p. 501). Drag your tanned and tired self to the **Blue Lagoon** of **Ölüdeniz,** near **Fethiye,** in **Turkey** (p. 964). Discover your inner beer connoisseur in the brewhouses of **Munich** (p. 454), and head to eastern **Berlin** (p. 402) for that city's best clubs. **Prague** (p. 249) and **Moscow** (p. 791) are Eastern Europe's hottest spots after sunset.

LET'S GO PICKS

BEST PLACE TO GET STEAMY: Pamper yourself in the ***hamams*** of İstanbul (p. 945), Stuttgart's **mineral baths** (p. 450), or a Finnish **sauna** (p. 307), then rinse off under Geneva's **Jet d'Eau** (p. 923).

BEST PLACE TO DAYDREAM: Contemplate your navel on Heidelberg's **Philosophenweg** (p. 448) or at desolate **Sagres** (p. 769), for centuries considered the end of the world.

BEST PLACE TO DREAM ON: Ogle Europe's hottest men and giant phalli (coincidence?) in **Malta** (p. 679).

BEST PLACE TO LOSE SLEEP: Party 'til dawn in the clubs of **Madrid** (p. 832), the jazz joints in **Prague,** (p. 249), and decadent **Juan-les-Pins** (p. 372).

BEST SUBWAY: The **Moscow Metro** (p. 799), one of the most beautiful in the world, is worth its own tour.

BEST PLACE TO PLAY: Find your inner child at **Tivoli** (p. 277), consult with the world's favorite fat man in **Santa Claus' Village** (p. 311), and go to pieces at **Legoland** (p. 285).

BEST PLACE TO SNAG A ROYAL: Mingle with blue bloods (or just feel like one) on the slopes of **Val d'Aran** (p. 880), at Sweden's **Kungliga Slottet** (p. 902), and on **The Mall** in London (p. 165).

BEST BOY BAND: The **Vienna Boys' Choir** wows fans every Sunday at the Hofburg in Vienna (p. 110).

BEST TAN LINES: Get tube top-ready at the nude (or semi-nude) beaches at **Lipari** (p. 651), **Cap d'Ail** (p. 378), and **Texel** (p. 704).

BEST PLACE TO MAKE A BET: The **Oracle at Delphi** (p. 484) offers advice on all matters, financial or otherwise.

SUGGESTED ITINERARIES

THE BASICS

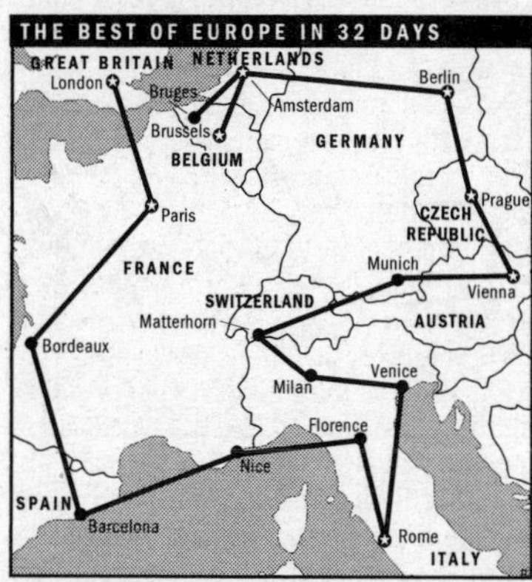

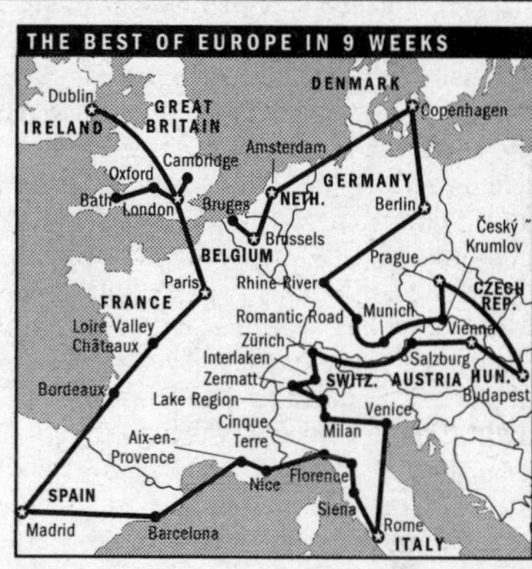

THE BEST OF EUROPE IN 32 DAYS (1-MONTH EURAILPASS) Start in **London,** spinning from theater to museum to club (4 days; p. 152). Chunnel to the sights, shops, and sweets of **Paris** (4 days; p. 319), then sample the fermented delicacies of **Bordeaux** (1 day; p. 360) en route to glittering **Barcelona** (2 days; p. 867). Hit the French Riviera hard in **Nice** (1 day; p. 373), then dive into Renaissance art in **Florence** (2 days; p. 629) and pull Adam's finger in **Rome** (3 days; p. 577). Float down **Venice's** canals by gondola (2 days; p. 602) and keep on keepin' on in the clubs of **Milan** (1 day; p. 615). Conquer the **Matterhorn** (1 day; p. 938), then recount your hiking adventures in the brewhouses of **Munich** (2 days; p. 454), followed by coffee in **Vienna** (2 days; p. 99). Join the tourist stampede to nonetheless enrapturing **Prague** (2 days; p. 249) then head up to sprawling, overwhelming **Berlin** (2 days; p. 402). Indulge in the goods in **Amsterdam** (2 days; p. 684), then finish off with a day in Tintin's **Brussels** (p. 131) or beautiful **Bruges** (p. 136).

THE BEST OF EUROPE IN 9 WEEKS (2-MONTH EURAILPASS) From **London** (4 days; p. 152), get studious for a day in **Oxford** (p. 186) or **Cambridge** (p. 191), then catch a cheap flight to stylish, energetic **Dublin** (2 days, p. 546). Back in England, sightsee in **Bath** (1 day; p. 191), then chunnel from London to the museums and cafes of **Paris** (4 days; p. 319). Ogle the gorgeous chateaux of the **Loire Valley** (1 day; p. 354), then warm up with a bottle of fine wine in **Bordeaux** (1 day; p. 360) before proceeding south to the all-night party in **Madrid** (2 days; p. 832). Marvel at the architectural gems of **Barcelona** (3 days; p. 867) then spend a day each in **Aix-en-Provence** (p. 368) and **Nice** (p. 373). Replenish in Italy's **Cinque Terre** (1 day; p. 625) and continue on to the orange roofs of **Florence** (2 days; p. 629). Stop at stunning **Siena** (1 day; p. 639) en route to **Rome** (3 days; p. 577), then wind through **Venice** (2 days; p. 602) on your way to posh **Milan** (1 day; p. 615) and the idyllic **Lake Region** (2 days; p. 613). Scale the Swiss Alps around **Zermatt** (1 day; p. 938) and **Interlaken** (1 day; p. 935), then do high culture in **Zürich** (1 day; p. 928) before indulging your passion for *The Sound of Music* in **Salzburg** (1 day; p. 112). After **Vienna** (2 days; p. 99), soak in the baths of **Budapest** (3 days; p. 512), then head to everybody's favorite city, **Prague** (3 days; p. 249), and everybody's new favorite city, **Český Krumlov** (1 day; p. 265). Love your beer in **Munich,** then take a sobering daytrip to **Dachau** (3 days; p. 454). Traverse the **Romantic Road** (2 days; p. 466), then cruise down the spectacular **Rhine River** (2 days; p. 434). From **Berlin** (3 days; p. 402), head north to cosmopolitan **Copenhagen** (2 days; p. 272) and continue on to **Amsterdam** (3 days; p. 684). Spend a day each in **Brussels** (p. 131) and **Bruges** (p. 136) to round out your trip.

REGIONAL ADD-ONS

THE BEST OF BRITAIN AND IRELAND

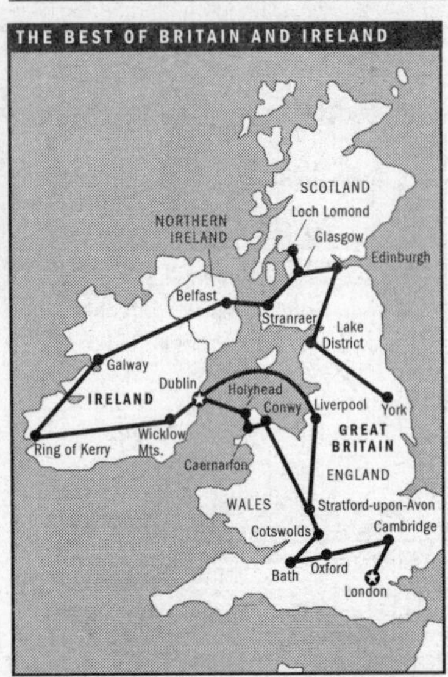

THE BEST OF SPAIN AND PORTUGAL

THE BEST OF BRITAIN AND IRELAND (21 DAYS) After visiting London, Bath, Cambridge, and Oxford on the two-month itinerary (see above), trek through the village-dotted **Cotswolds** (1 day; p. 189) to **Stratford-upon-Avon** (1 day; p. 190), Shakespeare's hometown, also near Warwick Castle. On to **Liverpool** (2 days; p. 196), home of the Beatles; or **Conwy** and **Caernarfon** (p. 205), known for their castles. Depending on which route you choose, cross the Irish Sea from either Liverpool or Holyhead (near Conwy and Caernarfon; p. 201) to **Dublin** (3 days; p. 546), home to James Joyce and Guinness. Answer the call of rural Ireland in the heather-covered **Wicklow Mountains** (1 day; p. 554) and the **Ring of Kerry** (2½ days; p. 559). **Galway** (1½ days; p. 562), a center of Irish culture, is also close to the limestone landscape of the Aran Islands. Then on to politically divided and exciting **Belfast** (2 days; p. 567). From there it's back across the Irish Sea to **Stranraer,** then on a train to energetic **Glasgow** (1 day; p. 212) and nearby **Loch Lomond.** Explore historic **Edinburgh** (3 days; p. 206) and the sublime **Lake District** (2 days; p. 198); **York** (1 day; p. 197) completes the southbound journey. Return to London to kick back with a West End play or a Guinness.

THE BEST OF SPAIN AND PORTUGAL (23 DAYS) Hop off the Paris-Madrid train at gorgeous **San Sebastián** (2 days; p. 883), then check out the new Guggenheim in **Bilbao** (1 day; p. 886) before having some urban fun in **Madrid** (3 days; p. 832). Take a daytrip to the winding streets of **Toledo** (1 day; p. 843), then cross the border into Portugal to marvel at the painted tiles in **Lisbon** (2½ days; p. 758). Bake in the sun along the Algarve in **Lagos** (2½ days; p. 768) before returning to Spain for **Seville**'s flower-filled plazas (2½ days; p. 853). Don't forget to see **Córdoba**'s stunning mosque (1 day; p. 849). Tan some more in **Marbella** (1½day; p. 860), then love the Alhambra in **Granada** (2 days; p. 861). In northeastern Spain, hit the sunny **Costa Brava** (p. 879; 2 days), the Dalí Museum in **Figueres** (1 day; p. 878), and medieval **Girona** (1 day; p. 879). Then continue with the two-month itinerary from **Barcelona** (p. 867).

THE BEST OF GREECE AND TURKEY (27-28 DAYS) Hop off the boot from **Brindisi** (p. 650) or **Bari,** where overnight ferries go to Greece (1 day). Get off at **Corfu** (1 day; p. 495), beloved by literary luminaries and partyers alike, then continue on to **Patras** (1 day; p. 486). Discover the "mysteries of love" in the ruins of **Corinth** (1 day; p. 489). On to chaotic **Athens,** a jumble of things ancient and modern (2 days; p. 477), then the Cyclades. Party all night long on **Mykonos** (p. 498), then daytrip to sacred **Delos** (p. 499)

BEST OF GREECE AND TURKEY

before continuing on to the earthly paradise of **Santorini** (total 4 days; p. 501). Catch the ferry to **Crete,** where chic **Iraklion** and **Knossos,** home to the Minotaur, await (2 days; p. 502). Base yourself in **Rethymno** or **Hania** and hike the spectacular **Samaria Gorge** (2 days; p. 503). Backtrack to Iraklion to catch the ferry to the Dodecanese, hitting historical **Rhodes** (2 days; p. 506) and partying in **Kos** (1 day; p. 506). Cross over to **Bodrum,** Turkey, the "Bedroom of the Mediterranean" (2 days; p. 962). From there, two routes diverge; they both meet up in **Cappadocia.** If you've come to see **ruins,** head up to **Kuşadasi** to check out the crumbling magnificence at **Ephesus** (1½ day; p. 960). Move on to the thermal springs of **Pamukkale** and **Aphrodisias** (2½ day; p. 962); then on to Cappadocia. Or, if you're into **beaches,** head from Bodrum to **Fethiye** and serene **Ölüdeniz** (1 day; p. 964) and the eternal flame of **Olimpos** (2 days; p. 965); then experience the surreal world of **Göreme** in Cappadocia (2 days; p. 968). Take an overnight bus to **İstanbul** and go a little crazy (3 days; p. 945) before heading home or linking up with the **Black Sea** itinerary.

THE BEST OF BALTIC EUROPE (22 DAYS) Take the ferry from Helsinki or the train from Central or Eastern Europe to reach **Tallinn's** charming medieval streets (2 days; p. 291), then relax on the tranquil and secluded **Estonian Islands** (4 days; p. 295). Move on to lively **Tartu,** the oldest city in the Baltics (2 days; p. 294), before immersing yourself in the Soviet-ness of **Riga** (2 days; p. 654). Swing over to **Klaipėda** in Lithuania and relax on the dreamy beach at **Nida** (2 day; p. 666). Continue to up-and-coming **Vilnius** (3 days; p. 662), one of the many "New Pragues," then get some shut-eye on the night train to **Moscow,** where you can survey Red Square and see history in action (4 days; p. 791). Cap it off spending some time in **St. Petersburg,** home of the ornate delights of the Hermitage (3 days; p. 802).

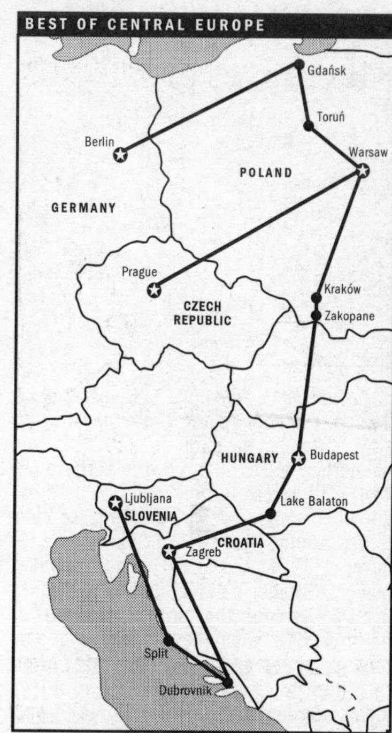

THE BEST OF CENTRAL EUROPE (22-24 DAYS) Link up from **Berlin** to **Gdańsk** (1 day; p. 744) stopping off in **Toruń,** the lovely home of Copernicus (1 day; p. 747) on the way to sprawling and chaotic **Warsaw** (3 days; p. 736). Or, skip Gdańsk and go directly from **Prague** to **Warsaw.** From there, trendy **Kraków** (3 days; p. 747) awaits, as does fabulous hiking in the Tatra Mountains surrounding **Zakopane** (2 days; p. 752). Vibrant **Budapest** is next (3 days; p. 512), then succumb to **Lake Balaton's** warm, shallow waters (2 days; p. 525). In Croatia, groove in hip, happening **Zagreb** (2 days; p. 236), then sample the delights of the Dalmatian Coast in **Dubrovnik** (3 days; p. 239) and **Split** (2 days; p. 238). Pass through delightful **Ljubljana** (2 days; p. 823) before linking back up with the two-month basic route by hopping on a train to Venice or Vienna.

THE BEST OF SCANDINAVIA (22 DAYS) From **Copenhagen** (p. 272), be true to thine own self with a daytrip (1 day) to the glorious castles of **Frederiksborg** (p. 280), **Roskilde** (p. 280), or **Elsinore** (p. 280). Cruise through **Odense** to the beautiful, quiet island of **Ærø** (3½ days; p. 283). Backtrack through Odense to Denmark's second city, **Århus** (2½ days; p. 284), then catch a ferry from Hirtshals to **Kristiansand,** Norway

(1 day; p. 727). Trek up to lovely **Bergen** (2 days; p. 717) before diving into the fjords (2 days); marvel at the natural wonders that are **Sognefjord** (p. 721) and **Geirangerfjord** (p. 724). Cut across to posh **Oslo** (3 days; p. 710) and sleep your way on the night train to **Stockholm,** the jewel of Scandinavia (2 days; p. 897). Take a daytrip to **Uppsala,** home of Sweden's oldest university (1 day; p. 905). Hop on the ferry to **Helsinki** (2 days; p. 300), where east meets west, and daytrip to **Porvoo** (1 day; p. 305). After returning to Stockholm, head south to friendly **Gothenburg** (1½ days; p. 909) and then take the ferry back to Copenhagen via **Malmö** (½ day; p. 907).

THE BEST OF THE BLACK SEA (19 DAYS) From **İstanbul,** discover the lovely beach town of **Sozopol** (2 days; p. 230) on the Bulgarian Black Sea coast. Journey through Sofia to **Bucharest,** once the gem of

Romania, but now a ghost of itself (3 days; p. 777). Detour from Bucharest to **Braşov,** located in the heart of Transylvania near Dracula's castle (2 days; p. 782). Truck to **Odessa,** the former USSR's party town (3 days; p. 979), then head via Simferopol to **Yalta** and its beaches (3 days; p. 979). Snooze on the night train to **Kiev,** where you can marvel at the bride industry and admire medieval castles (3 days; p. 974). Link back up with the more beaten path via transport to **Moscow** or **Warsaw** (1 day).

ESSENTIALS

WHEN TO GO

Give careful consideration to when you travel, because the timing of your trip can determine its success. Summer is the high season for traveling in Europe. *Everything* is crowded with tourists in July and August; June or September may be a better time to go. Additionally, climate can serve as a good guide for when to travel.

SEASONAL	JANUARY			APRIL			JULY			OCTOBER		
TEMP. (HI-LO), **precipitation**	°C	°F	in	°C	°F	in	°C	°F	in	°C	°F	in
Amsterdam	3.3	38	3.1	8.3	47	1.5	16.7	62	2.9	10.6	51	4.1
Athens	10	50	1.9	15	59	0.9	27.2	81	.2	19.4	67	2.1
Berlin	-0.6	31	1.6	7.8	46	1.6	18.3	65	2	9.4	49	1.0
Budapest	0.2	32.4	1.2	11.2	52.2	1.5	20.9	69.3	2.3	10.8	51.4	1.4
Copenhagen	0.6	33	1.7	6.1	43	1.6	16.7	62	2.6	9.4	49	2.1
Dublin	5.6	42	2.5	8.3	47	1.9	15.6	60	2.6	10.6	51	2.9
Istanbul	5.4	41.7	3.6	11.5	52.7	1.7	23.4	74.1	1	16	60.8	2.6
Kraków	-3.7	25.3	1.3	7.9	46.2	1.9	18.4	65.1	3.5	8.6	47.5	1.7
London	3.9	39	3.1	7.8	46	2.1	16.7	62	1.8	10.6	51	2.9
Madrid	5.6	42	1.8	11.7	53	1.8	24.4	76	.4	14.4	58	1.8
Moscow	-10.3	13.5	1.4	4.4	39.9	1.5	18.5	65.3	3.2	4.2	39.6	2
Paris	3.9	39	0.2	10	50	0.2	19.4	67	.21	11.7	53	0.2
Prague	-1.7	29	0.8	7.2	45	1.4	17.2	63	2.6	8.3	47	1.2
Rome	8.3	47	3.2	12.8	55	2.6	75	75	.6	17.8	64	4.5
Stockholm	-4.1	24.6	1.2	4.4	39.9	1.1	17.1	62.8	2.5	7.3	45.1	2
Vienna	0	32	1.5	9.4	49	2	20	68	2.9	10.6	51	1.9

DOCUMENTS AND FORMALITIES

Information on European **consular services** at home, as well as foreign consular services in Europe, is located in individual country chapters.

ENTRANCE REQUIREMENTS.

Passport (p. 9): Required for all citizens visiting any European country.

Visa (p. 12): Western European countries require visas for citizens of South Africa, but not for citizens of Australia, Canada, Ireland, New Zealand, the UK, or the US (for stays shorter than three months). Eastern European countries are more likely to require visas. Also, Russia, Belarus, and the Ukraine require invitations.

Inoculations (p. 22): Travelers to Europe are recommended to be up to date on vaccines for measles, mumps, rubella, diptheria, tetanus, pertussis, polio, haemophilus influenza B, hepatitis B, and hepatitis A.

Work Permit (p. 13): Required for all foreigners planning to work in Europe, except for citizens of EU member countries.

Driving Permit (p. 62): An International Driving Permit is required for all those planning to drive.

PASSPORTS

REQUIREMENTS. Citizens of Australia, Canada, Ireland, New Zealand, South Africa, the UK, and the US need valid passports to enter European countries and to re-enter their own countries. Most countries do not allow entrance if the holder's passport expires in under six months. Returning home with an expired passport is illegal, and may result in a fine.

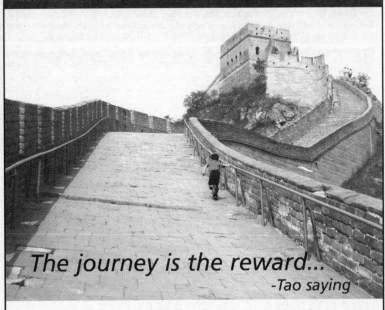

LOST PASSPORTS. If you lose your passport, immediately notify the local police and the nearest embassy or consulate of your home government. To expedite its replacement, you will need to know all information previously recorded and show ID and proof of citizenship. In some cases, a replacement may take weeks to process, and it may be valid only for a limited time. Any visas stamped in your old passport will be irretrievably lost. In an emergency, ask for immediate temporary traveling papers that will permit you to re-enter your home country. Your passport is a public document belonging to your nation's government. You may have to surrender it to a foreign government official, but if you don't get it back in a reasonable amount of time (24hr.), inform the nearest mission of your home country.

NEW PASSPORTS. File any new passport or renewal applications well in advance of your departure date. Most passport offices offer rush services for a steep fee. Citizens living abroad who need a passport or renewal should contact the nearest consular service of their home country.

ONE EUROPE. The idea of European unity has come a long way since 1958, when the European Economic Community (EEC) was created in order to promote solidarity and cooperation between its six founding states. Since then, the EEC has become the European Union (EU), with political, legal, and economic institutions spanning 15 member states: Austria, Belgium, Denmark, Finland, France, Germany, Greece, Ireland, Italy, Luxembourg, the Netherlands, Portugal, Spain, Sweden, and the UK.

What does this have to do with the average non-EU tourist? Well, the Schengen Treaty, fully implemented since 1995, has resulted in **freedom of movement** across 14 European countries–the entire EU minus Denmark, Ireland, and the UK, but plus Iceland and Norway. This means that border controls between participating countries have been abolished, and visa policies harmonized. While you're still required to carry a passport (or government-issued ID card for EU citizens) when crossing an internal border, once you've been admitted into one country, you're free to travel to all participating states. Britain and Ireland have also formed a **common travel area,** abolishing passport controls between the UK and the Republic of Ireland, meaning that the only times you'll see a border guard within the EU are traveling between the British Isles and the Continent–and of course, in and out of Denmark.

For more important consequences of the EU for travelers, see **The Euro** (p. 15) and **European Customs** (p. 14).

Australia: ☎ 13 12 32; email passports.australia@dfat.gov.au; www.dfat.gov.au/passports. Apply at a post office, passport office (in all state capitals and Newcastle), or overseas diplomatic mission. Passports AUS$128 (32-page) or AUS$192 (64-page); valid for 10 years. Children AUS$64 (32-page) or AUS$96 (64-page); valid for 5 years.

Canada: Canadian Passport Office, Department of Foreign Affairs and International Trade, Ottawa, ON K1A 0G3 (☎ (613) 994 35 00 or (800) 567 68 68; www.dfait-maeci.gc.ca/passport). Applications available at passport offices, Canadian missions, and post offices. Passports CDN$60; valid for 5 years (non-renewable).

Ireland: Pick up an application at a *Garda* station or post office, or request one from a passport office. Then apply by mail to the Department of Foreign Affairs, Passport Office, Molesworth St., Dublin 2 (☎ (01) 671 16 33; fax 671 10 92; www.irlgov.ie/iveagh), or the Passport Office, Irish Life Building, 1A South Mall, Cork (☎ (021) 27 25 25). Passports IR£45; valid for 10 years. Under 18 or over 65 IR£10; valid for 3 years.

New Zealand: Send applications to the Passport Office, Department of International Affairs, P.O. Box 10526, Wellington (☎ (0800) 22 50 50 or (4) 474 81 00; fax (4) 474 80 10; www.passports.govt.nz; email passports@dia.govt.nz). Standard processing time is 10 working days. Passports NZ$80; valid for 10 years. Children NZ$40; valid for 5 years. 3 day "urgent service" NZ$160; children NZ $120.

South Africa: Department of Home Affairs. Passports are issued only in Pretoria, but all applications must still be submitted or forwarded to the nearest South Afrmican consulate. Processing time is 3 months or more. Passports around SAR80; valid for 10 years. Under 16 around SAR60; valid for 5 years. For more information, check out http://usaembassy.southafrica.net/VisaForms/Passport/Passport2000.html.

UK: ☎ (0870) 521 04 10; www.open.gov.uk/ukpass/ukpass.htm. Get an application from a passport office, main post office, travel agent, or online (for UK residents only) at www.ukpa.gov.uk/forms/f_app_pack.htm. Then apply by mail to or in person at a passport office. Passports UK£28; valid for 10 years. Under 15 UK£14.80; valid for 5 years. The process takes about 4 weeks; faster service (by personal visit to the offices listed above) costs an additional £12.

US: ☎ (202) 647 05 18; www.travel.state.gov/passport_services.html. Apply at any federal or state courthouse, authorized post office, or US Passport Agency (in most major cities); see the "US Government, State Department" section of the telephone book or a post office for addresses. Processing takes 3-4 weeks. New passports US$60; valid for 10 years. Under 18 US$40; valid for 5 years. Passports may be renewed by mail or in person for US$40. Add US$35 for 3-day expedited service.

VISAS AND WORK PERMITS

VISAS. Some countries require a visa—a stamp, sticker, or insert in your passport specifying the purpose of your travel and the permitted duration of your stay—in addition to a valid passport for entrance. Most standard visas cost US$10-70, are valid for one month, and must be validated within six months to one year from the date of issue. Many countries are willing to grant double-entry visas for a premium. The **Center for International Business and Travel (CIBT;** ☎ (800) 929 24 28) secures visas for US citizens for travel to almost any country for a variable service charge.

The requirements in the chart below only apply to tourist stays shorter than three months. If you plan to stay longer than 90 days, or if you plan to work or study abroad, your requirements will differ. In any case, check with the nearest embassy or consulate of your desired destination for up-to-date info. US citizens can also consult www.pueblo.gsa.gov/cic_text/travel/foreign/foreignentryreqs.html..

VISA REQUIREMENTS

	AUS	CAN	IRE	NZ	SA	UK	US
BELARUS	Y[3]	Y[3]	Y[3]	Y[3]	Y[3]	Y[3]	Y[3]
BOSNIA	Y	N	N	Y	Y	N	N[1]
BULGARIA	Y	N[1]	N[1]	N[1]	Y	N[1]	N[1]
CZECH REPUBLIC	Y	N	N	N	Y	N	N[1]
ESTONIA	N	Y	N	N	Y	N	N
HUNGARY	Y	N	N	Y	Y	N	N
LATVIA	Y[2]	Y[2]	N	Y[2]	Y[2]	N	N
LITHUANIA	N	N	N	N	Y	N	N
MACEDONIA	Y	Y	N	Y	Y	N	Y
POLAND	Y	Y	N	Y	Y	N	N
ROMANIA	Y	Y	Y	Y	Y	Y	N[1]
RUSSIA	Y[3]	Y[3]	Y[3]	Y[3]	Y[3]	Y[3]	Y[3]
SLOVAKIA	N	N	Y	Y	N	N	Y
TURKEY	N	N	Y	N	N[1]	Y	Y
UKRAINE	Y[3]	Y[3]	Y[3]	Y[3]	Y[3]	Y[3]	Y[3]

KEY 1 tourists can stay up to 30 days without visa; **2** tourists can stay up to 10 days without visa; **3** invitation required

Note that not listed in this chart are **Austria, Belgium, Croatia, Denmark, Finland, France, Germany, Greece, Iceland, Italy, Luxembourg, the Netherlands, Norway, Portugal, Slovenia, Spain,** and **Sweden.** These countries require visas of South Africans, but not of nationals of Australia, Canada, Ireland, New Zealand, the UK, or the US (for stays shorter than three months). Also not listed are the **UK, Ireland, Malta,** and **Switzerland,** which do not require visas for any of the seven nationalities listed above (including South Africans) for stays shorter than 90 days. Travelers to **Andorra** should contact a French or Spanish embassy for more info, while those going to **Liechtenstein** should contact a Swiss embassy with any inquiries

INVITATIONS AND WORK PERMITS. In addition to a visa, **Belarus, Russia,** and **Ukraine** currently also require that visitors from Australia, Canada, Ireland, New Zealand, the UK, and the US obtain an invitation from a sponsoring individual or organization. Requirements change rapidly, so double-check. See individual chapters for info on how to acquire invitations. Visitors to any European country, with the exception of EU citizens in EU countries, who want the right to work will need a work permit (see **Alternatives to Tourism,** p. 71).

IDENTIFICATION

When you travel, always carry two or more forms of identification on your person, including at least one photo ID; a passport and a driver's license or birth certificate is usually adequate. Many establishments may require several IDs to cash traveler's checks. Never carry all your forms of ID together in case of theft or loss, and bring passport-size photos to affix to any IDs or passes you may acquire along the way.

STUDENT AND TEACHER IDENTIFICATION. The **International Student Identity Card (ISIC),** the most widely accepted form of student ID, provides discounts on sights, accommodations, food, and transport. The ISIC is preferable to an institution-specific card (such as a university ID) because it is more likely to be recognized and honored abroad. All cardholders have access to a 24-hour emergency helpline for medical, legal, and financial emergencies (in North America call (877) 370-ISIC, elsewhere call US collect +1 (715) 345 05 05), and US cardholders are also eligible for insurance benefits (see **Insurance,** p. 25). Many student travel agencies issue ISICs, including STA Travel in Australia and New Zealand; Travel CUTS in Canada; USIT in the Republic of Ireland and Northern Ireland; SASTS in South Africa; Campus Travel and STA Travel in the UK; and Council Travel (www.counciltravel.com/idcards/default.asp) and STA Travel in the US (see p. 41). The card is valid from September of one year to December of the following year and costs AUS$15, CDN$15, or US$20. Applicants must be degree-seeking students of a secondary or post-secondary school and must be at least 12 years of age. Because of the proliferation of fake ISICs, some services (particularly airlines) require additional proof of student identity, such as a school ID or a letter attesting to your student status, signed by your registrar and stamped with your school seal. The **International Teacher Identity Card (ITIC)** offers the same insurance coverage as well as similar, but limited, discounts. The fee is AUS$13, UK£5, or US$20. For more info, contact the **International Student Travel Confederation (ISTC),** Herengracht 479, 1017 BS Amsterdam, Netherlands (☎+31 (20) 421 28 00; fax 421 28 10; email istcinfo@istc.org; www.istc.org).

YOUTH IDENTIFICATION. The International Student Travel Confederation issues a card to travelers who are under 27, but are not students. This one-year **International Youth Travel Card** (**IYTC;** formerly the **GO 25** Card) offers many of the same benefits as the ISIC. Most organizations that sell the ISIC also sell the IYTC (US$20).

CUSTOMS

Upon entering a country, you must declare certain items from abroad and pay a duty on the value of those articles that exceeds that country's allowance. Note that goods and gifts purchased at **duty-free** shops abroad are not exempt from duty or sales tax at your point of return and must be declared as well; "duty-free" merely means that you need not pay a tax in the country of purchase. Upon returning home, you must similarly declare all articles acquired abroad and pay a duty on the value of articles in excess of your home country's allowance. In order to expedite your return, make a list of any valuables brought from home and register them with customs before traveling abroad, and keep receipts for all goods acquired abroad.

EUROPEAN CUSTOMS. Besides freedom of movement of people within the EU (see p. 11), travelers can also take advantage of the freedom of movement of goods. This means that there are no customs controls at internal EU borders (i.e., you can take the blue customs channel at the airport), and travelers are free to transport whatever legal substances they like as long as it is for their own personal (non-commercial) use–up to 800 cigarettes, 10L of spirits, 90L of wine (60L of sparkling wine), and 110L of beer. You should also be aware that **duty-free** was abolished on June 30, 1999 for travel between EU member states; however, travelers between the EU and the rest of the world still get a duty-free allowance when passing through customs.

FURTHER RESOURCES

Australia: Australian Customs National Information Line (in Australia call (01) 30 03 63, from elsewhere call +61 (2) 62 75 66 66; www.customs.gov.au).

Canada: Canadian Customs, 2265 St. Laurent Blvd., Ottawa, ON K1G 4K3 (☎ (800) 461 99 99 (24hr.) or (613) 993 05 34; www.revcan.ca).

Ireland: Customs Information Office, Irish Life Centre, Lower Abbey St., Dublin 1 (☎ (01) 878 88 11; fax 878 08 36; taxes@revenue.iol.ie; www.revenue.ie/customs.htm).

New Zealand: New Zealand Customhouse, 17-21 Whitmore St., Box 2218, Wellington (☎ (04) 473 60 99; fax 473 73 70; www.customs.govt.nz).

South Africa: Commissioner for Customs and Excise, Privat Bag X47, Pretoria 0001 (☎ (012) 314 99 11; fax 328 64 78; www.gov.za).

United Kingdom: Her Majesty's Customs and Excise, Passenger Enquiry Team, Wayfarer House, Great South West Road, Feltham, Middlesex TW14 8NP (☎ (020) 89 10 37 44; fax 89 10 39 33; www.hmce.gov.uk).

United States: US Customs Service, 1330 Pennsylvania Ave. NW, Washington, D.C. 20229 (☎ (202) 354 10 00; fax 354 10 10; www.customs.gov).

MONEY

CURRENCY AND EXCHANGE

As a general rule, it's cheaper to convert money in Europe than at home. However, you should bring enough foreign currency to last for the first 24 to 72 hours of a trip to avoid being penniless should you arrive after bank hours or on a holiday. Travelers from the US can get foreign currency from the comfort of home: **International Currency Express** (☎ (888) 278 66 28) delivers foreign currency or traveler's checks overnight (US$15) or second-day (US$12) at competitive exchange rates.

When changing money abroad, try to go only to banks or bureaux de change that have at most a 5% margin between their buy and sell prices. Since you lose money with every transaction, **convert large sums** (unless the currency is depreciating rapidly), **but no more than you'll need.**

If you use traveler's checks or bills, carry some in small denominations (the equivalent of US$50 or less) in case you are forced to exchange money at disadvantageous rates, but bring a range of denominations since charges may be levied per check cashed. Store your money in a variety of forms; at any given time carry some cash, some traveler's checks, and an ATM and/or credit card. All travelers should also consider carrying US dollars or German marks (about US$50 or DM95 worth), which are often preferred by local tellers.

THE EURO. Since 1999, the official currency of 12 members of the European Union—Austria, Belgium, Finland, France, Germany, Greece, Ireland, Italy, Luxembourg, the Netherlands, Portugal, and Spain—has been the euro. But you shouldn't throw out your francs, pesetas, and Deutschmarks just yet; actual euro banknotes and coins won't be available until January 1, 2002, and the old national currencies will remain legal tender for six months after that.

While you might not be able to pay for a coffee and get your change in euros yet, the currency has some important—and positive—consequences for travelers hitting more than one euro-zone country. For one thing, money-changers across the euro-zone are obliged to exchange money at the official, fixed rate (see below), and at no commission (although they may still charge a small service fee). So now you can change your guilders into escudos and your escudos into lire without losing fistfuls of money on every transaction. Second, euro-denominated traveler's checks allow you to pay for goods and services across the euro-zone, again at the official rate and commission-free.

The exchange rate between euro-zone currencies was permanently fixed on January 1, 1999 at EUR€1 = 40.3399BF (Belgian francs) = DM1.95583 (German marks) = 166.386PTAS (Spanish pesetas) = 6.55957F (French francs) = IR£0.787564 (Irish pounds) = L1936.27 (Italian liras) = 40.3399LUF (Luxembourg francs) = F2.20371 (Dutch guilders) = 13.7603AS (Austrian schillings) = 200.482$ (Portuguese escudos) = 5.94573MK (Finnish markka). (Greek Drachmas had not been fixed into the euro exchange rate at the time of publication). For more info, see www.europa.eu.int.

For **currency exchange information** please see the opening page of each country chapter. Check a large newspaper or the web (e.g. finance.yahoo.com or www.bloomberg.com) for the latest exchange rates.

TRAVELER'S CHECKS

Traveler's checks (**American Express** and **Visa** are the most recognized) are one of the safest and least troublesome means of carrying funds. Several agencies and banks sell them for a small commission. Each agency provides refunds if your checks are lost or stolen, and many provide additional services, such as toll-free refund hotlines abroad, emergency message services, and stolen credit card assistance.

While traveling, keep check receipts and a record of which checks you've cashed separate from the checks themselves. Also leave a list of check numbers with someone at home. Never countersign checks until you're ready to cash them, and always bring your passport with you to cash them. If your checks are lost or stolen, immediately contact a refund center (of the company that issued your checks) to be reimbursed; they may require a police report verifying the loss or theft. Less-touristed countries may not have refund centers at all, in which case you might have to wait to be reimbursed. Ask about toll-free refund hotlines and the location of refund centers when purchasing checks, and always carry emergency cash.

American Express: Call (800) 25 19 02 in Australia; in New Zealand (0800) 44 10 68; in the UK (0800) 52 13 13; in the US and Canada (800) 221 72 82. Elsewhere call US collect +1 (801) 964 66 65; www.aexp.com. Traveler's checks are available in ten currencies at 1-4% commission at AmEx offices and banks, commission-free at AAA offices. *Cheques for Two* can be signed by either of 2 people traveling together.

Citicorp: In the US and Canada call (800) 645 65 56; in Europe, the Middle East, or Africa call the UK +44 (020) 75 08 70 07; elsewhere call US collect +1 (813) 623 17 09. Traveler's checks available in 7 currencies at 1-2% commission. Call 24hr.

Thomas Cook MasterCard: In the US and Canada call (800) 223 73 73; in the UK call (0800) 62 21 01; elsewhere call UK collect +44 (1733) 31 89 50. Checks available in 13 currencies at 2% commission. Thomas Cook offices cash checks commission-free.

Visa: In the US call (800) 227 68 11; in the UK call (0800) 89 50 78; elsewhere call UK collect +44 (1733) 31 89 49. Call for the location of their nearest office.

CREDIT CARDS

Where they are accepted, credit cards often offer superior exchange rates—up to 5% better than the retail rate used by banks and other currency exchange establishments. Credit cards may also offer services such as insurance or emergency help, and are sometimes required to reserve hotel rooms or rental cars. **MasterCard** (a.k.a. EuroCard or Access in Europe) and Visa (a.k.a. Carte Bleue or Barclaycard) are the most welcomed; **American Express** cards work at some ATMs and at AmEx offices and major airports. However, budget travelers will probably find that few of the establishments they frequent will accept credit cards; aside from the occasional splurge, you will probably reserve use of your credit card for financial emergencies.

Credit cards are also useful for **cash advances,** which allow you to withdraw local currency from associated banks and ATMs throughout Europe instantly. However, transaction fees for all credit card advances (up to US$10 per advance, plus 2-3% extra on foreign transactions after conversion) tend to make credit cards a more costly way of withdrawing cash than ATMs or traveler's checks. In an emergency, however, the transaction fee may prove worth the cost. To be eligible for an advance, you'll need to get a **Personal Identification Number (PIN)** from your credit card company (see **Cash (ATM) Cards,** below). Be sure to check with your credit card company before you leave home, though; in certain circumstances companies have started to charge a foreign transaction fee.

CASH (ATM) CARDS

Cash cards—popularly called ATM cards—are widespread in Europe. Depending on the system that your home bank uses, you can most likely access your personal bank account from abroad. ATMs get the same wholesale exchange rate as credit cards, but there is often a limit on the amount of money you can withdraw per day (around US$500), and unfortunately computer networks sometimes fail. There is typically also a surcharge of US$1-5 per withdrawal. Be sure to memorize your PIN code in numeric form since machines elsewhere often don't have letters on their keys. Also, if your PIN is longer than four digits, ask your bank whether you need a new number. The two major international money networks are **Cirrus** (US ☎ (800) 424 77 87) and **PLUS** (US ☎ (800) 843 75 87). To locate ATMs in Europe, call the above numbers, or consult www.visa.com/pd/atm or www.mastercard.com/atm.

GETTING MONEY FROM HOME

AMERICAN EXPRESS. Cardholders can withdraw cash from their checking accounts at any of AmEx's major offices and many representative offices (up to US$1000 every 21 days; no service charge, no interest). AmEx "Express Cash" withdrawals from any AmEx ATM in Europe are automatically debited from the cardholder's checking account or line of credit. Green card holders may withdraw up to US$1000 in any seven-day period (2% transaction fee; minimum US$2.50, maximum US$20). To enroll in Express Cash, cardmembers may call (800) 227 46 69 in the US; elsewhere call the US collect +1 (336) 668 50 41.

WESTERN UNION. Travelers from Canada, the UK, and the US can wire money abroad through Western Union's money transfer services. In Canada, call (800) 235 00 00; in the UK, (0800) 83 38 33; in the US, (800) 325 60 00. The rates for sending cash are generally US$10-11 cheaper than with a credit card, and the money is usually available within an hour. Western Union maintains offices throughout Europe; to find the nearest location, consult www.westernunion.com.

US STATE DEPARTMENT (US CITIZENS ONLY). In dire emergencies only, the US State Department will forward money within hours to the nearest consular office, which will then disburse it according to instructions for a US$15 fee. Contact the Overseas Citizens Service, American Citizens Services, Consular Affairs, Room 4811, US Department of State, Washington, D.C. 20520 (☎ (202) 647 52 25; nights, Sundays, and holidays ☎ 647 40 00; http://travel.state.gov).

COSTS

The cost of your trip will vary considerably, depending on where you go, how you travel, and where you stay. The single biggest cost of your trip will probably be your round-trip (return) **airfare** to Europe (see p. 39); a **railpass** would be another major pre-departure expense (see p. 51). Before you go, spend some time calculating a reasonable per-day **budget** that will meet your needs. To give you a general idea, a bare-bones day in Western Europe (camping or sleeping in hostels, buying food at supermarkets) would cost about US$25-35, excluding the cost of a plane ticket and railpass; a slightly more comfortable day (sleeping in hostels and the occasional budget hotel, eating one meal a day at a restaurant, going out at night) would run US$35-50; and for a luxurious day, the sky's the limit. Countries such as Britain, Italy, and Switzerland tend to be more costly for tourists, while Spain and Greece are relatively inexpensive alternatives. You can expect to spend US$5-15 less per day in Eastern Europe or Turkey; similarly, if you will be traveling in Scandinavia, add on US$10-15 per day. If you're camping or traveling by campervan, knock off US$5-10, more if you plan to take advantage of free camping. For example, the typical first-time, under-26 traveler planning to spend most of his or her time in Western Europe and then tack on a quick jaunt into Eastern Europe, sleeping in hostels and traveling on a two-month unlimited Eurail pass, can probably expect to spend about US$2000, plus cost of plane fare (US$300-800), railpass (US$882), and a backpack (US$150-400). Also, don't forget to factor in emergency reserve funds (at least US$200) when planning how much money you'll need.

TIPS FOR STAYING ON A BUDGET. Considering that saving just a few dollars a day over the course of your trip might pay for days or weeks of additional travel, the art of penny-pinching is well worth learning. Learn to take advantage of freebies: for example, museums will typically be free once a week or once a month, and cities often host free open-air concerts and/or cultural events (especially in the summer). Bring a sleepsack (see p. 26) to save on sheet charges in European hostels, and do your **laundry** in the sink (unless you're explicitly prohibited from doing so). You can split **accommodations** costs (in hotels and some hostels) with trustworthy fellow travelers; multi-bed rooms almost always work out cheaper per person than singles. The same principle will also work for cutting down on the cost of **restaurant** meals. You can also buy food in supermarkets instead of eating out; you'd be surprised how tasty (and cheap) simple bread can be with cheese or spread.

TAXES

The European Union imposes a **value-added tax (VAT)** on goods and services purchased within the EU (usually included in the sticker price). Non-EU citizens may obtain a **refund** for taxes paid on retail goods, but not those on services. As the VAT in Europe ranges from 15 to 25%, you may find it worth the hassle to file for a refund. In order to do so, you must first obtain a Tax-free Shopping Cheque, available from shops sporting the blue, white, and silver Europe Tax-free Shopping logo, and then save the receipts from all of the purchases for which you want to be refunded. Upon leaving the last EU country on your itinerary, present your (unused) goods, invoices, and Tax-free Shopping Cheque to Customs for validation, then pick up an immediate cash refund at an ETS cash refund office or file for a refund once back home. Keep in mind that goods must be taken out of the country within three months of the end of the month of purchase, and that some stores require minimum purchase amounts to become eligible for refund. For more information on tax-free shopping, visit www.globalrefund.com.

SAFETY AND SECURITY

While tourists may be more vulnerable than the average individual, a few simple precautions will help you avoid problems. In countries like Russia and Turkey, you may need to take extra care. Crime in Russia, from petty robbery to murder, has been rising over the past decade, and terrorist attacks are a growing problem in

Turkey. There has been violence associated with the IRA and British peace keeping efforts in Northern Ireland which has been a problem area in recent years. Be aware that certain disgruntled groups, like the skinheads in Germany and Hungary, Basque terrorists in Spain, the Mafia in Sicily, and the *Romany* (also known as Gypsies) in Paris may pose a problem. See specific country introductions for more information, as well as **Specific Concerns** p. 67, and **Travel Advisories** p. 20.

PERSONAL SAFETY

To avoid unwanted attention, try to blend in. Respecting local customs (in many cases, dressing more conservatively) may placate would-be hecklers. Familiarize yourself with your surroundings before setting out, and look confident; if you must check a map on the street, duck into a shop. If you are traveling alone, be sure someone at home knows your itinerary, and **never admit that you're traveling alone.** When walking at night, stick to busy, well-lit streets and avoid dark alleyways. Do not attempt to cross through parks, parking lots, or other large, deserted areas. Look for children playing, women walking in the open, and other signs of an active community. If you feel uncomfortable, leave as quickly and directly as you can.

Trains are safe throughout most of Europe, and second-class travel is more than comfortable. **Overnight trains** are the most risky, as your vigilance is limited while you sleep. For tips on protecting your valuables on overnight transit, see p. 21. If you are using a **car,** learn local driving signals and wear a seatbelt. Study route maps before you hit the road, and if your car breaks down, wait for the police to assist you. For long drives, invest in a cellular phone and a roadside assistance program (see p. 62). Be sure to park your vehicle in a garage or well traveled area, and use a steering wheel locking device in larger cities. **Sleeping in your car** is one of the most dangerous (and often illegal) ways to get your rest. *Let's Go* does not recommend **hitchhiking** under any circumstances, particularly for women (see p. 51).

There is no sure-fire way to avoid threatening situations when you travel, but a good **self-defense course** will give you concrete ways to react to unwanted advances. **Impact, Prepare,** and **Model Mugging** can refer you to local self-defense courses in the US (☎ (800) 345 54 25) and Vancouver (☎ (604) 878 38 38). Workshops (2-3hr.) start at US$50; full courses run US$350-500. Both women and men are welcome.

TRAVEL ADVISORIES. The following government offices provide travel information and advisories by telephone, by fax, or via the web:

Australian Department of Foreign Affairs and Trade: www.dfat.gov.au.

Canadian Department of Foreign Affairs and International Trade (DFAIT): www.dfait-maeci.gc.ca. Call for their free booklet, *Bon Voyage...But.*

New Zealand Ministry of Foreign Affairs: www.mft.govt.nz/trav.html.

United Kingdom Foreign and Commonwealth Office: www.fco.gov.uk.

US Department of State: http://travel.state.gov. For *A Safe Trip Abroad,* call ☎(202) 512 18 00.

FINANCIAL SECURITY

PROTECTING YOUR VALUABLES

There are a few steps you can take to minimize the financial risk associated with traveling. First, **bring as little with you as possible.** Leave expensive watches, jewelry, cameras, and electronic equipment (like your Discman) at home; chances are you'd break them, lose them, or get sick of lugging them around anyway. Second, buy a few combination **padlocks** to secure your belongings either in your pack—which you should **never leave unattended**—or in a hostel or train station locker. Third, **carry as little cash as possible;** instead carry traveler's checks and ATM/credit cards, keeping them in a **money belt**—not a "fanny pack"—along with your passport and ID

Association, 1660 Duke St., Alexandria, VA 22314 (US ☎ (800) 232 34 72), offers copies of the article "Travel and Diabetes" and a multilingual diabetic ID card.

ON THE ROAD

ENVIRONMENTAL HAZARDS

Heat exhaustion and dehydration: While in Mediterranean countries such as Spain, Portugal, Greece, or Italy, where summer temperatures easily climb over 90°F (30°C), be aware of the possibility of heat exhaustion. Heat exhaustion is characterized by dehydration and salt deficiency, and can lead to fatigue, headaches, and wooziness. Drink plenty of fluids, eat salty foods (e.g. crackers), and limit dehydrating beverages (e.g. alcohol, coffee, tea, and soda). Continuous heat stress can eventually lead to **heatstroke,** characterized by a rising temperature, severe headache, and cessation of sweating. Victims should be cooled off with wet towels and taken to a doctor.

Hypothermia and frostbite: Europe is a continent of many climates, and in the Alps, temperatures can fall to the freezing point even in the summer months. A rapid drop in body temperature is the clearest sign of overexposure to cold. Victims may also shiver, feel exhausted, have poor coordination or slurred speech, hallucinate, or suffer amnesia. *Do not let hypothermia victims fall asleep,* or their body temperature will continue to drop. To avoid hypothermia, keep dry, wear layers, and stay out of the wind. When the temperature is below freezing, watch out for **frostbite.** If skin turns white, waxy, and cold, do not rub the area. Drink warm beverages, get dry, and slowly warm the area with dry fabric or steady body contact until a doctor is found.

High altitude: Allow your body a couple of days to adjust to less oxygen before exerting yourself. Note that alcohol is more potent and UV rays are stronger at high elevations.

INSECT-BORNE DISEASES

Many diseases are transmitted by insects—mainly mosquitoes, fleas, ticks, and lice. Be aware of insects in wet or forested areas, especially while hiking and camping. **Mosquitoes** are most active from dusk to dawn. Wear long pants and long sleeves, tuck long pants into socks, and buy a mosquito net. Use insect repellents such as DEET and soak or spray your gear with permethrin (licensed in the US for use on clothing). Natural repellents can make you smelly to insects, like vitamin B-12 or garlic pills. Calamine lotion or topical cortisones (like Cortaid) may stop itching. **Ticks**—responsible for Lyme and other diseases—are particularly dangerous in rural and forested regions. Pause periodically while walking to brush off ticks using a fine-toothed comb on your neck and scalp. Do not try to remove ticks by burning them or coating them with nail polish remover or petroleum jelly.

Tick-borne encephalitis: A viral infection of the central nervous system transmitted through tick bites and the consumption of unpasteurized dairy products. Occurs chiefly in wooded areas of Central and Western Europe. Symptoms can range from nothing to headaches and flu-like symptoms to swelling of the brain (encephalitis). A vaccine is available in Europe which provides protection for about three years, but the immunization schedule is impractical for most tourists.

Lyme disease: A bacterial infection carried by ticks and marked by a circular bull's-eye rash of 2 inches or more around the bite. Later symptoms include fever, headache, and aches and pains. Antibiotics are effective if administered early. Left untreated, Lyme disease can cause problems in joints, the heart, and the nervous system. If you find a tick, grasp the tick's head with tweezers as close to your skin as possible and apply slow, steady traction. Removing a tick within 24 hours greatly reduces risk of infection.

Leishmaniasis: A parasite transmitted by sand flies, leishmaniasis has been reported in Switzerland, Italy, Spain, and southern France. Common symptoms are fever, weakness, and swelling of the spleen. There is a treatment, but no vaccine.

FOOD- AND WATER-BORNE DISEASES

Unpeeled fruit and vegetables and tap water should be safe throughout most of Europe, particularly Western Europe, but may not be in parts of Turkey, Southern

Europe, or Eastern Europe. Remember to be cautious of ice cubes and anything washed in tap water, like salad. Other culprits are raw shellfish, unpasteurized milk, and sauces containing raw eggs. Buy bottled water, or purify your own water by bringing it to a rolling boil or treating it with **iodine tablets.**

Traveler's diarrhea: Results from drinking untreated water or eating uncooked foods; a temporary (and fairly common) reaction to the bacteria in new food ingredients. Symptoms include nausea, bloating, urgency, and malaise. Try quick-energy, non-sugary foods with protein and carbohydrates to keep your strength up. Over-the-counter anti-diarrheals (e.g. Immodium) may counteract the problems, but can complicate serious infections. The most dangerous side effect is dehydration; drink 8 oz. of water with ½ tsp. of sugar or honey and a pinch of salt, try uncaffeinated soft drinks, or munch on salted crackers. If you develop a fever or your symptoms don't go away after 4-5 days, consult a doctor. Consult a doctor for treatment of diarrhea in children.

Cholera: An intestinal disease caused by a bacteria found in contaminated food. A danger in the Russian Federation and the Ukraine. Symptoms include watery diarrhea, dehydration, vomiting, and muscle cramps. See a doctor immediately; if left untreated, it may be fatal. Antibiotics are available, but rehydration is most important.

Hepatitis A: A viral liver infection acquired primarily through contaminated water, but also through sexual contact. An intermediate risk in Eastern Europe. Symptoms include fatigue, fever, loss of appetite, nausea, dark urine, jaundice, vomiting, aches and pains, and light stools. Risk is highest in rural areas. Get the **vaccine** before leaving, p. 22.

Parasites: Microbes, tapeworms, etc. that hide in unsafe water and food. **Giardiasis,** for example, is acquired by drinking untreated water from streams or lakes all over the world (including Europe). Symptoms include swollen glands or lymph nodes, fever, rashes or itchiness, digestive problems, eye problems, and anemia. Boil water, wear shoes, avoid bugs, and eat only cooked food.

OTHER INFECTIOUS DISEASES

Rabies: Transmitted through the saliva of infected animals; fatal if untreated. By the time symptoms appear (thirst and muscle spasms), the disease is in its terminal stage. If you are bitten, wash the wound thoroughly, seek immediate medical care, and try to have the animal located. A rabies vaccine, which consists of 3 shots given over a 21-day period, is available but is only semi-effective.

Hepatitis B: A viral infection of the liver transmitted via bodily fluids or needle-sharing. Symptoms may not surface until years after infection. Vaccinations are recommended for health-care workers, sexually-active travelers, and anyone planning to seek medical treatment abroad. The 3-shot vaccination series must begin 6 mo. before traveling.

Hepatitis C: Like Hep B, but the mode of transmission differs. IV drug users, those with occupational exposure to blood, hemodialysis patients, and recipients of blood transfusions are at the highest risk, but the disease can also be spread through sexual contact or sharing items like razors and toothbrushes that may have traces of blood on them.

AIDS AND HIV

The virus that leads to **Acquired Immune Deficiency Syndrome (AIDS)** is most easily transmitted through direct blood-to-blood contact with an HIV-positive person, but is most commonly transmitted by sexual intercourse. Never share intravenous drug, tattooing, or other needles, and take precautions to avoid any blood transfusions or injections while abroad (if you do need medical care, ask to receive screened blood and sterilized equipment). Take along a supply of latex condoms, which are often difficult to find on the road. Some countries, including Luxembourg, screen incoming travelers for HIV, primarily those planning extended visits for work or study, and deny entrance to those who test HIV-positive. For detailed information on AIDS in Europe, call the US **Centers for Disease Control's** 24-hour hotline at (800) 342-AIDS (2437), or contact the **Joint United Nations Programme on HIV/AIDS (UNAIDS),** 20 av. Appia 20, CH-1211 Geneva 27, Switzerland (☎ +41 (22) 791 36 66; fax 791 41 87). Council Travel's brochure, *Travel Safe: AIDS and Interna-*

tional Travel, is available at all Council Travel offices and on their website (www.ciee.org/Isp/safety/travelsafe.htm).

WOMEN'S HEALTH

Tampons and **pads** are sometimes hard to find when traveling, and your preferred brand may not be available, so consider bringing supplies along. Reliable **contraceptive devices** may also be difficult to find; if you're on the pill or use a diaphragm, bring enough pills or contraceptive jelly, respectively, to allow for possible loss or extended stays. Availability and quality of condoms abroad also varies, so you also might want to bring your favorite brand if you plan to be sexually active.

If you need an **abortion,** contact the **International Planned Parenthood Federation,** European Regional Office, Regent's College Inner Circle, Regent's Park, London NW1 4NS (☎ (020) 74 87 79 00; fax 74 87 79 50). In Germany, contact Pro Familia: Deutsche Gesellschaft Fur Familienplanung, Sexualpädagogik und Sexualberatung Stresemann-allee 3, D-60596 Frankfurt am Main (☎ 49 (69) 63 90 02; fax 49 (69) 63 98 52); in France, the Mouvement Français pour le Planning Familial, 4 Square Saint Irenee, F-75011, Paris (☎ 33 (1) 48 07 29 10; fax 33 (1) 47 00 79 77); and in Italy, the Unione Italiana Centri Educazione Matrimoniale e Prematrimoniale (UICEMP), Via Eugenio Chiesa 1, Milan 20122 (☎ 39 (02) 54 10 20 20; fax 39 (02) 545 66 87).

INSURANCE

Travel insurance covers four basic areas: medical problems, property loss, trip cancellation/interruption, and emergency evacuation. Although your regular insurance policies may extend to travel-related accidents, consider travel insurance if the cost of potential trip cancellation/interruption or emergency medical evacuation is greater than you can absorb. Travel insurance generally runs about US$50 per week for full coverage, while trip cancellation/interruption may be purchased separately at a rate of about US$5.50 per US$100 of coverage.

Medical insurance (especially university policies) often covers costs incurred abroad; check with your provider. **US Medicare** does not cover foreign travel. **Canadians** are protected by their home province's health insurance plan for up to 90 days after leaving the country; check with the provincial Ministry of Health or Health Plan Headquarters for details. **Australians** traveling in the UK, the Netherlands, Sweden, Finland, Italy, and Malta are entitled to many of the services that they would receive at home as part of the Reciprocal Health Care Agreement. **Homeowners' insurance** (or your family's coverage) often covers theft during travel and loss of travel documents (passport, plane ticket, railpass, etc.) up to US$500. EU citizens should ask their insurer for an E111 form, which covers their emergency care in other EU countries. EU travelers to Great Britain do not need the E111 form, where the National Insurance system will provide free medical treatment.

ISIC and **ITIC** (see p. 13) provide basic insurance benefits, including US$100 per day of in-hospital sickness for up to 60 days, US$3000 of accident-related medical reimbursement, and US$25,000 for emergency medical transport. Cardholders have access to a toll-free 24-hour helpline for medical, legal, and financial emergencies overseas (in US and Canada call (800) 626 24 27; elsewhere call US collect +1 (713) 267 25 25). **American Express** (US ☎ (800) 528 48 00) grants most cardholders automatic car rental insurance (collision and theft, but not liability) and ground travel accident coverage of US$100,000 on flight purchases made with the card.

INSURANCE PROVIDERS. Council and **STA** (see p. 41) offer a range of plans that can supplement your basic coverage. Other private insurance providers in the **US and Canada** include: **Access America** (☎ (800) 284 83 00); **Berkely Group/Carefree Travel Insurance** (☎ (800) 323 31 49; www.berkely.com); **Globalcare Travel Insurance** (☎ (800) 821 24 88; www.globalcare-cocco.com); and **Travel Assistance International** (☎ (800) 821 28 28; www.worldwide-assistance.com). Providers in the **UK** include **Campus Travel** (☎ (01865) 25 80 00) and **Columbus Travel Insurance** (☎ (020) 73 75 00 11). In **Australia,** try **CIC Insurance** (☎ 92 02 80 00).

PACKING

Pack light: Lay out only what you absolutely need, then take half the clothes and twice the money. Any extra space left will be useful for any souvenirs or items you might pick up along the way. If you plan to do a lot of hiking, see **Outdoors,** p. 33.

IMPORTANT DOCUMENTS. Don't forget your **passport, traveler's checks, ATM** and/or **credit cards,** and adequate **ID** (see p. 13). Also check that you have any of the following that might apply to you: a **hosteling** membership card (see p. 29), **driver's license** (see p. 62), travel **insurance** forms, and/or **rail** or **bus pass** (see p. 51). It would be wise to make photocopies of all important documents to stash in a separate place, e.g. sewn into your pack, or to leave with family or friends back home.

LUGGAGE. If you plan to travel mostly by foot, a sturdy **frame backpack** is unbeatable (see p. 33.) Toting a **suitcase** or **trunk** is a very bad idea if you're going to be moving around a lot. A **daypack** (a small backpack or courier bag) is a must.

CLOTHING. No matter when you're traveling, it's always a good idea to bring a **warm jacket** or wool sweater, a **rain jacket** (Gore-Tex® is both waterproof and breathable), sturdy shoes or **hiking boots,** and **thick socks.** You will be particularly grateful for warm, waterproof clothing in Britain and Ireland, and northern continental Europe, where even summertime temperatures can hover around 60°F (15°C) and where rainfall is often generous. **Flip-flops** or waterproof sandals are crucial for grubby hostel showers. You may also want to add one dressier outfit if you have room. If you plan to visit any religious or cultural sites, remember that you'll need something besides tank tops and shorts to be respectful. Some churches, especially in Italy, Greece, and Spain, will not let women enter with bare shoulders—you can cover up with a scarf. In many cities in Spain, France, Italy, Germany, and Greece, the casual style is dressier than the North American standard.

SLEEPSACK. Some hostels require that you either provide your own linen or rent sheets from them. Save cash by making your own sleepsack: fold a full-size sheet in half the long way, then sew it closed along the long side and one of the short sides.

CONVERTERS AND ADAPTERS. In Europe, electricity is 220 volts AC (240V in Britain and Ireland), enough to fry any 110V North American appliance. 220/240V electrical appliances don't like 110V current, either. **Americans** and **Canadians** should buy an adapter (which changes the shape of the plug) and a converter (which changes the voltage). Don't make the mistake of using only an adapter (unless appliance instructions explicitly state otherwise). **New Zealanders** and **South Africans** (who both use 220V at home) as well as **Australians** (who use 240/250V) won't need a converter, but will need a set of adapters to use anything electrical.

WALK LIKE A EUROPEAN Europeans have an uncanny ability to pick tourists out of a crowd, perhaps because every American tourist is wearing khaki shorts, a white t-shirt, and a pair of Tevas. If you're ready to make the leap into Euro-chic, add this simple starter kit of must-haves to your wardrobe.

Adidas shirt: Preferably fluorescent stripes on black. Buy one that is too tight, and while you're at it get the matching windpants with chrome buttons from mid-shin down, to accommodate extremely large boots.

Asphyxiatingly tight jeans: Dark, with untapered leg. Ouch.

Really tight cargo pants: Thus negating the utility of all those pockets.

Hair gel: Men, your hair must be oiled back and appear clearly greasy.

The cell: A mobile phone is essential. If you can't afford one, no one will stop you from pretending. Buy a fake from a wandering cigarette-lighter salesman.

The **bottom line:** Banish that baggy attire to the bottom of your pack and, instead, choose anything tight enough to make breathing difficult.

TOILETRIES. Toothbrushes, towels, cold-water soap, talcum powder (to keep feet dry), deodorant, razors, tampons, and condoms are readily available in Europe, but if you're fond of particular brands, bring them along. **Contact lenses,** on the other hand, may be expensive and difficult to find, so bring enough extra pairs and solution for your entire trip. Also bring a copy of your prescription and your glasses, in case you need emergency replacements. If you use heat-disinfection, either switch temporarily to a chemical disinfection system (check first to make sure it's safe with your brand of lenses), or buy a converter (about US$20) to 220/240V.

FIRST-AID KIT. For a basic first-aid kit, pack bandages, aspirin or other painkiller, antibiotic cream, a thermometer, a Swiss Army knife, tweezers, moleskin, decongestant, motion-sickness remedy, diarrhea medication (Pepto Bismol or Immodium), antihistamines, sunscreen, insect repellent, and burn ointment.

FILM. Film and developing in Europe are expensive, so consider bringing enough film for your entire trip and then developing it at home. Amateur photographers may want to bring **disposable cameras** rather than an expensive permanent one. Despite disclaimers, airport security X-rays *can* fog film, so either buy a lead-lined pouch at a camera store or ask security to inspect it by hand. Always pack it in your carry-on luggage, since higher-intensity X-rays are used on checked luggage.

OTHER USEFUL ITEMS. For safety purposes, you should carry a **money belt** and bring a small **padlock.** Basic **outdoors equipment** (plastic screw-top water bottle, compass, waterproof matches, pocketknife, sunglasses, hat) may also prove useful. **Quick repairs** can be done on the road with a needle and thread; also consider bringing electrical tape for patching tears. Doing your **laundry** by hand (where it is allowed) is both cheaper and more convenient than doing it at a laundromat—bring detergent, a small rubber ball to stop up the sink, and string for a makeshift clothes line. **Other things** you're liable to forget: an umbrella; re-sealable plastic bags (for damp clothes, soap, food, shampoo, and other spillables); an alarm clock; safety pins; rubber bands; a flashlight; earplugs; garbage bags; and a small calculator.

ACCOMMODATIONS

HOSTELS

Europe in the summer is overrun by young budget travelers. Hostels are the hub of this subculture, allowing young people from all over the world to meet, find travel partners, and learn about places to visit. At US$10-25 per night, only camping is cheaper. Guests tend to be in their teens and 20s, but most hostels welcome all ages. In northern Europe, especially in Germany and Denmark, many hostels have special family rooms. In the average hostel, however, you and anywhere from one to 50 roommates will sleep on bunk beds in a gender-segregated room, with common bathrooms and a lounge down the hall. The hostel warden may be a laid-back student, a hippie dropout, or a crotchety disciplinarian. Hostels sometimes have kitchens, bike or moped rentals, storage areas, and/or laundry facilities.

However, some hostels close during certain daytime lockout hours (from morning to mid-afternoon), have a curfew (a distinct cramp in your style if you plan to rage in town), don't accept reservations, or impose a maximum stay. Conditions are generally spartan and crowded, and you may run into screaming pre-teen tour groups. Quality varies dramatically: some hostels are set in gorgeous castles, others in run-down barracks. You can typically rent sheets from hostels, or you can avoid the charge by making a sleepsack (see p. 26).

A HOSTELER'S BILL OF RIGHTS. Unless we state otherwise, you can assume that every hostel we list has certain standard features: no lockout, no curfew, free hot showers, secure luggage storage, and no key deposit.

HOSTELLING INTERNATIONAL

A **hostel membership** allows you to stay at hostels throughout Europe at unbeatable prices, and you usually need not be a youth to benefit (although some are only open to those under 26). Joining the youth hostel association in your own country (listed below) automatically grants you membership privileges in **Hostelling International (HI).** HI affiliates comply with given standards and regulations and normally display a blue triangle with the symbol of the national hostel association. *Hostelling International: Europe* (UK£7 or US$11; available from national hostelling associations) lists every HI-affiliated hostel in Europe and details the **International Booking Network (IBN),** through which you can book ahead for more than 300 hostels worldwide (US$5 per hostel; V, MC, D only; maximum 3-7 days advance notice required). To prepay and reserve ahead from home, call (02) 92 61 11 11 in Australia; (800) 663 57 77 in Canada; (1629) 58 14 18 in England and Wales; (1232) 32 47 33 in Northern Ireland; (01) 830 17 66 in the Republic of Ireland; (09) 303 95 24 in New Zealand; (541) 55 32 55 in Scotland; or (202) 783 61 61 in the US (www.hiayh.org/ushostel/reserva/ibn3.htm). If you want to make a reservation on less than three days' notice or are already in Europe, call the hostel where you want to stay directly.

Most HI hostels also honor **guest memberships**—you get a blank card with space for six validation stamps. Each night you pay a nonmember supplement (one-sixth the membership fee) and earn one guest stamp; get six stamps, and you're a member. This system works well in most of Europe, although in some countries you may need to remind the hostel reception. Most student travel agencies (see p. 41) sell HI cards, as do all of the national hostelling organizations listed below. For more info, see www.iyhf.org, www.hostels.com, or www.budgettravel.com/hostels.htm. All prices listed below are valid for **one-year memberships** unless otherwise noted.

Australian Youth Hostels Association (AYHA), 422 Kent St., Sydney NSW 2000 (☎ (02) 92 61 11 11; fax 92 61 19 69; www.yha.org.au). AUS$49, under 18 AUS$14.50.

Hostelling International-Canada (HI-C), 400-205 Catherine St., Ottawa, ON K2P 1C3 (☎ (800) 663 57 77 or (613) 237 78 84; fax 237 78 68; email info@hostellingintl.ca; www.hostellingintl.ca). CDN$25, under 18 CDN$12.

An Óige (Irish Youth Hostel Association), 61 Mountjoy St., Dublin 7 (☎ (1) 830 45 55; fax 830 58 08; email anoige@iol.ie; www.irelandyha.org). IR£10, under 18 IR£4.

Youth Hostels Association of New Zealand (YHANZ), P.O. Box 436, 173 Cashel St., Christchurch 1 (☎ (03) 379 99 70; fax 365 44 76; email info@yha.org.nz; www.yha.org.nz). NZ$40, ages 15-17 NZ$12, under 15 free.

Hostels Association of South Africa, 73 St. George's St. Mall, 3rd fl. P.O. Box 4402, Cape Town 8000 (☎ (021) 424 25 11; fax 424 41 19; email info@hisa.org.za; www.hisa.org.za). SAR50, under 18 SAR25, lifetime SAR250.

Scottish Youth Hostels Association (SYHA), 7 Glebe Crescent, Stirling FK8 2JA (☎ (01786) 89 14 00; fax 89 13 33; www.syha.org.uk). UK£6, under 18 UK£2.50.

Youth Hostels Association (England and Wales) Ltd., Trevelyan House, 8 St. Stephen's Hill, St. Albans, Hertfordshire AL1 2DY, UK (☎ (01727) 85 52 15; fax 84 41 26; www.yha.org.uk). UK£12, under 18 UK£6, families UK£24.

Hostelling International Northern Ireland (HINI), 22-32 Donegall Rd., Belfast BT12 5JN, Northern Ireland (☎ (01232) 32 47 33; fax 43 96 99; email info@hini.org.uk; www.hini.org.uk). UK£7, under 18 UK£3.

Hostelling International-American Youth Hostels (HI-AYH), 733 15th St. NW, #840, Washington, D.C. 20005 (☎ (202) 783 61 61 ext. 136; fax 783 61 71; email hiayhserv@hiayh.org; www.hiayh.org). US$25, under 18 free.

YMCAS

Young Men's Christian Association (YMCA) lodgings are usually cheaper than a hotel but more expensive than a hostel. Not all YMCA locations offer lodging; those that do are often located in urban downtowns. Many YMCAs accept women and families; some will not lodge those under 18 without parental permission.

ESSENTIALS

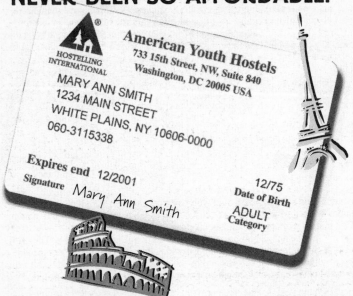

Y's Way International, 224 E. 47th St., New York, NY 10017 (☎ (212) 308 28 99; fax 308 31 61). For a small fee (US$3 in North America, US$5 elsewhere), this "booking service" makes reservations for YMCAs throughout Europe.

World Alliance of YMCAs, 12 Clos Belmont, 1208 Geneva, Switzerland (☎/fax +41 (22) 849 51 00; email office@ymca.int; www.ymca.int).

HOTELS, GUESTHOUSES, AND PENSIONS

Hotels are quite expensive in Britain, Switzerland, Austria, and northern Europe, where rock-bottom for one or two people is US$25 each. Elsewhere, couples can usually get by fairly well, as can larger groups. You'll typically share a hall bathroom; a private bathroom will cost extra, as may hot showers. In Britain and Ireland, a large breakfast is often included; elsewhere, a continental breakfast of a roll, jam, coffee or tea, and maybe an egg is served. Some hotels offer "full pension" (all meals) and "half pension" (no lunch). Guesthouses and pensions are often cheaper than hotels; in many countries, "pension" simply refers to a smaller, privately-owned and run hostel. If you make reservations in writing, indicate your night of arrival and the number of nights you plan to stay. The hotel will send you a confirmation and may request payment for the first night. Not all hotels take reservations, and few accept checks in foreign currency. Enclosing two International Reply Coupons will ensure a prompt reply (each US$1.05; available at any post office).

BED AND BREAKFASTS (B&BS)

For a cozy alternative to impersonal hotel rooms, B&Bs (private homes, yet more formal than the private rooms described above) range from the acceptable to the sublime. Hosts will sometimes go out of their way to be accommodating by giving personalized tours or offering home-cooked meals. On the other hand, many B&Bs do not provide phones, TVs, or private baths. The British and Irish version of the B&B is extra heavy on the bacon and eggs. Hometours International, Inc., P.O. Box 11503, Knoxville, TN 37939 (US ☎ (800) 367 46 68; http://thor.he.net/~hometour), offers catalogs of B&B listings in France, Italy, Portugal, Switzerland, Spain, and the UK, and also sells packets of B&B vouchers. For more info, see **Nerd World's Bed and Breakfasts by Region** (www.nerdworld.com/users/dstein/nw854), or try **Bed & Breakfast Central Information (BBCI),** P.O. Box 38279, Colorado Springs, CO 80937 (fax (719) 471 47 40; email bbci@bbonline.com; www.bbonline.com/bbci).

DORMS

Many colleges and universities open their residence halls to travelers when school is not in session—some do so even during term-time. These dorms are often close to student areas—good sources for information on things to do—and are usually very clean. Getting a room may take a couple of phone calls and require advanced planning, but rates tend to be low, and many offer free local calls. If you are a student or an intern in Paris, try contacting the Cité Universitaire, 19, bd. Jourdan, 75014 Paris (email marie-therese.texeraud@ciup.fr). For students, single rooms range from US$280-US$360/month. The University of London opens its residential halls to visiting students, often giving discounts for stays over 28 days. For more information, see http://www.lon.ac.uk/accom/site2000/VacationF.html.

HOME EXCHANGES AND HOME RENTALS

Home exchange offers the traveler various types of homes (houses, apartments, condominiums, villas, even castles in some cases), plus the opportunity to live like a native and to cut living costs. For more information and listings for European countries, contact **HomeExchange.Com** (☎ (805) 898 96 60; www.homeexchange.com/euother.html), **Intervac International Home Exchange** (www.intervac.com), or **The Invented City: International Home Exchange** (US ☎ (800) 788-CITY, elsewhere call US +1 (415) 252 11 41; www.invented-city.com). **Home rentals** are more expensive than exchanges, but they can be cheaper than comparably-serviced hotels. Both home

exchanges and rentals are ideal for families with children, or travelers with special dietary needs; you often get your own kitchen, maid service, TV, and telephones.

CAMPING AND THE OUTDOORS

Organized campgrounds exist just outside most European cities. Showers, bathrooms, and a small restaurant or store are common; some have more elaborate facilities. Prices are low, at US$5-15 per person, with additional charges for tents and/or cars, still making camping a much cheaper option than hostelling. **Free camping** allows you to camp in parks or public land (in some cases, such as Sweden, even on private land) for free. For information about camping, hiking, and biking, write or call the publishers and organizations listed below to receive a free catalog. Campers heading to Europe should consider buying an **International Camping Carnet,** which is required at a few campgrounds and provides discounts at others. It is available in North America from the Family Campers and RVers Association (email fcrv-nat@pce.net; www.fcrv.org) and in the UK from The Caravan Club (see below), but can usually also be bought on the spot.

USEFUL RESOURCES

Automobile Association, A.A. Publishing. Publishes the CD-ROM *A Guide to Camping and Caravanning in Britain and Europe* (UK£20). Order by phone: UK ☎0 800 389 27 95, 9am-5pm GMT; by fax, www.theaa.co.uk/bookshop/boocdr003.asp.

The Caravan Club, East Grinstead House, East Grinstead, West Sussex, RH19 1UA (UK ☎ (01342) 32 69 44; www.caravanclub.co.uk). Members receive a 700-page directory and handbook, discounts, and a monthly magazine (UK£27.50).

The European Federation of Campingsite Organisations, EFCO Secretariat, 6 Pullman Court, Great Western Road, Gloucester, GL 1 3 ND (UK ☎14 52 52 69 11; email efco@bhhpa.org.uk; www.campingeurope.com). The website has a comprehensive list of links to campsites in most European countries.

The Mountaineers Books, 1001 SW Klickitat Way #201, Seattle, WA 98134 (US ☎ (800) 553 44 53 or (206) 223 63 03; www.mountaineers.org).

CAMPING AND HIKING EQUIPMENT

Backpack: If you intend to do a lot of hiking, you should have a frame backpack. **Internal-frame packs** mold better to your back, keep a lower center of gravity, and flex adequately to allow you to hike difficult trails. **External-frame packs** are more comfortable for long hikes over even terrain, as they keep weight higher and distribute it more evenly. Whichever you choose, make sure your pack has a strong, padded hip-belt to transfer weight to your legs. Any serious backpacking requires a pack of at least 4000 in^3 (16,000cc), plus 500 in^3 for sleeping bags in internal-frame packs. Sturdy backpacks cost anywhere from US$125-420—this is one area in which it doesn't pay to economize. Fill up a pack with something heavy and walk around the store with it to get a sense of how it distributes weight before buying it. Either buy a **waterproof backpack cover,** or store all of your belongings in plastic bags inside your backpack.

Other Necessities: Be sure to wear hiking boots with good **ankle support.** They should fit snugly and comfortably over 1-2 pairs of wool socks and thin liner socks. Break in boots over several weeks to spare yourself from blisters. A **sleeping bag** and **tent** are necessities if you plan to camp at higher altitudes. **Synthetic** layers, like those made of polypropylene, and a **pile jacket** will keep you warm even when wet. A **"space blanket"** will help you to retain your body heat and doubles as a groundcloth (US$5-15). Plastic screw-top **water bottles** are virtually shatter- and leak-proof. Bring **water-purification tablets** (e.g. iodine) for when you can't boil water. Although most campgrounds provide campfire sites, you may want to bring a small **metal grate** or **grill** of your own. Since virtually every organized campground in Europe forbids fires or the gathering of firewood, you'll also need a **camp stove** (the classic Coleman starts at US$40) and a propane-filled **fuel bottle** to operate it. Don't forget a **first-aid kit, Swiss Army knife, insect repellent, calamine lotion,** and **waterproof matches** or a **lighter.**

WHERE TO BUY. The mail-order/online companies listed below offer lower prices than many retail stores, but keep in mind that a visit to a local camping or outdoors store will give you a better sense of items' look and weight.

Au vieux campeur, 48-50 r. des Ecoles, Paris 75005, France (☎01 53 10 48 48). One of the largest outdoors shops in France, with 18 separate boutiques in a one-block radius, outfitting for everything from ice-climbing to beachcombing. Open M-F 9am-6pm, Sa 9am-1pm.

Campmor, P.O. Box 700, Upper Saddle River, NJ 07458 (US ☎ (888) 226 76 67; elsewhere call US +1 (201) 825 83 00; www.campmor.com).

Discount Camping, 880 Main North Rd., Pooraka, South Australia 5095, Australia (☎ (08) 82 62 33 99; www.discountcamping.com.au).

Eastern Mountain Sports (EMS), 327 Jaffrey Rd., Peterborough, NH 03458, USA (☎ (888) 463 63 67 or (603) 924 72 31; www.shopems.com)

L.L. Bean, Freeport, ME 04033 (US and Canada ☎ (800) 441 57 13; UK ☎ (0800) 962 954; elsewhere, call US +1 (207) 552 68 78; www.llbean.com).

Mountain Designs, P.O. Box 1472, Fortitude Valley, Queensland 4006, Australia (☎ (07) 32 52 88 94; www.mountaindesign.com.au).

Recreational Equipment, Inc. (REI), Sumner, WA 98352, USA (☎ (800) 426 48 40 or (253) 891 25 00; www.rei.com).

YHA Adventure Shop, 14 Southampton St., London, WC2E 7HA, UK (☎ (020) 78 36 85 41). The main branch of one of Britain's largest outdoor equipment suppliers.

CAMPERS AND RVS

Renting an RV is always more expensive than tenting or hostelling, but it's cheaper than staying in hotels and renting a car (see **Rental Cars,** p. 63), and the convenience of bringing along your own bedroom, bathroom, and kitchen makes it an attractive option, especially for older travelers and families with children. Rates vary widely by region, season (July and August are the most expensive months), and RV type. Try contacting several different companies to compare vehicles and prices.

Auto Europe (US ☎ (800) 223 55 55; UK toll-free ☎ (0800) 89 98 93; www.autoeurope.com) rents RVs in Florence, London, Paris, Lyon, Marseilles, Hamburg, Frankfurt, Munich, Düsseldorf, Barcelona, and Madrid. Weekly rates for a 4-passenger RV range about US$1000-1300/600-800 in high/low season (cheaper in Germany).

FURTHER RESOURCES

Camping Your Way through Europe, Carol Mickelsen. Affordable Press (US$15).

Exploring Europe by RV, Dennis and Tina Jaffe. Globe Pequot (US$15).

Europe by Van and Motorhome, David Shore and Patty Campbell (US$14; ☎/fax (800) 659 52 22; email shorecam@aol.com; members.aol.com/europevan).

Great Outdoor Recreation Pages, www.gorp.com.

KEEPING IN TOUCH

MAIL

SENDING MAIL TO EUROPE

Australia: Allow 4-7 days for regular airmail to Europe. **EMS** can get a letter to Europe in 3-5 days for AUS$32. www.auspost.com.au/pac.

Canada: Allow 4-7 days for regular airmail to Europe. www.canadapost.ca/CPC2/common/rates/ratesgen.html#international.

Ireland: Allow 2-3 days for regular airmail to the UK, 3-4 days to the continent. **Swiftpost International** speeds letters for IR£2.30 plus normal airmail cost. www.letterpost.ie.

New Zealand: Allow 6-12 days for regular airmail to Europe. www.nzpost.co.nz/nzpost/inrates.

UK: Allow 3 days for airmail to the continent. UK Swiftair delivers letters a day faster for an extra UK£2.85 in addition to the airmail rate. www.royalmail.co.uk/calculator.

US: Allow 4-7 days for regular airmail to Europe. **US Express Mail** takes 2-3 days and costs US$19/23 (0.5/1 lb.). **US Global Priority Mail** delivers small/large flat-rate envelopes to Europe in 3-5 days for US$5/9.

Additionally, **Federal Express** (Australia ☎ 13 26 10; US and Canada ☎ (800) 247 47 47; New Zealand ☎ (0800) 73 33 39; UK ☎ (0800) 12 38 00) handles express mail services from most of the above countries to Europe; for example, they can get a letter from New York to Europe in two days for US$25.50.

RECEIVING MAIL IN EUROPE

There are several ways to pick up letters sent to you abroad by friends and family:

General Delivery: Mail can be sent via **Poste Restante** (French for General Delivery, and the acceptable term throughout most of Europe; *Lista de Correos* in Spanish, *Fermo Posta* in Italian, and *Postlagernde Briefe* in German) to almost any city or town in Europe with a post office. Address mail to be held: Jane DOE, *Poste Restante*, London SW1, United Kingdom. The mail goes to a special desk in the central post office, unless you specify a different post office by street address or postal code. It's best to use the largest post office in the area, since mail may be sent there regardless. It is usually safer and quicker, although more expensive, to send mail express or registered. Bring your passport (or other photo ID) for pick-up; there may be a small fee. If the clerks insist that there is nothing for you, have them check under your first name as well.

American Express: AmEx travel offices worldwide offer a free **Client Letter Service.** They will hold mail for up to 30 days and forward upon request. Address the letter in the same manner shown above, but with the address of the AmEx office. Some offices offer these services to non-cardholders (especially those with AmEx Travelers Cheques), but call ahead to confirm. *Let's Go* lists AmEx office locations for most large cities in **Practical Information** sections; get a free list from AmEx (US ☎ (800) 528 48 00).

SENDING MAIL HOME FROM EUROPE

Airmail from Western Europe to North America averages seven days; from Central or Eastern Europe, allow anywhere from seven days to three weeks (in Russia, Ukraine, and Belarus, you'll be lucky if mail leaves the post office at all). Times are more unpredictable from smaller towns. **Aerogrammes,** printed sheets that fold into envelopes and travel via airmail, are available at post offices. Most post offices will charge exorbitant fees or simply refuse to send aerogrammes with enclosures. In either case, it helps to write "airmail" (or *por avión, mit Luftpost, via aerea,* etc.) on the envelope, although *par avion* is generally understood. For exact postage for postcards and letters sent from Europe, see individual country introductions.

Surface mail is by far the cheapest and slowest way to send mail. It takes one to three months to cross the Atlantic and two to four to cross the Pacific—good for items you won't need to see for a while, such as souvenirs or other articles you've acquired along the way that are weighing down your pack.

TELEPHONES

CALLING HOME FROM EUROPE

A **calling card** is probably your cheapest bet. Calls are billed either collect or to your account. **To obtain a calling card** from your national telecommunications service before leaving home, contact one of the following:

Australia: Telstra Australia Direct (☎ 13 22 00).
Canada: Bell Canada **Canada Direct** (☎ (800) 565 47 08).
Ireland: Telecom Éireann **Ireland Direct** (☎ (800) 25 02 50).
New Zealand: Telecom New Zealand (☎ (0800) 00 00 00).
South Africa: Telkom South Africa (☎ 09 03).
UK: British Telecom **BT Direct** (☎ (800) 34 51 44).

ESSENTIALS

US: AT&T (☎ (888) 288 46 85), **Sprint** (☎ (800) 877 46 46), or **MCI** (☎ (800) 444 41 41). To **call home with a calling card,** contact the operator for your service provider in the appropriate country by dialing the toll-free access number provided in the Essentials chapter for each country under **Communications.** Keep in mind that phone cards can be problematic in Russia, Ukraine, Belarus, and Slovenia—double-check with your provider before setting out. You can usually make **direct international calls** from pay phones, but if you aren't using a calling card, you may need to drop your coins as quickly as your words. Where available, prepaid phone cards (see below) and occasionally major credit cards can be used for direct international calls, but they are still less cost-efficient. Placing a **collect call** through an international operator is a more expensive alternative. You can typically place collect calls through the service providers listed above, even if you don't possess one of their phone cards.

LOCAL CALLS WITHIN EUROPE

For **local calls,** the simplest way to call may be to use a coin-operated phone. However, much of Europe has switched to a **prepaid phone card** system, and in some countries you may have a hard time finding any coin-operated phones at all. Phone cards (usually available at newspaper kiosks and tobacco stores) carry a certain amount of phone time, measured in units. Investing in a phone card usually saves time and money in the long run; just use any leftover time on a call home before leaving the country. The computerized phone will tell you how much time, in units, you have left on your card. Another kind of prepaid telephone card comes with a Personal Identification Number (PIN) and a toll-free access number. Instead of inserting the card into the phone, you call the access number and follow the directions on the card. These cards can be used to make international as well as domestic calls. **Phone rates** are highest in the morning, lower in the evening, and lowest on Sundays and late at night.

To place **international calls** (to Europe from home or between countries in Europe), see the **inside back cover.**

TIME DIFFERENCES

Greenwich Mean Time (GMT) is five hours ahead of New York time, eight hours ahead of Vancouver and San Francisco time, two hours behind Johannesburg time, 10 hours behind Sydney time, and 12 hours behind Auckland time. Some countries (like Iceland) ignore **daylight savings time;** fall and spring switchover times vary. See specific country introductions and the **time zone map** in the Appendix (p. 981).

EMAIL AND INTERNET

Email has become the joy of backpackers worldwide, so it's no surprise that it has become a popular and easily accessible option in Europe as well. Although in some places it's possible to forge a remote link with your home server, usually this is slower and more expensive than taking advantage of free **web-based email accounts** (e.g., www.hotmail.com, www.yahoo.com, www.youpy.fr, mail.voila.fr, mail.wordwalla.com). Travelers with laptops can call an internet service provider via a **modem.** Long-distance phone cards specifically intended for such calls can defray normally high phone charges; check with your long-distance phone provider to see if it offers this option. **Internet cafés** and the occasional free internet terminal at a public library or university are listed in the **Orientation and Practical Information** sections of major cities. For lists of additional cybercafes in Europe, check out http://cybercaptive.com or www.cyberiacafe.net/cyberia/guide/ccafe.htm.

GETTING THERE

BY PLANE

When it comes to airfare, a little effort can save you a bundle. If your plans are flexible enough to deal with complex restrictions, courier fares are the cheapest. Tickets bought from consolidators and standby tickets are also good deals, but last-minute specials, airfare wars, and charter flights often beat these fares. The key is to hunt around, to be flexible, and to ask persistently about discounts. Students, seniors, and those under 26 should never pay full price for a ticket.

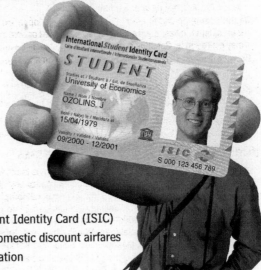

DETAILS AND TIPS

Timing: Airfares to Europe peak between mid-June and early Sept.; mid-Dec. to early Jan. can also be expensive. The cheapest times to travel are Nov. to mid-Dec. and early Jan. to Mar. Midweek (M-Th morning) round-trip flights run US$40-50 less than weekend flights, but are generally more crowded and are less likely to permit frequent flier upgrades. Traveling with an "open-return" ticket can be pricier than buying a fixed-return date ticket and paying later to change it.

Route: Round-trip flights are by far the cheapest; "open-jaw" (arriving in and departing from different cities, e.g. London-Paris and Rome-London) tickets tend to be pricier but may make sense. Patching one-way flights together is the most expensive way to travel.

Round-the-World (RTW): If Europe is only 1 stop on a more extensive globe-hop, consider a RTW ticket. Tickets usually include at least 5 stops and are valid for about a year; prices range US$1200-5000. Try **Northwest Airlines/KLM** (US ☎ (800) 225 25 25; www.nwa.com) or **Star Alliance,** a consortium of 8 airlines including United Airlines (US ☎ (800) 241 65 22; www.star-alliance.com).

Gateway Cities: Flights between capitals or regional hubs will offer the cheapest fares. The cheapest gateway cities in Europe are London, Paris, Amsterdam, and Frankfurt.

BUDGET AND STUDENT TRAVEL AGENCIES

usit world (www.usitworld.com). Over 50 **usit campus** branches in the UK (www.usitcampus.co.uk), including 52 Grosvenor Gardens, **London** SW1W 0AG (☎ (0870) 240 10 10); **Manchester** (☎ (0161) 273 17 21); and **Edinburgh** (☎ (0131) 668 33 03). Nearly 20 **usit now** offices in Ireland, including 19-21 Aston Quay, O'Connell Bridge, **Dublin** 2 (☎ (01) 602 1600; www.usitnow.ie), and **Belfast** (☎ (02890) 32 71 11; www.usitnow.com). Offices also in Athens, Auckland, Brussels, Frankfurt, Johannesburg, Lisbon, Luxembourg, Madrid, Paris, Sofia, and Warsaw.

Council Travel (www.counciltravel.com). US offices include: Emory Village, 1561 N. Decatur Rd., **Atlanta,** GA 30307 (☎ (404) 377 99 97); 273 Newbury St., **Boston,** MA 02116 (☎ (617) 266 19 26); 1160 N. State St., **Chicago,** IL 60610 (☎ (312) 951 05 85); 931 Westwood Blvd., Westwood, **Los Angeles,** CA 90024 (☎ (310) 208 35 51); 254 Greene St., **New York,** NY 10003 (☎ (212) 254 25 25); 530 Bush St., **San Francisco,** CA 94108 (☎ (415) 566 62 22); 424 Broadway Ave E., **Seattle,** WA 98102 (☎ (206) 329 45 67); and 3301 M St. NW, **Washington, D.C.** 20007 (☎ (202) 337 64 64). **For US cities not listed,** call (800) 2-COUNCIL (226 86 24). In the UK, 28A Poland St. (Oxford Circus), **London,** W1V 3DB (☎ (020) 74 37 77 67).

CTS Travel, 44 Goodge St., **London** W1 (☎ (020) 76 36 00 31; fax 76 37 53 28; email ctsinfo@ctstravel.com.uk).

STA Travel, 6560 Scottsdale Rd. #F100, Scottsdale, AZ 85253 (☎ (800) 777 01 12; fax (602) 922 07 93; www.sta-travel.com). A student and youth travel organization with over 150 offices worldwide. Ticket booking, travel insurance, railpasses, and more. US offices include: 297 Newbury St., **Boston,** MA 02115 (☎ (617) 266 60 14); 429 S. Dearborn St., **Chicago,** IL 60605 (☎ (312) 786 90 50); 7202 Melrose Ave., **Los Angeles,** CA 90046 (☎ (323) 934 87 22); 10 Downing St., **New York,** NY 10014 (☎ (212) 627 31 11); 4341 University Way NE, **Seattle,** WA 98105 (☎ (206) 633 50 00); 2401 Pennsylvania Ave., Ste. G, **Washington, D.C.** 20037 (☎ (202) 887 09 12); and 51 Grant Ave., **San Francisco,** CA 94108 (☎ (415) 391 84 07). In the UK, 11 Goodge St., **London** WIP 1FE (☎ (020) 74 36 77 79 for North American travel). In New Zealand, 10 High St., **Auckland** (☎ (09) 309 04 58). In Australia, 366 Lygon St., **Melbourne** Vic 3053 (☎ (03) 93 49 43 44).

Travel CUTS (Canadian Universities Travel Services Limited), 187 College St., **Toronto,** ON M5T 1P7 (☎ (416) 979 24 06; fax 979 81 67; www.travelcuts.com). 40 offices across Canada. Also in the UK, 295-A Regent St., **London** W1R 7YA (☎ (020) 72 55 19 44).

Wasteels, Platform 2, Victoria Station, **London** SW1V 1JT (☎ (020) 78 34 70 66; fax 76 30 76 28; www.wasteels.dk/uk). Huge chain in Europe. Sells BIJ tickets, which are discounted (30-45% off regular fare), and 2nd-class international point-to-point train tickets with unlimited stopovers for under 26ers (sold only in Europe).

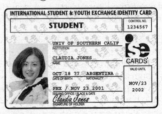

COMMERCIAL AIRLINES

The commercial airlines' lowest regular offer is the **APEX** (Advance Purchase Excursion) fare, which provides confirmed reservations and allows "open-jaw" tickets. Generally, reservations must be made seven to 21 days ahead of departure, with seven- to 14-day minimum-stay and up to 90-day maximum-stay restrictions. These fares carry hefty cancellation and change penalties (fees rise in summer). Book peak-season APEX fares early; by May you will have a hard time getting your desired departure date. Use **Microsoft Expedia** (expedia.msn.com) or **Travelocity** (www.travelocity.com) to get an idea of the lowest published fares, then use the resources outlined here to try and beat those fares. Low-season fares should be appreciably cheaper than the **high-season** (mid-June to Aug.) ones listed here.

TRAVELING FROM NORTH AMERICA

Basic round-trip fares to Europe range from roughly US$200-750: to Frankfurt, US$300-750; London, US$200-600; Paris, US$250-700. Standard commercial carriers like American (☎ (800) 433 73 00; www.aa.com) and United (☎ (800) 241 65 22; www.ual.com) will probably offer the most convenient flights, but they may not be the cheapest, unless you manage to grab a special promotion or airfare war ticket. You might find flying one of the following airlines a better deal, if any of their limited departure points is convenient for you.

Icelandair: ☎ (800) 223 55 00; www.icelandair.com. Stopovers in Iceland for no extra cost on most transatlantic flights. New York to Frankfurt May-Sept. US$470-710; Oct.-May US$370-$425. For last-minute offers, subscribe to their email *Lucky Fares*.

Finnair: ☎ (800) 950 50 00; www.us.finnair.com. Cheap round-trips from San Francisco, New York, and Toronto to Helsinki; connections throughout Europe.

Martinair: ☎ (800) 627 84 62; www.martinairusa.com. Fly from California or Florida to Amsterdam mid-June to mid-Aug. US$840; mid-Aug. to mid-June US$710.

TRAVELING FROM THE UK AND IRELAND

Because of the myriad carriers flying from the British Isles to the continent, we've only included discount airlines or those with cheap specials. The **Air Travel Advisory Bureau** in London (☎ (020) 76 36 50 00; www.atab.co.uk) provides referrals to travel agencies and consolidators that offer discounted airfares out of the UK.

Aer Lingus: Ireland ☎ (01) 886 88 88; www.aerlingus.ie. Return tickets from Dublin, Cork, Galway, Kerry, and Shannon to Amsterdam, Brussels, Düsseldorf, Frankfurt, Madrid, Milan, Munich, Paris, Rennes, Rome, Stockholm, and Zürich (IR£102-244).

British Midland Airways: UK ☎ (0870) 607 05 55; www.britishmidland.com. Departures from throughout the UK. London to Brussels (UK£68), Madrid (UK£98), Paris (UK£71), and Frankfurt (UK£172).

buzz: UK ☎ (0870) 240 70 70; www.buzzaway.com. A subsidiary of KLM. From London to Berlin, Frankfurt, Hamburg, Milan, Paris, and Vienna (UK£50-80). Tickets cannot be changed or refunded.

easyJet: UK ☎ (0870) 600 00 00; www.easyjet.com. London to Amsterdam, Athens, Barcelona, Geneva, Madrid, Nice, Palma, and Zurich (UK£47-136). Online tickets.

Go-Fly Limited: UK ☎ (0845) 605 43 21, elsewhere call UK +44 (1279) 66 63 88; www.go-fly.com. A subsidiary of British Airways. From London to Barcelona, Copenhagen, Edinburgh, Lisbon, Madrid, Naples, Prague, Rome, and Venice (UK£53-180).

KLM: UK ☎ (0870) 507 40 74; www.klmuk.com. Cheap return tickets from London and elsewhere to Amsterdam, Brussels, Frankfurt, Düsseldorf, Milan, Paris, and Rome.

Ryanair: Ireland ☎ (01) 812 12 12, UK (0870) 156 95 69; www.ryanair.ie. From Dublin, London, and Glasgow to destinations in France, Ireland, Italy, Scandinavia, and elsewhere. Deals from as low as UK£9 on limited weekend specials.

TRAVELING FROM AUSTRALIA AND NEW ZEALAND

Air New Zealand: New Zealand ☎ (0800) 35 22 66; www.airnz.co.nz. Auckland to London and Frankfurt.

Baden-Baden

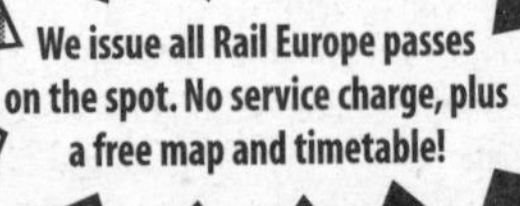
We issue all Rail Europe passes on the spot. No service charge, plus a free map and timetable!

Qantas Air: Australia ☎ 13 13 13, New Zealand 0800 808 767; www.qantas.com.au. Flights from Australia and New Zealand to London for around AUS$2400.

Singapore Air: Australia ☎ 13 10 11, New Zealand 0800 808 909; www.singaporeair.com. Flies from Auckland, Sydney, Melbourne, and Perth to Western Europe.

Thai Airways: Australia ☎ (1300) 65 19 60, New Zealand (09) 377 38 86; www.thaiair.com. Auckland, Sydney, and Melbourne to Amsterdam, Frankfurt, and London.

TRAVELING FROM SOUTH AFRICA

Air France: ☎ (011) 880 80 40; www.airfrance.com. Johannesburg to Paris; connections throughout Europe.

British Airways: ☎ (0860) 01 17 47; www.british-airways.com/regional/sa. Cape Town and Johannesburg to the UK and the rest of Europe from SAR3400.

Lufthansa: ☎ (011) 484 47 11; www.lufthansa.co.za. From Cape Town, Durban, and Johannesburg to Germany and elsewhere.

Virgin Atlantic (☎ (011) 340 34 00; www.virgin-atlantic.co.za) flies to London from both Cape Town and Johannesburg.

AIR COURIER FLIGHTS

Those who travel light should consider being a courier. Couriers help transport cargo on international flights by using their checked luggage space for freight. Generally, couriers must travel with carry-ons only and must deal with complex flight restrictions. Most flights are round-trip only, with short fixed-length stays (usually one week) and a limit of a one ticket per issue. Most of these flights also operate only out of major gateway cities, mostly in North America. Generally, you must be over 21 (in some cases 18), have a valid passport, and procure your own visa, if necessary. In summer, the most popular destinations usually require an advance reservation of about two weeks (you can usually book up to two months ahead). Super-discounted fares are common for "last-minute" flights (three to 14 days ahead).

TRAVELING FROM NORTH AMERICA

Round-trip courier fares from the US to Europe run about US$200-500. Most flights leave from New York, Los Angeles, San Francisco, or Miami in the US; and from Montreal, Toronto, or Vancouver in Canada. The first four organizations below provide their members with lists of opportunities and courier brokers worldwide for an annual fee (typically US$50-60). Alternatively, you can contact a courier broker (such as the last three listings) directly; most charge registration fees, but a few don't. Prices quoted below are **round-trip.**

Air Cargo Partners, 1983 Marcus Ave #108, Lake Success, NY 11042 (☎ (516) 358 20 25 or (888) VEX-MOVE; fax (516) 358 18 35). Eight US cities to Manchester and London. 90-day max. stay. Ages 19 and up. No registration fee.

Air Courier Association, 191 University Blvd #300, Denver CO 80206 (☎ (800) 282 12 02; elsewhere call US +1 (303) 215 90 00; www.aircourier.org). Ten departure cities throughout the US and Canada to Ireland, the UK, Copenhagen, and throughout Western Europe (high-season US$400-540). One-year US$29.

Global Delivery Systems, 147-25 176th St., Jamaica, NY 11434 (☎ (718) 995 73 00). From New York to Amsterdam, Copenhagen, Rome, Milan, Paris, and Madrid (US$250-650). Ages 18 and up. No registration fee.

International Association of Air Travel Couriers (IAATC), P.O. Box 1349, Lake Worth, FL 33460 (☎ (561) 582 83 20; fax 582 15 81; www.courier.org). New York to 9 Western European cities. Select other cities to London only. 18+. One-year US$45-50.

Global Courier Travel, P.O. Box 3051, Nederland, CO 80466 (www.globalcouriertraveler.com). Searchable online database. Six departure points along both coasts. Some one-way flights. One-year US$40, 2 people US$55.

NOW Voyager, 74 Varick St #307, New York, NY 10013 (☎ (212) 431 16 16; fax 219 17 53; www.nowvoyagertravel.com). New York to London (US$516); Amsterdam, Brussels,

WHOLE EARTH TRAVEL INC.
EUROPE
$169-$249 o/w*
U.S.A.
Hawaii $129
Coast to Coast $129
and more . . . .
TARGET FLIGHTS
Confirmed seats on all domestic and international destinations
MEXICO / CARIBBEAN
$199-$229 r/t*
FREE BROCHURE
East Coast : 1-800-326-2009
West Coast : 1-888-AIRHITCH
www.4cheapair.com
*plus departure taxes
BE FLEXIBLE
SAVE MONEY
AIRHITCH®

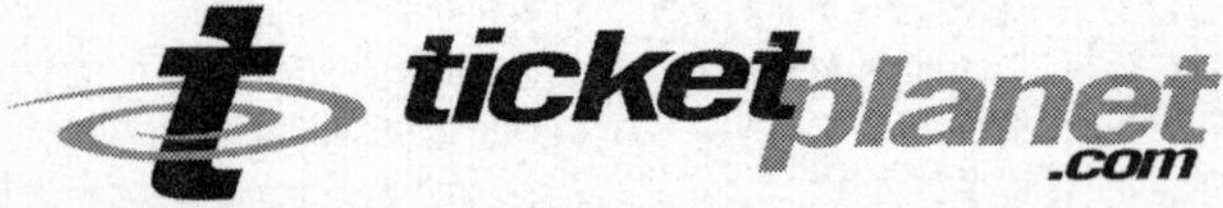

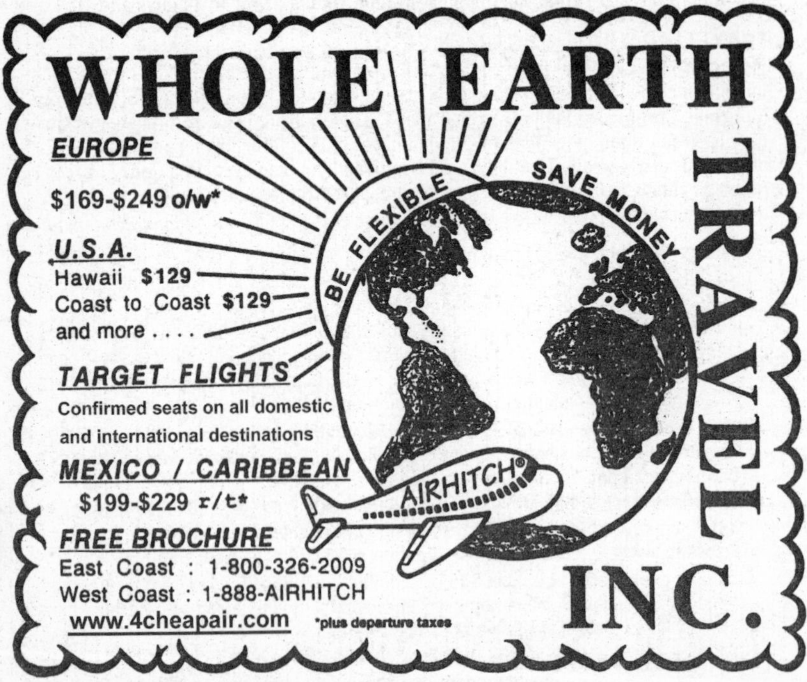

Copenhagen, and Dublin (US$499-649); and Paris, Madrid, Rome, and Milan (US$450-749). Usually one-week max. stay. Ages 18 and up. One-year US$50.

Worldwide Courier Association (☎ (800) 780 43 59, ext. 441; www.massiveweb.com). From New York, San Francisco, Los Angeles, and Chicago to Western Europe, including Milan, Madrid, and London (US$300-600). One-year US$58.

FROM THE UK, IRELAND, AUSTRALIA, AND NEW ZEALAND

Although the courier industry is most developed from North America, there are limited courier flights in other areas. The minimum age for couriers from the **UK** is usually 18. **Brave New World Enterprises,** P.O. Box 22212, London SE5 8WB (email guideinfo@nry.co.uk; www.nry.co.uk/bnw) publishes a directory of all the companies offering courier flights in the UK (UK£10, in electronic form UK£8). The **International Association of Air Travel Couriers** (see above) often offers courier flights from London to Budapest. **Global Courier Travel** (see above) also offers flights from London and Dublin to continental Europe, and often has listings from Sydney and Auckland to London and occasionally Frankfurt.

ESSENTIALS

STANDBY FLIGHTS

Traveling standby requires considerable flexibility in arrival and departure dates and cities. Companies dealing in standby flights sell vouchers rather than tickets, along with the promise to get you to your destination (or near your destination) within a certain window of time (typically one to five days). You call in before your specific window of time to hear your flight options and the probability that you will be able to board each flight. You then decide what flight you want to try to make, show up at the appropriate airport at the appropriate time, present your voucher, and board if space is available. Vouchers can usually be bought for both one-way and round-trip travel. You may receive a monetary refund only if every available flight within your date range is full; if you opt not to take an available (but perhaps less convenient) flight, you can only get credit toward future travel. Carefully read agreements with any company offering standby flights, as tricky fine print can leave you in a lurch. To check on a company's service record in the US, call the Better Business Bureau (☎ (212) 533 62 00). It is difficult to receive refunds, and clients' vouchers will not be honored when an airline fails to receive payment in time. One established standby company in the US is **Airhitch,** 2641 Broadway, third fl. #100, New York, NY 10025 (☎ (800) 326 20 09; fax 864 54 89; www.airhitch.org) and Los Angeles, CA (☎ (888) 247 44 82), which offers one-way flights to Europe from the Northeast (US$169), West Coast and Northwest (US$249), Midwest (US$219), and Southeast (US$189). Intracontinental connecting flights within the US or Europe cost US$79-139. Airhitch's head European office is in **Paris** (☎ +33 01 47 00 16 30); there's also one in **Amsterdam** (☎ +31 (20) 626 32 20).

TICKET CONSOLIDATORS

Ticket consolidators, or **"bucket shops,"** buy unsold tickets in bulk from commercial airlines and sell them at discounted rates. The best place to look is in the Sunday travel section of any major newspaper (such as the *New York Times*), where many bucket shops place tiny ads. Call quickly, as availability is typically extremely limited. Not all bucket shops are reliable, so insist on a receipt that gives full details of restrictions, refunds, and tickets, and pay by credit card (in spite of the 2-5% fee) so you can stop payment if you never receive your tickets. For more info, see www.travel-library.com/air-travel/consolidators.html or pick up Kelly Monaghan's *Air Travel's Bargain Basement* (Intrepid Traveler, US$10).

TRAVELING FROM NORTH AMERICA

Travel Avenue (☎ (800) 333 33 35; www.travelavenue.com) rebates commercial fares to or from the US (5% for over US$550) and will search for cheap flights from anywhere for a fee. **NOW Voyager** (see above) arranges discounted flights, mostly from New York, to Barcelona, London, Madrid, Milan, Paris, and Rome. At 17% off published fares, they are often as cheap as courier fares, and are considerably more

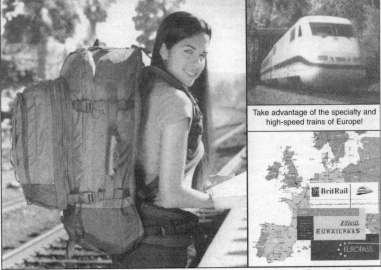

flexible. Other consolidators worth trying are **Interworld** (☎ (305) 443 49 29; fax 443 03 51); **Pennsylvania Travel** (☎ (800) 331 09 47); **Rebel** (☎ (800) 227 32 35; email travel@rebeltours.com; www.rebeltours.com); **Cheap Tickets** (☎ (800) 377 10 00; www.cheaptickets.com); and **Travac** (☎ (800) 872 88 00; fax (212) 714 90 63; www.travac.com). More consolidators on the web include the **Internet Travel Network** (www.itn.com); **Travel Information Services** (www.tiss.com); **TravelHUB** (www.travelhub.com); and **The Travel Site** (www.thetravelsite.com). Keep in mind that these are just suggestions to get you started in your research; *Let's Go* does not endorse any of these agencies. As always, be cautious, and research companies before you hand over your credit card number.

TRAVELING FROM THE UK, AUSTRALIA, AND NEW ZEALAND

In London, the **Air Travel Advisory Bureau** (☎ (020) 76 36 50 00; www.atab.co.uk) can provide names of reliable consolidators and discount flight specialists. Also look for ads in the Sunday papers. From Australia and New Zealand, look for consolidator ads in the travel section of the *Sydney Morning Herald* and other papers.

CHARTER FLIGHTS

Charters are flights a tour operator contracts with an airline to fly extra loads of passengers during peak season. Charters can sometimes be cheaper than flights on scheduled airlines, some operate nonstop, and restrictions on minimum advance-purchase and minimum stay are more lenient. However, charters fly less frequently than major airlines, make refunds particularly difficult, and are almost always fully booked. Schedules and itineraries may also change or be cancelled at the last moment (as late as 48hr. before the trip, and without a full refund), and check-in, boarding, and baggage claim are often much slower. Pay with a credit card if you can, and consider traveler's insurance against trip interruption.

FURTHER READING

The Worldwide Guide to Cheap Airfare, Michael McColl. Insider Publications (US$15).

Discount Airfares: The Insider's Guide, George Hobart. Priceless Publications (US$14).

The Official Airline Guide, an expensive tome available at many libraries, has flight schedules, fares, and reservation numbers.

Air Traveler's Handbook (www.cs.cmu.edu/afs/cs/user/mkant/Public/Travel/airfare.html).

BY CHUNNEL FROM THE UK

Traversing 27 miles under the sea, the Chunnel is undoubtedly the fastest, most convenient, and least scenic route from England to France.

BY TRAIN. **Eurostar,** Eurostar House, Waterloo Station, **London** SE1 8SE (UK ☎ (0990) 18 61 86; US ☎ (800) 387 67 82; elsewhere call UK +44 (1233) 61 75 75; www.eurostar.com, www.raileurope.com) runs a frequent train service between London and the continent. Over 17 departures per day to Paris (3hr., US$75-159, 2nd class) and 10 to Brussels (3hr., 50min., US$75-159, 2nd class). Some routes include stops at Ashford in England, and Calais and Lille in France. Book at major rail stations in the UK, at the office above, by phone, or on the web.

BY BUS. Both **Eurolines** and **Eurobus** provide bus service (see p. 61).

BY CAR. If traveling by car, **Eurotunnel** (UK ☎ (08000) 96 99 92; www.eurotunnel.co.uk) shuttles cars and passengers between Kent and Nord-Pas-de-Calais. Return fares range from UK£219-299 with car, UK£259-598 with campervan, and UK£119-299 for a trailer/caravan supplement. Same-day return costs UK£110-150, five-day return UK£139-195. Book online or via phone.

BY BOAT FROM THE UK AND IRELAND

The following fares listed are **one-way** for **adult foot passengers** unless otherwise noted. Although standard return fares are in most cases simply twice the one-way fare, **fixed-period returns** (usually within five days) are almost invariably cheaper. Ferries run **year-round** unless otherwise noted. **Bikes** are usually free, although you may have to pay up to UK£10 in high season. For a **camper/trailer** supplement, you will have to add UK£20-140 to the "with car" fare. If more than one price is quoted, the quote in UK£ is valid for departures from the UK. A directory of ferries in this region can be found at www.seaview.co.uk/ferries.html.

P&O Stena Line: UK ☎ (08706) 00 06 00; www.posl.com. **Dover** to **Calais** (1¼hr., every 45min.-1hr., 30 per day; UK£24).

Hoverspeed: UK ☎ (08702) 40 80 70; www.hoverspeed.co.uk. **Dover** to **Calais** (35-50min., 12 per day, UK£24-30) and **Ostend, Belgium** (2hr., 5 per day, UK£28). **Folkestone** to **Boulogne, France** (1hr., 4 per day, UK£24). **Newhaven** to **Dieppe, France** (2hr., 1-3 per day, UK£28).

SeaFrance: UK ☎ (08705) 71 17 11; www.seafrance.co.uk. **Dover** to **Calais** (1½hr., 15 per day, UK£15, with car UK£117).

Scandinavian Seaways: UK ☎ (0990) 44 43 33; www.scansea.com. **Harwich** to **Hamburg** (20hr., every other day, US$94-221) and **Esbjerg, Denmark** (22hr., every other day, US$131-270). **Newcastle** to **Amsterdam** (15hr., daily, US$94-221) and **Kristiansand, Norway** (18hr., twice a week, US$94-185), connecting from there to **Gothenburg, Sweden** (22hr.).

P&O European Ferries: UK ☎ (0870) 242 49 99; www.poef.com. **Portsmouth** to **Le Havre** and **Cherbourg** (both 5½hr., 1-7 per day, UK£20-33, with car UK£95-170) and **Bilbao** (35hr., 2 per week, UK£55-90, with car UK£160-295).

Brittany Ferries: UK ☎ (0870) 901 24 00; www.brittany-ferries.com. **Plymouth** to **Roscoff, France** (6hr., in summer 1-3 per day, off season 1 per week, UK£25-38) and **Santander, Spain** (24-30hr., 1-2 per week, return UK£80-145). **Portsmouth** to **St-Malo** (8¾hr., 1-2 per day, UK£26-45) and **Caen** (6hr., 1-3 per day, UK£24-40), France.

Poole to **Cherbourg** (4¼hr., 1-2 per day, UK£24-40). **Cork** to **Roscoff** (14hr., Apr.-Sept. 1 per week).

P&O North Sea Ferries: UK ☎ (01482) 37 71 77; www.ponsf.com/passeng/index.htm. Daily ferries from **Hull** to **Rotterdam, Netherlands** (13½hr.) and **Zeebrugge, Belgium** (14hr.). Both UK£38-48, with car UK£161-204. Online bookings.

Fjord Line: UK ☎ (0191) 296 13 13; www.fjordline.no. **Newcastle, England** to **Stavanger** (19hr.), connecting from there to **Bergen** (26hr., 2-3 per week, UK£44-224, vehicles UK£60-300, 50% discount for students, seniors, and children ages 4-15.) Also between western Norway and Denmark.

Irish Ferries: Ireland ☎ 189 031 31 31; UK ☎ (0807) 05 17 17 17; www.irishferries.ie. **Rosslare** to **Cherbourg** (19hr., 1-3 per week, IR£45-85); **Roscoff** (14½hr., Apr.-Sept. 1-2 per week, IR£40-80); and **Pembroke, England** (3¾hr., 2 per day, IR£16-25). **Holyhead, England** to **Dublin** (2-3¼hr., 5-6 per day, return IR£35-60, students IR£28-48).

Stena Line: UK ☎ (08705) 70 70 70; elsewhere call UK +44 (1233) 64 70 22; www.stenaline.co.uk. **Harwich, England** to **Hook of Holland** (3¾hr., 2 per day, UK£22). **Fishguard** to **Rosslare** (1½-3½hr., 2-4 per day, UK£16-34). **Holyhead** to **Dublin** (4hr., 2 per day, vehicles only, UK£30-35) and **Dún Laoghaire** (1½-3½hr., 4 per day, UK£20-30, students UK£16-28). **Stranraer** to **Belfast** (1¾-3¼hr., 5-9 per day, UK£20-25; Mar.-Jan.).

GETTING AROUND EUROPE

Fares on all modes of transportation are either **single** (one-way) or **return** (round-trip). Unless stated otherwise, *Let's Go* always lists single fares. Round-trip fares on trains and buses in most of Europe are simply double the one-way fare.

BY TRAIN

In most of Europe, trains are the fastest and easiest way to travel. Second-class travel is pleasant, and compartments, which seat two to six, are excellent places to meet fellow travelers. Trains, however, are not always safe; for safety tips, see p. 19. For long trips make sure you are on the correct car, as trains sometimes split at crossroads. Towns listed in parentheses on European train schedules require a train switch at the town listed immediately before the parentheses.

You can either buy a **railpass,** which allows you unlimited travel within a particular region for a given period of time, or rely on buying individual **point-to-point** tickets as you go. Almost all countries give students or youths (usually defined as those under 26) direct discounts on regular domestic rail tickets, and many also sell a student or youth card that provides 20-50% off all fares for up to a year.

RESERVATIONS. While seat reservations are required only for some trains (usually on major lines), you are not guaranteed a seat without one (US$10-15). Reservations are available on major trains as far as 60 days in advance (120 days for the Eurostar), and Europeans often reserve far ahead; you should strongly consider reserving during peak holiday and tourist seasons. While reservations for ICE trains are highly recommended, it will be necessary to purchase a **supplement** (US$10-50) or special fare for high-speed or -quality trains such as Spain's AVE, Cisalpino, Finland's Pendolino S220, Italy's ETR500 and Pendolino, all Thalys high-speed trains, and certain French TGVs. InterRail holders must also purchase supplements (US$10-25) for trains like EuroCity, InterCity, Sweden's X2000, and many French TGVs; these supplements are unnecessary for Eurailpass and Europass holders. Reservations are included in the cost of a Eurostar ticket.

OVERNIGHT TRAINS. Night trains have their advantages: you won't waste valuable daylight hours traveling, and you will be able to forego the hassle and considerable expense of securing a night's accommodation. However, night travel has its drawbacks as well: discomfort and sleepless nights are the most obvious; the scenery probably won't look as enticing in pitch black, either. **Sleeping accommodations** on trains differ from country to country, but typically you can either sleep upright in your seat (for free) or pay for a separate space. **Couchettes** (berths) typically have four to six seats per compartment (about US$27-37 per person); **sleepers** (beds) in

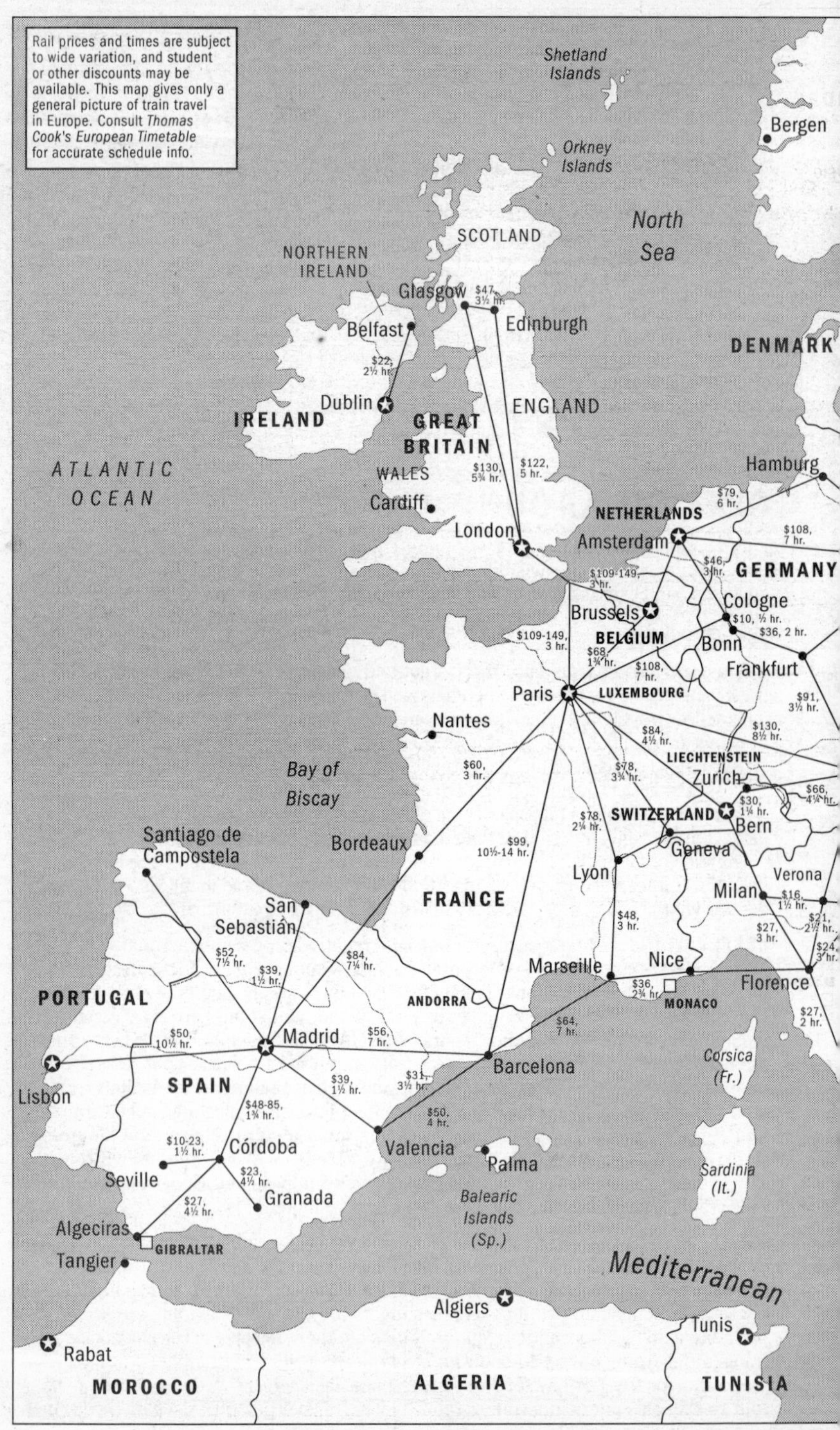
Rail prices and times are subject to wide variation, and student or other discounts may be available. This map gives only a general picture of train travel in Europe. Consult Thomas Cook's European Timetable for accurate schedule info.
Shetland Islands
Orkney Islands
Bergen
North Sea
SCOTLAND
NORTHERN IRELAND
Glasgow
$47, 3½ hr.
Edinburgh
Belfast
$22, 2½ hr.
DENMARK
Dublin
IRELAND
GREAT BRITAIN
ENGLAND
ATLANTIC OCEAN
WALES
$130, 5¾ hr.
$122, 5 hr.
Hamburg
Cardiff
$79, 6 hr.
NETHERLANDS
London
Amsterdam
$108, 7 hr.
$46, 3 hr.
GERMANY
$109-149, 3 hr.
Cologne
Brussels
$10, ½ hr.
$36, 2 hr.
$109-149, 3 hr.
BELGIUM
Bonn
$68, 1¾ hr.
$108, 7 hr.
Frankfurt
Paris
LUXEMBOURG
$91, 3½ hr.
Nantes
$130, 8½ hr.
$84, 4½ hr.
LIECHTENSTEIN
$60, 3 hr.
Bay of Biscay
$78, 3¾ hr.
Zurich
$66, 4¼ hr.
$30, 1¼ hr.
SWITZERLAND
Bern
$78, 2¼ hr.
Santiago de Campostela
Bordeaux
$99, 10½-14 hr.
Geneva
Lyon
Verona
Milan
$16, 1½ hr.
FRANCE
San Sebastián
$48, 3 hr.
$27, 3 hr.
$21, 2½ hr.
$24, 3 hr.
$52, 7½ hr.
$39, 1½ hr.
$84, 7¼ hr.
Nice
Marseille
Florence
PORTUGAL
$36, 2¾ hr.
MONACO
ANDORRA
$27, 2 hr.
$64, 7 hr.
$50, 10½ hr.
Madrid
$56, 7 hr.
Corsica (Fr.)
Barcelona
$39, 1½ hr.
$31, 3½ hr.
Lisbon
SPAIN
$48-85, 1¾ hr.
$50, 4 hr.
$10-23, 1½ hr.
Córdoba
Valencia
Palma
Seville
$23, 4½ hr.
Sardinia (It.)
$27, 4½ hr.
Granada
Balearic Islands (Sp.)
Algeciras
GIBRALTAR
Tangier
Mediterranean
Algiers
Tunis
Rabat
MOROCCO
ALGERIA
TUNISIA

Rail Planner
FINLAND
SWEDEN
ORWAY
ESTONIA
LATVIA
LITHUANIA
RUSSIA
BELARUS
POLAND
CZECH REPUBLIC
SLOVAKIA
AUSTRIA
HUNGARY
SLOVENIA
CROATIA
BOSNIA-HERZEGOVINA
YUGOSLAVIA
MONTENEGRO
UKRAINE
MOLDOVA
ROMANIA
BULGARIA
FYR MACEDONIA
ALBANIA
GREECE
TURKEY
ITALY
SAN MARINO
L. Onega
L. Ladoga
Gulf of
Baltic Sea
Dnieper River
Sea of Azov
Black Sea
Adriatic Sea
Ionian Sea
Aegean Sea
Sea of Crete
Sicily
Helsinki
St. Petersburg
Tallinn
Stockholm
Oslo
Göteborg
Malmö
Copenhagen
Riga
Moscow
Vilnius
Minsk
Gdańsk
Berlin
Poznań
Warsaw
Wrocław
Kraków
Prague
Lviv
Kiev
Kharkiv
Munich
Vienna
Bratislava
Budapest
Ljubljana
Zagreb
Venice
Belgrade
Bucharest
Chişinău
Odessa
Yalta
Sarajevo
Dubrovnik
Sofia
Istanbul
Ankara
Rome
Naples
Brindisi
Tiranë
Thessaloniki
Athens
Izmir
Palermo
Messina
Nicosia
$44, 5 hr.
$18, 8 hr.
$116, 6 hr.
$6-0, 4½ hr.
$9, 5 hr.
$12, 6-9 hr.
$32, 11 hr.
$40, 4¼ hr.
$17, 7½ hr.
$32, 17 hr.
$23, 10-14 hr.
$13, 5 hr.
$20-30, 15-17 hr.
$30, 7 hr.
$62, 2½ hr.
$7-12, 3-5 hr.
$29, 11 hr.
$27, 12 hr.
$31, 3¼ hr.
$19, 3¼ hr.
$61, 22-24 hr.
$99, 4 hr.
$21, 5 hr.
$32, 6½ hr.
$19, 2½ hr.
$19, 2 hr.
$47, 8½ hr.
$15, 10½ hr.
$3, 12 hr.
$59, 5¼ hr.
$45, 5 hr.
$37, 5 hr.
$6, 19 hr.
$66, 5 hr.
$14, 1 hr.
$47, 14 hr.
$34, 3½ hr.
$51, 6 hr.
$63, 6½ hr.
$27, 2 hr.
$38, 6 hr.
$86, 12 hr.
$17, 2½ hr.
$42, 10 hr.
$34, 10 hr.
$35, 12 hr.
$6-33, 6½-9½ hr.
$21, 2 hr.
$21, 5 hr.
$23, 2 hr.
$49, 6 hr.
$22, 3½ hr.

private sleeping cars offer more privacy and comfort, but are considerably more expensive (1st class: US$20-210; 2nd class: US$10-110). If you are using a railpass valid only for a restricted number of days, inspect train schedules to maximize the use of your pass: an overnight train or boat journey uses up only one of your travel days if it departs after 7pm (write in the next day's date on your pass).

SHOULD YOU BUY A RAILPASS? Railpasses were conceived to allow you to jump on any train in Europe, go wherever you want whenever you want, and change your plans at will. In practice, it's not so simple. You still must stand in line to validate your pass, pay for supplements, and fork over cash for seat and couchette reservations. More importantly, railpasses don't always pay off. Consult our **railplanner** (at the front of this book) to estimate the point-to-point cost of each leg of your journey; add them up and compare the total with the cost of a railpass. If you are planning to spend extensive time on trains hopping between big cities, a railpass will probably be worth it. But in many cases, especially if you are under 26, point-to-point tickets may prove a cheaper option.

You might find it tough to make your railpass pay for itself in Belgium, Greece, Ireland, Italy, Luxembourg, the Netherlands, Portugal, Spain, Eastern Europe, or the Balkans, where train fares are reasonable, distances short, or buses preferable. If, however, the total cost of your trips nears the price of the pass, the convenience of avoiding ticket lines might be worth the difference.

MULTINATIONAL RAILPASSES

EURAILPASS. Eurail is **valid** in most of Western Europe: Austria, Belgium, Denmark, Finland, France, Germany, Greece, Hungary, Italy, Luxembourg, the Netherlands, Norway, Portugal, the Republic of Ireland, Spain, Sweden, and Switzerland. It is **not valid** in the UK. Standard **Eurailpasses,** valid for a consecutive given number of days, are most suitable for those planning on spending extensive time on trains every few days. **Flexipasses,** valid for any 10 or 15 (not necessarily consecutive) days in a two-month period, are more cost-effective for those traveling longer distances less frequently. It often makes sense for holders of a flexipass to save their "flexidays" for expensive train rides and pay for cheaper fares out of pocket. **Saverpasses** provide first-class travel for travelers in groups of two to five (prices are per person). **Youthpasses** and **Youth Flexipasses** provide parallel second-class perks for those under 26.

EURAILPASSES	15 days	21 days	1 month	2 months	3 months
1st class Eurailpass	US$554	US$718	US$890	US$1260	US$1558
Eurail Saverpass	US$470	US$610	US$756	US$1072	US$1324
Eurail Youthpass	US$388	US$499	US$623	US$882	US$1089

EURAIL FLEXIPASSES	10 days in 2 months	15 days in 2 months
1st class Eurail Flexipass	US$654	US$862
Eurail Saver Flexipass	US$556	US$732
Eurail Youth Flexipass	US$458	US$599

Passholders receive a timetable for major routes and a map detailing ferry, steamer, bus, car rental, hotel, and Eurostar (see p. 49) discounts. **Eurail freebies** (excepting surcharges such as reservation fees and port taxes) include: discounts at Hilton International and Hertz Rent-a-Car; sightseeing cruises on the Rhine (Cologne-Mainz) and Mosel (Koblenz-Cochem), as well as Europabus rides down the Romantic Road (Frankfurt-Füssen; 75% off) and Castle Road (Mannheim-Heidelberg-Nuremberg) in **Germany**; ferries between **Italy** and **Sardinia** (Civitavecchia-Golfo Aranci), **Sicily** (Villa S. Giovanni-Messina), and **Greece** (Brindisi-Patras); between **Ireland** (Rosslare/Cork) and **France** (Cherbourg/Le Havre); and boat trips between **Sweden** and **Denmark** (Helsingborg-Helsingør), **Germany** and **Denmark** (Puttgarden-Rødby), **Germany** (Trelleborg-Sassnitz), and **Finland** (Ůmea/Sundsvall-Vaasa).

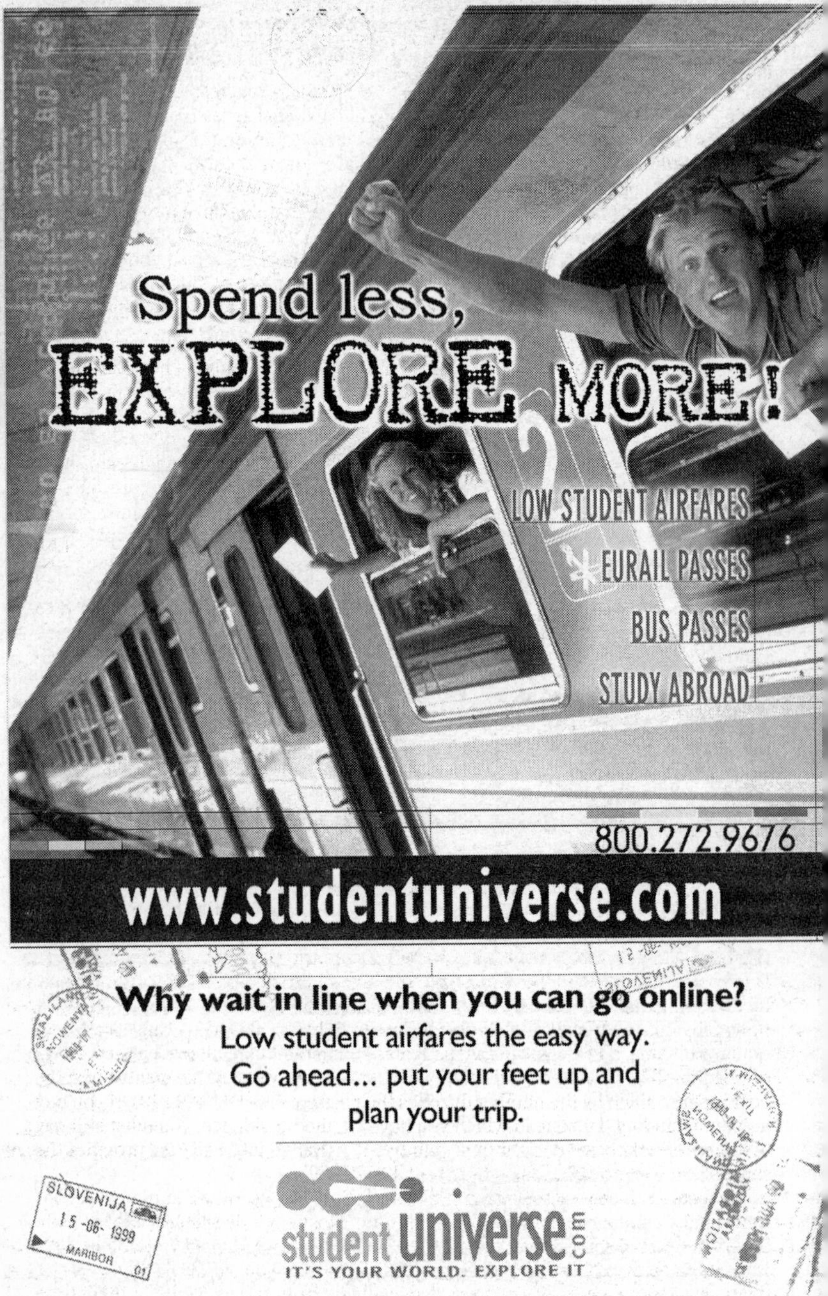

EUROPASS. The Europass is a slimmed-down version of the Eurailpass: it allows five to 15 days of unlimited travel in any two-month period within France, Germany, Italy, Spain, and Switzerland. **First-Class Europasses** (for individuals)/**Saverpasses** (for people traveling in groups of two to five) range from US$348/296 per person (five days) to US$728/620 (15 days). **Second-Class Youthpasses** for those ages 12-25 cost US$233-513. For a fee, you can add **additional zones** (Austria/Hungary; Belgium/Luxembourg/Netherlands; Greece Plus, including the ADN/HML ferry between Italy and Greece; and/or Portugal): $45 for one associated country, $78 for two. You are entitled to the same **freebies** afforded by the Eurailpass (see above), but only when they are within or between countries that you have purchased. Plan your itinerary before buying a Europass: it will save you money if your travels are confined to three to five adjacent Western European countries, or if you only want to go to large cities, but would be a waste if you plan lots of side-trips. If you're tempted to add many rail days and associate countries, consider a Eurailpass.

SHOPPING AROUND FOR A EURAIL OR EUROPASS. Railpasses and Europasses are designed by the EU itself, and are purchasable only by non-Europeans almost exclusively from non-European distributors. These passes must be sold at uniform prices determined by the EU. However, some travel agents tack on a US$10 handling fee, and others offer certain perks with purchase of a railpass, so shop around. Also, keep in mind that pass prices usually go up each year, so if you're planning to travel early in the year, save cash by purchasing before January 1 (you have three months from the purchase date to validate your pass in Europe).

It is best to buy your Eurail- or Europass before leaving; only a few places in major European cities sell them, and at a marked-up price. Once in Europe, you'd probably have to use a credit card to buy over the phone from a railpass agent in a non-EU country (one on the North American East Coast would be closest) who could send the pass to you by express mail. Eurailpasses are non-refundable once validated; if your pass is completely unused and invalidated and you have the original purchase documents, you can get an 85% refund from the place of purchase. You can get a replacement for a lost pass only if you have purchased insurance on it under the Pass Protection Plan (about US$12). Eurailpasses are available through travel agents, student travel agencies like STA and Council (see p. 41), and **Rail Europe,** 44 South Broadway, White Plains, NY 10601 (US ☎ (888) 382 72 45, fax (800) 432 13 29; Canada ☎ (800) 361 72 45, fax (905) 602 41 98; UK ☎ (0990) 84 88 48; www.raileurope.com); or **DER Travel Services,** 9501 W. Devon Ave #301, Rosemont, IL 60018 (US ☎ (888) 337 73 50; fax (800) 282 74 74; www.dertravel.com).

INTERRAIL PASS. If you have lived for at least six months in one of the European countries where InterRail Passes are valid, they prove an economical option. There are eight InterRail **zones:** A (Great Britain, Northern Ireland, Republic of Ireland), B (Finland, Norway, and Sweden), C (Austria, Denmark, Germany, and Switzerland), D (Croatia, Czech Republic, Hungary, Poland, and Slovakia), E (Belgium, France, Luxembourg, and the Netherlands), F (Morocco, Portugal, and Spain), G (Greece, Italy, Slovenia, and Turkey, including a Greece-Italy ferry), and H (Bulgaria, Macedonia, Romania, and Yugoslavia). The **Under 26 InterRail Card** allows either 22 days or one month of unlimited travel within one, two, three, or all of the eight zones; the cost is determined by the number of zones the pass covers (UK£129-219). If you buy a ticket including the zone in which you have claimed residence, you must still pay 50% fare for tickets inside your own country. The **Over 26 InterRail Card** provides the same service for travelers 26 and older (UK£179-309).

Passholders receive **discounts** on rail travel, Eurostar journeys, and most ferries to Ireland, Scandinavia, and the rest of Europe. Most exclude **supplements** for high-speed trains. For info and ticket sales in Europe contact **Student Travel Center,** 24 Rupert St., 1st fl., London W1V 7FN (☎ (020) 74 34 13 06; fax 77 34 38 36; www.student-travel-centre.com). Tickets are also available from travel agents or main train stations throughout Europe.

OTHER MULTINATIONAL PASSES. If your travels will be limited to one area, regional passes are often good values. The **ScanRail Pass,** which gives you unlimited rail travel in Denmark, Finland, Norway, and Sweden, is available both in the UK and the US (standard/under 26 passes for five days out of two months of second-class travel US$129/97; 10 days out of 2 months US$174/127; 21 consecutive days US$198/147). The **Benelux Tourrail Pass** for Belgium, the Netherlands, and Luxembourg is available in the UK, in the US (five days in one month second-class US$88, under 26 US$62; 50% discount for adults), and at train stations in Belgium and Luxembourg (but not the Netherlands). The **Balkan Flexipass,** which is valid for travel in Bulgaria, Greece, Macedonia, Montenegro, Romania, Serbia, and Turkey (five days in one month US$152, under 26 US$90). The **European East Pass** covers Austria, the Czech Republic, Hungary, Poland, and Slovakia (five days in one month US$205, plus US$23 a day for up to five additional days).

DOMESTIC RAILPASSES

If you are planning to spend a significant amount of time in one country or region, a national pass—valid on all rail lines of a country's rail company—would probably be more cost-effective than a multinational pass. But many national passes are limited, and don't provide the free or discounted travel on many private railways and ferries that Eurail does. However, several national and regional passes offer companion fares, allowing two adults traveling together to save about 50% on the price of one pass. Some of these passes can be bought only in Europe, some only outside of Europe; check with a railpass agent or with national tourist offices.

NATIONAL RAILPASSES. The domestic analogs of the Eurailpass, national railpasses are valid either for a given number of consecutive days or for a specific number of days within a given time period. Usually, they must be purchased before you leave. Although they will usually save frequent travelers some money, in some cases (particularly in Eastern Europe) you might find that they are actually a more expensive alternative to point-to-point tickets. National passes include the **Austrian Flexipass; BritIreland Flexipass** covering the UK and the Republic of Ireland; **Britrail Pass** for England, Scotland, and Wales; **Bulgarian Flexipass; Czech Flexipass; Finnrail Flexipass; France Flexipass; German Flexipass; Greek Flexipass; Holland Flexipass; Hungarian Flexipass;** Ireland's **Emerald Card, Irish Explorer,** and **Irish Rover; Italian Railpass** and **Flexipass; Norway Flexipass; Polrail Pass; Portuguese Flexipass; Romanian Flexipas; Freedom of Scotland Travelpass; Iberic Flexipass; Spain Flexipass; Sweden Railpass;** and **Swiss Railpass** and **Flexipass.** For more info, contact Rail Europe (see p. 57).

EURO DOMINO. Like the Interrail Pass, the Euro Domino pass is available to anyone who has lived in Europe for at least six months; it differs in that it is only valid in one country (which you designate upon buying the pass). It is available for 29 European countries as well as Morocco. Reservations must still be paid for separately. The Euro Domino pass is available for first- and second-class travel (with a special rate for under 26ers), for three to eight days of unlimited travel within a one-month period. Euro Domino is not valid on Eurostar or Thalys trains. **Supplements** for many high-speed (e.g., French TGV, German ICE, and Swedish X2000) trains are included (Spanish AVE is not), although you must still pay for **reservations** where they are compulsory (e.g., about 20F on the TGV). The pass must be bought within your country of residence (except for the Euro Domino Plus pass in the Netherlands, which also includes all bus, tram, and metro rides and can be bought in the Netherlands); each country has its own price for the pass. Inquire with your national rail company for more info.

REGIONAL PASSES. Another type of regional pass covers a specific area within a country or a round trip between any border and a particular destination; these are useful as supplements to your main pass. The **Prague Excursion Pass** is a common purchase for Eurailers, whose passes are not valid in the Czech Republic; it covers travel from any Czech border to Prague and back out of the country (round trip must be completed within seven days; second-class US$35, under 26 US$30). The

Copenhagen Sightseeing Pass is valid for Europass or German railpass holders from any German or Danish border to Copenhagen and back, while the **BritRail Southeast Pass** permits unlimited travel in southeast England (three out of eight days US$70).

RAIL-AND-DRIVE PASSES. In addition to simple railpasses, many countries (as well as Europass and Eurail) offer rail-and-drive passes, which combine car rental with rail travel—a good option for travelers who wish both to visit cities accessible by rail and to make side trips into the surrounding areas. Rail Europe (see above, p. 61) offers a EurailDrive Pass with four trains days and two rental days for between US$439 and US$529, depending on the car.

DISCOUNTED TICKETS

For travelers under 26, **BIJ** tickets (Billets Internationals de Jeunesse; a.k.a. **Wasteels, Eurotrain,** and **Route 26**) are a great alternative to railpasses. Available for international trips within Europe and for travel within France as well as most ferries, they knock 20-40% off regular second-class fares. Tickets are good for two months after purchase and allow stopovers along the normal direct route of the train journey. Issued for a specific international route between two points, they must be used in the direction and order of the designated route and must be bought in Europe. The equivalent for those over 26, **BIGT** tickets provide a 20-30% discount on first- and second-class international tickets for business travelers, temporary residents of Europe, and their families. Both types of tickets are available from European travel agents, at Wasteels or Eurotrain offices (usually in or near train stations), or directly at the ticket counter in some nations. For more info, contact **Wasteels,** Victoria Station, London SW1V 1JT (☎ (020) 78 34 70 66; fax 76 30 76 28).

FURTHER RESOURCES: TRAIN TRAVEL

Rail schedules: bahn.hafas.de/bin/db.w97/query.exe/en. A testament to German efficiency, with minute-by-minute itineraries and connection information.

Point-to-point fares: www.raileurope.com/us/rail/fares_schedules.index.htm. For a more convenient resource, see our **railplanner** at the front of this book.

European Railway Servers: home.wxs.nl/~grijns/timetables/time.html; mercurio.iet.unipi.it/home.html. Links to rail servers throughout Europe.

Thomas Cook European Timetable, updated monthly, covers all major and most minor train routes in Europe. In the US, order it from Forsyth Travel Library (US$28; ☎ (800) 367 79 84; www.forsyth.com). In Europe, find it at any Thomas Cook Money Exchange Center. Alternatively, buy directly from Thomas Cook (UK£10.10; UK ☎ (8705) 66 62 22; www.thomascook.com).

Info on rail travel and railpasses: www.eurorail.com.

Guide to European Railpasses, Rick Steves. Available online and by mail (US ☎ (425) 771 83 03; fax (425) 771 08 33; www.ricksteves.com). Free.

On the Rails Around Europe, Melissa Shales. Thomas Cook Ltd. (US$19).

Eurail and Train Travel Guide to Europe. Houghton Mifflin (US$15).

BY BUS

Although European trains and railpasses are extremely popular, in some cases buses are a better option. In Spain, Hungary, and the Baltics, the bus and train systems are on par; in Britain, Greece, Ireland, Portugal, and Turkey, bus networks are more extensive, efficient, and often more comfortable; and in Iceland and parts of northern Scandinavia, bus service is the only ground transportation available. In the rest of Europe, bus travel is a crapshoot; scattered offerings from private companies are often cheap, but sometimes unreliable. Amsterdam, Athens, Istanbul, London, Munich, and Oslo are centers for lines that offer long-distance rides across Europe. Often cheaper than railpasses, **international bus passes** typically allow unlimited travel on a hop-on, hop-off basis between major European cities. These services in general tend to be more popular among non-American backpackers. Note that **Eurobus,** a one-time UK-based bus service, is no longer in operation.

Eurolines, 4 Cardiff Rd., Luton, Bedfordshire L41 1PP (UK ☎ (0990) 14 32 19; fax (01582) 40 06 94); and 52 Grosvenor Gardens, London SW1W 0AU (☎ (020) 77 30 82 35; www.eurolines.co.uk or www.eurolines.com). The largest operator of Europe-wide coach services. Unlimited 30-day travel in peak/off-peak periods (UK£229/199, under 26 and over 60 UK£199/159) or 60-day (UK£279/249, under 26 and over 60 UK£249/199) travel between 48 major European cities in 21 countries.

Busabout, 258 Vauxhall Bridge Rd., London SW1V 1BS (☎ (017) 19 50 16 61; fax 19 50 16 62; www.busabout.com). Offers 5 interconnecting bus circuits covering 17 cities and towns in Europe. Pre-calls hotel reservations. Standard/student passes are valid for 15 days (US$259/229), 21 days (US$369/339), 1 month (US$489/439), 2 months (US$759/669), 3 months (US$929/839), or a season pass (US$1109/999).

BY CAR

Although travel by car might insulate you from backpacker culture, it will allow more flexibility and accessibility. While a single traveler won't save cash by renting a car, four typically will. Rail Europe and other railpass vendors offer rail-and-drive packages both for individual countries and all of Europe. Fly-and-drive packages are often available from travel agents or airline/rental agency partnerships.

Before setting off, know the laws of the countries in which you'll be driving (e.g., both seat belts and headlights must be on at all times in Scandinavia, and vehicles drive on the left in Ireland and the UK). For an informal primer on European road signs, conventions, and general driving guidelines, check out www.travlang.com/signs. Additionally, the **Association for Safe International Road Travel (ASIRT),** 11769 Gainsborough Rd., Potomac, MD 20854 (US ☎ (301) 983 52 52; fax 983 36 63; www.asirt.org; e-mail asirt@erols.com), can provide specific information about road conditions. ASIRT considers road travel (by car or bus) to be relatively **safe** in Denmark, Ireland, the Netherlands, Norway, Sweden, Switzerland, and the UK, and relatively **unsafe** in Turkey. Scandinavians and Western Europeans use unleaded **gas** almost exclusively, but it's not consistently available in Eastern Europe.

INTERNATIONAL DRIVING PERMIT (IDP)

If you plan to drive a car while abroad, you must be over 18 and have an International Driving Permit (IDP), although certain countries allow travelers to drive with a valid American or Canadian license for a limited number of months. It may be a good idea to get one anyway, in case you're in a situation (e.g., if you are in an accident or stranded in a smaller town) where the police do not know English; information on the IDP is printed in 10 languages, including French, German, Italian, Portuguese, Russian, Spanish, and Swedish.

Your IDP, valid for one year, must be issued in your own country before you depart. You must be 18 years old and have a valid driver's license. An application for an IDP usually requires one or two photos, a current local license, a passport (sometimes other identification is accepted), and a fee (generally about US$10).

Australia: Contact your local Royal Automobile Club (RAC) or the National Royal Motorist Association (NRMA; ☎ (08) 94 21 42 98; www.rac.com.au/travel). Permits AUS$15.

Canada: Contact any Canadian Automobile Association (CAA) branch, or write to CAA, 1145 Hunt Club Rd #200, Ottawa, Ontario, K1V 0Y3 (☎ (613) 247 01 17; fax 247 01 18; www.caa.ca/CAAInternet/travelservices/frames14.htm). Permits CDN$10.

Ireland: Contact the nearest Automobile Association (AA) office or write: AA Travel, 23 Suffolk St., Dublin 2 (☎ (01) 617 99 88). Permits IR£4.

New Zealand: Contact your local Automobile Association (AA), or write Auckland Central, 99 Albert St (☎ (09) 377 46 60; fax 302 20 37; www.nzaa.co.nz.). Permits NZ$10.

South Africa: Contact your local Automobile Association of South Africa office, or write the head office at P.O. Box 596, Johannesburg 2000 (☎ (011) 799 10 00; fax 799 10 10; www.aasa.co.za). Permits SAR30.78.

UK: Visit your local AA Shop. To find the location nearest you that issues the IDP, call (0990) 50 06 00; www.theaa.co.uk/motoringandtravel/idp/motidp002.asp. Permits UK£4.

US: Visit any American Automobile Association (AAA) office or write to AAA Florida, Travel Related Services, 1000 AAA Dr (mail stop 100), Heathrow, FL 32746 (☎ (407) 444 42 40; fax 444 73 80). You don't have to be a member to buy an IDP. Permits US$10. AAA Travel Related Services (☎ (800) 222 43 57) provides road maps and many travel guides free to members, and provides emergency road services and auto insurance.

CAR INSURANCE

Most credit cards cover standard insurance. If you rent, lease, or borrow a car, you will need a **green card,** or **International Insurance Certificate,** to prove that you have liability insurance. Obtain it through the car rental agency; most include coverage in their prices. If you lease a car, you can obtain a green card from the dealer. Some travel agents offer the card; it may also be available at border crossings. Verify whether your auto insurance applies abroad; even if it does, you will still need a green card to certify this to foreign officials. If you have a collision abroad, the accident will show up on your domestic records if you report it to your insurance company. Rental agencies might require you to purchase theft insurance in countries that they consider to have a high risk of auto theft (such as Italy).

ACQUIRING SOME WHEELS

RENTING A CAR. You can rent a car from a US-based firm (Alamo, Avis, Budget, or Hertz) with European offices, from a European-based company with local representatives (Europcar), or from a tour operator (Auto Europe or Europe By Car), which will arrange a rental for you from a European company at its own rates. Multinationals offer greater flexibility, but tour operators often strike better deals. Picking up your car in Belgium, Germany, or the Netherlands is usually cheaper than renting in Paris. Expect to pay at least US$80-400 per week, plus tax (5-25%). Reserve ahead and pay in advance if at all possible. It is always significantly less expensive to reserve a car from the US than from Europe. Always check if prices quoted include tax and collision insurance; some credit card companies cover the deductible on collision insurance, allowing their customers to decline the collision damage waiver. Ask about discounts and check the terms of insurance, particularly the size of the deductible. Rates are generally lowest in Belgium, Germany, Holland, and the UK, and highest in Scandinavia and Eastern Europe. Ask airlines about special fly-and-drive packages; you might get up to a week of free or discounted rental. Minimum age varies by country, but is usually 21-25. At most agencies, all that's needed to rent a car is a license from home and proof that you've had it for a year.

Car rental in Europe is available through the following agencies: **Auto Europe,** 39 Commercial St, P.O. Box 7006, Portland, ME 04112 (US ☎ (888) 223 55 55; fax (207) 842 22 22; www.autoeurope.com); **Avis** (US ☎ (800) 230 48 98; Canada ☎ (800) 272 58 71; UK ☎ (0870) 907 73 00; Australia ☎ (800) 22 55 33; www.avis.com); **Budget,** 4225 Naperville Rd., Lisle, IL 60532 (US ☎ (800) 527 07 00; Canada ☎ (800) 268 89 00; UK ☎ (0800) 18 11 81; Australia ☎ 1 300 36 28 48; www.budget.com); **Europe by Car,** One Rockefeller Plaza, New York, NY 10020 (US ☎ (800) 223 15 16 or (212) 581 30 40; www.europebycar.com); **Europcar,** 145 av. Malekoff, 75016 Paris (☎ (01) 55 66 84 84); US ☎ (877) 940 69 00; Canada ☎ (800) 227 73 68; www.europcar.com); **Hertz** 225 Brae Boulevard, Park Ridge, NJ 07656 (US ☎ (800) 654 31 31; Canada ☎ (800) 263 06 00; UK ☎ (0870) 844 88 44; Australia ☎ 13 30 39; www.hertz.com); and **Kemwel Holiday Autos** (US ☎ (800) 576 15 90; international ☎ 914 825 31 00; www.kemwel.com).

LEASING A CAR. For longer than 17 days, leasing can be cheaper than renting; it is often the only option for those ages 18 to 21. The cheapest leases are agreements to buy the car and then sell it back to the manufacturer at a prearranged price. As far as you're concerned, though, it's a lease and doesn't entail enormous financial transactions. Leases generally include insurance coverage and are not taxed. The most affordable ones usually originate in Belgium, France, or Germany. Expect to pay around US$1100-1800 (depending on the size of car) for 60 days. Contact **Auto Europe, Europe by Car,** or **Kemwel Holiday Autos** (see above) before you go.

BUYING A CAR. If you're brave and know what you're doing, buying a used car or van in Europe and selling it just before you leave can provide the cheapest wheels for longer trips. Check with consulates for import-export laws concerning used vehicles, registration, and safety and emission standards.

BY PLANE

Although flying is almost invariably more expensive than traveling by train, if you are short on time (or flush with cash) you might consider it. Student travel agencies sell cheap tickets, and budget fares are frequently available in the spring and summer on high-volume routes between northern Europe and resort areas in Greece, Italy, and Spain; consult budget travel agents and local newspapers. For info on cheap flights from Britain to the continent, see **Traveling from the UK,** p. 43.

In addition, a number of European airlines offer coupon packets that considerably discount the cost of each flight leg. Most are only available as tack-ons to their transatlantic passengers, but some are available as stand-alone offers. Most must be purchased before departure, so research in advance.

Europe by Air: US ☎ (888) 387 24 79, auto faxback (512) 404 12 91; Australia ☎ (02) 92 85 68 88; New Zealand ☎ (09) 309 80 94; www.europebyair.com. Passes, good for point-to-point flights on 16 partner airlines to 130 European cities, mostly in Western Europe but including Moscow and the Balkans. Must be purchased prior to departure; available only to non-European residents (3 passes min., no max.). US$99 each, excluding airport tax.

Alitalia: US ☎ (800) 223 57 30; www.alitaliausa.com. Program available to North Americans who fly into Milan or Rome on Alitalia. Allows passengers to tack on 3 coupons good for flights to 30 airports in Europe and North Africa, mostly in major cities. US$299; each additional ticket US$100; must be accompanied with a transcontinental flight on Alitalia or airline partner Continental.

Austrian Airlines: US ☎ (800) 843 00 02; www.austrianair.com/specials/visit-europe-fares.html. "Visit Europe Fares," good to cities served by AA and partner airlines, is available in the US to AA transatlantic passengers (3 min., 6max.). US$100 each.

Lufthansa: US ☎ (800) 399 58 38; www.lufthansa-usa.com/special_offers/discover_europe.html. "Discover Europe" is available to US travelers booked on a transatlantic Lufthansa flight or flying into Germany on a US carrier (3 coupons min.). US$170 each; up to six additional tickets.

SAS: US ☎ (800) 221 23 50; www.flysas.com/airpass.html. Visit Europe Air Pass—one-way coupons for travel within Scandinavia, the Baltics, or all of Europe US$75-105. Most are available only to transatlantic SAS passengers, but partner carrier passengers may qualify. Up to 8 passes. Call for details.

KLM/Northwest: US ☎ (800) 800 15 04; www.nwaworldvacations.com. "Passport to Europe," available to US transatlantic passengers on either airline, connects 90 European cities (mostly Western European, but including a few Eastern European and North African destinations; 3 min., 12 max.). US$100 each.

Iberia: US ☎ (800) 772 46 42; www.iberia.com/ibusa/special.htm#europass. "EuroPass" allows North American Iberia passengers to Spain to tack on at least 2 additional destinations from the 35 they serve. Most US$125 each; some US$155 each.

BY BOAT

Most European ferries are quite comfortable; the cheapest ticket typically still includes a reclining chair or couchette. Fares jump sharply in July and August. Ask for discounts: ISIC holders can often get student fares, and Eurailpass holders get many reductions and free trips (for examples of popular freebies, see p. 55). You'll occasionally have to pay a port tax (under US$10). For more info, consult the *Official Steamship Guide International* (available at travel agents), or www.youra.com/ferry or home.wxs.nl/~grijns/seatravel/ferries.html.

ENGLISH CHANNEL AND IRISH SEA FERRIES

Ferries are frequent and dependable. The main route across the **English Channel,** from England to France, is Dover-Calais. The main ferry port on the southern coast of England is Portsmouth, with connections to France and Spain. Ferries also cross the **Irish Sea,** connecting Northern Ireland with Scotland and England, and the Republic of Ireland with Wales. For more information on sailing (or hovering) in this region, see **By Boat from the UK and Ireland,** p. 49.

ESSENTIALS

NORTH AND BALTIC SEA FERRIES

Ferries in the **North Sea** are reliable and go everywhere. For information on ferries heading across the North Sea to and from the UK, see p. 49. **Baltic Sea** ferries service routes between Poland and Scandinavia.

Polferries: Sweden ☎46 (40) 12 17 00; fax 97 03 70; www.polferries.se. **Copenhagen** (10hr.) and **Malmö, Sweden** (4½hr.) to **Świnoujście, Poland.** Also **Oxelösund-Stockholm** to **Gdańsk** (18½hr.).

Color Line: Norway ☎47 81 00 08 11; fax 83 07 76; www.colorline.com. **Oslo** to **Kiel, Germany** (19½hr., 1 per day, large price range depending on cabin type). **Hirtshals, Denmark** to **Oslo** (8½hr., 1-4 per day, US$24-60), **Kristiansand** (2½-4½hr., 2-5 per day, US$24-60), and **Moss** (7-9hr, usually 1-2 per day, US$24-60), Norway. Also **Frederikshavn, Denmark** to **Moss** (6¼-11hr., 1-2 per day, US$24-60). Seniors and ages 4-15 50% off, except in high season. Prices higher on weekends and in high season.

Silja Line: Finland ☎358 (090) 71 44 00; www.silja.com. **Helsinki** to **Stockholm** (15hr., 1 per day), **Tallinn** (3hr., June to mid-Sept. 3-7 per week), and **Rostock, Germany** (23-25hr., June to mid-Sept. 3 per week). **Turku** to **Stockholm** (10hr., Jan. to June 2 per day). Also **Vaasa, Finland** to **Umeå, Sweden** (1-2 per day).

Scandinavian Seaways: See p. 49. **Copenhagen** to **Oslo** (16hr., 1 per day, US$133-US$305, 50% off with Eurail).

MEDITERRANEAN AND AEGEAN FERRIES

Mediterranean ferries may be the most glamorous, but they can also be the most rocky. Ferries run from Spain to Morocco, from Italy to Tunisia, and from France to Morocco and Tunisia. Reservations are recommended, especially in July and August. Bring toilet paper. Ferries run on erratic schedules, with similar routes and varying prices. Shop around, and beware of dinky, unreliable companies that don't take reservations. Ferries float across the **Adriatic** from Ancona and Bari, Italy to Split and Dubrovnik, respectively, in Croatia.

Ferries also run across the **Aegean,** from Ancona, Italy to Patras, Greece (19hr.), and from Bari, Italy to Igoumenitsa (9hr.) and Patras (15hr.), Greece. **Eurail** is valid on certain ferries between Brindisi, Italy and Corfu (8hr.), Igoumenitsa, and Patras, Greece. Countless ferry companies operate these routes simultaneously; see specific country chapters for more information. The Paleologos Travel Agency website (www.ferries.gr) contains an extensive database of Greek ferries, with connections to Italy, Cyprus, Israel, and Turkey.

Hydrofoils (Flying Dolphins) are a tempting alternative. They run relatively more frequently and reliably than ferries at twice their speed, but cost twice as much.

FURTHER RESOURCES

Official Steamship Guide International (available at your travel agent).

Online ferry guides: www.youra.com/ferry; home.wxs.nl/~grijns/seatravel/ferries.html.

BY BICYCLE

Biking is one of the key elements of the classic budget Eurovoyage. With the proliferation of mountain bikes, you can do some serious natural sightseeing. Many airlines will count your bike as your second free piece of luggage; a few charge extra (US$60-110 one-way). Bikes must be packed in a cardboard box with the pedals and front wheel detached; many airlines sell bike boxes at the airport (US$10). Most ferries let you take your bike for free or for a nominal fee, and you can always ship your bike on trains. Renting a bike beats bringing your own if your touring will be confined to one or two regions. Some youth hostels rent bicycles for low prices. In Switzerland, train stations rent bikes and often allow you to drop them off elsewhere; check train stations throughout Europe for similar deals. In addition to **panniers** in which you can pack your luggage, you'll need a good **helmet** (US$25-50) and a good U-shaped **Citadel** or **Kryptonite lock** (from US$30). For equipment, **Bike Nashbar,** 4111 Simon Rd, Youngstown, OH 44512 (US ☎ (800) 627 42 27; www.nashbar.com), beats all competitors' offers and ships anywhere in the US or Canada. For more country-specific books on biking through France, Germany, Ireland, or the UK, or to purchase the more general *Europe by Bike*, by Karen and Terry Whitehall (US$15), try **Mountaineers Books,** 1001 S.W. Klickitat Way #201, Seattle, WA 98134 (US ☎ (800) 553 44 53 or (206) 223 63 03; www.mountaineersbooks.org).

Blue Marble Travel (Canada ☎ (519) 624 24 94; France ☎ 01 42 36 02 34; US ☎ (800) 258 86 89 or (973) 326 95 33; www.bluemarble.org) offers bike tours for small groups for those ages 20 to 50 through the Alps, Austria, Belgium, France, Germany, Italy, Luxemburg, Portugal, Scandinavia, and Spain. **CBT Tours,** 415 W. Fullerton #1003, Chicago, IL 60614 (US ☎ (800) 736 24 53) or (312) 475 06 25; www.cbttours.com), offers full-package one-week biking, mountain biking, and hiking tours that are easily combined (around US$250 per day).

BY MOPED AND MOTORCYCLE

Motorized bikes don't use much gas, can be put on trains and ferries, and are a good compromise between the high cost of car travel and the limited range of bicycles. However, they're uncomfortable for long distances, dangerous in the rain, and unpredictable on rough roads and gravel. Always wear a helmet, and never ride with a backpack. If you've never been on a moped before, a twisting Alpine road is not the place to start. Expect to pay about US$20-35 per day; try auto repair shops, and remember to bargain. Motorcycles can be much more expensive and normally require a license, but are better for long distances. Before renting, ask if the quoted price includes tax and insurance, or you may be hit with an unexpected additional fee. Avoid handing your passport over as a deposit; if you have an accident or mechanical failure you may not get it back until you cover all repairs. Pay ahead of time instead. For more information, try **Europe by Motorcycle,** by Gregory Frazier (Arrowstar Publishing, US$20).

BY THUMB

Let's Go strongly urges you to consider the risks before you choose to hitch. We do not recommend hitching as a safe means of transportation, and none of the information presented here is intended to do so.

Hitching means entrusting your life to a random person who happens to stop for you on the road and risking theft, assault, sexual harassment, and unsafe driving. In spite of this, there are advantages to hitching when it is safe: it allows you to meet local people and get where you're going, especially in northern Europe and Ireland, where public transportation is sketchy. The choice, however, remains yours.

Britain and Ireland are probably the easiest places in Europe to get a lift. Hitching in Scandinavia is slow but steady. Long-distance hitching in the developed countries of northwestern Europe demands close attention to expressway junctions, rest stop locations, and often a destination sign. Hitching in southern Europe is generally mediocre; France is the worst. In some Central and Eastern European countries, the line between hitching and taking a taxi is quite thin.

Safety-minded hitchers avoid getting in the back of a two-door car (or any car they wouldn't be able to get out of in a hurry) and never let go of their backpacks. If they ever feel threatened, they insist on being let off immediately. Acting as if they are going to open the car door or vomit on the upholstery will usually get a driver to stop. Hitchhiking at night is particularly dangerous; experienced hitchers stand in well-lit places, and expect drivers to be wary of nocturnal thumbers.

For women traveling alone, hitching is just too dangerous. A man and a woman are a safer combination, two men will have a harder time, and three will go nowhere. Where one stands is vital. Experienced hitchers pick a spot outside of built-up areas, where drivers can stop, return to the road without causing an accident, and have time to look over potential passengers as they approach. Hitching (or even standing) on super-highways is usually illegal: one may only thumb at rest stops or at the entrance ramps to highways. In the **Practical Information** section of many cities, *Let's Go* lists the tram or bus lines that take travelers to strategic hitching points. Finally, success will depend on appearance. Successful hitchers travel light and stack their belongings in a compact but visible cluster. Most Europeans signal with an open hand rather than a thumb; many write their destination on a sign in large, bold letters and draw a smiley-face under it. Drivers prefer hitchers who are neat and wholesome. No one stops for anyone wearing sunglasses.

Many European countries offer a ride service (listed in the **Practical Information** for major cities), a cross between hitchhiking and ride boards, which pairs drivers with riders; the fee varies according to destination. **Eurostop International** (**Verband der Deutschen Mitfahrzentralen** in Germany and **Allostop** in France) is one of the largest. Riders and drivers enter their names on the Internet through the **Taxistop** website (www.taxistop.be) or at **Hitchhikers** (www.hitchhikers.org). Not all organizations screen drivers and riders; ask in advance.

SPECIFIC CONCERNS

WOMEN TRAVELERS

Women exploring on their own inevitably face some additional safety concerns, but you can be adventurous without taking undue risks. If you are concerned, consider staying in hostels that offer single rooms that lock from the inside or in religious organizations with rooms for women only. Communal showers in some hostels are safer than others; check them before settling in. Stick to centrally located accommodations and avoid solitary late-night treks or metro rides.

When traveling, always carry extra money for a phone call, bus, or taxi. **Hitching** is never safe for women, even for two women traveling together. Choose train compartments occupied by other women or couples; ask the conductor to put together a women-only compartment if he or she doesn't offer to do so first. Approach older women or couples for directions if you're lost or uneasy.

Dress conservatively, especially in rural areas. Wearing a conspicuous **wedding band** may help prevent unwanted overtures. Some travelers report that carrying pictures of a "husband" or "children" is extremely useful to help document marriage status. Even a mention of a husband waiting back at the hotel may be enough in some places to discount your potentially vulnerable, unattached appearance.

Your best answer to verbal harassment is no answer at all; feigning deafness, sitting motionless, and staring straight ahead will do a world of good that reactions usually don't achieve. The extremely persistent can often be dissuaded by a firm, loud, and very public "Go away!" in the appropriate language. Don't hesitate to seek out a police officer or a passerby if you are being harassed. Memorize the emergency numbers in places you visit, and consider carrying a whistle or airhorn on your keychain. A **self-defense course** will not only prepare you for a potential attack, but will also raise your level of awareness of your surroundings and your confidence (see p. 20). Women also face some specific health concerns when traveling (see p. 25). **Journeywoman** (www.journeywoman.com) posts an online newsletter and a variety of other resources for female travelers.

FURTHER READING

A Journey of One's Own: Uncommon Advice for the Independent Woman Traveler, Thalia Zepatos. Eighth Mountain Press (US$17).

Adventures in Good Company: The Complete Guide to Women's Tours and Outdoor Trips, Thalia Zepatos. Eighth Mountain Press (US$17).

Travelers' Tales: Gutsy Women, Travel Tips and Wisdom for the Road, Marybeth Bond. Traveler's Tales (US$8).

TRAVELING ALONE

There are many benefits to traveling alone, among them greater independence and more opportunities to interact with the residents of the region you're visiting. On the other hand, any solo traveler is a more vulnerable to harassment and street theft. Lone travelers need to be well-organized and look confident at all times. Try not to stand out as a tourist, and be especially careful in deserted or very crowded areas. If questioned, never admit that you are traveling alone. Maintain regular contact with someone at home who knows your itinerary.

A number of organizations also supply information for solo travelers, and others find travel companions for those who don't want to go alone. Here are a few:

The Single Traveler Newsletter, P.O. Box 682, Ross, CA 94957 (US ☎ (415) 389 02 27; 6 issues US$29).

American International Homestays, P.O. Box 1754, Nederland, CO 80466 (US ☎ (800) 876 20 48; www.spectravel.com/homes). Lodgings with host families in Austria, Belgium, France, Spain, and E. Europe.

Connecting: Solo Traveler Network, P.O. Box 29088, Delmont RPO, Vancouver, BC V6J 5C2 (Canada ☎ (604) 737 77 91; www.cstn.org). Membership US$28-40.

Travel Companion Exchange, P.O. Box 833, Amityville, NY 11701 (US ☎ (800) 392 12 56 or ☎ (631) 454 08 80; www.whytravelalone.com). Newsletter links up travel partners (subscription US$48). Membership $159.

OLDER TRAVELERS

Senior citizens are eligible for a wide range of discounts on transportation, museums, movies, theaters, concerts, restaurants, and accommodations. If you don't see a senior citizen price listed, ask, and you might be delightfully surprised.

ElderTreks, 597 Markham St., Toronto, ON M6G 2L7 (☎ (800) 741 79 56 or (416) 588 50 00; fax 588 98 39; email eldertreks@eldertreks.com; www.eldertreks.com). Adventure travel programs for the 50+ traveler in Finland, Iceland, and Turkey.

Elderhostel, 75 Federal St., Boston, MA 02110, USA (☎ (617) 426 77 88 or (877) 426 80 56; www.elderhostel.org). Organizes one- to four-week "educational adventures" throughout Europe on varied subjects for those 55+.

The Mature Traveler, P.O. Box 50400, Reno, NV 89513, USA (☎ (775) 786 74 19, credit card orders (800) 460 66 76). Deals, discounts, and travel packages for the 50+ traveler. Subscription $30.

Walking the World, P.O. Box 1186, Fort Collins, CO 80522, USA (☎ 1 (800) 340 92 55 or (970) 498 05 00; email walktworld@aol.com; www.walkingtheworld.com). Organizes trips for 50+ travelers to Britain, the Czech Republic, France, Greece, Ireland, Italy, Norway, Portugal, and Switzerland.

FURTHER READING

No Problem! Worldwise Tips for Mature Adventurers, Janice Kenyon. Orca Book Publishers (US$16).

A Senior's Guide to Healthy Travel, Donald L. Sullivan. Career Press (US$15).

Unbelievably Good Deals and Great Adventures That You Absolutely Can't Get Unless You're Over 50, Joan Rattner Heilman. Contemporary Books (US$13).

BISEXUAL, GAY, AND LESBIAN TRAVELERS

Attitudes toward bisexual, gay, and lesbian travelers vary; acceptance is generally highest in the Netherlands and particularly low in Turkey. The contact organizations, mail-order bookstores, and publishers below, as well as the newsletter published by **Out and About** (www.planetout.com), address specific travel concerns.

Gay's the Word, 66 Marchmont St., London WC1N 1AB (☎ (020) 72 78 76 54; email sales@gaystheword.co.uk; www.gaystheword.co.uk). The largest gay and lesbian bookshop in the UK, with both fiction and non-fiction titles. Mail-order service available.

Giovanni's Room, 345 S. 12th St., Philadelphia, PA 19107, USA (☎ (215) 923 29 60; fax 923 08 13; www.queerbooks.com). An international lesbian/feminist and gay bookstore with mail-order service (carries many of the publications listed below).

International Gay and Lesbian Travel Association, 4331 N. Federal Hwy., #304, Fort Lauderdale, FL 33308, USA (☎ (954) 776 26 26; fax 776 33 03; www.iglta.com). An organization of over 1350 companies serving gay and lesbian travelers worldwide.

International Lesbian and Gay Association (ILGA), 81, r. Marché-au-Charbon, B-1000 Brussels, Belgium (tel./fax +32 (2) 502 24 71; www.ilga.org). Not a travel service; provides political information, such as homosexuality laws of individual countries.

FURTHER READING

Spartacus International Gay Guide. Bruno Gmunder Verlag. (US$33).

Damron Men's Guide, Damron's Accommodations, Damron's Amsterdam Guide, and *The Women's Traveller.* Damron Travel Guides (US$10-19). For more info, call US ☎ (415) 255 04 04 or (800) 462 66 54 or check their website (www.damron.com).

Ferrari Guides' Gay Travel A to Z, Ferrari Guides' Men's Travel in Your Pocket, Ferrari Guides' Women's Travel in Your Pocket, and *Ferrari Guides' Inn Places.* Ferrari Guides (US$14-16). For more info, call (602) 863 24 08 or (800) 962 29 12 or try www.q-net.com.

The Gay Vacation Guide: The Best Trips and How to Plan Them, Mark Chesnut. Citadel Press (US$15).

TRAVELERS WITH DISABILITIES

Countries vary in accessibility to travelers with disabilities. Some tourist boards provide directories on the accessibility of various accommodations and transportation services; or, contact institutions of interest directly. Those with disabilities should inform airlines and hotels of their disabilities when making arrangements for travel; some time may be needed to prepare special accommodations. Call ahead to restaurants, hotels, parks, and other facilities to find out about ramps, door widths, the dimensions of elevators, etc. **Guide dog owners** should inquire as to the specific quarantine policies of each destination country. At the very least, they will need to provide a certificate of immunization against rabies.

Rail is probably the most convenient form of travel for disabled travelers in Europe: many stations have ramps, and some trains have wheelchair lifts, special seating areas, and specially equipped toilets. Large stations in Britain are equipped with wheelchair facilities, and the French national railroad offers wheelchair compartments on all TGV (high speed) and Conrail trains. All Eurostar, some InterCity (IC) and EuroCity (EC) trains are wheelchair-accessible, and CityNightLine trains, French TGV (high speed), and Conrail trains feature special compartments. The countries with the most **wheelchair-accessible rail networks** are: Denmark (IC and Lyn trains), Finland, France (TGVs and other long-distance trains), Germany (ICE, EC, IC, and IR trains), Italy (all Pendolino and many EC and IC trains), the Netherlands (most trains), the Republic of Ireland (most major trains), Spain, Sweden (X2000s, most IC and IR trains), and Switzerland (all IC, most EC, and some regional trains). Austria, Poland, and Great Britain offer accessibility on selected routes. Bulgaria, the Czech Republic, Greece, Hungary, Romania, Slovakia, and Turkey's rail systems have limited wheelchair accessibility. Some major **car rental** agencies (Hertz, Avis, and National) may offer hand-controlled vehicles.

USEFUL ORGANIZATIONS

Mobility International USA (MIUSA), P.O. Box 10767, Eugene, OR 97440, USA (☎ (541) 343 12 84 voice and TDD; fax 343 68 12; email info@miusa.org; www.miusa.org). Sells *A World of Options: A Guide to International Educational Exchange, Community Service, and Travel for Persons with Disabilities* (US$35).

Moss Rehab Hospital Travel Information Service (☎ (215) 456 96 00 or (800) CALL-MOSS; email netstaff@mossresourcenet.org; www.mossresourcenet.org). An information resource center on travel-related concerns for those with disabilities.

Society for the Advancement of Travel for the Handicapped (SATH), 347 Fifth Ave., #610, New York, NY 10016 (☎ (212) 447 72 84; www.sath.org). An advocacy group that publishes the quarterly travel magazine *OPEN WORLD* (free for members, US$13 for nonmembers). Also publishes a wide range of info sheets on disability travel facilitation and destinations. Annual membership US$45, students and seniors US$30.

TOUR AGENCIES

Directions Unlimited, 123 Green Ln., Bedford Hills, NY 10507, USA (☎ (914) 241 17 00 or (800) 533 53 43; www.travel-cruises.com). Specializes in arranging individual and group vacations, tours, and cruises for the physically disabled.

The Guided Tour Inc., 7900 Old York Rd., #114B, Elkins Park, PA 19027, USA (☎ (800) 783 58 41 or (215) 782 13 70; www.guidedtour.com). Organizes travel programs for persons with developmental and physical challenges around Ireland, London, and Rome.

FURTHER READING

Access in London, Gordon Couch. Cimino Publishing Group (US$12).

Access in Paris, Gordon Couch. Quiller Press (US$12).

Resource Directory for the Disabled, Richard Neil Shrout. Facts on file (US$45).

Wheelchair Through Europe, Annie Mackin. Graphic Language Press (US ☎ (760) 944 95 94; email niteowl@cts.com; US$13).

MINORITY TRAVELERS

In general, minority travelers will find a high level of tolerance in large cities; small towns and the countryside are more unpredictable. Western Europe tends to be more tolerant than Eastern Europe. *Romany* (Gypsies) encounter the most hostility throughout Eastern Europe, and travelers with darker skin of any nationality might be mistaken for *Romany* and face unpleasant consequences. Other minority travelers, especially those of African or Asian descent, will usually meet with more curiosity than hostility; travelers of Arab ethnicity may also be treated more suspiciously, especially in France. Skinheads are on the rise in Eastern Europe, and minority travelers, especially Jews and blacks, should regard them with caution. Anti-Semitism is still a problem in many countries, including Poland and the former Soviet Union; it is generally best to be discreet about your religion. Travelers should use common sense—someone who flashes money around will become a target regardless of any racial or religious differences.

TRAVELERS WITH CHILDREN

Family vacations often require that you slow your pace and always require that you plan ahead. When choosing an accommodation, call ahead and make sure it's child-friendly. Be sure that your child carries some sort of ID in case of an emergency or in case he or she gets lost.

Children under two generally fly for 10% of the adult airfare on international flights (this does not necessarily include a seat). International fares are usually discounted 25% for children from two to 11.

FURTHER READING

Backpacking with Babies and Small Children, Goldie Silverman. Wilderness Press (US$10).

Take Your Kids to Europe, Cynthia W. Harriman. Globe Pequot (US$17).

How to take Great Trips with Your Kids, Sanford and Jane Portnoy. Harvard Common Press (US $10).

Have Kid, Will Travel: 101 Survival Strategies for Vacationing With Babies and Young Children, Claire and Lucille Tristram. Andrews and McMeel (US$9).

Adventuring with Children: An Inspirational Guide to World Travel and the Outdoors, Nan Jeffrey. Avalon House Publishing ($15).

DIETARY CONCERNS

Vegetarians should have no problem in most of Europe. Travelers who keep **kosher** should contact synagogues for information on kosher restaurants. Your own synagogue or college Hillel should have access to lists of Jewish institutions. If you are strict in your observance, you might have to prepare your own food on the road. **The Jewish Travel Guide,** which lists synagogues, kosher restaurants, and Jewish institutions in over 100 countries, is available in Europe from Vallentine Mitchell Publishers, Newbury House 890-900, Eastern Ave., Newbury Park, Ilford, Essex IG2 7HH, UK (☎ (020) 85 99 88 66; fax 85 99 09 84) and in the US ($16.95 + $4 S&H) from ISBS, 5804 NE Hassallo St., Portland, OR 97213 (☎ (800) 944 61 90).

The Vegetarian Society of the UK (VSUK), Parkdale, Dunham Rd, Altringham, Cheshire WA14 4QG (☎ (0161) 925 20 00; fax 926 91 82; www.vegsoc.org).

North American Vegetarian Society, P.O. Box 72, Dolgeville, NY 13329 (US ☎ (518) 568 79 70, fax (518) 568 79 79; email navs@telenet.com; www.navs-online.org).

FURTHER READING

The Jewish Travel Guide 2001 lists synagogues and kosher restaurants in 80 countries. Ed. Michael Zaidner. Vallentine-Mitchell Publishers (US$17).

The Vegan Travel Guide: UK and Southern Ireland. Book Publishing Co. (US$15).

The Vegetarian Traveler: Where to Stay if You're Vegetarian, Jed Civic. Larson Pub. (US$16).

Europe on 10 Salads a Day, Greg and Mary Jane Edwards. Mustang Publishing. (US$10/ UK£9).

ALTERNATIVES TO TOURISM

STUDYING ABROAD

Whether you seek a college semester abroad, a summer of foreign-language immersion, or a top-notch cooking school, you are sure to find a program tailored to your needs. Most American undergraduates enroll in programs sponsored by US universities. However, if your language skills are already decent, local universities can be much cheaper (although getting credit may be more difficult); enrolling directly in one usually involves passing a language-proficiency test.

Studying abroad in Europe usually requires a special study **visa,** issued for a duration longer than a tourist visa. Applying for such a visa usually requires proof of admission to an appropriate university or program. In some countries, student status will affect your right to work. Information on visa and other requirements should be available from foreign embassies at home.

STUDY ABROAD ORGANIZATIONS

American Institute for Foreign Study, College Division, River Plaza, 9 West Broad St., Stamford, CT 06902, USA (☎ (800) 727 24 37, ext. 5163; www.aifsabroad.com). Organizes high school and college study programs at universities in Austria, the Czech Republic, France, Great Britain, Ireland, Italy, the Netherlands, Russia, and Spain.

Association of Commonwealth Universities (ACU), John Foster House, 36 Gordon Sq., London WC1H OPF (☎ (020) 73 87 85 72; www.acu.ac.uk). Publishes information about Commonwealth universities.

Beaver College Center for Education Abroad, 450 S. Easton Rd., Glenside, PA 19038, USA (☎ (888) 232 83 79; www.beaver.edu/cea). Operates programs in Western Europe. Costs range from $1900 (summer) to $20,000 (full-year).

Central College Abroad, Office of International Education, 812 University, Pella, IA 50219, USA (☎ (800) 831 36 29 or (515) 628 52 84; studyabroad.com/central). Offers semester- and year-long programs. US$25 application fee.

School for International Training, College Semester Abroad, Admissions, Kipling Rd., P.O. Box 676, Brattleboro, VT 05302, USA (☎ (800) 336 16 16 or (802) 258 32 67; www.sit.edu). Semester- and year-long programs in Europe run US$9500-12,900. Also runs the **Experiment in International Living** (☎ (800) 345 29 29; fax (802) 258 34 28; email eil@worldlearning.org), three- to five-week summer programs that offer high-school students cross-cultural homestays, community service, ecological adventure, and language training cost US$1900-5000.

Council on International Educational Exchange (CIEE), 205 East 42nd St., New York, NY 10017 (☎ (888) 268 62 45 or (800) 407 88 39; fax (212) 822 27 99; www.ciee.org/study) sponsors work, volunteer, academic, and internship programs in Britain, France, Ireland, Italy, and Spain. Non-US residents should locate their country's CIEE office number on the website.

International Association for the Exchange of Students for Technical Experience (IAESTE), 10400 Little Patuxent Pkwy. #250, Columbia, MD 21044, USA (☎ (410) 997 30 68; www.aipt.org). Operates 8- to 12-week programs in Austria, Britain, Eastern Europe, France, Germany, Greece, Ireland, Italy, Spain, Switzerland, and Turkey for college students who have completed 2 years of technical study. US$50 application fee.

LANGUAGE SCHOOLS

Eurocentres, 101 N. Union St #300, Alexandria, VA 22314, USA (☎ (800) 648 48 09 or (703) 684 14 94; fax 684 14 95; www.eurocentres.com) or Head Office, Seestr. 247, CH-8038 Zurich, Switzerland (☎+41 (411) 485 50 40; email info@eurocentres.com). Language programs for beginning to advanced students with homestays in Britain, France, Germany, Italy, Russia, and Spain run approximately US$1132.

Language Immersion Institute, 75 South Manheim Blvd., The College at New Paltz, New Paltz, NY 12561, USA (☎ (914) 257 35 00; www.newpaltz.edu/lii). 2-week summer language courses and some overseas courses. Program fees are about US$295 for a weekend or US$750 per 2 weeks.

World Exchange, Ltd., White Birch Rd, Putnam Valley, NY 10579 (US ☎ (800) 444 39 24; fax 528 91 87; www.worldexchange.org), offers 1- to 4-week language-based homestay programs offered in France or Spain (up to 14 days US$850; 15-28 days US$1,150).

Languages Abroad, 502-99 Avenue Road, Toronto, Ontario M5R-2G5 (US ☎ (800) 219 99 24, ☎ (416) 925 59 90; fax 925 59 90; www.languagesabroad.com), organizes 2-16 week language and culture immersion programs, and arranges for homestays or apartments in Austria, France, Germany, Greece, Italy, Portugal, Russia, Spain, Switzerland, and Turkey for US$545-6400. Must be 18+. Registration fee US$100.

LanguagesPLUS, 317 Adelaide St. W., Suite 900, Toronto, Ontario M5V-1P9 (US ☎ (888) 526 47 58, ☎ (416) 925 71 17; fax 925 59 90; www.languagesplus.com), runs 1-36-week programs in France, Germany, Italy, and Spain from US$470-5000 that include tuition, accommodations with host families or apartments, and activities. 18+.

FURTHER READING AND RESOURCES

www.studyabroad.com

Academic Year Abroad 2000/2001. Institute of International Education Books (US$43).

Vacation Study Abroad 2000/2001. Institute of International Education Books (US$43).

Peterson's Study Abroad 2001. Peterson's (US$30).

WORKING ABROAD

There's no better way to immerse yourself in a foreign culture than to become part of its economy. **European Union citizens** can work in any EU country; if your parents were born in an EU country, you may be able to claim dual citizenship or the right to a permit (note that in some cases citizenship entails compulsory military service). Officially, **non-EU citizens** can hold a job in Europe only with a **work permit,** obtained by your employer, usually demonstrating that you have skills that locals lack. Working in Eastern Europe often requires both a work permit and a visa. In some countries, a particular visa called a "visa with work permit" is required, although this document (contrary to the name) actually does *not* include a work permit; in order to apply for one of these special visas (issued from the nearest consulate or embassy like any other visa), you must first acquire a work permit from the Labor Bureau of the country in question. Temporary jobs that can be more easily found include au pair, English teacher, agriculture worker, or waiter. Look for help wanted ads in local newspapers, at federally run employment offices, at university foreign language courses, and American chambers of commerce.

If you are a full-time student at a US university, the simplest way to get a job abroad in France, Germany, Ireland, Italy, or Spain is through work permit programs run by the **Council on International Educational Exchange** (p. 73). For a US$300-400 application fee, Council can procure three- to six-month work permits. European friends can expedite permits or arrange work-for-accommodations swaps.

AU PAIR ORGANIZATIONS

Accord Cultural Exchange, 750 La Playa, San Francisco, CA 94121, USA (☎ (415) 386 62 03; www.cognitext.com/accord). US$40 application fee.

interExchange, 161 Sixth Ave., New York, NY 10013 (☎ (212) 924 04 46; fax 924 05 75; www.interexchange.org). Participants except in the Netherlands must speak the local language.

Childcare International, Ltd., Trafalgar House, Grenville Pl., London NW7 3SA (☎ (020) 89 06 31 16; fax 89 06 34 61; www.childint.co.uk), offers au pair positions in Austria, Belgium, Croatia, the Czech Republic, Denmark, Finland, France, Germany, Hungary, Iceland, Italy, the Netherlands, Norway, Spain, Switzerland, and Turkey. UK£100 application fee.

TEACHING ENGLISH

International Schools Services, Educational Staffing Program, P.O. Box 5910, Princeton, NJ 08543, USA (☎ (609) 452 09 90; fax 452 26 90; www.iss.edu). Recruits teachers and administrators for American and English schools in Europe. Applicants must have a bachelor's degree and 2 years of experience. Nonrefundable US$150 application fee.

Office of Overseas Schools, US Department of State, Room H328, SA-1, Washington, D.C. 20522 (☎ (202) 261 82 00; fax 261 82 24; www.state.gov/www/about_state/schools/). Keeps a comprehensive list of schools abroad and agencies that arrange placement for Americans to teach abroad.

OTHER

Willing Workers on Organic Farms (WWOOF), P.O. Box 2675, Lewes, England BN7 1RB (www.phdcc.com/sites/wwoof). Membership allows you to exchange work for room and board at organic farms in Austria, Britain, Denmark, Finland, France, Germany, Hungary, Ireland, Italy, and Switzerland. Check the website for membership fees.

Archaeological Institute of America, 656 Beacon St., Boston, MA 02215 (US ☎ (617) 353 93 61; fax 353 65 50; www.archaeological.org). Puts out a list of field sites in Italy, France, Greece, and Turkey (nonmembers US$16), available from Kendall/Hunt Publishing, 4050 Westmark Dr., Dubuque, IA 52002 (☎ (800) 228 08 10).

VOLUNTEERING

Volunteer jobs are readily available, and many provide room and board in exchange for labor. You can sometimes avoid high application fees by contacting the individual workcamps directly.

Earthwatch, 680 Mt. Auburn St., Box 403, Watertown, MA 02272, USA (☎ (800) 776 01 88 or ☎ (617) 926 82 00; www.earthwatch.org). Arranges 1- to 3-week programs to promote conservation of natural resources. Programs average US$1600.

Habitat for Humanity International, 121 Habitat St., Americus, GA 31709, USA (☎ (800) 334 33 08; www.habitat.org). Offers international opportunities to live with and build houses in a host community. Costs range US$1200-3500.

Peace Corps, Office of Volunteer Recruitment and Selection, 1111 20th St. NW, Washington, D.C. 20526 (☎ (800) 424 85 80; www.peacecorps.gov). Opportunities in 78 developing nations including much of Eastern Europe. Volunteers must be US citizens ages 18+ willing to make a 2-year commitment, plus three months of training. A bachelor's degree is usually required.

Service Civil International Voluntary Service (SCI-IVS), 814 NE 40th St., Seattle, WA 98105, USA (☎/fax (206) 545 65 85; www.sci-ivs.org). Arranges placement in workcamps in Europe for those 18+. Registration fee US$125.

Volunteers for Peace, 1034 Tiffany Rd., Belmont, VT 05730, USA (☎ (802) 259 27 59; www.vfp.org). A nonprofit organization that arranges speedy placement in a 2- to 3-week, 10- to 20- person workcamps in Europe mostly during the summer. Annual *International Workcamp Directory* US$20. Registration fee US$200. Free newsletter.

FURTHER READING

International Jobs: Where they Are, How to Get Them, Eric Koocher. Perseus Books (US$17).

How to Get a Job in Europe, Robert Sanborn. Surrey Books (US$22).

Work Abroad: The Complete Guide to Finding a Job Overseas, Clayton Hubbs. Transitions Abroad (US$16).

International Directory of Voluntary Work, Louise Whetter. Vacation Work Publications (US$16).

Overseas Summer Jobs 2001, Work Your Way Around the World, and *The Directory of Jobs and Careers Abroad.* Peterson's (US$17-18 each).

OTHER RESOURCES

Let's Go tries to cover all aspects of budget travel, but we can't include *everything.* Listed below are books, organizations, and websites for your own research.

TRAVEL PUBLISHERS & BOOKSTORES

Hippocrene Books, Inc., 171 Madison Ave., New York, NY 10016 (☎ (212) 685 43 71; orders ☎ (718) 454 23 66; fax 454 13 91; www.hippocrenebooks.com), publishes travel guides, as well as foreign language dictionaries and learning guides.

Hunter Publishing, 821 L South King St., Leesburg, VA 20175 (☎/fax (703) 777 89 07; www.hunterpublishing.com), offers an extensive catalog of travel books, guides, maps, and hotel guides for Europe.

Rand McNally, 150 S. Wacker Dr., Chicago, IL 60606 (☎ (800) 275 72 63, ☎ (312) 332 20 09; fax 443 95 40; email store@randmcnally.com; www.randmcnally.com), publishes a number of comprehensive road atlases (US$10).

Travel Books & Language Center, Inc., 4437 Wisconsin Ave. NW, Washington, D.C. 20016 (☎ (800) 220 26 65, (202) 237 13 22; fax 237 60 22; www.bookweb.org/bookstore/travelbks), sells travel aids, language cassettes, dictionaries, travel books, atlases, and maps. No web orders.

Bon Voyage!, 2069 W. Bullard Ave., Fresno, CA 93711-1200 (☎ (800) 995 97 16, elsewhere call US (559) 447 84 41; fax 266 64 60; www.bon-voyage-travel.com), sells videos, travel gear, and railpasses. Free newsletter.

THE WORLD WIDE WEB

Almost every aspect of budget travel is accessible via the web. In minutes, you can reserve a room in France, get travel advice from others who have just returned from Europe, or find out how much a train from Barcelona to Rome costs. Listed here are some budget travel sites to start off your surfing; other relevant web sites are listed throughout the book. Because web site turnover is high, use search engines (such as www.yahoo.com) to strike out on your own. But in doing so, keep in mind that most travel web sites exist simply to get your money.

LEARNING THE ART OF BUDGET TRAVEL

Backpacker's Ultimate Guide: www.bugeurope.com. Tips on packing, transportation, hostels, cultural events, and key destinations.

Backpack Europe: www.backpackeurope.com. Helpful packing list, travel tips, information on work and study abroad, a bulletin board, and useful links.

How to See the World: www.artoftravel.com. A compendium of great travel tips, from cheap flights to self defense to interacting with local culture.

TripSpot: www.tripspot.com/europefeature.htm. An outline of links to help plan trips, transportation, sleeping accommodations, and packing.

Rec. Travel Library: www.travel-library.com. A fantastic set of links for general information and personal travelogues.

Shoestring Travel: www.stratpub.com. An e-zine focusing on budget travel.

COUNTRY-SPECIFIC INFORMATION

CIA World Factbook: www.odci.gov/cia/publications/factbook/index.html. Tons of vital statistics on European geography, governments, economies, and politics.

Foreign Language for Travelers: www.travlang.com. Provides free online translating dictionaries and lists of phrases in European languages from Albanian to Yiddish.

DESTINATION GUIDES

MyTravelGuide: www.mytravelguide.com. Country overviews, with everything from history to transportation to local newspapers. Free travel newsletter.

Geographia: www.geographia.com. Describes highlights and attractions of the various European countries.

Atevo Travel: www.atevo.com/guides/destinations. Detailed introductions, transportation tips, and suggested itineraries. Free travel newsletter.

Columbus Travel Guides: www.travel-guides.com/navigate/region/eur.asp. Well-organized site with practical information on geography, government, communication, health precautions, economy, and useful addresses.

LeisurePlanet: www.leisureplanet.com/TravelGuides. Good country-specific background with coverage of sites and basic practical information.

CNN: www.cnn.com/travel/city.guides. Detailed information about services, sites, shopping, dining, nightlife, and recreation in the major cities of Europe.

In Your Pocket: www.inyourpocket.com. Extensive virtual guides to select Baltic and Eastern European cities.

LINKS TO EUROPEAN TOURISM PAGES

TravelPage: www.travelpage.com. Links to official tourist office sites throughout Europe.

Lycos: cityguide.lycos.com/europe. General introductions to cities and regions throughout Europe, accompanied by links to applicable histories, news, and local tourism sites.

PlanetRider: www.planetrider.com/Europe-index.cfm. A subjective list of links to the "best" websites covering the culture and tourist attractions of major European cities.

AND OUR PERSONAL FAVORITE...

Let's Go: www.letsgo.com. Our website features photos and streaming video, info about our books, a travel forum buzzing with stories and tips, and helpful links.

FURTHER READING: SURFING THE WEB

How to Plan Your Dream Vacation Using the Web, by Elizabeth Dempsey. Coriolis Group (US$25).

Nettravel: How Travelers Use the Internet (US$25) and *Internet Travel Planner* (US$19), by Michael Shapiro. O'Reilly & Associates and Globe Pequot Press.

Travel Planning Online for Dummies, by Noah Vadnai. IDG Books (US$25).

Ten Minute Guide to Travel Planning on the Net, by Thomas Pack. QUE. (US$15).

300 Incredible Things for Travelers on the Internet, by Ken Leebow. 300Incredible.com. (US$9).

PRICES (US$), TRAVEL TIMES, AND DISTANCES (KM) BY TRAIN

	Amsterdam	Barcelona	Berlin	Brussels	Budapest	Copenhagen	Florence	Kraków	Madrid	Milan	Munich	Paris	Prague	Rome	Warsaw	Venice	Vienna	Zürich
Amsterdam		1773	673	246	1620	807	1540	1358	2013	1053	885	554	1044	1789	1240	1662	1249	990
Barcelona	$204; 16½hr.[1]		2193	1679	2267	2096	1493	n/a	728	1044	1335	1219	2583	1443	2776	1363	2000	1160
Berlin	$117; 7hr.	$314 27¼hr.[1]		836	993	841	1253	681	2633	1271	679	1174	408	1650	795	1234	772	963
Brussels	$42; 2½hr.	$182; 14hr.[1]	$138; 11hr.		1191	904	1722	n/a	1771	664	877	460	1049	1848	1631	1201	1346	613
Budapest	$248; 17½hr.[1]	$259; 26½hr.[1]	$104; 13hr.	$215; 16½hr.[1]		1260	1146	592	3112	1156	735	1653	621	1275	940	705	267	1023
Copenhagen	$166; 14hr.	n/a	$104; 7½hr.	$178; 12hr.	n/a		1890	n/a	2575	1608	1235	759	651	2106	1268	n/a	1052	1268
Florence	$227; 18½hr.[1]	$116; 19hr.[1]	$185; 17½hr.	$181; 16hr.[1]	$123; 14½hr.[1]	$299; 19½hr.[1]		1287	1936	316	655	1137	1094	316	n/a	257	879	1109
Kraków	$155; 15½hr.[1]	n/a	$38; 8hr.	n/a	$49; 10½hr.	n/a	$126; 21½hr.[1]		n/a	n/a	885	1898	534	n/a	320	n/a	418	1320
Madrid	$215; 17½hr.[1]	$56; 7hr.	$291; 25¼hr.[1]	$201; 15hr.[1]	$351; 31¼hr.[1]	$379; 27¾[1]	$176; 25hr.[1]	n/a		1535	2349	1459	2823	1880	2961	1806	2849	2073
Milan	$206; 14½hr.	$107; 13hr.	$183; 17½hr.[1]	$137; 12hr.	$127; 15¾hr.[1]	$297; 22hr.	$31; 3½hr.	n/a	$170; 25¼hr.[1]		592	953	1031	632	1497	267	889	293
Munich	$155; 9½hr.	$204; 16¾hr.[1]	$115; 10hr.	$143; 8½hr.	$93; 8hr.	$222; 10½hr.[1]	$72; 9hr.	$111; 15hr.[1]	$257; 24hr.	$68; 7½hr.		923	439	971	1201	577	469	354
Paris	$94; 4¼hr.	$110; 12¼hr.	$197; 12hr.	$72; 1¾hr.	$218; 18hr.	$231; 15¼hr.	$133; 12½hr.	$238; 23¼hr.[1]	$133; 13¼hr.	$94; 7½hr.	$128; 8½hr.		1364	1585	1690	1220	1390	614
Prague	$175; 12½hr.[1]	$280; 27¼hr.[1]	$58; 5½hr.	$159; 13½hr.[1]	$59; 7¾hr.	$161; 12¼hr.	$146; 15hr.[1]	$47; 8½hr.	$319; 28¼hr.[1]	$130; 13½hr.[1]	$74 6hr.	$186; 15hr.		1410	762	700	407	767
Rome	$272; 20hr.[1]	$143; 21¼hr.[1]	$207; 20¼hr.[1]	$174; 18¾hr.[1]	$124; 25hr.[1]	$332; 25hr.[1]	$31; 1¾hr.	n/a	$192; 30½hr.[1]	$49; 4½hr.	$92; 10¼hr.	$158; 14½hr.	$154; 16¼hr.[1]		2255	573	1203	979
Warsaw	$154; 13hr.[1]	$348; 34½hr.[1]	$37; 6hr.	$175; 17¼hr.[1]	$57; 11¼hr.[1]	$144; 13½hr.[1]	n/a	$19; 2¾hr.	n/a	n/a	$112; 16½hr.[1]	$194; 19hr.[1]	$50; 10½hr.	$152; 24hr.		1303	673	1600
Venice	$222; 17hr.[1]	$141; 22hr.[1]	$255; 17hr.	$161; 15¼hr.[1]	$87; 13hr.	$280; 22hr	$28; 2¾hr.	n/a	$189; 30½hr.[1]	$24; 3hr.	$69; 7hr.	$137; 12½hr.	$110; 13½hr.	$46; 4¾hr.	$121; 17¼hr.[1]		630	614
Vienna	$196; 13hr.[1]	$221; 23hr.	$92; 10hr.	$181; 15hr.[1]	$38; 3hr.	$265; 17½hr.[1]	$85; 11½hr.	$44; 10hr.	$324; 28¼hr.[1]	$89; 12¾hr.	$67; 5hr.	$191; 15hr.	$46; 5hr.	$102; 13hr.	$51; 8¼hr.	$68; 9hr.		902
Zürich	$166; 9hr.	$128; 13hr.	$191; 8hr.[1]	$98; 8hr.	$120; 13½hr.	$277; 15hr.[1]	$83; 8hr.	$144; 19¼hr.[1]	$213; 21½hr.[1]	$61; 3¾hr.	$70; 4¼hr.	$80; 8¼hr.	$123; 11½hr.	$99; 8¼hr.	$217; 20¼hr.[1]	$81; 8hr.	$100; 9¼hr.	

1 These routes require a change of trains. Travel times do not include layover.

EUROPEAN CULTURE FROM ATHENS TO ABBA

Europe is a cultural cornucopia, yielding fruits of literature, art, and music that continue to shape the Western worldview with their ageless beauty. Forget politics—here are the artistic and intellectual movements that forged a continent. For the historical lowdown, refer to the **timeline,** p. 89. For more country-specific details, check out the fabulous *Let's Go* regional guides.

CLASSICAL GREECE

Western culture began to flower in the fertile soil of **Classical Greece,** which peaked around 500-400 BC. Sparring city-states clashed in war; held competitions in athletics, art, and drama; and spun myths of magnificent, mischievous gods that are still widely read today. The story of the Greeks begins with the Dorian invasion in the 12th century BC. These supposed descendents of **Hercules** drove out the original inhabitants, mostly remnants of the earlier Mycenaean civilization. The cultures of the Dorians, most famously of **Sparta** (p. 487), and the Ionians, who became **Athenians,** mingled in the fascinating mixture of Classical Greece. In architecture, for example, the artistic values of the Dorians—simplicity, stark monumentality—fused with the elaborate elegance of Ionian styles. The **Parthenon** (p. 482) in Athens, Classical Greece's most enduring architectural contribution, marries Ionic columns with a massive Doric exterior.

Also from Ionia came the famed intellectual tradition of **Athens** (p. 477), which primarily concerned itself with geography and the state of nature but also produced the two great historians of antiquity. **Herodotus,** in his *History*, chronicled the Greco-Persian Wars of 499-479 BC. **Thucydides** wrote another detailed historical work, the *History of the Peloponnesian War* between Athens and Sparta from 431-404 BC. The foundations of Western philosophy were laid first by **Socrates,** then by **Plato** and **Aristotle,** who developed the concept of the ideal state in the *Republic* and the *Politics*, respectively. The great dramatists of the age contributed works whose themes of **tragedy** (Aeschylus, Sophocles, and Euripides) and **comedy** (Aristophanes and Menander) still resonate on modern stages. The literary big daddy of ancient Greece, however, was undoubtedly **Homer.** His *Iliad* and *Odyssey* are generally regarded as the most important poems in the European classical tradition, telling of the war against **Troy,** a city that was once considered only Homeric legend but whose remains (dating back to the 12th or 13th century BC) were uncovered in Western Turkey (p. 958).

Hellenic Greek culture was spread throughout the known world by the heroic warrior and leader **Alexander.** Soon labeled the Great, Alexander conquered the Greeks, then moved against Persia in the east. In his hugely successful military career, he named several cities after himself, one for his horse Bucephalus, and demanded to be named a god. (The Spartans reportedly responded, "Since Alexander wishes to be a god, let him be a god.") His empire, which shattered when he died in 323 BC, brought the world from Spain to India into a common interchange of objects and ideas that would be crucial in the course of human history.

THE ROMAN EMPIRE

Rome (p. 577) began as a Republic, formed after the Etruscan invasion in 509 BC. Spanning all of Western Europe as far north as Scotland, the entire Mediterranean basin, and most of Northern Africa, the empire lasted over four hundred years. The Romans established a "dual-kingship" of two consuls, appointed yearly by a **Senate** with whom they shared power. This mighty governmental structure ruled all of civilized Europe and kept a **Pax Romana,** or "Roman peace," for 200 years through a combination of strength and efficiency. The legal **Code of Justinian** was enforced by the massive, disciplined, and well-equipped Roman army, and has formed the basis of many revised legal codes.

The Romans adapted many Greek architectural principles, but conducted building projects on a grander scale than was possible for the Greeks. Their feats of public engineering—roads, bridges, aqueducts, and dams—were the first large-scale mass infrastructure projects and were so well-made that many are still used two thousand years later. The basis of Roman architecture was the **rounded arch,** used in structures like basilicas and amphitheaters (or the Colosseum, p. 588).

While the Roman literary scene arguably did not equal that of the Greeks, Classical **Latin** was established as a serious vehicle for literary expression. The Republican senator, orator, and philosopher **Cicero** left scores of recorded speeches, while **Livy** and **Tacitus** set forth comprehensive histories of Rome. **Petronius** and **Suetonius** penned tomes on the decadent, scandalous lives of Nero and the first twelve Roman emperors, respectively. In poetry, **Virgil** connected Troy and Rome through the travels of Aeneas in the *Aeneid*, and **Ovid** waxed romantic in the *Amores* and the *Metamorphoses.* The wise philosopher-king Emperor **Marcus Aurelius** wrote his *Meditations* (c. AD 167), an important work of **Stoic** philosophy.

Rome evolved into a Christian state when **Emperor Constantine I** assumed power in the early years of the 3rd century. Constantine converted to Christianity in 312, and during his reign extended tolerance to Christians in the **Edict of Milan.** He also oversaw the completion of the **Basilica of Maxentius** (p. 587), which at one time housed a gargantuan statue of the Emperor himself.

THE MIDDLE AGES

The order of the Western Roman Empire was disrupted when the **Visigoths** rolled into Rome in 410, and Germanic tribes crowned their own emperor in 476. In the wake of these invasions, most forms of organized government broke down and Europe sank into **feudalism,** a many-layered system of allegiance and service in exchange for protection. This model, without urban centers or any meaningful pan-European culture, led to the political and cultural stagnation of Europe.

With the collapse of non-religious authority following the fall of the empire, **the Christian Church** assumed great power and influence. The Church had come to be based in Rome and structurally mimicked the hierarchy of the Empire. (The pope paralleled the emperor, with a "senate" of cardinals and regional bishops ruling over religious "provinces" called dioceses.) After the fall of the Western Empire, the Church remained one of the few bastions of knowledge and civilization in the broken West. Even during the **Dark Ages,** or High Middle Ages, **monasteries** (under the Rule of St. Benedict, which set forth rules for life in religious communities) remained storehouses of knowledge and learning. At a time of almost no painting or sculpture, Christian monks continued to produce intricate **illuminated manuscripts,** Church documents decorated with elaborate and colorful designs and often supplemented by gold plate within their pages. The scholarly and ascetic force of monasticism became a powerful and reaching influence in European society, spreading to Kiev in 1050 and Moscow in 1354. (The Romanian monasteries of Bukovina, five hundred years old, are painted with brilliant frescoes, p. 784.)

In addition to the literary and decorative efforts of monks, the later medieval Church was the source of all meaningful philosophy of the Middle Ages. **Scholasticism,** typified most clearly by **St. Thomas Aquinas,** was a masterwork of rational synthesis. Aquinas combined the ancient teachings of Aristotle (whom he often referred to simply as "Reason"), the Church Fathers, and the Bible. By resolving apparent contradictions and fitting the teachings of these three revered sources together, he did much to support Christianity and advance Western thought.

It took the great conquests of **Charlemagne,** king of the Franks, to shake up Europe in the Dark Ages. Founder of the **Carolingian dynasty,** Charlemagne brought most of Europe under his command, including modern-day France, Germany, and Italy. He was crowned Holy Roman Emperor by the Pope on Christmas Day, 800, and during his 14-year reign strived to make his empire a superior cultural force. Although unable to read or write well himself, Charlemagne had books read aloud to him and learned what he could of astronomy and mathematics. He attracted scholars to his court and was instrumental as well in religious artistic life, instituting **Gregorian chant** across the churches and worship sites in the Empire.

Charlemagne's kingdom was quickly divided by his three surviving sons at his death, and Europe began to splinter politically. Following political breakup came a return to part of the cultural devastation of the Dark Ages. And while the **Crusades** of later generations helped bring Christendom together somewhat (especially when Pope Urban II called the first Crusade in 1095), these military migrations were under the loose authority of a religious leader. The Crusades, despite their folly, did help reinvigorate Europe by establishing contact with the superior technology and learning of civilizations in the East.

THE BYZANTINE EMPIRE

For a thousand years after the Western Roman Empire crumbled, plunging half the continent into the Dark Ages, the Eastern **Byzantine Empire** continued to flourish in autocratic might. Emperors in the East were very closely connected to the Christian Church, and their authority (generally greater than that of their western counterparts) was endowed with a limited divinity. Byzantine art was almost entirely religious and reflected the spiritual, hierarchical worldview of the East, in which individual facial features are symbolically de-emphasized and tradition is of primary importance. Visual art was based not on three-dimensional forms but rather on flat areas of color, achieving a certain stylistic sophistication. Iconographic **frescoes** (water-based paintings on plaster, usually wall murals) and **mosaics** (decorations made with small pieces of colored tile) covered the interiors of Byzantine **basilicas.** These works depicted Biblical scenes or the dominant figure of the Father surrounded by angels and saints; particularly stunning mosaics adorn the **Euphrasius Basilica** in Poreč, Croatia (p. 232). Byzantine religious art spread to the rest of the Eastern empire with the growth of Orthodoxy, and was transmitted through trade and conquest to Italy, where it influenced the **Renaissance.**

Literature and music were also inextricably tied to religion. **Illuminated manuscripts** (see above) aided in the dispersal of Byzantine iconography across Eastern Europe. Unison Byzantine **chant** most likely descended from Hebrew and early Christian liturgies in Syria, and was written in **neumatic notation**, an approximate notational system that served mostly as a memory aid.

THE RENAISSANCE

Both the visits of Westerners to the East in the Crusades and the westward migration of Eastern scholars after the fall of Constantinople (with Classical documents in hand) planted the seeds of a revival of Classical values of culture and learning. As feudalism declined in Europe—replaced by national kings and a rising class of townspeople and merchants—a tremendous flowering of art and culture began in Italy, one so great that later scholars would call it the rebirth, or the **Renaissance.**

The driving ideological force of the Renaissance was **humanism,** which elevated man from a compliant soul yearning for Heaven to a striving body eager for the promises of this life. This revival of the values of ancient Greece and Rome corresponded with a gradual decline in the cultural power of the Church. The Italian poet **Dante Alighieri** used the **vernacular** (spoken) language, rather than formal Church Latin; his *Divine Comedy* puts a new spin on medieval religious themes. The master of Italian classical prose was **Boccaccio,** whose *Decameron* (written from 1348-1353) is an earthy and playful satire of ten Florentines.

The three greatest figures in Renaissance art emerged around the turn of the 15th century. **Leonardo da Vinci** (1452-1519), a Florentine artist, scientist, and engineer, typified more than anyone else the kaleidoscopic spirit of the Renaissance. His sketchbooks, written in a quirky mirror-script, are filled with designs for inventions and detailed pictures of human and animal anatomy. His oil paintings (like the **Mona Lisa,** on display at the Louvre, p. 338) and frescoes (most notably **The Last Supper,** at the Chiesa di Santa Maria delle Grazie, p. 619) are among the most highly considered works in Western art.

Michelangelo Buonarroti (1475-1564) was considered the greatest living artist by his contemporaries, and is still esteemed among history's finest. Michelangelo was foremost a sculptor, although he was proficient and prolific in several media; his most famous work is probably the **Sistine Chapel ceiling** (p. 596). Pope Julius II famously bullied the gentle artist into painting his chapel, coercing him with a stick. At Florence stands Michelangelo's **David,** the statue of the Biblical king majestically looming eighteen feet tall (at the Accademia, p. 636).

The third master was **Raphael,** dubbed the "prince of the painters" as much for his peaceful demeanor as for the technical perfection of his figures. Schooled partly in Florence, Raphael too was employed by Pope Julius II, along with Michelangelo and the architect Donato Bramante. The set of frescoes painted for Julius's papal apartments (at the Vatican, p. 596) are among his greatest works. One series, the Stanza della Segnatura, includes his **School of Athens,** a masterwork of balance and fluidity that does not sacrifice the individuality of any of its subjects. The work portrays the great philosophers of history conversing in a setting based on the new plans for St. Peter's but named after the seat of Classical thought.

Music, too, benefited from papal patronage. The Sistine Choir, governed by the Pope, helped transform traditional, single-voice Gregorian chant into the **polyphonic** (many-voiced) music of the Renaissance. Composer **Josquin des Prez** (1445-1521) introduced innovations to the religious choral form known as the motet, and hinted at the beginnings of modern harmony. **Palestrina** (1525-1584) followed in his footsteps, becoming the personal composer of a string of Popes in Rome.

THE REFORMATION

From 1492 to 1521, the reigning Popes were decadent and irreligious. The monstrous Alexander VI, a member of the politically and ecclesiastically influential **Borgia** family, shamelessly advanced the political career of his vicious nephew Cesare. Julius II, while a patron of the arts, was more a warrior than a cleric. The aloof Leo X instituted a policy of papal indulgences whereby Christians could pay for forgiveness of past sins or sins of their relatives in purgatory; this money was then used to finance the building of St. Peter's Cathedral in Rome. Leo X was one of four popes to come from the **Medici** clan, the greatest ruling family of Florence whose activities ranged from banking and politicking to the patronage of artists.

Such unseemly papal behavior outraged the pious German monk **Martin Luther,** who on October 31, 1519, expressed his discontent by posting his famous **95 Theses** on the door of the Castle Church, Wittenberg (p. 425). The resulting **Reformation,** as the movement came to be known, plunged Europe into more than a hundred years of war and debate, displacing artistic creativity and expression with the sobriety of sound Biblical faith and honest Christian humility. The belly button of the Reformation, the **Cathédrale de St-Pierre** (in Geneva, p. 923), was once resplendent with popish baubles but was stripped by the Swiss Reformer **John Calvin** to its present austere state. Although artistically joyless, the Reformation did sow the seeds of the **Enlightenment** by insisting on reasonable discourse, valued so heavily by Classical philosophers. And so, while the Reformation pruned the flower of Rome, it also helped the West along to its next stage of growth, the budding of democracy and modernization.

THE BAROQUE AND ROCOCO

The stylistically complex artistic phase known as the **Baroque** emerged around 1600. The prevailing social structure at the time consisted of absolute monarchies and an expanding middle class eager to provide patronage. Baroque architecture emphasized monumentality, dramatic layout, and rich interiors as a testament to the power of centralized states. The shockingly gold-encrusted palace and gardens at **Versailles** (p. 345), declared France's official royal residence in 1682, are particularly decadent remnants of the Baroque. Built by France's Sun King, **Louis XIV**, Versailles became the model for royal palaces in many European countries.

A renewed interest in nature, as well as an expansion of knowledge due to exploration and scientific developments, also characterized the Baroque. Beginning in the 1490's, European efforts to find a sea trade route to Cathay had opened up the New World to the **Age of Exploration.** The **British** and **Dutch East India Companies,** founded at the turn of the century, facilitated trade and cultural exchange with these distant and exotic countries. The invention of the **telescope** in Holland and **Galileo Galilei**'s findings helped confirm that the Earth orbited the sun, refuting the Church's teaching that all celestial bodies revolved around the Earth. This increasingly complex view of the natural world, as well as man's less significant place in it, emerged in artistic themes and subjects. Landscapes, often featuring tiny figures in a vast natural scene, became the dominant genre in 17th-century art.

The flourishing of the Baroque reached musical forms as well, witnessing the emergence of the **sonata, concerto, overture,** and **opera. Claudio Monteverdi** and **Jean-Baptiste Lully** (who, according to legend, died after impaling his foot with a conducting stick) gained fame in Italy and France, while **Georg Friedrich Händel** and **Johann Sebastian Bach** were major figures of sacred Baroque music in Germany.

The eighteenth century brought a taste for refinement and elegance to European culture, and the drama of the Baroque mellowed into a graceful **Rococo** style. Munich (p. 454) is home to several fine examples of Rococo architecture, especially in the subtle details of the Amalienburg park and Residenztheater of the **Schloss Nymphenburg.** The light and highly ornamental style of Rococo music influenced the early works of **Joseph Haydn** and **Wolfgang Amadeus Mozart.**

THE ENLIGHTENMENT

The artistic innovations of the Baroque and Rococo roughly preceded an intellectual movement referred to as the **Enlightenment,** or Age of Reason, which spurred revolutionary developments in philosophical literature. The Enlightenment was birthed by earlier trends in European cultural history: humanism's celebration of human intellectual power, the revival of Classical values during the Renaissance, and the Reformation's reliance on logic to question church authority. These movements also produced a rise in the status and influence of scientists and mathematicians. In particular, **Isaac Newton**'s mathematical equations defining the motions of the planets hinted that man could understand the universe through logic and reason, which came to be exalted as the keys to truth and understanding. The prominent thinkers of the time, the **philosophes,** championed the use of reason for social improvement and self-understanding.

The most important work of the Enlightenment was Denis Diderot's **Encyclopedia** (1751-1772), the first attempt at compiling all human knowledge in a logical form. While Diderot's work collected knowledge, the *Meditations* of **René Descartes** ("I think, therefore I am") introduced a philosophy of doubt that questioned all knowledge. Philosophers like **John Locke, Jean-Jacques Rousseau, Montesquieu,** and **Voltaire** critiqued authoritarian states and advanced the concept of political democracy, while **Thomas Hobbes**' *Leviathan* advocated an absolute monarchy to protect men from their naturally destructive state. In Italy, **Cesare Beccaria**'s 1764 *On Crimes and Punishments* radically altered attitudes toward the European justice system, leading many countries to abolish torture. The German philosopher **Gotthold Lessing** encouraged religious tolerance for Jews in his work *Nathan the Wise*, which separated human excellence from religious affiliation.

NEO-CLASSICISM

Just as the Enlightenment grew from past movements, **Neo-Classicism,** an emerging movement in art and architecture, drew on ancient Roman and Greek styles.

In the mid-18th century, Europe reacted against the intricacy of the Baroque and Rococo periods in favor of a simpler Classical model stressing clear form and simple content. In architecture and sculpture, this new focus emerged through a close imitation of ancient works, while architects wrestled with applying ancient principles to modern materials. The French palaces on the **Place de la Concorde** (p. 337) and the **Panthéon** (p. 336), as well as Madrid's royal **Palacio Real** (p. 839), embody the Neo-Classical values of harmony, proportion, and congruence.

Neo-Classicism seeped into all aspects of European high society and extreme politeness became standard, especially at court. The art of the period centered mostly on restrained portraits of nobility that eulogized their subjects, much as ancient artists had done. In France, **Watteau** gained prominence, and **Joshua Reynolds** became famous in England, also helping to found the **Royal Academy of Arts** (at Piccadilly in London, p. 166) in 1768. The literary leaders of the Classicist revival included the dramatist **Jean Racine** and the English writers **John Dryden** and **Alexander Pope.** And in music, instrumental works dominated for the first time in history; composers like **Joseph Haydn, Wolfgang Amadeus Mozart,** and **Ludwig van Beethoven** shaped its highly ordered rhythmic structures and polished melodies.

THE FRENCH REVOLUTION

Influenced by the Enlightenment, European intellectuals came to regard certain social institutions, such as absolutism and supernatural religiosity, with skepticism. Despite this philosophical challenge, some governments continued to operate as despotically as they had for past centuries, most notably Louis XVI's **divine right monarchy** in France, breeding tension between ideology and oppressive reality. The **French Revolution** began in 1789 with the **Tennis Court Oath,** which marked the non-privileged peoples' determination to end divine right monarchy and replace it with a constitutional monarchy. The revolution grew increasingly intense as an angry mob of Parisians stormed the **Bastille** (p. 337) on July 14, a date that remains a French national holiday. In 1792, the French monarchy was abolished and in 1793, Louis XVI was executed at the present-day Place de la Concorde. Immediately after the execution of the King, the **Reign of Terror** (1793-1794), facilitated by the invention of the **guillotine,** resulted in the execution of thousands of moderates and potential enemies. A notoriously corrupt government, the **Directory,** lasted from 1795-1799, until **Napoleon Bonaparte** established the **Consulate** and proclaimed himself "Emperor of the French." **Jacques-Louis David,** the most important artistic chronicler of the Revolution, captured Napoleon's triumphant rise to power in *The Coronation of Napoleon* (now at the Louvre, p. 338).

Not simply a historical event, the French Revolution profoundly affected intellectual, philosophical, and political life in the 19th century, particularly in Britain. Revolutionary values initially corresponded to the Enlightenment concept of reason triumphing over superstition and privilege, an ideal supported by liberals and radicals like **Thomas Paine** and **William Blake.** The Reign of Terror, however, revealed to many the flaws in their optimistic Enlightenment thought. The French Revolution also spurred great literary works, such as the **Declaration of the Rights of Man** set forth by the National Assembly (a revolutionary parliament) in 1789, which stated the equality of all members of the human race.

ROMANTICISM

The perils of the Revolution and France's unstable political situation sent it to the back of the pack during the **Industrial Revolution,** which was permanently changing the face of Europe in the early 1800s. However, the dynamics of the revolutionary era, combined with the Napoleonic brand of militarism spreading throughout Europe, did inspire a new mode of art called **Romanticism.** Characterized by boldness of color and composition, Romanticism offered a challenge to Neo-Classicism by rejecting the ideas of order, harmony, and reason, stressing instead the irrational and the emotional—much like the French Revolution itself. **Francisco**

Goya, a Spanish painter, depicted the horror of Napoleon's 1808 invasion of Spain in "The Third of May" (in the **Museo del Prado** in Madrid, p. 840). In France, **Eugène Delacroix**'s 1830 painting "Liberty Guiding the People" (in the Louvre, p. 338) depicts the rise of Louis Philippe, who from 1830-1845 supported the upper bourgeoisie rather than the aristocracy. In addition to political and military themes, Romanticism also stressed a deep appreciation of nature and a more sensitive understanding of human personalities and moods; the works of the great English Romantic landscape painters **J.M.W. Turner** and **John Constable** portray the dynamics and passion of the natural world; extensive collections of both artists' work are at the **Tate Gallery of British Art** in London (p. 172).

Romanticism originally grew out of literature, drawing its name from an appreciation of the medieval romance, a highly emotional genre of adventurous tale that emphasized individual heroism. The watershed event launching Romanticism in Britain, with its emphasis on nature and powerful feelings, is generally considered to be the joint publication of *Lyrical Ballads* in 1798 by **William Wordsworth** and **Samuel Taylor Coleridge.** Wordsworth's later colleagues were plagued by early deaths: **John Keats** died of tuberculosis at 26, while **Percy Bysshe Shelley** drowned off the Tuscan coast at 29. **Lord Byron**'s *Don Juan* (1819-24), meanwhile, established him as the heartthrob of the age. The greatest German Romantic was **Johann von Goethe,** whose lyrics possessed a revolutionary immediacy and drew on rediscovered folk songs and ballads. Romanticism in France crystallized in the works of **Victor Hugo;** with masterpieces like his *Les Misérables,* the novel flourished for the first time as a primary mode of literary expression.

The music of the Romantic period stretched and expanded forms like the nocturne, intermezzo, prelude, and mazurka to achieve intensely personal, emotional expression. **Frédéric Chopin, Felix Mendelssohn,** and **Franz Liszt** achieved unprecedented harmonic creativity and pyrotechnic virtuosity. Romantic opera developed in Italy and peaked under **Giuseppe Verdi;** in Germany, it reached grandiose heights in the works of **Richard Wagner.** A strong sense of nationalism, another Romantic trend, was reflected in the works of composers like the Czechs **Antonín Dvořák** and **Bedřich Smetana** and the Norwegian **Edvard Grieg.**

IMPRESSIONISM

The late 19th and early 20th centuries witnessed the development of a predominantly French movement referred to as **Impressionism.** Its artistic leaders, including **Claude Monet, Pierre-Auguste Renoir, Camille Pissaro, Edouard Manet,** and **Edgar Degas** (famous for his renderings of ballet dancers), rejected the historical and literary overtones of the Romantic period. For the first time, the artists' perspectives and personal representations, rather than depictive realism, were emphasized. Painting technique attempted to capture the fleeting effects of light and color using individually juxtaposed brushstrokes, and forms lost their clear outlines, reflecting instead transient, spontaneous outdoor conditions. The moniker "Impressionists" was initially a derisive label derived by critics from Monet's 1872 work, *Impression: Sunrise,* but was quickly embraced by the artists themselves.

The Impressionist movement progressed in a more abstract direction with the **Post-Impressionists,** including **Vincent van Gogh, Paul Cézanne, Georges Seurat,** and **Henri de Toulouse-Lautrec.** (The world's largest van Gogh collection is in the Van Gogh Museum in Amsterdam, p. 692.) The Post-Impressionists retained the brilliant palette and the freedom in subject matter of their predecessors, but were more daring and innovative in their technique, style, and artistic interpretations of a given subject. **Paul Gauguin** incorporated exotic foreign elements into his works, a trend also reflected in, for example, the influence of the Balinese gamelan on Impressionist music. (The **Age of Imperialism,** while primarily a vehicle for paternalism and exploitation by Western European powers in Africa and Asia, also facilitated a certain amount of cultural exchange.) The works of Impressionist composers like **Claude Debussy** and **Maurice Ravel** display a dissolution in regular forms and structures, instead relying on fragile harmonies and evocative melodies.

WORLD WAR I

At the turn of the century, Europe had split into two power alignments: the **Triple Alliance** of Germany, Austria-Hungary, and Italy, and the **Triple Entente** of Great Britain, France, and Russia, thus setting the stage for "The Great War." Tensions exploded on June 28, 1914 when a young Slav nationalist assassinated the heir to the Austro-Hungarian throne, Archduke Francis Ferdinand, during his visit to Sarajevo. (The corner of Obala Kulina Bana and Zelenih Beretki in Sarajevo commemorates the event, p. 145). In the following months, Austria-Hungary declared war on Serbia, and France, Germany, Russia, Belgium, Great Britain, Montenegro, Serbia, and Turkey issued war declarations of their own. Most Eastern European nations fought with the Alliance, but the Baltic nations divided their alliances.

After over four years of conflict, Germany and its allies could no longer continue to fight. The creation of **trench warfare** (in which troops shovel out deep ditches and fight from fixed positions), along with advances in heavy artillery, wreaked destruction on an unprecedented scale; almost one-eighth of the 70 million troops massed for the war were killed. In January, 1919, an assembly of all major national leaders, excluding Germany, Austria-Hungary, and Soviet Russia, convened in Paris to discuss the future of Europe and draw up five peace treaties. The treaty with Germany, signed on June 28, was dubbed the **Treaty of Versailles,** having been drawn up in the famed Bourbon palace (p. 345). Article 231 of the treaty forced Germany to bear all responsibility for the war and established a system of **reparations.** With such an economic burden placed on Germany's shoulders, international tensions lingered for the next few decades.

WAR AND INTERWAR MOVEMENTS

Shaped by global hostilities, revolutionary artistic movements thrived before, during, and after the war. **Dadaism,** derived from a word meaning "hobby-horse" in French, was born as an art form in Zurich in 1916. Its artists and writers injected a strong sense of nihilism into works such as *Sept Manifestes Dada* (*Seven Dada Manifestos*) by Romanian **Tristan Tzara** and the drawing collection *Ecce Homo* by **George Grosz.** (Castel DADA, a Zurich disco, now sits where Cabaret Voltaire popularized the movement, p. 931). When Dadaism spread to Berlin in 1917, it assumed a more political tone with the rise of the **photomontage** technique, which juxtaposes photographs and text. Dadaism found a literary outlet in Paris, where **Louis Aragon** and others incorporated its "anti-art" concerns with senseless death and the dismal reality of bourgeois values into their writings. By 1922, however, many of these artists had abandoned Dadaism in favor of less antagonistic art.

Art took a turn for the weird with the advent of **Surrealism,** which rejected rationalism in favor of a more positive fusion of fantasy and reality, a "surreality." Paris especially nurtured the movement, heavily influenced by the theories of **Sigmund Freud,** the father of **psychoanalysis.** An Austrian neurologist, Freud became fascinated by the psyche (which he divided into the id, ego, and superego) and the significance of dream analysis, which he outlined in *The Interpretation of Dreams.* Freud was the first Western scientist to postulate both the subconscious and a mind-body connection; the Surrealists, led by the poet and critic **André Breton** (who published *The Surrealist Manifesto* in 1924), explored the art of the subconscious, striving to be free of the constraints of the conscious world. Highly influential painters like **René Magritte, Salvador Dalí, Joan Miró,** and **Max Ernst** often transformed regular scenes into alien dreamworlds. Surrealist writings featured word pairings based on thought association rather than logic.

Surrealism's formalized, content-based contemporary was **Cubism,** which found popularity earlier in the century through the work of **Pablo Picasso** and **Georges Braque.** Cubists disposed of perspective and the concept of realism in order to accentuate the two-dimensional character of paintings, often resulting in simplified, more monochrome works. The Exposition Internationale des Arts Décoratifs held in Paris in 1925, helped **Art Deco,** a Cubist-influenced style, to establish a significant following. Artists strove to achieve a sophisticated elegance using sleek lines; one of the foremost Art Deco designers was **Alfons Mucha,** who was a principal advertiser of the actress Sarah Bernhardt and who donated several works to the city of Prague (p. 249). Usually crafted from man-made materials like plastics and vita-glass, Art Deco objects lauded the beauty of machinery and modernity.

European culture in the early 20th century began also to be heavily influenced by its counterpart across the Atlantic. The American **Jazz Age** of the 1920s did not take long to spread to Europe, as musicians like **Stéphane Grappelli** and **Django Reinhardt** gained popularity in the 1930s. African-American performers reveled in this new trend; notably, **Josephine Baker** achieved phenomenal success as a dancer at Paris' **Folies-Bergères.** American **expatriate** writers like **Ernest Hemingway, Gertrude Stein,** and **F. Scott Fitzgerald** imported a sense of crisis and alienation to the cafes of Paris in the early years of the 20th century. Some of these expatriates, along with Europeans like the German **Franz Kafka** and the Norwegian **Knut Hamsun,** ushered in **Modernism,** a pessimistic, apathetic move away from realism and the social world. Modernism in both poetry and prose was characterized by disruptive devices creating a fragmented, non-chronological effect.

WORLD WAR II

Europe suffered severe economic problems immediately after WWI. Even as renewed prosperity arrived in the late 1920s, encouraging the growth of mass culture, Weimar Republic films like **Fritz Lang**'s *Metropolis* reflected the public's skepticism of government and bureaucracy. The Great Depression spread from America to Europe in 1929, damaging a fragile Germany still smarting from the Treaty of Versailles. In turbulent, unhappy times, the Nazi party was able to build its power base until 1933, when party leader **Adolph Hitler** headed the government.

Hitler used cultural control to cement his influence on the German citizenry. **Joseph Goebbels,** head of the Nazi Ministry of Propaganda, manipulated art forms, especially films, to reinforce Nazi ideology. (His bunker still exists in Berlin, p. 402). Films like **Leni Riefenstahl**'s *Triumph of the Will* (1935), which depicts a Nazi rally at Nuremberg (p. 464), exalted Hitler and glamorized the Aryan image. Foreign influence was discouraged because it deviated from the German "Volk," or people. This anti-foreigner spirit translated into the persecution of "asocials": Jews, homosexuals, gypsies, and other groups who were harassed and persecuted under Nazi rule. When Germany invaded Poland in 1939, Britain and France declared war on the aggressors, and the asocials were shipped to concentration camps like Auschwitz and Birkenau (p. 752) to starve or meet death in gas chambers. As Hitler's "final solution," the **Holocaust** ultimately resulted in the deaths of at least six million Jews, almost completely eliminating the Jewish communities of Poland, Slovakia, Hungary, Lithuania, Moldova, Odessa, and the Czech Republic.

Civilian and military losses in the war are estimated at 50 to 60 million, with Eastern Europe suffering the heaviest casualties. Warsaw, Budapest, and Belgrade were utterly ruined. Berlin and London were also heavily damaged; a plaque in the floor of **St. Paul's Cathedral** in London (p. 167) honors the volunteer firemen who staved off its destruction; St. Paul's endured fifty-one firebombs in one night at the height of the blitz. The Allied victors, in contrast to their post-WWI policies, were not vindictive. Although war criminals were tried at Nuremberg in 1945-1946, Germany's penalties under the **Marshall Plan** were not severe. European nations concerned themselves with helping their beleaguered peoples through times of economic crisis and all of the Western European countries eventually adopted the idea of a welfare state. Many countries with colonies also had to forfeit these territories, leaving 800 million people worldwide with newfound independence.

CONTEMPORARY MOVEMENTS

With post-war rebuilding on the agenda, most countries backed away from cultural affairs to concentrate on pressing domestic matters. In cinema, for example,

Europe lagged behind the burgeoning American industry. Nonetheless, European cinema produced some legendary work: Italy, which had surrendered relatively early, took the lead with **neorealism,** the mimicking of a documentary style. Italy's directorial star was **Federico Fellini,** who began as a neorealist before moving into the surrealism of his later works. France also boasted a cutting-edge cinema scene; 1950s new wave directors like **Louis Malle, Francois Truffaut,** and **Jean-Luc Goddard** exemplified the **auteur** style of rapid cuts and experimental images.

The 1960s brought social and cultural upheaval to the continent, highlighted by 1968 rallies staged by students in Paris and Prague against oppressive government regimes. The American rock craze, like the jazz influx in the 1920s, stimulated similar musical trends across the ocean. British bands like the **Beatles** and **Rolling Stones** hit it big at home and went on to build international fame. Women's movements also experienced a boost in the 1960s, with Simone de Beauvoir's *The Second Sex* (1949) emerging as the handbook of the era. De Beauvoir was also a close friend of **Jean-Paul Sartre,** whose **Existentialist** movement held that life, in itself, is meaningless; only by choosing and then committing yourself to a cause could existence take on a purpose. His *Being and Nothingness* became a kind of Existentialist manifesto, declaring that God is dead and that it is the absurd that governs our lives. **Post-modernism,** coined in 1975 by **Charles Jencks,** reacted against the positivism and universalism of Modernism by emphasizing pluralism over structure and grand narrative. Originally associated with avant-garde trends in art and architecture, Post-modernism also spread to literature, social science theory, and critical philosophy. The **Structuralist** movement used signs and codes to seek out larger fundamental structures in everything, whether texts, objects, or events. Structuralism was intimately tied to similar strands of thought in linguistics, psychology, and anthropology, notably the work of French anthropologist **Claude Lévi-Strauss,** whose postulation of the universal structure of the human mind led him to view cultures in terms of relations among their structural elements.

The advent of **Eurodisco** and **Europop** in the 1970s brought fame to groups such as **ABBA,** the campy Swedish quartet that scored 18 number one hits in Europe, and the German group **Kraftwerk,** whose album **Autobahn** garnered international acclaim. A heavy synth-pop sound influenced much European music in the 1980s, including **Depeche Mode,** the **Pet Shop Boys,** and **Falco.** Chicago-based house music, with its heavily electronic, high-tempo style, found a foothold in Europe in 1986, but interest soon swung to acid house. Accompanying this new musical movement, the drug **Ecstasy** (MDMA) ingrained itself into British rave culture.

The late 1980s witnessed the final days of Communism across Eastern Europe. In 1985, Mikhail Gorbachev came into power in the Soviet Union with two key policies: **glasnost** (openness) and **perestroika** (restructuring). The new freedom of political expression led to a snowballing of dissidence, disapproval, and revolt that finally erupted in 1989 with a series of revolutions throughout Eastern Europe. Sparked by the Polish election of **Lech Wałęsa** and his **Solidarity** party, intense pressure for reform also toppled Communist regimes in Hungary, East Germany, Czechoslovakia, Bulgaria, and Romania. The symbolic end of Communism came with the 1989 **fall of the Berlin Wall** (p. 406), and in 1991, newly-elected President and noted populist **Boris Yeltsin** saw the Communist regime and the Soviet Union finally collapse after the failure of a hard-line Communist coup. Since then, the former Soviet republics have experimented with democracy and capitalism, with mixed results. The **first Soviet McDonald's** (p. 795) is a testament to the influence of Western culture on the increasingly democratic landscape of Eastern Europe.

The 2000 introduction of the **Euro,** a unified European currency, in part signified a move to re-solidify a cultural, political, and economic European identity. The currency is descended from the European Economic Community that formed in the years after World War II in order to provide for free circulation of goods, labor, and capital. The present **European Union** includes Austria, Belgium, Denmark, France, Germany, Greece, Ireland, Italy, Luxembourg, Netherlands, Portugal, Spain, and Great Britain; by January 1, 2002, the switchover from national currencies to euros will be complete (see whitebox, p. 15).

TIMELINE

ANCIENT CIV.

2500-1300 BC: Minoan civilization in Crete.

2500-500 BC: Early Greek civilization.

509 BC: Beginning of Roman Republic.

500-200 BC: Classical and Hellenistic Greece.

44 BC: Assassination of Julius Caesar.

27 BC - AD 293: Imperial Rome.

293: Diocletian splits the Roman Empire between East and West.

312-337: Constantine the Great reunifies the Roman Empire, with its capital at Byzantium (later known as Constantinople). Christianity becomes the new state religion.

360-450: Huns invade Russia and Europe; Visigoths, Vandals, and other barbarians attack the Roman Empire.

EARLY MIDDLE AGES

476: Theodoric and the Ostrogoths invade Italy. Barbarian chief Odoacer assumes the title of King of Italy—traditionally considered the fall of the Western Empire.

527-565: Byzantine emperor Justinian the Great recaptures North Africa, southern Spain, and Italy. The Justinian Code, the most influential legal text in European history, compiles Roman laws.

622-650: Islam spreads through the Middle East, North Africa, and Asia Minor.

719: Arabs complete their conquest of Spain.

790: Vikings begin to attack the British Isles.

800: Charlemagne is crowned Holy Roman Emperor by the Pope. The Carolingian Empire, which stretches from the Atlantic to the Adriatic and the Baltic, incorporates universal Christianity and Roman administration with Frankish military might.

843: Following the death of Charlemagne's son, Louis the Pious, the Carolingian Empire is divided among his three sons, decentralizing power and leading to the rise of local lords.

867-1059: Macedonian dynasty rules Byzantine Empire and starts to recover lands from Muslims.

962: Otto I founds Holy Roman Empire anew in Germany.

996: Hugh Capet takes the French throne; Capetian dynasty of France is founded.

HIGH MIDDLE AGES

1066: Harold of the Saxons is defeated at the Battle of Normandy by William I of Normandy. Traditionally considered the beginning of English history.

1095-99: Pope Urban II calls for the freeing of the Holy Land from Muslim occupation; Jerusalem recaptured by First Crusade.

1095-1291: Holy Wars: the seven Crusades.

1215: England's King John forced to sign the Magna Carta, the "great charter" guaranteeing the rights of the English nobility and generally considered the first document of modern democracy.

1233: Spanish Inquisition begins.

1223-1241: Genghis Khan leads Mongols in invasion of Russia; takes Kiev, Silesia, Poland, and Hungary.

1284-97: Welsh defeated by England's Edward I; Scots rebel.

1299: Ottoman Empire founded in Turkey.

1337-1452: Hundred Years' War between England and France. The English win early battles, but are eventually expelled from all of northwestern France outside of Calais.

1347-52: The Black Plague sweeps across Europe. Twenty-five million people, between one-half and one-third of Europe's population, die. Episodes recur through 1771.

1356: Holy Roman Emperor Charles IV's "Golden Bull" edict officially recognizes various German princes and kings as rulers; the empire breaks up into a number of large kingdoms and duchies.

1378-1417: The Great Schism: Popes fight for control of the Roman Catholic Church—one in Avignon, France and one in Rome. The election of an Italian cardinal during the Council of Constance finally ends the schism, but papal authority remains weak.

THE RENAISSANCE

1450: Florence becomes the center of the Renaissance. Johannes Gutenberg invents printing press.

1453: The Byzantine Empire shifts to the Ottoman control with the fall of Constantinople, which the Turks rename Istanbul.

1455-85: English Houses of York and Lancaster feud in the War of the Roses. Henry Tudor (of Lancaster, a.k.a. Henry VII) defeats his opponents and inaugurates the Tudor dynasty in England.

1462-1505: Ivan III (the Great) rules as the first tsar in Russia; he expands to the north and west and drives out the Mongols.

1469: Ferdinand of Aragon and Isabella of Castile marry to unite Spain.

1490s: Beginning of the Age of Exploration.

1492: Unified Spain expels Jews and Muslims. Christopher Columbus lands on San Salvador in the West Indies.

EUROPEAN CULTURE

REFORMATION AND COUNTERREFORMATION

1516-56: Charles V becomes heir to both the Austrian and Spanish branches of the Habsburg family. Enters into dynastic struggles with Francis I of France and Henry VIII.

1517: Reformation begins in Germany with Martin Luther's *95 Theses;* Luther will be excommunicated in 1521.

1520-66: Height of Ottoman Empire under Süleyman I (the Magnificent).

1527: Holy Roman Empire attacks Rome, imprisons Pope Clement VII; this event is often considered the end of the Italian Renaissance.

1534: Henry VIII divorces Catherine of Aragon, breaks with the church of Rome, and declares himself head of the Protestant Church in England, beginning the English Reformation.

1536-41: The Reformation reaches Norway, Denmark, and then Scotland.

1543: Copernicus' *Concerning the Revolutions of the Celestial Spheres* is published. It rejects the Aristotelian view of the universe in favor of one with the sun at the center.

1545-1563: Council of Trent, keystone of the Catholic Counterreformation, upholds justification by faith, confirms the true Scriptures, and reaffirms the seven sacraments along with the Eucharist.

1547: Ivan IV (the Terrible) becomes tsar of Russia and battles with Boyars (nobles) for power.

1553: Death of Edward VI (successor to King Henry VII). His successor, Queen (Bloody) Mary I, restores the Catholic Church in England.

1555: Peace of Augsburg: Charles V grants the princes of Germany the right to establish the religion of their own people, Catholic or Lutheran.

WARS OF RELIGION

1556: Holy Roman Emperor Charles V divides power between brother Ferdinand I (Austrian Habsburg lands) and son Philip II (Spain, Netherlands). Spain is the greatest power in Europe.

1558-1603: Reign of Queen Elizabeth I after death of Mary I; restores Anglican Church in England.

1572: Saint Bartholomew's Day Massacre of French Huguenots in Paris.

1587: Mary, Queen of Scots, is executed.

1588: The Spanish Armada is defeated by the English, signalling Spain's decline.

1594: Henry IV, crowned King of France, establishes Bourbon dynasty and ends French wars of religion. Henry's Edict of Nantes (1598) grants limited toleration to French Huguenots.

1600: Danish astronomer Tycho Brahe moves to Prague and works with Johannes Kepler, who postulates three laws of planetary motion in line with the Copernican view.

1610-43: Louis XII of France is guided by chief minister Cardinal Richelieu, who preaches *raison d'état* (reason of state), placing the needs of the national above those of the nobility.

1616-33: Galileo is condemned by the pope, and then by the Inquisition, for teaching that the sun is at the center of the universe.

1618-1648: Thirty Years' War: Struggle between the Roman Catholic Church, Habsburg Holy Roman Empire, and German Protestant towns. The Peace of Westphalia (1648) grants the member-states of the Holy Roman Empire full sovereignty. Germany's population is cut in half due to war and pestilence. Spain acknowledges the independence of the Netherlands.

SCIENTIFIC REVOLUTION

1640-88: Frederick William, the Great Elector of Brandenburg-Prussia, inherits a weakened collection of territories, but develops them into an efficient state bureaucracy based in military might.

1642-60: England plunges into civil war between Cavaliers (Loyalists to King Charles I) and Roundheads (many Puritans and others loyal to Parliament). After Charles I is executed (1649), Oliver Cromwell dissolves the Rump Parliament and declares himself Lord Protector (1653). Soon after his death (1658), Charles II takes the throne, restoring the Stuart line (1660).

1643: Louis XIV, the Sun King, becomes King of France, although chief minister Cardinal Mazarin exerts real power until 1661. Colbert, Louis's chief minister for finance, builds up the navy, reforms legal codes, and establishes national academies of culture. France, the richest and most populous European state, becomes the greatest nation in Europe; French replaces Latin as the universal European tongue. Louis begins dynastic wars that will continue through 1715.

1666: Plague in England and the Great Fire of London. Isaac Newton begins developing his theories of optics, calculus, and planetary motion.

1682-1725: Peter I (the Great) in Russia campaigns to westernize Russia and introduces great military reforms (conscription, military schools, meritocracy). After the Battle of Poltava (1709), Russia gradually replaces Sweden as the dominant power in the Baltics.

1685: Louis XIV revokes the Edict of Nantes of 1598.

1688: Glorious Revolution in England. Catholic James II flees to France and William, Prince of Orange, and Mary, James' daughter, ascend to the throne with very little bloodshed. The Declaration of Rights (1689) asserts the fundamental principles of constitutional monarchy.

1700-1800: Industrial Revolution kicks off in Northern England: invention of steam engine, spinning mill, spinning jenny. Factory manufacturing becomes a symbol of the industrial age.

1700-1721: Great Northern War: Saxony, Poland, Brandenburg-Prussia, Hannover, Denmark, and Russia ally to attack Sweden; Sweden loses lands in Germany, Poland, and the Baltics.

1701-1714: War of the Spanish Succession: upon Spanish Habsburg Charles II's death, Austria and Britain fight France and Germany to keep Louis XIV's son, Philip V, off the Spanish throne. The Treaty of Utrecht (1713) allows him to rule but prevents him from merging his empire with France. Spain cedes half of Italy and the Spanish Netherlands to Austria.

AGE OF ENLIGHTENMENT

1707: The Act of Union joins England, Scotland, and Wales in the United Kingdom of Great Britain

1740-1786: Frederick II's (the Great) enlightened reforms enhance the efficiency of the Prussian absolutist state. The Prussian and Austrian states vie for power.

1740-1748: War of the Austrian Succession: Frederick II invades and wins Habsburg Silesia.

1751-1770s: Denis Diderot's *Encyclopedia,* the greatest work of the Enlightenment, is published; it constitutes the first attempt at a compilation of all the world's knowledge.

1756-1763: Seven Years' War: Austria and France put aside long standing differences to join forces against Prussia and Britain. Battle spreads to North America, the Caribbean, and India.

1772-95: Poland is carved up between Austria, Prussia, and Russia over the course of three partitions (1772, 1793, 1795).

1780s: Enlightened despots Maria Theresa and son Joseph II of Austria abolish serfdom and improve conditions of rural life; Catherine the Great clarifies the rights of the Russian nobility, although there is virtually no change in the life of the masses. Critics in France condemn the king's despotism, high taxes to finance foreign wars, and the decadence of the court.

FRENCH REVOLUTION AND NAPOLEON

1789: French Revolution: The Third Estate of the Estates-Genéral declares itself a "National Assembly" (June 20) and takes the so-called Tennis Court Oath to demand limits on the king's authority (June 23). Crowds storm the Bastille (July 14). The National Assembly formally abolishes the "feudal regime" (August 4) and authors a declaration of rights and a new constitution.

1791-93: Louis XVI tries to flee France, but is caught at the border; the Revolution enters a second, more radical phase. The monarchy is overthrown and is replaced by a republic.

1793: Louis XVI is tried and hanged. The Jacobin-dominated government collapses into a dictatorship that brings on "the Terror," famed for its use of the guillotine. The Committee of Public Safety, led by Maximilien Robespierre, executes all perceived counter-revolutionaries.

1794-99: Moderate Jacobins and others, afraid they might be next to be "purged," overthrow the dictatorship and establish the "Directory," a second try at representative government. Robespierre is guillotined. High society returns to France, but instability remains.

1799: Sieyès and Napoleon Bonaparte overthrow the Directory and found the Consulat (1799).

1799-1814: After designating himself "consul for life" (1802) and then emperor (1804), Napoleon suffers a disastrous naval defeat by Great Britain at the Battle of Trafalgar (1805), but gains significant lands on the continent. He abolishes the Holy Roman Empire, dismembers Prussia, and captures Habsburg Vienna. The Napoleonic Code (1804) defines property rights, declares all people equal before the law, and affirms the freedoms of religion and work. After wars with Britain and Spain, his Grand Army is disastrously defeated in Russia (1812). Russian, Prussian, British, and Austrian allied forces sweep into Paris, and Napoleon abdicates (1814).

1814: Bourbon rule is restored in France with Louis XVIII. The Treaty of Paris leaves France with its lands as of November 1792.

INDUSTRIAL REVOLUTION

1800-1850: The Industrial Revolution, born in England in the 18th century, spreads throughout Western Europe. Life expectancy, population, and urbanization all increase.

1815-1848: Liberal revolts in Spain, Portugal, Italy, Germany, and Poland.

1825-55: Reign of Nicholas I in Russia. The Decembrist revolt during his accession (1825) fails.

1830: The "July Revolution" in France places liberal Louis-Philippe on the throne rather than continue the Bourbon dynasty, encouraging liberal and nationalist movements elsewhere.

1830-50: Origins of socialism and experimentation with utopian societies.

1831: Belgium wins autonomy from the Netherlands.

1832: Greece's independence is recognized by the Turks.

1832-46: The British Reform Act of 1832 grants one out of every five adult male citizens suffrage. Additional reforms abolish slavery and limited child labor (1833).

1837-1901: Queen Victoria of Britain leads the Victorian Age of reform.

NATIONAL UNIFICATION

1848-49: "A springtime of nationalities": Prussians, Austrians, Germans, Italians, Poles, Czechs, Hungarians, and South Slavs demand liberal and national reforms. The February Revolution in France ends with the abdication of Louis-Philippe and the declaration of the Second French Republic; Louis Napoleon Bonaparte, Napoleon's nephew, is elected president. Only Britain and Russia remain untouched by revolution.

1851: Louis Napoleon dissolves the National Assembly, stages a coup, and declares himself Emperor Napoleon III. He further centralizes French economic and political power and oversees the rebuilding of Paris.

1853-56: Crimean War: Russians, British-French-Piedmontese, and Austrian troops clash over Russian influence of Constantinople; Russia capitulates.

1855-81: Reign of Tsar Alexander II; the tsar abolishes serfdom in Russia (1861).

1859-70: Unification of Italy: led by King Victor Emmanuel II, Count Camillo di Cavour, Giuseppe Mazzini, and Giuseppe Garibaldi.

1866-1871: Otto von Bismarck appointed Prime Minister of Prussia under Frederick William. Bismarck unifies the new German Empire, including lands acquired in the Austro-Prussian War (1866) and Franco-Prussian War (1870-71; includes Alsace-Lorraine).

1867: Dual Monarchy of Austria-Hungary is created. The British Reform Bill of 1867 grants the vote to the head of each household, doubling the number of voters in Britain.

INDUSTRIALIZATION AND IMPERIALISM

1870-1914: Second Industrial Revolution and rapid industrialization: inventions include electricity, the sewing machine, the telephone, and the automobile; living standards rise dramatically.

1880-1914: Age of Imperialism: the scramble for Africa and Asia.

1882: Germany, Austria-Hungary, and Italy form the Triple Alliance to unite against Russian conquests; the system of alliances later contributes to WWI.

1890s: Sigmund Freud develops the method of psychoanalysis.

1905: Albert Einstein's *Special Theory of Relativity* is published. France and Britain, previously steadfast rivals, join Russia in the Triple Entente alliance. Norway gains independence from Sweden. The First Moroccan Crisis tests English-French resolve in light of German demands in French-dominated Morocco. In the Russian Revolution of this year, troops fire at marchers on "Bloody Sunday"; the tsar is soon forced to grant a parliament and to promise civil rights.

1908: Bosnian Crisis: Austro-Hungarian government announces annexation of Bosnia-Herzegovina, in violation of the 1878 Congress of Berlin. Russia is outraged, but unwilling to go to war.

1909-11: Second Moroccan Crisis: France establishes a virtual protectorate in Morocco, violating the Algeciras agreements of 1906, but appeases Germany with territory in the French Congo.

WORLD WAR I

1914: Austro-Hungarian Archduke Franz Ferdinand is assassinated in Sarajevo by Serb nationalists (June 28). Austria hands Serb officials a lengthy ultimatum (July 23); when all points are not met, it declares war on Serbia (July 28). World War I breaks out between Austria-Hungary and Germany (Italy remains neutral) and France, Britain, and Russia.

1917: The United States enters the war on the Allied side (April). Russia withdraws from the war after October Revolution (due to revised calendar, in November), in which the Bolsheviks seize power; the Treaty of Brest-Litovsk yields lands to Germany.

1918: WWI ends with Allied victory.

1918-21: Civil war breaks out in Russia between the Bolsheviks and Mensheviks; the Bolsheviks, led by Vladimir Ilyich Lenin and Leon Trotsky, are victorious. The Communist International (Comintern) is founded to assist revolutions in other countries.

1919: The "Big Four" at the Treaty of Versailles (Orlando of Italy, Lloyd George of Britain, Clemenceau of France, and Wilson of the US) assign blame to Germany; the weak new Weimar Republic is forced to assume the financial burden of the war. Germany, Austria-Hungary, and Russia all lose extensive territories. The idealistic League of Nations is formed by US President Wilson to arbitrate future international disputes, but is not ratified by the US or Russian governments.

INTERWAR YEARS

1920: Adolf Hitler rises to the head of the nationalist German Workers' Party, which he renames the National Socialist German Workers' (Nazi) Party.

1921-23: German inflation spirals out of control. The American Dawes Plan (1924) extends the schedule for the payment of war reparations; the German economy improves.

1922: The Union of Soviet Socialist Republics is created, including Russia, Belarus, and Ukraine. "Il Duce" Benito Mussolini becomes prime minister of the first fascist government, in Italy. The Irish Free State is formed; Northern Ireland remains a part of the UK.

1923: French and Belgian troops occupy the mine-rich Ruhr Valley to force reparation payments from the Germans; they withdraw after nine months.

1924: Death of Lenin.

1925: Hitler's *Mein Kampf (My Struggle)* is published, predicting that Germany will rearm, then conquer *Lebensraum* (living space) at the expense of "inferior" Slavic peoples.

1927: Dictator Joseph Stalin assumes power in Russia; his arrests and "purges" target rivals and opponents. German economy collapses.

1929: Stock market crash on Wall Street exacerbates European economic woes. German Prime Minister Gustav Stresemann dies in the same month, heightening political instability and lending to the rise of Nazism.

1930: Nazis and Communists gain seats in the German Reichstag, although Social Democrats retain the plurality.

1930s: Dictatorships exist in Portugal, Spain, Germany, Italy, Austria, Hungary, Yugoslavia, Greece, Turkey, Bulgaria, Romania, Poland, Lithuania, Latvia, Estonia, and the USSR. Only France, Switzerland, Britain, Ireland, Benelux, Scandinavia, and Czechoslovakia remain democracies.

1931: King Alfonso XIII of Spain is overthrown; Spain becomes a republic.

1932: The Nazi Party becomes the largest in the Reichstag.

1933: Hitler is appointed chancellor, forming the 17th and last Weimar government. The Enabling Act extends the "emergency" powers of the Nazi Party and transfers power from the legislative to the executive branch. Hitler bans all parties but the Nazis and implements a totalitarian state.

1935-36: The Nuremberg Laws strip Jews of citizenship and force them to wear yellow Stars of David as identification. Hitler defies the Treaty of Versailles by beginning steady rearmament and moving into the demilitarized Rhineland. Hitler signs a pact forming the "Axis" with Mussolini and the "Anti-Comintern" Pact with Japan.

1936-39: The Spanish Civil War pits loyalists against nationalists, led by General Francisco Franco, and is perceived as a struggle against international fascism. Britain, Ireland, and France support the loyalists but remain neutral; German and Italian aid to Franco's troops proves decisive.

WORLD WAR II

1938: *Kristallnacht* (Night of Broken Glass): Nazis destroy Jewish stores, homes, and synagogues throughout Germany, and beat and imprison thousands of Jews. Hitler declares the unification *(Anschluß)* of Austria and Germany. At the Munich Conference, the other Great Powers appease Hitler with the Sudetenland and other territory in exchange for a promise of no further expansion.

1939: The Nazis occupy Czechoslovakia. Hitler signs a non-aggression pact with Russia, then invades Poland, starting WWII. Hitler unveils his "Final Solution": the annihilation of European Jews.

1940: The Nazis capture Paris and set up the puppet Vichy government in Southern France. Hitler contemplates invading Britain, but is put off by Nazi defeat in the air Battle of Britain.

1941: The US enters the war after the bombing of Pearl Harbor by the Japanese. The Nazis renege on their non-aggression pact by invading Russia; German troops freeze in the Russian winter.

1941-45: Six million Jews die in the Holocaust.

1943: The tide turns in favor of the Allies, as German troops go on the defensive at Stalingrad in the Soviet Union and in North Africa. The Allies invade southern Italy; Mussolini signs an armistice, and Allies continue to fight the Germans in Italy.

1944: D-Day (June 6): Allied troops invade Normandy coast. By August, the Allies take Paris and de Gaulle's government is recognized.

1945: Yalta Conference (February): Churchill, Roosevelt, and Stalin formulate the UN, plan the final defeat and occupation of Nazi Germany, and determine spheres of influence in post-war Europe; Stalin promises free elections throughout Eastern Europe. Adolf Hitler commits suicide (April). Potsdam Conference: Churchill, Truman, and Stalin set up four occupation zones (the fourth for the French) in Germany, Berlin, Austria, and Vienna.

COLD WAR

1946-1990: Decolonialization of Africa, the Middle East, the Indian subcontinent, and SE Asia

1948-49: US airlift to Berlin; beginning of Cold War tension between the USSR and the US.

1949: The Soviet-occupied zone of East Germany becomes the German Democratic Republic; the American, British, and French zones in the West become the German Federal Republic. Twelve nations sign the North Atlantic Treaty Organization (NATO) to counter Soviet aggression.

1953: Death of Stalin.

1955-64: After winning the power struggle in Russia, Nikita Khrushchev offers brief respite from the censorship of the Stalinist era, but the Communist Party retains power.

1956: Soviet intervention crushes the Hungarian Uprising against Communism. Suez Canal Crisis: Nasser of Egypt announces nationalization of the Suez Canal, demanding an end to British and French colonialism.

1957: USSR successfully launches Sputnik, the first man-made satellite to orbit the Earth; Cold War tensions heighten.

1961: Construction of the Berlin Wall between East and West Berlin.

1962: The Cuban Missile Crisis brings the US and the Soviet Union to the brink of nuclear war.

1967: Creation of the European Community (including France, Benelux, Italy, and West Germany) eliminates tariffs between partners. They are later joined by other powers (Britain, Denmark, and Ireland in 1973; Greece in 1981; Spain and Portugal in 1986; Eastern Germany in 1990; Austria, Sweden, and Finland in 1995).

1968: Massive student protests in Paris; Soviets clamp down on the reformist "Prague Spring" in Czechoslovakia.

1970s: Greece, Portugal, and Spain undergo democratization following the collapse of the Greek government and the deaths of the Portuguese and Spanish dictators Salazar and Franco.

1985: Head of state Mikhail Gorbachev initiates bold economic and political reforms in the USSR.

1986: Unit 4 of the Chernobyl nuclear power station, in north-central Ukraine, experienced a brief but powerful surge the system couldn't control. Wind blew the radioactive gases over the surrounding region and as far away as Sweden. The USSR evacuates 116,000.

POST-WAR EUROPE

1989: The election of Lech Wałęsa and his Solidarity party; the fall of the Berlin Wall, symbolizing the fall of communism in Eastern Europe; the "Velvet Revolution" of Czechoslovakia; the violent overthrow of dictator Nicolae Ceausescu in Romania, and the fall of Communist regimes in Bulgaria, Romania, and Albania symbolize the fall of the Iron Curtain.

1991: Boris Yeltsin is elected President of the "Russian Federation" and moves to initiate a Russian market economy. A failed coup d'état accelerates the collapse of the USSR; the republics one by one begin to declare their independence. Gorbachev resigns (December 25).

1992: Treaty of Maastricht: 12 members of the EC and six other European states forge a European Economic Area, eliminating national barriers for the movement of goods and services, workers, and capital.

1995: The fall of the Communists in Yugoslavia leads to civil war between Croats, Muslims, and Serbs.

1998-99: Fighting between ethnic Albanians and ethnic Serbs in the Serbian province of Kosovo leads to eventual NATO bombing of selected targets in Yugoslavia.

1999-2000: Russians fight independence-seeking Chechen rebels in the province of Chechnya, resuming the fighting of 1994-96.

ANDORRA

Welcome to Andorra (pop. 65,000; 464 sq. km), the forgotten country sandwiched between France and Spain. The serenity of this Pyrenean nation's stunning landscapes vies for attention with its neon-lit streets. Catalán is the official **language,** but French and Spanish are widely spoken. With no **currency,** all establishments must accept both Spanish and French currencies, although *pesetas* are more prevalent. Because of Andorra's diminutive size, one day can include sniffing aisles of duty-free perfume, hiking through a pine-scented valley, and relaxing in a luxury spa. **Phones** require an STA *teletarjeta* (telecard) available at the tourist office, post office, or kiosk (500ptas). You cannot make collect calls, and AT&T does not have an international access code. **Directory assistance:** ☎111. **Country code:** ☎376.

GETTING THERE AND GETTING AROUND. The only way to get to Andorra is by **car** or **bus,** as the country has no airport or train station. All traffic from France must enter through the town of **Pas de la Casa;** the Spanish gateway town is **La Seu d'Urgell. Andor-Inter/Samar buses** (Madrid ☎91 468 41 90; Toulouse ☎61 58 14 53; Andorra ☎82 62 89) connect Andorra la Vella to **Madrid** (9hr.; M, Th, and Su; 4900ptas), while **Alsina Graells** (☎82 73 79) and **Eurolines** (☎82 11 38) run to **Barcelona** (3-4hr., 10-11 per day, 2800-2850ptas). To go anywhere else in Spain, take a **La Hispano-Andorra bus** (☎82 13 72) from Andorra la Vella to La Seu d'Urgell (30min., 5-7 per day, 340ptas) and change there for an Alsina Graells bus. Efficient **intercity buses** (100-300ptas) connect the villages; all Andorra la Vella buses make every stop, so just look at the direction sign in the front window of the bus.

ANDORRA LA VELLA. Andorra la Vella (pop. 20,000), the capital, is little more than a cluttered road flanked by duty-free shops. All buses go to the **Estació d'Autobusos,** on C. Bonaventura Riberaygua. To get to the **tourist office** on Av. Dr. Villanova from the bus stop on Av. Princep Benlloch, continue east (away from Spain) just past the *plaça* on your left and take Av. Dr. Villanova down to the right. (Open July-Sept. M-F 9am-9pm, Sa 9am-1pm and 3-7pm, Su 10am-1pm; Oct.-June M-Sa 10am-1pm and 3-7pm, Su 10am-1pm.) Send **email** from **La Cibertec,** C. Bonaventura Riberaygua. (600ptas per 30min. Open M-Sa 10am-1pm and 3:30-9pm.) Dream of duty-free cheese at **Pensió La Rosa,** Antic C. Major, 18, off Av. Princep Benlloch. (☎82 18 10. Singles 2000ptas; doubles 3500ptas.) Drool at the chocolate bars at the **supermarket** in **Grans Magatzems Pyrénées,** Av. Meritxell, 11. (Open Sept.-July M-F 9:30am-8pm, Sa 9:30am-9pm, Su 9:30am-7pm; Aug. M-Sa 9:30am-9pm and Su 9:30am-7pm.)

ELSEWHERE IN ANDORRA. "Elsewhere" is where to go in Andorra. An extensive system of **hiking trails,** including the *Grandes-Randonnées* #7 and 11, traverse the tiny country; most are easy enough for even the least-seasoned outdoor enthusiasts. Pick up the *Sports Activities* brochure at the tourist office (free), for itineraries and potential routes. The masses also flock to Andorra's four outstanding **ski resorts,** all of which rent equipment; contact **SKI Andorra** (☎86 43 89) or pick up the tourist office's winter edition of *Andorra: The Pyrenean Country* for more info.

Ordino (pop. 2500; alt. 1304m), 5km northeast of La Massana, is convenient for hiking and skiing adventures. The **tourist office** is on C. Nou Desvio. (☎73 70 80. Open July-Aug. M-Sa 8am-7pm, Su 9am-5pm; Sept.-June M-Sa 9am-1pm and 3-7pm, Su 9am-1pm.) Ordino is best as a daytrip as there are no budget accommodations.

The tiny town of **Canillo** (pop. 952; 1562m), in the center of the country, suffers from the same architectural short-sightedness as the rest of Andorra, but is surrounded by fine scenery and great **skiing. Soldeu-El Tarter** (☎89 05 01) occupies 840 hectares of skiable area between Andorra la Vella and Pas de la Casa, France; **free buses** transport skiers from hotels in Canillo. **Hotel Comerç,** on the road to Andorra La Vella, with bare rooms at bare prices, is the nearest budget place to snooze. (☎85 10 20. Singles 1500ptas; doubles 3000ptas.

AUSTRIA (ÖSTERREICH)

AUSTRIAN SCHILLINGS

US$1 = 16.00AS	10AS = US$0.62
CDN$1 = 10.81AS	10AS = CDN$0.93
UK£1 = 22.43AS	10AS = UK£0.45
IR£1 = 17.47AS	10AS = IR£0.57
AUS$1 = 8.95AS	10AS = AUS$1.12
NZ$1 = 6.83AS	10AS = NZ$1.46
SAR1 = 2.24AS	10AS = SAR4.46
EUR€1 = 13.76AS	10AS = EUR€0.73

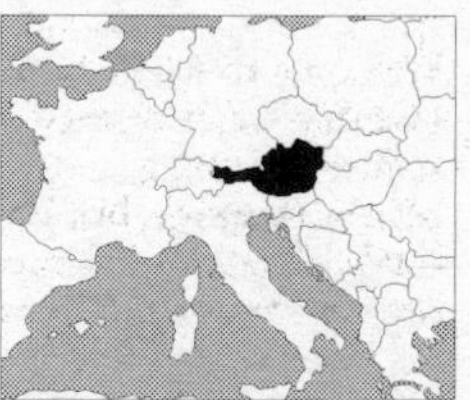

Country code: 43. **International dialing prefix:** 00 (from Vienna, **900**). From outside Austria, dial int'l dialing prefix (see inside back cover) + 43 + city code + local number. To call **Vienna** from outside Austria, dial int'l dialing prefix + 43 + 1 + local number.

The mighty Austro-Hungarian Empire may have crumbled after World War I, but Austria remains a complex, multi-ethnic country. Drawing on centuries of Habsburg political maneuvering, Austria has become a skillful mediator between Eastern and Western Europe, connecting Germany, Switzerland, and Italy with Slovenia, Hungary, Slovakia, and the Czech Republic. But Austria is more renowned for its brilliant artists, writers, and musicians. From Gustav Klimt's *Jugendstil* paintings to Arthur Schnitzler's dark insights into imperial decadence to Beethoven's thundering symphonies, Austria has had an indelible impact on Western art and literature. Austria owes its contemporary glory to the overpowering Alpine landscape that hovers over the remnants of its tumultuous past. A mention of Austria evokes images of onion-domed churches set against snow-capped Alpine peaks, lush meadows of wildflowers, dark forests, and mighty castles.

For extensive and entertaining information on Austria's attractions, pick up a copy of *Let's Go: Austria & Switzerland 2001.*

FACTS AND FIGURES

Official Name: Republic of Austria.

Government: Federal Republic.

Capital: Vienna.

Land Area: 83,858 sq. km.

Geography: Rolling terrain by the Danube river valley in the northeastern regions, otherwise mountainous.

Climate: Varies with altitude. Cool summers, and cold winters with rain in the lowlands and snow in the mountains.

Major Cities: Vienna, Salzburg, Innsbruck, Graz, Linz, Klagenfurt.

Population: 8,200,000.

Languages: German.

Religions: Roman Catholic (80%), Protestant (5%).

Income Per Capita: US$22,700.

Major Exports: Construction, machinery, agriculture.

DISCOVER AUSTRIA

In Austria's capital, **Vienna,** soak up cafe culture, stare down works by Klimt and other Secessionist artists, and listen to a world-famous opera or orchestra for a mere pittance (p. 99). An easy stopover between Vienna and Munich, **Salzburg** was home to both the von Trapp family and Mozart—some travelers find the overabundance of kitsch a tad overwhelming (p. 112). Between Vienna and Salzburg lies the backpacker hot spot, the relaxing hostel in **Grünau** (p. 118). Hike around historic **Hallstatt** in the nearby **Salzkammergut** region (p. 117), or explore the natural pleasures of the **Hohe Tauern National Park,** including the **Krimml Waterfalls** (p. 119). Farther west, **Innsbruck** is a fantastic jumping off point for skiers and hikers into the snow-capped peaks of the Tyrolean Alps (p. 120). For superior skiing, head to **Kitzbühel** (p. 123). For sunbathing, try the banks of the Bodensee near **Bregenz** (p. 124).

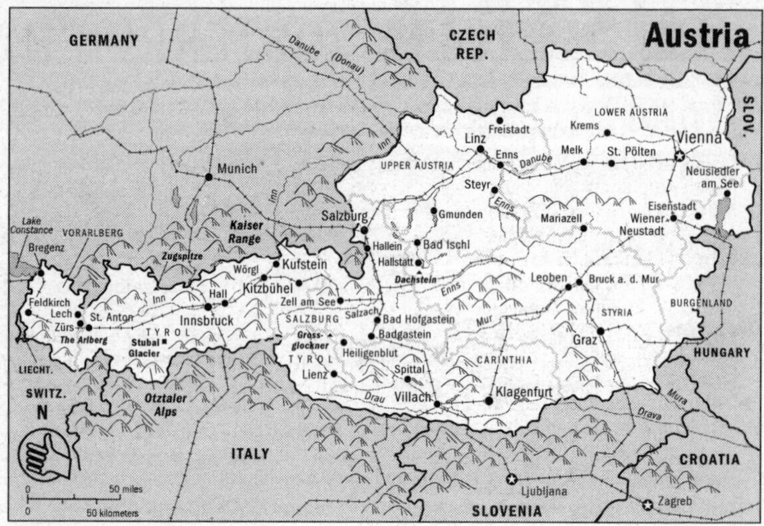

ESSENTIALS

WHEN TO GO

November to March is peak ski season, so prices in western Austria double and travelers need reservations months in advance. The situation reverses in the summer, when the flatter, eastern half fills with vacationers. Sights and accommodations are cheaper and less crowded in the shoulder season (May-June, Sept.-Oct.). But some Alpine resorts close in May and June—call ahead. The Vienna State Opera, the Vienna Boy's Choir, and many major theaters throughout Austria don't have any performances during July and August.

DOCUMENTS AND FORMALITIES

For citizens of the EU, Australia, Canada, New Zealand, and the US, just a valid passport is required for stays of less than three months; visas are required for working or studying in Austria. South Africans must have a visa and a valid passport for all stays. For more information, visit www.bmaa.gv.at/embassy/uk/index.html.en.

EMBASSIES AND CONSULATES

Embassies and consulates of other countries in Austria are all in **Vienna** (see p. 100).

Austrian Embassies at Home: Australia, 12 Talbot St., Forrest, Canberra ACT 2603 (☎ (02) 62 95 15 33; fax 62 39 67 51; email austria@dynamite.com.au); **consulates** in Adelaide, Brisbane, Melbourne, and Sydney; **Canada,** 445 Wilbrod St., Ottawa, ON KIN 6M7 (☎ (613) 789 14 44; fax 789 34 31; email embassy@austro.org; www.austro.org); **consulates** in Montréal, Toronto, and Vancouver; **Ireland,** 15 Ailesbury Court Apts., 93 Ailesbury Rd., Dublin 4 (☎ (01) 269 45 77 or 269 14 51; fax 283 08 60); **New Zealand,** Consular General, 22-4 Garrett St., Wellington (☎ (04) 801 97 09); for visas or passports, contact Australian office; **South Africa,** 1109 Duncan St., Momentum Office Park, 0011 Brooklyn, Pretoria; Post: P.O. Box 95572, 0145 Waterkloof, Pretoria (☎012 462 483; email saembvie@ins.at); **consulates** in Johannesburg and Capetown; **UK,** 18 Belgrave Mews West, London SW1 X 8HU (☎ (0207) 235 37 31; fax 344 02 92; www.austria.org.uk); **consulate** in Edinburgh; **US,** 3524 International Court NW, Washington DC 20008-3035 (☎ (202) 895 67 00; fax 895 67 50); **consulates** in Chicago, Los Angeles, and New York.

GETTING AROUND

BY PLANE. The only major international airport is **Vienna's** Schwechat Flughafen. European flights also land in Salzburg, Graz, Innsbruck, and Klagenfurt. From the UK, **buzz** flies to Vienna. (☎ (0870) 240 70 70; www.buzzaway.com. UK£50-80.)

BY TRAIN. The **Österreichische Bundesbahn (ÖBB),** Austria's federal railroad, operates frequent and fast trains. The ÖBB publishes the yearly *Fahrpläne Kursbuch Bahn-Inland,* a compilation of all transportation schedules (100AS). **Eurail, InterRail,** and **Europe East** passes are valid. The **Austrian Railpass** allows three days of travel within any 15-day period on all rail lines, including Wolfgangsee ferries and private rail lines, and entitles holders to 50% off on bike rental at train stations and on DDSG steamers between Passau, Linz, and Vienna (second-class US$104, up to five additional days US$16 each). The one-month **Bundesnetzkarte** (National Network Pass), sold only in Austria, allows unlimited domestic train travel, including Wolfgangsee ferries and private rail lines, as well as half-price tickets for Bodensee and Danube ferries (second-class 4000AS, first-class 6000AS). The **Kilometer Bank,** sold only in Austria, involves prepurchasing a given number of kilometers' worth of travel, which can be used by one to six people traveling together on trips of over 70km one-way in first or second class. For **rail info,** dial ☎ 017 17.

BY BUS. The efficient Austrian bus system consists mainly of orange **BundesBuses,** which cover areas inaccessible by train. They cost as much as trains, and **railpasses** are not valid. You can buy discounted tickets, valid for one week, for any particular route. A **Mehrfahrtenkarte** gives you six tickets for the price of five. For more **bus information,** dial ☎ (0222) 711 01 within Austria (from outside Austria ☎ (1) 711 01).

BY FERRY. Private ferries are offered on most lakes, while the **DDSG** runs boats on the Danube between Vienna and Krems, Melk, Passau, Bratislava, and Budapest.

BY CAR. Driving is a convenient way to see Austria's more isolated regions. The roads are generally very good and well-marked, and Austrian drivers are quite careful. Austrians drive on the right side of the road. Be aware that Austrian law tolerates only a very minimal blood-alcohol level. **Drivers** must purchase a permit/sticker at Austria's border to place on the windshield (70AS per week) at the border or face a US$130 fine. If renting a car, it is usually cheaper to do so in Germany.

BY BIKE AND BY THUMB. Bicycling is a great way to travel; the roads are fairly level and many companies and train stations rent bikes (generally 150AS per day, 90AS with a railpass or valid train ticket from that day). If you get a bike at a train station, you can return it to any participating station. The *Gepäckbeförderung* symbol (a little bicycle) on departure schedules means that bikes are allowed in the baggage car. If your bike breaks down, some auto clubs may rescue you; try the **Austrian Automobile, Motorcycle, and Touring Club (ÖAMTC)** (☎ 120) or **ARBÖ** (☎ 123).

Austria is a rough place to **hitchhike**—Austrians rarely stop, and many mountain roads are all but deserted. Generally, hitchhikers stand on highway *Knoten* (on-ramps) and wait. *Let's Go* does not recommend hitchhiking. For a more certain ride, **Mitfahrzentrale** offices in larger cities match travelers with drivers for a fee.

TOURIST SERVICES AND MONEY

EMERGENCY. Police: ☎ 133. **Ambulance:** ☎ 144. **Fire:** ☎ 122.

TOURIST OFFICES. Virtually every town has a **tourist office** marked by a green **"i"** sign. Most brochures are available in English. The website for Austrian tourism is www.experienceaustria.com.

Tourist Boards at Home: Australia, 1st fl., 36 Carrington St., Sydney, NSW 2000 (☎ (02) 92 99 36 21; fax 92 99 38 08); **Canada,** 2 Bloor St. East #3330, Toronto, ON M4W 1A8 (☎ (416) 967 33 81; fax 967 41 01); **UK,** 14 Cork St., London W1X 1PF (☎ (020) 76 29 04 61; fax 74 99 60 38); **US,** 500 Fifth Ave., #800, P.O. Box 1142, New York, NY 10108-1142 (☎ (212) 944 68 80; fax 730 45 68; email antonyc@ibm.net.

MONEY. Austria's unit of currency is the **Schilling,** abbreviated as **AS, ÖS,** or simply **S.** Each *Schilling* is subdivided into 100 **Groschen (g).** Coins come in 2, 5, 10, and 50g, and 1, 5, 10, and 20AS denominations. Bills come in 20, 50, 100, 500, 1000, and 5000AS amounts. Currency exchange is easiest at ATMs, train stations, and post offices, where rates are the same as or close to bank rates. Expect to spend between US$25 and US$50 per person per day for lodging and food. **Accommodations** start at about US$15, while a basic sit-down meal costs around US$12. Menus say whether service is included (*Preise inclusive* or *Bedienung inclusiv*); if it is, you don't have to **tip.** If not, tip up to 10%. Restaurants expect you to seat yourself, and servers will not bring the bill until you ask for it. Don't leave tips on the table. Say *Zahlen bitte* (TSAHL-en BIT-uh) to ask for your bill. Some restaurants charge for each piece of bread that you eat during your meal. Don't expect to bargain in shops or markets, except at flea markets and the Naschmarkt in Vienna. Austria has a 20-34% **value-added tax** (VAT), applied to all purchases of books, clothing, souvenir items, art items, jewelry, perfume, alcohol, cigarettes, etc. You can get it refunded if the total is at least 1000AS (US$95) at one store.

BUSINESS HOURS. Most **stores** close M-F noon-3pm, Sa afternoons, and Su. Many **museums** are closed M. **Banks** usually open M-F 8am-12:30pm and 2-4:30pm.

ACCOMMODATIONS AND CAMPING

HOSTELS. Even the least appealing of Austria's tidy **youth hostels** *(Jugendherbergen)* are tolerable. Most hostels charge US$12-25 per night for dorms. Many hostels are somewhat cramped and offer little privacy. Austria has two independent organizations which run the over 80 HI hostels in the country; the ÖJHV and the ÖJHW. Non-HI members can stay in these hostels but are usually charged a surcharge.

HOTELS. Hotels are usually expensive. If you're on a tight budget, look for *Zimmer Frei* or *Privatzimmer* signs, which advertise rooms in private homes for US$10-25. Pensions and *Gästehäuser* are often within the budget traveler's range.

CAMPING. Prices are 50-70AS per person and 25-60AS per tent, plus a 8-10AS tax.

SKIING AND HIKING

Western Austria provides some of the world's best skiing and hiking; Innsbruck and Kitzbühel in Tirol are covered in lifts. High-season runs from mid-December to mid-January and from February to March. An extensive network of trails and Alpine refuges makes Austria's Alps as accessible as they are gorgeous. A **Österreichischer Alpenverein (ÖAV)** membership grants half-price at a series of mountain **huts** across the Tirol and throughout Austria, all a day's hike apart from each other. For info, contact Österreichischer Alpenverein, Willhelm-Greil-Str. 15, A-6010 Innsbruck (☎ (512) 58 78 28). Membership (US$55, students under 25 US$40, plus US$10 one-time fee) also includes use of **Deutscher Alpenverein** (German Alpine Club) huts.

FOOD AND DRINK

Loaded with fat, salt, and cholesterol, traditional Austrian cuisine is a cardiologist's nightmare, but tasty. Staple ingredients include *Schweinefleisch* (pork), *Kalbsfleisch* (veal), *Wurst* (sausage), *Eier* (eggs), *Käse* (cheese), *Brot* (bread), and *Kartoffeln/Erdäpfel* (potatoes). Austria's best-known dish is *Wienerschnitzel*, a meat cutlet (usually veal or pork) fried in butter with bread crumbs. Vegetarians should look for *Spätzle* (homemade noodles), *Eierschwammerln* (tiny yellow mushrooms), or anything with the word "Vegi" in it. The best discount supermarkets are **Billa** and **Hofer,** where you can buy cheap bags of *Semmeln* (rolls) and fruits and veggies. Natives nurse their sweet tooths at *Café-Konditoreien* with *Kaffee und Kuchen* (coffee and cake). Try *Sacher Torte*, a rich chocolate pastry layered with marmalade; *Linzer Torte*, a light yellow cake embedded with currant jam; *Apfelstrudel;* or any pastry. Austrian beers are outstanding—try *Stiegl Bier*, a Salzburg brew, *Zipfer Bier* from upper Austria, and *Gösser Bier* from Graz. Austria imports lots of Budweiser (the famous Czech *Budvar*, not the American brew).

COMMUNICATION

MAIL. Domestic service takes 1-2 days. **Airmail** to North America takes 5-7 days, but it can take up to 2 weeks to Australia and New Zealand. Mark all mail "mit Flugpost" or "par avion." The cheapest option is to send **aerogrammes.** *Poste Restante* letters to: First name SURNAME, Postlagernde Briefe, A-1010 Vienna, Austria.

TELEPHONES. You can usually make international calls from pay phones, but **phone cards** *(Wertkarten)*, available at post offices, train stations, and *Tabak/Trafik* (50 or 100AS) are better. The cheapest way to call abroad collect is to go to a post office and ask for *Zurückruf*, or "return call," and have your party call you back. **International direct dial** numbers include: **AT&T** ☎022 90 30 11; **BT Direct** ☎0800 20 02 09; **Canada Direct** ☎0800 20 02 17; **MCI WorldPhone Direct** ☎022 90 30 12; **Sprint Global One** ☎0800 20 02 36; **Telkom South Africa Direct** ☎022 90 30 27.

INTERNET ACCESS. Most towns have Internet access for 50-100AS per hr.

LANGUAGE. German is the official language. English is the most common second language, but any effort to use German is appreciated. Outside of cities and among older residents, English is less common. *Grüss Gott* is the typical greeting.

HOLIDAYS AND FESTIVALS

Holidays: New Year's Day (Jan. 1-2); Epiphany (Jan. 6); Good Friday (Apr. 2); Easter Monday (Apr. 5); Labor Day (May 1); Ascension (June 1); Whitmonday (June 12); Corpus Christi (June 22); Assumption Day (Aug. 15); Austrian National Day (Oct. 26); All Saints' Day (Nov. 1); Immaculate Conception (Dec. 8); and Christmas (Dec. 25-26).

Festivals: Just about everything closes down on public holidays, so plan accordingly. Austrians celebrate **Fasching** (Carneval) during the first 2 weeks of February. Austria's most famous summer **music festivals** are the **Wiener Festwochen** (mid-May to mid-June) and the **Salzburger Festspiele** (late July to late Aug.).

VIENNA (WIEN) ☎0222

Vienna oozes culture, thanks to its inspired musical tradition (Mozart, Beethoven, Schubert, Strauss, Brahms), imperial wealth, and Baroque art and architecture. But it was with reason that satirist Karl Kraus once dubbed Vienna—birthplace of psychoanalysis, atonal music, functionalist architecture, Zionism, and Nazism—a "laboratory for world destruction." Vienna's *fin de siècle* heyday carried the seeds of its decay—the Viennese self-mockingly called it the "merry apocalypse" as they stared down their own dissolution over coffee. The whipped cream and smooth veneer of waltz music concealed a darker reality found in Freud's theories, Kafka's writings, and Mahler's symphonies. While the city has been known as a quiet showplace for its many treasures, the city is attempting to reestablish itself as the political, cultural, and economic gateway to Eastern Europe.

GETTING THERE AND GETTING AROUND

Flights: Wien-Schwechat Flughafen (☎700 72 22 31), 18km from Vienna's center, is the home of **Austrian Airlines** (☎17 89; www.aua.com; open M-F 8am-7pm, Sa-Su 8am-5pm). The S-7 connects the airport ("Flughafen/Wolfsthal"; every 30min., 38AS; Eurail not valid) to "Wien Mitte/Landstr." on the U-3 or U-4 lines. **Vienna Airport Lines Shuttle Buses** run from the airport to the City Air Terminal 24hr. (opposite "Wien Mitte/Landstr."; every 20-30min., 70AS).

Trains: Info ☎17 17 (24hr.); schedules online at www.bahn.at. Three main stations:

Westbahnhof, XV, Mariahilferstr. 132, primarily runs trains west. To: **Salzburg** (3hr., every hr., 430AS); **Budapest** (3-4hr., 6 per day, 420AS); **Munich** (4½hr., 5 per day, 788AS); **Innsbruck** (6hr., every 2hr., 660AS); **Zurich** (9¼hr., 3 per day, 1122AS); **Amsterdam** (14hr., 1 per day, 2276AS); **Berlin** (11hr., 1 per day, 1678AS); and **Paris** (14hr., 2 per day, 2096AS).

Südbahnhof, X, Wiedner Gürtel 1a, sends trains mostly south, but also east. To: **Bratislava** (1hr., 3 per day, 166AS); **Prague** (4½hr., 3 per day, 550AS); **Rome** (13¾hr., 2 per day, 1352AS); **Kraków** (7-8hr., 2 per day, 496AS); **Berlin** (9¼hr., 1 per day, 1160AS); and **Venice** (9-10hr., 3 per day, 880AS). Also to destinations in **Poland, Germany, Russia, Turkey, Greece,** and **Spain.**

Franz-Josefs Bahnhof, IX, Althamstr. 10, handles mostly commuter trains.

Ferries: DDSG Donaureisen (☎58 88 00; www.ddsg-blue-danube.at) sails the Danube. 130-690AS; 20% off with Eurail or ISIC. Summer ferries depart every Su from Reichbrücke (take U-1).

Public Transportation: Info ☎580 00, ☎790 91 05 for directions; www.wiennet.at/efa. Excellent **U-Bahn** (subway), **bus, Straßenbahn** (tram), and **S-Bahn** (elevated train) systems cover the city. **Single-fare** 22AS if purchased on a bus; 19AS in advance at ticket offices, *Tabak,* or U-Bahn station *Automaten.* The ticket includes transfers; punch it upon boarding the first vehicle of your journey and don't punch again if you transfer, or it will be invalid (fine 560AS). The following **passes** are available: **24-hour** 60AS, **3-day "rover"** 150AS, **7-day** 155AS (valid from M 9am to following M 9am). The 3-day **Vienna Card** (210AS) includes unlimited public transit as well as discounts at museums and sights. Regular trams and subways stop 12:30-5am, but **nightbuses** run every 30min. along most tram, subway, and major bus routes ("N" designates bus stops; 15AS; passes not valid). **Maps** (15AS) and night bus schedules are in U-Bahn stations.

Taxis: ☎313 00, 401 00, 601 60, 814 00, or 910 91. Stands at Westbahnhof, Südbahnhof, and Karlspl. Base fare 27AS; 14AS per km. Surcharges: Su and 11pm-6am 27AS; heavy luggage or taxis called by radiophone 13-26AS.

Hitchhiking: For Salzburg, the highway leading to the *Autobahn* is 10km past U-4: Hütteldorf. Hitchers going south ride tram #67 to the end and wait at the rotary near Laaerberg. **Mitfahrzentrale Wien,** VIII, Daung. 1a (☎408 22 10), off Laudong., organizes ride-sharing. To **Salzburg** (210AS), **Prague** (450AS). Open M-F 8am-noon and 2-7pm, Sa-Su 1-3pm. *Let's Go* does not endorse hitching.

Bike Rental: At **Wien Nord** and the **Westbahnhof.** 150AS per day, 90AS with train ticket from day of arrival. **Pedal Power,** II, Ausstellungsstr. 3 (☎729 72 34). 60AS per hr., 300AS per half-day. **Bike tours** of the city (180-280AS). Open May-Sept. 8am-8pm. Pick up *Vienna By Bike* at the tourist office.

ORIENTATION AND PRACTICAL INFORMATION

Vienna is divided into 23 *Bezirke* (districts). The first district is the city center, *innere Stadt* or **Innenstadt** (inner city), bounded by the name-changing **Ringstraße** (the site of the old city fortifications) and the Danube. Many of Vienna's major attractions lie along the southern section of the Ring, around the Hofburg (Imperial Palace), among them the **Kunsthistorisches Museum,** the **Rathaus,** and the **Burggarten,** and the **Staatsoper** (Opera House). Districts two through nine radiate clockwise from the center between the Ring and the larger, concentric **Gürtel** ("belt"), beyond which further districts similarly radiate clockwise. Street signs indicate the district numbers in Roman numerals. *Let's Go* includes these district numbers before street addresses. At night avoid the fifth, 10th, and 14th districts, as well as Landstraßer Hauptstr., Prater Park, and sections of the **Gürtel** (the red-light district). Also, be careful by the U-Bahn station in Karlspl., home to pushers.

TOURIST AND FINANCIAL SERVICES

Tourist Office: Main Office, I, Am Albertinaplatz. 1, right behind the Opera House. Books 300-400AS rooms (40AS fee plus deposit), and has a excellent, free map. Open daily 9am-7pm (www.info.wien.at). **Branch** at the **Westbahnhof. Jugend-Info Wien** (Vienna Youth Information Service), in the Bellaria-Passage (☎17 99). Enter at "Dr.-Karl-Renner-Ring/Bellaria" (tram #1, 2, 46, 49, D, or J) or U-2/U-3: Volkstheater. Get *Jugend in Wien.* Open M-Sa noon-7pm.

Embassies: Australia, IV, Mattiellistr. 2-4 (☎51 28 58 00), behind Karlskirche. Open M-Th 9am-1pm and 2-5pm, F 9am-1pm. **Canada,** I, Laurenzerburg 2, 3rd fl. (☎531 38, ext. 3000). Open M-F 8:30am-12:30pm and 1:30-3:30pm. **Ireland,** III, Hilton Center, Landstraßer Hauptstr. 21, 6th fl. (☎71 54 24 60; fax 713 60 04). Open M-F 9:30-11:30am and 1:30-4pm. **New Zealand,** XIX, Springsiedleg. 28 (☎318 85 05; fax 318 67 17). **South Africa,** XIX, Sandg. 33 (☎32 06 49 30). Open M-F 8:30am-noon. **UK,** III, Jauresg. 12 (☎71 61 30; fax 716 13 29 99), near Schloß Belvedere. Open M-F 9am-5pm. **US,** IX, Boltzmanng. 16, off Währingerstr. (☎313 39; staffed M-F 8:30am-noon and 1-5pm). Open M-F 8:30am-noon.

Currency Exchange: ATMs have the best rates and usually accept Cirrus, Eurocard, V, and MC. **Banks** and **airport exchanges** use official rates (commission on checks 65AS, cash 10AS). Most open M-W and F 8am-12:30pm and 1:30-3pm, Th until 5:30pm.

American Express: I, Kärntnerstr. 21-23 (☎515 40), down the street from Stephanspl. Mail held. Open M-F 9am-5:30pm, Sa 9am-noon.

AUSTRIA

LOCAL SERVICES

Luggage Storage: Lockers at all train stations 30-50AS per 24hr.

English-Language Bookstores: Shakespeare & Company, I, Sterng. 2 (☎535 50 53). Eclectic and intelligent. Open M-F 9am-7pm, Sa 9am-5pm.

Bisexual, Gay, and Lesbian Services: Rosa Lila Villa, VI, Linke Wienzeile 102 (☎586 81 50). Counseling, library, and nightlife info. Open M-F 5-8pm. Pick up the monthly magazines *Extra* (German-language) and *Bussi* (free at any gay bar, cafe, or club), or the straight but hip *Falter* newspaper.

Laundromat: Schnell und Sauber, VII, Westbahnhofstr. 60 (☎524 64 60); U-6: Burgg. Stadthalle. Wash 60AS for 6kg. Soap included. Spin-dry 10AS. Open 24hr.

Public Showers: At Westbahnhof in Friseursalon Navratil downstairs from subway passage. Well-maintained. 30min. 54AS, with soap and towel 66AS. Su 10AS extra.

EMERGENCY AND COMMUNICATIONS

Emergencies: Police: ☎133. **Ambulance:** ☎144. **Fire:** ☎122.

Medical Assistance: Allgemeines Krankenhaus, IX, Währinger Gürtel 18-20 (☎404 00 19 64). **Emergency care:** ☎141. Consulates provide lists of English-speaking physicians. **Fachärzte Lugeck** (☎512 18 18) has English-speaking doctors and nurses 24hr. daily. **24hr. pharmacies:** ☎15 50.

Crisis Hotlines: Rape Crisis Hotline: ☎717 19 (24hr.). **Suicide Hotline:** ☎713 33 74.

Internet Access: Amadeus Media Café, I, Kärntnerstr. 19, on the 5th fl. of Steffl department store. Free. Open M-F 9:30am-7pm, Sa 9:30am-5pm. **Libro,** XXII, Donauzentrum. Free. Open Su-F 7am-7pm, Sa 9am-5pm.

Post Offices: Hauptpostamt, I, Fleischmarkt 19. Open 24hr. Address mail to be held: SURNAME, First name, *Postlagernde Briefe;* Hauptpostamt, Fleischmarkt 19, **A-1010** Wien, Austria.

ACCOMMODATIONS AND CAMPING

High season (June-Sept.) room hunting is vicious; reserve five days ahead or arrive before 9am for a same-day spot. If your choice is full, ask for a waiting list slot. University dorms convert into hostels (July-Sept.). One-star *Pensionen* in the seventh, eighth, and ninth districts have singles from 350AS and doubles from 500AS.

HOSTELS

Wombats City Hostel, XV, Grangaße 6 (☎879 23 36; email wombats@chello.at). From Westbahnhof, turn right out of the Außer Mariahilfer Straße exit, take the 6th right on Rosinagaße, and take your 2nd left. Brand new hostel with immaculate rooms, private baths, and in-the-know staff. Internet (60AS per hour). Inline skate and bike rental (both 100AS per day). Breakfast 35AS. Laundry. 2-6 bedrooms 175-245AS.

Believe It or Not, VII, Myrtheng. 10, #14 (☎526 46 58). From Westbahnhof, take U-6 (dir. Heiligenstadt) to "Burgg./Stadthalle," then bus #48A (dir. Ring) to "Neubaug." Backtrack a block on Burgg. and turn right on Myrtheng. (15min.). From Südbahnhof, take bus #13A (dir. Skodag./Alerstr.) to "Kellermanng." Walk left on Neustiftg. and left again on Myrtheng. Fab caretaker gives crash-course on Vienna. Kitchen. Reception 8am-1pm. Lockout 10:30am-12:30pm. Easter-Oct. 160AS; Nov.-Easter 110AS.

AUSTRIA

Hostel Ruthensteiner (HI), XV, Robert-Hamerlingg. 24 (☎893 42 02 or 893 27 96; email hostel.ruthensteiner@telecom.at), 5min. from the Westbahnhof. Turn right out of the Mariahilfer Straße exit, left on Haidmannsg., and right on Robert-Hammerlingg. Gorgeous courtyard. Kitchen. Internet (100AS per hr.). 4-night max. stay. Reception 24hr. Summer dorm 125AS; dorms 145-169AS; doubles 235AS.

Myrthengasse (HI), VII, Myrtheng. 7, opposite Believe It or Not, and **Neustiftgasse (HI),** VII, Neustiftg. 85 (both ☎523 63 16; email hostel@chello.at). Simple hostels 20min. from the *Innenstadt.* Breakfast included. Laundry. Reception at Myrtheng. 7am-11:30pm. Curfew 1am. Lockout 9am-2pm. 170-215AS. Nonmembers add 40AS.

Hostel Panda, VII, Kaiserstr. 77, 3rd fl. (☎522 53 53). From Westbahnhof, take tram #5 to "Burgg." From Südbahnhof, take tram #18 to "Westbahnhof". Fun and eclectic hostel in an old-fashioned Austrian apartment building. Kitchen and TVs. Lockers; bring a lock. Easter-Oct. 160AS; Nov.-Easter 110AS; add 50AS for one-night stay.

Hostel Zöhrer, IX, Skodagasstr. 26 (☎406 07 30; email zoehrer.com). From Westbahnhof take tram #5 to "Laudong." Go right on Daung. and walk a block to Skodog. From Südbahnhof, take bus #13a to "Alserstr., Skodag." Caring staff. Breakfast included. Kitchen. Lockout 11am-2pm. Dorms 170AS; doubles 460AS; triples 690AS.

Kolpingfamilie Wien-Meidling (HI), XIII, Bendlg. 10-12 (☎813 54 87; fax 812 21 30). U-6: Niederhofstr.; go right on Niederhofstr. and take the 4th right onto Bendlg. Well-lit and modern in a quiet neighborhood. Breakfast 55AS. Reception 6am-midnight. Check-out 9am. Lockout midnight-4am. Dorms 150-195AS. Nonmembers add 40AS.

Schloßherberge am Wilhelminenberg (HI), XVI, Savoyenstr. 2 (☎485 85 03, ext. 700; email SHB@wigast.com). U-6: Thaliastr.; tram #46 (dir. Joachimsthalerpl.) to "Maroltingerg," or tram #44 from Schottentor to "Wilhelminenstr." Then take bus #146B or #46B to "Schloß Wilhelminenberg" and follow the signs. Magnificent views. Breakfast included. Laundry. Reception 7am-11pm. Lockout 9am-2pm. Curfew midnight. 225AS.

Jugendgästehaus Wien Brigittenau (HI), XX, Friedrich-Engels-Pl. 24 (☎332 82 94 or 330 05 98), 25min. from city center. Take U-1 or U-4 to "Schwedenpl.," then tram N to "Floridsdorferbrücke/Friedrich-Engels-Pl." Breakfast included. 5-night max. stay. Reception 24hr. Lockout 9am-1pm. Dorms 130-250AS.

Central Vienna

ACCOMMODATIONS

Studenten Wohnheim der Hochschule für Musik, 1

UNIVERSITY DORMS

Porzellaneum der Wiener Universität, IX, Porzellang. 30 (☎31 77 28 20; fax 31 77 28 30), 10min. from the Ring. From Westbahnhof, take tram #5 to "Franz-Josefs Bahnhof," then tram D (dir. Südbahnhof) to "Fürsteng." From Südbahnhof, take tram D (dir. Nußdorf) to "Fürsteng." Reception 24hr. Singles 190AS; doubles 380AS; quads 760AS.

Rudolfinum, IV, Mayerhofg. 3 (☎505 53 84). U-1: Taubstummeng. Good location. Breakfast included. Reception 24hr. Singles 270AS; doubles 480AS; triples 600AS.

Gästehaus Pfeilgasse, VIII, Pfeilg. 6 (☎401 74; fax 401 76 20; email acahot@academia-hotels.co.at). U-2: Lerchenfelderstr.; go right, then right on Lange Gasse, and left on Pfeilg. Breakfast included. Singles 270AS; doubles 480AS; triples 600AS.

Katholisches Studentenhaus, XIX, Peter-Jordanstr. 29 (☎/fax 34 74 73 12). From Westbahnhof, take U-6 (dir. Heiligenstadt) to "Nußdorferstr.," then bus #35A or tram #38 to "Hardtg." and turn left. From Südbahnhof, take tram D to "Schottentor," then tram #38 to "Hardtg." Laid-back ambiance. Singles 250AS; doubles 400AS.

HOTELS AND PENSIONS

Lauria Apartments, VII, Kaiserstr. 77, #8 (☎522 25 55). From Südbahnhof, take tram #18 to "Westbahnhof," then tram #5 to "Burgg." Near the city center. TVs and kitchens. 2-night min. for reservations. Credit cards accepted for non-dorms. Dorms 160AS; singles 480AS; doubles 530-700AS; triples 700-800AS; quads 850-940AS.

Pension Kraml, VI, Brauerg. 5 (☎587 85 88), by the *Innenstadt* and Naschmarkt. U-3: Zierierg.; exit onto Otto-Bauerg., take 1st left and 1st right. From Südbahnhof, take bus #13A to Esterhazyg. and walk up Brauerg. Spacious rooms. Singles 310AS; doubles 560-760AS; triples 720-930AS. Apartment for 3-5 1120-1250AS.

CAMPING

Wien-West, Hüttelbergstr. 80 (☎914 23 14), 8km from the city center. From U-4: Hütteldorf take bus #14B or 152 (dir. Campingpl.) to "Wien West." Laundry, and cooking facilities. Reception 7:30am-9:30pm. Closed Feb. July-Aug. 75AS per person, Sept.-June 68AS; 40-45AS per tent; 2-person cabins 250AS; 4-person cabins 400-440AS.

FOOD AND COFFEE

Viennese cuisine reflects the Habsburg patchwork empire: *Knödeln* (Czech dumplings) and *Ungarische Gulaschsuppe* (Hungarian spicy beef stew) show Eastern European influence, and even *Wienerschnitzel* (fried and breaded veal cutlets) is probably from Milan. Vienna is renowned for desserts as high in price as in calories, but residents maintain that the sumptuous treats are worth every *Groschen*. Gorge on *Sacher Torte*, *Imperial Torte*, and *Apfelstrudel*. *Gästehäuser*, *Imbiße* (food stands), and *Beisln* (pubs) have cheap meals. Places near **Kärntnerstr.** tend to be pricey—try north of the university near the Votivkirche (U-2: Schottentor), where **Universitätsstr.** and **Währingerstr.** meet, or the area around the **Rechte** and **Linke Wienzeile** near Naschmarkt (U-4: Kettenbrückeg.). The **Naschmarkt** is full of vendors selling snacks to feed the shoppers at Vienna's premier flea market (Sa-Su). Buy groceries at **Billa, Hofer,** and **Spar** (most closed Su).

RESTAURANTS

OH Pot, OH Pot, IX, Währingerstr. 22. U-2: Schottentor. Adorable Spanish joint with amazingly good namesake "pots" (stew-like concoctions of veggies or meat), 72-110AS. Open M-F 11am-midnight, Sa-Su 6pm-midnight.

Brezelg'wölb, I, Lederhof 9, near Am Hof. Nestled in a tiny side street, this old-fashioned *Backstube* serves excellent, hearty Viennese cuisine. Lunch around 100AS. Open daily 11:30am-1am, hot food until midnight.

Bizi Pizza, I, Rotenturmstr. 4, by Stephanspl. Pizza for a pittance (60-75AS), or pasta (65-75AS) whipped up before your eyes. Also at Franz-Josefs-Kai; Mariahilferstr. 22-24; and X, Favoritenstr. 105. All open daily 11am-11:30pm.

MMM...COFFEE There is a steadfast rule for the Vienna coffeehouse—the drink matters, but the atmosphere *really* matters. In the 19th-century, artists, writers, and thinkers fled poorly heated apartments to surround themselves with the dark wood and velvet of coffeehouses, ordering cups of coffee and staying long into the night, composing operettas, writing books, and distracting each other with talk. The bourgeoisie followed suit, and the coffeehouse soon became the living room of the city—where Peter Altenberg, "the cafe writer," scribbled lines; Kokoschka grumbled alone; exiles Vladimir Lenin and Leon Trotsky played chess; Theodor Herzl made plans for a Zionist Israel; and Kafka journeyed from Prague to visit the Herrenhof. The original literary cafe was Café Griensteidl. After it was demolished in 1897, the torch passed first to Café Central and then to Café Herrenhof. Cafes still exist under these names, but only Café Central looks the way it originally did. The best places today resist overhauls, succumbing to a noble, comfortable decrepitude.

Hungerkünstler, VI, Gumpendorfstr. 48. Exceptional food in a mellow atmosphere. Entrees average 90AS. Open daily 11am-2am.

Tunnel, VIII, Florianig. 39. U-2: Rathaus; with the Rathaus behind you, head right on Landesgerichtstr. and left on Florianig. Funky decor, live music, and cheap Austrian, Italian, and Middle Eastern food. Lunch *Menüs* 45AS. Open 10am-2am.

Rosenberger Markt, I, Mayserderg. 2, behind the Sacher Hotel. Large and chaotic subterranean buffet with a gargantuan selection of salad (29-64AS), fruit salad, waffles (55AS), antipasti, potatoes, and pasta. Open daily 10:30am-11pm.

COFFEEHOUSES AND KONDITOREIEN

The quintessential Viennese coffee is the *Melange;* you can order every coffee as a *Kleiner* (small) or *Grosser* (large), *Brauner* (brown, with milk) or *Schwarzer* (black). Most cafes serve hot food, but don't order it (except pastries) with coffee. The most serious dictate of coffeehouse etiquette is lingering. The waiter *(Herr Ober)* will serve you when you sit, then leave you to sip and brood. Vienna's *Konditoreien*, as traditional as its coffee shops, focus on pastries rather than coffee.

Café Hawelka, I, Dorotheerg. 6, off Grabe, three blocks from the Stephansdom. With dusty wallpaper, dark wood, and old red-striped velvet sofas, this legendary cafe is glorious. *Melange* 37AS. Open M and W-Sa 8am-2am, Su 4pm-2am.

Café Central, I, at Herreng. and Strauchg. inside Palais Ferstel. Theodor Herzl, Sigmund Freud, Vladimir Ilych Ulianov (a.k.a. Lenin), and Leon Trotsky hung out here. Piano 4-7pm. Open M-Sa 8am-8pm, Su 10am-6pm.

Demel, I, Kohlmarkt 14, 5min. from the Stephansdom down Graben. The most luxurious *Konditorei*, Demel's was confectioner to the imperial court until the empire dissolved. Confections 40-50AS. Open 10am-7pm.

Café Sperl, VI, Gumpendorferstr. 11. U-2: Babenbergstr.; walk a block down Getreidemarkt and turn right on Gumpendorferstr. One of Vienna's oldest and most beautiful cafes. Cake 35-45AS. Open M-Sa 7am-11pm, Su 3-11pm; July-Aug. closed Su.

Café Griensteidl, I Michaelerpl. 6, down the street from Café Central toward the Hofburg. Vienna's first literary cafe retains an intellectual flair. Open daily 8am-11:30pm.

Café Savoy, VI, Linke Wienzeile 36, is a camp *fin de siècle* cafe with dark wood and decrepit gold trim. A large gay and lesbian crowd moves in to make this a lively nightspot on weekends. Open M-F 5pm-2am, Sa 9am-2am.

SIGHTS

Viennese streets are by turns startling, scuzzy, and grandiose; the best way to see the city is simply to get lost. To wander in a more organized manner, get the brochure *Vienna from A to Z* (50AS with Vienna Card) or *Walks in Vienna*, both at the tourist office. Organized tours run 130AS; some require additional admission fees to sites. **Vienna Bike,** IX, Wasag., runs **cycling tours.** (☎319 12 58. 2-3hr., 280AS.) Another great way to see the city is to ride around the Ring on trams #1 or 2.

THE RINGSTRAßE

In 1857, Emperor Franz Josef commissioned this boulevard, which defines the boundaries of the inner city, to replace the medieval city walls. Freud walked the 2½ mi. circuit of the Ring every day during his lunch break; it took two hours. Extending south from the Danube Canal, **Schottenring** leads to the twin spires of the **Votivkirche,** a neo-Gothic wonder surrounded by rose gardens. The next stretch, **Karl-Lueger Ring,** runs from the **Universität Wien** to Rathausplatz, the inner city's largest square. The fluted arches of the **Rathaus** (town hall) and the Neoclassical, sculpture-adorned **Parlament** (Parliament) building mark **Dr. Karl-Renner Ring.** On **Burgring,** opposite the Hofburg, stand two of Vienna's largest museums, the **Kunsthistorisches Museum** (Museum of Art History) and the **Naturhistorisches Museum** (Museum of Natural History; see **Museums,** p. 109). From the Burggarten, **Opernring/Kärntnerring** heads to Schwarzenbergstr., marked by an equestrian statue. The **Staatsoper** (State Opera) dominates the Opernring. Originally completed in 1869, it was meticulously restored following heavy WWII damage. Former directors include Gustav Mahler, Richard Strauss, and Lorin Maazel. The cheapest way to partake of its fabulous gold, crystal, and red-velvet interior is to see an opera—standing room tickets are 50AS. *(Take U-1, U-2, U-4, or tram #1, 2, J, or D to "Karlsplatz" and take the Staatsoper exit. Tours July-Aug. at 10, 11am, 1, 2, and 3pm; May-June and Sept.-Oct. at 1, 2, and 3pm; Nov.-Apr. at 2 and 3pm. 60AS, students 45AS.)* The Schubertring/Stubenring, which heads back to the Danube Canal, borders **Stadtpark** (City Park).

INSIDE THE RING

The **Innere Stadt** (Inner City), enclosed by the **Ringstraße** and the **Danube Canal,** is Vienna's social and geographical center. With palaces, theaters, tenements, and toilet bowls designed by master architects, it's a gallery of the history of aesthetics, from Baroque to *Jugendstil*.

AUSTRIA

NEAR STEPHANSPLATZ. This active square is at the heart of Vienna in the shadow of the city's most treasured symbol, the Gothic **Stephansdom,** whose smoothly tapered **South Tower** has become Vienna's emblem. Climb its 343 steps for a 360° view of Vienna. Photographs inside chronicle the painstaking process of reconstruction following WWII damages. Downstairs in the **catacombs,** skeletons of thousands of plague victims line the walls, while another *Gruft* stores Habsburg remains. *(U-1 or U-3: Stephansplatz. Cathedral tours in English M-Sa 10:30am and 3pm, Su 3pm; 40AS. Spectacular evening tour July-Sept. Sa 7pm; 100AS. South Tower open 9am-5:30pm; 30AS. Gruft tours M-Sa 10, 11, 11:30am, 2, 2:30, 3:30, 4, and 4:30pm; Su 2, 2:30, 3:30, 4, and 4:30pm; 50AS.)* Running straight out of Stephansplatz is **Graben,** a main pedestrian street with Baroque, *Biedermeier*, *Jugendstil*, and postmodern trends, including the **Ankerhaus** (#10) and the red-marble **Grabenhof** by Otto Wagner. Heading up Seilergasse from Graben brings you to the spectacular **Neuer Markt,** where a graceful fountain and the 17th-century **Kapuzinerkirche** (Church of the Capuchin Friars) await. The church houses an imperial **Gruft** (vault), a series of subterranean rooms whose coffins contain the remains (minus heart and entrails) of all the Habsburg rulers since 1633. *(Open 9:30am-4pm. 30AS.)*

FROM STEPHANSPLATZ TO JUDEN PLATZ. From Stephanspl., head up Rotenturmstr. and turn left onto **Hoher Markt,** the center of town (used as a market and execution site) during the Middle Ages. It served a convenient double-duty as a market and execution site. Its biggest draw is the magnificent *Jugendstil* **Ankeruhr** (clock), which features 12 historical figures (including Emperor Marcus Aurelius, Maria Theresia, and Josef Haydn) rotating past the old Viennese coat of arms; one 3m figure appears per hour, but show up at noon to see all of them in succession. Peek under the bridge to see depictions of Adam, Eve, an angel, and the devil. The square is also the heart of the Roman encampment **Vindobona,** where Marcus Aurelius penned his *Meditations*. The remains lie below the shopping arcade on the south side of the square. *(Open Sa-Su 11am-1pm. 25AS.)* From Hoher Markt, follow Wipplingerstr. west (right) to the impressive Baroque facade of the **Böhmische Hofkanzlei** (Bohemian Court Chancellory), the seat of Austria's Constitutional Court. The **Altes Rathaus,** directly across the street, today houses the **Austrian Resistance Museum** and various temporary exhibits. *(On Friedrich-Schmidt-Pl. ☎525 50. Open M, W, and Th 9am-5pm. Tours M, W, and F 1pm. Free.)* Turn left directly after the *Hofkanzlei* to get to the **Judenplatz,** the site of the city's first Jewish ghetto. Turn left on Seitenstetteng. to reach the Jewish **Stadttempel,** the only one of Vienna's 94 synagogues to escape Nazi destruction during **Kristallnacht** (Night of Broken Glass) on November 9-10, 1938; it was only spared because it was concealed from the street. An armed guard now patrols the synagogue as a precaution against repeats of the 1983 terrorist attack, which killed three people. *(Seitenstetteng. 2-4. Take your passport. Open Su-F. Free.)* Continue up Seitenstetteng. to **Judengasse** (Jew Lane), a remnant of the old Jewish ghetto.

FROM AM HOF TO MICHAELERPLATZ. On the other side of Judenpl., Drahtg. opens into the grand courtyard **Am Hof,** a medieval jousting square that now houses the **Kirche am Hof** (Church of the Nine Choirs of Angels), built from 1386-1662. Roman ruins show that Am Hof has been popular for a while. From Am Hof turn right on Bognerstr. to **Freyung,** an uneven square used for public executions in the Middle Ages. Freyung is linked to **Herrengasse,** home to Vienna's nobility during the Hapsburg era. Heading right on Herreng. brings you to the Italianate **Palais Ferstel,** home to **Café Central** (see p. 105), for "those who want to be alone in the company of others." Head left down Herreng. and turn right on Landhausg. to reach the peaceful **Minoritenplatz,** home of the 14th-century **Minoritenkirche.** The Church's tower was destroyed during the Turkish siege of Vienna in 1529. On the south side of the square stands the **Bundeskanzleramt** (Federal Chancery), where the Congress of Vienna met in 1815 and Chancellor Engelbert Dollfuss was assassinated in 1934. Follow Schauflerg. to the left and you'll run into **Michaelerplatz,** named for the unassuming **Michaelerkirche** (St. Michael's Church) on its eastern side. Leopold "the Glorious" Babenburg purportedly founded the church in gratitude for his safe return from the Crusades. *(Open May-Oct. M-Sa 10:30am-4:30pm, Su 1-5pm. 25AS.)* In the middle of Michaelerpl. are further excavations of Roman Vienna, **Vindobona.** A reconstructed **Café Griensteidl** is on the side of the square, inviting visitors to imagine themselves drinking coffee alongside *fin de siècle* writers Arthur Schnitzler and Hugo von Hofmannsthal. The square is dominated by the green, neo-Baroque, **Michaelertor,** the main gate of the Hofburg.

THE HOFBURG. The sprawling Hofburg was the Habsburgs' winter residence until their 700-year reign ended in 1918. It experienced periods of neglect when various emperors chose to live in other palaces, such as Schönbrunn, but it remained the symbol of the family's power. Today, it houses the office of the Austrian President.

Perhaps the best way to get an overview of the Hofburg is to walk around the perimeter. The **Stallburg** (Palace Stables), accessible via Josefspl., is home to the Royal Lipizzaner stallions of the **Spanische Reitschule** (Spanish Riding School). The cheapest way to get a glimpse of the famous steeds is to watch them train. *(Mid-Feb. to June and Nov. to mid-Dec. Tu-F 10am-noon; early Feb. M-Sa 10am-noon, except when the horses tour. Tickets sold at the door at Josefspl., Gate 2, from about 8:30am. 100AS.)* Continue down Augustinerstr. to reach the 14th-century Gothic **Augustinerkirche,** where the hearts of the Habsburgs rest in peace in the **Herzgrüftel** (Little Heart Crypt). *(Open M-Sa 10am-6pm, Su 1-6pm.)* The **Albertina,** the southern wing of the Hofburg, has a film museum and the celebrated **Collection of Graphic Arts,** with an array of old political cartoons and drawings by Dürer, Michelangelo, da Vinci, Raphael, Cézanne, and Schiele. *(Open Tu-Sa 10am-5pm. 70AS.)*

Head up to Michaelerpl. The wooden door on the right as you enter the Hofburg via the Michaelertor leads to the **Kaiserappartements,** the former quarters of Emperor Franz Josef (1848-1916) and Empress Elisabeth (1838-1898). *(Open daily 9am-4:30pm. 80AS.)* As you continue through the Michaelertor, enter the courtyard **In der Burg** (within the fortress). Through the red-and-black-striped **Schweizertor** (Swiss Gate) on the left and up the stairs to the right is the Gothic **Burgkapelle,** where the heavenly **Wiener Sängerknaben** (Vienna Boys' Choir) graces Mass-goers (see **Music,** p. 110). Below the Burgkapelle is the **Schatzkammer** (Treasury), which displays the Habsburg jewels, the crowns of the Holy Roman and Austrian Empires,

Imperial christening robes, and a tooth that reportedly belonged to John the Baptist. *(Open W-M 10am-6pm. 80AS, students 50AS. One English tour per day; 30AS.)* The passageway at the rear of In der Burg opens up onto **Heldenplatz** (Heroes' Square). To the left is the vast **Neue Burg** (New Fortress). The **Österreichische Nationalbibliothek** (Austrian National Library) has an outstanding museum of papyruses, scriptures, and musical manuscripts. *(Open May 7-Oct. 26 M-W and F-Sa 10am-4pm, Th 10am-7pm, Su 10am-1pm; Nov.-Apr. M-Sa 10am-1pm. May-Nov. 60AS, students 40AS; Nov.-Apr. 40AS.)*

OUTSIDE THE RING

KARLSPLATZ AND RESSELPARK. *(Take U-1, U-2, U-4, or any number of trams to "Karlsplatz" and exit toward Resselpark.)* **Karlsplatz,** within the **Resselpark,** is home to the city's most impressive Baroque church. The **Karlskirche,** in the southeast corner of the park, combines a Neoclassical portico with a Baroque dome; the gorgeous interior has colorful ceiling frescoes and a sunburst altar. *(Open M-Sa 9-11:30am and 1-5pm, Su 1-5pm. Free.)* The **Historisches Museum der Stadt Wien,** to the left of the Karlskirche, stands across the square from the blocky yellow-and-blue **Kunsthalle** (see **Museums,** below). Above one side of the square, a terrace links the *Jugendstil* **Karlsplatz Stadtbahn Pavilions,** designed in 1899 by **Otto Wagner,** the architect primarily responsible for Vienna's *Jugendstil* face. Visible to the north across Lothringerstr., between Karlsplatz and the Ring, from the pavilions are the **Künstlerhaus,** the traditional home of Vienna's artistic community, from which the Secession artists seceded in 1897 (see **Museums,** below) and the **Musikverein,** home of the **Vienna Philharmonic Orchestra** (see **Music,** below). Northwest of the Resselpark across Friedrichstr. stands the nemesis of the Künstlerhaus, the **Secession Building,** whose restrained decoration, and gilded dome were intended to clash with the Historicist Ringstraße. The door's inscription reads: *Der Zeit, ihre Kunst; der Kunst, ihre Freiheit* (To the age, its art; to art, its freedom). The Secession exhibits of 1898-1903, which attracted cutting-edge artists, were led by Gustav Klimt, whose painting *Nuda Veritas* (Naked Truth) became the icon of a new aesthetic ideal.

SCHLOß BELVEDERE. The landscaped gardens of **Schloß Belvedere,** IV, originally the summer residence **Prince Eugene of Savoy,** Austria's greatest military hero, lie southeast of the center. The Belvedere summer palace, initially only what is now the **Untere** (Lower) **Belvedere,** was a gift from the emperor; Eugene later added the more opulent **Obere** (Upper) **Belvedere.** The grounds of the palace, which stretch from the Schwarzenberg Palace to the Südbahnhof, contain spectacular sphinx-filled gardens and excellent museums. *(Take tram D to "Schwarzenberg," tram #71 one stop past Schwarzenbergpl., or walk from Südbahnhof.)*

SCHLOß SCHÖNBRUNN. Belvedere pales in comparison to **Schloß Schönbrunn,** XIII, the former Imperial summer residence. Tours of some of the palace's 1500 rooms reveal the elaborate taste of Maria Theresia's era. The frescoes lining the **Great Gallery** once witnessed the Congress of Vienna, which loved a good party after a long day of divvying up the continent. A six-year-old Mozart played in the **Hall of Mirrors.** The **Millions Room** wins the prize for excess, with Oriental miniatures covering its walls. Even more impressive than the palace are the classical **gardens** behind it, designed by Emperor Josef II, that are nearly four times the length of the palace. The gardens are an orchestration of various elements, ranging from a sprawling **zoo** to the massive stone **Neptunbrunnen** (Neptune fountain) and bogus **Roman ruins.** Walk past the **flower sculptures** to reach Schönbrunn's labyrinths, rose gardens, and nature preserves. *(U-4: Schönbrunn. Apartments open daily Apr.-Oct. 8:30am-5pm; Nov.-Mar. 8:30am-4:30pm. 22-room Imperial Tour 95AS, students 85AS; more worthwhile 44-room Grand Tour 125AS, 110AS. Audio guide included. Gardens open 6am-dusk; free.)*

ZENTRALFRIEDHOF. Death doesn't get any better than at the massive Zentralfriedhof (Cemetery). Graves of the famous, infamous, and unknown spread out in a grid from the church at the center. The cemetery is the place to pay respects to your favorite Viennese decomposer: **Tor II** (the second gate) leads to Beethoven, Wolf, Strauss, Schönberg, Moser, and an honorary monument to Mozart. (His true resting place is an unmarked pauper's grave in the **Cemetery of St. Mark,** III, Leberstr. 6-8.)

Tor I leads to the **Jewish Cemetery** and Arthur Schnitzler's burial plot. Many of the headstones are cracked, broken, lying prone, or neglected because the families of most of the dead are no longer in Austria. Various structures throughout this portion of the burial grounds memorialize the millions slaughtered in Nazi death camps. *(XI, Simmeringer Hauptstr. 234. Take tram #71 from Schwarzenbergpl. or tram #72 from Schlachthausg. The tram stops at each of the 3 main gates; Tor II is the main entrance. Or take S-7 to "Zentralfriedhof," which stops along the southwest wall of the cemetery. Open May-Aug. 7am-7pm; Mar.-Apr. and Sept.-Oct. 7am-6pm; Nov.-Feb. 8am-5pm. 38AS.)*

MUSEUMS

Vienna owes its selection of masterpieces to the acquisitive Habsburgs, as well as the city's crop of art schools and world-class artists. All city-run museums are free Friday mornings; check out the tourist office's free *Museums* brochure. The **Messepalast,** Museumspl. 1/5, originally the imperial barracks, opens this year as the **MuseumsQuartier** (☎523 58 81; www.mqw.at). The modern complex houses the **Leopold Museum** (which holds one of Austria's most significant collections, including a number of valuable Schieles), a **Museum of Modern Art**, and a new **Kunsthalle.**

ART MUSEUMS

Kunsthistorisches Museum (Museum of Art History; ☎52 52 40), off the Burgring. Take U-2 or U-3 to "Volkstheater." The world's 4th-largest art collection oozes with 15th- to 18th-century Venetian and Flemish paintings, including Breughels and Rembrandts, and ancient art. The lobby's Klimt mural depicts artistic progress from the classical era to the 19th century in the Historicist style he would later attack. Open Tu-Su 10am-6pm. 120AS, students 80AS. English tours in summer 11am and 3pm (30AS).

Österreichische Gallerie (Austrian Gallery), III, Prinz-Eugen-Str. 27 (☎79 55 70), in the Belvedere Palace. Walk from the Südbahnhof or take tram D, #566, 567, 666, 668, or 766 to "Prinz-Eugen-Str." 19th- to 20th-century Austrian art and famous Secessionist works by Schiele, Kokoschka, and Klimt (*The Kiss*) in the **Upper Belvedere.** The **Lower Belvedere** has the **Baroque Museum** and the **Museum of Medieval Austrian Art.** Both open Tu-Su 10am-6pm. Joint ticket 60AS, students 40AS. English tours 11am.

Museum Moderner Kunst (Museum of Modern Art; ☎317 69 00; www.MMKSLW.or.at) has two locations. **Liechtenstein Palace,** IX, Fürsteng. 1, holds work by 20th-century masters—Magritte, Picasso, Miró, Kandinsky, Pollock, Warhol, and Klee. Take tram D (dir. Nußdorf) to "Fürsteng." The **20er Haus,** III, Arsenalstr. 1, opposite the Südbahnhof, has influential 60s and 70s work and a great sculpture garden. Open Tu-W and F-Su 10am-6pm, Th 10am-8pm. Each museum 60AS, students 40AS; both 80AS, 60AS.

Österreiches Museum für Angewandte Kunst (a.k.a. MAK, Austrian Museum of Applied Art; ☎712 80 80), Stubenring 5. Take U-3 to "Stubentor." Dedicated to the beauty of design from the smooth curves of Thonet bentwood chairs to the intricate designs of Venetian glass. Open Tu-W and F-Su 10am-6pm, Th 10am-9pm. 90AS, students 45AS.

Akademie der Bildende Kunst (Academy of Fine Arts), I, Schillerpl. 3 (☎58 81 62 25), near Karlspl. Excellent collection, including Hieronymus Bosch's *Last Judgment* and works by Peter Paul Rubens. Open Tu-Su 10am-4pm. 50AS, students 20AS.

Secession Building, I, Friedrichstr. 12 (☎587 53 07), on the western side of Karlspl. Originally built to give the pioneers of modern art, including Klimt, Kokoschka, and Gauguin, space to hang artwork that didn't conform to *Künstlerhaus* standards. Substantial contemporary works are exhibited now. Klimt's 30km *Beethoven Frieze*—a visual interpretation of Beethoven's *Ninth Symphony*—is also displayed. Open Tu-W and F-Su 10am-6pm, Th 10am-8pm. 60AS, students 40AS.

Künstlerhaus, Karlspl. 5 (☎587 96 63). Once home to the Viennese artistic establishment. Now it invites temporary exhibits, usually of recent, non-European art. The theater hosts **film festivals.** Open Th 10am-9pm, F-W 10am-6pm. 90AS, students 60AS.

OTHER MUSEUMS

Museum für Völkerkunde, I, in the Neue Burg on Heldenpl. U-2 or U-3: Volkstheater. Admire Benin bronzes, West African Dan heads, and Montezuma's feathered head-dress, gathered by Habsburg agents during their travels. Art and artifacts from Africa, the Americas, the Middle East, and the Far East. Open W-M 10am-4pm. 50AS, students 30AS. Free May 16, Oct. 26, Dec. 10, and Dec. 24.

Historisches Museum der Stadt Wien (Historical Museum of the City of Vienna), IV, Karlspl. 5 (☎505 87 47), to the left of the Karlskirche. Amazing collection of historical artifacts and paintings documenting Vienna's evolution from a Roman encampment through the Turkish siege, and the subsequent 640 years of Habsburg rule. Also contains a number of Seccesionist gems by Schiele and Klimt. Open Tu-Su 9am-6pm. 50AS, students 25AS; free F 9am-noon.

Sigmund Freud Haus, IX, Bergg. 19 (☎319 15 96), near the Votivkirche. U-2: Schottentor; walk up Währingerstr. to Bergg. Freud's home from 1891 until the *Anschluß.* Lots of photos and documents, including his report cards and circumcision certificate. Open July-Sept. 9am-6pm; Oct.-June 9am-4pm. 60AS, students 40AS. Tours 75AS.

ENTERTAINMENT

MUSIC. Vienna's musical history is full of big names: Mozart, Beethoven, and Haydn created the First Viennese School; a century later, Schönberg, Webern, and Berg teamed up to form the Second Viennese School. Vienna presents performances ranging from the above-average to the sublime, with many surprisingly accessible to budget travelers. The **Staatsoper,** one of the world's top three opera houses, performs about 300 times from September through June. **Standing-room tickets** grant cheap access to world-class opera; more pricey **last-minute student tickets** go on sale 30 minutes before curtain. (Standing-room tickets 30-50AS. Arrive 2-3hr. early in high season. The standing-room line forms inside the side door on the western side of the Opera, by Operng. Formal dress unnecessary, but no shorts. Student tickets 100-150AS. Line up to the left inside the main entrance at least 1hr. before curtain; ISIC not valid, bring a university ID.) Advance tickets (120-2150AS) go on sale a week ahead at the **Bundestheaterkasse,** I, Hanuschg. 3, around the corner from the opera. (☎514 44 29 60. Open M-F 8am-6pm, Sa-Su 9am-noon. ISIC not valid for student discounts.) The world-famous **Wiener Philharmoniker** (Vienna Philharmonic Orchestra) has been directed by the world's finest conductors, including Gustav Mahler and Leonard Bernstein. Performances take place in the **Musikverein,** I, Dumbastr. 3, on the northeast side of Karlspl. (☎505 81 90. Box office open Sept.-June M-F 9am-7:30pm, Sa 9am-5pm. Standing-room tickets available; prices vary.) The prepubescent prodigies of the 500-year-old **Vienna Boys' Choir** perform Sundays at 9:15am (mid-Sept. to June) in the **Burgkapelle** (Royal Chapel) of the Hofburg. Standing room is free, but arrive before 8am.

FESTIVALS. Vienna hosts an array of annual festivals, mostly musical; check the tourist office's monthly calendar. The **Vienna Festival** has a diverse program of exhibitions, plays, and concerts. (☎589 22 22; fax 589 22 49; www.festwochen.or.at. Mid-May to mid-June.) The Staatsoper and Volkstheater host the annual **Jazzfest Wien** (☎503 56 47; www.jazzfestwien.at) during the first weeks of July. Don't miss the **Rathausplatz Music Film Festival** in July and August, in the Rathauspl. at dusk, during which taped operas, ballets, and concerts enrapture audiences.

NIGHTLIFE

Vienna is a great place to party, whether you're looking for a quiet evening with a glass of wine or a wild night in a disco full of black-clad Euro musclemen and drag queens. U-1 or U-4: Schwedenplatz is just blocks from the **Bermuda Dreieck** (Triangle), so dubbed both for the three-block area it covers and for the tipsy revelers who lose their way here and never make it home. If your vision isn't foggy yet, head down **Rotenturmstr.** toward the Stephansdom, or check out the cellar bars of smooth, dark **Bäckerstr.** Just outside the Ring, the streets off **Burgg.** and **Stiftg.** in the seventh district and the university quarter (eighth and ninth districts) can be good places of refuge when the summer crowd in the Triangle feels too pubescent or touristy. As usual, the best nights are Friday and Saturday, beginning around 1am. For the scoop on raves, concerts, and parties, grab the fliers at swanky cafes around town or pick up a copy of the indispensable *Falter* (28AS) for listings of everything from opera and theater to punk concerts to the gay and lesbian scene.

U-4, XII, Schönbrunnerstr. 222. U-4: Meidling Hauptstr. Two dance areas, multiple bars, and rotating theme nights. Th Gay Heaven Night. Cover 100AS. Open daily 11pm-5am.

Flex Halle, I, Donaulände/Augartenbrücke, near the Schottenring U-Bahn station. Small club with bands and chemically enhanced dancing. Cover 70-150AS. Open 8pm-4am.

Cato, I, Tiefer Graben 19. U-3: Herreng.; walk down to Strauchg., turn right, and continue to Tiefer Graben. Laid-back, super-comfortable bar—enjoy the music, Art-Deco decor, and delicious champagne cocktails. Open Su-Th 6pm-2am, F-Sa 6pm-4am.

Santo Spirito Bar, I, Kumpfg. 7. From Stephanspl., walk down Singerstr. and turn left onto Kumpfg. Pays homage to conductors. Open 6pm until people leave. Closed in July.

Volksgarten Disco, I, Burgring 1. U-2 or U-3: Volkstheater. A "park club," where hip-hop, soul, funk, and house converge with nature. Cover 80-180AS. Open Th-Su 10pm-5am.

Chelsea, VIII, Lerchenfeldergürtel under the U-Bahn between Thaliastr. and Josefstädterstr. Vienna's haven for live underground music. Cover 60-200AS. Open daily 7pm-4am.

Objektiv, VII, Kirchbergg. 26. U-2 or U-3: Volkstheater; walk two blocks down Burgg. and turn right on Kirchbergg. Decorated with stoves and sewing machines. Lively local crowd and cheap drinks. Happy hour daily 11pm-1am. Open M-Sa 6pm-2am, Su 6pm-1am.

Why Not, I, Tiefer Graben 22 (☎535 11 58). Relaxed gay and lesbian bar/disco with a chill chatting venue and a hip-hop-happening subterranean black-box dance floor. Sa drink specials (43AS). Cover 100AS. Open F-Sa 10pm-4am, Su 9pm-2am.

EXCURSION FROM VIENNA: MELK

The enormous yellow mass of Melk's **monastery** floats over dark blue Danube waters and stucco houses of the village below in one of Austria's most surreal vistas. The monastery, a renowned ecclesiastical force in the medieval world for its famed library and learned monks, still reports directly to the Pope. Visitors can tour the secular wing, full of informative exhibits and Baroque optical tricks. The grand church features the jeweled **Melker Kreuz** (Melk Cross). (☎523 12 52. Open daily Apr. 15-Nov. 15 9am-5pm, Nov. 16-Apr.14 9am-6pm. 100AS, students 40AS, tour 30AS. English tour 3pm 30AS. English audio guide 40AS.) **Trains** head to Vienna's Westbahnhof (1½hr., 156AS). To reach the **tourist office,** Babenbergstr. 1 (☎523 07 32), walk down Bahnhofstr. and Bahng.; turn right at Rathauspl. and stay to your right until Abbe-Stadler-G. **Postal code:** A-3390. ☎**02752.**

SOUTHERN AUSTRIA

GRAZ ☎0316

Despite its dignified medieval and Baroque past, Graz (pop. 240,000), Austria's second-largest city, remains deliciously tourist-free. The **Altstadt** packs classical arches and domes into its twisting streets; **Sporgaße** winds past cafes and street musicians. From the tourist office, walk left up Herreng./Sackstr. to Schloßbergpl. and climb the **Schloßstiege,** zigzagging up the stone steps built by Russian prisoners during WWI, to the top of the manicured greenery of the **Schloßberg.** The **Landhaus,** which houses the tourist office, is a sight in itself, remodeled in 1557 in masterful Lombard style. The **Landeszeughaus** (Provincial Arsenal), Herreng. 16, details the history of the arsenal and has enough spears, muskets, and armor to outfit 28,000 burly mercenaries. (Open Apr.-Oct. M-F 9am-5pm, Sa-Su 9am-1pm. 70AS, students 50AS.) The solemn 17th-century Habsburg **Mausoleum,** on Burgg., by the cathedral, is one of the finest examples of Austrian Mannerism. (Open M-Sa 10am-noon and 1:30-3:30pm. 10AS.) Down the street, Graz's **Opernhaus,** at Opernring and Burgg., sells standing-room opera tickets an hour before curtain. In 2001, *Evita* will grace the stage. (☎80 08. 360-1490AS; student rush 150AS; standing-room from 45AS.)

Trains (☎17 17) run frequently from the center of Europapl. across the river to: Vienna (3¾hr., 330AS); Salzburg (4¼hr., 430AS); Innsbruck (6¼hr., 560AS); and Munich (6¼hr., 720AS). Go down Annenstr. and cross the Hauptbrücke (bridge) to reach the central Hauptpl. Turn right on Herreng. to get to the **tourist office** at #16 in the Landhaus, which lists *Privatzimmer* from 150-300AS. (☎807 50; fax 807 55 15; www.graztourismus.at. Open in summer M-F 9am-7pm, Sa 9am-6pm, Su 10am-3pm; off season M-F 9am-6pm, Sa 9am-3pm, Su 10am-3pm. Tours 2½hr., daily June-Sept. 2:30pm, Oct.-May Sa only; 75AS.) From the station head right on Eggenberger Gürtel, turn left at Josef-Huber-Gasse, and take the first right to reach the **Jugendgästehaus Graz (HI),** Idlhofg. 74. (☎71 48 76; fax 71 48 76 88. Breakfast included. Laundry. Internet. Reception 7am-11pm. Dorms 220AS; singles 320AS; doubles 540AS; overflow mattresses 155AS.) On the way you'll pass the **Hotel Strasser,** Eggenberger Gürtel 11, five minutes from the station on the left. (☎71 39 77; fax 71 68 56. Breakfast included. Singles 360-480AS; doubles 580-660AS; triples 840AS; quads 1000AS.) Cheap student hangouts line **Zinzendorfg.** by the university. The hub of after hours activity is the so-called **Bermuda Triangle,** an area of the old city behind Hauptpl., bordered by Mehlpl., Färberg., and Prokopiag. **Postal code:** A-8010.

SALZBURG ☎0662

At no point in Salzburg will you see children running through the city singing about a "needle pulling thread," but you may see hordes of tourists doing just that—perhaps slightly less gracefully. More than a movie set, wedged between mountains and dotted with church spires, medieval turrets, and splendid palaces, Salzburg offers spectacular sights and the rich musical culture that once nurtured Mozart.

GETTING THERE AND GETTING AROUND

Trains: Hauptbahnhof, Südtirolerpl. (☎017 17). Frequent trains to: **Munich** (2hr., 316AS); **Innsbruck** (2hr., 370AS); **Vienna** (3½hr., 430AS); **Graz** (4½hr., 430AS); **Zurich** (6hr., 888AS); **Venice** (6hr., 560AS); **Budapest** (6½hr., 750AS); and **Prague** (7hr., 860AS; via Linz). Ticket office open 24hr. **Luggage storage:** Lockers 30-50AS per 2 days; luggage check 30AS per piece per day. Open 6am-10pm.

Public Transportation: Lokalbahnhof (☎87 21 45), by the train station. Cheap tickets are available from *Tabaks* (single ride 20AS, day pass 40AS); purchase 5 single-ride tickets from vending machines at bus stops for 75AS or buy single tickets on the bus. Punch your ticket when you board or face a 500AS fine. Bus service ends at 11:30pm.

Bike Rental: Climb every mountain and ford every stream with a bicycle from the train station, counter #3 (☎88 87 31 63). 150AS per day, 90AS with same-day train ticket.

Hitchhiking: Hitchers headed to Innsbruck, Munich, or most of Italy allegedly take bus #77 to the German border; for Vienna or Venice, they take bus #29 (dir. Forellenwegsiedlung) or bus #15 (dir. Bergheim) to Autobahn entrances at "Schmiedlingerstr." or "Grüner Wald," respectively. *Let's Go* does not recommend hitchhiking.

ORIENTATION AND PRACTICAL INFORMATION

Just across from the German border, Salzburg straddles the **Salzach River.** The **Altstadt** (old city) and the heavily touristed pedestrian district share the west bank; the **Neustadt** (new city), with the central **Mirabellplatz** is on the east. Head left from the Hauptbahnhof, and follow Rainerstr. under the tunnel to Mirabellpl. (15min.).

Tourist Office, Mozartpl. 5 (☎888 98 73 30; fax 889 87 342; www.salzburginfo.or.at), in the Altstadt. From the train station, take bus #5, 6, 51, 55 to "Mozartsteg." Or, turn left on Rainerstr., go to the end, cross Staatsbrücke, then continue upstream along the west bank. Updates travelers on hostel vacancies and sells the **Salzburg Card,** good for admission to all museums and sights as well as unlimited public transport (24hr. 225AS, 48hr. 300AS, 72hr. 390AS). The free hotel maps are exactly the same as the 10AS city map. Open July-Aug. 8:30am-8pm; Sept.-June 9am-6pm. **Branch** at platform #2a of the train station. Open M-Sa 9:15am-9pm.

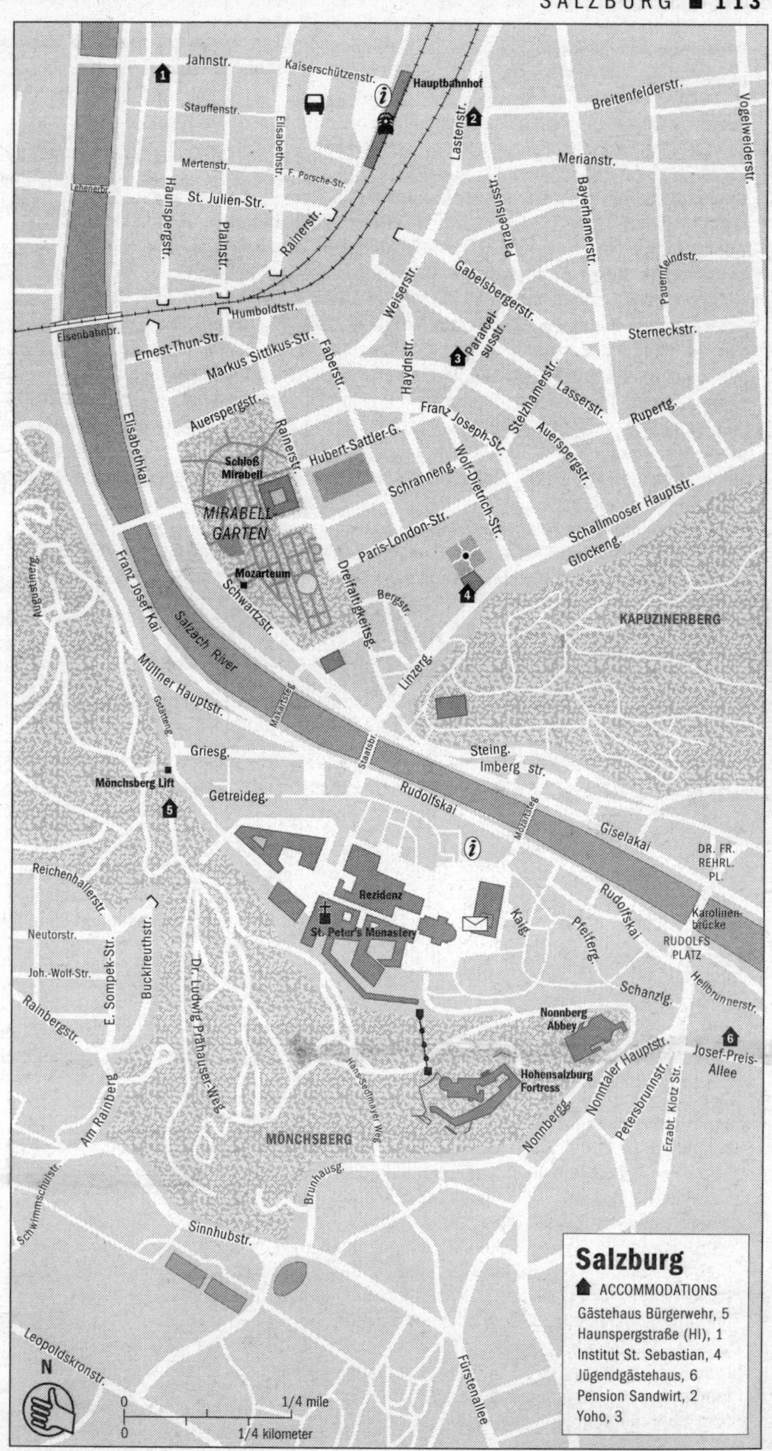
Salzburg
ACCOMMODATIONS
Gästehaus Bürgerwehr, 5
Haunspergstraße (HI), 1
Institut St. Sebastian, 4
Jügendgästehaus, 6
Pension Sandwirt, 2
Yoho, 3
Hauptbahnhof
Schloß Mirabell
MIRABELL-GARTEN
Mozarteum
KAPUZINERBERG
Mönchsberg Lift
Rezidenz
St. Peter's Monastery
Nonnberg Abbey
Hohensalzburg Fortress
MÖNCHSBERG
Salzach River
1/4 mile
1/4 kilometer

Consulates: South Africa, Buchenweg 14 (☎/fax 62 20 35). Open M-F 8am-1pm and 2-5pm. **UK,** Alter Markt 4 (☎84 81 33; fax 84 55 63). Open M-F 9am-noon. **US,** Alter Markt 1/3 (☎84 87 76; fax 84 97 77), in the Altstadt. Open M, W, and F 9am-noon.

Currency Exchange: Most banks open M-F 8am-12:30pm and 2-4:30pm. **Rieger Bank,** at Alter Markt and Getreideg. Open July-Aug. M-F 9am-7:30pm, Sa 9am-6pm, Su 10am-5pm; Sept.-June M-F 9am-6pm, Sa 9am-3pm, Su 10am-5pm.

Gay and Lesbian Services: Frauenkulturzentrum (Women's Center), Elisabethstr. 11 (☎87 16 39). Open M 10am-12:30pm. **Homosexual Initiative of Salzburg** (HOSI), Müllner Hauptstr. 11 (☎43 59 27). Cafe-bar open F from 9pm and Sa from 8pm.

Laundromat: Norge Exquisit Textil Reinigung, Paris-Lodronstr. 16 (☎87 63 81), at Wolf-Dietrich-Str. Wash and dry 82AS, soap 28AS. Open M-F 7:30am-4pm, Sa 8-10am.

Emergencies: Police: ☎133. Headquarters at Alpenstr. 90 (☎63 83). **Ambulance:** ☎144. **Fire:** ☎122.

Pharmacies: Elisabeth-Apotheke, Elisabethstr. 1 (☎87 14 84), near the train station. Pharmacies in the city center are open M-F 8am-6pm, Sa 8am-noon. There are always 3 pharmacies open for emergencies; check the list on the door of any closed pharmacy.

Medical Assistance: Hospital, Dr. Franz-Rebirl-Pl. 5 (☎658 00).

Internet Access: Cybercafé, Gstätteng. 29 (☎84 26 16 22). 80AS per hr. Open W-Th 2-11pm, F-Su 2pm-1am.

Post Office: Mail your brown paper packages tied up with strings or exchange money at the Hauptbahnhof (☎889 70). Open 6am-11pm. Address mail to be held: *Postlagernde Briefe* für First name SURNAME, Bahnhofspostamt, **A-5020** Salzburg, Austria.

ACCOMMODATIONS AND CAMPING

Housing in Salzburg is even more expensive than in Vienna; most affordable options lie on the edge of town. Ask for the tourist office's list of **private rooms** or the *Hotel Plan* (with hostel info). From mid-May to mid-September, hostels fill by mid-afternoon; call ahead. Also reserve ahead during the *Festspiele.*

HOSTELS, DORMS, AND CAMPING

Gästehaus Bürgerwehr, Mönchsberg 19c (☎84 17 29). Take bus #1 (dir. Maxglan) to "Mönchsberglift," walk through the stone arch on the left, and take the Mönchsberglift (elevator; runs 9am-11pm, 27AS round-trip). Turn right from the summit, climb the steps, and follow signs for "Gästehaus Naturfreundehaus" for a princely view on a pauper's budget. Breakfast 30AS. Showers 10AS per 4min. Sheets 20AS. Reception 8am-9pm. Curfew 1am. Reserve ahead. Open May to mid-Sept. 120AS.

International Youth Hotel (YoHo), Paracelsusstr. 9 (☎87 96 49), off Franz-Josef-Str. Head left from the train station, turn left on Gabelsbergerstr. through the tunnel, and turn right on Paracelsusstr. (7min.). Showers 10AS for 6min. Lockers 10AS. Reception 8am-noon. Theoretical curfew 1am. Dorms 150-200AS; doubles 400AS; quads 680AS.

Institut St. Sebastian, Linzerg. 41 (☎87 13 86; fax 87 13 86 85). From the station, take bus #1, 5, 6, 51, or 55 to Mirabellpl. Continue until Bergstr. Turn left, then left again at the end on Linzerg., and head through the arch on the left before the church. Kitchen. Breakfast included. Laundry 40AS. Reception in summer 7:30am-noon and 1-10pm, in winter 8am-noon and 4-9pm. Dorms (Oct.-June only) 180AS, with sheets 210AS; singles 330-390AS; doubles 500-680AS; triples 870AS; quads 1000-1080AS.

Eduard-Heinrich-Haus (HI), Eduard-Heinrich-Str. 2 (☎62 59 76). Bus #51 (dir. Salzburg-Süd) to "Polizeidirektion," continue down Billrothstr., turn left on the Robert-Stolz-Promenade footpath, take the 1st right, and it's on the left. Kitchen, laundry, and small gym. Breakfast included. Reception 7-9am and 5-11pm. Lockout 9am-5pm. Curfew 11pm-midnight. 186AS; nonmembers 226AS.

Camping Stadtblick, Rauchenbichlerstr. 21 (☎45 06 52). By car, take exit "Salzburg-Nord" off A1. Take bus #51 to "Itzling-Pflanzmann," walk up Rauchenbichlerstr. over the footbridge, and go right along the path. Laundry. Open Mar. 20-Oct. 31. 65AS per person; 20AS per tent; 4-person mobile home with fridge and stove 100AS per person.

PRIVATZIMMER AND PENSIONS

Privatzimmer on **Kasern Berg** are outside Salzburg, so the tourist office can't officially recommend them. All northbound regional trains run to Kasern Berg (4min., every 30min. 6:17am-11:17pm, 20AS; Eurail valid). Get off at "Salzburg-Maria Plain" and walk uphill. Traditional rooms await guests of **Germana Kapeller,** at Kasem Berg 64. (☎45 66 71. Breakfast included. Doubles 400AS; triples 510-600AS.) **Haus Christine,** Panoramaweg 3 (☎/fax 45 67 73), offers spacious rooms set back 16m from Kasem Berg on a gravel road. Next door, **Haus Matilda Lindner** (☎/fax 45 66 81) is run by Christine's sister. (For both call for pickup from the station. 180-200AS.)

FOOD

Beer gardens and **Konditoreien** (pastry shops) invite outdoor meals. The local specialty is *Salzburger Nockerl,* a large soufflé of egg whites, sugar, and raspberry filling baked into three mounds representing the three hills of Salzburg. World-famous **Mozartkugeln** ("Mozart balls") are hazelnuts covered with marzipan and nougat dipped in chocolate. Escape the tourist throng with a tasty *Menü* at **Restaurant Zur Bürgerwehr-Einkehr,** by the Gästehaus Bügerwehr. (Open Apr.-Oct. Sa-Th 11:30am-8:45pm.) **Café im Künstlerhaus,** Helbrunnerstr. 3, is a low-key cafe. (Local bands play Tu and Th. Sa lesbian night. Open M-Sa 11am-11pm.) The culturally schizophrenic **Shakespeare** serves everything from *Wienerschnitzel* to wonton soup. (Open M-F 11:30am-2:30pm and 6pm-midnight, Sa 6pm-midnight, Su open from 11am.) Supermarkets line the Mirabellpl. side of the river. Look for **SPAR;** the giant **EuroSpar** sprawls next to the train station and bus terminal.

SIGHTS

THE NEUSTADT

SCHLOß MIRABELL AND MIRABELLGARTEN. The **Schloß Mirabell** was built by Archbishop Wolf Dietrich, who, despite a vow of celibacy needed to house his mistress and their 10 children. Today it hosts the city government. *(Mirabellpl. Open M-F 7am-4pm.)* Behind the palace, the **Mirabellgarten** boasts extravagant flower beds and groomed shrubs. Maria von Trapp and clan once stopped here for a rendition of "Do-Re-Mi." From the garden, look for the moss-covered shack called the **Zauberflötenhäuschen,** where Mozart allegedly composed *The Magic Flute* in five months.

MOZARTS WOHNHAUS. Down the street from the Mozarteum stands the composer's home from 1773 to 1780. The house reopened on the composer's 240th birthday (January 27, 1996) following post-WWII renovations, with expanded displays and audio samples. *(Makartpl. 8. ☎88 34 54 40. Open daily 10am-5:30pm. 65AS.)*

KAPUZINERKLOSTER AND SEBASTIANSKIRCHE. At the crest of the **Kapuzinerberg,** to the south of the Neustadt, stands the simple 16th-century **Kapuzinerkloster** (Capuchin Monastery), built by Wolf Dietrich. *(From the Mirabellgarten or Mozarts Wohnhaus, follow Dreifaltigkeitsg. south to its intersection with Linzerg., head under the stone arch on the right side of Linzerg. 14, and follow the tiny stone staircase up.)* The graveyard in the nearby **Sebastianskirche** has Wolf Dietrich's gaudy mausoleum and the tombs of Mozart's wife and father. *(Lizerg. 41. Open Apr.-Oct. 9am-7pm, Nov.-Mar. 9am-4pm.)*

THE ALTSTADT

Winding pathways sit on the other side of the Salzach. The **Getreidegaße,** one of Salzburg's best-preserved streets, has wrought-iron signs from the Middle Ages.

MOZARTS GEBURTSHAUS AND UNIVERSITÄTSKIRCHE. Mozart's **birthplace** has an impressive collection of his belongings and a supposed lock of his hair. *(Getreideg. 9. Open July-Aug. 9am-6:30pm; Sept.-June 9am-5:30pm. 70AS, students 55AS.)* The **Universitätskirche**, among Europe's largest Baroque chapels, is directly behind the house. Its dome stands over the daily farmer's market in **Universitätspl.**

TOSCANINIHOF TO THE DOM. Steps lead from **Toscaninihof,** the courtyard of **St. Peter's Monastery,** up the Mönchseberg cliffs. **Stiftskirche St. Peter,** a Romanesque basilica in the 1100s, was remodeled in Rococo style in the 18th century. *(Open daily 9am-12:15pm and 2:30-6:30pm.)* Through the arch and right of the church is the **Petersfriedhof,** a cemetery from the 1600s that served as the model for the one where Rolf blew the whistle on the von Trapps. *(Open daily Apr.-Sept. 6:30am-7pm; Oct.-Mar. 6:30am-6pm.)* At the end of the cemetery against the mountains are the **Katakomben** (catacombs), cave-like rooms where Christians allegedly worshipped in secret as early as AD 250. *(Open in summer Tu-Su 10:30am-4pm; in winter W-Su 10:30am-3:30pm. 12AS, students 8AS.)* The exit at the other end from the Stiftskirche leads into Kapitelpl., bordered by the huge **Dom** (cathedral), where Mozart was christened in 1756 and later worked as *Konzertmeister* and court organist.

RESIDENZ. Visit the stunning Baroque **Prunkräume** (state rooms), which house a three-dimensional ceiling fresco by Rottmayr. A **gallery** exhibits 16th- to 19th-century art. *(Residenzpl. 1. Open daily 9am-5pm. 91AS, students 70AS. Audio guide included. Gallery open Apr.-Sept. 10am-5pm; Oct.-Mar. Su-Tu and Th-Sa 10am-5pm. 50AS, students 40AS.)*

HOHENSALZBURG FORTRESS. Built between 1077 and 1681 by the ruling archbishops, the **Festung Hohensalzburg** looms from atop Mönchsberg as Europe's largest preserved castle. Walk through torture chambers, Gothic state rooms, and an impregnable watchtower. *(Take the trail or the Festungsbahn funicular up to the fortress from the Festungsg. Funicular runs every 10min. 9am-9pm; Oct.-Apr. 9am-5pm. Ascent 66AS, 76AS round-trip; includes entrance to fortress.)* The **Burg Museum** displays medieval torture instruments. *(Fortress open July-Oct. 8:30am-7pm; Nov.-Mar. 9am-5pm; Apr.-June 9am-6pm. 42AS. Museum open daily 9am-5pm. Joint ticket including castle tour, museum, and fortress 84AS.)* Down the hill and to the right of the fortress, **Nonnberg Abbey** (where Maria von Trapp lived) remains a private monastic complex.

MUSICAL ENTERTAINMENT

Ever since Max Reinhardt, Richard Strauss, and Hugo von Hofmannsthal founded the **Salzburger Festspiele** (Festivals) in 1920, performances have overrun Salzburg from late July to the end of August. Festival programs are available at any tourist office for 10AS. For tickets, contact the **Festspiele Kartenbüro** (☎804 55 79; fax 804 57 60; www.salzburgfestival.at), by early January. Under-26ers can try for subscription tickets (2-4 tickets for 200-300AS each); write eight months ahead to *Direktion der Salzburger Festspiele*, attn: Ulrich Hauschild, Hofstallg. 1, A-5020 Salzburg. Or, try the **Fest zur Eröffungsfest** (Opening Day Festival), when events are either cheap or free and admission is on a first-come, first-served basis.

Many other concerts and events occur across the city. Students of the **Mozarteum** (music conservatory) perform concerts on a rotating schedule (available at the tourist office). For tickets, contact **Kartenbüro Mozarteum,** Postfach 156, Theaterg. 2. (☎87 31 54; fax 87 29 96. Open M-Th 9am-2pm, F 9am-4pm.) For a lot more kitsch, you can enjoy knicker-clad musicians with powdered hair performing **Mozart Serenaden** in the Gothic Hall on Burgerspitalg. 2. (Daily in summer 8:30pm, off season 7:30pm; 200-420AS.) For info and tickets, contact **Konzertdirektion Nerat,** A-5020 Salzburg, Lieferinger Hauptstr. 136 (☎43 68 70; fax 43 69 70). In July and August, **outdoor opera** rings out from the Mirabellgarten's historical hedge-theater (330-560AS, students 190AS). Tickets are available from the **box office** in Schloß Mirabell. (☎84 85 86; fax 84 47 47. Open M-F 9am-5:30pm.) The Mirabellgarten hosts various **outdoor performances** throughout the summer. The tourist office has info, but strolling through in the evening might be just as effective in seeing what's going on.

NIGHTLIFE

Beer gardens *(Biergärten)* cluster in the city center by the Salzach River. Altstadt nightclubs (especially along Gstätteng. and near Chiemseeg.) attract younger types and tourists; the other side of the river has a more mature atmosphere. From the

Altstadt, follow the footpath from Hanuschpl. downstream, go left up the stairs past the Riverside Café, cross Müllner Hauptstr., walk uphill, and take the first left to the legendary **Augustiner Bräu,** Augustinerg. 4, where great beer brewed by the Müllner Kloster is poured into massive steins from even more massive wooden kegs. (☎43 12 46. Beer 1L 68AS; tip the tap-*meister* 4AS. Open M-F 3-11pm, Sa-Su 2:30-11pm.) Get cozy with a drink at **Vis à Vis,** Rudolfskai 24. (Open Su-Th 8am-4pm, F-Sa 8pm-5am.) **Zweistein,** Giselakai 9, rocks at night. (Open M-W 6pm-4am, Th-F 6pm-5am, Sa 2pm-5am, Su 2pm-4am.) **Pub Passage,** Rudolfskai 22-26, under the Radisson Hotel by the Mozartsteg bridge, is a promenade of bars, each with its own gimmick. **Schwarze Katze,** Frudiele, Auerspergstr. 45, opens for night owls. (Tu-Sa 4am-noon.)

EXCURSIONS FROM SALZBURG

LUSTSCHLOß HELLBRUNN AND UNTERSBERG PEAK. To the south lies **Lustschloß Hellbrunn,** a pleasure dome for Wolf Dietrich's nephew, the Archbishop Markus Sittikus. The estate includes a palace, fish ponds, hedge gardens, the "I-Am-Sixteen-Going-On-Seventeen" gazebo, and the **Wasserspiele** (water games). Archbishop Markus amused himself with elaborate water-powered figurines and booby-traps that could spout water on his drunken guests. (☎820 00 30. Open July-Aug. 9am-10pm; May-June and Sept. 9am-5:30pm; Apr. and Oct. 9am-4:30pm. Compulsory tours 40AS, students 30AS. Compulsory *Wasserspiele* tour 80AS, 65AS. Both 100AS, 80AS.) Take **bus** #55 (dir. Anif) from Salzburg's train station, Mirabellpl., or Mozartsteg to "Hellbrunn," or bike down Hellbrunner Allee (40min.).

Bus #55 continues to the luscious **Untersberg peak,** where Charlemagne supposedly rests underground, prepared to return and reign over Europe once again when needed. Dozens of **hikes** carve through color-soaked meadows, with mountains hovering in the distance. The **Eishöhlen** (ice caves) are only a 1½-hour climb from the peak. A **cable car** glides over Salzburg to the summit. (Runs July-Sept. Su-Tu and Th-Sa 8:30am-5:30pm, W 8:30am-8pm; Mar.-June and Oct. 9am-5pm; Dec.-Feb. 10am-4pm. Ascent 130AS, descent 110AS, 215AS round-trip.) ☎**0662.**

THE SALZKAMMERGUT. Check out salt mines, ice caves, and **The Treehouse** hostel in the Salzkammergut, accessible by train or bus from Salzburg (see below).

HOHE TAUERN NATIONAL PARK. Conquer Europe's largest national park, boasting the **Krimml Waterfalls** and the spectacular **Großglocknerstraße** (see p. 118).

WESTERN AUSTRIA

THE SALZKAMMERGUT

The *Salzkammergut* was named for the salt mines that once underwrote Salzburg's architectural treasures; now, the white gold of the smooth lakes and furrowed mountains is no longer salt, but sunshine on sparkling water and snow. The **Salzkammergut Card** (65AS at tourist offices) grants 25% off on most attractions. The area is easily navigable, with 2000km of paths and 12 cable cars and chairlifts. **Buses** (☎167 from Salzburg) are the way to travel into and throughout the region.

HALLSTATT ☎06134

Beautiful but tiny Hallstatt (pop. 1400) teeters on the banks of the **Hallstättersee**, surrounded by the sheer Dachstein mountains. In the 19th century, it was the site of an immense Iron Age archaeological find; the **Prähistorisches Museum,** across from the tourist office, as well as the **Heimatmuseum** around the corner, exhibit some of the treasures. (Both open daily Apr. and Oct. 10am-4pm; May-Sept. 10am-6pm. Joint ticket 50AS, students 25AS.) The fascinating charnel house next to St. Michael's Chapel at the **Pfarrkirche** is a bizarre repository of the skeletons of villagers dating to the 16th century. (Open daily May-Sept. 10am-6pm. 10AS, students 5AS.) Tours of the 2500-year-old **Salzbergwerke,** the world's oldest saltworks, include a zip down a mining slide on a burlap sack down to an eerie lake deep inside the mountain. (Open June to mid-Sept. 9:30am-4:30pm; Apr.-May and mid-Sept. to Oct. 9:30am-3pm. 1½hr. tours in English. 140AS, students 70AS.) Climb the path near the Pfarrkirche to the top (1hr.), or follow the black signs with yellow eyes to the **Salzbergbahn** station at the south end of town. (Salzbergbahn runs daily June to mid-Sept. 9am-6pm; Apr.-May and mid-Sept. to Oct. 9am-4:30pm. 65AS, round-trip 105AS.) Pick up the tourist office guide (90AS) detailing 38 **hikes,** and a **mountain bike** map (35AS) to explore the trails leading into the Echental valley. A 1½-hour walk leads to the **Waldbachstub waterfall.** Turn right on Seestr. from the tourist office and follow the brown "Malerweg" signs, then follow the "Waldbachstrub" sign.

Buses go to Hallstatt from Salzburg (130AS). **Trains** arrive across the lake from downtown (210AS); **ferries** (25AS; last ferry 6:46pm) shuttle passengers across. The **tourist office,** Seestr. 169, finds rooms. (☎82 08; fax 83 52; www.tiscover.com/hallstatt. Open July-Aug. M-F 9am-5pm, Sa 10am-2pm; Sept.-June M-F 9am-noon and 2-5pm.) To reach the **Gästehaus Zur Mühle,** Kirchenweg 36, from the tourist office, walk uphill toward the Heimatmuseum, then swing right at the end of the Platz; it's through the little tunnel on the left, by the waterfall. (☎83 18. Showers and locker included with 200AS deposit. Sheets 35AS. Reception 8am-2pm and 4-10pm. 115AS.) **Frühstückspension Sarstein,** Gosaumühlstr. 83, offers vistas of the lake and village. From the tourist office, walk left on Seestr. for 10 minutes; it will be on the right. (☎82 17. Breakfast included. Showers 10AS per 10min. 200-270AS; add 20AS for one-night stay.) **Camping Klausner-Höll,** Lahnstr. 6, is three blocks past the Seestr. bus stop. (☎83 22. Breakfast 65-110AS. Showers included. Laundry 100AS. Gate closed daily noon-2:30pm and 10pm-7am. Open mid-Apr. to mid-Oct. 65AS per person; 45AS per tent; 35AS per car.) **Konsum supermarket** is across from the main bus stop. (Open M-F 7:30am-noon and 3-6pm, Sa 7:30am-noon.) **Postal code:** A-4830.

EXCURSION FROM HALLSTATT: DACHSTEIN ICE CAVES. In **Obertraun,** eerie ice caves testify to the geological hyperactivity that forged the area's natural beauty. (☎84 00. Open daily May to mid-Oct. 9am-5pm. Either cave 90AS, together 150AS; children 45AS, 75AS.) Take the **bus** (25AS) from Seestr. to the Dachstein **cable car** station, then ride 1350m up to "Schönbergalm" (round-trip 170AS.)

GRÜNAU ☎07616

Nestled in the **Totes Gebirge** (Dead Mountains) is the backpacker's dream resort, **The Treehouse,** Schindlbachstr. 525. Settle into your room (with private shower and goosedown blankets), and take advantage of the many amenities. Adventures include **paragliding** (900AS), **canyoning** (650AS), **rafting** (590AS), **bungee jumping** (990AS; Sa-Su only), and **horseback riding** (100AS per hr.). Rent a **mountain bike** (70AS per day) or ask to be dropped off at a nearby mountain or lake with a map so you can **hike** home. For winter visits, the **ski lift** is five minutes away (200AS); borrow snow gear for free and rent skis for 120AS or a snowboard for 150AS. (☎84 99; email treehousehotel@hotmail.com; www.hostels.com/treehouse. Breakfast included. Dorms 180AS; doubles 220AS per person; triples 210AS; quads 190AS. V, MC, AmEx.) **Regional trains** come from Wels, on the Vienna-Salzburg rail line (1hr., every 2hr., 80AS). Call ahead for pick-up from the station.

HOHE TAUERN NATIONAL PARK

Europe's largest national park, it encompasses 246 glaciers and 304 mountains over 3000m. The **Glocknergruppe,** in the heart of the park, has Austria's highest peak, the **Großglockner** (3798m). The main attractions are the **Krimml Waterfalls** and the spectacular mountain road **Großglocknerstraße** (a.k.a. Bundesstr. 107).

GETTING THERE AND GETTING AROUND. Two **train** lines service towns near the park: a rail line from **Zell am See** runs west along the northern border of the park, terminating in **Krimml** (1¾hr., 100AS); another runs from **Salzburg** to **Bad-**

gastein in the southwest corner of the park (1½hr., every 2hr. 7:14am-8:15pm, 170AS). **Buses** connect to and traverse the park, terminating in the center at **Franz-Josefs-Höhe;** from Zell am See (2hr., June 19-Oct. 10 1-2 per day, 145AS). Check the brochure *Der BundesBus ist Wanderfreundlich* (available at bus stations in Zell am See and tourist offices). The spectacular **Großglocknerstraße,** one of the world's most beautiful highways, winds 50km through silent Alpine valleys, meadows of wildflowers, tumbling waterfalls, and huge glaciers between Zell am See and Lienz (about 5hr.). You can traverse the Großglocknerstr. in a **tour bus** or **rental car,** but the public **bus** service is good. Heavy snow forces the Großglocknerstr. to close from October to April. For road conditions, call ☎22 12. ☎**04824.**

ZELL AM SEE ☎06542

Conquer the gorgeous peaks surrounding Zell am See (TSELL-am-ZAY) on one of the five **cable cars.** The BundesBus (dir. Schmittenhöhebahn/Sonnenalmbahn Talstation) goes to the **Schmittenhöhebahn,** 2km north of town on Schmittenstr. (Runs mid-July to late Oct. every 30min. 8:30am-5pm. 185AS; round-trip 240AS.) The **Zeller Bergbahn** (780-1411m) is in town, at Schmittenstr. and Gartenstr. (Runs daily mid-June to mid-Sept. 9am-5pm. 110AS; round-trip 150AS.) The Schmittenhöhe lift has brochures on **hikes.** For more hiking info, grab a *Wanderplan.* The **Zell/Kaprun Ski Pass** covers Zell and nearby Kaprun. A free bus connects them every 10 minutes from late December to mid-April. (2-day 740-780AS, students 670-720AS.) The **Kitzsteinhorn** mountain (3203m) and its glacier in Kaprun offer **year-round skiing.** (Day pass 270AS. Equipment rental runs 255AS per day.)

Trains (☎73 21 43 57) arrive at Bahnhofstr. and Salzmannstr. from: Kitzbühel (45min., 108AS); Salzburg (1½hr., 150AS); Innsbruck (2hr., 260AS); and Vienna (5hr., 520AS). From the station, turn right and follow the "i" by the stairs on the left to reach the **tourist office,** Brucker Bundesstr. 3. (☎770; fax 720 32; email zell@gold.at. Open July to mid-Sept. and mid-Dec. to Mar. M-F 8am-6pm, Sa 8am-noon and 4-6pm, Su 10am-noon; Apr.-June and Sept. to mid-Dec. M-F 8am-noon and 2-6pm, Sa 9am-noon.) To reach the lakeside **Haus der Jugend (HI),** Seespitzstr. 13, and its large rooms with bath, exit the station toward the lake ("Zum See"), turn right, walk along the footpath, and turn left at the end on Seespitzstr. (15min.). (☎571 85; email hostel-zell-se@salzburg.co.at. Breakfast included. Reception 7-9am and 4-10pm. Check-out 9am. Lockout noon-4pm. Open Dec.-Oct. Reserve ahead. 165AS first night, 140AS thereafter.) **SPAR supermarket** is at Brucker Bundesstr. 4. (Open M-Th 8am-7pm, F 8am-7:30pm, Sa 7:30am-5pm.) **Postal code:** A-5700.

FRANZ-JOSEFS-HÖHE AND PASTERZE GLACIER. Großglocknerstr. buses from Zell am See, Lienz, and Heiligenblut terminate at **Franz-Josefs-Höhe,** a observation center above the **Pasterze glacier.** The hordes of visitors can't detract from the sight of the glacier's icy tongue extending down the valley. In good weather, you can glimpse the summit of the **Großglockner.** The **park office** in the parking area has a free mini-museum and organizes daily walks around the glacier—call for prices and times. (☎27 27. Open daily 10am-4pm.) The **Gletscherbahn funicular** runs from Franz-Josefs-Höhe down to the glacier, where you can walk 100m on its hard-packed surface. (Runs daily May 21-Oct. 10 9am-2pm. 98AS round-trip.) Take the *Panoramaweg* up the hill to the **Swarovski Observation Center,** with binoculars and telescopes for viewing the surrounding terrain; keep an eye out for marmots and other animals indigenous to the park. (Open daily 10am-4pm. Free.) ☎**04842.**

KRIMML WATERFALLS AND TOWN. A path leads from the mini mountain town of **Krimml** to the **Wasserfälle**—three roaring cascades totaling over 400m in height. **Buses** from Zell am See (1½hr., 110AS) drop you at the start of the path to the falls (get off at "Maustelle Ort"). The **Pinzgauer Lokalbahn** train arrives in town from Zell am See (1¾hr., 100AS; Swisspass and Eurail valid); catch the **bus** (20AS) across the street or walk 3km along the path to the falls. (Falls 8am-6pm 15AS; otherwise free.) **ÖAV Information** is by the ticket booth. (☎72 12. Open May-Oct. M-Sa 11am-4pm.) The **tourist office** is downhill from the "Krimml Ort" bus stop. (☎72 39. Open M-F 8am-noon and 2:30-5:30pm, Sa 9-11am). ☎**06564.**

HEILIGENBLUT. The cheapest base for exploring is Heiligenblut ("Holy Blood"). The **tourist office,** by the bus stop, has info on park transport. (☎20 01 21. Open M-F 8:30am-noon and 2:30-6pm, Sa 9am-noon and 4-6pm; July-Aug. M-F 8:30am-6pm.) Take the path from behind the bus stop parking lot to **Jugendherberge (HI),** Hof 36,. (☎/fax 22 59. Breakfast included. Reception May-Sept. 7-10am and 5-10pm. Curfew 10pm. Members only; 190AS.) **Pension Bergkristall** has rooms with balconies. (☎20 05. Breakfast included. 300AS-420AS.) **Buses** arrive from Franz-Josefs-Höhe (30min., 4 per day, 47AS) and Zell am See (2½hr., 3 per day, 145AS). ☎**04824.**

INNSBRUCK ☎0512

Innsbruck, the site of two Olympic Games, is surrounded by massive, snow-capped peaks. The Tyrolean Alps await skiers and hikers; while in town, the Altstadt's streets are peppered with fancy facades and remnants of the Habsburg Empire.

GETTING THERE AND GETTING AROUND

Trains: Hauptbahnhof, Südtirolerpl. (☎17 17). To: **Munich** (2hr., 11 per day, 350AS); **Salzburg** (3hr., 11 per day, 360AS); **Zurich** (4hr., 8 per day, 600AS); **Venice** (7hr., 5 per day, 424AS); and **Vienna** Westbahnhof (7hr., 12 per day, 660AS).

Buses: Bundesbuses (☎503 43 82) leave from the station on Sterzingerstr., next to the Hauptbahnhof, to destinations throughout Tyrol.

Public Transportation: The main bus station is in front of the Hauptbahnhof. Buy single-ride (21AS), 24hr. (35AS), or 4-ride (61AS) tickets from any driver or *Tabak* and punch them as you board (400AS fine for riding without a validated ticket). Most buses stop running around 10:30-11:30pm, but each night the *Nachtbus* heads through Marktpl. at 11:47pm and 1:17am, by Maria-Theresien-Str.

Bike and Ski Rental: Rent **bikes** at the Hauptbahnhof (☎503 53 95). 90-200AS per day. Open Apr. to early Nov. **Skischule Innsbruck,** Leopoldstr. 4 (☎58 17 42). Skis, boots, poles, and insurance 270AS.

ORIENTATION AND PRACTICAL INFORMATION

The city center lies between the **Inn River** and the train tracks. Turn right from the Hauptbahnhof on Brunecker Str., left on Museumstr., and left on Burggraben to reach the **Altstadt** and the tourist office. **Maria-Theresien-Str.,** the city's main thoroughfare, leads south from the Altstadt; Marktgraben leads west across the river to the **University district.** Most sights are near the Altstadt.

Tourist Offices: Innsbruck Information Office, Burggraben 3, 3rd fl. (☎598 50; fax 598 07; www.tiscover.com/innsbruck). Open M-F 8am-6pm, Sa 8am-noon. **Innsbruck-Information** (email ibk.ticket@netway.at) is in the same building. Open daily 9am-6pm. The **Innsbruck Card,** sold at both, allows admission to many sights and unlimited transportation (24hr. 230AS, 48hr. 300AS, 72hr. 370AS; children 50% off). **Österreichischer Alpenverein,** Wilhelm-Greil-Str. 15 (☎595 47; fax 57 55 28). Info and discounts for hikers. Membership 530AS, ages 18-25 390AS. Open M-F 9am-1pm and 2-5pm.

American Express: Brixnerstr. 3 (☎58 24 91). Open M-F 9am-noon and 1-5:30pm.

Internet Access: Internet Corner, Bruneckerstr. 12 (☎59 42 72 61), across from the train station. 1.5AS per min. Open daily 9am-11pm.

Laundromat: Bubblepoint Waschsalon, Andreas-Hofer-Str. 37, at the corner of Franz-Fischer-Str. Wash 55-120AS. Open M-F 8am-10pm, Sa-Su 8am-8pm.

Emergencies: Police: ☎133. Headquarters at Kaiserjägerstr. 8 (☎590 00). **Ambulance:** ☎144 or 142. **Fire:** ☎122. **Mountain Rescue:** ☎140.

Post Office: Maximilianstr. 2, a few blocks straight ahead from the station. Open M-F 7am-11pm, Sa 7am-9pm, Su 8am-9pm. Address mail to be held: *Postlagernde Briefe* für First Name SURNAME, Hauptpostamt, Maximilianstr. 2, **A-6020** Innsbruck, Austria.

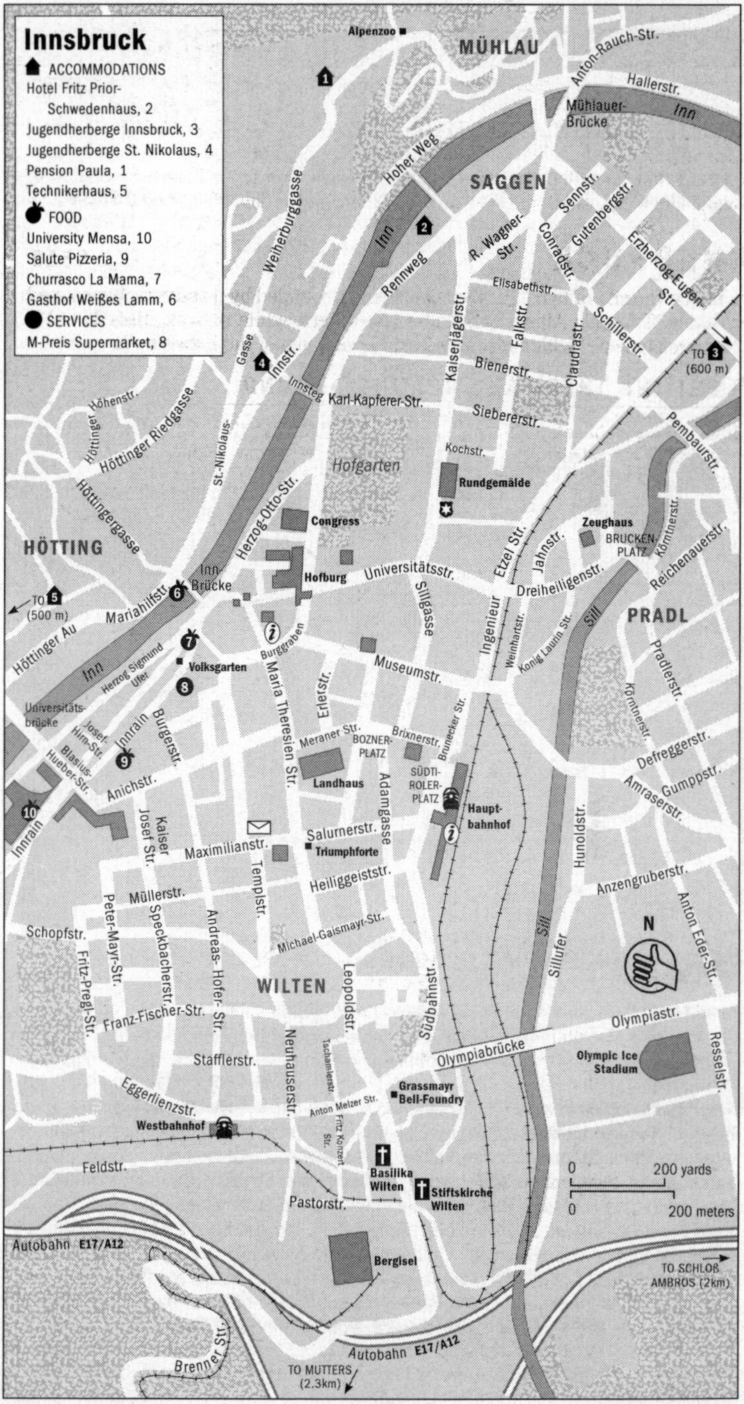

Innsbruck

ACCOMMODATIONS

Hotel Fritz Prior-Schwedenhaus, 2
Jugendherberge Innsbruck, 3
Jugendherberge St. Nikolaus, 4
Pension Paula, 1
Technikerhaus, 5

FOOD

University Mensa, 10
Salute Pizzeria, 9
Churrasco La Mama, 7
Gasthof Weißes Lamm, 6

SERVICES

M-Preis Supermarket, 8

Alpenzoo
MÜHLAU
Anton-Rauch-Str.
Hallerstr.
Inn
Mühlauer-Brücke
Hoher Weg
Weiherburggasse
SAGGEN
Sennstr.
Gutenbergstr.
Erzherzog-Eugen-Str.
R. Wagner-Str.
Conradstr.
Rennweg
Elisabethstr.
Schillerstr.
Kaiserjägerstr.
Falkstr.
Claudiastr.
TO 3 (600 m)
Gasse
Innstr.
Bienerstr.
Innsteg
Karl-Kapferer-Str.
Siebererstr.
Pembaurstr.
Höhenstr.
Höttinger
Höttinger Riedgasse
St.-Nikolaus-
Kochstr.
Hofgarten
Rundgemälde
Höttingergasse
Herzog-Otto-Str.
Congress
Zeughaus
BRUCKEN-PLATZ
Körnerstr.
Reichenauerstr.
HÖTTING
Jahnstr.
Etzel Str.
Inn-Brücke
Hofburg
Universitätsstr.
Dreiheiligenstr.
TO 5 (500 m)
Mariahilfstr.
Sillgasse
Ingenieur
Weinhartstr.
Konig Laurin Str.
Sill
PRADL
Höttinger Au
Burggraben
Herzog Sigmund Ufer
Volksgarten
Maria Theresien Str.
Museumstr.
Pradlerstr.
Universitäts-brücke
Innrain
Josef-Hirn-Str.
Burgerstr.
Erlerstr.
Meraner Str.
BOZNER-PLATZ
Brixnerstr.
Brunecker Str.
Körntnerstr.
Blasius-Hueber-Str.
Landhaus
SÜDTI-ROLER-PLATZ
Haupt-bahnhof
Defreggerstr.
Gumppstr.
Amraserstr.
Anichstr.
Kaiser Josef Str.
Adamgasse
Salurnerstr.
Maximilianstr.
Triumphforte
Heiliggeiststr.
Hunoldstr.
Anzengruberstr.
Müllerstr.
Templstr.
Peter-Mayr-Str.
Speckbacherstr.
Andreas-Hofer-Str.
Michael-Gaismayr-Str.
Schopfstr.
Fritz-Pregl-Str.
Anton Eder-Str.
N
WILTEN
Leopoldstr.
Südbahnstr.
Sillufer
Franz-Fischer-Str.
Olympiastr.
Neuhauserstr.
Olympiabrücke
Olympic Ice Stadium
Resselstr.
Stafflerstr.
Tschamlerstr.
Grassmayr Bell-Foundry
Eggerlienzstr.
Anton Melzer Str.
Westbahnhof
Fritz Konzert Str.
Feldstr.
Basilika Wilten
Stiftskirche Wilten
0 200 yards
0 200 meters
Pastorstr.
Autobahn E17/A12
Bergisel
TO SCHLOß AMBROS (2km)
Autobahn E17/A12
Brenner Str.
TO MUTTERS (2.3km)

AUSTRIA

ACCOMMODATIONS, CAMPING, AND FOOD

Hostel beds are scarce in June, when **Jugendherberge Innsbruck** and **Jugendherberge St. Niklaus** (☎28 65 15) are the only hostels open. In July and August, student dorms ease the crunch; try **Internationales Studentenhaus,** Recheng. 7 (☎50 15 92).

Haus Wolf, Dorfstr. 48 (☎54 86 73), in Mutters. Take the Stubaitalbahn tram (26AS; last tram 10:30pm) from the 3rd island in front of the Hauptbahnhof to "Birchfeld," and continue in the same direction down Dorfstr. (30min.). Let proprietor Titti Wolf spoil you with attention and gigantic breakfasts. Singles 170AS; doubles 340AS; triples 510AS.

Pension Paula, Weiherburgg. 15 (☎29 22 62; fax 29 30 17; email pensionpaula@telering.at). Take bus K to "St. Nikolaus," then walk uphill. Bright rooms with antique furniture. Breakfast included. Singles 340-440AS; doubles 560-680AS; triples 750-920AS.

Hostel Fritz Prior-Schwedenhaus (HI), Rennweg 17b (☎58 58 14; fax 585 81 44; email youth.hostel@tirol.at). Follow directions to the Altstadt, but go right on Burggraben, which becomes Rennweg. Breakfast 45AS. Sheets 20AS. Reception 7-9am and 5-10:30pm. Lockout 9am-5pm. Curfew 10:30pm; ask for a key. Open July-Aug. and Dec. 27-Jan. 5. Reservations held until 6pm. Dorms 125AS; doubles 250AS; triples 495AS.

Jugendherberge Innsbruck (HI), Reichenauer Str. 147 (☎34 61 79; fax 34 61 79 12; email yhibk@tirol.com). Take bus R to "König-Laurin Str." from the train station then bus O to "Jugendherberge." Breakfast 85AS. Laundry 45AS. Reception Sept.-June 5-10pm, July-Aug. 3-10pm. Lockout 10am-5pm. Curfew 11pm; ask for a key. Phone reservations held until 6pm. Dorms 155-190AS first night, 125-160AS thereafter; 2-bed rooms 220AS, 190AS. July-Aug. singles 360AS; doubles 520AS. Nonmembers add 40AS.

Camping Innsbruck Kranebitten, Kranebitter Allee 214 (☎28 41 80). Take bus LK from Bozner Platz (a block down Brixner Str. from the Bahnhof) to "Klammstr." (20min.). At night, take bus O to "Lohbachsiedlung" and switch to the LK. Walk downhill to the right and follow the road. Shower included. Laundry. Reception 8am-1pm. 75AS per person, 40AS per tent, 40AS per car. Tent rental 75-110AS per person.

Innstr. has ethnic restaurants, *Schnitzel Stuben*, and grocers. Look for **M-Preis Supermarkets** in front of the train station, on Maximilianstr. by the arch, and at Innrain 15. (Open M-Th 7:30am-6:30pm, F 7:30am-7:30pm, Sa 7:30am-5pm.) Indulge in Indian food at **Shere Punjab,** Innstr. 19. (Two daily *menüs* 65-75AS. Open M-F 11:30am-2:30pm and 5:50-11pm.) **Churrasco la Mamma,** Innrain 2, has river views by the bridge. (Pasta 82-134AS. Brick-oven pizza 74-112AS. Open 9am-midnight.) **Gasthof Weißes Lamm,** Mariahilfstr. 12, 2nd fl., serves homestyle Tyrolean fare. (Soup, entree, and salad 85-115AS. Open M-W and F-Su 11:30am-2pm and 6-10pm.)

SIGHTS AND OUTDOORS

ALTSTADT. Inside the **Goldenes Dachl** (Little Golden Roof) on Herzog-Friedrich-Str., the tiny **Maximilianeum Museum** commemorates Innsbruck's favorite emperor, who ruled from 1490 to 1519 using his smarts (and well-timed marriages) to create an empire whose size was exceeded only by that of his nose. *(Open May-Sept. 10am-6pm; Oct.-Apr. Tu-Su 10am-12:30pm and 2-5pm. 50AS, students 20AS. Commentary recording included.)* Lined with pastel-colored Baroque buildings, **Maria-Theresien-Straße** begins with the **Triumphpforte** (Triumphal Arch) by the Altstadt and runs south past the **Annasäule** (Anna Column). Off Maria-Theresien-Str., down Museumstr., is the **Tiroler Landesmuseum Ferdinandeum,** with a large regional collection. *(Open May-Sept. M-W and F-Su 10am-5pm, Th 10am-9pm; Oct.-Apr. Tu-Su 10am-noon and 2-5pm, Su 10am-1pm. 60AS, 30AS.)* A block behind the Goldenes Dachl rise the twin towers of the **Dom St. Jakob** (remodeled 1717-24), displaying *trompe l'oeil* ceiling murals by C.D. Asam depicting the life of St. James, and an altar painting by Cranach the Elder. *(Open daily Apr.-Sept. 8am-7:30pm; Oct.-Mar. 8am-6:30pm. Free.)* Behind the Dom and to the right is the entrance to the grand **Hofburg** (Imperial Palace), whose imposing furniture and large portraits—including one of Empress Maria Theresia's youngest daughter, Marie Antoinette (head intact)—fill sumptuously decorated rooms. *(Open daily 9am-5pm. 75AS, students 45AS. Tours in German 11am and 2pm.)* Across Rennweg sits the

Hofkirche (Imperial Church), with 28 larger-than-life bronze statues of Habsburg saints and Roman emperors, some by Dürer. An intricate sarcophagus within is decorated with scenes from Maximilian I's life, although he was buried near Vienna because the monument was not completed as he wished. The **Tiroler Volkskunstmuseum** (Tyrolean Handicrafts Museum) shares the same building. *(Church open daily 9am-5pm. 30AS, students 20AS. Museum open M-Sa 9am-5pm, Su 9am-noon. 60AS, students 35AS.)* In the other direction up Rennweg lies the **Hofgarten** (Imperial Garden), a manicured park complete with an outdoor chess set.

SCHLOß AMBRAS. One of the most beautiful Renaissance castles in Austria, Schloß Ambras was built by Archduke Ferdinand of Tyrol in the late 16th century. The museum within showcases good-as-new casts of armor, paintings by Velázquez and Titian, and Archduke Ferdinand's *Wunderkammer* (Cabinet of Curiosities). The walls of the Spanish Hall, Ambras' most famous room, are covered with mythological scenes and portraits of Tyrol's princes. *(Schloßstr. 20, in a park southeast of the city. Take tram #6 (dir. Igls) to "Tummelpl./Schloß Ambras" and follow the signs; or, take the shuttle bus that departs every hr. from Maria-Theresien-Str. opposite McDonalds. Open Su-M and W-Sa 10am-5pm. 90AS, children and students 50AS. Tours 30AS.)*

HIKING AND SKIING. A **Club Innsbruck** membership (available at accommodations) grants access to a **hiking** program that provides guides, transportation, and equipment at no additional cost; it also grants discounts on **ski** passes and provides free shuttles to suburban slopes. The **Patscherkofelbahn** in Igls takes hikers up beautiful trails to the **Alpine Garden,** Europe's highest botanical garden. *(Runs daily 9am-4:30pm. 120AS, round-trip 200AS. Open June-Sept. 9:30am-4pm. Free.)* The tourist office offers the **Innsbruck Gletscher Ski Pass,** valid for the region's 62 lifts (3-day 1260AS, Club Innsbruck members 1050AS); **equipment rental** (Alpine 270AS per day, cross-country 160AS); and **glacier skiing** (1-day in summer 170-280AS, in winter 420AS; add 270AS for ski rental; 599AS package includes bus, lift, and rental).

ENTERTAINMENT

At the corner of the Hofgarten, the Congress Center and Tiroler Landestheater (☎52 07 44) host festivals and concerts. The **university quarter** is a mecca for late-night revelry. The **Viaduktbögen** contains a stretch of theme bars along Ingenieur-Etzel-Str. East meets West at ultra-hip **Jimmy's,** Wilhelm-Greilstr. 17, by Landhauspl. (Beer 35-46AS. Open M-F 11am-1am, Sa-Su 7pm-1am.) **Treibhaus,** Angerzellg. 8, is Innsbruck's favorite alterna-teen hangout. Sift through their flyers for info on club and rave events. (Open daily 10am-1am.) Cozy **Die Alte Piccolo Bar,** Seilerg. 2, attracts a primarily gay male crowd. (Open Th-Tu 10pm-4am.)

EXCURSION FROM INNSBRUCK: KITZBÜHEL

Kitzbühel offers casinos and pubs, but most visitors head straight for the mountains. The **Ski Circus** is one of the best ski areas in the world. A one-day **ski pass** grants passage on 64 lifts and the shuttle buses connecting them. (Purchase passes at any of the lifts. High season 390-420AS.) **Renting** downhill **ski equipment** runs 170-500AS per day; **lessons** cost 500AS, **snowboards** 180-350AS. For summer visitors, more than 70 **hiking trails** snake up the mountains; get to the **Kampenweg** and **Hochetzkogel** trails via the Bichlalm bus (every hr., 26AS) or a two-hour climb. The **Kitzbüheler Hornbahn lift** (90AS) ascends to the **Alpenblumengarten,** where more than 120 different types of flowers bloom. (Open late May to mid-Oct. 8:30am-5pm.) Take advantage of the tourist office's **mountain hikes.** (Mid-May to mid-Oct. M-F at 8:45am from the tourist office. 90AS; free with **guest card,** except for cable car rides.) **Mountain bike trails** abound; rent bikes from **Stanger Radsport,** Josef-Pirchl-str. 42. (☎625 49. 250AS per day. Open M-F 8am-noon and 1-6pm, Sa 9am-noon.)

Trains (☎640 55 13 85) arrive from Innsbruck (1hr.-1½hr., 150AS) and Salzburg (1½hr., 200AS). The **tourist office,** Hinterstadt 18, by the Rathaus in the Fußgängerzone, has free hiking maps. (☎62 15 50; www.kitzbuehel.com. Open July-Sept. and mid-Dec. to late Apr. M-F 8:30am-6:30pm, Sa 8:30am-noon and 4-6pm, Su 10am-noon and 4-6pm; Oct. to mid-Dec. and late Apr. to June M-F 8:30am-12:30pm and

2:30-6pm.) The **Hotel Kaiser,** Bahnhofstr. 2, is by the Hauptbahnhof. (☎647 09. Laundry. Sometimes closed off season; call ahead. In summer 200AS; more in winter.) Take the train to "Schwarzsee," and follow the tracks around the back of the lake to **Camping Schwarzsee,** Reitherstr. 24. (☎62 80 60. 95AS per person plus 7AS tax; 98AS per tent; 90-100AS per caravan.) Shop at **SPAR supermarket,** Bichlstr. 22, at Ehrenbachg. (Open M-F 8am-7pm, Sa 7:30am-1pm.) **Postal code:** A-6370. ☎ **05356.**

BREGENZ ☎05574

When missionaries glimpsed the gray-green waters of the Bodensee (Lake Constance), they dubbed their find "Bregenz" (Golden Bowl). The area still awes visitors, who hike the Bregenzerwald and explore the historic **Oberstadt** (Old City). The wooden **Martinturm** rules the Oberstadt with Europe's largest onion dome. Next door is the **Martinskirche,** filled with 14th-century frescoes. Hike up Schloßbergstr. to the **St. Gallus Pfarrkirche,** a white stucco sanctuary that glows under lavish gold ornaments and a detailed painted ceiling. From the tourist office, walk down the *Fußgängerzone* (pedestrian zone) to reach the avant-garde **Kunsthaus Bregenz.** (Open Tu-W and F-Su 10am-6pm, Th 10am-9pm. 60AS, students 40AS.) The **Pfänderbahn** cable car leaves from the top of Schillerstr. and sways up the Pfänder Mountain for a panorama view spanning the Black Forest and Switzerland. (Runs daily 9am-7pm every 30min. 70AS, round-trip 125AS.) The town's main attraction is the **Bodensee,** where groomed waterfront paths surround fantastic playgrounds and paddle boat rental shops. Hop a ferry to the **Blumeninsel Mainau** (Mainau Flower Isle) to tour the island's castle, tropical palm collection, butterfly house, and gardens. (Ferries depart daily May-Sept. 9:20, 10:20, and 11:25am; return 2:50, 4:15, and 4:55pm. Round-trip 293AS. Admission 127AS.)

Trains go to: Lindau, Germany (10min.; see p. 454); St. Gallen (45min., 100AS); Zurich (2¼hr., 284AS); and Innsbruck (2¼hr., 300AS). Local **BundesBuses** also depart from the station. For hotel reservations (30AS), head to the **tourist office,** Bahnhofstr. 14. (☎495 90; fax 49 59 59; email tourismus@bregenz.at.) The new **Jugendgästehaus (HI),** Mehrerauerstr. 3-5, offers spic-'n'-span rooms and Internet access. From the train station, cross the bridge, pass the skateboard half-pipe, and look for yellow brick. (☎428 67; fax 428 67 88; email bregenz@jgh.at. Breakfast included. 237-277AS.) Two blocks behind the post office, **Pension Gunz** offers homey rooms. (☎436 57. Breakfast included. Singles 340AS; doubles 600AS. 30AS fee for 1-night stays.) **Camping Lamm** is at Mehrerauerstr. 50-51. (☎717 01. 50AS per person; children 25AS; tents 35-45AS; cars 35AS.) **Postal code:** A-6900.

BELARUS (БЕЛАРУСЬ)

BELARUSSIAN RUBLES

US$1 = 930BR	1000BR = US$1.10
CDN$1 = 630BR	1000BR = CDN$1.60
UK£1 = 1400BR	1000BR = UK£0.71
IR£1 = 1000BR	1000BR = IR£1.00
AUS$1 = 540BR	1000BR = AUS$1.85
NZ$1 = 400BR	1000BR = NZ$2.50
SAR1 = 130BR	1000BR = SAR17.70
DM1 = 420BR	1000BR = DM2.40
EUR€1 = 821BR	1000BR = EUR€1.23

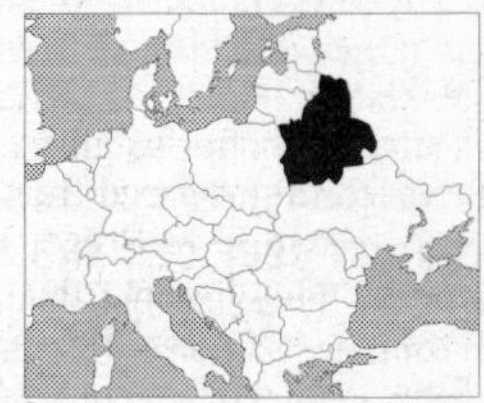

Country code: 375. **International dialing prefix:** 810. From outside Belarus, dial int'l dialing prefix (see inside back cover) + 375 + city code + local number.

For as long as anyone can remember, Belarus has been the backwater of someone else's empire, and today it remains the black sheep of Eastern Europe. Flattened by the Nazis from 1941 to 1945 and exploited by the Soviets from 1946 to 1990, the country seems to have lost its sense of self. Belarus today is a collection of sprawling Soviet urban landscapes surrounded by unspoiled forest villages. For those willing to endure the difficulties inherent in traveling in Belarus, the country offers a fascinating look at a conflicted but slowly emerging national feeling; others should look to countries better prepared for foreign consumption.

Lift the Belarussian curtain of your mind with *Let's Go: Eastern Europe 2001.*

FACTS AND FIGURES

Official Name: Republic of Belarus.
Government: Republic.
Capital: Minsk.
Land Area: 207,600 sq. km.
Climate: Cold winters, cool and moist summers. Be prepared for rain all year.
Population: 10,401,784.
Language: Belarussian, Russian.
Religions: Eastern Orthodox (80%), other (20%).
Average Income Per Capita: US$5200.

ESSENTIALS

DOCUMENTS AND FORMALITIES. To visit Belarus, you must secure an invitation and a visa. If you have an acquaintance in Belarus who can provide you with an official invitation, you may obtain a 90-day single-entry (5-day service US$50; next-day US$100) or multiple-entry (5-day processing US$170; next-day US$340) visa at an embassy or consulate. Those without contacts can turn to **Russia House** (see **Russia,** p. 787), which will get you an invitation and visa in five business days (US$225; 3-day processing US$275; next-day US$325). **Host Families Association (HOFA)** provides invitations for its guests (see **Russia,** p. 787). You may also obtain an invitation through a **Belintourist** office. Transit visas (US$20-30), valid for 48 hours, are issued at a consulate and theoretically at the border, but avoid the latter option anywhere other than Brest. Embassies and consulates of other countries are all in **Minsk** (see p. 126). At home, contact: **Canada,** 130 Albert St., Suite 600, Ottawa, ON, K1R 5G4 (☎ (613) 223 99 94; fax 233 85 00); **UK,** 6 Kensington Ct., London, W8 5DL (☎ (171) 937 32 88; fax 361 00 05); **US,** 1619 New Hampshire Ave. NW, Washington, DC 20009 (☎ (202) 986 16 04, visa ☎ 986 16 06; fax 986 18 05).

GETTING THERE AND GETTING AROUND. You can **fly** into Minsk on **Belavia,** Belarus's national airline (*if* you trust the old planes) from many European capitals. **LOT** also flies from Warsaw, and **Lufthansa** has daily flights from Frankfurt. Leaving Belarus by air can be a nightmare, as customs officials are wont to rip through your bags. Be aware that some international **train** tickets must be paid partly in US dollars and partly in Belarussian rubles. All immigration and customs are done on the trains. Tickets for same-day trains within Belarus are purchased at the station. **Eurail** is not valid. Information booths in the stations charge 5BR per inquiry; it's better to ask a cashier. For **city buses,** buy tickets at a kiosk (or from the driver for a surcharge) and punch them on board.

TOURIST SERVICES AND MONEY. In an **emergency,** call ☎03, or ☎01 for **fire** and ☎02 for the **police. Belintourist** (Белінтурист) is all that's left of the once omnipotent Intourist, but does not cater to budget travelers. Hotel Belarus and Hotel Yubilyenaya in Minsk have **private travel agencies.** Be sure to carry plenty of hard **cash;** US dollars, Deutschmarks, and Russian rubles are preferred. There are few **ATMs** outside Minsk, and most bank clerks scratch their heads at the mention of "traveler's checks." Some hotels accept **credit cards,** mostly AmEx and Visa. Belarussian rubles are impossible to exchange abroad. Inflation is rampant, so we list many prices in US$. Posted prices in Belarus often drop the final three zeros and *Let's Go* prices follow that convention. Bills printed in 2000 and later also omit the zeros, but the old bills remain in circulation and are difficult to distinguish from the new ones.

ACCOMMODATIONS AND CAMPING. Keep all receipts from hotels; you may have to show them to the authorities to avoid fines when leaving Belarus. **Hotels** are very cheap for Belarussians, outrageous for foreigners, and in-between for CIS member countries. The desk clerks will ask where you are from and request your passport, making it impossible to pass as a native. Some **private hotels** don't accept foreigners at all, but those that do are usually much cheaper and friendlier than the Soviet dinosaurs. To find a **private room,** look around for postings at train stations, or ask taxi drivers, who may know of a lead. The *babushki* at train stations might quote high prices, but they'll be willing to feed and house you for US$10 or less.

HEALTH AND SAFETY. Today, more than 10 years after the 1986 **Chernobyl** accident, it is safe to travel through the formerly contaminated areas. None of the cities *Let's Go* covers are in affected regions. It is important to be aware of a few safety considerations. Avoid inexpensive **dairy products,** which likely come from contaminated areas—opt instead for something German or Dutch—and stay away from **mushrooms** and **berries,** which tend to collect radioactivity. Drink only bottled **water;** tap water, especially in the southeast, may be contaminated.

COMMUNICATION. Avoid the **mail** system at all costs. **Local calls** require tokens sold at kiosks or magnetic cards, available at the post office, train station, and some hotels (200-500BR). **International calls** must be placed at the telephone office and paid for in advance, in cash. Write down the number you're calling and say "Ya hatchoo po-ZVAH-neet" ("I'd like to call...") followed by the name of the country; pay with exact change. Calls to the US and Western Europe cost US$1-3 per minute. **International direct dial** numbers include: **AT&T,** ☎880 01 01; **Australia Direct,** ☎810; **BT Direct,** ☎88 00 44; **Canada Direct,** ☎810 80 01 11; **MCI,** ☎880 01 03; and **Sprint,** ☎880 01 02 from Grodna, Brest, Minsk, and Vitebsk; ☎810 80 01 02 from Gomel and Mogilev.

HOLIDAYS AND FESTIVALS. Orthodox Christmas (Jan. 7); International Women's Day (Mar. 8); Constitution Day (Mar. 15); Catholic Easter (Apr. 15-16); Victory Day and Mother's Day (May 9); Independence Day (July 3); Remembrance Day (Nov. 2); October Revolution Day (Nov. 7); Catholic Christmas (Dec. 25).

MINSK (МІНСК) ☎0172

If you're looking for the supreme Soviet city, skip Moscow and head to Minsk (pop. 1.7 million), where the fall of Communism has been a reluctant shuffle rather than a wanton gallop west. With imaginary political reforms and concrete everywhere, not to mention the Minsk police on the prowl, everyone is asking if Belarussian authorities are really giving Minsk a new face, or just a new facade.

PRACTICAL INFORMATION AND ACCOMMODATIONS. **Trains** depart from **Tsentralny Vakzal** (Центральный Вакзал; ☎220 99 89 and 596 54 10), on Privakzalnaya pl., for Vilnius (4½hr., 3 per day, US$8-14); Warsaw (12hr., 3-5 per day, US$13 and 12,500,000BR); Berlin (1 per day, US$40 and 22,000,000BR); Moscow (14hr., 14-17 per day, US$20); Kiev (14hr., 1-3 per day, US$12); Prague (1 per day, US$60 and 12,500,000BR); and St. Petersburg (3 per day, US$14). Buy tickets at **Belintourist,** pr. Masherava 19. **Buses** go from **Avtovakzal Tsentralny** (Автовакзал Центральный), vul. Babruyskaya 6 (Бабруйская; ☎227 78 20), to the right of the train station, to Prague (6 per day, US$20) and Vilnius (4hr., 4 per day, US$11.50). From the train station, go up vul. Leningradskaya and left on Svyardlova (Свярдлова) to **pl. Nezalezhnastsi** (Independence Sq; Незалежнасці), connected by pr. F. Skoriny (Францішка Скарыны) to pl. Peramohi (Перамогі). **Belintourist** (Белінтуріст), pr. Masherava 19 (Машэрава), is next to Hotel Yubileynaya; pr. Masherava is perpendicular to pr. F. Skoriny. (☎226 94 85. M: Nemiga. Open M-F 8am-5:30pm.) **Embassies: Russia,** vul. Staravilenskaya 48 (Старавіленская; ☎250 36 65); **UK,** vul. Karla Marxa 37 (Карла Маркса; ☎229 23 03); **Ukraine,** vul. Kirava 17, #306 (☎227 27 96); and **US,** vul. Staravilenskaya 46 (☎231 50 00; open M-F 9am-5:30pm). All **phone numbers** have seven digits and start with a "2," so for six-digit numbers, add an initial "2"; but for some phones you have to drop the first "2." For **Internet** access, go to the **post office,** Pr. F. Skoriny 10. (US$1 per hr. Open daily 8am-8pm.) Sleep over at **Gastsinitsa Svisloch** (Гасцініца Свіслочь), vul. Kirava 13 for comfortable rooms in a great location. (☎220 97 83. M-red: pl. Nezalezhnastsi (пл. Незалежнасці). Singles 13,720,000-19,600,000BR.) From M-red: Park Chelyuskintsev (Парк Челюскинцев), take a right on the street in front of you that runs perpendicular to the main road to reach **Gastsinitsa Druzhba** (Дружба), vul. Tolbukhina 3. (☎266 24 81. Reserve ahead. Bed in a triple US$8.)

SIGHTS AND ENTERTAINMENT. After most of Minsk's buildings were obliterated in WWII, the city was rebuilt in high Soviet style. A block north of the train stations, grand buildings of State loom at **pl. Nezalezhnastsi,** formerly pl. Lenina (M-red: pl. Nezalezhnastsi; пл. Незалежнасці), the symbol of Belarussian independence. A few pre-War jewels remain, mainly in the **Old Town** quarter on the other side of the Svisloch, as well as a few churches. The **Church of St. Simon,** Savetskaya 15 (M-blue: Frunzenskaja; Фрунэенская), wards against dragons at pl. Nezalezhnastsi while pl. Svobody is home to the dazzling 17th-century **Cathedral of the Holy Spirit** (Svetadukha Kafedralny Sobor; Светадуха Кафедралный Собор), vul. Mefodiya 3 (M-blue: Nyamiha; Няміга). The **Jewish memorial stone,** vul. Zaslavskaya, commemorates the more than 5000 Jews who were shot and buried here by the Nazis in 1941 (M-blue: Nyamiha; Няміга). Lovely **parks** line the banks of the Svislac east of the Old Town. The **National Arts Museum** (Нацыянальны Мастацкі Музей Рэспублікі Беларусь; Natsyanalny Mastatski Muzey Raspubliki Belarus), pr. Lenina 20 (Леніна), brims with fantastic Russian and Belarussian art. (Open W-M 11am-7pm. 250BR.) The grim **Museum of the Great Patriotic War** (Muzey Velikoy Otechestvennoy Voyny; Музей Великой Отечественной Войны) is at pr. Skoriny 25a. (M-red: pl. Peramohi; пл. Перамогі. Open Tu-Su 10am-7pm. 250,00BR.) The monument of **Victory Square** disrupts vul. F. Skoriny before continuing to the **Opera and Ballet Theater,** vul. E. Pashkevich 23 (Пашкевіч), one of the best ballets in the former USSR. (☎234 06 66. Tickets under US$5. M-blue: Nyamiha; Няміга.)

BELGIUM
(BELGIQUE, BELGIË)

BELGIAN FRANCS

US$1 = 46.95BF	10BF = US$0.21
CDN$1 = 31.72BF	10BF = CDN$0.32
UK£1 = 66.10BF	10BF = UK£0.15
IR£1 = 51.22BF	10BF = IR£0.20
AUS$1 = 26.38BF	10BF = AUS$0.38
NZ$1 = 20.20BF	10BF = NZ$0.50
SAR1 = 6.59BF	10BF = SAR 1.52
EUR€1 = 40.34BF	10BF = EUR€0.25

Country code: 32. **International dialing prefix:** 00. From outside Belgium, dial int'l dialing prefix (see inside back cover) + 32 + city code + local number.

Situated between France, Germany, and the Netherlands, Belgium rubs shoulders with some of Europe's most powerful cultural and intellectual traditions. By comparison, travelers too often mistake Belgium's subtlety for boredom, but its castle-dotted countryside provides a beautiful escape for hikers and bikers, and its cities offer some of Europe's finest art and architecture. Antwerp thrives with commerce, and Brussels, the capital and home to NATO and the European Union, buzzes with international decision-makers making news. The nearby cultural treasures of Bruges and Ghent await discovery. The first stop on the military tours of many aspiring European conquerors—and today still the first stop of military history buffs—Belgium bears the scars of a troubled history. But today, Belgium's Flemish art, French Gothic architecture, and warm embrace of the Euro reaffirm the border-free identity of the new Europe. Some tension persists between the Flemish-speaking nationalists of Flanders and the French-speaking area of Wallonie to the south. But some things transcend politics: from the Ardennes forests to the white sands of the North Sea coast, Belgium's beauty is even richer than its chocolate.

FACTS AND FIGURES

Official Name: Kingdom of Belgium.
Government: Federal Constitutional Monarchy.
Capital: Brussels.
Land Area: 30,528 sq. km.
Geography: Low-lying, with the hilly Ardennes in the southeast.
Climate: Maritime climate; cool summers (May-Sept.), damp winters (Nov.-Feb.).
Major Cities: Brussels, Antwerp, Ghent, Charleroi, Liège.
Population: 10,208,000. Urban 97%, rural 3%.
Language: Dutch, French, German.
Religions: Roman Catholic (88%), Muslim, other Christian, Jewish, other (12%).
Average Income: US$26,440 per capita.
Major Exports: Machinery, chemicals, and diamonds.

DISCOVER BELGIUM

Start out in the northern region of Flanders; take in the old city and diverse museums of **Brussels** (p. 131), then spend at least two days in the real Belgian gem of **Bruges** (p. 136), a majestic town with a Gothic beauty unparalleled elsewhere in Europe. Spend a day in bustling **Antwerp** (p. 140) and a day (and definitely a night) with the students in **Ghent** (p. 141), then head south to the Wallonie region for a day or two of biking and exploration in and around **Namur** and **Dinant** (see p. 142).

ESSENTIALS

WHEN TO GO

Belgium, temperate and rainy, is best visited May to September, when temperatures average 13-21°C (54-72°F). Winter temperatures average 0-5°C (32-43°F). Bring a sweater and umbrella whenever you go.

DOCUMENTS AND FORMALITIES

Visas are generally not required for tourist stays under three months; South African citizens are the exception. All foreign embassies are in **Brussels** (see p. 131).

EMBASSIES AND CONSULATES

Belgian Embassies at Home: Australia, 19 Arkana St., Yarralumba, Canberra, ACT 2600 (☎ (02) 62 73 25 01; fax 62 73 33 92); **Canada,** 80 Elgin St., Ottawa, ON K1P 1B7 (☎ (613) 236 72 67; fax 236 78 82); **Ireland,** 2 Shrewsbury Rd., Ballsbridge, Dublin (☎ (353) 1 269 20 82; fax (353) 1 283 84 88); **New Zealand,** 1-3 Willeston St., Wellington (☎ (04) 472 95 58); **South Africa,** 625 Leyds St., Muckleneuk, Pretoria 0002 (☎ (012) 44 32 01; fax 44 32 16); **UK,** 103-105 Eaton Sq., London SW1W 9AB (☎ (020) 74 70 37 00; www.belgium-embassy.co.uk); **US,** 3330 Garfield St. NW, Washington, DC 20008 (☎ (202) 333 69 00; fax 333 30 79).

GETTING THERE AND GETTING AROUND

BY PLANE. Several major airlines fly into **Brussels** from Europe, North America, and Africa. **Sabena Belgian World Airlines** (Belgium ☎ (02) 723 62 19; US ☎ (800) 955 20 00; www.sabena.com) has cheap last-minute deals.

BY TRAIN. The **Belgian Rail** (www.sncb.be) network traverses the country in 4hr. **Eurostar** trains connect Brussels to London's Waterloo Station (1¾hr). **Thalys** trains run from Brussels to Paris (1¼hr.) and also serve other cities in Belgium as well as parts of Germany and the Netherlands (Belgium ☎ (09) 00 10 177, US or Canada ☎ 1 800 456 72 45). **Eurail** is valid in Belgium (US ☎ 1 800 4EURAIL, Canada ☎ 1 800 361 RAIL). The **Benelux Tourrail Pass** covers five days of travel in Belgium, the Netherlands, and Luxembourg in a one-month period (6510BF, under 27 4368BF), but

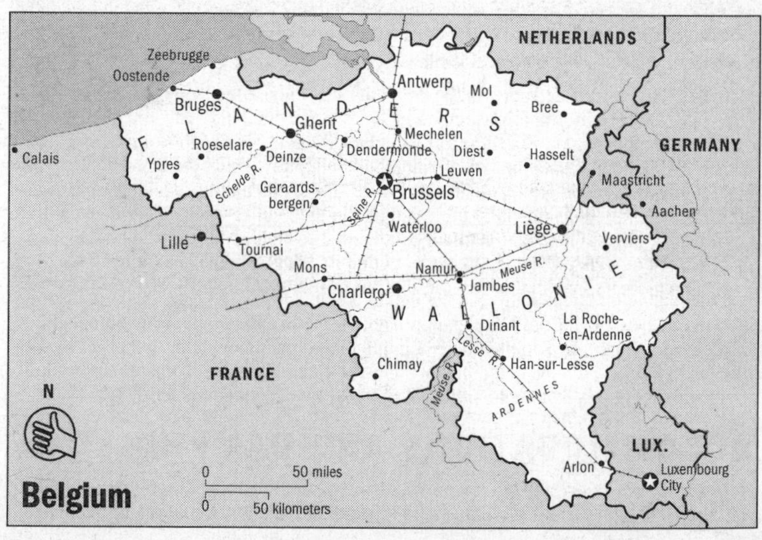

Belgium

BELGIUM

doesn't always make economic sense. The best deal for travelers under 26 may be the **Go Pass,** which allows 10 trips over six months in Belgium and may be used by more than one person at a time (1490BF). For travelers over 26, the **Pass 9+** allows 10 trips in Belgium after 9am (2200BF). Tourist offices sell 24-hour passes, which cover all municipal transport in the country (150BF).

BY BUS. Buses are used primarily for municipal transport (40-50BF); intercity buses are only slightly cheaper than trains and are far less convenient.

BY FERRY. P&O European Ferries (UK ☎ 0 14 82 79 51 41, email info.uk@ponsf.com; Belgium ☎ (050) 54 34 30; email info.be@ponsf.com) cross the Channel from **Zeebrugge,** north of Bruges, to **Hull, England** (14hr.), near York (see p. 197). **Ostend Lines** (☎ (059) 55 99 55) crosses from Ostend to **Ramsgate, England,** two hours from London's Victoria Station (8 per day; July-Aug. 599BF; Sept.-June 499BF).

BY CAR. Belgium honors most foreign licenses, including those from Australia, Canada, the EU, and the US. **Speed limits** are 120kph on motorways, 90kph on main roads, and 50kph elsewhere. Gas is about 40BF per liter. For info or help, contact the **Touring Club de Belgique (TCB),** r. de la Loi 44, Brussels 1040 (☎ (02) 233 22 11), or the **Royal Automobile Club de Belgique,** r. d'Arlon 53, Brussels 1040 (☎ (02) 287 09 11).

BY BIKE AND BY THUMB. Biking is popular, and many roads have bike lanes (which you are required to use). When you see two paths next to the street, the one nearer the street is for bicycles and mopeds, while the one nearer the storefronts is for pedestrians. Bike rental is available at many train stations. **Hitchhiking** is neither popular nor reported as safe in Belgium, but hitchers still report a fair amount of success in some areas. *Let's Go* does not recommend hitchhiking.

TOURIST SERVICES AND MONEY

EMERGENCY. Police: ☎ 101. **Ambulance:** ☎ 105. **Fire:** ☎ 100.

TOURIST OFFICES. Bureaux de Tourisme, marked by green-and-white "i" signs, are supplemented by **Info-Jeunes/Info-Jeugd,** a service that helps young people secure accommodations. For info, contact the **Belgian Tourist Board,** Grasmarkt 63, B-1000 Brussels (☎ (02) 504 03 90; www.tourism-belgium.net). The weekly English-language *Bulletin* (85BF at newsstands) lists everything from movies to job openings.

Tourist Offices at Home: Canada, P.O. Box 760, Succursale NDG, Montréal, Quebec H4A 3S2 (☎ (514) 484 35 94; fax 489 89 65). **UK,** 31 Peper St., London E14 9RW (fax (020) 74 58 00 45). **US,** 780 Third Ave. 1501, New York, NY 10017 (☎ (212) 758 81 30; fax 355 76 75; www.visitbelgium.com).

MONEY. The unit of currency is the **Belgian franc;** bills come in 100, 200, 500, 1000, 2000 and 10,000 denominations, coins in 1, 5, 20 and 50. There are 100 centimes in one franc. Expect to pay 750-1200BF for a hotel room, 350-550BF for a hostel, 150-400BF for a cheap restaurant meal, and 100-300BF for a day's supermarket fare. A bare-bones day in Belgium might cost US$12-25, a more comfortable day US$30-40. Service charges are usually included in the price in restaurants and taxis, but **tip** for exceptional service. Bathroom attendants usually receive 10-20BF. Belgium's **VAT** (generally 21%) is always included in price; refunds (usually 17% of the purchase price) are available for a minimum purchase of 5000BF per invoice.

BUSINESS HOURS. Banks are usually open M-F 9am-3:30pm or 4pm, some with a lunch break. Stores are open M-Sa 10am-6pm. Most sights open Su but are closed M except in Bruges, where museums are closed Tu or W. Most stores close on holidays; museums stay open except for Christmas, New Year's, and Armistice Day.

ACCOMMODATIONS AND CAMPING

Hotels in Belgium are fairly expensive, with "trench-bottom" singles from 800BF and doubles 1000-1100BF. Belgium's 31 **HI youth hostels,** which charge about 405BF per night, are generally modern, but **private hostels** are often cheaper and nicer. Pick up *Budget Holidays* or *Camping* at any tourist office for listings. **Campgrounds** charge about 130BF per night. An **international camping card** is not required.

FOOD AND DRINK

Belgian cuisine can be wonderful, but a native dish may cost as much as a night in a hotel. Steamed mussels *(moules)*, a Belgian delicacy, are usually tasty and reasonably affordable (around 430BF per pot). Other specialities include *lapin* (rabbit) and *canard* (duck). Belgian beer is a national pride and a national pastime; more varieties (over 500) are produced here than in any other country. Try Leffe, Kwak, Devel, cherry-flavored *kriek*, and the wheat-based *lambric doux*. Leave room for Belgium's *gaufres* (waffles)—soft, warm, glazed ones on the street (50BF) and bigger, crispier ones piled high with toppings at cafes (80-200BF)—and famous Godiva and Leonidas chocolates.

COMMUNICATION

MAIL. A postcard or letter (up to 20g) sent to a destination within the European Union costs 30BF, to the rest of the world 34BF. Most post offices are open M-F 9am to 4 or 6pm (sometimes with a midday break) and some Saturday mornings.

TELEPHONES. Most phones require a 200BF phone card, available at PTT offices and magazine stands. Coin-operated phones are more expensive and require either 5BF or 20BF coins. Calls are cheapest from 6:30pm to 8am and Saturday to Sunday. For **operator assistance** within Benelux, ☎13 07; for **international assistance,** ☎13 04 (10BF). **International direct dial** numbers include: **AT&T Direct,** ☎0800 100 10; **Australia Direct,** ☎0800 100 61; **BT Direct,** ☎0800 100 24; **Canada Direct,** ☎0800 100 19; **Ireland Direct,** ☎0800 110 353; **MCI WorldPhone,** ☎0800 100 12; **New Zealand Direct,** ☎0800 104 23; **Sprint Access,** ☎0800 100 14; **Telekom South Africa Direct,** ☎0800 100 27.

LANGUAGE. French (spoken in Brussels and Wallonie) and German. Most people, especially in Flanders, speak English. Dutch (a slightly different variety than is heard in the Netherlands) is also commonly heard. For the basics, see p. 981.

HOLIDAYS AND FESTIVALS

Holidays: New Year's Day (Jan. 1); Easter (Apr. 23); Easter Monday (Apr. 24); Labor Day (May 1); Ascension Day (June 1); Whit Sunday (June 11); Whit Monday (June 12); Independence Day (July 21); Assumption Day (Aug. 15); All Saints Day (Nov. 1); Armistice Day (Nov. 11); Christmas (Dec. 25).

Festivals: Ghent hosts the **Gentse Feesten** (July 21-31) and, this year, the 500th birthday of native-born Keizer Karel (Charles V); see p. 141. Wallonie hosts a slew of quirky and creative festivals, including the **Festival of Fairground Arts** (late May), **Les Jeux Nautiques** (early Aug.), and the **International French-language Film Festival** (early Sept.) in Namur, and the **International Bathtub Regatta** (mid-Aug.) in Dinant.

BRUSSELS (BRUXELLES, BRUSSEL) ☎02

Despite Brussels' association with NATO and the European Union, the stodgy diplomats in suits are constantly outdone by Brussels' two boy heroes: Tintin and the Mannekin Pis. In the late 1920s, cartoonist Hergé created Tintin, who, with his faithful dog Snowy, righted international wrongs long before Brussels became the capital of the EU. The cherubic Mannekin Pis perpetually pees three blocks from the Grand-Place, spoiling the formality of international politics. The museums of Brussels display Flemish masters, modern art, and antique sculptures, but you don't need to go inside for a visual feast—the restaurants, lounges, and movie theaters enliven the city in architect Victor Horta's art nouveau style.

GETTING THERE AND GETTING AROUND

Flights: Brussels International Airport (☎090 07 00 00). **Trains** go there from Gare du Midi (25min., every 20min., 90BF), stopping at Gare Centrale and Gare du Nord.

Trains: ☎515 20 00. All international trains stop at **Gare du Midi Zuid;** most also stop at **Gare du Nord** (near the Botanical Gardens) or **Gare Centrale** (near the Grand-Place). To: **Antwerp** (30min., 200BF); **Bruges** (45min., 390BF); **Paris** (1½hr., 2180BF, under 26 1000BF); **Amsterdam** (2½hr., 1310BF, 640BF); **Cologne** (2¾hr., 2320BF); and **Luxembourg City** (2¾hr., 1860BF). **Eurostar** goes to **London** (1¾hr., from 6200BF, 2100BF).

Buses: Société des Transports Intercommunaux Bruxellois (STIB), at 20 Galeries de la Toison d'Or, 6th fl. (☎515 30 64, schedule info ☎515 20 00). Open M-F 7:30am-5:30pm, Sa 8am-4pm.

Public Transportation: Runs daily 6am-midnight. 1hr. tickets (50BF) valid on **buses,** the **Métro (M),** and **trams. Day pass** 140BF. **10-trip pass** 350BF.

Hitchhiking: *Let's Go* does not recommend hitchhiking. Hitchers headed to **Antwerp** and **Amsterdam** take tram #52 or 92 from Gare du Midi or Gare du Nord to Heysel; **Ghent, Bruges,** and **Oostende,** bus #85 from the Bourse to the stop before the terminus, then follow E40 signs; **Paris,** tram #52, 55, or 91 to r. de Stalle, then walk toward the E19.

ORIENTATION AND PRACTICAL INFORMATION

Most major attractions cluster around the three train stations, between the **Bourse** (Stock Market) to the west and the **Parc de Bruxelles** to the east, around the **Grand-Place.** Two **Métro** lines circle the city, and efficient trams run north to south. A **tourist passport** (300BF at the TIB and bookshops) includes two days of public transit, a map, and reduced museum prices.

Tourist Offices: National, 63 r. du Marché aux Herbes (☎504 03 90), 1 block from the Grand-Place. Books rooms and gives out the free weekly *What's On.* Open daily 9am-6pm. **TIB (Tourist Information Brussels;** ☎513 89 40), on the Grand-Place, in the Town Hall, has free walking tour info. Open July-Aug. M-F 9am-6pm; May-June and Sept.-Oct. M-F 9am-6pm, Sa-Su 9am-1pm and 2-6pm; Nov.-Apr. Su only 9am-1pm.

Budget Travel: Infor-Jeunes, 9A r. St. Catherine (☎514 41 11). Info for young travelers. Open M-F 10am-5pm.

Embassies: Australia, 6-8 r. Guimard, 1040 (☎231 05 00; fax 230 68 02); **Canada,** 2 av. Tervueren, 1040 (☎741 06 11; fax 448 00 00); **Ireland,** 89/93 r. Froissart, 1040 (☎230 53 37; fax 230 53 12); **New Zealand,** 47 bd. du Régent, 1000 (☎513 48 56); **South Africa,** 26 r. de la Loi (☎285 44 02), generally open M-F 9am-5pm; **UK,** 85 r. Arlon (☎287 62 11; fax 287 63 55); **US,** 27 bd. du Régent, 1000 (embassy ☎508 21 11; consulate ☎508 25 32; fax 511 96 52; www.usinfo.be), open M-F 9am-noon.

Currency Exchange: Many booths near the Grand-Place (open until 11pm). Most banks and booths charge 100-150BF to cash checks. **Goffin,** R. du Marché aux Herbes 88 (☎502 23 82), charges 2% on travelers checks over 200BF. Open daily 9am-11pm.

Gay and Lesbian Services: Call ☎733 10 24 for info on local events. Staffed Tu 8-10pm, W 8-11pm, F-8-11pm.

Laundromat: Salon Lavoir, 5 r. Haute, around the corner from the Jeugdherberg Bruegel. M: Gare Centrale. Wash and dry 240BF. Open daily 7am-11pm.

Emergencies: Ambulance or **first aid:** ☎100. **Police:** ☎101.

Pharmacies: Neos-Bourse Pharmacie (☎218 06 40), bd. Anspach at r. du Marché-aux-Polets. M: Bourse. Open M-F 8:30am-6:30pm, Sa 9am-6:30pm.

Medical Assistance: Free Clinic, 154a chaussée de Wavre (☎512 13 14). Actually, you'll have to pay (600Fr). Open M-F 9am-6pm. **Medical Services,** ☎479 18 18. 24hr.

Internet Access: Point.Net, 16 petite r. des Bouchers, off Marché-Aux-Herbes, near the Grand-Place. Students 100BF per 30min. Open M-Sa 10am-7pm, Su 10am-6pm.

Post Office: (☎226 20 17) pl. de la Monnaie, Centre Monnaie, 2nd fl. M: de Brouckère. Open M-F 8am-7pm, Sa 9:30am-3pm. Address mail to be held: First name SURNAME, *Poste Restante,* Pl. de la Monnaie, **1000,** Bruxelles, Belgium.

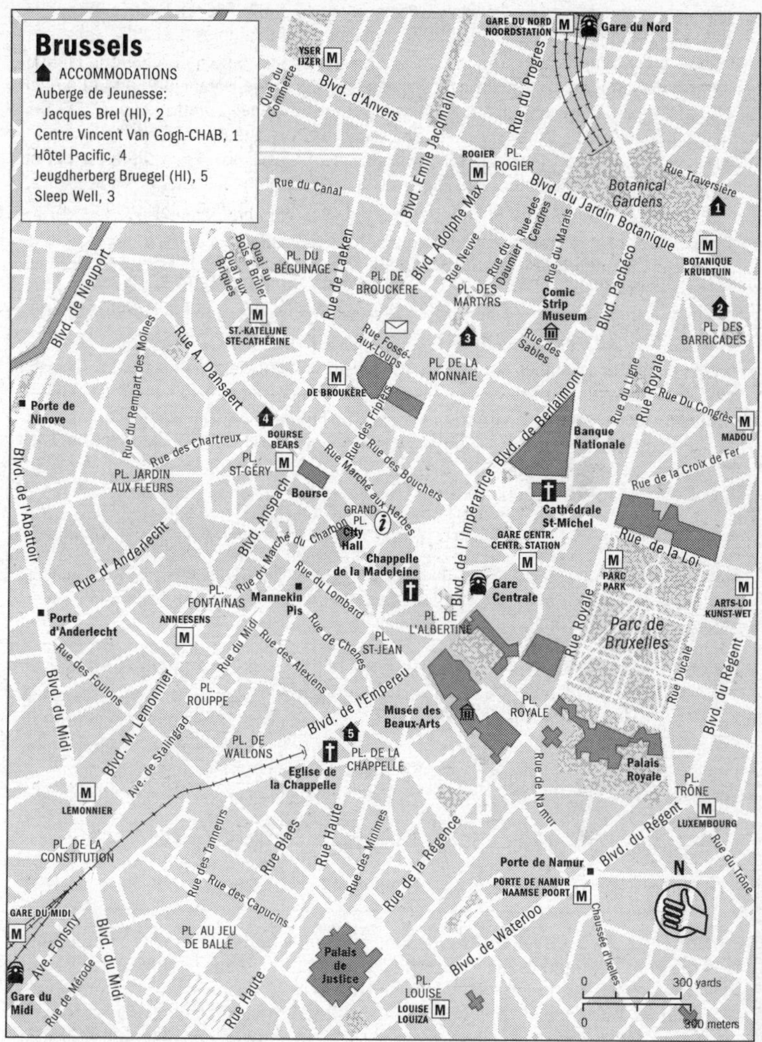

ACCOMMODATIONS AND CAMPING

Hotels and hostels are generally very well-kept; staffs at the five hostels will call each other if prospective guests arrive and they are booked.

Hôtel Pacific, 57 r. Antoine Dansaert (☎511 84 59). M: Bourse; cross bd. Anspach. Excellent location, basic rooms. Showers 100BF. Breakfast included. Reception 7am-midnight. Curfew midnight. Singles 1100BF; doubles 1800-2250BF; triples 2550BF.

Sleep Well, 23 r. du Damier (☎218 50 50; info@sleepwell.be), near Gare du Nord. M:Rogier; go right on the bd. du Jardin Botanique and turn right on r. des Cendres, which turns into r. Damier. Internet. Lockout 10am-4pm. Curfew 4am. Dorms 350-510BF; singles 695BF; doubles 1140BF; triples 1500BF.

Auberge de Jeunesse "Jacques Brel" (HI), 30 r. de la Sablonnière (☎218 01 87), on pl. des Barricades. M: Botanique; walk straight toward the church tower on R. Royal and turn right onto Sablonière. Spacious rooms. Dinner 295BF. Sheets 125BF. Reception 8am-1am. Dorms 430BF; singles 820BF; doubles 1200BF; triples 1530BF.

Centre Vincent Van Gogh-CHAB, 8 r. Traversière (☎217 01 58; chab@ping.be). M: Botanique; exit on R. Royale, head right (as you face the Jardin Botanique), and turn right on r. Traversière. Lively bar and garden. Internet 50BF per 15min. Laundry 180BF. Reception 7am-2am. Dorms 340-480BF; singles 700BF; doubles 1120-1160BF.

Jeugdherberg Bruegel (HI), 2 Heilige Geeststr. (☎511 04 36). From the back exit of Gare Centrale, go right on bd. de l'Empereur and take the 2nd left after Pl. de la Justice. Sheets 130BF. Reception 7am-1am. Lockout 10am-2pm. Curfew 1am. Dorms 430BF; singles 820BF; doubles 1200BF; quads 2040BF.

Camping: Paul Rosmant, 52 Warandeberg (☎782 10 09), in Wezembeek-Oppem. Métro 1B: Kraainem, or bus #30 to "Sint-Peterspl."; on Su, Métro 1B: Stockel, then tram #39 to "Marcelisstr." Reception 9am-12:30pm and 2-10pm. Open Apr.-Oct. 250BF per person.

FOOD

Restaurants cluster around the **Grand-Place;** for cheap food, try the arcade across from the back entrance to the Central Station. Seafood abounds on **rue des Bouchers,** north of the *place*. **Quai aux Briques,** in the Ste-Catherine area behind pl. St-Gery, offers cheaper seafood. South of the *place*, the **rue du Marché-aux-Fromages** is lined with Greek eateries. The **Belgaufras** has hot waffles (50-80BF). Load up at **GB supermarket,** 248 r. Vierge Noire. (M: Bourse. Open M-F 9am-7pm, Sa 10am-6pm.)

Hemispheres, r. de l'Ecuver 65, 2 doors down from Arcadi Coffeeshop. Libyan, Turkish, Chinese, and Indian cuisine convene. Vegetarian meals 280-400BF. Open M-F noon-3pm and 6:30-10:30pm, Sa 6:30pm-midnight.

Arcadi Coffeeshop, r. d'Arenberg 1b. Small cafe specializing in homemade quiche (180BF) and lots of veggie options. Open M-F 7:30am-11pm, Sa-Su 10am-11pm.

Léon, r. des Bouchers 18. Brussels' landmark for seafood; popular with locals and tourists alike. Mussels and chips (around 600BF) can serve two. (Open daily noon-11pm.)

L'Ecole Buissonnière, r. de Traversière 13, opposite the CHAB hostel. M: Botanique. Belgian fare; 3-course menus for 350BF. Open M-F noon-2:30pm and 6:30-10pm.

Ultième Hallutinatie, r. Royale 316. A splendid stained glass art nouveau house and garden. Salads, pastas, and omelettes in the Tavern from 250BF. Open M-F noon-2:30pm and 6pm-midnight, Sa noon-2:30pm and 6pm-1am.

SIGHTS

GRAND-PLACE AND ENVIRONS. One look and you'll understand why Victor Hugo called the gold-trimmed **Grand-Place** "the most beautiful square in the world." Built in the 15th century and ravaged by French troops in 1695, the square was restored to its original splendor in four years. A daily flower market and feverish tourist activity add color. The best sight in town is the light show, when 800 multi-colored flood lights give the **Town Hall** on the Grand-Place a man-made glow accompanied by booming classical music. *(Apr.-Aug. and Dec. daily around 10 or 11pm.)* Three blocks behind the Town Hall on r. de l'Etuve at r. du Chêne is Brussels' most giggled-at sight, the **Mannekin Pis,** a statue of an impudent boy (with an apparently infinite bladder) steadily urinating. One story goes that a 17th-century mayor promised to build a statue where his lost son was found; another says it commemorates a boy who defused a bomb. Each day the statue dons a costume representing an organization or group with a little hole for you-know-what. *(Free, he's always peeing.)*

ART MUSEUMS. The **Musées Royaux des Beaux Arts** houses a huge collection of the Flemish masters, including Brueghel the Elder's *Fall of Icarus* and works by Rubens. The collection is divided into four main color-coded wings; the **Musée d'Art Ancien** is in the green wing. Also check out the contemporary collection in the **Musée d'Art Moderne;** the green tour includes works by Miró, Picasso, and Brussels-based Magritte, as well as Jacque-Louis David's *Death of Marat*. *(R. de la*

Régence 3. M: Parc or port de Namur, a block south of the Parc. Open Tu-Su 10am-5pm. 150BF, students 100BF. 1st W of each month free 1-5pm.) The enormous **Musées Royaux d'Art et d'Histoire** covers a wide variety of periods and parts—Roman torsos without heads, Syrian heads without torsos, and Egyptian caskets with feet. From Mérode, walk straight through the arch, turn left, go past the doors that appear to be the entrance, and turn left again for the real entrance. *(10 parc du Cinquantenaire. M: Mérode. Open Tu-Su 10am-5pm. 150BF, students 100BF.)* Early 20th-century art nouveau master Baron Victor Horta's home, today the **Musée Horta,** is an elegant example of Brussels' architectural claim to fame. *(25 r. Américaine. M: Louise; walk down Av. Louise, bear right on r. Charleroi, and turn left on r. Américaine. Open Tu-Su 2-5:30pm. 200BF.)*

BELGIAN COMIC STRIP CENTRE. This museum in the "Comic Strip Capital of the World" displays hundreds of Belgian comics. The **museum-library** features a reproduction of Tintin's rocket ship and works by over 700 artists. An English guidebook is available at the ticket desk. *(20 r. des Sables. M: Rogier. From Sleep Well, turn left with the hostel at your back, walk to the end of the street, turn left, walk to the end of the street, turn right, and make your first left onto r. des Sables. Open Tu-Su 10am–6pm. 200BF.)*

ATOMIUM AND BRUPARCK ENTERTAINMENT COMPLEX. The **Atomium,** a monument of aluminum and steel built for the 1958 World's Fair, represents a cubic iron crystal structure magnified 165 billion times to a height of 102m. Today it houses a **science museum** featuring fauna and minerals from around the world. The Atomium towers over the **Bruparck entertainment complex,** home of the **Kinepolis cinema and Imax,** the largest movie theater in Europe. *(www.atomium.be. M: Huysel. on tram #81. Atomium open daily Apr.-Aug. 9am-7:30pm; Sept.-Mar. 10am-5:30pm. 200BF. Imax info and movie listings ☎09 00 55 55, reservations ☎474 26 00. Movies from 300BF.)*

OTHER SIGHTS. Stroll through the glorious **Galerie St. Hubert,** one block behind the Grand-Place, to window shop for everything from umbrellas to marzipan frogs. Built over the course of six centuries, the magnificent Gothic **Saints Michel et Gudule Cathedral** mixes in a little Romanesque and modern architecture for fun. *(Pl. St-Gudule, north of Central Station. Open daily 8am-7pm. Free.)* Wander the charming hills of **Sablon,** home to antique markets, art galleries, and lazy cafes, and **le Jeu de Balles,** where you can practice the fine art of bargaining at the morning **flea market.** For a lazy afternoon, try the **Botanical Gardens** on R. Royale. *(Open daily 10am-10pm. Free.)*

ENTERTAINMENT

For info on events, snag a copy of *What's On*. Brussels' theatrical flagship is the beautiful **Théâtre Royal de la Monnaie,** on pl. de la Monnaie. (M: de Brouckère; ☎229 12 00; 300-3000BF.) Renowned throughout the world for its opera and ballet, the theater had a performance of the opera *Muette de Portici* in August 1830 that inspired the audience to leave the theater early, take to the streets, and begin the revolt that led to Belgium's independence. The tourist office has schedules and tickets. Experience a distinctly Belgian art form at the **Theatre Toone,** 21 Petite r. des Bouchers, a 170-year-old puppet theater. (☎511 71 37. Shows in French, German, Flemish, and English by request. 400BF, students 250BF.) In summer, **concerts** are on the **Grand-Place,** the **Place de la Monnaie,** and in the **Parc de Bruxelles.**

BELGIUM

NIGHTLIFE

The scene in Brussels ranges from sharing a drink with old gents to glamming it up in outdoor cafes and lounges. Take caution if you are walking from a disco in the south back to the Gare du Nord late at night. The most stylish coffeeshops surround the **Pl. St-Gèry,** behind the Bourse. At night the **Grand-Place,** the **Bourse,** and environs come to life with street performers and live concerts. The club scene changes very quickly—ask at bars and check *What's On* for the best spots. The 19th-century puppet theater **Poechenellekelder,** r. de Chêne 5, across from the Mannekin Pis, features a nice selection of Belgian beers. (Open daily noon-midnight, F-Sa until 1 or 2am.) **La Mort Subite,** 7 r. Montagne-aux-Herbes-Potagères, across from the Arcadi Coffeeshop (open daily 10am-2am), and **La Bécasse,** r. de Tabora 11 (open daily 10am-midnight), are two of Brussels' oldest and best-known cafes, specializing in *lambric*, a local wheat beer (50-90BF). **Le Fuse,** 208 r. Blaes, is one of Belgium's trendiest clubs. (Open daily 10pm-late.) Gay men socialize in a mellow atmosphere at **L'Incognito,** 36 r. des Pierres. (Beer 60F. Open daily 4pm-dawn.)

EXCURSIONS FROM BRUSSELS

WATERLOO. Napoleon was caught with both hands in his shirt at Waterloo (well, even ABBA couldn't escape if they wanted to), south of Brussels. Modern residents are more likely to have their hands in your pockets, as fans of the diminutive dictator shell out big bucks for the town's little slice of history. **The Lion's Mound,** 5km outside of town, is a huge hill overlooking the battlefield; nearby, the Visitor's Center offers a panoramic painting of the battle and a brief movie about Waterloo. A reenactment of the Battle is scheduled for June 16-17, 2001. (Open daily Apr.-Sept. 9:30am-6:30pm; Oct. 9:30am-5:30pm; Nov.-Feb. 10:30am-4pm; Mar. 10:30am-5pm. Mound 40BF, with movie and panorama 305BF.) In the center of Waterloo, **Musée Wellington,** chausée de Bruxelles 147, was Wellington's headquarters and has artifacts from the battle. (Open daily Apr.-Oct. 9:30am-6:30pm; Nov.-Mar. 10:30am-5pm. 100BF, students 80BF.) **Bus** W leaves pl. Rouppe near Brussels' Gare Midi (every 50min., 100F) and stops at Waterloo Church, across the street from Musée Wellington, at a gas station near Lion's Mound, and at the train station in Braine L'Alleud. Belgian Railways offers a **B-excursion ticket** for round-trip transit between Brussels Midi (also available from Brussels Nord) and Braine L'Alleud, a bus pass from Braine L'Alleud to Waterloo, and entrance to all sights (710BF, students 660BF).

MECHELEN (MALINES). Historically the ecclesiastical capital of Belgium, Mechelen is known today for its clamorous bells and grim contribution to the Holocaust. Down Consciencestr. from the station, the **Grote Markt** is lined with early Renaissance buildings, including the **Stadhuis** (city hall) and the stately **St. Rumbold's Cathedral.** (Stadhuis open M-Sa 8:30am-5:30pm, Su 2-5:30pm.) Boasting an institute where students still learn to play the **carillon** (a set of 49 bells), the cathedral offers concerts (M and Sa 11:30am, Su 3pm; June 15-Sept. also M 8:30pm). **St. Rumbold's Tower** rises 97m over Grote Markt and contains two carillons; you can climb the bell tower an hour before performances. (M 2:15pm and 7:15pm. 100BF.) The 18th-century military barracks used during the Holocaust as a temporary camp for Belgian and Dutch Jews en route to Auschwitz-Birkenau now houses the **Museum of Nazi Deportation and Resistance.** From the Grote Markt, head down Merodestr., left on St. Janstr., and right on Stassartstr. (Open Su-Th 10am-5pm, F 10am-1pm. Free.) **Buses** arrive in Mechelen from Brussels and Antwerp (both 15min., 120BF). The **tourist office** is in the Stadhuis and finds rooms for free. (☎29 76 55. Open Easter-Oct. M-F 8am-6pm, Sa-Su 9:30am-12:30pm and 1:30-5pm; June-Sept. M until 7pm; Nov.-Easter reduced hours.) **Postal code:** 2800. ☎**015.**

FLANDERS (VLAANDEREN)

Boogie in Antwerp, bask in Bruges, and satisfy your castle cravings with Ghent's Gravensteen in Flanders, the Flemish-speaking part of Belgium. The three major cities will sate your chocolate lust with praline shops galore, and offer up a wealth of Renaissance splendor. Flanders' Golden Age was during the 16th century, when its commercial centers were among the largest in Europe and its innovative artists motivated the Northern Renaissance. The friendly, multilingual folks in Flanders today take more pride in their region than in Belgium as a whole.

BRUGES (BRUGGE) ☎050

The capital of Flanders is one of the most beautiful cities in Europe, and tourists know it: famed for its lace, the home of Jan van Eyck has become the largest tourist

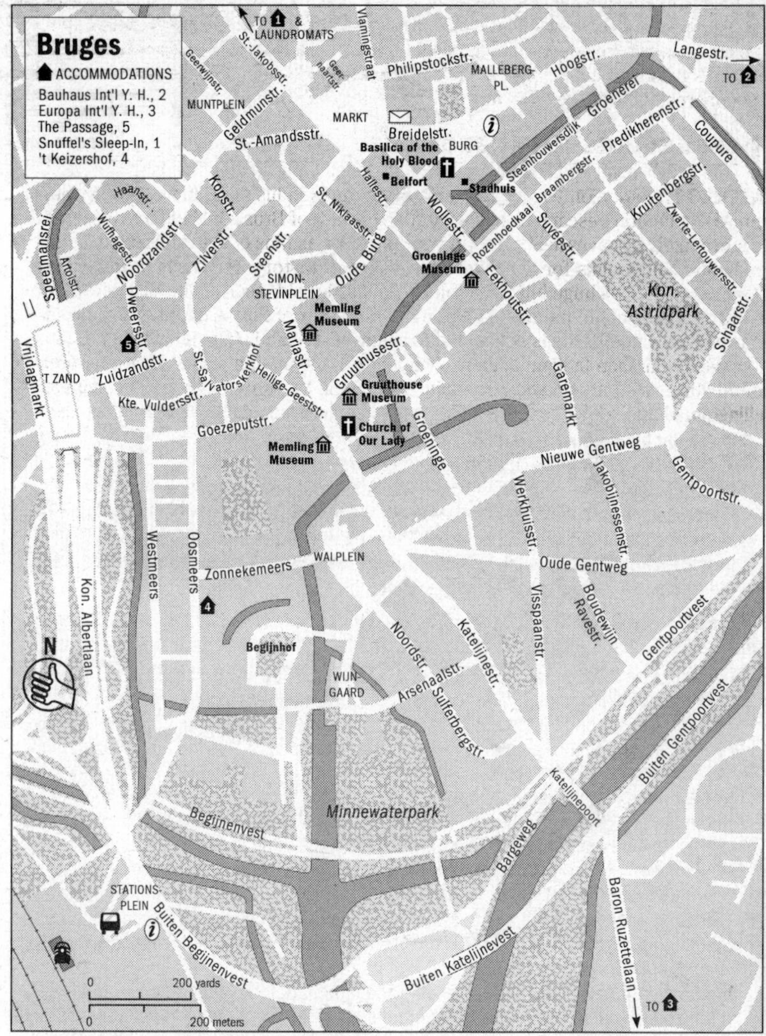

attraction in the country. The entire city remains one of the best-preserved examples of Northern Renaissance architecture, with a beauty that belies the destruction it sustained in World War I; eight decades after the war, farmers still uncover 200 tons of artillery every year as they plough their fields.

GETTING THERE AND GETTING AWAY

Trains: Depart from **Stationsplein** (☎38 23 82), 15min. south of the city center. To: **Brussels** (1hr., 380BF); **Antwerp** (1hr., 395BF); and **Ghent** (25min., 175BF).

Bike Rental: At the train station; 345BF per day, 500BF deposit. **'t Koffieboontje,** Hallestr. 4 (☎33 80 27), off the Markt by the belfry. 325BF per day, students 200BF. Open daily 9am-10pm.

Hitchhiking: Those hitching to Brussels reportedly take bus #7 to St. Michiels or pick up the highway behind the train station. *Let's Go* does not recommend hitchhiking.

ORIENTATION AND PRACTICAL INFORMATION

Bruges is enclosed by a circular canal, with the train station just beyond its southern extreme. Its historic district is entirely navigable on foot. The dizzying **Belfort** (belfry) towers high at the center of town, presiding over the handsome **Markt.**

Tourist Offices: Burg 11 (☎44 86 86; www.bruges.be), behind the Markt. Head left from the station to 't Zand square, right on Zuidzandstr., and right on Breidelstr. through the Markt. Books rooms (400BF deposit). Open Apr.-Sept. M-F 9:30am-6:30pm, Sa-Su 10am-noon and 2-6:30pm; Oct.-Mar. M-F 9:30am-5pm, Sa-Su 9:30am-1pm and 2-5:30pm. **Branch** at the train station open 10:30am-1:15pm and 2-5:30pm.

Tours: Quasimodo Tours (☎37 04 70), leads excellent bike and bus tours to windmills, castles, and WWII bunkers. Bike tours depart daily mid-Mar.-Sept. from the tourist office at the Burg; 650BF, under 26 550BF. The Triple Treat trip stops on M, W, F at medieval castles, with chocolate, waffles, and beer thrown in. 1500BF, under 26 1200BF.

Currency Exchange: Everywhere around the Markt. **Goffin,** 2 Steenstr., has good rates (2% commission on traveler's checks, min. 200BF transaction). Open daily 9am-8pm.

Luggage Storage: At the train station; 80BF. **Lockers** at the tourist office; 50BF.

Laundromat: Belfort, Ezelstr. 51, next to Snuffel's Sleep-In (see p. 138). Wash 100-140BF, dry 200-300BF. Open daily 7am-10pm.

Emergencies: ☎100. **Police:** ☎101. Police station at Hauwerstr. 7 (☎44 88 44).

Internet Access: The Coffee Link, Mariastr. 38 (☎34 99 73), in the Oud Sint-Jon Historic Hospital. 60BF per 15min. Open M-Sa 10am-9:30pm, Su 1:30-6:30pm.

Post Office: Hoedenmakerst. 2. Address mail to be held: First name SURNAME, *Poste Restante*, Hoedenmakerst. 2, Brugge **8000.**

ACCOMMODATIONS AND CAMPING

The Passage, Dweerstr. 26 (☎34 02 32). Take any bus from the station to St. Salvators, turn left onto Zuidzandstr., and the 1st right onto Dweerstr. Or, walk from the station to 't Zand, go right on Zuidzandstr., and take the 1st left. Airy rooms and an ideal location. Breakfast 100BF. Reception 8:30am-midnight. Closed each Jan. for renovations. Dorms 450BF; singles 900BF; doubles 1400BF.

't Keizershof, Oostmeers 126 (☎33 87 28; email hotel.keizerhof@weant2move.be). From the station, walk to the traffic lights on the left, cross the street, and follow signs to the Memling Museum and Oud St. Jan. The hotel is on your left. Pretty rooms on a quiet street. Singles 950BF; doubles 1400BF; triples 2100BF; quads 2500BF.

Charlie Rockets, 19 Hoogstr. (☎33 06 60), 3min. from the Burg and Markt. This bar and upstairs youth hostel has a distinctly American feel, comfortable dorms, and clean bathrooms. Breakfast 100BF for dorms. Laundry 150BF. Internet. Reception 8am-4am. Dorms 495BF; doubles 1500BF.

Bauhaus International Youth Hotel, Langestr. 133-137 (☎34 10 93; email bauhaus@bauhaus.be). Take bus #6 from the station to Kruispoort and tell the driver your destination (40BF). Internet cafe. Breakfast 60BF. Reception 8am-2am. Dorms 380BF; singles 550-850BF; doubles 1000-1300BF; triples 1350-1800BF.

Europa International Youth Hostel (HI), Baron Ruzettelaan 143 (☎35 26 79). Quiet, away from the Markt and the nightlife. Turn right from the station and follow Buiten Katelijnevest to Baron Ruzettelaan (15min.). Breakfast included. Sheets 125BF. Key deposit 100BF. Reception 7:30-10am and 1-11pm. 420BF; nonmembers 520BF.

Snuffel's Sleep-In, Ezelstr. 49 (☎33 31 33; snuffel@flanderscoast.be). From the Markt, follow Sint-Jakobstr., which becomes Ezelstr. (10min.). Breakfast 80BF. Internet. Reception 8am-2am. Snug dorms 350-390BF; quads 1960BF.

Camping: St-Michiel, Tillegemstr. (☎38 08 19), 25min. from the Markt. Or, take bus #7 from the station. 110BF per person; 130BF per tent; 130BF per car.

FOOD

To avoid high prices, look a block or two away from the city center. Splurge on a pot of Belgium's famous *mosselen* (mussels), which for 450-500BF often includes appetizers and dessert, even in the Markt. Excellent, reasonably priced vegetarian and healthy food restaurants cluster around the Markt; get veggie lunches at **The Lotus,** Wappenmakerstr. 5. From the Markt, take the third left off Philipstockstr. (310-330BF. Open mid-Aug. to mid-July M-Sa 11:45am-2pm.) The **Gran Kaffee De Passage,** Dweerstr. 26-28, serves traditional Belgian cuisine. (Open daily 5pm-late.) On Friday morning, cross the river from the Burg and turn left to buy fresh seafood at the celebrated **Vismarkt.** For even cheaper fare, head to **Nopri Supermarket,** Noordzandstr. 4, just off 't Zand. (Open M-Sa 9:30am-6:30pm.)

SIGHTS

Small enough to be covered by short walks and lined with gorgeous canals and Renaissance streets, Bruges is best seen on foot. The tourist office leads **walking tours** (July-Aug. daily 3pm; 150BF). **Boat tours** also ply Bruges' canals (every 30min., 190BF); ask at the tourist office or pick up tickets at the booth on the bridge between Wollestr. and Dijver. The **museum combination ticket** covers the Gruuthuse, Groeninge Museum, Arentshuis, and Memling (500BF).

MARKT AND BURG. Over the **Markt** looms the 88m medieval bell tower of the **Belfort;** its dizzying 366 steps afford a great view, and at night, it serves as the city's torch. *(Open daily 9:30am-5pm. 100BF, students 80BF. Bell concerts M, W, and Sa 9pm, Su 2:15pm.)* Behind the Markt, the **Burg** square is dominated by the flamboyant Gothic facade of the **Stadhuis** (City Hall), filled with paintings and wood carvings. Upstairs is a gilded hall where many Bruges residents still get married. *(Open daily 9:30am-5pm. 150BF.)* Hidden in the corner of the Burg next to the Stadhuis, the **Basilica of the Holy Blood** supposedly houses the blood of Christ. *(Open daily Apr.-Sept. 9:30am-noon and 2-6pm; Oct.-Mar. 10am-noon and 2-4pm; closed W afternoon. 40BF.)*

MUSEUMS. From the Burg, follow Wollestr. left and head right on Dijver to reach the **Groeninge Museum,** a comprehensive collection of Belgian and Dutch paintings from the last six centuries, featuring works by Bruges-based Jan Van Eyck, Bruges-born Hans Memling, and the master of medieval macabre, Hieronymous Bosch. *(Dijver 12. Open daily in summer 9:30am-5pm; closed Tu in winter. 250BF. Last tickets sold at 4:30pm.)* Next door, the **Gruuthuse Museum,** in the lavish 15th-century home of beer magnates, houses an amazing collection of weapons, tapestries, musical instruments, and coins dating back to the 6th century. *(Dijver 17. Open Apr.-Sept. daily 9:30am-5pm; Oct.-Mar. W-M 9:30am-5pm. 130BF, students 100BF.)* Continue as Dijver becomes Gruuthusestr. and walk under the stone archway to the **Memling Museum,** Mariastr. 38, housed in St. John's Hospital, one of the oldest surviving medieval hospitals in Europe. The collection is scheduled to reopen in mid-2001. *(Open daily in summer 9:30am-5pm; closed W in winter. 100BF.)*

OTHER SIGHTS. The **Church of Our Lady,** at Mariastr. and Gruuthusestr. near the Groeninge Museum, contains Michelangelo's *Madonna and Child,* as well as medieval frescoed tombs and the mausoleums of Mary of Burgundy and Charles the Bold. *(Open daily 9:30am-5pm. Church free; tombs 100BF.)* From the church, turn left and stroll along the Mariastr., then turn right on Stoofstr., where you will come to Walplein; cross the footbridge to enter the **Beguinage,** a grassy cove encircled by the residences of cloistered women in medieval times and inhabited today by three Benedictine sisters. *(Free.)* The 230-year-old **Sint-Janshuismolen** windmill is still used to grind flour. From the Burg, follow Hoogstr., which becomes Langestr., and turn left at the end on Kruisvest. *(Open daily May-Sept. 9:30am-12:30pm and 1:30-5pm. 40BF.)*

 NIGHTLIFE

The best nighttime entertainment consists of wandering through the city's romantic streets and over its cobblestone bridges, but if that isn't enough, sample 300 varieties of beer at **'t Brugs Beertje,** Kemelstr. 5, off Steenstr. (Open Th-Tu 4pm-1am.) Next door, the **Dreupelhuisje** serves tantalizingly fruity *jenever*, a flavored Dutch gin; be aware that the 21 different flavors mask a high alcohol content. (Open Su-Th 6pm-1am, W 4pm-1am, F-Sa 4pm-2am.) **Rikka Rock,** on 't Zand, is popular with local twenty-somethings. (No cover. Open 24hr.) Continue next door at **The Break,** 't Zand 9, for pulsing music and glam patrons. (No cover. Open daily 1pm to late.)

 BEACHES NEAR BRUGES

The towns along Belgium's North Sea coast win fans for their **beaches. Zeebrugge** is little more than a port, but **Ostend** (Oostende) and **Knokke** have cute beaches and stores, one hour by bike and 15 minutes by train from Bruges. For info on **ferries** from Zeebrugge and Ostend to the UK, see p. 49. Get ferry tickets from travel agents, at ports, or in the Oostende train station. **Trains** go from Bruges to: Zeebrugge (every hr., 80BF); Ostend (3 per hr., 110BF); and Knokke (2 per hr., 100BF).

ANTWERP (ANTWERPEN, ANVERS) ☎03

Home to the Golden Age master painter Rubens, Antwerp today is a distinctly cosmopolitan city. Along the Meir, the main drag, a hearty plethora of fine Belgian chocolates tempts; in the bars that cluster at the end of the Meir, beer flows cheaply, fuelling the dusk-til-dawn nightlife that throbs at modern Antwerp's core.

PRACTICAL INFORMATION AND ACCOMMODATIONS. Trains go to: Brussels (50min., 200BF); Rotterdam (1½hr., 700BF); and Amsterdam (2hr., 970BF). To get from the station to the **tourist office,** Grote Markt 15, turn left on De Keyserlei, which becomes Meir, curve right at Meirburg on Eiermarkt, and head straight across Groenpl. around the cathedral. (☎232 01 03; fax 231 19 37. Open M-Sa 9am-6pm, Su 9am-5pm.) For the **Jeugdherberg Op-Sinjoorke (HI),** Eric Sasselaan 2, take tram #2 (dir. Hoboken) to "Bouwcentrum," walk towards the fountain, make your first left, then a right after the standing man statue, go to the end of the street, turn left, and cross the bridge. (☎238 02 73. Breakfast included. Sheets 125BF. Lockout 10am-3pm. Dorms 520BF, members 420BF; doubles 585BF.) **Globetrotter's Nest,** Vlagstr. 25, is cozy, but slightly spartan. (☎236 99 28. Breakfast included. Sheets 100BF. Dorms 400-430BF; doubles 1200BF.) Near the Jeugdherberg Op-Sinjoorke, **camp** at **Sted. Kamp Vogelzangan.** Follow the directions to the hostel; when you get off the tram facing the Bouwcentrum, turn right and walk away from the fountain, cross the street, take your first left, and go through the gates. (☎238 57 17. Open Apr. 1-Sept. 30. 65BF per person; 35BF per tent, 85BF with electricity; 35BF per car.) **Postal code:** 2000.

SIGHTS AND ENTERTAINMENT. Many of Antwerp's best sights are free. Fanciful Art Nouveau mansions built in the city's Golden Age line the **Cogels Osylei. Centraal Station** itself is beautiful; note also the buildings along the **Meir.** The dignified Renaissance **Stadhuis** (City Hall) is in the *oude stad* (old city) in Grote Markt. (☎203 95 33. Call for frequent tour times. 30BF.) The nearby **Kathedraal van Onze-Lieve-Vrouw,** Groenpl. 21, has a showy Gothic tower and Flemish masterpieces, including Rubens' *Descent from the Cross.* (Open M-F 10am-5pm, Sa 10am-3pm, Su 1-4pm. 70BF.) The little-known **Mayer van den Bergh Museum,** Lange Gasthuisstr. 19, harbors Brueghel's *Mad Meg.* (☎232 42 37. Open Tu-Su 10am-4:45pm. 100BF.) Antwerp's favorite son built the stunning **Rubens Huis,** Wapper 9, off Meir, and filled it with art. (☎201 15 55. Open Tu-Su 10am-4:45pm. 100BF.) The **Royal Museum of Fine Art,** Leopold De Waelpl. 1-9, has one of the world's best collections of Old Flemish Master paintings. (Open Tu-Su 10am-5pm. 150BF, students 120BF; F free.)

Get *Play* at the tourist office for information on Antwerp's 300 bars and nightclubs. DJs spin house in near-rave conditions at **Café d'Anvers,** Verversrui 15. (Cover 200BF. Open Sa-Su after midnight.) The streets behind the cathedral throb at night; **Bierland,** Korte Nieuwstr. 28, is a popular student hangout. (Open daily 9am-late.) Next to the cathedral, over 600 Flemish religious figurines bump elbows with curious drinkers at **Elfde Gebod,** Torfburg 10. (☎289 34 66. Beer 70-120BF. Open daily noon-1am, weekends until 2am.) Sample local *elixir d'Anvers* at the candlelit **Pelgrom,** Pelgrimstr. 15. (Open daily noon-late.) Gay bars and discos cluster on **Van Schoonhovenstr.,** just north of Centraal Station. Closer to Grote Markt, a mixed crowd parties at gay-friendly **in de Roscam,** Vrijdagmarkt 12. (Open daily 6am-2am.)

GHENT (GENT) ☎09

Ghent lives and breathes industrial pride. The magnificent Socialist Working-people's Building, constructed with dues collected by textile workers at the turn of the century, evokes the workers' long, glorious struggle for freedom from the sweatshops. One victory came in 1860, when workers got a week of vacation—a victory still celebrated as the **Gentse Feesten** (Ghent festivities; July 14-23, 2001), also called "10 Days Off," with street performers, live music, rides, and great food and beer.

PRACTICAL INFO, ACCOMMODATIONS, AND FOOD. **Trains** run from Sint-Pietersstation (accessible by tram #1 or 12) to Bruges (20min., 175BF) and Brussels (40min., 245BF). The **tourist office** is in the basement of the belfry. (☎266 52 32. Open daily Apr.-Oct. 9:30am-6:30pm; Nov.-Mar. 9:30am-4:30pm.) **The Hotel Flandria,** Barrestraat 3, offers big breakfasts. (☎223 06 26; www.flandria-centrum.be. Reception 7am-9pm. Doubles from 1400-1800BF.) **De Draeke (HI),** St-Widostr. 11, is in the shadow of a castle. From the station, take tram #1, 10, or 11 to Gravensteen (15min.); head left, then right on Gewad and right again on St-Widostr. (☎233 70 50. Breakfast included. Sheets 125BF. Reception 7:30am-11pm. Dorms 510BF; singles 820BF; doubles 1200BF; nonmembers add 100BF.) To get to **Camping Blaarmeersen,** Zuiderlaan 12, take bus #9 from Sint-Pietersstation and ask to be connected to bus #38 to Blaarmeersen. When you get off, take the first left to the end. (☎221 53 99. Open Mar. to mid-Oct. 130BF per person; 140BF per tent; 70BF per car.) Good meals run about 200BF; try **Korenmarkt,** in front of the post office; **Vrijdagmarkt,** a few blocks from the town hall; and **St-Pietersnieuwstr.,** by the university. Students eat at **Magazyne,** Bredestraat 159, for cheap, hearty fare in the historic disctrict. (Lunch noon-2pm, dinner 6-10pm.) **Postal code:** 9000.

SIGHTS AND ENTERTAINMENT. Lovers of fine architecture relish Ghent's city center. The revered **Gravensteen** is a sprawling medieval fortress and 19th-century textile factory. (Open Apr.-Sept. 3 9am-6pm, last ticket sale 5:15pm; Sept. 4-Mar. 31 9am-5pm. 200BF, students 100BF.) Wind your way up the towering **Belfort** (belfry) for some Hitchcockian vertigo. (Open mid-Mar. to mid.Nov. 10am-12:30pm and 2-5:30pm. 100BF.) The **Stadhuis** (town hall) juxtaposes Gothic and Renaissance architecture. A block away on Limburgstr., the 14th- to 16th-century **Sint-Baafskathedraal** boasts Van Eyck's *Adoration of the Mystic Lamb*, also known as the *Ghent Altarpiece.* (Cathedral open daily 8:30am-6pm; free. Altarpiece open M-Sa 9:30am-4:30pm, Su 1-4:30pm; 100BF, includes audio tour.) Head to Citadel Park, near the city center, for the **Museum voor Schone Kunsten's** (Museum of Fine Arts) strong Flemish collection (open Tu-Su 9:30am-5pm; 100BF, students 50BF; free during festivities) and the contemporary art of the **Stedelijk Museum voor Actuele Kunst** (**SMAK;** open Tu-Su 10am-6pm; 200BF, students 150BF).

From October to July 15, scholars cavort in the cafes and discos near the university restaurant on **Overpoortstr.** The huge Art Deco bar **Vooruit,** on St-Pietersnieuwstr., was once the meeting place of the Socialist Party, and was later occupied by Nazis in WWII. (Open mid-Aug. to mid-July Su-Th 11:30am-2am, F-Sa 11:30am-3am.) Beer lovers flock to **Dulle Grief,** on the Vrijdagmarkt, for the 1.2-liter "Max." (Open daily noon-12:30am, Su noon-7pm, M 5:30pm-12:30am.) The **Gentse Feesten** (☎269 09 45) brings 11 nights of international DJs to a different host club each year.

WALLONIE

Although Wallonie lacks the world-class cities of the north, the castle-dotted **Ardennes** offer a relaxing hideaway, with excellent hiking trails and cool caves. Gorgeous train lines sweep through peaceful farmland in the southeast corner. Although nature lovers will want to spend a night in this part of the region, urban addicts can enjoy the scenery en route to Brussels, Paris, or Luxembourg City.

NAMUR ☎081

Quiet Namur, in the heart of Wallonie, is close to **hiking, biking, caving,** and **kayaking** options that make it the best base for exploring the wilderness of the Ardennes. The foreboding **citadel,** atop a rocky hill to the south, was built by the Spanish in the Middle Ages, expanded by the Dutch in the 19th century, witness to a bloody battle in WWI, and occupied until 1978. Hike or take a **mini-bus** (every hr., 40BF) from the tourist office at Sq. Leopold and r. de Grognon. (Open daily 11am-5pm. 210BF.)

Trains link Namur to Brussels (1hr., 245BF). One **tourist office** is a few blocks left of the train station at pl. de la Gare, facing r. Godefroid, and another is in the **Hôtel de Ville.** (Train station office ☎22 28 59, Hôtel de Ville ☎24 64 44; www.ville.namur.be. Both open daily 9:30am-6pm.) To reach the friendly **Auberge Félicien Rops (HI),** 8 av. Félicien Rops, take bus #3 directly to the door, or take bus #4 and ask to be let off. (☎22 36 88. Breakfast included. Sheets 100BF. Laundry 240BF. Bikes 500BF per day. Reception 7:30am-1am. Dorms 440BF; singles 820BF; doubles 1210BF; nonmembers add 100BF.) To **camp** at **Les Trieux,** 99 r. des Tris, 6km away in Malonne, take bus #6. (☎44 55 83. Open Apr.-Oct. 85BF per person, 85BF per tent.) Try the regional Ardennes ham (from 70F) at one of the sandwich stands throughout the city, or stop at the **Match supermarket** in the city center.

EXCURSION FROM NAMUR: DINANT. Dinant is a good launching pad for climbing and kayaking excursions, with an imposing **citadel** rising over the town. Explore on your own, or ride the cable car up and follow along with one of the French tours. (Citadel open daily 10am-6pm. 19F.) Or, explore Dinant's **underground caves**—go with a guide and bring a sweater to the chilly, cascade-filled **Grotte Merveilleuse,** rt. de Phillippeville 142. To reach the Grotte from the citadel, cross the bridge and take the second left onto Rt. de Phillippeville. (☎22 22 10. Open daily Apr.-Oct. 10am-6pm, Mar. and Nov. 11am-5pm. Tours 190BF.) **Dakota Raid Adventure,** r. Saint Roch 17, leads rock-climbing trips. (☎22 32 43. Open daily 10am-5pm.) Reach Dinant by **train** (15min., 130BF) or **bike** from Namur; on summer weekends, take a cruise (3½hr.) on the Meuse River. The **tourist office** is at Quai Cadoux 8. (☎22 28 70; www.maison-du-tourisme.net.) With your back to the train station, turn right, take your first left, and then take your next left. ☎**082.**

BOSNIA-HERZEGOVINA

CONVERTIBLE MARKS (KM)

US$1 = 2.20KM	1KM = US$0.45
CDN$1 = 1.50KM	1KM = CDN$0.67
UK£1 = 3.20KM	1KM = UK£0.31
IR£1 = 2.50KM	1KM = IR£0.40
AUS$1 = 1.30KM	1KM = AUS$0.77
NZ$1 = 0.94KM	1KM = NZ$1.10
SAR1 = 0.32KM	1KM = SAR3.27
DM1 = 1.00KM	1KM = DM1.00
HRV KUNA1 = 0.26KM	1KM = HRV KUNA3.90
EUR€1 = 1.96KM	1KM = EUR€0.51

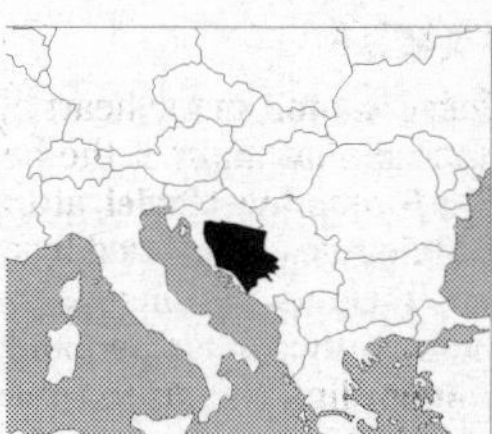

Country code: 387. **International dialing prefix:** 00. From outside Bosnia-Herzegovina, dial int'l dialing prefix (see inside back cover) + 387 + city code + local number.

The mountainous centerpiece of the former Yugoslavia, Bosnia-Herzegovina (herts-uh-GOH-vih-nah) has defied the odds and the centuries to stand as an independent nation today. Bosnia's distinctiveness—and its troubles—spring from its self-proclaimed role as a mixing ground for Muslims, Croats, and Serbs. In Sarajevo, its cosmopolitan capital, that ideal is at least verbally maintained, but ethnic problems continue in the countryside. The country is marked by rolling hills and sparkling rivers, but its lush valleys are now punctuated with abandoned houses and gaping rooftops. The past decade has been brutal, with a bloody war broadcast nightly to the world and much of the population displaced. Bosnia's future is uncertain, particularly with the imminent withdrawal of NATO troops, but its resilient people are optimistic. In this period of post-Dayton peace, rebuilding is slowly underway. Learn more about Bosnia's past and present in *Let's Go: Eastern Europe 2001*.

In August 1999, the US State Department reiterated its **Travel Warning** against unnecessary travel to Bosnia, particularly the Republika Srpska. For more info and the most recent updates, see travel.state.gov/travelwarnings.html.

FACTS AND FIGURES

Official Name: Bosnia and Herzegovina.
Government: Emerging democracy.
Capital: Sarajevo.
Geography: Mountainous, plains in the north; 20km of coastline.
Climate: Mild continental and rainy; cold winters, hot summers. Visit in summer.
Land Area: 51,233km.
Population: 3,482,000 (40% Serbs, 38% Bosnians, 22% Croats).
Languages: Bosnian, Serbian, Croatian.
Religions: Muslim (40%), Orthodox (31%), Catholic (15%), Protestant (4%), other (10%).
Income per capita: US$1720.

ESSENTIALS

DOCUMENTS AND FORMALITIES

Citizens of Canada, Ireland, the UK, and the US may visit Bosnia visa-free for up to one month; **visas** are required for citizens of Australia, New Zealand, and South Africa. There are occasional police checkpoints within Bosnia; register with your embassy upon arrival, and keep your papers with you at all times.

EMBASSIES AND CONSULATES

Embassies and consulates of other countries in Bosnia and Herzegovina are all in **Sarajevo** (see p. 145).

Bosnian Embassies at Home: Australia, 27 State Circle, Forest, Canberra ACT 2603 (☎ (0612) 62 39 59 55; fax 62 39 57 93); **UK,** 320 Regent St., London W1R 5AB (☎ (020) 72 55 37 58; fax 72 55 37 60; email bosnia@embassy_london.ision.co.uk); **US,** 2109 E St. NW, Washington, D.C. 20037 (☎ (202) 337 15 00; fax 337 15 02; www.bosnianembassy.org).

GETTING THERE AND AROUND

Buses are reliable, clean, and not very crowded, but brace yourself for Balkan driving. Buses run daily between Sarajevo and Dubrovnik, and Split and Zagreb, with the first route being the most popular one into the country. Commercial **plane** service into Sarajevo is limited and expensive: **Lufthansa** (US ☎ (800) 399 58 38; www.lufthansa.com), **Croatia Airlines** (☎ +385 (1) 487 27 27;www.croatiaairlines.hr), and **Swiss Air** (US ☎ (800) 221 47 50; www.swissair.com) service Sarajevo. **Railways** are not functional and should not be considered an option. **Eurail** is not valid. Because of road hazards, you should avoid **driving. Biking** and **hitchhiking** are also uncommon and inadvisable.

TOURIST SERVICES AND MONEY

EMERGENCY. Police: ☎ 92. **Fire:** ☎ 93. **Emergency:** ☎ 94.

MONEY. The new Bosnian currency, the **convertible mark (KM),** was introduced in the summer of 1998. It is fixed to the **Deutschmark** at a 1:1 exchange rate. Deutschmarks can be changed directly into convertible marks for no commission at most Sarajevo banks. The Bosnian dinar is not a valid currency. The Croatian **kuna** was named an official Bosnian currency in the summer of 1997; while not legal tender in Sarajevo, it is accepted in the western (Croatian) area of divided Mostar. Change your money back to Deutschmarks when you leave; it is inconvertible outside Bosnia. **Banks** are the best places to exchange money. **Traveler's checks** can be cashed at some Sarajevo banks. There are **no ATMs** in Bosnia. Most restaurants accept credit cards; Visa is best for getting **cash advances.** If your itinerary lies outside of Sarajevo, bring Deutschmarks with you. Accommodations are fairly pricey, at US$15-30; food remains affordable at US$2-5 per meal. **Tip** waitstaff only for excellent service; the amount is up to you.

ACCOMMODATIONS AND CAMPING

Housing prices are stabilizing in Bosnia and Herzegovian. A room in a **pension** costs as little as 30KM, and relatively cheap **private rooms** (30-50KM) are available all over. Discounts are usually available for longer stays. **Camping** is not an option.

HEALTH AND SAFETY

Outside Sarajevo, **do NOT set foot off the pavement** under any circumstances. Even in Sarajevo, stay on paved roads and hard-covered surfaces. Do not pick up any objects on the ground. Millions of **landmines** and **unexploded ordinance** (UXOs) cover the country, many on **road shoulders** and in **abandoned houses.** The **Mine Action Center (MAC),** Zmaja od Bosne 8 (☎ 66 73 10 and 20 12 99; fax 66 73 11), has info.

In Sarajevo, finding medical help and supplies is not a problem; your embassy is your best resource. Peacekeeping operations have brought English-speaking doctors, but not insurance; **cash** is the only method of payment. All drugs are sold at pharmacies, while basic hygiene products are sold at many drugstores.

COMMUNICATION

Yellow-and-white "PTT" signs indicate **post offices.** Few towns outside the capital have mail service. Mail to Australia, Canada, New Zealand, the US, and South Africa, usually takes 1-2 weeks, somewhat less time to Ireland and the UK. **Postcards** cost 1KM to mail. **Poste Restante** is unavailable. **Telephones** are troublesome and

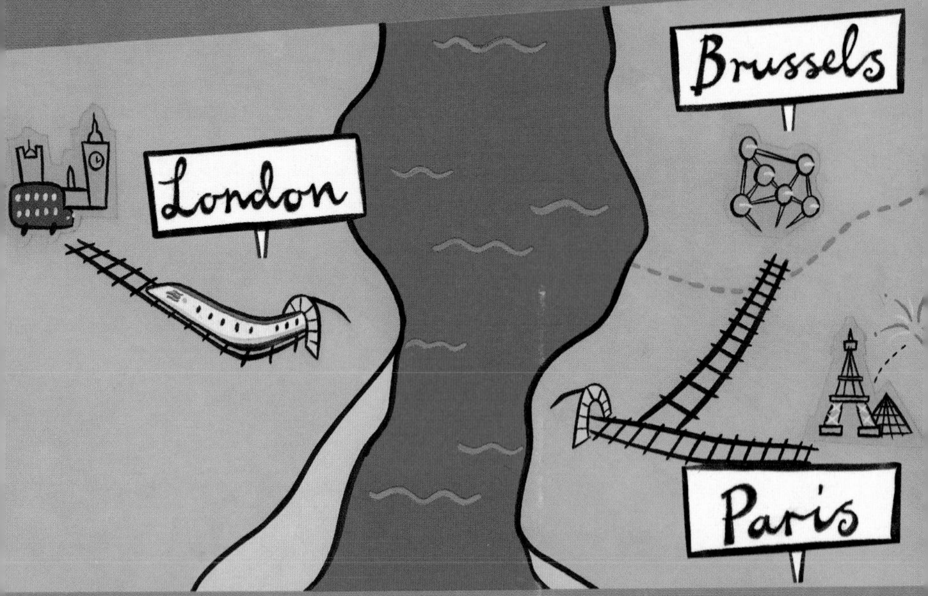

expensive; the best option is to call collect from the Sarajevo post office. Calling the UK is roughly 3.50KM per minute, the US 5KM, but prices vary. **International direct dialing numbers** include **AT&T Direct,** ☎00 800 0010.

HOLIDAYS AND FESTIVALS

Bosnia celebrates many Catholic, Orthodox, and Muslim religious holidays; *Let's Go* does not list them all, as most are days of observance, not public holidays.

Holidays: New Year's (Jan. 1); Orthodox Christmas (Jan.7); Republic Day (Jan. 9); Orthodox New Year's (Jan. 14); Independence Day (Mar. 1); Catholic Easter (Apr. 15); Orthodox Easter (Apr. 30); Labor Day (May 1); St. George's Day (May 6); Vidovdan (June 28); Petrovdan (July 12); Ilindan (Aug. 2); Velika gospa (Aug. 15); Assumption (Aug. 28); National Day (Nov. 25); Catholic Christmas (Dec. 25).

SARAJEVO ☎071

Sarajevo defies cliché; to define the city by its bullet holes is to reduce it to its television presence. Perhaps wary of CNN stereotyping, the city remains largely aloof to the short-term visitor, and tensions are on the rise with the recent influx of refugees. But it is just that sort of elusiveness that makes finding the real Sarajevo—the city loved so passionately by its residents—all the more rewarding.

The following outlying areas of Sarajevo are at particular risk for **mines:** Grbavica, Lukavica, Illidža, and Dobrinja.

PRACTICAL INFO, ACCOMMODATIONS, AND FOOD. **Buses** (☎53 87 02) go from Kranjćevića 9, behind the Holiday Inn at the corner with Halida Kajtaza, to: Dubrovnik (7hr., 2 per day, 41KM); Split (8hr., 4per day, 36KM); Zagreb (9hr., 4 per day, 51KM); Vienna (12hr., 2 per week, 81KM); and Frankfurt (15hr., 1 per day, 190KM). The city's main street is **Maršala Tita.** To reach the **tourist bureau,** Zelenih Beretki 22a, bear right on Maršala Tita past the eternal flame, continue until you see the Catholic church on your left, turn right down Strosmajerova, then left onto Zelenih Beretki. (☎53 26 06. Open M-F 8:30am-noon and 2-4pm.) Most accommodations owners will register your passport number with the police, but visitors planning to stay longer than one month in Bosnia should register at their embassy. **Embassies: Australians** should contact the embassy in Vienna (see p. 101); **Canada,** Logavina 7 (☎44 79 00; open M-F 8:30am-noon and 1-5pm); citizens of **New Zealand** should contact the embassy in Rome (see p. 574); **UK,** Tina Ujevića 8 (☎44 44 29; open M-F 8:30am-5pm); and **US,** Alipašina 43 (☎44 57 00; open M-F 9am-1pm). **Central Profit Bank,** Zelenih Beretki 24, changes money. (Open M-F 8am-7:30pm, Sa 8am-3pm.) There are **no ATMs** in Sarajevo, like the rest of Bosnia. Relatively cheap **private rooms** (40-70KM) are all over; ask a taxi driver at the station if you arrive late. From Maršala Tita, go left at the eternal flame and walk two blocks past the market to get to **Prenoćište "Konak,"** Mula Mustafe Bašeskije 48, on the right. (☎53 35 06. Reception 24hr. Singles 40KM; doubles 60KM.) For an authentic Bosnian meal, scour the Turkish Quarter for **Čevabdžinića** shops; 3KM buys a *čevapčici* (nicknamed *čevaps*), lamb sausages encased in *somun*, Bosnia's tasty, elastic flat bread. **Postal code:** 71000.

SIGHTS. The **eternal flame,** where Maršala Tita splits into Ferhadija and Mula Mustafe Bašeskije, has burned on and off since 1945 as a memorial to all Sarajevans

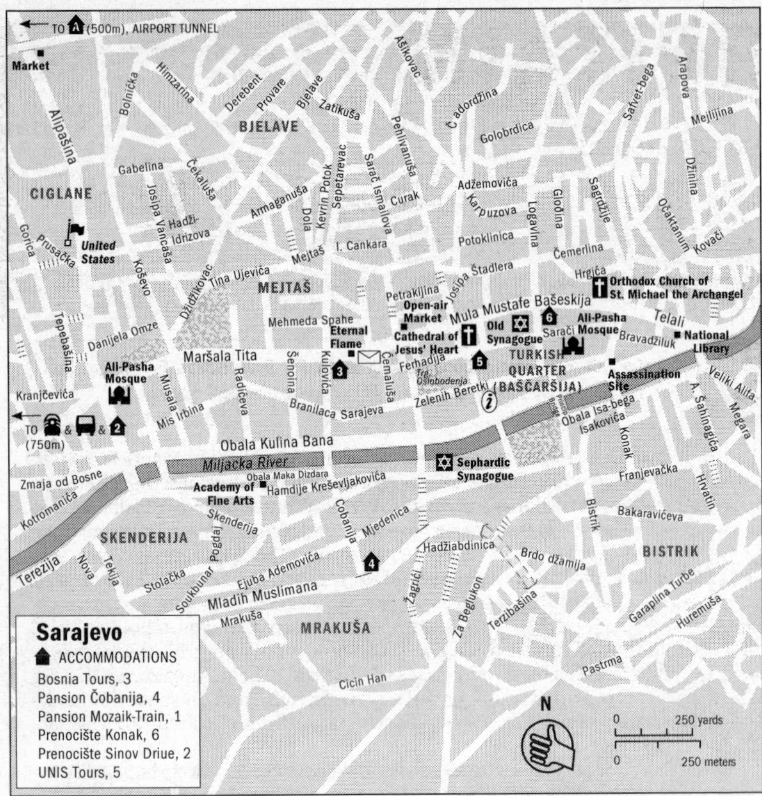

who died in WWII; its homage to South Slav unity now seems painfully ironic. Steady reconstruction has hidden most signs of the recent four-year siege within the city center, but **Sarajevo Roses**—red fillings of grenade holes where people died—are still visible on many streets. The glaring **treeline** in the hills marks the front lines; Bosnians trapped in Sarajevo cut down all the available wood for winter heat. From Maršala Tita, walk toward the river to **Obala Kulina Bana** and turn left to find the **National Library,** at the tip of the Turkish Quarter. Once the most beautiful building in the city, its remains are now smothered in scaffolding. At the second bridge on Obala Kulina Bana, walking from the National Library toward the center, Serbian terrorist Gavrilo Princip shot the Austrian Archduke Franz Ferdinand on June 28, 1914—the **assassination** triggered the build-up to WWI.

Many different religions huddle together in Central Sarajevo as a constant reminder of the diversity that tore the country apart. Walk left at the flame on Ferhadija, which becomes Sarači, to find the 16th-century **Gazi Husrev-Bey mosque,** Sarači 12, perhaps Sarajevo's most famous building. The interior is closed for repairs, but prayer continues in the beautiful courtyard. Surrounding the mosque are the low, red-roofed buildings that make up Baščaršija, the **Turkish Quarter.** The main Orthodox church, **Saborna,** is also closed, but the old **Orthodox Church of St. Michael the Archangel,** on Mula Mustafe Bašeskije, remains open. (Open daily 7am-6pm.) The 1889 **Cathedral of Jesus' Heart** (Katedrala Srce Isusovo), on Ferhadija, designed by Josipa Vancasa, is the spiritual center for local Catholics. (English mass every Sunday at noon.) The **National Museum** and the **History Museum** are at Zmaja od Bosne 3 and 5, respectively. The former is among the Balkans' most famous museums, the latter used to contain historical relics but now houses modern art, much pertaining to the war. (National Museum Open Tu, Th, and Su 10am-2pm; W 11am-7pm. 5KM, students 1KM. History Museum Open M-F 11am-2pm and 6-9pm, Sa-Su 9am-1pm. Free.)

BRITAIN

BRITISH POUNDS

US$1 = UK£0.71	UK£1 = US$1.41
CDN$1 =UK£0.48	UK£1 = CDN$2.08
IR£1 = UK£0.78	UK£1 = IR£1.28
AUS$1 = UK£0.40	UK£1 = AUS$2.52
NZ$1 = UK£0.30	UK£1 = NZ$3.30
SAR1 = UK£0.10	UK£1 = SAR10.03
EUR€1= UK£0.61	UK£1 = EUR€1.63

Country code: 44. **International dialing prefix:** 00. From outside Britain, dial int'l dialing prefix (see inside back cover) + 44 + city code + local number.

The past century has not been kind to the Empire. After Britain founded modern democracy, led the Industrial Revolution, spread colonies around the globe, and helped stave off a Nazi Europe in World War II, a former colony displaced it as the world's economic power. While overseas colonies claimed independence one by one, the Empire frayed at home: most of Ireland won independence in 1921, and Scotland and Wales were promised regional autonomy in 1975. Today, the troubles in Northern Ireland underscore the problems of union and nationalism associated with empire. Travelers should be aware that names hold political force. "Great Britain" refers to England, Scotland, and Wales; it's neither accurate nor polite to call a Scot or Welshman "English." The political term "United Kingdom" refers to these nations as well as Northern Ireland. Because of distinctions in laws and currency, *Let's Go* uses the term "Britain" to refer to England, Scotland, and Wales.

At first glance, anglophone Britain may not seem quite exotic enough for travelers aching to dive into the unknown. The sonnets of Shakespeare, the theories of Adam Smith and Isaac Newton, the philosophy of John Locke, the literature of Virginia Woolf, Charles Dickens, and George Orwell, even the lyrics of John Lennon go to show that strong British threads have been woven into the cultural and historical tapestry of the recent Western world. Despite all this, Britain is less familiar than it appears—look beyond London and allow time for medieval castles, rugged coasts, eerie prehistoric monuments, and wild islands that hearken back to another era.

For more detailed, exhilarating coverage of Britain and London, pore over *Let's Go: Britain & Ireland 2001* or *Let's Go: London 2001*.

FACTS AND FIGURES

Official Name: United Kingdom of Great Britain and Northern Ireland.

Government: Constitutional monarchy.

Capital: London.

Land Area: 241,590 sq. km.

Geography: Mostly rugged hills and low moutains; plains in the south.

Climate: Temperate; summer 55-70°F (12-21°C); winter 36-41°F (2-7°C); often overcast.

Major Cities: Manchester, Liverpool, Cardiff, Glasgow, Edinburgh.

Population: 59,113,439.

Language: English, Welsh, Scottish Gaelic.

Religions: Anglican (46%), Roman Catholic (15%), other (39%).

Average Income Per Capita: US$21,200.

Major Exports: Manufactured goods, machinery, fuels, foodstuffs.

DISCOVER BRITAIN

London is brimming with cultural wonders—wonders from other cultures, that is. The British and the Victoria & Albert Museums testify to the avarice of Empire. While in the capital, don't miss a trip to the Globe Theater to revisit the London of Shakespeare's time (p. 152). Southwest of London, **Winchester** offers a massive Norman cathedral and celebrates native daughter Jane Austen (p. 183), while prehistoric **Stonehenge** (p. 184) and the massive cathedral at **Salisbury** are close by (p. 183). Farther west in the Cornish Coast, **Newquay** is Britain's contribution to surfer culture (p. 185). Back toward London, **Oxford** (p. 186) and **Cambridge** (p. 191) battle to see who's smarter, while **Stratford-Upon-Avon** (p. 190) is Shakespeare-crazy. Near Oxford, **Blenheim Palace** is almost oppressive in its opulence (p. 189). Walk from pretty village to pretty village in the **Cotswolds** (p. 189), then hit **Bath,** which once offered Roman-style healing baths to the rich and famous of Georgian England (p. 191). In nearby Wales, cavort with the sheep and commune with nature in **Snowdonia National Park** (p. 204) and enjoy the theaters of **Cardiff** (p. 201). Back in England, **Liverpool** basks in Beatles mania (p. 196). After exploring industrial **Manchester** (p. 195) and its raucous nightlife, you can escape to the dramatic **Lake District National Park,** filled with rugged hills and windswept fells (p. 198). To munch on haggis and live out your wildest *Braveheart* fantasies, head farther north to Scotland. Enjoy the cultural capitals of **Edinburgh** (p. 206) and **Glasgow** (p. 212), then take the low road to the bonnie, bonnie banks of **Loch Lomond** (p. 217) followed by a journey to the highlands of beautiful **Isle of Skye** (p. 218) and the famed **Loch Ness,** where Nessie awaits (p. 219).

ESSENTIALS

DOCUMENTS AND FORMALITIES

EU citizens do not need a visa to enter Britain or Ireland. For visits of less than six months, citizens of Australia, Canada, New Zealand, South Africa, and the US do not need a visa to enter.

EMBASSIES AND CONSULATES

Embassies and consulates of other countries in Britain are in **London** (p. 152).

British Embassies at Home: Australia, Commonwealth Ave., Yarralumla, Canberra, ACT 2600 (☎ (02) 6270 66 66; fax (02) 6273 32 36; www.uk.emb.gov.au); **Canada,** 80 Elgin St., Ottawa, K1P 5K7 (☎ (613) 237 15 30; www.britain-in-canada.org); **Ireland,** 29 Merrion Rd., Ballsbridge, Dublin 4 (☎ (01) 205 37 00; www.britishembassy.ie); **New Zealand,** 44 Hill St., Thorndon, Wellington 1 (☎ (64) (4) 472 60 49; www.brithighcomm.org.nz); **South Africa Embassy,** 91 Parliament St., Cape Town 8001 (☎ (27) (21) 461 72 20) and 255 Hill St., Arcadia 0083, Pretoria (☎ (012) 483 12 00; www.britain.org.za); **US,** 3100 Massachusetts Ave. NW, Washington, D.C. 20008 (☎ (202) 588 65 00; www.britainusa.com/bis/embassy/embassy.stm).

GETTING AROUND

BY PLANE. Most flights into Britain that originate outside Europe land at **London's Heathrow** and **Gatwick** airports. Flights from Europe also hit **Luton** and **Stansted,** near London, as well as **Cardiff, Liverpool, Manchester, Edinburgh,** and **Glasgow.**

BY TRAIN. There is no longer a single national rail company, although the various companies are often still referred to under the umbrella of "British Rail." Prices and schedules often change: find up-to-date information from **National Rail Inquiries** (☎ (08457) 48 49 50), or online at **Railtrack** (www.railtrack.co.uk; no price information). Rail service in Britain is extensive (and expensive). The **BritRail Pass,** available to non-British travelers outside Britain, allows unlimited travel in England, Wales, and Scotland (8-day US$265, under 26 US$215; 22-day US$505, under 26 US$355). The one-year **Young Person's Railcard,** which grants 33% off most fares in

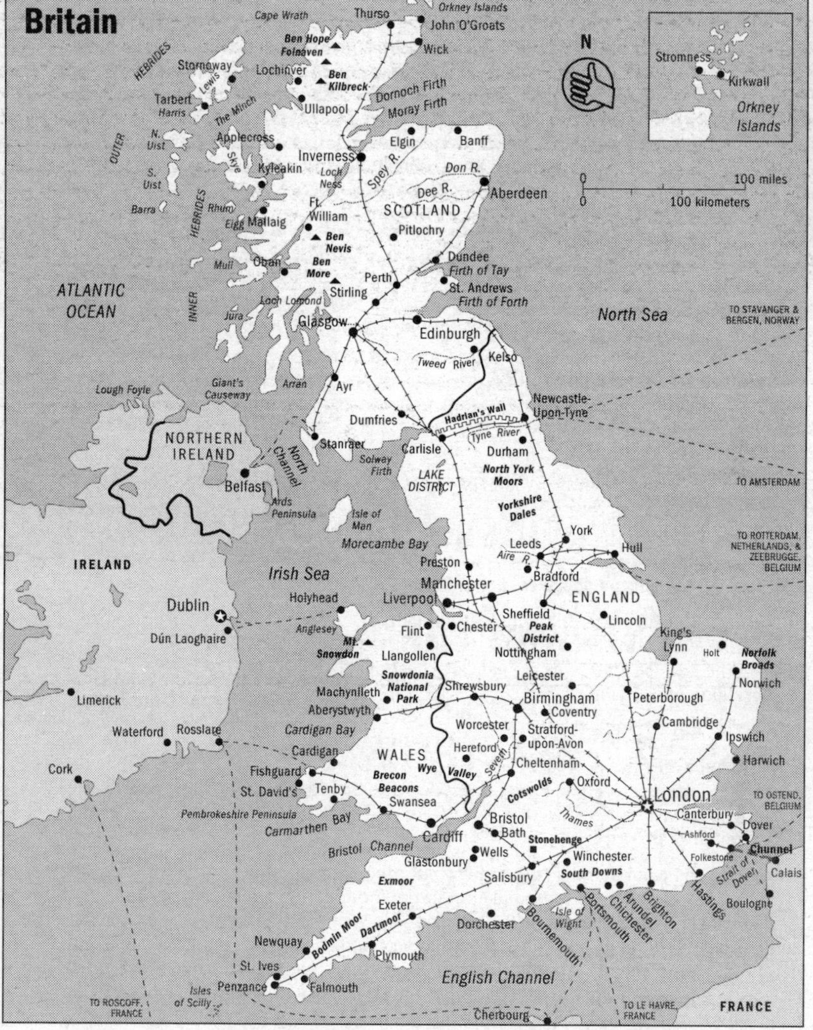

addition to discounts on some ferries, is available to those ages 16 to 25, and to full-time students at British universities over age 23 (£18) at major British Rail Travel Centres in the UK. **Eurail** is not valid in Britain.

BY BUS. Long-distance coach travel in Britain is more extensive than in most European countries and is the cheapest option. **National Express** (☎ (08705) 80 80 80; www.nationalexpress.co.uk) is the principal operator of long-distance coach services in Britain, although **Scottish Citylink** (tel. (08705) 50 50 50) has extensive coverage in Scotland. **Discount Coachcards** are available for seniors (over 50), students, and young persons (ages 16-25) for £8 and reduce fares on National Express by about 30%. For those planning a lot of coach travel, the **Tourist Trail Pass** offers unlimited travel for a number of days within a given period (2 days out of 3 £49, students, seniors, and children £39; 5 out of 10 £85, £69; 7 out of 21 £120, £94; 14 out of 30 £187, £143).

BY FERRY. Numerous ferry lines ply the route across the English Channel; the most popular crossing is from **Dover** to **Calais, France.** Always ask about reduced fares—an HI card or ISIC with Travelsave stamps might mean a 25 to 50% discount. Book ahead June through August. Other routes between the Continent and England include Bergen, Norway to Lerwick or Newcastle; Esbjerg, Denmark to Harwich; Göteborg, Sweden to Harwich or Newcastle; Hamburg, Germany to Harwich or Newcastle; Oostende, Belgium to Ramsgate, near Dover; and Hook of Holland to Harwich. For info on boats from **Wales** to **Dublin** and **Rosslare, Ireland,** see p. 201; from **Scotland** to **Belfast,** see p. 554; from **England** to the **Continent,** see p. 177.

BY CAR. Brits drive on the left side of the road; enter traffic circles by turning left as well. **Gas,** usually called petrol, averages about US$4 per gallon. **Roads** are generally well maintained, but parking in London is impossible and traffic is slow. In Britain, rotaries are called "roundabouts," overpasses are "flyovers," traffic jams are "tail-backs," and the breakdown lane is the "lay-by." The trunk of a car is the "boot."

BY BIKE AND BY THUMB. Much of Britain's countryside is well suited for **biking.** Many cities and villages have bike rental shops and maps of local cycle routes; ask at the tourist office. Large-scale Ordnance Survey maps detail the extensive system of long-distance **hiking** paths. Tourist offices and National Park Information Centres can provide extra information about routes. *Let's Go* does not recommend **hitchhiking;** it is illegal on motorways (roads labeled "M") and always risky.

TOURIST SERVICES AND MONEY

EMERGENCY. Police, ambulance, fire: ☎999.

TOURIST OFFICES. The **British Tourist Authority** (BTA; www.visitbritain.com) is an umbrella organization coordinating the activities of the separate UK tourist boards outside the UK. **Tourist Boards at home** are: **Australia,** Level 16, Gateway, 1 Macquarie Pl., Circular Quay, Sydney NSW 2000 (☎ (02) 93 77 44 00; www.visitbritain.com/au); **Canada,** Air Transat Bldg., 5915 Airport Rd., Suite 120, Mississauga, ON L4V 1T1 (☎ (888) 847 48 85 or (905) 405 18 40; www.visitbritain.com/ca); **New Zealand,** 17th Fl., Fay Richwhite Building, 151 Queen Street, Auckland 1 (☎ (09) 303 14 46); **South Africa,** Lancaster Gate, Hyde Park Ln., Hyde Park, Sandton 2196 (☎ (011) 325 03 43); **US,** 551 Fifth Ave. #701, New York, NY 10176 (☎ (800) 462 27 48 or (212) 986 22 00; www.travelbritain.org).

MONEY. The **Pound Sterling** is the main unit of currency in the United Kingdom. It is divided into 100 pence, issued in standard denominations of 1p, 2p, 5p, 10p, 20p, 50p, and £1 in coins, and £5, £10, £20, and £50 in notes. Scotland uses a £1 note, and you may see the discontinued £2 coin. Scotland has its own bank notes, which can be used interchangeably with English currency, though you may have difficulty using Scottish £1 notes outside Scotland. Expect to spend anywhere from £15-30 per person per day, depending on where you choose to visit. Accommodations start at about £6 a night for a bed in a **hostel** in rural areas, or £12 per night in a **B&B,** while a basic sit-down **meal** at a pub costs about £5. London in particular is a budget-buster, with £25-35 a day being the bare minimum for accommodations, food, and transport. **Tips** in restaurants are usually included in the bill, sometimes as a "service charge." If gratuity is not included then you should tip 10-15%. Tipping the barman in pubs is not at all expected, though a waiter or waitress should be tipped. Taxi drivers should receive a 10% tip, and bellhops and chambermaids usually expect somewhere between £1 and £3. Aside from open-air markets, don't expect to barter anywhere else, including hostels, taxis, and tour guides. Britain has a 17.5% **Value Added Tax (VAT),** a sales tax applied to everything except food, books, medicine, and children's clothing. The tax is included within the price indicated—no extra expenses should be added at the register.

ACCOMMODATIONS AND CAMPING

HOSTELS. Youth hostels in Britain are run by the **Youth Hostels Association (YHA) of England and Wales** and the **Scottish Youth Hostels Association (SYHA), An Óige** (an OYJ). Unless noted as "self-catering," the YHA hostels listed in *Let's Go* (not including SYHA ones) offer cooked meals at standard rates—breakfast £3.20, small/standard packed lunch £2.80/£3.65, evening meal £4.15 (or £4.80 for a three-course meal in some hostels), and children's meals (breakfast £1.75, lunch or dinner £2.70). In Britain, a bed in a hostel will cost around £6 in rural areas, £12 in larger cities, and £13-20 in London.

BED AND BREAKFASTS. For a cozier alternative to impersonal hotel rooms, B&Bs and guest houses (often private homes with rooms available to travelers) range from the acceptable to the sublime. **Bed and Breakfast (GB),** 94-96 Bell St., Henley-on-Thames, Oxon, England RG9 1XS (☎ (01491) 578803), is a reservation service which covers England, Scotland, Wales, and Ireland. It books rooms for a minimum deposit of £30, which is not refundable, but can be deducted from the total price of your stay.

CAMPING. Campsites tend to be privately owned, with basic ones costing £3 per person, and posh ones costing up to £10 per person. It is illegal to camp in national parks, since much of their land is privately owned.

FOOD AND DRINK

British cuisine's deservedly lackluster reputation redeems itself in a few areas. Britain is largely a nation of carnivores; the best native dishes are roasts—beef, lamb, and Wiltshire hams. And meat isn't just for dinner; the British like their famed breakfasts meaty and cholesterol-filled. Before you leave the country, you must try any of the sweet, glorious British puddings. The "ploughman's lunch" (a product of a 60s advertising campaign) consists of cheese, bread, relish, chutney, and a tomato. Fish and chips are traditionally drowned in vinegar and salt. Caffs (full meals £5-6) are the British equivalent of US diners. To escape English food, try Chinese, Greek, or especially Indian cuisine. British **"tea"** refers both to a drink and a social ritual. Tea the drink is served strong and milky; if you want it any other way, say so in advance. Tea the social can be a meal unto itself. Afternoon high tea as served in rural Britain includes cooked meats, salad, sandwiches, and pastries. Cream tea, a specialty of Cornwall and Devon, includes toast, shortbread, crumpets, scones, jam, and clotted cream.

FLAKES AND SMARTIES British food has character (of one sort or another), and the traditional menu is a mad hodgepodge of candy, crisps, yeasts, and squashes. Britain has a greater variety of **candy** for sale than most countries. Brands to watch out for include Flake by Cadbury, Crunchies (made out of honeycombed magic), and the ever-popular Smarties. Watch out for the orange ones–they're made of orange chocolate. Potato chips, or **crisps** as they are known in England, are not just salted, but come in a range of flavors, including Prawn Cocktail, Beef, Chicken, and Fruit 'n' Spice. All this sugar and salt can be washed down with pineapple-and-grapefruit-flavored soda Lilt or a can of Ribena, a red currant syrup which has to be diluted with water. This latter beverage belongs to a family of drinks known as **squash,** all of which are diluted before consumption. But the food that expatriate Britons miss most is **Marmite,** a yeast extract which is spread on bread or toast. If you weren't fed Marmite as a baby, you'll never appreciate it; most babies don't either.

COMMUNICATION

MAIL. Airmail letters under 1 oz. between North America and Britain or Ireland take 3-5 days and cost US$1 or CDN$0.95. From Australia, airmail takes 5-7 days (postage AUS$1.20 for small letters up to 20g, AUS$1.50 for large letters up to 20g). Envelopes should be marked "air mail" or "par avion" to avoid having letters sent by sea. Address *Poste Restante* letters to the post office, highlighting the last name. For example: First name SURNAME, Poste Restante, New Bond St. Post Office, Bath BA1 1A5, United Kingdom.

TELEPHONES. Public pay phones in Britain are mostly run by **British Telecom (BT);** The BT phonecard, available in denominations from £2-20, is probably a useful purchase, since BT phones tend to be omnipresent. Public phones charge a minimum of 10p for calls, and don't accept 1p, 2p, or 5p coins. For **directory inquiries,** which are free from payphones, call 192 in Britain. **International direct dial numbers** include: **AT&T,** ☎ (0800) 89 00 11; **BT Direct,** ☎ (0800) 34 51 44; **Canada Direct,** ☎ (0800) 89 00 16; **MCI WorldPhone Direct,** ☎ (0800) 89 02 22; **Sprint Global One,** ☎ (0800) 89 08 77; **Telkom South Africa Direct,** ☎ (0800) 89 00 27.

INTERNET ACCESS. Britain is one of the world's most wired countries, and cybercafes can usually be found in larger cities. They cost £4-6 an hour, but often you can pay only for time used, not for the whole hour. On-line guides to cybercafes in Britain and Ireland that are updated daily include **The Cybercafe Search Engine** (http://cybercaptive.com) and **Cybercafes.com** (www.cybercafes.com).

HOLIDAYS AND FESTIVALS

Holidays: New Year's Day (Jan. 1); Good Friday (Apr. 21); Easter Sunday and Monday; May Day (May 1); May 29 (bank holiday); and Christmas (Dec. 25-26). Scotland also kicks back on Jan. 2 and Aug. 7 (both bank holidays).

Festivals: The largest festival in the world is the **Edinburgh International Festival** (Aug.). Manchester's Gay Village hosts **Mardi Gras** (late Aug.). Muddy fun abounds at the **Glastonbury Festival.**

ENGLAND

A land where there is the promise of a cup of tea just beyond even the darkest moor, England, for better or worse, has determined the meaning of "civilized" for many peoples and cultures. England is now the heart of "Cool Britannia," a young, fashionable image of a country looking forward. The avant-garde has emerged from behind the sensible plaid skirts of the mainstream and taken center stage. But traditionalists can rest easy; for all the metropolitan moving and shaking, around the corner there are a handful of quaint towns, dozen of picturesque castles, and a score of comforting cups of teas.

LONDON ☎020

No longer the sole domain of bobbies and Beefeaters, princes, and Parliament, eclectic London welcomes everyone, from tea-drinking Royal-watchers to black-clad Soho types. The stereotypical Londoner is almost impossible to define: both the snooty Kensington resident and the owner of an Indian takeaway in the East End hold equal claim to the title. The city itself is equally difficult to categorize, as administrative capital of Britain, financial center of Europe, and a world leader in the arts. London will not disappoint as a tweed heaven, but you need only look at the array of hip restaurants or the queues in front of clubs to realize why it's Austin Powers's hometown. Despite the city's costly lodgings and food, its top-quality theater, museums, and galleries remain very much within the reach of any traveler.

For an absolutely smashing little book, check out *Let's Go: London 2001*.

GETTING THERE AND AWAY

Flights: Heathrow Airport (☎87 59 43 21; www.baa.co.uk) is the world's busiest airport. The **Heathrow Express** (www.heathrowexpress.com) train goes between Heathrow terminals 1-4 and Paddington Station (every 15min. 5:10am-11:40pm, £12). From **Gatwick Airport** (☎ (01293) 53 53 53), take the BR Gatwick Express train to Victoria Station (35min., every 15-30min. 24hr., £8.50). **National Express** (☎ (08705) 80 80 80) buses run from Victoria Station to Gatwick (1hr., every hr. 5:05am-8:20pm, £8.50). **Taxis** take twice as long and cost 5 times as much.

Trains: London has 8 major stations: **Charing Cross** (serves south England); **Euston** (the north and northwest, including Birmingham, Glasgow, Holyhead, Inverness, Liverpool, and Manchester); **King's Cross** (the north and northeast, including Cambridge, Edinburgh, Leeds, Newcastle, and York); **Liverpool St.** (East Anglia, including Colchester, Ipswich, and Norwich, as well as Stansted Airport); **Paddington** (the west, including Oxford, the southwest, including Bristol, and South Wales, including Cardiff); **St. Pancras** (the Midlands, including Nottingham and Sheffield); **Victoria** (the south, including Brighton, Canterbury, Dover, and Hastings, as well as Gatwick Airport); and **Waterloo** (the south and southwest, including Portsmouth and Salisbury, and the continent). All stations are linked by the Underground. Get info at station ticket offices, tourist offices, or from the **National Rail Inquires Line** (☎ (0345) 48 49 50; www.britrail.com).

Buses: Long-distance buses (known as **coaches** in the UK) arrive in London at **Victoria Coach Station,** 164 Buckingham Palace Rd. SW1 (☎77 30 34 66; Tube: Victoria). **National Express** (☎ (08705) 80 80 80; www.nationalexpress.co.uk), is the principal operator of long-distance coach services in Britain. **Eurolines** (☎ (01582) 40 45 11) runs coaches into Victoria from Europe.

GETTING AROUND

Public Transportation: London is divided into 6 concentric transport zones; fares depend on the distance and number of zones crossed. The 24hr. help line (☎72 22 12 34) helps plan subway and bus travel. The **Underground** (or **Tube**) is fast, efficient, and crowded. Open daily 6am-midnight. A single adult ticket costs between £1.50 and £3.50, with most central London trips costing £1.50 to £1.80. Trips to, from, or within Zone 1 cost £1; any trip within outer London (not traveling in Zone 1) costs £0.70. Buy your ticket before you board and pass it through automatic gates at both ends of your journey. The **Travelcard,** a must for budget travelers, is valid on the Underground, regular buses, British Rail (Network SouthEast), and the Docklands Light Railway. Available in 1-day, 1-week, and 1-month increments from any station; some restrictions apply. Refer also to the **Underground map** at the back of this book. The **bus** network is divided into 4 zones. **Night buses** ("N") run frequently throughout London 11:30pm-6am; all pass through Trafalgar Sq. Pick up free maps and guides at **London Transport Information Centres** (look for the lower-case "i" logo on signs) at the following Tube stations: Euston, Victoria, King's Cross, Liverpool St., Oxford Circus, Piccadilly, and St. James's Park; you can also find them at Heathrow Terminals 1, 2, and 4.

Taxis: A light signifies that they're empty. Fares are steep and a 10% tip is standard. You can call a radio dispatcher for a taxi (☎72 72 02 72), but beware that you may be charged extra for ordering by phone.

ORIENTATION

Central London, on the north side of the Thames, bounded roughly by the Underground's Circle Line, contains most major sights. Within Central London, the vaguely defined **West End,** south of Oxford St., incorporates the understated elegance of **Mayfair,** the shopping streets around **Oxford Circus,** the theaters and tourist traps of **Piccadilly Circus** and **Leicester Square,** bohemian **Soho, Covent Garden,** and London's unofficial center, **Trafalgar Square.** East of the West End lies **Holborn,** the center of legal activity, and **Fleet Street,** journalists' traditional haunt. North of Oxford St. are literary **Bloomsbury** and embassy-filled **Marylebone.** To the southwest

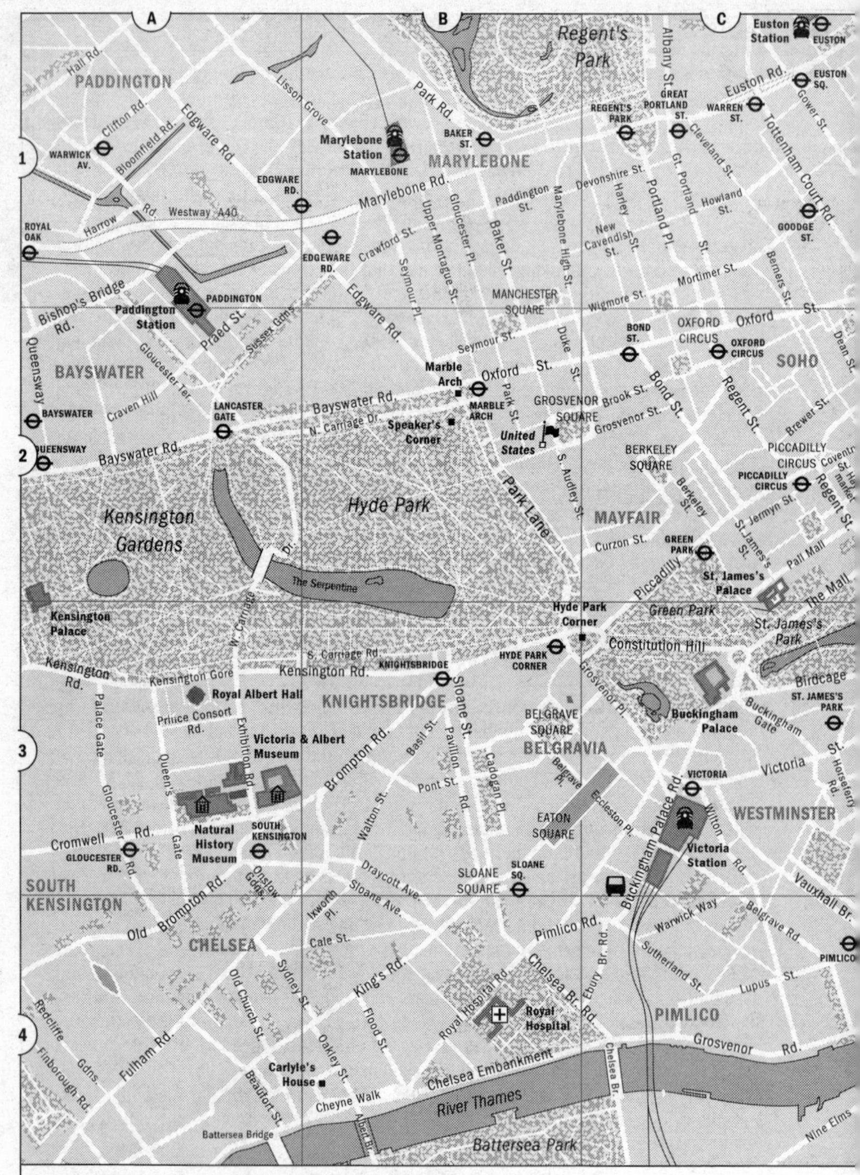

Central London: Major Street Finder

Albert Embankment **D4**
Aldersgate **E1**
Aldwych **D2**
Audley(N&S) **B2**
Baker St **B1**
Bayswater Rd **A2**
Beech St/Chiswell St **E1**
Belgrave Pl **B3**
Beaufort **A4**
Belgrave Rd **C4**
Berkeley St **C2**
Birdcage Walk **C3**
Bishops Br. Rd **A1**
Bishopsgate **F1**
Blackfriars Rd **E2**
Bloomsbury Way **D1**
Bond St (New&Old) **C2**
Bow St/Lancaster Pl **D2**
Brompton Rd **B3**
Buckingham Gate **C3**
Buckingham Palace Rd **C3**
Cannon St **F2**
Chancery Ln **D1**
Charing Cross Rd **D2**
Charterhouse St **E1**
Cheapside **E2**
Chelsea Br. Rd **B4**
Chelsea Embankment **B4**
Cheyne Walk **B4**
City Rd **F1**
Clerkenwell Rd **E1**
Constitution Hill **C3**
Cornhill/Leadenhall St **F2**
Coventry/Cranbourne **D2**
Craven Hill Rd/Praed St **A2**
Cromwell Rd **A3**
Curzon St **C2**
Drury Ln **D2**
Eastcheap/Great Tower **F2**
Eccleston Pl **C3**

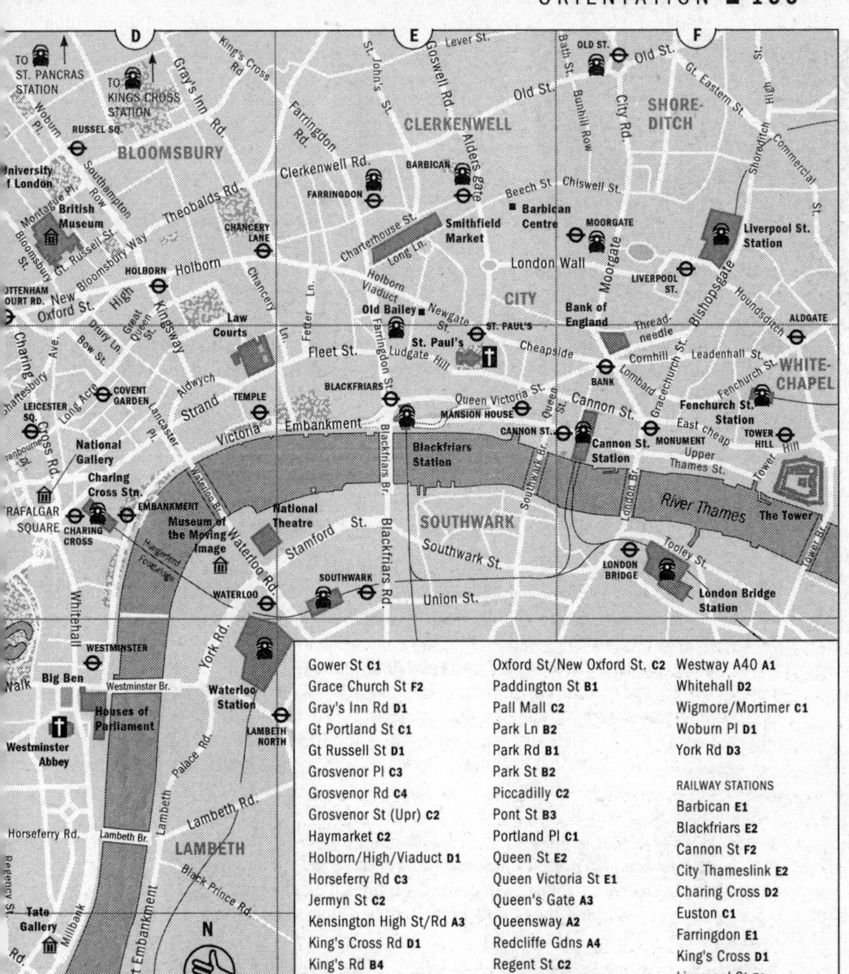

Edgware Rd **A1**
Euston Rd **C1**
Exhibition Rd **A3**
Farringdon Rd **E1**
Fenchurch/Aldgate **F2**
Fleet St **E2**
Fulham Rd **A4**
Gloucester Pl **B1**
Gloucester Rd **A3**
Goswell Rd **E1**
Gower St **C1**
Grace Church St **F2**
Gray's Inn Rd **D1**
Gt Portland St **C1**
Gt Russell St **D1**
Grosvenor Pl **C3**
Grosvenor Rd **C4**
Grosvenor St (Upr) **C2**
Haymarket **C2**
Holborn/High/Viaduct **D1**
Horseferry Rd **C3**
Jermyn St **C2**
Kensington High St/Rd **A3**
King's Cross Rd **D1**
King's Rd **B4**
Kingsway **D2**
Knightsbridge **B3**
Lambeth Palace Rd **D3**
Lisson Grove **A1**
Lombard St **F2**
London Wall **E1**
Long Acre/Grt Queen **D2**
Long Ln **E1**
Ludgate Hill **E2**
Marylebone High St **B1**
Marylebone Rd **B1**
Millbank **D4**
Montague Pl **D1**
Moorgate **F1**
New Bridge St **E2**
New Cavendish **C1**
Newgate St **E1**
Nine Elms Ln **C4**
Oakley St **B4**
Old St **F1**
Old Brompton Rd **A4**
Onslow Sq/St **A3**
Oxford St/New Oxford St. **C2**
Paddington St **B1**
Pall Mall **C2**
Park Ln **B2**
Park Rd **B1**
Park St **B2**
Piccadilly **C2**
Pont St **B3**
Portland Pl **C1**
Queen St **E2**
Queen Victoria St **E1**
Queen's Gate **A3**
Queensway **A2**
Redcliffe Gdns **A4**
Regent St **C2**
Royal Hospital Rd **B4**
St. James's St **C2**
Seymour Pl **A1**
Seymour St **A2**
Shaftesbury Ave **C2**
Sloane/Lwr Sloane **B3**
Southampton Row **D1**
Southwark Bridge Rd **E2**
Southwark Rd **E2**
Stamford St **E2**
Strand **D2**
Sydney St **A4**
Thames St(Upr&Lwr) **F2**
The Mall **C2**
Theobald's Rd **D1**
Threadneedle St **F2**
Tottenham Ct Rd **C1**
Vauxhall Br. Rd **C4**
Victoria Embankment **D2**
Victoria St **C3**
Warwick Way **C4**
Waterloo Rd **E1**
Westway A40 **A1**
Whitehall **D2**
Wigmore/Mortimer **C1**
Woburn Pl **D1**
York Rd **D3**

RAILWAY STATIONS

Barbican **E1**
Blackfriars **E2**
Cannon St **F2**
City Thameslink **E2**
Charing Cross **D2**
Euston **C1**
Farringdon **E1**
King's Cross **D1**
Liverpool St **F1**
London Bridge **F2**
Marylebone **B1**
Moorgate **F1**
Old St. **F1**
Paddington **A2**
St Pancras **D1**
Victoria **C3**
Waterloo East **E2**
Waterloo **D3**

BRIDGES

Albert **B4**
Battersea **A4**
Blackfriars **E2**
Chelsea **C4**
Hungerford Footbridge **D2**
Lambeth **D3**
London Bridge **F2**
Southwark **E2**
Tower Bridge **F2**
Waterloo **D2**
Westminster **D3**

are posh **Knightsbridge, Kensington,** and **Belgravia,** and to the west lie the vibrant **Notting Hill** and **Bayswater** districts. Around the southeastern corner of the Circle Line is the **City,** which refers to the ancient and much smaller "City of London," which covers only one of the 620 sq. mi. of today's Greater London. Today the City is the financial nerve center of London, with the **Tower of London** at its eastern edge and **St. Paul's Cathedral** nearby. Farther east is the ethnically diverse, working-class **East End.** Back west along the river and the southern part of the Circle Line is the district of **Westminster,** just south of the West End, where you'll find **Buckingham Palace,** the **Houses of Parliament,** and **Westminster Abbey.** Trendy residential districts stretch to the north, including **Hampstead** and **Highgate,** graced by Hampstead Heath. The most useful navigational aids are street atlases, such as *London A to Z* (the "A to Zed"), *ABC Street Atlas,* Nicholson's *London Streetfinder,* or *Let's Go Map Guide: London.* Refer also to the **color maps** at the back of this book. London is divided into boroughs and into postal code areas, whose letters stand for compass directions. The borough name and postal code appear at the bottom of most street signs; *Let's Go* lists postal codes in addresses.

PRACTICAL INFORMATION

TOURIST, FINANCIAL, AND LOCAL SERVICES

British Travel Centre, 12 Regent St. (☎88 46 90 00). Tube: Piccadilly Circus. Run by the British Tourist Authority and ideal for travelers bound for destinations outside London. £5 surcharge for accommodations booking and a required deposit (1 night or 15% of the total stay; does not book for hostels). Open M-F 9am-6:30pm, Sa-Su 10am-4pm.

London Tourist Board Information Centre, Victoria Station Forecourt, SW1 (☎ (0839) 12 34 32; £0.39-.49 per min.). Tube: Victoria. Offers information on London and England and an accommodations service (☎79 32 20 20, fax 79 32 20 21). £5 booking fee, plus 15% refundable deposit; MC, V. Open Apr.-Nov. daily 8am-7pm; Dec.-Mar. M-Sa 8am-7pm, Su 8am-5pm. Additional tourist offices located at: **Heathrow Airport** (open daily Apr.-Nov. 9am-6pm; Dec.-Mar. 9am-5pm) and **Liverpool St. Underground Station** (open M 8:15am-7pm, Tu-Sa 8:15am-6pm, Su 8:30am-4:45pm).

Embassies: Australia, Australia House, The Strand, WC2 (☎73 79 43 34). Tube: Aldwych or Temple. Open M-F 9:30am-3:30pm. **Canada,** MacDonald House, 1 Grosvenor Sq., W1 (☎72 58 66 00). Tube: Bond St. or Oxford Circus. **Ireland,** 17 Grosvenor Pl., SW1 (☎72 35 21 71). Tube: Hyde Park Corner. Open M-F 9:30am-4:30pm. **New Zealand,** New Zealand House, 80 Haymarket, SW1 (☎7930 8422). Open M-F 10am-noon and 2-4pm. **South Africa,** South Africa House, Trafalgar Sq., WC2 (☎74 51 72 99). Tube: Charing Cross. Consular services M-F 8:45am-12:45pm. **US,** 24 Grosvenor Sq., W1 (☎74 99 90 00). Tube: Bond St. Phones answered 24hr.

Currency Exchange: The best rates are at **High St.** banks, including **Barclay's, Lloyd's, National Westminster (NatWest),** and **HSBC (Midland).**

American Express: Throughout London; call ☎ (0800) 52 13 13 for the closest one.

Gay and Lesbian Services: London Lesbian and Gay Switchboard (☎78 37 73 24). 24hr. advice and support service.

EMERGENCY AND COMMUNICATIONS

Emergency (Medical, Police, and Fire): ☎999; no coins required.

Dental Care: Eastman Dental Hospital (☎79 15 10 00).

Medical Assistance: In an emergency, you can be treated at no charge in the Accidents and Emergencies (A&E; also known as casualty) ward of a hospital. The following have 24hr. walk-in A&E departments: **Royal London Hospital,** Whitechapel Rd., E1 (☎73 77 70 00). Tube: Whitechapel. **Royal Free Hospital,** Pond St., NW3 (☎77 94 05 00). Tube: Belsize Park. Rail: Hampstead Heath. **Charing Cross Hospital,** Fulham Palace Rd. (entrance on St. Dunstan's Rd.), W6 (☎88 46 12 34). Tube: Baron's Court or Hammersmith. **St. Thomas' Hospital,** Lambeth Palace Rd., SE1 (☎79 28 92 92). Tube:

Westminster. **University College Hospital,** Gower St. (entrance on Grafton Way), WC1 (☎73 87 93 00). Tube: Euston or Warren St.

Pharmacies: Every police station keeps a list of emergency doctors and chemists in its area. Listings are under "Chemists" in the Yellow Pages. **Bliss Chemists,** 5 Marble Arch, W1 (☎77 23 61 16), is open daily including public holidays, 9am-midnight.

Police: Stations in every district of London. **Headquarters,** New Scotland Yard, Broadway, SW1 (☎72 30 12 12). Tube: St. James's Park. **West End Central,** 10 Vine St., W1 (☎74 37 12 12). Tube: Piccadilly Circus. For emergencies, dial ☎999.

Samaritans: (☎77 34 28 00; ☎ (0345) 90 90 90). 24hr. crisis hotline.

Internet Access: Cybercafes punctuate London. Get connected at **easyEverything,** 9-13 Wilson Rd., W1 (☎74 82 95 02), directly opposite Victoria station. Tube: Victoria. This dirt-cheap (£1 per hr.) Internet emporium has over 400 terminals. Cafe serves coffee (espresso £0.80) and sandwiches (chicken tikka £2.25). Open daily 24hr.

Post Office: Post offices are everywhere; call ☎ (0345) 22 33 44 to find the nearest one. When sending mail to the UK, be sure to write the postal district: London has 7 King's Roads, 8 Queen's Roads, and 2 Mandela Streets. The main office is the **Trafalgar Square Post Office,** 24-28 William IV St., **WC2N 4DL** (☎74 84 93 04; Tube: Charing Cross). Open M-Th and Sa 8am-8pm, F 8:30am-8pm. All mail sent *Poste Restante* or general delivery to unspecified post offices ends up here. Address mail to be sent: First name SURNAME, Poste Restante, London SW1, United Kingdom.

ACCOMMODATIONS

Reserve rooms in advance for summer—landing in London without reservations is like landing on a bicycle with no seat. B&Bs are a bargain for groups of two or more, but hostels are the cheapest (and most social) option for small groups. Accommodations in the **City** are scarce, with most available space gobbled up by offices. However, many sights are nearby and the region is well served by the Tube and buses, particularly on weekdays.

YHA HOSTELS

Youth Hostel Association hostels are restricted to members of **Hostelling International** and its affiliated **Youth Hostel Association of England and Wales** (☎ (0870) 870 88 88; www.yha.org.uk). You can join at YHA London Headquarters or at the hostels themselves for £12, under 18 £6. An **International Guest Pass** (£1.90) permits nonmembers not residents of England or Wales to stay at hostels, often at slightly higher rates. Buy six guest passes and you automatically become a full member. Hostels are not always able to accommodate every written request for reservations, much less on-the-spot inquiries, but they frequently hold a few beds available—it's always worth checking. To secure a place, show up as early as possible and expect to stand in line, book in advance with a credit card at the number or website above, or write to the warden of the individual hostel.

All hostels are equipped with large **lockers** that require a padlock. Bring your own, or purchase one from the hostel for £3. London hostels do not charge for sheets or sleeping bags, and most have laundry facilities and some kitchen equipment. Theater tickets and discounted attraction tickets are available.

YHA Hampstead Heath, 4 Wellgarth Rd., NW11 (☎84 58 90 54; fax 82 09 05 46; email hampstead@yha.org.uk). Tube: Golders Green, then bus #210 or 268 toward Hampstead; or, turn left from the station onto North End Rd., then left again onto Wellgarth Rd. (10min.). A beautiful, sprawling hostel. Kitchen and laundry. Restaurant. Reception 24hr. Book in advance. Dorms £19.70, under 18 £17.30; doubles £35; triples £51.95; quads £68.95; quints £85.95; 6-bed rooms £100.

YHA City of London, 36 Carter Ln., EC4 (☎72 36 49 65; fax 72 36 76 81). Tube: St. Paul's. Sleep in quiet comfort a stone's throw from St. Paul's. Scrupulously clean, with luggage storage, currency exchange, laundry, Internet (£5 per hr.), and theater box office. Reception 7am-11pm. Dorms £18.70-24.10; singles £26.80, under 18 £23.30; doubles £52.10, £44.60; private rooms £50-135, families £40-120.

YHA Holland House, Holland Walk, W8 (☎79 37 07 48; fax 73 76 06 67; email hollandhouse@yha.org.uk). Tube: High St. Kensington or Holland Park. Clean, spacious rooms with lockers–bring a padlock. Breakfast included. Laundry and kitchen facilities. Luggage storage. Reception 24hr. £19.95, under 18 £17.95.

YHA King's Cross/St. Pancras, 79-81 Euston Rd. (☎73 88 99 98; fax 73 88 67 66; email stpancras@yha.org.uk). Tube: King's Cross/St. Pancras. Many family rooms. Premium rooms include bathroom, TV, and coffee/tea facilities. English breakfast included. Luggage storage. Laundry, Internet, and kitchen facilities. Max. 1-week stay. Dorms £23, under 18 £19.70; doubles £40-53; quads £80-100; quints £100.

PRIVATE HOSTELS

Private hostels don't require HI/YHA membership, serve a youthful clientele, and usually have single-sex rooms. Curfews are rare, and the dorms are usually cheaper. Almost all accept major credit cards.

International Student House, 229 Great Portland St., W1 (☎76 31 83 00; fax 76 31 83 15). Tube: Great Portland St. At the foot of Regent's Park, across the street from the Tube station. Films, concerts, discos, athletic contests, expeditions, and parties. Laundry facilities, currency exchange. Breakfast included. Dorms (without breakfast) £10; singles £31, with ISIC £24.50; doubles £45, £39; triples £60; quads £70.

Ashlee House, 261-65 Gray's Inn Rd. (☎78 33 94 00; fax 78 33 67 77; email info@ashleehouse.co.uk; www.ashleehouse.co.uk). Tube: King's Cross. Clean, bright rooms within easy walking distance of King's Cross (which is good and bad). Some rooms have skylights; all have washbasins and central heating. No hot water noon-6pm. Generous breakfast included. Secure luggage room, laundry, kitchens, and Internet access. Sheets provided. Reception 24hr. Check-out 10am. Dorms Apr.-Oct. £15-19, Nov.-Mar. £13-17; doubles £44, 48.

Central University of Iowa Hostel, 7 Bedford Pl. (☎/fax 75 80 11 21). Tube: Tottenham Court Rd. or Russell Sq. On a quiet street near the British Museum. Spartan, narrow dorm rooms with bunk beds and washbasins. Continental breakfast included. Laundry facilities, towels and linen, TV lounge. Key deposit £10. Reception 9am-10:30pm. Open May 20-Aug. 20. Dorms £20; doubles £44.

Tonbridge Club, 120 Cromer St. (☎78 37 44 06). Tube: King's Cross/St. Pancras. Follow Euston Rd. toward the British Library and turn left onto Judd St.; the hostel is 3 blocks down on the left. Students and foreigners only. Clean, no-frills. Men in basement gym, women in karate-club hall. Pool tables, TV, video games. Blankets and foam pads provided. Lockout 9am-9pm, lights out 11:30pm. Curfew midnight. Floor space £5.

HALLS OF RESIDENCE

London's universities rent out rooms in their **halls of residence,** which are generally the cheapest single rooms available, particularly if you have a student ID. Rooms tend to be spartan but clean. The halls usually offer rooms to individuals for two or three months over the summer, and during the long Easter break in the spring. Some halls reserve a few rooms for travelers year-round. Calling ahead is advisable. The **King's Campus Vacation Bureau,** 127 Stanford St., SE1 (☎79 28 37 77), controls bookings for a number of University of London residence halls, all available from early June to mid-September.

High Holborn Residence, 178 High Holborn, WC1 (☎73 79 55 89; fax 73 79 56 40). Tube: Holborn. Comfortable, modern, and well-located. Laundry. Excellent wheelchair facilities. English breakfast included. Open mid-June to Sept. (peak rates in July). Singles £27-34; doubles £46-57, with bath £56-67; triples with bath £66-77.

Wellington Hall, 71 Vincent Sq. (☎78 34 47 40; fax 72 33 77 09; reservations ☎79 28 37 77). Tube: Victoria. An Edwardian building on a beautiful square near Victoria Station. TV lounge, library, and bar. English breakfast included. Laundry. Open Easter and mid-June to mid-Sept. Singles £26; doubles £40. 10% discount for stays over a week.

Queen Alexandra's House, Kensington Gore (☎75 89 11 20; fax 75 89 31 77). Tube: South Kensington. **Women only.** Kitchen, laundry, sitting room, and 20 music rooms.

Common bathrooms. No visitors 11pm-10am. Breakfast included. 2-night min. stay. Write weeks in advance for a booking form; fax is best. Cozy singles £25; stays over 2 weeks £150 per week upon availability, including breakfast and dinner. No credit cards.

John Adams Hall, 15-23 Endsleigh St., WC1 (☎73 87 40 86; fax 73 83 01 64; email jah@ioe.ac.uk). Tube: Euston Sq. An elegant Georgian building with small, wrought-iron balconies. Singles are small and simple. TV lounge, pianos. Laundry. English breakfast included. Open July-Sept. and Easter. Singles £24, twins £42, triples £59. Discounts for students, stays of 6 nights or more, and in the off season.

BED AND BREAKFASTS

All B&Bs listed serve full English breakfasts and accept credit cards unless otherwise noted.

WESTMINSTER

The area near Victoria Station is full of budget hotels; hotels closer to Pimlico are nicer than those around Victoria.

Luna and Simone Hotel, 47-49 Belgrave Rd. (☎78 34 58 97; fax 78 28 24 74; email lunasimone@talk21.com). Tube: Victoria. The area's best; all rooms with TV, phones, and hair dryers. Book a month ahead. Singles £28-34; doubles £48-60, with bath £50-75; triples £65-80, with shower £75-95. 10% discount for long stays. Winter discount.

Melbourne House, 79 Belgrave Rd. (☎78 28 35 16; fax 78 28 71 20; email melbourne.househotel@virgin.net). Tube: Pimlico. An extraordinarily well-kept establishment. Spacious, nonsmoking rooms with TV, phone, and hot pot. Luggage storage. Book ahead with credit card. Singles £30, with bath £50-55; doubles with bath £70-75; triples with bath £90-95; quads with bath £100-110. Cash preferred.

Alexander Hotel, 13 Belgrave Rd. (☎78 34 97 38; fax 76 30 96 30). Tube: Pimlico. Slightly crunched rooms but attractive and sparkling. All with satellite TV, radio, and private bath. TV lounge. Check-out 11am. Singles £45; doubles £60-65; triples £75-80; family rooms £80-110. Winter discount.

Dover Hotel, 42/44 Belgrave Rd. (☎78 21 90 85; fax 78 34 64 25; email dover@rooms.demon.co.uk). Tube: Pimlico. Clean rooms with bathrooms. Singles £40-55; doubles £50-70; triples £60-75; quads £70-100; quints £80-110.

KENSINGTON, KNIGHTSBRIDGE, AND CHELSEA

Kensington is not the cheapest part of town; still, it's close to the stunning array of museums that line the southwest side of Hyde Park, as well as the huge department stores in Knightsbridge.

Abbey House Hotel, 11 Vicarage Gate (☎77 27 25 94). Tube: High St. Kensington. After you check in, the owners (who live in-house) or an assistant will spend 20min. giving you an introduction to London. The hotel achieves a level of comfort unrivaled at these prices. Reception 8:30am-10pm. Book far ahead. Singles £43; doubles £68; triples £85; quads £95; quints £105. Weekly rates in winter only. No credit cards.

Vicarage Hotel, 10 Vicarage Gate (☎72 29 40 30; fax 77 92 59 89; email reception@londonvicaragehotel.com). Tube: High St. Kensington. Stately foyer and breakfast room surpassed only by comfortable bedrooms and spotless bathrooms. Singles £45; doubles £74, with bath and TV £98; triples £90; family rooms £98. No credit cards.

Swiss House Hotel, 171 Old Brompton Rd. (☎73 73 27 69; fax 73 73 49 83; email recep@swiss-hh.demon.co.uk). Tube: Gloucester Rd. A beautiful, plant-filled B&B. Internet. All rooms have showers. Free continental breakfast; English breakfast £6. Reception open M-F 7:30am-11pm, Sa-Su 8am-11pm. Singles £46, with toilet £65; doubles with bath £80-90; triples with bath £104; quads with bath £118. 5% discount for stays over a week in the off season. 5% discount for cash payments.

MARYLEBONE AND BLOOMSBURY

A few hotels can be found near Marble Arch, in the sidestreets off Edgware Rd. Numerous night buses serve the area, convenient to Oxford St., Regent's Park, and the British Museum. The residential streets are lined with B&Bs, halls of residence, and hostels. The closer to the King's Cross, St. Pancras, and Euston train-station triumvirate, the dodgier the neighborhood tends to be, especially after dark.

Arosfa Hotel, 83 Gower St. (☎/fax 76 36 21 15). Tube: Tottenham Court Rd. Spacious rooms and immaculate facilities. All rooms with TV and sink. No smoking. Singles £35; doubles £48, with bath £63; triples £65, £76; quads with bath £88.

Euro Hotel, 51-53 Cartwright Gdns., WC1 (☎73 87 43 21; fax 73 83 50 44; email reception@eurohotel.co.uk). Tube: Russell Sq. Large, high-ceilinged rooms with cable TV, radio, kettle, phone, and sink. Free email. Singles £46, with bath £68; doubles £65, £85; triples £79, £99; quads £88, £108. Under 13 sharing with adults £10.

Ridgemount Hotel, 65-67 Gower St. (☎76 36 11 41; fax 76 36 25 58). Tube: Tottenham Court Rd. Charming staff keep the loyal guests happy and the well-kept hotel radiantly clean. Snug singles with TVs. Laundry service £3. Book ahead. Singles £32, with shower £43; doubles £48, £62; triples £63, £75; quads £72, £86; quints £78, £89.

The Langland Hotel, 29-31 Gower St. (☎76 36 58 01; fax 75 80 22 27; email sarah@langlandhotel.freeserve.co.uk). Tube: Euston. Renovations have added bathrooms to many of the rooms and TVs to all. Cable-TV lounge with comfy blue sofas. Laundry. Winter and long-term student discounts. Singles £40; doubles £50, with bath £70; triples £70; quads £90; quints £110.

Mentone Hotel, 54-56 Cartwright Gdns. (☎73 87 39 27; fax 73 88 46 71; email mentonehotel@compuserve.com). Tube: Russell Sq. Bright, cheery place. Airport shuttle available with advance reservation (from Heathrow £24, Gatwick £40, Luton £34, Stansted £43). Singles £42, with bath £60; doubles with bath £79; triples with bath £90; quads with bath £99. Reduced rates for longer stays Dec.-Apr.

EARL'S COURT

West of Kensington, this area feeds on the budget tourist trade, spewing forth travel agencies, souvenir shops, and bureaux de change; some streets seem solely populated by B&Bs and hostels. The area has a vibrant gay and lesbian population and is tremendously popular with Aussie travelers, gaining the nickname "Kangaroo Valley" in the 1970s. Be careful at night. Beware of over-eager guides willing to lead you from the station to a hostel. Some B&Bs in the area conceal grimy rooms behind fancy lobbies and well-dressed staff; ask to see a room.

Oxford Hotel, 24 Penywern Rd. (☎73 70 11 61; fax 73 73 82 56; email oxfordhotel@btinternet.com). Clean rooms installed with new beds and repainted every year. Stylish dining room and bar. Luggage storage and safe. Reception 24hr. Reserve ahead. Singles £34-47; doubles £53-63; triples £63-73; quads £75-85; quints £95-£105. Winter and weekly rates may be 10-15% lower.

Mowbray Court Hotel, 28-32 Penywern Rd. (☎73 73 82 85; fax 73 70 56 93; email mowbraycrthot@hotmail.com). Staff this helpful is a rarity in London; wake-up calls, tour arrangements, taxicabs, theater bookings, and dry cleaning. Internet. Reserve ahead. Singles £45, with bath £52; doubles £56, £67; triples £69, £80; quads £84, £95; quints £100, £110; 6-bed rooms £115, £125. Negotiable discounts.

Beaver Hotel, 57-59 Philbeach Gdns. (☎73 73 45 53; fax 7373 45 55). Warm and welcoming–plush lounge with wood floors and cable TV. All rooms with desks, phones, and hair dryers. Spotless bathrooms. Wheelchair accessible. Parking £5. Reserve several weeks ahead. Singles £38, with bath £55; doubles £45, £80; triples with bath £90.

Philbeach Hotel, 30-31 Philbeach Gdns. (☎73 73 12 44; fax 72 44 01 49). England's largest gay B&B, popular with men, women, and everything in between. Internet access. Breakfast included. Book ahead. Singles £30-50, with shower £50-60; doubles £65, with bath £85; triples £75, £90;

FOOD

Savoring the booty of imperialism needn't be a guilty pleasure; imports from former colonies have spiced up London's stodgy kitchens. The city is perhaps most famous for its **Indian restaurants,** the true British food (the cheapest cluster around Westbourne Grove near Bayswater, Euston Sq., and Brick Ln. in the East End), but food from various corners of the globe is everywhere. The wealth of international restaurants shouldn't deter you from sampling Britain's own cuisine. **Pubs** are a solid choice for meat dishes, while **fish-and-chip shops** and **kebab shops** are on nearly every corner. They vary little in price but can be miles apart in quality; look for queues out the door and hop in line. **Jacket potatoes,** baked potatoes stuffed with goodies, make a filling, quick lunch. The "New British" label applies to restaurants that blend continental influences with British staples to form a tasty, if pricey, cuisine.

RESTAURANTS

THE CITY OF LONDON

Futures!, 8 Botolph Alley (☎ 76 23 45 29). Tube: Monument. Off Botolph Ln. Fresh takeaway veggie breakfast and lunch. Quiche £3.40; spinach pizza £1.85. **Branch** in Exchange Sq., behind Liverpool St. Open M-F 7:30-10am and 11:30am-3pm.

The Place Below, in St. Mary-le-Bow crypt, Cheapside (☎ 73 29 07 89). Tube: St. Paul's. Generous vegetarian dishes served to City executives in an impressive church crypt. The 2nd dining room moonlights as an ecclesiastical court, where the Archbishop of Canterbury still settles cases pertaining to Anglican law and swears in new bishops a few times a year. Quiche and salad £6, takeaway £4.20. Significant takeaway discount. £2 discount 11:30am-noon. Open M-F 7:30am-2:30pm.

Sushi & Sozai, 51a Queen Victoria St. (☎ 73 32 01 08). Tube: Mansion House. A cheap sushi stand. Medium sushi £4; large sushi £5. Hot Japanese dishes, including deep-fried pork cutlet and egg on rice, £3. Open M-F 11am-3pm.

COVENT GARDEN AND SOHO

Belgo Centraal, 50 Earlham St. (☎ 78 13 22 33). Tube: Covent Garden. Waiters in monk's cowls and great specials make this one of Covent Garden's most popular restaurants. During "Beat the Clock" (M-F 6-7:30pm), the time you order is the cost of your meal. Open M-Sa noon-11:30pm, Su noon-10:30pm.

World Food Cafe, 14-15 Neal's Yd. (☎ 73 79 02 98). Tube: Covent Garden. A bit pricier than similar veggie-loving enclaves, but worth it. Features an array of *meze,* light meals, and appetizing platters (£6-8). Open M-Sa noon-5pm.

Yo! Sushi, 52 Poland St. (☎ 72 87 04 43). Tube: Oxford Circus. As much an eating experience as a restaurant; diners pluck their dishes from a central conveyer belt. Plates are color-coded by price (£1.50-3.50). An electronic drink cart makes its way behind diners, delivering liquid delights. Open daily noon-midnight.

Don Zoko, 15 Kingley St. (☎ 77 34 19 74). Tube: Oxford Circus. *Don Zoko* means "rock bottom," and its prices are just that. Sushi £2-4, dishes £3-6.50, beer £1.60-3.90, sake £3.50-5.50. Open M-F noon-2:30pm and 6-10:30pm; Sa-Su 6-10:30pm.

Lok Ho Fook, 4-5 Gerrard St. (☎ 74 37 20 01). Tube: Leicester Sq. Busy place with good prices and a welcoming atmosphere. Extensive selection of seafood, noodles, and vegetarian dishes £4-8. Dim sum (£1.40-1.60) made to order, not paraded on carts. Not to be confused with the nearby and more expensive Lee Ho Fook. Dim sum served until 6pm. Open daily noon-11:45pm.

WESTMINSTER

Al-Fresco (☎ 72 33 82 98). Tube: Victoria. Trendy variations on old standbys. Jacket potato with brie £2.75. Fresh melon juice £1.70. Panini sandwiches £2.80. Open M-F 8am-5:30pm, Sa-Su 9am-4:30pm.

Goya, 34 Lupus St. (☎ 79 76 53 09). Tube: Pimlico. Corner tapas bar popular with locals for sipping drinks and munching Spanish snacks. Outdoor tables filled on summer nights. Tapas £2.50-4.50. Hearty garlic chicken £4.20. Open daily noon-midnight.

KENSINGTON, KNIGHTSBRIDGE, AND CHELSEA

New Culture Revolution, 305 King's Rd. (☎73 52 92 81). Tube: Sloane Sq. Take a great leap forward and enjoy delicious north Chinese food, mostly noodles and dumplings. Open daily noon-11pm. **Branches:** 43 Parkway (☎72 67 27 00; Tube: Camden Town); Notting Hill; and 42 Duncan St. (☎78 33 90 83; Tube: Angel).

Café Floris, 5 Harrington Rd. (☎75 89 32 76). Tube: High St. Kensington. A bustling cafe offering large, fresh sandwiches (£1.60-2.90) and filling breakfasts. Colossal all-day breakfast special £3.50. Min. purchase £3 noon-3pm. Open daily 6am-7pm.

Rotisserie Jules, 6-8 Bute St. (☎75 84 06 00). Tube: High St. Kensington. This lively restaurant serves free-range poultry. Dishes from £4.95. Open daily noon-11:30pm. **Branches:** 338 King's Rd. and 133 Notting Hill Gate.

NOTTING HILL, BAYSWATER, AND HYDE PARK

The Grain Shop, 269a Portobello Rd. (☎72 29 55 71). Tube: Ladbroke Grove. This takeaway sells a surprisingly large array of foods. Organic whole grain breads baked daily on the premises £0.90-£1.90 per loaf. Main dishes from £2.40. Vegan brownies £1. Groceries also available, many organic. Open M-Sa 9:30am-6pm.

Cockney's Pie & Mash, 314 Portobello Rd. (☎89 60 94 09). Tube: Ladbroke Grove. Cheap, no-nonsense pie and mash (£1.85), with portions of eel (F-Sa only) for a mere £2.70. Open Tu-Sa 11:30am-5:30pm.

Mandola, 139 Westbourne Grove (☎72 29 63 91). Tube: Bayswater. Simply put, it rocks. A tiny diner that has rapidly shot into trendy eating notoriety, but hasn't raised its prices to match. Salads £3, main dishes £4-8. To finish, try the date mousse (£2.40) and Sudanese coffee, in a traditional pot (£3.50; serves 2). Takeaway available. Open M-Sa noon-11:30pm, Su noon-10:30pm.

Royal China, 13 Queensway (☎72 21 25 35). Tube: Bayswater. For the full Cantonese experience, try the steamed duck's tongue (£1.80) or the marinated chicken feet (£1.80). Generous dishes £10-15. Dim sum served M-Sa noon-5pm, Su 11am-5pm. Open M-Th noon-11pm, F-Sa noon-11:30pm, Su 11am-10pm.

MARYLEBONE AND BLOOMSBURY

Mandalay, 444 Edgware Rd. (☎72 58 36 96). Tube: Edgware Rd. This Burmese restaurant is so consistently good it only needs word of mouth to attract customers. Friendly owners. Set lunches include curry and rice £3.50; curry, rice, dessert, and coffee £5.90. Open M-Sa noon-3pm and 6-11pm; last orders 2:30pm and 10:30pm.

Wagamama, 4A Streatham St. (☎73 23 92 23). Tube: Tottenham Ct. Rd. If a restaurant could be a London must-see on the level of Buckingham Palace, this would be it. The waitstaff radio orders to the kitchen and diners slurp happily from massive bowls of ramen at long tables, like extras from *Tampopo.* Noodles in various combinations and permutations, all obscenely tasty (£5-7.25). Open M-Sa noon-11pm, Su 12:30-10pm. **Branches** in Piccadilly, Soho, Camden Town, and Kensington.

Diwana Bhel Poori House, 121 Drummond St. (☎73 87 55 56). Tube: Warren St. The specialty is *thali* (an assortment of vegetables, rices, sauces, breads, and desserts; £4.50-6.20). The "Chef's Special" is served on weekdays with rice for £4.80. Lunch buffet (noon-2:30pm, £4.50) includes 4 vegetable dishes, rice, savories, and dessert. Open daily noon-11:30pm.

EAST LONDON

Arkansas Cafe, Old Spitalfields Market. (☎73 77 69 99). Tube: Aldgate East. This may not give you a taste of jolly old England, but the Brits flock here in droves. Schooled in the art of flesh in Louisiana, Bubba uses nothing but free-range, happy-while-it-lasted meat, and the results are to die for. If your arteries block on-site, the Royal London Hospital is nearby. Open M-F noon-2:30pm, Su noon-4pm.

Spitz, 109 Commercial St. (☎72 47 97 47). Tube: Aldgate East. Inside Spitalfields Market, this elegant bar serves delicious lunches from £5. During the weekend, there is live music upstairs, with an emphasis on folk, jazz, and klezmer. Open daily 11am-midnight.

NORTH LONDON

Tartuf, 88 Upper St. (☎72 88 09 54). Tube: Angel. A convivial Alsatian place serving *tartes flambées,* similar to pizzas on very thin crusts, but much tastier. All-you-can-eat *tartes* £8.90. £4.90 "lunch express" (before 3pm) gets you a savory and a sweet *tarte*. Open M-F noon-2:30pm and 5:45-11:30pm, Sa noon-11:30pm, Su noon-11pm.

Le Mercury, 140a Upper St. (☎73 54 40 88). Tube: Angel. This French restaurant feels like the quintessential Islington gourmet bistro, but with astoundingly low prices. All main courses, including honey-roasted breast of duck, £5.85. Lunch and dinner 3-course *prix fixe* menu changes daily. Kids eat Sunday Roast free. Reservations recommended for evening. Open daily 11am-1am.

PUBS AND BARS

Shoreditch Electricity Showrooms, 39a Hoxton Sq. (☎77 39 69 34). Tube: Old St. Where the super-cool go. Cocktails £6, beers from £2.30. Open Tu and W noon-11pm, Th noon-midnight, F-Sa noon-1am, Su noon-10:30pm.

Prospect of Whitby, 57 Wapping Wall (☎74 81 10 95). Tube: Wapping. Open ceilings and flagstone bar in a building dating from 1520 pale next to the glorious Thamescape. Lunch served noon-2:30pm, dinner 6-9pm. Open M-F 11:30am-3pm and 5:30pm-11pm, Sa 11:30am-11pm, Su noon-10:30pm.

Filthy MacNasty's Whiskey Café, 68 Amwell St. (☎78 37 60 67). Tube: Angel. Renowned for traditional Irish music Su, and one of Shane Macgowan's favorite pubs. Live readings and music every M and W-Th. Guinness £2.20. Open daily noon-11pm.

Cubana, 48 Lower Marsh. (☎79 28 87 78). Tube: Waterloo. Staff keep people happy with spiky cocktails, live salsa W nights, a cheap and intriguing menu (crab and papaya salad £6.95), and a wide selection of edible cigars. Open M-Sa noon-midnight.

Freud, 198 Shaftesbury Ave. (☎72 40 99 33). Tube: Covent Garden. Cheaper than an hour on the couch. Open M-Sa 11am-11pm, Su noon-10:30pm. No credit cards.

Crown and Anchor, 22 Neal St. (☎78 36 56 49). Tube: Covent Garden. One of Covent Garden's most popular pubs. Open M-Sa 11am-11pm, Su noon-10:30pm.

192, 192 Kensington Park Rd. (☎72 29 04 82). Tube: Ladbroke Grove. Despite its repeated mention in the *Bridget Jones* books, this wine bar is worth a visit. Wines £2.60-6 per glass. Open M-Sa 12:30-11:30pm, Su 12:30-11pm.

Bread and Roses, 68 Clapham Manor St. (☎74 98 17 79). Tube: Clapham Common. With socialist roots, Bread and Roses has a history of liquoring up the people. Primarily trad pub that has great beers (Smile's Workers' Ale £2) and often hosts theater and music; call for a schedule. Open M-Sa 11am-11pm, Su noon-10:30pm.

SIGHTS

London's landmarks annually face an onslaught of around five million visitors. Sightseers who don't qualify for student or senior discounts may want to consider the **London for Less** card, issued by Metropolis International (☎89 64 42 42), which grants discounts on attractions, theaters, restaurants, and hotels, and is available at all BTA offices (4-person 8-day card £13). Many **bus tours** are "hop-on hop-off," allowing you to stop at the sights you find particularly fascinating and rejoin later. Be sure to ask how often buses circle through the route. **Walking tours** can fill in the specifics that bus tours zoom past; among the best are **The Original London Walks** (☎76 24 39 78), which cover specific topics such as Legal London, Jack the Ripper, or Spies and Spycatchers in two hours. **Historical Tours of London** are also popular (☎86 68 40 19; £5, students and seniors £4); for more options, *Time Out* lists walks in its "Around Town" section. A cheaper way to see the city is from the top of an ordinary double-decker bus; you'll miss the commentary, but gain authentic London experience. Bus #11 cruises the city's main sights, passing Chelsea, Sloane Sq., Victoria, Westminster Abbey, the Houses of Parliament, Whitehall, Trafalgar Sq., St. Paul's, and various stops in the City. If glancing at London from the top of a bus is unsatisfactory and hoofing it seems daunting, a tour led by **The London Bicycle Tour Company** may be the happy medium. (☎79 28 68 38. Tours £11.90.)

WESTMINSTER AND WHITEHALL

The city of Westminster, now a borough of London, once served as haven to a seething nest of criminals seeking sanctuary in the Abbey. For the past 100 years, Westminster has been the center of political and religious power in England.

WESTMINSTER ABBEY

Parliament Sq. Tube: Westminster or St. James's Park. ☎ 72 22 51 52; www.westminster-abbey.org. "Supertours" include admission to the Abbey and all sights inside (reservations ☎ 72 22 71 10), offered Nov.-Mar. M-Th 10, 11am, 2, and 3pm, F 10, 11am, and 2pm, Sa 10, 11am, and 12:30pm; Apr.-Oct. also M-F 10:30am and 2:30pm. £10. Audio tour £3. Open M-F 9am–4:45pm, Sa 9am-2:45pm; last admission 1hr. before closing. £5, students and UK seniors £3, ages 11-16 £2, families £10. Evensong 5pm M-Tu and Th-F, and 3pm Sa-Su. Organ recitals in summer on Tu at 6:30pm. Reservations ☎ 72 22 51 52, or write to the Concert Secretary, 20 Dean's Yard, SW1P 3PA. £6, students £4.

The site of every royal coronation since 1066, Westminster Abbey's significance is secular as well as sacred. Controlled by the Crown and not the Church of England, the Abbey is the temple of England's civic religion. Only the **Pyx Chamber** and the **Norman Undercroft** (now the Westminster Abbey Undercroft Museum) survive from the original structure, which was consecrated by King Edward the Confessor on December 28, 1065. Most of the present Abbey was erected under Henry III in the 13th century, and the post-1850 North Entrance is the latest addition.

The **north transept** contains memorials to Prime Ministers Disraeli and Gladstone. Kings' tombs surround the **Shrine of St. Edward** and lead to the **Lady Chapel.** Henry VII and his wife Elizabeth lie at the end of the chapel, and nearby is the stone that once marked Cromwell's grave. Protestant Queen Elizabeth I and the Catholic cousin she ordered beheaded, Mary Queen of Scots, are buried on opposite sides of the Henry VII chapel (in the north and south aisles, respectively). At the exit of the Lady Chapel stands the **Coronation Chair,** which used to rest on the Stone of Scone.

A number of monarchs from Henry III to George II are interred in the **Chapel.** Edward I had himself placed in an unsealed crypt, in case he was needed to fight the Scots; his mummy was used as a standard by the English army in Scotland. The **Poets' Corner** begins with Geoffrey Chaucer, who was originally buried in the Abbey in 1400—the short Gothic tomb you see today in the east wall of the transept was not erected until 1556. The **south transept** is graced with the graves of Samuel Johnson and actor David Garrick, as well as busts of William Wordsworth, Samuel Taylor Coleridge, and Robert Burns. The **High Altar,** between the North and South transepts, has long been the scene of coronations, royal weddings, and funerals. The **Scientists' Corner** holds a memorial to Sir Isaac Newton, which sits next to the grave of Lord Kelvin. Past the cloisters, in the Abbey's narrow nave, the highest in England, a slab of black Belgian marble marks the **Grave of the Unknown Warrior.** Here the body of a World War I soldier is buried in soil from the battlefields of France, with an oration written in letters made from melted bullets.

THE HOUSES OF PARLIAMENT

Parliament Sq. Tube: Westminster. Public tours offered early Aug. to mid-Sept. M-Sa 9:30am-4:15pm. £3.50; tickets go on sale in mid-June and must be booked in advance from Ticketmaster (☎ 73 44 99 66; www.ticketmaster.co.uk). For foreign-language tours book 4 weeks ahead. At other times of the year, UK residents should contact their MP or a friendly Lord; tours normally available M-Th 9:30am-noon and F 3:30-5:30pm. Overseas visitors can request tours through the Parliamentary Education Unit, Norman Shaw Building (North), London SW1A 2TT (☎ 72 19 30 00; edunit@parliament.uk); tours are limited to 16 people and offered only F 3:30-5:30pm, so book far ahead. Government business may lead to cancellation of tours at any time.

For the classic view of the Houses of Parliament, as captured by Claude Monet, walk about halfway over Westminster Bridge, preferably at dusk. Like the government offices along Whitehall, the Houses of Parliament occupy the former site of a royal palace. Only **Jewel Tower** (see below) and **Westminster Hall** (to the left of St. Stephen's entrance on St. Margaret St.) survive from the original building, which was destroyed by a fire in 1834. Sir Charles Barry and A.W.N. Pugin won a competition for the design of the new houses. The immense complex blankets eight acres and includes more than 1000 rooms and 100 staircases. Space is nevertheless so scarce that Members of Parliament (MPs) have neither private offices nor staff, and the archives—the originals of every Act of Parliament passed since 1497—are stuffed into **Victoria Tower,** the large tower to the south. A flag flown from the tower indicates that Parliament is in session. **Big Ben** is not the famous northernmost clock tower but rather the 14-ton bell that tolls the hours. Ben is most likely named after the rotund Sir Benjamin Hall, who served as Commissioner of Works when the bell was cast and hung in 1858.

HOUSE OF COMMONS' GALLERY. You can watch MPs at work from the House of Commons Gallery for "Distinguished and Ordinary Strangers." If you don't have an advance booking (see below), arrive early and wait at the public entrance at St. Stephen's gate; keep left (the right-hand queue is for the Lords). Weekdays after 6pm and Fridays are the least crowded; afternoon waits can be as long as two hours. *(☎72 19 42 72. Gallery open M-W 2:30-10:30pm, Th 11:30am-7:30pm, F normally 9:30am to around 3pm. For advance tickets, UK residents should contact their MP; overseas visitors must apply for a Card of Introduction from their Embassy or High Commission in London. Book at least a month in advance. Free.)*

HOUSE OF LORDS' GALLERY. To see real live Lords in action, go through the Central Lobby, and pass through the Peers' corridor, bedecked by MPs with scenes of Charles I's downfall. *(☎72 19 31 07. Keep right in the queue at St. Stephen's entrance. Open M-W 2:30pm-rise, Th from 3pm, occasionally F 11am. Free.)*

10 DOWNING STREET

The Prime Minister's headquarters lies just steps up Parliament St. from the Houses of Parliament. The exterior of "Number Ten" is decidedly unimpressive, but behind the famous door spreads an extensive political network. The Chancellor of the Exchequer forges economic policy from 11 Downing St., while the Chief Whip of the House of Commons plans Party campaigns at #12. Tony Blair's family is too big for #10, so he's moved into #11. *(Tube: Westminster.)*

THE MALL AND ST. JAMES'S

BUCKINGHAM PALACE. When a freshly-crowned Victoria moved from St. James's Palace in 1837, Buckingham Palace, built in 1825 by John Nash, had faulty drains and a host of other difficulties. Improvements were made, and now the monarch calls it home. The 20th-century facade on The Mall is impressive, but the Palace's best side, the garden front, is seldom seen by ordinary visitors, as it is protected by the 40-acre spread where the Queen holds garden parties. Visitors are allowed in the **Blue Drawing Room,** the **Throne Room,** the **Picture Gallery** (filled with pictures by Rubens, Rembrandt, and Van Dyck), and the **Music Room** (where Mendelssohn played for Queen Victoria), among other stately rooms. *(Buckingham Palace Rd. Tube: Victoria, Green Park, or St. James's Park. Recorded info ☎77 99 23 31, info office ☎78 39 13 77; tickets before the opening dates ☎73 21 22 33; www.royal.gov.uk. Open daily Aug.-Sept. 9:30am-4:30pm. £10.50, seniors £8, under 17 £5.)* Although public support for the royal family has waned considerably in the past years, tourist enthusiasm for the fur-capped Buckingham guards has not. The **Changing of the Guard** ceremony takes place daily from April to June; the rest of the year, it occurs on odd-numbered dates. *(To witness the spectacle, show up well before 11:30am and stand directly in front of the palace. You can also watch along the routes of the troops prior to their arrival at the palace (10:40-11:25am) between the Victoria Memorial and St. James's Palace or along Birdcage Walk.)*

THE MALL. Bordered by St. James's Park and Green Park to the south and Piccadilly to the north, The Mall begins at Cockspur St., off Trafalgar Sq., and leads to Buckingham Palace. Every Sunday it is pedestrian-only. Nearby, **St. James's Street** runs into stately **Pall Mall.** *(Tube: Charing Cross, Green Park, or St. James's Park.)*

ST. JAMES'S PALACE AND PARK. A residence of the monarchy from 1660 to 1668 and again from 1715 to 1837, **St. James's Palace** is now the home of Prince Charles, while his grandmother, the Queen Mum, bunks next door at Clarence House. The palace is closed to the public except for Inigo Jones' **Queen's Chapel,** built in 1626, open for Sunday services at 8:30 and 11am. *(Tube: Green Park. Just north of Buckingham Palace and The Mall, up Stable Yard or Marlborough Rd.)* **St. James's Park** was declared London's first royal park in 1532. Lawn chairs must be rented, but don't bother finding the attendants; sit and they'll find you. *(£0.70 per 4hr.)*

TRAFALGAR SQUARE AND PICCADILLY

TRAFALGAR SQUARE. Trafalgar Sq. slopes from the **National Gallery** (see p. 171) into the center of a vicious traffic roundabout. **Nelson's Column** commands the square, with four majestic, beloved lions guarding the base. The monument and square commemorate Admiral Horatio Nelson, killed during his triumph over Napoleon's navy off Trafalgar—the monument's reliefs were cast from French cannons. *(Tube: Charing Cross.)*

ST. MARTIN-IN-THE-FIELDS. Designer James Gibbs topped the templar classicism of this 18th-century church with a Gothic steeple. The dreary coffins have been cleared from the **crypt** to make room for a gallery, a book shop, a brass rubbing center, and a cafe. *(Trafalgar Sq. ☎ 79 30 00 89; www.stmartin-in-the-fields.org. Free concerts M-Tu and F 1:05pm. Reserve seats for evening concerts online; by phone M-F 10am-4pm ☎ 78 39 83 62, or in the bookstore, open M-W 10am-6pm and Th-Sa 10am-7:30pm. Cafe open M-Sa 10am-8pm, Su noon-6pm. Brass rubbing center open M-Sa 10am-6pm, Su noon-6pm.)*

PICCADILLY CIRCUS. Five of the West End's major arteries (Piccadilly, Regent St., Shaftesbury Ave., and the Haymarket) merge and swirl around Piccadilly Circus; at times it seems as though the entire tourist population of London has decided to bask in the lurid neon signs. The central focus of the Circus is the **statue of Eros,** by Lord Shaftesbury; Eros originally pointed his bow and arrow down Shaftesbury Ave., but recent restoration work has put his aim significantly off.

COVENT GARDEN AND SOHO

The cafes, pubs, upscale shops, and slick crowds animating Covent Garden today belie the square's medieval beginnings as a literal "convent garden" where monks grew vegetables. *(Tube: Covent Garden.)* For centuries, nearby Soho was London's red-light district of prostitutes and sex shows; today it overflows with artists and club kids, while the gay-owned restaurants and bars of **Old Compton Street** have turned Soho into the heart of gay London. *(Tube: Tottenham Ct. Rd. or Leicester Sq.)*

CARNABY STREET. Running parallel to Regent St., this notorious hotbed of 1960s sex, fashion, and Mods is the heart of "Swinging' London." Chic boutiques and bohemian stores mix with stalls of junky souvenirs. *(Tube: Oxford Circus.)*

LEICESTER SQUARE. Just south of Shaftesbury Ave., between Piccadilly Circus and Charing Cross Rd., lies this entertainment nexus of cinemas, clubs, and street entertainers. A large queue marks the **half-price ticket booth** (see p. 174) where same-day theater tickets are sold for a number of shows. *(Tube: Leicester Sq.)*

CHINATOWN. Cantonese immigrants first arrived in Britain as cooks on British ships, then Chinatown swelled with immigrants from Hong Kong. The streets spout Chinese signs and pagoda-like phone booths. The vibrant **Chinese New Year Festival** takes place at the beginning of February. *(Tube: Leicester Sq.)*

THEATRE ROYAL AND ROYAL OPERA HOUSE. Representing a long tradition of theater in the Covent Garden area, the **Theatre Royal,** with an entrance on Catherine St., dates from 1812. The **Royal Opera House,** on Bow St., began as a theater for concerts and plays in 1732 and currently houses the Royal Opera and Royal Ballet companies. *(Tube: Covent Garden.)*

ROYAL COURTS OF JUSTICE. The Strand and Fleet St. meet at this elaborate Gothic structure—easily mistaken for a cathedral—designed in 1874 for the Supreme Court of Judicature. At the Strand entrance, displays explain the court system. *(Tube: Temple. ☎ 79 47 60 00. Open M-F 9am-4:30pm.)*

THE STRAND AND FLEET STREET

THE STRAND. Built to connect the City with Westminster Palace and Parliament, the area is now a center of education in London. The thoroughfare curves from Trafalgar Sq. past many theaters to Aldwych. *(Tube: Holborn or Charing Cross.)*

KING'S COLLEGE AND LONDON SCHOOL OF ECONOMICS. As you stroll away from the Courts of Justice on Houghton St., two of London's top educational institutions come into view. **King's College** stands opposite the prestigious **London School of Economics (LSE),** a 60s center for student radicalism. *(Tube: Holborn.)*

ST. CLEMENT DANES. The melodious bells of this handsome church get their 15 seconds of fame in the nursery rhyme "Oranges and lemons, say the bells of St. Clement's." Designed by Christopher Wren in 1682, today it is the official church of the Royal Air Force. *(On The Strand, east of St. Mary-le-Strand's. Tube: Temple. ☎72 42 82 82. Open daily 8am-5pm. Bells ring daily 9am, noon, 3, and 6pm.)*

THE CITY OF LONDON

Until the 18th century, the City of London *was* London. Today, the tiny (1 sq. mi.) City is the financial center of Europe. When 350,000 commuters go home each weekday, they leave behind a resident population of only 6000. The City hums on weekdays, is dead on Saturdays, and seems downright ghostly on Sundays. The massive **Bank of England** controls the country's finances, and the **Stock Exchange** makes (or breaks) the nation's fortune. *(Tube: Bank.)*

ST. PAUL'S CATHEDRAL

Tube: St. Paul's. Open M-Sa 8:30am-4pm. Dome open M-Sa 9:30am-4pm. Ground floor and crypt wheelchair accessible. 1½hr. "Supertours" depart at 11, 11:30am, 1:30, and 2pm; £2.50, students and seniors £2, children £1. 45min. audio tours available 8:45am-3:30pm; £3.50, students £3. Admission to cathedral, galleries, and crypt £5, students and seniors £4, children £2.50. Evensong M-Sa at 5pm (about 45min.).

St. Paul's, topped by its beautiful Neoclassical dome, is arguably the most stunning architectural sight in London, a physical and spiritual symbol of the city. Sir Christopher Wren's enormous (157m by 76m) creation dominates its surroundings, even as modern challengers spring up around it. The current edifice is the fifth cathedral dedicated to St. Paul to stand on the site; the first was founded in AD 604 and was destroyed by fire. The fourth and most massive cathedral, now referred to as "Old St. Paul's," was a medieval structure built by the Normans and one of the largest in Europe, topped by a spire ascending 150m (the current spire tops out at 111m). Falling into almost complete neglect in the 16th century, the cathedral became more of a marketplace than a church. Wren had already started drawing up his grand scheme in 1666 when the Great Fire demolished the cathedral, giving him the opportunity to build from scratch.

Above the marble **High Altar** looms the crowning glory, the ceiling mosaic of *Christ Seated in Majesty*. Farther into the church, the north quire aisle holds *Mother and Child*, a modern sculpture of the Madonna and Child by Henry Moore. Behind the altar you'll find the **American Memorial Chapel,** dedicated to the 28,000 US soldiers based in Britain who died during World War II. Climbing to any of the three levels within the dome rewards the stout of heart, leg, and soul. Over 250 steps lead to the **Whispering Gallery,** on the inside base of the dome. It's a perfect resounding chamber: whisper into the wall, and a friend on the other side should be able to hear you. A farther 119 steps up, the first external view beckons from the **Stone Gallery,** only to be eclipsed 152 steps later by the panorama from the **Golden Gallery** atop the dome.

THE TOWER OF LONDON

Tube: Tower Hill or DLR: Tower Gateway. ☎77 09 07 65; www.hrp.org.uk/tol/indextol.htm. Yeoman Warders ("Beefeaters") lead free tours every 30min. starting 9:30am M-Sa, Su 10am, plus 8 daily themed tours. Audio tours available in 7 languages; £2. Frequent exhibitions, ceremonies, and re-enactments of historic events; call for details. For tickets to the Ceremony of the Keys, the 700-year-old nightly ritual locking of the gates, write 6 weeks in advance to the Ceremony of the Keys, Waterloo Block, HM Tower of London, EC3N 4AB, with the full name of those attending and a choice of dates, enclosing a stamped addressed envelope or international response coupon; free. Tower open Mar.-Oct. M-Sa 9am-5pm, Su 10am-5pm; Nov.-Feb. M-Sa 9am-4pm, Su 10am-4pm; last ticket sold at 4pm. £11, students and seniors £8.30, ages 5-15 £7.30, families £33. Avoid long queues by buying tickets in advance or from Tube stations.

The oldest continuously occupied fortress in Europe, "The Tower" was founded by William the Conqueror in 1066 to provide protection for and from his subjects. Richard the Lionheart began the construction of additional defenses around the original White Tower in 1189, and further work by Henry III and Edward I brought the Tower close to its present condition. Now 20 towers stand behind its walls, all connected by massive walls and gateways, forming fortifications disheartening to visitors even today. The **Outer Ward,** which sports a precariously hung portcullis, witnessed the execution of German spies in WWII. The password, required for entry here after hours, has been changed every day since 1327. Along the outer wall, **St. Thomas's Tower** (named after Thomas à Becket) tops the evocative **Traitors' Gate,** through which boats once brought the condemned to the Tower. Completed in 1097, the **White Tower** overpowers all the fortifications that were later built around it, and houses an expansive display from the **Royal Armouries** and a display of **Instruments of Torture.** Since the 1190s, this tower has sounded the curfew bell each night. Henry III lived in the adjacent **Wakefield Tower,** the second-largest in the complex. The line at the **Jewel House** (where the Crown Jewels are stored) is a miracle of crowd management. The **Imperial State Crown** and the **Sceptre with the Cross** feature the Stars of Africa, cut from the Cullinan Diamond. **St. Edward's Crown,** made for Charles II in 1661, is only worn during coronations. Look for the **Queen Mother's Crown,** which contains the Koh-I-Noor diamond. Legend claims the diamond brings luck—to women only.

TOWER BRIDGE

A granite-and-steel structure reminiscent of a castle with a drawbridge, the bridge is a symbol of the city. The **Tower Bridge Experience** explains the bridge's genesis through the eyes of its designers. *(Tube: Tower Hill; follow signs. ☎74 03 37 61. Open daily Apr.-Oct. 10am-6:30pm; Nov.-Mar. 9:30am-6pm. £6.25.)*

LLOYD'S

This 1986 building supplies the most startling architectural clash in the City, with ducts, lifts, and chutes straight out of the future; it seems not so much a building as a vertical street. The **Lutine Bell** is still occasionally rung—once for bad insurance news, twice for good. *(Off Leadenhall St. Tube: Monument.)*

HYDE PARK AND ENVIRONS

HYDE PARK AND KENSINGTON GARDENS. The lakes and green lawns of Hyde Park and the contiguous Kensington Gardens, the "Lungs of London," comprise the largest open area (1 sq. mi.) in the city center. *(Tube: Hyde Park Corner or Marble Arch. Park open daily 5am-midnight. Gardens open daily dawn-dusk. Free.)*

KENSINGTON PALACE. At the far west of the Gardens is Kensington, originally the residence of King William III and Queen Mary II. The birthplace of Queen Victoria, and most recently home to the late Princess Diana, Kensington has moved in and out of vogue with the Royal Family. *(Tube: High St. Kensington. ☎79 37 95 61. Tours 1¼hr., May-Sept. M-Sa every hr. 10am-5pm. £8.50, students £6.70.)*

SPEAKERS' CORNER. On summer evenings and on Sundays, proselytizers, politicos, and flat-out crazies assemble to dispense the fruits of their knowledge to whomever will bite. *(Tube: Marble Arch. In the northeastern corner of Hyde Park.)*

NOTTING HILL AND PORTOBELLO ROAD. Simultaneously shabby and extravagant, Notting Hill pulses with chaotic energy. Portobello Rd. is the commercial heart of Notting Hill's bustling activity. Antique stores and galleries line the southern end of Portobello near the Notting Hill Gate Tube station; near Lancaster Rd.

and the Westway (the overhead highway), vendors sell clothing, collector's vinyl, and trinkets. *(Tube: Notting Hill Gate; turn on Pembridge Rd. from the station, and Portobello Rd. is the 3rd left.)*

HARRODS. Simply put, this is *the* store in London, perhaps in the world. The sales (July and January) get so crazy that the police bring out a whole detail to deal with the shoppers. *(87-135 Brompton Rd. ☎77 30 12 34. Tube: Knightsbridge. Open M-Tu and Sa 10am-6pm, W-F 10am-7pm.)*

NORTH LONDON

221B BAKER STREET. The area's most fondly remembered resident is Sherlock Holmes who, although fictitious, still receives 50 letters per week addressed to his residence at 221b Baker St. The **Sherlock Holmes Museum,** 239 Baker St., thrills with a re-creation of the detective's lodgings. *(Tube: Baker St.)*

REGENT'S PARK. North of Baker St. and south of Camden Town, the 500-acre, wide open Regent's Park is one of London's most beautiful spaces. The park contains well-kept lawns, broad walkways (including Broad Walk), playing fields, and scores of sunbathers. It also houses the **London Zoo.** *(Tube: Regent's Park, Great Portland St., Baker St., or Camden Town. ☎74 86 79 05; constabulary ☎79 35 12 59. Open 6am-dusk.)*

CAMDEN TOWN. At the time of the canal's construction in the 19th century, Camden Town was a solid working-class district spliced with railways and covered in soot. Camden Town today hosts **Camden Market,** where hundreds of merchants set up stands that draw swarms of bargain-seekers. *(Tube: Camden Town.)*

DICKENS HOUSE. Charles Dickens lived here from 1837 to 1839, scribbling parts of *Nicholas Nickleby*, *Barnaby Rudge*, and *Oliver Twist*. Now a four-floor museum and a library of Dickens paraphernalia, the house holds an array of prints, photographs, manuscripts, and letters. *(48 Doughty St., east of Russell Sq. and parallel to Gray's Inn Rd. Tube: Russell Sq. or Chancery Ln. Open M-Sa 10am-5pm. £3.50, students £2.50.)*

HAMPSTEAD HEATH. The most fabulous green space in the metropolis is the perfect place to get lost in vast meadows and woodlands and forget the hustle and bustle of the city with carefree picnickers, kite-flyers, and anglers. At night, the Heath, particularly West Heath, becomes one of the city's oldest gay cruising areas. On a hot day, take a dip in the murky waters of **Kenwood Ladies' Pond, Highgate Men's Pond,** or the **Mixed Bathing Pond.** *(Tube: Hampstead. Rail: Hampstead Heath. Pools open in summer 7-9:30am and 10am-7pm; off season 7-10am. £3, students £1; free before 10am.)*

HIGHGATE. To the northeast of Hampstead lies Highgate. While not the home of glittering literati like Hampstead, it does contain one of London's most well-known cemeteries and Karl Marx's final resting place. To get a feel for Highgate (and a good glimpse of London), climb Highgate Hill, London's highest at 424 ft. above the Thames. *(Tube to Archway (not Highgate), then bus #210 to Highgate Village. From Hampstead, it's a 45min. walk across the Heath, more or less parallel to Spaniard's Rd.)*

EAST LONDON

THE EAST END

Tube: Aldgate East. To reach Brick Ln., go left up Whitechapel as you exit the Tube station, then turn left onto Osbourne St., which becomes Brick Ln.

A large working-class English population moved into the East End during the Industrial Revolution, followed by a wave of Jewish immigrants fleeing persecution in Eastern Europe, who settled around **Whitechapel.** The most recent wave of immigrants to join the East End consists of London artists; their work occasionally hangs in the **Whitechapel Art Gallery** (see **Museums,** p. 173). At the heart of the Muslim Bangladeshi community is **Brick Lane,** lined with Indian and Bangladeshi restaurants, colorful textile shops, and grocers. Stalls selling everything from leather jackets to salt beef sandwiches flank Brick Ln. and **Petticoat Lane.** Nearby on 82-92 Whitechapel Rd., the **East London Mosque,** London's first, testifies to the size of the Muslim community.

BEVIS MARKS SYNAGOGUE. The city's oldest standing synagogue sits at Bevis Marks and Heneage Ln. The congregation traces its roots back to Spanish and Portuguese Jews who inhabited the area as early as 1657. Rabbi Menashe Ben Israel founded the synagogue in 1701, 435 years after Jews were first expelled from England. *(Tube: Aldgate. From Aldgate High St. turn right onto Houndsditch; Creechurch Ln. on the left leads to Bevis Marks. ☎ 76 26 12 74. Tours Su-W and F noon; call in advance. Open Su-M, W, and F 11:30am-1pm, Tu 10:30am-4pm. Entrance donation £1.)*

DOCKLANDS. Docklands proper covers 55 mi. of waterfront from the Tower of London to Greenwich. The center of the new 8.5 sq. mi. development is on the **Isle of Dogs,** the spit of land defined by a sharp U-shaped bend in the Thames. To the east lie the **Royal Docks,** once the center of one of history's proudest trading empires. **Canary Wharf,** at a towering 800 ft., is Britain's tallest edifice and the jewel of Docklands, visible from almost anywhere in London. *(DLR: Canary Wharf.)* Getting off at Shadwell station, you'll see **St. George-in-the-East,** an old working-class community. Drab housing, dusty streets, traditional pubs, cafes, and pie-and-mash shops stand in the throes of a major transformation brought on by an infusion of Bengali immigrants. *(☎ 74 81 13 45. Open daily 9am-5pm.)*

THE SOUTH BANK AND LAMBETH

OXO TOWER AND GABRIEL'S WHARF. The most colorful changes in the South Bank landscape have resulted from the unflagging efforts of a nonprofit development company, **Coin Street Community Builders (CSCB).** The nearby **Museum Of...** and the **gallery@oxo** are succeeding in their aim to provide a democratic artistic forum. *(Between Waterloo and Blackfriars Bridges on Barge House St. Tube: Blackfriars or Waterloo.)*

ROSE AND GLOBE THEATRES. Shakespeare's and Marlowe's plays were performed at the Rose, which was built in 1587. Remnants of the Rose, discovered during construction in 1989, are displayed underneath a new office block at Park St. and Rose Alley. The remains of Shakespeare's **Globe Theatre** (see p. 174) were discovered just months after those of the Rose. The space itself is not only a wonderful reconstruction, but also a unique experience in theater-going. *(New Globe Walk, Bankside. Tube: London Bridge. ☎ 79 02 14 00. 45min. tours available May-Sept. M 9am-6pm, Tu-Su 9am-noon; Oct.-Apr. daily 10am-5pm. £6, seniors and students £5, children £4.)*

SOUTHWARK CATHEDRAL. The cathedral, an endearing remnant of ecclesiastical power, is probably the most striking Gothic church in the city after Westminster Abbey. It is certainly the oldest, having been the site of a nunnery as early as AD 606. Ed Shakespeare, brother of Bill, was buried in the church in 1607 and lies beneath a stained-glass window depicting his sibling's characters. (*Montague Close. ☎ 73 67 67 12; www.dswark.org. Tube: London Bridge. Open M-F 8am-6pm. Evensong Su 3pm. Free. Photo permit £1, video permit £5.)*

MILLENNIUM DOME. This enormous white structure cost £7 million, but Londoners still aren't sure what exactly it does. Word is that Japanese investors plan to turn it into an amusement park. *(Tube: North Greenwich. Reserve tickets by calling ☎ (0870) 606 20 00, or at www.dome2000.co.uk. There are also plans to run a link from the East India DLR station. £20, students £16.50.)*

YE OLDE ROAD RAGE Ever wonder why the British drive on the left side of the road? Tradition. The days of chivalry had their own set of traffic regulations, and the cardinal rule stated: "Never point your sword at another as you pass." To do so was considered an insult more extreme than certain hand gestures of modern-day motorists. Since most knights carried their weapons on their left side, etiquette required them to face their left flanks to the outside of the road. This custom endures today in Britain, resulting in the observed traffic pattern. Just as in the days of Lancelot, present-day drivers on the wrong side of the road risk both life and pride; the British love to laugh as foreign drivers try hopelessly to make turns and park.

WEST LONDON

KEW GARDENS. The perfect antidote to central London, the Royal Botanic Gardens at Kew provide a breath of fresh air. Yet another example of the Empire's collecting frenzy, the 124-acre park houses the living bank of a research collection with millions of DNA samples and seeds and thousands of plants and flowers. (*Tube: Richmond, or take a Westminster Passenger Association (☎79 30 47 21; www.wpsa.co.uk) boat from Westminster Pier (Tube: Westminster). £8, round-trip £12, ages 5-15 £3.50, £6. Info office open May-Sept. M-Sa 10am-5pm, Su 10:30am-1:30pm; Oct.-Apr. M-Sa 10am-5pm.*

HAMPTON COURT PALACE. Although a monarch hasn't lived here since George II moved out over 200 years ago, Hampton Court Palace continues to exude regal charm. Six miles down the Thames from Richmond, the brick palace housed over 1500 court members at its height. The 60 marvelous acres of the **Palace Gardens** are open and free, and contain celebrated amusements, including the **maze,** a hedgerow labyrinth first planted in 1714. *(Take the train to Hampton Court from Waterloo (32min.; every 30min.; round-trip £4, £3.50 with zone 2-6 Travelcard) and walk the 2min. to the palace, or take the tube to Richmond and take the R68 bus (£0.70). ☎87 81 95 00; www.hrp.org.uk. Wheelchairs and electric buggies available from West Gate.)*

MUSEUMS

London's museums distinguish themselves as some of the best in the world; many are also free. The **London Go See Card** allows unlimited access to 13 participating museums for three or seven days. The card can be purchased at any of the participating museums (the V&A, the Science Museum, the Natural History Museum, the Royal Academy of Arts, the Hayward Gallery, the Design Museum, the London Transport Museum, the Museum of London, the Museum of the Moving Image, and the Courtauld Institute), but will afford you substantial discounts only if you plan to visit *many* museums, or if you plan to visit a particularly expensive museum more than once. (3-day card £16, families £32; 7-day card £26, £50.)

BRITISH MUSEUM

Great Russell St., rear entrance on Montague St. ☎73 23 82 99; www.britishmuseum.ac.uk. Tube: Tottenham Court Rd., Goodge St., Russell Sq., or Holborn. 1½hr. highlights tours M-Sa 10:30, 11am, 1:30, 2:30pm; Su 12:30, 1:30, 2:30, and 4pm; £7, students and under 16 £4. 1hr. focus tours depart M-Sa 1pm from upstairs, M-Sa 3:30pm and Su 4:30pm downstairs; £5, £3. Visually-impaired travelers should inquire about tactile exhibits and touch-tours. Open M-Sa 10am-5pm, Su noon-6pm. Free; suggested donation £2. Special exhibits £4, students £3.

Founded in 1753, the British Museum began with the personal collection of Sir Hans Sloane. Robert Smirke drew up the design of the current Neoclassical building in 1824; construction took 30 years. The outstanding **Egyptian collection** contains the **Rosetta Stone,** the head of Ramses II, and a how-to guide to mummification. The **Greek exhibits** are dominated by the **Elgin Marbles,** 5th-century BC reliefs from the Parthenon, now residing in the spacious Duveen Gallery; other Hellenic highlights include the complete Ionic facade of the **Nereid Monument,** one of the female caryatid columns from the Acropolis. The **Romano-Britain** section includes the **Mindenhall Treasure,** a magnificent collection of 4th-century silver tableware. Nearby lies **Lindow Man,** an Iron Age Celt sacrificed in a gruesome ritual and preserved in a peat bog. The **Sutton Hoo Ship Burial,** an Anglo-Saxon ship buried (and subsequently dug up) in Suffolk complete with an unknown king, is the centerpiece of the Medieval galleries. Gallery 33 is dedicated to the **Asian collections;** the Chinese collection is renowned for its ancient Shang bronzes and fine porcelains, and the Indian and Southeast Asian exhibits include the largest collection of Indian religious sculpture outside of India. Downstairs by the Montague St. entrance, don't miss the **Islamic art gallery** with its tiles, ceramics and other treasures from all over the Muslim world.

NATIONAL GALLERY

Trafalgar Sq. Tube: Charing Cross, Leicester Sq., or Piccadilly Circus. ☎77 47 28 85; www.nationalgallery.org.uk. A free Art Bus shuttles between the National Gallery, the Tate

Britain, and the Tate Modern (mid-May to Sept. 2 per hr. 10am-6pm). Tours start from the Sainsbury Wing info desk M-Tu and Th-Su at 11:30am and 2:30pm and W 11:30am, 2:30 and 6:30pm; tours for the visually impaired 3rd Sa of each month 11:30am; sign-language tour 1st Sa of month 11:30am. Audioguides are available at the main entrance and Sainsbury Wing foyer; donation requested. Orange St. and Sainsbury Wing entrances wheelchair accessible. Open Th-Tu 10am-6pm, W 10am-9pm. Permanent collection free.

The National Gallery maintains one of the world's finest collections of Western art from the Middle Ages to the end of the 19th century, divvied up chronologically among four distinct wings. You could spend days ambling through the maze of galleries; if you're pressed for time and know what you want to see, the high-tech **Micro Gallery,** in the Sainsbury wing, will guide you through the collection on-line and print out a personalized tour of the paintings you want to see.

The **Sainsbury Wing,** the newest part of the Gallery, holds the oldest part of the collection, most of which are devotional works created between 1260 and 1510. Paintings from 1510 to 1600 are found in the **West Wing,** left of the Trafalgar Sq. entrance. The **North Wing** holds 17th-century Italian, Spanish, Flemish, and French paintings, including 12 Rembrandts. The **East Wing,** to the right of the main entrance, is devoted to painting from 1700 to 1900, including a strong English collection.

TATE MODERN

Sumner St., Bankside. Tube: Southwark. ☎78 87 80 00; www.tate.org.uk. A free Art Bus shuttles between the National Gallery, the Tate Britain, and the Tate Modern (mid-May to Sept. every 30min. 10am-6pm). Daily highlights tours at 10:30, 11:30am, 2:30, 3:30pm; free. Call for schedule of special talks; free. Audioguide £1. Wheelchair access; 6 wheelchairs can be reserved at ☎78 87 88 88. Guide dogs welcome. Open Su-Th 10am-6pm, F-Sa 10pm-10pm. Cafe 7 open F-Sa until 11pm. Permanent collection free.

While other millennium projects struggled to pull in the crowds, the Tate became an instant landmark upon its opening in May 2000. Crowds snaked around London's first large-scale museum dedicated entirely to modern art, housed in a stunning converted power station designed by Giles Gilbert Scott. The Swiss firm Herzog and de Meuron renovated the building and have turned the old turbine room into an immense top-lit cavern 155m long and 35m high while preserving the old power station's industrial feel. Tate Modern's controversial curatorial method groups works thematically rather than chronologically.

TATE BRITAIN

Millbank. Tube: Pimlico. ☎78 87 80 08, recorded info ☎78 87 80 00; www.tate.org.uk. Museum tour M-F 12:30pm, Sa 3pm; Turner collection tour M-F 11:30am. Audio tour £3, students £2. Touch tours for visually impaired visitors ☎78 87 87 25. Open daily 10am-5:50pm. Free.

With the opening of the new Tate Modern (above), the original Tate has now been renamed the Tate Britain, and holds a superb collection of British works from the 16th century to the present day. The collection starts with a room at the far end of the gallery devoted to 16th- and 17th-century painting. The **parade of Constables** includes the famous views of Salisbury Cathedral, and a number of Hampstead scenes dotted with red saddle splashes. Don't miss the visionary works of William Blake, or the haunting images of Sir John Everett Millais, a founder of the Pre-Raphaelite Brotherhood. The Tate's chronologically ordered displays have been supplemented by thematic arrangements.

NATIONAL PORTRAIT GALLERY

St. Martin's Pl., opposite St.-Martin-in-the-Fields. Tube: Charing Cross or Leicester Sq. ☎73 06 00 55, recorded info ☎73 12 24 63; www.npg.org.uk. Frequent free daytime lectures. Evening lectures Th 7pm (£3, students £2); concerts F 7pm (mostly free). Orange St. entrance is wheelchair accessible. Audioguide available in entrance hall; suggested donation £3, ID or credit card deposit required. Open M-W 10am-6pm, Th-F 10am-9pm, Sa-Su 10am-6pm. Free, excluding temporary exhibits.

This unofficial Who's Who in Britain began in 1856 as "the fulfillment of a patriotic and moral ideal"—namely to showcase Britain's most officially noteworthy citizens. The museum's principle of looking "to the celebrity of the person represented, rather than to the merit of the artist" does not seem to have affected the quality of the works displayed. The sleek new **Ondaatje wing** opened in May 2000, housing the oldest works in a suite of climate-controlled top-floor rooms. The **Elizabethan portraits** hang in a room modeled after a Tudor long gallery; the dark walls and dramatic fiber-optic backlighting highlight pictures such as William Scrot's astonishing distorted-perspective portrait of Edward VI, designed to be viewed from an extreme angle. The Gallery normally commissions three new portraits a year; new backs against the wall for 2000 include stage director and physician Jonathan Miller, author Doris Lessing, and tycoon Richard Branson.

VICTORIA AND ALBERT

Cromwell Rd. Tube: South Kensington. ☎ 79 42 20 00; www.vam.ac.uk. Wheelchair access at the side entrance on Exhibition Rd.; call ahead (☎ 79 42 20 00). 1hr. tours leave every hr. from the Cromwell St. info desk M 12:30-3:30pm, Tu-Su 10:30am-3:30pm. Open M-Tu and Th-Su 10am-5:45pm, W 10am-5:45pm and 6:30-9:30pm. £5, seniors £3; students, disabled, and under 15 free. Free for everyone daily 4:30-5:45pm. Night openings (select galleries only) £3. Season ticket for all 3 South Kensington museums (the V&A, the Science, and the Natural History) £29, two adults £49.50, students £16.

Founded in 1852 to encourage excellence in art and design, the original curators were deluged with objects from around the world. The 150-odd galleries arrange items either by time and place or by material and style. The popular **dress collection** traces fashion, focusing mainly on women's wear, from the 16th century to the present. Persian carpets and Moroccan rugs distinguish the V&A's collection of **Islamic Art,** including the large, breathtaking Persian Ardabil carpet. The **Asian collections** are particularly formidable. On Sundays, the New Restaurant hosts a jazz brunch, with live music accompanying either an English breakfast or lunch. **Late View,** late night openings (most summer W and occasional F), feature lectures, live performances, guest DJs, and a bar.

OTHER MUSEUMS

The Courtauld Gallery (☎ 78 48 25 26), at Somerset House, on The Strand, WC2, opposite the corner of Aldwych and The Strand. Tube: Temple, Embankment, Charing Cross, or Covent Garden. Intimate 11-room gallery with world-famous masterpieces, mostly Impressionist and post-Impressionist. Open M-Sa 10am-6pm, Su 2-6pm. £4, students and seniors £2; M half-price.

Sir John Soane's Museum, 13 Lincoln's Inn Fields, WC2 (☎ 74 05 21 07). Tube: Holborn. Soane was an architect's architect, but the idiosyncratic home he designed for himself will intrigue everyone. Artifacts on display include Hogarth paintings and the massive sarcophagus of Seti I. Open Tu-Sa 10am-5pm; free. Tours Sa 2:30pm.

Madame Tussaud's (☎ (0870) 400 30 00), on Marylebone Rd., NW1. Tube: Baker St. The classic waxwork museum, founded by an emigré aristocrat who made life-size models of French nobility. Beat horrific lines by going very early or very late. A green dome shelters the adjacent **Planetarium.** Both open in summer M-F 9am-5:30pm, Sa-Su 9:30am-5:30pm. £11.50, combined entry with planetarium £13.95.

Whitechapel Art Gallery, Whitechapel High St., E1 (☎ 73 77 78 88). Tube: Aldgate East. Whitechapel's sunny galleries contain no permanent collections, but host some of Britain's (and the Continent's) most daring exhibitions of contemporary art. Wheelchair accessible. Gallery open Tu and Th-Su 11am-5pm, W 11am-8pm. Free.

Museum of London, 150 London Wall, EC2 (☎ 76 00 36 99 or ☎ 76 00 08 07; email info@museum-london.org.uk). Tube: St. Paul's or Barbican. Tells London's story from its origins to the present. Wheelchair accessible. Open Tu-Sa 10am-5:50pm, Su noon-5:50pm, last admission 5:30pm. £5, students and seniors £3, under 17 free.

Science Museum (☎ (0870) 870 48 68), on Exhibition Rd., SW7. Tube: South Kensington. Closet science geeks will be outed as they enter this wonderland of diagrammed motors, springs, and spaceships. Introductory exhibit romps through a "synopsis" of science since 6000 BC. Numerous exhibits geared toward the under-12 sector. Open daily 10am-6pm. £6.95, students £3.50; free for all after 4:30pm.

Wallace Collection, in Hertford House in Manchester Sq., W1. Tube: Bond St. Founded by various Marquises of Hertford and the illegitimate son of the fourth Marquis, Sir Richard Wallace, this collection defines the adjective "sumptuous." Also home to the largest weaponry collection outside the Tower of London. Open M-Sa 10am-5pm, Su 2-5pm. Tours M-Tu and Th-F 1pm, W and Sa 11:30am and 1pm, Su 3pm. Free.

ENTERTAINMENT

On any given day or night in London, you can choose from world-class theater, dance, comedy, sports, and countless unclassifiable happenings. Check out the listings in *Time Out* (£1.80) and *What's On* (£1.30). **Kidsline** provides info on children's events. (☎72 22 80 70. Open M-F 4-6pm.) **Artsline** handles queries about disabled access at venues across London. (☎73 88 22 27. Open M-F 9:30am-5:30pm.)

THEATER

The **Leicester Square Half-Price Ticket Booth** sells tickets at half price (plus £1.50-2 reservation fee) on the day of the performance, but carries them only for the West End, the Barbican, and the National Theatre. Tickets are sold from the top of the pile, which means you can't choose seats, and the priciest seats are sold first. Lines are particularly long on Saturdays. (Open M-Sa noon-6:30pm, Su noon-3pm; cash only.) Your next best bet for low prices is to schlep to a theater's box office where day seats, standbys, or student-rate tickets are often available. Major **repertory theaters** are listed below; for other venues, especially those with constant repertoires, check *Time Out*. For popular **musicals,** you should book far in advance.

Royal Shakespeare Company, Barbican Centre, Silk St. (☎76 38 88 91; www.barbican.org.uk). Tube: Barbican or Moorgate. The RSC makes its London home in the 2 theatres of the Barbican Centre. Forward-leaning balconies in the **Barbicon Theatre** guarantee that none of the 1166 seats sit farther than 65 ft. from center stage, and every seat gives a clear view. **The Pit** provides a more intimate (200-seat) setting. Tickets for the main stage £7.50-24; weekday matinees £6-13; Saturday matinees and previews £8-18. Student and senior standby available in person or by phone from 9am on the day of performance; £8 (1 per person). There are always several sign-language and audio-described performances during each run. Box office open daily 9am-8pm.

Royal National Theatre, South Bank Centre (☎74 52 34 00; www.nt-online.org). Tube: Waterloo. As you might expect from the "National" part of the name, the RNT's brilliant repertory company puts on a bit of everything on its 3 stages. Backstage tours M-Sa £4.75, students £3.75. Book ahead; call for times. Box office open M-Sa 10am-8pm.

Olivier and **Lyttelton:** Tickets £10-32, day seats (available from 10am on day of performance) £10-14, general standby seats (available 2hr. before show) £12-16, student standby (available 45min. before show) £8-10, standing £4.50-6. Discounted admission for those in wheelchairs (all seats £15-16) and for other disabled people (£8-16). Discounted seats to matinees for under-18s (all seats £9-10) and seniors (£13-14).

Cottesloe: Tickets £10-22. Discounted admission for those in wheelchairs and the visually impaired (all seats £15) and for other disabled people (£8-15). Discounted entry to matinees for under-18s (£9) and seniors (£13).

Shakespeare's Globe Theatre, New Globe Walk, Bankside (☎74 01 99 19 or Ticketmaster ☎73 16 47 03). Tube: London Bridge. Using this reconstruction of the original Globe (where the Bard himself put on some plays) the company employs the 3-tiered open-air space well. Purchase spots on the wooden benches or stand through a performance as a "groundling." However, groundlings should prepare for the possibility of rain: umbrellas are prohibited because they impede sight lines. Shows take place May-Sept. Wheelchair access. Box office open M-Sa 10am-8pm, until 6pm by phone.

FILM

The **Empire** (☎ (0870) 603 45 67) and **Odeon Leicester Sq.** are London's biggest cinemas. The following cinemas offer independent, foreign, and classic films:

The Prince Charles, Leicester Pl. (☎77 34 91 27; www.princecharlescinema.com). Tube: Leicester Sq. A Soho institution: 4 shows daily (generally second runs and a few classics) for only £2-3.50. Originator of hot trend *Sing-a-Long-a-Sound-of-Music*, where von Trappists dress as everything from nuns to "Ray, a drop of golden sun." (F 7:30pm, £12.50; Su 2pm, £10; children always £8.) Catch the *Rocky Horror Picture Show,* complete with a live troupe, every F at 11:45pm; £6, students £3.

Gate Cinema, 87 Notting Hill Gate (☎77 27 40 43). Tube: Notting Hill Gate. A Victorian-interior 240-seater with an arthouse selection. £6.50, M-F first film before 3pm £3.50, M-F before 6pm and late shows F and Sa, students and seniors £3.

CLASSICAL MUSIC, OPERA, AND BALLET

Barbican Hall, Barbican Centre, Silk St. (☎76 38 88 91; 24hr. recorded info ☎73 82 72 72; www.barbican.org.uk). Tube: Barbican or Moorgate. The venerable **London Symphony Orchestra** (www.lso.co.uk) inhabits this modern hall with superb acoustics. LSO concerts £6.50-35, under 16 £3. Student and senior standby tickets sold shortly before the performance; £6-8. Prices may vary for other concerts. Box office open 9am-8pm.

Royal Albert Hall, Kensington Gore (☎75 89 82 12; www.royalalberthall.com). Tube: South Kensington or Knightsbridge (buses #9, 10, and 52 go by the Hall from either station). London's premier concert hall, seating 5300. The **Proms** (BBC Henry Wood Promenade Concerts) never fail to enliven London summers with concerts every day for 8 weeks from mid-July to mid-Sept. All the Proms are also broadcast live on BBC Radio 3, 90-93 FM. £5-60. Over 1000 standing tickets in the Arena (the floor of the hall) and the Gallery (the very top of the hall) are available 1hr. before each concert for just £3, but be ready to queue for longer. Box office open daily 9am-9pm.

Royal Opera House, at Covent Garden, Box St. (☎73 04 40 00). The newly refurbished stage hosts the **Royal Opera** and the **Royal Ballet.** All works at the English National Opera are sung in English. Call the box office, 48 Floral St. (Tube: Covent Garden) for ticket prices. Open M-Sa 10am-7pm.

NIGHTLIFE

CLUBS

Avoid the glitzy clubs in Leicester Sq. (e.g. **Equinox** and **Hippodrome**), which are crowded with out-of-town youth looking to get lucky. *Time Out* is the undisputed scene cop, and their starred picks of the day are usually a safe bet. Many clubs have after-hours parties called "chill outs," usually 6am-noon. The **tube** shuts down shortly after midnight and **black cabs** are especially hard to find when clubs are closing. Some late-night frolickers catch **"minicabs,"** unmarked cars that sometimes wait outside clubs; negotiate a price before you get in, and be wary of riding alone. It's advisable to arrange transportation in advance or acquaint yourself with the extensive network of **night buses** (information ☎ 72 22 12 34).

The Aquarium, 256 Old St., EC1 (☎72 51 61 36). Tube: Old Street. Ultra-trendy club comes complete with swimming pool for club kids to take a dip. Cover £5-15. Open Th 9am-3pm, F (garage) 10pm-4am, Sa (house) 10am-5pm.

Bar Rumba, 35 Shaftesbury Ave., W1 (☎72 87 27 15). Tube: Piccadilly Circus. Brilliant nights out in a cozy underground space. Cover £4-12. Open M-Tu and Th-F 10pm-3am, W 10pm-3:30am, Sa 10pm-4am, Su 8pm-1:30am.

The Fridge, on Town Hall Parade, Brixton Hill, SW2 (☎73 26 51 00). Tube: Brixton. Outside the station, cross the street, walk left, walk up Brixton Hill Rd., and look for the long line. Converted cinema hosts some of the most popular nights in London. Cover £8-12. Open F-Sa 10pm-6am. Head next-door for the after party at the **Fridge Bar.**

The Hanover Grand, 6 Hanover St., W1 (☎74 99 79 77). Tube: Oxford Circus. Multiple floors crammed full of well-dressed people. Getting in, however, may take ages–plan to go early, even on weekdays. Cover £3-15. Open W (hiphop and UK garage) 10:30pm-3:30am, F (garage) 10pm-4am, and Sa (house) 10:30pm-5:30am.

The Astoria (LA1), 157 Charing Cross Rd., WC2 (☎74 34 04 03). Tube: Tottenham Court Rd. From the station, take Charing Cross towards Soho. Megavenue hosts frequent live acts as well as Jeremy Joseph's popular *G.A.Y.* In the basement is the **LA2,** whose Sa *Carwash* requires a costume and a love of the 1970s. Cover £7-14.

Bagleys, York Way, N1 (☎72 78 27 77). Tube: King's Cross. This former movie studio is London's biggest club venue (capacity 3000). Four cavernous rooms with garage, house and old school raves. Cover £10-14. Open F 10pm-6am, Sa 10pm-8am. **Be careful around King's Cross at night.**

Notting Hill Arts Club, 21 Notting Hill Gate, W11 (☎74 60 44 59). Tube: Notting Hill Gate. Hard beats fill the basement dance floor. Soul, Latin, jazz, house. Cover £3-5 M-Sa after 8pm, Su after 7pm. Open M-Sa 5pm-1am, Su 4-11pm.

Ministry of Sound, 103 Gaunt St., SE1 (☎73 78 65 28; www.ministryofsound.co.uk). Tube: Elephant and Castle. Take the exit for South Bank University. The granddaddy of all serious clubbing. Cover £10-15. Open F 10:30pm-6:30am, Sa midnight-9am.

Turnmills, 63B Clerkenwell Rd., EC1 (☎72 50 34 09). Tube: Farringdon. Walk up Turnmill St. and turn right onto Clerkenwell Rd. *Trad* gets kickin' at 3am and keeps on kickin' until noon. Get there early or late to avoid long queues, or reserve in advance. Cover £10. Open F-Sa 3am-noon.

Ronnie Scott's, 47 Frith St., W1 (☎74 39 07 47; fax 74 37 50 81). Tube: Leicester Sq. or Piccadilly Circus. The most famous jazz club in London and one of the oldest in the world has seen the likes of Ella Fitzgerald and Dizzy Gillespie. Reservations essential. Cover £15 M-Th, £20 F-Sa; students £9 M-W. Box office open M-Sa 11am-6pm. Music M-Sa 9:45pm-2:30am. Open M-Sa 8:30pm-3am, Su 7:30-11:30pm.

The Africa Centre, 38 King St., WC2 (☎78 36 19 73). Tube: Covent Garden. Art center by day, den of funk by night. African and samba music at the "Lompopo Club" most F, some Sa. Cover £7-8 in advance, £10 at the door. Open F and Sa 9pm-3am.

GAY AND LESBIAN NIGHTLIFE

London has a very visible gay scene, ranging from flamboyant to mainstream. *Time Out* has a section devoted to gay listings, and gay newspapers include *Capital Gay* (free, caters to men), *Pink Paper*, and *Shebang* (for women). *Gay Times* (£3) is the British counterpart to the *Advocate; Diva* (£2) is a monthly lesbian mag. Islington, Earl's Ct., and Soho (especially **Old Compton St.**) are all gay-friendly areas. For more details about London's gay and lesbian nightlife scene, check out *Boyz* (www.boyz.co.uk) or *QX* (www.qxmag.co.uk), available free at many gay bars.

"Atelier," Thursday at **The End,** 18 West Central St., WC1 (☎74 19 91 99). Tube: Tottenham Court Rd. Dressing up is essential. Cover £5, free with flyer from pre-party at **Manto,** 30 Old Compton St.

The Black Cap, 171 Camden High St., NW1 (☎74 28 27 21). Tube: Camden Town. North London's best-known drag bar. Live shows every night attract a mixed male and female crowd. When the shows aren't on, a DJ plays Top 40. M "oldies and trash" night is a favorite. Cover Tu-Sa £2-4, free before 11pm. Open M-Th 9pm-2am, F-Sa 9pm-3am, Su noon-3pm and 7pm-midnight.

The Box, Seven Dials, 32-34 Monmouth St., WC2 (☎72 40 58 28). Tube: Covent Garden or Leicester Sq. Intimate and stylish gay/mixed bar and brasserie. Menus change to match the season (main courses £6-9). Fun, hip clientele of both sexes and all races. The dance floor downstairs makes this an excellent venue for a night of dancing and drinking (lager £2.50). Open M-Sa 11am-11pm, Su 7-10:30pm.

Freedom, 60-66 Wardour St., W1 (☎77 34 00 71). Tube: Piccadilly Circus. A very trendy (look the part!) cafe-bar that draws in a mixed crowd for cocktails. DJs and dancing space below.

EXCURSIONS FROM LONDON

OXBRIDGE. Don your academic regalia for a day in the intellectual meccas of **Oxford** (p. 186) and **Cambridge** (p. 191), both an hour from London by train.

BRIGHTON. Just over an hour from London by train, indulge in a "dirty weekend" in **Brighton** (p. 181).

SALISBURY AND CANTERBURY. Make like a pilgrim and head to **Canterbury** (p. 180) or ponder the beyond at **Salisbury Cathedral** and **Stonehenge** (p. 183), all under two hours from London by train.

SOUTHERN ENGLAND

Sprawling toward the continent, the landscape of southern England simultaneously asserts Britain's island heritage and belies a continental link deeper than the Chunnel. Early Britons settled the counties of Kent, Sussex, and Hampshire from across the English Channel, and William the Conqueror left his mark upon the downsland in the form of awe-inspiring cathedrals. But Geoffrey Chaucer, Jane Austen, Charles Dickens, E.M. Forster, and Virginia Woolf—all staples of modern British culture—also all drew inspiration from these lands. To the west, the counties of Somerset, Avon, and Wiltshire boast Salisbury's medieval cathedral, the Roman Baths at Bath, and the forever-mysterious Stonehenge.

FERRIES AND TRAINS TO FRANCE, SPAIN, AND BELGIUM

Ferries chug from **Portsmouth** (p. 181) to **St. Malo** (p. 352) and **Caen, France** (p. 348); from **Folkestone** to **Boulogne, France** (p. 316) and from **Newhaven** to **Dieppe, France** (p. 348). Travelers with cars can head through the **Chunnel** (from Dover to Calais) on **Le Shuttle.** For detailed info on over- and underwater transport options to the continent, see p. 51.

BATH ☎01225

A visit to the elegant Georgian city of Bath (pop. 83,000) remains *de rigueur*, even though today it's more of a museum (or a museum gift shop) than a resort. But expensive trinkets can't conceal the fact that Bath, immortalized by Austen and Dickens, once stood second only to London as the social capital of England.

PRACTICAL INFO, ACCOMMODATIONS, AND FOOD. **Trains** head frequently to Bristol (15min., £4.60); London's Paddington Station (1½hr., £34); and Exeter (1¼hr., £21.50). National Express **buses** (☎ (08705) 80 80 80) run to Oxford (2hr., 6 per day, £12) and London's Victoria Station (3hr., 9 per day, £11.50). Both arrive near the southern end of Manvers St.; walk to the Terrace Walk roundabout and turn left on York St. to reach the **tourist office,** in Abbey Churchyard. (☎47 71 01; email tourism@bathnes.gov.uk. Open May-Sept. M-Sa 9:30am-6pm, Su 10am-4pm; Oct.-Apr. M-Sa 9am-5pm, Su 10am-4pm.)

B&Bs (from £18) cluster on **Pulteney Rd., Pulteney** and **Crescent Gardens,** and **Widcombe Hill.** The **YHA youth hostel,** on Bathwick Hill, is in a mansion 20 minutes above the city; catch Badgerline bus #18 (dir. University) from the station or the Orange Grove rotary (round-trip £1). (☎46 56 74; fax 48 29 47. Breakfast £3.10. TV. Laundry. £10.15.) The **International Backpackers Hostel,** 13 Pierrepont St., is up the street from the stations and is three blocks from the baths. (☎44 67 87; email info@backpackers-uk.demon.co.uk. Breakfast £1.50. Laundry. Internet. £12.) Cross Pulteney Bridge and go through Pulteney Gardens to get to **Toad Hall Guest House,** 6 Lime Grove. (☎42 32 54. £20 per person.) To reach **Newton Mill Camping,** 2½ mi. west on Newton Rd., take bus #5 from the bus station (round-trip £1.60) to Twerton and ask to be let off at the campsite. (☎33 39 09. 2 people, tent, and car £11.) **Guildhall Market** is between High St. and Grand Parade. (Open M-Sa 8am-5:30pm.) **Tilleys Bistro,** 3 North Parade Passage, has French and English fare. (Open M-Sa noon-2:30pm and 6:30-11pm, Su 6:30-10:30pm.) **The Pump Room,** in Abbey Courtyard, holds a monopoly on Bath Spa mineral water (£0.45). **Postal code:** BA1 1A5.

SIGHTS AND ENTERTAINMENT. Once the spot for naughty sightings, the **Roman Baths** are now a must-see for all. Most of the visible complex is not actually

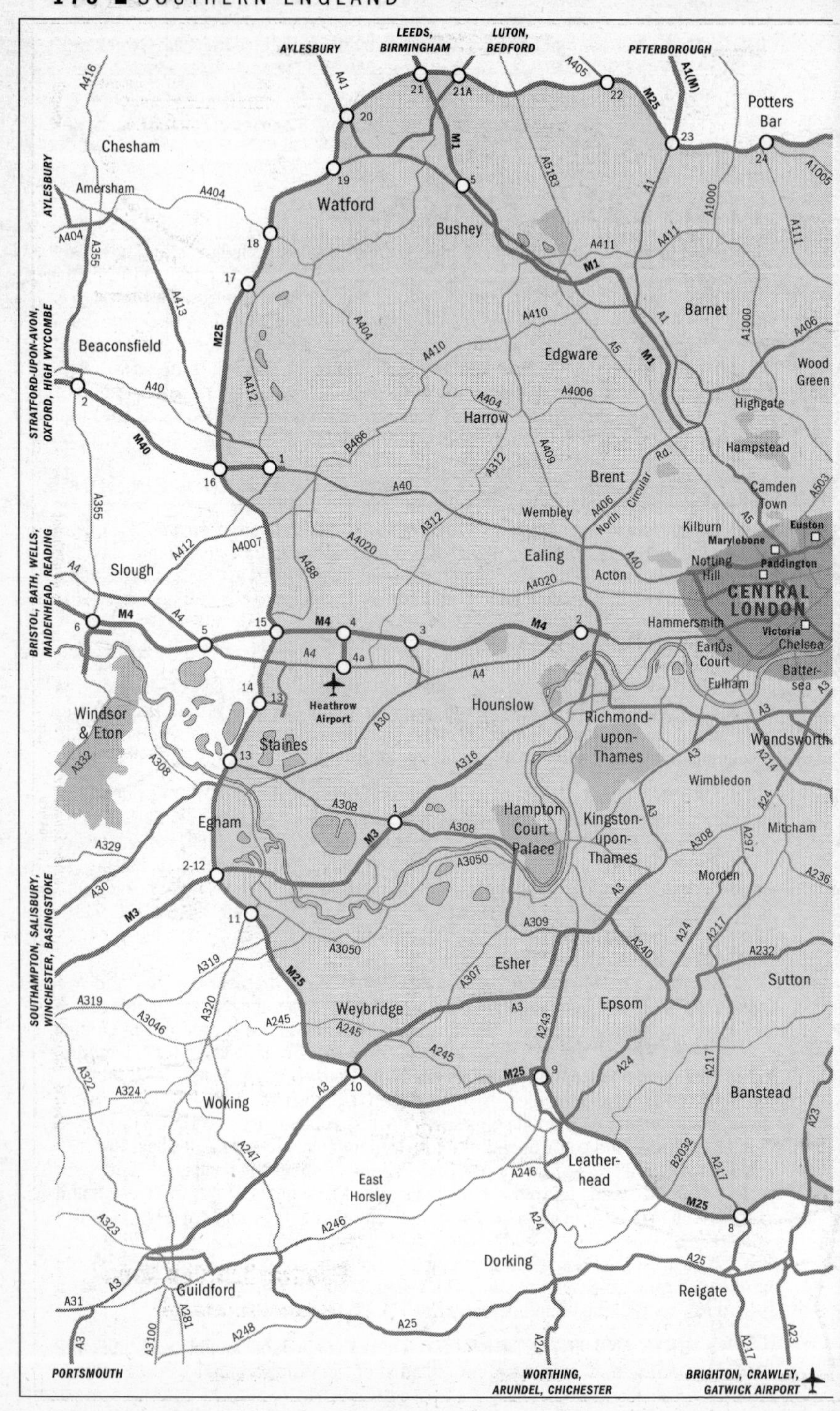

AYLESBURY
LEEDS, BIRMINGHAM
LUTON, BEDFORD
PETERBOROUGH
Potters Bar
Chesham
Amersham
AYLESBURY
Watford
Bushey
STRATFORD-UPON-AVON, OXFORD, HIGH WYCOMBE
Beaconsfield
Barnet
Edgware
Wood Green
Highgate
Harrow
Hampstead
Brent
Camden Town
Wembley
Kilburn
Euston
Marylebone
BRISTOL, BATH, WELLS, MAIDENHEAD, READING
Slough
Ealing
Notting Hill
Paddington
Acton
CENTRAL LONDON
Hammersmith
Victoria
Chelsea
Earl's Court
Batter-sea
Fulham
Heathrow Airport
Windsor & Eton
Hounslow
Richmond-upon-Thames
Staines
Wandsworth
Wimbledon
Egham
Hampton Court Palace
Kingston-upon-Thames
Mitcham
Morden
SOUTHAMPTON, SALISBURY, WINCHESTER, BASINGSTOKE
Esher
Sutton
Weybridge
Epsom
Woking
Banstead
Leather-head
East Horsley
Dorking
Guildford
Reigate
PORTSMOUTH
WORTHING, ARUNDEL, CHICHESTER
BRIGHTON, CRAWLEY, GATWICK AIRPORT

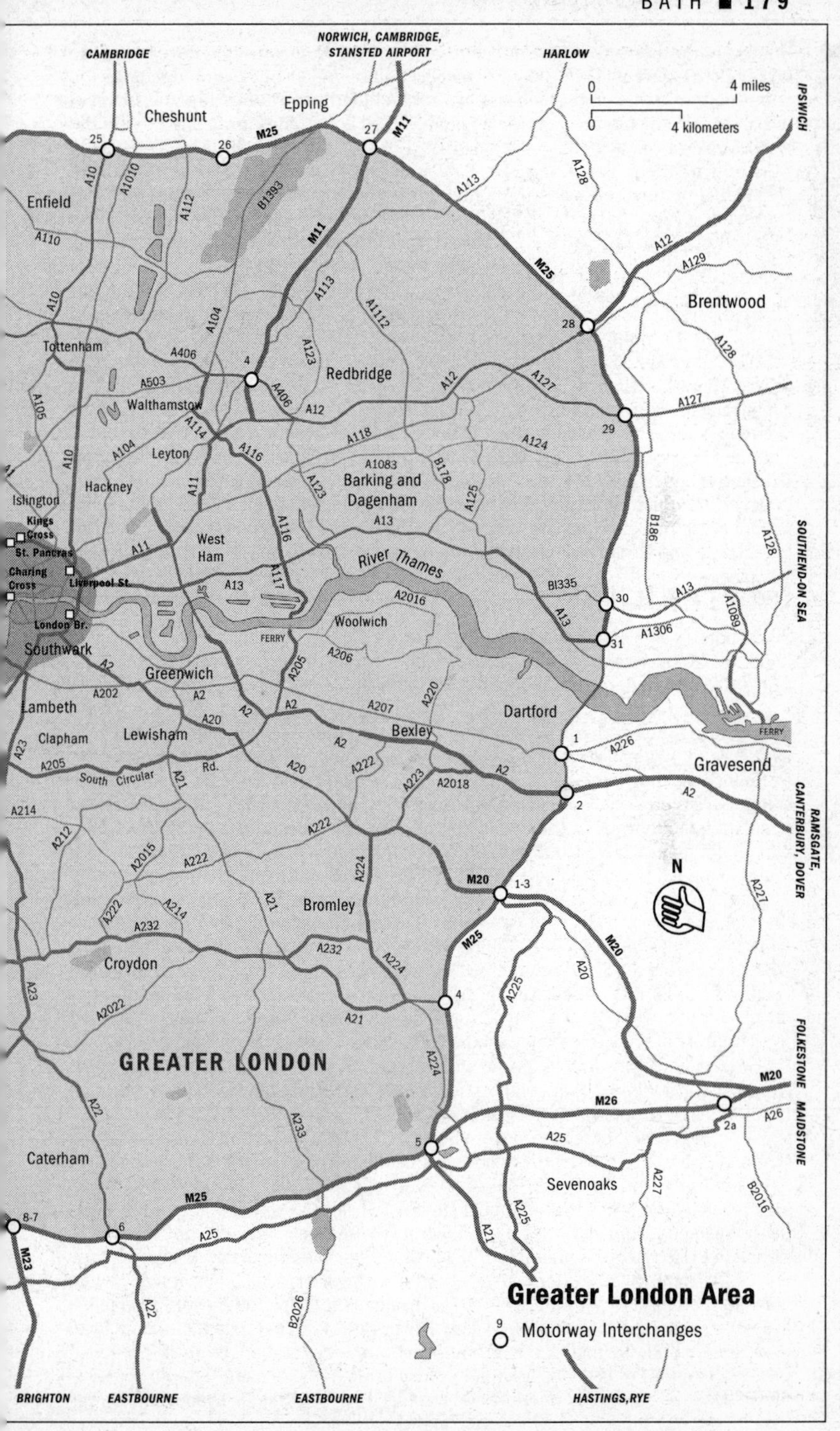
Greater London Area
Motorway Interchanges
GREATER LONDON
CAMBRIDGE
NORWICH, CAMBRIDGE, STANSTED AIRPORT
HARLOW
IPSWICH
SOUTHEND-ON SEA
RAMSGATE, CANTERBURY, DOVER
FOLKESTONE
MAIDSTONE
BRIGHTON
EASTBOURNE
EASTBOURNE
HASTINGS, RYE
0 4 miles
0 4 kilometers
N
Cheshunt
Epping
Enfield
Tottenham
Walthamstow
Redbridge
Brentwood
Leyton
Hackney
Islington
Kings Cross
St. Pancras
Charing Cross
Liverpool St.
London Br.
Southwark
West Ham
Barking and Dagenham
River Thames
Woolwich
FERRY
Greenwich
Lambeth
Clapham
Lewisham
Bexley
Dartford
Gravesend
South Circular Rd.
Bromley
Croydon
Caterham
Sevenoaks
M25
M11
M20
M26
M23

Roman, but rather reflects Georgian dreams of what Romans might have built. The **Roman Baths Museum** underneath reveals genuine Roman Baths and highlights the complexity of Roman engineering, which included central heating and internal plumbing. Recovered artifacts, scale models, and hot springs bring back to life the Roman spa city Aquae Salis, first unearthed in 1880 by sewer diggers. (Open daily Apr.-July and Sept. 9am-6pm; Aug. 9am-6pm and 8-10pm; Oct.-Mar. 9:30am-5pm. £6.70.) Penny pinchers can view one bath in the complex by entering (for free) through the **Pump Room** on Stall St. (see above). Next to the baths, the towering 15th-century **Bath Abbey** has a whimsical west facade with several angels climbing ladders up to heaven—and, curiously enough, two climbing down. (Open M-Sa 9am-4:30pm, Su 1-2:30pm and 4:30-5:30pm. £1.50.) Head north up Stall St., turn left on Westgate St., and turn right on Saw Close to reach Queen Sq., where Jane Austen lived at #13. Continue up Gay St. to **The Circus,** where Thomas Gainsborough, William Pitt, and David Livingstone once lived. To the left down Brock St. is the **Royal Crescent,** a half-moon of Georgian townhouses bordering **Royal Victoria Park.** The **botanical gardens** within nurture 5000 species of plants. (Open M-Sa 9am-dusk, Su 10am-dusk. Free.) Backtrack down Brock St. and bear left at The Circus (or take a right at The Circus from Gay St.) to reach Bennett St. and the dazzling **Museum of Costume,** which will satisfy any fashion fetishist. (Open daily 10am-5pm. £3.90; joint ticket with Roman Baths £8.70.) The laid-back **Paragon Wine Bar,** 1A The Paragon, is a fantastic place to kick back, while the **The Pig and Fiddle** pub, on the corner of Saracen St. and Broad St., packs in a rowdy young crowd.

CANTERBURY ☎01227

Six hundred years ago in his famed *Canterbury Tales*, Chaucer saw enough irony in droves of tourists to capture them in verse, writing of the medieval pilgrims who flocked from London to the **Canterbury Cathedral.** Archbishop Thomas à Becket was beheaded here in 1170 after an irate Henry II allegedly asked, "Will no one rid me of this troublesome priest?" (Open Easter-Sept. M-Sa 9am-6:30pm, Su 12:30-2:30pm and 4:30-5:30pm; Oct.-Easter M-Sa 9am-5pm, Su 12:30-2:30pm and 4:30-5:30pm. Evensong services M-F 5:30pm, Sa 3:15pm, Su 6:30pm. £3, students and seniors £2. Audio tour £2.50.) **The Canterbury Tales,** on St. Margaret's St., is a museum simulating the journey of Chaucer's pilgrims; the gap-toothed Wife of Bath and her waxen companions bust out with an abbreviated, Modern English version of the Tales. (Open July-Aug. daily 9am-5:30pm; Mar.-June and Sept.-Oct. daily 9:30am-5:30pm; Nov.-Feb. Su-F 10am-4:30pm, Sa 9:30am-5:30pm. £5.50, students and children £4.60.) On Stour St., the **Canterbury Heritage Museum** tells the town's history from medieval times to WWII. (Open June-Oct. M-Sa 10:30am-5pm, Su 1:30-5pm; Nov.-May closed Su. £2.40, students £1.60, family of five £5.30.) To see two of South England's most storied castles, head 12 mi. southeast to **Deal. Deal Castle** was designed by Henry VIII as a coastal fortification; **Walmer Castle** has been converted from military bastion to country estate. **Trains** leave regularly from Canterbury (£3).

For those not traveling by horse with a group of verbally gifted pilgrims, **trains** from London's Victoria Station arrive at Canterbury's **East Station,** while trains from London's Charing Cross and Waterloo Stations arrive at **West Station** (1½hr., £15.30). Stagecoach **buses** leave from St. George's Ln. for London's Victoria Coach Station (1¾hr., £8). The **Tourist Information Centre,** 34 St. Margaret's St., stocks free mini-guides to Canterbury. (☎76 65 67. Open daily Apr.-Aug. 9:30am-5:30pm; Sept.-Mar. 9:30am-5pm.) Surf the **Internet** at **Library,** 18 High St., for a free one-hour booking; manage the four-day wait by calling ahead. **B&Bs** cluster near both train stations, on London Rd., Whitstable Rd., and High St. The **Hampton House,** 40 New Dover Rd. (☎46 49 12), offers quiet, luxurious rooms for £20-25 per person, while **Let's Stay,** 26 New Dover Rd. (☎46 36 28), has beds for £10; both serve full English breakfasts. The **YHA youth hostel,** 54 New Dover Rd., is three-quarters of a mile from East Station and one-half of a mile southeast of the bus station. (☎46 29 11; fax 47 07 52. Lockers £1 plus deposit. Laundry. Reception 7:30-10am and 1-11pm. Reserve ahead. Call for off-season openings. £11, under 18 £7.40.) **The Camping and Caravan-**

ning Club, on Bekesbourne Ln., has good facilities. (☎46 32 16. Summer £5.30 per person, winter £3.75; £4.30 pitch fee.) **High St.** is crowded with pubs, restaurants, and fast-food joints. For **groceries,** head to **Safeway,** on St. George's Pl. (Open M-Th and Sa 8am-8pm, F 8am-9pm, Su 10am-4pm.) **Patrick Casey's,** on Butchery Ln., will warm you up with traditional Irish food and bitters. **Postal code:** CT1 2BA.

BRIGHTON ☎01273

According to legend, the future King George IV scuttled into Brighton (pop. 250,000) for some un-kingly behavior around 1784. Today, Brighton is still the unrivaled home of the "dirty weekend"—it sparkles with a risqué, tawdry luster all its own. Before indulging, check out England's long-time obsession with the Far East at the excessively ornate **Royal Pavilion,** on Pavilion Parade, next to Old Steine. (Open daily June-Sept. 10am-6pm; Oct.-May 10am-5pm. £4.90, students £3.55, families £12.80. Guided tours 11:30am and 2:30pm; £1.25, audio tour £1.) Around the corner on Church St. stands the **Brighton Museum and Art Gallery,** with paintings, English pottery, and a wild Art Deco and Art Nouveau collection. Leer at Salvador Dalí's sexy red sofa, *Mae West's Lips.* (Open M-Tu and Th-Sa 10am-5pm, Su 2-5pm. Free.) Before heading out to the rocky **beach,** stroll the **Lanes,** a jumble of 17th-century streets forming the heart of Old Brighton. Brighton brims with nightlife options; pick up *The Punter* or *What's On* (at music stores, news agents, and pubs) for tips. Brighton is also *the* gay nightlife spot in Britain outside London; pick up *Gay Times* (£2.50) or *Capital Gay.* Drink at **Fortune of War,** 157 King's Rd. Arches (open M-Sa 10:30am-11pm and Su 11am-10:30pm), or **The Squid,** 78 Middle St. (open M-F 5-11pm, Sa 3-11pm, and Su 3-10:30pm). Most clubs are open M-Sa 10pm-2am; many offer student discounts on weeknights but raise prices weekends. **Paradox** and **Event II,** on West St., are popular, and the converted WWII tunnels of **Zap Club,** on King's Rd., provide space for dirty dancing. **The Beach,** 171-181 King's Rd. Arches, produces some of the beachfront's biggest beats, while **Casablanca,** on Middle St., plays live jazz to a mostly student crowd.

Trains (☎ (0345) 48 49 50) roll to London (1¼hr., 6 per hr., £9.90) and Portsmouth (1½hr., 1 per day, £11.70, round-trip £12.30). National Express **buses** (☎38 37 44) head to London (2hr., 15 per day, return £8). The **tourist office** is at 10 Bartholomew Sq. (☎ (0906) 711 22 55. Open M-Tu and Th-F 9am-5pm, W and Sa 10am-5pm.) The rowdy **Brighton Backpackers Hostel,** 75-76 Middle St., is the best place to meet other backpackers. (☎77 77 17; fax 88 77 88; email stay@brightonbackpackers.com. Linens included. Internet £1.50 per 30min. Dorms £10-11, weekly £55-60; doubles £25.) **Baggies Back-packers,** 33 Oriental Pl., has mellow vibes and exquisite murals. Head west of West Pier along King's Rd.; Oriental Pl. is on the right. (☎73 37 40. Dorms £10; doubles £25.) To get to the **YHA youth hostel,** on Patcham Pl., 4 mi. away, take Patcham bus #5 or 5A from Old Steine in front of the Royal Pavilion to the Black Lion Hotel. (☎55 61 96. Curfew 11pm. Breakfast £3. £10.15.) For cheap food, try the fish-and-chip shops along the beach or north of the Lanes; also try **Food for Friends,** 17a-18 Prince Albert St., for well-seasoned vegetarian fare. ("Taster" special, £5.20. Open M-Sa 8am-10pm, Su 9:15am-10pm.) Or head to **Safeway,** 6 St. James St., and prepare your own food. (☎57 03 63. Open M-W 8am-8pm, Th-Sa 8am-9pm, Su 10am-4pm.) **Postal code:** BN1 1BA.

GLASTONBURY ☎01458

The reputed birthplace of Christianity in England and the seat of Arthurian myth, Glastonbury (pop. 6900) has evolved into an intersection of Christianity and mysticism. Present-day pagan pilgrimage site **Glastonbury Tor** is supposedly the site of the mystical Isle of Avalon, where the Messiah is slated to return. To make the trek up to the Tor, turn right at the top of High St., continue up to Chilkwell St., turn left onto Wellhouse Ln., and take the first right up the hill (buses in summer £0.50). On your way down, visit the **Chalice Well,** on the corner of Welhouse Ln., the supposed resting place of the Holy Grail. (Open daily Easter-Oct. 10am-6pm; Nov.-Feb. 1-4pm. £1.50.) Back in town, the ruins of **Glastonbury Abbey,** England's oldest Christian

A CASTLE FIT FOR A HORSE George IV loved his horses, but not as much as he loved himself. Before the Royal Pavilion was rebuilt, the grounds housed a building for George's fleet of horses and army of attendants. Accommodations for all these beasts and their servants required an enormous structure (designed in the style of Indian architecture), and Brighton's citizens jokingly whispered that the horses lived better than the Prince. Bridled by such remarks and spurred to action, George nagged his architects to design an even more impressive home in the same Eastern style; he would not be outflanked by his own stallions. Several years and a modern equivalent of £20 million later, the Royal Pavilion took shape, allowing George to jockey for the respect he desired and reclaim his title as the stud of Brighton.

building foundation, stands behind the archway on Magdalene St. (Open daily June-Aug. 9am-6pm; Sept.-May 9:30am-6pm. £3, students £2.50.) Although no trains serve Glastonbury, Baker's Dolphin **buses** (☎ (01934) 61 60 00) run from London (3¼hr., 1 per day, round-trip £5), while Badgerline buses (☎ (01225) 46 44 46) run from Bath (round-trip £3.90; change at Wells). From the bus stop, turn right on High St. to reach the **tourist office,** The Tribunal, 9 High St. (☎83 29 54. Open Apr.-Sept. Su-Th 10am-5pm, F-Sa 10am-5:30pm; Oct.-Mar. Su-Th 10am-4pm.) **Glastonbury Backpackers,** in the Crown Hotel on Market Pl., contributes its own splashes of color to the city's tie-dye. (☎83 33 53. Internet. Dorms £10; doubles £26.) Sleep in comfort at **Blake House,** 3 Bove Town. (☎83 16 80. £19.) **Postal code:** BA6 9HG.

PORTSMOUTH ☎023

Set Victorian prudery against prostitutes, drunkards, and a lot of bloody cursing sailors, and you have a basic 900-year history of Portsmouth (pop. 190,500). On the sea, visitors relive D-Day, explore warships, and learn of the days when Britannia ruled the seas. War buffs and historians will plunge headfirst into the unparalleled **Naval Heritage Centre,** in the Naval Base, which houses a virtual armada of Britain's most storied ships. The center includes Henry VIII's **Mary Rose,** the only 16th-century warship on display anywhere in the world. Although Henry was particularly fond of her, she—like many women with whom Henry associated—died before her time, sinking after setting sail from Portsmouth in July 1545. Napoleon would roll in his mini grave if he knew that the **HMS Victory,** the ship that clinched Britain's reputation as king of the waves when it defeated his fleet at the Battle of Trafalgar in 1805, is still afloat. (Ticket lists tour time slot.) Although eclipsed by its neighbor, the iron-clad **HMS Warrior** provides an intriguing companion to the *Victory.* The five galleries of the **Royal Naval Museum** fill the historical gaps between the three ships. The entrance is next to the tourist office on The Hard—follow the signs to Portsmouth Historic Ships. (Ships open daily 10am-5pm. £6, students £5.20.)

For info on **ferries** to France, see p. 49. **Trains** (☎ (0345) 48 49 50) run to Southsea Station, on Commercial Rd., from: Chichester (40min., 2 per hr., round-trip £4.90); London's Waterloo Station (1½hr., 3 per hr., £19, round-trip £19.10); and Salisbury (2hr., every hr., £8.25). National Express **buses** (☎ (08705) 80 80 80) arrive at The Hard Interchange, next to the Harbour station, from London (2½hr., every hr., £10.50) and Salisbury (2hr., 1 per day, £8.25). The **tourist office** is on The Hard; there's a **branch** next to the train station. (☎92 82 67 22. Open daily 9:30am-5:45pm.) Moderately priced **B&Bs** (around £20) clutter **Southsea,** 1½ mi. east of The Hard along the coast. **Birchwood Guest House,** 44 Waverly Rd., offers bright, spacious rooms and an ample breakfast. (☎92 81 13 37. £16-25 per person.) Take any bus to Cosham (#1, 3, or 40) to the police station and follow the signs for the **YHA youth hostel** at Wymering Manor, on Old Wymering Ln., off Medina Rd., in Cosham. (☎92 37 56 61. Lockout 10am-5pm. Curfew 11pm. Open Feb.-Aug. daily; Sept.-Nov. F-Sa. £9.15.) The **Tesco supermarket,** on Craswell St., is near the town center. (Open M-Th 8am-8pm, F 8am-9pm, Sa 8am-7pm, Su 10am-4pm.) **Pubs** near The Hard provide weary sailors with galley fare and bottles of gin. **Postal code:** PO1 1AA.

WINCHESTER ☎01962

The glory of Winchester (pop. 32,000) stretches back into the distant past. William the Conqueror deemed it the center of his kingdom and both Jane Austen and John Keats lived and wrote in town. Duck through the archway, pass through the square, and behold the 900-year-old **Winchester Cathedral,** 5 The Close. Famed for its nave, the cathedral (556 ft.) is the longest medieval building in Europe; the interior holds magnificent tiles and Jane Austen's tomb. The **Norman crypt,** supposedly the oldest in England, can only be viewed in the summer and by guided tour. The 12th-century Winchester Bible resides in the library. (Open daily 7:15am-5:30pm; East End closes 5pm. Tours 10am-3pm. Suggested donation £3, students £2.) Fifteen miles north of Winchester is the meek village of **Chawton,** where Jane Austen lived. It was in her **cottage** that she penned *Pride and Prejudice, Emma, Northanger Abbey,* and *Persuasion.* Take Hampshire **bus #X64** (M-Sa 11 per day, round-trip £4.50), or the London and Country **bus #65** on Sundays; ask to be let off at the Chawton roundabout and follow the brown signs. (☎ (01420) 832 62. Open Mar.-Dec. daily 11am-4:30pm; Jan.-Feb. Sa-Su 11am-4:30pm. £2.50.)

Trains (☎ (0345) 48 49 50) arrive at Winchester's Station Hill, at City Rd. and Sussex St., from Chichester (50min., every hr., £9.50); London's Waterloo Station (1hr., 2 per hr., £16.60); and Portsmouth (1hr., every hr., £7). To get there from the train station, head down City Rd., right on Jewry St., and left on High St. (10min.). National Express **buses** (☎ (08705) 80 80 80) go to London (1½hr., 7 per day, £12); Hampshire Stagecoach (☎ (01256) 46 45 01) goes to Salisbury (#68; 1½hr., 7 per day, roundtrip £4.45) and Portsmouth (#69; 1½hr., 12 per day, roundtrip £4.45). The **tourist information centre,** at The Guildhall, Broadway, is by the statue of Alfred the Great. (☎84 05 00; fax 85 03 48. Open June-Sept. M-Sa 10am-6pm, Su 11am-2pm; Oct.-May M-Sa 10am-5pm.) The lovely home of **Mrs. P. Patton,** 12 Christchurch Rd., between St. James Ln. and Beaufort Rd., is five minutes from the cathedral. (☎85 42 72. Singles £22-25; doubles £30-35.) Go past the Alfred statue, across the bridge, and left before Cricketers Pub to reach the **YHA youth hostel,** 1 Water Ln. (☎85 37 23. Kitchen. Lockout 10am-5pm. Curfew 11pm. Open July-Aug. daily; mid-Feb. to June and Sept.-Oct. Tu-Sa. £9.15.) **Royal Oak,** on Royal Oak Passage, next to the Godbegot House off High St., claims to be the kingdom's oldest. (Open daily 11am-11pm.) Get **groceries** at **Sainsbury,** on Middle Brook St., off High St. (Open M-Th 8am-6:30pm, F 8am-9pm, Sa 7:30am-6pm.) **Postal code:** SO23 8WA.

SALISBURY ☎01722

Salisbury (pop. 103,000) revolves around **Salisbury Cathedral,** a famous pilgrimage site whose spire rises a neck-straining 404 ft. The pillars literally bend inward under 6400 tons of limestone; if a pillar rings when you knock on it, you should probably move away. (Open June-Aug. M-Sa 7am-8:15pm, Su 7am-6:15pm; Sept.-May daily 7am-6:15pm. Donation £3, students £2. Tours May-Sept. M-Sa 9:30am-4:45pm, Su 4-6:15pm; Oct. M-Sa same hours; Nov.-Feb. M-Sa 10am-4pm. Free. Roof and tower tours May-Sept. M-Sa 11am, 2 and 3pm, Su 4:30pm; June-Aug. M-Sa also 6:30pm. £3.) One of four surviving copies of the Magna Carta rests in the **Chapter House.** (Open June-Aug. M-Sa 9:30am-7:45pm, Su 9:30am-5:30pm; Sept.-May daily 9:30am-5:30pm. Free.)

Trains arrive on South Western Rd. from Winchester (1½hr., every hr., £10.60) and London (1½hr., every hr., £22-30). National Express **buses** (☎08705) 80 80 80) pull into 8 Endless St. from London's Victoria Station (2¾hr., 4 per day, £11.50); Wilts & Dorset buses (☎33 68 55) arrive from Bath (#X4; 2hr., 6 per day, £3). The **tourist information centre** is on Fish Row in the Guildhall, in Market Sq.; turn left on South Western Rd., bear right on Fisherton St., continue on Bridge St., cross the bridge onto High St., and walk straight on Silver St., which becomes Butcher Row and Fish Row (10-15min.). From the bus station, head left on Endless St., which (shockingly) ends and becomes Queen St., and turn right at the first old building to the right to enter Fish Row. (☎33 49 56; fax 42 20 59. Open July-Aug. M-Sa 9:30am-7pm, Su 10:30am-4:30pm; June and Sept. M-Sa 9:30am-6pm, Su 10:30am-4:30pm; Oct.-May M-

Sa 9:30am-5:30pm.) To get from the bus station to lodgings at **The Old Bakery,** 35 Bedwin St., head two blocks up Rollestone St. and turn left onto Bedwin St. (☎32 01 00. £15-20; with full breakfast £18-25. Backpackers' cottage £15 per person; with continental breakfast £17.) From the tourist information center, head left on Fish Row, right on Queen St., left on Milford St., and straight under the overpass to find the **YHA youth hostel,** in Milford Hill House, on Milford Hill. (☎32 75 72; fax 33 04 46. Dorms £9.85-10.85.) They also have **camping.** (Call ahead. Lockout 10am-1pm. Curfew 11:30pm. £4.70 per person.) **Sainsbury's supermarket** is at The Maltings. (Open M-Th 8am-8pm, F 8am-9pm, Sa 7:30am-7pm, Su 10am-4pm.) **Postal code:** SP1 1AB.

EXCURSION FROM SALISBURY: STONEHENGE. The 22-foot boulders of Stonehenge, which weigh up to 45 tons, date from about 1500 BC. Various stories attribute the monument to Druids, Phoenicians, Merlin, Mycenaean Greeks, Björk, giants, Romans, Smurfs, Masai, Danes, and aliens. In any case, their methods continue to elude both archaeologists and supermarket tabloids. For centuries, religious devotees have come for its mystical karmic energies, building temples and leaving us to marvel at the awe-inspiring, impressive nature of the site. You can languidly admire Stonehenge for free from nearby Amesbury Hill, 1½ mi. up the A303, or pay admission at the site. (☎ (01980) 62 53 68. Open daily June-Aug. 9am-7pm; mid-Mar. to May and Sept. to mid-Oct. 9:30am-6pm; mid-Oct. to mid-Mar. 9:30am-4pm. £4, students £3.) Wilts & Dorset **buses** (☎33 68 55) connect from Salisbury's center and train station (40min., round-trip £4.80).

EXETER ☎01392

Besieged by William the Conqueror in 1068 and flattened by German bombs in 1942, Exeter (pop. 110,000), has undergone frantic rebuilding, resulting in an odd mixture of the venerable and the banal: ruins punctuate parking lots and department store cash registers ring atop medieval catacombs. **Exeter Cathedral** was heavily damaged in WWII but still retains exquisite detail. The cathedral library's **Exeter Book** is the richest treasury of early Anglo-Saxon poetry in the world. (Cathedral open daily 7am-6:30pm; library open M-F 2-5pm. Evensong M-F 5:30pm, Sa-Su 3pm. Tours Apr.-Oct. M-F 11:30am and 2:30pm, Sa 11am. Suggested donation £2.50.) Six-hundred-year-old **underground passages** are accessible from the Romangate Passage next to Boots on High St. (Open July-Sept. M-Sa 10am-5:30pm; Oct.-June Tu-F 2-5pm, Sa 10am-5pm. Tours £3.50, students £2.50.)

Trains arrive in Exeter from London Paddington Station (2½hr., 2 per day, £39) and London Waterloo Station (3hr., 6 per day, £38.30). From St. David's Station, follow the footpath in front, turn right onto St. David's Hill (which becomes Iron Bridge and North St.), and turn left on High St. National Express **buses** (☎ (08705) 80 80 80) pull into Paris St., off High St. just outside the city walls, from London's Victoria Coach Station (4hr., every 1½hr., round-trip £16) and Bath (2¾hr., 3 per day, £13); walk through the arcade to Sidwell St. and turn left to reach High St. The **tourist office,** in the Civic Centre, in the City Council Building on Paris St., is behind the bus station. (☎26 57 00. Open M-Sa 9am-5pm, Su 10am-4pm.) To reach the **YHA youth hostel,** 47 Countess Wear Rd., 2 mi. away down Topsham Rd., take minibus K or T from High St. to the Countess Wear Post Office (£0.97), follow Exe Vale Rd. to the end, and turn left. (☎87 33 29. Breakfast £3.10. Reception 8-10am and 5-10pm. £10.15; **camping** about £5.) Pack a picnic at **Sainsbury's supermarket,** in the Guildhall Shopping Centre off High St. (Open M-W and F 8am-6:30pm, Th 8am-7pm, Sa 7:30am-6pm, Su 10:30am-4:30pm.) **Postal code:** EX1 1AA.

THE CORNISH COAST

PENZANCE. Penzance is the very model of an ancient English pirate town: waterlogged and unabashed. A Benedictine monastery was built on the spot where St. Michael dropped by in AD 495, and today **St. Michael's Mount** sits offshore where it offers 30-story views. (Open Apr.-Oct. M-F 10:30am-5:30pm; in summer usually also Sa-Su; Nov.-Mar. in nice weather. £4.40.) A causeway links the mount to the island; or, take ferry bus #2 or 2A to Marazion (M-Sa 3 per hr., round-trip £0.80) and catch a ferry during high tide (round-trip £1.40). **Trains** (☎ (0345) 48 49 50) go to: London (5½hr., every hr., £54); Plymouth (2hr., every hr., £10); and Exeter (3hr., every hr., £18.60). National Express (☎ (08705) 80 80 80) **buses** go to Plymouth (3hr., 2 per hr., £6) and London (8hr., 8 per day, £27). Between the two stations is the **tourist office,** on Station Rd. (☎36 22 07. Open in summer M-F 9am-5pm, Sa 9am-4pm, Su 10am-1pm; off season M-F 9am-5pm, Sa 10am-1pm.) To get to the **YHA Penzance,** Castle Horneck, walk 30 minutes up Market Jew and Alverton St., then take the right fork with the signs for Castle Horneck. (☎36 26 66; email penzance@yha.org.uk. Kitchen. Laundry. Reception 3-11pm. Lockout 10am-1pm. £10.85. **Camping** £5.) **The Turk's Head,** 49 Chapel St., is a 13th-century pub (Penzance's oldest), sacked by Spanish pirates in 1595. ☎**01736.**

ST. IVES. St. Ives (pop. 11,100) perches 10 mi. north of Penzance, on a spit of land lined by pastel beaches and azure waters. Virginia Woolf too was bewitched by the energy of the Atlantic at St. Ives: her masterpiece *To the Lighthouse* is thought to refer to the Godrevy Lighthouse in the distance. Whether you seek the perfect subject or the perfect strip of sand, St. Ives has it, if hidden beneath a veneer of postcards and ice cream cones. Some **trains** (☎ (08457) 484950) on the Plymouth-Penzance line run directly to **Penzance** (3-6 per day), but most connect via **St. Erth** (10min., 2 per hr., £3) Western National **buses** go to Penzance (3 per hr., off season M-Sa only, £2.50) and Newquay. National Express (☎ (08705) 80 80 80) stops in St. Ives between Plymouth and Penzance (6 per day). The **tourist office** is in the Guildhall on Street-an-Pol. From the stations, walk down to the foot of Tregenna Hill and turn right on Street-an-Pol. (☎79 62 97. Open in summer M-Sa 9:30am-6pm, Su 10am-1pm; off season closed Sa-Su.) **St. Ives International Backpackers,** The Stenmack, fills a renovated 19th-century Methodist church. (☎/fax 79 94 44. Internet. £8-12.) Places to camp abound in nearby **Hayle;** try **Trevalgan Camping Park** (☎79 64 33). **Fore St.** is packed with small bakeries. Many places also sell Cornish cream teas (a pot of tea with scones, jam, and Cornish clotted cream). ☎**01736.**

NEWQUAY. An outpost of surfer subculture, Newquay (NEW-key) lures the bald, the bleached-blond, and even the blue to its surf and pubs. Winds descend on **Fistral Beach** with a vengeance, creating what some consider the best surfing conditions in all of Europe. The enticing **Lusty Glaze Beach** beckons from the bay side. The party beast stirs around 9pm and reigns into the wee hours. Drink up at **The Red Lion,** on North Quay Hill, at Tower Rd. and Fore St., then ride the wave down Fore St. to **Sailors.** (Cover £4-10.) Go on and shake what your momma gave you at **Bertie's,** on East St. (Open until 1am.) From the **train station,** just off Cliff Rd., trains go to Plymouth (2hr., every hr., £8.10) and Penzance (2hr., every hr., £10.30). From the **bus station,** 1 East St., Western National runs to St. Ives (2hr., June-Sept. 1 per day, £4.90). National Express (☎ (08705) 80 80 80) buses run to London (5¾hr., 3 per day, £26.50). With your back to the train station, go four blocks left to reach the **tourist office,** on Marcus Hill. (☎85 40 22. Open in summer M-Sa 9am-6pm, Su 9am-4pm; off season reduced hours.) **Newquay International Backpackers,** 69-73 Tower Rd., offers free shuttle service to its sister hostel in St. Ives. (☎87 93 66; email backpacker@dial.pipex.com. Internet. £10.) ☎**01637.**

EAST ANGLIA AND THE MIDLANDS

The plush farmlands of **East Anglia** stretch northeast from London, cloaking the counties of Cambridgeshire, Norfolk, and Suffolk. While the area is still characterized by its rustic beauty, the **Midlands** to the west are known for the mills that sprang up in the Industrial Revolution.

OXFORD ☎01865

Almost a millennium of scholarship lies behind Oxford—22 British Prime Ministers were educated here, as well as numerous other world leaders. Today, it is a scramble of rumbling trucks, screeching brakes, and pedestrians shoving past one another in the streets. But the academic pilgrim can still find places to pay homage: the basement room of Blackwell's bookshop, the impeccable gallery of the Ashmolean Museum, and the perfectly maintained quadrangles of Oxford's 39 colleges help the town retain an irrepressible grandeur.

PRACTICAL INFO, ACCOMMODATIONS, AND FOOD. **Trains** (☎(0345) 48 49 50; recording ☎79 44 22) run from Park End St., west of Carfax, to London's Pattington Station (1hr., every 15-30min., round-trip £14.80). **Buses** depart from Gloucester Green; follow the arrows up Cornmarket St. from Carfax. **Oxford CityLink** (☎78 54 00) connects London's Victoria Station (1¾hr., 1-4 per hr., round-trip £7.50, students £6.50) with Gatwick and Heathrow. **National Express** (☎ (08705) 80 80 80) offers domestic routes. Most **local service buses** board on the streets around Carfax and have fares around £0.70. Beside the bus station, the **tourist office** sells accommodations lists for 60p and maps for £1, and books rooms for a £2.50 fee. (☎72 68 71; fax 24 02 61. Walking tours £4.50. Open M-Sa 9:30am-5pm, Su 10am-3:30pm.) You can access the **Internet** at **Pickwick Papers,** 90 Gloucester Green, next to the bus station. (£1 per 15min. Open daily 4:30am-6:30pm.)

In summer, book at least a week ahead. **B&Bs** line the main roads out of town; take Cityline **buses** or walk 15-45 minutes. More B&Bs are located in the 300s on **Banbury Rd.** (take bus #2A, 2C, or 2D); cheaper ones lie in the 200s and 300s on **Iffley Rd.** (bus #4), between 250 and 350 on **Cowley Rd.** (buses #51 or 52), and on **Abingdon Rd.** in South Oxford (bus #16). Expect to pay £20-25. **Oxford Backpacker's Hotel,** 9a Hythe Bridge St., has nonstop music in the common room. (☎72 17 61. Kitchen. Laundry. Internet. Guests must show passport. £11-12.) To get to the **YHA Youth Hostel,** 32 Jack Straw's Ln., Headington, take bus #13 heading away from Carfax on High St., ask the driver to stop at Jack Straw's Ln., and walk 8 minutes up the hill. (☎76 29 97; fax 76 94 02. Kitchen. Laundry. Lockers. £10.85, students £9.85.) **Bravalla,** 242 Iffley Rd., has six sunny rooms with baths and TVs. (☎24 13 26; fax 25 05 11. Sign breakfast board the night before. Singles £35; doubles £50.) Lincoln College dorms with shaggy green carpets are available at **Old Mitre Rooms,** 4b Turl St. (☎27 98 21; fax 27 99 63. Open July to early Sept. Singles £24; twins £44, with bath £48.50; triples and family rooms £58, £63.) Walk 20 minutes or take the "Rose Hill" bus from the bus station, train station, or Carfax Tower to reach **Heather House,** 192 Iffley Rd. (☎/fax 24 97 57. Singles £25; doubles with bath £48.) Take any Abingdon bus across Folly Bridge to reach **Newton House,** 82-84 Abingdon Rd., ½ mi. from the town center. (☎24 05 61. Doubles £44-58; varies with season.) **Oxford Camping and Caravaning,** 426 Abingdon Rd., behind the Touchwoods camping store, has 84 sites. (☎24 40 88. 2-night max. stay for nonmembers of the Camping and Caravaning Society. Toilet and laundry facilities. Showers free. £5-6.25 per tent.)

Oxford students fed up with cafeteria grub keep cheap restaurants in business. After hours, **kebab vans** roam around Broad St., High St., Queen St., and St. Aldate's St. Across Magdalen Bridge, try restaurants along the first four blocks of **Cowley Rd. Cafe CoCo,** 23 Cowley Rd., has a lively atmosphere and a great Mediterranean menu. (Entrees £5.95-8.50. Open daily 10am-11pm.) **The Nosebag,** 6-8 St. Michael's St., has a gourmet-grade menu served cafeteria-style. (Lunch under £6.50, dinner under £8. Open M 9:30am-5:30pm, Tu-Th 9:30am-10pm, F-Sa 9:30am-10:30pm, Su 9:30am-9pm.) **Chiang Mai,** 130a High St., tucked down an alley, is a popular Thai restaurant with plenty of veggie options. (Entrees £5.50-9. Jungles curry with wild rabbit £7. Open M-Sa noon-2:30pm and 6-11pm, Su noon-3pm and 6-10pm.) Near Magdalen College, **Harvey's of Oxford,** 58 High St., has great takeout. (Cherry-apple flapjacks 85p; carrot cake £1.25; large sandwiches £1.60-3. Open M-F 8am-7pm, Sa 8am-6pm, Su 8:30am-6pm.) **Heroes,** 8 Ship St., is filled with students feeding on sandwiches,

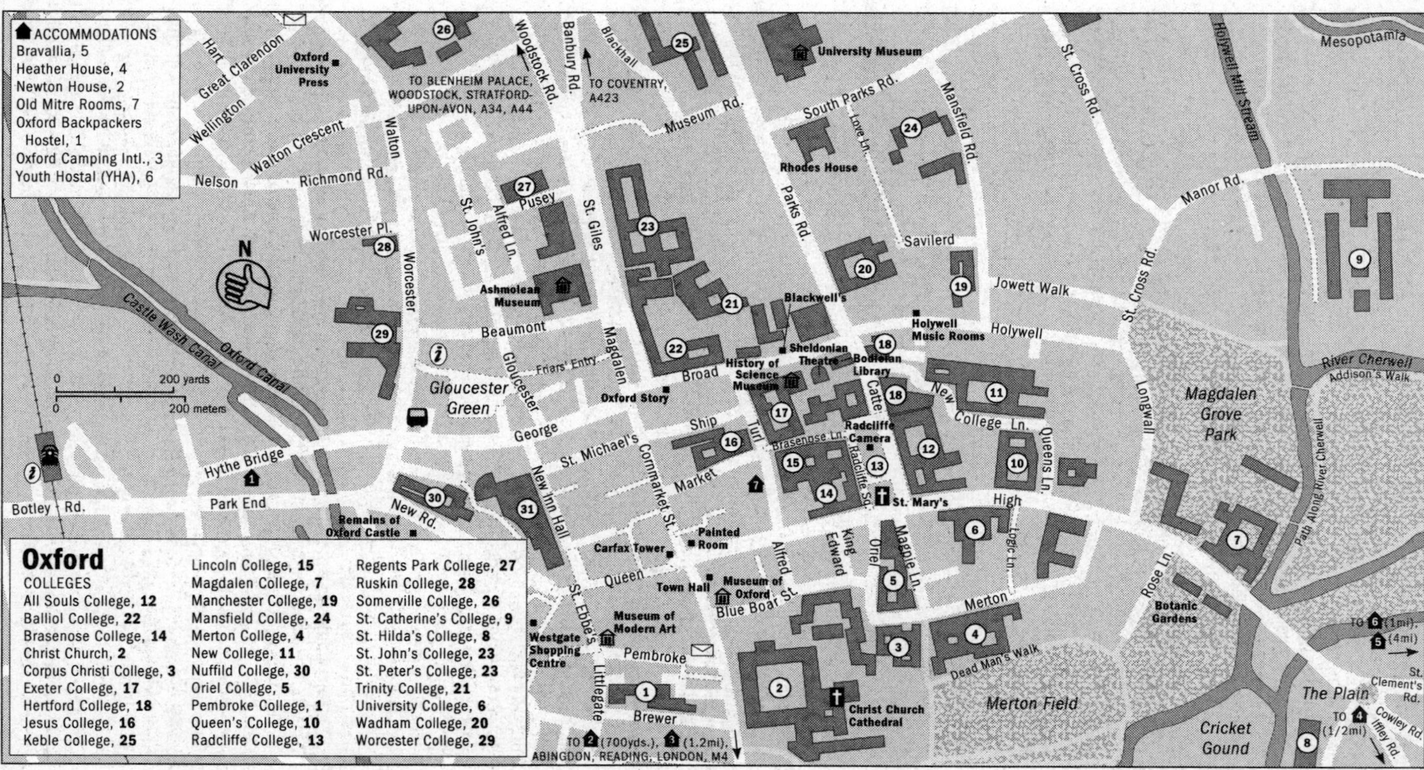
ACCOMMODATIONS
Bravallia, 5
Heather House, 4
Newton House, 2
Old Mitre Rooms, 7
Oxford Backpackers Hostel, 1
Oxford Camping Intl., 3
Youth Hostal (YHA), 6
Oxford
COLLEGES
All Souls College, 12
Balliol College, 22
Brasenose College, 14
Christ Church, 2
Corpus Christi College, 3
Exeter College, 17
Hertford College, 18
Jesus College, 16
Keble College, 25
Lincoln College, 15
Magdalen College, 7
Manchester College, 19
Mansfield College, 24
Merton College, 4
New College, 11
Nuffild College, 30
Oriel College, 5
Pembroke College, 1
Queen's College, 10
Radcliffe College, 13
Regents Park College, 27
Ruskin College, 28
Somerville College, 26
St. Catherine's College, 9
St. Hilda's College, 8
St. John's College, 23
St. Peter's College, 23
Trinity College, 21
University College, 6
Wadham College, 20
Worcester College, 29
Hart
Great Clarendon
Wellington
Oxford University Press
Woodstock Rd.
Banbury Rd.
Blackhall
TO BLENHEIM PALACE, WOODSTOCK, STRATFORD-UPON-AVON, A34, A44
TO COVENTRY, A423
University Museum
Mesopotamia
St. Cross Rd.
Holywell Mill Stream
South Parks Rd.
Mansfield Rd.
Museum Rd.
Walton Crescent
Walton
Nelson
Richmond Rd.
Rhodes House
Love Ln.
Manor Rd.
Pusey
St. John's
Alfred Ln.
St. Giles
Parks Rd.
Worcester Pl.
Savilerd
N
Worcester
Ashmolean Museum
Blackwell's
Jowett Walk
Castle Wash Canal
Oxford Canal
Holywell Music Rooms
Holywell
Beaumont
Magdalen
Sheldonian Theatre
Bodleian Library
History of Science Museum
Friars' Entry
Broad
River Cherwell
Addison's Walk
0 200 yards
0 200 meters
Gloucester Green
Gloucester
Oxford Story
Catte
New College Ln.
Longwall
Magdalen Grove Park
George
Ship
Turl
Radcliffe Camera
Queens Ln.
Brasenose Ln.
Radcliffe Sq.
Path Along River Cherwell
St. Michael's
Hythe Bridge
Cornmarket St.
Market
St. Mary's
High
Botley Rd.
Park End
New Rd.
New Inn Hall
Remains of Oxford Castle
Painted Room
Carfax Tower
Alfred
King Edward
Oriel
Magpie Ln.
Logic Ln.
Rose Ln.
Queen
Town Hall
Museum of Oxford
Blue Boar St.
Merton
Botanic Gardens
St. Ebbe's
Museum of Modern Art
Westgate Shopping Centre
Pembroke
Dead Man's Walk
TO 6 (1mi), 5 (4mi)
St. Clement's Rd.
Littlegate
Christ Church Cathedral
Merton Field
The Plain
Brewer
TO 4 (1/2mi)
Cowley Rd.
Iffley Rd.
Cricket Gound
TO 2 (700yds.), 3 (1.2mi), ABINGDON, READING, LONDON, M4

meats and cheeses, and freshly baked breads. (Open M-F 8am-7pm, Sa 8:30am-5pm, Su 10am-5pm.) **Covered Market,** between Market St. and Carfax, sells produce, deli goods, and breads. (Open M-Sa 8am-5:30pm.) **Postal code:** OX1 1ZZ.

SIGHTS. King Henry II founded Britain's first university in 1167; today, Oxford's alumni register reads like a who's who of British history, literature, and philosophy. Oxford University's three favorite literary sons include Lewis Carroll, C.S. Lewis, and J.R.R. Tolkien. The tourist office's *Welcome to Oxford* guide (£2) lists the colleges' public visiting hours. In Carfax, hike up the 99 steps of **Carfax Tower** for an overview of the city. (Open daily Apr.-Oct. 10am-5:30pm; Nov.-Mar. 10am-3:30pm. £1.20.) Just down St. Aldate's St. from Carfax, Christ Church College has Oxford's grandest quad and its most socially distinguished students. The **Christ Church Chapel** is also Oxford's cathedral. The Reverend Charles Dodgson (better known as Lewis Carroll) was friendly with Dean Liddell of Christ Church—and friendlier with his daughter, Alice. (Open M-Sa 9:30am-5:30pm, Su 1-5pm. £2.50, students £1.50. Services Su 8, 10, 11:15am, 6pm; weekdays 7:30am, 6pm.) The **Botanic Garden** cultivates a sumptuous array of plants that have flourished for three centuries. The path connecting the Botanic Garden to the Christ Church Meadow provides a beautiful view of the Thames. From Carfax, head down High St.; the garden is on the right. (Open daily Apr.-Sept. 9am-5pm; Oct.-Mar. 9am-4:30pm. Admission late June to early Sept. £2, children free; free mid-Sept. to mid-June.) North of Carfax, the imposing **Ashmolean Museum,** Beaumont St., houses works by Leonardo, Monet, Manet, van Gogh, Michelangelo, Rodin, and Matisse, while the **Cast Gallery,** behind the museum, exhibits over 250 casts of Greek sculptures—the finest classical collection outside London. From Carfax, head up Cornmarket St., which becomes Magdalen St.; Beaumont St. is on the left. (Both museum and gallery open Tu-Sa 10am-5pm, Su 2-5pm. Free.) **Bodleian Library,** Catte St., is Oxford's principal reading and research library, with over five million books; no one has ever been permitted to check one out. Take High St. and turn left on Catte. (Open M-F 9am-6pm, Sa 9am-1pm. £3.50.) Next to the Bodleian, the **Sheldonian Theatre** is a Roman-style jewel of an auditorium, where graduation ceremonies are conducted in Latin. The cupola affords an inspiring view of Oxford's spires. (Open M-Sa 10am-12:30pm and 2-4:30pm. £1.50, children £1.) You could browse for days at **Blackwell's Bookstore,** on Broad St., which (according to Guinness) is the world's largest room devoted to bookselling. (Open M-Sa 9am-6pm, Su 11am-5pm.) Oscar Wilde attended **Magdalen** (MAUD-lin) **College,** considered by many to be Oxford's most handsome college. (Open July-Sept. M-F noon-6pm, Sa-Su 2-6pm; Oct.-June daily 2-5pm. Apr.-Sept. £2, students £1; Oct.-Mar. free.)

ENTERTAINMENT AND NIGHTLIFE. Punting on the river Thames (known in Oxford as the Isis) or on the River Cherwell (CHAR-wul) is a traditional Oxford pasttime. Punters receive a tall pole, a small oar, and an advisory against falling into the water. Don't be surprised if you suddenly come across **Parson's Pleasure,** a small riverside area where men sometimes sunbathe nude. **Magdalen Bridge Boat Co.,** Magdalen Bridge, east of Carfax along High St., rents boats from March to November. (☎20 26 43. M-F £9 per hr., Sa-Su £10 per hr.; deposit £20 plus ID. Open daily 10am-9pm.) Music and drama at Oxford are cherished arts. Attend a concert or Evensong service at one of the colleges (the **New College Choir** is one of the best boy choirs around) or a performance at the **Holywell Music Rooms,** the oldest in the country. The **Oxford Playhouse,** 11-12 Beaumont St., is a venue for bands, dance troupes, and the Oxford Stage Company. (☎79 86 00. Tickets from £6, standby tickets available for seniors and students.) During summer, college **theater groups** stage productions in local gardens and cloisters. The **City of Oxford Orchestra,** the city's professional orchestra, gives monthly concerts in the Sheldonian Theatre. (☎74 44 57. Tickets £10-15; 25% student discount.)

Pubs far outnumber colleges in Oxford. Sprawling underneath the city, the 13th-century **Turf Tavern** on Bath Pl., off Holywell St., is Oxford's unofficial student union. (Open M-Sa 11am-11pm, Su 11am-10:30pm. Kitchen open noon-8pm.) **The Eagle and Child,** 49 St. Giles St., moistened the tongues of C.S. Lewis and J.R.R. Tolkien for 25 years; *The Chronicles of Narnia* and *The Hobbit* were first read aloud here. (Open M-Sa 11am-11pm, Su noon-10:30pm.) **The King's Arms,** Holywell St, draws in a huge young crowd. (Open M-Sa 10:30am-11pm, Su 10:30am-10:30pm.) Although pubs in Oxford tend to close down by 11pm, nightlife can last until 3am; grab *This Month in Oxford* at the tourist office. For starters, check out **The Westgate Pub,** Park End St. (Dance music until 2am on F and Sa, jazz on M, comedy on Tu.) **Walton St.** and **Cowley Rd.** host late-night clubs, as well as a fascinating jumble of ethnic restaurants, used bookstores, and offbeat shops.

EXCURSION FROM OXFORD: BLENHEIM PALACE

The largest private home in England and one of the loveliest, **Blenheim** (BLEN-em) **Palace** features sprawling grounds, a lake, and a fantastic garden. While attending a party here, Winston Churchill's mother gave birth to the future Prime Minister in a closet; his grave rests nearby in the village churchyard of **Bladon.** The palace rent is a single French franc, payable each year to the Crown—not a bad deal for a palace with 187 furnished rooms. Blenheim's full glory is on display in Kenneth Branagh's 1996 *Hamlet.* (☎ (01993) 81 10 91. Open daily mid-Mar. to Oct. 10:30am-5:30pm; grounds daily open year-round 9am-9pm. £9, students £7.) Blenheim sprawls in **Woodstock,** 8 mi. north of Oxford on the A44. Stagecoach Express **buses** (☎ (01865) 77 22 50) run to Blenheim Palace from Gloucester Green station in Oxford (20min., return £3.50); the same route also goes to Stratford and Birmingham.

THE COTSWOLDS

Stretching across western England—bounded by Banbury in the northeast, Bradford-upon-Avon in the southwest, Cheltenham in the north, and Malmesbury in the south—the Cotswolds' verdant, vivid hills enfold tiny towns barely touched by modern life. These old Roman settlements and Saxon villages, hewn from the famed Cotswold stone, demand a place on any itinerary, although their relative inaccessibility via public transportation means extra effort to get there.

GETTING THERE AND GETTING AROUND. Useful **gateway cities** are Cheltenham, Oxford, and Bath. **Trains** to Cheltenham arrive from: London (2½hr., every hr., £31.50); Bath (1½hr., every hr., £11.10); and Exeter (2hr., every 2hr., £28.50). National Express **buses** (☎ (08705) 80 80 80) also arrive from London (3hr., every hr., £10.50); Stratford-upon-Avon (1hr., 2 per day, £7.50); and Exeter (3½hr., every 2hr., £18). For connections to Oxford, see p. 186; for connections to **Bath,** see p. 191.

From Cheltenham, Oxford, and Bath, **trains** zip to **Moreton-in-Marsh** (from Oxford £6.70) and **Charlbury** (£3.40)—the only two villages in the Cotswolds with train stations. Several **bus** companies cover the Cotswolds, but most routes are very infrequent (1-2 per week). Two unusually regular services run from Cheltenham; **Pulham's Coaches** (☎ (01451) 82 03 69) run to Moreton via **Bourton-on-the-Water** and **Stow-on-the-Wold** (50min., M-Sa 7 per day, £1.50); **Castleway's Coaches** (☎ (01242) 60 29 49) depart for Broadway via Winchcombe (50min., M-Sa 4 per day, £1.80). Snag the indispensable *Connection* timetable from any bus station or tourist office, and the Cheltenham tourist office's *Getting There from Cheltenham.*

Local roads are perfect for **biking;** the closely spaced villages make ideal watering holes. **Country Lanes Cycle Center** rents bikes at the Moreton-on-the-Marsh train station. (☎ (01608) 65 00 65. Gear and maps included. Call ahead. Open daily 9:30am-5:30pm. £14 per day.) Experience the Cotswolds as the English have for centuries by treading well-worn **footpaths** from village to village. **Cotswold Way,** spanning 100 mi. from Bath to Chipping Camden, gives **hikers** glorious vistas of hills and dales. The *Cotswold Way Handbook* (£2) lists **B&Bs** along the Cotswold Way. There are **hostels** in Charlbury (☎/fax (01608) 81 02 02; tourist office open Apr.-June daily,

July-Aug. M-Sa, Feb.-Mar. and Sept.-Oct. W-Su, and Jan. F-Su), Slimbridge, and Stow-on-the-Wold with dorms from £8.35. Most **campsites** are close to Cheltenham; Bourton-on-the-Water, Stow-on-the-Wold, and Moreton-on-the-Marsh also have places to put your Tent-on-the-Ground. The *Gloucestershire Caravan and Camping Guide* is free at local tourist centers.

STOW-ON-THE-WOLD, WINCHCOMBE, AND CIRENCESTER. Stow-on-the-Wold is a sleepy town with fine views of the surrounding countryside and cold winds. The **tourist office** is in Hollis House on The Square. (☎ (01451) 83 10 82. Open Easter-Oct. M-Sa 9:30am-5:30pm, Su 10:30am-4pm; Nov.-Easter M-Sa 9:30am-4:30pm.) The **YHA youth hostel** stands just a few yards from the village's authentic stocks. (☎ (01451) 83 04 97. Open daily Apr.-Oct. £10.85, students £9.85.)

West of Stow-on-the-Wold and 6 mi. north of Cheltenham on the A46, **Sudeley Castle,** once the manor of King Ethelred the Unready, enserfs the town of **Winchcombe.** (Open daily Apr.-Oct. 10:30am-5pm. £6.) Just 1½ mi. southwest of Sudeley Castle lies **Belas Knap,** a 4000-year-old burial mound, proving that the area was inhabited in prehistoric times. The **tourist office** is in Town Hall, near Cheltenham. (☎ (01242) 60 29 25. Open Apr.-Oct. M-Sa 10am-5pm, Su 10am-4pm.)

Sometimes regarded as the region's capital, **Cirencester** is the site of Corinium, an important Roman town founded in AD 49. Its **Corinium Museum,** on Park St., houses a formidable collection of Roman artifacts. (Open Apr.-Oct. M-Sa 10am-5pm, Su 2-5pm; Nov.-Mar. Tu-Sa 10am-5pm, Su 2-5pm. £2.50, students £1.) The **tourist office** is in Corn Hall, on Market Pl. (☎ (01285) 65 41 80. Open Apr.-Oct. M 9:45am-5:30pm, Tu-Sa 9:30am-5:30pm; Nov.-Mar. daily 9:30am-5pm.) The **Cirencester Parish Church,** Gloucestershire's largest parish church, is a "wool church," meaning the money to build it was endowed by wealthy local wool merchants. (Open daily 10am-5pm.) On Fridays, the town turns into a mad **antique marketplace.**

STRATFORD-UPON-AVON ☎01789

Native son William Shakespeare has spawned a veritable industry; the vaguest of connections to the Bard are exploited here to their full potential. But at rare moments, beyond the "Will Power" t-shirts and the tour bus exhaust, the essence of Shakespeare does lurk in Stratford: in the groves of the former Forest of Arden and in the pin-drop silence before a soliloquy in the Royal Shakespeare Theatre.

JOURNEY'S END. Thames **trains** roll in from: London's Paddington Station (2¼hr., 7-10 per day, round-trip £22.50); Warwick (25min., £2.60); and Birmingham (1hr., £3.60). National Express runs **buses** from London's Victoria Station (3hr., 12 per day, round-trip £4); Stagecoach runs from Oxford (round-trip £5.25); and Cambridge Coach connects to Cambridge (round-trip £16, students £12).

HERE CEASE MORE QUESTIONS. The **tourist office,** Bridgefoot, across Warwick Rd. at Bridge St. toward the waterside park, has a free accommodation guide. (☎29 31 27. Open Apr.-Oct. M-Sa 9am-6pm, Su 11am-5pm; Nov.-Mar. M-Sa 9am-5pm.) Romeo and Juliet would have lived happily ever after if they'd had email; surf the **Internet** at **Java Café,** 28 Greenhill St. (£3 per 30min., £5 per hr.; students £2.50, £4.) **Postal code:** CV37 6PU.

TO SLEEP, PERCHANCE TO DREAM. To B&B or not to B&B? This hamlet has tons of them (£15-26), but 'tis nobler in summer to make reservations. The nearest hostel is more than 2 mi. away, and the cost is comparable to many B&Bs after adding in round-trip bus fare. Keep an eye out for B&Bs on **Grove Rd., Evesham Pl.,** and **Evesham Rd. Bradbourne Guest House,** 44 Shipston Rd., is a recently redecorated Tudor-style home eight minutes from the town center. (☎20 41 78. Singles £25-30; doubles £44-48.) Warm and attentive proprietors consider **The Hollies,** 16 Evesham Pl., their labor of love. (☎26 68 57. Doubles £35, with bath £45.) The **Stratford Backpackers Hotel,** 33 Greenhill St., is conveniently located across the bridge from the train station, and has clean rooms, a common room, and kitchen. (☎26 38 38. £12.) The **YHA youth hostel,** Hemmingford House, on Wellesbourne Rd., Alveston, has large, attractive grounds; take bus #X18 (every hr., £1.70) from Bridge St., opposite the McDonald's. (☎29 70 93. Breakfast included. Reception 7am-midnight. £14.05, students £13.05.) **Riverside Caravan Park,** Tiddington Rd., 1 mi. east of Stratford on B4086, provides beautiful but sometimes crowded sunset views of the Avon. (☎29 23 12. Open Easter-Oct. Tent and 2 people £7, each additional person £1.)

FOOD OF LOVE. **Hussain's Indian Cuisine,** 6a Chapel St., has fantastic chicken *tikka masala;* keep an eye out for regular Ben Kingsley. (Lunch £6, entrees from £6. Open Th-Su 12:30-2:30pm and 5pm-midnight.) Drink deep ere you depart at the **Dirty Duck Pub,** on Waterside. (Traditional pub lunch £3-9; dinner £6-18. Open M-Sa 11am-11pm, Su noon-10:30pm.) To get to the **Safeway supermarket** on Alcester Rd., take the Avon shuttle from the town center, or just cross the bridge past the rail station. (Open M-Th and Sa 8am-9pm, F 8am-10pm, Su 10am-4pm.)

THE GILDED MONUMENTS. Bardolatry peaks around 2pm, so hit any Will-centered sights before 11am or after 4pm. Fanatics can buy a **combination ticket** (£12, students £11) for admission to five official Shakespeare properties: **Shakespeare's Birthplace, Anne Hathaway's cottage** (1 mi. away), **Mary Arden's House** and **Countryside Museum** (4 mi. away), **New Place** and **Nash's House,** and **Hall's Croft.** For a smaller dose, buy a **Shakespeare's Town Heritage Trail ticket** (£7.50, students £6.50), which covers all three sights in town. **Shakespeare's Birthplace,** Henley St., is equal parts period recreation and Shakespeare life-and-work exhibition. (Open Mar. 20-Oct. 19 M-Sa 9am-5pm, Su 9:30am-5pm; Oct. 20-Mar. 19 M-Sa 9:30am-4pm, Su 10am-4pm. £5.50.) **New Place,** on High St., was Stratford's hippest address when Shakespeare bought it in 1597. The remains of the foundation can be viewed from **Nash's House,** which belonged to the 1st husband of Shakespeare's granddaughter and last descendant, Elizabeth. **Hall's Croft** and **Mary Arden's House** bank on their tenuous connections to the Bard's extended family. Finally, pay homage to Shakespeare's little, little grave, in the **Holy Trinity Church,** on Trinity St. (£0.60, students £0.40.)

THE PLAY'S THE THING. Get thee to a performance at the world-famous **Royal Shakespeare Company;** recent sons include Kenneth Branagh and Ralph Fiennes. Tickets (£5-40) for all three theaters—the Royal Shakespeare Theatre, the Swan Theatre, and The Other Place—are sold through the box office in the foyer of the Royal Shakespeare Theatre, on Waterside. (☎40 34 03; 24hr. recording ☎40 34 04. Open M-Sa 9am-8pm. Arrive at least 20min. before opening for same-day sales; student and senior standbys for £8-12 exist in principle.)

EXCURSION FROM STRATFORD: WARWICK CASTLE. One of England's finest medieval castles, Warwick makes an excellent daytrip. Climb the 530 steps up the towers of Warwick and see the countryside unfold like a fairy tale kingdom of hobbits and elves. The dungeons are filled with life-size wax figures of people preparing for battle, while "knights" and "craftsmen" talk about their trades. (Open daily Apr.-Oct. 10am-6pm; Nov.-Mar. 10am-5pm. £11, students £7.85.) **Trains** arrive from Stratford (20min., round-trip £4) and Birmingham (40min., round-trip £4.70).

CAMBRIDGE ☎01223

Cambridge (pop. 105,000) is steadfastly determined to remain a city under its academic robes—the tourist office "manages," rather than encourages, visitors. Most colleges close to visitors during official quiet periods in May and early June, but when exams end, cobblestoned Cambridge explodes in gin-soaked glee. May Week (in mid-June, naturally) hosts a dizzying schedule of cocktail parties.

PRACTICAL INFO, ACCOMMODATIONS, AND FOOD. **Trains** (☎ (0345) 48 49 50) run from Station Rd. to London's King Cross and London's Liverpool St. (1¼hr., 2 per hr., £14.50). **Buses** run from Drummer St.; **National Express** (☎ (01604) 62 00 77) goes to London's Victoria Station (2hr., 17 per day, from £8) and **Stagecoach Express** runs to Oxford (2¾hr., £7). The **tourist office,** on Wheeler St., is just south of the marketplace and books rooms for a £3 fee. (☎ 32 26 40; fax 45 75 88; www.cambridge.gov.uk/leisure/tourism. Walking tour £7. Open Apr.-Oct. and Nov.-Mar. M-F 10am-5:30pm, Sa 10am-5pm.) Access the **Internet** at **CBI,** 32 Mill Rd., near the hostel. (10p per min. Open M-Sa 10am-8pm, Su 11am-7pm. Also at 5-7 Norfolk St. Open daily 8am-11pm.)

Many of the **B&Bs** around **Portugal St.** and **Tenison Rd.** are open only in July and August. Check the list at the tourist office, or pick up their guide to accommodations (50p). Two blocks from the train station, **Tenison Towers Guest House,** 148 Tenison Rd., is impeccable. (☎ 56 65 11. Singles £22; doubles £42.) **Warkworth Guest House,** Warkworth Terr., near the bus station, offers sunny rooms and packed lunches on request. (☎ 36 36 82. Singles £25-30; doubles £50-55.) **Mrs. McCann,** 40 Warkworth St., offers comfortable twin rooms with TVs. (☎ 31 40 98. Breakfast included. £16-18.) Twenty minutes from the center, **Home from Home B&B,** Liz Fasano, 39 Milton Rd., has sparkling rooms and a welcoming hostess. (☎ 32 35 55. Breakfast included. Call ahead with credit card. Singles £30; doubles £40.) The **YHA Youth Hostel,** 97 Tenison Rd., has a welcoming atmosphere. (☎ 35 46 01; fax 31 27 80. Kitchen. Laundry. TV lounge. 3- to 4-bed rooms. £15.10; students £11.40.) **Cambridge YMCA,** Gonville Pl., between the train station and town center, has clean rooms. (☎ 35 69 98. Breakfast included. Singles £22.65; doubles £37.) Take Cambus #118 from the Drummer St. bus station to reach **Highfield Farm Camping Park,** Long Rd., Comberton. (☎ 26 23 08. Showers. Laundry. £6.25-7 per tent; £7.25-8.75 with car.)

Cantabrigians are too busy learning Latin to flavor their food, so try the fruit and vegetables at **Market Sq.** (Open M-Sa 9:30am-4:30pm.) **Groceries** are available at **Sainsbury's,** 44 Sidney St. (Open M-F 8am-9pm, Sa 7:30am-9pm, Su 11am-5pm.) **The Little Tea Room,** 1 All Saints' Passage, off Trinity St., serves a "post-tutorial tea." (Open M-Sa 10am-5:30pm, Su 1-5:30pm.) Foreigners and beautiful people meet for cappuccino and quiche at **Clowns Coffee Bar,** 54 King St. (Open daily 7:30am-midnight.) **Postal code:** CB2 3AA.

SIGHTS AND ENTERTAINMENT. Cambridge is an architect's dream—it packs some of the most breathtaking examples of English architecture into less than 1 sq. mi. It's most exciting during the university's three eight-week terms: Michaelmas (Oct.-Dec.), Lent (Jan.-Mar.), and Easter (Apr.-June). **Trinity College** houses the stunning **Wren Library,** Trinity St., which keeps such notable treasures as A.A. Milne's handwritten manuscript of *Winnie the Pooh.* (Chapel and courtyard open daily 10am-5pm; library open M-F noon-2pm; both closed during exams. £1.75.) **King's College,** south of Trinity on King's Parade, is E.M. Forster's alma mater. Rubens's magnificent *Adoration of the Magi* hangs behind the altar of the college's spectacular Gothic chapel. (College open M-F 9:30am-4:30pm, Su 9:30am-2:30pm. Tours arranged through the tourist office. £3.50, students £2.50.) A welcome break from the academia of the colleges, the **Fitzwilliam Museum,** Trumpington St., 10 minutes from King's College, boasts a hoard of Egyptian, Chinese, Japanese, and Greek treasures that only the Brits could have assembled. (Open Tu-Sa 10am-5pm, Su 2:15-5pm. Guided tours Sa 2:30pm. £3 donation requested. Tours £3.) Today you can sip tea at **The Orchard,** on Mill Way, where these luminaries once discussed the ways of the world. Start the delightful walk there by crossing the Silver St. Bridge in Cambridge and following Newnham Rd. until it turns into Grantchester St.; at the dead end, take a right onto Grantchester Meadows and follow it to the footpath. Pick up *The Orchard* from the tourist office for inspiration.

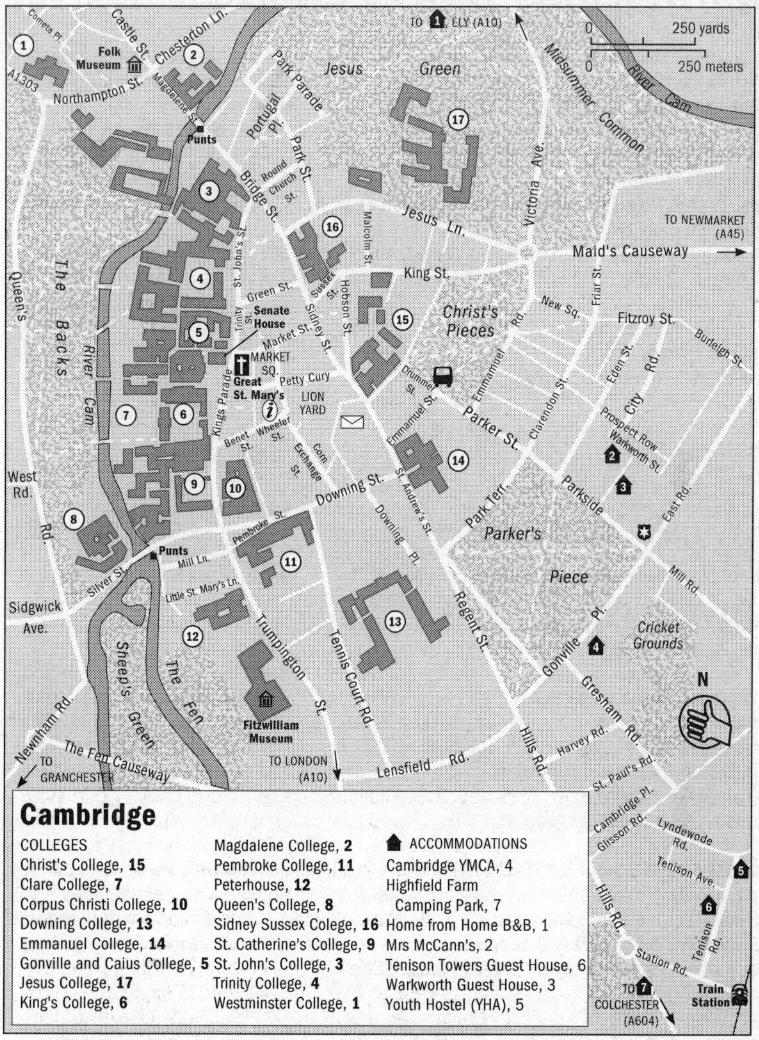

The best source of info on student activities is the student newspaper *Varsity;* the tourist office's free *Cambridge Nightlife Guide* is also helpful. **Punts** (gondola-like boats) are a favorite form of entertainment in Cambridge. Beware that punt-bombing—jumping from bridges into the river alongside a punt, thereby tipping its occupants into the Cam—has evolved into an art form. **Tyrell's,** at Magdalene Bridge, rents boats for £8 an hour plus a £40 deposit. Even more traditional than punting is **pub-crawling;** Cambridge hangouts offer good pub-crawling year-round, although they lose some of their character (and their best customers) in summer. **The Eagle,** Benet St., is the oldest pub in Cambridge.

NORTHERN ENGLAND

Cradled between the Pennines and the North Sea, the Northeast attracts with its calm coast and rich national parkland, including some of the most beautifully desolate areas in England. Extensive paths lace the gray and purple moors that captured the imagination of the Brontës and the emerald dales that figure so prominently in the stories of James Herriot.

PEAK DISTRICT NATIONAL PARK

Britain's first national park, wedged between industrial giants Manchester, Sheffield, and Nottingham, serves as a 555 sq. mi. playground for its 17 million urban neighbors. In the northern Dark Peak area, deep *groughs* (gullies) gouge the hard peat moorland against a backdrop of gloomy cliffs, and well-marked footpaths lead over rocky hillsides to village clusters. Abandoned milestones, derelict lead mines, and country homes are scattered throughout the southern White Peak.

Contact the **Peak District National Park Office,** Aldern House, Barlow Rd., Bakewell DE4 5AE (☎ (01629) 81 62 00), for more info. The **National Park Information Centres** at **Bakewell** (see below), **Castleton** (☎/fax (01433) 62 06 79), and **Edale** (☎ (01433) 67 02 07) offer walking guides; you can also inquire at **tourist offices** in **Buxton** (☎ (01298) 251 06) and **Matlock Bath** (☎ (01629) 550 82). Many farmers allow camping on their land if you leave no trace of your stay. **YHA youth hostels** in the park cost from £7.50-10.15 and can be found in **Bakewell** (see below), **Buxton** (☎/fax (01298) 222 87), **Castleton** (see below), **Edale** (see below), and **Matlock** (☎ (01629) 58 29 83). There are 13 **YHA Camping Barns** (£3.35 per night) in the park; book ahead at the **Camping Barns Reservation Office** (☎ (01200) 42 01 02; fax 42 01 03), 6 King St., Clitheroe, Lancashire, BB7 2EP. The park runs six **Cycle Hire Centres** (£9 per day); call **Ashbourne** (☎/fax (01335) 34 31 56) or **Hayfield** (☎ (01663) 74 62 22) for info.

GETTING THERE AND GETTING AROUND. The invaluable *Peak District Timetable* (£0.60; available in all Peak tourist offices) has transport routes and a map. Two **rail** lines originate in **Manchester** and enter the park from the west: one stops at **Buxton** near the park's edge (1hr., every hr., £5.30), and the other crosses the park via **Edale, Hope** (near Castleton), and **Hathersage** (1½hr., 9-15 per day, £6.30-10.40) on its way to **Sheffield.** From the south, a train heads from **Nottingham** to **Matlock,** on the park's southeastern edge. Trent **bus** TP (Transpeak; ☎ (01298) 230 98) serves the southern half of the park, stopping at **Buxton, Bakewell, Matlock,** and **Derby** (3hr., every 2hr.) between Manchester and Nottingham. A one-day **Wayfarer** pass (£6.60) covers unlimited train and bus travel within Greater Manchester, including most of the Peak District.

BAKEWELL, EDALE, AND CASTLETON. The Southern Peak is better served by public transportation than its northern counterpart, and is consequently more trampled. Thirty miles southeast of Manchester, **Bakewell** is the best base for exploration. Near several scenic walks through the White Peaks, the town is known for its Bakewell pudding, created when a flustered cook erred making a tart. Bakewell's **National Park Information Center** is at the corner of Bridge and Market St. (☎ (01629) 81 32 27). The small and cozy **YHA youth hostel,** Fly Hill, is five minutes from the town center. (☎/fax (01629) 81 23 13. Open Apr.-Oct. M-Sa; Nov.-Mar. F-Sa. £7.50.) **Postal code:** DE45 1EF.

The northern Dark Peak area contains some of the wildest and most rugged hill country in England. **Edale** offers little in the way of civilization other than a church, cafe, pub, school, and nearby **youth hostel** (☎ (01433) 67 03 02). Its surroundings, however, are arguably the most spectacular in northern England. The National Park Authority's *8 Walks Around Edale* (£1.20) details nearby **hiking** trails (1½-8½ mi.). Stay at the hostel (see above) or **camp** at **Fieldhead,** behind the tourist office. (☎ (01433) 67 03 86. £3.25 per person.) From Edale, the 3½mi. hike to **Castleton** affords a breathtaking view of the dark gritstone **Edale Valley** (Dark Peak) and the lighter limestone **Hope Valley** (White Peak) to the south. Castleton's river-carved limestone engulfs several famous caverns; **Treak Cliff Cavern** holds breathtaking stalagtite chambers and massive seams of the Blue John Stone. (Tours every 12min. £5, students and YHA members £4.) Stay at the excellent **YHA youth hostel** (☎ (01433) 62 02 35; open Feb. to late Dec.; £12.95) or **Cryer House,** across from the tourist office (☎ (01433) 62 02 44; doubles £42).

MANCHESTER ☎0161

The Industrial Revolution transformed the once unremarkable village of Manchester into a northern hub, now Britain's second-largest city. With few comely corners and fewer budget accommodations in the city center, Manchester—which attracts with its pulsing nightlife and vibrant arts scene—proves that you don't have to be pretty to be popular.

PRACTICAL INFO, ACCOMMODATIONS, AND FOOD. **Trains** leave **Piccadilly Station,** on London Rd., and **Victoria Station,** on Victoria St., for: York (40min., 2 per hr., £15.80); Liverpool (50min., 2 per hr., £6.95); Chester (1hr., every hr., £8.50); and London Euston (2½hr., every hr., £84.50). **Piccadilly Bus Station** consists of about 50 bus stops around Piccadilly Gardens; pick up a free route map at the tourist office. National Express **buses** (☎ (08705) 80 80 80) go from Chorlton St., two blocks south and one east of Piccadilly, to Liverpool (50min., every hr., £4) and London (4-5hr., 7 per day, £15). The **Manchester Visitor Centre,** in the Town Hall Extension, is on Lloyd St., off St. Peter's Sq. (☎234 31 57; info ☎ (0891) 71 55 33. Open M-Sa 10am-5:30pm, Su 11am-4pm.) You can check **email** at **interc@fe,** Piccadilly Sq., on the first floor of the Debenhams. (£1.50 per 30min. Open M and W-F 9:30am-5:30pm, Tu 10am-5:30pm, Sa 9am-5:30pm, Su 11am-4:30pm.)

Take bus #33 from Piccadilly Gardens towards Wigan or walk 10 minutes down Liverpool Rd. from the Deansgate train station to reach the sleek **YHA Manchester,** Potato Wharf, Castlefield, behind the Castlefield Hotel on Liverpool Rd. (☎839 99 60; email manchester@yha.org.uk. Breakfast included. Lockers £1-2. Kitchen. Laundry. Internet. Reception 7am-11:30pm. £17.40, students £13.10.) To get to the friendly **Woodies Backpackers Hostel,** 19 Blossom St., Ancoats, walk five minutes up Newton St. from Piccadilly Gardens and cross Great Ancoats St.; it's just past the Duke of Edinburgh pub. (☎/fax 228 34 56. Kitchen. Laundry. £12.) **Cornerhouse Café,** 70 Oxford St., is part of the trendy Cornerhouse Arts Center. (Entrees from £3.50. Open daily 11am-8:30pm; kitchen open noon-2:30pm and 5-7pm; bar open M-Sa noon-11pm, Su noon-10:30pm.) A **Tesco supermarket** is on Market St. (Open M-Sa 8am-8pm, Su 11am-5pm.) **Postal code:** M2 2AA.

SIGHTS AND ENTERTAINMENT. The exception to Manchester's generally unremarkable buildings is the neo-Gothic **Manchester Town Hall,** on St. Peter's Sq., behind the tourist office. Nearby, the domed **Central Library** houses one of the largest municipal libraries in Europe, including the UK's second-largest Judaica collection. (Open M-Th 10am-8pm, F-Sa 10am-5pm.) In the **Museum of Science and Industry,** on Liverpool Rd. in Castlefield, working steam engines provide a dramatic vision of Britain's industrialization. (Open daily 10am-5pm. £5, students £3.) At the **Manchester United Museum and Tour Centre,** on Sir Matt Busby Way, at the Old Trafford football stadium, you can learn all about Manchester United, England's best-known, loved, and reviled football team. Follow the signs up Warwick Rd. from the "Old Trafford" Metrolink stop. (Open daily 9am-5pm. £4.50. Tours £3.) One of Manchester's biggest draws is its artistic community, most notably its theater and music scenes; the **Royal Exchange Theatre,** on St. Ann's Sq., regularly puts on Shakespeare and original works. (☎833 98 33. M-Th and Sa tickets £7-23; student discounts available. Box office open M-Sa 9:30am-7:30pm.) Come nightfall, try the cafe-bar **Temple of Convenience,** 100 Great Bridgewater St., off Oxford St. (Open daily 11am-11pm.) One of the players in Manchester's trendsetting club scene is **Generation X,** 11/13 New Wakefield St., off Oxford St. (Cover after 11pm £2. Open F-Sa until 2am, Su noon-10:30pm.) Northeast of Princess St., the **Gay Village** rings merrily at night. Bars line **Canal St.;** purple **Manto's** at #46 draws all ages, sexes, and orientations to its Saturday night/Sunday morning "Breakfast Club." (Cover £2. Open daily 2-6am.)

BRITAIN

LIVERPOOL ☎0151

On the banks of the Mersey, Liverpool's history is rooted in its docks. Today, Liverpool (pop. 520,000) boasts two huge cathedrals, a dynamic arts scene, wild nightlife, and—oh yeah—the Beatles.

TICKET TO RIDE. **Trains** (☎ (08457) 48 49 50) leave Liverpool's Lime St. Station for: Manchester (1½hr., 2 per hr., £6.50); Birmingham (2hr., every hr., £24); London Euston (2hr., every hr., £45); Edinburgh (4hr., every 2hr., £41.60); and Glasgow (4½hr., every hr., £38.90). National Express **buses** (☎ (08705) 80 80 80) go from Norton St. Coach Station to: Manchester (1hr., every hr., £4); Birmingham (2½hr., 6 per day, round-trip £12.50); and London (4-5hr., 6 per day, £15, round-trip £24). The Isle of Man Steam Packet Company (☎ (08705) 52 35 23) runs **ferries** to Dublin.

HELP! The main **tourist office,** in Merseyside Welcome Centre in Queen Sq., sells a map guide (£1), and a *Beatles Map* (£2.50), books beds for a 10% deposit, and organizes bus (from £4) and walking (£1) tours. (☎709 36 31; fax 708 02 04. Open M-Sa 10am-5:30pm, Su 10am-4:30pm.) **Phil Hughes** runs an excellent Beatles bus tour. (☎228 45 65. £9.) The **Central Library,** William Brown St., has **Internet** access. (Open M-Sa 9am-5:30pm. £1 per 30min.) **Postal code:** L1 1AA.

HARD DAY'S NIGHT. Budget hotels are mostly on **Lord Nelson St.,** next to the train station, and **Mt. Pleasant,** one block from Brownlow Hill. **Embassie Youth Hostel,** 1 Falkner Sq., 15-20 minutes from the bus or train station at the end of Canning St., has laundry, TV, pool table, kitchen, and all the toast and jam you can eat. (☎707 10 89. £12.50.) **YWCA,** 1 Rodney St., just off Mt. Pleasant, has renovated rooms in a lively neighborhood. (☎709 77 91. Kitchen. £12.) The new **YHA youth hostel,** 24 Tabley St., The Wapping, is ideally located. From the train station, follow the signs to Albert Dock, turn left on Strand St., and it's on the left. (☎709 88 88; fax 709 04 17; email liverpool@yha.org.uk. Laundry, kitchen. £17.40. V, MC.)

STRAWBERRY FIELDS FOREVER. Trendy vegetarian cafes and reasonably priced Indian restaurants line **Bold St.,** while cheap takeout clusters on **Hardnon St.** and **Berry St.** The **Kwik Save supermarket** sits at 58 Hanover St. (Open M-Tu 8:30am-6pm, W-Sa 8:30am-6:30pm.) The **Metz Cafe-Bar,** Rainford Gardens, off Matthew St., serves reasonably priced lunch combos (£4.25) in a candlelit underground room. (Open M-Th noon-midnight, Su noon-10:30pm.)

MAGICAL MYSTERY TOUR. **Albert Dock,** at the western end of Hanover St., is a series of Victorian warehouses transformed into a complex of restaurants and museums. Don't miss the impressive collection of modern art at a branch of London's **Tate Gallery.** (Open Tu-Su 10am-6pm. Free; some special exhibits £3, students £1.) Also at Albert Dock, **The Beatles Story** pays tribute to the group's work with John Lennon's white piano, a recreation of the Cavern Club, and, of course, a yellow submarine. (Open daily Apr.-Oct. 10am-6pm; Nov.-Mar. 10am-5pm. £7, students £5.) The **Metropolitan Cathedral of Christ the King,** Mt. Pleasant, with its gorgeous neon-blue stained glass, resembles a rocket launcher. (Open daily 8am-6pm; in winter M-Sa 8am-6pm, Su 8am-5pm. Free.) In contrast, the Anglican **Liverpool Cathedral** on Upper Duke St. boasts the highest Gothic arches ever built, the largest vault and organ, and the highest and heaviest bells in the world. Climb to the top of the 300-foot tower for a view stretching to North Wales. (Cathedral open daily 9am-6pm. Free. Tower open daily 11am-4pm. £2.) The elegant **Walker Art Gallery,** William Brown St., houses an impressive variety of art (open M-Sa 10am-5pm, Su noon-5pm; £3), while the **Bluecoat Centre,** tucked off School Ln., is Liverpool's center for the arts (gallery open Tu-Sa 10:30am-5pm).

LONELY HEARTS CLUB BAND. Almost every Liverpool street teems with pubs; **Slater St.** in particular brims with £1 pints. **The Jacaranda,** Slater St., site of the Beatles' first paid gig, has live bands and a small dance floor. (Open M-Th 8pm-2am,

F-Sa noon-2am.) John Lennon once said that the worst thing about fame was "not being able to get a quiet pint at the Phil." The rest of us can sip in solitude at **The Philharmonic,** 36 Hope St. (Drafts £1.60. Open M-Sa 11:30am-11pm, Su 7-10:30pm.)

Try *Ink*, at the tourist office, for up-to-date arts and nightlife info. **Cream,** in Wolstonholme Sq. off Parr St., is Liverpool's world-renowned superclub. (Open Sa and the last F of every month. Cover £11.) **The Cavern Club,** 10 Matthew St., is on the site where the fab four gained prominence; today it plays regular club music (M and F-Sa 9pm-2am; free before 10pm) and showcases live music (Sa 2-6pm). At the end of August, a **Beatles Convention** draws pop fans from around the world.

YORK ☎01904

More high-tech than the Roman with his long spear, more aggressive than the Viking with his broad sword, more accurate than the Norman with his strong bow—she is the Tourist with her zoom camera. Unlike those before her, she invades for neither wealth nor power: she comes for York's history, medieval thoroughfares, the Georgian townhouses, and the largest Gothic cathedral in Britain.

PRACTICAL INFO, ACCOMMODATIONS, AND FOOD. **Trains** run from Station Rd. to: Newcastle (1hr., 2 per hr., £14.90); Manchester (1½hr., 2 per hr., £16.20); London's King's Cross Station (2hr., 2 per hr., £56); and Edinburgh (2-3hr., every hr., £48). National Express **buses** (☎ (08705) 80 80 80) depart from Rougier St. for Manchester (3hr., 6 per day, £7.75); London (4hr., 6 per day, £16.50); and Edinburgh (5hr., 2 per day, £21). To reach the **tourist office,** in De Grey Rooms, Exhibition Sq., follow Station Rd., which turns into Museum St. and leads over the bridge, and turn left on St. Leonards Pl. (☎62 17 56. Open daily June-Oct. 9am-6pm; Nov.-May 9am-5pm.) Check your **email** at **The Gateway Internet Café,** 26 Swinegate. (£3 per 30min. Open M-Sa 10am-11pm, Su noon-4pm.)

Competition for inexpensive **B&Bs** (from £16) can be fierce in summer; try side streets along Bootham/Clifton or The Mount area (past the train station and down Blossom St.) The **Avenue Guest House,** 6 The Avenue, ¾ mi. down Bootham/Clifton, is immaculate. From the train station, take the river footpath to the bottom of The Avenue. (☎62 05 75. Singles £15-17; doubles £28-40.) To reach the **Foss Bank Guest House,** 16 Huntington Rd., follow Goodramgate/Monkgate from King's Sq. and turn left on Huntington. (☎63 55 48. Singles £17-19; doubles £18.50-22.) **York Backpackers,** 88-90 Micklegate (☎/fax 62 77 20) and **York Youth Hostel,** 11-15 Bishophill Senior (☎62 59 04), have cheap dorms (£9-12) and friendly bars near the station. For the former, follow Station Rd. left, enter the city walls via Rougier St., which becomes George Hudson St., and turn right on Mickelgate; for the latter, walk right on Queen St., turn left on Mickelgate, and turn right on Trinity Ln., which becomes Bishophill. Expensive tea rooms, mid-priced bistros, fudge shops, and cheap eateries are everywhere. **Betty's,** 6-8 St. Helen's Sq., serves tea, sweets, and entrees (£3-8). (Open daily 9am-9pm.) Shop for produce at the **Newgate Market,** between Parliament St. and the Shambles. (Open Apr.-Dec. M-Sa 9am-5pm, Su 9am-4:30pm; Jan.-Mar. M-Sa 9am-5pm.) **Postal code:** YO1 2DA.

SIGHTS AND ENTERTAINMENT. The best introduction to the city is a 2½ mi. walk along its medieval walls; sign up for a **walking tour** at the tourist office. The **Association of Voluntary Guides** runs a good architectural tour (2hr.); meet in front of the York City Art Gallery opposite the tourist office. (Daily June-Aug. 10:15am, 2:15, and 7pm; Apr.-May and Sept.-Oct. 10:15am and 2:15pm; Nov.-Mar. 10:15am. Free.) The tourist stampede abates in the early morning and toward dusk, but everyone and everything converges at the enormous **York Minster,** built between 1220 and 1470. Half of all the medieval stained glass in England glitters here; the **Great East Window** depicts the beginning and end of the world in over a hundred scenes. Climb 275 steps to the top of the **Central Tower** for a view of York's red roofs. (Cathedral open daily in summer 7am-8:30pm; off-season 7am-6pm; £3 suggested. Tower open daily 9:30am-6:30pm; £2.50.) The **York Castle Museum,** in Minster Yard, by the river and Skeldergate Bridge, is Britain's premier showcase devoted to everyday life.

(Open daily Apr.-Oct. 9:30am-5pm; Nov.-Mar. 9:30am-4:30pm. £4.95, students £3.50.) In the gardens off Museum St., peacocks strut among the haunting ruins of **St. Mary's Abbey,** once the most influential Benedictine monastery in northern England. There are more pubs in the center of York than gargoyles on the east wall of the Minster; for entertainment options, pick up *What's On* or *Evening Entertainment* from the tourist office.

EXCURSIONS FROM YORK: CASTLE HOWARD AND DURHAM CITY. The breathtaking **Castle Howard** presides over 1½ sq. mi. of stunning gardens, fountains, and lakes. (☎ (01653) 64 83 33. Open daily mid-Mar. to Oct. 11am-4:45pm. Grounds open daily mid-Mar. to Jan. 10am-6:30pm. £7, students £6.50.) Yorkshire Coastliner **bus** #842 runs half-day trips from the train station to the castle (£4).

Nearby **Durham City** holds England's greatest Norman edifice, the **Durham Cathedral.** The view from the **tower** is worth the 325-step climb. (Cathedral open daily May-Sept. 7:30am-8pm; Oct.-Apr. 7:30am-6pm. Tower open mid-Apr. to Sept. 9:30am-4pm; Oct. to mid-Apr. M-Sa 10am-3pm. £2.50 suggested.) Across the cathedral green, **Durham Castle** was once a defensive fortress. **Trains** (☎ (0191) 232 62 62) run from York (1hr., 2 per hr., £17).

NEWCASTLE-UPON-TYNE ☎0191

Hardworking Newcastle is legendary for its pub and club scene. While you can still see straight, explore the masterful **Tyne Bridge,** neighboring **Castle Keep,** and the fine holdings of the **Laing Art Gallery.** (Castle open Apr.-Sept. Tu-Su 9:30am-5:30pm; Oct.-Mar. daily 9:30am-4:30pm. £1.50, students £0.50. Museum open M-Sa 10am-5pm, Su 2-5pm. Free.) At night, the rowdy area of **Bigg Market** frowns on under-dressed student types, but milder pubs include **Blackie Boy,** 11 Groatmarket, and **Macey's,** 31 Groatmarket. The **Quayside** (Metro: Central Station) is slightly more relaxed and student-friendly; try **The Red House,** 32 Sandhill. Revelers sway even before they've imbibed at **The Tuxedo Royale,** a boat/dance club under the Tyne Bridge. (Open M and W-Sa 7:30pm-2am.) Gays and lesbians flock to the corner of Waterloo and Sunderland St. to drink at **The Village** and dance at **Powerhouse.** (Pub open daily noon-11pm. Club open M and Th 10pm-2am, Tu-W 11pm-1am, F-Sa 10pm-3am.)

Trains (☎ (08457) 48 49 50) leave for Edinburgh (1½hr., 16-23 per day, £31) and London (3hr., every hr., £72). National Express **buses** (☎(08705) 80 80 80) leave Percy St. for Edinburgh (3hr., round-trip £18.50) and London (6hr., round-trip £29.50) as well. The **tourist office,** 132 Grainger St., facing Grey's Monument, has maps. (☎277 80 00. Open M-Sa 9:30am-6pm, Th 9:30am-8pm.) To get to the crowded **YHA youth hostel,** 107 Jesmond Rd., take the metro to Jesmond and turn left on Jesmond Rd. (☎281 25 70; fax 281 87 79. Breakfast £2.80. Lockout 10am-5pm. Curfew 11pm. Open Feb.-Nov. £9.75-10.85.) **The Brighton Guest House,** 47-51 Brighton Grove, is cheap and cheery. Take bus #10, 34-36, or 38 from the train station, or bus #12, 39, or 40 from Blackett St. in the town center. (☎273 36 00. Breakfast included. £16-22.) **Don Vito's,** 82 Pilgrim St., stands out among the many Italian eateries. (Open M-F 11:45am-2pm and 5-10pm, Sa 11:45am-10:30pm.) **Postal code:** NE1 7AB.

LAKE DISTRICT NATIONAL PARK

In the Lake District, quite possibly the most beautiful place in England, mountainsides plummet down to shores gently embraced by lapping waves, and water winds its way in every direction. The area's jagged peaks and windswept fells stand in desolate splendor, except in July and August, when outdoor enthusiasts outnumber water molecules. Use **Windermere, Ambleside, Grasmere,** and **Keswick** as bases from which to ascend into the hills—the farther west you go from the **A591** connecting these towns, the more countryside you'll have to yourself.

The **National Park Visitor Centre** is in **Brockhole,** halfway between Windermere and Ambleside. (☎(015394) 466 01. Open daily Easter-Oct. daily 10am-5pm; Oct.-Easter Sa-Su 10am-5pm.) **National Park Information Centres** dispense info on the camping-barn network and book accommodations. While **B&Bs** line every street in every

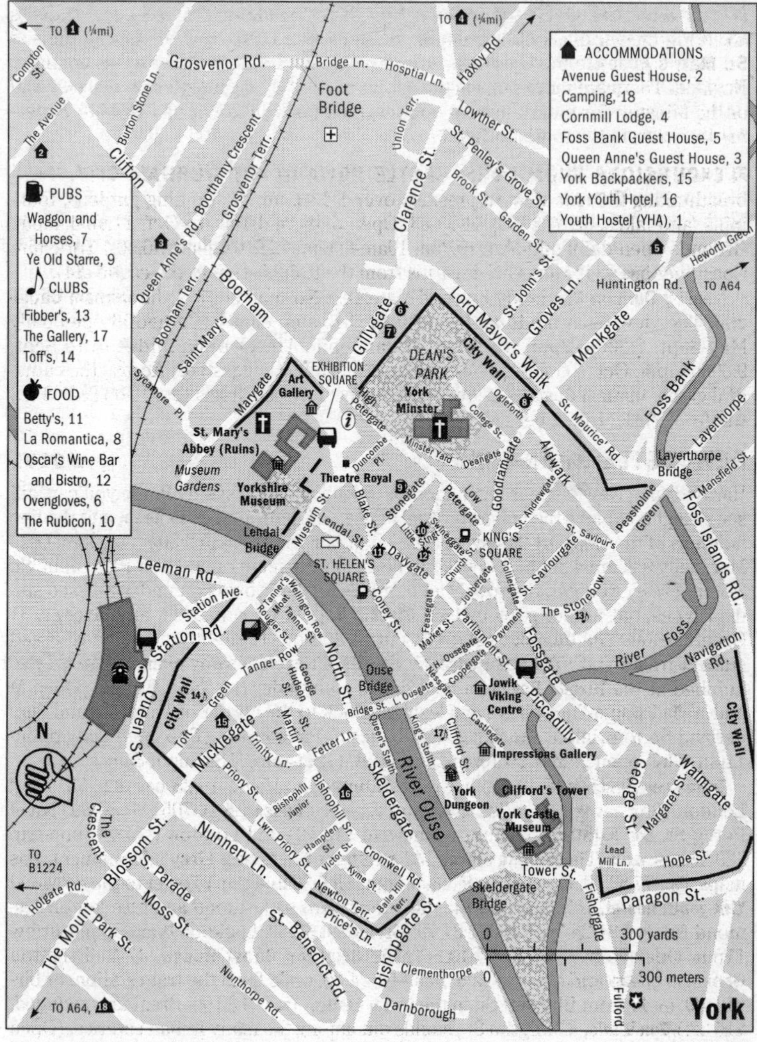

town (£15-20) and the region has the highest concentration of youth hostels in the world, lodgings do fill up in July and August; book ahead.

GETTING THERE AND GETTING AROUND. Two rail lines (☎ (08457) 48 49 50) flank the park: the south-north **Preston-Lancaster-Carlisle** line skirts the park's eastern edge, while the **Barrow-Carlisle** line serves the western coast. On the former, **Oxenholme,** on the southeastern edge of the Lake District, and **Penrith,** to the northeast, are accessible from: **Manchester's** Piccadilly Station (2hr., 5-7 per day, £14); **Edinburgh** (2½-3hr., 6 per day, £31.50); and **London's** Euston Station (4-5hr., 11-16 per day, £58.30). From Oxenholme, a short branch line covers the 10 mi. to **Windermere** (20min., every hr., £3.20). **National Express buses** (☎ (08705) 808 80) go directly to Windermere from **Manchester** (3hr., 1 per day, £14) and **London** (7½hr., 1 per day, £24), and continue north through **Ambleside** and **Grasmere** to **Keswick. Stagecoach Cumberland buses** (☎ (01946) 632 22) serve over 25 towns and villages within the district; pick up the essential *Lakeland Explorer* at any tourist office. An **Explorer** ticket offers unlimited all-day travel on all area Stagecoach buses (£5.50). The Ambleside YHA Youth Hostel offers a convenient **minibus service** (☎ (015394) 323 04; £2.50) between hostels as well as free service from the Windermere train station to the Windermere and Ambleside hostels. Potential cyclists can get **bike rental** info at tourist offices; *Ordnance Survey Cycle Tours* (£10) has route maps.

WINDERMERE AND BOWNESS. **Windermere** and sidekick **Bowness-on-Windermere** fill with vacationers in summer, when sailboats and waterskiers swarm over Lake Windermere. **Windermere Lake Cruises** runs the **Lake Information Centre** (☎433 60; fax 434 68), at the north end of Bowness Pier, which provides maps, rents rowboats and motorboats, and books lake cruises. From Easter to October, boats sail north to Waterhead Pier in Ambleside (30min., 2 per hr., round-trip £5.70) and south to Lakeside (40min., every hr., round-trip £5.90). The **train station** sends Lakeland Experience **buses** to Bowness (#599; 3 per hr., £1). The **tourist office** is next door. (☎464 99. Open daily July-Aug. 9am-7:30pm; Easter-June and Sept.-Oct. 9am-6pm; Nov.-Easter 9am-5pm.) The local **National Park Information Centre,** on Glebe Rd., is beside Bowness Pier. (☎428 95. Open daily July-Aug. 9:30am-6pm; Apr.-June and Sept.-Oct. 9am-5:30pm; Nov.-Mar. F-Su 10am-4:30pm.) To get to the spacious **YHA youth hostel,** on High Cross, Bridge Ln., Troutbeck, 1 mi. north of Windermere off A591, take the Ambleside bus to Troutbeck Bridge and walk ¾ mi. uphill, or catch the YHA shuttle from the train station. (☎435 43; email windermere@yha.org.uk. Bike rental. Open mid-Feb. to Oct. £9.80.) To reach the social **Lake District Backpackers Hostel,** on High St., look for the sign on the right as you descend the hill from the train station (2min.) or call for free pick-up. (☎463 74. Reception 9am-1pm and 5-9pm. £9.50) **Camp** at **Limefitt Park,** 4½ mi. north of the pier on A592, below the Kirkstone path. (☎323 00. £3 per person; 2 people with tent and car £12.) ☎**015394.**

AMBLESIDE. About a mile north of Lake Windermere, Ambleside has adapted to the tourist influx without selling its soul. You can't go wrong **hiking** in any direction near Ambleside; however, hidden trail markings, steep slopes, and weather-sensitive visibility all necessitate a good map and compass. Excellent guided **walks** leave from National Park and tourist offices. The top of **Loughrigg,** 2½ mi. from Ambleside (3½ mi. circuit descent), provides a view of higher surrounding fells. For gentler, shorter hikes, *Ambleside Walks in the Countryside* (£0.30) lists three easy walks from the town center. Lakeslink **bus** #555 (☎322 31; every hr.) rolls into Kelsick Rd. from Windermere, Grasmere, and Keswick. The **tourist office** is on Church St. (☎325 82. Open daily 9am-5:30pm.) To reach the **National Park Information Centre,** Waterside, walk south on Lake or Borrans Rd. from town to the pier. (☎327 29. Open daily Easter-Oct. 9:30am-6pm.) Bus #555 also stops in front of the superb **Ambleside YHA Youth Hostel,** 1 mi. south of Ambleside and 3 mi. north of Windermere, on the northern shore of Windermere Lake. (☎323 04; email ambleside@yha.org.uk. Bike rental. Nov.-Feb. curfew midnight. £11.15.) ☎**015394.**

GRASMERE. The peace that Wordsworth enjoyed in the village of Grasmere is still apparent on quiet mornings. The 17th-century **Dove Cottage,** 10 minutes from the center of town, was Wordsworth's home from 1799 to 1808, and remains almost exactly as he left it; next door is the outstanding **Wordsworth Museum.** (Both open daily mid-Feb. to mid-Jan. 9:30am-5pm. £5, students £4.20.) The **Wordsworth Walk** (6 mi.) circumnavigates the two lakes of the Rothay River, passing the poet's grave, Dove Cottage, and **Rydal Mount,** where the poet lived until his death. (Open daily Mar.-Oct. 9:30am-5pm; Nov.-Feb. W-M 10am-4pm. £3.75, students £3.25.) **Bus** #555 stops in Grasmere every hour on its way south to Ambleside or north to Keswick; bus #599 stops every 20 minutes. The combined **tourist office** and **National Park Information Centre** lies on Redbank Rd. (☎352 45. Open daily Easter-Oct. 9:30am-5:30pm; Nov.-Easter F-Su 10am-4pm.) **Grasmere YHA** (☎353 16; fax 357 98; email grasmerebh@yha.org.uk) is split into two buildings: **Butterlip How (YHA)** and **Thorney How (YHA).** To reach **Butterlip How,** on Easedale Rd., follow the road to Easedale for 150 yd. and turn right down the sign-posted drive. (Open Apr.-Oct.

daily; Nov.-Jan. F-Sa; Feb.-Mar Tu-Sa. £11.90.) To reach **Thorney How,** follow Easedale Rd. ½ mi. out of town, turn right at the fork, and look for it ¼ mi. down on the left. (Open Apr.-Sept. daily; mid-Feb. to Mar. and Oct.-Dec. Th-M.) Sarah Nelson's famed Grasmere Gingerbread, a staple since 1854, is a steal at £0.22 in **Church Cottage,** outside St. Oswald's Church. (Open Easter-Nov. M-Sa 9:15am-5:30pm, Su 12:30-5:30pm; Dec.-Easter M-Sa 9:15am-5pm, Su 12:30-5pm.) ☎ **015394.**

KESWICK. Between towering Skiddaw peak and the north edge of Lake Derwentwater, Keswick (KEZ-ick) rivals Windermere as the Lake District's tourist capital but surpasses it in charm. One of the best ridge hikes in the Lake District begins only a mile from Keswick: ascend the **Cat Bells** from the west shore of Derwent Water at Hawes End and stroll a gentle 3 mi. atop the ridge, passing **Maiden Moor** and **Eel Crags** on the way to **Dale Head,** one of the highest peaks in the area. Then, descend via the saddle-shaped Honister Pass to reach Seatoller (10-12 mi. total). The **National Park Information Centre,** in Moot Hall, is behind the clock tower in Market Sq. (☎ 726 45. Open daily Aug. 9:30am-6pm; Sept.-July 9:30am-5:30pm.) From the tourist office, bear left down Station Rd. and follow the signs to the stellar **Keswick YHA Youth Hostel**. (☎ 724 84; email keswick@yha.org.uk. Kitchen. Curfew 11:30pm. Open mid-Feb. to late Dec. £10.15.) It's worth the 2 mi. ride south on B5289 (bus #79; every hr.) to Seatoller to stay at the **Derwentwater YHA Youth Hostel,** in Barrow House, Borrowdale, where you can relax by its waterfall. (☎ 772 46. Open Jan.-Oct. £10.15.) **Camp** at **Castlerigg Hall,** southeast of Keswick on A591. (☎ 724 37. Showers £0.50. Open Apr.-Nov. £2.70-3.20 per person; £1 per car.) ☎ **017687.**

WALES

Wales borders England, but if many of the 2.9 million Welsh people had their way, it would be floating miles away. Wales clings steadfastly to its Celtic heritage, continuing a centuries-old struggle for independence. Travelers come for the miles of sandy beaches, grassy cliffs, and dramatic mountains that typify the rich landscape of this corner of Britain, or to scan the numerous castles that dot the towns, remnants of centuries of warfare with England.

FERRIES TO IRELAND

Irish Ferries (☎ (0990) 17 17 17; www.irishferries.co.uk) runs to **Dublin, Ireland** from **Holyhead** (2hr.; round-trip £40-50, students £30-38). **Stena Line** (☎ (08705) 70 70 70; www.stenaline.co.uk), runs to **Dún Laoghaire** (near Dublin), from **Holyhead** (1½hr.; round-trip £40-50, students £32-40). **Swansea Cork Ferries** (☎ (01792) 456116) run from King's Dock, Swansea to Cork, Ireland (June £27; July-Sept. £34).

CARDIFF (CAERDYDD) ☎ 029

Cardiff (pop. 340,000) burst on the scene in the late 19th century as the main shipping center of Welsh coal; at its height, it was the world's busiest port. Today, the buzzing capital of Wales brims with theaters and clubs as well as remnants of its past. The flamboyant **Cardiff Castle** was restored in mock-medieval style, with a different theme for each room; climb the steps of the Norman keep for a sweeping view of town. (Open daily Mar.-Oct. 9:30am-6pm; Nov.-Feb. 9:30am-4:30pm. £5, children £3, families £14.) The **National Museum and Gallery of Wales** has a collection of Western European art and an audio-visual exhibit on "The Evolution of Wales." (Open Tu-Su 10am-5pm. £4.50, children free.)

National Express **buses** (☎ (08705) 80 80 80) roll to Cardiff from London's Victoria Station (3¼hr., 12 per day, £14) and Manchester (5½hr., 11 per day, £25). **Trains** (☎ (08457) 48 49 50) arrive behind the bus station from Bath (1-1½hr., 3 per hr., £11.90) and London (2hr., every hr., £37). The **tourist office,** on Wood St., opposite the bus station, books B&Bs and has maps. (☎ 20 22 72 81. Open July-Aug. M-Sa

9am-6pm, Su 10am-4pm; Sept.-June M-Sa 9am-5pm, Su 10am-4pm.) **Cardiff Internet Cafe** is at 15-17 Wyndham Arcade, off St. Mary's St. (£1.50 per 15min. Open 24hrs.)

The best B&Bs are off Cathedral Rd. (take bus #32 or walk 15min. from the castle). To get to the colorful **Cardiff International Backpacker,** 98 Neville St., from the train station, go down Wood St., cross the river, turn right on Fitzham Embankment, and turn left at the end of the road onto Despenser St. After dark, call for pick-up from the station. (☎20 34 55 77; fax 20 23 04 04. Dorms £13.50; doubles £35; triples £41.) The Victorian **Central Market** is in the arcade between St. Mary St. and Trinity St. (Open M-Sa 9am-5pm.) **The Prince of Wales,** at the corner of St. Mary's St. and Wood St., offers great food and atmosphere (open M-Sa 11am-11pm, Su noon-10:30pm.) Cardiff's specialty, **Brains S.A.** (Special Ale), known by locals as "Brains Skull Attack," is proudly served in many local pubs. Head to the **Clwb Ifor Bach** (the Welsh Club), 11 Womanby St., for dancing and the local music scene. (Cover £2-8. Open M-Th until 2am, F-Sa until 3am.) **Postal code:** CF10 2SJ.

WYE VALLEY

Wordsworth once came to the Wye Valley (Afon Gwy) to escape the "fever of the world"; the region's tranquility has since been disturbed by a feverish tourist trade. Nonetheless, much of this region remains unsullied. Below Monmouth, moving past Wordsworth's "steep cliffs," "orchard tufts," and "pastoral farms," the Wye brings green to the door of even the larger towns.

GETTING THERE AND GETTING AROUND. The valley is best entered from the south, at Chepstow. **Trains** chug from Cardiff northeast to Chepstow (40min., 7-8 per day, £5.20) and Hereford (1hr., every hr., £11.70), the closest train station to Hay-on-Wye. National Express buses (☎ (08705) 80 80 80) run to Chepstow from Cardiff (50min., 5 per day, £3.25) and London (2¼hr., 10 per day, £16.50). Bus service in the region is rare on Sundays. Pick up the indispensable *Discover the Wye Valley on Foot and by Bus* at any Wye tourist office. Stagecoach Red and White bus #69 loops between Chepstow, Tintern, and Monmouth (4-8 per day). One-day Roverbus passes (£5) save money if you take more than one bus a day.

Hikers enjoy walks of all difficulties and lengths. The **Wye Valley Walk** heads north from Chepstow and passes the abbey at Tintern, the cathedral at Hereford, and the breathtaking vista at Symonds Yat en route to Hay-on-Wye and Prestatyn. Across the river, the **Offa's Dyke Path** runs the entire length of the English-Welsh border, providing 177 mi. of hiking trails.

CHEPSTOW AND TINTERN. Chepstow's strategic position at the mouth of the river and the base of the English border made it an important fortification and commerce center in Norman times. **Chepstow Castle,** built by a comrade of William the Conqueror, is Britain's oldest stone castle, and offers awesome views of the Wye River. (Open June-Sept. daily 9:30am-6pm; Nov.-Mar. M-Sa 9:30am-5pm, Su 11am-4pm; Apr.-May and Oct. daily 9:30am-5pm. £3, students £2.) **Trains** arrive at Station Rd.; **buses** stop above the town gate in front of the Somerfield supermarket. Ask about bus tickets at **The Travel House,** 9 Moor St. (☎62 30 31). The **tourist office** is in the castle parking lot. (☎62 37 72; www.chepstow.co.uk. Open daily Apr.-Sept. 10am-5:15pm; Oct.-Mar. 10:30am-3:30pm.) Take bus #69 to the hostel near Tintern (see below), or stay in Chepstow at **Lower Hardwick House,** on Mt. Pleasant, 300 yards up the hill from the bus station. (☎62 21 62. Singles £18; doubles £30-36; **camping** £5 per tent.) **Postal code:** NP6 5DA. **☎01291.**

Five miles north of Chepstow on the A466, the haunting arches of **Tintern Abbey** shade crowds of tourists in the summer and, according to Wordsworth's famous poem written just a few miles north, "connect the landscape with the quiet of the sky." (☎68 92 51. Open June-Sept. daily 9:30am-6pm; Apr.-May and Oct. daily 9:30am-5pm; Nov.-Mar. M-Sa 9:30am-4pm, Su 11am-4pm. £2.40, students £1.90.) Near the iron footbridge, paths lead to **Offa's Dyke** (45min.) and the **Devil's Pulpit** (1hr.). A mile north of the abbey, the **Old Station** houses the **info service.** (☎68 95 66.

Open Apr.-Oct. daily 10:30am-5:30pm.) The **YHA youth hostel,** 4 mi. northeast of Tintern, occupies a 13th-century castle complete with dungeon. (☎ (01594) 53 02 72; fax 53 08 49. £10.85, under 18 £7.40.) **Postal code:** NP6 6SB. **☎01291.**

HEREFORD AND HAY-ON-WYE. Ideal for excursions into Wales, **Hereford** (pop. 60,000) also draws its own visitors with its 11th-century **cathedral** and the 13th-century **Mappa Mundi** within—a map of the world drawn on animal skin around 1290. (Open Th-Tu until Evensong at 5:30pm, W all day. Mappa Mundi shown May-Sept. M-Sa 10am-4:15pm, Su 11am-3:15pm; Oct.-Apr. M-Sa 11am-3:15pm. £4, students £3.) The helpful staff at the **tourist office,** 1 King St., in front of the cathedral, books beds for a 10% deposit. (☎26 84 30. Open May-Sept. M-Sa 9am-5pm, Su 10am-4pm.) The T-junction at the end of **Bodenham Rd.** hosts many of the cheaper B&Bs in town (around £16). Otherwise, try the B&B **Holly Tree,** 19-21 Barton Rd. (☎35 78 45. Singles £20; doubles £40.) **Postal code:** HR4 9HQ. **☎01432.**

Bookseller Richard Booth transformed **Hay-on-Wye** into the world-renowned "Town of Books." Forty secondhand and antiquarian book shops attract browsers, and a 10-day **literary festival** in late May brings luminaries like Toni Morrison and P.D. James to give readings. The **tourist information center,** on Oxford Rd., books beds for a £2 fee. (☎82 01 44. Open daily Apr.-Oct. 10am-1pm and 2-5pm; Nov.-Mar. 11am-1pm and 2-4pm.) **The Bear,** Bear St., has traditional rooms and breakfast. (☎82 13 02; fax 82 05 06. Singles £22; doubles £27.) **Postal code:** HR3 5AE. **☎01497.**

BRECON BEACONS NATIONAL PARK

Brecon Beacons National Park encompasses 519 dramatic square miles divided into four regions. The fringe towns of Brecon and Abergavenny facilitate access to the park. **Trains** (☎ (08457) 48 49 50) run from **London**'s Paddington Station to **Abergavenny** at the park's southeastern corner, as well as to **Merthyr Tydfil** on the southern edge. **National Express** (☎ (08705) 80 80 80) bus #509 runs once a day to **Brecon,** on the northern side of the park, from London and Cardiff. **Stagecoach Red and White** (☎ (01633) 26 63 36) crosses the park en route to **Brecon** from: **Cardiff** via **Merthyr Tydfil** (#43, changing to #X4; 1½hr., M-Sa 5 per day, £5-7); **Swansea** (#63, 1½hr., M-Sa 3 per day, Su 4 per day, £3.70); and **Hereford** via **Hay-on-Wye** (#39, M-Sa 5 per day; **Yeomans** (☎ (01432) 35 62 01) bus #40 runs the same route, Su 2 per day; £3-4).

Just north of the mountains, **Brecon** is the best hiking base. Buses arrive at The Bulwark, the central square. The **tourist office** is in the parking lot. (☎ (01497) 62 31 56. Pass through Bethel Sq. off Lion St. Open daily in summer 10am-6pm, winter 9:30am-5:30pm.) Only three minutes from town, The Watton is ripe with **B&Bs** (£17-20). **Camp** at **Brynich Caravan Park,** 1½ mi. east of town on the A40, signposted from the A40-A470 roundabout. (☎ (01874) 62 33 25. Showers and laundry. Open Mar.-Oct. £6.50-7.50 per person, £4 per walk-in.)

At the park's center, the **Brecon Beacons** lure hikers with pastoral slopes and barren peaks. Since many paths are unmarked, Landranger Ordnance Survey **maps 12** and **13** (£6.50 each) are essential to navigate the park. From the Mountain Center, a one-hour stroll among daredevil sheep and panoramic views ends at the scant remains of an **Iron Age fort.** The most convenient route to the top of **Pen-y-Fan** (pen-uh-van; 2907 ft.) begins at **Storey Arms,** a large parking lot and bus stop 5 mi. south of Libanus on A470. A more pleasant hiking route starts in **Llanfaes,** a western suburb of Brecon, and passes **Llyn Cwm Llwch** (HLIN koom hlooch), a 2000-foot-deep glacial pool. Follow Ffrwdgrech Rd. in Llanfaesm until you reach a fork; take the middle branch after the first bridge, where the trail begins.

In the **Waterfall District,** forest rivers tumble through rapids, gorges, and spectacular falls near **Ystradfellte** (uh-strahd-FELTH-tuh), 7 mi. southwest of the Beacons. The **YHA Ystradfellte** is the best base. (☎ (01639) 72 03 01. Open Apr. to mid-July and Sept.-Oct. F-Tu; mid-July to Aug. daily. Dorms £8.10, under 18 £5.65.) Follow marked paths from Gwann Hepste and stand on the cliff face behind the **Sgwdyr Elra** waterfall. To the west near **Abercave,** the **Dan-yr-Ogof Showcaves** impress with enormous stalagmites. (☎ (01639) 73 02 84, 24hr. ☎73 08 01. Open Apr.-Oct. 10:30am-

3pm, later in summer. Tours every 20min; £7.50.) **Stagecoach Red and White** bus #63 stops at the hostel, caves, and country park en route from Brecon.

Located in the easternmost section of the park, the **Black Mountains** are a group of lofty ridges that offer 80 sq. mi. of solitude linked by ridge walks. The Ordnance Survey Outdoor Leisure **map 13** costs £6.50. Begin forays from **Crickhowell,** or travel the eastern boundary along **Offa's Dyke Path,** which is dotted with a handful of impressive ruins. There is almost no public transportation along valley routes, but **Stagecoach Red and White** bus #39 descends the north side of the Black Mountains.

ABERYSTWYTH ☎01970

Halfway down the sweeping Cardigan Bay coastline, the university town of Aberystwyth (Abber-RIST-with) offers easy access to Wales and its pubs as you wait for your connection. The **National Library of Wales,** off Penglais Rd., houses the earliest surviving manuscript of *The Canterbury Tales* and almost every written book in Welsh pertaining to Wales. (Open M-F 9:30am-6pm, Sa 9:30am-5pm. Free.) Aberystwyth's beachfront and promenade remain as they were in Victorian times. If you have a spare half-day, don't miss the steam engine ride on the **Vale of Rheidol Railway** through mountains and the waterfalls and gorges of **Jacob's Ladder.** (☎62 58 19. Runs year-round. Call for daily schedule. £10.50, accompanied children £1.) The **train station,** on Alexandria Rd., is at the receiving end of the main rail line from England into central Wales. For destinations on the scenic Cambrian Coast to the north, change at **Machynlleth** (30min., £4.60). **Arriva Cymru** (☎ (08706) 08 26 08) covers buses in the region; call for schedules. The **tourist office,** in Lisburne House on Terrace Rd., has info on **B&Bs.** (☎61 21 25. Open July-Aug. daily 9am-6pm; Sept.-June M-Sa 10am-5pm.) To get to the **YHA Borth,** 9 mi. north in Borth, take the **train** to Borth Station (10min., 8-12 per day, £1.50) or take Crosville **bus** #511 or 512. (☎87 14 98. Open Apr.-Aug. daily; Sept. M-Sa; Oct. and Mar. Tu-Sa. £9.80, students £6.75.) In town, **Mrs. E. V. Williams,** 28 Bridge St., offers delicious cakes along with comfortable beds. (☎61 25 50. £15.) Eat and drink at **The Academy,** St. James Sq., a chapel converted into a lively student pub. (Open M-Sa 11am-11pm, Su 11am-10:30pm.)

SNOWDONIA NATIONAL PARK

Stretching from forested Machynlleth in the south to sand-strewn Conwy in the north, the 840 sheep-dotted sq. mi. of Snowdonia National Park accommodate droves of visitors with untrammeled corners and quiet hikes. Known in Welsh as *Eryri* (Place of Eagles), Snowdonia's upper reaches are as barren and lonesome as the name suggests; the park also embraces dark pine forests, deep glacial lakes, sun-pierced coves, and shimmering estuaries. **Mount Snowden** (3560 ft.) is the highest peak in England and Wales and the most popular destination in the park.

Tourist offices and **National Park Information Centers** stock walk leaflets and sell Ordnance Survey Maps (£5.25-6.50), with directions to the eight wonderful **YHA youth hostels** in the park. Weather on Snowdonia's exposed mountains shifts unpredictably; arm yourself with layers of clothing. Check www.gwynedd.gov.uk for bus schedules and tourist info.

GETTING THERE AND GETTING AROUND. **Trains** (☎ (08457) 48 49 50) stop at several large towns on the park's outskirts, including **Bangor** and **Conwy.** The **Conwy Valley Line** runs through the park from **Llandudno,** near Conwy, through **Betws-y-Coed** to **Blaenau Ffestiniog** (2-10 per day, round-trip £14.20). Buses run to the interior from these towns, as well as others near the edge of the park, like **Caernarfon** (see p. 205). At Blaenau Ffestiniog, the Valley Conwy Line connects with the narrow-gauge **Ffestiniog Railway** (☎ (01766) 51 23 40), which romps through the mountains to Porthmadog, meeting up with Cambrian Coaster service to **Llanberis** and **Aberystwyth** (see p. 204). Pick up the indispensable *Gwynedd Public Transport Maps and Timetables* at any tourist office.

HARLECH. On the Cambrian coast, south of the Llŷn Peninsula and the foothills of Snowdonia, tiny Harlech clings to a steep hillside. **Harlech Castle,** a World Heritage Site, crowns a 200-foot rock with sweeping views of Snowdonia and the bay. (Open daily June-Sept. 9:30am-6pm; Apr.-May and Oct. 9:30am-5pm; Nov.-Mar. M-Sa 9:30am-4pm, Su 11am-4pm. £3, students £2.) The **tourist office,** in Gwyddfor House, Stryd Fawr, doubles as the **Snowdonia National Park Information Centre.** (☎/fax 78 06 58. Open daily Apr.-Oct. 10am-1pm and 2-6pm.) The **YHA Llanbedr,** 4 mi. south of town, is the closest hostel; take the 10-minute train ride to "Llanbedr" or ride bus #38 and ask to be let off at the hostel. (☎ (01341) 24 12 87. Open daily May-Aug.; mid-Feb. to Apr. and Sept.-Oct. Th-M; Jan. to mid-Feb. F-Su. £9.) ☎**01766.**

LLYN PENINSULA ☎01766

The Llyn has been a hotspot for tourism since the Middle Ages, when crowds of religious pilgrims tramped through on their way to Bardsey Island, off the peninsula's wild western tip. Now sun worshippers make the trek to the endless, sandy beaches lining the southern coast. **Porthmadog,** on the southeastern part of the peninsula, is its main gateway; Cambrian Coaster **trains** arrive from Aberystwyth (3-5 per day, £11.80), while other trains arrive through the adjacent Snowdonia National Park (see above). This travel hub's principal attraction is the **Ffestiniog Railway,** which runs from Harbour Station on High St. into the hills of Snowdonia (1hr., 2-10 per day, £13.80; runs mid-Feb. to Nov.). The **tourist office** is at the opposite end of High St., by the harbor. (☎51 29 81. Open daily Easter-Oct. 10am-6pm; Nov.-Easter 9:30am-5pm.) Sleep comfortably in Lawrence of Arabia's first home at **Snowdon Backpackers,** on Church St., 10 minutes from the train station. (☎51 53 54; fax 51 53 64. £12.50.) **Portmeirion,** 2 mi. east of Porthmadog, proves an eccentric bastion of Italy-fixation, with Mediterranean courtyards, pastel houses, palm trees, and exotic statues that constitute an otherworldly diversion from Wales' standard castles and cottages. (Open daily 9:30am-5:30pm. £4.50, students £3.60; reduced admission Nov.-Mar.) **Bus** #98 runs from Porthmadog to Minffordd, a scenic 30 minutes from Portmeirion, as does the Cambrian Coaster **train.**

NORTHERN COAST

CAERNARFON. Perched on the edge of the Menai Strait, Caernarfon (car-NAR-von) lures visitors with North Wales' grandest medieval castle. Built by Edward I beginning in 1283, the **Caernarfon Castle** was left unfinished when Edward ran out of money and was distracted by revolting Scots. (Open June-Sept. daily 9:30am-6pm; Apr.-May and Oct. daily 9:30am-5pm; Nov.-Mar. M-Sa 9:30am-4pm, Su 11am-4pm. £4.20, students £3.20.) **Buses** arrive on Penllyn; Arriva Cymru (☎ (08706) 08 26 08) runs from Bangor (#5, 5A, 5B, and 5X; £1.55) and Conwy (£2.85). The **tourist office,** on Castle St., is opposite the castle gate. (☎67 22 32. Open Apr.-Oct. daily 10am-6pm; Nov.-Mar. Th-Tu 9:30am-4:30pm.) Stay in comfy bunks at **Totter's Hostel,** 2 High St., at the end of the street toward the strait. (☎67 29 63. £10.) Watch the sunset, pint in hand, from **Anglesey Arms,** on the Promenade just below the castle. (Open M-Sa 11am-11pm, Su noon-10:30pm.) ☎**01286.**

CONWY. The central attraction of this modern tourist mecca is the 13th-century **Conwy castle,** built as another link in Edward I's rings of fortresses. (Open June-Sept. daily 9:30am-6pm; Apr.-May and Oct. daily 9:30am-5pm; Nov.-Mar. M-Sa 9:30am-4pm, Su 11am-4pm. £3.50, students £2.50.) Arriva Cymru **buses** #5 and 5X from Caernarfon and Bangor stop along the main streets in Conwy. National Express rolls in from: Chester (2hr., 1 per day, £15); Manchester (3½hr., 1 per day, £10.75); and London (7hr., 1 per day, £19). The **tourist office** is at the entrance to the castle. (☎59 22 48. Open daily Mar.-Oct. noon-6pm; Nov.-Mar. 10am-4pm.) From Lancaster Sq., head down Bangor Rd., turn left up Mt. Pleasant, and turn right at the top of the hill to get to the **YHA Conwy,** Larkhill, on Sychnant Pass Rd. (☎59 35 71; fax 59 35 80. Open mid-Feb. to Dec. £11.90, under 18 £8.20.) ☎**01492.**

ISLE OF ANGLESEY ☎01248

The ancient Isle of Anglesey, whose Welsh name means "Mona, the mother of Wales," attracts visitors to the prehistoric ruins and eerie Celtic burial mounds set in its flat landscape. Less prehistoric is **Beaumaris Castle,** the last of Edward I's Welsh fortresses and today a World Heritage site. (Open June-Sept. daily 9:30am-6pm; Apr.-May and Oct. daily 9:30am-5pm; Nov.-Mar. M-Sa 9:30am-4pm, Su 11am-4pm. £2.20, students £1.70.) **Bangor,** on the mainland, is probably the best hub for the island. For info on **ferries** to Dublin and Dún Laoghaire, Ireland from **Holyhead,** see p. 546. Get to Holyhead via **train** (☎ (08457) 48 49 50) from Bangor (30min., £5.05); Chester (1½hr., £16.15); or London (6hr., £57.30).

SCOTLAND

At its best, Scotland is a world apart, a defiantly distinct nation within the United Kingdom with a culture and world view all its own. Exuberant Glasgow boasts a mind-bending nightlife, and Edinburgh is the festive epicenter of Scottish culture. A little over half the land size of England but with a tenth of its population, Scotland possesses open spaces and natural splendor its southern neighbor cannot rival. The heather-covered mountains and glassy lochs of the west coast and luminescent mists of the Hebrides demand worship; the farmlands to the south and the rolling river valleys of the east coast display a gentler beauty; and the frayed northwestern coast remains one of the last stretches of true wilderness in Europe.

GETTING THERE AND GETTING AROUND

Hop-on, hop-off bus tours are often a good way to reach more inaccessible areas: try **Haggis,** 60 High St., Edinburgh EH1 1NB (☎ (0131) 557 9393; www.radicaltravel.com; day tour £19; 3-day £79; 6-day £139; Flexitour from £69); **MacBackpackers,** 105 High St., Edinburgh EH1 1SG (☎ (0131) 558 9900; www.macbackpackers.com; 3-7 day tours £55-129).

EDINBURGH ☎0131

Framed by rolling hills and the blue Firth of Forth, Edinburgh (ED-din-bur-ra; pop. 500,000) is the jewel of Scotland. The country's capital since the 12th century, the seeds of Reformation were sown in the 16th century when John Knox became the minister of the High Kirk of St. Giles. An outpouring of talent later made the city a capital of the Enlightenment: the philosopher David Hume presided over a republic of letters that fostered both Adam Smith's invisible hand and the literary wanderings of Sir Walter Scott. Today, Edinburgh Castle stands watch over literary ghosts, exuberant festivals, and the omnipresent pint of dark ale.

GETTING THERE AND GETTING AROUND

Flights: Edinburgh International Airport, 7 mi. west of the city center (☎333 10 00). **LRT's Airlink 100** (☎555 63 63; £3.30) and **Edinburgh Airbus Express** (☎556 22 44; £3.60) go to the airport (25min.); both depart from Waverley Bridge every 10-15min.

Trains: Waverley Station (☎ (0345) 48 49 50), near the center of town between North and Waverley Bridges. To: **Glasgow** (1hr., 2 per hr., £7.30); **Aberdeen** (2½hr., every hr., £32.80); and **London's** King's Cross (5hr., every 30min. 9am-3pm, £70-86).

Buses: The **south side of St. Andrew Sq.,** 3 blocks from the east end of Princes St., serves as a temporary bus station until 2002. (☎ (08705) 50 59 50.) **Scottish Citylink** (☎ (0990) 50 50 50) serves: **Glasgow** (2 per hr., £3); **Inverness** (every hr., £13.50); and **Aberdeen** (every hr., £14.50). **National Express** goes to **London** twice daily (£22).

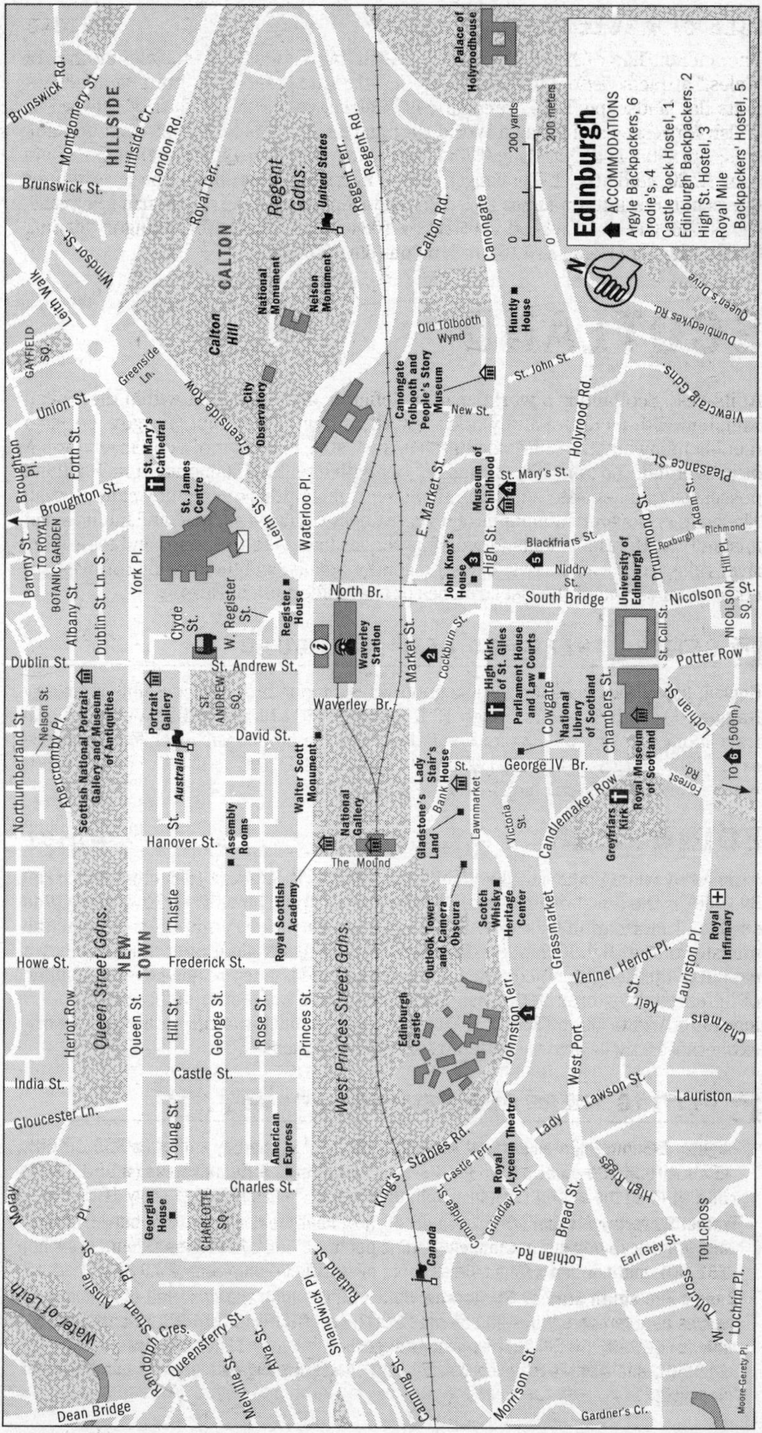

Edinburgh

ACCOMMODATIONS

- Argyle Backpackers, 6
- Brodie's, 4
- Castle Rock Hostel, 1
- Edinburgh Backpackers, 2
- High St. Hostel, 3
- Royal Mile Backpackers' Hostel, 5

0 — 200 yards

0 — 200 meters

Bike Rental: Edinburgh Rent-a-Bike, 29 Blackfriars St. (☎556 55 60), off High St. Bikes £5-15 per day. City tours and Highland safaris also available. Open daily July-Sept. 9am-9pm; Oct.-June 10am-6pm.

Hitchhiking: *Let's Go* does not recommend hitching. Those who choose to hitch to Newcastle, York, or Durham often take bus #15, 26, or 43 to Musselburgh and the A1; to other points south, bus #4 or 15 to Fairmilehead and the A702 to Biggar. To points north, one can take bus #18 or 40 to Barnton and the Forth Rd. Bridge.

ORIENTATION AND PRACTICAL INFORMATION

Princes St. is the main road in the **New Town,** in the northern section of the city; the **Royal Mile** (Lawnmarket, High St., and Canongate) is the axis of the **Old Town,** connecting the hilltop Edinburgh Castle and Holyrood Palace. **North Bridge, Waverley Bridge,** and **The Mound** connect the Old and New Towns.

Tourist Office: Edinburgh and Scotland Information Centre, Waverley Market, 3 Princes St. (☎473 38 00), next to Waverley Station. Books rooms (£3, with 10% deposit). Sells bus, tour, and theater tickets. Open July-Aug. M-Sa 9am-8pm, Su 10am-8pm; May-June and Sept. M-Sa 9am-7pm, Su 10am-7pm; Oct.-Apr. M-Sa 9am-6pm, Su 10am-6pm.

Budget Travel Services: Radical Travel Center, 60 High St. (☎557 93 93), is geared for backpackers. Open daily 8am-7pm. **Edinburgh Travel Centre,** in Potterow Union, Bristo Sq. (☎668 22 21) and at 92 South Clerk St. (☎667 94 88). Both open M-W and F 9am-5:30pm, Th 10am-5:30pm, Sa 10am-1pm.

American Express: 139 Princes St (☎718 25 03), 5 long blocks west of Waverley Station. Mail held. Open M-F 9am-5:30pm, Sa 9am-4pm.

Gay and Lesbian Services: Gay and Lesbian Switchboard, ☎556 40 49. Pick up *Gay Information* at the tourist office or *Gay Scotland* at bookstores.

Emergency: Dial ☎999; no coins required. **Police,** 5 Fettes Ave. (☎311 31 31).

Crisis Lines: Rape Crisis Center, ☎556 94 37. Staffed M-W and F 7-9pm, Th 1-3pm, Sa 9:30-11am.

Hospital: Royal Infirmary of Edinburgh, 1 Lauriston Pl. (☎536 10 00 or 536 40 40 for emergencies). From The Mound, take bus #23 or 27.

Post Office: Main office at 8-10 St. James Centre (☎556 95 46). Address mail to be held: First Name SURNAME, *Poste Restante,* GPO, 8-10 St. James Centre, Edinburgh **EH1 3SR,** Scotland, UK. Open M 9am-5:30pm, Tu-F 8:30am-5:30pm, Sa 8:30am-6pm.

Internet Access: easyEverything, 58 Rose St. (☎220 35 77), is the undisputed champion of cheap Internet access. Rates fluctuate, but £1 can often get you as much as 3hr. of emailing. Open daily 24hr.

ACCOMMODATIONS

Edinburgh is crammed with backpacker hostels, but especially in festival season (late July to early Sept.), there are few available rooms; book ahead. The tourist office has free hostel lists and finds rooms (£3 with 10% deposit). Most of Edinburgh's countless **B&Bs** are clustered in three areas: **Bruntsfield** to the southwest, **Newington** in the southeast, and **Leith** in the northeast.

Brodie's Backpacker Hostel, 12 High St. (☎556 67 70), at St. Mary's St. Relaxed environment. Only 50 beds, so book ahead. Laundry. Reception open 7am-midnight. Sept.-July M-Th £12, F-Su £13.50; higher in Aug.

Edinburgh Backpackers, 65 Cockburn St. (☎220 17 17, reservations ☎221 00 22), just off the Royal Mile. From North Bridge, turn right on High St. and take the 1st right. Organizes legendary pub crawls most Tu in summer. Pool table, TV, Internet access (£1.50 per 15min.), and showers. Reception 24hr. Dorms £12, £14 in Aug.

Argyle Backpackers, 14 Argyle Pl. (☎667 99 91; email argylr@aol.co.uk), south of the Meadows and the Royal Mile. From the train station, take bus #40 or 41 from The Mound to Melville Dr. Or, walk left and turn left on Waverley Bridge; walk straight, across the Royal Mile, over the George IV Br., veering right onto Forrest Rd. and through the park. Charming rooms and lounge with TV. Reception 9am-11pm. Check-out 10:30am. Dorms £10-15; doubles and twins £15-20.

Castle Rock Hostel, 15 Johnston Terr. (☎225 96 66). Walk toward the Castle on Royal Mile, then turn left on Johnston Terr. Gigantic hostel with views of the castle. Breakfast £1.60. Laundry £2.50. Internet £1.80 per 30min. Reception 24hr. £10.50-12.

Royal Mile Backpackers, 105 High St. (☎557 61 20). Walk down High St. from Cockburn St.; this new hostel is directly opposite the yellow Telecom Center. Go upstairs and veer left. Free High St. walking tours, pub crawls, and movies. £10.50-12.

High St. Hostel, 8 Blackfriars St. (☎557 39 84). Edinburgh's original hostel lacks a bit of the polish of the affiliated Royal Mile and Castle Rock hostels, but you can enjoy a pool table, TV, and movies. £10.50-12.

Edinburgh Caravans (☎312 68 74), Marine Dr., by the Forth. Take bus #28A from Frederick St. off Princes St. (90p). Toilets, showers, and a shop. Open Apr.-Oct. £4 per person, £3 per tent, £1.50 per car.

FOOD

You can get haggis cheap in many pubs; most offer student and hosteler discounts in the early evening. **South Clerk St.** and **Lothian Rd.** have tons of shops offering reasonably priced Chinese or Indian food. For **groceries,** try **Sainsbury's Central** on S. St. David St., just north of the Scott monument. (Open M-Sa 7am-9pm, Su 9am-8pm.)

The Basement, 10a-12a Broughton St. (☎557 00 97). Menu, packed with vegetarian dishes, as well as Thai and Mexican specialties, changes daily. Candle-lit, cavernous environment attracts lively crowd. Kitchen open daily noon-10pm; drinks served later.

The Last Drop, 72-74 Grassmarket. "Haggis, tatties, and neeps" (haggis, potatoes, and turnips) in meat and veggie versions. Entire menu (save the steak) is £2.95 for students and hostelers until 7:30pm. Packed pub at night. Open daily 10am-2am.

Ndebele, 57 Home St. (☎221 11 41). Named after a southern African tribe, it serves copious amounts of exotic grub for under £5. Daily African special and a huge array of African and South American coffees and juices. Open daily 10am-10pm.

The City Cafe, 19 Blair St. (☎220 01 25), off the Royal Mile behind the Tron Kirk. Serves venison burgers (£4-6) and incredible shakes immortalized in *Trainspotting*. Club downstairs (see **Nightlife,** p. 211). Food served until 10pm. Open daily 11am-1am.

Kebab Mahal, 7 Nicolson Sq. (☎667 52 14). Chicken *tikka masala* is the specialty (£5.25) but try the kebabs (£2.25-4.50). Open Su-Th noon-midnight, F-Sa until 2am.

The Black Medicine Coffee Co., 2 Nicolson St. (☎622 72 09). Native American decor surrounds a mellow student crowd. Live music Th-Su in late afternoon. Sandwiches and pastries (£1-4). Open daily 8am-8pm.

SIGHTS

The Royal Mile (Lawnmarket, High St., Canongate) defines the length of the Old Town. Defended by Edinburgh Castle at the top of the hill and the Palace of Holyroodhouse at the bottom, the Old Town once packed thousands of inhabitants into a few square miles—evident in the narrow shopfronts and 13-story slum buildings—but today the street is more the domain of tourists than slum lords.

HAGGIS: WHAT'S IN THERE? Although restaurants throughout Scotland produce steaming plates of haggis for eager tourists, we at *Let's Go* think everyone should know what's inside that strange-looking bundle before taking the plunge. An age-old recipe calls for the following: the large stomach bag of a sheep, the small (knight's hood) bag, the pluck (including lungs, liver, and heart), beef, suet, oatmeal, onions, pepper, and salt. Today's haggis is available conveniently canned and includes lamb, lamb offal, oatmeal, wheat flour, beef, suet, onions, salt, spices, stock, and liquor (1%). Restaurants may serve it in non-traditional forms as well: unbagged, like a sloppy joe; vegetarian; and deep-fried in batter and grease. Mmmm...

EDINBURGH CASTLE. Crowning the top of the Royal Mile, most of the structures in the castle are the result of rebuilding in recent centuries. Inside, **St. Margaret's Chapel,** a 12th-century Norman church, is believed to be the oldest structure in Edinburgh. The castle also displays the 15th-century Scottish Crown Jewels and the legendary Stone of Scone. *(At the western end of the Royal Mile. Open daily Apr.-Sept. 9:30am-6pm; Oct.-Mar. 9:30am-5pm. £7.)*

ALONG THE ROYAL MILE. Near the Castle, through Milne's Close, you can watch the new **Scottish Parliament** in the temporary **Debating Chamber.** *(Open Sept.-June, W 2:30-5:30pm, Th 9:30am-12:30pm and 2:30-5:30pm. Free.)* You can also reserve tickets in the nearby **Visitor Centre,** at the corner of the Royal Mile and the George IV Bridge. *(☎348 50 00; bookings ☎348 54 11; www.scottish.parliament.uk. Open Sept.-June M and F 10am-5pm, Tu-Th 9am-5pm; July-Aug. M-F 10am-5pm. Free.)* Nearby, **Lady Stair's House,** a 17th-century townhouse, contains the **Writer's Museum,** with memorabilia and manuscripts belonging to three of Scotland's greatest literary figures: Robert Burns, Sir Walter Scott, and Robert Louis Stevenson. *(Through the passage at 477 Lawnmarket St. Open M-Sa 10am-5pm; during Festival Su 2-5pm. Free.)* The **High Kirk of St. Giles** (St. Giles Cathedral), Scotland's principal church, was pressed into service as an Episcopal cathedral twice in the country's turbulent religious history. From the pulpit, John Knox delivered the fiery Presbyterian sermons that drove Mary, Queen of Scots, into exile. Now it offers free concerts year-round. *(Where Lawnmarket becomes High St., opposite Parliament. Open Easter to mid-Sept. M-F 9am-7pm, Sa 9am-5pm, Su 1-5pm; mid-Sept. to Easter M-Sa 9am-5pm, Su 1-5pm. Donation £1.)* The 17th-century **Canongate Kirk** is the resting place of economist Adam Smith; royals in residence also worship here. **Canongate,** the steep hill at the end of the Mile, has three museums, including one with children's toys. *(All open M-Sa 10am-5pm; during Festival also Su 2-5pm. Free.)*

PALACE OF HOLYROODHOUSE. Once the home of Mary, Queen of Scots, this spectacular Stuart palace, dating from the 16th and 17th centuries, is now Queen Elizabeth II's official residence in Scotland. Behind the palace lies the 12th-century abbey ransacked during the Reformation. *(At the eastern end of the Royal Mile. Open Apr.-Oct. daily 9:30am-5:15pm; Nov.-Mar. M-Sa 9:30am-3:45pm; closed during official residences in late May and late June to early July. £6.)*

THE NEW TOWN. The New Town is a masterpiece of Georgian planning. James Craig, a then 23-year-old architect, won the city planning contest in 1767 with the design you see today: the three main parallel streets (Queen, George, and Princes) form a rectangular, symmetrical gridiron linking two large squares (Charlotte and St. Andrew). The design reflected the Scottish Enlightenment's belief in order. Enlighten yourself by viewing the premier works of art in the four galleries within the **National Galleries of Scotland.** *(All open M-Sa 10am-5pm, Su noon-5pm. Free; special charges for some exhibits.)* A shuttle runs between the four stops: the **National Gallery of Scotland,** which houses a collection of Renaissance, Romantic, and Impressionist works; the **Scottish National Portrait Gallery,** 1 Queen St., which mounts the mugs of famous Scots; the **Scottish National Gallery of Modern Art,** 75 Belford Rd., and the **Dean Gallery,** 73 Belford Rd., both of which specialize in Surrealist and Dada art. A crucial stop on your stroll through the New Town is the elegant **Georgian House,** a restored townhouse. *(7 Charlotte Sq. From Princes St., turn right on Charlotte St. and take your 2nd left. Open Apr.-Oct. M-Sa 10am-5pm, Su 2-5pm. £5, students £3.50.)* The **Walter Scott Monument** is a grotesque Gothic "steeple without a church" containing statues of Scott and his dog. Climb the winding 287-step staircase for an eagle's-eye view of Princes St. Gardens, the castle, and Old Town's Market St. *(On Princes St., between The Mound and Waverley Bridge. Open M-Sa Apr.-Sept. 9am-6pm; Oct.-Mar. 9am-3pm. £2.)*

GARDENS AND PARKS. You're depriving yourself of quite an experience if you don't climb **Arthur's Seat,** the extinct volcano at the east end of the city with a glorious view of the city and the Highlands. Along with the **Salisbury Crags,** it rises from the vast **Holyrood Park,** east of the Royal Mile. For more views, try the even easier **Calton Hill,** just past the east end of Princes St., which also boasts a towering **Nelson Monument.** Or, to see beautiful scenery without a hike, you can explore the lovely **Royal Botanic Gardens,** north of the city center. Walk north along Hanover St. from Princes St., or take bus #23 or 27. *(☎552 71 71. Open daily Apr.-Aug. 9:30am-7pm; Mar. and Sept. 9:30am-6pm; Feb. and Oct. 9:30-5pm; Nov.-Jan. 9:30-4pm. Free.)*

ENTERTAINMENT

The summer season overflows with music in the gardens and many theater and film events around town. For details on pubs and clubs, pick up *The List* (£1.95).

WALKING TOURS. Popular with tourists, the most worthwhile walking tour is perhaps the **McEwan's 80/- Edinburgh Literary Pub Tour,** a two-hour, alcohol-friendly crash course in Scottish literature led by professional actors. (☎226 66 65. £7, children and students £5.)

THEATER AND MUSIC. The **Festival Theatre,** 13-29 Nicholson St., stages ballet and opera, while the affiliated **King's Theatre,** 2 Leven St., promotes serious and comedic fare, musicals, and opera. Same-day seats (£5.50) for the Festival Theatre go on sale daily at 10am. (☎529 60 00. Box office open daily 11am-6pm.) Scottish bands and country dancing abound after 7pm at the **Ross Open-Air Theatre** (☎529 41 47), under the tent in Princes St. Gardens. The **Filmhouse,** 88 Lothian Rd., offers quality European, art house, and Hollywood cinema. (☎228 26 88. Tickets £1.20-5.20.)

FESTIVALS. For a few weeks in August, Edinburgh hosts the spectacular **Edinburgh International Festival** (Aug. 12-Sept. 1 in 2001), featuring a kaleidoscopic program of music, drama, dance, and art. Tickets (£4-44) are sold beginning in April, but you can usually get tickets at the door; look for half-price tickets after 1pm on performance days. For tickets and a schedule, contact **The HUB,** Edinburgh's Festival Centre, Casthehill, Edinburgh EH1 2NE. It's the church-like structure just downhill from the castle. Around the festival has grown a more spontaneous **Fringe Festival** (Aug. 5-27 in 2001), which now includes over 500 amateur and professional companies presenting theater, comedy, children's shows, folk and classical music, poetry, dance, and opera events that budget travelers may find more suitable for their wallets (usually free-£5). Contact the **Fringe Festival Office,** 180 High St., Edinburgh EH1 1QS. (☎226 52 57, bookings 226 51 38; www.edfringe.com. Box office open Sept.-June M-F 10am-6pm; July M-Sa 10am-6pm; Aug. daily 10am-6pm.) Another August festival is the **Military Tattoo,** a spectacle of military bands, bagpipes, and drums, considered by some to be the highlight of the month. For tickets (£8-20), contact the **Tattoo Ticket Sale Office,** 33-34 Market St. (☎225 11 88; fax 225 86 27. Open M-F 10am-4:30pm or until the show. Shows M-Sa.)

NIGHTLIFE. If you can't find a pub in Edinburgh, you're not looking hard enough. Edinburgh credibly claims to have the highest density of pubs anywhere in Europe. **The Tron,** 9 Hunter Sq. (☎226 09 31), off High St., is smashingly popular with drunk youths and usually has live music on its three hopping floors. (Open daily 11:30am-1am and later.) The new **Espionage Bar and Club Complex,** Victoria St., has five floors of trendy partying in exotic settings. (No cover, but long lines. Open Su-Th 5pm-3am, F-Sa 5pm-4am.) The young and tightly clad frequent **The Three Sisters,** 139 Cowgate, a packed indoor/outdoor pub and meat market. (Open daily 9am-1am.) **The City Cafe,** 19 Blair St., across the street from The Tron, has a smoky bar and pool tables upstairs, and a dance club below (see **Food,** p. 209).

EXCURSIONS FROM EDINBURGH

GLASGOW. Less than an hour from Edinburgh by train, Glasgow exudes trendy creativity and energy without attracting too many tourists (p. 212).

STIRLING. **Stirling Castle** and the **Wallace Monument Tower** (in honor of William Wallace of *Braveheart* fame) await only 50 minutes from Edinburgh (p. 215).

ST. ANDREWS. After a two-hour train ride, you can tee off at St. Andrews (p. 215).

GLASGOW

☎0141

Although it has traditionally suffered a reputation of industrial lackluster, Glasgow, Scotland's largest city (pop. 675,000), today thrives with renewed energy, a flourishing economy, and a passion for football. The millions of pounds the city has poured into the arts are reflected in its free museums, extensive galleries, and first-rate theaters; the West End oozes with trendy creativity and energy. And while it rivals its sister to the east in cultural attractions, Glasgow also remains much less touristed.

GETTING THERE AND GETTING AROUND

Flights: Glasgow Airport (☎887 11 11), 10 mi. west in Abbotsinch. Citylink buses connect to **Buchanan Station** (20min., 2 per hr., £3).

Trains: Two main stations.

Central Station, on Gordon St. U: St. Enoch. To: **Stranraer** (2½hr., 3-8 per day, £15.30). **London-King's Cross** (5-6hr., 5-20 per day, £50).

Queen St. Station, on George Sq. U: Buchanan St. To: **Edinburgh** (50min., 2 per hr., £7.30); **Aberdeen** (2½hr., 11-24 per day, £36.40); and **Inverness** (3¼hr., 5 per day, £29.90). Bus #398 runs between the 2 stations (4 per hr., 50p).

Buses: Buchanan Station (☎332 71 33), on North Hanover St., 2 blocks north of Queen St. Station. **Scottish Citylink** (☎ (08705) 50 50 50) to: **Edinburgh** (50min., 2-4 per hr., £3); **Oban** (3hr., 2-4 per day, £10.70); **Inverness** (3½-4½hr., every hr., £12.80); and **Aberdeen** (4hr., 12-24 per day, £14.50). **National Express** (☎ (08705) 80 80 80) buses arrive daily from **London** (8-18hr., every hr., £22, round-trip £31).

Public Transportation: The circular **Underground (U)** subway line, a.k.a. the "Clockwork Orange" runs M-Sa 6:30am-midnight, Su 11am-6pm. Single-fare £0.80. Wave wildly to stop **buses,** and carry exact change. Single-fare £0.45-.95.

ORIENTATION AND PRACTICAL INFORMATION

George Sq. is the physical center of town. Sections of **Sauchiehall St.** (SAW-kee-hall), **Argyle St.,** and **Buchanan St.** are pedestrian areas. **Charing Cross,** in the northwest, where Bath St. crosses the M8, is used as a general landmark. The vibrant **West End** revolves around **Byres Rd.** and **Glasgow University,** 1 mi. northwest of the city center. To reach the **tourist office** from Central Station, exit on Union St., turn left, walk two blocks, turn right on St. Vincent St., and go three-and-a-half blocks. From **Queen St. Station,** exit onto George St., and cross George Sq. From the **Buchanan Bus Station,** exit on North Hanover St. and follow it right to George Sq.

Tourist Office: 11 George Sq. (☎204 44 00; fax 221 35 24), off George Sq. U: Buchanan St. Books rooms for £2 fee plus 10% deposit. **Walking tours** depart M-Sa 6pm, Su 10:30am (1½hr.; £5, students £4). Open July-Aug. M-Sa 9am-8pm, Su 10am-6pm; June and Sept. M-Sa 9am-7pm, Su 10am-6pm; Oct.-May M-Sa 9am-6pm.

Budget Travel: STA Travel, 184 Byres Rd. (☎338 60 00). Open M-Tu and F 9:30am-5:30pm, W 10:30am-5:30pm, Th 9:30am-7pm, Sa 11am-5pm.

American Express: 115 Hope St. (☎221 43 66). Open July-Aug. M-F 8:30am-5:30pm, Sa 9am-5pm; Sept.-June M-F 8:30am-5:30pm, Sa 9am-noon.

Laundromat: Coin-Op Laundromat, 39/41 Bank St. (☎339 89 53). U: Kelvin Bridge. Open M-F 9am-7:30pm, Sa-Su 9am-5pm.

Emergency: ☎999; no coins required. **Police** on Stewart St. (☎532 30 00).

Medical Assistance: Glasgow Royal Infirmary, 84-106 Castle St. (☎211 40 00).

Internet Access: The Internet Café, 569 Sauchiehall St. Open M-Th 9am-11pm, F-Su 9am-7pm. (☎564 10 52). £3 per 30min., students £2.50.

Post Office: 47 St. Vincent St. Open M-F 8:30am-5:45pm, Sa 9am-5:30pm. Address mail to be held: First name SURNAME, *Poste Restante,* 47 St. Vincent St., **G2 5QX** Glasgow, UK.

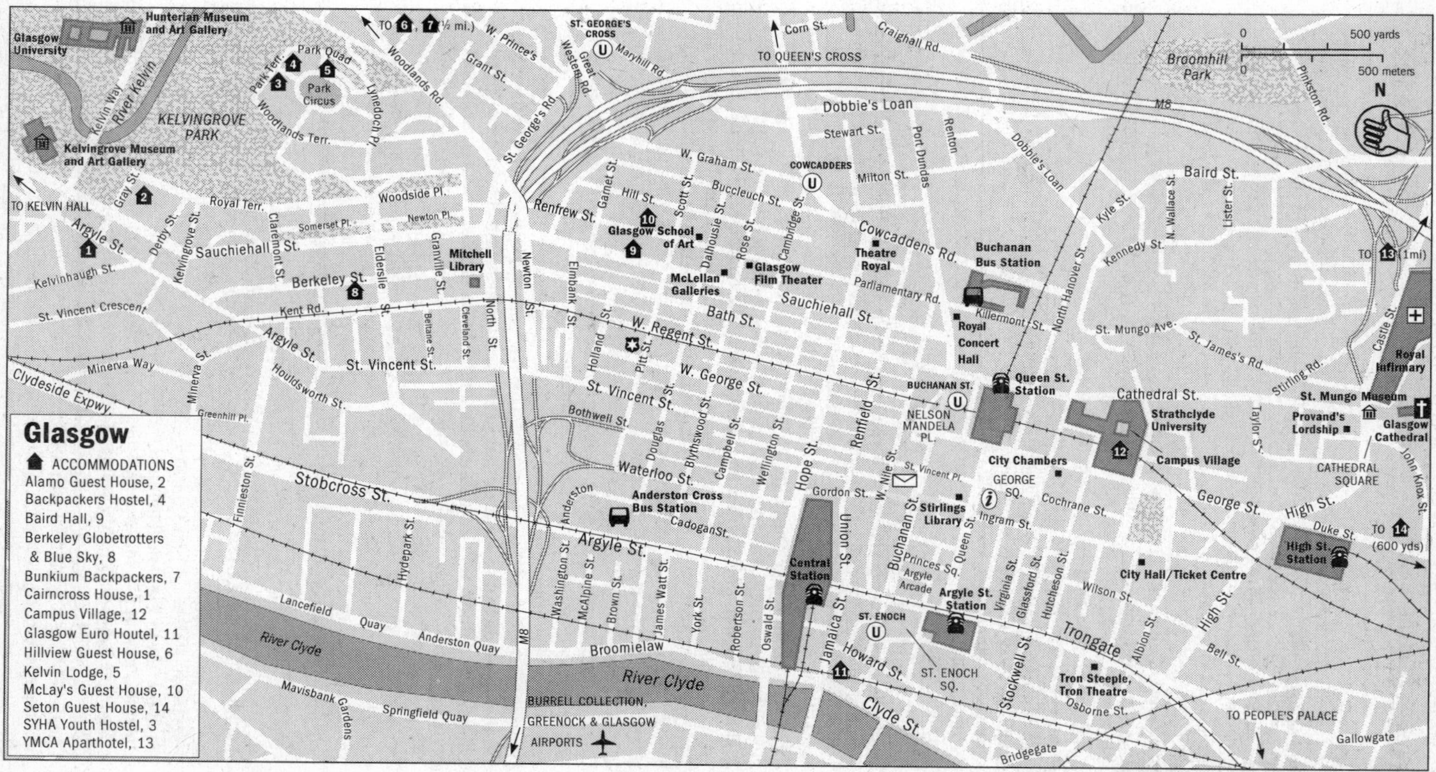
Glasgow
ACCOMMODATIONS
Alamo Guest House, 2
Backpackers Hostel, 4
Baird Hall, 9
Berkeley Globetrotters & Blue Sky, 8
Bunkium Backpackers, 7
Cairncross House, 1
Campus Village, 12
Glasgow Euro Houtel, 11
Hillview Guest House, 6
Kelvin Lodge, 5
McLay's Guest House, 10
Seton Guest House, 14
SYHA Youth Hostel, 3
YMCA Aparthotel, 13
500 yards
500 meters
N
Broomhill Park
Pinkston Rd.
Royal Infirmary
Glasgow Cathedral
St. Mungo Museum
Provand's Lordship
CATHEDRAL SQUARE
High St. Station
Strathclyde University
Campus Village
Queen St. Station
Buchanan Bus Station
Royal Concert Hall
City Chambers
GEORGE SQ.
City Hall/Ticket Centre
Tron Steeple, Tron Theatre
Trongate
Argyle St. Station
ST. ENOCH SQ.
Stirlings Library
Princes Sq.
Argyle Arcade
Central Station
Theatre Royal
Glasgow Film Theater
McLellan Galleries
Glasgow School of Art
Anderston Cross Bus Station
Mitchell Library
River Clyde
KELVINGROVE PARK
Kelvingrove Museum and Art Gallery
Hunterian Museum and Art Gallery
Glasgow University
TO KELVIN HALL
TO QUEEN'S CROSS
TO PEOPLE'S PALACE
BURRELL COLLECTION, GREENOCK & GLASGOW AIRPORTS
Sauchiehall St.
Argyle St.
St. Vincent St.
W. George St.
W. Regent St.
Bath St.
Renfrew St.
Buchanan St.
Hope St.
Union St.
Clyde St.
Stobcross St.
Broomielaw
Clydeside Expwy
Woodlands Rd.
Cowcaddens Rd.
Dobbie's Loan
M8

ACCOMMODATIONS AND FOOD

Reserve B&Bs and hostels in advance, especially in August. Last-minute planners may consider calling **SYHA Loch Lomond** (see p. 217). Most B&Bs cluster on **Great Western Rd.,** in the university area, or near **Westercraigs Rd.,** east of the Necropolis.

Bunkum Backpackers, 26 Hillhead St. (☎/fax 581 44 81). Spacious dorms minutes from the West End. Kitchen. Laundry. Internet. £9.

Glasgow Backpackers Hostel, 17 Park Terr. (☎332 90 99). U: St. George's Cross. Clean, friendly, and extremely social. Open July-Sept. Dorms £10.50; twins £24.

SYHA Youth Hostel, 7-8 Park Terr. (☎332 30 04; fax 331 50 07). U: St. George's Cross. From Central Station, take bus #44 or 59 from Hope St. and ask for the 1st stop on Woodlands Rd., then follow the signs. From Queen St. or Buchanan Stations, catch bus #11 from Bath St. Breakfast included. Kitchen. Laundry. £12.25-13.75.

Kelvin Lodge Backpackers Hostel/B&B, 8 Park Circus. (☎331 20 00; email contact@backpackersglasgow.co.uk). Large rooms with TV and telephone. B&Bs open July-Sept.; doubles £20. Year-round dorms £11; twins £30.

Glasgow Euro Hostel, (☎446 00 66; email info@euro-hostels.com), corner of Clyde St. and Jamaica St., opposite Central Station. Excellent location. Breakfast included. Kitchen. Laundry. Internet. £13.75.

The area bordered by **Otago St.** in the west, **St. George's Rd.** in the east, and along **Great Western Rd., Woodlands Rd.,** and **Eldon St.** brims with cheap kebab 'n' curry joints. **Byres Rd.** and **Ashton Ln.,** a tiny cobblestone alley parallel to Byres Rd., thrive with cheap, trendy cafes and bistros. **Insomnia Café,** 38/40 Woodlands Rd., near the hostels, is the hip place to gorge, day or night. (Cafe and adjoining deli open 24hr.) **The Bay Tree Vegetarian Café,** 403 Great Western Rd., at Park Rd., also near the hostels (cut through Kelvingrove Park), offers pitas with hummus and salad for £3.50-4.50. (Open M-Sa 9am-9pm, Su 9am-8pm.) **La Focaccia,** 291 Byres Rd., has excellent pizzas and sandwiches on fresh foccaccia (£2.40). **The Willow Tea Room,** 217 Sauchiehall St., upstairs from Henderson the Jewellers, is a Glasgow landmark. Sip 28 kinds of tea. (£1.20-1.45 per pot. High tea £7.75. Open M-Sa 9:30am-4:30pm, Su noon-4:15pm.) **Woodlands Grocers** is at 110 Woodlands Rd. (Open 24hr.) There's also a **Safeway** at 373 Byres Rd. (Open M-Sa 8am-8pm, Su 9am-7pm.)

SIGHTS

The red-paved **George Square** marks the busiest part of the city. The **City Chambers,** on the east side of the square, conceal an ornate marble interior in Italian Renaissance style. (Open M-F. Tours 10:30am and 2:30pm.) Follow George St. from the square and take a left on High St., which becomes Castle St., to reach the Gothic **Glasgow Cathedral,** the only full-scale cathedral spared the fury of the 16th-century Scottish Reformation. (Open Apr.-Sept. M-Sa 9:30am-6pm, Su 2-5pm; Oct.-Mar. M-Sa 9:30am-4pm, Su 2-4pm. Free.) On the same street is the **St. Mungo Museum of Religious Life and Art,** 2 Castle St., which surveys every religion from Anglicanism to Yoruba. (Open M-Sa 10am-5pm, Su 11am-5pm. Free.) Behind the cathedral is the spectacular **Necropolis,** a terrifying hilltop cemetery filled with broken tombstones. (Free.) In the West End, the large, wooded **Kelvingrove Park** lies on the banks of the cold River Kelvin. In the southwest corner of the park, at Argyle and Sauchiehall St., sits the magnificent, spired **Kelvingrove Art Gallery and Museum,** which shelters works by van Gogh, Monet, and Rembrandt. (U: Kelvin Hall. Open M-Th and Sa 10am-5pm, F and Su 11am-5pm. Free.) Farther west rises the Gothic central spire of the **University of Glasgow.** The main building is on University Ave., which runs into Byres Rd. While you are walking through the campus, which has churned out 57 Nobel laureates, stop by the **Hunterian Museum** or the **Hunterian Art Gallery,** across the street. (U: Hillhead. Open M-Sa 9:30-5pm. Free.) Several buildings designed by Charles Rennie Mackintosh, Scotland's most famous architect, are open to the public; the **Glasgow School of Art,** 167 Renfrew St., south of the river, reflects a uniquely Glaswegian Modernist style. (Tours M-F 11am and 2pm, Sa 10:30am. £5, students

£3.) Shop 'til you drop at **Princes Sq.,** 48 Buchanan St., a gorgeous high-end shopping mall and the classiest place to shop outside of London. If your wallet has any life left in it, hit **Sauchiehall St.,** which also hosts shops and art galleries.

ENTERTAINMENT

The infamous **Byers Rd.** pub crawl passes the Glasgow University area, starting at Tennant's Bar and heading toward the River Clyde. **Uisge Beatha,** 232 Woodlands Rd., serves over 100 malt whiskys costing between £1.85 and £35. (Open M-Th 11am-11pm, F-Sa 11am-midnight, Su 12:30-11pm.) The **Cul de Sac Bar,** 46 Ashton Ln., hosts an artsy, fun crowd of pre-clubbers. (Open M-Sa 9am-midnight, Su noon-midnight.) **Russell Bar-Café,** 77 Byres Rd., is a log cabin with live DJs and meal deals. (Open Su-Th 11am-11pm, F-Sa 11am-midnight.) The longest continuous bar in the UK is at **Horseshoe Bar,** 17-21 Drury St. (Open M-Sa 8am-midnight, Su 12:30pm-midnight.) Look for skeletons just outside the second-floor windows of club **Archaos,** 25 Queen St. (Cover £3-8. Open Th-F and Su 11pm-3am, Sa 11pm-3:30am.) **Sub Club,** 22 Jamaica St., has legendary "sub-culture Saturdays." (Cover Th-F and Su £3-6, Sa £8. Open Th-F and Su 11pm-3am, Sa 11pm-3:30am.)

STIRLING ☎01786

The third point of a strategic triangle with Glasgow and Edinburgh, Stirling has historically presided over the region's north-south movement; it was once said that he who controlled Stirling controlled Scotland. At the 1297 Battle of Stirling Bridge, **William Wallace** (of *Braveheart* fame) overpowered the English army, enabling Robert the Bruce to finally overthrow the English in 1314 at **Bannockburn,** 2 mi. south of town, and lead Scotland to 400 years of independence. The **Stirling Castle** possesses prim gardens and superb views of the Forth Valley that belie its militant and murderous past. (Open daily Apr.-Oct. 9:30am-6pm; Nov.-Mar. 9:30am-5pm. £6. Tours free.) The castle also contains the fascinating **Regimental Museum of the Argyll and Sutherland Highlanders.** (Open Easter-Sept. M-Sa 10am-5:45pm, Su 11am-4:45pm; Oct.-Easter daily 10am-4:15pm. Free.) The 19th-century **Wallace Monument Tower,** on Hillfouts Rd., 1½ mi. from town, offers incredible views atop a set of wind-whipped stairs. (Open daily July-Aug. 9:30am-6:30pm; June and Sept. 10am-6pm; Mar.-May and Oct. 10am-5pm; Nov.-Feb. 10am-4pm. £3.30, students £3.05.)

Trains run from Goosecroft Rd. (☎ (08457) 48 49 50) to: Glasgow (30min., 1-3 per hr., £4.10); Edinburgh (50min., 2 per hr., £5); Aberdeen (2hr., every hr., £30); and Inverness (3hr., 4 per day, £28.90). National Express **buses** leave from Goosecroft Rd. to Inverness (every hr., £11.20) and Glasgow (2-3 per hr., £3.40). The **Stirling Visitor Centre** is next to the castle. (☎46 25 17. Open daily July-Aug. 9am-6:30pm; Apr.-June and Sept.-Oct. 9:30am-6pm; Nov.-Mar. 9:30am-5pm.) **SYHA Stirling,** on St. John St., halfway up the hill to the castle, occupies the shell of the first Separatist Church in Stirling. In summer, overflow singles in the **Union St. Annexe,** normally University of Stirling dorms, are the same prices as the hostel. (☎47 34 42. Reception 7:30am-11pm. Curfew 2am. £12.75-13.75.) **Postal code:** FK8 2BP.

ST. ANDREWS ☎01334

In St. Andrews, golf is the game; the rules of the sport were even formally established here. The **Old Course,** a frequent site of the British Open, is a golf pilgrim's Canterbury. (Reservations ☎46 66 66 or fax 47 70 36; or, enter the on-the-spot lottery for starting times. £80 per round.) For the financially challenged, **Balgove Course** offers 9 holes for £7. If you've neglected to bring your clubs along, the **British Golf Museum,** next to the Old Course, details the ancient origins of golf. (Open daily Easter-Oct. 9:30am-5:30pm; Nov.-Easter Th-M 11am-3pm. £3.75, students £2.75.) Despite the onslaught of pastel and polyester, one need not worship the wedge—or the pompom-bearing, hat-clad putt-putt enthusiasts St. Andrews attracts—to love this city; its medieval streets and castle ruins transcend even golf. Although today it's only a shell, pilgrims in the Middle Ages journeyed to **St. Andrews Cathedral** to pray at the Saint's Shrine. Nearby, **St. Andrews Castle** maintains secret tunnels, bottle-shaped dungeons, and high stone walls to keep rebellious heretics out or in. (Cathedral and castle open daily Apr.-Sept. 9:30am-6:30pm; Oct.-Mar. 9:30am-4:30pm. Joint ticket £3.75.) Scotland's oldest university, **St. Andrews,** which lies just west of the castle between North St. and The Scores, will receive the royal treatment when **Prince William** beautifies its campus.

Fife Scottish **buses** (☎47 42 38) pull in from Edinburgh (bus X59 or X60; 2hr., every hr., £5.70, students £3.60) and Glasgow (X24 to Glenrothes, then transfer to X58-X60; 2hr., 12 per day, £5.50). From Aberdeen or Inverness, take a CityLink bus to Dundee (every hr.) and transfer to Fife Scottish bus #95 (£2.40, students £1.60) to St. Andrews. **Trains** (☎ (0345) 55 00 33) stop 5 mi. away at **Leuchars** (from Edinburgh 1hr., every hr., £8.10), where buses (X59, X60, and #95; £1) depart for St. Andrews. To get to the **tourist office,** 70 Market St., from the bus station, slice right on City Rd. and take the first left. (☎47 20 21; fax 47 84 22; www.standrews.co.uk. Open May-June and Sept. M-Sa 9:30am-6pm, Su 11am-5pm; July-Aug. M-Sa 9:30am-7pm, Su 11am-6pm; Oct.-Mar. M-Sa 9:30am-5pm.) Get on the **Internet** at **Costa Coffee,** 83 Market St. (£1.50 per 15min. Open M-Sa 8am-8pm, Su 10am-8pm.) The tourist office has **B&B** lists (many B&Bs line Murray Pl. and Murray Park near the bus station), but a night's lodging will cost upwards of £17. Making St. Andrews a daytrip from Edinburgh is the most affordable option. **Postal code:** KY16 9UL.

FORT WILLIAM AND BEN NEVIS ☎01397

With a slew of beautiful lakes and valleys, **Fort William** makes an excellent base for mountain excursions to **Ben Nevis** (4406 ft.), the highest peak in Britain. To ascend the well-beaten trail from Fort William to the summit, go half a mile north on the A82 and follow signs (5-6hr. round-trip). **Trains** arrive in Fort William from Glasgow's Queen St. Station (2-4 per day, £20) and London's Euston Station (12hr., 3 per day, £89). Skye-Ways **buses** (☎ (01599) 53 43 28) run to Glasgow (3hr., 4 per day, £11.20); Scottish Citylink (☎ (08705) 50 50 50) goes to Inverness (2hr., 5-6 per day, £6.50) and Edinburgh (6hr., 2 per day). Buses and trains leave from the northern end of High St.; nearby, the **tourist office** provides info on the West Highlands. (☎70 37 81; email fortwilliam@host.co.uk. Open mid-June to mid-July M-Sa 9am-7pm, Su 10am-6pm; mid-July to Aug. M-Sa 9am-8:30pm, Su 9am-6pm; Sept.-Oct. M-Sa 9am-6pm, Su 10am-5:30pm; Nov.-Mar. M-Sa 9am-5pm, Su 10am-4pm; Mar.-June M-Sa 9am-6pm, Su 10am-4pm.) By far the best place to stay within striking distance of Ben Nevis is the comfy **Farr Cottage Accommodation and Activity Center** in Corpach. (☎77 23 15; fax 77 22 47. Kitchen. Laundry. Internet. £11.) To get there, take the train two stops north of Fort William or take the bus from High St. (10min., 1-3 per hr., 80p). The **Fort William Backpackers Guesthouse,** on Alma Rd., is five minutes from the Fort William train station. (☎70 07 11. Curfew 2am. £10-11.) The **Glen Nevis Caravan & Camping Park,** on Glen Nevis Rd., is half a mile before the SYHA hostel. (☎70 21 91. Showers included. Open mid-Mar. to Oct. Tent and 2 people £8.70.)

INVERNESS AND LOCH NESS ☎01463

The charms of Inverness, like the Loch Ness monster herself, are somewhat elusive, but you won't be disappointed. In town, disillusionment awaits those who remember Inverness as the home of Shakespeare's *Macbeth.* Nothing of the "Auld Castlehill" remains; the present reconstructed **castle** looks like it was made out of pink Legos this very morning (tours Easter-Nov. £3). In 1746 the Jacobite cause died on **Culloden Battlefield,** east of Inverness; take **bus** #12 from the post office (£1.10). One and a half miles south of Culloden, the stone circles of the **Cairns of Clava,** mounds of rough stones, recall Bronze Age civilizations. **Cawdor Castle** has been the home of the Cawdors since the 15th century; don't miss the maze. (Open May to Sept. daily 10am-5:30pm. £5.50, students £4.50.) And, of course, no trip to Inverness would be complete without taking in the deep and mysterious **Loch Ness,** which guards its secrets 5 mi. south of Inverness. In AD 565, St. Columba repelled a savage sea beast as it attacked a monk; whether a prehistoric leftover, giant seasnake, or cosmic wanderer, the monster has captivated the imagination of the world ever since. **Jacobite Cruises** (☎73 12 02; £11.90, students £9.90) and other tour agencies are the most convenient ways to see the loch, as well as nearby **Urquhart Castle** and **monster exhibitions.** Even if you don't see the real monster, vendors are all too happy to sell you a cute stuffed one.

Trains (☎ (08457) 48 49 50) run from Academy St., in Station Sq., to Aberdeen (2¼hr., 7-10 per day, £17.80) and to Edinburgh and Glasgow (both 3½hr., 5-7 per day, £30-42.60). Scottish Citylink **buses** (☎ (08705) 50 50 50) run from Farraline Park, off Academy St., to: Aberdeen (3½hr., 1-2 per day, £9); Edinburgh (4hr., 8-10 per day, £12.80); and Glasgow (4-4½hr., 10-12 per day, £12.80). The **Highland County Tourist Trail Day Rover bus** allows unlimited travel to most sights near Inverness (July-Aug.; 7 per day; £6, students £4). To reach the **tourist office**, Castle Wynd, from the stations, turn left on Academy St., right on Union St., and left on Church St. (☎23 43 53. Open mid-June to Aug. M-Sa 9am-7pm, Su 10am-6pm; Sept. to mid-June M-Sa 9am-5pm, Su 10am-4pm.) Facing the tourist office, go left on Bridge St. and right on Castle St., which leads to Culduthel Rd. and the **Inverness Student Hotel,** at #8. (☎23 65 56. Kitchen. Laundry. Reception 6:30am-2:30am. Check-out 10:30am. £10-11.) The **Bazpackers Backpackers Hotel** is next door at #4. (☎71 76 63. Kitchen. Reception 7:30am-midnight. Check-out 10:30am. Dorms £8.50-10; doubles £24-28.)

LOCH LOMOND AND THE TROSSACHS

LOCH LOMOND. With Britain's largest inland freshwater body as its base, the landscape of Loch Lomond is filled with lush bays, thickly wooded islands, and bare hills. Hikers on the northeastern edge of Loch Lomond are rewarded with stunning views, quiet splendor, and small beaches. The **West Highland Way** snakes along the entire eastern side of the Loch, stretching 95 mi. from Milngavie north to Fort William. **Balloch,** at the southern tip of Loch Lomond, is the major town in the area. Across the River Leven, the **Balloch Castle Country Park** provides 200 acres of gorgeous grounds, as well as a 19th-century castle housing a **Visitor's Centre.** Look for the pixies in **Fairy Glen.** (Park open daily dawn-dusk. Visitor's Centre open Easter-Oct. daily 10am-6pm. Free.) **Sweeney's Cruises** (☎75 23 76) boat tours depart from the tourist office side of the River Leven (1hr., every hr., £4.80).

Trains arrive on Balloch Rd., opposite the tourist office, from Glasgow's Queen St. Station (45min., 2 per hr., £3.10). Citylink **buses** (☎ (08705) 80 80 80) #926, 975, and 976 arrive from Glasgow (3-5 per day); First Midland (☎ (01324) 61 37 77) travels from Stirling (1½hr., 3 per day). Buses arrive a few minutes down Balloch Rd., across the bridge to the left of the **tourist office,** in Old Station Building. (☎75 35 33. Open daily July-Sept. 9:30am-7pm; June 9:30am-6pm; Apr.-May and Oct. 10am-5pm.) **B&Bs** congregate on **Balloch Rd. SYHA Loch Lomond,** in a 19th-century castle-like building 2 mi. north of town, is one of Scotland's largest hostels. (☎85 02 26. Open early Mar. to Oct. £12.25-13.25.) To reach the **SYHA Rowardennan,** the first hostel along the West Highland Way, take the Inverberg ferry (☎ (01301) 70 23 56; May-Sept. 3 per day, £4) across the Loch to Rowardennan. (☎ (01360) 87 02 59. Curfew 11:30pm. Open Mar.-Oct. £9.25.) The **Tullichewan Caravan and Camping Site,** on Old Luss Rd., is up Balloch Rd. from the tourist office. (☎75 94 75. Reception 8:30am-10pm. Tent and 2 people £6.50-9; with car £8.50-12.50.) ☎ **01389.**

TROSSACHS. The gentle mountains and lakes of the Trossachs form the northern boundary of central Scotland. A road for walkers and cyclists traces the Loch's shoreline; tourists drop like flies after half a mile, leaving the Loch's joys to more hardy travelers. The **Steamship Sir Walter Scott** (☎37 63 16) steams between Loch Katrine's Trossachs Pier and Stronachlachar. (Apr.-Oct. 2-3 per day, £4.60-6.) Only a few buses each day go to the area's two main towns, **Aberfoyle** and **Callander.** Citylink **bus** #974 runs through Edinburgh and Stirling to Fort William, stopping in Callander (1 per day). The Trossachs Trundler is a 1950s-style bus that creaks to Callander, Aberfoyle, and Trossachs Pier in time for the sailing of the *Sir Walter Scott* (July-Sept. Su-F 4 per day, £8). Bus #59 from Stirling connects with the Trundler in Callander. Call the **Stirling Council Public Transport Helpline** (☎ (01786) 44 27 07) for info. **Trossachs Cycle Hire,** on the pier, rents bikes. (☎38 26 14. £12 per day. Open daily Apr.-Oct. 8:30am-5:30pm.) ☎ **01877.**

BRITAIN

THE INNER HEBRIDES

ISLE OF SKYE. Often described as the jewel in the Hebridean crown, Skye radiates splendor from the serrated peaks of the Cuillin Hills to the rugged northern tip of the Trotternish Peninsula. Touring Skye takes effort; pick up the *Public Transport Guide to Skye and the Western Isles* (£1) at a tourist office. **Buses** on the island are infrequent; **biking** and **hiking** are better options. **MacBackpackers** in Kyleakin (☎ (01599) 53 45 10) offers **mini-bus day tours** (£15) and a **Skye Trekker Tour,** an outdoor experience with all camping equipment provided (2 days, £30).

The **Skye Bridge** links **Kyle of Lochalsh,** the last stop on the mainland before the Isle, with Kyleakin (Kyle-ACK-in), on Skye's southeastern tail fin. On the mainland side perches the made-for-postcard **Eilean Donan Castle,** which struck a pose for the movie *Highlander*. To get there, take the bus (dir. Inverness; £2.50) from Kyle of Lochalsh. (Open daily Apr.-Oct. M-Sa 9am-5:30pm; July-Sept. also Su 10am-4pm. £3.75, students £3.) Scottish Citylink **buses** (☎ (01599) 53 43 28) run daily to Kyleakin from: Fort William (2hr., 3 per day, £10.70); Inverness (2½hr., 2 per day, £9.80); and Glasgow (5½hr., 3 per day, £17.50). **Trains** (☎ (08457) 48 49 50) arrive from Inverness (2½hr., 2-4 per day, £15). The **train station** (☎ (01599) 53 42 05) is near the pier and the **tourist office.** (☎ (01599) 53 42 76. Open Apr.-Oct. M-Sa 9am-5:30pm; July-Sept. also Su 10am-4pm.) **Caledonian-MacBrayne ferries** (☎ 46 24 03) also sail to Skye from **Mallaig,** at the end of the West Highland rail line from Glasgow and Fort William (M-Sa 6-7 per day, June-Aug. Su also, £2.70). **Cuchulainn's Backpackers Hostel,** (☎ (01599) 53 44 92), in Kyle of Lochalsh offers rooms for £9.

When you're ready to skip the mainland and dive into Skye, traverse the 1½ m. footpath or take the **shuttle bus** (2 per hr., £0.65) across the Skye Bridge. Over the bridge, quiet **Kyleakin** harbor is resplendent at sunset. A slippery scramble leads to the small ruins of **Castle Moil;** cross the bridge behind the SYHA hostel, turn left, follow the road to the pier, and take the gravel path. Lodgings cluster alongside the park a few hundred yards from the pier; to the right is the comfy **Skye Backpackers.** (☎ (01599) 53 45 10. Laundry. Curfew 2am. £10-11.)

West of Kyleakin, the smooth, conical Red Cuillin and the rough, craggy Black Cuillin Hills meet in **Sligachan,** where paths wind their way up the mountains. If you plan to scale some peaks, stay at the **SYHA Glenbrittle** in Glenbrittle near the southwest coast, where expert mountaineers can give you advice on exploring the area. (☎ (01478) 64 02 78. Open Apr.-Sept. £8.50.) Campers should head to the **Glenbrittle Campsite.** (☎ (01478) 64 04 04. Open Mar.-Oct. £3.50 per person.) Take Highland Country **bus** #360 from Portree and Sligachan to Grenbrittle (M-Sa 2 per day).

In northern Skye is the island's capital, **Portree** (pop. 2500). Buses run from Portree to **Dunvegan Castle,** the seat of the MacLeod clan. The castle holds the **Fairy Flag,** more than 1300 years old and swathed in clan legend, although looking rather tattered of late. (Open daily late Mar. to Oct. 10am-5:30pm; Nov.-Mar. 11am-4pm. £5.20, students £4.60.) **Buses** stop at Somerled Sq. The busy **tourist office** is in the old jail on Bank St., a block from the harbor. (☎ (01478) 61 21 37. Open July-Aug. M-Sa 9am-8pm, Su 10am-5pm; Sept.-June M-Sa 9am-5pm.) The **Portee Independent Hostel** is right off Somerled Sq. (☎ (01478) 61 37 37. Dorms £8.50-9.50; twins £21.)

THE OUTER HEBRIDES

The magical Outer Hebridean archipelago is not just extraordinarily sublime, but also astoundingly ancient. Much of its exposed rock has existed for about three billion years, more than half as long as the planet, and inhabitants of the island in the distant past have left behind a rich sediment of tombs, standing stones (including the remarkable stone circle at Callanish on Lewis), and Neolithic remains. The vehemently Calvinist islands of Lewis and Harris observe the Sabbath strictly: all shops and restaurants close and public transportation stops on Sundays. Television and tourism are diluting some local customs, but the islands are remote enough to retain much of their charm, and Gaelic is still heard on the streets.

GETTING THERE AND GETTING AROUND. Four major **Caledonian MacBrayne ferries** (☎ (01475) 65 01 00) serve the Western Isles—from **Oban** to **Barra** and **South Uist,** from **Mallaig** to **South Uist,** from **Skye** to **Harris,** and from **Ullapool** to **Lewis.** Ferries and infrequent **buses** connect the islands, and **hitchers** and **cyclists** enjoy success except during frequent rain storms. *Let's Go* does not recommend hitchhiking. Except in bilingual Stornoway and Benbecula, all road signs are in Gaelic. Tourist offices often carry translation keys, and *Let's Go* lists the Gaelic place names after the English ones where necessary. For up-to-date transport info, consult the *Skye and Western Isles Public Transport Travel Guide* (£1 at tourist offices).

LEWIS AND HARRIS. The island of Lewis (Leodhas) is famous for its atmosphere: pure light and drifting mists off the Atlantic Ocean shroud the untouched miles of moorland and small lakes in quiet luminescence. The unearthly setting is ideal for exploring the island's many archaeological sites, most notably the **Callanish Stones,** an extraordinary Bronze Age circle. **Buses** on the W2 route from Stornoway run past the stones at Calanais (M-Sa 5 per day). Caledonian MacBrayne **ferries** from Ullapool on the mainland serve **Stornoway** (Steornobhaigh; pop. 8000), the largest town in northwestern Scotland (M-Sa 2-3 per day, £12.70, round-trip £21.75). To get from the ferry terminal to the **tourist office,** 26 Cromwell St., turn right from the ferry terminal, then hang a left on Cromwell St. (☎70 30 88. Open Apr.-Sept. M-Sa 9am-6pm and to meet the late ferries; Oct.-Mar. M-Sa 9am-5pm.) Lay your head and wax your board at the new **Fair Haven Hostel,** at the intersection of Francis and Keith St., over the surf shop. (☎70 58 62. £10.) ☎**01851.**

Although **Harris** (Na Hearadh) is technically part of the same island as Lewis, it is an entirely different world. Lewis is mainly flat and watery, while Harris, formed by volcanic gneiss, has the ruggedness more characteristic of Scotland. Toward the west coast, the barricade of the **Forest of Harris** (actually a treeless mountain range) descends to brilliant crescents of yellow beaches bordered by indigo waters and *machair*—sea meadows of green grass and summer flowers. **Ferries** serve **Tarbert** (An Tairbeart), the biggest town on Harris, from Uig on Skye (M-Sa 1-2 per day, £8.30, round-trip £14.20). Pick up essential Ordnance Survey hiking maps at the **tourist office,** on Pier Rd. (☎50 20 11. Open early Apr. to mid-Oct. M-Sa 9am-5pm and for late ferry arrivals.) For a good night's sleep, walk up the hill behind the comfy **Rockview Bunkhouse,** Main St. (☎50 22 11. £9.) ☎**01859.**

BULGARIA (БЪЛГАРИЯ)

BULGARIA

LEVA (BGL)

US$1 = 2.20LV	1LV = US$0.46
CDN$1 = 1.50LV	1LV = CDN$0.68
UK£1 = 3.20LV	1LV = UK£0.32
IR£1 = 2.50LV	1LV = IR£0.40
AUS$1 = 1.20LV	1LV = AUS$0.80
NZ$1 = 0.93LV	1LV = NZ$1.10
SAR1 = 0.31LV	1LV = SAR3.20
DM1 = 1.00LV	1LV = DM1.00
EUR€1 = 1.96LV	1LV = EUR€0.51

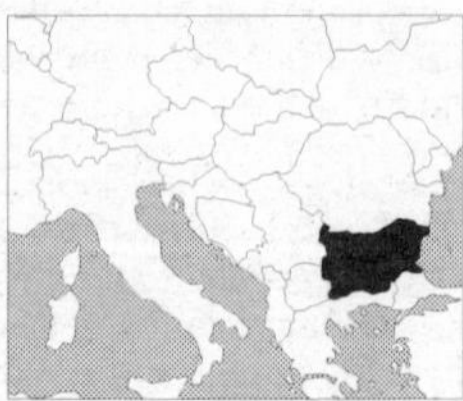

Country code: 359. **International dialing prefix:** 00. From outside Bulgaria, dial int'l dialing prefix (see inside back cover) + 359 + city code + local number.

Bulgaria is blessed with a lush countryside, rich in natural resources and ancient tradition. The history of the Bulgarian people, centered around oppression and struggle, has not matched the beauty of their nation. Once the most powerful state in the Balkans and the progenitor of the Cyrillic alphabet, Bulgaria spent 500 years under Ottoman Turk rule. These years yielded minarets, underground monasteries, and, finally, the National Revival of the 19th century, when much of the majestic, very European architecture now gracing its cities was built. Today, Bulgaria struggles with a flagging economy and a lack of western attention, problems only heightened by the recent Balkan wars. As a result, the country has gone unnoticed by most travelers, and its people—slowly emerging from under the rubble of Communism—are too poor to package all they have to offer.

For more detailed coverage of Bulgaria, grab *Let's Go: Eastern Europe 2001.*

FACTS AND FIGURES

Official Name: Republic of Bulgaria.

Government: Parliamentary democracy.

Capital: Sofia (1.2 million).

Land Area: 110,550 sq. km.

Geography: Mountains to the west, and plans to the east.

Climate: Temperate; cold, damp winters; hot, dry summers.

Major Cities: Sofia, Varna, Burgas, Ruse.

Population: 8,195,000.

Language: Bulgarian.

Religions: Bulgarian Orthodox (85%), Muslim (13%), other (2%).

Average Income Per Capita: US$4300.

Major Exports: Machinery and equipment; metals, minerals, and fuels; chemicals and plastics.

DISCOVER BULGARIA

Bulgaria is a great stopover between Western Europe and Greece or Turkey. Start in **Sofia** (p. 224), where more than 1500 years of Orthodox Churches and cobblestone alleyways hide among the city's vast boulevards. **Plovdiv** (p. 228) shelters Roman ruins and fabulous art museums and is only 30 minutes from the splendid **Bachkovo Monastery** (p. 229). Nestled in the highest mountains on the Balkan Peninsula, **Rila Monastery** (p. 228) is the masterpiece of Bulgarian religious art. Whether you're reveling with sun-scorched discoers or lounging on deserted beaches, no visit to Bulgaria is complete without a sojourn on the **Black Sea Coast** (p. 230), a summer wonderland. On your way to the coast from western Bulgaria, be sure to stop in **Veliko Turnovo** (p. 229), the most beautiful town in the country.

ESSENTIALS

WHEN TO GO

The best time to visit the Black Sea Coast is summer. For everywhere else, spring and fall weather is ideal. Year-round it's milder than other Balkan countries due to the proximity of the Mediterranean and Black Sea coasts; winter can be quite cold.

DOCUMENTS AND FORMALITIES

Citizens of Australia, Canada, the EU, New Zealand, and the US may visit Bulgaria visa-free for up to 30 days. Citizens of South Africa and anyone planning to stay more than 30 days must obtain a 90-day visa from their local embassy or consulate. Single-entry visas are US$53 (in 10 days), US$68 (in 5 days), and US$88 (overnight; only available if US citizen). Multiple-entry visas cost US$123, transit (valid for 24hrs.) US$43, and double transit (valid for 24hrs.) US$63. Visas may be extended at a police stations before the date of expiration, though the cost is likely to be high.

EMBASSIES AND CONSULATES

Embassies and consulates of other countries in Bulgaria are all in **Sofia** (see p. 196).

Bulgarian Embassies at home: Australia, 4 Carlotta Rd., Double Bay, Sydney, NSW 2028; postal address P.O. Box 1000, Double Bay, NSW 1360 (☎ (02) 9327 7581; fax 9327 8067; email bgconsul@ihug.com.au); **Canada,** 325 Stewart St., Ottawa, ON K1N 6K5 (☎ (613) 789 32 15; fax 789 35 24); **South Africa,** 1071 Church St., Hatfield, Pretoria; P.O. Box 32569, Arcadia (☎ (012) 342 37 20; fax 342 37 21; email embulgsa@iafrica.com); **UK,** 186-188 Queensgate, London SW7 5HL (☎ (020) 75 84 94 00; fax 75 84 49 48); **US,** 1621 22nd St. NW, Washington, D.C. 20008 (☎ (202) 387 01 74 or 387 79 69 for consular matters; fax 234-7973; email office@bulgaria-embassy.org or bgconsul@wizard.net for consular matters; www.bulgaria-embassy.org).

GETTING AROUND

BY PLANE. Balkan Bulgarian Airlines (☎ (0)2 98 44 89; www.balkan.com) flies to several large cities worldwide. Its domestic fares are fairly cheap (Sofia-Varna: US$41, round-trip US$71).

BY TRAIN. Bulgarian trains run to Hungary, Romania, and Turkey and are better for transportation in the north and sometimes in the south; **Rila** is the main international train company. The train system is comprehensive but slow, crowded, and old. There are three types of trains: *ekspres* (express; експрес), *burz* (fast; бърз), and *putnicheski* (slow; пътнически). Avoid *putnicheski* like the plague—they stop at anything that looks inhabited, even if only by goats. *Purva klasa* (first-class seating; първа класа) is very similar to *vtora klasa* (second class; втора класа), and not worth the extra money. Some useful words: *vlak* (train; влак); *avtobus* (bus; автобус); *gara* (station; гара); *peron* (platform; перон); *kolovoz* (track; коловоз); *bilet* (ticket; билет); *zaminavashti* (departure; заминаващи); *pristigashti* (arrival; пристигащи); and *ne/pushachi* (non-/smoking; не/пушачи).

BY BUS. Buses head north from Ruse, and to Istanbul from anywhere on the Black Sea Coast and are better for travel in eastern and western Bulgaria. Bus trips are more comfortable, quicker, and only slightly more expensive than trains. For long distances, **Group Travel** and **Etap** offer modern buses at prices 50% higher than trains. Buy a seat from the agency office or pay when boarding. Grueling local buses stop everywhere. *Let's Go* does not recommend that travelers take direct buses from Bulgaria to Central and Western Europe; they all go through former Yugoslavia; go up to Bucharest and begin your journey westward from there.

BY CAR AND BY TAXI. Major car rental companies such as **Hertz** and **EuroDollar** are in most large cities. The cheapest cars average US$70-80 per day. In Sofia, **Odysseia** rents reliable cars for US$15 per day. Be prepared for poor driving and unfamiliar signs. Yellow **taxis** are everywhere. Refuse to pay in dollars and insist on a metered ride *("sus apparata")*; ask the distance and price per km to do your own calculations. Some Black Sea towns can only be reached by taxi.

BY BIKE AND BY THUMB. Biking is uncommon as it is nearly impossible to rent a bicycle. Hitchhiking is risky, but some claim it yields a refreshing taste of *gostelyubivnost* (hospitality) to those who are cautious, polite, and patient. *Let's Go* does not recommend hitchhiking.

TOURIST SERVICES AND MONEY

EMERGENCY. **Police:** ☎166. **Ambulance:** ☎150. **Fire:** ☎160.

TOURIST OFFICES. Bolstering tourism is not really a priority for Bulgaria. **Balkantourist,** the state chain under communism, has been humbled by privatization. In big hotels you can often find an English-speaking receptionist and **maps** to purchase.

MONEY. The **lev** (lv; plural *leva*) is the standard monetary unit. It's illegal to exchange money on the street. Private banks and **exchange bureaus** are best for exchanging money. The latter tend to have extended hours and better rates, but may not change anything other than dollars. **Traveler's checks** can usually only be cashed at banks. Banks also give Visa **cash advances. Credit cards** are rarely accepted except in larger hotels and expensive resorts. **ATMs** are usually inconspicuous, but major banks have them either inside or nearby, as do many post offices; ATMs accept Cirrus, MC, and Visa. It is illegal to exchange currency on the street. Bulgaria has recently tied its currency to the Deutschmark; 1 *leva* always equals 1 DM. Staying in **campgrounds** and shopping at grocery stores in Bulgaria will run you about US$10; a comfortable day (staying in hostels/hotels and eating out) won't cost more than US$20. Food from restaurants average 6lv per meal. **Tipping** is not obligatory, as most people just round up to the nearest leva, but 10% doesn't hurt, especially in Sofia. A 7-10% service charge will occasionally be added for you; always double check the bill or the menu. Tipping taxi drivers usually means rounding up to the nearest half-leva. Bargaining for fares is not done, but make sure there is a meter or agree on a price.

BUSINESS HOURS. Businesses open at 8 or 9am and take a one-hour lunch break between 11am and 2pm. Train and bus cashiers and post office attendants take occasional 15-minute coffee breaks—be patient. **Banks** are usually open 8:30am to 4pm, but some close at 2pm. *Vseki den* (every day; всеки ден) usually means Monday through Friday, and "non-stop" doesn't guarantee a place will be open 24hr.

ACCOMMODATIONS AND CAMPING

Upon crossing the border, citizens of South Africa may receive a statistical card to document where they sleep. If you don't get a card at all, don't worry. Ask hotels or private room bureaus to stamp your passport or a receipt-like paper that you can show upon border re-crossing (if they ask for it a fine could be levied if you don't have it). If staying with friends, register with the Bulgarian Registration Office.

HOTELS AND HOSTELS. Bulgarian **hotels** are classed on a star system and licensed by the Government Committee on Tourism; rooms in one-star hotels are almost identical to those in two- and three-star hotels, but have no private bathrooms. Expect to pay US$15-50 per night, although foreigners are always charged more. The majority of Bulgarian **youth hostels** are in the countryside and are popular with student groups; many give ISIC discounts, and almost all provide bedding.

OTHER LOCAL ACCOMMODATIONS AND CAMPING. Private rooms (частни квартири) can be arranged through Balkantourist or other tourist offices for US$5-15 per night. It is also common for people to offer private accommodations in train and bus stations. In crowded locations, such as the Black Sea in summer, this may be your only chance to get a room. *Babushki* are the safest; bargain them down. Outside major towns, most **campgrounds** provide spartan bungalows and tent space.

FOOD AND DRINK

Kiosks sell *kebabcheta* (sausage burgers; кебабчета), sandwiches, pizzas, and *banitsa sus sirene* (cheese-filled pastries; баница със сирене). Fruit and vegetables are sold in a *plod-zelenchuk* (fruit store; плод-зеленчук), *pazar* (market; пазар), or on the street. Try *shopska salata* (шопска салата), a mix of tomatoes, peppers, and cucumbers with feta cheese. *Tarator* (таратор), a cold soup made with yogurt, cucumber, garlic, and sometimes walnuts, is also tasty. Vegetarian options with eggs (omelettes; омлети) and cheese are ubiquitous. Bulgarians are known for cheese and yogurt. Baklava and *sladoled* (ice cream; сладолед) are sold in *sladkarnitsy* (сладкарницы). In restaurants, seat yourself and directly ask for the bill.

COMMUNICATION

MAIL. Sending a **letter** abroad costs 0.60lv for any European destination, 0.80lv for the US, and 0.80-1.00lv for Australia, New Zealand, or South Africa; note that a Bulgarian return address is required to do so. Mail can be received in Bulgaria general delivery through *Poste Restante*, though it is unreliable at best.

TELEPHONES. Making international **telephone** calls from Bulgaria can be a challenge. Payphones are ludicrously expensive; opt for the phones in a telephone office. If you must make an **international call** from a pay phone with a card, purchase the 400 unit card. Units run out quickly. To call **collect,** dial ☎01 23 for an international operator. The Bulgarian phrase for collect call is *za tyahna smetka* (за тяхна сметка). For **local calls,** it's best to buy a phone card. There are two brands: **Bulfon** (orange) and **Mobika** (blue), which work only at telephones of the same brand sold at kiosks, restaurants, shops, and post offices. (400 units=20lv; 200 units=12lv; 100 units=7.50lv; 50 units=4.90lv.) In Sofia or Varna, calls to the U.S. average US$2 per minute, but expect to pay as much as US$4 per minute at hotels. **International direct dial** numbers include: **AT&T Direct,** ☎00 800 0010; **BT Direct,** ☎00 800 99 44; **Canada Direct,** ☎00 800 1359; **MCI,** ☎00800 001; and **Sprint,** ☎00 800 1010.

INTERNET ACCESS. Email is becoming more widespread in Bulgaria; sending a message is around 1-2lv per hour.

LANGUAGES. Bulgarian is a South Slavic language similar to Russian. **English** is increasingly spoken by young people and in tourist areas. **German** is understood in many places. It's advisable to learn the Cyrillic alphabet.

YES AND NO Bulgarians shake their heads to indicate "yes" and "no" in the opposite directions from Brits and Yanks. For the uncoordinated, it's easier to just hold your head still and say *dah* or *neh.*

HOLIDAYS

Holidays: New Year's (Jan. 1); Orthodox Christmas (Jan. 7); 1878 Liberation Day (Mar. 3); Orthodox Good Friday (Apr. 13); Orthodox Easter (Apr. 15); Labor Day (May 1); Cyrillic Alphabet Day, St. George's Day, and Bulgarian Army Day (May 24); Day of Union (Sept. 6); Independence Day (Sept. 22); Bulgarian Culture Celebration (Nov. 1); Catholic Christmas (Dec. 24-25).

SOFIA (СОФИЯ) ☎02

To find the "culture" in Sofia (pop. 1.4 million) you may have to sift through pairs of fake Nikes to locate the handmade lace at a bazaar, or dodge trams and cars on the way to the theater, but it's well worth the effort. Fifteen hundred years of majestic churches are not quite dwarfed by Soviet-era concrete blocks, and 19th-century elegance is gracefully weathering the fast food invasion.

GETTING THERE AND GETTING AROUND

Flights: Airport Sofia (☎79 80 35). Take bus #84 (0.30lv), to the left as you exit international arrivals, to the city center.

Trains: Tsentralna Gara (Централна Гара; Central Train Station), north of the city center on Knyaginya Maria Luiza St. (Мария Луиза). Trams (0.30lv) #1 and 7 go to pl. Sv. Nedelya (Пл. Св. Неделя); trams #9 and 12 down Hristo Botev (Христо Ботев); buses (0.30lv) #85, 213, 305, and 313 to the station. The **ticket office** (☎843 42 80) is downstairs in front of the NDK. Open M-F 7am-7pm, Sa 7am-2pm. To: **Burgas** (7½hr., 6 per day, 9lv); **Plovdiv** (2½hr., 15 per day, 3.80lv); **Athens** (6 per day, 60lv); **Bucharest** (6 per day, 37lv); **Budapest** (1 per day, 85lv); and **Īstanbul** (4 per day, 46lv).

Buses: Ovcha Kupel (Овча Купел), along Tsar Boris III bul. (Цар Борис III), reachable by tram #5 or 19 (away from Vitosha). Buses go to: **Athens** (3 per day, 66lv); **Budapest** (3 per day, 80lv); and **Istanbul** (2 per day, 72lv). **Private buses** leave from the parking lot opposite the Central Train Station, and are cheap and fast: **Group Travel** (☎32 01 22) has a kiosk in the parking lot that sends buses to Burgas, Veliko Tarnovo, and Varna. Geared to tourists. Open daily 7am-5:30pm and 6-7:30pm.

Local Transportation: Trams, trolleybuses, and **buses** cost 0.30lv per ride. **Day-pass** 1000lv; **5-day pass** 4400lv. Buy tickets at kiosks with signs saying "билети" (tickets; *bileti*) or from the driver, then punch them in the machines between the bus windows to avoid a 10lv fine. Backpackers may be expected to buy a separate ticket for a large pack. Officially run 5am-1am, but rides are scarce after 9pm.

Taxis: Softaxi (☎12 84), **OK Taxi** (☎973 21 21), and **INEX** (☎919 19). From the airport, don't pay more than 20lv to the city center. Fares are 0.32-0.40lv per km (and rising with gas prices), and 0.45lv per km after 10pm, when it's really wise to take a cab.

ORIENTATION AND PRACTICAL INFORMATION

The city center, **pl. Sveta Nedelya** (пл. Света Неделя), is marked by the green roof of the Tsurkva Sv. Nedelya, the Sheraton Hotel, and Tsentralen Universalen Magazin (TSUM). **Bul. Knyaginya Maria Luiza** (Княгиня Мария Луиза) connects pl. Sveta Nedelya to the train station. Trams #1 and 7 run from the train station through pl. Sveta Nedelya and up **bul. Vitosha** (Витоша), a main shopping and nightlife thoroughfare. Vitosha links pl. Sveta Nedelya to **pl. Bulgaria** and the huge, concrete **National Palace of Culture** (Национален Дворец Култура; NDK; Natsionalen Dvorets Kultura). Historical **bul. Tsar Osvoboditel** (бул. Цар Освободител; Tsar the Liberator) heads to the **university** and the hottest spots for dancing and drinking in Sofia.

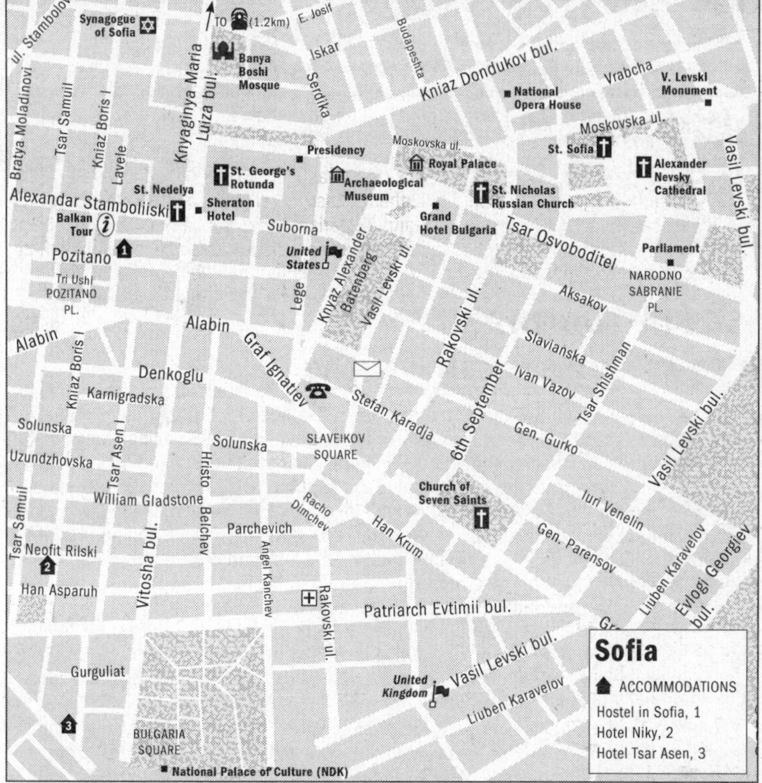

The monthly **Sofia City Guide** (free, available at the Sheraton Hotel) is a great English publication with loads of tourist information. **Maps** are also available in the lobby of the Sheraton Hotel and where books are sold—try Slaveikov Square (пл. Славйков) on Graf Ignatiev (Граф Игнатиев).

TOURIST, FINANCIAL, AND LOCAL SERVICES

Tourist Office: Odysseia-In, Stambolysky bul. 20-V (Страмболийски; ☎989 05 38 and 981 05 60; email odysseia@omega.bg). From pl. Sv. Nedelya, head down Stambolysky and take the 2nd right on Lavele; Odysseia is halfway down on the left, 2 floors up. A great resource. Open M-F 9am-7pm, Sa 10am-4pm. Consultation 5lv per 30min.

Embassies: Australians, Canadians, and **New Zealanders** should contact the British embassy. **South Africans** should contact the embassy in Athens (see p. 480). **UK,** bul. (*not* ul.) Vasil Levski 38 (☎980 12 20 and 980 12 21). Open M-Th 8:30am-12:30pm and 1:30-5pm, F 8:30am-1pm. **US,** ul. Suborna 1a (Съборна; ☎980 52 41). Consular section at Kapitan Andreev 1 (Капитан Андреев; ☎963 00 89), behind NDK. Americans should register with the consular section upon arrival in Bulgaria. Open M-Th 2-4pm; open for emergencies M-F 9am-5pm.

Currency Exchange: Bulbank (Булбанк), pl. Sv. Nedelya 7, cashes traveler's checks for a 0.5% commission and gives Visa cash advances for a 4% commission. Open M-F 8:30am-4pm. ATMs are everywhere.

American Express: Aksakov 5 (Аксаков; ☎986 58 37; fax 980 88 89). Mail held for members. Open M-F 9am-6pm, Sa 9am-2:30pm.

Luggage Storage: Downstairs at the Central Train Station. Look for "гардероб" *(garderob)* signs. 0.50lv per piece. Open daily 5:30am-midnight.

EMERGENCY AND COMMUNICATIONS

Emergency: Ambulance, ☎150. **Fire,** ☎160. **Police,** ☎166.

Pharmacy: All over town; just look for the word Аптека (*Apteka*).

Medical Assistance: State-owned hospitals offer foreigners free emergency aid. **Pirogov Emergency Hospital,** Gen. Totleben bul. 21 (Ген. Тотлебен; ☎515 31), opposite Hotel Rodina. Take trolleybus #5 or 19 from the city center. Open 24hr.

Telephones: Ul. Stefan Karadzha 6 (Стефан Караджа), near the post office. Use 50lv coins for local calls. Bulgarian phone cards also sold here. Open 24hr.

Internet Access: Club Cyberia, Stephan Karadzha 18B (☎988 73 50). 2lv per hr. Open daily 10am-midnight. **ICN** (☎088 24 10 76), in NDK. 4lv per hr. Open daily 9am-10:30pm.

Post Office: Gen. Gurko 6 (Гурко). International mailing at window #7. *Poste Restante* for 1.20lv. Open M-F 7am-8:30pm. Address mail to be held: First name SURNAME, *Poste Restante,* Gen. Gurko 6, Sofia **1000,** Bulgaria.

ACCOMMODATIONS AND FOOD

Hotels are rarely worth the exorbitant price—if the hostel is full, **private rooms** are often the best option. Camping is another inexpensive choice; **Camping Vrana** (☎78 12 13) is 10km from the city center on E-80, and **Cherniya Kos** (☎57 11 29) is 11km away on E-79. Check with **Odysseia-In** (see **Tourist Office,** above) for both options. A friendly staff awaits at **Hostel in Sofia** (a.k.a. Naska's Home for Weary Travelers), Pozitano 16 (Позитано). From pl. St. Nedelya, walk down Vitosha, and go right on Pozitano. (☎/fax 989 15 04. Breakfast included. Communal showers and toilet. Kitchen. Reception 5pm-noon. Check-out noon. US$10.) **Hotel Niky** is on Neofit Rilski 16, off Vitosha (Витоша). (☎51 19 15. Communal showers and toilet. Singles US$22; doubles US$40. 10% student discount.) From St. Nicholas Church, walk toward the NDK on Tsar Asen; ring the doorbell of **Hotel Tsar Asen** (Цар Асен), Tsar Asen 68, on the right before Gen. M. Skobelev Bul. (Ген. М. Скобелев). (☎54 78 01. Private showers. Singles US$28; doubles US$34.)

From fast food to Bulgarian specialties, cheap meals are easy to find. In general, meals at restaurants run from 6-10lv, but vendors will fill you up for 2lv. **Vitosha** abounds with 24-hour supermarkets. In summer, an **outdoor market** lines the sides of Graf Ignatiev (Граф Игнатиев), past Slaveikov Square (Пл. Славейков), near the Church of Seven Saints. The first floor of TZUM (at pl. Sv. Nedelya) has a large international **grocery store. Murphy's Irish Pub,** Karnigradska 6 (Кьрниградска), is a real Irish pub that attracts an international crowd. (☎980 28 70. Entrees 4-9lv. Murphy's pint 4lv. Open daily 10:30am-10:30pm.) **Trops House** (Тропс Кьща), Saborna 11, is a convenient and quick restaurant with surprisingly good cafeteria-style food. (Entrees 1-2lv. Open daily 8am-9:30pm.) For the best ice cream in town (by far), visit **Jimmy's,** Angel Kunchev 11 (Ангел Кьнчев; 0.50lv per scoop).

SIGHTS

PL. ALEXANDER NEVSKY. In the city center stands Sofia's pride and joy, the gold-domed **Cathedral of St. Alexander Nevsky** (Sv. Aleksandr Nevsky; Св. Александр Невски), which was erected in memory of the 200,000 Russians who died in the 1877-1878 Russo-Turkish War. Through a separate entrance left of the main church, the **crypt** houses a spectacular array of painted icons and religious artifacts, the richest collection of its kind in Bulgaria. *(Cathedral open daily 7:30am-7pm; free. Crypt open W-M 10:30am-6:30pm. 3lv, students 1.5lv.)* At the **markets** surrounding the square, antiques, Soviet paraphernalia, and handmade crafts are sold; Bulgarian *babushki* offer handmade lace and embroidery.

AROUND PL. SVETA NEDELYA. The focal point of Sofia is the **Cathedral of St. Nedelya** (Katedralen Hram Sv. Nedelya; Катедрален Храм Св. Неделя), filled with soot-blackened frescoes. The church is a reconstruction of a 14th-century original destroyed by a bomb in an attempt on Tsar Boris III's life in 1925; the tsar escaped, but the cupola buried 190 generals and politicians. *(Open daily 7am-6:30pm.)* In the courtyard behind the Sheraton Hotel stands the 4th-century **St. George's Rotunda** (Sv. Georgi; Св. Георги). One of Sofia's most venerable churches, it is accompanied by a former Roman bath and the remains of the ancient town of Serdica. *(Open daily 8am-6pm.)* In the underpass between pl. Sv. Nedelya and TSUM, the tiny, 14th-century **Church of St. Petya of Samardzhiyska** (Tsurkva Hram Sv. Petya Samardzhiyska; Църква Храм Св. Петя Самарджийска) contains fascinating layers of frescoes on the upper walls and ceiling and is rumored to have originally held the bones of Vasil Levsky, Bulgaria's national hero. *(Open Nov.-Apr. M-Sa 9:30am-6pm, Su 9am-noon; May-Oct. M-Sa 8am-7pm, Su 9am-noon. 5lv; tours 10lv.)* Walk up bul. Maria Luiza and take a left on Tsar Simeon to reach the **Synagogue of Sofia** (Sofiaski Synagoga; Софийска Синагога), a beautifully renovated synagogue, where a museum upstairs outlines the history of Jews in Bulgaria. *(Open Su-F 9am-5pm, Sa 10am-6:30pm. Weekly service Sa 6:30pm. Donations accepted.)*

BULGARIA

ALONG BUL. TSAR OSVOBODITEL. Historical bul. Tsar Osvoboditel is weighted down on the ends by the **House of Parliament** and the **Royal Palace.** Midway sits the 1913 Russian **Church of St. Nicholas** (Sv. Nikolai; Св. Николай), with five Russian Orthodox-style onion domes. *(Open daily 8am-6pm.)*

NATIONAL PALACE OF CULTURE. Opened in 1981 to celebrate Bulgaria's 13th centennial, the monstrous NDK (Natsionalen Dvorets Kultura; Национален Дворец Култура) is a barracks of culture, with restaurants, theaters, and movie halls that show subtitled American movies. Buy tickets (approx. 5lv) from the ticket office (биллетни център) to the left of the main entrance. *(In Yuzhen Park. From pl. Sveta Nedelya, walk down bul. Vitosha to bul. Patriarch Evtimy and enter the park. The palace is at its far end. Open daily 8:30am-7pm.)*

MUSEUMS. From St. Nedelya, head down Suborna and take your first left on Lege to reach the **National Archaeological Museum** (Arheologicheski Muzey; Археологически Музей), which houses items from Thracian, Greek, Roman, and Turkish settlements from the past 2000 years. *(Open Tu-Su 10am-6pm.)* The Royal Palace houses the **National Museum of Ethnography** (Natsionalen Etnograficheski Muzey; Национален Етнографически), which details the role of Armenians in Bulgaria. *(Open Tu-Su 10am-5pm. 3lv, students 1.50lv.)* It also houses the **National Art Gallery** (Natsionalna Hudozhestvena Galeriya; Национална Художествена Галерийа), the best art museum in Bulgaria. *(Open Tu-Su 10am-6pm. 3000lv, students 1.50lv.)*

ENTERTAINMENT

The main **opera** and **theater** seasons run from September to June; good theater seats are sometimes less than US$1. (☎987 70 11, 987 14 66, and 981 14 67. Box office open daily 9am-7pm. No performances M.) You can get tickets for the **Ivan Vazov National Theater** at Rakovski 98 (☎07 23 03). Cinemas often show subtitled Hollywood movies—try Vitosha 62 and pl. Vasil Levski 1.

While nightlife in Sofia does not consume the entire city, the scene is getting wilder every year. Smartly dressed Sofians roam the main streets, filling the outdoor bars along **bul. Vitosha** and the cafes around the **NDK.** Most nightlife centers around bul. Vitosha or, for the younger set, the University of Sofia at the intersection of **Vasil Levski** and **Tsar Osvoboditel.** When out on the town, be careful: the mafia runs the show. From Vitosha, heading toward the NDK, turn left on Alabin (Алабин), veer right on Graf Ignatiev, and turn left at pl. Slaveykov (with McDonald's) into the courtyard to reach lively **Biraria Luciano** (Бирария Лучано), Slaveykov 9 (Славейков), which has beer (1-3lv) from seven different countries. (Open daily noon-11pm.) Enter **Bibloteka** (Виблиотека), in St. Cyril and Methodius Library, from Obhorishte. Sing karaoke to American songs while surrounded by reproductions of essays and old leather books. (Cover 3lv. Open W-Sa 11pm-5am.) **Spartakus** (Спартакус), in the underpass past the pl. Narodno Subranie, leading toward Vasil Levski, keeps its somewhat exclusive gay and straight clientele happy with thumping techno and intense strobe light. Speaking English and explaining your exotic (foreign) origins should get you in. (Cover 3lv. Open daily 11pm-late.) **Dali,** behind the University on Krakra, is the best Latin club in Sofia, with plenty of room to spin and swivel. (Cover for men 3lv. Women free. Open daily until 6am.)

EXCURSIONS FROM SOFIA

RILA MONASTERY. Holy Ivan of Rila built the 10th-century Rila Monastery (Rilski Manastir; Рилски Манастир), Bulgaria's largest and most famous monastery, as a refuge from the lascivious outer world. Moved to its current location in the 14th century, the monastery sheltered the arts of icon painting and manuscript copying during the Byzantine and Ottoman occupations, and remained an oasis of Bulgarian culture for five centuries. Today's monastery was built between 1834 and 1837; little remains from the earlier structure. Examine the 1200 brilliantly colored **frescoes** (on the central chapel), or check out the **museum.** (Open daily 8:30am-4:30pm. 5lv, students 3lv. Sporadic English tours 15lv.) The quickest way to get to Rila Town is to take a **bus** from Novotel Europa in Sofia to Blagoevgrad (2hr., 8-10 per day, 3.80lv), then from Blagoevgrad to Rila Town (45min., every hr., 2lv). From Rila Town, catch the bus up to the monastery (45min., 3 per day, 1.10lv). **Hotel Tsarev Vrukh** (Царев Врьх) is a new hotel with luxury facilities. (☎/fax 22 80. Breakfast US$2. US$14.) The hotel is 50m down the path that follows the river from behind the monastery. Inquire at room #170 in the monastery about staying in a spartan, but heated, **monastery cell.** (☎22 08. Curfew midnight. 30lv.) Behind the monastery is a cluster of restaurants, cafes, snack bars, and a small mini-market. ☎**07054.**

KOPRIVSHTITSA. Todor Kableshkov's movement for rebellion against Ottoman rule started in this little town, tucked away in the Sredna Gora mountains. Today, the town is a center of historical cultural life, where the National Revival period of 125 years ago is still well-preserved in its buildings. If you miss the folk festivals, beginning in May and continuing through mid-August, the preserved **National Revival houses** are the thing to see. Many homes of the leaders of the 1876 Uprising have become **museums,** and all are easy to find with a map from the tourist office. The most notable is the 1845 **Todor Kableshkov Museum-House** (Kushta-muzey Todor Kableshkov; Къща-музей Тодор Каблешков), which has an impressive facade, ingeniously carved ceilings, and the hero's personal possessions. (Open Tu-Su 8am-noon and 1:30-5:30pm.) **Trains** come from Sofia (2hr., 5 per day, 2.40lv) and **Plovdiv** via **Karlovo** (3½hr., 3 per day, 2.30lv). Take a bus (15min., 0.70lv) from the train station to reach the train center, and get off at the **bus station** (a wooden building), which posts bus and train schedules. To reach the **main square,** backtrack along the river bisecting town. The **tourist office,** in the main square, has an invaluable (2lv) **map** with a guide to museums, monuments, and places to stay and eat.

PLOVDIV (ПЛОВДИВ) ☎032

While Plovdiv is smaller than Sofia, it is widely hailed as the cultural capital of Bulgaria. In the convoluted Old Town, National Revival houses protrude over the cobblestones below, windows stare into alleys at impossible angles, and churches and mosques hide in secluded corners.

PRACTICAL INFO, ACCOMMODATIONS, AND FOOD. Trains arrive from: Sofia (2½hr., 14 per day, 3.90lv); Burgas (5hr., 7 per day, 6.20lv); and Varna (5½hr., 3 per day, 8.10lv). Buy tickets at **Rila,** bul. Hristo Botev 31a. (☎44 61 20. Open M-F 8am-7pm, Sa 8am-4pm.) **Buses** arrive from Sofia (2hr., every hr., 6lv) at Yug (Юг) station, Hristo Botev 47 (Христо Ботев), diagonally across from the train station. **Traffic Express** (Трафик Экспрес; ☎26 57 90), in the station, services the Black Sea coast. **Puldin Tours** (Пълдин), bul. Bulgaria 106 (България), finds rooms (US$13-16), arranges tours, and changes money. From the train station, ride trolley #2 or 102 (200lv) nine stops to bul. Bulgaria and backtrack a block. (☎55 38 48. Open M-F 9am-5:30pm; until 9pm during fairs.) An up-to-date map is essential—

street vendors sell good Cyrillic ones for 3lv. Check **email** at **Voo Doo Net,** Stan Knyaz Aleksander 3, near the mosque, up two flights. (1lv per hr. Open 24hr.) It is important to make reservations for rooms in Plovdiv in the summer. **Hostel Touristicheski Dom** (Туристически Дом), P.R. Slaveykov 5 (П.Р. Славейков), is in the Old Town (Stari Grad; Стари Град). From Knyaz Aleksandr (Княз Александр), take Patriarch Evtimii (Патриарх Евтимий) into town, passing under Tsar Boris, and hang a left on Slaveykov. (☎63 32 11. Curfew 11pm. 22lv.) From Rodopi bus station, head away from the train track on Dimitar Talev (Димитър Талив), and take the second right after Nikola Vapstarov (Никола Вапцаров) to **Hotel Feniks** (Феникс), Silivria 18A (Силиврия); it's a 20-minute walk. (☎77 48 51. US$15.) **Postal code:** 4000.

SIGHTS AND ENTERTAINMENT. Most of Plovdiv's historic and cultural treasures are concentrated in the three hills (the **Trimondium**) of the Old Town. Take a right off Knyaz Aleksandr (Княз Александр) to Stanislav Dospevski (Станислав Доспевски), turn right at the end of the street, and take the stairs to the left to reach the second-century Roman **amphitheater** (Antichen Teatr; Античен Театр), a marble masterpiece. (Open daily 8am-dark. 2lv.) It currently serves as a popular venue for concerts and shows, hosting the **Festival of the Arts** (Walt Whitman would be proud) in the summer and early fall, and the **Opera Festival** in June. Return to Knyaz Aleksandr and follow it to the end to pl. Dzhumaya (Джумая), home to the **Dzhumaya Mosque** (Dzhumaya Dzhamiya; Джамия; services daily at 6pm) and the ancient **Philipoplis Stadium.** The gladiator's entrance is still intact and a restaurant-cafe serves traditional Bulgarian food on the stadium's tiers. (Entrees 2-8lv. Open daily 11am-midnight.) At the end of Suborna (Съборна), the **Museum of Ethnography** (Etnografski Muzey; Етнографски Музей) displays Bulgarian artifacts. (Open Tu-Su 9am-noon and 2-5pm. 3lv, students 0.20lv.) At night, head to the fountainside cafe in **Tsentralni Park** (Централни Парк), by pl. Tsentralen (пл. Централен).

EXCURSION FROM PLOVDIV: BACHKOVO MONASTERY. About 28km south of Plovdiv, in the plush green Rodopi mountain slopes, is Bulgaria's second-largest monastery, **Bachkovo Monastery** (Bachkovski Manastir; Бачковски Манастир), built in the 11th century. The main church is home to the **icon of the Virgin Mary and Child** (ikona Sveta Bogoroditsa; икона Света Богородица), which is said to have miraculous healing power. (Open daily 8am-dark.) **Buses** run from Plovdiv's Yug station to Asenovgrad (25min., 21 per day, 0.60lv), as do **trains** (25min., every hr., 0.80lv). From Asenovgrad's bus station, catch a bus to the monastery (2nd stop; 20min., every 30min., 0.50lv).

VELIKO TARNOVO (ВЕЛИКО ТЪРНОВО) ☎062

Veliko Turnovo has been watching over Bulgaria for 5000 years—its residents led the national uprising against Byzantine rule in 1185, and its fortress walls and battle towers have stood since it was the capital of Bulgaria's Second Kingdom. The remains of the **Tsarevets** (Царевец), a fortress that once housed a cathedral and royal palace, stretch across a hilltop above the city. (Open daily Apr.-Sept. 8am-7pm; Oct. 8am-6pm; Nov.-Mar. 9am-5pm. 4lv, students 2lv.) At the top is the **Church of the Ascension** (Tsurkva Vuzneseniegospodne; Църква Възнесениегосподне), restored in 1981 on the 13th centennial of the Bulgarian state. Near the fortress off ul. Ivan Vazov (Иван Вазов), the **National Revival Museum** (Muzey na Vuzrazhdaneto; Музей на Възраждането) documents Bulgaria's 19th-century cultural and religious resurgence. (Open daily 8am-noon and 1-5:30pm. 4lv, students 2lv. English tours 3lv.) On summer evenings, there is often a **sound and light show** above Tsarvets Hill: lasers play out Bulgaria's history symbolically on the fortress ruins. (30min. Show starts between 9:45 and 10pm.)

Most **trains** stop at nearby **Gorna Oryahovitsa** (Горна Оряховица; 30 min., 0.50lv), where they then leave for Burgas (6 per day, 5½hr., 5.80lv) and Sofia (8 per day, 7760lv). City buses #7 and 10 go from the station to the town center. Bookstores along **Rakovski** (Раковски), the small street two minutes from Hotel Trapezitsa on the way to Hotel Comfort, have good maps (3lv). **Rila Travel Bureau** is down Hristo

Botev on the left. (Open M-F 9am-5:30pm.) Check **email** up the stairs and to the right of **La Scalla, Pizzeria Italian.** (2lv per hr. Open 24hr.) **Hotel Trapezitsa (HI)** (Хотел Трапезица), Stefan Stambolov 79, is an excellent hostel with clean rooms. From the town center, walk down Nevvisimost toward the post office and follow the street right. (☎220 61. 14lv; nonmembers 18lv.) **Hotel Comfort** (Комфорт), Panayot Tipografov 5 (Панайот Типографов), has an amazing view of Tsarvets. From Stambolov, walk left on Rakovski (Раковски), turn left on the small square, and look for the street sign. (☎287 28. US$15, students US$11.) **Postal code:** 5000.

BLACK SEA COAST

The Black Sea, the most popular destination in Bulgaria for foreign and native vacationers alike, bundles centuries-old, thumbnail-sized fishing villages with clear, secluded bays, energetic seaside towns, and resorts designed to suck hard currency. In between, you'll find warm, sandy beaches in the south and rockier, white-cliffed shores to the north. You're bound to run into more English speakers than in any other part of Bulgaria, along with higher—though still reasonable—prices.

VARNA (ВАРНА) ☎52

Varna's appeal centers on its extensive **beaches** and Mediterranean-like climate, while the highly-regarded summer arts and music festival draws eager audiences. The beaches stretch north from the train station and are separated from bul. Primorsky by seaside gardens. The well-preserved **Roman Thermal Baths** (Rimski Termi; Римски Терми) stand on San Stefano in the city's old quarter, **Grutska Makhala.** (Гръцка Махала. Open Tu-Su 10am-5pm. 1lv.) In the park behind Maria Luiza, the **Archaeological Museum** (Археологически Музей; Arkheologicheski Muzey) traces the country's history from the Early Stone Age, with artifacts from the past 100,000 years. (Open Tu-Sa 10am-5pm. 2lv, students 1lv. English guide 5lv.) Both the **National Revival Museum,** which sits just off pl. Ekzarkh Yossif (Екзарх Йосиф; open Tu-Su 10am-5pm; 1.50lv), and the **Ethnographic Museum** (Етнографски Музей; Etnografski Muzey), at Sofronii Vrachanski 22 (Софроний Врачански; ☎63 05 88; open Tu-Sa 10am-5pm), maintain displays of 19th-century folk crafts in well-preserved buildings from Bulgaria's historic National Revival Period. Varna is home to many special arts events; for a complete seasonal schedule, tickets, and information, check the **International Advertisement Office** (☎23 72 84), two floors below the main entrance of the Community House of Art.

Trains, near the commercial port by the shore, go to: Gorna Oryahovitza (3hr., 6 per day, 5.55lv); Plovdiv (5½hr., 3 per day, 8lv); and Sofia (7hr., 7 per day, 12.10-17.90lv). **Buses,** at Ul. Vladislav Varenchik (Владислав Варенчик), go to Burgas (3hr., 6 per day, 5.50lv). The **American Express in Megatours,** in the Hotel Cherno More, Slivnitsa 33, is good for tourist information. (Open June-Sept. M-F 9am-7pm, Sa 9am-2pm; Oct.-May M-F 9am-6pm, Sa 9am-2pm.) Get on the **Internet** at **The Game Club,** off Pl. Nezivisimost on Musala. (Мусала. 2lv per hr. Open 24hr.) **Solvex,** near track #4 at the train station, finds rooms for US$6-10 per person. (☎60 58 61. Open daily in summer 6am-10pm.) **Hotel Trite Delfina** (Трите Делфина; Three Dolphins), at ul. Gabrovo 27, is close to the train station. Go up Simeon from the train station and take a right on Gabrovo. (☎60 09 11. Singles US$20; doubles US$25.)

BURGAS. Burgas (BOOR-gahs; Бургас) is a transport hub for the Southern Black Sea Coast. The **bus** and **train stations** are near the port at **Garov pl.** (Гаров). **Trains** go to Sofia via Plovdiv (7hr., 7 per day, 9.50lv); **buses** serve the Black Sea Coast (Varna: 2½hr., 6 per day, 5.50lv), while cheaper **minibuses** run to the coastal resorts from the opposite end of the bus station from the train station. Many smaller resorts don't have places to change money; **Bulbank,** across the street from Hotel Bulgaria on Aleksandrovska, cashes traveler's checks and has an **ATM.** (Open M-F 8:30am-4pm.) If you stay the night here, secure a room at the change bureau at Bogoridi 14, on the corner of Lermontov. (Лермонтов. ☎71 42. Open M-F 8am-8pm, Sa 9am-8pm. US$6-10.) Or, go to **Hotel Mirage** (Мираж), Lermontov 18; from the station, go up

Aleksandrovska, take a right on Bogoridi, pass the Hotel Bulgaria, and take the first left on Lermontov. (☎92 10 19. Doubles US$25-28; triples US$33.) ☎**056.**

NESEBUR. Nesebur (Несебър), a museum town atop the peninsula at the south end of Sunny Beach, is a break from sand and sun. The town has successfully preserved its charm. A walk through its ancient **Stari Grad** begins with the 3rd-century stone **fortress walls.** The Byzantine **gate** and **port** date from the 5th century. The **Archaeological Museum** (Arheologicheski Muzey; Археологически Музей), to the right of the town gate, exhibits ancient ceramics and icons. (☎460 18. Open May-Oct. daily 9am-1:30pm and 2-7:30pm; Nov.-Apr. M-F 9am-9pm. 2.10lv, students 0.85lv. English tour 4lv.) The 11th-century **New Metropolitan Church of St. Stephen** (Tsurkvata Sveti Stefan; Църквата Свети Стефан) is plastered in well preserved 16th-century frescoes. From the town center, continue down Mesembria and take a right on Ribarska. (Open June-Sept. 7am-7:30pm. 1.70lv, students 0.85lv.) Along the harbor, steet kiosks sells fruit and nuts or small meals. Get to Nesebur by **bus** from Burgas (40min., every 40min., 2lv). ☎**0554.**

SOZOPOL. Sozopol (soh-ZO-pohl; Созопол), settled in 610 BC, is Bulgaria's oldest Black Sea town. Once the resort of choice for Bulgaria's artistic community, it still caters to a creative set and is quieter and cheaper than its neighbors. Take a **boat cruise** (15lv per boat) from the seaport behind the bus station and get a closer look at the two nearby islands, **St. Peter** and **St. Ivan.** The best time to go is around sunset. To explore some of Sozopol's less-crowded **beaches,** rent a motorbike near the bus station and cruise along the shoreline. (10lv per hr.) **Buses** arrive from Burgas (45min., every 30min., 1.70lv). Turn left on **Apolonia** (Аполония) to reach **Stari Grad** (Old Town). To get to **Novi Grad** (New Town), go right through the park and turn left on Republikanska (Републиканска). The tourist bureau **Lotos,** at the bus station, arranges **private rooms.** (☎22 82. US$7 per person. Open daily 8am-8pm.) ☎**5514.**

CROATIA (HRVATSKA)

KUNA

US$1 = 8.40KN	10KN = US$1.20
CDN$1 = 5.70KN	10KN = CDN$1.80
UK£1 = 12.00KN	10KN = UK£0.81
IR£1 = 9.60KN	10KN = IR£1.00
AUS$1 = 4.85KN	10KN = AUS$2.10
NZ$1 = 3.60KN	10KN = NZ$2.80
SAR1 = 1.20KN	10KN = SAR8.30
DM1 = 3.90KN	10KN = DM2.60
EUR€1 = 7.63KN	10KN = EUR€1.33

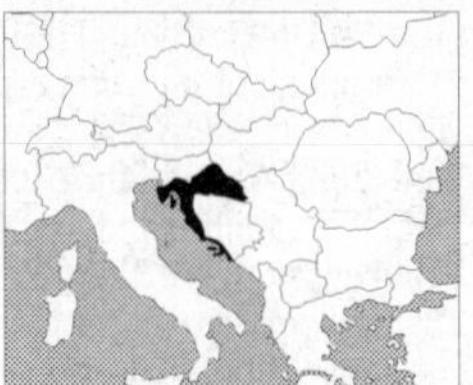

Country code: 385. **International dialing prefix:** 00. From outside Croatia, dial int'l dialing prefix (see inside back cover) + 385 + city code + local number.

Croatia is a land of unearthly beauty. Traced with thick forests, wispy plains, underground streams, and the translucent sea, it has served for centuries as a summer playground for visitors. Positioned at the convergence of the Mediterranean, the Alps, and the Pannonian plain, Croatia has also been situated on dangerous divides—between the Frankish and Byzantine empires in the 9th century, the Catholic and Orthodox churches since the 11th century, Christian Europe and Islamic Turkey from the 15th to the 19th centuries, and its own fractious ethnic groups in the past decade. Dancing in the nightclubs of Dubrovnik or lounging on the beaches in Pula, it's easy to forget the tensions that have played out here in the past. Independent for the first time in 800 years, Croatians are finally free to enjoy the extraordinary landscape in peace.

For sparkling coverage of Croatia, refer to *Let's Go: Eastern Europe 2001*.

FACTS AND FIGURES

Official Name: Republic of Croatia.

Government: Presidential/parliamentary democracy.

Capital: Zagreb.

Land Area: 56,538 sq. km.

Geography: Mountainous coast with numerous islands; lowlands in the north.

Climate: Hot summers and cold winters; mild winters, dry summers along coast.

Population: 4,677,000 (78% Croats, 12% Serbs, 1% Bosniaks, 9% other).

Languages: Croatian.

Religions: Catholic (77%), Orthodox (11%), Muslim (1%), other (11%).

Income Per Capita: US$5100.

Major Exports: Textiles, chemicals, foodstuffs, fuels.

Major Cities: Zagreb, Split, Dubrovnik.

DISCOVER CROATIA

With Mediterranean beaches, mind-boggling Roman ruins, and happening cities, Croatia is worth the extra effort it takes to get there. Start in the capital, **Zagreb,** with its alluring mix of Habsburg splendor, Mediterranean relaxation, and the hippest cafe scene in the Balkans (p. 236). Croatia's most impressive ruins are in **Pula,** the 2000-year-old heart of Istria (p. 237). The true highlight of Croatia, however, is the fabled **Dalmatian Coast,** one of the Mediterranean's most dazzling natural spectacles, where pristine beaches and azure waters mingle (p. 238); bask in **Split** on the central coast (p. 238). George Bernard Shaw called **Dubrovnik** "paradise on earth" for its stunning seascapes and walled city center (p. 239).

ESSENTIALS

WHEN TO GO

Croatia's mild Mediterranean climate means that there is no wrong time to visit. The high season (July to Aug.) may bring crowds to the coast; going in June or September will reward visitors with lower prices and more breathing room.

DOCUMENTS AND FORMALITIES

Citizens of Australia, Canada, Ireland, New Zealand, the UK, and the US do not need **visas** for stays of up to 90 days. Visas are required of South African citizens. All visitors must register with the police within two days of arrival, regardless of their length of stay. Hotels, campsites, and accommodations agencies should automatically register you, but those staying with friends or in private rooms must do so themselves to avoid fines or expulsion. Police may check passports anywhere.

EMBASSIES AND CONSULATES

Embassies and consulates of other countries in Croatia are all in **Zagreb** (p. 236).

Croatian Embassies at Home: Australia, 14 Jindalee Crescent, O'Malley, Canberra ACT 2606 (☎ (06) 286 69 88; fax 286 35 44); **Canada,** 229 Chapel St., Ottawa, ON K1N 7Y6 (☎ (613) 562 78 20; www.croatiaemb.net); **New Zealand Consulate,** 131 Lincoln

Rd., Henderson, P.O. Box 83200, Edmonton, Auckland (☎ (09) 836 55 81; fax 836 54 81); **South Africa,** 1160 Church St., Colbyn, Pretoria; P.O. Box 11335, Hatfield 0028 (☎ (012) 342 12 06; fax 342 18 19); **UK,** 21 Conway St., London W1P 5HL (☎ (020) 73 87 20 22; fax 73 87 09 36); **US,** 2343 Massachusetts Ave. NW, Washington, D.C. 20008 (☎ (202) 588 58 99; www.croatiaemb.org).

GETTING THERE AND GETTING AROUND

BY PLANE. **Zagreb** is Croatia's main entry point; **Croatia Airlines** (☎ +385 (1) 487 27 27; www.croatiaairlines.hr) often continues to Dubrovnik and Split. Rijeka, Zadar, and Pula also have international airports.

BY TRAIN, BY BUS, AND BY CAR. Trains are *very* slow, and nonexistent south of Split. *Odlazak* means departures, *dolazak* arrivals. **Eurail** is not valid. For domestic travel, **buses** are the best option. Tickets are cheaper if you buy them on board. You can **rent a car** in larger cities, but parking can be expensive, rural roads are in poor condition, and in the Krajina region and other conflict areas, drivers should be wary of off-road land mines. **Speed limits** are 50 kph in cities, and 130 kph on highways. Contact the **Croatian Autoclub (HAK;** ☎ (01) 464 08 00; www.hak.hr) for further info.

BY FERRY. If you're on the coast, take one of the **ferries** run by **Jadrolinija.** Boats sail the Rijeka-Split-Dubrovnik route with islands stops en route. Ferries also float from **Split** (p. 238) to **Ancona,** Italy (p. 643), and from **Dubrovnik** (p. 239) to **Bari,** Italy.

BY THUMB. Hitchhiking in Croatia is highly discouraged.

TOURIST SERVICES AND MONEY

EMERGENCY. **Police:** ☎ 92. **Ambulance:** ☎ 94. **Fire:** ☎ 93.

TOURIST OFFICES. Even the smallest towns have a branch of the excellent, English-speaking **state-run tourist board** (*turistička zajednica;* www.htz.hr). Private accommodations are handled by private tourist agencies *(turistička/putnička agencija)*, the largest of which is the ubiquitous **Atlas** with branches in every major city.

MONEY. Most banks, tourist offices, hotels, and transportation stations exchange currency and traveler's checks. Banks usually have the best rates. Croatia's monetary unit is the **kuna** (kn), which is divided into 100 lipa and is virtually impossible to exchange abroad, except in Hungary and Slovenia. Neither South African rand nor Irish pounds are exchangeable in Croatia. **ATMs** *(bankomat)* are common. Most banks give MC/Visa **cash advances,** and credit cards are widely accepted. A basic day in Croatia runs about US$25 per day. **Tipping** is not expected, but you may round up to the nearest whole kuna; in some cases, the establishment will do it for you—check your change. Always try **bargaining.** If purchases exceed 500kn per bill, you may reclaim the **VAT** (PDV); ask the salesperson for form PDV-P. On leaving Croatia, the receipt has to be verified by the Croatian Customs Service. A PDV refund can be obtained within six months where the goods were purchased, or by posting the verified receipt back to the shop.

BUSINESS HOURS. Shops and banks are usually open between Monday and Friday 8am and 8pm, and on Saturday mornings. Most stores close for a long lunch.

ACCOMMODATIONS AND CAMPING

Two words: **private rooms.** Apart from the country's five **youth hostels** (in Zagreb, Pula, Zadar, Dubrovnik, and Punat) and **camping** (bring your own tent), they are the only affordable option. Look for *sobe* signs, especially near transportation stations. Agencies generally charge 30-50% more if you stay less than three nights. All accommodations are subject to a **tourist tax** of 5-10kn. If you opt for a hotel, call a few days in advance, especially during the summer. For info on HI hostels around Croatia, contact the **Croatian Youth Hostel Association** in Zagreb (☎482 92 94; fax 482 92 96; email hfhs@alf.tel.hr). Wherever you stay, hot water is ephemeral at best.

HEALTH AND SAFETY

Although Croatia is no longer at war, travel to the Slavonia and Krajina regions remains dangerous due to **unexploded mines. Crime** is rare. **Pharmacies** are generally well stocked with Western products. Croatians are friendly toward foreigners and sometimes a little too friendly to female travelers; going out in public with a companion will help ward off unwanted displays of machismo. Croatians are just beginning to accept **homosexuality;** discretion may be wise.

FOOD AND DRINK

Cuisine *à la* Hrvatska is defined by the country's geography; in continental Croatia around and east of Zagreb, typically heavy Slavic meals predominate, while on the coast, seafood blends with Italian pasta dishes. *Purica s mlincima* (turkey with pasta) is the regional dish near Zagreb, and spicy *Slavonian kulen* is considered one of the world's best sausages by the panel of fat German men who decide such things. Along the coast, try *lignje* (squid) or *Dalmatinski pršut* (Dalmatian smoked ham). The oysters from Ston Bay have received a number of awards; *slane sardele* (salted sardines) are a tasty (and cheaper) substitute. *Grešak varivo* (green bean stew), *tikvice va lešo* (steamed zucchini in olive oil), and *grah salata* (beans and onion salad) are meatless favorites. Croatia also offers excellent **wines;** price is usually the best indicator of quality. Mix red wine with tap water to get the popular *bevanda*, and white with carbonated water to get *gemišt*. *Karlovačko* and *Ožujsko* are the most popular beers, especially with fishermen.

COMMUNICATION

MAIL. Mail from the US arrives in 7 days or less; if addressed to *Poste Restante*, it will be held for 90 days at the main (not always the most central) post office. *Avionski* and *zrakoplovom* both mean **"airmail"** in Croatian.

TELEPHONES. Post offices usually have **public phones;** pay after you talk. All phones on the street require **phone cards** (*telekarta*), sold at all newsstands and post offices. Fifty "impulses" cost 23kn (1 impulse equals 3min. domestic, 36 seconds international; 50% discount 10pm-7am, Su, and holidays). Calls to the US are expensive (20kn per min.). **International direct dial numbers** include: **AT&T Direct** (☎0800 22 01 11); **BT Direct** (☎0800 22 00 44); **Canada Direct** (☎0800 22 01 01); **MCI WorldPhone** (☎0800 22 01 12); **Sprint** (☎0800 22 01 13). Technically, this operator assistance is free, but some phones demand a *telekarta* card.

LANGUAGES. Croats speak **Croatian** and write in Roman characters. Street designations on maps often differ from those on signs by "-va" or "-a" because of grammatical declensions. In Zagreb and most tourist offices, some people know **English,** but the most common language on the coast is **Italian.**

HOLIDAYS AND FESTIVALS

Holidays: New Year's Day (Jan. 1); Holy Trinity (Jan. 6); Catholic Easter (Apr. 23-24); Labor Day (May 1); Independence Day (May 30); Croatian National Uprising Day (June 22); Homeland Gratitude Day (Aug. 5); Feast of the Assumption (Aug. 15); All Saints' Day (Nov. 1); and Catholic Christmas (Dec. 25-26).

Festivals: Folklore fetishists flock to Zagreb for the **International Folklore Festival** (July 19-23), the premier gathering of European folk dancers and singing groups. The **Zagreb Summer Festival** (July 1-Aug. 15) hosts open-air concerts and theatrical performances. Wild **carnival celebrations,** including weekly masked balls (*maškare*), are held from mid-

Jan. to Ash Wednesday (the end of Feb. at the latest) on Korčula. The **Festival of Sword Dances** (Festival Viteških Igara) takes place each July in Korčula. During the **Dubrovnik Summer Festival** (July 10-Aug. 25), the city transforms into a cultural mecca, featuring theater, ballet, opera, classical music, and jazz.

ZAGREB ☎01

Zagreb (pop. 1 million) initially reminds a visitor of its unfortunate past with scars from recent wars with Serbia. But a stroll through its blooming gardens and Habsburg architecture shows it to be a place of great beauty, despite its troubling past. Fortunately for the visitor, Zagreb is in the midst of a vibrant rebirth.

PRACTICAL INFO, ACCOMMODATIONS, AND FOOD. Trains leave the **Glavni Kolodvor** station, Trg kralja Tomislava 12 (domestic ☎98 30; international ☎457 32 38), for: Ljubljana (2½hr., 5 per day, 87kn); Vienna (6½hr., 2 per day, 347kn); Budapest (7hr., 4 per day, 210kn); and Zurich (8hr., 1 per day, 680kn). To reach the main square, **Trg bana Josipa Jelačića,** with your back to the train station, walk across the street, staying along the left side of the park until it ends, and follow Praška. **Buses** (☎ (060) 31 33 33) head from **Autobusni Kolodvor,** Držićeva, to: Ljubljana (2hr., 3 per day, 70kn); Vienna (8hr., 2 per day, 180-190kn); and Sarajevo (9hr., 5per day, 207kn). Exit on Držićeva, turn left toward the bridge, and the main square will be on the left. The **tourist office** is at Trg b. Jelačića 11. (☎481 40 51. Open M-F 8:30am-8pm, Sa 10am-6pm, Su 10am-2pm.) All foreigners staying in private accommodations must register at their point of arrival within two days. In Zagreb, register at the **Department of Foreign Visitors** at the police station, Petrinjska 30, Room 101; use Form 14. (☎456 31 11. Open M-F 8am-2pm.) Hotels and hostels register guests automatically, bypassing this frustrating process. Get **Internet** access at **Art Net Club,** Prekadoviceva 25. (20kn per hr. Open daily 9am-11pm.)

Rooms in Zagreb are expensive. **Omladinski Turistićki Centar (HI),** Petrinjska 77, is perfectly located; from the train station, walk right on Branimirova, and Petrinjska will be on your left. (☎484 12 61; fax 484 12 69. Dorms 67kn, non-members 72kn; singles 149kn, with bath 202kn; doubles 204kn, 274kn.) **Hotel Ilica,** Ilica 102, has a friendly staff and satellite TVs in every room. From the train station, take tram #6 (dir. Črnomerec) to the second stop on Ilica. (☎377 75 22. Breakfast included. Singles 299kn; doubles 399kn; 3-person apts. 639kn; 4-person apts. 779kn.) **Baltazar,** Nova Ves 4, has expensive but magnificent local specialties in a very Croatian environment. (Entrees 30-70kn. Open daily 1pm-midnight.) There are **grocery** stores throughout the city, including **Konzum,** at Britanski Trg. 12. (Open M-F 7am-8pm, Sa 7am-9pm, Su 8am-1pm.) **Postal code:** 10000.

SIGHTS. Start your exploration of Zagreb by riding the funicular (uspinjača; 2kn), which connects Donji Grad and Gornji Grad from Tomiceva. From Trg b. Jelačica, walk down Ilica; Tomiceva will be on your right. **Lotrščak Tower** provides a spectacular view of the city. The Baroque masterpiece **St. Catherine's Church** is in the square to the right of the tower. Follow ul. Cirilometodska to Markov Trg. The colorful tiles of Gothic **St. Mark's Church** (Crkva sv. Marka) depict the coats of arms of Croatia, Dalmatia, and Slavonia on the left and of Zagreb on the right. The church also contains works by Ivan Meštrovic, Croatia's most famous sculptor. Follow ul. Kamenita to the **Stone Gate** (Kamenita Vrata), the only gate left from the original Gradec city walls. **Kaptol** hill is dominated by the 11th-century **Cathedral of the Assumption of the Virgin Mary** and its striking neo-Gothic bell towers. (Open M-Sa 10am-5pm, Su and holy days 1-5pm. Free.) Take an eight-minute bus ride from Kaptol to Mirogoj #1, the country's largest and most stunning cemetery. (Open M-F 6am-8pm, Su 7:30am-6pm. Free.) Zagreb's museums house Croatia's best artwork: the **Gallery of Modern Art,** Herbranga 1, displays 20th-century paintings. (Open M-Sa 10am-6pm, Su 10am-1pm. 20kn, students 10kn.) The **Ivan Meštrovic Foundation,** Mletačka 8, shows off the work of the master sculptor. (Open Tu-F 9am-2pm, Sa 10am-6pm. 10kn, students 5kn.)

ENTERTAINMENT AND NIGHTLIFE. Festival season opens with a concert by the **Vienna Symphony Orchestra** in April 2001, and a week of **contemporary dance** in May. Streets fill with performances of all kinds in the second week in June for the fifth-annual Zagreb street festival **Cest is d'Best** (the streets are the best). **Eurokaz,** a festival of avant-garde European theater, takes place annually at the end of June. Folklore fetishists will flock to Zagreb in July 2001, for the **International Folklore Festival,** the premier gathering of European folk dancers and singing groups. July and August host open-air concerts and theatrical performances during the **Zagreb Summer Festival;** some of the best concerts take place in the Muzejski Prostor Atrium, Jezuitski trg 4 (☎27 89 57). There is also a huge, annual **International Puppet Festival** at the beginning of September. The **Zagreb Jazz Fair** at the BP Club, Teslina 7, hosts Croatia's best jazz artists during October. **Zagreb Fest,** a pop festival, in November, attracts rock bands from all over Europe. A local favorite, the **Portugizac wine festival** at the end of October brings out revelers of all ages to end the festival season. For up-to-date information and schedules contact the **Zagreb Convetion Bureau** (☎481 43 43; fax 481 49 49; www.zagreb-convention.hr).

Dance and swim at the lakeside club **Aquarius,** Lake Jarun. To get there, take tram #117 to Srednjaci (third stop), turn around, cross the street, and follow one of the dirt paths to the lake, and walk along the boardwalk to the left until you reach the last building. (Cover 30kn. Open W-Su 10pm-4am.) Mix with locals and their beer at **Bulldog,** Bogoviceva 6. (Open M-Th and Su 9pm-1am, F-Sa 9pm-2am.)

NORTHERN COAST

As you head from Zagreb toward the coast, you'll approach the islands of the **Gulf of Kvarner,** blessed by long summers and gentle coastal breezes. Rab is one of the least touristed of the bunch. Farther north along the coast lies **Croatian Istria,** home to Pula, where the Mediterranean laps at the foot of the Alps. Today, the region seems almost more Italian than Croatian in language, tradition, and culture. Perhaps this has always been the case: colorful ancient fishing ports, countless craggy coves, and the deep blue-green hues of the sea led a Roman chronicler almost 2000 years ago to remark, "In Istria, Roman patricians feel like gods."

PULA ☎052

If you only get to visit one city in Istria, it should be Pula—not only for its fantastic beaches, but also for its winding medieval corridors, appealing cafes, and breathtaking first-century Roman **amphitheater** (the 2nd-largest in the world). From the bus station, take a left on Istarska to get there. (Open daily 7:30am-9pm. 16kn, students 8kn.) Follow Istarska in the opposite direction from the station to the **Arch of the Sergians** (Slavoluk obitelji Sergi), which dates from 29 BC; go through the gates and down bustling **ul. Sergijevaca** to the **Forum,** which holds the **Temple of Augustus** (Augustov hram), built between 2 BC and AD 14. Buy a bus ticket from any kiosk (8kn) and take bus #1 to the Stója campground or bus #2 toward the hostel to reach Pula's **beaches. Trains** (☎54 11 33 and 54 19 82) roll into the station at Kolodvorska 5 from Zagreb (7hr., 4 per day, 120-188kn) and Ljubljana (7½hr., 1 per day, 130kn). **Buses** (☎21 89 28), run from the station at Matta Balotta 6 to Trieste, Italy (3¾hr., 4 per day, 100kn) and Zagreb (5-6hr., 15 per day, 112kn). From the train station, facing the sea, walk left on Kolodvoska for five minutes, right at the amphitheater on Istarska to Giardini, past the bus stops in the garden, and right through the Arch of the Sergians to **Sergijevaca,** the main street. The **tourist office** is near the forum. (Open daily 9am-8pm.) Travel agencies help find **private rooms;** try **Arenaturist,** Giardini 4. (☎21 86 96; email arenaturist@pu.tel.hr.) To get to the **Omladinski Hostel (HI),** Zaljev Valsaline 4, walk right from the bus station on Istarska, take bus #2 (dir. Veruda) from the small park on Giardini to the last stop, and follow the signs. (☎39 11 33; email hfhspuls@pu.tel.hr. Breakfast included. 63-80kn.) **Postal code:** 52100.

THE FLASHY AND THE FLESHY Part of the coastline from Poreč south to Rovinj holds the title of the world's longest stretch of naturist, or nude, beaches, many of which are owned privately by naturist camps. Anyone interesting in getting naked should take off their clothes. Anyone interested in getting naked with other people should ask at any of the naturist camps to apply for a naturist membership card, as entrance to the camps is not permitted without one. No special attributes or equipment are necessary to obtain the card, though men are not allowed into the camps alone, even with membership.

NEAR PULA: BRIJUNI ARCHIPELAGO. To anyone remotely interested in Yugoslav history, a visit to beautiful Brijuni is essential. The largest island in the archipelago, **Veli Brijun** has been the site of a Roman resort, a Venetian colony, a cure for malaria, and the residence of former Yugoslav president Josip Bro° Tito. To see the island, you should get a guided tour. The **Brijuni Agency,** Brijunska 10, in Fazana, has the lowest rates. (]52 58 83 and 52 58 82; email np-brijuni®pu.tel.hr. Round-trip ferry and a 4hr. tour 160kn. One tour per day at 11:30am; call the day before to reserve a spot. Open daily 8am-8pm.) To get to Fazana, take a local bus from the station on Istarske Divizije in Pula (20min., every hr., 10kn).

RAB ☎051

An extraordinarily beautiful town whose narrow streets and whitewashed stone houses seem to rise out of the sea, Rab will seduce you with its beaches and buildings. A stroll along Gornja ul. runs from the remains of **St. John's Church** (Crkva sv. Jvana), an outstanding Roman basilica, to **St. Justine's Church** (Crkva sv. Justine), which houses a museum of Christian art. (Open daily 9am-noon and 7:30-10pm. 7kn.) Sunsets from the top of **St. Mary's Bell Tower,** circa 13th century, are truly stupendous. (Open daily 10am-1pm and 7:30-10pm.) The 12th-century **Virgin Mary Cathedral** (Katedrala Djevice Marije) and nearby 14th-century **St. Anthony's Monastery** (Samostan sv. Antuna) lie farther down Gornja ul. Rab's greatest assets are its **beaches,** scattered all over the island; ask at the tourist office for transport info. **Buses** arrive from Zagreb (5½hr., 3 per day, 121kn). The **tourist office** is on the other side of the bus station. (☎77 11 11. Open daily 8am-10pm.) **Katurbo,** M. de Dominisa, between the bus station and the town center, arranges **private rooms.** (☎/fax 72 44 95. Open daily 7:30am-10pm. Singles 50-80kn; 2-person studio 260-260kn. 30% surcharge on stays less than 3 nights. Tourist tax 4.50-7.60kn.) Walk along the bay to reach **Camping Padova,** 2km east of the bus station. (☎72 43 55; fax 72 45 31. 22kn per person; 20kn per tent; daily tax 7kn; registration fee 4kn.) A **supermarket** is in the basement of **Merkur,** Palit 71, across from the tourist office. (Open M-Sa 6:30am-9pm, Su 6:30-11am.) **Postal code:** 51280.

DALMATIAN COAST

Stretching from the Rijeka harbor to Dubrovnik in the south, Croatia's coast is a stunning seascape of hospitable locals and unfathomable beauty. With more than 1100 islands (only 66 of which are inhabited), Dalmatia boasts the Mediterranean's largest archipelago and cleanest waters, bronze beaches, and Roman ruins.

SPLIT ☎021

The aesthetic appeal of Split's female population is rivaled only by the geography and architecture of this palace-city by the sea. The **Stari Grad** (Old Town), wedged between a high mountain range and palm-lined waterfront, sprawls around a luxurious **palace** where Roman Emperor Diocletian, known for his violent persecution of Christians, used to summer. The **cellars** of the city are located near the entrance to the palace, under a flag just past the line of taxis on the waterfront; turn in either direction to wander around this labyrinth, with its archaeological and modern art displays. (Open M-F 10am-1pm and 6-8pm, Sa 10am-1pm. 6kn.) Through the cellars and up the stairs is the open-air **peristyle,** a colonnaded square, and the open-domed **vestibule,** which serves as the backstage during the **Summer Festival.** (Free during the day.) The **cathedral** on the right side of the peristyle was originally the mausoleum of Diocletian. (Open daily 7am-noon and 4-7pm.) A 25-minute walk away along the waterfront, the **Meštrović Gallery,** Setaliste Ivana Meštrovica 46, features a mind-blowing collection of Croatia's most famous modern sculptor. (Open in summer Tu-Sa 10am-6pm, Su 10am-3pm; off season Tu-Sa 10am-4pm, Su 10am-2pm. 15kn, students 10kn. English booklet 5kn.)

Trains (☎32 85 25) go from Obala kneza Domagoja 10 to: Zagreb (7½hr., 4 per day, 65kn); Ljubljana (12hr., 2 per week, 152kn); and Budapest (16hr., 1 per night, 225kn). **Buses** (☎34 50 47) go to: Dubrovnik (4½hr., 15 per day, 65-84kn); Sarajevo (7½hr., 6 per day, 143kn); Zagreb (8hr., every 30min., 86-113kn); and Ljubljana (11hr., 1 per day, 193kn). **Ferries** (☎35 53 99) chug to Dubrovnik (8hr., 5 per week, 139kn) and Ancona, Italy (10hr., 4 per week, 311kn). The **train** and **bus stations** lie across from the ferry terminal on Obala kneza Domagoja. From the train or bus station, follow Obala kneza Domagoja to the waterside mouthful **Obala hrvatskog narodnog preporoda,** which runs roughly east-west. The **tourist office** is at Obala hrv. narodnog preporoda 12. (☎34 21 42. Open M-F 7:30am-8pm, Sa 8am-3pm.) The **Daluma Travel Agency,** Obala kneza domagoja 1, helps find **private rooms.** (☎33 84 84; email daluma-st@st.tel.hr. May-Oct. singles 100kn, doubles 200kn; Nov.-Apr. 80kn, 160kn. Open M-F 8am-8pm, Sa 8am-12:30pm.) To get from the stations to a bed at **Prenoćište Slavija,** Buvinova 2, follow Obala hrv. narodnog preporoda, turn right on Trg Braće Radića, go right on Mihovilova širina, and go up the stairs in the left-hand corner. (☎34 70 53; fax 59 15 58. Breakfast included. Singles 180-220kn; doubles 210-260kn; triples 250-300kn; quads 280-360kn.) There is a **supermarket** at Svačićeva 4. (Open daily 7am-10pm.) **Postal code:** 21000.

CROATIA

KORČULA ☎020

The central Dalmatian island of Korčula (KOR-chu-lah), stretching parallel to the nearby mainland, is full of exceptional grace and culture. Its sacred monuments and churches date from the time of the Apostles, and its **Festival of Sword Dances** (July 5-Aug. 23, 2001; tickets available at tourist office or hotel reception desks; 40kn) give it a distinctive personality. Korčula can be reached by **buses,** which board a short ferry to the mainland and head to: Dubrovnik (3½hr., 1 per day, 58kn); Sarajevo (6½hr., 4 per week, 145kn); and Zagreb (11-13hr., 1 per day, 190kn). **Ferries** run to Dubrovnik (3½hr., 5 per week, 64kn). To get to the **tourist office,** face the water and walk left around the peninsula to Hotel Korčula; the office is next door. (☎71 57 01; fax 71 58 66. Open M-Sa 8am-3pm and 4-9pm.) **Private rooms** are the only budget accommodations available; **Marko Polo,** Biline 5, will arrange one for you. (☎71 54 00; fax 71 58 00; email marko-polo-tours@du.tel.hr. Singles 76-192kn; doubles 100-212kn; triples 140-272kn. Tourist tax 4.50-7kn. Open daily 8am-10pm.) **Postal code:** 20260.

DUBROVNIK ☎020

George Bernard Shaw said that "those who seek Paradise on earth should come to Dubrovnik." He wasn't far off the mark—if you make it as far south as Dubrovnik, you might never leave. Nearly scarless despite recent wars, Dubrovnik captivates visitors with azure waters and copper sunsets atop 14th-century city walls.

PRACTICAL INFO, ACCOMMODATIONS, AND FOOD. Jadrolinija **ferries** (☎41 80 00) leave from opposite Obala S. Radića 40 for Split (8hr., 1 per day, 80kn) and Bari, Italy (9hr., 2 per week, 270kn). **Buses** (☎35 70 88) go to: Split (4½hr., 14 per day, 47-85kn); Sarajevo (6hr., 2 per day, 163kn); Zagreb (11hr., 8 per day, 173kn); and Trieste (15hr., 1 per day, 225kn). To reach Stari Grad, face the bus station, walk around the building, turn left on ul. Ante Starčević, and follow it uphill to the Old Town's western entrance (30min.). Or, to reach the ferry terminal, head left (with your back to the bus station) and then bear right. To get

BUT IT'S SO CHEAP Descending wearily from the ferry or bus in Dubrovnik, you will hear chants of *sobe!*, *rooms!*, and *zimmer!* from the throngs of ladies done up in their Sunday best. While the prospect of a place to lie down with an appealing price tag may seem ideal, there are a few considerations to keep in mind before you tramp off with the lady of your choice. If Dubrovnik is your first stop in Croatia, you must **register with the police.** If the rooms you see are sanctioned by the tourist bureau—that is, if a stamped and signed document with the price listed is posted in the room, then you're good to go. If there is no such paper posted, do not stay, as they cannot register you. If the police find you unregistered for any reason, you will receive a large fine. Besides that, rooms that have not been inspected by the tourist bureau may not meet the bureau requirements—hot water and clean sheets, for example. So, pick your woman wisely.

to the **tourist office,** C. Zuzorić 1/2, walk to the end of Placa, turn right at St. Blasius' Church and the coffee shop Gradska Kavana, and take the first right. (☎42 63 03. Open M-Sa 8am-3pm, Sa 9am-1pm, Su 9am-noon.) For two people a **private room** is cheapest (singles 100-150kn; doubles 120-180kn); arrange one through the tourist office or **Atlas,** on Lučrica 1, next to St. Blasius' Church. (☎44 25 28; www.atlas-croatia.com. Open in summer M-Sa 8am-9pm, Su 9am-1pm; off season M-Sa 8am-7pm.) For cheaper rooms, try your luck with the women around the ferry and bus terminals, but bear in mind the warning below. The **HI youth hostel** at b. Josipa Jelačića 15/17 is one of the best in Croatia. From the bus station, walk up ul. Ante Starčević, turn right after 10 minutes at the lights, turn right on b. Josipa Jelačića, and look for the hidden HI sign on your left right before #17. (☎42 32 41. Breakfast included. Check-out 10am. Curfew 2am. Open May-Dec. 65-87kn.) Call ahead to the cozy **Begović Boarding House,** Primorska 17, for a ride from the station. Or, from the bus station, take bus #6 toward Dubrava and tell the driver to let you off at Post Office Lapud; facing the pedestrian walkway, turn right at the intersection, bear left, turn right onto Primorska, and continue to the top of the hill. (☎42 85 63. Reserve at least 10 days in advance. 75-85kn.) **Marco Polo,** Lučarica 6, is a local favorite that serves meat dishes for 45-76kn. (Open daily 10am-midnight.) Behind St. Blasius' Church, on Gunduliceva Poljana, you'll find an open **market. Mediator supermarket,** Od puča 4, faces the market. (Open M-Sa 6:30am-9pm, Su 7am-9pm.) **Postal code:** 20000.

SIGHTS. The most impressive legacy of this former naval city-state are the staggering **city walls** (gradske zidine), the entrance to which lies just inside the Pile Gate on the left. Make sure you have a camera and an hour for the 2km walk along the top. (Open daily 8am-sunset. 10kn, children 5kn.) The beautiful Renaissance **Franciscan Monastery** (Franjevački samostan), next to the city wall entrance on Placa, houses the oldest working pharmacy in Croatia and a pharmaceutical museum. (Open daily 9am-6pm. 5kn.) The **Renaissance Sponza Palace** and its bell tower mark the end of Placa and house the city archives. (Open daily 10am-2pm and 7-11pm. 5kn.) Across from the Sponza Palace stands the **Church of St. Blasius** (Crkva sv. Vlaha), who can be seen in statues adorning nearly every 10m of the city walls. (Open daily 9am-noon and 6-9pm.) The **Dominican Monastery** (Dominikanski samostan), Sv. Dominikanska 4, between the city walls and the Old Port, is still home to monks of the order. Inside, you'll find a museum comprising the cloister and sacristy, as well as most of Dubrovnik's religious art. (Open daily 9am-6pm. Museum 5kn.) Behind the Church of St. Blasius on Drzićeva Poljana stands another Renaissance prize, the **Rector's Palace** (Knežev Dvor), which houses 16th- and 18th-century weaponry, paintings, coins, and furniture. (Open M-Sa 9am-7pm. 10kn, students 5kn.) The **Cathedral** (riznica) dominates Bunićeva Poljana. Its treasury holds saintly relics, including the "Diapers of Jesus," which date to the year 0 and are from Jerusalem. (Open daily 8am-5pm. 5kn.) The 4000 Bosnian Muslims in Dubrovnik come to pray at the tiny

Islamic Mosque, Miha Pracata 3, the eighth street off Placa from the Pile Gate. (Open daily 10am-1pm and 8-9pm.) Around the corner from the mosque is the 19th-century **Serbian Orthodox Church,** Od Puča 8, and its Museum of Icons (Muzej Ikona). (Open M-Sa 9am-1pm. 10kn.)

ENTERTAINMENT AND NIGHTLIFE. In summer, the **Dubrovnik Summer Festival** (Dubrovački Ljetni Festival; ☎ (02) 42 88 64; July 10-Aug. 15, 2001) turns the city into a cultural mecca for theater, ballet, opera, classical music, and jazz lovers. Head to the island of **Lokrum** for a **nude beach;** ferries run from the Old Port (15min., 2 per hr. 9am-8pm, round-trip 20kn). Once there, take a break from the sun to stroll through the **botanical garden** and look back on Dubrovnik from the fortress.

Dubrovnik is by far the liveliest Croatian city at night. Locales boast a wide variety of music, you can almost always find a live band in the summer, and most importantly, many bars will stay open until 4 or 5am every night. Crowds gravitate in a few areas; often, they overflow from **Stari Grad** and the cafes on **Buničeva Poljana.** Another great center of nightlife is outside the city walls on **B. Josipa Jelačica** by the youth hostel, otherwise known as **Bourbon Street.**

As tempting as it may be to stroll in the hills above **Dubrovnik** or to wander down unpaved paths on **Lopud** island, both may still be laced with **landmines;** stick to the paved paths and beach.

EXCURSION FROM DUBROVNIK: LOPUD ISLAND

Less than an hour from Dubrovnik, Lopud is an enchanting island of the Elafiti Archipelago. The tiny village, dotted with white buildings, chapels, and parks, stretches along the island's waterfront (*obala*). Currently under renovation, **Dorđič Mayneri** remains among the most beautiful parks in Croatia. Signs from Kavana Dubrava on the waterfront point to the **museum,** the meeting place for tours of the church, museum, and monastery. (Tours Th 9am.) The island's absolute highlight is its **beach, Plaza Šunj.** Arguably the best beach in Croatia, it has all the qualities that most places on the Dalmatian Coast lack: sand, waves, and a secluded cove.

Ferries run from Dubrovnik to the Elafiti islands (50min., 1-2 per day, round-trip 25kn). The beach is on the opposite side of the island from the village. On the road between the high wall and the palm park, look for the "Konoba Barbara" sign and turn off the road onto a large path. Ignore small paths branching off; when the path forks, keep right.

CYPRUS (ΚΥΠΡΟΣ)

CYPRUS POUNDS

US$1 = £0.67	1£ = US$1.50
CDN$1 = £0.45	1£ = CDN$2.22
EUR€1 = £0.57	1£ = EUR€1.74
UK£1 =£0.94	1£ = UK£1.07
IR£1 = £0.73	1£ = IR£1.37
AUS$1 = £0.37	1£ = AUS$0.27
NZ$1 = £0.29	1£ = NZ$3.49
SAR1 = £0.09	1£ = SAR10.68
GRDR100 = £0.17	1£ = GRDR590.21

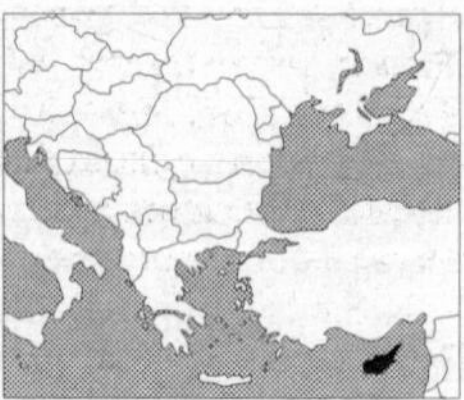

Country code: 357. **International dialing prefix:** 080. From outside Cyprus, dial int'l dialing prefix (see inside back cover) + 357 + city code + local number.

CYPRUS

Aphrodite blessed Cyprus with an abundance of natural beauty, from the sandy beaches of Agia Napa to the serene Troodos Mountains. After long-standing territorial disputes and a Turkish invasion, the island was left partitioned in 1974 among Greeks in the south and Turks in the north, divided by the UN-manned Green Line. Restrictions prohibit travel from north to south except for tourists making short daytrips across the Green Line in Nicosia. *Let's Go: Europe* only includes coverage of southern Cyprus; for more coverage of this lovely isle, dig *Let's Go: Greece 2000.* Journeys to northern Cyprus require careful planning and must begin in Turkey. For info on northern Cyprus, see *Let's Go: Turkey 2000.*

ESSENTIALS

EMBASSIES

Passports are required of all visitors to Cyprus; citizens of South Africa (but not Australia, Canada, Ireland, New Zealand, the UK, or the US) need **visas.** Foreign embassies and consulates are all located in **Nicosia.**

Cypriot Embassies at Home: Australia, 30 Beale Cr., Deakin Canberra ACT 2600 (☎ 62 81 08 32; fax 62 81 08 60); **Canada,** Toronto, 365 Bloor St. E., Suite 1010, Box #43, ON M4W 3L4 (☎ (416) 944 09 98; fax 944 91 49); Montréal, 2930 Rue Edouard Mont Petit, Suite PH2, QC H3T 1J7 (☎ (514) 735 72 33); **Greece,** Odos Irodotou 16, Athens (☎ 723 27 27; fax 723 19 27); **UK,** 93 Park St., London W1Y 4ET (☎ (0171) 499 82 72; fax 491 06 91); **US,** 2211 R St. NW, Washington, D.C. 20008 (☎ (202) 462 57 72; fax 483 67 10).

GETTING THERE AND GETTING AROUND

Olympic Airlines (US ☎ (800) 223 12 26; Cyprus ☎ (02) 46 21 01), **Egypt Air** (US ☎ (800) 334 67 87), and **Cyprus Airways** (US ☎ (212) 714 21 90; Cyprus ☎ (02) 44 30 54) offer **flights** to the Republic of Cyprus. Student fare from Athens is about US$150 roundtrip. The international airports are in **Paphos** and **Larnaka.** An island-wide **bus schedule** is available at tourist offices. Another affordable option is **shared taxis;** each taxi seats four to seven passengers. (Taxis run every 30min. M-Sa 5:45am-7:30pm, Su 7am-6:30pm; in winter M-Sa 5:45am-6:30pm, Su 7am-5:30pm. £2.10-5.50.) After 7pm, transportation is limited to private taxis. By **ferry,** both **Limassol** and **Larnaka** are accessible from a number of points, including **Rhodes, Crete,** and **Hafia, Israel.** Schedules are available at the ports; expect to pay around £45 for a ferry to Cyprus, a few pounds more if your trip begins in Israel.

TOURIST SERVICES AND TELEPHONES

> **!** Dial ☎ **199** for **ambulance, fire,** or **police** in Cyprus. **192** for **night pharmacies.**

Tourist offices in Cyprus (in **Limassol, Nicosia, Larnaka, Paphos, Polis, Agia Napa,** and **Platres**) are extremely helpful and efficient. The **Cyprus Tourism Organization (CTO),** P.O. Box 4535, Limassol 19, Nicosia CY 1390 (☎ (02) 337 715; fax 331 644; email cto@cyta.com.cy), provides free maps and info on buses, museums, and events. A helpful publication available at tourist offices is *The Cyprus Traveler's Handbook* (free). Officials generally speak English, Greek, German, and French.

In Southern Cyprus, direct overseas calls can be made from all public phones. **Telecards** are available in denominations of £2, £3, £5, and £10 and are sold at banks and kiosks. Private phones in hotels may have a 10% surcharge.

LARNAKA (Λαρνακα) ☎04

Although many tourists come to Larnaka for its **beaches,** the wonders of its **archaeological digs** are more impressive. Larnaka was built over the 13th-century BC city of **Kition** and retains monuments from its long history. The **temple** complex of Kition is the oldest spot in Larnaka. (Open M-F 7:30am-5pm. £0.75.) The remains of Lazarus, the biblical figure who rose from the dead, lie in the **Church of Agios Lazarus,** one block west of the fortress. (Open daily 8am-12:30pm and 3:30-6:30pm. £0.50. Modest dress required.) The private **Pierides Foundation Museum,** 4 Zinonos Kitieos, showcases artifacts spanning 3000 years of Cypriot history. (Open M-F 9am-1pm and 3-6pm, Sa 9am-1pm, Su 11am-1pm. 18+. £1.) Two kilometers west of Larnaka Airport, the **Hala Sultan Tekke Mosque** houses the tomb of Umm Haram, Muhammad's maternal aunt. Take bus #19 to Kiti (15min.; £0.50), then walk 1km from the "Tekke." (Open daily in summer 7:30am-7:30pm. Free.) At night, check out the beachfront pubs and eateries on **Athinon.** If you're disappointed by Larnaka's dusty shores, daytrip to **Agia Napa** (Αγια Ναπα), a tourist resort with white, sandy beaches and a raucous nightlife; hop on a **bus** (5-10 per day, £1) from Larnaka. **Cinderella Flats,** on Makarios Ave. in Agia Napa, above the leather shop, is close to nightlife. (☎ 72 21 48. Singles £14; doubles £16.)

Most **flights** to Cyprus land at the Larnaka airport; take **bus** #19 (M-Sa in summer 6:20am-7pm; in winter 6:20am-5:45pm; £0.50) or a taxi (£3-5) to the town center. **Buses** leave from Athinon for Nicosia (4-6 per day, £2) and Limassol (3-4 per day, £1.70). One **tourist office** is at the airport (☎ 64 30 00; open 24hr.); another is at Pl. Vasileos Pavlou (☎ 65 43 22; hours vary). The **Youth Hostel (HI),** Nikolaou Rossou 27, in Pl. Ag. Lazarus, is in a former mosque. (☎ 62 11 88. £4.) **Postal codes:** 6900, 6902.

LIMASSOL (Λεμεσος) ☎05

Limassol is a transport hub and the point of arrival or departure by sea. **Poseidon Lines** (☎ 74 56 66; open M-F 8am-noon and 3-5pm, Sa 10am-2pm) and **Salamis Tours** (☎ 35 55 55) run ferries to: **Haifa, Israel** (11hr., 2 per week, £50); **Rhodes, Greece** (18hr., 2 per week, £44); and **Piraeus via Rhodes** (45hr., 2 per week, £47). **Buses** traverse the island (check times with the tourist office): **KEMEK** (☎ 74 75 32), 400m north of the castle at the corner of Irinis and Enosis, serves Nicosia (M-F 5 per day, Sa 3 per day; £1.50) and Paphos (6-10 per week, M-Sa 9am, £1.50); **Kallenos** (☎ 65 48 50) heads for Larnaka (M-Sa 3-4 per day, £1.70). **Service taxis** are a more personal but expensive option, running 6am-6:30pm to Nicosia (£3.45), Larnaka (£3), and Paphos (£2.50). Contact **Makris** (☎ 36 55 50). **Postal code:** 3900.

TROODOS (Τροοδος) AND PLATRES (Πλατρες) ☎05

With crisp mountain air, authentic village life, and Byzantine churches tucked among its pine-covered mountains, the Troodos are the perfect escape for hikers who wish to avoid Cyprus' summer heat. In winter, **Mt. Olympus,** the highest point in Cyprus (1951m), is host to hundreds of skiers.

Platres is an inexpensive base for exploring the Troodos Mountains. The town of **Troodos** is 10km (and a £5 taxi ride) from Platres. Four spectacular hikes originate near Troodos; maps are available at all tourist offices. From Troodos, **Artemis** begins 200m up the road to Prodromos. The circular trail wraps around **Mt. Olympus** for 7km (3½ hr.), providing majestic views of Cyprus. From the Troodos post office, the **Atalante** trail mimics the Artemis trail at a lower altitude. A fresh mountain spring 3km into the hike sustains the photo-happy. The 3km **Persephone** trail leaves from the coffee shop in Pl. Troodos and gradually descends to a divine lookout point among huge limestone slabs. The **Kaledonia** trail, the shortest of the four, begins 2km from Troodos on the road to Platres, passes the **Kaledonia Falls,** and ends at the **Psilo Dentro** restaurant near Platres. Platres is fairly accessible by public transportation, although bus schedules change frequently and often run 30 minutes late. **Zingas Bus** (☎463 989) in **Lefkosia** (South Nicosia), runs to Platres (M-Sa 12:15pm, £2) on a reservation basis. The **tourist office,** at 4820 Pano Platres, is left of the parking lot in the *plateia* (square). (☎421 316. Open M-F 9am-3:30pm, Sa 9am-2:30pm.) From the post office, go down the hill and left to find the simple rooms at the **Kallithea Hotel.** (☎421 746. Breakfast included. Doubles £11.)

PAPHOS (Παφος) ☎06

Travelers flock to Paphos' celebrated blend of limestone remnants and sandy shores. The upper section of town, **Ktima Paphos,** referred to simply as "Paphos," centers around Pl. Kennedy, while the lower **Kato Paphos** hosts the city's nightlife. Kato Paphos features over 2000 sq. meters of mosaic floors, depicting scenes from Greek mythology and daily life, in the 2nd-century **House of Dionysus,** the **House of Theseus,** and the **House of Aion.** (Open daily 7:30am-7:30pm. £1.) Ag. Pavlou holds the musty **Catacombs,** including a chapel with deteriorating Byzantine frescoes dedicated to **St. Solomoni** (Hannah). **St. Paul** was whipped for preaching Christianity at **St. Paul's Pillar.** The **Tomb of the Kings,** a World Heritage site, is 2km up the road of the same name; take bus #15. Local aristocracy, not kings, were interred in the tombs. (Open 8am-7:30pm. £0.75.) Ktima Paphos boasts the **Paphos Archaeology Museum** (open M-F 7:30am-2:30pm and 3-5pm, Sa-Su 10am-1pm; £0.75), the **Ethnographic Museum,** Exo Vrysi 1 (open M-Sa 9am-6pm, Su 10am-1pm; £1), and the **Byzantine Museum,** 25th Martiou 26 (open M-F 9am-5pm, Sa 9am-1pm; £1).

Nea Amoroza Co. buses, Pallikaridi 79 (☎23 68 22), in Pl. Kennedy, go to **Polis** (M-F, 10 per day, £1). Contact **Travel&Express** (☎23 31 81 or ☎077 74 74), on Eagorou, for service **taxis** to Limassol (every 30min., M-Sa 5:45am-6:30pm, Su 7am-5:30pm; £2.50). The **tourist office** is at Gladstone 3. (☎23 28 1. Open M-Tu and Th-F 8:15am-2:30pm and 3-5:15pm, W and Sa 8:15am-1:30pm.) **Triaron Hotel Guest House** is at Makarios 99. (☎23 21 93. Singles £5; doubles £7.) To get to the **Youth Hostel (HI),** El. Venizelou 45, leave the *plateia* on Pallikaridi, walk until Venizelou, then turn right. (☎23 25 88. 1st night £5; additional nights £4.) Nightlife centers around **Agias Napas,** a couple blocks inland from the waterfront in Kato Paphos.

CZECH REPUBLIC
(ČESKÁ REPUBLIKA)

KORUNA (CSK)

US$1 = 39KČ	10KČ = US$0.25
CDN$1 = 27KČ	10KČ = CDN$0.37
UK£1 = 58KČ	10KČ = UK£0.17
IR£1 = 45KČ	10KČ = IR£0.22
AUS$1 = 23KČ	10KČ = AUS$0.44
NZ$1 = 17KČ	10KČ = NZ$0.59
SAR1 = 5.70KČ	10KČ = SAR0.18
DM1 = 18KČ	10KČ = DM0.55
EUR€1 = 35KČ	10KČ = EUR€0.28

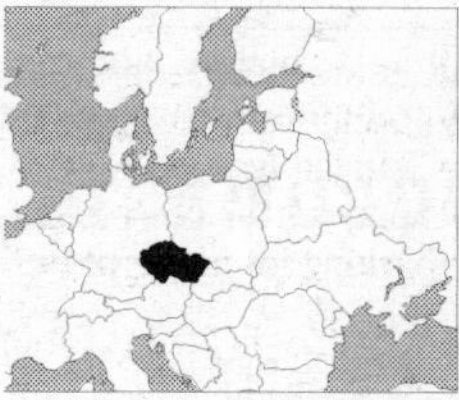

Country code: 420. **International dialing prefix:** 00. From outside the Czech Republic, dial int'l dialing prefix (see inside back cover) + 420 + city code + local number.

In November of 1989, following the demise of Communist governments in Hungary and Poland and the fall of the Berlin Wall, Czechs peacefully threw off the Communists and chose dissident playwright Václav Havel to lead them westward. Havel attempted to preserve the Czech-Slovak union, but on New Year's Day, 1993, after more than 75 years of relatively calm coexistence, the two nations split bloodlessly. Czechs for the most part are embracing westernization, although the notion of self-determination is relatively new to them. From the Holy Roman Empire through the Nazis and Soviets, foreigners have driven Czech internal affairs; even the 1968 Prague Spring was frozen by the iron rumble of Soviet tanks. The Czechs, unlike many of their neighbors, have rarely fought back as countries have marched through their borders; as a result, their towns and cities are among the best-preserved in Europe. Today, they face a different kind of invasion, as tourists sweep in to savor the magnificent capital, charming locals, and the world's best beer.

Check out the Czech Republic in *Let's Go: Eastern Europe 2001*.

FACTS AND FIGURES

Official Name: Czech Republic.

Government: Parliamentary Democracy.

Capital: Prague.

Land Area: 78,864 sq. km.

Geography: Plateaus and mountains.

Climate: Temperate; cool summers, cold, cloudy, humid winters.

Major Cities: Prague, Brno, Ostrava.

Population: 10.3 million.

Languages: Czech.

Religions: Catholic (39%), Protestant (4%).

Average Income: US$11,300.

Major Exports: Machinery and transport equipment, other manufactured goods.

DISCOVER THE CZECH REPUBLIC

Everything you've heard is true: from the medieval alleys of Staré Město and the fabulous Baroque and art nouveau architecture to the world's best (and cheapest) beer, **Prague** is the starlet of Central Europe (p. 249). An interesting (if spooky) daytrip awaits in nearby **Kutná Hora** (p. 263), where femurs and crania hang from the ceilings and chandeliers. In Western Bohemia, international hipsters flock to **Karlovy Vary** (p. 264) every summer for its film festival and its

Becherovka, a local herb liqueur with "curative powers" rivaled only by those of the many local hot springs. In Southern Bohemia, **Český Krumlov** (p. 265), everybody's favorite town, charms visitors with its 13th-century castle, a medieval summer festival, and the best nightlife this side of the Vltava.

ESSENTIALS

WHEN TO GO

Spring and fall are the best times to visit, although spring can be rainy. Summer is drier, but the crowds mob the country. Winters are very cold, damp, and snowy.

DOCUMENTS AND FORMALITIES

Americans may visit the Czech Republic without a **visa** for up to 30 days, Irish and New Zealand citizens for up to 90 days, and Canadian and UK citizens for up to 180 days. Australians and South Africans must obtain 30-day tourist visas. Visas are available at an embassy or consulate, but not at the border. Single-entry visas cost US$28 for Australians, and US$22 for citizens of most other countries, while 90-day multiple-entry visas cost US$28 for Australians, US$84 for citizens of most other countries. Prices for single and double-entry transit visas are the same as those for other single-entry visas. A multiple-entry transit visa costs US$84. The maximum stay in the Czech Republic is five days per transit visa; all transit visas are valid for 90 days. Travelers on a visa must register with the Czech Immigration Police within three days of arrival; guests in hotels are registered automatically.

EMBASSIES AND CONSULATES

All foreign embassies are in **Prague** (see p. 252).

Czech Embassies at Home: Australia, 38 Culgoa Circuit, O'Malley, Canberra, ACT 2606 (☎ (02) 62 90 13 86; fax 62 90 00 06;canberra@embassy.mzv.cz); **Canada,** 541 Sussex Dr., Ottawa, ON K1N 6Z6 (☎ (613) 562 38 75; fax 562 38 78; email ottowa@embassy.mzv.cz); **Ireland,** 57 Northumberland Rd., Ballsbridge, Dublin 4 (☎ (3531) 668 11 35; fax 668 16 60); **New Zealand** (honorary consul), 48 Hair St., Wainuiomata, Wellington (☎/fax (644) 564 60 01); **South Africa,** 936 Pretorius St., Arcadia, Pretoria; P.O. Box 3326, Pretoria 0001 (☎ (012) 342 34 77; fax 43 20 33); **UK,** 26 Kensington Palace Gardens, London W8 4QY (☎ (020) 72 43 11 15; fax 77 27 96 54; london@embassy.mzv.cz); **US,** 3900 Spring of Freedom St. NW, Washington, D.C. 20008 (☎ (202) 274 91 00; fax 966 85 40; www.czech.cz/washington/).

GETTING THERE AND GETTING AROUND

BY PLANE. Air France, British Airways, ČSA, Delta, KLM, Lufthansa, and **Swissair** are among the major carriers into Prague.

BY TRAIN. The most economical way to enter the country is by **train. Eastrail** is accepted in the Czech Republic, but **Eurail** is valid only with a special supplement. The fastest trains are *EuroCity* and *InterCity* (*expresní*, marked in blue on schedules). *Rychlík* trains, also known as *zrychlený vlak*, are fast domestic trains, marked in red on schedules. Avoid slow *osobní* trains, marked in white. **ČSD,** the national transportation company, publishes the monster *Jízdní řád* train schedule (74Kč), which has a two-page English explanation. *Odjezdy* (departures) are printed in train stations on yellow posters, *příjezdy* (arrivals) on white. Seat reservations (*místenka;* 10Kč) are recommended on express and international trains and for all first-class seating; snag them at the counter with a boxed "R."

BY BUS. Buses are the preferred means of domestic travel, but are inefficient for crossing borders. **ČSAD** runs national and international bus lines. Consult the timetables posted at stations or buy your own bus schedule (25Kč) from kiosks.

BY CAR, BY BIKE, AND BY THUMB. It is not necessary to have an International Driving Permit, but having one won't hurt. **Speed limits** in residential areas are 50kph, on expressways 130kph, and 90kph on all other roads. Always park in guarded lots, as there is a high incidence of car theft. The blood alcohol limit is **zero.** In an **emergency,** dial ☎ 1230 or ☎ 1240, or contact **Ustřední Automotoklub ČR (UAMK),** Na Štrži, 146 01, Praha 4 (☎ (02) 61 10 41 11; fax 43 14 21; www.uamk.cz). For help planning your trip, contact **Autoturist,** at the same address (☎ (2) 61 10 43 33). **Biking** is common in Southern Bohemia; roads and bike trails are in good condition and motorists yield bikers the right of way. You can rent bikes from most hotels and hostels and through major tourist offices. **Hitchhikers** report success in the Czech Republic. *Let's Go* does not recommend hitchhiking.

TOURIST SERVICES AND MONEY

EMERGENCIES. Fire: ☎ 150. **Ambulance:** ☎ 155. **Police:** ☎ 158.

TOURIST OFFICES. CKM, a junior affiliate of the communist dinosaur Čedok, is helpful for the budget and student traveler, serving as a clearinghouse for youth hostel beds and issuing ISICs and HI cards. **Municipal tourist offices** in major cities provide printed matter on sights and cultural events, as well as lists of hostels and hotels. If they're nice, they might even book you a room.

MONEY. The Czech unit of currency is the **koruna** (crown), plural *koruny* (Kč). **ATMs** are everywhere—look for the red and black "Bankomat" signs—and offer the best exchange rates available. **Traveler's checks** can be exchanged almost everywhere, if at times for an obscene commission. **Komerční banka** and **Česká spořitelna** are common bank chains. Mastercard and Visa are accepted at most expensive places, but rarely at hostels.

A bare-bones day in the Czech Republic (sleeping in campgrounds, shopping at grocery stores) will run US$10; a more extravagant day (hostels/hotels, eating in restaurants) costs no more than US$25. To **tip,** add about 10% to the cost of your meal and tell the waiter the new amount; don't leave a few *koruny* on the table, as it is considered offensive. Visitors can apply for **value added tax** (VAT) reimbursement when leaving the country. The minimum price of a single item to be refunded is 1000Kč. Refunds are available for of all purchases made within 30 days prior to their departure from the country. Foreigners must claim the reimbursement at the store where they bought the goods within three months after the day of purchase.

THE WORLD'S MOST DIFFICULT SOUND Not quite a Spanish "r" and simply not the Polish "rz" (e.g., the second "g" in "garage"), Czech's own linguistic blue note, the letter "ř," lies excruciatingly in between. Although many of Prague's expats would sacrifice a month of Saturdays at Jo's Bar to utter the elusive sound just once, few manage more than a strangely trilled whistle. Most foreigners resign themselves to using the "ž" (akin to the Polish "rz") in its place, but what we consider a subtle difference often confuses Czechs. For all those linguistic daredevils in the audience, here's a surefire method of tackling the randy Mr. Ř: roll your tongue and quickly follow with a "ž", then repeat. Oh, yeah—and start when you're two.

BUSINESS HOURS. **Banks** are roughly open Monday to Friday 8am to 4pm. **Shops** are open Monday-Friday 9am-5pm and Saturday 9am-noon. Nearly all **museums** and **galleries** close on Mondays, and **theaters** rarely perform regular shows in December and from late June to early September.

ACCOMMODATIONS AND CAMPING

Hostels, particularly in **university dorms,** are the cheapest option in July and August; two- to four-bed rooms are 200-300Kč per person. CKM's **Junior Hotels** (year-round hostels giving discounts to ISIC and HI cardholders) are comfortable but often full. **Private hostels** have broken the CKM monopoly. **Pensions** are the next most affordable option; expect to pay 600Kč, including breakfast. Reserve at least one week ahead from June to September in Prague, Český Krumlov, and Brno. **Private homes** are not nearly as popular (or as cheap) as in the rest of Eastern Europe; scan train stations for *Zimmer frei* signs. Outside Prague, **local tourist offices** and **CKM/GTS** book rooms, with private agencies around train and bus stations. **Campgrounds** are strewn throughout the countryside, most only open mid-May to September. *Ubytování v ČSR,* in decodable Czech, lists all the hotels, hostels, huts, and campgrounds in Bohemia and Moravia.

CZECH REPUBLIC

FOOD AND DRINK

Anyone in the mood for true Czech cuisine should start learning to pronounce *knedlíky* (KNED-lee-kee). These thick, pasty loaves of dough serve as staples of Czech meals. The Czech national meal is *vepřové* (roast pork), *knedlíky*, and *zelí* (known as *vepřo-knedlo-zelo*), but *guláš* (stew) runs a close second. The main food groups are *hovězí* (beef), *sekaná pečeně* (meatloaf), *klobása* (sausage), and *brambory* (potatoes). If you're in a hurry, get *párky* (frankfurters) at a *bufet*, *samoobsluha*, or *občerstvení*, all food stands. **Vegetarian** restaurants serve *šopský salát* (salad with feta cheese) and other *bez masa* (meatless) dishes; at most restaurants, however, vegetarians will be limited to *smaženy sýr* (fried cheese). Ask for *káva espresso* rather than *káva* to avoid the mud Czechs call coffee. The most beloved dessert is *koláč*—a tart with poppy-seed jam or sweet cheese. The most prominent beer is *Plzeňský Prazdroj* (Pilsner Urquell), although many Czechs are loyal to *Budvar* or *Krušovice.*

COMMUNICATION

MAIL. The Czech Republic's **postal system** has embraced capitalist efficiency; letters reach the US in less than 10 days. A postcard to the US costs 8Kč, to Australia 7Kč. When sending by **air mail,** stress that you want it to go on a *plane (letecky)*. Go to the customs office to send packages heavier than 2kg abroad. **Mail** can be received general delivery through *Poste Restante.*

TELEPHONES. To make a call, seek out the blue card phones (150Kč per 50 units) rather than playing Sisyphus to a coin phone's giant boulder. Calls run 31Kč per minute to the **UK;** 63Kč per minute to **Australia, Canada,** or the **US;** and 94Kč per minute to **New Zealand.** Making calls abroad through an operator doesn't require a card—just dial one of these toll-free numbers. The international operator is at ☎013 15; for lower rates, try: **AT&T Direct** ☎00 42 00 01 01; **BT Direct** ☎00 42 00 44 01; **MCI WorldPhone** ☎00 42 00 01 12; **Canada Direct** ☎00 42 00 01 51; **Sprint** ☎00 42 08 71 87.

LANGUAGES. Russian *was* every student's mandatory second language, but these days, **English** will earn you more friends. A few **German** phrases go further, but might gain you some enemies. To gain some survival-level savvy in Czech, see p. 981.

HOLIDAYS AND FESTIVALS

Holidays: New Year's Day (Jan. 1); Catholic Easter (Apr. 15); May Day (May 1); Liberation Day (May 8); Cyril and Methodius Day (July 5); Jan Hus Day (July 6); St. Wenceslas Day (Sept. 28); 1918 Republic Day (Oct. 28); Student Day (Day of Fight for Freedom and Democracy, Nov. 17); and Catholic Christmas (Dec. 24-26).

Festivals: The **Prague Spring Festival,** Prague, May 12-June 3, attracts international music lovers in hordes. Music also fills the streets in Český Krumlov for their **International Music Festival** in early August. Film lovers flock to the **Karlovy Vary International Film Festival** in July.

PRAGUE (PRAHA) ☎02

According to legend, Countes Libuše stood above the Vltava and declared, "I see a city whose glory will touch the stars; it shall be called Praha (threshold)." Medieval kings, benefactors, and architects fulfilled the prophecy, building soaring cathedrals and lavish palaces that reflected Prague's status as capital of the Holy Roman Empire. Yet legends of demons, occult forces, and a maze of alleys lent this "city of dreams" a dark side that inspired Franz Kafka's tales of paranoia. Since the fall of the Iron Curtain, hordes of Euro-trotting foreigners have flooded the city. In summer, tourists pack streets so tightly that crowd-surfing seems a viable way to travel; sometimes the only way off the Charles Bridge is to jump. Yet walk a few blocks from any of the major sights and you'll be lost among cobblestone alleys and looming churches; head to an outlying metro stop and you'll find haggling *babičky*, supermodel-esque natives, and not a backpack in sight.

Prague continues to reform its phone system. Businesses often receive no more than three weeks' notice before their numbers change. The four- to eight-digit numbers provided in these listings are the least likely to be obsolete by the time you read this–but things change fast.

GETTING THERE AND GETTING AROUND

Flights: Ruzyně Airport (☎20 11 11 11), 20km northwest of the city. Take bus #119 to Metro A: Dejvická (runs daily 5am-midnight; 12Kč, plus 6Kč per piece of large luggage); buy tickets from kiosks or machines. Late at night, take night tram #51 to "Divoká Šárka," then night bus #510 to the center. **Airport buses** (☎20 11 42 96) go every 30min. from outside Metro stops at Nám. Republiky (90Kč) and Dejvická (60Kč). Taxis to the airport are extremely expensive.

Trains: ☎24 22 42 00; international ☎24 61 52 49. Prague has 4 main terminals:

Hlavní Nádraží (Main Station): ☎24 22 42 00. Metro C: Hlavní nádraží. The largest station. **BIJ Wasteels** (☎24 61 74 54; fax 24 22 18 72), 2nd fl., to the right of the stairs, sells discount international tickets to those under 26 and books *couchettes*. Open in summer M-F 7:30am-8pm, Sa 8-11:30am and 12:30-3pm; off-season M-F 8:30am-6pm.

Holešovice: ☎24 61 72 65. Metro C: Nádraží Holešovice. Services most international destinations. Buy **BIJ Wasteels** and regular train tickets from the **Czech Railways Travel Agency** (☎80 08 05). Open M-F 9am-5pm; Sa-Su 8am-4pm. To: **Vienna**

(4½hr., 3 per day, 780Kč); **Berlin** (5hr., 5 per day, 1580Kč); **Bratislava** (5½hr., 7 per day, 300Kč); **Munich** (6hr., 3 per day, 1450Kč); **Kraków** (8½hr., 3 per day, 1000Kč); **Warsaw** (9½hr., 3 per day, 670Kč); **Budapest** (10hr., 5 per day, 1290Kč); and **Moscow** (30hr., 1 per day, 2500Kč).

Masarykovo: ☎24 61 72 60. Metro B: Nám. Republiky. On the corner of Hybernská and Havlíčkova. Serves domestic destinations.

Smíchov: ☎24 61 72 55. Metro B: Smíchovské nádraží. Opposite Vyšehrad. Also serves domestic destinations.

Buses: ČSAD has several bus stations. The biggest is **Florenc,** Křižíkova 4 (☎24 21 49 90). Metro B,C: Florenc. Staff rarely speaks English. Info office open M-F 6am-9pm, Sa 6am-6pm, Su 8am-8pm. Buy tickets in advance, as they often sell out. To: **Berlin** (6hr., 1 per day, 1040Kč); **Vienna** (8½hr., 1 per day, 870Kč); and **Sofia** (26hr., 4 per day, 1850Kč). Students may get 10% discount. The **Tourbus** office upstairs (☎24 21 02 21) sells tickets for Eurolines and airport buses. Open M-F 8am-8pm, Sa-Su 9am-8pm.

Public Transportation: Buy tickets for the **metro, tram,** or **bus** from newsstands and *tabák* kiosks, machines in stations, or **DP** (*Dopravní Podnik;* transport authority) kiosks. The basic 8Kč ticket is good for 15min. (or 4 stops on the metro); 12Kč is valid for 1hr. during the day, 1½hr. 8pm-5am, with unlimited connections on the entire network in any one direction. Large bags and bikes require an extra 6Kč ticket. Validate your ticket in the machines above the escalators or face a 200Kč fine. The **metro's** 3 lines run daily 5am-midnight: A is green on the maps, B yellow, C red. **Night trams** #51-58 and **buses** run all night after the last metro and can be picked up at the Charles Bridge; look for the dark blue signs at bus stops.

Taxis: Taxi Praha (☎85 77 or 10 87) or **AAA** (☎24 32 24 32). Both open 24hr. Taxi drivers are notorious scam artists. Check that the meter is set to zero, and ask the driver to start it *("Zapněte taximetr").* Always ask for a receipt *("Prosím, dejte mi paragon")* with distance traveled and price paid. If the driver doesn't write the receipt or set the meter to zero, you aren't obligated to pay. Set rate 25Kč, plus 13Kč per km.

ORIENTATION AND PRACTICAL INFORMATION

Straddling the river **Vltava,** Prague is a gigantic mess of suburbs and labyrinthine medieval streets. Fortunately, nearly everything of interest lies within the compact, walkable downtown. The river Vltava runs south-northeast through central Prague and separates the **Staré Město** (Old Town) and the **Nové Město** (New Town) from **Malá Strana** (Lesser Side). On the right bank of the river, the Old Town's **Staroměstské náměstí** (Old Town Square) is the focal point of the city. From the square, the elegant **Pařížská ulice** (Paris Street) leads north into **Josefov,** the old Jewish ghetto; unfortunately, all that remains are six synagogues and the Old Jewish Cemetery. In the opposite direction from Pařížská lies **Nové Město.** It houses **Václavské náměstí** (Wenceslas Square), the administrative and commercial heart of the city. West of Staroměstské nám., **Karlův most** (Charles Bridge) traverses the Vltava and connects the Old Town with **Malostranské náměstí** (Lesser Town Square). **Pražský Hrad** (Prague Castle) sits on the **Hradčany** hilltop above Malostranské nám.

Prague's main train station, Hlavní nádraží, and Florenc bus station sit in the northeastern corner of Václavské nám. All train and bus terminals are on or near the excellent metro system. To get to Staroměstské nám., take the Metro A line to Staroměstská and walk down Kaprova away from the river. *Tabák* stands and bookstores sell the indexed *plán města* (map); this, along with the English-language weekly *The Prague Post*, is essential for visitors.

TOURIST AND FINANCIAL SERVICES

Tourist Offices: Green "i"s mark tourist information. **Pražská Informační Služba** (Prague Info Service), in the Old Town Hall (☎24 48 25 62; English ☎54 44 44). **Branches** at Na příkopě 20, Hlavní nádraží, and in the tower on the Malá Strana side of the Charles Bridge. All open in summer M-F 9am-7pm, Sa-Su 9am-6pm; off season M-F 9am-6pm, Sa-Su 9am-5pm.

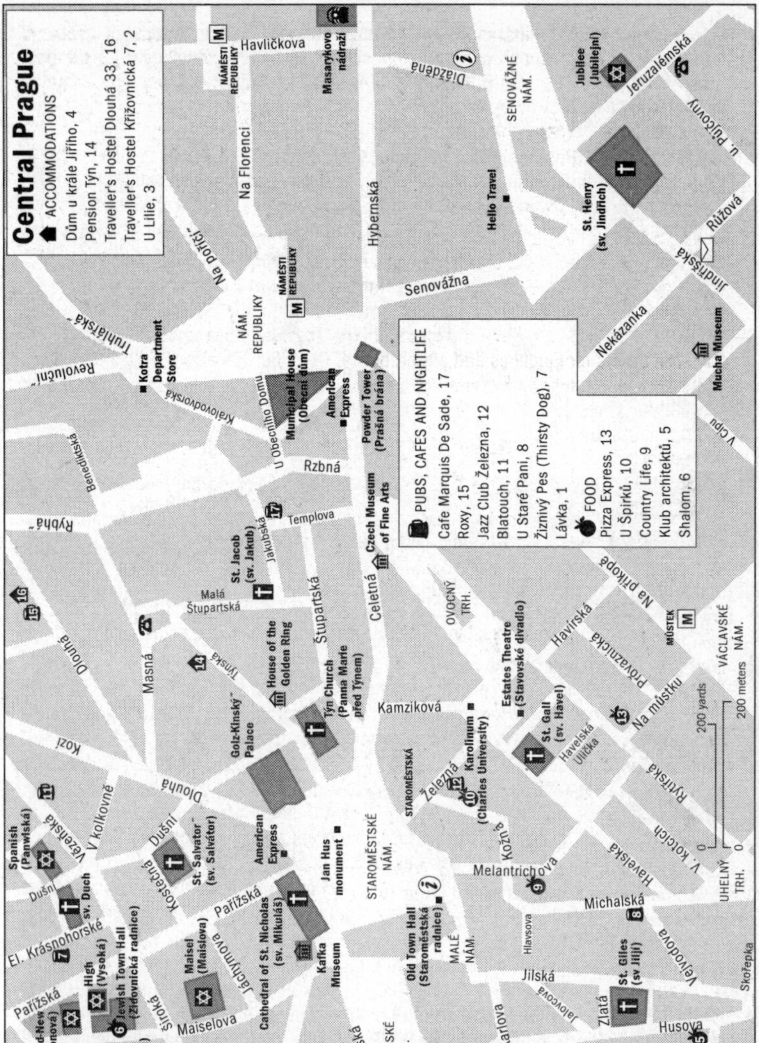

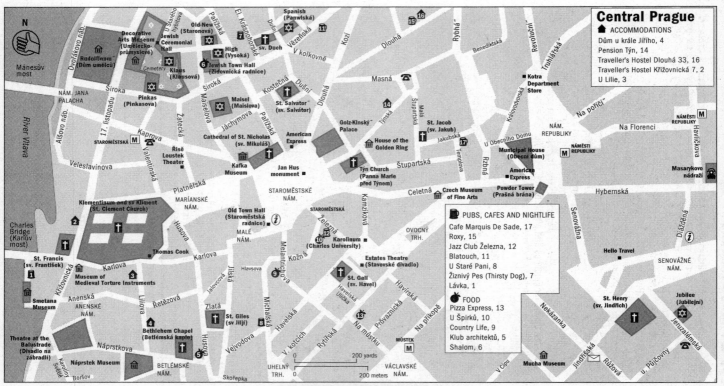

Central Prague

ACCOMMODATIONS

Dům u krále Jiřího, 4
Pension Týn, 14
Traveller's Hostel Dlouhá 33, 16
Traveller's Hostel Křižovnická 7, 2
U Lilie, 3

PUBS, CAFES AND NIGHTLIFE

Cafe Marquis De Sade, 17
Roxy, 15
Jazz Club Železna, 12
Blatouch, 11
U Staré Pani, 8
Žiznivý Pes (Thirsty Dog), 7
Lávka, 1

FOOD

Pizza Express, 13
U Špirků, 10
Country Life, 9
Klub architektů, 5
Shalom, 6

N
Mánesův most
River Vltava
Charles Bridge (Karlův most)
Dvořákovo náb.
Alšovo náb.
NÁM. JANA PALACHA
Rudolfinum (Dům umělců)
Decorative Arts Museum (Umělecko-průmyslové)
Jewish Ceremonial Hall
U Starého hřbitova
Cemetery
Klaus (Klausová)
Pinkas (Pinkasova)
Old-New (Staronová)
High (Vysoká)
Jewish Town Hall (Židovnická radnice)
Pařížská
El. Krásnohorské
Dušní
sv. Duch
Spanish (Panwiská)
Vězeňská
V kolkovně
Kozí
Dlouhá
Rybná
Benediktská
Revoluční
Truhlářská
Široká
Maiselova
Maisel (Maislova)
Kostečná
St. Salvator (sv. Salvátor)
Jáchymova
17. listopadu
STAROMĚSTSKÁ
Kaprova
Žatecká
Valentinská
Říše Loustek Theater
Veleslavínova
Cathedral of St. Nicholas (sv. Mikuláš)
Kafka Museum
American Express
Jan Hus monument
Golz-Kinský Palace
Týnská
House of the Golden Ring
Týn Church (Panna Marie před Týnem)
Masná
Malá Štupartská
Štupartská
St. Jacob (sv. Jakub)
Jakubská
Templova
Rzbná
U Obecního Domu
Králodvorská
Kotra Department Store
Na poříčí
NÁM. REPUBLIKY
NÁMĚSTI REPUBLIKY
Na Florenci
Havlíčkova
Municipal House (Obecní dům)
American Express
Powder Tower (Prašná brána)
Masarykovo nádraží
Hybernská
Celetná
Czech Museum of Fine Arts
Platnéřská
MARÍANSKÉ NÁM.
STAROMĚSTSKÉ NÁM.
Old Town Hall (Staroměstská radnice)
MALÉ NÁM.
Klementinum and sv Kliment (St. Clement Church)
Husova
Thomas Cook
Karlova
St. Francis (sv. František)
Křižovnická
Museum of Medieval Torture Instruments
Smetana Museum
Anenská
ANENSKÉ NÁM.
Liliova
Řetězová
Zlatá
St. Giles (sv Jiljí)
Jalovcová
Jilská
Hlavsova
Melantrichova
Michalská
Kožná
Železná
Karolinum (Charles University)
Kamzíková
OVOCNÝ TRH.
Estates Theatre (Stavovské divadlo)
St. Gall (sv. Havel)
Havelská Ulička
Havelská
V. kotcích
Rytířská
Na můstku
Provaznická
Havířská
Na příkopě
MŮSTEK
VÁCLAVSKÉ NÁM.
UHELNÝ TRH.
Bethlehem Chapel (Betlémská kaple)
Vejvodova
Skořepka
BETLÉMSKÉ NÁM.
Náprstkova
Náprstek Museum
Theatre at the Balustrade (Divadlo na zábradlí)
Karolíny Světlé
Boršov
0 200 yards
0 200 meters
Senovážna
Dlážděná
Hello Travel
SENOVÁŽNÉ NÁM.
St. Henry (sv. Jindřich)
Jubilee (Jubilejní)
Jeruzalémská
Nekázanka
Jindřišská
Růžová
u. Půjčovny
V Cípu
Mucha Museum

CZECH REPUBLIC

Budget Travel: CKM, Jindřišská 28 (☎24 23 02 18; email ckmprg@mbox.vol.cz). Metro A,B: Můstek. Budget air tickets for those under 26. Also books lodgings in Prague from 350Kč. Open M-Th 10am-6pm, F 10am-4pm. **STA Travel,** Široká 15. Metro A: Staroměstsksá; walk away from the river on Kaprova, left onto Valentinská, right onto Široká. Open M-F 8:30am-5:30pm.

Passport Office: Foreigner police headquarters, Olšanská 2 (☎683 17 39). Metro A: Flora; turn right on Jičínská with the cemetery on your right, then right on Olšanská. Or, take tram #9 from Václavské nám. toward Spojovací and get off at Olšanská. For visa extensions, get a 90Kč stamp inside, line up in front of doors 2-12, and prepare to wait up to 2hr. Little English spoken. Open M-Tu and Th 7:30-11:30am and 12:30-2:30pm, W 7:30-11:30am and 12:30-5pm, F 7:30am-noon.

Embassies: Australia (☎24 31 00 71) and **New Zealand** (☎25 41 98) have consulates, but citizens should contact the UK embassy in an emergency. **Canada,** Mickiewiczova 6 (☎24 31 11 08). Metro A: Hradčanská. Open M-F 8am-noon and 2-4pm. **Hungary,** Badeního 1 (☎36 50 41). Metro A: Hradčanská. Open M-W and F 9am-noon. **Ireland,** Tržiště 13 (☎53 09 11). Metro A: Malostranská. Open M-F 9:30am-12:30pm and 2:30-4:30pm. **Poland,** Váldštejnská nám. 8 (☎57 32 06 78). Metro A: Malostranská. Open M-F 7am-noon. **Russia,** Pod Kaštany 1 (☎38 19 40). Metro A: Hradčanská. Open M, W, and F 9am-1pm. **Slovakia,** Pod Hradební 1 (☎32 05 21). Metro A: Dejvická. Open M-F 8:30am-noon. **South Africa,** Ruská 65 (☎67 31 11 14). Metro A: Flora. Open M-F 9am-noon. **UK,** Thunovská 14 (☎57 32 03 55). Metro A: Malostranská. Open M-F 9am-noon. **US,** Tržiště 15 (☎57 53 06 63; emergency ☎53 12 00). Metro A: Malostranská. From Malostranská nám., head down Karmelitská and take a right onto Tržiště. Open M-F 8am-1pm and 2-4:30pm.

Currency Exchange: AmEx and **Thomas Cook** traveler's checks can be cashed commission-free at their respective offices. Exchange counters are everywhere with wildly varying rates. **Chequepoints** may be the only ones open when you need cash, but usually charge a 3% commission. **Komerční banka,** Na pĺíkopw 33 (☎24 43 21 11), buys notes and checks for a 2% commission. Open M-F 8am-5pm. **ATMs** ("Bankomats") abound and offer the best rates, but sometimes charge large fees.

American Express: Václavské nám. 56, (☎22 80 02 37). Metro A,C: Muzeum. **ATM** outside takes AmEx cards. Cashes AmEx checks commission-free and grants V, MC cash advances for a 3% commission. Open July-Sept. M-F 9am-6pm, Sa 9am-2pm; Oct.-June M-F 9am-5pm, Sa 9am-noon. **Branches:** Mostecká 12 (near the Charles Bridge; open daily 9:30am-7:30pm), Celetná 17, and Staroměstské nám. 5.

Thomas Cook: Národní třída 28 (☎21 10 52 76). Cashes Cook checks commission-free. V, MC cash advances. Open M-F 9am-7pm, Sa 9am-6pm, and Su 10am-6pm. **Branch:** Karlova 3. Open daily 10am-10pm.

LOCAL SERVICES

Luggage Storage: Lockers in all train and bus stations take two 5Kč coins. If these are full, or if you need to store your cargo longer than 24hr., use the luggage offices to the left in the basement of **Hlavní nádraží** (15-30Kč per day; open 24hr.) and halfway up the stairs at **Florenc** (10-25Kč per day; open daily 5am-11pm).

English Bookstore: The Globe Bookstore, Pštrossova 6 (☎/fax 24 91 62 64). Metro B: Národní třída. Exit left onto Spálená, right onto Ostrovní, left to Pštrossova. Free Internet access. Open Su-Th 10am-midnight, F-Sa 10-1am.

Laundromat: Laundry Kings, Dejvická 16 (☎312 37 43), one block from Metro A: Hradčanská. Cross the tram *and* railroad tracks and turn left. Wash 60Kč per 6kg; dry 15Kč per 8min. Soap 10-20Kč. **Beer** 17Kč. Open M-F 6am-10pm, Sa-Su 8am-10pm.

EMERGENCY AND COMMUNICATIONS

Medical Assistance: Na Homolce (Hospital for Foreigners), Roentgenova 2 (☎52 92 21 74; after-hours ☎57 21 11 11). Open M-F 8am-4pm; offers 24hr. emergency service.

Pharmacy: "U Anděla," Štefánikova 6 (☎57 32 09 18). Metro B: Anděl. Open 24hr.

Internet Access: Prague is Internet Nirvana. **Terminal Bar,** Soukenická 6 (☎21 87 19 99). Metro B: Nám. Republiky. 1.5Kč per min. Open M-Th and Su 11am-1am, F-Sa

11am-3am. **Café Electra,** Rašínovo nábřeží 62 (☎297 038). Metro B: Karlovo nám. 80Kč per hr. Open M-F 9am-midnight, Sa-Su 11am-midnight.

Telephones: Phone cards sell for 175Kč per 50 units at kiosks, post offices, and some exchange places; don't let kiosks rip you off.

Post Office: Jindřišská 14. Metro A, B: Můstek (☎21 13 15 20). Get stamps at window #11; letters and small parcels at windows #12-14; *Poste Restante* at window #17. To send large boxes go to booths #3-9. Open daily 7am-8pm. Address mail to be held: First name SURNAME, POSTE RESTANTE, Jindřišská 14, **110 00** Praha 1, Czech Republic.

ACCOMMODATIONS

While hotel prices rise higher than your wildest fears, the glutted hostel market has stabilized prices around 270-420Kč per night. Reservations are a good idea; rooms in smaller hostels must be reserved at least two days in advance. Most accommodations have 24-hour reception and require check-in after 2pm, check-out by 10am. A few bare-bones hotels are still cheap, and a growing number of Prague residents are renting rooms. Sleeping on the streets is too dangerous to consider.

ACCOMMODATIONS AGENCIES

The going rate for apartments hovers around 600-1200Kč, depending on proximity to the city center; you can haggle with the hawkers. This is usually safe, but if you're wary of bargaining on the street, try a private agency. Ask where the nearest tram, bus, or metro stop is, and don't pay until you know what you're getting; ask for details in writing. You can often pay in US dollars or German marks, but prices are lower if you pay in Czech crowns. **Hello Travel Ltd.,** Senovážné nám. 3, metro B: Nám Republiky, arranges housing. (☎24 21 26 47. 500-1500Kč per person in summer, off season 400-1200Kč. Pay in Czech crowns, German marks, or with V, MC, or AmEx. Open M-F 8am-7pm.) **Ave.,** Hlavní nádraží, second fl. of station, next to the stairs on the far left, offers hundreds of rooms from 800Kč per person and books hostels from 300Kč. (☎24 22 35 21. Open daily 6am-11pm. V, MC, AmEx.)

HOSTELS

If you're schlepping a backpack in Hlavní nádraží or Holešovice, you *will* be bombarded by hostel runners trying to coerce you back to their hostel. Many are university dorms that free up from June to August, and often you'll be offered transport to the room—an easy option for those arriving in the middle of the night without a reservation. If you prefer more than just a place to sleep, smaller places are a better alternative. It's best to phone the night before you arrive or at 10am when they know who's checking out. **Vinohrady** is a residential district about 15 minutes southeast of the city center.

A ROOM WITHOUT A VIEW At decisive points in European history, unlucky men tend to fall from Prague's window ledges. The Hussite wars began on July 30, 1419, after Catholic councillors were thrown to the mob from the New Town Hall on Karlovo nám. The Thirty Years' War devastated Europe after Habsburg officials were tossed from the windows of Prague Castle's Bohemian Chancellery into a heap of steaming manure on May 23, 1618. These first and second defenestrations echo down the ages, but two more falls this century have continued the macabre tradition. On March 10, 1948, liberal foreign minister Jan Masaryk fell to his death from the top floor of his ministry just two weeks after the Communist takeover; murder was always suspected, but never proven. On Feb. 3, 1997, Bohumil Hrabal, age 82, popular author of *I Served the King of England* and *Closely-Observed Trains,* fell from the fifth floor of his hospital window and died in his pajamas. Nothing unusual here, except that two of his books describe people committing suicide—by jumping out of fifth-floor windows.

Hostel Boathouse, Lodnická (☎/fax 402 10 76), south of the city center. From Hlavní nádraží, Karlovo nám., Staré Město, or the Charles Bridge, take tram #3 south toward Sídliště and get off at "Černý Kůň" (20min.). From Holešovice, take tram #17. From the tram stop, follow the yellow signs down to the Vltava. As Věra the owner says, "This isn't a hostel; it's a crazy house." Nurturing home/summer camp. Breakfast 50Kč. Laundry. 2-night min. stay. Call ahead; if they're full, Věra might find space. Dorms 290Kč.

Penzion v podzámčí, V podzámčí 27 (☎/fax 41 44 46 09), south of the city center. From Metro C: Budějovická, take bus #192 to the 3rd stop–ask the driver to stop at Nad Rybníky. The homiest hostel in Prague. Kitchen. Incredible laundry service (they iron your socks!) 100Kč per load. Dorms 280Kč; doubles 640Kč; triples 900Kč.

Domov Mládeže, Dykova 20 (☎/fax 22 51 25 97 or 22 51 17 77), in Vinohrady. Metro A: Jiřího z Poděbrad. Follow Nitranská and turn left on Dykova; it's 2 blocks down on the right. So peaceful you might forget you're in Prague. Breakfast included. Dorms 430Kč; double 650Kč. Sister hostels: **Amadeus,** Slavojova 108/8. Metro C: Vyšehrad; descend the bridge to Čiklova, turn left, and it's on the left. **Máchova,** Máchova 11. Metro A: Nám. Míru; walk down Ruská and turn right on Máchova. **Košická,** Košická 12. Metro A: Nám. Míru. All hostels have the same phone number and prices.

Hostel U Melounu (At the Watermelon), Ke Karlovu 7 (☎/fax 24 91 83 22), in Nové Město. Metro C: I.P. Pavlova; follow Sokolská to Na Bojišti and turn left at the street's end onto Ke Karlovu. A historic building with great facilities. Breakfast included. Dorms 380Kč; singles 450Kč; double 840Kč. 100Kč discount with ISIC.

Traveller's Hostels, in Staré Město. These summertime big-dorm specialists round up travelers at bus and train stations and herd them into one of six central hostels for lots of beds and beer. At all, breakfast is included and Internet access is available (27Kč per 15min.). Dlouhá 33 (☎24 82 66 62; fax 24 82 66 65). Metro B: Nám Republiky. Follow Revoluční toward the river, turn left on Dlouhá, on the right. Unbeatable location; in the same building as the Roxy, but with good soundproofing. Dorms 350-380Kč; doubles 1100Kč; triples 1290Kč. Husova 3 (☎24 21 53 26). Metro B: Národní třída; turn right on Spálená (which becomes Na Perštýně after Národní), then Husova. Dorms 400Kč. Křížovnická 7 (☎232 09 87). Metro A: Staroměstská. Dorms 230Kč. Střelecký ostrov (☎24 91 01 88), on an island off Most Legií. Metro B: Národní třída. Dorms 300Kč. Růžová 5 (☎24 21 69 71). Metro C: Hlavní nádraží. Dorms 220Kč.

Pension Týn, Týnská 19 (☎/fax 24 80 83 33; backpacker@razdva.cz), near the Staré Město. Metro A: Staroměstská. From Old Town Square, head down Dlouhá, then bear right at Masná and right onto Týnská. A quiet getaway conveniently located in the center of the Old Town. Immaculate facilities. Dorms 400Kč; singles 1000Kč; doubles 1200Kč.

Strahov Complex, Vaníčkova 5 (☎52 71 90), west of the city center. Metro A: Dejvická; take bus #217 or 143 to Koleje Strahov. Next to the enormous stadium, Strahov is known as the "hostel ghetto"–10 concrete blocks, open all year to accommodate the hordes. Not very convenient, but there's always space. Singles 300Kč; doubles 440Kč. Students 180Kč each in any room.

Hotel Standart, Přístavní 2 (☎87 52 58; fax 80 67 52), north of the city center. Metro C: Vltavská; take tram #1 toward Spojavací, #3 toward Lehovec, #14 toward Vozovna Kobylisy, or #25 toward Střelničná. Turn left onto Přístavní. Very quiet neighborhood. Breakfast included. Singles 350Kč, nonmembers 620Kč; doubles 700Kč, 800Kč; triples 1050Kč, 1100Kč; quads 1300Kč. 100Kč per person for 1-night stays.

HOTELS AND PENSIONS

Budget hotels are now scarce. Beware of hotels that may try to bill you for a more expensive room than the one in which you stayed; some cheap establishments require reservations up to a month in advance, but many refuse reservations altogether. Call first, then confirm by fax with a credit card.

B&B U Oty (Ota's House), Radlická 188 (☎/fax 57 21 53 23), west of the center. Metro B: Radlická; exit left and go right 400m up the slope. Charming, English-speaking Ota will make your stay a pleasure. Kitchen. Laundry. Singles 700Kč; doubles 770Kč; triples 990Kč; quads 1250Kč. One-night surcharge 100Kč.

Pension Unitas/Cloister Inn, Bartolomějská 9 (☎24 21 10 20; email unitas@cloister-inn.cz), in **Staré Město.** Metro B: Národní třída; cross Národní, head down Na Perštýně away from Tesco, and turn left on Bartolomějská. Once the site of Beethoven performances, this was where Václav Havel was incarcerated. Breakfast included. Singles 1020Kč; doubles 1200Kč; triples 1650Kč.

Dům U krále Jiřího, Liliová 10 (☎22 22 09 25; email kral.jiri@telecom.cz), in **Staré Město.** Metro A: Staroměstská; exit onto Nám. Jana Palacha, walk down Křížovnická toward the Charles Bridge, turn left onto Karlova, and Liliová is the 1st right. Gorgeous rooms with private bath. Buffet breakfast included. Singles 1700Kč, 1500Kč off season; doubles 2900Kč, 2700Kč.

U Lilie, Liliová 15 (☎22 22 04 32; fax 22 22 06 41), in **Staré Město.** Metro A: Staroměstská; follow directions to U krále Jiřího (above). TV. Breakfast included. Singles 1700Kč; doubles 3400Kč, with bath 4600Kč.

CAMPING

Campsites have taken over both the outskirts and the centrally located Vltava islands. Bungalows must be reserved in advance, but tent space is generally available without prior notice. Tourist offices sell a guide to sites near the city (15Kč).

Císařská louka, on a peninsula on the Vltava. Metro B: Smíchovské nádraží; then take tram #12 (dir. Hlubočepy) to Lihovar and go toward the river. Or, take the ferry from Smíchovské nádraží. **Caravan Park** (☎54 50 64) is near the ferry. 90-140Kč per tent, plus 95Kč per person. Singles 365Kč; doubles 630Kč; triples 945Kč. **Caravan Camping** (☎/fax 54 01 29) is near the tram. 90-120Kč per tent, 110Kč per person.

Sokol Troja, Trojská 171 (☎/fax 83 85 04 86), north of the center in the Troja district. Metro C: Nádraží Holešovice; take bus #112 to "Kazanka," the 4th stop. At least 4 nearly identical places line the same road. Tents 105-130Kč, plus 100Kč per person. Dorms 250Kč; bungalows 230Kč per person.

Na Vlachovce, Zenklova 217 (☎/fax 688 04 28). Take bus #102 or 175 from Nádraží Holešovice toward Okrouhlická, get off, and continue in the same direction. Breakfast included. Reserve a week ahead. Romantic 2-person "barrels" 400Kč. Attached doubles with bath 975Kč.

FOOD

The nearer you are to **Staroměstské nám.**, the **Charles Bridge** (Karlův most), and **Václavské nám.**, the more you'll pay; away from the center, you can get pork, cabbage, dumplings, and a half-liter of beer for 50Kč. Check your bill carefully; you'll pay for everything the waiter brings to the table. Outlying Metro stops become markets in the summer. **Tesco,** Národní třída 26, has **groceries** right next to Metro B: Národní třída. (Open M-F 7am-8pm, Sa 8am-7pm, Su 9am-7pm.) Look for the **daily market** where Havelská and Melantrichova meet in Staré Město. After a night out, grab a *párek v rohlíku* (hot dog) or a *smažený sýr* (fried cheese sandwich) from a Václavské nám. vendor, or a gyro from a stand on Spálená or Vodičkova. Or, make a morning of it and uncover the developing late-night eating scene.

RESTAURANTS

Universal, V jirchářích 6 (☎24 91 81 82), in Nové Město. Metro B: Národní třída; turn left onto Spálená and right on Myslíkova, then right on Křemencova. A transplanted California-style eatery with huge, fresh salads (97-143Kč). Open daily 11:30am-1am.

Velryba (The Whale), Opatovická 24 (☎24 91 23 91), in Nové Město. Metro B: Národní třída; exit to left, then right onto Ostrovní, and left onto Opatovická. Relaxed cafe-restaurant with a chic gallery in back. International and Czech dishes (38-155Kč) and adventurous veggie platters. Open daily 11am-2am.

Bar bar, Všehrdova 17 (☎53 29 41), in Malá Strana. Metro A: Malostranská; follow the tram tracks down Letenská Malostranské nám. and Karmelitská; turn left on Všehrdova after the museum. The stuttering eatery has a good vibe, good music, and 40 varieties of good whiskey (from 55Kč). Open daily noon-midnight.

U Špirků, Kožná ulička 12 (☎24 23 84 20), in Staré Město. Metro A: Staroměstská; with your back to the astronomical clock on Staroměstské nám. go down Melantrichova and take the 1st left onto Kožná. Some of the city's best and cheapest food in a spacious pub. Main dishes 89-138Kč. Open daily 11am-midnight.

Lotos, Platnéřská 13 (☎/fax 232 23 90), in Staré Město. Metro A: Staroměstská; go left down Valentinská and turn right on Platnélská. Vegetarian Czech restaurant with organic menu (60-140Kč). 0.5L wheat-yeast Pilsner 33Kč. Open daily 11am-10pm.

Klub architektů, Betlémské nám. 52 (☎24 40 12 14), in Staré Město. Metro B: Národní třída. Exit the station to the right, keep walking, and take a left. A 12th-century cellar thrust into the 20th century. Veggie options 80-90Kč; meat dishes 120-130Kč. Open daily 11:30am-midnight.

Shalom, Maiselova 18 (☎23 1 90 02), in Staré Město. Metro A: Staroměstská; follow Kaprova away from the river and go left on Maiselova. Fine kosher lunches inside a synagogue. You'll need to buy tickets for lunch at the Legacy Tours, the travel agent across the road. Set menu 220-520Kč. Open M-Sa 11:30am-2pm.

Góvinda Vegetarian Club, Soukenická 27 (☎24 81 66 31). Metro B: Nám. Republiky. Restaurant upstairs at the back of building. Delicious vegetarian dishes (about 70Kč). *Bhagavad Gitá* lectures Wednesdays 6:30pm. Open M-Sa 11am-5:30pm.

Malostranská Restaurace, Karmelitská 25 (☎57 53 14 18), in Malá Strana. Metro A: Malostranská; go down Klárov, then right on Letenská, and at Malostranské nám. go across to Karmelitská. Chairs spill out onto the street from the vaulted interior. Czech entrees 70-80Kč. Open M-F 10am-midnight, Sa 11am-midnight.

Restaurace U Pravdů, Žitná 15 (☎29 95 92). Metro B: Karlovo nám. Popular Czech lunch spot. Main dishes 80-149Kč. Open M-F 10am-11pm, Sa-Su 11am-11pm.

Radost FX, Bělehradská 120 (☎24 25 47 76), is a late-night veggie cafe. Metro C: I.P. Pavlova. Imaginative entrees 150Kč. Open Su-Th 11am-late, F-Sa 11am-later.

Iron Door, Michalská 13., provides trendy atmosphere and an international menu for the after-hours crowd. Beer 30Kč. Kitchen open daily until 3am.

CAFES AND TEAHOUSES

When Prague journalists are bored, they churn out yet another "Whatever happened to cafe life?" feature. The answer: it turned into *čajovna* (teahouse) culture.

U malého Glena, Karmelitská 23. Metro A: Malostranská; take tram #12 to Malostranské nám. With the motto "Eat, Drink, Drink Some More," they've got consumption down to a science. Killer margaritas 80Kč. Nightly jazz or blues 9pm. Cover 60-120Kč. Open daily 10am-2am; Su brunch 10am-3pm.

Dobrá Čajovna U Čajovníka (Good Tearoom), Boršov 2. Metro A: Staroměstská; follow Křížovnická past the Charles Bridge and bear left onto Karoliny Světlé; Boršov is tiny and on the left. Knock at the door and wait to be let in. 90 teas from all over the world (12-150Kč) and good snacks (eggplant dip 55Kč). Open M-Sa 10am-midnight, Su noon-midnight.

Jazz Café 14, Opatovická 14. Metro B: Národní třída. Perpetually filled with smoke and twenty-somethings. No live jazz, but photos and recordings of Louis and Miles are almost as good. Snacks (30Kč) and drinks (16Kč). Open daily noon-11pm.

The Globe Coffeehouse, Pštrossova 6. Metro B: Narodni Trida. At the Globe Bookstore (see p. 252). Tasty, strong black coffee (20Kč), gazpacho (35Kč), and English speakers working on a love connection (priceless). Open Su-Th 10am-midnight, F-Sa 10am-1am.

Kavárna Medúza, Belgická 17. Metro A: Nám. Míru. Walk down Rumunská and turn left at Belgická. Antique shop masquerading as a cafe. Fluffed-up Victorian seats and lots of coffee (19-30Kč). Open M-F 11am-1am.

SIGHTS

The only Central European city left entirely unscathed by either natural disaster or WWII, Prague at its center is a well-preserved combination of labyrinthine alleys and Baroque buildings. The flocks of tourists prove an amusing sight as well, but you can easily escape the packs by venturing away from **Staroměstské nám.,** the

Charles Bridge, and **Václavské nám.** Compact central Prague is best explored on foot. Don't leave without wandering the back alleys of **Josefov,** exploring the hills of **Vyšehrad,** and getting lost in the maze of **Malá Strana's** streets.

NOVÉ MĚSTO

Established in 1348 by Charles IV, Nové Město is not exactly new. But it's aged well; its wide boulevards and sprawling squares seem centuries ahead of their time.

WENCESLAS SQUARE (VÁCLAVSKÉ NÁMĚSTÍ). Not so much a square as a broad boulevard running through the center of Nové Město, Wenceslas Square owes its name to the Czech ruler and saint **Wenceslas** (Václav) whose statue sits in front of the **National Museum** (Národní muzeum). Lately, Wenceslas has presided over a century of turmoil and triumph, witnessing no fewer than five revolutions from his pedestal—the declaration of the new Czechoslovak state in 1918, the invasion of Hitler's troops, the arrival of Soviet tanks in 1968, Jan Palach setting himself on fire to protest the Soviet invasion, and the 1989 Velvet Revolution. The square sweeps down from the statue past department stores, overpriced discos, posh hotels, sausage stands, and trashy casinos. At the northern end of Wenceslas Square, near the Můstek Metro station, Art Nouveau design stares out from everything from lampposts to windowsills. The glass **Radio Prague Building,** behind the National Museum, was the scene of a tense battle during the Prague Spring, as citizens tried to protect the radio studios from Soviet tanks with a human barricade. *(Metro A, C: Muzeum.)*

FRANCISCAN GARDENS AND VELVET REVOLUTION MEMORIAL. Perhaps if the Franciscans took a break from talking to the birds, they could divulge how they managed to preserve the serene **rose garden** (Františkánská zahrada) in the heart of Prague's bustling commercial district. *(Metro A, B: Můstek; Metro B: Národní třída. Enter through the arch at Jungmannova and Národní. Open daily mid-Apr. to mid-Sept. 7am-10pm; mid-Sept. to mid-Oct. 8am-8pm; mid-Oct. to mid-Apr. 8am-7pm. Free.)* Under the arcades halfway down Národní třída stands a memorial to the hundreds of Prague's citizens beaten on November 17, 1989 during the **Velvet Revolution.**

THE DANCING HOUSE. Built by American architect Frank Gehry of Guggenheim-Bilbao fame, the undulating building at the corner of Resslova and Rašínovo nábřeží is called Fred and Ginger by Anglophones, and the Dancing House (Taneční dům) by Czechs. It opened in 1996, next to President Havel's former apartment building; he moved out when construction began. *(Metro B: Karlovo nám.)*

MUNICIPAL HOUSE (OBECNÍ DŮM). By far the most impressive Art Nouveau building in the city, the Municipal House (Obecní dům) captures the opulence of Prague's 19th-century cafe culture. *(Nám. Republiky 5. Metro B: Nám. Republiky. Open daily 10am-6pm.)*

STARÉ MĚSTO (OLD TOWN)

Settled in the 10th century, the narrow roads and Old World alleys of the Staré Město make it easy to get lost. But that's the best way to appreciate the neighborhood's charm.

CHARLES BRIDGE (KARLŮV MOST). Thronged with tourists and the hawkers who prey on them, this bridge is Prague's most recognizable landmark. Five years ago, the bridge's vendors peddled Red Army gear and dodgy black market currency deals; today, they sell watercolors of the bridge and other junk. The foundation stone of the bridge was laid at 5:31am on July 9, 1357, the most significant astrological point for Leo, the mascot of Bohemia (now, incidentally, the name of a Czech porn magazine). When darkness falls, the street musicians emerge, but the penalty for requesting "My Heart Will Go On" is being tied up in a goatskin and lowered into the Vltava. This same fate befell St. Jan Nepomucký when the hapless saint was tossed over the side of the bridge for faithfully guarding the queen's extramarital secrets from a suspicious King Wenceslas IV.

OLD TOWN SQUARE (STAROMĚSTSKÉ NÁMĚSTÍ). The heart of Staré Město is Old Town Square, surrounded by no fewer than eight magnificent towers. Next to the grassy knoll, Old Town Hall (Staroměstská radnice) is the multi-facaded building with a bit blown off the front. The building was partially demolished by the Nazis in the final week of WWII, receiving Prague's only visible damage from the war. *(Open daily in summer 9am-5:30pm. 30Kč, students 15Kč.)* Crowds gather on the hour to watch the wonderful astronomical clock *(orloj)* chime with its procession of apostles, a skeleton, and a thwarted Turk. *(Metro A: Staroměstská; Metro A, B: Můstek. Clock animated until 9pm.)* The Czech Republic's most famous martyred theologian, **Jan Hus,** hovers over Old Town Square in bronze effigy. Opposite the Old Town Hall, the spires of **Týn Church** (Matka Boží před Týnem) rise above a mass of medieval homes. The famous astronomer Tycho de Brahe is buried inside—he overindulged at one of Emperor Rudolf's lavish dinner parties, where it was unacceptable to leave the table unless the Emperor himself did so. When poor Tycho de Brahe needed to go (you know, *go*), he was forced to stay seated, and his bladder burst.

GOLTZ-KINSKÝ PALACE. The flowery 14th-century Goltz-Kinský Palace is the finest of Prague's Rococo buildings. It is also the official birthplace of Soviet Communism in the Czech Republic: on February 21, 1948, Klement Gottwald declared communism victorious from its balcony. *(On Staroměstské nám. at the corner of Dlouhá, next to Týn Church. Open Tu-F 10am-5pm; closes early in summer for daily concerts.)*

POWDER TOWER. The gothic Powder Tower (Prašná brána) looms at the edge of Nám. Republiky as the entrance to Staré Město. It is one of the only remaining of the eight original city gates. After a stint as a royal fortification, it was used primarily for gunpowder storage. A small history exhibit is inside, but skip it for a climb to the top. *(Metro B: Nám. Republiky. Open daily Apr.-Sept. 10am-6pm.)*

JOSEFOV

Metro A: Staroměstská. ☎231 71 91. Synagogues and museum open Su-F 9am-6pm. Closed for Jewish holidays. All sights except New Synagogue 450Kč, 330Kč. New Synagogue 200Kč, 140Kč. Museum only 280Kč, 200Kč.

Prague's historic Jewish neighborhood and the oldest Jewish settlement in Europe, Josefov lies north of Starométstské nám., along Maiselova and several sidestreets. In 1180, Prague's citizens built a 12-foot wall around the area. The closed city bred legends, many focusing on **Rabbi Loew ben Bezalel** (1512-1609) and his legendary *golem*—a mud creature that supposedly came to life to protect Prague's Jews. For the next 500 years, the city's Jews were exiled to this cramped ghetto, which was vacated in World War II when the residents were deported to death camps.

THE SYNAGOGUES. The **Maisel Synagogue** (Maiselova synagoga) exhibits treasures from the extensive collections of the Jewish Museum. *(On Maiselova, between Široká and Jáchymova.)* Turn left down Široká to reach the 16th-century **Pinkas Synagogue** (Pinkasova synagoga), converted in 1958 into a sobering memorial to the 77,000 Czech Jews killed in the Holocaust. Backtrack up Široká and go left on Maiselova to see the oldest operating synagogue in Europe, the 700-year-old **Old-New Synagogue** (Staronová synagoga). Further up Široká on Dušní is the ornate Moorish interior of the **Spanish Synagogue** (Španělská synagoga).

OLD JEWISH CEMETERY AND CEREMONY HALL. The Old Jewish Cemetery (Starý židovský hřbitov) remains Josefov's most popular attraction. Between the 14th and 18th centuries, 20,000 graves were laid in 12 layers. Rabbi Loew is buried by the wall directly opposite the entrance. *(At the corner of Široká and Žatecká.)* Originally a ceremonial hall for the Jewish Burial Society, Ceremony Hall (Obřadní dům) now houses the renowned exhibit "Children's Drawings from Terezín: 1942-44;" most of the young artists died at Auschwitz. *(On Červená, just off Maiselova.)*

MALÁ STRANA

The seedy hangout of criminals and counter-revolutionaries for nearly a century, the cobblestone streets of Malá Strana have become the most prized real estate on either side of the Vltava. The Malá Strana is centered around **Malostranské nám.** and its centerpiece, the Baroque **St. Nicholas' Cathedral** (Chrám sv. Mikuláš), whose towering dome is one of Prague's most notable landmarks. *(Metro A: Malostranská; then follow Letenská to Malostranské nám. Open daily 9am-4pm. 45Kč, students 15Kč.)* Along

Letenská, a wooden gate opens through a 10-meter wall into the beautiful **Wallenstein Garden** (Valdštejnská zahrada), one of Prague's best-kept secrets. *(Letenská 10. Metro A: Malostranská. Open daily May-Sept. 9am-7pm; Mar. 21-Apr. and Oct. 10am-6pm.)*

Hidden on Hroznová, a tiny street on Kampa Island, is a 1990s version of the infamous **John Lennon Wall.** The authorities kept trying to suppress it as part of the 1960s global peace movement, but it fell into disrepair and was plagued by unimaginative graffiti. In summer 1998, the wall was white-washed and is now covered with a prefab portrait of John Lennon and even less imaginative tourist graffiti. It still reminds you "all you need is love." *(Metro A: Malostranská; walk down U Lužického semináře to the Charles Bridge, descend the stairs leading to Na Kampě, make the 1st right onto Hroznová, and bear right close to the wall over the bridge onto Velkopřerovské nám.)*

Opposite the Malostranská metro stop, a plaque hidden in a lawn constitutes the **Charousková Memorial,** the only monument to those slain in the 1968 Prague Spring. It commemorates **Marie Charousková,** a graduate student who was machine-gunned by a Soviet soldier for refusing to remove a black ribbon protesting the invasion. Unlike other churches in Prague, the modest **Church of Our Lady Victorious** (Kostel Panna Marie Vítězná) is not notable for its exterior but for the famous wax statue of the **Infant Jesus of Prague** inside, said to bestow miracles on the faithful. *(Metro A: Malostranská; follow Letenská through Malostranské nám. and continue onto Karmelitská. Open M-F 8:30am-6:30pm, Sa 7:30am-8pm, Su 9am-9pm; off season same hours but Su 9am-8pm. Free.)*

PRAGUE CASTLE (PRAŽSKÝ HRAD)

Metro A: Hradčanská. Open daily Apr.-Oct. 9am-5pm, Nov.-May 9am-4pm. Buy tickets opposite St. Vitus' Cathedral, inside the castle walls. Three-day ticket valid at Royal Crypt, Cathedral and Powder Towers, Old Royal Palace, and Basilica of St. George. 120Kč, students 60Kč.

Prague Castle has been the seat of the Bohemian government since its founding 1000 years ago. From the metro, cross the tram tracks and turn left onto Tychonova, which leads to the newly renovated **Royal Summer Palace** (Královský letohrádek). The main **castle entrance** is at the other end of the 1534 **Royal Garden** (Královská zahrada), across the **Powder Bridge** (Prašný most). Before exploring, pass the main gate to see the **Šternberský Palace,** home of the National Gallery's European art collection. *(Open Tu-Su 10am-6pm. 90Kč, students 40Kč.)*

ST. VITUS' CATHEDRAL (KATEDRÁLA SV. VÍTA). Inside the castle walls stands Prague Castle's centerpiece, the colossal St. Vitus' Cathedral, which may look Gothic but in fact was only finished in 1929—600 years after construction began. The cathedral's stained-glass windows were created by some of the most gifted Czech artists; Alphonse Mucha's brilliant depiction of St. Ludmila and Wenceslas is the most recognizable and haunting. To the right of the high altar stands the **tomb of sv. Jan Nepomucký** (of Charles Bridge fame), 3m of solid, glistening silver weighing 1800kg. In the main church, the walls of **St. Wenceslas's Chapel** (Svatováclavská kaple) are lined with precious stones and a painting cycle depicting the legend of this saint. Climb the 287 steps of the **Cathedral Tower** for the best view of the city.

OLD ROYAL PALACE (STARÝ KRÁLOVSKÝ PALÁC). The Old Royal Palace, to the right of the cathedral behind the Old Provost's House and the statue of St. George, houses the lengthy expanse of the **Vladislav Hall,** which once hosted jousting competitions. Upstairs is the **Chancellery of Bohemia,** where on May 23, 1618, angry Protestants flung two Habsburg officials (and their secretary) through the windows in the defenistration of Prague, which triggered the bloody Thirty Years' War.

ST. GEORGE'S BASILICA AND AROUND. Behind the cathedral and across the courtyard from the Old Royal Palace stand the Romanesque St. George's Basilica (Bazilika sv. Jiří) and its adjacent convent. The convent houses the **National Gallery of Bohemian Art,** with art ranging from Gothic to Baroque. *(Open Tu-Su 10am-6pm. 90Kč, students 40Kč.)* The Old Royal Palace street **Jiřská** begins to the right of the basilica. Halfway down, the tiny **Golden Lane** (Zlatá ulička) heads off to the right; alchemists once worked here, and Kafka later lived at #22. Back on Jiřská, after passing out of the Prague Castle between the two armed sentries, peer over the battlements on the right for a fine cityscape.

OUTER PRAGUE

The city's outskirts are packed with greenery, nifty churches, and panoramic vistas, all peacefully tucked away from the tourist hordes. **Petřín Gardens** (Petřínské sady), the largest in Prague, provide some of the most spectacular views of the city. A cable car from just above the intersection of Vítězná and Újezd goes to the top. *(8Kč; look for lanová dráha signs. Open daily 11am-6pm and 7-11pm.)* At the summit is a small Eiffel tower and a wacky labyrinth of mirrors at **Bludiště.** *(Open Tu-Su 10am-7pm. 20Kč, students 10Kč.)* **Vyšehrad** is the former haunt of Prague's 19th-century Romantics; quiet walkways wind between crumbling stone walls to one of the Czech Republic's most celebrated sites, **Vyšehrad Cemetery** (home to the remains of Dvořák). Even the Metro C: Vyšehrad stop has a movie-sweep vista of Prague.

MUSEUMS

Prague's magnificence isn't best reflected in its museums, which often have striking facades but mediocre collections. But the city is victim to many rainy days, and it has a few public museums that shelter interesting and quirky collections.

HOUSE OF THE GOLDEN RING (DŮM U ZLATÉHO PRSTENU). Behind Týn Church, at Týnská 6, the House of the Golden Ring houses an astounding collection of 20th-century Czech art. *(☎24 82 80 04. Metro A: Staroěwstská. Open Tu-Su 10am-6pm. 60Kč, students 30Kč; 1st Tu of each month free.)*

NATIONAL GALLERY (NÁRODNÍ GALERIE). The massive National Gallery collection is spread around nine different locations; the notable **Šternberský palác** and **Klášter sv. Jiří** are in the **Prague Castle** (see p. 259). **St. Agnes' Cloister** (Klášter sv. Anežky) is the other major branch of the National Gallery, with a collection of 19th-century Czech art, but it's undergoing renovation, and its collection has been moved to the **Trade Fair Palace and the Gallery of Modern Art** (Veletržní palác a Galerie moderního umění), which also exhibits 20th-century Czech art. *(Dukelských hrdinů 47. Metro C: Vltavská. ☎24 30 11 11. Both open Tu-W and F-Su 10am-6pm, Th 10am-9pm. 90Kč, students 40Kč.)*

THE CZECH MUSEUM OF FINE ARTS (ČESKÉ MUZEUM VÝTVARNÝCH UMĚNÍ). At Celetná 34, itself one of Prague's best examples of Cubist architecture, the Museum of Fine Arts contains a complementary collection of Czech Cubism. *(☎24 21 17 31. Metro A: Nám. Republiky. Open Tu-Su 10am-6pm. 40Kč, students 10Kč.)*

ENTERTAINMENT

For concerts and performances, consult *The Prague Post*, *Threshold*, or *Do města-Downtown* (the latter two are free at many cafes and restaurants). Most performances start at 7pm and offer unsold tickets one half hour before show time. From mid-May to early June, the **Prague Spring Festival** draws musicians from around the world. For tickets (400-3500Kč), try **Bohemia Ticket International,** Malé nám. 13, next to Čedok. (☎24 22 78 32. Open M-F 9am-5pm, Sa 9am-2pm.) The **National Theater** (Národní divadlo), Národní třída 2/4, features drama, opera, and ballet. (☎24 90 14 19. Metro B: Národní třída. Tickets 100-1000Kč. Box office open M-F 10am-6pm, Sa-Su 10am-12:30pm and 3-6pm, and 30min. before performances.) **Estates Theater** (Stavovské divadlo), Ovocný trh 1, is left from the pedestrian Na Příkopě (☎24 91 34 37; Metro A, B: Můstek) Where *Don Giovanni* premiered many years ago, it now performs mostly classic theater. Head to the box office of the National Theater, or turn up 30 minutes before the show.

NIGHTLIFE

The most authentic way to experience Prague at night is in an alcoholic fog. With some of the best beers in the world on tap, pubs and beer halls are understandably the city's favorite form of nighttime entertainment. These days, however, authentic pub experiences are restricted to the suburbs and outlying metro stops; nearly everything in central Prague has been overrun by tourists. Prague is not a clubbing city, although there are enough dance clubs pumping out ABBA and techno to satisfy any Eurotrash cravings; more popular are the city's many excellent jazz and rock clubs. Otherwise, you can always retreat to the Charles Bridge to sing along with aspiring Brit-pop guitarists into the wee hours. The monthly *Amigo* (39Kč) is the most thorough guide to gay life in the Czech Republic and Slovakia, with a lot in English. *Gayčko* (59Kč) is a glossier piece of work mostly in Czech.

BARS

U Fleků, Křemencova 11. Metro B: Národní třída; turn right on Spálená away from Národní, right on Myslíkova, and right on Křemencova. The oldest brewhouse in Prague (1491). A steep 50Kč per 0.4L of beer. Open daily 9am-11pm.

Kozička (The Little Goat), Kozí 1. Metro A: Staroměstské; take Dlouhá from the northeast corner of the square, then left onto Kozí, and look for the iron goat. This giant cellar bar is always packed; you'll know why after your first 0.5L of *Krušovice* (25Kč). Czech twenty-somethings stay all night. Open M-F noon-4am, Sa-Su 4pm-4am.

Iron Door, Michalská 13. Metro B: Národní třída; go down Spálená, turn right onto Národní, and left onto Perlová through the intersection until it becomes Michalská. A trendy spot serving everything from Czech favorites to Japanese sushi. Beer 30Kč. Kitchen open daily until 3am.

Vinárna U Sude, Vodičkova 10. Metro A, B: Můstek; cross Václavské nám. to Vodičkova, follow the curve left, and it's on your left. Infinite labyrinth of cavernous cellars. Red wine 110Kč per 1L. Open M-F 11am-midnight, Sa-Su 2pm-midnight.

Le Châpeau Rouge, Jakubská 2. Metro B: Náměstí Republiky; walk through the Powder Tower to Celetná, turn right on Templová, and look for the corner of Templová and Jakubská. The Châpeau recharges the tired souls of travelers by fulfilling all of their earthly needs. Non-stop techno-rock keeps the place pumping until the wee hours. Open M-Th noon-3am, F noon-4am, Sa 4pm-4am, Su 4am-2am.

Cafe Marquis de Sade, Templová 8. Metro B: Nám Republiky; go by the Powder Tower to Celetná; turn right on Templová. Live music Th. Beer 35Kč. Open daily 11am-2am.

Újezd, Újezd 18. Metro B: Národní třída; exit onto Národní, turn left toward the river, cross the Legií bridge, continue straight on Vítězná, and turn right on Újezd. Mecca of mellowness. DJ or live acid jazz 3 times a week. Beer 22Kč. Open daily 11am-4am.

Molly Malone's, U obecního dvora 4. Metro A: Staroměstská; turn right on Křižonvická away from the Charles Bridge, turn right after Nám. Jana Palacha on Široká, which veers left and becomes Vězeňská, and turn left at the end. *Staropramen* beer 30Kč; pint of Guinness 70Kč (cheaper than in Ireland). Open Su-Th noon-1am, F-Sa noon-2am.

Zanzibar, Saská 6 (cell ☎0602 75 24 74). Metro A: Malostranská; head down Nostecká toward the Charles Bridge, turn right on Lázeňská, and left on Saská. The classiest place to see and be seen among Czech cocktail lovers. The tastiest, priciest and most extensive cocktails this side of the Vltava (120-150Kč). Cuban cigars (600-1200Kč). Reserve on weekends. Open daily 5pm-3am.

Jo's Bar and Garáž, Malostranské nám. 7. Metro A: Malostranská. If you can't bear the idea that the people at the next table might not speak English, all-Anglophone Jo's Bar is the perfect spot for you. With new ownership, the bar is getting better. *Staropramen* 30Kč. Open daily 11am-2am, dancing later.

Jáma (The Hollow), V jámě 7. Metro A,C: Muzeum. Hidden off Vodičkova. The closest thing Prague has to a real sports bar, Jáma attracts a diverse but largely foreign crowd. Watch American sports live via satellite. Open daily 11am-1am.

CLUBS AND DISCOS

Roxy, Dlouhá 33. Metro B: Nám. Republiky; walk up Revoluční toward the river and turn left on Dlouhá. Hip locals and in-the-know tourists dance the night away to experimental DJs. Cover from 150-200Kč. Open daily July-Aug. 9pm-late, Sept.-June Tu-Su 9pm-late.

U staré paní, Michalská 9. Metro A, B: Můstek; walk down Na můstku at the end of Václavské nám., continue on Melantrichova, turn left on Havelská, then right on Michalská. Some of Prague's finest jazz vocalists in a dark and classy venue. Shows nightly 9pm-midnight. Cover 160Kč, includes one drink. Open daily 7pm-1am.

ABSINTHE BUT NOT FORGOTTEN Shrouded in Bohemian mystique and taboo, this translucent turquoise fire-water is a force to be reckoned with. Although absinthe has been banned in all but three countries this century due to allegations of opium-lacing and fatal hallucinations, Czechs have had a long love affair with the liquor. It has been the mainstay spirit of the Prague intelligentsia since Kafka's days, and during WWII every Czech adult was rationed 0.5L per month. Today's backpackers, who apparently will drink anything, have discovered the liquor, which at its strongest can be 160 proof. The bravest and most seasoned expats sip it on the rocks, but for the most snapshot-worthy ritual douse a spoonful of sugar in the alcohol, torch it with a match until the sugar caramelizes and the alcohol burns off, and dump the residue into your glass.

U střelce, Karolíny Světlé 12. Metro B: Národní třída. Under the archway on the right. Gay club that draws a diverse crowd for its F and Sa night cabarets. Cover 80Kč. Open W and F-Sa 9:30pm-5am.

Radost FX, Bělehradská 120. Metro C: I.P. Pavlova. Heavily touristed, but still plays badass techno, jungle, and house music. Creative drinks. Cover from 80-150Kč. Open M-Sa 10pm-late. Restaurant upstairs open until 5am.

Palác Akropolis, Kubelíkova 27. Metro A: Jiřího z Poděbrad; head down Slavíkova and turn right onto Kubelíkova. Live bands several times a week. Top Czech act *Psí vojáci* are occasional visitors. Open daily 10pm-5am.

A Club, Milíčova 25. Metro C: Hlavní nádraží. Take tram #5 toward Harfa, #9 toward Spojovací, or #26 toward Nádraží Hostivař; get off at Lipanská. A lesbian nightspot, but men are welcome. Beer 20Kč. Open daily 7pm-sunrise.

Lávka, Novotného lávka 1. Tourists from around the world make Prague memories under the Charles Bridge. Cover from 50Kč. Open daily 10pm-late.

Club Bílý Koníček, Staroměstské nám. 20. A 12th-century cellar transformed into a popular dance spot. Expensive drinks. No cover. Open daily 9pm-5am.

CZECH REPUBLIC

EXCURSIONS FROM PRAGUE

TEREZÍN (THERESIENSTADT). In 1941, Terezín became a concentration camp; by 1942, the entire pre-war civilian population had been evacuated. Nazi propaganda films successfully touted the area as an almost idyllic spa resort where Jews were "allowed" to educate their young, partake in arts and recreation, and live a "fulfilling" life. In reality, 35,000 died here, some of starvation and disease, others at the hands of brutal guards. Another 85,000 Jews were transported to death camps in the east, primarily Auschwitz. The **Ghetto Museum,** on Komenského in town, sets Terezín in the wider Nazi context. (☎78 25 77. Open daily Apr.-Sept. 9am-6pm; Oct.-Mar. 9am-5:30pm. 130Kč, students 100Kč; combined with Small Fortress 150Kč, 110Kč. English tours 240Kč.) You can explore the **Small Fortress** (Malá Peunost) east of town across the river. (Open daily Apr.-Sept. 8am-6pm; Oct.-Mar. 8am-4:30pm.) The furnaces and autopsy lab at the **Jewish cemetery** and **crematorium** are as they were 50 years ago, with the addition of tributes left by the victims' ancestors. Men should cover their heads. (Open Mar.-Nov. Su-F 10am-5pm.) The **bus** from Prague's Florenc station (1hr., every 1-2hr., 59Kč) stops by the central square, where the **tourist office** sells a 29Kč map. (Open daily until 6pm.) ☎**0416.**

KARLŠTEJN. A patriotic gem of the Bohemian countryside, Karlštejn is a walled and turreted fortress built by Charles IV to house his crown jewels and holy relics. (☎68 16 17. Open July-Aug. Tu-Su 9am-6pm; May-June and Sept. 9am-5pm; Apr. and Oct. 9am-4pm; Nov.-Dec. 9am-3pm. English tours 50min.; 7-8 per day; 200Kč, students 100Kč.) The **Chapel of the Holy Cross** is decorated with inlaid precious stones and 128 apocalyptic paintings by medieval Master Theodorik.

(Open Tu-Su 9am-5pm. Mandatory tours 200Kč, in English 600Kč.) Find out if they've finished restoring the chapel before setting out. Karlštejn is most easily reached by **train** from Hlavní nádraží or Praha-Smíchov (45min., every hr., 27Kč). Turn right out of the station, go left over the modern bridge, and walk to the village (2min.). ☎**0311.**

KONOPIŠTĚ. The mighty castle Konopiště (KOH-no-peesh-tyeh), south of Prague in **Benešov,** boasts more than 300,000 taxidermied animals, an eternal tribute to Archduke Franz Ferdinand's shooting prowess. His collection of ivory pistols and armor used in 16th-century Italian theater astounds as well. (Open Tu-F 9am-12:30pm and 1-3pm, Sa-Su 1-4pm. 70Kč, students 35Kč; tours 120Kč, 70Kč. Tours of the Archduke's private rooms 130Kč, in English 250Kč.) **Buses** run from Prague's Florenc station to Benešov (1hr., 7 per day, 59Kč). From the station, turn left on Nádražní, go left over the bridge, continue on Konopištská, bear left at the fork, and follow the road to the castle.

KUTNÁ HORA. East of Prague, the former mining town of Kutná Hora (Mining Mountain) has a history as morbid as the **bone church** that has made the city famous. After 13th-century monks sprinkled soil from the Biblical Golgotha Cemetery on Kutná Hora's own cemetery, the rich and superstitious grew quite keen to be buried there, and it soon became overcrowded. Neighbors started to complain about the stench by the 15th century, so the Cistercian order built a chapel and started cramming in bodies. In a fit of whimsy, the monk in charge began designing flowers out of pelvises and crania. He never finished, but the artist František Rint eventually completed the project in 1870 with flying butt-bones, femur crosses, and a grotesque chandelier made from every bone in the human body. (Open daily Apr.-Oct. 8am-6pm; Nov.-Mar. 9am-noon and 1-4pm. 30Kč, students 15Kč.) Take a **bus** (1½hr., 6 per day, 46Kč) from Prague's Florenc station, then walk or take a local bus to Sedlec Tabák (2km) and follow the signs for the chapel.

ČESKÝ RÁJ NATIONAL PRESERVE. The sandstone **Prachov rocks** (Prachovské skály) in the 2.4 sq. km Český Raj (Czech Paradise) National Preserve were formed by the sedimentation of sandstone, marl, and slate on the bottom of the Mesozoic sea. High, narrow towers and pillars separated by deep, cramped gorges make for stellar climbing and hiking and stunning views. The rocks also boast the ruins of the 14th-century rock castle **Pařez** and the rock pond **Pelíšek.** (Open daily Apr.-Oct. 8am-5pm; swimming in rock pond May-Aug. 25Kč, students 10Kč.) The 588 acres of the park are interwoven by a dense network of **trails;** green signs mark the roundabout route, yellow the most challenging trails, and red the extremely long "Golden Trail," which connects Prachovské skály to **Hrubá Skála,** a rock town surrounding a hilltop castle where hikers enjoy the best view of the sandstone rocks. From the Hrubá Skála castle, the red trails leads up to what remains of **Valdštejn** (Wallenstein) castle.

Buses run from Prague's Florenc station to **Jičín** (1½hr., every hr., 92Kč), where other buses go to Prachovské skály and Český Ráj (15min., every hr., 9Kč). You can also take the fairly easy yellow trail (8km) that starts at the Rumcjas Motel in Jičin. From Valdštejn nám., turn onto Palackého, and go left on Jiraskova (which turns into Kollárova). When you reach the bus stop at Prachovské skály, take a right at the fork; a 10 minute walk brings you to the ticket office by the rocks.

WEST AND SOUTH BOHEMIA

Bursting at the seams with curative springs, West Bohemia is the Czech mecca for those in search of a good bath. Over the centuries, emperors and intellectuals alike have soaked in the waters of Karlovy Vary (Carlsbad in German). South Bohemia is a rustic Eden, a scenic ensemble of scattered villages, unspoiled brooks, virgin forests, and castle ruins. Low hills and plentiful attractions have made the region a favorite for wildlife-watching, castle-traipsing, and *Budvar*-guzzling cyclists.

KARLOVY VARY (CARLSBAD) ☎017

A stroll into Karlovy Vary's spa district or up into the hills reveals why this lovely town developed into one of the great "salons" of Europe, frequented by Johann Sebastian Bach, Peter the Great, Sigmund Freud, and Karl Marx. It was once a vacation spot for Holy Roman Emperor Karel IV; these days, older Germans seeking the therapeutic powers of the springs are the main vacationers.

PRACTICAL INFO, ACCOMMODATIONS, AND FOOD. **Trains** go from **Horní nádraží,** northwest of town, to Prague (4½hr. plus a 1-2hr. layover in Chomutov, 4-5 per day, 152Kč). To reach the town center from the train station, take bus #11 or 13 (8Kč) to the end. Faster **buses** zoom from **Dolní nádraží,** on Západní, to Prague (2½hr., 25 per day, 89-130Kč). Buy tickets at the **ČSAD office,** Dr. Engla 6. (Open M 6am-6pm, Tu-F 8am-6pm, Sa 8am-noon, Su 12:30-6pm.) To get to the town center from the bus station, turn left on Západní, continue past the Becher building, and bear right on T. G. Masaryka, which runs parallel to Bechera, the other main thoroughfare. **Karlovarský Autorent,** Nám. Dr. Horákové 18, books doubles in private homes for 1000Kč. (☎322 28 33. Open M-F 9am-5pm, Sa-Su 9am-1pm.) Follow the directions from the bus and train stations to T.G. Masaryka and bear right at the post office to find **Pension Kosmos,** Zahradní 39, in the center of the spa district. (☎322 04 73; fax 322 31 68. Singles 440-750Kč; doubles 720-1340Kč.) Luxurious **Pension Romania,** Zahradní 49, is next to the post office at the intersection with T.G. Masaryka. (☎322 28 22. Breakfast included. 850-930Kč per person, students 680-745Kč.) Karlovy Vary is known for its sweet *oplatky* (spa wafers); try them at a street vendor (5Kč). The almost **Vegetarian Restaurant,** I.P. Pavlova 25, has great veggie dishes. (Fruit kebab 45Kč. Open daily 11am-midnight.) A **supermarket,** Horova 1, is in the large building with the "Městská tržnice" sign over the local bus station. (Open M-F 6am-7pm, Sa 7am-5pm, Su 9am-5pm. V, MC.) **Postal code:** 36001.

SIGHTS AND ENTERTAINMENT. The spa district officially begins with the Victorian **Bath 5** (Lázně 5), Smetanovy Sady 1, across the street from the post office, marked by flowers displaying the date. (Thermal baths 300Kč. Underwater massages 420Kč. Open M-F 8am-9pm, Sa 8am-6pm, Su 10am-6pm. Massages M-F 3-9pm, Sa-Su 10am-6pm.) The pedestrian **Mlýnské nábř.** meanders alongside the Teplá beneath shady trees. **Bath 3** lies to the right, just before **Freedom Spring** (Pramen svobody). Next door, the imposing **Mill Colonnade** (Mlýnská kolonáda) shelters five different springs. The **Zawojski House,** Trižiště 9, now the Živnostenská Banka, is a gorgeous cream-and-gold Art Nouveau building. The **Vřídlo spring,** Karlovy Vary's hottest and highest-shooting spring, inside the **Vřídlo Colonnade** (Vřídelní kolonáda), spouts 30L of 72° Celsius water each second. (Open daily 6am-6:30pm.) Follow Stará Louka until signs point you to the **funicular,** which leads to the 555m **Diana Observatory** (Rozhledna) and a magnificent panorama of the city. (Funicular runs every 15min. 9am-7pm. 25Kč, round-trip 40Kč. Tower open 9am-7pm. 10Kč.) **Propaganda,** Jaltská 5, off Bechera, attracts a hip, young crowd with live music and a trendy blue-steel interior. (Mixed drinks 40-100Kč. Open daily 5pm-late.)

ČESKÉ BUDĚJOVICE ☎038

No amount of beer will ever help you correctly pronounce České Budějovice (CHESS-kay BOOD-yeh-yoh-vee-tsay). The town was known as Budweis in the 19th century, when it inspired the name of the popular but pale North American Budweiser bearing little relation to the malty local *Budvar.* Surrounded by Renaissance and Baroque buildings, cobblestone **Nám. Otakara II** is the largest square in the country. The 72m **Black Tower** (Černá věž) in one corner looms over the town. Beware: the treacherous stairs are difficult even for the sober. (Open July-Aug. daily 10am-6pm; Sept.-Oct. and Apr.-June Tu-Su 10am-6pm. 10Kč.) Tours of the city's most famous attraction, the **Budweiser Brewery,** Karoliny Světlé 4, can be arranged for groups of six or more through the tourist office (100Kč per person). Take bus #2 or 4 from the center of town to the brewery.

THIS BUD'S FOR EU Many Yankees, having tasted the malty goodness of a *Budvar* brew, return home to find it conspicuously unavailable. What's up? The answer lies in a tale of trademarks and town names. České Budějovice (Budweis in German) had been brewing its own style of lager for centuries when the Anheuser-Busch brewery in St. Louis came out with its Budweiser-style beer in 1876. Not until the 1890s, however, did the Budějovice Pivovar (Brewery) begin producing a beer labeled "Budweiser." International trademark conflicts ensued, and in 1911 the companies signed a non-competition agreement: *Budvar* got markets in Europe and Anheuser-Busch took North America. But Anheuser-Busch attempted to buy a controlling interest in the makers of *Budvar*, to which the Czech government summarily replied: "nyeh." *Budvar* lobbied to make the "Budweiser" a designation as exclusive as that of "Champagne," meaning that any brand sold in the EU under that name would have to come from the Budweiser region. But a 2000 ruling ended the 89-year conflict and gave both Anheuser-Busch and *Budvar* the right to sell their brand in the UK.

Trains travel to Nádražní 12 from Prague (2½hr., 12 per day, 114Kč) and Brno (4½hr., 2 per day, 152Kč). The TIC **tourist office,** Nám. Otakara II 26, books central private rooms from 230Kč. (☎/fax 635 25 89. Open May-Sept. M-F 8am-6:30pm, Sa 8am-4:30pm, Su 9am-4:30pm; Oct.-Apr. M-F 8am-6pm, Sa 8am-4:30pm.) To get to the center of town from the station, walk right on Nádražní, turn left at the first crosswalk, and follow the pedestrian street, Lannova třída, as it becomes Kanovnická and pours into the square. From the bus station, opposite and to the left of the train station, take bus #1, 14, or 17 five stops to "U parku" and continue 150m along the side street that branches off to the right behind the bus stop to get to the friendly **Penzion U Výstaviště,** U Výstaviště 17. (☎724 01 48. 1 night 250Kč, subsequent nights 200Kč.) The University of South Bohemia **dorms,** Studentská 19, are open to tourists July through September. Take tram #1 from the bus station five stops to "U parku"; backtrack down Husova, then take the second right on Studentská. (☎777 44 00. Doubles 260-300Kč.) **Večerka grocery** is at Palackého 10; enter on Hroznova. (Open M-F 7am-8pm, Sa 7am-1pm, Su 8am-8pm.) Sample Czech cuisine at **Restaurace U paní Emy,** Široká 25, by the main square. (Tábor steak 95Kč, veggie dishes 50-70Kč. Open M-Th 10:30am-1am, F-Sa 10:30am-3am, Sa noon-11pm.) **Postal code:** 370 01.

ČESKÝ KRUMLOV ☎0337

The worst part about Český Krumlov (TSCHes-kee KRUM-lov) is leaving. Weaving medieval streets, cobblestone promenades, and Bohemia's second-largest castle make the gorgeous, UNESCO-protected town one of the most popular spots in Eastern Europe. Come for a day, but you're destined to stay for weeks.

PRACTICAL INFO, ACCOMMODATIONS, AND FOOD. Frequent **buses** arrive from České Budějovice (30-45min., 7-31 per day, 22-24Kč). From the station, head to the upper street (near stops #20-25), turn right (with the station to your back), follow the small dirt path that veers left and heads uphill, turn right on Kaplická, cross the highway at the light, and head straight onto Horní, which brings you to Nám. Svornosti. The **tourist office,** Nám Svornosti 1, books pension rooms (from 600Kč) as well as cheaper private rooms. (☎71 16 50. Open daily 9am-6pm.) Log onto the **Internet** at the tourist office (10Kč per 10min.) or at **Internet Café,** in the castle courtyard (30Kč per 15min.). To get to the awesome **U vodníka,** Po vodě 55, or **Krumlov House,** Rooseveltova 68, both run by an American expat couple, follow the directions above from the station and turn left onto Rooseveltova after the light (just before the bridge). From there, follow the signs to U vodníka or continue down the street to Krumlov House. (☎71 19 35; email vodnik@ck.bohem-net.cz. Laundry. Bike rental. Dorms 200Kč; doubles 500Kč.) To get to **Hostel Skippy,** Plešivecká 123, follow the directions above from the station, but turn left at the light onto the highway, cross the river, and bear right on Plešivecká. (☎72 83 80. Laundry. Bike rental. Dorms 175Kč; doubles 400Kč.) Get **groceries** at **SPAR,** Linecká 49. (Open M-Sa 7am-6pm, Su 9am-6pm.) **Postal code:** 38101.

SIGHTS AND ENTERTAINMENT. The stone courtyards of the **castle,** perched high above the town, are free to the public. Two tours cover different parts of the lavish interior, including a frescoed ballroom, a splendid Baroque theater, and Renaissance-style rooms. The **galleries of the crypts** showcase local artists' sculptures and ceramics. Ascend the 162 steps of the **tower** for a fabulous view. (Castle open June-Aug. Tu-Su 9am-6pm; May and Sept. Tu-Su 9am-5pm; Apr. and Oct. Tu-Su 9am-4pm. 1hr. tours in English 150Kč, students 75Kč. Crypts open May-Oct. Tu-Su 10am-5pm; July-Aug. daily 10am-5pm. 30Kč, students 20Kč. Tower open daily May-Sept. 9am-6pm; Apr. and Oct. 11am-3pm. 30Kč, students 20Kč.) The Austrian painter Egon Schiele (1890-1918) lived in Český Krumlov for a while—until the citizens ran him out for painting burghers' daughters in the nude. Decades later, the **Egon Schiele International Cultural Center,** Široká 70-72, displays his work, along with paintings by other 20th-century Central European artists. (Open daily 10am-6pm. 120Kč, students 60Kč.) Borrow an **inner tube** from your hostel to spend a lazy day drifting down the Vltava, or hike up into the hills to go **horseback riding** at **Jezdecký klub Slupenec,** Slupenec 1; from the town center, follow Horní to the highway, take the second left on Křížová, and follow the red trail up to Slupenec. (☎71 10 53. Open Tu-Sa 9am-6pm. 220Kč per hr. Call ahead.) Rent a **bike** (300Kč per day) from **Globtour Vltava,** Kájovská 62, to cruise the Bohemian countryside **Zlatá Koruna,** a monastery built in 1263, is a great trip. Throw 'em back at **U Hada** (Snake Bar), Rybárška 37 (open daily 7pm-3am) or **U baby,** at Rooseveltova 66.

MORAVIA

Wine-making Moravia makes up the easternmost third of the Czech Republic. Home of the country's finest folk-singing tradition and two of its leading universities, it's also the birthplace of a number of notables, including Tomáš G. Masaryk, Czechoslovakia's founder and first president, and psychoanalyst Sigmund Freud. Gregor Mendel founded modern genetics in his pea-garden in a Brno monastery.

BRNO ☎05

The second-largest city in the Czech Republic, Brno (berh-NO) is a mecca of business and industry, and its streets show it: scores of "erotic club" sirens call out to lonely men, and restaurant prices have corporate expense accounts in mind. The city also offers an extensive array of Gothic and Baroque churches and splendidly cheap opera. While not as scenic or touristy as other places in the Czech Republic, Brno lets travelers experience a living Czech city.

PRACTICAL INFO, ACCOMMODATIONS, AND FOOD. **Trains** (☎42 21 48 03) go to: Bratislava (2hr., 9 per day, 115Kč); Vienna (2hr., 1 per day, 525Kč); Prague (3hr., 16 per day, 164-224Kč); and Budapest (4½hr., 2 per day, 872Kč). From the main exit, cross the three tram lines on Nádražní to Masarykova to reach the main square, **Nám. Svobody. Buses** (☎43 21 77 33) leave from Zvonařka, down Plotní from the train station, for Vienna (2½hr., 3 per day, 250Kč) and Prague (3hr., 112-116Kč). To get from the bus to the train station, follow Plotní as it becomes Dornych, and turn left onto Nádražni. The **tourist office** (Kulturní a informační centrum města Brna), Radnická 8, off Zelný trh, books rooms (from 400Kč) and hostels (200Kč). Follow the directions above from the train station, then take a left off Masarykova on Květinářska just before Svobody. (☎42 21 10 90; fax 42 21 07 58. Open M-F 8am-6pm, Sa-Su 9am-5pm.) **@InternetCafé** is at Lidická 17. (2Kč per min. Open M-F 10am-10pm, Sa-Su 2-10pm.) From the train station, head up Masarykova and turn right on Josefská, which leads to Novobranská and the new **Hotel Astorka,** at #3. (☎42 51 03 70; fax 42 51 01 06; email astorka@jamu.cz. Doubles 840Kč per person, students 420Kč; triples 945Kč, 472.50Kč.) Take tram #9 or 12 from the train station to the end at "Komárov," continue on Hněvkovského, and turn left on the unmarked Pompova (the second-to-last turn before the railroad overpass) to find **Interservis (HI),** Lomená 48. (☎/fax 45 23 42 32. Dorms 260Kč, students 230Kč; with breakfast 310Kč, 270Kč.) A **Tesco supermarket** is behind the train station. (Open M-F 7am-8pm, Sa 7am-7pm, Su 8am-6pm.) **Postal code:** 60200.

SIGHTS AND ENTERTAINMENT. If you like macabre morbidity, try the **Capuchin Monastery Crypt** (Hrobka Kapucínského kláštera), just left of Masarykova from the train station, where monks have embalmed more than 100 of their 18th-century brothers. (☎42 21 23 32. Open M-Sa 9am-noon and 2-4:30pm, Su 11-noon and 2-4:30pm. 40Kč, students 20Kč.) On Petrov Hill, just south of Zelný trh and across the square from the town hall, the overachieving bells of **Peter and Paul Cathedral** (Biskupská katedrála sv. Petra a Pavla) strike noon at 11am. Allegedly Brno was saved from the Swedish siege one day in 1645, when the besieging general told his army he would withdraw if they hadn't captured the town by noon. The folks of Brno rang the bells early, and the Swedes slunk away. (Cathedral open daily 8am-6pm; tower open daily 10am-6pm. Church free. Tower 20Kč, students 15Kč. Crypt 20Kč, students 15Kč.) In the heart of Old Brno, the High Gothic **Basilica of the Assumption of the Virgin Mary** (Basilika Nanebevzetí Panny Marie) houses the 13th-century Black Madonna, the Czech Republic's oldest wooden icon, which supposedly held off the Swedes in 1645. (Open M-Sa 5-7:15pm, Su also 7am-12:15pm and 5-7:15pm.) The monastery next door was home to **Johann Gregor Mendel,** father of modern genetics. The **Mendelianum,** Mendlovo nám. 1a, documents his life and work. (Open daily July-Aug. 9am-6pm; Sept.-June 8am-5pm. 8Kč, students 4Kč.)

EXCURSION FROM BRNO OR ČESKÉ BUDĚJOVICE: TELČ. The Italian aura of Telč (TELCH) is a result of the trip the town's ruler took to Genoa in 1546, and the battalion of Italian artists and craftsmen he brought back with him. As you step over the cobblestone footbridge to the main square—flanked by long arcades of peach gables, lime-green Baroque bays, and time-worn terra-cotta roofs—it's easy to see why UNESCO designated the gingerbread town a World Heritage Monument. Browse the porticos for Bohemian glass figurines, watch the children from neighboring towns sing folk songs and dance in traditional Czech attire every Sunday, and definitely don't miss a tour of the castles: *trasa A* leads you through Renaissance hallways, through the old chapel, and under extravagant ceilings; *trasa B* leads through rooms decorated in later styles. (Open Tu-Su May-Aug. 9-noon and 1-5pm; Mar.-Apr. and Sept.-Oct. 9am-noon and 1-4pm. Tours 60Kč, students 30Kč.) You can rent a **rowboat** from **Půjčovná lodí,** on the shore, to view the castle and town from the swan-filled lake. (Open daily June 20-Aug. 10am-7pm. 20Kč per 30min.) **Buses** running between Brno and České Budějovice stop at Telč (2hr., 8 per day, 70-80Kč). From the station, follow the pedestrian path, turn right on Tyršova, then left on Masarykovo, and pass under the archway on the right to reach the square, Nám. Zachariáše z Hradce. The **tourist office,** Nám. Zachariáše z Hradce 10 (☎724 31 45; fax 724 35 57), books private rooms.

DENMARK (DANMARK)

DANISH KRONER

US$1 = 8.69KR	10KR = US$1.15
CDN$1 = 5.87KR	10KR = CDN$1.70
UK£1 = 12.22KR	10KR = UK£0.82
IR£1 = 9.49KR	10KR = IR£1.05
AUS$1 = 4.88KR	10KR = AUS$2.05
NZ$1 = 3.74KR	10KR = NZ$2.67
SAR1 = 1.22KR	10KR = SAR8.19
EUR€1 = 7.47KR	10KR = EUR€1.34

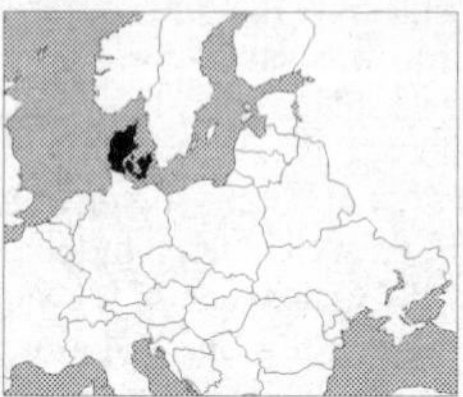

Country code: 45. **International dialing prefix:** 00. Denmark has no city codes. From outside Denmark, dial int'l dialing prefix (see inside back cover) + 45 + local number.

Like Thumbelina, the heroine of native son Hans Christian Andersen's fairy tales, Denmark has a tremendous personality crammed into a tiny body. Danes delight in their eccentric traditions, such as burning witches in effigy on Midsummer's Eve, dancing around the Christmas tree, and eating pickled herring on New Year's Day. Although Danes are justifiably proud of their fertile farmlands, beech forests, chalk cliffs, and sand dunes, their sense of self-criticism is reflected in the Danish literary canon: the more famous voices are Søren Kierkegaard, Hans Christian Andersen, and Isak Dinesen. Denmark is also the cultural and geographic bridge between Scandinavia and continental Europe. From the 13th to 16th centuries, the Danish crown ruled an empire uniting Norway, Sweden, Iceland, and parts of Germany. Christianity, the Protestant Reformation, and the socialist movements of the late 19th century entered Scandinavia via Denmark. Today, Denmark has a progressive youth culture that beckons travelers to the pristine beaches of Funen and the hip pub scene in Copenhagen. Home to the famous beers Carlsberg and Tuborg, this gentle country knows how to have a good time. Contrary to the suggestion of a certain English playwright, very little seems to be rotten in the state of Denmark.

FACTS AND FIGURES

Official Name: Kingdom of Denmark.

Government: Constitutional Monarchy.

Capital: Copenhagen.

Land Area: 43,075 sq. km.

Geography: Coast and islands; rolling plains.

Climate: Temperate, overcast with humidity; mild winters and cool summers.

Major Cities: Copenhagen, Aalborg, Århus, Esbjerg, Odense.

Population: 5,360,000. Urban 85%, Rural 15%.

Language: Danish, Faroese, Greenlandic.

Religion: Evangelical Lutheran (91%), other Protestant and Roman Catholic (2%).

Average Income Per Capita: US$23,300.

Major Exports: Machinery, meat, fuels, and dairy products.

DISCOVER DENMARK

Begin in chic, progressive **Copenhagen,** where you can cruise the canals, party until dawn, and ponder Kierkegaard (p. 272). Daytrip north to the fabulous **Louisiana**

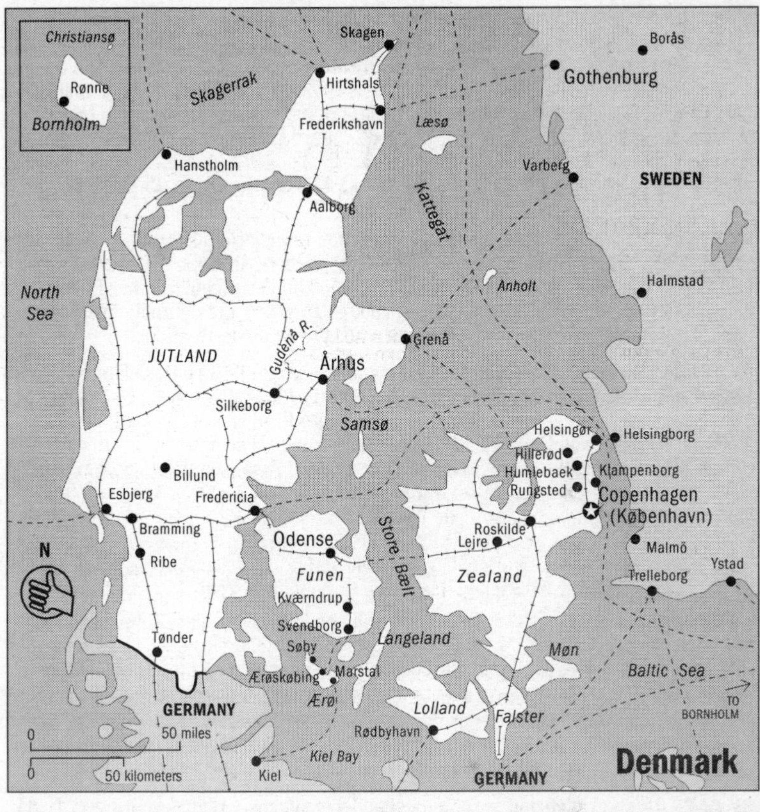

museum and **Elsinore,** Hamlet's castle, or shoot south to **Roskilde** and the fascinating Viking Ship Museum (p. 280). If you time it right, you'll hit the massive Roskilde Festival, when rock takes over the city. For the best beaches in Denmark, ferry to the island of **Bornholm** (p. 281). Move west over the Storebæltsbro bridge to Funen and **Odense** (p. 282), the hometown of Hans Christian Andersen, then head south to the stunning 16th-century castle **Egeskov Slot** (p. 283). From the southern end of Funen, hop on a ferry to the idyllic island of **Ærø** (p. 283), a throwback to the Denmark of several centuries ago. Cross the Lillebælt to Jutland, where laid-back **Århus** delights with students and culture (p. 284), then play with blocks at nearby **Legoland** (p. 285). On your way back down south, stop in historic **Ribe** (p. 287).

ESSENTIALS

DOCUMENTS AND FORMALITIES

South Africans need a **visa** to enter Denmark for tourist visits; nationals of Australia, Canada, New Zealand, and the US do not for visits shorter than three months.

EMBASSIES AND CONSULATES

Foreign embassies and consulates in Denmark are in **Copenhagen** (p. 272).

Danish Embassies at Home: Australia, 15 Hunter St., Yarralumla, ACT 2600 (☎ (02) 62 73 21 95; fax 62 73 38 64); **Canada,** 47 Clarence St., #450, Ottawa, ON K1N 9K1 (☎ (613)

562 18 11; fax 562 18 12); **Ireland,** 121 St. Stephen's Green, Dublin 2 (☎ (01) 475 64 04; fax 478 45 36); **New Zealand,** 273 Bleakhouse Rd., Howick, P.O. Box 619, Auckland 1 (☎ (09) 537 30 99; fax 537 30 67); **South Africa,** 8th fl., Sanlam Centre, corner of Pretorius and Andries St; P.O. Box 2942, Pretoria 0001 (☎ (012) 322 05 95; fax 322 05 96); **UK,** 55 Sloane St., London SW1X 9SR (☎ (020) 73 33 02 00; www.denmark.org.uk); **US,** 3200 Whitehaven St. NW, Washington, DC 20008 (☎ (202) 234-4300; www.denmarkemb.org).

GETTING THERE AND GETTING AROUND

BY PLANE. The airport in **Copenhagen** handles international flights from cities around the world, mostly by SAS, Delta, United, British Airways, Air France, KLM, Lufthansa, and Swissair. **Billund Airport** in Jutland handles flights to other European cities. **SAS** (Scandinavian Airlines; US ☎ (800) 437 58 04), the national airline company, offers youth, spouse, and senior discounts to some destinations.

BY TRAIN AND BY BUS. Eurail is valid on all state-run **DSB** routes. The *buy-in-Scandinavia* **Scanrail Pass** allows five days within 15 (1390kr, under 26 1040kr) or 21 consecutive days (2110kr, 1585kr) of unlimited rail travel through Denmark, Norway, Sweden, and Finland, as well as many free or discounted ferry rides. This differs from the *buy-outside-Scandinavia* **Scanrail Pass** (see p. 59). Seat reservations, compulsory on many international trains (20-68kr), can be made at central stations or by phone. For domestic info, call ☎70 13 14 15; for international info, ☎70 13 14 16. Remote towns are typically served by **buses** from the nearest train station. The national **bus** network is very reliable and fairly cheap. You can take buses or trains over the new **Østersund bridge** from Copenhagen from Malmö, Sweden.

BY FERRY. Railpasses earn discounts or free rides on many Scandinavian ferries. The free *Vi Rejser* newspaper, at tourist offices, can help you sort out the dozens of smaller ferries that serve Denmark's outlying islands. For info on ferries from **Copenhagen** to **Norway, Sweden, Poland,** and **Bornholm,** see p. 273. Bornholm is also served by other international ferry routes (see p. 281). **Ærø,** reachable by boat from southern Funen (see p. 283), is connected by boat to **Kiel, Germany** (see p. 283). For more on connections from **Jutland** to **England, Sweden,** and **Norway,** see p. 284.

BY CAR. Roads are **toll-free,** except for the **Storebæltsbro** (Great Belt Bridge; 210kr) and the Øresund bridge (around 300kr). **Car rental** is around US$75 per day, plus insurance and a per-kilometer fee; to rent a car, you must be at least 20 years old (in some cases 25). **Speed limits** are 50kph (30mph) in urban areas, 80kph (50mph) on highways, and 110kph (68mph) on motorways. **Service centers** for motorists, called *Info-terias*, are spaced along Danish highways. Most **gas stations** in Denmark are open for self-service from 6 or 7am to 9pm or midnight; gas averages 6.50kr per liter. For more info on driving in Denmark, contact the **Forenede Danske Motorejere (FDM),** Firskovvej 32, Box 500, DK-2800 Lyngby (☎45 27 07 07; www.fdm.dk).

BY BIKE AND BY THUMB. Flat terrain and well-marked urban and rural bike paths make Denmark a cyclist's dream. You can **rent bikes** (40-55kr per day) from some tourist offices, rental shops, and a few train stations in North Zealand. The **Dansk Cyklist Førbund** (Danish Cycle Federation), Rømersg. 7, 1362 Copenhagen K (☎33 32 31 21; www.dcf.dk), can hook you up with longer-term rentals. For info on bringing your bike on a train (which costs 50kr or less), pick up *Bikes and Trains* at any train station. **Hitchhiking** is legal in Denmark, but is, as usual, risky. *Let's Go* does not recommend hitchhiking.

TOURIST SERVICES AND MONEY

EMERGENCY. Police: ☎112. **Ambulance:** ☎112. **Fire:** ☎112.

TOURIST OFFICES. Contact the **main tourist board** in Denmark at Vesterbrogade 6D, 1620 Copenhagen V (☎33 11 14 15; email dt@dt.dk). **Use It** in Copenhagen offers many excellent services, particularly for budget travelers (see p. 274).

Tourist Boards at Home: US, 655 Third Ave., New York, NY 10017 (☎ (212) 949 2333; www.dt.dk); **UK,** 55 Sloane St., London SW1X 9SY (☎ (020) 72 59 59 57; www.dt.dk).

MONEY. The Danish monetary unit is the **kroner** (kr), divided into 100 *øre.* Denmark has a high cost of living; expect to spend from US$30 (hostels and supermarkets) to US$60 (cheap hotels and restaurants) per day. Take advantage of buffet restaurants, which offer all-you-can-eat buffet lunches for around 50kr. The easiest way to get cash is from **ATMs: Cirrus** and **PLUS** cash cards are widely accepted, and many machines give advances on credit cards. There are no hard and fast rules about **tipping,** but it's always polite to round up to the nearest 10kr in restaurants and for taxis. In general, service at restaurants is included in the bill. Tipping up to 15% is becoming common in Copenhagen. Bargaining is not common. Denmark has one of the highest **VATs** in Europe, a flat 25% on just about everything except food. You can get a VAT refund upon leaving the country if you have spent at least US$95 in one store.

BUSINESS HOURS. Shops are normally open Monday-Thursday from about 9 or 10am to 6pm, and Friday until 7 or 8pm; they are also usually open Saturday mornings (Copenhagen shops stay open all day Saturday). Regular **banking** hours are Monday-Wednesday and Friday 9:30am-4pm, Thursday 9:30am-6pm.

ACCOMMODATIONS AND CAMPING

HOSTELS. Denmark's 101 **HI youth hostels** *(vandrerhjem)* are cheap (less than 100kr per night; nonmembers add 25kr), well-run, and have no age limit. The one- to five-star rating system doesn't take lovely settings, friendly owners, or serendipitous encounters into account, but higher-rated hostels may have in-room bathrooms and longer opening hours. Sheets cost about 40kr more. All-you-can-eat breakfasts usually run 40kr. Reception desks normally take a break from noon to 4pm and close for the day between 9 and 11pm. Reservations are required in winter and highly recommended in summer, especially near beaches. For more info, contact the **Danish Youth Hostel Association** (☎31 31 36 12; fax 31 31 36 26; email ldv@danhostel.dk; www.danhostel.dk).

OTHER LOCAL ACCOMMODATIONS. Denmark's hotels are generally expensive (250-850kr per night). Many tourist offices book rooms in **private homes** (125-175kr), which are often in the suburbs.

CAMPING. Denmark's 525 official **campgrounds** (about 60kr per person) rank from one-star (toilets and drinking water) to three-star (showers and laundry) to five-star (swimming, restaurants, and stoves). You'll either need a Danish **camping pass,** available at all campgrounds and valid for one year (45kr, families 75kr, groups 120kr), or an **international camping card.** The **Danish Camping Council** (*Campingrådet;* ☎39 27 80 44) sells *Camping Denmark* and passes. The Danish Youth Hostel Association's free *Camping/Youth and Family Hostels* is also adequate. Sleeping in train stations, in parks, and on public property is illegal.

FOOD AND DRINK

A "Danish" in Denmark is a *wienerbrød* ("Viennese bread"), found in bakeries alongside other flaky treats. For more substantial fare, Danes favor small, open-faced sandwiches called *smørrebrød.* For cheap eats, look for lunch specials *(dagens ret)* and all-you-can-eat buffets (*spis alt du kan* or *tag selv buffet*). Beer *(Øl)* is usually served as a *lille* or *stor fadøl* (0.25L or 0.5L draft), but bottled beer tends to be cheaper. National brews are **Carlsberg** and **Tuborg.** The drinking age in bars in Denmark is 18, but many clubs have higher age limits; you must be 15 to buy beer and wine in stores. Many **vegetarian** *(vegetarret)* options are the result of Indian and Mediterranean influences, but salads and veggies *(grøntsaker)* can be found on most menus. For more on being veggie in Denmark, contact **Dansk Vegetarforening,** Borups Allé 131, 2000 Frederiksberg (☎38 34 24 48).

COMMUNICATION

MAIL. Mailing a postcard or letter to Australia, Canada, New Zealand, the US, or South Africa costs 8kr; to elsewhere in Europe, 4.50kr. Domestic postage is 4kr. *Poste Restante* is available at main post offices, and is free. Government-issued picture IDs are often requested.

TELEPHONES. Denmark has **no city codes;** include all digits for local *and* international calls. Pay phones are split fairly evenly between card- and coin-operated. Buy phone cards at post offices or kiosks (30 units 30kr; 53 units 50kr; 110 units 100kr). Even if you are dialing a toll-free number, you must use a phone card; you will not, however, be charged. For domestic directory info, call ☎118; international info, ☎113; collect calls, ☎141. **International direct dial** numbers include: **AT&T,** ☎80 01 00 10; **Sprint,** ☎80 01 08 77; **MCI WorldPhone Direct,** ☎80 01 00 22; **Canada Direct,** ☎80 01 00 11; **BT Direct,** ☎80 01 02 90; **Ireland Direct,** ☎80 01 03 53; **Australia Direct,** ☎80 01 00 61; **Telecom New Zealand,** ☎80 01 00 64; and **Telkom South Africa,** ☎80 01 00 27.

LANGUAGE. The Danish add *æ* (like the "e" in "egg"), *ø* (like the "i" in "first"), and *å* (sometimes written as *aa;* like the "o" in "lord") to the end of the alphabet; thus Århus follows Viborg in an alphabetical list. Knowing *ikke* ("not") will help you figure out signs like "No smoking" *(ikke-ryger); åben/lukket* (O-ben/loock-eh) means open/closed. Nearly all Danes speak English, but a few Danish words might help break the ice: try *skål* (skoal), or "cheers." Danish has a distinctive glottal stop known as a *stød.* To gain some insight into the Danish language, see p. 981.

HOLIDAYS AND FESTIVALS

Holidays: Easter (Apr. 15); Common Prayer Day (May 11); Ascension Day (May 24); Whit Sunday and Monday (June 3-4); Constitution Day (June 5); Midsummer (June 22-23); Christmas (Dec. 24-26); and New Year's Eve (Dec. 31).

Festivals: Danes celebrate **Fastelavn** (Carneval) in Feb. and Mar. In May, the **Copenhagen Jazz Festival** does a week of concerts, many free. The **Roskilde Festival** is an immense open-air music festival held in Roskilde in June (see p. 280).

COPENHAGEN (KØBENHAVN)

Despite the swan ponds and cobblestone clichés that Hans Christian Andersen's fairy-tale imagery brings to mind, Denmark's capital is a fast-paced modern city that offers cafes to rival Paris's, nightlife to rival London's, and style to rival New York's—all at half the cost of Oslo or Stockholm. Some of the most beautiful (and best-dressed) people on the planet can be seen walking down Strøget, the pedestrian zone. Though studded with elaborate past and present royal palaces, Copenhagen is a cosmopolitan city where angelic blond children walk to school with their Inuit, Turkish, Greek, Vietnamese, and Ethiopian classmates. But if you still crave Andersen's Copenhagen, the *Lille Havfrue* (Little Mermaid), Tivoli, and Nyhavn's Hanseatic gingerbread houses are also yours to discover.

GETTING THERE AND GETTING AROUND

Flights: Kastrup Airport (☎32 47 47 47 or 32 54 17 01). S-trains connect the airport to Central Station (12min., every 20min., 18kr).

Trains: Trains stop at **Hovedbanegården.** Domestic travel ☎70 13 14 15; international ☎70 13 14 16. To: **Hamburg** (4hr., 5 per day, 425kr, under 26 320kr); **Stockholm** (9hr., 4-5 per day, 700kr, 540kr); **Oslo** (9hr., 3 per day, 740kr, 530kr); and **Berlin** (9hr., 1 per day, 895kr, 580kr). **Reservations** mandatory (20kr). For cheaper travel to **Gothenburg, Stockholm, Oslo,** and **Östersund, Sweden,** buy a **Scanrabat** ticket a week ahead; you must reserve. The **InterRail Center** in the station offers a lounge, phones, showers (10kr), a stove, maps, free luggage storage, and free condoms to BIJ, Scanrail, and Eurail holders. Open June to mid-Sept. daily 6:30-10:30am and 4-10pm.

Public Transportation: Bus info ☎36 13 14 15 (daily 7am-9:30pm); **train** info ☎33 14 17 01 (daily 7am-9pm). **S-trains** (subways and suburban trains) and **buses** run M-Sa 5am-12:30am, Su 6am-12:30am and operate on a zone system; 2 zones cover central Copenhagen, and 7 get you to Helsingør. 2-zone **tickets** run 12kr; add 6kr per additional zone. The cheaper **rabatkort** (rebate card), available from kiosks and bus drivers, gets you 10 "clips," each good for one journey within a specified number of zones; clip cards in the yellow machines at the front of the bus and in S-bahn stations at the beginning of your journey. The blue 2-zone *rabatkort* (80kr) can be clipped more than once for longer trips. Tickets and clips allow 1hr. of transfers. The **24hr. pass** grants unlimited bus and train transport in greater Copenhagen (70kr); buy at the Tivoli tourist office or any train station. **Railpasses,** including **Eurail,** are good on S-trains but not buses. **Night buses** run on different routes during the remaining hours and charge double fare. A North Zealand public transport map (5kr) is available at the bus info center on Rådhuspladsen. The **Copenhagen Card,** sold in hotels, tourist offices, and train stations, grants unlimited travel in North Zealand, discounts on ferries to Sweden, and admission to most sights (24hr. 155kr, 48hr. 255kr, 72hr. 320kr), but isn't always worth it unless you plan to ride the bus religiously and see several museums a day.

Ferries: Scandinavian Seaways (☎33 42 33 42; fax 33 42 33 41) departs daily at 5pm for **Oslo** (16hr., 480-735kr, under 26 315-570kr; Eurail and Scanrail 50% off). Trains to **Sweden** cross over on the **Helsingør-Helsingborg** ferry at no extra charge. Hourly **hydrofoils** (☎33 12 80 88) to **Malmö** go from Havnegade, at the end of Nyhavn (40min., 19-49kr). Both **Flyvebådene** and **Pilen** run hourly hydrofoils to Malmö from 9am-11pm (45min., 50kr). **Polferries** (☎33 11 46 45; fax 33 11 95 78) set out Su, M, and W 8am, and Th and F 7:30pm from Nordre Toldbod, 12A (off Esplanaden) to **Świnoujście, Poland** (10hr., 340kr, with ISIC 285kr). **Bornholmstrafikken** (☎33 13 18 66; fax 33 93 18 66) goes to **Bornholm** (7hr., 1-2 per day, 189kr).

Taxis: ☎35 35 35 35, ☎38 77 77 77, or ☎38 10 10 10. Base fare 22kr; add 8kr per km 7am-4pm, 10kr per km 4pm-7am. From Central Station to airport costs 150kr.

Bike Rental: City Bike lends bikes for free. Deposit 20kr at any of 150 bike racks citywide and retrieve the coin upon return at any rack. **Københavns Cykler,** Reventlowsgade 11 (☎33 33 86 13), rents for 50kr per day, 225kr per week; 300kr deposit. Open July-Aug. M-F 8am-6pm, Sa 9am-1pm, Su 10am-1pm; Sept.-June closed Su.

Hitchhiking: *Let's Go* does not recommend hitchhiking. Try **Use It's** ride-sharing boards (see **Tourist Office,** below) instead.

ORIENTATION

Copenhagen lies on the east coast of the island of **Zealand** (Sjælland), across the sound (Øresund) from Malmö, Sweden. The new 17-mile **Øresund bridge and tunnel,** opened July 1, 2000, established the first "fixed link" between the two countries. Copenhagen's **Hovedbanegården** (Central Station) lies near the city's heart. North of the station, **Vesterbrogade** passes **Tivoli** and **Rådhuspladsen** (the central square and terminus of most bus lines), then cuts through the city center as **Strøget** (STROY-yet), the world's longest pedestrian thoroughfare. Outlying districts fan out from the center: **Østerbro** is affluent, while working-class **Nørrebro** draws students and locals into a bustling and cheerful neighborhood culture and nightlife. **Vesterbro** has Copenhagen's red-light district (near the train station, on Istegade) and should be regarded with caution at night, but is nevertheless an up-and-coming neighborhood with multi-cultural flair. **Christianshavn** is known as "little Amsterdam" for its waterways and, in its south-central half, the hippie-hash artists' colony **Christiania.** For an informative, entertaining tour of medieval Copenhagen, join the **night watchman** on his rounds; tours leave from Gråbrødre Toru (June-Aug. F 9 or 10pm).

PRACTICAL INFORMATION

TOURIST AND FINANCIAL SERVICES

Tourist Office: Use It, Rådhusstr. 13 (☎33 73 06 20; www.useit.dk). From the station, follow Vesterbrog., cross Rådhuspladsen onto Frederiksbergg., and turn right on Rådhusstr. Indispensable and geared toward budget travelers. Pick up a copy of *Play Time,* a comprehensive guide to the city geared specifically to young budget travelers. Has daytime luggage storage, finds lodgings, holds mail. Open mid-June to mid-Sept. daily 9am-7pm; mid-Sept. to mid-June M-W 11am-4pm, Th 11am-6pm, F 11am-2pm.

Budget Travel: Wasteels Rejser, Skoubog. 6 (☎33 14 46 33). Open M-F 9am-7pm, Sa 10am-3pm. **Kilroy Travels,** Skinderg. 28 (☎33 11 00 44). Open M-F 10am-5:30pm, Sa 10am-2pm.

Embassies: Australia (consulate), Strand Boulevarden 122, 5th fl. (☎39 29 20 77; fax 39 29 60 77). **Canada,** Kristen Bernikowsg. 1 (☎33 48 32 00; fax 33 48 32 21). **Ireland,** Østerbaneg. 21 (☎35 42 32 33; fax 35 43 18 58). **New Zealanders** should contact their embassy in Brussels (see p. 132). **South Africa,** Gammel Vartovvej 8 (☎39 18 01 55; fax 39 18 40 06). **UK,** Kastelsvej 36-40 (☎35 44 52 00; fax 35 44 52 93). **US,** Dag Hammarskjölds Allé 24 (☎35 55 31 44; fax 35 43 02 23).

Currency Exchange: Forex, in Central Station. 25kr commission on cash, 15kr per traveler's check. Open daily 8am-9pm. At the **airport,** open daily 6:30am-8:30pm. Exchange bureaus on **Strøget** charge up to 10% commission. **Banks** cluster in the pedestrian district and on Vesterbrog., near the station; most charge 25kr commission.

LOCAL SERVICES

Luggage Storage: Free at **Use It** tourist office and most hostels. At **Central Station,** 20-35kr per 24hr. Open M-Sa 5:30am-1am and Su 6am-1am.

English Bookstores: Atheneum, Nørreg. 6. Open M-Th 9am-5:30pm, F 9am-6pm, Sa 10am-2pm. **Use It** tourist office offers a book swap.

Laundromats: Look for **Vascomat** and **Møntvask** chains. At Borgerg. 2, Nansensg. 39, and Istedg. 45. Wash and dry 40-50kr. Most open daily 7am-9pm.

Gay and Lesbian Services: National Association for Gay Men and Women, Teglgaardsstr. 13 (tel. 33 13 19 48). Small bookstore and library. Open M-F 5-7pm. The monthly *PAN Homoguide* lists clubs, cafes, and organizations, and is available at **PAN** (see p. 279). Also check out www.copenhagen-gay-life.dk and www.gayonline.dk. The Danish word for "gay" is *bøsser;* "lesbian" is *lesbiske.*

EMERGENCY AND COMMUNICATIONS

Emergencies: ☎112. **Police** headquarters are at Polititorvet (☎33 14 14 48).

Pharmacy: Steno Apotek, Vesterbrog. 6c (☎33 14 82 66). Open 24hr.; ring the bell.

Medical Assistance: Doctors on Call (☎33 93 63 00), open M-F 8am-4pm; after hours, call ☎38 88 60 41. Visits 120-350kr. **Emergency rooms** at **Sundby Hospital,** Kastrup 63 (☎32 34 32 34), and **Bispebjerg Hospital,** Bispebjerg Bakke 23 (☎35 31 35 31).

Post Office: Tietgensg. 35-39, **1500** København V, behind Central Station. Open M-F 11am-6pm, Sa 10am-1pm. **Branch office** in Central Station. Address mail to be held: First name SURNAME, *Poste Restante,* Main Post Office, Tietgensgade 35-39, **1500** Kobenhavn V, DENMARK. Mail also held at **Use It;** address mail to: First name SURNAME, Poste Restante, Use It, 13 Rådhusstræde, **1466** Copenhagen K.

Internet Access: Free at **Use It** and at **Copenhagen Hovedbibliotek** (Central Library), Krystalg. 15 (open M-F 10am-7pm, Sa 10am-2pm).

ACCOMMODATIONS AND CAMPING

København means "merchant's port" in Danish, but the lodgings that once housed emigré merchants disappeared ages ago, leaving in their wake lovely hostels and campgrounds, but few budget hotels. HI hostels fill early with large families and school groups; excellent amenities help compensate for remote locations. During

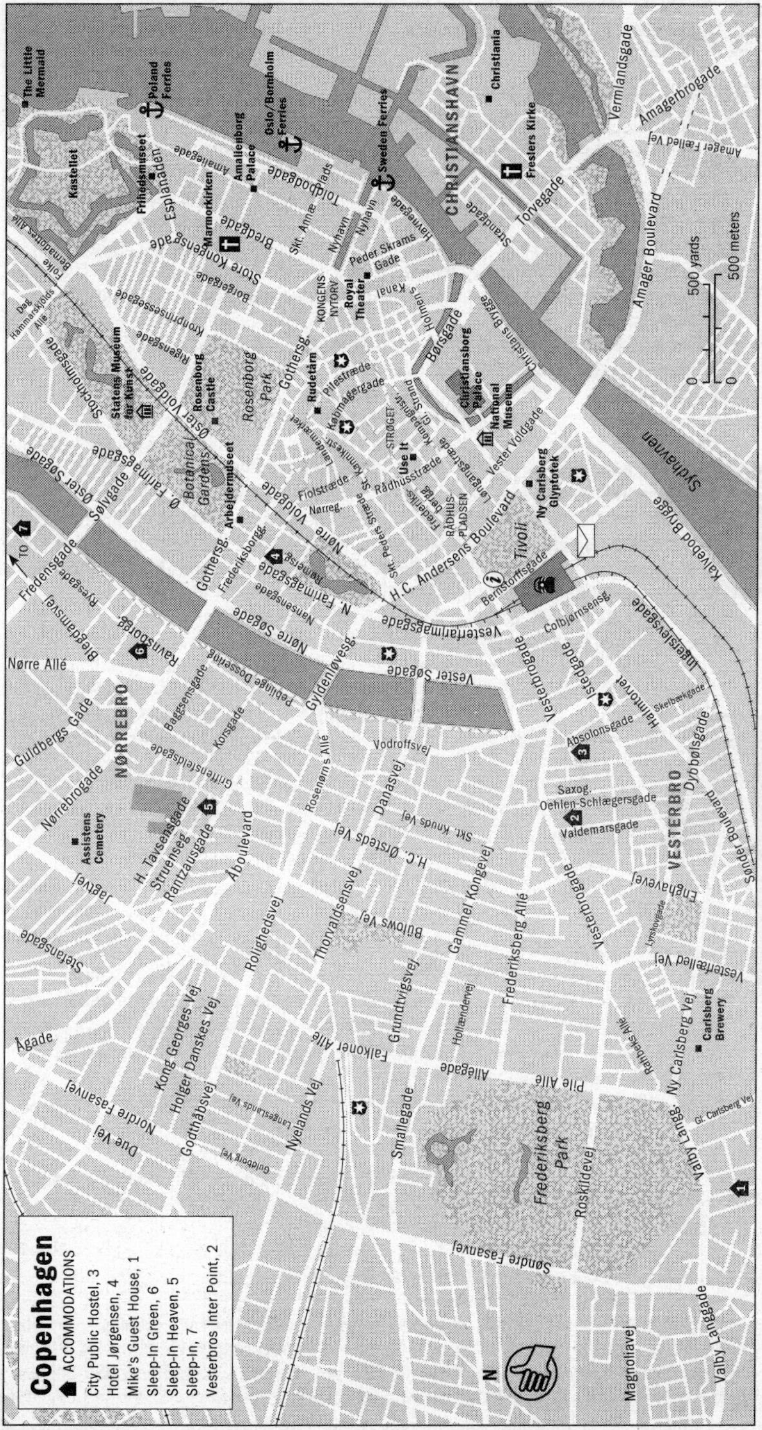

Copenhagen

ACCOMMODATIONS

City Public Hostel, 3
Hotel Jørgensen, 4
Mike's Guest House, 1
Sleep-In Green, 6
Sleep-In Heaven, 5
Sleep-In, 7
Vesterbros Inter Point, 2

holidays (such as the national vacation in early August) and the largest festivals, especially Karneval (mid-May), Roskilde (late June), and Copenhagen Jazz (late July), reserve rooms well in advance. The lodging of choice for young travelers, **Sleep-In** hostels are cheap and central.

Sleep-In Heaven, Struenseeg. 7 (☎35 35 46 48; email sleepinheaven@get2net.dk), in Nørrebro. Take bus #8 (dir. Tingbjerg) 5 stops to "Rantzausg."; continue in the same direction as the bus, then turn right on Kapelvej, left on Tavsensg., and left on (poorly marked) Struenseeg. Lively courtyard and lounge. Close to hip Skt. Hans Torv nightlife. Internet 20kr per 30min. Reception 24hr. Dorms 100kr; doubles 400kr.

Hotel Jørgensen, Rømersg. 11 (☎33 13 81 86), 25min. from Central Station, 5min. from Strøget, on a quiet street. S-train: Nørreport; walk along Frederiksborgg. and turn left on Rømersg. Cramped no-frills dorms, but central and friendly. Breakfast included. Sheets 30kr. Reception 24hr. Lockout 11am-3pm. No dorm reservations. July-Sept. dorms 115kr. Oct.-June dorms 100kr; singles 400kr; doubles from 500kr; quads 560kr.

City Public Hostel, Absalonsg. 8 (☎31 31 20 70), in the Vesterbro Youth Center. From the station, walk away from the Rådhuspladsen on Vesterbrog. and turn left on Absalonsg. Happening lounge and BBQ. Sheets 30kr. Kitchen. Reception 24hr. Open early May-late Aug. Dorms 110kr; with breakfast 130kr.

Sleep-In Green, Ravnsborgg. 18, Baghuset (☎35 37 77 77). Take bus #16 from the station *to* "Nørrebrog." Cozy, eco-friendly dorms outside the city center. Organic breakfast 30kr. Sheets 30kr. Reception 24hr. Check-out noon. Open late May-Sept. 85kr.

Mike's Guest House, Kirkevænget 13 (☎36 45 65 40). 10min. by bus or train from Central station; always call ahead. Clean, spacious rooms–some with private balconies—in a quiet neighborhood. Singles 200kr; doubles 290kr; triples 400kr.

Vesterbros Inter Point, Vesterbros KFUM (YMCA), Valdemarsg. 15 (☎33 31 15 74). From Central Station, walk east on Vesterbrog. and turn left. Super-friendly staff; homey atmosphere. Breakfast 25kr. Sheets 20kr. Kitchen. Reception 8:30-11:30am, 3:30-5:30pm, and 8pm-12:30am. Curfew 12:30am. Open late June-early Aug. 75kr.

Sleep-In, Blegdamsvej 132 (☎35 26 50 59). Bus #6: "Triangeln" or S-train: Østerport; walk 10min. up Hammerskjölds (across the square from the 7-11). Near the city center and Østerbro nightlife. Quantity over privacy at this popular (and noisy) warehouse of a hostel. Sheets 30kr. Kitchen. Reception 24hr. Lockout noon-4pm. Open July-Aug. 80kr.

Ajax, Bavnehøj Allé 30 (☎33 21 24 56). S-train A: Sydhavn; walk north on Enghavevej, turn left on Bavnehøj Allé, and look for signs on the right. Sheets 20kr. Kitchen. TV. Open July-Aug. Dorms 60kr; hostel tent 50kr; camp in your own tent 45kr.

København Vandrerhjem Bellahøj (HI), Herbergvejen 8 (☎38 28 97 15; email bellahoj@danhostel.dk), in Bellahøj. Take bus #11 from the station to "Primulavej." Large, modern hostel far from the city center. Breakfast 40kr. Sheets 30kr. Laundry 26kr. Reception 24hr. Open Mar. to mid-Jan. Dorms 90kr; doubles 240kr.

København Vandrerhjem Amager (HI), Vejlandsallé 200 (☎32 52 29 08). Take bus #46 (M-F 6am-5pm; at night, bus #96N) from Central Station or the S-train to "Valby," then take bus #37. Far from the city center in a huge nature reserve. Laundry 25kr. Kitchen. Sheets 30kr. Safe. Reception 24hr. Check-in 1-5pm. Open mid-Jan. to Nov. Dorms 90kr; nonmembers 110kr.

Bellahøj Camping, Hvidkildevej 66 (☎38 10 11 50), 5km from the city center. Take bus #11 to "Bellahøj." Shower included. Kitchen. Cafe and market. Reception 24hr. Open June-Aug. 57kr per person.

Absalon Camping, Korsdalsvej 132, Rødovre (☎36 41 06 00), 9km from the city center. From Central Station, take bus #5505. Kitchen, laundry, and store. 55kr per person, 8kr per tent; cabins 195kr plus 54kr per person.

FOOD

The Vikings once slobbered down mutton and salted fish in Copenhagen; today you can seek out more refined offerings. Around **Kongens Nytorv,** elegant cafes serve sandwiches *(smørrebrod)* for around 35kr. All-you-can-eat buffets (40-70kr) are popular, especially at Turkish, Indian, and Italian restaurants. The line between cafe and bar often blurs. In most cafes, you'll order at the bar and wait at your table for both food and drink; feel free to do so any time of day. **Fakta** and **Netto supermarkets** are budget fantasies; one is at Fiolstr. 7, north of Strøget (open M-F 9am-7pm, Sa 8am-5pm). High-class **Irma supermarkets** often offer a wide selection of organic foods. Open-air **markets** provide fresh fruits and veggies; try the one at Israels Plads near Nørreport Station. (Open M-Th 9am-5:30pm, F 9am-6:30pm, Sa 9am-3pm.) **Fruit stalls** line Strøget and the side streets to the north.

Nyhavns Færgekro, Nyhavn 5. Upscale fisherman's cottage atmosphere along the canal. Lunch on 10 varieties of all-you-can-eat herring (78kr). Dinner 155kr; lunch is cheaper, with 50-60kr sandwiches. Open daily 11:30am-11:30pm.

Den Grønne Kælder, Pilestr. 48. Popular, classy vegetarian and vegan dining. Hummus 18-35kr. Veggie burgers 30kr. Open M-Sa 11am-10pm.

Café Klimt, Fredericksborg. 29, From Strøget, turn on Købmagerg. and exit the pedestrian zone, crossing Nørre Voldg, which becomes Frederiksborgg. The food and the atmosphere are as imaginative as the cafe's namesake. Great brunch 11am-4pm. Main dishes 60-90kr. Open daily 11am-midnight.

Kafe Kys, Læderstr. 7, on a quiet street running south of and parallel to Strøget. Sandwiches 40-60k. Beer 35kr. Open M-Th 11am-1am, F-Sa 11am-2am, Su noon-10pm.

Café Nemoland, at the end of Pusher St., in Christiania. This chill cafe makes a perfect mid-afternoon pitstop. Cheap drinks and sandwich fare. Open 10am-midnight.

Café Norden, Østerg. 61, on Strøget and Nicolaj Plads, in sight of the fountain. A French-style cafe with the best vantage point on Strøget. Crepes 59-62kr; sandwiches 16-58kr; pastries 15-40kr. Open daily 9am-midnight.

Café Europa, Amagertorv, on Nicolaj Plads opposite Café Norden. If Norden is the place to see, trendy Europa is the place to be seen. Sandwiches 23-44kr. Beer 45kr per pint. Great coffee. Open M-W 9am-midnight, Th-Sa 9am-1am.

SIGHTS

Compact Copenhagen is best seen by foot or bike; pick up a free **city bike** (see p. 273) to survey its stunning architecture. Various **tours** are detailed in Use It's *Playtime* and tourist office brochures. The squares along the lively pedestrian **Strøget,** which divides the city center, are **Nytorv, Nicolaj Plads,** and **Kungens Nytorv.** Opposite Kungens Nytorv is **Nyhavn,** the "new port" where Hans Christian Andersen wrote his first fairy tale, lined with Hanseatic houses and sailing boats. There are several canal tours, but **Netto boats** offers the best value (late Apr. to mid-Sept. every 20min. 10am-5pm; 20kr). **Bus #6** travels through Vesterbro, Rådhuspladsen, alongside Stroget, and on to Østerbro, acting as a comprehensive sight-seeing guide to the city.

CITY CENTER. The first sight you'll see as you exit the train station is **Tivoli,** the famed 19th-century amusement park, which delights with botanical gardens, marching toy soldiers, and rides. Wednesday and weekend nights culminate with music and fireworks. An increasingly popular Christmas market is open at Tivoli mid-November through mid-December. *(Vesterbrog. 3. Open late Apr. to mid-Sept. Su-Th 11am-midnight, F-Sa 11am-1am. Children's rides open 11:30am, others 12:30pm. 45kr; before 1pm 35kr. Single-ride tickets 10-20kr. Ride pass 168kr.)* From Central Station, turn right on Bernstorffsg. and left on Tietgensg. to partake of the ancient and Impressionist art and sculpture at the beautiful **Ny Carlsberg Glyptoket.** *(Dantes Plads 7. Open Tu-Su 10am-4pm. 30kr; free W and Su or with ISIC.)* Continue along Tietgensg., which becomes Stormg., to dive into Denmark's Viking treasures and other tidbits of its cultural history at the **National Museum.** *(Ny Vestergade 10. Open Tu-Su 10am-5pm. 40kr, students 30kr; W free.)* **Christiansborg Castle,** Prins Jørgens Gård, features subterranean ruins, royal reception rooms, and the *Folketing* (Parliament) chambers. To get there, continue down Tietgensg. from the city center until you cross the canal. *(Tours May-Sept. daily 11am and 3pm; June-Aug. 11am, 1, and 3pm; Oct.-Apr. Tu-Th and Sa-Su 11am and 3pm; 40kr. Ruins 20kr. Ask about the free Parliament tours.)*

CHRISTIANSHAVN. In the southern section of Christianshavn, the "free city" of **Christiania,** founded in 1971 by youthful squatters in abandoned military barracks, is inhabited by a thriving group of artists and alterna-thinkers carrying '70s activism and free love into the new millennium. Come Christmas, there is a fabulous market with curiosities from all over the world. Hash and marijuana are for sale on "Pusher St." (joints 20-50kr), but they are **illegal.** Possession of even small amounts can get you arrested. Always ask before taking pictures, **never** take pictures on Pusher St. itself, and exercise caution in the area at night. *(From Central Station, turn right on Bernstorffs, left on Tietgensg.; continue as it changes names and bear right along the water. After crossing the water, turn left on Prinsesseg.)* Climb the golden spire of **Vor Frelsers Kirke** (Our Savior's Church) for a great view. *(Sankt Annæg. 29. Turn left off Prinsesseg. Church open daily Mar.-Nov. 9am-4:30pm, Dec.-Feb. 10am-2pm; free. Tower open Mar.-Nov. 9am-4:30pm; 20kr.)*

FREDERIKSTADEN. Edvard Eriksen's **den Lille Havfrue** (The Little Mermaid) tiny but touristed statue at the opening of the harbor honors favorite son Hans Christian Andersen. *(S-train: Østerport; turn left out of the station, left on Folke Bernadottes Allé, right after passing a canal, and follow it to the ocean. Open daily 6am-dusk.)* Retrace your steps and turn left to cross the moat to **Kastellet,** a 17th-century fortress-turned-park. Cross through Kastellet to the **Frihedsmuseet** (Resistance Museum), which chronicles the Nazi occupation from 1940 to 1945. The fascinating museum documents Denmark's efforts to rescue its Jews and its period of acceptance of German "protection," when the Danish government arrested anti-Nazi saboteurs. *(At Churchillparken. Open May to early Sept. Tu-Sa 10am-4pm, Su 10am-5pm; mid-Sept. to Apr. Tu-Sa 11am-3pm, Su 11am-4pm. Free.)* From the museum, walk south down Amalieng. to reach the lovely **Amalienborg Palace,** residence of Queen Margarethe II and the royal family; most of the interior is closed to the public, but you can see the apartments of Christian VII. The changing of the palace guard takes place at noon on the brick plaza. *(Open daily June-Aug. 10am-4pm; May and Sept.-Oct. 11am-4pm; Jan.-Apr. Tu-Su 11am-4pm. 35kr.)* The 19th-century **Marmokirken** (Marble Church), opposite the palace, features an ornate interior and Europe's third-largest dome. *(Church open M-Tu and Th-Sa 10:30am-4:30pm, W 10:30am-6:30pm, Su noon-4:30pm; free. Dome 20kr.)*

A few blocks north, **Statens Museum for Kunst** (State Museum of Fine Arts) displays an eclectic collection in a beautifully designed building. From the church, head away from Amalienborg, go left on Store Kongensg., turn right on Dronningrnd Tværg., and take an immediate right and then left onto Sølvg. *(Sølvg. 48-50. Open Tu-Su 10am-5pm. 40kr.)* Opposite the museum, **Rosenborg Slot** (Rosenborg Palace and Gardens) hoards royal treasures, including the crown jewels. *(Øster Volg. 4A. Open daily May-Sept. 10am-4pm; Oct. 11am-3pm; Nov.-Apr. Tu-Su 11am-2pm. 45kr.)*

OTHER SIGHTS. For legalized substance abuse, a trip to the **Carlsberg Brewery** will reward you with a wealth of knowledge and, more importantly, free samples. *(Ny Carlsbergvej 140. Take bus #6 west from Rådhuspladsen to Valby Langg. Open M-F 10am-3pm. Free.)* If the breweries haven't confused your senses enough, play with science at the hands-on **Experimentarium.** *(Tuborg Havnevej 7. Take bus #6 north from Rådhuspladsen. Open late June to mid-Aug. daily 10am-5pm; late Aug. to early June M and W-F 9am-5pm, Tu 9am-9pm, Sa-Su 11am-5pm. 79kr, students 61kr.)*

ENTERTAINMENT

For events, consult *Copenhagen This Week* (free at hostels and tourist offices), or pick up *Use It News* from Use It. The **Royal Theater** is home to the world-famous Royal Danish Ballet. For same-day half-price tickets, head to the **Tivoli ticket office,** Vesterbrog. 3. (☎33 15 10 12. Open daily mid-Apr. to mid-Sept. 9am-9pm; mid-Sept. to mid-Apr. 9am-7pm. Royal theater tickets available at 4 or 5pm, others at noon.) Call **Arte,** Hvidkildevej 64 (☎38 88 22 22), to ask about student discounts. The relaxed **Kul-Kaféen,** Teglgårdsstr. 5, is a great place to see live performers and get info on music, dance, and theater. (Open M-Sa 11am-midnight.) During the world-class **Copenhagen Jazz Festival** (mid-July; ☎33 93 20 13; www.cjf.dk), the city teems with free outdoor concerts complementing the more refined venues. In anticipation of the summer blowout, the **Swingin' Copenhagen** festival sets the city grooving to traditional jazz (www.swingin-copenhagen.dk), and **Copenhagen Autumn Jazz** in early November keeps the city bopping long after summer is gone.

NIGHTLIFE

Copenhagen's weekends often begin on Wednesday, and nights rock until 5am; "morning pubs" that open when the clubs close let you party around the clock. On Thursday, most bars and clubs have reduced covers and cheap drinks. The central pedestrian district reverberates with crowded bars and discos; **Kongens Nytorv** has fancier joints. Many buy beer at a supermarket and head to the boats and cafes of **Nyhavn** for its salty charisma. The **Scala** complex, opposite Tivoli, has many bars and restaurants; students enliven the cheaper bars in the **Nørrebro** area. Copenhagen's gay and lesbian scene is one of Europe's best, and gay Danish men and women report equal comfort in straight establishments.

Rust, Guldbergsg. 8, in the Nørreboro. Twenty-somethings pack this disco with an underground feel. Long lines by 1am. Open Tu-Su 10pm-5am. Cover 50kr; free before 11pm.

Café Pavillionen, on Borgmester Jensens Allé, in Fælleaparken. Summer-only, outdoor cafe. Local bands 8-10pm, plus a disco W-Sa 10pm-5am. On Mondays, enjoy a concert 2:30-5pm. Tango lessons and dancing 5pm-midnight. No cover.

Park, Østerbrog. 79, in Østerbro. Lose your inhibitions and your friends in this enormous club with 2 packed dance floors, live music hall, and rooftop patio. Pints 40kr. No tennis shoes. Cover F-Sa 50kr. Open Su-W 10am-2am, Th 10am-4am, F-Sa 10am-5am.

Enzo, Nørreg. 41. Doll yourself up and dance with a young stylish crowd. Dress code. 21+. Cover 60kr. Open F-Sa 10:30pm-5:30am.

Sabor Latino, Vester Voldg. 85. Groove to hot Latin beats and enjoy free salsa and merengue lessons at 10pm. Cover 35-50kr. Open Th 9pm-3am, F-Sa 9pm-5am.

IN Bar, Nørreg 1. Dance on the speakers! No, wait, drink *cheap* and then dance on the speakers! Th cover 30kr; F-Sa cover 150kr, includes open bar. Su-W 18+; Th-Sa 20+. Open Su-Th 10pm-5am, F-Sa 10pm-10am.

JazzHouse, Niels Hemmingsens G. 10 (www.jazzhouse.dk). Turn left off Strøget from Gammeltorv (closer to Råhuspladsen) and Nytorv. Copenhagen's premiere jazz venue makes for a sophisticated and potentially expensive evening. Check the calendar for prices. Concerts Su-Th 8:30pm, F-Sa 9:30pm. Club open midnight-5am.

PAN Club and Café, Knabrostr. 3. Gay cafe, bar, and disco. Publishes the *Homoguide*. Cover Th 20kr; F-Sa 50kr. Cafe opens daily 8pm, disco 11pm. Both stay open late.

Sebastian Bar and Café, 10 Hyskenstr., off Strøget. The city's best-known gay and lesbian bar. *Homoguide* available. Happy hour 5-9pm. Open daily noon-2am.

EXCURSIONS FROM COPENHAGEN

Stunning castles, white sand beaches, and a world-class museum hide in North, Central, and South Zealand, all within easy reach of Copenhagen by train. A northern train route (every 20min.) offers easy access to many attractive daytrips that lie within an hour of Copenhagen in North Zealand.

RUNGSTED AND HUMLEBÆK. In North Zealand, the quiet harbor town of **Rungsted** (30min., 40kr or 4 clips on the blue *rabatkort*), where Karen Blixen (pseudonym Isak Dinesen) wrote *Out of Africa*, houses the author's abode, personal effects, and grave at the **Karen Blixen Museum,** Rungsted Strandvej 111. From the station, turn left on Stationsvej, right on Rungstedsvej, and left on Rungsted Strandvej. (Open May-Sept. daily 10am-5pm; Oct.-Apr. W-F 1-4pm, Sa-Su 11am-4pm. 30kr.) **Humlebæk** (45min., 38.50kr or 4 clips), farther up the coast, distinguishes itself with the spectacular **Louisiana Museum of Modern Art,** named for the three wives (all named Louisa) of the estate's original owner. The museum contains works by Picasso, Warhol, Lichtenstein, Calder, and other 20th-century masters; the building and its sculpture-studded grounds overlooking the sea are themselves worth the trip. Follow signs 1.5km north from the Humlebæk station or snag bus #388. (Open Th-M 10am-5pm, W 10am-10pm. 60kr, students 50kr.)

HELSINGØR AND HORNBÆK. At the end of the northern line lies **Helsingør** (1hr.), evidence of the Danish monarchy's fondness for lavish architecture. In a region famous for castles, the most famous is the 15th-century **Kronborg Slot** in Helsingør, also known as **Elsinore,** the setting for Shakespeare's *Hamlet* (although neither the historical "Amled" nor the Bard ever visited Kronborg). Viking chief Holger Danske is buried in the castle's spooky dungeon; legend has it that he still rises to face any threat to Denmark's safety. The castle also houses the **Danish Maritime Museum,** which contains the world's oldest sea biscuit, from 1853. From the train station, turn left and follow the signs on the waterfront to the castle. (Open May-Sept. daily 10:30am-5pm; Apr. and Oct. Tu-Su 11am-4pm; Nov.-Mar. Tu-Su 11am-3pm. 45kr.) The **tourist office,** inside **Kulturhuset,** books rooms (25kr fee). The large gray building across the street from the station is the Kulturhuset; the entrance is around the corner. (☎49 21 13 33. Open mid-June to Aug. M-Th 9am-5pm, F-Sa 10am-6pm, Su 10am-3pm; Sept. to mid-June M-F 9am-4pm, Sa 10am-1pm.)

Hornbæk offers beautiful beaches where you can see Danes at their aesthetic best. There's a wild **harbor festival** on the fourth weekend in July. **Bus** #340 and the **train** outside the station run from Helsingør to Hornbæk (20min., 20kr).

HILLERØD AND FREDENSBORG. Another northern route brings you to **Hillerød** (at the end of S-train lines A and E via Lyngby; 40min., 42kr), home of the moated **Frederiksborg Slot,** arguably the most impressive of North Zealand's castles, with exquisite gardens and brick ramparts. Free concerts are given Thursdays at 1:30pm on the famous 1610 **Esaias Compenius organ** in the chapel. To get there from the station, cross the street onto Vibekeg. and follow the signs. (Open daily Apr.-Oct. 10am-5pm; Nov.-Mar. 11am-3pm. 40kr, students 10kr.) A final stop on the northern castle tour is **Fredensborg Castle,** on the "Lille Nord" rail line connecting Hillerød and Helsingør, at the Fredensborg stop. Built in 1722, the castle still serves as the spring and fall royal residence. (Castle open daily July 1-5pm; 10kr. Park open year-round; free.) Sleep with (well, near) the royals and enjoy a fantastic palace garden view at **Fredensborg Youth Hostel (HI),** Østrupvej 3, 1km from the train station. (☎48 48 03 15. Sheets 45kr. Reception 7am-9pm. 100kr, nonmembers 120kr.)

DENMARK

ROSKILDE. In Central Zealand, Roskilde (25-30min., 38.50kr or 4 clips) served as Denmark's first capital when King Harald Bluetooth built the country's first Christian church here in 980. Several Danish monarchs repose in the ornate sarcophagi of **Roskilde Domkirke.** (Open Apr.-Sept. M-F 9am-4:45pm, Sa 9am-noon, Su 12:30-4:45pm; Oct.-Mar. M-F 9am-4:45pm, Sa 12:30-3:45pm. Concerts June-Aug. Th 8pm. 12kr, students 6kr.) The **Viking Ship Museum,** on Strandengen along the harbor, houses remnants of five trade ships and warships sunk circa 1060 and salvaged in the late 1960s. In summer, book a ride on a Viking longboat, but be prepared to take an oar—Viking conquest is no spectator sport! From the tourist office, walk to the cathedral and downhill through the park. (Open daily May-Sept. 9am-5pm; Oct.-Apr. 10am-4pm. May-Sept. 50kr; Oct.-Apr. 50kr. Boat trip 40kr; book ahead.) Roskilde hosts one of Europe's largest **music festivals,** drawing over 90,000 fans with bands such as REM, U2, Radiohead, Smashing Pumpkins, and Metallica. (June 28-30, 2001; ☎46 36 66 13; www.roskilde-festival.dk.)

The **tourist office,** Gullandsstr. 15, sells festival tickets and books rooms for a 25kr fee. From the train station, turn left on Jernbaneg., right on Allehelgansg., and left again on Barchog. (☎46 35 27 00. Open Apr.-June M-F 9am-5pm, Sa 10am-1pm; July-Aug. M-F 9am-6pm, Sa 9am-3pm, Su 10am-2pm; Sept.-Mar. M-Th 9am-5pm, F 9am-4pm, Sa 10am-1pm.) The **HI youth hostel,** Hørhusene 61, is on the harbor next to the Viking museum shipyard. The gorgeous, modern facility is always booked during the festival. (☎46 35 21 84. Reception 9am-noon and 4-8pm. Open Feb.-Dec. 90kr; nonmembers 115kr.) To camp by the beach at **Roskilde Camping,** Baunehøjvej 7,

4km north of town, take bus #603 towards Veddelev. (☎46 75 79 96. Reception 8am-10pm. Open Apr. to mid-Sept. 50kr per person.)

KLAMPENBORG AND CHARLOTTENLUND. Klampenborg and Charlottenlund, on the coastal line (and at the end of S-train line C), feature **topless beaches.** Though less ornate than Tivoli, **Bakken** in Dyrehaven, Klampenborg, the world's oldest amusement park, delivers more thrills. From the Klampenborg train station, turn left, cross the overpass, and head through the park. (Open daily Mar. 25-Aug. 11am-midnight. Rides start at 2pm; 10-25kr each.) Bakken borders the **Jægersborg Deer Park,** the royal family's former hunting grounds, still home to their **Eremitage** summer chateau, miles of wooded paths, and more than 2000 red deer.

MØN. To see what Andersen called one of the most beautiful spots in Denmark, head south of Copenhagen (2hr.) to the isle of Møn's white cliffs. Locals travel to Møn to spend quiet days shopping in the villages and exploring the gorgeous chalk cliffs and the cottage-strewn pastoral landscape. Take the **train** from Copenhagen to Vordingborg, then **bus** #62 or 64 to Stege. Once on the island, you can take bus #54 to Møn Klint. Plan carefully: only three buses go to the island and back each day, and the last often leaves Møn before 4pm. For more info, contact the **Møns Turistbureau,** Storeg. 2, in Stege. (☎55 81 44 11. Open June 15-Aug. M-F 10am-6pm, Sa 9am-6pm, Su 10am-noon; Sept.-June 14 M-F 10am-5pm, Sa 9am-noon.)

BORNHOLM

Gorgeous Bornholm island bathes in the most sun in Denmark, luring vacationers to its world-class beaches and pleasant fishing villages. Ideal for avid bikers and nature-lovers, its red-roofed cliffside villas may seem southern European, but the flowers and half-timbered houses are undeniably Danish. Bornholm's unique **round churches** were both places of worship and fortresses for waiting out pirate attacks.

GETTING THERE AND GETTING AROUND. Beaches cover the southern tip of the island at **Dueodde.** Of the four towns, **Østerlars** is the largest and **Nylors** the best-preserved. Ferries arrive in **Rønne,** Bornholm's capital, from Denmark, Sweden, Germany, and Poland. **Bornholmsbussen** (☎44 68 44 00) offers combo bus/ferry routes from Copenhagen (5½hr., 190kr). **Bornholmstrafikken** (☎56 91 07 66) runs daily ferries (2½hr., 98-122kr) and more frequent **catamarans** (1½hr., 150kr) from Ystad, Sweden, one hour southeast of Malmö (both 50% off with Scanrail); Bornholmstrafikken also sails from Copenhagen (6hr., 1-2 per day, 208kr) and Sassnitz-Mukran, Germany (2hr., 1 per day, 50-100kr). **Scandlines** also runs from Sassnitz-Mukran to Bornholm (3¾hr., 1 per day, 495kr). In July and August, **Polferries** (☎56 95 10 69) sails between Rønne and Świnoujście, Poland (6hr., 180kr). Bornholm has an efficient local BAT **bus** service (10-clip *Rabatkort* 64kr, 24hr. card 90kr). There are numerous **cycling** paths; pick up a guide at the tourist office in Rønne.

RØNNE. Amid cafes and cobblestone streets, tiny Rønne, on the southwest coast, is Bornholm's principal port. Walking through the restored town, it's hard to visualize the devastation wrought by relentless bombing in WWII. Rent a **bike** from **Bornholms Cykeludlejning,** Ndr. Kystvej 5. (55kr per day. Open May-Sept. daily 7am-4pm and 8:30-9pm.) The **tourist office,** Nordre Kystvej 3, behind the gas station by the Bornholmstrafikken terminal, books private rooms for 140kr. (☎56 95 95 00. Open mid-June to mid-Aug. M-Sa 9:30am-6pm, Su 10am-4pm; mid-Aug. to mid-June M-F 9am-4pm, Sa 10am-1pm.) Next door to one of Bornholm's famous round churches, in a quiet, wooded area near Rønne, sits the cabana-like **HI youth hostel,** Arsenalvej 12. From the ferry terminal, walk along Munch Petersens Vej, bear left on Zahrtmannsvej, turn right at the roundabout onto Søndre Allé, right on Arsenalvej, and then follow the signs. (☎56 95 13 40. Breakfast 45kr. Laundry. Kitchen. Call ahead. 100kr.) **Galløkken Camping** is at Strandvejen 4. (☎56 95 23 20. Open mid-May to Aug. 52kr per person.) Get **groceries** at **Kvickly,** in the Snellemark Centret opposite the tourist office (open M-Th 9:30am-6pm, F 9:30am-7pm, Sa 9:30am-2pm), or visit the second-floor **cafeteria** (open M-F 9am-7pm, Sa 9am-4pm). **Postal code:** 3700.

SANDVIG-ALLINGE. On the tip of the spectacular northern coast, this small town's white sand **beaches** attract bikers and bathers. A few kilometers from town down Hammershusvej, **Hammershus** is northern Europe's largest castle ruin. Take bus #3 or 9 to reach Bornholm's most popular round church, **Østerlars Rundkirke,** near Sandvig in the village. (Open Apr.-Aug. M-Sa 9am-5pm.) The **Nordbornholms Turistbureau,** Kirkeg. 4, is in Allinge. (☎56 48 00 01. Open June-Aug. M-F 9am-5pm, Sa 10am-3pm; Sept.-May M-F 9am-5pm, Sa 10am-noon.) Just outside Sandvig is the **Sandvig Vandrerhjem (HI),** Hammershusvej 94. (☎56 48 03 62. Members only; sells HI cards. Reception 9:30-11am and 4:30-5:15pm. Open Apr.-Oct. 110kr.) **Sandvig Familie Camping,** Sandlinien 5, has sites on the sea. (☎56 48 04 47. Reception 8am-10pm. Open Apr.-Oct. 45kr per person, 10kr per tent.)

FUNEN (FYN)

Situated between Zealand to the east and the Jutland Peninsula to the west, the island of Funen is Denmark's garden. This remote bread basket is no longer isolated from the rest of Denmark—a bridge and tunnel now connect it to Zealand. Pick up maps of the **bike paths** covering the island at Funen tourist offices (75kr).

ODENSE

Visiting the hometown of Hans Christian Andersen, who once said, "To travel is to live!," may reveal the roots of his belief. Odense (OH-n-sa), Denmark's third-largest city, warrants only a short visit. At **H.C. Andersens Hus,** Hans Jensens Stræde 37-45, you can learn about the author's eccentricities and see free performances of his work. From the tourist office, walk right on Vesterg. to Torveg., turn left, and right on Hans Jensens Str. (Performances June 19-July 30 11am, 1, and 3pm. Museum open mid-June to Aug. daily 9am-7pm; Sept. to mid-June Tu-Su 10am-4pm. 30kr.) A few scraps of Andersen's own ugly-duckling childhood are on display at **H.C. Andersens Barndomshjem** (Childhood Home), Munkemøllestræde 3-5. (Open mid-June to Aug. daily 10am-4pm; Sept. to mid-June Tu-Su 11am-3pm. 10kr.) Next to the main H. C. Anderson Hus, don headphones and listen to the work of another great Dane at the **Carl Nielsen Museum,** Claus Bergs Gade 11. (Open June-Aug. Tu-Su 10am-4pm; off season reduced hours. 15kr.) Walk back to the tourist office and all the way down Vesterg., the main pedestrian drag, to the outstanding **Brandts Klædefabrik,** Brandts Passage 37 and 43. This former factory houses a modern art gallery, the **Museum of Photographic Art,** and the **Danish Press/Graphic Arts Museum.** (All open June-Aug. daily 10am-5pm; Sept.-May Tu-Su 10am-5pm. 30kr, 25kr, and 25kr, respectively; joint ticket 50kr.) The **Fyns Kunstmuseum,** Jernbaneg. 13, features Danish art. (Open Tu-Su 10am-4pm. 25kr.) **Ringe,** 30km away, hosts the rock-and-folk-music **Midtfyns Festival** (early July), which has featured the Eurythmics, Macy Gray, Moby, and the Counting Crows. (☎62 62 58 24; www.mf.dk).

Buses depart behind the train station (11kr). Ask the driver for an *omstigning*, a ticket valid for 1hr. The **tourist office,** on Rådhuspladsen, books rooms (125-175kr per person) for a 25kr fee and sells the **Odense Adventure Pass,** good for museum admission, discounts on plays, and unlimited public transport (24hr. 85kr; 48hr. 125kr). From the train station, take Nørreg., which becomes Asylgade, turn left at the end on Vesterg. (☎66 12 75 20. Open June 15-Aug. M-Sa 9am-7pm, Su 10am-5pm; Sept.-June 14 M-F 9:30am-4:30pm, Sa 10am-1pm.) The **library** in the station has free **Internet.** (Open May-Sept. M-Th 10am-7pm, F 10am-4pm, Sa 10am-2pm; Oct.-Apr. M-Th 10am-7pm, F-Su 10am-4pm.) The brand new **Danhostel Odense City (HI)** is attached to the station. (☎63 11 04 25. Reception open 8am-noon and 4-8pm. Call ahead. Dorms 140kr; singles 330kr; doubles 400kr; triples 480kr.) To camp next to the Fruens Boge park at **DCU Camping,** Odensevej 102, take bus #41 or 81. (☎66 11 47 02. Reception 7am-10pm. Open late Mar.-Sept. 50kr per person.) Get **groceries** at **Aktiv Super,** at Nørreg. and Skulkenborg. (Open M-F 9am-7pm, Sa 8:30am-4pm, Su noon-4pm.) **Postal code:** 5000.

EXCURSION FROM ODENSE: EGESKOV SLOT. About 30 minutes south of Odense on the Svendborg rail line is the town of **Kværndrup** and **Egeskov Slot,** a stunning 16th-century castle that appears to float on the surrounding lake (it's actually supported by 12,000 oak piles). Spend at least two hours in the magnificently preserved Renaissance interior and the equally splendid grounds, which include a large bamboo labyrinth. On summer Sundays at 5pm, classical concerts resound in the **Knight Hall.** (Open daily May-June and Aug.-Sept. 10am-5pm; July 10am-6pm. 50kr. Grounds open daily May and Sept. 10am-5pm; June and Aug. 10am-6pm; July 10am-8pm. 60kr.) To get to Egeskov, exit the Svendborg-bound **train** at Kværndrup; go right from the station until you reach Bøjdenvej, the main road. Wait for **bus** #920 (every hr., 11kr), or turn right and walk 2km through wheat fields to the castle.

SVENDBORG

On Funen's south coast, an hour from Odense by train, **Svendborg** is a beautiful harbor town and a departure point for ferries to the south Funen islands. Near Svendborg on an adjacent island, the regal 17th-century estate of **Valdemars Slot,** built by Christian IV for his son, holds a new **yachting museum** and a **beach.** (Open May-Sept. daily 10am-5pm; Apr. and early Oct. Sa-Su 10am-5pm. Castle 50kr, museum 25kr; joint ticket 65kr.) Cruise there on the antique passenger steamer **M/S Helge,** which leaves from Jensens Mole, behind the train station (1hr., 4 per day, round-trip 55kr).

Ferries to Ærø (see below) leave from behind the train station. The **tourist office,** on the Centrum Pladsen, books ferries and lodgings. From the train station, turn left on Toldbodvej and right on Brogade, which becomes Gerritsg. The office is at the top. (☎62 21 09 80. Open late June-Aug. M-F 9am-7pm, Sa 9am-3pm; Sept. to mid-June M-F 9:30am-5:30pm, Sa 9:30am-1pm.) To get from the station to the five-star, family-oriented **HI youth hostel,** Vesterg. 45, turn left on Jernbaneg. and again on Valdemarsg., which becomes Vesterg. (☎62 21 66 99. Breakfast, sheets, and laundry 40kr each. Kitchen. Bikes 50kr per day. Reception 8am-8pm. Check-out 9:30am. 100kr; overflow mattresses on the floor 50kr.) **Carlsberg Camping,** Sundbrovej 19, is across the sound on Tåsinge. (☎62 22 53 84. 51kr. Reception 8am-10pm. Open May-Oct.) **Jette's Diner,** at Kullinggade 1 between the train station and the docks, puts a Danish spin on diner fare. (Open daily noon-midnight.) **Postal code:** 5700.

ÆRØ

The wheat fields, harbors, and cobblestone hamlets of Ærø (EH-ruh), a small island off the south coast of Funen, quietly preserve an earlier era in Danish history. Here cows, rather than real estate developers, lay claim to the beautiful land.

GETTING THERE AND GETTING AROUND. Several **trains** from Odense to **Svendborg** are timed to meet the **ferry** (☎62 52 40 00) from Svendborg to **Ærøskøbing** (1¼hr., 6 per day, 75kr, round-trip 115kr; buy tickets on board). From **Mommark,** on Jutland, **Ærø-Als** (☎62 58 17 17) sails to **Søby** (1hr.; Apr.-Sept. 2-5 per day, Oct.-Mar. Sa-Su only; 60kr), on Ærø's northwestern shore. **Bus** #990 travels between Ærøskøbing, Marstal, and Søby (16kr), but Ærø is best seen by **bike.**

ÆRØSKØBING. The town of Ærøskøbing appears today almost as it did 200 years ago thanks to economic stagnation followed by conservation efforts. Rosebushes and half-timbered houses attract tourist yachts from Sweden and Germany as well as vacationing Danes, but you don't have to get too far out of town to find your own serene spot. The **tourist office,** opposite the ferry landing, arranges private rooms for 170kr. (☎62 52 13 00. Open June 15-Aug. M-F 9am-5pm, Sa 9am-2pm, Su 10am-noon; Sept.-June 14 M-F 9am-4pm, Sa 8:45-11:45am.) To get from the landing to the **HI youth hostel,** Smedevejen 15, walk left on Smedeg., which becomes Nørreg., Østerg., and finally Smedevejen. (☎62 52 10 44. Breakfast 40kr. Sheets 35kr. Reception 8am-noon and 4-8pm. Check-in by 5pm or call ahead. Reserve far in advance. Open Apr. to mid-Oct. 90kr; nonmembers 115kr.) **Ærøskøbing Camping,** Sygehusvejen 40b, is 10 minutes to the right as you leave the ferry. (☎62 52 18 54. Reception 8am-1pm and

3-9pm. Open May-Sept. 46kr per person.) **Emerko supermarket** is at Statene 3; walking uphill from the ferry on Vesterg., turn right on Sluttergyden, which becomes Statene. (Open M-Th 9am-5pm, F 9am-6pm, Sa 9am-4pm, Su 10am-4pm.) Rent a **bike** at the hostel or campground (40-50kr per day) to explore the towns of **Marstal** and **Søby,** on the more remote shores of the island.

JUTLAND (JYLLAND)

Homeland of the Jutes who joined the Anglos and Saxons in the conquest of England, the Jutland peninsula is Denmark's largest landmass. Beaches and campgrounds mark the peninsula as prime summer vacation territory, while rolling hills, marshland, and sparse forests add color and variety. Jutland may be a bit out of the way, but you can take a weekend beach fling there without denting your budget.

FERRIES TO ENGLAND, NORWAY, AND SWEDEN

From **Esbjerg,** on Jutland's west coast, **DFDF** sails to **Harwich, England** (18hr., 3-4 per week). If you need to stay, try the **HI youth hostel,** Gammel Vade Vej 80. (☎75 12 42 58; fax 75 13 68 33. Reception 8am-noon and 4-7pm. Open Feb.-Dec. 85kr; non-members 110kr.) From **Frederikshavn,** on the northern tip of Jutland, **Stena Line** ferries (☎96 20 02 00; in Sweden ☎ (0340) 690 900) leave for **Gothenburg, Sweden** (2-3¼hr., 110-150kr, round-trip 200-230kr; 50% off with Scanrail), **Oslo** (10hr., 350kr, round-trip 400kr; 50% off with Scanrail), and other points in Norway. **SeaCat** (☎96 20 32 00) offers cheaper service to **Gothenburg** (2hr., 3 per day, 110-130kr). **Color Line** (☎99 56 20 00) sails to **Oslo** (316-352kr; 50% off with Scanrail). Boats also go from **Hirtshals,** on the northern tip of Jutland, to **Oslo** (12½hr., from 160kr) and **Kristiansand, Norway** (2½-4½hr., in summer from 200kr); and from **Hanstholm,** on the northwestern coast of Jutland, to **Bergen, Norway** (15½hr., 300-680kr; round-trip 10% off).

DENMARK

ÅRHUS

Århus (ORE-hoos), Denmark's second-largest city and a Danish favorite, bills itself as "the world's smallest big city." Studded with impressive museums and architectural gems from prehistoric times through the 21st century, the city is a visual treat. Many travelers to this manageably sized and laid-back student and cultural center find themselves agreeing that size doesn't matter.

PRACTICAL INFO, ACCOMMODATIONS, AND FOOD. You can reach Århus by **train** from Aalborg (2hr.) and Copenhagen (3hr.). The **tourist office,** in the town hall, books **private rooms** (125-175kr; no fee) and sells the **Århus Passport,** which includes unlimited public transit and admission to most museums and sights (1-day 88kr, 2-day 110kr). If you're only interested in one or two museums, consider the **Tourist Punch Ticket** (45kr), which provides unlimited bus transportation (24hr.). To find the office, turn left as you exit the train station, take the first right, and walk to the building with the clock tower. (☎89 40 67 00; www.aarhus-tourist.dk. Open late June-early Sept. M-F 9:30am-6pm, Sa 9:30am-5pm, Su 9:30am-1pm; early Sept.-Apr. M-F 9:30am-4:30pm, Sa 10am-1pm; May to mid-June M-F 9:30am-5pm, Sa 10am-1pm.) Most public buses leave from the train station or outside the tourist office. The main **library,** at Mølleparken, has free **Internet** access. (Open May-Aug. M-Th 10am-7pm, F 10am-6pm, Sa 10am-2pm; Sept.-Apr. M 10am-10pm, Tu-Th 10am-8pm, F 10am-6pm, Sa 10am-2pm.)

The hip backpacker hang-out, **Århus City Sleep-In,** Havneg. 20, is 10 minutes from the train station, in the middle of the city's nightlife. Walk out of the train station and follow Ryesg., which becomes Sønderg., all the way to the canal. Take the steps or elevator down to Aboulevarden, turn right, walk to the end, and turn left on Havneg. (☎86 19 20 55; email sleep-in@mail1.stofanet.dk. Breakfast 30kr. Sheets 30kr; deposit 30kr. Kitchen. Laundry 25kr. Key deposit 50kr. Bikes 50kr per day;

deposit 200kr. Reception 24hr. Check-out noon. Dorms 85kr; doubles 240-280kr.) **Pavillonen (HI),** Marienlundsvej 10, is in the Risskov forest, 3km from the city center and five minutes from the beach. Take bus #1, 6, 9, 16, or 56 to Marienlund, then walk 300m into the park. (☎86 16 72 98. Breakfast 40kr. Sheets 30kr. Laundry. Reception 7:30-10am and 4-11pm. Dorms 85kr, nonmembers 110kr; doubles 240-280kr.) Beautiful **Blommehavenn Camping Århus,** Ørneredevej 35, in the Marselisborg forest, is by a beach and the royal family's summer residence. In summer, take bus #19 from the station to the grounds; in winter, take bus #6 to Hørhavevej. (☎86 27 02 07. Reception Apr.-early Sept. 7am-10pm; mid-Sept. to Mar. 8am-8pm. In summer 50kr per person, 15kr per tent.) **Den Grønne Hjørne,** Frederiksg. 60, has an all-you-can-eat Danish buffet (59-79kr). From the tourist office, turn left on Radhuspl., and then an immediate right. (Open M-Sa 11:30am-10pm, Su 5-10pm.) Get **groceries** at **Fakta,** Østerg. 8-12. (Open M-F 9am-7pm, Sa 9am-4pm.) **Postal code:** 8100.

SIGHTS AND ENTERTAINMENT. In the town center, the 13th-century **Århus Domkirke** (cathedral) dominates Bispetorv and the pedestrian streets that fan out around its Gothic walls. (Open May-Sept. M-Sa 9:30am-4pm; Oct.-Apr. 10am-3pm. Free.) Next door, reclaim herstory at the **Women's Museum,** Domkirkeplads 5, where provocative exhibits chronicle women throughout time. (Open June-Aug. daily 10am-5pm; Sept.-May Tu-Su 10am-4pm. 20kr.) Just west of the town center lies **Den Gamle By,** an open-air museum displaying a collection of Danish buildings from the Renaissance through the 20th century. (Open June-Aug. 9am-6pm, Apr.-May and Sept.-Oct. 10am-5pm, Nov.-Dec. 10am-4pm, Jan.-Mar. 11am-3pm. 55kr. Free after hours.) **Åboulevarden,** lined with trendy cafes, makes a perfect mid-afternoon stop for beer and sunshine. The **Århus Kunstmuseum,** on Vennelystparken, has a fine collection of Danish Golden Age paintings. (Open Tu-Su 10am-5pm. 30kr.)

Just outside town lies the spectacular **Moesgård Museum of Prehistory,** which chronicles Århus's history from 4000 BC through the Viking age. Two millennia ago, the casualties of infighting were entombed in a nearby bog and mummified by its antiseptic acidity. Today you can visit the **Grauballe Man,** the only perfectly preserved **bog person.** Take bus #6 from the train station to the end. (Open Mar.-Sept. daily 10am-5pm; Oct.-Feb. Tu-Su 10am-4pm. 35kr.) Save time for the **Prehistoric Trail,** which leads from behind the museum to a sandy **beach** (3km). In summer, bus #19 (last bus 10:18pm) returns from the beach to the Århus station. The exquisite rose garden of **Marselisborg Castle,** Queen Margarethe II's summer getaway, is open to the public. From the train station, take bus #1, 18, or 19. (Palace closed in July and whenever else the Queen is in residence.)

Århus hosts an acclaimed jazz festival in late July (☎89 31 82 10; www.jazzfest.dk). The **Århus Festuge** (☎89 31 82 70; www.aarhusfestuge.dk) is a rollicking celebration of theater, dance, and music. You can visit a smaller version of Tivoli, the **Tivoli Friheden,** at Skovbrynet. Take bus #1, 4, 6, 8, 18, or 19. (Open daily June 19-Aug. 8 1-11pm; Apr. 19-June 18 and Aug. 9-15 2-10pm. 35kr.) At night, chill at the jazz club **Bent J,** Nørre Allé 66, which jams Monday evenings and occasionally on other weekdays as well. **Valdemar,** Store Torv 4, is a popular disco in the city center. (No cover. 23+. Open Th 11pm-5am, F-Sa 10pm-5am.) The **Pan Club,** Jægergårdsg. 42, has a cafe, bar, and largely gay and lesbian dance club. (Cafe open M-Th 6pm-midnight, F-Su 8pm-5am. Club cover F-Sa 45kr; open W-Sa 11pm-4am.) **Aboulevarden** rocks at night, too; many bars offer live music and drink specials.

EXCURSION FROM ÅRHUS: LEGOLAND. **Billund** is renowned as the home of Legoland, an amusement park built of 40 million Lego pieces. More than just baby-babble, "Lego" is an abbreviation of *leg godt* (have fun playing). Don't skip the impressive indoor exhibitions. Unfortunately, private buses make Legoland a bit expensive. To get there, take the train from Århus to **Vejle** (45min., every hr.), then bus #912 or 44 (dir. Legoland). A joint ticket for the bus and park (including rides) costs 165kr. (☎76 50 00 55; www.legoland.dk. Open daily late June-Aug. 10am-9pm; Apr. to mid-June and Sept.-Oct. 10am-8pm; rides close 2hr. earlier.)

AALBORG

The site of the earliest known Viking settlement, Aalborg (OLE-borg) is Denmark's fourth-largest city. Aalborg's spotless streets and white church garnered the title of "Europe's Tidiest City" in 1990 and brought it even farther from its unkempt Viking origins. Check out these rowdy precursors at **Lindholm Høje,** Vendilavej 11, which has 700 graves and a museum of Viking life. To reach the site, take bus #6 (13kr) from outside the tourist office. (Site open daily dawn-dusk. Museum open Apr. to mid-Oct. daily 10am-5pm; late Oct. to mid-Mar. Tu-Su 10am-4pm. 20kr.) The frescoed 15th-century **Monastery of the Holy Ghost,** on C.W. Obelsplads, is Denmark's oldest welfare institution. From the tourist office, cross the street and head down Adelg. The monastery is on the right. (English tours late June to mid-Aug. Tu and Th 1:30pm. 25kr.) The **Budolfi Church,** on Algade, has a brilliantly colored interior with ringing carillon. From the tourist office, turn left onto Østerågade and right on Algade. (Open M-F 9am-4pm, Sa 9am-2pm.) For serious rollercoasters, visit **Tivoliland,** on Karolinelundsvej. From the tourist office, turn left on Østerågade, turn right on Nytorv, and follow it until you see the rides. (Open May-Sept. daily noon to 8 or 10pm. 40kr; full-day 160kr.) From the station, cross the street and J.F.K. Plads, then turn left on Boulevarden, which becomes Østerågade, to find the **tourist office,** Østerågade 8. (☎98 12 60 22. Open mid-June to mid-Aug. M-F 9am-6pm, Sa 10am-5pm; mid-Aug. to mid-June M-F 9am-4:30pm, Sa 9am-1pm.) **Aalborg Vandrerhjem and Camping (HI),** Skydebanevej 50, has cabins with modern facilities next to a beautiful fjord. Take bus #2, 8, or 9 (dir. Fjordparken) to the end. (☎98 11 60 44; fax 98 12 47 11. Laundry. Reception late June to mid-Aug. 7:30am-11pm; late Jan. to mid-June and early Aug. to mid-Dec. 8am-noon and 4-9pm. Hostel 75kr, non-members 100kr; camping 49kr.) Bars and restaurants line **Jomfru Ane Gade;** from the tourist office, turn right on Østeragade and left onto Bispensg. Jomfru Ane Gade will be on your right. **Postal code:** 9000.

FREDERIKSHAVN

Despite noble efforts to showcase its endearing streets and hospitality, Frederikshavn is best known and used for its **ferry** links (see p. 284). The **tourist office,** Brotorvet 1, inside the Stena Line terminal south of the rail station, reserves rooms for a 25kr fee. (☎98 42 32 66; fax 98 42 12 99. Open mid-June to mid-Aug. M-Sa 8:15am-7pm, Su 11am-7pm; mid-Aug. to mid-June M-Sa 9am-4pm.) From the tourist office, walk left 10 minutes to reach the bus and train stations. The **HI youth hostel,** Buhlsvej 6, is packed with a mixed crowd. From the bus or train stations, walk right, then follow the signs. (15min. ☎98 42 14 75; fax 98 42 65 22. Reception in summer 7am-noon and 4-9pm. Always call ahead. Open Feb.-Dec. 60kr, non-members 85kr.) **Nordstrand Camping** is at Apholmenvej 40. (☎98 42 93 50; fax 98 43 47 85. Open Apr.-Sept.15. 52kr per person, 30kr per tent.) **Postal code:** 9900.

SKAGEN

Perched on Denmark's northernmost tip, sunny Skagen (SKAY-en) is a beautiful summer retreat amid long stretches of sea and white-sand dunes. The powerful currents of the North and Baltic Seas collide at **Grenen.** Don't try to swim in these dangerous waters; every year some hapless soul is carried out to sea. To get to Grenen, take bus #79 or 99 from the Skagen station to **Gammel** (11kr) or walk 3km down Fyrvej; turn left out of the train station and bear left when the road forks. In summer, you can climb the lighthouse tower for an amazing view of Grenen (5kr). The spectacular **Råberg Mile** sand dunes, formed by a 16th-century storm, migrate 15m east each year. From here, you can swim along 60km of **beaches,** where the endless summer light attracted Denmark's most famous late-19th-century painters. Their works are displayed in the wonderful **Skagen Museum,** Brøndumsvej 4. (Open June-Aug. daily 10am-6pm; off season reduced hours. 40kr.) You can also tour the artists' homes at **Michael og Anna Archers Hus,** Markvej 2-4, and **Holger Drachmanns Hus,** Hans Baghsvej 21. Skagen has a large annual **Dixieland music festival** in late June (free-150kr); contact the tourist office for more info.

The **tourist office** is in the train station. (☎98 44 13 77; fax 98 45 02 94. Open June-Aug. M-Sa 9am-7pm, Su 10am-2pm; Sept.-May reduced hours.) Nordjyllands Trafikselskab (☎98 44 21 33) runs **buses** and **trains** from Frederikshavn to Skagen (1hr., 33kr; with Scanrail 50% off). The **Skagen Ny Vandrerhjem,** Rolighedsvej. 2, is wildly popular among vacationing Danish families. From the station, turn right on Chr. X's Vej, which turns into Frederikshshavnvej, and turn left on Rolighedsvej. (☎98 44 22 00; fax 98 44 22 55. Reception 9am-noon and 4-6pm. Call ahead. Open Mar.-Nov. 75-85kr, non-members 100-110kr.) Most **campgrounds** are open late April to mid-September (55kr per person); try **Grenen** (☎98 44 25 46; fax 98 44 65 46) or **Østerklit** (☎/fax 98 44 31 23), near the city center. Call ahead for both campgrounds.

RIBE

Well aware of their town's historic value, the town government of Ribe forged preservation laws forcing residents to maintain the character of their houses and to live in them year-round. The result is a magnificently preserved medieval town, situated beautifully on the salt plains near Jutland's west coast. Ribe is particularly proud of the arrival of migratory storks who always roost on the roof of the Town Hall. For a great view of the birds and the surrounding landscape, climb the 248 steps through the clockwork and huge bells of the 12th-century **cathedral** tower. (Open June-Aug. M-Sa 10am-6pm, Su noon-6pm; May and Sept. M-Sa 10am-5pm, Su noon-6pm; Apr. and Oct. daily 11am-4pm; Nov.-Mar. daily 11am-3pm. 10kr.) Next to the **Rådhus** (Old Town Hall), Van Støckens Plads, a former debtor's prison houses a small museum on medieval torture. (Open June-Aug. daily 1-3pm; May and Sept. M-F 1-3pm. 15kr.) Follow the **night watchman** on his rounds for an English or Danish tour of town beginning in Torvet, the main square. (35min. June-Aug. 8 and 10pm; May and Sept. 10pm. Free.) Ribe's **Vikinger,** Udin Plads 1, houses artifacts recovered from an excavation of the town, once an important Viking trading post. To get the full story on the Vikings, sit through the hourly film, in English, Danish, and German. (Open Apr.-June and Sept.-Oct. daily 10am-4pm; July-Aug. daily 10am-6pm; Nov.-Mar. Tu-Su 10am-4pm. 45kr.) South of town, the open-air **Ribe Vikingcenter,** Lustrupvej 4, recreates a Viking town. (Open May-June and Sept. M-F 11am-4pm, July-Aug. daily 11am-4pm. 45kr.) The **Vadehavscentret** (Wadden Sea Center), Okholmvej 5, Vestervedsted, offers tours of the local marshes. Take bus #711. (☎75 44 61 61. Open daily Apr.-Oct. 10am-5pm; Feb.-Mar. and Nov. 10am-3pm. 35kr.)

Trains to Ribe run from Bramming (25min., 4-5 per day, 25kr). The **tourist office,** Torvet 3, arranges accommodations for 20kr. From the train station, walk down Dagmarsg., to the left of the Viking museum; it'll be on your right in the main square. (☎75 42 15 00. Open July-Aug. M-F 9:30am-5:30pm, Sa 10am-5pm, Su 10am-2pm; Apr.-June and Sept.-Oct. M-F 9am-5pm, Sa 10am-2pm; Nov.-Mar. M-F 9am-4:30pm, Sa 10am-1pm.) The central **Ribe Vandrerhjen (HI),** Sct. Pedersg. 16, offers bike rental (50kr per day) and a gorgeous view of the flatlands. From the station, cross the Viking Museum parking lot, bear right, walk down Sct. Nicolaj G. to the end, turn right on Saltg., and immediately left on Sct. Peters G. (☎75 42 06 20. Sheets 36kr. Reception 8am-noon and 4-8pm; longer hours May-Sept. Open Feb.-Nov. 100kr, nonmembers 125kr.) **Ribe Camping,** Farupvej 2, is 1.5km from the town center. (☎75 41 07 77. 50kr per person; 2-person cabins 175kr.) **Supermarkets** are around Seminarievej near the hostel; most are open M-F 10am-6pm, Sa 10am-4pm.

ESTONIA (EESTI)

ESTONIAN KROONS

US$1 = 17EEK	10EEK = US$0.57
CDN$1 = 12EEK	10EEK = CDN$0.85
UK£1 = 25EEK	10EEK = UK£0.39
IR£1 = 20EK	10EEK = IR£0.50
AUS$1 = 10EEK	10EEK = AUS$9.90
NZ$1 = 7.50EEK	10EEK = NZ$1.30
SAR1 = 2.50EEK	10EEK = SAR4.00
DM1 = 8.00EEK	10EEK = DM1.25
EUR€1 = 15.65EEK	10EEK = EUR€0.64

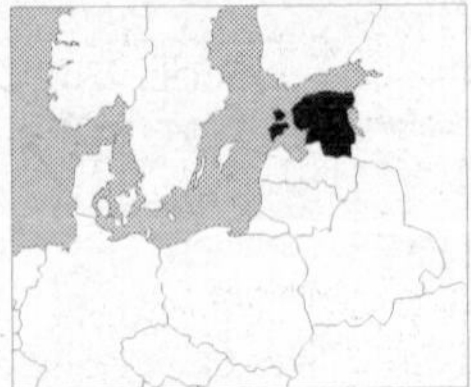

Country code: 372. **International dialing prefix:** 800. From outside Estonia, dial int'l dialing prefix (see inside back cover) + 372 + city code + local number.

The small Baltic state of Estonia has been dominated for centuries by outside powers, most recently the Soviet Union, which imposed a foreign Slavic culture on the Estonians' Balto-Finnic lifestyle. Happy to shuck its Soviet past, Estonia has been quick to revive its historical and cultural ties to its Nordic neighbors, as Finnish money (and tourists) revitalize the nation. German cars, cellular phones, designer shops, and ever more stylish youngsters indicate that Estonia is benefiting from its transition to democracy and capitalism. Material trappings mask the declining living standards common outside big cities, but having overcome successive centuries of domination by Danes, Swedes, and Russians, Estonians are now proudly ready to take their place as members of modern Europe.

Eager for extra Estonian excitement? Examine *Let's Go: Eastern Europe 2001*.

FACTS AND FIGURES

Official Name: Republic of Estonia.

Government: Parliamentary democracy.

Capital: Tallinn.

Land Area: 45,226 sq. km.

Geography: Lowlands, marshes.

Climate: Maritime; wet, moderate winters, cool summers.

Major Cities: Tallinn, Tartu, Pärnu.

Population: 1,400,000 (65% Estonian, 28% Russian, 7% other).

Language: Estonian (official), Russian, Ukrainian, English, Finnish.

Religions: Evangelical Lutheran, Russian Orthodox, Estonian Orthodox.

Average Income Per Capita: US$5500.

Major Exports: Machinery and appliances, wood products, textiles, food.

ESSENTIALS

WHEN TO GO

The best time to visit is May-September. Though it's quite far north, Estonia's climate is relatively mild due to its proximity to water. Winters can be very severe.

DOCUMENTS AND FORMALITIES

Citizens of Australia, Ireland, New Zealand, and the US can visit Estonia **visa-free** for up to 90 days in a six-month period, UK citizens for 180 days in a year. Canadians and South Africans must obtain a visa at the nearest consulate. You may also use a Latvian or Lithuanian visa to enter the country. Single-entry visas (valid for 30 days)

are US$13, multiple-entry (length of validity varies with consulate) US$61. Single-entry transit visas (72hr.) cost US$13, double-transit (72hr.) US$19. Single-entry urgent visas (issued within 48hr.) are US$25. To get an extension, contact the visa department of the **Immigration Department,** Endla 4, in Tallinn (☎612 69 79). For more information, consult the **Estonian Ministry of Foreign Affairs** (www.vm.ee).

EMBASSIES AND CONSULATES

Embassies and consulates of other countries in Estonia are all in **Tallinn** (p. 291).

Estonian Embassies at Home: Australia, 86 Louisa Rd., Birchgrove NSW, 2041 (☎ (02) 98 10 74 68; fax 98 18 17 79); **Canada,** 958 Broadview Ave., Toronto, ON M4K 2R6 (☎ (416) 461 07 64; fax 461 03 53); **Ireland,** Merlyn Park 24, Ballsbridge, Dublin 4 (☎ (01) 269 15 52; fax 260 51 19; email asjur@gofree.indigo.ie); **South Africa** (consulate), 16 Hofmeyer St., Welgemoed, Belville, 7530 (☎ (021) 913 38 50; fax 913 25 79); **UK,** 16 Hyde Park Gate, London SW7 5DG (☎ (020) 75 89 34 28; fax 75 89 34 30; email tvaravas@estonia.gov.uk; www.estonia.gov.uk); **US,** 2131 Massachusetts Ave. NW, Washington, D.C. 20008 (☎ (202) 588 01 01; fax 588 01 08; email info@estemb.org; www.estemb.org).

GETTING THERE AND GETTING AROUND

BY PLANE, TRAIN, BUS, AND FERRY. Finnair (www.finnair.com) offers flights from New York and London to **Tallinn.** If you're coming from Russia or a Baltic state, **trains** may be cheaper than ferries, but expect more red tape during border crossings. Domestic **buses** are cheaper and more efficient than trains. During the school year (Sept.-June 25), student bus tickets are half-price. Several **ferry lines** connect to Tallinn's harbor (☎631 85 50); see **Tallinn: Ferries,** p. 291. It is easiest and cheapest to enter Estonia by ferry from Finland or Sweden (200-300EEK).

BY CAR. Driving conditions are passable. Expressways are in good condition; other roads are plagued by potholes and gravel. Americans need International Driving Permits; European licenses are sufficient. Drivers can be quite aggressive. **Speed limits** are 50kph in cities and 70 to 100kph on expressways. Park in guarded lots; Estonia has high rates of auto theft. Car **rentals** are 350-900EEK.

BY BIKE AND BY THUMB. On the islands, **bike rentals** (100EEK per day) are an excellent means of exploration. *Let's Go* does not recommend hitchhiking. Those who choose to do so should stretch out an open hand. Or, call the agency **Vismutar** (☎ (8290) 010 50) and leave your name, number, destination, and time of departure; they will match you with a driver going in your direction 24hr. before you leave.

TOURIST SERVICES AND MONEY

EMERGENCY. Fire, Police, and **Ambulance:** ☎ 112. In Tallinn, add a leading 0.

TOURIST OFFICES. Larger towns and cities in Estonia have well-equipped, English-speaking **tourist offices** (www.tourism.ee) that often arrange tours and make reservations. Smaller information booths, marked with a green "i," sell maps and have brochures.

MONEY. Estonia uses the **kroon** (EEK), divided into 100 **senti** and tied to the Deutschmark. **Hansapank** and **Eesti Ühispank,** the biggest and most stable banks, cash **traveler's checks.** Many establishments take Visa and MasterCard. **ATMs** are common. When purchasing items in a shop, cash is not passed between hands, but placed in a small tray on counter tops. No one **tips** in Estonia, although a service charge might be included in the bill.

BUSINESS HOURS. Most **businesses** are open Monday-Friday from 9 or 10am to 6 or 7pm and Saturday 10am to 2 or 3pm. Some **food shops** stay open until 10pm or later and are also open on Sunday. Businesses take hour-long breaks at noon, 1, or 2pm. **Banks** are open Monday-Friday from 9am-4pm.

ACCOMMODATIONS AND CAMPING

Tourist offices have accommodations listings and can often arrange beds. There is little distinction between hotels, hostels, and guesthouses. Some **hostels** are part of larger hotels, so ask for the cheaper rooms. For info on HI hostels, contact the **Estonian Youth Hostel Association,** Tatari (☎ 646 14 57; fax 646 15 95; email eyha@online.ee). Some upscale hotels have hall toilets and showers, and many provide **laundry** services for a fee. **Homestays** are common and cheap, but the cheapest hostels can be a better deal. The word *võõrastemaja* (**guest house**) in a place's name implies that it is less expensive. There are **campgrounds** throughout Estonia.

FOOD AND DRINK

While *schnitel* (a breaded, fried pork fillet) still appears on nearly every menu, salads, pasta, pizza, curries and more innovative meat preparation can now be found. Estonian specialties include the Baltic *seljanka* meat stew and *pelmenid* dumplings, plus smoked salmon and trout. Pancakes with cheese curd and berries are a delicious dessert. If you visit the islands, try picking up some *Hiumaa leib*; a loaf of this black bread easily weighs a kilo. **Beer** (*õlu*) is the national drink for good reason—not only is it inexpensive, but it's also delicious and high-quality. The national brand *Saku* is excellent, as is the darker *Saku Tume.*

COMMUNICATION

MAIL. An airmail **letter** and **postcards** costs 5.50EEK to Europe, 6.50EEK to the EU, and 8EEK to the rest of the world. Mail can be received general delivery through *Poste Restante.*

TELEPHONES. Telephone calls are paid for with **digital cards,** available at banks or newspaper kiosks. Cards come in 30, 50, and 100EEK. **International long-distance** calls can be made at post offices. Calls to the Baltic states cost 5EEK per minute, to Russia 10EEK per minute. Phoning the US is quite expensive: US$1-4 per minute. **There are two phone systems** in Tallinn: digital and cellular, each with its own area code. Calling to a cell phone always requires an area code (note that all calls within Estonia must be prefaced by the 8 which we list in parentheses in front of city codes.) To call Tallinn from outside Estonia on the digital system, first dial 372. To call a cell phone in Estonia, dial 37 25. To call out of Estonia, dial 00, the country code, the city code (if there is one), and the number. To call Eesti Telefon's **information number** is ☎07. For help, call the English-speaking **Ekspress Hotline** (☎0 11 88). **International direct dial** numbers include: **AT&T Direct** (☎80 08 00 10 01); **BT Direct** (☎800 800 104 41); and **Canada Direct** (☎800 800 10 11).

LANGUAGES. Estonian is a Finno-Ugric language, with 14 cases and all sorts of letters. Estonians speak the best **English** in the Baltic states; most young people also know **Finnish** or **Swedish,** but **German** is more common among the older set and in resort towns like Pärnu, Saaremaa, and Tartu. **Russian** used to be mandatory, but Estonians are usually averse to using it. Try English first, making it clear you're not Russian, then switch to Russian if necessary. The exception to this is along the border in eastern Estonia, where many prefer Russian.

HOLIDAYS AND FESTIVALS

Holidays: New Year's Day (Jan. 1); Independence Day (1918; Feb. 24); Good Friday (Apr. 13); Catholic Easter (Apr. 15); Spring Day (May 1); Whit Sunday (June 11); Victory Day (Battle of Võnnu, 1919; June 23); Jaanipäev (St. John's Day, Midsummer; June 24); Restoration of Independence (Aug. 20); Christmas (Dec. 25-26).

Festivals: Old Town Days (early June), in Tallinn, host open-air concerts throughout Vanalinn. The first week of July provides just one more excuse (as if one were necessary) to loose the taps in Tallinn bars, as **Beersummer** celebrates all things hoppy.

TALLINN ☎(8)2

The most renowned town of the German Hanseatic League in the 14th and 15th centuries, Tallinn is beginning to boom once again. Although its drab outskirts remain squalid, as if frozen in Soviet rule, Tallinn's cosmopolitan shops and fashionable youngsters complement the capital's ancient beauty and charming serenity.

GETTING THERE AND GETTING AROUND

Trains: Toompuiestee 35 (☎615 68 51). Trams #1 and 2 connect the station to Hotel Viru. English-speaking information desk. To: **Rīga** (9hr., 155EEK); **St. Petersburg** (10hr., 1 per day, 155EEK); and **Warsaw** (27hr., 1 per day, 519EEK).

Buses: Lastekodu 46 (☎601 03 86), 1.5km southeast of Vanalinn. Take trams #2 or 4 or bus #22 to the city center. Buy tickets at the station or from the driver. Buses–frequent and cheap–are the best way to travel domestically or internationally. To: **Rīga** (5-6hr., 4 per day, 180EEK); **St. Petersburg** (10hr., 4 per day, 200EEK); and **Vilnius** (10hr., 2 per day, 300EEK).

Ferries: At the end of Sadama (☎631 85 50), 15min. from the city center. The following steam to **Helsinki: Nordic Jet Line,** Terminal C (☎613 70 00; fax 613 72 22; 1½hr., 6 per day, 430-510EEK); **Tallinn Express,** Terminal D (☎632 83 20; fax 631 83 25; 1½hr., 3 per day, 225-775EEK); **Eckerö Line,** Terminal B (☎631 86 06; fax 631 86 61; 3½hr., 1 per day, 205EEK, students 165EEK); and **Silja Line,** Terminal D (☎631 83 31; fax 631 82 64; 3½-8½hr., 2 per day, 270-410EEK).

Public Transportation: Buses, trams, and **trolleybuses** cover the entire metropolitan area 6am-midnight. Buy tickets (*talong*; 10EEK) from kiosks around town and validate them in the metal boxes on board (460EEK fine for riding without a valid ticket).

Taxis: Find a *Takso* stand. Or, call ☎612 00 00, 655 60 00, 644 24 42, or 627 55 55. Check the cab for a meter and expect to pay 4-6EEK per km.

ORIENTATION AND PRACTICAL INFORMATION

The ring around Tallinn's egg-shaped **Vanalinn** (Old Town) is made up of **Rannamäe tee, Mere pst., Pärnu mnt., Kaarli pst.,** and **Toompuiestee.** The old town has two sections: **All-linn,** or Lower Town, which is the larger, busier section, and **Toompea,** a rocky fortified hill. Enter Vanalinn through the 15th-century **Viru värarad,** the main gates in the city wall, 500m from **Hotel Viru,** Tallinn's central landmark. To get to Vanalinn from the **ferry terminal,** walk 15 minutes along Sadama, which turns into Põhja pst., and turn left on Pikk through **Paks Margareeta** (Fat Margaret) gate. From the train station, cross under Toompuiestee and continue straight on **Nunne;** turn left on Pikk and right on Kinga to get to **Raekoja pl.,** the center of All-linn.

Tourist Office: Raekoja pl. 10 (☎694 69 46; www.tallinn.ee). *Tallinn in Your Pocket* 19EEK. Open M-F 9am-5pm, Sa-Su 10am-4pm. **Branch,** Sadama 25, at the harbor (Terminal A). Open daily 8am-4:30pm. The **Tallinn Card** covers a city tour, transportation, and entry to most museums (1-day 195EEK, 2-day 270EEK, 3-day 325EEK).

Embassies: Canada, Toomkooli 13 (☎627 33 11; fax 627 33 12). Open M, W, and F 9am-noon. **Latvia,** Tõnismägi 10 (☎46 13 13; fax 31 13 66). Open M-F 10am-noon. **Russia,** Pikk 19 (☎646 41 69; fax 646 41 78). Open M-F 9am-noon. **UK,** Wismari 6 (☎67 47 00; fax 67 47 23). Open Tu-Th 2:30-4:30pm. **US,** Kentmanni 20 (☎631 20 21; fax 631 20 25). Open M-F 8:30am-5:30pm.

Currency Exchange: Eesti Ühispank, in the same building as the main post office, changes money. **ATMs** are on nearly every street in Vanalinn.

American Express: Suur-Karja 15, 10140. (☎626 62 62; fax 626 62 12). Mail held and cash advances granted for members. Open M-F 9am-6pm; in summer M-F 9am-6pm and Sa 10am-5pm.

Luggage Storage: At the bus station, checked baggage 4-12EEK per day. Open daily 6:30-11am, 11:30am-7:30pm, and 8-10:30pm.

Emergencies: Ambulance, Fire, and **Police:** ☎0112.

Pharmacy: Tallinna Linnaapteek, Pärnu mnt. 10 (☎644 22 62). Open M-F 8am-8pm, Sa 9am-4pm, Su 10am-3pm.

Internet Access: Cafe ENTER, Gonsiori 4 (☎626 73 67), diagonally left of the side of Hotel Cero that doesn't face the post office. 60EEK per hr. Open daily 10am-midnight.

Post Office: Narva mnt. 1, 2nd fl., opposite Hotel Viru (☎625 73 00). Open M-F 7:30am-8pm, Sa 8am-6pm. Address mail to be held: First name SURNAME, Narva mnt. 1, Tallinn **0001,** Estonia.

ACCOMMODATIONS AND FOOD

Hostels fill fast, so book ahead. In a bind, ask at the bus station about beds there (doubles 340EEK). **Resastra,** Mere 4 (☎641 22 91), finds rooms in private homes.

Hostel Vana Tom (Formerly Hotell Küün, The Barn), Väike-Karja 1, 2nd fl. (☎/fax 631 32 52), in Vanalinn. From Raekoja pl., follow Vanaturu kael, turn right on Vana turg, left on Suur-Karja, and bear left; the sparkling hostel is through an arch on the left. Sheets 20EEK. Laundry. Dorms 195EEK; doubles 550EEK. HI members get 15EEK discount.

Hotell Gasthaus Eeslitall, Dunkri 4, 2nd fl. (☎631 37 55; fax 631 32 10), just off Raekoja pl. Colorful, clean rooms. Breakfast 36EEK. Singles 450EEK; doubles 585EEK.

Pääsu Hotell, Sõpruse pst. 182 (☎652 00 34), in Mustamäe. Take trolleybus #4 from the train station or trolleybus #2, 3, or 9 from the city center to "Linnu tee." Backtrack, hang a left on Linnu tee, left on Nirgi, and follow the signs. Comfortable rooms with TVs and fridges. Breakfast included. Singles 360EEK; doubles 460EEK; triples 540EEK.

For cheap food, the best option may be local pubs. Most are good; try **Dubliner,** on Suur Karja next to the hostel, whose name belies the cuisine, ranging from Italian pasta to Indian curries. **Merevaikus,** Rahukohtu 5, at the top of Toompea, has great views and inexpensive cafe food. (Crepes, salads, soups, and herring with potatoes 30-50EEK. Entrees 75-100EEK. Open daily 11am-11pm.) **Eeslitall** (Donkey Stable;

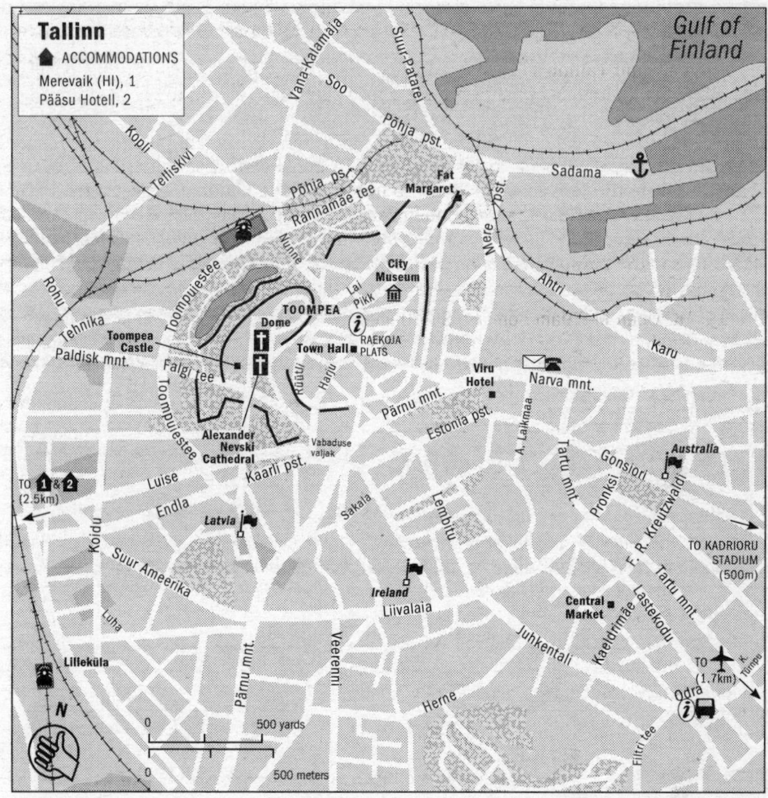

☎631 37 55), Dunkri 4/6, serves American and Balto-Russian fare in a building that's housed restaurants since 1362. (Meals around 140EEK. Open Su-Th 11am-11pm, F-Sa 11am-1am.) **Spar supermarket,** Aia 7, is by the Viru gates. (Open daily 9am-9pm.)

SIGHTS

VANALINN (OLD TOWN)

ALL-LINN. Enter the Old Town through Viru värarad; up Viru lies Europe's oldest town square, **Town Hall Square** (Raekoja pl.), where beer flows in outdoor cafes and local troupes perform in summer. **Old Thomas** (Vana Toomas), the 16th-century cast-iron weathervane figurine of Tallinn's legendary defender, tops the 14th-century *raekoja. (Open daily 9am-5pm. Tours 30EEK.)* Head up Mündi on the north side of the square and turn right on Pühavaimu to reach the 14th-century **Church of the Holy Ghost** (Pühavaimu kirik), which has an intricate 17th-century wooden clock. *(Open M-Sa 10am-4:30pm. Free concerts M 6pm.)* Continue down Pühavaimu and turn left on Vene to reach the **Dominican Cloister** (Dominiiklaste Klooster), founded in 1246. *(Vene 16. Open daily 11am-7pm. 25EEK.)* Continue up Vene, turn left on Olevimägi, and turn right on Pikk for a view of the medieval city's north towers. At the end of Pikk, in the squat tower known as **Fat Margaret** (Paks Margareeta), the **Maritime Museum** (Meremuuseum) examines Tallinn's port history. *(Pikk 70. Open W-Su 10am-6pm. 15EEK, students 7EEK.)* Head to the other end of Pikk and turn left on Rataskaevu to see **St. Nicholas' Church** (Niguliste kirik) and its mighty spire. *(Open W-F 10am-6pm, Sa-Su 11:30am-6:30pm. 15EEK.)* The 1475 **Peek in the Kitchen Tower** (Kiek in de Kök) offers a fun and fact-filled journey through medieval Tallinn in six floors. *(Komandandi 2. Open Tu-F 10:30am-5:30pm, Sa-Su 11am-4:30pm. 10EEK, students and seniors 5EEK.)*

TOOMPEA. From Raekoja pl., head down Kullassepa, right on Niguliste, and uphill on Lühike jalg to reach Toompea's **Castle Square** (Lossi pl.), dominated by the Russian minarets of golden **Aleksander Nevsky Cathedral.** *(Open daily 8am-7pm. Services 9am and 6pm.)* Directly behind **Toompea Castle,** the current seat of the Estonian Parliament (closed to the public), an Estonian flag tops **Tall Hermann** (Pikk Hermann), Tallinn's tallest tower and most impressive medieval fortification. As you face the tower, turn right on Toom-Kooli and turn right at the **Dome Church** (Toomkirik) to get to the **Art Museum** (Eesti Kunstimuuseum), which displays Estonian art from the 1800s to the 1940s. *(Kiriku pl. 1. Open W-Su 11am-6pm. 10EEK, students and seniors 5EEK.)*

ROCCA-AL-MARE

On the peninsula of Rocca-al-Mare, 10km west of the city center, the **Estonian Open-Air Museum** is full of 18th- to 20th-century wooden mills and homesteads, collected from all over Estonia and rebuilt in the park. Estonian folk troupes perform here regularly. *(Vabaõhumuuseumi 12. From Tallinn's train station, take bus #21 or 21a (25min.). Open daily May-Oct. 10am-8pm; in winter 10am-6pm. 25EEK, students and seniors 9EEK.)*

ENTERTAINMENT AND NIGHTLIFE

Pick up *Tallinn This Week* (free) at the tourist office. **Estonia Theater,** Estonia pst. 4, offers opera, ballet, musicals, and chamber music. (Ticket office open daily noon-7pm.) **Eesti Kontsert,** Estonia pst. 4, features almost nightly classical music. (Box office open M-F noon-7pm, Sa-Su noon-5pm. Student tickets 30EEK.) During **Old Town Days** (usually the last week of May to the 1st week of June), the city fills with open-air concerts. The first week of July brings **Beersummer,** a celebration of the good stuff. On summer Sundays, Tallinn converges on the **beach** of **Pirita,** a few kilometers from the city center (bus #1, 1a, 8, or 114).

Vanalinn is packed with pubs that offer a great night out. One relaxed and classy joint is **Nimega Baar** (Bar With No Name), Suur Karja 13. (Beer 32EEK. Open M-Th 11am-2am, F-Sa 11am-4am, Su noon-2am.) Or, for a late night dance party, try **Hollywood,** Vanna-Post 8, which spins house and techno. (Beer 30EEK. W ladies' night. 21+. Cover up to 100EEK. Open W-Sa 10pm-5am.)

TARTU ☎(8)7

ESTONIA

Tartu may be the oldest city in the Baltics and the second-largest in Estonia (pop. 101,900), but its youthful population and nightlife keeps it intimate and lively. From the 1775 **Town Hall Square** (Raekoja plats), follow Ülikooli from behind the town hall to the must-see **Tartu University** (Tartu Ülikool). Farther up Ülikooli (which becomes Jaani), **St. John's Church** (Jaani-kirik), Lutsu 16/24, holds hundreds of figures of saints and martyrs. On **Cathedral Hill** (Toomemägi), marvel at the ruins of the 15th-century **Cathedral of St. Peter and Paul** (Toomkirik). At night, try **Wilde Bar,** Vallikraavi 4, where the crowd chugs Irish beer. (Beer 25EEK. Live music F and Sa nights. Open Su-Tu noon-midnight, W-Th noon-1am, F-Sa noon-2am.)

Buses (☎47 72 27) go from Turu 2, at Riia and Turu, 300m southeast of Raekoja pl. along Vabaduse, to: Tallinn (2-5hr., 44 per day, 85-90EEK); Rīga (5hr., 1 per day, 150EEK); and St. Petersburg (10hr., 2 per day, 160EEK). Buses #5 and 6 run from the train station to the city center and then to the bus station. **Trains,** generally worse than buses, go from Vaksali 6 (☎37 32 20), at Kuperjanovi and Vaksali, 1.5km from the city center, to Tallinn (3hr., 5 per day, 70EEK) and Moscow (18hr., 1 per day, 284EEK, *coupé* 416EEK). From the bus station, follow Riia mnt. and turn right on Ülikoali to Raekoja pl. and the **tourist office,** Raekoja pl. 14. (☎/fax 43 21 41. Open M-F 10am-6pm, Sa 10am-3pm.) **Hostel Tartu (HI),** Soola 3, is in the center of town opposite the bus station. (☎43 20 91; fax 43 30 41. Sauna 140EEK per hr. Check-out noon. Members 200EEK. Nonmembers singles 410-670EEK; doubles 720-990EEK.) The **Tartu Kaubamaja supermarket,** is at Riia 2. (Open M-F 10am-8pm, Sa 10am-6pm, Su 11am-5pm.) **Postal code:** 51003.

COPS AND ROBBERS Mention hooliganism at soccer matches to most people, and visions of pub brawls between drunk, starved fans come to mind. The relation between ne'er-do-wells and the world's most popular sport, however, is a global phenomenon, as seen by the annual match between the punks and the police in **Kuressaare** (see below). Someone had the bright idea a few years back to put these mortal foes together on the pitch to let out their aggressions. Since then, every June, the cops in their blue shirts and badges and the punks with their rainbow mohawks have had at each other with a flurry of slide tackles and obscenities. The quality of the footballing is usually rather poor, a fact only compounded by the keg of beer on the punks' sideline. Nonetheless, the game is a town spectacle, with almost everyone there supporting the underdogs against the long foot of the law.

ESTONIAN ISLANDS

Worried about providing an easy escape route to the West, the Soviets once cordoned these islands off from foreigners and Estonians; they now remain a preserve for all that is distinctive about Estonia.

SAAREMAA. Kuressaare, the largest city of the island of Saaremaa, is making a comeback with summer influxes of young Estonians. Head south from Raekoja pl. along Lossi, through the park, and across the moat to reach the **Bishopric Castle** (Piiskopilinnus). Inside, the eclectic collection of the **Saaremaa Regional Museum** chronicles the islands' history. (Open May-Aug. daily 11am-7pm; Sept.-Apr. W-Su 11am-7pm. 30EEK, students 15EEK.) Rent a **bike** at **Raatapood,** Tallinna 26 (☎571 18), near the bus station (120EEK per day), and pedal southwest to the **beaches** in southwest Saaremaa (8-12km from Kuressaare) or to the **Kaarma Church** in east Saaremaa. Direct **buses** (☎573 80) leave from Pihtla tee 2, at the corner of Tallinna, for **Tallinn** (4hr., 7 per day, 150EEK) and **Pärnu** (3hr., 2 per day, 115EEK). The **tourist office,** Tallinna 2, is inside the town hall. (☎/fax 331 20. Open May to mid-Sept. M-Sa 9am-7pm, Su 10am-3pm; mid-Sept. to Apr. M-F 9am-5pm.) Sleep at **Mardi Öömaja,** Vallimaa 5a (☎/fax 332 85; singles 150EEK; doubles 200EEK), or at the school hostel **Hariduse 13A** (☎543 88; fax 572 26; 65-80EEK per person). **☎(8)245.**

HIIUMAA. By restricting access to Hiiumaa (HEE-you-ma) for 50 years, the Soviets unwittingly preserved the island's rare plant and animal species. **Kärdla,** the island's biggest city, contains as many creeks and trees as houses. You can **hike** or **camp** in the **West-Estonian Islands Biosphere Reserve,** which hosts more than two-thirds of all Estonia's plant species. Other interesting sights lie along the coast; rent a **bike** (100EEK) from **Kertu Sport,** Vabrikuväljak 1, across the bridge from the bus station in Kärdla. (☎963 73. Open M-F 10am-6pm, Sa 10am-3pm.) Don't miss the tiny island of **Kassair,** attached to Hiumaa by a land bridge. **Ferries** run between north Saaremaa's Triigi port and south Hiiumaa's Sõru port (1hr., 2 per day, 20EEK). Direct **buses** run from Sadama 13 (☎320 77), north of Kärdla's main square, Keskväljak, to Tallinn (4hr., 3 per day, 115EEK). **Postal code:** 92411. **☎(8)246.**

FINLAND (SUOMI)

FINNISH MARKKA

US$1 = 6.92MK	1MK = US$0.14
CDN$1 = 4.67MK	1MK = CDN$0.21
UK£1 = 9.70MK	1MK = UK£0.10
IR£1 = 7.55MK	1MK = IR£0.132
AUS$1 = 3.87MK	1MK = AUS$0.26
NZ$1 = 2.95MK	1MK = NZ$0.34
SAR1 = 0.97MK	1MK = SAR1.03
EUR€1 = 5.95MK	1MK = EUR€0.168

Country code: 358. **International dialing prefix:** 00. From outside Finland, dial the int'l dialing prefix (see inside back cover) + 358 + city code + local number.

Between the Scandinavian peninsula and the Russian wilderness, Finland is a land of coniferous trees, astounding summer clouds, and five million taciturn souls. "Finnish design" is synonymous with architectural excellence; outside Helsinki, wilderness reigns. Glistening lakes peek from lush forests, wooden shacks dot the west coast, and the Åland Islands are a biker's paradise. The Lake District in southeast Finland invites sailing and skiing. Lapland, in the north, boasts rugged terrain and rolling fells, boundless wilderness, and Finland's indigenous Sami people.

After seven centuries in the crossfire of warring Swedish and Russian empires, Finland experienced an extensive 19th-century romantic nationalist awakening largely nurtured by the *Kalevala* folk epic, Jean Sibelius' inspirational symphonies, and Akseli Gallen-Kallela's mythic paintings. In the years since, Finland has labored to maintain a delicate Nordic neutrality. Its cultural influences are felt most strongly geographically: the east tends to be more Russian, the west more Swedish.

FACTS AND FIGURES

Official Name: Republic of Finland.

Government: Republic.

Capital: Helsinki.

Land Area: 305,000 sq. km.

Geography: Plains, with lakes and hills.

Climate: Temperate but cold; in some places subarctic.

Major Cities: Tampere, Turku, Oulu.

Population: 5,160,000. Urban 65%, Rural 35%.

Languages: Finnish, Swedish.

Religions: Evangelical Lutheran (89%), Greek Orthodox (1%), none (9%).

Income Per Capita: US$20,100.

Major Exports: Machinery, chemicals, metals, timber, paper.

DISCOVER FINLAND

Perched on the edge of Scandinavia and Russia, **Helsinki** (p. 300) mixes Orthodox cathedrals and Lutheran churches, sleek 20th-century architecture, and grand 19th-century avenues. Daytrip to oft-photographed **Porvoo** (p. 305) and seaside **Hanko** (p. 306) before heading westward to **Turku,** Finland's oldest city (p. 310). Check out **Moomin World** in nearby Naantali (p. 311) before ferrying to the lovely **Åland Islands** (p. 306). **Savonlinna** in the Lake District was once a tsarist resort (p. 309). Finish the trip in **Lapland,** where you can sit in Santa's lap and frolic with reindeer (p. 311).

ESSENTIALS

WHEN TO GO

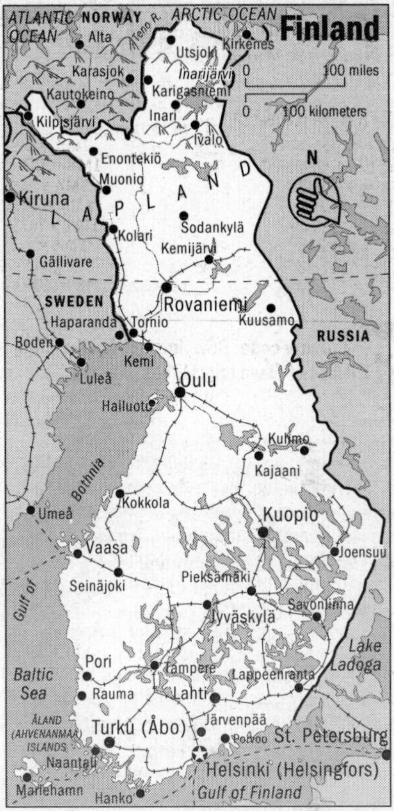

The long days of Finnish summers make for a tourist's dream; even night owls get out in the light of the midnight sun. After coming out of the two-month *kaamos* (polar night), without any sunlight, winter fanatics start hitting the slopes in early February; the skiing continues into March and April.

DOCUMENTS AND FORMALITIES

South Africans need a **visa** to enter as short-stay tourists; citizens of Australia, New Zealand, Canada, the UK, Ireland, and the US can visit Scandinavia for up to 90 days without a visa. For more than 90 days in any combination of Finland, Iceland, Norway, and Sweden, you will need a visa.

EMBASSIES AND CONSULATES

Embassies and consulates of other countries in Finland are in **Helsinki** (see p. 229).

Finnish Embassies at Home: Australia, 10 Darwin Ave., Yarralumla, ACT 2600 (☎ (02) 62 73 38 00; fax 62 73 36 03); **Canada,** 55 Metcalfe St., Suite 850, Ottawa ON, K1P 6L5 (☎(613) 236 23 89; fax 238 14 74; email finembott@synapse.net); **South Africa,** P.O. Box 443, Pretoria 0001 (☎(012) 343 02 75; fax 343 30 95); **Ireland,** Russell House, Stokes Pl., St. Stephen's Green, Dublin 2 (☎(01) 478 13 44); **UK:** 38 Chesham Pl., London SW1X 8HW (☎(020) 78 38 62 00; fax 72 35 36 80); **US:** 3301 Massachusetts Ave., NW, Washington, DC 20008 (☎(202) 298 58 00; www.finland.org).

GETTING THERE AND AROUND

BY PLANE. Finnair (toll-free in Finland ☎0203 140 160; English 24hr. info ☎818 83 83; fax (09) 818 87 35; www.finnair.com) flies from 50 international cities and covers the domestic market. Contact them in **Australia,** Avion House, 249-251 Pulteney St., Adelaide SA 5000 (☎(08) 83 06 84 11; fax 83 06 84 39); in **New Zealand,** Trust Bank Building, 229 Queen St., 6th fl., Auckland (☎(09) 308 33 65; fax 308 33 88); or in the **US,** 20 Park Plaza, Suite 912, Boston, MA 02116 (☎(617) 482-4952 or 800-950-5000; fax (617) 482-5932). Finnair gives a domestic discount of up to 50% for ages 17-24, and has summer and snow rates that reduce fares by up to 60%.

BY TRAIN. Eurail is valid in Finland. The national rail company is **VR Ltd., Finnish Railways,** P.O.Box 488, 00101 Helsinki (fax (03) 072 1700; www.vr.fi/heo/english/heo.htm). Efficient trains run at typical Nordic prices (Turku to Helsinki 100mk, Helsinki to Rovaniemi 340mk); seat reservations (20-30mk) are not required except on **InterCity** trains. The *buy-in-Scandinavia* **Scanrail Pass** allows unlimited rail travel through Denmark, Norway, Sweden, Finland, and many free or 20-50% discounted ferry rides. (5 days within 15 days 1523mk, under 26 1148mk, 60+ 1356mk; 21 consecutive days 1725mk, under 26 1749mk, 60+ 1534mk.) This differs from the *buy-outside-Scandinavia* **Scanrail Pass** (see **Essentials,** p. 59). A **Finnrail Pass** gives one month of unlimited rail travel. (3 days 620mk, 5 days 830mk, 10 days 1120mk.)

BY BUS. Buses cost the same as or more than trains, and often take longer. But they are the only way to reach some smaller towns and travel in northern Finland. **Onni Vilkas Ltd** (www.onnivilkas.planet.fi/pietarie.ht) runs a daily bus between **Helsinki** and **St. Petersburg,** as well as domestic service. **Expressbus** covers a lot of Finland (www.expressbus.com). For bus info, call ☎02 00 40 00 (6.34mk per min.). ISIC cardholders can buy a **student card** (32mk plus passport-sized photo), that discounts tickets by 50%, from bus stations. With student ID, drivers will give the student discount. Railpasses are valid on **VR Ltd. Buses** when trains are not in service.

BY FERRY. Viking Line (Helsinki ☎ (09) 123 51, fax 17 55 51; Stockholm ☎ (08) 452 40 00, fax 452 40 75) steams from **Stockholm** to: **Helsinki** (15hr., 230mk, students 180mk; off season 130mk, students 100mk); **Mariehamn** on **Åland** (6½hr., 68mk, students 55mk); and **Turku** (11-12hr., 199mk, students 159mk; off season 127mk, 87mk). Scanrail holders get 50% off on Viking; Eurailers ride free. **Silja Line** (Helsinki ☎ (09) 180 41, fax 180 4402; Stockholm ☎ (46) 666 3512; fax (46) 8 611 9162; Turku ☎(02) 335 6244; www.silja.com/english) sails from **Stockholm** to: **Helsinki** (15hr., from 245mk); **Mariehamn** (5½hr., 125mk, students 115mk); and **Turku** (11hr., 2 per day, from 110mk, students from 85mk). For Eurailers, Stockholm to Helsinki is 145mk and to Turku at night is 100mk (10mk during the day.) **Birka Lines** (Mariehamn ☎ (018) 270 27; Stockholm ☎ (08) 702 72 30; email info@birkacruises.com) launches *Princess* daily from **Stockholm** to **Mariehamn** (24hr., 125mk).

BY CAR. Driving conditions are good, but be wary of snow and ice in winter, and reindeer crossings. Drive on the right side of the road. Drinking and driving laws result in fines and/or imprisonment for violators. For car **rentals,** contact **Europcar** (☎(09) 75 15 57 00; fax 75 15 54 54; www.europcar.com) or **Hertz** (☎(09) 16 67 13 00; fax 16 67 13 82; www.hertz.com); both charge about 2400mk per week.

BY BIKE AND BY THUMB. Finland has 10,000km of **cycling** paths. Some campgrounds, hostels, and tourist offices rent bikes. Rates average 30-70mk per day or 190mk per week. **Hitchhikers** find more rides in Finland than elsewhere in Scandinavia; truck drivers may be likely to stop. *Let's Go* does not recommend hitchhiking.

TOURIST SERVICES AND MONEY

EMERGENCY. Police: ☎122. **Ambulance:** ☎123. **Fire:** ☎124.

TOURIST OFFICES. The helpful **Finnish tourist boards** offer a comprehensive website (www.mek.fi). Contact the tourist office of the region you plan to visit.

Finnish Tourist Boards at Home: Australia (Representative Office), 81 York St., Level 4, Sydney NSW 2000 (☎(02) 92 90 19 50; fax 92 90 19 81); **Canada** (Representative Office), P.O. Box 246, Station Q, Toronto, ON M4T 2M1 (☎(416) 964-9159; fax 964-1524); **UK,** 30-35 Pall Mall, London SW1Y 5LP (☎(020) 78 39 40 48; fax 73 21 06 96); **US,** 655 Third Ave., New York, NY 10017 (☎(212) 885-9700; fax 885-9739).

MONEY. Finland's currency unit is the markka, also known as the Finnish mark or Finmark (mk or FIM). There are 100 *pennia* in a *markka.* Banks exchange currency and accept ATM cards. ATMs offer the best exchange rates. Orange "Otto" bank machines accept Cirrus, MC, Visa, and ATM cards. **Food costs** run 60-100mk per day. Meals generally cost at least 30mk. Restaurants include a 14-15% **gratuity** in the meal price, but leave some coins if the service was particularly good. Round the fare up for cab drivers. A normal tip for bellhops, train porters, and sauna and cloakroom attendants is 5mk. The **Value Added Tax** (VAT) is 22%, 17% on food, and

8% on select services. For VAT refund or general info, contact **Global Refund Finland Oy,** Salamonkatu 17A, 00101 Helsinki (☎020 355 432; www.globalrefund.com).

BUSINESS HOURS. Most shops close M-F at 5 or 6pm (10pm in Helsinki), and Sa at 2 or 3pm. Urban supermarkets may stay open until 9pm, Sa 6pm. Shops may also be open June-Aug. on Su. Kiosks sell basic food, snacks, and toiletries until 9 or 10pm. Banks are typically open M-F 9:15am-4:15pm.

ACCOMMODATIONS AND CAMPING

Finland has more than 120 **youth hostels** (*retkeilymaja*; RET-kay-loo-MAH-yah); 70 are open all year. Prices average 60-150mk; non-HI-members add 15mk. Most have laundry and a kitchen; some have saunas, rent bicycles, boats, and ski equipment.

HOSTELS. The **Finnish Youth Hostel Association** (Suomen Retkeilymaja-järjestö-SRM) is at Yrjönkatu 38B, 00100 Helsinki (☎(09) 565 71 50; info line 060 092 484, 2.85mk per min.; fax 565 715 10; email info@srm.inet.fi; www.srmnet.org).

HOTELS. Hotels are often exorbitant (over 250mk); *kesähotelli* (summer hotels) operate June-Aug. and offer accommodation for around 40-110mk. The **Finland Tourism Board** (www.finland-tourism.com/mek_page4.html) keeps a database of booking agencies for year-round and summer hotels.

OTHER LOCAL ACCOMMODATIONS. **Private room** rental is not particularly common, but local tourist offices may help you find the cheapest accommodations.

CAMPING. Without permission it is illegal to camp outside campsites. About 360 campgrounds dapple the country; 200 to the Finnish Travel Association's national network (tent sites 25-90mk per night; *mökit* (small cottages) from 150mk). Seventy are open year-round. Finnish or International Camping Cards (FICC) earn discounts at most campgrounds. Buy a membership card from camping sites (20mk per family). For a campground guide, contact the **Finnish Travel Association/Camping Department,** Atomitie 5C, 00370 Helsinki (☎(09) 622 62 80; fax 654 3 58).

FOOD AND DRINK

A *kahvila* serves food, coffee, and beer; a *grilli* is a fast-food stand. A *ravintola* (restaurant) covers the spectrum from cafeterias to pubs. The best budget dining is at common **all-you-can-eat lunch buffets** (35-45mk), often found at otherwise pricier restaurants. Kebab and pizza joints are cheap, although quality varies (small pizza or kebab plate from 25mk). The cheapest **supermarkets** are **Alepa, Euromarket, Valintalo,** and any type of **K market.** The Finns are proud of their fish, including *kirjolohi* (rainbow trout), *silakka* (Baltic herring), and *lohi* (salmon) cured, pickled, smoked, poached, or baked. Finnish dietary staples include rye bread, potatoes, sour milk, Karelian pastries, and stretchy yogurt, *viili*. Reindeer meat, roasted or in a stew, is on some menus. Finnish caviar is superb, often served with sour cream and chopped onions. In summer, blueberries, cranberries, lingonberries, and, in the far north, Arctic cloudberries are picked for desserts, wines, vodka, and other liquors. You must be 18 to purchase beer and wine, and 20 for hard liquor; the age limit in bars and pubs is usually 18 but can be as high as 25. Beer *(olut)* is divided into groups. *Olut* IV is the strongest and most expensive (at least 25mk per 0.5L). *Olut* III (the best value) is slightly weaker and cheaper (18-20mk). Outside bars and restaurants, all alcohol stronger than *Olut* III must be purchased at state-run **Alko liquor** stores; expect lines before Midsummer as everyone prepares for drunken revelry. For "cheers," Finns say *"hi," "kippis,"* or the Scandinavian *"skal."*

COMMUNICATION

MAIL. Mail service is fast and efficient. Post offices are open M-F from 9am until 5 or 6pm. First-class and priority postal rates for **postcards** and **letters** under 20g is

3.20mk to other EU countries; 2.70mk to non-EU European countries; 6.30mk for letters and 3.40mk for postcards going outside Europe. Domestic letters and postcards under 50g cost 3mk. **Post Restante** can be sent to any town's main post office.

TELEPHONES. To make a long-distance call within Finland, dial 0 and the number. Local and long-distance calls within Finland usually cost 3mk; many pay phones take 1-, 5-, and 10mk coins. **Phone cards** are available from R-kiosks and post offices in 30-, 50-, 70-, and 100mk denominations. "Sonera" or "Nonstop" cards work nationwide; other cards only work in one city. There are two types of phone cards: those inserted vertically and those inserted horizontally. Check the pay phone you plan to use before purchasing a card. Also, some pay phones block toll-free calls. Some card telephones take credit cards. For **domestic information,** call ☎118. For **international information,** call ☎020 208. **International direct dialing** numbers include: **AT&T,** ☎0800 100 10; **Sprint,** ☎0800 11 02 84; **MCI WorldPhone Direct,** ☎08001 102 80; **Canada Direct,** ☎0800 11 00 11; **BT Direct,** ☎0800 11 04 40; **Ireland Direct,** ☎0800 11 03 53; **Australia Direct,** ☎0800 11 00 610; and **Telkom South Africa Direct,** ☎0800 11 02 70.

LANGUAGES. Finnish, a Finno-Ugric language, is spoken by 93% of the population, while Swedish, the official second language, is spoken by 6%. Many Finns speak English, but fluency decreases in the north. Sami (Lappish) is the tongue of about 1700 people. Some town names modify form on train and bus schedules due to a lack of prepositions in Finland. For example, "To Helsinki" is "Helsinkiin"; "From Helsinki" is "Helsingistä." For useful phrases, see p. 981.

HOLIDAYS AND FESTIVALS

Holidays: Epiphany (Jan. 6), Good Friday (Apr. 13), May Day (May 1), Ascension Day (May 24), Midsummer (June 22-23), All Saints' Day (Nov. 3), Independence Day (Dec. 6), Christmas Day (Dec. 25), and Boxing Day (Dec. 26). Many stores and museums, as well as all banks and post offices, are closed for Easter (Apr. 15-16), Christmas (Dec. 24-26), and New Year's Day. During Midsummer, when Finns party all night to the light of *kokko* (bonfires) and the midnight sun, virtually the entire country shuts down.

Festivals: The **Helsinki Festival** (mid-Aug. to early Sept., p. 300) presents concerts, dance, theater, and opera. Savonlinna's **Opera Festival** (early July-early Aug., p. 309), is in Olavinlinna Castle. **Naantali** has a Chamber Music Festival (June, p. 311).

HELSINKI (HELSINGFORS) ☎09

With all the appeal and none of the grime of a big city, Helsinki's broad avenues, grand architecture, and green parks make it a model of 19th-century city planning. The city also distinguishes itself with a decidedly multicultural flair: Lutheran and Russian Orthodox cathedrals stand almost face-to-face, and youthful energy mingles with old world charm. Baltic Sea produce fills the marketplaces and restaurants, while St. Petersburg and Tallinn are only a short cruise away.

GETTING THERE AND GETTING AROUND

Flights: Helsinki-Vantaa Airport (☎96 00 81 00; 3.40mk per min.) **Buses** #615 (more direct) and 616 run frequently between the airport and the train station square (15mk). A **Finnair bus** shuttles between the airport and the Finnair building at Asemaaukio 3, next to the train station (35min., every 20min. 5am-midnight, 27mk).

Trains: (☎707 57 06, or 03 02 72 09 00.) To: **Tampere** (2hr., 6am-10pm, 100mk); **Turku** (2hr., 12 per day, 100mk); **Rovaniemi** (10hr., 8 per day, 340mk); **St. Petersburg** (7hr., 2 per day, 284mk); and **Moscow** (15hr., daily at 5:34pm, 485mk).

Buses: (☎02 00 40 10. For Espoo and Vantaa buses, ☎010 01 11.) The station is between Salomonkatu and Simonkatu; from the Mannerheimintie side of the train station, head down Postikatu past the statue of Mannerheim. Cross Mannerheimintie onto

Salomonkatu and the station will be to your left. To: **Lahti** (1½hr., 2 per hr., 93mk); **Tampere** (2½hr., every hr., 100mk); and **Turku** (2½hr., 2 per hr., 114mk).

Ferries: For route options, see p. 298. **Silja Line,** Mannerheimintie 2 (☎980 07 45 52 or 091 80 41). Take tram #3B or 3T from the city center to the Olympic terminal. **Viking Line,** Mannerheimintie 14 (☎12 35 77). **Tallink,** Erottajankatu 19 (☎22 82 12 77). Viking Line and **Finnjet** (contact Silja Line) depart from Katajanokka Island, east of Kauppatori (take tram #2 or 4). Silja Line sails from South Harbor, south of Kauppatori (take tram #3T).

Local Transportation: (☎010 01 11; 2mk per call.) The metro, trams, and buses run roughly 5:30am-11pm. (Some major tram and bus lines, including tram #3T, continue until 1:30am.) There is only one metro line, which runs approximately east to west, 10 tram lines, and many more bus lines. Night buses, marked with an N, run after 1:30am. You can buy single-fare tickets on buses and trams or from machines at the metro station (15mk); 10-trip tickets (120mk) are available at R-kiosks and at the **City Transport** office in the Rautatientori metro station (open M-Th 7:30am-6pm, F 7:30am-4pm; closes 1hr. later in winter). Tickets are valid for 1hr. (transfers free); punch your ticket on board. The **Tourist Ticket,** a convenient bargain for a 5-day stay, is available at City Transport and tourist offices and provides unlimited bus, tram, metro, and local train transit (1-day 25mk, 3-day 50mk, 5-day 75mk; half-price for children).

ORIENTATION AND PRACTICAL INFORMATION

Sea surrounds Helsinki on the east and west, and the city center is bisected by two lakes. Water shapes everything in the Finnish capital, from relaxing city beaches to gorgeous parks around the lakes. Helsinki's main street, **Mannerheimintie,** passes between the bus and train stations on its way to the city center, eventually crossing **Esplanadi.** This tree-lined promenade leads east to **Kauppatori** (Market Square) and the beautiful South Harbor. Both Finnish and Swedish are used on all street signs and maps. *Let's Go* uses the Finnish names in all listings and maps.

TOURIST, FINANCIAL, AND LOCAL SERVICES

Tourist Offices: City Tourist Office, Pohjoisesplanadi 19 (☎169 37 57; fax 169 38 39; www.hel.fi). From the train station, walk 2 blocks south on Keskuskatu and turn left on Pohjoisesplanadi. Open May-Sept. M-F 9am-7pm, Sa-Su 9am-3pm; Oct.-Apr. M-F 9am-5pm, Sa 9am-3pm. The **Finnish Tourist Board,** Eteläesplanadi 4 (☎41 76 93 00; fax 41 76 93 01; www.mek.fi), has info on all of Finland. Open June-Aug. M-F 9:00am-5pm, Sa 10am-2pm; Sept.-May M-F 8:30am-4pm. **Hotellikeskus** (Hotel Booking Center; ☎22 88 14 00; fax 22 88 14 99), in the train station, books rooms for a fee of 30mk in person, but free by phone or email. Open June-Aug. M-F 9am-7pm, Sa-Su 10am-6pm; Sept.-May M-F 9am-5pm. The **Helsinki Card,** sold at the tourist office, Hotellikeskus, central R-kiosks, and most hotels, provides museum discounts and unlimited local transportation (1-day 130mk, 3-day 190mk).

Embassies: Canada, Pohjoisesplanadi 25B (☎17 11 41). Open M-F 8:30am-noon and 1-4:30pm. **Estonia,** Itäinen Puistotie 10 (☎622 02 88). **Ireland,** Erottajankatu 7A (☎64 60 06). **Latvia,** Armfeltintie 10 (☎476 47 20). **Lithuania,** Rauhankatu 13A (☎60 82 10). **Poland,** Armas Lindgrenintie 21 (☎684 80 77). **Russia,** Tehtaankatu 1B (☎66 18 76). **South Africa,** Rahapajankatu 1A 5 (☎68 60 31 00). **UK,** Itäinen Puistotie 17 (☎22 86 51 00). Also handles diplomatic matters for **Australians** and **New Zealanders.** Open M-F 8:30am-5pm. **US,** Itäinen Puistotie 14A (☎17 19 31). Open M-F 8:30am-5pm, 9am-noon for consulate. By appointment only.

Currency Exchange: Exchange, Kaivokatu 6, across from the train station. No fee for cash exchange, but 30mk fee for up to six traveler's checks. Open M-F 8am-8pm, Sa 10am-4pm. The five Helsinki **Forex** offices are a good choice (10mk/US$ exchange). Hours vary but the Rautatieasema/Jvgstn location in the train station is open 7am-9pm.

Luggage Storage: Train station lockers 10mk per day.

Laundromat: Easywash, Runeberginkatu 47 (☎40 69 82). Open M-Th 10am-9pm, F 10am-6pm, Sa 10am-4pm.

EMERGENCY AND COMMUNICATIONS

Emergencies: ☎112. **Police:** ☎100 22.

Pharmacy: Yliopiston Apteekki, Mannerheimintie 96 (☎41 78 03 00). Open 24hr.

Medical Assistance: Aleksin lääkäriasema, Mannerheimintie 8 (☎77 50 84 00).

Internet Access: Cable Book Library, Mannerheimintie 22-24, in the Lasipalatsi mall directly across from the bus station. Open M-Th 10am-8pm, Su noon-6pm.

Post Office: Mannerheiminaukio 1A (☎020 451 44 00). Open M-F 9am-6pm. Address mail to be held: First name SURNAME, *Poste Restante,* Mannerheiminaukio 1A, 00100 Helsinki, Finland. Open M-F 7am-9pm, Sa 9am-6pm, Su 11am-9pm.

ACCOMMODATIONS AND CAMPING

Helsinki hotels tend to be expensive, but budget hostels are often quite nice. In June and July, it's wise to make reservations. Most hostels offer laundry facilities and provide breakfast for a fee. Extra summer hostels are open from June to August: try **Hotel Satakunta (HI),** Lapinrinne 1A (☎69 58 51; fax 694 22 26), and **Academica (HI),** Hietaniemenkatu 14A (☎13 11 43 34; fax 44 12 01).

Hotel Erottanjanpuisto (HI), Uudenmaankatu 9 (☎64 21 69; fax 680 27 57). Turn right from the train station, left onto Mannerheimintie, and bear right onto Erottajankatu; Uudenmaankatu is on the right. The well-kept accommodations are posh but pricey. Breakfast 25-35mk. Lockers 5mk. Laundry 40mk. Kitchen. Reception 24hr. Check-in 10pm, check-out 1pm. In summer, dorms 145mk, singles 260mk, doubles 320mk; off season 140mk, 250mk, 300mk; nonmembers add 15mk.

Finnapartments Fenno, Franzeninkatu 26 (☎773 16 61; fax 701 68 89). From the train station, turn left, follow Kaisaniemenkatu, and bear left onto Unioninkatu (which becomes Siltasaarenkatu); or catch the metro to Hakaniemi. Then head right on Porthaninkatu (the street diagonal from the WWII memorial), turn left onto Fleminginkatu, then left again. Alternatively, take tram #3T to Kallion virastotalo. The neighborhood is not the best, but the clean accommodations are super-cheap. Sauna. Economy singles have radio, sink and fridge (180 mk); apartments also include kitchenette and private bath. Singles 270mk; doubles 350mk.

Eurohostel (HI), Linnankatu 9, Katajanokka (☎622 04 70; fax 65 50 44; email euroh@icon.fi; www.eurohostel.fi). 200m from the Viking Line/Finnjet ferry terminal. From the train station, head right to Mannerheimintie, and take tram #2 to Mastokatu; or tram #4 to Munkkiniemi (both dir. Katajanokka). From Uspensky Cathedral, head down Kanavankatu, turn left on Pikku Satamankatu, and bear right on Linnankatu. The largest hostel in Finland, with bright rooms, non-smoking floors, and sauna. Kitchen and cafe. Reception 24hr. Accepts email reservations. Singles 180mk; doubles 210mk; triples 315mk. Nonmembers add 15-17mk each. Student discounts in winter.

Stadion Hostel (HI), Pohj. Stadiontie 3B (☎49 60 71; fax 49 64 66). Take tram #7A, 4, or 10 from by the train station, behind Sokos on Mannerheimintie, to the Ooppera stop. Continue on Mannerheimintie, then right on Toivonkatu. The hostel, on the far side of the Stadium, is converted athletic space with sports memorabilia popular with school groups. Kitchen. Breakfast 25mk. Paper sheets 15mk. Cotton Sheets 25mk. Laundry 15mk. Reception June-early Sept. 7am-3am; mid-Sept. to May 8-10am and 4pm-2am. Lockout 10am-4pm. Dorms 65mk; doubles 180mk. Nonmembers add 15mk each.

Rastila Camping (☎31 65 51), 12km east of the city center. Take the metro east to Rastila (a Vuosaari, not Mellunmäki train); the campsite is 100m away to the right. Toilets, showers, and washing and cooking facilities. Reception 24hr. Camping 50mk per single, 80mk for 2-6 people; 2-person cabins 220mk, 4-person cabins 360mk. Rastila also recently opened a summer **hostel:** singles 150mk; doubles 220mk; triples 315mk.

FOOD

Escape pricey restaurants at **Alepa supermarket,** under the train station (open M-F 7:30-am-10pm, Sa 9am-10pm, Su 10am-10pm) or at **open-air markets** at **Kauppatori,** by

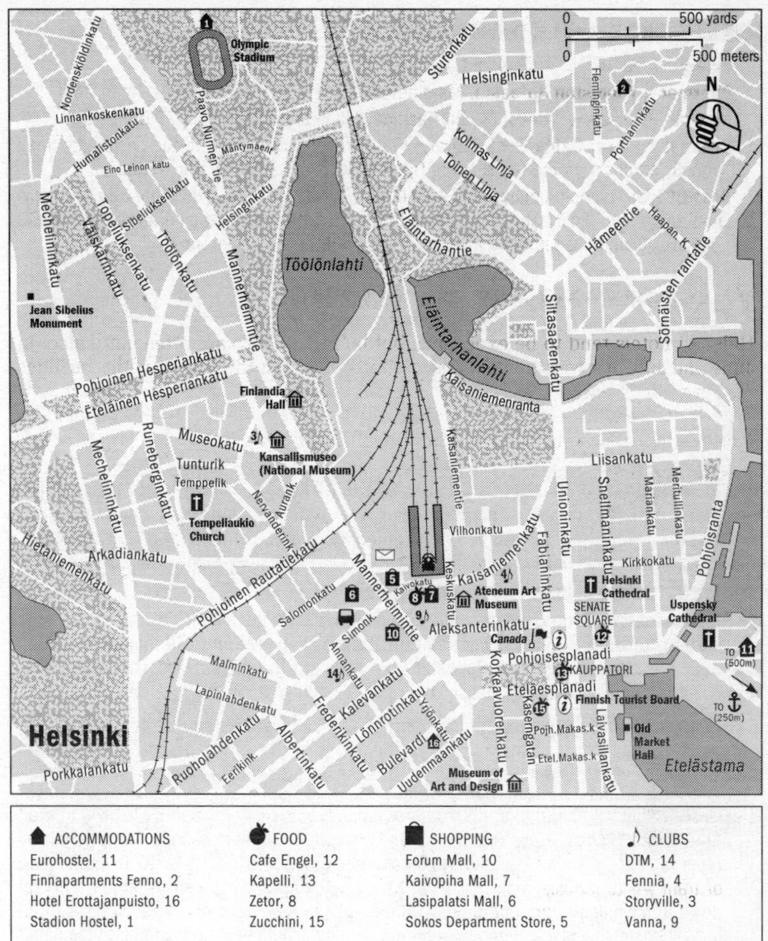

the port (open June-Aug. M-Sa 7am-2pm and 4-8pm; Sept.-May M-F 7am-2pm) or the nearby **Vanha Kauppahalli** (Old Market Hall; open M-F 8am-8pm, Sa 8am-3pm.)

Zetor, Kaivokatu 10, in Kaivopiha, the mall directly opposite the train station. Food, dancing, and tractors. Sit on a log stump to enjoy tiny fried fish. Entrees 40-100mk. Beer 26mk. Open Su-M 3pm-1am, Tu-Th 3pm-3am, F 3pm-4am, and Sa 1pm-4 am.

Café Engel, Aleksanterinkatu 26, in Senate Square. Light fare for the budding intellectual crowd. Try the variety of coffees (from 12mk) and cakes (from 25mk). Open M-F 7:45am-midnight, Sa 9:30am-midnight, Su 11am-midnight.

Golden Rax Pizza Buffet, in Forum, opposite the post office. All-you-can-eat pasta and pizza bargain extravaganza (43mk). Open M-Sa 11am-9pm, and Su 12am-9pm.

Kappeli, Eteläesplanadi 1, at the Unionkatu end of Esplanadi park. The distinctive yellow building has catered to trendies since 1837. Not cheap, but a great spot for people-watching. Entrees 60-120mk. Open M-Th 9am-2am, F-Sa 9am-3am, Su 9am-1am.

Zucchini, Fabianinkatu 4, near the tourist office. A casual *kasvisravintola* (vegetarian restaurant) that serves a daily lunch special with salad and bread (42mk). Dense veggie bread and tasty quinoa. Open M-F 11am-4pm.

SIGHTS

Home to a bold new designs and polished Neoclassical works, Helsinki proves famed Finnish architect Alvar Aalto's statement, "Architecture is our form of expression because our language is so impossible." Much of the layout and architecture of the old center, however, is the brainchild of a German. After Helsinki became the capital of the Grand Duchy of Finland in 1812, Carl Engel designed a grand city modeled after St. Petersburg. **Tram #3T** circles past the major attractions in an hour, offering the cheapest city tour. Better yet, walk—most sights are packed within 2km of the train station. Pick up *See Helsinki on Foot* from the Helsinki tourist office. Helsinki's beautiful parks are must-sees, especially the promenade along **Töölönlahti,** which blooms with lilacs in the summer, and **Tahtitorninvuori** (Observatory Park), overlooking Uspensky Cathedral.

SENAATIN TORI (SENATE SQUARE). The square and its gleaming white **Tuomiokirkko** (Dome Church, officially known as Cathedral) showcase Engel's work and exemplify the splendor of Finland's Russian period. *(On the corner of Aleksanterinkatu and Unioninkatu in the city center. Open June-Aug. M-Sa 9am-6pm, Su noon- 8pm; Sept.-May Su-F 10am-4pm, Sa 10am-6pm.)*

USPENSKINKATEDRAADI (USPENSKY ORTHODOX CATHEDRAL). Mainly known for its red and gold cupolas and great spires, which jut prominently out of the city skyline, the Cathedral also has an ornate interior. *(Follow Esplanadi down to Kauppatori. Interior open M and W-F 9:30am-4pm, Tu 9:30am-6pm, Sa 9am-4pm, Su noon-3pm.)*

SUOMEN KANSALLISMUSEO (NATIONAL MUSEUM OF FINLAND). The museum displays intriguing bits of Finnish culture, from Gypsy and Sami costumes to *ryijyt* (rugs), as well as a magnificent roof mural by Akseli Gallen-Kallela. *(Up the street from the Finnish Parliament House. Open T-W 11am-8pm and Th-Su 11am-6pm. Call ☎94 05 01 or consult the board outside the museum.)*

OTHER MUSEUMS. Ateneum Taidemuseo, Finland's largest art museum, features a comprehensive look at Finnish art from the 1700s to the 1960s. *(Kaivokatu 2, opposite the train station. Open Tu and F 9am-6pm, W-Th 9am-8pm, Sa-Su 11am-5pm. 15mk, students 10mk; special exhibits 30-35mk.)* **Kiasma,** aptly named for the crossing over stage in mitosis, houses great modern art from Finnish and international artists in a funky silver building. *(Mannerheiminaukio 2. Open Tu 9am-5pm, W-Su 10am-10pm. 25mk, students 20mk.)* Even the stairs in the **Museum of Art and Design,** a showcase of Finnish and international design, are a mesh masterpiece. *(Korkeavuorenkatu 23. Open M-Su 11am-6pm; in winter, closed Mondays. 40mk, students 20mk.)*

FINLANDIA TALO. The magnificent white marble concert hall stands as a testament to the skill of the Finnish architect Alvar Aalto, who also designed the interior and furnishings. *(☎402 41. Mannerheimintie 13E. Tours 25mk, children 15mk.)*

TEMPPELIAUKIO KIRKKO. Designed in 1969 by Tuomo and Timo Suomalainen, this inspiring church is built into a hill of rock, with only the roof visible from the outside. Inside, its huge dome ceiling appears to be supported by rays of sunshine. *(Lutherinkatu 3. Walk away from the main post office near the train station on Paasikivenaudio, which becomes Arkadiagatan, then turn right on Fredrikinatu; you'll end up in the square where the church is buried. Open M-F 10am-8pm, Sa 10am-6pm, Su noon-1:30pm and 3:30pm-6pm. Services in English Su 2pm.)*

JEAN SIBELIUS MONUMENT. Dedicated in 1967 by sculptor Eila Hiltunen to one of the 20th century's greatest composers, the Sibelius monument looks like a cloud of organ pipes ascending to heaven. A well-touristed spot in a scenic area, the monument and its surrounding park makes a great place for an afternoon picnic. *(On Mechelininkatu in Sibelius Park. Catch bus #24, dir. Seurasaari, from Mannerheimintie; get off at Rasjasaarentie and the monument will be behind you and to the left.)*

SUOMENLINNA. This 18th-century Swedish military fortification consists of five interconnected islands used by the Swedes to repel attacks on Helsinki. The old fortress's dark passageways are exciting to explore, and the island's museums are worth a visit; check out the model ship collection of the Ehrensvärd and the submarine Vesikko. *(Most museums open in summer 10am-5pm; Mar.-May Sa-Su 11am-4pm. 10mk, students 5mk; some museums have additional admission. Ferries depart from Market Square every hr. 8am-11pm; round-trip 25mk.)*

SEURASAARI. A quick walk across the beautiful white bridge from the mainland brings you to the many paths of the island of Seurasaari, lined by old churches and farmsteads transplanted from all over the country. An open-air museum allows entrance into many of the island's historical buildings. Visit during Midsummer to witness the *kokko* (bonfires) and Finnish revelry in its full splendor. *(Take bus #24 from Erottaja, outside the Swedish Theater, to the last stop. The island is always open for hiking. Museum open M-F 9am-3pm, Sa-Su 11am-5pm. 20mk; children free.)*

NIGHTLIFE

Sway to afternoon music in **Esplanadi** (the park between Pohjoiesplanadi and Eteläesplanadi) or party with a younger crowd at **Kaivopuisto park** (on the corner of Puistokatu and Ehrenstromintie in the southern part of town) or **Hietaniemi beach.** (From Mannerheimintie, head down Hesperiankatu to the western shore.) The free English-language papers *Helsinki This Week*, *Helsinki Happens*, and *City* list popular cafes, bars, nightclubs, and events. Finland actually enforces the drinking age—but you will see younger folks drinking. Many clubs have a 22 age minimum. Bouncers and cover charges usually relax on weeknights; speaking English may help. With the exception of licensed restaurants and bars, the state-run liquor store **Alko** has a monopoly on sales of alcohol more potent than light beer. (Branch at Mannerheimintie 1, in Kaivopiha across from the train station. Open M-F 9am-8pm, Sa 9am-6pm.) Euro-pop at **Fennia,** Mikonkatu 17, opposite the train station. (22+. Cover 30mk. Open M-F 11pm-4am, Sa-Su 8pm-4am.) Sip 80-proof on the terrace at **Vanha** (Old Students' House), Mannerheimintie 3. The wide selection includes 130 beers. (Beer from 25mk. Cover up to 150mk for live bands. Open M-F 10am-2am, Sa 10am-4am, Su noon-midnight.) **Storyville,** Museokatu 8, near the National Museum, has live jazz and blues after 10pm. (Jazz club open 8pm-4am. Bar upstairs open M-Su 7pm-4am.) **DTM** (Don't Tell Mama), Annankatu 32, has a gay and mixed crowd. (20+. Open Su-Th 10pm-4am, F-Sa 9pm-4am.) **Decadenz,** a shop in the Forum, stocks flyers with rave info. Open M-F 10am-9pm, Sa 9am-6pm, Su 2pm-8pm.

EXCURSIONS FROM HELSINKI

PORVOO. Porvoo's picturesque cobblestone roads wind around historic wooden houses along the River Porvoo. The nation's second-largest town (pop. 44,000), and one of its most photographed, Porvoo is located on Old King Rd., which continues from Helsinki to Russia. In 1809, Tsar Alexander I granted Finland autonomy at the Porvoo **cathedral** in the old town. (Open May-Sept. M-F 10am-6pm, Sa 10am-2pm, Su 2pm-5pm; Oct.-Apr. Tu-F 10am-2pm, Su-M 2-4pm. Free.) The former home of **Johan Ludvig Runeberg,** Aleksanterinkatu 3, is now a museum memorializing the beloved Finnish poet who lived in Porvoo in the mid-19th century. Admission includes a sculpture exhibition by Walter Runeburg, the poet's son, at Aleksanterinkatu 5. (House open May-Aug. M-Sa 10am-4pm, Su 11am-5pm; Sept.-Apr. W-Sa 10am-4pm, Su 11am-5pm. 15mk. Exhibition open same hours in summer; in winter W-Su 11am-3pm.) Eat a *Runeberginpulla*, a cylindrical pastry immortalized as the poet's favorite breakfast. The **Tea and Coffee Shop Helmi**, Välikatu 7, has 19th-century appeal. (Open May-Aug. M-F 11am-10pm, Sa-Su 10am-10pm; Sept.-Apr. M, W, Th, and Su 11am-7pm, F-Sa 11am-9pm.) **Buses** roll into Porvoo from Helsinki (1hr., every 30min., 45mk). The helpful **tourist office,** Rihkamakatu 4, has free maps. (☎58 01 45; www.porvoo.fi. Open in summer M-F 10am-4:30pm, Sa 10am-2pm; in winter, M-F 9am-4:30pm, Sa 10am-2pm.) **Porvoo Camping Kokonniemi,** Linnankoskenkatu 1-3, 1.5km from the town center, has a sauna, laundry, and cooking facilities. (☎523

0012. Cross the footbridge on Jokikatu, near the corner of Lundinkatu, and turn left onto the asphalt path. The camping area is 15 minutes away. Shower included. Call ahead. Open June-Aug. 90 mk per tent; cabins from 345 mk.) ☎ **019.**

HANKO. The seaside resort of Hanko juts out into a beautiful rocky archipelago. Great villas lining Hanko's miles of coastland reflect the decadence of the now-vanished Russian nobility. Choose from over 30km of **beaches;** those along Appelgrenintie are the most popular. **Buses** arrive from Helsinki (2¼hr., 7 per day, 148mk), as do **trains,** which run less frequently (171mk). The **tourist office,** Raatihuoneentori 5, has free maps and helps find rooms. (☎220 34 11; fax 248 58 21. Open summer M-F 9am-5pm, Sa 10am-2pm; winter M-F 8am-4pm.) **Ari's Snack Bar** rents **bikes;** look for the "100% Welcome" sign in the Guest Harbor (10mk per hr., 50mk per day). Many **guest houses** are in former villas along Appelgrenintie; try **Villa Doris** at #23 for ocean views. (☎248 12 28. 80-200mk.) **Hanko Camping Silversand,** on Hopeahietikko 2.5km northeast of the town center, has a beach and offers tent sites and RV hookups right on the ocean. Follow Santalantie from town and turn left on Lähteentie. (☎248 55 00. Laundry. Open June 1-Aug. 20. 45mk per person; tent or car 90mk; cabins from 365mk.) The cafe at **Neljän Tuulen Tupa** (The House of the Four Winds) was once owned by Finnish war hero, Marshal Mannerheim, and is a peaceful place to watch the ocean. (Sandwiches 16mk, cakes from 15mk.) Follow Appelgrenintie until the sign for the House leading down a dirt path called Långsanda (15min.). ☎ **019.**

ÅLAND ISLANDS (AHVENANMAA) ☎018

Åland is a series of 6500 peaceful islands that were part of Sweden until 1809. The "Åland question" burned until the early 1900s; after Finland gained independence in 1917, there was an Ålander movement to rejoin Sweden. The question was settled on June 9, 1921: Åland was to remain part of Finland but with considerable of autonomy. Åland has its own flag, parliament, and postal system. While Autonomy Day is still celebrated, the only Åland question visitors are likely to ask is how to enjoy the shining sun, flower-covered winding bike paths, and rose-colored roads.

GETTING THERE AND GETTING AROUND

For info on traveling to Mariehamn on the **Viking Line** or **Silja Line,** see **Getting Around Europe: By Ferry,** p. 64. **Birka Lines** launches its *Princess* daily from Stockholm to Mariehamn. (Mariehamn ☎270 27, in Stockholm ☎(08) 702 72 30; email info@birkacruises.com. 24hr., 125mk.) **Inter-island ferries** are free for foot passengers and cyclists; passengers with cars pay 30-40mk (200mk if landing on Åland, Uårdö, or the mainland). **Ferry** and **bus** schedules are at the Mariehamn tourist office. The main island, Åland, with extensive paths and wide roads, is best explored by **bike. RoNo Rent,** facing the ferry terminal in Mariehamn in the Eastern harbor, rents bikes for 30mk, mopeds for 200mk, and boats from 220mk. (☎128 21. Open daily June-Aug. 9am-5pm and 6-7pm; May and Sept. call for hours.) The other islands are accessible from Mariehamn by a combo of ferries, buses, and bikes.

MARIEHAMN. On the south coast of the main island, Mariehamn (pop. 10,500) is the only actual *town* in Åland. Stock up on groceries, as most of the island consists of small campgrounds, beaches, and a few cafes. Although the outdoors are spectacular, the town itself has some interesting sights. The **Åland Art Museum** and **Åland Museum,** at Stadshusparken off Storagatan, display Åland's historical and cultural richness. (Open W-M 10am-4pm, Tu 10am-8pm. 15mk, students 10mk.) Visible from the ferry terminal, the smallish **Sjöfartsmuseum** displays its collection of mastheads and recovered booty. The adjacent moored ship **Pommern** recreates the high seas experience. (Both open May-June and Aug. 9am-5pm; July 9am-7pm. Pommern also Sept.-Oct. 10am-4pm. Free tours in English. 25mk for one museum, 40mk for both.)

For maps and info, head to the **tourist office,** Storagatan 8. From the ferry terminal, go left up Hamngatan and turn right on Storagatan. (☎240 00; fax 242 65; www.info.aland.fi. Open daily June-Aug. 9am-6pm; Sept.-May M-F 9am-4pm, S

NAKED NORTHERNERS True to the stories, the sauna is an integral part of almost every Finn's life. More than simply a place to cleanse oneself thoroughly after a shower, saunas have developed a certain mystique and are immortalized in *Kalevala,* the Finnish national epic. Associated with cleanliness, strength, and endurance, there are over 1.5 million saunas in Finland, or one for every three people. Modern saunas are found in every hotel, most hostels, and many campgrounds. These wooden rooms reach temperatures around 88°C, so hot that no metal parts may be exposed, lest the bathers be burned. Water thrown on heated stones brings humidity as high as 100%. Finland's electricity use skyrockets on Friday and Saturday evenings, when hundreds of thousands of saunas are heated.

10am-4pm.) **Ålandsresor,** Torggatan 2, books rooms and cottages (from 120mk) for all the islands for a 35mk fee. (☎280 40; fax 283 80; www.alandsresor.fi. Open M-F 8:30am-5pm. Book ahead.) Docked at the Eastern harbor, the boat **Alida** offers sardine-sized rooms. (☎137 55. Reception 8am-10pm. Open May-Sept. Doubles 200mk.) **Gröna Uddens Camping** is 10 minutes down Skillnadsgatan from the town center. (☎211 21. Shower included. Laundry. Open mid-May to Aug. 25mk.) Inflated restaurant prices make **supermarkets** alluring; try **Fokus** at Torggatan 14 (open M-F 9am-6pm, Sa 9am-4pm), or **Mathis Hallen**, on the corner of Norragaten and Ålandsvagen (open M-F 9am-7pm, Sa 9am-4pm, Su 11am-4pm). Cafes and pizza joints are the only real bargains. **Café Nero,** in an old warehouse at Strandgatan 12, covers baked potatoes with your choice of toppings and creamy garlic salad dressing for 30mk. (Open M-Th 10am-11pm, F 10am-midnight, Sa 11am-midnight, Su noon-10pm.) Next door, the Finnish chain **Koti Pizza,** serves personal pizzas from 23mk. **Café Julius,** Torggatan 10, serves the island's specialty, *Alands Pannkaka* (a custardy thin cake with berry sauce and whipped cream), for 12mk. (Open daily 9am-9pm.) **The Upstairs Pub,** upstairs from Café Nero, has a terrace, dancing, cushy armchairs, and a stunning view of the sound. (Open daily 5pm-4am.)

SUND. Northeast of Mariehamn lies the province of Sund. **Bike** along the cycling route to Godby or take **bus #4** (30min., 8 per day, 17mk) to "Kastelholm" and see the 13th-century **Kastelholms Slott,** with the prison room where mad King Erik XIV was kept during his bout with lead poisoning. (☎43 21 50. Open daily May-Oct. 10am-4pm; in winter by appointment. 25mk, students 17mk. Includes guided tour; English tours usually available.) Up the hill, the **Vita Björn** museum features prison cells through the centuries, up to 1975. (Open May-Sept. same hours as castle. 6mk, students 4mk.) An open-air homestead museum, **Jan Karlsgården,** boasts over 30 authentic wooden buildings culled from various parts of Åland, on a gorgeous plot of land. (Open daily May-Sept. 10am-5pm. Free.) Ten kilometers down the road in **Bomarsund** is a tsarist Russian fortress destroyed by British and French forces during the Crimean War (bus #4; 23mk from Mariehamn, 10mk from Kastelholm). **Puttes Camping** (☎440 16; fax 440 47), at Bomarsund, has a kitchen, laundry, and **bike and boat rental.** From the Prästö bridge, the campground is 100m to the right.

PORI ☎02

Each July the coastal town of Pori overflows with tourists attending the **Pori Jazz Festival,** which attracts varied acts from Big Bad Voodoo Daddy to Kool and the Gang. (Info ☎626 22 00; tickets ☎626 22 15; www.porijazz.fi. Tickets 80-660mk.) Head to the **Pori Art Museum,** on the corner of Etelärantakatu and Raatihuonekatu, for Finnish and international modern art. (Open Tu-Su 11am-6pm, W 11am-8pm. 20mk, students 8mk.) Walk by the river to view beautiful architecture and spectacular greenery or get out to **Yyteri** beach and **Repossaari,** the fishing village. **Trains** run from Tampere (1¾hr., 6 per day, 76mk) and Helsinki (4hr, 6 per day, 132mk). **Buses** roll in from Turku (2hr., 14 per day, 55mk). The **tourist office,** Hallituskatu 9A, is attractively designed by Carl Engel. (☎621 12 73; fax 621 12 75.) A student dorm in winter, the **Youth Hostel Tekunkorpi** is far from town, but the walk past the jogging park is lovely. Take bus #30 or 40 (15min., 11mk) to the corner of Professorintie and Korpraalintie and walk 750m up Teknikantie. (☎634 84 00. Singles with breakfast 180mk; doubles with breakfast 260mk, without breakfast 190mk; quads 300mk. HI members subtract 15mk.) At **Hudson Bay Restaurant,** Yrjönkatu 10, roses accompany the Finnish lunch special. (38mk. Lunch from 10:45am-3pm. Open M-Tu 10:45am-8pm, W-Th 10:45am-10pm, F-Sa 10:45am-11pm, Su noon-9pm.)

LAHTI ☎03

A sporty lakeside city, Lahti (pop. 100,000) combines scenic lakeside vistas with a bustling marketplace. At its prime during the snowy season as a world class ski-jumping and cross-country ski venue, Lahti will be hosting the 2001 Nordic Games. Ride the slow elevator to the top of the **"Big Hill"** at Lahti's **Sports Center.** (Open May-Aug. Chairlift to the foot of Big Hill open daily 11am-5:30pm; 15mk. Elevator to the top open daily 9am-5:30pm; 20mk.) The **Ski Museum** adjacent to the Sports Center has ski-jump and biathalon simulators (☎814 45 23. Open M-F 10am-5pm, Sa-Su 11am-5pm). **Cross-country ski trails** (150km), also good for a hike, radiate from the complex. Closer to town, the **Church of the Cross,** Kirkkokatu 4, is a must see for Aalto architecture lovers with its cool, graceful interior. (Open daily 10am-3pm.)

Lahti is a transportation hub. **Buses** depart for Jyväskylä (3hr., 122mk) and Savonlinna (4hr., 153mk). **Trains** speed to: Helsinki (1½hr., 64mk); Tampere (2hr., 90mk); Savonlinna (3½hr., 82mk); and St. Petersburg, Russia (5hr., 228mk). The **tourist office** is at Aleksanterinkatu 16, 2nd fl. (☎814 45 66; fax 814 45 64; email matkailu@lahti.fi; www.lahti.fi. Open M-F 9am-4pm.) **Lahden Kansanopisto hostel (HI),** Harjukatu 46, student housing used as a hostel in summer, houses three people per spacious room, complete with balconies. From the train station, walk north on Vesijärvenkatu one block and then right on Harjukatu. (☎878 11 81; fax 878 12 34. Reception M-F 8am-9pm, Sa-Su 8am-noon and 4-9pm. Open June-Aug. Dorms 80mk; singles 160m. Nonmembers add 15mk.) **Hostel Patria,** Vesijarvenkatu 3, is tidy but small. (☎782 37 83; fax 03 782 37 93. Breakfast 25mk. Singles 160mk, with extra bed 220mk; doubles 250 mk; triples 290.) The idyllic **Mukkula Tourist Center** has a **campground.** (☎874 14 00. Tents 40-70mk; 4-person cabins 220-450mk). Take bus #30 from stop D1 at Market Square, on the side closest to The Church of the Cross (3 per hr., 12mk). For a cheap bite, the ubiquitous **Golden Rax** pizza buffet (see Helsinki listing) is across from the huge 20 Rautatienkatu sign. (Open M-F 11am-9pm.) Meals in **Market Square** (Kauppatori, between Rauhankatu and Rautatienkatu) come with a side of people-watching. **Bellmanni,** Kauppakatu 9, has hearty Finnish favorites. (Daily lunch special 28mk with salad and bread. Open M-F 10am-1am.) **Open House** in Hotelli Cumulus, Vapaudenkatu 24, hosts live bands. (Cover from 40mk. Open W-F 11pm-4am, Sa 10pm-4am, Su 11pm-4am.)

TAMPERE ☎03

Once Finland's most industrialized city, smokestacks puncture Tampere's skyline, but the city does not lack culture. With museums at every turn, energetic nightlife, frequent cultural festivals, and beaches, Tampere is worth a short stay.

PRACTICAL INFO, ACCOMMODATIONS, AND FOOD. **Trains** head south to Helsinki (2hr., 12 per day, 190mk) and Turku (2hr., 10 per day, 172mk), and north to Oulu (5hr., 8 per day, 273mk). **Boats** (☎212 48 04) cruise to Ruovesi (4½hr.; Tu, Th, and Sa; 167mk) and beyond to Virrat (7½hr., 226mk) or to Hämeenlinna (8hr., 1 per day, 202mk). The **tourist office,** Verkatehtaankatu 2, and its army zipping around town on green scooters, is happy to help. From the train station, walk up Hämeenkatu, turn left before the bridge, and look for the sign. (☎31 46 68 00; fax 31 46 64 63; email touristbureau@tampere.fi; www.tampere.fi. Open June-Aug. M-F 8:30am-8pm, Sa-Su 10am-5pm; Sept.-May M-F 8:30am-5pm.)

Tampeeren NNKY (HI), Tuomiokirkonkatu 12 (☎254 40 20; fax 254 40 22), offers amazing rooms with balconies facing the cathedral. From the train station, walk down Hämeenkatu and make a right onto Tumoiokirkoukatu. (Sheets 30mk.

Reception 8-10am and 4-11pm. Dorms 60-70mk; singles 140mk; doubles 200mk. Nonmembers add 15mk.) Overlooking Lake Pyhäjärvi 5km southwest, **Camping Härmälä** is accessible by bus #1. (☎265 13 55. Open late May to late Aug. 45mk per person, families 90mk; cabins 170mk-310mk.) Sample *mustamakkara*, a Tampere sausage made with flour and cow's blood, at the ever-popular **Market Hall** (Kauppahalli), Hämeenkatu 19. (Open M-Th 8am-5pm, F 8am-5:30pm, Sa 8am-3pm.) Finnish Tex-Mex, the pub **Zarillo,** Otovalankatu 9, serves burritos (35mk) and fajitas from 55mk. (Open M-Tu 5-10pm, W-Sa 4pm-midnight, Su 5-11pm.) Chow on pizza and pasta—served with the usual cream sauce—at **Napoli**, Aleksanterinkatu 31. (Lunch specials 35-39mk. Open M-Th 11am-9pm, F-Sa 11am-10pm, Su noon-9pm.)

SIGHTS AND ENTERTAINMENT. Tampere has some of the wackiest museums in Europe. A defiant proletarian spirit burns at the last existing **Lenin Museum,** Hämeenpuisto 28, 3rd fl. The museum and its founders, the **Finnish-Soviet Friendship Society,** share the building where the first conference of Lenin's revolutionary party was held and where Lenin and Stalin first met. (Open M-F 9am-6pm, Sa-Su 11am-4pm. 15mk, students 10mk.) The **Amuri Museum,** Makasiininkatu 12, which presents the cramped living quarters of 25 workers and their families between 1882 and 1973. (Open mid-May to mid-Sept. Tu-Su 10am-6pm. 20mk, students 5mk.) The **Spy Museum,** Hatanpäänvaltatie 42, the first of its kind in Scandanavia, exhibits a variety of sneaky devices. (Open May-Aug M-F noon-6pm, Sa-Su 10am-4pm; Sept.-Apr. M-F 4pm-7pm, Sa-Su 10am-4pm. 35mk, students 25mk.) For fun without espionage, the **Moominvalley Museum,** Hämeenpuisto 20 in the City Library, has some of Tove Jansson's original works and tiny Moomin on display in doll houses. (Open M-F 9am-5pm, Sa-Su 10am-6pm; Sept.-May closed M. 20mk, students and children 5mk.) For java junkies, the **Coffee Cup Museum**, Pispalanvaltatie 2, displays an eclectic collection. (Open Tu-F 11am-6pm, Sa 11am-3pm. 10mk, students 5mk.) The **Pyynikki** forest park offers walking trails and great views of the Näsijärvi and Pyhäjärvi lakes. Take the stairs or ride an elevator to the top of the observation tower for a panoramic view. (Bus #27. Open daily 9am-8pm. 5mk.) For an even more spectacular sight, take the elevator up the 124m **Näsinuela** in the **Särkänniemi** amusement complex. (Open 11am-midnight. 20mk.) Other Särkänniemi attractions include an amusement park, a dolphinarium, a children's zoo, and a planetarium. Tampere also has two **cathedrals,** the **Orthodox cathedral,** Tummiokirkonkatu 27, evocative of St. Basil's in Russia with its onion domes, (Open May-Aug. M-F 10am-12:30pm and 1-4pm, Sa 10am-3pm, Su 1-4pm.) and the **Lutheran cathedral**, featuring once-controversial interior murals by Hugo Simberg and Magnus Ecknell. (Open daily May-Aug. 9am-6pm; Sept.-Apr. 11am-3pm.) The quirky **Short Film Festival** (☎213 00 34), in early March, features works from 30 countries. August brings the **International Theater Festival,** transforming parks and streets into stages. (☎214 09 92; tampere.fi/festival/theatre). A walk through **Koskipuisto** in the evening reveals throngs of youngsters, awaiting the evening's revelry.

SAVONLINNA ☎015

Savonlinna perches atop a chain of islands connected by picturesque bridges. The tsarist aristocracy was the first to discover Savonlinna's potential as a vacation spot, and soon turned it into a fashionable spa town. The elegant **Olavinlinna Castle,** built to reinforce the Swedish-Finnish border with Russia in 1475, impresses with its towering spires and high vaulted ceilings. From the Market Square, follow the docks along the water and hug Linnankatu as it winds between old wooden houses until you reach the castle. (Open daily June to mid-Aug. 10am-5pm; mid-Aug. to May 10am-3pm. 25mk, students 15mk. Admission includes multilingual tours every hr.) Performers and spectators alike flock to Savonlinna's **International Opera Festival** (☎47 67 50; www.operafestival.fi) in early July. The **beaches** of the island of **Sulosaari** are a welcome retreat from the hordes of tourists in town for the festival. Cross the footbridge behind Market Square, walk past the baths, and cross a footbridge for a stunning view. **Trains** run to Savonlinna from Helsinki (5hr., 4 per day, 200mk); hop off at "Savonlinna-Kauppatori" in the center of town rather than the distant "Savonlinna." The **tourist office,** Puistokatu 1, across the bridge from the market, books rooms. (☎51 75 10; fax 517 51 23. Open daily June-Aug. 8am-6pm; Sept.-May M-F 9am-4pm.) **Vuorilinna Hostel (HI),** on Kylpylaitoksentie, Kasinosaari, is sandwiched between luxurious baths and casinos of old. (☎739 50; fax 27 25 24. Kitchen. Reception 7am-11pm. Open June-Aug. Dorms 105mk; singles 270mk; doubles 330mk; nonmembers add 15mk each.) Bus #3 runs every hour from the bus station to **Vuohimäki Camping,** 7km out of town. (☎53 73 53. Reception M-Th 8am-11pm, F-Sa 8am-midnight, Su 9am-10pm. Open early June to late Aug. 45mk per person; 85mk per tent, 75mk with camping card; 295-379mk per cabin.)

NEAR SAVONLINNA. The largest wooden church in the world, seating over 3000, was constructed in the late 1800s in **Kerimäki** (pop. 5000), after the town decided that a church for only 1500 would not do. (Open June 1-11 10am-5pm, June 12-Aug. 15 10am-6pm, Aug. 16-31 10am-4pm. Free.) Take the **bus** to Kerimäki from Savonlinna (35min., 24mk); the church will be visible from there. About half an hour from Savonlinna by rail, the **Retretti Art Center** has 3000 square meters of exhibition space inside huge caves. (Open daily May-June 10am-5pm, July 10am-6pm; exhibitions 1 hr. later. 75mk, students and seniors 60mk, children 30mk.)

TURKU (ÅBO) ☎02

Turku (pop. 163,000), Finland's oldest city, became capital in 1809 when Tsar Alexander I snatched Finland from Sweden and granted it autonomy. After the capital moved to Helsinki in 1812, the worst fire in Scandinavian history devoured Turku's wooden buildings. Despite this, Turku flourishes as a cultural and academic center.

PRACTICAL INFO, ACCOMMODATIONS, AND FOOD. **Trains** arrive from Helsinki (2hr., 12 per day, 120mk-140mk). **Viking** and **Silja Line ferries** depart for Åland and Stockholm (see **By Ferry,** p. 298); to get to the terminal at the southwestern end of Linnankatu, hop the train (3 per day) to the *satama* (harbor) or catch bus #1 from Market Square (10mk). The **tourist office,** Aurakatu 2, has accommodations info. (☎262 74 44; fax 251 03 90; www.turku.fi. Open M-F 8:30am-6pm, Sa-Su 9am-4pm.) Check **email** at the **library,** Linnankatu 2, 2nd fl. (Open M-F 10am-8pm. Free.) The **Hostel Turku (HI),** Linnankatu 39, is on the river between the ferry terminals and the train station. From the station, walk west four blocks on Ratapihankatu, take a left on Puistokatu to the river, and make a right on Linnankatu. From the ferry, walk 20 minutes up Linnankatu. (☎262 76 80; fax 262 76 75. Breakfast 23mk. Sheets 30mk. Laundry 5mk. Dorms 45mk; singles 105mk; doubles 140mk. Nonmembers add 15mk.) For immaculate rooms and immaculate reception, try nun-run **Bridgettine Sisters' Guesthouse,** Ursininkatu 15A, near the corner of Puutarhakatu. (☎250 19 10, fax 250 30 78. Singles with bath 210mk; doubles with bath 320mk.) **Ruissalo Camping** (☎262 76 81) on Ruissalo Island, is open in summer. Produce fills **Kauppatori** (open M-Sa 7am-2pm) or **Kauppahalli,** on Eerikinkatu, Market Hall (open M-Th 8am-5pm, F 8am-6pm, Sa 8am-2pm); or, head to **Valintalo supermarket,** Eerikinkatu 19. (Open M-F 9am-9pm, Sa 9am-6pm.)

SIGHTS AND ENTERTAINMENT. Turku surrounds the river Aura, and most of the sights are within meters of its banks. The **Turku Cathedral** towers above Tuomiokirkkotori (Cathedral Square). (Open daily mid-Apr. to mid-Sept. 9am-8pm; mid-Sept. to mid-Apr. 9am-7pm.) The 700-year-old **Turun Linna** (Turku Castle), about 3km from the town center, contains a **historical museum** with dark passageways, medieval artifacts, and Iron Age dioramas. Catch the #1 bus (10mk) from Market Square. (Open mid-Apr. to mid-Sept. daily 10am-6pm; mid-Sept. to mid-Apr. M 1-7pm, Tu-Su 10am-3pm. 30mk, students 20mk.) **Luostarinmäki,** the only neighborhood to survive the 1827 fire, now houses an open-air **handicrafts museum** with over 30 workshops. (Open mid-Apr. to mid-Sept. daily 10am-6pm; mid-Sept. to mid-Apr. Tu-Su 10am-3pm. 20mk, students 15mk.) The collections of the **Turan Taidemuseo** (Art Museum), including vibrant *Kalevala* paintings by Akseli Gallen-Kallela, are temporarily being housed on Vartiovuorenmaki in a building designed by Carl

Engel. (Open Apr.-Sept. Tu and F-Sa 10am-4pm, W-Th 10am-7pm, Su 11am-6pm; Oct.-Mar. Tu-W and F-Sa 10am-4pm, Th 10am-7pm, Su 11am-6pm. 30mk, students 20mk.) **Aboa Vetus Ars Nova** combines modern art and archeology in the Rettig palace, a 1928 building refurbished and filled with modern art as Ars Nova; while a new museum protects the old buildings as Aboa Vetus. (Open May-Sept. M-Su 11am-7pm; Jan.-Apr. Th-Su 11am-7pm. 50mk, students 35mk for both museums; each museum 35mk, students 30mk.) **Dynamo,** Linnankatu 7, gets down to funk, soul, ska, and techno. (Cover from 15mk for live music. Open in summer Su-Th 9pm-3am, F-Sa until 4am; winter, closed Su-Tu.) Turku proper hosts **Down by the Laituri,** a music and city festival that lasts several days in June. (☎250 44 20, www.dbtl.fi.) Ruissalo Island in Turku hosts **Ruisrock,** Finland's oldest and largest rock festival, which attracts names like Björk, the Beastie Boys, David Bowie, and Sting. (☎(06) 001 04 95; www.ruisrock.fi).

EXCURSION FROM TURKU: NAANTALI (NÅDENDAL)

Naantali, a sleepy enclave of old wooden houses 15km west of Turku, is awakened each summer by vacationing Finns. Mannerheiminkatu leads to the **Old Town,** where some buildings date to the late 18th century. Across the harbor is the Finnish president's fortress-like summer home, **Kultaranta;** if the flag's up, keep an eye out for her. The tourist office offers tours of the park around the home daily from late June to mid-August (☎435 08 50). A bus leaves from the office daily at 10am (45mk, children 25mk) or from the park's main gate at 2pm and 3pm (30mk, children 15mk). The main attraction is **Moomin World,** a harborside fantasy theme park. (☎511 11 11. Open daily June to mid-Aug. 10am-7pm. 80mk, children 60mk.) The **Naantali Music Festival** (☎434 53 63; www.naantalimusic.com) brings chamber music in early June. Perhaps the most traditional Naantali summer event is **Sleepyhead Day** (July 27), when the residents of Naantali get up at 6am, wake anyone still sleeping, and, dressed in carnival costumes, proceed to crown the year's Sleepyhead and throw him or her into the harbor. **Buses** #11 and 110 run to Naantali from the marketplace in Turku (25min., 19mk). The **tourist office,** Kaivotori 2, helps find accommodations. From the bus station, walk southwest on Tullikatu to Kaivokatu and go right 300m; it will be on the left. (☎435 08 50; fax 435 08 52; www.travel.fi/naantali. Open daily June to mid-Aug. 9am-7pm; mid-Aug. to May M-F 9am-4pm.) ☎**02.**

ROVANIEMI ☎016

Just south of the Arctic Circle and home to the world's favorite jolly fat man, the capital of Finnish Lapland is a popular spot for tourists of all ages and nationalities. Now an entirely modern city, the old Rovaniemi is forever lost, burned to the ground by retreating German soldiers in 1944. Completely redesigned by Alvar Aalto, the city has become the perfect place to start exploring Arctic culture and nature. Fulfill childhood fantasies any time of year at **Santa Claus's Village** to meet jolly St. Nick himself. When he's in his office, you can shop, view reindeer or huskies, and stand on the Arctic Circle. Take bus #8 from the train station (15mk, round-trip 26mk) to the Arctic Circle Center. (Open daily Jan.-June 10am-5pm, June to mid-Aug. 9am-8pm, mid-Aug. to Sept. 9am-6pm, Oct.-Nov. 10am-5pm, Dec. 9am-7pm.) Santa's **theme park** is 2km away. Take the bus (12mk) to the park from the village. (30mk, rides extra.) The **Arktikum** center, Pohjoisranta 4, houses the **Arctic Science Center** and the **Provincial Museum of Lapland,** a multimedia wonderland of information on Arctic peoples, culture, landscapes, and wildlife. (Open daily May to mid-June and late Aug. 10am-6pm; mid-June to mid-Aug. 10am-7pm; Sept.-Apr. Tu-Su 10am-6pm. 50mk, students 40mk.) The **Ranua Wildlife Park,** 60km south of Rovaniemi, has 3km of paths through areas of fenced-in Arctic elk, bears, and wolves. Doe-eyed reindeer lovers should skip the gift shop, which sells Rudolph's fur, skin, and munchy-crunchy ribs. (☎355 19 21. Open daily May and mid-Aug. to Sept. 10am-6pm, June to mid-Aug. 9am-8pm, Oct.-Apr. 10am-4pm. 60mk, children 50mk.) Ranua is also a great area for **cloudberry-picking**—get maps at the tourist office near the entrance. Take bus #6 from Rovaniemi (1hr., M-F 6 per day, 65mk).

Four **trains** per day roll into Rovaniemi from Helsinki via Oulu (340mk). **Buses** run to destinations throughout northern Finland, with connections to Norway and Murmansk, Russia. The staff of the **tourist office,** Koskikatu 1, combs the town on yellow mopeds. If you don't spot them at the train station, head right on Ratakatu, pass the post office, go under the bridge onto Hallituskatu, turn left on Korkalonkatu, and continue right on Koskikatu to the river. (☎34 62 70; www.rovaniemi.fi. Open June-Aug. M-F 8am-6pm, Sa-Su 10am-4pm; Sept.-May M-F 8am-4pm.) **Lapland Safaris,** Koskikatu 1 (☎331 12 00), offers cruises (2hr., 210mk), rafting (3hr., 430mk), and Husky and snowmobile safaris (3-6hr., 350-780mk). To get to the **HI youth hostel,** Hallituskatu 16, follow the directions to Hallituskatu. The bargain place is a bit spartan. (☎34 46 44. Reception, showers, and kitchen 6-10am and 5-9:45pm. 75mk, nonmembers 95mk.) **Ounaskoski Camping** is across the river, next to a rocky beach. (☎34 53 04. Open June-Aug. 65mk, 60mk with camping card.) Chomp on a Big Mac (32mk) at the world's northernmost **McDonald's,** Poromiehenkata 3. (Open M-Th 10:30am-10pm, F-Sa 10:30-midnight, Su 11am-10pm.) **Monte Rose,** Pekankatu 9, in City Hotel, serves a Lapland treat, sauteed reindeer and lingonberry sauce over mashed potatoes, for 95mk. (Open M-Tu 10am-11pm, W-Th 10am-midnight, F 10am-1am, Sa noon-1am, Su 1-11pm.) Check out nightlife on **Koskikatu.**

OULU ☎08

Flower-lined avenues and warm winds give Oulu a southern feel. On the Gulf of Bothnia, **Nallikari**'s seemingly endless beaches and crystal-clear waters goad everyone into a dip. Take **bus** #5 from Otto Karhin Park or Nallikari (12mk). The adjacent **Nallikari Camping** has colorful bungalows. (☎55 86 13 50. 50mk per person; 4-person cabins 130-300mk.) Closer to the city center, the azure sea at **Pikisaari,** an island lined with multi-colored cottages, is ideal for picnics; take the footbridge at the end of Kaarlenväylä. Across from Pikisaari is the boisterous **marketplace,** lined with worn warehouses housing cafes and gift stores (corner of Rantakatu and Kaarlenväylä). A 15-minute ride away on bus #19 (12mk), 5m cactuses, gigantic banana plants, and other exotic flora flourish in the glass pyramids of the University of Oulu's **Botanical Gardens**. (Kaitoväylä 5. Pyramids open June-Aug. Tu-F 8am-4pm, Sa-Su 10am-4pm; Sept.-May Tu-F 8am-3pm, Sa-Su noon-3pm. 10mk. Open-air gardens open daily in summer 8am-9pm; off season 7am-5pm, snow willing. Free.) The **Tietomaa,** Nahkatehtaankatu 6, has interactive science exhibits, a huge IMAX theater, and pants made for the world's heaviest man. (Open daily May-Aug. 10am-6pm; July 10am-8pm; Sept.-Apr. M-F 10am-4pm, Sa-Su 10am-6pm. 60mk.)

All **trains** between northern and southern Finland pass through Oulu, heading for Helsinki (8hr., 5 per day, 292mk) and north to Rovaniemi (8-10 per day, 2½ hr., 116mk). The **tourist office,** Torikatu 10, provides info on the entire Ostrobothnia region. Take Hallituskatu, the broad avenue perpendicular to the train station, up to the second left after passing through the park. (☎55 84 13 30; fax 55 84 17 11; www.ouka.fi. Open M-F 9am-4pm.) Hard bodies abound at **Uni Hostel (HI),** Kajaanintie 36, as it shares facilities with the Fitness Palace. Facing away from the train station, go right on Rantatienkatu, turn right, and go under the bridge onto Kajaanintie. Follow the Uni Hostel sign to the far end of a building complex. (☎88 03 311; fax 88 03 754. Kitchens. Open June-Aug. Dorms 75mk, nonmembers 90mk; singles 220mk; doubles 290mk.) Nightlife revolves around **Rotuaari,** the pavilion on **Kirkkokatu,** and the terraces lining **Otto Karhin Park** on Hallituskatu.

FRANCE

FRENCH FRANCS

US$1 = 7.61F	1F = US$0.13
CDN$1 = 4.25F	1F = CDN$0.24
UK£1 = 10.71F	1F = UK£0.09
IR£1 = 8.33F	1F = IR£0.12
AUS$1 = 4.25F	1F = AUS$0.24
NZ$1 = 3.24F	1F = NZ$0.31
SAR1= 1.07F	1F = SAR0.94
EUR€1 = 6.56F	1F = EUR€0.152

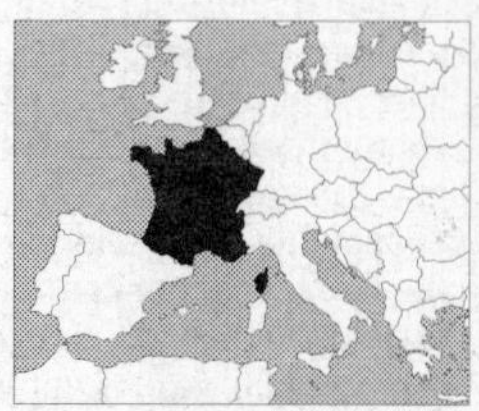

Country code: 33. **International dialing prefix:** 00. France has no city codes. From outside France, dial int'l dialing prefix (see inside back cover) + 33 + local number.

Conventional preconceptions of France focus on sensual pleasures: the vineyards of Bordeaux and Burgundy, the elaborate dishes of Dijon, the sandy expanses of the Riviera, and the crisp Alpine air. France welcomes over 70 million visitors to its cities, chateaux, mountains, and beaches each year, making it the most popular tourist destination in the world. To the French, it is only natural that outsiders should flock to their beloved homeland, so steeped in history, rich in art and architecture, and magnificently endowed with beautiful, diverse landscapes. The fruits of France include the philosophies of Voltaire, Sartre, and Derrida; the rich literature of Hugo, Proust, and Camus; and the visionary art of Rodin, Monet, and Degas. From the trendsetting opulence of Louis XIV and Versailles to the great Revolution of 1789, from the ambition of Napoleon to the birth of existentialism and postmodernism, the French for many centuries occupied the driver's seat of history. While France no longer controls the course of world events, it has nonetheless secured a spot as one of the most influential forces in the course of Western history.

If you too are smitten by France, pick up a copy of *Let's Go: France 2001* for more fact- and flavor-filled coverage.

FACTS AND FIGURES

Official Name: French Republic.

Government: Republic.

Capital: Paris.

Land Area: 545,630 sq. km.

Geography: Mostly plains in north and west; mountainous in south and east.

Climate: Mild summers and cool winters; along Mediterranean, hot summers.

Major Cities: Lyon, Nice, Marseille.

Population: 59,329,691.

Language: French.

Religions: Roman Catholic (90%).

Average Income Per Capita: US$23,300.

Major Exports: Machinery and transportation equipment, chemicals, iron and steel products.

DISCOVER FRANCE

Paris—ah, Paris. Aside from the requisite croissant-munching, elusive-smile-admiring, tower-climbing activities that occupy most visitors' time, don't miss the exquisite **Sainte Chapelle,** Gothic architecture's finest jewel (p. 335). A stroll down the **Champs-Elysées** (p. 337), through the studenty **Latin Quarter** (p. 335), or in medieval **Montmartre** (p. 338) will give you a good feel for the city, with stops along the way for **Notre-Dame** (p. 334) and the **Musée d'Orsay** (p. 339). When you've had your fill of the city, be sure to squeeze in a daytrip to the epitome of Gothic style, the *cathédrale* in **Chartres** (p. 346) and ornate **Versailles** (p. 345). Northwest of Paris lies

Rouen, home to a cathedral that so entranced Claude Monet that he painted it time and time again (p. 347). Rouen was the capital of William the Conqueror before he conquered England in 1066—the whole story unfolds on the Bayeux Tapestry in nearby **Bayeux** (p. 349), which itself serves as a good base for exploring the **D-Day beaches** of Normandy (p. 349). The majestic abbey of **Mont-St-Michel** rises from the sea above shifting sands between Normandy and Brittany (p. 350), while the chateau-studded **Loire Valley** brings visitors back to the days of royal intrigue and opulence (p. 356). The *vieille ville* of **Carcassonne,** in Languedoc-Roussillon, is surrounded by spectacular medieval ramparts (p. 365). To see Provence's **Camargue,** an untamed flatland of bulls, wild horses, and flamingoes, base yourself in **Arles,** whose picturesque streets once enchanted van Gogh (p. 367). Arles also has the largest Roman amphitheater in France, but its sister in **Nîmes** is even more well preserved (p. 366). Seven popes who called nearby **Avignon** home in the 15th century left behind an impressive palace (p. 366). Just to the south beckons the **French Riviera:** while **Nice,** with its excellent museums and nightlife, is the first stop on most itineraries (p. 373), its rocky beaches may send some to other destinations along the Riviera (p. 369). **Marseille** (p. 369) offers wild nightlife and easy access to wine-filled **Bordeaux** (p. 360). The main attraction at France's most famous beach towns, **Cannes** (p. 371) and **St-Tropez** (p. 370), isn't the sun—you go for the stars. For a rugged Alpine experience, head to **Chamonix,** in the shadow of Mont Blanc, which features fantastic skiing and mountain climbing (p. 383). To the north, French and German culture intermingle in Alsace-Lorraine, where **Strasbourg,** home to one of France's finest Gothic cathedrals and the beginning of **La Route du Vin,** stands (p. 390).

ESSENTIALS

WHEN TO GO

Give careful consideration to when you travel, because the timing of your trip can determine its success. Summer is the high season for traveling in Europe. *Everything* is crowded with tourists in July and August; June or September may be a better time to go. Also consider the seasonal weather when you plan to travel.

DOCUMENTS AND FORMALITIES

For stays shorter than 90 days, citizens of Australia, Canada, the EU, New Zealand, and the US don't require visas; South Africans do (30-day visas 165F; 90-day 195-230F). For stays longer than 90 days, all non-EU citizens require long-stay visas (650F). Non-EU nationals cannot work in France without a **work permit,** which requires a contract of employment; nor can they **study** without a **student visa,** which requires proofs of admission to a French university, financial independence, and medical insurance. For **au pair** and **teaching assistant** jobs, special rules apply; check with your local consulate.

EMBASSIES AND CONSULATES

Embassies and consulates of other countries in France are all in **Paris** (p. 321).

French Embassies at Home: Australia, Consulate General, Level 26, St. Martins Tower, 31 Market St., Sydney NSW 2000 (☎ (02) 92 61 57 79); **Canada,** Consulate General, 130 Bloor St. W., #401, Toronto, ON M5S 1N5 (☎ (416) 925 82 33; Consulate General, 1100-1130 West Pender St., Vancouver, BC V6E 4A4 (☎ (604) 681 43 45; www.consulfrancevancouver.org); **Ireland,** Consulate Section, 36 Ailesbury Rd., Ballsbridge, Dublin 4 (☎ (01) 260 16 66; www.ambafrance.ie); **New Zealand,** 34-42 Manners St., P.O. Box 11-343, Wellington (☎ (04) 802 77 93; www.ambafrance.net.nz); **South Africa,** 807 George Ave., Arcadia, Pretoria 0083 (☎ (12) 429 70 30; www.france.co.za); **UK,** Consulate General, 21 Cromwell Rd., London SW7 2EN (☎

(020) 78 38 20 00; www.ambafrance.org.uk); **US,** Consulate General, 4101 Reservoir Rd., NW, Washington, DC 20007 (☎ (202) 944 60 00; www.france-consulat.org/dc/dc.html); Consulate General, 934 5th Ave., New York, NY 10021 (☎ (212) 606 36 00).

GETTING AROUND

BY PLANE. The two major international airports in Paris are **Charles de Gaulle** (to the north) and **Orly** (to the south). For info on cheap flights from the UK, see p. 43.

BY TRAIN. The **SNCF** (*Société Nationale de Chemins de Fer;* ☎08 36 35 35 35; www.sncf.fr) manages one of Europe's most efficient rail networks. Timetables are complicated but well organized, with color-designated periods: low-traffic periods are blue *(période bleue)*, while peak times are white *(période blanche)* or red *(période rouge)*. Traveling in blue periods makes you eligible for reductions called **tarifs Découvertes,** often up to 25%; the *Découverte 12-25* discount is available to those ages 12-25 for any blue-period travel. Tickets must be validated in the orange machine at the entrance to the platforms at the *gare* (train station). Seat **reservations,** recommended for international trips, are mandatory on EuroCity (EC), InterCity (IC), and TGV *(train à grande vitesse)* trains. All three require a ticket supplement (US$3-18; railpass-holders exempt) and reservation fee (US$2-3). **TGV** trains, the fastest in the world, run from Paris to major cities in France, as well as to Geneva and Lausanne, Switzerland. **Rapide** trains are slower, and local **Express** trains are, oddly, the slowest option. The **Eurostar** provides rapid connections to London and Brussels (see p. 49).

Eurail is valid in France. The SNCF's **France Railpass** grants three days of unlimited rail travel in France during any 30-day period (US$175; companion travelers $140 each; up to 6 extra days $30 each); the parallel **Youthpass** provides those under 26 with four days of unlimited travel within a two-month period ($158; up to 6 extra days $26 each). The **France Rail 'n' Drive pass** combines three days of rail travel with two days of car rental (US$255; companion travelers $187 each; extra rail days $30 each, extra car days $50).

BY BUS. Within France, long-distance buses are a secondary transportation choice; service is rare and infrequent compared to that in most other European countries. However, in some regions buses can be indispensable for reaching out-of-the-way towns. Bus services operated by the SNCF accept railpasses. *Gare routière* is French for "bus station."

BY FERRY. Ferries across the English Channel *(la Manche)* link France to England and Ireland. The most common route is that from **Dover** (p. 49) to **Calais,** run by **P&O Stena Line, SeaFrance,** and **Hoverspeed** (☎03 21 46 14 54). Other ferries go from **Boulogne-sur-Mer** to **Folkestone, England** on **Hoverspeed** (☎03 21 30 80 40); from **Cherbourg** (p. 350) to **Rosslare, Ireland** (see p. 555) on **Irish Ferries, Portsmouth** (p. 181) on **P&O European Ferries,** and **Poole** on **Brittany Ferries;** from **Dieppe** (p. 348) to **Newhaven, England** on **P&O Stena Line;** from **Le Havre** (p. 348) to **Portsmouth** (p. 181) on **P&O European Ferries** (☎02 35 19 78 50); and from **Roscoff** to **Plymouth** and **Cork** (p. 556) on **Brittany Ferries,** and **Rosslare** and **Cork** on **Irish Ferries** (☎02 98 61 17 17). **Eurail** is valid on boats to Ireland (excluding 30F port tax). Students usually receive a 10% discount. For **schedules** and **prices** on English Channel ferries, see p. 49. For info on ferries from **Nice** and **Marseille** to **Corsica,** see p. 379.

BY CHANNEL TUNNEL. Though still dogged by huge debts, the Chunnel is increasing in popularity every year as people overcome their fear of traveling 27 mi. under the sea. Undoubtedly the fastest and most convenient route from England to France, the Chunnel offers two types of passenger service. Eurostar is the high-speed train which links London to Paris and Brussels, with stops at Ashford in England and Calais and Lille in France. (Reservations in UK ☎01233 61 75 75; in France ☎01 49 70 01 75; www.eurostar.co.uk. Eurostar tickets can also be bought at most major travel agents.) *Le Shuttle* is a drive-on train service which ferries cars and coaches between Folkestone and Calais. (In UK ☎ (0800) 096 9992; in France ☎03 21 00 61 00; www.eurotunnel.co.uk.)

BY CAR. Thanks to high *autoroute* tolls, France maintains its roads well, but the landscape itself often makes the roads a menace, especially in Corsica. The numerous and pricey tolls (from Paris to Marseille, for instance, costs 267F) combine with expensive gasoline (*essence sans plomb*, or unleaded, at about 6F per liter) to make driving a very expensive mode of transportation.

BY BIKE AND BY THUMB. Of all Europeans, the French may be alone in loving cycling more than football. French drivers usually accommodate bikers on the wide country roads, and many cities banish cars from select streets each Sunday. Renting a bike beats bringing your own if your touring will be confined to one or two regions (50-120F per day).

Many consider France the hardest country in Europe to get a lift. *Let's Go* does not recommend hitchhiking. In major cities there are ride-sharing organizations that pair drivers and riders. Contact **Eurostop International** (**Allostop** in France; www.ecritel.fr/allostop/). Not all organizations screen drivers and riders.

TOURIST SERVICES AND MONEY

EMERGENCY. Police: ☎122. **Ambulance:** ☎123. **Fire:** ☎124.

TOURIST OFFICES. The extensive French tourism support network revolves around **syndicats d'initiative** and **offices de tourisme** (in the smallest towns, the **Mai-**

rie, the mayor's office, deals with tourist concerns), all of which *Let's Go* labels "tourist office." All three distribute maps and pamphlets, help you find accommodations, and suggest excursions to the countryside. For up-to-date events and regional info, try www.francetourism.com.

MONEY. The national currency of France is the **franc français** or French Franc (abbreviated to FF or F). Each franc is divided into 100 **centimes.** The franc is available in brightly colored 20F, 50F, 100F, 200F and 500F notes, smart two-tone 10F and 20F coins, and silvery 1F, 2F, 5F coins and pale copper 5, 10, 20, and 50 *centimes* pieces. If you stay in **hostels** and prepare your own food, expect to spend about 100-140F per person per day. A double room in a hostel starts at about 130F, and a decent sit-down meal with wine starts at about 65F.

By law, **service** must be included at all restaurants, bars, and cafes in France. It is not unheard of to leave extra *monnaie* (change) at a cafe or bar, maybe a franc or two per drink; exceptionally good service may be rewarded with a 5-10% tip. Otherwise, tipping is only expected for taxis and hairdressers; 10-15% is the norm. **Bargaining** is appropriate at flea markets *(marchés aux puces)*. Most purchases in France include a 20.6% **value-added tax** (**TVA** is the French acronym, **VAT** the English). Non-EU residents (including EU citizens who reside outside the EU) who are in France for less than 6 months can reclaim 17.1% of the purchase price on goods over 1200F bought in one store. Only certain stores participate in this **vente en détaxe** refund process; ask before you buy.

ACCOMMODATIONS AND CAMPING

HOSTELS. Hostels generally offer dormitory accommodations in large single-sex rooms with 6-10 beds, though some have as many as 60. At the other end of the scale, many offer private singles and doubles. They sometimes have kitchens and utensils for your use, bike rental, storage areas, and laundry facilities. There can be drawbacks: some hostels close during certain daytime "lockout" hours, have a curfew, don't accept reservations, and/or impose a maximum stay. In France, a bed in a hostel will average around 60-90F. If you plan on doing a lot of hosteling, it is definitely worth joining **Hostelling International (HI)** before you leave home (p. 29). Many hostels in France are HI affiliates; members get lower rates and can reserve in advance, often through the **International Booking Network.**

HOTELS. Two or more people traveling together will often save money by staying in cheap hotels rather than hostels. The French government employs a hotel ratings system which runs from zero to four stars. Most hotels listed by *Let's Go* have zero stars or one, with a smattering of two stars, but are chosen and ranked according to qualities such as charm, convenience, and value for money.

CAMPING. After three thousand years of settled history, true wilderness in France is hard to find. It's **illegal to camp** in most public spaces, including and especially national parks. Instead, look forward to organized *campings* (campsites), where you'll share your splendid isolation with vacationing families, bawling French babies, and all manner of programmed fun. Most campsites have toilets, showers, and electrical outlets, though you may have to pay extra for such luxuries (10-40F); you'll often need to pay a supplement for your car, too (20-50F). Otherwise, expect to pay 50-90F per site.

FOOD AND DRINK

French chefs cook for one of the most finicky clienteles in the world. Traditionally, a complete French dinner includes an *apértif* (pre-dinner drink), an *entrée* (appetizer), a *plat* (main course), salad, cheese, dessert, coffee, and a *digestif* (after-dinner drink). The French usually take wine with their meals; *boisson comprise* entitles you to a free drink (usually wine) with your meal. In restaurants, *menus* (fixed-price three-course meals) begin at 60F. Service is usually included *(service compris)*. Be careful when ordering *à la carte; l'addition* (the check) may exceed your weekly budget. Do as the French do; go from one specialty shop to another to assemble a picnic, or find a *marché* (outdoor market). Cafes are a forum for long chats, but you pay to sit and watch the world go by: drinks and food are often more expensive if served in the dining room or outside rather than at the bar. *Boulangeries*, *pâtisseries*, and *confiseries* tempt with bread, pastries, and candy, respectively; *charcuteries* sell cooked meats. For **supermarket** shopping, look for **Carrefour, Casino, Monoprix, Prisunic, Stoc,** and **Rallye.** Local markets are picturesque and animated, and often offer better quality than supermarkets.

COMMUNICATION

MAIL. Airmail letters under 1 oz. between the US and France take four to seven days and cost US$1. Letters from Canada cost CDN$0.95 for 20g. Allow at least five working days from Australia (postage AUS$1 for up to 20g) and three days from Britain (postage UK£0.30 for up to 20g). Envelopes should be marked *"par avion"* (airmail) to avoid having letters sent by sea. Mail can be held for pick-up through **Poste Restante** (French for General Delivery) to almost any city or town with a post office. Address letters to: SURNAME, First name; Poste Restante: Recette Principale; [5-digit postal code] TOWN; FRANCE. Mark the envelope HOLD.

TELEPHONES. All French telephone numbers are ten digits in length; there are no city codes. When calling from abroad, drop the leading zero of the local number. To operate payphones, buy a *télécarte* (telephone card), available in denominations of 41F and 98F at train stations, post offices, and *tabacs*. Phone numbers starting with 0800 are toll-free; those starting with just 08 charge high rates. To call collect, tell the operator *"en PCV"* (ahn-pay-say-VAY). **Operator,** ☎ 10. **Directory assistance,** ☎ 12. **International operator,** ☎ 00 33 11. **International direct dial** numbers include: **AT&T,** ☎ 888 288 46 85; **BT Direct,** ☎ 800 34 51 44; **Canada Direct,** ☎ 800 565 47 08; **MCI,** ☎ 800 444 41 41; **Sprint,** ☎ 800 877 46 46; **Telecom Éireann Ireland Direct,** ☎ 800 25 02 50; **Telecom New Zealand,** ☎ 0800 00 00 00; **Telkom South Africa,** ☎ 09 03; and **Telstra Australia Direct,** ☎ 13 22 00.

INTERNET ACCESS. Most large towns in France have a cybercafe. Rates and speed of connection vary widely; occasionally there are free terminals in technologically-oriented museums or exhibition spaces. **Cybercafé Guide** (www.cyberiacafe.net/cyberia/guide/ccafe.htm#working_france) lists cybercafes in France.

HOLIDAYS AND FESTIVALS

Holidays: Le Jour de l'an (St-Sébastian; New Year; Jan. 1); Le lundi de Pâques (Easter Monday; Apr. 5); La Fête du Travail (Labor Day; May 1); L'Anniversaire de la Liberation (celebrates the Liberation in 1944; May 8); L'Ascension (Ascension day; June 1); Le lundi de Pentecôte (Whitmonday; June 12); La Fête Nationale (Bastille Day; July 14); L'Assomption (Feast of the Assumption; Aug. 15); La Toussaint (All Saints' Day; Nov. 1); L'Armistice 1918 (Armistice Day; Nov. 11); and Le Noël (Christmas; Dec. 25).

NO PRÉSERVATIFS ADDED Having invented the French kiss and the French tickler, the speakers of the language of love have long had *savoir faire* in all things sexual–safety included. French pharmacies provide 24-hour condom (*préservatif* or *capote*) dispensers. In wonderful French style, they unabashedly adorn the sides of buildings on public streets and vending machines in the Métro. When dining out, don't ask for foods without *préservatifs* or mistake your raspberry compote for a *capote*. Funny looks will greet you, as the French have not yet caught on to the international craze for condom-eating, and will think you a bit odd.

Festivals: Most festivals, like **fête du cinema** and **fête de la musique** (late June, when musicians rule the streets), are in summer. The **Cannes Film Festival** (May; www.festival-cannes.com) is mostly for directors and stars, but provides good people-watching. The **Festival d'Avignon** (July-Aug.; www.festival-avignon.com/gbindex3.html) is famous for its theater. **Bastille Day** (July 14) is marked by military parades and fireworks nationwide. Although you may not be competing in the **Tour de France** (3rd or 4th Su in July; www.letour.fr), you'll enjoy all the hype. A **Vineyard Festival** (Sept., in Nice; www.nice-coteazur.org/americain/tourisme/vigne/index.html) celebrates the grape harvest with music, parades, and wine tastings. Nice and Nantes celebrate **Carnaval** in the last week or two before Ash Wednesday (culminating with Mardi Gras celebrations).

PARIS

Paris is an ancient, infamous, and lovely tourist trap. It is a living city full of beautiful people, stunning art, and excellent clothes. It is open air markets, manicured parks, and romantic sidestreets; it is sitting for hours outside at a cafe.

From the world's best bistros to the hottest of *haute couture*, from the old stone of Notre-Dame to the futuristic motions of the Parc de la Villette, from the relics of the first millennium to the celebration of the second, Paris boldly presents itself as both a harbor of tradition and a place of impulse. You can't conquer Paris, old or new, in one week or in 30 years, but you can certainly get acquainted with the *grande dame* of world capitals.

For dazzling coverage of Paris and its environs, snag *Let's Go: Paris 2001*.

GETTING THERE AND AWAY

Flights: For info call the 24hr. English-speaking information center (☎48 62 22 80) or look it up on the web at www.parisairports.com.

Trains: There are six main stations.

Gare du Nord: M: Gare du Nord. Serves northern France, Belgium, the Netherlands, Britain, and northern Germany. To: **Brussels** (2hr., 287F); **Amsterdam** (5hr., 378F); **Cologne/Köln** (5-6hr., 364F); and **Copenhagen** (16hr., 1265F). The **Eurostar** (☎01 49 70 01 75; see p. 49) departs here for **London** (3hr., 360-740F).

Gare de l'Est: M: Gare de l'Est. To eastern France, Austria, Luxembourg, southern Germany, and northern Switzerland. To: **Munich** (8hr., 685F) and **Vienna** (14hr., 970F).

Gare de Lyon: M: Gare de Lyon. Handles trains to southeastern France, parts of Switzerland, Italy, and Greece. To: **Geneva** (3½hr., 508F) and **Rome** (12hr., 630F).

Gare d'Austerlitz: M: Gare d'Austerlitz. Serves the Loire Valley, southwestern France, Spain, and Portugal. To: **Barcelona** (9hr., 500-800F) and **Madrid** (12-13hr., 530-850F).

Gare St-Lazare: M: Gare St-Lazare. Serves Normandy. To: **Rouen** (1hr., 103F).

Gare de Montparnasse: M: Montparnasse-Bienvenüe. Serves Brittany; also the point of departure for southbound **TGV** high-speed trains.

Buses: Gare Routière Internationale du Paris-Gallieni, 28, av. du Général de Gaulle (☎01 49 72 51 51), Bagnolet. M: Gallieni.

GETTING AROUND

Public Transportation: The efficient **Métropolitain,** or **Métro (M),** runs 5:30am-12:30am. Lines are numbered but are generally referred to by their final destinations; connections are called *correspondences.* **Single-fare tickets** within the city cost 8F; a **carnet** (packet) of 10 costs 52F. Buy extras for times when ticket booths are closed (after 10pm) and hold on to your ticket until you exit. The **RER** (Réseau Express Régional), the commuter train to the suburbs, serves as an express subway within central Paris; changing to and getting off the RER requires sticking your validated ticket into a turnstile. Watch the signboards next to the RER tracks and check that your stop is lit up before riding. **Buses** use the same 8F tickets (bought on the bus; validate in the machine by the driver), but transferring requires a new ticket. Buses run 7am-8:30pm,

Autobus du Soir until 1am, and *Noctambus* (3-4 tickets) every hr. 1:30-5:30am at stops marked with the bug-eyed moon between the Châtelet stop and the *portes* (city exits). The **Paris Visite** pass grants unlimited travel on the Métro, RER, and buses, along with other discounts (2-day 70F). The **Mobilis** pass covers the Métro, RER, and buses only (1-day 32F). To qualify for a weekly *(hebdomadaire)* **Coupon Vert,** valid from M (75F), bring a photo ID to the ticket counter to get the necessary **Carte Orange.** Refer to the **color maps** of Paris' transit network at the end of this book.

Taxis: ☎01 47 39 47 39. Cab stands are near train stations and major bus stops. 3-person max. Taxis are pricey (13F plus 4-8F per km), and even pricier if you don't speak French. The meter starts running when you phone.

Car Rental: Rent-a-Car, 79, r. de Bercy, 12ème (☎01 43 45 98 99). Open M-Sa 8:30am-7pm.

Bike Rental: Paris à vélo, c'est sympa! 37, bd. Bourdon, 4ème (☎01 48 87 60 01). M: Bastille. Rentals available with a 2500F (or credit card) deposit. 24hr. rental 150F; 9am-7pm 80F; half-day (9am-2pm or 2-7pm) 60F.

Hitchhiking: *Let's Go* does not recommend hitchhiking. Don't waste time at the *portes* of the city, as traffic there is too heavy for cars to stop. **Allostop-Provoya,** 8, r. Rochambeau, 9ème (☎01 53 20 42 42), matches drivers and riders. M: Cadet. To **Geneva** (188F) and **Frankfurt** (about 197F). Open M-F 9am-7:30pm, Sa 9am-1pm and 2-6pm.

ORIENTATION

The **Ile de la Cité** and **Ile St-Louis** sit at the geographical center of the city, while the **Seine,** flowing east to west, splits Paris into two large expanses: the **Rive Gauche** (Left Bank) to the south and the **Rive Droite** (Right Bank) to the north. The Left Bank, with its older architecture and narrow streets, has traditionally been considered bohemian and intellectual, while the Right Bank, with its grand avenues and designer shops, is more chi-chi. Administratively, Paris is divided into 20 **arrondissements** (districts) that spiral clockwise around the Louvre. Areas of interest are compact and central, and sketchier neighborhoods tend to lie on the outskirts of town. Refer also to this book's **color maps** of the city.

RIVE GAUCHE (LEFT BANK). The **Latin Quarter,** encompassing the 5ème and parts of the 6ème around the **Sorbonne** and the **Ecole des Beaux-Arts,** has been home to students for centuries; the animated **bd. St-Michel** is the boundary between the two *arrondissements.* The area around east-west **bd. St-Germain,** which crosses bd. St-Michel just south of pl. St-Michel in the 6ème, is known as **St-Germain des Prés.** To the west, the gold-domed **Invalides** and the stern Neoclassical **Ecole Militaire,** which faces the **Eiffel Tower** across the **Champ-de-Mars,** recall the military past of the 7ème and northern 15ème, now full of traveling businesspeople. South of the Latin Quarter, **Montparnasse,** in the 14ème, eastern 15ème, and southwestern 6ème, lolls in the shadow of its tower. The glamorous **bd. du Montparnasse** belies the more residential districts around it. The eastern Left Bank, comprising the 13ème, is the city's newest up-and-coming hotspot, centered on the **pl. d'Italie.**

RIVE DROITE (RIGHT BANK). The **Louvre** and **r. de Rivoli** occupy the sight- and tourist-packed 1er and the more business-oriented 2ème. The crooked streets of **Marais,** in the 3ème and 4ème, escaped Baron Haussmann's redesign of ancient Paris and now support many diverse communities. From **pl. de la Concorde,** at the western end of the 1er, **av. des Champs-Elysées** bisects the 8ème as it sweeps up toward the **Arc de Triomphe** at **Charles de Gaulle-Etoile.** South of the Etoile, money old and new chinks in the exclusive 16ème, bordered to the west by the **Bois de Boulogne** park and to the east by the Seine and the **Trocadéro,** which faces the Eiffel Tower across the river. Back toward central Paris, the 9ème, just north of the 2ème, is defined by the sumptuous **Opéra.** East of the 9ème, the 10ème hosts cheap lodgings and the **Gares du Nord** and **de l'Est.** The 10ème, 3ème, and the happening 11ème (which peaks with the nightlife of **Bastille**) meet at **pl. de la République.** South of Bastille, the 12ème surrounds the **Gare de Lyon,** petering out at the **Bois de Vincennes.** East of Bastille, the party atmosphere gives way to the quieter, more residential 20ème and 19ème, while the 18ème is home to **Montmartre,** capped by the **Sacré-Cœur.** To the east, the 17ème starts in the red-light district of **Pigalle** and bd. de Clichy, growing more elegant toward the Etoile, the **Opéra Garnier,** and the 16ème. Continuing west along the *grande axe* defined by the Champs-Elysées, the skyscrapers of **La Défense,** Paris' newest quarter, are across the Seine from the Bois de Boulogne.

PRACTICAL INFORMATION

TOURIST AND FINANCIAL SERVICES

Tourist Offices: Bureau d'Accueil Central, 127, av. des Champs-Elysées, 8ème (☎08 36 68 31 12; 23F per min.). M: Charles-de-Gaulle-Etoile. Mobbed. Open daily 9am-8pm. **Branches** at Gare de Lyon (open M-Sa 8am-8pm) and the Orly (open daily 6am-11:30pm) and Charles de Gaulle (open daily 7am-10pm) airports.

Budget Travel: Office de Tourisme Universitaire (OTU), 119, r. St-Martin, 4ème (☎01 40 29 12 12), opposite the Centre Pompidou. M: Rambuteau. Sells ISICs and discounted student plane, train, and bus tickets; books hostel and hotel rooms for a 10F fee. Open M-F 10am-6:30pm, Sa 10am-5pm. Also at 139, bd. St-Michel, 5ème (☎01 44 41 74 74). M: Port-Royal. Open M-F 10am-6:30pm. **Council Travel,** 1 pl. Odéon, 6ème (☎01 44 41 89 80). M: Odéon. Sells ISICs, plane tickets, and train tickets (including BIJ/Eurotrain). Open M-F 9:30am-6:30pm, Sa 10am-5pm.

Embassies: Australia, 4, r. Jean-Rey, 15ème (☎01 40 59 33 00; www.austgov.fr). M: Bir-Hakeim. Open M-F 9:15am-noon and 2-4:30pm. **Canada,** 35, av. Montaigne, 8ème (☎01 44 43 29 00). M: Franklin-Roosevelt or Alma-Marceau. Open M-F 9am-noon and 2-5pm. **Ireland,** 12, av. Foch, 16ème (☎01 44 17 67 48). M: Argentine. Open M-F 9:30am-noon. **New Zealand,** 7ter, r. Léonard de Vinci, 16ème (☎01 45 00 24 11). M: Victor-Hugo. Open M-F 9am-1pm and 2-5:30pm. **South Africa,** 59, quai d'Orsay, 7ème (☎01 53 59 23 23). M: Invalides. Open M-F 9am-noon. **UK,** 35, r. du Faubourg-St-Honoré, 8ème (☎01 44 51 31 00). M: Concorde. Open M-F 9:30am-12:30pm and 2:30-5pm. Consulate Section, 18bis, r. d'Anjou, 8ème (☎01 44 51 31 02; www.amb-grande-bretagne.fr). Open M-F 9:30am-12:30pm and 2:30-5pm. **US,** 2, av. Gabriel, 8ème (☎01 43 12 22 22). M: Concorde. Open M-F 9am-6pm. Consulate General, 2, r. St-Florentin, 8ème (☎01 43 12 22 22). Open M-F 9am-3pm.

Currency Exchange: Hotels, train stations, and airports offer poor rates but have extended hours; Gare de Lyon, Gare du Nord, and both airports have booths open 6:30am-10:30pm. Most **ATMs** accept **Visa** and **MasterCard** ("EC"). Crédit Lyonnais ATMs take **AmEx;** Crédit Mutuel and Crédit Agricole ATMs are on the **Cirrus** network; and most Visa ATMs accept **PLUS**-network cards.

American Express: 11, r. Scribe, 9ème (☎01 47 77 79 33), opposite the rear of the Opéra. M: Opéra. Poor rates; long lines. Mail held for cardholders and AmEx Travelers Cheques holders; otherwise 5F per inquiry. Open M-F 9am-6:30pm, Sa 10am-5:30pm.

LOCAL SERVICES

Bookstores: Gibert Jeune, 5, pl. St-Michel, 5ème. M: St-Michel. The best bookstore in town, with several departments along bd. St-Michel. Books in all languages for all tastes. Open M-Sa 9:30am-7:30pm. **Shakespeare and Co.,** 37, r. de la Bûcherie, 5ème, across the Seine from Notre-Dame. M: St-Michel. No relation to Sylvia Beach's 1920s bookstore. Quirky, wide-ranging selection of new and used books. Open daily noon-midnight.

Gay and Lesbian Services: Centre Gai et Lesbien, 3, r. Keller, 11ème (☎01 43 57 21 47). M: Ledru Rollin. Info hub of all gay services and associations in Paris. English spoken. Open M-Sa 2-8pm, Su 2-7pm. **Les Mots à la Bouche,** 6, r. Ste-Croix-de-la-Bretonnerie, 4ème (☎01 42 78 88 30). M: St-Paul or Hôtel-de-Ville. Gay/lesbian bookstore with info on current events. Open M-Th 11am-11pm, F-Sa 11am-midnight, Su 2-8pm.

Laundromats: Most *laveries* charge about 5F for 8-12min. in the dryer *(séchoir)* and 2-5F for detergent. **LaveauClaire,** 119, r. Charenton, 11ème. Wash 18F per 6kg. Open daily 7am-9pm. **Lavage,** 69, r. de Bac, 6ème. Wash 25F per 6kg. Open daily 7:30am-9pm. **Laverie Primus,** 87, r. Didot, 14ème. Wash 25F per 7kg.

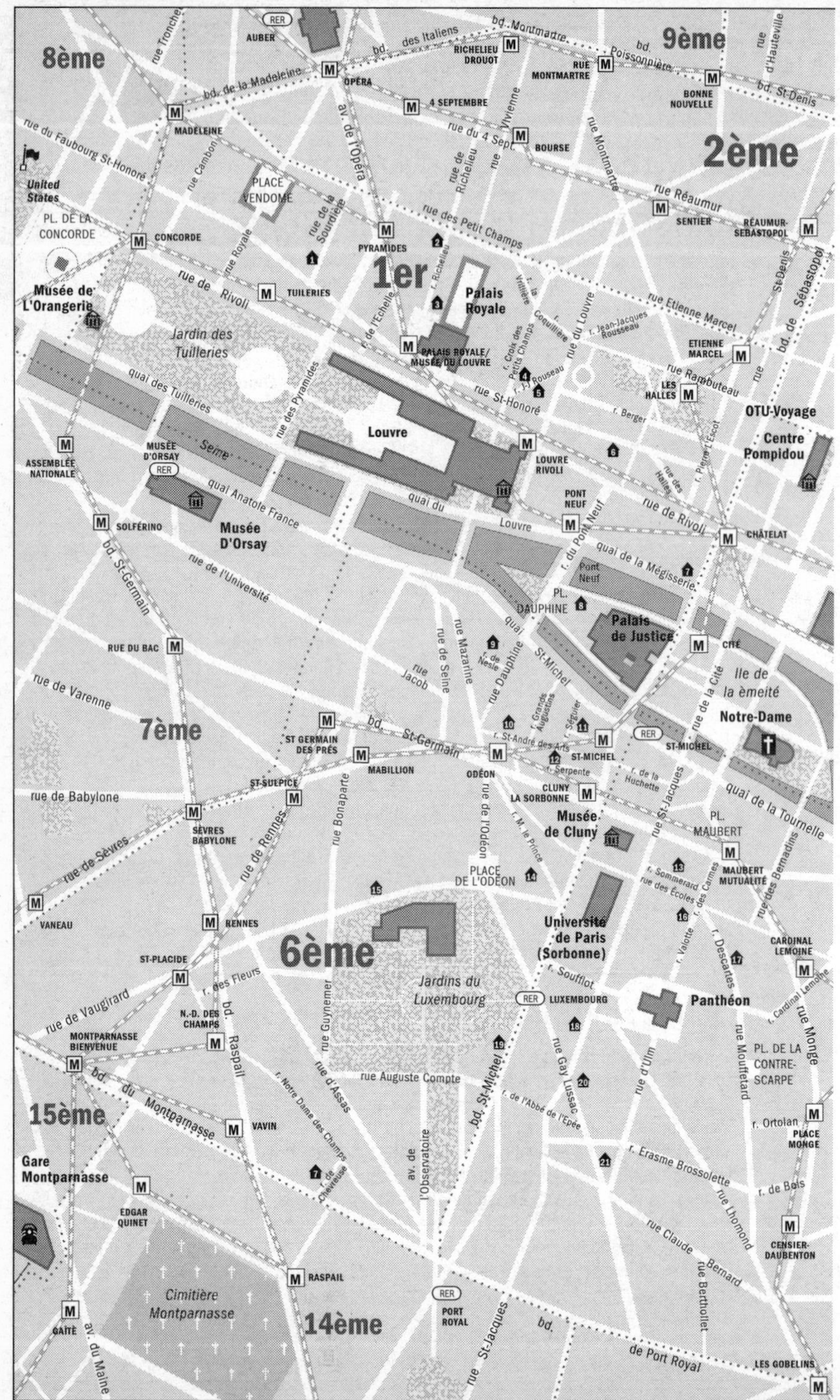
8ème
9ème
2ème
1er
7ème
6ème
15ème
14ème
AUBER
RER
bd. des Italiens
bd. Montmartre
RICHELIEU DROUOT
RUE MONTMARTRE
bd. Poissonnière
rue d'Hauteville
BONNE NOUVELLE
bd. St-Denis
rue Tronchet
bd. de la Madeleine
OPÉRA
MADELEINE
4 SEPTEMBRE
av. de l'Opéra
rue du 4 Sept.
rue Vivienne
BOURSE
rue de Richelieu
rue Montmartre
rue du Faubourg St-Honoré
rue Cambon
PLACE VENDOME
United States
PL. DE LA CONCORDE
CONCORDE
rue de la Sourdière
PYRAMIDES
rue des Petit Champs
rue Réaumur
SENTIER
RÉAUMUR-SÉBASTOPOL
rue Royale
rue de Rivoli
TUILERIES
Palais Royale
Musée de L'Orangerie
Jardin des Tuilleries
r. de l'Echelle
r. Richelieu
r. la Vrillière
r. Coquillière
rue du Louvre
r. Jean-Jacques Rousseau
rue Etienne Marcel
rue St-Denis
bd. de Sébastopol
ETIENNE MARCEL
PALAIS ROYALE/ MUSÉE DU LOUVRE
r. Croix des Petits Champs
r. J-J Rousseau
rue Rambuteau
LES HALLES
quai des Tuilleries
rue des Pyramides
rue St-Honoré
r. Berger
OTU-Voyage
Louvre
Centre Pompidou
r. Pierre-l'Escot
rue des Halles
ASSEMBLÉE NATIONALE
MUSÉE D'ORSAY
Seine
LOUVRE RIVOLI
quai Anatole France
quai du Louvre
PONT NEUF
rue de Rivoli
CHÂTELAT
SOLFÉRINO
Musée D'Orsay
r. du Pont Neuf
quai de la Mégisserie
bd. St-Germain
rue de l'Université
Pont Neuf
PL. DAUPHINE
Palais de Justice
quai St-Michel
CITÉ
RUE DU BAC
rue Jacob
rue de Seine
rue Mazarine
r. de Nesle
rue Dauphine
Ile de la èmeité
rue de Varenne
r. Grands Augustins
r. Séguier
rue de la Cité
Notre-Dame
ST GERMAIN DES PRÉS
bd. St-Germain
r. St-André des Arts
ST-MICHEL
MABILLION
ODÉON
r. Serpente
r. de la Huchette
ST-SULPICE
CLUNY LA SORBONNE
quai de la Tournelle
rue de Babylone
rue Bonaparte
rue de l'Odéon
Musée de Cluny
rue St-Jacques
PL. MAUBERT
SÈVRES BABYLONE
rue de Rennes
r. M. le Prince
rue de Sèvres
PLACE DE L'ODÉON
r. Sommerard
rue des Écoles
r. des Carmes
MAUBERT MUTUALITÉ
rue des Bernadins
VANEAU
RENNES
Universite de Paris (Sorbonne)
r. Valette
r. Descartes
CARDINAL LEMOINE
ST-PLACIDE
r. des Fleurs
Jardins du Luxembourg
r. Soufflot
rue Cardinal Lemoine
rue de Vaugirard
N.-D. DES CHAMPS
RER
LUXEMBOURG
Panthéon
rue Monge
MONTPARNASSE BIENVENUE
bd. Raspail
rue Guynemer
rue Gay Lussac
rue d'Ulm
rue Mouffetard
PL. DE LA CONTRE-SCARPE
bd. du Montparnasse
r. Notre Dame des Champs
rue d'Assas
rue Auguste Compte
bd. St-Michel
r. de l'Abbé de l'Epée
VAVIN
r. Ortolan
PLACE MONGE
Gare Montparnasse
r. de Chevreuse
av. de l'Observatoire
r. Erasme Brossolette
r. de Bois
rue Lhomond
EDGAR QUINET
rue Claude Bernard
CENSIER-DAUBENTON
RASPAIL
Cimitière Montparnasse
RER
PORT ROYAL
rue Berthollet
GAITÉ
av. du Maine
14ème
rue St-Jacques
bd. de Port Royal
LES GOBELINS

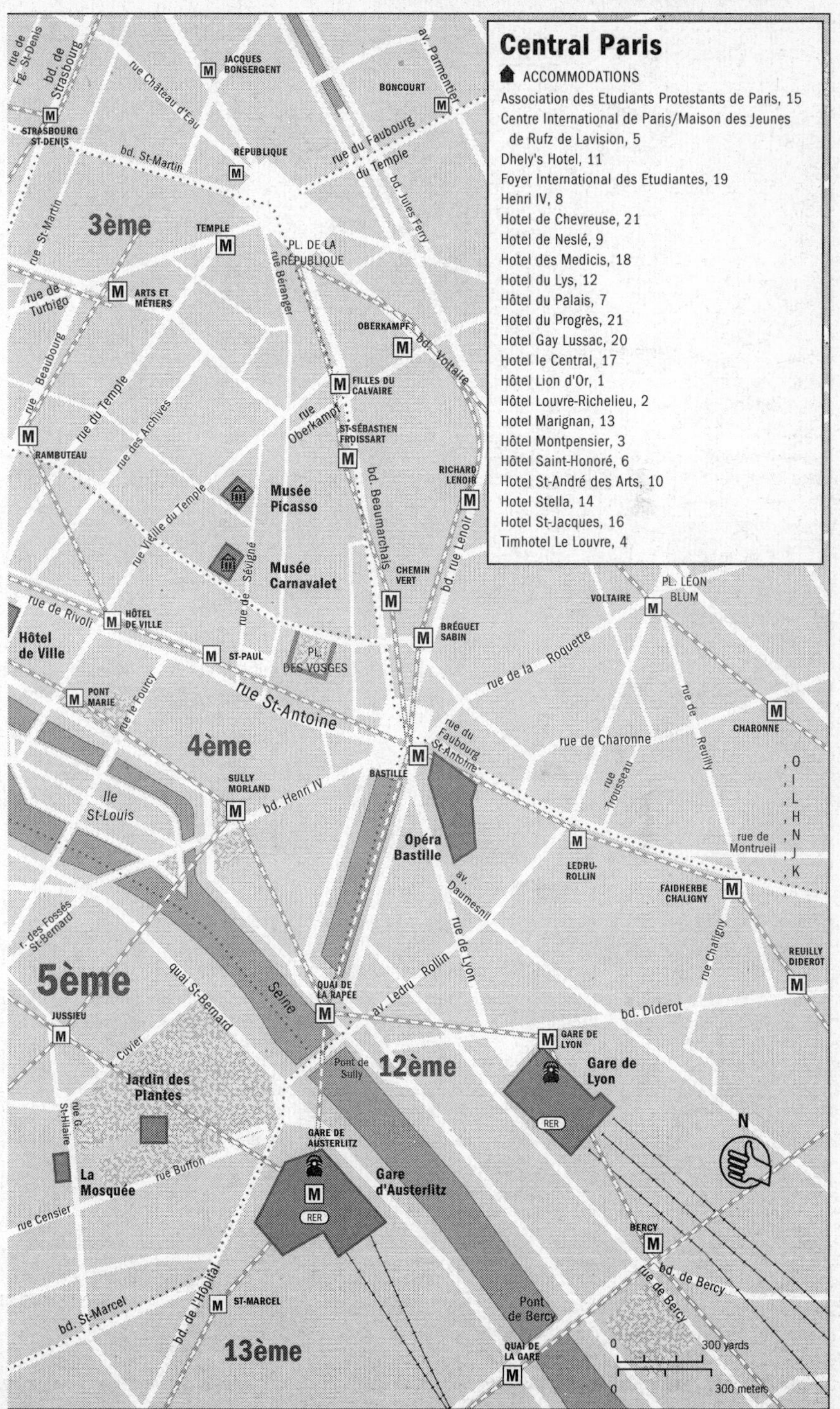
Central Paris
ACCOMMODATIONS
Association des Etudiants Protestants de Paris, 15
Centre International de Paris/Maison des Jeunes de Rufz de Lavision, 5
Dhely's Hotel, 11
Foyer International des Etudiantes, 19
Henri IV, 8
Hotel de Chevreuse, 21
Hotel de Neslé, 9
Hotel des Medicis, 18
Hotel du Lys, 12
Hôtel du Palais, 7
Hotel du Progrès, 21
Hotel Gay Lussac, 20
Hotel le Central, 17
Hôtel Lion d'Or, 1
Hôtel Louvre-Richelieu, 2
Hotel Marignan, 13
Hôtel Montpensier, 3
Hôtel Saint-Honoré, 6
Hotel St-André des Arts, 10
Hotel Stella, 14
Hotel St-Jacques, 16
Timhotel Le Louvre, 4
3ème
4ème
5ème
12ème
13ème
Musée Picasso
Musée Carnavalet
Hôtel de Ville
Ile St-Louis
Opéra Bastille
Jardin des Plantes
La Mosquée
Gare d'Austerlitz
Gare de Lyon
PL. DE LA RÉPUBLIQUE
PL. DES VOSGES
PL. LÉON BLUM
JACQUES BONSERGENT
BONCOURT
STRASBOURG ST-DENIS
RÉPUBLIQUE
TEMPLE
ARTS ET MÉTIERS
OBERKAMPF
FILLES DU CALVAIRE
ST-SÉBASTIEN FROISSART
RAMBUTEAU
RICHARD LENOIR
CHEMIN VERT
HÔTEL DE VILLE
ST-PAUL
BRÉGUET SABIN
VOLTAIRE
PONT MARIE
SULLY MORLAND
BASTILLE
CHARONNE
LEDRU-ROLLIN
FAIDHERBE CHALIGNY
REUILLY DIDEROT
QUAI DE LA RAPÉE
JUSSIEU
GARE DE LYON
GARE DE AUSTERLITZ
BERCY
ST-MARCEL
QUAI DE LA GARE
rue de Fg. St-Denis
bd. de Strasbourg
rue Château d'Eau
av. Parmentier
bd. St-Martin
rue du Faubourg du Temple
bd. Jules Ferry
rue St-Martin
rue Béranger
rue de Turbigo
rue Beaubourg
bd. Voltaire
rue du Temple
rue des Archives
rue Oberkampf
bd. Beaumarchais
rue Vieille du Temple
rue de Sévigné
bd. rue Lenoir
rue de Rivoli
rue de la Roquette
rue St-Antoine
rue le Fourcy
rue du Faubourg St-Antoine
rue de Charonne
rue de Reuilly
rue Trousseau
bd. Henri IV
rue de Montreuil
av. Daumesnil
r. des Fossés St-Bernard
rue de Lyon
rue Chaligny
quai St-Bernard
Seine
av. Ledru Rollin
bd. Diderot
Cuvier
Pont de Sully
rue G. St-Hilaire
rue Buffon
rue Censier
bd. de l'Hôpital
bd. St-Marcel
Pont de Bercy
bd. de Bercy
rue de Bercy
RER
N
0
300 yards
300 meters

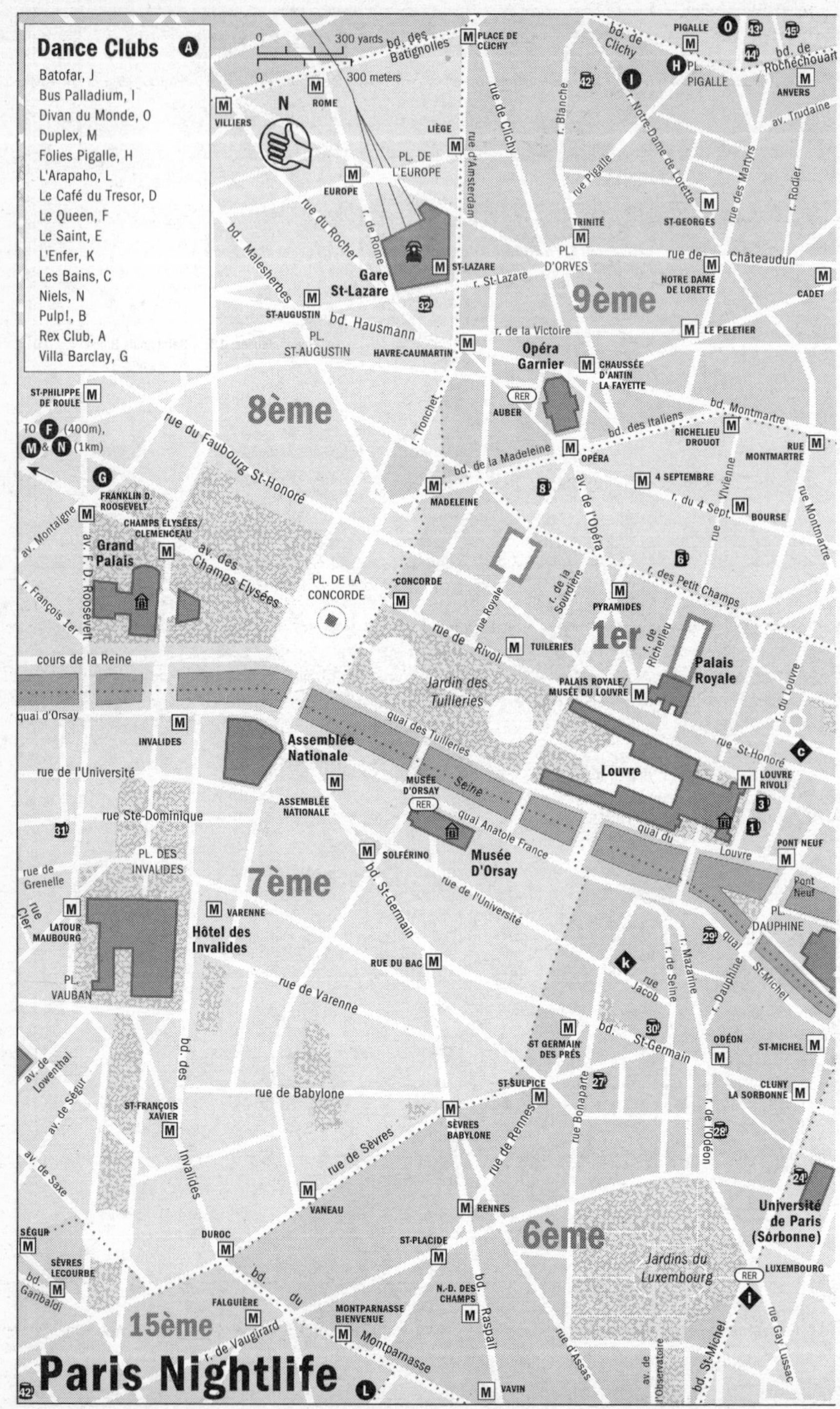

Dance Clubs A
Batofar, J
Bus Palladium, I
Divan du Monde, O
Duplex, M
Folies Pigalle, H
L'Arapaho, L
Le Café du Tresor, D
Le Queen, F
Le Saint, E
L'Enfer, K
Les Bains, C
Niels, N
Pulp!, B
Rex Club, A
Villa Barclay, G
Paris Nightlife
8ème
9ème
1er
7ème
6ème
15ème
Gare St-Lazare
Opéra Garnier
Grand Palais
PL. DE LA CONCORDE
Jardin des Tuilleries
Palais Royale
Louvre
Assemblée Nationale
Musée D'Orsay
Hôtel des Invalides
Université de Paris (Sorbonne)
Jardins du Luxembourg
Seine
TO F (400m), M & N (1km)
0 300 yards
0 300 meters

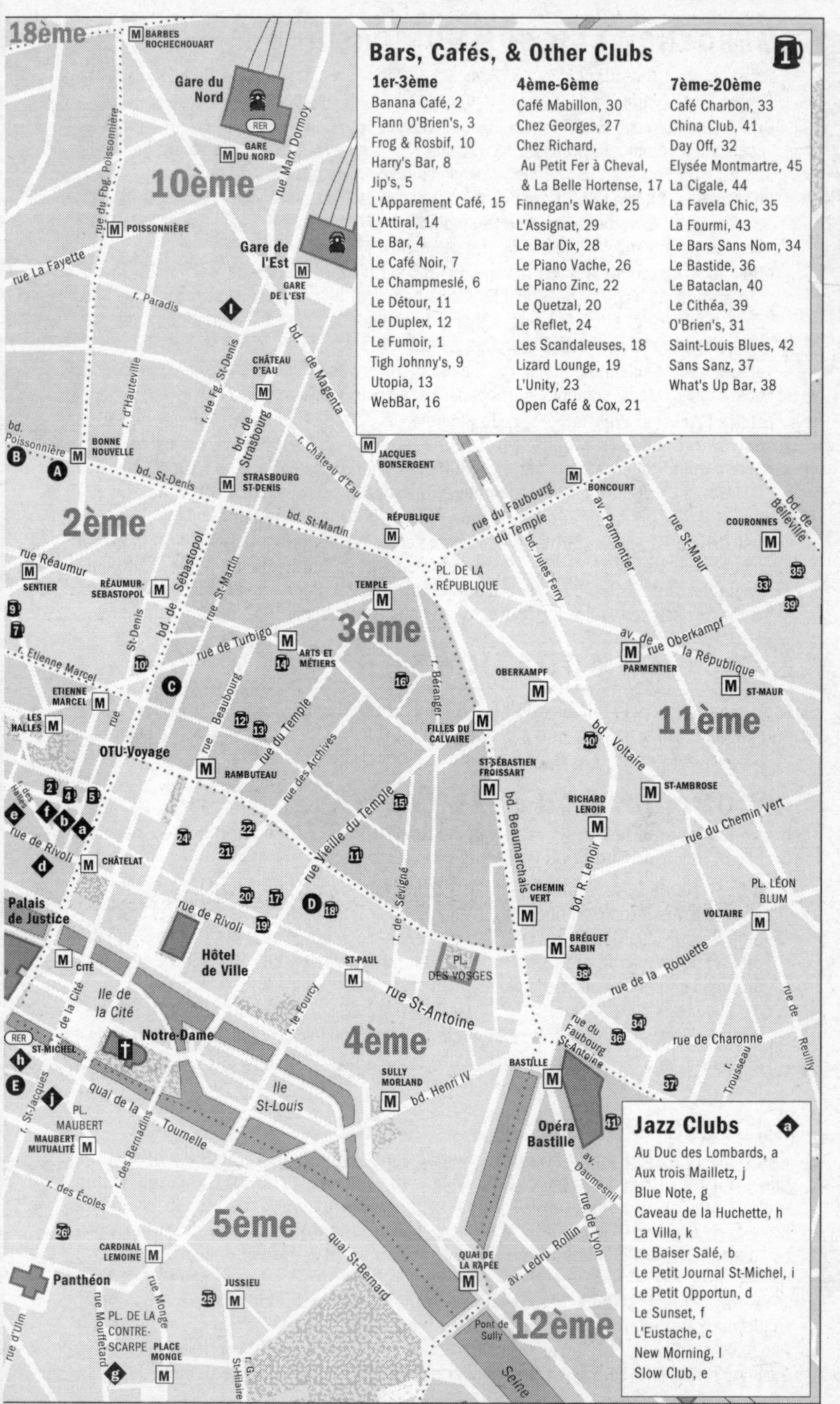
Bars, Cafés, & Other Clubs
1er-3ème
Banana Café, 2
Flann O'Brien's, 3
Frog & Rosbif, 10
Harry's Bar, 8
Jip's, 5
L'Apparement Café, 15
L'Attiral, 14
Le Bar, 4
Le Café Noir, 7
Le Champmeslé, 6
Le Détour, 11
Le Duplex, 12
Le Fumoir, 1
Tigh Johnny's, 9
Utopia, 13
WebBar, 16
4ème-6ème
Café Mabillon, 30
Chez Georges, 27
Chez Richard,
Au Petit Fer à Cheval,
& La Belle Hortense, 17
Finnegan's Wake, 25
L'Assignat, 29
Le Bar Dix, 28
Le Piano Vache, 26
Le Piano Zinc, 22
Le Quetzal, 20
Le Reflet, 24
Les Scandaleuses, 18
Lizard Lounge, 19
L'Unity, 23
Open Café & Cox, 21
7ème-20ème
Café Charbon, 33
China Club, 41
Day Off, 32
Elysée Montmartre, 45
La Cigale, 44
La Favela Chic, 35
La Fourmi, 43
Le Bars Sans Nom, 34
Le Bastide, 36
Le Bataclan, 40
Le Cithéa, 39
O'Brien's, 31
Saint-Louis Blues, 42
Sans Sanz, 37
What's Up Bar, 38
Jazz Clubs
Au Duc des Lombards, a
Aux trois Mailletz, j
Blue Note, g
Caveau de la Huchette, h
La Villa, k
Le Baiser Salé, b
Le Petit Journal St-Michel, i
Le Petit Opportun, d
Le Sunset, f
L'Eustache, c
New Morning, l
Slow Club, e
18ème
BARBES ROCHECHOUART
Gare du Nord
RER
GARE DU NORD
10ème
rue Marx Dormoy
rue du Fbg. Poissonnière
POISSONNIÈRE
Gare de l'Est
GARE DE L'EST
rue La Fayette
r. Paradis
CHÂTEAU D'EAU
bd. de Magenta
r. de Fg. St-Denis
bd. de Strasbourg
r. d'Hauteville
bd. Poissonnière
BONNE NOUVELLE
bd. St-Denis
r. Château d'Eau
JACQUES BONSERGENT
STRASBOURG ST-DENIS
BONCOURT
2ème
bd. St-Martin
RÉPUBLIQUE
rue du Faubourg du Temple
av. Parmentier
rue St-Maur
COURONNES
bd. de Belleville
rue Réaumur
SENTIER
RÉAUMUR-SEBASTOPOL
bd. de Sébastopol
rue St-Martin
PL. DE LA RÉPUBLIQUE
bd. Jules Ferry
TEMPLE
3ème
St-Denis
r. Etienne Marcel
rue de Turbigo
ARTS ET MÉTIERS
av. de la République
rue Oberkampf
PARMENTIER
OBERKAMPF
ST-MAUR
ETIENNE MARCEL
rue Beaubourg
r. Béranger
11ème
LES HALLES
rue du Temple
FILLES DU CALVAIRE
bd. Voltaire
OTU-Voyage
rue des Archives
RAMBUTEAU
ST-SÉBASTIEN FROISSART
ST-AMBROSE
r. des Halles
bd. Beaumarchais
RICHARD LENOIR
rue Vieille du Temple
rue du Chemin Vert
rue de Rivoli
CHÂTELAT
bd. R. Lenoir
r. de Sévigné
CHEMIN VERT
PL. LÉON BLUM
Palais de Justice
VOLTAIRE
Hôtel de Ville
BRÉGUET SABIN
CITÉ
ST-PAUL
PL. DES VOSGES
rue de la Roquette
Ile de la Cité
rue St-Antoine
r. de la Cité
r. le Fourcy
rue du Faubourg St-Antoine
rue de Reuilly
Notre-Dame
4ème
rue de Charonne
ST-MICHEL
BASTILLE
r. Trousseau
SULLY MORLAND
bd. Henri IV
Ile St-Louis
r. St-Jacques
quai de la Tournelle
PL. MAUBERT
MAUBERT MUTUALITÉ
Opéra Bastille
av. Daumesnil
r. des Bernadins
r. des Écoles
rue de Lyon
5ème
av. Ledru Rollin
quai St-Bernard
CARDINAL LEMOINE
QUAI DE LA RAPÉE
Panthéon
rue Monge
JUSSIEU
rue d'Ulm
rue Mouffetard
PL. DE LA CONTRE-SCARPE
PLACE MONGE
r. G. St-Hilaire
Pont de Sully
12ème
Seine

EMERGENCY AND COMMUNICATIONS

Emergencies: Ambulance: ☎15. **Fire:** ☎18. **Police:** ☎17. For non-emergencies, head to the local *gendarmerie* (police force) in each *arrondissement*.

Crisis Lines: Rape, SOS Viol (☎ (0800) 05 95 95). Call free anywhere in France for counseling (medical and legal, too). Open M-F 10am-7pm. **SOS Friendship** (☎01 47 23 80 80). For depressed, lonely English-speakers. Open daily 3-11pm.

Pharmacies: Pharmacie Dhéry, 84, av. des Champs-Elysées, 8ème (☎01 45 62 02 41). M: George V. **Grande Pharmacie Daumesnil,** 6, pl. Félix-Eboué, 12ème (☎01 43 43 19 03). M: Daumesnil; visible as you exit the Métro. All open 24hr.

Medical Assistance: Hôpital Americain, 63, bd. Victor Hugo (☎01 46 41 25 25), in the suburb of Neuilly. M: Porte Maillot; then take bus #82 to the end of the line. English-speaking, but much pricier than French hospitals. The full gamut of specialists, including state-of-the-art facilities and dental services.

Telephones: To use the phones, you'll need to buy a **phone card** *(télécarte), available* at post offices, Métro stations, and *tabacs*. For **directory info,** call ☎12.

Internet Access: WebBar, 23, r. de Picardie, 3ème. M: République. 40F per hr., 300F per 10hr. Open M-F 8:30am-2am, Sa-Su 11am-2am. **Cyber Cube,** 5, r. Mignon, 6ème. 1F per min. Students 200F per 5hr., 300F per 10hr. Open M-Sa 10am-10pm. Also 12, r. Daval, 11ème. M: Bastille. **Luxembourg Micro,** 83, bd. St-Michel, 5ème. RER: Luxembourg. 0.75F per min., 23F per 30min., 45F per hr. Open M-Sa 9am-9pm.

Post Office: 52, r. du Louvre, 1er. M: Châtelet-les-Halles. Open daily 7am-6:20am. For postal info, call ☎01 40 28 20 40. Address mail to be held: First name SURNAME, *Poste Restante*, 52, r. du Louvre, **75001** Paris, France. **Postal code:** 750xx, where "xx" is the *arrondissement* (e.g., 75003 for any address in the 3ème).

ACCOMMODATIONS

High season in Paris falls around Easter and from May to October, peaking in July and August. Most hostels and *foyers* (student dorms) include the **taxe de séjour** (1-5F per person per day) in their listed prices, but some hotels do not.

ACCOMMODATION SERVICES

If you haven't made a reservation in advance, tourist offices and some organizations can help find and book rooms.

La Centrale de Réservations (FUAJ-HI), 4, bd. Jules Ferry, 11ème (☎01 43 57 02 60). M: République; follow r. du Fbg. du Temple away from pl. de la République, cross the park that divides bd. Jules Ferry, and it's a half-block up on your left. Offers same-day reservations in affiliated hostels (115F) and budget hotels. Show up early. Also arranges excursions and sells plane/bus tickets. Open 24hr.

OTU-Voyage, 119, r. St-Martin, 4ème (☎01 40 29 12 12), across the pedestrian mall from the Pompidou. Guarantees same-day "decent and low-cost lodging" (10F fee). Full price due with reservation. English spoken. Open Sa 10am-5pm. Also at 2, r. Malus, 5ème (☎01 44 41 74 74). M: Place Monge. Open M-F 10am-6:30pm.

HOSTELS, FOYERS, AND HOTELS

Paris' hostels skip many standard restrictions—sleep sheets, curfews, and the like—but they do tend to have (flexible) maximum stays. The six HI hostels within the city are for members only. The rest of Paris' dorm-style beds are either private hostels or *foyers*, often quieter and more private than regular hostels. Hotels may be the most practical accommodations for the majority of travelers. Groups of two to four may also find hotels more economical than hostels. Expect to pay at least 160F for a single, 200-400F for a double in the cheapest, luckiest of circumstances. In cheaper hotels, few rooms have private baths; hall showers can cost 15-25F per use. Rooms fill quickly after morning check-out (generally 10am-noon), so arrive early or reserve ahead. Most hotels accept reservations with a credit card deposit.

1ER AND 2ÈME: LOUVRE-PALAIS ROYAL

Central to the **Louvre,** the **Tuileries,** the **Seine,** and the ritzy **pl. Vendôme,** this area still has a few budget hotels. Avoid r. St-Denis.

Centre International de Paris (BVJ)/Paris Louvre, 20, r. J.-J. Rousseau (☎01 53 00 90 90). M: Louvre or Palais-Royal. Bright, dorm-style rooms with 2-10 each. Internet 1F per min. Breakfast and showers included. Reservations by phone up to 1 week in advance. Rooms held only 10min. after expected check-in time; call if late. 130F.

Hôtel Montpensier, 12, r. de Richelieu (☎01 42 96 28 50). M: Palais-Royal. Lofty elegance welcomes the clientele. Shower 25F. Reserve 4 weeks in advance in high season. Singles with toilet 295F; doubles with toilet 305F; rooms with toilet and shower 435F, with toilet, bath, and sink 515F. Extra bed 80F.

Hotel Vivienne, 40, r. Vivienne (☎01 42 33 13 26; fax 01 40 41 98 19). M: R. Montmartre. A touch of refinement in budget digs. Some rooms with balconies. Breakfast 40F. Singles with shower 390F; doubles with bath 490F, with shower 470F.

Maison des Jeunes de Rufz de Lavison, 18, r. J.-J. Rousseau (☎01 45 08 02 10). M: Louvre or Palais-Royal. Quiet, spacious, sunny rooms for 50 students. Flower-filled courtyard. Breakfast and showers included. 4-night min. stay. Reception 9am-7pm. Reservations require 1-night's payment. Singles 160F; doubles 280F.

Hôtel du Palais, 2, quai de la Mégisserie (☎01 42 36 98 25). M: Châtelet. All rooms (except on the top floor) have views of the Seine and Left Bank. Reserve 3 weeks in advance. Singles 283-353F; doubles 326-386F; triples 429F; large quad 462F; quint with 2-sink bathroom and huge windows 535F. Extra bed 70F.

Hôtel Lion d'Or, 5, r. de la Sourdière (☎01 42 60 79 04; www.123france.com). M: Tuileries or Pyramides. You'll hear the bells toll from nearby Eglise St-Roch but little else. Phone and TV. Reserve 1 month in advance. 5% discount for stays of more than 3 nights. Singles 380-480F; doubles with shower 480-560F; triples with shower 560F, with bath and toilet 680F. Extra bed 60F.

Hôtel Saint-Honoré, 85, r. St-Honoré (☎01 42 36 20 38; fax 42 21 44 08). M: Louvre, Châtelet, or Les Halles. Recently renovated. All rooms with full bath and TV. Breakfast 29F. Reserve by fax or phone and confirm the night before. Singles 290F; doubles 410F, with bathtub 450F; triples and quads 490F.

Hôtel Bonne Nouvelle, 17, r. Beauregard (☎01 45 08 42 42; fax 01 40 26 05 81). M: Bonne Nouvelle. Rooms on the top floor boast rooftop views and skylights; all have a TV and tidy bathroom. Breakfast 30F. Reserve with credit card. Singles 330-390F; doubles 380-430F; triples 500-600F; quads 590-690F.

3ÈME AND 4ÈME: THE MARAIS

The Marais' 17th-century mansions now house budget hotels close to the **Centre Pompidou** and the **Ile St-Louis;** the area is also convenient for sampling nightlife, as Paris' night buses converge in the 4*ème* at M: Châtelet.

Hôtel des Jeunes (**MIJE;** ☎01 42 74 23 45; www.mije.com) books beds in Le Fourcy, Le Fauconnier, and Maubuisson (see below), 3 small hostels located on cobblestone streets in old Marais residences. No smoking. Ages 18-30 only. 7-day max. stay. Reception 7am-1am. Lockout noon-3pm. Curfew 1am. Breakfast, shower, and sheets included. Arrive before noon (call in advance if you'll be late). Reserve 1 month in advance. Reception M-F 11:30am-1:30pm and 6:30-8:30pm. 4- to 9-bed dorms 140F; singles 240F; doubles 350F; triples 465F.

Le Fourcy, 6, r. de Fourcy. M: St-Paul or Pont Marie. From M: St-Paul, walk opposite the traffic for a few meters down r. François-Miron and turn left on r. de Fourcy. Light sleepers should avoid rooms on the social courtyard. Internet 1F per min.

Le Fauconnier, 11, r. du Fauconnier. M: St-Paul or Pont Marie. From M: St-Paul, take r. du Prevôt, turn left on r. Charlemagne, and turn right on r. du Fauconnier. Ivy-covered building steps away from the Seine and Ile St-Louis. Spacious 4-bed rooms, some singles and doubles.

Maubuisson, 12, r. des Barres. M: Hôtel-de-Ville or Pont Marie. From M: Pont Marie, walk opposite traffic on r. de l'Hôtel de Ville and turn right on r. des Barres. A half-timbered former girls' convent. Smaller 2- to 7-bed rooms with nice views.

Hôtel du Séjour, 36, r. du Grenier St-Lazare (☎01 48 87 40 36). M: Etienne-Marcel or Rambuteau. Clean, bright rooms. Showers 20F. Reception 7am-10:30pm. Singles 180F-200F; doubles 280F, with shower and toilet 340F; third person 150F extra.

Grand Hôtel Jeanne d'Arc, 3, r. de Jarente (☎01 48 87 62 11; www.hoteljeanne-darc.com). M: St-Paul or Bastille. Jeanne d'Arc blesses her visionary rooms with baths and TVs. Two rooms on the ground floor wheelchair accessible. Reserve 2 months in advance. Singles 325F; doubles 330-660F; triples 600F; quads 660F. Extra bed 75F.

Hôtel de Roubaix, 6, r. Greneta (☎01 42 72 89 91). M: Réaumur-Sébastopol or Arts-et-Métiers. Helpful staff, clean rooms, and new bathrooms. All rooms with bath, telephone, locker, and TV. Some with balconies. Breakfast included. Singles 310-330F; doubles 380-410F; triples 430-490F; quads 520F; quints 550F.

Hôtel Bellevue et du Chariot d'Or, 39, r. de Turbigo (☎01 48 87 45 60; fax 01 48 87 95 04). M: Etienne-Marcel. Belle Epoque lobby, with bar and breakfast room. Clean and modern rooms. All have phones, TVs, toilets, and baths. Singles 315F; doubles 350F; triples 425F; quads 460F.

Castex Hôtel, 5, r. Castex (☎01 42 72 31 52; fax 01 42 72 57 91). M: Bastille or Sully-Morland. Modern stucco decor; all rooms with telephone and sink. TV room. Check-in 1pm. Reserve by sending a fax with a credit card number 1 month in advance. Singles 240-320F; doubles 320-360F; triples 460F. Extra bed 70F.

Hôtel de Nice, 42bis, r. de Rivoli (☎01 42 78 55 29; fax 01 42 78 36 07). M: Hôtel-de-Ville. Nice, nice rooms feature vintage catalogue illustrations, TVs, toilets, showers, and phones. A few have balconies with great views. Rooms ready at 2pm, but leave your bags earlier. Check-out 11am. Reserve by fax or phone with deposit 1 month ahead for summer. Singles 380F; doubles 550F; triples 680F. Extra bed 130F.

Hôtel Andréa, 3, r. St-Bon (☎01 42 78 43 93; fax 01 44 61 28 36). M: Hôtel-de-Ville. Two blocks from Châtelet. Clean, comfortable rooms with phones. Top floor rooms have balconies. Breakfast 30F. Hall showers 20F. Reserve 3 weeks in advance by fax or by phone with credit card. Singles 250F, with toilet and shower 325F; doubles 260F, with toilet and shower 360F; triples 435F; quads 500F.

5ÈME AND 6ÈME: THE LATIN QUARTER AND ST-GERMAIN-DES-PRÉS

The lively *quartier latin* and St-Germain-des-Prés offer proximity to the **Notre-Dame,** the **Panthéon,** the **Jardin du Luxembourg,** and the bustling student cafe culture.

Centre International de Paris (BVJ): Paris Quartier Latin, 44, r. des Bernardins (☎01 43 29 34 80; fax 53 00 90 91). M: Maubert-Mutualité. Immense, ultra-modern hostel with a shiny cafeteria. Showers in rooms. Lockers 10F. Check-in before 2:30pm. Check-out 9am. Reserve well in advance, or arrive at 9am to check for often available rooms. 138 beds. 5- and 6-person dorms 130F; singles 160F; doubles 140F per person.

Hôtel St-Jacques, 35, r. des Ecoles (☎01 44 07 45 45). M: Maubert-Mutualité. Elegant rooms at reasonable rates, with balconies and TVs. Singles 260F, with shower and toilet 480F; doubles 420-610F; triples 680F.

Young and Happy (Y&H) Hostel, 80, r. Mouffetard (☎01 45 35 09 53; email smile@youngandhappy.fr). M: Monge. In the heart of the student quarter. Basic but cheerful. Sheets 15F. Towels 5F. Commission-free currency exchange. Laundry nearby. Lockout 11am-5pm. Curfew 2am. Dorms 127F, off season 107F; doubles 127F.

Hôtel d'Esmeralda, 4, r. St-Julien-le-Pauvre (☎01 43 54 19 20; fax 01 40 51 00 68). M: Maubert-Mutualité. Turn left on r. des Carmes, then left on r. des Ecoles. Regal rooms at reasonable rates, with balconies, windows, and TVs. Breakfast 35F. Singles 250F, with shower and toilet 480F; doubles 420-580F; triples 560-650F.

Hôtel de Neslé, 7, r. du Neslé (☎01 43 54 62 41). M: Odéon. Fantastical and absolutely sparkling. For a treat, book the double room with Turkish *hamam* steam bath (600F). Singles 300-378F; doubles 400-600F; triples 478-675F.

Dhely's Hotel, 22, r. de l'Hirondelle (☎01 43 26 58 25). M: St-Michel. Wood paneling, flower boxes, modern facilities, and quiet location. Hall showers 25F. Reserve well in advance. Singles 258-338F, with shower 428F; doubles 376F, 466F; triples 516F, 606F. Extra bed 100F.

Hôtel du Lys, 23, r. Serpente (☎01 43 26 97 57; fax 01 44 07 34 90). M: Odéon or St-Michel. Floral decorating theme and skylights give this hotel an English country house feel. All rooms with bath or shower and TV. Singles 490F; doubles 520F; triples 620F.

Hôtel de Chevreuse, 3, r. de Chevreuse (☎01 43 20 93 16; fax 01 43 21 43 72). M: Vavin. Clean, quiet rooms with TVs. Breakfast 35F. Reserve one week ahead and confirm by fax. Singles 235F; doubles 295F-395F; triples 535F.

Hôtel des Argonauts, 12, r. de la Huchette (☎01 43 54 09 82; fax 01 44 07 18 84). M: St-Michel. Above a Greek restaurant with the same name. Clean, modern rooms. Courtyard rooms are quiet. Breakfast 25F. Singles with shower 250F; doubles with shower and bath 350-400F.

Hotel Stella, 41, r. Monsieur-le-Prince (☎01 40 51 00 25; fax 01 43 54 97 28). M: Odéon. Homey hotel with antique woodwork. All rooms with shower and toilet. Reserve in advance with deposit; no credit cards. Singles 250F; doubles 300F; triples 450F; quads 500F.

7ÈME: EIFFEL TOWER AND LES INVALIDES

Hôtel du Champs de Mars, 7, r. du Champ de Mars (☎01 45 51 52 30; email stg@club-internet.fr; www.adx.fr/hotel-du-champ-de-mars.com). M: Ecole-Militaire. Reserve 1 month ahead. Singles with shower 390F, with large bed and bath 425F; doubles with shower 430F, with bath 460F; triples with bath 550F.

Grand Hôtel Lévêque, 29, r. Cler (☎01 47 05 49 15; email info@hotelleveque.com; www.hotel-leveque.com). M: Ecole-Militaire. 3-star quality: clean and cheery. Satellite TV, phone, ceiling fan and computer plug in all rooms. Reserve 1 month ahead. Singles 300F; doubles with shower and toilet 400-420F, with twin beds, shower, and toilet 420-470F; triples with shower and toilet 580F.

Hôtel Malar, 29, r. Malar (☎01 45 51 38 46). M: Latou-Maubourg. Elegantly furnished rooms with matching bathrooms. Breakfast 40F. Reserve in advance. Singles 480F, with shower 440F; doubles 520F, with shower 480F. Extra bed 100F.

Hôtel Eiffel Rive Gauche, 6, r. du Gros Caillou (☎01 45 51 24 56; email eiffel@easynet.fr; www.france-hotel-guide.com/h75007/eifriv.htm). M: Ecole-Militaire. On a quiet street, this family-run hotel is a favorite of anglophone travelers. Rooms have cable TV, phone; upper floors see top of Eiffel Tower. Breakfast buffet 40F. Hall showers 15F. Singles 240-435F; doubles 280-480F; triples 460-570F. Extra bed 90F.

Hôtel de la Paix, 19, r. du Gros-Caillou (☎01 45 51 86 17). M: Ecole-Militaire. Across from Hôtel Eiffel Rive Gauche (above), it's the cheapest of the bunch. Reserve 1 week ahead. Singles 180F, with shower 280F; doubles with shower 320F, with bath 350-395F; triple 500F. Extra bed 100F. French traveler's checks or cash only.

Hotel Amelie, 5, r. Amelie (☎01 45 51 74 75; e-mail RESA@hotel-AMELIE.COM.) M: Latour-Maubourg or Invalides. Welcoming, on a charming back street. Reserve 2 weeks in advance. Singles with shower 440F; doubles with shower 480F, with twin beds and shower 540F, with bath 540F.

8ÈME: CHAMPS-ELYSÉES

Foyer de Chaillot, 28, av. George V (☎01 47 23 35 32). M: George V. Take the elevator to the foyer on the 3rd floor. Cheerful, well-equipped, modern rooms, in an upscale dorm-like environment for **women only.** Dinner included M-F. Doubles 7100F per month; after a stay of two months, you can request a single for 3550F per month.

Hôtel Europe-Liège, 8, r. de Moscou (☎01 42 94 01 51). M: Liège. Reasonably priced hotel with newly painted rooms. 2 wheelchair accessible rooms on the ground floor. Breakfast 37F. Singles 390F; doubles 500F.

9ÈME: OPÉRA

The northern part of the 9ème mixes pumping nightlife with a red-light district; avoid M: Pigalle, M: Barbès-Rochechouart, and bd. de Clichy.

Hôtel Chopin, 10, bd. Montmartre, or 46, passage Jouffroy (☎01 47 70 58 10). M: Grands Boulevards. Inside a spectacular old passage lined with shops. A cut above most budget hotels. TV, phone, and fans. Singles with shower 355F, with bath 405-455F; doubles with bath 450-520F; triples with bath 595F.

Hôtel Beauharnais, 51, r. de la Victoire (☎01 48 74 71 13). M: Le Peletier. Look for flower boxes, since there is no Hôtel sign and the lobby looks like a sitting room. All rooms have shower. Doubles 320F; triples 490F; quads 550F; quints 640F.

Woodstock Hostel, 48, r. Rodier (☎01 48 78 87 76; www.woodstock.fr; email flowers@woodstock.fr). M: Anvers or Gare du Nord. A fun hostel with character and a great international staff. Communal kitchen, deposit box, Internet, and fax access. Showers free (and clean). Call ahead to reserve a room. 4-person dorms Apr.-Oct. 117F, Sept.-Mar. 77F; doubles 137F, 87F.

11ÈME AND 12ÈME: LA BASTILLE AND RÉPUBLIQUE

Convenient to hopping nightlife, but take caution in the area at night.

Auberge de Jeunesse "Jules Ferry" (HI), 8, bd. Jules Ferry (☎01 43 57 55 60). M: République. Clean rooms with bunk beds, sinks, mirrors, and tiled floors. Doubles with big beds. Party atmosphere. Breakfast and showers included. Lockers 10F. Sheets 5F. Laundry 20F wash, 10F dry. Week-long max. stay. Airport shuttle 89F. Internet access in lobby 1F per min. Lockout 10am-2pm. If there are no vacancies, the hostel can book you in another nearby hostel. 4- to 6-bed dorms 120F; doubles 250F.

Mistral Hôtel, 3, r. Chaligny (☎01 46 28 10 20). M: Reuilly-Diderot. One of the best deals in Paris. Each room is unique. Hall showers 15F. Call to reserve 2 weeks in advance. Singles 208F, with shower 253F; 1-bed doubles 216F, with shower 266F; 2-bed doubles with shower 296F; triples with bath 349F; quads with bath 412F.

Hôtel Rhetia, 3, r. du Général Blaise (☎01 47 00 47 18). M: Voltaire or Saint-Ambroise. Aging furnishings and narrow single beds. Hall showers 10F. Reception 7:30am-10pm. Singles 180F, with shower 290F; doubles 190F, 240F; triples 240F, 290F.

Hotel Moderne, 121, r. de Chemin-Vert (☎01 47 00 54 05; email modern.hotel@wanadoo.fr; www.modern-hotel.fr). M: Père Lachaise. Newly renovated, with modern furnishings and clean bathrooms. Reserve with credit card. Singles 250-290F; doubles 290-350F; quads 510F. Extra bed 80F.

Plessis Hôtel, 25, r. du Grand Prieuré (☎01 47 00 13 38). M: Oberkampf. Five floors of clean, bright rooms. Rooms with showers have hair dryers, fans, TVs, and balconies. Lounge with TV and vending machines. "American" breakfast 38F. Open Sept-July. Singles 195-295F; doubles 215-350F.

14ÈME AND 15ÈME: MONTPARNASSE

Just south of the Latin Quarter, Montparnasse mixes intellectual charm with thriving commercial centers and cafes.

Three Ducks Hostel, 6, pl. Etienne Pernet (☎01 48 42 04 05; fax 01 48 42 99 99). M: Félix Faure. Aimed at young fun-seekers, with a 2am curfew and an in-house bar. Kitchen, lockers, and nearby laundromat. Breakfast and shower included. Sheets 15F. Towels 5F. Reserve with credit card deposit. Mar.-Oct. 117F; Nov.-Feb. 97F.

Hôtel de Blois, 5, r. des Plantes (☎01 45 40 99 48; fax 01 45 40 45 62). M: Mouton-Duvernet. Classy interior, with ornate ceiling carvings and an iron spiral staircase. Breakfast 27F. Reserve 10 days ahead. Singles 230F; doubles 240-360F; triples 360F.

CISP "Kellerman," 17, bd. Kellerman (☎01 44 16 37 38; www.cisp.asso.fr). M: Porte d'Italie. This 392-bed hostel resembles a spaceship on stilts. Impeccably clean with TV room, laundry, and cafeteria (open daily noon-1:30pm and 6:30-9:30pm). Bunk beds. Breakfast included. Lockout 1:30-6:30pm. Wheelchair accessible. Good for last-minute reservations. Dorms 101-126F; singles 146F, with bath 196F.

FOOD

For most Parisians, life is about eating. Scratch that. Life *is* eating. Establishments range from the famous repositories of *haute cuisine* to corner *brasseries*. Inexpensive bistros and *crêperies* offer the breads, cheeses, wines, *pâtés*, *pôtages*, and pastries central to French cuisine. *Gauche* or gourmet, French or foreign, you'll find it in Paris. **CROUS (Centre Regional des Oeuvres Universitaires et Scolaires),** 39, av. Georges Bernanos, 5ème, has info on university restaurants. (☎01 40 51 37 10. M: Port-Royal. Open M-F 9am-5pm.) To assemble a picnic, visit the specialty shops of the **Marché Montorgeuil,** 2ème, **r. Mouffetard,** 5ème, or the **Marché Bastille,** on bd. Richard-Lenoir (M: Bastille; open Th and Su 7am-1:30pm).

RESTAURANTS

1ER AND 2ÈME: LOUVRE-PALAIS ROYAL

Cheap options surround **Les Halles,** 1er and 2ème. Near the **Louvre,** the small streets of the 2ème teem with traditional bistros.

Jules, 62, r. Jean-Jacques Rousseau (☎01 40 28 99 04). M: Les Halles. Subtle blend of modern and traditional French cooking; selections change by season. 4-course *menu* 120F. Open M-F noon-2:30pm and 7-10:30pm.

Les Noces de Jeannette, 14, r. Favart, and 9, r. d'Amboise (☎01 42 96 36 89). M: Richelieu Drouot. Impress your date. *Menu du Bistro* (162F). Open daily noon-1:30pm and 7-9:30pm.

Le Dénicheur, 4, r. Tiquetonne (☎01 42 21 31 01). M: Etienne-Marcel. Diner turned disco/junkyard cafe. 2-course *menu* 50-55F; 3-course 70F. Brunch 85F. Open daily noon-3:30pm and 7:30pm-1am.

La Victoire Suprême du Coeur, 41, r. des Bourdonnais (☎01 40 41 93 95). M: Châtelet. Run by the devotees of guru Sri Chinmoy. Vegetarian, and very tasty. All-day 3-course *formule* 89F. Open M-F noon-2:30pm and 6:30-10pm, Sa noon-10pm.

3ÈME AND 4ÈME: THE MARAIS

The Marais offers chic bistros, kosher delis, and couple-friendly cafes, serving *brûnch,* a meal invented by gay men in the 7th century.

Chez Omar, 47, r. de Bretagne (☎01 42 72 36 26). M: Arts et Métiers. One of the better Middle Eastern places in town. Couscous 60F; lamb 70-98F; chicken 70F. Open M-F noon-2:45pm and 7pm-midnight, Sa 7pm-midnight.

Au Petit Fer à Cheval, 30, r. Vieille-du-Temple (☎01 42 72 47 47). M: Hôtel-de-Ville or St-Paul. An oasis of *chèvre,* kir, and *Gauloises.* Sandwiches 20-32F; desserts 25-34F. Open daily 9am-2am; food served noon-1:15am.

Le Réconfort, 37, r. de Poitou (☎01 42 76 06 36). M: St-Sébastien-Froissart. Swank French, Indian, and Middle Eastern cuisine. Lunch *menu* 69-89F. Open M-F noon-2pm and 8:15-11pm, Sa 8:15-11pm.

En Attendant Pablo, 78, r. Vieille-du-Temple (☎01 42 74 34 65). M: Hôtel de Ville. Intimate. Enormous salads 58F. Lunch *menu* 65F; brunch 89-109F. Fruit juice 26-28F; chocolate pastries 30F. Open W-Su noon-6pm.

Taxi Jaune, 13, r. Chapon (☎01 42 76 00 40). M: Arts-et-Métiers. Eclectic and taxi-themed *entrées* 35F, *plats* 85F. Lunch *menu* 72F. Open M-F noon-2:30pm and 7:30pm-2am; food served until 10:15pm.

Les Philosophes, 28, r. Vieille-du-Temple (☎01 48 87 49 64; www.cafeine.com). M: Hôtel-de-Ville. Veggie options 50-58F; sandwiches 20-32F. Open daily 9am-2am.

5ÈME AND 6ÈME: THE LATIN QUARTER AND ST-GERMAIN-DES-PRÉS

Cheap, touristy restaurants of dubious quality cluster around **r. de la Huchette** and **r. Galande.** Walk uphill toward the **Sorbonne** to find more local establishments. Tiny restaurants with rock-bottom prices jockey for space and customers in the quadrangle bounded by **bd. St-Germain, bd. St-Michel, r. de Seine,** and the **Seine. R. de Buci** harbors bargain Greek restaurants and a rambling street market, while **r. Gregoire de Tours** has cheap, greasy restaurants. More options are near Odéon.

Savannah Café, 27, r. Descartes (☎01 43 29 45 77). M: Cardinal Lemoine. Lebanese food and other "selections from around the world." Happy hour (7-8pm) dinner *menu* 99F; regular *Ménu Gastronomique* 139F. Open M-Sa 7-11pm.

Le Machon d'Henri, 8, r. Guisarde (☎01 43 29 08 70). M: Mabillon. Classic Left Bank bistro has *gigot d'agneau* and *gratin dauphinois*. Appetizers 35-40F; *plats* 70-80F; dinner *menu* 160F. Open daily noon-2:30pm and 7-11:30pm.

La Crêpe Rit du Clown, 6, r. des Canettes (☎01 46 34 01 02). M: Mabillon. If you fear clowns, let tasty, inexpensive crepes revive you. *Formule* 69F; crepes 35-42F; salads start at 24F. Open M-Sa noon-11:30pm.

Comptoir Méditerranée, 42, r. Cardinal Lemoine (☎01 43 25 29 08). M: Cardinal Lemoine. Lebanese specialties. Make your own plate (4 items 32F, 6 items 48F). Open M-Sa 11am-10pm.

Au Jardin des Pâtés, 4, r. Lacépède (☎01 43 31 50 71). M: Jussieu. Organic gourmet pastas with a variety of vegetables and sauces. Appetizers 19-31F; main dishes 47-77F. Open daily noon-2:30pm and 7-11pm.

7ÈME: EIFFEL TOWER AND LES INVALIDES

The 7ème is not budget; the restaurants below are worth the small splurge.

Le Lotus Blanc, 45, r. de Bourgogne (☎01 45 55 18 89). M: Varenne. Vietnamese specialties. Lunch *formule expresse* 59F. Reservations encouraged. Closed Aug. 12-19. Open M-Sa noon-2:30pm and 7-10:30pm.

Le Club des Poètes, 30, r. de Bourgogne (☎01 47 05 06 03). M: Varenne. Not cheap (dinner with wine 120-150F), but fun. Poetry readings at 10pm. Lunch *menu* 77-87F. Drinks 90F, students 45F. Open M-Sa noon-3pm and 8pm-1am.

Chez Lucie, 15, r. Augereau (☎01 45 55 08 74). M: Ecole-Militaire. Inventive cuisine from Martinique, including gumbo, crab, and chicken with lime and ginger. 3-course *menu* 98 and 148F; *plats* 65-98F. Open M-Sa noon-2:30pm and 7:30-11:30pm.

8ÈME: CHAMPS-ELYSÉES

The 8ème is as glamorous and expensive as it gets. If you're not interested in such extravagance, there are some affordable restaurants around r. La Boétie.

Antoine's: Les Sandwiches des 5 Continents, 31, r. de Ponthieu (☎01 42 89 44 20). M: Franklin D. Roosevelt. 41F meal (panini, yogurt, and a drink) on bread that is probably worth that amount on its own. Open M-Sa 8am-7pm.

Restaurant LaMaline, 40, r. Ponthieu (☎01 45 63 14 14). M: Franklin D. Roosevelt. A simple, incandescent restaurant named after a poem by Aurthur Rimbaud. 2-course *menu* 150F. Open daily 7:30pm-11pm.

Bankok, 28, r. de Moscou (☎01 43 87 62 56) M: Rome. Talented Thai chef and a choice of meats cooked in coconut milk, curry, or satay sauce (82-128F). Plenty of vegetarian options. Open 10:30am-2am; lunch noon-3pm; dinner 7pm-midnight.

9ÈME: OPÉRA

Except for a few gems, meals close to the Opéra cater to the after-theater and movie crowd and can be quite expensive. For truly cheap deals, head farther north. **R. Faubourg-Montmartre** is crammed with cheap sandwich and pizza places.

Le Bistro de Gala, 45, r. Faubourg-Montmartre (☎01 40 22 90 55). *Menu* is a commitment at 170F, but definitely worth it. Open M-F noon-2:30pm and 7-11:30pm, Sa 7-11:30pm.

Haynes Bar, 3, r. Clauzel (☎01 48 78 40 63). M: St-Georges. The first African-American-owned restaurant in Paris (1949). Very generous portions under 100F. Closed Aug. Open Tu-Sa 7pm-midnight.

Pizzéria King Salomon, 46, r. Richer (☎01 42 46 31 22). M: Cadet or Bonne Nouvelle. A popular kosher pizzeria. Individual pizzas 42-62F. Open Su-Th 11:30am-3pm and 6:30pm-midnight, Su 6:30-11:30pm.

11ÈME: LA BASTILLE

Although Bastille swells with fast-food joints, reasonably priced tapas, African, Asian, and French spots lie on **r. Charonne, r. Keller, r. de Lappe,** and **r. Oberkampf.**

La Ville de Jagannath, 101, r. St-Maur (☎01 43 55 80 81). M: St-Maur. Lunchtime means "world cuisine"; switch to platters of vegetarian Indian food for dinner. Basic *menu* 90F (with tangy basmati, two creamy curries, and balls of cheese and spinach kofta) will do. Open Tu-Sa noon-2:30pm, Su-Th 7:30-11:30pm, F-Sa 7:30-12:30pm.

Chez Paul, 13, r. de Charonne (☎01 47 00 34 57). M: Bastille. From succulent salmon to peppercorn steak (78F), Paul dishes a menu to make your palate sing. Open daily Sept.-July noon-2:30pm and 7pm-2am; food served until 12:30am.

13ÈME, 14ÈME, AND 15ÈME: BUTTE AUX CAILLES AND MONTPARNASSE

The 13*ème* is a budget dream. Scores of Asian restaurants cluster in Paris's **Chinatown",** south of pl. d'Italie on av. de Choisy. A large North African community huddles near the St-Marcel Métro. The 14*ème* is bordered at the top by the busy bd. du Montparnasse, which is lined with restaurants ranging from Tex-Mex chains to classic cafes. **R. du Montparnasse,** which intersects with the boulevard, teems with reasonably priced *crêperies*. The r. Daguerre is lined with vegetarian-friendly restaurants. Good-value restaurants cluster on r. Didot, r. du Commerce, r. de Vaugirard, bd. de Grenelle, and Gare Montparnasse.

Café du Commerce, 39, r. des Cinq Diamants (☎01 53 62 91 04). M: Pl. d'Italie. Funky place with a fruit-i-ful menu. Dinner *menus* (65-120F). Lunch *menu* 50F. Open daily noon-3pm (service until 2:30pm) and 7pm-2am (service until 1am).

Chez Foong, 32, r. Frémicourt (☎01 45 67 36 99). M: Cambronne. Superb Malaysian kitchen. 3-course lunch and dinner *menus* 85F (M-F). Worth the trek. Open M-Sa noon-2:30pm and 7-11pm.

Au P'tit Cahoua, 39, bd. St-Marcel (☎01 47 07 24 42). M: St-Marcel. Under a tent worlds away from Paris, this kitchen spins fabulous Maghrébin meals. The lunch *menu* (65F) offers tabouli or *briouats au thon* (tuna in a flaky pastry), chicken, olive, and lemon tajine, or couscous merguez (a spicy sausage). Open M-F and Su noon-2:30pm and 7:30-11pm, Sa 7:30-11pm.

Chez Papa, 6, r. Gassendi (☎01 43 22 41 19). M: Denfert-Rochereau. In this delish eatery, Papa-nalia is the name of the game. The best deal is the massive *salade boyarde*. *Menu* served until 9pm Su-Th (55F). Also in the 8*ème* (29, r. de l'Arcade), 10*ème* (206, r. Lafayette), and 15*ème* (101, r. de la Croix Nivert). Open M-Sa 10am-1am.

18ÈME: MONTMARTRE

During the siege of Paris in 1814, Russian cossacks occupied **Montmartre;** the restaurants where they grabbed quick bites between battles became known as bistros (Russian for "quick"). The Russians were replaced by hungry tourists, particularly around **pl. du Tertre** and **pl. St-Pierre.** Be cautious in the area, particularly at night. Charming bistros and cafes are common between **r. des Abbesses** and **r. Lepic.**

Chez Ginette, 101, r. Caulaincourt (☎01 46 06 01 49). M: Lamarck-Caulaincourt. Upstairs from the Métro. Inventive and inexpensive French cooking, like monkfish with prawn sauce (100F). Closed Aug. Open M-Sa noon-2:30pm and 7:30pm-2am.

Le Soleil Gourmand, 10, r. Ravignan (☎01 42 51 00 50). M: Abbesses. 5-cheese tart with salad (58F); oriental seafood salad (65F); house-baked cakes (30-44F). Open daily 12:30-2:30pm and 8:30-11pm.

FRANCE

CAFES

French cafes conjure up images of tortured writers and lingering afternoons. Popular drinks include coffee, wine, *citron pressé* (fresh-squeezed lemon juice), tea, and spring, mineral, and soda water. Cafes also serve affordable light lunches and snacks. It's cheaper at the counter (*comptoir* or *zinc*) than in the seating area.

Le Fumoir, 6, r. de l'Admiral Coligny (☎01 42 92 05 05). M: Louvre. Drink in deep green leather sofas. Best brunch in Paris 120F; coffee 15F. Open daily 11am-2am.

Café de l'Industrie, 16, r. St-Sabin (☎01 47 00 13 53). M: Breguet-Sabin. Huge and happening cafe pays tribute to the lighter side of Colonialism. Coffee 10F; salads 45-58F. Prices increase 4F after 10pm. Open Su-F 10am-2am.

L'Apparemment Café, 18, r. des Coutures St-Gervais (☎01 48 87 12 22). M: St-Paul. Next to the Picasso Museum. Coffee 12F; designer salads 45F. Open M-F noon-2am, Sa 4pm-2am, Su 12:30pm-midnight.

Le Marais Plus, 20, r. des Francs-Bourgeois (☎01 48 87 01 40). Relaxed *salon de thé* and funky gift and book shop. Open daily noon-7pm.

Les Enfants Gâtés, 43, r. des Francs-Bourgeois (☎01 42 77 07 63). M: St-Paul. "Spoiled children" is a sexy and lovable spot to linger. Coffee 15F; brunch 95-170F. Food served all day. Open W-M 11am-8pm.

Café Beaubourg, 43, r. St-Merri (☎01 48 87 63 96). M: Hôtel-de-Ville. Draws models, tourists, families, and comrades for people-watching across from Centre Pompidou. Coffee 16F; hot chocolate 26F; breakfast 65F; brunch 110F. Open M-Th and Su 8am-1am, F-Sa 8am-2am.

Café de la Mosquée, 39, r. Geoffrey St-Hilaire (☎01 43 31 38 20). M: Censier Daubenton. In the Mosquée de Paris. Delicate tiles, white-marble floors, and tropical shade. Mint tea (10F) and Maghrébin pastries (10F). Open daily 10am-midnight.

Le Séléct, 99, bd. du Montparnasse (☎01 45 48 38 24). M: Vavin. Trotsky, Satie, Breton, Cocteau, and Picasso all frequented this art deco bistro. Coffee 6.50F at the counter; *café au lait* 35F; tea 22-25F; hot chocolate 35F. Open daily 7am-3am.

Aux Deux Magots, 6, pl. St-Germain-des-Prés (☎01 45 48 55 25). M: St-Germain-des-Prés. Home to literati since 1885 and named after Chinese porcelain figures, not fly larva. Coffee 23F; pastries 12-24F. Open daily 7am-1:30am.

Café de Flore, 172, bd. St-Germain (☎01 45 48 55 26). M: St-Germain-des-Prés. Sartre composed *Being and Nothingness* here; Apollinaire, Picasso, Breton, and Thurber just sipped brew. Espresso 24F; *salade Flore* 68F; pastries 31-50F. Open daily 7am-2am.

SIGHTS

In a few hours, you can walk from the heart of the Marais in the east to the Eiffel Tower in the west, passing most major monuments along the way. Try to reserve a day for wandering; you don't have a true sense of Paris until you know how close medieval Notre-Dame is to the modern Centre Pompidou, or the *quartier latin* of students to the Louvre of kings. After dark, spotlights illuminate everything from the Panthéon to the Eiffel Tower, Notre-Dame to the Obélisque.

ILE DE LA CITÉ AND ILE ST-LOUIS

ILE DE LA CITÉ. If any place could be called the heart of Paris, it is this island in the river. In the 3rd century BC, when it was inhabited by the *Parisii*, a Gallic tribe of hunters, sailors, and fishermen, the Ile de la Cité was all there was to Paris. Although the city has expanded in all directions, all distance-points in France are measured from *kilomètre zéro*, a sundial on the ground in front of Notre-Dame.

CATHÉDRALE DE NOTRE-DAME DE PARIS

M: St-Michel-Notre-Dame; exit on the island side. From the Left Bank, cross the Pont au Double and turn right. Open M-F 8am-6:45pm, Sa-Su 8am-7:45pm. Towers open Apr.-Sept.

10am-6pm; Oct.-Mar. 10am-5pm; free. Treasury open M-Sa 9:30am-6pm; 15F, students 10F. Crypt open daily Apr.-Sept. 10am-6pm; Oct.-Mar. 10am-5pm; 35F, students 23F. Tours in English leave from the booth to the right of the entrance; W and Th noon, Sa 2:30pm; free.

This 12th- to 14th-century cathedral, begun under Bishop Maurice Sully, is one of the most famous and beautiful examples of medieval architecture. After the Revolution, the building fell into disrepair and was even used to shelter livestock until Victor Hugo's 1831 novel *Notre-Dame-de-Paris* (a.k.a. *The Hunchback of Notre Dame*) inspired citizens to lobby for restoration. Architect Eugène Viollet-le-Duc made subsequent modifications, including the addition of the spire and the gargoyles. The intricately carved, apocalyptic facade, and soaring, apparently weightless walls (effects produced by brilliant Gothic engineering and optical illusions) are inspiring even for the church-weary. The cathedral's biggest draws are its enormous stained-glass **rose windows** that dominate the north and south ends of the transept. A claustrophobic staircase inside the towers leads to a spectacular perch from which weather-worn gargoyles survey the city.

STE-CHAPELLE AND CONCIERGERIE. Within the courtyard of the **Palais de Justice,** which has harbored Paris' district courts since the 13th century, the opulent, Gothic **Ste-Chapelle** was built by Saint Louis (Louis IX) to house his most precious possession, Christ's crown of thorns (now in Notre-Dame). The chapel contains some of the most beautiful stained glass in the world. *(M: Cité; take r. du Lutèce away from Notre-Dame to bd. du Palais. Open daily Apr.-Sept. 9:30am-6:30pm; Oct.-Mar. 10am-5pm. 35F; joint ticket with Conciergerie 50F, under 26 23F.)* The **Conciergerie,** around the corner from Ste-Chapelle, was one of Paris' most famous prisons; Marie-Antoinette and Robespierre were imprisoned here during the Revolution. *(1, quai de l'Horloge. M: Cité. ☎01 53 73 78 50. Open daily Apr.-Sept. 9:30am-6:30pm; Oct.-Mar. 10am-5pm. 35F, students 23F. Guided tours in French 11am and 3pm; free. For tours in English, call in advance.)*

ILE ST-LOUIS. The Ile St-Louis is home to some of Paris' most privileged elite, such as the Rothschilds and Pompidou's widow, and former home to other super-famous folks, including Voltaire, Baudelaire, and Marie Curie. At night, the island glows in the light of cast-iron lamps and candlelit bistros. Look for Paris' best ice cream at Ile St-Louis' **Berthillon,** 31, r. St-Louis-en-Ile. *(Across the Pont St-Louis from Notre-Dame; also across the Pont Marie from M: Pont Marie. Berthillon open Sept.-July 14; take-out W-Su 10am-8pm; eat-in W-F 1-8pm, Sa-Su 2-8pm. Also closed 2 weeks in both Feb. and Apr.)*

THE LATIN QUARTER AND ST-GERMAIN-DES-PRÉS

The autumn influx of Parisian students is the prime cultural preservative of the *quartier latin*, so named because prestigious *lycées* and universities taught in Latin until 1798. Since the violent student riots in protest of the outmoded university system in May 1968, many artists and intellectuals have migrated to the less expensive outer *arrondissements*, and the *haute bourgeoisie* has moved in. The 5ème still presents the most diverse array of bookstores, cinemas, bars, and jazz clubs in the city. Designer shops and fascinating galleries line **St-Germain-des-Prés.**

CAFES. Cafes along bd. St-Germain have long been gathering places for literary and artistic notables such as Hemingway and Mallarmé. **Aux Deux Magots,** 6 pl. St-Germain-des-Prés, named for two porcelain figures that adorned a store selling Chinese silk and imports on the same spot in the 19th century, quickly became a favorite hangout of Verlaine and Rimbaud, later attracting Breton, Artaud, and Picasso as well. The **Café de Flore,** 172, bd. St-Germain, established in 1890, was made famous in the 1940s and 50s by literati Sartre and Camus, who favored its wood-burning stoves over their cold apartments. *(M: St-Germain-des-Prés.)*

BOULEVARD ST-MICHEL AND ENVIRONS. At the center of the Latin Quarter, bd. St-Michel, which divides the 5ème and 6ème, is filled with cafes, restaurants, bookstores, and clothing stores. **Place St-Michel,** at its northern tip, is packed with students, often engaged in typically Parisian protests, and lots of tourists. *(M: St-Michel.)*

JARDIN DU LUXEMBOURG. South along bd. St-Michel, the formal French gardens of the Jardin du Luxembourg are fabulous for strolling, reading, and watching the famous *guignol* puppet theater. *(RER: Luxembourg; exit onto bd. St-Michel. The main entrance is on bd. St-Michel. Open daily Apr.-Oct. 7:30am-9:30pm; Nov.-Mar. 8:15am-5pm.)*

PANTHÉON. The **crypt** of the Panthéon, which occupies the highest point on the Left Bank, houses the tombs of Voltaire, Rousseau, Victor Hugo, Emile Zola, Jean Jaurès, and Louis Braille; you can spy each tomb from behind locked gates. The **dome** features uninspiring Neoclassical frescoes. *(On pl. du Panthéon, east of the Jardin du Luxembourg. M: Cardinal Lemoine; follow r. du Cardinal Lemoine uphill and turn right on r. Clovis. Or, from RER: Luxembourg, head north on bd. St-Michel and turn right on r. Soufflot. Open daily 10am-6:30pm; last admission 5:45pm. 35F, students 23F.)*

EGLISE ST-GERMAIN-DES-PRÉS. Scarred by centuries of weather, revolution, and war, the Eglise St-Germain-des-Prés, which dates from 1163, is the oldest standing church in Paris. *(3, pl. St-Germain-des-Prés. M: St-Germain-des-Prés. Open daily 8am-7:45pm.)*

JARDIN DES PLANTES. Opened in 1640 to grow medicinal plants for King Louis XIII, the garden now features natural science museums and a **zoo,** which Parisians raided for food during the Prussian siege of 1871. *(On pl. Valhubert. M: Jussieu; follow r. Jussieu southeast along the university building.)*

MOSQUÉE DE PARIS. The cool courtyards and ornate archways of this mosque provide a soothing setting for prayer, mint tea, or an afternoon in the *hamam*. *(On pl. du Puits de l'Ermite. M: Jussieu; take r. Linné, turn right on r. Lacépède, and left on r. de Quatrefages. Open June-Aug. Sa-Th 9am-noon and 2-6pm. Tours 15F, students 10F.)*

THE EIFFEL TOWER AND INVALIDES

EIFFEL TOWER. Built in 1889 as the centerpiece of the World's Fair, the Tour Eiffel has come to symbolize the city. Despite criticism, tacky souvenirs, and Gustave Eiffel's own sentiment that "France is the only country in the world with a 300m flagpole," the tower is unfailingly elegant and commands an excellent view of the city. At night, it will impress even the most jaded tourist. *(M: Bir Hakeim; follow bd. de Grenelle to the Seine and turn right on quai Branly. Or, from RER: Champ de Mars-Tour Eiffel, follow quai Branly. Open daily June-Aug. 9am-midnight; Sept.-May 9:30am-11pm. Lift closes 10:30pm; to 1st fl. 21F, 2nd fl. 43F, 3rd fl. 60F. Stairs to 1st and 2nd floors 15F.)*

INVALIDES. The tree-lined **Esplanade des Invalides** runs from the grand **Pont Alexandre III** to the gold-leaf dome crowning the **Hôtel des Invalides.** The Hôtel, built under Louis XIV for veterans, now houses the **Musée de l'Armée** and **Napoleon's Tomb.** Nearby, on r. Varenne, is the **Musée Rodin.** *(M: Invalides, Latour Maubourg, or Varenne.)*

THE LOUVRE, OPÉRA, MARAIS, AND BASTILLE

AROUND THE LOUVRE. World-famous art museum and former residence of kings, the **Louvre** (p. 338) occupies one-seventh of the 1er *arrondissement*. Le Jardin des Tuileries, at the western foot of the Louvre, was commissioned by Catherine de Médici in 1564 and improved by André Le Notre (designer of the gardens at Versailles) in 1649. *(M: Tuileries. Open daily Apr.-Sept. 7am-9pm; Oct.-Mar. 7:30am-7:30pm. Free tours in English at varying times from the Arc de Triomphe du Carrousel.)* Three blocks north along r. de Castiglione, Place Vendôme hides 20th-century offices and luxury shops behind 17th-century facades. Look out for Napoleon atop the column in the center of the *place*—he's the one in the toga. *(M: Tuileries or Concorde.)* The Palais-Royal was commissioned in 1632 by Cardinal Richelieu, who gave it to Louis XIII. In 1784, the elegant buildings enclosing the palace's formal garden became *galeries*, the prototype of a shopping mall. The revolutions of 1789, 1830, and 1848 all began with angry crowds in the same garden. *(M: Palais-Royal/Musée du Louvre or Louvre-Rivoli.)*

OPÉRA. North of the Louvre, Charles Garnier's grandiose **Opéra** was built under Napoleon III in the eclectic style of the Second Empire. Gobelin tapestries, gilded mosaics, a 1964 Marc Chagall ceiling, and a six-ton chandelier adorn the magnificent interior. *(M: Opéra. Open daily in summer 10am-6pm; off season 10am-5pm. 30F, students 20F. Tours in English in summer daily at noon; off season varies. 60F, students 45F.)*

MARAIS. This area, made up of the 3ème and 4ème *arrondissements*, became the most chic place to live with Henri IV's construction of the elegant **place des Vosges** at the beginning of the 17th century; several remaining mansions now house museums. Today, the small streets of the Marais house the city's Jewish and gay communities as well as fun, hip restaurants and shops. At the confluence of the 1er, 2ème, 3ème, and 4ème, artists, musicians, and pickpockets gather at the **Centre Pompidou,** which looms like a colorful factory over the vast cobblestoned *place.* Linger in the day, but be cautious at night. *(M: Rambuteau; take r. Rambuteau to Pl. Georges Pompidou. Or, from M: Chatelet-Les Halles, take r. Rambuteau or r. Aubry le Boucher.)*

BASTILLE. Farther east, Charles V built the Bastille prison to guard the eastern entrance to his capital. When it became a state prison under Louis XIII, it housed religious heretics and political undesirables. On July 14, 1789, revolutionaries stormed the Bastille, searching for gunpowder and political prisoners. By 1792, nothing was left of the prison but its outline on the *place.* On July 14, 1989, François Mitterrand inaugurated the glittering **Opéra Bastille** to celebrate the destruction of Charles' fortress. *(120, r. de Lyon. M: Bastille. Tours daily 1pm. 50F, students 30F.)*

CHAMPS-ELYSÉES, BOIS DE BOULOGNE, AND LA DÉFENSE

PLACE DE LA CONCORDE. Paris' most famous public square lies at the western edge of the Tuileries. Constructed between 1757 and 1777 to hold a monument to Louis XV, the area soon became the *place de la Révolution,* site of a guillotine that severed 1343 heads. After the Reign of Terror, the square was optimistically renamed (*concorde* means "peace"). The huge, rose-granite, 13th-century BC **Obélisque de Luxor** depicts the deeds of Ramses II. Given to Charles X by the Viceroy of Egypt in 1829, it is Paris' oldest monument. *(M: Concorde.)*

ARC DE TRIOMPHE. Stretching west, the **avenue des Champs-Elysées** is lined with luxury shops, *haute couture* boutiques, cafes, and cinemas. The avenue is the work of Baron Haussmann, who was commissioned by Napoleon III to convert Paris into a grand capital with broad avenues, wide sidewalks, new parks, elegant housing, and sanitary sewers. In 1806, Napoleon commissioned the **Arc de Triomphe,** at the western terminus of the Champs-Elysées, in honor of his Grande Armée. In 1940, Parisians were brought to tears as Nazis goose-stepped through the Arc; on August 26, 1944, British, American, and French troops liberating the city from Nazi occupation marched through to the roaring cheers of thousands. The terrace at the top has a fabulous view. *(On pl. Charles de Gaulle. M: Charles-de-Gaulle-Etoile. Open daily Apr.-Sept. 9:30am-10:30pm; Oct.-Mar. 10am-6pm. 40F, under 26 25F.)*

BOIS DE BOULOGNE. Avenue Foch, one of Haussmann's finest creations, runs from the Arc de Triomphe to the Bois de Boulogne. Popular by day for picnicking, the park is a risky choice at night—until recently it was home to many drug dealers and prostitutes. *(16ème. M: Porte Maillot, Sablons, Pont de Neuilly, or Porte Dauphine.)*

MERDE! The French have a love affair with their dogs, and nearly 500,000 pooches call Paris home. According to official figures, the dogs of Paris leave over 11 tons of *déjections canines* on Paris' streets per day. Sidewalks are veritable minefields; experienced Parisians keep one eye on the ground. Since 1977, the Paris government has been campaigning–under the title *"La lutte contre les pollutions canines"* (The Fight Against Canine Pollution)–to encourage people to have their best friends defecate in street gutters. Inspiring slogans include "Teach him the gutter" and "If you love Paris, don't let him do that!" Clean-up efforts are now aided by a technological triumph called the *Caninette,* or more informally the *Motocrotte* (crapmobile), hybrid motorcycle/vacuum cleaners. If you have the misfortune of stepping into some *crotte de chien,* hope it's with your left foot; according to Parisian superstition, it's good luck.

LA DÉFENSE. Outside the city limits, the skyscrapers and modern architecture of La Défense make up Paris' newest (unofficial) *arrondissement*, home to the headquarters of 14 of France's top 20 corporations. The **Grande Arche,** inaugurated in 1989, completes the *axe historique* running through the Louvre, pl. de la Concorde, and the Arc de Triomphe. There's yet another stunning view from the top. Trees, shops, and sculptures by Miró and Calder line the esplanade. *(M: La Défense, zone 2; RER, zone 3. Open daily 10am-7pm; last entrance 6pm. 43F, students 33F.)*

MONTMARTRE AND PÈRE-LACHAISE

BASILIQUE DU SACRÉ-COEUR. The Basilique du Sacré-Coeur crowns the **butte Montmartre** like an enormous white meringue. Its onion dome is visible from almost anywhere in the city, and its 112m bell tower is the highest point in Paris, offering a view that stretches out to 50km. *(35, r. du Chevalier de la Barre, 18ème. M: Château-Rouge, Abbesses, or Anvers. From Anvers, take r. de Steinkerque off bd. de Rochechouart and climb the steps. Open daily 7am-11pm; free. Dome and crypt open daily 9am-6pm; each 15F, students 8F.)* Nearby, **place du Tertre** features touristy outdoor cafes and sketch artists.

CIMETIÈRE PÈRE-LACHAISE. The Cimetière Père-Lachaise holds the remains of Balzac, Colette, Seurat, Danton, David, Delacroix, La Fontaine, Haussmann, Molière, Proust, and Sarah Bernhardt within its peaceful, winding paths and elaborate sarcophagi. Foreigners buried here include Chopin, Modigliani, Gertrude Stein, and Oscar Wilde, but the most visited grave is Jim Morrison's. French Leftists make ceremonious pilgrimage to the **Mur des Fédérés** (Wall of the Federals), where 147 revolutionary *Communards* were executed and buried. *(16, r. du Repos, 20ème. M: Père-Lachaise. Open Mar.-Oct. M-F 8am-6pm, Sa 8:30am-6pm, Su 9am-6pm; Nov.-Feb. M-F 8am-5:30pm, Sa 8:30am-5:30pm, Su 9am-5:30pm. Free.)*

MUSEUMS

For updated info, check the bimonthly *Paris Museums and Monuments*, available at the Champs-Elysées tourist office. The weekly *Pariscope* and *L'Officiel des Spectacles* list museum hours and temporary exhibits. The **Carte Musées et Monuments** grants entry to 65 Paris museums without waiting in line; it is available at major museums and Métro stations (1-day 80F, 3-day 160F, 5-day 240F).

MUSÉE DU LOUVRE

☎01 40 20 51 51. M: Palais-Royal/Musée du Louvre, 1er. Open M and W 9am-9:45pm, Th-Su 9am-6pm. Before 3pm 45F, after 3pm and Su 26F; 1st Su of each month free. Tours in English M and W-Sa 17F.

A short list of the Louvre's masterpieces includes the Code of Hammurabi, the *Venus de Milo*, the *Winged Victory of Samothrace*, Vermeer's *Lacemaker*, and Delacroix's *Liberty Leading the People*. Oh, and there's that lady with the mysterious smile—the *Mona Lisa*. Enter through I.M. Pei's controversial glass **Pyramid** in the Cour Napoléon, or skip lines by entering directly from the Métro. When visiting the Louvre, strategy is everything. Think like a four-star general: the goal is to come and see without being conquered. The Louvre is organized into three different wings: **Sully, Richelieu,** and **Denon.** Each is divided into different sections according to the artwork's date, national origin, and medium. The color-coding and room numbers on the free maps correspond to the colors and numbers on the plaques at the entrances to every room within the wing.

The **Italian Renaissance collection,** on the first floor of the Denon wing, is rivaled only by that of the Uffizi museum in Florence. Look for Raphael's *Portrait of Balthazar Castiglione* and Titian's *Man with a Glove*. Titian's *Fête Champêtre* inspired Manet's *Déjeuner sur l'Herbe* (see Musée d'Orsay, below). Bought by François I during the artist's visit to Paris, Leonardo da Vinci's *Mona Lisa* smiles mysteriously at millions of guests each year. Don't overlook her remarkable neighbors—da Vinci's *Virgin of the Rocks* displays the *sfumato* smoky technique for which he is famous. The *Venus de Milo* and the *Winged Victory of Samothrace* are the tip of the Greek, Etruscan, and Roman antiquities iceberg.

MUSÉE D'ORSAY

62, r. de Lille, 7ème. ☎01 40 49 48 48. RER: Musée d'Orsay. Open June 20-Sept. 20 Tu-W and F-Su 9am-5:45pm, Th 9am-9:30pm; Sept. 21-June 19 opens 10am. 40F, under 26 and Su 30F.

While it's considered the premier Impressionist museum, the Musée d'Orsay is dedicated to presenting all major artistic movements between 1848 and WWI. On the ground floor, works from Classicism and Proto-Impressionism are on display, including Edouard Manet's *Olympia*, which caused a scandal when it was unveiled in 1865. The first room of the upper level features Manet's *Déjeuner sur l'Herbe*. Other highlights include: Monet's *La Gare St-Lazare* and *Cathédrale de Rouen* series, Renoir's *Le bal du Moulin de la Galette*, Edgar Dégas's *La classe de danse*, Whistler's *Portrait of the Artist's Mother*, and paintings by Alfred Sisley, Camille Pissaro, and Berthe Morisot. More than a dozen diverse works by Vincent Van Gogh follow, including his tormented *Portrait de l'Artiste*. Paul Cézanne's still lifes, portraits, and landscapes experiment with the soft colors and geometric planes that would open the door to Cubism.

OTHER MUSEUMS

Musée Rodin, 77, r. de Varenne, **7ème** (☎01 44 18 61 10). M: Varenne; take bd. des Invalides away from the Seine and turn left on r. de Varenne. The 18th-century Hôtel Biron holds hundred of sculptures by Auguste Rodin (and his lover, Camille Claudel), including the *Gates of Hell, The Thinker*, the *Burghers of Calais*, and *The Kiss*. Open Tu-Su Apr.-Sept. 9:30am-5:45pm; Oct.-Mar. 9:30am-4:45pm. 28F, students and Su 18F.

La Villette, 19ème. M: Porte de la Villette or Porte de Pantin. A vast urban renewal project that encloses a landscaped park, a huge science museum (open M-Sa 10am-6pm, Su 10am-7pm; 50F), an Omnimax cinema (57F), a conservatory, a jazz club, a concert/theater space, and a high-tech music museum (open Tu-Th noon-6pm, F-Sa noon-7:30pm, Su 10am-6pm; 35F, students 25F).

Musée de l'Orangerie, 1er (☎01 42 97 8 16). M: Concorde. Houses Renoirs, Cézannes, Rousseaus, Matisses, and Picassos, but is most famous for Monet's 8 gigantic *Water Lilies*. **Closed until December 2002.** Open W-M 10am-5pm. 30F, under 25 18F.

Galérie Nationale du Jeu de Paume, 1er (☎01 47 03 12 50), opposite the Musée de l'Orangerie in the Tuileries. M: Concorde. Hosts changing contemporary art exhibitions. Open Tu noon-9:30pm, W-F noon-7pm, Sa-Su 10am-7pm. 38F, students under 26 28F.

Musée Carnavalet, 23, r. de Sévigné, **3ème** (☎01 42 72 21 13). M: Chemin-Vert; take r. St-Gilles, which becomes r. du Parc Royal, to r. de Sévigné. In a 16th-century *hôtel particulier*, Carnavalet traces Paris' history from its very origins and guards Voltaire and Rousseau's writing supplies. Open Tu-Su 10am-5:40pm. 30F, students 20F.

Musée Picasso, 5, r. de Thorigny, **3ème** (☎01 42 71 63 15). M: Chemin-Vert; from bd. Beaumarchais, take r. St-Gilles, which becomes r. du Parc Royal, then bear right at pl. de Thorigny. Catalogs Picasso's life and career from his early work in Barcelona to his Cubist and Surrealist years in Paris and his Neoclassical work on the Riviera. Open W-M Apr.-Sept. 9:30am-6pm; Oct.-Mar. 9:30am-5:30pm. 30F, under 26 and Su 20F.

Centre National d'Art et de Culture Georges-Pompidou (**Palais Beaubourg;** ☎01 44 78 12 33), **4ème**. M: Rambuteau. This inside-out building has inspired debate since its inauguration in 1977. Its exhibit halls, library, and superb museum collections (including the **Musée National d'Art Moderne**) are very fine. The wacky exterior, with chaotic colored piping and ventilation ducts (blue for air, green for water, yellow for electricity, red for heating), is an appropriate shell for the collection of Fauves, Cubists, and Pop and Conceptual art. Open June 20-Sept. 20 Tu-W and F-Su 9am-6pm, Th 9am-9:30pm; Sept. 21-June 19 Tu-W and F-Su 10am-5:45pm, Th 10am-9:45pm. Last ticket sales 30min. before closing. 40F, ages 18-25 and all on Su 30F, under 18 free. 90min. English tours in English Tu-Sa, 36F.

Musée de Cluny, 6, pl. Paul-Painlevé, **5ème** (☎01 43 25 62 00). M: Cluny-Sorbonne; follow bd. St-Michel away from the Seine and turn left on r. P. Sarrazin. One of the world's finest collections of medieval art, housed in a medieval monastery built on top of Roman baths. *La Dame et La Licorne* (The Lady and the Unicorn) is one of the most beautiful extant medieval tapestry series. Open W-M 9:15am-5:45pm. 30F, under 25 and Su 20F.

Institut du Monde Arabe, 23, quai St-Bernard, **5ème** (☎01 40 51 38 38). M: Jussieu; take r. Jussieu away from r. Linné and turn right on r. des Fossés St-Bernard, which leads to quai St-Bernard. Features art from the Maghreb and the Near and Middle East. The riverside facade is shaped like a boat, representing the migration of Arabs to France; the opposite side has camera-lens windows with Arabic motifs that open and close to control the amount of sunlight in the museum. Open Tu-Su 10am-6pm. 25F.

The Invalides Museums, Esplanades des Invalides, **7ème** (☎01 44 42 37 72). M: Invalides. The resting place of Napoleon also hosts the **Musée de l'Armée,** which celebrates French military history, and the **Musée de l'Ordre de la Libération** (entrance on bd. de Latour-Maubourg), which tells the story of those who fought for the liberation of France. Open daily Apr.-Sept. 10am-6pm; Oct.-Mar. 10am-5pm. 38F, students under 26 28F. In the *cour d'honneur,* the **Musée d'Histoire Contemporaine** (☎01 44 42 54 91 or 01 44 42 38 39) probes current events. 30F, students 20F.

Musée d'Art Moderne de la Ville de Paris, 11, av. du Président Wilson, in the Palais de Tokyo, **16ème** (☎01 53 6740 00). M: Iéna; from pl. d'Iéna, take av. du Président Wilson to pl. de Tokyo. Paris' second-best collection (after the Pompidou) of 20th-century art, with works by Matisse *(The Dance)* and Picasso *(The Jester);* temporary exhibits vary. Open Tu-F 10am-5:30pm, Sa-Su 10am-6:45pm. 30-45F, students 20-35F.

Musée Marmottan Monet, 2, r. Louis-Boilly, **16ème** (☎01 44 96 50 33). M: La Muette; follow Chaussée de la Muette (av. du Ranelagh) through the Jardin du Ranelagh, turn right on av. Raphaël, then left on r. L. Boilly. This hunting-lodge-turned-stately-mansion features an eclectic collection of Empire furniture, Impressionist Monet and Renoir canvases, and medieval illuminations. Open Tu-Su 10am-5pm. 40F, students 25F.

ENTERTAINMENT

Paris' cabarets, cinemas, theaters, and concert halls satisfy all tastes and desires. The bibles of Paris entertainment, the weekly *Pariscope* (3F) and the *Officiel des Spectacles* (2F), on sale at any kiosk or *tabac,* have every conceivable listing. *Pariscope* includes an English-language pull-out section. When going out, remember that some popular nightlife areas, such as Pigalle, Gare St-Lazare, and Beaubourg, are not always safe. To avoid expensive late-night taxis, keep an eye on the time and hop on the Métro before it closes at 12:30am.

CABARET

Au Lapin Agile, 22, r. des Saules, **18ème** (☎01 46 06 85 87). M: Lamarck-Coulaincourt. Turn right on r. Lamarck, then right again up r. des Saules. Picasso, Verlaine, Renoir, and Apollinaire hung out here during the heyday of Montmartre; now a mainly tourist audience crowds in for comical poems and songs. Originally called the *Cabaret des Assassins,* when the artist André Gill painted a rabbit on the theater's facade, it came to be known as *le lapin à Gill* (Gill's Rabbit), a name that eventually morphed into *Le lapin agile* (the nimble rabbit). Shows Tu-Su at 9:15pm. Admission and 1st drink 130F, students 90F. Subsequent drinks 30-45F.

Caveau de la République, 1, bd. St-Martin, **3ème** (☎01 42 78 44 45). M: République. A Parisian crowd fills the 482 seats of this 96 year-old venue for political satire. Shows consist of 6 separate comedy and song acts; the sequence is called the *tour de champs* (tour of the field). Good French skills and knowledge of French politics needed to get the gags. Tickets sold up to 6 days in advance, daily 11am-6pm. Shows mid-Sept. to June Tu-Sa 9pm, Su 3:30pm. Admission M-Th 145F, F-Sa 180F, Tu-Th students 85F and over 60 110F.

THEATER

Bouffes du Nord, 37bis, bd. de la Chapelle, **10ème** (☎01 46 07 34 50). M: La Chapelle. This experimental theater, headed by the British director Peter Brook, produces cutting-edge performances and occasional productions in English. Closed July and Aug. Box office open M-Sa 11am-6pm. Tickets 70-140F. Wheelchair accessible.

La Comédie Française, 2, r. de Richelieu, **1er** (☎01 44 58 15 15; www.comedie-francaise.fr). M: Palais-Royal. Founded by Molière, now the granddaddy of all French theaters. Expect wildly gesticulated slapstick farce; you don't need to speak French to understand the jokes. Performances take place in the 892-seat Salle Richelieu. Expect several plays by Molière in the coming season. Box office open daily 11am-6pm. Tickets 70-190F, under 27 65F (remainders). Rush tickets (30F) available 45min. before show; line up an hour in advance. They also have special package deals, often for students under a certain age, with reduced prices for tickets to 3 plays or more; call for details. The *comédiens français* also mount plays in the 330-seat **Théâtre du Vieux Colombier,** 21, r. des Vieux Colombiers, **6ème** (☎01 44 39 87 00). M: St-Sulpice. Tickets 160F, 60+ 110F; student rush tickets (65F) sold 45min. before performances, available to students under 27 and anyone under 25.

Odéon Théâtre de l'Europe, 1, pl. Odéon, **6ème** (☎01 44 41 36 36; www.theatre-odeon.fr). M: Odéon. Programs in this elegant Neoclassical building range from classical to avant-garde, but the Odéon specializes in foreign plays in their original language. 1042 seats. **Petit Odéon** is an affiliate with 82 seats. In 2000-2001, the theatre will present the poetry of Robert Wilson and Lou Reed, *Medea* by Euripides, and *L'Avare* by Molière. Open Sept.-July. Box office open M-Sa 11am-6:30pm. Tickets 30-180F for most shows; student rush tickets 50F, available 90min. before performance. Petit Odéon 70F, students 50F. Call ahead for wheelchair access.

FILM

Musée du Louvre, 1er (☎01 40 20 51 86; schedules and reservation ☎01 40 20 52 99). M: Louvre. Art films, films on art, and silent movies. 25-70F, students 15-50F. Open Sept.-June.

Les Trois Luxembourg, 67, r. Monsieur-le-Prince, **6ème** (☎01 46 33 97 77). M: Odéon. High-quality independent, classic, and foreign films, all in V.O. Purchase tickets early. 40F, students 30F.

Action Christine, 4, r. Christine, **6ème** (☎01 43 29 11 30). M: Odéon. Off r. Dauphine. Eclectic, international selection of art and cult films from the '40s and '50s. Always V.O. 40F, early show (usually 6 or 7pm) 25F; M and students 30F.

Dôme IMAX, pl. de la Défense (☎08 36 67 06 06; 2.23F/min.). M: Grande Arche de la Défense. The big dome to the right with your back to the Grand Arche. IMAX cinema. Documentaries in French, but who listens to an IMAX anyway? 55F; students, seniors, and under 16 40F. For 2 shows 75F; students, seniors, and under 16 65F.

 SHOPPING BY ARRONDISSEMENT

1ER AND 2ÈME: ÉTIENNE-MARCEL AND LES HALLES

Sugar and spice, and all things naughty. Fabrics are a little cheaper here, and the style is younger. At the **agnés b.** empire on r. du Jour, the black classics still rule, and **Claude Pierlot** at 3, r. de Turbigo, does button-up cardigans with a well-bred touch. The stores on r. Etienne Marcel and r. Tiquetonne are best for technicolor clubwear and outrageously sexy outfits. (M: Etienne-Marcel.) **Forum Les Halles** (a subterranean shopping mall located just south of the Etienne Marcel area) and the streets that surround it outfit shoppers in the full urban warrior aesthetic.

4ÈME AND THE LOWER 3ÈME: MARAIS

The Marais trades streetwise edge for a consistent line-up of affordable, trendy boutiques. Mid-priced clothing chains, independent designer shops, and vintage stores line **r. Vieille-du-Temple, r. de Sévigne, r. Roi de Sicile,** and **r. des Rosiers.** Lifestyle shops line **r. de Bourg-Tibourg** and **r. des Francs-Bourgeois.** The best selection of affordable-chic men's wear in Paris can be found here, especially along **r. Ste-Croix-de-la-Bretonnerie.** Most stores are open late on weekdays and on Sundays. (M: St-Paul or Hôtel-de-Ville.)

6ÈME AND EASTERN BORDER OF 7ÈME: ST-GERMAIN-DES-PRÉS

Post-intellectual, materialistic St-Germain-des-Prés, particularly the triangle bordered by bd. St-Germain, r. St-Sulpice and r. des Saints-Pères, is saturated with high-budget names. *(M: St Germain des Pres.)* But don't just settle for *lécher les vitrines* (window shopping; literally, licking the windows)—r. du Four hosts fun and affordable designers such as **Paul and Joe** (#40; ☎01 45 44 97 70; open daily 11am-7:30pm) and **Sinéquanone** (#16; ☎01 56 24 27 74; open M-Sa 10am-7:30pm). Closer to the Jardin du Luxembourg, calm r. de Fleurus has **A.P.C.**, as well as the interesting designs of **t***** at #7. *(M: St-Placide.)* In the 7ème, visit r. de Pré-aux-Clercs and r. de Grenelle to ogle avant-garde jewelry at **Stella Cadente,** #22. In general, the 7ème is very expensive, but there are some impressive little boutiques around the Bon Marché department store on r. de Sevres and on r. du Cherche Midi. *(M: Vaneau, Duroc, Sèvres-Babylone, R. du Bac.)*

NIGHTLIFE

The primary leisure pastime of Parisians, as they would have it, is fomenting revolution and burning buildings. Actually, their nighttime pleasures tend more toward drinking, relaxing, and people-watching. For those new to the town, the exclusive nightlife scene will probably feel like a tough nut to crack, but there are definitely alternatives to the mega-trendy and mega-expensive. Those looking for live music, especially jazz, are in for a heavenly time. Those on the prowl for dancing may be at first frustrated by Paris' rather closed (and sometimes downright nasty) club scene, but *Let's Go* tries to list places that are tolerant of non-models. If you'd rather just drink and watch the world go by, Parisian bars—and the cafes that blend into bars at sundown—won't disappoint.

1ER AND 2ÈME: LOUVRE-PALAIS ROYAL

Le Fumoir, 6, r. de l'Admiral Coligny (☎01 42 92 05 05). M: Louvre. As cool by night as it is by day. Extra dry martini 58F. See **Cafes,** p. 334.

Flann O'Brien's, 6, r. Bailleul (☎01 42 60 13 58). M: Louvre-Rivoli. From the Métro, walk away from the Seine on r. du Louvre and make the first right after crossing r. de Rivoli. Arguably the best Irish bar in Paris. Ask about the live music schedule. Open daily 4pm-2am.

Frog & Rosbif, 116, r. St-Denis (☎01 42 36 34 73). M: Etienne-Marcel. At the corner of r. St-Denis and r. Tiquetonne. As if a slice of High Street had been plugged in next to the peep shows. Open daily noon-2am.

Rex Club, 5, bd. Poissonnière (☎01 42 36 10 96). M: Bonne-Nouvelle. A non-selective club which presents a most selective DJ line-up. Large dance floor and lots of seats. Open Tu-Sa 11:30pm-6am.

3ÈME AND 4ÈME: THE MARAIS

La Belle Hortense, 31, r. Vieille-du-Temple (☎01 48 04 71 60). M: St-Paul. Walk in the direction of traffic along r. de Rivoli and turn right onto r. Vieille-du-Temple. Wide wine selection from 18F per glass, 90F per bottle. Walls of books (literature, art, philosophy) and some really mellow music to go with your merlot. Frequent exhibits, readings, and discussions in the small leather-couch-filled back room. Open daily 1pm-2am.

Le Détour, 5, r. Elizéver (☎01 40 29 44 04). M: St-Paul. Swank, neo-couchical lounge beats with soul, jazz, and deep house. Hookahs (strawberry, apple, or apricot tobacco) 35F. Cocktails 50F, beer 18F. Open daily 7pm-1:30am.

Utopia, 15 r. Michel Le Comte (☎01 42 71 63 43). M: Rambuteau. Displaying the slogan *le bar des filles qui bougent* (the bar for girls who move), Utopia boasts house beats, pool, pinball, and occasional out-there dress-up parties. Beer 18F. Happy hour M-W 5-8pm. Open M-Sa 5pm-2am.

Les Bains, 7, r. du Bourg l'Abbé (☎01 48 87 01 80). M: Réaumur-Sébastopol or Etienne-Marcel. Ultraselective, super-crowded, and expensive. Used to be a public bath, visited at least once by Marcel Proust. More recently visited by Mike Tyson, Madonna, and Jack Nicholson. Cover and 1st drink M-F 100F; Sa-Su 120F. Subsequent drinks 70F. Open daily 11:30pm-6am.

Le Café du Trésor, 5, r. du Trésor (☎01 44 78 06 60). M: St-Paul. Walk along r. de Rivoli in the direction of traffic, turn right onto r. Vieille-du-Temple, and right onto the pedestrian r. du Trésor. Color, boom, style, and youth. DJs spin house, deep house, and funk Th-Sa 8pm-1:30am. Open daily 9am-2am; food served M-F 12:30-3pm and 7:30-10:30pm, Sa-Su 12:30-10:30pm.

Chez Richard, 37, r. Vieille-du-Temple (☎01 42 74 31 65). M: Hôtel-de-Ville. Inside a courtyard off r. Vieille-du-Temple, this super-sexy bar and lounge screams drama. The secret: on a slow night (read: not the weekend) it's an ideal chill spot, with hip bartenders and smooth beats. Beer 22-40F, cocktails 50-60F. Open daily 5pm-2am.

5ÈME AND 6ÈME: THE LATIN QUARTER AND ST-GERMAIN-DES-PRÉS

Le Reflet, 6, r. Champollion (☎01 43 29 97 27). M: Cluny-La Sorbonne. Walk away from the river on bd. St-Michel, make a left on r. des Ecoles, and take the 1st right. Small, low key, and crowded with student and younger Frenchies. Beer 11-16F, cocktails 12-32F at bar. Open M-Sa 10am-2am, Su noon-2am.

Le Bar Dix, 10, r. de l'Odéon (☎01 43 26 66 83). M: Odéon. From the Métro, walk against traffic on bv. St-Germain and make a left on r. de l'Odéon. A classic student hangout. Open daily 6pm-2am.

Chez Georges, 11, r. des Cannettes (☎01 43 26 79 15). M: Mabillon. From the Métro, walk down r. du Four and make a left on r. des Cannettes. Former cabaret. Upstairs open Tu-Sa noon-2am, cellar open 10pm-2am. Closed Aug.

Le Piano Vache, 8, r. Laplace (☎01 46 33 75 03). M: Cardinal Lemoine or Maubert-Mutualité. From the Métro, walk up r. de la Montagne Saint Geneviève and make a right on r. Laplace. Relaxed student atmosphere. Beer 20-30F, cocktails 40F. Open July-Aug. M-F 6pm-2am, Sa-Su 9pm-2am; Sept.-June M-F noon-2am, Sa-Su 9pm-2am.

Finnegan's Wake, 9, r. des Boulangers (☎01 46 34 23 65). M: Cardinal Lemoine. From the Métro, walk up r. des Boulangers to this Irish pub set in a renovated ancient wine cellar with low, black-beamed ceilings. Have a pint (25-35F) with the boisterous crowd and soak up some Irish culture. Open M-F 11am-2am, Sa-Su 6pm-2am.

7ÈME: EIFFEL TOWER AND LES INVALIDES

O'Brien's, 77, r. St-Dominique (☎01 45 51 75 87). M. Latour-Maubourg. Handsome Irish pub. Open M-Th 6pm-2am, F-Su 4pm-2am.

Master's Bar, 64, av. Bosquet (☎01 45 51 08 99). M: Ecole-Militaire. Here you'll find the Frenchman who's not averse to Anglo-American culture. Open M-F noon-2am, Sa 7pm-2am.

8ÈME AND 9ÈME: CHAMPS-ELYSÉES AND OPÉRA

Chesterfield Cafe, 124, r. de la Boétie (☎01 42 25 18 06) M: Franklin D. Roosevelt. Walk toward the Arc on the Champs-Elysées; r. de la Boétie is the 2nd street on your right. Friendly American bar with first-class live music. Open daily 10am-5am.

Bus Palladium, 6, r. Fontaine (☎01 53 21 07 33). M: Pigalle. The classiest of the mainstream clubs, Le Bus fills with a young and trendy crowd who rock the party that rocks the ex-rock 'n' roll club. Cover 100F. Free for ladies Tu; free for all W. Drinks 60F. Open Tu-Sa 11pm-6am.

Le Queen, 102, av. des Champs-Elysées (☎01 53 89 08 90). Her majesty is one of the cheapest and most fashionable clubs in town, and thus the toughest to get in to—especially for women. M disco; W "Respect"; Th house; F-Sa house; Su "Overkitsch." Cover Su-Th 50F, F-Sa 100F. All drinks 50F. Open daily midnight to dawn.

11ÈME AND 12ÈME: PLACE DE LA BASTILLE AND RÉPUBLIQUE

Café Charbon, 109, r. Oberkampf (☎01 43 57 55 13). M: Parmentier or Ménilmontant. A spacious bar that proudly wears traces of its *fin-de-siècle* dance hall days, but still manages to pack in the punters. Open 9pm-2am.

Le Bar Sans Nom, 49, r. de Lappe (☎01 48 05 59 36). M: Bastille. Dim, jazzy lounge famous for its inventive cocktails. Open M-Sa 7pm-2am.

What's Up Bar, 15, r. Daval (☎01 48 05 88 33). M: Bastille. From the Métro, walk north on bd. Richard Lenoir and make a right on r. Duval. One of those rare Paris miracles: a place that is (almost always) free and funky. Cover F-Sa 50F. Drinks 25-50F.

China Club, 50, r. de Charenton (☎01 43 43 82 02). M: Ledru-Rollin or Bastille. Swank Hong Kong club with a speakeasy-style cellar and lacquered *fumoir chinois* look. Open M-Th 7pm-2am, F-Sa 7pm-3am.

13ÈME: BUTTE AUX CAILLES

Les Oiseaux de Passage, 7, passage Barrault (☎01 45 89 72 42). M: Corvisart. From r. de la Butte aux Cailles, turn right on r. des Cinq Diamants, then left on passage Barrault. Young, hip, and laid-back. Art openings, live music, board games, and theme evenings, including "silent discussion night." Open M-F 11am-2am, Sa-Su 4pm-2am.

Batofar, facing 11, Quai François-Mauriac (☎01 56 29 10 33). M: Quai de la Gare. A club on a light-boat! Friendly industrial environment. Open in summer Tu-Su 6pm-2am.

La Folie en Tête, 33, r. de la Butte aux Cailles (☎01 45 80 65 99). M: Corvisart. *The* artsy axis mundi of the 13*ème*. Magazines, writing workshops, and musical instruments. Crowded concerts on Sa nights. Open M-Sa 5pm-2am.

16ÈME: CHARLES-DE-GAULLE-ETOILE

L'Etoile, 12, r. de Presbourg (☎01 45 00 78 70). M: Charles-de-Gaulle-Etoile. Just across from the entrance to Duplex on av. Foch. Vibrant techno, hip-hop, and funk from DJ Jean-Jean from St-Tropé. Entrance and drink 100F. Open daily 11:30pm to dawn.

Duplex, 2bis, av. Foch (☎01 45 00 93 93). M: Charles-de-Gaulle-Etoile. Walk around the Arc to this chic nightclub where young glamouratzi party to techno-fied pop, funk, and occasionally hip-hop. Club open Tu-Su midnight-dawn.

17ÈME AND 18ÈME: MONTMARTRE

L'Endroit, 67, pl. du Dr-Félix-Lobligeois (☎01 42 29 50 00). M: Rome. Follow r. Boursault to r. Legendre and make a right. The purveyor of cool in work-a-day Batignolles. Open daily noon-2am.

Chez Camille, 8, r. Ravignan (☎01 46 06 05 78). M: Abbesses. From the Métro, walk down r. de la Veuville and make a left on r. Drevet, then another left on r. Gabrielle, which becomes r. Ravignan. Small and trendy bar with a pretty terrace looking down the *butte* to the Invalides dome. Open M-Sa noon-2am.

La Cigale, 120, bd. Rochechouart (☎01 49 25 89 99). M: Pigalle. The Métro puts you right on bd. Rochechouart. One of the two large rock clubs in Pigalle, seating 2000 for international indie, punk, and hard-core bands. Music starts 8:30pm.

Elysée Montmartre, 72, bd. Rochechouart (☎01 44 92 45 42). M: Anvers. The Métro lets you out right on bd. Rochechouart. The biggest-name rock, reggae, and rap venue in a neighborhood fixture.

JAZZ

Au Duc des Lombards, 42, r. des Lombards, 1*er* (☎01 42 33 22 88). M: Châtelet. From r. des Halles, walk down r. de la Ferronerie and make a right on r. St-Denis and another right on r. des Lombards. The best in French jazz with occasional American soloists, and hot items in world music. Cover 80-100F, music students 50-80F. Music starts either 8:30pm or 10pm and wails on until 3am (4am on weekends). Open daily 7:30pm-4am.

Le Baiser Salé, 58, r. des Lombards, 1*er* (☎01 42 33 37 71). M: Châtelet. From r. des Halles, walk down r. de la Ferronerie and make a right on r. St-Denis and another right on r. des Lombards. Lower-key than Lombards. Cuban, African, and Antillean music featured together with modern jazz and funk. Open daily 4pm-dawn.

Le Petit Opportun, 15, r. des Lavandières-Ste-Opportune, 1er (☎01 42 36 01 36). M: Châtelet. From the Métro, walk down r. des Halles and take a right onto r. des Lavandières-Ste-Opportune. Some of the best modern jazz around. Cover 50-80F. Drinks 30-60F. Open Sept.-July Tu-Sa 9pm-5am; music begins at 10:30pm.

GAY AND LESBIAN NIGHTLIFE

Paris' gay and lesbian life centers on the **Marais** (3ème and 4ème), with most establishments clustering around **r. Vieille-du-Temple, r. Ste-Croix de la Bretonnerie,** and **r. des Archives.** For the most comprehensive listing of gay and lesbian establishments and services, consult *Guide Gai* (79F at any kiosk).

Banana Café, 13-15 r. de la Ferronerie (☎01 42 33 35 31), 1er. M: Châtelet. From the Porte du Pont Neuf of Les Halles, go straight, then left on r. St-Honoré; r. de la Ferronerie is straight ahead past the Châtelet Métro stop. Most popular gay bar in the 1er. Open daily 4pm-dawn.

Le Champmeslé, 4, r. Chabanais (☎01 42 96 85 20), 2ème. M: Pyramides or Quatre Septembre. From the Métro, walk down av. de l'Opéra and make a right on r. des Petits Champs. Make another right onto r. Cabanais. This comfy lesbian bar is Paris's oldest and most famous. No cover. Open M-W 5pm-2am, Th-Sa 5pm-5am.

Le Duplex, 25, r. Michel Le Comte (☎01 42 72 80 86), 3ème. M: Rambuteau. This gay bar d'art has a funky mezzanine, yet feels small and intimate. Not an exclusively male bar, but few women hang out here. Beer 15F. Open daily 8pm-2am.

Les Scandaleuses, 8, r. des Ecouffes (☎01 48 87 39 26), 4ème. M: St-Paul. Walk along r. de Rivoli in the direction of traffic and turn right onto r. des Ecouffes. A vibrant, ultra-hip lesbian bar set to techno beats. Men welcome if accompanied by women. Beer 22F. Happy hour 6-8pm. Open daily 6pm-2am.

Open Café, 17, r. des Archives (☎01 42 72 26 18). M: Hôtel-de-Ville. Recently redone, the Open Café is the most popular of the Marais gay bars. Beer 18F, cocktails 35F. Happy hour 6-8pm. Open daily 11am-2am; Su brunch (70-105F).

EXCURSIONS FROM PARIS

VERSAILLES. Louis XIV, the Sun King, built and held court at Versailles' extraordinary palace, 12km west of Paris. The incredibly lavish chateau embodies the extravagance of the Old Regime, especially in the **Hall of Mirrors** and fountain-filled **gardens.** (Chateau open May-Sept. Tu-Su 9am-6:30pm; Oct.-Apr. 9am-5:30pm. 45F, after 3:30pm and under 26 35F (entrance A). Audio (1hr., 25F) and guided tours (1-2hr., 25-50F) available at entrances C and D, respectively. Gardens open daily sunrise-sundown. Free. Fountains turned on for special displays mid-Apr. to mid-Oct. Sa-Su 3:30-5:30pm.) A **shuttle** (roundtrip 33F) runs behind the palace to the **Grand** and **Petit Trianons,** and to Marie Antoinette's farm fantasy, the **Hameau.** (Both Trianons open Tu-Sa Nov.-Mar. noon-5:30pm; Apr.-Oct. noon-6pm; 30F, reduced 20F.)

Take any **RER C5 train** beginning with a "V" from M: Invalides to the Versailles Rive Gauche station (30-40min., every 15min., round-trip 28F). Buy your RER ticket before getting to the platform; a Métro ticket will not get you through the RER turnstiles at Versailles.

CHÂTEAU DE FONTAINEBLEAU. The Château de Fontainebleau achieves the grandeur of Versailles with a unique charm. François I and Napoleon stand out among the parade of post-Renaissance kings who lived here; the former was responsible for the dazzling ballrooms lined with work from Michelangelo's school, the latter restored the post-Revolution dilapidation to a home befitting an emperor. In the long **Galerie de François I,** the most famous room at Fontainebleau, muscular figures by Il Rosso illustrate mythological tales of heroism. Since the 17th century, every queen and empress of France has slept in the gold and green **Queen's Bed Chamber**. The **Musée Napoléon** features a collection of the Emperor's personal toothbrush, his tiny shoes, his field tent, and state gifts. (Castle open July-Aug. W-M 9:30am-6pm; May-June and Sept.-Oct. W-M 9:30am-5pm; Nov.-Apr. W-M 9:30am-12:30pm and 2-5pm. 35F; students, seniors, and Su 23F.)

From the Gare de Lyon in Paris, **trains** run to Fontainebleau (45min., every hr., round trip 94F). The castle is a 30-minute walk or a 10-minute bus ride away.

CHARTRES. Chartres' stunning **Cathédrale Notre-Dame** is one of the most beautiful surviving creations of the Middle Ages. Arguably the finest example of early Gothic architecture in Europe, the cathedral retains several of its original 12th-century stained-glass windows; the rest of the windows and the magnificent sculptures on the main portals date from the 13th century, as does the carved floor in the rear of the nave. You can only enter the **crypt,** which dates back to the 9th century, from La Crypte, opposite the cathedral's south entrance. (Open Apr.-Sept. M-Sa 9am-7pm, Su 9:30am-5:30pm; Oct.-Mar. M-Sa 10am-6pm, Su 10am-1pm and 2:30-4:30pm. 1¼hr. tours in English Apr.-Jan. M-Sa noon and 2:45pm. 30F, students 20F.)

Trains run from Paris' Gare Montparnasse (1hr., every hr., round-trip 142F, under 26 108F). From the station, walk straight, turn left into the pl. de Châtelet, turn right on r. Ste-Même, then turn left on r. Jean Moulin.

DISNEYLAND. It's a small, small world, and Disney is hell-bent on making it even smaller. When Euro-Disney opened in 1992, it was met by jeers, but resistance subsided once it was renamed Disneyland Paris and started serving wine. Everything in Disneyland Paris is in English and French. (www.disneylandparis.com. Open in summer daily 9am-11pm; in winter hours vary. Buy *passeports* (tickets) on Disneyland Hotel's ground floor, at the Paris tourist office, or at any major station on RER line A. Open Apr.-Sept. and Dec. 23-Jan. 7, 220F; Oct.-Dec. 22 and Jan. 8-Mar., 175F.)

From Paris, take the **RER A4** "Marne-la-Vallée" to the last stop, "Marne-la-Vallée/Chessy" (45min., every 30min., round-trip 76F); the last train back leaves at 12:22am, but arrives after the Métro closes. Eurailers can take the **TGV** from Roissy/Charles de Gaulle Airport to the park in 15 minutes.

GIVERNY. Today, Monet's house and gardens in Giverny are maintained by the **Fondation Claude Monet.** From April to July, Giverny overflows with roses, holly hocks, poppies, and the heady scent of honeysuckle. The water lilies, the Japanese bridge, and the weeping willows look like, well, Monets. Monet's thatched-roof house holds his collection of 18th- and 19th-century Japanese prints. (Open Apr.-Oct. Tu-Su 10am-6pm. 35F, students and ages 12-18 25F. Gardens only 25F.)

Trains (☎08 36 35 35 35) run from Paris-St-Lazare to Vernon, the station nearest Giverny (round-trip 132F). When you purchase your ticket from St-Lazare, check the timetables or ask for the **bus** schedules for travel from Vernon to Giverny. (Buses ☎02 32 71 06 39. 10min.; 4-6 per day; 12F, round-trip 20F.) Taxis in front of the train station are another option (65F, weekends 80F).

ROUEN. Enchanting **Rouen** is home to the cathedral that captivated Monet over and over again, just 1½ hours from Paris by train. (p. 347).

LYON. Sample the cuisine and nightlife of France's second-largest city, a two-hour train ride away (p. 384).

BAYEUX. A convenient base for exploring the D-Day beaches, **Bayeux** also contains a stunning tapestry, 2½ hours from Paris by train (p. 349).

NORTHWEST FRANCE

Since the beginning of history, the fate of northwestern France has been caught up with that of its neighbor across the Channel. Even today, although Gauls, Celts, Franks, and Normans no longer clash in battle over the region's treasures, waves of peaceful invaders continue to flock to the chateaux of the Loire Valley, the craggy cliffs of Brittany, and the D-Day beaches and incomparable Mont-St-Michel in Normandy. But beyond these must-see sights lie a wealth of small towns, rugged coastline, and idyllic islands that have yet to succumb to the lures of mass tourism.

NORMANDY (NORMANDIE)

Fertile Normandy is a land of fields, fishing villages, and cathedrals. Vikings seized the region in the 9th century, and invasions have twice secured Normandy's place in military history: in 1066, William of Normandy conquered England; on D-Day, June 6, 1944, Allied armies began the liberation of France on Normandy's beaches.

ROUEN

Best known as the city that burned Joan of Arc and bored Emma Bovary, Rouen (pop. 400,000) is no provincial hayseed town. The city enjoyed prosperity and status from the 10th through 12th centuries as the capital of the Norman empire, and was later immortalized in Monet's multiple renditions of the cathedral.

PRACTICAL INFO, ACCOMMODATIONS, AND FOOD. **Trains** chug to Paris (1½hr., every hr., 104F) and Lille (3hr., 2 per day, 161F). From the station, walk down r. Jeanne d'Arc and turn left to reach pl. de la Cathédrale and the **tourist office,** 25, pl. de la Cathédrale. (☎02 32 08 32 40; fax 02 32 08 32 44. Open May-Sept. M-Sa 9am-7pm, Su 9:30am-12:30pm and 2:30-6pm; Oct.-Mar. M-Sa 9am-6pm, Su 10am-1pm.) Check **email** at **Place Net,** 37, r. de la République, near the Eglise St-Maclou. (37F per hr. Open M 1-9pm, Tu-Sa 11am-9pm, Su 2-8pm.) To reach the **Hôtel Normandya,** 32, r. du Cordier, head straight down r. Jeanne d'Arc from the station and left on r. Donjon to r. du Cordier. (☎02 35 71 46 15. Shower 10F. Reception 8am-8pm. Singles and doubles 130-150F.) **Hôtel des Arcades,** 52, r. de Carmes, is comfy but pricier. (☎02 35 70 10 30; fax 02 35 70 08 91. Breakfast 32F. Reception 7am-8pm. Singles and doubles 150-245F.) Cheap eateries crowd **pl. du Vieux-Marché** and the **Gros Horloge** area. **Natural Gourmand'grain,** 3, r. du Petit Salut, off pl. de la Cathédrale, has organic veggie food. (*Menu* 72F. Open Tu-Sa noon-3pm; takeout 4-7pm.) **Monoprix supermarket** is at 73-83, r. du Gros Horloge. (Open M-Sa 8:30am-9pm.) **Postal code:** 76000.

SIGHTS AND ENTERTAINMENT. The most famous of Rouen's "hundred spires" are those of the **Cathédrale de Notre-Dame,** in pl. de la Cathédrale, with the tallest tower in France (151m). The facade incorporates nearly every style of Gothic architecture; don't miss the stained glass in its **Chapelle St-Jean de la Nef.** (Open M-Sa 8am-7pm, Su 8am-6pm.) Behind the cathedral, the flamboyant **Eglise St-Maclou,** in pl. Barthélémy, features an elaborately carved pipe organ. (Open M-Sa 10am-noon and 2-5:30pm, Su 3-5:30pm.) A poorly marked passageway at 186, r. de Martainville leads to the **Aitre St-Maclou,** which served as the church's charnel house and cemetery through the later Middle Ages; a 15th-century frieze depicts the plague years. Visitors gape at the cadaver of a cat entombed alive to exorcise spirits. (Open daily 8am-8pm. Free.) Joan of Arc died on **place du Vieux Marché,** to the left as you exit the station on r. du Donjon. A cross marks the spot near the unsightly **Eglise Ste-Jeanne d'Arc,** designed to resemble an overturned Viking boat. A block up r. Jeanne d'Arc, the **Musée des Beaux-Arts,** on pl. Verdrel, houses an excellent collection of European masters from the 16th to 20th centuries, including Monet and Renoir. (Open W-M 10am-6pm; in summer 1-6pm. 20F, ages 18-25 13F.) The **Musée Flaubert et d'Histoire de la Médecine,** 51, r. de Lecat, far west of the art museum in pl. de la Madeleine next to the Hôtel-Dieu hospital, which showcases a gruesome array of medical instruments—including gallstone crushers and a battlefield amputation kit—as well as writer Gustave Flaubert's possessions. (Open Tu 10am-6pm, W-Sa 10am-noon and 2-6pm. 12F, students free.)

NORMANDY COAST

FÉCAMP. The port town of Fécamp (pop. 20,000) is one of the jewels of the High Normandy coast, with a scenic beach and two architectural marvels. The magnificent, Renaissance-inspired **Palais Bénédictine,** 110, r. Alexandre Le Grand, houses impressive collections of medieval and Renaissance religious artifacts and is famous for its monk-produced after-dinner liqueur. (Open daily July-Sept. 9:30am-6pm; off season reduced hours. 29F.) The 12th- to 13th-century **Abbatiale de la Trinité** houses an even rarer liquid: the relic of the *précieux-sang,* a fig trunk that allegedly carried a few drops of Christ's blood to the shores of Fécamp in the 6th century. **Trains** arrive from: Le Havre (45min., 5 per day, 43F); Rouen (1¼hr., 6 per day, 69F); and Paris (2½hr., 6 per day, 148F). The **tourist office,** 113, r. Alexandre Le Grand, books rooms for a 10F fee. From the station, head right on r. St-Etienne as it becomes r. de Mer and then left at Palais Bénédictine; it's opposite the entrance. (☎02 35 28 51 01. Open May-June and Sept. M-F 9am-12:15pm and 1:45-6pm, Sa 10am-noon and 2:30-6:30pm, Su 10am-noon and 2-6pm; July-Aug. M-F 10am-6pm; Oct.-Mar. M-F 9am-12:15pm and 1:45-6pm.) **Hôtel Martin,** 18, pl. St-Etienne, has cheery rooms. (☎02 35 28 23 82. Reception 7:30am-11pm, closed Su night and M. Singles and doubles 150-200F.) **Marché-Plus supermarket** is at 83, quai Berigny. (Open M-Sa 7am-9pm, Su 9am-1pm.)

LE HAVRE. An elegy to concrete, Le Havre (pop. 200,000) can brag of being France's largest transatlantic port and little else—get in and get out. For info on **ferries** to Portsmouth, see p. 49. **Trains** (☎02 35 98 50 50) leave from cours de la République for: Rouen (50min., 13 per day, 72F); Fécamp via Etretat (1hr., 9 per day, 43F); and Paris (2hr., 8 per day, 151F). If you must stay in town, **Hôtel Jeanne d'Arc,** 91, r. Emile Zola, offers homey rooms with TVs and phones. (☎02 35 21 67 27; fax 02 35 41 26 83. Breakfast 20F. Singles 135-150F; doubles 150-200F.) Stock up for the ferry ride at **Monoprix,** 38-40, av. René-Coty. (Open M-F 8:30am-8:30pm.)

CAEN

Although Allied bombing leveled three quarters of its buildings in WWII, Caen has since restored its architectural treasures and revitalized its tourist industry. Its biggest draw is the powerful **Mémorial de Caen,** in the northwestern corner of the city, which includes footage of WWII, displays on pre-war Europe and the Battle of Normandy, and a haunting testimonial to the victims of the Holocaust. Take bus #17 to "Mémorial." (Open daily July-Aug. 9am-8pm; Feb. 15-June and Sept.-Oct. 9am-7pm; Nov.-Jan. 4 and Jan. 20-Feb. 14 9am-6pm. 74F, students 65F, veterans free.) Opposite the tourist office looms the dingy **Cathédrale St-Pierre,** which awes visitors with its intricate carvings. (Open M-Sa 8am-6pm, Su 9:30am-12:30pm.) The ruins of William's **chateau** dominate the same area. Inside, the **Musée des Beaux-Arts** contains a fine selection of 16th- and 17th-century Flemish works and 19th-century Impressionist paintings. (Chateau open daily May-Sept. 6am-1am; Oct.-Apr. 6am-7:30pm. Museum open W-M 9:30am-6pm. 25F, students 15F; W free.) From the castle walls on r. de Geôle, turn left on r. Bosnières to reach the romantic **Jardin des Plantes,** on pl. Blot. (Open daily June-Aug. 8am-dusk; Sept.-May 8am-5:30pm.) The **Abbatiale St-Etienne,** twins with the **Abbaye aux Hommes,** off r. Guillaume le Conquérant, holds William the Conqueror's tomb. (Open daily 8:15am-noon and 2-7:30pm.)

Trains (☎08 36 35 35 35) run to: Rouen (2hr., 5 per day, 116F); Paris (2½hr., 12 per day, 156F); Rennes (3hr., 3 per day, 167F); and Tours (3½hr., 2 per day, 169F). CTAC city **buses** (6.40F) run from the station to near pl. St-Pierre and the **tourist office.** (☎02 31 27 14 14; fax 02 31 27 14 18. Open July-Aug. M-Sa 9:30am-7pm, Su 10am-1pm and 2-5pm; Sept.-June M-Sa 10am-1pm and 2-6pm, Su 9:30am-1pm.) The popular but far-away **Auberge de Jeunesse (HI),** 68bis, r. Eustache-Restout, is at Foyer Robert Reme. Take a right from the train station, take your second right on r. de Vaucelles, walk one block, and catch bus #5 or 17 (dir. Fleury or Grâce de Dieu) from the stop on your left to "Lycée Fresnel." (☎02 31 52 19 96; fax 02 31 84 29 49. Breakfast 10F. Sheets 15F. Reception 5-10pm. 62F.) For rooms near the *centre* *ville*, try **Hôtel de la Paix,** 14, r. Neuve-St-Jean. (☎02 31 86 18 99; fax 02 31 38 20 74. Breakfast 28F. Singles 140-175F; doubles 160-195F; triples 240-260F.) **Terrain Municipal,** on rte. de Louvigny, has gorgeous riverside **campsites.** Take bus #13 (dir. Louvigny) to "Camping." (☎02 31 73 60 92. Reception 9am-noon and 5-8pm. Open May-Sept. 18F per person; 10F per tent; 10F per car.) Ethnic restaurants, *crêperies*, and *brasseries* line the **quartier Vaugueux** near the chateau as well as the streets between **Église St-Pierre** and **Église St-Jean.** Get your grocery fix at **Monoprix supermarket,** 45, bd. du Maréchal Leclerc. (Open M-Sa 8am-8:30pm.) Caen's old streets pulsate by moonlight, especially around **r. de Bras, r. des Croisiers,** and **r. St-Pierre. Postal code:** 14000 (specify "Gambetta" for *Poste Restante*).

BAYEUX

Beautiful Bayeux (pop. 15,000) is an ideal base for exploring the nearby D-Day beaches. But visitors should not overlook its **Tapisserie de Bayeux** (Bayeux tapestry), a 900-year-old, 70m embroidery that relates the tale of William the Bastard's invasion of England and his earning of a snazzier name—"the Conqueror." The tapestry is displayed in the **Centre Guillaume le Conquérant,** on r. de Nesmond. (Open daily May-Aug. 9am-7pm; mid-Mar. to Apr. and Sept. to mid-Oct. 9am-6:30pm; mid-Oct. to mid-Mar. 9:30am-12:30pm and 2-6pm. 40F, students 18F.) Nearby is the original home of the tapestry, the extraordinary **Cathédrale Notre-Dame.** (Open July-Aug. M-Sa 8am-7pm, Su 9am-7pm; Sept.-June M-Sa 8:30am-noon and 2:30-7pm, Su 9am-12:15pm and 2:30-7pm.) Across bd. Fabian Ware, near the **Musée de la Bataille de Normandie** (open May to mid-Sept. 9:30am-6:30pm; mid-Sept. to Apr. 10am-12:30pm and 2-6pm; closed early Jan.; 33F, students 16F), the **British Cemetery** reveals a white expanse of graves of soldiers who fell in Normandy.

Trains (☎02 31 92 80 50) arrive at pl. de la Gare from: Caen (20min., 13 per day, 31F); Cherbourg (1hr., 10 per day, 81F); and Paris (2½hr., 13 per day, 171F). To reach the **tourist office,** pont St-Jean, turn left on the highway (bd. Sadi-Carnot), bear right, follow the signs to the *centre ville*, and follow r. Larcher to r. St-Martin. (☎02 31 51 28 28. Open June-Sept. 15 M-Sa 9am-noon and 2-6pm, Su 9:30am-noon and 2:30-6pm; Sept. 16-May M-Sa 9am-noon and 2-6pm.) To get from the station to **Centre d'Accueil Municipal,** 21, r. des Marettes, follow bd. Sadi-Carnot and bear left at the rotary onto bd. Maréchal Leclerc, which becomes bd. Fabien Ware. (☎02 31 92 08 19. Breakfast 15F. Reception 7am-8pm. 75F.) From the tourist office, turn right onto r. St-Martin (which changes names) and turn left onto r. General de Dais to reach the **Family Home/Auberge de Jeuness (HI),** 39, r. General de Dais. (☎02 31 92 15 22; fax 02 31 92 55 72. Breakfast included. Kitchen. Laundry. 95F.) Follow r. Genas Duhomme and head straight on av. de la Vallée des Prés for **Camping Municipal,** on bd. d'Eindhoven. (☎02 31 92 08 43. Open mid-Mar. to Sept. 18F per person; 22F per tent, 22F per car.) Get **groceries** at **Proxi,** on pl. St-Patrice. (Open Tu-Sa 7:30am-12:30pm and 2:30-7:30pm, Su 9am-12:30pm.) **Postal code:** 14400.

D-DAY BEACHES

On June 6, 1944, over a million Allied soldiers invaded the beaches of Normandy—code-named Utah and Omaha (American), Gold and Sword (British), and Juno (Canadian). Today, reminders of the battle can be clearly seen in sobering gravestones, remnants of German bunkers, and the pockmarked landscape.

The beaches/sights lie from west to east as follows: **Utah Beach, Pointe du Hoc, Omaha Beach, Arromanches/Gold Beach** (just northeast of Bayeux), **Juno Beach,** and **Sword Beach** (just north of Caen). **Bus Verts** (☎02 31 44 74 44), which leaves from Caen or Bayeux, covers most of the region. **Victory Tours,** château de Lingerolles, runs half- and full-day tours in English from the Bayeux tourist office. (☎02 31 51 98 14. Half-day tours depart 12:30pm; full-day tours depart 9:15am. 175F; 300F.)

UTAH BEACH. At Utah Beach, near Ste-Marie du Mont, the Americans headed the western flank of the invasion. The **Musée du Débarquement** shows how 836,000 troops, 220,000 vehicles, and 725,000 tons of equipment came ashore. (☎02 33 71 53

35. Open June-Sept. daily 9:30am-6:30pm; May and Oct. daily 9:30am-12:30pm and 2-6:30pm; Nov.-Apr. Sa-Su 10am-12:30pm and 2-5:30pm. 28F, students 23F.) The beach and museum are accessible only by car or by foot from Ste-Mère-Eglise. Take a **train** from Bayeux to Caretan (20min., 5-6 per day) and then a **bus** from Caretan (15min., 1 per day) to Ste-Mère-Eglise.

POINTE DU HOC, OMAHA BEACH, AND GOLD BEACH. The most difficult landing was that of the First US Infantry Division at **Pointe du Hoc.** The grassy area beyond the cliffs is still marked by deep pits; one of the still-extant German bunkers has been turned into a memorial. Next to **Colleville-sur-Mer** and east of the Pointe du Hoc is **Omaha Beach,** memorialized in the movie *Saving Private Ryan,* where almost 10,000 graves stretch over the 172-acre **American Cemetery.** (Open daily Apr.-Nov. 8am-6pm; Dec.-Mar. 9am-5pm.) Ten kilometers north of Bayeux and just east of Omaha is **Arromanches,** a small town at the center of **Gold Beach,** where the British built the artificial **Port Winston** in a single day to provide shelter while the Allies unloaded their supplies. The **Musée du Débarquement** on the beach uses detailed models to show the beach as it once was. (Open daily May-Aug. 9am-7pm; Apr. and Sept. 9am-6pm; Oct. and Mar. 9:30am-5:30pm; Nov.-Dec. and Feb. 10am-5pm. 35F, students 22F.) The **Arromanches 360° Cinéma** combines images of modern Normandy with those of D-Day. Turn left on r. de la Batterie from the museum and follow the steps up. (☎02 31 22 30 30. Open daily June-Aug. 9:40am-6:40pm; Apr.-May and Sept.-Oct. 10:10am-5:40pm; Dec. and Feb. 10:10am-4:40pm; Mar. and Nov. 10:10am-5:10pm. 24F, ages 10-18 21F.) The **D-Day Line** of Bus Verts runs from Caen and Bayeux to Arromanches, the American Cemetery, and Pointe du Hoc. (July-Aug. 1 per day; departs 9:30am, returns 5:50pm. 100F.)

JUNO BEACH AND SWORD BEACH. East of Arromanches lies **Juno Beach,** the landing site of the Canadian forces. The **Canadian Cemetery** is at **Bény-sur-Mer-Reviers.** In **Ouistreham,** the **No. 4 Commando Museum,** on pl. Alfred Thomas, tells the story of French troops who participated in the attack on Sword Beach. (Open Apr.-Sept. 10:30am-6pm. 25F, students 15F.) **Bus** Verts line 20 links Caen to Bény-sur-Mer-Riviers, while line 1 runs from Caen to Ouistreham.

CHERBOURG

On the northern tip of the Cotentin peninsula, Cherbourg (pop. 28,000) was the "Gateway to France," serving as the major supply port following the D-Day offensive of 1944. Today, the island is visited by ferry lines that shuttle tourists from France to England and Ireland. **Ferries,** which leave from bd. Maritime northeast of the *centre ville*, connect to Rosslare, Portsmouth, and Poole (see p. 49). **Trains** (☎02 33 44 18 74) serve Bayeux (1hr., 8 per day, 81F); Caen (1½hr., 10 per day, 99F); Rouen (4½hr., 4 per day, 182F); and Paris (3hr., 7 per day, 218F). To get to the station, go left at the roundabout onto av. A. Briand and follow it as it becomes av. Carnot; it's at the end of the canal right off av. Carnot on av. Millet (25min.). A **shuttle bus** connects the ferry and train station. To reach the **tourist office** (20min.), turn right from the ferry terminal onto bd. Felix Amiot, go straight at the roundabout, make a right across the canal; it will be on your left. (☎02 33 93 52 02. Open in summer M-Sa 9am-6:30pm; off season M-F 9am-noon and 2-6pm, Sa 9am-noon.)

MONT-SAINT-MICHEL

Rising abruptly from the sea, the island of Mont-St-Michel is visible for miles. The Mont is a dazzling labyrinth of stone arches, spires, and stairways that climb up to the **abbey,** balanced precariously on the jutting rock. To reach the abbey entrance (the departure point for tours), walk along the ramparts and the twisting **Grande Rue,** a pedestrian street filled with souvenir stands and restaurants. (Open daily May-Sept. 9am-5:30pm; Oct.-Apr. 9:30am-4:30pm. 45F, under 26 26F. Audio tour 30F. 6 1hr. tours in English per day; free.) The descent to the frigid **crypts** beneath the church leads to its dark, chilly foundations, where walls are up to 2m thick. **La Merveille,** an intricate 13th-century cloister, encloses a seemingly endless web of passageways and chambers. The Mont is most stunning at night, particularly from the causeway entrance, but there is no late-night public transport off the island. Mont-St-Michel is best visited as a daytrip via Courriers Bretons **bus** (☎ 02 33 60 11 43) from St-Malo (1½hr., 2-4 per day, 55F) or Rennes (1½hr., 1-6 per day, 65F).

BRITTANY (BRETAGNE)

Lined with spectacular beaches, misty, almost apocalyptic headlands, and cliffs gnawed by the sea into long crags and inlets, the peninsula of Brittany has always tugged away from mainland France, self-consciously maintaining its Celtic heritage. Present-day Breton culture has its roots in the 5th to the 7th centuries, when Britons fled Anglo-Saxon invaders. In the centuries that followed, the Britons fought for and retained their independence from Frankish, Norman, French, and English invaders, uniting with France only after the last Duchess ceded it to her husband in 1532. Traditions are fiercely guarded, and lilting *Brezhoneg* (Breton) is spoken energetically at pubs and ports in the western part of the province.

RENNES

The administrative center of Brittany and an academic center with two major universities, Rennes (pop. 205,000) possesses Parisian sophistication mixed with traditional Breton charm. A 1720 fire destroyed much of the city, but the lovely *vieille ville* remained intact and today teems with hip cafes and bars. A popular stopover between Paris and Mont-St-Michel, Rennes merits a weekend excursion on its own.

PRACTICAL INFO, ACCOMMODATIONS, AND FOOD. **Trains** (☎ 02 99 29 11 92) arrive on the south side of the river, opposite the town center, from: St-Malo (1hr., 14 per day, 70F); Nantes (1¼-2hr., 10 per day, 114F); Brest (2hr., every hr., 175F); Paris (2hr., every hr., 289-349F); Caen (3hr., 2 per day, 167F); Bordeaux (6hr., 30 per day, 290F direct, 546F through Paris); and Marseille (8hr., 13 per day via Paris, approx. 560F). **Buses** (☎ 02 99 30 87 80) leave from the left of the train station, as you face its north entrance, for Angers (3hr., 1-3 per day, 95F) and Mont-St-Michel (2½hr., 1-2 per day, 64F.) The **tourist office,** 11, r. pont Saint-Yves, has free maps and event listings. From the station, take av. Jean Janvier, turn left on quai Chateaubriand and walk along the river, turn right on r. George Dottin, and then right on r. Saint-Yves. (☎ 02 99 67 11 11. Open M-Sa 9am-7pm, Su 11am-6pm.) Surf the **Internet** at **Cyberspirit,** 22, r. de la Visitation. (25F per 30min., 5F per sent email. Open M 2-9pm, Tu-W noon-9pm, Th-F noon-10pm, Sa 2-10pm.)

To get to the **Auberge de Jeunesse (HI),** 10-12, Canal St-Martin, take bus #1 toward Centre Commercial Nord to Hôtel Dieu, continue down the road, turn right on r. de St-Malo, cross the canal, and turn right at the intersection. (☎ 02 99 33 22 33; fax 02 99 59 06 21. Breakfast included. Reception daily 7am-11pm. Dorms 89F; singles 130F.) **Hôtel Venezia,** 27, r. Dupont des Loges, off quai Richemont, is in a great location; take av. Jean Janvier from the train station and turn right on r. Dupont des Loges. (☎ 02 99 30 36 56; fax 02 99 30 78 78. Singles 130F; doubles 160-220F.) To reach **Camping Municipal des Gayeulles** from r. Gambetta, turn right on r. Victor Hugo, which becomes r. de Paris; from there take bus #3 to the campsite in Parc les Gayeulles. (☎ 02 99 36 91 22; fax 02 99 35 32 80. Shower 5F. 14F per person, 12F per tent, 5F per car.) Rennes is a *gourmand*'s dream—seek out your fancy on **rues St-Malo, St-Georges, Ste-Melaine,** or in **pl. St-Michel.** There is a **supermarket** in the Galeries-Lafayette on quai Duguay-Trouin. (Open M-Sa 9am-8pm.) **Postal code:** 35000.

SIGHTS AND ENTERTAINMENT. The **Musée des Beaux-Arts,** 20, quai Emile Zola, houses a small but eclectic collection ranging from Picasso to Egyptian pottery. (Open W-M 10am-noon and 2-6pm. Tours July-Aug. W and F 2:30pm. 20F; students, children, and senior citizens 10F.) Sculptures and fountains grace the labyrinthine **Jardin du Thabor,** reputedly one of the most beautiful gardens in France. (Open June-Sept. daily 7am-9:30pm.) In the *vieille ville*, the **Cathédrale St-Pierre**

boasts a magnificent chandeliered ceiling. (Open daily 9am-noon and 2-5pm.) Across the street from the cathedral, down r. Porte Mordelaise, stands the **Porte Mordelaise,** the last remaining piece of the city's medieval wall. In early July, the **Tombées de la Nuit** festival (☎02 99 67 11 11; fax 02 99 30 88 88; www.ville-rennes.fr) brings nine days of nonstop music, theater, partying, and dancing. *Rennais* nightlife centers around **pl. Ste-Anne** and **pl. St-Michel.** The club **Le Zing,** 5, pl. des Lices, hits its stride at 1am (open 4pm-3am).

ST-MALO

St-Malo (pop. 52,000) is the ultimate oceanside getaway—and everybody knows it. Tourists converge on its miles of warm, sandy **beaches** and crystalline blue waters, as well as its historic *centre ville.* The best view of St-Malo is from its **ramparts**—enter the walled city through the Porte St-Vincent and follow the stairs up on the right. **Trains** run from pl. de l'Hermine to Dinan (1hr., 8 per day, 46F); Rennes (1hr., 8-12 per day, 68F); and Paris (5hr., 3 per day, 294F). As you exit the station, cross bd. de la République and follow esplanade St-Vincent straight to the **tourist office.** (☎02 99 56 64 48. Open July-Aug. M-Sa 8:30am-8pm, Su 10am-7pm; June and Sept. M-Sa 9am-12:30pm and 1:30-7pm, Su 10am-12:30pm and 2:30-6pm; Easter-May M-Sa 9am-12:30pm and 1:30-6pm.) **Auberge de Jeunesse/Centre de Rencontres Internationales (HI),** 37, av. du Révérend Père Umbricht, is three blocks from the beach; it's 30 minutes from the station. Follow bd. de la République right from the station, turn right on av. Ernest Renan, turn left on r. Guen (which becomes av. de Moka), turn right on av. Pasteur, which becomes av. du Révérend Père Umbricht, and keep right. (☎02 99 40 29 80; fax 02 99 40 29 02. Reception 8am-noon and 6-8pm. Lockout 10am-5pm. Rooms 77-119F.) For **Hôtel Gambetta,** 40, bd. Gambetta, head toward the hostel and look for bd. Gambetta off av. du Révérend Père Umbricht. (☎02 99 56 54 70. Showers 16F. Breakfast 30F. Singles 110-220F; doubles 140-260F. V, MC.) **Stoc supermarket,** on av. Pasteur, is near the hostel. (Open M-F 8:30am-1pm and 3-7:30pm, Sa 8:30am-7:30pm, Su 9:30am-noon.) **Postal code:** 35400.

DINAN

Splendid and tranquil, Dinan (pop. 10,000) may be the best-preserved medieval town in Brittany; 15th-century houses inhabited by traditional artisans line the cobblestoned streets of the *vieille ville.* The 13th-century **Porte du Guichet** is the entrance to the **Château de la Duchesse Anne.** Climb the steps to the terrace to look out over the town, or inspect the galleries of the **Tour de Coëtquen,** which include a spooky subterranean room full of tomb sculptures. (Complex open daily June to mid-Oct. 10am-6:30pm; mid-Oct. to mid-Nov. and mid-Mar. to May W-M 10am-noon and 2-6pm; mid-Nov. to Dec. and Feb. 7 to mid-Mar. W-M 1:30-5:30pm. 25F.) On the other side of the ramparts from the chateau is the entrance to the **Jardin du Val Cocherel,** a creative park with a larger-than-life checkerboard and small zoo. (Open 8am-7:30pm.) From port St-Louis, turn right onto r. du Général de Gaulle and go down the Promenade de la Duchesse Anne to reach the **Basilica St-Saveur Jardin Anglais** and the **Jardin Anglais,** a simple sculpted garden.

Trains run to Rennes (1¼hr., 8 per day, 73F) and Paris (3hr., 8 per day, 316F). To get from the station to the **tourist office,** 6, r. de l'Horloge, bear left across the plaza onto r. Carnot, turn right on r. Thiers, which leads to pl. Duclos; enter the *vielle ville* through Grande Rue on the left (which becomes r. da la Lainerie), turn right on r. de la Poissonerie, and the office is on the left. (☎96 87 69 76. Open June-Sept. M-Sa 9am-7pm, Su 10am-noon and 3-5pm; Oct.-May M-Sa 8:30am-12:30pm and 2-6pm. Walking tours daily July-Aug. 10am and 3pm; 25F.) To walk to the wonderful **Auberge de Jeunesse (HI),** on Moulin du Méen in Vallée de la Fontaine-des-Eaux, turn left as you exit the station, head left across the tracks, turn right, follow the tracks and signs downhill, and turn right after 1.5km onto a wooded lane (30min.). (☎96 39 10 83; fax 96 39 10 62. Sheets 17F. Breakfast 19F. Reception daily June-Sept. 8am-midnight; Oct.-Dec. and Feb.-May 9-11pm. Curfew midnight. 50F.) **Hôtel du Théâtre,** 2, r. Ste-Claire, is opposite the tourist office. (☎96 39 06 91. Breakfast 25F. Singles 85F; doubles 120-160F; triples 210F.) Get **groceries** at **Monoprix,** on r. de la Ferronnerie. (Open M-F 9am-12:30pm and 2:30-7:30pm, Sa 9am-7pm.) Inexpensive *brasseries* lie near **r. de la Ferronnerie** and **pl. des Merciers. Postal code:** 22100.

CÔTE D'EMERAUDE AND CÔTE DE GRANITE ROSE

FRANCE

ST-BRIEUC. There's not much to see in St-Brieuc, but situated between the Côte d'Emeraude and the Côte de Granite Rose, it's a perfect base for daytrips to the scenic countryside. **Trains** arrive from Dinan (1hr., 2-3 per day, 64F) and Rennes (1hr., 15 per day, 92F). From the station, walk down r. de la Gare and bear right at the fork to reach the pl. de la Résistance and the **tourist office,** 7, r. St-Gouéno. (☎02 96 33 32 50. Open July-Aug. M-Sa 9am-7pm, Su 10am-1pm; Sept.-June M-Sa 9am-noon and 1:30-6:30pm.) Take bus #3 (dir. le Village) to the **Auberge de Jeunesse (HI),** in a 15th-century house outside of town. (☎02 96 78 70 70. Call ahead. 72F.)

CAP FRÉHEL. Northeast of St-Brieuc, the rust-hued cliffs of Cap Fréhel—a landscape artist's dream—mark this northern point of the Côte d'Emeraude. Catch a CAT **bus** from St-Brieuc (1½hr., July-Aug. 5 per day, 44F) and follow the red-and-white-striped markers along the well-marked GR34 trail on the edge of the peninsula. The 13th-century **Fort La Latte** boasts drawbridges and a hair-raising view of the Cap (1½hr.). To reach the barracks-like **Auberge de Jeunesse Cap Fréhel (HI),** in la Ville Hadrieux, in Kerivet, from the bus station (35min.), walk toward Plévenon on the D16, then follow the inconspicuous signs with the fir-tree hostel symbol. (May-Sept. 15. ☎41 48 98; Sept. 16-Apr. ☎02 98 78 70 70. Breakfast 19F. Sheets 17F. Lockout noon-5:30pm. Open May-Sept. 45F. **Camping** 27F.) If you ask at St-Brieuc's hostel, you can leave a **rented bike** (48F per half-day) at Cap Fréhel, or vice-versa.

PAIMPOL. Northwest of St-Brieuc at the end of the Côte de Granite Rose, Paimpol offers access to nearby islands, beaches, and hiking. **Buses** run to the dramatic pink granite **Pointe de l'Arcouest** (15min., 5 per day, 17.50F), 6km north of Paimpol. **Trains** (1hr., 4-5 per day, 68F) and CAT **buses** (1¼hr., 3-7 per day, 42F) arrive in Paimpol from St-Brieuc. From the station, go straight on r. du 18 Juin and turn right on r. de l'Oise, which becomes r. St-Vincent, to reach the **tourist office,** on pl. de la République. (☎02 96 20 83 16. Open July-Aug. M-Sa 9am-7:30pm, Su 10am-1pm; Sept.-June reduced hours.) To get to the **Auberge de Jeunesse/Gîte d'Étape (HI)** from the station (20min.), turn left on av. Général de Gaulle, right onto r. du Marne, left at the next light, follow r. Bécot, bear right on r. de Pen Ar Run, and turn left at the end. (☎02 96 20 83 60. Breakfast 19F. Sheets 17F. Check-in until 9pm. 48F. **Camping** 27F.)

BREST

Although it is often used only as a base for exploring northwest Brittany, Brest (pop. 154,000) is a lively home to boisterous sailors and students at Brittany's second largest university. Brest's **chateau** was the only building in town to survive WWII and is now the world's oldest active military institution. You can only enter the chateau through the **Musée de la Marine,** a museum on local maritime history, which occupies most of the sprawling fortress. (Open W-M 9:15am-noon and 2-6pm. 29F, students 19F.) The impressive **Océanopolis Brest,** port de Plaisance, has space-age exhibits on marine life, biodiversity, and conservation. Take bus #7 diagonally opposite the station to "Océanopolis." (Bus every 30min. until 7:30pm. Museum open daily June-Sept. 9am-7pm; Oct.-May 9am-6pm. 90F.)

Trains (☎02 98 31 51 72) arrive from Rennes (1½hr., 15 per day, 170F) and Nantes (4hr., 6 per day, 221F). From the station, av. Georges Clemenceau leads to the pl. de la Liberté, at the intersection of the main r. de Siam and Jean Jaurès, and the **tourist office.** (☎02 98 44 24 96; fax 02 98 44 53 73. Open mid-June to mid-Sept. M-Sa 9:30am-12:30pm and 2-6:30pm, Su 10am-noon and 2-4pm; mid-Sept. to mid-June M-Sa 10am-12:30pm and 2-6pm.) To get to the **Auberge de Jeunesse (HI),** r. de Kerbriant, 4km away, take bus #7 diagonally opposite the station to "Port de Plaisance" (6.30F; last bus M-Sa 7:30pm, Su 6pm); facing the port, take your first right, then another right. (☎02 98 41 90 41; fax 02 98 41 82 66. Breakfast included. Reception M-F 7-9am and 6-8pm, Sa-Su 7-10am and 5-8pm. Lockout 10am-5pm. Curfew July-Aug. midnight; Sept.-June 11pm; ask for a key. 72F.) **Camping du Goulet** is 6km from Brest and 1km from the sea; take bus #14 to "Le Cosquer." (☎02 98 45 86 84. Shower included. Laundry. 18F per person, 21F per tent.) For **groceries,** try the **Monoprix,** on r. de Siam. (Open M-Sa 8:30am-7:30pm.) **Postal code:** 29200 (29279 for *Poste Restante*).

CROZON PENINSULA

With spectacular scenery, rugged terrain, and few inhabitants, the Crozon Peninsula *(Presqu'île de Crozon)* merits the effort required to get there, especially for hikers and bikers seeking a challenge. **Crozon** is a good base for exploring the peninsula; from Brest, take a Vedettes Armoricaines combo **boat/shuttle** (☎02 98 44 44 04; Apr.-Oct. 3 per day, 57F) or Transports Salaun **bus** (☎02 98 27 02 02; 1¼hr., 2-3 per day, 58F). Buses stop at the Crozon **tourist office.** (☎02 98 27 07 92; fax 02 98 27 24 89. Open July-Aug. M-Sa 9:15am-7pm, Su 10am-7pm, Sept.-June M-Sa 9:30am-noon and 2-6pm.) **Presqu'île Loisirs,** across the street, rents indispensable **bikes.** (☎02 98 27 00 09. 40F per half-day, 60F per day, 350F per week. Open July-Aug. M-Sa 9am-noon and 2-7pm, Su 9am-noon; Sept.-June Tu-Sa 9am-noon and 2-7 pm.) The peninsula has four **gîtes d'étape** (hostels; 50F) on the way to Ronscanvel from Crozon; look for the white sign for **Lescoat** on your left, along with a little brown bed sign. **Hôtel du Clos St-Yves,** 61, r. Alsace Lorraine, has decent rooms. From the bus stop, with the tourist office on your right, go left on r. St-Yves and right on r. Alsace Lorraine. (☎02 98 27 00 10; fax 02 98 26 19 21. Breakfast 35F. Doubles 184-300F; 60-80F per extra person.)

CAMARET. The **Alignements de Lagatjar,** rocky monoliths believed to have been sun-worshiping sites from 2500 BC, are just a few minutes on D8 from Camaret by bike or foot (look for signs to the left of the Hôtel le Styvel). Behind them, the ruins of **Château de St-Pol Roux** afford a magnificent view of the bay. A path winds to the **Pointe de Penhir,** 3.5km away on D8. From the Camaret bus stop, take a left and backtrack to the **tourist office,** on your right. (☎02 98 27 29 49. Open June-Sept. M-W and F-Sa 10am-noon and 3-6pm.) **Hôtel Vauban,** 4 quai du Styvel, is right on the port. (☎02 98 27 91 36l; fax 02 98 27 96 34. Breakfast 30F. Reception open 24hr. Open Feb.-Dec. Singles or doubles with toilet and sink 160F, with shower 180-280F, with bathtub 250F. Extra bed 50F.) A **bus** connects Camaret to Crozon (4-6 per day, 11F).

MORGAT. From Crozon, you can walk or bike the 3km to Morgat, passing splendid **beaches** along the way, or take the infrequent Vedettes Armoricaines **shuttle.** To walk from the Crozon bus stop to Morgat, turn left onto r. St-Yves, right on r. Alsace Lorraine, and left on bd. de la France Libre. The **tourist office** is along this path on the right. (☎02 98 27 29 49. Open June-Sept. M-W and F-Sa 10am-noon and 3-6pm.) **Hikers** can take the 14km path along the cliffs overlooking the ocean from Morgat port to **Cap de la Chèvre** for ocean views. **Camping du Bouis** is 1.5km out of town on the way to the Cap. (☎02 98 26 12 53. Reception July-Aug. 8am-noon and 2-10pm; Easter-June and Sept. 10am-noon and 6:30-dinner. Open Easter-Sept. 35F, 2 people 68F; 15F per additional person.)

LOIRE VALLEY (VAL DE LOIRE)

Between Paris and Brittany is the fertile valley of the Loire, France's longest and most celebrated river. The valley seems to overflow with chateaux, ranging from dilapidated medieval fortresses to elegant Renaissance homes. Some date back to the 9th century, but most were built in the 16th and 17th centuries when French monarchs left Paris for the countryside around Tours to hunt and attend to state duties. **Tours** is the region's rail hub, although the chateaux Sully-sur-Loire, Chambord, and Cheverny aren't accessible by train. Infrequent public transit from larger cities can strand travelers. Train stations distribute the invaluable *Les Châteaux de la Loire en Train Eté* and *Châteaux pour Train et Vélo* with train schedules and bike and car rental info, which are the best ways to experience the region.

ORLÉANS

Fast-paced Orléans (pop. 200,000) is defined by Joan of Arc, the statues dedicated to her, and the nearby chateau. The stained-glass windows of the stunning **Cathédrale Ste-Croix,** in pl. Ste-Croix, depict Joan's dramatic story, from her liberation of the city to the flames that consumed her. (Open daily May-Sept. 9:15am-noon and 2:15-6pm; Oct.-Apr. 9:15am-noon and 2:15-5pm.) The **Musée des Beaux-Arts,** 1, r. Ferdinand Rabier, has a fine collection of Italian, Flemish, Dutch, and French works spanning the last five centuries. (Open Th-Sa 10am-6pm, Tu and Su 11am-6pm, W 10am-8pm. 20F, students 10F.) The **Maison de Jeanne d'Arc,** 3, pl. de Gaulle, off pl. du Martroi, celebrates the life and times of Orléans' favorite liberator. (Open Tu-Su May-Oct. 10am-noon and 2-6pm; Nov.-Apr. 2-6pm. 13F, students 6.50F.) A daytrip down the Loire lies the region's second-oldest castle, the imposing 14th-century fortress **Sully-sur-Loire,** accessible by bus from the bus station, 2, r. Marcel Proust, which is connected by an overpass to the Gare d'Orleans train station.

Trains arrive from: Blois (30min., 12 per day, 53-89F); Tours (1hr., 12 per day, 178F); and Paris (1¼hr., 3 per hr., 92F). To get to the **tourist office,** 6, pl. Albert 1er, from the station, ascend into the mall and turn right; it's on the left as you exit the mall. (☎02 38 24 05 05. Open July-Aug. M-Sa 9am-7pm, Su 9:30am-12:30pm and 3-6:30pm; Apr.-June and Sept. M-Sa 9am-7pm, Su 10am-noon; Oct.-Mar. M-Sa 9am-6:30pm, Su 10am-noon.) The **Auberge de Jeunesse (HI),** 1, bd. de la Motte, is in a beautiful old mansion between the highway and river. Take bus RS (dir. Rosette) or SY (dir. Concyr/La Bolière) from pl. d'Arc to "Pont Bourgogne"; head down bd. de la Motte; it will be at the end on the right. (☎02 38 53 60 03. Breakfast 21F. Sheets 16F. Reception 9am-noon and 5-10pm. 100F, under 26 70F.) **Carrefour,** in the back of the mall at pl. d'Arc, has **groceries.** (Open M-Sa 8:30am-9pm.) **Postal code:** 45000.

BLOIS

Blois (pop. 60,000) relishes its position as gateway to the Loire Valley and welcomes visitors with bucolic charm. Home to monarchs Louis XII and François I, Blois' **chateau** was the Versailles of the late 15th and early 16th centuries; today it houses museums. (Open daily July-Aug. 9am-8pm; mid-Mar. to June and Sept. 9am-6:30pm; Oct. to mid-Mar. 9am-12:30pm and 2-5:30pm. 35F, students 20F.) Although Blois has plenty of sights, the hilly streets and ancient staircases of its **vielle ville** (outlined in the tourist office's walking guide) may be more memorable.

Trains run to: Orléans (30min., 14 per day, 53F); Tours (1hr., 10 per day, 53F); and Paris (1¾hr., 8 per day, 123F), but not to most chateaux. **Point Bus,** 2, pl. Victor Hugo (☎02 54 78 15 66), sends buses to Chambord and Cheverny. Or, rent a **bike** from **Atelier Cycles,** 44, Levée des Tuileries (☎02 54 74 30 13), and pedal for an hour. The **tourist office,** 3, av. Jean Laigret, can point the way. (☎02 54 90 41 41; www.loiredeschateaux.com. Open mid-Apr. to mid-Oct. Su-M 10am-7pm, Tu-Sa 9am-7pm; mid-Oct. to mid-Apr. M 10am-12:30pm and 2-6pm, Tu-Sa from 9am.) Five kilometers west is the **Auberge de Jeunesse (HI),** 18, r. de l'Hôtel Pasquier. To get there from the tourist office, follow r. Porte Côté, then r. Denis Papin to the river, and take bus #4 (dir. Les Grouets) to the end. (☎/fax 02 54 78 27 21. Breakfast 19F. Reception 6:45-10am and 6-10:30pm. Lockout 10am-6pm. Curfew 10:30pm. Open Mar.-Nov. 15. 41F.) The rustic **Auberge de Jeunesse Verte (HI),** convenient for Chambord visitors, is 11km away in Montivault; take TLC bus #1 (dir. Beaugency). (☎02 54 20 56 78. Open July-Aug. 45F. **Camping** 27F.) **Hôtel du Bellay,** 12, r. des Minimes, at the top of porte Chartraine is next to the *centre ville*. (☎02 54 78 23 62. Breakfast 25F. Singles 130-170F; doubles 135-185F; triples 240F; quads 280F.) Sumptuous *pavé du roi* (chocolate-almond cookies) and *malices du loup* (orange peels in chocolate) entice pedestrians from *pâtisseries* along **r. Denis Papin.** For those who cling foolishly to the dinner-before-dessert convention, homespun restaurants line **r. St-Lubin, r. Drussy,** and **pl. Ploids du Roi,** near the cathedral. **Postal code:** 41000.

EXCURSIONS FROM BLOIS: CHAMBORD AND CHEVERNY. Built to satisfy François I's egomania, **Chambord** is the largest and most extravagant of the Loire chateaux. Seven hundred of François I's trademark stone salamanders are stamped throughout this "hunting lodge," whose 440 rooms kept him and his hounds warm with 365 fireplaces. A double-helix staircase dominates the castle's center. (Open daily July-Aug. 9am-6:45pm; Apr.-June and Sept. 9:30am-6:15pm; Oct.-Mar. 9:30am-5:15pm. 42F, under 26 26F.) Take TLC **bus** #2 from Blois (45min., 20F); hop on the TLC **Chambord-Cheverny bus circuit** (50-65F to both chateaux plus reduced admission); or **bike** from Blois (1hr.; take the D956 south 2-3km, then go left on the D33).

Cheverny, accessible by bus (see above) or bike from Blois (take the D956 south), showcases leather walls, Delft vases, and an elaborate royal bedchamber. (☎02 54 79 96 29. Open daily June to mid-Sept. 9:15am-6:45pm; Apr.-May 9:15am-noon and 2:15-6:30pm; late Sept. 9:30am-noon and 2:15-6pm; Mar. and Oct. 9:30am-noon and 2:15-5:30pm; Nov.-Feb. 9:30am-noon and 2:15-5pm. 38F, students 27F.)

AMBOISE

The battlements of the 15th-century chateau at **Amboise** stretch out protectively across the hill above the town. Two of the four kings who lived here also met their end here: Charles V tripped over a torchbearer and burned himself alive, and the equally clumsy, four-foot-tall Charles VIII bumped his head on a *really* low door and died a few hours later. Today, the jewel of the grounds is the late 15th-century **Chapelle St-Hubert;** a plaque inside marks **Leonardo da Vinci's** final resting place. (Open daily Apr.-June 9am-6:30pm; July-Aug. 9am-7:30pm; mid-Mar. and Sept.-Oct. 9am-6pm; Feb. to mid-Mar. and Nov. 9am-noon and 2-5:30pm; Dec.-Jan. 9am-noon and 2-5pm. 40F, students 33F.) After being invited to France by François I, Leonardo spent his last four years at **Clos Lucé** manor. Today, its main attraction is a collection of 40 of his inventions, built with the materials that would have been available during da Vinci's times. (Open daily July-Aug. 9am-8pm, Apr.-June and Sept.-Oct. 9am-7pm; Nov.-Mar. 9am-6pm; Jan. 10am-5pm. 38F, students 29F.)

Trains run from bd. Gambetta to: Tours (20min., 14 per day, 28F); Blois (20min., 15 per day, 34F); Orléans (1hr., 14 per day, 76F); and Paris (2¼hr., 5 per day, 140F). To reach the **tourist office,** on quai du Général de Gaulle, follow r. Jules-Ferry from the station and cross both bridges past the Île d'Or. (Open July-Aug., M-Sa 9am-8pm, Su 10am-noon and 3-6pm; Sept.-June M-Sa 9am-12:30pm and 2-6pm, Su 10am-noon.) The **Centre International de Séjour (HI) Charles Péguy,** on Ile d'Or, sits on an island in the middle of the Loire. (☎02 47 57 06 36. Breakfast 15F. Sheets 18F. Reception M-F 3-7pm. 50F.) **Postal code:** 35400.

TOURS

While Tours boasts fabulous nightlife and great food, it's best used as a base for its surrounding chateaux (see below). The **Cathédrale St-Gatien,** on r. Jules Simon, has dazzling stained glass. (Open daily 9am-7pm.) At the **Musée du Gemmail,** 7, r. du Murier, *gemmail*-works (in which shards of brightly colored glass and enamel are fused) by Picasso and Braque glow in rooms of dark velvet. (Open Easter-Oct. Tu-Su 10am-noon and 2-6:30pm; mid-Nov. to Easter Sa-Su 10am-noon and 2-6:30pm. 30F, students 20F.) **Trains** run to Paris (1-2¼hr., 6-7 per day, 160-261F) and Bordeaux (2½hr., 6 per day, 226F). The **tourist office,** 78/82, r. Bernard Palissy, books rooms and leads a historical tour. (☎02 47 70 37 37; fax 02 47 61 14 22. Open mid-Apr. to mid-Oct. M-Sa 8:30am-6pm, Su 10-12:30pm and 2:30-5pm; mid-Oct. to mid-Apr. M-Sa 9:30am-12:30pm and 1:30-6pm, Su 9:30am-12:30pm.) **Foyer des Jeunes Travailleurs,** 24, r. Bernard Palissy, is centrally located. (☎02 47 60 51 51. Meals 46F. Membership 20F. Singles 100F; doubles 160F.) **Hotel Regina,** 2, r. Pimbert, is near the happening r. Colbert. (☎02 47 05 25 36; fax 02 47 66 08 72. Singles 110-175F; doubles 140-240F.) **Pl. Plumereau** is your best bet for great restaurants, cafes, and bars. **Taverne de l'Homme Tranquille,** 22, r. du grande Marché, has tasty entrees in large portions. (Open daily noon-2pm and 7-10:30pm.) **Postal code:** 37000.

EXCURSIONS FROM TOURS: LOIRE CHATEAUX

Several companies offer **bus tours** of the Loire's chateaux, including: **Saint-Eloi Excursions** (☎02 47 37 08 04); **Touraine Evasion** (☎06 07 39 13 31); and **Sillione Val** (☎02 47 59 13 14). Half-day tours run 100-150F and full-day tours run 200-300F, excluding admission. Also consider renting a **car** or **bike. ADA,** 49, bd. Thiers (☎02 47 64 94 94), rents cars from 240F per day; **Amster Cycles,** 5, r. du Rempart (☎02 47 61 22 23), rents bikes from 80F the first day and 45 thereafter.

VILLANDRY. Villandry maintains fantastic **gardens** with waterfalls, vine-covered walkways, and over 120,000 plants, but the chateau itself is of less historical interest than its regal cousins. (☎02 47 50 02 09. Open daily June-Aug. 9:30am-7:30pm; Sept.-May 9am-dusk. 33F, students 22F.) Villandry is hard to get to; take the **train** from Tours to Savonnières (10min., 4 per day, 17F) and walk 4km along the Loire. **Cyclists** follow the D16, **drivers** take the D7.

LOCHES. The walled medieval town of Loches surrounds its grand chateau, which has two distinct structures at opposite ends of a hill. To the north, the 11th-century **donjon** (keep) and watchtowers went from keeping enemies out to putting them up when Louis XI turned it into a state prison, complete with suspended cages. To the north, the **Logis Royal** housed French kings from the 12th to 15th centuries. (Open daily July to mid-Sept. 9am-7pm; mid-Mar. to June and late Sept. 9:30am-1pm and 2:30-7pm; Feb. to mid-Mar. and Oct. 9:30am-1pm and 2:30-6pm. Joint ticket 32F, students 22F.) **Buses** run from the Tours train station to Loches (50min.; 4 per day; 47F, pay on board); nine **trains** also make the trip (1hr., 47F).

CHENONCEAU. A series of women designers created the exquisite beauty of Chateau Chenonceau, site of many a wild Renaissance party. The bridge over the river Cher that connects two sections of the chateau also marked the border between annexed and Vichy France during WWII. Chenonceau's beautiful setting makes it the most touristed of the chateaux. (☎02 47 23 90 07. Open mid-Mar. to mid-Sept. daily 9am-7pm; call for off-season hours. 50F, students 40F.) **Trains** from Tours roll into the station 2km away (45min., 3 per day, 36F). To reach the chateau from the station, cross the tracks, turn right, and follow the blue signs.

AZAY-LE-RIDEAU. Lounging on an island in the Indre, Azay-le-Rideau gazes peacefully at its reflection. Intended to rival Chambord in beauty, Azay succeeded so well that François I seized the chateau before its third wing was completed. Azay's flamboyant style is apparent in the ornate second-floor staircase. (☎02 47 45 42 04. Open daily July-Aug. 9am-7pm; Apr.-June and Sept.-Oct. 9:30am-6pm; Nov.-Mar. 9:30am-12:30pm and 2-5:30pm. 35F, under 26 23F. English audio guides 26F.) **Trains** run from Tours to Azay-le-Rideau town, 2km away (30min., 3 per day, 28F). **Buses** run from Tours' train station to the tourist office, 1km from the train station (45min.; M-Sa 3 per day, Su 1 per day; one-way 29F; pay on the bus).

ANGERS

From behind the massive stone walls of the 13th-century **Château d'Angers,** on pl. Kennedy, the Dukes of Anjou ruled the surrounding countryside and an island across the Channel (known today as Britain). Although Angers is dominated by a lively student population and vibrant pedestrian sector, its tradition as Europe's capital of tapestry remains strong. The 14th-century **Tapisserie de l'Apocalypse** within, the world's largest tapestry masterpiece, depicts the Book of Revelations. (Open daily June to mid-Sept. 9:30am-7pm; mid-Sept. to Oct. and Lent-May 10am-6pm; Nov.-Lent 10am-5pm. 35F, students 23F.) Angers' second woven masterpiece, the **Chant du Monde** ("Song of the World"), in the **Musée Jean Lurçat,** 4, bd. Arago, illustrates a symbolic journey through human destiny. (Open mid-June to mid-Sept. daily 9am-6:30pm and mid-Sept. to mid-June Tu-Su 10am-noon and 2-6pm. 20F.) The **Gallerie David D'Angers,** near the tourist office on 37bis, r. Toussaint, houses the magnificent 19th-century sculptor's work in the glass-topped **Toussaint Abbey.**

(Open mid-June to mid-Sept. daily 9am-6:30pm; mid-Sept. to mid-June Tu-Su 10am-noon and 2-6pm. 10F.) A 25F **ticket,** sold at the tourist office and museums, gives admission to five museums and the 50F *billet jumelé* includes chateau admission.

Trains roll from r. de la Gare to: Tours (1hr., 7 per day, 84F); Orléans (3-4hr., 6 per day, 166F); and Paris (2-4hr., 3 per day, 242F). **Buses** go from pl. de la République to Rennes (3hr., 2 per day, 97F). To get from the station to the **tourist office,** on pl. Kennedy, exit straight onto r. de la Gare, turn right on pl. de la Visitation onto r. Talot, turn left on bd. du Roi-René, and continue until you hit the plaza. (☎02 41 23 51 11; fax 02 41 23 51 66. Open June-Sept. M-Sa 9am-7pm, Su 10am-6pm; Oct.-May M-Sa 9am-12:30pm and 2-6:30pm.) To get to the **Centre d'Accueil du Lac de Maine (HI),** 49, av. du Maine, take bus #6 or 16 to "Accueil Lac de Maine," turn around and cross the street, and follow signs on the right-hand side. (☎02 41 22 32 10; fax 02 41 22 32 11. Breakfast included. Doubles 198F; quads 336F.) **Royal Hôtel,** on r. d'Iéna, off pl. de la Visitation, has spacious rooms and great decor. (☎02 41 88 30 25; fax 02 41 81 05 75. Breakfast 28-32F. Singles 110-210F; doubles 150-250F.) Cheap international food is available along **r. St-Laud.** Get **groceries** in the basement of **Galerie Lafayette,** at the corner of r. d'Alsace and pl. du Ralliement. (Open M-Sa 9am-7pm.) **Postal code:** 49052 (specify "Angers-Ralliement" for *Poste Restante*).

SOUTHWEST FRANCE

Caught between the wild Atlantic surf and the calm brilliance of the Mediterranean, southwestern France holds a hand of aces beneath its demure poker face. Gastronomes will delight in the wines of Bordeaux and the delicacies of Gascony, paleontologists will rejoice in the prehistoric surplus of Périgord, hikers will thrill at the vistas of the Pyrénées, and heat-seekers will find sun throughout the vast expanses of sand and surf on both coasts. The most geographically and culturally diverse of France's four corners, the Southwest is home to Basques in the west and Catalans in the east, both proudly guarding their ancient traditions.

PÉRIGORD AND AQUITAINE

The images of Périgord and Aquitaine are seductive: green countryside splashed with yellow sunflowers, white chalk cliffs, golden wine, and plates of black truffles. First settled 150,000 years ago, the area around Les Eyzies-de-Tayac has turned up more stone-age artifacts—tools, bones, weapons, cave paintings, and etchings—than any other place on earth.

PÉRIGUEUX

Encircled by the river Isle, Périgueux (pop. 37,700) preserves significant architecture in both the medieval-Renaissance and Gallo-Roman halves of the town. The city is also a good base for visiting local prehistoric caves. The *vieille ville* sports Renaissance architecture, and the multi-domed **Cathédrale St-Front** combines styles of several eras. (Open daily 8am-7:30pm.) The **Tour de Vésone** is a remarkable ruin; it was a *cella*, the holiest place and center of worship of a Roman temple. (Open daily Apr.-Sept. 7:30am-9pm; Oct.-Mar. 7:30am-6:30pm.)

Trains run to: Bordeaux (1½hr., 7 per day, 99F); Toulouse (4hr., 8hr., 177-184F); and Paris (4-6hr., 12 per day, 278F; change at Limoges). The **tourist office,** 26, pl. Francheville, has free walking tour maps. From the station, turn right on r. Denis Papin, bear left on r. des Mobiles-de-Coulmierts (which becomes r. du Président Wilson), pass r. Guillier (which leads to the Roman ruins), and take the next right. (☎05 53 53 10 63; fax 05 53 09 02 70. Open July-Aug. M-Sa 9am-7pm, Su 10am-6pm; Sept.-June M-Sa 9am-6pm.) To reach the beds of **Au Bon Coin/Chez Pierrot,** 8, r. Chanzy, turn right down r. Denis Papin after you cross the train station parking lot. (☎05 53 53 43 22. Breakfast 25F. Reception M-Sa. Singles and doubles 110-130F.)

From the train station, turn right onto r. Denis Papin, follow it as it becomes r. Chanzy, turn left on av. Cavignac, turn right down r. Emile, and then left to get to the **Foyer des Jeunes Travailleurs Résidence Lakanal,** off bd. Lakanal. (☎05 53 06 81 40. Breakfast included. Reception M-F 24hr.; closed Su 3-5pm. Dorms 73F; singles 80F.) **Monoprix supermarket** is on pl. de la République. (Open M-Sa 8:30am-8pm.) **Postal code:** 24070 (24017 for *Poste Restante*).

SARLAT

The golden medieval and renaissance buildings of Sarlat (pop. 10,700) have caught the eye of movie producers, as well as tourists—Gérard Depardieu's greatest cinematic *tour de force* before *My Father the Hero*, *Cyrano de Bergerac*, was filmed here. Today, its narrow 14th- and 15th-century streets fill with flea markets, dancing violinists, and purveyors of *gâteaux aux noix* (cakes with nuts) and golden Monbazillac wines. **Trains** go to Bordeaux (2½hr., 4 per day, 119F) and Périgueux (3hr., 1 per day, 75F). Stop by the **tourist office,** on pl. de la Liberté. (☎05 53 31 45 45. Open May-Sept. M-Sa 9am-7pm, Su 10am-noon and 2-6pm; Oct.-Apr. M-Sa 9am-noon and 2-6pm.) Sarlat's **Auberge de Jeunesse,** 77, av. de Selves, is 30 minutes from the train station but only 10 minutes from the *vieille ville.* Go straight along r. de la République (which becomes av. Gambetta), bear left at the fork onto av. de Selves. (☎05 53 59 47 59. Sheets 16F. **Camping** 35F. Open mid-Mar. to Nov. Reserve ahead. Dorms 50-55F.) **Champion supermarket** is near the hostel on rte. de Montignac; continue following av. de Selves away from the *centre ville.* (Open M-Sa 9am-7:30pm, Su 9am-noon.) **Postal code:** 24200.

EXCURSIONS FROM SARLAT AND PÉRIGUEUX: CAVE PAINTINGS. The most spectacular cave paintings yet discovered hide in the **caves of Lascaux,** near the town of **Montignac,** 25km north of Sarlat. Discovered in 1940 by a few teenagers and their dog, the caves were closed in 1963 after it was found that the oohs and aahs of millions of tourists had fostered algae and micro-stalactites, ravaging the paintings. **Lascaux II** duplicates every inch of the original cave, in the same pigments used 17,000 years ago. Although the reproduction may lack ancient awe and mystery, the caves—filled with paintings of five-meter-tall bulls, horses, and bison—nevertheless manage to inspire a wonder all their own. (Open May-Aug. daily 9am-7pm; Apr. and Sept.-Oct. Tu-Su 9am-6pm; Jan. 26-Mar. and Nov.-Jan. 4 Tu-Su 10am-12:30pm and 1:30-5:30pm. 50F.) The machine near the **tourist office** (☎05 53 51 96 23), on pl. Bertram-de-Born, sells tickets. Reserve a week or two ahead for the 45-minute tours (in French or English). One **bus** for Montignac leaves Périgueux each night (1½hr., 40F); two CFTA buses per day run each morning from Sarlat in July and August (30min., 27F) and return in early evening.

At the **Grotte de Font-de-Gaume,** 1km outside **Les Eyzies-de-Tayac** on the D47, 15,000-year-old horses, bison, and woolly mammoths line the cave walls. (☎05 53 06 86 00. Open Tu-Th Apr.-Sept. 9am-noon and 2-6pm; Mar. and Oct. 9:30am-noon and 2-5:30pm; Nov.-Feb. 10am-noon and 2-5pm. 35F, under 26 23F, art students free.)

EXCURSION FROM SARLAT: THE DORDOGNE VALLEY. Steep, craggy cliffs overlook the Dordogne River, 15km south of Sarlat. Numerous chateaux keep watch over tourists in canoes, on bikes, and in cars; by avoiding the major towns, it's also possible to find solitude. Ten kilometers southwest of Sarlat, the town of **Castelnaud-La Chapelle** snoozes in the shadow of its crumbling, pale-yellow-stone chateau, a fortress of the 12th to 15th centuries, and now the most visited castle in Aquitaine. **Domme,** the best-defended of the Dordogne Valley's villages, was built by King Philippe III (Philippe the Bold) in 1280 on a high dome of solid rock. *Chambres d'hôte* provide cheap farmhouse **accommodations** near the historic sites; ask at any tourist office for lists of *hôtes* and campgrounds. To get to and around the valley, you'll need to rent a car or be prepared for a good bike workout—the hills are steep but manageable. You can reach chateaux by **excursion buses** leaving Sarlat. **Hep!** (☎05 53 28 10 04), on pl. Pasteur, and **CFTA Périgord,** 21, r. de Cahors (☎05 53 59 01 48), run convenient but expensive **buses** each day.

BORDEAUX

Enveloped by emerald vineyards, Bordeaux (pop. 700,000) toasts the violet wine that made it famous. Not just a temple to wine connoisseurs, the city also has spirited nightclubs, a stunning opera house, and some of France's best food.

PRACTICAL INFO, ACCOMMODATIONS, AND FOOD. **Trains** depart for: Toulouse (2½hr., 11 per day, 165F); Paris (3½hr., 15-25 per day, 345F); and Nice (9½hr., 5 per day, 428F). From the train station, take bus #7 or 8 (dir. Grand Théâtre) to pl. Gambetta and walk toward the Monument des Girondins to the **tourist office,** 12, cours du 30 Juillet, which arranges winery tours. (☎05 56 00 66 00; fax 05 56 00 66 01; www.bordeaux-tourisme.com. Open May-Sept. M-Sa 9am-8pm, Su 9am-7pm; Oct.-Apr. M-Sa 9am-7pm, Su 9:45am-6pm.) **Wasteels,** 13, pl. de Casablanca opposite the station, sells BIJ tickets. (☎08 03 88 70 22. Open M-F 9am-noon and 2-7pm, Sa 9am-1pm and 2-6pm.) **American Express** is at 14, cours de l'Intendance. (☎05 56 00 63 36. Open M-F 8:45am-noon and 1:30-5:30pm.) Get **Internet** access at **A.E.C.,** in the Cité Mondiale off quai des Chartrons. (☎05 56 01 76 76. Open M-Th 2-6pm, F 2-5pm. Free, but limited to 1hr. per day.) **Postal code:** 33065.

Hôtel Boulan, 22, r. Boulan, welcomes backpackers with spic-and-span rooms. Take bus #7 or 8 to pl. Gambetta, follow r. Bouffard, and turn right onto r. Boulan. (☎05 56 52 23 62; fax 05 05 56 44 91. Breakfast 20F. Reception 24hr. Singles 101F, with shower 121F; doubles 112F, 142F. V, MC.) While it undergoes renovation, the **Auberge de Jeunesse (HI),** 22, cours Barbey, has a temporary hostel at 208, cours de l'Argonne, a 10-minute walk from pl. de la Victoire. At night, take bus #7 or 8 to pl. de la Victoire, then bus F, U, G, #20, or 21 and ask the driver to stop at the hostel. Call ahead. (☎05 56 91 59 51; fax 05 56 94 02 98. Sheets 18F. 3-day max. stay. 72F for first night, then 62F.) Young travelers flock to **Hôtel Studio,** 26, r. Huguerie. Walk one block down r. Georges Clemenceau from the pl. Gambetta, and half a block to the left on the r. Huguerie. (☎05 56 48 00 14; fax 05 56 81 25 71. Breakfast 20F. Internet 15F per hr. Singles 98-135F; doubles 120-160F; triples 180F.) **Hôtel la Boétie,** 4, r. de la Boétie, between pl. Gambetta and the Musée des Beaux-Arts, has rooms with TVs and showers. (☎05 56 81 76 68; fax 05 56 81 24 72. Singles 120F; doubles 135F.) Just opposite the train station are the clean rooms of **Hôtel Regina,** 34, r. Charles Domercq. (☎05 56 91 66 07. Open 24hr. Singles 145-205F; doubles 185-225F.)

Living in the *région de bien manger et de bien vivre* (region of fine eating and living), *Bordelais* take their food as seriously as their wine. Hunt around **r. St-Remi** and **pl. St-Pierre** for splendid regional specialties, including oysters, *foie gras*, beef braised in wine sauce, and *canelé de Bordeaux* (a cake created in 1519). Descend into the cool cellar of **Baud et Millet,** 19, r. Huguerie, off pl. Tourny, for all-you-can-eat cheese. (105F. Open M-Sa 9am-midnight. V, MC, AmEx.) The helpful English-speaking waitstaff at the elegant and romantic **La Casuccia,** 49, r. St-Rémi, serves French and Italian delicacies from 85F. (Open daily for lunch from 11:30am, for dinner 7pm-midnight. V, MC.) Stock up at **Auchan supermarket,** at the Centre Meriadeck on r. Claude Bonnier. (Open M-Sa 8:30am-10pm.) Locals buy their wine at **Vinothèque,** 8, cours du 30 Juillet. (Open M-Sa 9:15am-7:30pm.)

SIGHTS AND ENTERTAINMENT. Work your way into the center of town from the tourist office; start with the elaborate fountains of the **Monument aux Girondins,** commemorating French Revolutionary leaders from regions bordering the wide Gironde river for which they were named. Retrace your steps to the **Grand Théâtre,** on the other side of the tourist office, and watch a play, concert, or opera. (Tickets 35F, students 20F.) Follow r. Sainte Catherine from the pl. de la Comédie facing the theater to reach the stunning Gothic **Cathédrale St-André,** in pl. Pey-Berland. (Open daily Apr.-Oct. 7:30-11:30am and 2-6:30pm; Nov.-Mar. M-F 7:30-11:30am and 2-6:30pm. 25F, under 25 and seniors 15F.) Walking down the river along cours d'Alsace, turn left onto quai Richelieu and pass the 15th-century **Porte de Calihau,** on pl. de Palais, commemorating Charles VIII. Two blocks beyond lies the **place de la Bourse,** with pillars and fountains reflecting Bordeaux's grandeur. On the left, the

Musée National des Douanes traces the dangerous lives of customs officers. (Open daily Apr.-Sept. 10am-noon and 1-6pm; Oct.-Mar. M-Sa 10am-noon and 1-5pm. 20F, students and seniors 10F.) Turn left at the cours du Médoc for a wine-based conclusion to your tour. **Vinorama de Bourdeaux,** 12, cours du Médoc, is filled with elaborate dioramas and wine samples. (Open June-Sept. Tu-Sa 10:30am-12:30pm and 2:30-6:30pm, Su 2-6:30pm; Oct.-May Tu-F 2-6:30pm, Sa 10:30am-12:30pm and 2:30-6:30pm. 35F, 15F without tasting.) Or, make a trip to the **Maison du Vin/CIVB,** 1, cours du 30 Juillet, where you can sample—at a price—any of the bottles displayed at the bar. The two-hour "Initiation to Wine Tasting" course, available in English, explores wine evaluation methods through tasting some of the more outstanding vintages of the region. (Open M-Th 8:30am-6pm, F 8:30am-5:30pm.) Just 35km from Bordeaux are the **St-Émilion vineyards,** whose viticulters have been refining their techniques since Roman times. The **Maison du Vin de St-Émilion,** pl. Pierre Meyrat, offers a one-hour wine course focused on local wines. (Open Mar.-July and Sept.-Nov. M-Sa 10am-12:30pm and 2-6:30pm, Su 10am-12:30pm and 2:30-6:30pm; Aug. daily 10am-7pm; Dec.-Feb. daily 10am-12:30pm and 2:30-6pm. Wine course offered mid-July to mid-Sept. 11am; 100F.) **Trains** run from Bordeaux to St-Émilion. (30min., 2 per day, 66F. The only return is at 6:30pm.)

For an overview of Bordeaux nightlife, pick up a free copy of *Clubs and Concerts* at the tourist office, or purchase the biweekly magazine *Bordeaux Plus* (2F) at a magazine stand. **Chika Kafée,** 3, r. Duffour-Dubergier, attracts boisterous students with its dance floor, bar, and pool table. (Open M-Sa 9pm-2am.)

THE BASQUE COUNTRY

In the southwest corner of France and spilling into northern Spain and the Pyrénées, the Basque Country is home to the *Euzkadi*, or Basque, people. For millennia, since before the arrival the Celts in Europe, the Basques have lived in this triangle between the Pyrénées and the Atlantic, speaking a language that linguists are still at a loss to classify. Long renowned as fierce fighters, the Basques continue to struggle today, striving to win independence for their long-suffering homeland.

BAYONNE

Bayonne (pop. 43,000) is a grand port with small town appeal. The twin steeples of the 13th-century **Cathédrale Ste-Marie** needle the sky. (Open M-Sa 7am-noon and 3-7pm, Su 3:30-10pm.) Highlights of the **Musée Bonnat,** 5, r. Jacques Laffitte, in Petit-Bayonne, include works by Rubens, El Greco, and Goya. (Open W-M 10am-12:30pm and 2-6pm. 20F, students 10F.)

Trains (☎05 59 55 50 50) depart from the station, pl. de la République, to: Bordeaux (1½-2½hr., 9 per day, 130-189F); Toulouse (4hr., 5 per day, 190F); and San Sebastián, Spain (1½hr.; change at Hendaye). Trains run between Bayonne and Biarritz (10min., 10-22 per day, 12F), but the local **bus** network provides more comprehensive (and usually cheaper) regional transit. Local STAB buses depart from the Hôtel de Ville, running to Anglet and Biarritz (every 30-40min., last bus M-Sa 8pm, Su 7pm). Tickets cost 7.50F; packets of 10 cost 62F. The **tourist office,** on pl. des Basques, has maps and finds rooms. From the train station, take the middle fork onto pl. de la République, veer right over pont St-Esprit, pass through pl. Réduit, cross pont Mayou, turn right on r. Bernède (which becomes av. Bonnat), and turn left on pl. des Basques. (☎05 59 46 01 46; fax 05 59 59 37 55. Open July-Aug. M-Sa 9am-7pm, Su 10am-1pm; Sept.-June M-F 9am-6:30pm, Sa 10am-6pm.) Decent lodgings dot the area around the train station and pl. Paul Bert. The **Hôtel Paris-Madrid,** on pl. de la Gare, has cozy rooms and English-speaking owners. (☎05 59 55 13 98; fax 05 59 55 07 22. Breakfast 25F. Reception daily 6am-12:30am. Rooms 95-180F.) To get to **Camping de la Chêneraie,** take bus #1 from the station to Leclerc supermarket; catch the bus (5 per hr.) for the remaining 2km. (Reception Easter-June and Sept. 8:30am-noon and 5-7:30pm; July-Aug. 8am-10pm. 26F per person; 58F per tent or car.) Find groceries at **Monoprix supermarket,** 8, r. Orbe. (Open M-F 8:30am-7:30pm, Sa 8am-7:30pm.)

EXCURSION FROM BAYONNE: ST-JEAN-DE-PORT. The village of St-Jean-Pied-de-Port, historically an important crossroads for religious travelers, still hosts a continual procession of pilgrims on their way to Spain. Its narrow, cobblestone streets wind through the *haute ville* to a dilapidated fortress, offering ever-expanding views of rolling green hills and red-tiled roofs. **Trains** arrive from Bayonne (1hr., 5 per day, 47F). Rent **bikes** at **Garazi Cycles,** 1, pl. St-Laurent. (☎05 59 37 21 79. 120F per day, 150F per weekend. Passport deposit. Open M-Sa 8:30am-noon and 3-6pm.) From the station, turn right on av. Renaud, follow it up the slope until av. de Gaulle, and turn right to reach the **tourist office,** 14, av. de Gaulle. (☎05 59 37 03 57; fax 05 59 37 34 91. Open July-Aug. M-Sa 9am-12:30pm and 2-7pm, Su 10:30am-12:30pm and 3-6pm; Sept.-June M-F 9am-noon and 2-7pm, Sa 9am-noon and 2-6pm.)

BIARRITZ

Biarritz (pop. 29,000) is not a budget dream, but its free **beaches** make a daytrip *de luxe*—you too can sunbathe where Napoleon III, Bismarck, and Queen Victoria summered. At the **Grande Plage,** you'll find a wealth of surfers and bathers, and just to the north at the less-crowded **plage Miramar,** bathers repose *au naturel.* A short **hike** to **Pointe St-Martin** affords a priceless view. **BASC Subaquatique,** near Plateau de l'Atalaye (☎05 59 24 80 40), organizes **scuba** excursions in summer for 155F. **Trains** roll into **Biarritz-la-Négresse,** 3km out of town; hop on blue bus #2 (dir. Bayonne via Biarritz) or green bus #9 (dir. Biarritz HDV) to get to the *centre ville.* Or, get off the train in Bayonne and hop on STAB **bus** #1 or 2 to the central Hôtel de Ville (30min.). The **tourist office,** 1, sq. d'Ixelles, helps find accommodations and dispenses events listings. (☎05 59 22 37 10; fax 05 59 24 14 19. Open daily July-Aug. 8am-8pm; Sept.-June 9am-6:45pm.) The **Auberge de Jeunesse (HI),** 8, r. de Chiquito de Cambo, has a friendly staff and lakefront location. From the train station, turn left up the hill, left at the rotary, and follow r. de Movettes to the right; the hostel is across the street at the bottom of the hill. (☎05 59 41 76 00; fax 05 59 41 76 07. Breakfast included. Sheets 25F. Doubles 85F per person; triples and quads 76F.) **Hôtel Barnetche,** 5bis, r. Charles-Floquet, has homemade croissants for breakfast. (☎05 59 24 22 25; fax 05 59 24 98 71. Obligatory breakfast 35F; in Aug., obligatory half-pension 100F. Reception 7:30am-10:30pm. Open May-Sept. Doubles 170-360F; triples and quads 150F per person.) **Shopi,** 2, r. du Centre, off r. Gambetta, has **groceries.** (Open July-Aug. M-Sa 8:45am-12:25pm and 3-7:10pm, Su 8:45am-1pm; Sept.-June closed Su.)

EXCURSION FROM BIARRITZ: ST-JEAN-DE-LUZ. The vibrant seaport of St-Jean-de-Luz lures visitors with the **Maison Louis XIV,** pl. Louis XIV, which temporarily housed the Sun King. (Obligatory tours every 30min. Open July-Aug. M-Sa 10:30am-noon and 2:30-6:30pm, Su 2:30-6:30pm; Sept.-June closes 1 hr. earlier.) The village's earlier days of piracy funded its unique buildings, exemplified in the **Église St-Jean-Baptiste,** r. Gambetta, built to resemble a fishing boat. **Trains** roll in to bd. du Cdt. Passicot from Biarritz (15min., 10 per day, 17F) and Bayonne (30min., 7 per day, 26F). ATCRB **buses** (☎05 59 08 00 33), across from the train station, also run to Biarritz (7-13 per day, 18F) and Bayonne (7-13 per day, 23F). The **tourist office** is at Pl. Foch. (☎05 59 26 03 16; fax 05 59 26 21 47. Open July-Aug. M-Sa 9am-8pm, Su 10:30am-1pm and 3-7pm; Sept.-June M-Sa 9am-12:30pm and 2-7pm.)

GASCONY AND THE PYRÉNÉES

South of Aquitaine, the forests recede and the mountains of Gascony begin, shielded from the Atlantic by the Basque Country. Both Gascons and Basques are descended from the people the Romans called *Vascones.* They differ in that Gascony was more amenable to outside influences, and Gascons have long considered themselves French. Today, people come to Gascony to be healed; millions of believers descend on Lourdes hoping for miracle cures while thousands of others undergo scarcely more scientific treatments in the many *thermes* of the Pyrénées.

LOURDES

In 1858, 14-year-old Bernadette Soubirous saw the first of what would total 18 visions of the Virgin Mary in the Massabielle grotto in Lourdes (pop. 16,300). "The Lady" made a healing spring appear, and today five million rosary-toting faithful make pilgrimages here annually. To get from the tourist office to the **Caverne des Apparitions (La Grotte)** and the two **basilicas** above, follow av. de la Gare, turn left on bd. de la Grotte, and follow it across the river (10min.). **Processions** depart daily from the grotto at 5pm and 8:45pm from the **Basilica Pius the X,** an underground stadium-sized chamber. (Grotto open daily 5am-midnight. Dress modestly. Basilicas open daily Easter-Oct. 6am-7pm; Nov.-Easter 8am-6pm.)

Lourdes is accessible by **train** via Bayonne (2hr., 5 per day, 106F); Toulouse (2½hr., 8 per day, 125F); and Bordeaux (3hr., 7 per day, 182F). To get to the **tourist office,** on pl. Peyramale, from the station, turn right on av. de la Gare, bear left on av. Marasin, and look to the right (5min.). (☎05 62 42 77 40; fax 05 62 94 60 95; email lourdes@sudfr.com. Open May to mid-Oct. M-Sa 9am-7pm, Su 10am-6pm; mid-Oct. to mid-Mar. M-Sa 9am-noon and 2-6pm; daily mid-Mar. to Apr. 9am-12:30pm and 1:30-7pm, Su 10am-6pm.) To find the clean and comfortable **Hôtel Saint-Sylve,** 9, r. de la Fontaine, follow av. Helios away from the train station as it curves down the hill, bear left on r. du Callat, turn left onto r. Basse from bd. du Lapacca, and take your second right onto r. de la Fontaine. (☎/fax 05 62 94 63 48. Breakfast 25F. Shower 15F. Call ahead if arriving late. Open Apr.-Oct. Singles 75F, with shower 120F; doubles 140F, with shower 170F; triples 210F; quads 260F.) **Camping de la Poste,** 26, r. de Langelle, is just a few minutes from the center of town. (☎05 62 94 40 35. Shower 8F. Open Easter to mid-Oct. 15F per person; 21F per site.) Save a few francs by heading to **Prisunic supermarket,** 9, pl. du Champ-Commun. (Open M-Sa 8:30am-12:30pm and 2-7:30pm, Su 8am-noon.) **Postal code:** 65100.

CAUTERETS

Nestled in a breathtaking valley on the edge of the **Parc National des Pyrénées Occidentales** is tiny Cauterets. Most visitors come to take advantage of the hiking and skiing; for easy access to the mountains, ride the **Téléphérique du Lys** from the parking lot across from the *gare* (56F round-trip). Head to the **tourist office,** on pl. Foch, for info on sights in town. (☎05 62 92 50 27; fax 05 62 92 59 12; www.cauterets.com. Open daily July-Aug. 9am-7pm; Sept.-June 9am-12:30pm and 2-6:30pm.) For good **hiking info** and **maps,** head to **Parc National Office** (☎05 62 92 52 56), in Maison du Parc, on pl. de la Gare. **Skilys,** rte. de Pierrefitte (☎05 62 92 52 10), pl. de la Gare, has guides for hire and rents **bike, mountain,** and **ski equipment.** SNCF **buses** (Eurail valid) run from Lourdes to Cauterets (1hr., 6 per day, 39F). The rustic **Gîte d'Etape UCJG,** av. du Docteur Domer, is near the town center. From the Parc National Office, cross the parking lot and street, and turn left up the hill; the Gîte is just beyond the tennis courts. (☎05 62 92 52 95. Associated with the Protestant church, but open to all. Reception open daily; hours vary. Call ahead. 40-55F.) The covered **Halles market,** in the center of town on av. du Général Leclerc, has fresh produce. (Open daily 8:30am-12:30pm and 2:30-7:30pm.) **Postal code:** 65110.

EXCURSIONS FROM CAUTERETS: LUZ AND THE PYRÉNÉES. The **Parc National des Pyrénées** soothes with sulfur springs, frustrates with unattainable peaks, and awes visitors with mountain biking, hiking, and skiing opportunities. It is crucial to procure a good map before setting off on a trail. Pick up maps for intermediate hikes at sporting goods stores, or go to the friendly and helpful **Parc National Office** (see above), which has *Promenades en Montagne* maps (40F) of 15 different trails beginning and ending in Cauterets, all labeled with estimated duration (from 1hr. to 2 days) and difficulty. From Cauterets, the **Grand Randonée 10 (GR 10)** meanders across the Pyrénées, connecting to **Luz-St-Saveur** over the mountain and on to **Gavarnie,** another day's hike up the valley. Circling counterclockwise from Cauterets to Luz-St-Sauveur, the **Refuges Des Oulettes** (2152m) is the first shelter past the **Lac de Gaube,** which you can find on the IGN map. (☎62 92 62 97. Open

June-Sept. 80F.) Dipping into the **Vallée Lutour,** the **Refuge Estom** rests peacefully near **Lac d'Estom.** (In summer ☎05 62 92 72 93, off season ☎05 62 92 75 07. 60-70F.)

LANGUEDOC-ROUSSILLON

Languedoc and Roussillon, rugged lands with roots as much Spanish as French, have never been comfortable with Parisian authority. Once, an immense region called Occitania (today Languedoc) stretched from the Rhine to the foothills of the Pyrénées. Its people spoke the *langue d'oc*, not the *langue d'oïl* spoken in northern France, which evolved into modern French. The region was eventually integrated into the French kingdom, and the Cathar religion, popular among Occitanians, was severely persecuted by the Crown and Church. The *langue d'oc* faded, and in 1539, the *langue d'oïl* became official. Latent nationalism lingers on, however. Many speak Catalán, a relative of the *langue d'oc*, and look to Barcelona, rather than Paris, for guidance.

TOULOUSE

When all of France starts to look alike, rose-tinted Toulouse (pop. 350,000) provides a breath of fresh air with its eclectic architecture, squares, gardens, and fountains. Once a center for the bloody persecution of Protestants by the French kings—culminating in the St. Bartholomew's Day Massacre of 1572—today Toulouse is the prosperous capital of the French aerospace industry, and its economic prosperity is reflected in its clean streets and shining edifices.

PRACTICAL INFO, ACCOMMODATIONS, AND FOOD. **Trains** (☎08 36 35 36 15) head to: Bordeaux (2-3hr., 14 per day, 165F); Marseille (4½hr., 8 per day, 241F); Lyon (6½hr., 3-4 per day, 304F); and Paris (8-9hr., 4 per day, 365-498F). To reach the **tourist office,** at Donjon du Capitôle on r. Lafayette in sq. Charles de Gaulle, from the station, turn left along the canal, right on allée Jean Jaurès, bear right around pl. Wilson, and turn right on r. Lafayette; it's in a park near r. d'Alsace-Lorraine. (☎05 61 11 02 22; www.mairie-toulouse.fr. Open May-Sept. M-Sa 9am-7pm, Su 10am-1pm and 2-6:30pm; Oct.-Apr. M-F 9am-6pm, Sa 9am-12:30pm and 2-6pm, Su 10am-12:30pm and 2-5pm.) **Blodstation,** 42, r. Pargaminières, provides **Internet** access. (35F per hr. Open M-Sa noon-midnight, Su 2-8pm.)

To reach the spacious and well located **Hôtel des Arts,** 1bis, r. Cantegril, at r. des Arts near pl. St-Georges, take the Métro (dir. Basso Cambo) to "Pl. Esquirol"; follow r. du Metz away from the river, and turn left after three blocks. (☎05 61 23 36 21; fax 05 61 12 22 37. Breakfast 25F. Shower 15F. Reserve ahead. Singles 80-140F; doubles 125-160F; triples and quads 150-180F.) **Hôtel Beauséjour,** 4, r. Caffarelli, is just off allée Jean Jaurès. (☎/fax 05 61 62 77 59. Breakfast 23F. Showers 10F. Reception until 11pm. Singles and doubles 109-150F.) **Camp** at **Pont de Rupé,** 21, chemin du Pont de Rupé, at av. des Etats-Unis. Take bus #59 (dir. Camping) to "Rupé" or drive north on N20. (☎05 61 70 07 35. Laundry. 50F; 2 people 60F; 16F per additional person.) **Markets** line **pl. des Carmes, pl. Victor Hugo,** and **bd. de Strasbourg** (open Tu-Su 6am-1pm); inexpensive eateries cover **r. du Taur** and **pl. Wilson. Postal code:** 31000.

SIGHTS AND ENTERTAINMENT. Toulouse's most central monument, the **Capitole,** is a red-brick palace next to the tourist office. (Open M-F 8:30am-noon and 1:30-7pm, Sa-Su 10am-noon and 2-6pm. Free.) Just up r. du Taur from pl. du Capitole is the **Eglise Notre-Dame-du-Taur,** so named because it marks the spot where the priest Saturninus died in AD 250 after being tied to the tail of a wild bull by pagans. (Open daily July-Sept. 9am-6:30pm; Oct.-June 8am-noon and 2-6pm.) Continuing on r. du Taur leads to the **Basilique St-Sernin,** the longest Romanesque structure in the world; its **crypt** houses ecclesiastical relics gathered from Charlemagne's time. (Open July-Sept. M-Sa 9am-6:30pm, Su 9am-7:30pm; Oct.-June M-Sa 8:30-11:45am and 2-5:45pm, Su 9am-12:30pm and 2-7:30pm. Free. Tours 35F. Crypt 10F.) Backtrack to the pl. du Capitole, take a right on r. Romiguières, and turn left on r. Lakanal to get to the 13th-century **Les Jacobins,** an excellent example of the southern Gothic style. A modest crypt inside its **cloister** contains the ashes of St. Thomas Aquinas. (Open daily 9am-7pm. Cloister 14F.) Nearby on a side street off r. du Rome, the jumbled fragments of Toulouse's past come together at the **Musée de Vieux Toulouse,** 7, r. de May. (Open June-Sept. M-Sa 3-6pm. 10F, students 5F.) Retracing your steps back r. de Metz, which you'll arrive at the newly restored **Hôtel d'Assézat,** at pl. d'Assézat on r. de Metz, which houses the **Fondation Bemberg,** with an impressive collection of Bonnards, Dufys, Pisarros, and Gauguins. (Open Tu and F-Su 10am-6pm, Th 10am-9pm. 30F.) Toulouse has something to please almost any nocturnal whim, although nightlife is liveliest when students are in town. Numerous cafes flank **pl. St-Georges** and **pl. du Capitole,** and late-night bars line **r. St-Rome** and **r. des Filatiers.**

CARCASSONNE

Carcassonne (pop. 45,000) has had a rough go of it. Attacked at various times by Romans, Visigoths, and Moors, Europe's largest fortress has come to exemplify stalwart opposition in the face of the enemy. The backdrop for the movie *Robin Hood: Prince of Thieves* (1991), the *cité* is bombarded today—by tourists. Constructed as a palace in the 12th century, the **Château Comtal** was transformed into a citadel following submission to royal control in 1226. (Open daily June-Sept. 9am-7:30pm; Apr.-May and Oct. 9am-7pm; Nov.-Mar. 9:30am-5pm. 35F, under 26 23F.) In the *basse ville*, the **Cathédrale St-Michel,** r. Voltaire, has 14th-century fortifications. (Open M-Sa 7am-noon and 2-7pm, Su 9:30am-noon.) Although nightlife is limited, several bars and cafes along **r. Omer Sarraut** and **pl. Verdun** offer some excitement. For two weeks in early August, Carcassonne returns to the Middle Ages for the **Spectacles Médiévaux** (www.terredhistoire.com).

Trains (☎04 68 71 79 14) arrive behind Jardin St-Chenier from: Toulouse (50min., 24 per day, 74F); Nîmes (2½hr., 12 per day, 139F); Marseille (3hr., every 2hr., 201F); and Nice (6hr., 5 per day, 297F). Shops, hotels, and the train station are located in the *basse ville;* walk 30 minutes uphill or catch the *navette* in front of the station (every 30min.) to reach the *cité* or the campsite. To reach the **tourist office,** 15, bd. Camille Pelletan, pl. Gambetta, from the train station, walk over the canal on r. Clemenceau, turn left on r. de la Liberté, and right on bd. Jean Jaurès. (☎04 68 10 24 30; fax 04 68 10 24 38. Open daily July-Aug. 9am-7pm; Sept.-June 9am-12:15pm and 1:45-6:30pm.) The **Auberge de Jeunesse (HI),** on r. de Vicomte Trencavel, is in the middle of the *cité.* (☎04 68 25 23 16; fax 04 68 71 14 84. Breakfast included. Sheets 17F. Laundry 30F. Reception 24hr. Members only. 74F.) **Le Cathare,** 53, r. Jean Bringer, has cozy, bright rooms. (☎04 68 25 65 92. Breakfast 27F. English spoken. Singles and doubles 120-170F; triples 200F.) The region's speciality is *cassoulet* (a stew of white beans, herbs, and meat). On **r. du Plo,** 55-60F *menus* abound; try a dessert at one of the many outdoor *crêperies* in **pl. Marcou. Postal code:** 11000 (11012 for *Poste Restante*).

SOUTHEAST FRANCE

Heavy with the fragrance of lavender and wild herbs, the air in the southeast of France brings a piercing vitality to the landscape, a sense of eternal youth that today draws aging movie stars just as once it drew artists like van Gogh and Cézanne. A panacea for the weary traveler, southeastern France has it all, from some of the best skiing and hiking in the world to the most glamorous beach resorts, from unspoiled villages and natural parks to astoundingly well-preserved reminders of earlier ages.

PROVENCE

At the southern end of the Rhône River, where it cascades into the Mediterranean, lie the gorgeous Rhône Valley towns of Provence. From Arles's majestic Roman arena to the lively Festival d'Avignon to the lingering footsteps of Cézanne in Aix-en-Provence, rich cultural life abounds.

AVIGNON

The city of Avignon (pop. 100,000) has danced with cultural and artistic brilliance ever since it temporarily snatched the papacy away from Rome some 700 years ago. Film festivals, street musicians, and Europe's most prestigious theatrical gathering keep this university town shining. The massive 14th-century **Palais des Papes** is the largest Gothic palace in Europe, and hosts an annual art exhibition in May through September. (Open daily July-Sept. 9am-8pm; Apr.-June and Oct. 9am-7pm; Nov.-Mar. 9:30am-5:45pm. Palace or exhibition 46F; combined ticket 56F. Audioguide included.) During the **Festival d'Avignon,** a theater festival also known as the **IN** (early July-early Aug.), Gregorian chanters pull an all-nighter with *Odyssey*-readers and African dancers. (☎04 90 14 14 14 for tickets or info. Some ticketed events free, but others up to 200F. Reservations accepted from mid-June; 10F fee per ticket. Tickets also available 45min. before shows; 50% student discount.)

From the train station, walk through porte de la République onto cours Jean Jaurès to reach the **tourist office** at #41. (☎04 32 74 32 74; fax 04 90 82 95 03. Open Apr.-Sept. M-F 9am-6pm, Sa-Su 9am-1pm and 2-5pm; Oct.-Mar. 10am-noon; during festival M-Sa 10am-8pm and Su 10am-5pm.) Access the **Internet** at **Cyberdrome,** 68, r. Guillaume Puy. (50F per hr. Open M-Sa 8am-midnight, Su 2-10pm.) The **Foyer YMCA/UCJG,** 7bis chemin de la Justice, is across the river in Villeneuve. From the station, turn left and follow the city wall, cross the second bridge (pont Daladier), and turn left on chemin de la Justice (30min.). Or, take bus #10 (dir. Les Angles-Grand Angles) to "Général Leclerc" or bus #11 (dir. Villeneuve-Grand Terme) to "Pont d'Avignon." (☎04 90 25 46 20; fax 04 90 25 30 64; email ymca@avignon.com. Breakfast 25F. Reception daily 8:30am-6pm. Reserve ahead. 136-170F.) To get to **Foyer Bagatelle,** on Ile de la Barthelasse, follow the directions above, cross pont Daladier, and it's on the right (10min.); or, take bus #10 or 11 (same directions as above) to "La Barthelasse." (☎04 90 86 30 39; fax 04 90 27 16 23. Breakfast 20F. Dorms 65F; doubles 140F. **Camping** 18-24F per person, 10-16F per tent.) A **Codec supermarket** is on r. de la République. (Open M-Sa 8:30am-8pm.) **Postal code:** 84000.

NÎMES

Established as a Roman colony, Nîmes (pop. 135,000) is home to a durable textile once imported by Lévi-Strauss for Californian gold-diggers. Its name is a truncated form of the French phrase "de Nîmes" (from Nîmes): denim. The magnificent **Les Arènes** (Roman amphitheater) was built in the first century AD for gory animal and gladiatorial combats; it's open for visits, but the best way to experience it is to attend a bullfight or concert. (Open daily in summer 9am-6:30pm; off season 9am-5:30pm. 28F, students 20F.) The exquisitely sculpted **Maison Carré** (Square House) is actually a rectangular temple, built in the first century BC. (Open in summer daily 9am-noon and 2:30-7pm; off season 9am-12:30pm and 2-6pm. Free.) If you're tired or hot, head from the Maison down pl. Foch to the left along the canals to relax by the beautiful fountains of the **Jardins de la Fontaine,** which also house the Roman ruins of the **Temple de Diane** and the **Tour Magne.** (Garden and temple open Apr.-Sept. 15 daily 7:30am-10pm; Sept.16-Mar. 7:30am-6:30pm; Nov.-Mar. 8am-7pm. Free. *Tour* open July-Aug. daily 9am-7pm; Sept.-June 9am-5pm. 15F, students 12F.) Thirty minutes from Nîmes by bus is the Roman **Pont du Gard,** an aqueduct carrying water to Nîmes from the **Eure springs** near Uzès. The engineering masterpiece winds for 50km despite only a 17m total fall in altitude, and was completed without the use of mortar. **Buses** run to the Pont du Gard from Nîmes (30min., 2-5 per day, 31F).

Trains chug from bd. Talabot to: Arles (30min., 10 per day, 41F); Marseille (1¼hr., 6 per day, 96F); and Toulouse (3hr., 10 per day, 184F). **Buses** (☎04 66 29 52 00) depart behind the train station for Avignon (1½hr., 2-8 per day, 44F). To get from the stations to the **tourist office,** 6, r. Auguste, follow av. Feuchères, veer left around the park and clockwise around the arena, then head straight on bd. Victor Hugo; it's off pl. Comédie. (☎04 66 67 29 11; fax 04 66 21 81 04. Open May-June and Sept. M-F 8am-7pm, Sa 9am-7pm, Su 10am-6pm; July-Aug. M-F 8am-8pm, Sa 9am-7pm, Su 10am-6pm; Oct.-Apr. M-F 8:30am-7pm, Sa 9am-7pm, Su 10am-6pm.) The relaxed

Auberge de Jeunesse (HI), 257, chemin de l'Auberge de la Jeunesse, off chemin de la Cigale 4.5km from quai de la Fontaine, is far but newly renovated. Take bus #2 (dir. Alès or Villeverte) to "Stade, Route d'Alès" and follow the signs uphill; after the buses stop running, call for pickup. (☎04 66 68 03 20; fax 04 66 68 03 21. Sheets 17F. Breakfast 19F. 53F.) **Camping** is at Domaine de la Bastide, on rte. de Générac. (☎66 38 09 32. 45-50F. Caravan with electricity 65F per person.) Stock up at **Marché U supermarket,** 19, r. d'Alès, downhill from the hostel. (Open M-Sa 8am-12:45pm and 3:30-8pm.) **Postal code:** 30000 (30006 for *Poste Restante*).

ARLES

Roman ruins dot Arles (pop. 35,000), a Provence favorite. **Les Arènes,** the largest surviving amphitheater in France, and the **Théâtre Antique,** a ruined theater strewn with carved stone, are both still in use—the former for bullfights, the latter for plays. (Both 20F, students 15F.) The city's Roman past comes back to life in the ultramodern **Musée d'Arles Antique,** on av. de la 1ère DFL. (☎04 90 18 88 88. Open daily Mar.-Oct. 9am-7pm; Nov.-Feb. 10am-5pm. 35F, students 25F, children 5F.) **Les Alyscamps,** one of the most famous ancient burial grounds, is mentioned in *Dante's Inferno*. (☎04 90 49 36 87. From av. des Alyscamps, cross the tracks and follow the canal. Call for hours.) The calming courtyard of the **Cloître** (cloister) **St-Trophime** is a medieval gem. (20F, students 14F.) The passion of Arles' *corridas* (bullfights) lured Picasso here, while van Gogh spent two years (and an ear) in Arles; both have left enduring impressions (and post-impressions) on the city. *Arles et Vincent* (5F at the tourist office) explains the markers at the spots where van Gogh's easel once stood. The **Fondation Van Gogh,** 26, Rond-Point des Arènes, houses tributes to the master by artists, poets, and composers. (Open Apr.-Oct. 15 daily 10am-7pm; Oct. 16-Mar. Tu-Su 9:30am-noon and 2-5:30pm. 30F, students and children 20F.) The city celebrates **Fête d'Arles** in costume the last weekend in June and the first in July.

Trains roll to: Avignon (30min., M-Sa 21 per day, 36F); Nîmes (30min., M-Sa 15 per day, 41F); Marseille (1hr., M-Sa 8 per day, 71F); and Montpellier (1hr., M-Sa 15 per day, 75F). Next to the station, **buses** (☎04 90 49 38 01) depart for Nîmes (50min., M-Sa 5 per day, 35F) and Avignon (45min., M-Sa 5 per day, 43F). To get to the **tourist office,** on esplanade Charles de Gaulle at bd. des Lices, turn left from the station, walk to pl. Lamartine, turn left, and follow bd. Emile Courbes (10min.), then cross and turn right on bd. des Lices. (☎04 90 18 41 20; fax 04 90 18 41 29. Open Apr.-Sept. daily 9am-8:45pm; Oct.-Mar. M-Sa 9am-5:45pm, Su 10am-noon.) To get from the tourist office to the **Auberge de Jeunesse (HI),** on av. Maréchal Foch, cross bd. des Lices, walk down av. des Alyscamps, and follow the signs. (20min. from town. ☎04 90 96 18 25; fax 04 90 96 31 26. Breakfast included. Reception 7-10am and 5pm-midnight. Lockout 10am-5pm. Curfew 11:30pm, during festival 1-2am. Call ahead Apr.-June. First night 80F, additional nights 68F.) Or, try the **Hôtel Gauguin,** 5, pl. Voltaire (☎04 90 96 14 35; fax 04 90 18 98 87; breakfast 25F; singles and doubles 160-220F; triples 260F), and friendly **Hôtel Mirador,** 3, r. Voltaire (☎04 90 96 28 05; fax 04 90 96 59 89; breakfast 28F; singles and doubles with shower 190F). Take bus #2 from bd. des Lices (dir. Pont de Crau) to "Graveaux" to **Camping-City,** 67, rte. de Crau. (☎04 90 93 08 86. Open Apr.-Sept. 25F per person and per site, 18F per car.) **Monoprix supermarket** is on pl. Lamartine near the station. (Open M-Th and Sa 8:30am-7:30pm, F 8:30am-8pm.) Try cafes in **pl. du Forum** or **pl. Voltaire,** which has music on W in summer. **Postal code:** 13200.

EXCURSION FROM ARLES: THE CAMARGUE. Between Arles and the Mediterranean coast stretches the Camargue. Pink flamingos, black bulls, and the famous white Camargue horses roam freely across this flat expanse of protected wild marshland. Aspiring botanists and zoologists should stop at the **Centre d'Information de Ginès** along D570, which distributes info on the region's unusual flora and fauna. (☎04 90 97 86 32. Open Apr.-Sept. daily 9am-6pm; Oct.-Mar. Sa-Th 9:30am-5pm.) Next door, the **Parc Ornithologique de Pont de Gau** provides a sanctuary for birds of prey and flamingos. (☎04 90 97 82 62. Open daily Apr.-Sept. 9am-dusk; Oct.-Mar. 10am-dusk. 35F, children 18F.) The best way to see the Camargue is on **horse-**

back; call the **Association Camarguaise de Tourisme Equestre** for more info. (☎04 90 97 86 32. 80F per hr., 200-230F per 3hr., 350F per day.) Wear long pants and sturdy shoes. **Jeep safaris** (☎04 66 53 04 99; 200F per 2hr., 220F per 4hr.) and **boat trips** (☎04 90 97 84 72; 1½hr., 60F) are also options. **Bicycle touring** is a great way to see the area, although trails may be difficult; **trail maps** indicating length, difficulty, and dangerous spots are available from the Les Stes-Maries-de-la-Mer **tourist office,** 5, av. Van Gogh (☎04 90 97 82 55). From Arles, take a **bus** (dir. Stes-Maries-de-la-Mer) to "Pont du Gau" (1hr., 7 per day, 36.50F). Contact **Les Cars de Camargue** (☎04 90 96 36 25) for more info.

AIX-EN-PROVENCE

Famous for its festivals and fountains, Aix (pronounced "X"; pop. 150,000) panders to tourists without being spoiled by them. Once home to artists such as Paul Cézanne, Victor Vasarely, and Emile Zola, today a large student population keeps the city on the cultural cutting edge. The **Chemin de Cézanne,** on 9, av. Paul Cézanne, features a self-guided walking tour devoted to the artist, and includes sites like his studio. (Open daily Apr.-Sept. 10am-noon and 2:30-6pm; Oct.-Mar. 10am-noon and 2-5pm. 25F, students 10F.) The **Fondation Vasarely,** on av. Marcel-Pagnol in quartier du Jas de Bouffan, designed by artist Victor Vasarely, is a must-see for modern art fans. (Open in summer M-F 10am-1pm and 2-7pm, Sa-Su 10am-7pm; off season 9:30am-1pm and 2-6pm. 35F, students 20F.) **Cathédrale St-Sauveur,** on r. Gaston de Saporta, is a dramatic melange of Romanesque, Gothic, and Baroque carvings and reliefs. (Open daily 8am-noon and 2-6pm.) Aix's **International Music Festival,** June through July, features operas and concerts. (☎04 42 17 34 34. Tickets 100-350F. Reserve months early for a good seat.) Aix also hosts a two-week **Jazz Festival** beginning in early July (tickets 80-150F) followed by a two-week **Dance Festival** (tickets 80-150F, students 60-120F). The **Office des Fêtes et de la Culture** (☎04 42 96 27 79), on Espace Forbin, 1, pl. John Rewald, has festival info. Partying is a year-round pastime in Aix. Bars line the **Forum des Cardeurs,** behind the Hôtel de Ville. **Le Scat,** 11, r. Verrerie (☎04 42 23 00 23), has a pub, club, and live music. (Open M-Sa after 11pm. Concerts 80F.) **Bistro Aixois,** 37 Cours Sextius (☎04 42 27 50 10), off la Rotonde, packs students and bands. (Open daily 6:30pm-3 or 4am. V, MC.)

Trains (☎08 36 35 35 35), at the end of av. Victor Hugo, run almost exclusively to Marseille (35min., 21 trains a day, 38F). **Buses** (☎04 42 91 26 80), Av. de l'Europe, run to Marseille (30min., every 10min., 26F) and Avignon (2hr., 4 per day, 80F). From the train station, follow av. Victor Hugo (bear left at the fork) until it feeds into La Rotonde. On the left is the **tourist office,** 2, pl. du Général de Gaulle, which books rooms for free, sells a city museum pass (40F), and has city maps and useful guides like "Bienvenue." (☎04 42 16 11 61. Open July-Aug. M-Sa 8:30am-10pm, Su 10am-1pm and 2-6pm; Sept.-Jun. M-Sa 8:30am-7pm, Su 10am-1pm and 2-6pm.) You can surf the **Internet** at **Hublot Cyber Cafe,** 17, r. Paul Bert. (☎04 42 21 37 31. 45F per hr., 25F 7-8pm. Open M-F 9am-8pm, Sa-Su 10am-8pm.) To get to the **Auberge de Jeunesse (HI),** 3, av. Marcel Pagnol, in quartier du Jas de Bouffan, follow av. de Belges from La Rotonde, turn right on av. de l'Europe, bear left at the first roundabout after the overpass, climb the hill, and it's on the left (35min.). Or, take bus #4 (bus A on weekends; every 15-30min. until 8pm; 7F) from La Rotonde to Vasarely. (☎04 42 20 15 99. 69F. Breakfast included. Sheets 11F. Laundry 35F. Reception before noon or after 5pm. Lockout 9:30am-4pm. Midnight curfew. No kitchen.) **Hôtel des Arts,** 69, bd. Carnot, has compact modern rooms with showers, toilets, TVs, and phones. (☎04 42 38 11 70. Singles and doubles 149-205F. V, MC.) To **camp** at **Arc-en-Ciel,** on rte. de Nice, take bus #3 from La Rotonde to Trois Sautets. (☎04 42 26 14 28. Pool and hot showers. 35F per person, 31F per tent.) Restaurants abound in Aix; eating on the cours Mirabeau is more expensive than in the pl. des Cardeurs and pl. Ramus. Try **markets** on pl. de la Madeleine (open Tu, Th, and Sa 7am-1pm) and pl. Richelme (open daily 7am-1pm) to save money without skimping on taste. Stock up at **Casino supermarket,** 3, cours d'Orbitelle (open M-Sa 8am-1pm and 4-8pm), and 1, av. de Lattre de Tassigny (M-Sa 8:30am-8:30pm). **Postal code:** 13100.

FRENCH RIVIERA (CÔTE D'AZUR)

Paradises are made to be lost. Between Marseille and the Italian border, the sun-drenched beaches and warm waters of the Mediterranean form the backdrop for this fabled playground of the rich and famous—F. Scott Fitzgerald, Cole Porter, Picasso, Renoir, and Matisse are among those who flocked to the coast in its heyday. The area today is crammed with as many low-budget tourists as high-handed millionaires, but the Riviera's seductive loveliness has been its undoing, as shrewd developers have turned the coast's beauty into big business. Many French condemn the Riviera as a mere shadow of its former self.

Every woman who has traveled on the Riviera has a story to tell about men in the big beach towns. Unsolicited pick-up techniques range from subtle invitations to more, uh, bare displays of interest. Brush them off with a biting *"laissez-moi tranquille!"* ("leave me alone") or stony indifference, but don't be shy about enlisting the help of passersby or the police to fend off Mediterranean Don Juans.

MARSEILLE

France's third-largest city, Marseille (pop. 900,000) is like the *bouillabaisse* soup for which it is famous: steaming hot and pungently spiced, with a little bit of everything mixed in. A mix of wild nightclubs, beaches, islands, gardens, and big-city adventure, Marseille bites its thumb at the manicured nails of Monaco and displays a rare and astounding cultural melange along with gritty urban intensity.

PRACTICAL INFO, ACCOMMODATIONS, AND FOOD. **Trains** (☎08 36 35 35 35) run to: Nice (2¾hr., every hr., 149F); Lyon (3½hr., 9 per day, 209F); and Paris (4¾hr., 12 per day, 413F). **Buses** (☎04 91 08 16 40) serve: Aix-en-Provence (5 per hr., 25F); Avignon (2hr., 5 per day, 89F); Cannes (2¼-3hr., 4 per day, 122F); Nice (2¾hr., 4 per day, 136F); and Arles (2-3hr., 7 per day, 85F). **SNCM,** 61, bd. des Dames (☎08 36 67 95 00), runs **ferries** to Corsica (640-720F round-trip, students 12% discount) and Sardinia (750-850F). The **tourist office,** 4, La Canebière, offers free maps and accommodation services. (☎04 91 13 89 00. Open July-Aug. daily 9am-8pm; Oct.-June M-Sa 9am-7pm, Su and holidays 10am-5pm.) The tourist office **annex** is at the train station. (☎04 91 50 59 18. Open July-Aug. daily 10am-5pm; Sept.-June M-F 10am-1pm and 1:30-5pm.) Access the **Internet** at **InfoCafe,** 1, quai Rive Neuve. (35F per hr. Open M-Sa 9am-11pm, Su 2-7pm.) **Hôtel du Palais,** 26, r. Breteuil, has large, redone rooms. From the *vieux port,* head down quai des Belges, which turns into cours J. Ballard and then r. Breteuil. (☎04 91 37 78 86. Breakfast 30F. Singles with shower 195F; doubles 230-280F; triples with bath 300F. V, MC.) To reach the **Auberge de Jeunesse Bonneveine (HI),** on impasse Bonfils off av. J. Vidal, take metro line #2 to "Rond-Point du Prado," and transfer onto bus #44 to pl. Bonnefon. Walk toward the rond-point, turn left at J. Vidal, and turn onto impasse Bonfils after #47. (☎04 91 17 63 30. Breakfast included. Sheets 17F. Lockers 10F per day. Reception daily 6am-1am. Closed Jan. 72F in summer, 69F in spring, 65F in winter; doubles 93F. V, MC.) **Hôtel Béarn,** 63, r. Sylvabelle, has spacious rooms. (☎04 91 37 75 83. Breakfast 25F. Singles with shower 104F; doubles 138F; triples 262F. V, MC.) For the diverse dining scene, poke around the *vieux port,* especially **pl. Thiars** and the **cours Estienne d'Orves,** where meals come for 60F; the city's trademark *bouillabaisse* is available there for a decent price. North African restaurants cluster in the *quartiers* around the **Canebière,** and offer dishes for 40F. Head up to **cours Julien,** northeast of the harbor, for a more artsy crowd and cheap fare. **Ce Soleil Donne,** 70, cours Julien, has exotic dishes like kangaroo and pineapple for 59F, and attracts a young clientele. You can pick up **groceries** at **BAZE supermarket,** on La Canebière. (Open M-Sa 8:30am-8pm.) **Postal code:** 13001.

SIGHTS AND ENTERTAINMENT. To truly experience Marseille, wander through its diverse collection of neighborhoods. **La Canebière** separates the city into north and south, funneling into the *vieux port* to the west and becoming bland urban sprawl to the east. North of the *vieux port* and west of bd. République, working-class residents of varied ethnicities pile onto the hilltop neighborhood of **Le Panier,** where the original Greek city stood. East of Le Panier, the dilapidated buildings of the **Belsunce Quarter** (between cours Belsunce and bd. Athens) houses the city's Arab and African communities; this area is not safe at night. East of the *vieux port*, **rues de Rome, St-Ferreol,** and **Paradis** and nearby squares contain large shops and upscale restaurants. Past r. de Rome near La Canebière, narrow streets teem with peerless intensity in the colorful African markets. Farther southeast, **cours Julien** is a funky neighborhood whose book and music stores and eclectic restaurants converge to create a distinct counterculture feel. After exploring Marseille's neighborhoods, follow r. Breteuil from the *vieux port*, turn right on bd. Vauban, and turn right again on r. Fort du Sanctuaire to reach the majestic 19th-century **Basilique de Notre Dame de la Garde;** the battle-scarred church offers a beautiful view of the city and holds a golden statue of the Madonna known as "the good mother." (Open daily in summer 7am-8pm; off season 7am-7pm. Free.) The imposing **Abbaye St-Victor,** on r. Sainte at the end of quai de Rive Neuve, holds eerie catacombs as well as pagan and Christian relics. (Open daily 8:30am-6:30pm. Crypts 10F.) **Musée Cantini,** 19, r. Grignan, exhibits memorable art from Fauvism to the present-day. (Open Tu-Su June-Sept. 11am-6pm; Oct.-May 10am-5pm. 15-20F, students half-price, over 65 or under 10 free.) Bus #83 ("Rond Pont du Prado") from the *vieux port* runs to Marseille's **beaches;** get off just after the statue of David (25min.). Nightlife centers around cours Julien and pl. Thiers. **Trolleybus,** 24, quai de Rive Neuve, is a megaclub with a discotheque built around two boule-courts. (Cover Sa 60F, including one drink. Open in summer W-Sa 11pm-7am, off season Th-Sa 11pm-7am.)

ST-TROPEZ

Nowhere does the sparkling glitz and glamour of the Riviera shine more than in St-Tropez. While other towns along the coast cling to past glories, *St-Trop d'Aise* (St. Too-Much-Luxury) religiously devotes itself to the holy trinity of sun, sand, and big boats. The free **navette municipale** leaves from pl. des Lices four times per day to **Les Salins,** a secluded sunspot, and **plage Tahiti** ("Capon-Pinet"), the first of the popular **plages des Pampelonne.** A break from your tan, **La Musée de l'Annonciade,** pl. Grammont, houses the stunning Fauvist and neo-Impressionist paintings that first brought St-Tropez fame. (Open W-M June-Sept. 10am-noon and 3-7pm; Oct. and Dec.-May 10am-noon and 2-6pm. 30F, students 15F.)

Les Bateaux de St-Raphaël **ferries,** at the *vieux* port, sail in to St-Tropez from St-Raphaël. (☎04 94 95 17 46. 50min; 2-5 per day; 70F, round-trip 110F.) Sodetrav **buses** leave from av. Général Leclerc for St-Raphaël. (☎04 94 97 88 51. 2hr., 8-15 per day, 51F.) The **tourist office,** on quai Jean Jaurès, has schedules of the *navette municipale* and a *Manifestations* guide that lists local events. (☎04 94 97 45 21; fax 04 94 97 82 66. Open June-Sept. M-F 8:30am-11pm; May and Oct. daily 9am-8pm.) Budget hotels do not exist in St-Tropez, and the closest youth hostel is in Fréjus. **Camping** is the cheapest option, but you'll need reservations. Try **Les Prairies de la Mer,** Port Grimaud, which you can reach by a ferry (30F, 55F round-trip) that goes to St-Tropez 15 minutes before every hour. (Open Apr.-Oct. July-Aug. Person and tent 82F, two people 84F, with car 115F; Apr.-June and Sept.-Oct. 23F lower.) The **vieux port** and the streets behind the waterfront are the hub of culinary activity. To be charmingly rustic and do it yourself, duck into **Prisunic supermarket,** 7, av. du Général Leclerc. (Open in summer M-Sa 8am-8pm, Su 8:30am-8pm; off season M-Sa 8am-8pm.) In summer, restaurant-bar **Bodega de Papagayo,** on the old port, and nightclub **Le Papagayo** are magnets for tanned youth. (Cover 100F. Open W-M.)

ST-RAPHAËL AND FRÉJUS

The twin cities of St-Raphaël and Fréjus may not have trendy boutiques like St- Tropez, but they still enchant visitors with an unpretentious ambiance, sunny beaches, and a rich history. In **St-Raphaël,** the **boardwalk** turns into a carnival; golden **beaches** stretch along the coast, and the first weekend in July brings the **Competition International de Jazz New Orleans** (☎04 98 11 89 00). In Fréjus, the **Roman amphitheater,** on r.

Henri Vadon, holds rock concerts and bullfights. The **Musée Archeologique Municipal,** on pl. Calvini, has a stunning sculpture. (Open M and W-Sa Apr.-Oct. 10am-1pm and 2:30-6:30pm; Nov.-Mar. 10am-noon and 1:30-5:30pm. Free.) The **Fréjus Episcopal Buildings,** on pl. Formige, contain spectacular detailed cloisters. (Open Tu-Su Apr.-Sept. 9am-7pm; Oct.-Mar. 9am-noon and 2-5pm. 25F.)

St-Raphaël sends **trains** every 30 minutes to Cannes (25min., 34F) and Nice (50min., 56F). **Buses** leave from behind the train station in St-Raphaël for: Fréjus (20min., every 30min., 8.50F); Cannes (70min., 8 per day, 34.50F); and Nice (1¼hr., 1 per day, 15 per day, 51F). The **tourist office** in St-Raphaël is opposite the train station. (☎04 94 19 52 52; fax 04 94 83 85 40. Open daily June-Sept. 9am-7pm; Oct.-May M-Sa 9am-12:30pm and 2-6:30pm.) To reach **Le Touring,** 1, quai Albert 1er, take your third right after the station. (☎04 94 95 01 72; fax 04 94 95 86 09. Closed mid-Nov. to mid-Dec. Ask for the 150F economy single. Singles and doubles with one bed 190-300F; triples 420F.) In Fréjus, take av. du 15ème Corps d'Armée from the tourist office, then turn left on chemin de Councillier after the next roundabout to reach the **Auberge de Jeunesse de St-Raphaël-Fréjus (HI),** chemin du Councillier. From St-Raphaël, a shuttle bus (8.50F) leaves quai #7 of the bus station for the hostel at 6pm. (☎04 94 52 93 93; fax 04 94 53 25 86. Breakfast included. Sheets 17F. Lockout 10am-6pm. Curfew 11:30pm. 67F; châtelet 82F.) St. Raphaël's **Monoprix supermarket** is on 14, bd. de Félix Martin, off av. Alphonse Karr near the train station. (Open M-Sa 8:30am-7:30pm.) **Postal codes:** St-Raphaël 83700; Fréjus 83600.

CANNES

Classic Riviera images materialize in Cannes (pop. 78,000), a favorite stopover for the international jet set. Less exclusive than St-Tropez, Cannes still allows even ungroomed budget travelers to tan like the stars. In May, the spotlights turn on and the red carpets roll out for the **Festival International du Film,** which imports Hollywood's *crème de la crème.* None of the festival's 350 screenings are open to the public, but the sidewalk show is free. The best window-shopping along the Riviera lies along **r. d'Antibes** and **bd. de la Croisette.** Farther west, the **Castre Cathédrale** and its courtyard stand on the hill on which *vieux Cannes* was built. Of Cannes' three **casinos,** the most accessible is **Le Casino Croisette,** 1, jetée Albert Eduoard, next to the Palais des Festivals, with slots, blackjack, and roulette. (Gambling daily 7:30pm-4am; open for slots at 10am. No shorts, jeans, or t-shirts. 18+.) See live blues and Irish folk music at **Morrison's,** 10, r. Teisseire, a rowdy Irish pub. (Beer from 18F. Music starts at 10pm. Open 5pm-2:30am.) Dance until dawn at **Jane's,** 38, r. des Serbes, in the Hôtel Gray d'Albion. (Cover and 1 drink Th and F before midnight 50F, Sa-Su 100F; Su women free.) **Whisky à Go Go,** 115, av. de Lérins, revs it up nightly by Palm Beach (100F; open F-Sa 11pm-dawn); look nearby for the popular **Mocambo,** which sets up during July and August.

Coastal **trains** run every 30 minutes to: St-Raphaël (25min., 34F); Antibes (15min., 14F); Nice (35min., 32F); and Monaco (1hr., 46F). Hourly trains run to Marseille (2hr., 6:30am-11:05pm, 133F). TGV trains go to Paris via Marseille (450-540F). The **tourist office,** 1, bd. de la Croisette, has maps and guides. (☎04 93 39 24 53; fax 04 92 99 84 23. Open daily July-Aug. 9am-6pm; Sept.-June M-F 9am-7pm, Sa-Su 9am-6pm.) **La centrale de reservation** (☎04 97 06 53 07) arranges **hotel reservations.** Access the **Internet** at **Cyber-Cafe Institut Riviera Lanuge,** 26, r. de Mimont. (10F per 15min.; 35F per hr. Open M-Sa 9am-11pm, Su 2-11pm.) Plan accommodations in advance; for the film festival, you'll need to book at least a year in advance and pay triple the rate. **Centre International de Séjour de Cannes (HI),** 35, av. de Vallauris, has 6-bunk dorms in a sunny mansion. Avoid the underground passageway from the station at night; instead, turn left on bd. Jean Jaures, left on bd. de la République, and right on av. de Vallauris. (☎/fax 04 93 99 26 79. First breakfast free, then 10F. Laundry 25F. Reception daily 8am-1pm and 3-11:30pm. Curfew 2am. Sept.-Apr. 70F; May-Aug. 80F.) As you exit the station, turn right on bd. Carnot, right on av. 11 November, and left onto av. Galliéni to reach **Auberge de Jeunesse—Le Chalit,** 27, av. Maréchal Galliéni. (☎/fax 93 99 22 11. Sheets 17F. Reception daily in summer 8:30am-1pm and 5-8pm; in winter 9am-noon and 1-8pm. Lockout 10:30am-5pm. Cancel 2 days in advance. Dorms 90F.) To reach **Hôtel Mimont,** 39, r. de

Mimont, turn left on bd. de la République from the station, and turn left on r. de Mimont. Modern, clean rooms with showers and TV. (☎04 93 39 51 64; fax 04 93 99 65 35. Breakfast 30F. Reception daily 7:30am-11pm. Singles 170F, with toilet 190F; doubles 220F, 230F; triples 295F. Extra person 65F. V, MC, AmEx.) **Camp** at **Le Grand Saule,** 24, bd. Jean Moulin, in nearby Ranguin; take bus #9 (dir. Grasse; 7.70F) from pl. de l'Hôtel de Ville. (☎04 93 90 55 10. Apr.-May, June, and Sept. 60F for one person, 92F for two people and tent, car 19F; July-Aug. 80F for one person, 170F for two people and tent, 19F extra for car.) Save your francs at **Champion supermarket,** 6, r. Meynadier. (Open M-Sa in summer 8:45am-7:40pm; off season 9am-7:30pm.) Reasonably priced restaurants abound in the pedestrian zone around **r. Meynadier. Postal code:** 06400.

ANTIBES-JUAN-LES-PINS

Although joined as one in the city of Antibes-Juan-les-Pins (pop. 70,000), Antibes and Juan-les-Pins are 3km apart and use separate train stations and tourist offices.

ANTIBES. More serene than Nice, **Antibes** is clean and pleasant, with sandy beaches and interesting museums. Lately, Antibes has been inundated with young, globe-trotting "yachtees" looking for lucrative work—a phenomenon that has helped turn the city into an increasingly popular beach town. After lounging in the sun, visitors can retreat to the charming *vielle ville.* The **Musée Picasso,** in the Château Grimaldi on pl. Mariejol, displays works by the master and his contemporaries. (Open Tu-Su June-Sept. 10am-6pm; Oct.-May 10am-noon and 2-6pm. 30F, students 18F.) **Trains** leave from av. Robert Soleau for: Cannes (30min., every 30min., 14F); Nice (30min., every 30min., 22F); and Marseille (2½hr., 15 per day, 139F). Exit the station, turn right on av. Robert Soleau, and follow the "Maison du Tourisme" signs to the **tourist office,** 11, pl. de Gaulle. (☎04 92 90 53 00. Open July-Aug. daily 8:45am-7:30pm; Sept.-June M-F 9am-12:30pm and 2-6pm, Sa 9am-noon and 2-6pm.) To get to the **Hôtel Jabotte,** 13, av. Max Maurey, follow bd. Albert 1*er* from pl. de Gaulle to its end, turn right on Maréchal Leclerc, and walk along the beach for 10 minutes; or, take the *bus gratuit* (free), which leaves every hour and stops at the beach. (☎04 93 61 45 89; fax 04 93 61 07 04. Breakfast 30F. Singles and doubles 200-400F; triples 350-550F; quads 620-820F.) **Postal code:** 06600.

JUAN-LES-PINS. In Juan-les-Pins, Antibes' younger, hipper, and more hedonistic sibling, boutiques remain open until midnight, cafes until 2am, and nightclubs until past dawn. The streets are packed with those seeking the sea, sun, and sex (the order varies), and nightclubs pulse with promises of decadence. Pickpockets also abound, so never leave belongings out of your sight. Cafes are much cheaper than nightclubs and are almost as lively, so even the most miserly traveler can join in the nightly bash. *Discothèques* are generally open from 11pm to 5am. (Covers around 100F; includes 1 drink). Le Village, 1, bd. de la Pinède, has a notoriously lively dance floor. Check out the psychedelic Whiskey à Go Go, on la Pinède, or Le Duc, at the intersection of av. Maupassant and bd. Wilson. Or, join the crowds piling onto the patio of hip Che Café, 1, bd. de la Pinède. Trains arrive from Cannes (10min., every 20min., 12F) and Nice (30min., every 20min.). To get from Antibes' pl. du Général de Gaulle to Juan-les-Pins by foot, follow bd. Wilson, which runs right into the center of town (about 1.5km). Rather than make the post-party trek back to Antibes, take a right out of the train station and stay at Hôtel Trianon, 14, av. de L'Estérel. (☎04 93 61 18 11. Breakfast 30F. Doubles 215-260F; triples 260-280F.)

A NOSE FOR BUSINESS What does it take to make it in the perfume world? A good Nose—at least, that's what the *haute couture* master perfumers are called. Noses train for 15 years before extracting an essence; by the time they're ready to mix a scent, which can take up to two years, the sniffing students have memorized around 2000 smells. With only a handful in the world, Noses are hot commodities and are required by contract to protect their precious snouts. Alcohol, smoking, and eating spicy foods—in France, the ultimate sacrifices—are strictly forbidden.

FRANCE

NICE

Sun-drenched and spicy, Nice sparkles as the Riviera's unofficial capital, a rite of passage for young travelers. The city's pumping nightlife, top-notch museums, and bustling beaches enhance its native *Provençal* charms: flowery, palm-lined boulevards, casual affluence, and sea breezes. During **Carnaval** (the second half of February), visitors and *Niçois* alike ring in spring with wild revelry, grotesque costumes, and raucous song and dance. Prepare to have more fun than you'll remember.

GETTING THERE AND GETTING AROUND

Trains: Gare SNCF Nice-Ville (☎04 92 14 81 62), on av. Thiers. Office open M-Sa 8am-6:30pm, Su 8:30-11:15am and 2-6pm. To: **Monaco** (25min., every 10-30min., 22F); **Antibes** (30min., every 10-30min., 22F); **Cannes** (40min., every 15-45min., 32F); **Marseille** (2¾hr., every 30-90min., 149F); **Lyon** (6hr., 11 per day, 304F); **Bordeaux** (10¼hr., 3 per day, 440F); and **Paris** (7hr., 2-4 per day, 485F).

Buses: 5, bd. Jean Jaurès (☎04 93 85 61 81). Tickets sold M-Sa 6:30am-8pm and on buses. To **Monaco** (30min., 3-4 per hr., 17-20F) and **Cannes** (1½hr., 3 per hr., 32F).

Ferries: SNCM (☎04 93 13 66 66), on quai du Commerce. Take bus #1 or 2 (dir. Port) from pl. Masséna. Open M-F 8am-7pm, Sa 8am-noon. To **Corsica** (see p. 379).

Public Transportation: Sunbus, 10, av. Félix Faure (☎04 93 16 52 10), near pl. Leclerc and pl. Masséna. 8.5F per ride; 10-ticket *carnet* 55F. Bus passes (day pass 22F, 5-day 85F, 7-day 110F) are well worth it. Bus #12 runs between the train station, pl. Masséna, and the beach every 12min.

Bike and Scooter Rental: JML Location, 34, av. Auber (☎04 93 16 07 00), opposite the train station. Bikes 70F per day, 300F per wk.; scooters 220F, 1350-2250F. 1500F credit card required for deposit. Open M-F 8am-1pm and 2-6:30pm, Sa 8am-1pm.

ORIENTATION AND PRACTICAL INFORMATION

As you exit the train station, **av. Jean-Médecin** to the left and **bd. Gambetta** to the right run to the beach. **Pl. Masséna** is 10 minutes down av. Jean-Médecin. Along the coast, **Promenade des Anglais** is a people-watching paradise. To the southeast, past av. Jean Médecin and toward the bus station, pulsates **Vieux Nice** (Old Nice). Women should avoid walking alone after sundown, and everyone should be cautious at night around the train station, in *Vieux Nice*, and on the Promenade des Anglais.

Tourist Office: (☎04 93 87 07 07; fax 04 93 16 85 16; www.nice-coteazur.org), on av. Thiers, beside the train station. Makes same-day hotel reservations; go in the morning. Open daily mid-June to mid-Sept. 7:30am-8pm; mid-Sept. to mid-June 8am-7pm.

Currency Exchange: Cambio, 17, av. Thiers (☎04 93 88 56 80), opposite the train station. No commission. Open daily 7am-midnight.

American Express: 11, Promenade des Anglais (☎04 93 16 53 53; fax 04 93 16 51 67), at r. des Congrès. **ATM** machine. Open daily 9am-9pm.

Luggage Storage: At the train station. 30F per day. Lockers 15-20F. Open daily 7am-11:30pm.

Laundromat: Laverie Niçoise, 1, r. d'Italie, next to Basilique Notre-Dame. Wash 50F per 15kg. Open M-Sa 8:30am-12:30pm and 2:30-7:30pm, Su 8:30am-1pm.

Emergency: ☎17. **Medical emergency:** ☎15.

Police: ☎04 93 17 22 22. At the opposite end of bd. M. Foch from bd. Jean-Médecin.

Pharmacy: 7, r. Masséna (☎04 93 87 78 94). Open 24hr.

Post Office: 21, av. Thiers (☎04 93 82 65 22), near the train station. Open M-F 8am-7pm, Sa 8am-noon. 24hr. **ATM.** Address mail to be held: First name SURNAME, *Poste Restante,* Recette Principale, Nice **06000,** France.

Internet Access: Organic Café, 16, r. Paganini. Mention *Let's Go* and pay 10F per 15min., 34F per hr. Open daily 9am-10pm. **Web Nice,** 25bis, Promenade des Anglais. 25F per 30min., 50F per hr. Open Tu-Su 10:30am-8:30pm.

ACCOMMODATIONS

To sleep easy, come to Nice with reservations. Affordable places surround the train station, but without reservations, you might join the legions outside the station, which moonlights as one of the largest and most dangerous bedrooms in France.

Hôtel Les Orangiers, 10bis, av. Durante (☎04 93 87 51 41; fax 04 93 82 57 82). Bright rooms, most with showers and fridges. English spoken. Free beach-mat loan and luggage storage. Breakfast 20F. Closed Nov. In summer, dorms 85F; singles 95-100F; doubles 210-230F; triples 270-300F; quads 360F.

Hôtel Baccarat, 39, r. d'Angleterre (☎04 93 88 35 73; fax 04 93 16 14 25). Large, well-kept rooms with showers. Friendly staff creates a homey ambiance. Morning crêpes 12F, coffee and croissant 10F. Reception 24hr. Remember your reservation code. Dorms 87F; singles 177F; doubles 220F.

Hôtel Belle Meunière, 21, av. Durante (☎04 93 88 66 15; fax 04 93 82 51 75), on a street facing the train station. A converted mansion with courtyard and gardens. Breakfast included. Dorms 112F; doubles with shower 280F; triples 336F.

Hôtel des Flandres, 6, r. de Belgique (☎04 93 88 78 94; fax 04 93 88 74 90). Large rooms and bathrooms. Breakfast 28F. Reception 24hr. Free luggage storage. Dorms 100F; singles 200F; doubles 280-300F; triples 360F; quads 380-420F. Extra bed 70F.

Hôtel Notre Dame, 22, r. de la Russie (☎04 93 88 70 44; fax 04 93 81 27 63), at the corner of r. d'Italie. Spotless, quiet rooms with phones and pleasant decor. Breakfast 25F. Singles 200F; doubles 250F; triples 320F; quads 380F; extra bed 60F.

Relais International de la Jeunesse "Clairvallon," 26, av. Scudéri (☎04 93 81 27 63; fax 04 93 53 35 88), in Cimiez, 4km out of town. Take bus #15 (dir. Rimiez; 20min., every 10min.) from the train station or pl. Masséna to "Scudéri"; then head uphill to the right and take your 1st left. You and 160 buddies in the luxurious villa of a dead marquis. Tennis and basketball courts. Lovely TV and dining rooms. Breakfast included. Check-in 5pm. Lockout 9:30am-5pm. Curfew 11pm. 75F.

Hôtel Petit Trianon, 11, r. Paradis (☎04 93 87 50 46). Turn left off the pedestrian r. Masséna. Large, elegant rooms close to the beach, markets, and *Vieux Nice*. Showers 10F. Breakfast 25F. Singles 100F; doubles 200F; triples 300F.

Hôtel Little Masséna, 22, r. Masséna (☎/fax 04 93 87 72 34). Small but comfortable rooms with TV and kitchenette on a pedestrian street. Singles and doubles 150-250F. Extra bed 30F. Prices 10-30F cheaper in off season.

Hôtel Au Picardy, 10, bd. Jean-Jaurès (☎04 93 85 75 51), across from the bus station. Excellent proximity to *Vieux Nice*. Breakfast 17F. Singles 130-180; doubles 200-250F; triples and quads 230-290F. Extra bed 45F.

Auberge de Jeunesse (HI; ☎04 93 89 23 64; fax 04 92 04 03 10), on rte. Forestière du Mont-Alban, 4km out of town. From the bus station, take bus #14 (dir. Mont Baron; M-F every 15min., Sa-Su every 30min.; both until 7:30pm) to "l'Auberge." From the train station, take bus #17 and tell the driver you need to switch to the #14. Otherwise walk from the train station: turn left, then right on av. Jean-Médecin, left on bd. Jaurès, right on r. Barla, and follow the signs (50min.). Breakfast included. Kitchen. Lockout 10am-5pm. Curfew 12:30am. 68F.

FOOD

Nice offers a smorgasbord of seafood, Asian cuisine, and Italian gastronomic delights. *Vieux Nice* is crowded and touristy, but good eats are easy to find. Stock up at the **Prisunic supermarket,** 42, av. Jean-Médecin. (Open M-Sa 8:30am-8:30pm.)

Acchiardo, 38, r. Droite, in *Vieux Nice*. Pastas from 36F are immensely popular with a loyal local clientele. Open M-F noon-1:30pm and 7-9:30pm, Sa noon-1:30am.

Lou Pilha Leva, 13, r. du Collet. A wonderful, cheap way to try a lot of *niçois* food. Pizzas, *socca* (an olive-oil-flavored chickpea bread), and *pissaladière* (anchovy and olive pizza) all 10-23F. Hard-to-resist *moules* (mussels) 37F. Open daily 8am-11pm.

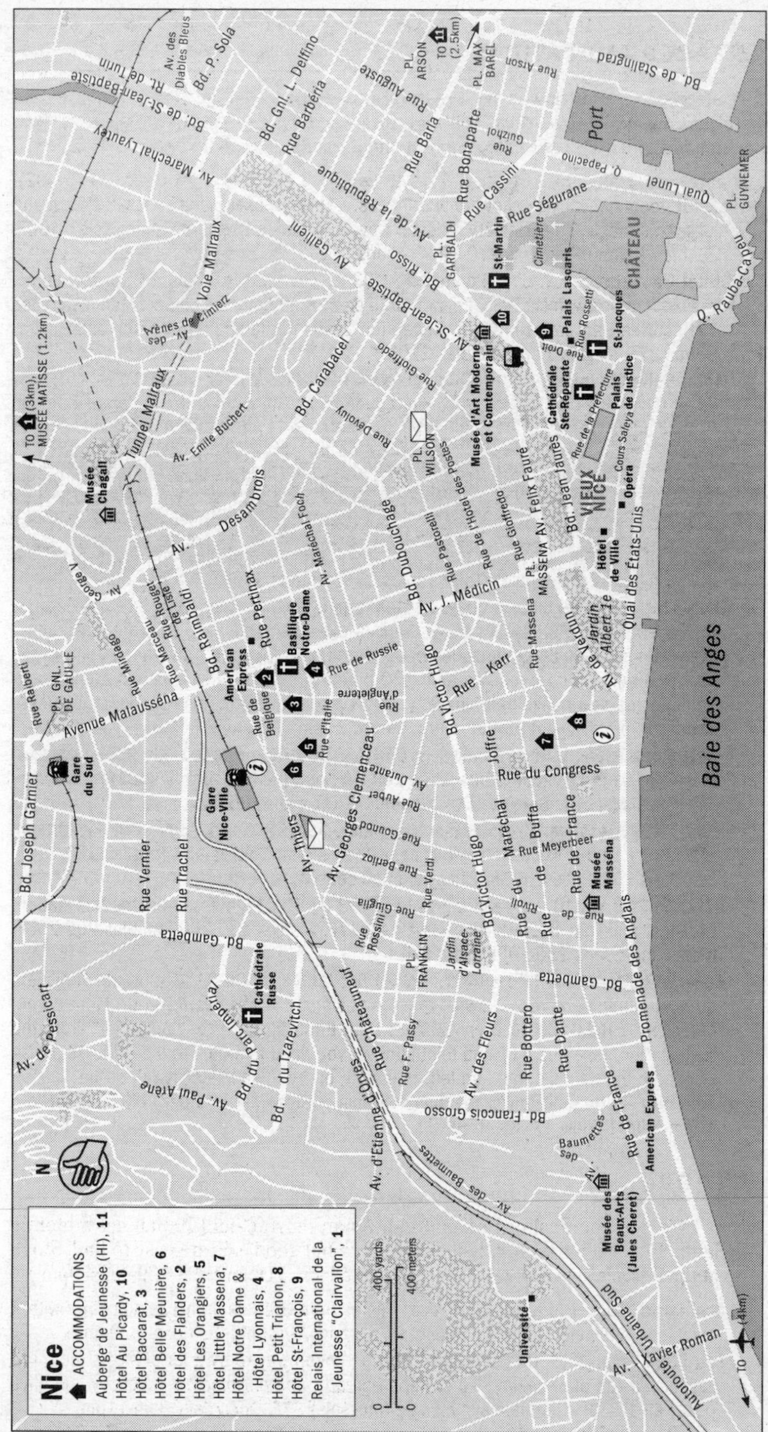
Nice
ACCOMMODATIONS
Auberge de Jeunesse (HI), 11
Hôtel Au Picardy, 10
Hôtel Baccarat, 3
Hôtel Belle Meunière, 6
Hôtel des Flanders, 2
Hôtel Les Orangiers, 5
Hôtel Little Massena, 7
Hôtel Notre Dame & Hôtel Lyonnais, 4
Hôtel Petit Trianon, 8
Hôtel St-François, 9
Relais International de la Jeunesse "Clairvallon", 1
400 yards
400 meters
N
Baie des Anges
Promenade des Anglais
Quai des États-Unis
Gare Nice-Ville
Gare du Sud
VIEUX NICE
CHÂTEAU
Port
Musée Chagall
MUSÉE MATISSE (1.2km)
Musée d'Art Moderne et Contemporain
Musée Masséna
Musée des Beaux-Arts (Jules Cheret)
Cathédrale Russe
Basilique Notre-Dame
Cathédrale Ste-Réparate
Palais Lascaris
Palais de Justice
American Express
Hôtel de Ville
Opéra
Université
Av. Jean Médecin
Bd. Gambetta
Av. Malausséna
Bd. Jean Jaurès
Av. de la République
Bd. Victor Hugo
Rue de France
Av. Georges Clemenceau
Autoroute Urbaine Sud
Av. Xavier Roman

Indyana, 11, r. Gustave de Loye. Trendy French fare with an Asian twist. Salads and entrees are self-contained meals, especially the sushi-maki platter big enough for two (148F). Open M-Sa for lunch and dinner. V, MC.

La Merenda, 4, r. de la Terrasse. Unlike other restaurants, doesn't cater to tourists; outsiders might feel unwelcome. The brave can savor the creations of a culinary master who left a four-star hotel to open this totem to *niçoise* cuisine (40-75F).

SIGHTS

Nice's **Promenade des Anglais,** named after the English expatriates who had it built, is a sight in itself. Despite the dreams you've had about Nice's beach, the hard reality is an endless stretch of smooth rocks; bring a beach mat. Follow the Promenade east of bd. Jean Jaurès to visit **Vieux Nice**'s labyrinthine streets, containing buildings of considerable historical significance. Or, continue to **Le Château,** a flowery hillside park crowned by the remains of an 11th-century cathedral. (Open daily 7am-8pm.)

Even burn-hard sunbathers will have a hard time passing up Nice's first-class museums. Northeast of the train station off bd. Cimiez, find the moving **Musée National Marc Chagall,** av. du Dr. Ménard, the largest public collection of his works. (15min. from the train station, or take bus #15: "Rimiez" and "Les Sources." Open July-Sept. W-M 10am-5:50pm, Oct.-June W-M 10am-4:50pm. 20-30F.) Farther up the hill, an impressive collection of Matisse's Riviera work is housed in the **Musée Matisse,** 1634, av. des Arènes de Cimiez. The artist lived in Nice from 1917-1954 because of the special quality of its light. (Take bus #15, 17, 20, or 22 to "Arènes." Open W-F Apr.-Sept. 10am-6pm; Oct.-Mar. 10am-5pm. 25F, students 20F.) Matisse, along with Raoul Duffy, is buried nearby in a cemetery beside the **Monastère Cimiez,** which contains a museum devoted to Franciscan art. (Museum open M-Sa 10am-noon and 3-6pm; cemetery open daily 8am-6pm.) Far to the northwest, the onion-domed **Cathédrale Orthodoxe Russe St-Nicolas,** west of bd. Gambetta near the train station, is a reminder of the days when the Côte d'Azur was a favorite retreat for Russian nobility. (Open daily June-Aug. 9am-noon and 2:30-6pm; Sept.-May 9:30am-noon and 2:30-5pm. 15F, students 12F.) Closer to *Vieux Nice,* the **Musée d'Art Moderne et d'Art Contemporain,** on Promenade des Arts at the intersection of av. St-Jean Baptiste and Traverse Garibaldi, features avant-garde works by French and American provacateurs. (Take bus #5: "St-Charles" from the station to "Garibaldi." 20F, students 10F. Open W-M 10am-6pm.) The **Musée des Beaux-Arts,** 33, av. Baumettes, off bd. François Grosso just north of the Promenade des Anglais, exhibits the work of Fragonard, Monet, Sisley, Bonnard, and Degas, as well as sculptures by Rodin and Carpeaux. Take bus #38 from the train station to "Chéret" or bus #12 to "Grosso." (Open Tu-Su 10am-noon and 2-6pm. 25F, students 15F.)

ENTERTAINMENT AND NIGHTLIFE

Nice's **Jazz Festival,** in mid-July at the Parc et Arènes de Cimiez near the Musée Matisse, attracts world-famous jazz and non-jazz musicians. Last year's lineup included Lou Reed and Herbie Hancock. (☎04 93 21 68 12; fax 04 93 18 07 92. Tickets 50-250F.) **FNAC,** 24, av. Jean-Médecin, in the Nice Etoile shopping center, sells tickets.

Nice guys do finish last—here the party crowd swings long after the folks in nearby St-Tropez and Antibes are asleep. The bars and nightclubs around r. Masséna and *Vieux Nice* jump to jazz and rock. However, the areas around *Vieux Nice* and the Promenade des Anglais can be dangerous at night. The dress code at all bars and clubs is simple: look good. Most will turn you away for wearing shorts, sandals, a t-shirt, or a baseball cap. Men usually wear gray or black, and women wear tight clothing. But don't go over the top or you'll stick out like a sore thumb.

De Klomp, 6, r. Mascoinat. A Dutch pub with a friendly ambiance and mixed crowd. Try one of their 40 whiskeys (from 30F) or 18 beers on tap (pint 40F). Live music nightly from salsa to jazz. Gay-friendly. Open M-Sa 5:30pm-2:30am.

Le Bar des Deux Frères, 1, r. du Moulin. Hip, local favorite guarantees a good time. A young, funky crowd throws back tequila (20F) and beer (15F) amid lasers and graffitied walls. Open in summer daily 9pm-2 or 3am; winter Tu-Sa 9pm-2 or 3am.

La Suite, 2, r. Brea. A well-dressed crowd packs Nice's most chic club. Come with a pretty girl and you're sure to get in. Cover 60F. Th free. Open Th-Sa 11pm-2:30am.

La Palousa, 29, r. Alphonse Karr at the corner of r. Georges Clemenceau. A huge dance floor fills with a casual crowd dancing to disco and Latin. Beer 50F. Cover 100F; free for women on F until 1am. Open in summer Th-Su 11pm-dawn; in winter F-Sa 11pm-dawn.

THE CORNICHES: NICE TO MONACO

Rocky shores, pebble beaches, and luxurious villas glow along the coast between hectic Nice and high-rolling Monaco. More relaxing than their glamorous neighbors, these tiny towns are like freshwater pearls—similar in brilliance, yet gratifyingly unique, with interesting museums, architectural finds, and breathtaking countrysides. The train offers a glimpse of the coast up close, while bus rides on the high roads provide bird's-eye views of the steep cliffs and crashing sea below.

GETTING THERE AND GETTING AROUND. Trains run between Nice and Monaco hourly and stop at (from west to east): Villefranche-sur-Mer (7min., 10F); Beaulieu-sur-Mer (10min., 12F); Eze-sur-Mer (16min., 13F); and Cap D'Ail (20min., 16F). **RCA buses** (☎04 93 85 64 44), which depart from Nice's *gare routière*, run the route more frequently; RCA #111 leaves Nice and stops in Villefranche-sur-Mer. Three buses continue on to St-Jean-Cap-Ferrat; #117 runs between Nice and Villefranche-sur-Mer 11 times daily; and #112 runs seven times per day (3 on Su) between Nice and Monte-Carlo, stopping in Èze-le-Village. **RCA and Broch** (☎04 93 31 10 52 or 04 93 07 63 28) run every hour between Nice and: Villefranche-sur-Mer (10min., 8.50F); Beaulieu-sur-Mer (20min., 12F); Èze-le-Village (25min., 15F); Cap d'Ail (30min., 17F); Monaco-Ville (40min., 20F); and Monte-Carlo (45 min., 20F). Most tickets include free same-day return.

VILLEFRANCHE-SUR-MER. Narrow streets and pastel houses have enchanted Aldous Huxley, Katherine Mansfield, and a bevy of other writers. Strolling from the train station along quai Ponchardier, a sign to the *vieille ville* points toward the spooky and dungeonesque 13th-century **r. Obscure,** which has been layered with so many homes and shops that the only light comes from iron chandeliers hanging from the street's "ceiling." The **tourist office,** on Jardin François Binon, gives out free maps and info on sights. (☎04 93 01 73 68; fax 04 93 76 63 65. Open July-Aug. daily 9am-7pm; mid-Sept. to June M-Sa 9am-noon and 2-6pm.)

ST-JEAN-CAP-FERRAT. A lovely town with an even lovelier beach, St-Jean-Cap-Ferrat is the trump card of the Riviera. Consider taking the bus or train to Beaulieu and then walking to St-Jean-Cap-Ferrat (25min.); the walk leads you along a seaside path full of lavish villas and secluded rocky beaches. The **Fondation Ephrussi di Rothschild**—a stunning Italianate villa with an impressive, eclectic collection of artwork—is the town's main draw, and the best sight between Nice and Monaco. (Open July-Aug. daily 10am-7pm; Sept.-Oct. and mid-Feb. to June daily 10am-6pm; Nov. to mid-Feb. M-F 2-6pm, Sa-Su 10am-6pm. 49F, students 37F.) The town's beautiful and untouristed **beaches** merit the area's nickname *Presqu'île des Rêves* (Peninsula of Dreams), and are mostly frequented by local families.

EZE-LE-VILLAGE. This imposing medieval town (the center of the larger Eze-sur-Mer) features the **Porte des Maures,** which served as a portal for a surprise attack by the Moors, and the newly renovated Baroque **Eglise Paroissial,** decorated with Christian and Egyptian symbols. (Open daily 9am-noon and 2-6pm.) The best views go to those who venture 40 minutes up the **Sentier Friedrich Nietzsche,** a windy trail whose namesake found inspiration here for the third part of *Thus Spake Zarathustra;* the trail begins in Eze Bord-du-Mer, 100m east of the train station and tourist office, and ends near the base of the medieval city, by the Fragonard *parfumerie.*

CAP D'AIL. With 3km of cliff-framed seashore, **Les Pissarelles** draws dozens of **nudists,** while **plage Mala** is frequented by more modest folk. Free maps and lists of daytrips are available from the **tourist office,** 87bis, av. de 3 Septembre. To walk from the train station (20min.), turn right uphill at the village, continue on av. de la Gare, and turn right on r. du 4 Septembre. (☎04 93 78 02 33. Open M-Sa 9am-12:30pm and 2-6pm.) The **Relais International de la Jeunesse,** on bd. de la Mer, is on the beachfront. (☎04 93 78 18 58 Breakfast included. 3-night max. stay when busy. Lockout 9:30am-5pm. Curfew midnight. 70F.)

MONACO AND MONTE-CARLO

Named for a temple to Hercules reputedly built on its site, Monaco has indeed become a shrine to wealth of Herculean proportions. The world's playground for the rich and famous, this resourceless principality was actually in danger of going under until 1865, when a Frenchman built the casino that ensured that the Monagasques never pay another cent in taxes. ☎ **Country code:** 377. **International dialing prefix:** 00.

ORIENTATION AND PRACTICAL INFORMATION. Trains run to: Nice (20min., every 30min., 20F); Antibes (1hr., every 30min., 38F); Cannes (1¼hr., every 30min., 46F); and Menton (15min., every 30min., 13F). From the station, turn right on av. du Port and left on bd. Albert 1[er], overlooking the harbor. On the right is the *quartier* of **Monaco-Ville,** with its *vieille ville* and the palace; to the left rises the fabled *quartier* of **Monte-Carlo** and the casino. Five public transportation routes (☎93 50 62 41) connect the entire hilly town every 11 minutes; bus #4 links the train station to the Casino in Monte-Carlo. Buy tickets on board (8.50F). The tourist office, 2a bd. des Moulins, near the casino, makes reservations and gives out maps of the city for no charge. (☎92 16 61 16; fax 92 16 60 00. Open M-Sa 9am-7pm, Su 10am-noon.) Access the **Internet** at **Stars 'N' Bars,** 6 Quai Antoine 1er. (Open daily 10am-1:30am.) **Postal code:** 06500.

ACCOMMODATIONS AND FOOD. To afford a room in Monaco, you'll either need to seduce royalty or win big. For an absolute steal, check out the **Centre de la Jeunesse Princesse Stéphanie,** 24 av. Prince Pierre (☎93 50 83 20; fax 93 25 29 82). From the train station, follow the signs for **Le Rocher/Fontveille** to the av. Prince Pierre exit, and walk 100m uphill to the hostel. (Breakfast included. Sheets free with ID deposit. Laundry 30F. Must be aged 16-31. 5-day max. stay July-Aug.; 7-day Sept.-June. Reception July-Aug. 31 7am-1am; Sept. 1-June 7am-midnight. 80F, cash only.) Stop by the lively **fruit and flower market** on pl. d'Armes (open daily 6am-1pm) at the end of av. Prince Pierre or the huge **Carrefour supermarket** (☎92 05 57 00; open M-Sa 8:30am-10pm) in Fontvieille's shopping plaza. From the av. Prince Pierre station exit, turn right and then right again onto r. de la Colle until you reach pl. du Canton; cross the street, and head down the escalator.

SIGHTS, ENTERTAINMENT, AND NIGHTLIFE. The **Monte-Carlo Casino** glows with 19th-century extravagance; even non-gamblers should admire its red velvet curtains, gilded ceilings, and gold and crystal chandeliers. The slot machines open at 2pm, while blackjack, craps, and roulette (25F minimum) open at noon. If you need to start your gambling fix before noon, head next door to the **Café de Paris** (opens 10am). Peeking at the *salons privés*, where such French games as *chemin de fer* and *trente et quarante* begin at noon, will cost you 50-100F. All casinos have dress codes (no shorts, sneakers, sandals, or jeans), but you'll only win respect in a jacket and tie. Guards are strict about the 21 age minimum; bring a passport as proof. Even if you've lost your shirt at the casino, you can still admire the royal robes at the **Palais Princier,** the sometime home of Prince Rainier and his tabloid-darling family. When the flag is down, the prince is away and visitors can tour the lavish palace; of special interest to American patriots is the chamber where England's King George III died. (Open June-Sept. 9:30am-6pm; Oct. 10am-5pm. 30F, students 20F before 5pm.) Next door, the **Cathédrale de Monaco**

contains the tombs of former princes of Monaco; Princess Grace lies in a tomb behind the altar marked simply with her Latinized name, "Patritia Gracia." (Pl. St-Martin. Open daily Mar.-Oct. 7am-7pm; Nov.-Feb. 7am-6pm. Free.) The mouthful **Exhibition of H.S.H. the Prince of Monaco's Private Collection of Classic Cars** on les Terraces de Fontvielle showcases 105 of the most glamorous cars ever made. (Open daily Dec.-Oct. 10am-6pm. 30F, students 15F.) Head to av. St-Martin to see the **Musée Océanographique,** which was once directed by Jacques Cousteau and holds the most exotic and bizarre oceanic species. The museum itself is an architectural wonder, built out of 100,000 tons of white stone on the edge of a cliff. (Open daily July-Aug. 9am-8pm; Apr.-June and Sept. 9am-7pm; Oct. and Mar. 9:30am-7pm; Nov.-Feb. 10am-6pm. 60F, students and ages 6-18 30F.) To be part of Monaco's night scene, stop by **La Rascasse** on Quai Antoine 1er. This all-night bar delivers live rock music in a raucous atmosphere while Fabio look-a-likes serve drinks until 6am to a mixed crowd of playboys and painters. (Beer 30-55F. Live music starts around midnight. No cover. Open M-Sa from 6pm.) If you're looking for a more subdued atmosphere, Quai Antoine 1er also features **Stars 'N' Bars,** a restaurant/bar that attracts cosmopolitan locals and European tourists despite its American allegiance. Put on tight clothes, slick your hair, and dance, groove, and pop 'til you drop. (Open 10am-11pm; disco open F-Sa midnight-5am. W is salsa night; free lessons.)

CORSICA (LA CORSE)

A Corsican children's story goes something like this: On the sixth day, God made Corsica. He mixed the turquoise waters of the Mediterranean, the snow-capped splendor of the Alps, and the golden sunshine of the Riviera to create the island the Greeks called *Kallysté* (the most beautiful).

GETTING THERE AND GETTING AROUND. **Air France** and **Compagnie Corse** fly to **Bastia** and **Ajaccio** from: **Paris** (1065F, students 880F); **Marseille** (1202F, students 822F); and **Lyon** (from 865F, students 781F). Or, fly from **Lille** to **Bastia** (from 1200F, students 1070F). **Ferries** to Corsica can be rough and aren't much cheaper than flights. The **Société National Maritime Corse Méditerranée (SNCM)** sails to **Bastia, Calvi,** and **Ajaccio** from **Marseille** (256-292F, under 25 224-256F) and **Nice** (213-243F, under 25 186-213F). **Corsica Ferries** travels from **Livorno** and **Savona, Italy** to **Bastia** (140-220F). Ferries also bridge the gap from **Bonifacio,** at the southern tip of the island, to **Sardinia, Italy.**

Train service in Corsica is slow and limited to the half of the island north of Ajaccio; **railpasses** are not valid. **Eurocorse Voyages buses** (☎04 95 21 06 30) are neither cheaper nor more frequent, but provide more comprehensive service. **Hiking** is the best way to explore the island's mountainous interior. The longest marked route, **GR20,** is an extremely difficult 14- to 15-day trail (200km) traversing the island. The **Parc Naturel Régional de la Corse,** 2 Sargent Casalonga, in Ajaccio (☎04 95 51 79 10; fax 04 95 21 88 17), publishes maps and a guide to *gîtes d'étapes*.

AJACCIO

Ajaccio (pop. 60,000) grew rich in history and culture from its love affair with Napoleon. The **Musée National de la Maison Bonaparte,** on r. St-Charles, between r. Bonaparte and r. Roi-de-Rome, contains original furnishings, like his smaller-than-average bed. (Open Apr.-Sept. M 2-6pm, Tu-Su 9am-noon and 2-6pm; Oct.-Mar. M 2-4:45pm, Tu-Su 10am-noon and 2-4:45pm. 22F, ages 18-25 15F.) When Napoleon's uncle Fesch, who amassed a fortune as a merchant during the Revolution, became a cardinal, he used the booty to collect Renaissance art. Inside the **Musée Fesch,** 50-52 r. Cardinal Fesch, you'll find a collection including works by Raphael, Botticelli, and Titian. Within the complex is the **Chapelle Impériale,** the final resting place of most of the Bonaparte family—though Napoleon himself is buried in a modest Parisian tomb. (Open Apr.-June and Sept. M 1-5:15pm, T-F 9:15am-12:15pm and 2:15-5:15pm; July-Aug. M 1:30-6pm, Tu-Th 9am-6:30pm, F 9am-midnight, Sa 10:30am-6pm; Oct.-Mar. T-Sa 9:15am-12:15pm and 2:15-5:15pm. Museum 35F, students 25F; chapel 10F, students 5F.)

From the **airport,** shuttle bus #8 (☎04 95 23 11 03; 26F) runs hourly to the bus station. **Trains** (☎04 95 23 11 03) chug from pl. de la Gare, off bd. Sampiero beside the port, to Bastia (4hr., 4 per day, 124F) and Calvi via Ponte Leccia (4½hr., 2 per day, 145F). Eurocorse Voyages **buses** (☎04 95 21 06 30) go from **quai L'Herminier** (☎04 95 51 55 45) to Bastia (3hr., 110F) via Corte (1½hr., 65F), while Autocars Les Beux Voyages (☎04 95 65 15 02) runs to Calvi (3½hr., 1 per day, 135F). The **tourist office** is at 3 bd. du roi Jérôme. (☎04 95 51 53 03. Open May-June M-Sa 8am-7pm, Su 9am-1pm; July-Sept. M-Sa 8am-8:30pm, Su 9am-1pm; Nov.-Mar. M-Sa 8am-6pm, Su 9am-1pm.) **Hôtel Kallisté,** 51 cours Napoléon, has comfortable, well-designed rooms. (☎04 95 51 34 45; fax 04 95 21 79 00. Singles 240-340F; doubles 280-390F; triples 360-520F; quads 400-650F.) **Hôtel Bella Vista** is on bd. Lantivy. (☎04 95 21 07 97; fax 04 95 21 81 88. Breakfast 25F. Singles 230-270F; doubles 240-280F; triples 300-340F; quads 390F.) **Monoprix supermarket** is at 31 cours Napoléon. (Open M-Sa 8:30am-7:30pm.)

BONIFACIO (BONIFAZIU)

A unique inhabited landscape on the island, the fortified town of Bonifacio sits like a sand castle above limestone cliffs. It is a marvel of both man-made and natural architecture; consider taking a **boat tour** with one of the companies at the port (65F). Les Vedettes Christina (☎04 95 73 09 77), on the port, offers a **ferry** service to **Les Iles Levezzi,** a natural reserve where you can tan all day, then take a cliffside tour on the way back (100F). To explore the *ville haute,* head up the steep **Rastello steps,** the wide staircase halfway down the port, where excellent views of the ridged cliffs to the east await. (Open daily 9:30am-8:30pm. 10F.) Continue up St-Roch to the lookout at **Porte des Gênes,** a drawbridge built by invaders. Then walk to the **pl. du Marche** to see Bonifacio's famous cliffs.

Eurocorse Voyages (☎04 95 21 06 30) runs **buses** between Bonaficio and Ajaccio (3½hr., 2-3 per day, 125F) as well as Porto Vecchio (30min., 4 per day, 45F), where connections can be made to Bastia. To reach the **tourist office,** at the corner of av. de Gaulle and r. F. Scamaroni, walk along the port and then up the stairs before the *gare maritime.* (☎04 95 73 11 88. Open May to mid-Oct. daily 9am-8pm; mid-Oct. to Apr. M-F 9am-noon and 2-6pm, Sa 9am-noon.) Finding affordable rooms is difficult in summer; avoid visiting in August, when prices soar and vacancies plummet. Try **Hôtel des Étrangers,** av. Sylvère Bohn. (☎04 95 73 01 09; fax 04 95 73 16 97. Singles and doubles 236-396F; triples 350-420F; quads 390-480F.) The most reasonable option is **camping:** wooded and spacious **Cavallo Morto** offers "chalets" for 4-6 people and "studios" for 1-2 people with kitchen and showers. (Studios 200-350F; chalets 350-600F; camping 28-34F per person; tent and car each 10-13F; electricity 17F.)

CALVI

With its sandy beaches, warm turquoise waters, misty mountains, and nearly 2400 hours of sunshine per year, Calvi could well be paradise—although no benevolent god would charge these rates. Visit the alluring **citadel** at the end of the day and bask in the setting sun. Gorgeous sand and water stretch as far as the eye can see; 6km of **public beaches** dotted by rocky coves wind around the coast. Eurocourse **Trains** (☎04 95 65 00 61) go from pl. de la Gare, on av. de la République near Port de Plaisance, to Bastia (3hr., 2 per day, 95F) and Corte (2½hr., 2 per day, 79F). **Buses** stop at pl. Porteuse d'Eau Agence. Voyages buses (☎04 95 46 06 83), on av. Wilson, run to Bastia (1¼hr., M-Sa 2 per day, 55F) and Ajaccio (1¾hr., M-Sa 2 per day, 65F). To reach the **tourist office,** at Port de Plaisance, exit from the back of the train station, turn left (facing the beach), and follow the signs. (☎04 95 65 16 67. Open May M-Sa 9am-6:30pm; July to mid-Sept. daily 9am-8pm; mid-Sept. to Apr. M-F 9am-noon and 2-5:30pm, Sa 9am-noon.) To get to the isolated but beautiful **Relais International de la Jeunesse U Carabellu,** exit the station, turn left on av. de la République, turn right at rte. de Pietra-Maggiore, follow the signs 5km up the mountain, continue straight past Bella Vista camping, and bear right at the stop sign. (☎04 95 65 14 16. Breakfast included. Sheets 20F. Open Mar.-Oct. 85F.) **BVJ Corsotel** is on av. de la République. (☎04 95 65 14 15; fax 04 95 65 33 72. Breakfast 30F. Reception 24hr. Open Apr.-Oct.

100F.) **Camp** at **International,** on RN 197, close to the beach past Super U and Hotel L'Onda. (☎04 95 65 01 75. Open Apr.-Oct. 33F per person, 18F per tent, 10F per car.)

BASTIA AND CAP CORSE

Corsica's second largest city and France's second largest port, **Bastia** (pop. 45,000) is more than just a transport hub. You'll feel like you're inside a gem at the silk-lined **Oratoire de L'Immaculée Conception,** down r. Napoleon, which was once the site of the English parliament. The Genovese extended their power over the island from the **Citadel,** also called Terra Nova; it now houses several museums. Head north to Miomo on bus #4, which leaves every hour from pl. St-Nicholas, to reach enchanting **Erbalunga beach** (20min., 12F) and **Marina di Siscu** (30min., 14F). **Buses** connect to the **airport** in **Bastia-Poretta** from pl. de la Gare (30min., 50F). **Trains** (☎04 95 32 80 61) leave pl. de la Gare for Calvi (3hr., 2 per day, 95F) and Ajaccio (4hr., 4 per day, 124F). Eurocorse **buses** (☎04 95 21 06 30) also run to Ajaccio (3hr., 2 per day, 111F). The **tourist office** is on pl. St-Nicholas. (☎04 95 55 96 96; fax 04 95 31 80 34. Open June-Sept. M-Sa 8am-8pm; daily Oct.-May 8am-noon and 2-6pm.) Stay at **Hôtel Central,** 3, r. Miot. (☎04 95 31 71 12. Breakfast 35F. Singles 200-300F; doubles 200-400F; extra bed 70F.) **Les Orangiers camping** is 4km north in Miomo. (☎04 95 33 24 09. Open May-Sept. 25F per person, 13F per tent, 10F per car.) **SPAR supermarket** is at 14, r. César Campinchini. (Open M-Sa 7:30am-1pm and 6-9pm, Su 7:30am-1pm.)

The **Cap Corse** peninsula stretches north from Bastia, a necklace of tiny former fishing villages strung together by a narrow road of perilous curves and breathtaking views. The Cap is a dream for **hikers;** every jungle forest and cliff lays claim to some decaying Genoan tower or hilltop chapel. **Transports Michéle** (☎04 95 34 64 03), in Ersa at the top of the peninsula, offers full-day tours of the Cap, departing from 1, r. de Nouveau Port in Bastia (July-Sept. 10 M-Sa 9am; 84F), but the cheapest way to see Cap Corse is to take **bus** #4 from pl. St-Nicolas in Bastia; nicely ask the driver to drop you off wherever you feel the urge to explore. The bus also goes to **Erbalunga** (see above); you will never want to leave.

CORTE

"The heart of Corsica," Corte is enfolded amid huge, sheer cliffs and snow-capped peaks, appearing from a distance like a fairy-tale illustration. Corsica's intellectual center, Corte houses the island's only university, and students (2600 of its 6000 residents) keep prices fairly low. The town's *vieille ville*—with its steep, nearly inaccessible topography and stone citadel—has always been a bastion of Corsican patriotism. At the top of the *vieille ville*, the focus of the **Citadel** is the brand new **La Musée de la Corse.** The museum also provides entrance to the higher fortifications of the citadel. (☎04 95 45 25 45. Museum open June 20-Sept. 20 daily 10am-8pm; Sept. 21-Nov. Tu-Su 10am-6pm; Dec.-Mar. Tu-Sa 10am-6pm; Apr.-June 20 T-Su 10am-6pm. Citadel closes 1hr. before the museum. 35F, students 20F.) Countless trails through the area's mountains and valleys are spectacular. Choose from **hiking** (call tourist office for trail maps), **biking** (though there are no bike rentals in town), and **horse riding** (☎04 95 46 24 55; 90F per hr., 200F per half-day, 400F per day).

Trains (☎04 95 46 00 97) run to: Bastia (1¾hr., 5 per day, 59F); Calvi via Ponte-Leccia (2½hr., 2 per day, 79F); and Ajaccio (2½hr., 4 per day, 66F). Eurocorse Voyages (☎04 95 46 06 83) runs **buses** to Bastia (1¼hr., M-Sa 2 per day, 55F) and Ajaccio (1¾hr., M-Sa 2 per day, 65F). To reach the *centre ville* from the train station, turn right on the D14 (alias av. Jean Nicoli), cross two bridges, and follow the road until it ends at **cours Paoli,** Corte's main drag. A left turn on the busy street leads to beautiful **pl. Paoli,** the town center; at the top-right corner, climb stairwayed r. Scolisca to reach the citadel and the **tourist office.** (☎04 95 46 26 70. Open May-June M-Sa 9am-1pm and 2-7pm; July-Aug. daily 9am-1pm and 2-7pm; Sept.-Apr. M-F 9am-noon and 2-6pm.) In the summer, students can stay in university housing for 100F per night; contact **CROUS,** 7 av. Jean Nicoli, before you arrive to find out where to check in. (☎04 95 45 21 00. Open M-F 9am-noon and 2-3:30pm.) The **Gîte d'Etape: U Tavignanu,** on Chemin de Balari, offers a peaceful farmhouse and shaded **campsites** 20 minutes away. Turn left out of the station and bear right when the road forks, initially following allée du 9 Septembre and then the signs at the base of the Citadel. (☎04 95 46 16 85. Dorms 80F with breakfast; half-pension 160F. Camping 24F per person, 12F per tent.) The huge **Casino supermarket** is on allée du 9 Septembre. (Open M-Sa 8:30am-12:30pm and 3-8pm, Sa 9:30am-12:30pm.) **Postal code:** 20250.

THE ALPS

Nature's architecture is the real attraction of the Alps. The curves of the Chartreuse Valley rise to rugged crags in the Vercors range and ultimately crescendo into Europe's highest peak, Mont Blanc. **Hiking trails** are clearly marked, and winter **skiers** enjoy some of the world's most challenging slopes. The cheapest months for skiing are January, March, and April; most resorts close in October and November. **FUAJ** (☎01 43 57 02 60; www.fuaj.org), the French Youth Hostel Federation, offers skiing and sports packages.

TGV **trains** will whisk you from Paris to Grenoble or Annecy; from there, it's either slow trains, slow special mountain trains, or (more often) torturously slow **buses.** The farther into the mountains you want to get, the harder it is to get there, although service is at least twice as frequent in ski season (Dec.-Apr.).

GRENOBLE

Grenoble (pop. 160,000) hosts the eccentric cafes, dusty bookshops, and shaggy radicals you'll find in any university town, but it also boasts the snow-capped peaks and sapphire-blue lakes cherished by hikers, skiers, bikers, and aesthetes alike.

PRACTICAL INFO, ACCOMMODATIONS, AND FOOD. **Trains** arrive in Grenoble at pl. de la Gare from: Lyon (1½hr., 16 per day, 97F); Annecy (2hr., 9 per day, 89F); Paris (3¼hr., 8 per day, 371-459F); Marseille (3½hr., 15 per day, 202F); and Nice (6½hr., 10 per day, 301F). **Buses** leave from the left of the station for Geneva (3hr., 1 per day, 151F) and Chamonix (3hr., 1 per day, 161F). From the station it's a 10-minute walk. Turn right into pl. de la Gare, take the third left on av. Alsace-Lorraine, and follow the tram tracks on r. Félix Poulat and r. Blanchard to reach the **tourist office,** 14, r. de la République. (☎04 76 42 41 41; fax 04 76 00 18 98. Open daily 9am-7pm.) To get from the station to the **Auberge de Jeunesse (HI),** 10, av. du Grésivaudan, 4km away in Echirolles, follow the tram tracks down av. Alsace-Lorraine, turn right on cours Jean Jaurès, and take bus #8 (dir. Pont Rouge) to "La Quinzaine"; it's behind the Casino supermarket. (☎04 76 09 33 52; fax 04 76 09 38 99. Breakfast included. Sheets 17F. Laundry 30F. Reception M-Sa 7:30am-11pm, Su 7:30-10am and 5:30-11pm. Singles 110F; doubles 85F per person.) To reach **Le Foyer de l'Etudiante,** 4, r. Ste-Ursule, follow pl. Ste-Claire from the tourist office to pl. Notre-Dame, and take r. du Vieux Temple on the far right. (☎04 76 42 00 84; fax 04 76 44 96 67. Laundry 19F. Min. 2-night stay. Reception 24hr. Women only mid-Sept. to mid-June. Dorms 50F; singles 90F; doubles 140F.) **Hôtel de la Poste,** 25, r. de la Poste, has amazing rooms near the pedestrian zone. (☎04 76 46 67 25. Breakfast 28F. Singles 100-130F; doubles 130-200; triples 190F; quads 220F.) To reach **Camping Les 3 Pucelles,** 58, r. des Allobroges, in Seyssins, take tram A to "Fontaine," then bus #51 (dir. Les Nalettes) to "Mas des Iles." (☎04 76 96 45 73. Call ahead in summer. 45F per person, 45F tent per person, 45F per car.) **La Galerie Rome,** 1, r. Trois-Cloitres, has flawless cuisine. (Open Tu-Su for lunch and dinner.) **Prisunic,** opposite the tourist office, stocks **groceries.** (Open M-Sa 8:30am-7:30pm.) **Postal code:** 38000.

SIGHTS AND THE OUTDOORS. **Téléphériques** (lifts) depart from quai Stéphane-Jay for the 16th-century **Bastille,** a fort which hovers above town. (Lifts run every 10min., July-Aug. M 9:15am-12:30am, Tu-Su 9am-11pm; Sept. M 11am-11:45pm, Tu-Sa 9:15am-11:45pm, Su 9:15am-7:25pm; off season shuts down earlier.) Enjoy the views from the top, then descend via the **Parc Guy Pape,** which crisscrosses through the fortress and deposits you just across the river from the train station. The **Musée Dauphinois,** 30, r. Maurice Gignoux, toward the bottom of the

Bastille hill on the north bank of the Isère, has futuristic exhibits. (Open May-Oct. W-M 10am-7pm; Nov.-Apr. 10am-6pm. 20F, students 10F.) Grenoble's major attraction is its proximity to the slopes. The biggest and most developed **ski areas** lie in the **Oisans** to the east; the **Alpe d'Huez** boasts 220km of trails (lift tickets 197F per day). The **Belledonne** region, northeast of Grenoble, lacks the towering heights of the Oisans but is cheaper. **Chamrousse** is its biggest and most popular ski area (lift tickets 136F per day), and has a **youth hostel** (☎89 91 31). Only 30 minutes from Grenoble by **bus** (50F), the resort makes an ideal daytrip in summer.

CHAMONIX

In other Alpine towns, the peaks provide harmless backdrops; in Chamonix (pop. 20,000), daggers of mammoth glaciers seem to reach down and menace the village. Just west of Mont Blanc, Europe's highest peak (4807m), this site of the first Winter Olympics (1924) has exploited its surroundings since 19th-century gentleman-climbers scaled the peaks in crewneck sweaters.

PRACTICAL INFO, ACCOMMODATIONS, AND FOOD. **Trains** (☎04 50 53 00 44) go to: Annecy (2½hr., 6 per day, 105F); Geneva (2½hr., 4 per day, 118F); Lyon (4hr., 4 per day, 185F); and Paris (6½hr., 6 per day, 500F). Société Alpes Transports **buses** (☎04 50 53 01 15) depart from the train station for: Geneva (1½hr., 2 per day, 170F); Annecy (2¼hr., 1 per day, 95F); and Grenoble (3hr., 1 per day, 161F). **Local buses** connect with ski slopes and hiking trails (7.50F). From the station, follow av. Michel Croz, turn left on r. du Dr. Paccard, and take the first right to reach the pl. de l'Eglise (5min.) and the **tourist office,** 85, pl. du Triangle de l'Amitié. (☎04 50 53 00 24; fax 04 50 53 58 90. Open daily July-Aug. and Dec.-Feb. 8:30am-7:30pm; Mar-June and Sept.-Nov. 9am-noon and 2-6pm.) **Compagnie des Guides,** in Maison de la Montagne on pl. de l'Eglise, will help plan **hiking** adventures. (☎04 50 53 22 08. Open daily Jan.-Mar. and July-Aug. 8:30am-noon and 3:30-7:30pm; Sept.-Dec. and Apr.-June Tu-Sa 10am-noon and 5-7pm.) Chamonix's *gîtes* (mountain hostels) and dorms are a budget traveler's dream if you can get a bed; call in advance. The **Auberge de Jeunesse (HI),** 127, montée Jacques Balmat, in Les Pèlerins at the base of the Glacier de Bossons, offers all-inclusive winter **ski packages.** Take the bus from pl. de l'Eglise (dir. Les Houches) to "Pèlerins Ecole" (7F) and follow the signs uphill, or take the train to "Les Pèlerins" and follow the signs. (☎04 50 53 14 52; fax 04 50 55 92 34. Breakfast 29F. Sheets 19F. Bike rental. Reception 8am-noon and 5-10pm. Dorms 78F; singles 93-113F; doubles 184-204F. Ski packages 2500-3500F per week.) **Red Mountain Lodge,** 435, r. Joseph-Vallot, is friendly and cozy. (☎04 50 53 94 97. Breakfast included. Dorms 100F; doubles and triples 120-160F.) To reach **Le Chamoniard Volant,** 45, rte. de la Frasse, from the station, turn right, go under the bridge, turn right across the tracks, left on chemin des Cristalliers, and right on rte. de la Frasse. (☎04 50 53 14 09; fax 04 50 53 23 25. Sheets 20F. Reception 10am-10pm. Dorms 70F.) The **Super U,** 117, r. Joseph Vallot, has **groceries.** (Open M-Sa 8:15am-7:30pm, Su 8:30am-noon.) **Postal code:** 74400.

HIKING AND OUTDOORS. Whether you've come to climb up the mountains or to ski down them, you're in for a challenge. The **Téléphérique de l'Aiguille du Midi** (☎04 50 53 30 80; reservations ☎04 50 53 40 00) offers a pricey, knuckle-whitening ascent over forests and snowy cliffs to a needlepoint peak at the top. A ride to the top reveals a fantastic panorama from 3842m. Bring your passport to continue by gondola to **Helbronner, Italy** for views of three countries, the **Matterhorn,** and **Mont Blanc,** as well as the opportunity to picnic on a glacier (round trip 200F). In summer, you can **hike** two hours to **La Mer de Glace,** a glacier that slides 30m per year.

Sunken in a valley, Chamonix is surrounded by skiable mountains. To the south, **Le Tour-Col. de Balme** (☎04 50 54 00 58), above the village of **Le Tour,** cuddles up to the Swiss border and provides sunny intermediate slopes (lift tickets 148F per day). On the northern side of the valley, **Le Brevent** (☎04 50 53 13 18), a proving ground for experts, has also expanded its slopes for beginners and intermediates (lift tickets 230F per day). Wherever you go, be cautious—people die on the mountains.

ANNECY

With narrow cobblestone streets, winding canals, and a turreted castle, all bordering Europe's purest lake, Annecy appears more like a fairy-tale fabrication than a modern city. The **Palais de l'Ile** is a 13th-century fortress once occupied by the counts of Geneva. Across from the tourist office, the grassy **Champs de mars** are connected to the manicured **Jardins de l'Europe** by the **Pont des Amours** (Bridge of Love). Although it may be hard to tear yourself away from the city's cosmetic charms, a **bike ride** or **hike** through nearby Alpine forests will prove that Annecy is also a natural beauty. One of the best hikes begins at the **Basilique de la Visitiation,** near the hostel. Ten kilometers west of Annecy, the impressive **Gorges du Fier** draws many visitors. (Hiking info ☎04 50 46 23 07.)

Trains (☎08 36 35 35 35) arrive at pl. de la Gare from: Grenoble (1½hr., 9 per day, 89F); Lyon (2hr., 6 per day, 115F); Chamonix (2¼hr., 7 per day, 106F); Paris (4hr., 6 per day, 363F); and Nice (8hr., 2 per day, 345F). Voyages Frossard **buses** (☎04 50 45 73 90) leave from next to the station for Geneva (1¼hr., 6 per day, 53F) and Lyon (3½hr., 2 per day, 92F). From the train station, take the underground passage to r. Vaugelas, follow the street left for four blocks, and enter the modern Bonlieu shopping mall to reach the **tourist office,** 1, r. Jean Jaurès, in pl. de la Libération. (☎04 50 45 00 33; fax 04 50 51 87 20. Open July-Aug. M-Sa 9am-6:30pm, Su 9am-12:30pm and 1:45-6:30pm; Sept.-June daily 9am-12:30pm and 1:45-6pm.) In summer, you can reach the **Auberge de Jeunesse "La Grande Jeanne" (HI),** on rte. de Semnoz, via a Ligne d'Ete bus (dir. Semnoz) from the station (7F); otherwise, take bus #1 (dir. Marquisats) from the station to "Hôtel de Police," turn right on av. du Tresum, and follow signs pointing to Semnoz. (☎04 50 45 33 19; fax 04 50 52 77 52. Breakfast included. Sheets 17F. Kitchen. Laundry. Reception 7am-midnight. 74F.) From the station, exit left, walk around the station to av. Berthollet, and turn left again on av. de Cran to reach the **Hôtel Savoyard** at #41. (☎04 50 57 08 08. Breakfast 20F. Singles and doubles 124-224F; triples 156F; quads 268F.) **Camp** at 8 rte. de Semnoz, near the youth hostel. (☎04 50 45 48 30; fax 04 50 45 55 56. Laundry. Reception Apr.-Aug. daily 8am-10pm; off season ring the bell. Open mid-Apr. to mid-Oct. 60F per tent and 2 people, 17F per car.) A **Prisunic supermarket** fills the better part of pl. de Notre-Dame. (Open M-Sa 8:30am-7:30pm.) **Postal code:** 74000.

CENTRAL FRANCE

Central France is often overlooked by tourists speeding south from Paris toward the attractions of the coasts. Thanks to the benign neglect engendered by its smokestack reputation, most of the region has escaped the deleterious effects of mass tourism; still continuing in its traditional lifestyle, it is here that cliché meets reality. With medieval abbeys, *grands vins*, outstanding cuisine, unspoiled countryside, and magnificent chateaux, this is France in all its preconceived glory.

LYON

France's second-largest city is second in little else. With industrial and culinary *savoir faire*, Lyon (pop. 1.5 million) has established itself as a cultural and economic alternative to Paris; despite its historical reputation for bourgeois snobbery, Lyon is friendlier and more relaxed than the capital city.

GETTING THERE AND GETTING AROUND

Trains (Eurolines; ☎04 72 56 95 30) are faster and cheaper than buses, going to: Grenoble (1¼hr., 15 per day, 96F); Paris (2hr., 20 per day, 312-388F); Dijon (2hr., 15 per day, 132F); Marseille (3hr., 13 per day, 205F); and Nice (6hr., 15 per day, 299F). Trains to Lyon stop only at Gare de la Part-Dieu, in the business district on the east bank of the Rhône. For **bus** info, call ☎04 72 77 63 03 or 04 72 61 72 61. **TCL** (☎04 78 71 70 00), at both train stations and major Métro stops, sells **public transportation**

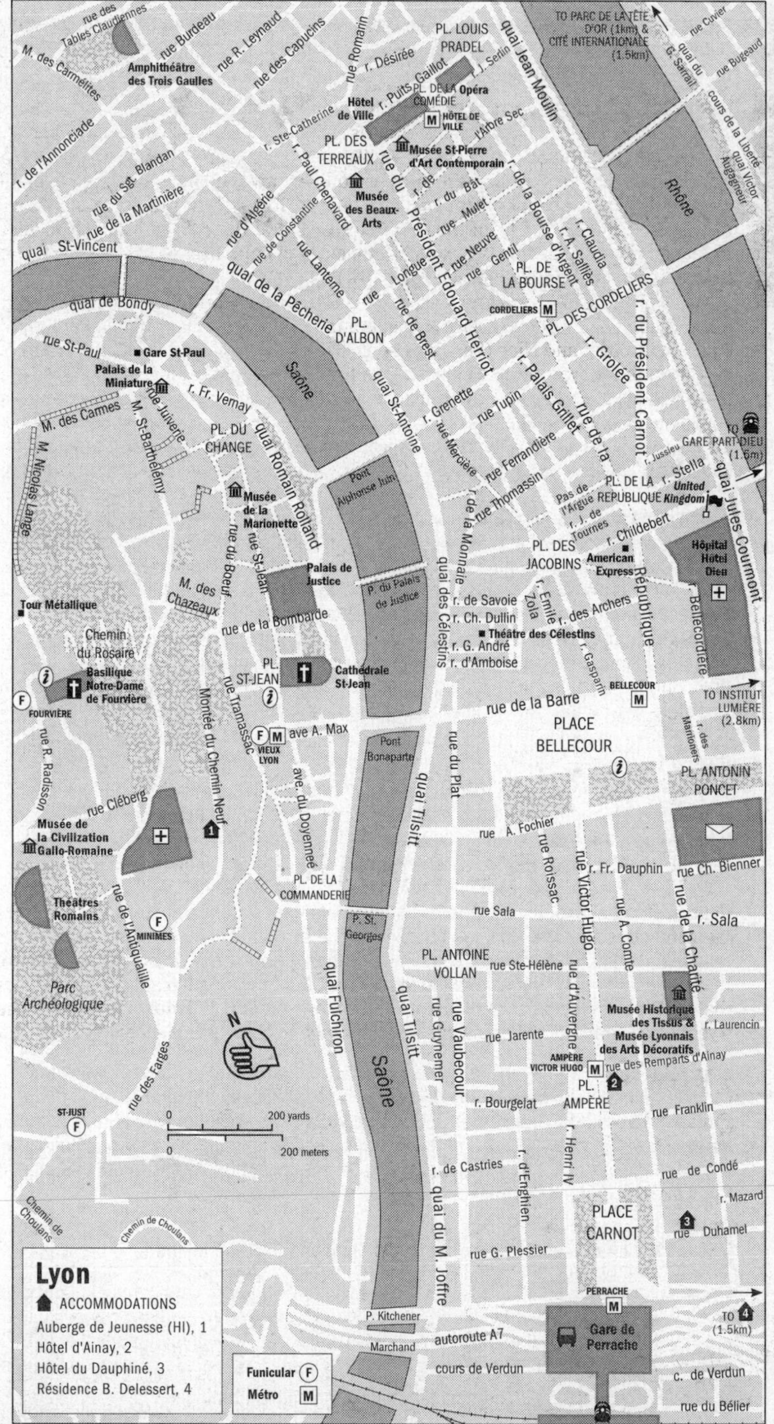
Lyon
ACCOMMODATIONS
Auberge de Jeunesse (HI), 1
Hôtel d'Ainay, 2
Hôtel du Dauphiné, 3
Résidence B. Delessert, 4
Funicular
Métro
Amphithéâtre des Trois Gaulles
Hôtel de Ville
Opéra
PL. LOUIS PRADEL
PL. DES TERREAUX
Musée St-Pierre d'Art Contemporain
Musée des Beaux-Arts
TO PARC DE LA TÊTE D'OR (1km) & CITÉ INTERNATIONALE (1.5km)
Rhône
Saône
PL. DE LA BOURSE
CORDELIERS
PL. DES CORDELIERS
PL. D'ALBON
Gare St-Paul
Palais de la Miniature
PL. DU CHANGE
Musée de la Marionette
Palais de Justice
TO GARE PART-DIEU (1.5m)
PL. DE LA REPUBLIQUE
United Kingdom
Hôpital Hôtel Dieu
PL. DES JACOBINS
American Express
Tour Métallique
Théâtre des Célestins
Basilique Notre-Dame de Fourvière
FOURVIÈRE
PL. ST-JEAN
Cathédrale St-Jean
VIEUX LYON
BELLECOUR
PLACE BELLECOUR
TO INSTITUT LUMIÈRE (2.8km)
PL. ANTONIN PONCET
Musée de la Civilization Gallo-Romaine
Théâtres Romains
MINIMES
Parc Archéologique
PL. DE LA COMMANDERIE
PL. ANTOINE VOLLAN
Musée Historique des Tissus & Musée Lyonnais des Arts Décoratifs
AMPÈRE VICTOR HUGO
PL. AMPÈRE
ST-JUST
200 yards
200 meters
PLACE CARNOT
PERRACHE
Gare de Perrache
TO (1.5km)
autoroute A7
cours de Verdun
quai St-Vincent
quai de Bondy
quai de la Pêcherie
quai St-Antoine
quai Romain Rolland
quai des Célestins
quai Tilsitt
quai Fulchiron
quai du M. Joffre
quai Jean Moulin
quai Jules Courmont
rue du Président Edouard Herriot
r. du Président Carnot
rue de la République
rue de la Barre
rue Victor Hugo
rue de la Charité
rue St-Jean
rue du Boeuf
Montée du Chemin Neuf
rue de l'Antiquaille
rue des Farges

tickets for 8F and a *carnet* of 10 for 68F (students 58F); the full-day *Ticket Liberté* (24F), good for unlimited public transport, is sold at tourist and TCL offices. The Métro runs 5am-midnight, and buses run 5am-9pm.

ORIENTATION AND PRACTICAL INFORMATION

Lyon is divided into nine **arrondissements** (districts). The **Saône** (to the west) and the **Rhône** (to the east) rivers run north-south through the city. West of the Saône, **Fourvière Hill** and its basilica overlook *vieux Lyon* (5ème). Between the two rivers lies the *centre ville*, home to the **Perrache** train station, **pl. Bellecour** (2ème) and the old **Terraux** neighborhood (1er); the **Croix-Rousse** (1er and 4ème) lies farther north. East of the Rhône (3ème and 6-8ème) lies the **Part-Dieu** train station (3ème), its commercial complex, and most of the city's population.

The **tourist office,** located at pl. Bellecour in the Pavilion, offers maps with museum listings (5F), a hotel reservation office, city tours (50-60F, students 25-35F), and the *Lyon City Card*, which grants admission to 14 museums and 1 day of public transport, for 90F. (☎ 04 72 77 69 69. Open May-Oct. M-Sa 9am-7pm, Su 10am-7pm; Nov.-Apr. daily 10am-6pm.) Check **email** at **Station-Internet,** 4, r. du President Carnot, 2ème. (40F per hr., students 30F. Open M-Sa 10am-7pm.) **Postal codes:** 690000-69009; the last digit indicates *arrondissement*.

ACCOMMODATIONS

As a financial center, Lyon's beds are booked during the work week, but vacancies open up on weekends. The off season is actually July and August. Inexpensive hotels cluster east of **pl. Carnot** near Perrache and north of **pl. des Terreaux.**

Auberge de Jeunesse (HI), 41/45 Montée du Chemin Neuf, **5ème** (☎ 04 78 15 05 50; fax 04 78 15 05 51). M: Vieux Lyon. Or walk west from pl. Bellecour, cross pont Bonaparte, turn right at pl. St-Jean and left on r. de la Bombarde; follow the hairpin left turn on Montée du Chemin Neuf, and walk uphill for a room with a view (15min.). Breakfast included. Sheets 17F. Bar, kitchen. Internet. Reception 24hr. Members only. 71F.

Hôtel St-Vincet, 9, r. Pareille, **1er** (☎ 04 78 27 22 56; fax 04 78 30 92 87), just off Quai St-Vincent. Simple, elegant rooms close to Lyon's nightlife. Breakfast 30F. Reserve ahead. English, German, and Italian spoken. Singles 180-230F; doubles 230-270F.

Hôtel d'Ainay, 14, r. des Remparts d'Ainay, **2ème** (☎ 04 78 42 43 42; fax 04 72 77 51 90). M: Ampère-Victor Hugo. English spoken. Breakfast 25F. Shower 15F. Reception 7am-10pm. Singles from 140F, with shower from 205F; doubles 175F, 235F.

FOOD

The stars adorning Lyon's restaurants confirm the city's reputation as the culinary capital of Western civilization. Cozy *bouchons*, descendants of inns, serve *andouillettes* (sausages made of cow intestines) and other local treats in the **Terreaux** district, 1er, and along **r. Mercière,** 2ème. Finish off your dinner with *torte tatin* (think upside-down apple pie) or *cocons* (chocolates wrapped in marzipan). Ethnic restaurants cluster off **r. de la République,** 2ème. **Prisunic supermarket** is on r. de la République, in pl. des Cordeliers, 2ème. (Open M-Sa 8:30am-8:30pm.)

Chez Mounier, 3, r. des Marronniers, **2ème.** This tiny place satisfies a discriminating local clientele with generous traditional specialties. 4-course *menus* 61-96F. Open Tu-Sa noon-2pm and 7-10:30pm, Su noon-2pm.

Saveurs Indiennes, 68, r. St-Jean, **5ème.** M: Vieux Lyon. Indo-Pakistani 3-course menus 65 or 95F; vegetarian 85F. Open W-Su noon-2pm and 7-11pm; M and Tu 7-11pm.

Les Paves de St-Jean, 23, r. Saint-Jean, **5ème.** M: Vieux Lyon. Boisterous, with dishes like *terrine maison* (homemade pate) and *quenelles* (fish dumpling). 3-course lunch menu 50F; other menus from 68F. Open daily noon-2pm and 7-11:30pm.

Chabert et Fils, 11, r. des Marronniers, **2ème.** One of the better known *bouchons* in Lyon. *Museau de bœuf* (snout of cattle) and *andouillettes* (sausages) are on the 99F *menu*. Lunch *menus* 50-80F. Open daily noon-2pm and 7-11pm.

Chez Carlo, 22, r. du Palais Grillet, **2ème.** Locals call it the best pasta and pizza in town (50-55F). Open Tu-Sa noon-2pm and 7-11pm, Su noon-2pm.

SIGHTS

VIEUX LYON. *(M: Vieux Lyon.)* Along the Saône at the bottom of the Fourvière Hill, the cobblestone streets of *vieux Lyon* are lined with cafes and magnificent medieval and Renaissance **townhouses.** The townhouses are graced with *traboules*, tunnels that lead from the street through a maze of courtyards. Colorful *hôtels particuliers*, with delicate carvings, shaded courtyards, and ornate turrets, are the result of wealth accrued over 400 years from the silk and publishing industries. The 12th-century **Cathédrale St-Jean** is where Henri IV met and married Marie de Médici in 1600. *(Pl. St-Jean. Open M-F 8am-noon and 2-7:30pm, Sa-Su 2-5pm. Free.)*

FOURVIÈRE AND ROMAN LYON. *(M: Fourvière.)* From the corner of r. du Bœuf and de la Bombarde, northwest of the cathedral, ascend the stairs and then follow the rose-lined **chemin de la Rosarie** up the **Fourvière Hill,** the nucleus of Roman Lyon. You can also take the **funiculaire** from the head of av. Max, off pl. St-Jean, to the top of the hill *(runs until 10pm; 8F)*. From there you can admire the view from the **Esplanade Fourvière,** where a model of the cityscape points out local landmarks. Behind the Esplanade is the **Basilique Notre-Dame de Fourvière,** with multicolored mosaics, gilded pillars, and elaborate carvings. On the left down the hill as you exit the church, you'll see signs for the **Musée Gallo-Romain,** which displays mosaics, helmets, swords, jewelry, and a bronze tablet inscribed with a speech by Lyon native Emperor Claudius. *(17, r. Cléberg. Open W-Su 9:30am-noon and 2-6pm. 20F, students 10F.)*

LE PRESQU'ÎLE AND LES TERREAUX. Monumental squares, statues, and fountains mark the **Presqu'île,** the lively area between the Rhône and the Saône. The heart is **pl. Bellecour,** a sea of red gravel with shops and flower stalls. The movie theaters and rushing crowds along **r. de la République,** which runs north from pl. Bellecour, establish the street as the urban aorta of Lyon. It terminates at **pl. Louis Pradel** in the 1*er*, at the tip of the **Terreaux** district. Opposite the spectacular 17th-century **Hôtel de Ville** (Town Hall), on pl. Louis Pradel, stands the **Musée des Beaux-Arts,** with a collection of French paintings, works by Spanish and Dutch masters, an Italian Renaissance wing, and a sculpture garden. *(On pl. des Terreaux. Open M 1-6pm, W-Su 10:30am-noon and 2-5:50pm. 25F, students 13F.)*

EAST OF THE RHÔNE AND MODERN LYON. The **Centre d'Histoire de la Résistance et de la Déportation** has documents, photos, and films of the Lyon-based resistance to the Nazis. *(14, av. Bertholet, 7ème. From Perrache, walk east over pont Gallieni; or take bus #11, 26, 32, or 39. Open W-Su 9am-5:15pm. 25F, students 13F.)* The **Musée d'Art Contemporain,** in the futuristic Cité Internationale de Lyon, has an extensive collection. *(On quai Charles de Gaulle, 6ème. M: Masséna or bus #4. Open W-Su noon-7pm. 25F, students 13F.)* The **Cité** itself is a sight; the super-modern complex houses offices, shops, theaters, and—don't jaywalk—Interpol's world headquarters.

FESTIVALS AND NIGHTLIFE

FESTIVALS. In summer, Lyon bursts with festivals and special events. Highlights are the **Fête de la Musique** (June 21), when performers take over the city streets, and the **Bastille Day** celebration (July 14). **Les Nuits de Fourvière** is a two-month summer festival held in the ancient Théâtre Romain, featuring both pop and classical concerts and plays. Buy tickets at the FNAC shop on r. de la République.

NIGHTLIFE. Nightlife in Lyon is fast and furious. Pound 10F tequilas with the crowd at **L'Abreuvoir,** 18, r. Ste-Catherine. (Open M-Th and Su 6pm-1am, F-Sa 6pm-2am.) **Le Chantier,** 20, r. Ste-Catherine, is a bit classier; slip down the spiral slide to reach the dance floor downstairs. (Live music W-Sa. Nominal cover. Open Tu-Sa 9pm-3am.) The city's best and most accessible late-night spots are a strip of **river-**

boat dance clubs by the east bank of the Rhône. Student-only **Le Fish,** opposite 21, quai Augagneur, has theme nights with salsa, jungle, house, and disco in a swank floater. (60-80F includes 1 drink; free before 11pm F-Sa. Open W-Sa 10pm-5am.)

BURGUNDY (BOURGOGNE)

Drunk on the power of their Duchy, the rulers of Burgundy made so bold as to challenge the French monarchy during the 15th century. Shifting alliances during the Hundred Years' War brought them lands as far north as the Netherlands, but Louis XI took advantage of the death of the last duke, Charles the Bold, to annex Burgundy to France. Today, Burgundy's fame rests on more peaceful foundations, as the home of some of the world's finest wines. Even cheaper wines can be superb, and dishes like *coq au vin* and *bœuf bourguinon* have made this region a capital in the hearts of Epicureans both in France and elsewhere.

DIJON

Dijon (pop. 160,000) is renowned for its snobbery in France, and its mustard everywhere else. The city is richly endowed with late medieval and early modern architecture, museums, a marvelous culinary tradition, and fine wines. The diverse **Musée des Beaux-Arts** occupies the east wing of the colossal **Palais des Ducs de Bourgogne,** in pl. de la Libération at the center of the *vieille ville.* (Open W-M 10am-6pm. 22F, students free; Su free.) At the **Église Notre-Dame,** in pl. Notre-Dame, admire the facade of gargoyles and rub the owl on the left side of the exterior for good luck. The Renaissance facade of the **Église St-Michel,** in pl. St-Michel, has been beautifully restored. The **Jardin de l'Arquebuse,** 1, av. Albert 1er, provides a welcome retreat from Dijon's churches and monuments with reflecting pools and arboretum. (Open daily July-Sept. 7:30am-8pm; Oct.-Feb. 7:30am-5:30pm; Mar.-June 7:30am-7pm.) A trip to the **Grey Poupon** store, 32, r. de la Liberté, where *moutarde au vin* has been made since 1777, should be more than a mere condiment to any Dijon excursion.

Trains from Cours de la Gare, at the end of av. Maréchal Foch, go to Lyon (2hr., 10 per day, 140F) and Paris (1½hr., 14 per day, 382F). The **tourist office,** on pl. Darcy, is a straight shot down av. Maréchal Foch from the station. (☎03 80 44 11 44. Open daily July-Aug. 9am-8pm; Sept.-June 9am-7pm.) Students can stay at the **Foyer International d'Étudiants,** 6, r. Maréchal Leclerc, which offers huge singles. Take bus #4 from pl. Darcy (dir. St-Apollinaire) to "Parc des Sports" to get there. (☎03 80 71 70 00; fax 03 80 71 60 48. Reception 24hr. 90F.) To catch up to the huge **Auberge de Jeunesse (HI),** 1, av. Champollion, take bus #5 (bus A at night) from pl. Grangier to "Epirey." (☎03 80 72 95 20. Breakfast included. Reception 24hr. Dorms 72-82F; singles with shower 140F; singles, doubles, and triples 155F per person.) **Hôtel Montchapet,** 26-28, r. Jacques Cellerier, north of av. Première Armée Française off Pl. Darcy, has homey rooms and lots of students. (☎03 80 53 95 00. Breakfast 33F. Reception 7am-10:30pm. Singles 150-215F; doubles 215-245F; triples 340F; quads 370F.) **R. Berbisey** and **Monge** host a variety of low- to mid-priced restaurants. Get your Grey Poupon at the **supermarket** downstairs in the **Galeries Lafayette,** 41, r. de la Liberté. (Open M-Sa 9am-7:15pm.) **Postal code:** 21000 (21031 for *Poste Restante*).

EXCURSION FROM DIJON: BEAUNE. The well-touristed town of **Beaune,** just south of Dijon on the Lyon rail line (25min., 21 per day, 38F), has poured out wine for centuries. Surrounded by the famous Côte de Beaune vineyards, the town itself is packed with wineries offering free tastings. The largest of the cellars belongs to **Patriarche Père et Fils,** 5-7, r. du Collège; stairs descend from the altar of an 18th-century chapel to a labyrinth of corridors packed with 10 million bottles. (☎03 80 24 53 78. Open daily 9:30-11:30am and 2-5:30pm. 50F.) The **tourist office,** 1, r. de l'Hôtel-Dieu, lists *caves* in the region offering tours. (☎03 80 26 21 30. Open June 9 to mid-Sept. M-Sa 9am-8pm, Su 9am-7pm; mid-Sept. to mid-Nov. M-Th 10am-6:30pm, F-Sa 9:30am-7pm, Su 10am-6pm; mid-Nov. to Apr. M-F and Su 10am-6pm, Sa 9:30am-6pm; Apr.-June 8 M-Th 9:30am-7pm, F-Sa 9:30am-8pm, Su 9:30am-6pm.)

BOURGES

Bourges (pop. 76,000) is proud of its Berry culture, with its fine regional wines and exquisite dinner platters; the city also features a medieval *vielle ville* and cobblestone streets lined with Gothic turrets. Bourges lies in the shadow of the **Cathédrale St-Étienne,** graced with stunning 13th-century handiwork in the cathedral, **tower,** and **crypt.** To get there from the train station, follow av. H. Laudier (which turns into av. Jean Jaurès), bear left onto r. du Commerce and continue straight on r. Moyenne. (Open daily July-Aug. 8am-9pm; June and Sept. 8:30am-7:30pm; Oct.-May 8:30am-6:30pm. Crypt and tower open daily 9am-6pm; unguided visits 2-7pm only. 32F, students 21F; 30F *billet jumelé* includes entrance to the Palais Jacques Coeur.) The **Palais Jacques-Coeur,** former home of Charles VII's financial minister, reveals lavish carvings. (Open July-Aug. 9am-6pm; Apr.-June and Sept. 9am-noon and 2-6pm; Oct.-Mar. 9am-noon and 2-5pm. Tours in French every hr. 32F, ages 18-24 21F. English text available.) A **pedestrian tour** is available from the **tourist office,** 21, r. Victor Hugo, near the cathedral. (☎02 48 23 02 60. Open M-Sa 9am-7pm, Su 10am-7pm.) Make sure to catch the **promenade des Remparts,** between r. Bourbonnoux and Molière, which winds past Roman ramparts and back gardens.

Trains leave for Tours (1½hr., 10 per day, 123F) and Paris (2½hr., 5per day, 153F). To get to the **Auberge de Jeunesse (HI),** 22, r. Henri Sellier, from the station, follow ac. H. Laudier (which becomes av. Jean Jaurès), bear left onto r. du Commerce, bear right on r. des Arènes (which becomes r. Fernault), cross at the intersection to r. René Ménard and follow it to the right, and turn left at r. Henri Sellier (25min.). (☎02 48 24 58 09. Reception M-F 8am-noon and 2pm-1am, Sa-Su 8am-noon and 5-10pm. 48F.) To reach the skateboard mecca of Europe, otherwise known as the **Centre International de Séjour, "La Charmille,"** 17, r. Félix-Chédin, cross the footbridge from the station over the tracks and head up r. Félix-Chédin. (☎02 48 23 07 40. Singles 98F; for 2 or more 72F per person.) Outdoor tables pack **pl. Gordaine** and **r. Borbonnoux,** while sandwich shops line **r. Moyenne** and **Mirebeau.** The huge **Leclerc supermarket** is on r. Prado off bd. Juranville. (Open M-F 9am-7:30pm, Sa 8:30am-7:30pm.) For late-night relaxing, try the pedestrian core of the *centre ville.* **Postal code:** 18000 (18012 "Bourges Cedex" for *Poste Restante*).

EASTERN FRANCE

Commonly ignored by travelers except as a rest stop between France and the rest of Europe, the "frontier regions" of the northeast represent the last outpost of French tourism. Sprawling clockwise from the Chunnel terminus to the mountainous Swiss border, the regions of Flanders, Champagne, Alsace, Lorraine, and Franche-Comté have been memorialized as battlefields since the Middle Ages, and for many travelers the northeast is of interest for primarily historical reasons. Yet the fields and cellars of Champagne, the wine towns surrounding Strasbourg, and the splendid hiking trails in the Jura mountains suggest other motives for visiting the area. Furthermore, the bloody history of these regions has done more than leave behind solemn monuments—it has left behind a culturally independent region, as fascinating as any in France.

ALSACE, LORRAINE, AND FRANCHE-COMTÉ

Heavily influenced by its tumultuous history, the northeastern frontier of France has been defined by its place as the prize in the ceaseless border wars between France and Germany. The entire region maintains a fascinating blend of local dialects, cuisine, and architecture. Germanic influences are most apparent in its cuisine, which pairs baguettes and fine wine with sauerkraut and heavy German meats, bringing an element of heartiness to traditional delicacies.

STRASBOURG

Just a few kilometers from the Franco-German border, Strasbourg (pop. 260,000) has spent much of its history being annexed by one side or another. Today the city is a symbol of French-German détente: German is often heard on its streets, and as many *Winstubs* line its squares as *pâtisseries*. With Brussels, Strasbourg is also joint center of the European Union. With half-timbered houses and flower-lined canals, the city makes a fantastic stopover.

PRACTICAL INFO, ACCOMMODATIONS, AND FOOD. Strasbourg is a major rail hub. **Trains** (☎03 88 22 50 50) go to: Luxembourg (2½hr., 14 per day, 160F); Frankfurt (3hr., 18 per day, 218F); Zurich (3hr., 18 per day, 218F); and Paris (4hr., 16 per day, 220F). The **tourist office,** 17, pl. de la Cathédrale, makes reservations for 10F. (☎88 52 28 28. Open June-Sept. M-Sa 9am-7pm, Su 9am-6pm; daily Oct.-May.) Rent **bikes** at **Vélocation,** 4, r. du Maire Kuss, near the train station. (☎03 88 52 01 01. 20F per half-day, 30F per day.) Get on the **Internet** at **Cybermaniak,** on r. du Fosse des Treize. (30F per hr. Open Tu and Th-Su 2pm-midnight, W 9am-noon.)

Make reservations or arrive early to find reasonable accommodations. **CIARUS (Centre International d'Accueil de Strasbourg),** 7, r. Finkmatt, has sparkling rooms, a social atmosphere, a TV, and Internet access. From the train station, take r. du Maire-Kuss to the canal, turn left, and follow quais St-Jean, Kléber, and r. Finkmatt; turn left on r. Finkmatt, and it's on the left (15min.). (☎03 88 15 27 88; fax 03 88 15 27 89; email ciarus@media-net.fr. Breakfast 20F. Reception 24hr. Check-in 3:30pm. Check-out 9am. Curfew 1am. Dorms 92-124F; singles 206F.) **Auberge de Jeunesse René Cassin (HI),** 9, r. de l'Auberge de Jeunesse, 2km from the train station, has clean but slightly worn rooms in a beautiful setting. From the station, go up r. de Maire-Kuss, turn right on quai St-Jean (which becomes quai Altoffer), and turn right on r. Ste-Marguerite to get to the bus station. From "Ste-Marguerite," take bus #3 (dir. Holtzheim-Entzheim Ouest) or 23 (dir. Illkirch) to "Auberge de Jeunesse." (☎03 88 30 26 46; fax 03 88 30 35 16. Breakfast included. Sheets 18F. Reception 7am-12:30pm, 1:30-7:30pm, and 8:30-11pm. Curfew 1am. Open Feb.-Dec. Dorms 73F; singles 149F; doubles 200F; nonmembers add 19F per person. **Camping** 42F.) **Auberge de Jeunesse,** Centre International de Rencontres du parc du Rhin, r. des Cavaliers, has spacious rooms looking over the Rhine. Take the tram to "Homme de Fer," then bus #2 to "Pont du Rhin;" it's around the tourist office. (☎03 88 45 54 20; fax 88 45 54 21. Breakfast included. Sheets 17F. Reception 7am-12:30pm. Curfew 1am. Dorms 73F; Sept.-Oct. and Mar.-May 86F; nonmembers 19F more.)

Winstubs are informal places traditionally affiliated with wineries that serve Alsatian specialties such as *choucroute garnie* (spiced sauerkraut served with meats)—try the **La Petite France** neighborhood, especially along r. des Dentelles and petite r. des Dentelles. Explore **pl. de la Cathédrale, r. Mercière,** or **r. du Vieil Hôpital** for restaurants, and **pl. Marché Gayot,** hidden off r. des Frères, for lively cafes. For **groceries,** swing by the **ATAC Supermarket,** 47, r. des Grandes Arcades, off pl. Kléber. (Open M-Sa 8:30am-8pm.)

SIGHTS AND ENTERTAINMENT. The ornate Gothic **Cathédrale de Strasbourg** sends its tower 142m skyward. Inside, the **Horloge Astronomique** demonstrates the wizardry of 16th-century Swiss clockmakers. While you wait for the clock to strut its stuff—apostles troop out of the clockface while a cock crows to greet St. Peter (daily at 12:30pm)—check out the **Pilier des Anges** (Angels' Pillar), a masterpiece of Gothic sculpture. You can climb the **tower** in front of the clock to follow in the footsteps of young Goethe, who scaled its 330 steps regularly to cure his fear of heights. (Cathedral open M-Sa 7-11:40am and 12:45-7pm, Su 12:45-6pm. Tickets for the clock go on sale at 8:30am in the cathedral and at 11:45am at the south entrance; 5F. Tower open daily 9am-6:30pm; 20F, children 10F.) **Palais Rohan,** 2, pl. du Château, houses a trio of small museums: the **Musée des Beaux-Arts, Musée des Arts Décoratifs,** and **Musée Archéologique.** (20F each; combined ticket for all three 40F, students 20F.) Take bus #23, 30, or 72 to "L'Orangerie" to see, predictably, **l'Orange-**

rie, Strasbourg's largest park; there are free concerts in summer (Th-Tu 8:30pm) at the Pavillion Joséphine. Across the canal from **La Petite France,** in the southwest corner of the *centre ville*, lies the spectacular collection of the new **Musée d'Art Moderne et Contemporain,** 1, pl. Hans Jean Arp, ranging from Impressionist to the avant-garde. (Open Tu-W, F-Su 11am-7pm, Th noon-10pm. 30F, students 20F.)

LA ROUTE DU VIN

Since the High Middle Ages, the wines of Alsace have been highly prized—and highly priced—across Europe. The vineyards of Alsace flourish along a corridor of 170km known as La Route du Vin (Wine Route) that begins at **Strasbourg** and stretches south along the foothills of the Vosges, passing through (from north to south) Molsheim, Obernai, Barr, Sélestat, Kintzheim, Riquewihr, Kaysersberg, Colmar, Eguisheim, and Guebwille along the way to **Mulhouse.** Hordes of tourists are drawn each year to explore the beautifully preserved medieval villages along the route—and, of course, for the free *dégustations* (tastings) along the way.

Colmar and **Sélestat** offer excellent bases and fascinating sights of their own; but don't miss out on smaller, less-touristed villages. The most accessible towns from Strasbourg are **Molsheim,** a medieval university center, and **Barr,** with an intricate old town and a vineyard trail that leads up through the hills. The more famous towns lie to the south: the most visited sight in Alsace, the **Château de Haut Koenigsbourg,** towers over **Kintzheim;** and the 16th-century walled hamlet of **Riquewihr,** the Route's most touristed village, is home to many of Alsace's best-known wine firms.

If you're in Strasbourg and are contemplating a detour along the Wine Route, drop by the **Departmental Tourist Office,** 9, r. du Dôme. (☎03 88 15 45 80. Open M 10am-noon and 2-6pm, Tu-F 9:30am-noon and 2-6pm, Sa 10am-1pm and 2-6pm.)

GETTING THERE AND GETTING AROUND. Strasbourg, the northern terminus of the Wine Route, is a major rail hub, easily accessible from France, Germany, and Luxembourg. Trains from Strasbourg hit many of the towns along the northern half of the Route, including: **Molsheim** (30min., 23F); **Barr** (50min., 35F); and **Sélestat** (30min., 42F). You can also go directly from Strasbourg to **Colmar** (40min., 57F), although wine lovers are more likely to get there via train from Sélestat (20min., 24F). **Bus** lines pepper the southern half of the Route, running from Colmar to **Kaysersberg** (20min., 12F); **Riquewihr** (30min., 15-20F); and many other small towns on the Route. From Mulhouse, leap into Switzerland from nearby **Basel** (20min., 36F), return to **Strasbourg** (1hr., 85F, or go to **Paris** (4½hr., 9 per day, 275F).

SÉLESTAT. Sélestat (pop. 17,200), between Colmar and Strasbourg, is often overlooked by tourists on their way between the two larger cities. Founded in 1452, the **Bibliothèque Humaniste,** 1, r. de la Bibliothèque, contains a fascinating collection of ancient documents, reflecting Sélestat's 15th-century status as a center of humanist learning. (Open July-Aug. M and W-F 9am-noon and 2-6pm, Sa-Su 9am-noon and 2-5pm; Sept.-June M and W-F 9am-noon and 2-6pm. 20F.) The **tourist office,** 10, bd. Gén. Leclerc, in the Commanderie St-Jean, rents **bikes.** (☎03 88 58 87 20; fax 03 88 92 88 63. 35F per 2hr., 50F per half-day, 80F per day. Open May-Sept. M-F 9am-12:30pm and 1:30-7pm, Sa 9am-noon and 2-5pm, Su 9am-3pm; Oct.-Apr. M-F 8:30am-noon and 1:30-6pm, Sa 9am-noon and 2-5pm.) The **Hôtel de l'Ill,** 13, r. des Bateliers, off bd. des Thiers, has bright rooms in a lovely building. (☎03 88 92 91 09. Breakfast 30F. Reception daily 7am-3pm and 5-11pm. Singles 140-150F; doubles 180-220F; triples with shower and bathroom 400F.) **Camping Les Cigognes** is outside the ramparts on the south edge of the *vieille ville.* (☎03 88 92 03 98. Reception July-Aug. 2-10pm; May-June and Sept.-Oct 7:30am-noon and 2-8pm; closed Nov.-Apr. July-Aug. 60F per site and 1 person, 80F for 2 or 3 people; May-June and Sept.-Oct. 50F, 70F.) You'll find food along **r. des Chevaliers** and **r. de l'Hôpital. Postal code:** 67600.

COLMAR. Colmar (pop. 65,000) feels distinctly unlike the rest of France, a reminder that it hasn't always been a part of the country. Its crooked lanes and pastel houses lend it a calm atmosphere despite packs of summer tourists. The collection at the **Musée Unterlinden,** 1, r. d'Unterlinden, ranges from Romanesque to Renaissance—its crown jewel, Grünewald's *Issenheim Altarpiece*, alone justifies a visit. (Open Apr.-Oct. daily 9am-6pm; Nov.-Mar. W-M 10am-5pm. 35F, students 25F.) The **Eglise des Dominicains,** on pl. des Dominicains, houses Colmar's other major masterpiece, Schongauer's *Virgin in the Rose Bower*. (Open daily 10am-12:45pm and 3-5:45pm. 8F, students 6F.)

To get to the **tourist office,** 4, r. d'Unterlinden, from the train station, turn left on av. de la République (which becomes r. Kléber) and follow it to the right to pl. Unterlinden. (☎03 89 20 68 92; email accueil@ot-colmar.fr. Open July-Aug. M-Sa 9am-7pm, Su 9:30am-2pm; Apr.-June and Sept.-Oct. M-Sa 9am-6pm, Su 10am-2pm; Nov.-Mar. M-Sa 9am-noon and 2-6pm, Su 10am-2pm.) To reach the **Auberge de Jeunesse (HI),** 2, r. Pasteur, take bus #4 (dir. Logelbach) to "Pont Rouge." (☎03 89 80 57 39. Breakfast 20F. Sheets 9F. Reception July-Aug. 7-10am and 5pm-midnight; Sept.-June 5-11pm. Curfew midnight. Lockout 10am-5pm. No reservations. Closed Dec. 15-Jan. 15. Dorms 48F; singles 78F; doubles 156F. V, MC.) Take bus #1 (dir. Horbourg-Wihr) to "Plage d'Ill" for **Camping de l'Ill,** on rte. Horbourg-Wihr. (☎03 89 41 15 94. Reception July-Aug. M-F 7am-9pm, Sa-Su 8am-noon and 2-10pm; daily Feb.-June and Sept.-Nov. 8am-noon and 2-8pm. Open Feb.-Nov. Adults 18F, children under 10 10F; tent 10F; site 20F.) Stock up at **Monoprix supermarket,** on pl. Unterlinden. (Open M-F 8am-8:30pm, Sa 8am-7:55pm.) *Brasseries* with canal-side terraces abound in **La Petite Venise** and the **Quartier des Tanneurs. Postal code:** 68000.

BESANÇON

Since Julius Caesar founded a military post here in 58 BC, Besançon (pop. 120,000) has intrigued military strategists with its geographically protected location. Now a university town known for its prosperity as France's watch-making capital, Besançon fascinates its young population with an energetic abundance of nightlife.

PRACTICAL INFO, ACCOMMODATIONS, AND FOOD. Trains chug to the station, on av. de la Paix (☎08 36 35 35 35), from: Dijon (1hr., 6 per day, 74F); Paris's Gare de Lyon station (2hr., 7 per day, 318F); and Strasbourg (3hr., 10 per day, 163F). From the station, head downhill and cross onto av. Maréchal Foch, then continue downhill and to the left (as it becomes av. de l'Helvétie) until you reach pl. de la Première Armée Française. The *vieille ville* is across the pont de la République; the **tourist office,** 2, pl. de la Première Armée Française, is in the park to the right. (☎03 81 80 92 55; www.besancon.com. Open April to mid-June and late Sept. M 10am-7pm, Tu-Sa 9am-7pm; mid-June to mid-Sept. M 10am-7pm, Tu-Sa 9am-7pm, Su 10am-noon and 3-5pm; Oct.-Mar. M 10am-6pm, Tu-Sa 9am-6pm.) Surf the **Internet** at **Rom Collection,** 22, r. du Lycée. (1F per min., 50F per hr.) To get to **Foyer Mixte de Jeunes Travailleurs (HI),** 48, r. des Cras, turn left from the station on av. de la Paix (which becomes r. de Belfort) and left again on r. Marie-Louise (which turns into r. des Cras); the hostel is uphill on the right (total 25min.). Or take bus #7 from pl. Flore off r. de Belfort on av. Carnot (dir. Orchamps; 3 per hr.) to Oiseaux. (☎03 81 40 32 00; fax 03 81 40 32 01. Breakfast and sheets included. Reception 9am-8pm. No reservations; arrive early. Singles 100F, 90F next night; doubles 160F, 140F next night.) An eclectic group of student-oriented restaurants line **r. Claude-Pouillet.** Pick up **groceries** at **Monoprix,** 12, Grande Rue. (Open M-Sa 8:30am-9pm.) **La Boîte à Sandwiches,** 21 r. du Lycée, off r. Pasteur, serves scrumptious sandwiches (11-30F) and salads (15-35F) simultaneously. (Open M-Sa 11:30am-2:30pm and 6:30pm-midnight.) At **Au Gourmand,** 5 r. Megevand, patrons dine on hearty rice and pasta dishes with provincial cheeses (35-50F) amid delightful decorations. (Open M-F 11am-2pm and 6:45-9pm.) **Postal code:** 25000 (25031 "Besançon-Cedex" for *Poste Restante*).

SIGHTS AND ENTERTAINMENT. The elegant Renaissance buildings gracing the *vieille ville* provide plenty of eye candy during a casual stroll around town, but the city's true delights lie high above in the **citadel,** designed by Louis XIV's architect, Vauban. It's a grueling trek uphill from town, but the view and the three museums inside are worth it. Within the citadel, the **Musée de la Résistance et de la Déportation** chronicles the Nazis' rise to power and the German occupation of France; other sights include a natural history museum, a zoo, an aquarium, and a folk arts museum. Access to the first level, including manicured lawns and a breathtaking panorama, is free. (At the end of r. des Fusillés de la Résistance. Grounds open daily July-Aug. 9am-7pm; Apr.-June and Sept.-Oct. 9am-6pm; Nov.-Mar. 10am-5pm. Museums open daily in summer 9am-6pm; off season 10am-5pm. Admission to inner fortress and all museums 40F, students 30F.) The **Cathédrale St-Jean,** perched on the hill beneath the citadel, mixes architectural styles from the 12th to 18th centuries and is crowned by the intricate 19th-century **Horloge Astronomique.** (Open W-M 9am-7pm. Free. Tours of clock 15F, children 9F.) The **Musée des Beaux-Arts,** on pl. de la Révolution, houses an exceptional collection ranging from ancient Egyptian treasures to artwork by Matisse. (Open W-M 9:30am-6pm. 21F, students free; Su and holidays free for all.) Small bars and *brasseries* line **rues Pasteur** and **Bersot.** Every night of the week, local students pack bars and discos, particularly the three dance floors at **Le Queen,** 8, av. de Chardonnet. (Open W-Th 10:30pm-4am, F-Sa 10:30pm-5am.) Shoot pool at the surprisingly hip **Pop Hall,** 26, r. Proudhon across from the post office; even the decorations in its bathrooms will amaze you. (Open M-Th 3pm-1am, Sa 3pm-2am, Su 6pm-2am.)

EXCURSION FROM BESANÇON: PONTARLIER AND THE JURA. The quiet town of **Pontarlier** (840m) makes a good base for reaching greater heights in the Haut-Jura mountains. The Jura are most famed for cross-country **skiing;** over 60km of trails wind around the city. (Day pass 30F, ages 10-16 20F.) The closest Alpine ski area is **Le Larmont** (☎03 81 46 55 20). **Sport et Neige,** 4, r. de la République (☎03 81 39 04 69), rents skis (50F per day). In summer, **fishing, hiking,** and **mountain biking** are popular. Rent a **bike** (80F per day) from **Cycles Pernet,** 23, r. de la République. (☎03 81 46 48 00. Open Tu-Sa 9am-noon and 2-7pm.) **Monts Jura buses,** 9, r. Proudhon, in Besançon (☎03 81 39 88 80), run to Pontarlier (55min., 6 per day, 51F). The **tourist office,** 14bis, r. de la Gare, has info on outdoor activities and sells hiking and topographical maps. (☎03 81 46 48 33; fax 03 81 46 83 32. Maps 12-58F.) **L'Auberge de Pontarlier (HI),** 2, r. Jouffroy, is clean and central. (☎03 81 39 06 57; fax 03 81 39 24 34. Breakfast 19F. Sheets 17F. Reception 8am-noon and 5:30-10pm. Reserve ahead. Members only. 49F; private rooms 79F.) **Postal code:** 25300.

NANCY

Nancy (pop. 100,000) is a model of 18th-century classicism, with broad plazas, wrought-iron grillwork, and cascading fountains. More than just a pretty face, the city reigns as the cultural and intellectual heart of Lorraine. The **place Stanislas** wraps Baroque gilded-iron arms around a statue of the "Good Duke" Stanislas Lesczynski, a dethroned Polish king relocated to Lorraine by his son-in-law Louis XV. Pass through the five-arch **Arc de Triomphe** to the tree-lined pl. de la Carrière, whose northern end segues into the relaxing **Parc de la Pépinière.** The park's aromatic **Roseraie** beckons with roses from around the world. The eye-grabbing **Musée de l'École de Nancy** holds dramatic sculptures, glass work, and furniture that redefine everyday objects. To get there, take bus #5 (dir. Vandoeuvre Cheminots) to "Nancy Thermal." (Open M 2-6pm and W-Su 10:30am-6pm. 35F; students 25F and W free; free 1st Su of each month.)

Trains roll to and from Metz (40min., 24 per day, 51F); Strasbourg (1hr., 19 per day, 110F); and Paris (3hr., 14 per day, 209F). The **tourist office,** on pl. Stanislas, is to the right as you enter from r. Stanislas; ask for the invaluable *Le Fil d'Ariane* guide. (☎03 83 35 22 41; fax 03 83 35 90 10. Open Apr.-Sept. M-Sa 9am-7pm, Su 10am-5pm; Oct.-May M-Sa 9am-6pm, Su 10am-1pm.) Access the **Internet** at **Voyager** on r. St-Jean. (5F per 1-5min.; 1F each additional min. Open M-Sa 9am-midnight, Su 2-11pm.) **Centre d'Accueil de Remicourt (HI),** 149, r. de Vandoeuvre, is in Villiers-lès-Nancy, 4km away. From the station, take bus #26 (dir. Villiers Clairlieu; 2 per hr.; last bus 8pm) to "St-Fiacre"; head downhill from the stop, turn right on r. de Vandoeuvre, walk uphill, and follow the signs. (☎03 83 27 73 67.

Breakfast included. Reception 9am-noon and 2-5pm. 3- to 4-bed dorms 80F; doubles with shower and toilet 95F.) **Hôtel de l'Académie,** 7, r. des Michottes, is between the station and pl. Stanislas. (☎03 83 35 52 31. Breakfast 22F. Reception M-Sa 24hr, Su noon-4:30pm. Singles and doubles 140-200F; extra bed 40F.) Restaurants cluster around **r. des Maréchaux. Postal code:** 54000 (54039 "Nancy-RP" for *Poste Restante*).

CHAMPAGNE AND THE NORTH

John Maynard Keynes once remarked that his major regret in life was not having consumed enough champagne; a trip through the rolling vineyards and fertile plains of Champagne promises many opportunities not to repeat his mistake. The moniker *champagne* is fiercely guarded; the name can be applied only to wines made from regional grapes and produced according to a rigorous, time-honored method. Farther north, a different sparkling drink holds sway; in Flanders, by the Belgian border, beer is the order of the day, to be quaffed with lots of mussels. The northern corner of the country is the final frontier of tourist-free France, perhaps because of the scars the Channel coast bears from WWII and its aftermath. But as you flee the ferry ports, don't overlook the hidden treasures of the North, including the intriguing Flemish culture of Arras and the world-class art collections of Lille.

REIMS

Reims (pop. 185,000) delights with the bubbly champagne of its fabulous *caves*, the beauty of architectural masterpieces, and its royal history. The famed **Cathédrale de Notre-Dame,** built with golden limestone quarried in the Champagne *caves*, features a set of sea-blue stained-glass windows by Marc Chagall. (Open daily 7:30am-7:30pm. Tours July-Aug. M-Sa 10:30am, 2:30, and 4:30pm, Su 11am, 2:30, and 4:30pm; Mar.-June and Oct. less frequently. 35F, under 26 20F.) Enter the **Palais du Tau** through the cathedral for dazzling robes and sacramental objects from the crowning of Charles X. (Pl. du Cardinal Luçon. Open July-Aug. daily 9:30am-6:30pm; Sept. to mid-Nov. and mid-Mar. to June daily 9:30am-12:30pm and 2-6pm; mid-Nov. to mid-Mar. M-F 10am-noon and 2-5pm, Sa-Su 10am-noon and 2-6pm. 32F, students 21F.) Four hundred kilometers of *crayères* (Roman chalk quarries) wind underground through the countryside around Reims, along with more recently dug tunnels sheltering bottles emblazoned with the great names of Champagne—Pommery, Piper-Heidsieck, Mumm, and Taittinger. The tourist office (see below) has a list of **caves** open to the public; many offer tours by appointment only, so call ahead. The most elegant tour is at **Pommery,** 5, pl. du Général Gouraud. (☎03 26 61 62 56. By appointment mid-Mar to Oct. daily 11am-5pm; Nov.-Mar. M-F 11am-5pm. 40F, students 20F.) **Pl. Drouet d'Erlon** is crowded with cafes and bars open until 3am.

Trains (☎03 26 78 60 60) leave from bd. Joffre to Paris (1½hr., 11 per day, 121F). To get to the **tourist office,** 2, r. Guillaume de Machault, from the station, follow the right-hand curve of the rotary to pl. d'Erlon, and turn left on r. de Vesle, turn right on r. du Tresor; it's on the left before the cathedral. (☎03 26 77 45 25; fax 02 36 77 45 27. Open mid-Apr. to mid-Oct. M-Sa 9am-7pm, Su 10am-5pm; mid-Oct. to mid-Apr. M-Sa 9am-6pm, Su 10am-5pm.) To get to the **Auberge de Jeunesse (HI),** on chaussée Bocquaine (15min.), from the station, cross the park, turn right on bd. Général Leclerc, cross the first bridge (pont de Vesle), and take your first left. (☎03 26 40 52 60. Breakfast 18F. Reception 24hr. Singles 89-129F; doubles and triples 69-119F per person. Non-members 10F fee.) **Au Bon Accueil,** 31, r. Thillois, is off pl. d'Erlon. (☎03 26 88 55 74. Breakfast 25F. Reception 24hr. Singles 80-150F; doubles 140-220F.) **Pl. Drouet d'Erlon** brims with *boulangeries*, cheap cafes, and restaurants. **Monoprix supermarket** is at the corner of r. de Vesle and r. de Talleyrand. (Open M-Sa 8:30am-9pm.) **Postal code:** 51100.

EXCURSION FROM REIMS: EPERNAY. Unlike the more metropolitan Reims, neighboring Epernay (pop. 30,000) strips away all urban distractions and devotes itself heart and soul to the production of the bubbly. **Av. de Champagne,** one of the richest streets in the world, is distinguished by its mansions, lush gardens, and monumental champagne firms. Swanky **Moët & Chandon,** 20, av. de Champagne, produces the king of all wines: Dom Perignon. (☎ 03 26 51 20 20. Open Apr.-Nov. 15 daily 9:30-11:30am and 2-4:30pm; Nov. 19-Mar. 14 closed Sa-Su. Tours with tasting 40F.) **Mercier,** 70, av. de Champagne, gives fascinating 30-minute tours in roller-coaster-like cars. (☎ 03 26 51 22 22. Open Mar.-Nov. M-F 9:30-11:30am and 2-4:30pm, Sa-Su until 5pm; Dec.-Mar. closed Tu-W. Tours 30F.) Frequent **trains** arrive at cour de la Gare from Reims (25min., 14 per day, 33F). From the station, walk straight through pl. Mendès and one block up r. Gambetta to reach the town center at pl. de la République; from there, turn left on av. de Champagne to reach the **tourist office,** 7, av. de Champagne, and the myriad *caves*.

GERMANY (DEUTSCHLAND)

DEUTSCHMARKS

US$1 = DM2.28	1DM = US$0.44
CDN$1 = DM1.54	1DM = CDN$0.65
UK£1 = DM3.20	1DM = UK£0.31
IR£1 = DM2.48F	1DM = IR£0.40
AUS$1 = DM1.28	1DM = AUS$0.78
NZ$1 = DM0.98	1DM = NZ$1.02
SAR1 = DM0.32	1DM = SAR3.13
EURO€1 = DM1.96	1DM = EURO€0.51

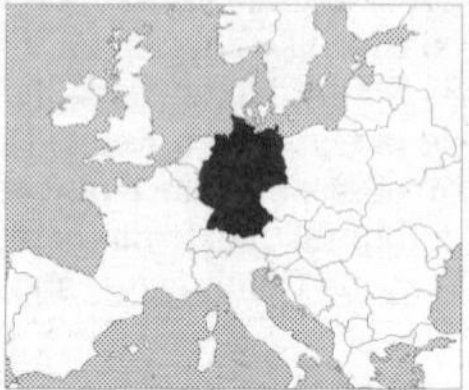

Country code: 49. **International dialing prefix:** 00. From outside Germany, dial int'l dialing prefix (see inside back cover) + 49 + city code + local number.

After centuries of war, fragmentation, occupation, and division and a decade after the fall of the Berlin Wall, Germany now finds itself a wealthy nation at the forefront of European and global politics. The nation's history is a parable for life in the modern era, encapsulating all of the promises and betrayals of the 20th century and exposing the fissures beneath the veneer of Western civilization.

Germany has always been a wellspring of revolutionaries and innovators, for better and for worse—Germans must grapple with the fact that the cradle of Bach, Beethoven, Goethe, Kant, and Nietzsche also spawned Hitler's Dachau and Buchenwald. While combatting this incongruous legacy, modern Germans must also come to terms with the issues spawned by the country's remarkably quick reunification. In the wake of Europe's most recent revolutions, Germany's pivotal role between East and West is even more important than it was during the Cold War, yet efforts to provide leadership on the Continent have been hampered by Germany's internal identity crises. Nevertheless, the country assumes an increasingly assertive role in the global community, and as it enters the next millennium, it remains the dominant economic power on the Continent.

For more comprehensive coverage, treat yourself to *Let's Go: Germany 2001*.

FACTS AND FIGURES

Official Name: Federal Republic of Germany.

Government: Federal Republic.

Capital: Berlin.

Land Area: 357,021 sq. km.

Geography: Lowlands in north, uplands in center, Bavarian Alps in south.

Climate: Temperate and marine; cool, cloudy, wet winters and summers.

Major Cities: Berlin, Hamburg, Munich, Cologne, Frankfurt.

Population: 82.1 million.

Language: German.

Religions: Lutheran (41%), Catholic (34%), Muslim (3%).

Average Income: US$22,700.

Major Exports: Iron, steel, coal, cement, chemicals, machinery, and vehicles.

DISCOVER GERMANY

Berlin's myriad cultural and historical treasures, not to mention its chaotic nightlife, sprawl over an area eight times the size of Paris (see p. 402). **Dresden** is nearly as intense, with a jumping nightlife and exquisite palaces and museums (see p. 418).

Daytrip to the tiny villages of **Saxon Switzerland,** a surefire way to satisfy your *Wanderlust* (see p. 422). **Weimar** rests solidly on the cultural heritage of Goethe, the Bauhaus movement, and Germany's first liberal constitution (see p. 423). To the north, reckless **Hamburg,** Germany's second-largest city, fuses the burliness of a port town with cosmopolitan flair (see p. 427), while **Cologne,** near the Belgian and Dutch borders, is home to Germany's largest, most poignant cathedral and pounding nightlife (see p. 434). To the south, **Koblenz** is the gateway to the castles and wine towns of the **Rhine** (see p. 443) and **Mosel** (see p. 445) **Valleys.** Farther south, Germany's oldest, most prestigious, and most scenic university sits below the brooding ruins of **Heidelberg's** castle (see p. 446). From there, live out your favorite Brothers Grimm fairy tales in the **Black Forest,** from the winding alleys of **Freiburg** to the mountain-top lakes of **Titisee** and **Schluchsee** (see p. 451). Or, conquer the so-called **Romantic Road** (see p. 466), which snakes along the western edge of Bavaria from **Würzburg** to **Füssen** and is epitomized by the kitschy yet fascinating medieval city of **Rothenburg** (see p. 467). At the southern end of the trail lie the Mad King Ludwig's **Royal Castles** (see p. 468). And no trip to Germany would be complete without visiting the Bavarian capital of **Munich,** which takes bucolic merriment to a frothy head with its excellent museums and jovial beer halls (see p. 454).

ESSENTIALS

WHEN TO GO

Germany's climate is temperate, with rain year-round (especially in summer). The cloudy, temperate months of May, June, and Sept. are the best time to go, as there are fewer tourists and the weather is pleasant. Germans head to vacation spots en masse in early July with the onset of school vacations. Winter sports gear up November to April; skiing high season is mid-December to March.

DOCUMENTS AND FORMALITIES

Germany requires **visas** of South Africans, but not of nationals of Australia, Canada, the EU, New Zealand, or the US for stays of shorter than three months.

EMBASSIES AND CONSULATES

All foreign embassies in Germany are in **Berlin** (p. 402).

German Embassies at Home: Australia, 119 Empire Circuit, Yarralumla, Canberra, ACT 2600 (☎ (02) 62 70 19 11; fax 62 70 19 51); **Canada,** 1 Waverly St., Ottawa, ON K2P 0T8 (☎613 232 11 01; email 100566.2620@compuserve.com). **Ireland,** 31 Trimleston Ave., Booterstown, Blackrock, Co. Dublin (☎ (012) 69 30 11; fax 269 39 46). **New Zealand,** 90-92 Hobson St., Thorndon, Wellington (☎ (04) 473 60 63; fax 473 60 69). **South Africa,** 180 Blackwood St., Arcadia, Pretoria, 0083 (☎ (012) 427 89 00; fax 343 94 01). **UK,** 23 Belgrave Sq., London SW1X 8PZ (☎ (020) 78 24 13 00; fax 78 24 14 35). **US,** 4645 Reservoir Rd. NW, Washington, D.C. 20007-1998 (☎ (202) 298 40 00; fax 298 42 49; www.germany-info.org).

GETTING THERE AND GETTING AROUND

BY PLANE. Most flights land in Frankfurt; Berlin, Munich, and Hamburg also have international airports. **Lufthansa,** the national airline, has the most flights in and out of the country, although they're not always the cheapest option. For cheap fares, look into **Icelandair** flights to neighboring Luxembourg; from there, it's only three hours by train to Cologne and four hours to Frankfurt. Flying within Germany is usually more expensive and less convenient than taking the train.

BY TRAIN. The **Deutsche Bahn (DB)** network (in Germany ☎ (0180) 599 66 33; http://bahn.hafas.de or www.bahn.de) is Europe's best, and also one of the most expensive. **RE** (RegionalExpress) and slower **RB** (Regionalbahn) trains connect neighboring cities, while **IR** (InterRegio) trains cover larger networks between cities. **D** trains serve international routes. **EC** (EuroCity) and **IC** (InterCity) trains zoom along between major cities hourly 6am-10pm. The futuristic **ICE** (InterCityExpress) trains run at speeds up to 280kph. You must purchase a **Zuschlag** (supplement) to ride an ICE, IC, or EC train (DM7 from the station, DM9 on the train).

The **German Railpass** allows unlimited travel for four to 10 days within a four-week period. Non-Europeans can purchase German Railpasses in their home countries and (with a passport) in major German train stations (2nd-class 5-day pass US$196, 10-day US$306). The **German Rail Youth Pass** is for tourists under 26 (5-day US$156, 9-day US$198), and the second-class **Twin Pass** is for two adults traveling together (5-day US$294, 10-day US$459). Travelers under 26 can purchase **TwenTickets,** which knock 20-60% off fares over DM10; be sure to let your ticket agent know your age. A **Schönes-Wochenende-Ticket** offers unlimited travel to up to five people on any of the slower trains (*not* ICE, IC, EC, D, or IR) from 12:01am Saturday until 2am on Monday (DM35). Single travelers often find larger groups who are amenable to sharing their ticket, either free or for a fraction of the purchase cost. The **Guten-Abend-Ticket** is an excellent deal for long-distance night travel and entitles its holders to travel anywhere (*not* on InterCityNight or CityNightLines) in Germany between 7pm and 2am (2nd class DM59, with ICE surcharge DM69; 1st class DM99, DM109; F and Su DM15 extra).

A great option for those making frequent and extensive use of German trains for more than one month, the **Bahncard** is valid for one year and entitles you to a 50% discount on all trains. Passes are available at major train stations and require a passport-sized photo (2nd-class DM260; ages 17-22, over 60, or any student under 27 DM130; students under 17 DM65.)

Eurail is valid in Germany and provides free passage on urban S-Bahns and DB buses, but not U-Bahns. **Public transit** is excellent, and comes in four types: the **Straßenbahn** (streetcar), **S-Bahn** (surface commuter rail), **U-Bahn** (underground subway), and regular **buses.** Consider buying a day card *(Tageskarte)* or multiple-ride ticket *(Mehrfahrkarte);* they usually pay for themselves quickly.

BY BUS. Bus service between cities and to outlying areas runs from the local **Zentralomnibusbahnhof (ZOB),** which is usually close to the main train station. Buses are often slightly more expensive than trains for comparable distances. Railpasses are not valid on any buses other than a few run by Deutsche Bahn.

BY FERRY. Ferries in the **North** and **Baltic Seas** are reliable and go everywhere. Ferries run from Hamburg, Kiel, Travemünde, Rostock, and Saßnitz to England, Scandinavia, Poland, the Baltic States, and Russia. See **Hamburg** (p. 427) and **Rostock** (p. 426) for detailed information.

BY CAR. German road conditions are generally excellent. Yes, it's true, there is no set speed limit on the **Autobahn,** only a recommendation of 130kph (81mph). Germans drive *fast.* Watch for signs indicating right-of-way (usually designated by a yellow triangle). The Autobahn is indicated by an intuitive "A" on signs; secondary highways, where the speed limit is usually 100kph, are accompanied by signs bearing a "B." Germans drive on the right side of the road. In cities and towns, **speed limits** hover around 30-60kph (31mph). Germans use unleaded gas almost exclusively; prices run around DM7 per gallon, or about DM1.80 per liter.

BY BIKE AND BY THUMB. **Bikes** are sight-seeing power tools; Germany makes it easy with its wealth of trails and bike tours. Cities and towns usually have designated bike lanes. For information about bike routes, regulations, and maps, contact **Allgemeiner Deutscher Fahrrad-Club,** Postfach 10 77 47, 28077 Bremen. A bike tour guidebook, including extensive maps, is available from **Deutsches Jugendherbergswerk (DJH)** (☎ (05231) 740 10). Although *Let's Go* does not recommend **hitchhiking,** it is permitted and quite common on the Autobahn. Hitchers may stand only at rest stops, gas stations, and in front of the Autobahn signs at on-ramps. **Mitfahrzentralen** pair up drivers and riders, who pay the agency a fee for the match and then negotiate the payment agreement with their driver.

TOURIST SERVICES AND MONEY

EMERGENCY. Police: ☎ 110. **Ambulance and Fire:** ☎ 112.

TOURIST OFFICES. Every city in Germany has a **tourist office,** usually located near the train station *(Hauptbahnhof)* or central square *(Marktplatz).* All are marked by a thick lowercase **"i"** sign. The offices often book rooms for a small fee.

MONEY. The **deutsche Mark** or **Deutschmark** (abbreviated DM) is the unit of currency in Germany. It is one of the most stable and respected currencies in the world; in most markets in Eastern Europe, "hard currency" means US dollars and

Deutschmarks exclusively. One DM equals 100 Pfennig (Pf). Coins come in denominations of 1, 2, 5, 10, and 50Pf, and DM1, 2, and 5. Bills come in DM5, 10, 20, 50, 100, 200, 500, and 1000. If you stay in **hostels** and prepare your own food, expect to spend anywhere from US$25-50 per person per day. **Hotels** start at about US$25 per night; a basic sit-down meal costs at least US$6. **Tipping** is not as common in Germany as elsewhere—most Germans only tip DM1-2 in restaurants and bars, or when they are the beneficiary of a service, such as a taxi ride. Note that tips in Germany are not left lying on the table, but handed directly to the server when you pay. If you don't want any change, say *Das stimmt so* (das SHTIMMT so). Germans rarely bargain except at flea markets. Most goods and services bought in Germany will automatically include a **VAT** of 15%. In German, this is called the *Mehrwertsteuer* **(MwSt).** Non-EU citizens can get the VAT refunded for large purchases of goods. At the point of purchase, ask for a Tax-Free Shopping Cheque, then have it stamped at customs upon leaving the country or at a customs authority. The goods must remain unused until you leave the country.

BUSINESS HOURS. **Bank hours** can seem random; a typical work week might be M-W and F 9am-12:30pm and 2:30-4pm, Th 9am-12:30pm and 2:30-5pm. **Store hours** are usually M-F 9am-6:30pm, Sa 9am-2pm. Some stores remain open until 8:30pm on Th and until 4pm on the first Sa of each month.

ACCOMMODATIONS AND CAMPING

HOSTELS. Germany currently has about **600 hostels**—more than any other nation on Earth. Hostelling in Germany is overseen by **Deutsches Jugendherbergswerk (DJH)** Postfach 1462, 32704 Detmold, Germany (☎ (05231) 740 10; fax 74 01 84). DJH has recently initiated a growing number of **Jugendgästehäuser,** youth guest-houses that have more facilities, and attract slightly older guests. DJH publishes *Jugendherbergen in Deutschland* (DM14.80), a guide to all federated German hostels. The cheapest accommodations are places with **Pension, Gasthof, Gästehaus,** or **Hotel-Garni** in the name. Breakfast *(Frühstück)* is almost always included.

PRIVATE ROOMS. The best bet for a cheap bed is often a **private room** *(Privatzimmer),* which tend to be much quieter than hostels and bring you in direct contact with the local population. Costs generally run DM20-50 per person. Reserve rooms through the local tourist office or through a private **Zimmervermittlung** (room-booking office), for free or for a DM2-8 fee.

CAMPING. The German love of the outdoors is evidenced by the 2,600 **campsites** that dot the outskirts of even the most major cities. Camping costs DM3-10 per person, with additional charges for tents and vehicles. Blue signs with a black tent on a white background indicate official sites. **Deutscher Camping-Club (DCC),** Mandlstr. 28, 80802 München (☎ (089) 380 14 20) has more information, and the National Tourist Office distributes a free map, *Camping in Germany.*

FOOD AND DRINK

German delights include *Schnitzel* (a lightly fried veal cutlet), *Spätzle* (a southern noodle), and *Kartoffeln* (potatoes). The typical German *Frühstück* (breakfast) consists of coffee or tea with *Brötchen* (rolls), bread, *Wurst* (cold sausage), and cheese. The main meal of the day, *Mittagessen* (lunch), includes soup, broiled sausage or roasted meat, potatoes or dumplings, and a salad or *Gemüsebeilage* (vegetable side dish). *Abendessen* or *Abendbrot* (dinner) is a reprise of breakfast, only beer replaces coffee and the selection of meats and cheese is wider. Many older Germans indulge in a daily ritual of *Kaffee und Kuchen* (coffee and cakes) at 3 or 4pm. Seat yourself at restaurants. To eat on the cheap, stick to the daily *Tagesmenü*, buy food in supermarkets; or, if you have a student ID, head to a university *Mensa* (cafeteria). Fast-food *Imbiß* stands also provide cheap fare; try the delicious Turkish *Döner*, something like a gyro. The average German beer is maltier and more "bread-like" than Czech, Dutch, or American beers; an affectionate German slang term for beer is *Flüßige Brot* ("liquid bread").

COMMUNICATION

MAIL. Mail can be sent through **Poste Restante** *(Postlagernde Briefe)* to almost any German city or town with a post office. The mail will go to the main post office unless you specify a post office by street address or postal code.

TELEPHONES. Most public phones only accept **telephone cards.** Telephones in transport hubs and near major attractions sometimes give you the option of paying by **credit card.** You can pick up a **Telefonkarte** (phone card) in post offices, at a *Kiosk* (newsstand), or at selected Deutsche Bahn counters in major train stations. The cards come in DM12, DM24, and DM50 denominations. To place **inter-city calls,** dial the **Vorwahl** (area code), including the first zero, followed by the **Rufnummer** (telephone number). The smaller the city, the more digits in the city code; telephone numbers can have anywhere from three to ten digits. The **national information number** is ☎ 11 833. For **international information,** call ☎ 118 34. **Phone rates** tend to be highest in the morning and afternoon, lower in the evening, and lowest after 9pm and on Sundays and holidays. **International direct dial numbers** include: **AT&T,** ☎ (0800) 225 52 88; **Sprint,** ☎ (0800) 888 00 13; **MCI WorldPhone Direct,** ☎ (0800) 888 80 00; **Canada Direct,** ☎ (0800) 888 00 14; **BT Direct:** ☎ (0130) 80 01 44; **Ireland Direct,** ☎ (0800) 180 00 27; **Australia Direct,** ☎ (0130) 80 00 61; **Telecom New Zealand Direct,** ☎ (0130) 80 00 64; and **Telkom South Africa Direct,** ☎ (0800) 180 00 27.

INTERNET ACCESS. Most German cities as well as a surprising number of smaller towns have at least one Internet cafe, where patrons can surf the web to the tune of DM3-7 per 30 minutes. Some German universities have banks of computers hooked up to the Internet in their libraries, although ostensibly for student use.

LANGUAGE. English language ability is common in Western Germany, but less so in the East. The letter **ß** is equivalent to a double *s*. For German tips, see p. 981.

Violent crime is less common in Germany than in most countries, but it exists, especially in big cities like Frankfurt and Berlin, as well as in economically depressed regions of Eastern Germany. Most neo-Nazis and skinheads subscribe to a traditional uniform of flight jackets, white short-sleeved shirts, and tight jeans rolled up high over high-cut combat boots. Skinheads also tend to follow a shoelace code, with white supremacists and neo-Nazis wearing white laces and anti-gay skinheads wearing pink laces. Left-wing, anti-Nazi "S.H.A.R.P.s" (Skinheads Against Racial Prejudice) also exist; they favor red laces.

HOLIDAYS AND FESTIVALS

Holidays: Epiphany (Jan. 6), Ash Wednesday (Mar. 8), Good Friday (Apr. 21), Easter Sunday and Monday (Apr. 23-24), Labor Day (May 1), Ascension Day (June 1), Whit Sunday (June 11), Whit Monday (June 12), Corpus Christi (June 22), Assumption Day (Aug. 15), Day of German Unity (Oct. 3), Reformation Day (Nov. 1), All Saint's Day (Nov. 1), and Christmas (Dec. 25-26).

Festivals: Check out the **Fasching** in Munich (Jan. 7-Mar.7), **Berlinale Film Festival** (Feb. 9-20), **Karneval** in Cologne (Mar. 2-7), **Hafensgeburtstag** in Hamburg (May 5-7), **International Film Festival** in Munich (late June), **Christopher St. Day** in Berlin and other major cities (late June to early July), **Love Parade** in Berlin (early July), **Bach Festival** in Leipzig (July 21-30), **Wagner Festspiele** in Bayreuth (July 25-Aug. 28), **Wine Festival** in Stuttgart (Aug. 24-Sept. 3), **Oktoberfest** in Munich (Sept. 16-Oct. 1), and **Christmas Market** in Nuremberg (Dec. 24-27).

BERLIN ☎030

Berliners live like there is no tomorrow, and this penchant for shortsighted excess shows itself in all aspects of the city's existence, from its grandiose building endeavors to the party-til-dawn atmosphere that remains in its smoky nightclubs. Projects are underway to transform it from the Allied-bombed and occupied city of the post-WWII years into a sparkling metropolis ready to serve again as Germany's capital. Berlin has always been dynamic; never in its history has it assumed a static identity, nor has it ever seemed "complete." The fall of the physical and psychological division between East and West Berlin in 1989 symbolized the end of the Cold War, and Berlin was officially reunited (along with the rest of Germany) to widespread celebration on October 3, 1990. It remains to be seen whether the brilliantly colored, magnificently varied neighborhoods that contain Berlin's true vitality will be affected by the presence of a complete and usable city center, or whether they will maintain the individuality that has resulted from the consistent lack of a true nexus over the past 50 years.

GETTING THERE AND GETTING AROUND

Flights: ☎ (0180) 500 01 86 for all airports. **Flughafen Tegel** is Western Berlin's main airport. Take express bus X9 from Bahnhof Zoo, bus #109 from Jakob-Kaiser-Pl. on U7, or bus #128 from Kurt-Schumacher-Pl. on U6. **Flughafen Tempelhof** handles domestic and European travel. Take U6 to Pl. der Luftbrücke. **Flughafen Schönefeld,** southeast of Berlin, is used for international flights. Take S45 or 9 to "Flughafen Berlin Schönefeld," or bus #171 from Rudow on U7.

Trains: Deutsche Bahn ☎ (0180) 599 66 33. While construction continues on the *Megabahnhof* of the future at Lehrter Stadtbahnhof, trains to and from Berlin are serviced by **Zoologischer Garten** (almost always called **Bahnhof Zoo**) in the West and **Ostbahnhof** (formerly the Hauptbahnhof) in the East. Trains also connect to **Schönefeld** airport and stop at **Oranienburg, Spandau,** and **Potsdam** before entering the city. Every hour to: **Dresden** (2hr., DM59); **Leipzig** (2hr., DM58); **Hamburg** (2½hr., DM81); **Rostock** (2¾hr., DM65); **Frankfurt** (4hr., DM207); **Köln** (4¼hr., DM190); **Prague** (5hr., DM127); **Amsterdam** (6½hr., DM203); **Munich** (7½hr., DM249); **Brussels** (7½hr., DM217); **Copenhagen** (7½hr., DM188); **Paris** (9hr., DM287); **Zurich** (9hr.); **Vienna** (11½hr.); **Budapest** (12hr.); and **Rome** (21hr.).

Buses: ZOB, the central bus station (☎301 80 28), is by the *Funkturm* near Kaiserdamm. Take U2 to "Kaiserdamm" or S4, 45, or 46 to "Witzleben." Check *Zitty* and *Tip* for deals on long-distance buses, or call **Gulliver's** travel agency (☎78 10 21). To **Paris** (10hr., DM109) and **Vienna** (10½hr., DM79).

Public Transportation: It is impossible to tour Berlin on foot—fortunately, the extensive **bus, Straßenbahn** (streetcar), **U-Bahn** (subway), and **S-Bahn** (surface rail) systems are safe and quick. Berlin is divided into 3 transit zones. **Zone A** encompasses downtown, including Tempelhof airport. Almost everything else falls into **Zone B,** while **Zone C** contains the outlying areas, including Potsdam and Oranienburg. An **AB ticket** is the best deal, as you can buy regional Bahn tickets for the outlying areas. A single ticket for the combined network (*Langstrecke* AB or BC, DM3.90; or *Ganzstrecke* ABC, DM4.20) is good for 2hr. All tickets must be canceled in the validation box marked *hier entwerten* before boarding. With the high cost of single tickets, it usually makes sense to buy a transit pass. A **Tageskarte** (AB DM7.80, ABC DM8.50) is valid from the time of cancellation until 3am the next day. A **Gruppentageskarte** (AB DM20, ABC DM22.50) allows up to 5 people to travel together on the same ticket. The **WelcomeCard** (DM32) is valid for 72hr. The **7-Tage-Karte** (AB DM40, ABC DM48) is good for 7 days. For longer stays, an **Umweltkarte Standard** (AB DM99, ABC DM120) is valid for one calendar month. U- and S-Bahn lines generally do not run from 1-4am, although the **U9** and **U12** run all night F and Sa. **Night buses** (numbers preceded by an "N") centered on Bahnhof Zoo run about every 20-30min.; pick up the free *Nachtliniennetz* map at the BVG pavilion.

Taxis: ☎26 10 26. Women may request a female driver. City trips can go up to DM40.

Car Rental: The **Mietwagenservice,** counter #21 in Bahnhof Zoo's *Reisezentrum,* represents Avis, Hertz, Europacar, and Sixt. Open daily 4:45am-11pm.

Bike Rental: Hackescher Markt Fahrradstation, downstairs at the Hackescher Markt S-Bahn stop; also try the red trailer off the **Lustgarten** (DM5 per day). Take S3, 5, 7, 75, or 9 to "Hackescher Markt" for both locations. The government's **bikecity** program rents bikes (DM5-10 per day). The main rental station is at **Waldenserstr. 2-4,** U9: "Turmstr." Open M-Th 7:30am-4pm, F 7:30am-2:30pm.

Hitchhiking: *Let's Go* does not recommend hitchhiking. It is illegal to hitch at rest stops or on the highway. To the west and south (Hannover, Munich, Weimar, Leipzig) take S1 or 7 to Wannsee, then bus #211 to the Autobahn entrance ramp. To the north (Hamburg, Rostock) ride S25 to Hennigsdorf, then walk 50m to the bridge on the right, or ask for the location of the *Trampenplatz.* **City Netz,** Joachimstaler Str. 17 (☎ 194 44) has a **ride-share** database. Take U15 or 9 to "Kurfürstendamm." To Hamburg or Hannover DM12, Frankfurt DM17, Munich DM18. Open M-F 9am-8pm, Sa-Su 9am-7pm.

GERMANY

ORIENTATION

Berlin is an immense conglomeration (eight times the size of Paris) of what were once two separate cities. The former East contains most landmarks and historic sites. The former West is still the commercial heart of united Berlin, lying at one end of the **Tiergarten** park and centered around the **Bahnhof Zoo** and **Kurfürstendamm** (Ku'damm for short). It is marked by the bombed-out **Kaiser-Wilhelm-Gedächtniskirche,** next to the boxy **Europa-Center,** one of the few "skyscrapers" in Western Berlin. A star of streets radiates from **Breitscheidpl.;** to the west run **Hardenbergstr., Kantstr.,** and Berlin's great commercial boulevard, the Kurfürstendamm. About a kilometer down Kantstr. lies **Savignyplatz,** one of many pleasant squares in **Charlottenburg,** home to cafes, restaurants, and *Pensionen.* Southeast of the Ku'damm, **Schöneberg** is a residential neighborhood renowned for its cafe culture and as the traditional nexus of the city's gay and lesbian community. Farther south, **Dahlem** houses Western Berlin's largest university and museum complex.

The grand, tree-lined **Str. des 17. Juni** runs west-east through the Tiergarten to the triumphant **Brandenburg Gate,** which opens out onto **Pariser Platz.** Heading south from the Brandenburg Gate and the nearby **Reichstag,** Ebertstr. runs haphazardly through construction sites to **Potsdamer Platz.** To the east, the gate opens onto **Unter den Linden,** Berlin's most famous boulevard and the site of many historic buildings. The *Linden* empties into socialist-realist **Alexanderplatz,** the center of the East's growing commercial district and the home of Berlin's most visible landmark, the **Fernsehturm.** Southeast of the Mitte lies **Kreuzberg,** a district home to a mix of radical leftists, Turks, punks, and homosexuals. Once confined to West Berlin's outer limits, Kreuzberg today finds itself bordering reunited Berlin's city center. The **Spree River** snakes west-east through the center of Berlin, forming the northern border of the Tiergarten and splitting just east of Unter den Linden to close off the **Museuminsel** (Museum Island). The **Wannsee, Tegeler See,** and **Heiligensee** lap against the city's west side and are connected by narrow canals.

If you're planning to stay more than a few days in Berlin, the blue-and-yellow **Falk Plan** (available at most kiosks and bookstores) is an indispensable and convenient city map that includes a street index and unfolds like a book (DM11).

SAFETY PRECAUTION! With thriving minority communities, Berlin is the most tolerant city in Germany. The media has sensationalized the new wave of Nazi extremism perhaps more than necessary; among major cities, Berlin in fact has the fewest hate crimes per capita.There are only an estimated 750 neo-Nazi skinheads in Berlin. However, there are still a few areas in which people of color, gays, or lesbians should be cautious—the outlying areas in the eastern suburbs, particularly Bahnhof Lichtenberg, are best avoided late at night. If you see dark-colored combat boots with white laces, exercise caution, but do not panic.

PRACTICAL INFORMATION

TOURIST AND FINANCIAL SERVICES

Tourist Office: Tourist offices (www.berlin.de.) sell a useful **city map** (DM1) and give out the free **Liniennetz map.** They also book same-day **hotel rooms** (from DM50) for a DM5 fee. **EurAide,** in Bahnhof Zoo, doles out multilingual info. Facing the Reisezentrum, go left and down the passage on your right. Open daily 8am-noon and 1-6pm. **Berlin Tourismus** (☎25 00 25) reserves **rooms. Europa-Center** has an entrance on Budapester Str. From the Bahnhof Zoo, walk along Budapester Str. past the Kaiser-Wilhelm-Gedächtniskirche; it's on the right. Open M-Sa 8:30am-8:30pm, Su 10am-6:30pm.

Tours: Berlin Walks (☎301 91 94) offers a range of English tours, including **Infamous Third Reich Sites, Jewish Life in Berlin,** and **Discover Berlin** (3-7hr.; tours depart at 10am from the taxi stand in front of Bahnhof Zoo; Discover Berlin in summer also 2:30pm; all tours DM18, under 26 DM14. Get tickets at Euraide). **Insider Tour** provides a thorough historical narrative and hits all the major sights (3½hr.; departs from the McDonald's by Bahnhof Zoo; late Mar. to Nov. daily at 10am and 2:30pm; DM15).

Budget Travel: STA, Goethestr. 73 (☎311 09 50). U2: Ernst-Reuter-Pl. Open M-W and F 10am-6pm, Th 10am-8pm. **Kilroy Travels,** Hardenbergstr. 9 (☎31 000 40; www.kilroytravels.de), across from the Technische Universität, 2 blocks from Bahnhof Zoo.

Embassies and Consulates: The locations of embassies and consulates remain in flux. The **Auswärtiges Amt Dienststelle Berlin,** Werderscher Markt (☎20 18 60), has the latest info. U2: Hausvogteipl. **Australia,** Friedrichstr. 200 (☎880 08 80). U2 or 6: Stadtmitte. Or, try Uhlandstr. 181-183 (☎880 08 80; fax 88 00 88 99). U15: Uhlandstr. Open M-F 9am-noon. **Canada,** Friedrichstr. 95, International Trade Center, 12th fl. (☎20 31 20; fax 20 31 25 90). S1, 2, 25, 3, 5, 7, 75 or 9 or U6 to Friedrichstr. Open M-F 9am-noon. **Ireland,** Friedrichstr. 200 (☎22 07 20). Open M-F 9:30am-noon, 2:30-4:45pm. **New Zealand,** Friedrichstr. 60. U6 to Oranienburger Tor. **South Africa** (consulate), Douglasstr. 9 (☎82 50 11 or 825 27 11; fax 826 65 43). S7: Grunewald. Open M-F 9am-noon. **UK,** Unter den Linden 32-34 (☎20 18 40; fax 20 18 41 58). S1, 2, 25, 3, 5, 7, 75 or 9 or U6 to Friedrichstr. Open M-F 9am-4pm. **US Citizens Service,** Clayallee 170 (☎832 92 33, after hours ☎830 50; fax 831 49 26). U1 to Oskar-Helene-Heim. Open M-F 8:30am-noon; telephones staffed M-F 2-4pm. **US,** Neustädtische Kirchstr. 4-5 (☎238 51 74; fax 238 62 90). S1, 2, 25, 3, 5, 7, 75 or 9 or U6 to Friedrichstr. Open 8:30am-5:30pm by appointment only.

Currency Exchange: The **Wechselstube** at Joachimstaler Str. 1-3 (☎882 10 86), near Bahnhof Zoo, has good rates and no commission. Open M-F 8am-8pm, Sa 9am-3pm. **ReiseBank,** at Bahnhof Zoo (☎881 71 17; open daily 7am-10pm) and Ostbahnhof (☎296 43 93; open M-F 7am-10pm, Sa 7am-6pm, Su 8am-4pm) has poorer rates. **Berliner Sparkasse** and **Deutsche Bank** have branches everywhere; their ATMs usually accept V and MC. **Citibank** has branches with **24hr. ATMs** at Kurfürstendamm 72, Wittenbergpl. 1, Wilmersdorfer Str. 133, and Karl-Marx-Allee 153.

American Express: Bayreuther Str. 23 (☎21 49 83 63). U1, 15, or 2 to Wittenbergpl. Mail held, banking services. Open M-F 9am-6pm, Sa 10am-1pm. **Branch office,** Friedrichstr. 172 (☎20 17 40 12). U6 to Französische Str. Open M-F 9am-5:30pm, Sa 10am-1pm.

LOCAL SERVICES

Luggage Storage: In **Bahnhof Zoo** and **Ostbahnhof.** Lockers DM2-4 per day; 72hr. max. Also at **Bahnhof Lichtenberg** and **Alexanderplatz.** Lockers DM2 per day; 24hr. max.

English Bookstores: Marga Schoeler Bücherstube, Knesebeckstr. 33 (☎881 11 12), at Mommsenstr., between Savignypl. and the Ku'damm. S3, 5, 7, 75, or 9 to Savignypl. Open M-W 9:30am-7pm, Th-F 9:30am-8pm, Sa 9:30am-4pm.

Laundromat: Wasch Centers, Leibnizstr. 72, in Charlottenburg (U7: Wilmersdorfer Str.); Wexstr. 34, in Schöneberg (U9: Bundespl.); Bergmannstr. 109 in Kreuzberg (U7: Gneisenaustr.); Behmstr. 12, in the Mitte (S1, 2, or 25 or U8 to Gesundbrunnen. All open daily 6am-11pm.

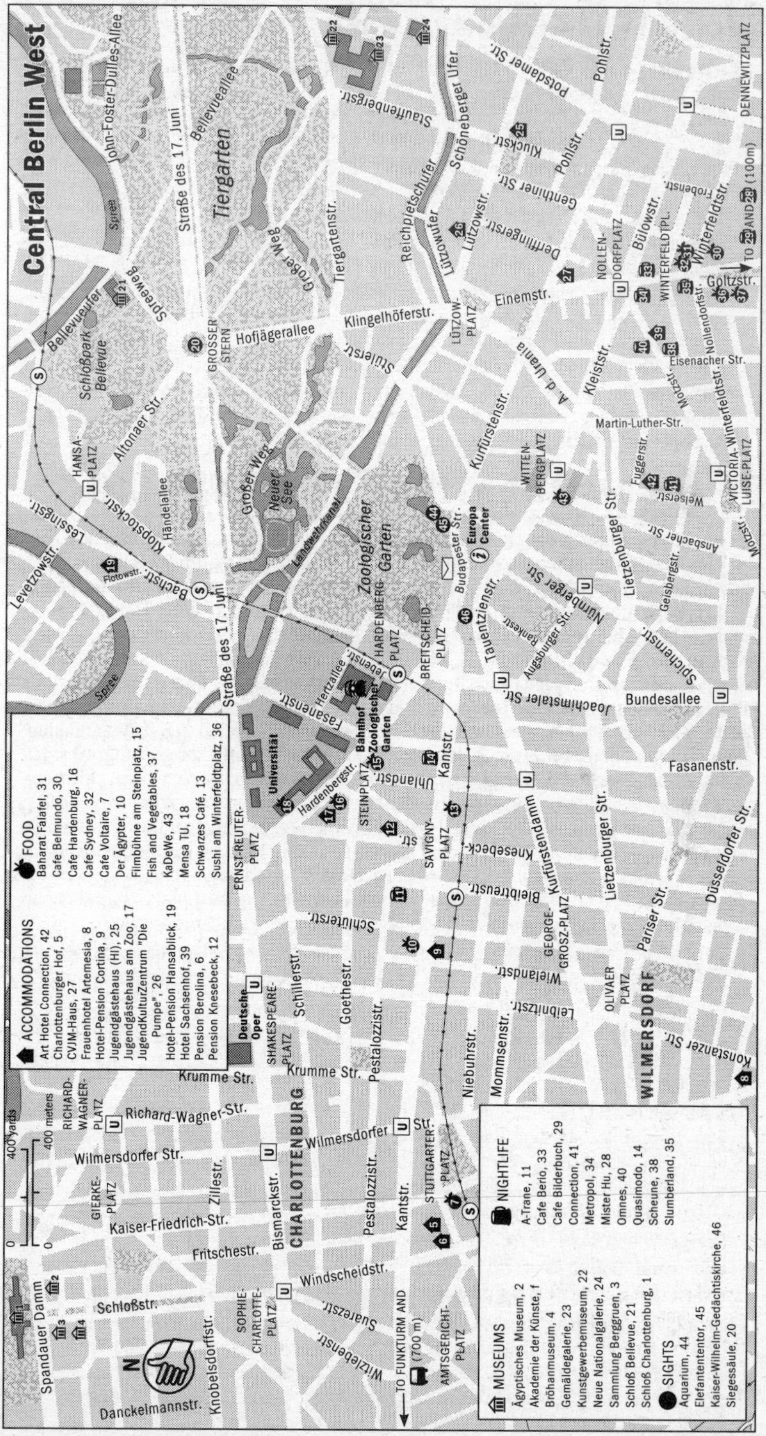

GERMANY

Central Berlin West

ACCOMMODATIONS
- Art Hotel Connection, 42
- Charlottenburger Hof, 5
- CVJM-Haus, 27
- Frauenhotel Artemesia, 8
- Hotel-Pension Cortina, 9
- Jugendgästehaus (HI), 25
- Jugendgästehaus am Zoo, 17
- JugendKulturZentrum "Die Pumpe", 26
- Hotel-Pension Hansablick, 19
- Hotel Sachsenhof, 39
- Pension Berolina, 6
- Pension Knesebeck, 12

FOOD
- Baharat Falafel, 31
- Cafe Belmundo, 30
- Cafe Hardenburg, 16
- Cafe Sydney, 32
- Cafe Voltaire, 7
- Der Ägypter, 10
- Filmbühne am Steinplatz, 15
- Fish and Vegetables, 37
- KaDeWe, 43
- Mensa TU, 18
- Schwarzes Café, 13
- Sushi am Winterfeldtplatz, 36

NIGHTLIFE
- A-Trane, 11
- Cafe Berio, 33
- Cafe Bilderbuch, 29
- Connection, 41
- Metropol, 34
- Mister Hu, 28
- Omnes, 40
- Quasimodo, 14
- Scheune, 38
- Slumberland, 35

MUSEUMS
- Ägyptisches Museum, 2
- Akademie der Künste, f
- Bröhanmuseum, 4
- Gemäldegalerie, 23
- Kunstgewerbemuseum, 22
- Neue Nationalgalerie, 24
- Sammlung Berggruen, 3
- Schloß Bellevue, 21
- Schloß Charlottenburg, 1

SIGHTS
- Aquarium, 44
- Elefantentor, 45
- Kaiser-Wilhelm-Gedächtniskirche, 46
- Siegessäule, 20

EMERGENCY AND COMMUNICATIONS

Emergency: ☎112. **Police,** Pl. der Luftbrücke 6 (☎110). U6: Pl. der Luftbrücke.

Crisis Lines: American Hotline, ☎ (0177) 814 15 10. **Sexual Assault,** ☎251 28 28. Open Tu and Th 6-9pm, Su noon-2pm. **Drug Crisis,** ☎192 37. Open M-F 8:30am-10pm, Sa-Su 2-9:30pm. **Schwules Überfall** (gay bashing), ☎216 33 36. Open daily 6-9pm.

Pharmacies: Europa-Apotheke, Tauentzienstr. 9-12 (☎261 41 42), near the Europa Center and Bahnhof Zoo. Open M-F 9am-8pm, Sa 9am-4pm. Closed pharmacies post signs directing you to the nearest open one. For **late-night pharmacies,** call ☎011 89.

Medical Assistance: The US and UK embassies list English-speaking doctors. **Emergency Doctor** (☎31 00 31) and **Emergency Dentist** (☎89 00 43 33). Both 24hr.

Internet Access: Cyberb@r, Joachimstaler Str. 5-6, near the Bahnhof Zoo, Karstadt Sport store, 2nd fl. DM5 per 30min. **Webtimes,** Chausseestr. 8, in Mitte. U6: Oranienburger Tor. DM7 per hr. Open M-F 9am-midnight, Sa and Su 10am-midnight. **Website,** Joachimstaler Str. 41. Berlin's trendiest cybercafe. Open daily 10am-late.

Post Office: Budapester Str. 42, opposite the Europa-Center near Bahnhof Zoo. Open M-Sa 8am-midnight, Su 10am-midnight. Address mail to be held: First name SURNAME, Postlagernd, Postamt in der Budapester Str. 42, **10787** Berlin.

ACCOMMODATIONS AND CAMPING

For stays longer than a couple of days or on weekends, reservations are essential. For the **Love Parade,** call at least two months early. For DM5, tourist offices will find you a room (singles from DM70, doubles from DM100). There are over 4000 **private rooms** in the city; the majority are controlled by the tourist offices (singles from DM80; doubles from DM100). The tourist offices have the pamphlet *Accommodations, Youth Hostels, and Camping Places in Berlin,* which lists hostels and inexpensive guest houses and hotels in English and German (DM1). For visits over four days, the various **Mitwohnzentralen** can arrange for you to house-sit or sublet an apartment. Contact **Home Company Mitwohnzentrale,** Joachimstaler Str. 17. (☎194 45. U9 or 15 to Kurfürstendamm. Open M-F 9am-6pm, Sa 11am-2pm.) **Hostels** in Berlin fall into three categories: HI-affiliated, state-owned *Jugendherbergen* and *Jugendgästehäuser;* large, privately-owned hostels; and smaller, more off-beat private hostels. State-run hostels often impose a **curfew.** Large, well-equipped private hostels are located near the train stations and major nightlife areas. Many small *Pensionen* and hotels are within the means of budget travelers; most establishments listed in *Let's Go* are amenable to *Mehrbettzimmer,* extra beds moved into a large double or triple. The best place to find cheap rooms is **Charlottenburg,** especially around Savignypl. and Wilmersdorfer Str.

MITTE

Circus, Rosa-Luxemburg-Str. 39-41 (☎28 39 14 33; email circus@mind.de). U2 to Rosa-Luxemburg-Pl. Circus defines hostel hipness, offering cheap Internet access and a disco ball in the lobby. Sheets DM4. Bike rental DM12 per day. Reservations in summer are a must and should be confirmed a day before arrival. Dorms DM25; singles DM45; doubles DM 80; triples DM105; quads DM160.

Clubhouse Hostel, Kalkscheunenstr. 2 (☎28 09 79 79). S1, 2, or 25 to Oranienburger Str., or U6 to Oranienburger Tor. Enter the courtyard from Johannisstr. 2 or Kalkscheunestr. Breakfast DM7. Internet DM1 per 5min. Call at least 2-3 days ahead. Dorms DM25-30; singles DM50; doubles DM80.

Mitte's Backpacker Hostel, Chausseestr. 102 (☎262 51 40; email backpacker@snafu.de). U6 to Zinnowitzer Str. Internet. Sheets DM5. Bikes DM10-12 per day. Reception 7am-9:30pm. Dorms DM25; doubles DM38; triples DM30; quads DM28.

SCHÖNEBERG–TIERGARTEN–WILMERSDORF

Jugendgästehaus (HI), Kluckstr. 3 (☎261 10 97). From Bahnhof Zoo, take bus #129 (dir. Hermannpl.) to Gedenkstätte, or U1 to Kurfürstenstr., then walk up Potsdamer Str., go left on Pohlstr., and right on Kluckstr. Breakfast and sheets included. Internet, laundry, and bike rental. Key deposit DM10. Curfew midnight; stragglers admitted every 30min. 12:30-6am. Lockout 9am-1pm. Dorms DM43, under 27 DM34.

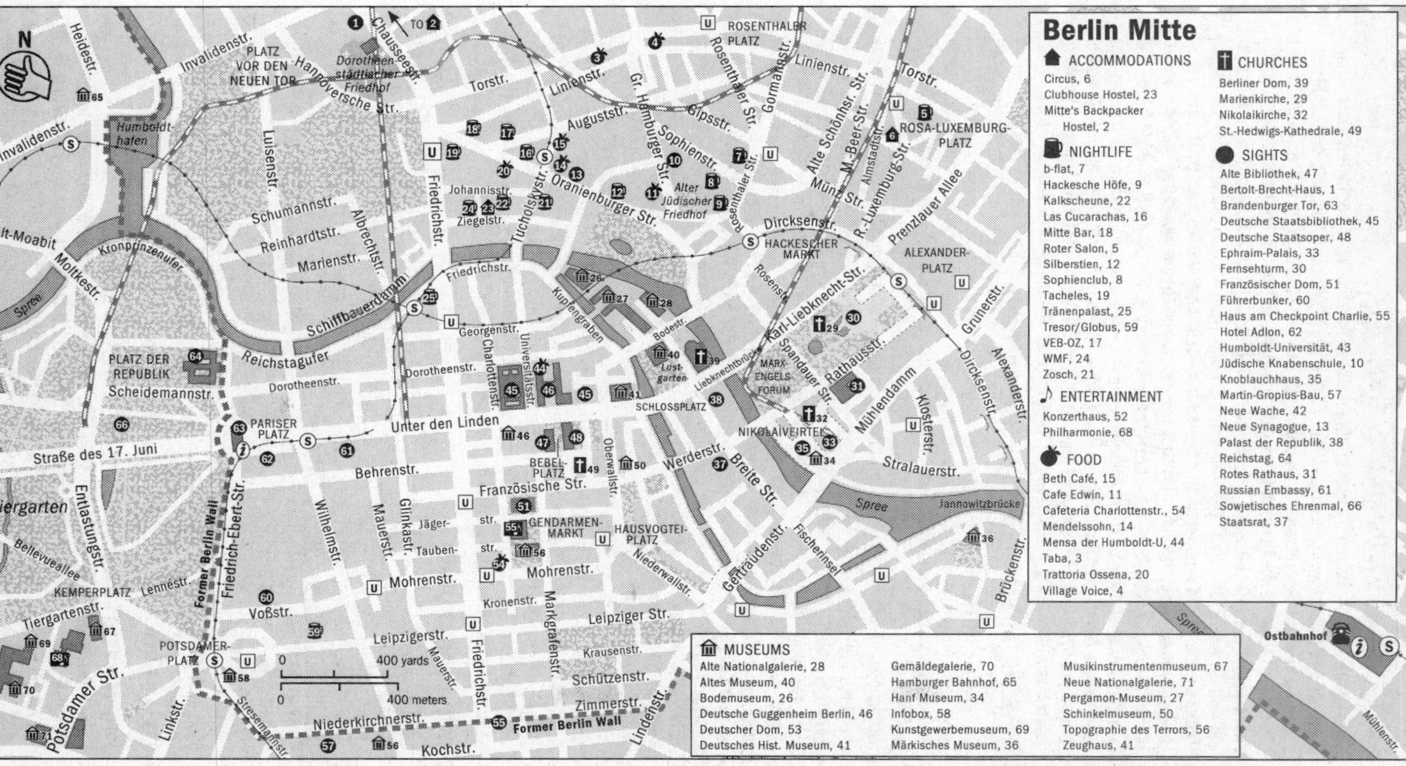
Berlin Mitte
ACCOMMODATIONS
Circus, 6
Clubhouse Hostel, 23
Mitte's Backpacker Hostel, 2
NIGHTLIFE
b-flat, 7
Hackesche Höfe, 9
Kalkscheune, 22
Las Cucarachas, 16
Mitte Bar, 18
Roter Salon, 5
Silberstien, 12
Sophienclub, 8
Tacheles, 19
Tränenpalast, 25
Tresor/Globus, 59
VEB-OZ, 17
WMF, 24
Zosch, 21
ENTERTAINMENT
Konzerthaus, 52
Philharmonie, 68
FOOD
Beth Café, 15
Cafe Edwin, 11
Cafeteria Charlottenstr., 54
Mendelssohn, 14
Mensa der Humboldt-U, 44
Taba, 3
Trattoria Ossena, 20
Village Voice, 4
CHURCHES
Berliner Dom, 39
Marienkirche, 29
Nikolaikirche, 32
St.-Hedwigs-Kathedrale, 49
SIGHTS
Alte Bibliothek, 47
Bertolt-Brecht-Haus, 1
Brandenburger Tor, 63
Deutsche Staatsbibliothek, 45
Deutsche Staatsoper, 48
Ephraim-Palais, 33
Fernsehturm, 30
Französischer Dom, 51
Führerbunker, 60
Haus am Checkpoint Charlie, 55
Hotel Adlon, 62
Humboldt-Universität, 43
Jüdische Knabenschule, 10
Knoblauchhaus, 35
Martin-Gropius-Bau, 57
Neue Wache, 42
Neue Synagogue, 13
Palast der Republik, 38
Reichstag, 64
Rotes Rathaus, 31
Russian Embassy, 61
Sowjetisches Ehrenmal, 66
Staatsrat, 37
MUSEUMS
Alte Nationalgalerie, 28
Altes Museum, 40
Bodemuseum, 26
Deutsche Guggenheim Berlin, 46
Deutscher Dom, 53
Deutsches Hist. Museum, 41
Gemäldegalerie, 70
Hamburger Bahnhof, 65
Hanf Museum, 34
Infobox, 58
Kunstgewerbemuseum, 69
Märkisches Museum, 36
Musikinstrumentenmuseum, 67
Neue Nationalgalerie, 71
Pergamon-Museum, 27
Schinkelmuseum, 50
Topographie des Terrors, 56
Zeughaus, 41
0 400 yards
0 400 meters
Former Berlin Wall

Studentenhotel Meininger 10, Meiningerstr. 10 (☎78 71 74 14; email info@studentenhotel.de). U4, bus #146 or N46 to Rathaus Schöneberg. Walk toward the Rathaus on Freiherr-vom-Stein-Str., turn left onto Martin-Luther-Str., and right on Meiningerstr. Breakfast included. Dorms DM25; singles DM66; doubles DM44; 3- to 6-bed rooms DM40.

Jugendgästehaus Feurigstraße, Feurigstr. 63 (☎781 52 11). U7 to Kleistpark, or bus #204 or 348 to Kaiser-Wilhelm-Pl. Walk down Hauptstr., turn left onto Kollonenstr., and right onto Feurigstr. Close to the Schöneberg bar scene. Breakfast included. Dorms DM27-40; singles DM55; doubles DM50.

Hotel-Pension München, Güntzelstr. 62 (☎857 91 20; email hotel-pension.muenchen@arcormail.de). U9 to Güntzelstr. Clean rooms with cable TV and phones. Breakfast DM10. Check-out 11am. Written reservations. Singles DM66-70, with shower DM95-110; doubles DM80-90, with bath DM115-130.

Hotel Sachsenhof, Motzstr. 7 (☎216 20 74). U1, 2, 4, or 15 to Nollendorfpl. A lovely old house near Nollendorfpl. cafes and gay nightlife. Breakfast DM10. Call ahead between 7am and 11pm. Singles DM57, with shower DM65; doubles DM99-146, DM126-156.

GERMANY

FRIEDRICHSHAIN AND PRENZLAUER BERG

Frederik's Hostel, Str. der Pariser Kommune 35 (☎29 66 94 50 or 29 66 94 51; www.frederiks.de). U5 to Weberwiese or S3, 5, 7, 75 or 9 to Ostbahnhof. From the U-Bahn, exit on Karl-Marx-Allee and turn left on Str. der Pariser Kommune. From Ostbahnhof, walk to the farthest exit along the train tracks; with your back to station, walk straight along Str. der Pariser Kommune. Breakfast DM6. Sheets DM5. Large kitchen. Internet. Reception 24hr. Dorms DM23-29; singles DM59; doubles DM78.

Odyssee, Grünberger Str. 23 (☎29 00 00 81; www.hostel-berlin.de). U5 to Frankfurter Tor. Bar open until dawn. Internet DM3 per 15min. Breakfast DM5. Reserve ahead. Dorms DM24-26; doubles DM36; quads DM32.

Lette'm Sleep Hostel, Lettestr. 7 (☎44 73 36 23). U2: Eberswalder Str. The 1st hostel in Prenzlauer Berg, near Kollwitzpl. Internet DM1 per 5min. Dorms DM26-35.

TEGEL

Backpacker's Paradise, Ziekowstr. 161 (☎433 86 40). S25 to Tegel or U6 to Alt-Tegel, then bus #222 or night bus #N22 to Titusweg. Campfire every night. Breakfast DM3. Lockers DM1. Laundry DM5. Open late June-Aug. DM10 gets you a blanket and thermal pad under a tent; add DM3 for a summer camp-like cot.

Jugendherberge Ernst Reuter (HI), Hermsdorfer Damm 48-50 (☎404 16 10). S25 to Tegel or U6 to Alt-Tegel, then bus #125 or night bus N25 (dir. Frohnau/Invalidensiedlung) to Jugendherberge. Breakfast and sheets included. Laundry DM8. Key deposit DM20. Closed Dec. DM35; members and under 27 DM28.

CHARLOTTENBURG

Charlottenburger Hof, Stuttgarter Pl. 14 (☎32 90 70). S3, 5, 7, 75, or 9 to Charlottenburg or U7 to Wilmersdorfer Str. The art-themed decor of this hotel could pass for a gallery. Laundry DM5. All rooms have phones and TVs; some doubles with balconies and whirlpools. Singles DM80-120; doubles DM110-160; quads DM160-220.

Hotel-Pension Cortina, Kantstr. 140 (☎313 90 59). S3, 5, 7, 9, or 75 to Savignypl. Bright rooms with a friendly staff and a great location. Breakfast included. Reception 24hr. Dorms DM35-60; singles DM60-90; doubles DM90-150.

Pension Berolina, Stuttgarter Pl. 17 (☎32 70 90 72). S3, 5, 7, 75, or 9 to Charlottenburg or U7 to Wilmersdorferstr. Spartan rooms near the S-Bahn station. Singles DM60; doubles DM80; triples DM90; quads DM100; quints DM110.

KREUZBERG

Bax Pax, Skalitzer Str. 104 (☎69 51 83 22; email info@baxpax.de). U1 or 15 to Görlitzer Bahnhof, across the street. Fuzzy blue carpets, sparkling bathrooms, and an ultra-friendly staff. Sheets DM5. Reception 7am-10pm. DM25-30.

Die Fabrik, Schlesische Str. 18 (☎611 71 16; email info@diefabrik.com). U1 or 15 to Schlesisches Tor, or night bus N65 to Taborstr. Within walking distance of Kreuzberg's nightlife. Breakfast DM10. Bike rental DM20 per day. Reserve ahead. Dorms DM30; singles DM66; doubles DM94; triples DM120; quads DM144.

Hotel Transit, Hagelberger Str. 53-54 (☎789 04 70). U6 or 7 or night bus N19 to Mehringdamm. Party hard and crash in this stylin' *Pension.* Breakfast included. Singles DM90; doubles DM105; triples DM140; quads DM180; *Mehrbettzimmer* DM33.

Pension Kreuzberg, Großbeerenstr. 64 (☎251 13 62). U6 or 7 or night bus N19 to Mehringdamm. Breakfast included. Reception 8am-10pm. Singles DM75; doubles DM98; *Mehrbettzimmer* DM44 per person.

CAMPING

Deutscher Camping-Club runs the following campgrounds. For reservations, write to Deutscher Camping-Club Berlin, Geisbergstr. 11, 10777 Berlin. Or, call ahead (☎218 60 71). Both sites charge DM9.70 per person, DM4.60 per child, DM7.20 per tent, and DM12.70 per trailer.

Dreilinden (☎805 12 01). S7 to Griebnitzsee, then walk back between the station and lake. Surrounded on 3 sides by the vestiges of the Berlin Wall. Open Mar.-Oct.

Kladow, Krampnitzer Weg 111-117 (☎365 27 97). U7 to Rathaus Spandau, then bus #135 (dir. Alt-Kladow) to the end. Switch to bus #234 to Krampnitzer Weg/Selbitzerstr. A store, restaurant, and a swimmable lake. Open year-round.

FOOD

Food in Berlin is a tasty surprise; its Turkish, Indian, Thai and Italian immigrants bring a wide variety of quality ethnic food to restaurants and stands throughout the city. Berlin's most notable home-grown option is the sweet **Berliner Weiße mit Schuß,** a concoction of wheat beer with a shot of syrup. A lot of typical Berlin street food is Turkish, and almost every street has its own Turkish *Imbiß* or restaurant. **Aldi, Plus, Edeka,** and **Penny Markt** are the cheapest supermarket chains, and are usually open Monday to Friday 9am-6pm and Saturday 9am-4pm. At Bahnhof Zoo, **Ullrich am Zoo,** below the S-Bahn tracks, and **Nimm's Mit,** near the Reisezentrum, have longer hours. (Open daily 6am-10pm.) The best **open-air market** fires up Saturday mornings on Winterfeldtpl.

AROUND ORANIENBURGER STRAßE

Taba, Torstr. 164. U8 to Rosenthaler Pl. A lively, happening place with good Brazilian cuisine. Live music F, Sa, and Su, disco every Sa midnight-4am. Open W-Su from 7pm.

Trattoria Ossena, Oranienburger Str. 65. S1, 2, or 25 to Oranienburger Str. Substantial fare in the form of delicious Italian pastas and enormous pizzas. Most meals under DM20, many (especially pizzas) large enough to feed two. Open daily from 5pm.

Café Beth, Tucholskystr. 40, just off Auguststr. S1, 2, or 25 to Oranienburger Str. Kosher restaurant in the Scheunenviertel with a generous selection of kosher wines. Open M-Th and Su 11am-10pm, F 11am-5pm; in winter M-Th and Su 11am-10pm, F 11am-3pm.

AROUND BAHNHOF ZOO

KaDeWe, Tauentzienstr. 21-24. U1, 2, or 15 to Wittenbergpl. Indulge in confectionery wonders, sample flavorful Italian *antipasto,* enjoy a glass of wine, or just get lost among the maze of counters. Open M-F 9:30am-8pm, Sa 9am-4pm.

Mensa TU, Hardenbergstr. 34. Bus #145 to Steinpl., or walk 10min. from Bahnhof Zoo. The mightiest of Berlin's *Mensen* serves decent food, including good vegetarian dishes. Meals DM4-5 for students, others DM6-7. Cafeteria downstairs has longer hours and higher prices. *Mensa* open M-F 11:15am-2:30pm. Cafeteria open M-F 8am-7:45pm.

Filmbühne am Steinplatz, Hardenbergstr. 12. This cafe in an independent cinema has an eclectic and extensive but generally inexpensive menu. Open M-Sa 9am-3am, Su 9am-2am. Films DM11, Mondays DM8.50. Call ☎312 90 12 for film info.

Café Hardenberg, Hardenbergstr. 10. Opposite the TU's *Mensa,* but with a lot more atmosphere. Breakfast day or night DM5-12. Open M-F 9am-1am, Sa-Su 9am-2am.

SCHÖNEBERG

Baharat Falafel, Winterfeldtstr. 37. U1, 2, 4, or 15 to Nollendorfpl. Enjoy falafel (DM6-7) and wash it all down with fresh-squeezed *Gute-Laune Saft* (good mood juice). Open daily 11am-2am. Closed last week in July.

Bua Luang, Vorbergstr. 10a. U7 to Kleistpark. Thai food in a quiet, residential neighborhood. Open daily 2pm-midnight.

Café Sidney, Winterfeldtstr. 40. U1, 2, 4 or 15 to Nollendorfpl. With vaguely Australian interior decor, Sidney tries for worldly trendiness. Breakfast from DM7 and baguettes with tomato and mozzarella for DM6.50. A wide variety of drinks plus two pool tables in the back make it a good evening destination.

KREUZBERG

Amrit, Oranienstr. 202-203. U1 or 15 to "Görlitzer Bahnhof." Perhaps the best Indian food in Berlin. Fabulous vegetarian dishes like *Alu Saag* (DM12.50) and spicy meat dishes; try *Chicken Saag* (DM13.50). Open M-Th and Su noon-1am, F-Sa noon-2am.

Café V, Lausitzer Pl. 12. U1 or 15 to Görlitzer Bahnhof. Berlin's oldest vegetarian restaurant. Some entrees are vegan-friendly, and fish entrees are also available. Try the *Auberginem-Tofu-Mosakka.* Open daily 10am-2am.

PRENZLAUER BERG-FRIEDRICHSHAIN

Sergena, Pappalallee 19. Amazing food with slightly exotic flavors. Artichoke and cheese dish DM10, range of salads DM4-13. Open M-Th 3pm-1am, F-Su 2pm-1am.

Chop Bar, Pappalallee 29. A friendly African restaurant. Substantial vegetarian options DM14-16. Entrees DM12. Open daily 6pm-midnight.

Ostwind, Husemannstr. 13. U2 to Senefelderpl. Chinese food that bridges East and West. Indulge in the dim sum. Open M-Th 6pm-1am, F-Sa 10am-1am.

Die Krähe, Kollwitzstr. 84, off Kollwitzpl. U2 to Senefelderpl. White tablecloths and tasteful decor create a garden-like feel. Breakfast under DM10, salads DM12. Popular Su buffet DM13.50. Open M-Th 5:30pm-2am, F-Sa 5:30pm-3am, Su 10:30am-2am.

SIGHTS

The sights below are organized by *Bezirk* (district), radiating from Mitte. Many of central Berlin's major sights lie along the route of **bus #100,** which travels from Bahnhof Zoo to Prenzlauer Berg, passing the Siegessäule, Brandenburg Gate, Unter den Linden, the Berliner Dom, and Alexanderpl. along the way.

MITTE

Formerly the heart of Imperial Berlin, Mitte contains some of Berlin's most magnificent sights and museums. Much of the neighborhood languished in disuse and disrepair during GDR days, but now that the government is back in town, Mitte ("center") is once again living up to its name, as embassies and national institutes pour back into the area's rapidly-renovating streets. **Unter den Linden,** once one of Europe's best-known boulevards and the spine of old Berlin, runs east from the Brandenburg Gate to Alexanderpl. via Bebelpl., and is best reached by taking S1, 2, or 25 to Unter den Linden and heading east; alternatively, bus #100 runs the length of the boulevard every 4-6 minutes. The remainder of sights in this section lie between Under den Linden and the former Berlin Wall to the south.

BRANDENBURGER TOR. For decades a barricaded gateway to nowhere, today the Brandenburg Gate is the most powerful emblem of reunited Berlin. In the center of the city, it was in no-man's land during the time of the Wall. It opens east onto **Pariser Platz** and Unter den Linden and west onto the Tiergarten and Straße des 17. Juni. All but a few of the venerable buildings near the gate have been destroyed, but a reconstruction effort centered on the gate has already revived pre-war staples, like the **Hotel Adlon,** once the premier address for visiting dignitaries and celebrities.

NEUE WACHE. The new guard house was designed by Prussian architect Karl Friedrich Schinkel in the unrepentant Neoclassical style. During the GDR era, it was known as the "Monument to the Victims of Fascism and Militarism," and, ironically, was guarded by East German soldiers. After reunification, the building was reopened in 1993 as a war memorial. The remains of an unknown soldier and an unknown concentration camp victim are buried inside with earth from the Nazi concentration camps, as well as from the battlefields of Stalingrad, El Alamein, and Normandy. *(Unter den Linden 4. Open daily 10am-6pm.)*

BEBELPLATZ. It was here on May 10, 1933 that Nazi students burned nearly 20,000 books by "subversive" authors such as Heinrich Heine and Sigmund Freud—both Jews. The building with the curved facade is the **Alte Bibliothek,** once the royal library. On the other side of the square is the handsome **Deutsche Staatsoper,** fully rebuilt from original sketches by Knobelsdorff. The distinctive blue dome at the end of the square belongs to the **St-Hedwigs-Kathedrale.** Built in 1773 as the first Catholic church erected in Berlin after the Reformation, it was burnt to a crisp by American bombers in 1943 and rebuilt in the 1950s. *(Cathedral open M-F 10am-5pm, Sa 10am-4:30pm, Su 1-5pm. Free.)* Next door, the **Bundeshauptstadt Berlin** has an exhibit on the new construction. *(Behrenstr. 39. ☎ 20 08 32 34. Open daily 9am-5:30pm. Free.)*

LUSTGARTEN AND MUSEUMINSEL. Continuing east, Unter den Linden passes by the **Museuminsel** (Museum Island), home to four major museums (see **Museums,** p. 414) and the **Berliner Dom.** The many-domed cathedral, built during the reign of Kaiser Wilhelm II, recently emerged from 20 years of restoration for damage sustained in a 1944 air raid. *(Open daily 9am-7:30pm. Dom DM5, students DM3. Dom, tower, and galleries DM8, DM5. Free organ recitals W-F 3pm. Frequent concerts in summer; buy tickets in the church or call ☎ 20 26 91 36 for information.)*

ALEXANDERPLATZ AND FERNSEHTURM. On the other side of Museuminsel, Unter den Linden becomes Karl-Liebknecht-Str. and leads to the monolithic **Alexanderplatz.** Formerly the frantic heart of Weimar Berlin, the plaza was transformed in East German times into an urban wasteland of fountains and pre-fab office buildings. *(Take S3, 5, 7, 75, or 9 or U2, 5, or 8 to Alexanderpl.)* South of Alexanderpl. rises the **Fernsehturm** TV tower, the tallest structure in Berlin (365m). A truly awkward piece of design intended to show off the new heights achieved through communism, it looks more like something out of the Jetsons. The view from the top (the spherical node 203m up the spike) is magnificent. *(Open daily Mar.-Oct. 9am-1am; Nov.-Feb. 10am-midnight. DM10, under 16 DM5.)*

SCHEUNENVIERTEL. Northwest of Alexanderpl. lies the **Scheunenviertel,** once the center of Berlin's Orthodox Jewish community, today better known for its teeming masses of outdoor cafes. The past few years have seen the opening of several Judaica-oriented bookstores and kosher restaurants. *(S1, 2, or 25 to Oranienburger Str. or U6 to Oranienburger Tor.)* The huge, oriental-style **Neue Synagoge** was used for worship until 1940, when the Nazis occupied it and used it for storage. The synagogue was destroyed by bombing, but its beautiful, gold-laced domes were rebuilt and opened to the public in 1995. The interior houses an exhibit chronicling the synagogue's history in addition to temporary exhibits on the history of Berlin's Jews. *(Oranienburger Str. 30. ☎ 28 40 13 16. Open M-Th and Su 10am-6pm, F 10am-2pm. Museum DM5, students DM3. Dome DM3, DM2.)*

GENDARMENMARKT. Berlin's most impressive ensemble of 19th-century buildings is a few blocks south of Unter den Linden on the **Gendarmenmarkt,** also known as the French Quarter after it became the main settlement for Protestant Huguenots in the 18th century. Note the **Deutscher Dom, Französischer Dom,** and **Konzerthaus am Gendarmenmarkt.** *(U2 to Französische Str. or U2 or 6 to Stadtmitte.)*

POTSDAMER PLATZ AND FÜHRERBUNKER. Heading south along Ebertstr. from the Brandenburg Gate will bring you to **Potsdamer Platz,** built under Friedrich Wilhelm I with the primary purpose of moving troops quickly. After reunification, the square became the new commercial center of Berlin. The half-finished buildings, sand lots, and newly constructed facades of glass and steel create a landscape that is both a product and symbol of the master plans for a new Berlin; the completion date has been pushed back to 2004. *(S1, 2, or 25 or U2 to Potsdamer Pl.)*

Near Potsdamer Pl. lies the unmarked site of the **Führerbunker,** where Hitler married Eva Braun and later ended his life. In macabre irony, the actual bunker site is now a playground (behind the record store at Wilhelmstr. 92); tourists often mistakenly head for the visible bunker at the southern edge of Potsdamer Pl.

BERTOLT-BRECHT-HAUS. If any single man personifies the maelstrom of political and aesthetic contradictions that is Berlin, it is **Bertolt Brecht,** who called the city home. Brecht lived and worked in the house near the intersection with Schlegelstr. from 1953 to 1956. If you understand German, take the guided tour, given in flamboyant Brechtian style. *(Chausseestr. 125. ☎283 05 70 44. U6 to Zinnowitzer Str. Mandatory tours every 30min. Tu-W and F 10-11:30am, Th 10-11:30am and 5-6:30pm, Sa 9:30am-1:30pm. Tours every hr. Su 11am-6pm. DM4, students DM2.)*

TIERGARTEN

In the center of Berlin, the lush **Tiergarten** stretches from Bahnhof Zoo to the Brandenburg Gate and was formerly used by Prussian monarchs as a hunting and parade ground. Today the Tiergarten is filled with strolling families by day and cruising gay men at night. **Straße des 17. Juni** bisects the park, connecting Ernst-Reuter-Pl. to the Brandenburg Gate. The 70m **Siegessäule** (Victory Column) in the heart of the park, topped by a gilded statue of winged victory, commemorates Prussia's humiliating defeat of France in 1870. Climb the monument's 285 steps to the top for a panorama of the city. *(Take bus #100, 187, or 341 to Großer Stern. Open Apr.-Nov. M 1-6pm, Tu-Su 9am-6pm. DM2, students DM1.)*

THE REICHSTAG. North of the Brandenburg Gate sits the stone-gray **Reichstag,** former seat of the parliaments of the German Empire and the Weimar Republic, and current home of Germany's governing body, the Bundestag. In the summer of 1995, the husband-and-wife team **Christo** and **Jeanne-Claude** wrapped the dignified building in 120,000 yards of shimmery metallic fabric. After the wrapping was torn down, a giant glass dome was constructed around an upside-down solar cone that powers the building. A walkway spirals up the inside of the dome, leading visitors to the top of the cone. *(Open daily 8am-midnight; last entrance at 10pm. Free.)*

KU'DAMM—CHARLOTTENBURG—SCHÖNEBERG

The borough of Charlottenburg, one of the wealthiest areas in Berlin, includes the area between the Spree River and the **Ku'damm,** Berlin's biggest and fanciest shopping strip. South of the Ku'damm, Schöneberg is a pleasant, middle-class residential district, the birthplace of Marlene Dietrich, and home to the more affluent segments of Berlin's gay and lesbian community.

BAHNHOF ZOO. During the city's division, West Berlin centered around **Bahnhof Zoo,** the station that inspired U2's "Zoo TV" tour (the U2 line runs through the station). The area surrounding the station is a spectacular wasteland of department stores and peepshows intermingled with souvenir shops and G-rated attractions. Across Bahnhof Zoo and through the corral of bus depots, the renowned **Zoologischer Garten** is one of the best zoos in the world, with many animals displayed in open-air habitats instead of cages. *(Open daily May-Sept. 9am-6:30pm; Oct.-Feb. 9am-5pm; Mar.-Apr. 9am-5:30pm. DM13, students DM11.)* Next door is the excellent **Aquarium,** whose pride and joy is its 450kg **Komodo dragon,** the world's largest reptile, a gift to Germany from Indonesia. *(Budapester Str. 32. Open daily 9am-6pm. Aquarium DM12, students DM10. Combination ticket to the zoo and aquarium DM21, students DM17.)*

KAISER-WILHELM-GEDÄCHTNISKIRCHE. Nicknamed "the rotten tooth," the shattered church stands as a quiet reminder of the destruction caused during WWII. Built in 1852 in a Romanesque-Byzantine style, the church has an equally striking interior, with colorful mosaics covering the ceiling, floors, and walls, all bathed in a dim blue glow from stained-glass blocks. *(☎218 50 23. Open daily 9am-7pm.)*

KADEWE. This largest department store in mainland Europe (an abbreviation of *Kaufhaus des Westens*, or "Department Store of the West") is the temple of consumerism in commercial Berlin. For the tens of thousands of product-starved former East Germans who flooded Western Berlin following the fall of the Wall,

KaDeWe *was* the West—prompting warnings such as, "OK now, we're going in. Just act normal." The food department, sixth floor, has to be seen to be believed. *(Wittenbergpl. at Tauentzienstr. 21-24. Open M-F 9:30am-8pm, Sa 9am-4pm.)*

SCHLOSS CHARLOTTENBURG. The broad, bright Baroque palace commissioned by Friedrich I for his second wife, Sophie-Charlotte, lies on the northern edge of Charlottenburg. Its buildings include the **Neringbau** (or **Altes Schloß**), the palace proper, which contains many rooms filled with historical furnishings; the **Schinkel-Pavilion,** a museum dedicated to Prussian architect Karl Friedrich Schinkel; **Belvedere,** a small building housing the royal family's porcelain collection; and the **Mausoleum,** the final resting spot for most of the family. The **Galerie der Romantik,** a state museum housing Berlin's first-rate collection of German Romantic paintings, is located in a side wing (see **Museums**). The carefully manicured **Schloßgarten** behind the main buildings is an elysium of small lakes, footbridges, and fountains. *(Bus #145 from Bahnhof Zoo to Luisenpl./Schloß Charlottenburg or U7 to Richard-Wagner-Pl; walk down Otto-Suhr-Allee. Altes Schloß open Tu-F 9am-5pm, Sa-Su 10am-5pm. DM8, DM4. Schinkel-Pavilion open Tu-Su 10am-5pm. DM3, DM2. Belvedere open Apr.-Oct. Tu-Su 10am-5pm; Nov.-Mar. Tu-F noon-4pm and Sa-Su noon-5pm. DM3, DM2. Mausoleum open Apr.-Oct. Tu-Su 10am-noon and 1-5pm. DM3, DM2. Schloßgarten open Tu-Su 6am-9pm. Free. Ticket to entire complex DM15, DM10, under 14 free. Family card DM25.)*

KREUZBERG—FRIEDRICHSHAIN—LICHTENBERG

Kreuzberg is the indisputable center of Berlin's alternative *Szene*, an eclectic mix of ethnicities, punks, lots of graffiti, and a thriving gay and lesbian community. Kreuzberg has long been proud of its diverse population and liberal leanings: this is the place to see anti-Nazi graffiti and left-wing revolutionary slogans (in English, Turkish, Russian, Spanish, and German). Much of the area was occupied by *Hausbesetzer* (squatters) in the 1960s and '70s. A conservative city government decided to forcibly evict the illegal residents in the early '80s, provoking riots and throwing the city into total consternation.

HAUS AM CHECKPOINT CHARLIE. A fascinating exhibition on the site of the famous border-crossing point with an uneasy mixture of blatant Western tourist kitsch and didactic Eastern earnestness, the Haus is one of Berlin's most popular tourist attractions. The ground floor holds a pricey snack bar and a ticket desk buried under piles of Wall-related books, stickers, and postcards. The upper floors are a giant collage of artworks, newspaper clippings, and photographs, along with all types of devices used to get over, under, or through the wall. *(Friedrichstr. 44. U6 or bus #129 to Kochstr. ☎251 10 31. Museum open daily 9am-10pm. DM8, students DM5. Films M-F at 5:30 and 7:30pm, Sa-Su at 4:30, 6, and 7pm.)*

EAST SIDE GALLERY. The longest remaining portion of the Wall, this 1.3km stretch of cement and asbestos slabs also serves as one of the world's largest open-air art galleries. The murals are the efforts of an international group of artists who gathered in 1989 to celebrate reunification. In 1999, with the wall still standing, the same artists repainted their work. *(Along Mühlenstr. Take S3, 5, 6, 7, 75, or 9 or U1 or 15 to Warschauer Str. and walk back toward the river. Open 24hr.)*

FORSCHUNGS- UND GEDENKSTÄTTE NORMANNENSTRAßE. In the suburb of Lichtenberg stands perhaps the most hated and feared building of the GDR regime—the headquarters of the East German secret police, the **Staatssicherheit** or **Stasi.** The building once contained six million individual dossiers on citizens of the GDR, a country of only 16 million people. Since a 1991 law returned the records to their subjects, the "Horror-Files" have rocked Germany, exposing informants—and wrecking careers, marriages, and friendships—at all levels of society. The exhibit displays the offices of Erich Mielke (the loathed Minister for State Security from 1957-1989), a collection of tiny microphones and hidden cameras used for surveillance, and a GDR Stasi shrine full of Lenin busts. *(Ruschestr. 103, Haus 1. U5 to Magdalenenstr. From the station's Ruschestr. exit, walk up Ruschestr. and take a right on Normannenstr. ☎553 68 54. Open Tu-F 11am-6pm, Sa-Su 2-6pm. DM5, students DM3.75.)*

MUSEUMS

Berlin is one of the world's great museum cities, with collections spanning all subjects and eras. The **Staatliche Museen Preußischer Kulturbesitz (SMPK)** runs the four major complexes that form the hub of the city's museum culture—**Charlottenburg** (bus #145 from Bahnhof Zoo to Luisenpl./Schloß Charlottenburg, or U7 to Richard-Wagner-Pl.; then walk down Otto-Suhr-Allee), **Dahlem** (U1 to Dahlem-Dorf), **Museuminsel** (S3, 5, 7, 9 or 75 to Hackescher Markt, or bus #100 to Lustgarten), and the **Kulturforum** (S1, 2, or 25 or U2 to Potsdamer Pl.; walk down Potsdamer Str.). Entrance prices for these museums are standardized; a single admission costs DM4, students DM2. A *Tageskarte* (DM8, students DM4) is valid for all SMPK museums on the day of purchase; the *Wochenkarte* (DM25, students DM12.50) is valid for the whole week. Admission is free the first Sunday of every month.

Pergamon Museum, Kupfergraben. One of the world's great ancient history museums. Named for Pergamon, the city from which the enormous **Altar of Zeus** (180 BC) that fills its main exhibit hall was taken, the museum features huge pieces of ancient Mediterranean and Near Eastern artifacts. Open Tu-Su 9am-6pm. *Tageskarte* required.

Altes Museum, at the far end of the Lustgarten. The lower level contains the *Antikensammlung,* a permanent collection of ancient Greco-Roman decorative art. Upstairs, see the greatest hits of the **Alte Nationalgalerie** while their true home is renovated. Open Tu-Su 9am-6pm. *Tageskarte* valid while the Alte Nationalgalerie collection remains there.

Ägyptisches Museum, Schloßstr. 70 (☎20 90 55 55). Across Spandauer Damm from the palace. This stern Neoclassical building contains a famous collection of ancient Egyptian art. The most popular item is the stunning 3300-year-old bust of **Queen Nefertiti** (1350 BC), thought by many to be the most beautiful representation of a woman in the world. Open Tu-Su 10am-6pm. DM8, students DM4.

Sammlung Berggruen, Schloßstr. 1 (☎326 95 80). Five floors offer a substantial collection of Picasso's work, including numerous sketches, some of which from when the artist was only 16. The top floor exhibits a collection of Paul Klee's paintings and Alberto Giacometti's sculptures. Open Tu-F 10am-6pm, Sa-Su 11am-6pm. DM8, students DM4.

Deutsche Guggenheim Berlin, Unter den Linden 13-15 (☎20 20 93 13). In a newly renovated building across the street from the *Staatsbibliothek,* this joint venture between the Deutsche Bank and the Guggenheim Foundation in New York features contemporary avant-garde art. Open daily 11am-8pm, Th-F 11am-10pm. DM8, students DM5; M free.

Deutsches Historisches Museum, Unter den Linden 2 (☎20 30 40), in the Zeughaus. S3, 5, 7, 75, or 9 to Hackescher Markt. Until renovations are completed in 2002, the museum is housed in the Kronprinzenpalais across the street. Traces German history from the Neanderthal period to the Nazis. Large quantities of GDR art in the "painting-of-a-happy-faced-worker" period are present. Open M-Tu and Th-Su 10am-6pm. Free.

Infobox, Leipziger Pl. 21. S1, 2, or 25 or U2 to Potsdamer Pl. Everything you ever wanted to know about Europe's largest construction site. The exhibits change regularly as building progresses, and address topics such as environmental concerns and the "mushroom concept," the overall idea behind the changes to the transportation systems. Open M-W and F-Su 9am-7pm, Th 9am-9pm. Tours every hr. 10am-4pm. Free.

Gemäldegalerie, (☎20 90 55 55), in the Tiergarten-Kulturforum, on Matthäikirchpl. One of Germany's most famous museums, it houses an enormous collection by Italian, German, Dutch, and Flemish masters, including works by Rembrandt, Bruegel, Rubens, Vermeer, Raphael, Titian, Botticelli, and Dürer. Open Tu-Su 10am-6pm, Th until 10 pm.

Neue National Gallerie, Potsdamer Str. 50 (☎266 26 62). Past the Kulturforum. This sleek building, designed by Mies van der Rohe, houses interesting temporary exhibits upstairs; the permanent collection downstairs includes works by Warhol, Munch, Kirchner, Pechstein, Beckmann, and Ernst. Open Tu-F 10am-6pm and Sa-Su 11am-6pm. SMPK prices for permanent collection; DM12, students DM6 for the whole museum.

Hamburger Bahnhof Museum für Gegenwart, Invalidenstr. 50-51 (☎397 83 11). S3, 5, 7, 75, or 9 to Lehrter Stadtbahnhof or U6 to Zinnowitzer Str. Berlin's foremost collection of contemporary art features some cheerfully amusing works by Warhol, and a few neat multimedia installations. Open Tu-W and F 10am-6pm, Th 10am-10pm, Sa-Su 11am-6pm. DM10, students DM5. Tours Sa-Su at 3pm.

Bauhaus-Archiv Museum für Gestaltung, Klingelhöferstr. 14. Bus #100 or 187 to Stülerstr. A building designed by Bauhaus founder Walter Gropius devoted to the school's development, along with a collection of paintings by Kandinsky and Klee. Open M and W-Su 10am-5pm. DM5, students DM2.50; M free.

Topographie des Terrors, (☎25 48 67 03), at the corner of Niederkirchnerstr. and Wilhelmstr. S1 or 2, or U2 to Potsdamer Pl. Built on the ruins of a Gestapo kitchen, the comprehensive exhibit of photographs, documents, and German texts details the Nazi rise to power and the atrocities that occurred during the war. Open Tu-Su 10am-6pm. Free.

ENTERTAINMENT

Berlin has one of the most vibrant cultural scenes in the world: exhibitions, concerts, plays, and dance performances abound. Festivals celebrating everything from Chinese film to West African music spice up the regular offerings. Always ask about student discounts; most theaters and concert halls offer up to 50% off, but only if you buy at *Abendkassen* (evening box offices), which generally open one hour before performance. Look for theater and concert listings in the monthly *Konzerte und Theater in Berlin und Brandenburg* (free) and *Berlin Programm* (DM2.80), as well as in the biweekly *Zitty* and *Tip*. **Hekticket,** on Hardenbergstr. next to the Zoo-Palast cineplex, sells last-minute half-price tickets. (☎230 99 30. Open M-F 9am-8pm, Sa 10am-8pm, Su 4-8pm.) **Berliner Festspiele,** Budapester Str. 48-50, has tickets for a variety of shows and concerts. (☎25 48 92 50; www.berlinerfestspiele.de. Open M-F 10am-6pm, Su 10am-2pm.)

CONCERTS AND OPERA. Berlin reaches its musical zenith during the **Berliner Festwochen,** which draws the world's best orchestras and soloists in September. The **Berliner Jazztage** in November also brings crowds. In mid-July, the **Bachtage** offers an intense week of classical music, while every Saturday night in August, the **Sommer Festspiele** turns the Ku'damm into a multi-faceted concert hall for punk, steel-drum, and folk groups. **Berliner Philharmonisches Orchester,** Matthäikirchstr. 1, is one of the world's finest. Check for last-minute seats an hour before curtain. (☎25 48 81 32. U2, S1, 2, or 25: Potsdamer Pl., then head up Potsdamer Str. Tickets from DM14-26; sold M-F 3:30-6pm, Sa-Su 11am-2pm.) **Deutsche Oper Berlin,** Bismarckstr. 35, is Berlin's best opera. (Info ☎341 02 49, tickets ☎343 84 01, toll-free ☎0 800 248 98 42. U2: Deutsche Oper. Student discounts available 1 week or less before shows. Tickets DM15-140. Evening tickets available 1hr. before show. Box office open M-Sa from 11am until 1hr. before show, Su 10am-2pm.)

THEATER AND FILM. In addition to the best German-language theater in the world, Berlin also has a lively English-language theater scene. Look for listings in *Zitty* or *Tip* that say *in englischer Sprache* (in English). The **Deutsches Theater,** Schumannstr. 13a, offers everything from Büchner to Mamet to Ibsen. (☎28 44 12 25. Tickets DM15-25. Box office open M-Sa 11am-6:30pm, Su 3-6:30pm.) **Hebbel-Theater,** Stresemannstr. 29, is the most avant of the avant-garde theaters in Berlin. (☎25 90 04 27. Order tickets by phone M-Su 4-7pm or show up 1hr. before performance.) The hip **Berliner Ensemble,** Bertolt-Brecht-Pl. 1, was established by Bertolt Brecht. (☎282 31 60. Tickets DM12-40, 50% student discount available 1hr. before performance. Box office open M-Sa 11am-6pm, Su 3-6pm.) Berlin is a movie-loving town; it hosts the international **Berlinale** film festival (Feb. 7-18, 2001), and on any night in Berlin you can choose from 100 different films. *O.F.* next to a movie listing means original version (i.e., not dubbed); *O.m.U.* means original version with German subtitles. Numerous cineplexes offer the chance to see dubbed Hollywood blockbusters. **UCI Kinowelt Zoo-Palast,** Hardenbergstr. 29a (☎25 41 47 77), near Bahnhof Zoo, is one of the biggest and most popular, with more than a dozen screens. Mondays, Tuesdays, or Wednesdays are *Kinotage* at most movie theaters, with reduced prices. Bring a student ID for discounts.

NIGHTLIFE

This is the section of *Let's Go: Europe* where we dance.

Berlin's nightlife is **absolute madness,** a round-the-clock cauldron of debauchery that may terrify the faint of heart. Bars typically open around 6pm; as they wind down around 1am, the pace picks up and the smoke machines kick in at the clubs, which groove till dawn, when a variety of after-parties and 24-hour cafes keep up the seemingly perpetual motion. From 1am to 4am, take advantage of the **night buses** and **U9** and **12,** which run all night on Fridays and Saturdays; normal transit resumes after 4:30am. In addition to *Tip* and *Zitty*, the free *030*, in hostels, cafes and bars, is a good reference for bands and dance venues.

Western Berlin has a variety of scenes. **Savignyplatz** offers refined, laid-back cafes in one of Berlin's oldest (and richest) neighborhoods. The **Eastern Kreuzberg** scene is in a strong Turkish community, with a dizzying array of radically alternative clubs and bars centering around Oranienstr. and radiating outward several blocks, with gay and lesbian establishments around Muskauerstr. Berlin's best clubs are in **Eastern Berlin,** centering around Orangienburgerstr. in **Mitte** (not to be confused with Kreuzberg's Oranienstr.). If at all possible, try to hit (or, if you're prone to bouts of claustrophobia, avoid) Berlin during the **Love Parade,** usually the second weekend of July, when the city just says "yes" to everything. Note also that Berlin has **de-criminalized marijuana possession** of up to eight grams. Smoking it in public has not been officially accepted, though it's becoming more common in some clubs. *Let's Go* does not recommend puffing smoke rings at police officers.

SO36, Oranienstr. 190. U1, 12, or 15 to Görlitzer Bahnhof or night bus N29 to Heinrichpl. Berlin's *truly* mixed club, with hip heteros, gays, and lesbians grooving to a mish-mash of wild genres. Cover varies. Open after 11pm.

Tresor/Globus, Leipziger Str. 126a. U2 or S1, 2, or 25 or night bus N5, N29 or N52 to Potsdamer Pl. Packed wall-to-wall with enthusiastic ravers. Cover W DM5, F DM10, Sa DM15-20. Open W and F-Sa 11pm-6am.

Insel der Jugend, Alt-Treptow 6. S4, 6, 8, or 9 to Treptower Park, then bus #166, 167, or 265 or night bus N65 to Alt-Treptow. In the Spree River. Its 3 floors of dancing have the feel of a fishbowl with fluorescent silver foil and netting. Cover Th-Sa DM5-15. Open W after 7pm, Th after 9pm, F-Sa after 10pm.

Tacheles, Oranienburger Str. 53-56. U6 to "Oranienburger Tor" or S1, 2, or 25 to Oranienburger Str. or night bus N6 or N84. A playground for artists, punks, and curious tourists. Hosts art galleries, a *Biergarten,* **Cafe Zapata,** and vicious raves. Open daily 24hr.

KulturBrauerei, Knaackstr. 97. U2 to Eberswalder Str. This small village of *kultur* houses numerous different stages and dance floors, with everything from hard-core *Ostrock* and disco to techno, reggae, and *Schlager*. Cover DM3-5. Open Tu and Th-Su after 10pm.

Café Silberstein, Oranienburger Str. 27. S1, 2, or 25 to Oranienburger Str. Sushi served late and a lively student crowd. Open daily after 10am; sushi served M-Th 4pm-midnight, F 4pm-2am, Sa noon-2am, Su noon-midnight.

KitKat Club, Glogauer Str. 2. U1, 12, or 15 to Görlitzer Bahnhof or night bus N29. People with varying degrees of clothing, some copulating, some just digging the cool trance music. 4 primarily gay-lesbian events, including the Th cross-dressed **Fuck-Naked Sex Party** (men only!). Cover DM10-20. Open W-Su after 11pm. **After-hours party** (Su 8am-7pm) is popular, free, and more clothed.

Quasimodo, Kantstr. 12a. U2 or 12 or S3, 5, 7, 75, or 9 to Zoologischer Garten. A wide variety of artists play at this basement jazz venue; T and W are always a mere DM5, so students fill the club in the middle of the week. On weekends, cover ranges from free to DM40. Tickets available from 5pm or at Kant-Kasse ticket service (☎313 45 54). Club open every Tu, W, F, Sa from 9pm; other days occasionally.

WMF, Ziegelstr. 22. S1, 2, or 25 to Oranienburger Str. or U6 to Oranienburger Tor. It's like a house-party gone terribly wrong, or maybe terribly right. Drum 'n' bass, house, and techno. Sundays feature GMF, a gay tea dance. Cover DM15-25. Open W-Su after 11pm.

b-flat, Rosenthalerstr. 13. U8 to Rosenthalerpl. Acoustic music and jazz in a relaxed atmosphere. Cover varies; frequent student discounts of DM3-5. Open daily from 8pm; happy hour 9-10pm, blue hour 1-2am.

GAY AND LESBIAN NIGHTLIFE

Gay Berlin centers on **Nollendorf Platz,** where crowds are usually mixed and establishments range from friendly to cruisy. The gay information center **Mann-o-Meter,** Motzstr. 5, off Nollendorfpl., gives information on nightlife, activism, and gay or gay-friendly living arrangements (☎216 80 08. DM30-75 pernight). Pick up a copy of the amazingly comprehensive *Siegessäule* (free), named after one of Berlin's most prominent phallic monuments. Late June is the high point of the queer calendar, culminating in the ecstatic, champagne-soaked floats of the **Christopher Street Day (CSD)** parade, a six-hour street party drawing more than 250,000 revelers.

Omnes, Motzstr. 8. U1, 15, 2, or 4 to Nollendorfpl. A mainly male gay bar, its hours accommodate early-morning revelers. Open M-F from 8am, Sa and Su from 5am.

Rose's, Oranienstr. 187. Mixed gay and lesbian clientele kicks it amid flashing red lights and glitter. Lots of glitter. Open daily 10pm-6am.

Schoko-Café, Mariannenstr. 6. Lesbian central; a cafe with a cultural center upstairs, billiards, and dancing every 2nd Sa of the month (10pm). Open M-Th and Su 5pm-1am year-round, plus F-Sa noon-1am in the summer.

Connection, Fuggerstr. 33. U1, 15, or 2 to Wittenbergpl. Sketchy, sketchy, sketchy. The name says it all. Cover DM12 including one drink. Open M-Th 10pm-1am, F-Sa 10pm-6am, Su 2pm-2am. First weekend of the month mixed, otherwise men only.

GERMANY

EXCURSIONS FROM BERLIN

POTSDAM. Visitors disappointed by Berlin's gritty, distinctly unroyal demeanor could do no better than to head to nearby Potsdam, the glittering city of Frederick II (the Great). From 1921 through WWII, Potsdam was Germany's "Little Hollywood," and in 1945 the Allies divided up Germany at the Potsdam Conference. The 600-acre **Park Sanssouci,** with countless marble fountains, exotic pavilions, and Baroque castles, is a monument to Frederick the Great's scattered aesthetic tastes. A **day ticket** grants access to all of the park's four castles (DM20, students DM15). At one end of the long **Hauptallee** (central path) stands the Versailles-esque **Schloß Sanssouci,** where Frederick escaped his wife and drowned his sorrows. (☎969 41 90. Open Tu-Su Apr.-Oct. 9am-5pm; Nov.-Mar. 9am-4pm. DM10, students DM5.) At the opposite end is the largest castle, the 200-room **Neues Palais,** built by Frederick to demonstrate Prussia's power. (☎969 42 55. Open Su-Th Apr.-Oct. 9am-5pm; Nov.-Mar. 9am-4pm. DM6, students DM4.) The most exotic of the park's pavilions is the gilded **Chinesisches Teehaus** (DM2). Potsdam's second park, the **Neuer Garten,** contains several former royal residences. Built in the style of an English country manor, **Schloß Cecilienhof** hosted the signers of the 1945 Potsdam Treaty. To get there, take **bus** #694 to Cecilienhof or streetcar #92 to Alleestr. (☎969 42 44. Open Tu-Su 9am-noon and 12:30-5pm. DM6, with tour DM8; students DM4).

S7 runs to Potsdam-Stadt (in Zone C) from Berlin's Bahnhof Zoo (30min., DM4.20). The **tourist office,** Friedrich-Ebert-Str. 5, between the Alter Markt and Pl. der Einheit streetcar stops, books rooms (DM20-40 per person) for a DM5 fee. (☎(0331) 27 55 80. Open Apr.-Oct. M-F 9am-6pm, Sa 10am-4pm, Su 10am-2pm; Nov.-Mar. M-F 10am-6pm, Sa-Su 10am-2pm.)

DRESDEN. Check out August the Strong's collection in the **Zwinger** and other world-class attractions in **Dresden,** only two hours from Berlin by train (p. 418).

LEIPZIG. Once the stomping grounds of Goethe, Nietzsche, and Leibniz, **Leipzig** (2-3hr. from Berlin by train) now blazes with a student-oriented scene (p. 422).

EASTERN GERMANY

Sachsen (Saxony) is known primarily for Dresden and Leipzig, the largest cities in Eastern Germany after Berlin. However, the entire region offers a fascinating historical and cultural diversity that reveals a great deal about life in the former East. The castles around Dresden attest to the bombastic history of Sachsen's decadent Electors, while the socialist monuments of Chemnitz and the shapeless architecture of other major cities depict the former world of the GDR. On the eastern edge of Sachsen, the mountain ranges of the *Sächsiche Schweiz* and the *Zittauer Gebirge* are a respite from the aesthetic violence created by East Germany's city planners. Sachsen is also home to the Sorbs, Germany's only national minority, whose presence lends a Slavic air to many of the region's eastern towns.

DRESDEN ☎0351

Dresden pulses with an intensity that is both vicious and sublime. The city was one of the cultural capitals of pre-war Germany; sadly, Allied bombings claimed over 50,000 lives and destroyed 75% of the city center. Dresden today engages visitors with spectacular ruins amid world-class museums and partially reconstructed palaces and churches, it is entering the new millennium as a dynamic metropolis propelled by a history of cultural turbulence.

GETTING THERE AND GETTING AROUND

Trains: Hauptbahnhof (☎ (0180) 599 66 33). To: **Leipzig** (1½hr., 34 per day, DM33); **Berlin** (2hr., 15 per day, DM52); **Frankfurt** (6hr., 14 per day, DM136); **Munich** (8hr., 24 per day, DM148); **Budapest** (11hr., 4 per day, DM125); **Prague** (3hr., 12 per day, DM38); and **Warsaw** (8hr., 8 per day, DM55). **Bahnhof Dresden Neustadt** sits across the Elbe, sending trains primarily to other cities in Eastern Germany.

Public Transportation: Dresden is sprawling–even for short visits, familiarize yourself with the transport lines. **Single-ride** DM2.90; 4 or fewer stops DM1.80. **Day pass** DM8; **weekly pass** DM25, students DM19. Most major lines run every hour after midnight. Dresden's **S-Bahn** network reaches from Meißen (DM7.70) to Schöna by the Czech border (DM7.70). Buy tickets from *Automaten* in the *Hauptbahnhof* and validate them in the red contraptions as you board; insert the ticket and press *hard.*

Hitchhiking: *Let's Go* does not recommend hitchhiking. Hitchers stand by "Autobahn" signs at on-ramps. To **Berlin:** streetcar #3 or 13 to "Liststr.," then bus #81 to "Olter." To **Prague** or **Frankfurt:** bus #72 or 88 to "Luga," or bus #76, 85, or 87 to "Lockwitz."

ORIENTATION AND PRACTICAL INFORMATION

Dresden is bisected by the Elbe. The **Altstadt** lies on the same side as the Hauptbahnhof; **Neustadt,** to the north, escaped most of the bombing, making it one of the oldest parts of the city. Many of Dresden's main attractions are centered between the **Altmarkt** and the **Elbe,** five minutes from the Neustadt.

Tourist Office: Two locations: **Prager Str.,** across from the Hauptbahnhof (☎49 19 20), and **Theaterpl.,** in the Schinkelwache in front of the Semper-Oper. Sells the **Dresden Card,** which provides 48hr. of public transit and free or reduced entry at many museums (DM26). Both open M-F 10am-6pm, Sa-Su 10am-2pm.

Currency Exchange: ReiseBank, in the train station. 2.5-4.5% commission, depending on amount; DM7.50 for traveler's checks. Open M-F 7:30am-7:30pm, Sa 8am-noon and 12:30-4pm, Su 9am-1pm. After hours, try the self-service machine; rates are poor.

American Express: Hoyerswerdaer Str. 20 (☎80 70 30), in the Neustadt near Rosa-Luxemburg-Pl. Money sent and mail held. Open M-F 7:30am-6pm.

Luggage Storage: At both train stations. Lockers DM2-4. Storage DM4 per piece per 24hr. Open M-F 6am-10pm, Sa 6am-9pm.

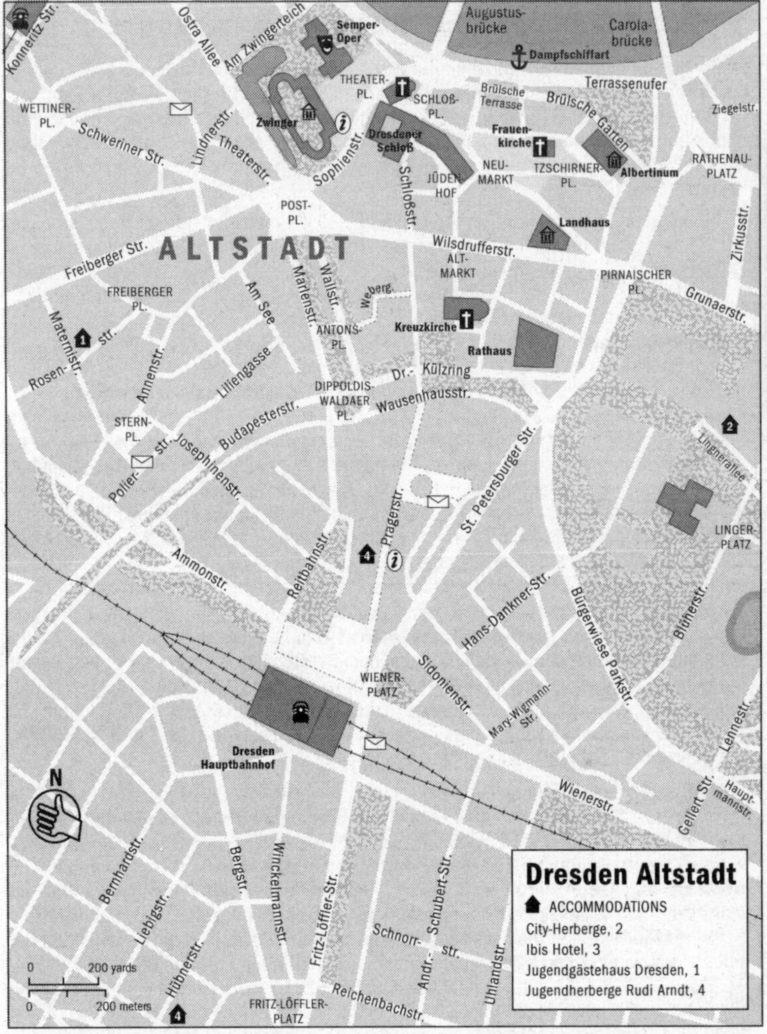

Laundromat: Groove Station, Katharinenstr. 11-13. Wash, dry, and cup o' joe DM8. Browse leather, tattoos, or piercing options. Open Su-F 11am-2am, Sa 10am-late.

Emergency: Police: ☎ 110. **Ambulance and Fire:** ☎ 112.

Pharmacy: Apctheke Prager Straße, Prager Str. 3 (☎425 08). Open M-F 8:30am-7pm, Sa 8:30am-4pm. After hours, a sign indicates the nearest open pharmacies.

Internet Access: Upd@te, Louisenstr. 30, near Die Boofe (see **Accommodations**). DM10 per hr. Open M-F noon-8pm, Sa noon-2pm.

Post Office: Hauptpostamt, Königsbrücker Str. 21/29 (☎819 13 70), in Neustadt. Open M-F 8am-7pm, Sa 8am-1pm. **Postamt 72,** St. Petersburger Str. 26, is near the tourist office. Open M-F 8:30am-8pm, Sa 8:30am-noon. Address mail to be held: *Postlagernde Briefe* für First name SURNAME, Hauptpostamt, **D-01099** Dresden, Germany.

ACCOMMODATIONS, CAMPING, AND FOOD

New hotels and hostels are constantly being planned, built, and opened in Dresden; but come the weekend, it's hard to find anything with a good location. Regular hotels often have an excess available rooms, meaning that you can find same-day deals at some of the hotels on Prager Str. The tourist office can facilitate stays in private rooms and provide information on other accommodation options.

Mondpalast Backpacker, Katharinenstr. 11-13 (☎/fax 804 60 61). From Bahnhof Neustadt, walk down Antonstr. and turn left onto Königsbrücker Str. Cross the street and turn right on Katharinenstr. (10min.). Created by backpackers for backpackers, it's the hippest place in town. Breakfast DM8. Sheets DM5. Reception 24hr. Internet DM12 per hr. Call ahead. Dorms DM25-DM27; doubles DM62.

Hostel Die Boofe, Louisenstr. 20 (☎801 33 61). This new hostel offers immaculate rooms and cushy beds. Bike rental DM10. Sheets DM5. Breakfast DM8. Reception 24hr. Reserve ahead. Dorms DM27; doubles DM79 with sheets and breakfast.

Jugendherberge Dresden Rudi Arndt (HI), Hübnerstr. 11 (☎471 06 67). Streetcar #5 (dir. Südvorstadt) or #3 (dir. Plauen) to "Nürnberger Platz." Continue down Nürnberger Str. and turn right onto Hübnerstr.; the hostel is on the right. Or, from Hauptbahnhof, walk down Fritz-Löffler-Str., bear right onto Münchener Str., turn right on Eisenstuckstr. and walk two blocks. Convenient location and friendly atmosphere make up for small rooms. Sheets DM5. HI members only. Check-in 3pm-1am. Curfew 1am. Reservations recommended. DM30, under 27 DM25.

Jugendgästehaus Dresden (HI), Maternistr. 22 (☎49 26 20). Exit the Hauptbahnhof at Prager Str. and turn left, following Ammonstr. to Freiberger Str. Turn right and right again onto Maternistr. A glimpse into pre-fab hotel living, the hostel attracts lots of school groups. Breakfast and sheets included. Check-in after 4pm. Check-out 9:30am. Rooms with sinks DM38 per person, with shower DM45; singles DM15 extra.

Camping: Campingplatz Altfranken, Otto-Harzer-Str. 2 (☎410 24 00). From the Hauptbahnhof, take streetcar #17 (dir. Gorbitz) to "Tharandter Str.," then bus #90 to "Altfranken." Reception 24hr. DM10 per tent.

Unfortunately, the surge in Dresden tourism has raised food prices, particularly in the *Altstadt*. The cheapest eats are at supermarkets or *Imbiß* stands along Prager Str. Most restaurants in the *Altstadt* cater almost exclusively to tourists; those in search of authenticity will probably prefer something outside the city center. The **Neustadt,** between Albertpl. and Alaunpl., spawns a new bar every few weeks and rules the roost of quirky ethnic and student-friendly restaurants. The free monthly *Spot*, available at the tourist office, details culinary options. Try the tasty "mix & match" *tapas* at **El Perro Borracho,** Alaunstr. 70. (All main courses DM12. Open M-F 11:30am-1am, Sa-Su 10am-1am.) **Blumenau,** Louisenstr. 67, offers the perfect setting for *Milchkaffee* mornings, or an evening drink. (Most dishes run DM6-10. Breakfast DM5-11. Open daily 10am-3am.

SIGHTS

Consider buying the **Tageskarte** (DM12, students and seniors DM7), which covers one-day admission to the Albertinum museums, the Schloß, most of the Zwinger, and a number of other sights. The **Dresden Card** (see above) also includes free or reduced entrance to many of the major museums.

ZWINGER AND SEMPER-OPER. The extravagant collection of Friedrich August I (the Strong), Prince Elector of Saxony and King of Poland, is housed in the magnificent **Zwinger** palace, designed by August's senior architect, Matthäus Daniel Pöppelmann, and championed as a triumph of Baroque design. The palace narrowly escaped destruction in the 1945 bombings; workers are busy restoring it to aesthetic perfection. In the Semper wing is the **Gemäldegalerie Alte Meister,** a world-class collection of paintings from 1400-1800. *(Open Tu-Su 10am-6pm. DM7, students and* *seniors DM4. Tours F and Su at 4pm. DM1.)* Across from the gallery is the **Rüstkammer,** a collection of chain mail and other courtly toys. *(Same hours as Gemäldegalerie. DM3, students and seniors DM2; covered by admission to Gemäldegalerie.)* The famed **Semper-Oper** reverberates with the same glorious luxury as the Semper wing of the Zwinger. *(Theaterpl. 2. DM9, students DM6. Almost daily tours; check times at the main entrance.)*

DRESDENER SCHLOß. Across from the Zwinger, the residence of Sachsen's Electors and emperors is nearly restored from the 1945 bombings. The 100m **Hausmannsturm** exhibits photographs and texts (available in English) discussing the bombings; the top floor offers a 360° view of the city. *(Open Apr.-Oct. Tu-Su 10am-6pm. DM5, students and seniors DM3.)* The **Katholische Hofkirche** (Catholic royal church) used to be connected to the Schloß. The back right corner shelters an altar dedicated to bombing victims. *(Open M-Th 9am-5pm, F 1-5pm, Sa 10:30am-4pm, Su noon-4pm. Free.)* If you've been mistaking Friedrich the Earnest for Friedrich the Pugnacious, stop by the **Fürstenzug** (Procession of Electors) along Augustusstr., a mural (102m) made of 24,000 Meißen china tiles, depicting the Saxon rulers from 1123 to 1904. On the Elbe, the **Brühlsche Terrasse** offers prime photo opportunities.

KREUZKIRCHE. After being leveled four times, in 1669 and 1897 by fire, in 1760 with the Seven Years War, and in 1945 by the bombing, the Kreuzkirche's interior remains in a damaged state, with rough plaster columns and half-headed cherubs serving as powerful reminders of the war's destruction. The tower offers a bird's eye view of downtown Dresden. *(An der Kreuzkirche 6. Open in summer M-Tu and Th-F 10am-5:30pm, W and Sa 10am-4:30pm, Su noon-4:30pm; in winter M-F 10am-4:30pm, Sa 10am-3:30pm, Su noon-4:30pm. Free. Tower closes 30min. earlier. DM2, children DM1.)*

NEUSTADT. Across the magnificent **Augustusbrücke,** Hauptstr. is home to the **Goldener Reiter,** a gold-plated statue of August the Strong atop a steed in pompous glory. At the other end of Hauptstr., **Albertplatz** is the gateway to the Neustadt scene.

SCHLACHTHOFRINGE. The **Schlachthofringe** (Slaughterhouse Circle) is a 1910 housing complex used during WWII as a P.O.W. camp. Neglected by the tourist industry, the buildings have been left to waste away. So it goes. Novelist Kurt Vonnegut was imprisoned here during the bombing of Dresden, inspiring his masterpiece *Slaughterhouse-Five*. *(Take bus #82 to "Ostragehege.")*

ALBERTINUM. The **Gemäldegalerie der Neuen Meister** combines a solid ensemble of tried-and-true German and French Impressionists with a collection of Expressionists and Neue Sachlichkeit modernist works, including Otto Dix's renowned "War" triptych. *(Open Su-W and F-Sa 10am-6pm. DM7, students and seniors DM4; includes admission to Grünes Gewölbe, an assemblage of Saxon trifles, upstairs.)*

STADTMUSEUM. In the 18th-century **Landhaus,** the museum tells the story of the city since the 13th century. A colorful collection of 20th-century memorabilia completes the tale, from bomb shells from 1945 to a collection of protest signs from the 1989 demonstrations. *(Wilsdruffer Str. 2, near Pirnaischer Pl. Open May-Sept. M-Tu, Th, and Sa-Su 10am-6pm, W 10am-8pm; Oct.-Apr. Sa-Th 10am-6pm. DM4, students DM2.)*

NIGHTLIFE

Dresden's nightlife scene is young and dynamic; the **Neustadt,** roughly bounded by Königsbrücker Str., Bischofsweg, Kamenzerstr., and Albertpl., is its thumping heart. At last count over 50 bars packed the area; *Kneipen Surfer* lists all of them. Peruse the back of *SAX* (DM2.50) at the tourist office or any bar for upcoming concerts and dances. **Scheune,** Alaunstr. 36-40, is the granddaddy of the Neustadt scene; its eclectic dance floor specializes in obscure world music. (Cover varies. Club open from 8pm. Bar open M-F 11am-2am, Sa-Su 10am-2am.) **DownTown,** Katharinenstr. 11-13, below the Mondpalast hostel, keeps the beat going fast and furious as Dresden's young and energetic scene grooves to techno. (F house and techno, Sa funk and occasional live music. Cover DM7, students DM5. Open 10pm-5am.) **Mona Lisa,** Louisenstr., on the corner of Kamenzerstr., chills nightly as DJs spin techno. (Happy hour 7-9pm. Open daily from 7pm.)

EXCURSIONS FROM DRESDEN

MEIßEN. Meißen, 30km from Dresden, is another testament to the frivolity of August the Strong. In 1710, the Saxon Elector contracted severe *Porzellankrankheit* (the porcelain "bug," still afflicting tourists today) and turned the city's defunct castle into a porcelain-manufacturing base. The factory was once more tightly guarded than KGB headquarters to prevent competitors from learning its techniques; today anyone can tour the **Staatliche Porzellan-Manufaktur,** Talstr. 9. You can peruse finished products in the **Schauhalle** (DM9, students DM7), but the real fun lies in the high-tech tour of the **Schauwerkstatt** (show workshop), which demonstrates the manufacturing process. (Open daily 9am-6pm. DM5. English tapes available.) The **Albrechtsburg** castle and cathedral overlook the city. (Open daily Mar.-Oct. 10am-6pm; Nov.-Feb. 10am-5pm. Last entry 30min. before closing. DM6, students DM43.) From the station, walk to Bahnhofstr., follow the Elbe to the Elbbrücke, cross it, continue to the Markt, and turn right onto Burgstr.; at the end, stairs lead to the right up to Albrechtsburg. Next door looms the **Meißener Dom,** a Gothic cathedral which satisfies visitors with four 13th-century statues by the Naumburg Master, a triptych by Cranach the Elder, and the metal grave coverings of the Wettins. (Open daily Apr.-Oct. 9am-6pm; Nov.-Mar. 10am-4pm. Last entry 30min. before closing. DM3.50, students DM2.50.) Reach Meißen from Dresden by **train** (45min., DM7.70). The **tourist office,** Markt 3, is across from the church, and finds private rooms (DM25-55) for a DM4 fee. (☎419 40. Open Apr.-Oct. M-F 10am-6:30pm, Sa-Su 10am-3pm; Nov.-Mar. M-F 10am-6pm, Sa 10am-3pm.) **☎03521.**

SAXON SWITZERLAND. The *Sächsische Schweiz*—so dubbed because of its stunning, Swiss-like landscape—is one of Germany's most popular vacation spots. Breathtaking **hikes** wind up into the hills of this national park, connecting the towns. Two trails link **Wehlen** to **Rathen;** the more impressive one climbs the famous **Bastei cliffs. Rathen** boasts the **Felsenbühne,** a beautiful open-air theater, with 2000 seats carved into a cliff. (Open 8am until 2hr. before each event, and 1hr. after the event until 8pm.) Tickets and schedules are available from the **Theaterkasse,** on the way to the theater. (☎ (035024) 77 70; fax (035024) 77 735. DM6-39.) The small village of **Hohnstein** is linked to Rathen by two hikes through one of the park's most stunning valleys; be sure to stop at the **Hockstein,** an outcropping with a spectacular view of the valley below. Above the town of **Königstein** looms an impressive **fortress,** which has huge walls built into stone spires. (Open daily Apr.-Sept. 9am-8pm; Oct. 9am-6pm; Nov.-Mar. 9am-5pm. DM7, students and seniors DM5.) Paths also lead from the town to the challenging 415m **Lilienstein** (1½hr.). To get there, take the **ferry** (DM1.30) and the first right after getting off.

Saxon Switzerland is accessible by Dresden's **S-Bahn #1,** which stops at (west to east) Pirna, Wehlen, Rathen, Königstein, and Bad Schandau. A **ferry,** the **Sächsische Dampfschiffart,** also connects the towns. From **Bad Schandau,** cross the river by ferry (DM1.30) and hop on the **S-Bahn** back to Dresden (50min., every 30min., DM7.70), or head to Prague (2hr., DM30.60). Each town has its own **tourist office;** further info is available from the **Tourismusverband Sächsische Schweiz,** Am Bahnhof 6, Bad Schandau (☎/fax 49 50), or the **Nationalpark-Verwaltung,** An der Elbe 4, Bad Schandau (☎900 60; fax 900 66). To hit more than one town in a day, ask at a **Deutsche Bahn** desk about the **Tageskarte** (DM8, families DM12), or buy one from any *Fahrausweis* machine. These passes allow unlimited travel on the S-Bahn, buses, and many ferries for a 24-hour period. **☎035022.**

LEIPZIG ☎0341

A boom town bursting with style, Leipzig jumps out from the calm Eastern German landscape in a fiery blaze of nowNowNOW. The *Uni*-culture, spawned by more than 20,000 students, creates an aura of youthful vitality as it did when Goethe, Nietzsche, and Leibnitz stalked these ivory towers.

PRACTICAL INFO, ACCOMMODATIONS, AND FOOD. **Trains** run to: Dresden (1½hr., every hr., DM26); Berlin (2-3hr., every hr., DM46); Frankfurt (5hr., every 2 hr., DM90); and Munich (7hr., every hr., DM113). To reach the **tourist office,** Richard-Wagner-Str. 1, walk across Willy-Brandt-Pl. in front of the station and turn left at Richard-Wagner-Str. (☎710 42 60; email lipsia@aol.com. Open M-F 8am-8pm, Sa 8am-4pm.) Check **email** at **Café le bit,** Kohlgartenstr. 2, right off Friedrich-List-Pl. (First 30min. free; DM2 each additional 15min. Open M-F 8:30am-3am, Sa 10am-late, Su 10am-1am.) The best budget lodgings in Leipzig are cheap pensions or **private rooms** (singles from DM40; doubles from DM70). Consult the tourist office or **Leipziger Allerlei,** which lists all accommodations. To reach the **Jugendherberge Leipzig Centrum (HI),** Volksgartenstr. 24, take streetcar #17, 37, or 57 (dir. Thekla or Schönefeld) to "Löbauer Str.," walk past the supermarket along Löbauer Str., and turn right on Volksgartenstr. (☎245 70 11. Breakfast included. Sheets DM6. Reception 2:30-11pm. DM29, under 27 DM24.) **Campingplatz Am Auensee,** Gustav-Esche-Str. 5, in nearby Wahren, is a budget alternative. From the station, take streetcar #11 or 28 (dir. Wahren) to "Rathaus Wahren"; turn left at the Rathaus and follow the twisting main road for 10 minutes. (☎465 16 00. Reception M-Sa 6am-9:30pm, Su 6am-8:30pm. DM8 per person; DM5 per car; DM12 per caravan. Small 2-bed hut DM30; large hut with shower DM60.) The Innenstadt is well-supplied with *Imbiß* stands, bistros, and restaurants. A **Kaiser's supermarket** pops up on the Brühl, near Sachsenpl. (Open M-F 7am-8pm, Sa 7am-4pm.) **Postal code:** 04109.

SIGHTS AND ENTERTAINMENT. The colorful **Marktplatz** contains the **Altes Rathaus,** where you'll find the **Stadtgeschichtliches Museum Leipzig.** (Open Tu 2-8pm, W-Su 10am-6pm. DM5, students DM2.50.) Moving away from the Markt on Grimmaischestr. leads you to the temporary home of Leipzig's **Museum der Bildenden Künste,** Grimmaische Str. 1-7, behind the Rathaus, including an excellent collection of 19th-century German paintings. (Open Tu and Th-Su 10am-6pm, W 1-9:30pm. DM5, students and seniors DM2.50.) Across the street is the **Zeitgeschichtliches Forum,** which holds a well-designed exhibit on the histories of Leipzig and Germany from WWII to the present. (Open Tu-F 9am-6pm, Sa-Su 10am-6pm. Free.) Nikolaistr. will take you to the **Nikolaikirche,** where Bach's *St. John Passion* was premiered and where the 1989 *Montagdemos* (Monday demonstrations) pushed for the fall of Communism. Returning to the Markt and following Grimmaischestr. to Thomasg. will bring you to the **Thomaskirche,** where Bach worked for the last 27 years of his career. (Church open daily in summer 9am-6pm; in winter 9am-5pm. Boys choir performances F 6pm, Sa 3pm, Su during services.) Across the street is the **Johann-Sebastian-Bach-Museum,** which depicts Bach's time in Leipzig. (Open daily 10am-5pm. DM4, students and seniors DM2.50.) Head back on Thomasg., then turn right on Dittrichring to reach the fascinating **Museum der "Runden Ecke,"** which describes the history, doctrine, and tools of the feared secret police. (Open W-Su 2-6pm. Free.) A streetcar ride out of the city on #15 or 21 will take you to the **Volkerschlachtdenkmal,** a monument to the soldiers who died in the 1813 "Battle of the Nations," where Napoleon suffered an important defeat. (Open daily Apr.-Oct. 10am-6pm; Nov.-Mar. 10am-4pm. DM6, students DM3.)

Leipzig's nightlife centers around its cafes, most of which have outdoor seating in the summer. **Barfußgäßchen,** off the Markt, hosts the most popular cafes, while more can be found on **Gottschedstraße** and **Bosestraße.** Dance clubs abound across Dittrichring from the Markt, and on **Karl-Liebknecht-Straße.** The **Leipzig University Moritzbastei** serves as dance club, cafe, Biergarten, and outdoor movie theatre.

WEIMAR ☎03643

Named one of Europe's cultural capitals in 1999, Weimar is one of the most renovated cities in the former East Germany. Once home to literary giants Schiller and Goethe, Weimar is also the source of the Bauhaus architectural movement and was the capital of Germany's unstable post-WWI republic. The **Goethehaus** and **Goethe-Nationalmuseum,** Frauenplan 1, show off the immaculately preserved private chambers where the writer entertained, composed, studied, and died. (Open Tu-Su mid-Mar. to mid-Oct. 9am-7pm; mid-Oct. to mid-Mar. 9am-4pm. Expect to wait up to 2hr. on summer afternoons. DM8, students and seniors DM5, children DM2.50.) Head up Schillerstr. to Theaterpl. and the **Deutsches Nationaltheater,** Am Palais 3. The theater that gave Goethe his start still regularly presents *Faust*. The Weimar Constitution was also concocted in this building. Across the way is the **Bauhaus-Museum,** Am Palais 3, which covers the history of the Bauhaus architectural school. (Open Tu-Su Apr.-Oct. 10am-6pm; Nov.-Mar. 10am-4:30pm. DM5, students and seniors DM3.) Heading out of the city center toward the train station on Karl-Liebknecht-Str. brings you to the **Neues Museum Weimar,** Weimarpl. 4, at Rathenaupl., with a quirky collection of contemporary art. (Open Tu-Su 10am-6pm. DM6, students and children DM3.) Head away from the city in the opposite direction to find the **Nietzsche Archiv,** Hummboldtstr. 36. Nietzsche lived his last crazy years here, and after his death, his sister Elisabeth based the archive on her warped, Nazi-friendly version of his philosophy. (Open Tu-Su mid-Mar. to mid-Oct. 1-6pm; mid-Oct. to mid-Mar. 1-4pm. DM4, students and seniors DM3.) Goethe and Schiller lie side by side in a decorated tomb in the **Historischer Friedhof.** (Cemetery open daily Mar.-Sept. 8am-9pm; Oct.-Feb. 8am-6pm. Tomb open daily mid-Mar. to mid-Oct. 9am-7pm; mid-Oct. to mid-Mar. M and W-Su 9am-4pm. DM4, students and seniors DM3.) On the far slopes of the Goethe-landscaped **Park an der Ilm,** on Corona-Schöfer-Str. flanking the river, is the poet's **Gartenhaus.** (Open M-W and Su mid-Mar. to mid-Oct. 9am-7pm; mid-Oct. to mid-Mar. 9am-4pm. DM5, students and seniors DM2.50.)

Trains head to: Erfurt (15min., 4 per hr., DM7.60); Jena (20min., 2 per hr., DM9.80); Eisenach (1hr., 3 per hr., DM19.40); Leipzig (1½hr., every 2 hr., DM24.40); Dresden (3hr., every hr., DM65); and Frankfurt (3hr., every hr., DM78). To reach the city center, head down Carl-August-Allee to Karl-Liebknecht-Str., which leads to Goethepl. (15min.). From Goethpl., follow Geleitstr. as it curves right and leads to a statue; the entrance to the student-run **Jugendhotel Hababusch,** Geleitstr. 4, is in the ivy-covered corner. (☎85 07 37; www.uni-weimar.de/yh. Kitchen. Reception 24hr. Dorms DM15 per person; doubles DM40.) The **Jugendherberge Germania (HI),** Carl-August-Allee 13, is downhill from the train station. (☎85 04 90. Sheets DM7. Reception 24hr. Members only. DM30, under 27 DM25.) A **Rewe supermarket** is in the basement of the **Handelhaus zu Weimar,** on Theaterpl. (Open M-F 7am-8pm, Sa 7am-4pm.) The **Bauhaus University Mensa** (cafeteria), Marienstr. 13/15 near the park, serves cheap food to students. (Open M-F 11am-2pm.) **Postal code:** 99423.

EXCURSION FROM WEIMAR: BUCHENWALD. Two hundred fifty thousand Jews, Gypsies, homosexuals, Communists, and political prisoners were imprisoned and murdered by the Nazis at the labor camp of Buchenwald during WWII, now the **Nationale Mahnmal und Gedenkstätte Buchenwald** (☎ (03643) 43 00). Many Jews were sent here, but after 1942, most were deported to Auschwitz; the camp mostly served to detain and murder political enemies of Nazism and prisoners of war. After "liberation," Soviet authorities used the site from 1945 to 1950 as an internment camp in which more than 28,000 Germans, mostly Nazi war criminals and opponents of the Communist regime, were held; an exhibit detailing the Soviet abuses opened in 1997. A museum at the **KZ-Lager,** the remnants of the camp, documents the histories of Buchenwald (1937-45) and of Nazism. On the other side of the hilltop from the KZ-Lager are the GDR-designed **Mahnmal** (memorial) and **Glockenturm** (bell tower). A path leads through the woods, emerging at a two-way fork in the road. Head right, past the parking lot and bus stop, and continue as the street curves left (20min.). To reach the camp, catch **bus** #6 from Weimar's train station or Goethepl.; check that the bus goes to "Gedenkenstätte Buchenwald," rather than "Ettersburg" (M-F every hr., Sa-Su every 2hr.). Buses back to Weimar stop at the KZ-Lager parking lot and next to the Glockenturm. There is an **information center** near the bus stop at Buchenwald. (Exhibits and information open Tu-Su May-Sept. 9:45am-5:15pm; Oct.-Apr. 8:45am-4:15pm; outdoor area open daily until sundown.)

EISENACH ☎03691

Birthplace of Johann Sebastian Bach and home-in-exile to Martin Luther, Eisenach boasts impressive humanist credentials. High above its half-timbered houses, the **Wartburg fortress** sheltered the excommunicated Luther (disguised as a noble named Junker Jörg) in 1521 while he worked on his German translation of the Bible. (Open daily Mar.-Oct. 8:30am-5pm; Nov.-Feb. 9am-3:30pm. Mandatory German tour every 10min.; DM11, seniors DM8, students and children DM6.) From the station, stroll down **Wartburgerallee** and trudge up one of the steep **footpaths** (30min.), or catch a **tour bus** (every hr. 9am-5pm; DM1.50, round-trip DM2.50). A turn off Wartburgallee down Grimmelg. will bring you to the **Bachhaus,** Frauenplan 21, where the composer was born in 1685. Frequent presentations include anecdotes about Bach's life and spellbinding musical interludes. (Open Apr.-Sept. M noon-5:45pm, Tu-Su 9am-5:45pm.; Oct.-Mar. M 1-4:45pm, Tu-Su 9am-4:45pm. DM5, students DM4.) Town life centers on the **Markt,** where the **Georgenkirche** witnessed a few of Luther's sermons and Bach's baptism. (Open M-Sa 10am-12:30pm and 2-5pm, Su after services.) Up the street from the Markt, the latticed **Lutherhaus,** Lutherpl. 8., was young Martin's home in his schoolboy days. (Open daily Apr.-Oct. 9am-5pm; Nov.-Mar. 10am-5pm. DM5, seniors DM4, students DM2.)

Frequent **trains** run to Weimar (1hr., DM19.50) and Kassel (1½hr., DM27). The **tourist office,** Markt 2, books rooms (DM30-40) for free and offers daily tours (2pm, DM5). From the train station, walk on Bahnhofstr. through the tunnel and angle left until you turn right onto the pedestrian Karlstr. (☎67 02 60. Open M 10am-6pm, Tu-F 9am-6pm, Sa-Su 10am-2pm.) The **Jugendherberge Artur Becker (HI),** Mariental 24, is in a comfortable villa beyond the Schloß. From the station, walk down Bahnhofstr. to Wartburger Allee, which runs into Mariental, continue past the pond, and it'll be on your right (35min.). Or, take bus #3 (dir. Mariental) to Lilienstr.; signs point the way 100m past the stop. (☎74 32 59. Breakfast included. Sheets DM7. Reception 4-9pm. DM30, under 27 DM25.) The excellent **Gasthof Storchenturm,** Georgenstr. 43, has a restaurant, *Biergarten*, and quiet rooms. (☎21 52 50. Breakfast DM7.50. Singles DM45; doubles DM70.) To **camp** at **Am Altenberger See,** 10km from town, catch the bus (dir. Bad Liebenstein; M-F 14 per day, Sa-Su 3 per day) from the train station and tell the driver your destination. (☎21 56 37. Reception 8am-1pm and 3-10pm. DM7 per person; DM5 per tent; DM2 per car.) Get **groceries** at the **Edeka** on Johannispl. (Open M-F 7am-7pm, Sa 7am-2pm.) **Postal code:** 99817.

WITTENBERG ☎03491

The Protestant Reformation, which initiated centuries of religious conflict, began quietly in Wittenberg on October 13, 1517, when local professor and priest Martin Luther nailed his *95 Thesen* to the wooden door of the Schloßkirche. All the major sights lie along **Collegienstr.** The **Lutherhalle** at #54 was Luther's home from 1508, and today houses a museum chronicling the history of the Reformation. (Open daily 9am-6pm. DM7, students DM4.) Turn right from the Lutherhalle and stroll down to Lutherstr. to behold the oak tree under which Luther defiantly burned a papal bull (a decree of excommunication, not a Catholic beast). Farther down the street, as Collegienstr. becomes Schloßstr., is the **Schloßkirche,** crowned by a sumptuous Baroque cupola, which holds a copy of the complaints that Luther nailed to its doors. (Open May-Oct. M 2-5pm, Tu-Sa 10am-5pm, Su 11:30am-3:30pm; Nov.-Apr. M 2-4pm, Tu-Sa 10am-4pm, Su 11:30am-4pm. Free.)

Trains arrive from Leipzig (1hr., every 2hr., DM16) and Berlin (1½hr., every 2hr., DM39). To get to the pedestrian zone from the station, go straight out of the main building, or left from the bus stop, walk down the street and follow the curve to the right. The Lutherhalle will appear on the left. Follow Collegienstr.; and at the other end of the pedestrian zone is the **tourist office,** Schloßpl. 2, which books rooms (DM25-75) for a DM3 fee. (☎49 86 10. Open M-F 9:30am-5:30pm, Sa 10am-3pm, Su 11am-4pm.) Cross the street from the tourist office and walk straight into the castle's enclosure, then trek up the spiraling stairs to the right to reach the

Jugendherberge (HI), in the castle. (☎/fax 40 32 55. Breakfast included. Sheets DM6. Reception 5-10pm. Reserve ahead. DM26, under 27 DM21.) **City-Kauf supermarket** is by the tourist office. (Open M-F 7am-6:30pm, Sa 8am-12:30pm.) **Postal code:** 06886.

DESSAU ☎0340

Founded as a medieval fortress in 1341, Dessau has long been a breeding ground for creative genius, from the schizophrenic sounds of composer Kurt Weill to Bauhaus, one of the most significant architectural movements of the 20th century. The **Bauhaus,** Gropiusallee 38, houses rotating design exhibits. To get there from the station, turn left and go up the steps, then head left over the railroad tracks. Veer left at the first street onto Kleiststr., then right onto Bauhausstr. Or, take bus E or K to "Bauhaus." (Building open 24hr. Free. Exhibitions open Tu-Su 10am-5pm. DM8, students DM6.) A left from the Bauhaus entrance, a right on Gropiusallee, and a left on Ebertallee brings you to the **Kurt-Weill-Zentrum,** Ebertallee 63, the first in the row of **Meisterhäuser,** three houses designed by Gropius. (Meisterhäuser open Tu-Su 10am-5pm. DM8, students DM5.) A **combination ticket** to the Bauhaus and the Meisterhäuser costs DM12, students DM8. Get a **map** of all of Dessau's Bauhaus architecture at the tourist office or the Bauhaus building.

Trains depart for Wittenberg (35min., every 2hr., DM10); Leipzig (1hr., every 2hr., DM15); and Berlin (2hr., every hr., DM33). To reach the **tourist office,** Zerbster Str. 2c, take streetcar #1 or 2 from the station to "Hauptpost," walk toward the Rathaus-Center, veer left on Ratsg., and take the first right. (☎204 14 42; www.dessau.de. Open Apr.-Oct. M-F 9am-7pm, Sa 9am-1pm; Nov.-Mar. M-F 9am-6pm, Sa 10am-1pm.) Enjoy black and white dreams of architectural utopias in the **Bauhaus school building.** For directions from the station, see above. (☎650 83 18. Reservations recommended; call and ask for Frau Oede. Otherwise, knock on room 318. Singles DM30; doubles DM50.) Hip **Klub im Bauhaus** in the Bauhaus school basement lets you indulge in angst over a light meal. Eat *Anarchistenfrühstück* (anarchist's breakfast) while pondering the imminent revolution. (Open M-F 8am-midnight, Sa 10am-midnight, Su 10am-6pm.) **Postal code:** 06844.

NORTHERN GERMANY

Once a favored vacation spot for East Germans, **Mecklenburg-Vorpommern,** the northeasternmost portion of Germany, has suffered economic depression in recent years. To the west, Schleswig-Holstein, which borders Denmark, became a Prussian province in 1867 as part of Bismarck's unification plan, and although it chose to remain part of Germany after WWI, it retains close ties with Scandinavia. To the west, Bremen is Germany's smallest *Land,* a small pocket within Niedersachsen.

ROSTOCK ☎0381

Rostock is poised to regain much of its prosperity as the former GDR's largest port, showing how scars can heal. On August 24, 1992, a hostel for foreigners seeking political asylum was set ablaze by neo-Nazi youths; today, the neo-Nazi presence is almost invisible—it is the left-leaning student crowd that takes center stage. Tourists on the way to the beach or Scandinavia pause in Rostock for the beautiful buildings, lively nightlife, and cosmopolitan feel. Much of 13th-century Rostock remains intact, including its main pedestrian zone, **Kröpeliner Straße,** lined by restored buildings that reflect the city's past as a center of Hanseatic trade. A beast of a brick basilica, the **Marienkiche,** is near the main square at the Steintor end of Kröpeliner Str. (Open M-Sa 10am-5pm, Su 11am-noon.)

Trains (☎493 44 54) connect to: Schwerin (1hr., every hr., DM22.20); Berlin (2½hr., DM65); Hamburg (3hr., DM76.20); and Dresden (7hr., DM118). **Ferries** leave for Scandinavia from the Überseehafen docks. **TT-Linie** (☎67 07 90) chugs to Trelleborg, Sweden (5hr.; 6 per day; DM50, students and children DM25); **Scandlines Europa GT Links** (☎34 34 35; fax 670 66 71) sails to Gedser, Denmark (2hr., 8 per day; Th-Su DM8, M-W DM5, children DM2.50). To get from the station to the **tourist office,** Neuer Markt 3, take streetcar #11 or 12 to "Steintor"; it's in the same building as the post office. (☎194 33. Open May-Sept. M-F 10am-7pm, Sa-Su 10am-4pm; Oct.-Apr. M-F 10am-5pm, Sa-Su 10am-4pm.) Ride the Internet at **Surfing 'inn,** on the third floor of the Galleria Kauphof on Lange Str. (DM3 per 30min. Open M-F 9am-8pm, Sa 9am-6pm.) Both of Rostock's hostels are far from town and in somewhat dangerous neighborhoods, but the tourist office arranges private rooms (DM30-40). To get to the **Jugendherberge Rostock-Warnemünde (HI),** Parkstr. 46, take the S-Bahn (dir. Warnemünde) to the end, cross the bridge, and head straight on Kirchenstr. as it becomes Mühlenstr., then Parkstr. Or, ride the S-Bahn to "Warnemünde Werft," then take bus #36 (dir. "Warnemünde-Strand") to Parkstr. (☎54 81 70. Breakfast included. Sheets DM7. Reception 8-9am, 2:30-5pm, and 7-10pm. Curfew 10pm. Doubles DM30.50, under 27 DM25.50.) There's a **market** on Seinstr. (open M-F 8am-5pm, Sa 8am-1pm), and bakeries on **Kröpeliner Str.** have sandwiches. **Postal code:** 18055.

HAMBURG ☎040

The largest port city in Germany, Hamburg is a reckless coupling of the progressive and the perverse. In 1618, Hamburg gained the status of Free Imperial City, beginning a tradition of autonomy that continues today. Since WWII, Hamburg has seen an active conservation movement to restore buildings damaged in war, as well as infamous riots in the early 80s. Today, Hamburg expresses its restlessness less violently, channeling the energy of contemporary artists, intellectuals, and reveling party-goers who live it up in Germany's self-declared "capital of lust."

GETTING THERE AND GETTING AROUND

Trains: The **Hauptbahnhof,** on Glockengießerwall, handles connections to: **Berlin** (2¾hr., every hr., DM93); **Frankfurt** (3¾hr., every hr., DM191); **Hannover** (1½hr., 3 per hr., DM70); **Munich** (6hr., every hr., DM260); **Amsterdam** (5½hr., 3 per day, DM105); and **Copenhagen** (6hr., 3 per day, DM102). Open daily 5:30am-11pm. Most trains to and from **Schleswig-Holstein** stop only at **Altona** station, in the west of the city.

Buses: The **ZOB,** across from the Hauptbahnhof. To: **Berlin** (2½hr., 8 per day, DM41); **Copenhagen** (6hr., 2 per day, DM63); and **Paris** (15hr., 1 per day, DM115). **Polenreisen** goes to **Poland.** Open M-F 9am-8pm, Sa 9:30am-1:30pm and 4-8pm, Su 4-8pm.

Ferries: DFDS Seaways, Van-der-Smissen-Str. 4 (☎389 03 71), west of the Fischmarkt (S-Bahn #1 or 3 to "Königstr."), sails to **England, Ireland, Copenhagen,** and **Amsterdam.** Open M-F 10am-4:30pm; phone reservations M-F 9am-6pm, Sa 9am-2pm. **Käpitan Prüsse** offers harbor cruises. (☎31 31 30. Every 30min., DM15.) **HADAG** cruises to outlying areas from pier 2. (☎311 70 70. Every 30min. 9:30am-6pm.) **Scandinavian Seaways** (☎389 03 71; fax 38 90 31 41) sets sail for **Harwich, England** (20hr., from DM152); **Ireland; Copenhagen;** and **Oslo.**

Public Transportation: HVV operates an efficient U-Bahn, S-Bahn, and bus network. Single ride (DM1.80); 1-day pass (DM9.50); 3-day pass (DM23.30).

ORIENTATION AND PRACTICAL INFORMATION

The city center sits between the **Elbe** River and the **Außenalster** and **Binnenalster** Lakes. Most major sights lie between the **St. Pauli Landungsbrücken** port in the west and the **Hauptbahnhof** in the east. The **Hanseviertel** quarter is thick with banks, shops, and art galleries. North of the center, the **university** dominates the **Dammtor** area. West of the university, the **Sternschanze** hosts a politically active community of artists, squatters, and Turks. The **Altona** district was once an independent Danish city. Down south in **St. Pauli,** the raucous **Fischmarkt** (fish market) is juxtaposed with the equally wild **Reeperbahn,** home to Hamburg's infamous sex trade.

Tourist Offices: The **Hauptbahnhof office** (☎30 05 12 00; www.hamburg-tourism.de), near the Kirchenallee exit, books rooms for DM6. Open M-F 6am-10pm, Sa-Su 7am-

10pm. The **St. Pauli Landungsbrücken office** (☎30 05 12 00) is between piers 4 and 5 (take U-Bahn #3 to Landungsbrücke). Open daily 10am-7pm. Buy the **Hamburg Card,** which provides unlimited access to public transportation, admission to most museums, and discounts on bus and boat tours (1-day DM12.50; 3-day DM26). The **Group Card** provides the same deals for up to five people (1-day DM24; 3-day DM42).

Currency Exchange: ReiseBank, on the 2nd floor of the Hauptbahnhof near the Kirchenallee exit. Arranges Western Union money transfers, cashes traveler's checks, and exchanges money for a DM5 fee. Open daily 7:30am-10pm.

American Express: Ballindamm 39, 20095 Hamburg (☎30 39 38 11 12). Mail held for card-members up to 4 weeks; all banking services. Open M-F 9am-6pm, Sa 10am-1pm.

Gay and Lesbian Resources: Hein und Fiete, Pulverteich 21 (☎24 03 33). Open M-F 4-9pm, Sa 4-7pm. **Magnus-Hirschfeld-Centrum,** Borgweg 8 (☎279 00 69). U3 or bus #108 to Borgweg. Open M and F 2-6pm, Tu-W 7-10pm; cafe open daily 5pm-midnight.

Laundromat: Schnell und Sauber, Grindelallee 158, in the university district. S21 or 31 to "Dammtor." Wash DM6, dry DM1. Open daily 7am-10pm.

Emergency: Police: ☎110. **Fire** and **ambulance:** ☎112.

Post Office: Großer Burstah 3. Open M-F 8am-6pm, Sa 8am-noon. Address mail to be held: *Postlagernde Briefe* für First Name SURNAME, Hauptpostamt, **20099** Hamburg, Germany. **Branch** at the Kirchenallee exit of the Hauptbahnhof.

Internet Access: Cyberb@r, 3rd fl. of the gigantic **Karstadt** department store on Mönckebergstr. DM5 per 30min. Open M-F 9am-8pm, Sa 9am-4pm.

ACCOMMODATIONS AND CAMPING

Hamburg's accommodations tend to be tawdry with few comforts. A slew of relatively cheap *Pensionen* line Steindamm, Steintorweg, Bremer Weg, and Bremer Reihe, around the **Hauptbahnhof.** Consult the tourist office's free *Hotelführer.*

Instant Sleep, Max-Brauer-Allee 277 (☎43 18 23 10). S21 or 31, or U3 to "Sternschanze." From the station go straight on Schanzenstr., left on Altonaer Str. and follow it until it becomes Max-Brauer-Allee. Internet (15min. DM2.50), kitchen, and laundry. Sheets DM5. Reception 9am-2pm. Dorms DM27; singles DM35; doubles DM80.

Schanzenstern Übernachtungs-und Gasthaus, Bartelsstr. 12 (☎439 84 41). S21 or 31, or U3 to "Sternschanze." Take a left onto Schanzenstr., right on Susannenstr., and left on Bartelsstr. In an electrifying neighborhood of students and left-wing dissenters. Reserve in summer and New Year's. Dorms DM33; singles DM60; doubles DM90.

Jugendherberge auf dem Stintfang (HI), Alfred-Wegener-Weg 5 (☎31 34 88). S1, 2, or 3, or U3 to "Landungsbrücke." A convenient location near the Reeperbahn and a beautiful view of the harbor compensate for the regimental house rules. Internet access. Same-sex halls. Reception 12:30pm-1am. Lockout 9:30-11:30am. Curfew 1am. Call ahead. Dorms DM34.50; singles DM60. Non-members add DM6.

Hotel Florida, Spielbudenpl. 22 (☎31 43 94). U3 to "St. Pauli," or S1 or 3 to "Reeperbahn." Small but clean rooms adjacent to Hamburg's biggest clubs. Breakfast included. Singles DM60; doubles DM95; triples DM135.

Hotel Alt-Nürnberg, Steintorweg 15 (☎24 60 24). From the station, go right on Kirchenallee and left onto Steintorweg. Heidi-themed decor in the somewhat sketchy Hauptbahnhof neighborhood. Each room with telephone, some with TV. Call ahead. Singles DM60, with shower DM90; doubles DM90, DM130.

Camping: Campingplatz Rosemarie Buchholz, Kieler Str. 374 (☎540 45 32). From Altona station, take bus #182 or 183 to "Basselweg," then walk 100m with traffic. Reception 8am-noon and 2-10pm. DM7 per person; DM12.50 per tent.

FOOD

The most culinarily interesting area is **Sternschanze,** where Turkish fruit stands, Asian *Imbiße*, and avant-garde cafes tempt with good food and atmosphere. **Schulterblatt, Susannenstr., and Schanzenstr.** host funky cafes and restaurants. Cheaper establishments abound in the university area, especially along **Rentzelstr.,**

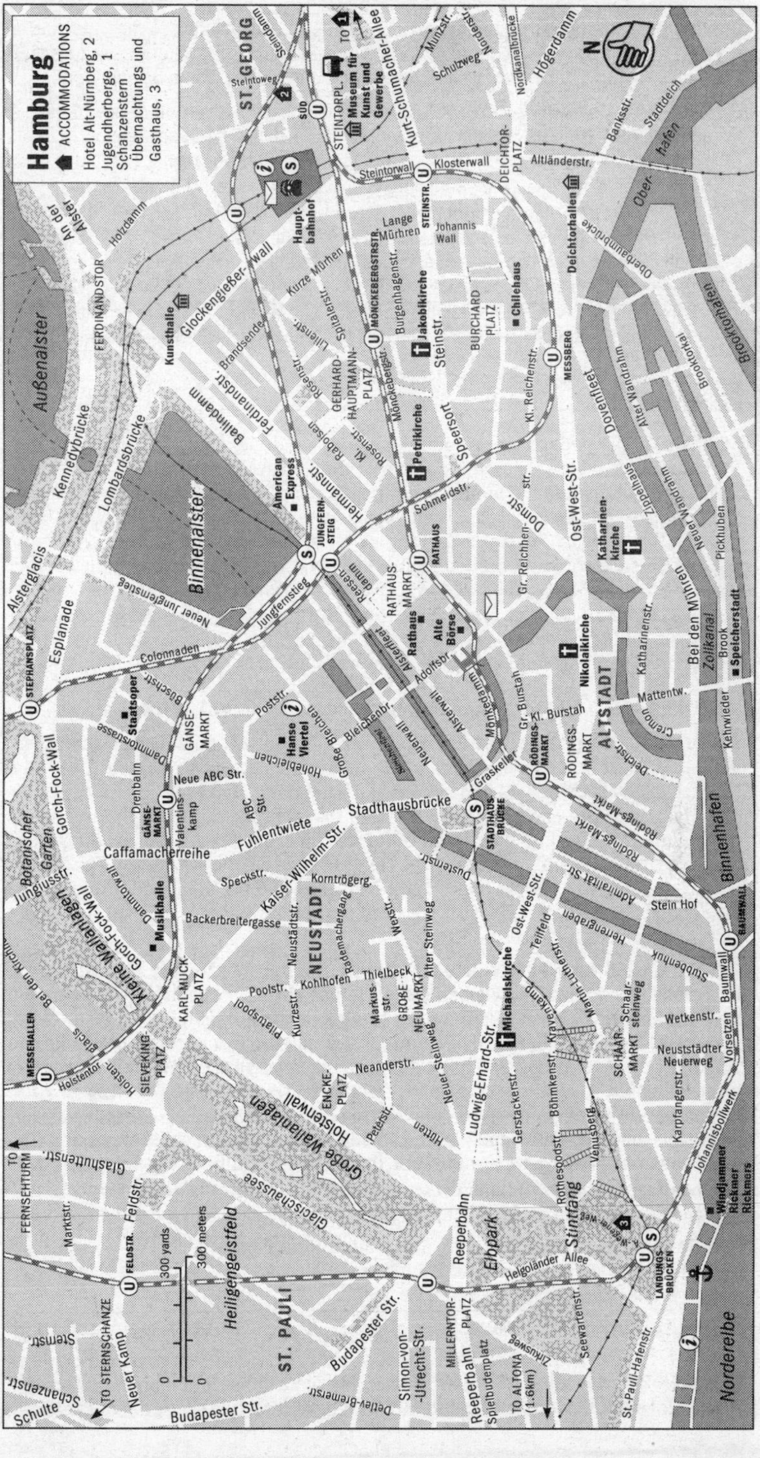

Hamburg

ACCOMMODATIONS

Hotel Alt-Nürnberg, 2
Jugendherberge, 1
Schanzenstern Übernachtungs und Gasthaus, 3

ST. GEORG · ALTSTADT · NEUSTADT · ST. PAULI

Außenalster · Binnenalster · Norderelbe · Binnenhafen · Oberhafen · Zollkanal · Elbpark · Heiligengeistfeld · Große Wallanlagen · Kleine Wallanlagen · Botanischer Garten · Stintfang

Hauptbahnhof · Kunsthalle · Museum für Kunst und Gewerbe · Deichtorhallen · Chilehaus · Jakobikirche · Petrikirche · Rathaus · Alte Börse · Nikolaikirche · Katharinenkirche · Speicherstadt · Michaelskirche · Musikhalle · Staatsoper · Hanse Viertel · American Express · Windjammer Rickmer Rickmers

TO FERNSEHTURM · TO STERNSCHANZE · TO ALTONA (1.6km)

0 300 yards · 0 300 meters

Grindelhof, and Grindelallee. In **Altona,** the pedestrian zone leading to the train station is packed with ethnic food stands and produce shops. The market in Altona's Mercado mall includes a **Safeway supermarket.** (Open M-F 10am-8pm, Sa 9am-4pm.)

Noodles, Schanzenstr. 2-4. Serves up innovative pastas and veggie dishes. Breakfast from DM7.50. Beer DM5. Open M-Th and Su 10am-1am, F-Sa 10am-3am.

Machwitz, Schanzenstr. 121. Hip students in a funky interior. Dishes DM12-17. Open Su-Th 10am-4am, F-Sa 10am-8am. Kitchen closes Su-Th midnight, F-Sa 2am.

Geo Pizza aus dem Holzbackofen, Beim Schlump 27. U2 or 3 to "Schlump." Delectable pizzas (DM9-16) and a large vegetarian selection. The Inferno Pizza (DM11.80-13.80), topped with an incendiary mix of jalapeños, red peppers, beef, onions, salsa, and corn, transforms diners into fire-belching beasts. Open M-F 5pm-1am, Sa-Su 11am-1am.

Asia Imbiß Bok, Bartelstr. 29. *Imbiß* ("snack") is a misnomer–this joint serves filling Thai, Korean, and Chinese cuisine (DM10-17). Open daily 11:30am-11:30pm.

SIGHTS

ALTSTADT. The pedestrian shopping zone along Mönckebergstr. pours out into Rathausmarkt, where the copper spires of the **Rathaus** (town hall), a richly ornamented, neo-Renaissance monstrosity, rise above the city center. *(Tours in German every 30min. M-Th 10am-3pm, F-Su 10am-1pm. Tours in English every hr. M-Th 10:15am-3:15pm, F-Su 10:15am-1:15pm.)* Nearby, a zig-zagging maze of canals and bridges centers on the **Alte Börse,** Germany's first stock market. Over the **Tröstbrücke** rest the somber ruins of **St. Nikolaikirche,** flattened by a 1943 air raid and left unrestored as a memorial to the horrors of war. From the church, turn right on Ost-West-Str. and continue on Ludwig-Erhard-Str. to reach the gargantuan 18th-century **Große Michaelskirche,** the granddaddy of all Hamburg churches, affectionately referred to as "der Michael." *(Open Apr.-Sept. M-Sa 9am-6pm, Su 11:30am-5:30pm; Oct.-Mar. M-Sa 10am-4:30pm, Su 11:30am-4:30pm. DM1. Organ music daily Apr.-Aug. at noon and 5pm.)*

ST. PAULI LANDUNGSBRÜCKEN. Hamburg's harbor **St. Pauli Landungsbrücken,** the largest port in Germany, lights up at night with ships from all over the world. More than 100,000 dockers and sailors work the ports, and their presence permeates Hamburg. The elevator to the **Old Elbe Tunnel** protrudes through the floor of the building behind Pier 6; with all of its machinery exposed, the building looks like a Nautilus machine for the gods. Head farther west to reach the **Fischmarkt,** where charismatic vendors haul in and hawk huge amounts of fish, produce, and other goods. *(Take the U- or S-Bahn to "Landungsbrücken" or S-Bahn to "Königstr." Market open Su in summer 6-10am; off season 7-10am.)*

ALSTER LAKES AND PLANTEN UN BLOMEN. To the west of the Alster near the university, the **Planten un Blomen** park features dozens of meticulously planned and trimmed flowerbeds surrounding two lakes and a handful of outdoor cafes. From May to September, daily performances ranging from Irish step-dancing to Hamburg's police orchestra shake the outdoor **Musikpavillon; Wasserlichtkonzerte** feature lighted fountain arrangements to music. *(Wasserlichtkonzerte daily May-Aug. 10pm; Sept. 9pm. Cafes open 7am-11pm.)* North of the center, the two **Alster lakes** bordered by tree-lined paths and parks, provide refuge from crowded Hamburg. Elegant promenades and commercial facades surround **Binnenalster,** while windsurfers, sailboats, and paddle boats dominate the larger **Außenalster.**

ALTONAER BALKON. Ships from the four corners of the world pass under the **Altonaer Balkon.** The tops of the bluffs upstream from the harbor have been converted into a popular flower-covered park and scenic overlook. *(S3, 31, or 1 to "Altona." Walk south along Max-Brauer-Allee until you hit the overlook.)*

GEDENKSTÄTTE JANUSZ-KORCZAK-SCHULE. This school is a memorial to 20 Jewish children brought here from Auschwitz for "testing," murdered by the SS only hours before Allied troops arrived. Visitors can plant a rose for the children in the flower garden, where the children's photographs line the fence. *(Bullenhuser*

Damm 92. S21: Rothenburgsort; follow the signs to Bullenhuser Damm along Ausschlaeger Bildeich and across a bridge; the school is 200m down. Open Su 10am-7pm and Th 2-8pm. Free.)

MUSEUMS. The dozens of museums in Hamburg range from the erotic to the Victorian. The first-rate **Hamburger Kunsthalle** holds an extensive and dazzling collection spanning medieval to modern art. *(Glockengießerwall 1. Turn left from the "City" exit of the Hauptbahnhof and cross the street. Open Tu-W and F-Su 10am-6pm, Th 10am-9pm. DM15, students DM12.)* Hamburg's contemporary art scene resides in the two buildings of the **Deichtorhallen Hamburg,** whose exhibits showcase up-and-coming artists. *(Deichtorstr. 1-2. U1: Steinstr.; then follow the signs. Open Tu-Su 11am-6pm, Sa-Su 10am-6pm. Each building DM10, students DM8.)* Follow the silver sperm painted on the floor through four floors of tactful iniquity at the **Erotic Art Museum.** *(Nobistor 12 and Bernhard-Nocht-Str. 69. S1 or 3: Reeperbahn. Open Tu-Su 10am-midnight. DM15, groups DM10.)*

ENTERTAINMENT AND NIGHTLIFE

MUSIC AND THEATER. As the cultural capital of the North, Hamburg showers the arts with money and attention. Federal and municipal subsidies lower ticket prices significantly, and most box offices and concert halls offer generous student discounts. The **Staatsoper,** Dammtorstr. 28, houses one of the best opera companies in Germany, tending toward the modern, but also playing a steady stream of Bizet and Puccini. (Take U1 to "Stephanspl." ☎ 35 17 21. Tickets from DM7. Open M-F 10am-6:30pm, Sa 10am-2pm.) Orchestras abound—the **Philharmonie, Norddeutscher Rundfunk Symphony,** and **Hamburg Symphonia** all perform at the **Musikhalle** on Johans-Brahms-Pl. (☎ 34 69 20. Take U2 to "Gänsemarkt" or "Messehallen.") The **English Theater,** Lerchenfeld 14, entertains with English-language productions. (☎ 227 70 89. U2 to "Mundsgurg." Performances M-Sa 7:30pm; matinees Tu and F 11am.) In July and August, many theaters close down to make way for the **Hamburger Sommer** arts festival; pick up a schedule at any kiosk. The techno frenzy called **G-Move** (www.g-move.com) grooves into town in early June.

NIGHTLIFE. Sternschanze, St. Pauli, and Altona monopolize Hamburg's crazy nightlife. The infamous **Reeperbahn,** a long boulevard that makes Las Vegas look like Sunday church, is the spinal cord of St. Pauli; sex shops, strip joints, peep shows, and other establishments seeking to satisfy every libidinal desire compete for space along the sidewalks. **Herbertstr.,** Hamburg's only remaining legalized prostitution strip, runs parallel to the Reeperbahn, and is open only to men over 18. The prostitutes flaunting their flesh on Herbertstr. are licensed professionals required to undergo health inspections, while the streetwalkers are venereal roulette wheels. Students trying to avoid the hypersexed Reeperbahn head north to the spiffy streets of **Sternschanze,** centered around cafes and weekend extravaganzas of an alternative flavor. Much of Hamburg's gay scene is located in the **St. Georg** area, near Berliner Tor. Gay and straight bars here are more welcoming and classier than those in the Reeperbahn. *Szene,* available at newsstands (DM5), lists events and parties. *Hinnerk* lists gay and lesbian events.

The **Mojo Club,** Reeperbahn 1, has more attitude than it knows what to do with. The attached **Jazz Café** features acid jazz. (Cover DM12 on weekends. Usually open 11pm-4am.) The graffiti-covered **Rote Flora,** Schulterblatt 71, is the nucleus of the Sternschanze scene. (☎ 439 54 13. Cover from DM8 on weekends. Opening times vary.) **Absolute,** Hans-Albers-Pl. 15, is a popular gay club that spins unrelenting house. (Cover DM10. Open after 11pm.) The Beatles played downstairs at **Große Freiheit 36/Kaiser Keller,** Große Freiheit 36. Today, everyone from Ziggy Marley to Matchbox Twenty stomps about on the big stage upstairs. (☎ 31 77 78. Call for show times and ticket prices, DM5-30, for the upstairs stage. Basement opens at 10pm; students admitted to the downstairs for free on Tu. Große Freiheit 36 opening hours vary. Kaiser Keller open from 10pm.)

LÜBECK ☎0451

With a skyline of Neoclassical townhouses punctuated by 13th-century copper spires, Lübeck is Schleswig-Holstein's most beautiful city. Between the Altstadt and the train station is the city's symbol, the massive **Holstentor.** The centerpiece of the Altstadt is the **Rathaus,** a 13th-century structure of glazed bricks. (Open M-F 9:30am-6pm, Sa-Su 10am-2pm. Tours M-F 11am and noon. DM4, students DM2.) The **Marienkirche,** begun in the Romanesque style but finished as a Gothic cathedral, houses the world's largest mechanical organ. A reproduction of the church's famous **Totentanzbild** mural depicts the plague era. (Open daily in summer 10am-6pm, off season 10am-4pm. Free. Organ concerts daily at noon, and Tu 6:30pm, Th 8pm, Sa 6:30pm. DM9, students DM6.) Opposite the Marienkirche is the **Buddenbrookhaus,** Mengstr. 4, the childhood home of writers Heinrich and Thomas Mann and today a museum dedicated to their lives and work. (Open daily 10am-5pm. DM8, students DM5.) At the **Behnhaus** and **Drägerhaus** museums, Königstr. 11, modern art clashes with an 18th-century Neoclassical townhouse. (Open Apr.-Sept. Tu-Su 10am-5pm; Oct.-May 10am-4pm. DM5, students DM3; free 1st F of each month.)

Frequent **trains** arrive from: Hamburg (45min., 2 per hr., DM17); Rostock (1¾hr., every hr., DM37); and Berlin (3¼hr., every hr., DM97). Skip absurdly expensive services at the train station tourist office; instead, try the **tourist office** in the Altstadt, Breitestr. 62. (☎122 54 13. Open M-F 9:30am-7pm, Sa-Su 10am-3pm.) From the station, walk past the **Holstentor,** turn left on An der Untertrave, and turn right on Beckergrube (which becomes Pfaffstr. and then Glockengießerstr.) to reach the **Rucksack Hotel,** Kanalstr. 70. (☎70 68 92. Breakfast DM8. Sheets DM6. Kitchen. Reception 9am-1pm and 4-10pm. Dorms DM24-26; doubles with bath DM80; quads DM112-136.) From the station head for the Holstentor, cross the river, make a left on An der Untertrave, and go right on Mengstr. to reach the conveniently located **Jugendgästehaus Lübeck (HI),** Mengstr. 33. (☎702 03 99. Reception 7:30am-noon, 1:15-6pm, and 7:15pm-midnight. Members only. Doubles DM84, under 26 DM66; triples and quads DM86-158.) A local specialty is **Lübecker Marzipan;** the confectionery **I.G. Niederegger,** Breitestr. 89, across from the Rathaus, makes the exquisite sugar and almond candy in the shape of pigs, jellyfish, and even the town gate. (Open M-F 9am-7pm, Sa 9am-6pm, Su 10am-4pm.) The hip waitstaff at **Tipasa,** Schlumacherstr. 12-14, serves students in the *Biergarten* out back. (Open Su-Th noon-1am, F-Sa noon-2am.) A **Co-op supermarket** is at the corner of Sandstr. and Schmiedstr. (Open M-F 8:30am-7pm, Sa 9am-4pm.) **Postal code:** 23552.

SCHLESWIG ☎04621

Schleswig, at the southern end of the **Schlei inlet,** has idyllic fishing settlements, a 16th-century castle, and extensive museum collections. Towering over the Altstadt is the 12th-century **St. Petri-Dom,** renowned for its intricately carved 16th-century **Bordesholmer Altar.** (Open May-Sept. M-Th and Sa 9am-5pm, F 9am-3pm, Su 1-5pm; Oct.-Apr. M-Th and Sa 10am-4pm, F 10am-3pm, Su 1-4pm.) A 20-minute walk along the harbor from the Altstadt, the 18th-century **Schloß Gottorf** houses the **Landesmuseen,** a treasure trove of Dutch, Danish, and Art Deco works. On the other side of the castle, the **Kreuzstall** and adjacent buildings house the **Museum des 20 Jahrhunderts,** a collection devoted to the artists of the *Brücke* school. The park surrounding the castle is an **outdoor contemporary sculpture museum.** (All open daily Mar.-Oct. 9am-5pm; Nov.-Feb. 9:30am-4pm. DM9, students DM5.) If you long to see the remains of a civilization of tall attractive people, **ferries** (DM2.50) travel from the Stadthafen near the Dom to the **Wikinger Museum Haithabu.** The museum, next to a former Viking settlement, covers all aspects of Viking life. (Open daily Apr.-Oct. 9am-5pm; Nov.-Mar. Tu-Su 9am-4pm. DM5, students DM3, families DM12.)

Schleswig's **train station** is 20 minutes south of the city center; to get there, take bus #1, 2, 4, or 5 from the stop outside the **bus terminal** (ZOB), close to the Altstadt (DM1.90). **Trains** go hourly to Kiel and Hamburg (via Neumünster). The **tourist office,** Plessenstr. 7, is up the street from the harbor; from the ZOB, walk down Plessenstr. toward the water. (☎98 16 16; reservations ☎98 16 17. Open May-

Sept. M-F 9am-12:30pm and 1:30-5pm, Sa 9am-noon; Oct.-Apr. M-Th 9am-12:30pm and 1:30-5pm, F 9am-12:30pm.) The **Jugendherberge (HI),** Spielkoppel 1, is near the center of town. With your back to the ZOB, walk right along Königstr., turn right onto Poststr. (which becomes Moltkestr.), turn left on Bellmannstr., and follow it to Spielkoppel on your left. (☎238 93. Breakfast included. Sheets DM7. Reception 7am-1pm and 5-11pm. Curfew 11pm. DM26, under 27 DM21.) The **Wikinger Campingplatz,** Am Haithabu, is across the inlet from the Altstadt. (☎324 50. DM6 per person.) Try the fresh and cheap seafood at the *Imbiße* by the **Stadthafen. Postal code:** 24837.

CENTRAL GERMANY

Stretching from the North Sea to the hills of central Germany, Lower-Saxony has two distinct flavors: the majority of the *Land* is broad, agricultural plain, but along the coast, descendants of the Frisians run fishing boats along foggy marshland. On the Dutch and Belgian borders, North Rhine-Westphalia, with 17 million inhabitants and the mighty Ruhr Valley, is the most heavily populated and economically powerful area in Germany. While the region's squalor may have inspired the philosophy of Karl Marx and Friedrich Engels, its natural beauty and Cologne and Düsseldorf's intellectual energy also spurred the muses of Goethe, Heine, and Böll. Hesse, known prior to the 20th century primarily as a source for mercenary soldiers (many hired by King George III to put down an unruly gang of colonials in 1776), is today the busiest commercial area in the country, led by the banking metropolis of Frankfurt. Fortunately, the medieval delights and Baroque elegance of areas outside the city remain blessedly off the beaten path.

HANOVER (HANNOVER) ☎0511

Despite its relatively small size, Hannover puts on a show of culture and cosmopolitan charm. As the most important railway center in northwestern Germany and Lower Saxony's cultural and political capital, the city's myriad attractions lure travelers out of the Berlin-Hamburg-Köln triangle. To fully experience Hannover, follow the **Red Thread,** a 4km walking tour marked by a painted red line connecting all the sights. Painstakingly recreated after World War II, the **Neues Rathaus** towers outside the Altstadt. Take the elevator to the top of the dome (DM3, students DM2) for a view of the Machsee and Hannover's skyline. (Open Apr.-Oct. M-F 9:30am-5:30pm, Sa-Su 10am-5pm.) The **Kestner-Museum,** Trammpl. 3, next to the Neues Rathaus, exhibits the decorative arts of medieval and Renaissance Europe as well as ancient Egypt, Greece, and Rome. (Open Tu, Th, and Sa 11am-6pm, W 11am-8pm. DM5, students DM3; F free.) Behind the Rathaus, on the shores of the Machsee, the **Sprengel Museum,** on Kurt-Schwitters-Pl., shows off works by Turrell, Dali, Picasso, Magritte, and Antes. (Open Tu 10am-8pm, W-Su 10am-6pm. DM7, students DM3.50.) Near the University district, the **Herrenhausen Gardens** contain tree-lined avenues, Europe's highest garden fountain (80m), and an indoor rain forest. Take U4 (dir. Garbsen) or U5 toward Stoeken. (Gardens open Apr.-Oct. M-Tu 8am-8pm, W-Su 8am-10pm; Nov.-Mar. daily 8am-dusk. DM3. Fountains open M-F 11am-noon and 3-5pm, Sa-Su 11am-noon and 2-5pm. DM3.)

Trains leave frequently for: Hamburg (1½hr., DM40-62); Berlin (2½hr., DM62-101); Köln (2hr., DM60-104); Frankfurt (3hr., DM77-130); Munich (9hr., DM190-215); and Amsterdam (4½-5hr., DM80). From the station, turn right (facing the rear of the king's steed) to reach the **tourist office,** Ernst-August-Pl. 2. (☎116 84 97 10. Open M-F 9am-7pm, Sa 9:30am-3pm.) Note that the hostel and *Naturfreundehäuser* are situated on the outskirts of town, where walkways are deserted and poorly lit; use caution late at night. To reach the renovated **Jugendherberge Hannover (HI),** Ferdinand-Wilhelm-Fricke-Weg 1, take U3 or U7 (dir. Wettbergen) to "Fischerhof/Fachhochschule"; cross the tracks, walk through the parking lot, follow the path as it curves, cross the street, go over the red footbridge, and turn right. (☎131 76 74. Reception 7:30-11:30pm. DM32-34, under 27 DM5 less.) To reach **Naturfreundehaus Stadtheim,** Hermann-Bahlsen-Allee 8, take U3 (dir. Lahe) or U7 (dir. Fasanenkrug) to "Spannhagengarten"; backtrack 15m to the intersection, follow Hermann-Bahlsen-Allee left for five minutes, and follow the sign to your right down the paved road. (☎69 14 93. Breakfast included. Reception 8am-noon and 3-10pm. DM49.) At **Uwe's Hannenfaß Hannover,** Knochenhauerstr. 36, steaming *Niedersachsenschmaus* (DM8.90), a potato casserole, steadies the stomach, while the house-brewed *Hannen Alt* (DM5.40) lightens the head. (Open M-Sa noon-2am, Su 3pm-2am.) **Spar supermarkets** sit by the Lister Meile and Kröpcke U-Bahn stops. (Open M-F 7am-7pm, Sa 8am-2pm.) **The Loft,** Georgstr. 50b, near Kröpcke, draws students on the weekends. (Open M-Th and Su 9pm-2am, F-Sa 9pm-5am.) **Postal code:** 30159.

COLOGNE (KÖLN) ☎0221

Founded as a Roman colony (*colonia*, hence Köln) in AD 48, Cologne gained fame and fortune in the Middle Ages as an elite university town and an important trade hub. While most of the inner city was destroyed in WWII, the magnificent Gothic cathedral survived no fewer than 14 bombings and remains Cologne's main attraction. Today, tourists come to see this symbol of Cologne's rebirth, participate in indulgent celebrations, and sample the burgeoning fine arts scene.

GETTING THERE AND GETTING AROUND

Trains: From the **Hauptbahnhof** to: **Düsseldorf** (1hr., 5 per hr., DM12.60, students DM10); **Frankfurt** (2hr., 3-4 per hr., DM61, students DM49); **Brussels** (2½hr., every 2hr., DM54.80); **Hamburg** (5hr., 3 per hr., DM123, students DM98); **Amsterdam** (2½hr., every hr., DM79); **Paris** (4hr., every 2hr., DM190.80); **Berlin** (6½hr., every 2hr., DM172, students DM138); **Munich** (6hr., 5 per hr., DM173, students DM138); and **Dresden** (7hr., 2 per hr., DM191, students DM153).

Ferries: Köln-Düsseldorfer (☎208 83 18) begins its ever-popular Rhine cruises here. Students 50% off; most trips (excluding hydrofoils) covered by Eurail.

Public Transportation: VRS (Verkehrsverbund Rhein-Sieg) offices have free maps of the S- and U-Bahn, bus, and streetcar lines; one is downstairs in the train station near the U-Bahn. **Single-fare tickets** DM2.20-14.50; **day pass** DM9.50.

ORIENTATION AND PRACTICAL INFORMATION

The city center lies along the west bank of the **Rhine** River. The Altstadt is split into **Altstadt-Nord,** near the Hauptbahnhof, and **Altstadt-Süd,** south of the Severinsbrücke.

Tourist Office: Verkehrsamt, Unter Fettenhennen 19 (☎221 33 45; fax 221 33 20; www.koeln.de), opposite the Dom. Books rooms (DM6). Open May-Oct. M-Sa 8am-10:30pm, Su 9am-10:30pm; Nov.-Apr. M-Sa 8am-9pm, Su 9:30am-7pm.

Currency Exchange: An office at the **train station** is open daily 7am-9pm, but the service charges are lower at the **post office** (see below).

Gay and Lesbian Services: Schulz Schwulen-und Lesbenzentrum, Kartäuserwall 18 (☎93 18 80 80), near Chlodwigpl. Info, movies, youth activities, library, and popular cafe. The tourist office also offers a "Gay City Map" with listings and locations of gay-friendly hotels, bars, and clubs.

Laundry: Eco-Express, on Richard-Wagner-Str. Wash DM6; soap included. Dry DM1 per 10min. Open M-Sa 6am-11pm.

Emergency: Police: ☎110. **Fire** and **ambulance:** ☎112.

Pharmacy: Dom-Apotheke, Komödienstr. 5 (☎257 67 54), near the station. Posts a list of after-hours pharmacies outside. English spoken. Open M-F 8am-6:30pm, Sa 9am-1pm.

Internet Access: FuturePoint, Richmodstr. 13. DM2 per 15min. Open daily 9am-1am.

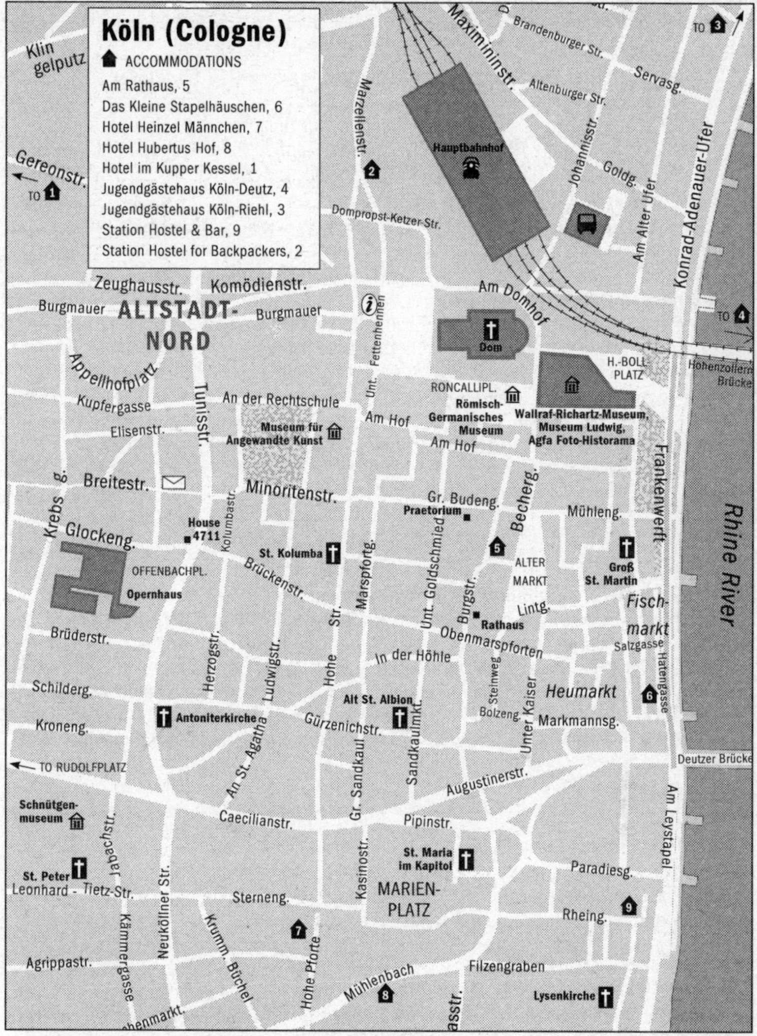

Post Office: Hauptpostamt, at the corner of Breite Str. and Auf der Ruhr. Address mail to be held: *Postlagernde Briefe* für First name SURNAME, Hauptpostamt, **50667** Köln, Germany. Open M-F 8am-8pm, Sa 8am-4pm.

ACCOMMODATIONS AND CAMPING

Most hotels fill up in spring and fall when conventions roll in, and the two hostels are nearly always booked from June to September and during Karneval. Call ahead.

Station Hostel and Bar, Rheing. 34-36 (☎23 02 47; email station@t-online.de). The new addition to the Station hostel family with larger and cleaner rooms. Reception all day except 1-5pm. Singles DM50; doubles DM80; triples DM108; quads DM132.

Jansen Pension, Richard-Wagner-Str. 18 (☎25 18 75). Take U1, U6-7, U15, U17, or U19 to "Rudolfplatz," then follow Richard-Wagner-Str. A Victorian townhouse with pleasant rooms. Breakfast included. Singles DM55-70; doubles DM110.

Station Hostel for Backpackers, Marzellenstr. 44-48 (☎912 53 01; fax 912 53 03; email station@t-online.de). From the station, walk one block along Dompropst-Ketzer-Str. and turn right on Marzellenstr. Independent hostel with a relaxed atmosphere. Sheets DM3. Laundry DM6. Internet access. Reception 24hr. Call by 3pm to confirm reservations. Dorms DM27; singles DM40; doubles DM70.

Jugendherberge Köln-Deutz (HI), Siegesstr. 5a (☎81 47 11; fax 88 44 25), over the Hohenzollernbrücke. Take S6, S11, or S12 to "Köln-Deutz"; from the main exit, go down Neuhöfferstr. and take the 1st right. Breakfast included. Laundry free; soap DM1. Reception 11am-1am. Curfew 1am. Call ahead. DM37, under 27 DM33.

Jugendgästehaus Köln-Riehl (HI), An der Schanz 14 (☎76 70 81; fax 76 15 55), on the Rhine north of the zoo. U6 (dir. Ebertplatz/Mülheim) to Boltensternstr. Or walk north along the Rhine on Konrad-Adenauer-Ufer until it becomes An der Schanz (40min.). Breakfast included. Reception 24hr. Call ahead. Dorms DM38.50; singles DM63.50.

Campingplatz Poll, Weidenweg (☎83 19 66), on the Rhine southeast of the Altstadt. Take U16 to Marienburg, then cross the Rodenkirchener Brücke. Reception 8am-noon and 5-8pm. Open Apr.-Oct. DM8 per person, DM4 per tent, DM4 per car.

FOOD

Cologne cuisine includes scrumptious *Rievekoochen* (potato pancakes) dunked in *Apfelmus* (applesauce) and smooth **Kölsch** beer. Cafes and cheap restaurants line **Zülpicherstr.** (U7 or U9: Zülpicher Pl.). Mid-priced ethnic restaurants lie around the perimeter of the Altstadt, particularly from **Hohenzollernring** to **Hohenstaufenring;** the city's best cheap eats are in the Turkish district on **Weideng.** Patrons enjoy German specialties at **Brauhaus Früh am Dom,** Am Hof 12-14. (Meals DM9-30. Open daily 8am-midnight.) Breakfast (from DM5.50) is served until 4pm at **Café Waschsalon,** Ehrenstr. 77. (Open M-Th 8am-1am, F 8am-3am, Sa 10am-3am, Su 10am-1am.) Pick up **groceries** at **Mini-Mal,** Hohenstaufenring 30. (Open M-F 8am-8pm, Sa 8am-4pm.)

SIGHTS

DOM. Visitors exiting Cologne's train station are immediately treated to the beauty, power, and sorrow of Germany's greatest cathedral. Six centuries in the making, the cathedral was finally completed in 1880 in High Gothic style. The stunning stained-glass windows cast a harlequin display of colored light over the interior. To the right of the center altar is the **Dombild triptych,** a masterful 15th-century painting and gilded altarpiece. Look for the brightly shining **Shrine of the Magi,** a reliquary of the Three Kings in blinding gold brought to the city in 1164; the 976 **Gero crucifix,** the oldest intact sculpture of *Christus patiens* (depicting a crucified Christ with eyes shut); and Rubens' *Crucifixion of St. Peter.* A mere 509 steps lead to the top of the **Südturm** (south tower); catch your breath 400 steps up at the Glockenstube, where the 24-ton **Der große Peter,** the world's heaviest swinging bell, roosts. *(Cathedral open daily 6am-7pm. Free. Tours in German M-Sa 11am and 12:30, 2, and 3:30pm, Su 2 and 3:30pm; DM6, students DM3. Tours in English M-Sa 10:30am and 2:30pm, Su 2:30pm; DM7, students DM4. Tower open daily May-Sept. 9am-6pm; Mar.-Apr. and Oct. 9am-5pm; Nov.-Feb. 9am-4pm. DM3, students DM1.50.)*

GROß ST. MARTIN. Along with the cathedral, **Groß St. Martin** defines the legendary Rhine panorama of Cologne. The renovated church was reopened in 1985 after near-destruction in WWII. *(An Groß St. Martin 9, south of the cathedral near the Fischmarkt. Open M-F 10:15am-6pm, Sa 10am-12:30pm and 1:30-6pm, Su 2-4pm. Free.)*

HOUSE #4711. This unobtrusively named sight yields the water **Eau de Cologne,** once prescribed as a drinkable curative, which made the town a household name. Be sure your bottle says *Echt kölnisch Wasser* ("real Cologne water"), or look for

INSULTS FOR SALE The concept of free speech in Germany does not imply *cost-free* speech—dropping insults will unload your wallet in no time. Public humiliation in Germany carries such destructive force that officials have created an insult price list; offended or drunk budget travelers should beware. The heaviest fines are incurred by tongue-flappers who put down a police officer's respectability: belting out *Trottel in Uniform* (fool in uniform) or *Idiot* costs DM3000, while the lesser insult *Dumme Kuh* (dumb cow) requires a mere DM1200 payoff. The budget traveler's insult, *Holzkopf* (woodheaded), goes for DM1500. Equivalent insults in English are not exempt; stories abound of policemen who've doled out thousands of *Marks* in fines to tourists who think that Germans don't understand what "asshole" means. Prices, of course, are subject to change, you idiot.

the "4711" label. The house today is a boutique, with a small fountain continually dispensing the scented water. *(Glockeng, at the intersection with Tunisstr. From Hohe Str., turn right on Brückenstr., which becomes Glockeng. Open M-F 9:30am-8pm, Sa 9:30am-4pm.)*

RÖMISCHES PRAETORIUM UND KANAL. Classical historians and *Gladiator* fans will be impressed by the excavated ruins of these former Roman military headquarters. *(From the Rathaus, take a right toward the swarm of hotels and then a left onto Kleine Budeng. Open Tu-F 10am-4pm, Sa-Su 11am-4pm. DM3, students DM1.50.)*

MUSEUMS. The major museums are free with the **Köln Tourismus Card.** Between the cathedral and the Hohenzollernbrücke, the cultural center on **Heinrich-Böll-Platz** houses three complementary collections. The **Wallraf-Richartz Museum** features masterpieces from the Italian Renaissance to the French Impressionists; the **Museum Ludwig** spans Impressionism, Picasso, Dalí, Liechtenstein, Warhol, and art whose glue has yet to dry; and the **Agfa Foto-Historama** chronicles chemical art of the last 150 years. *(Bischofsgartenstr. 1. Open Tu 10am-8pm, W-F 10am-6pm, Sa-Su 11am-6pm. Tours Tu 6pm, W 4:30pm, Sa-Su 11:30am. DM10, students DM5.)* Better than Willy Wonka's Chocolate Factory, the **Schokoladenmuseum** allows you to salivate at every step of the chocolate production process. Resist the urge to drool and wait for the free, but small, samples. *(Rheinauhafen 1a, near the Severinsbrücke. From the station, walk right along the Rhine, head under the Deutzer Brücke, and take the 1st footbridge. Open M-F 10am-6pm, Sa-Su 11am-7pm. Last entry 1hr. before closing. DM10, students DM5. Tours Sa 2 and 4pm, Su 11:30am, 2 and 4pm; DM3.)*

ENTERTAINMENT AND NIGHTLIFE

Cologne becomes a living spectacle during **Karneval,** a week-long pre-Lent festival celebrated in the hedonistic spirit of the city's Roman past. The weekend builds up to a bacchanalian parade on **Rosenmontag,** the last Monday before Lent (Feb. 26), when everyone is in costume and gets and gives dozens of *Bützchen* (kisses on a stranger's cheek). Pick up the *Karneval* booklet at the tourist office.

Students congregate in the *Bermuda-Dreieck* (triangle), bounded by **Zülpicherstr., Zülpicherpl., Roonstr.,** and **Luxemburgstr.** Gay nightlife runs up **Matthiasstr.** to **Mühlenbach, Hohe Pforte, Marienpl.,** and up to **Heumarkt** by the Deutzer Brücke. The tradition of Bacchus is still practiced in Cologne; at the *Brauhaüser,* waiters will bring drink after drink unless you cover your glass with a coaster. **Das Ding,** Hohenstaufenring, is a popular bar and disco for students. (Cover DM8. Open M and W 9pm-2am, Tu and Th-Su 9pm-3am.) Legendary *Kölsch* is brewed on the premises and at **Päffgen-Brauerei,** Friesenstr. 64-66. (Open daily 10am-midnight.) **Papa Joe's Jazzlokal,** Buttermarkt 37, features high-caliber live jazz and New Orleans atmosphere. (Open M-Sa 7pm-2am, Su 3:30-11pm.) You'll be livin' la **Taco Loco** at Zülpicherstr. 4a, with happy "hour" daily 6-8pm and tasty margaritas. (Open M-Th and Su 10am-2am, F-Sa 10am-3am.) **Vampire,** Rathenaupl. 5, is a gay and lesbian bar with a laid-back atmosphere. (Open Tu-Th and Su 8pm-1am; disco F-Sa 8pm-3am.)

BONN ☎0228

Derisively called the *Hauptdorf* (capital village), Bonn has been Germany's whipping boy for 50 years just because it's not Berlin. Bonn made it big by chance, because postwar chancellor Konrad Adenauer had a house in the suburbs. The Bundestag packed up and moved back to Berlin in 1999, but Bonn remains a worthy destination with several museums, a bustling Altstadt, and a respected university.

PRACTICAL INFO, ACCOMMODATIONS, AND FOOD. **Trains** run to: Cologne (30min., 6 per hr., DM10); Koblenz (1hr., 3 per hr., DM14.80); and Frankfurt (1½hr., every hr., DM59). The **tourist office** is on Windeckstr. 2, on Münsterpl. near the cathedral, in a passageway. (☎77 50 00. Open M-F 9am-6:30pm, Sa 9am-4pm, Su 10am-2pm.) Take bus #621 (dir. Ippendorf Altenheim) to "Jugendgästehaus" to get to the **Jugendgästehaus Bonn-Venusberg (HI),** Haager Weg 42. (☎28 99 70; fax 289 97 14; email jgh-bonn@t-online.de. Breakfast included. Laundry DM10. Reception 9am-1am. Curfew 1am. DM39.) Or, splurge on the stately **Hotel Hofgarten,** Fritz-Tillman-Str. 7. From the station turn right onto Maximilianstr., continue on Kaiserstr., and then turn left on Fritz-Tillman-Str. (☎22 34 82; fax 21 39 02. Breakfast included. Call ahead. Singles DM60-140; doubles DM125-185.) To reach **Campingplatz Genienaue,** Im Frankenkeller 49, take U16 or U63 to "Rheinallee," then bus #613 (dir. Giselherstr.) to "Guntherstr."; turn left on Guntherstr. and right on Frankenkeller. (☎34 49 49. Reception 9am-noon and 3-10pm. DM8 per person, DM5-8 per tent.) **Cafe-Bistro Bonngoût,** Remigiusplatz 2-4, serves generous meals. (Huge breakfasts for DM8-18. Open M-Sa 9am-1am, Su 10am-1am.) There is a **supermarket** in the Kaufhof basement on Münsterpl. (Open M-F 9:30am-8pm, Sa 9am-4pm.) **Postal code:** 53111.

SIGHTS AND ENTERTAINMENT. The **Beethoven Geburtshaus** (birthplace), Bonng. 20, has a fantastic collection of the composer's personal effects, from his primitive hearing aids to his first violin. (Open Apr.-Sept. M-Sa 10am-6pm, Su 11am-4pm; Oct.-Mar. M-Sa 10am-5pm, Su 11am-4pm. DM8, students DM6.) The castles and most museums lie just outside the inner city. The **Kurfürstliches Schloß,** a huge 18th-century palace, is now the center of Bonn's university. The Schloß is the gateway to the refreshing **Hofgarten** and **Stadtgarten,** filled with students and punks. Down the Poppelsdorfer Allee promenade, the 18th-century **Poppelsdorfer Schloß** sports a French facade, an Italian courtyard, and **botanical gardens.** (Gardens open Apr.-Sept. M-F 9am-6pm, Su 9am-1pm; Oct.-Mar. M-F 9am-4pm, Su 9am-1pm. M-F free, Su DM1.) The **Bonncard** provides public transport and admission to most of the **Museum Mile** (U16, U63, or U66: "Heussallee" or "Museum Koenig"). The **Kunstmuseum Bonn,** Friedrich-Ebert-Allee 2, has superb Expressionist and contemporary German art. (Open Tu and Th-Su 10am-6pm, W 10am-7pm. DM5, students DM3.) The art in the **Kunst- und Ausstellungshalle der BRD,** Friedrich-Ebert-Allee 4, is even newer. (Open Tu-W 10am-9pm, Th-Su 10am-7pm. DM10, students DM5.) The futuristic **Haus der Geschichte,** Adenauerallee 250, one block from the Kunstmuseum Bonn, offers an interactive look at German history. (Open Tu-Su 9am-7pm. Free.) Cultural and entertainment listings are in *Schnüss*. The **Jazz Galerie,** Oxfordstr. 24, is a jumping bar and disco and a hub for jazz and rock concerts. (Cover DM13 with 2 drinks. Concerts DM10-20. Open M-Th and Su 9pm-3am, F-Sa 9pm-4am.)

AACHEN ☎0241

Charlemagne made Aachen—at the meeting of Germany, the Netherlands and Belgium—the capital of his Frankish empire in the 8th century; his palace and cathedral are Aachen's main attractions. The neo-Byzantine **Dom** (cathedral) is in the city center. The king himself (well, part of him) now lies in the casket behind the altar. (Open daily 7am-7pm. Tours M 11am and noon; Tu-F 11am, noon, 1, 2:30, and 3:30pm; Sa-Su 12:30, 1:30, 2:30, and 3:30pm. DM3.) The **Schatzkammer,** a treasury that holds a gold-plated solid silver bust of Charlemagne (actually encasing his skull), is around the corner to the right from the Dom, tucked into the Klosterg. (Open M 10am-1pm, Tu-W and F-Su 10am-6pm, Th 10am-9pm. DM5, students DM3.) A large clown in drag greets visitors at the **Ludwigforum für Internationale Kunst,**

Jülicherstr. 97-109. A converted Bauhaus umbrella factory, the Ludwigforum has a cutting-edge collection of current greats, like Jeff Koons' gigantic sex dolls, and soon-to-be-greats, such as a Marge Simpson stone fertility doll. (Open Tu and Th 10am-5pm, W and F 10am-8pm, Sa-Su 11am-5pm. DM6, students DM3.)

Trains chug from Aachen to: Cologne (1hr., 2-3 per hr., DM20); Brussels (2hr., every hr., DM51); and Amsterdam (4hr., 1-2 per hr., DM102). To get from the station to the **tourist office,** on Friedrich-Wilhelm-Pl. in the Atrium Elisenbrunnen, cross the street, head up Bahnhofstr., turn left on Theaterstr., then right onto Kapuzinergraben, which leads to Friedrich-Wilhelm-Pl. (☎180 29 60; fax 180 29 31. Open M-F 9am-6pm, Sa 9am-2pm.) The **Euroregionales Jugendgästehaus (HI),** Maria-Theresia-Allee 260, is more like a hotel than a hostel. From the station, walk left on Lagerhausstr. until it intersects Karmeliterstr. and Mozartstr., then take bus #2 (dir. Preusswald) to Ronheide or #12 (dir. Diepenbendem) to Colynshof. (☎711 10 11. Breakfast buffet included. Curfew 1am. DM38.50.) Aachen's Altstadt is filled with cafes and *biergartens*, especially along Pontstr. leading away from the Rathaus pl. **Pera,** Marienbongard 2, serves up Mediterranean dishes in a classy setting. (☎409 37 80. Open daily 11am-1am.) **Plus,** Marienbongard 27, off Pontstr., stocks **groceries.** (Open M-F 8am-8pm, Sa 8am-4pm.) The **post office** is by the train station, on Kpuzinergraben. (Open M-F 9am-6pm, Sa 9am-1pm.) **Postal code:** 52064.

GERMANY

DÜSSELDORF ☎0211

Düsseldorf is a stately metropolis with the best nightlife on the majestic Rhein. By day, crowds line the Königsallee (also known as the Kö), a kilometer-long fashion runway that sweeps down both sides of the old town moat. At night, propriety (and sobriety) are cast aside as Düsseldorfers flock to the Altstadt's 500 pubs, trading monocles and Rolexes for beer goggles and a good time.

ORIENTATION AND PRACTICAL INFORMATION. Trains run from the Hauptbahnhof to: Frankfurt (3hr., 3 per hr., DM79, students DM65); Amsterdam (3hr., every hr., DM55); Brussels (3¼hr., every hr., DM59); Hamburg (3½hr.; 2 per hr.; DM116, students DM93); Berlin (4hr.; 1-2 per hr.; DM170, students DM137); Paris (4½hr., 7 per day, DM140); and Munich (6hr.; 2-3 per hr.; DM184, students DM147). To Aachen or Cologne/Köln, the **S-Bahn** is cheaper. The **tourist office,** Konrad-Adenauer-Pl., books rooms (from DM55) for a DM5 fee. Walk up and to the right from the Hauptbahnhof. (☎17 20 20; www.duesseldorf.de. Open M-F 8:30am-6pm, Sa 9am-12:30pm. Room booking M-Sa 8am-8pm, Su 2-8pm.) **Telenet-Center,** Fritz-Vomfeldestr. 34, offers **Internet** access. (DM3 for 30min. Open daily 9am-11pm.) Fairly cheap hotels populate the seedy train station neighborhood. The **Jugendgästehaus Düsseldorf (HI),** Düsseldorferstr. 1 has an unbeatable location just over the Rheinkniebrücke from the Altstadt. Take U70 or U74-77: Lügpl., then walk 500m down Kaiser-Wilhelm-Ring. (☎55 73 10; jgh-duesseldorf@t-online.de. Reception 7am-1pm. Curfew 1am, but doors open every hr. 2-6am. DM42, under 27 DM38.) To reach **Hotel Schaum,** Gustav-Poengsenstr. 63, exit the train station going left along Graf-Adolfstr. Take your first left and follow the tracks to Gustav-Poengsenstr. (☎311 65 10. Singles DM60, with bath DM80; doubles DM100-120.) **Hotel Bristol,** Aderstr. 8, one block south of Graf-Adolfstr. at the bottom tip of Königsallee, has large, newly-renovated rooms. (☎37 07 50. Singles DM75-95; doubles DM120-140.) **Camp** at **Kleiner Torfbruch.** Take the S-Bahn to Düsseldorf Geresheim, then bus #735 (dir. Stamesberg) to Seeweb. (☎899 20 38. DM7.50 per person; DM10 per tent.) Pizzerias, *Döner* stands, and Chinese eateries stretch from **Heinrich-Heine-Allee** to the banks of the Rhine in the Altstadt. The **Markt** on Karlspl. offers shoppers plenty of foreign fruits and a local favorite, *Sauerbraten* (pickled beef). An **Olto Mess supermarket** is on Karlspl. in the Altstadt. (Open M-F 8am-8pm, Sa 8am-4pm.)

SIGHTS, ENTERTAINMENT, AND NIGHTLIFE. The glitzy **Königsallee,** just outside the Altstadt, embodies the vitality and glamour of Düsseldorf. At the upper end of the Kö, the **Hofgarten park** is an oasis of green in the urban landscape. The Neoclassical **Ratinger Tor gate,** halfway down the park, opens onto Heinrich-

Heine-Allee. At the nearby **Kunstsammlung Nordrhein-Westfalen,** skylights lavish sunshine on Surrealists, Expressionists, and especially Paul Klee. (Grabbepl. 5. U70, U75-76, or U78-79: Heinrich-Heine-Allee, then walk north 2 blocks. Open Tu-Th and Sa-Su 10am-6pm, F 10am-8pm. Tours Su 11am, W 3:30pm, and F 6pm. DM5, students DM3. Special exhibits DM12, students DM8.) Across the square is the **Kunsthalle,** a forum for a variety of modern exhibits. (Grabbepl. 4. Open Tu-Su 11am-6pm. DM10, students DM7.) At the far end of the Hofgarten, the **Kunstmuseum Düsseldorf** balances Baroque and Romantic art with a 20th-century collection. (Ehrenhof 5. Open Tu-Su 11am-6pm. Tours Su 11am. DM5, students and children DM2.50.) The **ArtTicket** (DM20) includes entry to all museums, available at the tourist office or any museum. Pay homage to Düsseldorf's poet son at the **Heinrich-Heine-Institut,** Bilker Str. 12-14, with a collection of manuscripts and an unsettling death mask. (Open Tu-Su 11am-5pm, Sa 1-5pm. DM4, students DM2.) The **Schloß Benrath** sits in the suburbs of Düsseldorf, built 200 years ago as a pleasure palace for Elector Karl Theodor. (S-Bahn #6 (dir. Köln) to Benrath. Castle open Tu-Su 10am-5pm. DM7, students DM3.50.) North on the Rhine but still within Düsseldorf dwell the ruins of Emperor Friedrich's palace in the tiny town of **Kaiserwerth.** Take U79 to Klemenspl., then follow Kaiserwerther Markt to the Rhein and walk another 150m.

Folklore holds that Düsseldorf's 500 pubs make up *die längste Theke der Welt* ("the longest bar in the world"). Whether or not that's true, pubs in the Altstadt are standing-room-only by 6pm, and foot traffic is shoulder to shoulder by nightfall—it's nearly impossible to see where one pub ends and the next begins. **Bolkerstr.** is packed nightly with street performers of the musical and party-scene varieties. Pick up *Prinz* (DM5) for tips on hotspots. **Pam-Pam,** Bokerstr. 34, is a disco overflowing by midnight. Dance the night away to house, rock, pop, and plenty of American music. (Open F-Sa 10pm-dawn.) **Zum Uel,** Ratingerstr. 16, is packed with locals, giving it a quintessential beer-hall flavor. (*Schlösser Alt* beer DM2.80 for 0.2L. Open M-Tu, Th, and Su 10am-1am, W and F 10am-3am.)

FRANKFURT AM MAIN ☎069

International offices, skyscrapers, and luxury cars at every intersection hint at Frankfurt's commercial vitality. Known as "Bankfurt" or "Mainhattan," Frankfurt is home to the central bank of the European Union and plays an integral economic role in Europe. Most of the city was destroyed in WWII, but its concrete architecture exudes glitz nevertheless. The city government spends more on cultural attractions and tourism than any other German city, and consequently Frankfurt features several renowned museums. If all this isn't enough to make you visit, the likelihood of passing through Frankfurt's highly trafficked train station or airport probably is.

GETTING THERE AND GETTING AROUND

Flights: Flughafen Rhein-Main (☎69 01). S-Bahn #14 and 15 travel to the Hauptbahnhof every 15min. Buy tickets (DM6.10) from the green *Automaten* marked *Fahrkarten.*

Trains: ☎ (0180) 599 66 33. To: **Cologne/Köln** (2½hr.; 2 per hr.; DM70, under 26 DM61); **Munich** (3½-4½hr.; 2 per hr.; DM212, DM118); **Berlin** (5-6hr.; 2 per hr.; DM207, DM166); **Hamburg** (6hr.; 2 per hr.; DM191, DM153); **Amsterdam** (5hr., every 2 hr., DM126.50); **Paris** (6-8hr.; every 2 hr.; DM140, DM115); and **Rome** (15hr., every hr., DM228). Trains to Köln, Munich, and Hamburg also depart from the airport.

Public Transportation: Runs until about 1 am. Refer to the color **subway** map in the front of this guide. **Tageskarte** passes provide unlimited transportation on the U-Bahn, S-Bahn, streetcars, and buses (valid until midnight on the day of purchase); buy one from an *Automat* (DM8.50). **Single-ride** tickets valid for 1 hr. in one direction, including transfers (DM2.10, rush hour DM2.90). **Eurail** valid only on S-Bahn.

ORIENTATION AND PRACTICAL INFORMATION

The Hauptbahnhof (train station) lies at the end of Frankfurt's red-light district; walk 20 minutes down Kaiserstr. or Münchener Str. to reach the **Altstadt** (old city) and the **Römerberg** (U4: Römer). To the north, the commercial **Zeil** stretches from **Hauptwache** (S1-6 or S8: Hauptwache) to **Konstablerwache** (1 stop farther). Students and cafes cluster in **Bockenheim** (U6-7: Bockenheimer Warte). South of the Main River, **Sachsenhausen** (U1-3: Schweizer Pl.) draws pub-crawlers and museum-goers.

Tourist Office: (☎21 23 88 00; www.frankfurt-tourismus.de). In the Hauptbahnhof. Has maps (DM1-2), books rooms (DM5), and sells the **Frankfurt Card** (1-day DM12, 2-day DM19), which grants unlimited travel on all trains and buses and 50% off admission to 15 museums. Open M-F 8am-9pm, Sa-Su 9am-6pm.

American Express: Kaiserstr. 8 (☎21 93 88 60; fax 21 93 88 66; 24hr. hotline ☎97 97 10 00.) Open M-F 9:30am-6pm, Sa 9:30am-12:30pm.

English Bookstores: Süssman's Presse und Buch, Zeil 127 (☎131 07 51). Open M-W and F 9am-7pm, Th 9am-8pm, Sa 9am-4pm.

Laundromat: Schnell & Sauber, Wallstr. 8, near the hostel in Sachsenhausen. Wash and dry DM6. Open daily 6am-11pm. **Miele Washworld,** Moselstr. 17. DM7. Open daily 8am-11pm.

Emergency: ☎110. **Fire** and **Ambulance:** ☎112.

Pharmacy: In the Einkaufs passage of the Hauptbahnhof (☎23 30 47; emergencies ☎192 92.) Open M-F 6:30am-9pm, Sa 8am-9pm, Su and holidays 9am-8pm.

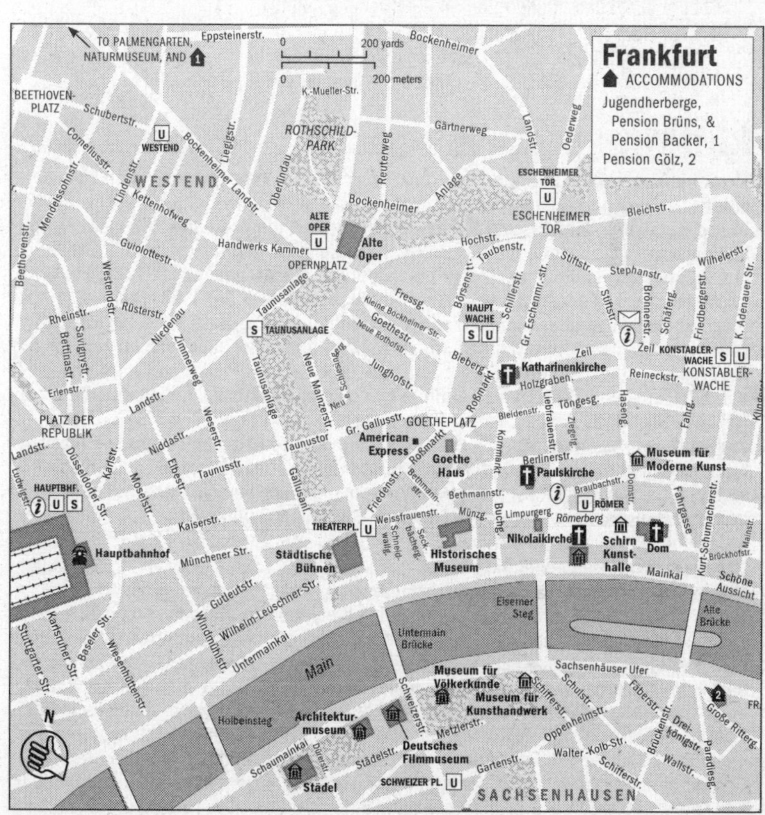

Internet Access: Alpha, in the Hauptbahnhof. DM1 per 4min. **Telemark,** Elisabethen Str. 45-47. DM 6 per 30 min., DM5 with hotel discount. Open 10am-10pm.

Post Office: Zeil 90 (☎13 81 26 21), in the *Hertie* department store. U- or S-Bahn: "Hauptwache." Open M-F 9:30am-8pm, Sa 9am-4pm. Address mail to be held: *Postlagernde Briefe* für First name SURNAME, Hauptpostamt, **60313** Frankfurt, Germany.

ACCOMMODATIONS

Frankfurt's hotel industry has adopted the motto "show me the money." However, there are a few reasonable options in the Westend/University area, and you can ask pensions about cheaper, shower-less rooms. If all else fails, the hostel in Mainz is less than 45 minutes away (take S14; see p. 444).

Pension Bruns, Mendelssohnstr. 42. (☎74 88 96; fax 74 88 46). From the Hauptbahnhof, head left on Düsseldorfer Str., right on Beethovenstr., and right again at the circle on Mendelssohnstr. (10-15min.). Spacious rooms with phone and TV. Breakfast included. Showers DM2. Call ahead. Doubles DM79; triples DM105; quads DM140.

Jugendherberge (HI), Deutschherrnufer 12 (☎610 01 50; fax 61 00 15 99; www.jugendherberge_frankfurt.de). Take bus #46 from the Hauptbahnhof to "Frankensteiner Pl." Turn left at the river and it's at the end of the block. After 7:30pm M-F, 5:45pm Sa, and 5pm Su, take S2-6 to "Lokalbahnhof," go down Darmstädter Landstr. with your back to the train bridge, bear right onto Dreieichstr., and turn left along the river. Borders the Sachsenhausen pub and museum district; lively and busy with students and fellow travelers. Breakfast included. Reception 24hr. Check-in after noon. Check-out 9:30am. Curfew 2am. DM33, under 27 DM27.

Pension Backer, Mendelssohnstr. 92 (☎74 79 92), past Pension Bruns (see above). U6 (dir. Heerstr.) or U7 (dir. Hausen): Westend. The best value in town. Breakfast included. Showers DM3. Singles DM25-50; doubles DM60; triples DM78.

FOOD

Regional specialties include *Handkäse mit Musik* (cheese curd with onions—Goethe's favorite), *grüne Sosse* (green sauce with various herbs, served over boiled eggs or potatoes), and *Äpfelwein* (apple wine; also called *Ebbelwei*). The cheapest grub surrounds the university in **Bockenheim** and nearby parts of **Westend** (U6-7: Bockenheimer Warte), and many pubs in **Sachsenhausen** (U1-3: Schweizer Pl.) serve food at decent prices. The German dishes (DM5-27) and liters of *Äpfelwein* at **Adolf Wagner,** Schweizer Str. 71, in Sachsenhausen, keep patrons jolly, rowdy, and loyal. (Open daily 11am-1am.) **Zum Gemalten Haus,** Schweizer Str. 67, four doors down, has treated generations of locals to *Wurst* and home-brewed wine. (DM13. Open W-Su 10am-midnight.) The **Kleinmarkthalle,** on Haseng. between Berliner Str. and Töngeg., hosts cutthroat competition between bakery, butcher, and fruit and vegetable stands—and has the prices to prove it. (Open M-F 7:30am-6pm, Sa 7:30am-4pm.) Get **groceries** at **HL Markt,** Dreieichstr. 56, near Frankensteiner Pl. (open M-F 8am-8pm, Sa 8am-4pm), or **Tengelmann,** Münchener Str. 37, near the Hauptbahnhof (open M-F 8:30am-7:30pm, Su 8am-2pm).

SIGHTS

Much of Frankfurt's historic splendor lives on only in memories and in reconstructed monuments nostalgic for the time before the 1944 bombing. At the center of the **Altstadt** is **Römerberg** square (U-Bahn: Römer), which sports reconstructed half-timbered architecture and a medieval fountain. At the west end of the Römerberg, the gables of **Römer** have marked the site of Frankfurt's city hall since 1405. East of the reconstructed Römerberg stands the only building in the city that survived the bombings: the red sandstone Gothic **Dom** (cathedral), the site of coronation ceremonies from 1562 to 1792. The **museum** within contains intricate chalices and the venerated robes of the imperial Electors. (Cathedral open daily 9am-noon and 2-6pm. Museum open Tu-F 10am-5pm, Sa-Su 11am-5pm. DM3, students DM1.) South of the Römerberg, the **Alte Nikolaikirche** raises its considerably more modest, pinkish spires. (Open daily Apr.-Sept. 10am-8pm; Oct.-Mar. 10am-6pm. Free.) The **Museum für Moderne Kunst,** Domstr. 10, just a few blocks north of the Dom, is spectacular; it houses a stunning modern art collection, including works by Claes Oldenburg, Roy Liechtenstein, and Jasper Johns. (Open Tu and Th-Su 10am-5pm, W 10am-8pm. DM10, students DM5; W free.) The **Museumsufer,** on the Schaumainkai along the south bank of the Main between the Eiserner Steg and the Friedensbrücke, hosts an eclectic collection of museums, including the **Deutsches Filmmuseum,** Schaumainkai 41. (Open Tu, Th-F, and Su 10am-5pm, W 10am-8pm, Sa 2-8pm. Tours Su 3pm. DM5, students DM2.50; W free.)

ENTERTAINMENT AND NIGHTLIFE

Frankfurt excels at entertainment and nightlife. The **Alte Oper,** Opernpl. (☎134 04 00; U6 or 7 to "Alte Oper"), offers a full range of classical music, while the **Städtische Bühne,** Untermainanlage 11 (☎21 23 71 33; U1, 2, 3, or 4 to "Theaterpl."), mounts ballets and operas. Shows and schedules are detailed in several publications, including *Fritz* and *Strandgut* (free at the tourist office), and the *Journal Frankfurt* (DM3.30), available at any newsstand. Or, call **Frankfurt Ticket** (☎134 04 00). The **Jazzkeller,** Kleine Bockenheimerstr. 18a, is a Frankfurt jazz institution. (Cover DM20. Open Tu-Su 9pm-3am.) For a night out, head to the **Alt-Sachsenhausen** district between Brückenstr. and Dreieichstr., home to a huge number of rowdy pubs and taverns specializing in *Äpfelwein*. The narrow, cobblestoned streets centering on **Grosse** and **Kleine Rittergasse** teem with canopied cafes, bars, and gregarious Irish pubs. Frankfurt has a number of thriving discos and prominent techno DJs, mostly in the commercial district around Zeil. In general, you're better off coming after midnight. Wear something dressier than jeans to try your luck with the neurotic bouncers; cover charges run DM10-20. **U60311,** Roßmarkt, on the corner of Goethepl., is popular with the young and trendy; the lines start at 10pm on Friday. (Cover DM15-30. Open M-F 10pm-10am, Sa-Su 10pm-6am.) **Blue Angel,** Brönnerstr. 17, is one of the liveliest gay men's clubs around. Ring the bell to be let in. (Cover DM11 includes drinks F-Sa. Open daily 11pm-4am.) **Das Opium,** Broennerstr. 7, houses an enormous disco ball that lights up a spacious, fleshy dance floor. (Cover DM12-20. Open Th-Sa 10pm-4am.)

SOUTHWEST GERMANY

The valleys, castles, and wine towns of Rhineland-Palatinate (Rheinland-Pfalz) form a visual feast as the Mosel curls downstream to the soft, castle-backed shores of the Rhine Valley. Centuries of literature, from the *Nibelungenlied* to the Lorelei revelry, attest to its beauty. The Rhineland also provides a literal feast: a rich agricultural tradition keeps produce in abundance, and the many vineyards in the Rhine and Mosel Valleys produce sweet, delicious wines. Two of the most prominent of German icons—the Brothers Grimm and the Mercedes-Benz—face off in Baden-Württemberg, where the bucolic, traditional hinterlands of the Black Forest contrast with the region's modern industrial cities.

RHINE VALLEY (RHEINTAL)

The Rhine River may run from Switzerland to the North Sea, but in the popular imagination it exists only in the 80km of the Rhine Gorge stretching from Bonn to north of Mainz. This is the Rhine of legends: sailors' nightmares, poets' dreams, and often the center of rhetorical storms of nationalism.

GETTING THERE AND GETTING AROUND. The Rhine Valley runs north from **Mainz,** easily accessible from Frankfurt, to **Bonn** (see p. 438), just south of **Köln** (Cologne) via **Bacharach, St. Goarshausen** and **St. Goar,** and **Koblenz.** Two different train lines (one on each bank) traverse this fabled stretch; **Eurail** is valid on trips between Cologne and Mainz. If you're willing to put up with lots of tourists, **boats** are probably the best way to see the sights. The **Köln-Düsseldorfer** (KD) and **Bingen-Rüdesheimer** lines cover the Mainz-Koblenz stretch three times per day in summer, while shorter trips are more frequent.

MAINZ. At the heart of Mainz, the capital of the Rhineland-Palatinate, lies the colossal sandstone **Martinsdom,** the resting place of the archbishops of Mainz. (Open Apr.-Sept. M-F 9am-6:30pm, Sa 9am-4pm, Su 12:45-3pm and 4-6:30pm; Oct.-Mar. M-F 9am-5pm, Sa 9am-4pm, Su 12:45-3pm and 4-5pm. Free.) Johannes Gutenberg, Mainz's favorite son and the father of movable type, is immortalized at the fascinating **Gutenberg Museum,** Liebfrauenpl. 5., across from the Dom. The museum contains several Gutenberg Bibles and a working replica of his original press. (Open Tu-Su 10am-5pm. DM6, students DM3.) On a hill several blocks south of the Altstadt stands the **Stephanskirche,** noted for its stunning stained-glass windows by Marc Chagall. From the Dom, take Ludwigstr. until it ends at Schillerpl. and follow Gaustr. up the hill to the church. (Open daily 10am-noon and 2-5pm. Free.)

Köln-Düsseldorf **ferries** (☎23 28 00) depart from the wharfs on the other side of the Rathaus. The **tourist office** finds rooms (from DM50) for a DM5 fee. (☎28 62 10; www.info-mainz.de. Open M-F 9am-6pm, Sa 9am-1pm.) The **Jugendgästehaus (HI),** Otto-Brunfels-Schneise 4, is in Weisenau in a corner of the Volkspark; take bus #22, 62, 63, or 92 to "Jugendherberge/Viktorstift." (☎853 32. Breakfast included. Reception 7am-midnight. Doubles DM39.40; 4 to 6-bed rooms DM120-180.) Near the Dom, the **Central Café,** on the corner of Rheinstr. and Heug., cooks up traditional German fare for under DM15. (Open M-Th and Su 10am-midnight, F-Sa 10am-1am.) The **Domplatz** in the Altstadt turns into an outdoor produce market. (Open Tu, F, and Sa in summer.) **Postal code:** 55001. **☎06131.**

BACHARACH. On the west bank of the Rhine, the gorgeous hidden gem of Bacharach brims with *Weinkeller* and *Weinstuben* (wine cellars and pubs) that do justice to its name—"altar to Bacchus." Find love, sweet love, at **Die Weinstube,** Oberstr. 63, behind the stunning **Altes Haus** in the center of town. Also off Oberstr. is the 14th-century **Wernerkapelle,** ghost-like remains of a red sandstone chapel that took 140 years to build but only a few hours to destroy in the Palatinate War of Succession in 1689; climb the steps next to the late-Romanesque Peterskirche. The **tourist office,** Oberstr. 45, in the post office, is five minutes from the station on the right. (☎91 93 03; fax 91 93 04. Open Apr.-Oct. M-F 9am-5pm, Sa 10am-4pm; Nov.-Mar. M-F 9am-1pm and 1:30-5pm, Sa 10am-1pm.) Hostels get no better than the unbelievable **Jugendherberge Stahleck (HI),** a gorgeous 12th-century castle with a panoramic view of the Rhine Valley. From the station, turn left at the Peterskirche and take any of the marked paths leading up the hill for 20 minutes. (☎12 66; fax 26 84. Breakfast included. Curfew 10pm. Call ahead. DM25.90, doubles 31.90.) To reach **Campingplatz Bacharach,** directly on the Rhine, turn right from the station (heading downhill toward the river) and walk 10 minutes south. (☎17 52. DM8 per person; DM5 per tent.) **☎06743.**

KOBLENZ. The beauty of Koblenz—or perhaps its strategic position at the convergence of the Rhine and the Mosel—has attracted Roman, French, Prussian, and German conquerors for the past 2000 years. Before reunification, the city served as a large munitions dump, but now the only pyrotechnics are during the **Rhein in Flammen** (Rhine in Flames) fireworks festival each August. Koblenz's sights cluster in the **Markt** and the **Deutsches Eck** (German Corner), a peninsula where the rivers meet that supposedly saw the birth of Germany when the Teutonic Order of Knights settled here in 1216. The **Mahnmal der Deutschen Einheit** (Monument to German Unity) on the right was erected in 1897 in honor of Kaiser Wilhelm I's forced reconciliation of the German Empire. Behind the Mahnmal, walk through the peaceful **Blumenhof** to the **Museum Ludwig im Deutschherrenhaus,** Danziger Freiheit 1, which mainly features contemporary French art. (Open Tu-Sa 10:30am-5pm, Su 11am-6pm. DM5, students DM3.) Much of Koblenz's *Altstadt* was flattened during WWII, but several churches have been carefully restored. The 12th-century **Florin-**

skirche was used as a military encampment by Napoleon in the 19th century (open daily 11am-5pm), while the stunning **Liebfrauenkirche** features oval Baroque towers, emerald- and sapphire-colored stained glass, and intricate ceiling latticework. (Open M-Sa 8am-6pm, Su 9am-12:30pm and 6-8pm. In summer, open Su 9am-8pm.) For a better view, head across the river to the **Festung Ehrenbreitstein,** a fortress at the city's highest point. The Prussians used it to accommodate French troops in past centuries; today, the German state uses it to accommodate you. (Non-hostel guests DM2, students DM1. Tours DM6.)

Trains go to Mainz (1hr., 3 per hr., DM25); Cologne/Köln (1hr., 3-4 per hr., DM25); Trier (2hr., every hr., DM30); and Frankfurt (2hr., 2 per hr., DM36). Take a sharp left from the station for the **tourist office,** Löhrstr. 141. (☎313 04; fax 100 43 88. Open M-F 9am-8pm, Sa-Su 10am-8pm.) The **Jugendherberge Koblenz (HI),** in the Festung, reveals a breathtaking view of Koblenz and the Rhine and Mosel Valleys. Take bus #9 or 10 across from the tourist office to "Charlottenstr." and continue along the Rhine side of the mountain on the main road following the DJH signs. (☎737 37; fax 70 27 07. Breakfast included. Reception 7:30am-11:30pm. Curfew 11:30pm. DM26, doubles DM32.) The **chairlift** is a block away from the hostel in the same direction. (Runs daily Mar.-Sept. 9am-5:50pm. DM4; round-trip DM6, non-hostel guests DM9.) Ferries (DM1) cross the Mosel to **Campingplatz Rhein-Mosel,** Am Neuendorfer Eck. (☎827 19. Reception 8am-noon and 2-8pm. Open Apr.-Oct. 15. DM6.50 per person, DM5 per tent.) **Marktstübchen,** Am Markt 220, at the bottom of the hill from the hostel, serves real German food at real budget prices. (Open M-Tu, Th, and Sa-Su 11am-midnight, W 11am-2pm, F 4pm-1am.) **Plus supermarket** is at Roonstr. 49-51. (Open M-F 8:30am-7pm and Sa 8am-2pm.) **Postal code:** 65068. **☎0261.**

MOSEL VALLEY (MOSELTAL)

The Mosel meanders slowly past the sun-drenched hills, picturesque towns, and ancient castles of the gently cut Mosel Valley before it surrenders to the Rhine at Koblenz. The valley's slopes aren't as dramatic as the Rhine's narrow gorge, but the arresting landscape, castles, and vineyards easily compensate.

GETTING THERE AND GETTING AROUND. The Mosel Valley runs northeast from **Trier,** just 45 minutes from **Luxembourg City** by train (see p. 670), to **Koblenz,** where it bisects the Rhine Valley (see p. 443), passing **Beilstein** and **Cochem** en route. The **train** line between Trier and Cochem passes through serene but unremarkable countryside and is better traversed by **boat, bus,** or **bicycle;** the route from Cochem to Koblenz hugs the Mosel and offers spectacular views. Although **passenger boats** no longer make the complete Koblenz-Trier run, several companies run daily trips along shorter stretches in summer.

TRIER ☎0651

The oldest town in Germany, Trier was founded by the Romans during the reign of Augustus, and had its heyday in the 4th century as the capital of the Western Roman Empire and Emperor Constantine's residence.

PRACTICAL INFO, ACCOMMODATIONS, AND FOOD. Trains go to Luxembourg City (45min., every hr., DM15); Cologne (2½hr., 2 per hr.); and Koblenz (1¾hr., 2 per hr., DM30). **Tourist-Information** (☎97 80 80; www.trier.de), in the shadow of the Porta Nigra, offers daily tours in English at 1:30pm (DM10, children DM3) and sells the **Trier Card** (DM21), which offers admission to six museums, free bus fare, and discounts on the Roman ruins, tours, and theater performances over a three-day period (DM21, family card DM39). Head down Theodor-Heuss-Allee or Christophstr. from the station. (Open Jan.-Feb. M-F 10am-5pm, Sa 9am-1pm; Mar. M-Sa 9am-6pm, Su 9am-1pm; Apr.-Oct. M-Sa 9am-6:30pm, Su 9am-3:30pm; Nov.-Dec. M-Sa 9am-6pm, Su 9am-3:30pm.) The **Jugendhotel/Jugendgästehaus Kolpinghaus,** Dietrichstr. 42, is one block off the Hauptmarkt. (☎97 52 50. Breakfast included. Reception 8am-11pm. Call ahead. Dorms DM27; singles DM39;

doubles DM80.) To reach the **Jugendgästehaus (HI),** An der Jugendherberge 4, take bus #2 or 87 (dir. "Trierweilerweg" or "Pfalzel/Quint") from the station to "Zur Laubener Ufer," and walk 10 minutes downstream along the river. (☎ 14 66 20 or 292 92; fax 146 62 30. Breakfast included. Reception 7am-midnight. Singles DM54; doubles DM79; quads DM120.) For **groceries,** check out **Plus** near the Hauptmarkt, Brotstr. 54. (Open M-F 8:30am-7pm, Sa 8:30am-4pm.) **Postal code:** 54292.

SIGHTS AND ENTERTAINMENT. The city's most impressive Roman remnant is the massive 2nd-century **Porta Nigra** (Black Gate), named for the centuries of grime that have blackened the originally light yellow sandstone facade. Simeonstr. leads to the **Hauptmarkt,** near which the 11th-century **Dom** shelters archbishops' tombs and the reputed **Tunica Christi** (Holy Robe of Christ), brought from Jerusalem to Trier around AD 300 by St. Helena, mother of Emperor Constantine. (Open daily Apr.-Oct. 6:30am-6pm, Nov.-Mar. 6:30am-5:30pm. Free.) Just south of the Dom, the **Basilika** was originally the location of Emperor Constantine's throne room. (Open M-Sa 9am-6pm, Su 11:30am-6pm. Free.) The ruins of the **Kaiserthermen,** the Roman baths where Constantine once scrubbed himself, lie down Am Palastgarten from the Basilica. Head left on Olewiger Str. to reach the 2nd-century **amphitheater,** which once hosted demonstrations of spectacular and gruesome ways to inflict pain (and death) on humans and animals for crowds of up to 20,000. (All Roman sights open daily Palm Sunday to Sept. 9am-6pm; Oct.-Nov. and Jan. to Palm Sunday 9am-5pm; Dec. 10am-4pm. DM4, students DM2; the amphitheater is closed in Dec. 1-day combination passes for all Roman monuments DM9, students DM4.50.) From back in the Hauptmarkt, head down Fleischstr. to make a pilgrimage to the **Karl-Marx-Haus,** Brückenstr. 10, where little Karl first walked, talked, and dreamed of labor alienation. (Open Apr.-Oct. M 1-6pm, Tu-Su 10am-6pm; Nov.-Mar. M 2-5pm, Tu-Su 10am-1pm and 2-5pm. DM3, students DM2.)

EXCURSIONS FROM TRIER: COCHEM AND BEILSTEIN. Busloads of tourists devour the quaintness of **Cochem,** a nostalgic wine-making village. The 11th-century **castle** was destroyed in 1689 by Louis XIV's French troops, but was rebuilt in 1868 as a neo-Gothic villa; make the 15-minute climb up Schloßstr. from the Marktpl. (Frequent 40min. tours in German; English translations available. Open daily mid-Mar. to Oct. 9am-5pm, Nov.-Dec. 11am-5pm. DM7, students DM6, children DM3.) **Trains** run to Trier (1hr., 2 per hr., DM17).

Ten kilometers upstream from Cochem lies **Beilstein,** the smallest official town in Germany. **Burg Metternich** is the resident castle; the French sacked it in 1689, but the view from the tower is still spectacular. (Open daily Apr.-Oct. 9am-6pm. DM3, students DM2, children DM1.) The Baroque **Karmelitenkirche** has the 16th-century **Schwarze Madonna von Beilstein.** (Open daily 9am-8pm.) **Bus** #8060 runs to Beilstein from Cochem's Endertpl. or train station (15min., 3-14 per day, DM4.90). The passenger **boats** of Personnenschiffahrt Kolb also float to Beilstein. (☎ (02673) 15 15. 1hr., May-Oct. 4 per day. DM18 round-trip.)

HEIDELBERG ☎06221

Believe the tourist propaganda—Heidelberg truly shines. In 1386, the sages of Heidelberg turned from illuminating manuscripts to illuminating young German minds when they founded Germany's first and greatest university. Set against wooded hills along the Neckar River, the town and its crumbling *Schloß* have exerted a magnetic pull over numerous writers and artists, including Mark Twain, Goethe, and Hugo, and today draw thousands of shutter-clicking tourists daily.

GETTING THERE AND GETTING AROUND

Trains: To: **Stuttgart** (40min., every hr., DM31, reduced DM25); **Frankfurt** (40min., 2 per hr., DM23.40, reduced DM18.80); and **Mannheim** (10min., 5 per hr., DM7.80).

Public Transportation: Single-ride tickets DM3.30. 24hr. **day passes** valid for up to 5 people on all streetcars and buses (DM10.50); buy them at the tourist office.

Hitchhiking: *Let's Go* does not recommend hitchhiking. Hitchers walk to the western end of Bergheimer Str. **Mitfahrzentrale,** Bergheimer Str. 125 (☎246 46), organizes ride-sharing. To Cologne/Köln DM28, Hamburg DM54, Paris DM51, Freiburg DM24. Open M-F 9am-5pm; Apr.-Oct. also Sa 9am-noon.

ORIENTATION AND PRACTICAL INFORMATION

Most of Heidelberg's attractions are clustered in the eastern part of the city, along the southern bank of the Neckar. To get from the train station to the **Altstadt,** take any bus or streetcar to "Bismarckpl.," where **Hauptstraße** leads to the heart of the city. The two-day **Heidelberg Card** includes unlimited use of public transit and admission to most sights (DM19.80 from the tourist office).

Tourist Office: Tourist Information (☎13 88 121; www.cvb.heidelberg.de), in front of the station. Books **rooms** (from DM70) with 8% deposit for DM5. Open Mar.-Dec. M-Sa 9am-7pm, Su 10am-6pm; Jan.-Feb. closed Su. Pick up *Meier* (DM2) or *Heidelberg Aktuell* (DM1) for events info. **Branches** at the Schloß (☎211 44; open daily 9am-5pm; closed in winter) and at Neckarmünzpl. (open daily in summer 9am-6:30pm).

Currency Exchange: Change cash at the **Sparkassen** on Universitätspl. and Bismarckpl., or try the exchange office in the train station. Open M-Sa 7am-8:30pm, Su 9am-1pm.

American Express: Brückenkopfstr. 1 (☎450 517; fax 45 55 84), at the north end of Theodor-Heuss-Brücke. Open M-F 10am-6pm, Sa 9am-1pm.

Emergency: ☎110. **Police:** Römerstr. 2-4 (☎990). **Fire** and **Ambulance:** ☎112.

Internet Access: Café Gecko, Bergheimer Str. 8 (☎60 45 20). DM4 per 30min. Open S-Th 9am-1am, F 9am-2am, Sa 9am-3am. **La Tapa,** Steing. 16 (☎18 35 11). DM1.50 for 10 min. Open M, Tu, and Th-Sa 11am-8pm, Su noon-5pm.

Post Office: Sofienstr. 8-10 (☎91 24 10). Open daily 9am-6:30pm. Address mail to be held: *Postlagernde Briefe* für First name SURNAME, **69115** Heidelberg, Germany.

ACCOMMODATIONS, CAMPING, AND FOOD

In summer, reserve ahead or arrive early. If you get stuck, try the **hostels** in nearby **Neckargemünd** (10min.; ☎ (06223) 21 33); **Mannheim** (20min.; ☎ (0621) 82 27 18); **Zwingenberg** (35min.; ☎ (06251) 759 38); and **Eberbach** (25min.; ☎ (06271) 25 93).

Jugendherberge (HI), Tiergartenstr. 5 (☎41 20 66; fax 40 25 59). From Bismarckpl. or the station, take bus #33 (dir. "Zoo-Sportzentrum") to "Jugendherberge." In peak season, it's advisable to fax your reservation. Sheets DM5.50. Reception until 11:30pm. Lockout 9am-1pm. Members only. DM24, 26+ DM28.

Hotel-Pension Elite, Bunsenstr. 15 (☎257 33 or 257 34; fax 16 39 49). From Bismarckpl., follow Rohrbacher Str. away from the river, turn right on Bunsenstr. Nice rooms with bath and TV. Breakfast included. With *Let's Go:* single DM75; doubles DM85 for one, DM100 for two, DM20 for each extra person. DM5 credit card surcharge.

Jeske Hotel, Mittelbadg. 2 (☎237 33). From the station, take bus #33 (dir. "Ziegelhausen") or 11 (dir. "Karlstor") to "Rathaus/Kornmark"; Mittelbadg. is the 2nd left off the square. The best value in Heidelberg in an unbeatable location. Reservations only accepted 1hr. in advance. Call ahead; opening times may vary. Doubles DM52.

Camping Haide (☎ (06223) 21 11), between Ziegelhausen and Neckargemünd. Take bus #35 to "Orthopädisches Klinik," cross the river, turn right, and it's on the right. Reception 8am-noon and 4:30-7:30pm. Open Apr.-Oct. DM14.50-20 per person; DM2 per car; cabins DM14.50-20.

Get cheap grub at **Handelshof supermarket,** Kurfürsten-Anlage 60, 200m straight down from the station on the right. (Open M-F 7:30am-8pm, Sa 7:30am-4pm.) There is a **fruit market** on Marktpl. on Wednesdays and Saturdays. Appetizing aromas of Chinese food emanate from **Großer Wok,** Bergheimer Str. 1a, near Bismarckpl. (Entrees DM4-13. Open Su-Th 11am-11pm, F-Sa 11am-midnight.) Some traditional German dishes (DM8-15) at **Goldener Anker,** Untere Neckar 52, near the river and the Alte Brücke, are affordable. (Open M-Sa 6pm-midnight.)

GERMANY

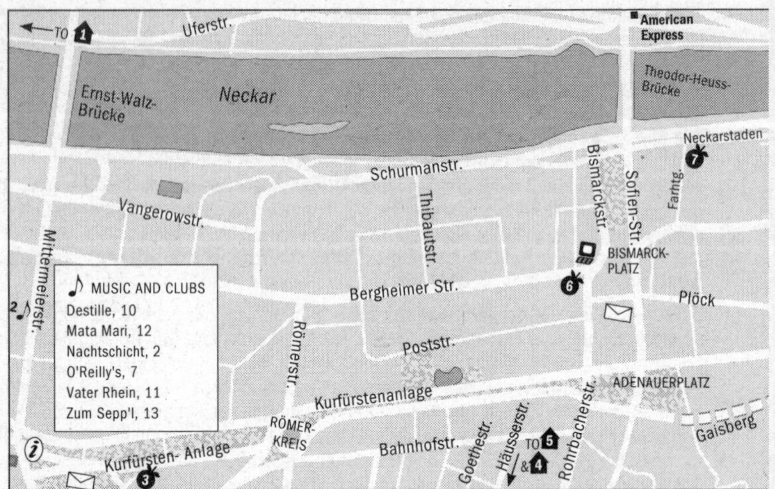

SIGHTS

HEIDELBERGER SCHLOSS. The ramparts of Heidelberg's aging castle, the jewel in the crown of an already striking city, preside over the Altstadt. After 1329, it served as the home of the prince Electors, but was later thrice destroyed—twice by war (1622 and 1693) and once by lightning (1764). The castle's regal state of disrepair is best viewed from the Philosophenweg across the Neckar. *(Walk uphill from the base of the castle or take the Bergbahn cable car from the "Bergbahn/Rathaus" bus stop, round-trip DM4.70. Trams take off from the Kornmarkt parking lot every 10min., 9am-7:45pm. Castle ☎ 53 84 14 or 538 40. Obligatory daily tours in English leave every hr. from 11:15am-3:15pm; DM4, students DM2. Grounds open daily 8am-dusk. DM3, students DM1.50.)*

MARKTPLATZ AND UNIVERSITÄT. The Altstadt centers on the cobblestone **Marktplatz,** where accused witches and heretics were burned at the stake in the 15th century; today, tourists recline on legions of plastic chairs. Heidelberg's two oldest structures border the square: the 14th-century **Heiliggeistkirche** (Church of the Holy Spirit), where residents hid during Louis XIV's invasion, and **Haus Zum Ritter,** opposite the church. *(Church open M-Sa 11am-5pm, Su 1-5pm. Free.)* Five blocks down Hauptstr., a stone-lion fountain oversees the oldest remaining buildings of the **Alte Universität** (Old University), established in 1368. Here, Clemens Brentano compiled a folk poetry collection that led to the Brothers Grimm's prose compilation, and Max Weber transformed sociology into a legitimate academic subject.

KURPFÄLZISCHES MUSEUM. The museum is crammed with artifacts such as the jawbone of an unfortunate *homo Heidelbergensis*, a.k.a. "Heidelberg man," one of the oldest humans ever discovered. Elsewhere in the museum stand well-preserved works of art by Dürer and a spectacular archaeology exhibit. *(Hauptstr. 97. Open Tu and Th-Su 10am-5pm, W 10am-9pm. DM5, students DM3; Su DM3, students DM2.)*

PHILOSOPHENWEG. If train schedules haven't given you enough time to contemplate the Other, or if you just need a romantic place to kiss the Other, follow in the footsteps of Hegel and Weber on the "philosopher's path." A high path opposite the Neckar from the Altstadt, the Philosophenweg offers the best views of the city and traverses the **Heiligenberg** (mountain). The ruins of the 9th-century **St. Michael Basilika,** the 13th-century **Stefanskloster,** and an **amphitheater** built under Hitler in 1934, all lie atop the mountain on the site of an ancient Celtic gathering place. *(Take streetcar #1 or 3 to "Tiefburg," a castle in neighboring Handschuhsheim, to begin the hike upwards, or use the footpath to the west of Karl-Theodor-Brücke.)*

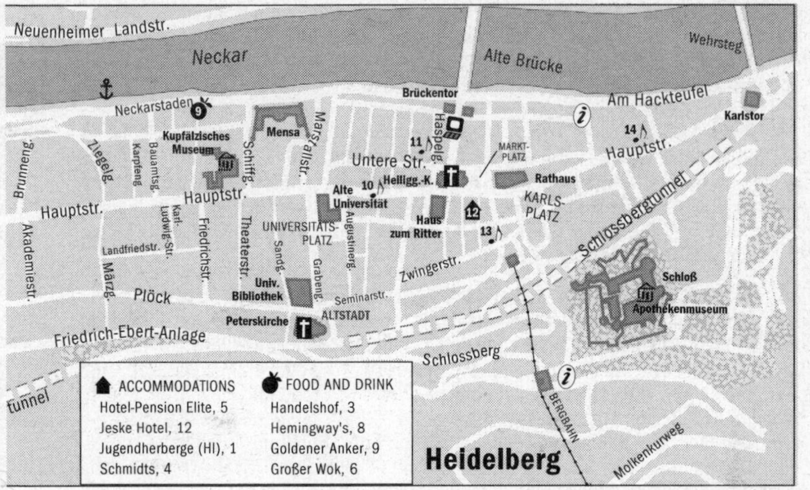

NIGHTLIFE

For info on Heidelberg festivals and events, call **InfoLife** (☎60 45 20). Most popular nightspots fan out from **Marktplatz** or line **Hauptstraße; Unter Straße,** on the Neckar side of the Heiliggeistkirche, boasts the most bars. Students converge at **VaterRhein,** Untere Neckarstr. 20-22, to chill among the vintage 1950s ads that decorate the wood-paneled walls. (Pilsner DM4.50. Open daily 8pm-3am.) Across the river, try **O'Reilly's,** on the corner of Brückenkopfstr. and Uferstr. (Guinness DM7.50 for half a liter. Open M-F 5pm-1am, Sa-Su 1pm-3am.) **Nachtschicht** is in the Landfried-Komplex. Take Mittermaierstr. past the metal dinosaur; take the first left onto Alte Eppenheimerstr. and enter the parking lot 100m on the right. The club offers a variety of music in a basement that resembles an abandoned warehouse. (DM6. students half-price on W and F. Open W-Sa 10pm-4am.)

EXCURSIONS FROM HEIDELBERG: THE NECKAR VALLEY

The Neckar Valley (Neckartal), a scenic stretch of narrow, thickly wooded ridges along the Neckar River, encompasses several medieval **castles,** forming part of the **Burgenstraße** that stretches from Mannheim to Prague. One of the best ways to explore the valley is by **biking** along the well-maintained 85km route from **Heilbronn** to **Heidelberg,** which are also connected by two rail lines. At the northern end of the valley, 14km upstream from Heidelberg, **Neckarsteinach** is renowned for its four 12th- to 13th-century medieval castles, all within 3km of one another along the northern bank of the Neckar River. The two westernmost castles stand in ruins, while the two to the east stand in splendor. Although the latter two are not open to the public, the beautiful views make for a great daytrip. The castles are accessible via the **Burgenweg** (castle path); from the Neckarsteinach **train station** (15min. from Heidelberg), turn right on Bahnhofstr., turn left on Hauptstr., follow the bend in the road, then climb the brick *Schloßsteige* (castle steps) that lead up to the right. The **tourist office,** Hauptstr. 7, inside the Rathaus, is on the way to the *Schloßsteige.* (Open M-W 8am-noon and 1:30-3:30pm, Th 8am-noon and 1:30-5pm, F 8am-noon.)

Until the recent tourist influx, **Bad Wimpfen,** downstream from Heilbronn, was one of southwest Germany's best-kept secrets. The well-preserved **Altstadt** is 10 minutes from the ornately Gothic train station; follow Karl-Ulrich-Str., or take the steep hiking trail to the right of the station. Easily accessible points on the ancient battlements along the northern side of the old **castle walls** offer incredible views of the valley and the surrounding countryside. The **tourist office** is in the train station. (☎ (07063) 972 00. Open M-F 9am-1pm and 2-5pm, Sa-Su 10am-noon and 2-4pm.)

STUTTGART ☎0711

Leave your half-timbered houses and *lederhosen* at home; corporate thoroughbreds Porsche and Daimler-Chrysler disqualify Stuttgart from the slow lane. Blown to bits in WWII, Stuttgart was rebuilt in a completely modern and supremely uninspiring style, but the green hills of the Neckar provide welcome tranquility to the busy capital of Baden-Württemberg.

PRACTICAL INFO, ACCOMMODATIONS, AND FOOD. Trains (☎ (0180) 599 66 33) run from Stuttgart, the transportation hub of southwestern Germany, to: Frankfurt (1½hr., every hr., DM88); Munich (2½hr., every hr., DM73); Basel (3hr., every hr., DM85); Berlin (5½hr., every 2hr., DM256); and Paris (6hr., 3 per day, DM136). The **tourist office,** I-Punkt, Königstr. 1, is next to the escalator down to the Klett-Passage. (☎222 80; www.stuttgart-tourist.de. Open May-Oct. M-F 9:30am-8:30pm, Sa 9:30am-6pm, Su 11am-6pm; Nov.-Apr. M-F 9:30am-8:30pm, Sa 9:30am-6pm, Su 1-6pm.) For info on youth travel or the youth scene, head to **tips 'n' trips,** Rotebühlpl. 26, in the U-Bahn passage at Rotebühlpl. (☎222 27 30. Internet DM5 per hr. for students. Open M-F noon-7pm, Sa 10am-2pm.) To reach the spotless **Jugendgästehaus Stuttgart,** Richard-Wagner-Str. 2, take streetcar #15 (dir. Ruhbank) to "Bubenbad." Continue in the direction of the streetcar on the right side of the street and veer right around the corner. (☎24 11 32. Breakfast included. Key deposit DM20. Reception M-F 9am-8pm, Sa-Su 11am-8pm. Singles DM40-50; DM35 per extra person.) To get to the **Jugendherberge Stuttgart (HI),** Haußmannstr. 27, take the "ZOB" exit from the Klett-Passage and walk through the Schloßgarten. Exit to the right of the statue, continue up the path past the police station, and climb the staircase on Schnützerstr. (☎24 15 83. Breakfast included. Sheets DM5.50. Reception 7-9am and noon-11:30pm. Curfew 11:30pm. Call ahead. DM29, under 27 DM24.) Sample the amazing variety of vegetarian fare served cafeteria-style at **Iden,** Eberhardstr. 1. (U-Bahn to "Rathaus." Open M-F 11am-9pm, Sa 10:30am-5pm.) For **groceries,** head to the basement of **Kaufhof,** on Eberhardstr. near the end of Königstr. (Open M-F 9am-8pm, Sa 9am-4pm.) **Postal code:** 70001.

SIGHTS AND ENTERTAINMENT. At Stuttgart's core lies an enormous pedestrian zone, centered on **Königstraße** and the smaller **Calwerstraße.** The main municipal park, the tranquil **Schloßgarten,** runs south from the station to the elegant Baroque **Neues Schloß.** The north end of the park contains the **Rosensteinpark** and **Wilhelma,** Stuttgart's zoo and botanical garden. (Open daily Mar.-Oct. 8:15am-5pm; Nov.-Feb. 8:15am-4pm. DM14, students DM7; Nov.-Feb. reduced.) Behind the Schloßgarten is the superb **Staatsgalerie Stuttgart,** Konrade-Adenaur-Str. 30-32, containing works by Picasso, Kandinsky, Beckmann, and Dalí. Take U1, 4, 9, or 11 to "Staatsgalerie." (Open W and F-Su 10am-6pm, Tu and Th 10am-8pm. DM5, students DM3.) For artistry of a different sort, the high-tech **Mercedes-Benz Museum** traces the luxury automobile from its inception to modern experimental models. Take S1 to "Daimlerstadion," go left under the bridge, and follow the signs. (Open Tu-Su 9am-5pm. Free.) The soothing waters of Stuttgart's **mineral baths** are an ideal remedy for budget travel exhaustion. The **Mineralbad Leuze,** Am Leuzebad 2-6, has spectacular facilities. Take the U-Bahn to "Wilhelma." (☎216 42 10. Open daily 6am-9pm. Day card DM25, students DM16. Swim cap required.) Once refreshed, join the noise and the crowd at **Palast der Republik,** Friedrichstr. 27. (Drinks DM4-12. Open M-W 11am-2am, Th-Sa 11am-3am, Su 3pm-2am; in winter M-W and Su 11am-1am, Th-Sa 11am-2am.) Or, head to **Zap,** Hauptstätter Str. 40, in Josef-Hirn-Pl., for hip-hop, house, and soul. (Cover DM8-15. Open Tu 9pm-3am, W-Su 10pm-4am.)

BLACK FOREST (SCHWARZWALD)

The German cultural consciousness has always dreamt of the dark, from early fairy tales to Franz Kafka's disturbing fiction. Nowhere do such nightmarish thoughts come to life better than in the Black Forest, a tangled expanse in southwestern Baden-Württemberg named for the eerie gloom under its evergreen canopy. Inspiration for the tale of Hänsel and Gretel, the region now attracts hikers and skiers with more than just bread crumbs.

GETTING THERE AND GETTING AROUND. The main entry points to the Black Forest are **Freiburg** in the center (see p. 452); **Baden-Baden** to the northwest; **Stuttgart** to the east (see p. 450); and **Basel, Switzerland** to the southwest (see p. 926). Only one **train** penetrates the interior; **bus** service is more thorough, albeit slow and less frequent. The **Freiburg tourist office** (☎ (0761) 368 90 90; fax 37 00 37) is the best place to gather information about the Black Forest.

TITISEE AND SCHLUCHSEE. The touristed **Titisee** (TEE-tee-zay) is only 30 minutes by train from Freiburg (dir. Seebrugg) via the scenic Höllental (Hell's Valley). The **tourist office,** Strandbadstr. 4, dispenses maps of nearby hiking trails (DM1-15). From the station, turn left on Parkstr., go left at the intersection, and make a quick right following the road. (☎980 40. Open July-Sept. M-F 8am-6pm, Sa 9am-noon and 3-5pm, Su 10am-noon; Oct.-June M-F 9am-noon and 1:30-5:30pm.) **Hiking trails** start in front of the office; consider the placid **Seerundweg,** or keep going along Strandbadstr. and turn right on Alte Poststr. for more challenging trails. **☎07651.**

Schluchsee, to the south, is home to a slew of first-rate **hiking trails.** The **Seerundweg** circumvents the lake (18km, about 4hr.); more difficult trails depart from the **Sportplatz** parking lot, 15 minutes up Dresselbacher Str. **Trains** run from Titisee to Schluchsee (30min., every hr.). From the station, turn right, walk through the underpass, and turn left on Kirchsteige to reach the **tourist office,** at the corner of Fischbacher Str. and Lindenstr. (☎77 32. Open May-Sept. M-F 8am-6pm, Sa-Su 10am-noon; Oct.-Apr. M-F 8am-noon and 2-6pm.) The **Jugendherberge Schluchsee-Wolfsgrund (HI),** Im Wolfsgrund 28, has stunning lake views. From the station, cross the tracks, hop the fence, and follow the path right over the bridge. (☎329. May-Oct. DM2-3 *Kurtaxe.* Laundry. Reception closed 2-5pm. Curfew 11pm. DM30, under 27 DM25.) Walk left up Bahnhofstr., continue on Freiburger Str., turn left on Sägackerweg, go past Am Waldrain, and go left again to the **Campingplatz Wolfsgrund.** (☎573. DM9.50 per person; DM10 per site.) Get **groceries** at **Schmidt's Markt,** Im Rappennest 2. (Open M-F 7:30am-8pm, Sa 7:30am-4pm.) **☎07656.**

ST. PETER AND ST. MÄRGEN. North of Titisee and 17km east of Freiburg, twin villages **St. Peter** and **St. Märgen** lie between cow-speckled hills in the High Black Forest. **Bus** #7216 runs from Freiburg to St. Märgen via St. Peter; you can also take any **train** on the Freiburg-Neustadt line to "Kirchzarten" (3rd stop), then take bus #7216 to St. Peter (only half continue to St. Märgen; check with the driver). An easy but very scenic 8km path leads from **St. Peter,** surrounded by cherry orchards, to St. Märgen; follow the blue diamonds of the *Panoramaweg.* From in front of St. Peter's **Klosterkirche,** make a sharp right alongside it—don't cross the stream and the main road—heading for Jägerhaus, and cross the highway. St. Peter's **tourist office,** in the Klosterhof, lists rooms from DM25. Get off the bus at "Zähringer Eck"; it's right in front of the church. (☎91 02 24; fax 91 02 44. Open June-Oct. M-F 8am-noon and 2-5pm, Sa 11am-1pm; Nov.-May M-F 8am-noon and 2-5pm.) **☎07660.**

With links to all major Black Forest trails and a number of gorgeous day hikes, **St. Märgen** rightfully calls itself a *Wanderparadies* (hiking paradise). One of the more challenging trails leads to the **Zweibach waterfall;** follow the yellow signs with a black dot (16km, 4hr.). To reach the trail from the town center, walk downhill along Feldbergstr., turn left on Landfeldweg, and follow signs for *Rankmühle.* The **tourist office,** in the Rathaus, 100m from the "Post" bus stop, has good hiking and biking maps (DM5), and finds rooms for free. (☎91 18 17; fax 91 18 40. Open June-Aug. M-

F 8am-noon and 2-5pm, Sa 10am-noon; Sept.-Oct. and Jan.-May M-F 8am-noon and 2-5pm; Nov.-Dec. M-F 8am-noon.) ☎07669.

TRIBERG. The residents of touristy **Triberg** gush over the **Gutacher Wasserfall,** Germany's highest **waterfall,** a series of bright cascades tumbling 163m down moss-covered rocks. The idyllic hike through lush pines trees surpasses the actual falls. In the park follow the *Kulturweg* signs to the **Wallfahrtskirche,** continue on Kroneckweg, and follow the *Panoramaweg* signs for an excellent view of the Black Forest valley. (Park admission DM2.50, students DM1.) **Trains** chug to Triberg from Freiburg (1¾hr., every hr., DM32). To get from the station to the **tourist office,** in the Kurhaus, cross the bridge, go under it, head up steep Fréjusstr. (which becomes Hauptstr.), pass the Marktpl., and turn left at the Hotel Pfaff. (☎95 32 30. Open May-Sept. M-F 9am-5pm, Sa 10am-noon; Oct.-Apr. M-F 9am-5pm.) The sparkling **Jugendherberge (HI),** Rohrbacher Str. 35, requires a masochistic 30-minute climb up Friedrichstr. (which becomes Rohrbacher Str.) from the tourist office. (☎41 10. Sheets DM6. Reception 5-7pm and at 9:45pm. Call ahead. DM30, under 27 DM25.) The **Hotel Zum Bären,** Hauptstr. 10, is closer to the center and the park entrance. (☎44 93. Breakfast included. Singles DM37-45; doubles DM66-84.) ☎07722.

GERMANY

FREIBURG IM BREISGAU ☎0761

Freiburg may be the "metropolis" of the Schwarzwald, but it has yet to succumb to hectic urban rhythms. Its relaxed air results not only from persistent French influence and hordes of students, but also from the surrounding hills, brimming with greenery and fantastic hiking.

PRACTICAL INFO, ACCOMMODATIONS, AND FOOD. Trains arrive from: Basel, Switzerland (45min., 1-2 per hr., DM14-17); Stuttgart (1½hr., every hr., DM49-61); and Strasbourg, France (1¾hr.; every hr., DM21-27). The **tourist office,** Rotteckring 14, is down Eisenbahnstr. from the station. (☎388 18 82. Open June-Sept. M-F 9:30am-8pm, Sa 9:30am-5pm, Su 10am-noon; Oct.-May M-F 9:30am-8pm, Sa 9:30am-2pm, Su 10am-noon.) Check your **email** at the **Internet-Café,** in the **Kaufhof** department store on Dreherstr. and Schusterstr. (DM3 per 30min. Open M-F 9:30am-8pm, Sa 9am-4pm.) To reach the **Jugendherberge (HI),** Kartäuserstr. 151, take streetcar #1 (dir. Littenweiler) to Römerhof, cross the tracks, backtrack 20m, walk 10 minutes down Fritz-Geiges-Str., cross the stream, and follow the footpath to the right. (☎676 56. Reception 7am-9am and 1-10pm. Curfew 1am. Members only. DM33, under 27 DM28.) **Pension Gisela,** Am Vogelbach 27, offers quiet studio apartments. Take bus #10 (dir. Padua-Allee) to Hofackerstr., then double back a block and turn left, walk 250m, and turn right on Hasenweg before the train tracks. (☎89 78 980. Breakfast included. Singles DM60-70; doubles from DM90.) **Hotel Zum Löwen,** Breisgauer Str. 62, doesn't feel like a budget hotel. Take streetcar #1 to Padua-Allee, backtrack 30m along the tracks, and walk five minutes down Breigauerstr. (☎809 72 20. Breakfast included. Singles DM50-70; doubles DM90-130.) **Campground Hirzberg,** Kartäuserstr. 9, is near the city. Take streetcar #1 (dir. Lassbergstr.) to Stadthalle; go left via the underpass, walk straight (north) on Hirzbergstr., cross the Max-Miller-Steg bridge, and take a left at the street. (☎350 54. Laundry. DM9 per person; DM6-8 per tent; summer tent rentals DM10-15.) **Brennessel,** Eschholzstr. 17, is a spunky student tavern with funk, jazz, and cheap chow. (Open M-Sa 6pm-1am, Su 5pm-1am.) Load up at **Edeka ActivMarkt,** Eisenbahnstr. 39. (Open M-F 8am-8pm, Sa 8am-2pm.) **Postal code:** 79098.

SIGHTS AND ENTERTAINMENT. Freiburg's pride and joy is the majestic 13th- to 16th-century **Münster,** a stone cathedral with a 116m spire and a tower with the oldest bell in Germany. (Cathedral open M-Sa 10am-6pm, Su 1-6pm. Tower open May-Oct. M-F 9:30am-5pm, Su 1-5pm; Nov.-Apr. Tu-Sa 9:30am-5pm, Su 1-5pm. DM2.50, students DM1.50.) Two medieval gates—the **Schwabentor** and the **Martinstor**—stand within a few blocks of one another in the southeast corner of the Altstadt. From the Schwabentor, take the pedestrian overpass across the heavily trafficked Schloßbergring to climb the **Schloßberg** for an excellent view of the city. The **Adelhausermusem Natur- und Völkerkunde,** Gerberau 32, covers animals, vegetables, and minerals, and has an ambitious anthropological exhibit. (Open Tu-Su 10am-5pm. Free.) The **Museum für Neue Kunst** (Museum of Modern Art), Marienstr. 10a, near the Schwabentor, displays the work of 20th-century German artists such as Otto Dix. (English guide available. Open Tu-Su 10am-5pm. Free.) The narrow streams around town are **Bächle,** used as swift-flowing gutters in medieval times.

Call ahead to get a one-hour tour at the **Brauerei Ganter,** Schwarzwaldstr. 43; tours track the production process of the malt beverage; the grand finale has food and lots of beer on one of the factory buildings. (☎218 51 81. Tu and Th 1:30pm. Free.) For less structured entertainment, Freiburg's nightlife revolves around the **Martinstor** near the university. **Exit,** Kaiser-Josef-Str. 248, inspires people to do just the opposite. (Cover DM6. Th and Sa students free; ISIC not accepted. Open M and W-Th 10pm-3am, F-Sa 10pm-4am.) **Jazzhaus,** Schnewlingstr. 1, features live performances almost every night. (☎349 73. Cover from DM10. Open M-Th and Su 10pm-3:30am, F-Sa 8pm-3am; call for tickets or show up after 7pm.)

GERMANY

LAKE CONSTANCE (BODENSEE)

Germany has long suffered from a Mediterranean complex, and the single strip of land along the Bodensee in southern Baden-Württemberg provides an opportunity to fulfill Italian fantasies and satisfy Grecian longings with a thoroughly un-German ease. With the snow-dusted Swiss and Austrian Alps in the background, the Bodensee is one of Germany's most stunning destinations.

KONSTANZ ☎07531

Narrow streets in this elegant university city, among the few German cities to have escaped Allied bombing in WWII, wind around the beautifully painted Baroque and Renaissance facades in the town center. The **Münster** has a soaring 76m Gothic spire and a display of ancient religious objects, although the tower is unfortunately being renovated through 2003. (Open M-Sa 10am-6pm, Su noon-6:30pm. Free.) Wander down **Seestraße,** near the yacht harbor on the lake, or down **Rheinsteig,** along the Rhine, for picturesque promenades, or rent a **paddle boat** or **rowboat** at **Am Gondelhafen.** (Open Apr.-Oct. daily 10am-dusk. DM12-16 per hr.). Take bus #5 to reach **Strandbad Horn,** Konstanz's most popular **public beach,** with a nude sunbathing section modestly enclosed by hedges.

Trains arrive from: Zürich (1¼hr.); Freiburg (2½hr., DM43); and Stuttgart (3hr., DM56). The **tourist office,** Bahnhofspl. 13, is to the right of the train station. Ask about the **Gästekarte** (DM1.50 per day), which provides unlimited bus transit in Konstanz and reduced admission to some sights for those staying two nights or more. (☎13 30 30. Open Apr.-Oct. M-F 9am-6:30pm, Sa 9am-1pm; Nov.-Mar. M-F 9am-noon and 2-5pm.) Reserve ahead for the marvelous **Jugendherberge Kreuzlingen (HI),** Promenadenstr. 7, which is actually in Switzerland but is closer to downtown Konstanz than the other hostel. From the station, turn left, cross the metal bridge over the tracks, turn right, go through the parking lot to checkpoint "Klein Venedig," bear left along Seestr., continue straight on the gravel path instead of following the sharp curve right, go past the gate and goats, then head right through the castle parking lot and up the hill. (From Germany ☎00 41 (71) 688 26 63; from Switzerland ☎ (071) 688 26 63. Breakfast included. Reception 8-9:30am and 5-9pm. Curfew 11pm. Open Mar.-Nov. 23SFr/DM28.) **Jugendherberge "Otto-Moericke-Turm" (HI),** Zur Allmannshöhe 18, is less luxurious, but has a great view. Take bus #4 from the station to "Jugendherberge" (7th stop), backtrack and head straight down Zur Allmannshöhe. (☎322 60. Breakfast and dinner included. Sheets DM6. Reception Apr.-Oct. 3-10pm; Nov.-Mar. 5-10pm. Curfew 10pm. Lockout 9:30am-noon. Call ahead. DM42, under 27 DM37; members only.) Get **groceries** at **Edeka,** at Münzg. near Fischmarkt. (Open M-F 8am-8pm, Sa 8am-4pm.) **Postal code:** 78462.

LINDAU IM BODENSEE ☎08382

Tourists come to soak in Lindau's balmy climate and wander among the 14th-century gabled houses along **Maximilianstr.** The **Cavazzen-Haus** in the Marktpl. holds the **Stadtmuseum,** including a collection of mechanized musical instruments. (Open Apr.-Oct. Tu-Su 10am-noon and 2-5pm. DM5, students DM3.) Roulette wheels spin and wallets thin at the **Spielbank** (casino) by the Seebrücke. (☎50 51. No jeans, tie required after 5pm. Bring passport. 21+. DM5. Open daily 3pm-3am.) The largest of Lindau's four **beaches** is **Eichwald,** a 30-minute walk away from town with your back to the island along Uferweg. (Open M-F 9:30am-7:30pm, Sa-Su 9am-8pm. DM5.) To reach the quieter **Lindenhofbad,** take bus #1 or 2 to Anheggerstr. and then bus #4 to Alwind. (Open daily 10am-8pm. DM4, students DM3.) You can rent a **boat** on the left of the casino, next to the bridge. (Open daily mid-Mar. to mid.-Sept. 9am-9pm. Rowboats DM12; paddle boats DM14-18; motorboat DM45.)

Trains run to Konstanz (2hr., DM28), as do **ferries** (3½hr., 3-6 per day, DM18.80). The **tourist office,** Ludwigstr. 68, is across from the train station. (☎26 00 30; www.lindau-tourismus.de. Open mid-June to early Sept. M-Sa 9am-1pm and 2-7pm; May to mid-June and Sept. M-F 9am-1pm and 2-6pm, Sa 9am-1pm; Apr. and Oct. M-F 9am-1pm and 2-5pm, Sa 9am-1pm; Nov.-Mar. M-F 9am-noon and 2-5pm.) The spectacular **Jugendherberge (HI),** Herbergsweg 11, lies across the Seebrücke off Bregenzer Str. (☎967 10. Breakfast included. Reception 7am-midnight. Curfew midnight. Under 27 and families with young children only. Dorms DM29.) **Park-Camping Lindau Am See,** Frauenhofer Str. 20, is 3km east of the island on the mainland; take bus #1 or 2 to Anheggerstr., then bus #3 (dir. Zech) to the end of the line. (☎722 36. DM9.50 per person; DM4 per tent. *Kurtaxe* DM1.50.) Pick up **groceries** at **Plus,** in the basement of the department store at the corner of In der Grub and Cramerg. (Open M-F 8:30am-6:30pm, Sa 8am-1pm.) **Postal code:** 88131

BAVARIA (BAYERN)

Bavaria is the Germany of Teutonic myth, Wagnerian opera, and the Brothers Grimm fairy tales. From the Baroque cities along the Danube to Mad King Ludwig's castles high in the Alps, the region draws more tourists than any other part of the country. Most foreigners' notions of Germany are inextricably tied to this land of *Biergartens* and *Lederhosen;* mostly rural, Catholic, and conservative, it contrasts sharply with the rest of the country. Local authorities still use Bavaria's proper name, *Freistaat Bayern* (Free State of Bavaria), and its traditions and dialect have been preserved. Residents have always been Bavarians first and Germans second.

REMINDER. HI-affiliated hostels in Bavaria do not admit guests over age 26, although an exception is usually made for those with young children.

MUNICH (MÜNCHEN) ☎089

The capital and cultural center of Bavaria, Munich is a sprawling, relatively liberal metropolis in the midst of solidly conservative southern Germany. The two cities of Munich and Berlin express the split German character: Munich's sensual merriment—most obvious during the wild *Fasching* (Jan. 7-Feb. 27, 2001) and the legendary *Oktoberfest* (Sept. 22-Oct. 7, 2001)—contrasts with Berlin's fragmented, avant-garde sensibility. Since the Bavarian Golden Age of the 18th and 19th centuries and the devastation of WWII (when less than 3% of the city was left intact), Munich has proved resilient, and today basks in Western German postwar economic glory. World-class museums, handsome parks and buildings, and a rambunctious arts scene create a city of astonishing vitality.

GETTING THERE AND GETTING AROUND

Flights: Flughafen München (☎97 52 13 13). S-Bahn #8 connects the airport to the Hauptbahnhof every 20min. DM15.20 or 8 strips on the *Streifenkarte*. A **Lufthansa shuttle bus** runs the same route with a pickup at the Nordfriedhof U-Bahn stop in Schwabing. Buses leave from Arnulfstr., on the northern side of the train station, every 20min. 6:50am-7:50pm, and return from Terminal A *(Zentralbereich)* and Terminal D every 20min. 7:55am-8:55pm. DM16, round-trip DM26.

Trains: The **Hauptbahnhof** (☎22 33 12 56, info ☎ (0180) 599 66 33). Station open 6am-10:30pm. To: **Berlin** (7½hr., 2 per hr., DM277, youth DM222); **Frankfurt** (3½hr., 3 per hr., DM147, DM118); **Cologne** (6hr., 2 per hr., DM173, DM138); **Hamburg** (6hr., 2 per hr., DM268, DM214); **Amsterdam** (9hr., every hr., DM248, DM198); **Innsbruck** (2hr., every hr., DM48, DM37); **Paris** (10hr., DM194, DM156); **Prague** (8½hr., 6 per day, DM113, DM85); **Salzburg** (1¾hr., every hr., DM41, DM30); **Vienna** (5hr., every hr., DM106, DM82); **Zürich** (5hr., every 2 hr., DM110, DM85).

Public Transportation: MVV runs Su-Th 5am-12:30am, F-Sa 5am-2am. Eurail, Inter-Rail, and German passes valid on the S-Bahn only. Buy tickets at blue *MVV-Fahrausweise* machines and validate them in the "E" boxes before entering the platform. Transit maps are at the tourist office, EurAide, and MVV counters in the train station. A *Streifenkarte* (11-strip ticket) costs DM16 and can be used by more than 1 person. **Single ride** DM3.80 or 2 strips; **Kurzstrecke** (short trip) tickets DM1.90 or 1 strip, valid for 2 stops on the U- or S-Bahn, or 4 stops on a streetcar or bus. Cancel 2 strips per zone beyond the city center. **Single-Tageskarte** (single-day ticket) DM9, valid for 1 day. **Partner-Tageskarte** (DM14) can be used by 2 adults, 4 children under 18, and a dog for 1 day. Consider the **3-Day Pass** (DM22) or the **München Welcome Card,** available at the tourist office and in many hotels and valid for public transportation (1-day DM12; 3-day DM29; group ticket for up to 5 DM42). The card includes a 50% discount on many museums and on Radius bike rental (see below), and can be purchased at the MVV office behind tracks #31 and 32 in the Hauptbahnhof.

Taxis: Taxi-Zentrale (☎216 11 or 194 10) in front of the station and throughout the city.

Car Rental: Swing, Schellingstr. 139 (☎523 20 05). Prices from DM45 per day. **Avis** (☎550 12 12), **Europcar/National** (☎550 13 41), **Hertz** (☎550 22 56), and **Sixt Budget** (☎550 24 47) have offices upstairs in the station. Prices from DM130 per day.

Bike Rental: Radius Bikes (☎59 61 13), in the Hauptbahnhof, behind the lockers opposite tracks #30-31. From DM5 per hr., DM25 per day, DM75 per week. Deposit DM100, passport, or credit card. Students and Eurailpass holders receive a 10% discount. Open daily May to mid-Oct. 10am-6pm.

Hitchhiking: *Let's Go* does not recommend hitchhiking. For ride-sharing, scan the bulletin boards in the **Mensa,** Leopoldstr. 13. Hitchers try *Autobahn* on-ramps; standing behind the blue sign with the white auto incurs a fine. To: **Salzburg,** take U1 or 2 to "Karl-Preis-Platz"; **Stuttgart,** take streetcar #17 to "Amalienburgstr." or S2 to "Obermenzing," then bus #73 or 75 to "Blutenburg"; **Nürnberg** and **Berlin,** take U6 to "Studentenstadt" and walk 500m to the Frankfurter Ring; **Bodensee** and **Switzerland,** take U4 or 5 to "Heimeranpl.," then bus #33 to "Siegenburger Str."

ORIENTATION

Munich's center is encircled by the main **Ring** and quartered by two thoroughfares which cross at the **Marienplatz** and meet the traffic rings at **Karlsplatz** (a.k.a. **Stachus**) in the west, **Isartorplatz** in the east, **Odeonsplatz** in the north, and **Sendlinger Tor** in the south. The **Hauptbahnhof** is west of Karlspl. East of the Isartor, the **Isar** flows south-north by the city center. To get to Marienpl. from the station, go straight on Bayerstr. to Karlspl. and continue through Karlstor to Neuhauser Str., which becomes Kaufingerstr. before it reaches Marienpl. Or, take S1-8 (two stops from the Hauptbahnhof, dir. Ostbahnhof) to Marienpl.

The **Residenz** palace sprawls at Odeonspl.; **Ludwigstraße** stretches north from there toward the university district before turning into **Leopoldstraße,** and heading farther toward **Schwabing.** This district, also known as "Schwabylon," is student country. To the east of Schwabing sprawls the **Englischer Garten;** to the west is the **Olympiazentrum,** constructed for the 1972 Olympic games and surrounded by the verdant **Olympiapark.** Farther west sits the posh **Nymphenburg,** built around the **Schloß Nymphenburg.** Southwest of Marienpl., **Sendlinger Str.** leads to the Sendlinger Tor. From there, Lindwurmstr. goes to Goethepl., from which Mozartstr. runs to **Theresienwiese,** site of Oktoberfest.

PRACTICAL INFORMATION

TOURIST AND FINANCIAL SERVICES

Tourist Offices: Fremdenverkehrsamt (☎23 33 02 57; www.munich-tourist.de), in front of the train station. Books rooms for free with 10-15% deposit. Purchase the **München Welcome Card** here (see **Public Transportation,** above). **EurAide in English** (☎59 38 89; www.euraide.de), along track #11 (room 3) of the Hauptbahnhof. Open June-Oktoberfest daily 7:45am-noon and 1-6pm; Oct.-Apr. M-F 8am-noon and 1-4pm, Sa 8am-noon; May daily 7:45am-noon and 1-4:30pm.

Consulates: Canada, Tal 29 (☎219 95 70); **Ireland,** Mauerkircherstr. 1a (☎98 57 23); **South Africa,** Sendlinger-Tor-Pl. 5 (☎231 16 30); **UK,** Bürkleinstr. 10, 4th fl. (☎21 10 90); **US:** Königinstr. 5 (☎288 80).

Budget Travel: Council Travel, Adalbertstr. 32 (☎38 83 89 70), near the university. Open M-F 10am-1pm and 2-6:30pm, Sa 10am-3pm. **DER Reisebüro** (☎55 14 02 00; www.der.de) in the Hauptbahnhof. Open M-F 9:30am-6pm and Sa 10am-1pm.

Currency Exchange: ReiseBank (☎551 08 37) has a branch in front of the main entrance to the train station on Bahnhofpl. (open daily 6am-11pm), and another around the corner from EurAide at track #11 (open M-Sa 7:30am-7:15pm, Su 9:30am-12:30pm and 1-4:45pm). Western Union services available.

American Express: Promenadepl. 6 (24hr. ☎(0130) 85 31 00; or 29 09 00), in Hotel Bayerischer Hof. Open M-F 9am-5:30pm, Sa 9:30am-12:30pm. **Branch** at Kaufingerstr. 24 (☎22 80 13 87), by the Frauenkirche. Open M-F 9am-6pm, Sa 10am-2pm.

LOCAL SERVICES

Luggage Storage: At the **train station** (*Gepäckaufbewahrung*). Open M-F 6:30am-11pm, Sa-Su 7:30am-10pm. DM4 per piece per day. Lockers in the main hall and opposite tracks #16, 24, and 28-36. DM2-4 per 24hr.

Gay and Lesbian Resources: Gay services information (☎260 30 56). **Lesbian information** in the **LeTra Lesbentraum,** Angertorstr. 3 (☎725 42 72). Phones staffed M and W 2:30-5pm; Tu 10:30am-1pm; Th 7-9pm.

Ticket Agencies: To order **tickets by phone** call **München Ticket** (☎54 81 81 81).

Laundromat: City SB-Waschcenter, Paul-Heyse-Str. 21. From the station, turn right on Bayerstr., then left on Paul-Heyse-Str. Wash DM6, dry DM1 per 10min. Open daily 7am-11pm. **Münz Waschsalon,** Amalienstr. 61, near the university. Wash DM6.20, soap DM1, dry DM1 per 10min. Open M-F 8am-6:30pm, Sa 8am-1pm.

EMERGENCY AND COMMUNICATIONS

Emergency: Police: ☎110. **Ambulance** and **Fire:** ☎112. **Medical:** ☎59 44 75.

Pharmacy: Bahnhof-Apotheke, Bahnhofpl. 2 (☎59 41 19), outside the train station. Open M-F 8am-6:30pm, Sa 8am-2pm. Call ☎59 44 75 for 24hr. service (in German).

Medical Assistance: Klinikum Rechts der Isar, across the river on Ismaninger Str. U4 or 5 to "Max-Weber-Platz." UK and US consulates carry lists of English-speaking doctors.

Internet Access: Times Square Internet Café, Bayerstr. 10a, on the south side of the train station. DM4.50 per 15min. **Internet-Café,** Nymphenburger Str. 145, on the corner of Landshuter Allee. U1 to "Rotkreuzplatz." Free with pasta (DM5.30-7.50) or pizza (DM5.50-8.50); otherwise, DM5 per 30min. Open daily 11am-4am.

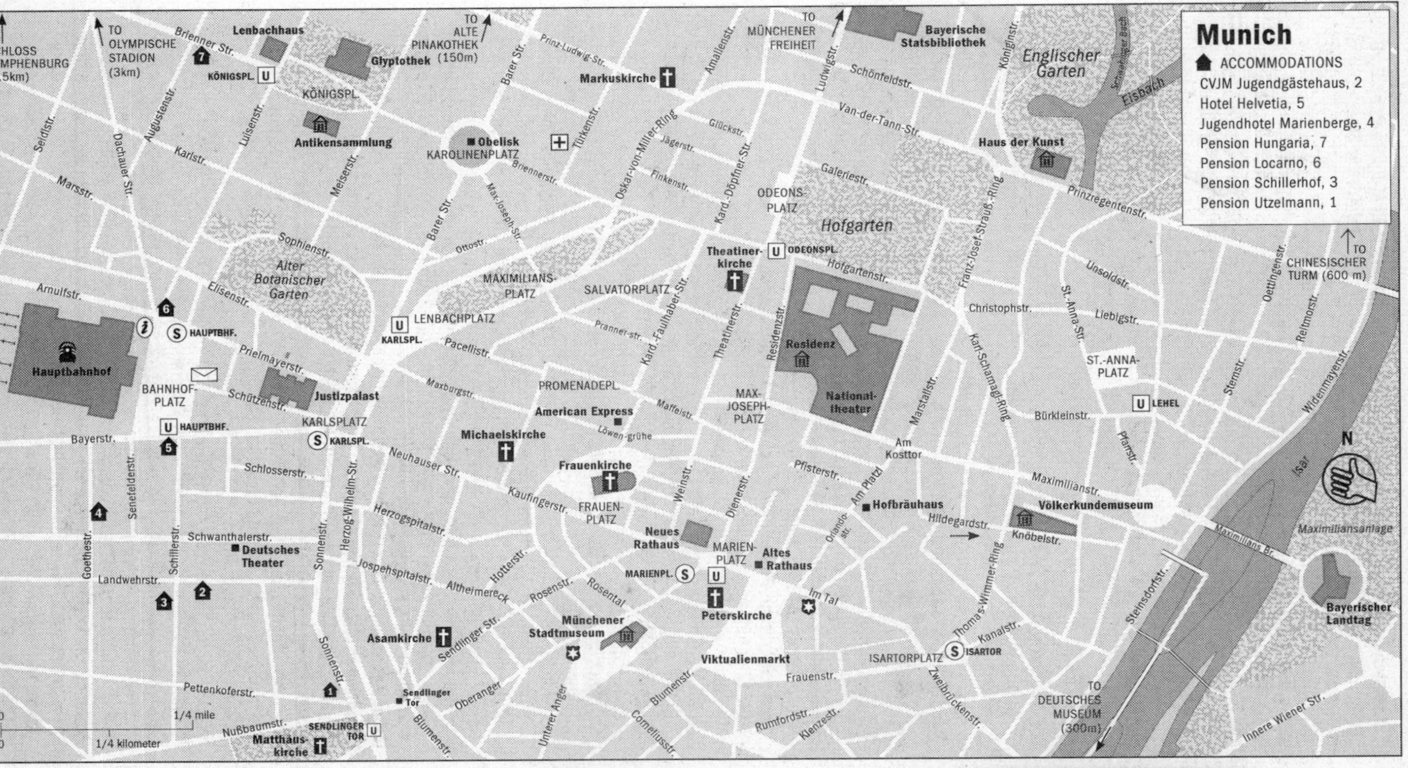
Munich
ACCOMMODATIONS
CVJM Jugendgästehaus, 2
Hotel Helvetia, 5
Jugendhotel Marienberge, 4
Pension Hungaria, 7
Pension Locarno, 6
Pension Schillerhof, 3
Pension Utzelmann, 1
TO SCHLOSS NYMPHENBURG (4.5km)
TO OLYMPISCHE STADION (3km)
Lenbachhaus
Glyptothek
TO ALTE PINAKOTHEK (150m)
KÖNIGSPL.
Antikensammlung
Obelisk
KAROLINENPLATZ
Markuskirche
TO MÜNCHENER FREIHEIT
Bayerische Statsbibliothek
Englischer Garten
Haus der Kunst
ODEONSPLATZ
Hofgarten
Theatiner-kirche
ODEONSPL.
TO CHINESISCHER TURM (600 m)
Alter Botanischer Garten
MAXIMILIANSPLATZ
SALVATORPLATZ
Residenz
National-theater
ST.-ANNA-PLATZ
LEHEL
Hauptbahnhof
HAUPTBHF.
LENBACHPLATZ
KARLSPL.
BAHNHOFPLATZ
Justizpalast
PROMENADEPL.
American Express
MAX-JOSEPH-PLATZ
KARLSPLATZ
Michaelskirche
Frauenkirche
FRAUENPLATZ
Hofbräuhaus
Völkerkundemuseum
Deutsches Theater
Neues Rathaus
MARIENPLATZ
Altes Rathaus
MARIENPL.
Peterskirche
Münchener Stadtmuseum
Asamkirche
Viktualienmarkt
ISARTORPLATZ
ISARTOR
Bayerischer Landtag
Maximiliansanlage
Isar
N
Sendlinger Tor
SENDLINGER TOR
Matthäuskirche
TO DEUTSCHES MUSEUM (300m)
1/4 mile
1/4 kilometer

Post Office: Across from the Hauptbahnhof on Bahnhofpl. Open M-F 7am-8pm, Sa 8am-4pm, Su 9am-3pm. Address mail to be held: *Postlagernde Briefe* für First name SURNAME, Hauptpostamt, München **80335,** Germany.

ACCOMMODATIONS AND CAMPING

Munich accommodations are usually seedy, expensive, or booked solid; during Oktoberfest, only the last category exists. In summer, call before noon or book a few weeks ahead. If planning an extended stay, consult the *Mitwohnzentrale*, or try bargaining with a *Pension* owner. Remember: **Bavarian HI hostels do not accept guests over age 26.** Don't even think of sleeping in public areas, including the Hauptbahnhof; police patrol frequently all night long.

HOSTELS

Euro Youth Hotel, Senefelderstr. 5 (☎59 90 88 11; www.euro-youth-hotel.de). From the Bahnhofspl. exit of the Hauptbahnhof, make a right on Bayerstr. and a left on Senefelderstr. Breakfast buffet DM7.90. Laundry DM6. Dorms DM29; doubles DM42, with shower, telephone, and breakfast DM60; triples and quads DM36.

Jugendlager Kapuzinerhölzl ("The Tent"), In den Kirschen 30 (☎141 43 00; www.the-tent.de). Streetcar #17 from the Hauptbahnhof (dir. Amalienburgstr.) to "Botanischer Garten"; go straight on Franz-Schrank-Str. and left at In den Kirschen. Sleep under a big circus tent on a wooden floor. Laundry DM4. Internet DM2 per 15min. Free city tours (W 9am). Passport required as deposit. Open mid-June to Aug. DM15 for foam pad, blankets, bathrooms, shower (not necessarily warm), breakfast, and enthusiastic management; beds DM19. **Camping** DM8 per person; DM8 per site.

Jugendherberge Pullach Burg Schwaneck (HI), Burgweg 4-6 (☎793 06 43), in a castle 12km outside the city center. S7 (dir. Wolfratshausen) to "Pullach." Exit the station on the Munich side and walk toward the soccer field down Margarethenstr.; follow signs (8min.). Breakfast included. Dinner DM8. Reception 4-11pm. Curfew 11:30pm. Dorms DM23; singles DM37.50; doubles DM35.50 per person; quads DM26 per person.

Jugendherberge München (HI), Wendl-Dietrich-Str. 20 (☎13 11 56; email jhmuenchen@djh-bayern.de). U1 (dir. Westfriedhof) to "Rotkreuzpl." Go down Wendl-Dietrich-Str. to the left of the *Schwestern Schule* building; the entrance is on the right. The most "central" HI hostel, 3km from the city. Safes available. Breakfast and sheets included. Bike rental DM24. Mandatory DM20 key deposit. Reception 24hr. Check-in after 11am, but lines form before 9am. Reservations only accepted a week in advance; if you get one, arrive by 6pm or call ahead. Men-only dorm DM25; coed dorms DM30.

4 you münchen, Hirtenstr. 18 (☎552 16 60; www.the4you.de), near the Hauptbahnhof. Exit at Arnulfstr., go left, right onto Pfefferstr., then left on Hirtenstr. Breakfast buffet DM8. Sheets DM5. Key deposit DM20. Dorms DM26-32; singles DM56; doubles DM40. Over 27 15% surcharge. In adjoining hotel, singles with bath DM79; doubles with bath DM129; extra bed DM49.

Jugendgästehaus Thalkirchen (HI), Miesingstr. 4 (☎723 65 50; email BineMunich@aol.com). U1 or 2 to "Sendlinger Tor," then U3 (dir. Fürstenrieder West) to "Thalkirchen." Take the Thalkirchnerpl. exit and follow Schäftlarnstr. toward Innsbruck and bear right around the curve, then follow Frauenbergstr. and head left on Münchner Str. Breakfast and sheets included. Laundry DM10. Reception 7am-1am. Check-in 2-6pm. Curfew 1am. Dorms DM37.50; singles DM42.50.

CVJM Jugendgästehaus, Landwehrstr. 13 (☎552 14 10; fax 550 42 82; email info@cvjm-muenchen.org). Take the Bayerstr. exit from the train station, head down Goethestr. or Schillerstr. and take the 2nd left onto Landwehrstr. Central location with modern rooms. Coed rooms for married couples only. Breakfast included. Reception 8am-12:30am. Curfew 12:30am-7am. Reservations can be made a year ahead. Closed during Easter and Dec. 20-Jan. 7. Singles DM53; doubles DM90; triples DM126. Rates lower Dec.-Feb., higher during Oktoberfest. Over 26 16% surcharge.

Jump In, Hochstr. 51 (☎48 95 34 37; www.jump-in.net), a new place founded by a brother and sister tired of impersonal hostels. S1-8 to "Rosenheimer Pl.," then take the

Gasteig exit to the left and walk left on Hochstr. (10min.). Or, take streetcar #27 or bus #51 to "Ostfriedhof." Every room with sink. Sheets DM5. Laundry DM5. Reception 10am-noon and 5-10pm. Mattresses DM29; beds DM35; doubles DM39.

Haus International, Elisabethstr. 87 (☎12 00 60). U2 (dir. Feldmoching) to "Hohenzollernpl.," then streetcar #12 (dir. Romanplatz) or bus #33 (dir. Aidenbachstr.) to "Barbarastr." The beige building behind the BP gas station. Free indoor pool, small beer garden, TV room, and groovy disco with bar. Singles DM55, with bath DM85; doubles DM98, with shower DM138; triples DM144; quads DM180; quints DM210.

HOTELS AND PENSIONEN

Hotel Helvetia, Schillerstr. 6 (☎590 68 50; email hotel-helvetia@t-online.de), next to Vereinsbank, to the right of the station. Friendliest hotel in Munich. Breakfast included. Singles DM55-65; doubles DM72-95, with shower DM99-115; triples DM105-126.

Hotel Kurpfalz, Schwanthaler Str. 121 (☎540 98 60; www.munich-hotels.com). Exit the station on Bayerstr., turn right and walk 5-6 blocks down Bayerstr., veer left onto Holzapfelstr., and make a right onto Schwanthaler Str. (10min.). Or, take streetcar #18 or 19 to "Holzapfelstr." Satellite TVs, phones, private baths, and hardwood furniture in all rooms. Breakfast buffet included. Free email; Internet surfing DM5 per 30min. Singles from DM89; doubles from DM109; triples (doubles with cots) DM165.

Hotel-Pension Utzelmann, Pettenkoferstr. 6 (☎59 48 89). From the station, walk 4 blocks down Schillerstr. and go left on Pettenkofer. Breakfast included. Reception 7am-10pm. Singles DM55, with shower DM95, with bath DM130; doubles DM98, DM115, DM150; triples DM140, DM160, DM180; quads DM170, with shower DM190.

Pension Locarno, Bahnhofspl. 5 (☎55 51 64; www.deutschland-hotel.de/muc/locarno.htm). From the station's main entrance walk left across Bahnhofspl. and look for the "Pension" sign. Reception Su-M 7:30am-midnight, Tu-Sa 7:30am-5am. Singles DM55-75; doubles DM85; triples DM125; quads DM140.

Pension Schillerhof, Schillerstr. 21 (☎59 42 70; www.hotel-schillerhof.de). Exit onto Bahnhofpl. from the station, turn right, and walk 2 blocks down Schillerstr. Breakfast included. Reception 6am-10pm. Reservations can be made online. Singles DM60-80; doubles DM90-120; extra bed DM20. Oktoberfest surcharge DM25-40 per person.

Pension Central, Bayerstr. 55 (☎543 98 46). Go right out the Bayerstr. exit of the station. Reception 24hr. Singles DM65, with bath DM75; doubles DM95, DM110-120; triples DM120; quads DM160-180; quints DM200-220.

Pension Frank, Schellingstr. 24 (☎28 14 51; www.pension-frank.de). U3 or 6 to "Universität." Take the Schellingstr. exit, then the first right onto Schellingstr. Fabulous location for cafe and bookstore aficionados. Breakfast included. Reception 7:30am-10pm. Check-out 11am. Dorms DM40; singles DM55-65; doubles DM95.

Pension am Kaiserplatz, Kaiserpl. 12 (☎34 91 90). Near tons of nightlife—good location if you doubt your sense of direction after a couple of beers. U3 or 6 to "Münchener Freiheit." Take the escalator to Herzogstr., then go left 3 blocks to Viktoriastr. Take a left at Viktoriastr.; it's at the end of the street on the right (10min.). Breakfast included. Reception 7am-9pm. Dorms DM40; singles DM59; doubles DM89, with shower DM99-105; each additional person DM40.

Pension Geiger, Steinheilstr. 1 (☎52 15 56). U2 to "Theresienstr." Exit on Augustenstr. S.O. and walk down Theresienstr. toward Kopierladen München. Take a right on Enhuberstr. and a left on Steinheilstr.; enter through the double doors on the right. Family-run in a quiet neighborhood. Showers DM2. Reception (2 floors up) 8am-9pm. Arrive by 6pm or call. Closed Dec. 24-Jan. 31. Singles DM55-DM80; doubles DM98-DM108.

CAMPING

Campingplatz Thalkirchen, Zentralländstr. 49 (☎723 17 07). U1 or 2 to "Sendlinger Tor," then #3 to "Thalkirchen," and change to bus #57 (20min.). From the bus stop, cross the street on the left and take a right onto the footpath next to the road. Jogging and bike paths. Showers DM2. Laundry. Curfew 11pm. Open mid-Mar. to late Oct. DM8.40 per person, DM2.50 per child under 14; DM5.50-7 per tent; DM8.50 per car.

FOOD

The **Viktualienmarkt,** south of Marienpl., is Munich's gastronomic center. (Open M-F 10am-8pm, Sa 8am-4pm.) To sink your fangs into an authentic Bavarian lunch, grab a *Brez'n* (pretzel) and spread it with *Leberwurst* or cheese (DM5-6). The university district off **Ludwigstraße** is unpretentiously hip. Many reasonably-priced restaurants and cafes cluster on **Schellingstr., Amalienstr.,** and **Türkenstr.** Ride U3 or 6 to "Universität." *Munich Found* (DM4) and *Prinz* (DM5) list restaurants, cafes, and bars. Fruit and vegetable **markets** are held throughout the city, many on Bayerstr. **Plus supermarket,** Schellingstr. 38 (open M-F 8:30am-7pm, Sa 8am-3pm) and **A&P Tengelmann,** in the Karlspl. subway station, meet **grocery** needs. From the Hauptbahnhof, walk east on Bayerstr., make a right onto Sonnenstr., and enter the U-Bahn after Schlosserstr. (Open M-F 8:30am-8pm, Sa 8am-4pm.)

Marché, Neuhauser Str., between Karlspl. and Marienpl. The top floor of this monstrous eatery offers cafeteria-style, make-your-own-meal displays. Great vegetarian selections. Top floor open 11am-10pm, bottom floor open 8am-11pm.

Weißes Bräuhaus, Tal 7, across from McDonalds at the end of Marienpl. Brimming with traditional Bavarian dishes (DM8.90-25). Open daily 7:30am-midnight.

News Bar, Amalienstr. 55, at the corner of Schellingstr. Trendy cafe serving large portions at reasonable prices. Crepes DM12-14. Open daily 7:30am-2am.

Türkenhof, Türkenstr. 78, offers a wide selection of global cuisine. Immensely popular with the low-key student population. Variable daily menu with numerous veggie options; entrees DM10.80-15.80. Open M-Th and Su 11am-1am, F-Sa 11am-2am.

Beim Sedlmayr, Westenriederstr. 14, off the Viktualienmarkt. Anyone craving *Weißwurst* (DM7) will love this slice of Bavaria. Specials DM7-27. Beer DM5.70 for 0.5L. Open daily 9am-10pm. Kitchen open M-F 11am-9pm, Sa 8am-4pm.

Schelling Salon, Schellingstr. 54. Founded in 1872, this pool joint has racked the balls of Lenin, Rilke, and Hitler. Offerings include breakfast (DM5.50-9.50), *Wurst* (DM6-7), and a free **billiard museum.** Open Th-M 6:30am-1am; museum open at night Sa-Su.

Gollier, Gollierstr. 83. U4 or 5 or S7 or 27 to "Heimeranpl.," then walk 2 blocks north on Garmischer Str. and turn left on Gollierstr. Delicious vegetarian fare (DM6-19). Open M-F noon-3pm and 5pm-midnight, Sa 5pm-midnight, Su 10am-midnight.

BEER, BEER, AND MORE BEER

To most visitors, Munich means beer. There are four main types of beer served in Munich: **Helles** and **Dunkles,** delicious light and dark beers; **Weißbier,** a cloudy blond wheat beer; and **Radler** ("cyclist's brew"), half beer and half lemon soda. The six great Munich labels are *Augustiner, Hacker-Pschorr, Hofbräu, Löwenbräu, Paulaner,* and *Spaten-Franziskaner;* most restaurants will serve only one. Munich's beer typically has a 3.5% alcohol content. The longest beer festival in the world, and an incredibly popular one, is Munich's **Oktoberfest** (Sept. 22-Oct. 7, 2001), at **Theresienwiese** (U4 or 5).

Hirschgarten, Hirschgarten 1. U1 to "Rotkreuzpl.," then streetcar #12 to "Romanpl." The largest beer garden in Europe (seating 9000) is boisterous and pleasant, but somewhat remote. *Maß* DM9.30. Open daily 9am-midnight; kitchen open until 10pm.

Augustinerkeller, Arnulfstr. 52, at Zirkus-Krone-Str. S1-8 to "Hackerbrücke." Founded in 1824, Augustiner is viewed by most Müncheners as the finest beer garden in town. *Maß* DM10.50. Open daily 10:30am-midnight or 1am.

Hofbräuhaus, Am Platzl 9, 2 blocks from Marienpl. In 1589, Bavarian Duke Wilhelm the Pious founded the Hofbräuhaus for the worship of Germany's most revered beverages. 15,000-30,000L of beer are sold per day. Maß DM11.40. Open daily 9am-midnight.

Am Seehaus, Kleinhesselohe 3. U6 to "Dietlindenstr.," then bus #44 (dir. Giesing) to "Osterwaldstr." On the Kleinhesseloher See in the Englischer Garten. Beloved by locals for the lack of tourists. *Maß* (DM11). Open M-F 11am-midnight, Sa-Su 10am-midnight. Beer garden closes at 11pm.

Taxisgarten, Taxisstr. 12. U1 to "Rotkreuzpl.," then bus #83 or 177 to "Gern," and walk one block east on Tizianstr. One of few places that serves a green variety of the normally orange *Obazer* (a mix of cheeses, DM3.80). *Maß* DM10.20. Open daily 11am-11pm.

SIGHTS

MARIENPLATZ AND ENVIRONS. Sacred stone edifices dot the area around Marienpl., the social nexus of Munich. An ornate 17th-century monument dedicated to the Virgin Mary, the **Mariensäule** commemorates the resistance of the city when fighting against the Swedes during the Thirty Years War. At the neo-Gothic **Neues Rathaus,** the **Glockenspiel** chimes with a display of jousting knights and dancing coopers. *(Daily 11am, noon, and 5pm.)* At bedtime *(9pm),* a mechanical watchman marches out and the Guardian Angel escorts the town's symbol, the *Münchner Kindl* (Munich Child) to bed. *(Tower open M-F 9am-7pm, Sa-Su 10am-7pm. DM3, under 18 DM1.50.)* The **Altes Rathaus** tower, to the right of the Neues Rathaus, displays all of Munich's coats of arms since its inception as a city, except the swastika-bearing one from the Nazi era. One block toward the Hauptbahnhof on Kaufingerstr., the onion-domed towers of the 15th-century **Frauenkirche** are among Munich's most notable landmarks. *(Open Apr.-Oct. M-Sa 10am-5pm. DM4, students DM2.)*

SOUTH OF MARIENPLATZ. The golden interior of the 11th-century **Peterskirche,** just south of Marienpl., was Baroquified in the 18th century. Over 300 steps scale the tower, dubbed *"Alter Peter"* by locals. *(Rindermarkt and Peterspl. Open M-Sa 9am-5pm, Su 10am-7pm. DM2.50, students DM1.50.)* Mad King Ludwig (of castle fame) rests with 40-odd other Wittelsbachs in the crypt of the 16th-century Jesuit **Michaelskirche.** *(On Neuhauser Str. Crypt open M-F 9:30am-4:30pm, Sa 9:30am-2:30pm. DM2, students and under 16 DM1.)* Farther along Sendlinger Str. lies the Rococo **Asamkirche,** named for the Asam brothers, who promised God to build the church if they survived a shipwreck. They did. *(Sendlinger Str. 32. Tours June-Sept. Sa at noon. DM5.)*

RESIDENZ. Down the pedestrian zone from Odeonspl., the richly decorated **Residenz** (palace) forms the material vestiges of the Wittelsbach dynasty. The grounds now house several museums, a beautifully landscaped **Hofgarten,** and a bejeweled **Schatzkammer,** or treasury. *(Open Apr. to mid-Oct. M-W and F-Su 9am-6pm, Th 9am-8pm; late Oct. to Mar. daily 10am-4pm. Last admission 1 hr. before closing. DM8; students, seniors, and groups DM6, children under 15 free with adult.)* The **Residenzmuseum** comprises the former Wittelsbach apartments and State Rooms, a collection of European porcelain, and a 17th-century court chapel. German tours of the Residenzmuseum meet just outside the museum entrance. The walls of the museum's **Ahnengalerie,** hung with 120 "family portraits," trace the royal lineage in an unusual manner. *(Max-Joseph-pl. 3. U3-6 to Odeonspl. Same hours as Schatzkammer. DM8, students and children DM6. Residenzmuseum tours Su and W 11am, Tu and Sa 2pm. DM8, Su DM10. Combination ticket to Schatzkammer and Residenzmuseum DM14, students and seniors DM11.)*

SCHLOß NYMPHENBURG. After 10 years of trying for an heir, Ludwig I celebrated the birth of his son Maximilian in 1662 by erecting an elaborate summer playground. Check out the "Gallery of Beauties"—whenever a woman caught Ludwig's fancy, he would have her portrait painted. A few lakes and four manors also inhabit the palace grounds. *(Streetcar #17, dir. Amalienburgstr. Palace open Apr. to mid-Oct. M-W and F-Su 9am-6pm, Th 9am-8pm; late Oct. to Mar. daily 10am-4pm. Schloß DM7, students DM5; entire complex DM15, students DM12. Grounds open until 9:30pm. Free.)*

ENGLISCHER GARTEN. On sunny days, all of Munich flocks here to bike, fly kites, play badminton, or ride horseback. The grounds contain a Japanese tea house, Chinese pagoda, and Greek temple, as well as nude sunbathing areas, marked "FKK" on signs and maps. Nudity + lots of *Bratwurst* and *Bier* = consider yourself warned. Head to the bridge on Prinzregentenstr., near the Staatsgalerie Moderner Kunst, to watch Müncheners surf the rapids of the artificial Eisbach river.

MUSEUMS

Munich is a supreme museum city, and many of the city's offerings would require days for exhaustive perusal. A day pass (DM30) to all of Munich's museums is sold at the tourist office and at many larger museums. All museums in Königspl. are accessible from U2: Königspl.

KÖNIGSPLATZ

Alte Pinakothek, Barerstr. 27. Commissioned by King Ludwig I, the last of the passionate Wittelsbacher art collectors, this world-renowned hall houses Munich's most precious collection—including works by Titian, da Vinci, Raphael, Dürer, Rembrandt, and Rubens. Open Tu and W-Su 10am-5pm, Th 10am-8pm. DM7, students DM4; combination ticket for the Alte and the Neue Pinakothek DM12, students DM6.

Neue Pinakothek, Barerstr. 29, next to the Alte Pinakothek. Sleek space for 18th- to 20th-century works by van Gogh, Klimt, Cézanne, and Manet. Open W and F-M 10am-5pm, Th 10am-8pm. Same prices as Alte Pinakothek.

Glyptothek, Königspl. 3. Features 2400-year-old pediment figures from the Temple of Aphaea as well as Etruscan and Roman sculptures. Open Tu-W and F-Su 10am-5pm, Th 10am-8pm. DM6, students DM3.50. Tours Th at 6pm; free. Combination ticket for the Glyptothek and the Antikensammlung DM10, students DM5.

Antikensammlung, Königspl. 1, across from the Glyptothek. Flaunts a first-rate flock of vases and the other half of Munich's finest collection of ancient Greek and Etruscan pottery and jewelry. Open Tu and Th-Su 10am-5pm, W 10am-8pm. DM6, students DM3.50. Tours W at 6pm; free. Closed for renovations until Apr. 2001.

ELSEWHERE IN MUNICH

Deutsches Museum, Museumsinsel 1. S1-8: Isartor, or streetcar #18 to "Deutsches Museum." One of the world's best science and technology museums. Fascinating exhibits include the work bench upon which Otto Hahn split his first atom, and labyrinthine mining tunnels. Open daily 9am-5pm. DM12, students DM5.

BMW Museum, Petuelring 130. U3 to "Olympiazentrum." The ultimate driving museum features a fetching display of past, present, and future products of Bavaria's second-favorite export. Open daily 9am-5pm. Last entry 4pm. DM5.50, students DM4.

ZAM: Zentrum für Aussergewöhnliche Museen, (Center for Unusual Museums), Westenriederstr. 41. S1-8: Isartor, or streetcar #17 or 18. Holds such treasures as the Padlock Museum, the Museum of Easter Rabbits, and the Chamberpot Museum. Open daily 10am-6pm. DM8, students and children DM5.

ENTERTAINMENT

Munich's cultural cachet rivals the world's best. Theater offerings range from dramatic classics at the **Residenztheater** and **Volkstheater** to comic opera at the **Staatstheater am Gärtnerplatz** to experimental works at the **Theater im Marstall** in Nymphenburg (standing room tickets around DM10). Scores of small fringe theaters, cabaret stages, art cinemas, and artsy pubs cluster in **Schwabing.** Munich's July **opera festival** is held in the **Bayerische Staatsoper,** Maximilianstr. 11 (☎21 85 19 30 or ☎21 85 19 19); take U3-6 to "Odeonspl." or streetcar #19 to "Nationaltheater." During the regular season, standing and student tickets (DM7-20) to the numerous operas and ballets are sold at Maximilianstr. 11 (☎26 46 20), behind the opera house, or one hour before performances at the side entrance on Maximilianstr. (Box office open M-F 10am-6pm, Sa 10am-1pm. No performances Aug. to mid-Sept.) The opera festival is accompanied by a concert series in the Nymphenburg and Schleißheim palaces. The *Monatsprogramm* (DM2.50) lists schedules for all of Munich's stages, museums, and festivals.

NIGHTLIFE

Munich throws together Bavarian *Gemütlichkeit* and trendy cliquishness, the latter represented by *Schicki-Mickis*—club-going, coiffed and scented specimens of both sexes. A nighttime odyssey begins at one of Munich's beer gardens or beer halls; the alcohol keeps flowing at cafes and bars, which, except for Friday and Saturday nights, shut off their taps at 1am. The discos and dance clubs, sedate before midnight, rage relentlessly until 4am. The trendy bars, cafes, cabarets, and discos plugged into **Leopoldstr.** in **Schwabing** draw tourists from all over Europe. **Münchener Freiheit** is the most famous (and touristy) bar/cafe district. Grab *Munich Found, In München,* or *Prinz* at newsstands to find out what's up. Munich's gay scene centers in the **Golden Triangle,** stretching from south of the Sendlinger Tor through the Viktualienmarkt/Gärtnerpl. to the Isartor. Pick up *Rosa Seiten* at **Max&Milian Bookstore,** Ickstattstr. 2 (open M-F 10:30am-2pm and 3:30-8pm, Sa 11am-4pm), or at any gay locale for listings of gay nightlife and services.

Kunstpark Ost, Grafinger Str. 6. U5 or S1-8 to "Ostbahnhof"; follow signs for the "Kunstpark Ost" exit, turn right onto Friedenstr. and then left onto Grafinger Str. This huge complex with 40 different venues swarms with young people dancing the night away. Try the psychedelic-trance **Natraj Temple** (open F-Sa), the alternative cocktail and disco joint **K41** (open nightly), the very chill cigars and drinks mecca **Cohibar** (open W-Sa), or the risqué South American rock bar **Titty Twister** (open W-Sa).

Nachtwerk and Club, Landesberger Str. 185. Streetcar #18 or 19 or bus #83 to "Lautensackstr." The older, larger **Nachtwerk** spins mainstream dance tunes in a packed warehouse. Its little sister **Club** offers rock, trip-hop, house and acid jazz grooves. Cover for both DM10. Open daily 10pm-4am.

Reactor, Domagkstr. 33, in the Alabamahalle. U6: Alte Heide. With three other discos on a former military base in Schwabing. Techno and German oldies. Open F-Sa 9pm-4am.

Master's Home, Frauenstr. 11. U3 or 6 or S1-8 to Marienpl. A tremendous stuffed peacock greets visitors to the subterranean bar and *faux* private home. Mixed drinks DM11.50. Open daily 6:30pm-3am.

Lux, Reichenbachstr. 37. U-Bahn to "Frauenhofer." Large pastel asterisks decorate the walls of this popular hang-out. Drinks DM8-20. Open M-Th 6pm-1am, F-Sa 8pm-2am.

EXCURSIONS FROM MUNICH

DACHAU. At the entrance to Dachau, the first concentration camp and the model for the Nazi network of 3000 other camps, a photograph of one of Hitler's book burnings is accompanied by Heinrich Heine's prophetic words: "Once they burn books, they will end up burning people." The camp walls, gas chamber, and crematorium have been restored in a chillingly sparse memorial to the 206,000 prisoners who were interned here from 1933 to 1945. The **museum** examines pre-1930 anti-Semitism, the rise of Nazism, and the lives of prisoners through photographs, documents, and artifacts. Most exhibits have short English captions. (Open Tu-Su 9am-5pm. Films 22min.; screened in English at noon, 2, and 3:30pm.) Excellent English **tours** leave from the museum (July daily 12:30pm, Aug.-June Sa-Su and holidays 12:30pm; DM5 donation). From Munich, take **S2** (dir. Petershausen) to "Dachau" (20min.; DM7.60, or 4 strips on the *Streifenkarte*), then **bus** #724 (dir. Kraütgarten) or 726 (dir. Kopernikusstr.) from the station to "KZ-Gedenkstätte" (10min., DM1.90 or one strip). **☎08131.**

AUGSBURG. For a taste of the Romantic Road, **Augsburg**'s *Függerei* awaits 30 minutes by train from the city (see p. 468).

THE CHIEMSEE. The islands, meadows, forests, and marshland of the **Chiemsee** beckon only one hour from Munich by train (see p. 471).

THE BAVARIAN ALPS. The **Bavarian Alps** offer forested slopes and crazy King Ludwig's fabulous castles, only two hours from Munich by train (see p. 468).

NUREMBERG (NÜRNBERG) ☎091

Nuremberg is inextricably bound to a darker past. The city hosted the massive annual Nazi party rallies (1933-38) and lent its name to the 1935 Racial Purity Laws; Allies later chose it as the site of the post-WWII war crimes trials to foster a sense of justice. Although 90% of the city was demolished in 1945, today it is a model of postwar prosperity and is forging an identity as the *Stadt der Menschenrechte* (City of Human Rights), known for its toy fair and Christmas market, sausages and gingerbread, and association with Albrecht Dürer.

PRACTICAL INFO, ACCOMMODATIONS, AND FOOD. **Trains** run to: Würzburg (1hr., 2 per hr., DM28-42); Regensburg (1hr., every 2hr., DM27-34); Munich (2½hr., every hr., DM54-74); Stuttgart (2¾hr., 6 per day, DM54); Frankfurt (3hr., every hr., DM73-80); Berlin (6hr., every 2hr., DM142); and Prague (5hr., 2 per day, DM72.40). The **tourist office** is in the train station. (☎233 61 31; www.nuernberg.de. Open M-Sa 9am-7pm.) Check **email** at **Internetcafé M@x,** Färberstr. 11, fourth fl. (Before 3pm DM5 per hr.; after 3pm DM5 per 30min., DM9 per hr. Open M-Sa noon-1am, Su 4pm-midnight.) The friendly **Jugendgästehaus (HI),** Burg 2, is perched in a castle above the city. From the station, cross Frauentorgraben, turn right, walk along the outside of the city walls to Königstor, follow Königstr. through Lorenzerpl. over the bridge to the Hauptmarkt (10min.), head toward the golden fountain on the far left, bear right on Burgstr., and huff and puff up the hill. (☎230 93 60. Reception 7am-1am. Curfew 1am. Reserve ahead. Dorms DM30; singles DM60; doubles DM72.) From the station, take the underground passage to Königstr. and turn left on Frauentormauerstr; follow the town wall, then bear right onto Hintere Sterng. to the **Gasthof Schwänlein,** Hintere Sterng. 11. (☎22 51 62; fax 241 90 08. Breakfast included. Reserve by fax or mail. Singles DM40-60; doubles DM75-90.) Pitch your tent at **Campingpark Nürnberg,** Hans-Kalb-Str. 56, southwest of the soccer stadium in Volkspark Dutzendteich. Take S2 (dir. Freucht/Altdorf) to Frankenstadion. (☎981 27 17. Reception 2-10pm. Call ahead. Closed Nov. DM8.75 per person; DM5-10 per tent.) Try some of Nuremberg's famous *Rostbratwurst* (sausage) at **Bratwursthäusle,** Rathauspl. 1, next to the Sebalduskirche. (Open M-Sa 10am-10:30pm.) **Edeka,** Hauptmarkt 12, near the Frauenkirche, has **groceries.** (Open M-F 8:30am-7pm, Sa 8am-3pm.) **Postal code:** 90402.

SIGHTS. Allied bombing left little of Nuremberg for posterity; its churches, castle, and other buildings have all been reconstructed. In the Altstadt near the train station is the walled-in **Handwerkerhof,** a tourist trap masked as a historical attraction; head up **Königstraße** for the real sights. The Gothic **Lorenzkirche** on Lorenzpl. features a 20m tabernacle with delicate stone tendrils that curl up into the ceiling. (Open M-Sa 9am-5pm, Su 1-4pm. German tours in summer M-F 11am and 2pm; in winter M-F 2pm. Free.) Across the river on **Hauptmarktplatz** are the **Frauenkirche** (open M-Sa 9am-6pm, Su 12:30-6pm) and the **Schöner Brunnen** (Beautiful Fountain), with 40 imaginatively carved figures. Walk uphill from the fountain to the **Rathaus,** built in early Baroque style with a little Renaissance Classicism thrown in. The **Lochgefängnisse** (dungeons) beneath contain medieval torture instruments. (Open Tu-Su 10am-4:30pm. Obligatory tours every 30min. DM4, students DM2.) Across from the Rathaus is the Protestant **Sebalduskirche,** which houses the remains of St. Sebaldus for 364 days a year; on the 365th, they're paraded around town. (Open daily June-Aug. 9:30am-8pm; Mar.-May and Sept.-Dec. 9:30am-6pm; Jan.-Feb. 9:30am-4pm.) Atop the hill, the **Kaiserburg** (Emperor's fortress), Nuremberg's symbol, offers the best view of the city. Every Holy Roman Emperor after Konrad III spent at least his first day in office here. (Open daily Apr.-Sept. 9am-6pm; Oct.-Mar. 10am-4pm. Tours every 30min. DM10, students DM8.)

The ruins of **Dutzendteich Park,** site of the Nazi Party Congress rallies of 1934 and 1935 (which drew more than a million citizens), remind visitors of Germany's darker history. The unfinished **Kongresshalle** is at the north end of the Volkspark; the 2km **Große Straße** was designed not only as a marching grounds for Nazi troops, but also as a symbolic link between Hitler and the Kaisers of German history. The **Zeppelinwiese,** a field across the Großer Dutzendteich lake from the Kongresshalle, contains the **Tribüne,** the massive marble platform from which Hitler addressed throngs of listeners. The poles along the field, which once supported enormous banners, were made famous in Leni Riefenstahl's film *Triumph des Willens* (Triumph of the Will) immortalizing the 1935 rally in one of the most terrifying and enduring depictions of the Fascist aesthetic. The exhibit *Faszination und Gewalt* (Fascination and Terror), in the **Golden Hall** at the rear of the Tribüne, covers the rise of the Third Reich and the war crimes trials. (Open mid-May to Oct. Tu-Su 10am-6pm. DM5, students DM4.) To reach the park, take S2 (dir. Freucht/Altdorf) to Dutzendteich, take the middle exit, head down the stairs, turn left, turn left again after Strandcafé Wanner, and follow the path.

BAMBERG ☎0951

Packed with sights but largely overlooked by travelers, this city on the Regnitz boasts one of the most beautiful Altstadts in Bavaria. The residents of Bamberg are proud of their picturesque home, and they celebrate by drinking an astounding amount of beer—330L per capita annually, the highest consumption rate in the world. The 15th-century **Altes Rathaus** guards the middle of the river with its half-timbered, half-Baroque facade and Rococo tower. (Open Tu-Su 9:30am-4:30pm.) Across the river and up the hill, the 11th-century **Dom** (cathedral) contains the 13th-century equestrian statue of the **Bamberger Reiter** (Bamberg Knight) as well as the **Diözesanmuseum,** which contains the **Domschatz** and the perfectly preserved garments of 10th- to 12th-century saints, popes, and Kaisers. (Open daily Apr.-Oct. 8am-6pm; Nov.-Mar. 8am-5pm. Museum DM4, students DM2.) Opposite the cathedral, the **Neue Residenz** boasts lavish furnishings and a primrose garden. Admission to the museum, which houses art from 1600-1703, includes a tour of the palace's parade rooms. (Open daily Apr.-Sept. 9am-6pm, Oct.-Mar. 10am-4pm. Last entry 30min. before closing. DM6, students and seniors DM4.)

Trains arrive at Ludwigstr. from: Nuremberg (1hr., 3 per hr., DM17); Würzburg (1¼hr., 2 per hr., DM27); Munich (2½-4hr., 1-2 per hr., DM71-88); and Frankfurt (3¼hr., every hr., DM65-71). To reach the Altstadt from the station, take any city bus to "ZOB"; or, walk down Luitpoldstr., cross the canal, walk straight on Willy-Lessing-Str., turn right at Schönleinspl. onto Lange Str., and turn left on Obere Brückestr., which leads through the archway of the Rathaus (25-30min.). Once through the Rathaus, take two lefts and recross the Regnitz on the wooden footbridge; the **tourist office,** Geyerwörthstr. 3, is on the right under the arches. (☎87 11 61. Open Apr.-Oct. and Dec. M-F 9am-6pm, Sa 9am-3pm, Su 10am-2pm; Nov.-Mar. and Jan.-Mar. M-F 9am-6pm, Sa 9am-3pm.) To reach the **Jugendherberge Wolfsschlucht (HI),** Oberer Leinritt 70, take bus #18 (dir. Bug) to Rodelbahn. (☎560 02 or 563 44. Breakfast included. Reception 7am-1pm and 5-10pm. Open mid-Jan. to mid-Dec. DM21.) To get from the station to **Bamberger Weißbierhaus,** Obere Königstr. 38, turn left off Luitpoldstr. before the river. (☎255 03. Breakfast included. Reception 9am-midnight. Singles DM39; doubles DM70, with shower DM80.) **Edeka,** Lange Str. 14, sells **groceries.** (Open M-F 8:30am-7pm, Sa 7:30am-4pm.) **Postal code:** 96052.

BAYREUTH ☎0921

Once you've turned off Tristanstr. onto Isoldenstr. and passed Walküreg., there will be little doubt that you're in Bayreuth (Buy-ROIT), the adopted home of **Richard Wagner** and site of the annual **Bayreuth Festspiele** (July 25-Aug. 28), a pilgrimage of BMW-driving devotees basking in his operatic glory. Tickets sell out several years in advance (DM40-300; write to Bayreuther Festspiele, 95402 Bayreuth). The avid fan can tour Wagner's house (Haus Wahnfried), now the **Richard Wagner Museum,** Richard-Wagner-Str. 48. (Open Apr.-Oct. M, W, and F 9am-5pm, Tu and Th 9am-8pm; Nov.-Mar. daily 10am-5pm. DM4, students DM2.) Reach Bayreuth by **train** from: Nuremberg (change at Lichtenfels; 1hr., DM24.60); Bamberg (1½hr., DM24.60); and Regensburg (2hr., DM40). The **tourist office,** Luitpoldpl. 9, is four blocks to the left of the station. (☎885 88. Open M-F 9am-6pm, Sa 9:30am-1pm.) To reach the friendly, hyper-efficient **Jugendherberge (HI),** Universitätsstr. 28, past the Hofgarten, walk down Ludwigstr. from the city center, turn left on Friedrichstr., and veer left onto Jean-Paul-Str., which merges with Universitätsstr. Or, take bus #4 (DM2.70) from the Marktpl. to Mensa, walk out of the *Uni* onto Universitätstr., and turn left. (☎76 43 80. Breakfast included. Sheets DM5.50. Reception 7am-noon and 5-9:30pm. Lockout 9:30-11am. Open Mar. to mid-Dec. DM21.) **Postal code:** 95444.

ROMANTIC ROAD (ROMANTISCHE STRAßE)

The landscape between Würzburg and Füssen is spread like a mammoth picnic: plates of circular cities, castles in tasty shades of lemon and mint, and dense forests of healthy greenery. The German tourist industry christened the area the Romantic Road in 1950, and it has since become the most visited road in Germany.

GETTING THERE AND GETTING AROUND. Although Deutsche Bahn's **Europabus** is the most popular way to see the Romantic Road, it's also inflexible—there is only one bus in each direction per day. The **Frankfurt-Munich** route runs north-south via Würzburg, Rothenburg ob der Tauber, Dinkelsbühl, Nördlingen, and Augsburg, leaving Frankfurt at 8am and Munich at 9am. The **Dinkelsbühl-Füssen** route, also north-south, stops at Augsburg, Wieskirche, and Hohenschwangau and Neuschwanstein, leaving Dinkesbühl at 4:15pm and Füssen at 8am. Check schedules at any tourist office. Europabus is relatively expensive (Frankfurt to Munich DM121; Dinkelsbühl to Hohenschwangau or Füssen DM61), but students and under 26ers get 10% off, under 12 and over 60 50% off, and Eurailers and German Pass holders 75% off. For information or reservations, contact **Deutsche Touring** (☎ (069) 79 03 50; www.deutsche-touring.com) or the **Romantische Straße Arbeitsgemeinschaft** (☎ (09851) 902 71; www.romantischestrasse.de).

Trains are faster and cheaper, and run to every town except Dinkelsbühl. Or, take the opportunity for a **bike** journey; with campgrounds 10 to 20km apart. Drop by any tourist office for cycling maps and campground info.

WÜRZBURG. Surrounded by vineyards and bisected by the Main River, Würzburg is a famous university town, the center of the Franconian wine region, and a scenic portal to the Romantic Road. The striking 12th-century **Marienburg Fortress,** the symbol of the city, keeps vigil on a hillside across the Main. (Tours Tu-F 11am, 2, and 3pm, Sa-Su every hr. 10am-4pm; DM4, students and seniors DM3.) Inside, note the 11th-century **Marienkirche** (containing the bones of early Christian martyrs), the **Bergfried** watchtower (and the **Hole of Fear** dungeon underneath), the **Fürstengarten,** and the 102m **Brunnentempel,** which supplied the castle with water. Artifacts from the lives of the prince-bishops and a display on the destruction of Würzburg at the end of WWII grace the **Fürstenbau Museum.** (Open Tu-Su Apr. to mid-Oct. 9am-6pm; mid-Oct. to Mar. 10am-4pm; last entry 30min. before closing. DM5, students DM4.) Outside the main fortress, the Baroque arsenal houses the **Mainfränkishes Museum,** with statues by Tilman Riemenschneider, the Master of Würzburg. (Open Tu-Su Apr.-Oct. 10am-6pm; Nov.-Mar. 10am-4pm. DM5, students DM2.50, under 14 free. Both museums DM8.) Climb the footpath to the fortress, which starts a short distance from the statue-lined **Alte Mainbrücke,** or take bus #9 from the train station. The **Residenz** palace, on Residenzpl., is a Baroque masterpiece housing the largest ceiling fresco in the world. The **Residenzhofkirche** is astounding: the gilded moldings and pink marble are a Baroque fantasy. (Palace and church open daily Apr. to mid-Oct. 9am-6pm; mid-Oct. to Mar. 10am-4pm. Last entry 30min. before closing. DM8, students and seniors DM6. Church free).

Trains roll in from: Rothenburg (1hr., every hr., DM17); Frankfurt (2hr., 2 per hr., DM38); and Munich (2½hr., every hr., DM76). **Europabuses** (see p. 466) also go to Rothenburg (DM29) and Munich (DM89). The **tourist office** is in Haus zum Falken on the Marktpl. (☎37 23 98. Open M-F 10am-6pm, Sa 10am-2pm; Apr.-Oct. M-F 10am-6pm, Sa 10am-2pm, Su 10am-2pm.) The **Jugendgästehaus (HI),** Burkarderstr. 44, is across the river from downtown; take streetcar #3 (dir. Heidingsfeld) or 5 (dir. Heuchelhof) to Löwenbrücke, backtrack, go down the stairs with the *Jugendher-*

berge/Kapelle sign, turn right, and go through the tunnel. (☎425 90. Reception 24hr. Check-in 5-10pm. DM33.) **Gasthof Goldener Hahn,** Marktg. 7, is off the Markt. (☎519 41. Singles DM50-85; doubles DM150.) Get **groceries** at **Kupsch,** Kaiserstr. 5, near Barbarossapl. (Open M-F 8am-8pm, Sa 8am-4pm.) **Postal code:** 97070. **☎0931.**

ROTHENBURG OB DER TAUBER. Although Rothenburg is *the* Romantic Road-stop, touched by just about everyone, it's probably your only chance to see a walled medieval city without a single modern building, thanks to strict preservation laws. The lantern- and spear-bearing **"night watchman"** leads a nightly **tour** that's more entertaining than educational; meet at the Rathaus. (English at 8pm; DM6. German at 9:30pm; DM5.) On the Marktpl. stands the Renaissance **Rathaus,** whose 60m tower affords a nice view of the town. (Rathaus open daily 8am-6pm; free. Tower open Apr.-Oct. daily 9:30am-12:30pm and 1-5pm; Nov.-Mar. M-F 9:30am-12:30pm, Sa-Su noon-3pm. DM2, children DM1.) The **Jakobskirche,** Klosterg. 15, is famed for its **Altar of the Holy Blood** by Tilman Riemenschneider, its 5500-pipe organ, and its 14th-century stained-glass windows. (Open Apr.-Oct. M-Sa 9am-5:30pm, Su 10:30am-5:30pm; Dec. daily 10am-5pm; Nov. and Jan.-Mar. daily 10am-noon and 2-4pm. DM2.50, students DM1. German tours Apr.-Oct. 11am and 2pm. Free.) The disturbing yet fascinating **Medieval Crime Museum,** Burgg. 3, houses exhibits on torture instruments and "eye for an eye" jurisprudence. (Open daily Apr.-Oct. 9:30am-6pm; Nov. and Jan.-Mar. 2-4pm; Dec. 10am-4pm. DM5, students DM4, children DM3.) Head to Käthe Wohlfahrt's **Christkindlmarkt** (Christ Child Market), Herrng. 2, and the more extensive **Weihnachtsdorf** (Christmas Village), Herrng. 1, to explore Rothenburg's obsession with Christmas. (Open mid-May to Dec. M-F 9am-6:30pm, Sa 9am-4pm, Su 11am-6pm; Jan. to mid-May M-F 9am-6:30pm, Sa 9am-4pm.)

Trains arrive hourly at **Steinach** from Würzburg (40min., DM15.40) and Munich (3hr., DM60); change there for Rothenburg (15min., DM3.30). The **Europabus** leaves from the Busbahnhof, next to the train station. To reach the **tourist office,** Marktpl. 2, go left from the station and bear right on Ansbacher Str. (☎404 92. Open May-Oct. M-F 9am-12:30pm and 1-6pm, Sa-Su 10am-3pm; Nov.-Apr. M-F 9am-12:30pm and 1-5pm, Sa 10am-1pm.) To get from the tourist office to the fantastic **Jugendherberge Rossmühle (HI),** Mühlacker 1, go left down Obere Schmiedg. and look for the small, white *Jugendherberge* sign to the right. (☎941 60; email jhrothen@aol.com. Breakfast and sheets included. Reception 7am-midnight. Check-in until 10pm. DM28.) You're almost obligated to try Rothenburg's heart-stopping *Schneeballen* (snowballs), balls of fried dough covered in powdered sugar; modern varieties are dipped in chocolate or nuts, with marzipan or amaretto centers. Wash them down with milk from **Kupsch supermarket,** on Röderg., inside the city wall as you enter town. (Open M-F 8am-7pm, Sa 8am-2pm.) **Postal code:** 91541. **☎09861.**

DINKELSBÜHL AND NÖRDLINGEN. Forty-five kilometers south of Rothenburg, **Dinkelsbühl** boasts medieval half-timbered houses, a climbable 16th-century church tower, and a navigable town wall with gateways, towers, and moats. Regional **buses** go from the town's Bahnhof to Rothenburg (M-F 9 per day, Sa-Su 1-3 per day; transfer at Dombühl or Feuchtwangen; DM11.40) and Nördlingen (M-F 7 per day, Sa-Su 4-5 per day). The **Europabus** (see p. 466) also serves Dinkelsbühl. From the stop, turn right on Luitpoldsr. and left through the Wörnitz Tor into the Altstadt; the **tourist office** is on the Marktpl. (☎902 40. Open Apr.-Oct. M-F 9am-noon and 2-6pm, Sa 10am-1pm and 2-6pm, Su 10am-1pm; Nov.-Mar. M-F 9am-noon and 2-5pm, Sa 10am-1pm.) From there, head west down Segringer Str. and take a right on Bauhofstr. after the Rathaus; at the first bus stop, swing left on Koppeng. to snooze at the **Jugendherberge (HI),** Koppeng. 10. (☎95 09. Breakfast included. Sheets DM5.50. Reception 5-7pm. Curfew 11pm. Open Mar.-Oct. DM20-24.) **☎09851.**

The only town in Germany with original walls are complete that can be entirely navigated, **Nördlingen** is built on the spot where a meteorite crashed 15 million years ago. Climb up the 90m Gothic bell tower **Daniel** for a view of the town and countryside below. (Open daily Apr.-Oct. 9am-8pm; Nov.-Mar. 9am-5:30pm. DM3, under 17 DM2.) **Trains** arrive from Augsburg (1¼hr., every hr., DM20) and Nuremberg (2hr., every 2hr., DM35); change at Donauwörth for both. **Buses** also run from Dinkelsbühl to Nördlingen (45min., 8 per day, DM7.50). The **Europabus** (p. 466) also stops daily at Nördlingen's Rathaus (southbound 4:55pm, northbound 12:15pm). The **tourist office** is at Marktpl. 2. (☎43 80. Open Easter-Oct. M-Th 9am-6pm, F 9am-4:30pm, Sa 9:30am-1pm; Nov.-Easter M-Th 9am-5pm, F 9am-3:30pm.) From Marktpl., follow Baldinger Str. outside the city walls to the **Jugendherberge,** Kaiserwiese 1, on your right in the parking lot one cross-street beyond the walls. (☎27 18 16. Reception 8-10am and 4:30-7pm. Curfew 10pm. Open Mar.-Oct. DM18.) **☎09081.**

AUGSBURG. Founded by Caesar Augustus in 15 BC, Augsburg was the financial center of the Holy Roman Empire and a major commercial city by the end of the 15th century. The town owed its success and prestige mainly to the Fuggers, an Augsburg banking family; Jakob Fugger "the Rich," personal financier to the Hapsburg Emperors, founded the **Fuggerei** quarter, the first welfare housing project in the world, in 1519; elderly residents today still only pay the equivalent of a "Rhine Guilder" (DM1.72) in rent annually. To reach the Fuggerei from the **Rathaus,** on Maximilianstr., walk behind the Perlachturm tower on Perlachberg, which becomes Barfüsserstr. and finally Jakoberstr., and turn right under the archway. Fugger lived in the **Fugger Haus,** Maximilianstr. 36-38, where a 1518 dispute between Martin Luther and Cardinal Cajetan ensured church schism. Luther stayed in the **St. Anna Kirche,** on Annastr. near Königspl., where he convinced Prior Frosch to pioneer the Reformation in Augsburg. (Open Tu-Su 10am-12:30pm and 3-6pm.) Down Hoher Weg to the left from the Rathaus sits the Gothic **Hoher Dom,** the regional bishop's seat. (Open M-Sa 6am-5pm. German tours M-Sa 10:15am-4pm.)

Trains arrive from: Munich (45min., 4-5 per hr., DM17-30); Stuttgart (1¾hr., 2 per hr., DM66); Nuremberg (2hr., 2 per hr., DM45); Würzburg (2hr., every hr., DM76); and Zurich (5hr., 2 per hr.). The ubiquitous **Europabus** (see p. 466) stops at the train station. The **tourist office,** Bahnhofstr. 7, 300m from the station, books rooms (DM30-40) for a DM3 fee. (☎50 20 70. Open M-F 9am-6pm.) A **branch** on Rathauspl. has longer hours; from the station, walk to the end of Bahnhofstr., turn left at Königspl. on Annastr., take the third right, and Rathauspl. is on the left. (☎502 07 24. Open Apr.-Sept. M-F 9am-6pm, Sa 10am-4pm, Su 10am-1pm; Oct.-Mar. M-F 9am-6pm, Sa 10am-1pm.) To get from the station to the **Jugendherberge (HI),** Beim Pfaffenkeller 3, walk up Prinzregentenstr. as it curves to the right, turn left at Karolinenstr., turn right at the cathedral on Innere Pfaffeng., and bear left on Beim Pfaffenkeller. (☎339 09. Breakfast included. Reception 7-9am and 5-10pm. Curfew 1am. Closed Jan. Call ahead. DM25, under 27 DM21.) Stock up on **groceries** at the **market** on the Stadtmarkt, two blocks west of Rathauspl. (M-F 7am-7pm and Sa 7am-3pm), or **Penny Markt,** Maximilianstr. 71, a few blocks south of the Rathaus. (Open M-F 8am-8pm, Sa 8am-4pm.) **Postal code:** 86150. **☎0821.**

BAVARIAN ALPS (BAYERISCHE ALPEN)

A series of snow-covered peaks and forested slopes stretching from southeast Germany across Austria and into Italy are visible on a clear day from Munich. It was in this rugged, magical terrain that Ludwig II of Bavaria, the certifiably batty "Fairy Tale King," built his theatrical palaces. Even today, residents of the area authentically, even nonchalantly, sport *Lederhosen* on their habitual hikes.

FÜSSEN. A brightly painted toenail at the tip of the Alpine foothills, Füssen's hiking trails, access to ski resorts, and proximity to Ludwig's famed **Königsschlösser** (p. 469) lures legions year-round. Reminders of Ludwig linger in Füssen's architectural wonders. The inner walls of the **Hohes Schloß** courtyard scream royalty with their arresting windows and towers; inside the castle walls, peruse the late Gothic and Renaissance art collection of the **Staatsgalerie.** (Open Tu-Su Apr.-Oct. 11am-4pm; Nov.-Mar. 2-4pm. DM5, students and seniors DM4, under 14 free.) Below the castle rests the 8th-century **Mangkirche,** abbey, and crypt. (Tours July-Sept. Tu and Th 4pm, Sa 10:30am; May-June and Oct. Tu 4pm and Sa 10:30am; Jan.-Apr. Sa 10:30am.) The **Stadtmuseum** in the abbey details the history, art, and culture of the

LUD-WIGGING OUT After Queen Marie bore Maximilian II two healthy sons, there was no reason to expect the fall of the Bavarian royal family—but it was soon to come. Otto, the younger son, developed schizophrenia as a young adult, leaving Ludwig to carry on the family name. In 1864, Ludwig assumed the throne at the tender age of 18, a shockingly handsome lad naïve in the world of politics. A zany visionary and Wagner fanatic, he squandered his private fortune (and bankrupted Bavaria) creating majestic castles, manifestations of his fantasyland. In 1886, a band of nobles and bureaucrats deposed Ludwig and imprisoned him in Schloß Berg on the Starnberger See. Three days later, the King and a loyal advisor were found dead in the lake under mysterious circumstances—suicide? murder? a failed escape? You can step into Ludwig's batty psyche at Schloß Neuschwanstein (see p. 469), Schloß Linderhof (see p. 470), and Schloß Herrenchiemsee (see p. 471).

region. Inside the **Annenkapelle,** skeleton-decked panels depict the *Totentanz*, or "death dance." (Museum open Tu-Su Apr.-Oct. 11am-4pm, Nov.-Mar. 2-4pm. DM5, children and students DM4.) The **Kombikarte** allows admission to both the Stadtmuseum and Staatsgalerie for DM6. Northeast of Füssen, torrents of light bathe the splendid Rococo pilgrimage church **Wieskirche.** (Church in the Meadows. Open daily 8am-7pm.) Bus #9715 leaves daily at 12:25, 1:05, 3:25, and 4:35pm and returns at 3:15 and 3:50pm (1hr., DM7.80; round-trip *Tagesticket* DM10).

Trains arrive in Füssen from Munich (2hr., every hr., DM36) and Augsburg (2hr., every 2hr., DM28). To get from the station to the **tourist office,** Kaiser-Maximilian-Pl. 1, walk the length of Bahnhofstr. and head straight on Luitpoldstr. to the big yellow building. (☎938 50; www.fuessen.de. Open Apr.-Sept. M-F 8:30am-6:30pm, Sa 9am-12:30pm, Su 10am-noon; Oct.-Mar. M-F 9am-5pm, Sa 10am-noon.) The **Jugendherberge (HI),** Mariahilfer Str. 5, has a lovely location. Turn right from the station and follow the railroad tracks for 10 minutes. (☎77 54. Sheets DM5.50. Reception 7-9am, 5-7pm, and 8-10pm. Open Dec.-Oct. Reserve ahead. DM21; add DM1.50 tax.) Get **groceries** at **Plus supermarket,** on the corner of Bahnhofstr. and Luitpoldstr. (Open M-F 8:30am-6:30pm, Sa 8am-2pm.) **Postal code:** 87629. **☎08362.**

NEUSCHWANSTEIN AND HOHENSCHWANGAU. Ludwig II's desperate building spree across Bavaria peaked with the glitzy **Schloß Neuschwanstein,** built from 1869 to 1886, now Germany's most clichéd tourist attraction and the inspiration for Disneyland's Cinderella Castle. The young Ludwig II lived a mere 173 days within the extravagant edifice. The completed chambers (63 remain unfinished) include a Byzantine throne room, a small artificial grotto, and an immense hall built expressly for Wagnerian opera performances. Ludwig grew up in (and watched his own creation of Neuschwanstein being created from) the bright-yellow, neo-Gothic **Schloß Hohenschwangau** across the way. Hohenschwangau is a bit less touristed than its cousin, but the rooms actually appear to have been lived in. The castle houses Wagner's piano and a loaf of bread from the 1830s. (Both open Apr.-Sept. 9am-6pm, Oct.-Mar. 10am-4pm. Mandatory tours of each castle DM14, students and children DM12; combination tickets DM26, DM22.) Consider spending the rest of the day **hiking** around the spectacular environs. For the fairy godmother of all views, hike up to the **Marienbrücke,** which spans the dramatic **Pöllat gorge** behind the Schloß Neuschwanstein (10min.).

Bus #9713 (marked "Königsschlösser; 2 per hr., DM2.50) runs to the castles from Füssen's train station. Separate paths lead to the castles. A less touristed path to Hohenschwangau is path #17, which meanders from the left side of the information booth through the forest (10min.). To Neuschwanstein, take the short but steep path #32, from Car Park D (25min.). A *Tagesticket* (DM13) entitles castle-hoppers to unlimited regional bus travel (including the ride to Linderhof); buy it from the driver. Tickets for both castles may be purchased at the **Ticket-Service Center,** Alpseestr. 12 (☎ (08362) 93 08 30; www.ticket-center-hohenschwangau.de), about 100m south of the Hohenschwangau bus stop. Arrive early to avoid lines, or reserve tickets for a DM3 per person fee.

LINDERHOF. East of Neuschwanstein and Hohenschwangau lies the exquisite **Schloß Linderhof,** Ludwig II's compact hunting palace, which (like Schloß Herrenchiemsee) reflected Ludwig's obsession with France's Louis XIV (the Sun King). The exterior, though not as pristine as Neuschwanstein's, is bathed in gold. The royal bedchamber, the largest room in the castle, is unbelievably lush, with gold leaf and a colossal, 454kg crystal chandelier. Even more impressive than the palace is the surrounding **park.** Paths originating at the swan lake at the park entrance weave through the ornately landscaped grounds, which include an enormous, artificial **grotto** swathed in red and blue floodlights (good taste was perhaps not one of Ludwig's strengths) and the **Hunding-Hütte,** modeled after a scene in Wagner's *Die Walküre.* (Castle open Apr.-Sept. daily 9am-6pm; Oct.-Mar. 10am-4pm. Mandatory tour Apr.-Sept. DM11, seniors and students DM9; Oct.-Mar. DM8, DM6. Park open Apr.-Sept.; free.) **Bus** #9622 runs between Oberammergau and the park (20min., every hr., round-trip DM9.20; last return bus 6:40pm). Oberammergau is accessible by **bus** from Füssen (#1084; 1½hr., 8 per day, DM12.50) and by **train** from Munich (1¾hr., every hr., DM25.60; change at Murnau).

HYPERTRAVEL TO THE CASTLES. Seeing all three of the royal castles on a daytrip from Munich requires fancy footwork and good connections (and can only be done M-F). Take the 6:50am train from Munich to Buchloe and transfer to the 7:46am to Füssen. Arriving in Füssen at 8:57am, hop on bus #9713 at 9:15am to the Königsschlösser. Arriving at 9:23am, you'll have almost four hours to fight the lines at Hohenschwangau and Neuschwanstein before you catch bus #1084 at 1:13pm to Oberammergau (changing in Steingaden), and from Oberammergau bus #9622 at 3:05pm to Schloß Linderhof. You can indulge in the surrounding opulence until 5:35pm, but then it'll be time to mount bus #9622 back to Oberammergau. You'll arrive at 6pm with plenty of time to catch the 6:08pm train to Murnau, where you'll change trains at 6:47pm and hopefully grab a *Löwenbräu* at 7:55pm back in Munich. Check your schedule with a timetable before departing. A simpler option, particularly if you don't have a railpass, is to sign on with **EurAide** for a castle tour (see p. 456).

BERCHTESGADEN. In the southeastern Bavarian Alps, Berchtesgaden wins admiration for its natural beauty, yet is equally well-known for a more sinister attraction: Hitler's **Kehlsteinhaus** (Eagle's Nest), so named by the American troops who occupied it after WWII. The stone resort house, now a restaurant with a spectacular view from the 1834m mountain peak, was built for the *Führer*'s 50th birthday. (Open daily May-Oct.; closes for snow.) Buy the round-trip ticket to Kehlstein from the Bahnhof in Berchtesgaden (DM27.90); once there, reserve your spot on a return bus at the booth when you get off. (Returns to Hintereck and Berchtesgaden every 30min.; last return at 5:05pm. 35-minute English tour of Kehlstein daily at 10:30 and 11:40am. DM7, children free.)

Hourly **trains** run to: Bad Reichenhall (30min., DM6); Salzburg via Freilassing (1hr., DM12.20); and Munich via Freilassing (2½hr., DM48). The Berchtesgaden **tourist office,** Königsseer Str. 2, is opposite the train station in an off-white building with blue shutters. (☎96 71 50; www.berchtesgadener-land.com. Open M-F 8am-6pm, Sa 9am-3pm.) The **Jugendherberge (HI),** Gebirgsjägerstr. 52, is a 30-minute walk uphill from the station. Turn right from the station and follow Ramsauer Str. on the left for 15 minutes, then take the first right on Gmündbrücke, and follow the signs up the steep gravel path on the left. Or, take bus #9539 (dir. "Strub Kaserne") to "Jugendherberge." (☎943 70. Breakfast included. Sheets DM5.50. Reception 8am-noon and 5-7pm. Check-in until 10pm. Curfew midnight. Closed Nov.-Dec. 26. DM20; add DM3 *Kurtaxe.*) Turn right from the tourist center to pick up **groceries** at the **Edeka Markt,** Königsseer Str. 22. (Open M-F 7:30am-6pm, Sa 7:30am-noon.) **Postal code:** 83471. **☎08652.**

HIKING NEAR BERCHTESGADEN. From Berchtesgaden, the 5.5km path to the **Königssee** winds through fields of flowers, across bubbling brooks, and past several beer gardens, offering a heart-stopping view of the Alps. From the Berchtesgaden train station, cross the street, take a right and a quick left over the bridge, and turn left at the stone wall. **Bus** #9541 also runs from near the train station to Königssee (round-trip DM7.20). Once you arrive, walk down Seestr. and look for the **Nationalpark Informationstelle** to your left, which has hiking info. Continue down Seestr. to reach the dock, where **Bayerische Seen Schiffahrt** cruises depart for points throughout the Königssee. Twenty kilometers southwest of Berchtesgaden, a network of hiking trails radiates from **Ramsau,** a heaven for hikers, kayakers, cyclists, skiers, and all appreciators of Mother Nature. Ramsau is a great base for exploring **Berchtesgaden National Park.** The **tourist office,** Im Tal 2, has trail maps and hiking info. (☎ (08657) 275. Open M-F 8am-12:30pm and 2:30-6:30pm, Sa 8am-12:30pm.) From Berchtesgaden, **bus** #9546 (15min., DM3.80) runs hourly to Ramsau.

THE CHIEMSEE

For almost 2000 years, artists, architects, and musicians have chosen the Chiemsee as the setting for their masterpieces. Its islands, meadows, forests, marshland, and mountains first lured the 9th-century builders of the **Raueninsel cloisters,** then the eccentric King Ludwig II, who built the fairy-tale **Königsschloß Herrenchiemsee.**

PRIEN AM CHIEMSEE. Prien, on the northwest corner of the Chiemsee, is a good base from which to ferry to the islands. **Trains** (☎28 74) arrive at the station, a few blocks from the city center from Salzburg (40min., every hr., DM34) and Munich (1hr., every hr., DM36). The **tourist office,** Alte Rathausstr. 11, finds private rooms (DM30-45) for free. (☎690 50. Open M-F 8:30am-6pm, Sa 9am-noon.) The **Jugendherberge (HI),** Carl-Braun-Str. 66, is 15 minutes from the station—head right on Seestr. and turn left on Staudenstr., which becomes Carl-Braun-Str. (☎687 70. Breakfast included. Sheets DM5.50. Reception 8-9am, 5-7pm, and 9:30-10pm. Lockout 9am-1pm. Curfew 10pm. Open early Feb. to Nov. DM25.) For **Campingplatz Hofbauer,** Bernauerstr. 110, turn left on Seestr. from the station, turn left at the next intersection, and walk for 30 minutes along Bernauerstr., heading out of town. (☎41 36. Open Apr.-Oct. DM10.50 per person; DM10 per tent and car.) Grab **groceries** at **HL Markt,** Seestr. 11. (Open M-F 8am-8pm, Sa 8am-4pm.) **☎08051.**

HERRENINSEL AND FRAUENINSEL. The fabulously overwrought **Königsschloß Herrenchiemsee** is on **Herreninsel** (Gentlemen's Island). Ludwig bankrupted Bavaria building this place, a shameless attempt to be bigger, better, and more extravagant than Versailles. A few barren rooms (abandoned after the cash ran out) contrast with the ornate completed portion. (Open daily Apr.-Sept. 9am-6pm; Oct.-Mar. 10am-4pm. Obligatory tour DM11, students DM9. German tours every 10min.; English tours 10:30, 11:30am, 1, 2, 3, and 4pm.) **Fraueninsel** (Ladies' Island), home to the nunnery that complemented the former monastery on Herreninsel, offers subtler pleasures. With no room for cars, only footpaths wander through this miniature world of fishermen and nuns. The 8th-century Merovingian **Cross of Bischofhofen** is on display in **Michaelskapelle** above the **Torhalle** (Gate), the oldest surviving part of the cloister. (Open June-Sept. *Torhalle* DM8, *Michaelskapelle* DM2.) **Ferries** run from Prien to Herreninsel and Fraueninsel (every hr. 6:40am-7:30pm; round-trip to Herreninsel DM10, under 15 DM5; to Fraueninsel or to both islands DM12.50). To get to the ferry port, turn right from the main entrance of the Prien train station and follow Seestr. for 20 minutes, or hop on the green *Chiemseebahn* from the station (9:40am-6:15pm, round-trip including ship passage DM16.50).

REGENSBURG ☎0941

Neither Regensburg's greatness nor its Roman structures crumbled with Rome. Instead, Regensburg flourished as the first capital of Bayern, then the seat of the Holy Roman Empire's parliament, and finally the site of the first German parliament, which lives on in the **Reichstagsmuseum** in the Gothic **Altes Rathaus.** (German tours every 30-60min. English tours May-Sept. M-Sa 3:15pm. DM5, students DM2.50.) The high Gothic **Dom St. Peter,** a few blocks away on Dompl., dazzles with richly colored stained glass. The **Domschatz** inside contains gold and jewels bought by the Regensburg bishops back in the days of indulgences. (Cathedral open daily Apr.-Oct. 6:30am-6pm; Nov.-Mar. 6:30am-5pm. Free. 2hr. tours May-Oct. M-Sa 10, 11am, and 2pm, Su noon and 2pm; Nov.-Apr. M-Sa 11am, Su noon. DM5, students DM3. *Domschatz* open Apr.-Nov. Tu-Sa 10am-5pm, Su noon-5pm; Dec.-Mar. F-Sa 10am-4pm, Su noon-4pm. DM2, students DM1.50.)

Trains chug to: Nürnberg (1-1½hr., 1-2 per hr., DM27); Passau (1-1½hr., every hr., DM32); and Munich (1½hr., every hr., DM38). To get from the station to the **tourist office,** in the Altes Rathaus, walk down Maximilianstr., turn left on Grasg. (which turns into Obermünsterstr.), turn right at the end on Obere Bachg., and continue on Untere Bachg. (☎507 44 10. Open Nov.-Mar. M-F 8:30am-6pm, Sa 9am-4pm, Su 9:30am-2:30pm; Apr.-Oct. M-F 8:30am-6pm, Sa 9am-4pm, Su 9:30am-4pm.) To get from the station to the **Jugendherberge (HI),** Wöhrdstr. 60, walk to the end of Maximilianstr., turn right at the *Apotheke* on Pflugg., turn immediately left at the *Optik* sign on Erhardig., take the steps down at the end, walk left over the Eiserne Brücke (bridge), then veer right onto Wöhrdstr. Or, take bus #3, 8, or 9 to Eisstadion. (☎574 02. Breakfast included. Reception 6am-1am. DM28.) **Historische Wurstküche,** Thundorfer Str., next to the Steinerne Brücke, is a 12th-century beer garden. (Open Apr.-Oct. daily 8am-7pm; Nov.-Mar. M-Sa 8am-7pm, Su 8am-3pm.) Buy **groceries** at **GM Markt,** Untere Bachg. 2 on the way to the tourist office from the station. (Open M-F 8am-8pm, Sa 8am-4pm.) **Postal code:** 93047.

PASSAU ☎0851

Eiscafes, monasteries, and art galleries dot this beautiful Baroque *Dreiflüssestadt* (three-river city), which sits at the meeting point of the Danube, Inn, and Ilz Rivers. The architecture peaks in the sublime **Stephansdom** (St. Stephen's Cathedral), where hundreds of cherubs sprawl across the ceiling and the world's largest church organ (17,774 pipes) looms above the choir. (Open 7:30-10:45am and 12:30-6pm. Free. Organ concerts May-Oct. M-Sa noon DM4, students DM2; Th 7:30pm DM10, DM5.) Behind the cathedral, the **Domschatz** (Cathedral Treasury) of the **Residenz** houses an extravagant collection of gold and tapestries. (Open Easter-Oct. M-Sa 10am-4pm. DM2, students DM1.) The 13th-century Gothic **Rathaus** contains a stunning Great Hall. (Open Apr.-Oct. 10am-4pm. DM2, students DM1.) Over the **Luipoldbrücke** (bridge) is the former palace of the Bishopric, the **Veste Oberhaus.** (Open early Apr.-Oct. M-F 9am-5pm, Sa-Su 10am-6pm; Nov.-Mar. Tu-Su 9am-5pm.) It now houses the **Cultural History Museum.** (DM7, students DM4.)

Trains (☎ (0180) 599 66 33) go from Bahnhofstr. to: Regensburg (1-2hr., every hr., DM32); Nürnberg (2hr., every 2hr., DM60); Munich (2hr., every hr., DM52); Frankfurt (4½hr., every 2hr., DM74-131); and Vienna (3½hr., 1-2 per hr.). To get to the **tourist office,** Rathauspl. 3, walk right down Bahnhofstr., downhill across Ludwigspl. to Ludwigstr., which becomes Rindermarkt, Steinweg, and Große Messerg.; continue straight on Schusterg. and turn left on Schrottg. to reach Rathauspl. The staff books rooms and provides accommodations info. (☎95 59 80; www.passau.de. Open Easter to mid-Oct. M-F 8:30am-6pm, Sa-Su 9:30am-3pm; late Oct. to Easter M-Th 8:30am-5pm, F 8:30am-4pm.) The **Jugendherberge (HI),** Veste Oberhaus 125, is in a castle above the Danube. Cross the bridge downstream of the Rathaus, ignore the sign pointing up the steps, and instead continue right along the curve through the lefthand tunnel, head up the steep driveway to your left, bear left, walk through the yellow house, and take a right to the hostel. (☎413 51. Breakfast included. Sheets DM5.50. Reception 7-11:30am. Check-in 4-11:30pm. Curfew 11:30pm. DM22.) The **Rotel Inn** has tiny rooms over the Danube. Walk down the steps in front of the station and through the tunnel toward the hotel, shaped like a sleeping man. (☎951 60. Reception 24hr. Singles DM35; doubles DM50.) Get **groceries** at **Edeka,** on Ludwigstr. at Grabeng. (open M-F 8am-8pm, Sa 7:30am-4pm), and **SuperSpar,** Residenzpl. 13 (open M-F 7:30am-6pm, Sa 7:30am-12:30pm). **Postal code:** 94032.

GREECE (ΕΛΛΑΣ)

GREEK DRACHMAS

US$1 = 394DR	100DR = US$0.25
CDN$1 = 266DR	100DR = CDN$0.38
UK£1 = 554DR	100DR = UK£0.18
IR£1 = 429DR	100DR = IR£0.29
AUS$1 = 221DR	100DR = AUS$0.45
NZ$1 = 169DR	100DR = NZ$0.59
SAR1 = 55.30DR	100DR = SAR1.81
EUR€1 = 338DR	100DR = EUR€0.29

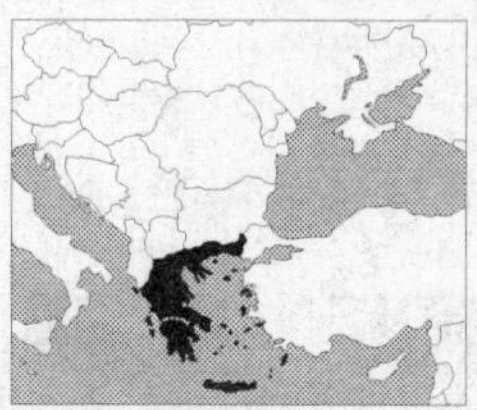

Country code: 30. **International dialing prefix:** 00. From outside Greece, dial int'l dialing prefix (see inside back cover) + 30 + city code + local number.

GREECE

Greece is both a place and a state of soul. The intensely rational beauty that inspired the ancients continues to call countless backpackers to commune with the universe as they wander the unearthed temples, theaters, palaces, and stadia of lost civilizations. The memory of Dionysus, god of the vine, still fuels the islands, in a blur of sun, sand, and sex, framed in the blues of the clear sky and the golds of the endless beach. In Greece's austere hills, monks and hermits pray in millennia-old structures, offering hospitality to the wanderers who seek them out. Over the centuries, Greece has stood at the crossroads of Europe and Asia, and 400 years under the Ottoman Turks left a spice in Greek food, an eastern flair in the strains of its *bouzouki* music, and minaret tips in its skylines. Greece emerged independent in 1821, and today, as the country moves toward the European Monetary Union and overhauls its infrastructure for the 2004 Summer Olympics in Athens, development has accelerated at a blistering pace. Still, above the concrete resorts and growling tour buses, the wind's lonely, persistent whistle reminds you that Greece remains oracles' ground. For more coverage of Greece, check out *Let's Go: Greece 2000.*

FACTS AND FIGURES

Official Name: Hellenic Republic.

Government: Parliamentary Republic.

Capital: Athens.

Land Area: 131,957 sq. km.

Climate: Sunny, hot, and humid summers, cool winters (50°F). October to March is the rainy season.

Major cities: Athens and Thessaloniki.

Population: 10.7 million.

Language: Greek.

Religion: Greek Orthodox (98%).

Income per capita: US$8,870.

Major Industries: Tourism, fishing, agriculture.

Geography: Mountains with fertile coasts and many small islands.

DISCOVER GREECE

Launch your Greek adventure in the urban sprawl of **Athens** (p. 477), with visits to the Acropolis and the National Museum, a daytrip to Cape Sounion, a sunset atop Lycavittos, and a night out clubbing in Glyfada. Then swing into the Peloponnese: whisper tragic secrets at the theater of **Epidavros** (p. 489) before a sunset stroll among the mansions of **Nafplion** (p. 488). Dash west to **Olympia** (p. 486) for your own Olympic footrace beside the ruins, then ferry from Patras to **Corfu** (p. 495), an isle lovingly immortalized by cultural luminaries (Edward Lear, Oscar Wilde) and wild partyers. Back on the mainland, soak up Greece's second city, **Thessaloniki** (p. 491), where trendy shops neighbor some of Byzantium's most precious ruins. Climb the cliffside **Monasteries of Meteora** (p. 490), then commune with the ancient gods at **Mt. Olympus** (p. 490) and at the fortune-telling Oracle of **Delphi** (p. 484). Hop a ferry from Athens to **Crete,** where the mythical Minotaur munched men (**Knossos,** p. 503); Europe's longest gorge, **Samaria** (p. 504), and unparalleled Mediterranean beaches await to the west. Recharge on the white cliffside buildings and black sand beaches of **Santorini** (p. 501), then party for days and nights on **Mykonos** (p. 498); repent with a visit to the Temple of Apollo on the sacred isle of **Delos** (p. 499).

ESSENTIALS

WHEN TO GO

June through August is **high season** in Greece; consider visiting during May or September, when the weather is beautiful and the crowds thinner. The **off season,** from mid-September through May, offers cheaper airfares and lodging, but many sights and accommodations have shorter hours or close altogether. Facilities and sights close and ferries run considerably less frequently in winter, although ski areas at Mt. Parnassos, Mt. Pelion, and Metsovo beckon winter visitors.

DOCUMENTS AND FORMALITIES

South Africans need a **visa** to enter Greece; citizens of Australia, New Zealand, Canada, the UK, Ireland, and the US can visit for up to 90 days without a visa. Other countries' **embassies and consulates** in Greece are in **Athens** (p. 477).

Greek Embassies and Consulates at Home: Australia, 9 Turrana St., Yarralumla, Canberra, ACT 26000 (☎ (02) 62 73 30 11; fax 62 73 26 20); **Canada,** 76-80 MacLaren St., Ottawa, ON K2P 0K6 (☎ (613) 238 62 71; fax 238 56 76); **Ireland,** 1 Upper Pembroke St., Dublin 2 (☎ (01) 67 67 25 45; fax 661 88 92); **New Zealand** (consulate), 57 Willeston St., 10th Fl., Box 24066, Wellington (☎ (04) 473 77 75 or 473 77 76; fax 473 74 41; **South Africa,** 995 Pretorius St., Arcadia, 0083, Pretoria (☎ (012) 437 35 13; fax 43 43 13); **UK,** 1a Holland Park, London W113TP (☎ (0171) 229 38 50; fax 229 72 21); **US,** 2221 Massachusetts Ave. NW, Washington, D.C. 20008 (☎ (202) 939 58 00; fax 939 58 24; email greece@greekembassy.org).

GETTING THERE AND GETTING AROUND

BY PLANE. Flying from northern European cities is a popular way of getting to Greece. From North America, an indirect flight through **Brussels** or **Luxembourg** may cost less than a flight going directly to **Athens. Olympic Airways,** 96-100 Singrou St., 11741 Athens (☎ (01) 926 7221), serves many large cities and islands within Greece, and also operates efficient and reasonably priced flights between many islands. These flights are often booked weeks in advance in summer.

BY TRAIN. A number of relatively cheap (and slow) international train routes connect Athens, Thessaloniki, and Larisa to most European cities. Count on at least a three-day journey from **Trieste** or **Vienna** to **Athens.** Train service in Greece is limited and sometimes uncomfortable, and no lines go to the western coast. The more extensive and reliable **bus** system is a better way to get around the country; if you must travel by rail, the new express intercity trains are well worth the price. **Eurail** passes are valid. **Hellenic Railways Organization (OSE)** connects Athens to other major Greek cities. In Greece, call ☎ 145 or ☎ 147 for schedules and prices.

BY BUS. Fast, extensive, and reasonably priced, buses are the best alternative for travel within Greece; most are run through **KTEL.** Smaller towns may use cafes as bus stops—ask for a schedule. **Confirm your destination** with the driver; signs may be wrong. Along the road, little blue signs marked with white buses or the word **ΣΤΑΣΗ** indicate stops. Drivers usually stop anywhere if you flag them down; let him know in advance where you want to get off; if your stop is passed, yell "Stasi!"

BY FERRY. A popular way to get to Greece is by **ferry** from Italy. Boats travel from **Ancona** and **Brindisi** to **Corfu** (10hr.), **Igoumenitsa** (12hr.), and **Patras** (20hr.), for L50,000 to 105,000 (US$31-66; low season L22,000-45,000 or US$13-29). If you plan to travel from Brindisi in summer, make reservations and arrive at the port well before your departure time. **Rhodes** connects by ferry to **Marmaris,** Turkey; **Limassol,** Cyprus (18,500-22,000dr); and **Haifa,** Israel (28,500-33,000dr in low season). If you plan a trip to Turkey, keep in mind that Greeks aren't too excited to help with travel there; gather info outside of the country. ISIC holders can often get student fares, and Eurail pass holders get many reductions and free trips. You'll pay the port tax (L10,000, or US$6.25, in Brindisi) and a high season supplementary fee of L19,000 (US$12). Schedules are irregular and exasperating, and misinformation is common. Arrive early to avoid literally missing the boat. To avoid hassles, go to the **limenarheio** (port police)—every port has one, and all carry ferry schedules. **Flying dolphins** (hydrofoils) run at double speed and twice the price.

BY CAR AND MOPED. Cars are a luxury in Greece, where public transportation is nonexistent after 7pm; mopeds are vastly more popular, especially among young people. Ferries carry cars if you pay a transport fee. Drivers must be comfortable with a stick shift transmission (for cars), hairpin turns on winding mountain roads, reckless drivers (especially in Athens), and the Greek alphabet—signs in Greek appear roughly 100m before the transliterated versions. Rental agencies may quote low daily rates that exclude the 20% tax and **Collision Damage Waiver (CDW)** insurance (2500dr per day), then hit you with hidden fees for returning with less than a full tank, a drop-off charge of 1.5-2.5dr per km, or 100km per day minimum mileage.

Most companies won't let you drive the car outside Greece. The **Automobile and Touring Club of Greece (ELPA),** Messogion 395, Athens 11527 (☎606 8800), provides assistance, reciprocal membership to foreign auto club members, 24-hour emergency road assistance (☎104), and an information line. (☎174 in Athens, ☎01 60 68 838 elsewhere in Greece. Open M-F 7am-3pm.) **Moped** and car rental places proliferate in almost every town. **Taxis** are available in larger towns and cities to take you anywhere for several hundred drachmas; most gather near the central *plateia* or along the waterfront. Expect to pay much higher rates at night.

TOURIST SERVICES AND MONEY

EMERGENCY. Police: ☎100. **Hospital:** ☎106. **Emergency:** ☎166.

TOURIST OFFICES. Tourism is overseen by two national organizations: the **Greek National Tourist Organization (GNTO)** and the **tourist police** *(touristiki astinomia).* The GNTO main office is at 2 Amerikis St., Athens (☎ (01) 327 1300). The GNTO is known as **EOT** in Greek. The **tourist police** (in Athens ☎171, elsewhere ☎922 7777) deal with more local and immediate problems: where to find a room, what the bus schedule is, or what to do when you've lost your passport.

MONEY. Greek drachmas (abbreviated "dr") are issued in paper notes (100, 200, 500, 1000, 5000, and 10,000dr) and coins (5, 10, 20, 50, and 100dr). It's cheaper to convert money in Greece and Cyprus than at home. Banks in Greece charge 2% commission on traveler's checks, with a 50dr minimum and a 4500dr maximum.

A bare-bones day in Greece costs about US$35. Camping can save about US$10-15 per day. A day with more creature comforts runs US$50. With **tipping,** the more informal the venue, the more flexible the price. Don't tip taxis. At all but the ritziest restaurants, service is included in the bill; instead of adding a tip, round your bill up—a few hundred drachmas at most. Feel free to **bargain** for *domatia* prices and at street markets; the more formal the store or hotel, the less acceptable it is to bargain.

BUSINESS HOURS. Businesses generally open in the early morning and close in the hot afternoon hours, to reopen in the evening. On **Sundays** and **holidays** most businesses are closed; opening hours aren't strict, but are at the owner's whim.

ACCOMMODATIONS AND CAMPING

Lodging in Greece is a bargain. Only one **hostel** in Greece is HI; the non-HI hostels are in most cases still safe and reputable. Hostel curfews are strict, and may leave you on the street. **Domatia** (rooms to let in Greeks' homes) are an attractive, perfectly dependable option; they're cheap and offer you a truly local experience. Often you'll be approached by locals as you enter town or disembark from your boat, or a tourist offices lists all domatia in town. Have the proprietors point out their establishment on a map before trekking there, and agree on a price before taking a room. **Hotel** prices are regulated, though the owners may push you to take the most expensive room. Check your bill carefully, and threaten to contact the tourist police if you think you are being cheated. **GNTO** offices usually have a list of inexpensive accommodations. Greece hosts plenty of **campgrounds,** which rent tents or even cabins for extremely low prices. Bring a sleeping bag if you plan to camp.

FOOD AND DRINK

Recent medical studies have highlighted the Greek diet as a model for healthy eating because of its reliance on unsaturated olive oil and vegetables. Penny-pinching carnivores will thank Zeus for lamb, chicken, or beef *souvlaki* and hot-off-the-spit *gyros* stuffed into a pita. Vegetarians can also eat their fill for cheap: try the feta-piled *horiatiki* (Greek salad), savory pastries like *spanakopita* (cheese pie, a pastry full of feta) and *tiropita* (spinach pie), and the fresh fruits and vegetables found at markets and vendor stands in most cities. Greek-style liquid relaxation typically involves a few basic options: the old standbys are *ouzo* (a Greek spirit that will earn your respect) and grainy Greek coffee. A Greek restaurant is known as a *taverna* or *estiatorio;* a grill is a *psistaria.* Don't be suspicious of restaurants without menus; this is common. Waiters will ask you if you want salad, appetizers, or the works, so be careful not to wind up with mountains of food, since Greek portions tend to be large. Service is always included in the check, but it is customary to leave a few drachmas as an extra tip.

COMMUNICATION

MAIL. Letters can be sent **general delivery** to almost any Greek city or town with a post office. Address **Poste Restante** letters to: First name SURNAME, Poste Restante, Vathy, Ithaka, Greece. Mail goes to a special desk in the central post office, unless you specify differently. Letters from Europe generally take at least three days to arrive; from the US, South Africa, and Australia airmail takes 7-10 days.

TELEPHONES. To make calls in Greece, you'll need a **prepaid phone card,** available at street side kiosks and *peripteros.* Time is measured in minutes or talk units (e.g. 1 unit=1min.). The card usually has a toll-free access telephone number and a **personal identification number (PIN).** Phone rates are highest in the morning, lower in the evening, and lowest on Sunday and late at night. National phone service long-distance rates can be exorbitant—use a calling card to call home. Simply contact your service provider's Greek operator: **AT&T:** ☎00 800 13 11; **Sprint:** ☎00 900 14 11; **MCI WorldPhone Direct:** ☎00 800 12 11; **Canada Direct:** ☎00 800 16 11; **BT Direct:** ☎00 800 44 11; **Ireland Direct:** ☎155 11 74.

LANGUAGE. Although many Greeks in Athens and other heavily touristed areas—particularly young people—speak English, rural Greeks rarely do. For the basics, see p. 981. Transliterating from Greek to English can cause some confusion: for instance, Φ and φ can be spelled *ph* or *f.* Greek body language will help you avoid misunderstandings. To say no, Greeks lift their heads back abruptly while raising their eyebrows; they emphatically nod once to say yes. A hand waving up and down that seems to say "stay there" actually means "come."

HOLIDAYS AND FESTIVALS

Almost everything shuts down during holidays, so be aware of them.

Holidays: Feast of St. Basil/New Year's Day (Jan. 1); Epiphany (Jan. 6); First Sunday in Lent (Mar. 18); Greek Independence Day (Mar. 25); Good Friday (Apr. 13); Easter (Apr. 25); St. George's Day (Apr. 23); Labor Day (May 1); Ascension (May 25); Pentecost (June 4); Feast of the Assumption (Aug. 15); The Virgin Mary's Birthday (Sept. 8); Feast of St. Demetrius (Oct. 26); National Anniversary of Greek Independence (Oct. 28); Commemoration of an uprising of Greek university students (Nov. 17); Christmas (Dec. 25).

Festivals: Starting on Feb. 25 of this year, three weeks of feasting and dancing at Carnival will precede the Lenten fast.

ATHENS (Αθηνα) ☎01

One minute of dodging the packs of mopeds in Pl. Syndagma will prove that Athens—the sprawling work of centuries—refuses to become a museum. Athens's historical skeletons aren't bottled in the closet: they jut up through the modern city in glowing white marble. The Acropolis looms larger than life over the city, a perpetual reminder of ancient glory, and Byzantine churches recall an era of foreign invaders. The reborn democracy of the past two centuries has revived the city in a wave of madcap construction: the conflicted, oddly adolescent metropolis gutted its crumbling medieval mansions to become a dense concrete jungle. Crowded, noisy, polluted, and totally alive, Athens will maroon you in traffic at 2am on a Tuesday. A new subway system should be completed for the 2004 Olympic Summer

Games. Still, civil engineers refuse to "destroy everything in the name of the underground," picking their way among subterranean antiquities, cisterns, and the springs of lost, ancient rivers that sleep beneath the city.

GETTING THERE AND GETTING AROUND

Flights: The airport's **East Terminal** handles all international flights, the **West Terminal** receives Olympic Airways flights, and the **New Charter Terminal** takes charter flights. Express **bus** #901 (40min.; every 20min. 7:10am-9pm, 12 per night 9:50pm-6:45am; 250dr, after 11:30pm 500dr) connects to Pl. Syndagma and Stadiou near Pl. Omonia. A **taxi** costs 2500-4000dr (add 50dr for heavy luggage and 300dr from the airport).

Trains: ☎145 or 147. **Larissis Train Station** (☎529 8837) serves northern Greece and the rest of Europe. To: **Thessaloniki** (7¼hr., 10 per day, 4100-5850dr); **İstanbul** (15hr., 1 per day, 20,000dr, must change trains and wait 1hr. at border); and **Sofia** (16,000dr) via **Bucharest** and **Budapest** (34hr. total, 40,000dr). Trolley bus #1 runs from the station to Panepistimiou in Pl. Syndagma (every 10min., 120dr). The **Peloponnese Train Station** (☎513 1601) serves **Patras** (1580dr) and the Peloponnese. To get to the station from Larissis, exit to your right and go over the footbridge; from Panepistimiou, take bus #057 (every 15min., 120dr).

Buses: Terminal A, Kifissou 100 (☎512 4910). To: **Patras** (3hr., 30 per day, 3650dr); **Thessaloniki** (7½hr., 6 per day, 8200dr); and the Peloponnese. Take blue bus #051 (every 15min., 120dr) from the corner of Zinonos and Menandrou near Pl. Omonia. **Terminal B,** Liossion 260 (M-F ☎831 7153), serves central Greece. Take blue bus #024 from Amalias and Panepistimiou. From the **Peloponnese Train Station** (see above), **Hellenic Railway (OSE;** ☎362 4402) runs to **Sofia** and **İstanbul.**

Ferries and Hydrofoils: Ferries to Crete and the Cyclades, and the Northeast Aegean and Dodecanese Islands dock at the Athenian suburb of **Piraeus** (Port Authority ☎422 6000). **Hydrofoils** to the mainland, Sporades, and Cyclades also depart from **Zea** near Piraeus. See **Piraeus,** p. 485. For info on other ferries, see **By Ferry,** p. 475.

Public Transportation: Purchase tickets for the blue **buses** (designated by 3-digit numbers) or yellow **trolleys** (1-2 digits) from any street kiosk (120dr) and validate them in the orange machines on board. The **metro** (every 5min. 5am-midnight) is under construction; branches stretch from Piraeus Harbor to Kifissia in northern Athens. Buy tickets at booths or automatic machines (120dr) and keep them, or face a 1500dr fine.

Taxis: Hail your taxi by shouting your destination—not the street address, but the area (e.g. "Kolonaki"). Base fare 250dr, plus 66dr per km within the city limits, 130dr outside. Be sure the meter is turned on, and ask how much the fare will be in advance.

ORIENTATION AND PRACTICAL INFORMATION

Pl. Syndagma is the center of modern Athens. Budget travel offices, eateries, and hostels line **Nikis** and **Filellinon,** which run south from Pl. Syndagma into the eastern part of **Plaka** (bounded by the Acropolis to the southwest and the Temple of Olympian Zeus to the southeast), the center of the old city and temporary home to most tourists. **Monastiraki,** mostly known for its hodge-podge flea market, lies west of Pl. Syndagma. Northwest of Pl. Syndagma, **Pl. Omonia** (which has become increasingly unsafe) is the site of the city's main subway station. North of Pl. Syndagma and east of Omonia, hip **Exarhia** brims with students, while east of Pl. Sydagma lies the glitzy area of **Kolonaki.** Southeast of Pl. Syndagma is large, quiet **Pangrati.** A 30-minute ride to the south is **Glyfada,** a seaside suburb where the bacchanalians party. Be aware that Athenian streets often have multiple spellings or names.

Tourist Office: Central office and information booth at Amerikis 2 (☎331 0561 or 331 0562; fax 325 2815; www.areianet.gr/infoxenios/GNTO), off Stadiou near Pl. Syndagma. City maps and transportation info. Open M-F 9am-9pm, Sa-Su 10am-9pm.

Budget Travel: International Student Youth Travel Service Limited, Nikis 11 (☎322 1267; fax 322 1531), sells ID cards and has student rates for European transport. Open M-F 9am-5pm, Sa 9am-1pm.

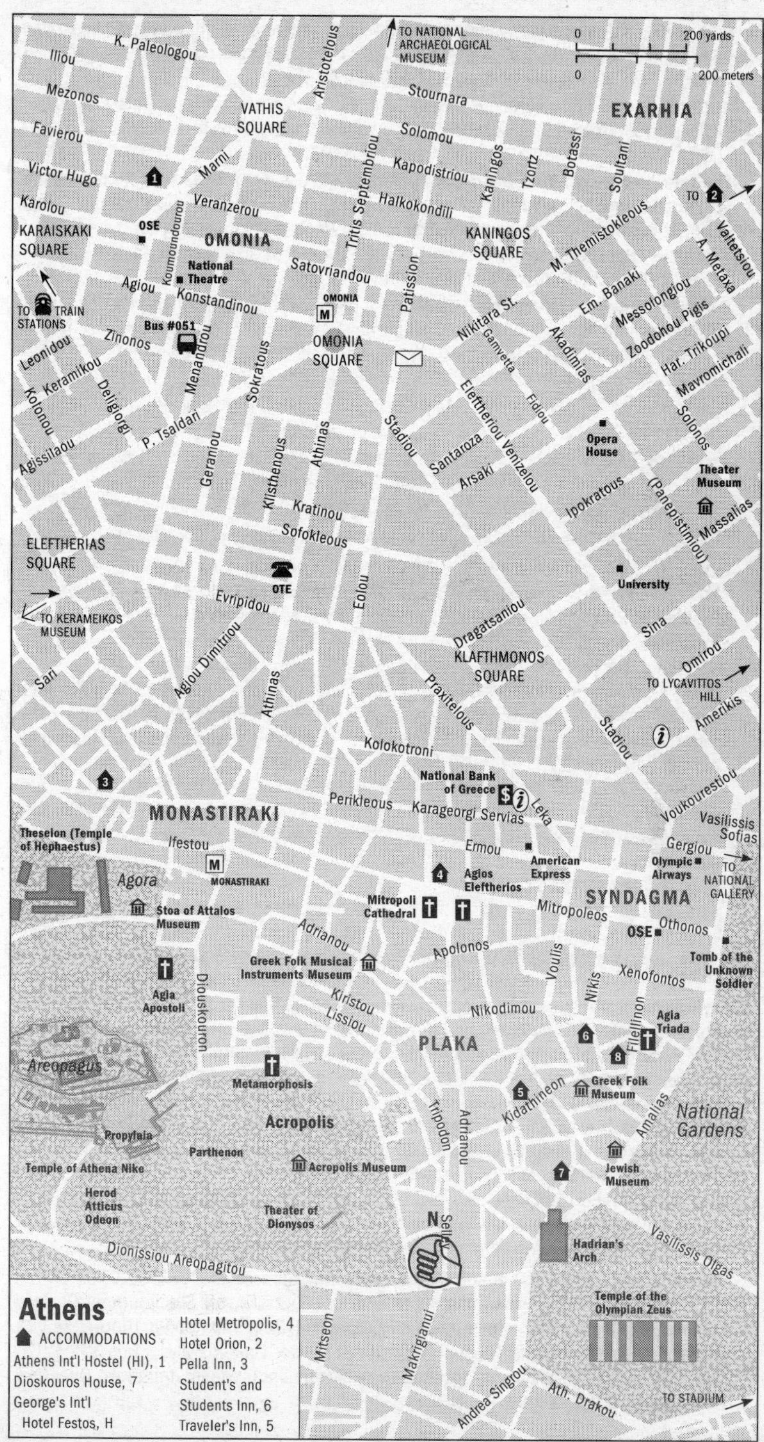
Athens
ACCOMMODATIONS
Athens Int'l Hostel (HI), 1
Dioskouros House, 7
George's Int'l Hotel Festos, H
Hotel Metropolis, 4
Hotel Orion, 2
Pella Inn, 3
Student's and Students Inn, 6
Traveler's Inn, 5
TO NATIONAL ARCHAEOLOGICAL MUSEUM
0 200 yards
0 200 meters
EXARHIA
VATHIS SQUARE
OMONIA
KARAISKAKI SQUARE
OSE
National Theatre
TO TRAIN STATIONS
Bus #051
OMONIA
OMONIA SQUARE
KANINGOS SQUARE
Opera House
Theater Museum
ELEFTHERIAS SQUARE
TO KERAMEIKOS MUSEUM
OTE
University
KLAFTHMONOS SQUARE
TO LYCAVITTOS HILL
National Bank of Greece
MONASTIRAKI
Theseion (Temple of Hephaestus)
Agora
MONASTIRAKI
Stoa of Attalos Museum
Agios Eleftherios
American Express
Olympic Airways
TO NATIONAL GALLERY
SYNDAGMA
Mitropoli Cathedral
OSE
Tomb of the Unknown Soldier
Greek Folk Musical Instruments Museum
Agia Apostoli
Agia Triada
PLAKA
Areopagus
Metamorphosis
Greek Folk Museum
National Gardens
Acropolis
Propylaia
Parthenon
Acropolis Museum
Temple of Athena Nike
Jewish Museum
Herod Atticus Odeon
Theater of Dionysos
Hadrian's Arch
Temple of the Olympian Zeus
TO STADIUM
K. Paleologou
Iliou
Mezonos
Favierou
Victor Hugo
Karolou
Aristotelous
Stournara
Solomou
Kapodistriou
Halkokondili
Marni
Veranzerou
Koumoundourou
Tritis Septembriou
Kaningos
Tzortz
Botassi
Soultani
Valtetsiou
A. Metaxa
M. Themistokleous
Satovriandou
Agiou Konstandinou
Patission
Em. Banaki
Messolongiou
Zoodohou Pigis
Har. Trikoupi
Mavromichali
Zinonos
Menandrou
Leonidou
Keramikou
Kolonou
Deligiorgi
Sokratous
Nikitara St.
Gamvetta
Akadimias
Fidiou
Solonos
P. Tsaldari
Geraniou
Athinas
Stadiou
Santaroza
Eleftheriou Venizelou
Agissilaou
Klisthenous
Arsaki
Ipokratous
(Panepistimiou)
Massalias
Kratinou
Sofokleous
Evripidou
Eolou
Dragatsaniou
Sina
Omirou
Agiou Dimitriou
Sari
Praxitelous
Stadiou
Amerikis
Kolokotroni
Perikleous
Karageorgi Servias
Leka
Voukourestiou
Vasilissis Sofias
Ifestou
Ermou
Gergiou
Mitropoleos
Adrianou
Apolonos
Othonos
Voulis
Xenofontos
Nikis
Dioskouron
Kiristou
Lissiou
Nikodimou
Filellinon
Kidathineon
Amalias
Tripodon
Adrianou
Sellei
Vasilissis Olgas
Dionissiou Areopagitou
Mitseon
Makrigianni
Andrea Singrou
Ath. Drakou

GREECE

Embassies: Australia, D. Soutsou 37 (☎644 7303). Open M-F 8:30am-12:30pm. **Canada,** Ioannou Genadiou 4 (☎725 4011 or 727 3400). Open M-F 8:30am-12:30pm. **Ireland,** Vas. Konstandinou 7 (☎723 2771). Open M-F 9am-3pm. **South Africa,** Kifissias 60 (☎680 6645). Open M-F 8am-1pm. **Turkey,** Vas. Georgiou B. 8 (☎724 5915). Open M-F 8:30am-12:30pm. **UK,** Ploutarchou 1 (☎727 2600). **US,** Vas. Sofias 91 (☎721 2951; www.usisathens.gr). Open M-F 8:30am-5pm.

Currency Exchange: National Bank of Greece, Karageorgi Servias 2, in Pl. Syndagma. Open for currency exchange M-Th 3:30-6:30pm, F 3-6:30pm, Sa 9am-3pm, Su 9am-1pm. 24hr. **ATMs** are available all over the city, including Pl. Syndagma.

American Express: Ermou 2 (☎324 4975 or 324 4979), above McDonald's in Pl. Syndagma. Open M-F 8:30am-4pm, Sa 8:30am-1:30pm.

Luggage Storage: At the **airport.** 1000dr per piece per day; hang on to your ticket stub. Also at several offices on **Nikis** and **Filellinon** for 500dr per piece per day.

English-Language Bookstore: Eleftheroudakis Book Store, Panepistimiou 17 (☎331 4180) and Nikkis 4. Open M and W 9am-4pm, Tu and Th-F 9am-8:30pm, Sa 9am-3pm.

Laundromats: The Greek word for laundry is *plinitirio,* but most signs say "Laundry." Try **Angelou Geront 10** in Plaka (2000dr) or **Kolokinthous 41 and Leonidou** (2300dr).

Emergencies: Police: ☎100. **Doctors:** ☎105. **Ambulance:** ☎166. **Tourist Police:** ☎171. **Poison Control:** ☎779 3777. **AIDS Help Line:** ☎772 2222.

Pharmacies: Check the daily *Athens News* (300dr) for the night pharmacy schedule.

Medical Assistance: The Greek word for hospital is *nosokomio;* operator ☎131. A **public hospital** is at Evangelismou 45-47 (☎722 0101), near Kolonaki.

Telephones: OTE, Patission 85 (☎821 4449 or 823 7040). Open M-F 7am-9pm, Sa 8am-3pm, Su 9am-2pm. Most phone booths require **telephone cards,** sold at OTE offices, street kiosks, and tourist shops (1000, 7000, or 11,500dr). Push the "i" button on the phones for instructions in English. Domestic operator in English ☎151.

Internet Access: Deligrece Internet Cafe, Akadimias 87 (☎330 2929). 1000dr per hr.; minimum 15min. Open daily 7:30am-midnight. **Sofokleous.com Internet Cafe,** Stadiou 5 (☎324 8105), just up Stadiou from Pl. Syndagma. 1500dr per hr., minimum 15min. for 500dr. Open daily 10am-10pm.

Post Office: Pl. Syndagma (☎322 6253), on the corner of Mitropolis. Open M-F 7:30am-8pm, Sa 7:30am-2pm, Su 9am-1pm. Address mail to be held: First name SURNAME, Pl. Syndagma Post Office, Athens, Greece **11702.**

ACCOMMODATIONS

Although some hawkers at the station rent decent, nearby places, others lure tourists to expensive, distant dumps; be sure to set a price and to have the place pointed out on a map before departing. Men should beware "friendly barkeeps" who may lead them to a brothel. Many budget options cluster in central **Plaka** and **Syndagma,** although women will have to ward off Plaka's catcalling *kamakia* (literally "octopus spears"). Cheap lodgings abound in **Omonia,** but the area isn't very safe at night. **Prices below are valid for summer;** subtract around 500-1000dr per person off-season (Sept.-May). Prices, like much else in Greece, are highly flexible; don't expect these figures to be exact. Note that hotel owners can legally add a 10% surcharge if you stay fewer than three nights. Athens has no camping.

Student's and Traveler's Inn, Kidathineon 16 (☎324 4808 or 324 8802; email Students-inn@ath.forthnet.gr), in **Plaka.** Great location with young backpackers. Internet access. Breakfast 1000-1500dr. Singles 8000-9000dr; doubles 10,000-11,000dr; triples 12,000-13,500dr; quads 14,000-16,000dr. 10% discount with ISIC.

Hotel Dryades, Dryadon 4 (☎382 7116 or 330 2387), in **Exarhia.** Some of Athens's nicest accommodations, with large rooms and private baths. Breakfast 1500dr. Singles 10,000dr; doubles 14,000dr; triples 17,000dr.

Pella Inn, Karaiskaki 1 (☎325 0598; fax 325 0598). Walk 10min. down Ermou from Pl. Syndagma; 2 blocks from the **Monastiraki** subway station. Breakfast 800dr. Dorms

3000dr; singles 6000-8000dr; doubles 6000-13,000dr; triples 9000dr; quads 10,000. 20% discount for *Let's Go* users.

Hotel Metropolis, Mitropoleos 46 (☎321 7871 or 321 7469), opposite Mitropoli Cathedral, in **Plaka.** Newly renovated. A step up from others in the area at a great price. Singles with bath 8000dr; doubles 12,000dr.

Hotel Orion, Em. Benaki 105 (☎382 7362 or 382 0191; fax 380 51 93) in **Exarhia.** From Pl. Omonia, walk up Em. Benaki or take bus #230 from Pl. Syndagma. Filled with hip travelers intent on seeing more than Athens's tourist magnets. Breakfast 1500dr. Singles 7000dr; doubles 9000dr; triples 11,000dr.

Dioskouros House, Pitakou 6 (☎324 8165), on the southwest corner of the National Gardens by the Temple of Olympian Zeus in **Plaka.** Secluded outdoor bar serves breakfast (500dr) and drinks until 11pm. Singles 7000-9000dr; doubles 8000-10,000dr; triples 12,000-15,000dr.

Hotel Festos, Filellinon 18 (☎323 2455; email consolas@hol.gr), in **Syndagma.** Backpacker-friendly. Breakfast 500dr. Dorms 2000-3500dr; singles 5000-7000dr; doubles 6000-8000dr; triples 12,000dr; quads 14,000dr.

Athens International Hostel (HI), Victor Hugo 16 (☎523 4170; fax 523 4015), in **Omonia.** Go down Tritis Septembriou from Pl. Omonia and go left on Veranzerou until it becomes Victor Hugo. Continental crowd packs Greece's only HI-affiliated youth hostel. HI membership required (4200dr). Full kitchen. Sheets included. Hot water 6-10am and 6-10pm. Internet access (1200dr per hr.) across the street. Dorms 1720dr.

GREECE

FOOD

Athens offers a melange of stands, open-air cafes, side-street *tavernas*, and intriguingly dim restaurants. Cheap fast food abounds in Syndagma and Omonia—try *souvlaki* (250-400dr), served either on a *kalamaki* (skewer) or wrapped in *pita; tost* (a grilled sandwich of variable ingredients, usually ham and cheese, around 350dr); *tiropita* (hot cheese pie, 300dr); or *spanakopita* (hot spinach pie, 300dr). A *koulouri* (a doughnut-shaped, sesame-coated roll) makes for a quick breakfast (50-100dr). Pick up basic groceries at a **minimarket** on Nikis.

Pluto, Plutarchou 38 (☎724 4713), in **Kolonaki.** Owner and chef extraordinaire Constantine has a unique restaurant with ambience and a great international menu. Don't miss the divine seafood risotto. Open daily 1-5pm and 9pm-2:30am.

Oineas, Aisopou 9 (☎321 5614), off Karaisaki by the Pella Inn. The best food in **Monastiraki.** Nostalgic Greek posters and old Singer sewing machine ads adorn the walls, and the menu is just as quirky. Interesting entrees 1400-5000dr. Open Tu-Su 11am-2am.

O Barba Giannis, Em. Benaki 94 (☎330 0185), in **Exarhia.** From Syndagma, take Stadiou and go right on Em. Benaki. Greek students, execs, and artists enjoy vegetarian, meat, and fish entrees (950-1500dr). Open daily 9am-1am; closed Su in summer.

O Platanos, Diogenous 4 (☎322 0666), on a street parallel to Adrianou in **Plaka.** A *Platanos* tree towers over the table-filled courtyard. Greek specialty veal with potatoes, rice, or *fricasse* 1800dr. Open M-Sa noon-4:30pm and 8pm-midnight.

Healthy Food Vegetarian Restaurant, Panepistimiou 57 (☎321 0966), in **Omonia.** Wholesomeness to make a souvlaki stand blush. Everything's made fresh. Try the potato carrot pie 400dr, breakfast *mueslix* 950dr, and the scrumptious carrot apple juice 500-600dr. Open M-F 8am-9:30pm, Sa 8am-8:30pm, Su 10am-3:30pm.

Dafni Taverna, Ionlianou 65 (☎821 3914), in **Omonia.** From Pl. Victoria, go down Aristotelous and right on Ionlianou. Grapevine-shaded courtyard walled by barrels of *retsina;* a classic. Traditional Greek entrees from 1500dr. Open daily noon-1am.

Dia Tafta, Adrianou 37 (☎321 2347), near the Agora in **Monastiraki.** A huge bar snakes through Dia Tafta, with more popular street-side tables. Fresh Greek salad 1700dr, platters for four 3500-6500dr. Open daily 9:30am-1:30am.

Savas, Mitropoleos 86 (☎324 5048), off Ermouin **Monastiraki.** A budget eater's take-out dream. Heavenly gyros 350dr. 1500dr extra to sit. Open daily 8am-3am.

SIGHTS

THE ACROPOLIS

The main entrance is on the west side of the Acropolis. Areopagitou to the south and Theorias in western Plaka (follow the sporadic signs) both lead to the entrance. Alternatively, exit the Agora (see below) to the south, following the path uphill, and then turn right. ☎321 0219. Open in summer 8am-6:30pm; off-season 8am-2pm. 2000dr, students 1000dr; includes the Acropolis Museum. The marble can be slippery, so wear shoes with good traction.

Perched on a rocky plateau above the city, the Acropolis has been Athens's highlight since the 5th century BC. At the center, the Parthenon towers over the Aegean and Attic Plains, the ultimate achievement of Athens's classical glory. Although each Greek *polis* had an *acropolis* ("high city"), Athens's magnificent example has effectively monopolized the name. Today, the hilltop's remarkable (if scaffolded) ruins grace otherwise rubble-strewn grounds.

BEULÉ GATE AND PROPYLAEA. The ramp that led to the Acropolis in classical times no longer exists; today's visitors make the five-minute climb to the ticket window, enter through the crumbling Roman **Beulé Gate** (added in the 3rd century AD), and continue through **Propylaea,** which formed the towering entrance in ancient times. The middle gate of the Propylaea opened onto the **Panathenaic Way,** an east-west route cutting across the middle of the Acropolis that was once traveled by Panathenaic processions venerating the goddess Athena.

TEMPLES OF ATHENA NIKE AND ATHENA PROMACHOS. On the right after leaving the Propylaea, the tiny Temple of Athena Nike, at the cliff's edge, was built during a respite from the Peloponnesian War, the Peace of Nikias (421-415 BC). It once housed a winged statue of the goddess; allegedly, frenzied Athenians who feared that their deity (and peace) would flee the city one day clipped the statue's wings. In a similar vein, the foundation to your left as you continue along the Panathenaic Way once supported a statue of Athena Promachos; when the statue lost its spear hundreds of years later, the inhabitants interpreted her outstretched hand as an invitation to invaders and smashed it to pieces.

ERECHTHEION. The Erechtheion, to the left down the Panathenaic Way, was finished in 406 BC, just prior to Athens' defeat by Sparta. The unique two-level structure was dedicated to Athena, Poseidon, and Erechtheus. Its southern portico, facing the Parthenon, is supported by six much-photographed casts of **caryatids,** sculpted column-women—see the originals in the Acropolis Museum.

PARTHENON. Looming over the hillside, the Parthenon (Virgin's Apartment) keeps vigil over the city. The crowning glory of Pericles' project to beautify Athens, it was designed by the architect Aktinos, who added two extra columns to the usual six in a Doric-style temple. The Parthenon also features other subtle irregularities: the upward bowing of the temple's *stylobate* (pedestal) and the slight swelling of its columns compensated for the optical illusion by which, from a distance, straight lines appear to bend. Its elegant lines reflect the ancient Greek obsession with proportion: everything from its layout to its sculpted details follow a four-to-nine ratio.

ACROPOLIS MUSEUM. Footsteps away from the Parthenon, the museum contains a superb collection of sculptures, including five of the original Erechtheion Caryatids (the sixth accompanies the original entablature in the British Museum, p. 171). Most treasures date from the period of transition between Archaic and Classical Greek art (550-400 BC): compare the stylized, entranced faces and frozen poses of Archaic sculptures such as the famous **Moschophoros** (calf-bearer) to the more human, idealized Classical pieces, like the perfectly balanced, curvaceous **Kritias** boy. Unfortunately, only a few pieces from the Parthenon are here—former British ambassador Lord Elgin helped himself to the rest. (*Open M noon-6:30pm, Tu-Su 8am-6:30pm; in winter M 11am-2pm, Tu-Su 8am-2pm.*)

SOUTHERN SLOPE. From the southwest corner of the Acropolis, you can look down on the reconstructed **Odeon of Herodes Atticus,** a still-functioning theater dating from the Roman Period (AD 160). Admire the ruins of the classical Greek **Asclepion** and **Stoa of Eumenes II** as you continue east to the **Theater of Dionysus,** which dates from the 4th century BC and once hosted dramas by Aeschylus and Sophocles and comedies by Aristophanes for audiences of up to 17,000. *(Main entrance on Dionissiou Areopagitou, but you can also enter from the Acropolis, just above the Herodes Atticus theater. Open Tu-Su 8:30am-2:30pm. 500dr, students 250dr.)*

OTHER SIGHTS

ANCIENT AGORA. The **Athenian Agora,** at the foot of the Acropolis, was the administrative center and marketplace of Athens from the 6th century BC to the late Roman Period (5th-6th centuries AD). The **Temple of Hephaestos,** on a hill in the northwest corner, is one of the best-preserved Classical temples in Greece, especially notable for its friezes depicting the tales of Hercules and Theseus. To the south, the elongated **Stoa of Attalos,** a multi-purpose building for shops, shelter, and gatherings, was rebuilt between 1953 and 1956 and now houses the **Agora Museum,** which contains a number of relics from the site. *(Enter from Pl. Thission, from Adrianou, or as you come down from the Acropolis. Open Tu-Su 8:30am-3pm. 1200dr, students 600dr.)*

GREECE

MOUNT LYCAVITTOS. Don't miss the view from the top of **Mt. Lycavittos,** the biggest of Athens' seven hills. The best time to ascend is sunset, when you can catch a last glimpse of Athens in daylight and watch the city light up. Using the Acropolis as your point of reference, you'll see Monastiraki, Omonia, and Exarhia to your right, then continue spinning clockwise to delight in the flashy lights and music of Lycavittos Theater, several parks, the Panathenaic Olympic Stadium, the National Gardens, and the Temple of Olympian Zeus. *(Hike 15min. to the top, or take the funicular from near the end of Ploutarchou in Kolonaki. Departs every 10-15min., round-trip 1000dr.)*

MUSEUMS. One of the world's finest collections of classical sculpture, ceramics, and bronzework lies in the **National Archaeological Museum.** The *Mask of Agamemnon* from Heinrich Schliemann's Mycenae digs and the huge bronze statue of Poseidon are must-sees. *(Patission 44, also called Oktovriou 28. Walk from Pl. Syndagma up Stadiou and turn right on Patission (20min.). Open Apr.-Oct. M 12:30-7pm, Tu-Su 8am-5pm; Nov.-Mar. M 11am-5pm, Tu-F 8am-5pm, Sa-Su 8:30am-3pm. 2000dr, students 1000dr; free Su and holidays.)* The **National Gallery** (Alexander Soutzos Museum) exhibits works by Greek artists, including El Greco, and some international artists. *(Vas. Konstandinou 50. Open M and W-Sa 9am-3pm, Su 10am-2pm. 1000-1500dr, students 500dr.)*

NEAR PLATEIA SYNDAGMA. Walk along the tranquil paths of the pleasant **National Gardens,** adjacent to Pl. Syndagma. *(Open daily dawn-dusk. Women should avoid coming here alone.)* Don't miss the changing of the guard in front of the **Parliament** building. Unlike their British equivalents, *evzones* occasionally wink, smile, or even say "I love you" to tourists. *(Two sets of guards perform every hour on the hour. Catch a more pomp-filled version—with a complete troop of guards and a band—on Su at 10:45am.)*

HADRIAN'S ARCH AND TEMPLE OF OLYMPIAN ZEUS. Hadrian's Arch marked the 2nd-century boundary between the ancient city of Theseus and the new city built by Hadrian. Next to the arch, fifteen majestic columns are all that remain of the Temple of Olympian Zeus, the largest temple ever built in Greece. *(Vas. Olgas at Amalias, southwest of the National Gardens. Open Tu-Su 8am-3pm. 500dr, students 300dr.)*

ENTERTAINMENT AND NIGHTLIFE

FESTIVALS. The **Athens Festival** runs annually from June until September, featuring classical theater groups at the Odeon of Herodes Atticus, at the Lycavittos Theater, and in Epidavros. The Greek Orchestra regularly plays during this festival, and visiting artists have ranged from the Bolshoi Ballet to the Talking Heads. The **Festival Office,** Stadiou 4 (☎322 1459), sells tickets for 3000-5000dr.

THE IRONY OF ORACLES The Delphic Oracle was famed for giving obscure, deceptive, metaphorical answers. Many a suppliant went home more confused than he came, having failed to draw meaning from the answer—or, worse still, having drawn the wrong meaning. In the 6th century BC, King Croesus of Sardis, ruler of most of Asia Minor, came to the Oracle to ask about the threat the Persians posed to his kingdom. The Oracle's answer: "A great empire will be destroyed." Croesus returned to Sardis thinking that he would conquer the Persian Empire; it was not until he watched his own kingdom and capital fall that he realized the fallen empire was his own. Similar stories show that the Oracle's nature was not simply to answer questions, but, as was once inscribed on the Temple of Apollo, to "know thyself."

MARKETS. The bazaar-like **Athens Flea Market,** adjacent to Pl. Monastiraki, hawks a potpourri of second-hand junk, costly antiques, and everything in between. (Open M, W, and Sa-Su 8am-3pm, Tu and Th-F 8am-8pm.) On Sundays, the flea market overflows the square and fills Athinas, and a huge indoor-outdoor **food market** lines the sides of Athinas between Evripidou and Sofokleous. The **meat market** is huge, and not for the faint of heart. (Open M-Sa 8am-2pm.)

FILM, CAFES, AND BARS. Enjoy your own *cinema paradiso* at the open-air movie theater **Cine Paris,** Kidatheneon 22 (☎322 2071). Check *Athens News* for showtimes (tickets 2000dr). For a livelier night, head to **Kolonaki** and its cafe-by-day-bar-by-night establishments. Millioni St. by **Jackson Hall** is just the right spot for homesick Americans and Yankophiles. **Jazz in Jazz,** Deinokratous 4, lures mellow Athenian Bacchants with endless old jazz records and spontaneous swing dancing. (Cover 1500dr with one drink. Open noon-3am.) In **Pl. Exarhia,** the **Cafe Floral** sells fredo cappuccinos (900dr). In **Plaka,** colorful **Bretto's,** Kidatheneon 41, distills its own liqueur. (Open daily 10am-midnight.) **Bee,** at Miaoli and Themidos, off Ermou in **Monastiraki,** is a hub of the artistic scene. (Open daily noon-3am.)

CLUBS. In summer, hip Athenians head to the seaside clubs in **Glyfada** (past the airport). Go for glam; shorts *don't* pass through these doors. Cover ranges from 3000-5000dr, and drinks are ridiculously pricey: beers are 1500-2000dr, cocktails 2000-3000dr. Cafe-bars proliferate on **Vouliagmenis,** Glyfada's main drag; clubs are just down the beach. Try **King Size** and **Bedside,** Poseidonos Beach 5; **Camel Club,** Pergamon 25, for rock; and **+ Soda,** on Poseidonos Beach, for after-hours (post-3am) fun. For **gay clubs** (primarily male), try the northern end of Singrou or Lembessi, off Singrou. To get to Glyfada, take bus A3 (240dr) from Pl. Syndagma to the last stop and cab it to your club of choice. Taxi fare back is 2500-3000dr.

EXCURSIONS FROM ATHENS

TEMPLE OF POSEIDON. The **Temple of Poseidon** has for centuries been a dazzling white landmark for sailors at sea, and also offers fantastic views of the blue, blue Aegean. The original temple was constructed around 600 BC, destroyed by the Persians in 480 BC, and rebuilt by Pericles in 440 BC. The 16 remaining Doric columns sit on a promontory at **Cape Sounion** (Ακρωτηριο Σουνιο), 65km from Athens. (☎39 363. Open daily 10am-sunset. 800dr, students 400dr, EU students free.) Two **bus** routes run to Cape Sounion from Athens; the shorter and more scenic route begins at the Mavromateon 14 stop near Areos Park in Athens (2hr.; every hr. 6:30am-6:30pm, last bus back 8pm, 1300dr).

DELPHI. Troubled denizens of the ancient world journeyed to the Oracle of Apollo at Delphi (Δελφοι), where the Pythia (a priestess of Apollo) gave them profound, if cryptic, advice. Today, tourists flock to modern Delphi (pop. 2500) for its fascinating ruins. Visit early in the morning. **Buses** leave Athens for Delphi from Terminal B at Liossion 260 (3½hr., 6 per day, 3100dr). Railpass holders can take the **train** to **Livadia** and catch the bus (2hr., 10 per day, 1500dr). From the bus station at the western end of Delphi, walk east on Pavlou toward Athens (with the mountain edge on your right) to reach the **tourist office,** 12 Friderikis, in the town hall. (Open M-F 7:30am-2:30pm.) Continue east down Pavlou to reach the oracle site.

MARATHON. Gasping out two words—*Νικη ημιν*, "Victory to us"—messenger Phidippides announced the Athenian victory over the Persians in the bloody 490 BC battle of Marathon (Μαραθωνας); he collapsed and died immediately after. His 42km sprint to Athens remains legendary, and today runners trace his Marathon route twice annually, beginning at a commemorative plaque. Others reach Marathon by **bus** from Mavromateon 29 by Areos Park in Athens (1½hr., every hr. 5:30am-10:30pm, 700dr). The town itself isn't very inspiring, but the five-room **Archaeological Museum** is packed with exciting finds. Ask the driver to let you off at the sign ("Mouseion and Marathonas"), then follow the signs 2km through farmlands (bear right at the one unlabeled fork in the road) to the end of the paved road, 114 Plateion. (Open Tu-Su 8:30am-3pm. 1000dr, students 500dr, EU, classics, and archaeology students free.)

FERRIES FROM ATHENS: PIRAEUS

A far cry from the charm of Plato's *Republic*—set in Piraeus (Πειραιας, "Port") at the height of Athenian power—modern Piraeus is best appreciated only as a point of departure to the Greek isles. **Ferries** go to most inhabited Greek islands (except the Sporades and Ionian Islands): **Ios** (7½hr., 5090dr); **Iraklion** (10hr., departs 7:30 and 8am, 6400dr), **Hania** (10hr., departs 8:30pm, 5400dr), and **Rethymno** (10hr., departs 7:30pm, 6500dr) on **Crete; Limassol, Cyprus; Mykonos** (6hr., 2 per day, 4800dr); **Naxos** and **Paros** (6hr., 3 per day, 4800dr); **Rhodes** (16hr., departs 2 and 4pm, 8600dr); and **Santorini** (9hr., 5630dr). **Minoan Flying Dolphins** (☎428 0001) run hydrofoils roughly twice as fast and twice as costly as ferries; they run to the mainland, Sporades, and Cyclades from the port of **Zea** on the opposite site of the peninsula, 10 minutes down any of the roads off Akti Miaouli. Long-distance **trains** for **Patras** and the **Peloponnese** leave daily from the train station on **Akti Kalimassioti;** trains to northern Greece leave daily from the station on **Ag. Dimitriou** across the harbor.

From Athens, take the **metro** to the last southbound stop (20min.). The **tourist office** in the metro station offers advice. (☎412 1181 or 412 1172. Open daily 6am-8pm.) From the stop, head left facing the water down Akti Kalimassioti, which becomes Akti Poseidonos, and bear right onto Akti Miaouli. Larger ferries dock at Akti Miaouli; small **ferries** depart from Akti Poseidonos; international ferries dock at the end of Akti Miaouli toward the Customs House.

THE PELOPONNESE (Πελοποννησος)

Connected to the mainland by the narrow isthmus of Corinth, the Peloponnese holds the majority of Greece's best archaeological sites: Mycenae, Olympia, Corinth, Messene, Mystras, and Epidavros are all here. You'll look out on some of the country's most stunning landscapes, from the barren crags of the Mani to the forested peaks and flowered fields of Arcadia. Brushy, sun-warmed, and sparsely populated, the Peloponnese remains an outpost of traditional Greek village life.

FERRIES TO ITALY AND CRETE

Boats go from **Patras** to **Brindisi** (6000-8000dr, plus 2200dr port tax), **Trieste, Bari, Ancona,** and **Venice, Italy.** The trip to or from Brindisi is free for **Eurail** holders on certain ferry lines. Check the travel offices on Iroön Polytechniou and Othonas Amplias in Patras to consult about tickets, and ask about discounts for those under 25. Ferries also sail from **Gythion** to **Crete** (7hr., 4900dr).

PATRAS (Πατρας) ☎061

Sprawling Patras, Greece's third-largest city, serves primarily as a transportation hub, but the port transforms into one big dance floor during **Carnival** (mid-Jan. to Ash Wednesday). During the rest of the year, spend your layover in the lower city or climbing the 13th-century **Venetian Castle** steps. (Open daily 8am-7pm. Free.) Follow the water to the west end of town to reach **Agios Andreas,** the largest Orthodox cathedral in Greece. (Open daily 9am-dusk.) Sweet black grapes age into *Mavrodaphne* wine at the nationally renowned **Achaïa Clauss winery.** (Take bus #7 from the intersection of Kolokotroni and Kanakari.)

Trains (☎639 109) also go from Othonos Amalias to: **Athens** (8 per day, 1600-3000dr); **Olympia** (2hr., 8 per day, 820-1220dr) via **Pyrgos;** and **Kalamata** (4½hr., 2 per day, 1500dr). KTEL **buses** (☎623 886) go from Othonos Amalias, between Aratou and Zaïmi, to: **Athens** (3hr., 28 per day, 3800dr); **Kalamata** (1hr., 2 per day, 4350dr); **Thessaloniki** (3 per day, 8800dr); and **Tripoli** (4hr., 2 per day, 3250dr). Daily **ferries** go to **Corfu** (6-8hr., 5800dr) and **Ithaka** (3¾hr., 3500dr) via **Kephalonia** (3hr., 3200dr). For ferries to **Italy,** see above. From the docks, turn right after leaving customs and follow Iroön Polytechniou, which becomes Othonos Amalias, to find the town center. **Eurail** holders should head to **HML** (☎452 521), on Iroön Polytechniou near customs, for ferry tickets. **Strintzis Tours,** Othonas Amalias 14, is also helpful. (☎622 602. Open daily 9am-11pm.) The **tourist office** is on the waterfront at the entrance to customs. (☎430 195. Open M-F 7am-9pm.) **Rocky Raccoon Online Café,** Gerokostopoulou 56, has **Internet** access. (1500dr per hr. Open daily 9am-3am.) Hotels dot **Ag. Andreas,** one block up from the waterfront. **Pension Nicos,** Patreos 3, is two blocks from the water. (☎221 643. Singles 4000dr; doubles 6500dr.) **Postal code:** 26001.

OLYMPIA (Ολυμπια) ☎0624

Beginning in 776 BC, leaders of rival Greek city-states shed their armor every four years and flocked to Olympia to make offerings to the gods and enjoy the Olympic games. Today, the remains of a gymnasium, palaestra, stadium, and several temples remain scattered around **Ancient Olympia,** although they are not labeled or particularly well-preserved. Follow the main road five minutes out of town to reach the ruins and museum. Dominating the site, called the **Altis,** is the gigantic **Temple of Zeus,** which once held a statue of the god by Phidias so beautiful that it was considered one of the **seven wonders of the ancient world.** On the north edge of the Altis lie the remains of the **Temple of Hera** (c. 600 BC), the ruins' best-preserved structure and the site of the lighting of the **Olympic flame.** Opposite the site, the **New Museum** houses a vast array of sculpture, including the Nike of Paionios, the **Hermes of Praxiteles,** the pedimental sculptures from the Temple of Zeus, and fun military spoils. (Site open daily 8am-7pm. Museum open M noon-7pm, Tu-Su 8am-7pm. Joint ticket 2000dr; separately 1200dr each, students 600dr; EU students free.)

In New Olympia, **buses** run from opposite the tourist info booth to **Tripoli** (4hr., 3 per day, 2500dr). The **tourist office,** on Kondili, is on the east side of town, toward the ruins. (☎23 100. Open M-F 8am-9pm, Sa 10am-5pm.) A conveniently located **youth hostel** is at Kondili 18. (☎25 580. Breakfast 600dr. Check-out 10:30am. Lockout 10:30am-noon. Dorms 1700dr.) **Pension Poseidon,** two blocks uphill on Kondili from the National Bank, rents rooms and serves Greek food. (Singles 5000-6000dr; doubles 7500dr; triples 9000dr. Entrees about 1500dr.) **Camping Diana** is farther uphill on Kondili from Pension Poseidon. (☎22 314. 1600dr per person; 1200-1600dr per tent; 1000dr per car.) **Postal code:** 27065.

TRIPOLI (Τριπολη) AND ENVIRONS ☎071

Tripoli itself is a transport hub, and offers little more. **Trains** go to: **Corinth** (2½hr., 4 per day, 900dr); **Kalamata** (2½hr., 4 per day, 840dr); and **Athens** (4hr., 4 per day, 1500dr). **Buses** from Pl. Kolokotronis, east of the center, go to **Athens** (3hr., 14 per day, 3200dr). The **KTEL Messinia and Laconia** depot is across from the train station and sends buses to **Sparta** (1hr., 10 per day, 1000dr) and **Patras** (3hr., 2 per day, 3100dr). Crash at **Hotel Alex,** Vas. Georgios 26, between Pl. Kolokotronis and Pl. Agios Vasiliou. (☎223 465. Singles 7000dr; doubles 10-14,000dr.) **Postal code:** 22100.

EXCURSIONS FROM TRIPOLI: DIMITSANA AND STEMNITSA. West of Tripoli, the enticing villages of Dimitsana (Δημητσανα) and Stemnitsa (Στεμνιτσα) are good bases for **hiking** in the idyllic, rugged countryside. **Dimitsana** has been a center of Greek learning and revolutionary activity since the 16th century. **Buses** pull in on Labardopoulou from Tripoli (1½hr., 1-3 per day, 1200dr). Buses to **Tripoli** and **Olympia** make frequent stops in Karkalou, 20 minutes away by taxi (1000dr). **Private rooms** are basically the only option—they're like bed and breakfasts. Walking through the *plateia*, take the last right before the road bends to the left to the gorgeous rooms in the home of **Basilis Tsiapa.** (☎31 583. Singles 9000dr; doubles 10,000dr.) Rooms to let are also available above the **grocery store** in the main square. From Dimitsana, a beautiful 11km stroll along the road (or a 1000dr taxi ride) will bring you to **Stemnitsa,** whose narrow, cobblestone streets betray medieval roots. Many consider the town to be the most beautiful in Greece. The splendid **Hotel Triokolonion** is left of the main road from Dimitsana. (☎81 297. Breakfast included. Call ahead. Singles 7800dr; doubles 10,600dr.) ☎**0795.**

KALAMATA (Καλαματα) AND MESSENE (Μεσσηνια) ☎0721

Kalamata, like Tripoli, is more important as a transport hub (to the southern Peloponnese) than a place to visit. The well-preserved, massive-walled ruins of **Ancient Messene** in nearby **Mavromati,** are some of Greece's most impressive archaeological finds. (Open daily 8:30am-3pm. 500dr, students 300dr, EU students free.) Buses run to Mavromati from Kalamata (1hr., 2 per day M-Sa, 500dr). **Trains** run from Sideromikou Stathmou to: **Tripoli** (2½hr., 840dr); **Olympia** (3hr., 900dr); **Corinth** (5¼hr., 1640dr); **Patras** (5½hr., 4 per day, 1500dr); and **Athens** (7hr., 4 per day, 2160dr). **Buses** arrive in Kalamata from: **Sparta** (2hr., 2 per day, 1150dr); **Tripoli** (2hr., 1550dr); **Corinth** (3hr., 3000dr); **Patras** (4hr., 2 per day, 4150dr); and **Athens** (4hr., 11 per day, 4400dr). From the bus station, take a taxi to the center (500-700dr), or go down Artemidos, turn right on Iatropoulou just before the post office, and follow it to Aristomenous; to the left is the old town and the waterfront is to the right. From the train station, turn right on Frantzi at the end of Pl. Georgiou and walk a few blocks to reach the town center. To get to **Hotel Nevada,** Santa Rosa 9, take bus #1 and get off as soon as it turns left along the water. (☎82 429. Singles 5000dr; doubles 7000dr; triples 8000dr.) **Postal code:** 24100.

EXCURSIONS FROM KALAMATA: PYLOS AND METHONI. Unspoiled **Pylos** (Πυλος) offers up its beaches, palace, and two fortresses. **Nestor's Palace,** where Nestor met Telemachus in Homer's *Odyssey*, was built in the 13th century BC. To see the site, still under excavation, take the bus to Kyparissia and get off at the palace (40min., 300dr). **Buses** arrive in Pylos from **Kalamata** (1½hr., 9 per day, 950dr). Look for **Rooms to Let** signs as the bus descends into town (singles 4000-6000dr; doubles 6000-10,000dr). Buses continue to nearby **Methoni** (Μεθωνη; 15min., 7 per day, 250dr), where hibiscus-lined streets wind around the 13th-century **Venetian fortress,** a mini city. (Open M-Sa 8am-8pm, Su 9am-8pm. Free.) Near the end of the lower road, make a left (heading toward the *plateia*) to find the **Hotel Galini.** (☎31 467. Singles 7000dr; doubles 10,000dr.) ☎**0723.**

SPARTA (Σπαρτη) AND MYSTRAS (Μυστρας) ☎0731

While **Ancient Sparta** has been immortalized in the annals of military history, the modern version is noted mostly for its olive oil and orange trees, and as a base for visits to **Mystras,** 6km away. **Buses** arrive in Sparta from: **Gythion** (1hr., 5 per day, 800dr); **Tripoli** (1hr., 1100dr); **Areopolis** (1½hr., 4 per day, 1300dr); **Corinth** (2hr., 2400dr); **Monemvassia** (2hr., 3 per day, 1800dr); **Kalamata** (2hr., 2 per day, 1150dr); and **Athens** (3½hr., 9 per day, 3800dr). To reach the town center from the bus station, walk 10 blocks west on Lykourgou; the **tourist office** is to the left of the town hall in the *plateia*. (☎24 852. Open daily 8am-2pm.) **Hotel Laconia** is conveniently located on Paleologou. (☎28 952. Singles 6000-8000dr; doubles 9000-10,000dr.)

Once the religious center of Byzantium and the locus of Constantinople's rule over the Peloponnese, **Mystras** and its extraordinary ruins reveal a city of Byzantine churches, chapels, and monasteries. Don't miss the beautiful **Metropolis of St.**

Demetrios on the lower tier, with its flowery courtyard and museum of architectural fragments. At the extreme left of the lower tier, every inch of the **Church of Peribleptos** is bathed in exquisitely detailed religious paintings; despite Ottoman vandalization, the church is still Mystras' most stunning relic. (Open daily 8am-7pm; in winter 8:30am-3pm. 1200dr, students 600dr, EU students free.) **Buses** from **Sparta** to Mystras stop at the corner of Lykourgou and Kythonigou (20min., 9 per day, 250dr), two blocks past the town *plateia* away from the main bus station.

GYTHION (Γυθειο) AND AREOPOLIS (Αρεοπολη) ☎0733

Once plagued by violent family feuds and savage piracy, the sparsely settled **Mani** (Μανη) province derives its name from *manis*, Greek for wrath or fury; history has affirmed its etymological roots many times. Today, fiery Maniot rage is cooled by a coastal breeze. **Gythion,** the "Gateway to the Mani," is the liveliest town in the region, near lovely sand and stone beaches. A tiny causeway connects to the island of **Marathonisi,** where Paris and Helen consummated their ill-fated love. **Buses** arrive at the north end of the waterfront from: **Athens** (4hr., 6 per day, 4700dr); **Corinth** (3hr., 3350dr); **Kalamata** (2 per day, 2050dr); **Sparta** (1hr., 850dr); and **Tripoli** (2hr., 1850dr). **Ferries** sail from the quay near **Pl. Mavromichali,** in the middle of the waterfront. To explore the hard-to-reach parts of Mani, rent a **moped** at **Moto Makis Rent-A-Moped,** on the waterfront near the causeway. (5000dr per day. Open daily 8:30am-8:30pm.) **Xenia Karlaftis Rooms,** on the water 20m from the causeway, rent spacious rooms with gracious service. (☎22 719. Kitchen. Laundry. Singles 5000dr; doubles 6000dr; triples 7000dr.) For **Meltemi Camping,** 4km south of town toward Areopolis, take a city bus (4 per day) or a taxi for 900dr. (☎22 833. 1500dr per person; 1300dr per tent; 850dr per car.) **Postal code:** 23200.

GREECE

From **Areopolis,** along the western coast of Mani, you can visit the spectacular **Vlihada Cave** (Σπηλαιο Πυργος Διρυου), 4km from town. The 30-minute **boat ride** down the cave's subterranean river passes a forest of stalagmites; the cave is believed to extend all the way to Sparta. (Open daily June-Sept. 8am-5pm; Oct.-May 8am-2:45pm. 3500dr.) A 250dr bus to the caves leaves **Areopolis** at 11am and returns at 12:45pm. **Buses** stop in Areopolis' main *plateia* from: **Athens** (6hr., 5000dr); **Gythion** (30min., 4 per day, 500dr); **Kalamata** (2½hr., 2 per day, 1400dr); and **Sparta** (1½hr., 1300dr). To sleep at **Tsimova,** turn left at the end of Kapetan Matapan. (☎51 301. Singles 6000dr; doubles 8000dr; triples 12,000dr.)

MONEMVASIA (Μονεμβασια) AND GEFYRA (Γεφυρα) ☎0732

The city of Monemvasia, a major Peloponnesian tourist sight, has an other-worldly quality. No cars or bikes pass the city's only gate; pack horses bear groceries into the city, where narrow streets hide stairways, child-sized doors, and flowered courtyards. From the Monemvasia gate, a cobblestone main street winds past tourist shops and restaurants to the town square. At the edge of the cliffs perches the oft-photographed 12th-century **Agia Sofia;** navigate the maze of streets to the edge of town farthest from the sea, where a path climbs the side of the cliff to the church. Stay in the more modern and cheaper **Gefyra;** from there, it's a 20min. walk down 23 Iouliou along the waterfront to the causeway, where an orange **bus** runs to Monemvasia (July-Aug. every 10min., 100dr). **Buses** leave Gefyra from 23 Iouliou for: **Corinth** (5hr., 3 per day, 4450dr); **Sparta** (2½hr., 3 per day, 1900dr); and **Tripoli** (4hr., 3 per day, 2950dr). The *domatia* along the waterfront are your best bet (doubles 5000-8000dr). **Hotel Sophos** has better prices than most hotels. (☎61 360. Singles 8000dr; doubles 10,000dr.) **Camping Paradise** is 3.5km along the water on the mainland. (☎61 123. 1400dr per person; 900-1200dr per tent; 950dr per car.) **To Limanaki,** beside the harbor on the mainland, serves tasty Greek favorites.

NAFPLION (Ναυπλιο) ☎0752

Nafplion is the perfect base to play archaeologist, though the Venetian fortresses, *plateias*, Old Town, and pebble beach may entice you away from the ruins. The town's crown jewel is the 18th-century **Palamidi Fortress,** with spectacular views of the town. To get there, walk the 3km road, or take 999 grueling steps up from

Arvanitias, across the park from the bus station. (Open M-F 8am-6pm, Sa-Su 8:30am-3pm; off-season daily 8:30am-3pm. 800dr, students 400dr, EU students free.) **Buses** arrive on Singrou, near the base of the Palamidi fortress, from **Athens** (3hr., 16 per day, 2650dr) and **Corinth** (2hr., 1100dr). To reach Bouboulinas, the waterfront, walk left from the station as you exit and follow Singrou to the harbor—the **Old Town** is on your left. The **tourist office** is on 25 Martiou across from the OTE. (☎24 444. Open daily 9am-1pm and 4-8pm.) To enjoy the rooftop views of **Dimitris Bekas' Domatia** in the old town, turn up the stairs on Kokinou and follow the sign for rooms off Staikopoulou; climb to the top, turn left, and go up another 50 steps. (☎24 594. Singles 5000dr; doubles 7000dr.) In the new town, try **Hotel Artemis** on Argos. (☎27 862. Singles 6000dr; doubles 8000dr.) **Taverna O Vasiles,** on Staikopoulou above the *plateia*, serves yummy rabbit (1650dr). **Postal code:** 21100.

EXCURSIONS FROM NAFPLION: MYCENAE AND EPIDAVROS. Greece's supreme city from 1600 to 1100 BC, **Mycenae** (Μυκηνες) was once ruled by Agamemnon, leader of the attacking forces in the Trojan War, gorily detailed in Homer's *Iliad*. Most of the site's treasures are in Athens, but the remaining **Lion's Gate** and the **Treasury of Atreus** are among the most celebrated archaeological finds. (Open daily Apr.-Sept. 8am-7pm; Oct.-Mar. 8am-5pm. 1500dr, students 800dr, EU students free. Keep your ticket or pay again at Agamemnon's tomb.) Join the illustrious ranks of Heinrich Schliemann, Woolf, Debussy, Faulkner, Agatha Christie, and Ginsberg, who have all stayed at **Hotel Belle Helene;** it also serves as a bus stop on the main road. (☎76 225. Singles 7000dr; doubles 10,000dr; triples 12,000dr.) **Trains** run from **Athens** to Fihtia via **Corinth** (5 per day). From Fihtia, take the Corinth-Argos road and follow the signs to Mycenae to reach the site. **Buses** roll in from **Nafplion** (30min., 4 per day, 600dr); others from **Athens** (2½hr., 15 per day, 1800dr) stop at **Fihtia,** 1.5km away.

The grand **Theater of Epidavros** (Επιδαυρος), built in the early 2nd century BC, is the highlight of the ancient site, and held 14,000 folks at its height. Henry Miller wrote that he heard "the great heart of the world" beat here; the incredible acoustics allow you to stand at the top row of seats and hear a match light on stage. (Open daily 7:30am-7pm. 1500dr, students 800dr, EU students free.) From late June to mid-August, the **Epidavros Theater Festival** brings performances of classical Greek plays (it'll all be Greek to you) on Friday or Saturday nights. Shows are at 9pm; purchase tickets at the site, in advance in Athens, at the Athens Festival Box Office (☎ (01) 322 1459), or at Nafplion's bus station (tickets 4000-6000dr, students 2000dr). **Buses** arrive in Epidavros from **Nafplion** (1hr., 4 per day, 600dr). **☎0751.**

CORINTH (Κορινθος) ☎0741

Most visitors to the Peloponnese stop first at New Corinth, where a green bus drives 7km from Koliatsou, near Kolokotroni, to the ruins of **Ancient Corinth** (20min., every hr. 6am-9pm, 300dr), at the base of the **Acrocorinth.** Columns and other remnants lie around the courtyard of the excellent **museum** in fascinating chaos. As you exit the museum, the 6th-century BC **Temple of Apollo** is down the stairs to the left. The **fortress** at the top of Acrocorinth is a 1½-hour walk only for the truly dedicated; at the summit, the largely-intact **Temple to Aphrodite** once initiated disciples into the "mysteries of love." (Museum and site open daily 8am-7pm; in winter 8am-5pm. Combined 1200dr, students 600dr.) Hired **taxis** (☎31 464) from New Corinth will wait at the site for an hour (4000dr).

Frequent **buses** stop in New Corinth two blocks inland, at Ermou and Koliatsou, from **Athens** (1½hr., 32 per day, 1750dr) and **Loutraki** (20min., 2 per hr., 320dr). To get to **Sparta** or other points south, take the Loutraki bus to the Corinth Canal and pick up the Athens bus to Sparta. **Trains** go to **Athens** (2hr., 14 per day, 900dr) and **Patras** (2½hr., 8 per day, 1150dr). To get to the waterfront from the train station, turn left out of the building onto Demokratias and take the first right onto Damaskinou. **Hotel Akti,** 3 Ethnikis Antistasis, is near the waterfront. (☎23 337. Singles 4000dr; doubles 8000dr.) To get to **Camping Korinth Beach,** 3km away, catch a bus (every 30min., 210dr) on Kollatsou, near Kolokotroni, and look for the signs. (☎27 920. 1400dr per person; 850dr per tent.)

CENTRAL AND NORTHERN GREECE

Under 19th-century Ottoman rule, the provinces of Sterea Ellada, Thessaly, Epirus, Macedonia, and Thrace acquired a Byzantine flavor; forgotten mountain-goat paths lead to these Byzantine treasures. Along the way, you'll encounter glorious mountain-top vistas over silvery olive groves, fruit trees, and patchwork farmland.

OSIOS LOUKAS (Οσιος Λουκας) ☎0267

Osios Loukas delights the eye with its mountain vistas and stunning Byzantine architecture. The exquisite monastery, built in the 10th and 11th centuries and still in use today, overlooks Boeotia and Phokis from the green slopes of Mt. Elikon more than 1700m above sea level. Gold-laden mosaics, vibrant frescoes, and intricate brick- and stonework adorn Osios Loukas, the most famous and perhaps the most gorgeous monastery in Greece. Dress modestly (long skirts for women, long pants for men, no bare shoulders). Two churches are at the site: the **katholikon,** on the right after the museum, built in AD 1011 and dedicated to the monastery's founding saint, Osios Loukas, is more impressive; the smaller **Church of the Panagia** (Church of the Virgin Mary) holds the dried body of the saint himself in a glass coffin. A **crypt,** accessible from an entrance on the south of the katholikon, has stunning frescoes and is not to be missed. (☎22 797. Open daily May 3 to Sept. 15 8am-2pm and 4-7pm; Sept. 16 to May 2 8am-5pm. 800dr, seniors 600dr, under 18 and students with ID free.) Take a car, moped, or **taxi** (☎ (0267) 22 322; around 5000dr one-way) or walk 9km on the hilly, narrow road from the town of Distomo.

GREECE

METEORA (Μετεωρα) ☎0432

Southwest of Olympus lie the majestic, iron-gray pinnacles of the Meteora rock formations, bedecked by 24 exquisite, gravity-defying Byzantine **monasteries.** (Open Apr.-Sept. Sa-Su and W 9am-12:30pm and 3:20-6pm. 500dr per monastery. Dress modestly; women in skirts; men in pants; no bare shoulders. No photography.) The **Grand Meteoron Monastery** is the oldest, largest, and most important of the monasteries, with brilliant frescoes of the Roman persecution of Christians. The monastery also houses a **Folk Museum.** The library of **Varlaam Monastery** contains 200 manuscripts, some housed in the museum, including a miniature Bible from 960. The most popular base for exploring Meteora is the town of **Kalambaka** (Καλαμ πακα). There will be **no train service** to Kalambaka through at least summer 2001 due to construction of new rail lines, but **buses** arrive from: **Athens** (5hr., 8 per day, 5500dr); **Patras** (6hr., 2 per week, 5800dr); and **Thessaloniki** (3hr., 6 per day, 3700dr). From the bus station, walk past the taxi stand and uphill to reach the small central square. Local buses depart from Kalambaka for Meteora (20min., 2 per day, 250dr); a **taxi** costs about 1500dr. Most people walk the 6km downhill back to town, visiting the monasteries along the way. **Koka Roka** offers an awe-inspiring view of Meteora; from the central square, follow Vlachara until it ends, then bear left and follow the signs to Kanari for 15 minutes. (☎24 554. 3500dr per person without bath. With bath, singles 6000dr; doubles 8000dr; triples 10,000dr.) **Camping** is also a popular option; campsites line the roads in all directions out of town. **Postal code:** 42200.

MOUNT OLYMPUS (Ολυμπος Ορος) ☎0352

Erupting out of the Thermaic Gulf, the height (nearly 3000m) and formidable slopes of Mt. Olympus once so awed the ancients that they envisioned it as their gods' home. A network of well-maintained **hiking** trails now makes the summit accessible to just about anyone with sturdy legs and a taste for adventure, although you may yearn for a pair of Hermes' winged sandals. From **Litohoro,** one route is to hike up via **Prionia,** stay at a refuge, and climb to the summit the next day. You could stay another night and walk down the next day to **Diastavrosi** (about 3-4hr.), or pass by the refuges and arrive at Diastavrosi in late afternoon. There is no bus to the trailheads from **Litohoro,** so you'll have to walk or drive the asphalt road. A **taxi** costs about 6000dr to Prionia or 1500dr to Diastavrosi. You'll want to make your ascent between May and October, when Persephone returns to Olympus from the Underworld and her mother, Demeter, warms the earth. **Mytikas,** the tallest peak, is inaccessible without special equipment before June. There are three **refuges** near the summits where you can find lodgings. **Trains** (☎22 522) run from **Athens** (7hr., 3 per day, 3500dr) and **Thessaloniki** (1½hr., 5 per day, 850dr) to the Litohoro station; from there walk 1km to the **bus stop** to catch a 5km ride into town (20min., 13 per day, 250dr). A **taxi** from the train station costs around 2000dr. Direct KTEL **buses** (☎81 271) run from **Athens** (6hr., 3 per day, 7400dr) and **Thessaloniki** (1½hr., 16 per day, 1750dr); they arrive at the station opposite the church in Litohoro's main *plateia*. Down Ag. Nikolaou from the bus stop is the town's **tourist office.** (☎83 100. Mountain maps 1000dr. Open daily 8:15am-9pm.) The most affordable hotel is the **Hotel Park,** Ag. Nikolaou 23, about 10m down from the *plateia*. (☎81 252. Singles 6500dr; doubles 8000dr; triples 9000dr.) **Camp** at **Olympus Zeus** (☎22 115 or 22 116) or **Olympus Beach** (☎22 112 or 22 113), on the beach 5km from town.

THE ZAGOROHORIA (Τα Ζαγοροχωια) ☎0653

The Zagorohoria is a cluster of 46 villages 36km north of Ioannina that surround the famed **Vikos Gorge.** Remarkable for their natural beauty and traditional architecture, the villages offer unparalleled hiking opportunities through the gorge and the surrounding Vikos-Aoös National Park. The complete absence of banks, post offices, and souvenir shops make them a welcome respite from more touristed areas. **Monodendri** can be reached by bus from Ioannina (45min.; M, W, and F 6am and 4:15pm; return 7am and 5pm; 750dr), and is the best starting point for hiking the Gorge—just follow the signs from the *plateia* below the main road. **Buses** run regularly to Zossimadon 4 in Ioannina from **Athens** (7hr., per day, 7500dr) and **Thessaloniki** (7hr., 6 per day, 6200dr). **Pension Monodendri,** up the road from the bus stop, has comfortable, traditional rooms over a *taverna* serving delicious food; the owners' son Mario is full of hiking information about the canyon and surrounding area. His parents can arrange a pick-up from the end of the hike. (☎71 300. Singles 5000dr, doubles 8000dr). At the other end of the six-hour hike lies the village of **Megalo Papingo,** the most developed Zagorian village, accessible by **bus** from **Ioannina** (1hr., 4 per week, 1200dr). Hotel prices are a bit stiffer in Megalo Papingo. The best deal is in the rooms above **Koulis Restaurant.** (☎41 138. Singles 9000dr; doubles 12,000dr.) Nikos at the restaurant has info on the gorge, nearby **Mt. Gamilia,** and **Mt. Astraka.**

According to the *Guinness Book of World Records,* the **Vikos Gorge,** with 900m deep walls only 1100m apart, is the steepest canyon on earth. Rusted iron deposits in the gorge's sedimentary rock give the walls an orange-pink sunset tint, even at high noon. The long hike through the gorge is impressive; the nearly vertical canyon-sides, to which throngs of trees cling stubbornly, tower hundreds of meters over your head. For directions through the Gorge, talk to Mario (see above).

THESSALONIKI (Θεσσαλονικη) ☎031

Thessaloniki is an elusive jumble of ancient, Byzantine, European, Turkish, Balkan, and contemporary Greek cultural and historical debris—pragmatic utility, frilly beauty, and tasteless chintz all mingle. A Byzantine-Turkish fortress oversees the old town, while modern mayhem encircles Byzantine churches, masking interiors of glimmering gold mosaics, masterful frescoes, and floating domes.

GETTING THERE AND GETTING AROUND

Trains: Main Terminal (☎517 517), on Monastiriou in the western part of the city. Take any bus down Egnatia (100dr). To: **Athens** (6-8hr., 10 per day, 4250dr); **İstanbul, Turkey** (13hr., 1 per day, 13,000dr); **Skopje, FYROM** (5hr., 1 per day, 5000dr); **Sofia, Bulgaria** (10½hr., 1 per day, 7000dr). **OSE** (☎518 113), at Aristotelous and Ermou, has tickets and schedules. Open M-Sa 8am-2:30pm.

Buses: Most **KTEL** buses depart from between the port and railway station or from north of the railway. To: **Athens** (6hr., 20 per day, 9000dr), from along Monastiriou; **Corinth**

(7½hr., 1 per day, 9200dr), from Monastiriou 69 (☎527 265); and **Patras** (8hr., 2 per day, 8250dr), from Monastiriou 87 (☎525 253). **International buses** (☎599 100) leave from the train station for **Sofia** (6hr., 4 per day, 5600dr) and **İstanbul** (12hr., 1 per day, 24,300dr).

Ferries and Hydrofoils: Buy tickets at **Karacharisis Travel and Shipping Agency,** Koundouriotou 8 (☎524 544; fax 532 289), on the corner. Open M-F 9am-9pm, Sa 9am-3pm. To: **Chios** (21hr., 3 per week, 8300dr); **Lesvos** (9hr., 2 per week, 8300dr); **Limnos** (7hr., 5 per week, 5300dr); **Mykonos** (16hr., 3 per week, 9200dr); and **Samos** (14hr., 1 per week, 9500dr). **Flying Dolphins:** June-Sept. daily 8am and Th-M usually 4:30pm. To **Skiathos** (3¾hr., 8500dr) and **Skopelos** (4½hr., 9300dr). **Crete Air Travel,** Dragoumi 1 (☎547 407), opposite the port, sells Flying Dolphin tickets. Open M-F 8:30am-9pm, Sa 8:30am-3pm, Su 9am-3pm.

Public Transportation: Many **buses** (100dr) traverse the city. Buses #8, 10, 11, and 31 run up and down Egnatia. Buy tickets at kiosks or ticket booths at major stations.

GREECE

ORIENTATION AND PRACTICAL INFORMATION

Egnatia, an old Roman highway, runs down the middle of town and is home to the cheapest hotels. Running parallel to the water, the main streets are **Ermou, Tsimiski, Mitropoleos,** and **Nikis,** which runs along the waterfront. Inland from Egnatia is **Ag. Dimitriou** and the **Old Town** beyond. Intersecting these and leading from the water into town are **I. Dragoumi, El. Venizelou, Aristotelous, Ag. Sophias,** and **Eth. Aminis.**

Tourist Office: EOT, Pl. Aristotelous (☎271 888; fax 265 504), 1 block from the water. Open M-F 9am-9pm, Sa 10am-6pm, Su 10am-5pm; reduced hours in winter.

Consulates: Bulgaria, N. Manou 12 (☎829 210). Open M-F 10am-noon. **Cyprus,** L. Nikis 37 (☎260 611). Open M-F 9am-1pm. **Turkey,** Ag. Dimitriou 151 (☎248 452). Open M-F 9am-noon. **UK,** Venizelou 8 (☎278 006). Open M-F 8am-1pm. **US,** Tsimiski 43 (☎242 900). Open M, W, and F 9am-noon.

Currency Exchange: Banks and **24hr. ATMs** line Tsimiski.

American Express: Memphis Travel, Aristotelous 3, 1st floor. (☎282 351). Cashes traveler's checks and changes currency. Open M-F 9:30am-3:30pm and Sa 9am-2pm.

Tourist Police: Dodekanissou 4, 5th fl. (☎554 870 or 554 871). Open 24hr. For the **general police,** call ☎553 800 or 100.

Telephones: OTE, Karolou Diehl 27 (☎221 899), at the corner of Ermou, 1 block east of Aristotelous. Open daily 7:15am-9:30pm.

Internet Access: Pl@net, 53 Alex. Svolou, across from the hostel. 10am-6pm 600dr per hr., 6pm-3am 800dr per hr. Open daily 10am-3am.

Post Office: On Aristotelous, just before Egnatia. Open M-F 7:30am-8pm, Sa 7:30am-2pm, Su 9am-1:30pm. Address mail to be held: First name SURNAME, Poste Restante, Pl. Aristotelous, Thessaloniki, **54101,** Greece.

ACCOMMODATIONS AND FOOD

Most budget hotels cluster along the western end of Egnatia, between Pl. Dimokratias (500m east of the train station) and Pl. Dikastiriou. Egnatia can be noisy and gritty, but you'll have to pay more elsewehere.

Hotel Augustos, Elenis Svoronou 4 (☎522 955; ☎/fax 522 500). From Egnatia, turn north at the Argo Hotel; it's straight ahead. The best budget deal in town. Some rooms with bath. Singles 5000-8000dr; doubles 7000-11,000dr; triples 13,000dr.

Youth Hostel, Alex. Svolou 44 (☎225 946; fax 262 208). Take bus #8, 10, 11, or 31 down Egnatia to Kamara (Arch of Galerius), walk toward the water, and turn left on Svolou. Lockout 11am-6:30pm. Reception 9-11am and 7-11pm. Open Mar.-Nov. 2500dr.

Hotel Acropolis, Tantalidou 4 (☎536 170). From Pl. Dimokratias, take the 2nd right off Egnatia after Dodekanissou. Quiet. Singles 5500dr; doubles 6500dr; triples 7500dr.

Hotel Averof, L. Sofou 24 (☎538 840; fax 543 194), at Egnatia. Friendly staff and communal TV room. Singles 6000-9000dr; doubles 8000-12,000dr.

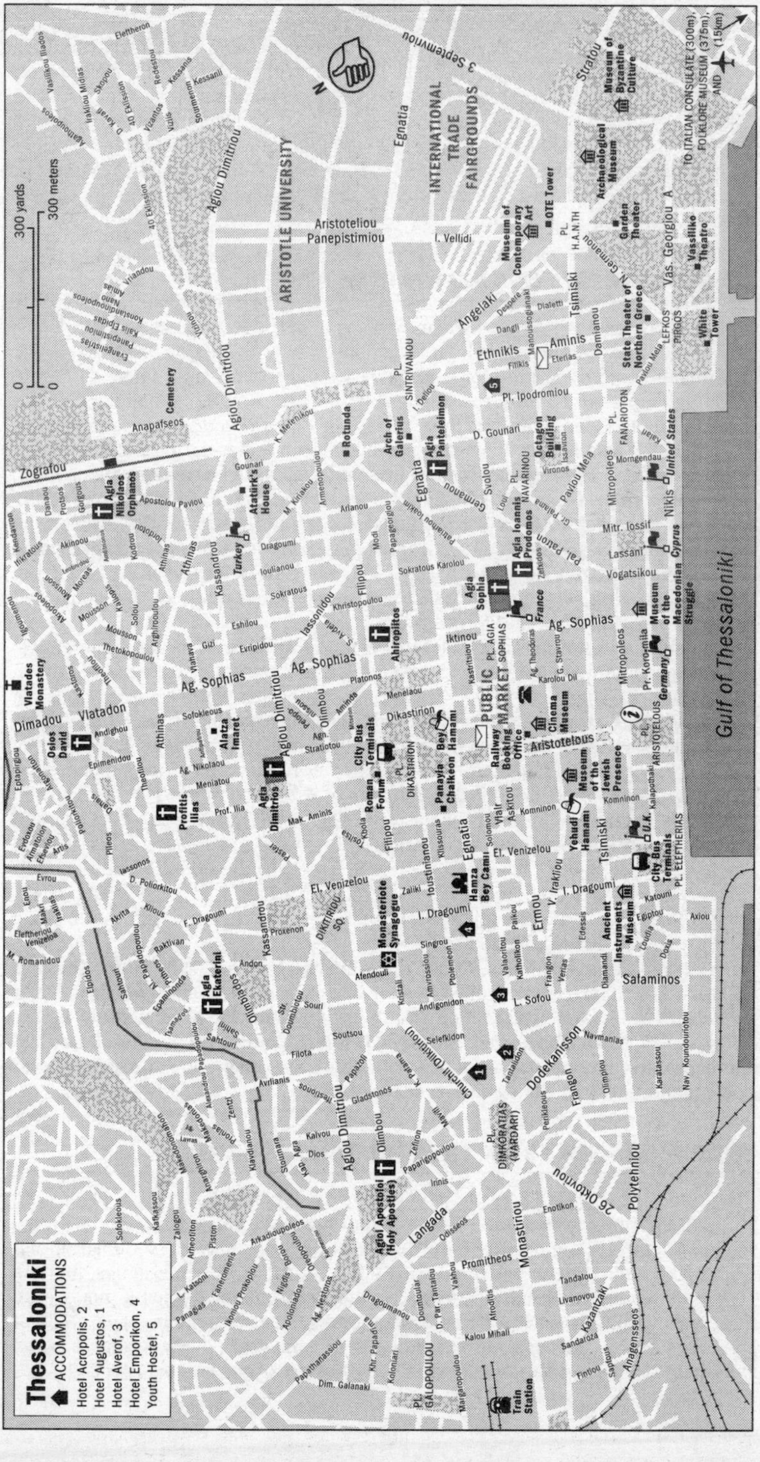

Thessaloniki

ACCOMMODATIONS

Hotel Acropolis, 2
Hotel Augustos, 1
Hotel Averof, 3
Hotel Emporikon, 4
Youth Hostel, 5

Most food can be found in tiny streets on both sides of Aristotelous; the innovative places a block down from Egnatia between Dragoumi and El. Venizelou cater to a younger clientele. **Open-air markets** are on Vati Kioutou, off Aristotelous between Irakliou and Egnatia. **Ouzeri Melathron,** in an alley between El. Venizelou and Dragoumi, has a humorous menu and delicious food. (Entrees 1150-3600dr.) **Ta Adelphi,** in Pl. Navarino, serves great meat dishes at good prices in a bustling atmosphere. (Entrees 980-2750dr. Open noon-midnight.) **Mesogeios,** Balanou 38, east of Aristotelous, a block south of Egnatia, is the area's largest *ouzeri*. (Entrees 1200-2200dr.)

SIGHTS AND ENTERTAINMENT

Salonica, Thessaloniki's former name, was vital to the Byzantines and Ottomans; its modern streets are littered with remnants from both. **Agios Dimitrios**, on Ag. Dimitriou north of Aristotelous, is the city's oldest and most famous church. Although most of its interior was gutted in the 1917 fire, the remaining mosaics are stunning. (Open daily 8am-8pm.) South of Egnatia on the square that bears its name, the **Agia Sophia Rotunda** became a church under the Byzantines. It was built to honor a Roman emperor but was later converted to a mosque; its walls, now under renovation, have some of the city's best mosaics. (Open daily 7am-2:30pm.) Head south to the **Arch of Galerius,** built in the 4th century AD, on the eastern end of Egnatia. Back west down Egnatia, don't miss the **Bey Hamamı,** where the Ottoman governor bathed, and the **Hamza Bey Camii,** across from Venezeliou. The 15th-century **Camii,** once a prominent mosque, was converted into a movie theater in the 20th century.

Thessaloniki's **Archaeological Museum** is full of artifacts from Neolithic tombs, mosaics from Roman houses, and dazzling Macedonian gold. Take bus #10 down Egnatia to Pl. Hanth. (Open M 12:30-7pm, Tu-Su 8am-7pm; reduced hours in winter. 1500dr, students and seniors 800dr.) Just across the street on 3 Septembriou, the **Museum of Byzantine Culture** has three huge rooms about Thessalonian daily life. (Open M 12:30-8pm, Tu-Su 8am-7pm; reduced in winter. 1000dr, students and seniors 500dr.) All that remains of a 15th-century Venetian seawall, the **White Tower** presides over the eastern edge of the waterfront. Once a site of bloody executions by Ottoman Janissaries, the tower now houses a collection of early Christian art. (Open Tu-Su 8am-3pm. Free.) In the middle of the marketplace west of Aristoteliou, on the first floor of Irakliou 26, the **Museum of the Jewish Presence** details the long history of Thessaloniki's Sephardic Jews. (Ring bell. Open M-F 10am-1:30pm. Free.)

There are three main hubs for late-night fun: the bars and cafes of the **Ladadika** district, the waterfront, and the open-air discos that throb near the airport exit (1000-2000dr by taxi). **Teatro,** 11km east of the city along the main highway, is very Greek, slick, and sophisticated. (Cover 3000dr includes one drink.) **Deka Dance** and **Privilege,** farther down the highway from Teatro, are other popular discos. (Cover 2500dr and 2000dr, includes one drink.)

EXCURSION FROM THESSALONIKI: VERGINA

The tombs of Vergina (Βεργινα), final home to ancient Macedonian royalty, lie only 30km from Thessaloniki. The principal site is the **museum,** located with the tombs themselves under the **Great Tumulus,** a huge man-made mount 12m tall and 110m wide. Check out the intricate gold work, brilliant frescoes, and the bones of **Alexander IV,** son of Alexander the Great, inside. (Open M noon-7pm, Tu-Su 8am-7pm; in winter Tu-Su 8:30am-3pm. 1200dr, students 600dr.) To get to Vergina, take the **bus** from Thessaloniki to **Veria** (2hr., every 30min., 1300dr) and from there take the "Alexandria" bus and get off in Vergina (20min., 9 per day, 300dr).

IONIAN ISLANDS (Νησια Του Ιονιου)

Even the most jaded travelers will gasp at the shimmering beauty of the gray-green olive groves and brilliant blues of the Ionian Islands. On Greece's western edge, the islands escaped Ottoman occupation, and were instead rolled over by the Venetians, British, French, and Russians. Each of these uninvited visitors left lasting cultural, commercial, and architectural imprints behind. Hundreds of ferry-hopping backpackers make the short trip from Italy, making the islands companionable.

FERRIES TO ITALY

Buy tickets early in high season and ask if the port tax (1500-2000dr) is included. **Eurail** passes are valid. Ferries run to **Corfu** from **Ancona** (21hr., 1 per day, 16-22,000dr); **Bari** (10hr., 3-4 per week, 9000dr); **Brindisi** (8hr., 4 per day, 7500-19,500dr); **Trieste** (24hr., 2 per week, 14,500-19,400dr); and **Venice** (26hr., 1 per day, 16-22,000dr). **Catamarans** go to **Corfu** from **Brindisi** (3¼hr., 18-27,000dr, under 28 5000-10,000dr less). In summer, ferries connect **Kephalonia** to **Brindisi, Venice,** and **Ancona.**

CORFU (Κερκυρα) ☎0661

Since Odysseus washed ashore and praised Corfu, the seas have brought crusaders, conquerors, and colonists to this verdant isle. While its beauty has brought perhaps too many tourists to the region, many inland villages and beach towns remain authentic. **Corfu Town** itself is lovely, and those who venture away from the city are even more greatly rewarded. **Paleokastritsa beach** rests among six coves and sea caves casting shadows over shades of blue. KTEL buses go to **Paleokastritsa** (45min., 10 per day, 650dr). South of Paleokastritsa is **Pelekas Town;** walk 30 minutes downhill to reach **Pelekas beach.** Bus #11 runs to Pelekas Town from Pl. Sanrocco (30min., 7 per day, 230dr). The more touristed **Glyfada beach,** 5km from Pelekas Town, is accessible by free shuttles from Pelekas and by KTEL buses from Pl. Sanrocco in Corfu Town (9400dr). Isolated **Moni Myrtidon** beach and the unofficial nude beach **Myrtiotissa** are also nearby. **Agios Gordios,** 10km south of Pelekas, offers impressive rock formations, a good beach, and the immensely popular (and frat-like) **Pink Palace Hotel.** On weekends, wild toga parties of Americans and Canadians at the "palace" conjure up scenes from *Animal House.* (☎53 103; fax 53 025. 7000-9000dr includes breakfast, dinner, ferry pick-up and drop-off, and nightclub.) Blue buses run to Agios Gordios from Pl. Sanrocco (45min., 7 per day, 300dr).

Ferries run from Corfu Town to: **Italy** (see above); **Kephalonia** (5hr., 1 per week, 5200dr); and **Patras** (9hr., 1-2 per day, 5800dr). KTEL inter-city **green buses** depart from just off I. Theotaki; municipal **blue buses** leave from Pl. Sanrocco. From the new port customs house, cross the intersection and walk 1km uphill on Avramiou, which becomes I. Theotoki, to reach **Pl. Sanrocco.** The **tourist office** is at the corner of R. Voulefton and I. Folila. (☎37 520. Open daily M-F 8am-2pm.) There's a branch in the new port customs house. (Open daily 6am-2pm.) The **Association of Owners of Private Rooms and Apartments in Corfu,** Polila 24, helps find private rooms. (☎26 133. Open M-F 8:30am-2pm and 5:30-8pm.) From the customs house to **Hotel Europa,** Giantsilio 10, cross the main street and make a right; Giantsilio is a tiny road on your left just after the road turns and becomes Napoleonta. (☎39 304. Singles 4000-5000dr; doubles 6000-7000dr; triples 8000dr.) **Supermarkets** are on I. Theotaki and in Pl. Sanrocco. (Open M-F 8am-9pm, Sa 8am-6pm.) **Postal code:** 49100.

KEPHALONIA (Κεφαλονια) ☎0671

Kephalonia's diverse natural landscape, endless beaches, and towering peaks make it famous. **Argostoli** (Αργοστολι), the capital and transport hub of Kephalonia and Ithaka, is a busy, noisy, ugly city with palm-lined, traffic-filled streets. Take a **bus** (☎22 281) to the countryside from the station at the southern end of the waterfront. The **tourist office** is beside the port authority. (☎22 248. Open in summer M-Sa 8am-2:30pm and 5:30-9:30pm; off-season M-F 8am-2pm.) To get from the waterfront to the main *plateia*, follow 21 Maiou (to the right of the station as you face inland) up two blocks. Private rooms are the cheapest option, although waterfront hotels are much nicer. Snappy **Hotel Tourist,** on the waterfront before the port authority, has great rooms for a low price. (☎22 510. Singles 7000dr; doubles 14,000dr.)

A small, pretty town on a harbor surrounded by steep, lush hills, **Sami** (Σαμη), 24km from Argostoli, offers white-pebble beaches, proximity to **Melissani Lake** and underground **Drograti Cave,** and a break from the bustle of Argostoli. **Ferries** sail to **Ithaka** (40min., 4 per day, 500dr) and **Patras** (1 per day, 3800dr). **Buses** arrive from **Argostoli** (4 per day, 500dr). **Hotel Kyma,** at the end of the *plateia* away from the water, has great views. (☎ (0674) 22 064. Singles 6000dr; doubles 8000-10,000dr.)

ITHAKA (Ιθακη) ☎0674

The least-touristed and perhaps most beautiful of the Ionian Islands, Ithaka (Ith-ah-KEE) is all too often passed over for the tourist havens of Corfu and Kephalonia. Those who discover Ithaka find pebbled, rocky hillsides and terraced olive groves. Ithaka was the kingdom that **Odysseus** left behind to fight the Trojan War (and star in *The Odyssey*), while his wife **Penelope** faithfully waited 20 years for his return. Ithaka's largest town and capital, **Vathy,** wraps around a circular bay skirted by steep, green hills. Those of poetic bent and sturdy footwear can climb to the **Cave of the Nymphs,** where Odysseus hid the treasure the Phoenicians gave him; bring a flashlight. **Ferries** connect Vathy to **Astakos** on the mainland (4hr., 9 per week, 1700dr). Boats also go from **Piso Aetos** (10min. taxi ride), on the southern side of Ithaka, to **Sami** on Kephalonia (45min., 4 per day, 500dr). **Ferry** schedules vary; check with **Delas Tours** (☎32 104; open daily 9am-2pm and 4-10pm) or **Polyctor Tours** (☎33 120; fax 33 130; open 9am-1:30pm and 3:30-10pm), both in the main square right off the water. Your best bet for accommodations is to stay in private *domatia*. **Camping** at **Dexa Beach,** Odysseus' mythological landing point, is free. **Taverna To Trexantiri** is the hands-down favorite among locals. **Postal code:** 28300.

The island's only **bus** runs north from Vathy, passing through the scenic villages of Lefki, Stavros, Platrithiai, Frikes (1hr., 350dr), and Kioni. Schedules are erratic, but buses usually run three times daily in high season. **Frikes** and **Kioni,** both with small, crystal-blue harbors on the northern coast of the island, are exceptionally beautiful. **Stavros** is high in the mountains on the way to Frikes and Kioni, and was allegedly once home to **Odysseus' Palace;** the site is now a small museum filled with excavated items from the site. (Hours vary. Free, but a small tip expected.)

THE SPORADES (Σποραδες)

The Sporades seem like a fairy-tale family. Greece's second-largest island, Evia, is the queen, and three of the Sporades are her princesses: quietly sophisticated Skopelos is the eldest, home to artists and jazz-filled harbors; Skiathos is the middle child, in a hurry to grow up and with the best party scene for miles; and innocent Alonnisos, the youngest, is a land of pristine wilderness and hiking trails. Skyros, in the east, is the grandmother, the keeper of the Old Ways.

GETTING THERE AND GETTING AROUND

From **Athens,** take the daily bus from the station at Liossion 260 to **Agios Konstantinos** (2½hr., 16 per day, 2650dr), where **Nomikos/Goutos Lines ferries** run to **Skiathos** (3½, 1-2 per day, 3300dr); **Skopelos** (4hr., 2 per day, 4100dr); and **Alonnisos** (5½hr., 8-9 per week, 4400dr). To reach **Skyros,** take a bus from Athens to **Kimi** (3½hr., 2 per day, 2600dr), between Evia and Linaria, then take a direct ferry (2 per day, 2300dr). **Flying Dolphins** follow similar routes and cost twice as much. **Ferries** and **hydrofoils** also connect the various islands. **Nomikos/Goutos ferries** (Skiathos ☎ (0427) 22 209; Skopelos ☎ (0424) 22 363) run from **Skiathos** to **Skopelos** (1½hr., 3-4 per day, 1400dr) and **Alonnisos** (2hr., 2-3 per day, 1900dr), and between **Skopelos** and **Alonnisos** (30min., 2 per day, 1100dr). **Skyros** is accessible from the other Sporades by Flying Dolphin (4-8 per week); to **Alonnisos** (1hr., 8000dr) and **Skiathos** (2¼hr., 8400dr).

SKIATHOS (Σκιαθος) ☎0427

Ski-A-Thos. To the Greeks it's Sporadic and to the Halkydians it's Little Mykonos, but to the middle-aged Brits who come here to let their hair down, it's Disco Heaven. Package tourists pack the streets of **Skiathos Town,** while budding writers populate the beaches and nature preserves. Buses leave the port in Skiathos Town for the southern **beaches** (every 15min., 320dr), including **Megali Ammos, Nostros, Vromolimnos, Kolios,** and **Trovlos.** The road and bus route end in **Koukounaries,** where the more secluded beaches begin, including the lovely, pine-wooded **Biotrope of Koukounaries,** the yellow, curved **Banana Beach,** and nude **Little Banana Beach.** *Domatia* abound, particularly on Evangelista, but in a pinch head to the **Rooms to Let Office,** in the wooden kiosk by the port. (☎22 990. Open daily 8:30am-midnight.) **Pension Danaos,** in an alley off Papadiamantis opposite the OTE, attracts a young backpacker crowd. (☎22 834. Open May-Sept. Singles 5000-10,000dr; doubles 8000-15,000dr.) **Camping Koukounaries** is on the bus route to Koukouniares. (☎49 250. 1800dr per person; 1000dr per tent; 750dr per car.) Eat at **Chris, Jan & Deborah's Daskalio Pub** with an English crowd; follow Papadiamantis to the kiosk and head right. (Entrees 2500-4000dr. Open May-Sept. Bar open 7pm-3am, food until 11pm.) Indulge at the countless bars in **Pl. Papadiamantis** or along **Polytechniou** or **Evangelista,** then dance all night long at the clubs on the far right side of the coast.

SKOPELOS (Σκοπελος) ☎0424

Relaxed Skopelos sits between the glitzy bacchanalia of Skiathos and the wilderness of Alonnisos. The pious head to the wooded hills, where the island's monasteries and shrines hide, and the fading sounds of *rembetika* (folk songs) still echo. Six **buses** per day leave from the stop left of the waterfront, facing inland, for **beaches** near **Stafilos, Agnondas, Milia,** and **Loutraki. Hiking trails** wind toward monasteries and beaches. The **Thalpo Travel Agency,** on the second floor behind Akteon Cafe, is up on everything from Flying Dolphins tickets to catching octopi. (☎22 947. Open daily May-Oct. 10am-9pm.) Take a *domatia* offer from the dock, or try the **Rooms and Apartments Association of Skopelos,** in the small wooden building near the dock. (☎24 567. Open daily 10am-2pm and 6-10pm.) **Pension Sotos,** 10m left of Thalpos Travel, is a well-located gem. (☎22 549. Doubles 6500-12,000dr; triples 9000-16,000dr.) You can find 350dr *gyros* on **Pl. Platanos. Postal code:** 37003.

ALONNISOS (Αλοννησος) ☎0424

Of the islands comprising Greece's new **National Marine Park,** only Alonnisos is inhabited. Most of the 25 small, remaining islets can be visited only by organized tour boats in summer; trips are advertised and sold along the harbor. Alonnisos' unexplored northern coast sends white sands into the sea, and **hiking trails** lace the high heartland; check the kiosk next to the ferry dock in **Patitiri** for an overview of walking routes. **Ikos Travel,** to the right from the center of the waterfront, finds rooms, books excursions, and sells ferry tickets. (☎65 320; fax 65 321. Open 6:15-7:15am, 9am-2:30pm, and 3-10pm.) The **Rooms to Let Office,** next to Ikos Travel, can help find *domatia.* (☎66 138. Open May-Oct. 9am-4pm.) **Panorama,** down the first alley on the left from Ikion Dolophon, rents bright rooms with private baths. (☎65 240. Doubles 6000-10,000dr.) **Artolikoudies,** marked by a yellow sign inland on Pelasgon, bakes delicious olive bread (400dr) and pastries.

Hikers may find the beautiful **Hora** (Old Town; Χωρα) a more convenient spot to snooze than Patitiri. The island's only **bus** runs between Hora and Patitiri (10min., 11 per day, 300dr); alternatively, walk uphill on Pelasgon from Patitiri and continue on the main road (1hr.). There is also a map of the island with hiking trails by the bus stop to the Hora. **Hiliadroma,** just up from the bus station behind the church, has brand new rooms. (☎65 814. Doubles 8000-10,000dr; triples 9000-12,000dr.)

SKYROS (Σκυρος) ☎0222

Skyros's hilly terrain once protected the island against pirates and now fights off modern culture. The islands remain traditional and separate, the last stand of ghosts and poets. The stark white, cubist **Skyros Town,** the capital, is a relic of prewar Greek life; old men sew sandals late into the evening as women embroider intricate patterns. Above Skyros Town, the 1000-year-old **Monastery of St. George** and the **Castle of Licomidus** command magnificent views of Skyrian sunsets. (Open daily Mar.-Aug. 7am-10pm, Sept.-Feb. 7:30am-6pm. Free.) The superb **Faltaits Museum,** up the stairs from Pl. Rupert Brooke in Skyros Town, boasts an incredible folk art collection. (Open Tu-Su 8:30am-3pm. 500dr.) **Ferries** arrive in the tiny western port of **Linaria** (2 per day), and are met by **buses** to Skyros Town (20min., 4 per day, 250dr); tell the driver where you're going. **Skyros Travel,** past the central *plateia* on Agoras, organizes boat and bus excursions and helps with accommodations. (☎91 123. Open daily 9:15am-2pm and 7-10pm.) For a local experience, bargain to stay in a traditional Skyrian house; the thick-walled treasure troves are brimming with Delft ceramics and Italian linens, purchased from pirates who conveniently looted much of the known world. The incredible **O Pappas Kai Ego** ("Grandpa and me"), toward the top of Agoras on the right, serves Skyrian specialties. (Entrees 850-2200dr. Open daily 8am-2pm and 7pm-late.) **Postal code:** 34007.

GREECE

THE CYCLADES (Κυκλαδες)

When people wax rhapsodic about the Greek islands, chances are they're talking about the Cyclades. Whatever your idea of Greece—peaceful cobblestone streets and whitewashed houses, breathtaking sunsets, scenic hikes, all-night revelry—you'll find it here. Although each island has quiet villages and untouched spots, in summer most are mobbed by backpackers convening for a post-Eurail party.

GETTING THERE AND GETTING AROUND

Ferries from **Piraeus/Athens** go to: **Ios** (7½hr., 5090dr); **Mykonos** (6hr., 2 per day, 4800dr); **Naxos** and **Paros** (6hr., 3 per day, 4800dr); and **Santorini** (9hr., 5630dr). Ferries from **Crete** connect to **Ios** (5hr., 1 per week, 4300dr) and **Naxos** (7hr., 2-3 per week, 4960dr). Ferries also run to **Paros** from **Samos** (6hr., 6 per week, 4050dr) and **Rhodes** (16hr., 1 per week, 6950dr). Faster, more expensive, Flying Dolphin **hydrofoils** run the same routes. Ferries and hydrofoils jump between islands, too.

MYKONOS (Μυκονος) ☎0289

Coveted by 18th-century pirates, chic Mykonos is still an object of lust for those seeking revelry, bacchanalian excess, and blond beaches amid rich history. Social life, both gay and straight, abounds, but it's not cheap—you'll need a wallet thicker than your *Let's Go* to afford all the festivities. You can mingle with the *kosmopolitikos* and then savor the beaches and labyrinthine streets of **Mykonos Town;** losing yourself in the colorful alleyways at dawn or dusk is one of the easiest, cheapest, and most exhilarating ways to experience the island. At every corner you'll stumble upon a tiny church or quiet corner glowing in ethereal Cycladic light. All Mykonos' beaches are nude, but the degree of bareness varies; the most daring are **Plati Yialos, Paradise Beach, Super Paradise Beach,** and **Elia. Buses** run from South Station to Plati Yialos (every 30min., 250dr), where you can catch *kaïkia* (little boats) to the other three beaches (around 400dr); direct buses also run to Paradise from South Station (every 30min., 250dr) and to Elia from North Station (30min., 8 per day, 330dr).

Ferries run to: **Naxos** (3hr., 1-2 per day, 1900dr); **Piraeus/Athens** (6hr., 2-3 per day, 5100dr); **Santorini** (6hr., 3 per week, 3500dr); and **Tinos** (45min., 3 per day, 1200dr). The helpful **tourist police** await at the ferry landing. (☎22 482. Open daily 8am-11pm.) Most budget travelers go to one of Mykonos's several festive campsites. There are information offices for **camping** (☎23 567), **hotels** (☎24 540), and **domatia** (☎24 860). **Paradise Beach Camping** is the liveliest place to stay in town. It's 6km from the port; take the bus (round-trip 250dr) or the free shuttle from the port. (☎22 852. 1300-2000dr per person; 900-1500dr per tent; 700-900dr per car; bungalows 3000-6000dr per person.) **Mykonos Camping,** on nearby Paraga Beach, is smaller, quieter, and cleaner. (1300-2000dr per person; 900-1100dr per tent; 1800-2500dr per tent rental; 2-person bungalow 8000-10,000dr.) **Hotel Apollon,** on the waterfront, is the oldest hotel in town. (☎22 223. Singles 9-14,000dr; doubles 11,500-16,000dr; triples 15-19,000dr.) You'll have to wait for a table at the **Dynasty Thai Chinese Restaurant,** on Pl. Lymni, by the cinema on Meletopoulou, but it's worth it. (Entrees 1650-2500dr. Open daily 6:30pm-12:45am.) The cheapest way to eat, though, is from fruit stands and groceries like **Mykonos Mini-Market** (☎24 897; open daily 7am-late) by South Station; generic creperies and *souvlaki* also abound around town. **Caprice Bar,** on the water in Little Venice, is popular and crowded. (Drinks 1500-2000dr. Open Su-Th 6:30pm-3:30am, F-Sa 6:30pm-4:30am.) Hum to cabaret tunes at groovy, sophisticated, mostly gay **Montparnasse Piano Bar,** Ag. Anargyron 24. (Drinks 1000-2000dr. Open daily 7pm-3am.) On Matogianni, **Pierro's,** reputedly the most happening place on Mykonos, was the first gay bar in Greece. (Beer 1500dr; cocktails 2500dr.) **Postal code:** 84600.

GREECE

EXCURSION FROM MYKONOS: DELOS. Delos (Δηλος), the sacred belly button at the center of the whirling Cyclades, is not to be missed. Delos holds the most famous sanctuary in the Cyclades, the **Temple of Apollo,** built to commemorate the birthplace of the god and his twin sister, Artemis. After several centuries of inhabitation, Delos was abandoned at the end of the 2nd century AD, taken over by legions of leaping lizards, huge spiderwebs, and members of the French School of Archaeology (just since 1873). The archaeological site, which occupies much of the small island, takes several days to explore completely, but highlights can be seen in under three hours. From the dock, head straight to the **Agora of the Competaliasts;** continue in the same direction and turn left onto the wide **Sacred Road** to reach the **Sanctuary of Apollo,** a collection of temples built in the god's honor from Mycenaean times to the 4th century BC. The **Great Temple of Apollo,** or **Temple of the Delians,** was completed at the end of the 4th century BC. Continue 50m straight past the end of the Sacred Road to the lovely **Terrace of the Lions.** The **museum,** next to the cafeteria, holds an assortment of finds. (Open daily Tu-Su 8am-3pm. 1200dr, students 600dr, EU students free.) From there, a path leads to the summit of **Mt. Kythnos,** where Zeus watched the birth of Apollo. **Boats** leave from the dock near **Mykonos Town,** not the dock for large ferries (35min.; Tu-Su every 30-45min.; round-trip 1900dr).

ANDROS (Ανδρος) ☎0282

The island of Andros has 300 beaches, each more breathtaking than the last, and is the perfect place for families or the visitor who delights in untrammeled ground and endless nights staring at the sea. The island also has an impressive collection of small museums that further add to its allure. The town of **Batsi** offers the best food and housing options along with the liveliest nightlife on the island. Tourists stroll along the waterfront at all hours, pausing for drinks at its many cafes. **Restaurant Sirocco,** at the top of the first set of steps on your left as you leave the beach (with the water to your right), provides an international menu. (Entrees 1000-2000dr. Open daily 6:30pm-midnight.) For drinking and music, try the waterfront **Skala** to the left of the *plateia*, or the **Capriccio Music Bar** right next to the Ionic Bank. **Buses** run to Andros Town (5-7 per day, 650dr) by way of Gavrio (5-7 day, 300dr).

Take a daytrip from Batsi to **Andros Town,** called Hora, a sophisticated village with Neoclassical architecture. The **Museum of Modern Art** displays works by 20th-century Greek sculptor Michael Tombros; don't miss the temporary exhibition space a little further downhill. (☎22 650. Open M, Th-Sa 10am-2pm and 6-8pm, Su 10am-2pm. 1000dr, students 500dr, EU students free.) Splash around beneath the Venetian arches below the **Maritime Museum,** at the end of the main road, just above the water. (Open M, W-Sa 10am-1pm and 6-8pm, Su 10am-1pm. Free.) Those yearning to explore Andros's exotic interior of ruins and waterfalls should contact **Cosmas** (mention his name in Andros Town or email earthmessage@icqmail.com); he leads weekend or scheduled hikes (2000-10,000dr including lunch). The **bus** from Gavrio/Batsi arrives at a *plateia* where taxis wait. A full schedule is posted in the outdoor waiting area. **Postal code:** 84500.

PAROS (Παρος) ☎0284

Paros, famed throughout antiquity for its pure white marble (sculpted into the Venus de Milo), today retains golden beaches and tangled whitewashed villages. The island strikes a balance between modern nightlife and Old World dignity, and gracefully absorbs hordes of summer tourists. Past the commercial surface of **Paroikia,** Paros' port and largest city, flower-filled streets wind through archways, by windmills and a historic basilica. Byzantine buffs will coo over **Panagia Ekatontapiliani** (Church of Our Lady of 100 Gates), which looms over Paroikia's *plateia* and houses three churches, cloisters, and a peaceful courtyard. Tradition holds that only 99 of the church's 100 doors can be counted—when the 100th appears, Constantinople will once again belong to Greece. (Open daily 8am-8:30pm. Dress modestly.) Ten kilometers south of town is the cool, spring-fed **Valley of the Butterflies** *(Petaloudes)*, home to an enormous congregation of brown-and-white-striped moths from June to late September. Take the bus from Paroikia toward Aliki and ask to be let off at the *petaloudes* (10min., 8 per day, 250dr); then follow the signs 2km up the steep, winding road to the entrance. (Open M-Sa 9am-8pm. 400dr.)

Ferries sail to **Ios** (2½hr., 7-9 per day, 2450dr) and **Santorini** (3½hr., 7-9 per day, 3080dr). **Polos Tours,** next to the OTE, has transportation schedules. (☎22 092; fax 21 983. Open daily 8am-1am.) Turn left from the dock and take a right after the ancient cemetery ruins to get to **Rena Rooms.** (☎/fax 22 220. Open Mar.-Nov. Doubles 6000-13,000dr; triples 9000-14,000dr; 20% *Let's Go* discount.) **Koula Camping** is 400m north of the dock across the street from the pebbly town beach. (☎22 081. 1500dr per person; 600dr per tent; 1000dr per car; 1000dr tent rental.) The psychedelic **Happy Green Cow,** a block inland off the *plateia* behind the National Bank, serves tasty veggie fare. (Open daily 7pm-midnight.) Find **Pirate Blues and Jazz** by heading away from the dock along the street marked by the National Bank on the *plateia.* (Beer 800dr. Open daily 7pm-3am.) **Postal code:** 84400.

NAXOS (Ναξος) ☎0285

The large, gleaming marble arch of a former temple of Apollo forms a worthy portal to the splendid, diverse island of Naxos. The largest of the Cyclades, its vast interior sprawls with olive groves, charming villages, and ruins. Old **Naxos Town** lies behind the waterfront shops, on the hill leading up to the **Venetian Castle.** Architecturally impressive itself, the new **Mitropolis Museum** surrounds the excavated 13th-century BC city. (Open Tu-Su 8am-2:30pm. Free.) The marble, 6th-century BC **Portara** archway, visible from the waterfront, is one of the few archaeological sites in Greece that you can climb all over—try midnight star-gazing. **Buses** run from the port (every 30min., 300dr) to nearby **beaches Ag. Georgios, Ag. Prokopios, Ag. Anna,** and **Plaka**—the hands-down favorite for nude frolicking. Rock and reggae play at **The Jam,** behind OTE. (Happy Hour 5-10pm. Open daily 7pm-3:30am.) **Cream,** the most popular dance club, is next to the Day-Night Bar, facing the harbor. (Cover 1500dr includes one drink. Open Su-Th 11pm-3:30am, F-Sa 11pm-even later.) Make sure to explore the stunning interior; **buses** run from Naxos Town to the small fishing village of **Apollonas,** on the northern tip, via a gorgeous coastal road (2hr., 3 per day, 1050dr). The exhilarating gems of the interior, like the vast, green olive grove of the **Tragea,** aren't serviced by buses; ask for **hiking** info at the tourist office.

Ferries go to: **Ios** (1½hr., 6 per day, 2200dr); **Mykonos** (2hr., 5 per week, 1740dr); **Paros** (1hr., 6-8 per day, 1400dr); and **Santorini** (3hr., 6 per day, 2900dr). The **tourist office** is 300m from the dock, past the private agencies, by the bus station. (☎24 358; fax 25 200. Open daily 8am-midnight. The **Rental Center** has **Internet** access in Pl. Protodikiou. (2500dr per hr. Open daily 8:30am-11pm.) **Pension Irene** is in newer Naxos, up the hill from Galini Restaurant, 300m from Ag. Georgios Beach. (☎23 169. Doubles 10,000dr; triples 12,000dr; quads 15,000dr.) **Hotel Panorama** in Old Naxos, is near Hotel Dionysos; follow the signs. (☎24 404. Singles 8000dr; doubles 14,000; triples 17,000.) Take a shuttle from the ferry or the frequent buses to Ag. Anna beach (2 per hr., 300dr) for **Maragas Camping.** (☎42 552. 900-1200dr per person; 300dr tent rental; doubles 6000-8000dr.) **Postal code:** 84300.

IOS (Ιος) ☎0286

Ios can be summed up in three words: frat party run amok. Alright, that was four—after a week on Ios, you won't be able to count either. It has everything your mother warned you about: people swimming less than 30 minutes after they've eaten, wine being swilled from the bottle at 3pm, drinking games all day long, men and women dancing madly in the streets, and oh so much more. The **port** (Yialos) is at one end; the **village** (Hora) sits above it on a hill. Frenzied **Mylopotas beach** awaits 3km farther. **Buses** shuttle between the port, village, and beach (every 10-20min., 230dr). Follow the main pedestrian path as it curves left through the *plateia* to reach **Blue Note,** where you can **get drunk** with lots of Swedes. Start your pub crawl by **getting drunk** at **Dubliner,** next to the bus stop (Guinness 600dr; open daily 8:30pm-3:30am), then migrate with the masses to nearby **Sweet Irish Dream,** near the "donkey steps," to **get drunk** and dance on tables after 2am (no cover before 1am). You can **get drunk** on "tequila slammers" (900dr) at the packed **Slammer Bar,** just uphill from the *plateia.* **Get drunk** to jazz and blues music at **Amadeus,** just through the main *plateia.* At **Fun Pub,** on the main road beyond the supermarket, watch movies and **get drunk.** In the village, take the uphill steps to the left (with your back to the bank) in the *plateia* and take the first left to reach **Francesco's,** where you can **get drunk** at the terrace bar. (☎/fax 91 223. Dorms 3000dr; doubles 6000-8000dr; triples 9000-12,000dr.) Or walk past the OTE and take the white archway to **Kolitsani View,** then **get drunk** at the poolside bar. (☎91 061. Doubles 15,000dr; triples 18,000dr.) Take some aspirin in the morning and head to the beach, where three **Mylopotas Water Sports Center** shacks along the beach offer free **windsurfing, waterskiing,** and **snorkeling lessons** with rental. (2000-5000dr per hr. Open daily Apr.-Oct.)

Ferries go to: **Crete** (5hr., 1 per week, 4300dr); **Mykonos** (4-5hr., 1 per day, 3300dr); **Naxos** (1½hr., 6-8 per day, 2100dr); **Paros** (2½hr., 5-6 per day, 2600dr); and **Santorini** (1¼hr., 4-6 per day, 1700dr). The **tourist office** is next to the bus stop. (☎91 135. Open daily 8am-midnight.) Many good, affordable rooms are in the village. To sleep with less noise near the port, try **Petros Place Hotel;** it's left down the waterfront, right before the beach. (☎91 421. Doubles 12-18,000dr; triples 15-18,000dr.) On the end of Mylopotas Beach, **Far Out Camping** has a bar. (☎92 301. Open Apr.-Sept. 1200dr per person; tent rental 300dr. Cabins 1500-2000dr; bungalows 2000-3000dr.) Try **Waves Indian Restaurant and International Cuisine**, to the left of the waterfront road as you get off the ferries. (Entrees 2000-2500dr. Opens at 10am for breakfast.) A **supermarket** is in the *plateia.* **Postal code:** 84001.

SANTORINI (Σαντορινη) ☎0286

Santorini's landscape is as dramatic as the volcanic eruption that laid waste to it 4500 years ago. Its eruptions—and startlingly beautiful black-sand beaches and mineral-rich fields—suggest it may be Plato's lost island of Atlantis. The center of activity on the island is the capital city **Fira.** Some visitors are shocked to step off the bus from the port and encounter the congested mess of glitzy shops, whizzing mopeds, and scads of tourists, but nothing can destroy the pleasure of the island's narrow streets and stunning sunsets. On the southwestern part of the island, the fascinating excavations at **Akrotiri,** a late Minoan city, are preserved virtually intact under layers of volcanic rock. (Open Tu-Su 8am-7pm. 1200dr, students 600dr.) **Buses** run to Akrotiri from Fira (16 per day, 400dr). Frequent buses also run from Fira to the **beaches** of **Perissa** (15min., 400dr) and **Kamari** (20min., 270dr) in the southeast. The former route stops along the way in **Pyrgos;** from there, you can hike to the **Profitias Ilias Monastery** (45min.) and continue to the ruins of **ancient Thira** (an additional 1½hr.), near Kamari. The theater, church, and forum of ancient Thira, the island's old capital, remain visible. (Open Tu-Su 8am-2pm.)

Ferries run to: **Ios** (1½hr., 3-5 per day, 1700dr); **Iraklion, Crete** (4hr., 1 per day, 3700dr); **Naxos** (4hr., 4-8 per day, 3000dr); **Mykonos** (7hr., 2 per week, 3600dr); and **Paros** (4½hr., 3-5 per day, 3200dr). Most land at **Athinios** harbor; frequent buses (30min., 380dr) connect to Fira. Share homemade wine with Petros at the **Pension Petros;** from the bus station, go one block up 25 Martiou, make a right, a left at the

GREECE

bottom of the hill, and the first right. (☎22 573; fax 22 615. Doubles 7000-16,000dr; triples 9000-19,000dr.) Head 300m north from the *plateia* for the **Thira Youth Hostel** (☎22 387; open Apr.-Oct.; dorms 1800-4000dr; doubles 5000-10,000dr), or follow the blue signs east from the *plateia* for **Santorini Camping** (☎22 944; open Apr.-Oct. 1500dr per person; 800dr per tent; 700dr per car). To bake on the sizzling black sand, stay at the **Youth Hostel Perissa-Anna,** between the first and second bus stops from Fira to Perissa. (☎82 182. Dorms 1200-16000dr; private rooms 2000-4000dr.) Back in Fira, the menu at **Nikolas Taverna** may be all Greek to you, but you can't go wrong; head uphill from the northwestern corner of the *plateia* and turn right at Hotel Tataki. (Open M-Sa noon-4pm and 6-11pm, Su 6-11pm.) The **Kira Thira Jazz Club** is across the street. (Open daily 9pm-late.) **Postal code:** 84700.

CRETE (Κρητη)

Greece's largest island embraces an infinite store of mosques, monasteries, mountain villages, gorges, grottoes, and beaches. Since 3000 BC, when the Minoans created their own language, script, and architecture, Crete has been a powerhouse. While Eastern Crete's resort towns seem to spring from the brains of British booking agents, the mountain-gripping highway winding from Malia to Agios Nikolaos and Sitia is absolutely spectacular. The vacation spots of Western Crete have grown around towns with rich histories and distinctive characters.

GETTING THERE AND GETTING AROUND

Olympic Airways and **Air Greece** connect **Athens:** to **Iraklion** (45min., 13-15 per day, 19,300-21,300dr) in the center; **Hania** (4 per day, 21,300dr) in the west; and **Sitia** (2-3 per week, 23,200dr) in the east. **Ferries** arrive in **Iraklion** from **Mykonos** (8½hr., 5 per week, 6000dr); **Naxos** (7hr., 3 per week, 5200dr); **Paros** (9hr., 7 per week, 5200dr); **Piraeus/Athens** (14hr., 3 per day, 7000dr); and **Santorini** (4hr., 2 per day, 3700dr). **Hydrofoils** service most destinations in half the time, but at double the price.

Crete is divided into four prefectures: Hania, Rethymno, Iraklion, and Lasithi. **Bus** networks are based on this division. Buses from **Iraklion** run west along the northern coast to **Rethymno** (1½hr., 18 per day, 1550dr) en route to **Hania** (from Iraklion 17 per day, 2900dr; from Rethymno 1600dr). Buses run from **Rethymno, Hania,** and **Iraklion** south to the **Samaria Gorge** (from Hania 4 per day, round-trip 2800dr). Buses also run east from **Iraklion** to **Heronissos** (45min.); **Malia** (from Iraklion 1hr., 800dr; from Heronissos 20min., 240dr); and **Agios Nikolaos** (from Iraklion 1½hr., 20 per day, 1450dr; from Malia 1½hr., 2 per hr., 800dr). Buses head to **Sitia** from **Agios Nikolaos** (1½hr., 4-6 per day, 1550dr) and from **Iraklion** (3¼hr., 4 per day, 2950dr).

IRAKLION (Ηρακλιο) ☎081

Crete's capital and the fifth-largest city in Greece, Iraklion sports a chic native population, a more diverse nightlife than nearby resorts, and an ideal location as a base to tour Crete. Off Pl. Eleftherias, the phenomenal **Archaeological Museum** has appropriated major finds from all over the island and presents a comprehensive island history from the Neolithic period to Roman times. (Open M 12:30-7pm and Tu-Su 8am-7pm. 1500dr, students 800dr, EU students free.) **Travel Hall Travel Agency,** Hatzimihali Yiannari 13, has info on **flights** to Athens and elsewhere. (☎341 862. Open M-Tu and Th-F 9am-4pm and 5:30-9pm, W 9am-5pm, Sa 9am-2pm.) **Boat** offices line 25 Augustou. There are several bus terminals in Iraklion. KTEL **Terminal A,** between the old city walls and the harbor near the waterfront, sends **buses** to Agios Nikolaos and Malia; the **Hania-Rethymno** terminal, which serves Hania, Rethymno, and other destinations, is opposite Terminal A, beside the ferry landing. The **tourist office,** Xanthoudidou 1, is opposite the Archaeological Museum in Pl. Eleftherias. (☎228 203. Open M-F 8am-2:30pm, July-Aug. also open evenings and Sa.) The **tourist police** are at 10 Dikeosinis. (☎283 190. Open daily 7am-11pm.) Check **email** at **Gallery Games Net,** on Korai 14, on the street past Dedalou away from Pl. Eleftherias. (500dr per 30min. Open daily 10am-midnight.)

Rent a Room Hellas, Handakos 24, is two blocks from El Greco Park. (☎288 851. Dorms 2200dr; doubles 4500-6000dr; triples 6000-8000dr.) To get from Pl. Venizelou to **Hotel Rea,** Kalimeraki, walk down Handakos and turn right. (☎223 638. Singles 6000-7500dr; doubles 7500-8500dr; triples 9000-10,500dr.) To get to the **Youth Hostel,** Vyronos 5, from the bus station, take a left on 25 Augustou (with the water on the right) and a right on Vyronos. (☎286 281. Curfew midnight. Dorms 2000dr; singles 3000-4000dr; doubles 5500-6000dr; triples 7000-8000dr.) The best show in town is the **open-air market** on 1866 street, starting near Pl. Venizelon. Walk down D. Beaufort for dancing at **Privilege Club** and **Yacht. Postal code:** 71001.

EXCURSION FROM IRAKLION: KNOSSOS. The excavations at Knossos, the most famous archaeological site in Crete, reveal the remains of a Minoan city that thrived here 3500 years ago. Sir Arthur Evans financed and supervised the excavations, and restored large parts of the **palace.** His work often crossed the line from preservation to artistic interpretation, but the site is impressive nonetheless. *(From Iraklion, take bus #2 from 25 Augustou or Pl. Eleftherias (every 20min., 260dr) and look for the signs. Open daily 8am-7pm; in winter 8am-5pm. 1500dr, students 800dr, EU students free.)*

RETHYMNO (Ρεθυμνο) ☎0831

Nowhere do reminders of the island's turbulent occupations mingle as magically as in **Rethymno**'s old city, near the cave famed as Zeus' birthplace. Arabic inscriptions lace the walls of the narrow streets, minarets highlight the skyline, and the 16th-century **Venetian fortress** (open Tu-Su 8am-8pm; 900dr) guards the scenic harbor. The **Rethymno-Hania bus station** (☎22 212) is south of the fortress on the water. Climb the stairs behind the bus station and go left on Igoumenou Gavriil, which becomes Kountouriotou, and turn left on Varda Kallergi to reach the waterfront. The **tourist office** is on El. Venizelou, by the waterfront. (☎29 148. Open M-F 8am-2:30pm.) Check **email** at **Cafe Galero** at Rimondi Fountain. (800dr for 30min., 1400dr for 1hr. Open daily 7am-3am.) To get from the station to the cheerful **Youth Hostel,** Tombazi 41-45, walk down Igoumenou Gavriil, take a left at the park traffic light, walk through the gate, and take your first right. (☎22 848. Sheets 150dr. Reception 8am-noon and 5-9pm. 1800dr.) **Olga's Pension,** Souliou 57, is off Antistassios. (☎53 206. Singles 5000-7000dr; doubles 7000-9000dr; triples 10,000-11,000dr.) Buses (170dr) shuttle from the station to **Elizabeth Camping,** 3km east of town. (☎28 694. Open mid-Apr. to Oct. 1650dr per person; 1100-1500dr per tent.) **Postal code:** 74100.

TAKE THE MAN-BULL BY THE HORNS The myth of **King Minos** begins with a crime of ingratitude. Poseidon, the sea god, had given him a white bull specifically to slaughter in the god's honor, but Minos neglected to axe the bull as promised. Aphrodite then set out for twisted retribution: she filled his wife **Pasiphaë** with a burning lust for the fine bull. Pasiphaë hired master engineer **Daedalus** to build a sexy cow costume to catch the bull's eye. After a (literal) roll in the hay, Pasiphaë gave birth to the hideous **Minotaur,** a fearsome beast with a bull's head, a man's body, and a taste for human flesh. Minos shut the beast into an inescapable **labyrinth** designed by Daedalus; to feed the monster, he taxed mainland Greece seven maidens and seven youths every year. The Minotaur gobbled the young 'uns year after year until dashing Athenian prince **Theseus** volunteered to be sacrificed. Theseus met, wooed, proposed to, and conspired to escape with **Ariadne,** Minos and Pasiphaë's all-human daughter. Ariadne gave Theseus a ball of string to find his way around the labyrinth; within the maze, he killed the monster, retraced his path, and escaped by ship with Ariadne. Theseus then ditched Ariadne on the beach of Naxos, Bacchus' favorite hangout. Men. Soon, Bacchus himself quieted Ariadne's grief and married her. Back in Crete, Minos imprisoned Daedalus and his son **Icarus** for their role in the whole mess. Resourceful Daedalus manufactured wax wings for them, going for the ultimate jailbreak. With freedom in sight, Icarus ignored dad's warning not to fly so close to the sun; his wings melted, and he plummeted to his death.

HIKING NEAR RETHYMNO: SAMARIA GORGE. The most popular excursion from Hania, Rethymno, and Iraklion is the five- to six-hour hike down the 16km Samaria Gorge, a spectacular ravine through the White Mountains, carved by rainwater over 14 million years. The gorge retains its allure despite being trampled by thousands of visitors: rare plants peek out from sheer rock walls, wild Cretan goats climb the hills, and endangered griffon vultures and golden eagles soar overhead. (Open daily May to mid-Oct. 6am-4pm. 1200dr.) For gorge info, call the **Hania Forest Service** (☎92 287). The trail starts at **Xyloskalo;** take the 6:15 or 8:30am **bus** from Hania to Xyloskalo (1½hr., 2 per day, 1400dr). **Hania,** whose proximity to the gorge allows the most flexibility concerning how early you start the trek, is accessible by **bus** from **Iraklion** (17 per day, 2900dr) or **Rethymno** (17 per day, 1600dr), or by **ferry** from **Piraeus/Athens** (9½hr., 1 per night, 5900-8600dr). The town of **Omalos** is also within striking distance of Samaria Gorge. **Buses** arrive in Omalos from **Iraklion** (5:30am, 3850dr) and **Rethymno** (6:15 and 7am, 2550dr). The trail ends in the town of **Agia Roumeli,** on the southern coast, where you can hop on a **boat** to **Hora Sfakion** (2 per day, 1500dr) and catch a waiting bus back to Hania (1600dr), Rethymno (1600dr), or Iraklion (3100dr). **☎0821.**

GREECE

SITIA (Σητεια) ☎0843

A winding drive east from **Agios Nikolaos** brings you to the fishing and port town of Sitia, where the wave of tourism slows to a trickle and pelicans walk the streets at dawn. The town's **beach** extends 3km to the east, while the hilltop **fortress** (open Tu-Su 8:30am-2:30pm; free) provides views of the town and bay. **Ferries** leave Sitia for: **Karpathos** (5hr., 3 per week, 3400dr); **Piraeus/Athens** (16-17hr., 5 per week, 7600dr) via **Agios Nikolaos** (1½hr., 1600dr); and **Rhodes** (12hr., 3 per week, 6000dr). With your back to the **bus station** (☎22 272), walk right, take your first right, then take your first left and follow Venizelou to the waterfront. From Polytechiou Sq., head right along the water to reach the **tourist office.** (☎28 300. Open M-F 9am-9pm, Sa-Su 10am-9pm.) To get to the **Youth Hostel,** Therissou 4, walk right from the bus station, go inland, follow signs for the major road to Iraklion and Agios Nikolaos, and bear left; or, call for a ride from the station. (☎22 693. Sheets 100dr. Dorms 1600dr; singles 2500dr; doubles 3500-4000dr; triples 4500-5000dr.) **Venus Rooms to Let** is at Kondilaki 60; walk up Kapetan Sifi from the main square and make your first right after the telephone office. (☎24 307. Doubles 4000-8000dr.) **Cretan House,** K. Karamanli 10, off the *plateia* and facing the water, serves Cretan entrees for around 1400dr. (Open daily 9am-1:30am.) Head to **Hot Summer,** way down the road to Palaikastro by the beach, after midnight. (Cover 1000dr.) **Postal code:** 72300

EXCURSION FROM SITIA: VAI BEACH. The beaches at **Vai,** to the east, used to be a secret refuge from Sitia's crowds. Today, bus loads of tourists roll in every day to swim at a smooth, blue-flag beach and rest in the shade of Europe's only indigenous palm tree forest. For more secluded bathing and a better beach, face the water and head left, up and over the craggy hill. **Buses** arrive from **Sitia** (1hr., 4-6 per day, 600dr) via **Palaikastro** (250dr).

EASTERN AEGEAN ISLANDS

The intricate, rocky coastlines and unassuming port towns of the **Northeastern Aegean Islands** enclose thickly wooded mountains that give way to unspoiled villages and beaches, and provide a taste of undiluted Greek culture just miles from the Turkish coast. The landscapes of the **Dodecanese** (Twelve Islands), southeast of the Northeastern Aegean Islands, reflect Greek history from the rise of Christianity to Mussolini's architectural style. In summer, tourists flock to Rhodes and Kos for raucous nightlife, while other islands are best for peaceful relaxation.

FERRIES TO TURKEY

Ferries run to: **Aivali** from **Lesvos** (16,000dr); **Kuşadası** from **Samos** (1¼hr., 2 per day, 9000-11,000dr); and **Bodrum** from **Kos** (round-trip 10-13,000dr). **Visas** must be bought at the border if you are staying the night in Turkey (citizens of the **US** US$45, the **UK** UK£10, **Ireland** IR£5). **Port taxes** are typically 3000dr.

SAMOS (Σαμος) ☎0273

Samos is perhaps the most beautiful and certainly the most touristed island in the Northeast Aegean. Many stop only briefly en route to **Kuşadası** and the ruins of **Ephesus** on the Turkish coast (see p. 961), but those who stay longer discover the quiet inland streets, palm trees, and red roof-covered hillside of **Samos Town** (Vathy), one of the Northeast Aegean's most attractive port cities. The phenomenal **Archaeological Museum** is behind the municipal gardens. (Open Tu-Su 8am-3pm. 800dr, students 400dr, EU students free.) The beach town of **Pythagorion,** the island's ancient capital, is 14km south of Samos Town. Near the town are the magnificent remains of Polykrates' 6th-century BC engineering projects: the **Tunnel of Eupalinos,** which diverted water from a natural spring to the city, a 40-meter-deep **harbor mole,** and the **Temple of Hera.** (Tunnel open Tu-Su 8:45am-2:45pm. 500dr, students 300dr, EU students free. Temple open Tu-Su 8:30am-3pm. 800dr, students 400dr.) Hourly **buses** arrive in Pythagorion from Samos Town (20min., 12 per day, 340dr).

Ferries arrive in Samos Town from: Lesvos (8hr., 1 per week, 4090dr); Mykonos (6hr., 4 per week, 5100dr); Naxos (6hr., 4-7 per week, 4900dr) via Paros (4370dr); and Piraeus/Athens (12hr., 2-3 per day, 6700dr) via Ikaria (2100dr). The **tourist office** is on a side street one block before Pl. Pythagoras. (Open July-Aug. M-Sa 8:30am-2pm.) Turn right at the end of the ferry dock on E. Stamatiadou before the Hotel Aiolis, then turn right on Manoli Kalomiri and left on Areos to get to the **Pension Avli,** Areos 2. (☎22 939. Open in summer only. Doubles 6000-7000dr.) Or, walk up the street to **Pension Dreams,** Areos 9. (☎28 601; fax 28 893. Singles 5000-6000dr; doubles 5000-7000dr; triples 6000-7500dr.) **Postal code:** 83100.

LESVOS (Λεσβος) ☎0251

Once home to the sensual poet Sappho, Lesvos is something of a mecca for lesbians paying homage to their etymological roots. Several artist colonies call the island home, as does Nobel Prize-winning poet Odysseus Elytis; the island is geographically diverse, with hot springs, petrified forests, and fabulous beaches. Most travelers pass through the modern **Mytilini,** the capital and central port city. The **Archaeological Museum,** Argiri Eftalioti 7, houses an impressive collection of the island's archaeological finds. (Open Tu-Su 8:30am-2pm. 500dr.)

Ferries go to: **Chios** (3hr., 1-2 per day, 3400dr); **Limnos** (5hr., 4 per week, 4400dr); **Piraeus/Athens** (12hr., 1-3 per day, 7200dr); and **Thessaloniki** (12hr., 2 per week, 8400dr). Book ferries at **NEL Lines,** Pavlou Koudoutrioti 67 (☎22 220), along the waterfront. The **tourist police,** in the passport control building at the ferry dock, offer maps and advice. (☎22 776. Open daily 7:15am-2:15pm and 5-8pm.) The **Rooms to Let** office is off the waterfront right after the Bank of Greece. (Singles 5000-6000dr; doubles 6000-8000dr. Open daily 9am-1pm.) Take an intercity bus from the station behind Agios Irinis Park, southwest of the harbor, to the north coast artist havens **Petras** and **Molyvos** (1½hr., 3-6 per day, 1400dr). The **Molyvos tourist office,** just up from the bus stop, helps find rooms. (☎71 347. Open daily Apr.-Oct. 7:30am-4pm.) Unhurried **Skala Eressou,** on the opposite end of the island, is the birthplace of Sappho. Its seemingly endless beaches attract archeologists, lesbians, poets, and families. **Sappho Travel,** one block from the bus stop before the waterfront, can help with accommodations and transportation. (☎52 140; www.lesvos.co.uk. Open daily May-Oct. 9am-11pm, in winter 9am-2pm and 5-9pm.) **Postal code:** 81100.

CHIOS (Χιος) ☎0271

As its striking volcanic beaches and medieval villages become more accessible, Chios is rising to new fame, attracting vacationers and package tourists hopping between Greece and the port of Çeşme in Turkey. **Pyrgi,** high in the hills 25km from **Chios Town,** is deeply striking, with fantastic black-and-white geometrical designs covering its buildings. Take a **bus** from Chios Town (8 per day, 620dr). Farther south, **Emborio**'s beige volcanic cliffs contrast with the black stones and deep-blue water below; **buses** run from Chios Town (4 per week, 720dr). **Ferries** go to **Lesvos** (3hr., 1 per week, 3400dr); **Piraeus/Athens** (8hr., 1-2 per day, 5800dr); and **Samos** (4hr., 3 per week, 3120dr). **Hatzelenis Tourist Agency,** at the end of the ferry dock, sells ferry tickets. (☎26 743 or 20 002; email mano2@otenet.gr.) To reach Chios Town's **tourist office,** Kanari 18, turn off the waterfront onto Kanari, walk toward the *plateia*, and look for the "i" sign. (☎44 344. Open Apr.-Oct. M-F 7am-2:30pm and 7-10pm, Sa 10am-1pm, Su 7-10pm; Nov.-Mar. M-F 7am-2:30pm.) **Chios Rooms,** 114 Leofores, offers bright rooms, some with a view; it's in a yellow building at the far right end of the waterfront. (☎20 198. Singles 4000-5000dr; doubles 5000-8000dr; triples 9000-10,000dr.) **Postal code:** 82100.

GREECE

RHODES (Ροδος) ☎0241

Although Rhodes is the tourism capital of the Dodecanese, the sandy beaches along its east coast, jagged cliffs skirting its west coast, and green mountains freckled with villages in the interior still retain their serenity. The island's most famous sight is one that no longer exists: the **Colossus of Rhodes,** a 35m bronze statue of Helios and one of the **seven wonders of the ancient world,** straddled the island's harbor and was destroyed by a 237 BC earthquake. The beautiful **City of Rhodes** has been the island's capital for over 20 centuries. The **Old Town,** surrounded by remnants of the 14th-century occupation by the Knights of St. John, lends the city a medieval flair. At the top of the hill looms the **Palace of the Grand Master,** with 300 rooms, moats, drawbridges, huge watchtowers, and colossal battlements. (Open M noon-7pm, Tu-Su 8am-7pm. 1200dr, students 600dr.) Down the hill, the former **Hospital of the Knights** is now the **Archaeological Museum** in nearby Pl. Argykastrou. (Open Tu-Su 8:30am-2:30pm. 800dr, students and seniors 400dr.) The **New Town** is nightlife central; **Orfanidou** is popularly known as **Bar Street.** Rowdy drinkers and beach bunnies daytrip to **Faliraki,** 15km south of the City of Rhodes; **excursion boats** to Faliraki stop along the way in **Lindos,** perhaps the island's most picturesque town, with whitewashed houses clustered beneath a castle-capped acropolis. See schedules and prices (from 3500dr) on the dock along the lower end of the Mandraki (waterfront). **Buses** also run to Faliraki (20 per day, 450dr) and Lindos (13 per day, 1000dr).

Ferries arrive in the City of Rhodes from: **Chios** (7000dr); **Crete** (1 per week, 6200dr); **Karpathos** (3 per week, 4400dr); **Kos** (2-3 per day, 4000dr); **Mykonos** (1 per week, 6800dr); **Paros** (1 per week, 6900dr); **Patmos** (1-2 per day, 5400dr); **Piraeus/Athens** (14hr., 1-4 per day, 9000dr); **Samos** (2 per week, 6500dr); and **Santorini** (1 per week, 5100dr). The **Greek National Tourist Office (EOT)** is up Papgou a few blocks from Pl. Rimini, at Makariou. (☎23 255. Open M-F 7:30am-3pm.) **Mama's Pension,** 28 Menecleous St., is off Sokratous, directly above Mike's Taverna. (☎25 359. Dorms 2500dr; doubles 6000dr.) **Pension Stathis** is at Omirou 60. (☎24 357. Dorms 2500dr; singles 6000dr; doubles 6000-8000dr.) Or, snooze in the New Town at the **New Village Inn,** Konstantopedos 10. (☎34 937. Singles 5000dr; doubles 8000dr.) **Yiannis,** Sokratous-Platonos 41, just off Sokratous away from the New Town, serves huge portions of Greek delights. (Open daily 10am-11pm or midnight.)

KOS (Κως) ☎0242

Rivalling Rhodes in sheer numbers of visitors, Kos draws a younger, louder, more intoxicated crowd. Don't be dismayed by the raucous bars and mammoth hotels; perseverance rewards you with quiet nooks and undiscovered golden beaches. In **Kos Town,** minarets of Ottoman mosques rise among massive walls of a Crusader fortress and scattered ruins from the Archaic, Classical, Hellenistic, and Roman eras. The ancient sanctuary of **Asclepion,** 4km west of Kos Town, is dedicated to the god of healing. In the 5th century BC, Hippocrates opened the world's first medical school here; today, doctors still take his oath. From the lowest level *(andiron)*, steps from the 3rd century BC lead to the 2nd-century AD **Temple of Apollo** and 4th-century BC **Minor Temple of Asclepios.** Sixty steps lead to the third *andiron*, with the forested remains of the **Main Temple of Asclepios** and a view of the ruins, Kos Town, and the Turkish coast. (Site open June-Sept. Tu-Su 8am-7pm. 800dr, students 400dr.) The site is easily reached by **bus** (15min., 16 per day). The best **beaches** stretch along Southern Kos up to Kardamene; the **bus** drops off at any of them.

Ferries run to: Patmos (4hr., 1-2 per day, 2800dr); Piraeus/Athens (11-15hr., 2-3 per day, 7500dr); and Rhodes (4hr., 2 per day, 3400dr). Walk left, facing inland, from the Castle to reach Vas. Georgios; the **tourist office** (☎24 460; fax 21 111) is at #1. It's best to find your own room, but if your boat docks in the middle of the night, you might have to go with Kos's notorious dock hawks. Take the first right off Megalou Alexandrou, on the back left corner of the first intersection, to get to **Pension Alexis,** Herodotou 9. (☎28 798. Doubles 5500-7000dr; triples 7500dr.) **Hotel Afendoulis,** Evrilpilou 1, is right down Vas. Georgiou near the beach. (☎/fax 25 321. Doubles 7500-9000dr.) **Kos Camping,** 3km southeast of the center, is accessible by bus from the city center every 30 minutes. (☎23 910. 1750dr per person, 800dr per tent; tent rental 1000dr.) Most bars are either in **Exarhia,** between Akti Koundouriotou and the ancient *agora*, or the more subdued **Porfiriou,** in the north near the beach. **Fashion Club,** Kanari 2 by the dolphin statue rotary, is huge and jumpin'. (Cover 2500dr; includes 1 drink.) **Hamam Club,** near the *agora* and next to the taxi station in Diagoras Square, was once a bathhouse. **Postal code:** 85300.

GREECE

PATMOS (Πατμος) ☎0247

The holy island of Patmos balances a weighty religious past with excellent beaches and traces of an artistic community. The white houses of **Hora** and the majestic walls of the **Monastery of St. John the Theologian** above are visible from all over the island. (Monastery and treasure museum open Tu-W 8am-1:30pm and 4-6pm, Th-M 8am-1:30pm. Treasury 1000dr; monastery free.) Hora is 4km from the colorful port town of **Skala;** take a bus (10min., 11 per day, 200dr) or taxi (1000dr) from Skala (walk left and follow the signs from the bus/taxi station), or tackle the steep hike. Halfway between the two is the **Apocalypsis Monastery** and the **Sacred Grotto of the Revelation,** where St. John dictated the Book of Revelation. (Open M, W, and F 8am-1:30pm; Tu, Th, and Su 8am-1:30pm and 4-6pm. Free. Dress modestly.)

Ferries arrive in Skala from: Kos (4hr., 2700dr); Piraeus/Athens (10hr., 6500dr); Rhodes (10hr., 5600dr); and Samos (4 per week, 1700dr). The **tourist office** is opposite the dock. (☎31 666. Open M-F 9am-3:30pm and 4-10:30pm, Sa 11am-1:30pm and 6:30-8pm.) **Jason's Rooms** are near the OTE, on the other side of the street. (☎31 832. Singles 5000dr; doubles 7000-10,000dr.) To get to **Flower Stefanos Camping** at **Meloi,** walk 2km right along the waterfront, facing inland, and follow the signs, or catch the free shuttle at the port. (☎31 821. Open May 15-Oct. 15. 1500dr per person; 750dr per tent; 750dr tent rental.)

HUNGARY (MAGYARORSZÁG)

FORINTS

US$1 = 290 FT (or HUF)	100FT = US$0.34
CDN$1 = 200FT	100FT =CDN$0.51
UK£1 = 430FT	100FT = UK£0.24
IR£1 = 330FT	100FT = IR£0.30
AUS$1 = 170FT	100FT = AUS$0.60
NZ$1 = 120FT	100FT = NZ$0.80
SAR1 = 42FT	100FT = SAR2.40
DM1 = 130FT	100FT = DM0.75
EUR€1 = 254FT	100FT = EUR€0.38

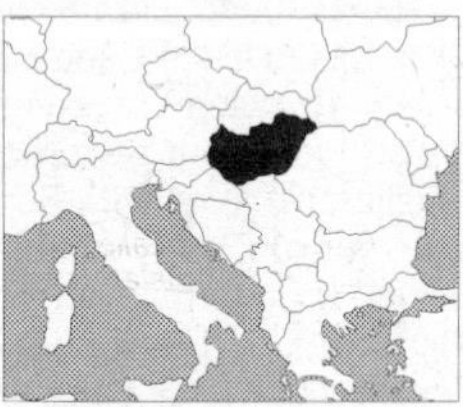

Country code: 36. **International dialing prefix:** 00. From outside Hungary, dial int'l dialing prefix (see inside back cover) + 36 + city code + local number.

Communism was a mere blip in Hungary's 1100-year history of repression and renewal. Today, the nation appears well at ease with its new-found capitalist identity. Although Budapest is Hungary's social and economic keystone, it by no means has a monopoly on cultural attractions; intriguing provincial capitals are within reach by train. With luscious wine valleys nestled in the northern hills, a rough and tumble cowboy plain in the south, and a bikini-worthy beach resort in the east, the beauty of the countryside should not be forsaken for a whirlwind tour of the capital. Otherwise, you'll have seen the heart of Hungary, but missed its soul entirely.

For everything Hungarian, ask to dance with *Let's Go: Eastern Europe 2001.*

FACTS AND FIGURES

Official Name: Republic of Hungary.

Government: Parliamentary democracy.

Capital: Budapest.

Land Area: 92,340 km.

Geography: Mostly plains; low mountains and hills on the Slovakian border.

Climate: Temperate; cold, cloudy, humid winters and warm summers.

Population: 9,971,000 (90% Magyar, 4% Roma, 3% German, 2% Serb.

Major Cities: Budapest, Eger, Szombathely, Debrecen, Pécs.

Language: Hungarian (Magyar).

Religions: Roman Catholic (68%), Calvinist (20%), Lutheran (5%), other (7%).

Income per capita: US$4340.

DISCOVER HUNGARY

Quickly being discovered as Central Europe's hippest and most cosmopolitan city, **Budapest** is the vibrant, fast-paced heart of Hungary (p. 512). Mosey on over to the relaxed villages of the **Danube Bend** (p. 522), then experience the alcoholic giddiness of Northern Hungary's fine vineyards. **Eger** is home to one of Hungary's most important castles, and the nearby Valley of the Beautiful Women attracts international discriminating drunks (p. 524). **Lake Balaton,** capital of the Hungarian summer, hosts a kitschy beach scene (p. 525). An escape from the thonged throngs of **Siófok's** Baywatch-esque Strand (p. 525), **Keszthely**—on the lake's western end—shelters a stunning palace and the world's largest radioactive thermal bath (p. 526).

ESSENTIALS

WHEN TO GO

The temperatures are most pleasant May to September. Budapest never feels crowded even in the high season, so time your visit to coincide with some of the summer festivals. Fall and spring can be a bit chillier, though with a sweater, it's quite nice. Winter tends to be very cold, and worth avoiding.

DOCUMENTS AND FORMALITIES

Citizens of Canada, Ireland, South Africa, the UK, and the US can visit Hungary without **visas** for 90 days, provided their passport does not expire within six months of their journey's end. Australians and New Zealanders must obtain 90-day tourist visas from a Hungarian embassy or consulate. For US residents, visas cost: single-entry US$40, double-entry US$75, multiple-entry US$180, and 48hr. transit US$38. Non-US residents pay US$65, US$100, US$200, and US$50. Visa processing takes a few days. Visa extensions are rare; apply at the Hungarian police.

EMBASSIES AND CONSULATES

All foreign embassies are in **Budapest** (see p. 512).

Hungarian Embassies at Home: Australia (consulate), Suite 405, Edgecliff Centre 203-233, New South Head Rd., Edgecliff, NSW 2027 (☎ (612) 93 28 78 59; fax 93 27 18 29); Canada, 299 Waverley St., Ottawa, ON K2P 0V9 (☎ (613) 230 27 17; fax 230 75 60; www.docuweb.ca/Hungary); New Zealand, 151 Orangi Kaupapa Rd., Wellington, 6005 (☎ (644) 938 04 27; fax 938 04 28; www.geocities.com/CapitolHill/Lobby/1958/ContentsEn.htm); South Africa, 959 Arcadia St., Hatfield, Arcadia; P.O. Box 27077, Sunnyside 0132 (☎ (012) 43 30 20; fax 430 30 29; email hunem@cis.co.za); UK, 35 Eaton Pl., London SW1X 8BY (☎ (020) 72 35 52 18; fax 78 23 13 48; www.huemblon.org.uk); US, 3910 Shoemaker St. NW, Washington, D.C. 20008 (☎ (202) 362 67 30; fax 966 81 35; www.hungaryemb.org).

GETTING THERE AND GETTING AROUND

BY PLANE. Hungary's national airline, **Malév** (US ☎ (800) 223 68 84; www.hungarianarilines.com) has daily direct flights from New York and London (both Gatwick and Heathrow) to Budapest.

BY TRAIN. Most trains *(vonat)* pass through Budapest and are generally reliable and inexpensive, although you should be cautious of theft on the Vienna-Budapest line. **Eurail** and **EastRail** are valid in Hungary. Students and those under 26 can be eligible for a 30% discount on train fares; ask ahead and be persistent. An **ISIC** gives discounts at IBUSZ, Express, and station ticket counters. Flash your card and repeat "student," or in Hungarian, *"diák"* (DEE-ahk). Book international tickets in advance. *Személyvonat* trains are slow; *gyorsvonat* (listed on schedules in red) cost the same and are twice as fast. Large towns are accessible by the blue *expressz* lines. Air-conditioned *InterCity* trains are fastest. A seat reservation *(potegy)* is required on trains labeled "R." While you can board an *InterCity* train without a reservation, the fine for doing so is 1000Ft; purchasing the reservation on board will double the price of the ticket. Some basic vocabulary words are: *érkezés* (arrival), *indulás* (departure), *vágány* (track), *állomás* or *pályaudvar* (station, abbreviated *pu.*), and *peron* (platform).

HUNGARY

BY BUS. The cheap, clean, and crowded bus system links many towns that have rail connections only to Budapest. The **Erzsébet tér** bus station in Budapest posts schedules and fares. *InterCity* bus tickets are purchased on board (arrive early if you want a seat). In larger cities, tickets for local transportation must be bought in advance from a newsstand and punched when you get on; there's a fine if you're caught without a ticket. In smaller cities, you pay when you board (usually 60Ft).

BY FERRY. The Danube **hydrofoil** goes from Budapest to Vienna via Bratislava; contact **Interticket Hungary** in the US (☎ (781) 275 57 52; www.interticket.com) or **MAHART Tours International** in Hungary (☎ (01) 318 17 43).

BY CAR. International Driving Permits are required of all non-Hungarian drivers. The national motorists' club is **Magyar Autóklub (MAK),** II, Rómer Flóris u. 4/a, 1024 Budapest (☎ (1) 345 18 00; www.autoklub.hu/us/index_us.html). For 24-hour MAK breakdown service, call ☎ 345 17 55 or ☎ 188.

BY BIKE AND BY THUMB. IBUSZ and Tourinform can provide brochures about cycling in Hungary that include maps, suggested tours, sights, accommodations, bike rental locations, repair shops, and border crossings. Always check the district as well as the kind of street: **út** is a major thoroughfare, **utca (u.)** a street, **körút (krt.)** a circular artery, and **tér** a square. *Let's Go* does not recommend hitchhiking.

TOURIST SERVICES AND MONEY

EMERGENCY. Ambulance: ☎ 104. **Fire:** ☎ 105. **Police:** ☎ 107.

TOURIST OFFICES. Tourinform (www.tourinform.hu) has branches in every county, and is generally the most useful tourist service in Hungary; they should be your first stop in any town. They can't make reservations, but they'll check on vacancies, usually in university dorms and private *panzió*. **IBUSZ** offices throughout the country book private rooms, exchange money, sell train tickets, and charter tours, and are generally best at helping with travel plans. Snare the pamphlet *Tourist Information: Hungary* and the monthly entertainment guides *Programme in Hungary* and *Budapest Panorama* (all free and in English). **Express,** the former national student travel bureau, handles hostels and changes money. Regional agencies are most helpful in the outlying areas. **Tourist bureaus** are generally open in summer M-Sa 8am-8pm.

MONEY. The national currency is the **forint,** divided into 100 **fillérs,** which are quickly disappearing from circulation. Keep US dollars or Deutschmarks for visas, international train tickets, and (less often) private accommodations. New Zealand and Australian dollars, as well as South African rand and Irish pounds, are not exchangeable. Rates are generally poor at exchange offices with extended hours. The maximum permissible commission for cash-to-cash exchange is 1%. Never change money on the street. **American Express** offices in Budapest and **IBUSZ** offices around the country convert **traveler's checks** to cash for a steep 6% commission; go to **OTP Bank** and **Postabank** offices. **Cash advances** are available at most OTP branches, but as **ATMs** increase, many banks no longer give them. Currency exchange machines are popping up all over and have excellent rates, although they are slow. **Credit cards** are accepted at expensive hotels and shops.

A basic day in Hungary runs about US$25. Rounding up the bill as a **tip** is standard for a job well done. In restaurants, hand the tip to the server when you pay; it's rude to leave it on the table. Foreigners are expected to tip 15%; locals never give more than 10%. Bathroom attendants get 30Ft. You can be refunded up to 16% of the **Value-Added Tax (AFA)** upon leaving Hungary for purchases exceeding 50,000Ft on a single invoice, bought within 90 days of leaving the country, and are unused. You must have a copy of your credit card receipt or documentation from when you exchanged currency.

ACCOMMODATIONS AND CAMPING

Many travelers stay in **private homes** booked through a tourist agency. Singles are scarce—it's worth finding a roommate, as solo travelers often pay for a double room. Agencies may try to foist their most expensive rooms on you. Outside Budapest, the best offices are region-specific (e.g. EgerTourist in Eger). After staying a few nights, you can make arrangements directly with the owner, thus saving yourself the agencies' 20-30% commission. **Panzió,** run out of private homes, are the next most common option, although not always the cheapest. **Hotels** exist in some towns, but most have disappeared. **Hosteling** is becoming more attractive, although it is rare outside Budapest; **HI cards** are increasingly useful. Sheets are rarely required. Many hostels can be booked through Express, the student travel agency, or the regional tourist office. From June-August, university **dorms** become hostels; inquire at Tourinform. There are more than 300 **campgrounds** are throughout Hungary open May-September. Tourist offices offer the annual free booklet *Camping Hungary.* For more info and maps, contact Tourinform in Budapest.

HEALTH AND SAFETY

Medical assistance is most easily obtained in Budapest, where embassies carry a list of Anglophone doctors; most hospitals staff English-speaking doctors. Outside Budapest, try to bring a Hungarian speaker with you. All medical services must be paid for in **cash. Tap water** is usually drinkable. Bottled water is available at every food store. Public bathrooms vary tremendously in cleanliness: pack soap, toilet paper, and a towel, and be prepared to pay the attendant 30Ft. Men should look for *Férfi*, and women for *Női* signs. **Pharmacies** *(gyógyszertar)* are well-stocked with Western brands. Violent **crime** in Hungary is low, but in larger cities, especially Budapest, foreign tourists are favorite targets of petty thieves and pickpockets.

FOOD AND DRINK

Hungarian food is more flavorful and varied than standard Eastern European fare. Paprika, Hungary's chief agricultural export, colors most dishes red. In Hungarian restaurants (*vendéglő* or *étterem*), begin with *halászlé*, a deliciously spicy fish stew. Alternately, try *gyümölesleves*, a cold fruit soup topped with whipped cream. The Hungarian national dish is *bográcsgulyás* (goulash), a stew of beef, onions, green pepper, tomatoes, potatoes, dumplings, and plenty of paprika. *Borjúpaprikás* is veal with paprika and potato-dumpling pasta. Vegetarians can find recourse in the tasty *rántott sajt* (fried cheese) and *gombapörkölt* (mushroom stew) on most menus. In general, Hungarian food is fried, and fresh vegetables other than peppers and cabbage are a rarity. In a *cukrászda* (confectionery), you can satisfy your sweet tooth cheaply. *Túrós rétes* is a chewy pastry pocket filled with sweetened cottage cheese. *Somlói galuska* is a fantastically rich sponge cake of chocolate, nuts, and cream, all soaked in rum. *Kávé* is espresso, served in thimble-sized cups and so strong your veins will be popping before you finish the first sip. *Unicum*, advertised as the national drink of Hungary, is a very fine herbal liqueur that Habsburg kings used to cure digestive ailments.

COMMUNICATION

MAIL. The Hungarian **mail** system is reliable; airmail *(légiposta)* takes 5-10 days to the US and the rest of Europe, and two weeks to South Africa, New Zealand, and Australia. Mailing a **postcard** from Hungary costs 80Ft to Australia, Canada, New Zealand, the US, or South Africa; to Ireland and the UK, 65Ft. **Letters** cost 100-110Ft. If you're mailing to a Hungarian citizen, the family name precedes the given name, hence "LASTNAME, Firstname." Mail can be received through *Poste Restante.*

HUNGARY

TELEPHONES. For intercity calls, wait for the tone and dial slowly; "06" goes before the phone code. **International calls** require red phones or new, digital-display blue ones. Blue phones tend to cut you off after three to nine minutes. Phones often require **phone cards** *(telefonkártya)*, available at kiosks, train stations, and post offices (800Ft or 1600Ft). Direct calls can also be made from Budapest's phone office. To call **collect**, dial ☎190 for the international operator. To reach international carriers, put in a 10Ft and a 20Ft coin (which you get back), dial 00, wait for the second tone, then dial the **international direct dialing number: AT&T Direct** (☎06 80 00 11 11); **BT Direct** (☎06 (wait for dial tone) 80 00 44 11); **Canada Direct** (☎06 80 00 12 11); **MCI WorldPhone** (☎00 80 00 14 11); **Sprint** (☎00 80 00 18 77).

LANGUAGES. Hungarian belongs to the Finno-Ugric branch of the Ugric language family, and is related distantly to Turkish and even more distantly to Estonian and Finnish. It is also spoken by minorities in Slovakia, Romania, and Yugoslavia. After Hungarian and **German, English** is Hungary's third language.

HOLIDAYS AND FESTIVALS

Holidays: New Year's Day (Jan. 1); National Day (Mar. 15); Catholic Easter (Apr. 23-24); Labor Day (May 1); Whit Sunday (June 11); Whit Monday (June 12); Constitution Day (St. Stephen's Day; Aug. 20); Republic Day (1956; Aug. 23); Christmas (Dec. 25-26).

Festivals: The best of all worlds come together in the last two weeks of March for the **Budapest Spring Festival,** a showcase of Hungary's premier musicians and actors. Óbudai island in Budapest hosts the week-long **Sziget Festival** (mid-Aug.), Europe's biggest open-air rock festival. An international folk-dance festival, **Eger Vintage Days,** is held daily in the beginning of September.

BUDAPEST ☎1

A cosmopolitan capital and the stronghold of Magyar nationalism, Budapest awakened from its 40 years in a Communist cocoon with the same pride that rebuilt the city from the rubble of WWII and endured the Soviet invasion of 1956. No toyland Prague, Budapest is bigger, dirtier, and more vibrant with an architectural majesty befitting the Habsburg Empire's number-two city. The grace of its buildings is matched only by the energy running through its streets. Although neon lights and legions of tourists have added a new twist to the Budapest rhapsody, the city remains one of Eastern Europe's most sophisticated tunes.

ORIENTATION AND PRACTICAL INFORMATION

The formerly separate cities of Buda and Pest (PESHT), separated by the **Duna** (Danube) river, have combined to form modern Budapest. On the west bank, elegant **Buda** inspires countless artists with its hilltop citadel, trees, and cobblestone **Castle District,** while bustling **Pest,** on the east bank, is the heart of the modern city. Three bridges link the two halves: **Széchenyi lánchíd,** slender, white **Erzsébet híd,** and green **Szabadság híd. Moszkva tér** (Moscow Square), just down the northern slope of the Castle District, is Budapest's bus and tram transportation hub. **Batthyány tér,** opposite the **Parliament** (Országház) building, is one Metro stop past the Danube in Buda, and is the starting point of the **HÉV commuter railway.** Budapest's three **Metro** lines (M1, M2, and M3) converge at **Deák tér,** at the core of Pest's loosely concentric boulevards, next to the main international bus terminal at **Erzsébet tér.** Two blocks west toward the river lies **Vörösmarty tér.** As you face the statue of Mihály Vörösmarty, the main pedestrian shopping zone, **Váci u.,** is to the right.

Budapest is divided into 23 **districts;** "I" indicates Central Buda, while "V" means downtown Pest. Because many streets have shed their Communist labels, an up-to-date **map** is essential; pick up a free one at American Express or Tourinform, or buy the *Belváros Idegenforgalmi Térképe* at any Metro stop (199Ft).

HUNGARY

GETTING THERE AND GETTING AROUND

Flights: Ferihegy Airport (☎296 96 96; info ☎29 67 15 or 296 70 00). Terminal 2A is for Malév (Hungarian airlines) international flights; terminal 2B is for foreign airlines. **Centrum buses** go to Erzsébet tér (45min., every 30min. 5:30am-9pm, 500Ft), but the **Ferihegy/red** bus #93, followed by the M3 to Köbanya-Kispest (50min.), is cheapest.

Trains: ☎461 54 00. Most international trains arrive at **Keleti pu.;** some from Prague end at **Nyugati pu.** or **Déli pu.** Each station has schedules for the others. To: **Vienna** (3hr., 17 per day, 7150Ft, 700Ft reservation fee); **Prague** (EC train 7hr., 5 per day, 13,600Ft; night train 9hr., 1 per day, 12,100Ft; 800Ft reservation fee); **Warsaw** (11hr., 2 per day, 12,900Ft, 2000Ft reservation fee); **Berlin** (12hr., 1 per day, 20,400Ft; night train 15hr., 1 per day, 35,200Ft; 2500Ft reservation fee); and **Bucharest** (14hr., 7 per day, 12,000Ft). The daily **Orient Express** stops on its way from **Paris** to **Īstanbul.** Prices vary widely. Students and under 26 get 33% discount on international tickets; indicate *diák* (DEE-ak; student). **International Ticket Office,** Keleti pu. Open daily 7am-6pm. **MÁV Hungarian Railways,** VI, Andrássy út 35 (☎/fax 322 84 05), and at all stations. Open Apr.-Sept. M-F 9am-6pm; Oct.-Mar. 9am-5pm.

Buses: ☎117 29 66. Most buses to Western Europe leave from **Volánbusz main station,** V, Erzsébet tér (international ticket office ☎317 25 62; fax 266 54 19). M1-3: Deák tér. Open M-F 6am-6pm, Sa 6:30am-4pm. Buses to much of Eastern Europe depart from **Népstadion,** Hungária körút 48/52 (☎252 18 96). M2: Népstadion. To: **Vienna** (3½hr., 5 per week, 5190Ft); **Prague** (8½hr., 1-3 per week, 9900Ft); and **Berlin** (14½hr., 2-5 per week, 16,110Ft).

Public Transportation: Subways, buses, and **trams** are inexpensive, convenient, and easy to navigate. The **Metro** has three lines: yellow (M1), red (M2), and blue (M3). Most tourist maps include Metro lines, but pick up the *Budapest közlekedési hálózata* (Network Map of Budapest Transport; 250Ft) at any Metro station to navigate the buses. **Night transit** ("É") runs midnight-5am along major routes; buses 7É and 78É follow the M2 route, while 14É follows M3. Blue **single-fare tickets** for all public transport (one-way on one line 95Ft) are sold in Metro stations, in *Trafik* shops, and by some sidewalk vendors; punch them in the orange boxes at the gate of the Metro or on buses and trams and punch a new ticket when you change lines, or face a 1360-3000Ft fine. **1-day passes** 740Ft; **3-day** 1500Ft; **1-week** 1850Ft.

Taxis: Often a rip-off; check that the meter is on, and negotiate a price ahead of time. **Budataxi** (☎233 33 33) has the best rates. 90-100Ft per km.

TOURIST AND FINANCIAL SERVICES

Tourist Offices: All sell the **Budapest Card** (Budapest Kártya), which provides unlimited public transport, museum admission, and discounts at shops and restaurants (2-day 2800Ft, 3-day 3400Ft). **Vista Travel Center,** Pauley Ede 7 (☎267 86 03). M1-3: Deák tér; exit on Bajcsy-Zsilinszky út. The multilingual staff arranges lodgings and books train, plane, and bus tickets. Open M-F 9am-6:30pm, Sa 9am-2:30pm. **IBUSZ,** V, Ferenciek tér 10 (☎485 27 00). M3: Ferenciek tér. Books discounted tickets and sightseeing packages and finds lodgings. Open M-F 8:15am-6pm, Sa 9am-1pm.

Embassies and Consulates: Australia, XII, Királyhágo tér 8/9 (☎457 97 77). M2: Déli pu.; then take bus #21. Open M-Th 9am-5pm, F 9am-2pm, Sa-Su 9am-noon. **Canada,** XII, Budakeszi út 32 (☎275 12 00). Take bus #158 from Moszkva tér to the end. Open M-F 9am-noon. **South Africa,** VII, Rákóczi út 1/3 (☎266 21 48). **UK,** V, Harmincad u. 6 (☎266 28 88), off the corner of Vörösmarty tér. M1: Vörösmarty tér. Open M-F 9:30am-noon and 2:30-4pm. **US,** V, Szabadság tér 12 (☎267 45 55; emergency ☎266 93 31). M2: Kossuth Lajos; walk 2 blocks down Akademia and turn on Zoltán. Open M and W 8:30-11am, Tu and Th-F 8:30-10:30am. **New Zealand** and **Irish** nationals should contact the UK embassy.

Currency Exchange: Magyar Külkereskedelmi Bank, V, Szent István tér 11 (☎269 09 22). M1-3: Deák tér, at the basilica's entrance. One of the few to grant V, MC cash advances (no commission; go inside if you don't have a PIN) and cash traveler's checks in US$ (2% commission, US$20 minimum). Outdoor Cirrus/MC/Visa **ATM.** Open M-Th 8am-4:30pm and F 8am-3pm.

American Express: V, Deák Ferenc u. 10 (☎235 43 30; fax 267 20 28), next to Hotel Kempinski. M1: Vörösmarty tér. No commission on traveler's checks cashed in Ft; variable commission on those cashed in US$. AmEx cash advances in Ft. Mail held for members and checkholders. AmEx **ATM.** Open June-Sept. M-F 9am-6:30pm, Sa-Su 9am-5:30pm; Oct.-May M-F 9am-5:30pm, Sa 9am-2pm.

LOCAL SERVICES

Luggage storage: Lockers at all three **train stations** 200Ft. Nyugati pu. also has a luggage desk in the waiting room; 140-280Ft per day.

English Bookstore: Bestsellers KFT, V, Október 6 u. 11 (☎/fax 312 12 95), near the intersection with Arany János u. M1-3: Deák tér or M1: Vörösmarts tér. Lit, pop novels, magazines, and travel guides. Open M-F 9am-6:30pm, Sa 10am-5pm, Su 10am-4pm.

Gay and Lesbian Services: Gay Switchboard Budapest (☎ (0630) 32 33 34; http://ourworld.compuserve.com/homepages/budapest), provides a comprehensive gay guide on the internet and a daily Info-Hotline service to assist gay tourists in Budapest.

Laundromats: Irisz Szalon, V, Városház u. 3/5 (☎317 20 92). M3: Ferenciek tére. Wash 1100Ft per 7kg; dry 450Ft per 15min. Open M-F 7am-7pm, Sa 7am-1pm.

EMERGENCY AND COMMUNICATIONS

Police: ☎107. **Ambulance:** ☎104. **Fire:** ☎105.

Tourist Police: Kulföldiket Elenörzö Osztály (KEO), VI, Városligeti Fasor 46/48 (☎443 50 00). M1: Hősök tér; go 3 blocks up Dózsa György út and turn right. Open Tu 8:30am-noon and 2-6pm, W 8:30am-1pm, Th 10am-6pm, F 8:30am-12:30pm.

24hr. Pharmacies: II, Frankel L. út 22 (☎212 44 06); III, Szentendrei út 2/A (☎388 65 28); IV, Pozsonyi u. 19 (☎389 40 79); VII, Rákóczi út 39 (☎314 36 95); IX, Boráras tér 3 (☎21 07 43); X-XII, Alkotás u. 1/B (☎355 46 91). At night, call the number on the door or ring the bell; you will be charged a slight fee.

Medical Assistance: Falck Személyi Olvosi Szolgálat (SOS) KFT, II, Kapy út 49/B (☎200 01 00 and 275 15 35). First aid free for foreigners. Open 24hr. The US embassy lists English-speaking doctors.

Internet Access: Cybercafes litter the city, but reserve well ahead of time and avoid peak afternoon hours; or, try a wired hostel. **Telephone,** Petőfi Sandor u. 17. M1-3: Deák tér. Expect to wait at least 1hr. 300Ft per 30min. Open M-F 9am-8pm, Sa 10am-3pm. **Vista Travel Center** (see above). Shorter wait. 11Ft per min. Open M-F 8am-11pm, Sa-Su 10am-11pm.

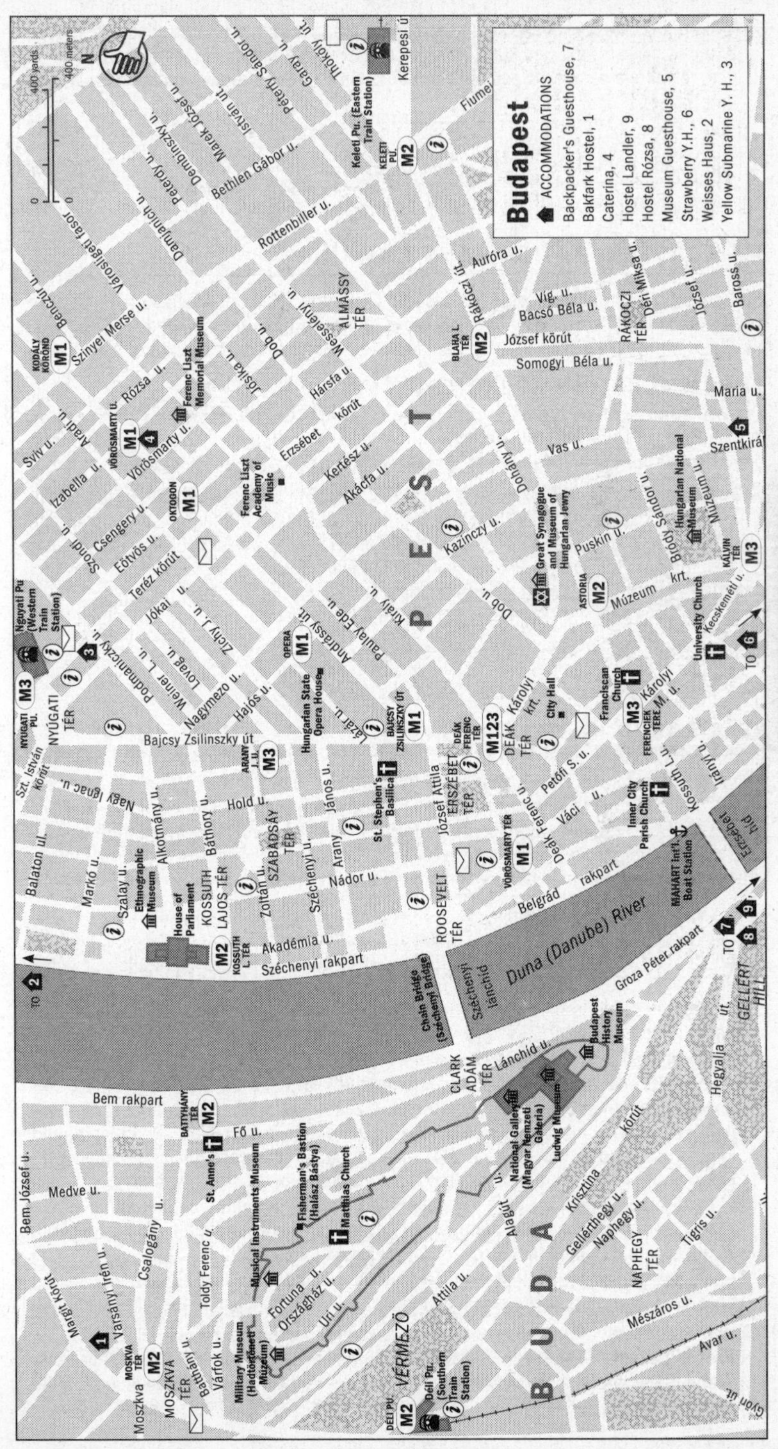
Budapest
ACCOMMODATIONS
Backpacker's Guesthouse, 7
Bakfark Hostel, 1
Caterina, 4
Hostel Landler, 9
Hostel Rózsa, 8
Museum Guesthouse, 5
Strawberry Y.H., 6
Weisses Haus, 2
Yellow Submarine Y. H., 3
PEST
BUDA
Duna (Danube) River
Chain Bridge (Széchenyi Bridge)
House of Parliament
St. Stephen's Basilica
Hungarian State Opera House
Great Synagogue and Museum of Hungarian Jewry
Hungarian National Museum
Budapest History Museum
National Gallery (Magyar Nemzeti Galéria)
Ludwig Museum
Matthias Church
Fisherman's Bastion (Halász Bástya)
Keleti Pu. (Eastern Train Station)
Nyugati Pu (Western Train Station)
Déli Pu. (Southern Train Station)
GELLÉRT HILL

Telephones: Most phones use **phone cards,** available at newsstands, post offices, and Metro stations. 50-unit card 800Ft, 120-unit card 1800Ft. **Telephone** (see above) offers fax and telephone services. Open M-F 8am-8pm, Sa 9am-3pm. **Domestic operator** ☎ 191; **International operator** ☎ 190.

Post Office: V, Városház u. 18 (☎318 48 11). Open M-F 8am-8pm, Sa 8am-2pm. Address mail to be held: SURNAME, First name, *Poste Restante,* V, Városház u. 18, **1052** Budapest, Hungary. **Branches** at Nyugati pu., VI, Teréz krt. 105/107, and Keleti pu. VIII, Baross tér 11/C. All open M-F 8am-9pm, Sa 8am-2pm.

ACCOMMODATIONS AND CAMPING

Call ahead in summer, or stash your pack while you seek out a bed for the night to save yourself blisters. Travelers arriving at Keleti pu. enter a feeding frenzy as hawkers elbow their way to tourists; take their promises with a grain of salt.

ACCOMMODATION AGENCIES

Private rooms, slightly more expensive than hostels (2000-5000Ft per person, depending on location and bathroom quality), usually offer what hostels can't: peace, quiet, and private showers. Arrive early, bring cash, and haggle stubbornly.

Budapest Tourist, I, Deli Pálaudrar (☎212 46 25). Singles in Central Pest 5000-7000Ft; doubles 6000-10,000Ft; triples 6000-12,000Ft. Off season prices considerably lower. Also rents apartments for stays longer than 1 week. 3000-7000Ft per day, less for stays longer than 2 months. Open M-F 9am-5pm.

IBUSZ, V, Ferenciek tér 10 (☎485 27 00). M3: Ferenciek tér. Base price plus 1050Ft per day. Doubles 3500Ft; triples 4500Ft; quads 5000Ft. Open M-F 8:15am-6pm.

Non-Stop Hotel Service, V, Apáczai Csere J. u. 1 (☎318 48 48; fax 317 90 99), M1: Vörösmarty tér. Rooms in Pest. Singles 6000Ft; doubles from 6000Ft off season, 7500Ft in summer; triples from 7000Ft, 8000Ft. Open 24hr.

HUNGARY

YEAR-ROUND HOSTELS

Budapest's hostels are generally social centers, with no curfews and beer- and music-filled common rooms that often prove more alluring than the city's bars and clubs. Most, including university dorms, operate under the auspices of the Hungarian Youth Hostel Association; representatives wear HI t-shirts. Beware theft in hostels; always keep your belongings in lockers, or take all valuables with you. Unless otherwise noted, all have luggage storage, kitchens, and TV in the common room.

Backpacker's Guesthouse, XI, Takács Menyhért u. 33 (☎/fax 385 89 46; backpackguest@hotmail.com), in **Buda,** 12min. from central Pest. From Keleti pu., take bus #7 or 7A toward Buda; get off at Tétenyi u. (5 stops past the river), walk back under the railway bridge, turn left, and go down the 3rd street on the right. Packed, clean bathrooms; Gen-X slacker guests; and superb CD and video collections. Internet 15Ft per min. Reception 24hr. Reserve 1 or 2 weeks in advance. 5- to 8-bed dorms 1600Ft; small dorm 1900Ft; double 4800Ft.

Station Guest House (HI), XIV, Mexikói út 36/B (☎221 88 64; email station@mail.matav.hu), in **Pest.** From Keleti pu., take bus #7 to Hungária Körút, walk under the railway pass, take an immediate right on Mexikói út, walk for 2 blocks, and look for the HI logo. Provide paints for guests to graffiti the walls. Billiards, satellite TV, liquor at the reception, and live music twice a week. Ask for a kitchen floor room if you plan to sleep. Breakfast 300Ft. Laundry 600Ft per 4kg. Internet 20Ft per min. Reserve ahead or end up on an attic mattress. Dorms in attic 1200-1400Ft; 6- to 8-bed 1400-2000Ft; 2- to 3-bed dorms 2200-2800Ft. Nonmembers add 200Ft.

Yellow Submarine Youth Hostel, VI, Teréz Körút 56, 3rd fl. (☎/fax 331 98 96). Across from Nyugati pu. Big, bright rooms and friendly staff. Large kitchen. Breakfast included. Laundry 500Ft. Check-out 9am. Dorms 2200-3800Ft; doubles 7000Ft. 10% off with HI.

Royal Youth Guesthouse, VIII, Német ut. 13. M2: Blaha Lujza tér; walk down Jószef Körú, take a left at the far end of Rájcócz tér, and take the 2nd right. Smaller and cozier than most. Laundry 1000Ft. Internet 400Ft per hr. 4-6 bed dorms 1800Ft; doubles 2800Ft.

SUMMER HOSTELS

Many university dorms, mostly near Móricz Zsigmond Körtér, morph into hostels in July and August. They typically have kitchens and a common room TV.

Hostel Bakfark, I, Bakfark u. 1/3 (☎343 0748), in **Buda.** M2: Moszkva tér; go along Margit krt. with Burger King to the right and take the 1st unmarked street after Mammut. Some of the most comfortable hostel rooms in town. Sparkling showers. Check-out 10am. Reserve ahead. Open June 15-Aug. Dorms 2700Ft; 300Ft less with HI.

Strawberry Youth Hostels, IX, Ráday u. 43/45 (☎218 47 66) and Kinizsi u. 2/6 (☎217 30 33), in **Pest.** M3: Kálvin tér; walk down Vámház krt. with Hotel Mercure on the right, and take a left after one block. Big, sunny bunk-less rooms with fridge, drying rack, and a view of the building next door. Small pub downstairs; ask for a 3rd fl. room if you're not into heavy bass. Free Keleti pu. pickup. Laundry 400Ft. Check-out 10am. Open June 29-Sept. 1. Doubles 3200Ft; triples and quads 2900Ft. 10% off with HI.

Hostel Landler, XI, Bartók Béla út 17 (☎463 36 21), in **Buda.** Take bus #7 or 7A across the river, get off at Géllert, and turn on Bartók Béla út away from the river. Lived-in college dorms. Some English spoken. Laundry. Check-out 9am. Open July 5-Sept. 5. Singles 4800Ft; doubles 3200Ft; triples and quads 2900Ft. 10% off with HI.

Hostel Rózsa, XI, Bercsényi u. 28/30 (☎463 42 50), in Buda. M2: Blaha Lujzatér; then take tram #4 and get off 3 stops after the river. Squeaky clean (but curtainless) showers. Refrigerators in all rooms. Laundry 160Ft; bring detergent. Free transport from bus or train station. Open July-Sept. 5. Doubles 3200Ft. 10% off with HI.

HUNGARY

GUESTHOUSES

Guesthouses and rooms in private homes lend a personal touch for about the same price as hostels. Owners prowl for guests in Keleti pu., but often carry cell phones for reservations.

Museum Guesthouse, VIII, Mikszáth Kálmán tér 4, 1st fl. (☎318 95 08 and 318 21 95), in **Pest.** M3: Kálvin tér; take the left exit from the stop onto Baross u., take the left branch at the fork, go to the far right corner at the open square, and ring the buzzer at gate #4. In the heart of a hopping bar scene, with a laid-back atmosphere. Run by young, hostel-style management. Internet 1000Ft per hr., free after 6pm. Laundry 1000Ft. Reception 24hr. Check-out 10am. Reserve the morning of your stay. 1800Ft.

Caterina, VI, Andrássy út 47, 3rd fl., apt. #18, in **Pest;** ring bell #11. (☎291 95 38; email caterina@mail.inext.hu). M1: Oktogon; or trams #4 and 6. Across from Burger King. Grandmother-style house–no curfew, but quiet hours. Internet 550Ft per 30min. Laundry 700Ft per 5kg. Reception 24hr. Check-out 9am. Lockout 10am-2pm. Reserve by email. Dorms 2000Ft; doubles 2700Ft; triples 2000Ft; 6-bed room US$60.

Weisses Haus, III, Erdőalja út 11 (☎/fax 387 82 36). M3: Árpád híd; then take tram #1 to Floriantér and #137 to Iskola. A family-owned villa in a nice neighborhood 30min. from the city center. Breakfast included. Some English spoken. Laundry 1000Ft per 4kg. No curfew, but bus #137 stops at 11:30pm. Doubles US$20.

CAMPING

Zugligeti "Niche" Camping, XII, Zugligeti út 101 (☎/fax 200 83 46). Take bus #158 from "Moszkva tér" to the last stop. Communal showers and a safe. English spoken. Electricity 500Ft. 850Ft per person, 500-900Ft per tent, 700 per car.

Római Camping, III, Szentendrei út 189 (☎368 62 60; fax 250 04 26). M2: Batthyány tér; take the HÉV to "Római fürdő" and walk 100m toward the river. A huge 3-star site. Swimming pool 300Ft. Open mid-Apr. to mid-Oct. Tents 1950Ft; bungalows with cold water 1350-2000Ft. 10% off with HI.

FOOD

Even the most expensive restaurants in Budapest may fall within your budget, but eating at family joints can be tastier and more fun. A 10% tip is generally expected, and another 10% if your meal is accompanied by live music. Seek out the *kifőzés* or *vendéglő* in your neighborhood for a taste of Hungarian life. For the less adventurous, the **world's largest Burger King** is on Oktogon. **Non-Stop** stores and corner markets are the best options for **groceries.** The king of them all is **Grand Market Hall,** IX, Fövamtér 1/3, next to Szabadság híd (M3: Kálvin Tér). First built in 1897, the hall's 10,000 sq. m of market stalls make it a tourist attraction in itself.

RESTAURANTS

Fatâl Restaurant, V, Váci út 67 (☎266 26 07), in **Pest.** Packs them in for large and hearty Hungarian meals. Giant, carefully garnished main courses from 860Ft. Reservations only. Open daily 11:30am-2am.

Marquis de Salade, VI, Hajós u. 43 (☎302 40 86), in **Pest.** M3: Arany János; at the corner of Bajcsy-Zsilinszky út. Chic cuisine served by waiters clad head-to-toe in black. Elaborate opium-den decor. Dishes from Azerbaijan, France, India, Italy, Japan, and Hungary. Main dishes 700-2200Ft. Open daily noon-midnight.

Söröző a Szent Jupáthoz, II, Retek u. 16 (☎212 29 23), in **Buda.** M2: Moszkva tér. Huge tables, menus, and portions. Main dishes 600-1700Ft. Open 24hr.

Marcello's, XI, Bartók Béla út 40 (☎466 62 31), in **Buda.** Just before Móricz Zsigmond Körtér, on the river side. With imported "cigarette" bread-sticks, fresh flowers, classy high-heeled waitresses, and real tomato sauce (a rarity in Budapest), this place is pizza all grown up. Pizzas 480-650Ft. Reservations recommended. Open M-Sa noon-10pm.

Falafel Faloda, VI, Paulay Ede u. 53 (☎267 95 67), in **Pest.** M1: Opera; cross Andrássy, head straight on Hajós u., and turn left on Paulay Ede. Fast food at its best: make-your-own-falafel with real tahini and fresh vegetables. Sandwiches 360Ft; salads 350-420Ft. Open M-F 10am-8pm, Sa 10am-6pm.

Paksi Halászcsárda, II, Margit Körút 14 (☎212 55 99), in **Buda.** Tram #4 or 6 to Margit Híd. Dimly lit, elegant restaurant where red wine and collared shirts rule the roost. Well-executed Hungarian standbys. Main dishes 760-2500Ft. Open daily noon-midnight.

CAFES

Cafes in Budapest are living museums of a bygone era. Once the pretentious haunts of Budapest's literary, intellectual, and cultural elite, as well as its political dissidents, the cafes now serve cheap and absurdly rich pastries.

Művész Kávéház, VI, Andrássy út 29 (☎352 13 37). M1: Opera. Diagonally across from the Opera. The name means "artist cafe," and the title fits. Cell-phoning Italians, Hungarian grandmothers, and starving artists all come here. Enjoy cakes (200Ft) and cappuccino (190Ft) on the terrace. Open daily 9am-midnight.

Cafe New York, VII, Erzsébet krt. 9-11 (☎322 38 49). M2: Blaha Lujza tér. This symbol of the *fin-de-siècle* Golden Age fell into disrepair under communism, but has been restored with exquisite velvet, gold and marble. Ice cream and coffee delights priced accordingly (750-1150Ft). Pastries 300-550Ft. Open daily 10am-midnight.

Ruszwurm, I, Szentháromság u. 7 (☎375 52 84), just off the square on Várhegy in the Castle District. The sweets that once attracted Habsburgs now draw packs of tourists. Homemade ice cream 60Ft; chocolate cake 220Ft. Open daily 10am-7pm.

SIGHTS

In 1896, Hungary's 1000th birthday bash prompted the construction of what are today Budapest's most prominent sights—a testament to the optimism of a capital on the verge of its Golden Age. Among the works commissioned by the Habsburgs were **Heroes' Square** (Hősök tere), **Liberty Bridge** (Szbadság híd), and **Vajdahunyad Castle** (Vajdahunyad vár). The domes of the **Parliament** (Országház) and **St. Stephen's Basilica** (Szent István Bazilika) are both 96m high—references to the historic date. A great way to see the sights, get a feel for the city, and meet other travelers are **The Absolute Walking Tours,** which meet daily at 9:30am and 1:30pm at Déak tér and 10am and 2pm from the Heroes' Square. (Tours last 2½-5½hr. 2500-5500Ft.)

BUDA

Buda is older, more conservative, and more disjointed than its sister, but with the city's best parks, lush hills, and Danube islands, it is no less worth exploring. The **Castle District** lies atop **Castle Hill** and contains the bulk of Buda's sights. South of Castle Hill, also on the banks of the Danube, lies **Gellért Hill.**

CASTLE DISTRICT. Towering above the Danube, the **Castle District** has been razed three times in its 800-year history, most recently in 1945. With its winding, statue-filled streets, breathtaking views, and magnificent hodge-podge of architectural styles, the UNESCO-protected district now appears much as it did in Habsburg times (although today it's much more touristed). Although bullet holes in the **castle** facade still recall the 1956 Uprising, the reconstructed palace today houses a number of fine museums. *(I, Szent Gyurgy tŭr 2, on Castle Hill. M2: Moszkva tŭr; walk up to the hill on V6rfok u. and enter the castle at Vienna Gate (Becsi kapu). Alternatively, take the funicular (sikly) from the Buda side of the Széchenyi Chain Bridge. Cable car runs daily 7:30am-10:30pm; closed 2nd and 4th M of each month; ascent 300Ft, descent 250Ft. The upper lift station sits inside the castle walls near the National Gallery.)*

MATTHIAS CHURCH AND FISHERMAN'S BASTION. The multi-colored roof of the neo-Gothic **Matthias Church** (Mátyás templom), which was converted into a mosque when Ottoman armies seized Buda in 1541 (and re-converted 145 years later when the Habsburgs defeated the Turks), is one of the most photographed sights in Budapest. Descend the stairway to the right of the altar to enter the **crypt** and **treasury.** *(On Castle Hill. From the Vienna Gate, walk straight down Fortuna u. From the cable car, turn right on Színház and veer left on Tárnok u. High mass with full orchestra and choir Su 7, 8:30, 10am, noon, and 8:30pm. Treasury open daily 9:30am-5:30pm; 200Ft.)* Behind St. Matthias Church is the grand equestrian monument of King Stephen bearing his trademark double cross in front of the **Fisherman's Bastion** (Halászbástya). The view across the Danube from the squat, fairy-tale **tower** is stunning. *(Tu-Su 200Ft; M free.)*

GELLÉRT HILL. The Pope sent Bishop Gellért to the coronation of King Stephen, the first Christian Hungarian monarch, to assist in the conversion of the Magyars; those unconvinced by his message gave the hill its name (Gellért-hegy) by hurling the good bishop to his death from the top. The **Liberation Monument** (Szabadság Szobor), created to honor Soviet soldiers who died "liberating" Hungary, looks over Budapest from atop the hill. The view from the top of the adjoining **Citadel,** built as a symbol of Habsburg power after the foiled 1848 revolution, is especially spectacular at night. At the base of the hill sits the **Gellért Hotel and Baths** (see **Thermal Baths,** p. 521), Budapest's most famous Turkish Bath. *(To ascend the hill, take tram #18 or 19 to Hotel Gellért; follow Szaby Verjték u. to Jubileumi Park, continuing on the marked paths to the summit. Or, take bus #27 to the top; get off at Búsuly Juhász and walk 5min. to the peak.)*

PEST

The winding streets of Pest were constructed in the 19th century and today host European chain stores, corporations and banks, and myriad monuments. The old **Inner City** (Belváros), rooted in the pedestrian **Váci u.** and **Vörösmarty tér,** is a crowded tourist strip with street vendors hawking overpriced wares.

PARLIAMENT. Pest's riverbank sports a string of luxury hotels leading to its magnificent Neo-Gothic **Parliament** (Országház), modeled after Britain's. The massive structure has always been too big for Hungary's government; today, the legislature uses only 12%. *(M2: Kossuth Lajos tér. Mandatory tours in English M-F 10am and 2pm, Sa-Su 10am. 900Ft, students 500Ft. Purchase tickets at gate #10 and enter at gate #12.)*

LIKE A TROUBLED BRIDGE OVER WATER

The citizens of Budapest are justly proud of the bridges that bind Buda to Pest. The four great lions that have guarded the Széchenyi Chain Bridge (Széchenyi lánchíd) since 1849 make the bridge one of Budapest's most recognizable. These beasts were created by János Marschalkó in a naturalistic style, with the tongues resting far back in their gaping mouths. The anatomical correctness of their new mascots did not impress Budapestians—distraught by public laughter over the seemingly missing tongues, Marschalkó jumped from the bridge to his death. Another version of the story has the king reprimanding Marschalkó, with the same result. *Let's Go* does not recommend sculpting lions without visible tongues.

ST. STEPHEN'S BASILICA. The city's largest church (Sz. István Bazilika) was decimated by Allied bombs in WWII. Its neo-Renaissance facade remains under reconstruction, but the ornate interior continues to attract both tourists and worshippers. The **Panorama Tower** offers an amazing 360° view, but the highlight is St. Stephen's mummified right hand, one of Hungary's most revered religious relics, on public display. For the devout and the macabre, a 100Ft donation dropped in the box will light up the religious relic for two minutes of closer inspection. *(M1-3: Deák tér. Basilica and museum open May-Oct. M-Sa 9am-5pm; Nov.-Apr. M-Sa 10am-4pm, Su 1-5pm. Tower open daily June-Aug. 9:30am-6pm; Sept.-Oct. 10am-5:30pm; Apr.-May 10am-4:30pm. 400Ft, students 300Ft.)*

SYNAGOGUE. Much of the artwork in Pest's Moorish synagogue (zsinagóga), the largest active synagogue in Europe and the second-largest in the world, is unfortunately blocked from view, as it has been under renovation since 1988. In back is the **Holocaust Memorial,** an enormous metal tree that sits above a mass grave for thousands of Jews killed near the end of WWII. *(M2: Astoria. At the corner of Doh6ny u. and Wesselényi u. Open May-Oct. M-Th 10am-5pm, F 10am-3pm, Su 10am-2pm; Nov.-Apr. M-F 10am-3pm, Su 10am-1pm. 500Ft.)*

HUNGARY

ANDRÁSSY ÚT & HEROES' SQUARE. Hungary's grandest boulevard, Andrássy út extends from **Erzsébet tér** in downtown Pest to **Heroes' Square** (Hősök tere) to the northeast. Perhaps the most vivid reminder of Budapest's Golden Age is the **Hungarian National Opera House** (Magyar Állami Operaház), whose gilded interior glows on performance nights. If you can't see an opera, take a tour. *(Andrássy út 22. M1: Opera. ☎332 81 97. Tours in English daily 3 and 4pm. 900Ft, students 450Ft. 20% discount with Budapest card.)* At the Heroes' Square end of Andrássy út, the **Millenium Monument** (Millenniumi emlékmű) commemorates the nation's most prominent leaders. Right off Heroes' Square is the **Museum of Fine Arts** (see **Museums,** below).

CITY PARK. The **Városliget** is home to a zoo, a circus, a run-down amusement park, and the lakeside **Vajdahunyad Castle** (Vajdahunyad Vár), whose Disney-esque collage of Romanesque, Gothic, Renaissance, and Baroque styles is intended to chronicle the history of Hungarian architecture. Outside the castle broods the hooded statue of **Anonymous,** the secretive scribe to whom we owe much of our knowledge of medieval Hungary. Rent a **rowboat** or **ice skates** on the lake next to the castle, or a **bike-trolley** to navigate the paths. *(M1: Széchenyi Fürdő. Boats and bike-trolleys rented June to mid-Sept. M-F 10am-8pm, Sa-Su 9am-8pm; ice skates rented daily Nov.-Mar. 9am-1pm and 4-8pm. Boats 400Ft per 30min. Ice skates and bike-trolleys 300Ft per 30min.)*

MUSEUMS

Buda Castle (☎375 75 33), on Castle Hill (see above). **Wing A** contains the **Museum of Contemporary Art** (Kortárs Művészeti Múzeum) and the **Ludwig Museum** upstairs, devoted to Warhol, Lichtenstein, and other modern masters. **Wings B-D** hold the **Hungarian National Gallery** (Magyar Nemzeti Galéria), a hoard of Hungarian paintings and sculptures. Artifacts from the 1242 castle, revealed by WWII bombings, lie in the **Budapest History Museum** (Budapesti Történeti Múzeum) in **Wing E.** Wings A-D open Tu-Su 10am-6pm. Wing A 400Ft, students 200Ft. Wings B-D 400Ft together, students 200Ft. Wing E open May 16-Sept. 15 daily 10am-6pm; Sept. 16-Oct. 31 and Mar.-May 15 W-M 10am-6pm; Nov.-Feb. 28 W-M 10am-4pm; 400Ft, students 200Ft.

Museum of Fine Arts (Szépművészeti Múzeum), XIV, Dózsa György út 41 (☎343 97 59). M1: Hősök tere. A simply spectacular collection; from Raphael to Rembrandt, Gaugin to Goya, these are the paintings you've never seen but shouldn't miss. Open Tu-Su 10am-5:30pm. 500Ft, students 200Ft. Tours for up to 5 people 2000Ft.

Museum of Applied Arts (Iparművészeti Múzeum), IX, Üllői út 33-37 (☎217 52 22). M3: Ferenc körút. Tiffany glass, furniture, and excellent temporary exhibits highlighting specific crafts. Open Mar. 15-Oct. Tu-Su 10am-6pm; Nov.-Mar. 11 Tu-Su 10am-4pm. 300Ft, students 100Ft; national holidays free.

AN OFFER YOU CAN'T REFUSE Communism may be dead in Hungary, but the mafia is alive and well in post-Soviet Budapest. Don't look for the usual Adidas-clad, gold chain-bedecked thugs; Budapest's agent extraordinaire might wear plenty of gold, but she also wears a miniskirt and high-heeled shoes. You'll meet her—an English-speaking, Hungarian hottie known as the "consumption girl" —at a swank bar or on the street around Váci út. Things will start off smoothly as she suggests a new venue. Of course you join her. She asks you to buy her a drink, and of course you do. When the bill comes, it is accompanied at last by the men you'd expect from the post-Soviet mafia. US$1000 for a single Sloe Gin Fizz? It's no mistake, they assure you. And what do you give a 300lb. gorilla? Anything he wants. You *will* pay, because there is no recourse for the victimized. Ask to see the menu and there it is, written in black-and-white. Not enough cash in your wallet? Don't worry, the mafia has learned at least a few tricks from capitalism: they now accept major credit cards. The US Embassy has advised against patronizing a number of establishments in the Váci út area, including: Fontana Cabaret, Mephisto Café, Muskátli Eszpresszó, and Tropical Bar.

Jewish Museum (Zsidy Múzeum), VII, Dohány út 2 (☎342 89 49). M2: Astoria. Juxtaposes a celebration of Hungary's rich Jewish past with haunting photographs and documents from the Holocaust. Open M-F 10am-3pm, Su 10am-2pm. 500Ft, students 250Ft.

Hungarian National Museum (Magyar Nemzeti Múzeum), VIII, Múzeum krt. 14/16 (☎338 21 22). M3: Kálvin tér. Exhibits from the Hungarian Crown Jewels to Soviet propaganda guarded by a cheery Stalin. Open Mar. 15-Oct. 15 Tu-Su 10am-6pm; Oct. 16-Mar. 14 Tu-Su 10am-5pm. 400Ft, students 150Ft. Tours 500Ft.

ENTERTAINMENT

Programme in Hungary and *Budapest Panorama* (available at tourist offices) are the best English-language guides to entertainment; also try the "Style" section of the weekly English-language *Budapest Sun*.

THEATER, MUSIC, AND DANCE. The **Central Theater Booking Office,** VI, Andrássy út 18 (☎312 00 00), next to the Opera House (open M-F 10am-6pm) and at Moszkva tér 3 (☎212 56 78; open M-F 10am-6pm), sells commission-free tickets to most performances. For less than US$5, you can enjoy an opera in the splendor of the gilded, neo-Renaissance **State Opera House** (Magyar Allami Operahaz), VI, Andrássy út 22. The box office on the left side of the building sells cheaper, unclaimed tickets 30 minutes before showtime. Take M1 to "Opera." (Box office ☎353 01 70. Open M-Sa 11am-5pm, Su 2-5pm.) The **Philharmonic Orchestra,** Vörösmarty tér 1, has equally grand music (concerts almost nightly Sept.-June) in a slightly more modest venue. The ticket office is on the side of the square farthest from the river; look for the Jegyroda sign. (☎318 44 46. Open daily 9am-3pm. Tickets 1200-1700Ft, less on the day of show.)

THERMAL BATHS. To soak away weeks of city grime and crowded trains, sink into a **thermal bath,** the quintessential Budapest experience. The baths were first built in 1565 by a Turkish ruler who feared that a siege of Buda would prevent the population from bathing. Thanks to him, you get to dive in, too, and the services—from mud baths to massages—are cheap enough to warrant indulgence without guilt. Ž **Gellért,** XI, Kelenhegyi út 4/6, has indoor thermal baths segregated by sex, a rooftop sundeck, a huge outdoor pool, mudbaths, ultrasound, and the new "Thai massage" (7500Ft; reserve ahead). The staff is accustomed to tourists—this is the only spa with English signs. Take bus #7 or tram #47 or 49 to Hotel Gellért, at the base of Gellért Hill. (☎466 61 66. Thermal bath 1000Ft; with pool 1600Ft. 15-minute massage 1200Ft. Pools open daily May-Sept. 6am-6pm; Oct.-Apr. M-F 6am-6pm, Sa-Su 6am-4pm.) Indoor baths and an **outdoor swimming pool** attract the city's gentry to **Széchenyi Fürdő,** XIV, Állatkerti u. 11/14. (☎321 03 10. M1: Hősök tere. Swimsuit required. 500Ft, after 5pm 400Ft. Massage 1200Ft per 15min. Open May-Sept. daily 6am-7pm; Oct.-Apr. M-F 6am-7pm, Sa-Su 6am-5pm. Baths men-only July-Aug. Tu, Th, and Sa; women-only M, W, and F.)

NIGHTLIFE

After a few drinks in Budapest among the global-village alterna-teens, you may forget you're in Hungary. A virtually unenforced drinking age and cheap drinks may be the only cause for culture shock, although cover prices are rising. To find out what's going on where and when, pick up *Budapest Week* (126Ft). Gay life in Budapest is just beginning to make itself visible; it is safer to be discreet.

Undergrass, VI, Liszt Ferenc tér 10. M1: Oktogon. The hottest spot in Pest's trendiest area. A soundproof, glass door divides the hip bar from the equally packed disco, which spins funk and pop. Open daily 8pm-5am; disco Tu-Su 10pm.

Old Man's Pub, VII, Akácfa u. 13. M2: Blaha Lujza tér. Although the name implies otherwise, this crowd is still in the larval phase of yuppie-dom—clean-cut hip. Live blues and jazz every evening. Restaurant and "funky disco." Open M-Sa 3pm-4:30 or 5am.

Capella Cafe, V, Belgrád rakpart 23. With glow-in-the-dark grafitti and an underground atmosphere, this popular spot draws a mixed gay and straight crowd for a line-up that varies from transvestite lip-synchs to W night stripteases. Nightly shows at midnight. Women welcome. Cover 500Ft; 500Ft min. Open Tu-Su 9pm-5am.

Piaf, VI, Nagymező u. 25. A much-loved after hours place. You'll feel like a cliché but you won't care. Knock on the door to await the approval of the club's matron. 500Ft cover includes 1 drink. Open daily 10pm-6am, but don't come before 1am.

Club Seven, Akácfa u. 7. More upscale than the average Budapest club, but still crowded. Funk to soul to jazz to disco. No cover M-Fr; Sa-Su men 1000Ft, women free. Coffeehouse open 9pm-4am, restaurant 6pm-midnight, dance floor 10pm-5am.

Fat Mo's Speakeasy, V, Nyári Pal u. 11. M3: Kálvin tér. "Spitting prohibited" in this Depression-era bar. Drinking, however, isn't—14 varieties of beer on tap (0.5L 350-750Ft) and live jazz (Su, M, and Th 9-11pm) to make the booze flow quicker. Th-Sa DJ from 11:30pm. Open M-F noon-2am, Sa-Su 6pm-4am.

THE DANUBE BEND

North of Budapest, the Danube sweeps in a dramatic arc called the Danube Bend (Dunakanyar), deservedly one of the greatest tourist attractions in Hungary.

SZENTENDRE ☎26

By far the most tourist-thronged of the Danube Bend towns, Szentendre (sen-TEN-dreh) delights with narrow cobblestone streets, upscale art galleries, and pricey restaurants in its cheery squares. Head up **Church Hill** (Templomdomb), above the town center in Fő tér, home to a 13th-century Roman Catholic church. Just across Alkotmány u., the museum at the Baroque **Serbian Orthodox Church** (Szerb Ortodox Templom) displays religious art. (Open W-Su 10am-8pm. 200Ft.) The popular **Margit Kovács Museum,** Vastagh György u. 1, exhibits work by the 20th-century Hungarian artist Margit Kovács. (Open mid-Mar. to Oct. daily 10am-6pm; Nov. to mid-Mar. Th-Su 10am-4pm. 380Ft, students 150Ft.) The real thriller at the **Szabó Marzipan Museum and Confectionary,** Dumtsa Jenő u. 7, is the larger-than-life chocolate statue of Michael Jackson. (Open daily 10am-6pm. 150Ft.)

HÉV trains travel to Budapest's Batthyány tér (45min., every 10-15min., 118Ft). **Buses** run from Budapest's Árpád híd station (30min., every 20-40min., 172Ft), many going on to Esztergom (1½hr., 432Ft). The HÉV commuter train and bus station are 10 minutes from Fő tér; descend the stairs outside the bus station, go through the underpass, and head up Kossuth u. At the fork in the road, bear right onto Dumsta Jenő út, which leads to the 1763 **Plague Cross** in the town center. **MAHART boats** leave from a pier north of the town center; with the river on your right, walk along the water until you see the sign (15min.). In summer, boats float to Budapest (3 per day, 650Ft) and Esztergom (1 per day, 700Ft). **Tourinform,** Dumsta Jenő u. 22, is between the town center and the station. (☎31 79 65. Open in summer M-F 10am-1pm and1:30-5pm, Sa 9:30am-6:30pm, Su 10am-2pm; off season M-F 10am-1pm and 1:30-5pm.) **IBUSZ,** Bogdányi u. 11, will hook you up with a private double for 3000Ft. (☎361 81; fax 31 35 97. Open M-F 9am-4pm, Sa-Su 10am-3pm.) **Ilona Panzió,** Rákóczi Ferenc u. 11, is in the center of town. (☎31 35 99. Breakfast included. 3500Ft for 1 person; 4600Ft for 2.) **Pap-szigeti Camping** sits 1km north of the town center on its own island in the Danube. (☎31 06 97. Open May-Oct.15. Tent sites 2500Ft for 2; US$3.50 per extra person. 3-5 bed bungalows US$3-12 per person. Hostel singles, doubles, triples, and quads US$4-6. *Panzió* doubles with shower US$15.) A **supermarket** is by the train station. (Open M-F 9am-7pm, Sa-Su 10am-5pm.)

ESZTERGOM ☎33

One thousand years of religious history revolve around a solemn hilltop **cathedral** that makes Esztergom (ESS-ter-gom) "the Hungarian Rome," the center of Catholicism in Hungary. Climb to the **cupola** (100Ft) for the best view of the bend, then descend into the **crypt** to honor the remains of archbishops. (Open daily 9am-4:45pm. 50Ft.) The **Cathedral Treasury** (Kincstáv) to the right of the main altar has Hungary's most extensive ecclesiastical collection. (Open daily 9am-4:30pm. 200Ft; English-language guide 80Ft.) On a smaller scale, the red marble **Bakócz Chapel,** to the left of the altar, is a masterwork of Renaissance Tuscan craftsmanship. Beside the cathedral stands the 12th-century **Esztergom Palace** and its museum. (Open Tu-Su in summer 9am-4pm; in winter 10am-3:30pm. 200Ft, students 100Ft.) At the foot of the cathedral's hill, the **Christian Museum** (Keresztény Múzeum), Berenyi Zsigmond u. 2, houses exceptional religious art. (Open Tu-Su 10am-5:30pm. 200Ft.)

Trains go to Budapest (1½hr., 22 per day, 1206Ft). With the station to your back, turn left on the main street, then right on Kiss János Altábornagy út, which becomes Kossuth Lajos u., to reach the square. Catch **buses** three blocks away from Rákóczi tér, on Simor János u., to Budapest (2hr., 15 per day, 570Ft) and Szentendre (1½hr., every hr., 432Ft); the bus from Budapest departs from Budapest's M3: Árpád híd. From the bus station in Esztergom, walk up Simor János u. toward the street market to reach Rákóczi tér. **Grantours,** Széchenyi tér 25, at the edge of Rákóczi tér, will help locate central **panzió rooms** (doubles 8000Ft) or cheaper **private rooms.** (☎/fax 41 37 56. Open July-Aug. M-F 8am-6pm, Sa 9am-noon; Sept.-June M-F 8am-4pm, Sa 9am-noon.) **Platán Panzió,** Kis-Duna Sétány 11, is between Rákóczi tér and Primas Sziget. (☎41 13 55. Reception 24hr. Check-out 10am. Singles 2500Ft; doubles 4000Ft.) **Gran Camping,** Nagy-Duna Sétány, is in Primas Sziget, a park on the banks of the Danube. (☎40 25 13. 800Ft per person; 750Ft per tent.) **Szalma Csárda,** at Primas Sziget near the pier at the end of Gőzhajó u., serves fish straight from the Danube. (Main dishes 800-1600Ft. Open daily noon-10pm.) **Julius Meinl,** just off Rákóczi tér, sells **groceries**. (Open M-F 6:30am-6:30pm, Sa 6:30am-1pm.)

SOUTHERN TRANSDANUBIA

Framed by the Danube to the west, the Dráva to the south, and Lake Balaton to the north, Southern Transdanubia is known for its rolling hills, sunflower fields, mild climate, and good wine. Once the northernmost section of the Pannonian Plain, fine churches and elegant architecture lend this ancient region a charming Baroque air.

PÉCS ☎72

At the foot of the Mecsek mountains, Pécs's climate, vistas, and architecture captivate visitors. University students further fuel an intense nightlife, making Pécs one of Hungary's most worthwhile weekend excursions. The **Csontváry Museum,** Janus Pannonius u. 11, displays the works of Tivadar Csontváry Kosztka, a Romantic-Symbolist-Expressionist known as the Hungarian van Gogh. (☎31 05 44. Open Tu-Su 10am-6pm. 200Ft, students 150Ft.) Down the hill, in the center of nearby Széchenyi tér, the **Ghasi Khasim Pasha Inner City Parish Church** was once a Turkish mosque built on the site of an earlier church. This fusion of Christian and Muslim traditions has become an emblem of the city. (Open daily Apr. 16-Oct. 14 10am-4pm; Oct. 15-

Apr. 15 10am-noon.) Walk downhill from Széchenyi tér on Irgalmasok u. to Kossuth tér to find a third religion's house of worship—Pécs's stunning Romantic 1869 **Synagogue.** (Open Su-F 10-11:30am and noon-4pm. 100Ft, students 50Ft.)

The **train** station is just south of the historic district. Take bus #30, 32, or 33 from the town center. Trains arrive from **Budapest-Déli** station (3½hr., 3 per day, 1624Ft). **Buses,** at the Nagy Lajos Király út and Alsómalom u., go to **Budapest** (4½hr., 7 per day, 1750Ft). The **Tourinform** tourist office, Széchenyi tér 9, sells **phone cards.** (☎21 11 34. Hours vary by season, but always open M-Sa 9am-2pm.) Change money at **K & H Bank,** on the corner of Széchenyi tér and Jókai u. (Open 24hr. **ATM.**) For central accommodations, **private rooms** are the best budget option. **Szent Mór Kollégium,** 48-as tér 4, is central but slightly more expensive. Take bus #21 two stops from the main bus terminal. (☎21 11 99. Spiffy triples in a university. Open June-Aug. 1000Ft, students 700Ft.) **Hotel-Camping Mandulás,** Angyán János u., is the center of a camping complex with a post office and grocery store. Take bus #34 from the train station to the hills above the city. (☎31 59 81. Open Apr.-Oct. 600Ft per person, 500Ft per tent.) **Caflisch Cukrászda Café,** Király u. 32 (☎31 03 91), is the best and trendiest cafe in town. (Pastries from 79Ft. Open daily 8am-10pm.) At night, check out **Hard Rák Cafe,** Ipar u. 7. The name refers to the music, not the well-known chain. (Live music F-Sa in summer. Open M-Sa 7pm-6am.) **Postal code:** 7621.

EGER ☎36

When an Ottoman army once tried to seize Eger Castle, locals fended off the attackers with their special "bull's blood" wine. This legend figures prominently in Hungarian lore and remains alive today in the lively wine cellars of the Valley of Beautiful Women and the historical monuments scattered throughout the city.

PRACTICAL INFO, ACCOMMODATIONS, AND FOOD. Trains bound for Budapest-Keleti (2hr., 5 per day, 1050Ft) split in Hatvan; make sure you're in the right car. From the train station, turn right on Deák u., right on Kossuth Lajos u., left on Széchenyi u., and right on Érsek u. to get to **Dobó tér** (main square; 20min.). **Tourinform,** Dobó tér 2, has maps and lodgings info. (☎/fax 32 18 07. Open M-F 9am-6:30pm, Sa-Su 9:30am-1pm.) **OTP,** Széchenyi u. 2, grants credit card advances, cashes AmEx traveler's checks commission-free, and has a 24-hour **ATM.** (☎31 08 66. Exchange open M-Tu and Th-F 7:45am-5pm, W 7:45am-6pm.) Surf the **Internet** at **PC Club,** Mecset u. 2. (480Ft per hr. Open daily 10am-10pm.)

The best accommodations are **private rooms;** look for *Zimmer Frei* signs outside the city center, particularly on Almagyar u. and Mekcsey u. near the castle. **Eger Tourist,** Bajcsy-Zsilinszky u. 9, arranges private rooms for around 3000Ft per person. (☎41 17 24. Open M-F 9am-5pm.) It also runs the basic **Tourist Motel,** Mekcsey u. 2. (☎42 90 14. Doubles 2800-3600Ft; triples 3450-4350Ft; quads 4800-5600Ft.) Take bus #5, 11, or 12 north for 20 minutes to get to **Autós Caravan Camping,** Rákóczi u. 79; get off at the Shell station and look for signs. (Open mid-Apr. to mid-Oct. 320Ft per person; 250Ft per tent.) In the Valley of the Beautiful Women, **Kulacs Csárda Borozó's** vine-draped courtyard draws crowds. (☎31 13 75. Main dishes 720-1100Ft. Open Tu-Su noon-10pm.) An **ABC supermarket** is directly off Széchenyi u. between Sandor u. and Szt. Janos u. (Open M-F 6am-6:30pm, Sa 6am-9pm.) **Postal code:** 3300.

SIGHTS AND ENTERTAINMENT. Hungarians revere the medieval **Eger Castle,** where Dobó István and his 2000 men repelled the attacking Ottoman army. The Castle includes subterranean barracks, catacombs, a crypt, and a wine cellar. One ticket covers a picture gallery, the **Dobó István Castle Museum,** which displays excavated artifacts and an impressive array of weapons, and the **Dungeon Exhibition,** a collection of torture equipment that will inspire sadists and masochists alike. (Castle open daily 8am-8pm; museums open Tu-Su 9am-5pm. Castle 120Ft, students 60Ft. Museums 300Ft, students 150Ft. English tours 300Ft.) The nearby Rococo **Lyceum,** at the corner of Kossuth Lajos u. and Eszterházy tér, houses a **camera obscura** that projects a live picture of the surrounding town onto a table, providing a god-like view of the world. (Open Th-Su 9:30am-3:30pm. 200Ft, students 100Ft.)

After a morning exploring Eger's historical sights, spend the early evening in the wine cellars of the **Valley of Beautiful Women** (Szépasszonyvölgy). Samples are free, 0.1L shots run 30-50Ft, and 1L of wine costs about 300Ft. To reach the wine cellars, start on Széchenyi u. with Eger Cathedral to your right. Turn right on Kossuth Lajos u., left on Deák u. (contrary to the directions on the sign), and right on Telekessy u. (which becomes Király u.); continue for about 10 minutes, then bear left onto Szépasszonyvölgy. **Cellar #16** is usually still kicking when others have begun to close, probably because they serve the best *Medok* in the valley. Taste a glass of *Bikavér* at the less rowdy **Cellar #17** next door. Although the budget gospel dictates otherwise, the smart thing to do here is to enjoy all the samples you want, then buy a bottle of your favorite so the cellars can continue to give free tastings.

In summer, the city's **open-air baths** offer a desperately needed respite from the sweltering city. (Open May-Sept. M-F 6am-7:30pm, Sa-Su 8am-7pm, Oct.-Apr. daily 9am-7pm. Full day 320Ft, students and seniors 170Ft.) Eger celebrates its heritage for two weeks in late July and early August at the **Baroque Festival.** Nightly performances of operas, operettas, and medieval and Renaissance court music are held around the city. You can buy tickets (500-1000Ft) at the site of the performance.

EXCURSION FROM EGER: SZILVÁSVÁRAD. Szilvásvárad (SEAL-vash-vah-rod), a perfect daytrip from Eger, attracts horse and nature lovers alike. **Horse shows** (800Ft) kick into action on most weekends in the arena on Szalajka u. **Lipicai Stables** is the stud farm for the town's famed Lipizzaner breed. Walk away from the park entrance on Egri út, turn left on Enyves u., and follow signs to the farm. (☎35 51 55. Open daily 8:30am-noon and 2-4pm. 80Ft.) Many farms offer **horseback riding,** especially in July and August. **Péter Kovács,** Egri út 62 (☎35 53 43), rents horses (1500Ft per hr.) and two-horse carriages (4500Ft per hr.). **Hikers** should head to the nearby **Bükk mountains** and **Szalajka valley.** A 45-minute walk along the green trail will lead you to the park's most popular attraction, the **Fátyol waterfall;** a further 30-minute hike from the falls leads to the **Istálósk cave,** the Stone Age home to a bear-worshipping cult. **Trains** (1¼hr., 8 per day, 202Ft) and **buses** (45min., every hr., 260Ft) run to Szilvásvárad from Eger. From the train station (Szilvásvárad-Szalajkavölgy), follow Egri út to Szalajka u. directly to the national park. There is no actual bus station in town; simply get off at the second stop in Szilvásvárad (it's the next town after passing the concrete factories of Bükkszentmárton), on Egri út near Szalajka u. Stop by **Eger Tourinform** (see above) before heading out, as there is no tourist office. **☎36.**

HUNGARY

LAKE BALATON

A land of beaches and wine, the warm, shallow Lake Balaton has become one of the most visited vacation spots in Central Europe. A retreat since Roman times, Balaton (in Hungarian, "holiday") became a playground for the Central European elite in the late 19th century. Visitors delight in museums, hikes, wine, discos, and the lake itself. Be aware that storms roll in quickly. Amber lights on tall buildings give warnings: one revolution per second means swimmers must be within 100m.

SIÓFOK. Tourist offices are more densely packed in Siófok than any other Hungarian city, reflecting the demand of surf-starved tourists who descend every summer. Most attractions in Siófok pale in comparison with the **Strand,** a series of park-like lawns running to an extremely un-sandy concrete shoreline. There are public and private sections, the latter about 150Ft per person. **Nightclubs** of varying seediness line the lakefront and amphibious lounge lizards frolic to ABBA and the Bee Gees aboard MAHART **disco boats.** (Cover 800Ft. July 9-Aug. 21 nightly 7-9:30pm.) Buses depart every hour from the water tower to **Palace Disco,** Deák Ferenc Sérány 2, a party complex with discos, bars, two restaurants, and an open-air cocktail bar arranged around a brightly lit courtyard. (Cover 1000-3000Ft. Open 10pm-5am.)

From **Fő u.,** the town's main drag, **trains** go to Budapest (2½hr., every hr., 1040Ft); **express buses** *(gyorsjárat)* also head to Budapest (1½hr., 17 per day, 1048Ft) and Pécs (3hr., 4 per day, 1240Ft). **Tourinform,** Fő u. 41, in the base of the wooden water tower across from the train station, helps find rooms. (☎31 53 55. Open July-Aug. M-Sa 8am-8pm, Su 10am-noon; Sept.-June M-F 9am-4pm.) To get to comfy **Tuja Panzió,** Szent László u. 74, turn left as you leave the train station, cross the tracks as soon as you can, turn right onto Ady Endre u., left on Tátra u., and right on Szent László. (☎31 49 96. 3000Ft per person, off season 2000Ft.) Or try **Hotel Viola,** Bethlen Gabor u. 1, which has an English-speaking staff. From the bus or train stations, walk along Fő u. with the tracks on your right; cross at Bethlen G. u. (☎31 28 45. Breakfast included. Reception 24hr. Doubles 3100Ft.) **☎84.**

TIHANY. With its scenic hikes, charming cottages, and panoramic views, the Tihany (TEE-hahn) peninsula is the pearl of Balaton. The magnificent **Benedictine Abbey** (Bencés Apátság) draws over a million visitors annually. Luminous frescoes and intricate Baroque altars make the interior distinctly photo-worthy; with so many blinding flashes going off at once, you might need to take a picture to see it properly. (Open daily 9am-6pm. 200Ft, students 100Ft; Su free.) Continue along the panoramic walkway to **Echo Hill.** You can also **hike** across the Peninsula on one of the many well-marked trails; most hikes are only an hour or two. MAHART **ferries** are the fastest way to reach Tihany from **Siófok** (40min., every hr., 580Ft). To reach the town from the ferry pier and neighboring Strand, walk underneath the elevated road and follow the "Apátság" signs up the steep hill to the abbey. **☎87.**

KESZTHELY. At the lake's west tip, Keszthely (KESS-tay) is a holiday town with a real-life feel. It is also the proud home of the **Helikon Palace Museum** (Helikon Kastélymúzeum) in the **Festetics Palace** (Kastély). Built by one of the most powerful Austro-Hungarian families of the period, the storybook Baroque palace boasts fanciful architecture, the 90,000-volume **Helikon Library,** an exotic arms collection, and an exhibit of the Festetics porcelain pieces. The vast **English park** surrounds the museum. Follow Kossuth Lajos u. from Fő tér toward **Tourinform** until it becomes Kastély u. (Open Tu-Su 9am-5pm; ticket office closes at 4:30pm. 1300Ft, students 650Ft. Tours 3000Ft.) The rocky and swampy **Strand,** on the coast to the right as you exit the train station, attracts crowds in spite of the terrain. From the center, walk down Erzsébet u. as it curves right into Vörösmarty u.; go through the park on the left after the train tracks to the beach beyond (220Ft).

Intercity trains (express) run between Keszthely and Budapest (2½hr., 13 per day, 1392Ft). To reach the main square from the train station, walk straight up **Mártirok u.,** which ends in Kossuth Lajos u., turn right, and walk five minutes to Fő tér. **Tourinform,** Kossuth Lajos u. 28, sits on the palace side of Fő tér. (☎31 41 44. Open July-Aug. M-F 9am-5pm, Sa-Su 9am-1pm; Sept. and Apr.-June M-F 9am-4pm, Sa 9am-1pm; Oct.-Mar. M-F 8am-4pm, Sa 9am-1pm.) **Private rooms** are available through Tourinform (from 2500Ft). Pitch a tent at **Castrum Camping,** Móra Ferene u. 48. (☎31 21 20. July-Aug. 780Ft per person, 250Ft per tent. Sept.-June 390-650Ft per person, 520Ft per tent. Tax 250Ft.) **Postal code:** 8360. **☎83.**

GYŐR ☎96

The cobblestone inner city streets of Győr (DYUR) wind peacefully around a wealth of religious monuments, well-kept museums, and prime examples of 17th- and 18th-century architecture, while the city's lively population invigorates the old town. Most sights lie near the center of town. From the station, go right until you come to the bridge. Turn left just before the underpass, then cross the big street to pedestrian **Baross Gabor u.** Turn left on Kazinezy u. to reach Bécsi Kapu tér, the site of the yellow, 18th-century **Carmelite church.** Continue up Baross Gábor u. to the top of **Chapter Hill** (Káptalandomb), where you will find the **Episcopal Cathedral** (Székesegyház), with its Baroque interior and its Romanesque, Gothic, and Neoclassical exterior. Legend has it that the **Weeping Madonna of Győr** within wept blood for persecuted Irish Catholics on St. Patrick's Day in 1697. For more religious art, the fascinating **Ecclesiastical Treasury** (Egyházmegyei Kincstáv) hides at the end of an alley off the square. (Open daily 10am-4pm. 150Ft, students 75Ft.) For contemporary art, head down Baross Gábor u. and make a left on Szabadsajtó u. to reach the **Imre**

Parkó collection at Széchenyi tér 4; enter at Stelczer u. (Open Tu-Su 10am-6pm. 140Ft, students 70Ft.) Across the river from the town center is the popular **water park,** Czirákytér 1. Cross the main bridge from the city center at Jedlik Ányos, take a left on the other side, and walk along the sidewalk until you come to smaller footbridge on the left; cross it, and the park is to the left. (Open daily 8am-7pm. 400Ft, students 300Ft, children 200Ft; after 3pm 290Ft, students 200St.)

The **train station** lies five minutes from the inner city; the underpass that links the rail platforms leads to the **bus station.** Frequent **trains** go to Budapest (2½hr., 11 per day, 974Ft) and Vienna (2hr., 13 per day, 5116Ft). **Buses** go to Budapest (2½hr., every hr., 1144Ft). The **Tourinform kiosk,** Árpád u. 32, is at the corner of Baross Gabór u. (☎31 17 71. Open June-Aug. M-F 8am-8pm, Sa 9am-3pm, Su 9am-1pm; Sept.-May M-Sa 9am-4pm.) **Hotel Szárnyaskerék,** Vasut u. 5, is opposite the train station. (☎31 46 29. Doubles 4250-6600Ft.) **Matróz Restaurant,** Dunakapu tér 3, off Jedlik Ányos facing the river, fries up succulent fish dishes. (Entrees 380-790Ft. Open daily 9am-10pm.) For a Guinness (290-599Ft), head to **Dublin Gate Irish Pub,** Bécsikapu tér 8, across from the Carmelite Church. (Open M-Sa noon-midnight, Su noon-11pm.) **Kaiser's Supermarket** is at the corner of Arany János u. and Aradi vértanúk. (Open M 7:30am-7pm, Tu-F 6:30am-7pm, Sa 6:30am-2pm.) **Postal code:** 9021.

EXCURSION FROM GYŐR: ARCHABBEY OF PANNONHALMA. Visible at a distance from Győr, the hilltop **Archabbey of Pannonhalma** (Pannonhalmi Főapátság) has seen 10 centuries of destruction and rebuilding since it was established by the Benedictine order in 996. Continued additions to the working abbey illustrate the layers of (sometimes conflicting) influences on Hungarian religious art. Legend has it that if you fit into St. Steven's wooden throne in the Gothic-Romanesque crypt, you'll get your wish. Classical music concerts also take place frequently in the acoustic halls of the abbey; inquire at **Pax Tourist** (☎57 01 91). To see the abbey, join a tour group at the Pax Tourist office to the left of the entrance. English-speaking guides are available for the mandatory one-hour tour at 11am and 1pm in summer only. (Abbey open daily 8:30am-4pm. Tours every hr. Hungarian tour with English text 400Ft, students 120Ft; English tour 800Ft, students 400Ft. Pannonhalma is accessible from **Győr** on the **bus** leaving from stand #11 (45min., 7 per day, 216Ft). Ask for Pannonhalma vár and look for the huge gates. Some buses only go as far as the town; the abbey is 1km from there (15min.).

ICELAND (ÍSLAND)

ICELANDIC KRÓNUR

US$1 = 83.55IKR	100IKR = US$1.20
CDN$1 = 56.42IKR	100IKR = CDN$1.77
UK£1 = 117.52IKR	100IKR = UK£0.85
IR£1 = 91.51IKR	100IKR = IR£1.09
AUS$1 = 46.68IKR	100IKR = AUS$2.14
NZ$1 = 35.58IKR	100IKR = NZ$2.81
SAR1 = 11.71IKR	100IKR = SAR8.54
EUR€1 = 72.07IKR	100IKR = EUR€1.39

Country code: 354. **International dialing prefix:** 00. From outside *Iceland*, dial int'l dialing prefix (see inside back cover) + 354 + local number.

Forged by the power of still-active volcanoes, raked by the slow advance and retreat of glaciers, and whipped by wind, rain, and snow, Iceland's landscape is uniquely warped and contorted. Nature is the country's greatest attraction: few places allow visitors to walk across moonscapes created by lava rocks, dodge warm water shooting up from geysers, and sail across a glacial lagoon filled with icebergs. Vegetation is sparse, but life abounds in the sea and air, making coastal areas ideal for observing everything from blue whales to baby puffins.

Civilization has made a powerful mark on Iceland; the geothermal energy that causes numerous earthquakes now also provides hot water and electricity to Iceland's settlements, and a network of roads carved through seemingly inhospitable terrain connects even the smallest villages to larger cities. A booming tourist industry and an abundance of cell phones in trendy Reykjavík attest to the fact that physical isolation has not set the country behind the rest of Europe. However, Iceland's island status has allowed it to achieve such a high standard of living without losing its deeply-rooted sense of community and pristine natural surroundings.

FACTS AND FIGURES

Official Name: Republic of Iceland.

Government: Constitutional Republic.

Capital: Reykjavík.

Land Area: 103,000 sq. km.

Geography: Plateaus around mountains and glaciers; bays and fjords.

Climate: Cool summers and mild winters.

Major Cities: Hafnarfjörðhur, Höfn, Ísafjörðhur, Vík.

Population: 280,000.

Language: Icelandic; Danish, English, and German are also widely spoken.

Religions: Evangelical Lutheran (96%), other Protestant and Roman Catholic (4%).

Average Income Per Capita: US$31,000.

Major Exports: Fish, seafood products, animal products, and aluminum.

DISCOVER ICELAND

Spend a day exploring the heart of **Reykjavík**—feed the birds at Tjörnin and stroll along Laugavegur to appreciate the city's unique blend of natural beauty and modern convenience. To see the water wonders of **Gullfoss, Geysir,** and the **Blue Lagoon,** take the bus from the capital. After hanging out with elves in **Hafnarfjörður,** you can return to the city for coffee—or cocktails when the sun sets—in a cozy cafe. The power of Iceland's volanoes, and great hikes among jagged black cliffs, are available by ferry at the the **Westman Islands.**

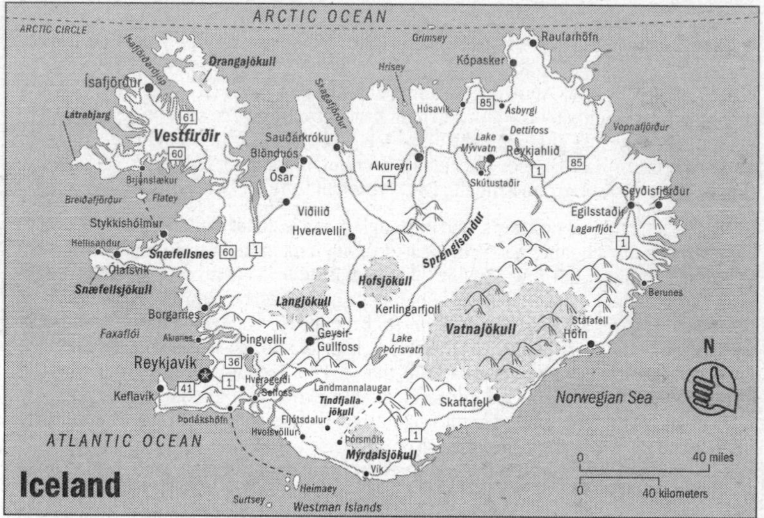

ESSENTIALS

WHEN TO GO

Tourist season starts in mid-June, but it really isn't high-season until July, when the interior opens up, snow almost disappears, and all the bus lines are running. In summer, the sun dips below the horizon for a few hours each night, but it never gets truly dark, and it's warm enough to camp and hike. The off-season tourist industry is picking up such that with warm clothing you could travel as late as October, but in winter there is very little sun. It rarely gets hotter than 60°F (16°C) in summer or dips below 20°F (-6°C) in winter.

ICELAND

DOCUMENTS AND FORMALITIES

South Africans need a **visa** for stays of any length. Citizens of Australia, New Zealand, Canada, the UK, Ireland, and the US can visit for up to 90 days without one, but this three-month period begins upon entry into any Scandinavian country; for a stay of more than 90 days in any combination of Finland, Iceland, Norway, and/or Sweden, you will need a visa.

EMBASSIES AND CONSULATES

Embassies and consulates of other countries in Iceland are in **Reykjavík** (see p. 450).

Icelandic Embassies at Home: Canada, 485 Broadview Ave., Ottawa, ON K2A 2L2 (☎ (613) 724 59 82; fax 724 12 09); **UK,** 1 Eaton Terr., London SW1W 8EY (☎ (020) 730 51 31; fax 730 16 83; www.iceland.org.uk); **US,** 1156 15th St. NW Suite 1200, Washington, D.C. 20005 (☎ (202) 265 66 53; fax 265 66 56; www.iceland.org).

GETTING AROUND

BY PLANE. Icelandair (US ☎ (800) 223 55 00) flies to **Reykjavík** year-round from the US and Europe. Icelandair charges no extra airfare for transatlantic travelers who stop over up to three days in the country in the Awesome Iceland Stopover Package—also ask about their "Take-A-Break" special offers. **SAS** from Copenhagen and **Lufthansa** from Frankfurt also fly to Iceland. Domestic-service **Flugfélag Islands** (☎750 30 30) fly between Reykjavík and Iceland's other major towns; tickets can be issued at BSÍ Travel. Another option is the **Air/Bus Rover** (fly one way, bus the other), offered jointly by the domestic air carriers and BSÍ Travel (June-Sept.; Reykjavík to Akureyri 9960Ikr; Reykjavík to Isafjörður 11,125 Ikr; Reykjavík to Höfn 11,485Ikr. Icelandair has some student discounts, including half-price on standby flights. Weather can ground flights; leave yourself time for delays.

BY BUS. Iceland has no trains, and although flying is faster and more comfortable, **buses** are usually cheaper and provide a close-up look at the terrain. Within Iceland, one tour company, **BSÍ Travel** (☎552 23 00; fax 552 99 73), with offices in the Reykjavík bus terminal, coordinates all schedules and prices. Schedules are available at hostels and tourist offices. The *Iceland 99* brochure lists selected bus schedules as well as tours and ferry routes; the *Leiðabók* lists all bus schedules and is a must for anyone traveling the **Ring Road;** a loop that circles Iceland, mainly following the 1414km **Highway 1,** with occasional arms radiating toward the coast. Buses run daily on each segment from mid-June through August, but frequency drops dramatically off season. Be warned: the going is slow since some roads are unpaved. The circle can be completed in three days, but to adequately explore, plan for a 10-day journey. Tickets are sold in the bus stations *(umferðarmiðstöð)* in Reykjavík and Akureyri, and can be purchased from the driver as you board the bus.

BSÍ sells passes that simplify bus travel greatly. The **Full Circle Passport** (16,100Ikr) lets travelers circle the island at their own pace on the Ring Road (available mid-May to Sept.). It only allows for continuous directional travel, so a traveler must continue either clockwise or counter-clockwise around the country. For an extra 7700Ikr, the pass (which has no time limitation) provides access to the Westfjords in the island's extreme northwest. The **Omnibus Passport** (available all year) gives a period of unlimited travel on all scheduled bus routes including non-Ring roads (1 week 17,600Ikr, 2 weeks 25,600Ikr, 3 weeks 32,800Ikr, 4 weeks 36,500Ikr); prices drop in the off season. Both passes give 5% discounts on many ferries, campgrounds, farms, *Hótel Edda* sleeping-bag dorms, and guided bus tours.

BY FERRY. The best way to see Iceland's rugged shores is on the car and passenger ferry, **Norröna,** Laugavegur 3 in Reykjavík (☎562 63 62; fax 552 94 50), which circles the North Atlantic via Seyðisfjörður, East Iceland; Tórshavn in the Faroe Islands; and from there goes to Hanstholm, Denmark. The ferry returns to Tórshavn before going to Bergen. Those journeying to Bergen and to Seyðisfjörður from Hanstholm have a three-day layover in the Faroe Islands. Students get a 25% discount on all trips. **Eimskip** (☎525 70 00) offers more expensive ferry rides on cargo ships from Reykjavík to Immingham, Rotterdam, and Hamburg.

BY CAR. In Iceland, travelers using **cars** (preferably 4-wheel-drive) have the most freedom. The country is overflowing with car rental *(bílaleiga)* companies. Prices average about 4900Ikr per day and 39Ikr per km after the first 100km for smaller cars, but are substantially higher for 4-wheel-drive vehicles (ask about special package deals). Some companies also require the purchase of insurance that can cost from 750-2000Ikr. **Geysir-Gullfoss,** Dugguvogur 10, offers the lowest rates. (☎568 88 88; fax 588 18 81. 3900 per day, 29Ikr per km after 100km, and a 1000Ikr insurance fee.) You are required to keep your headlights on at all times, wear a seatbelt, and drive only on marked roads. A **Green Card** or other proof of insurance is mandatory. Gas runs about US$1.25 per liter.

BY BIKE AND BY THUMB. Cycling is gaining popularity, but ferocious winds, driving rain, and nonexistent road shoulders make it difficult. Buses will carry bikes for a 500-1000Ikr fee, depending on the distance covered. **Trekking** is extremely arduous; well-marked trails are rare, but several suitable areas await the truly ambitious (ask the tourist office in Reykjavík for maps and more info). Determined **hitchers** try the roads in summer, but sparse traffic and harsh weather exacerbate the inherent risks of hitching. Nevertheless, for those who last, the ride usually does come (easily between Reykjavík and Akureyri; harder in the east and the south).

TOURIST SERVICES AND MONEY

EMERGENCY **Police:** ☎ 112. **Ambulance:** ☎ 112. **Fire:** ☎ 112.

TOURIST OFFICES. **Tourist offices** in large towns have schedules, maps, and brochures; check at hotel reception desks in smaller towns for local info. Must-haves are the free brochures *Around Iceland* (accommodation, restaurant, and museum listings for every town), *The Complete Iceland Map*, and the *Leiðabók* (with bus schedule). The tourist office in Iceland is at Bankastraeti 2, Rejkjavík (☎ 562 30 45; fax 562 30 57; www.icetourist.is).

Tourist Boards at Home: UK, 172 Tottenham Court Rd., London W1P 9LG (☎ (020) 73 88 53 46; fax. 387 57 11); **US,** 655 Third Ave., New York, NY 10017 (☎ (212) 885 97 00; fax 885 97 10; www.goiceland.org).

MONEY. Icleand's monetary unit is the **króna,** which is 100 **aurar.** There are 100Ikr, 50Ikr, 10Ikr, 5Ikr, and 1Ikr coins; notes are in denominations of 5000Ikr, 2000Ikr, 1000Ikr, and 500Ikr. **Costs** are sky-high: on average, a night in a hostel might cost you US$20; a budget hotel US$70-95; a budget restaurant meal US$10; and a day's worth of supermarket food US$25. **Tipping** is not customary in Iceland. **Value-added tax** is included in all posted prices. **VAT refunds** (of up to 15% of the retail price) are given if departing Iceland within 30 days after purchase. The amount bought must be at least 4,000 Ikr (VAT included) per receipt; goods must be unopened.

BUSINESS HOURS. Hours generally are M-F 9am-5pm (6pm in summer) and Sa mornings.

ACCOMMODATIONS AND CAMPING

HOSTELS. Iceland's 27 **HI youth hostels,** invariably clean and always with kitchens, are uniformly priced at 1250Ikr for members, 1500Ikr for nonmembers. Pick up the free *Hostelling in Iceland* brochure at tourist offices.

OTHER LOCAL ACCOMMODATIONS. **Sleeping-bag accommodations** *(svefnpokapláss)*—available on farms, at summer hotels, and in guesthouses *(gistiheimili)*—are relatively cheap (and generally you get at least a mattress). In early June, many schoolhouses become *Hótel Eddas*, which have sleeping-bag accommodations (no kitchens; 950-1500Ikr, 5% off for bus pass holders). Most also offer breakfast and beds (both *quite* expensive). Staying in a tiny farm or hostel can be the highlight of a trip, but the nearest bus may be 20km away and run once a week. Many remote lodgings will pick up tourists in the nearest town for a small fee.

CAMPING. In cities and nature reserves, **camping** is permitted only at designated campsites. Outside of official sites, camping is free but discouraged; watch out for *Tjaldstæði bönnuð* (No Camping) signs, and *always* ask at the nearest farm before you pitch a tent. Use gas burners; Iceland has no firewood, and it is illegal to burn the sparse vegetation. Always pack your trash out. **Official campsites** (summer only) range from rocky fields with cold water taps to the sumptuous facilities in Reykjavík. Upper-crust sites may cost 500Ikr per person; more basic ones start at about 250Ikr. Many offer discounts for students and bus pass holders.

FOOD AND DRINK

Icelandic cuisine celebrates animals foreigners might normally envision in a zoo or aquarium. Traditional foods include *lundar* (puffin), *rjúpa* (ptarmigan), and *selshreifar* (seal flippers). Fish and lamb are the most common components of authentic dishes, although more adventurous diners can try *svið* (singed and boiled sheep's head), *hrútspungur* (ram's testicles), or *hákarl* (rotten shark meat that has been buried underground). International cuisine also has a strong presence in Iceland, and Italian, American, and Chinese food are usually found even in smaller towns. If you just can't get down that last bite of puffin, rejoice: Iceland has some of the purest water in Europe. Beer costs 400-600Ikr at most pubs, cafes, and restaurants. The national drink is *Brennivín*, a type of schnapps known as "the Black Death". The rarely enforced drinking age is 20. Grocery stores are the way to go; virtually every town has a **Kaupfélag** (cooperative store) and often also a fast-food kiosk. Gas stations usually run a grill, and sell snacks. Grocery stores sometimes close for an hour at noon, especially outside Reykjavík. **Bonus** and **Netto** are cheaper alternatives to the more ubiquitous **Hagkaup** and **10-11.** Food is very expensive in Iceland; a *cheap* restaurant meal will cost at least 600Ikr.

COMMUNICATION

MAIL. Mailing a postcard/letter from Iceland costs 75Ikr to Australia, Canada, New Zealand, the US, or South Africa; to Ireland and the UK it costs 50Ikr. Post offices *(póstur)* are generally open Monday through Friday 8:30am to 4:30pm. Post offices and hostels hold mail.

TELEPHONES. Telephone *(sími)* offices are often in the same building as post offices. Pay phones take phone cards or 10 or 50Ikr pieces; local calls are 10Ikr. For the best prices, make calls from telephone offices; next best is a prepaid phone card. Before making an international call, deposit at least 10Ikr or insert a phone card (at the tourist office; 100 units 500Ikr). To reach the operator, call ☎115; for information, call ☎114. International direct dial numbers include: **AT&T,** ☎800 90 01; **Sprint,** ☎800 90 03; **MCI WorldPhone Direct,** ☎800 90 02; **Australia Direct,** ☎900 90 61; **Canada Direct,** ☎800 90 10; **BT Direct,** ☎800 90 44; **Ireland Direct,** ☎800 93 53; **Telecom New Zealand Direct,** ☎800 90 64.

INTERNET ACCESS. Internet access is widepsread in Iceland, although in small towns it may only be available in public libraries. In Reykjavík there are Internet cafes, generally charging about 250Ikr per half hour. Public libraries will often require a library card, but provide access free.

HOLIDAYS AND FESTIVALS

Holidays: New Year's (Jan. 1); Good Friday (Apr. 21); Easter (Apr. 23-24); Labor Day (May 1); Ascension Day (June 1); National Day (June 17); Whit Sunday and Monday (June 11-12); Commerce Day (Aug. 7); Christmas Eve and Day (Dec. 24-25); Boxing Day (Dec. 26); New Year's Eve (Dec. 31).

REYKJAVÍK

Reykjavík's character more than makes up for its modest size. Bold, modern architecture complements the backdrop of snow-dusted purple mountains, and the city's refreshingly clear air is matched by its sparkling streets and gardens (thanks to legions of youngsters who are required to work on municipal beautification projects in summer. There are geothermal pools throughout the city, and even the capital's homes are heated by geothermal steam. But don't conclude that Reykjavík (pop. 109,000) is a natural wonder untouched by civilization—its cellular phone-toting and platform shoe-donning inhabitants pride themselves on their modernity. Inviting and virtually crime-free, Reykjavík's only weaknesses are its often blustery weather and its high cost of living.

GETTING THERE AND GETTING AROUND

Flights: All international flights arrive at **Keflavík Airport,** 55km from Reykjavík. **Flybuses** (☎562 10 11; 700lkr) depart 45min. after each arrival for the domestic **Reykjavík Airport** and the adjacent Hótel Loftleiðir, just south of town, then proceed to Hotel Esja. To reach the city from Hótel Loftleiðir (15min.), cross the Hringbraut highway opposite the hotel, turn left, and follow the blue signs marked "City Center." Or take **bus #7** (every 30min., 150lkr) to Lækjartorg Square downtown. From Hotel Esja, take **bus #5** to Laekjartog Square. Flybuses pick up passengers from the Hótel Loftleiðir (2hr. before each flight departure) and the Grand Hotel Reykjavík (2½hr. before), as well as from the youth hostel (June-Aug. 4:45am and 1:15pm). Most hostels and guesthouses will arrange for guests to be picked up by the Flybus at no extra charge. The **Omnibus Pass** (but not Full Circle Passport) covers the Flybus; get a refund for your ride into town at BSÍ Travel (see below) or Reykjavík Excursions (in the Hotel Loftleiðir; open 24hr.).

Buses: Umferðarmiðstöð (also known as **BSÍ Station**), Vatnsmýrarvegur 10 (☎552 23 00), off Hringbraut near Reykjavík Airport. Walk 15-20min. south along the pond from city center, or take bus #7 or 8. Open daily 7am-11:30pm; tickets sold 7:30am-10pm. **BSÍ Travel** (☎552 23 00; fax 552 99 73), located inside the terminal, sells bus passes and tour packages. Open June 1-Aug. 31 M-F 7:30am-7pm, Sa-Su 7:30am-5pm; Sept. 1-May 31 M-F 9am-5pm.

Public Transportation: Strætisvagnar Reykjavíkur (**SVR;** ☎551 27 00) operates yellow city buses (150lkr). Pick up their brochures for visitors at tourist information booths or bus terminals for help in figuring out bus routes. Tickets are sold at 5 terminals, the **Radhus** (City Hall), and all municipal swimming pools; the two major terminals are Lækjartorg (open M-F 9am-6pm) and Hlemmur (open M-F 8am-6pm, Sa-Su noon-8pm). Buy packages of 8 adult fares or 20 youth fares (both 1000lkr) beforehand or buy tickets on the bus (exact change only). Ask the driver for a free transfer ticket (*skiptimiði;* valid for 30-45min.). *Around Reykjavík* has a map and schedule. Buses run every 20-30min. M-Sa 7am-midnight, Su and holidays 10am-midnight. Some night buses (rare and tricky to find) with limited routes run until 4am on weekends.

Taxis: BSR, Skolatröð 18 (☎561 00 00). 24-hour service. Tipping not customary.

Bike Rental: At the **youth hostel** (see below. 900lkr for 6hr., 1500lkr per day).

Hitchhiking: *Let's Go* does not recommend hitchhiking. Those hitching take buses #15, 10, or 110 to the east edge of town, then stand on Vesturlandsvegur to go north or Suðurlandsvegur to go southeast.

ICELAND

ORIENTATION AND PRACTICAL INFORMATION

Lækjartorg is old Reykjavík's main square. South of Lækjartorg are **Tjörnin** (the pond), the long-distance bus station (BSÍ terminal), and the Reykjavík Airport. Extending east and west from Lækjartorg square is the main thoroughfare, which becomes (from west to east) **Austurstræti, Bankastræti,** and **Laugavegur.** Pick up *Around Reykjavík* at the tourist office or around town (free), as well as the monthly *What's on in Reykjavík* for detailed information about exploring the city.

TOURIST AND FINANCIAL SERVICES

Tourist Office: Upplýsingamiðstöð Ferðamála í Íslandi, Bankastr. 2 (☎562 30 45), at Lækjartorg and Bankastr. **Branches** at the airport and City Hall. Open May 15-Sept. 15 daily 8:30am-7pm; Sept. 15-May 15 M-F 9am-5pm, Sa-Su noon-6pm.

Budget Travel: Ferðaskrifstofa Stúdenta (☎570 08 00; www.ist.is), Hringbraut, next to National Museum. Sells ISICs, railpasses, and bus passes. Open M-F 9am-5pm.

Embassies: Canada, Suðurlandsbraut 10, 3rd fl. (☎568 08 20; fax 568 08 99). Open M-F 8am-4pm. **Ireland,** Kringlan 7 (☎588 66 66; fax 588 65 64). Open M-F 8am-4pm. **South Africa,** P.O. Box 916 (☎520 33 00; fax 520 33 99). Open M-F 9am-5pm. **UK,** Laufásvegur 31 (☎550 51 00; fax 550 51 05). Open M-F 9am-noon. **US,** Laufásvegur 21 (☎562 91 00; fax 562 91 23). Open M-F 8am-12:30pm and 1:30-5pm.

Currency Exchange: Banks charge no commission; many are located on Austurstr. and Laugavegur. Most open M-F 9:15am-4pm.

LOCAL SERVICES

Camping Equipment: Sport Leigan (☎551 98 00), next to the BSÍ station. Open M-F 9am-6pm, F 9am-7pm, Sa 10am-3pm.

Luggage Storage: At the BSÍ terminal. 300Ikr per day, 600Ikr per week. Open M-F 7:30am-9:30pm, Sa 7:30am-2:30pm, Su 5-7pm (Su summer only).

English Bookstore: Mál og Menning, Laugavegur 18, at corner of Laugavegur and Vegemotstigur (☎515 25 00). Open M-F 9am-10pm, Sa-Su 10am-10pm. **Eymundsson,** on Austurstræti, opposite post office. Open M-F 9am-10pm, Sa 10am-10pm, Su 1-10pm.

Laundromat: Þvottahusið Emla, Barónsstígur 3 (☎552 74 99), just south of Hverfisg. Full service. 1300Ikr per load. Open M-F 8am-6pm. Many **hostels** also do laundry.

EMERGENCY AND COMMUNICATIONS

Emergencies: ☎112.

Police: Headquarters at Hverfisgata 113 (☎569 90 20). Downtown office at Tryggvagata 19 (☎56 90 25).

Pharmacies: Haaleitis Apótek, Haaleitisbraut 68 (☎581 21 01). Open 24hr. **Lyfja Apótek,** Laugavegur 16 (☎552 40 45). Carries contact lens supplies and beauty products. Open daily 9am-6pm.

Medical Assistance: National Hospital at Fossvogur (☎525 17 00), on Slettuvegur, has a 24hr. emergency ward. From the center of town, take bus #3, 5, 6, or 7.

Telephones: Public telephones are available at the tourist office, City Hall, and the post office. All phones require coins or a phone card (available at the tourist office and most convenience stores).

Internet Access: City Library, Đineholtsstr. 29A. Turn south onto Đineholtsstr from Bankast., pass the house marked "29" and enter the library through the side door. Sign up for half-hour slots (250Ikr without library cards). Open M-Th 10am-8pm, F 10am-7pm. The **BSÍ terminal** (see above) also offers Internet access (250Ikr per 30min.), as does **TopCafé** on Lækjarg. (250Ikr per 30min.; see below).

Post Office: ÍSLANDSPÓSTUR, Pósthússtr. 5, at Austurstr. (☎550 70 10). Address mail to be held: First name SURNAME, Poste Restante, ÍSLANDSPÓSTUR, Pósthússtr. 5, 101 Reykjavík, Iceland. Open M-F 8am-4:30pm.

ACCOMMODATIONS AND CAMPING

Many guesthouses offer "sleeping-bag accommodations" (a shared room and a nice bed with neither sheets nor blanket). A cheap hotel will cost at least 5000Ikr. Breakfast costs an extra 550-600Ikr; take advantage of Iceland's cheap cereal and yogurt instead. From mid-June through August, call ahead for reservations.

Hjálpræðisherinn Gisti-og Sjómannaheimili (Salvation Army Guest and Seamen's Home), Kirkjustr. 2 (☎561 32 03), in a pale yellow house one block north of the pond, at the corner of Kirkjustræti and Tjarnargata. Bustling with backpackers enjoying the fantastic location and friendly staff. Each floor has a common bathroom and shower. Kitchen available on the second floor. Sheets 400Ikr. Laundry 700Ikr. Reception 7am-1am; after hours ring the bell. Reserve ahead. Sleeping-bag accommodations 1600Ikr; singles 2900Ikr; doubles 3900Ikr.

Guesthouse Flókagata 1, Flókag. 1 (☎552 11 55; fax 562 03 55; email guesthouse@eyjar.is), entrance on Snorrabraut. Take bus #1 from BSÍ terminal. Pristine rooms, all with sinks, kettles, televisions, and refrigerators. Bathrooms and showers on each floor. Breakfast included. Reception 24hr. Open May 1-Sept. 30. Sleeping-bag accommodations 2400Ikr; singles 5500Ikr; doubles 7900Ikr.

Reykjavík Youth Hostel (HI), Sundlaugavegur 34 (☎553 81 10; fax 588 92 01). Take bus #5 from Lækjarg. to Sundlaugavegur. Clean and comfortable. Far from the city center, but located next to a huge geothermal pool. Kitchen. Bike rental. Luggage storage free. Sleeping bags allowed; sheets 400Ikr. Reception M-F 8am-midnight, Sa-Su 8am-

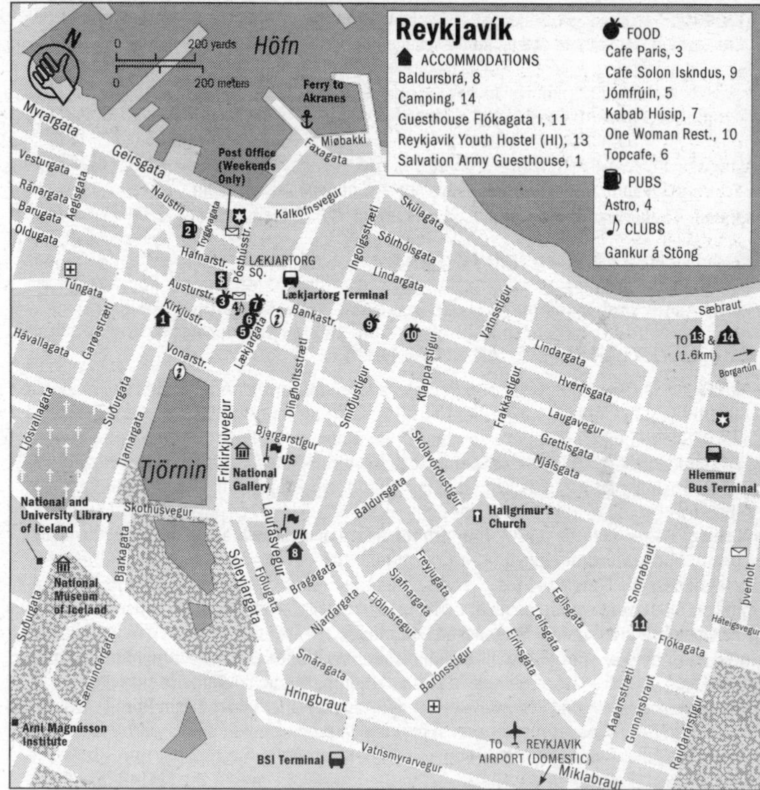

11am and 4pm-midnight; ring bell after hours. Dorms 1250Ikr, non-members 1500Ikr. Singles and doubles 600Ikr extra. Camping 350Ikr per person, 350Ikr per tent.

Baldursbrá, Laufásvegur 41 (☎552 66 46; fax 562 66 47; email heijfis@centrum.is). 5-7min. north of BSÍ terminal, 7-10min. south of city center. Spacious but cozy family-run guest house in a quiet residential neighborhood. Kitchen and television. Jacuzzi and sauna (200Ikr). Singles 5500Ikr, doubles 7500Ikr.

Camping Reykjavík (☎568 69 44), behind the Reykjavík youth hostel. Take bus #5 from city center. Campsite in a huge field near geothermal pool (200Ikr). Showers. Laundry. Open May 15-Sept. 15. 350Ikr per person, 350Ikr per tent; 2-bed cabins 3000Ikr.

FOOD

Hunting down affordable cuisine in Reykjavík can be a challenge. An authentic Icelandic meal featuring seafood, lamb, or puffin will cost at least 1000Ikr. Grocery stores are an affordable option, as are smaller convenience stores, which typically stay open until 10pm. Refer to **Nightlife** (p. 536) for cafes, which provide evening fun as well as daytime meals.

One Woman Restaurant, Laugavegur 20B, at the intersection with Klapparstígur. Delicious vegetarian fare in a soothing environment. Entrees 900Ikr, half portions 750Ikr (both include salad and bread). Open M-Sa 11:30am-2pm and 6-10pm, Su 6-10pm.

Jómfrúin, Lækjarg. 4. Casual Danish restaurant serves delectable open-faced sandwiches (500-1450Ikr). Beer 500-650Ikr. Open daily 11am-10pm.

Kebab Húsiþ, on the corner of Lækjarg. and Austurstr. Hearty vegetable, beef, or chicken kebabs on pita bread (320-590Ikr). Open M-Th 11:30am-midnight, F-Sa 11:30am-5am, Su 1pm-midnight.

TopCafé, Lækjarg. 3, on the upper floor of TopShop. This sleek cafe inside one of the city's hippest clothing stores serves everything from sushi to salad to smoothies, and provides internet access (250Ikr per half-hour) on some of the most modern-looking computer terminals known to man. Entrees 300-450Ikr. Coffee 190Ikr. Open M-W 10am-7pm, Th-F 10am-8pm, Sa 10am-6pm.

MARKETS

10-11, on Austurstr. next to the post office. Open daily 10am-11pm.

Bonus, Laugavegur 59. Open M-F noon-6:30pm, Sa 10am-4pm.

SIGHTS AND OUTDOORS

The **Reykjavík Card,** available at the tourist office, allows unlimited public transportation, entry to the geothermal pools around Reykjavík, and admission to many sights (1 day 900Ikr, 2 day 1200Ikr, 3 day 1500Ikr).

SIGHTS. The **Ásmundur Sveinsson Sculpture Museum,** on Sigtún, houses Sveinsson's sculptures and concrete monuments to the working man within a stunning domed gallery. (Take bus #5 from city center. Open daily May 1-Sept. 1 10am-4pm; Sept.1-May 1-4pm. 400Ikr.) The **Listasafn Íslands** (National Gallery of Iceland), Fríkirkjuvegur 7 on the east shore of Tjörnin displays small, rotating exhibits from the gallery's collection of Icelandic art. (Enter on Skálholtsstígur. Open Tu-Su 11am-5pm. 400Ikr, seniors 250; W free.) The **Árbaer Open-Air Folk Museum** on Ártúnsholt has exhibits chronicling Icelandic history, along with actors re-enacting Icelandic life during different time periods. (Take bus #10 or 110. Open in summer Tu-F 9am-5pm, Sa-Su 10am-6pm; in winter, open M, W, and F 1-2pm for guided tours. 300Ikr, students 150Ikr.) The **Arni Magnusson Institute,** at the intersection of Arnagarður and Suðurgata, displays medieval illustrated manuscripts of the Icelandic sagas. (Open June 1-Aug. 31 daily 1-5pm; Sept.-May Tu-F 2-4pm. 300Ikr; catalog included.)

Hallgrímskirkja (Hallgrímur's Church) offers a terrific view of Reykjavík and the surrounding ocean and mountains. The church's design was inspired by Iceland's natural basalt columns, and the soaring steeple is easily the highest point in Reykjavík. Turn off Laugavegur to Skólavörðustígur and continue to the church. (Open in summer, M-F 9am-6pm, Sa-Su 10am-6pm; in winter, daily 10am-6pm. Services Su 11am. 200Ikr for the elevator ride to the top.)

OUTDOORS AND HIKING. The outdoor **Laugardalslaug** is the largest of Reykjavík's geothermally heated pools, with a giant slide enjoyed by visitors of all ages. (On Sundlaugavegur next to the campground. Take bus #5 from city center. Open M-F 6:50am-10pm, Sa-Su 8am-8pm. 200Ikr.) Well-marked trails lead to the salmon-filled **Elliðaár river,** although highways spoil the scenery of some routes. Follow the river to **Lake Elliðavatn** and the **Heiðmörk reserve,** a popular picnic spot and photo stop.

Ferries run regularly to **Viðey Island** (schedules available at the tourist office and the BSÍ terminal), which on sunnier and warmer days provides excellent opportunities for hiking and picnicking. The island has been inhabited since the 10th century and boasts Iceland's 2nd-oldest church. Across the bay from Reykjavík looms **Mt. Esja,** which you can ascend via a well-kept trail in two to three hours. While the trail is not difficult, hikers are often assaulted by rain, hail, and snow, even in summer. (Take bus #10 or 110 to Artún and transfer to bus #20, exiting at Mógilsá. Bus #20 runs less frequently; consult a schedule before departing.)

NIGHTLIFE

Although Reykjavík's summer nights exist only between the midnight sunset and sunrise two hours later, there's still fun to be had. Unfortunately, you'll have to pay for it—cover charges can run 500-1000Ikr, and beer costs 500-650Ikr. The city's cafes (mostly located around Austurstr. and Laugavegur) are the hottest nightspots, transforming from quiet breakfast places to boisterous bars. *What's On in Reykjavík* (available at the tourist office) lists live cafe shows. While cafes domi-

ICELAND WAS THERE FIRST The year 2000 finally put to rest debate about who really discovered North America. While Columbus has traditionally gotten most of the credit, Icelander Leif Eriksson is now acknowledged as the first European ever to set foot in the new world, a millennium ago at L'Anse aux Meadows in eastern Canada. Disputes over the authenticity of the evidence for early Viking settlements in North America have been settled, and international magazines such as *Newsweek* and *National Geographic* have featured 'Leif the Lucky' and his Viking cohorts on their covers. The ruins of the farm built by his parents, Erik the Red and Thjóðhildur, have been turned into a living museum commemorating his birthplace near the village of Dalir in western Iceland. A Viking ship replica set sail in June from the west coast to retrace the Viking's route to Greenland and North America.

nate the city's nightlife, Reykjavík has its share of pubs and discos, ensuring that no Friday or Saturday night is ever a quiet one.

CAFES

Cafe Paris, Austurstr. 14, is packed from morning to night with people enjoying the steaming pots of coffee and intimate atmosphere. Coffee 150-250Ikr, beer 500-650Ikr, light entrees 400-800Ikr. Open M-F 8am-midnight, Sa-Su 10am-1am.

Cafe Sólon Íslandus, Bankastr. 7a. Students, literati, and the rest of the city's black-clad population congregate in this hip-yet-stately cafe. In summer, there is often live jazz upstairs (cover 1000Ikr). Coffee 220Ikr, beer 450-650Ikr. Salads and sandwiches from 860Ikr, mouth-watering bread and croissants 250-450Ikr. Children's menu available. Open M-Th 10am-1am, F-Su 10am-5am.

Kaffi Barinn, on Bergstatastr. near Laugavegur. Intimate, largely local crowd. Packed on weekend nights, especially after the DJ shows up on F and Sa. Coffee 200-250Ikr, beer 500-600Ikr. Open M-F 11am-1am, Sa noon-3am, Su 3pm-1am. Kitchen closed Sa-Su.

PUBS AND CLUBS

Gaukur á Stöng, Tryggvag. 22 (☎551 15 56), is Iceland's first pub and still one of its most popular nightspots. Live music after 11pm. Open Su-Th 6pm-1am, F-Sa until 3am.

Astro, Austurstr. 22 (☎552 92 22), next to the McDonald's. Draws a younger, magnificently dressed crowd just as hip as the green and purple color scheme. Stay a while and your eyes will begin to sting, either from the hazy smoke or the fact that everyone inside is so much more beautiful than you are. Open F-Sa 11pm-3am.

22, Laugavegur 22 (☎551 36 28), is an artsy hangout that attracts large crowds of students on weekends to its upstairs disco. Open M-Th noon-1am, F noon-3am, Sa 6pm-3am, Su 6pm-1am.

EXCURSIONS FROM REYKJAVÍK

Buses traverse the terrain from Reykjavík to various surrounding sights (mostly within an hour or two of downtown), but many opt for comprehensive scheduled tours instead. BSÍ's popular eight-hour **Golden Circle** guided bus tour departs from Hotel Loftleiðir in Reykjavík daily at 9am and covers Hveragerði, Kerið, Skálholt, Geysir, Gullfoss, and Þingvellir National Park (5100Ikr). Book ahead with **Reykjavík Excursions** (☎562 10 11). BSÍ also provides free pickup for customers at a number of other hotels and hostels around Reykjavík.

BLUE LAGOON. Southwest of Reykjavík lies paradise: a vast pool of geothermally heated water in the middle of a lava field. The lagoon's water is the run-off from a natural power plant that provides Reykjavík with electricity and heat by harnessing geothermal steam. The lagoon's unique concentrations of silica, minerals, and algae are thought to soothe skin diseases such as psoriasis, and silica mud sits in buckets around the pool's edge for bathers to slather on as they relax in the water. Despite its popularity with tourists, the Blue Lagoon offers magnificent relaxation with distinctive Icelandic personality. A **bus** runs from Reykjavík to the Blue Lagoon. 12,000Ikr round-trip. Departs daily 10:30am, 1:30pm, and 6pm; returns to Reykjavík at 12:35pm, 4:05pm, and 7:50pm. Three-hour admission to the lagoon is 700Ikr; bathing suits and towels 250Ikr.

ÞINGVELLIR NATIONAL PARK. Straddling the divide between the European and North American tectonic plates, Þingvellir National Park features some of Iceland's most impressive scenery and is only 50km east of its capital. The **Öxará River,** slicing through lumpy lava fields and jagged fissures, leads to the **Drekkingarhylur** (Drowning Pool), where convicted witches were once drowned, and to **Lake Þingvallavatn,** the largest lake in Iceland. The river's water purportedly foreshadows doom by changing into blood, and for one mysterious hour each year it is said to change to wine. Not far from its edge lies the site of Iceland's ancient parliament, the **Alþing,** which marked the beginning of the world's oldest parliamentary democracy. For almost nine centuries, Icelanders gathered once a year in the shadow of the **Lögberg** (Law Rock) to discuss matters of blood, money, and justice. A **bus** runs daily from Reykjavík to Þingvellir, dropping visitors off at an information center; from there walk 30-45 minutes along either the road or path to reach the lake and main historical sites. Runs May 20-Sept. 10. Departs 1:30pm and returns 5pm; 1200Ikr round-trip. The **information center** (☎482 26 60) sells maps (300Ikr). Open daily May-Sept. 8:50am-10pm; Oct.-Apr. 10am-5pm. There are **campgrounds** by the info center and the lake. 450Ikr per person; no showers.

GULLFOSS & GEYSIR. A glacial river plunging over 30m creates Gullfoss, the "Golden Falls." Cascading over two tiers to reach the gorge below, the falls send up billowing clouds of mist that drench visitors who stray too close to its edges. Uphill from the water, a small exhibit details the geology of the falls. Only 9km away is the **Geysir** area, a rocky, rugged tundra with steaming pools of hot water every few meters. Most pools merely bubble, and the Geysir itself, although the etymological parent of the word "geyser" and one of the world's largest, is now inactive. The energetic **Strokkur,** however, erupts every 5-10 minutes; look for the water beginning to swell, then take cover as it shoots up and out. Opposite the geysers, a **tourist shop** (open daily 10am-7pm) sells snacks and souvenirs, and **Hotel Geysir** (☎486 89 15; fax 486 87 15) offers a pool, panoramic views, and bus pass discounts (sleeping-bag accommodations 800-1500Ikr; singles and doubles 4600-5100Ikr, **camping** 350Ikr per person). A **bus** runs to both sites, stopping at Gullfoss for one hour and Geysir for two-and-a-half hours. The ride is lengthy and roundabout, but the beautiful destination is worth it. (3180Ikr round-trip. Departs daily June-Aug. at 8:30am and 12:30pm, returning at 2:30pm and 4:55pm from Geysir; Sept.-May departs M-Sa at 8:30am and returns at 2:30pm, Su at 12:30pm and returns at 4:40pm.)

HAFNARFJÖRÐUR. A historic trading village nestled among the lava fields of the Reykjanes peninsula, Hafnarfjörður was once an important European trading center and is now a mecca of both modern Icelandic culture and ancient traditions. **Hafnarborg,** Strandgata 34, hosts exhibits and concerts by Iceland's most prominent artists. (Open W-M noon-6pm.) A sculpture garden, **Viðistaðatun,** north along Strandgata to Hraunbrun (15min.), displays the works of international artists. (Open 24hr. Free.) **Hellisgerði,** the town park, is thought to be home to Iceland's largest **elf community;** construction sites are often relocated to avoid disturbing the magical inhabitants. The **tourist office,** Vesturgata 8, provides a *Hidden World* map that leads visitors to the haunts of elves, fairies, and other beings in Hellisgerði. (Open May 15-Sept. 15 M-F 8:30am-5:30pm, Sa-Su 9am-2pm; Sept. 15-May 15 M-F 1-4pm.) The **bus** to the Blue Lagoon stops at Hafnarfjörður. (Departs from the BSÍ terminal in Reykjavík daily at 10:30am, 1:30pm, and 6pm. Returns daily at 1:05pm, 4:35pm, and 8:30pm. 400Ikr.) Regional buses also connect the two cities. Take line #140 from the Lækjargata or Hlemmur bus terminals in Reykjavík to the station across from Hafnarfjörður's harbor. (Every 20-30min. 150Ikr.)

WESTMAN ISLANDS (VESTMANNAEYJAR)

Vaulting boldly from the depths of the North Atlantic, the black cliffs off the Westman Islands (named after the Irish slaves of the first Viking settlers) are the most recent products of the volcanic fury that created Iceland. These 16 jagged monoliths fascinate visitors and welcome thousands of seabirds from all over the north. **Heimaey** is the only inhabited island. The town of **Vestmannaeyjar,** which sprawls outward from the island's harbor, is one of the most important fishing ports in the country. The newest island, **Surtsey,** was the result of a volcanic explosion in 1963. An eruption of another sort, the three-day **Þjódhátíð** (People's Feast), held the first weekend in August, draws a hefty percentage of Reykjavík's livelier citizens to the island's shores for an annual festival of drinking and dancing. The rest of the year, Heimaey and its towns are quiet and subdued.

GETTING THERE. Getting to and from Vestmannaeyjar is relatively easy. **Flugfélag Islands** has daily **flights** from Reykjavík (one-way from 4265Ikr). A slower but much cheaper option is the **ferry** (☎481 28 00), a notoriously stomach-churning trip that begins in Þorlákshöfn. (3hr. Departs daily at noon; Th, F, and Su also 7pm. 1500Ikr. Return daily at 8:15am; Th, F, and Su also 3:30pm.) **Buses** from Reykjavík go to the dock from the BSÍ terminal one hour before departure (700Ikr).

PRACTICAL INFORMATION. Vestmannaeyjar's **tourist office** is at Vestmannabraut 38 (☎481 12 71), in the Samvinnuferðir-Landsyn travel agency. (Open June-Sept. M-F 9am-5pm, Sa-Su 1-5pm; Oct.-May M-F 9am-5pm.) Ask there about island **bus tours** (2 per day, 1600Ikr) and **boat tours** (1800Ikr).

ACCOMMODATIONS AND FOOD. The **Guesthouse Hreiðreið and Bolið,** Faxastigur 22 and Heiðarvegur 33 (☎481 10 45, fax 481 14 14), has two locations in town offering comfortable sleeping bag accommodations with kitchen facilities (1400Ikr). **Guesthouse Sunnoholl,** Vestmannabraut 28, houses visitors in both sleeping bags and made-up beds in a white house behind the hotel. (☎481 29 00; fax 481 16 96. Singles with sleeping bags 2300Ikr; doubles 3000Ikr; 500-1000Ikr more for beds.) The **campground,** 10 minutes west of town on Dalvegur near the golf course, has showers and cooking facilities. (☎481 20 75. 250Ikr per tent and per person). **K.A. supermarket** is on Strandavegur (open M-F 9am-6:30pm, Sa 9am-7pm, Su 10am-6pm) and **Voruval supermarket** is on Vestvegur (open daily 8am-7pm).

SIGHTS. In 1973, the fiery **Eldfell** volcano tore through the northern sector of **Heimaey** island, spewing glowing lava and hot ash in a surprise eruption that forced the population to flee in a dramatic overnight evacuation. When the eruption finally ceased five months later, the town was 20% smaller, but the island grew by the same amount. Nearly all of its former inhabitants returned, and the town underwent modernization. Today, visitors can observe the still-cooling lava that frames Vestmannaeyjar, the black and green mountains that shelter its harbor, and the chilling remnants of buildings half-crushed by the lava.

Hiking in the area is encouraged; the **tourist office** distributes a free map outlining hiking trails. The most spectacular spot is on the cliff's edge at **Há.** The view of the town below, the twin volcanic peaks across, and the snow-covered mainland afar is stunning. Both volcanic peaks also await intrepid hikers, but strong winds often make for rough going over the summits. Head to one of the country's two **aquariums** on Heiðarvegur (near the gas station on the second floor) to see some of the island's strange and wonderful sea creatures without venturing too close to the shore. (Open daily May-Sept. 11am-5pm; Sept.-Apr. Sa-Su 3-5pm. 200Ikr.)

REPUBLIC OF IRELAND

AND NORTHERN IRELAND

Although the Republic of Ireland and Northern Ireland are grouped together in this chapter for geographical reasons, no political statement is intended. For info on Northern Ireland's currency exchange rates and the like, see **Britain,** p. 147.

IRISH PUNT OR POUNDS

US$1 = £0.92	£1 = US$1.09
CDN$1 = £0.62	£1 = CDN$1.62
UK£1 = £1.28	£1 = UK£0.78
AUS$1 = £0.51	£1 = AUS$1.95
NZ$1 = £0.39	£1 = NZ$2.56
SAR1 = £0.13	£1 = SAR7.79
EUR€1 = £0.79	£1 = EUR€1.27

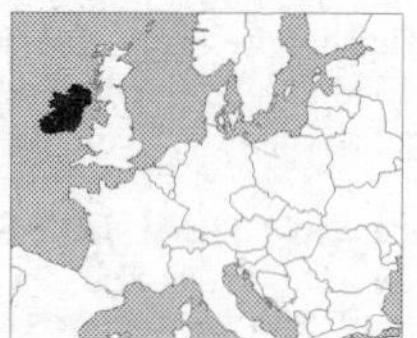

Country code: 353. **International dialing prefix:** 00. From outside the Republic of Ireland, dial int'l dialing prefix (see inside back cover) + 353 + city code + local number.

This largely agricultural island has retained its natural charm for thousands of centuries. Windswept scenery curls around the coast, and mountains punctuate interior expanses of bogland. The Irish language lives on in secluded areas known as *gaeltacht*, national papers, and literary works. Dublin and Belfast meanwhile have flowered into cosmopolitan cities, suffused with sophistication. But, like its natural beauty, centuries-old disputes refuse to die. The English suppressed the Catholic population after the Reformation and fighting eventually degenerated into civil war. The island split into the Irish Free State and Northern Ireland, which remained part of the UK. In 1949, the Free State proclaimed itself the independent Republic of Ireland (Éire), while the British kept control of Northern Ireland. In the 1960s, tensions in Northern Ireland between Catholic Nationalists and Protestant Unionists again erupted into violence. In 1998, the countries adopted a peace accord. 1999 and 2000 have seen the accord's fate fall into uncertainty, but negotiations continue in hopes of peace. For more detailed coverage, read *Let's Go: Ireland 2001.*

FACTS AND FIGURES: REPUBLIC OF IRELAND

Official Name: Éire.

Government: Parliamentary Democracy.

Capital: Dublin.

Land Area: 70,282 sq. km.

Geography: Glaciated, rocky terrain. Central plateau and bog-land flanked by coastal highlands.

Climate: Warmest and driest in the southeast, wettest in the West.

Major Cities: Dublin, Cork, Limerick.

Population: 3,647,000 (58% urban, 42% rural).

Languages: English, Irish.

Religions: Roman Catholic (95%), Protestant (3.4%), Jewish (0.1%).

Average Income Per Capita: $18,600.

Major Exports: Chemicals, data processing equipment, industrial machinery.

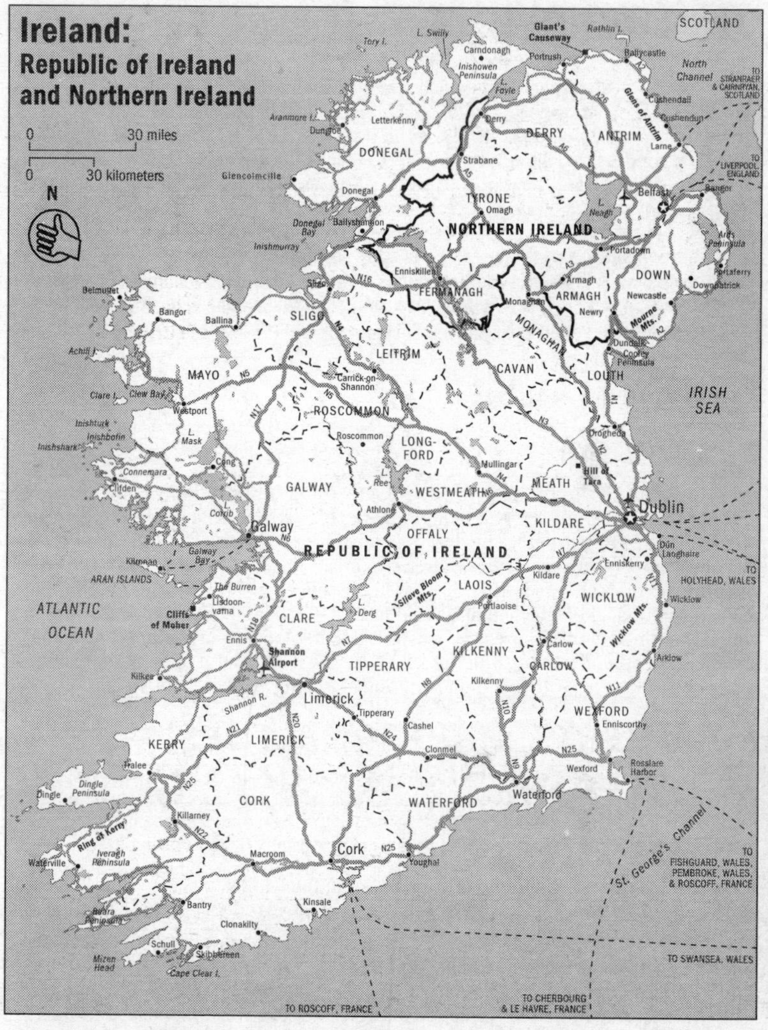

FACTS AND FIGURES: NORTHERN IRELAND

Official Name: Northern Ireland.

Government: Partial self-government (Home Rule) as part of the United Kingdom of Great Britain and Northern Ireland.

Capital: Belfast.

Land Area: 17,139 sq. km.

Geography: Primarily basalt plateau.

Climate: See Republic of Ireland.

Major Cities: Belfast, Derry.

Population: 1,577,836.

Languages: English, Irish.

Religions: Protestant (56%), Roman Catholic (44%).

Average Income Per Capita: $15,400.

Major Exports: Food, drink, tobacco, textiles and leather, transport equipment, electrical equipment and machinery.

DISCOVER IRELAND

Ireland is well-stocked with activities to suit the whims of hikers, bikers, aesthetes, poets, birdwatchers, musicians, and drinkers. Land in **Dublin** (p. 546) and explore this thousand-year-old city, a bastion of literary history and the stomping-ground of international hipsters. Take the train up to **Belfast** (p. 567) and contemplate its complex past, then catch the bus to **Giant's Causeway** (p. 571), a unique formation of rocks called the earth's eighth natural wonder. Ride the bus to **Donegal Town,** spend a night at a pub loving the trad, before climbing **Slieve League** (p. 565), Europe's tallest seacliffs. Next up is **Sligo** (p. 565), once the home of W.B. Yeats. From there, head to **Galway** (p. 562), an artsy student town that draws the island's best musicians. Relax in the picture-perfect **Ring of Kerry** (p. 559) and the **Killarney National Park** (p. 558), with its exquisite mountains, lakes, and wildlife. On the way back to Dublin, take a detour to **Kilkenny** (p. 555) and visit Ireland's oldest brewery..

ESSENTIALS

WHEN TO GO

Traveling during the off season (mid-Sept. to May) has benefits: airfares are cheaper, and you won't have to fend off flocks of fellow tourists. A thriving music scene fills pubs year-round. The acclaimed theater productions of Dublin and Belfast occur mostly during fall and winter. Countless music, film, arts, and, above all, region-specific festivals spring up practically every week. The flip side is that many attractions, hostels, bed and breakfasts (B&Bs), and tourist offices close in winter, and in some rural areas of western Ireland, local transportation drops off significantly or shuts down, and the sun goes down at around 5pm. Also, it's best to avoid traveling in Northern Ireland during Marching Season (July 4-12).

DOCUMENTS AND FORMALITIES

Citizens of Australia, Canada, EU countries, New Zealand, South Africa, the UK, and the US do not need **visas** to visit Ireland for stays shorter than three months.

EMBASSIES AND CONSULATES

All embassies for the Republic of Ireland are in **Dublin** (see p. 487). The **US** has a consulate in Belfast (see p. 506). For Northern Ireland's (United Kingdom's) Embassies, see Britain (p. 156).

Irish Embassies at Home: Australia, 20 Arkana St., Yarralumla ACT 2600 (☎ (02) 62 73 30 22); **Canada,** 130 Albert St., #1105, Ottawa, ON K1P 5G4 (☎ (613) 233 62 81); **South Africa,** Tubach Centre, 1234 Church St., 0083 Colbyn, Pretoria (☎ (012) 342 50 62); **UK,** 17 Grosvenor Pl., London SW1X 7HR (☎ (020) 72 35 21 71); **US,** 2234 Massachusetts Ave, NW, Washington, DC 20008 (☎ (202) 462 39 39; www.irelandemb.org/contact.html); **New Zealanders** should contact their embassy in Australia.

GETTING AROUND

BY PLANE. Flying to London and connecting to Ireland is often easier and cheaper. **Aer Lingus, British Airways, British Midlands,** and **Ryanair** offer **flights** from Britain (including Gatwick, Heathrow, Manchester, Birmingham, Liverpool, and Glasgow) and other cites to **Dublin, Shannon, Cork, Galway, Sligo, Waterford, Belfast,** and **Derry.** For info on cheap flights to Britain and the continent, see p. 39.

BY TRAIN. **Iarnród Éireann** (Irish Rail) is useful only for travel to urban areas, from which you'll need another form of transportation to reach Ireland's picturesque villages and wilds. While the **Eurailpass** is not accepted in Northern Ireland, it *is* accepted on trains (but not buses) in The Republic. The BritRail pass does not cover travel in Northern Ireland, but the month-long **BritRail+Ireland** works in both the North and the Republic with rail options and round-trip ferry service between Britain and Ireland (US$408-770). **Northern Ireland Railways** (☎ (01232) 899411; www.nirailways.co.uk) covers the northeastern coastal region well. The major line connects Dublin to Belfast. A valid **Northern Ireland Travelsave** stamp (UK£6, affixed to back of ISIC) will get you 50% off all trains and 15% discounts on bus fares over UK£1 within Northern Ireland. The **Freedom of Northern Ireland** ticket, allows unlimited travel by train and Ulsterbus, and can be purchased for seven consecutive days (UK£38), three consecutive days (UK£25), or one day (UK£10).

BY BUS. **Bus Éireann** (the Irish national bus company) reaches Britain and the continent by working with ferry services and the **Eurolines** bus company (UK ☎ (01582) 404 511; www.eurolines.com). Return (or round-trip) tickets are always a great value, as is the Éireann **Travel Save Stamp** (£8) if you are a student. A combined **Irish Explorer Rail/Bus** ticket allows unlimited travel eight out of 15 consecutive days on rail and bus lines (£100; children £50). Purchase Bus Éireann tickets at their main bus stations in transportation hubs (Dublin ☎ (01) 836 61 11).

Ulsterbus, Laganside, Belfast (☎ (44; from the Republic 048) 33 30 00; www.ulsterbus.co.uk), runs throughout Northern Ireland, where there are no private bus services. A **Freedom of Northern Ireland** bus and rail pass offers unlimited travel for one day (UK£10), or consecutive days (3-day pass UK£25, 7-day pass UK£38). The **Irish Rover** pass covers Bus Éireann and Ulsterbus services (unlimited travel for 3 out of 8 days £36, £18 child; for 8 out of 15 days £85, children £43; for 15 out of 30 £130, children £65). The **Emerald Card** offers unlimited travel on Ulsterbus; Northern Ireland Railways; Bus Éireann Expressway, Local, and City services in Dublin, Cork, Limerick, Galway, and Waterford; and intercity, DART, and suburban rail Iarnród Éireann services. The card works for eight out of 15 consecutive days (£115, children £58) or 15 out of 30 consecutive days (£200, children £100).

BY FERRY. Ferries journey between Britain and Ireland several times per day; tickets usually range £20-35. Traveling mid-week at night promises the cheapest fares. **An Óige (HI) members** receive up to a 20% discount on fares from Irish Ferries and Stena Sealink. **ISIC cardholders** with the **Travel Stamp** (see above) receive a 15% discount from Irish Ferries and an average 17% discount (variable among four routes) on StenaLine ferries. Bus tickets that include ferry connections between Britain and Ireland are available. Contact Bus Éireann for info. For more detailed ferry info on companies, routes, and prices, see p. 49.

BY CAR. Drivers in Ireland use the left side of the road, and have their steering-wheel on the right side of the car. Gas prices are high. Be particularly cautious at roundabouts (rotary interchanges)—give way to traffic from the right. Irish law requires drivers and passengers to wear seat belts—these laws are enforced. The general speed limit in the Republic is 90km per hr. (55 mph) on the open road and either 50km per hr. (30 mph) or 65km per hr. (40 mph) in town. The North's speed limits are 97km per hr. (60 mph) on single carriageways (non-divided highways), 113km per hr. (70 mph) on motorways (highways) and dual carriageways (divided highways), and usually 48km per hr. (30 mph) in urban areas. People under 21 cannot rent cars, and those under 23 often encounter difficulties. Prices range from £100-300 (plus VAT) per week with insurance and unlimited mileage.

BY BIKE, BY FOOT, AND BY THUMB. Much of the countryside is well suited for **cycling,** and towns throughout the island offer bike rental outlets. Ireland offers rugged hills and small mountains to its **hikers.** The **Wicklow Way,** a popular trail through mountainous Co. Wicklow, has hostels designed for hikers within a day's walk of each other and the **Ulster Way** encircles Northern Ireland with 560 mi. of marked trails. Irish drivers are usually **hitchhiker**-friendly, but there has been a recent backlash and *Let's Go* does not recommend hitching, especially in Northern Ireland.

TOURIST SERVICES AND MONEY

EMERGENCY: Police, ambulance, and **fire:** ☎ 999.

TOURIST OFFICES. Bord Fáilte (the **Irish Tourist Board**) operates a nationwide network. Most offices book rooms for a small fee (£1-3) and a 10% deposit, but fine hostels and B&Bs that are not "registered" can't be recommended. Bord Fáilte's central office is at Baggot St. Bridge, **Dublin** 2. In Ireland ☎ (1850) 230 330; in UK ☎ (020) 7493 3201; elsewhere ☎ (353) (01) 666 1258; www.ireland.travel.ie.

The **Northern Ireland Tourist Board** offers similar services at locations all over the North. The head office is at 59 North St., **Belfast,** BT1 1NB, Northern Ireland (☎ (44; from the Republic, 048) 246 609; fax 240 960; www.ni-tourism.com). **Dublin,** 16 Nassau St., Dublin 2 (☎ (01) 679 1977; CallSave (1850) 2302 30.) Tourist boards have brochures and *Where to Stay in Northern Ireland 2000* (UK£4).

Irish Tourist Boards at Home: Australia, 36 Carrington St., 5th level, Sydney, NSW 2000 (☎ (02) 9299 6177); **Canada,** 2 Bloor St. W, Toronto, ON M4W 3E2 (☎ (416) 925 63 68); **UK,** 150 New Bond St., London W1Y 0AQ (☎ (020) 74 93 32 01); **US,** 345 Park Ave., New York, NY 10154 (☎ (212) 418 08 00 or 1 (800) 223 64 70).

Northern Ireland Tourist Boards at home: Canada, 2 Bloor St. W., Toronto ON M4W3E2 (☎ (416) 925 63 68); **US,** 551 Fifth Ave, Room #701, New York, NY 10176 (☎ (800) 326 00 36); **UK,** British Travel Centre, 12 Lower Regent St., London SW1Y 4PQ (☎ (020) 7839 8417).

MONEY. The currency of the Irish Republic is the **Irish pound** (or **"punt"**), denoted £. It comes in the same denominations as the **British pound** (which is called **"sterling"** in Ireland) but has been worth a bit less recently. Legal tender in Northern Ireland is the British pound. Northern Ireland has its own bank notes, which are identical in value to English and Scottish notes of the same denominations. Although these notes are accepted in Northern Ireland, Northern Ireland bank notes are not accepted across the water. UK coins come in denominations of 1p, 2p, 5p, 10p, 20p, 50p, and £1. Residents of both nations refer to pounds as **"quid,"** never "quids." For exchange, only go to banks or bureaux de change that have less than a 5% margin between their buy and sell prices. ATMs and credit cards will often get you the best rates. The majority of towns have 24-hour **ATMs.**

If you stay in **hostels** and prepare your own food, expect to spend about US$18-30 per person per day. **Accommodations** start at about £8-10 per night for a bed while the cost for a basic sit-down meal begins around £6. Some restaurants figure a **service charge** into the bill; some even calculate it into the cost of the dishes. The menu often indicates whether or not service is included (ask if you're unsure). If the tip is not included, customers should leave 10-15%. Porters, parking-lot attendants, waitstaff, and hairdressers are usually tipped. Cab drivers are usually tipped 10%. Above all, **never tip the barman.** Ireland and Northern Ireland charge **Value Added Tax (VAT)** on most goods and some services. The VAT ranges from 0% on food and children's clothing to 17% in restaurants to 21% on other items, such as jewelry and clothing; VAT is usually included in listed prices. The British rate, applicable to Northern Ireland, is 17.5% on many services (such as hairdressers, hotels, restaurants, and car rental agencies) and on all goods (except books, medicine, and food). *Let's Go* prices include VAT. Refunds are available for non-EU citizens and for goods taken out of the country, but not for services.

ACCOMMODATIONS AND CAMPING

HOSTELS. Hostel dorms usually cost between £7-10, and breakfast is often included or can be added for £1-3. **An Óige,** the Irish Hostelling International affiliate, runs 34 spartan, out-of-the-way hostels. The North's HI affiliate is **HINI** (Hostelling International Northern Ireland; formerly **YHANI**), which operates eight nicer hostels. The *An Óige Handbook* details all An Óige and HINI hostels; its standard pricing system isn't always followed. Some hostels belong to

Independent Holiday Hostels (IHH); they have no lockout or curfew (with a few exceptions), accept all ages, don't require membership, and are approved by Bord Fáilte. Copious **B&Bs** provide a luxurious break; expect to pay £15-25 for singles and £20-36 for doubles. "Full Irish breakfasts" are often filling enough to get you through to dinner.

CAMPING. Camping in Irish State Forests and National Parks is not allowed; camping on public land is permissible only if there is no official campsite nearby. Most caravan and camping parks are open April through October, although some are open year-round. Pick up the *Caravan and Camping Ireland* guide from any Bord Fáilte office for info on camping in the Republic.

FOOD AND DRINK

Food is expensive, but the basics are simple and filling. "Take-away" (takeout) **fish and chips** shops are quick, greasy, and very popular. Many pubs serve food as well as drink; typical pub grub includes **Irish stew,** burgers, soup, and sandwiches. Soda bread is delicious and keeps well, and dairy products are addictive. Pubs are the forum for banter, singing, and *craic* (a good time). In the evenings, many pubs play impromptu or organized traditional music (trad). **Guinness,** a rich, dark stout, is Ireland's most revered brew. **Irish whiskey**, which Queen Elizabeth once claimed was her only true Irish friend, is sweeter than its Scotch counterpart (see p. 553). Irish monks invented whiskey, calling it *uisce beatha*, meaning "water of life." **Pubs** are usually open Monday to Saturday 10:30am to 11 or 11:30pm, Sunday 12:30 to 2pm and 4 to 11pm (in the North Su 12:30-2:30pm and 7-10pm).

COMMUNICATION

MAIL: To send a **postcard** or a **letter** (up to 25g) within Europe costs £0.32; to any other international destination, £0.45. Domestic postcards and letters cost £0.30. Mail can be sent **Poste Restante** to any post office. The mail will go to the central post office, unless you specify a post office by street address or postal code. Airmail letters take about a week between Ireland and North America.

TELEPHONES: Public phones accept **coins** and **pre-paid phone-cards.** In Northern Ireland, phones that accept pre-paid cards are generally marked with a yellow sign. Phone-cards are available at newsstands in the Republic, and at newsstands and post offices in the North. For an **international operator,** dial ☎114 in the Republic or ☎155 in Northern Ireland; **operator,** ☎10 and ☎100; **directory,** ☎1190 and ☎192. **International direct dial** numbers include: **AT&T** ☎ (1800) 550 000 in the Republic and ☎ (0800) 890 011 in Northern Ireland; **Australia Direct** ☎ (1800) 550 06 and ☎ (0800) 890 061; **British Telecom** ☎ (1800) 550 144 and ☎ (0800) 890 353; **Canada Direct** ☎ (1800) 555 001 and ☎ (0800) 890 016; **MCI World Ring** ☎ (1800) 551 001 and ☎ (0800) 890 222; **Telecom New Zealand** ☎ (1800) 550 064 and ☎ (0800) 890 064; **Telekom South Africa** ☎ (1800) 550 027 and ☎ (0800) 890 027.

INTERNET ACCESS. Try libraries and Internet cafes (usually £2-5 per 30min.).

HOLIDAYS AND FESTIVALS

Holidays: Much of Southern Ireland closes for holidays on January 1, St. Patrick's Day (Mar. 17), Good Friday (Apr. 2), Easter (Apr. 13-16), May 7, June 4, August 6, October 29, and Christmas (Dec. 25-26). Northern Ireland adds on May Day (May 1), Spring or Whitsun Holiday (May 28), Orange Day (June 12), and August 27.

Festivals: All of Ireland goes green for **St. Patrick's Day** (Mar. 17th). On **Bloomsday** (June 16) Dublin traipses about revering James Joyce (see p. 552).

DUBLIN ☎01

In a country known for a lackadaisical pace, Dublin, boasting nonstop theater, music, literary productions, and a diverse nightlife, stands out for its international style and boundless energy. The city and its suburbs, home to one-third of Ireland's population, are at the vanguard of the country's rapid social change. But despite Dublin's progressive pace and rocking nightlife, old Ireland still courses through its veins. Statues of great writers like Joyce, Swift, Burke, and Beckett pepper the streets. Beneath the urban bustle, majestic cathedrals and quaint pubs welcome visitors with Ireland's trademark friendliness and zeal.

GETTING THERE AND GETTING AROUND

Flights: Dublin Airport (☎844 49 00). Catch Dublin bus #41, 41B, or 41C (every 20min., £1.20) to Eden Quay in the city center. **Airport Express buses** (☎844 42 65) run to the Central Bus Station and O'Connell St. (30min., every 15-30min. 7am-11pm, £2.50). **Airlink** shuttles to the Central Bus Station and O'Connell St. (30-40min., every 10-15min., £3) as well as Heuston Station (50min., £3.50). A **taxi** to the city center costs £12-15. Beware traffic, even when planning on catching an express bus.

Trains: Irish Rail Information is at 35 Lower Abbey St. (☎836 62 22). Open M-F 9am-5pm, Sa 9am-1pm; recording after hours. Most inter-city trains arrive at **Heuston Station** (☎703 21 32), south of Victoria Quay and far west of the city center. Buses #26, 51, and 79 go to the center. To: **Limerick** (2¼hr., 9 per day, £16-25); **Galway** (2½hr., 4-5 per day, £13-22); **Waterford** (2½hr., 3-4 per day, £13); **Cork** (3½hr., 6-11 per day, £33.50); and **Tralee** (4½hr., 4-7 per day, £34). The other main terminus is **Connolly Station** (☎836 33 33), on Amiens St. by the Central Bus Station. To: **Belfast** (2¼hr., 5-8 per day, £18); **Wexford** and **Rosslare** (3hr., 2-3 per day, £11); and **Sligo** (3½hr., 3-4 per day, £14.50). **Pearse Station** is east of Trinity College on Pearse St.

Buses: Busáras Central Bus Station (☎836 61 11), on Store St., next to Connolly Station, sends off most inter-city buses. **Bus Éirann** runs to: **Belfast** (3hr., 4-7 per day, £10.50); **Rosslare Harbour** (3hr., 7-10 per day, £10); **Limerick** (3¼hr., 7-13 per day, £10); **Galway** (4hr., 14 per day, £9); and **Cork** (4½hr., 3-4 per day, £12). Bus #90 (every 10min., £0.85) makes the circuit of the train stations and Busáras.

Ferries: Stena Line pulls into **Dún Laoghaire,** a Dublin suburb, from **Holyhead, England;** DART shuttles incoming passengers to Connolly Station, Pearse Station, or Tara St. (£1.30). **Irish Ferries** (☎ (1890) 31 31 31; www.irishferries.ie) arrive from Holyhead at the Dublin Port (☎607 56 65). Buses #53 and 53A run from the Dublin Port to the Central Bus Station (every hr., 80p); **Dublin Bus** also goes from the city to meet outgoing ferries (£2-2.50). **Irish Rail** (see above) handles bookings for all of the above. **Merchant Ferries** runs a Dublin-Liverpool route (8hr.; 2 per day; £40, with car £150-170); book through **Gerry Feeney,** 19 Eden Quay (☎819 29 99).

Public Transportation: Dublin Bus, 59 Upper O'Connell St. Distressingly lime green. Fares £0.60-1.20. Buses run every 8-45min. daily 5am-11:30pm. Their **NiteLink** runs express routes to the suburbs (Th-Sa every hr. 11:30am-3:30am; £3, no passes valid). Timetables are available from newsagents and the above office. **Dublin Area Rapid Transportation (DART)** serves coastal suburbs from Howth to Greystones from Connolly Station (55p-£1.10). Runs daily 6:30am-11:30pm. Timetables available at many stations (£0.50). **Ramblers passes** offer unlimited bus transportation (1-day £3.50; 1-week £13, students £10; valid for the full week, starting Su, no matter when you buy the ticket). Other passes allow unlimited bus and suburban rail/DART transport.

Car Rental: Budget, 151 Lower Drumcondra Rd. (☎837 96 11), and at the airport. In summer from £35 per day, £165 per week; in winter £30, £140. Ages 23-75.

Bike Rental: Raleigh Rent-A-Bike (☎626 13 33), on Kylemore Rd. £10 per day, £40 per week; deposit £50. Limited one-way rental system for £10 surcharge.

ORIENTATION AND PRACTICAL INFORMATION

The **River Liffey** cuts Dublin in half from east to west. Better food, posh stores, and more famous sights reside on the **South Side,** while hostels and the bus station inhabit the cheaper **North Side.** Buying a map with a street index save time. Collins' superb *Handy Map of Dublin* (£4.64) is available at the tourist office. The names of the streets along the Liffey, called quays ("keys"), change every block. Each bridge has its own name, and streets change names as they cross. When streets split into "Upper" and "Lower" sections, "Lower" indicates closer proximity to the Liffey's mouth (east). Most attractions are in the area circumscribed by North and South Circular Rd., both of which frequently change names. **O'Connell St.,** three blocks west of the Central Bus Station, is the primary link between north and south Dublin; south of the Liffey, it becomes Westmoreland St., passes **Trinity College Dublin (TCD),** and becomes **Grafton St.,** an entertaining pedestrian zone. A block south of the Liffey, Fleet St. becomes **Temple Bar**—the name of a street and Dublin's liveliest nightspot. The **North Side** has the reputation of being a rougher part of town; on both sides of the river, avoid walking in unfamiliar areas at night.

TOURIST, FINANCIAL, AND LOCAL SERVICES

Tourist Offices: Dublin Tourist Centre, Suffolk St. (Ireland ☎ (1850) 23 03 30; UK ☎ (0171) 493 32 01; elsewhere ☎ (066) 979 20 83; www.visitdublin.com), in an old church. Exit Connolly Station on Talbot St., turn left at O'Connell St., cross the bridge, follow Westmoreland St. past TCD, and turn right on Suffolk St. Open July-Aug. M-Sa 9am-7pm, Su 10:30am-2:30pm; Sept.-June M-Sa 9am-6pm.

Budget Travel: Usit NOW (Irish Student Travel Agency), 19-21 Aston Quay (☎679 88 33), near O'Connell Bridge. ISICs, HI cards. Many discounts, especially for students and those under 26. Open M-W and F 9am-6pm, Th 9am-8pm, Sa 10am-5:30pm.

Embassies: Australia, 2nd fl., Fitzwilton House, Wilton Terr. (☎676 15 17). Open M-Th 8:30am-12:30pm and 1:30-4:30pm, F 9am-noon. **Canada,** 65 St. Stephen's Green South (☎478 19 88). Open M-F 9am-1pm and 2-4:30pm. **New Zealanders** should contact their embassy in London (☎ (44 020) 79 30 84 22). **South Africa,** 2nd fl., Alexandra House, Earlsfort Centre (☎661 55 53; email saembdub@iol.ie). Open M-F 8:30am-5pm. **UK,** 29 Merrion Rd. (☎269 52 11). Open M-F 9am-5pm. **US,** 42 Elgin Rd., Ballsbridge (☎668 87 77). Open M-F 8:30am-5pm.

American Express: 43 Nassau St. (☎679 90 00). Traveler's check refunds (☎618 55 88). Currency exchange and client mail held. Open M-F 9am-5pm.

Luggage Storage: Connolly, Heuston, and **Central Bus Stations.** £1.50-3.50 per day.

Gay and Lesbian Services: Gay Switchboard Dublin (☎872 10 55). Open Su-F 8-10pm. **Outhouse,** 65 William St. (☎670 63 77), has a library and cafe. The monthly *Gay Community News* has info on gay life and nightlife (free around Temple Bar).

Laundromat: The Laundry Shop, 191 Parnell St. (☎872 35 41), is nearest the Central Bus Station and hostels. Wash and dry £5. Open M-F 8pm-7pm, Sa 10am-6pm.

EMERGENCY AND COMMUNICATIONS

Emergency: ☎999 for **police, fire,** or **ambulance;** no coins required.

Crisis Lines: Tourist Victim Support, Harcourt Sq. (☎ (1800) 66 17 71). **Rape Crisis Centre,** 70 Lower Leeson St. (☎ (1800) 77 88 88).

Pharmacy: O'Connell's, 55 Lower O'Connell St. (☎873 04 27). Open M-Sa 8am-10pm, Su 10am-10pm. Other branches scattered around the city center, including Grafton St.

Internet Access: Machines and kiosks might not work; stick to Internet cafes. **Internet Exchange,** at various locations, including 146 Parnell St., Suffolk St. tourist office, and in the Granary in Temple Bar South. Open daily 9am-11pm. **Global Internet Café,** 8 Lower O'Connell St. £1.25 per 15min., students £1. Open M-F 8am-11pm, Sa 9am-11pm, Su noon-10pm.

Telephones: On every corner. Use phonecards, available at most newsstands, or coins. Directory information ☎118 11.

Post Office: General Post Office (**GPO;** ☎705 70 00), O'Connell St. *Poste Restante* at the *bureau de change* window. Open M-Sa 8am-8pm, Su 10am-6:30pm. Address mail to be held: First name SURNAME, *Poste Restante,* GPO, **Dublin 1,** Republic of Ireland.

ACCOMMODATIONS

Dublin's accommodations overflow, especially during Easter, holidays, and summer—reserve ahead. Most hostels cling to the center, on the north side. Dorms range from £8-15 per night. Hostel prices are listed for the high season; prices usually drop £1-2 between October and March. Quality **B&Bs** blanket the surrounding suburbs (most charge £16-30 per person); many cluster along **Upper** and **Lower Gardiner St.,** on **Sherriff St.,** and near **Parnell Sq. Phoenix Park** may tempt the desperate, but camping there is dangerous and illegal. Dublin Tourism's annual *Dublin Accommodation Guide* (£3) lists approved B&Bs and other accommodations.

HOSTELS AND CAMPING

Barnacle's Temple Bar House, 19 Temple Ln. (☎671 62 77; email templeba@barnacles.iol.ie). Excellent security and fantastic location right in Temple Bar. All rooms with bath. Breakfast included. June-Sept. dorms £11-15; doubles £20.

The Brewery Hostel, 22-23 Thomas St. (☎453 86 00; email breweryh@indigo.ie), next to Guinness, 20min. from Temple Bar. Follow Dame St. past Christ Church, or take bus #123. Social scene with patio, kitchen, and comfy lounge. Breakfast included. Laundry. All rooms with bath. Staff may offer you the nearby "overflow" hostel, which offers far less cleanliness and comfort. Dorms £10-12; singles £28; doubles £44; quads £60.

Avalon House (IHH), 55 Aungier St. (☎475 00 01; on-line booking at www.avalonhouse.ie), within stumbling distance of Temple Bar. Turn off Dame St. onto Great Georges St. (Aungier St.). Trans-continental travelers aplenty. Co-ed bathrooms and dorms. Breakfast included. Internet. Dorms £12.50-16.50; doubles £36-40.

Abbey Hostel, 29 Bachelor's Walk, O'Connell Bridge (☎878 07 00; email info@abbeyhostel.ie). Great location. Breakfast included. Internet £1 per 7min. Dorms £14-17.

Abraham House, 82-3 Lower Gardiner St. (☎855 06 00; email stay@abrahamhouse.ie). Clean rooms and all-important good bathrooms. Kitchen open until 10pm. Breakfast and towels included. Internet. Laundry £4. Dorms £9-15; doubles £40.

Globetrotter's Tourist Hostel (IHH), 46-7 Lower Gardiner St. (☎873 58 93; email gtrotter@indigo.ie). Luxury for the weary backpacker. Superb showers–just too few of them. Full Irish breakfast in included. Internet. £12-15.

Jacob's Inn, 21-28 Talbot Pl. (☎855 56 60), two blocks north of the Customs House. Cheery Rooms, all with bath, are clean to the point of sterility. Wheelchair accessible. Bed lockout 11am-3pm. Laundry. Dorms £11.25-17.50; doubles £43.

Ashfield House, 19-20 D'Olier St. (☎679 77 34), smack in Dublin's geographical center. Average beds, but beautiful common areas. All rooms with bath/shower. Breakfast included. Internet. Laundry. Dorms £12-18; singles £40. Weekend prices £1-2 higher.

Dublin International Youth Hostel (An Óige/HI), 61 Mountjoy St. (☎830 17 66). O'Connell St. changes names 3 times before reaching the left turn onto Mountjoy St. Welcome to the mothership; convent-turned-hostel with 365 beds. Shuttles to Temple Bar. Breakfast included. Wheelchair accessible. Dorms £10-14; doubles £29-30.

Celts House, 32 Blessington St. (☎830 06 57; email res@celtshouse.iol.ie). Comfy bunkbeds in a brightly painted, friendly atmosphere 15min. from the city center. Key deposit £5. Internet. Dorms £9-12.50; doubles £32-36.

Mount Eccles Court (M.E.C.), 42 North Great Georges St. (☎878 00 71). Walk up O'Connell, turn right on Parnell St., and take the 1st left. Impossibly spacious on a quiet street. Breakfast included. Dorms £8.50-13.50; doubles £36.

Camac Valley Tourist Caravan & Camping Park (☎464 06 44), on Naas Rd., in **Clondalkin,** near Corkagh Park. Take bus #69 from the city center (35min., £1.10). Store, laundry, and kitchen. Showers 50p. Laundry £3.50. Camping for hiker/cyclist £4-5.

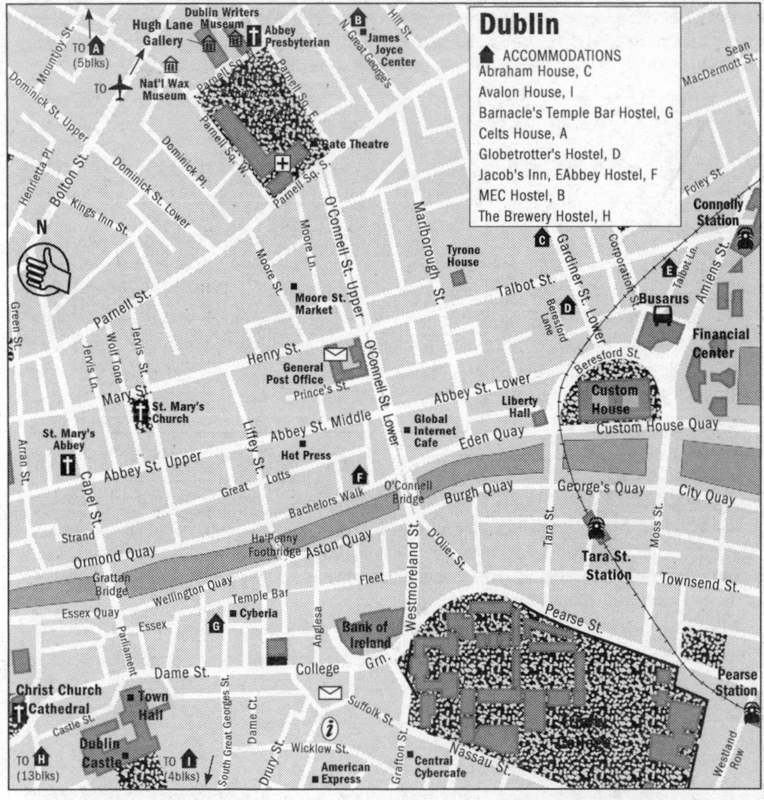

BED & BREAKFASTS

Parkway Guest House, 5 Gardiner Pl. (☎874 04 69). Well-located just off Gardiner St. High-ceilings, immaculate rooms, and friendly owners. Singles £23; doubles £36-48.

Mona B&B, 148 Clonliffe Rd. (☎837 67 23). Walk up O'Connell St., turn right on Dorset St., and turn right on Clonliffe (10min.). The proprietress, Mrs. Kathleen Greville, would "never refuse anyone tea and cakes!" Open May-Oct. Singles £17; doubles £36.

St. Aidan's B&B, 150 Clonliffe Rd. (☎837 67 50). Good beds, non-smoking rooms, and a relaxing atmosphere. Open Apr.-Sept. Singles £17; doubles £34-40.

Rita and Jim Casey, Villa Jude, 2 Church Ave. (☎668 49 82). Off Beach Rd. in Sandymount. Take bus #3 from Clery's on O'Connell St. to the first stop on Tritonville Rd. and backtrack a few yards. Mr. Casey is the Mayor of Sandymount, and this B&B specializes in royal treatment. Immaculate rooms with TVs. Singles £16; doubles £32.

Mrs. Dolores Abbot-Murphy, 14 Castle Park (☎269 84 13). Ask the bus #3 driver to drop you at Sandymount Green; continue past Browne's Deli and take the first left. Flowers bloomin' everywhere. Singles £23; doubles £38-44.

Charles Stewart Budget Accommodation, 5-6 Parnell Sq. (☎878 03 50). Full Irish breakfast included. Laundry £3. Singles £45; doubles £50.

FOOD

Wonderful and inexpensive eateries can be found in every neighborhood. Many restaurants have early bird dinner specials that halve the prices of entrees. Head to the open-air **Moore St. Market,** between Henry St. and Parnell St., to pick up fresh, cheap veggies. (Open M-Sa 7am-5pm.) The cheapest **supermarkets** are the **Dunnes**

Stores at: St. Stephen's Green Shopping Centre; the ILAC Centre, off Henry St.; and on North Earl St., off O'Connell. (Open M-W and F-Sa 8:30am-7pm, Th 8:30am-9pm, Su noon-6pm.) The **Temple Bar** area has creative eateries for every budget.

- **Café Irie,** on Fownes St., above the colorful Sé Sí Progressive. Probably the best value in Temple Bar: lip-smackingly good sandwich concoctions for under £3. Plenty of vegan options. Great coffee too. Open M-Sa 9am-8pm, Su noon-5:30pm.
- **Cornucopia,** 19 Wicklow St. Vegetarian horn of plenty with huge portions. Snacks around £1.50, meals around £5. Takeout too. Open M-W and F-Sa 9am-8pm, Th 9am-9pm.
- **La Mezza Luna,** 1 Temple Ln., at Dame St. (☎671 28 40). Celestial food. Roast-pepper-and-chicken crepe £8.50. £5 lunch specials noon-5pm. Open M-Th noon-11pm, F-Sa noon-11:30pm, Su noon-10:30pm.
- **Poco Loco,** 32 Parliament St., between Grattan Bridge and City Hall. Even the appetizers are filling. Enchiladas, burritos, chimichangas, and tacos £5.75. Vegetarian friendly. Open M-Tu 5-11pm, W-Th 5-11:30pm, F-Sa 5pm-midnight, Su 5-10pm.
- **Zaytoons,** 14-15 Parliament St. Big portions of Persian food served on platters of warm bread. Chicken kebab £3.50. Open M-W noon-3am, Th-Sa noon-4am, Su 2pm-3am.
- **Govinda's,** 4 Aungier St. Another fabulous vegetarian find with a relaxed Buddhist sensibility. The massive and yummy dinner special is only £4.95. Open M-Sa 11am-9pm.
- **Leo Burdock's,** 2 Werburgh St., uphill from Christ Church Cathedral. Takeout only. Their fish and chips are an institution (£3.20). Open M-Sa noon-midnight, Su 4pm-midnight.
- **The Winding Stair Bookshop and Cafe,** 40 Lower Ormond Quay, near the Ha'penny Bridge. Salads around £4; sandwiches £2. Open M-Sa 10:30am-5:30pm, Su 1-6pm.
- **Soup Dragon,** 168 Capel St. 10-12 soups per day and healthy juices, fruits, and breads. Soups £3-8.55. Open daily 8am-5:30pm.
- **Dail Bia,** 46 Kildare St. All-Irish restaurant. Delicious scones, cakes, and sandwiches. Many sandwiches under £3. Open M-Sa 7:30am-7pm.

SIGHTS

Most sights lie within a mile of O'Connell Bridge. The tourist office sells *Dublin's Top Visitor Attractions* and *Heritage Trails: Signpost Walking Tours of Dublin* (£2.50 each). The two-hour **Historical Walking Tour** is a Dublin crash course starting with the Celts. (☎878 02 27. May-Sept. M-F 11am and 3pm, Sa-Su 11am, noon, and 3pm; Oct.-Apr. F-Su noon. Meet at Trinity's front gate. £6, students £5.)

TRINITY COLLEGE TO ST. STEPHEN'S GREEN. Sprawling at the center of Dublin, **Trinity College** is the *alma mater* of Jonathan Swift, Thomas Moore, Samuel Beckett, and Oscar Wilde. The **Old Library,** built in 1712, houses the *Book of Kells* (circa AD 800), an illuminated four-volume edition of the Gospels; each page holds a dizzyingly intricate lattice of Celtic designs interwoven with text. *(Open June-Sept. M-Sa 9:30am-5pm, Su noon-4:30pm; Oct.-May M-Sa 9:30am-5pm, Su noon-4:30pm. £4.50, students £4.)* The **Trinity College Walking Tour** concentrates on University lore. *(June-Sept. every 45min. from the info booth in the front gate. March, Apr., and May, weekends only. 30min. £6, students £5; includes admission to the Old Library and the Book of Kells.)* South of the college, on the block between Kildare St. and Upper Merrion St., Irish history and culture reign. The **National Museum** protects the Ardagh Hoard, the Tara Brooch, and other artifacts from the last two millennia. Within the museum, the **Natural History Museum** presents a creepy collection, including a skeleton of the ancient Irish Elk, amoeba replicas, and jars of Irish tapeworms. The **National Museum of Decorative Arts and History,** Collins Barracks, explores Irish economic, social, and political history in Europe's oldest military barracks. *(The Museum Link bus runs from the National History Museum, on Kildare St., to Collins Barracks roughly every hour. All-day pass £2; one-way £0.85. Info for all three ☎677 74 44. All open Tu-Sa 10am-5pm, Su 2-5pm. Free.)* Portraits of Lady Gregory, Joyce, Shaw, and Yeats line the **National Gallery's** staircase; the museum also houses works by Brueghel, Caravaggio, Vermeer, Rembrandt, and El Greco. A Millennium wing, with a Centre for the Study of Irish Art, is opening this year. *(Merrion Sq. West. Open M-Sa 10am-5:30pm, Th 10am-8:30pm, Su 2-5pm. Tours Sa 3pm,*

Su 2:15, 3, and 4pm. Free.) Kildare, Dawson, and Grafton St. all lead from Trinity to **St. Stephen's Green.** Bequeathed to the city by the Guinness clan, this 22-acre park boasts arched bridges, a lake, gazebos, and a waterfall. On summer days, enjoy the outdoor performances near the old bandstand. *(Open M-Sa 8am-dusk, Su 10am-dusk.)*

TEMPLE BAR, DUBLIN CASTLE, AND THE CATHEDRALS. Between Dame St. and the Liffey, west of Trinity, the **Temple Bar** area bustles. Cheap cafes, hole-in-the-wall theaters, and used clothing and record stores line the streets. By this hipster scene is **Dublin Castle,** built in 1204 by King John on top of the first Viking settlement in Dubh Linn; it was the seat of English rule in Ireland for the next 700 years. *(Dame St., where it meets Parliament and Castle St. State Apartments open M-F 10am-5pm, Sa-Su 2-5pm. £3, students £2; Grounds free.)* Both of Dublin's two official cathedrals, **Christ Church Cathedral** and **St. Patrick's Cathedral,** are owned by the Church of Ireland, not the Catholic Church; since the Anglo-Irish aristocracy no longer exists, today they are considered more works of art than centers of worship. *(Christ Church is on Dame St. Open daily 10am-5:30pm. Donation of £2. St. Patrick's is down Nicholas St., which becomes Patrick St. Open Mar.-Oct. M-Sa 9am-6pm, Su 9-11am and 12:45-3pm and 4:15-6pm; Nov.-Feb. M-F 9am-6pm, Sa 9am-5pm, Su 10-11am and 12:45-3pm. £2, students £1.)*

GUINNESS BREWERY. Those craving alcoholic ambrosia are drawn to the giant Guinness Brewery. The **Hopstore** perpetuates the Guinness mystique and washes down tours with a pint of dark, creamy goodness, considered the best beer in the world. *(St. James Gate. The Hopstore is on Crane St. off James St. Take bus #51B or 78A from Aston Quay or bus #123 from O'Connell St. From Christ Church Cathedral, follow High St. west as it changes names to Cornmarket, Thomas and then James. Open Apr.-Sept. M-Sa 9:30am-5pm, Su 10:30am-4:30pm; Oct.-Mar. M-Sa 9:30am-4pm, Su noon-4pm. £5, students £4.)*

KILMAINHAM GAOL. "The cause for which I die has been rebaptized during this past week by the blood of as good men as ever trod God's earth," penned Sean MacDiarmada as he awaited execution for his role in the 1916 Easter Rising. Almost all of the rebels who fought in Ireland's struggle for independence from 1792 to 1921 were imprisoned at Kilmainham Gaol. Today the prison is a museum; tours wander through its chilly limestone corridors and haunting execution yard. *(Inchicore Rd. Take bus #51 or 79 from Aston Quay, or bus #51A from Lower Abbey St. Open Apr.-Sept. daily 9:30am-5pm; Oct.-Mar. M-F 9:30am-4pm, Su 10am-5pm. £3.50, students £1.50.)*

THE NORTH SIDE. The **Dublin Writer's Museum** introduces visitors to the city's rich literary legacy with manuscripts, memorabilia, and caricatures of pen-wielding Dubliners. *(18 Parnell Sq. North. Open June-Aug. M-F 10am-6pm, Sa 10am-5pm, Su 11am-5pm; Sept.-May M-Sa 10am-5pm. £3.10, students £2.89.)* At the heart of the up-and-coming Smithfield neighborhood is the **Old Jameson Distillery,** whose tours are more entertaining and less commercial than the ones at Guinness, and end with a glass of your choice of Irish whiskey; be quick to volunteer in the beginning and you'll get to sample a whole tray of different whiskeys. Feel the burn. *(Bow St. From O'Connell St., turn onto Henry St. and continue as it turns into Mary St., Mary Ln., and finally May Ln.; the warehouse is on a cobblestone street to the left. Tours daily 9:30am-5pm. £3.95, students £3.)*

THE PHIL Founded in 1684, Trinity College's University Philosophical Society is the oldest undergraduate student society in the world. With a current membership of 2000 students, "the Phil" counts Jonathan Swift, Oscar Wilde, Bram Stoker, and Samuel Beckett among its alumni. Throughout its existence, the Society has held debates and read papers every Thursday evening at 7:30pm. In 1734, three or four students threw rocks at the window of a young dean with a penchant for Draconian discipline, Edward Ford. He responded by shooting a gun vaguely in their direction. The students returned to their own rooms and loaded up on the pistols that—being responsible students—they kept there. In the ensuing shoot-out, Ford was mortally wounded. The students were promptly expelled from Trinity, but they avoided incarceration because the judge deemed the event merely a student prank that got out of hand.

ENTERTAINMENT

The *Event Guide* (free at the tourist office and Temple Bar restaurants) and *In Dublin* (£1.95) detail a smorgasbord of events. Hostel workers are also helpful for entertainment suggestions. *Hot Press* (£1.50) has the most up-to-date music listings, particularly for rock. Traditional music (trad) is an important element of the Irish culture and the Dublin music scene. The city's best pub for trad is **Cobblestones,** King St. North, in Smithfield, which has live shows every night, plus a trad session in the basement. The best small venue for live music, from rock to folk, is **Whelan's,** 25 Wexford St. Big deal bands frequent the **Baggot Inn,** 143 Baggot St. Hear classical music at the **National Concert Hall,** Earlsfort Terr. (☎671 15 33. Concerts July-Aug. £6-12, students £3-6.) Part of the National Theater, the **Abbey Theatre,** 26 Lower Abbey St., was founded in 1904 by Yeats and Lady Gregory to promote Irish culture and modernist theater. (☎878 72 22. Box office open M-Sa 10:30am-7pm. Tickets £10-17.50; student rate M-Th and Sa matinee £8.)

Dublin pretty much owns two days of the year. **St. Patrick's Day** (Mar. 17) and the half-week leading up to it host a city-wide carnival of concerts, fireworks, street theater, and intoxicated madness. (☎676 32 05; fax 676 32 08; www.paddyfest.ie.) The city returns to 1904 on **Bloomsday** (June 16), the day on which the action of Joyce's *Ulysses* takes place. Festivities are held all week long. The **James Joyce Cultural Center** (☎873 19 84) sponsors a reenactment of the funeral and wake, a lunch at Davy Byrne's, and a breakfast with Guinness.

NIGHTLIFE

PUBLIN

James Joyce once proposed that a "good puzzle would be to cross Dublin without passing a pub." A local radio station offered £100 to the first person to do it; the winner explained that you could take any route as long as you visited every pub along the way. The **Dublin Literary Pub Crawl** traces Dublin's liquid history in reference to its literary one. Meet at **The Duke,** 2 Duke St. (☎670 56 02. Tours depart Easter-Oct. M-Sa 7:30pm, Su noon and 7:30pm; Nov.-Easter Th-Sa 7:30pm, Su noon and 7:30pm. £6.50, students £5.50. Book at the door or at the Suffolk St. tourist office for £0.15 extra.) The **Let's Go Dublin Pub Crawl** begins early (say, noon) at the gates of TCD. Stroll up Grafton St., teeter to Camden St., stumble to South Great Georges St., and drag your soused self to Temple Bar. Be sure not to miss the following gems:

Mulligan's, 8 Poolbeg St., behind Burgh Quay off Tara St. Upholds its reputation as one of the best pint pourers in Dublin. The crowd consists mainly of middle-aged men. A taste of the typical Irish pub: low key and nothing fancy. Really.

The Stag's Head, 1 Dame Ct. Beautiful Victorian pub with stained glass, mirrors, and yes, a stag's head. The crowd dons everything from t-shirts to tuxes and spills out into the alleys. Truly excellent grub. Entrees around £5-7. Late bar Th-F until 12:30am.

The Globe, 11 South Great Georges St. Pretentious clientele? Maybe so, but it's a fine spot for relaxing with a Guinness or a frothy cappuccino. Meet the regular cast of amicable if somewhat freakish characters. Attached to the **Rí Rá** nightclub (see below).

The Porter House, 16-18 Parliament St. The largest selection of world beers in the country, and brews 8 different kinds of porter, stout, and ale. Late bar Th-F until 1:30am, Sa until midnight. Occasional trad, blues, and rock gigs.

The Palace, 21 Fleet St., behind Aston Quay. This classic neighborhood pub has old-fashioned wood paneling and close quarters; grab a comfy seat in the back room.

Messrs. Maguire, Burgh Quay. You'll find new worlds here, especially if you try the homemade microbrews. Try the spicy Weiss stout. Late bar W-Sa. Trad Su-Tu.

The Brazen Head, 20 North Bridge St., off Merchant's Quay. The city's oldest pub, established in 1198 as the first stop after the bridge on the way into the city. The courtyard is a pickup scene in summer. Nightly Irish music, weekend late bar until 12:30am.

KNOW YOUR WHISKEY Anyone who drinks whiskey as it's meant to be drunk—"neat," or straight—knows there's a huge difference between Irish whiskeys (Bushmills, Jameson, Power and Son, and the like), Scotch whiskys (spelled without an e), and American whiskeys. But what makes Irish whiskey *Irish?* The basic ingredients—water, barley (which becomes malt once processed), and heat—are the same; it's the quality of the ingredients, the way they're combined, and how the product is stored that give each product a distinct flavor. American whiskey is distilled once and stored in oak, scotch uses peat-smoked barley, and Irish whiskey is triple distilled. Individual distilleries will claim that their own variations make their product the best. The best way to understand the distinctions is to taste the various labels one after another—line up those shot glasses, sniff, and taste each one, having a sip of water between each brand. **"But I don't have the money to buy a shot of each brand,"** our readers whine. Well, get thee to a distillery tour and squeal, "Me! Me!" when the guide asks for volunteers. "Irish Whiskey Tasters" get to try no less than five Irish, two scotch, and one bourbon whiskey under the supervision of their highly trained guides.

CLUBLIN

The action typically starts after 11:30pm, when pubs close. Covers run £5-12, pints £3. To get home, take the **NiteLink bus** (1 per hour, Th-Sa 12:30-3:30am, £2.50), which runs from the corner of Westmoreland and College St. to the suburbs.

The Kitchen, The Clarence Hotel, Wellington Quay, Temple Bar. With 2 bars and a dance floor, this U2-owned club is the coolest spot in town. Often hard to get in with the VIPs there; dress to fit in with the rocker/model crowd. Cover £8-10; students £3-4 on Tu.

Rí-Rá, 1 Exchequer St., in the back of The Globe pub. Generally good music that steers clear of the pop and house extremes. Two floors, several bars, and more nooks and crannies than a crumpet. Open daily 11pm-2:30am. Cover £6-7.

PoD, 35 Harcourt St. Spanish-style decor meets hard-core dance music. As trendy as The Kitchen. The truly brave venture upstairs to **The Red Box,** a separate, more intense club. A warehouse atmosphere with brain-crushing music often spun by big name DJs. Cover £8-10; ladies free before midnight on Th; Th and Sa students £5.

Club M, Blooms Hotel, Anglesea St., Temple Bar. One of Dublin's largest clubs. Pseudo-cages occasionally host "exotic dancers" who inject naughtiness. Cover around £6.

EXCURSIONS FROM DUBLIN

HOWTH. The peninsula of Howth (rhymes with "both") dangles from the mainland in Edenesque isolation, less than 10 mi. from Dublin. A three-hour **cliff walk** rings the peninsula, passing heather and thousands of seabird nests. The best section is a hike (1hr.) between the harbor and the lighthouse. To get to the trailhead from town, turn left at the DART station and follow Harbour Rd. around the coast (20min.); or hike from the lighthouse. To reach the private **Howth Castle,** an awkwardly charming patchwork of styles, turn right as you exit the DART station and then left after a quarter-mile, at the entrance to the Deer Park Hotel. Farther up the hill, a path goes around the right side of the Deer Park Hotel to the fabulous **Rhododendron Gardens.** (Open 24hr. Free.) **Ireland's Eye island** once provided monks with religious sanctuary; now it's a bird haven. **Ireland's Eye Boat Trips** (☎831 42 00) jets passengers across the water from the east pier (15min.; every 30min. weather permitting; £5 return, students £3, children £2.50). To get to Howth, take a northbound DART **train** to the end (30min., 6 per hr., £1.15). Turn left out of the station to get to the **tourist office,** in the Old Courthouse on Harbour Rd. (Open May-Aug. M-F 11am-1pm and 1:30pm-5pm.) Snooze at **Gleann na Smól,** on the left at the end of Nashville Rd., off Thormanby Rd., which forks off upper Main St. and houses the main concentration of Howth's **B&Bs.** (☎832 29 36. Singles £25; doubles £38-42.) Bus #31B runs to **Hazelwood** and its comfy beds at the end of the cul-de-sac in the Thormanby Woods estate, 1 mi. up Thormanby Rd. (☎839 13 91. Singles £30; doubles £42.)

BOYNE VALLEY. Along the curves of the river between Slane and Drogheda lie 40 mind-boggling passage-tombs constructed by Neolithic people around the 4th millenium BC. The tombs, including **Newgrange, Dowth,** and **Knowth,** are archeological mysteries, although recent excavations are providing clues as to who exactly was entombed within their 80-ton rocks, carted over 40 mi. from the Wicklow mountains. Enter Newgrange through the **Brú na Bóinne Visitor Centre,** near Donore on the south side of the River Boyne, across from the tombs; prepare to wait. (☎ (041) 988 03 00. Open daily Mar.-Apr. 9:30am-5:30pm; May 9am-6:30pm; June to mid-Sept. 9am-7pm; late Sept. 9am-6:30pm; Oct. 9:30am-5:30pm; Nov.-Feb. 9:30am-5pm. Center and tour £3-7, students £1.25-3.25.) **Bus Éireann** shuttles to the Visitor Centre from Dublin (1½hr., round trip £10). The **Hill of Tara** was Ireland's spiritual and political center until the arrival of Christianity in the 4th century BC. Take any local bus to Navan and ask the driver to let you off at the road 1km from the site (45min., 37 per day, £6). Mel Gibson filmed scenes for *Braveheart* in the town of Trim at **Trim Castle,** built in 1172. You can take the tour, but you'll never take his freedom. (Open daily May-Oct. 10am-6pm. 35-45min. obligatory guided tours of the keep every 45min., limited to 15 people. No tour required to wander the grounds. Tour and grounds £2.50, students £1; grounds only £1, 40p.) **Bus Éireann** stops on Castle St. in front of the castle en route to **Dublin** (1½hr.; M-Sa 8 per day, Su 3 per day; £5). The **tourist office** is on Mill St. (☎ (046) 371 11. Open daily 10am-1pm and 2-5pm.)

SOUTHEAST IRELAND

Historically the power base of the Vikings and then the Normans, the influence of the Celts is faintest in southeast Ireland. While the nightlife rages south from Dublin through Kilkenny and Waterford, the daylight hours are most enjoyably spent exploring the beaches between Rosslare Harbour and Waterford, or traversing the scenic paths through Glendalough and the Wicklow Mountains.

FERRIES TO FRANCE AND BRITAIN

Irish Ferries sails from Rosslare Harbour to: Pembroke, Wales (4hr.); Roscoff, France (14½hr.); and Cherbourg, France (17½hr.). Ferries depart daily for Wales and every other day to France. For 24-hour information, dial ☎ 661 07 15 or call the desk at Rosslare Harbour. (☎ 331 58; fax 335 44; www.irishferries.com. To England Jan.-May and Oct.-Dec. £16; July-Aug. £20. Fares to France vary by season and by ship. Roughly £40 in winter; July-Aug. £80, students £66. Eurail passes earn a 50% discount on ferries to France.) **Stena Line** runs from Rosslare to Fishguard, Wales. (☎ 053 339 97. May-Sept. 3-4 per day. Adults from £29, students with ISIC from £23.)

THE WICKLOW MOUNTAINS. Over 2000 ft. high, covered by heather, and pleated by rivers, the Wicklow summits are home to grazing sheep and a few villagers. Smooth glacial valleys embrace the two lakes and the monastic ruins. The lush valley of **Glendalough** draws a summertime stream of coach tours filled with hikers and ruin-oglers. Admission, at the Visitor Centre, covers an exhibition, an audiovisual show, and a tour of the ruins. (☎ 453 24. Open daily June-Aug. 9am-6:30pm; Sept. to mid-Oct. 9:30am-6pm; mid-Oct. to mid-Mar. 9:30am-5pm; mid-Mar. to May 9:30am-6:30pm. Tours every 30min. £2, students and children £1.) The ruins themselves are free and always open. **St. Kevin's Bus Service** (☎ (01) 281 81 19) runs from Dublin's St. Stephen's Green West (2 per day; £6, round-trip £10) and returns from the glen in the evening (2-3 per day). The **tourist office** is across from the Glendalough Hotel. (☎ 456 88. Open mid-June to Sept. Tu 11am-1pm and 2-6pm, W-Su 10am-1pm and 2-6pm.) The **National Park Information Office,** between the two lakes, is the best source for hiking advice. (☎ 454 25. Open May-Aug. daily 10am-6pm; Apr. and Sept. Sa-Su 10am-6pm.) The **Glendaloch Hostel (An Óige/HI)** is five minutes past the Glendalough tourist office. (☎ 453 42. Laundry. Internet. Bike rental. Dorms £9-11; doubles £28-30.) For more affordable prices head to **Laragh** (LAR-a), 1 mi. up the road (10min.

from the Wicklow Way). Laragh has tons of **B&Bs,** as well as the **Wicklow Way Hostel.** (☎ (0404) 453 98. Dorms £7.) ☎**0404.**

ROSSLARE HARBOUR. Rosslare offers little charm, but it's an important link to Wales, France, and the Irish coast. **Trains** run from the ferry port to Limerick (2½hr., 1-2 per day, £12.50) via Waterford (1¼hr., £6) and Dublin (3hr., 3 per day, £11). **Buses** run twice per day via Waterford (£9.20) to: Galway (£17); Killarney (£16); and Tralee (£17); as well as to Cork (M-Sa 4 per day, £13.50); Limerick (2-3 per day, £13.50); and Dublin (3hr., 7-10 per day, £10). The Rosslare-Kilrane **tourist office** is 1 mi. from the harbor on Kilrane's Wexford Rd. (☎336 22. Open daily 10:30am-8pm.) To get to the **Rosslare Harbour Youth Hostel (HI),** on Goulding St., turn right at the top of the cliff, head left at the far corner of the Hotel Rosslare, and pass the **SuperValu supermarket** (open M-F 8am-7pm, Sa 8am-6pm, Su 9am-1pm) on the left. (☎333 99. Members only; buy a card for £1. Dorms £8; quads £36-40.) ☎**053.**

KILKENNY. Ireland's best-preserved medieval town, Kilkenny's 80 pubs and nine churches evoke a bygone era. Thirteenth-century **Kilkenny Castle,** restored to its former opulence, housed the Earls of Ormonde from the 1300s until 1935. (Open June-Sept. daily 9am-7pm; Apr.-May daily 10:30am-5:30pm; Oct.-Mar. Tu-Sa 10:30am-12:45pm and 2-5pm, Su 11am-12:45pm and 2-5pm. Mandatory tour £3.50, students £1.50.) **Tynan Walking Tours** provides the down-and-dirty on Kilkenny's folkloric tradition in an hour. (☎659 29. £3, students £2.50.) Climb the thin, 100-foot tower of **St. Canice's Cathedral,** up the hill off Dean St., for a panoramic view of the town. (Open Easter-Sept. M-Sa 9am-1pm and 2-6pm, Su 2-6pm; Oct.-Easter M-Sa 10am-1pm and 2-6pm, Su 2-6pm.) **Trains** (☎220 24) and **buses** (☎649 33) stop at Kilkenny MacDonagh Station on Dublin Rd.; buses also stop on Patrick St. in the city center. Trains go to Dublin (2hr., £11) and Waterford (45min., £5). Buses go to Cork (3hr., 2-3 per day, £10); Dublin (2hr., 5-6 per day, £7); Galway (5hr., 3-5 per day, £12); Rosslare Harbour (2hr., 3-6 per day, £10.50); and Waterford (1½hr., 1-2 per day, £5). From MacDonagh Station, turn left on John St. to reach The Parade, dominated by the castle on the left. The **tourist office,** Rose Inn St., has info on **B&Bs.** (☎515 00; fax 639 55. Open July-Aug. M-Sa 9am-8pm, Su 11am-1pm and 2-5pm; May-June and Sept. M-Sa 9am-6pm, Su 11am-1pm and 2-5pm; Apr. M-Sa 9am-6pm; Oct.-Mar. M-Sa 9am-5pm.) Check **email** at **Web Talk,** Rose Inn St., by the tourist office. (£1 per 10min.; £5 per hr. Open M-Sa 10am-9pm, Su 2am-8pm.) **Kilkenny Tourist Hostel (IHH),** 35 Parliament St., buzzes with activity. (☎635 41; email kilkennyhostel@tiniet.ie. Laundry £3. Dorms £8; doubles £21. Oct.-Apr. £1 less.) Buy **groceries** at **Dunnes Supermarket,** on Kieran St. (Open M-Tu and Sa 8:30am-7pm, W-F 8:30am-10pm, Su 10am-6pm.) **The Pump House,** 26 Parliament St., is a local fave (trad M-Th). ☎**056.**

WATERFORD. Behind an industrial facade of metal silos and cranes lie winding, narrow streets with pubs and shops. The town highlight is the **Waterford Crystal Factory,** 2 mi. away on the N25 (Cork Rd.). One-hour tours (every 15min.) show the transformation of molten goo into polished crystal. Catch bus #1 (dir. Kilbarry-Ballybeg; 2 per hr., £0.75) across from the Clock Tower. (☎37 33 11. Showroom open daily Apr.-Oct. 8:30am-6pm; Nov.-Mar. 9am-5pm; Jan.-Feb. 9am-5pm. Tours £3.50, students £2.) **The Crystal City Explorer** stops at the factory as well as the two other big sites: the **Waterford Treasures Museum** and the **Reginald Tower,** which has guarded the city since the 12th century. (☎38 22 09. £9.50 covers admission to all three.)

Trains (☎31 78 89) depart across the bridge, from the Quay; the **bus** (☎87 90 00) station is on the Quay across from the tourist office. **Trains** chug to: Kilkenny (40min., 3-5 per day, £5); Limerick (2¼hr., M-Sa 2 per day, £10); Dublin (2½hr., 3-5 per day, £12-15); and Rosslare Harbour (1hr., M-Sa 2 per day, £6.) **Buses** depart for: Kilkenny (1hr., 1-2 per day, £5); Limerick (2½hr., 4-5 per day, £10.50); Cork (2½hr., 5-8 per day, £10); Rosslare Harbour (1¼hr., 3-4 per day, £9.20); Galway (4¾hr., 5-8 per day, £13.50); and Dublin (2¾hr., 4-7 per day, £7). The **tourist office,** in The Granary at the intersection of the Quay and Hanover St., has maps. (☎87 58 23. Open Apr.-Oct. M-Sa 9am-6pm, July-Aug. also Su 11am-5pm; Nov.-Mar. M-Sa 9am-5pm.) Check **email** at **Voyager Internet Cafe,** in a mall at the intersection of Parnell and John

St. (Open M-Sa 11am-9pm, Su 3-9pm. £1.50 per 15min.) Spacious quarters await at **Barnacle's Viking House (IHH),** Coffee House Ln., Greyfriars, the Quay. Follow the Quay past the Clock Tower and post office. (☎85 38 27. Breakfast included. Dorms £7.50-8.50; doubles £13.50-15.50.) Get **groceries** at **Dunnes Store,** in the City Square Mall. (Open M-W 9am-7pm, Th-F 9am-9pm, Sa 9am-6pm, and Su noon-6pm.) **Pubs** cluster on the Quays, and John and Parnell St. **☎051.**

CASHEL. Cashel sprawls at the foot of the commanding 300-ft. **Rock of Cashel** (a.k.a. **St. Patrick's Rock**), a huge limestone outcropping topped by medieval buildings. (Open daily mid-June to mid-Sept. 9am-7:30pm; mid-Sept. to mid-Mar. 9:30am-4:30pm; mid-Mar. to mid.-June 9:30am-5:30pm. £3.50, students £1.50.) The two-towered **Cormac's Chapel,** consecrated in 1134, holds semi-restored Romanesque paintings. Down the cow path from the Rock lie the arch-filled ruins of **Hore Abbey,** built by Cistercian monks; the abbey is currently inhabited by sheep. **Bus Éireann** (☎621 21) leaves from Bianconi's Bistro, on Main St., for: Limerick (1hr., 4 per day, £8.80); Cork (1½hr., 3 per day, £8); and Dublin (3hr., 3 per day, £9). The **tourist office** is in the City Hall on Main St. (☎613 33. Open July-Aug. M-Sa 9:15am-6pm, Su 11am-5pm; Apr.-June and Sept. M-Sa 9:15am-6pm.) A few hundred yards from the ruins of Hore Abbey down Dundrum Rd. lies the stunning **O'Brien's Farmhouse Hostel.** (☎610 03. Laundry. Dorms £9-10; doubles £30; **camping** £4.50-5.) **Cashel Holiday Hostel (IHH),** 6 John St., is just off Main St. (☎623 30. Laundry. Internet. Dorms £8.50-10; private rooms £14-24.) **Centra Supermarket** is on Friar St. (Open daily 7am-11pm.) The *craic* is nightly at **Feehan's,** on Main St. **☎062.**

SOUTHWEST IRELAND

An astonishing landscape, from ocean-battered cliffs to mystic stretches of lakes and mountains, is matched by a momentous history. Outlaws and rebels once lurked in its hidden coves and glens. To escape the tourist mayhem, retreat to the quieter stretches along the Dingle Peninsula and Cork's southern coast.

FERRIES TO FRANCE AND BRITAIN

Cork-Swansea Ferries sails between Cork and Swansea, South Wales (10hr., 1 per day, £24-34, with car £95-189). Contact them at 52 South Mall, Cork (☎ (021) 427 11 66; fax 27 50 61; email scs.iol.ie) or in England (☎ (0044) 12 54 69 28 99). **Brittany Ferries** (brittany-ferries.com) sails from Cork to Roscoff, France (14hr.).

CORK CITY ☎021

Cork (pop. 150,000), Ireland's second-largest city, serves as the center of the southwest's sport, music, and arts scenes. Despite a tumultuous history, Cork has regularly rebuilt itself, and today a stroll along its pub-lined streets reveals grand architecture juxtaposed with many new commercial and industrial developments. Use Cork as a place to eat, drink, shop, and sleep while exploring the exquisite scenery of the surrounding countryside.

PRACTICAL INFO, ACCOMMODATIONS, AND FOOD. Trains leave from Kent Station, Lower Glanmire Rd. (☎450 67 66), across the river for Limerick (1½hr., £14); Killarney (2hr., £14); and Dublin (3hr., £33.50). **Buses** depart from Parnell Pl. (☎450 81 88), along Merchants' Quay, to Rosslare Harbor (4hr., £13.50); Dublin (4½hr., £13); and Belfast (7½hr., £20). **Brittany Ferries** (☎427 78 01) arranges **ferry** service to Roscoff, France from Ringaskiddy Terminal (☎427 50 61), eight miles south of the city (bus available every 30min., £3). **Cork-Swansea Ferries** connects to England daily (☎427 11 66; UK☎ (0044) 12 54 69 28 99). Pick up a map and sights guide (£1.50) at **Tourist House,** Grand Parade. (☎ 427 32 51. Open July-Aug. M-Sa 9:15am-5:30pm) Bring £1 coins for a 10-minute **Internet** surf at **The Favourite,** 122 Patrick St. (open daily 9am-10:30pm).

Sheila's Budget Accommodation Centre (IHH), 4 Belgrave Pl., by the intersection of Wellington Rd. and York St., lures visitors with a huge kitchen and a sauna. (☎450 55 62. Dorms £7-8.50; doubles from £21. Breakfast £1.50. Sheets 50p. **Internet** £2 per 20min. Reception 24hr.) **Cork City International Hostel, An Oige (HI)** is in a stately Victorian house at 1-2 Redclyffe, Western Rd. Take bus #8, which stops across the street, or walk 15 minutes from Grand Parade. (☎454 32 89. Dorms £8-14.50; doubles with bath £12.50. Breakfast £2. Reception 8am-midnight.) Prepare to be pampered at the B&B **Garnish House,** Western Rd. (☎427 51 11. Singles from £25; doubles from £40. Breakfast included. Free laundry. Restaurants and cafes cluster near the city center, especially between **Patrick St., Paul St.,** and **Oliver Plunkett St.** The biggest grocery store in town is **Tesco Supermarket** on Paul St. (open M-W and Sa 8:30am-8pm, Th-F 8:30am-10pm). The burgers, pizza, and grilled chicken at **Scoozi,** in the alley just off Winthrop Ave., will drive you wild. (Open M-Sa 9am-11pm, Su noon-10pm.) Scrumptious vegetarian delights await at the **Quay Co-op,** 24 Sullivan's Quay. (Restaurant open M-Sa 9am-9pm; store open 9am-6:15pm.)

SIGHTS AND ENTERTAINMENT. Downtown Cork is located on the tip of an arrow-shaped island in the River Lee; bridges link the island to Cork's residential south side and less affluent north side. Across the river to the north, walk up Shandon St. and take a right down unmarked Church St. to reach Cork's most famous landmark, **St. Ann's Church.** The church earned the nickname of "the four-faced liar" because the four tower clocks are notoriously out of sync with one another. (☎450 59 06. Open M-Sa 9:30am-5:30pm. £5, students and seniors £4.) Do not pass go before heading to the **Cork City Gaol,** where multimedia tours of the former prison and a walk through Cork's social history await; cross the bridge at the western end of Fitzgerald Park, turn right on Sunday's Well Rd., and follow the signs. (☎430 50 22. Open daily Mar.-Oct. 9:30am-6pm; Nov.-Feb. 10am-5pm. £4.50, students £3. Admission includes audio-tape tour.) After visiting the jail, taste liberty by wandering the grounds of the nearby **University College Cork,** on the riverbank along Western Rd. Three festivals come to Cork every October. The **Guiness Cork Jazz Festival** brings three days of free performances by big-name musicians (☎427 89 79). Book well ahead at hostels. Also popular are the week-long **International Film Festival** and **The Irish Gay and Lesbian Film Festival.**

Cork proudly produces both **Murphy's** and **Beamish,** which you can enjoy in the myriad of pubs along **Oliver Plunkett St., Union Quay,** and **South Main St.** A traditional pub is **An Spailpín Fánac,** at 28 South Main St. **The Lobby,** 1 Union Quay, arguably the most famous venue in Cork, gave some of Ireland's biggest folk acts their big breaks; it features live music nightly. (☎431 93 07. Occasional cover £3-5.) **The Western Star,** Western Rd. (a 25min. walk from the town center), lures a huge student crowd with its outdoor patio and free Friday and Saturday barbecues. **Gallaghers,** MacCurtain St., holds backpacker nights on Mondays and Tuesdays (3-pint pitchers £6). **Loafer's,** 26 Douglas St., is Cork's sole gay and lesbian pub (☎431 16 12). When the pubs close, the spotlight shifts to Cork's nightclubs. **Gorbys,** Oliver Plunkett St., features young groovers grinding. (Open W-Sa. Cover £2-5.) **Sir Henry's,** South Main St., packs three floors with sweaty bodies. (Open W-Sa. Cover £2-11.)

EXCURSION FROM CORK CITY: BLARNEY. Busloads of tourists eager for quintessential Irish scenery and a cold kiss head northwest of Cork to see **Blarney Castle** and its legendary **Blarney Stone,** which confers the gift of gab upon those who manage to smooch it while leaning over backwards. While crowds awaiting this opportunity clog the dank passageways, the top of the castle provides an airy and stunning view of the countryside. Try to come early in the morning. (☎438 52 52. Open June-Aug. 9am-7pm, Su 9:30am-5:30pm; Sept. M-Sa 9am-6:30pm, Su 9:30am-sundown; Oct.-Apr. M-Sa 9am-6pm, Su 9:30am-sundown; May M-Sa 9am-6:30pm, Su 9:30am-5:30pm. Last admission 30min. before closing. £3.50, seniors and students £2.50, children £1.) **Bus Éireann** runs buses from Cork (10-16 per day, return £2.50).

KINSALE. Affluent tourists come to swim, fish, and eat at Kinsale's famed and pricey 12 restaurants known as the "Good Food Circle." The attractions are cheaper. The star-shaped, 17th-century **Charles Fort** overlooks the town; follow the coastal **Scilly Walk** (30min.) from the end of Pearse St. (Open daily mid-June to mid-Sept. 9am-6pm; mid-Apr. to mid-June and mid-Sept. to mid-Oct. M-Sa 9am-5pm, Su 9:30am-5:30pm. £2, students £1.) Across the harbor, the grass-covered ruins of **James Fort** delight with panoramic views. (Open 24hr. Free.) The **Kinsale Regatta** is always a success. Marking the 500th anniversary of the battle of Kinsale, the 2001 **Kinsale Gourmet Festival** is celebrating with a Spanish theme this October. **Buses** arrive from **Cork** at the Esso station on the pier (40min., 3-10 per day, round-trip £3.80). The **tourist office,** Emmet Pl., is on the waterfront. (☎77 22 34. Open daily Mar.-Nov. 9am-6pm.) To get to the **Castlepark Marina Centre (IHH),** walk along the pier away from town for 10 minutes, turn left across Duggan Bridge, take a left past the bridge, and follow the road toward the harbor. (☎77 49 59. Open mid-Mar. to Dec. Dorms £8-9; doubles £10.) **Dempsey's Hostel (IHH)** is on Cork Rd. (☎77 21 24. Dorms £6; doubles £8.) **☎021.**

SCHULL AND THE MIZEN HEAD PENINSULA. The seaside hamlet of **Schull** is ideal for exploring Ireland's craggy, windswept, and beach-laden southwest tip. It's also a jumping-off point to the striking island of **Cape Clear.** (Ferry ☎391 35. June-Sept. 1-3 ferries per day, round-trip £9.) A calm harbor and numerous shipwrecks make **diving** ideal; the **Watersports Centre** rents gear. (☎285 54. Open M-Sa 9:30am-8:30pm.) Pick up the excellent *Schull Guide* from any store in town (£1.50). The immaculate **Schull Backpackers' Lodge (IHH),** Colla Rd., has **hiking** and **biking** maps and info. (☎286 81. Dorms £8; doubles £24-26; quads £32.) **Spar Market** is on Main St. (Open daily July-Sept. 7am-9pm; Oct.-June M-Sa 7am-8pm, Su 8am-8pm.) **Buses** arrive from Cork (1-2 per day, £13 round-trip) and Goleen (1-2 per day). Ireland ends at spectacular Mizen Head, whose cliffs rise to 700 ft. **Mizen Vision** has a small viewing platform on the southwesterly point of Ireland. **Betty's Bus Hire** offers tours of the Mizen via the scenic coast road. (☎284 10. £5. Call for hours.) Those who choose to accept the risks of **hitchhiking** often avoid poor public transport by waiting at the crossroads on Goleen Rd. outside of town. Confident **cyclists** can daytrip to Mizen Head (18 mi. from Schull). **☎028.**

KILLARNEY AND KILLARNEY NATIONAL PARK ☎064

The town of Killarney is just minutes from some of Ireland's most glorious natural scenery. The 37 sq. mi. **national park** outside town blends forested mountains with the famous Lakes of Killarney. **Muckross House,** 3 mi. south of Killarney on Kenmare Rd., is a massive 19th-century manor with a garden that blooms brilliantly each year. A path leads to the 60-foot **Torc Waterfall.** (House open daily July-Aug. 9am-7pm; Sept.-June 9am-6pm. £3.80, students £1.60.) Walk or drive to the 14th-century **Ross Castle** by taking a right on Ross Rd. off Muckross Rd., 2 mi. from Killarney; the numerous footpaths from Knockreer (out of town on New St.) are more scenic. (Open daily June-Aug. 9am-6:30pm; May-Sept. 10am-6pm; mid-Mar. to Apr. and Oct. 9am-5pm. Obligatory tour £3, students £1.25.) Bike around the **Gap of Dunlow,** which borders **Macgillycuddy's Reeks,** Ireland's highest mountain range. Hop on a **boat** from Ross Castle to the head of the Gap (£7; book at the tourist office). Head left over the stone bridge from Lord Brandon's Cottage, continue 2 mi. to the church, follow the hairpin turn, and huff the 1½ mi. to the top; your reward is a 7-mile coast downhill through the park's most breathtaking scenery. The 8-mile ride to Killarney (bear right after Kate Kearney's Cottage, turn left on the road to Fossa, and turn right on Killorglin Rd.) passes the ruins of **Dunloe Castle,** demolished by Cromwell's armies.

Trains arrive at the station (☎310 67) off East Avenue Rd., near Park Rd., from: Cork (2hr., 5 per day, roundtrip £9.50); Limerick (3hr., 3-4 per day, £15); and Dublin (3½hr., 4 per day, £33.50). **Buses** (☎300 11) rumble from Park Rd. to Cork (2hr., 3-7 per day, £9.40). **Bike rental** places abound. The **tourist office** is on Beech St., off New St. (☎316 33. Open July-Aug. M-Sa 9am-8pm, Su 10am-1pm and 2:15-6pm; June and Sept. M-Sa 9am-6pm, Su 10am-1pm and 2:15-6pm; Oct.-May M-Sa 9:15am-5:30pm.)

From either station, turn left on College St. and take a right past the courthouse to reach **The Súgán (IHH),** Lewis Rd., where exuberant management compensates for cramped quarters. (☎331 04. £9.) The immense **Neptune's (IHH),** Bishop's Ln., is up the first walkway off New St. on the right. (☎352 55. Dorms £7.50-9.50; doubles £20.) Call for a ride from either station to the **Aghadoe Hostel (An Óige/HI),** on Killorglin Rd. (☎312 40. Dorms £7.50-9.50; singles £10-12.) Pick up **groceries** at **Tesco,** in an arcade off New St. (Open M-W and Sa 8am-8pm, Th-F 8am-10pm, Su 10am-6pm.) **O'Conner's Traditional Pub,** 7 High St., mixes locals and tourists (trad M and Th).

RING OF KERRY

The Southwest's most beloved peninsula holds wee villages, ancient forts, and rugged mountains. Rewards await those who explore the landscape on foot or by bike.

GETTING THERE AND GETTING AROUND. The "Ring of Kerry" usually describes the entire **Iveragh Peninsula,** but it technically refers to the roads circumnavigating it. Prepackaged bus tours from **Killarney** stop in **Killorglin, Glenbeigh, Kells, Cahersiveen, Waterville, Caherdaniel, Sneem,** and **Moll's Gap** (£8 through a hostel; students £12 with 1-night stopover). Freer souls hop on the circuit run by **Bus Éireann,** which stops at the Ring's major towns (June-Sept. 2 per day): **Killorglin; Cahersiveen** (from Killorglin 50min., £5); **Waterville; Caherdaniel** (from Cahersiveen 1½hr., £3.10); **Sneem;** and **Killarney** (from Caherdaniel 1½hr., £7.30; from Cahersiveen 2½hr., £9).

CAHERSIVEEN. Cahersiveen (CARS-veen) is known as the birthplace of patriot Daniel "The Liberator" O'Connell, who won Catholic representation in Parliament in 1829. Two miles northwest of town across the bridge are the ruins of the **Ballycarbery Castle,** once held by O'Connell's ancestors. Past the castle turn-off, you can walk along the 10-foot-thick walls of **Cahergall Fort** or visit the small stone dwellings of **Leacanabuaile Fort. Cuas Crom Beach** and **White Strand Beach** are popular nearby swimming areas. The **Celtic Music Weekend** features free concerts in early August. The **tourist office** is in a former barracks on the road to the castle. (☎947 25 89. Open May to mid-Sept. M-F 10am-1pm and 2:15-6pm.) The welcoming **Sive Hostel (IHH)** is at 15 East End, Main St. (☎947 27 17. Dorms £8; doubles £20-25; camping £5 per person.) Equally fabulous is **Mortimer's Hostel,** Main St. (☎947 23 38. Dorms £7.) The town's 30 pubs may seem like a lot, but residents remember when there were 52.

Take a daytrip to quiet **Valentia Island,** where shady country roads link a handful of beehive huts, *ogham* stones, and small ruins. The views in between, across to the mountainous mainland, and over Dingle Bay, are reason enough to come to Ireland. You can **bike** to the island, connected by bridges on either end to the mainland, or take a short **ferry** (every 10min. 8:15am-7:30pm; cyclists £3, pedestrians £1.50.) from **Reenard Point,** 3 mi. west of Cahersiveen; a taxi to the ferry dock from Cahersiveen runs £4. Don't miss the **Skellig Rocks,** a stunning mass of rubble about 8 mi. off the shore of the Iveragh Peninsula. From your boat, **Little Skellig** will appear snow-capped, but it's actually covered with 22,000 crooning birds. Climb the vertigo-inducing 650 steps past puffins, kittiwakes, gannets, and petrels (a.k.a. birds) to reach a **monastery** built by 6th-century monks, whose beehive-like dwellings are still intact. Cahersiveen hostels and campground will arrange the stomach-churning **ferry** ride (45min.-1½hr.) for £20, including a ride to the dock. **☎066.**

CAHERDANIEL. There's little in the village of **Caherdaniel** to attract the Ring's droves of buses, but nearby **Derrynane Strand,** 1½ mi. away in Derrynane National Park, delights with 2 mi. of gorgeous beach ringed by picture perfect dunes. **Derrynane House,** signposted just up from the beach, was the cherished residence of Irish patriot Daniel O'Connell (see above). Trails lead from the house to gardens. (Open May-Sept. M-Sa 9am-6pm, Su 11am-7pm; Apr. and Oct. Tu-Su 1-5pm; Nov.-Mar. Sa-Su 1-5pm. £2, students £1.) Guests have the run of the house at **The Travellers' Rest Hostel.** (☎947 51 75. Breakfast £3. Dorms £8.50; doubles £20.) **☎066.**

DINGLE PENINSULA ☎066

For decades the Ring of Kerry's undertouristed counterpart, the gorgeous Dingle Peninsula, with spectacular cliffs and sweeping beaches, has remained more congested with ancient sites than tour buses. A *gaeltacht* to the west of Dingle Town preserves centuries-old Irish heritage preserved by generations of storytellers.

GETTING THERE AND GETTING AROUND. The best base for exploring the peninsula, which lies across the Dingle Bay from the Ring of Kerry to the south, is **Dingle Town,** easily reached from Tralee (1¼hr., 3-6 per day, £5.90). From **Dingle Town, Bus Éireann** runs west to **Ballydavid** (Tu and F 3 per day, round-trip £3.15) as well as **Dunquin** and **Ballyferriter** (in summer 2-4 per day, £2.30). In summer, buses also tour the south of the peninsula from Dingle (June-Sept. M-Sa 2 per day). A prepackaged **Dingle/Slea Head** tour runs from **Killarney** (M-Sa 2 per day, £12). There is no direct service to villages north of Dingle Town. Get detailed bus info from the Tralee station (☎712 35 66).

DINGLE TOWN. After scouring the peninsula for vistas and *ogham* stones, return to lively Dingle Town, adopted home of **Fungi the Dolphin** (a major focus of the tourist industry). **Sciúird Archaeology** tours (☎915 16 06) take you from the pier on a whirlwind bus tour of the area's ancient spots (3hr., 2 per day, £8; book ahead). **Morans** (☎915 11 55) runs great tours to Slea Head that stop by historical sites, film sets, and majestic views (£8; pickup at the Strand St. Esso). The **tourist office** is on Strand St. (☎915 11 88. Open June-Aug. M-Sa 9am-6pm, Su 10am-6pm; Sept.-Oct. and mid-Mar. to May M-Sa 9am-5pm.) **Ballintaggart Hostel (IHH),** 25 minutes east on Tralee Rd. in a stone mansion, is supposedly haunted by the wife of the Earl of Cork, who was strangled here. (☎915 14 54. Shuttle to town free. Dorms £8-10; doubles £30; off-season £1-2 less. **Camping** £4.) The laid-back **Grapevine Hostel** is on Dykegate St., off Main St., a short stagger from the town's pubs. (☎915 14 34. £8.50-10.50.) The pub **An Droichead Beag,** Lower Main St., has the best *trad* around. From Dingle Town, a winding cliff-side road runs north by way of the 1500 ft. **Connor Pass.** As the road twists downhill, a waterfall marks the base of **Pedlars Lake.**

SLEA HEAD AND DUNQUIN. Glorious Slea Head impresses with its jagged cliffs and crashing waves. Green hills, interrupted by rough stone walls and occasional sheep, suddenly break off into the foam-flecked sea. The best way to see the area in a day or less is to bike along **Slea Head Drive.** Past Dingle Town toward Slea Head sits the village of **Ventry** (Ceann Trá), home to a sandy beach and the huge beds of the **Ballybeag Hostel;** a regular shuttle runs to Dingle Town. (☎915 98 76; email balybeag@iol.ie. **Bike rental.** Laundry. £7.50-9.) The **Celtic and Prehistoric Museum,** down the road, houses an astounding collection. (☎915 99 41. Open Apr.-Oct. daily 10am-5pm, other times call ahead. £3, children £2.) North of Slea Head, the scattered settlement of **Dunquin** (Dún Chaoin) boasts **Kruger's,** purportedly Europe's westernmost pub. (☎915 61 27. Entrees around £6-8.) Its adjacent **B&B** has comfortable rooms (£17). On the road to Ballyferriter, the **Blasket Centre** has outstanding exhibits about the isolated Blasket Islands. (Open daily July-Aug. 10am-7pm; Easter-June and Sept.-Nov. 10am-6pm. £2.50, students £1.)

TRALEE. Residents proudly identify Tralee (pop. 20,000) as County Kerry's economic center and home to famed gardens. Ireland's second-largest museum, **Kerry the Kingdom,** Ashe Memorial Hall, Denny St., covers Irish history from 8000 BC to present. (Open daily Mar.-Oct. 10am-6pm; Nov.-Dec. noon-4:30pm. £5.50, students £4.75.) In late August, the renowned **Rose of Tralee Festival** brings a maelstrom of entertainment to town as lovely lasses compete for the "Rose of Tralee" title. **Trains** go to: Killarney (40min., 4-5 per day, £5.50); Cork (2½hr., 3-5 per day, £17); and Galway (3 per day, £33.50). **Buses** run to: Killarney (40min., 5-14 per day, £4.40); Limerick (2¼hr., 7 per day, £9); Cork (2½hr., 3-6 per day, £9.70); and Galway (4-6 per day, £13). To get to the **tourist office,** Ashe Memorial Hall, from either station, head into town on Edward St., turn right on Castle St. and left on Denny St. (☎712 12 88. Open

July-Aug. M-Sa 9am-7pm, Su 9am-6pm; May-June and Oct. M-Sa 9am-6pm; Oct.-Apr. M-F 9am-5pm.) Rooms in the well located **Courthouse Lodge (IHH),** 5 Church St., have toilets, showers, and sinks. (☎712 71 99. Dorms £9; singles £17, doubles £24.) Call for pick-up to the magnificent **Collis-Sandes House (IHH).** (☎712 86 58. Dorms £7.50-8.50; singles £15; doubles £23-25; triples £30-33; **camping** £4.) **☎066.**

WESTERN IRELAND

Even Dubliners will admit that the west is the "most Irish" part of Ireland. Hit hardest by the 19th-century potato famine, this land is miserable for farming, but it's a boon for hikers and bikers who enjoy the isolation of mountainous landscapes.

LIMERICK CITY. Despite a thriving trade in off-color poems, hard times in the 20th century spawned poverty. Industrial developments gave the city, with its 18th-century Georgian streets and parks, a dull and urban feel. But today it's thriving again. To reach the castle featured in *Monty Python and the Holy Grail*, **King John's Castle,** on Nicholas St., cross the Abbey River and turn left after St. Mary's Cathedral. (Open daily Mar.-Dec. 9:30am-6pm. £4.20, students £3.30.) **Trains** (☎31 55 55) leave Parnell St. for: Dublin (2hr., 9-10 per day, £27); Waterford (2hr., M-Sa 1-2, £13.50); and Cork (2½hr., 5-6 per day, £14). **Buses** (☎31 33 33) leave the train station for Cork (2hr., 14 per day, £9); Galway (2hr., 14 per day, £9); Tralee (2hr., 10 per day, £9); Waterford (2½hr., 6-7 per day, £9.70); and Dublin (3hr., 13 per day, £10). The **tourist office** is in the glass building on Arthurs Quay. From the station, walk down Davis St., right on O'Connell St., and left just before Arthurs Quay Mall. (☎31 75 22. Open July-Aug. M-F 9am-7pm, Sa-Su 9am-6pm; May-June and Sept.-Oct. M-Sa 9:30am-5:30pm; Nov.-Apr. M-F 9:30am-5:30pm, Sa 9:30am-1pm.) Snooze at **An Óige Hostel (HI),** 1 Pery Sq. (☎31 46 72. Dorms £6.50-7.50, non-members £7.50-8.50.) **Barrington Hostel (IHH),** George's Quay, offers a resplendent garden. (☎41 52 22. Laundry. Dorms £7.50; singles £11; doubles £15.) Get **groceries** at **Tesco** in Arthurs Quay Mall. (Open M-W and Sa 8:30am-8pm, Th-F 8:30am-10pm, Su noon-6pm.) **☎061.**

CLARE COAST. The Clare coast contains Europe's highest cliffs and strangest landscapes. **Ennis** is the main rail hub in the region. **Bus Éireann** (☎682 41 77) runs south-north from Kilkee to Galway; a **West Clare** line goes south-north from Kilkee to Milltown Malbay and Doolin. **Kilkee** features the spectacular **Westend Cliff Walk** and a famously fun pub crawl. The **Kilkee Hostel (HI),** among the pubs on O'Curry St., makes friends of strangers. (☎562 09. Sheets £0.50. Laundry £2. Dorms £8.) Just 20 mi. north of Kilkee and 2 mi. inland from Spanish Point beach is **Milltown Malbay,** the best place for Irish music. During **Willie Week** in early July, musicians and *craic* addicts converge for a week of nonstop sessions. For other accommodation options, try the **Station House** at the old railway station, which has huge beds. (☎840 08. Singles £20; doubles £35.) Just north of Milltown, the tiny seaside resort of **Lahinch,** also known as Ireland's surfing capital, sits on smooth sand in a crook of the bay. The comfortable **Lahinch Hostel,** on Church St., has a central, waterfront location. (☎708 10 40. Laundry £2. Bikes £7 per day. Call ahead in summer. Dorms £8-9; doubles £24.) The **Surf Shop,** along the promenade, rents foam surfboards and wet-suits. (☎708 15 43. Per hr., boards £3, wet suits £3, and boots £1. Open daily in summer 11am-6pm.) A 20-minute bus ride continues around the coast to the extraordinary **Cliffs of Moher,** justifiably one of Ireland's most famous sights. Standing 700 ft. above the Atlantic spray, peer below onto gulls circling limestone spires. Eight miles north up the coast, **Doolin** (pop. 200) is a rural backpackers' mecca. Its lower village is only a handful of buildings near the sea while the tiny upper village is a mile up the road. Doolin's three legendary pubs—**McDermott's** and **McGann's** in Upper Village and **O'Connor's** in the Lower— have fantastic trad sessions and tasty food. By the river between the two villages is the **Aille River Hostel (HI),** a small cottage with a groovy ambience. (☎707 42 60. Open mid-Mar. to mid-Nov. July-Aug. £7.50-8; Sept.-May £7.50. **Camping** £4.) Doolin is an easy bike ride from the Burren and the Cliffs; the **Doolin Bike Store** rents bikes. (☎707 42 82. £7 per day. Open daily 9am-8pm.) ☎**065.**

THE BURREN. If there were wild orchids, cantakerous cows, and B&Bs on the Moon, it would probably look a lot like the Burren. Its land comprises nearly 100 sq. miles and almost one-third of Co. Clare's coastline. Jagged gray hills resembling the rubble of destroyed skyscrapers, hidden depressions that open up into a labyrinth of caves, ruined churches and castles, thousands of miles of stone walls, ancient megaliths, and indigenous wildflowers abound. The best way to see the Burren is to walk or cycle it, but it's notoriously difficult to get around. Yellow arrows mark a 26-mile **hiking trail** from Liscannor to Ballyvaughan; Doolin and Kinvara are the best biking bases. All of the surrounding tourist offices (at Ennis, the Cliffs of Moher, and Kinvara) have maps of the region. **Bus Éireann** (☎682 41 77) connects Galway to towns in and near the Burren a few times a day in summer but infrequently during winter. Although cars plow through town on their way from Galway to the Burren, **Kinvara** (pop. 2300) is a well-kept secret with a well-preserved **medieval castle,** a vibrant artistic community, and pubs with character. **Johnston's Hostel (HI),** on Main St., uphill from the Quay area, is a relaxing haven. (☎ (091) 371 64. Sheets £1. Showers 50p. Laundry. Curfew 12:30am. Open June-Sept. Dorms £7.50; **camping** £4.50.)

GALWAY CITY ☎091

In the past few years, Galway (pop. 60,000) has earned a reputation as Ireland's cultural capital. With a mix of over 13,000 students at Galway's two major universities, a transient population of twenty-something Europeans, and waves of international backpackers, Galway has developed into one happening college town.

PRACTICAL INFO, ACCOMMODATIONS, AND FOOD. Direct **trains** (☎56 14 44) run to Dublin (3hr., 4-5 per day, £15-21); transfer at Athlone (£7.50-13.50) for all other cities. **Bus Éireann** (☎56 20 00) leaves for Dublin: (7-9 per day, £8); Cork (5 per day, £12); and Belfast (1-3 per day, £17). The main **tourist office,** Victoria Pl., is a block southeast of the bus and train stations at Eyre Sq. (☎56 30 81. Open July-Aug. daily 8:30am-7:45pm; May-June and Sept. daily 8:30am-5:45pm; Oct.-Apr. Su-F 9am-5:45pm, Sa 9am-12:45pm.) Check email at **Cyberzone,** The Old Malte Arcade, High St. (☎56 97 72. £5 per hr., £4 with student ID; includes coffee.) The **Salmon Weir Hostel,** west of Eyre Sq. on St. Vincent's Ave., encourages group pub-hopping excursions. (☎56 11 33. Open June-Aug. Laundry £4. Curfew 3am. Dorms £8.50-10.50; doubles £25.) **Great Western House (HI),** Eyre Sq., across from the station, approaches hostel heaven with its sauna and pool room. (☎56 11 50. Breakfast included. Bike rental. Internet. Laundry £5. Reception 24hr. Dorms £10-12.50; singles £18; doubles £32. Off season £1.50-3 cheaper.) **Kinlay House (HI),** on Merchant's Rd. across from the tourist office, is big, spotless, and secure. (☎56 52 44. Breakfast included. Internet. Laundry £3.50. July-Sept. dorms £10-12.50; singles £20; doubles £29, with bath £33. Less Oct.-June. 10% ISIC discount.) **Woodquay Hostel,** 23-24 Woodquay, is cute, comfy, and clean. (☎56 26 18. Dorms £10; double £25; quad £40.) **Barnacle's Quay Street Hostel (HI),** Quay St. (farther down Shop St.), has a fabulous location in pub central. (☎56 86 44. Laundry £5. Dorms £7.50-13.50; doubles £17.50. Less during off season.) For cheap food, head to the east bank; try Abbeygate St. and the blocks around **Quay, High,** and **Shop St.** On Saturday mornings, an **open market** sets up in front of St. Nicholas Church on Market St. with seafood, pastries, and fresh fruit. (Open 8am-1pm.) Pick up groceries at **Supervalu,** in the Eyre Sq. mall. (Open M-W and Sa 9am-6:30pm, Th-F 9am-9pm.)

SIGHTS AND ENTERTAINMENT. Galway's main attractions are its nightlife and setting as a starting point for trips to the Clare coast or the Connemara. Rent a **rowboat** from **Frank Dolan's,** 13 Riverside, Woodquay, and row/drift down the Corrib for great views of the city, countryside, and nearby castles (£3 per hr.). In mid-July, the **Galway Arts Festival** (☎58 38 00), Ireland's largest arts festival, brings *trad* musicians, rock groups, theater troupes, and filmmakers. Otherwise, rest up

IRELAND

for the long nights ahead. Choosing from the endless list of fantastic pubs is a challenge even for residents (nightclubs lag far behind in quality). The beautiful pubs along **Quay St.** generally cater to tourists and students. Try **Seaghan Ua Neachtain** (called **Knockton's**), one of the county's oldest and most genuine pubs, which hosts nightly *trad.* **The Quays,** built with the carved wood and stained-glass windows of an old church, is quite popular. (Cover £5. Open daily 10pm-1:30am.) Also in the Quay area, **Buskar Browne's/The Slate House,** between Cross St. and Kirwin's Ln., was a nunnery for 300 years before turning to the Dark Side; the medieval-themed **King's Head,** High St., has nightly live music and several bars; and **Taaffe's,** Shop St., packs 'em in for booze and *trad.* Pubs along **Dominick St.** (across the river from the Quay) are local faves; check out **Roisín Dubh** (The Black Rose), where big-name musicians hit the stage. **The Hole in the Wall** packs a hip late-night crowd in **Eyre Sq.,** while the huge **Skeffington Arms** is a pub crawl unto itself.

ARAN ISLANDS (OILEÁIN ÁRANN)

The harsh limestone landscapes of the Aran Islands guard the entrance to Galway Bay. Awesome Iron Age forts sit atop the stark cliffs while stone walls divide deserted fields. Islanders maintain the lifestyle they've had for centuries by fishing, speaking Irish, and producing traditional sweaters and *curraghs* (tar-bottomed boats). **Island Ferries** (☎ (091) 56 17 67, after hours 722 73) leaves from **Rossaveal** (return £15; return bus from Galway £4); **O'Brien Shipping/Doolin Ferries** (☎ (091) 56 72 83 in Galway, (065) 744 55 in Doolin) leaves from the Galway pier (return £12, students £9) and Doolin (return £15-20). Both have Galway tourist office booths.

Of the ruins, forts, churches, and holy wells that rise from the stony terrain of **Inishmore** (Inis Mór; pop. 900), the most amazing is the **Dún Aengus** ring fort, where a small wall surrounds a sheer 300-foot drop. The largest Aran Island, Inishmore is still fairly isolated despite a tourism increase. Ferries land at **Kilronan,** where the **tourist office** holds bags (£0.75) and changes money. (☎ (099) 612 63. Open Feb.-Nov. daily 10am-6:15pm.) The **Kilronan Hostel** has ocean views, a spotless kitchen, and a TV lounge. (☎ (099) 612 55. £8-9.) A free hostel minibus meets the ferries. The **Spar Market,** past the hostel, seems to be the island's social center. (Open M-Sa 9am-8pm, Su 10am-6pm.) Windswept **Inishmaan** (Inis Meáin; pop. 300) elevates solitude to its greatest form. **Inisheer** (Inis Oírr; pop. 300) the smallest island, is the least rugged and most budget-friendly. The **Brú Hostel (HI),** visible from the pier, is spacious with great views. (☎ (099) 750 24. Laundry. Dorms £8; singles £11; doubles £22.) A list of Inisheer's 19 B&Bs hangs on the window of the small tourist office.

CONNEMARA

A largely Gaelic-speaking region, comprised of a lacy net of inlets and islands, a rough gang of mountains, and stretches of bog, this region harbors some of Ireland's most breathtaking scenery. The jagged southern coastline teems with sinuous estuaries, safe beaches, and tidal causeways connecting to rocky islands.

CLIFDEN (AN CLOCHÁN). English-speaking Clifden has more amenities and modernities than its old-world neighbors. Its proximity to the region's scenic bogs and mountains attracts tourists, who enjoy the frenzied pub scene, shop in its arts and crafts studios, and use it as a base for exploring the region. The **Connemara Walking Center,** on Market St., runs tours of the bogs, mountains, and Inishbofin and Omey islands. (☎213 79. Open Mar.-Oct. M-Sa 10am-6pm. Tours Easter-Oct. 1-2 daily. £15-25.) **Bus Éireann** goes from the library on Market St. to Westport via Leenane (1½hr., late June-Aug. 1-2 per day) and Galway via Oughterard (2hr., 1-5 per day, £6.50); **Michael Nee** runs a bus from the courthouse to Galway (June-Sept. 3 per day, £5). To see the cliffs off 10-mile Sky Rd., rent a **bike** at **Mannion's,** Bridge St. (☎211 60. £7 per day, £40 per week; deposit £10. Open M-Sa 9:30am-6:30pm, Su 10am-1pm and 5-7pm.) The **tourist office** is on Galway Rd. (☎211 63. Open July-Aug. M-Sa 9:45am-5:45pm and Su noon-4pm; May-June and Sept. M-Sa 9:30am-5:30pm.) Check **email** at **Two Dog Cafe,** Church Hill. (Open M-Sa 10:30am-

7pm and Su 1-5pm.) **B&Bs** dot the streets (£18-20). The excellent **Clifden Town Hostel (IHH)** is on Market St. (☎210 76. Dorms £8; doubles £24; triples £30-33; quads £36; off season £1-2 less.) Head straight at the bottom of Market St. to **Brookside Hostel,** Hulk St. (☎218 12. Laundry. Dorms £8; doubles £18.) Tranquil **Shanaheever Campsite** is a little over 1 mi. away on Westport Rd. (☎210 18. £8 for 2 people and tent; £3 per additional person.) Get groceries at **O'Connor's Super-Valu,** on Market St. (Open M-F 9am-7pm, Su 10am-6pm.) Down pints along **Market St.,** in **The Square,** and on **Church Hill.** **☎095.**

CONNEMARA NATIONAL PARK. Connemara National Park occupies 7¾ sq. mi. of mountainous countryside that thousands of birds call home. The bogs covered by a screen of grass and flowers muddy everyone's shoes. The **Snuffaunboy Nature Trail** and the **Ellis Wood Trail** are easy hikes. More experienced hikers head for the **Twelve Bens** (*Na Benna Beola*, a.k.a. the Twelve Pins), a rugged range that reaches 2400 ft. There are no proper trails, but Jos Lynam's guidebook (£5) meticulously plots out 18 fantastic hikes through the Twelve Bens and the Maamturks. A tour of all 12 takes experienced walkers about 10hr. Biking the 40 mi. circle through Clifden, Letterfrack, and the Inagh Valley is breathtaking, but only appropriate for fit bikers. The **Visitors Centre** explains the fascinating differences between blanket bogs, raised bogs, turf, and heathland. Guides lead free **walks** (2hr.) over the hills and through the bogs. (☎410 54. Open daily July-Aug. 9:30am-6:30pm; June 10am-6:30pm; May and Sept. 10am-5:30pm. £2, students £1. Tours July-Aug. M, W, and F 10:30am.) The **Connemara Queen** sails from the Oceans Alive center, circling seals and deserted islands (7 per day; £8.50, students £6.50).

Tiny **Letterfrack** is the gateway to the park. The Galway-Clifden **bus** (M-Sa mid-June-Aug. 11 per week, Sept. to mid-June 4 per week) and the summertime Clifden-Westport bus (1-2 per day) stop at Letterfrack. Uphill from the Letterfrack intersection, the **Old Monastery Hostel** is exquisite. (☎411 32. Breakfast included. Laundry. Bikes £7 per day. Internet. Dorms £8-10.) The turn-off to the **Ben Lettery Hostel (An Óige/HI),** in Ballinafad, is 8 mi. east of Clifden. (☎511 36. £6.50-7.50.) **☎095.**

WESTPORT. One of the country's few planned towns, Westport (pop. 4300) still looks marvelous in its Georgian-period costume. Tourists savor beer at thriving pubs, drink tea at dapper cafes, and shop for hand-woven scarves. **Trains** arrive at the Altamont St. Station (☎252 53), five minutes up North Mall, from Dublin via Athlone (2-3 per day, £15). **Buses** leave from the Octagon on Mill St. for Galway (M-F 6 per day, £8.80). **Breheny & Sons,** on Castlebar St., rents **bikes.** (☎250 20. £5-7 per day, £35 per week; £30 deposit.) The **tourist office** is on James St. (☎257 11. Open Apr.-Oct. M-Sa 9am-12:45pm and 2-5:45pm; July-Aug. also Su 10am-6pm.) **B&Bs** are on the Castlebar and Altamont Rd. off North Mall (£18-20). **The Granary Hostel,** 1 mi. west of town on Louisburgh Rd., is near the entrance to Westport House. (☎259 03. Open Apr.-Oct. £6.) **Old Mill Holiday Hostel (IHH),** James St., is between The Octagon and the tourist office. (☎270 45. Sheets £1. Laundry. Kitchen. £7.) **SuperValu supermarket,** on Shop St. (open M-Sa 8:30am-9pm, Su 10am-6pm), keeps you from the crowds at **McCormack's** on Bridge St. (open M-Tu and Th-Sa 10am-6pm).

Conical **Croagh Patrick** rises 2510 ft. over Clew Bay. The summit has been revered since St. Patrick fasted for 40 days and nights in AD 441, arguing with angels and banishing snakes from Ireland. Climbers start at the 15th-century **Murrisk Abbey,** several miles west of Westport on the R395 toward Louisburgh (4hr. round-trip). **Buses** go to Murrisk (July-Aug. M-F 3 per day, Sept.-June M-Sa 2 per day), but **cabs** (☎271 71) for several people are cheaper and more convenient. **☎098.**

NORTHWEST IRELAND

The farmland of the upper Shannon region spans northward into County Sligo's mountains, lakes, and ancient monuments. A sliver of land connects County Sligo to County Donegal, a storehouse of genuine Irish tradition.

SLIGO. Since the turn of the century, Sligo has been a literary pilgrimage site for William Butler Yeats fans. The poet summered in town as a child, settled there as an adult, and set many of his poems around the area. The county remains as beautiful today as it was then. **Sligo Town,** the county's commercial center, goes wild at night with one of Ireland's most colorful pub scenes, and is an excellent base for exploring Yeat's haunts, most of which are at least a mile from the town center. In town, the 13th-century **Sligo Abbey,** Abbey St., is well-preserved. (Open daily in summer 9:30am-6:30pm. £1.50, students £0.60.) **The Niland Gallery,** Stephen St., houses an excellent modern Irish art collection along with some first editions of Yeats works. (Open Tu-Sa 10am-noon and 2-5pm. Free.) Yeats is buried in **Drumcliff churchyard,** on the N15, 4 mi. northwest of Sligo; his grave is to the left of the church door. **Buses** from Sligo to Derry stop at Drumcliff (10min.; 3-4 per day; round-trip £2.60).

Trains (☎698 88) go from McDiarmada Station on Lord Edward St. to Dublin via Carrick-on-Shannon and Mullingar (3 per day; £13.50). From the station, **buses** (☎600 66) fan out to: Galway (2½hr., 3-4 per day, £11); Westport (2½hr., 1-3 per day, £9.70); Derry (3hr., 3-6 per day, £10); Dublin (4hr., 4 per day, £9); and Belfast (4hr., 1-3 per day, £12.40). Turn left on Lord Edward St., then follow the signs right on Adelaid and around the corner to Temple St. to find the **tourist office,** at Temple and Charles St. (☎612 01. Open June-Aug. M-Sa 9am-8pm, Su 10am-6pm; Oct.-May M-F 9am-5pm.) **B&Bs** cluster on **Pearse Rd.,** on the south side of town. **Harbour House,** Finisklin Rd., is 10 minutes from the station. (☎715 47. Bikes £7. Dorms £10; private rooms £10.50 per person; singles £17.) Follow signs from the station to **Railway Hostel,** 1 Union Pl. (☎445 30. Dorms £6.50; private rooms £8 per person.) "Faery vats / Full of berries / And reddest stolen cherries" are not to be found in Sligo today, but **Quinnsworth Supermarket,** O'Connell St., will fulfill your food needs. (Open M-Tu 8:30am-7pm, W-F 8:30am-9pm, Sa 8:30am-7pm, Su 10am-6pm.) **☎071.**

DONEGAL COAST AND SLIEVE LEAGUE. The most remote and least Anglicized of Ireland's "scenic" provinces, Donegal escaped Ireland's widespread deforestation; vast wooded areas engulf many of its mountain chains, while the coastline alternates beaches with cliffs. Most travelers use **Donegal Town** as the county gateway. **Bus Éireann** (☎211 01) runs to: Sligo (1hr.; 3-7 per day); Dublin (4hr., 5 per day, £12); and Galway (4hr., 3-5 per day, £10). **McGeehan's Buses** (☎ (075) 461 50) drive to Dungloe and the Slieve League Peninsula towns (2 per day). Buses stop outside the Abbey Hotel on The Diamond; turn right from the hotel to reach the **tourist office,** just outside of The Diamond on Sligo Rd. (☎211 48; www.donegaltown.ie. Open July-Aug. M-Sa 9am-8pm, Su 10am-4pm; Sept.-Oct. and Easter-June M-F 9am-5pm, Sa 10am-2pm.) **Donegal Town Hostel (IHH)** is one half mile out on Killybegs Rd. (☎228 05. Reserve ahead. Dorms £7-7.50; doubles £17-18; **camping** £4 per person.)

West of Donegal Town lies the **Slieve League Peninsula,** which has some of Ireland's most stunning scenery and Europe's highest sea cliffs. The Bunglas Cliff's sheer 2000-foot drop is spectacular, and its landscape shows little evidence of human habitation. The few villages on the peninsula lie along the busy N56, which leads from Donegal Town and turns into the R63 as it approaches the western tip of the peninsula. Most Slieve League **hikers** stay in Kilcar or Glencolmcille, from which they can drive, bike, or walk (about 3hr.) to the mountain. **Bus Éireann** runs from Donegal Town to Glencolmcille and Dungloe, stopping in **Kilcar** and **Ardara** (2-3 per day), the gateway to Donegal's *gaeltacht* and a commercial base for many Donegal tweed weavers. Nearly 2 mi. out on the coast road from Kilcar to Carrick is the fabulous **Derrylahan Hostel (IHH);** call for pick-up. (☎380 79. Laundry. Dorms £7; private rooms £10; **camping** £4.) On the western top of the Slieve League peninsula, **Glencolmcille** (glen-kaul-um-KEEL) is renowned for its rolling hills, sandy coves between huge seacliffs, and handmade sweaters. On sunny days, the **Silver Strand** rewards with stunning views of the beach and surrounding rocky cliffs; from here, trek along the Slieve League. McGeehan's **buses** leave from Biddy's Bar for Kilcar and Letterkenny (1-2 per day). **Bus Éireann** also heads to Kilcar (3 per day). Snooze at the **Dooey Hostel.** (**IHO;** ☎301 30. Dorms £7; doubles £14; **camping** £4.) **☎073.**

IRELAND

DERRYVEAGH MOUNTAINS. Sandy beaches are isolated by the boglands and eerie stillness of the **Derryveagh Mountains.** On the eastern side of the mountains, **Glenveagh National Park** is 37 sq. mi. of forest glens, bogs, and herds of red deer. (☎ (074) 370 90. Open Mar.-Nov. daily 10am-6:30pm. £2, students £1.) The coastal road N56 twists and bends along the jagged edges where Donegal meets the sea, leading through spectacular scenery to **Crolly,** gateway to Mount Errigal and the legendary Poison Glen. From Crolly, Feda O'Donnell (☎481 14) has a daily **bus** to Galway and Donegal Town via Letterkenny; Swilly (Dungloe, ☎213 80) passes on its Dungloe-Derry route; John McGinley Coaches (☎ (074) 352 01) goes to Dublin; and O'Donnell Trans-Ulster Express (☎483 56) goes to Belfast. The Crolly and Dunlewy hostels are most convenient to the park. Just past Paddy Og's pub in Crolly, a sign points to **Screagan an Iolair Hill Hostel** (SCRAG an UH-ler), 4 mi. up a mountain road at **Tor** in the national park; turn left off the coastal road at the sign and follow Tor Rd. Trails through the **Derryveagh Mountains** begin at the hostel. (☎ 485 93. Laundry. Call ahead Nov.-Feb. Dorms £7.50, private rooms £9.) **☎075.**

LETTERKENNY. Letterkenny is a traffic-clogged mess; most tourists arrive just to make bus connections to the rest of Donegal, the Republic, and Northern Ireland. **Buses** leave from the roundabout at the junction of Port (Derry) and Pearse Rd. in front of the Letterkenny Shopping Center. **Bus Éireann** (☎213 09) runs a "Hills of Donegal" tour to Glenveigh National Park (M-Sa 11am, £13) as well as routes to: Derry (40min., 3-12per day, £5); Donegal Town (50min., £5.50); Sligo (2hr., 3 per day, £9.50); Galway (5hr., 3 per day, £12.50); and Dublin (5hr., 4 per day, £11). **Feda O'Donnell Coaches** (☎ (075) 481 14) drives to Galway (£10) via Donegal Town (2-3 per day, £5) and to Crolly (£5). **Northwest Busways** (☎ (077) 826 19) sends buses around the Inishowen Peninsula (3-4 per day). The **Chamber of Commerce Visitors Information Centre** is at 40 Port Rd. (☎248 66. Open M-F 9am-5pm.) **☎074.**

INISHOWEN PENINSULA AND MALIN HEAD. The Inishowen Peninsula is a mosaic of pristine mountains, forests, meadows, and white-sand beaches that reaches farther north than "the North." The **Inish Eoghain 100** road navigates the peninsula's perimeter, exactly 100 mi. The peninsula's most popular attraction is **Malin Head,** with its rocky coast and sky-high sand dunes, reputedly Europe's highest (over 100 ft.). The scattered town of Malin Head includes **Bamba's Crown,** the northernmost tip of Ireland, a tooth of dark rock rising up from the waves. The nearby beaches are covered with semi-precious stones. Lough Swilly **buses** (Buncrana, ☎613 40; 1½hr.; M, W, and F 2 per day, Sa 3 per day) and Northwest Buses (☎826 19; M-Sa 2 per day) run from Derry, the nearest city to Inishowen, to points on the peninsula including Malin Head. To get to the **Sandrock Holiday Hostel (IHO/IHH),** Port Ronan Pier, take the left fork off the Inish Eoghain 100, just before the Crossroads Inn. (☎702 89. Sheets £1. Laundry. Bikes £6 per day. £7.) **☎077.**

NORTHERN IRELAND

PHONE CODE	The regional code for all of Northern Ireland is 028. From outside Northern Ireland, call int'l dialing prefix (see inside back cover) + 44 (from the Republic, 048) + 28 + local number.

The predominantly calm tenor of life in the North has been overshadowed overseas by headlines concerning politics and bombs. Northern Ireland's natural beauty includes the Glens of Antrim's pockets of green and Giant's Causeway, one of the world's strangest geological sights. The ceasefires of recent years have allowed Belfast and Derry to develop into hip, pub-loving cities. Pub culture, urban neighborhoods, and tiny villages show everyday life in a divided but mostly peaceful society.

BELFAST

Belfast (pop. 330,000) is the center of the North's cultural, commercial, and political activity. West Belfast's famous sectarian murals are perhaps the most informative source on the effects of the Troubles (sectarian strife). The bar scene—a mix of Irish and British pub culture, with an international influence—entertains locals, foreigners, and students. Despite its reputation as a terrorist-riddled metropolis, the city feels more neighborly than most foreign—and even Irish—visitors expect.

GETTING THERE AND GETTING AROUND

Flights: Belfast International Airport (☎ (94) 42 28 88) in Aldergrove. **Airbus** (☎90 33 30 00) goes to the Europa (Glengall St.) bus station (M-Sa every 30min., Su every hr.; UK£5). From **Belfast City Airport, trains** go to Central Station (UK£1).

Trains: Central Station, East Bridge St. (☎90 89 94 00). To: **Dublin** (2hr., 5-8 per day, UK£17); and **Derry** (2½hr., 3-7 per day, UK£6.70). The **Centrelink** buses run to the city center, free with rail tickets.

Buses: Europa (Glengall St.) Station (☎90 32 00 00) serves the west and the Republic. To: **Derry** (1¾hr., 6-19 per day, UK£6.50); and **Dublin** (3hr., 4-7 per day, UK£10.50). **Laganside Station** (☎90 33 30 00) send buses to the east coast. The **Centrelink** bus connects both stations with the city center.

Ferries: SeaCat (☎52 35 23; www.seacat.co.uk) leaves for **Troon, Scotland** (2½hr.); **Heysham, England** (3¾hr.); and the **Isle of Man** from the terminal off Donegall Quay. Fares UK£10-30.

Local Transportation: The red **Citybus Network** (☎90 24 64 85), is supplemented by **Ulsterbus** "blue buses" to the suburbs. Single-fare within the city center UK£0.50. The **Centrelink** buses traverse the city (every 12min. M-F 7:25am-9:15pm, Sa 8:35am-9:15pm; UK£0.50, free with bus or rail ticket). Late **Nightlink** buses run to small towns outside Belfast 1am and 2:30am F-Sa (UK£3, available onboard).

Taxis: Value Cabs (☎90 23 00 00). Residents of West and North Belfast utilize the huge **black cabs**; some are metered, and some follow set routes (under UK£1 charge).

ORIENTATION AND PRACTICAL INFORMATION

Buses arrive at the Europa bus station on **Great Victoria St.** To the northeast is the **City Hall** in **Donegall Sq.** The stretch of Great Victoria St. south of the bus station to where it meets **Dublin Rd.** at **Shaftesbury Sq.** is known as the **Golden Mile. Botanic Ave.** and **Bradbury Pl.** (which becomes University Rd.) extend south from Shaftesbury Sq. into the student-friendly **Queen's University area.** The city center, Golden Mile, and the university area are relatively safe. **West Belfast** is more politically volatile. The Protestant neighborhood lies along **Shankill Rd.,** just north of the Catholic neighborhood, centered around **Falls Rd.** The **River Lagan** divides industrial **East Belfast** from the rest of the city. Use taxis after dark, particularly near the clubs and pubs of the northeast area.

Tourist Office: 59 North St., St. Anne's Court (☎90 24 66 09). 24hr. computerized info kiosk outside. Open July-Aug. M-F 9am-7pm, Sa 9am-5:15pm, Su noon-4pm; Sept.-June M 9:30am-5:15pm, Tu-Sa 9am-5:15pm.

Travel Agency: USIT, 13b The Fountain Centre, College St. (☎90 32 40 73), near Royal Ave. Open M and W-F 9:30am-5:30pm, Tu 10am-5:30pm, Sa 10am-1pm.

Consulates: US, Queens House, Queen St. (☎90 32 82 39). Open M-F 1-4pm.

Luggage Storage: For security reasons there is no luggage storage at airports or stations. Hostels will often store bags for guests who've stayed.

Bisexual, Gay, and Lesbian Information: Rainbow Project N.I., 33 Church Ln. (☎90 31 90 30). Open M-F 10am-4pm.

Laundry: The Laundry Room (Duds 'n Suds), Botanic Ave. (☎90 24 39 56). TV for the wait. Wash UK£1.95, dry UK£1.95; UK£1.80 each for students and seniors. Open M-F 8am-9pm, Sa 8am-6pm, Su noon-6pm. Last load 1½hr. before closing.

Emergency: ☎999; no coins required. **Police:** 65 Knock Rd. (☎90 65 02 22).

Hospitals: Belfast City Hospital, 9 Lisburn Rd. (☎90 32 92 41). From Shaftesbury Sq. follow Bradbury Pl. and take a right at the fork.

Internet Access: The **Belfast Central Library,** 122 Royal Ave. (☎90 24 32 33). Open M and Th 9:30am-8pm, Tu-W and F 9:30am-5:30pm, Sa 9:30am-1pm. 30min. of free email per day; UK£2 per hr. for web access.

Post Office: Central Post Office, 25 Castle Pl. (☎90 32 37 40). Open M-Sa 9am-5:30pm. Address mail to be held: First name SURNAME, *Poste Restante*, CPO, 25 Castle Pl, Belfast **BT1 1NB,** Northern Ireland.

ACCOMMODATIONS AND FOOD

Most budget accommodations are by Queen's University, south of the city center. You can catch a **Centrelink** bus to Shaftesbury Sq., or **Citybus** #59, 69-71, 84, or 85 from Donegall Sq. East to areas to the south. B&Bs occupy every other house on Eglantine Ave., off University Rd. just south of Queen's University.

The Ark (IHH), 18 University St. (☎90 32 96 26). From the Europa Hotel on Great Victoria St., head right; bear right onto Bradbury Pl. at Shaftesbury Sq., then fork left onto University Rd. University St. is the 4th left. Hard to leave. Belfast and Causeway tours. Laundry UK£4. Internet. Curfew 2am. Dorms UK£6.50-7.50; doubles UK£28.

Arnie's Backpackers (IHH), 63 Fitzwilliam St. (☎90 24 28 67). Follow the directions to the Ark above; Fitzwilliam St. is on your right across from the university. Relaxed atmosphere. Key deposit UK£2. Luggage storage. 4- to 6-bed dorms UK£7.50.

Belfast Hostel (YHANI/HI), 22 Donegall Rd. (☎90 31 54 35; www.hini.org.uk), off Shaftesbury Sq., near Sandy Row, a Loyalist area that has seen violence during marching season. Clean, modern rooms, some with bath. Laundry. Dorms UK£8-10.

Marine House, 30 Eglantine Ave. (☎90 66 28 28). B&B with hospitality and housekeeping standards high as its ceilings. Singles UK£22; doubles UK£40; triples UK£57.

The George, 9 Eglantine Ave. (☎90 68 32 12). Immaculately clean B&B with stained-glass windows. Rooms with shower and TV. Singles UK£22; doubles UK£44.

Dublin Rd., Botanic Ave., and the **Golden Mile** have the highest concentration of restaurants. The menu ranges from Thai to Cajun at **The Other Place,** 79 Botanic Ave, 133 Stranmillis Rd, and 537 Lisburn Rd. (All open M-Sa 8am-11pm.) **The Moghul,** 62A Botanic Ave., has an amazing Indian lunch buffet. (UK£4.95; M-F noon-2pm. Open for dinner M-Th 5-11:30pm, F-Sa 5-11:45pm, Su 5-10:30pm.) **Bookfinders,** 47 University Rd., is a smoky bookstore/art gallery/cafe. (Soup, bread, and sandwiches UK£2-3. Open M-Sa 10am-5:30pm.) **Spar** on Botanic Ave. has **groceries.** (Open 24hr.)

SIGHTS

DONEGALL SQUARE. The **Belfast City Hall** is the administrative and geographic center of Belfast. Its green copper dome (173 ft.) is visible from any point in the city. Check out the somber statues in the exterior garden. *(☎90 32 02 02, ext. 2346. Mandatory tours 1hr. June-Sept. M-F 10:30am, 11:30am, and 2:30pm; Sa 2:30pm. Oct.-May M-Sa 2:30pm. Free.)* The **Linen Hall Library** contains a comprehensive collection of Christmas cards, posters, hand bills, and newspaper articles related to the Troubles. *(☎90 32 17 07. 17 Donegall Sq. North. Open M-F 9:30am-5:30pm, Sa 9:30am-4pm.)*

CORNMARKET AND ST. ANNE'S CATHEDRAL. Just north of the city center, a shopping district envelops eight blocks around Castle St. and Royal Ave. This area has been a marketplace since Belfast's early days. Wander the **entries,** or tiny alleys, relics of old Belfast. **St. Anne's Cathedral,** also known as the **Belfast Cathedral,** was begun in 1899. Each of its interior pillars name Belfast's 10 fields of professionalism: Science, Industry, Healing, Agriculture, Music, Theology, Shipbuilding, Freemasonry, Art, and Womanhood (a nice enough profession, but the pay is lousy). *(On Donegall St., near the Tourist Office a few blocks from the city center. Open daily 9am-5pm.)*

THE GOLDEN MILE. This strip along Great Victoria St. contains many of Belfast's jewels, including the city's pride and joy, the **Grand Opera House,** which was cyclically bombed by the IRA, restored to its original splendor at enormous cost, and then bombed again. If there's not a rehearsal going on, they'll give you a tour. *(☎90 24 04 11. Ticket office open M-Sa 9:45am-5:30pm.)* The National Trust has restored the highly frequented **Crown Liquor Saloon,** 46 Great Victoria St., to a showcase of carved wood, gilded ceilings, and stained glass. Damaged by 32 bombs, the **Europa Hotel** has the dubious distinction of being "Europe's most bombed hotel."

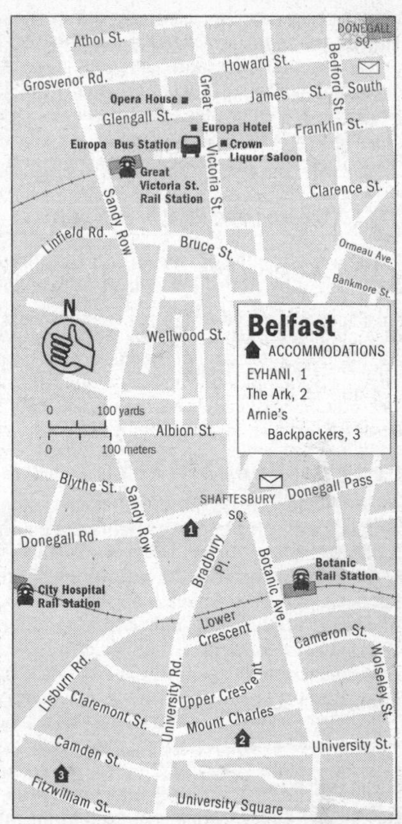

QUEEN'S UNIVERSITY AREA. The university was designed in 1849, modeled after Oxford's Magdalen College. *(University Rd. Visitors Centre ☎90 33 52 52. Open May.-Sept. M-Sa 10am-4pm, Oct.-Mar. M-F 10am-4pm.)* Bask in Belfast's occasional sun at the meticulously groomed **Botanic Gardens.** *(Open daily 8am-dusk. Free.)* The **Ulster Museum,** within the gardens, contains a hodgepodge of historical exhibits, antiquities, and artwork. (*☎90 38 30 00. Open M-F 10am-5pm, Sa 1-5pm, Su 2-5pm. Free.)*

WEST BELFAST AND THE MURALS. Separated from the rest of the city by the Westlink motorway, West Belfast has been historically rife with political tension. The Catholic and Protestant neighborhoods are grimly divided by the **peace line,** a gray and seemingly impenetrable wall. The streets display political murals. The Protestant Orangemen's marching season (in early July) is a risky time to visit, since the parades are underscored by mutual antagonism. **Black cab** tours, whose drivers are mostly residents of West Belfast, provide fascinating, if biased, commentary. *(Arrange tours through hostels; UK£6-7.)* Michael Johnston of **Black Taxi Tours,** gives witty, objective and independent presentations. *(☎90 64 22 64. UK£7.50.)*

IRELAND

ENTERTAINMENT AND NIGHTLIFE

Belfast's cultural events and performances are covered in the monthly *Arts Council Artslink* (free at the tourist office). Belfast's **theater** season runs from September to June. The **Grand Opera House,** on Great Victoria St., resounds with classical vocal music. Buy tickets at the box office, 2-4 Great Victoria St. (☎90 24 91 29. Tickets from UK£8; M-Th student rush tickets 50% off after noon.) The **Queen's University Festival** (☎90 66 76 87) in November draws artists in opera, film, and more.

Pubs close early; start crawling while the sun's still up. In Cornmarket, begin with an afternoon pint at Belfast's oldest pub, **White's Tavern,** Winecellar Entry, off High and Rosemary St. Stumble along Dublin Rd. and the Golden Mile, where some of the best pubs lie. Victorian town landmark **Crown Liquor Saloon,** 46 Great Victoria St., has been bombed 32 times. **Robinson's,** 38 Great Victoria St., hosts nightly trad sessions. **Lavery's,** 12 Bradbury Pl. offers three floors of unpretentious socializing. The bars near the university stay open the latest. **The Botanic Inn (the "Bot"),** 23 Malone Rd., and **The Eglantine Inn (the "Egg"),** 32 Malone Rd., are almost official extracurriculars. Explore the club scene at **The Manhattan,** 23-31 Bradbury Pl., exploding with gyrating twenty-somethings. Socialites head to **The Fly,** 5-6 Lower Crescent, a cool lounge. **The Kremlin,** 96 Donegall St., is the newest gay hotspot, and **The Crow's Nest,** 26 Skipper St., boasts frequent discos and karaoke. For info on nightlife, consult *The List*, available in the tourist office and most hostels.

EXCURSION FROM BELFAST: ULSTER FOLK MUSEUM

In **Holywood,** the **Ulster Folk Museum** and **Transport Museum** stretch over 176 acres. Established by Act of Parliament in the 1950s, the **Folk Museum,** which aims to preserve the way of life of Ulster's farmers, weavers, and craftspeople, contains over 30 buildings from the past three centuries. The **Transport Museum** and the **Railway Museum** are across the road. (☎90 42 84 28. Open July-Aug. M-Sa 10:30am-6pm, Su noon-6pm; Apr.-June and Sept. M-F 9:30am-5pm, Sa 10:30am-6pm, Su noon-6pm; Oct.-Mar. M-F 9:30am-4pm, Sa-Su 12:30-4:30pm. UK£4, students UK£2.50.) Frequent **buses** (45min.) and **trains** (30min.) stop by en route to **Bangor.**

DERRY (LONDONDERRY)

Although the Derry landscape was once razed by years of bombings, and violence still erupts occasionally during the Marching Season, the rebuilt city looks sparklingly new. Derry's **city walls,** 18 ft. high and 20 ft. thick, erected between 1614 and 1619, have never been breached, hence Derry's nickname "the Maiden City." The stone tower along the southeast wall past New Gate was built to protect **St. Columb's Cathedral,** off Bishop St., the symbolic focus of the city's Protestant defenders. (Open M-Sa Apr.-Oct. 9am-5pm, Nov.-Mar. 9am-4pm. UK£1 donation; chapterhouse UK£0.50.) At Union Hall Place, just inside Magazine Gate, the **Tower Museum's** engaging exhibits relay Derry's long history. (Open July-Aug. M-Sa 10am-5pm, Su 2pm-5pm; Sept.-June Tu-Sa 10am-5pm. Last entrance 4:30pm. UK£3.75, students UK£1.25.) Derry's residential neighborhoods, the Catholic **Bogside** and **Fountain Estate** (west of the city walls) and the Protestant **Waterside** (on the Foyle River's east bank) display brilliant murals. Bogside's **Free Derry Corner** and the **Bloody Sunday Memorial** commemorate the 1972 murder of 14 peaceful protestors by British soldiers.

Trains (☎71 34 22 28) arrive on Duke St., Waterside, on the east bank, from Belfast (2½hr., 4-7 per day, UK£7). A free **Rail-Link bus** connects the train station and the **bus station,** on Foyle St., between the walled city and the river. Ulsterbus (☎71 26 22 61) goes to Belfast (1½-3hr., 8-15 per day, UK£7.50) and Dublin (3-5 per day, UK£11). The **tourist office** is at 44 Foyle St. (☎71 26 72 84. Open July-Sept. M-F 9am-7pm, Sa 10am-6pm, Su 10am-5pm; Oct.-Easter M-F 9am-5pm; Easter-June M-F 9am-5pm, Sa 10am-5pm.) Go down Strand Rd. and turn left on Asylum Rd. just before the RUC station to reach the **Derry City Independent Hostel (Steve's Backpackers),** 4 Asylum Rd. (☎71 37 79 89. Laundry. Internet. UK£7.50.) **Derry City Youth Hostel (YHANI/HI),** is on Magazine St. inside the city walls. (☎71 28 41 00. Laundry. Check-out 10am. Reception 24hr. UK£7.50-£8.50, B&B with bath UK£15.) **Tesco supermarket** is on Strand Rd,. in the Quayside Shopping Center. (Open M-Sa 8:30am-9pm, Su 1-6pm.) For nightly trad, head to **Peadar O'Donnell's,** 53 Waterloo St. **Postal code:** BT48 6AA.

I'M TOO SEXY... The opulent homes of the local statesmen and merchants were once located within Derry's city walls. When the wealthy wives bought fancy dresses from London, they donned their new garb and strolled about on the city walls. The poverty-stricken residents of the Bogside looked at the ladies on the wall and were enraged at the decadent lifestyle on display, so a few of them wrote a letter to the London papers about the parading "cats." The London press were so amused by the nickname that it stuck, and the phrase "cat walk" fell into common usage.

IRELAND

GLENS OF ANTRIM

Nine lush green valleys, or "glens," slither from the hills and high moors of Co. Antrim down to the seashore. **Ulsterbus** (Belfast ☎90 32 00 11, Larne ☎28 27 23 45) #162 goes from Belfast to Waterfoot, Cushendall, and Cushendun (3-5 per day). The #252 Antrim Coaster stops at every coastal town from Belfast to Coleraine (2 per day). Cycling is glorious; rent a **bike** from the Cushendall Youth Hostel.

GLENARIFF. Antrim's broadest (and arguably most beautiful) glen, Glenariff, lies 4 mi. south of Waterfoot along Glenariff Rd. in the large **Glenariff Forest Park. Bus** #150 between Cushendun and Ballymena stops at the official park entrance (M-Sa 3-5 per day), but if you're walking from Waterfoot, you can enter the park 1½ mi. downhill of the official entrance by taking the road that branches left toward the Manor Lodge Restaurant. The stunning **Waterfall Trail** follows the cascading, fern-lined Glenariff River from the park entrance to the Manor Lodge. (☎21 75 87 69. Park open daily 10am-8pm. UK£3 per car or UK£1.50 per pedestrian.)

CUSHENDALL. Cushendall is the Glen's best base town. **Ulsterbus** #150 runs from Glenariff to Cushendall (M-Sa 3-5 per day); from July to August, the **Antrim Coaster** (#252) runs through Cushendall to Belfast (2 per day). The **tourist office,** 25 Mill St., is by the bus stop at the Cushendun end of town. (☎21 77 11 80. Open July-Sept. M-F 10am-1pm and 2-5:30pm, Sa 10am-1pm; Oct. to mid-Sept. and Mar.-June Tu-Sa 10am-1pm.) **Cushendall Youth Hostel (YHANI/HI),** 42 Layde Rd., is one half mile from town; take the left-hand (uphill) fork from Shore Rd. (☎21 77 13 44. Laundry. UK£8.50.) Or, sleep at **Glendale,** 46 Coast Rd. (☎21 77 14 95. UK£16.)

CAUSEWAY COAST

The northern coast shifts from lyrical into dramatic mode as sea-battered, 600-foot cliffs tower over white, wave-lapped beaches and give way to **Giant's Causeway.** In the summer, **Bushmills Bus** (Coleraine ☎70 43 33 34) goes between Coleraine, 5 mi. south of Portrush, and Giant's Causeway (July-Aug. 5 per day) and the Antrim Coaster #252 (Belfast, ☎90 33 30 00) runs up the coast from Belfast to Portstewart via every town listed here (2 per day).

BALLYCASTLE AND ENVIRONS. This bubbly seaside town is popular with Giant's Causeway-bound tourists. **Ulsterbus** #72 rides to Cushendall via Cushendun (50min., M-F 1 per day) and Antrim Coaster #252 runs to Belfast (2 per day). The **tourist office** is in Sheskburn House, 7 Mary St. (☎20 76 20 24. Open July-Aug. M-F 9:30am-7pm, Sa 10am-6pm, Su 2-6pm; Sept.-June M-F 9:30am-5pm.) Snooze at **Castle Hostel (IHH),** 62 Quay Rd. (☎20 76 23 37), or **Ballycastle Backpackers Hostel,** 4 North St. (☎70 26 36 12 or 07 77 32 37 89 01), next to the Marine Hotel. (Call ahead. Dorms UK£7-7.50; private rooms UK£8.50 per person.)

Off the coast at Ballycastle, **Rathlin Island** ("Fort of the Sea") is home to 20,000 puffins, the odd golden eagle, and 100 humans. Caledonian MacBrayne **ferries** sail from the Ballycastle pier, uphill from Quay Rd. on North St. (45min., 2-4 per day, round-trip UK£8). A minibus (☎20 76 39 09) drives to the **Kebble Bird Sanctuary** at the western tip of the island, 4½ mi. from the harbor (20min., every 45min., UK£2).

Five miles west of Ballycastle, the modest village of **Ballintoy** attracts the crowds on their way to teeny-tiny **Carrick-a-rede Island.** Cross the shaky, fishermen's **rope bridge** over the dizzying 100-foot drop to rocks and sea below; be extremely careful in windy weather. A sign marks the turn-off from the coastal road one half mile east of Ballintoy. Back in Ballintoy, the aptly titled **Sheep Island View Hostel (IHH),** 42A Main St., has soft beds and camping facilities. (☎20 76 93 91. Dorms UK£9.)

GIANT'S CAUSEWAY. Advertised as the eighth natural wonder of the world, Giant's Causeway is Northern Ireland's most famous sight. A spillage of 40,000 hexagonal basalt columns forms a 60-million-year-old honeycomb path from the foot of the cliffs into the sea. Many paths loop to and from the Causeway. A **bus** (every 15min., round-trip UK£1) runs there from the **Giant's Causeway Visitors Centre,** at the entrance to the Causeway from the car park. (☎20 73 18 55. Open daily June 10am-6pm; July-Aug. 10am-7pm; Mar.-May and Sept. 10am-5pm; Nov.-Feb. 10am-4:30pm.)

ITALY (ITALIA)

LIRE

US$1 = L2135 (LIRE)	L1000 = US$0.468
CDN$1 = L1447	L1000 = CDN$0.691
UK£1 = L3180	L1000 = UK£0.315
IR£1 = L2459	L1000 = IR£0.407
AUS$1 = L1262	L1000 = AUS$0.792
NZ$1 = L962	L1000 = NZ $1.04
SAR1 = L309	L1000 = SAR3.24
EUR€1 = L1936	L1000 = EUR€0.517

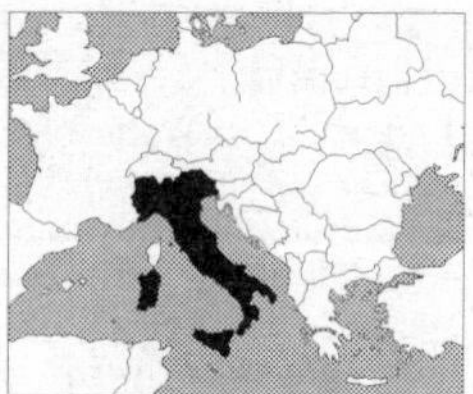

Country code: 39. **International dialing prefix:** 00. Italy has no city codes. From outside Italy, dial int'l dialing prefix + 39 + local number (drop the leading zero).

In the span of time between the stabbing of Julius Caesar and the acceptance of Italy into the European Monetary Union, the boot-shaped land-mass has undergone numerous transformations. Throughout its long, convoluted history, Italy has commanded the center stage of world events: first as the base for the ambitious Roman empire; later, as persecutor and popularizer of an upstart religion called Christianity; next as the center of the artistic and philosophical Renaissance; and finally as a world power that has changed governments more than 50 times since World War II. Italy has long been a prized international possession, both for its terrain and its key position. Countless invasions have left the land rich with examples of nearly every artistic era: Egyptian obelisks, Etruscan huts, Greek temples, Augustan arches, Byzantine mosaics, Renaissance *palazzi*, Baroque fountains, and fascist superstructures sprawl across the 19 regions. The fusion of these regions under one flag creates a vibrant patchwork of dialects, dress, customs, and artistic styles that separate the prosperous, industrialized north from the poorer, agricultural south.

Through it all, Italy has learned to enjoy the finer things in life, especially sumptuous culinary delights. From the meats of the Veneto to the cheeses of Sardinia and from perfect pasta to the creation of pizza, Italy has found that the best way to a country's happiness is through its stomach. When Italy isn't eating, it's loving. Its trademark language of romance inspires lovers to confess their *amore* from the rooftops of the world. Somewhere between the leisurely gondola rides and the fast techno nightclubs, you too will proclaim your love to Italy.

If you want to enjoy *la dolce vita*, check out *Let's Go: Italy 2001*.

FACTS AND FIGURES

Official Name: Italian Republic.

Government: Republic.

Capital: Rome.

Land Area: 294,020 sq. km.

Geography: Mostly rugged and mountainous; some plains and coastal lowlands.

Climate: Mediterranean; Alpine in the far north; hot and dry in the south.

Major Cities: Florence, Venice, Milan, Naples.

POPULATION: 56,735,130. Urban 67%, rural 33%

Language: Italian; some German.

Religions: Roman Catholic (98%), other (2%).

Average Income Per Capita: US$20,800.

Major Exports: Engineering products, textiles, production machinery, chemicals.

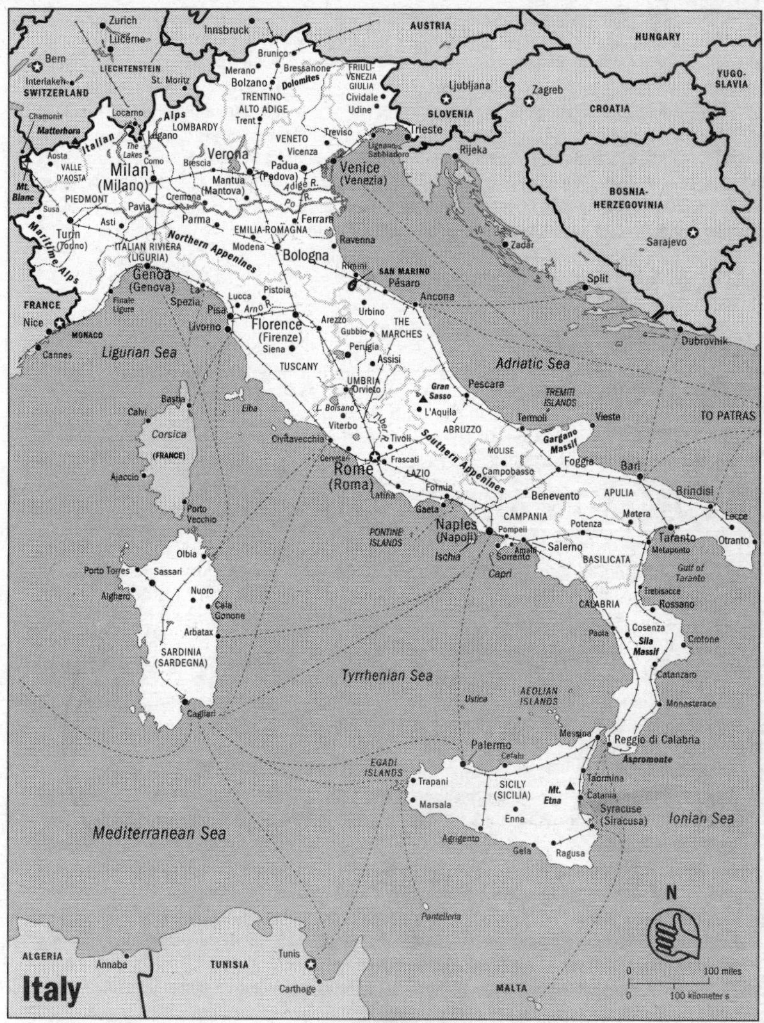

DISCOVER ITALY

The inevitable place to begin an Italian voyage is in **Rome,** where you can view the rubble of the toga-clad empire, the cathedrals of high Christianity, and the art of the Renaissance, then whizz around on a moped (p. 577). Shoot north to Umbria and shun worldly wealth à la St. Francis in **Assisi** (p. 641), before checking out the black-and-white *duomo* of stunning **Siena** (p. 639) and the medieval towers of **San Gimignano** (p. 640). Continue the northward jaunt to be enchanted by **Florence,** where burnt-orange roofs shelter incredible works by Renaissance grandmasters (p. 629). The Leaning Tower is in nearby **Pisa** (p. 640). Gritty **Genoa** is no postcard darling, but has personality and palaces (p. 622). You can see the mysterious shroud at **Turin** (p. 612) before reaching the five bright fishing villages of **Cinque Terre** on the Italian Riviera (p. 625). Away from the coast, the nightlife in **Milan** is unrivaled (p. 615), as is the beauty of **Lake Como** (p. 613). Dreamy **Verona** makes it easy to indulge your romantic, star-crossed side (p. 610) while nearby **Trent,** in the Dolomites, offers year-round skiing (p. 614). In **Venice** misty mornings give way to mystical *palazzi* (p. 602). For a change of pace, head to fresco-filled **Padua** (p. 610) and glittering **Ravenna,** a Byzantine treasure chest on the east coast (p. 628). Move inland to sample **Bologna's** culinary delights (p. 626) and work your way through **Naples** to satisfy pizza cravings (p. 643). A daytrip to **Pompeii** reveals Roman remains buried in AD 79 (p. 647). Next is captivating **Capri** (p. 649) and the **Amalfi Coast** (p. 647), framed by crystal-blue waters. Back in Naples, vibrant **Palermo,** the perfect start to Sicily, is accessible by ferry (p. 650). Round out your tour of Italy at the spectacular **Aeolian Islands** (p. 650), with a volcano and beaches of ebony sand.

ESSENTIALS

WHEN TO GO

Give careful consideration to when you travel, because the timing of your trip can determine its success. Summer is the high season for traveling in Europe; *everything* is crowded with tourists in June, July, and August. Late May or September is a better time to travel in Italy.

DOCUMENTS AND FORMALITIES

EU citizens need only carry a valid passport to enter Italy, and they may stay in the country for as long as they like. Citizens of Australia, Canada, New Zealand, South Africa, and the US need valid passports to enter Italy and to re-enter their own country, and do not need visitor visas for up to three months. Those wishing to stay in Italy for more than three months must apply for a *permesso di soggiorno* (residence permit) at a police station *(questura)*. For more info, contact the Italian embassy in your country.

EMBASSIES AND CONSULATES

Embassies and consulates of other countries in Italy are all in **Rome** (p. 577).

Italian Embassies at Home: Australia, 12 Grey St., Deakin, Canberra A.C.T. 2601 (☎ (02) 62 73 33 33; fax 62 73 42 23; email embassy@ambitalia.org.au); **Canada,** 275 Slater St., 21st fl., Ottawa, ON K1P 5H9 (☎ (613) 232 24 01; fax 233 14 84; www.italyincanada.com); **Ireland,** 63 Northumberland Rd., Dublin (☎ (3531) 660 17 44; fax 668 27 59; email italianembassy@tinet.ie); **New Zealand,** 34 Grant Rd., Wellington (☎ (04) 473 53 39; fax 472 72 55; email ambwell@xtra.co.nz); **South Africa,** 796 George Ave., Arcadia 0083, Pretoria (☎ (012) 43 55 41; fax 43 55 47; www.smartnet.co.za/ambital); **UK,** 14 Three Kings Yard, London W1Y 2EH (☎ (020) 73 12 22 00; fax 73 12 22 30; www.ambital.org.za); **US,** 1601 Fuller St. NW, Washington, DC 20009 (☎ (202) 328 55 00; fax 462 36 05; www.italyemb.org).

GETTING AROUND

BY PLANE. Rome's international airport (known as both Fiumicino and Leonardo da Vinci) is served by most major airlines. You can also fly into **Milan's** Malpensa or Linate Airports or **Florence's** international airport. **Alitalia** (US ☎ (800) 223 57 30; www.alitalia.it/eng) is Italy's national airline and may offer off-season youth fares.

BY TRAIN. The **Ferrovie dello Stato (FS;** national info ☎ 147 88 80 88; www.fs-on-line.com), the Italian State Railway, runs more or less on time and its network is comprehensive. A *locale* train stops at nearly every station; the *diretto* goes faster but serves fewer stations, while the *espresso* stops only at major stations. The *rapido*, an InterCity (IC) train, zips along but costs a bit more. If you plan to travel extensively in Italy and are under 26, the **Cartaverde** should be your first purchase (L40,000, valid for 1 year) which gives a 20% discount on state rail fare. **Eurail** is accepted, but if you are planning on extensive domestic travel you can look into the two-week **Italian Kilometric Ticket,** a cheaper alternative to the Eurail Pass. But since regular fares are cheap, these railpasses are seldom cost-effective. For more information, contact the **Italian State Railways** in the US (☎ (212) 730 21 21).

BY BUS. Intercity buses are convenient for shorter hauls off the main rail lines, and serve countryside points inaccessible by train. For **city buses,** buy tickets in *tabacchi*, newsstands, or kiosks, and validate them on board to avoid a fine.

BY FERRY. Ferry services at the ports of **Bari, Brindisi,** and **Ancona** (see p. 643) connect Italy to **Greece.** Boats from **Trieste** (see p. 611) serve the Istrian Peninsula as far south as **Croatia**'s Dalmatian Coast. Ferries also connect Italy's islands to the mainland. For **Sardinia,** boats go from **Genoa** (p. 622), **La Spezia** (p. 626), and **Naples** (p. 643). Travelers **to Sicily** take the ferry from **Naples** or **Reggio di Calabria** (p. 650).

BY CAR. Driving can be challenging in Rome, Milan, and Naples; congested traffic is more common in cities and in the north. An *Autostrada* (super-highway) has prohibitive tolls, and Italian driving is frightening. There is an extensive network of smaller highways: *strade statali* (national), *provinciali* (provincial), and *communali* (municipal). On three-lane roads, be aware that the center lane is for passing. Gas is about US$4 per gallon. **Mopeds** (L40-60,000 per day) can be a great way to see the islands and the more scenic areas of Italy, but can be disastrous in the rain and on rough roads. Call ☎ 116 if you have an emergency breakdown.

BY BIKE AND BY THUMB. Bicycling is a popular national sport, but bike trails are rare, drivers often reckless, and, except in the Po Valley, the terrain challenging. Although **hitchhiking** is relatively common, *Let's Go* urges travelers to consider the safety risks. Women should never hitchhike alone.

TOURIST SERVICES AND MONEY

EMERGENCY	**Police:** ☎ 112. **Ambulance:** ☎ 113. **Fire:** ☎ 115.

TOURIST OFFICES. In provincial capitals, look for the **Ente Provinciale per il Turismo (EPT)** or **Azienda di Promozione Turistica (APT)** for info on the entire province and the town. Local tourist offices, **Informazione e Assistenza ai Turisti (IAT)** and **Azienda Autonoma di Soggiorno e Turismo (AAST),** are generally the most useful. **Italian Government Tourist Boards (ENIT) at home** are: **Australia,** Level 26, 44 Market St., Sydney NSW 2000 (☎ (02) 92 62 16 66; fax (02) 92 62 57 45); **Canada,** 175 Bloor St. East, #907 South Tower, Toronto, Ontario M4W 3R9 (☎ (416) 925 48 87; fax 925 47 99; email initaly@ican.net); **UK,** 1 Princess St., London WIR 9AY (☎ (020) 74 08 12 54; fax 74 93 66 95; email Enitlond@globalnet.co.uk); **US,** 630 Fifth Ave. #1565, New York, NY 10111 (☎ (212) 245 56 18; fax 586 92 49; www.italiantourism.com).

MONEY. The **currency** in Italy is the *lira*. Banks tend to offer the best exchange rates. **Traveler's checks** are the safest way to carry funds; **credit cards** are useful, but cannot be used at many budget establishments. **ATMs** abound. A traveler staying in a **hostel** and preparing meals from supermarket supplies can expect to spend L40-120,000 a day. In touristed areas, a **service charge** will probably be added to restaurant and hotel bills; leave an additional 5-10%. Give taxi drivers 10%. The **value added tax** in Italy (known as IVA) ranges from 12-35%. Upon departure from the EU, non-EU citizens can get a refund of the VAT for purchases over L650,000.

BUSINESS HOURS. Nearly everything closes from around 1 to 3 or 4pm for siesta. Most museums are open 9am to 1pm and 3 to 6pm; some are open through lunch, however. Monday is often their *giorno di chiusura* (day of closure).

ACCOMMODATIONS AND CAMPING

HOSTELS. Associazione Italiana Alberghi per la Gioventù (AIG), the Italian **hostel** federation and affiliate of Hostelling International (HI), runs dozens of youth hostels *(ostelli per la gioventù)* across the country, especially in the north. A full list is available from most **EPT** and **CTS** offices and from many hostels. Prices average about L60,000 per night, including breakfast. Hostels are the best option for solo travelers (single rooms are relatively scarce in hotels), but curfews, lockouts, distant locations, and less-than-perfect security detract from their appeal. For more information, contact the **AIG office,** V. Cavour, 44 (☎06 487 11 52), in Rome.

HOTELS. Italian hotel rates are set by the state; hotel owners will need your passport to register you, don't be afraid to hand it over for a while (usually overnight), but ask for it as soon as you think you will need it. One-star *pensioni* are the best options. Prices fluctuate by region, but singles usually start around L50-60,000, doubles L70-80,000. By law, the price must be posted in each room; if it isn't, get it in writing. Check to see if breakfast and showers are additional and/or mandatory. A room with a private bath *(con bagno)* usually costs 30-50% more. A new breed of tourist office, the **Azienda di Promozione Turismo (APT),** provides lists of hotels that have paid to be listed; some of the hotels we recommend may not be on the list.

OTHER LOCAL ACCOMMODATIONS. Affittacamere (rooms to let in private residences) can be significantly less. Try to reach your destination and begin looking for accommodations before noon, especially in summer. If you must arrive late, call and reserve a day ahead. **B&Bs** generally run L60-400,000 for a single; www.bedandbreakfast.com lists options throughout Italy.

CAMPING. Camping sites tend to be loud, modern, and crowded. They cost around L8000 per person (or tent) plus L7000 per car, and cost much more near big cities.

FOOD AND DRINK

For simple, hearty, and inexpensive eating, try *alimentari* stores; they often prepare *panini* (sandwiches) with cold cuts and cheese: *Bel Paese*, *provolone*, *La Fontina*, or *mozzarella*. *Rosticcerie* sell hot food to take out and are often the cheapest option for a filling dinner. A *tavola calda* is a cheap, sit-down option. *Osterie*, *trattorie*, and *ristoranti* are, in ascending order, fancier and more expensive. They are usually open 12:30 to 2pm and 7 to 11pm (later in the south). Pizza can be sold by the *etto* (100g) or the *fetta* (slice) in a *pizza a taglio* place. In a sit-down pizzeria, you can order a whole round pizza. Menus in smaller restaurants are often incomplete or nonexistent; ask for the *piatti del giorno* (daily specials). A *menù turistico*, when offered, might run only L15-25,000 for a full meal, but variety is limited. Sit-down establishments often charge *pane e coperto* (bread and cover charge), usually around L2-3000. Check whether service is included *(servizio compreso)*. A full meal consists of an *antipasto* (appetizer), a *primo* (pasta or soup), a *secondo* (meat or fish) occasionally with a *contorno* (vegetable), and usually salad, fruit, and/or cheese. In the north, butter and cream sauces dominate. Rome and central Italy are notoriously spicy regions. Farther south, tomatoes play an increasingly significant role. Pastries also become sweeter toward the south. Coffee is another rich and varied focus of Italian life; espresso is to shoot, cappuccino is the breakfast beverage. *Caffè macchiato* ("spotted") is espresso with a touch of milk, while *latte macchiato* is milk with a splash of coffee. Wines from the north of Italy, such as the Piedmont's *Asti Spumante* or Verona's *Soave*, tend to be heavy and full-bodied; stronger, fruitier wines come from the hotter climate of south Italy and the islands. In almost every Italian town shops sell Italy's greatest contribution to civilization: *gelato* (ice cream).

COMMUNICATION

MAIL. Airmail letters under 1 oz. between North America and Italy take four to seven days and cost US$0.90 or CDN$1.35. Allow at least 7 days from Australia (postage AUS$1.52 for up to 1 oz.) and at least three days from Britain (postage UK£0.64 for up to 1 oz.). Envelopes should be marked "air mail" or "par avion." Since Italian mail is notoriously unreliable, it is usually safer and quicker to send mail express *(espresso)* or registered *(raccomandata)*. *Fermo Posta* is Italian for *Poste Restante*. When picking up your mail, bring a form of photo ID, preferably a passport.

TELEPHONES. Some phones take only coins—put more in than you think you'll need, or risk getting cut off. The most common type of phone accepts phone cards (L5000, L10,000, or L15,000 from *tabacchi*, newsstands, bars, post offices, and the occasional machine). A collect call is a *contassa a carico del destinatario* or *chiamata collect.* **International direct dial** numbers include: **AT&T,** ☎172 10 11; **Sprint,** ☎172 18 77; **MCI WorldPhone Direct,** ☎172 10 22; **Canada Direct,** ☎172 10 01; **BT Direct,** ☎172 00 44; **Ireland Direct,** ☎172 03 53; **Australia Direct,** ☎172 10 61; **Telecom New Zealand Direct,** ☎172 10 64; **Telkom South Africa Direct,** ☎172 10 27.

INTERNET ACCESS. Internet cafes are constantly popping up in Italian cities and larger towns. Universities and libraries may offer free Internet access. Italian cyberspots are listed on www.ecs.cafe/#list and www.cybercaptive.com.

HOLIDAYS AND FESTIVALS

Holidays: Italy closes on the following holidays: New Year's Day (Jan. 1); Epiphany (Jan. 6); Easter Sunday and Monday (Apr. 23-24); Liberation Day (Apr. 25); Labor Day (May 1); Assumption of the Virgin (Aug. 15); All Saints' Day (Nov. 1); Immaculate Conception (Dec. 8); Christmas Day (Dec. 25); and Santo Stefano (Dec. 26). August is vacation month for Italians; the cities shut down and empty out.

Festivals: The most common excuse for a local festival is the celebration of a religious event–a patron saint's day or the commemoration of a miracle. Most include parades, music, wine, obscene amounts of food, and boisterousness. Though **Jubilee 2001** will take place during the entire year, smaller local festivities add a unique flavor to any vacation. **Carnevale,** held in February during the 10 days before Lent, energizes Italian towns; in Venice, costumed Carnevale revelers fill the streets and canals (see p. 609). During **Scoppio del Carro,** held in Florence's P. del Duomo on Easter Sunday, Florentines set off a cart of explosives, following a tradition dating back to medieval times. On July 2 and Aug. 16, the **Palio** hits Siena (see p. 639), which celebrates the event with a horse race around the central *piazza.*

ROME (ROMA)

Italy's massive capital is an eruption of marble domes, noseless statues, and motorcycle dust. Rome is a sensory overload, rushing down the hills of Lazio to knock you down, leaving you gasping for air, and dying for more. The city and those it controlled were responsible for the development of over 2000 years of world history, art, architecture, politics, and literature. Rome has been the capital of kingdoms and republics; from this city, the Roman Empire defined the Western world, and from here, the Catholic Church spread its influence worldwide. For the traveler, there is so much to see, hear, eat, smell, and absorb that the city is both exhilarating and overwhelming. Never fear, however, because in *bella Roma*, everything is beautiful and everything tastes good. Liberate your senses from the pollution eroding the monuments and from the maniacal crush of motorcyclists, and enjoy the dizzying paradox that is the *Caput Mundi*, the Eternal City, Rome.

For more detailed information about Rome, curl up with *Let's Go: Rome 2001.*

GETTING THERE AND AWAY

Flights: Leonardo da Vinci International Airport (☎06 659 51), known as **Fiumicino,** handles most flights. The Termini train runs to **Stazione Termini** (30min.; 12 and 37min. past the hr. 7:37am-10:37pm; L16,000, L40,000 on board). After hours, take the blue COTRAL bus to Tiburtina (1:15, 2:15, 3:30, and 5am; L8000, pay on board). From Tiburtina, take bus #40N to Termini. Most charter flights arrive at Ciampino (☎06 79 49 41). To get to Rome, take COTRAL (about every 30min. 6:10am-11pm, L2000) to the Anagnina station on Metro Linea A.

Trains: The main station is **Termini.** To: **Naples** (2-2½hr., L18,600); **Florence** (2-3hr., L40,900); **Venice** (5hr., L66,000); and **Milan** (4½-8hr., L50,500). Trains arriving midnight-5am may arrive at Tiburtina or Ostiense; take bus #40N or 20N-21N to Termini.

GETTING AROUND

Public Transportation: The 2 **Metropolitana** subway lines meet at Termini and run 5:30am-11:30pm. **Buses** run 6am-midnight (there are limited late-night routes); board at the front or back and validate your ticket in the machine. Buy **tickets** (L1500) at *tabacchi*, newsstands, and station machines; they're valid for 1 Metro ride or unlimited bus travel within 1¼hr. of validation. **B.I.G. daily tickets** (L8000) and **C.I.S. weekly tickets** (L32,000) allow unlimited bus or train travel everywhere in Rome except Fiumicino. **Pickpockets are rampant on buses and trains.**

Taxis: Radiotaxi (☎06 35 70) and **Prontotaxi** (☎06 66 45). From city center to airport L70,000. Base fare L4500. Surcharges: night L5000; Su L2000; luggage L2000.

Car Rental: Avis (☎064 19 98; www.avis.com), **Europcar** (☎064 88 28 54; www.europcar.it), and **Maggiore** (☎062 29 15 30; www.maggiore.it).

Bike and Moped Rental: Scooters for Rent, V. della Purificazione 84 (☎064 88 54 85) off P. Barberini. Has bikes (L20,000 per day, L100,000 weekly) and mopeds (L50,000 per day, L250,000 weekly). Open daily in summer 9am-7pm.

ORIENTATION

The train station, **Termini,** is the arrival point for most visitors. **Via Nazionale** is the central artery connecting **Piazza della Repubblica** with **Piazza Venezia,** home to the immense wedding-cake-like **Vittorio Emanuele II monument.** West of P. Venezia, **Largo Argentina** marks the start of **C. Vittorio Emanuele,** which leads into Centro Storico, the medieval and Renaissance tangle of sights around the **Pantheon, Piazza Navona, Campo dei Fiori,** and **Piazza Farnese.** From P. Venezia, V. dei Fori Imperiale leads southeast to the **Forum** and **Colosseum,** south of which are the ruins of the **Baths of Caracalla** and the **Appian Way,** and the neighborhoods of southern Rome, the Aventine, Testaccio, Ostiense, and EUR. **Via del Corso** stretches from P. Venezia north to **Piazza del Popolo.** East of the Corso, fashionable streets border the **Piazza di Spagna** and, to the northeast, the **Villa Borghese.** South and east are the **Fontana di Trevi, Piazza Barberini,** and the **Quirinal Hill.** Across the Tiber to the north are **Vatican City,** and, to the south, **Trastevere,** the best neighborhood for wandering. Some people say Rome is impossible to navigate without a map. These people are correct. Using the free, ubiquitous **McDonald's** map will get you lost, although you may stumble upon a Big Mac. Instead, pick up a free map from a tourist office or *Let's Go*'s 30-page **map guide.** The invaluable **Roma Metro-Bus map** (L8000) is available at newsstands. Refer also to the **color maps** at the front of this book.

PRACTICAL INFORMATION

TOURIST AND FINANCIAL SERVICES

Tourist Agency: Enjoy Rome, V. Marghera 8a (☎06 445 68 90; www.enjoyrome.com). From Termini's middle concourse (between the trains and the ticket booths), exit right with the trains behind you, cross V. Marsala, and it's 3 blocks down V. Marghera. Owners answer questions in perfect English for free. Enjoy Rome arranges hotel accommodations and short-term apartments, offers Internet access, and runs a travel agency, booking transportation worldwide. They also run 3hr. English tours (L30,000 each; under 26 L25,000); a stroll through Trastevere and the Jewish Ghetto; a comprehensive bike tour (L35,000); a bus tour of Rome's famous cinematic areas (L50,000); and Pompeii bus trips (L70,000). **Branch** at V. Varese 39 (walk down V. Marghera another block and turn right). Open M-F 8:30am-2pm and 3:30-6:30pm, Sa 8:30am-2pm.

Embassies and Consulates: Australia, V. Alessandria 215 (☎06 85 27 21, emergency ☎800 87 77 90). Open M-Th 9am-5pm, F 9am-12:30pm. **Canada** (consulate), V. Zara 30 (☎06 44 59 84 21). Passport services open M-F 10am-noon and 2-4pm. Embassy, V. G. B. De Rossi 27 (☎06 44 59 81). **Ireland** (consulate), P. Campitelli 3 (☎06 697 91 21). Passport services open M-F 10am-12:30pm and 3-4:30pm. **New Zealand,** V.

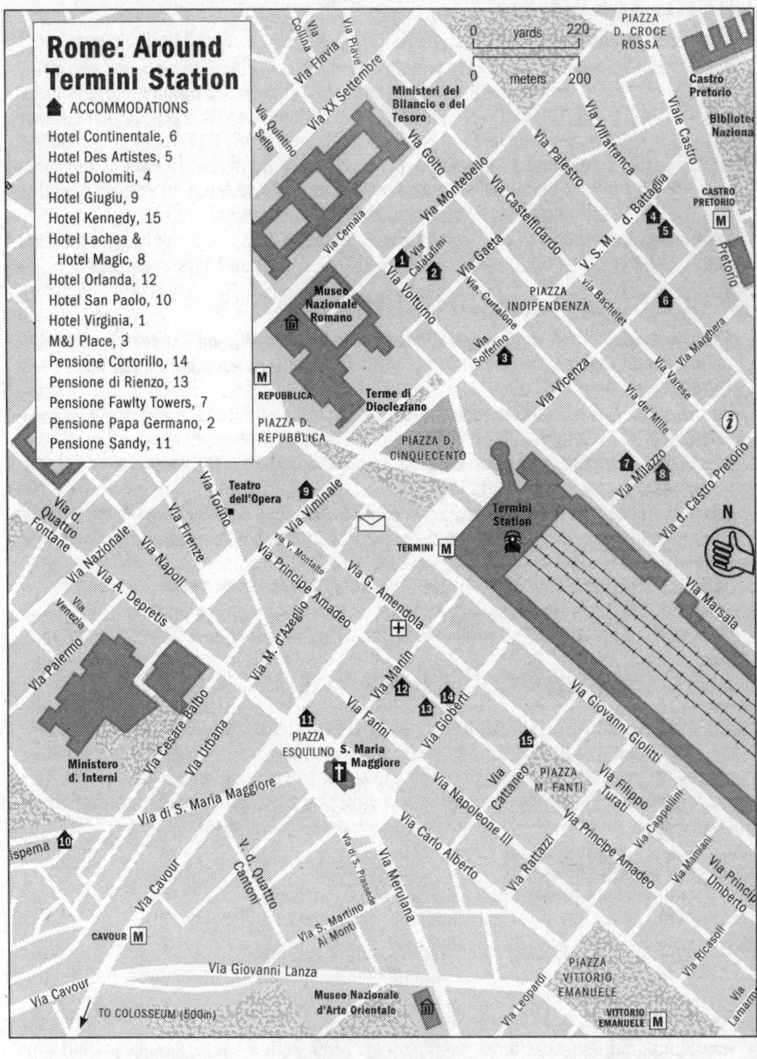

Zara 28 (☎064 41 71 71). Consular and passport services open M-F 9:30am-noon. Embassy services M-F 8:30am-12:45pm and 1:45-5pm. **South Africa,** V. Tanaro 14 (☎06 85 25 41). Open M-F 9am-noon. **UK,** V. XX Settembre 80a (☎064 82 54 41; consulate 06 42 20 26 00). Consular and passport services open M-F 9:15am-1:30pm. **US,** V. Veneto 119a (☎064 67 41). Passport and consular services open M-F 8:30-noon and 1:30-3:30pm. Visas M-F 8:30-10:30am.

American Express, P. di Spagna 38, 00187 Roma (☎066 76 41; lost or stolen cards and/or checks ☎067 22 81; fax 06 67 64 24 99). Open Sept.-July M-F 9am-7:30pm, Sa 9am-3pm; Aug. M-F 9am-6pm, Sa 9am-12:30pm.

Thomas Cook, P. Barberini 21a (☎064 82 80 82). Open M-Sa 9am-8pm, Su 9:30am-5pm. Branches at V. della Conciliazione 23-25 (☎06 68 30 04 35; open M-Sa 8:30am-6pm, Su 9am-5pm) and P. della Repubblica 65 (☎06 48 64 95; open M-F 9am-5pm with 1hr. lunch break, Sa 9am-1pm).

LOCAL SERVICES

Luggage Storage: In Termini, track #1. L5000 per 12hr. Open daily 7am-midnight.

English Bookstores: **Libreria Feltrinelli International,** V. V. E. Orlando 84-86 (☎064 82 78 78), by P. della Repubblica. Open daily 9am-7:30pm. **Anglo-American Bookshop,** V. della Vite 102 (☎066 79 52 22), south of the Spanish Steps. Open M-F 9am-1pm and 4-8pm, Sa 9am-1pm.

Bi-Gay-Lesbian Services: ARCI-GAY, V. Orvinio 2 (☎06 86 38 51 12) and V. Lariana 8 (☎068 55 55 22). **Circolo di Cultura Omosessuale Mario Mieli,** V. Corinto 5 (☎065 41 39 85; www.mariomieli.it). Open M-F 9am-1pm and 2-6pm; closed Aug.

Laundromat: OndaBlu, V. La Mora 7 (☎800 86 13 46). Many locations. Wash L6000 per 6.5kg load; dry L6000 per 6.5kg load; soap L1500. Open daily 8am-10pm.

EMERGENCY AND COMMUNICATIONS

Emergencies: Police: ☎113. **Carabinieri:** ☎112. **First Aid:** ☎118. **Ufficio Stranieri (Foreigners' Office),** V. Genova 2 (☎06 46 86 28 76), around the corner from Questura. Open 24hr.

Pharmacies: Farmacia Internazionale, P. Barberini 49 (☎064 87 11 95). V, MC. **Farmacia Piram,** V. Nazionale 228 (☎064 88 07 54). V, MC. Both open 24hr.

Medical Assistance: Policlinico Umberto I, V. le di Policlinico 155 (☎064 99 71). M:B-Policlinico. Free first aid. Open 24hr.

Internet Access: **Marco's Bar,** V. Varese 54, 3 blocks north of Termini. Cool music and a well-stocked bar. L5000 per hr. with *Let's Go*. Open daily 5:30am-2am.

Post Office: Main Office, P. S. Silvestro 19, (☎066 79 84 95). South of P. di Spagna. Address mail to be held: First name SURNAME, Palazzo delle Poste, *In Fermo Posta*, Roma **00186,** Italy. **Branch,** V. delle Terme di Diocleziano, 30 (☎064 74 56 02), next to Termini. Both open M-F 9am-6pm, Sa 9am-2pm. **Postal codes:** 00100 to 00200.

ACCOMMODATIONS AND CAMPING

Rome swells with tourists around Easter, from May to July, and in September. Prices vary widely with the time of year, and a proprietor's willingness to negotiate increases in proportion to length of stay, number of vacancies, and group size. Termini swarms with hotel scouts trying to bring you to their establishments. Watch out for sneaky imposters with fake badges, especially late at night.

CENTRO STORICO

If being a bit closer to the sights is worth it to you, then choosing Rome's medieval center over the area near Termini may be worth the higher prices.

Albergo Pomezia, V. dei Chiavari 12 (☎/fax 066 86 13 71). Behind S. Andrea della Valle. Rooms with phones and breakfast. Singles L70-100,000, with bath L100-170,000; doubles L100-170,000, L130-220,000; extra bed 35% surcharge.

Albergo della Lunetta, P. del Paradiso 68 (☎066 86 10 80; fax 066 89 20 28). First right off V. dei Chiavari. Rooms with phones; some abut a small, fern-filled courtyard. Singles L90,000, with bath L110,000; doubles L140,000, L190,000; triples L190,000, L240,000; quads L240,000, 300,000.

Albergo Abruzzi, P. della Rotonda 69 (☎066 79 20 21). 200 ft. from the Pantheon. Old-fashioned but clean. Singles L75-105,000; doubles L120-150,000; triples L200,000.

Hotel Piccolo, V. dei Chiavari 32 (☎066 89 23 30). Rooms with fans and phones. Breakfast L7000. Curfew 1am. Singles L100,000, with bath L120,000; doubles L120,000, L160,000; triples with bath L170,000; quads with bath L180,000.

Hotel Navona, V. dei Sediari 8, 1st fl. (☎066 86 42 03; fax 06 68 21 13 92). V. dei Canestrari from P. Navona. This 16th-century Borromini building has been a *pensione* for 150 years. Breakfast included. Check-out 10am. Singles L140,000; doubles with bath L190,000, with A/C L220,000; triples with bath L260,000.

Albergo del Sole, V. del Biscione 76 (☎06 68 80 68 73), off Campo dei Fiori. Allegedly Rome's oldest *pensione*. Modern rooms with phone, fan, TV, and fantastic antique furniture. Singles L110-160,000; doubles L150-230,000.

NEAR PIAZZA DI SPAGNA

Can you really put a price tag on living a few steps from Prada? John Keats couldn't.

Pensione Panda, V. della Croce 35 (☎066 78 01 79; www.webeco.it/hotelpanda). Painted, vaulted bathroom ceilings. Check-out 11am. In high season, singles L70-100,000; doubles L120-180,000; triples L180-210,000; quads L240-320,000.

Pensione Jonella, V. della Croce 41 (☎066 79 79 66; email jonella@lodgingitaly.com). Quiet, roomy, and cool even in summer. No reception; call ahead to arrange for someone to meet you when you arrive. Singles L100,000; doubles L120,000. Cash only.

Hotel Pensione Suisse S.A.S., V. Gregoriana 54 (☎066 78 36 49; fax 066 78 12 58). Old-fashioned furniture, comfy beds, fax, and phones. In-room breakfast included. Curfew 2am. Singles L135,000, with bath L155,000; doubles L165,000, L225,000; triples L285,000; quads L340,000. Half the bill may be paid by credit card.

Hotel Boccaccio, V. del Boccaccio 25 (☎064 88 59 62). M:A-Barberini. Friendly staff welcome you to an elegant decor with wood floors. Singles L80,000; doubles L110,000, with bath L150,000; triples L140,000, L180,000.

BORGO AND PRATI (NEAR VATICAN CITY)

Home to lots of priests and nuns, the Vatican and environs are pretty quiet at night.

Colors, V. Boezio 31 (☎/fax 066 87 40 30). M:A-Ottaviano. Take V. Cola di Rienzo to V. Terenzio. Sporting lots of amenities and a cool English-speaking staff, Colors offers clean rooms in the elegant Prati area. Kitchen, satellite TV, hair dryers, Internet, laundry service. Beautiful terrace open until 11:30pm. Dorms L30,000; doubles L110-140,000; triples L130-170,000. Reserve with credit card; payment in cash only.

Pensione Ottaviano, V. Ottaviano 6 (☎06 39 73 72 53; email gi.costantini@agora.stm.it). Satellite TV, individual lockers, fridges, a microwave, hot showers, free linens, and free email access for guests. Friendly Aussie and British staff and a lively backpacking clientele. Lockout 11am-2pm. Dorms L30,000, in winter L25,000; doubles L90,000, L60,000; triples L120,000.

Hotel Pensione Joli, V. Cola di Rienzo 243, 6th fl. (☎063 24 18 54; fax 06 324 18 93). Winding, blue-striped walls. All rooms with bath and telephone. Breakfast included. Singles L110,000; doubles L160,000; triples L215,000; quads L270,000.

Hotel Florida, V. Cola di Rienzo 243 (☎063 24 18 72). Floral carpets, floral bedspreads, floral wall decorations. Rooms with fans, TVs, phones, and hair dryers. Singles L120-140,000; doubles L180,000; triples L240,000; quads with bath L280,000.

Hotel Lady, V. Germanico 198, 4th fl. (☎063 24 21 12; fax 063 24 34 46). A boisterous, non-English-speaking Roman couple has been running this small *pensione* for 30 years. Phones in rooms. Singles L120,000; doubles L160,000, with bath L180,000.

TRASTEVERE

The streets of this artsy neighborhood come alive at night, and by day are filled with markets and working-class Romans going about their business.

Hotel Trastevere, V. Luciano Manara 25 (☎065 81 47 13, fax 065 88 10 16). Take a right off V. di Trastevere onto V. delle Fratte di Trastevere. Nine quiet rooms with graceful furniture, bath, TV, phone. Breakfast L10,000. Singles L120,000; doubles L150,000; triples L180,000; quads L200,000.

Hotel Carmel, V. G. Mameli 11 (☎065 80 99 21; email hotelcarmel@hotmail.com). Take a right on V. E. Morosini (V. G. Mameli) off V. di Trastevere. All rooms with bath and breakfast. Singles L100,000; doubles L150,000; triples L190,000; quads L220,000.

TERMINI AND SAN LORENZO

Welcome to budget traveler central. Be cautious south of Termini at night.

NORTH OF TERMINI

Pensione Fawlty Towers, V. Magenta 39 (☎/fax 064 45 03 74; www.enjoyrome.it/ftytwhtl.htm). From Termini, cross V. Marsala onto V. Marghera, and turn right onto V. Magenta. Fawlty Towers never fails to satisfy its customers. Common room with satellite

TV, library, refrigerator, microwave, and free Internet. Check-out 9am for dorms and 10am for private rooms. Dorm-style quads L30-35,000 (no children); singles L70-85,000; doubles L100-130,000; triples L140-155,000.

Hotel Des Artistes, V. Villafranca 20 (☎064 45 43 65; www.hoteldesartistes.com). From Termini, turn left on V. Marsala, right on V. Vicenza, then take the 5th left. Rooms with bathrooms, safes, fridges, and TVs. Reception 24hr. Dorms L35,000; singles L70,000; doubles L110-L170,000; triples L130-L210,000. In winter 20-30% off.

Pensione Papa Germano, V. Calatafimi 14a (☎06 48 69 19; fax 06 47 88 12 81; www.hotelpapagermano.it). From Termini, turn left onto V. Marsala. Internet. Check-out 11am. Singles L45-60,000; doubles L70-130,000; triples L100-150,000.

Hotel Dolomiti and **Hotel Lachea,** V. S. Martino della Battaglia 11 (☎064 95 72 56; fax 064 45 46 65; www.hotel-dolomiti.it). From Termini, turn left on V. Marsala, then right on V. Solferino (V. S. Martino della Battaglia). Breakfast L10,000. Check-out 11am. A/C L20,000 per night. Singles L75-120,000; doubles L85-180,000; triples 110-210,000; quads L140-230,000. 5-person rooms available at negotiable price.

Pensione Tizi, V. Collina 48 (☎064 82 01 28; fax 064 74 32 66). 10min. from the station. From V. XX Settembre, take V. Piave, then go left on V. Flavia. Breakfast L9000. Check-out 11am. Singles L70,000, with bath L90,000; doubles L90,000, L110,000; triples L120,000, L148,000; quads L160,000, L180,000.

Hotel Castelfidardo and **Hotel Lazzari,** V. Castelfidardo 31 (☎064 46 46 38; fax 064 94 13 78). Off V. XX Settmebre. Check-out 11am. Singles L70,000; doubles L95,000, with bath L120,000; triples L120-150,000; quads available.

Hotel Pensione Cathrine, V. Volturno 27 (☎06 48 36 34). From Termini, turn left onto V. Marsala (V. Volturno). Breakfast L10,000. Singles L75,000, with bath L100,000; doubles L100,000, L120,000; triples L160,000. *Let's Go* discount L10,000.

Hotel Adventure, V. Palestro 88 (☎064 46 90 26; fax 064 46 00 84; www.hoteladventure.com). Off V. Marghera. Rooms with bath, satellite TV, phones, safes, and breakfast. A/C L30,000. Doubles L140,000; triples L200,000. Extra bed L35,000.

SOUTH OF TERMINI (ESQUILINO)

Pensione di Rienzo, V. Principe Amedeo 79a (☎064 46 71 31 or 064 46 69 80). Plain, cheap, and good rooms. Breakfast L15,000. Check-out 10am. Singles L35-80,000, with bath up to L90,000; doubles L40-90,000, with bath up to L110,000.

Pensione Cortorillo, V. Principe Amedeo 79a, 5th fl. (☎064 46 69 34; fax 064 45 47 69). TV and full bath in all rooms. Breakfast included. Check-out 10am. Singles L100,000; doubles L70-100,000; triples 210,000; quads L280,000.

Hotel Kennedy, V. F. Turati 62-64 (☎064 46 53 73; email hotelkennedy@micanet.it). Bar, leather couches, and a library. Private baths, TV, and A/C. Breakfast included. Check-out 11am. Reservations by fax only. Singles L105,000; doubles L169-179,000; triples L299,000. 10% discount with *Let's Go*.

Hotel Il Castello, V. V. Amedeo II 9 (☎06 77 20 40 36; www.ilcastello.com). M:A-Manzoni. Take the 1st left off V. S. Quintino. A castle with small white rooms. Continental breakfast L5000. Check-out 10:30am. Dorms L30,000; singles L50-60,000; doubles L70-80,000, with bath L120-130,000; triples L105,000.

Hotel Orlanda, V. Principe Amedeo 76, 3rd fl. (☎064 88 01 24). At V. Gioberti. Breakfast included. Reception 24hr. Check-out 10am. A/C L20,000 extra. Singles L45-120,000; doubles L70-180,000; triples L90-220,000; quads L120-280,000.

Hotel Giu' Giu', V. del Viminale 8 (☎064 82 77 34; fax 06 48 91 26 16). In an elegant but fading *palazzo*. Breakfast L10,000. Check-out 10am. Singles L65,000; doubles L100,000, with bath L110,000; triples with bath L150,000; quads with bath L195,000.

WEST OF TERMINI

Hotel San Paolo, V. Panisperna 95 (☎064 74 52 13; email hsanpaolo@tin.it). From Termini, take V. Cavour, then take a right onto V. di S. Maria Maggiore (V. Panisperna). Check-out 10:30am. Singles L75,000; doubles L100-140,000; triples L135,000.

Pensione Sandy, V. Cavour, 136 4th fl. (☎064 88 45 85; www.sandyhostel.com). Past Santa Maria Maggiore. No sign; Hotel Valle is next door. Under the same ownership as Fawlty Towers. Internet free. Individual lockers. Dorms L25-30,000.

CAMPING

Camping on beaches, roads, and inconspicuous plots is illegal.

Seven Hills Village, V. Cassia 1216 (☎063 03 31 08 26; fax 063 03 31 00 39). 8km north of Rome. Take bus #907 from the Cipro-Musei Vaticani Metro(A), or bus #201 from P. Mancini. Ask where to get off–it's 3-4km past the GRA (the big highway that circles the city). From the stop, follow the country road about 1km until you see the sign. Bar, market, restaurant, *pizzeria,* disco, pool. Daily Vatican shuttles leave at 8 and 9:30am, round-trip L6000. Check-in 7am-11pm. L15,000 per person; L9000 per tent; L9000 per car; camper L16,000; bungalow L90-150,000. Open late Mar. to late Oct.

FOOD

Ancient Roman dinners were lavish, festive affairs lasting as long as 10 hours. Peacocks and flamingoes were served, while acrobats and fire-eaters distracted guests between courses of camels' feet and goat ears. Food orgies went on *ad nauseam,* literally—after gorging themselves, guests would retreat to a room called the *vomitorium,* throw it all up, and return to the party. Meals in Rome are still lengthy affairs, although they generally involve less vomiting. Restaurants tend to close between 3 and 7pm, so plan accordingly. **Cover prices** are bread charges. Get a taste of local produce at Rome's many outdoor **markets;** the largest are at P. Campo dei Fiori, P. Vittorio Emanuele II, and Piazza Navona, in via della Pace. **STANDA supermarkets** are at V. Cola di Rienzo 173 (near the Vatican), and V. di Trastevere 62.

RESTAURANTS

ANCIENT CITY

Despite its past glory, this area has yet to discover the noble concept of "affordable food." But along **V. dei Fori Imperiali,** several restaurants offer decent prices.

Taverna dei Quaranta, V. Claudia 24, off P. del Colosseo. Outdoor dining is amazing. 0.5L of wine L5000. Cover L3000. Open daily noon-3:30pm and 7:45pm-midnight.

I Buoni Amici, V. Aleardo Aleardi 4. From the Colosseum, take V. Labicana, turn right on V. Merulana, then left on V. A. Aleardi. *Linguine* with crayfish sauce L10,000. Cover L2500. Open M-Sa noon-3pm and 7-11:30pm.

CENTRO STORICO

The twisting streets of Rome's historic center offer many hidden gems. Expect to be serenaded by street performers, especially near P. Navona.

PIAZZA NAVONA

Pizzeria Pentola, V. Metastasio 21. Off P. di Campo Marzio. Try the truly, truly outrageous *Pizza dello chef* (spinach and parmesan), L13,000. Open daily noon-11pm.

Pizzeria Baffetto, V. del Governo Vecchio 114. At V. Sora. Once a meeting place for 60s radicals, Baffetto now overflows with those of the hungry persuasion. Cover L1000. Open M-F noon-3pm and 7:30pm-1am, Sa-Su noon-3pm and 7:30pm-2am.

Piedra del Sol, V. Rosini 6. Off V. di Campo Marzio. An Italian take on Mexican fare. *Chimichangas del Sol* L12,000. Open daily 12:30-3pm and 7:30pm-2am. Closed Aug.

CAMPO DEI FIORI AND THE JEWISH GHETTO

Trattoria da Sergio, V. delle Grotte 27 (☎066 54 66 69). Take V. dei Giubbonari and take your 1st right. Sergio offers honest-to-God Roman ambience and hearty portions of great food. Open M-Sa 12:30-3pm and 7pm-12:30am.

Trattoria Da Luigi, P. S. Cesarini 24 (☎066 86 59 46), near Chiesa Nuova. Enjoy inventive cuisine such as *tagliolini* with shrimp, asparagus, and tomato (L13,000). Great *antipasti* buffet. Cover L2000. Open Tu-Su 7pm-midnight.

Ristorante da Giggetto, V. del Portico d'Ottavio 21-22. Famed Giggetto has some of the city's finest cooking. If your food isn't spicy, sprinkle it with peppers picked from the potted pepper plants (free). Cover L3000. Open Tu-Su 12:30-3pm and 7:30-11pm.

Al 16, V. del Portico d'Ottavio 16. Near the Teatro di Marcello. Try the *Coda alla Vaccinara* (oxtail stew; L16,000). Cover L2500. Open W-M 12:30-3pm and 7:30-11pm.

La Pollarola, P. Pollarola 24-25, north of Campo dei Fiori. *"Si mangia bene e si spende giusto"* ("one eats well and pays a fair price"). Open M-Sa noon-3:30pm and 7:30pm-midnight.

PIAZZA DI SPAGNA

Although the Spanish Steps area may seem different from the less affluent environs of Termini, there is one big similarity—lots of bad food. The irony of it is that the same awful food here will be twice as much. Here are some exceptions:

Osteria dell'Ingegno, P. di Pietra, between the Trevi Fountain and the Pantheon. A modern take on Italian cuisine in an upscale setting. *Secondi* (L20-30,000) include a yummy tartar of fresh salmon and sea bass (L24,000). Risotto with asparagus tips, saffron, and parmesan L20,000. Cold eggplant soup with mint and yogurt L16,000. Huge salads L16-20,000. Open M-Sa noon-3pm and 7:30pm-midnight.

Trattoria da Settimio all'Arancio, V. dell'Arancio 50-52 (☎06 687 61 19). Take V. dei Condotti from P. di Spagna; take the 1st right after V. del Corso, then the 1st left. Excellent grilled *calamari* L18,000. Cover L2000. Open M-Sa 12:30-3pm and 7:30-11:30pm. Reservations accepted.

Centro Macrobiotico Italiano-Naturist Club, V. della Vite 14, 4th fl., just off V. del Corso. Fresh, well-seasoned macrobiotic and vegetarian fare in a breezy attic. *Primi* L10-12,000; *secondi* L12-18,000. Open M-F noon-3:30pm and 7:30-11pm.

BORGO & PRATI (NEAR VATICAN CITY)

Establishments near the Vatican serve mediocre sandwiches at hiked-up prices. For far better and much cheaper food, head a few blocks northeast.

Franchi, V. Cola di Rienzo 200-204 (☎066 87 46 51). Franchi ("Frankie") has been serving the happy folks of Prati superb sandwiches and other luxurious picnic supplies for nearly 50 years, and not an unsatisfied customer yet. Open M-Sa 8:15am-9pm.

Pizza Re, V. Oslavia 39. Serves some of Rome's best Neapolitan (thick crust) pizzas with every topping imaginable. Wonderful mousse and tiramisu. Lunch specials (pizza and drink) L11-13,000. Dinner L7-18,000. Takeout cheaper. Another location at V. di Ripetta 14, near P. de Popolo. Open M-Sa noon-3:30pm and 7:30-11pm, Su 7:30-11pm.

TRASTEVERE

By day, Trastevere's cobblestone streets rumble only with the sounds of children and Vespas, but when night falls, P. di Santa Maria di Trastevere is packed with expatriate hippies and their dogs, howling along with out-of-tune guitars.

Pizzeria San Calisto, P. S. Calisto 9a (☎065 81 82 56). Right off P. S. Maria in Trastevere. Massive *pizze* (L9-15,000) roam free at this busy neighborhood pizzeria. The *bruschetta* (L3-4000) alone is worth a postcard home. Open Tu-Su 7pm-midnight.

Augusto, P. de' Rienzi 15 (☎065 80 37 98). North of P. S. Maria in Trastevere. Enjoy the daily pasta specials at lunch (around L8000) and the *pollo arrosto con patate* (L10,500). The homemade desserts are out of this world, but you need to be assertive to get service. Open M-F 12:30-3pm and 8-11pm, Sa 12:30-3pm. Closed Aug.

Ristorante al Fontanone, P. Trilussa 46. North of P. S. Maria in Trastevere. Traditional Roman food. Open W-Su noon-2pm and 7-11pm. Closed mid-Aug. to early Sept.

Il Tulipano Nero, V. Roma Libera 15 (☎065 81 83 09). Right on V. E. Morosini off V. di Trastevere. Some of Rome's most innovative and biggest pizzas. Open Tu-Su 6pm-2am.

TERMINI

So you're near the train station, hungry, and in a hurry; this is no reason to subject yourself to the nightmare of a shady tourist trap offering a L10,000 "quick lunch."

La Cantinola da Livio, V. Calabria 26 (☎06 42 82 05 19). From V. XX Settembre, turn left on V. Piave, then take the 4th left onto V. Calabria. The spaghetti with seafood, caviar, tomato, and cream (L12,000) is transcendent. Lobster L120,000. Cover L1500. Open M-Sa 12:30-3pm and 7:20-11:30pm. Closed first 3 weeks of Aug.

Africa, V. Gaeta 26-28. Near P. Independenza. Excellent Ethiopian. Meat-filled *sambusas* L4500. *Zighini beghi* (roasted lamb in spicy sauce) L12,000. Cover L1500. Open M-Sa 8pm-midnight.

Trattoria da Bruno, V. Varese 29. From V. Marsala, walk 3 blocks down V. Milazzo and turn right onto V. Varese. *Tortellini* with cream and mushrooms L10,000. Homemade *gnocchi* L10,000. Open daily noon-3:30pm and 7-10:15pm. Closed Aug.

Gold Bar, P. del Viminale 1. Off V. A. Depretis. You won't find a seat during peak hours, for good reason. Entrees L4-5000. Open M-F noon-3pm.

SAN LORENZO

From Termini, walk south on V. Pretoriano to P. Tiburtino, or take bus #492 to Rome's funky university district. Women may find the walk uncomfortable at night.

Il Pulcino Ballerino, V. degli Equi 66-68. Off V. Tiburtina. Artsy scene and cuisine. *Tagliolini* in lemon cream sauce L12,000. Or, prepare your meal on a heated stone. Cover L1000. Open M-Sa 1-3:30pm and 8pm-midnight. Closed first week of Aug.

Arancia Blu, V. dei Latini 65 (☎064 45 41 05). Off V. Tiburtina. An elegant little vegetarian restaurant with elaborate dishes like *tonnarelli* with sheep cheese and truffles (L12,000). Extensive wine list. Open M-F noon-3pm and 7-11pm, Sa-Su 7-11pm.

Il Capellaio Matto, V. dei Marsi 25. From V. Tiburtina, take the 4th right off V. degli Equi. Vegetarians, rejoice! *Risotto al pepe verde* (rice with green peppercorn; L9000), unique salads, and crepes. Plenty of meat, too. Cover L1500. Open W-M 8pm-midnight.

TESTACCIO

Once home to a giant slaughterhouse, this working-class neighborhood is the center of Roman nightlife. Eateries offer just about every animal part imaginable.

Pizzeria Ficini, V. Luca della Robbia 23 (☎065 74 30 17). Take V. Luigi Vanvitelli off V. Marmorata, then the 1st left. A no-frills pizzeria befitting this working-class community. Pizzas (L6-8000). Calzone L8000. 1L wine L6000. Open Sept.-July Tu-Su 6-11:30pm.

Luna Piena, V. Luca della Robbia 15-17. Stupendous *carpaccio di salmone* appetizer L10,000. *Rigatoni con pagliata* L10,000. Open Th-Tu noon-3pm and 7:30-11:30pm.

Non Solo Pizza, V. Benjamino Franklin 11 (☎065 68 50 31). Not only pizza, but also kebab! Popular with students. Open 6:30pm-12:30am, in winter also noon-4:30pm.

Trattoria da Bucatino, V. Luca della Robbia 84-86. Take V. Luigi Vanvitelli off V. Marmorata, then the 1st left. Dishes involving animal entrails, as well as pasta, pizza, and seafood. Cover L2000. Open Tu-Su 12:30-3:30pm and 6:30-11:30pm. Closed Aug.

DESSERTS

Cheap *gelato* is as plentiful as leather pants. Look for *gelato* with very muted (hence natural) colors, or try some of our favorite *gelaterie* and other sweet-shops.

San Crispino, V. della Panetteria 42. Near P. di Trevi. Positively the world's best *gelato*. Don't miss the meringue, armagnac, and grapefruit flavors. Cups L3-10,000. Open M and W-Th noon-12:30am, F-Sa noon-1:30am, Su noon-midnight.

Tre Scalini, P. Navona 30. This chic, old-fashioned spot is famous for its *tartufo,* a hunk of truffled chocolate ice cream rolled in chocolate shavings (L5000 at the bar, L11,000 sitting). Bar open Th-Tu 9am-1:30am.

Giolitti, V. degli Uffici del Vicario, 40. From the Pantheon, follow V. del Pantheon to its end, take V. della Maddelena to its end, and turn right. *Gelato* in dozens of flavors. Festive and crowded at night. Cones L3-5000. Open daily 9am-1am. Nov.-Apr. closed M.

Forno del Ghetto, V. Portico d'Ottavia 1, in the Jewish Ghetto. Fabulous blueberry pies, buttery cookies, and more. Open Su-Th 8am-8pm, F 8am-5:30pm.

ENOTECHE (WINE BARS)

Roman wine bars range from laid-back and local to chic and international.

Trimani Wine Bar, V. Cernaia 37b (☎064 46 96 30). Near Termini, perpendicular to V. Volturno (V. Marsala). Pastas (L12,000), filling quiches, smoked fish, an impressive cheese board, and desserts (L9-12,000). Wines from L3500 a glass. Open M-Sa 11am-3:30pm and 6pm-12:30am. Reservations recommended for dinner.

La Bottega del Vino da Anacleto Bleve, V. S. Maria del Pianto 9a-11. Light pasta (L9-12,000) and a range of cheeses, smoked fish, and cured meats. Glasses begin at L4000. Open Tu and Sa 12:45-3pm, W-F 12:45-3pm and 8-10pm.

Bar Da Benito, V. dei Falegnami 14. Off P. Mattei in the Jewish Ghetto. A tiny shop lined with bottles and hordes of hungry workmen. One pasta is prepared each day (L6000), along with delicious *secondi.* Open M-Sa 6am-8pm; lunch noon-3:30pm. Closed Aug.

SIGHTS

Rome wasn't built in a day, and you can't see it in one, either. Ancient temples and forums, Renaissance basilicas, 280 fountains, and 981 churches cluster together in a city bursting with masterpieces from every era of Western civilization.

THE ANCIENT CITY

ROMAN FORUM

Main entrance: V. dei Fori Imperiali (between P. Venezia and the Colosseum). Other entrances are opposite the Colosseum (from here, you can reach the Palatine Hill, too) and at the Clivus Capitolinus, near P. del Campidoglio. M:B-Colosseo, or bus to P. Venezia. Open M-Sa 9am-7pm, Su 9am-1pm; in winter M-Sa 9am-1hr. before sunset, Su 9am-1hr. before sunset; sometimes closes M-F by 3pm, Su and holidays by noon. Free. Guided tour with archaeologist L6000; audioguide tour for Forum L7000 in English, French, German, Italian, Japanese, or Spanish; both available at main entrance.

The Forum was originally a marshland, prone to flooding from the Tiber, eschewed by Rome's Iron Age inhabitants (1000-900 BC) in favor of the Palatine Hill. In the 7th and 8th centuries BC, Etruscans and Greeks used the Forum as a weekly market. The soon-to-be-Romans founded a thatched-hut shantytown on the site in 753 BC, when Romulus and Sabine leader Titus Tatius met to end the war triggered by the rape of the Sabine women. The Forum bears witness to centuries of civic building, with layers excavated at random in a crumbling jumble. The entrance ramp leads to **Via Sacra,** Rome's oldest street.

CIVIC FORUM. The **Basilica Aemilia,** built in 179 BC, housed the guild of the *argentarii* (money changers). It was rebuilt several times after fires; in the pavement you can still see bronze marks from melted coins. Next to the Basilica Aemilia stands the **Curia,** or Senate House, one of the Forum's oldest buildings. It was converted to a church in AD 630 and restored by Mussolini. The Curia houses the **Plutei of Trajan,** two parapets that depict the burning of the tax registers and the distribution of food to poor children. The broad space in front of the Curia was the **Comitium,** where male citizens came to vote and representatives of the people gathered for public discussion. This space was also home to the **Twelve Tables,** bronze tablets upon which the codified laws of the Republic were inscribed. Bordering the Comitium is the large brick **Rostrum,** or speaker's platform, erected by Julius Caesar in 44 BC, just before his death. To the right, the hefty **Arch of Septimius Severus** was dedicated in AD 203 to celebrate that emperor's victories in the Middle East.

MARKET SQUARE. A number of shrines and sacred precincts, including the **Lapis Niger** (Black Stone), where Romulus was supposedly murdered by Republican senators, once graced the square in front of the Curia. Below the Lapis Niger rest the underground ruins of a 6th-century BC altar, along with a pyramidal pillar where the oldest known Latin inscription in Rome warns against defiling the shrine. In the square, the **Three Sacred Trees** of Rome—olive, fig, and grape—have been replanted by the Italian state. The newest part of the Forum is the **Column of Phocas,** erected in AD 608 for the visiting Byzantine emperor, Phocas.

LOWER FORUM. The three great temples of the lower Forum have been closed off for excavations and restoration; however, the eight columns of the **Temple of Saturn** have at last shed their scaffolding cloak. Built in the early 5th century BC, it was once the site of Saturnalia, a raucous winter bash where class and social distinctions were forgotten, masters served slaves, and all was permitted. Around the corner, rows of column bases are the remains of the **Basilica Julia,** a courthouse built by Julius Caesar in 54 BC. At the far end, three white marble columns mark the massive podium of the restored **Temple of Castor and Pollux.** The twin gods helped the Romans defeat the Etruscans at the Battle of Lake Regillus (496 BC), then appeared in the Forum to water their tired horses at the nearby **Basin of Juturna.** Down the road from the temple is the rectangular base of the **Temple of the Deified Julius,** which Augustus built in 29 BC to honor his murdered adoptive father (and, incidentally, to proclaim himself the son of a god). Augustus also built the **Arch of Augustus,** which framed V. Sacra. The circular building behind the Temple of the Deified Julius is the restored **Temple of Vesta,** dating back to the time of the Etruscans. In this temple, the Vestal Virgins tended the city's eternal, sacred fire, keeping it continuously lit for more than a thousand years.

UPPER FORUM. The **House of the Vestal Virgins** occupied the sprawling complex behind the Temple of Vesta. As long as they kept their vows of chastity, the virgins were among the most respected people in Ancient Rome. This esteem had a price; a virgin who strayed was buried alive with bread and a candle, allowing her to survive long enough to contemplate her sins. Statues of the priestesses, including one whose name was scraped away, reside in the central courtyard. The erased priestess is thought to have been Claudia, the Vestal Virgin who converted to Christianity at the end of the 4th century. Back on V. Sacra is the **Temple of Antoninus and Faustina** (right of the entrance ramp), which is unusually well preserved. In the 7th and 8th centuries, after attempts to pull the temple down, the **Church of San Lorenzo in Miranda** was built in its interior (you can see deep grooves at the top of the eight columns where cables were tied in futile attempts to tear it down). To the right lies the **necropolis,** where 8th-century BC graves have been uncovered, lending credence to the city's legendary founding date of 753 BC. Here V. Sacra runs over the **Cloaca Maxima,** an ancient sewer that still drains water from the valley.

VELIA. V. Sacra leads out of the Forum proper to the gargantuan **Basilica of Maxentius** (a.k.a. the **Basilica of Constantine**). Maxentius began construction of the basilica in AD 306, building until Constantine deposed him in 312 and completed the project. The middle apse once contained a gigantic statue of Constantine with a bronze body and marble head, legs, and arms. The uncovered remains, including a 6½ ft. long foot, are at the **Capitoline Museums** (see p. 597). The Baroque facade of the **Church of Santa Francesca Romana** (built over Hadrian's Temple to Venus—*Amor*—and Roma) hides the entrance to the **Antiquarium Forense,** a small museum displaying funerary urns and skeletons from the necropolis. (Open daily 9am-1pm. Free.) On the summit of the Velia, the road down from the Palatine, is the **Arch of Titus,** built in AD 81 by Domitian to celebrate his brother Titus, who destroyed Jerusalem. V. Sacra leads to an exit on the other side of the hill, an easy way to get to the Colosseum. The path in front of the arch climbs up to the Palatine Hill.

PALATINE HILL

Open M-Sa 9:30am-7:15pm, Su 9am-1pm; in winter M-Sa 9:30am-1hr. before sunset, Su 9am-1pm; sometimes closes M-F by 3pm, Su and holidays by noon. Last entrance 45min.

before closing. L12,000, EU citizens between 18 and 24 L6000, EU citizens under 18 and over 60 free. A 6-day ticket book is good for the 3 Musei Nazionali Romani, the Colosseum, and the Palatine Hill (L30,000).

Start at the stairs near the Forum's **Arch of Titus.** This plateau between the Tiber and the Forum was home to the she-wolf who suckled Romulus and Remus. During the Republic, the Palatine was the most fashionable residential quarter, where aristocrats and statesmen, including **Cicero** and **Marc Antony,** built their homes. Emperors capitalized on the hill's prestige by building progressively grander quarters. By the end of the first century, the imperial residence had swallowed up the hill, whose Latin name, *Palatium*, became synonymous with its palace. Throughout the garden complex, terraces provide breathtaking views. Lower down, excavations continue on the 9th-century BC village, the **Casa di Romulo.** Right of the village is the podium of the 191 BC **Temple of Cybele.** The stairs to the left lead to the **House of Livia,** which is connected to the **House of Augustus.** Livia, Augustus's wife, was the first Empress. Around the corner, the long, spooky **Cryptoporticus** connected Tiberius's palace with nearby buildings; it may actually have been built by Nero in one of his more paranoid moments. The path around the House of Augustus leads to the vast ruins of **Domitian**'s palace (AD 81-96), divided into two wings. The solemn **Domus Augustana** was the emperors' private space. The exterior walls are so high that archaeologists are unsure how they were roofed over. Nearby lies the **Domus Flavia,** site of a gigantic octagonal fountain. Between the Domus Augustana and the Domus Flavia stands the **Palatine Antiquarium,** which houses artifacts found in the Palatine excavations. *(30 people admitted every 20min. starting at 9:10am. Free.)* Outside on the right, the east wing contains the curious **Stadium Palatinum,** or Hippodrome, a sunken oval space decorated with fragments of porticoes, statues, and fountains.

FORI IMPERIALI

Across from the Republican Forum is a trove of temples, basilicas, and public squares from the first and 2nd centuries AD. Julius Caesar originally expanded in this direction (likely trying to undercut the Senate's prestige by moving the city center away from the Curia). In the 1930s, Mussolini cleared the area and built the V. dei Fori Imperiali through the remains. In 1999, Rome decided to remove the road and reconnect the forums; it's unclear when or how this will be done.

FORUM OF TRAJAN. Finished in AD 113, the complex celebrated the Emperor's Dacian campaign (in modern-day Romania). It included a huge equestrian statue of Trajan and a triumphal arch. At one end of the forum, 2500 legionnaires march their way up **Trajan's Column,** one of the best-preserved specimens of Roman relief-sculpture. The crowing statue is St. Peter, who replaced Trajan in 1588.

FORUMS. Across V. dei Fori Imperiali, in the shade of the Vittorio Emanuele II monument, lie the paltry remains of the **Forum of Caesar,** including the ruins of Julius Caesar's **Temple to Venus Genetrix** (from whom he claimed descent). Nearby, the gray tufa wall of the **Forum of Augustus** commemorates Augustus's victory over Caesar's murderers at the Battle of Philippi in 42 BC. The narrow, rectangular **Forum Transitorium** connected the Forum of Augustus with the Republican Forum. The only remnant of **Vespatian's Forum** is the **Church of Santi Cosma e Damiano** across V. Cavour, near the Roman Forum. *(Open daily 9am-1pm and 3-7pm.)*

OUTSIDE THE FORI

THE COLOSSEUM. The enduring symbol of the Eternal City—a hollowed-out ghost of travertine marble that dwarfs every other ruin—once held as many as 50,000 crazed spectators. Within 100 days of its AD 80 opening, 5000 wild beasts perished here. The slaughter went on for three centuries. The floor (now partially restored and open for special events) covers a labyrinth of brick cells, ramps, and elevators used to transport animals from cages to the arena. *(M:B-Colosseo. Open daily 9am-6:30pm; in winter 9am-1hr. before sunset. L10,000, EU citizens 18-24 L5000, EU citizens under 18 and over 60 free. A 6-day ticket book is good for the 3 Musei Nazionali Romani, the Colosseum, and the Palatine Hill, L30,000. Archaeologist tours L6000; audioguide L7000.)*

CIAO MEOW Thanks to a bizarre 1988 law, Rome's stray cats have the right to live where they're born. Today, there are 10,000 colonies, hundreds of which are fed by the city. Look for the felines among the ruins, especially near Largo Argentina.

ARCO DI CONSTANTINO. Between the Colosseum and the Palatine lies the **Arch of Constantine,** one of the area's best-preserved imperial monuments, which commemorates his victory at the Battle of the Milvian Bridge in AD 312. He used fragments from monuments of Trajan, Hadrian, and Marcus Aurelius to create the triple arch.

DOMUS AUREA. This park houses a portion of Nero's "Golden House." Having decided that he was a god, Nero had a divine house made. Within the palace was an **enclosed lake,** where the Colosseum now stands. Nero crowned it all with a statue of himself as the sun; the 35m *Colossus* was the largest bronze statue ever made, and where the Flavian Amphitheater got its nickname. When Nero committed suicide only five years after building his pleasure garden, the Flavian emperors replaced all traces of the palace with monuments. *(From the Colosseum, walk through the gates up V. della Domus Aurea and make the 1st right. ☎06 39 74 99 07. Open Tu-Su 9am-8pm. L10,000. A guard gives an Italian or English tour. A better bet is the audioguide, L3000. Italian tour with archaeologist L6000. Reservations recommended. L2000, L3000 for guided tour.)*

VELABRUM. The Velabrum is a flat flood plain south of the Jewish Ghetto. At the bend of V. del Portico d'Ottavia, a shattered pediment and a few ivy-covered columns are all that remain of the once magnificent **Portico d'Ottavia.** The stocky, gray **Teatro di Marcello** next door bears the name of Augustus's unfortunate nephew, whose sudden death remains a mystery. If the theater looks like a Colosseum copycat, think again—the exterior, completed in 11 BC, served as a model for the arena across town. Down V. di Teatro di Marcello, **Chiesa di San Nicola in Carcere** incorporates temples dedicated to Juno, Janus, and Spes. *(☎06 686 99 72; call for interior visits. Open Sept.-July M-Sa 7:30am-noon and 4-7pm.)* A block south on V. L. Petroselli, **Chiesa di Santa Maria in Cosmedin**'s porch holds the **Bocca della Verità,** the relief made famous in the film *Roman Holiday.* According to legend, the hoary face chomps on liars' hands. *(Portico open daily 9am-7pm. Church open daily 10am-1pm and 3-7pm.)*

CAPITOLINE HILL. Home to the original capitol, the **Monte Capitolino** is the seat of Rome's government. Michelangelo designed its **Piazza di Campidoglio,** home to the **Capitoline Museums** (see p. 597). Stairs lead to the rear of the 7th-century **Chiesa di Santa Maria in Aracoeli.** Its stunning **Cappella Bufalini** is home to the *Santo Bambino*, a cherubic statue (a replica; the real one was stolen) that receives letters from sick children. *(Open daily 9am-6pm.)* The gloomy **Mamertine Prison,** consecrated as the **Church of San Pietro in Carcere,** lies down the hill behind the church. Here, St. Peter baptized his captors with waters that flooded his cell. *(Open daily 9am-noon and 2:30-6pm. Donation requested.)* When Pope Paul III remodeled the hill for Charles V's visit, he had Michelangelo fashion the imposing statues of the twin warriors Castor and Pollux and brought the **statue of Marcus Aurelius** from the Lateran Palace. The statue resides in the courtyard of the **Palazzo dei Conservatori** to protect it from pollution—a copy crowns the piazza. *(From P. Venezia, face the Vittorio Emanuele II monument, walk around to the right to P. d'Aracoeli, and take the stairs.)*

CIRCUS MAXIMUS AND BATHS OF CARACALLA. Boxed in the valley between the Palatine and Aventine Hills, the **Circus Maximus** is just a grassy shadow of its former glory. After its construction in about 600 BC, 300,000 Romans gathered to watch chariots careen around the track. The remains of the **Baths of Caracalla** are the city's largest and best-preserved baths; some 1500 muddy Romans could sponge themselves off here. Note the beautiful mosaics that cover the floors in this proto-health club. *(M:B-Circo Massimo, or walk down V. di San Gregorio from the Colosseum. Circus is always open. To get to the baths, take V. delle Terme di Caracalla from the eastern end of the Circus. Baths open daily 9am-6pm; in winter 9am-1hr. before sunset. L8000.)*

CENTRO STORICO

PIAZZA VENEZIA AND VIA DEL CORSO

Following the line of the ancient V. Lata, the **Via del Corso** takes its name from its days as Rome's premier race course, running nearly a mile between P. del Popolo and the P. Venezia (not much more than a glorified traffic circle dominated by the **Vittorio Emanuele II monument**). The crumbling **Palazzo Venezia,** right of the piazza as you face the monument, was one of the city's earliest Renaissance palazzi. Mussolini delivered orations from its balcony. Off V. del Corso, the picturesque **Piazza Colonna** was named for the colossal **Colonna di Marco Aurelio,** designed like Trajan's earlier column. Sixtus V added the St. Paul statue in the 16th century. The northwest corner of the piazza flows into another piazza, dominated by Bernini's **Palazzo Montecitorio,** now the seat of the Chamber of Deputies. The obelisk in front was once the centerpiece of a giant sundial that was part of Augustus's Ara Pacis complex.

PIAZZA DELLA ROTONDA

THE PANTHEON. This temple has remained remarkably the same since it was erected nearly 2000 years ago. Architects still wonder how it was erected—its dome, a half-sphere constructed from poured concrete without the support of vaults, arches, or ribs, is the largest of its kind. Across the facade's architrave, an inscription reads "Marcus Agrippa made it in his third consulship." Indeed, Agrippa did build a temple here in 27 BC, dedicated to all the gods, but Hadrian tore it down in AD 119 and started from scratch. In 606, it was consecrated the **Church of Santa Maria ad Martyres,** its name to this day. *(Open June M-Sa 9am-7pm, Su 9am-1pm; July-Aug. M-Sa 9am-7:30pm, Su 9am-1pm; Oct.-May M-Sa 9am-4pm, Su 9am-1pm. Free.)*

OTHER SIGHTS. In front of the temple, Giacomo della Porta's late-Renaissance fountain supports an Egyptian **obelisk.** Around the left side of the Pantheon, another obelisk, perched on Bernini's curious elephant statue, marks the center of tiny **Piazza Minerva.** Behind the obelisk, the **Chiesa di Santa Maria Sopra Minerva** hides Renaissance masterpieces, including Michelangelo's *Christ Bearing the Cross* and a statue of St. Sebastian. The south transept houses the **Cappella Carafa,** home to a brilliant fresco cycle. *(Open M-Sa 7am-7pm, Su 7am-1pm and 3:30-7pm.)* From the upper left-hand corner of P. della Rotonda, V. Giustiniani intersects V. della Scrofa and V. della Dogana Vecchia. Here stands the **Chiesa di San Luigi dei Francesi,** the French National Church, home to three of Caravaggio's most famous works. *(Open F-W 7:30am-12:30pm and 3:30-7pm, Th 7:30am-12:30pm.)*

PIAZZA NAVONA

Bernini's **Fontana dei Quattro Fiumi** (Fountain of the Four Rivers) commands the center of posh P. Navona. Each of the river god statues represents one of the four continents of the globe (as they were thought of then): the Ganges for Asia, the Danube for Europe, the Nile for Africa (veiled, since the source of the river was unknown), and the Rio de la Plata for the Americas. At the ends of the piazza are the **Fontana del Moro** and the **Fontana di Nettuno,** designed by Giacomo della Porta in the 16th century and renovated by Bernini in 1653. Originally a stadium built by Domitian in AD 86, the area once saw wrestling matches and track and field events. It even hosted mock naval battles, for which the stadium was flooded and filled with fleets skippered by convicts. With a (relatively) new Borromini-designed exterior, the **Church of Sant'Agnese** dominates the western side of the piazza. Its attraction is the skull of its namesake saint, who was martyred in the stadium after refusing an arranged marriage. *(Open Tu-Sa 4:30-7pm, Su 10am-1pm.)* West of P. Navona, on nearby C. del Rinascimento, the **Chiesa di Sant'Ivo**'s corkscrew cupola hovers over the **Palazzo della Sapienza,** original home of the University of Rome.

CAMPO DEI FIORI

Campo dei Fiori lies across C. V. Emanuele II from P. Navona. During papal rule, the area was the site of countless executions. In the middle, a statue marks the spot of the death of **Giordano Bruno** (1548-1600). Philosophically out of sync with his time, Bruno sizzled at the stake in 1600 for taking Copernicus one step further—he argued that the universe had no center at all. Now colorful produce, fish, and flowers fill the **market** that springs up. M-Sa 6am-2pm. The huge, stately **Palazzo Farnese** dominates P. Farnese, south of the Campo. The first Counter-Reformation pope built this, the greatest of Rome's Renaissance palazzi. The French Embassy has rented it since 1635 for one *lira* per year, in exchange for office space in Paris's Hôtel Galiffet, home of the Italian Embassy. To the east of the palazzo is the Baroque facade of the **Palazzo Spada** and the collection of the **Galleria Spada**.

THE JEWISH GHETTO

Located across V. Arenula from Campo dei Fiori; take bus #64.

Rome's Jewish community is the oldest in Europe—Israelites came in 161 BC as ambassadors from Judas Maccabei, asking for help against invaders. The Ghetto, the tiny area to which Pope Paul IV confined the Jews in 1555, was abolished in 1870, but is still the center of the vibrant Jewish population of 16,000. **Piazza Mattei,** in the center of the ghetto, is home to the endearing 16th-century **Fontana delle Tartarughe.** Nearby is the **Church of Sant'Angelo in Pescheria,** installed inside the Portico d'Ottavia in 755 and named after the fish market that once flourished here. Jews were forced to attend mass here; they quietly resisted by stuffing their ears with wax. *(Open for prayer meetings W 5:30pm and Sa 5pm.)* On the Tiber near the Theater of Marcellus, the **Sinagoga Askenazita** incorporates Persian and Babylonian styles that consciously differ from Christian architecture. The temple houses a **museum** with Holocaust and religious artifacts. *(☎066 87 50 51. Temple open for services only, but you can tour the museum. Open July-Sept. M-Th 9am-7:30pm, F and Su 9am-1:30pm. No cameras. L10,000.)*

PIAZZA DI SPAGNA AND ENVIRONS

THE SPANISH STEPS. Designed by an Italian, funded by the French, named for the Spaniards, occupied by the British, and under the sway of American ambassador-at-large Ronald McDonald, the **Scalinata di Spagna** exude an international air. When the steps were built in 1725, hopeful artists' models flocked here dressed as the Madonna and Julius Caesar. Nowadays, hordes of young males descend to flirt with foreigners. The pink house to the right was the site of John Keats's 1821 death; it's now the **Keats-Shelley Memorial Museum.** *(Open May-Sept. M-F 9am-1pm, 3-6pm; Oct.-Apr. M-F 9am-1pm and 2:30-5:30pm. Admission L5000. Closed mid-July to mid-Aug.)*

FONTANA DI TREVI. Nicolo Salvi's (1697-1751) extravagant **Fontana di Trevi** emerges from the back wall of **Palazzo Poli,** dwarfing the narrow piazza. Legend has it that a traveler who throws a coin into the fountain is ensured a speedy return to Rome; tossing two will aid falling in love in Rome. Reality has it that coins damage the marble. Opposite the fountain is the Baroque **Chiesa dei Santi Vincenzo e Anastasio,** which preserves the hearts and lungs of popes from 1590-1903.

PIAZZA DEL POPOLO. P. del Popolo, once a favorite venue for public executions of heretics, is now the lively "people's square." In the center is the 3200-year-old **Obelisk of Pharaoh Ramses II,** which Augustus brought back as a souvenir from Egypt in the first century BC. Behind a simple early Renaissance shell, the **Chiesa di Santa Maria del Popolo** contains several Renaissance and Baroque masterpieces. *(Open daily 7am-noon and 4-7pm.)* The **Cappella della Rovere** holds Pinturicchio's *Adoration*, and two exquisite Caravaggios are in the **Cappella Cerasi.** Raphael designed the **Cappella Chigi** for the wealthy Sienese banker Agostino Chigi, reputedly once the world's richest man. At the southern end of the piazza are the 17th-century **twin churches** of Santa Maria di Montesano, on the left, with a facade by Bernini, and Santa Maria dei Miracoli.

PIAZZA BARBERINI. Rising from the hum of a busy rotary at the end of V. del Tritone, Bernini's **Fontana del Tritone** spouts over the piazza, which is also home to Bernini's **Fontana delle Api** (Bee Fountain). Maderno, Borromini, and Bernini all had a hand in the **Palazzo Barberini,** V. delle Quattro Fontane 13, home to the **Galleria Nazio-**

nale d'Arte Antica (see p. 597). Up V. V. Veneto on the right, at 27a, the severe Counter-Reformation **Church of L'Immaculata Concezione** houses the amazing **Capuchin Crypt,** where the bones of 4000 friars are artfully displayed. *(Open F-W 9am-noon and 3-6pm. L1000 minimum donation requested.)*

VILLA BORGHESE

In celebration of becoming a cardinal, Scipione Borghese built the **Villa Borghese** north of P. di Spagna and V. V. Veneto. Its huge park is home to three notable art museums: the world-renowned **Galleria Borghese** (see p. 597), the stark **Galleria Nazionale d'Arte Moderna** (see p. 598), and the intriguing **Museo Nazionale Etrusco di Villa Giulia** (see p. 597). The Borghese is also home to a second-rate but fun **zoo,** V. del Giardino Zoologico, 3. *(Open daily 9:30am-6pm; in winter 9:30am-5pm. L14,000, ages 4-12 L10,000, under 4 or over 60 free.)* North of the Borghese are the **Santa Priscilla catacombs,** V. Salaria, 430, before V. Antica crosses V. Ardeatina. Take bus #57 or 219 from Termini or bus #56 from V. del Tritone. Get off at P. Vescovio and walk down V. di Tor Fiorenza to P. di Priscilla. *(Open Tu-Su 8:30am-noon and 2:30-5pm. L10,000.)*

VATICAN CITY

M:A-Ottaviano or A-Cipro/Musei Vaticani. Or, take bus #64 or 492 from Termini or Largo Argentina, #62 from P. Barberini, or #23 from Testaccio. Try www.vatican.va for info on sights, events, and news. The Pilgrim Tourist Information Office, P. San Pietro, to the left as you face the basilica, serves as a tourist office and official souvenir shop; it conducts free English tours of the Basilica daily. Phone to arrange 2hr. tours of the otherwise inaccessible Vatican Gardens. Tours Mar.-Oct. M-Tu and Th-Sa 10am; Nov.-Feb. Sa 10am; L20,000. ☎06 69 88 44 66. Office open M-Sa 8:30am-7pm. Papal Audiences are held every W, when John Paul II greets up to 3000 pilgrims, usually at 10am behind the colonnade left of the basilica. For free tickets, stop by the Prefettura della Casa Pontificia (☎06 69 88 32 73) the day before the audience. The office is beyond the bronze doors to the right of the basilica (open M-Sa 9am-1pm). To secure tickets in advance, write to the Prefettura della Casa Pontificia, 00120 Città del Vaticano. Seating is limited, so arrive early.

Occupying 108.5 independent acres entirely within the boundaries of Rome, Vatican City is the last remnant of the Papal States. The Lateran Treaty of 1929, which allowed the Pope to maintain power over this tiny theocracy, requires the Church to remain neutral in Italian politics and Roman municipal affairs. As the spiritual leader for millions of Catholics around the world, however, the Pope's influence is immense. The nation preserves its independence by minting coins (Italian *lire* but with the Pope's face), running a separate postal system, and maintaining an army of Swiss Guards. And, while the Pope may not hold quite the influence he used to, his art collection in the **Vatican Museums** (see p. 596) is pretty daunting.

BASILICA DI SAN PIETRO (ST. PETER'S)

Open daily Apr.-Sept. 7am-7pm, Oct.-Mar. 7am-6pm. Mass M-Sa at 9, 10, and 11am, noon, and 5pm; Su 9, 10:30, and 11:30am, and 12:10, 1, 4, and 5:45pm. Multilingual confession available. Appropriate dress is always required in the basilica. Cover your knees and shoulders. No shorts, miniskirts, sleeveless shirts, or skimpy dresses are allowed, but jeans and t-shirts are acceptable for women and men.

PIAZZA AND FACADE. As you enter **Piazza San Pietro,** Bernini's colonnade draws you toward the church. The obelisk in the center is framed by two fountains; round porphyry disks set in the pavement between each fountain and the obelisk mark the spots where you should stand so that the quadruple rows of Bernini's colonnades visually resolve into one perfectly aligned row. One hundred and forty statues perch above on the colonnade. Those on the basilica represent Christ (in the center), John the Baptist, and the Apostles (except for Peter).

ENTRANCE AND PIETÀ. The pope opens the **Porta Sancta** (Holy Door), the last door on the right side of the entrance porch, every 25 years by knocking in the bricks with a silver hammer. The basilica itself rests on the reputed site of St. Peter's tomb, and a Christian structure has stood here since Constantine made

Christianity the state religion in the 4th century. The overwhelming interior of St. Peter's measures 186m by 137m along the transepts; metal lines on the marble floor mark the puny-by-comparison lengths of other major churches. To the right, Michelangelo's *Pietà* has been protected by bullet-proof glass since 1972, when an axe-wielding fiend attacked it, smashing Christ's nose and breaking Mary's hand.

INTERIOR. The crossing under the dome is anchored by four niches with statues of saints—Bernini's **San Longinus** is at the northeast. In the center, Bernini's bronze **baldacchino** (canopy) rises on spiral columns over the marble altar. The bronze bees are the symbol of the Barberini family, of which Bernini's patron Urban VIII was a member. In the apse is Bernini's **Cathedra Petri,** a Baroque reliquary housing the original throne in a riot of bronze and gold. Below the statue of St. Longinus, steps lead to the **Vatican Grottoes,** the resting place of many popes and saints.

CUPOLA. The entrance to the cupola is near the exit from the grottoes. Take an elevator to the interior or ascend 350 claustrophobic steps to the outdoor top ledge, which offers the best views in the city. *(Cupola closes 1¼hr. earlier than the basilica, and when the Pope is inside. On foot L7000, by elevator L8000.)*

CASTEL SANT'ANGELO

To enter, walk along the river with St. Peter's behind you and the towering castle to your left; signs will point you to the entrance. Open Tu-F and Su 9am-8pm, Sa 9am-midnight; in winter daily 9am-2pm. L10,000, EU citizens under 18 or over 60 free. Audio guide L7000 (in English, French, German, Italian, Japanese, and Spanish).

Built by Hadrian as a mausoleum for himself and his family, this hulking mass of brick and stone has served Popes as a fortress, prison, and palace. When the plague hit in 590, Pope Gregory the Great saw an angel at the top of the complex; when the plague abated, the edifice was rededicated to the angel. It contains a **museum of arms and artillery** and offers an incomparable view of Rome and the Vatican.

TRASTEVERE

Take bus #75 or 170 from Termini to V. Trastevere, or tram #13 from Largo Argentina.

Right off the Ponte Garibaldi stands the statue of the famous dialect poet, G. G. Belli, in the middle of his own piazza, bordering the busy P. Sonnino and marking the beginning of V. di Trastevere. On the left is the **Casa di Dante,** where readings of the *Divine Comedy* are held (Nov.-Mar. every Su). On V. di Santa Cecilia, behind the cars, through the gate, and beyond the courtyard full of roses, is the **Basilica di Santa Cecilia in Trastevere,** where Stefano Maderno's famous **statue of Santa Cecilia** lies under the altar. *(Open daily 8am-12:30pm and 2:30-7pm. Cloister open Tu and Th 10-11:30am, Su 11:30am-noon. Donation requested. Crypt L4000.)* From P. Sonnino, V. della Lungaretta leads west to P. di S. Maria in Trastevere, home to the **Chiesa di Santa Maria in Trastevere,** built in the 4th century by Pope Julius II. Although the church is being restored, the 12th-century mosaics in the apse and the chancel arch still glimmer in full splendor, depicting Jesus, Mary, and a bevy of saints and popes. *(Open daily 7:30am-7pm.)* North of the piazza are the Rococo **Galleria Corsini,** V. della Lungara 10, (see **Museo Nazionale dell'Arte Antica,** p. 597) and the **Villa Farnesina** across the street, the jewel of Trastevere. Baldassare Peruzzi built the villa for banker-philanthropist Agostino Chigi ("il Magnifico") between 1508-1511. The museum's frescoed walls are the main attraction. *(Open M-Sa 9am-1pm. L8000, under 18 L6000.)*

GIANICOLO

To reach the summit, take bus #41 from the Vatican, or ascend via the medieval V. Garibaldi from V. della Scala in Trastevere (about 10min.).

Atop the hill rests the **Chiesa di San Pietro in Montorio,** built on the spot believed to be the site of St. Peter's upside-down crucifixion. The church contains Sebastiano del Piombo's *Flagellation*, painted from designs by Michelangelo. Next door is Bramante's tiny **Tempietto,** constructed to commemorate Peter's martyrdom. *(Church and Tempietto open daily 9:30am-12:30pm and 4-6:30pm.)* Rome's **botanical gar-**

dens, at the end of V. Corsini, off V. della Lungara, at Largo Cristina di Svezia 24, contain a **garden for the blind** as well as a rose garden that supposedly holds the bush from which all the world's roses are descended. *(Grounds open Apr.-July and Sept. M-Sa 9am-6:30pm; Oct.-Mar. M-Sa 9am-5:30pm. Greenhouse open M-Sa 9am-12:30pm. Closed Aug. L4000, ages 6-11 L2000, under 6 free.)*

NEAR TERMINI

The sights in this very urban part of town are concentrated northwest of the station and to the south, near P. Vittorio Emanuele II, where an **outdoor market** is held daily.

NORTH OF TERMINI

BATHS OF DIOCLETIAN. From AD 298 to 306, 40,000 Christian slaves built these public baths, which could serve 3000 people. They contained a heated marble public toilet with seats for 30, pools of various temperatures, gymnasiums, art galleries, gardens, libraries, and concert halls. In 1561, Michelangelo undertook his last architectural work and converted the ruins into a church, the **Chiesa di Santa Maria degli Angeli.** In the floor leading from the east transept to the altar, a sundial has provided the standard time for Roman clocks for hundreds of years. *(Church open daily 7:30am-12:30pm and 4-6:30pm. Rotunda and baths open M-F 9am-2pm, Sa-Su 9am-1pm. Free.)*

PIAZZA DEL QUIRINALE. At the southeast end of V. del Quirinale, this piazza sits atop the tallest of Rome's hills. The President of the Republic officially resides in the imposing **Palazzo del Quirinale,** a Baroque collaboration by Bernini, Maderno, and Fontana. Down V. del Quirinale, V. Ferrara on the right leads down the steps to V. Milano. At the corner of V. Milano and V. Nazionale towers the **Palazzo delle Espozioni,** home to temporary art exhibitions. Farther along lies the marvelous facade of Borromini's **Chiesa di San Carlo alle Quattro Fontane.** *(Open M-F 9:30am-12:30pm and 4-6pm, Sa 9am-12:30pm; if the interior is closed, ring at the convent next door.)*

SOUTH OF TERMINI

BASILICA DI SANTA MARIA MAGGIORE. In 352, Pope Sixtus III commissioned the basilica when he saw that women were visiting a temple to the pagan mother-goddess Juno Lucina. Sixtus enthusiastically tore down the temple to build his new basilica, substituting a Christian cult for a pagan one and celebrating the Council of Ephesus's recent naming of Mary as the Mother of God. Most of the renowned mosaics inside were created to commemorate her radiant new status. To the right of the altar, a marble slab marks the **tomb of Bernini.** *(Four blocks down V. Cavour from Termini. Open daily 7am-7pm. Loggia open daily 9:30am-noon and 2-5:30pm. L5000.)*

CHURCH OF SANTA CROCE IN GERUSALEMME. This Rococo church draws pilgrims to its Fascist-era **Cappella delle Reliquie,** which contains fragments believed to be from the true cross. The eeriest relic hands down is the finger used by doubting St. Thomas to probe Christ's wounds. *(Take V. di S. Croce in Gerusalemme from the eastern end of P. V. Emanuele II. Open M-Sa 9:30am-noon and 3-6pm, Su and holidays 9:30am-noon and 2:30-5:30pm.)*

CHURCH OF SAN PIETRO IN VINCOLO. Dating from the 4th century, the church is named after the sacred chains (housed beneath the altar) with which Peter was supposedly bound after imprisonment on the Capitoline. Michelangelo's imposing **statue of Moses** presides regally over the church. *(M:B-Cavour. Walk southwest on V. Cavour toward the Forum. Take the stairs on your left. Open daily 7am-12:30pm and 3:30-7pm.)*

SOUTHERN ROME

The area south of the city center is a mix of wealthy and working-class neighborhoods, and is home to the city's best nightlife and some of its grandest churches.

CAELIAN HILL

Southeast of the Colosseum, the Caelian, along with the Esquiline, is the biggest of Rome's seven original hills. In ancient times, Nero built his decadent Domus Aurea between these hills. In the wake of its destruction, many of Rome's early churches were constructed here.

CHURCH OF SAN CLEMENTE. One of Rome's most intriguing churches incorporates centuries of handiwork into three layers: a 12th-century church on top of a 4th-century church, with an ancient **mithraeum** and sewers at the bottom. The upper church holds medieval mosaics. A fresco cycle by Masolino dating from the 1420s graces the **Chapel of Santa Caterina.** *(M:B-Colosseo. Turn left out of the station and walk east on V. Fori Imperiali (V. Labicana). Open M-Sa 9am-12:30pm and 3-6pm, Su and holidays 10am-12:30pm and 3-6pm. Lower basilica and mithraeum L5000.)*

CHIESA DI SAN GIOVANNI IN LATERANO. Founded by Constantine in 314, this immense cathedral is Rome's oldest Christian basilica and was the papal seat until the 14th century. The Gothic *baldacchino* over the altar houses the heads of **St. Peter** and **St. Paul.** Across the street is the **Scala Santa,** home of the so-called *acheropite* image, a depiction of Christ not created by human hand, and what are believed to be the 28 steps used by Jesus outside Pontius Pilate's house. *(M:A-San Giovanni or bus #16 from Termini. Church open daily 7am-7:30pm. Cloister open daily 9am-6pm; L4000. Scala Santa open Apr.-Sept. 6:15am-7:30pm, Oct.-Mar. 6:15am-6:30pm.)*

THE AVENTINE HILL

The easiest approach to the Aventine is up V. di Valle Murcia from the western end of the Circus Maximus. Make the climb to see Rome's swankiest homes and the famed **keyhole view** of St. Peter's through the yellow gate in P. dei Cavalieri di Malta.

APPIAN WAY

CHIESA DI SANTA MARIA IN PALMIS. In this church, St. Peter had a vision of Christ while fleeing from Rome; when Peter asked *"Domine Quo Vadis?"* ("Lord, where are you going?"), Christ replied that he was going to Rome to be crucified again because Peter had abandoned him. Guilt turned Peter around. *(At V. Appia Antica and V. Ardeatina. Take bus #218 from P. S. Giovanni. Open daily 9am-noon and 4-7pm.)*

CATACOMBS. Since burial inside the city walls was forbidden, fashionable ancient Romans made their final resting places along the Appian Way, while early Christians secretly dug maze-like **catacombs** underneath. **San Callisto** is Rome's largest catacomb, with nearly 22km of tunnels. It once held 16 popes, seven bishops, St. Cecilia, and 500,000 others. **Santa Domitilla** enjoys acclaim for its paintings, including a 3rd-century portrait of Christ and the Apostles. **San Sebastiano** was the temporary home of the bodies of Peter and Paul—or so ancient graffiti claims. *(Take bus #218 from P. di S. Giovanni to V. Ardeatina and V. delle Sette Chiese. At least 2 catacombs are open any given day 8:30am-5:30pm; in winter 8:30am-5pm. Admission to each L8000. In all 3, visitors follow a free tour in the language of their choice (every 20min.). S. Calisto: V. Appia Antica 110. Open M-Tu and Th-Su; in winter Th-Su only. Closed Feb. S. Domitilla: Facing V. Ardeatina from the exit of S. Callisto, cross the street and walk up V. delle Sette Chiese. Open W-M. Closed Jan. S. Sebastiano: V. Appia Antica 136. Open M-Sa. Closed Nov.)*

TESTACCIO

Metro:B-Piramide, or bus #27 from Termini.

This working-class district south of the Aventine centers on the forbidding **Porta San Paolo** (a remnant of the Aurelian defensive walls) and the huge **Piramide di Gaius Cestius.** By the pyramid is **Monte Testaccio** (from *testae* or pot shards), an ancient dumping ground for terra-cotta pots. The area is home to the **Protestant Cemetery,** where Keats is interred. From Testaccio, take bus #23 or 170 to the **Basilica di San Paolo Fuori le Mura,** the largest church in the city after St. Peter's. St. Paul is believed to be buried beneath the altar. Buy a bottle of monk-made **benedictine** (L13,000) in the gift shop. *(M:B-Basilica San Paolo. Open daily 7am-6:30pm, in winter 7am-6pm; cloister open 9am-1pm and 3-6:30pm, in winter 9am-1pm and 3-6pm.)*

EUR

South of Testaccio and Ostiense. M:B-EUR Fermi, or bus #714.

EUR (AY-oor) is an acronym for 1942's Universal Exposition of Rome that Mussolini intended as a showcase of Fascist achievement, where modern Rome was to impress the world with its identical square buildings. The center is P. Guglielmo Marconi's 1959 modernist **obelisk; EUR Museums** (see p. 598) are splayed around it.

ABBAZIA DELLE TRE FONTANE (ABBEY OF THE THREE FOUNTAINS). When St. Paul was beheaded here, his head bounced three times, allegedly creating a fountain on impact. The monks who live here sell their own eucalyptus liquor and divine chocolate. *(M:B-Laurentina. Walk ½ mi. north on V. Laurentina and turn right on V. di Acque Salve. It's at the bottom of the hill. Or, take bus #761 north from the Laurentina stop; ask to get off at V. di Acque Salve. Open M-Sa 11am-5pm, Su noon-5pm.)*

MUSEUMS

Etruscans, emperors, popes, and *condottiere* have been busily stuffing Rome's belly with artwork for several millennia, leaving behind a city teeming with galleries. Museums are generally closed holidays, Sunday afternoons, and all day Monday.

VATICAN MUSEUMS

About 10 blocks north of the right-hand side of P. San Pietro along the Vatican wall. From the Ottaviano Metro A stop, walk south several blocks to the Vatican wall and turn right. ☎06 69 88 33 33. Information and gift shop (with the very useful official guidebook, L12,000) on the ground level past the entrance. Valuable audio guide with information and amusing anecdotes, L8000. Most collections sport English and Italian labeling of some sort, although the descriptions become frustratingly sparse in certain galleries. All major galleries open Mar. 16-Oct. 30 M-F 8:45am-4:30pm, Sa 8:45am-1:45pm; Nov.-Mar. 15 M-Sa 8:45am-1:45pm. Last entrance 1hr. before closing. Closed on major religious holidays. L18,000, with ISIC card L12,000, children under 1m tall free. Free last Su of the month 8:45am-1:45pm. Most of the museum is wheelchair accessible, although less visited parts, such as the upper level of the Etruscan Museum, are not. Various galleries close without explanation; call ahead.

The Vatican Museums constitute one of the world's greatest and most comprehensive art collections. The entrance at V. Vaticano leads to the famous bronze double-helix ramp that climbs to the ticket office. Start your tour at the stellar **Museo Pio-Clementino,** the most fantastic collection of antique sculpture you will ever see. Two slobbering Molossian hounds guard the entrance to the **Stanza degli Animali,** a marble menagerie that reveals the importance of brutality in Roman pastimes. The Cabinet of Canova features the **Apollo Belvedere** and the unhappy **Laocoön** family. The last room of the gallery contains the enormous red **sarcofago di Sant'Elena,** Constantine's mother. From here, the Simonetti Stairway climbs to the **Museo Etrusco,** filled with artifacts from Tuscany and northern Lazio. On the landing is the **Stanza della Biga** and the **Galleria della Candelabra.** The long trudge to the Sistine Chapel begins here, passing through the **Galleria degli Arazzi** (tapestries), the **Galleria delle Mappe** (maps), the **Apartamento di Pio V** (where there is a shortcut to *la Sistina*), the **Stanza Sobieşki,** and the **Stanza della Immaculata Concezione;** from there, a door leads into the first of the four **Stanze di Rafaele,** apartments built for Pope Julius II in the 1510s. The **Stanza della Segnatura** features the *School of Athens*, considered Raphael's masterpiece. From here, a staircase leads to the brilliantly frescoed **Borgia Apartments** and the **Museum of Modern Religious Art.**

SISTINE CHAPEL. Since its completion in the 16th century, the Sistine Chapel (named for its founder, Pope Sixtus IV) has served as the chamber in which the College of Cardinals elects new popes. On the right, scenes from the life of Moses complement parallel scenes of Christ's life on the left. The cycle was completed between 1481 and 1483 under the direction of Perugino by a team of artists including Botticelli, Ghirlandaio, Roselli, Pinturicchio, Signorelli, and della Gatta. The simple compositions and vibrant colors of Michelangelo's unquestioned masterpiece hover above, each section depicting a story from Genesis. The scenes are framed by the famous *ignudi*, young nude males. Michelangelo's sublime *The Last Judgement*, painted 23 years after the ceiling, fills the altar wall.

PINACOTECA. This is one of Rome's best painting collections, with Filippo Lippi's *Coronation of the Virgin*, Perugino's *Madonna and Child*, Titian's *Madonna of San Nicoletta dei Frari*, and Raphael's *Transfiguration*. On the way from the Sistine Chapel, note the **Room of the Aldobrandini Marriage**'s rare ancient frescoes.

PRINCIPAL COLLECTIONS

GALLERIA BORGHESE. You only have two hours to visit this exquisite museum, so hurry! Room I houses Canova's sexy statue of **Paolina Borghese** portrayed as Venus triumphant. The next rooms display Bernini's most famous sculptures: magnificent **David,** who crouches in controlled aggression with his slingshot, **Apollo and Daphne,** the weightless body in **Rape of Proserpina,** and weary-looking Aeneas in **Eneo e Anchise.** Six **Caravaggio** paintings grace the side walls. The collection continues with works by **Rubens, Raphael, Il Sodoma,** and others, upstairs, accessible from the gardens around the back by a winding staircase. *(P. Scipione Borghese 5. M:A-Spagna. Or, take bus #910 from Termini to V. Pinciana or follow Villa Borghese exit signs and head left up the road to reach V. del Museo Borghese. Brown signs point the way. ☎068 54 85 77. Open Tu-F 9am-7:30pm, Sa 9am-11pm, Su and holidays 9am-8pm; entrance on the hr., 2hr. max.; last entrance 30min. before closing. L14,000, EU citizens ages 18-25 L8000, EU citizens under 18 and over 60 L2000. Tickets include the ground floor galleries and the Pinacoteca. Informative guidebook L20,000. Tickets may be reserved by phone or in person for an extra L2000.)*

MUSEO NAZIONALE ETRUSCO DI VILLA GIULIA. Highlights include a graceful sarcophagus of a man and wife in Room 9 and an Etruscan chariot and the petrified skeletons of two horses found beside it in Room 18. Upstairs, archaeologists have put together the fragments of the entire facade of an Etruscan temple, complete with terra-cotta gargoyles. Don't miss the famous Euphronios vase near the gift shop. *(In Villa Borghese at P. Villa Giulia 9. M:A-Flaminio, or bus #19 from P. Risorgimento or #52 from P. San Silvestro. Open June-Sept. Sa 9am-11pm; Oct.-May Tu-F, Su, and holidays 8:30am-7:30pm, Sa 9am-8pm. L8000. Audioguide L8000. Guidebook L20,000.)*

CAPITOLINE MUSEUMS. Founded in 1471 by Pope Sixtus IV, the world's oldest public museum houses collections of ancient sculpture among the world's largest, breathtaking frescoes, and a truly comprehensive assortment of 16th- and 17th-century Italian painting in the *pinoteca*. The Palazzo Nuovo contains the original statue of **Marcus Aurelius** that once stood in the center of the piazza. The sculpture rooms contain notables like *Dying Gaul*, *Satyr Resting* (the "Marble Faun" that inspired Hawthorne's book), and *Venus Prudens*. Across the piazza in the Palazzo dei Conservatori, see the fragments of the **Colossus of Constantine** and the famous **Capitoline Wolf,** an Etruscan statue that has symbolized the city of Rome since ancient times. *(Atop the Capitoline Hill behind the Vittorio Emanuele II monument. Open Tu-Su 10am-8pm, holidays 9am-1:30pm. Ticket office closes 30min. before museum. L15,000, with ISIC L11,000, Italian citizens under 18 or over 60 free. Guidebook L30,000; audioguide L7000; daily English tours L6000. Not wheelchair accessible.)*

MUSEO NAZIONALE D'ARTE ANTICA. This treasure trove is split between **Palazzo Barberini,** which holds art from the medieval through Baroque periods and **Galleria Corsini,** which holds a range of 17th- and 18th-century paintings. *(Museo Nazionale D'Arte Antica, V. delle Quattro Fontane 13, near P. Barberini; open Tu-Sa 9am-7pm, Su 9am-8pm; L12000, EU citizens 18-25 L7000, EU citizens under 18 or over 65 and students of art and architecture L2000. Galleria Corsini, V. della Lungara 10, opposite Villa Farnesina in Trastevere; open Tu-Su 9am-6pm; L8000, EU students L2000.)*

VILLA FARNESINA. Thought to be the wealthiest man in Europe, Agostino "il Magnifico" Chigi lived sumptuously and eccentrically in this villa. To the right of the entrance lies the breathtaking **Sala of Galatea,** mostly painted by the villa's architect, Baldassare Peruzzi, in 1511. The vault displays astrological signs that symbolically chart the stars at the moment of Agostino's birth. The masterpiece of the room is Raphael's **Triumph of Galatea.** Upstairs, the **Stanza delle Prospettive,** a fantasy room decorated by Peruzzi, offers views of Rome between *trompe l'oeil* columns. The adjacent **Stanza delle Nozze** (Marriage Room) is the real draw, with its extremely masterful fresco of Alexander the Great's marriage to the beautiful Roxanne by **Il Sodoma.** *(V. della Lungara 230, just across from Palazzo Corsini off Lungotevere Farnesina. Take bus #23. Open M-Sa 9am-1pm. L8000, under 18 L6000.)*

GALLERIA NAZIONALE D'ARTE MODERNA. Skip straight to the 20th-century wing to see Klimt's *The Three Ages of Man*, Modigliani's *Portrait of a Lady with a Collar*, and notable works by Giacometti, Mondrian, Braque, Duchamp, and de Chirico. *(In Villa Borghese, V. delle Belle Arti 131. Open Tu-Sa 9am-7pm, Su 9am-8pm. L12,000; discounts for art and architecture students. Wheelchair accessible.)*

GALLERIA SPADA. Time and good luck have left the palatial 17th-century apartments of Cardinal Bernardino Spada nearly intact. A visit to this small gallery offers a glimpse of the luxury surrounding Baroque courtly life. *(P. Capo di Ferro 13, south of Campo dei Fiori. Bus #64. ☎06 32 81 01. Open Tu-Sa 9am-7pm, Su 9am-12:30pm. L10,000, EU citizens under 18 and over 60 free. Call for reservations, L2000 extra.)*

MUSEI NAZIONALI ROMANI. The fascinating **Museo Nazionale Romano Palazzo Massimo,** Largo di Via Peretti 1, in the corner of P. dei Cinquecento, is devoted to the history of Roman art during the Empire and includes the **Lancellotti Discus Thrower,** a rare mosaic of Nero's, and ancient coins and jewelry. *(Open Tu-Su 9am-7pm. L12,000, EU citizens ages 18-24 L6000, EU citizens under 18 or over 60 free.)* Nearby, the **Museo Nazionale Romano Terme di Diocleziano,** P. dei Cinquecento 78, a beautifully renovated complex partly housed in the huge **Baths of Diocletian,** explores ancient cultures. *(Open Tu-Su 9am-7pm. L8000, EU citizens ages 18-24 L4000, EU citizens under 18 or over 60 free. Audioguide L6000; tour with archaeologist L10,000.)* Across town is the **Museo Nazionale Romano Palazzo Altemps,** P. S. Apollinaire 44, north of P. Navona. Ancient sculpture, including the 5th-century *Ludovisi Throne*, is its specialty. *(Open Tu-Su 9am-7pm. L10,000, EU citizens ages 18-24 L5000, EU citizens under 18 or over 60 free. A 6-day ticket book is good for all 3 museums, the Colosseum, and the Palatine Hill; L30,000.)*

EUR MUSEUMS. The expansive **Museo della Civiltà Romana,** P. Agnelli 10, contains exhibits on ancient Rome, including vast, intricate scale models of Republican and Imperial Rome and Trajan's Column. *(M:B-EUR, either stop. Walk north up V. Cristoforo Colombo, or take bus #714 from Termini. Open Tu-Sa 9am-7pm, Su 9am-1:30pm. L5000, under 18 or over 60 free.)* The smallest of the museums, the **Museo dell'Alto Medievo,** V. Lincoln 3, exhibits artifacts from the Dark Ages. *(Open M-Sa 9am-2pm, Su 9am-12:30pm. L4000, reduced price L2000, under 18 or over 65 free. Wheelchair accessible.)* The **Museo Nazionale delle Arti Tradizioni Popolari,** P. G. Marconi 8, preserves Italian folk art and replicas of traditional attire and farming equipment. *(Open Tu-Su 9am-8pm. L8000, reduced price L4000, under 18 or over 65 free.)* Finally, the **Museo Preistorico ed Etnografico Luigi Pigorini,** P. G. Marconi 14, contains an impressive collection of ethnographic artifacts, including the skull of the Guattari Neanderthal, found near Circeo. *(For guided tours in Italian, call ☎068 41 23 12. Open daily 9am-2pm. L8000, under 18 or over 65 free.)*

RECOMMENDED COLLECTIONS

Museo Centrale Termoelettrica Montemartini, V. Ostiense 106. M:B-Piramide. This turn-of-the-century electrical plant houses Classical sculpture. Open Tu-Su 10am-6pm. L8000, EU citizens ages 18-24 L4000, EU citizens under 18 or over 60 free.

Galleria Doria Pamphilj, P. del Collegio Romano 2. North of P. Venezia. The classical art here is quirkily arranged by size and theme. Seek out the masterpieces, such as Caravaggio's *Rest during the Flight in Egypt.* Open F-W 10am-5pm. L14,000, students and seniors L11,000. Audioguide included. Useful catalogue with a L10,000 deposit.

Museo Barracco, C. V. Emanuele II 166. Near Largo di Torre Argentina. This collection has some Greco-Roman art, but its Egyptian and Assyrian holdings are outstanding. Open Tu-Sa 9am-7pm, Su 9am-1pm. L3700, with ISIC L2500.

LIKE A VIRGIN Romulus and Remus may have learned the skills required to found Rome from their alternative upbringing. Legend claims that their mother, one of Rome's Vestal Virgins (the priestesses and protectors of the Eternal Flame), conceived the boys when she lost her virginity to Mars, the god of war. In a fury over the loss of her position, which in turn shamed the family name, her father killed her, and—in proper mythological form—left her twins Romulus and Remus to die on a mountaintop. Fortunately, a she-wolf *(La Lupa)* found and nursed the defenseless babes; the familial trio is commonly represented in artwork throughout Italy (most famously in a sculpture dating to 500 BC, located in the **Capitoline Museums,** p. 597). Interestingly, the word *lupa* is also used as slang for prostitute.

ENTERTAINMENT

Back in the day, when you were bored you could swing by the Colosseum to watch a man get mauled by a bear. Today, Romans seek other diversions. *Roma C'è* (with its English-language section) and *Time Out,* available at newsstands, have club, movie, and events listings. Small **classical music festivals** (mid-May to Aug.) are just part of the larger **Roma Estate** (www.romaestate.com), which starts with the **Festa Europea della Musica** at the end of June. In July, the **Accademia Nazionale di Santa Cecilia** (☎06 361 10 64, credit card reservations ☎06 68 80 10 44) holds concerts in the **Villa Giulia** in Villa Borghese. The **Theater of Marcellus,** near P. Venezia, hosts summer evening concerts (L30,000). Rome's most important theater, **Teatro Argentina,** V. di Torre Argentina 52, runs drama and music festivals year-round. (☎06 68 80 46 01. Box office open M-F 10am-2pm and 3-7pm, Sa 10am-2pm.) For information on English theater, check the tourist office or *Roma C'è.* The **San Lorenzo Sotto le Stelle** festival occurs at Villa Mercede, V. Tiburtina 113, with shows at 9am and 11pm (L8-10,000). In summer, especially July, **outdoor movie screenings** are held in various piazze and at the southern tip of Tiber Island. Theaters have **matinees** weekdays around 4:30 and 6:30pm, and all day Wednesday. **I Love Rome** (www.alfanet.it/welcomeItaly/roma/default.html) has a database of theaters and showtimes. "V.o." or "l.o." in listings means the movie (if foreign) is subtitled, not dubbed.

NIGHTLIFE

MUSIC CLUBS, DISCOS, AND JAZZ

Although discos can be a flashy good time, travelers must overcome some obstacles. You won't meet many non-Italians, the scene changes as often as Roman phone numbers, and many clubs flee beachward for the steaming summer to **Fregene, Ostia,** or **San Felice Circeo.** Check *Roma C'è* or *Time Out.*

Qube, V. Portonaccio 212. From P. di Porta Maggiore, take V. Prenestina east; turn left on V. Portonaccio. A warehouse-style disco. Plan to take a cab home. "Transmania," on Su, is one of the most popular gay nights. Cover L10-20,000. Open Th-Su 11pm-4am.

Alexanderplatz Jazz Club, V. Ostia 9. M:A-Ottaviano. From the station, head west on V. G. Cesare, take a right onto V. Leone IV, and the 1st left onto V. Ostia. A smoky 40s-style jazz joint, with a funky bar. Cocktails L12,000. Two-month pass required (L12,000). Open daily Sept.-June 9pm-2am. Shows start at 10:30pm.

Radio Londra Caffè, V. di Monte Testaccio 65b. Italian bands cover rock classics badly for an energetic, good-looking, young crowd. Pint of Carlsberg L7000. Pizza, *panini,* and hamburgers L8-12,000. Monthly pass L10,000. Open Su-F 9pm-3am, Sa 9pm-4am.

C.S.I.O.A. Villaggio Globale, Lungotevere Testaccio. Take bus #27 from Termini, get off before crossing the river, and turn left. Huge slaughterhouse hosting all things countercultural: music, films, art exhibits, etc. Women should be careful. Hours and cover vary.

Piper, V. Tagliamento 9 (☎068 41 44 59). North of Termini; take bus #319 to Tagliamento. 70s, rock, disco, and house and underground. Very gay-friendly. Cover L15-35,000 (includes 1 drink). Open Sa-Su 11pm-3am; in summer Su 11pm-3am.

ITALY

Alpheus, V. del Commercio 36 (☎065 74 78 26). Off V. Ostiense. Rome's most popular gay night, "Mucassassina," (literally, cow killer) F. Other nights live jazz, rock, folk, cabaret, and comedy. Cover L10-L20,000. Students free Th. Open Tu-Su 10pm-4:30am.

Dub Club, V. dei Funari 21a (☎06 68 80 50 24). In the Jewish Ghetto. A blue-lit underground, circular disco. Techno, funk, acid jazz, and exotica. Cover L10-20,000. Open Tu-F 11pm-4am, Sa-Su 11pm-6am. Things get rolling at 2am. Closed most of summer.

Berimbau, V. dei Fienaroli 30b (☎065 81 32 49). Live Brazilian music is followed by a raging Latin disco. Cover L10-25,000, includes 1 drink. Open W-Su 10:30pm-3:30am.

Testaccio Village, V. di Monte Testaccio 16 (☎06 57 28 76 61). Live, mostly local rock and pop from mid-June to mid-Sept. every night around 9pm.

PUBS

If you're longing for organized indoor drunkenness, head to Rome's countless pubs, many of which have an Irish theme. Drink prices often increase after 9pm.

Jonathan's Angels, V. della Fossa 16. Take V. del Governo Vecchio from Campo dei Fiori, turn left onto V. Parione, then head left toward the lights. Michelangelo's accomplishments pale before Jonathan's bathroom. Drinks L10-15,000. Open daily 4pm-2am.

Trinity College, V. del Collegio Romano 6, off V. del Corso by P. Venezia. Offers degrees in Guinness, Harp, and Heineken. Tuition L6-9000. Classes held daily noon-3am.

Pub Hallo'Ween, P. Tiburtino 31, in San Lorenzo, at the corner of V. Tiburtina and V. Marsala. Plastic skulls and fake spiderwebs abound. Drinks L6-10,000. Happy hour (free appetizers) 8:30-10pm. Open daily 8:30pm-2:30am. Closed Aug.

Abbey Theatre, V. del Governo Vecchio 51-53. Guinness L10,000. Happy hour daily 3-7pm. Open M-Th 10am-2am, F-Sa 10am-3am, Su 2:30pm-2am.

The Drunken Ship, Campo dei Fiori 20-21. Because you're proud to be an American, dammit. Happy hour daily 5-9pm, all night Tu. W 9-10pm is power hour–all the beer you can drink (L10,000). Beer L8000. Ask about the student discount on Heineken. Takeout window. Open daily 5pm-2am.

Caipirinha Pub-Café, V. del Gallo 10, off Campo dei Fiori. Serves up tropical drinks and Latin dancing. Cocktails around L10,000. Guinness L6000. Open daily 7pm-2am.

GAY AND LESBIAN NIGHTLIFE

Hangar, V. in Selci 69. M:B-Cavour. Near Termini. Hangar is considered the hot spot for gay nightlifers in Rome, attracting mostly 20-something men. Crowded, cool, and neon blue. M dirty movie night. Drinks L3-10,000. ARCI-GAY pass (L10,000) required; call **Circulo di Cultura Omosessuale Mario Mieli** (☎065 41 39 85). Open W-M 10:30pm-2am. Closed 3 weeks in Aug.

L'Alibi, V. Monte di Testaccio 39-44, in Testaccio. Bus #30N. Large, elegant, and diverse, with an expansive rooftop terrace. Especially in summer, this is *the* gay club. Underground, house, and retro. Mostly gay, although lesbians and straights are welcome. Cover L15-20,000; Th and Su free. Open W-Su 11pm-4:30am.

New Joli Coeur, V. Sirte 5. Off V. Eritrea, far from the city center, east of Villa Ada. The primary lesbian club. Take a cab. Retro music, with the occasional cabaret show or girl group. Women only. 1-drink minimum (L15-20,000). Open Sa 11pm-3am.

ITALY

EXCURSIONS FROM ROME

PONTINE ISLANDS. A stunning volcanic archipelago 60 miles off Anzio, these islands were once a haven for the notorious Saracen and Corsican pirates. Explore Ponza's cliff-sheltered beaches and grottoes on foot or rent a boat (from L80,000). Check **Ponza Mare,** on V. Banchina Nuova, for kayaks, paddle-boats, and pontoon **rentals** (☎077 18 06 79). At the port, look for offices offering *una gita* (JEE-tah) *a Palmarola* for a tour of Ponza's coastline and neighboring **Palmarola,** whose clear, turquoise water accentuates the white cliffs, tinted red by iron deposits and yellow by sulphur. The spectacular beach and white cliffs at **Chiai di Luna** are 10 minutes from Ponza's port. Turn left off the main road before the tunnel, then take the road to a path on the left. From Termini, take the train to Anzio (L5100) to catch a ferry. **CAREMAR** has Anzio and Ponza ferry offices. (Anzio ☎06 98 60 00 83, Ponza ☎077 18 05 65; summer only; 2½hr; 1-2 per day; round-trip L42,200.) **Linee Vetor** runs year-round hydrofoils to Ponza and Ventotene (Anzio ☎06 984 50 83, Ponza ☎077 18 05 49; 1½hr.; L35,000). The **Pro Loco Tourist Office** is in P. Carlo Pisacane off V. Dante at the far left of the port. (☎077 18 00 31. Open daily M-Sa 9am-12:50pm and 4-7:30pm, Su 9am-1pm.) Follow C. Pisacane until it becomes V. Dante (past the tunnel), and the **bus** station is to the left. Buses circle the island every 15-20 minutes until 1am (L1750, buy ticket on board). There are no official stops, so flag down buses along V. Panoramica. Budget accommodations are rare and **camping** is illegal; ask about private rooms with the tourist agency. **Pensione-Ristorante "Arcobaleno,"** V. Scotti D. Basso 6, offers great views and clean rooms. (☎077 18 03 15. Reservations are essential. Mandatory half-pension, but excellent food. L100-120,000 per person.)

TIVOLI. Horace, Catullus, Propertius, Maecenas, and many others retreated to villas lining the ravine in Tivoli. Spectacular terraces and fountains abound in the gardens of the castle-garden **Villa d'Este,** particularly the rows of grotesque faces spouting watery plumes, the **Grotto of Diana,** and the **Fontana della Civetta.** From P. Garibaldi, sneak your way through the gauntlet of souvenir stands in P. Trento down the path to the villa on your left. (Open daily May-Aug. 9am-6:45pm; Sept.-Apr. 9am-1hr. before dusk. Su closes 1½hr. earlier. L8000, EU citizens under 18 or over 60 free.) Follow V. di Sibilla across town to reach the **Villa Gregoriana,** a park with paths descending through scattered grottoes carved by rushing water, and walk past a series of lookouts over the cascades to the ancient **Temple of Vesta.** (Open June-Aug. Tu-Su 9:30am-7:30pm; Sept.-May Tu-Su 9:30am-1hr. before dusk. L3500, under 12 L1000.) From Tivoli proper, it's 5km to the remains of the **Villa Adriana.** From the P. Garibaldi newsstand, take the orange #4x bus (L1400; buy a return ticket). The villa is the largest and most expensive built in the Roman Empire, designed by Hadrian in the 2nd century in the styles of monuments that he had seen in his travels. (☎07 74 53 02 03. Open daily 9am-1½hr. before sunset. L8000.)

From Rome, take the Metro B to "Rebibbia" and exit the station to the COTRAL terminal above. **Buses** leave for Tivoli (35min., 3-5 per hr., L3000). The bus climbs to the center of Tivoli, making a stop beyond P. Garibaldi at P. delle Nazioni Unite. On the street leading away from P. Garibaldi, a big "I" on a round shack marks the information center and **tourist office.** (☎07 74 31 12 49. Open M-Sa 9:45am-3pm.)

ETRURIA AND LAKE BRACCIANO. Welcome to Etruscanland, former home of a mythologized tribe that dominated north-central Italy during the first millennium BC. Since the Etruscans' buildings were wood, only their carved-out tufa tombs survive. When Rome was just a few mud huts on the Palatine, Tarquin kings commanded the fledgling metropolis of **Tarquinia;** a subterranean **necropolis** lined with vibrant frescoes illustrates its history. Tomb paintings celebrate life, love, eating, drinking, and sport in the hilly countryside. The **Museo Nazionale,** in P. Cavourone, houses one of the best Etruscan art collections outside Rome. (Open Tu-Su 9am-7pm. Museum and necropolis L12000.) Take the bus marked "Cimitero" from Barriera S. Giusto or walk (15min.) to the necropolis. Head up C. V. Emanuele from P. Cavour and turn right on V. Porta Tarquinia. (Open 9am-1hr. before sunset.) **Trains** leave from Termini (1hr.; 11 per day, last train leaves Tarquinia at 10:12pm; L10,200). The **tourist office,** in P. Cavour, near the medieval walls, has info and bus schedules. (☎07 66 85 63 84. Open M-Sa 8am-2pm and 4-7pm.)

Lake Bracciano is Rome's nearest freshwater beach, an hour away by bus. Despite volcanic sand that may hurt your tush, the fresh air, cool water, and a lush and hilly surrounding landscape are worth visiting. The impressive 15th-century **Orsini-Odescalchi Castle** dominates town and offers stunning frescoes and stuffed wild boars. Bracciano's *trattorie* cook up mounds of fresh lake fish and eel. At the beach, a ferry ride across the lake to nearby Anguillara or Trevignano offers more spectacular scenery. See *Roma C'è* for listings of summertime classical concerts. By train, Anguillara and Bracciano are accessible by the Rome-Viterbo line from Rome's San Pietro station (every hr. 5:35am-9:45pm, last train to Rome 10:14pm; L5300).

THE VENETO

From the rocky foothills of the Dolomites to the fertile valleys of the Po River, the Veneto region has a geography as diverse as its historical influences. Once loosely linked under the Venetian Empire, these towns retained their cultural independence, and visitors are more likely to hear regional dialects than standard Italian when neighbors gossip across their geranium-bedecked windows. The sense of local culture and custom that remains strong within each town may surprise visitors lured to the area by Venice, the *bella* of the north.

VENICE (VENEZIA)

It is with good reason that Venetians call their city *La Serenissima* (the most serene); they awaken each morning to a city refreshingly free of cars and mopeds, as people make their way by foot or by boat through an ancient maze of narrow streets and winding canals. The serenity is broken only by tourists, who swarm in Venice's *campi* (squares) and thoroughfares, searching out the city's wealth of museums and landmarks. Two worlds collide as they cross paths with the locals living in the sparsely populated back streets of Cannaregio and the Ghetto; uniting them are the architectural gems of the city's glorious past and the intertwining canals, still the true arteries of this slowly sinking city.

GETTING THERE AND GETTING AROUND

The **train station** is on the northwest edge of the city; be sure to get off at Santa Lucia and *not* Mestre (on the mainland). **Buses** and **boats** arrive at Ple. Roma, across the Grand Canal from the train station. To get from either station to **Piazza San Marco** or the **Rialto Bridge,** take *vaporetto* #82 or walk, following the signs (40min.; exit left from the station onto Lista di Spagna).

Flights: Aeroporto Marco Polo (☎04 12 60 61 11; www.veniceairport.it), 5 mi. north of the city. Take the **ATVO shuttle** into the city (☎04 15 41 51 80; 30min., every 45min. 5:30am-8:40pm, L5000).

Trains: Stazione Venezia Santa Lucia. To: **Padua** (30min., 1-3 per hr., L4100); **Bologna** (2hr., 2 per hr., L15,000-20,000); **Florence** (3hr., every 2hr., L40,000); **Milan** (3hr., 1-2 per hr., L40,000); **Rome** (4-5hr., 5 per day, L64-75,000). **Lockers** by platform 1; L3000-4000 per 6hr.

Buses: ACTV, P. Roma (☎04 15 28 78 86), runs local buses and boats. **ACTV long distance carrier** buses run to nearby cities. Ticket office open daily 6:30am-midnight.

Public Transportation: The **Grand Canal** can be crossed on foot only at the Scalzi, Rialto, and Accademia *ponti* (bridges). Most **vaporetti** (water buses) run 24hr. (less frequently after 11pm). Single-ride L6000; round-trip L10,000. 24hr. **biglietto turistico** pass L18,000, 3-day L35,000 (L25,000 for Rolling Venice Cardholders; see **Tourist Offices**). Buy tickets from booths in front of *vaporetto* stops, automated machines at the ACTV office in Ple. Roma or at the Rialto stop, or the conductor; pick up extra *non timbrati* (non-validated) tickets for when the booths aren't open. Validate them yourself before boarding; there is a fine for riding without a valid ticket. **Lines #82** (faster) and **1** (slower) run from the station down the Grand and Giudecca Canals; **line N** goes from the Lido to the station, down the Giudecca Canal back to San Marco; **line #52** runs from the station through the Giudecca Canal to Lido and along the city's northern edge; and **line #12** goes from Fondamente Nuove to Murano, Burano, and Torcello.

ORIENTATION

Venice, spanning 118 bodies of land in a lagoon, connects to the mainland by a causeway at its northwestern edge. The Grand Canal snakes through the city, dividing it into **sestieri** (sixths, or districts; see the **color map** at the back of this book): **Cannaregio** includes the train station, Jewish Ghetto, and Cà d'Oro; **Castello** extends

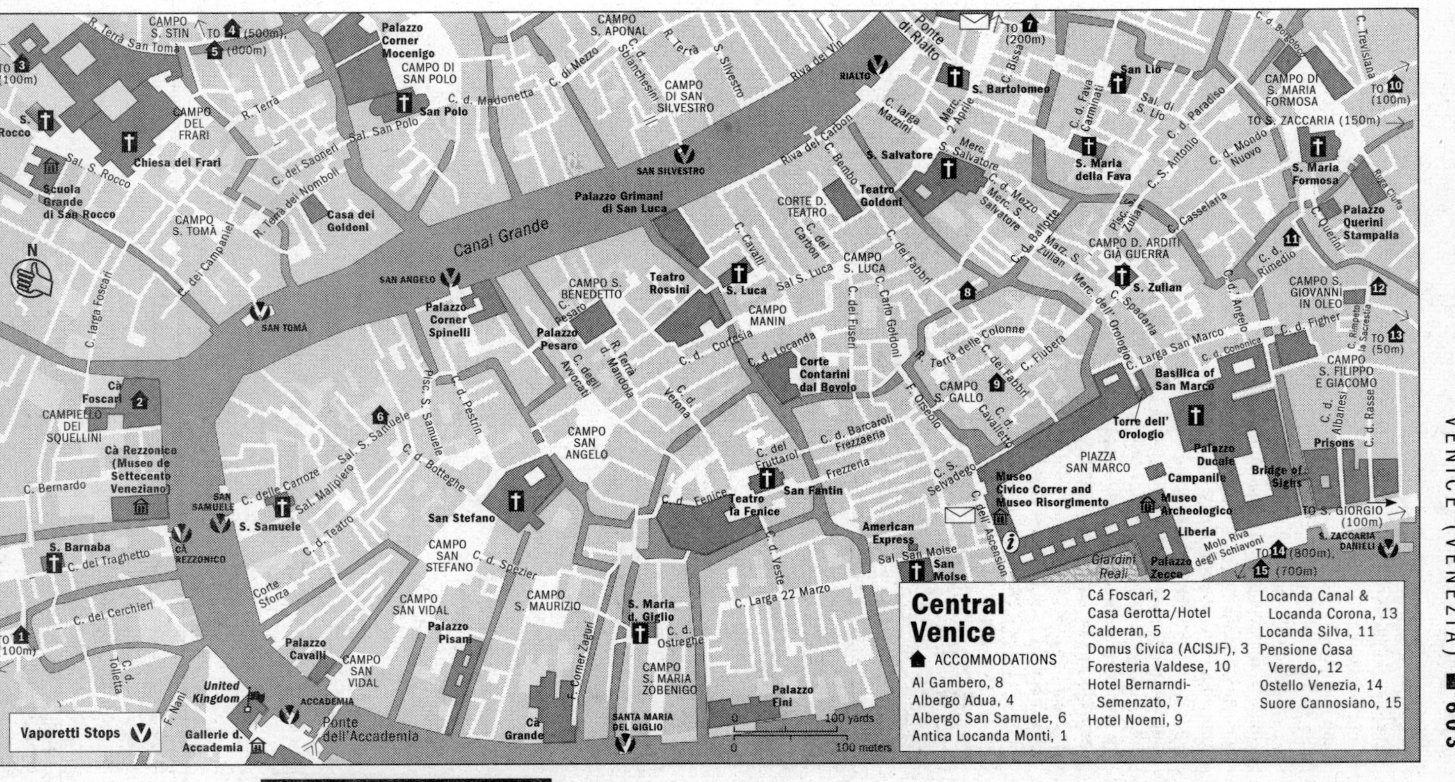
Central Venice
ACCOMMODATIONS
Al Gambero, 8
Albergo Adua, 4
Albergo San Samuele, 6
Antica Locanda Monti, 1
Cá Foscari, 2
Casa Gerotta/Hotel Calderan, 5
Domus Civica (ACISJF), 3
Foresteria Valdese, 10
Hotel Bernarndi-Semenzato, 7
Hotel Noemi, 9
Locanda Canal & Locanda Corona, 13
Locanda Silva, 11
Pensione Casa Vererdo, 12
Ostello Venezia, 14
Suore Cannosiano, 15
Vaporetti Stops
0
100 yards
100 meters
Canal Grande
PIAZZA SAN MARCO
Basilica of San Marco
Palazzo Ducale
Bridge of Sighs
Prisons
Campanile
Torre dell' Orologio
Museo Civico Correr and Museo Risorgimento
Museo Archeologico
Liberia
Palazzo Zecca
Giardini Reali
Ponte di Rialto
Ponte dell'Accademia
Gallerie d. Accademia
Teatro la Fenice
Teatro Goldoni
Teatro Rossini
Chiesa dei Frari
Scuola Grande di San Rocco
Cà Rezzonico (Museo de Settecento Veneziano)
Palazzo Grimani di San Luca
Corte Contarini dal Bovolo
San Stefano
American Express

east from Cannaregio toward the Arsenal; **San Marco** fills the area between P. S. Marco and the Grand Canal; **Dorsoduro** is across the Accademia bridge from S. Marco, swinging from the Salute church out to Giudecca and up to Cà Rezzonico; **San Polo** runs north from Dorsoduro to the Rialto Bridge; **Giudecca** lies just across the Canale della Giudecca, south of Dorsoduro; and **Santa Croce** lies between S. Polo to the east and the train station to the west. There are no individual street numbers within each *sestiere*—door numbers form one long, haphazard set. If *sestiere* boundaries are confusing, Venice's **parrochie** (parishes) provide a more defined idea of where you are, and *parrochia* signs, like *sestiere* signs, are painted on the sides of buildings. Venice is notoriously hard to navigate (you *will* get lost), but there are **yellow signs** throughout the city indicating certain landmarks: the **Rialto Bridge** (at the city center, between S. Marco and S. Polo); **Piazza San Marco** (south central, in S. Marco); the **Accademia** (southwest, in Dorsoduro), **Ferrovia** (the train station, northwest in Cannaregio); and **Ple. Roma** (in S. Croce).

PRACTICAL INFORMATION

TOURIST AND FINANCIAL SERVICES

Tourist Offices and Tours: APT, P. S. Marco 71/f (☎04 15 20 89 64), opposite the basilica. Open M-Sa 9:30am-3:30pm. **Branches** at the train station (☎/fax 041 71 90 78; open M-Sa 8am-7pm, Su 9:30am-3:30pm) and in the Lido, Gran Vle. 6a (☎04 15 26 57 21; open in high season M-Sa 10am-1pm). **Rolling Venice,** S. Marco 1529 (☎04 12 74 76 50), on Corte Contarina, sells the **Youth Discount Card** (L5000), which earns discounts at hotels, restaurants, and museums, as well as the **Rolling Venice vaporetto pass** (L25,000). Exit P. S. Marco opposite the basilica, turn right, follow the road left, continue through the building, look for the yellow "Comune di Venezia" signs, take a left, turn right, and go into the courtyard. Open M, W, and F 9am-1pm; Tu and Th 9am-1pm and 3-5pm. **Branch** (☎04 15 24 28 52) at the train station. Open July-Sept. 8am-8pm. **Enjoy Venice** (☎800 27 48 19 or 064 45 07 34) offers informative walking tours of the major sights. L30,000; under 26 L25,000. Tours leave in summer from Thomas Cook by the Rialto Bridge. M, W, and F at 10am; Tu, Th, and Sa at 1pm (call for winter hours).

Budget Travel: CTS, Dorsoduro 3252 (☎04 15 20 56 60; www.cts.it). From Campo S. Barnaba, cross the bridge nearest the church, then turn right at the end, left through the *piazza,* and left at the foot of the large bridge. Open M-F 9:30am-1:30pm and 3-7pm. **Transalpino** (☎/fax 041 71 66 00), next to the station, sells international train tickets. Open M-F 8:30am-12:30pm and 3-7pm, Sa 8:30am-12:30pm.

Currency Exchange: Banks and 24hr. **ATMs** line **Calle Larga XXII Marzo** (between P. S. Marco and the Accademia) and **Campo San Bartolomeo** (near the Rialto bridge).

American Express: Sal. S. Moise, S. Marco 1471 (☎800 87 20 00). Exit P. S. Marco away from the basilica, to the left. No commission; mediocre rates. Mail held for members and traveler's check customers. Open M-F 9am-8pm, Sa 9am-6pm.

Bookstore: Libreria Studium, S. Marco 337 (☎/fax 04 15 22 23 82). From P. S. Marco, head left along the basilica. Open M-Sa 9am-7:30pm.

EMERGENCY AND COMMUNICATIONS

Emergency: ☎113. **Police:** ☎112. **First Aid:** ☎118.

Police: Carabinieri, Castello 4693/a (☎04 15 20 47 77), in Campo S. Zaccaria.

Pharmacy: Farmacia Italo Inglese, Calle della Mandola, S. Marco 3717 (☎04 15 22 48 37), off Campo Manin. Open M-F 9am-12:30pm and 4:45-7:30pm, Sa 9am-12:45pm. Check the door of any pharmacy for night and weekend pharmacies, or consult *A Guest in Venice,* available at the tourist office.

Hospital: Ospedale Civile (☎04 15 29 41 11), Campo SS. Giovanni e Paolo.

Internet Access: Omniservice, Fond. d. Tolentini, S. Croce 220 (☎041 71 04 70). From the station, cross the Scalzi bridge, take a right, and turn left on Fond. d. Tolentini. L3000 per 15min. Open M-F 9am-1pm and 3-7pm, Sa 9:30am-12:30pm.

Post Office: S. Marco 5554 (☎04 12 71 71 11), on Salizzada Fontego d. Tedeschi, off Campo S. Bartolomeo. The palatial building is worth a visit. *Fermo Posta (Poste Restante)* at window #40. Address mail to be held: First name SURNAME, *In Fermo Posta,* Fontego dei Tedeschi, S. Marco 5554, **30124** Venice, Italy. Open M-Sa 8:10am-6pm.

ACCOMMODATIONS AND CAMPING

Rooms in Venice cost slightly more than elsewhere in Italy. Dorms are sometimes available without reservations, even in high season, but single rooms vanish quickly (make reservations up to a month in advance). In *pensioni,* watch out for L12,000 breakfasts and other rip-offs. Always agree on the price before taking a room. **AVA,** in the train station and at Ple. Roma 540d near the bus station (open daily 9am-10pm), books rooms for L1000 (☎04 15 22 22 64 for advance reservations), but proprietors are more willing to bargain in person. If you get desperate, ask the tourist office for info about the campgrounds at Mestre or head to the hostel in nearby Padua (see p. 610) or even Verona (see p. 610).

Cannaregio offers budget accommodations and a festive atmosphere, although the area is a 20- to 30-minute ride from most major sights. Accommodations in **San Marco,** surrounded by luxury hotels and Venice's main sights, are prime choices if you can get a reservation. **Dorsoduro** is a lively, less-touristed area between the Accademia and the Frari church. **Castello** provides lodging near the Rialto and the city center, a bit removed from the tourist hordes.

HOSTELS AND DORMITORIES

Foresteria Valdese, Castello 5170 (☎04 15 28 67 97; fax 04 12 41 62 38; email valdesi@doge.it). From the Rialto Bridge, head to Campo S. Bartolomeo, left to Salizzada S. Lio, and left on Calle Mondo Novo; enter Campo S. Maria Formosa and take Calle Lunga S. Maria Formosa over the 1st bridge. Amiable management and dazzling frescoed ceilings. Private rooms with TV. Breakfast included. Reception 9am-1pm and 6-8pm, Su 9am-1pm. Lockout 10am-1pm. Closed 2 weeks in Nov. Dorms L32-33,000; doubles L90-130,000; quads L164,000.

Ostello Venezia (HI), Fond. Giudecca Zitelle 86 (☎04 15 23 82 11), on Giudecca. *Vaporetto* #82 or 52: Zitelle. Institutional but friendly. Breakfast and sheets included. Reception 7-9:30am and 1:30-11:30pm. Lockout 9:30am-1:30pm. Curfew 11:30pm. IBN reservations only (see p. 29). Members only; HI cards sold. Dorms L27,000.

Domus Civica (ACISJF), S. Polo 3082 (☎041 72 11 03), between the Frari and Ple. Roma. From the station, cross the Scalzi bridge, turn right, hang a left on Fond. dei Tolentini, head left through the courtyard on Corte Amai, and it's a few blocks down on the right. Church-affiliated student housing offers rooms to tourists from mid-June to Sept. Ping-pong, TV, and piano. Check-in 7:30am-11:30pm. Curfew 11:30pm. Singles L47,000; doubles L84,000. 20% off with Rolling Venice or ISIC.

Suore Cannosiano, Fond. del Ponte Piccolo, Giudecca 428 (☎04 15 22 21 57). *Vaporetto* #82: Giudecca/Palanca; walk left over the bridge to get thee to this nunnery, managed by non-English-speaking nuns. Women only. Check-out 7:30-8:30am. Lockout noon-3pm. Strict curfew 10:30pm. Large dorms L23,000.

HOTELS

Casa Gerotto/Hotel Calderan, Campo S. Geremia 283 (☎041 71 55 62; ☎/fax 041 71 53 61), in **Cannaregio.** Turn left from the station (2min.). The city's best bargain and a backpacker's haven. Wonderful owners and huge, bright rooms, some with TV. Check-out 10am. Curfew 12:30-1am. Dorms L30,000; singles L50-60,000; doubles L80-130,000; triples L90-160,000; quads L135-200,000.

Hotel Bernardi-Semenzato, Campo S. Apostoli, Cannaregio 4366 (☎04 15 22 72 57; fax 04 15 22 24 24). *Vaporetto* #1: Cà d'Oro; turn right on Strada Nuova, left onto Calle del Duca, and right on Calle di Loca. Lovely rooms with Venetian antiques. Breakfast L6000. TV L5000 per day. Check-out 10:30am. Singles L60-95,000; doubles L95-130,000; triples L119-159,000; quads L140-180,000.

Pensione Casa Verardo, Castello 4765 (☎04 15 28 61 27; fax 04 15 23 27 65). *Vaporetto:* S. Zaccaria; take Calle degli Albanese to Campo SS. Filippo e Giacomo, cross the *campo,* and continue down Rimpetto la Sacrestia. Gorgeous rooms. Reserve with a one-night deposit. Singles L150,000; doubles L250,000. V, MC (require a 3-night min. stay).

Albergo Adua, Lista di Spagna, **Cannaregio** 233a (☎041 71 61 84; fax 04 12 44 01 62). Clean, attractive rooms. Breakfast L10,000. Curfew midnight. Singles L80,000, with bath L150,000; doubles L150,000, L210,000.

Albergo San Samuele, S. Marco 3358 (☎/fax 04 15 22 80 45). Follow Calle delle Botteghe from Campo S. Stefano (near the Accademia) and turn left on Salizzada S. Samuele. Colorful rooms. Reserve ahead. Singles L80,000; doubles L130-190,000.

Hotel Noemi, Calle dei Fabbri, **S. Marco** 909 (☎04 15 23 81 44; email hotelnoemi@tin.it). Take the 2nd archway from the Basilica di S. Marco and follow Calle dei Fabbri left (1min.). Reservations in writing. Singles L120,000; doubles L150-200,000; triples L185-280,000; quads L225-300,000. Cash only for 1-night stays.

Al Gambero, Calle dei Fabbri, **S. Marco** 4687 (☎04 15 22 43 84; email hotgamb@tin.it). Past Hotel Noemi (see above; 2min.). Singles L90,000-170,000; doubles L150-230,000; triples L200-300,000; quads L250-370,000.

Antica Locanda Montin, Fond. del Borgo, **Dorsoduro** 1147 (☎04 15 22 71 51; fax 04 15 20 02 55). *Vaporetto* #1: Cà Rezzonico; head straight to Campo S. Barnaba, then turn left under the archway, right at the iron sign, and left at the canal. Some rooms with terraces. Doubles L190-240,000.

Cà Foscari, Calle della Frescada, **Dorsoduro** 3887b (☎041 71 04 01; fax 041 71 08 17; email valtersc@tin.it). *Vaporetto* #1 or 82: S. Tomà; turn left at the dead end, cross the bridge, turn right, and take a left into the alleyway. Homey rooms. Curfew 1am. Rooms held until 2pm. Open Feb.-Nov. Singles L95,000; doubles L110,000; triples L141-186,000; quads L174-224,000.

Locanda Canal, Fond. del Remedio, **Castello** 4422c (☎04 15 23 45 38). From S. Marco, head under the clock tower, right on C. Larga S. Marco, left on Ramo dell'Anzolo, over the bridge, and left on Fond. del Remedio. Large rooms in a converted *palazzo.* Breakfast included. Shower L4000. Reserve with one-night deposit. Doubles L145-195,000; triples L175-235,000; quads L205-275,000.

Locanda Silva, Fond. del Remedio, **Castello** 4423 (☎04 15 22 76 43; fax 04 15 28 68 17), next to the Locanda Canal (see above). Simple, clean rooms painted in bright colors. Breakfast included. Open Feb. to mid-Nov. Singles L75,000; doubles L120-175,000; triples up to L225,000; quads L260,000.

Locanda Corona, Calle Corona, **Castello** 4464 (☎04 15 22 91 74). *Vaporetto:* S. Zaccharia; take Calle degli Albanese to Campo SS. Fillipo e Giacomo, continue on Rimpetto la Sacrestia, take the 1st right, and turn left on Calle Corona. Expensive breakfast. Closed Jan. Singles L59,000; doubles L85,000; triples L106,000.

CAMPING

Camping Miramare, Punta Sabbioni (☎041 96 61 50; fax 04 15 30 11 50). Take *vaporetto* #14 from P. S. Marco to "Punta Sabbioni" (40min.), then walk 700m along the beach to your right. 3-night min. stay. Open Apr. to mid-Nov. L9800 per person, L23,800 per tent; 4-person bungalow L62,000, 5-person L98,000.

Campeggio Fusina, V. Moranzani 79 (☎04 15 47 00 55), in Malcontenta. From Mestre, take bus #1. L11,000 per person; L7000 per tent; L25,000 per tent and car.

FOOD

In Venice, dining well on a budget requires exploration. Visit small side streets or any *osteria* or *bacaro* and create a meal from the vast display of *cicchetti* (chee-KET-ee; snacks), including meat- and cheese-filled pastries, seafood, rice, meat, and *tramezzini* (white bread with filling). Venetian cuisine is highly distinct; try the local seafood, which may include calamari, *polpo* (octopus), or shrimp.

The internationally renowned **Rialto markets,** once the center of trade for the Venetian Republic, abound on the S. Polo side of the Rialto Bridge every morning Monday through Saturday. Smaller **fruit and vegetable markets** set up in Cannaregio, on **Rio Terra S. Leonardo** by the Ponte delle Guglie, and in many *campi* throughout the city. **STANDA supermarket,** Strada Nuova, Cannaregio 3650, is near Campo S. Felice. (Open M-Sa 8:30am-7:20pm, Su 9am-7:20pm.)

Taverna San Trovaso, Fond. Nani, **Dorsoduro** 1016 (☎04 15 20 37 03). Young, enthusiastic staff serves great pastas and pizzas. *Primi* L10-15,000, *secondi* L15-27,000, pizzas L8-14,000. Cover L3000. Open Tu-Su noon-2:45pm and 7-9:45pm.

Oasi, Calle degli Albanese, **S. Marco** 4263/a (☎04 15 28 99 37), between the prisons and the Danieli Hotel. Enormous salads, delectable *frulatti,* and juices. Salads L8-17,000, *panini* L4-6000. Open Feb. to mid-Dec. M-Sa noon-3pm.

Do Mori, Calle dei Do Mori, **S. Polo** 429 (☎04 15 22 54 01), near the Rialto markets. Venice's oldest wine bar and an elegant place to grab a glass of local wine or a few *cicchetti* (from L2000). Standing room only. Open M-Sa 9am-9pm.

Due Colonne, Campo S. Agostin, **S. Polo** 2343 (☎04 15 24 06 85). Cross the bridge away from the Frari, turn left, cross into Campo S. Stin, turn right on Calle Dora, and cross the bridge. Variety of pizzas (L6-13,000). Cover L1500. Closed Aug. Open M-Sa 8am-3pm and 7-11pm; kitchen closes 1hr. earlier.

Vino, Vino, Ponte delle Veste, **S. Marco** 2007a (☎04 15 23 70 27). From Calle Larga XXII Marzo, turn onto Calle delle Veste. Wine bar with delicious, aromatic food. *Primi* L8000, *secondi* L15,000. Cover L1000. 10% off with Rolling Venice card. Open W-F and Su-M 10:30am-midnight, Sa 10:30am-1am.

Bacarro Jazz, S. Marco 5546 (☎04 15 28 52 49), across from the post office near the Rialto bridge. Patrons share plates of *cichetti* (L20,000) and relax to soothing jazz. Happy hour 2-7pm. Open Th-Tu 11am-2am.

Rosticceria San Bartomoleo, Calle della Bissa, **S. Marco** 5424/a (☎04 15 22 35 69). Follow the neon sign under the last archway on the left from Campo S. Bartolomeo. Loud music and a large selection of sandwiches and *cichetti*. Pasta L6500-9000, entrees L12-23,000. Cover L2500. Open Tu-Su 9:30am-9:30pm.

GELATERIE

La Boutique del Gelato, Salizzada S. Lio, **Castello** 5727 (☎04 15 22 32 83). Go. Go now. Enormous cones from L1500. Open daily Feb.-Nov. 10am-8:30pm.

Gelati Nico, Zattere, **Dorsoduro** 922 (☎04 15 22 52 93). Try *gianduiotto* (chocolate-hazelnut ice cream dunked in whipped cream). L2-4000. Open F-W 6:45am-11pm.

SIGHTS

Many churches enforce a strict dress code: shoulders and knees must be covered.

PIAZZA SAN MARCO TO THE RIALTO BRIDGE

PIAZZA SAN MARCO. The *piazza* is the city's pigeon-infested, *campanile*-punctuated nucleus. In contrast to the narrow, maze-like streets, it is an expanse of light and space, framed by museums and medieval buildings. Construction of the Basilica di San Marco began in the 9th century, when two Venetian merchants stole St. Mark's remains from Alexandria and hid them in a barrel of pork to sneak past Arab officials. The basilica's main treasure is the Pala d'Oro that rests behind the altar—a Veneto-Byzantine gold bas-relief encrusted with over 3000 precious gems. *(Basilica open M-Sa 9am-5pm, Su 1-5pm; illuminated 11:30am-12:30pm; free. Pala d'Oro open M-Sa 9:45am-5pm, Su 2-4:30pm; L1500-3000.)*

TORRE DELL'OROLOGIO. The 15th-century clock tower to the left of S. Marco indicates the hour, lunar phase, and ascending constellation. The brick campanile (bell tower; 96m) across the *piazza* originally served as a watchtower and lighthouse, and was rebuilt after a failed 1902 restoration project turned it into a pile of bricks. *(Elevator open daily 9am-7pm. L10,000.)*

PALAZZO DUCALE. To the right of the Basilica stands the Palazzo Ducale (Doge's Palace), once home to Venice's mayor and today the site of one of Venice's finest museums. Rebuilt in the 14th century after a fire, the palace epitomizes the Venetian Gothic with elegant arcades and light-colored stone cladding. *(Open daily Apr.-Oct. 9am-7pm; Nov.-Mar. 9am-5pm; last ticket sold 1½hr. before closing. Includes entry to Biblioteca Marciana and Museos Correr, Archeologico, Vetrario di Murano, and del Merletto di Burano. L18,000, students L10,000.)*

MUSEO CIVICO CORRER. Facing the palace, the Museo is dominated by Canova's neoclassical masterpieces, while the **Biblioteca Nazionale Marciana,** on the second floor, features frescoes by Titian and Tintoretto. *(Open daily Apr.-Sept. 9am-7pm; Oct.-Mar. 9am-5pm. Ticket office closes 1½hr. before museum. L18,000, students L10,000. Included with ticket to Palazzo Ducale.)*

CHIESA DI SAN ZACCARIA. The Gothic-Renaissance church holds one of the masterpieces of the Venetian Renaissance, Giovanni Bellini's *Virgin and Child Enthroned with Four Saints* (1505)—it's the second altar on the left. *(Vaporetto: S. Zaccaria. Or, from P. S. Marco, turn left along the water, cross the bridge, and turn left under the sottoportico. Open daily 10am-noon and 4-7pm. Free.)*

RIALTO BRIDGE. Constructed from 1588-91, the bridge arches over the Grand Canal, whose lacy, delicate *palazzi* testify to the city's wealthy history. To survey the main facades, ride *vaporetto* #82 from the station to P. S. Marco. The view at night, with dazzling reflections of light, is particularly impressive.

SAN POLO

BASILICA DI SANTA MARIA GLORIOSA DEI FRARI (I FRARI). The Gothic Basilica, begun in 1330, houses a moving wooden sculpture of St. John by Donatello, Bellini's *Madonna and Saints*, and Titian's famous *Assumption*—as well as the remains of Titian himself. *(Vaporetto: S. Tomà; follow the signs back to Campo dei Frari. Open M-Sa 9am-6pm, Su 1-6pm. L3000.)*

SCUOLA GRANDE DI SAN ROCCO

The *scuola* of Venice, a cross between guilds and religious fraternities, erected ornate "clubhouses" throughout the city; the most illustrious is the **Scuola Grande di San Rocco.** To view its 56 Tintorettos (which took him 23 years to paint) in chronological order, start on the second floor in the Sala dell'Albergo and follow the cycle downstairs. *(Behind I Frari in the Campo S. Rocco. Open daily in summer 9am-5:30pm; off season 10am-4pm. L9000, students L6000.)*

DORSODURO

CHIESA DI SANTA MARIA DELLA SALUTE. The theatrical *chiesa*, poised at the tip of Dorsoduro facing S. Marco, is a prime example of the Venetian Baroque. Survey the city from the old **customs house** next door, where ships sailing into Venice stopped to pay duties. *(Vaporetto: Salute. Open daily 9am-noon and 3-5:30pm. Free.)*

ACCADEMIA. The Accademia is a must-see for art lovers; its world-class collection includes the superb Bellini *Pala di San Giobbe*, Giorgione's enigmatic *Tempesta*, and Titian's last work, a brooding *Pietà*. *(Vaporetto: Accademia; or, walk across the Ponte dell'Accademia from S. Marco. ☎04 15 22 22 47. Open daily 9am-7pm. L12,000.)*

COLLEZIONE PEGGY GUGGENHEIM. The collection, in Guggenheim's former Palazzo Venier dei Leoni, includes works by Brancusi, Kandinsky, Picasso, Magritte, Rothko, Ernst, Pollock, and Dalí. *(Dorsoduro 701. Vaporetto: Accademia; turn left and follow the yellow signs to Calle S. Cristoforo. ☎04 12 40 54 11. Open M, W-F 10am-6pm, Sa 10am-10pm. L10,000, students with ISIC or Rolling Venice L8000, under 10 free.)*

NORTHERN VENICE

CHIESA DI SANTISSIMI GIOVANNI E PÁOLO (SAN ZANIPOLO). The *chiesa*, the largest Gothic church in the city, was built by the Dominican order from the mid-13th- to mid-15th centuries. The church contains a wonderful polyptych by Bellini, and outside stands a dignified equestrian statue, designed in 1479 by Verrochio, da Vinci's teacher. *(Vaporetto: Fond. Nuove; turn left and then right onto Fond. d. Mendicanti. Open M-Sa 7:30am-12:30pm and 3:30-7pm, Su 3-6pm. Free.)*

JEWISH GHETTO. In 1516, the Doge forced Venice's Jewish population into the old cannon-foundry area, coining the modern term "ghetto" (Venetian for "foundry"). Several synagogues are open for tours; one shares the **Museo Comunità Ebraica** building. *(Vaporetto: S. Marcuola; follow the signs straight ahead and then left into Campo d. Ghetto Nuovo. The museum is at Cannaregio 2899/b. Open Su-F June-Sept. 10am-7pm; Oct.-May 10am-4:30pm. L5000. Obligatory hourly tours for synagogues 40min. Museum and tour L9000.)*

GIUDECCA, SAN GIORGIO MAGGIORE, AND THE LAGOON. Many of Venice's most beautiful churches are a boat ride away from S. Marco. The **Chiesa di San Giorgio Maggiore,** an austere church of simple dignity, is across the lagoon on the island of the same name. *(Vaporetto #52 or 82: S. Giorgio Maggiore. ☎04 15 22 78 27. Open M-Sa 10am-12:30pm and 2:30-4:30pm.)* On the adjoining island of Giudecca is the famous **Redentore,** a church the Venetian Senate built to appease God and end the plague. *(Vaporetto #82 from S. Zaccaria: Redentore. Open M-Sa 10am-5pm, Su 1-5pm. L3000.)*

North of Venice stretches the **lagoon. San Michele** is Venice's cemetery island and the resting place of Ezra Pound, Igor Stravinsky, and Sergei Diaghilev. *(Vaporetto: Cimitero.)* **Murano** has been famed for its glass-blowing since 1292; **Burano** remains a traditional fishing village with colored facades; and rural **Torcello** boasts a Byzantine cathedral with magnificent medieval mosaics. *(For Murano, Burano, or Torcello, catch vaporetto #12 or 52 from S. Zaccaria or Fond. Nuove to "Faro.")* The **Lido** is Venice's beach island as well as the setting for Mann's *Death in Venice. (Vaporetto: Lido.)*

ENTERTAINMENT AND NIGHTLIFE

You won't have a true sense of Venice until you quietly slide down its canals in a gondola and pass its houses and *palazzi.* The rides are expensive; the minimum authorized rate starts at L120,000 for 45 minutes and increases after sunset. Rates are negotiable, but if you still can't afford it, try one of the city's *traghetti* (ferry gondolas that cross the Grand Canal at six points; L700).

The weekly *A Guest in Venice*, free at hotels and tourist offices, lists current festivals, concerts, and gallery exhibits. **Vivaldi** concerts occur almost nightly; talk to any of the costumed people scattered throughout town. During the 10 days before Ash Wednesday, Venice's famous **Carnevale** brings masked figures, camera-happy tourists, and outdoor concerts to the city. The famed **Biennale di Venezia** (☎04 12 41 10 58; www.labiennale.org) drowns the city with provocative contemporary international art every odd-numbered year.

Venetian nightlife is fairly quiet; even the liveliest places close around 1:30am. Students congregate in **Campo Santa Margherita** in Dorsoduro and around **Fond. della Misericordia** in Cannaregio. **Inishark Irish Pub,** Calle Mondo Novo, Castello 5787, is creatively decorated. (Open Tu-Su 6pm-2am.) Both Venetian and international students mingle at **Bar Salus,** Campo S. Margherita, Dorsoduro 2963. (Open M-Sa 7am-2am.) **Paradiso Perduto,** Fond. della Misericordia 2540, is a well-known bar, jazz club, and restaurant; from Strada Nuova, cross Campo S. Fosca and head straight over three bridges. (Open Th-Su 7pm-2am.) If you're starved for a *discoteca*, slink into **Casanova** and let modern-day Latin lovers show you their moves. (Theme and cover vary. Open daily 10pm-4am.)

EXCURSIONS FROM VENICE

VERONA. One of the most beautiful cities in Northern Italy, Verona is under two hours by train from Venice (p. 610).

TRIESTE. Once occupied by Austria, Trieste beckons with an intriguing Slavic flavor, just two hours by train from Venice (p. 611).

PADUA (PADOVA)

Brimming with art and student life, Padua is a treasury of strident frescoes, sculpture-lined piazze, and ethereal nighttime festivals. Art escapes the canvas, covering churches floor to ceiling, while high culture blends with a lively university scene.

PRACTICAL INFO, ACCOMMODATIONS, AND FOOD. Trains depart from P. Stazione for: Venice (30min., 3-4 per hr., L4100); Verona (1hr., 1-2 per hr., L7900); Bologna (1½hr., 1-2 per hr., L7900); and Milan (2½hr., 1-2 per hr., L20-31,500). The **bus station,** P. Boschetti (☎04 98 20 68 11), serves Venice (45min., 2 per hr., L5300). The **tourist office** is in the train station. (☎04 98 75 20 77; fax 04 98 75 50 88. Open M-Sa 9am-6pm, Su 9am-12:15pm.) The **Ostello Città di Padova (HI),** V. Aleardi 30, near Prato della Valle, has an English-speaking staff. Take bus #3 or 8 from the station. (☎04 98 75 22 19; fax 049 65 42 10. Breakfast and sheets included. Reception 7-9:30am and 2:30-11pm. Lockout 9:30am-4pm. Curfew 11pm. Reserve a week ahead. Dorms L24,000.) **Hotel Al Santo,** V. Santo 147, near the Basilica, has airy, well-kept rooms with phones. (☎04 98 75 21 31; fax 04 99 78 80 76. Open Feb. to mid-Dec. Singles L90,000; doubles L110,000; triples L130,000; quads L150-160,000.) **Taverna Nane della Giulia,** V.S. Sofia 1, fills with students and artists enjoying cheap food, fabulous wine and music. (Open Tu-Su 12:30-2:30pm and 7pm-1am.) **Postal code:** 35100.

SIGHTS AND ENTERTAINMENT. The one-year **Biglietto Unico** is valid at most of Padua's museums (L15,000, students L10,000; buy at the tourist office and participating sights). The **Cappella degli Scrovegni** (Arena Chapel) contains Giotto's breathtaking floor-to-ceiling fresco cycle, illustrating the lives of Mary, Jesus, and Mary's parents. Buy tickets at the adjoining **Musei Civici Eremitani,** which itself features a restored Giotto crucifix. (P. Eremitani 8. Open Feb.-Oct. Tu-Su 9am-7pm; Nov.-Jan. Tu-Su 9am-6pm. Chapel open daily Feb.-Dec. L10,000, students L7000.) Thousands of pilgrims are drawn to St. Anthony's jawbone and well-preserved tongue at the **Basilica di Sant'Antonio,** in P. del Santo, a medieval conglomeration of eight domes filled with devastatingly beautiful frescoes. (Open daily Apr.-Sept. 6:30am-8pm; Nov.-Mar. 6:30am-7pm. Dress code enforced.) In the center of P. del Santo stands Donatello's bronze equestrian **Gattamelata statue** of Erasmo da Narni (a.k.a. Gattamelata or Calico Cat), a general remembered for his agility and ferocity. Next door to the **duomo,** in P. Duomo, lies the 12th-century **Battistero,** perhaps the most beautiful of Padua's buildings. (Open daily in summer 9:30am-1:30pm and 3-7pm; off season 9:30am-1pm and 3-6pm. L3000, students L2000.) The **Palazzo della Ragione** (Law Courts), built in 1218, retains most of its original shape. Astrological signs line the walls, and to the right of the entrance sits the **Stone of Shame,** upon which partially clad debtors were forced to sit. (Open Jan.-Oct. Tu-Su 9am-7pm; Nov.-Dec. Tu-Su 9am-6pm. L10,000, students L6000.) Buildings of the ancient **university** are scattered throughout the city, but are centered in Palazzo Bó.

VERONA

A glorious combination of majestic Roman ruins, colorful Venetian facades, and orange rooftops, Verona is one of the most beautiful cities in Northern Italy. Gazing at the town from one of its many bridges at sunset sets the tone for romantic evenings befitting the home of *Romeo and Juliet.* Meanwhile, its artistic and historical treasures fill days with rewarding sightseeing.

PRACTICAL INFO, ACCOMMODATIONS, AND FOOD. Trains (☎04 58 00 08 61) go from P. XXV Aprile to: Venice (1¾hr., every hr., L10,800-17,000); Milan (2hr., every hr., L12,500); and Bologna (2hr., every 2hr., L10,500). The **tourist office,** in Piazza Brà, is off the plaza before Via D. Alpini. (☎04 58 06 86 80; fax 04 58 00 36 38. Open daily 10am-7pm.) Reserve lodgings ahead, especially in opera season (June 26-Aug. 30). The **Ostello della Gioventù (HI),** "Villa Francescatti," Salita Fontana del Ferro 15, in a renovated 16th-century villa with gorgeous gardens; from the station, take bus #73 or night bus #90 to P. Isolo, turn right, and follow the yellow signs uphill. (☎045 59 03 60; fax 04 58 00 91 27. Breakfast included. Max. night stay

5 nights. Check-in 5pm. Lockout 9am-5pm. Curfew 11pm; flexible for opera-goers. No reservations. Dorms L22,000.) Women can also try the beautiful **Casa della Giovane (ACISJF),** V. Pigna 7, 3rd fl., in the historic center of town. (☎045 59 68 80; fax 04 58 00 59 49. Reception 9am-11pm. Curfew 11pm; flexible for opera-goers. Dorms L22,000; singles L32,000; doubles L50,000.) To get to **Locanda Catullo,** Vco. Catullo 1, walk to V. Mazzini 40, turn onto V. Catullo, and turn left on Vco. Catullo. (☎04 58 00 27 86; fax 045 59 69 87. July-Sept. min. stay 3 nights. Singles L60,000; doubles L90-110,000; triples L135-165,000; quads L165-175,000.) Verona is famous for its wines—its dry white *soave* and red *valpolicella, bardolino,* and *recioto.* Prices in **P. Isolo** are cheaper than those in P. delle Erbe. For a large sampling, try **Oreste dal Zovo,** Vco. S. Marco in Foro 7/5, off C. Porta Borsari. **METÁ supermarket,** V. XX Settembre 81, can be reached by taking bus #11-14 or 51. (Open M-Tu and Th-Sa 8:30am-12:45pm and 3:45-7:30pm, W 8:30am-12:45pm.) **Postal code:** 37122.

SIGHTS AND ENTERTAINMENT. The physical and emotional heart of Verona is the majestic, pink-marble, first-century **Arena,** in P. Brà. (Open Tu-Su 9am-7pm; in opera season 9am-3pm. L6000, students L4000.) From P. Brà, V. Mazzini leads to the markets and stunning medieval architecture of **Piazza delle Erbe,** the former Roman forum. The 83m **Torre dei Lambertini,** down V. Capello from P. Erbe, offers perhaps the most stunning view of Verona. (Open Tu-Su 9:30am-6pm. Elevator L4000, students L3000. Stairs L3000; students L2000.) The **Giardino Giusti,** V. Giardino Giusti 2, is a magnificent 16th-century garden with a labyrinth of mythological statues. (Open daily Apr.-Sept. 9am-8pm; Oct.-Mar. 9am-dusk. L7000, students L3000.) The della Scala fortress, the **Castelvecchio,** down V. Roma from P. Brà, is filled with walkways, parapets, and an extensive art collection including Pisanello's *Madonna and Child.* (Open Tu-Su 9am-7pm. L6000, students L4000; 1st Su of each month free.) Thousands of tourists have immortalized **Casa di Giulietta** (Juliet's House), V. Cappello 23, where the Capulet family never really lived. Avoid wasting *lire* to stand on the balcony and view the few paintings inside. (Open Tu-Su 9am-7pm. L6000, students L4000; 1st Su of each month free.) From late June to late August, Verona resounds with arias, as tourists and singers from around the world descend on the Arena for the annual **Opera Festival.** (Info ☎04 58 00 51 51.)

FRIULI-VENEZIA GIULIA

Friuli-Venezia Giulia traditionally receives less than its fair share of recognition. James Joyce lived in Trieste for 12 years, during which he wrote most of *Ulysses;* Ernest Hemingway drew part the plot for *A Farewell to Arms* from the region's role in WWI; and Freud and Rilke both worked and wrote here. Trieste attracts tourists with the cheapest beach resorts on the Adriatic.

TRIESTE (TRIEST)

In the post-Napoleonic real estate grab, the Austrians snatched Trieste (pop. 230,000), a city that once rivaled Venice; after a little more ping-pong, the city became part of Italy in 1954, but still remains divided between its Slavic and Italian origins. Trieste's past lingers in its Neoclassical architecture, the Slavic nuances of its local cuisine, and the Slovenian still spoken in its streets. The grid-like 19th-century **Città Nuova,** between the waterfront and the Castello di S. Giusto, centers on the **Canale Grande.** Facing the canal from the south is the striking Serbian Orthodox **Chiesa di San Spiridione.** (Open Tu-Sa 9am-noon and 5-8pm. Dress modestly.) The ornate **Municipio** complements the **Piazza dell'Unità d'Italia,** the largest *piazza* in Italy. Trieste's Neoclassical architecture contrasts with its narrow, twisting alleys, reminiscent of its medieval and Roman history. The 15th-century Venetian **Castello di San Giusto** presides over **Capitoline Hill,** south of P. Unità, the city's historical center. (Castle open daily 9am-dusk.) Hilltop **Piazza della Cattedrale** overlooks the sea and downtown Trieste; from P. Goldoni, you can ascend the hill by way of the daunting 265 **Scala dei Giganti** (Steps of the Giants). The archaeological **Museo di Storia e d'Arte,** V. Cattedrale 15, is down the other side of the hill past the *duomo.* (Open Tu and Th-Su 9am-1pm. L3000.)

Trains (☎040 379 47 37) go from P. della Libertà 8, down C. Cavour from the quays, to: Venice (2hr., 2 per hr., L14,500); Milan (5hr., every hr., L34,500-50,000); Ljubljana (4 per day, L35,100); and Budapest (11hr., 2 per day, L120,000). The **tourist office** is on Riva III Novembre 9, along the quays near P. della Unita. (☎040 03 47 83 12; fax 347 83 20. Open M-Sa 9am-7pm, Su 10:30am-1pm and 4-7pm.) **Hotel Alabarda,** V. Valdirivo 22, has bright, spotless rooms. From P. Oberdan, go down V. XXX Ottobre and turn right onto V. Valdirivo. (☎040 63 02 69; fax 63 92 84; email albergoalabarda@tin.it. Singles L50,000; doubles L80-105,000; triples L94,000; quads L120,000.) To get from the station to **Ostello Tegeste (HI),** V. Miramare 331, on the seaside, take bus #36 (L1400) from across V. Miramare, the street on the left of the station as you exit, and ask the driver for the *ostello*. From the stop, walk back down the road toward Trieste and take the seaside fork toward Castle Miramare. (☎/fax 040 22 41 02. Breakfast and shower included. Reception daily 8am-11pm. Check-out 10am. Lockout 10am-1pm. Curfew 11:30pm. Dorms L20,000.) Stock up at **STANDA,** V. Battisti 15. (Open M 3:30-7:30pm, Tu-F 9am-1pm and 3:30-7:30pm, Sa 9am-7:30pm.) Get a great view of the square and excellent *primi* for L8-9000 at **Pizzeria Barattolo,** P.S. Antonio 2. (Open daily 8:30am-midnight). **Postal code:** 34100.

PIEDMONT (PIEMONTE)

Piedmont has been a politically influential region for centuries, as well as a fountainhead of fine food, wine, and nobility. After native-born Vittorio Emanuele II and Camillo Cavour united Italy, Turin served as its capital from 1861 to 1865.

TURIN (TORINO)

Turin, which will host the Winter Olympics in 2006, is primarily known for the Fiat Auto Company as well as one of the strangest relics of Christianity: the **Cattedrale di San Giovanni,** behind the Palazzo Reale, houses the **Holy Shroud of Turin.** When the chapel is closed, a life-size canvas copy of the shroud is on display. (Open daily 7am-12:30pm and 3-7pm. Free.) The **Museo Egizio,** in the **Palazzo dell'Accademia delle Scienze,** V. dell'Accademia delle Scienze 6, has a collection of Egyptian artifacts second only to the British Museum. (Open Tu-F and Su 8:30am-7:30pm, Sa 8:30am-11pm. L12,000.) One of Guarini's great Baroque palaces, the **Museo Nazionale del Risorgimento Italiano,** in the **Palazzo Carignano,** V. dell'Accademia delle Scienze 5, at various times housed both the first Italian parliament and Prince Vittorio Emanuele's cradle. Today the museum details Italy's unification, from 1800 to the early 1900s. (Open Tu-Su 9am-7pm. L8000, students L5000. Free tour Su 10-11:30am.)

Trains, C. Vittorio Emanuele, roll to: Milan (2hr., every hr., L21,600); Genoa (2hr., every hr., L14,500); and Venice (4½hr., 2 per day, L51,500). The **tourist office,** P. Castello 165, has free maps. (☎011 53 51 81. Open M-Sa 9:30am-7pm, Su 9:30am-3pm.) To get to the clean, comfortable, bright orange **Ostello Torino (HI),** V. Alby 1, take bus #52 (bus #64 on Su) from Stazione Porto Nuova to the 3rd stop after crossing the river. Go back up V. Thoveu, bear left onto V. Curreno, and turn left onto V. Gatti, which branches off onto V. Alby. (☎01 16 60 29 39; fax 01 16 60 44 45. Breakfast and

HOLY SHROUD, BATMAN! Called a hoax by some and a miracle by others, the holy shroud of Turin (a 1m by 4.5m piece of linen) was supposedly wrapped around Jesus' body in preparation for burial after his crucifixion. Although radiocarbon dating places the piece in the 12th century AD, uncanny evidence prevents the shroud's immediate dismissal. Visible on the cloth are outflows of blood: around the head (supposedly from the Crown of Thorns), all over the body (from scourging), and most importantly, on the wrists and feet (where the body was nailed to the cross). Scientists agree that the shroud was wrapped around the body of a 5'7" man who died by crucifixion, but whether it was Jesus remains a mystery. For Christian believers, the importance of the relic is captured by Pope Paul VI's words: "The Shroud is a document of Christ's love written in characters of blood."

sheets included. Laundry L10,000. Oct.-Apr. heat L2000 per day. Reception 7-10am and 3:30-11pm. Curfew 11:30pm. Open Feb.- late Dec. L22,000.) To **camp** at **Campeggio Villa Rey,** Strada Superiore Val S. Martino 27, take bus #61 north from the right side of the Porta Nuova until P. Vittorio, then take bus #54, and follow signs after the last stop. (☎ 01 18 19 01 17. Light L2500. Showers L1000. L7000 per person; L4-7000 per tent.) An open-air **market** sets up on P. della Repubblica. (Open M-F 8am-1pm, Sa 8am-6pm.) **Postal code:** 10100.

THE LAKES AND THE DOLOMITES

When Italy's monuments and museums start to blur together, escape to the natural beauty of the northern lakes and mountains. The Lake Country fueled Stendhal's descriptions of lakes, flowers, and mountains. In the province of Trentino-Alto Adige to the east, the Dolomite mountain range dominates the landscape, rising from Austrian-influenced valley communities to lofty peaks perfect for skiing and hiking. Activities from windsurfing to bar-hopping abound, but the lakeside lends itself most to relaxation.

LAKE COMO (LAGO DI COMO)

An otherworldly magnificence lingers over the northern reaches of Europe's deepest lake (410m), but peaceful Lake Como is not a figment of your imagination. Bougainvillea and lavish villas adorn the lake's craggy backdrop, warmed by the sun and cooled by lakeside breezes.

GETTING THERE AND GETTING AROUND. The only town on the lake accessible by train is its largest urban outpost, **Como,** on the southwestern tip of the lake. **Trains** roll in from Milan (1hr., every 30min., L9,000), while **buses** arrive from Bergamo (2hr., every 2hr., L8300). From Como, hourly **buses** run to towns in the **Central Lago** area, where the three prongs of the forked lake meet. **Bellaggio** (1hr., L5000), on the southern shore of the Centro Lago, is the favorite lake town of upper-crust Milanese society; steep streets lead to sidewalk cafes, silk shops, and the villas of Lombard aristocrats. **Varenna,** on the eastern shore, is more peaceful and scenic. The C10 bus runs along the western shore of the lake to **Menaggio** (1hr., L4700) and **Tremezzo,** which boasts the enormous azaleas and sculptures of **Villa Carlotta** (open Mar.-Oct.; L11,500, L6500 through the hostel) but is otherwise quiet. Once you've found a place to stay, you can spend the day zipping between the stores, gardens, villas, and wineries of the remaining towns on the lake by **ferry.**

COMO. For excellent hiking and stunning views, take the **funiculare** from the far end of Lungo Lario Trieste (every 15-30min.; round-trip L7200, through the hostel L5000) up to **Brunate.** To get from the station to the **tourist office,** P. Cavour 16, walk down the steps to V. Gallio, which becomes V. Garibaldi and leads to P. Cavour via P. Volta. (☎ 031 26 97 12. Open M-Sa 9am-1pm and 2:30-6pm.) **In Riva al Lago,** P. Matteoti 4, is a three-star hotel with immaculate rooms. (☎ 031 30 23 33. Breakfast 5000. Singles L45,000, with bath and TV L75,000; doubles L70,000-100,000.) Picnickers will appreciate the **G.S. supermarket,** on the corner of V. Fratelli Recchi and V. Fratelli Roselli. (Open M 2-8pm, Tu-Sa 8am-8pm, Su 10am-6pm.)

LAKE MAGGIORE (LAGO MAGGIORE)

Lacking the frenzy of its eastern neighbors, Lake Maggiore cradles similar temperate mountain waters and idyllic shores. The romantic resort town **Stresa** is only an hour from Milan by **train** (every hr.; L8200, IC supplement L6000). To get from the Stresa train station to the **tourist office,** V. Principe Tommaso 70/72, turn right and walk down the hill on V. Carducci, which becomes V. Gignous; V. Tommaso is on the left. (☎ 032 33 04 16. Open M-F 8:30am-12:30pm and 3-6:15pm.) To get to comfy beds at **Orsola Meublé,** V. Duchessa di Genova 45, turn right from the station, walk downhill, and turn left at the intersection. (☎ 032 33 10 87. Breakfast included. Singles L50-70,000; doubles L80-100,000.)

EXCURSION FROM LAKE MAGGIORE: BORROMEAN ISLANDS. Stresa and Pallanza are perfect stepping stones to the gorgeous **Borromean Islands.** Daily excursion tickets (L12,400 including travel to Laveno's train station) allow you to hop back and forth between either Stresa and Pallanza and the three islands—**Isola Bella, Isola Superiore dei Pescatori,** and **Isola Madre**. The islands boast lush, manicured botanical gardens, elegant villas, and an opulent Baroque palace.

LAKE GARDA (LAGO DI GARDA)

Garda, the ultimate resort destination for many Germans, has staggering mountains and breezy summers. **Desenzano,** the lake's southern transport hub, lies on the Milan-Venice line, 45 minutes from Verona, one hour from Milan, and two hours from Venice. From Desenzano, the other lake towns are accessible by bus and boat.

SIRMIONE. Along the lake shore, flashy Sirmione, with its beautifully situated medieval castle and extensive Roman ruins, you can easily fill a day with the holy trinity of dinner, shopping, and dessert. The 13th-century **Castello Scaligero** sits in the center of town. (Open Mar. to mid-Oct. Tu-Su 8:30am-7:30pm; Nov.-Feb. 9am-5pm. L8000.) **Buses** arrive hourly from Desenzano (20min., L2500) and Verona (1hr., L5000). **Battelli** (water steamers) run to: Desenzano (20min., L4500); Gardone (1¼hr., L10,000); and Riva (4hr., L14,100). The **Albergo Grifone,** V. Bisse 5, has a prime locale by the castle. (☎030 91 60 14; fax 030 91 65 48. Reserve ahead. Singles L50,000; doubles L88,000; L27,000 per extra bed.)

RIVA. Riva has few sights, but the town is livelier, the crowd younger, and the prices lower than other places on the lake. Travelers **swim, windsurf, hike,** and **climb** in the most stunning portion of the lake, where Alpine cliffs crash into the water. Riva is accessible by **bus** (☎0464 55 23 23) from Trent (2hr., 6 per day, L6000) and Verona (2hr., 11 per day, L9300). **Ferries** (☎030 914 95 11), on P. Matteoti, head to Sirmione (L13,900) and Gardone (L12,200). The **tourist office,** Giardini di Porta Orientale 8, is near the water. (☎0464 55 44 44. Open M-Sa 9am-noon and 3-6pm.) Snooze at the fabulous **Ostello Benacus (HI),** P. Cavour 9, in the center of town; from the bus station, walk down V. Trento, take V. Roma, turn left under the arch, and follow signs. (☎0464 55 49 11; fax 0464 55 65 54. Breakfast, sheets, and shower included. Reception daily 7-9am and 3pm-midnight. Reserve ahead. L22,000.)

THE DOLOMITES

Limestone spires shoot skyward from pine forests in the Dolomites. These amazing peaks—fantastic for hiking, skiing, and rock climbing—start west of Trent and extend north and east to Austria. With their sunny skies and powdery, light snow, the mountains offer very popular year-round downhill skiing.

TRENT. Between the Dolomites and the Veneto, Trent's pleasant, colorful streets offer a sampling of northern Italian life. At the edges of town are engaging walks set against a backdrop of dramatic limestone cliffs. The **Piazza del Duomo,** Trent's center and social heart, contains the city's best sights. The **Fontana del Nettuno** stands, trident in hand, in the center of the piazza. Nearby is the **Cattedrale di San Vigilio,** named for the patron saint of Trent. (Open daily 6:40am-12:15pm and 2:30-7:30pm.) Walk down V. Belenzani and head right on V. Roma to reach the well-preserved **Castello del Buonconsiglio.** (Open Apr.-Sept. Tu-Su 9am-noon and 2-5:30pm; Oct.-Mar. 9am-noon and 2-5pm. L9000, students L5000.) **Monte Bondone** rises majestically over Trent, a pleasant daytrip or overnight excursion. Catch the **cable car** (L1500) to **Sardagna** from Ponte di S. Lorenzo, between the train tracks and the river.

Trains head to: Bolzano (50min., every hr., L9400); Verona (1hr., every hr., L14,200); Venice (2½hr., L29,400); and Bologna (2½-3hr., 8 per day, L18,600). Atesina **buses** go from V. Pozzo, next to the train station, to Riva del Garda (1hr., every hr., L5500). The **tourist office,** on Via Manci, offers advice on biking, skiing, and hiking. (☎04 61 98 38 80; www.apt.trento.it. Open daily 9am-7pm.) From the station, turn right on V. Pozzo and left on V. Torre Vanga to get to **Ostello Giovane Europa (HI),**

V. Manzoni 17. (☎0461 23 45 67. Breakfast and sheets included. Reception 3:30-11pm. Check-out 9:30am. Curfew 11:30pm. Reserve ahead. Dorms L22,000; family rooms L22,000 per person.) **Hotel Venezia** is at P. Duomo 45. (☎/fax 04 61 23 41 14. Breakfast L12,000. Singles L55-65,000; doubles L95,000.)

BOLZANO. Bolzano's blend of Austrian and Italian influences and its prime location beneath vineyard-covered mountains make it a splendid stopover or base for exploring the Dolomites. The most compelling sight is the unbelievably well-preserved, 5200-year-old body of the **Ice Man.** (V. Museo 43. Open Tu-W and F-Su 10am-6pm, Th 10am-8pm. L13,000, students L7000.) The Gothic **duomo,** on P. Walther, is a dark and awesome sight, while the simple exterior of the **Chiesa dei Francescani,** on V. dei Francescani near P. Erbe, belies its splendid stained glass within. (Both churches open M-F 9:45am-noon and 2-5pm.) Take the bus from P. Walther to the frescoed **Castel Roncolo** for a spectacular view of the city. (Open Mar.-Nov. Tu-Su 10am-6pm; frescoes close 5pm. L2000.) **Trains** go to: Trent (1-2hr., 1-2 per hr., L5300); Verona (2hr., 1-2 per hr., L12,500); and Milan (3½hr., 3 per day, L24,300). Walk up V. Stazione from the train station, or V. Alto Adige from the bus stop, to reach the **tourist office,** P. Walther 8. (☎0471 30 70 00; fax 0471 98 01 28. Open M-F 9am-6:30pm, Sa 9am-12:30pm.) **Croce Bianca,** P. del Grano (Kornpl.) 3, has beds around the corner from P. Walther. (☎04 71 97 75 52. Singles L40,000; doubles L60-78,000; triples L90,000.)

LOMBARDY (LOMBARDIA)

In the past centuries, Roman generals, German emperors, and French kings have vied for control of Lombardy's rich agricultural wealth and fertile soil. Recently, Lombardy has become an even sturdier cornerstone of Italy's economy with increases in employment and industrial developments. While cosmopolitan Milan may bask in the spotlight of progress and glitz, don't neglect the rich culture and beauty of Bergamo, Mantua, or the nearby foothills of the Alps.

MILAN (MILANO)

Milan has embraced modernity more forcefully than any other major Italian city. Although it was the capital of the western Roman Empire from 286 to 402, Milan retains few reminders of that period. The pace of life is quick, and *il dolce di far niente* (the sweetness of doing nothing) is an unfamiliar taste. Although Milan's lifestyle has brought petty crime and drugs, the city remains vibrant and on the cutting edge of finance, fashion, and nighttime fun. For one week in March and September, models from all over the world gather here for the *Milano Collezioni.*

GETTING THERE AND GETTING AROUND

Flights: ☎02 74 85 22 00. **Malpensa Airport,** 45km away, handles intercontinental flights. **Malpensa Express** connects to MM1, 2: Cadorna (45min., L15,000). **Linate Airport,** 7km away, covers Europe. Take bus #73 from MM1: P. San Babila.

Trains: Stazione Centrale, P. Duca d'Aosta (☎02 01 47 88 80 88), on MM2. To: **Genoa** (1½hr., every hr., L24,500); **Turin** (2hr., every hr., L24,500); **Florence** (2½hr., every hr., L40,000); **Venice** (3hr., 21 per day, L36,000); and **Rome** (4½hr., every hr., L71,000). Office open daily 7am-9:30pm. **Luggage storage** L5000 per 12hr.

Buses: Stazione Centrale (see **Trains,** above). Intercity buses tend to be less convenient and more expensive than trains. **SAL, SIA, Autostradale,** and other carriers leave from P. Castello and nearby (MM1: Cairoli) for Turin, Lake Country, and Bergamo.

Public Transportation: The **subway** (Metropolitana Milanese, or **MM**) runs 6am-midnight. **ATM** (☎021 67 01 68 57 toll-free), in the MM1, 3 Duomo station, handles local transportation. Single-fare tickets (L1500) are good for 75min. of surface transportation. Day passes L5000, 2-day L9000. Info and ticket booths open M-Sa 7:15am-7:15pm. Keep extra tickets on hand since *tabacchi* close around 8pm.

ORIENTATION AND PRACTICAL INFORMATION

Milan's layout resembles a giant target, encircled by remnants of concentric ancient city walls. The **duomo** and **Galleria Vittorio Emanuele II** comprise the bull's-eye. From the train station, a scenic ride on bus #60 or a quick commute on MM3 will take you downtown. See our **color map** of Milan at the front of this book.

TOURIST, FINANCIAL, AND LOCAL SERVICES

Tourist Office: APT, V. Marconi 1 (☎02 72 52 43 00; fax 02 72 52 43 50), in the Palazzo di Turismo, to the right of the *duomo.* Useful museum guide (in Italian) and map. No room reservations, but will check for vacancies. Pick up *Milano: Where, When, How* and *Milano Mese* for info on activities and clubs. Open M-F 8:30am-8pm, Sa 9am-1pm and 2-7pm, Su 9am-1pm and 2-5pm. **Branch** at Stazione Centrale (☎02 72 52 43 70). Open M-Sa 9am-6pm, Su 9am-12:30pm and 1:30-6pm.

Budget Travel: CIT (☎02 86 37 01), in Galleria Vittorio Emanuele II. Open M-F 9am-7pm, Sa 9am-1pm and 2-6pm. **CTS,** V. S. Antonio 2 (☎02 58 30 41 21). Open M-F 9:30am-12:45pm and 2-6pm, Sa 9:30am-12:45pm. **Transalpino Tickets** (☎02 67 16 82 28; www.transalpino.com), next to the train office in Stazione Centrale. Discounts for age 26 and under. Open M-Sa 8am-8:30pm.

Currency Exchange: All **Banca d'America e d'Italia** and **Banca Nazionale del Lavoro** branches eagerly await your Visa card. Bank hours in Milan are usually M-F 8:30am-1:30pm and 2:30-4:30pm. **ATMs** abound.

American Express: V. Brera 3 (☎02 72 00 36 93), on the corner of V. dell'Orso. Holds mail free for AmEx members for 1 month and receives wired money (L2500 fee if over L150,000). Also **exchanges currency.** Open M-Th 9am-5:30pm, F 9am-5pm.

Laundromat: Vicolo Lavandai, V. le Monte Grappa 2 (MM2: Garibaldi). Wash or dry L6000 for 7kg. Open daily 8am-9pm.

EMERGENCY AND COMMUNICATIONS

Emergency: ☎118. **Police:** ☎113. **Ambulance:** ☎118.

Pharmacy: In Stazione Centrale (☎026 69 07 35). Open 24hr.

Hospital: Ospedale Maggiore di Milano, V. Francesco Sforza 35 (☎025 50 31).

Telephones: In Galleria Vittorio Emanuele II. Open daily 8am-7:30pm. Phones are also available in Stazione Centrale.

Internet Access: Mercedes Benz shop in Galleria Vitt. Emanuele II, on the left as you enter from the duomo. 15min. free. **El Pampero,** V. Gasparotto I (☎02 66 92 21), has a cafe, restaurant, and club. L10,000 per hr. Open daily 7am-3am.

Post Office: V. Cordusio 4 (☎028 69 20 69), near P. del Duomo. Address mail to be held: First name, SURNAME. *In Fermo Posta,* Ufficio Postale Centrale di Piazza Cordusio 4, Milano **20100,** Italia. Open M-F 8:30am-7:30pm, Sa 8:30am-1pm.

ACCOMMODATIONS AND CAMPING

It's always high season in Milan, except August, when mosquitoes outnumber humans. A decent single under L60,000 is a real find. Try east of the train station or the southern periphery of the city for the best deals.

Hotel Ca' Grande, V. Porpora 87 (☎/fax 02 26 14 40 01), 6 blocks from P. Loreto. MM1,2: Loreto, then take tram #33 to V. Ampere, 50m from the hotel. Wonderful proprietors and clean rooms with phones. The street below can be noisy. Breakfast included. Reception 24hr. Singles L70-90,000; doubles L110-130,000.

Hotel Ambra, V. Caccianino 10 (☎02 26 65 465). MM1,2: Loreto, then walk on V. Porpora for 10 blocks and turn right on V. Caccianino. Romantic atmosphere and spotless rooms with bath, TV, telephone. Breakfast L5000. Ask for key if going out at night. Reserve ahead. Singles L70,000; doubles L100,000; triples L140,000.

Hotel Sara, V. Sacchini 17 (☎02 20 17 73). MM1,2: Loreto, then take V. Porpora and turn right on V. Sacchini. Renovated hotel with simple rooms. Reception 24hr. Singles L55,000; doubles L80,000, with bath L100,000; triple with bath L120,000.

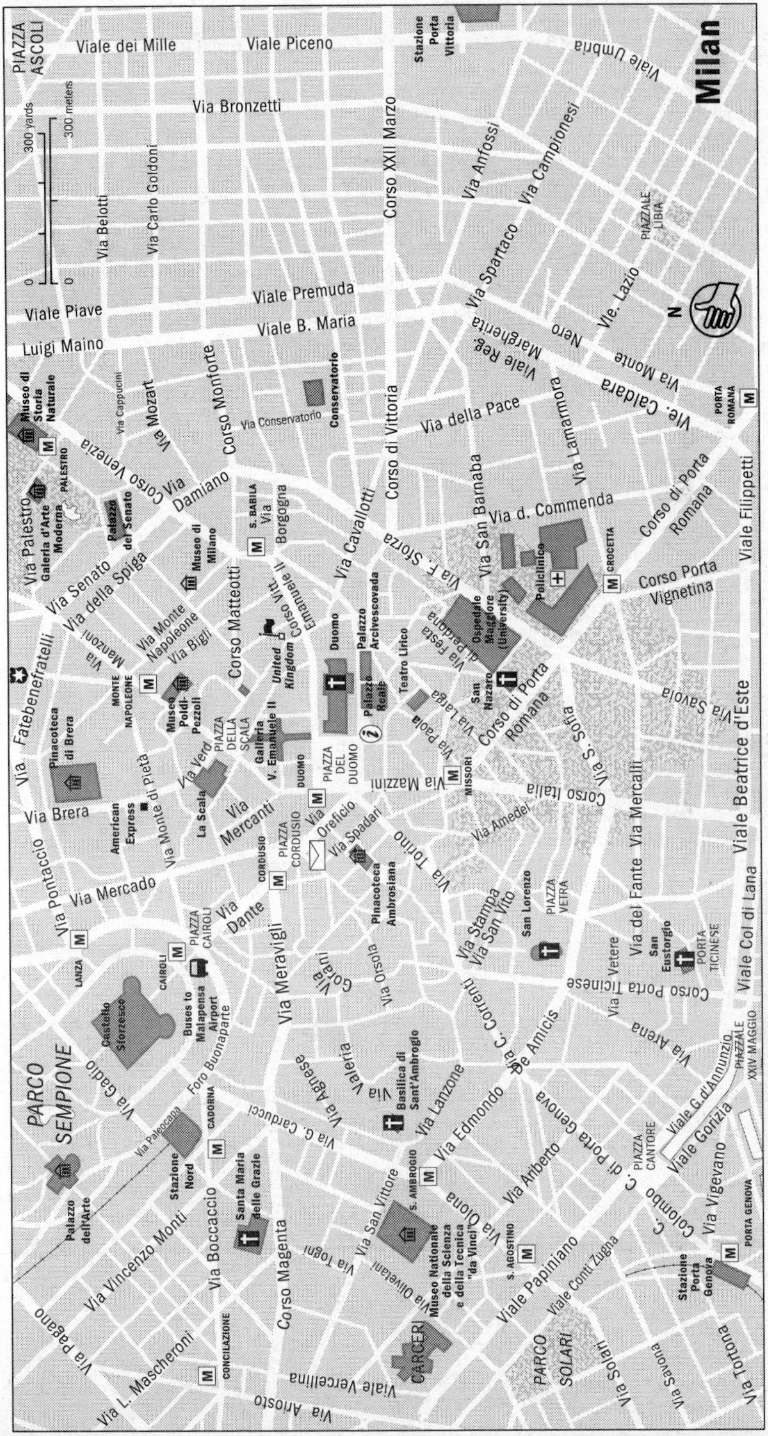
Milan
N
300 yards
300 meters
0
PARCO SEMPIONE
Palazzo dell'Arte
Castello Sforzesco
Buses to Malapensa Airport
Stazione Nord
CADORNA
Santa Maria delle Grazie
Museo Nationale della Scienza e della Tecnica "da Vinci"
S. AMBROGIO
Basilica di Sant'Ambrogio
CARCERI
Pinacoteca di Brera
American Express
La Scala
Galleria V. Emanuele II
PIAZZA DELLA SCALA
Museo Poldi-Pezzoli
MONTE NAPOLEONE
United Kingdom
Duomo
DUOMO
PIAZZA DEL DUOMO
Palazzo Reale
Palazzo Arcivescovado
Teatro Lirico
San Nazaro
MISSORI
Ospedale Maggiore (University)
Policlinico
CROCETTA
Museo di Milano
S. BABILA
Palazzo del Senato
Galleria d'Arte Moderna
PALESTRO
Museo di Storia Naturale
Conservatorio
Pinacoteca Ambrosiana
PIAZZA CORDUSIO
CORDUSIO
PIAZZA CAIROLI
CAIROLI
LANZA
San Lorenzo
PIAZZA VETRA
San Eustorgio
PORTA TICINESE
PIAZZALE XXIV MAGGIO
PIAZZA CANTORE
S. AGOSTINO
CONCILIAZIONE
PARCO SOLARI
Stazione Porta Genova
PORTA GENOVA
PORTA ROMANA
PIAZZALE LIBIA
Stazione Porta Vittoria
PIAZZA ASCOLI
Viale dei Mille
Viale Piceno
Via Bronzetti
Via Belotti
Via Carlo Goldoni
Viale Piave
Viale Premuda
Viale B. Maria
Luigi Maino
Corso Monforte
Via Mozart
Via Cappucini
Via Conservatorio
Corso XXII Marzo
Corso di Vittoria
Via della Pace
Via Anfossi
Via Campionesi
Via Spartaco
Viale Umbria
Vle. Lazio
Viale Reg. Margherita
Nero
Via Monte
Vle. Caldara
Via Lamarmora
Via San Barnaba
Via d. Commenda
Corso di Porta Romana
Corso Porta Vignetina
Viale Filippetti
Via F. Sforza
Via Cavallotti
Via Borgogna
Corso Vitt. Emanuele II
Corso Matteotti
Via Damiano
Corso Venezia
Via Palestro
Via Senato
Via della Spiga
Via Monte Napoleone
Via Bigli
Via Manzoni
Via Fatebenefratelli
Via Brera
Via Monte di Pietà
Via Verdi
Via Mercanti
Via Pontaccio
Via Mercado
Via Dante
Via Oreficio
Via Spadari
Via Torino
Via Mazzini
Via Paola
Via Larga
Via Festa d. Perdona
Via Amedei
Corso Italia
Via S. Sofia
Viale Savoia
Viale Beatrice d'Este
Via Mercalli
Via del Fante
Viale Col di Lana
Via Stampa
Via San Vito
Via Vetere
Corso Porta Ticinese
Via Arena
Viale G. d'Annunzio
Viale Gorizia
Via Vigevano
C. Colombo
C. di Porta Genova
Via Meravigli
Via Gorani
Via Orsola
Via C. Correnti
De Amicis
Via Edmondo
Via Lanzone
Via Valeria
Via Agnese
Via G. Carducci
Foro Buonaparte
Via Gadio
Via Paleocapa
Via Boccaccio
Via Vincenzo Monti
Corso Magenta
Via Togni
Via San Vittore
Via Olivetani
Via Olona
Via Alberto
Viale Papiniano
Viale Conti Zugna
Via Solari
Via Savona
Via Tortona
Via Pagano
Via L. Mascheroni
Viale Vercellina
Via Ariosto

Ostello Pietra Rotta (HI), V. Salmoiraghi 1 (☎02 39 26 70 95). MM1: QT8; walk to the right (so the round church is across the street and to your back) for 5min., and it's on your right. Breakfast included. 3-day max. stay. Reception 7-9:30am and 3:30pm-midnight, but no morning check-in. Curfew 11:30pm. Open Jan. 13-Dec. 20. Members only; HI cards L30,000. L26,000.

Hotel San Tomaso, V. Tunisia 6, 3rd fl. (☎/fax 02 29 51 47 47; email hotelsantomaso@tin.it). MM1: Porta Venezia; take the C. Buenos Aires exit and turn left at McDonald's. The exuberant proprietor runs the hotel *come sua casa*. Clean, renovated rooms with phone and TV. English spoken. Breakfast included. Reception 24hr. Singles L60,000; doubles with shower L100,000, with bath L120,000; triples L135,000; quads L200,000.

Hotel Kennedy, V. Tunisia 6, 6th fl. (☎02 29 40 09 34), above Hotel San Tomaso. MM1: Porta Venezia. Pristine rooms. Some English spoken. Check-out 10am. Ask for keys if going out late. Reserve ahead. Singles L60-70,000; doubles L100-130,000; triples L150,000; quads L160,000.

Hotel Rallye, V. B. Marcello 59 (☎/fax 02 29 53 12 09). MM1: Lima. Take V. Vitruvio for two blocks and turn left on V. Marcello. New, simple rooms with telephone and TV. Singles L65,000; doubles L110,000; triples L120,000.

Hotel Casa Mia, V. V. Veneto 30 (☎/fax 026 57 52 49). MM1: Porta Venezia or Repubblica. More upscale. 15 rooms, all with phone, TV, hair dryer, bath, and A/C. English spoken. Great continental breakfast included. Singles L85-100,000; doubles L120-150,000; triples L170-200,000.

Camping di Monza (☎020 39 38 77 71), in the park of the Villa Reale in Monza. Take a train or bus from Stazione Centrale to Monza, then a city bus. Hot showers L500. Call ahead. Open Apr.-Sept. L8000 per person and per tent; L15,000 per caravan.

FOOD

Like its fine *couture*, Milanese cuisine is sophisticated and overpriced. Specialties include *risotto giallo* (rice with saffron), *cotoletta alla milanese* (breaded veal cutlet with lemon), and *cazzouela* (a mixture of pork and cabbage). The largest **markets** are around V. Fauché and V. Papiniano on Saturdays and Tuesdays, and along P. Mirabello on Mondays and Thursdays. The **Fiera di Sinigallia,** a 400-year-old market extravaganza, occurs on Saturdays on the banks of the Darsena, a canal in the Navigli district (V. d'Annunzio). Splurge on a local pastry at **Sant'Ambroeus,** a Milanese culinary shrine, under the arcades at C. Matteotti 7. (Open daily 8am-8pm.) Pick up groceries near C. Buenos Aires at **Supermarket Regina Giovanna,** V. Regina Giovanna 34. (☎02 45 83 90 11. Open M-F 8am-9pm, Sa 8am-8pm.)

Brek, V. Lepetit 20, near Stazione Centrale; 2nd location in P. Cavour. Elegant self-serve restaurant. Fresh ingredients cooked into tasty dishes before your eyes. *Secondi* around L7500. Open M-Sa 11:30am-3pm and 6:30-10:30pm.

Peck, V. Cantù 3, off V. Orefici, two blocks from P. del Duomo. A premier *rosticceria* that sells pizza and pastries (L7500). Foreign currencies accepted. Open Tu-F 8:45am-2:30pm and 4-7:30pm, Sa 8:30am-1pm and 3:45-7:30pm, Su 8am-1pm.

Tarantella, V. le Abruzzi 35, just north of V. Plinio. MM1: Lima. Lively, elegant sidewalk dining. Try the pasta fresca (L12,000) or the pizza (L10,000). Secondi from L125,000. Open Sept.-July M-F noon-2:30pm and 7-11:30pm, Su 7-11:30pm.

Pizzeria Premiata, V. Alzaia Naviglio Grande 2. MM2: Porto Genova. From the metro, walk on V. Vigevano, turn right on V. Corsico, and left on V. Alzaia Naviglio Grande. Popular with students. *Pizze* from L9000, *primi* around L15,000. Open daily noon-2am.

Il Fondaco dei Mori, V. Solferino 33. MM2: Moscova; walk north to P. XXV Aprile, turn right onto Porta Nuova, and take your 2nd right onto V. Solferino. No sign; ring the bell. First Middle Eastern restaurant in Italy. Vegetarian lunch menu L14,000. Delicious dinner buffet L20,000. Try the mango or guava juice, or the excellent ginger coffee. Cover L3000. Open Tu-Su 12:30-3pm and 7:30pm-midnight.

Ristorante El Recreo, V. Scarlatti 7. MM1: Lima. Walk north on C. B. Aires and turn left on V. Scarlatti; it's on the 2nd block on the left. Romantic and hip atmosphere with merengue beats in background. Simple homemade Italian cuisine. *Pizze* L7500-13,000. Open Tu-Su noon-2:30pm and 7pm-11:30pm.

Le Briciole, V. Camperio 17, one block from V. Dante. MM1: Cairoli. Young clientele. Pizza L9-16,000. Spectacular *antipasto* buffet L13-22,000. Cover L3000. Open Tu-F and Su 12:15-2:30pm and 7:15-11:30pm, Sa 7:15-11:30pm.

SIGHTS

AROUND THE DUOMO. The Gothic **duomo** is the geographical and spiritual center of Milan. More than 3400 statues, 135 spires, and 96 gargoyles grace this third-largest church in the world. *(On P. del Duomo. Open June-Sept. daily 7am-5pm; Oct.-May 9am-4pm. Free. Roof access L6000, with elevator L8-9000.)* The **Museo d'Arte Contemporanea,** in Palazzo Reale to the right of the *duomo*, holds a fine permanent collection of 20th-century Italian art and a few Picassos. *(Open Tu-Su 9:30am-5:30pm. Free.)* Follow V. Torino from P. del Duomo, take a right on V. Spadari, and turn left on V. Cantù to get to the tiny but lovely **Pinacoteca Ambrosiana,** which houses 15th- to 17th-century art, including works by Botticelli, Leonardo, Raphael, Brueghel, and Caravaggio. *(P. Pio XI 2. Open Tu-Su 10am-5:30pm. L12,000, 65+ or under 18 L6000.)* Backtrack to the P. del Duomo and head into the **Galleria Vittorio Emanuele II,** to the left as you face the *duomo*, an arcade of cafes and shops with mosaic floors and walls that is now home to commercialized industry. On the other side of the gallery is the P. della Scala, home to the **Teatro alla Scala (La Scala),** the world's premier opera house, where Maria Callas became a legend. Enter through the **Museo Teatrale alla Scala,** which includes such memorabilia as Verdi's famous top hat. *(Open daily 9am-noon and 2-5:30pm. L6000. Construction planned until 2002.)* From La Scala, V. Verdi leads to V. Brera, another charming street lined with small, brightly-colored palaces and art galleries. The 17th-century **Pinacoteca di Brera** presents perhaps Milan's most impressive collection of paintings, with works by Caravaggio, Bellini, and Raphael. *(Open Tu-Sa 9am-7pm, Su 8:30am-11pm. L8000.)* Take the MM2: Lotto, and walk on V. Fed. Caprilli for five minutes to reach **Leonardo da Vinci's Horse,** a 24-foot bronze statue built from Leonardo's sketches. *(Open daily 9:30am-6:30pm. Free.)*

AROUND CASTELLO SFORZESCO. Restored since heavy bomb damage in 1943, the enormous **Castello Sforzesco,** northeast of the *duomo*, is one of Milan's best-known monuments. It houses Michelangelo's unfinished last work, *Pietà Rondanini*, and other excellent pieces. *(MM1: Cairoli. Open Tu-Su 9:30am-5:15pm. Free.)* The **Chiesa di Santa Maria delle Grazie** contains Leonardo da Vinci's *Last Supper*. The immensely famous fresco captures the apostles' reaction to Jesus' prophecy: "One of you will betray me." *(MM1,2: Cadorna; head down V. Carducci away from Castello Sforzesco and turn right on C. Magenta. Open Tu-F 9am-9pm, Su 8:15am-6:45pm. Arrive early or late to avoid a wait.)* From the church, head down V. Togni and turn left on V. S. Vittore to explore more da Vinci genius at the **Museo Nazionale della Scienza e della Tecnica "Leonardo da Vinci,"** which houses wooden models of the master's most ingenious and visionary inventions. *(V. S. Vittore 21, off V. Carducci. MM2: San Ambrogio. Open Tu-F 9:30am-4:50pm, Sa-Su 9:30am-6:20pm. L12,000.)*

CORSO PORTA TICINESE AND THE NAVIGLI. Head southeast on V. Torino from the *duomo* and left on C. Ticinese to reach the 4th-century **Chiesa di San Lorenzo Maggiore,** the oldest church in Milan. *(C. Ticinese. MM2: Porta Genova, then tram #3 from V. Torino. Open daily 7:30am-6:45pm.)* To the right of the church lies the **Cappella di Sant'Aquilino,** which contains a 5th-century mosaic of a beardless Christ among his apostles. *(L2000, students L1000.)* Farther down C. Ticinese stands the **Chiesa di Sant'Eustorgio,** founded in the 4th century to house the bones of the Magi, and taken to Cologne in 1164. *(MM2: Porta Genova; walk down V. Vigevano and turn left on C. Ticinese. Open W-M 9:30am-noon and 3:30-6pm.)* Near the front of the church is the 12th-century neoclassical **Arco di Porta Ticinese,** which serves as the northeastern gateway to the **Navigli** district. This "Venice of Lombardy," complete with canals, footbridges, open-air markets, and cafes, once constituted part of a canal system (whose original locks were designed by Leonardo da Vinci) used to transport tons of marble for the *duomo* and to link Milan to various northern cities and lakes.

GIARDINI PUBBLICI AND ENVIRONS. From the *duomo,* follow C. Vittorio Emanuele II and then C. Venezia northeast to reach the **Giardini Pubblici** (Public Gardens). The **Galleria d'Arte Moderna,** next to the gardens in the neoclassical Villa Comunale, displays important modern Lombard art and Impressionist works. When Napoleon lived here (1805-14), Milan was capital of his Kingdom of Italy. *(V. Palestro 16. MM2: Palestro. Open Tu-Su 9am-5:45pm. Free.)* The **Museo Civico di Storia Naturale** (Civic Museum of Natural History) in the gardens holds extensive geology and paleontology collections. *(C. Venezia 55. Open M-F 9am-6pm, Sa-Su 9:30am-6:30pm. Free.)*

ENTERTAINMENT AND NIGHTLIFE

While seats at the famed **La Scala** (☎ 02 72 00 37 44) are expensive, gallery seats may cost as little as L20,000, and 200 standing-room tickets (L10,000) go on sale 45 minutes before the show. (Opera season is Dec.-June; fewer shows July-Sept. Box office open daily noon-6pm.) If you've come to Milan to (window) **shop,** the city's most elegant boutiques are between the *duomo* and P. Babila, especially on **V. Monte Napoleone** and off P. S. Babila at V. della Spiga.

The nocturnal scene varies with the hour and the locale. A safe, chic, and very touristed district lies by **V. Brera,** northwest of the *duomo* and east of MM1: Cairoli, where you'll find art galleries, small clubs, restaurants, and an upscale thirtysomething crowd. Younger Milanese migrate to the areas around **C. Porta Ticinese** and **P. Vetra** (near Chiesa S. Lorenzo) to sip beer at one of the many *birrerie* (pubs). The highest concentration of bars and youth can be found in the wee hours of the morning in the **Navigli district.** (MM2: Porta Genova; then walk along V. Vigevano until it ends and veer right onto V. Naviglio Pavese.) Check any paper on Wednesday or Thursday for info on club and weekend events.

Scimmie, V. Sforza 49. A legendary, energetic bar. Different theme every night and frequent concerts; fusion, jazz, soul, and reggae dominate. Open daily 8pm-1:30am.

Bar Magenta, V. Carducci 13. A well-crafted Guinness bar with a crowd that often spills onto the sidewalk. Open Tu-Su 9am-3 or 5am.

Le Trottoir, at the intersection of T. Tivoli and C. Garibaldi. Take MM2: Lanza. A lively atmosphere with a different live band every night. Open daily 7pm-2:30am.

Artdeco, V. Lombro 7. MM1: Porta Venezia, then walk up C. Buenos Aires three blocks, turn right on V. Melzi, and walk three blocks on the left. Trendiest bar in Milan with 250 different colors of light. Dance after midnight. Open daily 7am-2am.

Lollapaloosa, C. Como 15. A wild crowd will have you dancing on the tables in no time. Cover (L15,000) includes a drink. Open Su-Th 7pm-2am, F-Sa 7pm-5:30am.

Grand Café Fashion, C. Porta Ticinese, on the corner of V. Vetere. A bar/restaurant/dance club with a stunningly beautiful crowd and velour leopard print couches. Open daily noon-3pm, 8pm-3:30am.

Old Fashion, on V. Camoens in Parco Sempione. Walk from P. Cadorna on the right in Via Paleocapa, which turns into V. E. Alemagna; the club is in the Palazzo dell'Arte. Music and fun for everyone; good DJs always bring a crowd. L25,000 cover includes one drink. Open F-Sa 11pm-4am.

Le Lephante, V. Melzi 22. MM2: Porta Venezia, then walk up C. B. Aires three blocks and take V. Melzi on the right. A mixed gay/straight crowd. Open Tu-Su 6:30pm-2am.

ITALY

EXCURSIONS FROM MILAN

BERGAMO. Bergamo's medieval palaces, fabulous art museum, and 12th-century basilica are only a one-hour train ride from Milan (p. 621).

LAKE COUNTRY. The magnificence of Lakes Como, Maggiore, and Garda lingers one hour from Milan by train (p. 613).

MANTUA (MANTOVA)

Mantua owes its literary fame to its most famous son, the poet Virgil. But the driving force that built the city's *centro storico* was not the punning wordsmith but the Gonzaga family. After ascending to power in 1328, the family revamped Mantua's small-town image by importing well-known artists and cultivating local talent. The cobblestone **Piazza Sordello** marks the center of a vast complex built by the Gonzaga family. Lined with grand *palazzi* and graceful churches, Mantua also provides easy passage to the surrounding lakes. During its lifetime, the huge **Palazzo Ducale,** which towers over the *piazza*, absorbed the Gothic Magna Domus *(duomo)* and **Palazzo del Capitano.** Inside, check out frescoes, tapestries, and gardens. Outside, signs point to the formidable **Castello di San Giorgio** (1390-1406), once a fortress before being absorbed by the *palazzo*, of which it is now a wing. (*Palazzo* open Tu-Su 8:45am-6:30pm. L12,000.) At the south end of the city, down V. P. Amedeo through P. Veneto and down Largo Parri, the opulent **Palazzo del Te,** built by Giulio Romano in 1534 as a suburban retreat for Francesco II Gonzaga, is widely considered the finest example of the Mannerist style, which strayed from classical ideals of harmonious design. (Open M 1-6pm, Tu-Su 9am-6pm. L12,000, students and children ages 12-18 L8000.) Opposite **Piazza delle Erbe,** just south of P. Sordello, is Alberti's **Chiesa di Sant'Andrea,** Mantua's most important Renaissance creation. (*Piazza* open 10am-12:30pm and 2:30-6:30pm; *chiesa* open daily 8am-noon and 3-6:30pm. Both free.) Walk from P. delle Erbe to P. Broletto and take V. Accademia until the end to reach the **Teatro Scientifico (Bibiena),** an acoustically marvelous theater straight out of a fairy tale.

Trains (☎03 76 32 16 47) go from P. Don Leoni to Verona (40min., every hr., L4100) and Milan (2hr., 9 per day, L16,000). From the station, head left on V. Solferino, through P. S. Francesco d'Assisi to V. Fratelli Bandiera, and right on V. Verdi to find the **tourist office,** P. Mantegna 6, next to **Chiesa di Sant'Andrea.** (☎03 76 36 32 53; fax 03 76 36 32 92. Open M-Sa 8:30am-12:30pm and 3-6pm.) **Hotel ABC,** P. Don Leoni 25, is opposite the station. (☎03 76 32 33 47; fax 03 76 32 23 29. Breakfast included. Singles from L50,000; doubles L90,000; triples L140,000.) **Antica Osteria ai Ranari,** V. Trieste 11, down V. Pomponazzo near Porta Catena, offers regional dishes. (*Primi* L8-10,000, *secondi* L10-15,000. Cover L2000. Closed for 3 weeks in late July and early Aug. Open Tu-Su noon-2:30pm and 7-11pm.) **Postal code:** 46100.

BERGAMO

A medieval city glistens from the hills over Bergamo, complete with palaces, churches, and a huge stone fortification. **Via Pignolo,** in the *città bassa* (lower city), winds past a succession of handsome 16th- to 18th-century palaces. Turning left onto V. S. Tomaso and then right to visit the astounding **Galleria dell'Accademia Carrara,** one of Italy's most important galleries, with works by Titian, Rubens, Breughel, and van Dyck. (Open W-M 9:30am-12:30pm and 2:30-5:30pm. L5000; Su free.) From there, the terraced **Via Noca** ascends to the *città alta* (upper city) through Porta Sant'Agostino. The 12th-century **Basilica di Santa Maria Maggiore** has an ornate Baroque interior and tapestries depicting biblical scenes. (Open May-Sept. M-F 9am-noon and 3-6pm, Sa-Su 8-10:30am and 3-6pm; Oct.-Apr. M-F 9am-noon and 3-4:30pm, Sa-Su 8-10:30am and 3-6pm. Free.) Head through the archway flanking P. Vecchia to P. del Duomo to reach the chapel **Cappella Colleoni.** (Open Tu-Su Mar.-Oct. 9am-12:30pm and 2-6:30pm; Nov.-Feb. 9am-12:30pm and 2:30-4:30pm. Free.) Stroll down V. Porta Dipinta to V. Gambito, which ends in **Piazza Vecchia,** a majestic ensemble of medieval and Renaissance buildings flanked by restaurants and cafes at the heart of the *città alta*. Climb the **Torre Civica** (L2000) for a marvelous view of Bergamo and the hills.

The train and bus stations and budget hotels are in the *città bassa*. **Trains** (1hr., L7200) and **buses** (L7500) pull into P. Marconi from Milan. To get to the **tourist office,** Vicolo Aquila Nera 2, in the *città alta*, take bus #1 or 1a to the funicular, then follow V. Gambito to P. Vecchia and turn right. (☎035 23 27 30; fax 035 24 29 94. Open daily 9am-12:30pm and 2-5:30pm.) Take bus #14 from Porto Nuova to "Leonardo da

Vinci" and walk uphill to reach the **Ostello della Gioventù di Bergamo (HI),** V. G. Ferraris 1. (☎035 34 30 38; fax 035 36 17 24. Breakfast included. Internet. Members only. Dorms L25,000; singles L35,000; doubles L60,000.) Take bus #5 or 7 from V. Angelo Maj, or walk for 20 minutes, to reach **Locanda Caironi,** V. Torretta 6B, off V. Gorgo Palazzo. (☎035 24 30 83. Singles L30,000; doubles L55,000.) In the *città bassa*, **Capolinea,** V. Giacomo Quarenghi 29, right off V. Zambonate, offers full meals from L15,000. (Open Tu-Sa 6:30pm-3am, Su 7pm-3am. Kitchen closes at midnight.) In the *città alta*, the prison-turned-communist-cafe **Circolino Cooperativa Città Alta,** V. S. Agata 19, features *bocce*, a view, and sandwiches, pizza, and salads for under L8000. (Open Th-Tu 8:30am-3am.) **Postal code:** 24122.

ITALIAN RIVIERA (LIGURIA)

The sun blazes down upon Liguria, the 350km stretch of Italian Riviera that graces the Mediterranean between France and Tuscany, forming the most famous and touristed area of the Italian coastline. Genoa divides the strip into the Riviera di Levante ("rising sun") to the east and the Riviera di Ponente ("setting sun") to the west. The **Cinque Terre** area, just to the west of La Spezia, is especially enchanting.

GETTING THERE AND GETTING AROUND

All the coastal towns are linked by the main **rail** line, which runs west from Genoa to Ventimiglia (near the French border) and east to La Spezia (near Tuscany), but slow local trains take hours to travel short distances. Frequent intercity **buses** pass through all major towns, and local buses run to inland hill-towns. **Boats** connect most resort towns. **Ferries** go from Genoa to Olbia, Sardinia, and Palermo, Sicily.

GENOA (GENOVA)

Urban, gritty Genoa has little in common with its picture-perfect resort neighbors. But flourishing trade in this port town in the 13th century allowed for the construction of parks and lavish palaces, and its financial glory was soon matched by the repute of its citizens, including Chistopher Columbus and Giuseppe Mazzini. Since falling into decline in the 18th century, modern Genoa has turned its attention from industry to the restoration of its bygone grandeur.

PRACTICAL INFO, ACCOMMODATIONS, AND FOOD. Trains go to Turin (2hr., 19 per day, L14,500-23,200) and Rome (5hr., 14 per day, L43,300-62,000). Most international trains arrive at **Stazione Principe,** on V. Acquaverde, northwest of the city center; take bus #19, 20, 30, 32, 35, or 41 to reach the central P. Ferrari, or take V. Balbi to V. Cairoli, and turn right on V. XXV Aprile at P. delle Fontane Marose. From **Stazione Brignole,** take bus #19 or 40; or, turn right to V. Fiume, and right onto V. XX Settembre. **Ferries** (see above) depart from the Ponte Assereto arm of the port; buy tickets at the **Stazione Marittima.** The APT **tourist office** is at Porto Antico, in P. Santa Maria. From the aquarium, walk toward the complex of buildings to the left. (☎01 02 48 71. Open daily 9am-6:30pm.) Log on at **Internet Village,** at V. Brigata Bisagno and C. Buenos Aires, across from P. Vittoria. (L15,000 per hr. Open 9am-1pm and 3-7pm.)

Ostello per la Gioventù (HI), V. Costanzi 120, has a cafeteria, TV, and a view of the city far below. From Stazione Principe, walk down V. Balbi to P. Delba Nunziata and catch bus #40 (every 15min.); tell the driver your destination. (☎/fax 01 02 42 24 57. Members only; HI card available. Breakfast included. Laundry L12,000 for 5kg. Reception 7-9am and 3:30pm-12:30am. Curfew midnight. L23,000.) **Albergo Carola,** V. Gropallo 4/12, has elegant rooms overlooking a garden. From Stazione Brignole, turn right on V. de Amicis, turn right when facing Albergo Astoria, and walk 20m. (☎01 08 39 13 40. Singles L45,000; doubles L65,000, with shower L75,000.) **Albergo Balbi,** V. Balbi 21/3, offers large, ornate rooms. (Breakfast L7000. Singles L35,0000, with bath L45,000; doubles L75,000,

L90,000; triples and quads add 30% per person. Student discount with ID.) **Camping** is popular; turn to the tourist office for info, as many campgrounds are booked solid. To reach **Villa Doria,** V. al Campeggio Villa Doria 15, take the train or bus #1-3 from P. Caricamento to Pegli, then walk or transfer to bus #93 up V. Vespucci. (☎01 06 96 96 00. L9000 per person; L10-13,000 per tent.) Genoa is famous for its *pesto* and *focaccia;* try **Trattoria da Maria,** V. Testa d'Oro 14r, off V. XXV Aprile, which has a new menu every day with dishes for L13,000. (Open Su-F noon-2:30pm and 7-9:30pm.) **Postal code:** 16100.

SIGHTS. Genoa's palaces are its most impressive aspect, along with its fine 16th- and 17th-century Flemish and Italian art acquired in its days of commercial power. **V. Balbi,** in the heart of the university quarter, contains some of the most lavish *palazzi* in Genoa. The 18th-century **Palazzo Reale,** V. Balbi 10, near Stazione Principe, is filled with rococo rooms bathed in gold and upholstered in red velvet. (Open M-Th 9:15am-1:45pm, F-Su 8:15am-7:15pm. L8000, under 18 and 60+ free.) Follow V. Balbi through P. della Nunziata and continue to L. Zecca, where V. Cairoli leads to **V. Garibaldi,** the most impressive street in Genoa, bedecked with elegant *palazzi* that once earned it the names "Golden Street" and "Street of Kings." The **Galleria di Palazzo Bianco,** V. Garibaldi 11, exhibits Ligurian, Dutch, and Flemish paintings. Across the street, the 17th-century **Galleria Palazzo Rosso,** V. Garibaldi 18, has magnificent furnishings in a lavishly frescoed interior. (Both open Tu and Th-F 9am-1pm, W and Sa 9am-7pm, Su 10am-6pm. L6000 each, L10,000 combined; Su free.) The **Villetta Di Negro,** on the hill farther down V. Garibaldi, features waterfalls, grottoes, and terraced gardens. Take V. M. Plaggio to P. Corvetto, then V. Roma to P. Ferrari, where V. Boetto leads to P. Matteotti and the **Palazzo Ducale,** the former home of the city's rulers. On the opposite corner stands the ornate **Chiesa del Gesù.** (Open daily 7:30am-noon and 4-6:30pm. Free.) Head past the *chiesa* down V. di Porta Soprana to V. Ravecca to reach the medieval twin-towered **Porta Soprana,** the supposed boyhood home of Christopher Columbus. Continue down V. Ravecca to reach the **Museo dell'Architettura e Scultura Ligure,** which features surviving art pieces from Genoa's history. (Open Tu-Sa 9am-7pm, Su 9am-12:30pm. L6000.) Off V. San Lorenzo, which emerges from O. Matteotti, the **Duomo (San Lorenzo)** has been around since the 9th century. (Open M-Sa 8am-7pm, Su 7am-7pm. Free.) The *duomo* lies on the southern edge of the **centro storico** (the historical center of town), a tangled web of alleys bordered by the port to the east, V. Garibaldi to the north, and P. Ferrari to the southeast. The neighborhood is home to some of Genoa's most notable monuments. Back on P. Matteotti, go down V. San Lorenzo toward the water, turn left on V. Chiabrera, and left on V. Di Mascherona to reach the **Chiesa Santa Maria di Castello,** a labyrinth of chapels, courtyards, cloisters, and crucifixes. (Open daily 9am-noon and 3:30-6:30pm.)

EXCURSION FROM GENOA: THE RIVIERA. Several idyllic Riviera towns (see below) are accessible from Genoa by train, including **Finale Ligure** (1hr.), **Santa Margherita Ligure** (40min.), and **Cinque Terre** (1½hr.).

RIVIERA DI PONENTE AND RIVIERA DI LEVANTE

FINALE LIGURE. A statue along the beachfront promenade holds a plaque that calls Finale the place for *Il riposo del popolo* (the people's rest). A prime spot to vacation from your vacation, Finale Ligure welcomes weary backpackers with soft sands, turquoise sea, and plenty of *gelato.* The city is divided into three sections: **Finalpia** to the east, **Finalmarina** in the center, and **Finalborgo** (the old city) inland to the northwest. Up a tough but fulfilling trail lies the ruined 13th-century **Castel Govone,** which offers a spectacular view of Finale. Skip the narrow strip of beach across from Hotel Boncardo, where you'll feel like a squished sardine; instead, walk east along V. Aurelia through the first tunnel and hang a quick right to a less populated **free beach.** SAR **buses** run from the train station to tiny and refreshingly tourist-free **Borgo Verezzi** (L1800), which delights with cool, peaceful streets and caves, as well as other nearby beachside towns.

Trains head to Genoa from P. Vittorio Veneto (1 hr., every hr., L6900). The IAT **tourist office** is at V.S. Pietro 14. (☎019 68 10 19; fax 019 68 18 04. Open M-Sa 9am-12:30pm and 3:30-7pm, Su 9am-noon.) **Castello Wuillerman (HI),** on V. Generale Caviglia, is well worth the tough hike. From the station, take a left onto V. Mazzini (which becomes V. Torino), turn left on V. degli Ulivi, and trudge up the daunting steps. (☎019 69 05 15. Breakfast and sheets included. Reception 7-10am and 5-10pm. Curfew 11:30pm. No phone reservations. Open Mar.15-Oct.15. L20,000.) For the convenient **Albergo Oasi,** V. San Cagna 25, veer left on V. Brunenghi from the station, walk through the underpass on your right to V. Silla, walk up the hill, and turn left at the intersection. (☎019 69 17 17. Open Easter-late Sept. No credit cards. Singles L45,000; doubles L90,000; extra beds L45,000.) To reach **Albergo San Marco,** V. della Concezione 22, walk straight down V. Saccone from the station and turn left on V. della Concezione. (☎019 69 25 33. Breakfast included. Open Easter-Sept. Singles L60,000; doubles L80,000.) To access **Camping Tahiti,** on V. Varese, take the bus from P. Vittorio Veneto (dir. Calvisio) to Bar Paradiso, cross the small bridge at Via Rossini, turn left, and walk along the river to V. Vanese. (☎019 60 06 00. Reception Easter-Oct.15 8am-8pm. L11,000 per person, L10,000 per tent; off season reduced.) Cheap restaurants lie inland along **V. Rossi** and **V. Roma. Simpatia Crai supermarket** is at V. Bruneghi 2a. (Open M-Sa 8am-12:30pm and 4-6:30pm.)

CAMOGLI. Postcard-perfect Camogli cascades with color. Sun-faded peach houses crowd the hilltop, red-and-turquoise boats bob in the water, piles of fishing nets cover the docks, and bright umbrellas dot the dark stone beaches. To reach the **beach,** turn left down the steep stairs 100m from the station (where a large blue sign points to Albergo La Camogliese). The stairs lead to V. Garibaldi; turn right off V. Garibaldi into the alley. **Trains** run on the Genoa-La Spezia line to: Santa Margherita (10min., 24 per day, L1900); Genoa (20min., 32 per day, L2700); and La Spezia (1½hr., 21per day, L6400). Golfo Paradiso **ferries,** V. Scalo 3 (☎01 85 77 20 91), near P. Colombo, go to Portofino (Sa-Su only; L14,000, round-trip L20,000) and Cinque Terre (L20,000); buy tickets on the dock. Head right from the station to find the **tourist office,** V. XX Settembre 33, which can help find rooms. (☎01 85 77 10 66. Open daily June-Sept. 8:30am-12:30pm and 3-7pm; Oct.-May M-Sa 9am-noon and 3:30-6:30pm, Su 9am-1pm.) Exit the station, walk down the long stairway to the right, and look for the sign to reach the joyful **Albergo La Camogliese,** V. Garibaldi 55. (☎01 85 77 14 02; fax 77 40 24. Breakfast L10,000. Reserve ahead. Singles L70-90,000; doubles L90-110,000.)

SANTA MARGHERITA LIGURE. Santa Margherita Ligure led a calm existence as a fishing village until the mid-20th century, when it fell into favor with Hollywood stars. Today, grace and glitz paint the shore, Art Deco lighting softens the pastel walls, and palm trees line the harbor. But the serenity of the town's early days still lingers; Santa Margherita Ligure's only attractions are leisure time and tranquility. If lapping waves don't invigorate your spirit, try the holy water in seashell basins at the **Basilica di Santa Margherita,** at P. Caprera. **Trains** along the Pisa-Genoa line go from P. Federico Raoul Nobili, at the top of V. Roma, to Genoa (40min., 2-3 per hr., L3600) and La Spezia (2 per hr., L6900) via Cinque Terre (1½hr., L5300). Tigullio **buses** (☎01 85 28 88 34) go from P. Vittorio Veneto to Portofino (20min., 3 per hr., L1600) and Camogli (30min., every hr., L2000). Tigullio **ferries,** V. Palestro 8/1b (☎01 85 28 15 98), have tours to Portofino (every hr.; L6000, round-trip L10,000) and Cinque Terre (July-Sept. daily; L25-30,000, round-trip L35-40,000). Turn right from the train station on V. Roma, left on C. Rainusso, and take a hard right onto V. XXV Aprile from Largo Giusti to find the **tourist office,** V. XXV Aprile 2b, which arranges lodging. (☎01 85 28 74 85. Open M-Sa 9am-12:30pm and 3-6pm, Su 9:30am-12:30pm.) **Hotel Riviera,** V. Belvedere 10, has spacious rooms. (☎/fax 01 85 28 74 03. Breakfast included. Singles L85-105,000; doubles L120-160,000; triples L165-210,000. V, MC; 10% discount with cash.) **Pensione Azalea,** V. Roma 60/V. Gramsci 89, is to the right of the train station. (☎01 85 28 61 60. Breakfast included. Doubles with bathroom L95,000.) **La Piadineria and Creperia,** V. Giuncheto 5, off P. Martiri della Libertà, serves huge sandwiches (L7-10,000) and more. (Open Easter-Oct. Tu-Sa 5:30pm-3am; July-Sept. M-Sa 5:30pm-3am and Su 12:30pm-3am.)

PORTOFINO. Secluded and exclusive, tiny Portofino—a great daytrip from Santa Margherita—has long been a playground for the financially advantaged. Yachts fill the harbor and chic boutiques line the streets, but both princes and paupers can enjoy the curvy shores and tiny bay. A one-hour walk along the ocean road offers the chance to scout out small rocky **beaches;** the beach at **Paraggi** (where the bus stops) is the area's only sandy beach. In town, follow the signs uphill from the bay to escape to the cool interior of the **Chiesa di San Giorgio.** A few minutes up the road toward the **castle** is a serene garden with sea views. (Open daily in summer 10am-6pm; off season 10am-5pm. L3000.) To get to town, take the bus to Portofino Mare (*not* Portofino Vetta). From P. Martiri della Libertà, Tigullio **buses** go to Santa Margherita (3 per hr., L1600); buy tickets at the green kiosk in P. Martiri della Libertà. **Ferries** also go to Santa Margherita (every hr. 9am-7pm, L6000) and Camogli (2 per day, L13,000). The **tourist office,** V. Roma 35, is on the way to the waterfront from the bus stop. (☎01 85 26 90 24. Open daily in summer 9:30am-1:30pm and 2-7pm; off season 9:30am-12:30pm and 2:30-5:30pm.)

CINQUE TERRE. The five bright fishing villages of Cinque Terre cling to a stretch of terraced hillsides and steep crumbling cliffs, a dazzling turquoise sea lapping against their shores. Savage cliffs and lush tropical vegetation surround the stone villages. You can hike through all five—Monterosso, Vernazza, Corniglia, Manarola, and Riomaggiore—in a few hours. **Monterosso** is the most developed, with sandy beaches and exciting nightlife; **Vernazza** is graced by a seaside piazza with colorful buildings and a busy harbor; **Corniglia** hovers high above the sea in peaceful solitude; **Manarola** has quiet streets and a spectacular swimming cove; and **Riomaggiore** has a tiny harbor and lots of rooms for rent. The best views are from the narrow goat paths that link the towns, winding through vineyards, streams, and dense foliage dotted with cacti and lemon trees. The best hike lies between Monterosso and Vernazza (1½hr.); the trail between Vernazza and Corniglia (2hr.) also leads through spectacular scenery. The area has two **public beaches**—one on the south side of Monterosso (to the left through the tunnel as you face the harbor) and the other between Corniglia and Manarola. **Guvano Beach,** a pebbly strip frequented by nudists, is through the tunnel at the base of the steps leading up to Corniglia (L5000). Tiny trails off the road to Vernazza lead to popular hidden coves.

The Genoa-La Spezia rail line connects the five towns; Monterosso is the most accessible. From the station on V. Fegina, at the north end of town, **trains** run to: La Spezia (20min., every 30min., L2300); Genoa (1½hr., every hr., L7000); Pisa (2½hr., every hr., L8500); Florence via Pisa (3½hr., every hr., L14,500); and Rome (7hr., every 2hr., L51,500). Trains also connect the five towns (5-20min., every 50min., L1700-2300). Reserve rooms several weeks in advance. **Private rooms** *(affittacamere)* are the cheapest, most plentiful options. To find Manarola's hostel, the **Albergo Della Gioventù-Ostello "Cinque Terre,"** V. B. Riccobaldi 21, turn right from the train station and go uphill (300m) to discover more fabulous amenities than can be believed. (☎01 87 92 02 15; fax 92 02 18; email ostello@cdh.it. Breakfast L5000. Laundry. Internet. Reception mid-Sept. to May 7-10am and 4pm-midnight; June to mid-Sept. 7-10am and 5pm-1am. Reserve 2 weeks ahead. Sept. 16-June 14 L25,000; June 15-Sept. 15 L30,000.) In Vernazza, ask in Trattoria Capitano about **Albergo Barbara,** P. Marconi 30, top floor, at the port. (☎01 87 81 23 98. Singles L70-80,000; doubles L80-100,000; triples L120,000; quads L140,000.) In Monterosso, try the **tourist office** (☎01 87 81 75 06)

LINGUINE LINGO For Italians, the desecration of pasta is a mortal sin. Pasta must be chosen correctly and cooked *al dente* (firm, literally "to the tooth"). The *spaghetti* family includes all variations that require twirling, from hollow cousins *bucatini* and *maccheroni* to the more delicate *capellini.* Flat *spaghetti* include *fettuccini, taglierini,* and *tagliatelle*. Short pasta tubes can be *penne,* cut diagonally and occasionally *rigate,* or (ribbed, *sedani* (curved), *rigatoni* (wider), or *cannelloni* (usually stuffed). *Fusilli* (corkscrews), *farfalle* (butterflies or bow-ties), and *ruote* (wheels) are fun and functional. Don't be alarmed if you see pastry displays labeled "pasta"; the Italian word refers to anything made of dough.

or **Hotel Souvenir,** V. Gioberti 24, the best deal in town. (☎01 87 81 75 95. Breakfast L10,000. L45,000.) To arrange private rooms in Riomaggiore, call **Robert Fazioli,** V. Colombo 94. (☎01 87 92 09 04. Doubles with bath L80,000.)

LA SPEZIA. A departure point for Corsica and an unavoidable transport hub for Cinque Terre, La Spezia is probably Italy's most beautiful port, with regal palms lining the promenade and citrus trees growing throught the parks. La Spezia lies on the Genoa-Pisa **train** line. **Happy Lines,** with a ticket kiosk on V. Italia, sends **ferries** to Corsica (round-trip L124,000, off season L84,000). **Navigazione Golfo dei Poeti,** V. Mazzini 21, run ferries to each village in Cinque Terre and Portovenereo (Easter-Nov. 4 per day; L20,000, round-trip L33,000); Capraia (5hr., July-Aug. round-trip L80,000); and Elba (3½hr., July-Aug. round-trip L80,000.) The **tourist office** (☎01 87 77 09 00), V. Mazzini 45, is at the port. To reach **Albergo Terminus,** V. Paleocapa 21, turn left out of the train station. (☎01 87 70 34 36; fax 01 87 70 00 79. Singles L40,000, with bath L55,000; doubles L65,000, L90,000; triples L70,000.)

EMILIA-ROMAGNA

Go to Florence, Venice, and Rome to sightsee, but come to Emilia-Romagna to eat. Italy's wealthiest wheat- and dairy-producing region covers the fertile plains of the Po River Valley, fostering the finest culinary traditions on the Italian Peninsula. Gorge yourself on Parmesan cheese and *prosciutto*, Bolognese fresh pasta and *mortadella*, and Ferrarese *salama* and *grana* cheese. Complement these dishes with regional wines like Parma's sparkling red *lambrusco*.

BOLOGNA

With just one forkful of Bologna's tortellini, it becomes clear that the city appreciates the better things in life. Bright facades lean on 700-year-old porticoes and cobblestone roads twist by churches, but the city's appeal extends far beyond aesthetics. Blessed with prosperity and Europe's oldest university, Bologna has developed an open-minded character; minority and gay political activism is strong. Apart from a formidable list of its university's graduates—including Dante, Petrarch, and Copernicus—the city prides itself on its great culinary heritage.

PRACTICAL INFO, ACCOMMODATIONS, AND FOOD. At the heart of northern Italy, Bologna is a rail hub for all major Italian cities and the Adriatic coast. **Trains** go to: Florence (1½hr., every 2hr., L8200-13,500); Venice (2hr., every hr., L14,000); Milan (3hr., 2-3 per hr., L18,000); and Rome (4hr., 1-2 per hr., L35,000). Arrive during the day, as the area near the station is not the safest. Buses #25 and 30 run between the station and the historic center at **P. Maggiore** (L1800). The **tourist office,** P. Maggiore 6, is next to the Palazzo Comunale. (☎051 23 96 60; fax 051 23 14 54; www.comune.bologna.it. Open M-Sa 9am-1pm and 2:30-7pm.) Check **email** at **Crazy Bull Café,** V. Montegrappa 11/e, off V. dell'Indipendenza near P. Maggiore. (L9000 per hr. Open Tu-Sa 10am-2am, Su 7:30pm-2am. Closed Aug.) Take V. Ugo Bassi from P. Maggiore and take the 3rd left to find the sparkling **Albergo Panorama,** V. Livraghi 1, 4th fl. (☎051 22 18 02; fax 051 26 63 60. Singles L75,000; doubles

L100,000; triples L125-145,000; quads L160,000.) Follow V. Rizzoli past the towers to V. S. Vitale to reach **Hotel San Vitale,** V. S. Vitale 94. (☎ 051 22 59 66; fax 051 23 93 96. Singles L90,000; doubles L110,000; triples L165,000.) To get to **Ostello due Torre San Sisto (HI),** V. Viadagola 5, off V. San Donato in the Località di San Sisto (6km from the city center), walk down V. dell'Indipendenza from the station, turn right on V. della Mille, catch bus #93 (every 30min.) on the left side of the road, ask the driver for "San Sisto," cross the street, and it's on the right. On Sunday, take bus #301 from the station. (☎/fax 051 50 18 10. Breakfast included. Reception 7am-midnight. Lockout 10am-3:30pm. Curfew midnight. L21,000; nonmembers L26,000.)

Bologna's namesake dish, *spaghetti alla bolognese*, has a hefty meat and tomato sauce. Scout **V. Augusto Righi, V. Piella,** and **V. Saragozza** for traditional *trattorie.* Locals chat over regional dishes like *tagliatelle* at **Trattoria Da Maro,** V. Broccaindosso 71d, off Strada Maggiore. (Cover L3000. Lunch L8-9000; dinner L10-12,000. Open M 8-10:15pm, Tu-Sa noon-2:30pm and 8-10:15pm.) **Nuova Pizzeria Gianna,** V.S. Stefano 76/a, serves pizza from L5000. (Open M-Sa for lunch and dinner.) **Il Gelatauro,** V. S. Vitale 82/b, dishes out cones from L3000. (Open June-Aug. Tu-Sa 11am-11pm.) A **supermarket PAM,** V. Marconi 26, is near V. Riva di Reno. (Open M-W and F-Sa 7:45am-7:45pm, Th 7:45am-1pm.)

SIGHTS AND ENTERTAINMENT. Twenty-five miles of porticoed buildings line the streets of Bologna. Tranquil **Piazza Maggiore** flaunts both Bologna's historical and modern-day wealth. **Basilica di San Petronio,** the city's *duomo*, was built to impress, but its pomp and pageantry allegedly drove a disgusted Martin Luther to reform religion in Germany. (Open M-Sa 7:15am-1pm and 2-6pm, Su 7:30am-1pm and 2-6:30pm.) **Palazzo Archiginnasio,** behind the church, was once a university building; the upstairs theater was built in 1637 to teach anatomy to local students. (Palazzo open M-F 9am-7pm, Sa 9am-2pm. Theater open M-Sa 9am-1pm. Both closed 2 weeks in Aug. Free.) The **Pinacoteca Nazionale,** V. delle Belle Arti 56, off V. Zamboni, traces the progress of Bolognese artists. (Open Tu-Sa 9am-1:50pm, Su 9am-12:50pm. L8000.) On the northern side of P. Maggiore is **Palazzo de Podestà,** remodeled by Fioravanti's son Aristotle, who later designed Moscow's Kremlin. Next to P. Maggiore, **Piazza del Nettuno** contains Giambologna's famous 16th-century fountain *Neptune and Attendants.* From P. Nettuno, go down V. Rizzoli to **Piazza Porta Ravegana,** where streets converge to form the medieval quarter. Two towers that constitute the city's emblem rise from the piazza; you can climb the **Torre degli Asinelli.** (Open daily in summer 9am-6pm; off season 9am-5pm. L5000.) Follow V. S. Stefano from V. Rizzoli to P. Santo Stefano, where four of the original seven churches of the Romanesque **Piazza Santo Stefano Church Complex** remain.

PARMA

Parma's loyalties lie with its excellent food: silky-smooth *prosciutto crudo*, sharp *parmigiano* cheese, and sweet, sparkling white Malvasia wine. Parma's artistic excellence goes beyond the kitchen, too: Giuseppe Verdi composed some of his greatest works here. From P. Garibaldi, follow Strada Cavour toward the train station and take the 3rd right on Strada al Duomo to reach the 11th-century Romanesque **duomo,** in P. del Duomo, one of the country's most vibrant cathedrals. Most spectacular is the **dome,** where Correggio's *Virgin* ascends to a golden heaven in a spiral of white robes, pink *putti*, and blue sky. The pink-and-white marble **baptistery** was built between the Romanesque and Gothic periods. (*Duomo* open daily 9am-noon and 3-7pm. Baptistery open daily 9am-12:30pm and 3-7pm. L5000, students L3000.) Behind the *duomo* is the frescoed dome of the **Chiesa di San Giovanni Evangelista,** designed by Correggio. (Open daily 9am-noon and 3-7pm.) From P. del Duomo, follow Strada al Duomo across Strada Cavour, continue one block down Strada Piscane, and cross P. della Pace to reach the monolithic **Palazzo della Pilotta,** Parma's artistic treasure chest, built in 1602, which today houses the excellent **Galleria Nazionale.** (Open daily 9am-2pm. L8000.)

Parma is on the Bologna-Milan rail line; **trains** go from P. Carlo Alberto della Chiesa to: Milan (1½hr., every hr., L11,600); Bologna (1hr., 2 per hr., L7700); and Florence (3hr., 7 per day, L26,300). Walk left from the station, right on V. Garibaldi, and left on V. Melloni to reach the **tourist office,** V. Melloni 1b. (☎/fax 05 21 23 47 35. Open M-W and F 9am-1pm and 3-7pm, Th 9am-7pm.) From the station, take bus #9 (L1300) and get off when the bus turns left on V. Martiri della Libertà (10min.) to get to the modern **Ostello Cittadella (HI),** on V. Passo Buole, in a corner of a 15th-century fortress. (☎05 21 96 14 34. 3-night max. stay. Lockout 9:30am-5pm. Curfew 11pm. Members only. Dorms L16,000.) **Camping** open Apr.-Oct. L11,150 per person; L21,000 per site.) **Locanda Lazzaro,** Borgo XX Marzo 14, is off V. della Repubblica, upstairs from the restaurant of the same name. (☎05 21 20 89 44. Reserve ahead. Singles L58-70,000; doubles L95,000.) **Supermarket 2B** is at V. XXII Luglio 27c. (Open M-W and F-Sa 8:30am-1pm and 4:30-8pm, Th 8:30am-1pm.) **Postal code:** 43100.

RAVENNA

Tired of fresco cycles? Enter a world of golden mosaics in Ravenna. Take V. Argentario from V. Cavour to reach the 6th-century **Basilica di San Vitale,** V. S. Vitale 17. An open courtyard leads to the glowing mosaics inside; those of the Emperor and Empress adorn the lower left and right panels of the apse, respectively. Behind San Vitale, the city's oldest and most interesting mosaics cover the glittering interior of the **Mausoleo di Galla Placidia.** (Both open daily Apr.-Sept. 9am-7pm; Oct.-Mar. 9:30am-4:30pm. Joint ticket L6000.) Take bus #4 or 44 from opposite the train station (L1300) to **Classe,** south of the city, to see the astounding mosaics at the **Chiesa di Sant'Apollinare in Classe.** (Open M-Sa 8:30am-7:30pm, Su 9am-1pm. L4000, Su free.) Much to Florence's dismay, Ravenna is also home to the **Tomb of Dante Alighieri,** its most popular sight. In the adjoining **Dante Museum,** his heaven and hell come alive in etchings, paintings, and sculptures. From P. del Popolo, cut through P. Garibaldi to V. Alighieri. (Tomb open daily 9am-7pm; free. Museum open Apr.-Sept. Tu-Su 9am-noon and 3:30-6pm; Oct.-Mar. Tu-Su 9am-noon. L3000.) A **comprehensive ticket** (L9000, students L7000; buy at participating sights) is valid at several sights, including the S. Vitale, S. Appolinare, and the Mausoleo. After looking at mosaics all day, buy some tiles from **Colori-Belle Arti,** P. Mameli 16, off Vle. Farini, and try your own hand. (☎054 43 73 87. Open M-Th 8:30am-12:30pm and 4-7:30pm.)

Trains (☎05 44 21 78 84) connect to Florence and Venice (1hr., every 1-2hr., L7400) and Ferrara (1hr., every 2hr., L6700). The train station is in P. Farini, at the east end of town. Follow Vle. Farini from the station to V. Diaz, which runs to the central P. del Popolo and the **tourist office,** V. Salara 8. (☎054 43 54 04. Open M-Sa 8:30am-7pm, Su 10am-4pm; in winter M-Sa 8:30am-6pm, Su 10am-4pm.) Walk down V. Farini and turn right at P. Mameli to **Albergo Al Giaciglio,** V. Rocca Brancaleone 42. (☎054 43 94 03. Closed 2 weeks in Dec. or Jan. Singles L45-55,000; doubles L65-85,000; triples L90-100,000.) Take bus #1 or 70 from V. Pallavicini at the station (L1300) to reach **Ostello Dante (HI),** V. Nicolodi 12. (☎/fax 05 44 42 11 64. Breakfast included. Internet. Reception 7-10am and 5-11:30pm. Lockout noon-3:30pm. Curfew 11:30pm. L22,000.)

FERRARA

Rome has its mopeds, Venice its boats, and Ferrara its bicycles. Old folks, young folks, and babies perched precariously on handlebars whirl through Ferrara's jumble of twisting medieval roads inaccessible to automobiles. **Bike** the tranquil, wooded concourse along the city's well-preserved, 9km **medieval wall,** which begins at the far end of C. Giovecca. Towered, turreted, and moated, **Castello Estense** stands precisely at the center of town. C. della Giovecca lies along the former route of the moat's feeder canal, separating the medieval section from the part planned by the d'Este's architect, Biagio Rosetti. (Open Tu-Su 9:30am-5:30pm. L8000, students L6000.) From the *castello*, take C. Martiri della Libertà to P. Cattedrale and the **duomo,** which contains the **Museo della Cattedrale.** (Cathedral open M-Sa 7:30am-noon and 3-6:30pm, Su 7:30am-12:30pm and 4-7:30pm. Museum open Tu-Sa 10am-noon and 3-5pm, Su and holidays 10am-noon and 4-6pm.) From Castello Estense, cross Largo Castello to C. Ercole I d'Este and walk to the corner of C. Rossetti to reach the **Palazzo Diamanti,** built in 1493, which outshines all other ducal residences. Inside, the **Pinacoteca Nazionale** contains many of the best Ferrarese works. (Open Tu-W and F-Sa 9am-2pm, Th 9am-7pm, Su and holidays 9am-1pm. L8000, students L4000.) Follow C. Ercole I d'Este behind the *castello* and turn right on C. Porta Mare to find the **Palazzo Massari,** C. Porta Mare 9, which now houses both the **Museo d'Arte Moderna e Contemporanea "Filippo de Pisis"** and, upstairs, the spectacular **Museo Ferrarese dell'Ottocentro/Museo Giovanni Boldini.** (Both open daily 9am-1pm and 3-6pm. Joint ticket L10,000.) From the *castello*, head down C. Giovecca, turn left on V. Montebello, and continue to V. Vigne to find the **Cimitero Ebraico** (Jewish Cemetery), where a monument commemorates Ferrarese Jews murdered at Auschwitz. (Open Su-F Apr.-Sept. 9am-6pm; Oct.-Mar. 9am-4:30pm.)

Ferrara is on the Bologna-Venice rail line; **trains** go to: Bologna (30min., 1-2 per hr., L4900); Padua (1hr., every hr., L7600); Venice (2hr., 1-2 per hr., L10,800); and Rome (3-4hr., 7 per day, L57,200). To get to the town center, head left from the station, then right on Vle. Costituzione, which becomes Vle. Cavour and runs to the Castello Estense at the center of town (1km). ACFT (☎05 32 59 94 92) and GGFP **buses** go from V. Rampari S. Paolo (most also leave from the train station) to Ferrara's beaches (1hr., 12 per day, L7600-8400) and Bologna (1½hr., 3-15 per day, L6000). The **tourist office** is in Castello Estense. (☎05 32 20 93 70; www.comune.fe.it. Open daily 9am-1pm and 2-6pm.) To reach the brand new **Ostella della Gioventù Estense (HI),** C.B. Rossetti 24, go down C. Ercole d'Este from the *castello*, or take bus #4C from the station and ask for the *castello* stop. (☎/fax 05 32 20 42 27. Reception 7-10am and 3:30-11:30pm. Lockout 10am-3:30pm. Curfew 11:40pm. L23,000.) From the *duomo*, head down C. Porta Reno, left on V. Ragno, and left on V. Vittoria to get to **Casa degli Artisti,** V. Vittoria 66, in the historic town center near P. Lampronti. (☎05 32 76 10 38. Singles L34,000; doubles L60-85,000.) Get **groceries** at the **Mercato Comunale,** on V. Mercato, off V. Garibaldi next to the *duomo*. (Open M-W 7am-1:30pm and 4:30-7:30pm, Th and Sa 7am-1:30pm, F 4:30-7:30pm.) In July and August, a free **Discobus** (☎05 32 59 94 11) runs every Saturday night between Ferrara and clubs; pick up flyers in the station. **Postal code:** 44100.

TUSCANY (TOSCANA)

Tuscany is the stuff of Italian dreams (and more than one Brits-in-Italy movie). With rolling hills blanketed in olive groves and grapevines, bright yellow fields of sunflowers, and inviting cobblestone streets, it's hard not to wax poetic. Tuscany's Renaissance culture became Italy's heritage, while its regional dialect, the language of Dante, Petrarch, and Machiavelli, has developed into modern textbook Italian. After a tumultuous medieval period of strife, Tuscany came under the astute (and despotic) rule of the Medici family, who commissioned huge *palazzi* and incredible art. Eventually, the ever-cavalier Tuscans watched their region decline into a cultural and political non-entity. Today, protected by centuries of relative serenity, Tuscany's eminence has returned with a thriving tourism industry.

FLORENCE (FIRENZE)

Surveying the glow of the setting sun over a sea of burnt-orange roofs and towering domes, one realizes that no other city offers so much beauty in such a small area. Florence evolved from a busy 13th-century wool- and silk-trading town plagued by civil strife into a center of political experimentation and artistic rebirth. Under Medici rule, Florentine Renaissance culture peaked in a flurry of splendid productivity: by the mid-15th century, the city was the unchallenged European capital of art, architecture, commerce, and political thought. Present-day Florence works hard to preserve its cultural legacy, but it's far from a lifeless museum: street graffiti quotes Marx and Malcolm X, businessmen whiz by on Vespas, children play soccer against the Duomo, and even the loneliest of back alleys hides a scintillating jewel.

GETTING THERE AND GETTING AROUND

Flights: Amerigo Vespucci Airport (☎05 53 06 17 00), in Peretola. Mostly domestic and charter flights. Orange ATAF **bus** #62 runs to the train station (L1500). **Galileo Galilei Airport** (☎055 50 07 07), in Pisa, has an info booth at platform 5 in the Florence train station. The **airport express** connects the station to Pisa (1hr., L8000).

Trains: Santa Maria Novella Station (☎05 51 47 880 88), across from S. Maria Novella. Info open daily 7am-9pm; take a number from the machine. After hours go to ticket window 20. Trains depart hourly to: **Bologna** (1hr., L14,200); **Rome** (2½hr., L35-40,000); **Venice** (3hr., L35,100); and **Milan** (3½hr., L39,700).

Buses: LAZZI, P. Adua 1-4r (☎055 21 51 55). To **Pisa** (L11,200). **SITA,** V. S. Caterina da Siena 15r (☎055 28 46 61). To **Siena** (1¼-2hr., L11,000).

Public Transportation: ATAF, outside the train station, runs orange city buses 6am-1am. **One-hour tickets** L1500, packet of 4 L5800; **3hr.** L2500; **24hr.** L6000; and **3-day** L11,100. Buy tickets at any newsstand, *tabacchi,* or automated ticket dispenser before boarding. Validate your ticket using the orange machine on board or risk a L75,000 fine. One-hour tickets are sold on the bus from 9pm-6am for L3000.

Taxis: ☎43 90, 47 98, or 42 42. Stands outside the train station.

Bike and Moped Rental: Alinari Noleggi, V. Guelfa 85r (☎055 28 05 00). Bikes L20-40,000 per day; mopeds L35-45,000 per day.

Hitchhiking: *Let's Go* does not recommend hitchhiking. Hitchers take the A-1 north to Bologna and Milan or the A-11 northwest to the Riviera and Genoa. Buses #29, 30, or 35 run from the station to the feeder near Peretola. For the A-1 south to Rome and to Siena, they take bus #31 or 32 from the station to Exit 23 ("Firenze Sud").

ORIENTATION AND PRACTICAL INFORMATION

From the train station, the city center is a short walk down V. de' Panzani and a left on V. de' Cerretani. Major arteries radiate from the Duomo and its two *piazze.* V. dei Calzaiuoli runs south from the Duomo to **Piazza della Signoria.** The parallel V. Roma to the west leads from P. S. Giovanni through **Piazza della Repubblica** to the Ponte Vecchio, which crosses the Arno to the **Oltrarno** district. East of and parallel to V. Roma, V. del Proconsolo runs south to the **Bargello.** Borgo S. Lorenzo (opposite V. Roma) runs north from P. S. Giovanni to **Piazza San Lorenzo,** and V. dei Servi leads northeast from P. del Duomo to the **Galleria dell'Accademia.**

Sights are scattered throughout Florence, but few lie beyond walking distance. **Florence's streets are numbered in red and black sequences.** Red numbers indicate commercial establishments and black (or blue) numbers denote residential addresses (including most sights and hotels). Black addresses appear in *Let's Go* as a numeral only, while red addresses are indicated with a subsequent "r." If you reach an address and it's not what you're looking for, you probably have the wrong color—just step back and look for the other sequence. See the **color map** at the front of this book for an overview of Florence and its sights.

TOURIST, FINANCIAL, AND LOCAL SERVICES

Tourist Offices: Consorzio ITA (☎055 28 28 93), in the train station by track 16. Suggest a price range, and they will find a room for L4,500-15,000 commission. Open daily 8:45am-8pm. **Informazione Turistica** (☎055 21 22 45), in P. della Stazione, is across the piazza from the main exit. Info on entertainment and cultural events. Open daily Apr.-Oct. 8:30am-7:30pm; Nov.-Mar. 8:15am-5:30pm.

Tours: Enjoy Florence (☎800 274 819 or 064 45 18 43) gives fast-paced, informative walking tours of the old city center, focusing on the history and culture of medieval and Renaissance Florence. Tours meet daily in summer at 10am in front of the Thomas Cook office at the Ponte Vecchio; reduced hours in winter. L30,000, under 26 L25,000.

Consulates: UK, Lungarno Corsini 2 (☎055 28 41 33). Open M-F 9:30am-12:30pm and 2:30-4:30pm. **US,** Lungarno Vespucci 38 (☎05 52 39 82 76), at V. Palestro, near

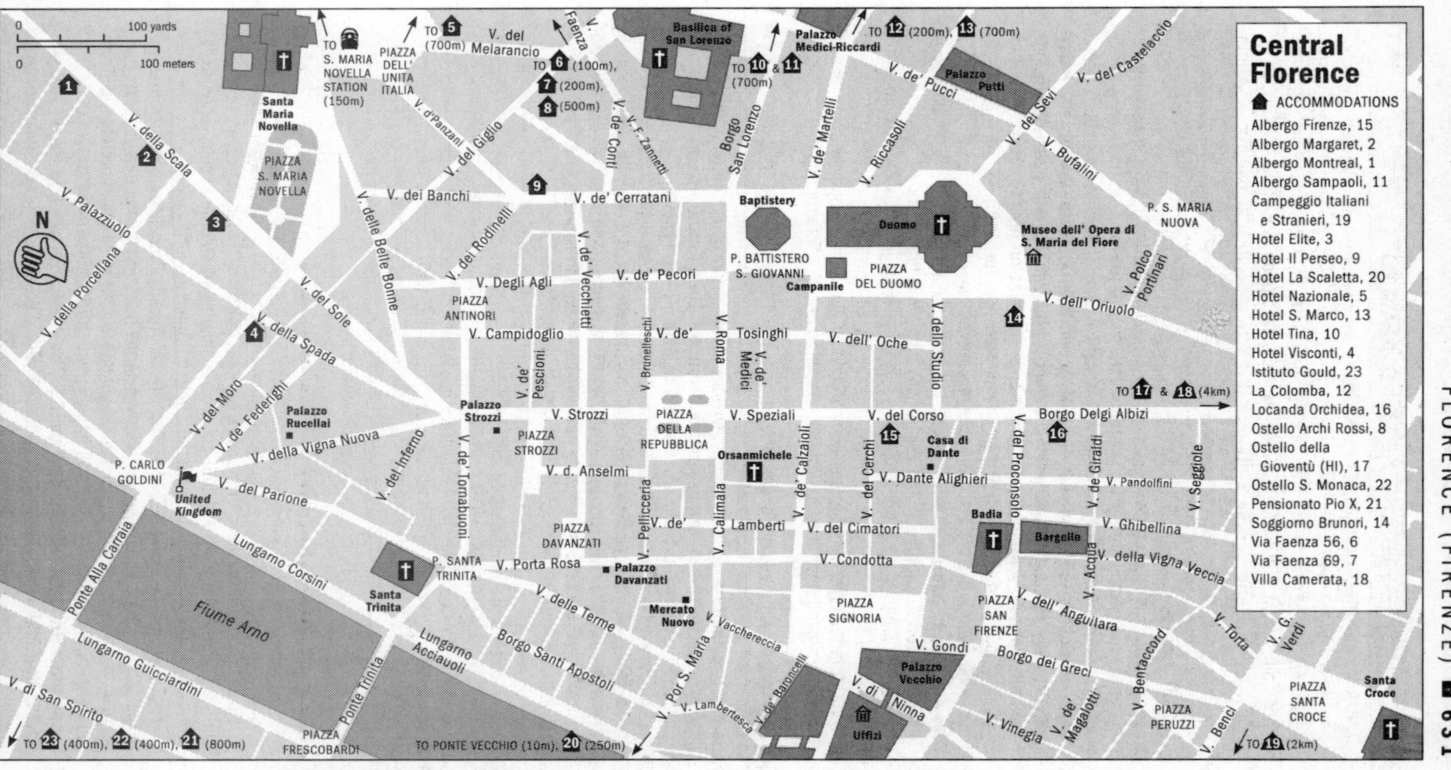
Central Florence
ACCOMMODATIONS
Albergo Firenze, 15
Albergo Margaret, 2
Albergo Montreal, 1
Albergo Sampaoli, 11
Campeggio Italiani e Stranieri, 19
Hotel Elite, 3
Hotel Il Perseo, 9
Hotel La Scaletta, 20
Hotel Nazionale, 5
Hotel S. Marco, 13
Hotel Tina, 10
Hotel Visconti, 4
Istituto Gould, 23
La Colomba, 12
Locanda Orchidea, 16
Ostello Archi Rossi, 8
Ostello della Gioventù (HI), 17
Ostello S. Monaca, 22
Pensionato Pio X, 21
Soggiorno Brunori, 14
Via Faenza 56, 6
Via Faenza 69, 7
Villa Camerata, 18

the station. Open M-F 9am-12:30pm and 2-4pm. **Canadians, Australians,** and **New Zealanders** should contact consulates in Rome or Milan.

Currency Exchange: Local banks offer the best rates. Most are open M-F 8:20am-1:20pm and 2:45-3:45pm, some also Sa morning. **ATMs** abound.

American Express: V. Dante Alighieri 20-22r (☎05 55 09 81). From the Duomo, walk down V. dei Calzaiuoli and turn left on V. dei Tavolini. Mail held; free for card- and check-holders, otherwise L3000 per inquiry. Open M-F 9am-5:30pm, Sa 9am-12:30pm.

Bookstores: Paperback Exchange, V. Fiesolana 31r (☎05 52 47 81 54), swaps books. Open mid-Mar. to mid-Nov. (closed 2-3 weeks in Aug.). M-Sa 9am-7:30pm; mid-Nov. to mid-Mar. Tu-Sa 9am-1pm and 3:30-7:30pm. **Feltrenelli International,** V. Cavour 12r (☎055 29 21 96), has French, German, and English books. Open M-Sa 9am-7:30pm.

Laundromat: Launderette, V. Guelfa 55r. Wash/dry L12,000. Open daily 8am-10pm.

EMERGENCY AND COMMUNICATIONS

Emergencies: ☎113. **Medical Emergency:** ☎118. **Fire:** ☎115. **Police:** ☎112.

Pharmacies: Farmacia Comunale (☎055 28 94 35), in the train station by track 16. **Molteni,** V. dei Calzaiuoli 7r (☎055 28 94 90). Both open 24hr.

Internet Access: Your Virtual Office, at V. Faenza 49, V. Guelfa 83, V. de' Neri 37, and Piazza Pitti 7-8. L6000 for 30min., students L5000. Open daily 10am-midnight.

Post Office: V. Pellicceria, off P. della Repubblica. Send packages from V. dei Sassetti 4. Address mail to be held: First name, SURNAME, *In Fermo Posta,* L'Ufficio Postale, V. Pellicceria, Firenze, **50100** Italy. Open M-F 8:15am-7pm, Sa 8:15am-12:30pm.

ACCOMMODATIONS

Florence abounds with one-star *pensioni* and private *affitta camere.* If you arrive late in the day, consult the accommodation service at the tourist office in the train station (see **Practical Information** above). Make reservations *(prenotazioni)* at least 10 days in advance during Easter or summer. Immediately cancel any reservations you decide not to keep; hotel owners are disgruntled with no-shows, and many no longer accept reservations for this reason. **Expect prices higher than those listed here;** rates uniformly increase by 10% or so every year.

The budget accommodations around the **Piazza Santa Maria Novella,** near the train station, are conveniently located near the Duomo. Although the central **Old City** is flooded by tourists, budget accommodations often provide great views of Florence's monuments or reside in Renaissance *palazzi.* Inexpensive budget hotels on and around **Via Nazionale,** off P. della Stazione in front of the station, cater to the disoriented; the area isn't big on ambience, but it's filled with cheap rooms. The area near **Piazza San Marco** is considerably calm and tourist-free given its proximity to the city center; to get there, turn right from the station, left on V. Nazionale, right on V. Guelfa, and left on V. Cavour. **Oltrarno,** across the river from the Duomo (10min.), offers a break from Florence's hustle and bustle.

HOSTELS

Ostello Archi Rossi, V. Faenza 94r (☎055 29 08 04; fax 05 52 30 26 01). Exit left from the station on V. Nazionale and turn left on V. Faenza. Floor-to-ceiling graffiti, TV, and patio brimming with young travelers. Breakfast L3-5000. Laundry L10,000. Lockout from room 9:30am, from hostel 11am. In summer, check in before 11am. Curfew 12:30am. No reservations. Dorms L23-28,000, with bath L25-40,000.

Istituto Gould, V. dei Serragli 49 (☎055 21 25 76; fax 055 28 02 74), in the **Oltrarno.** Exit the station by track 16, head right to P. della Stazione, walk to the left of the church, and continue through the P. S. Maria Novella and down V. dei Fossi, which becomes V. dei Serragli after the bridge (15min.). Spotless rooms. Reception M-F 9am-1pm and 3-7pm, Sa 9am-1pm. No check-in or check-out Sa afternoons or Su. Singles L48-55,000; doubles L72-78,000; triples L78-105,000; quads with bath L132,000.

Ostello Santa Monaca, V. S. Monaca 6 (☎055 26 83 38; fax 055 28 01 85; email info@ostello.it; www.ostello.it), off V. dei Serragli (see above) in the **Oltrarno.** Kitchen.

Laundry L12,000. 7-night max. stay. Reception 6am-1pm and 2pm-1am. Curfew 12:30am. Reserve in writing at least 3 days ahead. Crowded dorms L25,000.

Pensionato Pio X, V. dei Serragli 106 (☎/fax 055 22 50 44), past the Istituto Gould in **Oltrarno.** Quiet, clean rooms and comfortable lounges. Arrive before 9am. Check-out 9am. Curfew midnight. 2-night min. stay. No reservations. L25-30,000.

Ostello della Gioventù Europa Villa Camerata (HI), V. Augusto Righi 2-4 (☎055 60 14 51; fax 055 61 03 00). Take bus #17 from P. dell'Unità near the train station (25min.); ask the driver where to get off. Tidy and popular, in a gorgeous villa with *loggia* and gardens. Breakfast and sheets included. Laundry L10,000. Reception 1-11pm. Strict midnight curfew. Reserve in writing. If they're booked, sleep on a cot in their outdoor tent. L17,500. Dorms L25,000; nonmembers L30,000.

HOTELS

OLD CITY (NEAR THE DUOMO)

Locanda Orchidea, Borgo degli Albizi 11 (☎/fax 05 52 48 03 46), left off V. Proconsolo from the southeast corner of P. del Duomo. Some rooms open onto a garden. Reservations recommended. Singles L70,000; doubles L105,000; triples L150,000.

Albergo Brunetta, Borgo Pinti 5 (☎05 52 47 81 34). Central location and rooftop terrace with superb view. No rooms with bath, but free showers. Singles L65,000; doubles L85,000; triples L120,000. Cash only.

Hotel Il Perseo, V. de Cerretani 1 (☎055 21 25 04; fax 055 28 83 77), en route to the Duomo from the station, opposite the Feltrinelli bookstore. Enthusiastic owners and bright, immaculate rooms with fans. Bar and TV lounge. Breakfast included. Singles L85,000; doubles L135-155,000; triples L175-210,000. V, MC.

Soggiorno Brunori, V. del Proconsolo 5 (☎055 28 96 48). Simple rooms with an occasional balcony. Curfew 12:30am. Singles L60,000, with bath L80,000 (available only in winter); doubles L96-124,000; triples L130-168,000; quads L164-212,000.

AROUND PIAZZA SANTA MARIA NOVELLA

Hotel Giappone, V. de Banchi 1 (☎055 21 00 90; fax 055 29 28 77). Clean, comfortable rooms in a central location. Singles L80,000, with bath L90,000; doubles L110,000, L130,000; triples and quads L45,000 per person.

Tourist House, V. della Scala 1 (☎055 26 86 75; fax 055 28 25 52). All rooms with bath, TV, terrace, and breakfast. Singles L100,000; doubles L160,000.

Albergo Montreal, V. della Scala 43 (☎05 52 38 23 31; fax 055 28 74 91). Exit east from the station (left as you face the tracks), walk down V. degli Orti Oricellari, and turn left on V. della Scala. Cozy TV lounge and modern rooms. Curfew 1:30am. Singles L70,000; doubles L95-110,000; triples L150,000; quads L185,000.

Hotel Visconti, P. Ottaviani 1 (☎/fax 055 21 38 77). From P. S. Maria Novella, follow V. de' Fossi 1 block. Neoclassical decor, bar, and TV lounge. Breakfast in roof garden included. Singles L65,000, with bath L90,000; doubles L98,000, L140,000.

Hotel Elite, V. della Scala 12 (☎055 21 53 95; fax 055 21 38 32), past the Albergo Montreal Bubbly reception gives advice on sightseeing, eating, and playing. Breakfast L10,000. Singles L80-110,000; doubles L100-120,000.

Albergo Margaret, V. della Scala 25 (☎055 21 01 38), by the Albergo Montreal. Serene decor, kind staff, and beautiful rooms. Curfew midnight. June-Aug. singles L80-100,000; doubles L100-120,000; Sept.-May reduced.

AROUND PIAZZA SAN MARCO

Hotel Tina, V. S. Gallo 31 (☎055 48 35 19; fax 055 48 35 93). From P. S. Marco, follow V. XXII Aprile and turn right on V. S. Gallo. *Pensione* with high ceilings, new furniture, and amicable owners. Singles L80,000; doubles L100,000, with bath L130,000; triples with bath L140,000; quads with bath L160,000.

La Colomba, V. Cavour 21 (☎055 28 91 39; fax 055 28 43 23; email info@hotelcolomba.it), right off P. S. Marco. Clean rooms with phones, TVs, A/C, and fridges. Breakfast included. Singles L110-150,000; doubles L185-230,000.

Albergo Sampaoli, V. S. Gallo 14 (☎055 28 48 34), before the Hotel Tina (see above). Proprietress offers backpackers a "home away from home." Singles L90-100,000; doubles L110-160,000; extra bed L56,000. Reservations accepted 1-2 weeks ahead.

Hotel San Marco, V. Cavour 50 (☎/fax 055 28 42 35), off P. S. Marco. Modern, airy rooms. Breakfast included. Curfew 1:30am; ask for a key. Singles L80-100,000; doubles L110-140,000; triples with bath L200,000.

AROUND VIA NAZIONALE

Hotel Nazionale, V. Nazionale 22 (☎05 52 38 22 03), near P. della Indipendenza. Comfy beds in sunny rooms. Breakfast included. Curfew midnight; ask for a key. Singles L90-100,000; doubles L130-150,000; triples L250,000.

Via Faenza 56 houses six separate *pensioni*, among the best budget lodgings in the city. From the station, head up V. Nazionale and turn left on V. Faenza.

Pensione Azzi (☎055 21 38 06) styles itself as a *locanda degli artisti* (an artists' inn); all travelers enjoy the large rooms and terrace. Breakfast included. Singles L70,000; doubles L100-130,000.

Albergo Anna (☎05 52 39 83 22) has lovely singles and doubles with frescoes and fans.

Locanda Paola (☎055 21 36 82) has spartan doubles, some with views of Fiesole and the surrounding hills. Curfew 2am.

Albergo Merlini (☎055 21 28 48; fax 055 28 39 39) has some rooms with Duomo views. Breakfast L10,000. Curfew 1:30am. Singles L70,000; doubles L100-120,000.

Albergo Marini (☎055 28 48 24) boasts spotless rooms. Breakfast L8000. Singles L80-90,000; doubles L110-130,000; triples L130-150,000; quads L140-170,000. Cash only.

Albergo Armonia (☎055 21 11 46) decorates its rooms with American film posters. Singles L70,000; doubles L110,000; triples L135,000; quads L160,000.

Via Faenza 69 houses several accommodations. **Locanda Giovanna,** 4th fl. (☎05 52 38 13 53), has basic, well-kept rooms, some with garden views. Singles L50,000; doubles L75,000. Or, try **Locanda Pina** and **Albergo Nella,** 1st and 2nd fl. (☎05 52 65 43 46). Basic rooms. Free Internet. Singles L60,000; doubles L90-110,000.

OLTRARNO

Hotel La Scaletta, V. Guicciardini 13b (☎055 28 30 28; fax 055 28 95 62; email lascaletta@italyhotel.com). From the Duomo, head down V. Roma, which becomes V. Guicciardini after crossing the Ponte Vecchio. Beautiful rooms with antique furniture and rooftop terraces with spectacular views of the Boboli gardens. Breakfast included. Reception closes after midnight. Singles L80-160,000; doubles L160-220,000; triples with bath L250,000; quads with bath L260-280,000. V, MC.

CAMPING

Campeggio Michelangelo, V. Michelangelo 80 (☎05 56 81 19 77), beneath Ple. Michelangelo. Take bus #13 from the station (15min.; last bus 11:25pm). Crowded, but offers a spectacular panorama of Florence. Open Apr.-Nov. L10,000 per person; L9000 per tent; L7000 per car; L6000 per motorcycle.

Villa Camerata, V. A. Righi 2-4 (☎055 60 03 15), outside the HI hostel (see p. 632). Breakfast L2500. Reception daily 1pm-midnight. Check-out 7-10am. L8000 per person, L6800 with camping card; L8000 per small tent, L16,000 per large tent.

FOOD

Florence's hearty cuisine originated in the peasant fare of the surrounding countryside. Specialties include the Tuscan classics *minestra di fagioli* (white bean and garlic soup), *ribollita* (hearty bean, bread, and black cabbage stew), and *bistecca alla Fiorentina* (thick sirloin steak). Wine is a Florentine staple, and genuine *chianti classico* commands a premium price; a liter costs L7-10,000 in Florence's *trattorie*, while stores sell bottles for as little as L5000. The local dessert is *cantuccini di prato* (almond cookies made with egg yolks) dipped in *vinsanto* (a rich dessert wine made from raisins). *Gelato* is said to have been invented centuries ago by Florence's own Buontalenti family; as a tourist, it's your duty to sample the sweet. For lunch, visit a *rosticceria gastronomia*, peruse the city's pushcarts, or pick up fresh produce or meat at the **Mercato Centrale,** between V. Nazionale and Piazza S. Lorenzo. (Open June-Sept. M-Sa 7:30am-2pm; Oct.-May Sa 7am-2pm and 4-8pm.) To get to **STANDA supermarket,** V. Pietrapiana 1r, follow V. del Proconsolo from the Duomo, turn left on Borgo degli Albizi, and continue straight through P. G. Salvemini to V. Pietrapiana. (Open Tu-Sa 8:30am-9pm.)

OLD CITY (THE CENTER)

Acqua al Due, V. Vigna Vecchia 40r (☎055 28 41 70), behind the Bargello. Popular with young Italians. Serves Florentine specialties, including an excellent *assaggio* (L13,500). *Primi* L11,500-13,000; *secondi* from L12,000. Cover L2000. Open daily June-Sept. 7:30pm-1am; Oct.-May Tu-Su 8pm-1am. Reserve ahead.

Le Colonnine, V. dei Benci 6r (☎055 23 46 47), north of the Ponte alle Grazie. Delicious traditional fare. Pasta L10,000; *secondi* from L13,000. Famous *paella* "for 2" could feed a small army (L30,000). Open Tu-Su noon-2pm and 7pm-1am.

Il Latini, V. Palchetti 6r, north of the Ponte alla Carraia. Be prepared to wait for its delicious Tuscan classics. *Ribollita* L8000; *primi* L10-12,000; *secondi* L15-25,000. Cover L3000. Open Tu-Su noon-2:30pm and 7-10pm.

PIAZZE SANTA MARIA NOVELLA AND DEL MERCATO CENTRALE

Trattoria Contadino, V. Palazzuolo 71r. Filling, home-style meals. Lunch *menù* L16,000; dinner *menù* L20,000. Open M-Sa noon-3:30pm and 6pm-12:30am.

Trattoria da Zà-Zà, P. del Mercato Centrale 26r (☎055 21 54 11). A hopping *trattoria* with *tris* (veggie soup; L9000) and *tagliatelle al tartufo* (L11,000). Cover L2000 for outdoor dining. Reservations recommended. Open M-Sa noon-3pm and 7-11pm.

Trattoria da Garibaldi, P. del Mercato Centrale 38r (☎055 21 22 67). Locals flock to enjoy the fresh, inexpensive food. Daily *menù* L16,000. Cover L2000 for outdoor dining. Open M-Sa noon-3pm and 7-11pm.

OLTRARNO

Il Borgo Antico, P. S. Spirito 6r (☎055 21 04 37). An array of creative, tasty, and filling dishes. *Primi* L10,000; *secondi* L15-25,000. Cover L3000. Open daily 1-4pm and 6:30pm-1:30am. Reservations recommended.

Oltrarno Trattoria Casalinga, V. Michelozzi 9r (☎055 21 86 24), near P. S. Spirito. Delicious Tuscan specialties like *pasta al pastore* (L10,000). *Primi* L6-10,500; *secondi* L8-18,000. Cover L3000. Open M-Sa noon-2:30pm and 7-9:30pm.

GELATERIE

Vivoli, V. della Stinche 7 (☎055 29 23 34), behind the Bargello. The most famous Florentine *gelateria,* with the self-proclaimed "best ice cream in the world." Huge selection. Cups from L3000. Open 7am-1am.

Perchè No?, V. Tavolini 19r (☎05 52 39 89 69), off V. dei Calzaiuoli. Florence's oldest *gelateria*–try the chunky *nocciolosa.* Cones from L3000. Open in summer W-M 10am-1am; off season 10am-8pm.

SIGHTS

Florence's museums have recently doubled their prices (now L6-12,000 per venue) and no longer offer student discounts. In summer, watch for **Sere al Museo,** evenings when certain museums are free from 8:30 to 11pm. Additionally, don't miss Florence's churches, many of which are free treasuries of great art.

PIAZZA DEL DUOMO

DUOMO. The red brick of Florence's **Duomo,** the **Cattedrale di Santa Maria del Fiore,** at the center of P. del Duomo, is visible from virtually every part of the city. Filippo Brunelleschi dreamed up the ingenious technique that made building the sublime dome—at the time, the world's largest—possible: his revolutionary method of double-shelled construction utilized self-supporting interlocking bricks. Climb the 463 steps inside the dome to the **lantern,** or cupola, which offers an unparalleled view of the city. *(Duomo open M-Sa 10am-5pm, Su 1:30-5pm; first Sa of each month closes 3:30pm. Mass daily 7am-12:30pm and 5-7pm. Lantern open M-Sa 8:30am-7pm. L10,000.)* The top of the 82m-high **campanile** next to the Duomo has ineffably beautiful views. *(Open daily Apr.-Sept. 8:30am-6:50pm; Oct. 9am-5:20pm; Nov.-Mar. 9am-4:20pm. L10,000.)*

BATTISTERO. The **battistero** (baptistery) next to the Duomo, built between the 5th and 9th centuries, was the site of Dante's christening; its Byzantine-style mosaics inspired the details of his *Inferno*. The famous **bronze doors** were a product of intense competition among Florentine artists; Ghiberti was commissioned to forge the last set of doors. The products, reportedly dubbed the **Gates of Paradise** by Michelangelo, were nothing like Ghiberti's two earlier portals, as they exchanged his earlier 28-panel design for 10 large, gilded squares, each of which employs mathematical perspective to create the illusion of deep space. Under restoration since a 1966 flood, they will soon be housed in the Museo dell'Opera del Duomo. *(Open M-Sa noon-6:30pm, Su 9am-1:30pm. L5000. Mass 10:30, 11:30am.)*

MUSEO DELL'OPERA DEL DUOMO. Most of the Duomo's art resides behind the cathedral in the Museo dell'Opera del Duomo. Up the first flight of stairs is a late *Pietà* by Michelangelo, who, according to legend, destroyed Christ's left arm with a hammer in a fit of frustration; soon after, a diligent pupil touched up the work, leaving visible scars on parts of Mary Magdalene's head. The museum also houses four frames from the baptistery's *Gates of Paradise*. *(P. del Duomo 9. Open M-Sa 9:30am-6:30pm. L10,000. Tours in English in summer W-Th 4pm.)*

PIAZZA DELLA SIGNORIA AND ENVIRONS

From P. del Duomo, the bustling **Via dei Calzaiuoli,** one of the city's oldest streets, runs south through crowds and chic shops to P. della Signoria.

PIAZZA DELLA SIGNORIA. The *piazza*, a vast space by medieval standards, came into being in the 13th century. In 1497, religious leader and social critic Savonarola convinced Florentines to light the **Bonfire of the Vanities,** a grand roast that consumed some of Florence's best art, in the square. A year later, disillusioned citizens sent Savonarola up in smoke on the same spot, marked today by a granite disc. Monumental sculptures cluster in front of the *palazzo*, including Michelangelo's *David* (a copy now stands in place of the original). The awkward *Neptune* to the left of the Palazzo Vecchio so revolted Michelangelo that he insulted the artist: "Oh Ammannato, Ammannato, what lovely marble you have ruined!" The graceful 14th-century **Loggia dei Lanzi,** built as a stage for civic orators, became a misogynistic sculpture gallery under the Medici dukes.

PALAZZO VECCHIO. At the far end of the *piazza*, the area around the Palazzo Vecchio forms Florence's civic center. Arnolfo del Cambio designed this fortress-like *palazzo* in the late 13th century as the governmental seat. It later became the Medici family home, and in 1470 Michelozzo decorated the **courtyard** in Renaissance style. Inside are works by Michelangelo, da Vinci, and Bronzino. *(Open June-Aug. M and F 9am-11pm, Tu-W and Sa 9am-7pm, Th and Su 9am-2pm; Sept.-May M-W and F-Sa 9am-7pm, Th 9am-2pm, Su 9am-2pm.)*

THE UFFIZI. Vasari designed this palace in 1554 for the offices *(uffizi)* of Duke Cosimo's administration; today, it houses more first-class art per square inch than any other museum in the world. Botticelli, da Vinci, Michelangelo, Raphael, Titian, Giotto, Fra Angelico, Caravaggio, Bronzino, Cimabue, della Francesca, Bellini, even Dürer, Rubens, and Rembrandt—you name it, they have it. *(Extends from P. della Signoria to the Arno River. ☎055 21 83 41. Open Tu-Sa 8:30am-6:50pm, Su 8:30am-1:50pm. L12,000. Advance tickets spare hours of waiting but cost L2000 extra; call 050 47 19 60 to reserve with a credit card.)*

PONTE VECCHIO. From the Uffizi, follow V. Georgofili left and turn right along the river to reach the nearby **Ponte Vecchio** (Old Bridge). The oldest bridge in Florence, it replaced an older Roman version in 1345. In the 1500s, the Medici kicked out the butcheries and tanneries that lined the bridge—apparently, the odor of pig's blood and intestines offended powerful bankers on their way to work—and installed goldsmiths and diamond-carvers instead. Social criticism aside, the view of the bridge from the neighboring Ponte alle Grazie at sunset is heart-stopping, and the bridge itself buzzes with pedestrians and street performers, particularly at night.

BARGELLO. The heart of medieval Florence lies in this 13th-century fortress between the Duomo and P. della Signoria. Once the residence of the chief magistrate and later a brutal prison with public executions in the courtyard, it was restored in the 19th century and now houses the sculpture-filled **Museo Nazionale.** Donatello's bronze *David*, the first free-standing nude since antiquity, stands opposite the two bronze panels of the *Sacrifice of Isaac*, submitted by Ghiberti and Brunelleschi in the baptistery door competition. Michelangelo's early works, including *Bacchus*, *Brutus*, and *Apollo*, are on the ground floor. *(V. del Proconsolo 4. Open daily 8:30am-1:50pm; closed on the 1st, 3rd, and 5th Su and the 2nd and 4th M of each month. L8000.)*

SAN LORENZO AND FARTHER NORTH

BASILICA DI SAN LORENZO. The Medici, who lent the city the funds to build the church (designed in 1419 by Brunelleschi), retained artistic control over its construction. The family cunningly placed Cosimo Medici's grave in front of the high altar, making the entire church his personal mausoleum. Michelangelo designed the exterior, but—disgusted by Florentine politics—abandoned the project to study architecture in Rome. *(☎055 21 66 34. Open daily 7am-noon and 3:30-6:30pm.)*

To reach the **Cappelle dei Medici** (Medici Chapels), walk around to the back entrance on P. Madonna degli Aldobrandini. The **Cappella dei Principi** (Princes' Chapel) is a rare Baroque moment in Florence, while the **Sacrestia Nuova** (New Sacristy) reveals Michelangelo's study of Brunelleschi and holds two Medici tombs. *(Open M-Sa 8:30am-5pm, Su 8:30am-1:30pm; closed the 2nd and 4th Su and the 1st, 3rd, and 5th M of each month. L10,000.)*

ACCADEMIA. Michelangelo's triumphant *David* stands in self-assured perfection in a rotunda designed specifically for it. In the hallway stand Michelangelo's four *Prisoners;* the master left these intriguing statues intentionally unfinished, chipping away just enough to liberate the "living stone." *(V. Ricasoli 60, between the churches of San Marco and S. S. Annunziata. Open June-Aug. Tu-F 8:30am-9pm, Sa 8:30am-midnight, Su 8:30am-8pm; Sept.-May Tu-Su 8:30am-6:50pm. L15,000.)*

PIAZZA SANTA CROCE AND ENVIRONS

CHIESA DI SANTA CROCE. The ascetic Franciscans built arguably the city's most splendid church. Among the luminaries buried here are Machiavelli, Galileo, Michelangelo, who rests at the front of the right aisle in a tomb designed by Vasari, and humanist Leonardo Bruni, shown holding his precious *History of Florence* on a tomb designed by Bernardo Rossellino. Note also Donatello's gilded *Annunciation. (Open M-Sa 9:30am-5:30pm, Su and holidays 3-5:30pm.)*

THE OLTRARNO

Historically disdained by downtown Florentines, the far side of the Arno remains lively and unpretentious, even in high season.

PALAZZO PITTI. Luca Pitti, a nouveau-riche banker of the 15th century, built his *palazzo* east of Santo Spirito against the Boboli hill. The Medici acquired the *palazzo* and the hill in 1550 and enlarged everything possible. Today, it houses six museums, including the **Galleria Palatina.** The Galleria was one of only a few public galleries when it opened in 1833, and today houses Florence's most important art collection after the Uffizi. Works by Raphael, Titian, Andrea del Sarto, Caravaggio, and Rubens line the walls. Other museums display Medici family treasures, costumes, porcelain, carriages, and *Apartamenti Reale* (royal apartments)—lavish reminders of the time when the *palazzo* was the royal House of Savoy's living quarters. *(V. Guicciardini leads from Ponte Vecchio to the palazzo. Galleria Palatina open Su-F 8:30am-9pm, Sa 8:30am-midnight; L12,000. All other museums open 8:30am-1:50pm; closed on the 2nd and 4th Su of the month and the 1st, 3rd, and 5th M. L4000.)*

BOBOLI GARDENS. With geometrically sculpted hedges, contrasting groves of holly and cypress trees, and bubbling fountains, the elaborate gardens are an exquisite example of stylized Renaissance landscaping. You'll want to get lost (or picnic) in this sea of green, which stretches from behind the Palazzo Pitti all the way up the hill to the **Forte di Belvedere,** built for Grand Duke Ferdinand I and once the Medici fortress and treasury. The fort, a star-shaped construction by Buontalenti with a central *loggia* designed by Ammannati, now hosts summer exhibitions and tanning exhibitionism. *(From P. Santa Felicità, to the right as you face the Ponte Vecchio from the Palazzo Pitti, ascend Costa di S. Giorgio to reach the fortress. Gardens open daily June-Aug. 8:15am-7:30pm; Sept.-Oct. and Apr.-May 9am-6:30pm; Nov.-Feb. 9am-5pm; Mar. 8am-6pm. Closed 1st and last M of each month. L4000, EU citizens with passport L2000.)*

CHIESA DI SANTA MARIA DEL CARMINE. Inside, the **Brancacci Chapel** holds Masaccio's 15th-century frescoes, declared masterpieces even in their time. With such monumental works as the *Tribute Money*, this chapel became a school for many artists, including Michelangelo. *(Open M and W-Sa 10am-5pm, Su 1-5pm. L6000.)*

ENTERTAINMENT

In June, the *quartieri* of Florence turn out in costume to play their own medieval version of soccer, known as **calcio storico,** in which two teams of 27 players face off over a wooden ball in one of the city's *piazze.* Tickets (from L20,000) are sold at the box office. The **Festival of San Giovanni Battista** (June 24) features a tremendous fireworks display in Ple. Michelangelo (easily visible from the Arno) starting around 10pm. May starts the summer music festivals with the classical **Maggio Musicale.** The **Estate Fiesolana** (June-Aug.) fills the Roman theater in nearby Fiesole with concerts, opera, theater, ballet, and film. September brings the **Festa dell'Unità,** a concert series at Campi Bisenzia (take bus #30). On the **Festa del Grillo** (Festival of the Cricket; the 1st Sunday after Ascension Day), crickets in tiny wooden cages are hawked in the Cascine park to be released into the grass.

NIGHTLIFE

For info on what's hot in the nightlife scene, consult the monthly *Firenze Spettacolo* (L3000). Begin your nighttime *passeggiata* along V. dei Calzaiuoli and end it with coffee or *gelato* in a ritzy cafe on P. della Repubblica, where singers prance about the stage in front of **Bar Concerto.** In the Oltrarno, **P. San Spirito** has plenty of bars and restaurants, and live music in summer.

Amadeus, on V. dei Pescioni, two blocks from the Duomo. The "best German beer at the best price in town" is served here to a relaxed crowd. Open daily 4pm-1am.

Dolce Vita, in P. del Carmine. Open-air bar with tables on the beautiful *piazza.* Hip local *giovani* come for occasional live music. Open M-Sa 10pm-1:30am, Su 5pm-1:30am.

The William, V. Magliabechi 7/9/11r. New, trendy pub for Italians and tourists in the know. Rowdy and packed on weekends; mellower on weeknights. Open M-Sa 6pm-2am.

The Lion's Fountain, in P.G. Salvemini, down V. Proconsolo from the Duomo and left on Borgo degli Albizi. Friendly, English-speaking crowd. Open M-Th 6pm-2am, F 6pm-2:30am, Sa 3pm-2:30pm, Su 3pm-2am.

Angie's Pub, V. dei Neri 35r. Very Italian (despite the name). this pub caters mostly to students. Imported beer and cider from L4000. Open M-Sa noon-3pm and 7pm-1am.

Meccanò, V. degli Olmi 1, near Parco delle Cascinè. The most popular of Florence's discos among locals and tourists alike. Cover L25,000; includes 1 drink. Subsequent drinks L10,000. Open Tu-Sa 11pm-4am.

Central Park, in Parco della Cascinè. Open-air dance floor pulses with hip-hop, jungle, reggae, and something Italians call "dance rock." Open 9pm-late.

Blob, V. Vinegia 21r, behind the Palazzo Vecchio. DJs, movies, foosball, and an evening bar buffet. Talk to the club's manager about the AiCS card needed for admission; the card offers entry to over 20 establishments in Florence (L15,000). Open 6pm-late.

EXCURSIONS FROM FLORENCE

SIENA. You can't go wrong with any of the Tuscan towns surrounding Florence; make sure to absorb the gracious medieval architecture in Siena (see below), easily accessible by train from Florence (1½hr.).

SIENA

Many travelers rush directly from Rome to Florence, ignoring gorgeous, medieval Siena. But the city proudly celebrates a rich history in the arts, politics, and commerce. One of Italy's largest celebrations is the semiannual **Palio,** a wild horse race among the city's 17 competing districts.

PRACTICAL INFO, ACCOMMODATIONS, AND FOOD. From P. Rosselli, **trains** (☎05 77 28 01 15) go to Florence (1½hr., every hr., L8800) and Rome via Chiosi (2½hr., every hr., L31,400). Take **TRA-IN/SITA** bus #4, 7-10, 14, 17, or 77 from opposite the station to the central P. del Campo (L1400); buy tickets from vending machines. Express **TRA-IN/SITA buses** (☎05 77 20 42 45) link P. S. Domenico 1, near the heart of the city, with Florence (every hr., L12,000). The central **tourist office** is at Il Campo 56. (☎05 77 28 05 51; fax 05 77 27 06 76. Open Apr.-Oct. M-Sa 9am-7pm; Nov.-Mar. M-Sa 9am-7pm.) **Prenotazioni Alberghiere,** in P. S. Domenico, finds rooms for L3000. (☎05 77 28 80 84. Open Apr.-Oct. M-Sa 9am-8pm; Nov.-Mar. 9am-7pm.) Check **email** at **Internet Train,** V. Pantaneto 54. (Open M-F 10am-11pm, Su 4-9pm.) Tasteful **Albergo Tre Donzelle** is at V. Donzelle 5. (☎05 77 28 03 58. Flexible curfew 1am. Singles L50,000; doubles L80-100,000.) Take bus #15, 35, or 36 (20min.) from P. Gramsci, opposite the station, to reach the **Ostello della Gioventù "Guidoriccio" (HI),** V. Fiorentina 89, in Località Lo Stellino. (☎057 75 22 12. Breakfast included. Curfew 11:30pm. Dorms L24,000.) **Piccolo Hotel Etruria,** V. Donzelle 3, has immaculate, modern rooms. (☎05 77 28 80 88. Breakfast L7000. Curfew 12:30am. Singles L65-75,000; doubles with bath L112,000; triples with bath L156,000; quads L192,000.) To **camp** at **Colleverde,** Strada di Scacciapensieri 47, take bus #3 or 8 from P. Gramsci. (☎05 77 28 00 44. Open mid-Mar. to mid-Nov. L15,000 per person and tent.) Siena specializes in pastries such as *panforte,* a concoction of honey, almonds, and citron; indulge at **Bar/Pasticceria Nannini,** V. Banchi di Sopra 22-24. From P. del Duomo, take V. del Capitano to P. della Postierla and turn left on V. di Stalloreggi for **Osteria il Tamburino** at #11. (Cover L1000. *Primi* L8-15,000; *secondi* L10-25,000. Open M-Sa noon-2:30pm and 7-9:30pm.) **Consortio Agrario supermarket,** V. Pianigiani 5, is off P. Salimberi. (Open M-F 7:45am-1pm and 4:30-8pm, Sa 7:45am-1pm.) **Postal code:** 53100.

SIGHTS AND ENTERTAINMENT. The salmon-colored **Piazza del Campo** (Il Campo) is the focus of Sienese life; the **Fonte Gaia** is fed by the same aqueduct that Siena used in the 1300s. At the bottom, the **Torre del Mangia** clock tower looms over the graceful Gothic **Palazzo Pubblico.** (Palazzo and tower open July-Aug. daily 10am-11pm; Mar.-June and Sept.-Oct. M-Sa 9am-6pm, Su 9am-1:30pm; Nov.-Feb. daily 10am-6pm. Tower L10,000.) Inside, the **Museo Civico** contains excellent Gothic and early Renaissance painting; the **Sala del Mappamondo** and the **Sala della Pace** contain stellar works. (Same hours as the *palazzo.* L12,000, students L7000. Combined ticket with tower L18,000.) Siena's Gothic **duomo** was built on the edge of a hill; the apse would have been left hanging in mid-air if not for the construction of the lavishly decorated **baptistery** below. (Duomo open daily Jan. to mid-Mar. and Nov.-Dec. 7:30am-1:30pm and 2:30-5pm; mid-Mar. to Oct. 7:30am-7:30pm. Free. Baptistery open daily mid-Mar. to Oct. 9am-7:30pm; Nov. to mid-Mar. 10am-1pm and 2:30-5pm. L3000.) The **Libreria Piccolomini,** off the left aisle, holds frescoes and exquisite 15th-century musical scores. (Open mid-Mar. to Oct. 9am-7:30pm; Nov. to mid-Mar. 10am-1pm and 2:30-5pm. L2000.) To reach the *duomo,* face the Palazzo Pubblico and take the stairs nearest the Palazzo on the right; cross V. di Città and continue on the same twisting street. The **Museo dell'Opera della Metropolitana,** next to the cathedral, houses its overflow art. (Open mid-Mar. to Sept. 9am-7:30pm; Oct. 9am-6pm; Nov. to mid-Mar. 9am-

1:30pm. L6000.) The **biglietto cumulativo,** valid for three days, covers the baptistery, Piccolomini library, and Museo dell'Opera Metropolitana (L9500; in winter L8500).

The central event of the **Palio di Siena** (July 2 and Aug. 16) is a traditional bareback horse race around the packed P. del Campo. Get there three days early to watch the rambunctious horse selection in the *campo* (10am) and to pick a *contrada* (neighborhood) for which to root. For tickets and a list of rooms to let, write the tourist office by March; arrive without a reservation and you'll be on the streets.

EXCURSION FROM SIENA: SAN GIMIGNANO. The hilltop village of San Gimignano looks like an illumination from a medieval manuscript. Its famous towers earned its nickname as the *Città delle Belle Torri* (City of Beautiful Towers). Scale the **Torre Grossa,** the tallest remaining tower, attached to **Palazzo del Popolo,** for a panorama of Tuscany. (Torre open Mar.-Oct. daily 9:30am-7:20pm; Nov.-Feb. Sa-Th 10:30am-4:20pm. L8000, students 6000. Palazzo open Tu-Su 9am-7:30pm.) In the shadow of the Torre Grossa, the **Museo Civico** houses an amazing collection of Sienese and Florentine works. (Open same hours as *Torre Grossa.* L7000, students 5000. Combined with *Torre Grossa* L12,000, students L9000.) From the bus station, pass through the *porta,* climb the hill, and follow V. San Giovanni to the central P. della Cisterna and P. del Duomo. *Affitte camere* (doubles), at around L75,000, are a good alternative to overpriced hotels. Get a list from the **tourist office,** P. del Duomo 1 (☎05 88 94 00 08; open daily Mar.-Oct. 9am-1pm and 3-7pm; Nov.-Feb. 9am-1pm and 2-6pm), or the **Associazione Strutture Extralberghiere,** P. della Cisterna 6 (☎05 77 94 31 90; open daily Mar.-Nov. 9:30am-7:30pm). For the **Ostello di San Gimignano,** V. delle Fonti 1, turn off V. S. Matteo onto V. XX Settembre and follow the signs. (☎05 77 94 19 91. Breakfast and sheets included. Reception daily 7-9am and 5-11:30pm. Curfew 11:30pm. Open Mar.-Oct. Dorms L26,000. Cash only.) **Camp** at **Il Boschetto,** at Santa Lucia, 2.5km downhill from Porta S. Giovanni; a bus (L1500) runs from Porta S. Giovanni. (☎05 77 94 03 52. Hot showers included. Reception daily 8am-1pm, 3-8pm, and 9-11pm. Open Apr. to mid-Oct. L8500 per person and small tent.) A **market,** at V. S. Matteo 19, sells filling sandwiches and pasta. (Open Mar.-Oct. daily 9am-8pm; Nov.-Feb. M-W and F-Sa 9am-8pm, Th 9am-1pm.)

PISA

Tourism hasn't always been Pisa's prime industry: during the Middle Ages, the city was a major port with an empire extending to Corsica, Sardinia, and the Balearics. But when the Arno River silted up and the tower started leaning, the city's power and wealth declined accordingly. Today the city welcomes tourists and vendors to the **Piazza del Duomo,** also known as the **Campo dei Miracoli** (Field of Miracles), a grassy expanse enclosing the tower, *duomo,* baptistery, and Camposanto. An **all-inclusive ticket** to the Campo's sights costs L18,000. To reach the Campo from the train station, take bus #1 (L1500), or walk straight up V. Gramsci, through P. Vittorio Emanuele, and down C. Italia across the Arno, continue on V. Borgo Stretto, turn left on any street branching west, and continue through the old town. Begun in 1173, the famous **Leaning Tower** had reached a height of 10m when the soil beneath suddenly shifted; the tower slips 1-2mm every year. Visitors are no longer allowed to enter. The dazzling **duomo,** also on the Campo, is a treasury of fine art. (Open late Apr. to late Sept. 8am-7:45pm; off season reduced hours. L3000. Su mass free, but piety is a must.) Next door is the **baptistery,** whose acoustics allow an unamplified choir to be heard 2km away. (Open daily late Apr. to late Sept. 8am-7:45pm; off season 9am-4:40pm.) The adjoining **Camposanto,** a cloistered cemetery, has a series of haunting frescoes by an unidentified 14th-century artist known only as the "Master of the Triumph of Death." (Same hours as baptistery.) The **Museo delle Sinopie,** across the *piazza* from the Camposanto, displays preliminary fresco sketches by Traini, Veneziano, and Gaddi found during post-WWII restoration. Behind the tower is the **Museo dell'Opera del Duomo.** (Both open daily late Apr. to late Sept. 8am-7:45pm; off season 9am-4:40pm. Joint ticket L10,000, EU citizens free.) From the Campo, walk down V. S. Maria and over the bridge to the Gothic **Chiesa di Santa Maria della Spina,** whose bell tower supposedly holds a thorn from Christ's crown.

Trains (☎14 78 08 88) go from P. della Stazione, in the southern part of town, to Florence (1hr., every hr., L8000-10,000); the main coastal line serves Genoa (2½hr., L23,200) and Rome (3hr., L42,300). The **tourist office** is to the left as you exit the station. (☎05 04 22 91; www.turismo.toscana.it. Open daily May-Oct. 8am-8pm; Nov.-Apr. 9am-7pm.) The **Centro Turistico Madonna dell'Acqua Hostel,** V. Pietrasantina, 15, is 1km from the tower. Take bus #3 from the station (4 per hr.) and ask for the *ostello.* (☎050 89 06 22. Kitchen. Sheets L5000. Reception 6-11pm. Check-out 9am. Dorms L23,000; doubles L60,000; triples L90,000; quads L108,000.) The **Albergo Gronchi,** P. Archivescovado, 1, just off P. del Duomo, has frescoed ceilings. (☎050 56 18 23. Curfew midnight. Singles L35,000; doubles L58,000; triples L78,000; quads L98,000.) **Marcovaldo,** V. S. Martino, 47, has great food but no table service. (*Primi* L7000, *secondi* L10,000. Open M-Sa noon-10pm.) Get **groceries** at **Superal,** V. Pascoli, 6, just off C. Italia. (Open M-Sa 8am-8pm.) **Postal code:** 56100.

UMBRIA

Umbria is known as the "Green Heart of Italy," a land rich in natural beauty, encompassing wild woods and fertile plains, craggy gorges and tiny cobblestone villages. Christianity transformed Umbria's architecture and regional identity, turning it into a breeding ground for saints and religious movements; it was here that St. Francis of Assisi shamed the extravagant church with his humility.

PERUGIA

The extremely polite residents of Perugia may be trying to make up for two millennia of excessive nastiness, during which their ancestors regularly stoned each other. The city's most visited sights frame **Piazza IV Novembre,** on the north end. In the middle of the piazza the **Fontana Maggiore** is adorned with sculptures and bas-reliefs by Nicolà and Giovanni Pisano. The 13th-century **Palazzo dei Priori** impresses with the immense collection of the **Galleria Nazionale dell'Umbria,** C. Vannucci 19. (Open daily 9am-8pm; closed 1st M of each month. L8000.) Perugia's imposing Gothic **duomo** is also in the piazza. (Open daily 8am-noon and 4pm-dusk.) The **Basilica di San Pietro,** on C. Cavour, at the end of town past the Porta S. Pietro, maintains its original 10th-century layout. (Open daily 8am-noon and 4pm-dusk.)

The **FS train station,** P. V. Veneto, serves: Assisi (25min., every hr., L3200); Siena (every hr., L14,500); Florence (2½hr., every hr., from L14,500); and Rome (3hr., direct 2½hr.; L20,600). From the station, take bus #6, 7, or 9 to the central P. Italia (L1200), then take C. Vannucci to P. IV Novembre and the **tourist office,** in P. IV Novembre. (☎07 55 72 33 27. Open M-Sa 8:30am-1:30pm and 3:30-6:30pm, Su 9am-1pm.) To get from there to **Ostello della Gioventù/Centro Internazionale di Accoglienza per la Gioventù,** V. Bontempi 13, pass the *duomo* and P. Danti, take the farthest street right through P. Piccinino, and turn right on V. Bontempi. (☎07 55 72 28 80; email ostello@edisons.it. Sheets L2000. Kitchen. Lockout 9:30am-4pm. Curfew midnight. Open mid-Jan. to mid-Dec. L18,000.) **Albergo Anna,** V. dei Priori 48, off C. Vannucci, has clean, cool 17th-century rooms with great views. (☎07 55 73 63 04. Singles L50,000; doubles L80-100,000; triples L95-120,000.) **Trattoria Dal Mi Cocco,** C. Garibaldi 12, up from the University for Foreigners, offers an extremely generous L25,000 *menù.* (Open Tu-Su 1-2:30pm and 8:15-10:30pm.) The **COOP,** P. Matteoti 15, has **groceries.** (Open M-Sa 9am-8pm.) **Postal code:** 06100.

ASSISI

The undeniable jewel of Assisi, and even of Umbria, is the **Basilica di San Francesco,** which details the life of monk St. Francis with spectacular frescoes. From P. del Commune, take V. Portica. (Open Easter-Nov. M-Sa 6:30am-7pm, Su 6:30am-7:30pm; off season open daily 6:30am-6pm; no visits on Su morning or holidays.) The dramatic fortress **Rocca Maggiore** towers above town, offering panoramic views. (Open daily Sept.-June 10am-dusk, July-Aug. 9am-dusk. L5000, students L3500.) The pink and white **Basilica of Santa Chiara** is back in the town center. (Open M-F daily 7am-noon and 2-7pm.)

From the station near the Basilica Santa Maria degli Angeli, **trains** go to: Ancona (from L20,200); Florence (2 per day, L16,500); and Rome (1 per day, from L16,500); more frequent trains go to Rome via Foligno and to Florence via Ternotola. ASP **buses** run from P. Matteoti to Perugia (1½hr., 7 per day, L5000) and elsewhere in Umbria. From P. Matteotti, follow V. del Torrione, bear left in P. S. Rufino, and take V. S. Rufino to the town center. The **tourist office,** P. del Comune, is down V. Mazzini. (☎075 81 25 34; fax 075 81 37 27. Open M-F 8am-2pm and 3:30-6:30pm, Sa 9am-1pm and 3:30-6:30pm, Su 9am-1pm.) For **Ostello della Pace (HI),** V. di Valecchi 177, turn right out of the station, then left at the intersection on V. di Valecchi. (☎/fax 075 81 67 67. Breakfast included. Laundry. Reception 7-9:15am and 3:30-11:30pm. Check-out 9:30am. Reserve ahead. L22,-27,000.) Peaceful **Camere Annalisa Martini,** V. S. Gregorio 6, is in the medieval core of Assisi. (☎075 81 35 36. Laundry. Singles L38-40,000; doubles L58-60,000; triples L80,000.) **Postal code:** 06081.

THE MARCHES (LE MARCHE)

In the Marches, green foothills separate the gray shores of the Adriatic from the Apennine peaks and the traditional hill towns from the umbrella-laden beaches. Inland towns, easily accessible by train, rely on agriculture and preserve the region's historical legacy in the architectural remains of Gauls and Romans.

URBINO

Urbino's fairy-tale skyline, scattered with humble stone dwellings and an immense turreted palace, has changed little over the past 500 years. The city's most remarkable monument is the looming Renaissance **Palazzo Ducale** (Ducal Palace), in P. Rinascimento, though its facade is more thrilling than its interior. The central **courtyard** is the essence of Renaissance balance and proportion; to the left, stairs lead to the former private apartments of the Duke, which now house the **National Gallery of the Marches.** (Open M 8:30am-2pm, Tu-F 8:30am-7pm, Sa 8:30am-7pm and 8-11pm. L8000.) Walk back across P. della Repubblica and continue onto V. Raffaello to the **Casa di Rafaele,** at #57, now a museum that contains Raphael's earliest work, *Madonna e Bambino*. (Open M-Sa 9am-1pm and 3-7pm, Su 10am-1pm. L5000.)

Bucci **buses** (☎072 13 24 01) go from Borgo Mercatale to Rome (5hr., 1 per day, L30,000). Blue SOBET **buses** (☎22 23 33) run along the Bologna-Lecce rail line along the Adriatic coast. From there, a short walk uphill on V. G. Mazzini leads to **P. della Repubblica,** the city center. The **tourist office,** P. Rinascimento 1, is opposite the palace. (☎07 22 26 13. Open in summer M-Sa 9am-1pm and 3-7pm, Su 9am-1pm; off season M-Sa 9am-1pm and 3-6pm.) **Pensione Fosca,** V. Raffaello 67, top floor, has high-ceilinged rooms; reserve ahead to get a room. (☎07 22 32 96 22. Singles L40,000; doubles L60,000; triples L80,000.) The **Hotel San Giovanni,** V. Barocci 13, has a restaurant. (☎07 22 28 27. Open Aug.-June. Singles L35-53,000; doubles L50-80,000.) **Camping Pineta,** on V. San Donato, is 2km away in Cesane; take bus #4 or 7 from Borgo Mercatale and ask to get off at "camping." (☎/fax 07 22 47 10. Reception 9-11am and 3-10pm. Open Apr. to mid-Sept. L10,000 per person; L20,000 per tent.) **Supermarket Margherita** is at V. Raffaello 37. (Open M-Sa 7:30am-2pm and 4-8pm.)

EXTRA, EXTRA! Newspapers cover scandalous events, but in Southern Italy this phrase has literal meaning. The old newspapers that cover the windshields of parked cars often serve not to keep out the sun's heat but to conceal the more torrid heat produced from within. Beware, virgin eyes—it is the age-old art of *l'amore*.

ANCONA

Ancona is the center point of Italy's Adriatic Coast—a major port in a small, whimsical, and largely unexplored city. **Piazza Roma** is dotted with yellow and pink buildings, and **Piazza Cavour** is the heart of the town. **Adriatica** (☎071 20 49 15; www.adriatica.it), **Jadrolinija** (☎07 12 07 14 65; www.jadrolinija.hr/jadrolinija), and **SEM Maritime Co.** (☎071 20 40 90; www.sem.hr) send **ferries** to Croatia (from L66-80,000). **ANEK** (☎07 12 07 23 46) and **Strintzis** (☎207 10 68) ferries go to Greece (from L62-82,000); Strintzis also sends ferries to Venice. Ferry schedules and tickets are available at the Stazione Marittima; reserve ahead in July or August. **Trains** (☎07 14 24 74) arrive at P. Rosselli from: Bologna (2½hr., 1-2 per hr., from L18,600); Rome (3-4hr., 9 per day, L24,300-41,000); Milan (5hr., 24 per day, from L25,600); and Venice (5hr., 3 per day, from L26,300). Take bus #1 or 1/4 along the port past **Stazione Marittima** and up C. Stamira to reach P. Cavour. A branch of the **tourist office** is located in Stazione Marittima and provides ferry info. (Open June-Sept. M-Sa 8am-8pm, Su 8am-2pm.) From the train station, cross the *piazza*, turn left, then take the 1st right, and make a sharp right up the steps behind the newsstand to reach the new **Ostella della Gioventù,** V. Lamaticci 7. (☎/fax 07 14 22 57. Checkout 10am. L23,000.) **CONAD supermarket** is at V. Matteotti 115. (Open M-W and F 8:15am-1:30pm and 5-7:30pm, Th 8:15am-1:30pm, Sa 8:15am-12:45pm and 5-7:40pm.)

SOUTHERN ITALY

South of Rome, the sun gets brighter, the meals longer, and the passion more intense. The introduction to the *mezzogiorno* (Italian South) begins in Campania, the fertile crescent that cradles the Bay of Naples and hugs the Gulf of Salerno. In the shadow of Mount Vesuvius lie the famous Roman ruins of Pompeii, frozen in time in a bed of molten lava. In the Bay of Naples, Capri is Italy's answer to Fantasy Island, while the Amalfi Coast cuts a dramatic course down the lush Tyrrhenian shore. Though long subject to the negative stereotypes and prejudices of the more industrialized North, the region remains justly proud of its open-hearted populace, strong traditions, classical ruins, and relatively untouristed beaches.

NAPLES (NAPOLI)

Italy's 3rd-largest city is also its most chaotic: shouting merchants flood markets, stoplights are merely suggestions, and summer traffic jams clog the broiling city. But despite Naples's poverty and notorious pickpockets, the city's color and vitality, evident in the markets off V. Toledo and in the world's best pizza, defy its rough-edged image. In recent years, aggressive restoration has opened monuments and art treasures to the public for the first time, rewarding travelers with exquisite churches, artisans' workshops, and colorful *trattorie* in the narrowest of alleys.

GETTING THERE AND GETTING AROUND

Trains: Ferrovie dello Stato goes from Stazione Centrale to **Rome** (2hr., 38 per day, L18,600); **Brindisi** (5hr., 5 per day, L35,600); and **Milan** (8hr., 13 per day, L96,000). **Circumvesuviana** (☎08 17 72 24 44), also in the station, heads for local destinations.

Ferries: Depart from **Molo Angioino** and **Molo Beverello,** at the base of P. Municipio. From P. Garibaldi, take tram #1; from P. Municipio, take the R2 bus. **Caremar,** Molo Beverello (☎08 15 51 38 82), goes frequently to **Capri** and **Ischia** (both 1½hr., L9800-18,000). **Tirrenia Lines,** Molo Angioino (☎08 17 20 11 11), goes to **Palermo, Sicily** (11hr., 1 per day, L85,00) and **Cagliari, Sardinia** (15hr., 2 per week in summer, L98,000). L10,000 port tax. Schedules and prices change; check *Qui Napoli*.

Public Transportation: Giranapoli tickets (1½hr. L1500; full-day L4500) are valid on **buses, Metropolitana** (subway), **trams,** and **funiculars.**

Taxis: Cotana (☎08 15 70 70 70) or **Napoli** (☎08 15 56 02 02). Take metered taxis.

ORIENTATION AND PRACTICAL INFORMATION

The main train and bus terminals are in the immense **Piazza Garibaldi** on the east side of Naples. From P. Garibaldi, broad **Corso Umberto I** leads southwest to Piazza Bovi, from which Via De Pretis leads left to **Piazza Municipio,** the city center, and **Piazza Trieste e Trento** and **Piazza Plebiscito.** Below P. Municipio lie the **Stazione Marittima** ferry ports. From P. Trieste e Trento, **Via Toledo** (a.k.a. **Via Roma**) leads through the Spanish quarter to **Piazza Dante.** Make a right into the historic **Spaccanapoli** ("splitting Naples") district, which follows **Via dei Tribunali** through the middle of town. While violence is rare in Naples, petty theft is relatively common (unless you're in the Mafia, in which case the opposite is true). Always be careful.

Tourist Offices: EPT (☎081 26 87 79), at Stazione Centrale. Helps with hotels and ferries, but long lines. Grab a map and *Qui Napoli.* Open M-Sa 9am-8pm. **Branches** at P. dei Martiri 58 and Stazione Mergellina.

Consulates: South Africa, C. Umberto I (☎08 15 51 75 19). **UK,** V. Crispi 122 (☎081 66 35 11). M: P. Amedeo. Open July-Aug. M-F 8am-1:30pm; Sept.-June M-F 9am-12:30pm and 2:30-4pm. **US** (☎08 15 83 81 11; in emergency ☎081 03 37 94 50 83), in P. della Repubblica at the west end of Villa Comunale. Open M-F 8am-5pm.

Currency Exchange: Thomas Cook, P. Municipio 70 (☎08 15 51 83 99) and at the airport. Open M-F 9:30am-1pm and 3-6:30pm.

Emergencies: ☎113. **Ambulance:** ☎08 17 52 06 96.

Hospital: Cardarelli (☎08 17 47 11 11), north of town on the R4 bus line.

Police: ☎113 or 08 17 94 11 11. **Carabinieri:** ☎112. English spoken.

Internet Access: Internetbar, P. Bellini 74. L5000 per 30min. Open M-F 9am-2am and Sa-Su 9pm-2am. **Internet Multimedia,** Via Sapienza 43. L3000 per hr. Scanning, printing available. Open 9:30am-9:30pm.

Post Office: P. Matteotti, at V. Diaz (R2 line). Address mail to be held: First name, SURNAME, *In Fermo Posta,* P. Matteotti, Naples **80100,** Italy. Open M-F 8:15am-6pm, Sa 8:15am-noon.

ACCOMMODATIONS

The area near **P. Garibaldi** is packed with safe, comfortable hotels, while rooms are scarce in the historic district between P. Dante and the *duomo*. Be cautious: avoid hotels that solicit customers at the station, never give your passport until you've seen the room, agree on the price *before* unpacking, be alert for unexpected costs, and gauge how secure a lodging seems.

Casanova Hotel, V. Venezia 2 (☎081 26 82 87; email hcasanov@tin.it). From P. Garibaldi, follow V. Milano and turn left at the end. Clean, airy rooms, and a rooftop terrace. Breakfast L8000. Reserve ahead. V, MC, AmEx. Prices with *Let's Go:* singles L25,000; doubles L50,000, with bath L80,000; triples L100,000; quads L110,000.

Hotel Eden, C. Novara 9 (☎081 28 53 44). From the station, turn right and continue down the street; the large hotel is on the left. Breakfast L5000. V, MC, AmEx. Prices with *Let's Go:* singles L42,000; doubles L66,000; triples L90,000; quads L108,000.

Soggiorno Imperia, P. Miraglia 386 (☎081 45 93 47). Take the R2 from the train station, walk up V. Mezzocannone through P. S. Domenico Maggiore, and enter the first set of green doors to the left on P. Miraglia. Bright rooms in a 16th-century *palazzo.* Call ahead. Singles L35,000; doubles L55-65,000; triples L80,000.

6 Small Rooms, 18 Vio Diodata Lioy (☎08 17 90 13 78). Half a block north of P. Monteoliveto. New hotel with pleasant atmosphere. Kitchen. Breakfast included. No curfew. Dorms L30,000; private rooms L40,000 per person.

FOOD

Pizza-making is an art born in Naples; you can't go wrong. **Pizzeria Di Matteo,** V. Tribunali 94, near V. Duomo, draws a crowd of pizza lovers. President Clinton ate

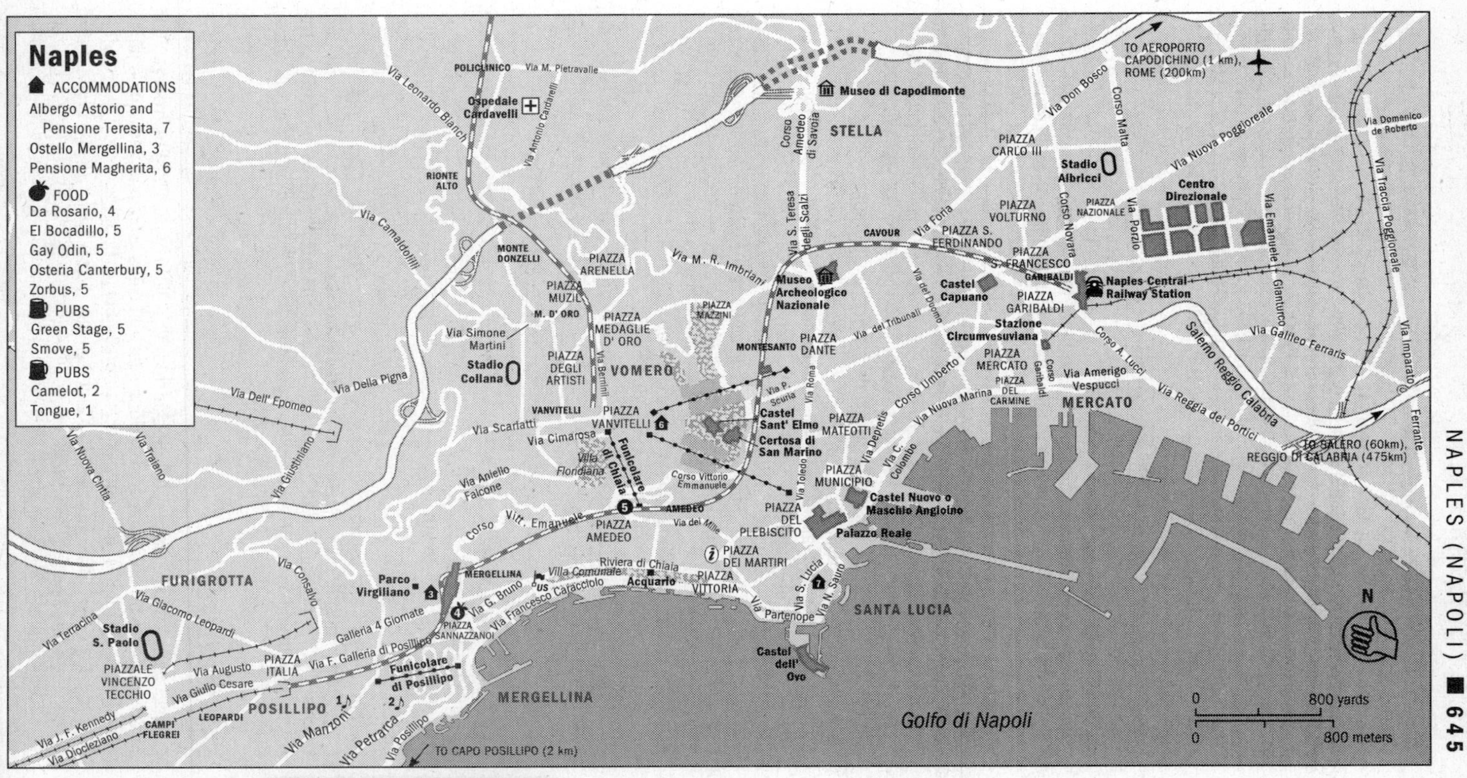
Naples
ACCOMMODATIONS
Albergo Astorio and Pensione Teresita, 7
Ostello Mergellina, 3
Pensione Magherita, 6
FOOD
Da Rosario, 4
El Bocadillo, 5
Gay Odin, 5
Osteria Canterbury, 5
Zorbus, 5
PUBS
Green Stage, 5
Smove, 5
PUBS
Camelot, 2
Tongue, 1
TO AEROPORTO CAPODICHINO (1 km), ROME (200km)
TO SALERO (60km), REGGIO DI CALABRIA (475km)
TO CAPO POSILLIPO (2 km)
Golfo di Napoli
N
800 yards
800 meters
Museo di Capodimonte
STELLA
Ospedale Cardavelli
POLICLINICO
RIONTE ALTO
MONTE DONZELLI
PIAZZA CARLO III
Stadio Albricci
Centro Direzionale
PIAZZA VOLTURNO
PIAZZA NAZIONALE
CAVOUR
PIAZZA S. FERDINANDO
PIAZZA S. FRANCESCO
GARIBALDI
Naples Central Railway Station
Museo Archeologico Nazionale
Castel Capuano
PIAZZA GARIBALDI
Stazione Circumvesuviana
PIAZZA ARENELLA
PIAZZA MUZIL
M. D' ORO
PIAZZA MEDAGLIE D' ORO
PIAZZA MAZZINI
MONTESANTO
PIAZZA DANTE
PIAZZA MERCATO
PIAZZA DEL CARMINE
MERCATO
Stadio Collana
PIAZZA DEGLI ARTISTI
VOMERO
VANVITELLI
PIAZZA VANVITELLI
Castel Sant' Elmo
Certosa di San Marino
PIAZZA MATEOTTI
Villa Floridiana
Funicolare di Chiaia
AMEDEO
PIAZZA AMEDEO
PIAZZA MUNICIPIO
Castel Nuovo o Maschio Angioino
PIAZZA DEL PLEBISCITO
Palazzo Reale
PIAZZA DEI MARTIRI
PIAZZA VITTORIA
FURIGROTTA
Parco Virgiliano
MERGELLINA
Villa Comunale
Acquario
SANTA LUCIA
Castel dell' Ovo
Stadio S. Paolo
PIAZZA SANNAZZANO
PIAZZA ITALIA
PIAZZALE VINCENZO TECCHIO
Funicolare di Posillipo
CAMPI FLEGREI
LEOPARDI
POSILLIPO
MERGELLINA
Via M. Pietravalle
Via Leonardo Bianchi
Via Antonio Cardarelli
Via Camaldolilli
Via Don Bosco
Corso Malta
Via Nuova Poggioreale
Via Domenico de Roberto
Via Traccia Poggioreale
Corso Amedeo di Savoia
Via S. Teresa degli Scalzi
Via M. R. Imbriani
Via Foria
Corso Novara
Via Porzio
Via Emanuele Gianturco
Via Galileo Ferraris
Salerno Reggio Calabria
Via Imparato
Ferrante
Via del Duomo
Via del Tribunali
Corso A. Lucci
Via Reggia dei Portici
Via Amerigo Vespucci
Corso Garibaldi
Corso Umberto I
Via Nuova Marina
Via Simone Martini
Via Bernini
Via Roma
Via P. Scuria
Via Della Pigna
Via Dell' Epomeo
Via Scarlatti
Via Cimarosa
Via Depretis
Via C. Colombo
Via Nuova Cintia
Via Traiano
Via Giustiniano
Via Aniello Falcone
Corso Vittorio Emanuele
Via Toledo
Corso Vitt. Emanuele
Via dei Mille
Riviera di Chiaia
Via Consalvo
Via Terracina
Via Giacomo Leopardi
Galleria 4 Giomate
Via G. Bruno
Via Francesco Caracciolo
Via Partenope
Via S. Lucia
Via N. Sauro
Via Augusto
Via F. Galleria di Posillipo
Via Giulio Cesare
Via J. F. Kennedy
Via Diocleziano
Via Manzoni
Via Petrarca
Via Posillipo

ITALY

here during the 1994 G-7 Conference and denies ever having had relations with the pizza. (*Margherita* L4000. Open M-Sa 9am-midnight.) To get to **Antica Pizzeria da Michele,** V. Cesare Sersale 1/3, walk up C. Umberto from P. Garibaldi and take the first right. Michele makes only two traditional pizzas, and he makes them right; *marinara* (tomato, garlic, oregano, and oil) and *margherita* (tomato, mozzarella, and basil). (L6000. Open M-Sa 8am-11pm.) Arguably the best pizza in Naples is at **Pizzeria Trianon da Ciro,** V. Pietro Colletta 42/44/46, a block off C. Umberto I. (L5500-12,500; 15% service charge. Open daily 10am-4:30pm and 6:30pm-midnight.) If you tire of pizza (who are we kidding?), head to the side streets around **P. Amedeo** for the beloved local *zuppa di cozze* (mussels in broth with octopus).

SIGHTS AND ENTERTAINMENT

MUSEO ARCHEOLOGICO NAZIONALE. This world-class collection houses exquisite treasures from Pompeii and Herculaneum, including the outstanding "Alexander Mosaic." The sculpture collection is also impressive. *(From M: P. Cavour, turn right and walk 2 blocks. Open M and W-F 9am-7:30pm, Sa-Su 9am-8pm. L15-60,000.)*

MUSEO AND GALLERIE DI CAPODIMONTE. This museum, in a royal *palazzo*, is surrounded by a pastoral park of woods and sprawling lawns. You can inspect the plush royal apartments, but the true gem is the **Farnese Collection,** with works by Bellini and Caravaggio. *(Take bus #110 from P. Garibaldi to Parco Capodimonte; enter by Portas Piccola or Grande. Open Tu-F 10am-7pm, Sa 10am-midnight, Su 9am-8pm. L14,000.)*

PALAZZO REALE AND CASTEL NUOVO. The 17th-century **Palazzo Reale** contains the **Museo di Palazzo Reale,** opulent royal apartments, and a fantastic view from the terrace of the **Royal Chapel.** The **Biblioteca Nazionale** stores 1.5 million volumes, including the scrolls from the **Villa dei Papiri** in Herculaneum. The **Teatro San Carlo** is reputed to top the acoustics in Milan's La Scala. *(Take the R2 bus from P. Garibaldi to P. Trieste e Trento and go around to the P. Plebiscito entrance. Open M-Tu and Th-F 9am-8pm. L8000.)* From P. Trieste e Trento, walk up V. Vittorio Emanuele III to P. Municipio for the five-turreted **Castel Nuovo,** built in 1286 by Charles II of Anjou. The double-arched entrance commemorates the arrival of Alphonse I of Aragon in Naples. Inside, admire the **Museo Civico.** *(Open M-Sa 9am-7pm. L10,000.)*

DUOMO. The main attraction of the 14th-century *duomo* is the **Capella del Tesoro di San Gennaro** on the right. A beautiful 17th-century bronze grille protects the high altar, which holds a gruesome display of relics with the saint's head and two vials of his coagulated blood. Supposedly, disaster will strike if the blood does not liquefy on the celebration of his *festa* (twice a year); miraculously, it always does. *(3 blocks up V. Duomo from C. Umberto I. Open M-F 9am-noon and 4:30-7pm, Sa-Su 9am-noon. Free.)*

SPACCANAPOLI. This renowned east-west neighborhood "splits" the city in two (reflected in its name) with its gorgeous architecture, meriting at least a 30-minute stroll. From P. Dante, walk through Porta Alba and P. Bellini before turning down V. dei Tribunali, which traces an old Roman road. Along V. dei Tribunali, you'll see the churches of **San Lorenzo Maggiore** and **San Paolo Maggiore.** Take a right on V. Duomo and another on V. San Biago into the heart of the area to meander past the **University of Naples** and the **Chiesa di San Domenico Maggiore,** where, according to legend, a painting once spoke to St. Thomas Aquinas. *(In P. S. Domenico Maggiore. Open daily 7:15am-12:15pm and 4:15-7:15pm. Free.)*

NIGHTLIFE

P. Vanvitelli in Vomero (take the funicular from V. Toledo or the C28 bus from P. Vittoria) is where the cool kids go. Outdoor bars and cafes are a popular choice in **P. Bellini** (near P. Dante). Pub-goers flock to **Green Stage,** P. S. Pasquale 15. From P. Amedeo, take V. Vittorio Colonna to V.S. Pasquale. (Open Tu-Th 7:30pm-3am, F-Su 7:30pm-4am.) **1799,** P. Bellini 70, mixes eerie trance music with dark decor. (Open Tu-Th 10am-1am, F-Su 10am-3am.) **Camelot,** V. Petrarca 101, in Posillipo, is a typical disco, with pop, house, and dance. (Cover L25,000. Open Oct.-May F-Sa midnight-4am.) **Tongue,** V. Manzoni 207, in Posillipo, features visiting DJs. (Take nightbus #404d from P. Garibaldi. Cover L25,000. Open Oct.-May F-Sa 11pm-4am.) **ARCI-Gay/Lesbica** (☎ 08 15 51 82 93) has information on gay and lesbian nights at local clubs.

EXCURSIONS FROM NAPLES

Mount Vesuvius, the only active volcano on the European continent, looms over the area east of Naples. Its infamous eruption in AD 79 buried the nearby Roman city of **Ercolano** (Herculaneum) in mud, and neighboring **Pompei** (Pompeii) in ashes.

POMPEII. Since 1748, excavations have unearthed a stunningly well-preserved picture of Roman daily life. The site hasn't changed much since then, and neither have the victims, whose ghastly remains were partially preserved by plaster casts in the hardened ash. Walk down V. D. Marina to reach the **Forum,** surrounded by a colonnade and once the commercial, civic, and religious center of the city. Exit the Forum through the upper end, by the cafeteria, and head right on V. della Fortuna to reach the **House of the Faun,** where a bronze dancing faun and the spectacular Alexander Mosaic (today in the Museo Archeologico Nazionale) were found. Continue on V. della Fortuna and turn left on V. dei Vettii to reach the **House of the Vettii,** on the left, and the most vivid frescoes in Pompeii. Back down V. dei Vettii, cross V. della Fortuna to V. Storto, turn left on V. degli Augustali, and take a quick right to reach a small **brothel** (the Lupenar). After 2000 years, it's still the most popular place in town. V. dei Teatri, across the street, leads to the oldest standing **amphitheater** in the world (80 BC), which once held up to 12,000 spectators. To get to the **Villa of the Mysteries,** the complex's best-preserved villa, head west on V. della Fortuna, right on V. Consolare, and all the way up Porta Ercolano. (Pompeii open daily in summer roughly 9am-7pm; off season 9am-3pm. L16,000.) Take the Circumvesuviana **train** from Naples or Sorrento to "Pompeii Scavi/Villa dei Mistert" (about L3000; Eurail passes not valid). To reach the site, head downhill and take your first left to the west (Porta Marina) entrance. To get to the **tourist office,** P. Porta Marina Inferiore 12, walk right from the station and continue to the bottom of the hill. (Open M-F 8am-3:30pm, Sa 8am-2pm.) Bring lunch and water.

HERCULANEUM. Herculaneum is 500m downhill from the "Ercolano" stop on the Circumvesuviana Line train (from Naples 20min., L2200). Stop at the **tourist office,** V. IV Novembre 84, to pick up a free **map.** The city is less excavated than Pompeii, but the 15-20 houses open to the public were so neatly dug up that the tour feels like an invasion of privacy. (Open daily 9am-1hr. before dusk. L16,000.)

MT. VESUVIUS. You can peer into the only active volcano on mainland Europe at Mt. Vesuvius. Trasporti Vesuviani **buses** (L6000; buy tickets on the bus) run from the Ercolano Circumvesuviana station to the crater. Although Vesuvius hasn't erupted since March 31, 1944 (scientists say volcanoes should erupt every 30 years), experts deem the trip safe.

AMALFI COAST. The dramatic scenery and pulsing nightlife of the towns on the Amalfi Coast are easily accessible from Naples by train, ferry, and bus (see p. 647).

BAY OF NAPLES. Only an hour away from Naples by ferry, the isles of Capri and Ischia tempt travelers with luscious beaches and enchanting grottos. (see p. 649).

AMALFI COAST

The beauty of the Amalfi coast is one of extremes and contrasts. Immense rugged cliffs plunge downwards into calm azure waters, while coastal towns climb the sides of narrow ravines. The picturesque villages provide stunning natural panoramas, delicious food, and throbbing nightlife.

GETTING THERE AND GETTING AROUND. The coast is accessible from Naples, Sorrento, Salerno, and the islands by **ferry** and blue SITA **bus. Trains** run directly to Salerno from Naples (45min., 32 per day, L5100-17,100); Rome (2½-3hr., 18 per day, L22-45,000); Florence (5½-6½hr., 7 per day, L49-79,000); and Venice (9hr., 1 per day, L64,000). They continue to Paestum (40min., 9 per day, L4700). From Salerno, Travelmar (☎089 87 31 90) runs **ferries** to Amalfi (1hr., 3 per day, L9000) via Positano (40min., L7000). From Sorrento, Linee Marittime Partenopee (☎081 878 14 30) **ferries** run to Amalfi (45min., 2 per day, L16,000) via Positano (30min., 7 per day, L13,000); and Capri (50min., 3 per day, L9000). From Amalfi they service Salerno (30min., 9 per day, L16,000).

AMALFI AND ATRANI. A small coastal ravine hides **Amalfi,** which nevertheless exudes noise and chaos worthy of a city many times its size. Visitors crowd the waterfront and admire the elegant, Moorish-influenced 9th-century **duomo,** rebuilt in the 19th century. **A'Scalinatella,** P. Umberto 12, has hostel beds and regular rooms all over Atrani and Amalfi. (☎089 87 19 30. Dorms L20-35,000; doubles L50-120,000; **camping** L15,000 per person.) To get to **Atrani,** a tiny ravine town unaltered by tourism, walk 10 minutes around the bend from Amalfi. Spectacular **hikes** lead through lemon groves and across mountain streams.

RAVELLO. Capping a promontory 330m above Amalfi, Ravello is ideal for quiet contemplation. The Moorish cloister and meandering gardens of **Villa Rufolo** (off P. Duomo) inspired Boccaccio's *Decameron* and Wagner's *Parsifal.* (Open daily 9am-dusk. L5000.) On the small road to the right, signs lead to the impressive **Villa Cimbrone,** where floral walkways and gardens hide temples and statued grottoes. Frequent **classical music concerts** punctuate Ravello's tranquility, especially in summer. The best rooms are at **Hotel Villa Amore.** (☎089 85 71 35. Breakfast included. Singles L80,000; doubles 120,000; off season L10,000 less.)

POSITANO. Cliffside homes and idiosyncratic locals began luring writers, artists, and actors to Positano in the early 1900s. Not surprisingly, the invention of the bikini here in 1959 heralded a marked increase in tourism. To see the large *pertusione* (hole) in **Montepertuso,** one of three perforated mountains in the world, hike 45 minutes uphill or take the bus (every hr., L1500) from any stop. Positano's **beaches** are also popular, and although boutiques may be a bit pricey, no one charges for window shopping. The **tourist office** (☎089 87 50 67) is below the *duomo.* **Ostello Brikette,** V. G. Marconi 358, 100m up the main coastal road to Sorrento from Vle. Pasitea, has incredible views from two large terraces. (☎/fax 089 87 58 57. Breakfast and sheets included. Dorms L35,000; doubles L100,000.) **Pensione Maria Luisa,** V. Fornillio 40, has seaside terraces. (☎/fax 089 87 50 23. Singles L60,000; doubles L100-120,000.) Prices in the town's restaurants reflect the high quality of the food. For a sit-down dinner, thrifty travelers head toward **Fornillo.**

SORRENTO. The most heavily touristed town on the peninsula, lively Sorrento makes a convenient base for daytrips around the Bay of Naples. Caremar **ferries** (☎08 18 07 30 77) go to Capri (50min., 3 per day, L9000). The **tourist office,** V. de Maio 35, is off P. Tasso. (☎08 18 07 40 33. Open Apr.-Sept. M-F 8:45am-7:45pm, Sa 8:45am-7:15pm; Oct.-Mar. M-Sa 8:30am-2pm and 4-6:15pm.) Halfway to the **free beach** at Punta del Capo on bus A, **Hotel Elios,** V. Capo 33, has comfy rooms. (☎08 18 78 18 12. Singles L45,000; doubles L80,000.) For extensive amenities, stay at **Hotel City,** C. Italia 221; turn left on C. Italia from the station. (☎08 18 77 22 10. Singles L75,000; doubles L120,000.) It's easy to find good, affordable food in Sorrento. **Davide,** V. Giuliani 39, off C. Italia two blocks from P. Tasso, has divine *gelato* and masterful mousse (55-80 flavors daily). After 10:30pm, a crowd gathers upstairs in the rooftop lemon grove above **The English Inn,** C. Italia 56.

SALERNO AND PAESTUM. Industrial **Salerno** is best used as a base for daytrips to nearby **Paestum,** the site of three spectacularly preserved **Doric buildings,** including the **Temple of Ceres,** the **Temple of Poseidon,** and the **basilica.** (Temples open daily 9am-1hr. before dusk. Closed 1st and 3rd M of each month. L8000.) Sleep in Salerno at the cheerful **Ostello della Gioventù "Irno" (HI),** V. Luigi Guercio 112; go left from the station on V. Torrione, then left under the bridge on V. Mobilio. (☎089 79 02 51. Breakfast included. Lockout 10:30am-3:30pm. Curfew 2am. L17,500.)

BAY OF NAPLES ISLANDS

CAPRI. The sheer bluffs, divine landscapes, and azure waters of Capri have beckoned wayfarers from the mainland since Roman times. **Capri town** is above the ports, while **Anacapri** sits higher up the mountain. From P. Umberto in Capri Town, V. Roma leads to Anacapri; **buses** also make the trip until 1:40am (taxi L20,000). The **Grotta Azzurra** (Blue Grotto) is a must-see—light enters the cavern through a hole in the rock under the water, causing the whole grotto to glow neon-blue. (Open Apr.-Oct. in good weather.) Take the bus from Capri to Anacapri and a second bus to the Grotto (L1700), or go by boat from Marina Grande (L8000). Upstairs from P. Vittoria in Anacapri, **Villa San Michele** has lush gardens, ancient sculptures, and a remarkable view of the island. (Open daily 9:30am-1hr. before dusk. L8000.) To appreciate Capri's Mediterranean beauty from higher ground, take the **chairlift** up Monte Solaro from P. Vittoria. (Open daily Mar.-Oct. 9:30am-1hr. before dusk. Round-trip L7000.) From P. Umberto in Capri take V. Longano, which becomes V. Tiberio, to **Villa Jovis** (1hr.), the most magnificent of the 12 villas that the emperor Tiberius scattered throughout Capri. (Open daily 9am-1hr. before dusk. L4000.)

Caremar **ferries** run from Marina Grande to Naples (1¼hr., 6 per day, L9800) and Sorrento (45min., 3 per day, L10,000). Linee Lauro sends **hydrofoils** to Ischia (40min., 1 per day, L20,000) and Sorrento (20min., 12 per day, L14,000); LineaJet hydrofoils go to Naples (40min., 11 per day, L17,000). The Capri **tourist office** (☎08 18 37 06 34) is at the end of Marina Grande; in Anacapri, it's at V. Orlandi 19a (☎08 18 37 15 24), to the right from the P. Vittoria bus stop. (Both open June-Sept. M-Sa 8:30am-8:30pm; Oct.-May 9am-1:30pm and 3:30-6:45pm.) In Anacapri, beautiful **Villa Eva,** V. La Fabbrica 8, will pick you up from P. Vittoria. (☎08 18 37 15 49; www.caprionline.com/villaeva. Breakfast included. Reserve ahead. Singles L50,000; doubles from L80,000; triples from L105,000; quads from L140,000.) From the last bus stop, follow the signs up the stairs to **Il Girasole,** V. Linciano 47. (☎08 18 37 23 51; fax 08 18 37 38 80. Prices with *Let's Go*: doubles from L105,000; triples L135-180,000.) In Capri, **Pensione Stella Maris,** V. Roma 27, is opposite the bus stop. (☎08 18 37 04 52; fax 08 18 37 86 62. Singles L100,000; doubles L120,000.) Get **groceries** at **STANDA** in Capri; head right at the fork at the end of V. Roma. (Open M-Sa 8:30am-1:30pm and 5-9pm, Su 9am-noon.) At night, dressed-to-kill Italians come out for Capri's *passegiatta;* bars in the streets around **P. Umberto** keep the music pumping late. Anacapri is cheaper and still loads of fun. **Postal code:** Capri: 80073; Anacapri: 80021.

ISCHIA. Across the bay from crowded Capri, larger, less glamorous Ischia (EES-kee-yah) offers luscious beaches, natural hot springs, ruins, forests, vineyards, and lemon groves. SEPSA **buses** #1, CD, and CS (every 20min., L1700, day pass L5200) follow the coast in a circular route, stopping at: **Ischia Porto,** a port formed by the crater of an extinct volcano; **Casamicciola Terme,** with a crowded beach and legendary thermal waters; **Lacco Ameno,** the oldest Greek settlement in the western Mediterranean; and finally, touristed **Forio,** which has lively bars. Caremar **ferries** (☎081 98 48 18) arrive from Naples (1½hr., 14 per day, L9800). **Linee Marittime Partenopee** (☎081 99 18 88) runs hydrofoils from Sorrento (L18,000). Stay in Ischia Porto only if you want to be close to the ferries, restaurants, and nightlife. Most *pensioni* are in Forio; **Pensione Di Lustro,** V. Filippo di Lustro 9, is near the beach. (☎081 99 71 63. Breakfast included. Doubles L90-120,000.) The **Ostello "Il Gabbiano" (HI),** Strada Statale Forio-Panza 162, between Forio and Panza, is accessible by bus #1, CS, or CD and has beach access. (☎081 90 94 22. Breakfast included. Lockout 10am-1pm. Curfew 12:30am. Open Apr.-Sept. Around L30,000.) **Camping Internazionale** is at V. Foschini 22, 15 minutes from the port. Take V. Alfredo de Luca from V. del Porto; bear right on V. Michele Mazzella at P. degi Eroi. (☎081 99 14 49. Open mid-Apr. to mid-Oct. L16,000 per person; L10,000 per tent; 2-person bungalows L80,000.)

SICILY (SICILIA)

With a history so steeped in chaos, catastrophe, and conquest, it's no wonder that the island of Sicily possesses such passionate volatility. The tempestuousness of Sicilian history and political life is matched only by the island's dramatic landscapes, dominated by craggy slopes. Entire cities have been destroyed in seismic and volcanic catastrophes, but those that have survived have lived up to the cliché and grown stronger; Sicilian pride is a testament to resilience during centuries of occupation and destruction.

GETTING THERE AND GETTING AROUND

Tirrenia ferries (Palermo ☎091 33 33 00) offers extensive service. From southern Italy, take a **train** to **Reggio di Calabria,** then the NGI or Meridiano **ferry** (40min., 12 per day, L1000) or Ferrovie Statale **hydrofoil** (☎09 65 86 35 40; 20min., 14 per day, L5000) to **Messina,** Sicily's transport hub. Ferries also go to **Palermo** from **Cagliari, Sardinia** (14hr., L60,500-107,000); **Naples** (11hr., 1 per day, L68-99,000); and **Genoa** (20hr., 6 per week, L123-181,000). **SAIS Trasporti** (☎09 16 17 11 41) and **SAIS** (☎09 16 16 60 28) buses serve destinations throughout the island, including Corleone (perhaps you've seen *The Godfather?*). **Trains** also chug to **Messina** directly from **Naples** (4½hr., 4 per day, L38,500) and **Rome** (9hr., 4 per day, L53,000). Trains continue west to **Palermo** (3½hr., 16 per day, L19,500) via **Milazzo** (L4500) and south to **Syracuse** (3hr., 12 per day, L16,000) via **Taormina** (1hr., 12 per day, L5500).

PALERMO

Sicily's capital, Palermo is notorious as the cradle of Italian organized crime; the city has recently begun cleaning up its politics and revitalizing its historic district. To get to the **Teatro Massimo,** where the climactic opera scene of *The Godfather Part III* was filmed, walk up V. Maqueda past the intersection of Quattro Canti and C. Vittorio Emanuele. (Open Tu-Su 10am-4pm for 20min. tours.) Up C. Vittorio Emanuele, the **Palazzo dei Normanni** contains the **Cappella Palatina,** with a carved stalactite ceiling and an incredible cycle of golden Byzantine mosaics. (Open M-Sa 9-11:45am and 3-4:45pm.) The **Cappuchin Catacombs** in P. Cappuccini are only for the strong of stomach. Eight thousand corpses in moth-eaten attire line the underground labyrinth. To get there, take bus #109 or 318 from the central station to P. Indipendenza and hop on bus #327. (Open M-Su 9am-noon and 3-5:30pm. L2500.)

Direct **trains** run from P. Giulio Cesare, at V. Roma and V. Maqueda, to Rome (11½hr., 4 per day, L67,000) and Milan (17½hr., 3 per day, L91,600). All four SAIS Trasporti **bus lines** are located on V. Balsamo, next to the train station. Ask one of the mini-offices for a combined metro and bus map. After purchasing tickets, ask exactly where your bus will arrive and its logo. The **tourist office,** P. Castelnuovo 34, is opposite Teatro Politeama; from the train station, take any bus showing "Politeama" on its overhead screen to P. Politeama, at the end of V. Maqueda. (☎09 16 05 83 51. Open M-F 8:30am-6pm, Sa 9am-2pm and 4-7pm, Su 9am-1pm.) Homey **Hotel Regina,** C. Vittorio Emanuele 316, is near V. Maqueda. (☎09 16 11 42 16. Kitchen. Singles L30-45,000; doubles L55-80,000.) To reach the **Petit Hotel,** V. Principe di Belmonte 84, take V. Roma from the train station, walk six blocks (past V. Cavour), and turn left. (☎091 32 36 16. Singles L35,000; doubles L65,000; triples L90,000.) **STANDA supermarket** is at V. Roma 59. (Open M 4-8pm, Tu and Th-Su 9am-1pm and 4-8pm, W 9am-1pm.) **Postal code:** 90100.

AEOLIAN ISLANDS (ISOLE EOLIE)

Home of the wind god Aeolus and the Sirens, the Aeolian (or Lipari) Islands, with their long, rocky beaches, boast some of Italy's last few stretches of unspoiled seashore. Volcanoes belching fire and smoke are often an easy hike from sea level.

LA FAMIGLIA Pin-striped suits, machine guns, horse heads, and the Godfather are a far cry from the reality of the Sicilian Mafia. The system has its roots in the *latifondi* (agricultural estates) of rural Sicily, where land managers and salaried militiamen (a.k.a. landlords and bouncers) protected their turf and people. Powerful because people owed them favors, strong because they supported one another, and feared because they did not hesitate to kill offenders, they founded a tradition that has dominated Sicilian life since the late 19th century. Since the mid-80s, the Italian government has worked to curtail Mafia influence, with visible results. Today Sicilians shy away from any Mafia discussion, referring to the system as *Cosa Nostra* (our thing).

GETTING THERE AND GETTING AROUND. The archipelago lies off Sicily, north of **Milazzo,** the principal embarkation point. Hop off a **train** from **Messina** (40min., 18 per day, L4500) or **Palermo** (3hr., L15,500) and onto an orange AST **bus** for the port (10min., every 30min., L1500). There, Navigazione Generale Italiana (☎09 09 28 40 91) and Siremar (☎09 09 28 32 42) **ferries** depart for: **Lipari** (2hr., L10,500-12,500); **Vulcano** (1½hr., L10-12,000); and **Stromboli** (5hr., L16,500-20,000). Siremar and SNAV (☎09 09 28 45 09) **hydrofoils** (*aliscafi*) make the trip in half the time but cost almost twice as much. All three have ticket offices on V. Dei Mille facing the port in Milazzo. Ferries leave for the islands less frequently from Naples' Molo Beverello port. Ferries between Lipari and Vulcano or Stromboli cost L4500.

LIPARI. Lipari, the largest and most developed island, makes a great base, with cheap hostels, great beaches, and hopping nightlife. The small promontory is crowned by a medieval **castello,** the site of an ancient Greek acropolis. The fortress shares its hill with an **archaeological park,** the **San Bartolo church,** and the superb **Museo Archeologico Eoliano,** where English captions explain Lipari's history and artifacts. (☎09 09 88 01 74. Open May-Oct. M-Su 9am-1:30pm and 4-7pm; Nov.-Apr. M-Su 9am-1:30pm and 3-6pm. L8000.) Rent a bike to explore the **beaches** or **pumice mines,** or find a fisherman willing to ferry you to the island's even tinier beaches. The popular **Spiaggia Bianca** and **Spiaggia Porticello** beaches are often the spot for semi-nude sunbathing; to get there, take the Lipari-Cavedi **bus** to Canneto.

The AAST **tourist office,** C. Vittorio Emanuele 202, is up the street from the ferry dock. (☎09 09 88 00 95; fax 09 09 81 11 90; email infocast@netnet.it. Open July-Aug. M-Sa 8am-2pm and 4-10pm, Su 8am-2pm; Sept.-June M-F 8am-2pm and 4:30-7:30pm, Sa 8am-2pm.) Down a quiet street in the center of town, **Casa Vittorio,** Vico Sparviero 15, offers a variety of rooms. (☎/fax 09 09 81 15 23. If the door is locked, continue to the end of the street and turn right; the owner lives at the red iron gate. May-July singles L30-40,000; doubles L60-70,000.) An exhilarating 20-minute scooter ride away, **Tivoli (Quatropani),** sits on the northwest cliffs 500m above the sea. (☎09 09 88 60 31. June L30,000; July L35,000; Aug. L40,000. Discounts for children.) **Camp** at **Baia Unci,** V. Marina Garibaldi 2, 2km from Lipari at the entrance to the hamlet of Canneto. (☎09 09 81 19 09; fax 09 09 81 17 15. Open mid-Mar. to mid-Oct. Reserve in Aug. June-Aug. L15-19,000 per person with tent.) Stock up at **UPIM supermarket,** C. Vittorio Emanuele 212. (Open M-Sa 8am-3:20pm and 4-11pm.) **Freeway Disco,** a lamp-lit pirate ship, leaves for Vulcano's Euro-disco from the Lipari docks. A mixed crowd bounces around on board until the early morning hours. (Purchase tickets at Salvatore's shorefront stand. L20,000.) **Postal code:** 98055.

STROMBOLI. Stromboli's active **volcano** spews orange cascades of lava and molten rock nightly (roughly every 10min.). From July to September, however, forget finding a room without a reservation. **Hiking** the *vulcano* on your own, particularly the descent, is illegal and dangerous, but **Guide Alpine Autorizzate** offers tours. (☎090 98 62 11. Tours depart from P. Vincenzo M, W, and Sa-Su 5:30pm; return midnight. L35,000.) Bring sturdy shoes, a flashlight, snacks, water, and warm clothes.

LATVIA (LATVIJA)

LATS

US$1 = 0.61LS (LATS)	1LS = US$1.60
CDN$1 = 0.41LS	1LS = CDN$2.40
UK£1 = 0.89LS	1LS = UK£1.10
IR£1 = 0.69LS	1LS = IR£1.40
AUS$1 = 0.35LS	1LS = AUS$2.80
NZ$1 = 0.26LS	1LS = NZ$3.80
SAR1 = 0.09LS	1LS = SAR11
DM1 = 0.28LS	1LS = DM3.60
EUR€1 = 0.55LS	1LS = EUR€1.84

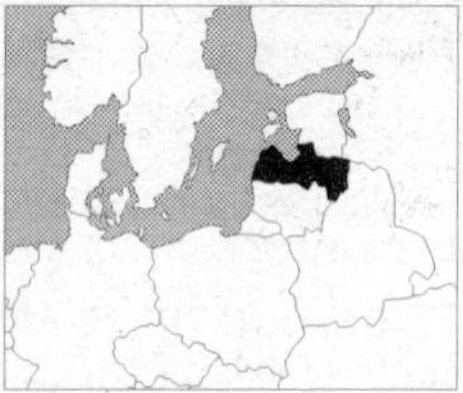

Country code: 371. **International dialing prefix:** 00. From outside Latvia, dial int'l dialing prefix (see inside back cover) + 371 + city code + local number.

With the smallest majority of natives of the three Baltic States, Latvia remains the least affluent and developed. Except for a brief period of independence that ended with WWII, Latvia was ruled by Germans, Swedes, and Russians from the 13th century until 1991. A half-century of Soviet occupation resulted in a mass exodus of Latvians and a huge influx of Russians. Attitudes toward the many Russians who still live in the country are softening, but evidence of national pride abounds, from patriotically renamed streets bleeding with crimson-and-white flags to a rediscovery of native holidays predating Christian invasions. Although the rest of the country is mostly a provincial expanse of green hills dominated by tall birches and pines, Rīga is a westernizing capital luring more and more international companies.

For more on Latvia's self re-discovery, snag *Let's Go: Eastern Europe 2001*.

FACTS AND FIGURES

Official Name: Republic of Latvia.
Government: Parliamentary democracy.
Capital: Rīga (pop. 874,000).
Land Area: 64,589 sq. km.
Geography: Low plain.
Climate: Maritime; wet, moderate winters, and temperate, pleasant summers.
Population: 2.4 million.
Languages: Latvian, Lithuanian, Russian.
Religions: Lutheran, Roman Catholic, Russian Orthodox.
Income Per Capita: US$4100.
Major Exports: Wood and wood products, machinery and equipment, metals.

ESSENTIALS

DOCUMENTS AND FORMALITIES

Irish, UK, and US citizens can visit Latvia for up to 90 days without a **visa.** Citizens of Australia, Canada, New Zealand, and South Africa require 90-day visas, obtainable at a Latvian consulate. Travelers may obtain 10-day visas at the airport in Rīga. Single-entry visas cost US$15; multiple-entry cost US$30 to US$75; 48-hour processing costs twice as much, 24-hour four times. For extensions, apply to the Department of Immigration and Citizenship, Raiņa bulv. 5 (☎721 91 81; fax 782 01 56).

EMBASSIES AND CONSULATES

All foreign embassies are in **Rīga** (see p. 654).

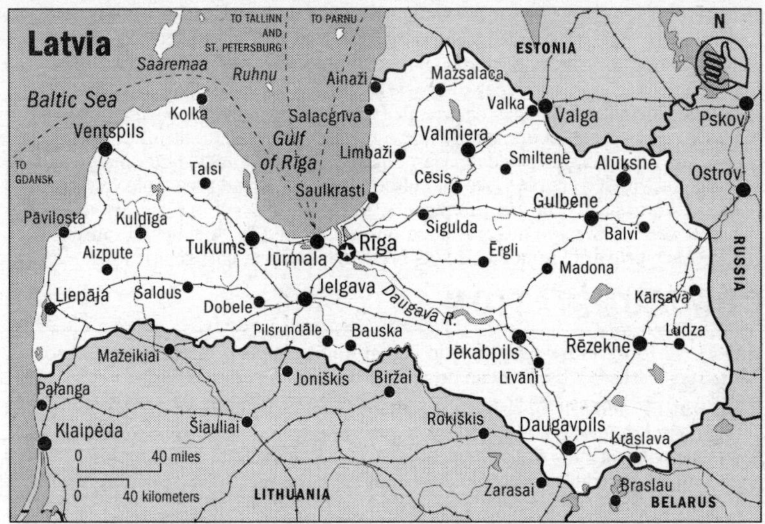

Latvian Embassies at Home: Australia, P.O. Box 457, Strathfield NSW 2135 (☎ (02) 97 44 59 81; fax 97 47 60 55); **Canada,** 280 Albert St. Ste. 300, Ottawa, ON K1P 5G8 (☎ (613) 238 60 14; fax 238 70 44; www.mgmacom.com~latemb/); **South Africa** (consulate), Bedford Centre, 17th fl., Bedfordview, P.O. Box 34, Cyrildene 2026, Johannesburg (☎(011) 614 22 43; fax 614 30 75); **UK,** 45 Nottingham Pl., London W1M 3FE (☎ (0171) 312 00 40; fax 312 00 42); **US,** 4325 17th St. NW, Washington, DC 20011 (☎ (202) 726 82 13; fax 726 67 85; www.latvia-usa.org).

GETTING THERE AND GETTING AROUND

Air Baltic, SAS, Finnair, Lufthansa, and others fly into Rīga's airport. **Trains** link Latvia to Berlin, Moscow, St. Petersburg, Tallinn, Lviv, Odessa, and Vilnius. Trains are cheap and efficient, but stations aren't well-marked, so get a map. The **suburban rail** system renders the entire country a suburb of Rīga. **Eurail** is not valid. Latvia's quicker **bus** network reaches Prague, Tallinn, Vilnius, and Warsaw. For daytrips from Rīga, you're best off taking the **electric train. Ferries** run to Rīga from Stockholm, Sweden and Kiel, Germany. **Hitchhiking** is common, but hitchers may be expected to pay. *Let's Go* does not recommend hitchhiking.

TOURIST SERVICES AND MONEY

In an **emergency,** call ☎01 for **fire,** ☎02 for the **police,** and ☎03 for **ambulance.** Look for the green "i" marking some **tourist offices,** which are rather scarce. Private tourist offices such as **Patricia** are much more helpful.The Latvian **currency** unit is the **Lat,** divided into 100 *santims.* There are many **ATMs** in Rīga linked to Cirrus, MC, and Visa, and at least one or two in larger towns. Larger businesses, restaurants, and hotels accept **MC** and **Visa. Traveler's checks** are harder to use; both AmEx and Thomas Cook can be converted in Rīga, but Thomas Cook is a safer bet outside the capital. It's often difficult to exchange currencies other than US dollars and Deutschmarks. If a **tip** is expected where you're dining, it will most often be included in the bill. Hostel beds run US$7-10, hotels US$10-15, and meals US$5-10.

ACCOMMODATIONS AND FOOD

College dormitories, which open to travelers in the summer, are often the cheapest places to sleep. In Rīga, **Patricia** arranges homestays and apartment rentals for around US$15 per night (see p. 655). Many towns have only one **hotel** (if any) in the budget range; expect to pay 3-15Ls per night.

Latvian food is heavy and starchy, but tasty. Big cities offer foreign cuisine, and Rīga is one of the easiest places to be a **vegetarian** in all the Baltics. Tasty national specialties include the holiday dish *zirņi* (gray peas with onions and smoked fat), *maizes zupa* (bread soup usually made from corn bread, and full of currants, cream, and other goodies), and the warming *Rīgas* (or *Melnais*) *balzams* (a black liquor great with ice cream, Coke, or coffee). Dark rye bread is a staple. Try *speķa rauši*, a warm pastry, or *biezpienmaize*, bread with sweet curds. Dark-colored *kaņepju sviests* (hemp butter) is good but too diluted for "medicinal" purposes. Latvian **beer,** primarily from the Aldaris brewery, is stellar, particularly *Porteris.*

COMMUNICATION

MAIL. Ask for *gaisa pastu* to send something by **airmail.** Letters abroad cost 0.40Ls, postcards 0.30Ls. **Mail** can be received through *Poste Restante.*

TELEPHONES. Most telephones take **phone cards** (available in 2, 3, 5, or 10Lt denominations) from post offices, telephone offices, and large state stores. Try to make **international** calls from a telephone office. The switch to digital phones has made calling incredibly complicated—sometimes you must dial a 2 before a number, sometimes a 7, and sometimes an 8 from an analog phone. To call abroad from an analog phone, dial 1, then 00, then the country code. From a digital phone, simply dial 00, then the country code. **International direct dial** numbers include **AT&T Direct,** ☎ 700 70 07 in Rīga, ☎ 827 00 70 07 otherwise, and **MCI,** ☎ 800 88 88.

LANGUAGES. Heavily influenced by German, Russian, Estonian, and Swedish, **Latvian** is one of two Baltic languages (the other is Lithuanian). **Russian** is in disfavor in the countryside but is more acceptable and widespread in Rīga. Many young Latvians study **English.** Older Latvians know some **German.**

HOLIDAYS AND FESTIVALS

Holidays: New Year's Day (Jan. 1); Good Friday (Apr. 11); Catholic Easter (Apr. 15-16); Labor Day (May 1); Memorial Day (May 31); Ligo (Midsummer Festival; June 23-24); Independence Day (1918; Nov. 18); Ziemsvetki (Christmas; Dec. 25-26); and New Year's Eve (Dec. 31).

RĪGA ☎ 02

The self-proclaimed capital of the Baltics, Rīga (pop. 825,000) envisions itself as the "Paris of the East," a city of museums, architecture, and diplomacy. Nonetheless, it feels more like Vegas than Paris, with 24-hour casinos on every street. While the city has a long way to go to becoming a major European capital, it has admirably established a new identity as the cultural and social center of the Baltics. Rīga promises to be the place to be in 2001 as it celebrates its 800th birthday in style.

GETTING THERE AND GETTING AROUND

Flights: Lidosta Rīga (☎ 720 70 09), 8km southwest. Take bus #22 from Gogol iela.

Trains: Centrālā Stacija (Central Station) Stacijas laukums (☎ 583 30 95), down the street from the bus station, behind the giant digital clock tower, with long-distance trains in the larger building to the left. To: **Vilnius** (8hr., 1 per day, 14Ls); **St. Petersburg** (13hr., 1 per day, 26Ls); and **Moscow** (15½hr., 2 per day, 32Ls).

Buses: Bus station (Autoosta), Prāgas 1, (☎ 721 36 11). 200m closer to the Daugava River than the train station, across the canal from the central market. To: **Tallinn** (5-6hr., 7 per day, 6-7Ls); **Vilnius** (6hr., 3 per day, 6Ls); and **Minsk** (10hr., 2 per day, 6.90Ls). **Eurolines** (☎ 721 40 80; fax 750 31 34), at the bus station right of the ticket windows, goes to **Warsaw** (14hr., 1 per day, 15Ls) and **Prague** (30hr., 1 per week, 38Ls). Open M-F 8am-7pm, Sa 9am-6pm.

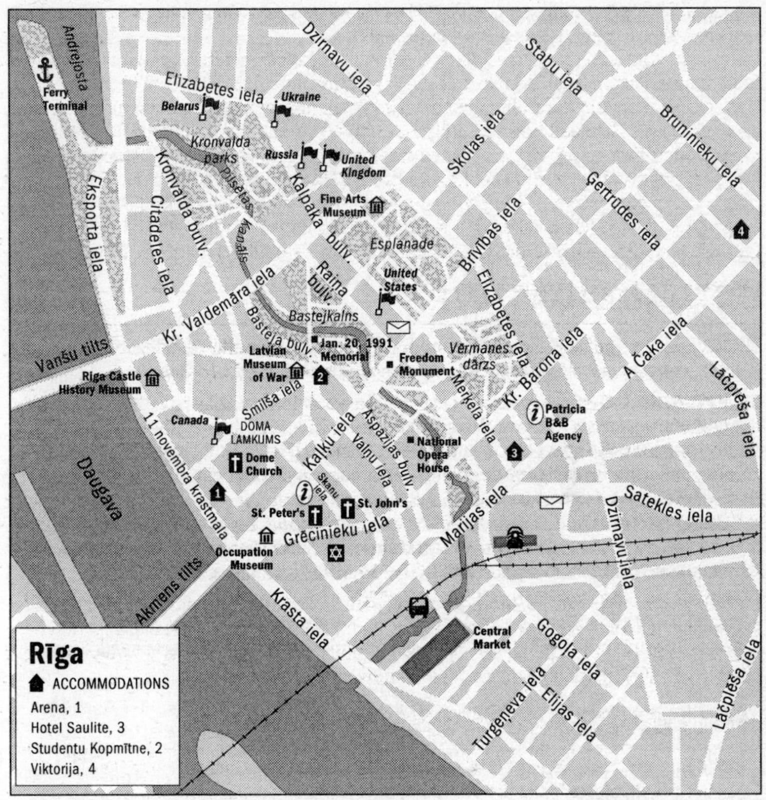

ORIENTATION AND PRACTICAL INFORMATION

The city is neatly divided in half by **Brīvības bulvāris,** which leads from the outskirts to the **Freedom Monument** in the center, continuing through **Vecrīga** (Old Rīga) as **Kaļķu iela.** With the trains behind you, turn left on the busy Marijas iela and right on any of the small streets beyond the canal to reach Vecrīga. For good **maps** and tons of info, pick up *Riga in Your Pocket* (0.60Ls) at kiosks, hotels, or travel agencies.

Tourist Office: Patricia, Elizabetes iela 22-26, 3rd fl. (☎925 67 31), 2 blocks from the train station. Arranges home stays in Vecrīga (US$15 per person) and can help with Russian visas (6-day US$80). Open M-F 9:15am-8pm, Sa-Su 10:15am-1pm.

Embassies: Belarus, Jēzusbaznīcas 12 (☎732 25 50; fax 732 28 91). Open M-F 8:30am-5pm. **Canada,** Doma laukums 4, 3rd and 4th fl. (☎722 63 15; fax 783 01 40). Open M-F 9am-3pm. **Estonia,** Skolas iela 13 (☎781 20 20; fax 781 20 29). Open M-Tu, Th-F 10am-1pm. **Lithuania,** Rūpniecības iela 24 (☎732 15 19; fax 732 15 89). Open M-F 9:30am-12:30pm. **Russia,** Antonijas iela 2 (☎721 25 79; fax 783 02 09). Open M-F 9am-5:30pm. **UK,** Alunāna iela 5 (☎733 81 26; fax 733 81 32). Open M-F 9am-1pm and 2-5pm. **US,** Raiņa bulv. 7 (☎721 00 05; fax 782 00 47). Open M-F 9am-noon and 2-4pm.

Currency Exchange: At any of the *Valutos Maiņa* kiosks or shops in the city. **Unibanka,** Kaļķu iela 13, with long hours, gives cash advances for a 4% commission and cashes AmEx and Thomas Cook traveler's checks for a 3% commission. **ATMs** are common.

Luggage Storage: In the bus station, on guarded racks near the Eurolines office (0.20Ls per 2hr. for 10kg). Open daily 6:30am-10:30pm. At the train station, **lockers** (0.60Ls) are in the tunnel under the long-distance tracks. Open daily 5am-1am.

Pharmacies: Mēness aptieka, Brīvības 121 (☎737 78 89). Open 24hr.

Internet Access: Internet Club, Kaļķu iela 10, 2nd fl. (☎750 35 95). This Internet addict's dream is open 24hr. 1.80Ls per hr. **Latnet,** Raiņa 29 (☎721 12 41). 0.22Ls per hr. Open M-Th 9am-6pm, F 9am-5pm.

Telephones: Brīvības bulv. 19 (☎701 87 38), or at the post office by the train station. Open 24hr.

Post Offices: Stacijas laukums 1 (☎701 88 04), near the train station. *Poste Restante* at window 2. Open M-F 8am-7pm, Sa 8am-4pm, Su 8am-4pm. Address mail to be held: First name SURNAME, *Poste Restante,* Stacijas laukums 1, Riga, **LV-1050** Latvia.

ACCOMMODATIONS AND FOOD

Rīga's prices for decent rooms are generally the highest in the Baltics. If you are interested in a **private room,** try your luck with **Patricia** (see **Tourist Office,** above).

Arena, Palasta iela 5 (☎722 85 83). Unmarked, by Dome Cathedral; the cheapest place in town. Open Apr.-Oct. 4Ls.

Studentu Kopmītne (Student Dormitories), Basteja bul. 10 (☎721 62 21). From the bus station, cross under the railroad tracks, take the pedestrian tunnel under the highway, and bear right on Aspazijei bul. (which becomes Basteja bul). Call ahead. Curfew midnight. 4-9Ls per person.

Saulite, Merķela iela 12 (☎722 45 46), directly opposite the train station. Spiral sea foam green staircase branches off to clean and communal toilets. English spoken. Shared shower 0.40Ls. Singles 6-16Ls; doubles 10-20Ls; triples 9-25Ls.

Viktorija, A. Čaka iela 55 (☎701 41 11; fax 701 41 40). Eight blocks from the trains on Marijas iela (which becomes Čaka iela), or 2 stops on trolleybus #11 or 18. More expensive, newly renovated rooms and old, cheaper rooms. Breakfast included. Singles 8-26Ls; doubles 10-38Ls.

Look for 24-hour food and liquor stores along **Elizabetes, Marijas,** and **Gertrūdes iela.** The **Centrālais Tirgus** (Central Market) is one of the largest in Europe. (Open M-Sa 8am-5pm, Su 8am-3pm.) Descend from the entrance on Arsenāla to **Alus Arsenāls,** Pils Laukums 4, for cheap, excellent Latvian cuisine. (Open daily 11am-midnight.)

SIGHTS

VECRĪGA (OLD RĪGA). Take time to peruse Vecrīga's winding streets and ponder its unusual architecture. From the top of the dark, 123m spire of **St. Peter's Church** (Sv. Pētera baznīca; c. 1209), you can see the entire city and the Baltic. *(On Kungu iela, off Kaļķu iela. Open Tu-Su 10am-7pm. Church free. Tower 1.50Ls, students 1Ls.)* Follow Skārņu iela, opposite the church, to Jāņa iela and the small **St. John's Church** (Sv. Jāņa baznīca); an alleyway on the left leads to **St. John's Courtyard** (Jāņa sēta), the oldest populated site in Rīga, where the city's first castle stood. *(Church open Tu-Su 11am-6pm.)* Follow Kungu iela across Kaļķu iela and take a right on Jauniela into cobblestone **Dome Square,** the home of Rīga's centerpiece, the **Dome Cathedral** (Doma baznīca), begun in 1226. *(Open Tu-F 1-5pm, Sa 10am-2pm. 0.50Ls. Concerts W and F 7pm.)* Follow Jēkaba iela to Smilšu iela to eight floors of fun and eight centuries of destruction at the **Latvian Museum of War** (Latvijas kara muzejs), Smilšu iela 20, inside the cannon-ball studded walls of the **Powder Tower,** Rīga's most interesting military site. *(Open Tu-Su 10am-6pm. 0.50Ls, students 0.25Ls. Foreign-language tours 3Ls.)*

LATVIA

FREEDOM MONUMENT AND ENVIRONS. In the center of the city stands the beloved **Freedom Monument** (Brivibas Piemineklis; affectionately known as "Milda"). *(At the corner of Raiņa bul. and Brīvības iela.)* Continuing along Kaļķu iela from the Freedom Monument toward the river, you'll see the **Latvian Riflemen Monument,** in honor of Lenin's famous bodyguards, one of the few Soviet monuments not torn down. Rising behind the statues are the black walls of the

Occupation Museum (Okupācijas muzejs), Strēlnieku laukums 1, perhaps the finest museum in the Baltics. The initial Soviet occupation is depicted so vividly that you can almost hear the Red Army marching through the streets of Rīga. *(Open daily 11am-5pm. Free.)* Just beyond the museums stands the unusual and magnificent **Blackheads House** (Ratslavkums 7). Built in 1344 and completely destroyed between the Nazis and the Soviets, it has been reconstructed in honor of Rīga's 800th birthday in 2001.

BASTEJKALNS. A central park near the old city moat **Pilsētas kanāls,** Bastejkalns houses ruins of the old city walls. Across and around the canal, five red stone slabs stand as memorials to the dead of January 20, 1991, when Soviet special forces stormed the Interior Ministry on Raiņa bul. At the north end of Bastejkalns, on Kr. Valdemāra iela, sits the **National Theater,** where Latvia first declared its independence on November 18, 1918. *(Open M-F 10am-7pm, Sa-Su 11am-6pm.)*

ENTERTAINMENT

Summer is the off season for ballet, opera, and theater; the rest of the year, purchase tickets at Teātra 10/12. (☎722 57 47. Open daily 10am-7pm.) The **Rīga Ballet** carries on the proud dancing tradition of native star Mikhail Baryshnikov. **Paddy Whelan's,** Grēcineku iela 4, is Rīga's first Irish pub. (Guinness 1.50Ls. Open Su-Th 10am-midnight and F-Sa 10am-2am.) Shiny **Vernisāža,** Tērbatas 2, carries club life into the 21st century. (Cover 5Ls. Open W-Su 11pm-6am.)

EXCURISIONS FROM RĪGA

DĀRZIŅI. The **Salaspils Memorial** marks the remains of the Kurtenhof concentration camp, which claimed 100,000 victims in the name of the Third Reich. The inscription over the entrance reads "Beyond this gate the earth moans." Four clusters of massive sculptures watch over the Way of Suffering, the circular path that connects barracks foundations. A black box covered in wreaths emits a low ticking sound, like the pulse of a beating heart. Green electric **trains** travel frequently from Rīga to Dārziņi (*not* "Salaspils" on the Krustpils line; 20-30min., 14 per day, 0.30Ls). Make sure the train will be stopping at Dārziņi before leaving Rīga.

JŪRMALA. Sun-bleached, powder-fine sand, warm waters, and boardwalks have drawn visitors to this narrow spit since the 19th century. Jūrmala (YOUR-ma-la; pop. 60,000) became a popular summer resort with the Soviet elite, and as a result, Latvian independence proved disastrous to the area. Nonetheless, Jūrmala is swiftly recovering, as crowds of tourists again discover its beaches and shops. Any of the coastal towns between **Bulduri** and **Dubulti** are popular for sunning and swimming, but if you're looking for Jūrmala's social center, go to **Majori.** Trainloads of people file to the beach or wander along **Jomas iela,** Majori's pedestrian street, lined with cafes, restaurants, and shops. From the train station, cross the road, walk through the cluster of trees in the small park, turn right, and you're there. The **tourist office** is at Jomas iela 42. (☎764 276 or 764 493; email jurmalainfo@mail.bkc.lv. Open M-F 9am-9pm.) Dining and drinking options abound along **Jomas iela.**

Lielupe, the town with beach access closest to Rīga, offers dramatic sand dunes. At the other end of Jūrmala, **Ķemeri** was once the Russian Empire's prime health resort. Therapeutic mud baths, sulfur water, and other cures have operated here since the mid-18th century. A handful of towns dot the coast; from Rīga, beachless **Priedaine** is the first train stop in Jūrmala; the tracks then pass over the Lielupe River and quickly run through Lielupe, Bulduri, Dzintari, Majori, Dubulti, Jaundubulti, Pumpuri, Melluži, Asari, and Vaivari before heading back inland to Sloka, Kudra, and Ķemeri. The **commuter rail** runs trains every 30 minutes in both directions from 5am to 11:30pm. Trips to **Majori** take 30 minutes and cost 0.40Ls. **Public buses** (0.18Ls) and **microbuses** (0.20-0.30Ls) also string together Jūrmala's towns.

LIECHTENSTEIN

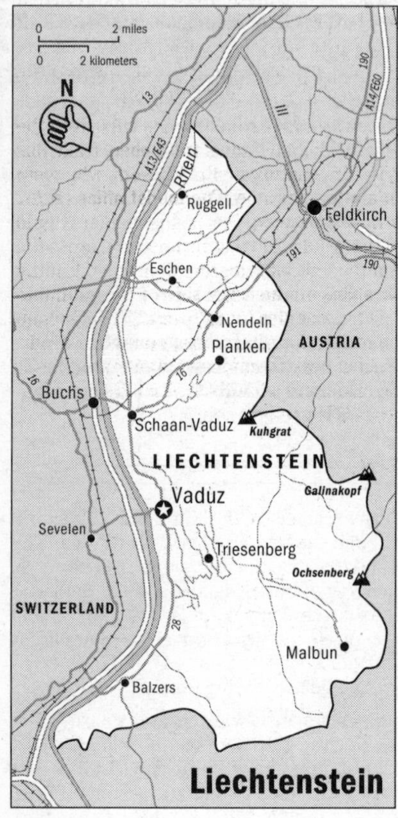

A recent tourist brochure for Liechtenstein (pop. 31,000) amusingly mislabeled the already tiny 160km² country as an even tinier 160m²; that's just about how much most tourists see of the world's only German-speaking monarchy, pausing only long enough to hastily record the visit in a passport and buy some postage stamps. But the cliff-hanging roads dotted with luxury cars are gateways to unspoiled mountains, a world away from the southern tourist traps. **Biking** is a dream in flatter areas, and efficient **postal buses** link all 11 villages (most trips 2.40-3.60SFr; 1-week pass 10SFr, students 5SFr; SwissPass valid). To enter the principality, catch a bus from Sargans or Buchs in Switzerland, or from Feldkirch in Austria (20min., 3.60SFr). German is the official **language,** but many residents also speak English, French, and an Alemannic dialect. The **currency** is the Swiss franc (SFr). **Country code:** 41. **Area code:** 075 (nationwide). **International dialing prefix**: 00. For the **police,** call ☎117, and for **medical emergencies,** call ☎144. **Postal code:** FL-9490.

VADUZ ☎075

More a hamlet than a national capital, Vaduz is not a budget-friendly place. Tourists travel in packs, scrambling furiously to find something worthy of a photo op. Your best bet for a Kodak moment is the 12th-century **Schloß Vaduz,** regal home to Hans-Adam II, Prince of Liechtenstein, above town. Philatelists (that's stamp collectors) flock to the **Briefmarkenmuseum** (Stamp Museum), Städtle 37. (Open daily Apr.-Oct. 10am-noon and 1:30-5:30pm; Nov.-Mar. 10am-noon and 1:30-5pm. Free.)

Liechtenstein's **national tourist office,** Städtle 37, up the hill from the Vaduz-Post bus stop, stamps passports (2SFr or 20AS) and gives advice on hiking, cycling, and skiing. (☎232 14 43. Open May-Sept. M-F 8am-noon and 1:30-5:30pm, Sa-Su 10am-noon and 1-4pm; Apr. and Oct. M-F 8am-noon and 1:30-5:30pm, Sa 9am-noon and 1-4pm; Nov.-May M-F 8am-noon and 1:30-5:30pm.) Take bus #1 (dir. Schaan) to get to the budget-friendly **Hotel Post** in nearby **Schaan,** behind the post office; the welcoming staff makes up for the train noise. (☎232 17 18. Breakfast included. Reception 8am-11pm. Singles 40-50SFr; doubles 80-100SFr.) Liechtenstein's sole hostel, **Jugendherberge (HI),** Untere

Rütig. 6, also in Schaan, is less service-oriented. Take bus #1 to "Mühleholz" and turn left down Marianumstr. (☎232 50 22; fax 232 58 56. Members only. Breakfast included. Laundry. Reception daily 7-9:30am and 5-10pm. Lockout 9:30am-5pm. Curfew 10pm; ask for key. Open Feb.-Oct. Dorms 26.30SFr; doubles 64.60SFr; family quads 113.20SFr.) Take bus #50/51 (dir. Schellenberg) to "Bendern" and walk past the village church to get to **Camping Bendern.** (☎373 12 11. Showers included. 7SFr per person, children 4SFr; tents 4SFr; cars 4SFr; tax 0.30SFr.) Buy **groceries** at **Migros,** Aulestr. 20, across from the tour bus parking lot. (Open M-F 8am-1pm and 1:30-6:30pm, Sa 8am-4pm, Su 9am-6pm.)

UPPER LIECHTENSTEIN. With gorgeous views and great hiking, the villages in the upper country are far more rewarding for visitors than Vaduz. **Triesenberg** (take bus #10), the principal town, was founded in the 13th century by the Walsers, who were fleeing the usual woes of overpopulation and intolerance. The **tourist office** (☎262 19 26) shares a building with the **Walser Heimatmuseum.** For a spectacular Alpine **hike** with views of the Rhine, take bus #30 (dir. Gaflei). From the bus stop, cross the street to the gravel road and the trail is on the left. **Malbun,** the hippest spot in the country, offers great **hiking** and affordable **skiing** on the other side of the mountain (day pass 33SFr, 6-day 136SFr). Contact the **tourist office** for info. (☎263 65 77. Open May-Oct. and Dec.-Apr. M-F 9am-noon and 1:30-5pm, Sa 9am-noon and 1-4pm.) Sleep in the excellent chalets, **Hotel Alpen** and **Hotel Galina;** reception for both is at the former. (☎263 11 81; fax 263 94 46. Breakfast included. Open mid-May to Oct. and mid-Dec. to Apr. Singles and doubles 40-90SFr per person.)

LITHUANIA (LIETUVA)

LITAI

US$1 = 4.00LT (LITAI)	1LT = US$0.25
CDN$1 = 2.70LT	1LT = CDN$0.37
UK£1 = 6.43LT	1LT = UK£0.17
IR£1 = 4.60LT	1LT = IR£0.22
AUS$1 = 2.30LT	1LT = AUS$0.43
NZ$1 = 1.70LT	1LT = NZ$0.58
SAR1 = 0.58LT	1LT = SAR1.70
DM1 = 1.80LT	1LT = DM0.54
EUR€1 = 3,52LT	1LT = EUR€0.28

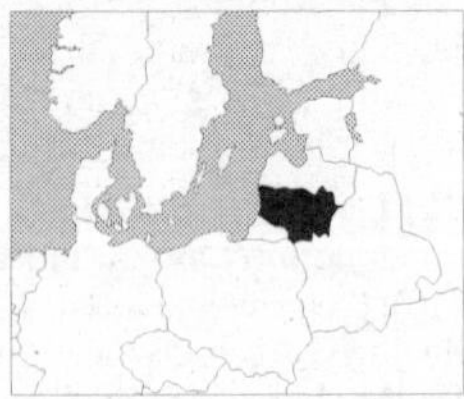

LITHUANIA

Country code: 370. **International dialing prefix:** 810. From outside Lithuania, dial int'l dialing prefix (see inside back cover) + 370 + city code + local number.

Once the largest country in Europe, stretching into modern-day Ukraine, Belarus, and Poland, Lithuania has since faced oppression from tsarist Russia, Nazi Germany, and Soviet Russia. The first Baltic nation to declare its independence from the USSR in 1990, Lithuania has become more Western with every passing year. Its spectacular capital city of Vilnius welcomes hordes of tourists into the largest old town in Europe, recently covered in a bright new coat of paint from city-wide renovations. In the other corner of the country, the mighty Baltic Sea washes up against Palanga and Kuršių Nerija, also called the Curonian Spit.

Tune in to *Let's Go: Eastern Europe 2001* for more madcap Lithuanian info.

FACTS AND FIGURES

Official Name: Republic of Lithuania.
Government: Parliamentary democracy.
Capital: Vilnius.
Land Area: 65,200 sq. km.
Geography: Lowlands with many lakes.
Climate: Rain, especially in winter; cold winters and moderate summers.
Major cities: Vilnius, Šiauliai, Klaipėda.
Population: 3.6 million (80.6% Lithuanian, 8.7% Russian, 7% Polish).
Languages: Lithuanian, Polish, Russian.
Religions: Roman Catholic (80%), Lutherans largest minority.
Major Exports: Machinery and equipment, mineral products, textiles.
Income Per Capita: US$4900.

DISCOVER LITHUANIA

Vilnius is touted as the "New Prague" for its thriving art scene and sprawling Old Town (p. 662); don't miss the nearby fairy-tale **Trakai Castle.** Sun, fun, and sea lions welcome visitors to **Klaipėda,** the Curonian Spit's premier beach town (p. 666).

ESSENTIALS

DOCUMENTS AND FORMALITIES

Citizens of Australia, Canada, Ireland, New Zealand, the UK, and the US do not need a **visa** for visits up to 90 days. Citizens of South Africa who have visas from Estonia or Latvia can use those to enter Lithuania; otherwise, regular 90-day visas are required. Obtain visas from the nearest embassy or consulate: single-entry visas cost US$20; multiple-entry visas US$50; transit visas (good for 48hr.) US$5. Obtaining a visa extension is tricky; try the **Immigration Service** in Vilnius, Virkių g. 3 #6 (☎75 64 53) or at the **Immigration Department,** Saltoniškių 19 (☎72 58 64).

EMBASSIES AND CONSULATES

Embassies and consulates of other countries in Lithuania are in **Vilnius** (see p. 662).

Lithuanian Embassies at Home: Australia (consulate), 47 Somers St., Burwood Victoria 3125 (☎ (03) 98 08 83 00; fax 98 08 83 00); **Canada** (consulate), 1573 Bloor W., Toronto, ON (☎ (416) 538 29 92); **South Africa** (consulate), Killarney Mall, 1st fl., Riviera Rd., Killarney Joh'annesburg; P.O. Box 1737, Houghton, 2041 (☎ (011) 486 36 60; fax 486 36 50); **UK,** 84 Gloucester Pl., London W1H 3HN (☎ (20) 74 86 64 01; fax 74 86 64 03; www.users.globalnet.co.uk/~lralon/); **US,** 2622 16th St. NW, Washington, DC 20009-4202 (☎ (202) 234 58 60; fax 328 04 66; www.ltembassyus.org).

GETTING THERE AND GETTING AROUND

Planes land in Vilnius from: **Warsaw** (1¼hr.); **Berlin** (2hr.); **Moscow** (2hr.); and **Stockholm** (2hr.). **Ferries** connect Klaipėda with German cities **Kiel** (34hr.) and **Muhkran** (18hr.). Vilnius, Kaunas, and Klaipėda are easily reached by **train** or **bus** from Belarus, Estonia, Latvia, Poland, and Russia. Domestically, **buses** are faster, more common, and only a bit more expensive than the often crowded **trains.** If you do ride the rails, two major lines cross Lithuania: one runs north-south from Latvia through Šiauliai and Kaunas to Poland, and the other runs east-west from Belarus through Vilnius and Kaunas to Kaliningrad.

TOURIST SERVICES AND MONEY

EMERGENCY. Fire: ☎ 01. **Police:** ☎ 02. **Emergency:** ☎ 03.

TOURIST OFFICES. Tourist offices are generally knowledgeable. **Litinterp** is the most helpful; they will reserve accommodations, usually without a surcharge. Vilnius, Kaunas, and Klaipėda each have an edition of the *In Your Pocket* series.

MONEY. The unit of **currency** is the **Litas** (1Lt=100 centų), plural Litai. Since 1994, it has been fixed to the US dollar at US$1 = 4Lt. It's difficult to exchange currencies other than US dollars and Deutschmarks. **Traveler's checks,** especially AmEx and Thomas Cook, can be cashed at most banks (usually for a 2-3% commission). **Cash advances** are available on Visa cards. **Vilniaus Bankas** accepts major credit cards and traveler's checks for a small commission. **ATMs,** especially Cirrus, are readily available in most cities. **Hostel beds** run US$6-8, hotels US$15-20, and **meals** US$4-6. **Tipping** is not expected, but some Lithuanians leave 10% for excellent service.

ACCOMMODATIONS

Lithuania has several **youth hostels,** with plans for more to open. HI membership is nominally required, but a LJNN guest card (US$3 at any of the hostels) will suffice. The head office in Vilnius has *Hostel Guide*, a handy booklet with info on bike and car rentals, reservations, and maps showing how to reach various hostels.

FOOD AND DRINK

Lithuanian cuisine is heavy and more often than not very greasy. Keeping a **vegetarian** or **kosher** diet will prove difficult, if not impossible. Restaurants serve various types of *blynai* (pancakes) with *mėsa* (meat) or *varške* (cheese). *Cepelinai* are heavy, potato-dough missiles of meat, cheese, and mushrooms, launched from street stands throughout Western Lithuania. *Šaltibarščiai* is a beet and cucumber soup prevalent in the east. *Karbonadas* is breaded pork fillet, and *koldunai* are meat dumplings. Lithuanian beer is very good. *Kalnapis* is popular in Vilnius and most of Lithuania, *Baltijos* reigns supreme around Klaipėda, and the award-winning *Utenos* is widely available. Lithuanian **vodka** *(degtinė)* is also very popular.

COMMUNICATION

MAIL. **Airmail** *(oro pastu)* letters abroad cost 1.70Lt, postcards 1.20Lt, and usually take about one week to reach the US. **EMS** international mail takes 3-5 days.

TELEPHONES. There are two kinds of public phones: rectangular ones accept magnetic strip cards and rounded ones accept chip cards. Both are sold at phone offices and many kiosks in denominations of 3.54Lt, 7.08Lt, and 28.32Lt. Calls to **Estonia** and **Latvia** cost 1.65Lt per minute; **Europe** 5.80Lt; and the **US** 7.32Lt. Most countries can be dialed directly. Dial 8, wait for the second tone, dial 10, then enter the country code and number. **International direct dialing** numbers include: **AT&T Direct,** ☎ (8) 80 09 28 00; **BT Direct,** ☎ (8) 80 09 00 44; **Canada,** ☎ (8) 80 09 10 04; and **Sprint Express,** ☎ (8) 80 09 10 04. For countries to which direct dialing is unavailable, dial 8, wait for the second tone, and dial 194 or 195 for English-speaking operators.

LANGUAGES. **Lithuanian** is one of only two Baltic languages (Latvian is the other). **Polish** is helpful in the south, **German** on the coast, and **Russian** most places. For phrases, see p. 981.

HOLIDAYS AND FESTIVALS

Holidays: New Year's Day (Jan. 1); Independence Day (1918; Feb. 16); Restoration of Lithuanian Statehood (Mar. 11); Catholic Easter (Apr. 15-16); Labor Day (May 1); Midsummer Night (June 23); Day of Statehood (July 6); All Saints' Day (Nov. 1); All Souls' Day (Nov. 2); Christmas (Dec. 24-25).

VILNIUS ☎(8)22

A majestic national capital, Vilnius (pop. 579,000) races into the 21st century alongside her Baltic sisters. To walk her winding and cobbled streets, lined with pastel gems of Baroque and Neoclassical architecture, is to be transported centuries back to a quieter time. By the 19th century, Vilnius's political perch had been supplanted by its significance as the "Jerusalem of Europe." With a population one-third Jewish, Vilnius bore the Jewish Enlightenment and many influential thinkers. Nearly all of Vilnius's Jews, however, were killed during WWII at the Paneriai death camp; after the war, what remained of Vilnius fell to the USSR. Today, Vilnius is on the rise. But with cafes and hostels filling up more and more with beer-guzzling expats, time is running out to get in on the secret of this Baltic beauty.

GETTING THERE AND GETTING AROUND

Flights: The airport *(oro uostas)*, Rodūnės Kelias 2 (☎30 66 66), is 5km south. Take bus #1 from the station or #2 from the Sparta stop of trolley bus #16 on Kauno g.

Trains: Geležinkelio Stotis, Geležinkelio g. 16 (☎33 00 86). Tickets for all trains are sold in the yellow addition left of the main station; windows #3 and 4 are specifically for trains to western Europe. All international trains (except those heading north) pass through Belarus; for visa info, see p. 125. To: **Rīga** (7½hr., 2 per day, *coupé* 72Lt); **Warsaw** (11hr., 1 per day, *coupé* 115Lt); **Moscow** (17hr., 3 per day, *coupé* 128Lt); **St. Petersburg** (18hr., 3 per day, *coupé* 110Lt); and **Berlin** (22hr., 1 per day, 317Lt).

Buses: Autobusų Stotis, Sodų g. 22 (☎26 24 82; reservations ☎26 29 77), opposite the train station. **Tarpmiestinė Salė** covers long-distance buses; windows #13-15 serve destinations outside the former Soviet Union. Open daily 7am-8pm. To: **Minsk** (5hr., 9

IT'S A SMALL GULAG AFTER ALL Apart from bringing freedom and opportunity for advancement to the millions formerly under its yoke, the fall of communism has left former Soviet states with a slew of statues to the leaders of the glorious revolution and no where to put them. Enter Viliumas Malinaukas, a Lithuanian entrepreneur (dare we say "beeznessman?") who wants to collect them all for a massive Soviet theme park. His plan to place the statues in a strip of filled bog land has already won the grace of the government, but not of all of the country. The older generation, which actually lived through communism, is particularly enraged at this plan to package their repression for tourists. And while Malinaukas claims that the park is meant to be educational, whether it's in good taste is another matter. Take, for example, the planned entrance to Leninland: a replica of the Vilnius train station from which thousands of Lithuanians were shipped to Siberia. Ooh-la-la.

per day, 19Lt); **Rīga** (6½hr., 5 per day, 30-40Lt); **Warsaw** (9½hr., 4 per day, 80Lt); and **Tallinn** (10hr., 2 per day, 81Lt).

Taxis: State Taxis (☎22 88 88). 1.30Lt per km. **Private taxis** show a green light in the windshield; agree on the fare before getting in. Taxis, especially private ones, have a nasty but deserved reputation for ripping off tourists.

ORIENTATION AND PRACTICAL INFORMATION

From the **train** or **bus stations**, walk east on **Geležinkelio g.** (right with your back to the train station), and turn left at the end to Aušros Vartų g., which leads downhill through the **Gates of Dawn** and into **Old Town** (Senamiestis). Aušros Vartų g. changes its name first to Didžioji g. and then Pilies g., before reaching the base of Gediminas Hill. Here, the **Gediminas Tower** of the **Higher Castle** presides over **Cathedral Square** (Arkikatedros aikštė) and the banks of the river **Neris. Gedimino pr.**, the commercial artery, leads west from the square in front of the cathedral's doors.

Tourist Offices: Tourist Information Centre, Pilies str. 42 (☎/fax 62 07 62). Sells *Vilnius in Your Pocket* (4Lt). Open M-F 9am-6pm, Sa noon-6pm.

Budget Travel: Lithuanian Student and Youth Travel, V. Basanavičiaus g. 30, #13 (☎22 13 73). Great deals for those under 27. Open M-F 8:30am-6pm, Sa 10am-2pm.

Embassies: Australia (consulate), Gaono 6 (☎/fax 22 33 69). **Belarus,** Mindaugo 13 (☎25 16 66); visas at Muitinės g. 41 (☎33 06 26). Open M-Tu and Th-F 8:15am-3:30pm. **Canada,** Gedimino pr. 64 (☎22 08 98). Open M and W 9am-noon. **Estonia** Michevičiaus g. 4a (☎75 79 70). Visas Tu-Th 10am-noon and 2:30-3:30pm. **Latvia** M.K. Čiurlionio g. 76 (☎23 12 60). Visas Tu and F 9am-noon. **Russia,** Latvių g. 53/54 (☎72 17 63; visas ☎72 38 93). Open M-F 8:30am-12:30pm and 2:30-5pm. **UK,** Antakalnio g. 2 (☎22 20 70). Open M-F 9-11am. **US,** Akmenų g. 6 (☎22 30 31). Open M-Th 8:30am-5:30pm.

Currency Exchange: Geležinkelio 6 (☎33 07 63), to the right facing the train station. Open 24hr. **Vilniaus Bankas,** Gedimino pr. 12, gives V, MC cash advances.

Pharmacy: Gedimino Vaistinė, Gedimino pr. 27 (☎61 06 08). Open 24hr.

Medical Assistance: Baltic-American Medical & Surgical Clinic, Antakalnio g. 124 (☎34 20 20), at Vilnius University Hospital. Open 24hr.

Internet Access: V002, Ašmenos 8 (☎79 18 6). 8Lt per hr. Open 8am-midnight. **Interneto Kavinė,** Gedimino pr. 4 (☎22 14 81). 8Lt per hr. Open daily 8am-8pm.

Post Office: Centrinis Paštas, Gedimino pr. 7 (☎61 67 59), west of Arkikatedros aikštė. Address mail to be held: First name SURNAME, Centrinis Paštas, Gedimino pr. 7, Vilnius **LT-2000,** Lietuva. Open M-F 7am-7pm, Sa 9am-4pm.

ACCOMMODATIONS

Old Town Hostel (HI), Aušros vartų g. 20-15a (☎62 53 57; email livijus@pub.osf.lt), 100m from the "Gates of Dawn" in the Old Town. Leaving the train station, turn right on Geležinkelio and left on Aušros Vartų; it's through the 1st arch on the right. Internet free. Laundry. Reception 7am-midnight. Dorms 32-34Lt; singles and doubles 40-60Lt.

Filaretai Youth Hostel (HI), Filaretų g. 17 (☎25 46 27; email filareta@post.omnitel.lt). Take bus #34 from right of the station (across from McDonald's) to the 7th stop (10min.). Cozy. Laundry 10Lt. Reception 7am-midnight. Curfew midnight-1am. 24-40Lt.

Litinterp, Bernardinų 7, #2 (☎22 38 50; fax 22 35 59; email litinterpşpost.omnitel.net). From the train station, turn right on Geležinkelio g., take the 3rd left on Aušros Vartv g., cross the square, follow Didžiolji g. as it turns into Pilies g., and turn right on Bernardinų. Breakfast included. Reception M-F 8:30am-5:30pm, Sa 8:30am-3:30pm. Reserve ahead. Singles 70-100Lt; doubles 120-140Lt; apartments 200Lt.

Jaunųjų Turistiu Centras, Polocko 7 (☎61 35 76). Take bus #34 from right of the station (across from McDonald's) to the 7th stop (10min.). *Very* clean bathrooms. Little English spoken. Dorms 20Lt.

FOOD

Inexpensive restaurants are popping up everywhere. A full meal can be as cheap as US$4-6, but quality and price are closely correlated. Check out translated menus before hitting a less Anglo-friendly establishment. French **Iki supermarkets** have several locations in Vilnius. Try **Ritos Smuklė** (Rita's Tavern), A. Goštauto g. 8 (take trolleybus #12, 13, or 17) for the funny menu and delicious food. Acorn coffee (3Lt) is really, really good. (Entrees 15-30Lt. Live folk music W-Th 7pm, F-Sa 8pm. Grill open M-F 5pm-midnight, Sa-Su noon-midnight.) Once a bomb shelter, **Ritos Slėptuvė** (Rita's Hideaway), A. Goštaulto g. 8 is now *the* place to go. After 4pm, it becomes a **bar.** (Meals 10Lt. Live music Su. Open M-Th 7am-2am, F 7am-6am, Sa 8am-6am, Su 8pm-2am.) **Stikliai Aludė** (Beer Bar), Gaono g. 7, is cozy, folksy, and yummy. (Entrees 16-28Lt. Excellent local brew 3-4.50Lt. Open daily noon-midnight.) **Cabare,** Mėsininiy 5/2, won't put on a dancing show, but does serve up authentic Lithuanian meals. (Entrees 12-16Lt. Open daily 10am-11pm.)

SIGHTS

With the largest Old Town in Eastern Europe, Vilnius has no shortage of architectural wonders or historic spots. The moment you reach the end of Geležinkelio g. and turn left, the 16th-century **Gates of Dawn** (Aušros Vartai), the only surviving portal of the old city walls, welcome you in.

OLD TOWN (SENAMIESTIS). Through the gates, enter the first door on the right to ascend the 17th-century **Chapel of the Gates of Dawn** (Aušros Vartų Koplyčia), packed with locals praying to the icon and selling holy paraphernalia. Head back to the street and through the doorway at the building's end to reach **St. Theresa's Church** (Šv. Teresės bažnyčia), known for its Baroque sculptures, multicolored arches, and frescoed ceiling. A few steps farther down, a gateway leads to the bright 17th-century **Church of the Holy Ghost** (Šv. Dvasios bažnyčia), seat of Lithuania's Russian Orthodox Archbishop. The street merges with the pedestrian **Pilies g.** and leads to the main entrance of **Vilnius University** (Vilniaus Universitetas), at Pilies g. and Šv. Jono g., founded in 1579. Follow Bernardinų g. off Pilies g., at the end stands **St. Anne's Church.** Napoleon was so taken by it that he wanted to carry it back to France on the palm of his hand. Continue north on Pilies g. to **Cathedral Square** (Arkikatedros aikštė), depicted on the 50Lt bill. Built on a pagan worship site, the Cathedral resembles a Greek temple. Behind the cathedral, walk up the Castle Hill path to **Gedimino tower** for a great view of Vilnius's spires. Off Pylimo, between Kalinausko 1 and 3, shoots up the most random monument on the continent, capped by a **bust of Frank Zappa** (installed in 1995).

THE OLD JEWISH QUARTER AND GENOCIDE MEMORIAL. Vilnius was once a center of Jewish life comparable to Warsaw and New York, with a Jewish population of 100,000 (in a city of 230,000) at the start of World War II. Nazi persecution left only 6000 survivors and only one of pre-war Vilnius's 105 **synagogues,** at Pylimo g. 39. The **Lithuanian State Jewish Museum,** housed in two buildings at Pylimo g. 4, offers a variety of exhibits about the vitality of Yiddish culture in Lithuania and the tragedy of the Holocaust. *(Open M-Th 9am-5pm, F 9am-4pm. Donation requested.)* The **Genocide Memorial,** Agrastų g. 15, is 10-15 minutes away by train in **Paneriai** (1.30Lt).

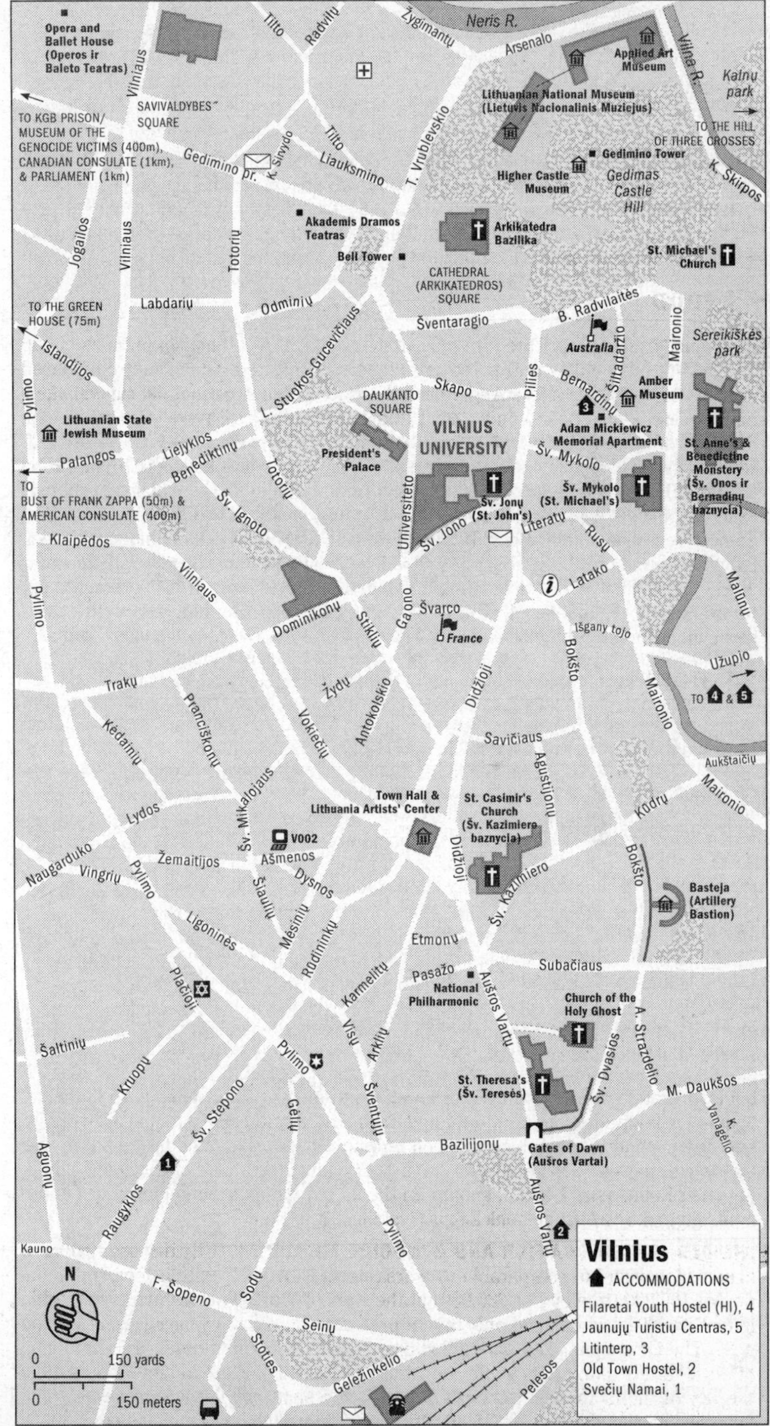

Opera and Ballet House (Operos ir Baleto Teatras)
Neris R.
Applied Art Museum
Lithuanian National Museum (Lietuvis Nacionalinis Muziejus)
Kalnų park
TO THE HILL OF THREE CROSSES
TO KGB PRISON/ MUSEUM OF THE GENOCIDE VICTIMS (400m), CANADIAN CONSULATE (1km), & PARLIAMENT (1km)
SAVIVALDYBES SQUARE
Gedimino Tower
Higher Castle Museum
Gedimas Castle Hill
Akademis Dramos Teatras
Arkikatedra Bazilika
Bell Tower
CATHEDRAL (ARKIKATEDROS) SQUARE
St. Michael's Church
TO THE GREEN HOUSE (75m)
Sereikiškės park
Australia
Amber Museum
DAUKANTO SQUARE
VILNIUS UNIVERSITY
Lithuanian State Jewish Museum
Adam Mickiewicz Memorial Apartment
President's Palace
St. Anne's & Benedictine Monstery (Šv. Onos ir Bernadinų baznycia)
Šv. Mykolo (St. Michael's)
Šv. Jonų (St. John's)
TO BUST OF FRANK ZAPPA (50m) & AMERICAN CONSULATE (400m)
France
TO 4 & 5
Town Hall & Lithuania Artists' Center
St. Casimir's Church (Šv. Kazimiero baznycia)
V002
Basteja (Artillery Bastion)
National Philharmonic
Church of the Holy Ghost
St. Theresa's (Šv. Teresės)
Gates of Dawn (Aušros Vartai)
N
0 150 yards
0 150 meters
Vilnius
ACCOMMODATIONS
Filaretai Youth Hostel (HI), 4
Jaunujų Turistiu Centras, 5
Litinterp, 3
Old Town Hostel, 2
Svečių Namai, 1

With your back to the train tracks, head right and follow Agrastų g. straight to the memorial. Between 1941 and 1944, 100,000 people, including 70,000 Jews, were shot, burned, and buried here. Paved paths connect the pits that served as mass graves. *(Open M and W-Sa 11am-6pm.)* For information on the Jewish Quarter or locating ancestors, visit the **Jewish Cultural Centre.** *(Лbaltiniv g. 12. ☎ 41 88 09.)*

MUSEUM OF GENOCIDE VICTIMS. Don't miss the Museum of Genocide Victims (Genocido Aukų Muziejus), in the old **KGB prison.** Originally constructed in 1899 as a Russian court, the Nazis turned it into a Gestapo headquarters during WWII. When the Soviets came to town, the building became Vilnius' KGB headquarters. One of the tour guides, G. Radžius, was once a prisoner in its cells; find someone to translate what he says. *(Gedimino pr. 40. Enter around the comer at Aukv g. 4. ☎ 62 24 49. Open Tu-Su 10am-4pm. Tours in Lithuanian and Russian, captions in English.)*

ENTERTAINMENT

In summer, music and dance festivals and pop concerts come to town; pick up *Vilnius in Your Pocket* or the paper *Lietuvos Rytas* for performances. New discos, bars, and clubs spring up daily to entertain the influx of foreigners and the city's younger crowd. Check out posters in the Old Town or wander down Gedimino prosp. toward the thumping music. Lithuanian hipsters Eduardas and Vladimiras organize a **gay disco** every Saturday night at a different venue; call for info. (☎ 828 72 58 79. Cover 15Lt. Usually open F-Sa 10pm-6am.) **The PUB (Prie Universiteto [Baras]),** Dominikonų g. 9, in the heart of the Old Town and near the university, is a traditional English pub with a heavy wooden interior and a cozy, 19th-century dungeon. (W night jazz, Su night disco. Cover 8Lt. Open daily 11am-2am.) **Savas Kampas** (Your Corner), Vokiečių g. 4, is a laid-back option for a more mature set listening to 60s, 70s, and 80s music. (Local bands F and Sa. Open daily midnight-3am.) Mingle with the locals at **Amatininskv Užeiga,** Didžiogi g. 19, #2. (Open M-F 8am-5am, Sa-Su 11am-5am.) **Naktinis Vilkas** (Night Wolf), Lukišų g. 3. features a local student crowd. (21+. Cover M-Sa 5-10Lt. Open daily 10pm-6am.)

NEAR VILNIUS: TRAKAI CASTLE

Trakai's magnificent lakes and fairy-tale castle have inspired legends and muses alike since its construction in the 15th century. With the defeat of the Teutonic order at the Battle of Grunewald, Trakai became the home of the Grand Duke and the capital of Lithuania. In 1665, the Tsar of Russia accomplished what the Germans could not—the Imperial Army plundered the town and razed the castle. Following a lengthy process of restoration from 1952 to 1980, five stories of red bricks now tower over some of the most beautiful lakes and woods in Lithuania. A combined admission ticket is valid for the Insular Castle's 30m brick **watchtower** and the **City and Castle History Museum.** Climb the watchtower's tight, circular staircases to the third floor for a magnificent view of the medieval courtyard below. The rooms in the tower chronicle the history of Lithuania after it came under the rule of tsarist Russia in 1795, as well as the history of the independent Lithuanian republic that existed between the wars. Across from the tower, the City and Castle History Museum features Lithuanian furniture from the 18th to 20th centuries, Bronius Kasperavicus's clock collection, handmade marble postal stampers, and an immense collection of tobacco and opium pipes. (Open daily 10am-7pm. 7Lt, students with ISIC and seniors 3.5Lt. Tours 40-50Lt, students 25Lt.) Apart from the historic sights, give yourself at least 30 minutes to wander around the island. With your back to the footbridge leading to the Insular Castle, walk left and explore the ruins of the Peninsular Castle and Dominican monastery.

Trakai, 28km east of Vilnius, is accessible by **bus** (1hr., over 25 per day, 2.90Lt; buy tickets on the bus). The last return is usually at 9:07pm. The easiest way to navigate Trakai is by **boat;** boat owners line the shore by the footbridge to the castle. Don't forget to bargain—the going rate is 5-7Lt per hr.

KLAIPĖDA ☎ (8)26

Guarding the Curonian Lagoon with its fortress on the tip of the Neringa peninsula, Klaipėda (klai-PAY-da; pop. 202,500), Lithuania's third-largest city, may be a little too strategically located for its own good. Briefly the Prussian capital in the 19th century, the town was handed to France in the 1919 Treaty of Versailles and served as a German U-boat base in WWII before being industrialized by the Soviets after the war. On mainland Klaipėda, the **Clock Museum** (Laikrodživ Muziejus), Liepv g. 12, is just the place for the perennially late to face punctuality. From S. Daukanto g., turn right on H. Manto and left on Liepv g. (Open Tu-Su 9am-5:30pm. 4Lt, students 2Lt. Tours 20Lt, foreign-language 40Lt.) **Klaipėda Theater** (Klaipėdos Dramos Teatras), Teatro aikštė, on the other side of Manto g., dominates the Old Town center. The theater is famed for being one of Wagner's favorite haunts. (☎31 44 53. Open W-Su 11am-7pm. 2Lt, students 1Lt.) **Smiltynė,** across the lagoon, houses the **Maritime Museum, Aquarium, and Dolphinarium** (Jurv muziejus ir Akvariumas), Tomo g. 10, in an 1860s fortress. (Open June-Aug. Tu-Su 11am-7pm; May and Sept. W-Su 11am-7pm; Oct.-Apr. Sa-Su 11am-6pm. 5Lt, students 3Lt.) Aquatic attractions are in **Kopgalis,** at the head of the Spit, 1.5km from the ferry landing. Forest paths lead west 500m to the **beaches.** The permanently moored **Meridianas,** Daués Krautinė (river bank), is a unique place to imbibe. (Cover 20-30Lt. Open daily 3pm-5am.)

LITHUANIA

Trains (☎31 36 76) go from Priestoties 1 to Vilnius (5hr., 3 per day, 40Lt). **Ferries** (☎31 42 57; info ☎31 11 57) run from Old Castle Port, Žveju 8, and connect with microbuses to Nida (1hr., 7Lt). The **tourist office,** Tomog. 2, sells maps, arranges tours, and provides tons of useful info. (☎41 21 86; fax 41 21 85; email kltic@taka.lt. Open M-F 8:30am-5pm; in summer also open Sa 9am-3pm.) **Litinterp,** S. Šimkaus g. 21/8, arranges **rooms.** (☎31 14 90; fax 21 98 62. Singles 70Lt; doubles 120Lt. Open M-F 8:30am-5:30pm, Sa 10am-3pm.) To reach the centrally located **Hotel Viktorija,** S. Šimkaus g. 2, head down H. manto from the stations, turn right onto Vytautog, and the hotel is on the corner to the left at the end of the block. (☎40 00 55; fax 41 21 47. Shower 3.50Lt. Singles 40-45Lt; doubles 60-120Lt.) To get to **Klaipėda Traveller's Guesthouse (HI),** Turgaus 3/4, in the Old Town, walk left from the train station (right from the bus station) down Trilapio, turn right on Liepu, and turn left on H. Manto, which crosses the river; Turgaus is the second left after the bridge. (☎21 49 35; email oldtown@takas.lt. Free beer and bike rental if you reserve by email. 32Lt; nonmembers 34Lt.) **Skandalas,** Kanto 44, serves all-out American cuisine and offers 30% off meals before 6pm. (Entrees 15-44Lt. Open daily noon-3am.) **IKI supermarket** is at M. Mažvyado 7. (Open daily 9am-10pm.) **Postal code:** LT-5800.

EXCURSION FROM KLAIPĖDA: NIDA. The magical rise of wind-swept, white sand dunes has long drawn summer vacationers to Nida (pop. 2000), only 3km north of the Kaliningrad region on the Curonian Spit. From the remains of the immense **sundial**—the highest point on the Spit—you can look down on the glorious vista of the dunes, the Curonian Lagoon, the Baltic, and even Russia. Walk along the **beach** or through forest paths to reach steps leading to surreal mountains and plains of white sand blowing gracefully into the sea from 100m above. From the center of town, walk along the promenade by the water and bear right on Skruzdynės g. to reach the renovated **Thomas Mann House** (Thomo Manno Namelis) at #17. Mann built the cottage in 1930 and wrote *Joseph and His Brothers* here, but had to give up the house when Hitler invaded. From Naglių 18, **microbuses** (☎523 34) run to Smiltynė (1hr., 7.50Lt); buy tickets on board. The last one (10pm) should get you there to catch the 11:15pm ferry back to mainland **Klaipėda.** The **Tourist Information Center,** Taikos g. 4, opposite the bus station, arranges **homestays** for a 5Lt service charge. (☎523 45; fax 523 44. Open June-Aug. M-Sa 10am-8pm, Su 10am-3pm; Sept.-May M-F 9am-noon and 1-7pm.) ☎ **(8)259.**

PLUNGING HEAD FIRST Legend has it the gorgeous and serene rippling waters surrounding Trakai Castle are more sinister than they seem. Lake Galvė derives its name from the Lithuanian word for "head." It seems Grand Duke Vytautas got a little carried away in his victory dance after defeating the Germanic crusaders of the Teutonic Order and spiked the head of a decapitated crusader into the lake's sparkling waters. The lake fell head over heels for this mortal morsel and now will not freeze before it takes its "head," usually a drowned drunkard or lost tourist.

LUXEMBOURG

LUXEMBOURG FRANCS

US$1 = 46.95LUF	10LUF = US$0.21
CDN$1 = 31.72LUF	10LUF = CDN$0.32
UK£1 = 66.10LUF	10LUF = UK£0.15
IR£1 = 51.22LUF	10LUF = IR£0.20
AUS$1 = 26.38LUF	10LUF = AUS$0.38
NZ$1 = 20.20LUF	10LUF = NZ$0.50
SAR1 = 6.59LUF	10LUF = SAR1.52
EUR€1 = 40.34LUF	10LUF = EUR€0.25

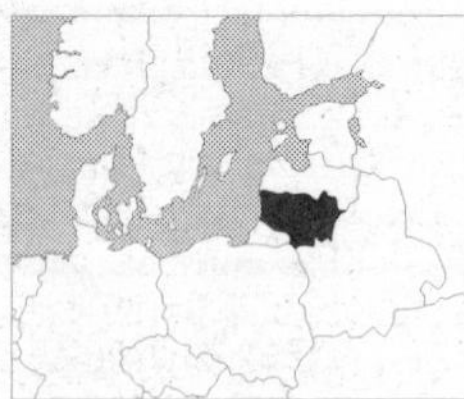

Country code: 352. **International dialing prefix:** 00. Luxembourg has no city codes. From outside Luxembourg, dial int'l dialing prefix (see inside back cover) + 352 + local number.

Too often overlooked by budget travelers, Luxembourg boasts beautiful hiking and impressive fortresses, remnants of successive waves of Burgundians, Spaniards, French, Austrians, and Germans. Only after the last French soldier returned home in 1867 and the Treaty of London restored its neutrality did Luxembourg begin to cultivate its current image of peacefulness. Today the wealthy nation is an independent constitutional monarchy, part of the European Union, and a tax haven for investors worldwide. From the wooded and hilly Ardennes in the north to the fertile vineyards of the Moselle Valley in the south, the country's unspoiled rural landscapes are a sharp contrast to the high-powered banking in the small capital city.

FACTS AND FIGURES

Official Name: Grand Duchy of Luxembourg.

Government: Constitutional monarchy.

Capital: Luxembourg City.

Land Area: 2586 sq. km.

Climate: Mild, with considerable precipitation. The sheltered Moselle Valley is sunnier than the rest of the duchy.

Population: 415,870.

Languages: French, German, Luxembourgian.

Religions: Roman Catholic (90%).

Income Per Capita: US$40,000.

Geography: Forested highlands in the north, several river valleys.

DISCOVER LUXEMBOURG

Luxembourg is a charming stopover between France or Belgium and Germany. **Luxembourg City** is arguably one of Europe's most beautiful capitals (p. 670). Your next stop should be **Vianden,** whose gorgeous chateau and outdoor opportunities make it well worth an overnight stay (p. 673). If you have extra time, consider daytripping to **Diekirch** (p. 674), or hiking and biking around **Echternach** (p. 674).

ESSENTIALS

DOCUMENTS AND FORMALITIES

Citizens of Australia, Canada, the EU, New Zealand, and the US need only a valid passport for stays of up to three months. South Africans require a short-stay visa.

EMBASSIES AND CONSULATES

All foreign embassies are located in **Luxembourg City** (see p. 670). Foreign embassies in **Brussels** also have jurisdiction over Luxembourg (see p. 131).

Luxembourg Embassies at Home: Australia (consulate), Level 12, 400 George St., Sydney NSW 2000 (☎ (02) 93 20 02 55; fax 92 62 40 80); **Canada** (consulate), 3877 Draper Ave, Montreal, PQ H4A 2N9 (☎ (514) 849 21 01); **South Africa** (consulate), P.O. Box 782922, Sandton 2146 (☎ (011) 463 17 44; 463 32 69); **UK,** 27 Wilton Crescent, London SW1X 8SD (☎ (020) 72 35 69 61; fax (020) 72 35 97 34); **US,** 2200 Massachusetts Ave. NW, Washington, DC 20008 (☎ (202) 265 41 71; fax 328 82 70).

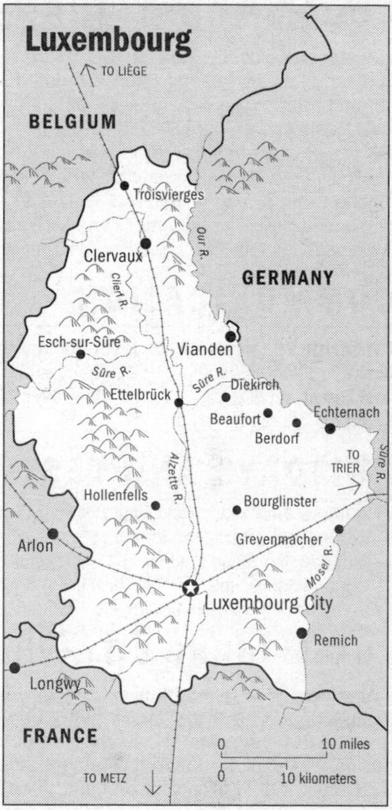

GETTING THERE AND GETTING AROUND

The Luxembourg City airport is serviced by **Luxair** (☎479 81, reservations ☎0800 20 00; www.luxair.lu). A **Benelux Tourrail Pass** allows five days of unlimited **train** travel in a one-month period (6400LUF, under 26 4400LF). The **Billet Réseau** (160LF), a network ticket, is good for one day of unlimited bus and train travel; even better is the **Luxembourg Card** (350 LUF), which covers unlimited transportation and most entrance fees. **Eurail** is valid. **Hiking** and **biking trails** run between Luxembourg City and Echternach, from Diekirch to Echternach and Vianden, and elsewhere. **Bikes** aren't permitted on buses, but are allowed on many trains for 40LF.

TOURIST SERVICES AND MONEY

TOURIST OFFICES. The **Luxembourg Card,** available from Easter to October at tourist offices, hostels, and many hotels and public transportation offices, provides unlimited transportation on national trains and buses and admission to 32 tourist sites (1-day 350LF, 2-day 600LF, 3-day 850LF). For more info, contact the **Luxembourg National Tourist Office,** P.O. Box 1001, 1010 Luxembourg (☎ (352) 42 82 82 210; fax 42 82 82 38; email tourism@ont.smtp.etat.lu; www.etat.lu/tourism).

MONEY. The currency is the Luxembourg **franc,** which is worth the same as Belgian *franc;* you can use Belgian money in Luxembourg, but not vice versa. Expect to pay 1200-1500LF for a hotel room, 435-650LF in a hostel, and 280-400LF for a restaurant meal. **Service** (15-20%) is included; tip taxi drivers 10%. The **value-added tax** is already included in most prices. Luxembourg's **VAT refund threshold** (US$85) is lower than most other EU countries; refunds are usually 13% of the purchase price.

ACCOMMODATIONS AND CAMPING

Luxembourg's 12 **HI youth hostels** *(Auberges de Jeunesse)* are busiest in late spring and early fall. Prices range from 435-650LF, under 27 355-650LF; nonmembers pay about 110LF extra. Breakfast is included, a packed lunch is 125LF, and dinner 260LF. Sheets are 125LF. Half of the hostels close from mid-November to mid-December, the other half from mid-January to mid-February. Contact **Centrale des Auberges de Jeunesse Luxembourgeoises** (☎22 55 88; email information@youthhostels.lu) for information. **Hotels** advertise 800-1500LF per night but sometimes try to persuade tourists to take more expensive rooms. **Campgrounds** abound, and most have hot showers. Two people with a tent will typically pay 200-360LF per night.

COMMUNICATION

TELEPHONES. International direct dial numbers include: **AT&T Direct,** ☎0800 01 11; **Australia Direct,** ☎0800 00 61; **BT Direct,** ☎0800 00 44; **Canada Direct,** ☎0800 01 19; **Ireland Direct,** ☎0800 89 35 30; **MCI WorldPhone,** ☎0800 01 12; **NZ Direct,** ☎0800 57 84; **Sprint Access,** ☎0800 01 15.

HOLIDAYS AND FESTIVALS

Holidays: New Year's Day (Jan. 1); Carnival (Feb. 26); Shrove Monday (Mar. 6); Easter (Apr. 15); Easter Monday (Apr. 16); May Day (May 1); Ascension Day (June 1); Whit Sunday and Monday (June 3-4); National Holiday (June 23); Assumption Day (Aug. 15); All Saints Holiday (Nov. 1); Christmas (Dec. 25); and Boxing Day (Dec. 26).

LUXEMBOURG CITY (VILLE DE LUXEMBOURG)

Rising above the ramparts of its medieval fortress and overlooking two lush river valleys, the 1000-year-old Luxembourg City (pop. 80,000) is one of the most attractive and dramatic capitals in Europe. Though it is home to thousands of foreign business executives due to its status as both an international banking capital and the center of the European Community, visitors find the city surprisingly relaxed.

GETTING THERE AND GETTING AROUND

Flights: Findel International Airport, 6km from the city. **Bus #9** (40LF) is cheaper and more frequent than the Luxair bus (every 20min., 150LF).

Trains: ☎49 90 49 90 (toll-free); www.cfl.lu. **Gare CFL,** av. de la Gare, near the foot of av. de la Liberté, 10min. south of the city center. To: **Brussels** (2¾hr.; 940LF, under 26 520LF); **Paris** (3½-4hr., 1560LF); **Frankfurt** (5hr.; 1720LF, under 26 1530LF); and **Amsterdam** (5¾hr.; 1680LF, under 26 1360LF).

Buses: Buy a **billet courte distance** (short-distance ticket) from the driver (single-fare 40LF, full-day 160LF), or pick up a package of 10 (320LF) at the train station.

Taxis: ☎48 22 33. 32LF per km. 10% premium 10pm-6am; 25% premium on Su. 700-800LF from the city center to the airport.

Bikes: Vélo en Ville, 8 r. Bisserwé (☎47 96 23). Open M-F 1-8pm, Sa-Su 9am-noon and 1-8pm. 250LF per half-day, 400LF per day. Under 26 20% discount.

ORIENTATION AND PRACTICAL INFORMATION

The old city centers around the **Place d'Armes** and hosts most museums, restaurants, and bars. Facing the tourist office, in the Town Hall, turn right down R. Chimay to reach **Blvd. Roosevelt.** To reach the museums, Grand Ducal Palace, and Boch Casemates, walk straight ahead from the tourist office onto **Rue Sigeroi**. The train station and the happening **rue de Hollerich** are south of the Pétrusse Valley.

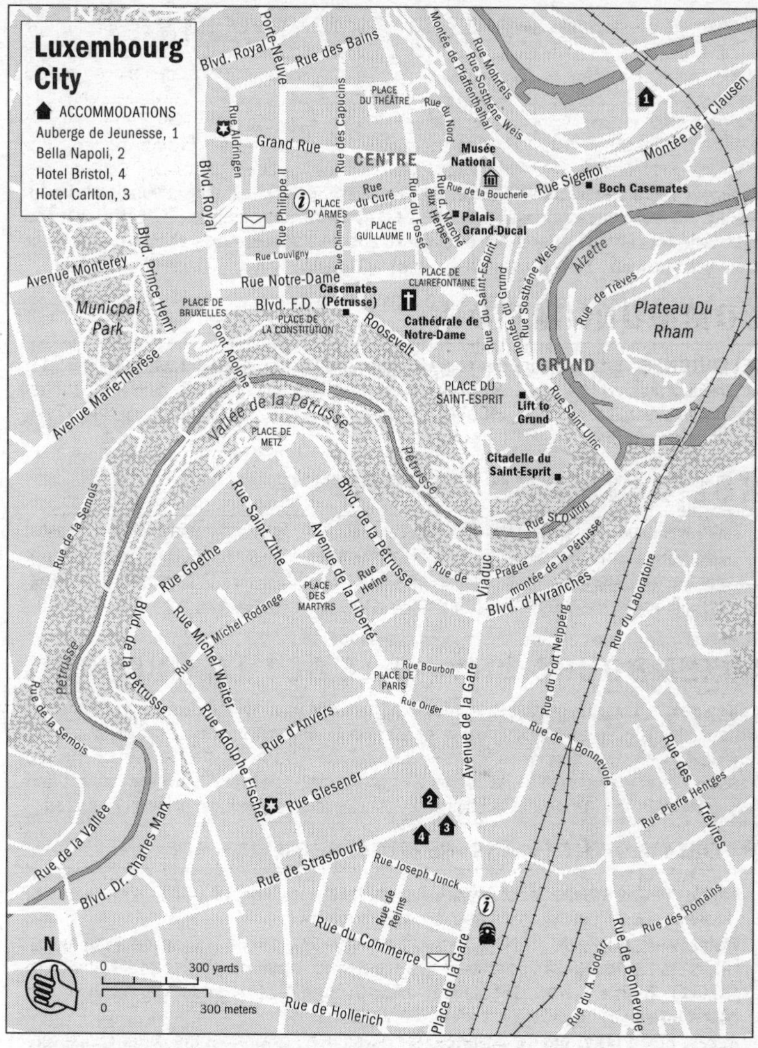

Tourist Offices: Grand Duchy National Tourist Office, in the train station (☎42 82 82 20; www.etat.lu/tourism). Open July-Sept. 9am-7pm; Oct.-June 9:15am-12:30pm and 1:45-6pm. **Municipal Tourist Office,** pl. d'Armes (☎22 28 09). Open Apr.-Sept. M-Sa 9am-7pm, Su 10am-6pm; Oct.-Mar. M-F 9am-6pm, Su 10am-6pm.

Embassies: Ireland, 28 r. d'Arlon (☎45 06 10; fax 45 88 20). Open M-F 10am-12:30pm and 2:30-5pm. **UK,** 14 bd. Roosevelt (☎22 98 64; fax 22 98 67). Open M-F 9am-12:30pm. **US,** 22 bd. E. Servais (☎46 01 23; fax 46 14 01). Open M-F 8:30am-12:30pm; visas M-Tu and Th-F 3:30-4:30pm. **Australians, Canadians, New Zealanders,** and **South Africans** should contact embassies in France or Belgium.

Laundromat: Quick Wash, 31 r. de Strasbourg, near the station. Wash and dry 390F. Open M-Sa 8:30am-6:30pm. Doing laundry is cheaper at the HI hostel (350F).

Emergencies: Police: ☎113. **Ambulance:** ☎112.

LUXEMBOURG

Pharmacy: Pharmacie Goedert, 5 pl. d'Armes (☎22 39 91). Open M 1-6:15pm, Tu-F 8am-6:15pm, Sa 8am-12:30pm. Check any pharmacy window for night pharmacy info.

Telephones: Outside post offices and at the train station. Coin-operated phones are rare; buy a 50-unit **phone card** (good for 50 local calls; 250LF).

Internet Access: Sparky's, 11a av. Monterey, (☎62 01 22 3), at the pl. d'Armes. 300LF per hr. Open daily 8am-8pm.

Post Office: R. Phillipine at pl. D'Armes and 38 pl. de la Gare, across the street, by the train station. Open M-F 6am-7pm, Sa 6am-noon. Address mail to be held: First name SURNAME, *Poste Restante,* Recette Principale, **L-1009** Luxembourg City, Luxembourg.

ACCOMMODATIONS AND CAMPING

Budget travelers have two basic options—the comparatively inexpensive, semi-posh accommodations near the train station (the city's unofficial red-light district), and the hostel, Luxembourg's overnight saviour.

Auberge de Jeunesse (HI), 2 r. du Fort Olisy (☎22 19 20; fax 22 33 60; email luxembourg@youthhostels.lu). Take bus #9 and ask to get off at the hostel stop; head under the bridge and turn right down the steep path. Breakfast included. Sheets 125LF. Laundry. Reception 7am-2am. Max 5-night stay in high season; reserve ahead. Dorms 520-580F, under 26 435-485LF; doubles 1340LF, 1140LF; nonmembers add 110LF.

Bella Napoli, 4 r. de Strasbourg (☎48 46 29). From the station, walk up av. de la Liberté and turn left on r. de Strasbourg (3 min.). Rooms with showers and toilets. Breakfast included. Reception 7am-1am. Singles 1500LF; doubles 1800LF; triples 2400LF.

Hotel Bristol, 11 r. de Strasbourg, opposite Bella Napoli. Comfortable rooms. Make sure to clarify what price you will be paying. Breakfast included. Singles 1500-2300LF; doubles 1900-2600LF.

Camping: Kockelscheuer (☎47 18 15). Bus #2 to Cloche d'Or/Kockelscheuer from the station. Showers included. Open Easter-Oct. 120LF per person, 140LF per tent.

FOOD

The area around **pl. d'Armes,** blanketed with outdoor terraces and frequent live music, teems with touristy fast-food options and pricey restaurants. **Restaurant Bacchus,** 32 r. Marché-aux-Herbes (☎47 13 97), down the street from the Grand Ducal palace, serves excellent pizza and pasta and is popular with locals, expats, and itinerants alike; reservations are recommended at night. (Open Tu-Su noon-10pm.) **Le Beaujolais,** 2a r. des Capucins, next to the tourist office, also offers reasonably priced Italian fare. (Open 11:30am-11:30pm.) **Giorgio,** 11 r. du Nord, has veggie options for 330LF. (Open M-Th 11:45am-2:30pm and 6:30-11:30pm, F-Sa 1:45-2:30pm and 6:30pm-midnight.) Stock up at **Nobilis supermarket,** 47 av. de la Gare. (Open M-F 9am-7:30pm, Sa 8:30am-6pm, Su 9am-1pm.)

SIGHTS

FORTRESSES AND THE OLD CITY. The 10th-century **Boch Casemates** fortress, part of Luxembourg's original castle, looms imposingly over the Alzette River Valley and offers a fantastic view of the Grund and the Clausen. The strategic stronghold was closed in 1867 when Luxembourg signed an act of neutrality, but was used during WWII to shelter 35,000 people. *(Entrance on r. Sigefroi just past the bridge leading to the hostel. Open daily Mar.-Oct. 10am-5pm. 70LF.)* The **Pétrusse Casemates** were built by the Spanish in the 1600s and later improved by the Austrians. *(Pl. de la Constitution. Mandatory tours every hr. 11am-4pm. Open July-Sept. 70LF, children 40LF.)* The tourist office has info on self-guided **walking tours** through the historic city center, including the self-guided **Wenzel Walk,** which leaves from the tourist office and winds around the walls of the old city and down into the casemates. *(One group tour per week Easter-Oct. Sa 3pm. Make reservations at tourist office. 240LF.)*

MUSEUMS. The **Luxembourg Card** (see p. 669) covers entrance to all museums in the city. The **All-in-One Ticket** covers five museums in two days (350LF at the Municipal Tourist Office). The eclectic collection at the **Musée National d'Histoire et d'Art** chronicles the various European empires that controlled Luxembourg. *(Marché-aux-Poissons, at r. Boucherie and Sigefroi. Open Tu-Su 10am-5pm. 100LF. Will partially close for renovations in 2001.)* The **Musée d'Histoire de la Ville de Luxembourg** explores the city's history through archived photographs, films, and music clips. *(14 r. du St-Esprit. Open Tu-Su 10am-6pm, Th 10am-8pm. 200LF, students 150LF. English guide available.)*

OTHER SIGHTS. Built as the city hall in 1574, the Renaissance **Grand Ducal Palace** became the official city residence of the Grand Duke in 1890. *(Tours mid-July to Sept. 2 M-Sa; inquire at the Municipal Tourist Office. 200LF.)* The nearby 16th-century **Notre Dame Cathedral** incorporates features of the Dutch Renaissance and early Baroque styles and houses the tombs of John the Blind, the 14th-century King of Bohemia and Count of Luxembourg, and other members of the Grand Ducal family. *(Entrance at bd. Roosevelt. Open Easter-Oct. M-F 10am-5pm, Sa 8am-6pm, Su 10am-6pm; Nov.-Easter M-F 10-11:30am and 2-5pm, Sa 8-11:30am and 2-5pm, Su 10am-5pm. Free.)*

ENTERTAINMENT

Pick up *La Semaine à Luxembourg* at the tourist office for event listings. In summer, there are almost nightly free **concerts** on the pl. d'Armes. On the Grand Duke's birthday (June 23), the city shuts down to host a large military and religious procession; the night before, the city erupts in street parties. Nocturnal debauchery centers on the valley in the **Grund** (take the elevator lift on pl. du St-Esprit), on **rue de Hollerich** near the train station, and in the **Clausen** neighborhood by the Mousel brewery. Check the monthly *Nightlife.lu*, available at most cafes and newsstands. Grab a Guinness with a young crowd across the river at **Scott's Pub,** Bisserwee 4. (Open daily 1pm-1am; dance floor open on weekends 8pm-1am.) Up the street in the Clausen, **Pygmalion,** 19 r. de la Tour Jacob Clausen, serves local beer for 120LF per pint. (Open Su-Th 5pm-1am, F-Sa 4pm-3am.)

EXCURSION FROM LUXEMBOURG CITY: GREVENMACHER

The **Moselle Valley** was discovered by French winemakers as a suitable substitute for the Champagne region and is renowned for its sparkling (often marked *méthode traditionelle*) and still wines such as *Riesling* and *Pinot Gris*. **Grevenmacher** is at the heart of the wine culture; begin with a tour of the **Bernard-Massard winery,** r. du Pont, to learn about the Champagne method and sample the product. From the bus stop, turn left on r. de Treves, left on r. de la Moselle, and right on rte. du Vin, then enter the *cave* through the gate and garden just under the bridge. (☎75 05 45. Open daily Apr.-Oct. 9:30am-6pm. 100LF.) A small, spectacular **Jardin des Papillons** (Butterfly Garden) lies in the other direction on rte. du Vin. (Open daily Apr. to mid-Oct. 9:30am-5pm. 180LF.) To get to Grevenmacher from Luxembourg City, take the **train** to Wasserbillig (40min.) and the **bus** to Grevenmacher. From the bus stop, turn left on r. de Treves, left on r. de la Moselle, and stop by the **tourist office,** 10 rte. du Vin, at the end of r. de la Moselle. (☎75 82 75. Open M-F 8am-noon and 2-5pm.)

THE ARDENNES

In 1944, the Battle of the Bulge mashed Luxembourg into slime and mud. Almost six decades later, the Ardennes forest is verdant once again, and its quiet towns, looming castles, and sobering WWII monuments attract anew.

VIANDEN. Hidden in the greenery of the dense Ardennes woods, the village of Vianden (pop. 1600), home to one of the most impressive castles in Western Europe, is not to be missed. While wealthy Europeans on weekend getaways whiz down Vianden's curvy streets in antique sportscars, backpackers **hike** and **kayak**

along the Sûre River, or **bike** to Diekirch (15-20min.) and Echternach (30min.). The **chateau,** a mix of Carolingian, Gothic, and Renaissance architecture, is filled with medieval armor, 16th-century furniture, and 17th-century tapestries. From April to May and September through October, the chateau hosts classical concerts on weekends. (☎83 41 08. Open daily Apr.-Sept. 10am-6pm.; Mar. and Oct. 10am-5pm; Nov.-Feb. 10am-4pm. 180LF. Concerts 300-500LF.) For a stellar view of the chateau, ride the **télésiège** (chairlift), 39 r. de Sanatorium, down the hill and across the river from the chateau. From the tourist office, cross the river, turn left on r. Victor Hugo, then left again on r. de Sanitorium. (Open daily Easter-June and Sept.-Oct. 10am-5pm, July and Aug. 10am-6pm. 90LF, round-trip 160LF.)

Buses arrive roughly hourly from Echternach and Ettelbrück via Diekirch. The **tourist office,** 1 r. du Vieux Marché, next to the main bus stop, has info on kayaking and **private rooms.** (☎83 42 57. Open in high season daily 9:30am-noon and 1-6pm; rest of year M-F 9:30am-noon and 2-6pm.) Rent **bikes** at **Beltendorf René.** (☎84 92 22. 550LF per day.) To reach the **HI youth hostel,** 3 montée du Château, from the bus stop or tourist office, follow the Grande Rue away from the river and head up the hill; branch off onto montée du Château and follow the signs. (☎83 41 77. Sheets 125LF. Reception 5-9pm. Lockout 10am-5pm. Curfew 11pm. Open mid-Mar. to mid-Nov. 455LF, under 26 375LF.) **Camp op dem Deich,** five minutes downstream from the tourist office, is in the shadow of the chateau. (☎83 43 75. Open Easter-Oct. 150LF per person, 150LF per tent.) Get **groceries** at **Economart,** 1 r. de la Gare. (Open M-Sa 8am-6pm and Su 10am-noon.)

LUXEMBOURG

DIEKIRCH. Between Vianden and Echternach lies Diekirch. The **National Museum of Military History,** 10 Bamertal, presents relics from WWII's Battle of the Bulge. (Open daily Apr.-Nov. 10am-6pm, Dec.-Mar. 2-6pm. 200LF, students 120LF.) Downhill from the museum, turn right onto Esplenade and right onto Zone Pietone to the 15th-century **Eglise Saint-Laurent**. (Open Tu-Su Easter-Oct. 10am-noon and 2-6pm.) **Trains** arrive hourly from Ettelbrück; **buses** roll in roughly every hour from Echternach. To get to the **tourist office,** 3 pl. de la Liberation, take the underground stairs to R. St. Antione, walk to the end, and go directly across the *place.* (☎80 30 23. Open daily 9am-5:30pm.) Across from the bus stop, stay at **Au Beau-Sejour**, 12 Esplenade. (☎80 34 03. Reception 8am-midnight. Singles 1500LF; doubles 2500LF.)

CLERVAUX. Northwest of Vianden and Diekirch, tiny Clervaux's **chateau** houses the striking **Family of Man** exhibition, a collection of over 500 pictures from 68 countries depicting the facets of human life and emotion compiled in 1955 by Luxembourg-born photographer Edward Steichen. (☎92 96 57. Open Mar.-Dec. Tu-Su 10am-noon and 1-6pm. 150LF, students 80LF.) To get to the chateau, turn left with your back to the train station and walk straight (10min.). Clervaux is on the Luxembourg City-Liège-Belgium rail line. The **tourist office,** in the castle, books rooms in **B&Bs.** (☎92 00 72. Open Apr.-June daily 2-5pm, July-Aug. daily 9:45-11:45am and 2-6pm, Sept.-Oct. M-Sa 9:45am-11:45am and 2-6pm.)

LITTLE SWITZERLAND (LE MULLERTHAL)

ECHTERNACH. A favored vacation spot of European families who **camp, bike,** and **hike,** the Lower-Sûre village of **Echternach** (pop. 4500) is famous for its millennia rock formations and seventh-century monastic center. In the Middle Ages, the monastic center was known for its illuminated manuscripts; several are at the 18th-century Benedictine **Abbaye.** From the bus station, turn left at the marketplace on r. de la Gare, take the last left, and walk past the basilica. (Open July-Aug. 10am-6pm, June and Sept. 10am-noon and 2-6pm, Oct.-May 10am-noon and 2-5pm. 80LF.) Echternach is accessible by **bus** from the Ardennes towns and Luxembourg City. The **tourist office** is on Porte St-Willibrord next to the abbey. (☎72 02 30. Open year-round M-F 9am-noon and 2-5pm; in high season open weekends.) To get from the bus station to the **youth hostel (HI),** 9 r. André Drechscher, turn left on av. de la Gare and make your last right. (☎72 01 58. Sheets 125LF. Reception 5-11pm. Lockout 10am-5pm. Closes 1 month in winter. 455LF, under 26 375LF.)

MACEDONIA (МАКЕДОНИЈА)

DENARS

US$1 = 60DN (DENARS)	10DN =US$0.17
CDN$1 = 41DN	10DN = CDN$0.24
UK£1 = 64DN	10DN = UK£0.16
IR£1 = 67DN	10DN =IR£0.15
AUS$1 = 35DN	10DN = AUS$0.29
NZ$1 = 26DN	10DN = NZ$0.38
SAR1 = 8.60DN	10DN = SAR1.16
DM1 = 27DN	10DN = DM0.37
EUR€1 = 53DN	10DN = EUR€0.19

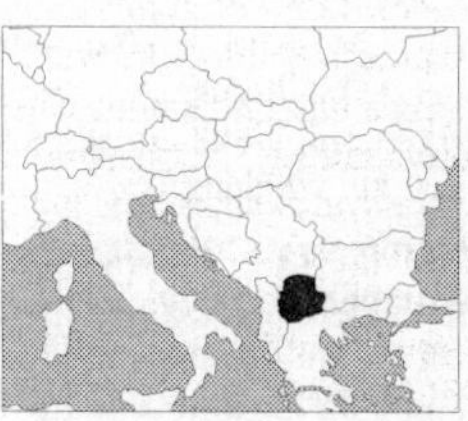

Country code: 389. **International dialing prefix:** 99. From outside Macedonia, dial int'l dialing prefix (see inside back cover) + 389 + city code + local number.

Although years of UN- and Greek-enforced trade embargoes damaged its economy, Macedonia is slowly regaining its place among southern European resorts. Its greater problem now may be the escalating unrest between the country's different ethnic groups. But Macedonia's historical and geographical treasures remain intact, accessible, and welcoming, from Skopje's nightlife to the spectacular mountain basin that is home to Lake Ohrid. For brevity's sake, *Let's Go* uses the name "Macedonia" to refer to the Former Yugoslav Republic of Macedonia. *Let's Go* does not endorse any perceived claims of the former Yugoslav Republic to the Greek territory of the same name. For more info, pick up *Let's Go: Eastern Europe 2001*.

FACTS AND FIGURES

Official Name: The Former Yugoslav Republic of Macedonia (FYROM).
Government: Emerging democracy.
Capital: Skopje.
Land Area: 25,333 sq. km.
Geography: Mountainous.
Climate: Dry in summer; snow in winter.
Population: 2 million.
Languages: Macedonian, Albanian.
Religions: Eastern Orthodox (67%), Muslim (30%).
Average Income Per Capita: US$1050.

ESSENTIALS

DOCUMENTS AND FORMALITIES. Irish, New Zealand, and UK citizens need only a valid **passport** to enter Macedonia. Citizens of Australia, Canada, and the US can obtain single-entry visas at the border or at the nearest Macedonian embassy or consulate. Fees should not exceed US$5.

EMBASSIES AND CONSULATES. All foreign embassies are in **Skopje** (see below). Macedonia's embassies at home include: **Canada,** 130 Albert St. Ottawa, K1M 5G4 ON (☎ (613) 234-3882; fax 233-1852); **UK,** Suite 10 Harcourt House 19a Cavendish Sq., London W1M 9AD (☎ (020) 74 99 51 52); **US,** 3050 K St., NW, Suite 210, Washington DC 20007 (☎ (202) 337-3063; fax (202) 337-3093).

GETTING THERE AND GETTING AROUND. Use both new and old street names when asking for directions. **Flights** to Macedonia land in the **Skopje Airport/Aerodrome Petrovec** (☎ 71 10 24), 23km from Skopje; Ohrid also has an airport, which stays open all year (Skopje's closes in winter). There are flights from Ohrid to

Greece. **Buses** and **trains** travel at comparable speed and comfort, but buses are usually more frequent. Domestic tickets may be purchased in *denars*, DM, or USD. International travel must be done through Skopje. **Taxis** are often the only way to get to a particular destination; settle the price before the ride. There are no bus or train connections from Ohrid to Greece. *Let's Go* does not recommend **hitchhiking.**

TOURIST SERVICES AND MONEY. In an **emergency,** call: ☎94 for an ambulance, ☎93 for the fire department, and ☎92 for the police. **Tourist bureaus** in Skopje and Ohrid give out maps, rent rooms, and sell train and airline tickets. The currency is the **denar,** which comes in notes of 10, 50, 100, 500, 1000, and the rare 5000dn, and in coins of 1, 2, and 5dn. The best rates are at **change bureaus,** the worst at hotels. **Traveler's checks** can only be cashed at banks. Most prices are given in **Deutschmarks (DM),** but most banks will accept US dollars or British pounds and cash **AmEx** traveler's checks. Few places take **credit cards;** some major hotels accept only cash. **ATMs** (scarce) accept MC and Cirrus. **Tipping** is appropriate in small amounts.

ACCOMMODATIONS AND CAMPING. Hotels and hostels take your passport at check-in: all accommodations are required to **register** passports with the police. In areas other than Lake Ohrid, **private rooms** are expensive (900dn) and difficult to find; check with the nearest tourist office. In the resorts, you'll be met by room-renting locals at the bus and train stations—prices improve with haggling (US$10-15). **Hotels** are expensive (4000-5000dn per person in summer). **Youth hostels** are rare. Many **campgrounds** are in a state of disarray; call ahead. Free-lance **camping** is popular, but you risk a fine and it's not safe. Camping in reserve areas is prohibited.

HEALTH AND SAFETY. Recent political events have made it inadvisable to enter Albania or Kosovo in Yugoslavia; even traveling near the border may be dangerous, due as much to bandits as to soldiers and occasional **landmines.**

FOOD AND DRINK. Macedonian food shows Serbian and Greek influences, as well as a love of sesame seeds. Kiosks sell grilled meats (skara; скара), especially small hamburgers (pleskavitsa; плескавица; 50dn) and burek (warm, filo-dough pastry stuffed with veggies, feta cheese, or meat; бурек; 30-35dn). Macedonian *chebubs* (чебаб) and hamburgers are often made of a mix of various meats that even the most die-hard carnivore may find challenging. You can buy fruits and vegetables at an outdoor market, or *pazar* (пазар). *Letnitsa* is a type of trout found only in Lake Ohrid. *Eyeyar* and *rindzur* are tomato-based pasta dishes. *Chorba* (a thick soup; чорба) is a popular morning snack. Wash it down with delicious Macedonian *vino* (вино) or *rakiya,* a grape or plum brandy. The water is drinkable.

COMMUNICATION. To make an international call with a calling card use an **international direct dial** number: **AT&T Direct,** ☎99 800 42 88; **BT Direct,** ☎99 800 00 44; **Canada Direct,** ☎99 800 42 77; or **MCI WorldPhone,** ☎99 800 42 66. Use phones at the post office for international calls. To get an international line, dial ☎99. Calls to the US average US$3-4 per minute. To make local calls from public phones, you must buy a microchip **phone card** (100 or 200dn) at a post office or kiosk. **Macedonian** is a south Slav language that uses the **Cyrillic** alphabet. **Russian** is understood, as are **Serbian** and **Croatian,** and **English** is becoming the second language of choice. Older Macedonians may reverse the Western **head movements** for "yes" and "no."

HOLIDAYS AND FESTIVALS. Holidays include: New Year's (Jan. 1-2); Orthodox Christmas (Jan. 7); Orthodox Easter (April 30-May 1); Labor Days (May 1-2); Ilinden Day (Aug. 1-3); Republic, or Constitution Day (Sept. 8); Partisan Day (Oct. 11).

SKOPJE (СКОПJЕ) ☎91

The rolling hills, tilled fields, and orange-roofed suburbs that surround Skopje lend the city a sense of rural serenity—an impression quickly corrected by the choking, smog-filled air in the nation's capital. In the last two years, the city has been filled with Kosovo-related humanitarian organizations using Skopje as a safe home base.

There are **landmines** in Skopje's immediate vicinity, particularly to the north at the border with Yugoslavia; stay on paved roads.

PRACTICAL INFO, ACCOMMODATIONS, AND FOOD. Trains, go from the *new* train station (Нова Железница Станица; Nova zheleznitsa stanitsa), bul. Jane Sandanski (Јане Сандански) to Belgrade (8hr., 3 per day, 1166dn) and Thessaloniki (6hr., 1 per day, 669dn). **Buses,** at the entrance to the Old Town, go to Ohrid (3½hr., 11 per day, 310dn). The **Skopje Tourist Information** (Скопје Туристичка Информација) is around the corner from the bus station. (☎11 68 54. Open July-Aug. M-F 8am-7pm, Sa 9am-4pm; off season M-F 9am-6pm, Sa 9am-4pm.) Change money at the **Komertsiyalna Banka** (Комерцијална Банка), in the gigantic white office building across from the bus station. Get on the **Internet** at **Cyberia Club,** Dimitrie Cupovski. (80dn per hr. Open daily 10am-4am.) Affordable accommodations abound, but many are occupied by Kosovo-related humanitarian workers. Cheap hotels (1000-3000dn) are usually booked. **Private rooms** are another option (800-1000dn); locals wait at the bus station. **"Ferealni Dom" Youth Hostel Skopje (HI),** Prolet 25 (Пролет), was recently renovated. From the train station, walk toward the river along Kuzman Yosifovski and take the second left. (☎11 48 49. Breakfast included. Dorms 1280dn, with ISIC 935dn; singles 1590dn, 1280dn.) Stara Charshiya's north end hosts a huge **vegetable market,** and the adjacent **Bitzpazar** (Битпазар) has everything else. **Pivnitsa An** (Пивница Ан) is down the steps and through the wooden gates in Stara Charshiya's fountain square. (Entrees 120-330dn. Open daily 9am-midnight.) **Postal code:** 91101.

SIGHTS AND ENTERTAINMENT. Most of Skopje's sights are near the bus station. The domes of the 15th-century **Turkish baths** (Даут-Пашин Амам; Daut-Pashim Amam), now an art gallery, are visible from the bus station. The baths serve as a gateway to the enchanting streets of the largely Albanian and Muslim **Old Bazaar** (Stara Charshiya). Climb the stairs on the left side of the shopping center "Most" and turn right onto Samoilova (Самоилова) until you reach a small square with a fountain. Up Samoilova, **Mustafa Pasha Mosque** (Мустафа Пашина џамија; Mustafa Pashina Jamiya), marks its 506th year. The mosque's key-holder will let you in any time he's around, usually between 5am and 10pm. Every Friday at 1pm, hundreds gather to listen to the preaching of *Hodzha,* or *Imam.* After hours, new clubs are always popping up in the park near the stadium (on the side opposite the river) and in the shopping center near the Swiss embassy on **bul. Makedonija.**

OHRID (ОХРИД) ☎096

Ohrid is Macedonia's premier summer resort, and possibly its most beautiful town. Thanks to UNESCO's protection, the architectural legacy of Yugoslav socialism is scarcely visible. To get to **Sveta Sofia** (Света Софиа), Ohrid's oldest church, take Kliment Ohridski toward the lake and turn right on Tsar Samoil (Цар Саммоил); the church is 300m up on the left. (Open Tu-Su 9am-10pm, although frequently closed on summer afternoons. 50dn, students 20dn.) Sveta Sofia also hosts performances for **Ohridsko Leto** (Охридско Лето; Ohrid Summer), Ohrid's annual classical music festival. (Mid-July to mid-Aug. ☎26 23 04.) Ohrid's best **beaches** are on the lake's eastern side, starting at Hotel Park, 5km from town. They get even better farther away, around Lagadin. **Water-taxis** transport sun-seekers from the shores of the town center (40dn per person; 300-500dn to hire a boat). Ohrid is filled with crowded bars blaring Eurocheese. For a mellower scene, chill out at Macedonia's first jazz club **Jazz Inn,** Kosta Abrash 74. (Open daily 10pm-sunrise.)

Buses go to Skopje (3½hr., 310dn). There are virtually no international buses out of Ohrid. The best transportation options out of Macedonia leave from Skopje. The **AD Galeb Bilyana** (АД Галеб-Билана), Partizanska 3 (☎224 94), in the bus station, finds **private rooms.** Get **Internet** access at **Cyber Cafe** on the corner of Mekodonski Prosvetiteli and Partizanska. (60dn per hr. Open 24hr.) The **gradsko pazarishte** (градско пазариште) sells fruits and vegetables daily between Gotse Delchev and Turistichka. In addition, *skara na kilo* stands are popping up all over Ohrid, where your choice cut of meat is cooked for you while you watch. **Postal code:** 96000.

MALTA

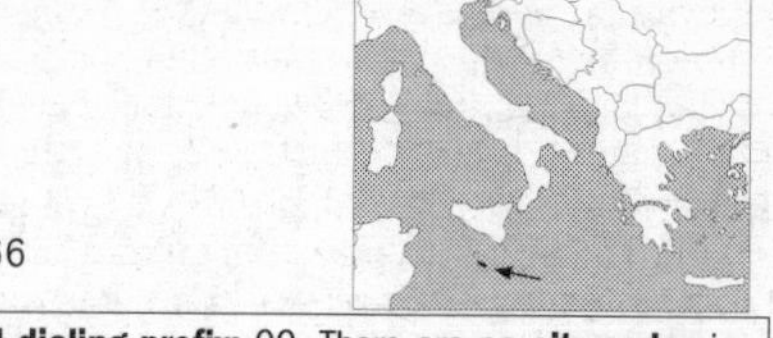

MALTESE LIRE

US$1 = LM0.442 UK£1 = LM0.666

Country code: 356. **International dialing prefix:** 00. There are no **city codes** in Malta. From outside Malta, dial int'l dialing prefix (see inside back cover) + 356 + local number.

Malta is a fairy-tale island whose past includes knights in shining armor, pirates, and the salvation of Christian Europe. Citizens of Australia, Canada, the EU, New Zealand, South Africa, and the US only need **visas** for stays longer than three months. Malta's official **languages** are Maltese and English. The **currency** is the **lira** (Lm), divided into 100 **cents** (¢). **Directory assistance:** ☎190.

GETTING THERE AND GETTING AROUND. **Island Seaway** (☎32 06 55) runs **ferries** from Catania in Sicily (Lm20) and Reggio di Calabria (at the big toe of Italy's boot; Lm25) to Valletta. **Virtu** (☎31 70 88) sends **catamarans** from Catania and Syracuse, Sicily. **Air Malta** (☎69 08 90) and **Alitalia** (☎24 67 82) fly from Rome and London; **NSTS Travel Service** in Valletta sells discounted fares (Lm35; see below). **Bus** #8 runs between the airport and Valletta (3 per hr., 6am-8pm, Lm0.11). For more transportation info, try www.maltayellowpages.com/malta/intro.htm.

VALLETTA. Malta's capital shows off the spectacular **St. John's Co-Cathedral,** with its inlaid marble tombs and works by Caravaggio. From the City Gate, go down Republic St. and turn right on St. John's St. (Open M-F 9:30am-12:45pm and 1:30-5:15pm, Sa 9:30am-12:45pm and 4-5pm. Lm1, students free with ISIC.) The **Lascaris War Rooms,** St. Ursula St., were used by Winston Churchill, Dwight Eisenhower, and other Allied greats for strategic planning in WWII. Take S. Ursula St. from Republic St. and follow the signs. (Open M-F 9:30am-4pm, Sa-Su 9:30am-12:30pm. Lm1.60, students Lm0.85.) The **National Art Museum,** on South St., has works by Maria Preti, who decorated the Co-Cathedral. (Open mid-June to Sept. daily 7:45am-2pm; Oct. to mid-June M-Sa 8:15am-5pm, Su 8:15am-4:15pm. Lm1, students free.) Beyond the cathedral is the **Grand Master's Palace,** home of Malta's rulers since 1575; stop by the tourist office for visiting hours. (State and armory rooms Lm1 each, students free.)

The **tourist office** is on Pope Pius V St., inside the City Gate to the right of the bus terminal. (☎23 77 47. Open Apr.-Oct. M-Sa 8:30am-6:30pm, Su 8:30am-1pm; Nov.-Mar. M-Sa 8:30am-6pm, Su 8:30am-1pm.) **NSTS Travel Service** is at 220 St. Paul's St. (☎24 49 83. Open May-Sept. M-F 9am-1pm and 3-6pm, Sa 9am-1pm; Oct.-Apr. M-F 9am-12:30pm and 2:30-5pm, Sa 9am-12:30pm.) To reach **Coronation Guest House,** 10 E. M. A. Vassalli St., turn left on South St. at the City Gate and descend the steps by the Osborne Hotel. (☎23 76 52. Breakfast included. Open June-Aug. and Oct.-Mar. Lm4-5.) The **Valletta Asti Guest House,** 18 St. Ursula St., is by the Upper Barracca Gardens. (☎23 95 06. Breakfast included. Lm5.50.) The **Hacienda Guest House,** 35 Wilga St., is near the **nightlife** in **Paceville, Sliema,** and **St. Julians.** (☎31 96 29. Breakfast included. Lm6.) Dance with Maltese men, who were named Europe's finest, at **Misfits,** in the White House Hotel on Triq Paceville. (Open daily 8pm-late.)

NEAR VALLETTA. The 9th-century fortifications in **Mdina** (em-DEE-na), once the island's capital, surround a well-preserved Baroque world. **St. Paul's Catacombs** were early Christian burial chambers. To reach Mdina, take **bus** #80 or 81 from Valletta. Near the end of bus route #38, **boats** (Lm2.50) leave the harbor for the phosphorescent **Blue Grotto.** The astonishing megalithic temples of **Mnajdra** and **Hagar Qim,** which has **giant phalli** structures up to 7m high, are 20 minutes away on foot. For **beaches,** try the crowded **Golden Bay** or quieter **Gnejna Bay** along the west coast (take bus #47 from Valletta or bus #652 from Sliema), the **Marfa** peninsula in the northwest (bus #50), or the **Pretty Bay** to the east (bus #11).

THE NETHERLANDS (NEDERLAND)

GUILDERS

US$1 = F2.56 (GUILDERS)	F1 = US$0.39
CDN$1 = F1.73	F1 = CDN$0.58
UK£1 = F3.61	F1 = UK£0.28
IR£1 = F2.80	F1 = IR£0.36
AUS$1 = F1.44	F1 = AUS$0.69
NZ$1 = F1.10	F1 = NZ$0.91
SAR1 = F0.36	F1 = SAR2.78
EUR€1 = F2.20	F1 = EUR€0.45

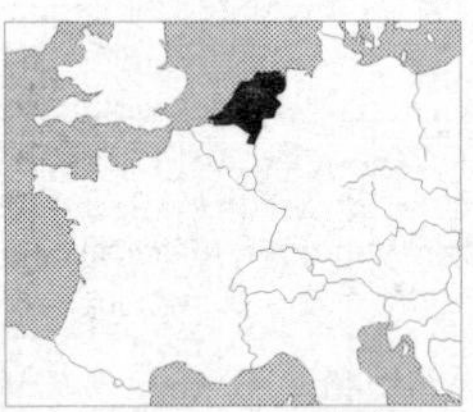

Country code: 31. **International dialing prefix:** 00. From outside the Netherlands, dial int'l dialing prefix (see inside back cover) + 31 + city code + local number.

The Dutch say that although God created the rest of the world, they created the Netherlands. The country is truly a masterful feat of engineering; since most of it is below sea level, vigorous pumping and a series of dikes created thousands of square kilometers of land known as *polders*, which now constitute most of the country's area, including Amsterdam. The Age of Exploration and the Dutch Golden Age crafted a prosperous nation able to support a thriving artistic community, including such masters as Rembrandt and Vermeer; at the same time, an atmosphere of freedom and tolerance spawned the philosophies of Descartes and Spinoza. Although devastated by two world wars, Dutch cities were rebuilt under the stark, modernist influence of Mondrian's de Stijl school and the architecture of Mies van der Rohe. Since the 1960s, the Dutch have continued to push the envelope, pioneering progressive policies regarding sexual identity, gender equality, birth control, and—as teenage tourists and hostile foreign drug officials know all too well—the legalization of soft drugs. The Netherlands' art, canal-lined towns, and Amsterdam's perpetual party draw hordes of travelers that double the country's population every summer.

FACTS AND FIGURES

Official Name: The Kingdom of The Netherlands.
Government: Constitutional Monarchy.
Capital: Amsterdam.
Land Area: 13,255 sq. km.
Geography: Mostly flat, reclaimed land from the sea.
Climate: Temperate, but with rainfall year-round.
Major Cities: Rotterdam, The Hague, Utrecht, Maastricht.
Population: 15,691,000.
Language: Dutch.
Religions: Catholic (32%), Protestant (23%), Muslim (4%).
Average Income Per Capita: US$32,824
Major Exports: Technology, food, and chemical products.

DISCOVER THE NETHERLANDS

Roll it, light it, then smoke it in **Amsterdam,** a hedonist's dream, with chill coffeeshops and breathtaking museums that overwhelm the senses (p. 684). Clear your head in the rustic Dutch countryside; the amazing **Hoge Veluwe National Park,** south-

east of Amsterdam, shelters within its 30,000 wooded acres one of the finest modern art museums in Europe (p. 703). Beautifully preserved **Leiden** (p. 699) and **Utrecht** (p. 702), less than 30 minutes away, delight with picturesque canals. Dutch politics and museums abound in **The Hague** (p. 700); for more innovative art and architecture, step into futuristic **Rotterdam** (p. 701). An afternoon in **Delft** (p. 701) provides a dose of small-town Dutch charm. Visit the sand dunes and isolated beaches of the tiny **Wadden Islands,** a biker's paradise (p. 704).

ESSENTIALS

WHEN TO GO

Mid-May to early October is the ideal time to visit, when day temperatures are generally 20-31°C (70-80°F), with nights around 10-20°C (50-60°F). However, it can be quite rainy; bring an umbrella. The tulip season runs from April to mid May.

DOCUMENTS AND FORMALITIES

South Africans must have a **visa** to enter; citizens of Australia, Canada, the EU, New Zealand, and the US do not need visas for stays shorter than three months.

EMBASSIES AND CONSULATES

All embassies and most consulates are in **The Hague** (p. 700). The **UK** and the **US** also have consulates in **Amsterdam** (p. 684).

Dutch Embassies at Home: Australia, 120 Empire Circuit, Yarralumba ACT 2600 (☎ (02) 62 73 31 11; fax 62 73 32 06); **Canada,** 350 Albert St., Suite 2020, Ottawa, ON K1R 1A4 (☎ (613) 237 50 30; fax 237 64 71); **Ireland,** 160 Merrion Rd., Dublin 4 (☎ (01) 269 34 44; fax 283 96 90); **New Zealand,** P.O. Box 840, Wellington (☎ (04) 471 63 90; fax 471 29 23); **South Africa,** P.O. Box 346, Cape Town 8000 (☎ (021) 421 56 60; fax 418 26 90); **UK,** 38 Hyde Park Gate, London SW7 5DP (☎ (020) 75 90 32 00; fax 75 81 34 58); **US,** 4200 Linnean Ave. NW, Washington, DC 20008 (☎ (202) 244 53 00; fax 362 34 30; www.netherlands-embassy.org).

GETTING THERE AND GETTING AROUND

BY PLANE. KLM Royal Dutch Airlines, Martinair, Continental, Delta, Northwest, United, and Singapore Airlines serve **Amsterdam's** Schiphol Airport. Amsterdam is a major hub for cheap transatlantic flights (seep. 684).

BY TRAIN. The national rail company is the efficient **Nederlandse Spoorwegen** (☎ (09) 00 92 92; www.ns.nl). Trains tends to be faster than buses. *Sneltreins* are the fastest; *stoptreins* make the most stops. One-way tickets are called *enkele reis;* normal round-trip tickets, *retour;* and day return tickets (valid only on day of purchase, but cheaper than normal round-trip tickets), *dagretour.* **Day Trip (Rail Idee)** programs, available at train stations, have reduced-price combo transportation/entrance fees. **Eurail** and **InterRail** (see p. 55) are valid. The **Holland Railpass** (US$52-98) is good for three or five travel days in any one-month period; although available in the US, it is cheaper in the Netherlands at DER Travel Service or RailEurope. The **Euro Domino Holland** card similarly allows three (f130, under 26 f100), five (f200, f150), or 10 days (f350, f275) of unlimited rail travel in any one-month period, but is only available to those who have lived in Europe for at least six months, and cannot be bought in the Netherlands (see p. 59). **One-day train passes** cost f45.25-75.50. The **Meerman's Kaart** grants one day of unlimited travel for two to six people (f114-192).

BY BUS. A nationalized fare system covers city buses, trams, and long-distance buses. The country is divided into zones; the number of strips on a **strippenkaart** (strip card) required depends on the number of zones through which you travel. The base charge within a city is two strips, and travel between towns costs from five to 20 strips. On buses, tell the driver your destination and he or she will cancel the correct number of strips; on trams and subways, stamp your own *strippenkaart* in a yellow box at the back of the tram or in the subway station. Bus and tram drivers sell two- (f3.50), three- (f4.75), and eight-strip tickets (f12), but they're *much* cheaper in bulk, available at public transit counters, tourist offices, post offices, and some tobacco shops and newsstands (15-strip f11.50, 45-strip f33.75). **Dagkaarten** (day tickets) are available for one to nine days (1-day f11). Riding without a ticket can result in a f60 fine plus the original cost of the ticket.

BY FERRY. Ferries traverse the North Sea, connecting **England** to the Netherlands. Boats arrive in **Hook of Holland** (3¾-8½hr.), near Delft and The Hague, from **Harwich,** northeast of London; in **Rotterdam** from **Hull** (13½hr.), near York (p. 197); and in **Amsterdam** from **Newcastle-upon-Tyne** (14hr.; p. 198). For more info, see p. 49.

BY CAR. The Netherlands has well-maintained roadways. On maps, a green "E" indicates international highways; a red "A," national highways; and small yellow signposts and "N," other main roads. **Speed limits** are 50kph in towns, 80kph outside, and 120kph on highways. Fuel prices per liter average about f2.30. The **Royal Dutch Touring Association** (ANWB) offers roadside assistance to members (☎ (06) 08 88). For more info, contact the ANWB at Wassenaarseweg 220, 2596 EC The Hague (☎ (070) 314 71 47), or Museumsplein 5, 1071 DJ Amsterdam (☎ (020) 673 08 44).

BY BIKE AND BY THUMB. Cycling is the way to go in the Netherlands—distances between cities are short, the countryside is absolutely flat, and most streets have separate bike lanes. Bikes run about f8 per day or f35 per week plus a f50-200 deposit (railpasses will often earn you a discount). Call the station a day ahead to reserve; phone numbers are listed in the free *Fiets en Trein*. For info, try www.visitholland.com. **Hitchhiking** is somewhat effective, but on the roads out of Amsterdam there is cutthroat competition. For more info about hitching, visit www.hitchhikers.org. *Let's Go* does not recommend hitchhiking.

TOURIST SERVICES AND MONEY

EMERGENCY. Police, Ambulance, and **Fire:** ☎112.

TOURIST OFFICES. VVV (vay-vay-vay) tourist offices are marked by triangular blue signs.

Tourist Offices at Home: Canada, 25 Adelaide St. E #710, Toronto ON H5C 1Y2 (☎ (416) 363 15 77; fax 363 14 70); **South Africa,** P.O. Box 781738, Sandton 2146 (☎ (11) 884 81 41; fax 883 55 73); **UK** and **Ireland,** P.O. Box 523, London SW1E 6NT (☎ (020) 79 31 06 61; fax 78 28 79 41); **US,** 355 Lexington Ave., New York, NY 10017 (☎ (888) 464 65 52; fax (212) 370 95 07; www.goholland.com).

MONEY. The Dutch currency is the **guilder,** made up of 100 cents. Coins include the *stuiver* (5¢), *dubbeltje* (10¢), *kwartje* (25¢), and *rijksdaalder* (f2.50). Post offices offer reasonable **currency exchange** rates; **GWK** often has the best rates and doesn't charge ISIC holders commission. Otherwise, expect a flat fee of about f5 and a 2.25% commission. A bare-bones day in the Netherlands will cost US$15-25; a slightly more comfortable day will run US$30-40. A 5-10% **gratuity** will generally be added to your hotel, restaurant and taxi bills. An additional 5% is common for superior service. **VAT** refunds in the Netherlands are usually 13.5%, and are available on purchases of more than f300 made during a single visit to a store.

BUSINESS HOURS. Banks open Monday-Friday 10am-4pm, sometimes also later Thursday. Stores are usually open Monday 1-6pm, Tuesday-Friday 9am-6pm, and Saturday 9am-5pm; some are open later Thursday-Friday.

ACCOMMODATIONS AND CAMPING

VVV offices supply accommodations lists and can nearly always reserve rooms (fee around f4). **Private rooms** cost about two-thirds as much as hotels, but are hard to find; check with the VVV. During July and August, many cities add about f2.50 tourist tax to all prices. The country's best values are the 35 **HI youth hostels,** run by the **NJHC (Dutch Youth Hostel Federation);** hostels are divided into three price categories based on quality. Most are exceedingly clean and modern and cost f28-33 for bed and breakfast, plus high season or prime location supplements (f1-3). The VVV has a hostel list, and the useful *Jeugdherbergen* brochure describes each one (both free). For more info, contact the NJHC at Prof. Tulppein 2, Amsterdam (☎ (020) 551 31 33; fax 623 49 86). Pick up a membership card at hostels (f30); nonmembers are charged an additional f5. **Camping** is available country-wide, but many sites are crowded and trailer-ridden in summer. An **international camping card** is not required.

FOOD AND DRINK

Pancakes, salted herring, and pea soup are Dutch specialties. Dutch cheeses transcend Gouda and Edam; try Leiden, the mild Belegen, and the creamy Kernhem. A typical breakfast consists of meat and cheese on bread and a soft boiled egg. For a hearty brunch, try *uitsmijter*, which packs in salad, ham, cheese, and fried eggs. At dinner, reap the benefits of Dutch imperialism: *rijsttafel* is an Indonesian specialty comprising up to 25 different dishes, including curried chicken or lamb with pineapple. *Pannenkoeken* is the traditional Dutch lunch of buttery, sugary, golden brown pancakes, topped with everything from ham and cheese to strawberries and whipped cream. Wash it down with a foamy glass of native Heineken or Amstel.

COMMUNICATION

MAIL. Post offices are generally open Monday-Friday 9am-5pm, and some are also open Saturday 9am-noon. Mailing a postcard or letter to the UK costs f1; to destinations outside Europe, postcards cost f1, letters (up to 20g) f1.60. Mail takes two to three days to the UK, four to six to North America, six to eight to Australia and New Zealand, and eight to 10 to South Africa.

TELEPHONES. When making international calls from pay phones, **phone cards** (in denominations of f10; available at post offices and train stations) are the most economical option. For **directory assistance,** dial ☎0900 8008 within the Netherlands or ☎06 04 18 from outside the country; for **collect calls,** dial ☎06 04 10. **International dial direct numbers** include: **AT&T,** ☎0800 022 91 11; **Sprint,** ☎0800 022 91 19; **Australia Direct,** ☎0800 022 20 61; **BT Direct,** ☎0800 022 04 44; **Canada Direct,** ☎0800 022 91 16; **Ireland Direct,** ☎0800 02 20 353; **MCI WorldPhone Direct,** ☎0800 022 91 22; **NZ Direct,** ☎0800 022 23 13; **Telekom South Africa Direct,** ☎0800 022 02 27.

LANGUAGE. Dutch is the official language of The Netherlands, although most natives speak English fluently. Dutch uses a guttural "g" sound for both "g" and "ch." "J" is usually pronounced as "y"; e.g., *hofje* is "hof-YUH." "Ui" is pronounced "ow," and the diphthong "ij" is best approximated in English as "ah" followed by a long "e." For more basic lingo, see p. 981.

HOLIDAYS AND FESTIVALS

Holidays: The major holidays in The Netherlands are: New Year's Day (Jan. 1); Good Friday (Apr. 13); Easter Monday (Apr. 16); Queen's Birthday (Apr. 29); Liberation Day (May 5); Ascension Day (June 1); Whit Monday (June 4); Christmas Day (Dec. 25); and Boxing Day (Dec. 26).

Festivals: Koninginnedag (Queen's Day; Apr. 30) features huge parties. The Hague hosts the huge North Sea Jazz Festival (July 13-15, 2001). The Holland Festival (in June) celebrates the nation's cultural diversity. Bloemen Corso (Flower Parade; 1st Sa in Sept.) runs from Aalsmeer to Amsterdam. Many historical canal houses and windmills open to the public for National Monument Day (2nd Sa in Sept.).

AMSTERDAM ☎020

Some say that the best vacation to Amsterdam is the one you can't remember. The city lives up to its reputation as a Never Never Land of bacchanalian excess: the aroma of cannabis wafts from coffeeshops and the city's infamous sex scene swathes itself in red lights. But one need not be naughty to enjoy Amsterdam; art enthusiasts will delight in the Rembrandts, Vermeers, and van Goghs, and romantics can stroll along endless streets and canals sparkling with reflected lights.

GETTING THERE AND GETTING AROUND

Flights: Schiphol Airport (SKIP-pull; ☎ (0900) 01 41; f1 per min.). **Trains** connect the airport to Centraal Station (20min., every 10min., f6.50).

Trains: Centraal Station, Stationspl. 1, at the end of the Damrak (international ☎ (0900) 92 96, domestic ☎ (0900) 92 92; f0.50 per min. Schedules at www.ns.nl/reisplan2a.asp). To: **Brussels** (3-4hr.); **Hamburg** (5hr.); **Frankfurt** (5¼-6hr.); **Paris** (8hr.); and **Berlin** (8hr.). Take a number and wait (up to 1hr. in summer). Info desk open 24hr.; international reservations daily 6:30am-11:30pm. **Lockers** f4-6.

Buses: Trains are quicker, but the **GVB** (Amsterdam's public transportation system) will direct you to a bus stop for destinations not on a rail line. **Muiderpoort** (2 blocks east of Oosterpark) sends buses east, **Marnixstation** (at the corner of Marnixstr. and Kinkerstr.) west, and the **Stationsplein depot** north and south.

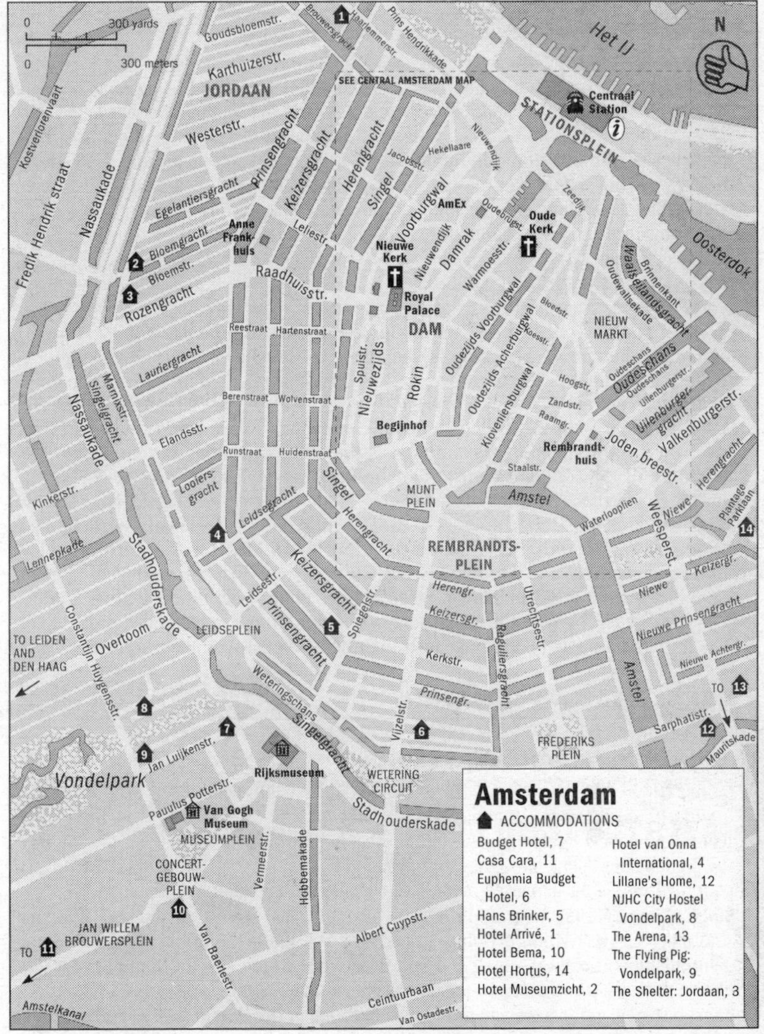

Public Transportation: GVB (☎ (06) 92 92), Stationspl., in front of Centraal Station. Open daily M-F 7am-9pm, Sa-Su 8am-9pm. Tram, metro, and bus lines radiate from Centraal Station. Trams are most convenient for inner-city travel; the metro goes to more distant neighborhoods. Last trams leave Centraal Station M-F midnight, Sa-Su 12:25am. Pick up a *nachtbussen* (night buses) schedule from the GVB office. The GVB offers **day tickets** for visitors to Amsterdam (1-day f11, 2-day f17, 3-day f22.) Don't buy *dagkaart* (day passes; f12) on the bus; the 45-strip *strippenkaart* (f35.25) is the best deal; it can be used on trams and buses throughout the Netherlands and is available at the VVV, the GVB, and many hostels.

Taxis: ☎ 677 77 77. Fares from f4.80 plus f2.80 per km or min. (more at night). Stands at the Dam, Spui, Nieuw Markt, Rembrantspl., Leidsepl., and Centraal Station.

Bike Rental: Beware rampant bike theft. All **train stations** rent bikes for f9.50 per day, f30 per week with a train ticket. **Damstraat Rent-a-Bike,** Pieter Jacobstr. 11 (☎ 625 50

29), is just off Damstr. near the Dam. Rentals f15 per day, f67 per week (plus a credit card slip); used bikes sold from f200. Open daily 9am-6pm.

Hitchhiking: Hitching is increasingly less common in the Netherlands, but it can be done, although *Let's Go* does not recommend it. Additionally, hitchhiking is not allowed on Dutch highways. Those heading to: **Utrecht,** central and southern Germany, and Belgium, take tram #25 to the end and start at the bridge; **Groningen** and northern Germany, take bus #56 to Prins Bernhardpl. or the metro to Amstel and start along Gooiseweg; **the Hague,** hop on tram #16 or 24 to Stadionpl. and start on the other side of the canal on Amstelveenseweg; **Haarlem** and **Noord Holland,** take bus #22 to Haarlemmerweg and start from Westerpark.

ORIENTATION

A series of roughly concentric canals ripple out from the **Centrum** (city center), resembling a giant horseshoe with its opening to the northeast. Emerging from Centraal Station, at the top of the horseshoe, you'll hit **Damrak,** which leads to the **Dam,** the main square. East of Damrak in the Centrum is Amsterdam's famed **red-light district,** bounded by Warmoestr., Gelderskade, and Oude Doelenstr. Don't head into the area until you've locked up your bags, either at the train station or at a hostel or hotel. South of the red-light district lies the **Rembrandtsplein.** The canals radiating around the Centrum (lined by streets of the same names) are **Singel, Herengracht, Keizergracht,** and **Prinsengracht.** West of the Centrum and beyond Prinsengracht, lies the **Jordaan,** an attractive residential neighborhood. Moving counterclockwise around Prinsengracht you'll hit the **Leidseplein,** which lies just across the canal from the **Museum District** and **Vondelpark.** Street names change capriciously; buy a good **map** of the city (f2.75-4) at the VVV tourist office or from a magazine stand. *Use It* (f4) includes a map, cheap lodgings info, an index of youth agencies, and city news.

PRACTICAL INFORMATION

TOURIST AND FINANCIAL SERVICES

Tourist Office: VVV, Stationspl. 10 (☎ (0900) 400 40 40; fax 625 28 69), to the left and in front of Centraal Station. Books rooms for a f4.50-6 fee. Sells maps, phone cards, excursions bookings, museum passes, and *strippenkaart.* Pick up *Day by Day* (f2), a fabulous listing of events. **Branches** at Centraal Station, platform 2, Leidsepl. 1, van Tuyll van Serooskerenweg (near Stadioplein), and the airport; all open daily.

Budget Travel: NBBS, Rokin 38 (☎624 09 89). Open mid-May to mid-Aug. M-F 9:30am-5:30pm, Sa 10am-4pm; mid-Aug. to mid-May M-F 9:30am-5:30pm, Sa 10am-3pm. **Budget Bus/Eurolines,** Rokin 10 (☎560 87 88). Open M-F 9:30am-5:30pm, Sa 10am-4pm. **Wasteels,** also on Rokin, has cheap plane tickets.

Consulates: All **embassies** and most consulates are in **The Hague** (see p. 700). Consulates: **UK,** Koningslaan 44 (☎676 43 43). Open M-F 9am-noon and 2-3:30pm. **US,** Museumpl. 19 (☎664 56 61). Open M-F 8:30am-noon and 1:30-4:30pm.

Currency Exchange: Best rates at **American Express** (see below). The **GWK** offices at Centraal Station and Schiphol have good rates, and charge students no commission for traveler's checks. Open 7am-11:30pm. **Change Express,** Kalverstr. 150 (open M-Sa 8:30am-8pm, Su 10:30am-6pm) or Leidestr. 106 (open daily 8am-11pm), has good rates and a 2.25% commission plus f7.50 fee.

American Express: Damrak 66 (☎520 77 77; fax 504 87 07). Excellent rates and no commission on traveler's checks. Mail held. AmEx ATM. Open M-F 9am-5pm, Sa 9am-noon. Beware the pickpockets in the neighborhood.

LOCAL SERVICES

English Bookstores: Bookstores line **Spui,** near Amsterdam University, which holds an open-air *Boekemarkt* F 10am-6pm. **American Book Center,** 185 Kalverstr. 10% student discount. Open M-W and F-Sa 10am-8pm, Th 10am-10pm, Su 11am-6pm.

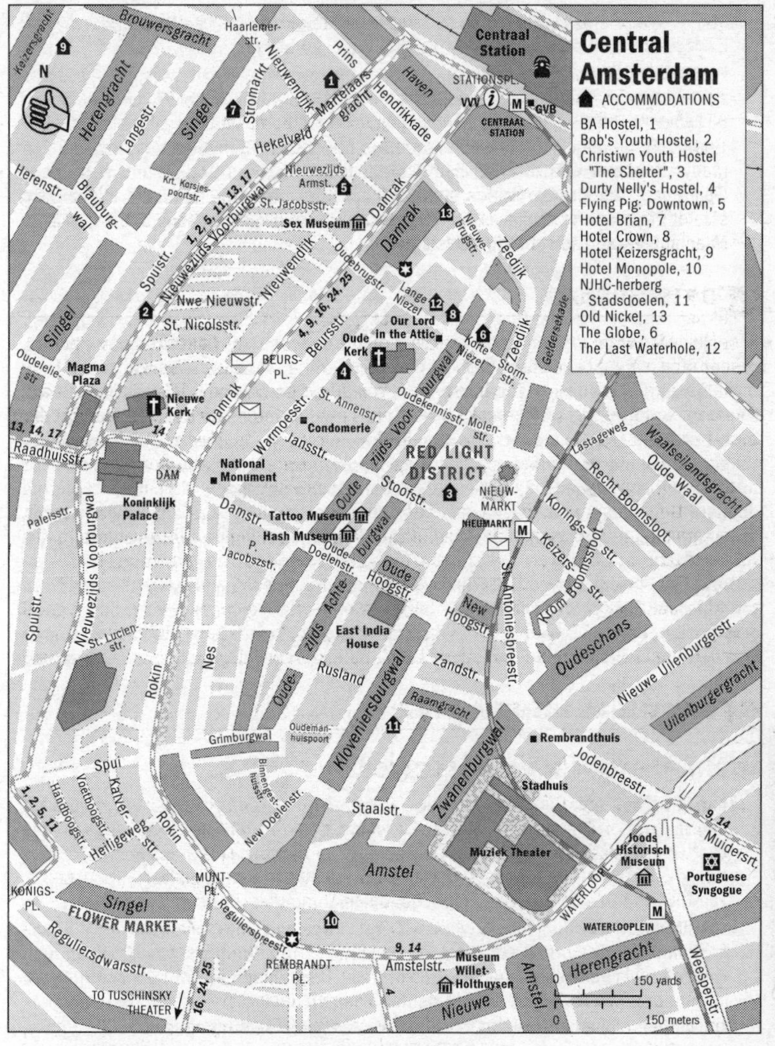

Gay and Lesbian Services: COC, Rozenstr. 14 (☎626 30 87), is the main source of info. Open M-F 10am-5pm. **Intermale,** Spuistr. 251 (☎625 00 09), is a gay bookstore. Open M 11am-6pm, Tu-W and F-Sa 10am-6pm, Th 11am-9pm. **Gay and Lesbian Switchboard** (☎623 65 65) runs daily 10am-10pm. In June, July, and Aug., also look for the **Pink Point** info booth behind the Homomonument at Westerkerk (☎412 44 63).

Laundry: Look for a *Wasserette* sign. **The Clean Brothers,** Kerkstr. 56. (☎622 02 73). Wash f8, dry f1 per 20min. Open daily 7am-9pm.

Condoms: Find the widest variety of colors, flavors, and styles at the **Condomerie,** Warmoesstr. 141, next to the red-light district. Open M-Sa 11am-6pm.

EMERGENCY AND COMMUNICATIONS

Emergencies: ☎112. **Police:** Elandsgracht 117 (☎559 91 11). Handles rape crisis.

Crisis Lines: General counseling at **Telephone Helpline** (☎675 75 75). Open 24hr. **Rape crisis hotline** (☎613 02 45). Open M-F 10:30am-11pm, Sa-Su 3:30-11pm. **Drug counseling,** Jellinek clinic (☎570 23 55). Open M-F 9am-5pm.

Pharmacies: Most open M-F 8:30am-5pm. When closed, each *apotheek* (pharmacy) posts a sign directing you to the nearest open one. After 11pm, call ☎694 87 09.

Medical Assistance: Tourist Medical Service (☎592 33 55). Open 24hr. **Academisch Medisch Centrum,** Meibergdreef 9 (☎566 91 11), near the Holendrecht metro stop. Free emergency medical care is at the **Kruispost,** Oudezijds Voorburgwal 129 (☎624 90 31). Open M-F 9:30am-12:30pm and 7-9:30pm. **STD Line** (☎555 58 22). Free clinic at Groenburgwal 44 with testing M-F 8-10:30am and 1:30-3:30pm.

Internet Access: Cybercafé, Nieuwendijk 19 (☎623 51 46). f1 per 10 min., f5 per hr. Open Su-Th 10am-1am, F-Sa 10am-3am. **Café ZoëZo,** Vijzelgracht 63 (☎330 67 67). f2 per 15min., f6 per hr. Open Su-Th 11am-midnight, F-Sa 11am-1am. **Easy Everything,** Reguliersbreestr. 22, in Rembrandtsplain next to the Tushinki Theatre. The largest Internet cafe in the world. Open 24hr.

Telephones: Call first and pay afterward at **Telehouse,** Raadhuisstr. 48-50, near the Dam (open 24hr.), or the **TeleTalk Center,** Leidsestr. 101, near the safer Leidsepl. (open daily 10am-midnight). Most public phones require prepaid phone cards, available at the tourist office, the post office, cigarette shops, and currency change offices. Coin phones can be found in hostels, hotels, and the post office.

Post Office: Singel 250-256 (☎556 33 11), at Raadhuisstr. behind the Dam. A Open M-W and F 9am-6pm, Th 9am-8pm, Sa 10am-1:30pm. Mail held downstairs available M-F 8am-7pm and Sa 9am-noon. Address mail to be held: First Name SURNAME, *Poste Restante,* Singel 250-256, Amsterdam **1016 AB,** The Netherlands.

ACCOMMODATIONS AND CAMPING

Accommodations closer to the **station** often have good security measures. Hostels and hotels in **Vondelpark** and the **Jordaan** are quieter and safer, near their share of bars and coffeeshops, close to large museums and the busy Leidsepl., and are only 15 minutes by foot or two minutes by train from the red-light district and city center. You can book spaces in **HI hostels** from any other HI hostel (free within the Netherlands, f4 elsewhere). Many other hostels do not accept dorm reservations, despite the crowds that swarm the city in June, July, and August. Call ahead, ask if there is a guest list, and plan to arrive from 9 to 10am in summer for places that adamantly will not take reservations. The hotels and hostels listed in the red-light district are often bars with beds over them; the exceptions merit their more favorable write-ups. Consider just how much pot, noise, and music you want to inhale before booking a bed, and always see accommodations under f30 before committing to them. If you tire of Amsterdam's intensity, consider staying in nearby **Edam** for a good dose of the Dutch countryside. VVV offices in every town book accommodations and **private rooms** for around f40 including booking fee.

LEIDSEPLEIN AND MUSEUMPLEIN

NJHC City Hostel Vondelpark (HI), Zandpad 5 (☎589 89 96; fax 589 89 55; www.njhc.org), bordering Vondelpark. Take tram #1, 2, or 5 from the station to Leidsepl., cross the canal, turn left at the Marriott, and take the 2nd right before the park entrance. Popular with all ages. Clean, spacious rooms and full baths. Breakfast included. Bike rental f10 per day. Reception 7am-12:30am. Avoid the park after dark. Dorms f34-38; doubles f108-158; quads f45-51 per person. Nonmembers add f5.

International Budget Hostel, Leidsegracht 76 (☎624 27 84; fax 626 18 39; email ibh@budgethostel.a2000.nl). Take tram #1, 2, or 5 to Prinsengracht, head right down Prinsengracht, turn left on Leidsegracht, and it's on your right with the red shutters. Well-located with simple, attractive rooms. Breakfast f2.50-8. In summer, 2-night min. stay. Reception 9am-11pm. Dorms f35-50; doubles f100-170.

The Flying Pig Palace, Vossiusstr. 46-47 (☎400 41 87; email palace@flyingpig.nl). Take tram #1, 2, or 5 from the station to Leidsepl., cross the canal, turn left at the Marriott, pass the Vondelpark entrance, and take the next right. This clean, vibrant hostel maintains a fun atmosphere in a beautiful location. Breakfast included. Kitchen and bar. Key deposit f10. Free Internet. Reception 8am-9pm. From f35.50.

Hans Brinker, Kerkstr. 136 (☎622 06 87; fax 638 20 60; www.hansbrinker.com). Take tram #1, 2, or 5 from the station, get off at Kerkstr., and it's 1 block down on the left. Clean, gigantic, and comparatively safe, with a bar and disco. Breakfast included. Key deposit f10. Reception 24hr. Dorms f42.50; singles f111; doubles f120-146; triples f186; quads/quints f150-200. Add f2.50 for 1-night stay.

The Golden Bear, Kerkstr. 37. (☎624 47 85; email hotel@goldenbear.nl). Take tram #1, 2, or 5 to Prinsengracht, walk back to Kerkstr. and turn left. Opened in 1948, the Golden Bear is thought to be the world's oldest openly gay hotel. Simple, sophisticated rooms with impeccably clean bathrooms. Mainly male couples, although lesbians are welcome as well. Breakfast included. Reception 8-11pm. Doubles f140; triples f225.

Hotel Wynnobel, Vossuisstr. 9 (☎662 22 98). Bordering the Vondel Park along the same street as the Flying Pig. A beautiful old bed and breakfast, truly from another era. Reception 7am-midnight. All rooms f60-75 per person.

Hotel Museumzicht, Luykenstr. 22 (☎671 29 54; fax 671 35 97). Take tram #2 or 5 from the station to Hobbemastr. Beautiful little hotel on a quiet street, with an unbelievable view of the Rijksmuseum. Breakfast included. Reception 8am-11pm. Singles f65-85; doubles f130-175; triples f180. 10-15% less off season.

Hotel Bellington, P.C Hooftstr. 78-80 (☎671 64 78; fax 671 86 37; email hotel-bellington@wxs.nl; www.hotel-beliington.com). Follow directions to Hotel Museumzicht. Hoftstr. is behind Lukenstr., toward the Leideplainl. A well-groomed hotel on one of Amsterdam's ritziest streets; 2-night stay preferred on weekends. Breakfast included. Reception 8am-5pm and 8-10pm. Doubles f130-200; triples f210-250.

Euphemia Budget Hotel, Fokke Simonszstr. 1-9 (☎622 90 45; email euphemiahotel@budgethotel.a2000.nl), 10min. from Leidsepl. Take tram #16, 24, or 25 to Wetering Circuit, backtrack on Vijzelstr., cross the canal, and turn right on Fokke Simonszstr. Officially gay-friendly. Breakfast f8.50. Reception until 11pm. Discounts for email reservations. Doubles f100-250; triples f120-240; quads f140-300.

RED-LIGHT DISTRICT AND REMBRANDTSPLEIN

NJHC-Herberg Stadsdoelen (HI), Kloveniersburgwal 97 (☎624 68 32; fax 639 10 35), between Nieuwmarkt and Rembrandtspl. Take tram #4, 9, 16, 24, or 25 to Muntpl., walk down Amstel, cross the green bridge, and it's 1 block up on the right. Lively lounge and casual atmosphere. Breakfast included. Laundry f11. Kitchen. Bike rental f12.50. Internet. Reception 7am-12:30am. f33.50; non-members add f5.

Flying Pig: Downtown, Nieuwendijk 100 (☎420 68 22; fax 421 08 02; email downtown@flyingpig.nl), just off Damrak. What Amsterdam myths are made of. Swap books or joints, party in the bar, or snuggle in the lounge. Breakfast included. Kitchen. Key deposit f10. Reception 24hr. Free Internet. Reserve at least a week ahead. Dorms f35.50-46.50; doubles f65; quads f49.50.

The Globe, Oudezijds Voorburgwal 3 (☎421 74 24; fax 421 74 23; email manager@theglobe.demon.nl). From the station, head toward Damrak, take the 2nd left on Nieuwezijds Brugsteeg, and the 2nd right on Oudezijds Voorburgwal. The hostel is across the 1st bridge on your left. Lively pub with live music F-Sa. Breakfast f7.50-15. Reception 24hr. Dorms f40, weekends f45; private rooms with bath f50-65 per person.

Durty Nelly's Hostel, Warmoesstr. 115/117 (☎638 01 25; fax. 633 44 01; email nellys@xs4all.nl). From the station, walk 2 blocks left of the Damrak. Above an Irish pub. Breakfast included. Reception 24hr. No reservations–arrive as close to 9am as possible. Dorms f35-40. Cash only.

BA Hotel, Martelaarsgracht 18 (☎638 71 19; fax 638 88 03; email india@cistron.nl). From the station, cross the bridge to Damrak, take a right on Prins Henrikkade, and the 1st left on Martelaarsgracht. Well-located, with a friendly staff and bar. No last-minute reservations; book ahead. Breakfast and map included. Key deposit f25. Reception 8am-midnight. On high-season weekends, 2-night min. stay. Dorms f25-45.

Christian Youth Hostel "The Shelter," Barndesteeg 21-25 (☎625 32 30), off the Nieuwmarkt (metro: Nieuwmarkt). Virtue amid the red lights. Cozy courtyard, religious slogans, and single-sex dorms. Breakfast included. Key deposit f10. Lockers f10. Curfew Su-Th midnight, F-Sa 1am. Reception 24hr. Dorms f28, off season f25.

Hotel Centrum, Warmoesstr. 15 (☎/fax 420 16 66; email centrum@xs4all.nl). Follow directions to The Old Quarter below. Keep the groove on in the downstairs bar. Reception 8am-1am. Singles f75; doubles f105; triples f150; quads f200.

Bob's Youth Hostel, Nieuwezijds Voorburgwal 92 (☎623 00 63), near Centraal Station. Take tram #1, 2, 5, or 13 to Nieuwezijds Kolk. No smoking in the rooms; you'll inhale enough on the stairs. Basic dorms and a chill atmosphere. Breakfast included. Key and locker deposit f25. Reception 8am-3am. No reservations or credit cards. Dorms f30. Nice doubles with kitchen and TV also available in separate building, f150.

The Greenhouse Effect, Warmoesstr. 55 (☎624 49 74; fax 427 70 06; www.the-greenhouse-effect.com). A bar, coffeeshop, and hotel wrapped up in one. Reception and breakfast in the bar; open Su-Th 9am-1am, F-Sa 9am-3am. Key deposit f50 or passport. Dorms f55; doubles from f160; triples from f190.

Hotel Brian, Singel 69 (☎624 46 61; fax 416 47 85; email hotelbrian@hotmail.com). On a quiet block only minutes from the city center; from Centraal Station turn right at the Victoria Hotel, proceed until turning right onto Singel. Small rooms in a very friendly and comfortable atmosphere. Breakfast included. TV lounge. Key deposit f25. Reception 8am-10:30pm. Dorms f40-50, off season f30-40. No credit cards.

Hotel Crown, Oudezijds Voorburgwal 21 (☎626 96 64; fax 420 64 73; www.web2day.com). Handsome dorms f65-90.

Old Nickel, Nieuwebrugsteeg 11 (☎624 19 12; fax 620 76 83). From Centraal Station, turn left onto Nieuwebrugst.; the Old Nick tavern is on the corner at Warmoestr. Breakfast included. Reception 8am-midnight. All rooms f45-65 per person.

Hotel Hortus, Plantage Parklaan 8 (☎625 99 96; fax 416 47 85). From the station, take tram #9 to Artis, backtrack on Plantage Middenlaan, and go left on Parklaan. Big-screen satellite TV and pool table. Breakfast included. Key deposit f25. Internet. Reception 8am-11pm. Dorms f40-50, off season f30-40.

Old Quarter, Warmoesstr. 20-22 (☎626 64 29; email info@oldquarter.a2000.nl.). Turn right onto Warmoesstr. from Old Nickel. The Old Nickel's larger, more-modern brother. Very clean accommodations with elevator accessibility. Reception 24hr. Downstairs bar has live music Th 9pm, F-Su 10pm. Doubles f125.

Hotel International, Warmoesstr. 1-3 (☎624 55 20; fax 624 45 01). Kitty corner to the Old Nickel. Simple accommodations in an old building. Breakfast included. Key deposit with passport or ID. Reception 8am-1am. Doubles f110-150; triples f150-225. Reduced in off season.

THE JORDAAN

Hotel van Onna, Bloemgracht 104 (☎626 58 01). Take tram #13 or 17 from the station to Westmarkt. Pleasant hotel with simple rooms and immaculate bathrooms. Breakfast included. Reception 8am-11pm. f80. No credit cards.

Anna's Youth Hostel, Spuistraat 6 (☎620 11 55). From Centraal Station, turn left onto Spuistr. Close to the station. 2-night min. stay with Sa night check-in. No drugs. Reception daily 8am-1pm and 5pm-3am. High season f35; off season weekdays f25, weekends f30. No credit cards.

The Shelter: Jordaan, Bloemstr. 179 (☎624 47 17; fax 627 61 37; email jordaan@shelter.nl). One street from Rozengracht (tram #13 or 17: Marnixstr.). Cheap, well-located Christian hostel. Few showers. Breakfast. Nightly Bible study. Age limit 15-35. Free Internet. Reception 7:30am-2am. Curfew 2am. Single-sex dorms f28.

CAMPING

Camping Zeeburg, Zuider-Ijdijk 20 (☎694 44 30), next to the Amsterdam Rijncanal. Take bus #22, tram #14, or night bus #79 (15min.) and walk 3min. Backpacker-oriented. Live music regularly. Reception July 8am-11pm; Aug.-June 9-11am and 5-9pm. f7.50 per person; f5 per tent. Showers f1.50.

Gaaspercamping, Loosdrechtdreef 7 (☎696 73 26; fax 696 93 69), in Gaasper Park. Take the metro (dir.: Gaasperplas) to the end, or night bus #75. Laundry f13. Reception 9am-9pm. Open mid-Mar. to Dec. f6.75 per person; f15 per tent. Showers f1.50.

FOOD

Dutch food ranges from the hopelessly bland to the oddly tasty. Dutch *pannenkoeken* (pancakes), similar to thick, unrolled crepes, are prepared as both main courses and sweet desserts and are the most savory Dutch dishes. If you're feeling adventurous, stop by a fish stall in summer to try herring—raw, salted, with a squeeze of lemon, and best when swallowed whole in one mouthful. Aside from the highlights of Holland proper, Surinamese, Indonesian, Chinese, and Indian food establishments are some of the best dining to be had in the city, often with the best vegetarian options. Cheap restaurants cluster around **Leidsepl., Rembrandtspl.,** and **Spui.** *Eetcafés*, especially in the Jordaan, serve cheap sandwiches (f4-9) and good meat-and-potatoes fare for f12-20. Bakeries sell inexpensive cheese croissants and magnificent breads along **Utrechtsestr.,** south of Prinsengracht.

Check out the **markets** on **Albert Cuypstr.,** behind the Heineken brewery. (Open M-Sa 10am-4:30pm.) The cheapest **groceries** are at **Aldi Supermarket,** Nieuwe Weteringstr., off Vijzelgracht, near the Heineken brewery. (Open M 11am-6pm, Tu-F 9am-6pm, Sa 8:30am-4pm.) **Albert Heijns** branches are at Koningspl. and 226 Nieuwezijds Voorburwal, beside the Magna Plaza. (Open M-Sa 8am-10pm, Su 11am-7pm.)

LEIDSEPLEIN, THE MUSEUM DISTRICT, AND THE JORDAAN

Balraj, Binnen Oranjestr. 1. Next to the Hotel Ramenas, this cozy Indian restaurant serves remarkably tender chicken dishes. Dinner from f17. Open daily 5-10pm.

Restaurant Semhar, Marnixstr. 259. From Leidsepl., take tram #1 to Bloemgracht. Eritrean-Ethiopian fare in a quiet corner restaurant. Open daily 1-11pm.

Bolhoed, Prinsengracht 60-62, across the canal from the Anne Frank Huis. Cafe with delicious vegan options. Salads and quiche f12-19. Open daily noon-10pm.

Esoterica, Overtoom 409. Incredible homemade vegetarian food by the Vondelpark. Indonesian specialities. Snacks and salads f5-9, meals f15-17. Open W-Su 2-10pm.

Harlem Drinks and Soul Food, Haarlemmerstr. 7. Jamaican, Surinamese, and soul food. Salads f12. Breakfast 8:30-11:30am. Open Su-Th 8:30am-1am, F-Sa 8:30am-3am.

Bojo, 51 Lange Leidsedwar. Delicious, heaping portions of Indonesian food, but with MSG. Meals f13-21. Open M-Th 4pm-2am, F 4pm-4am, Sa noon-4am, Su noon-2am.

Gary's Muffins, Prinsengracht 454. Small cafe bakes muffins (f2.50), cookies, brownies, and great bagel sandwiches (f4.25-9.75). Open M-Sa 8:30am-6pm. Late-night location at Reguliersdwarsstr. 53. Open noon-3am, F-Sa noon-4am.

Brasserie van Gogh, P.C. Hooftstr. 28, at the corner of Hobbemastr. Large menu and sunflower decor. Salads f18.50-24, baguettes f8.50-11.50. Open daily 9am-6pm.

Dionysos, Overtoom 176. From Leidsepl., walk right on the Stadhouderskade and Overtoom is on the left. Tasty Greek dishes from f12. Open daily 5-11pm.

RED-LIGHT DISTRICT AND REMBRANDTSPLEIN

Café Restaurant Turquoise, Wolvenstr. 30. Between Keizergracht and Hernegracht near the Spui. Turkish food and classy setting. Meals f19-26. Open daily 5pm-midnight.

Café de Jaren, Nieuwe Doelenstr. 20-22. Skim through a magazine/newspaper and chill in the large reading room, or sit outside and savor the view. Gourmet meals f18.50-28. Open Su-Th 10am-1am, F-Sa 10am-2am; kitchen closes 10:30pm.

Pannenkoekenhuis Upstairs, Grimburgwal 2. From Muntpl. tram stop, cross the bridge, walk along the Singel and turn right on Grimburgwal. A tiny nook with perhaps the best pancakes in the city. Open M-F noon-7pm, Sa noon-6pm, Su noon-5pm.

La Place, Muntpl. on the corner of Kalverstr. and Rokin, and at Vroom Dreesman, Kalverstr. 201. Vegetarian options abound along with meats cooked to order at this delectable buffet. Meals f20. Open M 11am-8pm, Tu-W 9:30am-8pm, Th 9:30am-9pm, F-Sa 9:30am-6pm, Su noon-6pm.

Downtown, Reguliersdwarsstr. 31. Small cafe popular with gay men. Cappucino f3.75; homemade quiche f7.75. Open daily 10am-7pm.

Keuhen Van 1870, Spuistr. 4. Serves traditional Dutch food at the cheapest prices around. *Prix fixe* f12.50. Open M-F 12:30-8pm, Sa-Su 4-9pm.

Kam Yin, Warmoesstr. 6. From Centraal Station, turn left on Nieuw Brugstreet, cross the bridge, and you're there. This Chinese/Surinamese landmark has a huge menu. Meals f8-16. Open daily noon-midnight.

SIGHTS

Amsterdam is fairly compact. **Circle Tram 20,** geared toward tourists, stops at 30 attractions in the city. (Runs every 10min. 9am-6pm. Day pass f11; buy on the tram or at VVV offices). The peaceful **Museumboot Canal Cruise** allows you to hop on and off along their loop from the VVV to the Anne Frank Huis, the Rijksmuseum, the Bloemenmarkt, Waterlooplein, and the old shipyard—buy tickets at any stop. (Departs every 30min. 10am-5pm, f25; pass also yields 10-50% off at all museums and is valid until noon the next day.) Or, rent a **canal bike.** (2 people f25 per hr., 4 people f40; f50 deposit. Pick-up and drop-off points at Westerkerk in the Jordaan, Weteringschans 24 at the Rijksmuseum, and Leidse Bosje at the Vondelpark. Open daily July-Aug. 10am-10pm; Sept.-June 10am-7:30pm). **Mike's Bike Tours** provide an entertaining introduction to the city and the surrounding countryside. (☎622 79 70. Reserve by phone. Tours start from the Rijksmuseum; adults f37, ages 4-12 f25; 10 or more f30 per person.) The **Museumkaart** grants discounts on admission to museums and transportation throughout the Netherlands (f55, under 25 f25; buy at museums throughout the Netherlands). The **Amsterdam Leisure Pass** includes a canal trip and admission to the Rijksmuseum, the Stedelijk Museum, and the Amsterdam Historical Museum (f41.50; buy at the VVV).

MUSEUM DISTRICT

VAN GOGH MUSEUM. The architecturally breathtaking **Van Gogh Museum** houses the largest collection of van Goghs in the world and a variety of 19th-century works by artists who influenced or were contemporaries of the master. Van Gogh's Japanese influence is proven by the sushi bar in the middle of the museum. *(Paulus Potterstr. 2. Take tram #2 or 5 from the station. Or, from the Rijksmuseum, walk a block down Museumstr. ☎570 52 52. Open daily 10am-6pm. f12.50. Audio tour f8.50.)*

STEDELIJK MUSEUM OF MODERN ART. Picasso, Pollock, de Kooning, Newman, Stella, Chagall, Malevich, and Ryman are all in the outstanding permanent collection. So too is Piet Mondrian; despite the modern master's later move to New York City, the Stedelijk chronicles his Dutch days with Post-Impressionist windmills. Up-and-coming contemporary work is also often shown. *(Paulus Potterstr. 13, next to the Van Gogh Museum. ☎573 29 11 or 573 27 37; www.stedelijk.nl. Open daily 11am-5pm. f10.)*

RIJKSMUSEUM (NATIONAL MUSEUM). It would be sinful to miss the Rijksmuseum's impressive collection of works by Rembrandt, Vermeer, Frans Hals, and Jan Steen. Follow the crowds to Rembrandt's famed militia portrait **The Night Watch,** in the Gallery of Honor, then proceed into Aria, the interactive computer room that can create a personalized museum map. Don't miss the doll house exhibits chronicling the boredom of rich married women in 18th-century Holland. *(On Stadhouderskade. Take tram #2 or 5 from the station. ☎674 70 47 for 24 hr. information. Open daily 10am-5pm. f12.50, f25 for additional exhibits.)*

HEINEKEN EXPERIENCE. *Cerveza, birra, bière*—in the Netherlands they call it Heineken, a name many Netherlanders revere more than the Royal Oranje family. Even the Queen and Alfred Heineken have cultivated a famous friendship in recent years. Tour this entirely refurbished museum, scheduled to reopen in April 2001. Get in line early: the sooner you take a tour, the more time you have to down the free beer. *(Stadhouderskade 78, off Ferdinand Bolstr. and down Stadhouderskade from the Rijksmuseum. ☎523 96 66; call for opening times. f10. Must be 18+ or with guardian.)*

REMBRANDTSPLEIN AND ENVIRONS

VERZETSMUSEUM (DUTCH RESISTANCE MUSEUM). In the heart of the Amsterdam's historically Jewish neighborhood, the museum brings the struggles and strategies of the Dutch Resistance Movement down to the local level; notes thrown to loved ones on trains to Auschwitz convey the extensive effort to keep networks alive, and a neighborhood tour tells how 150 Jewish people were successfully hidden in the lion cage in the Artis Zoo across the street. The 2001 exhibit will chronicle the post-war return of Dutch Jews held in concentration camps and gentry held by the Japanese in Indonesia. *(Plantage Kerklaan 61. Take tram #7, 9, or 14 to "Artis." Or, from the Synagogue, walk down Muiderstr., which becomes Plantage Middenlaan, and turn right on Plantage Kerklaan. ☎620 25 35. Open Tu-F 10am-5pm, Sa-Su noon-5pm. f9, students f4.)*

TUSCHINSKI THEATER. This fabulously ornate movie theater is one of Europe's first experiments in Art Deco. Although a group of drunk Nazis once started a fire in its cabaret, the theater survived WWII and has remained in operation for over 75 years. *(Reguliersbreestr., between Rembrandtspl. and Muntpl. ☎0900 202 53 50 for movie listings. Tours in summer Su-M 10:30am; f10. Screenings f14-38.)*

JOODS-PORTUGUESE SYNAGOGUE AND JOODS HISTORISCH MUSEUM. After being expelled from their country in the 15th century, a sizable number of Spanish and Portuguese Jews established a community in Amsterdam. In 1675, they built the large, handsome **Joods-Portuguese Synagogue.** The Dutch government protected the building from the Nazi torches by declaring it a national historic site. Across the street, the **Joods Historisch Museum (Jewish Historical Museum),** housed in three connected former synagogues, traces the history of the Dutch Jewish community. *(Jonas Daniel Meijerpl., at Waterloopl. Take tram #9 or 14. Synagogue open daily 10am-4pm. f7.50. Museum open daily 11am-5pm; resource center open daily 1pm-5pm. f8, students f4.)*

TROPENMUSEUM (MUSEUM OF THE TROPICS). Thanks to the Dutch East India company, this multimedia presentation of artifacts from Asia, Africa, and Latin America has especially fine Indonesian art and an engaging children's wing. It also hosts frequent film, food, and music festivals. *(Linnaeusstr. 2. Take tram #9 to "Artis," east of Waterloopl. ☎568 82 15. Open M-F 10am-5pm, Sa-Su noon-5pm. f15, students f10.)*

REMBRANDTHUIS. The master lived, worked, and taught in this recently renovated house until the city confiscated it for taxes; it holds 250 of Rembrandt's etchings and dry points, as well as many of his tools. *(Jodenbreestr. 4-6, at the corner of the Oudeschans Canal. Take tram #9 or 14. Open M-Sa 10am-5pm, Su 1-5pm. f12.50.)*

RED-LIGHT DISTRICT

While the red-light district is surprisingly liveable, woe to the uninformed: pushers, porn shops, and live sex theaters do brisk business. **Sex shows** (f10-50) consist of costumed, disaffected couples repeatedly acting out your "wildest" (i.e., choreographed) dreams. Red neon marks houses of legalized ill repute, where sex workers display themselves in windows. During the day, the red-light district is comparatively flaccid. As the sun goes down, people get braver, and the area much more stimulating (or disgusting, depending on your viewpoint). Cops patrol the district until midnight. Women may feel uncomfortable walking through this area, and all tourists are prime targets for pickpockets.

OUR LORD IN THE ATTIC. An oasis of piety hides in a 17th-century house known as the **Museum Amstelkring, Ons' Lieve Heer op Solder** ("Our Lord in the Attic"), where a Catholic priest, forbidden to practice his faith publicly during the Reformation, established a grand chapel in the attic. *(Oudezijds Voorburgwal 40, at the corner of Oudez. Armstr., 5min. from the station. Open Tu-F 10am-5pm, Sa-Su 1-5pm. f10, students f6.)*

THE VICES. For a historical, chemical, and agricultural breakdown of the wacky tobacky all over town, drop by the informative **Hash Marijuana Hemp Museum.** Although the museum collection is roughly 50% pro-pot pamphlets, posters, and propaganda for cannabis reform in the United States, the grow-room in back reminds you that you're still in Amsterdam. *(Open daily 11am-10pm. f12.50; seeds f20-275.)* **The Tattoo Museum**—the name says it all—displays designs, rituals, and tattoo-making tools from all over the world, plus a 2000-year-old mummified and tattooed arm found in Peru. *(Oudezijds Achterburgwal 130, next to the Hash Marijuana Hemp Museum. Open M-W noon-6pm, Th-Su 1am-7pm. f7.50, students with ID f5.)* See sex in every way you dreamed possible (and many you didn't) at the semi-tacky **Amsterdam Sex Museum,** which showcases an "only in Amsterdam" collection of erotic art and hard-core porn through the ages. *(Damrak 18, near the station. 18+. Open daily 10am-11:30pm. f6.)*

OTHER SIGHTS. A straight shot from Centraal Station, **Dam Square** contains some of the city's most interesting buildings. The former town hall, **Koninklijk Palace,** may be a symbol of 17th-century commercialism, but its majesty is topped by the stunning **Magna Plaza** mall next door, a 20th-century monument to commercialism. *(Palace at Dam 1; ☎620 40 60; call for hours. Plaza open Su-M 11am-7pm, Tu-Sa 9:30am-9pm.)*

THE JORDAAN

Lose the hordes in the narrow streets of the **Jordaan,** built as an artisan district in the Golden Age. Bounded roughly by Prinsengracht, Brouwersgracht, Marnixstr., and Lauriersgracht, and teeming with small cafes, galleries, and chocolate shops, the area is possibly the prettiest and most peaceful in the city. **Begijnhof** is a beautifully maintained grassy courtyard surrounded by 18th-century buildings that runs between Kalverstr. and the Spui. *(Open daily 10am-5pm. Free.)* For more nature, pick-up soccer, llama-grazing, and people-watching, relax in the sprawling **Vondelpark.**

ANNE FRANK HUIS. The tiny space where the young journal-keeper hid with her family from the Nazis until their capture in 1944 now has video interviews with Otto Frank, Anne's father, and Miep Gies, the woman who hid with the Franks. An interactive, multi-lingual CD-ROM exhibit provides extensive information about the Franks and their life in the Annex, and relates the Holocaust to current human rights issues. *(Prinsengracht 263, next to the Westerkerk. Take tram #13, 14, or 17. ☎556 71 00; www.annefrank.nl. Open daily 9am-9pm. f10.)* While you're there, check out the **Homomonument,** in front of the Westerkerk at the banks of the canal, a memorial to those persecuted through history for their sexual orientation.

ELSEWHERE IN AMSTERDAM

GRAFFITI ART. Some of the most exciting art in Amsterdam is free, painted on doors, walls, and trams. The **Vrankrijk** building, Spuistr. 216, and the area around **Mr. Visserplein,** near Waterloopl. and the Hortus Botannicus, prove that graffiti can be more than names and vulgar phrases. Continue the psychedelic survey at the **3D Hologram Store.** *(Grimburgwal 2, near Muntpl. Open Su-M 1-5:30pm, Tu-F noon-6pm, Sa noon-5:30pm.)*

MARKETS. An open-air art market takes place every Sunday in the **Spui,** where artists regularly present oils, etchings, sculptures, and jewelry, and where a book market occasionally yields rare editions and 17th-century Dutch romances. *(Art market open daily Mar.-Dec. 10am-6pm. Book market open F 10am-6pm.)* Pick up bulbs and blooms at the **Bloemenmarkt**. *(Open daily 8am-8pm.)* Mill with the masses at the famous flea market on **Waterlooplein,** where you can try your hand at bargaining for antiques, birds, or farm tools. *(Open M-Sa 9am-5pm.)*

ENTERTAINMENT

Pick up the monthly *Day by Day* (f4) from the VVV for comprehensive cultural listings. The mini-magazine *Boom!*, free at restaurants and cafes around the city, is full of tourist info; also try the free monthly *UITKRANT*. The **Amsterdams Uit Buro** (AUB), Leidsepl. 26, has fliers and other info and makes reservations for any cultural event. (☎0900 01 91; www.aub.nl. Open daily 10am-6pm.) The monthly *Culture and Camp* (f5) provides info on gay venues and events. The bi-monthly *Queer Fish* (f2.50) catalogues less mainstream concerts and parties.

CONCERTS. In summer, there are free performances Wednesday through Sunday at the **Vondelpark Openluchttheater** (☎673 14 99). Jazz and folk dominate, but children's theater, rock, political music, and mime also grab the limelight; check posters at park entrances. The **Royal Concertgebouw Orchestra,** at the Concertgebouw on Van Baerlestr., is one of the world's finest. (Take tram #316 to Museumplein. ☎671 83 45. Box office open daily 10am-7pm. Tickets from f35.) Sunday morning concerts (with guided tours 45min. before the performance) are cheaper. (Tours at 10:15am, f5; concerts at 11am, f25.) Organ concerts resound on summer Wednesdays at 8:15pm at **Westerkerk,** Prinsengracht 281, where Rembrandt is buried. There are also frequent concerts at **Nieuwe Kerk,** on the Dam (f5-12.50).

FILM AND THEATER. Check out the free **movieguide.nl** in pure pulp or on the web for listings. In the Vondelpark, head left from the main entrance on Stadhouderskade to see what's on at the stately **Filmmuseum** theater. (☎589 14 00; email fillmuseum@nhm.nl. Info open Tu-F 10am-5pm, Sa 11am-5pm.) Stop by the adjacent **Vertigo Cafe** even if you don't see a movie (see **Cafes and Bars,** below). Frequent English performances and cabarets are at the theater/cafe **Suikerhof,** Prinsengracht 381. (☎22 75 71. Open M-Sa from 5pm, Su from 2pm.) Make reservations for any cultural event at the **AUB** (see above) or at the VVV's theater desk, Stationspl. 10 (open M-Sa 10am-5pm). There's no escaping **Boom Chicago,** Leidepl. 12, opposite the Bulldog, an American comedy troupe that publishes *Boom!* and performs English improv sketches nightly. (Reservations ☎431 01 01. Performances Su-F at 8:15pm; doors open at 6pm. Box office open daily 10am-6pm. Tickets Su-Th f29.50, F-Sa f34.50; Su-F f5 off with *Boom!*.) The **Muziektheater,** in the Stadhuis (City Center) at Waterloopl., hosts the **Netherlands Opera** and the **National Ballet.** (☎625 54 55; www.muziektheater.nl. Box office open daily 1am-6pm and Su 11:30am-6pm. Opera tickets start at f50; student discount given. Ballet tickets from f25.)

FESTIVALS. Queen's Day (April 30) turns the city into a huge carnival; on the same day is the year's largest flea market. The **Holland Festival** in June, with dance, drama, and music, is closely followed by the **Summer Festival** of small theater companies in July. (Tickets f10-15. Call the Balie Theatre at ☎623 29 04 for info.) On the first weekend in August, gay pride comes out in street parties along Warmoesstr., Amstel, Kerkstr., and Reguliersdwarsstr., and in the outrageously fun **Gay Pride Parade,** when floats, boats, queens and jubilant queers take over the Prinsengracht. During **Uitmarket** weekend at the end of August, street theater, hundreds of free concerts around the Dam Square, and a book market along the Nieuwezijds Voorburgwal transform Amsterdam into a brilliant, raucous party.

COFFEESHOPS AND SMART SHOPS

The rumors are true: marijuana and hashish are legal in the Netherlands. Since soft drugs were decriminalized in 1996 and Mayor Patijn issued the first **coffeeshop** license, "coffeeshop" is no longer a euphemism for semi-shady spots dealing quasi-legal drugs. Coffeeshops don't just sell coffee, but also pot or hash; some even let you buy a drink and smoke your own stuff. **Don't be afraid to ask questions;** coffeeshop staffs are accustomed to explaining the different drugs to tourists. Look for the green and white "Coffeeshop BCD" sticker that certifies a coffeeshop's credibility. **Hash** comes in two varieties: **black** (like Afghani and Nepali; f10-24 per gram) and **blonde** (like Moroccan). **Marijuana** is also increasingly popular. You can legally possess up to 5g of marijuana or hash (the previous 30g limit was reduced in response to foreign criticism). Pot in Holland is very strong, and the Dutch tend to mix tobacco with their pot as well, so joints are harsher on your lungs; ask coffeeshop dealers if their joints are rolled with tobacco or are pure cannabis. Never smoke pot on the street; it's offensive to the Dutch. Pick up a free copy of the *BCD Official Coffeeshop Guide* for the pot-smoker's map of Amsterdam. **Never buy drugs from street dealers.** Remember that any drugs can be dangerous.

Also legal are **smart shops,** which peddle various **"herbal enhancers"** and **hallucinogens** that walk the line between soft and hard drugs. Some are alcohol-free and all have a strict no-hard-drugs policy. **All hard drugs are illegal**—possession is a serious crime. For legal info on drugs in Amsterdam, call the **Jellinek clinic** (☎570 23 55). If you or a friend experiences a bad trip, **don't hesitate to ask for help** or call ☎122, as you will not be arrested in Amsterdam for using.

Barney's Coffeeshop, Haarlemmerstr. 102 (☎625 97 61). Pot choices range from Thai for beginners (f5) to the killer Sweet Tooth (f17.50). Open daily 7am-8pm.

Baba, Warmoesstr. 64 (☎624 14 09). Head straight from Centraal Station, turn on Oudebrugs, and continue straight to the corner of Warmoesstr. Walk through the Hindu god Ganesh's threshold for hash brownies, spaceshakes, and grass muffins (f7.50). Open Su-Th 8:30am-1am, F-Sa 8am-1am.

De Rokerij, Amstelstr. 8, in the Muntpl. Also at Lange Leidsestr. 41 and Singel 8. A dark, largely untouristed coffeeshop with wrought-iron candlesticks and blue-and-gold-painted ceiling and walls. Strong pre-rolled joints for f6. Open daily noon-11pm.

The Greenhouse Effect, Warmoesstr. 53. A relaxed atmosphere with a friendly, knowledgeable staff. Spaceshake for f10. Open Su-Th 9am-1am, F-Sa 9am-3am.

Tweedy, Vondelstr. 104 (☎618 03 44), next to Cafe Vertigo at Vondelpark. Watch the game and smoke with locals after hanging out in the park. Open daily noon-midnight.

Conscious Dreams Kokopelli, Warmoestr. 12 (☎421 70 00). This smart shop is a good place to begin your psychedelic survey. Books, lava lamps, and a knowledgeable staff coat your trip: magic shrooms, oxygen, vitamins, and herbs. All drugs sold for 2 people. Open daily 11am-10pm.

Majic Mushroom Gallery, Spuistr. 249 (☎427 57 65) and Singel (☎422 78 48). Specializes in herbal ecstasy, relaxants, psychoactives, and energizers. Four kinds of shrooms f25-30. Catalogues available. Open Su-Th 11am-10pm, F-Sa 10am-10pm.

Homegrown Fantasy, Nieuwezijds Voorburgwal 87a (☎627 56 83). A smokeshop gallery specializing in weed. Art exhibitions change every six weeks. Not a place for novices. Bags f10-25, rolled joints f5, pure cannabis joints f7.50. Spacecakes f10, space bon bons f7.50. Open daily Su-Th 9am-midnight, F-Sa 9am-1am.

 NIGHTLIFE

CAFES AND BARS

Amsterdam's finest cafes are the old, wood-paneled *bruine kroegen* (brown cafes) of the **Jordaan,** many of which have canal-side seating along **Prinsengracht. Leidsepl.** is the liveliest nightspot, with coffeeshops, bars, and clubs galore. Dutch soap stars come to be seen and drink at reasonable prices at **Paladium** and **Raffles,** also in Leidsepl. **Rembrandtspl.** is the place to watch soccer and sing with drunk revelers. Gay bars line **Reguliersdwarsstr.,** which connects Muntpl. and Rembrandtspl., and **Kerkstr.,** five blocks north of Leidsepl. Most cafes open in the late morning and serve lunch and dinner; bars open at 10 or 11am and close at 1am during the week and 2 to 3am on Fridays and Saturdays.

Café 't Smalle, at the corner of Prinsengracht and Egelandiersgracht. Intimate, tiny bar founded in 1780. Famous pea soup served in winter for f8.50. Open Su-Th noon-12:15am, F-Sa noon-2am.

Café de Tuin, Tweede Tuindwarsstr. 13, attracts names from Dutch TV, radio, and film to its relaxed setting. Beer from f3.25. Open daily noon-2am.

Absinthe, Nieuwezijds Voorburgwal 171. Young and trendy, Absinthe looks and feels more like a chill mini-club than a typical Dutch bar. Shots of its namesake f7.50. Open Su-Th 8pm-3am, F-Sa 8pm-4am.

Saarein, Elandstr. 119. A gay-friendly bar in the Jordaan. Pool and pinball downstairs; books and women's magazines upstairs. Open Su-Th 5pm-1am, F-Sa 5pm-2am.

De Prins, Prinsengracht 124. A classic student bar in the Jordaan. No pot, no frills, but cool. Famous cheese fondue (f24). Open Su-Th 10am-1am, F-Sa 10am-2am.

Havana, Reguliersdwarsstr. 17-19. Glam it up in plush red velvet booths in this popular gay bar. Mainly men, but fun for women too. DJs upstairs on weekends. Bacardi f7.50. Open Su-Th 4pm-1am, F-Sa 4pm-3am.

Vive La Vie, Amstelstr. 7, at the corner of Rembrandtspl. Mixed gay bar especially for women; small, lively and extremely popular. Open Su-Th 3pm-1am, F-Sa 3pm-3am.

Cafe Vertigo, Vondelpark 3, adjacent to the Filmmuseum. Low lights and a chic crowd; head inside for a f4.50 glass of wine. Open daily 10am-1am.

NL Lounge, NZ Voorburgwal 169. Too cool for an outside sign, the trendy NL is the unmarked destination where slick, chic, sophisticated Amsterdam insiders come to mingle. Don't bother if you look under 26; try Time or Absinthe next door instead. Mixed drinks f12. Open Su-Th 8pm-3am, F-Sa 8pm-4am.

W.F. Fockink, 31 Pijlsteeg, in Dam Square. Largely untouristed, they've been brewing famous liquors for 400 years. f4 per glass, f35 per bottle. Open daily 3-9pm.

LIVE MUSIC

In Amsterdam, the lines blur between club life and live music; two top venues, the **Milky Way** and **Paradiso,** hold club discos after performances and on non-concert nights. Many aficionados argue that the soul of the music scene lies in the smaller cafes and bars. The **Jazzlijn** (☎626 77 64) provides info on local concerts. The **AUB** (see p. 694) has the **Pop & Jazz Uitlijst** and fliers for other free concerts. Many clubs expect you to buy an overpriced drink instead of charging a cover.

Paradiso, Weteringschans 6-8. Some of the foremost punk, new-wave, and reggae bands play in this former church where Lenny Kravitz got his big break and the Stones taped their latest live album. Tickets f10-50. Club nights W-Su.

Melkweg, Lijnbaasgracht 234a, in a warehouse off Leidsepl. Legendary nightspot has a cutting-edge aura. Live bands, theater, films, dance shows, and an art gallery make for sensory overload. f5 fee for concerts; tickets f20-60. Club night cover f10. Club nights F-Sa 1-5am. Box office open M-F 1-5pm, Sa-Su 4-6pm, and until 7:30pm on show days.

The Bimhuis, Oude Schans 73-77, near Waterloopl. (ticket reservations ☎62 13 61). The hub of Dutch jazz holds concerts W-Sa 9pm. Tickets f15-25, students f7.50. Su-Tu free jam sessions. Reservations daily 11pm-4pm. Box office opens at 8pm.

Maloe, Lijnbaansgracht 163. Vibrant crowds writhe to rock and blues. Cover f5 on live music nights, f2.50 on DJ Fridays. Open Su-Th 8pm-3am, F-Sa 8pm-4am.

Korsakoff, Lynbaansgr. 161. The leftovers of punk culture convene from Maloe. Alternative guitar and cheap beer by the bottle (f3.50) thrill in a three-story hall. Ring the bell, tip when you leave. Open Su and Th 10pm-3am, F-Sa 10pm-4am.

Bourbon Street Jazz & Blues Club, Leidsekruisstr. 6-8. Blues, soul, funk, and rock bands keep the crowds stocked every night. The Stones, B.B. King, and Sting have played this joint. Cover f5. Open Su-Th 10pm-4am, F-Sa 10pm-5am.

Alto, Korte Leidsedwarsstr. 115. A good place to be aloof in the Leidsepl. Live jazz and blues every night. No cover. Open Su-Th 9pm-3am, F-Sa 9pm-4am.

Winston Kingdom, Warmoesstr. 127. Offers nightly live music from acid rock to disco. Cover f7.50. Open Su-W 9pm-3am, Th-Sa 9pm-4am.

The Last Waterhole, Oudezijds Armsteeg 12. In the red-light district, the Waterhole also grooves to acid rock, disco, and everything else. Open Su-Th until 3am, F-Sa until 4am.

CLUBS AND DISCOS

Many clubs charge a membership fee in addition to cover, so the tab can be harsh. Be prepared for cocky doormen who live to turn away tourists; show up early or hope the bouncer thinks you're cute. As is the custom in Amsterdam, a promised tip of f10-20 (left on your way out) may help. There are pricey discos aplenty on **Prinsengracht,** near Leidsestr., and on **Lange Leidsedwarsstr.** Gay discos line **Amstelstr.** and **Reguliersdwarsstr.** and cater almost exclusively to men. **You II** is a popular lesbian club. Pick up a wallet-sized *Clu* guide, free at cafes and coffeeshops, for a club map of the city, and the free monthly *Gay and Night,* for info on gay parties.

Escape, Rembrandtspl. 11. Perhaps the most popular club in Amsterdam plays house, trance, disco, and dance classics. Beer f4.50, mixed drinks f13. Pricey cover (f25). Open W-Su 11pm-4am, F-Sa 11pm-5am.

Time, Nieuwezijds Voorburgwal 163-165. Young, trendy, and tourist-oriented, Time runs free shuttles to hostels. Chill dance floor topped by an upstairs lounge. Tu reggae night, W drum and bass, Th house, F progressive and trance, Sa house and funky techno. Cover f10-20. Open Su-Th 11pm-4am, F-Sa 11pm-5am.

MAZZO, Rozengracht 114, in the Jordaan. Artsy, experimental disco with red Victorian couches and lamp shades. Mixed drinks f10. Cover Su-F f10-12.50, Sa f15-20. Open Su-Th 11pm-4am, F-Sa 11pm-5am.

The iT, Amstelstr. 24. Leather, dry ice, and S&M make the iT Amsterdam's premier hardcore disco, specializing in house and trance. Innocence lost at rapid rates. Cover f15-25. Open Th and Su 11pm-4am, F-Sa 11pm-5am.

Exit, Reguliersdwarsstr. 42. One of the most popular gay discos in the Netherlands. Mostly men. Beer f5. Cover f10-12.50. Open Su-Th midnight-4am, F-Sa midnight-5am.

Dansen bij Jansen, Handboogstr. 11, near the Spui. Cheap, near the university, and popular with students. Beer f3 for a half-pint. Happy Hour Su-W 11pm-midnight. Cover Su-W f2.50, F f5, Sa f7.50. Open Su-Th 11pm-4am, F-Sa 11pm-5am.

You II, Amstel 178, near Rembrandtspl. Popular lesbian club has a circular bar in front opening onto a dance floor in back. Men allowed. Drinks f4-12. Su often karaoke night. Cover f10. Open Th and Su 10pm-4am, F-Sa 10pm-5am.

The Arena, Gravesandestr. 51-53. Take any metro to the third stop, night bus #76 or 77, or tram #9 to "Tropenmuseum"; turn right on Mauritskade and left on 's-Gravesandestr. 80s, 90s dance F from 11pm; f12.50. 60s, 70s dance Sa from 10pm; f15.

EXCURSIONS FROM AMSTERDAM

EDAM. Discover quaint cottages, peaceful parks, and lots of cheese and clogs in Edam. The 15th-century **Grote Kerk,** or St. Nicholaaskerk, is the largest three-ridged church in Europe and has exquisite stained-glass windows. (Open daily May-Sept. 2-4:30pm. Free.) Farmers still bring their famed cheese to **market** by horse and boat. (July-Aug. W 10am-12:30pm.) Rent a bike at **Ronald Schot,** Grote Kerkstr. 7/9, (☎37 21 55; f10 per day), and head to the source yourself. At the four cheese farms at **Alida Hoeve,** Zeddewed 1, Edam cheese is still hand-made. (Open daily 9am-6pm. Free samples.) If going by bike, leave Edam, and follow the bike path in the direction of Olendam and Amsterdam. Farther down the path from Alida Hoeve stands a towering **windmill.** (Open daily Apr.-Oct. 9:30am-4:30pm. f1 to climb to the top.) **Bus** #114 runs from Amsterdam's Centraal Station to Edam (30min., 7 strips). The **tourist office,** Kaizergracht 1, in the old town hall, helps find rooms (f35). To get there, take a left at the black bridge when you get off the bus, turn right, and follow Lingerzijde to the center of town. (☎31 51 25. Open Sept.-June M-Sa 10am-5pm, Su 1-5pm; July-Aug. M-Sa 10am-5pm, Su 1-5pm.) ☎**0299.**

UTRECHT. Just 25 minutes from Amsterdam by train, Utrecht is a popular daytrip; Its canals and prestigious university may coerce you into a longer stay (see p. 702).

HAARLEM ☎023

Surrounded by fields of tulips and daffodils and punctuated with Renaissance facades and placid canals, it's clear why Haarlem inspired native Frans Hals and other Golden Age Dutch artists. The **Grote Markt** (city center) pulsates with charming cafes, and the narrow cobblestone streets are filled with exquisite shops. The local 17th- and 18th-century *hofjes* (almshouses for elderly women), now private residences, feature elegant brickwork and idyllic courtyards. Along Kruisweg in the Grote Markt is the glorious medieval **Stadhuis** (Town Hall), originally the hunting lodge of the Count of Holland. The **Grote Kerk,** at the opposite end of the Markt, houses the mammoth Müller organ once played by an 11-year-old Mozart. (☎532 43 99. Open M-Sa 10am-4pm. f2.75.) From the church, turn left onto Damstr. and follow it until Spaarne, where you will find the **Teyler's Museum,** Spaarne 16. The Netherlands' oldest museum, it contains an eclectic assortment of scientific instruments, fossils, paintings, and drawings, including works by Raphael, Michelangelo, and Rembrandt. (☎531 90 10. Open Tu-Sa 10am-5pm, Su noon-5pm. f10, students f5.) The **Frans Hals Museum,** Groot Heiligland 62, is another almshouse; from the Teyler's, turn right, walk along the Zuider Buitenspaarne canal, turn right onto Kampverst., then left onto Groot Heiligland. The museum contains work by the portraitist and a collection of modern art. (☎511 57 75. Open M-Sa 11am-5pm, Su noon-5pm. f10, seniors f7.50, under 19 free.)

Reach Haarlem from Amsterdam by **train** (15min., f6.50) from Centraal Station or by **bus** #80 from Marnixstr., near Leidsepl. (2 per hr., 2 strips). The VVV **tourist office,** Stationspl. 1, finds private rooms (from f38) for a f10 fee. (☎ (0900) 616 16 00; www.vvvzk.nl; email info@vvvzk.nl. Open M-F 9am-5:30pm, Sa 10am-2pm.) The lively **NJHC-herberg Jan Gijzen (HI),** Jan Gijzenpad 3, is 3km from the station on the banks of a canal. Take bus #2 (dir. Haarlem-Nord) and tell the driver your destination. (☎537 37 93. Breakfast included. Key deposit f25 or passport. Non-NJHC members f42-46.) **Hotel Carillon,** Grote Markt 27, is ideally located, if not ideally priced. (☎531 05 91. Breakfast included. Reception and bar open 7:30am-1am. Singles f60-110; doubles f110-142.) To **camp** at **De Liede,** Lie Over 68, take bus #2 (dir. Zuiderpolder) and walk 10 minutes. (☎533 23 60. f6 per person; f5.50 per tent. In summer add f2.50 tax.) Try cafes in the **Grote Markt** for cheap meals.

EXCURSIONS FROM HAARLEM. The seaside town of **Zandvoort** boasts one of the **Holland Casinos** and two **nude beaches** south of town, along with more modest sands. Walk left when you hit the beach (30min.). A 30-minute walk in the opposite direction brings you to the hip **Blomendaal** beach, with the popular clubs **The NL Republic, Zomers, and Woodstock. Trains** arrive in Zandvoort from Haarlem (10min., round-trip f6). The VVV **tourist office,** Schoolpl. 1, in the town center, sells a lodgings guide (f2). Follow signs from the station. (☎571 79 47; fax 571 70 03. Generally open M-Sa 9am-5pm.) The **Hotel-Pension Noordzee,** Hogeweg 15, is 100m from the beach. (☎571 31 27. Breakfast included. Singles f55; doubles f90.)

Ninety million flowers are auctioned every day at the world's largest flower auction, in nearby **Aalsmeer.** Self-guided tours cover the auction's gargantuan warehouse and auction rooms. (☎ (0) 297 39 21 85; www.vba.nl. Open M-F 7:30am-11pm.) Take **bus** #140 (45min., every 30min.) from the Haarlem train station. The **Frans Roozen Gardens** bloom with 500 different types of flowers and plants. (Open Mar. to early Dec. M-F 9am-5pm. Tulip shows daily Apr.-May 8am-6pm. Flower shows free.) **Bus** #90 from Haarlem (dir. Den Haag) stops in front of the gardens (25min., every 30min.). For even more flowers, check out **Lisse** in late spring. The **Keukenhof** gardens become a kaleidoscope as over 5,000,000 bulbs come to life. (Open daily late Mar. to mid-May and Aug. 3-Sept. 17 8am-7:30pm; last entry 6pm. f19.) The **Zwarte Tulip Museum** details the history and science of tulip raising. (Open Tu-Su 1-5pm. f4.) Look for petals in motion at the **April flower parade** (April 21, 2001). Take **bus** #50 or 51 from the Haarlem train station; combo bus/museum tickets are available at the station (f21). The **tourist office** is at Grachtweg 53. (☎ (0252) 41 42 62. Open M noon-5pm, Tu-F 9am-5pm, Sa 9am-4pm.)

LEIDEN ☎071

Home to one of Europe's oldest and most prestigious universities, Leiden brims with bookstores, bicycles, museums, gated gardens, and hidden walkways. Rembrandt's birthplace and the site of the first **tulips,** Leiden is a picture-perfect gateway to flower country. Sharing a main gate with the *Academie* building is the university's 400-year-old garden, the **Hortus Botanicus,** Rapenburg 73, where the first Dutch tulips were grown. Its grassy location along the **Witte Singel** canal make it an ideal picnic spot. (Open daily Mar.-Nov. 10am-6pm; Dec.-Feb. Su-F 10am-4pm. f8.) Across the footbridge from the main gate to the Hortus, the **Rijksmuseum van Oudheden** (National Antiquities Museum), Rapenburg 28, harbors the restored Egyptian Temple of Taffeh, a gift removed from the reservoir basin of the Aswan

Dam. (☎516 31 63. Open Tu-F 10am-5pm, Sa-Su noon-5pm. f7, included in Museumkaart.) **Rijksmuseum voor Volkenkunde** (National Museum of Ethnology), Steenstr. 1, is one of the world's oldest anthropological museums, with fantastic artifacts from the Dutch East Indies. (☎516 88 00. Open Tu-F and Su 10am-5pm, Sa noon-5pm. f10, students f7.50.) Inspect the innards of a functioning windmill at the **Molenmuseum "De Valk,"** 2e Binnenvestgracht 1. (Open Tu-Sa 10am-5pm, Su 1-5pm. f5; included in Museumkaart.) The **Museum De Lakenhal,** Oude Singel 32, exhibits works by Rembrandt and Jan Steen. (☎516 53 60; www.lakenhal.demon.nl. Open Tu-Sa 10am-5pm, Su noon-5pm. f8, included in Museumkaart.)

Leiden is easily accessed by **train** from The Hague (20min., f5) or Amsterdam (30min., f12). The VVV **tourist office,** Stationsweg 2d, sells walking tour brochures (f1-4) and finds **private rooms** (f4.50). Head straight from the station and it'll be on the right. (3min. ☎ (0900) 222 23 33; fax 516 12 27; www.leiden.nl. Open June and Sept.-Mar. M-F 10am-6:30pm, Sa 10am-4:30pm; Apr.-May and July-Aug. M-F 10am-6:30pm, Sa 10am-4:30, Su 11am-3pm.) The **Hotel Pension Witte Singel,** Witte Singel 80, five minutes from Hortus Botanicus, has immaculate rooms. Take bus #43 to "Merenwijk" and tell the driver your destination. (☎512 45 92; fax 514 78 90; email wvanvriel@pensione-ws.demon.nl. Singles f60; doubles f93-120.) The Greek restaurant **Rhodos,** Turfmarkt 5, serves salads for f6-14. (Open daily 3pm-midnight.) Just off the Rapenburg, across from the Hortus, try escargot (f10) at the French-inspired **M'n Broer,** Kloksteeg 7. (Open daily 5pm-midnight.) The **VIV supermarket** is opposite the train station. (Open M-F 7am-9pm, Sa 9am-8pm, Su noon-7pm.)

THE HAGUE (DEN HAAG) ☎070

William II moved the royal residence to The Hague in 1248, spawning parliament buildings, museums, and sprawling parks. The **North Sea Jazz Festival** draws world-class musicians and 50,000 swinging fans. The rest of the year, The Hague is a hushed city where museum-gazing and embassy-sleuthing are the main attractions.

PRACTICAL INFO, ACCOMMODATIONS, AND FOOD. **Trains** depart Holland Spoor (HS) station (☎ (0900) 92 92) for Amsterdam (50min., f17) and Rotterdam (25min., f7.50); trains to HS usually continue to the larger Centraal Station. *Stoptrein* and trams #1, 9, and 12 connect the two stations. The VVV **tourist office,** Kon. Julianapl. 30, in front of Centraal Station next to the Hotel Sofitel, books rooms for f4. (☎ (0900) 340 35 05. Open Sept.-June M-F 9am-5:30pm, Sa 10am-5pm; July-Aug. M-F 9am-5:30pm, Sa 10am-5pm, and Su 11am-3pm.)

Most foreign **embassies** are located in The Hague: **Australia,** Carnegielaan 4, 2517 KH (☎310 82 00; fax 310 78 63; open M-F 8:45am-12:30pm); **Canada,** Sophialaan 7, 2514 JP (☎311 16 00; fax 311 16 20; open M-F 9am-1pm and 2-5:30pm); **Ireland,** 9 Dr. Kuyperstr., 2514 BA (☎363 09 93; fax 361 76 04; open M-F 10am-12:30pm and 2:30-5pm); **New Zealand** (consulate), Carnegielaan 10 (☎346 93 24; open M-F 9am-12:30pm and 1:30-5:30pm); **South Africa** (consulate), Wassenaarseweg 40, 2596 CJ (☎392 45 01; fax 346 06 69; open daily 9am-noon); **UK,** Lange Voorhout 10, 2514 ED (☎427 04 27; fax 427 03 45; open M-F 9am-1pm and 2:15-5:30pm); and the **US,** Lange Voorhout 102, 2514 EJ (☎310 92 09; fax 361 46 88; open M-F 8:15am-5pm).

To get from Centraal Station to the **NJHC City Hostel,** Scheepmakerstr. 27, take tram #1 (dir. Delft), 9 (dir. Vrederust), or 12 (dir. Duindrop) to "Rijswijkseplein" (2 strips); cross to the left in front of the tram, cross the big intersection, and Scheepmakerstr. is straight ahead. From Holland Spoor, turn right, follow the tram tracks, turn right at the big intersection, and Scheepmakerstr. is on your right. (3min. ☎ (070) 315 78 78; fax 315 78 77; email denhaag@njhc.org. Breakfast included. Dorms f35-40; doubles f80; non-members add f5.) Get a drink at the **Havana** bar and restaurant. (Beer f3.50; steak f17. Open daily 10:30am-1am.) For more vibrant nightlife, try the bars along the Boulevard in **Schevingenen,** 20 minutes away from the Hague Centraal station (or a pleasant 5km bike ride).

SIGHTS AND ENTERTAINMENT. For snippets of Dutch politics, visit the **Binnenhof,** the Hague's Parliament complex. Tours leave from Binnenhof 8A to the

13th-century **Ridderzaal** (Hall of Knights) and the chambers of the States General. (Open M-Sa 10:15am-4pm. f8.) Outside the north entrance of the Binnenhof, the 17th-century **Mauritshuis** features an impressive collection of Dutch paintings, including works by Rembrandt and Vermeer. (☎302 34 35. Open Tu-Sa 10am-5pm, Su 11am-5pm. f12.50.) The impressive modern art collection at the **Gemeentmuseum** includes Piet Mondrian's *Victory Boogie Woogie* and a contemporary fashion exhibit. Take tram #7 toward Staten Kwartier. (☎338 11 11. Open daily 10am-5pm. f12.50.) The **Peace Palace,** the opulent home of the International Court of Justice at Carnegiepl., 10 minutes from the Binnenhof, was donated by Andrew Carnegie during a bout of robber baron guilt. (Tours M-F 10, 11am, 2, 3, and 4pm. Book in advance through the tourist office. f5.) In addition to the **North Sea Jazz Festival,** The Hague also hosts **Parkpop,** Europe's largest free mainstream rock concert.

DELFT ☎015

A break from the drab urban cityscape, Delft's serene canvas gleams with exquisite details. The town is renowned for **Delftware,** blue-on-white china developed in the 16th century. Samples of the precious platters, and hourly demonstrations, await at **De Porceleyne Fles,** Rotterdamseweg 196. Take bus #63, 121, or 129 from the station to "Jaffalaan." Walk to the end of Jaffalaan, bear left, and cross the intersection. (☎251 20 30; www. royaldelft.com. Open Apr.-Oct. M-Sa 9am-5pm, Su 9:30am-5pm; Nov.-Apr. M-Sa 9am-5pm. f5.) In town, the **Nieuwe Kerk** on the central Markt holds the restored mausoleum of Dutch liberator William the Silent, along with his dog, who starved to death out of despair after his master died. Climb the 48-bell carillon for a view of old Delft. (Church open Apr.-Oct. M-Sa 9am-6pm; Nov.-Mar. M-F 11am-4pm, Sa 11am-5pm. f3. Tower closes 1hr. earlier. f3.) Built as a 15th-century nun's cloister, **Het Prinsenhof,** Sint Agathapl. 1, off Oude Singel, was William's abode until an assassin hired by Spain's Phillip II slew him in 1584. Today it houses paintings, tapestries, and pottery. (Open Tu-Sa 10am-5pm, Su 1-5pm. f5.) Wander among flowers and Delft's much-worshipped signature porcelain at the marketplace every Thursday. The VVV tourist office sells walking tour brochures (f4.95) outlining the possible footsteps of native son **Jan Vermeer,** the most mysterious of the great Dutch Golden Age triumvirate. **Rondvaart Delft,** Koornmkt. 113, offers canal rides. (☎212 63 85. Apr.-Oct. 10am-6pm. f8.75.)

Trains arrive from: The Hague (15min., f4); Leiden (30min., f6.50); and Amsterdam (1hr.). The VVV **tourist office,** Markt 85, books rooms (f3.50 fee plus 10% deposit). From the station, cross the bridge, turn left, go right at the first light, and follow signs to the Markt. (☎213 01 00; www.vvvdelft.nl. Open Apr.-Sept. M-Sa 9am-5:30pm, Su 11am-3pm; Oct.-May M-Sa 9am-5:30pm.) **Hotel Gastenkamers** has the best budget rooms in town. (Breakfast included. Reception 7am-10pm. Doubles f110-150; triples f195-245; quads f300.) To reach the unmarked **Van Leeuwen,** Achterom 143, exit straight from the station, cross four canals, and turn right on Achterom. (☎212 37 16. Singles f35; spacious doubles f70.) More affordable hotels are near the Markt. To **camp** on **Korftlaan** in the Delftse Hout area, take bus #64 to "Aan't Korft." (☎213 00 40. Laundry. Reception May to mid-Sept. 9am-10pm; mid-Sept. to Apr. 9am-6pm. f25 per tent.) Restaurants line **Volderstr.** and **Oude Delft.**

ROTTERDAM ☎010

After Rotterdam was annihilated in 1940, experimental architects looted it of Dutch charm, impregnating the city center with shimmering skyscrapers exuding an eerie, domineering presence. For a dramatic example of Rotterdam's eccentric designs (heavily influenced by the de Stijl school), check out the DNA-like **Kijks-Kubus** (cube houses) by Piet Blom; bus #70 offers tours. Take the metro to "Blaak," and they are immediately outside the station. (Open Mar.-Dec. daily 11am-5pm; Jan.-Feb. Sa-Su 11am-5pm. f3.50.) Try to decipher the architectural madness at the **Netherlands Architecture Institute,** Museumpark 25 (open Tu 10am-9pm, W-Sa 10am-5pm, Su 11am-5pm; f7.50), then refresh yourself with Rubens, van Gogh, Rembrandt, Rubinstein, Lichtenstein, Rothko, and Magritte across the street at the **Museum Boijmans van Beuningen,** Museumpark 18-20. Take the metro to "Eendractspl.," or take tram #4 or 5. (Open Tu-Sa 10am-5pm, Su 11am-5pm. f10.) The stately **Schielandshuis** (Historical Museum), Korte Hoogstr. 31, recounts the history of the city. (Open Tu-F 10am-5pm, Sa-Su 11am-5pm. f6.) Opposite the plaza, the powerful **Monument for the Destroyed City,** a statue of an anguished man with a hole in his heart, memorializes the 1940 bombing raid.

Trains run to: The Hague (20min., f7.50); Utrecht (45min., f15); and Amsterdam (1hr., f23). For **ferries** to Hull, England, see p. 682. The VVV **tourist office,** Coolsingel 67, opposite the *Stadhuis*, books rooms for f2.50-3.50. (☎414 40 65; f0.50 per min. Open M-Th 9:30am-6pm, F 9:30am-9pm, Sa 9:30am-5pm, Su noon-5pm.) **Use It,** Conradstr. 2, to the right of the station, dispenses backpacker-oriented advice. (☎240 91 58; www.jip.org/use-it. Open spring-fall Tu-Su 9am-6pm, in winter 9am-5pm.) To reach the comfy **NJHC City-Hostel Rotterdam (HI),** Rochussenstr. 107-109, take the metro to "Dijkzigt"; at the top of the escalator, go to Rochussenstr. and turn left. (☎436 57 63. Breakfast included. Sheets f7. Kitchen. Reception 7am-midnight. Dorms f29-37.50; doubles f80-100; nonmembers add f5.) To get from the station to the **Hotel Bienvenue,** Spoorsingel 24, exit through the back, walk straight along the canal, and look right (5min.) for comfortable rooms in a safe area. (☎466 93 94. Reception M-F 7:30am-9pm, Sa-Su 8am-9pm. Singles f86; doubles f105-135; triples f165-185; quads f200.) Eat around **Nieuwe Binnenweg** or in the **Oude Haven.** Buy **groceries** at **Albert Heyn,** Lijnbaanplein. From the VVV take two lefts and head toward the end of the Lijnbaan shopping plaza. (Open M-Th 8am-8pm, F 8am-9pm, Sa 8am-7pm, Su 1-6pm.) The **Oude Haven** and **Oostplein** brim with cafes and students, while mellow coffee shops line **Oude Binnenweg** and **Nieuwe Binnenweg.** Avoid the area west of **Dijkzigt.** In summer, musical festivals rock the city.

UTRECHT ☎030

Utrecht was the site of the **Peace of Utrecht,** one of the greatest peace treaties of all time, and now pulses with a vibrant student scene. The bars and restaurants around the **Oude Gracht** counter the anonymity of the hard-core club scene in Amsterdam. At the center of the old town stands the awe-inspiring Gothic **Domkerk,** begun in 1254 and finished 250 years later. Originally a Roman Catholic cathedral, its statues were defaced in the early 16th century by Calvinists. (Open May-Sept. M-F 10am-5pm, Sa 10am-3:30pm, Su 2-4pm; Oct.-Apr. M-F 11am-4pm, Sa 11am-3:30pm, Su 2-4pm. Free.) The **Domtoren,** originally attached to the cathedral but freestanding since a medieval tornado blew away the nave, is the highest tower in the Netherlands—on a clear day you can see Amsterdam. (Open M-Sa 10am-5pm, Su noon-5pm. f7.50.) Take bus #4 from Centraal Station to the **Rietveld Schroder House**; unveiled in 1924, it's designed like a Mondrian painting sprung to life. (Open W-Sa 11am-5pm, Su 12:30pm-5pm. Guided tours on request. f15.)

Trains from Amsterdam (25min., 3-6 per hr., round trip f19.75) arrive in the **Hoog Catharijne** mall; to get to the VVV **tourist office,** Vredenburg 90, exit the mall and follow the signs around the corner. (☎ (090) 04 14 14 14. Open M-F 9am-6pm, Sa 9am-5pm.) In a majestic manor house, the **Jeugdherberg Ridderhofstad (HI),** Rhijnauwenselaan 14, is one of the nicest hostels in the Netherlands. Take bus #41 from Centraal Station (12min., 3 strips) and tell the driver your destination; from the stop, cross the street, backtrack, turn right on Rhijnauwenselaan, and it's at the end of the road. (☎656 12 77. Breakfast included. Reception 8am-midnight. In summer f31.50; off season f28.75.) **Hostel Strowis,** Boothstraat 8, is 15 minutes from Centraal Station. (☎238 02 80; email strowis@xs4all.nl. Breakfast f7.50. Reception 24hr. Check-in before 1am. Dorms f20-25; doubles f80; triples f100.) Bring in dinner (f10) from the adjoining ACU vegetarian **Eetcafe,** around the corner at Voorstraat 71, which also has DJs and live music after 10pm on alternating nights. (Cover f3. Cafe open most weekdays 6-8pm.) To get to **Camping De Berekuil,** Ariënslaan 5-7, take bus #57 (2 strips) from the station and tell the driver your destination. (☎271 38 70. f8 per person; f8 per tent.) **De Winkel van Sinkel,** Oude Gracht 158, is a grand cafe whose popular bar pulses nightly and is the place to be seen in Utrecht. (Cover f20. Club open F-Sa midnight-5am.) Pick up a copy of *UiLoper* at bars or restaurants to scout the bar and cultural scene.

HOGE VELUWE NATIONAL PARK

Don't miss the impressive **Hoge Veluwe National Park** (HO-geh VEY-loo-wuh), a 13,000-acre preserve of woods, heath, dunes, red deer, and wild boars between Arnhem and Apeldoorn that shelters one of Europe's finest modern art museums. (Open daily Apr. 8am-8pm; May and Aug. 8am-9pm; June-July 8am-10pm; Sept. 9am-8pm; Oct. 9am-7pm; Nov.-Mar. 9am-5:30pm. No vehicular access May-Sept. after 8pm. Adults f8, children, 6-12 f4, under 6 free. Cars f8.50.) Deep in the park, the **Rijksmuseum Kröller-Müller** has troves of van Goghs from the Kroller-Muller family's outstanding collection, as well as key works by Seurat, Mondrian, Picasso, and Brancusi. The museum's striking sculpture garden, one of the largest in Europe, has exceptional work by Rodin, Bourdelle, and Hepworth. (Museum open Tu-Su 10am-5pm. Sculpture garden open daily 10am-4:30pm. f8.) Take one of the free **bikes** from outside the Kroller-Muller or the Koperen Kop **visitor center** to explore over 33km of paths winding through woods, along ponds, and amid sand dunes. (☎055 378 81 19. Visitor center open daily 10am-5pm.)

Arnhem, 15km from the park, is a good base. Stay at the **Jeugdherberg Alteveer (HI),** Diepenbrocklaan 27. Take bus #3 from the station (dir. Alteveer; 3 strips) to "Rijnstate Hospital." Facing the hospital, turn right and left on Cattepoelseweg. A sign at the brick path on your right points to the hostel. (☎ (026) 351 48 92. Breakfast included. Laundry f10. Reception 8am-11pm. Curfew 12:30am. f39.75; off season f36.25; nonmembers add f5.) Take bus #2 (dir. Haedaveld; 3 strips) to camp at **Kampeercentrum Arnhem,** Kemperbergerweg 771. (☎ (026) 445 61 00. Open Apr.-Oct. f16.50 per person; f21.50 for 2.) **Bus** #12 (Mar.-Oct.; round-trip f8) runs from the Arnhem station, stopping at the museum and visitor center (Tu-Su 10am-5pm); in winter, bus #107 (dir. Otterlo) stops in the park. After 6pm, take bus #2 to "Schaarsbergen" to get bikes.

MAASTRICHT ☎043

Situated on a narrow strip of land between Belgium and Germany, Maastricht (pop. 120,000) is one of the oldest cities in the Netherlands. Home of the prestigious **Jan van Eyck Academie of Art,** Maastricht has long been known for its abundance of art galleries and antique stores. The new **Bonnefantenmuseum,** 250 av. Ceramique, along the river, houses collections of archaeological artifacts, medieval sculpture, Northern Renaissance painting, and modern art. (Open Tu-Su 11am-5pm. f12.50.) Centuries of foreign threats culminated in an innovative subterranean defense system. The 20,000 passages of the **Mount Saint Peter Caves** were used as a siege shelter as late as WWII and contain inscriptions and artwork by generations of inhabitants. Mandatory tours depart from the cafe-restaurant Fort St. Pieter, Luikerweg 80; take bus #4 from the Markt. (Tours daily Apr. 22-May 7, June 1-12, July-Aug., and Oct. 14-29 at 3:30pm. f6.) The **Kazematten,** 10km of underground passageways constructed between 1575 and 1825 enabled locals to detect enemies and to make surprise attacks. From Vrijtmarkt, go toward Tongersepl. and follow the signs for Waldeck Bastion. (Tours July-Aug. daily 12:30pm and 2pm; Sept.-June Su 2pm. f6.) The **Natuurhistorich Museum,** De Bosuetplein 6-7, features a life-size replica of a Montasaurus. (Open M-F 10am-5pm, Sa and Su 2-5pm. f6.)

The **train station** is on the eastern side of town; buses run frequently to the Markt. **Trains** arrive from: Amsterdam (2½hr., f51); Koln (2hr., f38); and Brussels (2hr., f30.50). The VVV **tourist office,** Kleine Staat 1, is a block from the Markt at Het Dinghuis. From the Markt bus stop, walk toward the river and turn right on Muntstr. (☎325 21 21. Open May-Oct. M-Sa 9am-6pm, Su 11am-3pm; Nov.-Apr. M-F 9am-6pm, Sa 9am-5pm.) To get from the station to **Hostel Sportel de Dousberg (HI),** Dousbergweg 4, from the station, take bus #11 on weekdays, bus #22 on weeknights, bus #8 or 18 on Saturdays, or bus #28 after 6pm any day of the week to "De Dousberg." (☎346 67 77. Breakfast included. Curfew 1am. Dorms f38.15-43.15; doubles f113.50.) **Maison de Chene,** Boschstraat 104-106, sports cozy rooms in a great location just off the Markt. (☎321 35 23. Breakfast included. Singles f85-125; doubles f110-125.)

GRONINGEN ☎050

With 35,000 students and the nightlife to prove it, the small city of Groningen (KRO-ning-en; pop. 173,000) supports a number of eccentric museums and galleries, and trendy cafes. The town's spectacular **Groninger Museum,** a pastel assemblage of squares, cylinders, and slag metal, forms a bridge between the station and the city center. The multicolored, steel-trimmed galleries create a futuristic laboratory atmosphere for their wild contemporary art exhibits. (Open Tu-Su 10am-5pm. f12.) The 500-year-old **Martinitoren Tower** in the Grote Markt weathered the WWII bombing that left most of the city in ruins. (Open Apr.-Sept. daily noon-4:30pm; Oct.-Mar. Sa-Su noon-4:30pm. f3.) Escape Groningen's gray urbanity in the serene 16th-century **Prinsenhoftuin** (Princes' Court Gardens); the entrance is on the canal behind the Martinitoren. Sip one of 130 kinds of tea and other beverages at the tiny **Theeschenkerij Tea Hut** amid ivy-covered trellises and towering rose bushes. (Open Apr.-Sept.) Or, cool off in the **Noorderplantsoen Park,** host to the huge cultural **Noorderzon** (Northern Sun Festival) each August. Surrounding lakes and forests are within easy **biking** distance of town; rent a bike (f8 per day) at the station.

To reach the VVV **tourist office,** Ged. Kattendiep 6, turn right as you exit the station, cross the first bridge to your left, head straight through the Hereplein on Herestr., turn right at Ged. Zuderdiep, and veer left onto Ged. Kattendiep. (☎202 30 50. Open June-Aug. M-F 9am-6pm, Sa 10am-5pm; Sept.-May M-F 9am-5:30pm, Sa 10am-5pm.) To reach the funky **Simplon Youth Hotel,** Boterdiep 73, take bus #1 from the station and tell the driver your destination. (☎313 52 21. Breakfast f7.50. Sheets f4.50. Laundry. Reception 8am-noon and 3pm-2am. Lockout noon-3pm. f21.50.) **Het Pakhuis**, Peperstraat 8, serves a variety of ethnic dishes upstairs and mellow drinks at the cafe downstairs. (Restaurant open daily 6pm-11pm. Cafe open daily 9pm-4am.) Groningen's nightlife jams in a corner of the **Grote Markt** and along nearby **Poelstr.** and **Peperstr. Postal code:** 9725 BM. ☎**0900.**

WADDEN ISLANDS (WADDENEILANDEN)

Wadden means "mudflat" in Dutch, but sand is the defining characteristic of these islands: isolated beaches hide behind dune ridges with windblown manes of golden grass. Dutch vacationers are secretive about these gems; deserted, tulip-lined bike trails carve through vast, flat stretches of grazing land to the sea.

GETTING THERE AND GETTING AROUND. The islands arch clockwise from Amsterdam around northern Holland: Texel (closest to Amsterdam), Vlieland, Terschelling, Ameland, and Schiermonnikoog. To reach **Texel,** take the train from Amsterdam to **Den Helder** (70min., f20), bus #3 to the port, then a ferry to Texel (20min., every hr. 6am-9pm, round-trip f11). In summer, ferries link the rest of the islands. **Biking** is the easiest way to get around.

TEXEL. The largest of the Wadden Islands, **Texel** (TES-sel) can be a voyeur's paradise, with two popular **nude beaches** (south of Den Hoorn and off De Cocksdorp at paal 28) and **bird watching.** You can only visit the **nature reserves** on a guided tour; book in advance at **Ecomare Museum and Aquarium,** Ruyslaan 92, in De Koog, and specify English-speaking tours on land not requiring rubber boots. (☎31 77 41. 2hr. tours daily at 11am. f12.50.) The island's major villages are **Den Burg,** the beachfront **De Koog,** and **De Cocksdrop** to the north. To explore by **bike,** rent from **Verhuurbedrijf Heijne,** across from the ferry stop at Horntje. (f8 per day. Open daily Apr.-Oct. 9am-9pm; Nov.-Mar. 9am-6pm.) A **Texel Ticket** allows unlimited one-day bus travel on the island (runs mid-June to mid-Sept.; f7). The VVV **tourist office,** Emmaln 66, is in Den Burg. (☎31 28 47. Open M-Th 9am-6pm, F 9am-9pm, Sa 9am-5pm; July-Aug. also Su 10am-1:30pm.) Both **youth hostels (HI)** are easily accessible from the ferry; tell the bus driver your destination. Take bus #29 to the rural **Panorama,** Schansweg 7, 7km from the ferry and 3km from Den Burg's center. (☎31 54 41. Bikes f8 per day. Sheets f6.50. Reception 8:30am-10:30pm. f32.50-f37; nonmembers add f5.) **Campgrounds** are in De Koog (f4-7); ask at the tourist office. ☎**0222.**

NORWAY (NORGE)

NORWEGIAN KRONER

US$1 = 9.30KR	1KR = US$0.11
CDN$1 = 6.28KR	1KR = CDN$0.16
UK£1 = 13.09KR	1KR = UK£0.08
IR£1 = 10.19KR	1KR = IR£0.10
AUS$1 = 5.20KR	1KR = AUS$0.19
NZ$1 = 3.96KR	1KR = NZ$0.25
SAR1 = 1.30KR	1KR = SAR0.77
EUR€1 = 8.02KR	1KR = EUR€0.12

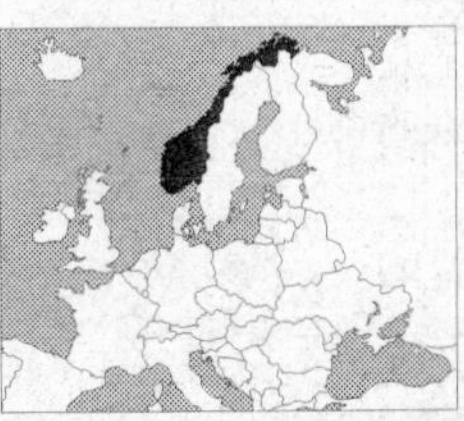

Country code: 47. **International dialing prefix:** 095. There are no city codes in Norway. From outside Norway, dial int'l dialing prefix (see inside back cover) + 47 + local number.

Norway is blessed with an abundance of natural beauty, from jagged, magnificent fjords to stunningly clear turquoise rivers and glacier-capped mountain ranges. Its long history manifests itself in its intimate relationship with the sea. The country's original seafarers were the Norse Vikings, who dominated a realm that used to span from the British Isles to southern Europe. In the 10th century, the country was unified under King Harald Hårfagre (the Fair-Haired), and Olav Haraldsson successfully imported Christianity. After the Viking's decline, Norway was annexed by Denmark and then Sweden. Though the country was politically dependent, the late 19th century saw Norway's rise to aesthetic prominence, nurturing artistic luminaries like Edvard Munch and Henrik Ibsen. After three decades of independence beginning in 1905, the country was subject to Nazi occupation during WWII. The psychological legacy left by the occupation is still strong today, and Norwegians are proud of the resistance movement that emerged during this period. In the years since WWII, Norway has developed into a modern welfare state. Although prices and taxes are among the world's highest, they translate into unparalleled social services, little class stratification, and a high standard of living. With only 4.5 million residents—aware of the nature around them—Norway's beauty is in good hands.

FACTS AND FIGURES

Official Name: Kingdom of Norway.
Government: Constitutional Monarchy.
Capital: Oslo.
Land Area: 308,000 sq. km.
Geography: Mostly coast and mountains; some valleys; arctic north.
Climate: Temperate coast; cold interior; rainy.
Major Cities: Bergen, Stavanger, Trondheim.
Population: 4,439,000.
Language: Norwegian.
Religions: Evangelical Lutheran (88%), other Protestant and Rom. Catholic (4%).
Average Income Per Capita: US$24,700.
Major Exports: Petroleum, machinery, fuels.

DISCOVER NORWAY

Cosmopolitan **Oslo** (p. 710), the first stop on most travelers' itineraries, swarms with lively cafes and museums. After you've exhausted the capital, hop on the gorgeous Oslo-Bergen rail line (p. 716) to fjord country. At the other end lies relaxed and cultural **Bergen,** a former Hanseatic stronghold with pointed gables lining the wharf (p. 717). If you only have one day to see the fjords, spend it exploring the **Sognefjord;** the popular **"Norway in a Nutshell"** (p. 720) tour, a daytip from Bergen, gives a glorious glimpse of fjord country's striking scenery. With more time for the fjords,

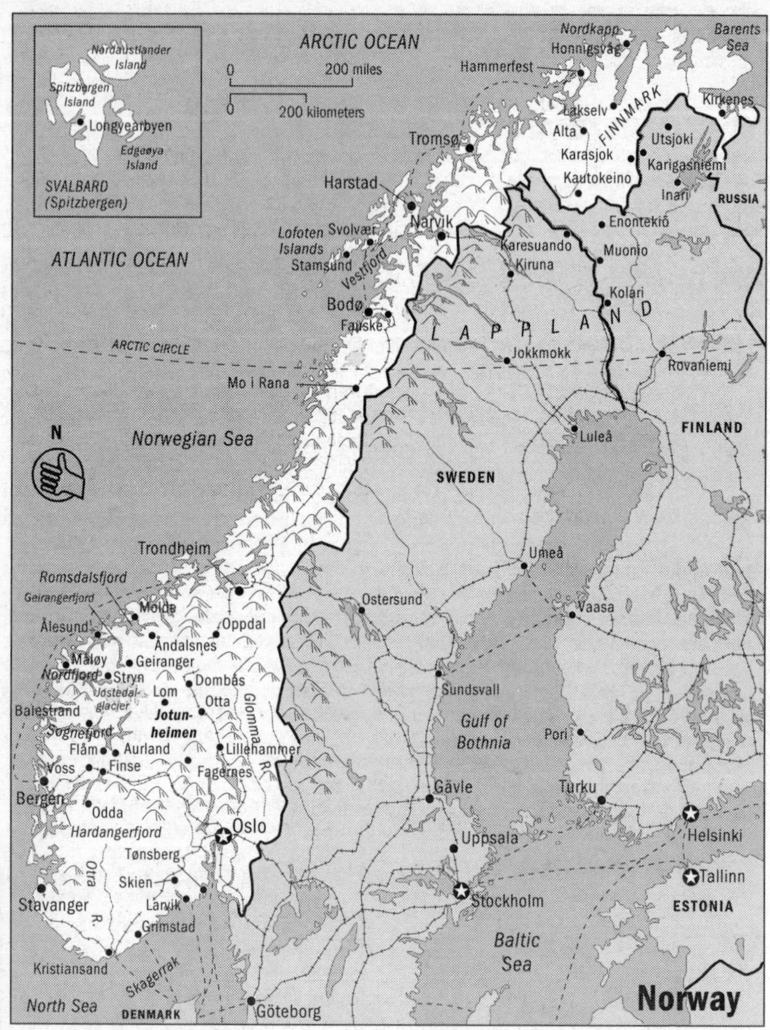

check out the **Jostedalsbreen Glacier** and nearby towns (p. 722) or head to **Hardangerfjord** (p. 721). **Trondheim,** at the northern end of fjord country, feels more authentic than tourist-oriented Bergen or Oslo (p. 726). If you have substantially more time in Norway, go north to the isolated **Lofoten Islands** (p. 729); or head to the southern coast and explore the lively cities of **Kristiansand** and **Stavanger.**

ESSENTIALS

WHEN TO GO

Everything is crowded with tourists in July and August; June or September may be a better time to go. Climate can also serve as a good guide for when to travel. Oslo averages 18°C (63°F) in July and -4°C (24°F) in January. In the north, average temperatures drop, and it is also wetter than the south and east. For a few weeks around the summer solstice (June 21), the area north of Bodø basks in the midnight sun. You stand the best chance of seeing the Northern Lights (Nov.-Feb.) from above the Arctic Circle. Skiing is best just before Easter.

DOCUMENTS AND FORMALITIES

Visas are not required for citizens of Australia, Canada, the EU, New Zealand, or the US for stays shorter than three months. These three months begin upon entry into any Nordic country; more than 90 days in any combination of Finland, Iceland, Norway, or Sweden requires a visa. South Africans need a visa for stays of any length.

EMBASSIES AND CONSULATES

Embassies and consulates of other countries in Norway are all in **Oslo** (see p. 710).

Norwegian Embassies at Home: Australia, 17 Hunter St., Yarralumla, Canberra ACT 2600 (☎ (26) 273 34 44; fax 273 36 69); **Canada,** 90 Sparks St., Ottawa, ON K1P 5B4 (☎ (613) 238 65 71; fax 238 27 65); **Ireland,** 34 Molesworth St., Dublin 2 (☎ (01) 662 18 00; fax 662 18 90); **New Zealand,** 61 Molesworth St., Wellington (☎ (04) 471 25 03); **South Africa,** 1166 Park St., Pretoria, 0083 (☎ (012) 323 47 90; fax 323 47 89); **UK,** 25 Belgrave Sq., London SW1X 8QD (☎ (171) 591 55 00; fax 245 69 93); **US:** 2720 34th St. NW, Washington DC 20008 (☎ (202) 333 60 00; fax 337 08 70; www.norway.org).

GETTING AROUND

BY PLANE. The main international airport is in **Oslo,** though a few flights land at **Trondheim** and **Bergen. SAS** (US ☎ (800) 221 23 50) flies to Norway, as does **Finnair** (US ☎ (800) 950 50 00) and **Icelandair** (US ☎ (800) 223 55 00). Those under 25 or students under 32 qualify for special youth fares that make **flying** an option for domestic travel, often cheaper than trains. **Braathens SAFE** (☎ 67 58 60 00) and **SAS** (☎ 81 00 33 00) both offer domestic standby tickets *(chance billets)*. Any trip ending either north or south of Trondheim is around 450kr one-way (both zones approx. 800kr).

BY TRAIN. Norway's train system includes an extensive commuter train network around Oslo and long distance lines running from Oslo to Bergen, to Stavanger via Kristiansand, and to Trondheim. From Trondheim, the northern lines run only as far north as Bodø, where buses take over. Trains farther north move along the Swedish line through Kiruna, ending at Narvik on the Norwegian coast. All stations have an info desk; regional schedules are avaible at the stations. Seat reservations are compulsory on many trains, including the new high-speed Signatur trains, which cover some departures on the long-distance lines (2nd-class 50kr).

Eurail is valid on all trains. The **Norway Railpass** grants unlimited travel within the country for three (1100kr), four (1364kr), or five (2002kr) days over the course of a month. The *buy-in-Scandinavia* **Scanrail Pass** allows five days within 15 (1575kr, under 26 1190kr) or 21 consecutive days (2510kr, under 26 1815kr) of unlimited rail travel through Scandinavia, as well as free or discounted ferry rides and reduced bus fares in Norway. This differs from the *buy-outside-Scandinavia* **Scanrail Pass** (see p. 59). Foreign students sometimes get the same discounts on domestic rail travel as Norwegian students. Off-peak green trains are always discounted.

BY BUS. Buses are quite expensive (about 1kr per km), but are the only land option north of Bodø and in the fjords. **Norway Bussekspress** (☎ 23 00 24 40) operates 75% of the domestic bus routes and publishes a free timetable *(Rutehefte)* containing schedules and prices. **Scanrail** and **InterRail** pass holders are entitled to a 50% discount on most bus routes, and students are entitled to a 25-50% discount on most routes—be insistent and follow the rules listed in the Norway Bussekspress booklet. **Bus passes,** valid for one (1375kr) or two (2200kr) weeks, are good deals for those exploring the fjords or the north.

BY FERRY. Car ferries *(ferjer)* are usually much cheaper (and slower) than the many **hydrofoils** *(hurtigbåte)* cruising the coasts and fjords; both often have student, Scanrail, and/or InterRail discounts. The **Hurtigruten** (the famed Coastal Steamer; see p. 717) takes six days for the fantastic voyage from **Bergen** to **Kirkenes** on the Russian border; there is one northbound and one southbound departure from each of its 34 stops per day. There are no railpass discounts, but students get 50% off. Generally buses and trains will be more affordable, but there are exceptions. For info on boats from **Oslo** to **Kiel, Germany; Hirtshals; Frederikshavn; Copenhagen, Denmark;** and **Helsingborg, Sweden** see p. 710. For boats from **Kristiansand** to **Hirtshals** or **Newcastle,** see p. 727. For ships connecting **Stavanger** and **Newcastle,** see p. 728. For ferries from **Bergen** to **Hanstholm, Denmark; Newcastle;** the **Faroe Islands;** the **Shetland Islands;** and **Iceland** see p. 717. For additional info on ferries to the UK, see p. 49.

BY CAR. Roads in Norway are in good condition, although they can be frighteningly narrow in some places and blind curves are extremely common. Drivers should remember to be cautious, especially on mountain roads and tunnels. Driving around the fjords can be frustrating, as only Nordfjord has a road that completely circumnavigates it; there are numerous car ferries, but check a timetable in advance to connect with boat departures. RVs are common. Rental cars are expensive, but for groups they can be more affordable than buying separate railpasses. **Gas** is prohibitively expensive at about 11-12kr per liter; stations are normally marked on maps, so plan carefully since distances between stations can be long. Vehicles are required to keep **headlights** on at all times. For maps, ask at local tourist offices or contact the **Sons of Norway** in the US and Canada at ☎ (800) 945-8851.

BY BIKE AND BY THUMB. Biking is becoming increasingly common. The beautiful scenery is rewarding for cyclists, although the hilly terrain can be rough on bikes. Contact **Syklistenes Landsforening** (Oslo ☎22 41 50 80) for more info. **Hitching** is notoriously difficult and discouraged by *Let's Go.* Some Norwegians hitch beyond the rail lines in northern Norway and the fjord areas of the west, but many others try for six hours and end up exactly where they started. Hitchers should bring several layers of clothing, rain gear, and a warm sleeping bag.

TOURIST SERVICES AND MONEY

EMERGENCY. Police: ☎110. **Ambulance:** ☎113. **Fire:** ☎112.

TOURIST OFFICES. Virtually every town and village has an ever-helpful **Turistinformasjon** office; look for a black or white lower-case **"i"** on a green sign. In July and the first half of August, all tourist offices are open daily; most have reduced hours the rest of the year. For more info, contact the **Norwegian Tourist Board,** P.O. Box 2893 Solli, N-0230 Oslo (☎ (47) 22 92 52 00; fax 22 56 05 05; www.tourist.no).

Tourist Boards at Home: UK, Charles House, 5 Regent St., London SW1Y 4LR (☎ (44) 20 78 39 62 55; fax 20 78 39 60 14); **US,** 655 Third Ave., Suite 1810, New York, NY 10017 (☎ (212) 885-9700; fax 885-9710).

MONEY. The Norwegian **kroner** (KR) is divided into 100 *øre.* Banks and large post offices change money, usually for a small commission and the best rates. **Prices** are sky-high throughout all of Norway. As a general rule, more isolated areas have even higher prices. The Lofoten Islands are especially pricey. A 15% **service charge** is often included in hotel bills, but it is customary to tip 10-15% for restaurant service. Taxi drivers are usually tipped a few kroner. **Value-added tax refunds** (10-17% of the price) are available for single-item purchases of more than 300kr in a single store in a single visit. Ask for a refund form when you make your purchase and then hand it in at the tax refund desk at the airport or ferry terminal when you leave the country.

BUSINESS HOURS. Business hours are short in summer, especially on Friday and in August, when Norwegians vacation. **Shop** hours are Monday-Friday 9am-5pm, Saturday 9am-1pm; hours may be extended on Thursday. It is rare to find any shops other than convenience stores or kiosks open on Sunday. **Banks** are generally open Monday-Wednesday and Friday 8:15am-3pm, Thursday 8:15am-5pm.

SAY CHEESE Cheese is a staple of almost every Norwegian kitchen, and most Norwegians eat at least one slice every day. The cheese slicer, a kitchen utensil used exclusively for cutting cheese, is even a Norwegian invention. The most frequently seen cheese varieties, Jarlsberg and Norvegia, are similar to other common European cheeses, such as Gouda and Havarti. However, Norway is unique in having *brunost*, or brown cheese, which is made from goat's milk. Unexpectedly sweet in flavor, with a taste similar to caramel, it is necessary for a truly Norwegian dining experience.

ACCOMMODATIONS AND CAMPING

HOSTELS. **HI youth hostels** *(vandrerhjem)* are run by **Norske Vandrerhjem,** Dronninggensgt. 26, in Oslo (☎23 13 93 00; fax 23 13 93 50). Beds run 80-170kr; another 25-60kr usually covers breakfast. Sheets typically cost 35-40kr per stay. Usually only rural or smaller hostels have curfews, and only a few are open year-round.

OTHER LOCAL ACCOMMODATIONS. Most tourist offices book **private rooms** (singles around 190kr, doubles 330kr).

CAMPING. When in Norway, **camp.** Norwegian law allows free camping anywhere on public land for up to two nights, provided that you keep 150m from all buildings and fences and leave no trace behind. **Den Norske Turistforening** (DNT; Norwegian Mountain Touring Association) sells excellent maps, offers guided hiking trips, and maintains more than 300 **mountain huts** *(hytter)* throughout the country. (☎22 82 28 22; www.turistforeningen.no. Membership cards available at DNT offices, huts, and tourist offices; 325kr, under 25 160kr. 75-145kr per night; nonmembers add 80kr.) Staffed huts, open around Easter and from late June to early September, serve meals. Unstaffed huts are open from late February until mid-October; you can pick up entrance keys (100kr deposit) from DNT and tourist offices. The DNT offices in Oslo (see p. 712) and Bergen (see p. 718) are particularly helpful. Official **campgrounds** charge 90-120kr per tent. Many also have two- to four-person cabins (450-800kr). Hot showers almost always cost extra.

FOOD AND DRINK

Eating in Norway is pricey; cuddle up to markets and bakeries. The supermarket chain **REMA 1000** generally has the best prices (usually open M-F 9am-8pm, Sa 9am-6pm). Join Norwegians at outdoor **markets** for cheap seafood and fruit, but be wary of the lookalike markets aimed at tourists. Many restaurants have cheap **dagens ret** (dish of the day) specials (full meal 60-70kr); otherwise, you'll rarely spend less than 100kr. All-you-can-eat buffets and self-service *kafeterias* are other less expensive options. Fish in Norway—cod, salmon, and herring—is fresh, good, and (relatively) cheap. National specialties include cheese *(ost)*; pork and veal meatballs *(kjøtkaker)* with boiled potatoes; and, for lusty carnivores, reindeer, ptarmigan (a type of bird), as well as the controversial whale meat *(kval)*. Norway grows divine berries. Come winter, you can also delight in dried fish *(lutefisk)*. In most Norwegian restaurants, alcohol is served only after 3pm and never on Sundays, although this is beginning to change in cities. Beer is very expensive (45kr for 0.5L in a bar). Alcohol is cheapest in supermarkets, but few towns permit the sale of alcohol outside of government-operated liquor stores.

COMMUNICATION

MAIL. Mailing a postcard/letter from Norway costs 7kr to regions outside of Europe. Sending mail within Europe costs 6kr.

TELEPHONES. Phone calls are expensive. There are three types of **public phones**; the black and gray phones accept 1, 5, 10, and 20kr coins; green phones accept only phone cards; and red phones accept coins, phone cards, and major credit cards. Local calls need at least 3kr; buying a **phone card** (*telekort;* 35, 90, or 210kr at Narvesen Kiosks and post offices) is more economical. Pay phones cost twice as much as calls from private lines; between 10pm-8am it's 15-20% cheaper. To make **domestic collect calls,** dial ☎117; **international collect calls,** ☎115. **International direct dial** numbers include: **AT&T,** ☎800 190 11; **Sprint,** ☎800 198 77; **MCI WorldPhone Direct,** ☎800 199 12; **Australia Direct,** ☎800 190 61; **Canada Direct,** ☎800 191 11; **BT Direct,** ☎800 199 44; **Ireland Direct,** ☎800 19 353, **Telecom New Zealand Direct,** ☎800 128 53; **Telkom South Africa Direct,** ☎800 199 27.

INTERNET ACCESS. Internet cafes abound in Norway's larger cities. While smaller cities don't usually have Internet cafes, most have a public library open on weekdays that offers free Internet access.

LANGUAGE. Norway is officially bilingual: the Danish-influenced **bokmål Norwegian** used in Oslo and the standardized **nynorsk Norwegian** based on the dialects of rural western Norway are both taught in schools. Another language, **Sami,** is spoken by the Same, the indigenous people of the north. Most Norwegians speak fluent English. For basic phrases and vocabulary in Norwegian, see p. 981.

HOLIDAYS AND FESTIVALS

Holidays: New Year's Day (Jan. 1); Easter Sunday and Monday (Apr. 23-24), May Day (May 1); National Independence Day (May 17); Ascension Day (June 1); Christmas Eve and Day (Dec. 24-25); Boxing Day (Dec. 26); and New Year's Eve (Dec. 31).

Festivals: The **Bergen Festival** in May offers world-class performances in music, dance, and theater. The **Norwegian Wood** (www.norwegianwood.no) rock festival in early June in Oslo features big-name rock bands, while the week-long **Quart** music festival in Kristiansund in early July attracts acts from Marilyn Manson to Ben Harper to Garbage. The mid-July **Molde Jazz Festival** pulls in the luminaries of jazz. **Midsummer Night,** June 23 in 2001, the longest day of the year, is celebrated with bonfires and huge parties.

OSLO

Verdant Oslo (pop. 500,000) bustles like a city twice its size, but feels as intimate as a small town. The Midnight Sun in summer and the extraordinary blue light in winter challenge the gloomy shadows found in the work of native artists Edvard Munch and Henrik Ibsen. In Oslo everything is spotless, timely, and expensive. But its urban edge—typified by classy cafes, cool boutiques, and beautiful Norwegians in tight, trendy clothes—is softened by nearby forests, islands, and lakes that hint at the splendor that lies farther west.

GETTING THERE AND GETTING AROUND

Flights: White SAS buses run every 15min. between **Gardermoen Airport** and the city (1hr., 80kr), with pick-up and drop-off at the bus and train stations, and the Radisson SAS Scandinavia hotel. Daily to airport 4:05am-10pm; from airport 5:15am-midnight.

Trains: Oslo Sentralstasjon (Oslo S; ☎81 50 08 88). Reduced fares *(minipriser)* available M-Th and Sa to major cities if you book 5 days ahead. Trains run to: **Stockholm** (7hr., 2 per day, 502kr, under 26 384kr); **Bergen** (7-8hr., 550kr); **Trondheim** (7-8hr., 640kr); and **Copenhagen** (10hr., 2 per day, 900kr, night train 490kr). Mandatory reservations 25kr for regular trains, 150kr for 1st class (meals included), and 50kr for 2nd class on *Signatur* trains running on the Oslo-Kristiansand and Oslo-Trondheim lines.

Buses: Norway Bussekspress, Schweigårdsgate 8 (☎23 00 24 40). Follow the signs from the train station through the Oslo Galleri Mall to the Bussterminalen Galleriet. Schedules at the terminal's information office. Students usually receive a 25% discount on fares; Interail and Scanrail pass holders usually receive a 50% reduction.

Ferries: Color Line (☎22 94 44 44; fax 22 83 20 96). To **Kiel, Germany** (20hr., from 470kr) and **Hirtshals, Denmark** (12½hr., daytime ferries from 160kr). 50% off with

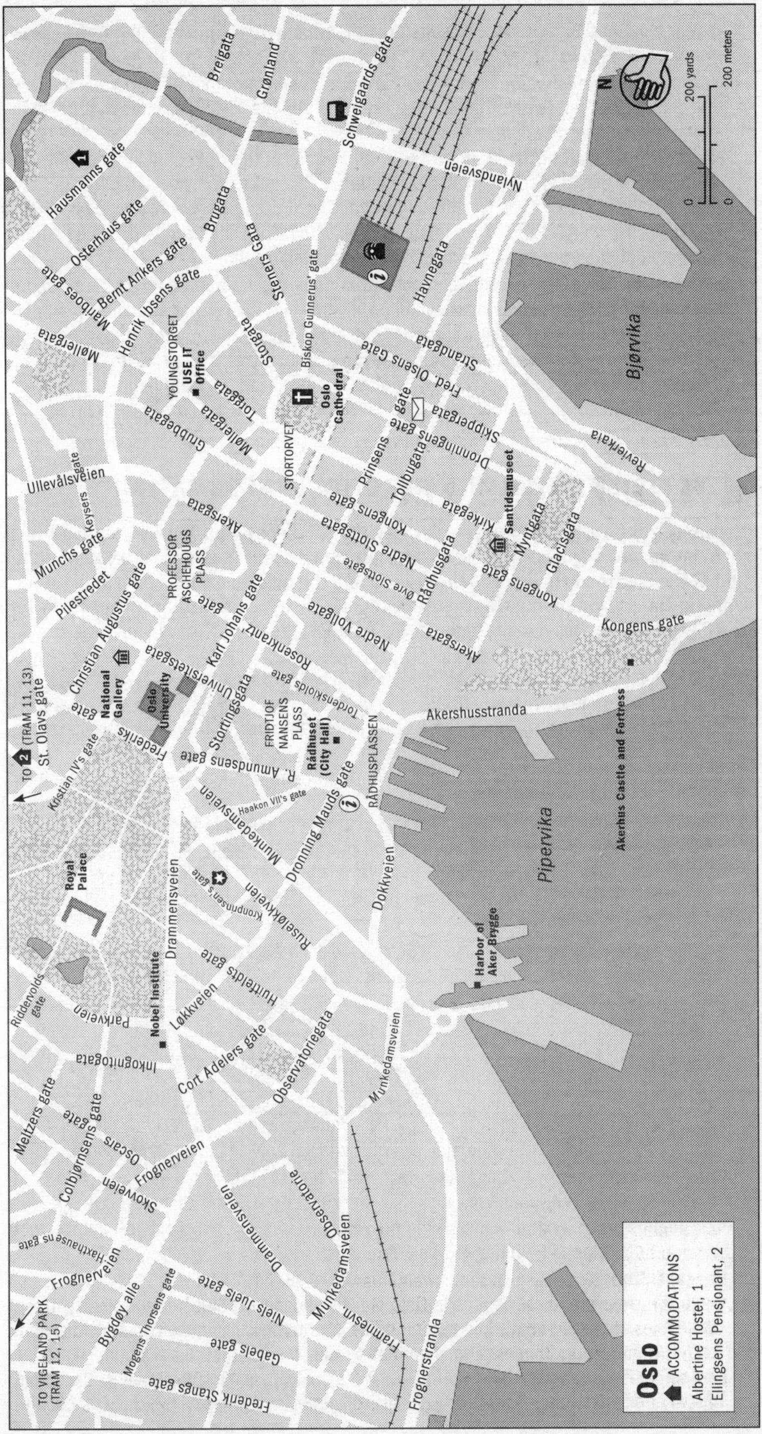

Oslo

ACCOMMODATIONS

Albertine Hostel, 1

Ellingsens Pensjonant, 2

NORWAY

Eurail, InterRail, or Scanrail; students 50% off from mid-Aug. to mid-June. **DFDS Scandinavian Seaways** (☎22 41 90 90; fax 22 41 38 38). To **Helsingborg, Sweden** (14hr.), and **Copenhagen** (16hr.) daily at 5pm (in summer from 560kr; students 25% off, with InterRail or Scanrail 50% off). Color Line departs from 20min. west of the train station; DFDS and Stena from 10min. south.

Public Transportation: Trafikanten (☎177), in front of the train station, has info; the tourist office also has comprehensive schedules. Bus, tram, subway, and ferry are 20kr per ride; 500-1000kr fines for traveling without valid ticket. **Dagskort** (day pass) 40kr; **7-day Card** 150kr; **Flexicard** (good for 8 trips) 120kr. The **Oslo Card** (see below) grants unlimited public transport. Late-night service runs midnight-5am.

Bike Rental: For info on cycling, contact **Syklistenes Landsforening** (☎22 41 50 80).

Hitchhiking: *Let's Go* does not recommend hitchhiking. Oslo is not a hitchhiker's paradise; the persistent go to gas stations and ask everyone who stops. Those heading southwest (E-18 to **Kristiansand** and **Stavanger**) take bus #31 or 32 to "Maritime." Hitchers to **Bergen** take bus #161 "Skui" to the last stop; to **Trondheim,** bus #32 or 321, or Metro #5 to "Grorudkrysset;" to **Sweden,** bus #81, 83, or 85 to "Bekkeleget" or local train "Ski" to "Nordstrand."

ORIENTATION AND PRACTICAL INFORMATION

Running south from Oslo to the *Slottet* (Royal Palace), **Karl Johans gate** is Oslo's main boulevard. Sights are packed in the city center near the **National Theater,** at the end of the **Slottsparken** between the station and the palace. And the excellent public transportation system makes it easy to reach those sights farther away. Don't be confused by the word *gate,* which simply means "street" in Norwegian.

TOURIST, FINANCIAL, AND LOCAL SERVICES

Tourist Offices: Main Tourist Office, Brynjulf Bullsplass 1 (☎23 11 78 84; fax 22 83 81 50; www.oslopro.no), near the Rådhus. Sells the **Oslo Card,** which covers public transit and admission to nearly all sights (1-day 180kr, 2-day 290kr, 3-day 410kr). Open daily June-Aug. 9am-7pm; Sept. M-Sa 9am-6pm; Oct.-May 9am-4pm. Info center at **Oslo S** books rooms from 360kr. Open daily 8am-11pm. **Den Norske Turistforening,** Storgata 3 (☎22 82 28 22; fax 22 82 28 23) has country-wide hiking info and maps. Open M-F 10am-4pm, Th 10am-6pm, Sa 10am-2pm. For **Use It,** Møllergata 3 (☎22 41 51 32; fax 22 42 63 71; www.unginfo.oslo.no), turn right four blocks up Karl Johans gt. from the station for youth-oriented info and the invaluable *Streetwise* guide. Open M-W and F 11am-5pm, Th 11am-6pm.

Budget Travel: Kilroy Travels, Nedre Slottsgt. 23 (☎23 10 23 10; fax 22 42 97 09; www.kilroytravels.com), has airline bargains. Open M-F 10am-6pm, Sa 10am-3pm.

Embassies: Australia (consulate), Jernbanetorget 2 (☎22 41 44 33; fax 22 42 26 83). **Canada,** Wergelandsveien 7 (☎22 99 53 00; fax 22 99 53 01). **Ireland,** Kirkeveien 7, P.O. Box 5683, Briskeby, N-0209 (☎22 56 33 10; fax 22 12 20 71). **South Africa** (consulate), Drammensveien 88c, P.O. Box 2822 Solli, N-0204 (☎22 44 79 10; fax 22 44 39 75). Open M-F 9am-noon. **UK,** Thomas Heftyesgt. 8, N-0244 (☎22 53 24 00; fax 22 43 40 05). Open M-F 9am-4pm. **US,** Drammensveien 18, N-0244 (☎22 44 85 50; fax 22 44 04 36; www.usembassy.no). Consular services open 9am-noon.

Currency Exchange: Available at the AmEx office and the main post office, as well as at the banks along Karl Johans gt.

American Express: Fridtjof Nansens Plass 6, N-0160 Oslo (☎22 98 37 35), across from the Rådhus. Open M-F 9am-5pm, Sa 10am-3pm.

Luggage Storage: Lockers at the train station. 25-40kr per 24hr.

Bookstore: Tanum Libris, Karl Johans gt. 37-41 (☎22 41 11 00), in the Paléet. Open M-F 10am-8pm, Sa 10am-5pm. **Norli Bokhandel,** Universitetsgaten 22-24, across from Oslo University, has complimentary coffee. Open M-F 9am-6pm, Sa 10am-4pm.

Laundromat: Look for the word *Myntvaskeri.* **Selvbetjent Vask,** Ullevålsveien 15. Wash 30kr per 20min. (soap included), dry 20kr per 30min. Open daily 8am-9pm.

Gay and Lesbian Services: The **Landsforeningen for Lesbiskog Homofil fri gjøring (LLH),** 2 St. Olavs plass (☎22 11 05 09; fax 22 20 24 05). Pick up *Blick* (30kr), a monthly newspaper with attractions and nightlife listings. Open M-F 9am-4pm.

EMERGENCY AND COMMUNICATIONS

Emergencies: Ambulance, ☎113. **Fire,** ☎110. **Police,** ☎112.

Pharmacy: Jernbanetorvets Apotek (☎22 41 24 82), opposite the train station. 24hr.

Medical Assistance: Oslo Kommunale Legevakt, Storgata 40 (☎22 11 70 70). 24hr.

Internet Access: Library, Henrik Ibsensgate 1. Sign up for free slots. Open Aug.-June M-F 10am-6pm, Sa 9am-3pm; July M-F 10am-3pm. Ask at Use It (see Tourist Offices, above) for *Nettkafeer i Oslo,* which lists Internet cafes in the city.

Post Office: Dronningens gt. 15 (☎23 14 78 02); enter at Prinsens gt. Address mail to be held: First name, SURNAME, *Poste Restante,* Dronningens gt. 15, N-0101 Oslo 1. Open M-F 8am-6pm, Sa 10am-3pm.

ACCOMMODATIONS AND CAMPING

Hostels in Oslo fill up quickly in the summer—make reservations, especially if traveling in a group. The **private rooms** arranged by **Use It** (see above) are a good deal; the later you show up, however, the less central your room (125kr, with sleeping bag 100kr). **Pensions** *(pensjonater)* are usually cheaper than hotels. Some **hotels** offer cheaper "last-minute" prices on vacant rooms through the tourist office. In principle, the Norwegian *allmansrett* gives you the right to **free camp,** but no one really camps on private lawns. Free camping is in the forest north of town as long as you avoid public areas; try the end of the Sognsvann line. Fires are not allowed.

Albertine Hostel, Storgata 55 (☎22 99 72 00; fax 22 99 72 20). Walk along Karl Johans gt. from the train station, around the cathedral, and up Storgata. Or take tram #10, 11, 12, 15, or 17 to "Hausmanns gate"; it's 100m up Storgata on the left, behind the Anker Hotel. New and beautifully furnished. Breakfast 50kr. Sheets 40kr. Reception 24hr. Open June 7-Aug. 24. Dorms 120kr; singles 360kr; doubles 380kr; quads 580kr.

Cochs Pensjonat, Parkveien 25 (☎23 33 24 00; fax 23 33 24 10), at Hegdehaugsveien. From the train station, walk 25min. along Karl Johans gt. through Slottsparken; or take tram #11 or 19 to the end of the park. Quiet rooms on the upper floors of a building overlooking the royal park. Singles 340kr; doubles 280-580kr; quads 700-820kr.

Ellingsens Pensjonat, Holtegata 25 (☎22 60 03 59; fax 22 60 99 21). Take tram #19 to "Briskeby." Unmarked gray house popular with backpackers, thanks to its central location and beautiful surroundings. Reception M-F 7:30am-10:30pm, Sa-Su 8am-10:30pm. Singles 290kr; doubles 470kr; doubles with bath 540kr; extra bed 100kr.

Oslo Vandrerhjem Haraldsheim (HI), Haraldsheimveien 4 (☎22 15 50 43 or 22 22 29 65; fax 22 22 10 25). Take tram #15 or 17, or the Flybus from the airport to "Sinsenkrysset"; follow the signs across the field and up the hill. Clean, comfortable rooms with a great view over the Oslofjord. Breakfast included. Sheets 45kr; no sleeping bags. Kitchen. Laundry. **Internet** 10kr for 15min. Reception 24hr. Lockout 10am-3pm. Dorms 160kr, non-members 185kr; singles 280kr; doubles 380kr.

Oslo Vandrerhjem Holtekilen (HI), Michelets vei 55 (☎67 51 80 40; fax 67 59 12 30). Take bus #151/161, 251/252, or 261 to "Kveldsroveien" (20min.), or take the local commuter train to "Stabekk." Popular, although quite far from central Oslo. Breakfast included. Reserve ahead. Open late May to late Aug. Dorms 165kr; singles 270kr; doubles 430kr; non-members add 25kr.

Ekeberg Camping, Ekebergveien 65 (☎22 19 85 68), 3km from town. Take tram #18/19 or bus #34A from the train station. Marvelous view. Cooking facilities, grocery store. Showers included. Open May 25-Aug. Tent for 2 people 120kr; extra person 40kr.

Bogstad Camping, Ankerveien 117 (☎22 50 76 80), on Bogstad Lake is beautiful, if far. Take bus #32 from the station (30min.). Reception 24hr. Open year-round. Tent for 2 people 130kr; tent for 4 people 160kr; extra person 20kr.

FOOD

Visitors should have no trouble finding authentic Norwegian meals or dishes from any part of the globe. Prices are high, however, and **grocery stores** may be the best option for those on a tight budget: try **Rema 1000,** Torggata 2-G (open M-F 9am-7pm, Sa 9am-6pm), or **Kiwi Supermarket,** on Storgata (open M-Sa 8am-11pm). You can eat out without hurting your wallet in the **Grønland** district east of the train station, in the international food court in **Paléet** shopping mall on Karl Johans gt., and at **lunch buffets** offered by most restaurants in the city center.

Coco Chalet, Prinsens gt. 21. Fabulous atmosphere and very popular. Get a magazine from the first floor and enjoy a light meal, coffee, or cake. Lunch 60-100kr; salads 89kr; dinner 90-180kr. Open M-Sa 11am-11pm.

Kaffistova, intersection of Rosenkrantz gt. and Kristian IV gt. Beautiful, cafeteria-style eatery with traditional Norwegian meat and fish dishes, porridges, and desserts. Vegetarian options. Entrees 80-100kr. Open M-F 9:30am-8pm, Sa-Su 10:30am-5pm.

Vegeta Vertshus, Munkedamsveien 3b, off Stortings gt. near the National Theater. Cafeteria-style vegeterian buffet and salad bar, including pizzas, veggie burgers, and various entrees. All-you-can-eat 125kr; large single serving 90kr; small single serving 80kr. Students 50kr Tu-F 3-8pm; 10% student discount at any other time. Open daily 11am-11pm; buffet closes at 10pm.

Café Sult, Thorvald Meyersgt. 26, in the trendy Gruner Løkka neighborhood north of the Albertine Hostel. Lunch 55-90kr; dinner 125-170kr. Open Tu-F 4pm-1am, Sa 11:30am-1am, Su 1pm-midnight.

Bagel and Juice, Haakon VII's gt. 5, near the Rådhus. Comfortable cafe serving bagel sandwiches (28kr with cream cheese, from 48kr with meat) and blended juice drinks (30-40kr). Becomes a popular bar after hours. Open M-Th 10am-12:30am, F-Sa 10am-2:30am, Su 11am-12:30am.

Lord Sandwich, Prinsens gt. 18. Serves tasty take-out sandwiches (35kr) made even tastier by the knowledge that they're the sweetest deal in town. Open M-F 8am-5:15pm.

SIGHTS

FROGNERPARKEN. Also called **Vigelandsparken.** Gustav Vigeland's powerful sculptures at Frognerparken depict each stage of the human life cycle and attract more than one million visitors annually, making it Norway's most visited attraction. The park is a playground of grassy knolls, duck ponds, and hosts concerts. *(Entrance on Kirkeveien. Take bus #20 or tram #12 or 15 to "Vigelandsparken." Open 24hr. Free.)*

EDVARD MUNCH. The **Munch Museum** has an outstanding collection of his unsettling paintings, lithographs, and photographs. *(Tøyengata 53. Take bus #20 to "Munch-museet," the subway to "Tøyen," or walk 10min. east from the train station. Open daily June to mid.-Sept. 10am-6pm; mid.-Sept. to May Tu-W and F-Sa 10am-4pm, Th and Su 10am-6pm. 60kr, students 30kr.)* His most famous work, "The Scream," is at the **Nasjonal Galleriet,** which houses a large collection of Scandinavian artwork. *(Universitetsgaten 13. Take tram #12, 13, or 19, or the subway to "Nationaltheatret." Open M, W, and F 10am-6pm, Th 10am-8pm, Sa 10am-4pm, Su 11am-4pm. Free.)* Next door at the **University** are Munch's massive "Sun" murals. *(Open M-F 9am-4pm. Free.)*

RÅDHUS (CITY HALL). The artists who painted the interior of the towering Rådhus during WWII did so in defiance of the orders of the Nazi occupiers and were punished by deportation to prison camps. The annual Nobel Peace Prize ceremony takes place here Dec. 10. *(South of the Nationaltheatret on Fridtjof Nansens plass, near the harbor. Open M-Sa 9am-4pm, Su noon-4pm. 25kr. Free tours M-F 10am, noon, and 2pm.)*

AKERSHUS CASTLE AND FORTRESS. Built in 1299, this waterfront complex was transformed into a Renaissance palace by Christian IV between 1637 and 1648. Explore dungeons, underground passages, and vast halls. *(Take bus #60 to "Bankplassen" or tram #10 or 15 to "Christianiatorv." Fortress open May to mid-Sept. M-Sa 8am-8pm, Su 10am-8pm; mid-Sept. to Apr. M-F 11am-4pm. Castle open May 5 to Sept. 15 M-F 10am-4pm, Su 12:30-4pm; mid to late Apr. and mid-Sept. to Oct. Su 12:30-4pm. Tours of the castle M-Sa 11am,*

1, and 3pm, and Su 1 and 3pm.) The powerful **Hjemmefrontmuseet** (Resistance Museum) in the fortress documents Norway's efforts to subvert Nazi occupation. *(Open mid-June to Aug. 8 M-Sa 10am-5pm, Su 11am-5pm; Sept.-June closes 1-2hr. earlier. 20kr.)*

BYGDØY. The peninsula of Bygdøy is right across the inlet from downtown Oslo; although mainly residential, it swarms with museums and even has a few beaches. The ferry stops first at the **Folkemuseet,** a massive outdoor museum featuring buildings from various eras and parts of the country, including the 13th-century *Stav* Church, one of the last of its kind in existence. *(Museumsveien 10. Walk up the hill leading away from the dock and follow signs to the right; or take the bus to "Folkemuseet." Open daily mid-May to mid-June and early to mid-Sept. 10am-5pm; daily mid-June to Aug. 10am-6pm; Jan. to mid-May and mid-Sept. to Dec. M-Sa 11am-3pm, Su 11am-4pm. 50kr.)* The three vessels of the impressive **Viking Ship Museum** include the 9th-century ring-prowed, dragon-keeled Oseberg burial barge. *(Open daily May-Aug. 9am-6pm; Sept. 11am-5pm; Apr. and Oct. 11am-4pm; Nov.-Mar. 11am-3pm. 30kr, students 10kr.)* At the ferry's second stop, "Bygdøynes," the **Polar Ship "Fram" Museum** chronicles the Arctic and Antarctic explorations of two of the most famous Norwegian explorers, Fridtjof Nansen and Roald Amundsen. *(Open daily in summer 9am-5:45pm; in winter reduced hours. 25kr, students 15kr.)* The popular **Huk Beach** lies just around the corner from the two museums; follow signs from the pier to reach it. Or, go bare as you dare at nude **Paradisbukten,** on the far side of the peninsula. *(To reach Bygdøy, take the commuter ferry Bygdøyfergene, which departs from pier 3 at Rådhusbryggen May-Sept. every 40min.; 20kr. Ferry info ☎22 20 07 15. Or, take bus #30 from Nationaltheatret to "Bygdøynes" or "Folkemuseet.")*

OTHER SIGHTS. The **Samtidsmuseet** (Museum of Contemporary Art) is near Akershus Fortress. *(Bankplassen 4. Open Tu, W, and F 10am-5pm, Th 10am-8pm, Sa 11am-4pm, Su 11am-5pm. 40kr, students and seniors 20kr; Th free.)* The **royal residence,** at the top of Karl Johans gt., is now open to the public following recent renovations. *(Guided tours in English are held daily at 2pm. Purchase tickets in advance from any post office. 55kr, students 45kr.)* You can also stop by the beautiful **Slottsparken** (Palace Park) nearby to see the changing of the guard, held daily at 1:30pm. *(Take tram #12, 15, or 19, or bus #30-32 or 45 to "Slottsparken.")* For a great panorama of **Oslofjord** and the city, head to the ski jump **Holmenkollen** at the **Ski Museum.** A simulator recreates the adrenaline rush of a four-minute, 130km-per-hour downhill ski run. *(Take subway #1 on the Frognerseteren line to "Holmenkollen." Open daily June-Aug. 9am-10pm; May and Sept. 10am-5pm; Sept.-Apr. 10am-4pm. Museum 60kr, students 50kr; simulator 45kr, with Oslo Card 35kr.)*

ENTERTAINMENT AND NIGHTLIFE

What's on in Oslo (free at tourist offices) details Oslo's "high culture," including the opera, symphony, and theater. **Filmenshus,** Dronningsgt. 16, is the center of Oslo's art film scene, while Hollywood flicks are screened at **Saga Cinema,** Stortingsgata 28. At **Nordic Black Theater,** Olaf Ryes plass 11 (☎22 38 12 62), immigrant and minority Norwegians stage social critiques in English. Big-name rock concerts take place at the **Rockefeller Music Hall,** Torggata. (☎22 20 32 32. 50-350kr.) All post offices sell concert and festival tickets.

In addition to the countless bars along **Karl Johans gt.** and the **Aker Brygge** harbor complex, Oslo boasts a number of nightclubs with busy DJs and live music. Dance to the house, rock, and funk of **Barock,** Univeritetsgt. 26. (Weekend cover 50kr. Open Th-Su 9pm-3am.) **So What!,** Grensen 9, is popular with a young, alternative crowd. (2-3 concerts per week. Cover 50kr. Open F-Sa 9pm-3:30am.) **Sikamikanico,** 2 Møllergata, is one of Oslo's hipper coffee bars, recently refurbished in psychedelic colors. (DJs Th-Sa. Open daily 4pm-3am.)

EXCURSIONS FROM OSLO

OSLOFJORD. The nearby islands of inner **Oslofjord** offer cheap, delightful daytrips. The ruins of a **Cistercian Abbey** lie on the landscaped island of **Hovedøya,** while **Langøyene** has Oslo's best **beach.** Take **bus** #29 from Oslo to **Vippetangen** (round-trip 40kr) to catch a ferry to either island.

DRØBAK. About an hour from Oslo by ferry, **Drøbak** has traditional wooden houses. The **ferry** to Drøbak leaves from in front of the Rådhus (round-trip 100kr).

FREDRIKSTAD. With an old city encircled by a massive wall, **Fredrikstad** is Norway's only fully-preserved fortified town. The town is on the Oslo **train** line toward Halden or Gothenburg (1¼hr.).

OUTDOORS. To bask in Norway's natural grandeur, take the Sognsvann subway from Nationaltheatret to the end of the line. **Use It**, the youth info center (p. 712) provides trail maps; in winter, ask the tourist office about cross-country ski rental. **Villmarkssenteret,** Christian Krohgs gt. 16, rents canoes and kayaks on the Akerselva river. (☎22 05 05 22. 300-400kr per 8hr., 350-450kr per day, 500-580kr per weekend.)

ALONG THE OSLO-BERGEN RAIL LINE

The seven-hour rail journey from Oslo to Bergen is one of the most famous scenic rides in the world. From Oslo, there are stops at **Finse, Myrdal** (the transfer point for the **Flåm railway**), and **Voss,** before the train finally pulls into Bergen.

FINSE. Wilderness junkies hop off at Finse and hike north for several beautiful days down the Aurlandsdal Valley to **Aurland,** 10km from Flåm. Be sure to ask about trail conditions before you set off at either the Finse station or the DNT in Oslo or Bergen. You can sleep all the way in evenly spaced DNT *hytter*. For maps, prices, and reservations, inquire at DNT in Oslo (☎22 82 28 22) or Bergen (☎55 32 22 30).

VOSS. Stretched along a glassy lake that reflects surrounding snow-capped mountains, Voss is an adventurer's dream. In winter, skiing is plentiful; in summer there's paragliding, horseback riding, and white water rafting. Book through the **Voss Adventure Center** (☎56 51 36 30), in a mini-golf hut behind the Park Hotel, and the **Voss Rafting Center** (☎56 51 05 25; www.bbb.no/rafting). **Trains** arrive from Oslo (5 per day, 450kr) and Bergen (10 per day, 125kr). **Buses** also run from Voss to Gudvangen (70min., 4-9 per day, 63kr) on the Sognefjord, and it is possible to make bus connections to Bergen, Oslo, and Lillehammer (ask at the station for more details). Trains and buses arrive at a central station near the downtown area; to get to the **tourist office,** Hestavangen 10, turn left as you exit the station and bear right at the fork by the church. (☎56 52 08 00; fax 56 52 08 01. Open June-Aug. M-Sa 9am-7pm, Su 2-7pm; Sept.-May M-F 9am-4pm.) Turn right as you exit the station and walk along the lakeside road to reach Voss's modern, well-equipped **HI youth hostel,** where you can admire the terrific view or relax in the sauna. (☎56 51 20 17. Canoe, rowboat, bike, and kayak rental. Reception 24hr. 180kr; nonmembers 200kr.) To reach **Voss Camping,** head left from the station, stick to the lake shore, and follow the road until you hit the campground pool. (☎56 51 15 97. Tent and 4 people 60kr.)

FLÅM AND THE FLÅM RAILWAY. The spectacular railway connecting **Myrdal** (a stop on the Oslo-Bergen line) to the tiny fjord town of Flåm is one of Norway's most famous attractions. Descending almost 864m in 55 minutes, the railway is an incredible feat of engineering, winding through tunnels past rushing waterfalls to the valley below. Be sure to see the magnificent **Kjosfossen falls** when the train makes its stop there. Alternatively, a 20km **hike** (4-5hr.) on well-tended paths from Myrdal to Flåm allows for extended lingering (and free camping) amid the rainbow-capped waterfalls and snowy mountain vistas. Flåm sits at the edge of the **Aurlandsfjord,** an inlet off the Sognefjord. During the day, the tiny town is heavily touristed; in the off season, the stunning surroundings make Flåm a terrific, soothing place to spend a night or two. The **tourist office** is in the large building beside the train station. (☎57 63 21 06. Open daily mid-June to mid-Aug. 8:30am-3:30pm and 4-8pm.)

THE FJORDS AND WEST COUNTRY

Spectacular views and summer's long days make fjord country irresistible to all types of travelers. Buses and ferries wind through this unique and scenic coastal region, and although transportation can be complicated, the scenery through the window is half the fun. **Bergen** is the major port for boats serving the region; **HSD express boats** (☎55 23 87 00; ticket office at Strandkaiterminalen) run to the Hardangerfjord, Stavanger, and points south of the city, while **Fylkesbaatane** (☎55 90 70 71; tickets also at Strandkaiterminalen) takes care of boat transport north into the Sognefjord and surrounding areas. Main **bus** departure points in the region are Bergen (see below), Sogndal (see p. 724), and Førde (a large town north of the Sognefjord with little scenery but a centrally located bus terminal); bus connections to almost all fjord towns can be reached through them. Call ☎177 for regional **transportation info;** tourist offices, boat terminals, and bus stations are able to help plan most routes through the fjords.

BERGEN

Vaunted as the "Gateway to the Fjords," Bergen is clean, compact, and stunningly beautiful, surrounded by forested mountains rising steeply from the fjords. Once Norway's capital and a center of trade in the Middle Ages, the city still claims a prominent commercial and intellectual standing. The lively student population and international influences make Bergen much more than just another scenic spot.

GETTING THERE AND GETTING AROUND

Trains: ☎81 50 08 88. Three trains daily to **Myrdal** (1¾-2½hr., 180kr) and **Oslo** (6½-7½hr., 550kr, mandatory seat reservations 25kr) via **Voss** (1hr., 125kr).

Buses: Bystasjonen, Strømgaten 8 (☎177, outside Bergen ☎55 55 90 70). Serves neighboring areas, the **Hardangerfjord** area, **Ålesund** (489kr, students 25% off), and **Oslo** (580kr; students 25% off). Ticket office open M-Sa 7am-6pm, Sa 7am-2pm.

Ferries: The **Hurtigruten** begins its journey along the coast to **Kirkenes** from **Bergen** (daily 10:30pm; May-Sept. 4858kr, reduced Oct.-Apr.; students 50% off). **Fjord Line,** on Skoltegrunnskaien (☎55 54 88 00), goes to **Hanstholm, Denmark** (15½hr., departs M, W, and F 4:30pm, from 680kr; off season from 300kr; round-trip 10% off) and **Newcastle, England** (25hr.; Tu-F and Su in summer, M and Th in winter; from 720kr in summer, from 440kr in winter; students 50% off). **Smyril Line,** Slottsgaten 1 (☎55 32 09 70; fax 55 96 02 72), departs for: the **Faroe Islands** (24hr., June-Aug. Tu 3pm, 840-1890kr); **Iceland** (40hr., 1840-3500kr); and the **Shetland Islands** (11hr., 690-1550kr; students 25% off). International ferries depart from **Skoltegrunnskaien,** 20min. past Bryggen along the right side of the harbor.

Public Transportation: Yellow and red buses chauffeur you around the city. 18kr per ride in city center, 25kr outside; free from the bus station into the center of town.

NORWAY

THE WORLD'S MOST BEAUTIFUL VOYAGE

While some might contest the title Norway has given to the sea journey along its coastline, few can deny the impression left by spectacular scenery drifting by the window. Known as the **"Hurtigruten,"** the coastal steamer's route begins in Bergen and ends at Kirkenes, on the Norwegian-Russian border. Although now primarily used as passenger cruise ships, the 11 vessels serving the route still carry out their historical function delivering supplies to its 34 ports of call along the sparsely populated western coast. Most passengers purchase a cabin and stay on board for the round-trip journey from Bergen; but with a north- and southbound ship stopping at all ports every day, the Hurtigruten provides a comfortable way for those traveling shorter distances to get from one place to the next. While rates tend to be more expensive than a bus or car ferry, discounts for students and seniors make a jaunt on the steamer more affordable for some, while others find that the first-class surroundings and freedom of movement aboard makes the higher fares a good value (p. 708). Financial matters aside, little can compare to seeing the midnight sun from a deck chair atop a a ship saililng along the coast–it is a spectacular experience worth the extra effort or money.

ORIENTATION AND PRACTICAL INFORMATION

The **train station** lies at the opposite end of the city center from the harbor, 10 minutes away. As you face the harbor, **Bryggen** (the extension of Kong Oscars gt.) and the town's most imposing mountains are to your right; most of the main buildings are to the left. The **Torget,** Bergen's famous outdoor market, is at the harbor's tip.

Tourist Office: Vågsalmenningen 1 (☎55 32 14 80; fax 55 32 14 64), just past the Torget. Books rooms and has free copies of the *Bergen Guide*. A special section in the office helps visitors plan travel through the fjords. The **Bergen Card** includes museum admissions and other discounts (1-day 150kr, 2-day 230kr). Open daily June-Aug. 8:30am-10pm; May and Sept. 9am-8pm; Oct.-Apr. M-Sa 9am-4pm. **DNT,** Tverrgt. 4-6 (☎55 32 22 30), off Marken, sells detailed topological maps for all of Norway and provides comprehensive hiking information. Open M-W and F 10am-4pm, Th 10am-6pm.

Currency Exchange: At the post office. After hours both tourist offices will change currency at a rate less favorable than the bank rate. No commission.

Luggage storage: At the train and bus stations. 20kr per day. Open daily 7am-11:50pm.

Emergencies: Fire: ☎110. **Police:** ☎112. **Ambulance:** ☎113.

Pharmacy: Apoteket Nordstjernen (☎55 21 83 84), on the 2nd fl. of the bus station. Open M-Sa 8am-midnight, Su 9:30am-midnight.

Medical Assistance: 24-hour Accident Clinic, Vestre Strømkai 19 (☎55 32 11 20).

Internet Access: Free at the **bibliotek** (public library) at Stromgata Vestre Strømkaien, though time is limited to 15min. Open M and Th 9am-7pm, Tu-W and F 9am-3pm, Sa 9am-2pm. Or, try **Netropolis,** Theatergaten 20. 30kr per 30min., 40kr per hr.

Post Office: Småstrandgt. (☎55 54 15 00). Open M-F 8am-6pm, Sa 9am-3pm. Address mail to be held: First name SURNAME, *Poste Restante*, **N-5014** Bergen, Norway.

ACCOMMODATIONS, CAMPING, AND FOOD

The tourist office books rooms (some with bathrooms) in private homes for a 25kr fee (40kr fee for 2 people; singles 185-210kr; doubles 295-430kr).

Intermission, Kalfarveien 8 (☎55 31 32 75). Head right from the train or bus station and right down Kong Oscars gt., which becomes Kalfarveien, and look for the white house on the left (5min.). Friendly staff and communal atmosphere. Free tea, cookies, and laundry. Breakfast 30kr; pack a lunch for 15kr. Reception 7-11am and 5pm-midnight, F-Sa until 1am. Lockout 11am-5pm. Curfew M-Th and Su midnight, F-Sa 1am. Reserve ahead. Open mid-June to mid-Aug. 95kr.

YMCA InterRail Center, Nedre Korskirkealmenningen 4 (☎55 31 72 52; fax 55 31 35 77). Exit the train or bus station and turn right, and head up the hill; then turn left onto Kong Oscars gt. and left again when you reach Nedre Korskirk (7-10min.). Crowded with backpackers, thanks to an excellent location. Kitchen. Laundry 40kr. Internet. Reception 7am-midnight. Lockout noon-4pm. Open June to mid-Sept. 100-150kr.

Montana Youth Hostel (HI), Johan Blyttsvei 30 (☎55 20 80 70; fax 55 20 80 75), 5km from the city center. Take bus #31 (dir. Lægdene; 17kr) from the post office to "Montana." Spacious modern hostel. Breakfast included. Sheets 40kr. Kitchen. Laundry. Reception 24hr. Lockout 10am-3pm. Dorms 135-170kr; doubles with bath 470kr.

Camping: Bergen Camping Park, Haukås om Åsane (☎55 24 88 08). 15kr per person, 70kr per tent. Or **free camp** on the far side of the hills above town. Pick up a map or ask for further info at the tourist office.

Bergen's culinary centerpiece is the **fish market** that springs up on the Torget, by the harbor; it's unclear, however, whether fish or tourists are the main haul. (Open in summer M-F 7am-4pm, Th 7am-7pm, Sa 7am-3pm; in off season opens later.) **Fellini,** Tverrgt., just off Marken, serves up Italian specialties and great pizza from 49kr. (Open M-Sa 2pm-midnight, Su 2-11pm.) Enjoy Norwegian cuisine with the older set at **Kaffistova til Ervingen,** Strandkaien 2B, on the 2nd fl. next to the harbor, a cafeteria-style joint with *dagens tilbur* (daily offer) including coffee and dessert for 99kr, soup with home-

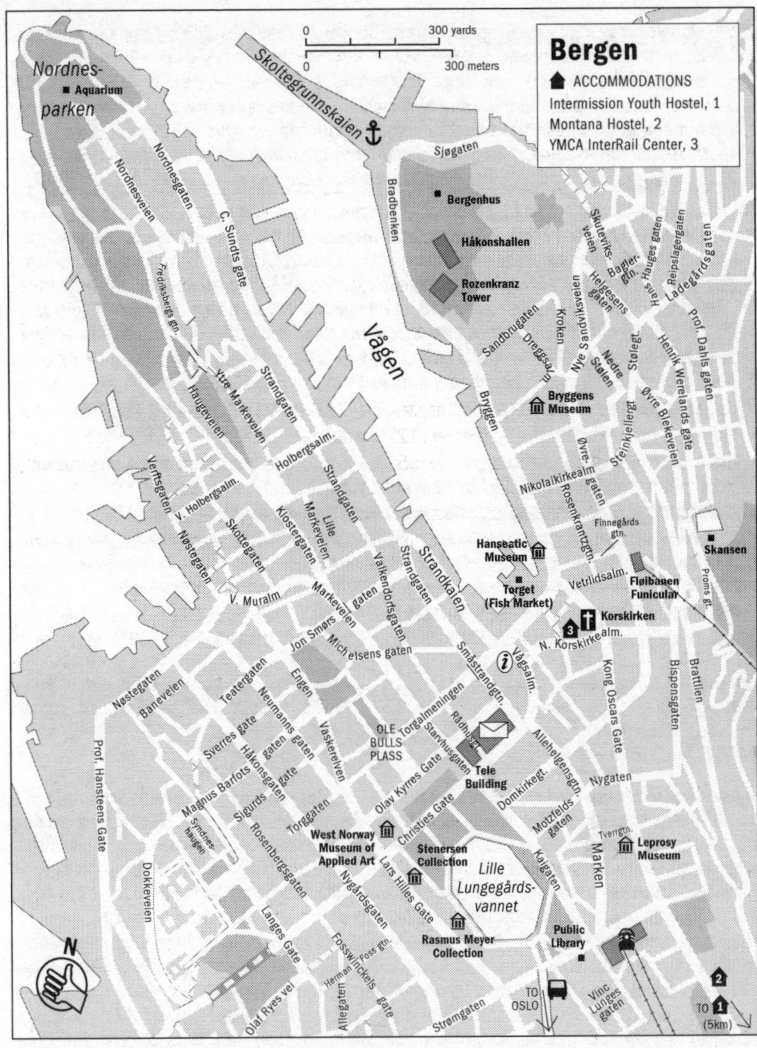

made bread for 35kr, and main dishes from 48kr. (Open M-F 8am-7pm, Sa 8am-5pm, Su noon-7pm.) Grab **groceries** at **Rimi,** Marken 3. (Open M-F 7am-9pm, Sa 7am-6pm.)

SIGHTS AND HIKING

BRYGGEN AND BERGENHUS. From the Torget, gazing down the right side of the harbor yields a view of **Bryggen**'s pointed gables. This row of medieval buildings has survived half a dozen disastrous fires and the explosion of a Nazi munitions ship, and is today listed by UNESCO as one of the world's most significant examples of the history and culture of the Middle Ages. The **Hanseatic Museum** contains secret compartments, mummified hanging fish, and an aura of gloom from the days when German merchants dominated European trade. *(At the end of Bryggen, near the Torget. Open daily June-Aug. 9am-5pm; Sept.-May 11am-2pm. May-Sept. 35kr; Oct.-Apr. 20kr.)* **Bryggens Museum** displays old costumes, runic inscriptions, and scenes from life in medieval Norway. *(3 Dreggsalm, behind a small park at the end of the Bryggen houses. Open May-Aug. daily 10am-5pm; Sept.-Apr. M-F 11am-3pm, Sa noon-3pm, Su noon-4pm. 30kr, students 15kr.)* The former city fortress, **Bergenhus,** teeters at the end of the quay, and the **Rosenkrantz Tower** stands adjacent in late medieval splendor. The 13th-century **Håkonshallen** is all that remains of the royal residence. *(At the far end of Bryggen; walk along the harbor away from the Torget. Hall and tower open daily mid-May to Aug. 10am-4pm; Sept. to mid-May hall open noon-3pm. Guided tours every hr. in summer. 20kr, students 10kr.)*

ART MUSEUMS AND GALLERIES. The **Rasmus Meyer Collection** provides a extensive overview of Norwegian Naturalists, Impressionists, and Expressionists, while the nearby **Stenersens Collection** features Munch and Picasso; both collections are branches of the **Bergen Art Museum.** *(7 and 3 Rasmus Meyers Allé, respectively. Both open mid-May to mid-Sept. daily 10am-5pm; mid-Sept. to mid-May Tu-Su 11am-5pm. Mid-May to mid-Sept. 35kr for both museums, temporary exhibits 15kr; mid-Sept. to mid-May 20kr.)* The **West Norway Museum of Applied Art** highlights stunning 20th-century Norwegian design. *(9 Nordahl Brunsgt. Open mid-May to mid-Sept. Tu-Su 11am-4pm; mid-Sept. to mid-May Tu-Sa noon-3pm, Th noon-6pm, Su noon-4pm. 30kr, students 20kr.)* Smaller, contemporary works line the intriguing **Galleri Nygaten.** *(Nygaten 5, off Kong Oscars gt. Open daily noon-4pm.)*

OTHER SIGHTS. The university has tastefully documented the history of the disease in a 19th-century hospital at the **Leprosy Museum.** *(Kong Oscars gt. 59. Open daily mid-May to Aug. 11am-3pm. 20kr, students 10kr.)* For an authentic taste of the city, explore the steep streets between the **Korskirken** church and the **Skansen** tower, and the **Sydneskleiben** and **Dragefjellsbarker** neighborhoods near the university campus; walk along Christies gt. west of the city center to where the street begins to slope steeply upward to get there. **Troldhaugen** (Troll Hill) was the summer villa of Edvard Grieg, Norway's most famous composer. The house still contains many of Grieg's belongings, including his Steinway piano, which is used at summer concerts in neighboring **Troldsalen Hall.** *(Hopsbroen, 8km south of Bergen. From the Bergen bus station, take any bus to "Hopsbroen," turn right, walk 200m, then turn left at Troldhaugsveien and follow the signs. Open daily Apr. 23-Sept. 30 9am-6pm; Oct.-Apr. 22 M-F 10am-2pm, Sa-Su noon-4pm. 50kr. Summer concerts W and Sa-Su; buy tickets at the tourist office from 150kr.)*

NORWAY IN A NUTSHELL. An immensely popular tour, "Norway in a Nutshell" combines a ride along the stunning rail line between **Myrdal** and **Flåm** *(55min., 8-10 per day; 115kr, with railpass 80kr)*, a cruise through the narrowest branches of the **Sognefjord** between Gudvangen and Flåm *(2hr., 2 per day; 156kr, students 50% off)*, and a twisting bus ride over the mountains from Gudvangen to Voss *(1¼hr., 4-8 per day, 63kr)*. The tour is unguided and extremely flexible, allowing "nutshellers" to complete the trip in one day or take stopovers at transfer points. From **Bergen,** most people take the train to Myrdal and begin the tour there, heading to Flåm, Gudvangen, and finally catching a train back to Bergen. Since Myrdal lies on the Oslo-Bergen rail line, the tour can also be done round-trip from **Oslo,** or while en route to another city. **Tickets** can be bought separately for each leg of the journey while traveling, or purchased in advance as a package from tourist offices and train stations in Oslo and Bergen *(560kr round-trip from Bergen, 1090kr round-trip from Oslo, 810kr from Bergen to Oslo)*. Railpass holders and students can get a better deal by purchasing individual tickets along the way.

FJORDS. Bergen is considered the capital of Norway's famous fjords, and many visitors use it as a launchpad for daytrips to the individual fjords (see below). **Bergen Fjord Sightseeing** offers tours of the fjords *(☎55 25 90 00. 4hr. Tickets are available at the tourist office or fish market pier.)*

HIKING. A vast archipelago spreads westward from Bergen, and towering mountains encroach from all other directions. Trails surrounding the city are well-kept and easily accessible. The **Fløibanen funicular** runs up **Mt. Fløyen** to a spectacular lookout point. *(From the Torget, follow Vetrlidsalm. east to the funicular. Runs Sept.-Apr. M-F 7:30am-11pm, Sa 8am-11pm, Su 9am-11pm; May-Aug. until midnight. Round-trip 40kr.)* At the summit, you can enjoy the spectacular views or join up with one of the many inter-

secting **hiking** trails that meander through a striking landscape dotted by massive boulders, springy moss, waterfalls, and ponds. A four-hour trail from Fløyen leads to the top of **Mt. Ulriken,** the highest peak above Bergen, and a panoramic view over the city, fjords, mountains, and nearby islands. Free concerts are held at the top of Mt. Ulriken on summer weekdays at 6pm. A **cable car** also runs to the top of Mt. Ulriken, and many choose to first ride to the top and then follow the hiking trails downward. *(Car runs daily every 7min. In summer 9am-9pm; in winter 10am-dusk. Round-trip 60kr.)* Pick up a **map** of the hills above Bergen at the DNT office.

ENTERTAINMENT

The city pulls out all the stops for the annual **Bergen International Festival** (☎55 21 61 50), a 12-day program of music, ballet, folklore, and drama, and the simultaneous **May Jazz Festival** in late May. The **Garage Bar,** at the corner of Nygårdsgaten and Christies gt., is Bergen's most popular rock club, with two pubs and a disco downstairs. (Cover 10kr Su-Th after 1am, 20kr F-Sa after 12:30am. Open M-Th 1pm-3am, F-Sa 1pm-3:30am, Su 3pm-3am.) The milder scene is on at **Café Opera,** Engen 18, a mellow cafe-restaurant that serves light meals and drinks; Thursdays nights sometime feature student theater, and weekends have dance music. (No cover. Open Su-M noon-1:30am, Tu-Th noon-3am, F-Sa noon-3:30am.) **Rick's,** Veiten 3, with a main entrance around the corner on Ole Bulls Plass, has three bars, a disco, and an upscale nightclub. (Cover 50kr F-Sa after 10:30pm. Open daily 10pm-3am.)

THE WESTERN FJORDS

HARDANGERFJORD

Slicing through one of Norway's fruit-growing regions, the steep banks of the Hardangerfjord, south of Bergen, are lined with orchards and waterfalls. Local tourist offices distribute the free *Hardanger Guide*, which provides detailed info about transportation and accommodations. At Bergen's tourist office, also find more info on **Hardanger Sunnhordlandske Dampskipsselskap (HSD;** ☎55 23 87 80), which offers day cruises through the Hardangerfjord, with stops at larger towns. Most tours depart from platform #21 at Bergen's bus station.

ROSENDAL. Perched at the mouth of the fjord, Rosendal is a good base for exploring nearby glaciers and waterfalls. The town itself is home to Norway's only **baronial manor** and its beautiful rose garden. Walking trails around the town will lead you to **Hattbergfossen,** the towering waterfall behind Rosendal. The tourist office runs a day-long tour that includes a visit to the nearby glacier and salmon farm (185kr). **Buses** from Bergen connect directly with **ferry** departures to Rosendal (2½hr., 1 per day, round-trip 265kr, students 180kr). The **tourist office,** next to the harbor, can help you find a place to stay. (☎53 48 42 80. Open daily June-Aug. 10am-6pm.)

EIDFJORD. Stampeding hikers can be heard in beautiful Eidfjord, 45km southeast of Voss on RV13, as they pass through this gateway to **Hardangervidda,** Norway's largest national park. Walk 1km from the town to see the **Viking Burial Place** in Hereid, or take the bus 20km to **Vøringstossen,** one of Norway's most famous waterfalls. **Ferries** arrive at Eidfjord from Bergen (5¾hr., 1 per day; round-trip 395kr, students 250kr; change from bus to ferry at Norteimsund). Duck into the **tourist office** for an info refill. (☎53 67 34 00. Open July M-F 9am-8pm, Sa 9am-6pm, Su noon-8pm; late June and Aug. M-Sa 9am-6pm; Sept. to mid-June M-F 8:30am-4pm.) Ask the tourist office to find you a bed (huts from 200kr), or try **Saebø Camping.** (☎53 66 59 27. 10kr per person, 50kr per tent, 250kr per cabin.)

SOGNEFJORD

The slender fingers of Sognefjord, the longest and deepest fjord in Europe, reach all the way to the foot of the Jotunheimen Mountains in central Norway. Sognefjord is just a short, stunning ride north of the rail line running west from Oslo, or a quick boat trip from Bergen. **Fylkesbaatane** (☎55 90 70 70) sends boats on daytrips to towns on the Sognefjord and back to Bergen, and offers day tours of the Sognefjord and Flåm valley. The boats depart from Strandkaiterminalen, and the tickets can be purchased both there and at Bergen's tourist office.

BALESTRAND. On the north side of Sognefjord, between Bergen and Flåm, Balestrand is ideal for fjord and glacier excursions. Enjoy the views of the fjord from the front of Balestrand's historic hotel near the quay. **Express boats** whiz from Balestrand up the **Fjærlandsfjord** to Fjærland (2 per day, 120kr, students 50% off), allowing for daytrips to the **Jostedal glacier. Hiking** in the area immediately around Balestrand is also excellent. Follow the blue-marked trail above the town to **Balastølen,** a mountain meadow with a great view of the fjord. Get maps and info at the **tourist office,** near the quay. (☎57 69 12 55. Open M-F 7:30am-9pm, Sa-Su 7:30am-6:30pm.) **Express boats** from Bergen serve Balestrand (4hr., 2 per day, 345kr; railpass holders and students 50% off). The gorgeous fjord-side **Kringsjå Hotel and Youth Hostel (HI)** is 100m up the hill behind town. (☎57 69 13 03. Breakfast included. Kitchen. Laundry. Open mid-June to mid-Aug. Dorms 165kr; doubles 400kr, nonmembers 195kr and 460kr.) **Sjøtun Camping,** 1km down the coastal road, has tent sites and huts. (☎57 69 12 23. Reception 9-10am, 6-7pm, and 9-10pm. Open June to mid-Sept. 15kr per person; 30kr per tent; 2-person hut from 150kr.)

EXCURSIONS FROM SOGNEFJORD: FJÆRLAND. With Balestrand perched at its mouth, Fjærlandsfjord branches off from Sognefjord in a thin northward line to the tiny town of **Fjærland,** which lies under the looming *Jostedalsbreen*, the Jostedal glacier (see below). The town is home to a number of fine hikes and an incongruous "book town"—a small village of 14 multilingual used book stores. The **Glacier Museum,** 3km outside town, shows a beautiful panoramic film about Jostedalsbreen and the surrounding national park. (Open daily June-Aug. 9am-7pm; Apr.-May and Sept.-Oct. 10am-4pm. 70kr.)

Express boats from Balestrand make the run to Fjærland (2 per day; 120kr, students 60kr). **Buses** (80kr) connect with boat arrival times and shuttle passengers to the Glacier Museum and, after a stopover, whisk them to view two offshoots of the Jostedal Glacier, then return them to Fjærland's harbor in time to catch the boat back to Balestrand. Tickets can be purchased on the boat or at the Balestrand tourist office. **Buses** run from Fjærland to: Sogndal (2-3 per day; 48kr, students 25% off); Førde (2-3 per day; 114kr, students 25% off); Bergen (4-8 per day; 235kr); Ålesund (4-8 per day; 304kr); and most destinations in the fjord region. Buses leave 200m up the road from the Glacier Museum on Route 5. Travelers just passing through Fjaerland should take the bus to the Glacier Museum one-way (16kr) to reach the stops; ask bus drivers for assistance in navigating bus connections if in doubt. The **tourist office** helps solve transportation woes and provides hiking maps and info about activities in the area. (☎57 69 32 33. Open daily May 29-Sept. 12 12:30-4pm.)

NORDFJORD AND JOSTEDALSBREEN GLACIER

Enveloping 800km of the area around **Nordfjord** in an icy cocoon, **Jostedalsbreen,** the Jostedal Glacier, is difficult to miss as it winds its way through mountain passes in frozen cascades of luminous blue. Nordfjord itself is less impressive than Geirangerfjord and Sognefjord, to the north and south, respectively; it's really more of a geographical entity around which you'll have to navigate than an object of direct interest, although spectacular scenery is in abundance. Jostedalsbreen, in contrast, is an increasingly popular destination, and a number of companies leading glacier walks have sprung up in recent years. Without a car, it's difficult to take advantage of the more substantial tours in the space of one day, as bus arrivals and departures are not often conveniently timed. However, shorter tours are convenient and make glacier-walking trips possible for backpackers. It is extremely dangerous to venture onto glaciers without a guide, as all glaciers have hidden soft spots and crevices.

STRYN (BRIKSDALSBREEN AND BØDALSBREEN). Stryn is wedged between the mountains near the inner end of Nordfjord, just northwest of the glacier. **Briks-**

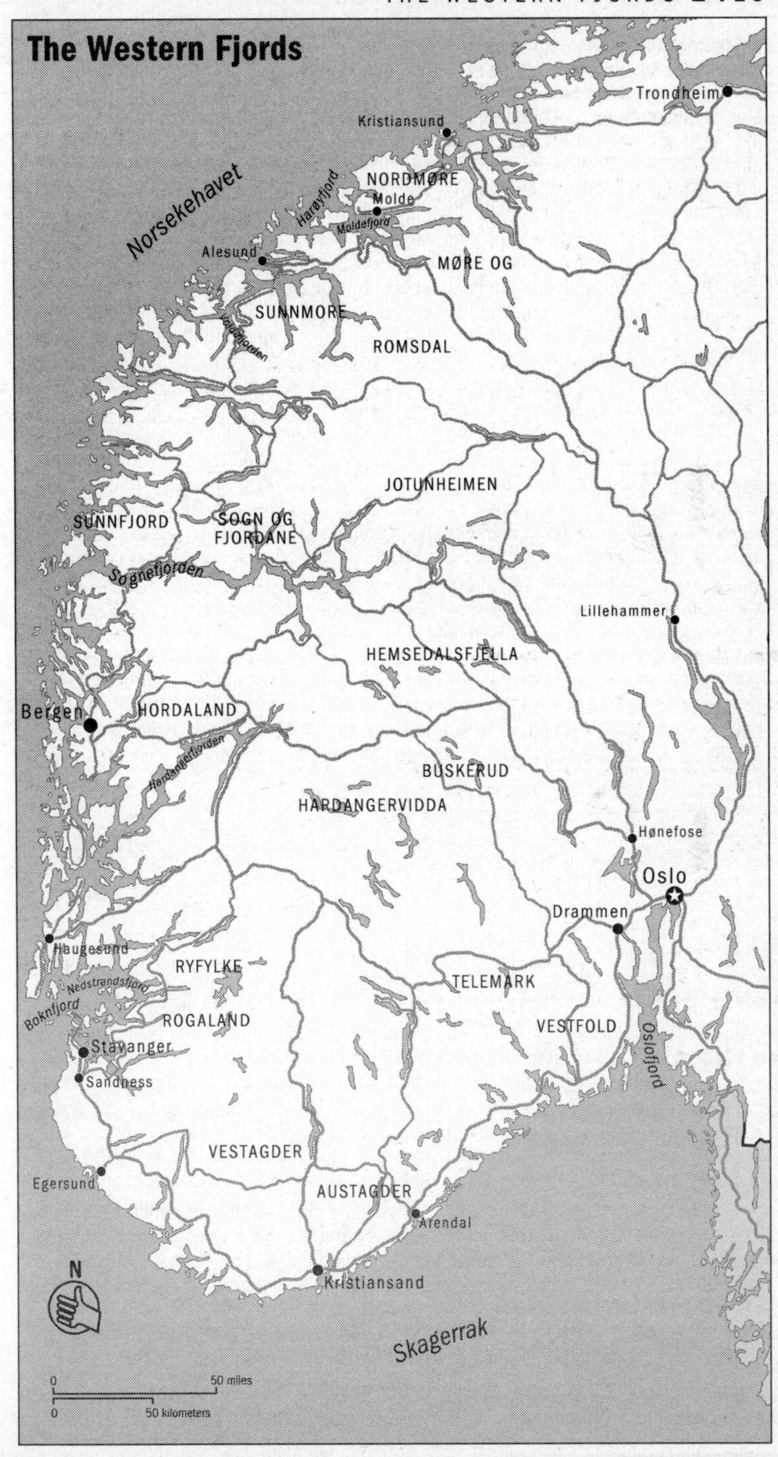
The Western Fjords
Trondheim
Kristiansund
Norsekehavet
Harøyfjord
NORDMØRE
Molde
Moldefjord
Alesund
MØRE OG
SUNNMORE
ROMSDAL
JOTUNHEIMEN
SUNNFJORD
SOGN OG
FJORDANE
Søgnefjorden
Lillehammer
HEMSEDALSFJELLA
Bergen
HORDALAND
Hardangerfjorden
BUSKERUD
HARDANGERVIDDA
Hønefose
Oslo
Drammen
Haugesund
RYFYLKE
Nedstrandsfjord
Boknfjord
TELEMARK
ROGALAND
VESTFOLD
Oslofjord
Stavanger
Sandness
VESTAGDER
Egersund
AUSTAGDER
Arendal
N
Kristiansand
Skagerrak
0
50 miles
0
50 kilometers

NORWAY

dal Breføring (☎57 87 68 00) and **Olden Aktiv** (☎57 87 38 88) run a variety of tours for different fitness and skill levels (200-400kr) on the nearby Briksdalsbreen arm of Jostedalsbreen. **Stryn Fjell-og Breførarlag** (☎57 87 79 93) runs longer, more intense hikes on **Bødalsbreen** (300-500kr), a different limb of the glacier. A **bus** (60kr) leaves Stryn daily at 10am for **Briksdal,** dropping passengers off at a mountain lodge where tickets and tour information are available; the meeting point for glacier walks is a mild half-hour walk from there. However, time is limited for car-less travelers: the return bus leaves Briksdal at 2pm, meaning that anyone relying on the bus for transport back can only spend an hour actually on the ice. The town is trying to remedy this situation, so inquire at the tourist office for the latest bus schedules. The more determined can camp in Briksdal's campgrounds or dish out the dough for a room at **Melkevoll Bretun,** the mountain lodge. (☎57 87 38 64; fax 57 87 38 90. Around 400kr.) Stryn itself is quite lively for a fjord-side town, especially in summer, when the downtown's outdoor cafes fill with tourists and locals alike. The town has excellent walking paths and is home to a popular summer **ski center.** (☎57 87 40 40. Open daily May-June and Aug.-Sept. 10am-4pm.)

Buses connect Stryn to **Otta** (220kr), which lies along the rail line, allowing connections to Åndalsnes, Trondheim, Lillehammer, and Oslo by train. Buses also come and go from Hellesylt on the Geirangerfjord (70kr), Ålesund (194kr), and Førde (156kr), where buses leaves for Bergen and all western fjord destinations; students get 25% off all fares, while railpass holders get 50% off. To get to the **tourist office,** on Walhallengen, walk past the Esso station, take the first road going left from the roundabout, and turn right on Walhallengen. (☎57 87 40 40. Open daily June 1-19 and Aug. 11-31 8:30am-6pm, June 20-Aug. 10 8:30am-8pm and Sept.-May M-F 8:30am-3:30pm.) The **youth hostel (HI)** is a hike up the hill behind town; rides can often be arranged if you call ahead. (☎57 87 11 06. Breakfast included. Laundry 30kr. Reception 8-11am and 4-11pm. Open June-Aug. Dorms 160kr, nonmembers 185kr; singles 250kr; doubles 400kr.) **Stryn Camping** is in the center of town. (☎57 87 11 36. Reception 8am-11pm. 120kr for tent and 1 person, 10kr per extra person.)

SOGNDAL (NIGARDSBREEN). Nestled on the coast of the Sognefjord, the town of Sogndal is another fine base for glacier walking, as well as a quiet spot to soak up the backdrop of water and mountains that makes Norway's fjords unique. The **Nigardsbreen** arm of Jostedalsbreen is nearby, virtually begging hikers to trek across its icy expanse. **Jostedal Breheimsenteret** (☎57 68 32 50) runs everything from one-hour outings to full-day jaunts (100-500kr). Buses (83kr) leave Sogndal for the glacier at 8:25am, with a return bus at 5pm. Fylkesbaatane **express boats** run to and from Bergen (420kr), Balestrand (100kr), and Flåm (140kr). Get ticket info at the tourist office and harbor; students get 50% off on all fares. Local **buses** head to Lom (3½hr., 2 per day, 169kr), where a connection can be made to Otta and the train lines. Norway Bussekspress buses leave for Fjaerland (30min., 5 per day, 48kr) and Førde (2-3hr., 4-8 per day, 162kr), which lead to all major bus routes (students 25% off all fares, railpass holders 50%). The **campground** at Nigardsbreen also has huts. (☎57 68 31 35. 10kr per person; 40kr per tent; 4-person huts 250kr.) Contact the **tourist office**, in the Sogndal Kulturhus at the corner of Gravensteingata and Hovevegen, for more info. (☎57 67 30 83. Open daily June 20-Aug. 20 M-F 9am-8pm, Sa 9am-5pm, Su 3-8pm; Aug. 21-June 19 M-F 9am-4pm.) The Sogndal **youth hostel (HI)** has a fjord-side spot and clean rooms east of the town center. From the bus station, turn left on Dalavegen, then left on Gravensteinsgata, follow it past the roundabout until it becomes Helgheimsvegen, and follow the signs. (☎57 67 20 33. Dorms 95kr; singles 160kr; doubles 220kr; nonmembers add 25kr.)

GEIRANGERFJORD

Though only 16km long, the narrow Geirangerfjord's cliffs and waterfalls make it one of Norway's most impressive natural attractions. While cruising through the green-blue water, watch for the **Seven Sisters** waterfalls and the spurting and gushing of the **Suitor** geyser opposite them. The Geirangerfjord can be reached from the north via the famous Tollstigen road from Åndalsnes, or by the bus from Ålesund that stops in Hellesylt. From the south, Stryn (see p. 722) has a direct bus connection to Hellesylt, but those departing from other fjord towns can easily reach this route by transferring buses in Førde. Hellesylt and Geiranger are connected by a stunning 1¼-hour ferry ride. During the summer months, the **Hurtigruten** coastal steamer sails into the fjord, connecting Geiranger to Ålesund by an unforgettable voyage on the coastal steamer (328kr, students and seniors 50% off).

GEIRANGER. Geiranger is dramatically ensconced on glorious Geirangerfjord's eastern terminus. An endpoint of the famous **Tollstigen** road with spectacular views and sheer inclines, the town is one of Norway's most visited destinations. Even the tourists don't overwhelm the area, which is truly picture-perfect. **Hiking** abounds in this charmed country; consider the hike to the path below the **Storseter Waterfall, Flydalsjuvet Cliff, Skageflå Farm,** or **Dalsnibba Mountain** (which you can also reach on the daily 10am bus from the church next to the hostel; returns 12:45pm; 90kr).

The **tourist office,** up from the ferry landing, helps find private rooms (from 200kr) for a 20kr fee. (☎ 70 26 30 99. Open daily late May to Aug. 9am-7pm.) **Geiranger Camping** is by the water, 500m past the ferry dock. (☎ 70 26 31 20. Showers 5kr per 3min. 10kr per person; 50kr per tent.) For the fantastic view of the fjord at **Vinjebakken Hostel,** follow the main road up the steep hill behind town. (☎ 70 26 32 05. Breakfast 50kr. Shower 10kr. Laundry 25kr. Reception 8-11am and 3pm-midnight. Check-out 11am. Open mid-June to mid-Aug. 125kr.) **Geiranger Fjordservice** cruises the fjord's chilly waters. (☎ 70 26 30 07. Cruises 1½hr. round-trip, June-Aug. 5 per day 10am-8pm; 70kr.) **Buses** run to Åndalsnes (3hr., 2 per day, 128kr, 50% off with railpass), allowing connections to Lillehammer, Oslo, and Trondheim.

HELLESYLT. Another way to see the fjord is to take the **ferry** connecting Geiranger with Hellesylt, the fjord's less touristy western base (1hr., 10 per day; 33kr, 50% Scanrail discount). To reach Hellesylt from the south, bus it from **Stryn** (2-3 per day; 70kr), or connect to this route by transferring buses at Førde, which is accessible from almost all fjord towns. From the north, take a bus from Åndalsnes or Ålesund. Hikers head for the famous **Troll's Path.** The **tourist office,** right on the ferry landing, provides hiking maps. (☎ 70 26 50 52. Open daily mid-June to mid-Aug. 10am-4pm.) The **Hellesylt Youth Hostel (HI),** up the steep hill along the road to Stranda, has a great view; take the path up the right side of the waterfall that thunders through town, hang a right at the top, and walk along the road 300m. If coming by bus ask the driver to let you off in front of the hostel. (☎ 70 26 51 28; fax 70 26 36 57. Reception June-July 10 and late Aug. 8am-noon and 5-11pm; July 10-Aug. 10 24hr. 100kr; non-members 125kr.) Walk 1km across the bridge from the dock and left to find **Hellesylt Camping.** (☎ 70 26 51 88. 15kr per person; 50kr per tent.)

ÅLESUND

The largest city between Bergen and Trondheim, Ålesund (OH-les-oond) is renowned for its art nouveau architecture and beautiful oceanside location. For a view of the splendid city and the distant mountains, gasp up the 418 steps to the **Aksla** viewpoint in the park near the city center; look for the stairs leading up to the park from the main pedestrian street, **Kongens gt.** Immerse yourself (almost literally!) in Ålesund's marine life at the **Atlantic Sea Park;** the innovative tanks are actually submerged in the ocean. Take bus #18 (20kr) from St. Olavs Pass to "Atlanterhavsparken." (Open June 15-Aug. 15 Su-F 10am-7pm, Sa 10am-5pm; Aug. 15-June 14 M-Sa 10am-4pm, Su noon-5pm. 75kr, students and seniors 60kr.) The **Sunnmøre Museum,** Borgundgavlen, displays old local fishing boats and a reconstructed Viking ship from AD 800. Take bus #13, 14, 18, or 24. (10min., 5kr. Open June 25-Aug. M-Sa 11am-4pm, Su noon-4pm; off season reduced hours. 50kr, students 35kr.) There's an old Viking site and 12th-century marble church on **Giske.** City buses travel through the tunnel connecting Ålesund and Giske (2hr., M-F 3 per day, 60-70kr). Contact **Runde Vandrerhjem (HI)** if you want to spend the night. (☎ 70 08 59 16. Dorms 100kr; singles 200kr; doubles 250kr.)

LAND OF THE TROLLS While Norwegians relish the unique light of the Scandinavian summer, some of the country's oldest inhabitants avoid it like the plague. The mythical trolls, made famous by plastic figurines sold around the world, are creatures of shadow and darkness; direct sunlight is thought to turn them to stone. Characterized by bushy tails, long noses, and four fingers and toes—unlike their commercial counterparts with fluorescent hair—Norwegian trolls live among the mountains, forests, and lakes. Despite their frightening appearance, trolls are supposedly the kindest of creatures. But tread softly through a troll's territory; with life spans stretching over hundreds of years, they have plenty of time to plot mischief against trespassers.

Buses run to and from Åndalsnes and connect with trains there (3 per day, 153kr; with railpass 50% off). Buses also travel to: Hellesylt (3 per day, 135kr; with railpass 50% off); Stryn (3 per day, 194kr); and Trondheim (2-4 per day, 435kr). The **Hurtigruten** also docks here twice daily in summer and once in winter (see p. 708). The **tourist office,** on Keiser Wilhelms gt., is opposite the bus station in the city hall. From St. Olavs Pass, head away from the pedestrian walkway along Notenesgata, follow it around the corner, turn left on Lorkenesgata, and left on Keiser Wilhelms gt. (☎70 15 76 00. Open June-Aug. M-F 8:30am-7pm, Sa 9am-5pm, Su 11am-5pm; Sept.-May M-F 8:30am-4pm.) The the beds of **Ålesund Vandrerhjem,** Parkg. 14, are five minutes from the bus station. (☎70 11 58 30. Breakfast included. Kitchen. Laundry. 170kr.) **Hansen Gaarden,** Kongensg. 14, has spotless, spacious rooms. (☎70 12 10 29. Kitchen. Laundry 15kr. Reception 8am-9pm. Open mid-June to Aug. 20. Doubles 320-340kr.) **Volsdalen Camping** is 2km out along the main highway next to a beach. Take bus #13, 14, 18, or 24 (11kr), turn right off the highway, follow the road down to the bottom of the stairs, cross the road, turn right and cross the overpass, and head 200m left. (☎/fax 70 12 58 90. Laundry 60kr. Reception 9am-9pm. Open May to mid-Sept. 10kr per person; 90kr per tent; cabins 290-490kr.)

TRONDHEIM

A thousand years ago, Viking kings turned Trondheim (then "Nidaros") into Norway's seat of power. Today, 20,000 slightly better-mannered students give the city a lively atmosphere, low prices, and a sense of quirkiness that other Norwegian cities can't quite match.

PRACTICAL INFO, ACCOMMODATIONS, AND FOOD. Trains come from Oslo (7-8hr., 4 per day, 665kr) and Stockholm (13hr., 2 per day, 810kr). **Long-distance buses** leave from the train station. **City buses** go from Munkeg., Dronningensg., and Olav Tryggvasong, and along Dronningensg. between Prinsensg. and Munkeg. (10kr within city center, 20kr to outlying regions). To get from the train station to the **tourist office,** Munkeg. 19, cross the bridge, walk six blocks down Søndreg., go right on Kongensg., and look to your left as you approach the roundabout. (☎73 80 76 60. Open July M-F 8:30am-10pm, Sa-Su 10am-8pm; June and early Aug. M-F 8:30am-8pm, Sa-Su 10am-6pm; late May and late Aug. M-F 8:30am-6pm, Sa-Su 10am-4pm; Sept. to early May M-F 9am-4pm.) **DNT,** Munkeg. 64, 2nd fl., has info on huts and trails. (☎73 52 38 08. Open M-W and F 9am-4pm, Th 9am-6pm.)

To get from the station to the lively **InterRail Center,** Elgeseterg. 1, in the Studentersenter, cross the bridge, then head right on Olav Tryggvasonsg., go left seven blocks down Prinsensg., cross the bridge, and it's on your left. Or, take bus #41, 44, 46, 48, 49, 52, or 63 (10kr) to "Samfundet." (☎73 89 95 38; email tirc@stud.ntnu.no. Breakfast included. Internet free. Open last weekend in June to last Tu in Aug. Sleeping-bag dorms 105kr.) For more peaceful lodging, walk up Lillegårdsbabakken to the student-run **Singsaker Sommerhotell,** Rogertsg. 1, near the Kristiansten Fortress. (☎73 89 31 00. Breakfast included. Sheets 30kr. Open early June to late Aug. Sleeping-bag dorms 125kr; singles 280kr; doubles 400kr; triples 670kr.) To reach the institutional but comfortable **Trondheim Vandrerhjem (HI),** Weidemannsvei 41, from the station, cross the bridge, head left on Olav Tryggvasonsg. across the bridge, bear left onto Innherredsvein, turn right on Nonneg., and left onto Weidemannsvei. (☎73 53 04 90. Breakfast included. Sheets 45kr. 160kr; nonmembers 185kr.) For a rare taste of excellent Asian food in Scandinavia, try **Phuc & Thinh Cafe** at Fjordgata 25; from the station, cross the river and turn right onto Fjordgata. (Dishes from 68kr. Open M-Sa 1-11pm, Su 1-10pm.) **Postal code:** 7000.

SIGHTS AND ENTERTAINMENT. The image of Olav Tryggvason, who founded Trondheim in 997, perches on a pillar over the main market square, **Torget.** Trondheim native King Olav Haraldsson, who died fighting to introduce Christianity to his country, was granted sainthood and became the icon of a Christian cult. Flocks of the faithful to St. Olav's grave prompted the construction of **Nidaros Cathedral,** the site of all Norwegian coronations and the repository of the crown jewels. (Open mid-June to mid-Aug. M-F 9am-6pm, Sa 9am-2pm, Su 1-4pm; May to mid-June and mid-Aug. to mid-Sept. M-F 9am-3pm, Sa 9am-2pm and 1-4pm; off season reduced hours. Cathedral 25kr, includes admission to Archbishop's Palace, below. Tower 5kr.) The **Archbishop's Palace** is the oldest secular building in Scandinavia. (Open mid-June to mid-Aug. M-Sa 10am-5pm, Su noon-5pm.) The **Hjemmefrontmuseet** details the development of the Norwegian army. (Open June-Aug. M-F 9am-3pm, Sa-Su 11am-4pm; Feb.-May and Sept.-Nov. Sa-Su 11am-4pm. Free.) The **Trondhjems Kunst Museum,** Bispeg. 7B, next to the cathedral, has a hallway devoted to Edvard Munch. (Open June-Aug. F-W 10am-4pm, Th 10am-6pm; Sept.-May Tu-Su noon-4pm. 30kr, students 20kr.) Across the **Gamle Bybru** (Old Town Bridge), the **old district,** where former fishing houses have been transformed into galleries and cafes, gives a taste of old Trondheim. To reach the bridge from the Torget, head toward the spires of Nidaros Cathedral, but turn left when you reach Bispegata and follow it around to the bridge. On the hill above the old district, the 1681 **Kristiansten Fortress** yields a splendid view. Borrow one of the 200 **city bicycles** parked at stations in town (deposit 20kr) and ride up the **bike lift** at the base of the Old Town Bridge (pick up a key-card at the tourist office; 100kr deposit).

SOUTHERN NORWAY

Norway's southern coast substitutes serenity for drama, and is the premier Norwegian summer holiday destination. *Skjærgard,* archipelagos of water-worn rock, hug the shore and stretch smoothly southward from Oslo to endless white beaches past Kristiansand. Fishing, hiking, rafting, and canoeing are popular in summer, while cross-country skiing reigns in winter.

NORWAY

KRISTIANSAND

Kristiansand attracts glacier- and winter-weary Norwegian tourists to its **beaches.** The city center's grid layout is easy to navigate: the harbor and train station sit at the bottom of the grid; **Markensgata,** the main street, is a block from the water; **Posebyen,** a well-preserved old town, begins two blocks farther away at Festningsgata.

PRACTICAL INFO, ACCOMMODATIONS, AND FOOD. Daily **trains** chug to Oslo (4½-5½hr., 480kr). Color Line **ferries** (☎81 00 08 11) run from **Kristiansand** to **Hirsthals, Denmark** (2½-4½hr., in summer from 200kr). Ferries also run from Kristiansand to the scenic **Skerries** (tiny islands and fjords; 150kr); for more info, ask at the **tourist office,** at Henrik Wegerlandsgt. and Vestre Strandsgt., opposite the train station. They can also arrange fishing trips and elk safaris in local forests. (☎38 12 13 14. Open mid-June to Aug. M-F 8am-8pm, Sa-Su noon-8pm; Sept. to mid-June M-F 8:30am-3:30pm.) The **Kristiansand Youth Hostel (HI),** Skansen 8, is 25 minutes from the harbor and train station. Walk away from the water until you reach Elvegata, turn right, and then left onto Skansen following the signs. (☎38 02 83 10. Breakfast buffet included. Kitchen. Laundry. Lockers. Reception mid-June to mid-Aug. 24hr.; mid-Aug. to mid-June 5-11pm. Dorms 170kr; singles 320kr; nonmembers add 25kr.) The noisy **Roligheden campground** is 45 minutes from town, or 15 minutes by bus #1 from the city center; ask the driver to let you off at the campground turn-off. (☎38 09 67 22. Showers 5kr per 3min. Open June-Aug. 20kr per person; 60kr per tent.) The area around Kristiansand's main street, **Markensgata,** one block north of the harbor and train station, is full of affordable bars, cafes, and restaurants. **Husholdnings,** on Gyldenløves gt. in the old town, serves authentic Norwegian cuisine. (Open M-F 9am-4pm; off season closes at 5pm.) The pub **Munch,** Kristian IV gt. 1, opposite the train station, is far more lively than the dark art of its namesake.

SIGHTS. The city's best-known attraction is **Dyreparken,** "the living park," which contains a zoo, an amusement park, and a circus. The zoo is considered to be one of Europe's best, and its animals roam freely. (Take bus #1 from the stop in front of the tourist office to "Dyreparken." Open June 3-Aug. 13 daily 10am-7pm; Aug. 14-May 19 M-F 10am-3:30pm, Sa-Su 10am-7pm; May 20-June 2 M-F 10am-5pm, Sa-Su 10am-7pm. Day pass June-Aug. 195kr, children 165kr, seniors 100kr; prices drop off season.) The open-air **Vest-Agder Fylkesmuseum,** Vigeveien 23b, showcases 17th-century southern Norwegian farmhouses and traditional folk dancing. (Take bus #2, 4, or 6 from H. Wergelandsgt. and ask the driver to let you off at the museum. Open mid-June to mid-Aug. M-Sa 10am-6pm, Su noon-6pm; mid-Aug. to mid-June Su noon-5pm. 30kr, students and seniors 10kr.) The remains of a Nazi bunker and the world's 2nd-largest cannon are on display at the **Kristiansand Kanonenmuseum.** (Take bus #1 from H. Wergelandsgt. Open mid-June to Aug. daily 11am-6pm; May to mid-June and Sept. W-Sa 11am-6pm. 50kr, students and seniors 20kr.) Scramble up the walls of the 17th-century circular stone **Christiansholm Fortress** for a great view of the beach and islands near the city. (Open daily mid-May to Sept. 9am-9pm.) In early July, Kristiansand hosts the **Quart Festival** (www.quart.yahoo.no), which draws major hip-hop, rock, and pop acts; headliners in 2000 included Moby, Macy Gray, and Counting Crows.

STAVANGER

Stavanger is a delightful port town with colorful wooden fishing houses along its pier and a daily fish market.

PRACTICAL INFO, ACCOMMODATIONS, AND FOOD. Trains pull in from Oslo (9hr., 4 per day, 700kr). Trains and buses arrive at Stavanger's central station; from the front entrance, walk around the pond and down the stairs to reach the harbor. **Flaggruten Catamarans** (☎51 86 87 80) speed to Bergen (4hr., 2-4 per day, 510kr, students 295kr; 50% off with Scanrail), arriving at a terminal on the eastern side of the city; exit the terminal through the main door and walk straight ahead along Kirkegata to reach the cathedral and town center. Three Fjordline **ferries** (☎51 52 45 45) per week go to Newcastle, England (18hr., July-Aug. from 980kr, Sept.-June around 400kr; prices vary by day and time), departing and arriving at a terminal on the western side of the harbor; walk along the water to reach the city center. The **tourist office,** Roskildetorget 1, is on the harbor next to the fish market. (☎51 85 92 00; fax 51 85 92 02. Open June-Aug. daily 9am-8pm; Sept.-May M-F 9am-4pm, Sa 9am-2pm.) **Rogalandsheimen Guesthouse,** Musegata 18, provides spacious accommodation in a centrally located manor house. Walk around the pond, bearing right past the train station; the guest house is one block up on the left. (☎/fax 51 53 37 60. Breakfast buffet included. Singles from 400kr; doubles from 500kr.) The **Mosvangen Vandrerhjem (HI),** Ibsensgt. 21, has a kitchen and free laundry. (☎51 87 29 00. Reception 7-11am and 5-10pm. 135kr; nonmembers 160kr.) Next door is **Mosvangen Camping.** (☎51 53 29 71. Open late May to early Sept. 10kr per person; 70kr per tent.) To reach either from the town center, take bus #130, 78-79, or 97 from in front of the cathedral (19kr). The **market** opposite the cathedral will satisfy most culinary needs; look for fresh Norwegian strawberries. (Open M-Sa 9am-5pm, Su closes earlier.) The jazz bar **Sting** is uphill from where Kirkegata and Breigata meet, east of the harbor in the old town. (Open M-Sa noon-3:30am, Su 3pm-2am. Live performances W-Sa 11pm-3:30am.) **Postal code:** 4000.

SIGHTS. On the eastern side of the harbor is **Gamle Stavanger,** a neighborhood of winding cobblestone streets restored to its prosperous 19th-century state. The

Gothic **Stavanger Domkirke** (cathedral) broods in medieval solemnity in the modern town center. (Open mid-May to mid-Sept. M-Sa 10am-7pm, Su 1-6pm; mid-Sept. to mid-May M-Tu 11am-6pm, W-Sa 10am-3pm. Free.) Despite its old-town charm, Stavanger is actually the driving force behind Norway's powerful oil industry. The multimedia exhibits at the recently opened **Norsk Oljemuseum** (Norwegian Petroleum Museum) cover everything from the manufacture of oil to the social change the industry has brought to modern Norway. (Walk along Kirkegata; the museum is to the right of the express boat terminal. Open May-Aug. daily 10am-7pm; Sept.-Apr. M-W and F-Sa 10am-5pm, Th and Su 10am-7pm. 60kr, students 30kr.) Feel like a Norse god, but don't tumble over the edge of **Pulpit Rock** (Preikestolen) in nearby **Lysefjord,** one of Norway's postcard darlings. To get there, take the 8:20 or 9:15am ferry to Tau (runs June 21-Sept. 7, 40min., 30kr), catch the waiting bus (45kr), and hike (2hr.). The return bus leaves at 4:15pm.

EASTERN NORWAY

The faster of the two train lines that shoot north from Oslo to Trondheim heads through the **Gudbrandsdalen** valley via Lillehammer. Farther up the valley, the **Rondane** and **Dovrefjell** mountain ranges offer hiking opportunities, while the truly breathtaking scenery is in the **Jotunheimen** mountains to the west.

LILLEHAMMER

The small city of Lillehammer gained an international reputation as host of the 1994 Winter Games. Lillehammer today still lives off its Olympic legacy: several billion kroner worth of state-of-the-art athletic facilities and new infrastructure, all constructed to harmonize with the mountainous environment. Håkons Hall, at the **Olympic Park,** the venue for the '94 ice-hockey competitions with a capacity of 10,000, now houses the **Norwegian Olympic Museum.** From the station, head two blocks uphill, turn left on Storgata, turn right on Tomtegata, go up the stairs, and follow the blue arrows. (Open mid-May to mid-Sept. daily 10am-6pm, mid-Sept. to mid-May Tu-Su 11am-4pm. 50kr, students 40kr.) You can climb up the infinite steps of an Olympic **ski jump** in sight of the museum spire (open daily June 17-Aug. 13 9am-8pm; Aug. 14-June 16 11am-4pm; 15kr) or give your spine a jolt on a **bobsled simulator** (40kr) at the bottom of the ski-jumping hills.

Daily **trains** run to Oslo (2½hr., 280kr) and Trondheim (4½hr., 475kr). Most restaurants and fast-food kiosks are around the pedestrian section of **Storgata,** two blocks uphill from the bus/train station. The **tourist office,** Elvegata 19, one block uphill from Storgata, has good info on hiking and attractions. (☎61 25 92 99. Open mid-June to mid-Aug. M-Sa 9am-7pm, Su 11am-6pm; mid-Aug. to mid-June M-F 9am-4pm, Sa 10am-2pm.) The comfy **Lillehammer Youth Hostel (HI)** is conveniently located on the top floor of the bus/train station. (☎61 26 25 66. Breakfast included. Dorms 170kr.) Try the popular lunch (49kr; 11am-3pm) or dinner (79kr; 3-10pm) specials at **Nikkers** cafe/pub, just before the tourist office on Elvegata.

LOFOTEN ISLANDS

The emerald and slate mountains of the Lofoten Islands thrust dramatically up from the ocean, sheltering fishing villages, bird colonies, and happy sheep. The panoramic ocean views and peaceful atmosphere make the islands a magical place to visit. As late as the 1950s, fisherfolk lived in the small *rorbuer*, yellow and red wooden shacks along the coast. Today, tourists book the *rorbuer* solid (90-300kr per person in groups of 4 or more).

GETTING THERE AND GETTING AROUND. The two best mainland springboards to the islands are **Bodø,** accessible by train from Trondheim (10hr., 680kr; mandatory seat reservations) and **Narvik,** reached by bus from Bodø (6-7hr., 362kr; students and railpass holders 50% off). From Bodø, the Lofotens can be reached by either **car ferry** (to Moskenes; 4hr., 122kr), **hydrofoil** (to Svolvær; 6hr., 306kr), **bus** (to Svolvær; 7hr., 279kr) or the **Hurtigruten coastal steamer** (to Stamsund; 4½hr., 306kr; and Svolvær; 6hr., 328kr). Within the islands, **buses** are the main form of transport; pick up the *Lofoten Trafikklag* bus timetable at tourist offices in Bodø, Narvik, or larger towns in the Lofotens. You can also dial ☎177 to reach a regional **transport info** desk. An **InterRail** pass gives 50% off routes within the islands; a **Scanrail** pass gets you a discount if your destination is on a rail line.

MOSKENES AND FLAKSTAD. Most of the **ferries** running to the islands from Bodø dock in **Moskenes,** the southernmost of the large Lofotens. The **tourist office,** by the ferry landing, has tours of the **Maelstrom,** one of the most dangerous currents in the world, and info on the **Refsuika caves** and their 3000-year-old drawings. (☎76 09 15 99. Open June 1-9 M-F 10am-5pm; June 22-Aug. 16 daily 10am-7pm.) **Adventure Rafting Lofoten** (☎76 09 20 00) runs similar tours in much smaller and more challenging rafts (300-650kr). Incoming ferry passengers usually head 5km south to **Å** (OH), a tiny fishing village at the end of E10 highway, via a bus that departs 5-15 minutes after boat landings. Half of Å's buildings comprise the open-air **Norsk Fiskeværsmuseum,** which depicts life in an old-fashioned fishing village. (Open mid-June to mid-Aug. daily 10am-6pm; mid-Aug. to mid-June M-F 10am-3:30pm. 40kr, students 30kr.) The **Å Vandrerhjem and Rorbuer** has bunks in 19th-century buildings. (☎76 09 11 21. Laundry. Rowboats and bikes 150kr per day. Reserve ahead. 125kr, nonmembers 150kr; *rorbuer* 550-1000kr.) To get to **Moskenes-Straumen Camping,** follow E10 until it stops at the edge of Å. (☎76 09 11 48. 10kr per person; 70kr per tent. Showers 5kr.) Or, **free camp** on the shores of the snow-fed lake behind town.

To the north, the next large island is **Flakstad,** centered on the hamlet of **Ramberg.** Flakstad's **hiking** trails are perhaps the best in the islands. The **tourist office** books doubles from 150kr; call ahead to secure an accommodation. (☎76 09 34 50. Open daily June 29-Aug. 10am-7pm.)

VESTVÅGØY AND AUSTVÅGØY. Farther north is **Vestvågøy,** whose magnificent **HI youth hostel,** in the hamlet of **Stamsund,** often convinces travelers to remain for weeks. (☎76 08 93 34. Laundry 30kr. Showers 5kr per 5min. Fishing gear 100kr deposit; rowboats free. Bikes. Open mid-Dec. to mid.-Oct. 80kr; *rorbuer* 400-600kr.) The **tourist office** sits at the coastal steamer and ferry dock. (☎76 08 97 92. Open daily mid-June to mid-Aug. 6-9:30pm.) Along the road north from Stamsund, between Leknes and Svolvær, **Borg** is the site of the largest Viking building ever found; the reconstructed longhouse holds a **Viking museum** staffed by costumed Norse folk who do full-scale reenactments. (Open daily mid-May to Sept. 21 10am-6pm. 80kr; Viking soup included.)

A ring of jagged peaks forms a dramatic backdrop to **Svolvær,** on the northernmost island of **Austvågøy.** The **tourist office** is by the ferry dock. (☎76 07 30 00. Open July to mid-Aug. M-F 9am-4pm and 5-9:30pm, Sa 9am-8pm, Su 10am-9:30pm.) To get to **Marinepollen Sjøhus,** head 15 minutes north along the E10 until Jektveien is on the right, or call ahead for pickup. (☎76 07 18 33. Fishing gear and rowboats free. Kitchen. 150kr.) **Svolvær Sjøhuscamping** offers rooms on stilts above the harbor; take the 3rd right from Torget on Vestfjordg. as you head away from the dock and tourist office. (☎/fax 76 07 03 36. Reception 8am-midnight. Doubles 350kr.) **Rimi,** at Torgg. and Storg., has **groceries.** (Open M-F 9am-8pm, Sa 9am-6pm.)

FARTHER NORTH

TROMSØ. Norway's fastest growing city, Tromsø comes to life when the summer midnight sun ends winter's perpetual darkness. **Polaria,** Norway's national info center for polar regions, shows a panoramic film that flies visitors over the island of Spitzbergen. After the film, visitors can explore a simulated arctic environment and the world's northernmost aquarium. (Open daily May-Aug. 10am-7pm; Sept.-Apr. noon-5pm. 70kr.) The **Arctic Cathedral,** on the mainland, contains one of the largest stained glass windows in Europe. Take bus #26-28, or walk across the bridge from the city center. (Open daily May and mid-Aug. to mid-Sept. 3-6pm; June to mid-Aug. 10am-8pm, Su 1-8pm. 20kr.) The **tourist office,** Storg. 61/63, books rooms in private homes for 25kr. (☎ 77 61 00 00. Open June to early Aug. M-F 8:30am-6pm, Sa-Su 10:30am-5pm; mid-Aug. to May M-F 8:30am-4pm.) Accessible from the Lofoten Islands, Tromsø can be reached by **bus** from Narvik (4½hr., 295kr).

ALTA AND HAMMERFEST. The road from Tromsø to **Alta,** Finnmark's largest town, is spectacular, with towering cliffs and an icy green expanse of sea. The **Alta Museum** displays stunning rock carvings from 2500 to 6200 years ago and boulders sporting painted figures. A **bus** runs to and from Tromsø (7-8hr., 330kr, plus a 50kr ferry) and Hammerfest (3hr., 185kr). At **Hammerfest,** the world's northernmost town, you can join the famous **Royal and Ancient Polar Bear Society** (150kr) against the backdrop of grazing reindeer in the streets; the only criterion is having visited Hammerfest, and members receive a certificate and a silver polar bear pin. Hammerfest is accessible by the northbound **Hurtigruten;** the southbound boat pulls in at 11:45am and departs at 1:15pm for Tromsø (650kr) on the way to Bergen. Daily **buses** also go to Alta (3hr., 185kr).

POLAND (POLSKA)

ZŁOTY, OR PLZ

US$1 = 4.40ZŁ	1ZŁ = US$0.23
CDN$1 = 3.00ZŁ	1ZŁ = CDN$0.34
UK£1 = 6.40ZŁ	1ZŁ = UK£0.16
IR£1 = 5.00ZŁ	1ZŁ = IR£0.20
AUS$1 = 2.50ZŁ	1ZŁ = AUS$0.40
NZ$1 = 1.90ZŁ	1ZŁ = NZ$0.53
SAR1 = 0.63ZŁ	1ZŁ = SAR 1.59
DM1 = 2.00ZŁ	1ZŁ = DM 0.50
EUR€1 = 3.91ZŁ	1ZŁ = EUR€0.26

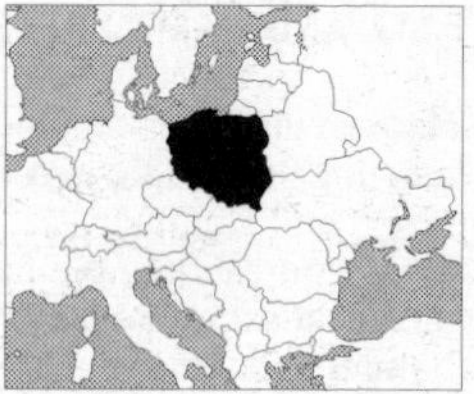

Country code: 48. **International dialing prefix:** 00. From outside Poland, dial int'l dialing prefix (see inside back cover) + 48 + city code + local number.

Poland has always been caught at the threshold of East and West, and its moments of freedom have been brief. From 1795 to 1918, Poland simply did not exist on any map of Europe, and its short spell of independence thereafter was brutally dissolved. Ravaged by World War II and viciously suppressed by Stalin and the USSR, Poland has at long last been given room to breathe, and its residents are not letting the opportunity slip by. The most prosperous of the "Baltic tigers," Poland now has a rapidly expanding GDP, a new membership in NATO, and a likely future membership in the EU. With their new wealth, the hospitable Poles have been returning to their cultural roots and repairing buildings destroyed in the wars, a trend popular with the growing legions of tourists that visit each year. Capitalism brought with it Western problems, like rising crime and unemployment, issues politicians have begun to recognize as serious. But there are few Poles complaining about the events of the past ten years. Political and economic freedoms have helped this rich culture to occupy its own skin once again, even if it's now wearing a pair of Levi's.

Even the Pope sometimes kicks back with a copy of *Let's Go: Eastern Europe 2001* for more detailed coverage of Poland.

FACTS AND FIGURES

Official Name: Republic of Poland.

Government: Republic.

Capital: Warsaw.

Land Area: 312,683 sq. km.

Geography: Plains, southern mountains.

Climate: Temperate; cold, cloudy, winters with frequent precipitation; mild summers with thundershowers.

Average Income Per Capita: US$6800.

Major Cities: Warsaw, Łódź, Kraków, Lublin, Poznań, Katowice, Gdańsk, Wrocław.

Population: 39 million.

Languages: Polish.

Religions: Roman Catholic (95%).

Major Exports: Manufactured goods and chemicals, machinery and equipment, mineral fuels.

DISCOVER POLAND

Over 19 million visitors flock annually to Poland's virgin forests, beautiful beaches, charming villages, spectacular castles, Old Towns, and museums. **Warsaw,** totally flattened in WWII, is a living testament to the effects of WWII and Communism, and a wild, energetic capital with plenty of cheap beer (except when the Pope's in town; p. 736). Much-adored **Kraków** is the only Polish city to make it to the 20th century unscathed by natural disaster or war, and now flaunts its magnificent castle and

perfectly preserved Old Town (p. 747). **Gdańsk** is the site of the start of WWII and of Poland's anti-Communist Solidarity movement in the 1980s (p. 744). On the Baltic Coast, **Sopot** shelters Poland's best beaches, while **Frombork** is home to more impressive castles (p. 746). In the south, in the heart of the High Tatras, the high-altitude fun of **Zakopane** pleases with ear-popping hikes, world-renowned music festivals, and a hefty dose of Tatran folk culture (p. 752).

ESSENTIALS

WHEN TO GO

Winters are dreary unless you're heading to the Tatras: anytime between November and February is ideal for skiing, and August is the perfect hiking month. Otherwise, summer and autumn are the best times to visit.

DOCUMENTS AND FORMALITIES

Citizens of Ireland and the US can travel to Poland without a **visa** for up to 90 days and UK citizens for up to 180 days. Australians, Canadians, New Zealanders, and South Africans need visas. Single-entry visas (valid for 180 days) cost US$60 (children and students under 26 pay US$45); multiple-entry visas cost US$100 (students US$75); and 48-hour transit visas cost US$20 (students US$15). Visas can only be obtained through an embassy or a consulate; no visas are available at the border. To extend your stay, apply at the local province office *(urząd wojewódzki)*, or in Warsaw to the Ministry of Internal Affairs at ul. Kruzca 5/11 (☎ (022) 625 59 04).

EMBASSIES AND CONSULATES

All embassies (www.polishworld.com/polemb) are in **Warsaw** (see p. 736); there are US and UK consulates in **Kraków** (see p. 747).

Polish Embassies at Home: Australia, 7 Turrana St., Yarralumla ACT 2600 Canberra (☎ (06) 273 12 08; fax 273 31 84; poland@clover.com.au); **Canada,** 443 Daly St., Ottawa, ON K1N 6H3 (☎ (613) 789 04 68; fax 789 12 18); **Ireland,** 5 Ailesbury Rd., Dublin 4 (☎ (01) 283 08 55; fax 283 75 62); **New Zealand,** 17 Upland Rd., Kelburn, Wellington (☎ (04) 71 24 56; fax 71 24 55; polishembassy@extra.co.nz); **South Africa,** 14 Amos St., Colbyn, Pretoria (☎ (012) 43 26 31; fax 43 26 08); during Parliamentary Session: 23 Hermina Ave., Constantia, Cape Town (☎ (021) 794 33 15; fax 794 47 99); **UK,** 47 Portland Pl., London W1N 4JH (☎ (020) 75 80 43 24; fax 73 23 40 18; www.poland-embassy.org.uk); **US,** 2640 16th St. NW, Washington, DC 20009 (☎ (202) 234 38 00; fax 328 62 71; email embpol@dgs.dgsys.com).

GETTING THERE AND GETTING AROUND

BY PLANE. LOT, British Airways, and Delta fly into Warsaw's **Okęcie Airport** from London, New York, Chicago, and Toronto (among other cities).

BY TRAIN. Eurail passes are not valid in Poland. **Almatur** offers ISIC holders a discount of 192zł. **Wasteels** tickets and **Eurotrain** passes, sold at Almatur, Orbis, and major train stations, get those under 26 40% off international train fares. For all but daytrips, **PKP trains** are preferable to and, for long hauls, usually cheaper than buses. Train stations have boards that list towns alphabetically, and posters that list trains chronologically. *Odjazdy* (departures) are in yellow; *przyjazdy* (arrivals) are in white. **InterCity** and *Ekspresowy* (express) trains are listed in red with an "IC" or "Ex" in front of the train number. *Pośpieszny* (direct; also in red) are almost as fast. *Osobowy* (in black) are the slowest but are 35% cheaper than *pośpieszny*. All InterCity, *ekspresowy*, and some *pośpieszny* trains require seat reservations; if you see a boxed R on the schedule, ask the clerk for a *miejscówka* (myay-SOOV-ka; reservation). Buy surcharged tickets on board from the *konduktor* before he or she finds (and fines) you. Most people purchase *normalny* tickets, while students and seniors buy *ulgowy* (half-price) tickets. Foreign travelers are not eligible for discounts; you risk a hefty fine by traveling with an *ulgowy* ticket without Polish ID. On Sundays, tickets cost 20% less. Train tickets are good only for the day they're issued. Allot time for long, slow lines or buy your ticket in advance at the station or an Orbis office. Stations are not announced and can be poorly marked.

BY BUS AND BY FERRY. PKS buses are cheapest and fastest for short trips. Like trains, there are *pośpieszny* (direct; marked in red) and *osobowy* (slow; in black). Purchase advance tickets at the bus station, and expect long lines. However, many tickets can only be bought from the driver. In the countryside, PKS markers (steering wheels that look like upside-down, yellow Mercedes-Benz symbols) indicate bus stops, but drivers will often stop if you flag them down. Traveling with a backpack can be a problem if the bus is full, since there are no storage compartments. **Ferries** run from Sweden and Denmark to Gdańsk (see p. 65).

BY CAR. Road conditions are generally safe, except at night and harvest season, when horse-drawn wagons carrying agricultural products pack the roads. For roadside assistance, contact **Polski Związek Motorowy (PZM),** ul. Solec 85, 00950 Warsaw (☎ (022) 849 93 61; fax 848 19 51; www.pzm.com.pl). For 24-hour PZM roadside assistance, dial ☎981. All PZM services are free for AAA members.

BY BIKE, BY TAXI, AND BY THUMB. Biking is relatively common; bicycle rentals are available through most tourist offices. **Taxi** drivers generally try to rip off foreigners; arrange the price before getting in or be sure the meter's on. The going rate is 1.50-2zł per km. Arrange cabs by phone rather than hailing one on the street. Though legal, **hitchhiking** is rare and more dangerous for foreigners. Hand-waving is the accepted sign. *Let's Go* does not recommend hitchhiking.

TOURIST SERVICES AND MONEY

EMERGENCY. Police: ☎997. **Fire:** ☎998. **Ambulance:** ☎999.

TOURIST OFFICES. City-specific offices are generally more helpful than the bigger chains. You can count on all offices to provide free info in English and to be of some help with accommodations for a nominal fee. **Orbis,** the state-sponsored travel bureau staffed by English speakers, operates luxury hotels and sells transportation tickets. **Almatur,** the Polish student travel organization, sells ISICs, helps find dorm rooms in summer, and sells student tickets. Both provide maps and brochures, as do **PTTK** and **IT** *(Informacji Turystycznej)* bureaus.

MONEY. The Polish **złoty**—plural *złote*—is fully convertible (1 *złoty* = 100 *grosze*). For cash, private **kantor** offices (except for those at the airport and train stations) offer better exchange rates than banks. **Bank PKO S.A.** also has fairly good exchange rates; they cash **traveler's checks** and give Visa and Mastercard **cash advances. ATMs** *(Bankomat)* are everywhere except the smallest villages. **MC** and **Visa** are the most widely accepted ATM networks. Budget accommodations rarely, if ever, accept **credit cards,** although some restaurants and pricier shops will. In restaurants, leave a 10% **tip** by telling the server how much change you want back. If you're paying with a credit card, give the tip in cash.

BUSINESS HOURS. Business hours tend to be Monday-Friday 10am-6pm and Saturday 9am-2pm. Saturday hours vary, as some shops in Poland distinguish "working" *(pracująca)* Saturdays, when they work longer hours, from "free" *(wolna)* ones, when hours are shorter. Very few stores or businesses are open on Sunday. **Museums** are generally open Tuesday to Sunday, 10am to 4pm. **Banks** are open Monday-Friday 9am-3 or 6pm.

ACCOMMODATIONS AND CAMPING

Grandmotherly **private room** owners drum up business at the train station or outside the tourist office. Private rooms are usually safe, clean, and convenient, but can be far from city centers. Expect to pay about US$10 per person. **Youth hostels** (*schronisko młodzieżowe*) abound and average 9-25zł per night. They are often booked solid, however, by school or tourist groups; call at least a week in advance. **PTSM** is the national hostel organization. **University dorms** transform into spartan budget housing in July and August; these are a good option in Kraków. The Warsaw office of **Almatur** can arrange stays in major cities. **PTTK** runs a number of hotels called **Dom Turysty,** which have multi-bed rooms as well as singles and doubles. Hotels generally cost 30-50zł per night. Many towns have a **Biuro Zakwaterowań,** which arranges stays in private homes. **Campsites** average US$2 per person; with a car, US$4. **Bungalows** are often available; a bed costs about US$5. *Polska Mapa Campingów* lists all campsites.

FOOD AND DRINK

Polish food favors meat, potatoes, cabbage, and butter. A Polish meal always starts with soup, usually *barszcz* (clear broth), *chłodnik* (a cold beet soup with buttermilk and hard-boiled eggs), *kapuśniak* (cabbage soup), or *żurek* (barley-flour soup loaded with eggs and sausage). Filling main courses include *gołąbki* (cabbage rolls stuffed with meat and rice), *kotlet schabowy* (pork cutlet), *naleśniki* (cream-topped crepes filled with cottage cheese or jam), and *pierogi* (dumplings with various fillings—meat, potato, cheese, blueberry). Poland bathes in beer, vodka, and spiced liquor. *Żywiec* is the most popular strong beer; *EB* is its excellent, gentler brother. Other available beers include *Okocim* and *Piast*. *Wódka* (vodka) ranges from wheat to potato. *Wyborowa*, *Żytnia*, and *Polonez* usually decorate private bars, while *Belweder* is Poland's proudest alcoholic export.

COMMUNICATION

MAIL. **Mail** is becoming increasingly efficient, although there are still incidents of theft. Airmail *(lotnicza)* usually takes a week to reach the US. For *Poste Restante*, put a "1" after the city name to ensure that it goes to the main post office. Letters abroad cost 1.60zl (air mail 1.80-2.20zl) for up to 20g. When picking up *Poste Restante*, you may have to pay a small fee (0.70-1zł) or show your passport.

TELEPHONES. **Card telephones** have become the public phone standard. Cards, which come in several denominations, are sold at post offices, *Telokomunikacja Polska* offices, and most kiosks. To make a **collect call,** write the name of the city or country and the number plus "*Rozmowa 'R'*" on a slip of paper, hand it to a post office clerk, and be patient. **International direct dial** numbers include: **AT&T Direct,** ☎00 80 01 11 11 11; **BT Direct,** ☎0, 080 04 41 11 44; **Canada Direct,** ☎00 80 01 11 41 18; **MCI WorldPhone,** ☎00 80 01 11 21 22; and **Sprint,** ☎00 80 01 11 31 15.

LANGUAGES. **Polish** varies little across the country; the exceptions are Kaszuby, with a Germanized dialect, and Karpaty, where the highlanders' accent is extraordinarily thick. In western Poland and Mazury, **German** is the most commonly known foreign language, although many Poles in big cities, especially students, will speak **English.** Try English and German before **Russian,** which many Poles show an aversion to speaking. Most Poles can understand **Czech** or **Slovak.** Students may also know **French.** For basic phrases in all these languages and more, see p. 981.

HOLIDAYS AND FESTIVALS

Holidays: New Year's Day (Jan. 1); Catholic Easter (Apr. 15-16); Labor Day (May 1); Constitution Day (May 3); Corpus Christi (June 14); Assumption Day (Aug. 15); Independence Day (1918; Nov. 11); Christmas (Dec. 25); Boxing Day (Dec. 26).

Festivals: Kraków is Poland's festival capital, especially in summer. Some of the most notable are the **International Short Film Festival** (late May), the **Festival of Jewish Culture** (early June), and the **Jazz Festival** (Oct.-Nov.).

WARSAW (WARSZAWA) ☎022

According to legend, Warsaw was created when a fisherman netted and released a mermaid *(syrena)* who promised that if he founded a city, she would protect it forever. In WWII alone, however, two-thirds of the population was killed and 83% of the city destroyed. Today, Warsaw is once again the world's largest Polish city (a title long held by Chicago) and is quickly throwing off its Soviet legacy to emerge as an important international business center. Skyscrapers are popping up all over, and the university infuses Warsaw with young blood, keeping energy high and the nightlife lively. All things considered, the *syrena* appears to have kept her promise.

GETTING THERE AND GETTING AROUND

Flights: Port Lotniczy Warszawa-Okęcie (Terminal 1), ul. Żwirki i Wigury. Take **bus** #175 (bus #611 after 11pm) to the city center; buy tickets at the Ruch kiosk in the departure hall or at the *kantor* outside. 2.40zł, students 1.20zł; extra tickets required for luggage and packs. Open M-F 7:30am-8pm.

Trains: Warszawa Centralna, al. Jerozolimskie 54 (☎825 50 00; international ☎620 45 12; domestic ☎620 03 61). English is rare; write down where and when you want to go, then ask *Który peron?* ("Which platform?"). Yellow signs list departures, white signs arrivals. To: **Kraków** (2½hr., 14-18 per day, 33-63zł); **Gdańsk** (3½-4½hr., 5-16 per day, 35-65zł); **Berlin** (7-8hr., 3 per day, 110zł); **Bratislava** (8hr., 2 per day, 136zł); **Budapest** (10hr., 2 per day, 190zł); **Vilnius** (12hr., 1 per day, 136zł); **Minsk** (12hr., 1 per day, 105zł); **Prague** (12-14hr., 3 per day, 153zł); **Kiev** (22-24hr., 2 per day, 147zł); **Moscow** (27-30hr., 3 per day, 250zł); and **St. Petersburg** (26hr., 1 per day, 160zł).

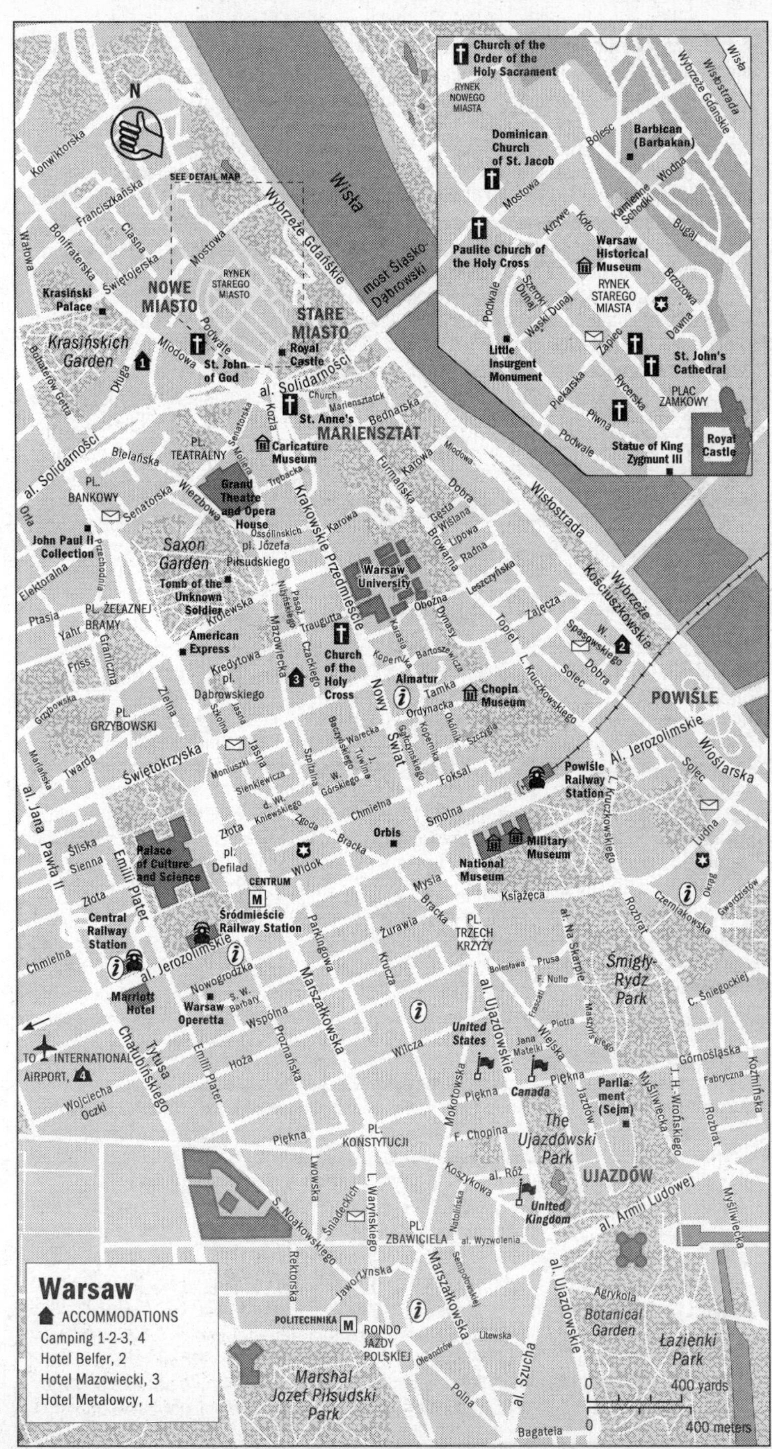
Warsaw
ACCOMMODATIONS
Camping 1-2-3, 4
Hotel Belfer, 2
Hotel Mazowiecki, 3
Hotel Metalowcy, 1
SEE DETAIL MAP
NOWE MIASTO
STARE MIASTO
MARIENSZTAT
POWIŚLE
UJAZDÓW
Wisła
Krasiński Palace
Krasińskich Garden
St. John of God
Royal Castle
St. Anne's Church
Caricature Museum
Grand Theatre and Opera House
John Paul II Collection
Saxon Garden
Tomb of the Unknown Soldier
American Express
Warsaw University
Church of the Holy Cross
Almatur
Chopin Museum
Powiśle Railway Station
Orbis
National Museum
Military Museum
Palace of Culture and Science
CENTRUM
Śródmieście Railway Station
Central Railway Station
Marriott Hotel
Warsaw Operetta
TO INTERNATIONAL AIRPORT, 4
United States
Canada
Parliament (Sejm)
The Ujazdówski Park
United Kingdom
Śmigły-Rydz Park
Botanical Garden
Łazienki Park
Marshal Jozef Piłsudski Park
POLITECHNIKA
RONDO JAZDY POLSKIEJ
PL. TRZECH KRZYŻY
PL. KONSTYTUCJI
PL. ZBAWICIELA
PL. TEATRALNY
PL. BANKOWY
PL. ŻELAZNEJ BRAMY
PL. GRZYBOWSKI
pl. Defilad
pl. Dąbrowskiego
pl. Józefa Piłsudskiego
al. Solidarności
al. Jerozolimskie
al. Jana Pawła II
al. Ujazdowskie
al. Armii Ludowej
Krakowskie Przedmieście
Nowy Świat
Marszałkowska
Świętokrzyska
Wybrzeże Gdańskie
Wybrzeże Kościuszkowskie
Wisłostrada
most Śląsko-Dąbrowski
Church of the Order of the Holy Sacrament
RYNEK NOWEGO MIASTA
Dominican Church of St. Jacob
Barbican (Barbakan)
Paulite Church of the Holy Cross
Warsaw Historical Museum
RYNEK STAREGO MIASTA
Little Insurgent Monument
St. John's Cathedral
PLAC ZAMKOWY
Statue of King Zygmunt III
0 400 yards
0 400 meters
N

WARNING: Theft is rising on overnight trains, especially to and from Berlin and Prague, and in train stations in Poland. Protect your property, and avoid sleeping on night trains (or trade off staying awake with any travel companions).

Buses: PKS Warszawa Zachodnia, al. Jerozolimskie 144 (☎822 48 11; international ☎823 55 70; domestic ☎94 33), in the same building as the Warszawa Zachodnia train station. For information on international bus tickets, check the **Centrum Podróży AURA** at the Zachodnia station. (☎823 68 58. Open daily 6am-9:30pm.) Buses depart for: **Copenhagen** (330zł), **London** (450zł), **Minsk** (84zł), **Paris** (399zł), **Prague** (94zł), and **Venice** (340zł). **PKS Warszawa Stadion,** on the other side of the river, sends buses east and south. **Polski Express,** al. Jana Pawła II (☎630 03 20), in a kiosk near Warsawa Centralna train station, offers fast, comfortable bus service to: **Gdańsk** (6hr., 2 per day, 37zł); **Kraków** (6hr., 2 per day, 33zł); and **Lublin** (3hr., 7 per day, 17zł).

Public Transportation: Rides on **trams** and **buses** (including express lines) 2.40zł, 1.20zł with ISIC; night buses 7.20zł; extra ticket required for large baggage. **Daily pass** 7.20zł, students 3.60zł. Buy tickets at kiosks or from the driver at night. Punch the end marked by the arrow and *tu kasować* in the machines on board. Bus #175 runs from the airport to Stare Miasto via the central train station, the town center, and ul. Nowy Świat. Bus #130 goes to Zachodnia Station, Centralna Station, and Wilanów in the south. Warsaw's single **Metro** line connects the southern border of town with the center (same prices).

Taxis: MPT Radio Taxi, ☎919. **Sawa Taxi,** ☎644 44 44. Overcharging is still a problem; call for pickup. State-run cabs with a mermaid sign are usually safe. Fares start at 4zł, plus 1.60zł per km; 2zł is the legal daytime max. per km, 2.40zł per km at night.

ORIENTATION AND PRACTICAL INFORMATION

The busy downtown area, **Śródmieście**, is on the west riverbank of the **Wisła River,** which bisects the city. In the middle of it all, **Warszawa Centralna,** the main train station, lies on **al. Jerozolimskie,** between **al. Jana Pawła II** and **ul. Emilii Plater.** From the vast marketplace of **Parade Square** (pl. Defilad), a short walk along al. Jerozolimskie leads to the large intersection with **ul. Marszałkowska,** one of the city's main north-south avenues. This busy street leads north to **Saxon Gardens** (Ogród Saski); the intersection serves as a major stop for most bus and tram lines. Al. Jerozolimskie continues east to the other main north-south avenue, **Trakt Królewski,** which intersects al. Jerozolimskie at **rondo Charles de Gaulle.** A left here runs north up **ul. Nowy Świat,** which becomes **ul. Krakowskie Przedmieście,** and leads directly to the **Old Town** (Stare Miasto) and the Royal Palace. A right at rondo Charles de Gaulle leads to **al. Ujazdowskie,** which leads down embassy row to the Łazienki Palace.

TOURIST AND FINANCIAL SERVICES

Tourist Offices: Informacja Turystyczna (IT), al. Jerozolimskie 54 (☎524 51 84; fax 654 24 47), in the main train station. Open M-F 8am-8pm, Sa-Su 9am-7pm. Also **pl. Zamkowy** 1/13 (☎635 18 81; fax 831 04 64), by the entrance to Stare Miasto across from the Royal Palace. Open M-F 9am-6pm, Sa 10am-6pm, Su 11am-6pm. Also at **Rynek Starego Miasta** 28, inside the Historical Museum. English-language *Warsaw Insider* (6zł) available. Open daily May-Sept. 8am-8pm; Oct.-Apr. 9am-6pm.

Budget Travel: Almatur, ul. Kopernika 23 (☎826 35 12; fax 826 35 07). International bus, ferry, and plane tickets at student discounts. Can arrange rooms in university **dorms** July-Aug. Open M-F 9am-7pm, Sa 10am-2pm.

Embassies: Most are near ul. Ujazdowskie. **Australia,** ul. Nowogrodska 11 (☎617 60 81). Open M-F 9am-1pm and 2-4pm. **Belarus,** ul. Ateńska 67 (☎617 32 12). Visa department open M-F 8am-4pm. **Canada,** al. Jerozolimskie 123, 5th floor (☎629 80 51). Open M-F 8am-4:30pm. **Russia,** ul. Belwederska 49, bldg. C (☎621 34 53). Open W and F 8am-1pm. **South Africa,** ul. Koszykowa 54 (☎625 62 28). Open M-F 9am-noon. **Ukraine,** al. Ujazdowskie 13 (☎625 01 27). Open M-F 10am-4pm. **UK,** al. Róż 1

(☎628 10 01). Open M-F 9am-noon and 2-4pm. **US,** al. Ujazdowskie 29/31 (☎628 30 41). Open M-F 8:30am-5pm; consular services 8:30am-noon.

Currency Exchange: Private *kantory* have the best rates. **24hr. exchange** is available at Warszawa Centralna and the airport. **Bank PKO S.A.,** pl. Bankowy 2 (☎637 10 61), in the blue skyscraper; ul. Mazowiecka 14 (☎661 25 59); and ul. Grójecka 1/3 (☎658 82 17), in Hotel Sobieski. AmEx/Visa **traveler's checks** are cashed into dollars or *złoty* for a 1-2% commission. V, MC **cash advances.** Open M-F 8am-6pm, Sa 10am-2pm. **ATMs** are at all listed branches.

American Express: ul. Krakowskie Przedmieście 11 (☎551 51 52). Cash and traveler's check exchange at no commission. Address *Poste Restante* mail to "American Express Travel," PL 00-069. Open M-F 9am-6pm.

LOCAL SERVICES

Luggage Storage: At Warszawa Centralna train station, below the main hall. Lockers 8-14zł per day. Open 24hr. In Zachodnia Station, 4zł for a big pack. Open daily 7am-7pm.

English Bookstore: American Bookstore, ul. Koszykowa 55 (☎660 56 37). A good but pricey selection. Open M-F 10am-7pm, Sa 11am-6pm.

Gay and Lesbian Information: Lambda Center Hotline (☎628 52 22). English spoken. Tu-W 6-9pm, F 4-10pm. Offices at Czerniakowska 178 (#16); call ahead. The **Ola Archive** (☎ (060) 465 6444; email olga@kki.net.pl) collects lesbian resources. Open M and Th 5-8pm.

Laundromat: ul. Karmelicka 17 (☎831 73 17). Take bus #180 from ul. Marszałkowska toward Żoliborz, get off at ul. Anielewicza, and go back one block. Wash and dry 23.10zł. Detergent 3zł. Open M-F 9am-5pm, Sa 9am-1pm. Call ahead. Some English spoken.

EMERGENCY AND COMMUNICATIONS

Emergencies: Ambulance: ☎999. **Fire:** ☎998. **Police:** ☎997.

Pharmacy: Apteka Grabowskiego (☎825 13 72), at the main train station. Open 24hr.

Medical Assistance: American Medical Center, ul. Wilcza 23 m. 29 (☎622 04 89; 24hr. emergency ☎06 02 24 30 24). Provides English-language referrals. General practice clinic open M-Sa 8am-6pm.

Telephones: At the post office; sells tokens and phone cards. **Directory assistance:** ☎913.

Internet Access: Planeta 8C8, ul. Królewska 2, just off Krakówskie Przedmieście. 5zł per 30min., 8zł per hr. Open M-F 10am-midnight, Su noon-8pm. **Casablanca,** ul. Krakówskie Przedmieście 4/6. 12zł per hr. Open M-Th 9:30am-1am, F 9:30am-2am, Sa 10am-2am, Su 10am-midnight. **Empik Zaprasza,** ul. Marszałkowska 104. 8zł per hr. Open M-Sa 9am-10pm, Su 11am-7pm.

Post Office: ul. Świętokrzyska 31/33 (☎827 00 52; info ☎826 75 11). Take a ticket at the entrance and wait in line. For stamps and letters, push "D"; for packages, push "F"; for *Poste Restante,* turn left into the other room, push "C" at the computer, and pick it up at window #12. Xerox and Fax bureau (fax 30 00 21) open 7am-10pm. Address mail to be held: First name SURNAME, *Poste Restante,* ul. Świętokrzyska 31/33, Warsaw 1, **00-001** Poland.

POLSKI PHONE HOME? After making a call from one of Warsaw's spiffy new magnetic card telephones, you may find yourself accosted by any number of locals—from young girls to elderly gentlemen—staring at your card longingly and bargaining at you in Polish like a used-car salesman. Before you write these poor souls off as free-loaders who couldn't bother to buy their own phone card, know that the opposite is more likely true: they probably have plenty of cards and are looking to add yours to their collection. If you need confirmation of this bizarre factoid, most collectors will whip out their collection with great pride if asked. The cards with pictures on the back are the most coveted; if you find you're holding the Honus Wagner of phone cards—a 1999 Pope John Paul II—you'll have to fend off an ugly mob to escape.

ACCOMMODATIONS AND CAMPING

Prices rise and rooms become scarce in the summer; call ahead, particularly for hostels. For help finding **private rooms,** check in with **Syrena,** ul. Krucza 17, off al. Jerozolimskie. (☎628 56 98. Open M-Sa 9am-7pm, Su 9am-5pm. Singles from 72zł; doubles from 96zł.) City tourist offices have accommodations lists.

Schronisko Młodzieżowe (HI), ul. Karolkowa 53a (☎632 88 29). Take tram #22 or 24 west from al. Jerozolimskie or the train station to "Okopowa." Cross at the corner near Pizza Hut, continue down al. Solidarności, and follow the green IYH signs. Dorms are often overrun by school groups. English spoken. Clean bathrooms. Lockout 10am-5pm. Dorms 22.50-28zł; singles 120-140zł; doubles 200zł; bed in a triple or quad 40zł.

Schronisko Młodzieżowe (HI), ul. Smolna 30, top floor (☎827 89 52), across from the National Museum. From the train station, take any eastbound tram to the 3rd stop, "Muzeum Narodowe." Great location, but extremely crowded all summer. Sheets 4zł. Lockout 10am-4pm. Curfew 11pm. 3-day max. stay. Call 2 weeks ahead. Dorms 21-28zł; singles 45zł; bed in a double or triple 38zł.

Schronisko Młodzieżowe "Agrykola," ul. Myśliwiecka 9 (☎622 91 10; fax 622 91 05). Near Kazienki Park. From Marszałkowska, take bus #107, 404 or 520 to "Rozbrat," continue on Rozbrat. The future of youth hostels. Breakfast included. Curfew midnight. Singles 200zł; doubles 250zł; triples and quads 60zł per person.

Schronisko Młodzieżowe (HI), ul. Międzyparkowa 4/6 (☎831 17 66). Near the river. Take tram #2, 6, or 18 north from ul. Marszałkowska to "K.K.S. Polonia"; continue down the road. Mostly school groups; attracts few foreigners. Sheets 5zł. Lockout 10am-5pm. Curfew 11pm. Open July-Aug. Call ahead. Dorms 30zł, under 26 12zł.

Hotel Metalowcy, ul. Długa 29 (☎831 40 21, ext. 29). Take bus #175 from the train station to "pl. Krasińskich," go back to ul. Długa, and turn right. Great location. Clean rooms and decent shared bathrooms. Singles 56zł; roomier doubles 88zł; quads with bath 155zł.

Hotel Mazowiecki, ul. Mazowiecka 10 (☎687 91 17). A little more than a block from ul. Krakowskie Przedmieście off ul. Świętokrzyska. One of the poshest budget hotels downtown. Check-in 4pm. Check-out 2pm. Singles 125zł; doubles 170zł; triples 210zł.

Hotel Belfer, ul. Wybrzeże Kościuszkowskie 31/33 (☎625 55 62). From the train station, take any tram east to "Most Poniatowskiego," then with the river on your right walk along ul. Wybrzeże Kościuszkowskie. Bright and roomy. Breakfast included. English spoken. Singles 122-165zł; doubles 165-188zł.

Camping "123," ul. Bitwy Warszawskiej 1920r. 15/17 (☎822 91 21), by the main bus station. Take bus #127, 130, or 517 to "Zachodnia," cross the street at the traffic circle and turn left to Bitwy Warszawskiej. English spoken. Guarded 24hr. 10zł per person, children 4-10 5zł; small site 8zł, large 10zł. Electricity 10zł.

FOOD

Food stands dot the square beneath the Palace of Culture and many more are by the train station. **Milk bars** *(bar mleczny)* or proletarian-style **cafeterias** are inexpensive and generally tasty options. There are 24-hour **supermarkets** at the central train station, as well as several late-night **delikatesy,** including those on ul. Nowy Świat 53 and al. Solidarnosci 82a. (☎826 03 22. Open daily 7am-5am.)

RESTAURANTS

Pod Samsonem, ul. Freta 3/5, between Stare Miasto and Nowe Miasto. Hearty Polish-Jewish cuisine to make you big and strong like Samson. Decorated with photos of prewar Jewish life. Meals 15-30zł. Open daily 10am-10pm.

Mata Hari, ul. Nowy Świat 52. Incredibly cheap, mostly Indian veggie dishes of the day, including a variety of samosas, soups, and calzones. Full meals under 10zł. Open M-F 11am-7pm, Sa 11am-5pm.

Bong Sen, ul. Poznańska 12, south of the train station on a road parallel to al. Marszałkowska. The decidedly Polish waitstaff won't create any illusion that you're in the Far East, but the food might fool you. Entrees 19-30zł. Open daily 11am-10pm.

Bar Mleczny Familijny, ul. Nowy Świat 39. A giant cafeteria version of a Polish grandmother's kitchen. Soups 1zł; meals 2-6zł. Open M-F 7am-8pm, Sa-Su 9am-5pm.

Restauracja Ekologiczna, "Nowe Miasto," Rynek Nowego Miasta 13/15. Healthy soups, crepes, and a variety of salads. Encores of Polish beer (0.5L *Zywiec* 9zł) and an international wine selection. Live music nightly 7-10pm. Open daily 10am-midnight.

CAFES

Pożegnanie z Afryka, ul. Freta 4/6. The name of this chain means "Out of Africa," though most types of coffee are actually South American; regardless, it's the best in town. Worth the wait for one of six tables. Coffee 7-8zł. Open daily 11am-9pm.

Antykwariat Cafe, ul. Żurawia 45, 2 blocks south of rondo de Gaulle. Book-lined, comfortable, and delicious. Coffee 6-8zł. Open M-F 10am-10pm, Sa-Su noon-10pm.

Kawiarnia Bazyliszek, Rynek Starego Miasta 9/11/13. A fancy cafe with relaxed outdoor seating. Great views of the restored splendor of Stare Miasto and the tourists here to see it. Tortes 7-10zł. Coffee 6-8zł. Open daily 11am-11pm.

SIGHTS

Razed beyond recognition during WWII, Warsaw was almost entirely rebuilt from the rubble. Thanks to the wonders of Soviet upkeep, though, most of the buildings look much older than their 50 years. As sights are spread out and some are quite distant from the center, the city requires time to explore.

STARE MIASTO AND NOWE MIASTO. Warsaw's postwar reconstruction shows its finest face in the narrow, cobblestone streets and colorful facades of the **Old Town** (Stare Miasto), at the very end of ul. Krakowskie Przedmieście in pl. Zamkowy. *(Take bus #175 or E3 from the city center to "Miodowa.")* At the right side of the entrance to Stare Miasto stands the impressive **Royal Castle** (Zamek Królewski). Burned down in September 1939 and plundered by the Nazis, the castle was elevated to martyrdom by Polish freedom fighters and ordinary Varsovions alike, many of whom risked their lives hiding priceless works in the hope they might one day be returned. Reconstructed from 1971 to 1984, today the castle houses the **Royal Castle Museum,** which showcases the world of Poland's kings through paintings, artifacts, and the stunning Royal Apartments. *(Pl. Zamkowy 4. ☎657 21 78. Open M 11am-4pm, Tu-Sa 10am-6pm, Su 11am-6pm; last entry 1hr. before closing. Tickets to the Royal Apartments ("Route 2") 12zł; students 6zl; Su free. Tours M-Sa 50zł.)* Just down ul. Świętojańska sits Warsaw's oldest church, the **Cathedral of St. John** (Anrchi-Katedra św. Jana), decimated in the 1944 Uprising but rebuilt after the war. *(Cathedral and crypts open daily dawn-dusk. Crypts 2zł, students 1zł.)* Ul. Świętojańska leads to the restored Renaissance and Baroque **Old Town Square** (Rynek Starego Miasta). A stone plaque at the entrance commemorates its reconstruction, finished in 1953-54, and recalls the square's prewar history. **Crooked Wheel** (Ul. Krzywe Koło) starts in the northeast corner of the *rynek* and leads to the restored **barbakan,** a rare example of 16th-century Polish fortification and a popular spot for locals and tourists alike to lounge. The *barbakan* opens onto ul. Freta, the edge of **Nowe Miasto.** In the district, which is only *relatively* Nowe, 18th- and 19th-century buildings stand shiny after expensive face-lifts repaired wartime destruction. The great physicist and chemist **Maria Skłodowska-Curie,** winner of two Nobel prizes, was born at ul. Freta 16 in 1867.

TRAKT KRÓLEWSKI (ROYAL WAY). The city's most attractive thoroughfare (named the Royal Way because it leads south toward Kraków, Poland's former capital) starts at **pl. Zamkowy,** at the entrance to Stare Miasto, and stretches 4km south, changing its name from **ul. Krakowskie Przedmieście** to **ul. Nowy Świat** to **al. Ujazdowskie.** On the left as you leave pl. Zamkowy, the 15th-century **St. Anne's Church** (Kościół św. Anny) looms. Rebuilt in Baroque style, its most striking feature is its gilded altar. *(Open daily dawn-dusk.)* **Fryderyk Chopin,** who spent his childhood in the neighborhood near ul. Krakowskie Przedmieście, gave his first public concert in **Pałac Radziwiłłów** (a.k.a. **Pałac Namiestnikowski**) 46/48, the building guarded by four stone lions; today, an armed guard stands watch alongside his feline counterparts outside the now-Polish presidential mansion. **Pałac Czapskich** was Chopin's last home before he left for France in 1830; today the palace houses **Chopin's Drawing Room** (Salonik Chopinów) and the **Academy of Fine Arts.** *(Ul. Krakowskie Przedmieście 5. Open M-F 10am-2pm. 3zł, students 2zł.)* Chopin died abroad at the age of 39 and was buried in Paris, but his heart belongs to Poland; it now rests in an urn in the **Holy Cross Church** (Kościół św. Krzyża), next to the Academy. If you haven't gotten enough of the mop-topped composer, waltz on over to the **Fryderyk Chopin Museum** (Muzeum Fryderyka Chopina), which has a small collection of original letters, scores, paintings, and keepsakes, including the great composer's last piano and a section of his first polonaise, penned when he was seven years old. *(Ul. Okólnik 1; enter from ul. Tamka. Open May-Sept. M, W, and F 10am-5pm, Th noon-6pm, Sa-Su 10am-2pm. 8zł, students 4zł. Audio guides 4zł.)*

The Royal Way continues down **ul. Nowy Świat,** the city's most fashionable street. Turn left just after rondo Charles de Gaulle to reach Poland's largest museum, the **National Museum** (Muzeum Narodowe). *(Al. Jerozolimskie 3. ☎629 30 93. Open Tu-W and F 10am-4pm, Th noon-5pm, Sa-Su 10am-5pm. 13zł, students 7zł; Sa free.)* Further down, the Royal Way turns into al. Ujazdowskie and runs alongside **Łazienki Park** (on your left). Near the entrance is the **Chopin Monument** (Pomnik Chopina), the site of free concerts every Sunday at noon and 4pm from spring to autumn. Farther into the park is the striking Neoclassical **Palace on Water** (Pałac na Wodzie), also called Pałac Łazienkowski, which houses galleries of 17th- and 18th-century art. *(Take bus #116 or 195 from ul. Nowy Świat or #119 from the city center south to Bagatela. Park open daily dawn-dusk. Palace open Tu-Su 9:30am-4pm. 11zł, students 8zł. Tours in English 55zł.)* Just north of the park, off ul. Agrykola, the exhibitions in the **Center of Contemporary Art** (Centrum Sztuki Wspólczesnej), al. Ujazdowskie 6, break all aesthetic barriers. *(Open Sa-Th 11am-5pm, F 11am-9pm. 8zl, students 4zl.)*

THE WARSAW GHETTO AND SYNAGOGUE. Still referred to as the Ghetto, the modern **Muranów** ("walled") neighborhood northwest of the city center holds few vestiges of the nearly 400,000 Jews—then one-third of the city's population—who lived here prior to WWII. The **Umschlagplatz,** at the corner of ul. Dzika and ul. Stawki was the railway platform where the Nazis gathered 300,000 of the Jews for transport to the death camps. *(Take tram #35 from ul. Marszałkowska to "Dzika." Or, follow ul. Freta out of the Rynek Starego Miasta on foot, continue as the street turns into Zakroczymska, turn left on Konwiktorska, and turn left on Muranowska, which becomes Stawki.)* With the monument that stands in its place to your left, continue down Stawki and turn right on ul. DuBois, which becomes ul. Zamenhofa; you will pass a stone monument marking the location of the command bunker of the 1943 ghetto uprising. Further on, in a large park to your right, note the large **Monument of the Ghetto Heroes** (Pomnik Bohaterów). Continue along ul. Zamenhofa for two blocks and then take a right on Dzielna. On the corner of Dzielna and Al. Jana Pawall, the **Museum of Pawiak Prison** (Muzeum Więzienia Pawiak) exhibits photographs and artifacts, including the artwork and poetry of many former prisoners. Over 100,000 Poles were imprisoned here from 1939-1944; 37,000 were executed and 60,000 were transferred to concentration camps. *(Ul. Dzielna 24/26. ☎831 13 17. Open W 9am-5pm, Th and Sa 9am-4pm, F 10am-5pm, Su 10am-4pm. English captions. Free; donation requested.)* Follow Al. Jana Pawall up to a left on ul. Anielewicza, and continue for five blocks to reach the **Jewish Cemetery** (Cmentarz Żydowski), in the western corner of Muranów. Thickly wooded and several kilometers long, the cemetery is the final resting place of 200,000 of Warsaw's Jews. *(You can also take tram #22 from the city center to "Cm. Żydowski." Open M-Th 9am-3pm, F 9am-1pm. 3zł.)* The beautifully reconstructed **Nożyk Synagogue** (Synagoga Nożyka), is a living remnant of Warsaw's Jewish life. The only synagogue to survive the war, today it serves as the spiritual home for the few hundred observant Jews who remain in Warsaw. *(Ul. Twarda 6, north of the Palace of Culture and Science (Pałac Kultury). From the central train station, take any tram north along ul. Jana*

Pawla II to "Rondo ONZ." Turn right on Twarda and left at the Jewish Theater (Teatr Żydowski). Or, from the tourist office, walk west down Świętokrzyska, turn right on Emilii Plater, and cross Twarda. ☎620 43 24 for a schedule of services. Open M-F 10am-3pm, Su 11am-3pm. 5zł.)

WILANÓW. After his coronation in 1677, King Jan III Sobieski bought the sleepy village of Milanowo, had its existing mansion rebuilt into a Baroque palace, and named the new residence Villa Nova *(Wilanów)*. Since 1805, **Pałac Wilanowski** has functioned both as a museum and as a residence for the highest-ranking guests of the Polish state. Inside are lovely frescoed rooms, countless 17th- to 19th-century portraits, and extravagant royal apartments. You can break off from the slow-moving Polish-language tour to explore on your own with the multilingual signs along the way. *(☎842 81 01. Take bus #180, 410, or 414 from ul. Marszałkowska, or bus #130 or 519 from the train station south to "Wilanów"; cross the street and the road to the palace will be to your right. Palace open June 15-Sept. 15 M and W-Sa 9:30am-2:30pm, Su 9:30am-4:30pm; Sept. 16-June 14 9:30am-2:30pm. 15zł, students 8zł; Th free. English tours 100zł; for groups of 6-35 20zł each. Garden open M and W-F 9:30am-dusk. 3zł, students 2zł.)* On the way out, take a left to see ads, art, and everything in between at the **Poster Museum.** *(Open Tu-F 10am-4pm, Sa-Su 10am-5pm. 7zł, students 5zł; W free.)*

ELSEWHERE IN CENTRAL WARSAW. The center of Warsaw's commercial district, southwest of Stare Miasto near the central train station, is dominated by the 70-story Stalinist Gothic **Palace of Culture and Science** (Pałac Kultury), ul. Marszałkowska. Locals claim the view from the top is the best in Warsaw. Why? Because it's the only place from which you can't see the building; the eyesore is reviled even more as a symbol of Soviet domination than for its aesthetics. Below, **Parade Square** (pl. Defilad), Europe's largest square (even bigger than Moscow's Red Square) swarms with freelance capitalists. Adjacent to **Saxon Garden** (Ogród Saski) is the **John Paul II Collection,** with over 400 works by artists including Dalí, Titian, Rembrandt, van Gogh, Goya, Renoir, and others. *(Pl. Bankowy 3/5. ☎620 21 81. Open Tu-Su 10am-5pm; last entry 4pm. 5zł, students 3zł.)*

ENTERTAINMENT AND NIGHTLIFE

After you've digested your dinner *pierogi* and *kiełbasa*, Warsaw is chock full o' excitement. To get the latest schedule of events, call the tourist info line (☎94 31). A large variety of pubs attract big crowds and often have live music, and cafes *(kawiarnie)* around Stare Miasto and ul. Nowy Świat serve late. In summer, large outdoor beer gardens complement the pub scene.

CONCERTS, OPERA, AND THEATER. Classical concerts fill Pałac na Wodzie in Łazienki on summer Saturdays. (Performances June-Sept. 4pm. 15zł, students 10zł.) Inquire about concerts at the **Warsaw Music Society** (Warszawskie Towarzystwo Muzyczne), ul. Morskie Oko 2. (☎849 68 56. Take tram #4, 18, 19, 35, or 36 to "Morskie Oko" from ul. Marszałkowska. Concerts frequent, but none in summer.) The **Warsaw Chamber Opera** (Warszawska Opera Kameralna), al. Solidarności 76B (☎831 22 40), hosts a Mozart festival each year in early summer, with performances throughout the city. The **Chopin Monument** (Pomnik Chopina), nearby in Łazienki Park, hosts free Sunday performances. (May-Oct. noon and 4pm.) **Teatr Wielki,** pl. Teatralny 1 (☎692 07 58), Warsaw's main opera and ballet hall, offers performances almost daily. **Sala Kongresowa** (☎620 49 80), in the Palace of Culture and Science on the train station side with the casino, hosts serious **jazz** and **rock** concerts with famous international bands; enter from ul. Emilii Plater. **Warsaw Summer Jazz Days** is in June. **Empik Megastore** sells rock concert tickets (☎625 12 19).

BARS AND NIGHTCLUBS. Drinks are pricey, but many pubs compensate with live music. The nightclub and dance scene shifts frequently; check posters around town. Gay life is a bit underground; call ☎628 52 22 for info. (Open Tu-W 6-9pm, F 4-10pm.) *Inaczej* and *Filo* list gay establishments. **Morgan's,** ul. Okólnik 1, with an entrance on ul. Tamka under the Chopin Museum, has the best Guinness in Poland, 0.5L for 15zł. (Live music some nights, but infrequently in summer. Open daily 2pm-midnight.) **Empik Pub,** ul. Nowy Swiat 15/17, in the basement of the Empike Megastore, is the place for blues in Warsaw. (No cover. Live music M-Sa 9pm, Su 8pm.) *The* nightclub is **Piekarnia,** ul. Mlocinska 11. The packed dance floor, sparse clothing, and expert DJs are so hip it hurts. (Cover F-Sa 25zł. Open F-Sa 10am-4am.)

EXCURSION FROM WARSAW

ŻELAZOWA WOLA. The birthplace of Fryderyk Chopin, Żelazowa Wola is a must see on any Coppin itinerary. The pianist's cottage and gardens reveal his origin. (10zł, students 5zł; park only 4zł, students 2zł.) The **museum** in the house (☎ (46) 863 33 00) recreates early 19th century living, with rooms devoted to each of Chopin's parents and the era in which they lived. The best reason to make the trip, however, is to catch a **concert** of the composer's works. From May to September, music fans gather to listen to Polish musicians perform. (Concerts Su at 11am and 3pm.) The schedule of music and performers, posted throughout Warsaw, is available at the Chopin museum (see p. 742). Concerts are free if you're content to listen from the park benches outside the music parlor. Seats in the parlor itself cost 30zł.

Two **buses** daily pass through Żelazowa Wola (53km west of Warsaw) but they aren't clearly marked; take the Wyszogrod bus. Żelazowa Wola is just a stop on the route (1¼hr., 6.70zł). Only the 9:45am bus arrives in time to time it all in.

GDAŃSK ☎058

The strategic location of Gdańsk (g-DAH-nsk) on the Baltic Coast and at the mouth of the Wisła has helped it flourish architecturally and culturally, and has put it at the forefront of Polish history for more than a millennium. Today, Gdańsk is a multifaceted gem, with a dizzying array of things to eat, drink, see, and do.

GETTING THERE AND AWAY

Trains: Gdańsk Główny, ul. Podwale Grodzkie 1 (☎301 11 12). To: **Warsaw** (4½hr., 18 per day, 60.18zł); **Kraków** (6½hr., 9 per day, 41.10zł); **Berlin** (8hr., 1 per day, 124.50zł); and **Prague** (14hr., 1 per day, 166zł). **Commuter trains (SKM)** run to Sopot (20min., every 20min., 2.50zł, students 1.25zł).

Buses: Ul. 3 Maja 12 (☎302 15 32), behind the train station via the underground passageway. To **Warsaw** (4½hr., 5 per day, 38zł) and **Berlin** (8½hr., 2 per week, 153zł).

Local Transportation: Buses and **trams** cost 1-3zł; **day-pass** 5zł. Prices rise at night. Students pay half-price, and baggage needs a ticket.

Taxis: Hallo Taxi, ☎91 97. **Super Hallo Taxi,** ☎301 91 91. 1.80zł per km.

ORIENTATION AND PRACTICAL INFORMATION

From the **Gdańsk Główny** train station, the city center lies a few blocks southeast, bordered on the west by **Wały Jagiełłońskie** and on the east by the **Motława.** Take the underpass in front of the train station, go right, exit the shopping center, then turn left on ul. Heweliusza. Turn right on ul. Rajska and follow the signs to **Główne Miasto** (Main Town), turning left on **ul. Długa.** Długa becomes **Długi Targ** as it widens near Motława. Gdańsk has a number of suburbs, all north of Główne Miasto.

Tourist Offices: IT Gdańsk, ul. Długa 45 (☎/fax 301 91 51), in Główne Miasto. Open daily June-Aug. 8am-8pm; Sept.-May 8am-6pm.

Budget Travel: Orbis, ul. Podwale Staromiejskie 96/97 (☎/fax 301 84 12). International and domestic ferry, train, and plane tickets. English tours of town. Open M-F 9am-5pm, Sa 10am-2pm. **Almatur,** ul. Długi Targ 11, 2nd fl. (☎301 29 31; email almatur@combidata.com.pl), in the Główne Miasto center. ISICs (35zł), info about youth and student hostels, ferries, and more. Open M-F 8:30am-5:30pm, Sa 10am-2pm.

Currency Exchange: The train station has a 24hr. *bureau de change* and an **ATM. Bank Gdański,** Wały Jagiełłońskie 14/16 (☎307 92 12), cashes traveler's checks for 1% commission and provides cash advances for no commission. Open M-F 9am-6pm.

Late Night Pharmacy: At the train station (☎346 25 40). Ring the bell 8pm-7:30am.

Internet Access: Rudy Kot Internet Music Café, ul. Garncarska 18/20 (☎301 86 49). Off Podwale Staromiejskie. 2.50zł per 30min.; 5zł per hr. Open daily 10am-midnight.

Post Office: ul. Długa 22/28 (☎301 88 53). *Poste Restante* is around the back, through a separate entrance. Open M-F 8am-8pm, Sa 9am-3pm. Address mail to be held: First name SURNAME, *Poste Restante,* Gdańsk 1, **80-801.**

ACCOMMODATIONS AND FOOD

Try to book ahead in summer or get a **private room** through **Gdańsk-Tourist** (Biuro Uslug Turystycznych), ul. Heweliusza 8, opposite the station. (☎301 26 34; fax 301 63 01. Singles 39-48zł; doubles 67-80zł. Open July-Aug. daily 8am-7:30pm; Sept.-June M-Sa 9am-5pm.) If you don't have luck inside, try one of the **elderly women** out front.

Schronisko Młodzieżowe (HI), ul. Wałowa 21 (☎301 23 13). Cross the street in front of the train station, head up ul. Heweliusza, turn left at ul. Łagiewniki, then right after the church onto Wałowa; the hostel is on the left. Sheets 3.21zł. Luggage storage 1zł. Lockout 10am-5pm. Curfew midnight. Dorms 16zł; singles and doubles 27-30zł.

Dom Studnck Angielski, ul. Chlebnicka 13/16 (☎301 28 16), 1 block off Długi Targ. Amazing location. Funky murals. Sheets 3zł. Open July-Aug. Singles 22zł, doubles 44zł.

Schronisko Młodzieżowe, ul. Grunwaldzka 244 (☎341 41 08). From the train station, take tram #6 or 12 north (to your left facing away from the station) and get off at "Abrahama", 14 stops later; you will see a complex of tram garages on the left (20-25min.). Turn right on ul. Abrahama, then right again on Grunwaldzka; the hostel is just ahead by the sports complex. Sheets 3zł. Luggage storage 1zł. Reception 5-9pm. Lockout 10am-5pm. Curfew 10pm. Dorms 21.40z; doubles 33.16-43.90zł.

Hotel Zaułek, ul. Ogarna 107/108 (☎301 41 69). Ogarna runs parallel to Długi Targ, 1 block farther when coming from the train station. Check-in and check-out noon. Singles 55zł; doubles 70zł; triples 90zł; quads 105zł; quints 120zł.

Hotel Dom Nauczyciela, ul. Uphagena 28 (☎/fax 341 49 17), in Gdańsk-Wrzeszcz. Take tram #6 or 12 north from the train station to "Miszewskiego" (7 stops). Turn right on ul. Miszewskiego and take the next right onto Uphagena; the hotel will be ahead on the left, across from the tennis courts. Check-in 2pm. Check-out noon. Singles 48-123zł; doubles 70-176zł; triples 96-105zł.

For fresh produce, try **Hala Targowa** on ul. Pańska, in the shadows of Kościół św. Katarzyny just off Podwale Staromiejskie. (Open M-F 9am-6pm, 1st and last Sa of the month 9am-3pm.) **Green Way Vegetarian Bar,** ul. Garncarska 4/6, creates stellar soups, samosas, stuffed pitas, and fruit juices. (Entrees 4-9zł. Open daily 10am-10pm.) Or, eat hearty, home style Polish food at **Bar Mleczny,** ul. Długa 33/34. (Full meals 5-10zł. Open M-F 7am-6pm, Sa-Su 9am-5pm.)

SIGHTS

GŁÓWNE MIASTO. Gdańsk was one of the first Polish cities to undergo an exhaustive postwar face-lift; only a few buildings have yet to be fully restored. The handsome market square, **Długi Targ,** forms the physical and social center of Główne Miasto, where the 16th-century facade of **Arthur's Court** (Dwór Artusa) faces out onto **Neptune Fountain** (Fontanna Neptuna). The court now houses a branch of the **Gdańsk History Museum** (Muzeum Historii Gdańska). Next to the fountain, where ul. Długa and Długi Targ meet, the 14th-century **town hall** (ratusz) houses another branch of the **Gdańsk History Museum.** Pay an extra 2zł to climb the **tower** for an incredible city view. *(Both museums open Tu and Th 11am-6pm, W 10am-4pm, F-Sa 10am-5pm, Su 11am-5pm. 5zł, students 2.50zł; W free.)* A block toward the train station is the world's largest brick cathedral, the 14th-century **Church of the Blessed Virgin Mary** (Kościół Najświętszej Marii Panny). Climb the 405 steps to the top of the steeple for a fantastic vista. *(Open M-Sa 9am-5:30pm. 300zł.)* The cobblestone ul. Mariacka leads to riverside ul. Długie Pobrzeże. The Gothic **Harbor Crane,** part of **Central Maritime Museum** (Centralne Muzeum Morskie), is along the left. *(Open daily 10am-6pm. 4zł, stu-*

dents 2.50zł.) The flags of Lech Wałęsa's trade union *Solidarność* fly high once again at the **Gdańsk Shipyard** (Stocznia Gdańska) and at the **Solidarity monument,** on pl. Solidarności, just north of the city center at the end of ul. Wały Piastowskie.

GDAŃSK-OLIWA. The most beautiful of Gdańsk's many suburbs, Oliwa provides a respite from the big city. From the city center take the commuter rail (15min., 2.50zł, students 1.25zł). Trams #6 and 12 get you there more slowly (30-35min.). From the Oliwa train station, go up ul. Poczty Gdańskiej, turn right on ul. Grundwaldzka, then left at the signs for the cathedral on ul. Rybińskiego. To the right you'll find the lush green shade and ponds of **Park Oliwski.** *(Open daily May-Sept. 5am-11pm; Mar.-Apr. and Oct. 5am-8pm.)* Within the park's gates is the oldest church in the Gdańsk area, the 13th-century **Oliwska Cathedral** (Katedra), which houses a magnificent 18th-century Rococo organ. (*Consult "Informator Turystyczney," at the tourist office for a complete schedule of daily concerts.)*

WESTERPLATTE. When Germany attacked on September 1, 1939, the little island **fort** guarding Gdańsk's harbor gained the unfortunate distinction of being the target of the first shots of WWII. Its defenders held out bravely for a week, until a lack of food and munitions forced them out. **Guardhouse #1** has been converted into a museum about the fateful day. *(Take bus #106 or 158 south from the train station to the last stop (20min.). Open May-Sept. 9am-dusk. 1.50zł, students 1zł.)* The path beyond the museum passes the ruins of a command building and, farther up, the massive **Memorial to the Heroes of the Coast** (Pomnik Obrońców Wybrzeża).

BRZEŹNO. For some fun at the **beach,** Brzeźno—though it may not be as trendy as Sopot—is perfect. What it does have over Sopot is **Park Brzeźnieński,** a wondrous escape full of tall pine trees. (*Take tram #13 north from the train station to the last stop, "Brzezno." Follow the footpath in the wooded area ahead to reach the beach.)*

NIGHTLIFE

NIGHTLIFE. Długi Targ rages as crowds of all ages pack the pubs, clubs, and beer gardens late into the evening. Near the intersection of ul. Podwale Staromiejskie and ul. Podmłyńska, **U7,** pl. Dominikański 7, has seven attractions: bowling, billiards, a sauna, a solarium, a shooting range, a fitness center, and of course, the bar. (Open daily 9am-midnight.) **Latający Holender Pub,** ul. Waly Jagiellońskie 2/4, near the end of ul. Długa, doubles as a coffeehouse. (Beer 6zł; coffee 4zł. Open daily noon-midnight.) The popular **Jazz Club,** ul. Długi Targ 39/40, is a great spot for live music on the weekends. (Cover 5zł for concerts. Open daily June-Aug. 10am until the last guest leaves; Sept.-May open from noon.)

EXCURSIONS FROM GDAŃSK: FROMBORK AND SOPOT

FROMBORK. Frombork is closely associated with the name and work of astronomer **Mikołaj Kopernik** (Copernicus), who lived here from 1510 until his death in 1543. In this little town Kopernik conducted most of his research and composed his revolutionary book, *De Revolutionibus Orbium Coelestium.* The tiny waterfront village surrounds a breathtaking cathedral complex perched majestically atop a hill. The *kasa* on the right after you cross the after you cross the wooden bridge sells tickets to **Muzeum Kopernika,** which houses copies of the great book and other odds and ends, the **cathedral** and its impressive **organ,** and the **tower.** (Museum open Tu-Su May-Sept. 9am-4:30pm; Oct.-Apr. 9am-3:30pm. 3zł, students 2zł. Cathedral open M-Sa 10am-6pm; Oct.-Apr. 9am-3:30pm. 2zł, students 1zł. Tower open daily May-Sept. 9:30am-5pm; Oct.-Apr. 9am-3:30pm. 3zł, students 2zł.) Reach Frombork by **bus** from Gdańsk (2hr., 5 per day, 10.90zł); buses depart from behind the Gdańsk train station via the underground passageway. The main **tourist office,** Globus, ul. Elbląska 2, sits across from the cathedral in the *rynek,* at the end of the path from the train station. (☎/fax 243 73 54. Open daily May-Sept. 7am-3pm.) ☎ **055.**

SOPOT. Sopot is a **beach** resort: white, sandy, big, and recreational. The most popular sands are at the end of ul. Monte Cassino, where the 512m **pier** (molo) begins.

(M-F 2.10zł, Sa-Su 2.80zł.) The **commuter rail** (SKM) connects Sopot to Gdańsk (20min., 2.50zł, students 1.25zł). Ul. Dworcowa begins at the train station and leads to the pedestrian ul. Monte Cassino, which runs along the sea to the pier. **Ferries** (☎551 12 93) go from the end of the pier to Gdańsk (1hr., 2 per day, round-trip 42zł, students 30zł). **IT,** ul. Dworcowa 4, by the train station, arranges **rooms.** (☎550 37 83. Singles 39zł; doubles 68zł; triples 90zł; quads 110zł. Accommodations bureau open M-F 8:30am-5pm, Sa-Su 9am-2pm.) Sopot is just beginning to realize that the fun doesn't have to end when the tide comes in, as seen by the growing number of street-side cafes, pubs, and discos along **ul. Monte Cassino.** ☎**058.**

TORUŃ ☎056

Toruń (pop. 210,000) bills itself as the birthplace and childhood home of Mikołaj Kopernik (a.k.a. Copernicus) the man who "stopped the sun and moved the earth." After wandering its cobblestone medieval streets, you might wonder why he ever left. The **Old Town** (Stare Miasto), commanding the right bank of the Wisła River, was constructed by the Teutonic Knights in the 13th century. Copernicus' birthplace, **Dom Kopernika,** ul. Kopernika 15/17, where he popped out on February 19, 1473, has been meticulously restored and wows tourists with 16th-century light shows. (Open Tu-Su 10am-4pm. 5zł, students 3zł.) The **Regional Museum** (Muzeum Okręgowe) is housed in the 14th-century **ratusz** (town hall), Rynek Staromiejski 1, in the center of the tourist district. (Open Tu-Su 10am-4pm. 3zł, students 2zł; Su free.) A city-wide burghers' revolt in 1454 led to the destruction of the **Teutonic Knights' Castle,** but the ruins on ul. Przedzamcze are still impressive. (Open daily 10am-6pm. 0.50zt.) The 50-foot **Leaning Tower,** Pod Krzywą Wieżą 17, was built in 1271 by a Teutonic knight as punishment for falling in love with a peasant girl. The **Cathedral of St. John the Baptist and St. John the Evangelist** (Bazylika Katedralna pw. św. Janów), at the corner of ul. Zeglarska, is the most impressive of the tall Gothic churches poking out of the low skyline. From there, it's a short walk across the *rynek* to ul. Panny Marii and the beautiful stained glass of the **Church of the Virgin Mary** (Kościół Św. Marii). After sunset, stroll along **Bulwar Filadelfijski** (named for Toruń's sister city, Philadelphia), where fishermen and couples line the stone steps.

The **train** station, across the Wisła River from the city center, serves: Gdańsk (3hr., 6 per day, 29.63zł); Warsaw (3½hr., 5 per day, 30.46zł); and Kraków (7hr., 3 per day, 37.70zł). Polski Express **buses** leave from pl. Teatralny for Warsaw (3½hr., 14 per day, 30-37zł) and Szczecin (5½hr., 2 per day, 36zł). The **IT tourist office,** Rynek Staromiejski 1, offers helpful advice in English and helps find lodgings. From the station, take city bus #22 or 27 to pl. Rapackiego (the first stop across the river), head through the little park area, and it's on your left. (☎621 09 31; fax 621 09 30; www.it.torun.pl. Open May-Aug. M and Sa 9am-4pm, Tu-F 9am-6pm, Su 9am-3pm; Sept.-Apr. M and Sa 9am-4pm, Tu-F 9am-6pm.) Check **email** at **Internet Club Jeremi,** Rynek Staromiejski 33. (5zł per hr. Open daily 24hr.) **Hotel Kopernik,** ul. Wola Zamkowa 16, by Rynek Nowomiejski, has bright, newly renovated rooms. (☎/fax 652 25 73. Check-in 2pm. Check-out noon. Singles 66-106zł; doubles 71-131zł.) To reach **PTTK Dom Wycieczkowy,** ul. Legionów 24, from the old town *rynek,* follow ul. Chelmińska past pl. Teatralny to the second right after the park and turn left onto ul Legionów. (☎/fax 622 38 55. Check-in 2pm. Check-out noon. Singles 60zł; doubles 70zł; triples 90zł; quads 122zł.) **Pizzeria Browarna,** ul. Mostowa 17, has huge portions of great food. (Pizza 8-21zł. Open daily 11am-midnight.) There is a 24-hour **grocery store** at ul. Chełmińska 22. **Postal code:** 87-100.

KRAKÓW ☎012

Kraków (KRAH-koof) only recently emerged as a trendy, international hot spot, but it has always figured prominently in Polish history. The city protected centuries of central European kings and astounding architectural achievements, many of which still stand in the colorful Old Town. Between the notorious Nowa Huta steelworks from the Stalinist era to the east and the Auschwitz-Birkenau death camp 70km to the west, Kraków has endured the darkness of the 20th century to earn UNESCO's protection as one of the world's 12 most important cultural monuments. Visitors agree, seeking out the hip pubs, clubs, and galleries in this ancient and modern city.

GETTING THERE AND GETTING AROUND

Flights: Balice airport (☎411 19 55), 15km west of the center. Connected to the main train station by northbound bus #152 or 208 (40min.) or express bus #502 (30min.).

Trains: Kraków Główny, pl. Kolejowy 1 (☎624 54 39). To: **Warsaw** (3hr., 30 per day, 50.69zł); **Bratislava** (8hr., 1 per day, 112zł); **Berlin** (8½hr., 2 per day, 110zł); **Prague** (8½hr., 1 per day, 145zł); **Vienna** (9hr., 2 per day, 149zł); **Lviv** (10½hr., 1 per day, 85zł); **Budapest** (11hr., 1 per day, 145zł); and **Kiev** (22hr., 1 per day, 180zł). Some trains to southeast Poland leave from **Kraków Płaszów,** pl. Dudzinskich 1 (☎933). Take the train from Kraków Główny or tram #3 or 13 from the center south to ul. Wielicka.

Buses: ☎936. On ul. Worcella, directly across from Kraków Główny. **Sindbad** (☎266 19 21), in the main hall, sells international tickets. Open M-F 9am-4:30pm. To: **Warsaw** (5hr., 4 per day, 40zł); **Lviv** (10hr., 1 per day, 50zł); **Budapest** (11hr., 2 per week, 116zł); **Prague** (11hr., 3 per week, 139zł); and **Berlin** (12hr., 3 per week, 142zł).

Public Transportation: Buy tickets at kiosks near **bus** and **tram** stops (2zł); punch them on board or face a fine. Large backpacks need their own tickets. **Day pass** 8zł.

Taxis: Express Taxi (☎644 41 11); **Hellou** (☎644 42 22); **Major** (☎636 33 33).

ORIENTATION

The true heart of the city, both for tourists and locals, is the huge **Main Market** (Rynek Główny), in the center of **Old Town** (Stare Miasto). Circling Stare Miasto are the **Planty** gardens and a ring of roads including Basztowa, Dunajewskiego, Podwale, and Westerplatte. South of the *rynek*, the gigantic **Wawel Castle** looms. The **Wista** river snakes past the castle and borders the old Jewish village of **Kazimierz,** which is accessible from the market by ul. Starowiślna. The **bus** and **train** stations are conveniently located just to the northeast of the Planty ring. To reach the *rynek* from either, follow the signs that read *do centrum;* they'll take you to Planty garden. A number of paths and streets cut from there to the square (10min.).

PRACTICAL INFORMATION

Tourist Offices: IT, ul. Pawia 10 (☎422 60 91). Sells the handy *Kraków in Your Pocket* (5zł). Open May-Oct. M-F 8am-6pm, Sa 9am-1pm; Nov.-Apr. M-F 8am-4pm.

Budget Travel: Orbis, Rynek Główny 41 (☎422 40 35; fax 422 28 85). Arranges trips to the Wieliczka and Auschwitz. English spoken. Open Apr.-Oct. M-F 9:30am-6pm, Sa 9am-2pm, Su 10am-2pm; Nov.-Mar. M-F 9am-6pm, Sa 9am-1pm.

Consulates: US, ul. Stolarska 9 (☎429 66 55; after-hours emergency ☎429 66 58). Open M-F 8:30am-4:30pm. Observes American holidays. **UK,** sw. Anny 9, 4th fl. (☎421 70 30). Open M-F 9am-4pm.

Currency Exchange: At *kantory,* Orbis, and hotels. Best rates far from train station.

American Express: Rynek Główny 41 (☎422 91 80), in the Orbis office (see above).

Luggage Storage: Kraków Główny. 1% of luggage value plus 3.90zł per day. Open 24hr.

English Bookstore: Szawal, ul. Długa 1. Open 10am-6pm, Sa 10am-2pm.

Laundromat: Ul. Piastowska 47, on the 1st floor of Hotel Piast. Wash 8zł; dry 8zł. Open M-Sa July-Aug. 8am-8pm; Sept.-June 10am-7pm.

Pharmacy: Apteka Pod Złotym Tygrysem, Szczepańska 1 (☎422 92 93). Open M-F and Su 8am-8pm, Sa 8am-2pm.

Medical Assistance: Medicover, ul. Krótka 1 (☎422 76 33; emergency ☎430 00 34). English-speaking staff. Open M-F 8am-8pm, Sa 9am-2pm.

Telephones: At the post office and opposite the train station, ul. Lubicz 4. Open 24hr.

Internet Access: Available at **Club U Louisa** (see **Entertainment,** p. 751) for 5zł per hr.

Post Office: Ul. Westerplatte 20 (☎422 51 63). *Poste Restante* at counters #1 and 3. Open M-F 7:30am-8:30pm, Sa 9am-2pm, Su 9-11am. Address mail to be held: First name SURNAME, Poste Restante, Kraków 1, **31-045,** Poland.

ACCOMMODATIONS

Call a couple of days ahead in summer. **Waweltur,** ul. Pawia 8, arranges **private rooms.** (☎422 16 40. Open M-F 8am-8pm, Sa 8am-2pm. Singles 75zł; doubles 128zł.) For private rooms, watch for signs or solicitors in the train station.

Schronisko Młodzieżowe (HI), ul. Oleandry 4 (☎633 88 22). Take tram #15 from the train station and get off when the main drag turns into ul. 3-go Maja. Take the 1st right up 3-go Maja. Flexible lock-out 10am-5pm. Curfew midnight. Dorms18-26zł.

Dom Wycieczkowy Pod Sokołem, ul Sokolska 17 (☎292 01 99). Take tram #8 or 10 from the train station toward "Kagiewniki" and get off at the 1st stop after the bridge. Head down the stairs. No curfew. 30zł.

Dom Studentcki Żaczek, ul. 3-go Maja 5 (☎633 54 77), opposite Hotel Cracovia. Take tram #15 to one stop after the museum. Good location, but the nearby disco may keep you up. Singles 60-70zł; doubles 70-110zł; triples 84-135zł.

Strawberry Youth Hostel, ul. Ractawicka 9 (☎636 15 00). Take tram #4, 8, or 13 from the train station to Urzędnicza, continue on foot, and take a right on Wowomiejska. Open July-Aug. 40zł.

Hotel Studentcki Piast, ul. Piastowska 47 (☎637 49 33). Take tram #4 or 12 from the train station to "Wawel." Walk in the direction of the tram to the 1st intersection and turn left. English spoken. Singles 50-85zł; doubles 74-110zł; triples with bath 120zł.

Hotel Mistia, ul. Szlak 73a (☎/fax 633 29 26), on the corner of ul. Warszawska. Cross to Ogrodova and follow it until you reach Warszawska, then take a right. Close to the city center. Breakfast included. Singles 90-130zł; doubles 110-150zł; triples 170zł.

Hotel Bydgoska 19, ul. Bydgoska 19 (☎636 80 00). Take tram #4 or 8 from the train station toward "Os. Bronowice Nowe" and get off at "Biprostal." Take the 1st left on al. Kijowska, walk 2 blocks, then take a right on Misjonarska. All rooms open July-Sept.; a few open year-round. Dorms 22zł; singles 45-90zł; doubles 58-112zł; triples 78-132zł.

FOOD

Many restaurants and cafes are on and around the *rynek*. **Grocery** stores surround the bus and train stations; more can be found near the *rynek*.

Chimera, ul. św. Anny 3. Cellar and ivy garden. The oldest and most famous salad joint in town. Salad 7-10zł. Live music nightly 8pm. Open M-Sa 9am-11pm, Su 9am-10pm.

Camelot, ul. św. Tomasza 17. Cafe popular with students, artists, and foreigners. Adorned with handcrafted wooden dolls and original paintings. Salads 14-18zł. Music or cabaret on W and F at 8pm. Open daily 9am-midnight.

Cafe Zakgtek, Grodzka 2. Great sandwiches (4-6zł) and salads. Breakfast 6zł. Open in summer M-Sa 8:30am-10pm; off season M-Sa 9am-7pm.

Jadłodajnia u Stasi, ul. Mikołajska 16. Famous for traditional Polish food. Open M-F 12:30pm until the food runs out–usually 4-5pm.

Vega Bar Restaurant, ul. św. Gertrudy 7. Elegant vegetarian eatery with dried chilies over the counter and lace-draped pianos. Salads, soups, and creative manipulations of traditional meat-based Polish cuisine (2-5zł). Open daily 9am-10pm.

Balaton, ul. Grodzka 37. Popular. Hungarian. Entrees 10-40zł. Open daily 9am-10pm.

Restauracja Ariel, ul. Szeroka 18 (☎/fax 421 79 20), in the old Jewish district, Kazimierz, 15min. south of the *rynek*. Non-kosher mix of Polish and Jewish cuisine. Music nightly 8pm; cover 20zł. Open daily 9am-midnight.

SIGHTS

At the center of the Stare Miasto spreads **Rynek Główny,** with seas of cafes and bars, not to mention tourists and Poles. The two towers of **St. Mary's Church** (Kościół Mariacki) were built by two brothers with different working styles: one hurried, the other deliberate. The hasty brother realized that the work of his careful sibling would put his own to shame, and killed him in a fit of jealousy. The murder weapon is on display in the Cloth Hall (see below). A trumpet call blares from the towers once in each direction every hour; its abrupt ending recalls the destruction of Kraków in 1241, when the invading Tartars are said to have shot down the trumpeter in the middle of his song. The Baroque interior of the church, with magnificent blues and golds, encases a 500-year-old wooden altarpiece that was dismantled by the Nazis and rediscovered by the Allies at the end of the war. *(At the corner of the rynek closest to the train station. Open daily noon-6pm. Altar 2.50zł, students 1.50zł.)* In the middle of the *rynek*, the yellow Italianate **Cloth Hall** (Sukiennice) houses vendors hawking souvenirs downstairs. Upstairs, in a gallery of the **National Museum** (Muzeum Narodowe), the art's a lot better. *(Open Tu-W and F-Su 10am-3:30pm, Th 10am-6pm. 5zł, students 2.50zł.)* Ul. Floriańska runs from the corner of the *rynek* closest to the train station to the **Barbakan,** the only remnant of the city's medieval fortifications. At the top of the street, **Floriańska Gate** (Brama Floriańska), the old entrance to the city, is the centerpiece of the only surviving remnant of the city wall. Walking down Grodzka from the corner of the *rynek* closest to **Wojciech's Church,** turn right one block down ul. Franciszkańka to the **Franciscan Church** (Kościół Franciszkański), which houses Stanisław Wyspiański's famed *God the Father: Let it Be* stained-glass window. Pope John Paul II resided across the street in the **Bishop's Palace** when he was still Cardinal Karol Wojtyła.

WAWEL CASTLE AND AROUND. **Wawel Castle** (Zamek Wawelski) is one of the finest pieces of architecture in Poland. Begun in the 10th century but remodeled during the 1500s, the castle contains 71 chambers, a magnificent sequence of 16th-century tapestries commissioned by the royal family, and a series of tapestries depicting the story of Noah's Ark, among many other treasures. The castle has been undergoing renovation, but all of the permanent exhibitions are open to the public. *(Castle open Tu and F 9:30am-4:30pm, W-Th 9:30am-3pm, Sa 9:30-3pm, Su 10am-3pm. Royal chambers 12zł, students 7zł; armory and treasury 10zł, students 6zł; W free.)* Next door, in the **Wawel Cathedral** (Katedra Wawelska), the native Krokovian Karol Wojtyła was archbishop before he became Pope. Earlier ages saw Poland's monarchs crowned and buried here. Climb the steep wooden stairs from the church to reach **Sigismund's Bell** (Dzwon Zygmunta). It sounds on major holidays and its tones echo for miles. *(Open May-Sept. M-Sa 9am-5:15pm, Su 12:15-5:15pm; Oct.-Apr. M-Sa 9am-3:15pm, Su 12:15pm-3:15pm. Cathedral free; tombs and bell 6zł, students 3zł.)* The entrance to **Dragon's Cave** (Smocza Jama), legendary dwelling of Kraków's special friend, hides in the complex's southwest corner. *(Open daily May-Sept. 10am-5pm. 2zł.)*

KAZIMIERZ. South of the Stare Miasto lies Kazimierz, for 600 years Kraków's **old Jewish quarter.** On the eve of WWII, 64,000 Jews lived in the Kraków area, many of them in Kazimierz, but Nazi policies forced most out. All were deported by March 1943, many to the nearby Płaszów (where parts of *Schindler's List* were filmed) and Auschwitz-Birkenau concentration camps. Kazimierz today is a focal point for the 5000 Jews living in Poland, and serves as a starting place for those seeking their ancestral roots. *(The walk from the rynek leads down ul. Sienna by St. Mary's Church, and opposite the statue of Adam Mickiewicz; ul. Sienna turns into Starowiślna. After 1km, turn right on Miodowa, then take the 1st left onto Szeroka.)* The tiny **Remuh Synagogue** is surrounded by **Remuh's Cemetery,** one of Poland's oldest Jewish cemeteries, with graves dating back to the plague of 1551-52 and a wall partially constructed from tombstones recovered after Nazi destruction. *(Szeroka 40. Open M-F 9am-4pm. 5zł, students 2zł. Services F dusk and Sa morning.)* Back on Szeroka is **Old Synagogue** (Stara Synagoga), Poland's oldest synagogue, and the one most emblematic of Jewish architecture. It now houses a **museum.** *(Szeroka 24. Open Mar.-Oct. W-Th and Sa-Su 9am-3pm, F 11am-6pm; Nov.-Feb. W-Th 9am-3pm, F 11am-5pm, Sa-Su 9am-4pm. Closed 1st weekend of every month; open the first M of every month. 6zł, students 4zł; W free.)* **The Center for Jewish Culture,** in the former Bene Emenu prayer house, operates a library, supports restoration efforts, and arranges heritage tours. *(Rabina Meiselsa 17, just off Mały Rynek. ☎42 35 58.)*

ENTERTAINMENT

The **Cultural Information Center,** ul. św. Jana 2, sells the comprehensive monthly guide *Karnet* (2zł) and tickets for upcoming events. (☎421 77 87; www.krakow2001.pl. Open M-F 10am-7pm, Sa 11am-7pm.) Festivals abound in Kraków, particularly in summer. Note the **International Short Film Festival** (late May), the **Festival of Jewish Culture** (early June), the **Street Theater Festival** (early July), and the **Jazz Festival** (Oct./Nov.). Classical music buffs will appreciate the regular performances at **Sala Filharmonia** (Philharmonic Hall), ul. Zwierzyniecka 1. (☎429 13 45 and 422 94 77. Box office open M-Th 2-7pm, F 2-7:30pm, Sa-Su 1hr. before performance.) The **opera** performs at the **J. Słowacki Theater,** Plac Św. Ducha 1. (☎422 43 22. Box office open M-Sa 11am-2pm and 3-7pm, Su 2hr. before performance.)

There's almost always good jazz around the *rynek.* **U Louisa,** Rynek Główny 13, draws a diverse crowd with good, loud jazz and blues on weekends. It also has a cybercafe with Internet access. (Beer 4-7.50zł. Cover for shows 5-10zł. Open daily 11am until the last guest leaves.) **Klub Kulturalny,** ul. Szewska 25, is unmarked and hidden below ground, hosting a slightly older crowd. (Beer 5zł. Open M-F noon-2am.) **Piec Art,** ul. Szewska 12, has reasonably priced food, a wide range of beers, and live music. (Beer 5zł. 5zł cover for jazz W at 8pm. Open 3pm until the last guest leaves.) **Free Pub,** ul. Sławkowska 4, is under the archway and down the stairs. It hosts mellow 20- and 30-somethings. (Beer 5zł. Open daily 4pm-late.)

EXCURSIONS FROM KRAKÓW

AUSCHWITZ-BIRKENAU. An estimated 1.5 million people, mostly Jews, were murdered—and thousands more suffered unthinkable horrors—in the Nazi concentration camps at **Auschwitz** (Oświęcim) and **Birkenau** (Brzezinka). The largest and most efficient of the death camps, their names are synonymous with the Nazi killing machine. The smaller **Konzentrationslager Auschwitz I** is located within the limits of the town of Oświęcim; the gates over the camp are inscribed with *Arbeit Macht Frei* (Work Makes You Free). Tours begin at the **museum** at Auschwitz; as you walk past the remnants of thousands of lives—suitcases, shoes, glasses, and more than 100,000 lb. of women's hair—the sheer enormity of the evil committed here comes into focus. There's an English-language **film** shown at 11am and 1pm, shot by the Soviet Army that liberated the camp on January 27, 1945. (Open daily June-Aug. 8am-7pm; May and Sept. 8am-6pm; Apr. and Oct. 8am-5pm; Mar. and Nov. to mid-Dec. 8am-4pm; mid-Dec. to Feb. 8am-3pm. 3½hr. tour in English daily at 11:30am. 20zł including price of film.) The starker and larger **Konzentrationslager Auschwitz II-Birkenau** lies in the countryside 3km from the original camp. A half-hour walk along a well-marked route or a quick **shuttle** ride from the parking lot of the Auschwitz museum (mid-Apr. to Oct., every hr. 11:30am-5:30pm, 1zł) will get you there. Birkenau was built later in the war, when the massive numbers of Jews, Roma, Slavs, homosexuals, disabled people, and other "inferiors" flooding Auschwitz necessitated a more brutally efficient means of killing. The site today is only a small section of the original camp; the remainder was destroyed by retreating Nazis trying to conceal their genocide. The train tracks, reconstructed after the liberation, lead to the ruins of the crematoria and gas chambers, where a memorial pays tribute to all those who died in the Auschwitz system. Near the monument lies a pond, still gray from the ashes deposited there half a century ago; fragments of bone can still be found in the area near the crematoria.

Buses from Kraków's central bus station go to Oświęcim (1½hr., 10 per day, 7zł). The bus back to Kraków leaves from the stop on the other side of the parking lot—go right out of the museum to reach it. Less convenient **trains** leave from Kraków Główny (1¾hr., 3 per day, 8.70zł) and from Kraków Plaszów, south of the town center. Buses #2-5 from the Oświęcim train station then connect to "Muzeum Oświęcim"; or, walk right as you exit the station, walk a block, turn left onto ul. Więźniów Oświęcimia, and walk 1.6km to Auschwitz, on the right.

WIELICZKA. A 1000-year-old **salt mine** sits at ul. Daniłowicza 10 in the tiny town of Wieliczka, 13km southeast of Kraków. Pious Poles carved the immense 20-chapel complex 100m underground entirely out of salt; in 1978, UNESCO declared the mine one of the 12 most priceless monuments in the world. The most spectacular cavern is the 60m by 11m **St. Kinga's Chapel,** complete with salty chandeliers, an altar, and relief works. (☎278 73 02 and 278 73 66; fax 278 73 33. Open daily mid-Apr. to mid-Oct. 7:30am-6:30pm; mid-Oct. to mid-Apr. 8am-4pm. Tours 30zł, students 20zł. English guide June-Aug.) Most of the travel companies, including **Orbis** (see p. 748), organize daily trips to the mines. But the easiest and cheapest way to go is to hop on one of the private **minibuses;** they depart from between the train and bus stations (every 15min., 2zł). Look for minibuses with "Wieliczka" on the door. In Wieliczka, follow the path of the former tracks, then the "*do kopalni*" signs.

ZAKOPANE ☎018

Set in a valley surrounded by jagged Tatran peaks and alpine meadows, Zakopane (ZAH-ko-PAH-neh; pop. 33,000), Poland's premier year-round resort, swells with hikers and skiers during peak seasons (Jan.-Feb. and July-Sept.). They come for the magnificent **Tatran National Park** (Tatrzański Park Narodowy), a terrific venue for outdoor adventure. Entrances to the park lie at the trailheads. (2zł, students 1zł. Keep your ticket.) The bus station (☎201 46 03) is on the corner of ul. Kościuszki and ul. Jagiellońska, across from the train station (☎201 45 04). **Trains** go to

Kraków Głowny (3½hr., 8 per day, 24zł) and Warsaw (8hr., 3 per day, 52zł). **Buses** go to: Kraków (2hr., 22 per day, 12zł); Warsaw (9hr., 1 per day, 48zł); and Poprad, Slovakia (2½hr., 2 per day, 15zł). Walk down ul. Kościuszki to reach the central ul. Krupówki (15min.). The fabulous **Tourist Agency Redykołka,** ul. Kościeliska 1 runs English language tours. (☎/fax 201 32 53. Open May-Oct. M-Sa 9am-5pm, Su 10am-5pm; Nov.-Apr. M-Sa 9am-5pm, Su 1-5pm.) When it's time to crash, look for *pokój*, *noclegi*, or *Zimmer* signs (25-30zł with some haggling). To get to **The Cukiers,** ul. Za Strugiem 10, scenic and convenient for hikers, turn right onto Krupówki, then left onto Kościeliska; ul. Za Strugiem is 10 minutes from the town center on the left. (☎206 66 29. Reserve 3 days in advance. Singles 40zł; doubles 60zł; triples 90zł.) **PTTK Dom Turysty,** ul. Zaruskiego 5, is a large chalet in the center of town. Walk right down ul. Kościuszki from the bus station; it turns into ul. Zaruskiego after the intersection with Krupówki. (☎206 32 07; fax 206 32 84. Reception 24hr. Check out 10am. Dorms 15-45zł.) **Postal code:** 34-500.

HIKING NEAR ZAKOPANE. To start hiking a bit closer to trails than Zakopane, catch a bus or minibus to **Kuźnice** (every 20min., 1.80zł), south of central Zakopane. Or, walk from the train station along ul. Jagiellonska, which becomes ul. Chałubińskiego, then continue down ul. Przewodników Tatrzańskich to catch the 1987m **Kasprowy Wierch** cable car. (Runs daily July-Aug. 7:30am-6:30pm; June and Sept. 7:30am-4pm; Oct. 7:30am-3pm. Round-trip 23zł, students 15zł) Before hiking, pick up the map *Tatrzański Park Narodowy: Mapa turystyczna* at a kiosk or bookstore. The mountain lake **Sea Eye** (Morskie Oko; 1406m) dazzles tourists each summer; take a bus from Zakopane's **bus station** (45min., 11 per day, 3.30zł) to Łysa Polana, or take a minibus (6-10zł) from opposite the bus station to begin the gentle 18km round-trip hike. **Dolina Kościeliska** (full day) offers an easy and lovely hike crossing the valley of Potok Kościeliski. A bus shuttles from Zakopane to Kiry (every 30min., 2zł) and the trailhead. **Valley of the Five Polish Lakes** (Dolina Pięciu Stawów Polskich) is one of the most beautiful hikes (full day; summer only). It starts at Kuźnice and follows the blue trail to Hala Gąsienicowa. After several steep ascents and descents, the blue trail ends at Morskie Oko. From here, it's a paved 9km to Łysa Polana and the bus back to Zakopane. **Mt. Giewont** (1895m; 6hr.) can be seen from most of the town. From Kuźnice, take the blue trail to the summit with the help of a few chains for a view of Zakopane, the Tatras, and Slovakia.

WROCŁAW ☎071

Since Wrocław's elaborate post-war and post-communist reconstructions, only photographs recall its destruction in WWII. Now, the city charms visitors with the antique grace of its many bridges, lush parks, and 19th-century buildings. The heart of the city, **Stare Miasto** (Old Town) centers around **Main Market Square** (Rynek Główny), the Renaissance and Gothic **ratusz** (town hall), and the **History Museum** (Muzeum Historyczne). One exhibit focuses entirely on **ul. Świdnicka,** a central street so beautiful that the Germans tried to have its cobblestones moved to their soil. (Open W-F 10am-4pm, Sa 11am-5pm, Su 10am-6pm. 4zł, students 2zł.) With your back to the town hall, bear left onto Kuźnicza, and turn right onto Kotlarska, which becomes ul. Purkyniego, to find the **Racławice Panorama** and **National Museum.** The enormous Panorama depicts the 18th-century peasant insurrection led by Tadeusz Kosiuszko against the Russian occupation. Audio guides are available in English. (☎344 23 44. Panorama and museum open Tu-Su 9am-4pm. Joint admission 15zł, students 10zł.) With your back to the town hall, bear left and go two blocks on Kuznicza, bear right on Kotlarska, which becomes ul. Purkyniego, turn left over Most Pokuju, and turn left again on Kard B. Kominka to reach pl. Katedralny and the stately **Cathedral of St. John the Baptist** (Katedra św. Jana Chrzciciela) on Cathedral Island (Ośtrów Tunski). Bearing right down Kapitalna brings you to the **Botanical Gardens** (Ogród Botaniczny), ul. Sienkiewicza 23. (Open daily 8am-6pm. 4zł, students 3zł.) The center of Wrocław's cultural life, the **University** (Uniwersytet Wrocławski), pl. Uniwersytecki 1, houses many architectural gems, the most impressive of which is **Aula Leopoldina,** an 18th-century lecture hall with magnificent frescoes. (Open M-Tu and Th-Su 10am-3:30pm. 2.5zł, students 1zł.)

Trains (☎368 83 33) go from Wrocław Głowny, ul. Piłsudskiego 105, to: Poznań (1hr., 21 per day, 27zł); Kraków (4hr., 11 per day, 32zł); Dresden (4½hr., 4 per day, 98zł); Warsaw (5hr., 9 per day, 37zł); Berlin (5½hr., 3 per day, 97zł); Prague (6½hr., 3 per day, 95zł); Budapest (12hr., 1 per day, 177zł); and Moscow (1 per day, 290zł). Buses leave from behind the train station; they are generally slower and more expensive. With your back to the train station, turn left on ul. Piłsudskiego, take your third right on ul. Świdnicka, and go past Kosciuszki pl. over the Podwale river to reach the main market square. **IT,** ul. Rynek 14, can help with rooms. (☎344 31 11; fax 44 29 62. Open in summer M-F 9am-6pm, Sa 9am-4pm; off season M-F 9am-5pm and Sa 10am-2pm.) Surf the **Internet** at **Cyberkawiarnia,** ul. Kuźnicza 29a. (6zł per hr. Open M-Sa 10am-10pm and Su 4-10pm.) The **HI youth hostel,** ul. Kołłątaja 20, is directly opposite the train station on the road perpendicular to ul. Piłsudskiego and is clean, secure-feeling, and spacious. (☎343 88 56. Lockout 10am-5pm. Curfew 10pm. Call ahead. Dorms and doubles 20zł per person.) **Postal code:** 50-900.

PORTUGAL

ESCUDOS

US$1 = 233.18	100$ = US$0.43
CDN$1 = 157.44$	100$ = CDN$0.64
UK£1 = 326.86$	100$ = UK£0.31
IR£1 = 254.56$	100$ = IR£0.39
AUS$1 = 130.40$	100$ = AUS$0.77
NZ$1 = 99.54$	100$ = NZ$1.00
SAR1 = 32.69$	100$ = SAR3.06
EUR€1 = 200.48$	100$ = EUR€0.50

Country code: 351. **International dialing prefix:** 00. There are no city codes in Portugal. From outside Portugal, dial int'l dialing prefix (see inside back cover) + 351 + local number.

In the era of Christopher Columbus, Vasco da Gama, and Magellan, Portugal was one of the world's most powerful nations, ruling a wealthy empire that stretched from America to Asia. Today, it is often overshadowed by its larger neighbor Spain. But while it shares the beaches, nightlife, and strong architectural heritage of the Iberian Peninsula, Portugal is culturally and geographically quite unique. It contains the most pristine wilderness areas in all of Europe and some villages in the northeast have not changed in over 800 years. Despite ongoing modernization in Lisbon and beyond, some of Portugal's age-old and rich traditions seem destined never to change—Porto's wines are as fine as ever, pristine beaches still line the Atlantic seaboard, and the country's loyal people continue to stand proud.

Let's Go: Spain & Portugal 2001 has more info on fabulous, vibrant Portugal.

FACTS AND FIGURES

Official Name: República Portuguesa.

Government: Constitutional Monarchy.

Capital: Lisbon.

Land Area: 92,389 sq. km.

Geography: Varied; miles of coast, dry plains, tall mountains, and fertile valleys.

Climate: Hot and dry May to Oct.; cooler and rainy Nov. to Apr.

Major Cities: Lisbon, Porto.

Population: 9,998,000; urban 36%, rural 64%.

Languages: Portuguese.

Religions: Christian (95%).

Income Per Capita: US$10,160.

Major Exports: Textiles, machinery, grain, and wine.

DISCOVER PORTUGAL

Most grand tours start at vibrant **Porto,** home of port, the strong dessert wine (p. 772). Continue on to the beach of **Figueira da Foz** (p. 772), then head inland for the thriving university town **Coimbra** (p. 770). Next, hit the sights, sounds, and cafes of fascinating **Lisbon** (p. 758). Climb to the castles of nearby **Sintra** (p. 765), then head south to the **Algarve** for wild nightlife, spectacular beaches, and luscious **Lagos** (p. 768). Nearby are **Sagres** (p. 769) and the glorious beach **Praia da Rocha** (p. 769).

ESSENTIALS

WHEN TO GO

Summer is high season, but the southern coast draws tourists March through November. In the off season, many hostels cut their prices by 50% or more, and reservations are seldom necessary. But while Lisbon and some of the larger towns (especially Coimbra, with its university) burst with vitality year-round, many smaller towns virtually shut down, and sights cut their hours nearly everywhere.

DOCUMENTS AND FORMALITIES

Citizens of the US, Canada, the UK, and New Zealand can visit visa-free for up to 90 days. Australian and South African citizens need a visa.

EMBASSIES AND CONSULATES

Australians can use their embassy in **France** (see p. 321); all other embassies are in **Lisbon** (see p. 760). Canada's consulate is in **Faro** and the UK's is in **Porto.**

Portugese Embassies at Home: Australia, 23 Culgoa Circuit, O'Malley, ACT 2603; mailing address P.O. Box 9092, Deakin, ACT 2600 (☎ (02) 62 90 17 33; fax 62 90 19 57); **Canada,** 645 Island Park Dr., Ottawa, ON K1Y 0B8 (☎ (613) 729 08 83; fax 729 42 36); **New Zealand,** refer to Embassy in Australia; **South Africa,** 599 Leyds St., Mucklenuk, Pretoria (☎ (012) 341 23 40; fax 341 39 75); **UK,** 11 Belgrave Sq., London SW1X 8PP (☎ (020) 72 35 53 31; fax 72 45 12 87); **US,** 2125 Kalorama Rd. NW, **Washington, D.C.** 20008 (☎ (202) 328 86 10; fax 462 37 26).

GETTING AROUND

BY PLANE. Most international airlines serve Lisbon; some go to Porto, Faro, and the Madeiras. Portugal's national airline **TAP Air Portugal** (in US and Canada ☎ (800) 221 7370; in UK ☎ (171) 828 20 92; in Lisbon ☎ 218 41 69 90; www.tap.pt) also serves international cities. The smaller **Portugália** (www.pga.pt) flies to Porto, Faro, Lisbon, major Spanish cities, and other Western European destinations. It has offices in Lisbon (☎ 218 42 55 00) and Manchester, UK (☎ (161) 489 50 40).

BY TRAIN. **Caminhos de Ferro Portugueses** is the national railway, but for travel outside of the Braga-Porto-Coimbra-Lisbon line, the bus is much better. Around Lisbon, though, local trains and commuter rails are fast and efficient. When you arrive in town, go to the ticket booth to check the departure schedule; trains often run at irregular hours, and posted schedules *(horarios)* are not always accurate. Unless you have a Eurailpass, the return on round-trip tickets must be used before 3am the following day. Anyone riding without a ticket is fined over 3500$. The Portugal Flexipass is not worth purchasing. **Eurail** is valid in Portugal.

BY BUS. Buses are cheap, frequent, and go to just about every town. **Rodoviária** (☎ 213 54 57 75), the national bus company, has recently been privatized. Each company name corresponds to a particular region, such as **Rodoviária Alentejo** or **Minho e Douro,** with notable exceptions such as **EVA** in the Algarve. There are other private companies, including **Cabanelas, AVIC,** and **Mafrense.** Be wary of stop-happy non-express buses in small regions. *Expressos* (express coach service) between major cities is very good; cheap city buses often run to nearby villages. Schedules are usually posted, but check with the ticket vendor to make sure they're accurate.

BY CAR. Portugal has a particularly high rate of automobile accidents. The highway system (IP) is good, but off the main arteries, the twisting roads are hard to negotiate. Speed limits are basically ignored, recklessness is common, and lighting can be inadequate. In-city parking is difficult. Buy **gas** in super (97 octane), normal (92 octane), or unleaded; prices are high by North American standards—140-170 *escudos* per liter. The national automobile association, the **Automóvel Clube de Portugal (ACP),** R. Rosa Araújo, 42, 1250 Lisbon (☎ 213 18 01 00), provides **breakdown** and **towing service** and 24-hour **first aid.**

BY THUMB: Beach-bound locals occasionally hitch but otherwise stick to buses. Rides are easiest to get between small towns. Best results are reputedly at gas stations by highways and rest stops. *Let's Go* does not recommend hitchhiking.

TOURIST SERVICES AND MONEY

EMERGENCY: Police, ambulance, or **fire:** ☎112

TOURIST OFFICES. The official tourism website is www.portugalinsite.pt. When in Portugal, stop by municipal and provincial tourist offices for maps and advice.

Tourist Boards at Home: Canada, 60 Bloor St. W, #1005, Toronto ON M4W 3B8 (☎(416) 921-7376; fax 921-1353); **Ireland,** 54 Dawson St., Dublin 2 (☎(01) 670 91 33; fax 670 91 41); **South Africa,** Sunnyside Ridge, 4th fl., Sunnyside Dr., Parktown, 2193 Johannesburg (☎(27) 114 84 34 87; fax 114 84 54 16); **UK,** 22-25A Sackville St., 2nd-4th fl., London W1X 2LY (☎(20) 74 94 14 41; fax 20 74 94 18 68); **US,** 590 Fifth Ave, 4th fl., New York, NY 10036-4704 (☎(212) 354 44 03; fax 764 61 37; www.portugal.org). Additional office in Washington, D.C. (☎ (202) 331-8222).

MONEY: The **currency** is the *escudo*, available in coins of 1, 2, 5, 10, 20, 50, 100, 200 and notes of 500, 1000, 2000, 5000, and 10,000. Sleeping in **hostels** and buying groceries can be done for about 5000$, or US$25. A more comfortable day can cost up to 8000 escudos, or US$40. **Tips** are customary only in fancy restaurants or hotels. Some restaurants include a 10% service charge. Taxi drivers only expect a tip after a long trip. **Bargaining** is uncommon, but try it at *mercados* (markets) or when room hunting. **Taxes** are included in all prices and are not redeemable upon departure.

ACCOMMODATIONS AND CAMPING

HOSTELS: Movijovem, Av. Duque de Ávila, 137, 1050 Lisbon (☎213 13 88 20; fax 213 52 14 66), is the Portuguese Hosteling International affiliate. A bed in a *pousada da juventude* (not to be confused with plush *pousadas*) costs 1200-2900$ (breakfast and sheets included). An **HI card** (3000$) is usually mandatory for HI hostels. To reserve a high season bed, get an **International Booking Voucher** from Movijovem (or your HI affiliate) and send it to the desired hostel at least a month in advance.

OTHER OPTIONS. Pensões (or *residencias*), are cheaper than hotels and only slightly more expensive (and much more common) than youth hostels. During the high season, many *pensões* do not take reservations, but for those that do, book a week ahead. **Hotels** tend to be pricey. When business is weak, try bargaining down in advance. **Quartos** are rooms in private residences, similar to Spain's *casas particulares*. These rooms may the only option in smaller towns (particularly in the south) or the cheapest one in bigger cities; tourist offices can usually help you. Prices can drop as much as 500-1000$ with bargaining.

CAMPING: There are over 150 **official campgrounds** *(parques de campismo)* with lots of amenities. Police are strict about illegal camping, so don't try it—especially by official campgrounds. Tourist offices stock the free *Portugal: Camping and Caravan Sites*, an official campgrounds guide. Or, write the **Federação Portuguesa de Campismo e Caravanismo,** Av. 5 de Outubro, 15-3, 950 Lisbon (☎218 12 69 00).

FOOD AND DRINK

Dishes are seasoned with olive oil, garlic, herbs, and sea salt, but few spices. The fish selection includes *chocos grelhados* (grilled cuttlefish), *linguado grelhado* (grilled sole), and *peixe espada* (swordfish). Cheese sandwiches (*sandes*) come on delectable bread. For **dessert,** try *pudim,* or *flan* (caramel custard). The hearty *almoço* (lunch) is eaten between noon and 2pm and *jantar* (dinner) between 8pm and midnight. **Meia dose** (half-portions) are often adequate; full portions may satisfy two. The **prato do dia** (special of the day) or **ementa** (menu) of appetizer, bread, entree, and dessert are filling. **Vinho do porto** (port) is a dessert in itself. **Madeira** wines have a unique "cooked" flavor. Coffees are **bica** (black espresso), **galão** (with milk, served in a glass), and **café com leite** (with milk, served in a cup).

COMMUNICATION

MAIL: **Air mail** *(via aerea)* takes a week within Europe, at least 10 days to reach the US or Canada, and over 2 weeks to reach Australia, New Zealand, and South Africa. **Registered** or **blue mail** and **EMS** (Express Mail) arrive more quickly but cost more. **Stamps** are available at post offices *(correios)* and stamp machines.

TELEPHONES: Phones accept **phone cards.** For the **Credifone** and **Telecom Portugal** systems, local calls cost 18$. Use a **calling card** for international calls. International direct dial numbers include: **AT&T,** ☎0800 80 01 28; **Sprint,** ☎800 800 187; **MCI World-Phone Direct,** ☎800 800 123; **Canada Direct,** ☎800 800 122; **BT Direct,** ☎800 800 440; **Eircom,** ☎800 800 353; **Australia Direct,** ☎800 800 610; **Telecom New Zealand Direct,** ☎800 800 640; and **Telkom South Africa Direct,** ☎800 800 270.

HOLIDAYS AND FESTIVALS

Holidays: New Year's (Jan. 1); Good Friday (Apr. 13); Liberation Day (Apr. 25); Labor Day (May 1); Corpus Christi (June 14) Assumption Day (Aug. 15); Republic Day (Oct. 5); All Saints Day (Nov. 1); Restoration of Independence (Dec. 1); Feast of the Immaculate Conception (Dec. 8); Christmas Eve (Dec. 24); Christmas (Dec. 25).

Festivals: All of Portugal will celebrate **Carnival** in mid-March and the **Holy Week** in mid-April. Coimbra holds the **Burning of the Ribbons** festival in early May, and Lisbon hosts the **Feira Internacional de Lisboa** in June. Coimbra's **Feira Popular** takes place the second week of July. For more info on Portuguese festivals, see www.portugal.org.

LISBON (LISBOA)

Lisbon, once the center of the world's richest and farthest-reaching empire, has overcome its social and political problems to reclaim its place as one of Europe's grandest cities. It has preserved tradition by renovating historic monuments and meticulously maintaining its black-and-white mosaic sidewalks, pastel facades, and medieval alleys. The 1998 World Expo sparked massive construction and a city-wide face-lift, while helping boost Lisbon to the forefront of European culture.

GETTING THERE AND GETTING AROUND

Flights: Aeroporto de Lisboa (☎218 41 37 00), on the city's northern edge. **Buses** #44 and 45 (20-40min., 165$) or the express **AeroBus** #91 (15min., every 20min., 460$) go to Pr. Restauradores from outside the terminal, to the right of where the road curves. A **taxi** to downtown costs about 2000$, plus a 300$ luggage fee.

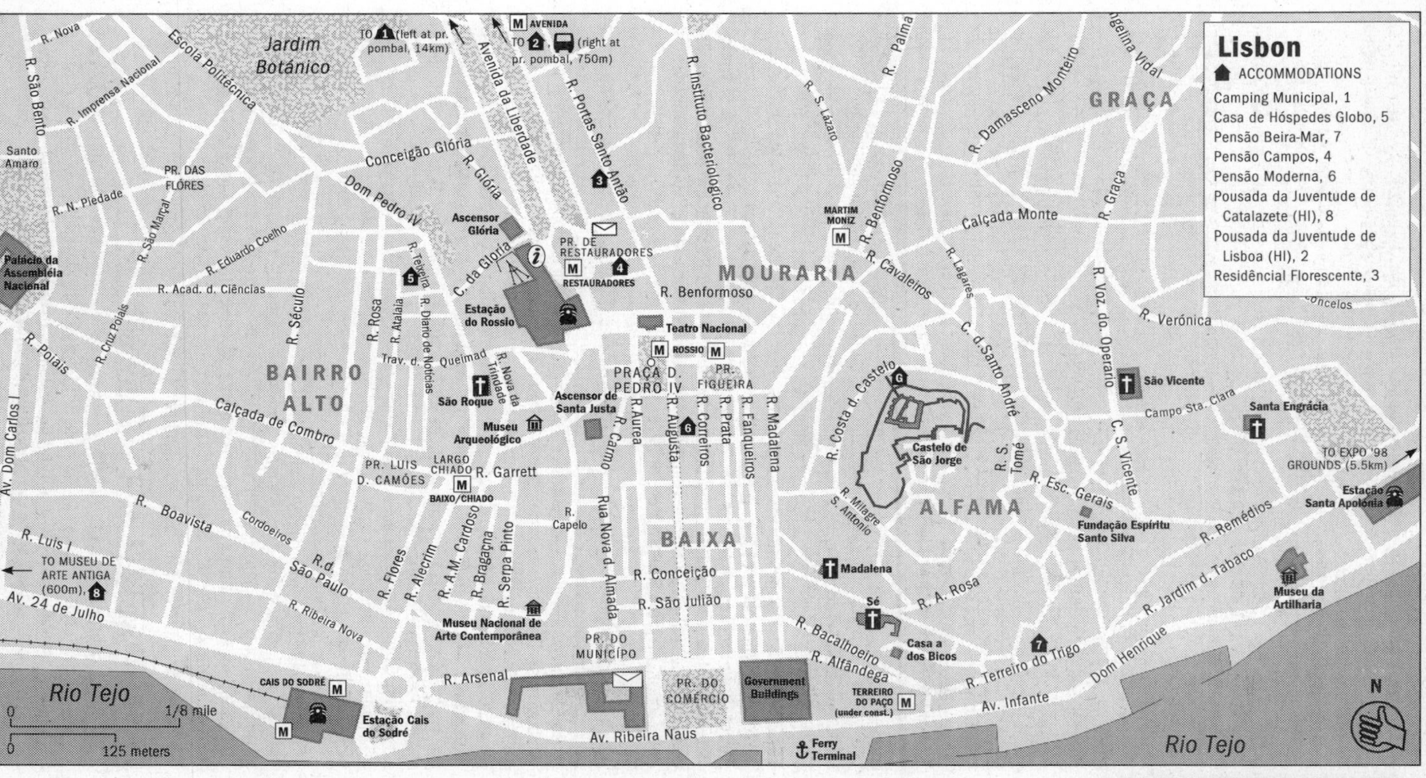

Lisbon
ACCOMMODATIONS
Camping Municipal, 1
Casa de Hóspedes Globo, 5
Pensão Beira-Mar, 7
Pensão Campos, 4
Pensão Moderna, 6
Pousada da Juventude de Catalazete (HI), 8
Pousada da Juventude de Lisboa (HI), 2
Residêncial Florescente, 3
R. Nova
R. São Bento
Jardim Botânico
TO 1 (left at pr. pombal, 14km)
AVENIDA
TO 2 (right at pr. pombal, 750m)
Escola Politécnica
R. Imprensa Nacional
Avenida da Liberdade
R. Portas Santo Antão
R. Instituto Bacteriologico
R. S. Lázaro
R. Palma
R. Damasceno Monteiro
GRAÇA
Santo Amaro
PR. DAS FLÓRES
R. N. Piedade
Conceigão Glória
R. Glória
Dom Pedro IV
R. São Marçal
R. Eduardo Coelho
Palácio da Assembléia Nacional
R. Acad. d. Ciências
Ascensor Glória
C. da Glória
PR. DE RESTAURADORES
RESTAURADORES
MARTIM MONIZ
R. Benformoso
Calçada Monte
R. Graça
MOURARIA
R. Cavaleiros
R. Lagares
R. Voz. do. Operario
R. Verónica
R. Teixeira
Estação do Rossio
R. Benformoso
Teatro Nacional
ROSSIO
R. Século
R. Rosa
R. Atalaia
R. Diario de Notícias
R. Cruz Poiais
R. Poiais
Trav. d. Queimad
R. Nova da Trindade
PRAÇA D. PEDRO IV
PR. FIGUEIRA
R. Costa d. Castelo
C. d.Santo André
São Vicente
Campo Sta. Clara
Santa Engrácia
BAIRRO ALTO
São Roque
Ascensor de Santa Justa
Calçada de Combro
Museu Arqueológico
R. Carmo
R.Aurea
R. Augusta
R. Correiros
R. Prata
R. Fanqueiros
R. Madalena
Castelo de São Jorge
R. S. Tomé
C. S. Vicente
TO EXPO '98 GROUNDS (5.5km)
Av. Dom Carlos I
PR. LUIS D. CAMÕES
LARGO CHIADO
R. Garrett
BAIXO/CHIADO
R. Esc. Gerais
Estação Santa Apolónia
R. Boavista
Cordoeiros
R. Capelo
R. Milagre S. Antonio
ALFAMA
Fundação Espíritu Santo Silva
R. Remédios
R. Luis I
TO MUSEU DE ARTE ANTIGA (600m), 8
R.d. São Paulo
R. Flores
R. Alecrim
R. A.M. Cardoso
R. Bragaçna
R. Serpa Pinto
Rua Nova d. Almada
BAIXA
R. Conceição
R. São Julião
Madalena
R. Jardim d. Tabaco
Museu da Artilharia
Av. 24 de Julho
R. Ribeira Nova
Museu Nacional de Arte Contemporânea
PR. DO MUNICÍPIO
Sé
R. A. Rosa
R. Bacalhoeiro
R. Alfândega
Casa a dos Bicos
R. Terreiro do Trigo
Dom Henrique
Rio Tejo
CAIS DO SODRÉ
R. Arsenal
PR. DO COMÉRCIO
Government Buildings
TERREIRO DO PAÇO (under const.)
Av. Infante
N
0
1/8 mile
125 meters
Estação Cais do Sodré
Av. Ribeira Naus
Ferry Terminal
Rio Tejo

Trains: Caminhos de Ferro Portuguêses (☎218 88 40 25 or 213 46 50 22; www.cp.pt). Five main stations, each serving different destinations. Portuguese trains are usually quite slow; buses are often a better choice.

Estação Santa Apolónia, on Av. Infante D. Henrique, east of the Alfama on the Rio Tejo, runs the international, northern, and eastern lines. Take bus #9, 39, or 46 to Pr. Restauradores and Estação Rossio. To: **Coimbra** (2½hr., 7 per day 8:05am-8:05pm, 1510-2700$); **Porto** (4½hr., 12 per day 7:55am-8:05pm, 2080-3700$); **Madrid** (10hr., 1 per day 10:05pm, 8200$); and **Paris** (21hr., 1 per day 6:05pm, 29,000$).

Estação Barreiro, across the Rio Tejo, goes south. Station accessible by ferry (included in train ticket) from the Terreiro do Paço dock off Pr. Comércio (30 min., every 30min.). To: **Évora** (2½hr., 7 per day 6:50am-11:50pm, 1200$); and **Lagos** (5½hr., 5 per day 7:35am-7:45pm, 2800$).

Estação Rossio, between Pr. Restauradores and Pr. Dom Pedro IV (Rossio), serves points west. M: Rossio or Restauradores. To **Sintra** (45min., every 10min. 6am-2am, 210$).

Estação Cais do Sodré, to the right of Pr. Comércio when walking from Baixa. M: Cais do Sodré. To **Belém** (10min., every 15min. 5:30am-2:50am, 140$).

Buses: Arco do Cego, on Av. João Crisóstomo. M: Saldanha; exit on Av. República, walk 1 block from the *praça*, turn right on Av. Dunque de Ávila, and right before the McDonald's. "Saldanha" buses (#36, 44, and 45) stop in the *praça* (165$). **Rede Expressos** (☎213 54 54 39) to: **Coimbra** (2½hr., 16 per day, 1500$); **Évora** (2hr., 13 per day, 1500$); **Porto** (4hr., 7 per day, 2300$); and **Lagos** (5hr., 9 per day, 2500$).

Public Transit: CARRIS (☎213 61 30 00) operates **buses, trams,** and **funiculars** (each 165$); *passe turistico* (tourist pass) good for unlimited CARRIS travel. 1-, 3-, 4-, and 7-day passes (460$, 1080$, 1760$, 2490$). The **Metro** (☎21 355 84 57) runs daily 6am-1am, though some stations close early (100$ per ride, 10 tickets 850$).

Taxis: Rádio Táxis de Lisboa (☎218 11 90 00), **Autocoope** (☎217 93 27 56), and **Teletáxi** (☎21 811 90 00) cluster along Av. Liberdade and Rossio. Luggage 300$.

ORIENTATION AND PRACTICAL INFORMATION

The center is the **Baixa,** the old business area, between the **Bairro Alto** and the **Alfama.** The Baixa's grid of mostly pedestrian streets is bordered to the north by Rossio (a.k.a. Praça Dom Pedro IV), adjacent to Praça da Figueira and Praça dos Restauradores (where airport buses stop and the tourist office is located); Av. da Liberdade runs north, uphill from Pr. Restauradores. At the Baixa's southern end is the **Praça do Comércio,** on the **Rio Tejo** (River Tagus). Along the river are the Expo '98 grounds, now called the **Parque das Nações** (Park of Nations), and the fast-growing **Alcantara** and **Docas** (docks) regions. **Alfama,** is the city's oldest district, a labyrinth of narrow alleys and stairways beneath the Castelo de São Jorge. Across the Baixa from Alfama is **Bairro Alto,** and its upscale shopping district, the **Chiado,** which is traversed by R. do Carmo and R. Garrett, where much of the city's nightlife is located.

TOURIST, FINANCIAL, AND LOCAL SERVICES

Tourist Office: Palácio da Foz (☎213 46 63 07), on Pr. Restauradores. M: Restauradores. Bus schedules, room listings, and free map. English spoken. Open daily 9am-8pm. **Branch** at the airport (☎218 49 43 23). Open daily 6am-2am.

Embassies: Canada, Av. Liberdade, 196-200, 3rd fl. (☎213 16 46 00; fax 213 16 46 91); **Ireland,** R. Imprensa à Estrela, 4th fl. (☎213 92 94 40; fax 213 97 73 63); **New Zealand,** Av. Antonio Agusto Aguiar, 122, 9th fl. (☎213 50 96 90; fax 213 47 20 04); **South Africa,** Av. Luis Bivar, 10 (☎213 53 50 41; fax 213 53 57 13); **UK,** R. São Bernardo, 33 (☎213 92 40 00; fax 213 92 41 85); **US,** Av. das Forças Armadas (☎217 26 91 09; fax 217 27 91 09).

American Express: Top Tours, Av. Duque de Loulé 108 (☎213 19 42 90). M: Marquês de Pombal; walk up Av. Liberdade toward the Marquês de Pombal statue and turn right. English spoken. Open M-F 9:30am-1pm and 2:30-6:30pm.

Luggage Storage: Estação Rossio, between Pr. Restauradores and Pr. Dom Pedro IV (Rossio). M: Rossio. Lockers 550$ per 48hr. Open daily 8:30am-11:30pm.

English Bookstore: Livraria Británica, R. Luis Fernandes 14-16 (☎213 42 84 72), in the Bairro Alto. Walk up R. São Pedro de Alcântara and go straight as it becomes R.

Dom Pedro V and then R. Escola Politécnica. Turn left on R. São Marcal, then right after 2 blocks onto R. Luis Fernandes. Open M-F 9:30am-7pm.

Laundromat: Lavatax, R. Francisco Sanches 65A (☎218 12 33 92). M: Arroios. Wash, dry, and fold 1100$ per 5kg. Open M-F 8:30am-1pm and 3-7pm, Sa 8:30am-1pm.

EMERGENCY AND COMMUNICATIONS

Emergency: ☎112. **Police:** R. Capelo, 3 (☎213 46 61 41). English spoken.

Pharmacy: ☎118. Night pharmacy info is posted on pharmacy doors.

Medical Assistance: British Hospital, R. Saraiva de Carvalho, 49 (☎213 95 50 67).

Post Office: Main office on Pr. Comércio. Open M-F 8:30am-6:30pm. **Branch** in Pr. Restauradores. Open M-F 8am-10pm, Sa-Su 9am-6pm. Address mail to be held: First name SURNAME, *Posta Restante,* Praça do Comércio, **1100** Lisbon, Portugal.

Internet Access: Web Café, R. Diário de Notícias, 126 (☎213 42 11 81). 300$ per 15min., 800$ per hr. Open daily 4pm-2am.

Telephones: Portugal Telecom, Pr. Dom Pedro IV, 68. M: Rossio. Open daily 8am-11pm. **Phone cards** come in 50 units (650$), 100 units (1300$), or 150 units (1900$). Buy them here or at bookstores and stationery stores.

ACCOMMODATIONS AND CAMPING

Expect to pay 3000-5000$ for a single, 5000-9000$ for a double; when in doubt, ask for a price list. During low or mid season prices generally drop—try bargaining the price down then. If you're dissatisfied, ask the owner for a *livro de reclamações* (complaints book)—they are required to give these to the tourist bureau. Most hotels are in the town center on **Av. Liberdade,** while in the **Baixa** budget *pensões* line the **Rossio** and **R. Prata, R. Correeiros,** and **R. Ouro.** Lodgings in the steep streets of **Alfama** or nightlife hot-spot **Bairro Alto** are closer to sights. If more central accommodations are full, head east along **Av. Almirante Reis.** Youth hostels are inconveniently located but super cheap, and have no curfew or lockout. At night, be careful in the Bairro Alto, the Alfama, and the Baixa; many streets are empty and poorly lit.

Residencial Estrela do Mondego, Calçada do Carmo, 25, 2nd fl. (☎213 24 08 40), in the **Baixa,** next to the Estação Rossio. Large, comfy rooms with phones, cable TV, and A/C. English spoken. Laundry 1500$. Singles with bath 5000$; doubles 6000-6500$; triples with bath 7000$; quads with bath 8000$.

Residencial Duas Nações, R. Vitória, 41 (☎213 46 07 10; fax 213 47 02 06), by R. Augusta, 2 blocks from M: Baixa-Chiado. Rooms at an affordable price. Breakfast included. English spoken. In summer, reserve a week ahead. With *Let's Go,* singles 3500$, with bath 6000$; doubles 4500$, 7500$; triples with bath 9000$.

Casa de Hóspedes Globo, R. Teixeira, 37 (☎/fax 213 46 22 79), in **Bairro Alto.** Take the funicular from Pr. Restauradores to the Parque São Pedro de Alcântra; from the park entrance, cross the street and turn right on R. Teixeira. Safe, convenient, and nice. English spoken. Reserve ahead. Singles 2500-4500; doubles 6000$; triples 6500$.

Pensão Campos, R. Jardim do Regedor, 24, 3rd fl. (☎213 46 28 64), in the **Baixa.** M: Restauradores. Between Pr. Restauradores and R. Portas de Santo Antão. Cozy rooms in a lively locale. Laundry 1500$. Singles 4000$; doubles 6000-7000$; triples 7000$.

Residencial Florescente, R. Portas de Santo Antão 99 (☎213 42 66 09; fax 213 42 77 33), in the **Baixa.** A block from Pr. Restauradores. Luxurious, with incredible views of Pr. Figueira. Laundry. Reserve 2 weeks ahead in summer. Singles 5000$, with bath 7000$; doubles 6000-8000$; triples 8000-12000$.

Pensão Ninho das Águias, R. Costa do Castelo, 74 (☎218 86 70 08), in the **Alfama.** From Pr. Figueira, take R. Madalena to Largo Adelino Costa and head up to R. Costa do Castelo. The spectacular views are worth the hike. Breakfast included. Reserve ahead. Singles 5000$; doubles 7500-8000$; triples 10,000$.

Pousada da Juventude de Lisboa (HI), R. Andrade Corvo, 46 (☎213 53 26 96; fax 213 53 75 41). M: Picoas; turn right and walk 1 block. Huge, ultra-clean, but inconvenient. Breakfast included. Lockers 300$. Reception 8am-midnight. Check-out 10:30am. Members only. June-Sept. dorms 2900$; doubles 6500$; Oct.-May 2000$, 5000$.

TASTES LIKE CHICKEN A few days in Portugal and you'll notice a national rooster obsession. A very special rooster, that is—*o galo de Barcelos* (the cock of Barcelos). This particular animal, with flowers and hearts on its wings and tail, may seem like a psychedelic symbol of sorts, but it actually serves an altogether nobler cause. Once upon a time in the sleepy town of Barcelos, an innocent man was condemned to die for a crime he didn't commit. As his last wish he asked to have dinner with the judge so that he could try one last time to prove his innocence. The judge, who was having roast chicken for dinner that night, obliged. When the man saw the chicken at dinner, he blurted out that the cock would crow to prove his innocence. And sure enough the *galo* did—or so the story goes—forever securing itself a special place in Portuguese folklore as a symbol of truth, justice and faith. A superhero of sorts.

Pousada da Juventude de Parque das Nações, R. de Moscavide, lote 4-71-01 (☎218 92 08 90; fax 218 92 08 91). M: Oriente. Go left from the station on Av. Dom João II, walking past the Park of Nations to R. de Moscavide. Internet. Breakfast included. Reception 8am-midnight. Wheelchair accessible. Reserve 1 week ahead in summer. June-Sept. dorms 2100$; doubles 5100$. Oct.-May dorms 1700$; doubles 4300$.

Parque de Campismo Municipal de Lisboa (☎217 60 20 61), on the road to Benfica. Take bus #43 from Rossio to the Parque Florestal Monsanto. Reception 9am-9pm. July-Aug. 840$ per person, 840$ per tent, 540$ per car; May-June and Sept. 760$, 750$, 480$; Oct.-Apr. 600$, 600$, 380$.

FOOD

Top off a *prato do dia* (daily special) with a scrumptious pastry from a *pastelaria*. The **Baixa** by the port, the area near the **Alfama,** and the **Bairro Alto** have cheap dining options. Specialties include *bacalhau cozido com grão e batatas* (cod, chickpeas, and potatoes). **Supermercado Celeiro,** R. 1 de Dezembro, 73, is near the Estação Rossio. (Open M-F 9am-8pm, Sa 9am-7pm.) **Mercado Ribeira** is an open-air market just outside Estação Cais do Sodré. (Take bus #40 or tram #15. Open M-Sa 6am-2pm.)

Hell's Kitchen, R. Atalaia, 176, in the **Bairro Alto.** From Pr. Restauradores, walk uphill on C. Glória to the top and go right on R. Atalaia. Heavenly hummus with pita 450$. Falafel and salad 1100$. Open Tu-Su 8pm-12:30am.

Casa da Té, R. D. Pedro V, 63, just past Parque de São Pedro de Alcântara in the **Bairro Alto,** near the corner of R. da Rosa. Tiny budget gold mine. Takeout available; perfect for park picnics. Entrees 750-900$. Open 8am-8pm.

Celeiro, R. 1 de Dezembro, 51. Take the 1st right off Estação Rossio and go 2 blocks. Seatless macrobiotic restaurant pleases vegetarians and meat-eaters alike with its creative and appetizing menu. Entrees 350-730$. Open M-F 9am-8pm, Sa 9am-6pm.

Restaurante Calcuta, R. do Norte, 17, near Lg. Camões in the **Bairro Alto.** Fancy but inexpensive selection of Indian dishes. Vegetarian entrees (rare in Portugal) 900-1000$. Meat entrees 1200-1600$. Open daily noon-3pm and 6:30-11pm.

Lua de Mel, R. da Prata, 242, on the corner of R. Santa Justa in the **Baixa.** Diner-style pastry shop. Pastries 110-160$. Open M-F 7am-9pm, Sa 7am-7pm.

SIGHTS

THE BAIXA. Start at Lisbon's heart—the **Rossio** (also known as the **Praça Dom Pedro IV**). Once a cattle market, the site of public executions, a bullfighting arena, and a carnival ground, the *praça* is now the domain of drink-sipping tourists and heart-stopping traffic whizzing around a statue of Dom Pedro IV. Past the train station, an obelisk and a sculpture of the "Spirit of Independence" in the **Praça dos Restauradores** commemorate Portugal's independence from Spain in 1640. The *praça* is the start of **Avenida da Liberdade,** Lisbon's most imposing, elegant promenade. Modeled after the wide boulevards of 19th-century Paris, this shady mile-long thoroughfare ends at **Praça do Marquês do Pombal**. On the other side of the Rossio from Pr. Restauradores, the **Baixa's** grid of pedestrian streets with wide mosaic sidewalks invites wandering. From the Baixa, all roads lead to **Praça do Comércio,** on the banks of the Rio Tejo, where several government ministries are housed.

BAIRRO ALTO. From the Baixa, walk uphill to the *bairro* or take the historic **Ascensor de Santa Justa,** a 1902 elevator in a Gothic wrought-iron tower. From the upper terrace, a narrow walkway leads under a huge flying buttress to the 14th-century **Igreja do Carmo,** whose roof was destroyed in the 1755 earthquake but whose dramatic Gothic arches remain. *(Elevator runs M-F 7am-11pm, Sa-Su 9am-11pm. 165$ one-way. Walkway usually open 7am-6pm. 100$.)* At the center of the **Chiado,** Biarro Alto's chic shopping neighborhood, Praça Camões joins Largo Chiado at the top of R. Garrett. To reach R. Garrett, turn left from the elevator, walk 1 block, and it's on the right. Half-mad Maria I, desiring a male heir, made fervent religious vows promising God anything if she were granted a son. When she bore a baby boy, she built the exquisitely ornate **Basílica da Estrêla.** *(On Pr. Estrêla. Take tram #28 from Pr. Comércio (165$). Open daily 8am-12:30pm and 3-7:30pm. Free.)* For a perfect picnic, walk up R. Misericórdia to the shady **Parque de São Pedro de Alcântara.** The European paintings at the **Museu Nacional de Arte Antiga** date to the 12th century. *(R. Janelas Verdes, Jardim 9 Abril. Walk 30min. down Av. Infante Santo from the Ascensor de Santa Justa. Buses #40 and 60 stop to the right of the museum exit and then head back to the Baixa. Open Tu 2-6pm, W-Su 10am-6pm. 600$, students 300$. Free Su before 2pm.)*

ALFAMA. Lisbon's medieval quarter slopes in tiers from the **Castelo de São Jorge,** facing the Rio Tejo. Between the Alfama and the Baixa is the **Mouraria** (Moorish quarter), established after the Crusaders expelled the Moors in 1147. Scenic **tram** #28 (165$) passes most sights; walking is the best way to navigate the neighborhood, but be careful of muggers. From Pr. Comércio, follow R. Alfandega two blocks, climb up R. Madalena, turn right after the church on Largo Madalena, follow R. Santo António da Sé, and follow the tram tracks to the richly ornamented 1812 **Igreja de Santo António da Sé.** *(Open daily 8am-7pm. Mass daily 11am, 5pm, and 7pm.)* Follow yellow signs to a spectacular ocean view from the top of the Alfama to the fifth-century **Castelo de São Jorge,** a Visigoth castle expanded by the Moors. *(Open daily Apr.-Sept. 9am-9pm; Oct.-Mar. 9am-7pm. Free.)*

SALDANHA. Lisbon's business center, this modern district has two excellent museums, both owned by the Fundação Gulbenkian. The **Museu Calouste Gulbenkian** houses oil tycoon Calouste Gulbenkian's collection, including an extensive array of ancient art as well as more modern European pieces. *(Av. Berna 45. M: Palhavã or S. Sebastião. Bus #16, 31, or 46. Open Tu-Su 10am-5pm. 500$, students and seniors Su morning free.)* The adjacent **Museu do Centro de Arte Moderna** has a sizable modern art collection, as well as beautiful gardens. *(On R. Dr. Nicolau Bettencourt. Open Tu-Su 10am-5pm. 500$, students and seniors Su morning free.)*

BELÉM. A pseudo-suburb of Lisbon, Belém showcases the opulence and extravagance of the Portuguese empire with well-maintained museums and historical sites. Take tram #15 from Pr. Comércio (20min., 165$), bus #28 or 43 from Pr. Figueira (20min., 165$), or the train from Estação Cais do Sodré (10min., every 15min., 140$). From the train station, cross the tracks and the street, then go left. The **Mosteiro dos Jerónimos,** on the banks of the Tejo, is to the right walking from the train station, through the public gardens. King Dom Manuel I established the monastery in 1502 to give thanks for Vasco da Gama's successful Indian voyage. *(Open Tu-Su 10am-5pm. 600$, students 300$. Cloisters open Tu-Su 10am-5pm. Free.)* Take the underpass beneath the highway to the **Torre de Belém** (10min.), with its panoramic views of Belém, the Tejo, and the Atlantic beyond. Surrounded by the ocean due to the receding shoreline, it's only accessible by a small bridge. *(Open Tu-Su 10am-6pm. 600$, students and seniors 300$.)* Do not leave Belém without trying the heavenly *pastéis de Belém* at **Pastéis de Belém,** R. Belém 84-92 (130-250$).

PARQUE DAS NAÇÕES (PARK OF NATIONS). The government took a chance on the former Expo '98 grounds, spending millions to convert it into the **Parque**

das Nações. The gamble paid off—the futuristic park is constantly packed. Take M: Oriente and enter through the **Centro Vasco de Gama** shopping mall to the center of the grounds. The biggest attraction is the **Pavilhão dos Oceanos**, the largest oceanarium in Europe. The 145m **Torre Vasco de Gama** offers spectacular views of the city. A **teleférico** (gondola) connects the two ends of the park. *(Shopping mall open daily 10am-midnight. Oceanarium open daily Apr.-Sept. 10am-7pm, Oct.-Mar. 10am-6pm. 1700$, under 18 or 65+ 900$. Torre open daily 10am-8pm; 500$, under 18 or 65+ 250$. Teleférico open M-F 11am-8pm, Sa-Su 10am-9pm; 500$, under 18 or 65+ 250$.)*

ENTERTAINMENT

Agenda Cultural and *Follow Me Lisboa*, free at kiosks in the Rossio, on R. Portas de Santo Antão, and at the tourist office, have info on arts events and bullfights. Lisbon's trademark is *fado*, an art combining singing and narrative poetry; *fadistas'* wailing expresses *saudade* (nostalgia and yearning). Listeners feel a "knife turning in their hearts." The Bairro Alto has many *fado* joints off R. Misericórdia and on streets by the Museu de São Roque; the prices alone may turn a knife in your heart. Various bars offer free performances. **Adega Machado,** R. Norte 91, draws locals as well as tourists. (Minimum consumption 2900$. Open Tu-Su 8pm-3am.) The famed 19th-century cafe **A Brasileira,** R. Garrett 120-122, is in the Bairro Alto's stylish Chiado neighborhood. (Coffee 80-300$. Mixed drinks 650-900$. Open daily 8pm-2am.) **Costa do Castelo,** Calçada Marquês de Tancos, 1-1B, just behind the Castelo in Alfama, is a small, self-consciously trendy bar/cafe with outdoor patio. (Sandwiches from 250$. Mixed drinks 300-700$. Open Tu-Su 12:30pm-2am.)

NIGHTLIFE

You can't go wrong along the **Bairro Alto's** R. Norte, R. Diario Notícias, and R. Atalaia, where small clubs and bars are packed into three short blocks, making club-hopping easy. The **Rato** area near the edge of Bairro Alto has a number of gay and lesbian clubs; also stop by the trendy places on **Av. 24 de Julho.** A recent in-spot is the revamped **Docas de Santo Amaro,** a strip of waterfront bars and clubs. It's best to cab it late at night. Dress to impress and come fashionably late (after 2am).

Memorial, R. Gustavo de Matos Sequeira 42A, one block from R. Escola Politécnica in the Bairro Alto. This lesbian disco-bar mixes all ages and orientations. 1000$; includes 2 beers or 1 mixed drink. Open Tu-Su 11pm-4am.

Trumps, R. Imprensa Nacional, 104B. Shirtless muscle boys bump and grind. Cover 1000$, minimum consumption 2000$. Open Tu-Su 11:30pm-6am.

Divina Comida, Largo Santa Martinho, 6-7, in the Alfama, is a bar that lives up to its name. Open M-Th 12:30pm-2am, F-Sa 12:30pm-3am.

Havana, Armazem 5. A crowded palm-treed club on the Docas de Santo Amaro. Beer 400$; mixed drinks 900$. Open M-Sa noon-4am; disco open M-Sa 11pm-4am.

Celtas & Iberos Irish Pub, Armazem 7. Guinness 600$. Open Tu-Su 12:30-3am.

Cosmos, Doca de Santo Amaro, Armazem. Torches, a patio, and techno welcome a crowd of twenty-somethings. Cover (2000$) includes four beers or two mixed drinks.

Salsa Latina, at the Gare Marítima de Alcântara. Live salsa swivels its hips. Beer 500$; mixed drinks 1000$. Open M-Th 8-11pm, F-Sa 8pm-1:30am.

EXCURSIONS FROM LISBON

ESTORIL AND CASCAIS. Glorious beaches draw sun-loving tourists and locals alike to Estoril and neighboring Cascais. For the beach-weary, the air conditioning of **Casino Estoril,** Europe's largest casino, is a welcome relief, and one can't help but marvel at the gaming palace. (☎214 66 77 00. Open daily 3pm-3am. No swim-wear, jeans, or shorts. 18+ for the slots, 21+ for the game room. Bring your passport.)

Trains from Lisbon's Estação do Sodré runs to Estoril (30min., about every 20min., 210$) and on to Cascais (also a pleasant 20min. seaside stroll along the

THE MAN WHO WOULD BE KING Although Portugal's chances of returning to a monarchy are slim, if it did, the Portuguese know who'd be king. He is Dom Duarte, a direct descendant of the royal crown. If you met him on the street in his home of Sintra (near his ancestor's castle), you would not recognize his royal heritage. A whiskered man with a round tummy, Duarte has a jovial disposition, a degree in engineering, and a great love for the people. In 1995, his popularity soared when he married Isabel, a young Spanish (!) noblewoman, 22 years his junior. It was once forbidden for a Portuguese monarch to marry any Spaniard, but this wedding was cheerfully applauded nationwide. Their eldest child, Afonso, is an adorable blond youth named for Portugal's first king. Afonso is said to have inherited his namesake's best traits; unfortunately, he will likely have to apply them in some other fashion.

promenade from Estoril). **Bus** #418 to Sintra departs from Av. Marginal, down the street from the train station (40min., every hr., 440$). From the station, cross Av. Marginal and head to the Estoril **tourist office** (left of the Casino on Arcadas do Parque) for a free map of both towns. (☎214 66 38 13. Open M-Sa 9am-7pm, Su 10am-6pm). Ask for help finding a room (from 5000$) at the Cascais **tourist office,** Av. dos Combatentes da Grande Guerra, 25. From the Cascais train station, cross the square and take a right onto Av. Valbom. Look for a small sign at Av. Combatantes. (☎214 86 82 04. Open July-Sept. 15 M-Sa 9am-8pm, Su 10am-6pm; Sept. 16-June M-Sa 9am-7pm, Su 10am-6pm).

SINTRA. With fairy-tale castles, enchanting gardens, and spectacular mountain vistas, Sintra (pop. 20,000) is a favorite among tour groups and backpackers alike. A mix of Moorish, Gothic, and Manueline styles, the **Palácio Nacional de Sintra,** in Pr. República, once was the summer residence of Moorish sultans and their harems. (☎219 10 68 40. Open Th-Tu 10am-5:30pm; closed on bank holidays. Buy tickets by 5pm. 600$, students 300$.) Perched on the mountain overlooking the old town, the **Castelo dos Mouros** provides stunning views of the mountains and coast. (Follow the blue signs 3km up the mountain or take bus #434, which runs to the top from the tourist office; 15min., every 30min., day-pass 600$. Castle open 10am-6pm. Free.) Farther uphill is the **Palácio Nacional da Pena**. With Arabic minarets and Russian onion domes, it looks like it belongs in Disney World. (Open Tu-Su July-Sept. 10am-6:30pm; Oct.-June 2-4:30pm. Mar.-Sept. 600$, students 400$; Oct.-Apr. 200$.)

Trains (☎219 23 26 05) arrive on Av. Dr. Miguel Bombarda from Lisbon's Estação Rossio (45min., every 15min., 200$). Stagecoach **buses** leave from outside the train station for Cascais (#417, 40min., every hr., 7:20am-8:30pm, 520$; also #403, 1hr., every 1-1½hr., 6:30am-7:55pm, 740$) and Estoril (#418, 40min., every hr., 6:50am-midnight, 440$). Down the street, Mafrense buses go to Ericeira (50min., every hr., 7:30am-9:30pm, 410$) with connections to points north. To get to the **tourist office** in Sintra-Vila from the bus station (on Av. Dr. Miguel Bombarda), turn left on Av. Bombarda, which becomes the winding Volta do Duche. Continue straight into the Praça da República; the Palácio Nacional de Sintra is ahead, and the tourist office is to the left. (☎219 23 11 57; fax 219 23 51 76. Pr. República, 23.) To reach the **Pousada da Juventude de Sintra (HI),** on Sta. Eufémia, take bus #434 from the train station to the Palácio da Pena. Walk through the palace garden to the hostel (look for signs). Or hike the 2km uphill to São Pedro, but beware the confusing *escadinha* (stair-alley) shortcut. (☎/fax 219 24 12 10. Reception daily 9am-noon and 6pm-midnight. Reservations recommended. Dorms 1500$; doubles 3500-3800$.)

ERICEIRA. Primarily a fishing village, Ericeira has become known for its spectacular beaches. The main beaches, **Praia do Sol** and **Praia do Norte,** crowd quickly; for something more secluded, stroll down the Largo da Feira toward Ribamar until you reach **Praia da Ribeira d'Ilhas,** with its rolling surf, dramatic tides, stunning sand dunes, and rock formations. If you stay, ask about rooms at the tourist office. Mafrense **buses** run from Lisbon's Campo Grande to Ericeira (1¼-1½hr., every hr. 6:30am-11:20pm, 720$); get off at the Centro Rodoviario Municipal (Ericeira's bus station). Buses from Ericeira run to Mafra (20min., every hr., 230$) and Sintra (50min., every hr., 410$). To get to the **tourist office,** R. Eduardo Burnay, 46 (☎261 86 31 22) from the station, cross the road, turn right onto Calçada do Rego, continue down R. Paroquial (to the right at the fork), and turn left after three blocks onto R. 5 de Outubro, which runs to Pr. República. The office is across the square.

MAFRA. One of Portugal's most impressive sights, the **Palácio Nacional de Mafra** is in this sleepy town. The massive 2000-room castle, including a cathedral-sized church, a monastery, a library, and a palace, took 50,000 workers 13 years (1717-1730) to complete. (Open W-M 10am-4:30pm; closed on national holidays. 600$, students 300$. Free tours in English at 11am and 2:30pm.) Mafrense **buses,** which also serve Lisbon's Campo Grande (1-1½hr., every hr., 540$) and Ericeira (20min., every hr., 230$), stop in front of the palace. Don't take the **train** from Lisbon's Estação Sta. Apolónia unless you want a two-hour walk to town.

CENTRAL PORTUGAL

Jagged cliffs and whitewashed fishing villages line the Costa de Prata (Silver Coast) of **Estremadura,** with beaches that rival even those in the Algarve. In the fertile region of the **Ribatejo** (Banks of the Tejo), lush greenery surrounds historic sights.

TOMAR

For centuries, the arcane Knights Templar—part monks, part warriors—plotted crusades from a monastery-fortress high above this small town. The **Convento de Cristo** complex was their mysterious headquarters. The structure was built in 1160, but some cloisters and other buildings were added later. The **Claustro dos Felipes** is a masterpiece of Renaissance architecture. Walk out of the tourist office, take the second right, bear left at the fork, and either follow the steep dirt path to the left or follow the cars up the road. (☎249 31 34 81. Open daily June-Sept. 9am-6pm; Oct.-May 9am-5pm. 600$, under 25 300$.) The **Sinagoga do Arco,** R. Dr. Joaquim Jaquinto, 73, houses the **Museu Luso-Hebraico,** with a collection of tombstones, inscriptions, and other reminders of Portugal's once-vibrant Jewish community. (Open daily 10am-1pm and 2-6pm. Free.) Hiking trails lead into the **Parque da Mata Nacional dos Sete Montes** from opposite the tourist office. (Open 10am-6pm. Free.)

Trains (☎249 31 28 15) go from Av. Combatentes da Grande Guerra, at the southern edge of town, to: Santarém (1hr., 18 per day, 520-840$); Lisbon (2hr., 18 per day, 1010-2040$); Coimbra (2½hr., 6 per day, 960-1200$); and Porto (4½hr., 7 per day, 1510-2210$). Rodoviaria Tejo **buses** (☎249 31 27 38) depart near the train station for: Santarém (1hr., 2 per day, 1150$); Lisbon (2hr., 4 per day, 1150$); Coimbra (2½hr., every day, 1450$); and Porto (4hr., every day, 1900$). From either station, go through the square onto Av. General Bernardo Raria, go left after four blocks on Av. Dr. Cândido Madureira, go to the end of the street, and look right for the **tourist office.** (☎249 32 24 27. Open daily June-Sept. 10am-8pm; Oct.-May 10am-6pm.) **Residencial União,** R. Serpa Pinto, 94, is between Pr. República and the bridge. (☎249 32 31 61. Breakfast included. Reception 8am-midnight. Call ahead July-Aug. Singles 4000$; doubles 6500-7000$; triples 7500-8000$.) The **market** is on the corner of Av. Norton de Matos and R. Santa Iria (Tu and Th-F 8am-2pm). **Postal code:** 2300.

EXCURSION FROM TOMAR: BATALHA. The only reason (but a good one) to visit Batalha (pop. 6000) is the flamboyant **Mosteiro de Santa Maria da Vitória.** Built by Dom João I in 1385 to commemorate his victory over the Spanish, the complex of cloisters and chapels remains one of Portugal's greatest monuments. To get to the monastery, enter through the church. (Open daily Apr.-Sept. 9am-6pm; Oct.-Mar. 9am-5pm. 600$, under 25 300$. Free Su before 2pm. Church free.) **Buses** run from a square across from the monastery to Tomar (1½hr., 3 per day, 520$) and Lisbon (2hr., 6 per day, 1200$). The **tourist office,** on Pr. Mouzinho de Albuquerque along R. Nossa Senhora do Caminho, stands opposite the unfinished chapels of the *mosteiro.* (☎244 76 51 80. Open daily May-Sept. 10am-1pm and 3-7pm; Oct.-Apr. 10am-1pm and 2-6pm.)

ÉVORA

Évora (pop. 54,000), considered Portugal's foremost showpiece of medieval architecture, is justly known as the "Museum City." Its picture-perfect streets wind past a Roman temple, an impressive cathedral, and a 16th-century university.

PRACTICAL INFO, ACCOMMODATIONS, AND FOOD. **Trains** (☎266 70 21 25) go from the end of R. Dr. Baronha to Lisbon (3hr., 5 per day, 1380$) and Porto (6½hr., 3 per day, 2650$). From the train station, take bus #6 (130$) from just down the tracks or hike up R. Dr. Baronha, which becomes R. República and leads to the central Pr. Giraldo (20min.). **Buses** (☎266 76 94 10) go from the continuation of R. Raimundo, 15 minutes downhill from Pr. Giraldo, past the gas station, to Lisbon (2-2½hr., 10 per day, 1550$) and Faro (5hr., 4 per day, 1900$). The **tourist office** is at Pr. Giraldo, 73. (☎266 70 26 71. Open Apr.-Oct. M-F 9am-7pm, Sa-Su 9am-12:30pm and 2-5:30pm; Oct.-Mar. daily 9am-12:30pm and 2-5:30pm.) Check **email** at **Oficin@,** R. Moeda, 27, off Pr. Giraldo. (500$ per hr. Open Apr.-Sept. Tu-F 8pm-3am, Sa 9pm-3am; Oct.-Mar. Tu-F 8pm-2am, Sa 9pm-2am.)

Pensões cluster around **Pr. Giraldo.** From the end of Pr. Giraldo opposite the church, walk down R. Miguel Bombarda to reach the **Pousada de Juventude (HI),** R. Miguel Bombarda, 40. (☎266 74 48 48. Reception 8am-midnight. Dorms 2000-2500$; doubles 5000-6000$.) **Movijem** (☎21 359 60 00) handles reservations for the hostel. From the tourist office, walk down the street and three blocks right to **Casa Palma,** R. Bernando Mato, 29-A, a backpacker fave. (☎266 70 35 60. Singles 2500-4500$; doubles 5000-7000$.) Bus #14 (M-F 20 per day, Sa 6 per day) goes from Pr. Giraldo to **Orbitur's Parque de Campismo de Évora,** on Estrada das Alcáçovas, which branches off the bottom of R. Raimundo. (☎266 70 51 90. Laundry. Reception 8am-10pm. 380-640$ per person; 300-640$ per tent; 330-550$ per car.) Many budget restaurants are near **Pr. Giraldo,** particularly along **R. Mercadores.** Try **Restaurante A Gruta,** Av. General Humberto Delgado, 2. (Open Su-F noon-3pm and 5-10:30pm.) Grab **groceries** at **Maxigrula,** R. João de Deus, 130. (Open M-Sa 9am-7pm.) **Postal code:** 7000.

SIGHTS AND ENTERTAINMENT. The city's most famous monument is the second-century **Roman temple,** on Largo do Vila Flor. Facing the temple is the **Igreja de São João Evangelista** (1485), its interior covered with dazzling *azulejos* (tiles); ask to see the hidden chambers. (Open Tu-Su 10am-12:30pm and 2-6pm. Church 500$, church and exhibition hall 850$.) From Pr. Giraldo, head up R. 5 de Outubro to the colossal 12th-century **cathedral;** the 12 apostles on the doorway are masterpieces of medieval Portuguese sculpture. The **Museu de Arte Sacra,** above the nave, has religious artifacts. (Cathedral open daily 9am-12:30pm and 2-5pm. Cloisters open daily 9am-noon and 2-4:30pm. Museum open Tu-Su 9am-noon and 2-4:30pm. Cloisters and museum 450$. Cathedral free.) Attached to the pleasant **Igreja Real de São Francisco,** the bizarre **Capela dos Ossos** (Chapel of Bones) was built out of the bones of 5000 people by three Franciscan monks. From Pr. Giraldo, follow R. República; the church is on the right and the chapel around back to the right of the main entrance. (Open M-Sa 9am-1pm and 2:30-6pm. Photography permit 50$. 100$, students 50$.) After sunset, **Fimdelinha** (End of the Line), Av. Combatentes de Grande Guerra, 56, plays a mix of music to a local crowd. (Cover 1000$, includes 2 beers. Open M-Sa 10pm-5am.) Take R. República outside the city walls and follow the street parallel to its continuation, by the termination of the railroad tracks. A Portuguese-style country fair accompanies the **Feira de São João** festival the last week of June.

ALGARVE

Behold the Algarve—a freak of nature, a desert on the sea, an inexhaustible vacationland where happy campers bask in the sun. Nearly 3000 hours of sunshine per year have transformed this one-time fishermen's backwater into one of Europe's favorite vacation spots. In July and August, tourists mob the resorts, packing the bars and discos from sunset until way past the all-too-early sunrise. In the off season, the resorts become pleasantly de-populated and the sun eases.

LAGOS

As the town's countless international expats will attest, Lagos (pop. 22,000) is a black hole: come for two days and you'll never leave. There isn't much beyond beaches and bars, but no one's complaining. You too may be tempted to stay.

GETTING THERE AND GETTING AROUND

Trains: ☎282 76 29 87. Across the river (over the metal drawbridge) from the town center. To **Évora** (6hr., 2 per day, 1930$) and **Lisbon** (4-4½hr., 6 per day, 2110-2280$).

Buses: EVA bus station (☎76 29 44), off Av. Descobrimentos, just past the train station bridge as you leave town. To: **Lisbon** (5hr., 9 per day, 2500-2600$); Sagres (1hr., 17 per day, 470$); and **Seville** (4¾hr.; 2 per day; 3000$).

ORIENTATION AND PRACTICAL INFORMATION

Avenida dos Descobrimentos, the main road, runs along the river. Exit left from the train station, cross the river, and hang a left on Av. Descobrimentos. From the bus station, go right on the main street and follow R. Portas de Portugal, which leads to the old town, **Praça Gil Eanes.** Most restaurants and lodgings hover near this *praça*, adjoining **R. 25 de Abril** and parallel **R. Cândido dos Reis.** Down Av. Descobrimentos, on the right, by the **fortaleza,** is **Praça Infante Dom Henrique** (or Praça República).

Tourist Office: ☎282 76 30 31. On R. Vasco de Gama, 10min. past the bus station going out of town on Av. Descobrimentos. Go through the traffic circle and past the gas station; it's on the left. Open daily 9:30am-12:30pm and 2-5:30pm.

Laundromat: Lavanderia Miele, Av. Descobrimentos, 27 (☎282 76 39 69). Wash and dry 1250$ per 5kg, 10kg for 1900$. Open M-F 9am-1pm and 3-7pm, Sa 9am-1pm.

Emergency: ☎112. **Police:** On R. General Alberto Silva (☎282 76 29 30).

Medical Assistance: Hospital (☎282 76 30 34), R. Castelo dos Governadores.

Internet Access: The Irish Rover, R. de Ferrador, 9 (☎282 76 80 33). 15min. 300$, 30min. 500$, 1hr. 900$. Open daily July-Sept. 2pm-2am, Oct.-June 6pm-2am.

Post Office: (☎282 77 02 50), on R. Portas de Portugal, between Pr. Gil Eanes and the river. Open M-F 9am-6pm. Address mail to be held: First name SURNAME, *Posta Restante,* Estação Portas de Portugal, **8600** Lagos, Portugal.

ACCOMMODATIONS, CAMPING, AND FOOD

Reserve at least a week ahead. Rooms in *casas particulares* run around 2000-3000$ per person in summer; haggle with owners at the train and bus stations. If full, the youth hostel will refer you to a *quarto* nearby for about the same price.

Pousada de Juventude de Lagos (HI), R. Lançarote de Freitas, 50 (☎282 76 19 70; fax 282 76 96 84). From Pr. República, follow the small street in the back-center 1 block until it becomes R. Lançarote de Freitas. Social and friendly. Breakfast included. Kitchen. Laundry. Internet 300$ per 30min. Reception 9am-1am. Check-out noon. Book summer reservations through **Movijovem** (☎213 59 60 00; fax 213 59 60 01). July-Sept. dorms 2500$, doubles with bath 4300$; Oct.-June 1700$, 3800$.

Residencial Rubi Mar, R. Barroca, 70 (☎282 76 31 65, ask for David; fax 282 76 77 49; email rubimar01@hotmail.com), off Pr. Gil Eanes. Well-located, quiet, and comfy. Breakfast included. Reserve ahead. Doubles 5500-8500$; quads 10,000-15,000$.

Residencial Gil Vicente, R. Gil Vicente, 26, 2nd fl. (☎/fax 282 76 29 82; email ggh@clix.pt), behind the youth hostel. Officially a "gay guest house" but open to anyone. High ceilings. Reception July-Aug. 24hr., Oct.-June 8am-9pm. Breakfast included. Reserve a month ahead in summer. Singles 3000-5000; doubles 5000-7000$.

Residencial Caravela, R. 25 de Abril, 8 (☎282 76 33 61). Small rooms, some with balconies. Breakfast included. Singles 4300$; doubles 6000-6500$; triples 9000$.

Camping: Many Europeans camp, so sites are crowded and expensive. **Camping Trindade** (☎282 76 38 93), just outside Lagos. Follow Av. Descobrimentos toward Sagres. 580$ per person; 630-735$ per tent; 620$ per car. **Camping Valverde** (☎282 78 92 11), 5km away. Showers. 790$ per person; 650-790$ per tent; 680$ per car.

Multilingual menus abound near **Pr. Gil Eanes** and **R. 25 de Abril,** but budget Portuguese is almost impossible to find. Get **Groceries** at **Supermercado São Toque,** on R. Portas de Portugal, opposite the post office. (Open July-Sept. M-F 9am-5pm, Sa 9am-7pm; Oct.-June M-F 9am-7:30pm, Sa 9am-7pm.) Hordes of backpackers enjoy 650$ meals at **Casa Rosa,** R. Ferrador, 22. (Open daily 7pm-2am.) Try the spicy dishes at **Mullen's,** R. Cãndido dos Reis, 86, which turns into a hot bar after dinner. (Entrees 1125-2225$. Open daily noon-2pm and 7-10:30pm. Bar closes at 2am.)

BEACHES AND NIGHTLIFE

Flat, smooth, sunbathing sands (crowded in summer, pristine in the off season) can be found at the 4km **Meia Praia,** across the river from town. Hop on the 30-second ferry near Pr. República (70$). For beautiful cliffs hiding less-crowded beaches and caves, follow Av. Descobrimentos toward Sagres to the **Praia de Pinhão** (20min.). A tad farther, **Praia Dona Ana** features the sculpted cliffs and grottos that appear on most Algarve postcards. The streets pick up as soon as the sun dips down, and by midnight the city's walls shake. The area between **Pr. Gil Eanes** and **Pr. Luis de Camões** is filled with cafes. **R. Cândido dos Reis, R. do Ferrador,** and the intersection of **R. 25 de Abril, R. Silva Lopes,** and **R. Soeiro da Costa** are crammed with bars. Down the street from the hostel, **Taverna Velha** (Old Tavern), R. Lançarote de Freitas, 34, holds happy hour from 9pm to midnight. (Open M-Sa 4pm-2am, Su 8pm-2am.) Resurrect at the **Phoenix Club,** R. São Gonçalo, 29, by the hostel. (Cover 1000$, includes 2 beers or 1 cocktail. Open daily 1-6am.) The DJ keeps **Whyte's Bar,** R. Ferrador, 7, packed all night. (Beer 500$. Open daily Oct.-June 8pm-2am, July-Sept. 7pm-2am.)

EXCURSIONS FROM LAGOS

SAGRES. Sagres was considered the end of the world for centuries. The windswept and barren cape plunges on all three sides into the Atlantic. Near the town lurks the **Fortaleza de Sagres,** the outpost where Prince Henry founded his famous **school of navigation.** (Open daily May-Sept. 10am-8:30pm; Oct.-Apr. 10am-6:30pm. 600$.) The striking **Cabo de São Vicente,** where Europe's second most powerful lighthouse shines over 100km out to sea, lies 6km to the west. To get there, take the bus from the main road (10min., M-F 3 per day, 180$). Or hike or bike past the several fortresses perched atop the cliffs. The most notable **beach** in the area is **Mareta,** at the bottom of the road from the town center, a sandy crescent flanked by rock formations jutting into the ocean. West of town, **Praia de Martinhal** and **Praia da Baleeira** have great windsurfing. At night, crowds head to **Água Salgada,** on R. Comandante Matoso. (Beer 200$, shots 350$. Open daily 10am-2am.) Next door, **O Dromedário** whips up innovative pizzas (740-1180$) and vegetarian dishes. (Open daily 10am-midnight; bar open until 2am; closed Jan.-Feb.)

EVA **buses** (☎282 76 29 44) run from Lagos (1hr., 17 per day, 7:15am-8:30pm, 470$). The **tourist office,** on R. Comandante Matoso, is up the street from the bus stop. (☎282 62 48 73. Open Tu-Sa 9:30am-12:30pm and 2-5:30pm.) **Turinfo,** in Pr. República, rents **bikes** (1900$ per day, 1200$ per half-day), does **laundry** (1300$ per load), and offers **currency exchange.** (☎282 62 00 03. Open daily 10am-1pm, 2-7pm.)

PRAIA DA ROCHA. A short jaunt from Lagos, this grand **beach** is perhaps the very best the Algarve has to offer. With vast expanses of sand, surfable waves, rocky red cliffs, and plenty of secluded coves, the beach has a well-deserved reputation (and crowds). From Lagos, take a **bus** to **Portimão** (40min., 14 per day, 360-450$), then switch at the station to the **Praia da Rocha bus** (10min., every 30min., 220$). The **tourist office** is at the end of R. Tomás Cabreina. (☎282 41 91 32. Open daily May-Sept. 9:30am-7pm; Oct.-Apr. M-F 9:30am-12:30pm and 2-5:30pm, Sa-Su 9:30am-12:30pm.)

TAVIRA

Farmers teasing police by riding their motor scooters over the **Roman pedestrian bridge** may be about as eventful as Tavira gets, but the relaxing haven is speckled with white houses, palm trees, and Baroque churches. Steps from the central **Pr. República** lead to the **Igreja da Misericórdia.** (Open daily 9:30am-noon and 2:30-5pm. Free.) Just beyond it, the remains of the city's **Castelo Mouro** (Moorish Castle) sit next to the **Santa Maria do Castelo.** (Both open daily 9am-5pm. Free.) The seven-arched Ponte Romana footbridge leads to the floral **Pr. 5 de Outubro.** Local **beaches,** such as **Araial do Barril,** are accessible year-round by the **bus** to Pedras D'el Rei (10min., 8 per day, 170$). To reach the great beach on **Ilha da Tavira,** an island 2km away, take the ferry from the end of Estrada das 4 Aguas, 20 minutes downstream (every 15min., round-trip 200$). EVA **buses** (☎281 32 25 46) leave from the station upstream from Pr. República for Faro (1hr., 11 per day, 435$). **Trains** (☎281 32 23 54) also head to Faro (40min., 17 per day, 300$). From the train station, catch the local TUT bus to the town center (10min., every 30min., 100$). The **tourist office,** R. Galeria, 9, is up the stairs off Pr. República. (☎281 32 25 11. Open M-Sa 9:30am-12:30pm and 2-5:30pm, Su 9:30am-12:30pm.) To get from Pr. República to the riverfront **Pensão Residencial Lagôas Bica,** R. Almirante Cândido dos Reis, 24, cross the footbridge, continue down R. A. Cabreira, turn right, and go down one block. (☎281 32 22 52. Singles 3000-3500$; doubles 4500-7000$) **Ilha de Tavira campground** is on the Ilha da Tavira. (See directions above. ☎281 32 50 21. Showers 100$. Reception 8am-11pm. Open May-Oct. 15. 430$ per person; 700-800$ per tent.) Try restaurants on **Pr. República** or opposite the garden on **R. José Pires Padinha. Postal code:** 8800.

FARO

The Algarve's capital, largest city, and transportation hub is untouristed despite its charm. Its **old town,** a medley of museums, handicraft shops, and ornate churches, begins at the **Arco da Vila,** a stone arch. In Largo Carmo, is the **Igreja de Nossa Senhora do Carmo** and its **Capela dos Ossos** (Chapel of Bones), a macabre bonanza of bones and skulls "borrowed" from the adjacent cemetery. (☎289 82 44 90. Open M-F 10am-1pm and 3-5pm, Sa 10am-1pm. Church free, chapel 120$.) Faro's rock-free **beach** hides on an islet off the coast. Take bus #16 from the bus station or the stop in front of the tourist office (5-10min., every hr., 170$).

Trains (☎289 80 17 26) run from Largo Estação to: Albufeira (45min., 14 per day, 300$); Lagos (2hr., 7 per day, 750$); Évora (5hr., 2 per day, 1650$); and Lisbon (5-6hr., 6 per day, 2280$). EVA **buses** (☎289 89 97 00) go from Av. República to Albufeira (1hr., 14 per day, 600$); Tavira (1hr., 11 per day, 435$); and Lagos (2hr., 8 per day, 720$). **Renex** (☎81 29 80) goes from across the street to Lisbon (4hr., 8per day, 2500$) and Porto (7½hr., 8 per day, 3500$); **Intersul** (☎289 89 97 70) runs to Seville (2800$). From the stations, turn right down Av. República along the harbor, then turn left past the garden to reach the **tourist office,** R. Misericórdia, 8, at the entrance to the old town. (☎289 80 36 04. Open daily June-Aug. 9:30am-7pm; Sept.-May 9:30am-5:30pm.) Head down Av. República from either station to the central Pr. Gomes, and take R. 1 de Maio to get to **Pensão Residencial Central,** Largo Terreiro Do Bispo, 12. (☎289 80 72 91. Singles 5000$; doubles 6500-7500$.) Enjoy coffee at a cafe along **R. Conselheiro Bívar,** off Pr. Gomes.

NORTHERN PORTUGAL

In the north, trellised vineyards for *porto* and *vinho verde* wines beckon connoisseurs, and *azulejo*-lined houses draw visitors to charming streets. The **Beira Litoral** (coastal region) begins with the resort of Figueira da Foz, while **Coimbra,** a bustling university city, overlooks the region from high above the Rio Mondego.

COIMBRA

The country's only university city from the mid-16th to the early 20th century, charming and vibrant Coimbra is a mecca for the country's youth.

PRACTICAL INFO, ACCOMMODATIONS, AND FOOD. **Trains** (☎239 83 49 98) from other regions stop only at **Estação Coimbra-B (Velha),** 3km northwest of town, while regional trains stop at both Coimbra-B and **Estação Coimbra-A (Nova),** two blocks from the lower town center. Frequent trains go to: Figueira da Foz (1¼hr., 290$); Porto (2hr., 1040$); and Lisbon (3hr., 1540-2700$). A train connects the two stations (5min., every 10min., 140$). **Buses** (☎239 82 70 81) go from Av. Fernão Magalhães, on the university side of the river 10 minutes from town, past Coimbra-A, to: Porto (1½hr., 10 per day, 1400$); Lisbon (2½hr., 17 per day, 1550$); Évora (4hr., 2 per day, 2000$); and Faro (8hr., 3 per day, 3000$). From the bus station, go right on Av. Fernão Magalhães to Coimbra-A, then walk upstream to Largo Portagem to the **tourist office.** (☎239 85 59 50. Open M-F 9am-7pm, Sa-Su 10am-1pm and 2:30-5:30pm.) Check **email** at **Museu Sandwich Bar,** R. da Matemática, 46, near the university. (600$ per hr. Open M-F 4-7pm and 10pm-3am, Sa 10pm-3am.)

To get from Coimbra-A or Largo Portagem to the welcoming **Pousada de Juventude de Coimbra (HI),** R. Henrique Seco, 14, walk uphill on R. Olímpio Nicolau Rui Fernandes to Pr. República, go up R. Lourenço Azevedo (left of the park), take the second right, and it's on the right. Or, take bus #2, 7, 8, 29, or 46 to Pr. República and walk. (☎239 82 29 55. Breakfast included. Kitchen. Laundry. Reception 8am-noon and 6pm-midnight. Dorms 1700-1900$; doubles 4300-4600$.) Follow R. Ferreira Borges as it becomes R. Visconde da Luz and leads to **Pensão Santa Cruz,** Pr. 8 de Maio, 21, 3rd floor. (☎/fax 239 82 61 97. Singles 4000$; doubles 6000$; triples 7500$.) Enter the **Municipal Campground** through the arch off Pr. 25 de Abril; take bus #5, 7, or 10 (dir. São José or Estádio) from Largo Portagem. (☎239 70 14 97. Reception May-Sept. 9am-10pm; Oct.-Apr. 9am-6pm. 237-474$ per person; 156-312$ per tent; 301-602$ per car.) The best cuisine lies around **R. Direita,** off Pr. 8 de Maio, on the side streets between the river and Largo Portagem, and around **Pr. República** in the university district. **Supermercado Minipreço,** R. António Granjo, 6C, is in the lower town center; turn left as you exit Coimbra-A and take another left. (Open M-Sa 8:30am-8pm, Su 9am-1pm and 3-7pm.) **Postal code:** 3000.

SIGHTS AND ENTERTAINMENT. Begin at the **Arco de Almedina,** a remnant of the Moorish town wall, a block uphill from Largo Portagem, which leads to the aptly-named R. Quebra-Costas (Back-Breaker Street). At the top looms the 12th-century Romanesque **Sé Velha** (Old Cathedral), with tombs and a cloister. (Open M-Th 10am-noon and 2-7:30pm, F-Su 10am-1pm. Cathedral free. Cloister 150$, students 100$.) Follow signs to the late-16th century **Sé Nova** (New Cathedral), built for the Jesuits. (Open Tu-Sa 9am-noon and 2-6:30pm. Free.) A few blocks away is the 16th-century **University of Coimbra.** The **Porta Férrea** (Iron Gate), off R. São Pedro, opens onto the old university, whose buildings were Portugal's de facto royal palace when Coimbra was the capital. (Open daily 9:30am-12:30pm and 2-5:30pm. 250$.) The stairs to the right lead to the **Sala dos Capelos** (Graduate's Hall), which houses portraits of Portugal's kings. (Open daily 9:30am-12:30pm and 2-5pm. 250$.) The **university chapel** and the gilded 18th-century **Biblioteca Joanina** lie past the clock tower; press the library buzzer to enter. (Open daily 9:30am-noon and 2-4:30pm. 250$, students free. All university sights 500$; buy tickets from the main quad office.) Back at Largo Portagem, follow R. Ferreira Borges as it becomes R. Visconde da Luz, which leads to Praça 8 de Maio, where the **Igreja de Santa Cruz** (Church of the Holy Cross) stands by the lively square. A splendid **sacristy** and **túmulos reals** (tombs) lie inside. (Open M-Sa 9am-noon and 2-4:45pm. 200$.)

Nightlife in Coimbra gets highest honors. After dinner, outdoor cafes around **Pr. República** buzz; try the **Café-Bar Cartola.** (Open M-Sa 8am-2am, Su 9am-1am.) **Via Latina,** R. Almeida Garrett, 1, around the corner and uphill from Pr. República, is hot in all senses of the word. (Open F-Sa midnight-8am.) **Bar 1910,** above a gymnasium on R. Simões Castro, does *fado*. (Open daily 11pm-4am.) In early May, graduates burn narrow ribbons they got as first-years and get wide ones in return during Coimbra's famed week-long festival, the **Queima das Fitas** (Burning of the Ribbons).

FIGUEIRA DA FOZ

The town's best features are its Sahara-like beach and its party scene. Bars and clubs line **Av. 25 de Abril,** around the tourist office. The **casino** complex, on R. Bernardo Lopes, is popular. (Casino open daily 3pm-3am. Club open July-Sept. daily 12:30am-6am; Oct.-June Th-Sa 12:30am-6am. Club cover 1000$; includes 2 beers.) **Trains** (☎233 42 83 16) leave near the bridge for: Coimbra (1hr., 27 per day, 290$); Porto (2¼hr., 8 per day, 1120$); and Lisbon (3½hr., 9 per day, 1510$). From there, walk with the river to the left on Av. Saraiva de Carvalho, which becomes R. 5 de Outubro then curves to the tourist office, Av. 25 de Abril (25min.). **Buses** (☎233 42 67 03) go to Lisbon (3hr., 4 per day, 1550$) and Faro (12hr., 2 per day, 3100$). Facing the church, turn right on R. Dr. Santos Rocha, walk 10 minutes toward the waterfront, and turn right on R. 5 de Outubro to reach the **tourist office.** (☎233 40 28 27. Open June-Sept. daily 9am-midnight; Oct.-May M-F 9am-5:30pm, Sa-Su 10am-12:30pm and 2:30-6:30pm.) Scour **R. Bernardo Lopes,** inland from Av. 25 de Abril, for cheap beds. **Pensão Central,** R. Bernardo Lopes, 36, 2nd floor, is near the casino. (☎233 42 23 08. Breakfast included. Singles 3000-5000$; doubles 4000-8000$; triples 6000-9000$.) Walk up Av. 25 de Abril with the beach to the left, turn right at the rotary on R. Alexandre Herculano, and turn left at Parque Santa Catarina to **camp** at the **Parque Municipal de Campismo da Figueira da Foz Municipal,** on Estrada Buarcos. (☎233 40 28 10. Reception June-Sept. 8am-8pm; Oct.-May 8am-7pm. Groups of 2 or more only. Showers 100$. 400$ per person; 300$ per tent and per car.) **Supermercado Ovo** is at R. A. Dinis and R. B. Lopes. (Open M-Sa 8am-8pm, Su 9am-2pm.)

PORTO (OPORTO)

Porto has more than just port wine. Situated on a gorge cut by the Douro River and designated one of Europe's two Cultural Capitals for 2001, Porto rivals Lisbon's vibrance and is reminiscent of more cosmopolitan metropolises.

PRACTICAL INFO, ACCOMMODATIONS, AND FOOD. From the main train station, **Estação de Campanhã** (☎225 36 41 41), east of the city center, **trains** go to Coimbra (1½hr., 17 per day, 1010-1040$) and Lisbon (4½hr., 14 per day, 2080-3700$). Trains connect to the **Estação de São Bento** (5min., 140$), a block from the central Pr. Liberdade. There is no central bus station. Garagem Atlântico **buses** leave from R. Alexandre Herculano, 366 (☎222 05 24 59) for Coimbra (1½hr., 11 per day, 1410$) and Lisbon (4hr., 12 per day, 2300$); Renex goes from R. Carmelitas, 32 (☎222 00 33 95) to Lagos (9½hr., 8 per day, 3500$). Get a map at the **tourist office,** R. Clube dos Fenianos, 25, off Pr. Liberdade. (Open daily July-Sept. 9am-7pm; Oct.-June M-F 9am-5:30pm.) A **branch** on R. Infante Dom Henrique, 63, is also open weekends 9:30am-4:30pm. Check **email** at **Portweb,** Pr. Gen. Humberto Delgado, 291, by the tourist office. (100-240$ per hr. Open M-Sa 9am-2am, Su 3pm-2am.)

To get from the station to the spacious **Residencial Paris,** R. Fábrica, 27-9, cross Pr. Liberdade and turn left on R. Dr. Artur de Magalhães Basto, which turns into R. Fábrica. (☎222 07 31 40. Breakfast included. Singles 3450-5300$; doubles 5100-7250$; triples 6600-9450$.) One block over from Av. Aliados lies the small and tidy **Pensão Porto Rico,** R. Almada, 237, 2nd fl. (☎223 39 46 90. Breakfast included. Singles 4500$; doubles 7500$; triples 9000$.) Facing the town hall, go up Av. dos Aliados, turn left onto R. Dr. Ricardo Jorge, which becomes R. Conceição, turn left on R. Oliveiras, and make a quick right to find **Pensão São Marino,** Pr. Carlos Alberto, 59. (☎223 32 54 99. Singles 4000-5000$; doubles 5500-6500$; triples 6500-7500$.) Take bus #6 from Pr. Liberdade (bus #54 at night) to **camp** at **Prelada,** on R. Monte dos Burgos, in Quinta da Prelada, 2km from the city center. (☎228 31 26 16. Reception 8am-1am. 620$ per person; 520$ per tent and per car.) Budget fare and rowdier environments prevail near Pr. Batalha on R. Cimo de Vila and R. Cativo. Doling out more *escudos* will land you tasty dishes; look near the river in the **Ribeira** district, on C. Ribeira, R. Reboleira, and R. Cima do Muro. Try the city's specialty, *tripas à moda do Porto* (tripe and beans). Do coffee (200-350$) at **Majestic Café,** R. Santa Catarina, 112. (Open M-Sa 9am-midnight.) The dirt-cheap dishes at **Churrasqueira**

Moura, R. Almada, 219, satisfy any stomach. (Half-portions 450-990$; full portions 450-1800$. Open M-Sa 9am-10pm.) Get **groceries** at **Mercado de Bolhão,** at R. Formosa and R. Sá de Bandeira. (Open M-F 8am-5pm, Sa 8am-1pm.) **Postal code:** 4000.

SIGHTS AND ENTERTAINMENT. First encounter Porto's rich stock of fine artwork at the collection of *azulejos* (tiles) in the **Estação São Bento.** Walk past the station and uphill on Av. Afonso Henriques to reach Porto's pride and joy, the 12th- to 13th-century Romanesque **Cathedral** (Sé). The *azulejo*-covered cloister was added in the 14th century. (Open M-Sa 9am-12:30pm and 2:30-6pm, Su 2:30-6pm. Cloister 250$.) From the station, follow signs down R. Mouzinho da Silveira to the **Palácio da Bolsa** (Stock Exchange), the epitome of 19th-century elegance. The ornate **Sala Árabe** (Arabic Hall) took 18 years to decorate. (Open daily 9am-7pm. Tours every 30min. 800$; main courtyard free.) Next door, the Gothic **Igreja de São Francisco** glitters with a gilded wooden interior. Under the floor, thousands of human bones are stored in preparation for Judgment Day. (Open M-Sa 9am-6pm. 500$, students 250$.) From Pr. Liberdade up R. Clérigos rises the granite **Torre dos Clérigos** (Tower of Clerics), adjoined to the **Igreja dos Clérigos.** (Tower open daily June-July 10am-12:30pm and 2-5:30pm. 200$; church free.) The rotating exhibits at the **Museu de Arte Contemporânea** crown 44 acres of sculpted gardens and fountains. Take bus #78 (30min., 180$) from Pr. Dom João I and ask the driver to stop at the museum. (Open Tu-W and F-Su 10am-7pm, Th 10am-10pm. Park closes at sundown. 800$; free Su before 2pm.) To get to Porto's dirty (but popular) **beach,** in the ritzy Foz district, take bus #1 from the São Bento train station (180$).

Fine and bounteous **port** wines are available for tasting at 20-odd port wine lodges, usually *gratuito* (free). The lodges are all across the river in Vila Nova da Gaia—from the Ribeira district, cross the lower level of the large bridge and head right. **Sandeman,** Lg. Miguel Bombarda, 3, with its costumed guides, is a good start (500$); **Cálem,** Av. Diogo Leite, 25, has a less-stilted tour, and the port is almost as good. **Quinta do Noval,** Av. Diogo Leite, 256, doesn't have tours, but there is plenty of free tasting in this breezy bar. **Taylor's,** R. do Choupelo, 250, up a huge hill, wins the inebriating (but highly unscientific) *Let's Go* poll for Porto's best port lodge. (Most open daily 10am-6pm.) Boogie to Brazilian and Latin tunes in the **Ribeira,** a few blocks downhill from the city center, over the bridge from Vila Nova de Gaia. **Pr. Ribeira, M. Bacalhoeiros,** and **R. Alfândega** harbor most bars and pubs. Bus #1 runs all night from Pr. Liberdade to the beach at Matosinhos via the club-happy **Foz** district. Try **Twins,** R. Passeio, 994, for house and dance music. (Cover 1000$. Open Tu-Sa midnight-4am.) The down-to-earth **Pub O Muro,** Muro dos Bacalhoeiros, 87-88, is in the Ribeira. (Open daily noon-2am.) **Discoteca Swing,** Praceta Eng. Amaro Costa, 766, by R. Júlio Dinis, has action for a mixed gay-straight crowd (cover 1000$).

THAT TOOK GUTS When native son Henry the Navigator geared up to conquer Cueta in the early 15th century, Porto's residents slaughtered their cattle, gave the meat to Prince Henry's fleet, and kept only the entrails. This dramatic generosity came in the wake of the Plague when food supplies were extremely crucial. The dish *tripàs a moda do Porto* commemorates their culinary sacrifice; to this day, the people of Porto are known as *tripeiros* (tripe-eaters). If you're feeling adventurous, try some of the tripe dishes, which locals—and few others—consider quite a delicacy.

ROMANIA (ROMÂNIA)

ROMANIAN LEI

US$1 = L23,000	L10,000 = US$0.43
CDN$1 = L16,000	L10,000 = CDN$0.64
UK£1 = L34,000	L10,000 = UK£0.30
IR£1 = L26,000	L10,000 = IR£0.38
AUS$1 = L13,000	L10,000 = AUS$0.75
NZ$1 = L10,000	L10,000 = NZ$1.00
SAR1 = L3300	L10,000 = SAR3.00
DM1 = L11,000	L10,000 = DM0.94
EUR€1 = L22,000	L10,000 = EUR€0.48

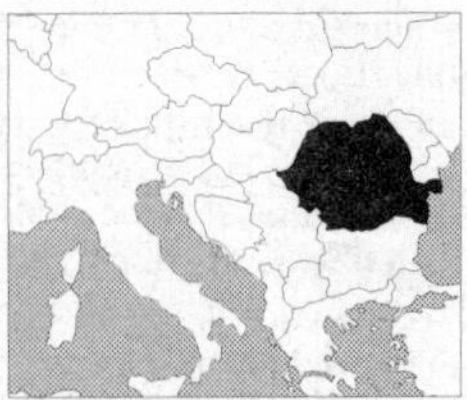

Country code: 40. **International dialing prefix:** 00. From outside Romania, dial int'l dialing prefix (see inside back cover) + 40 + city code + local number.

Romania, devastated by the lengthy reign of communist dictator Nicolae Ceauşescu, now suffers under a government incapable of bridging its gaps with the West. The resulting state of flux has left the country disheartened, as the tourist industry flounders and presents sights less attractive than those of its more westernized neighbors. Bucharest, the center of the country's political and cultural existence, has been swallowed by concrete apartment blocks and sterile communist squares. However, visitors who manage to avoid the beaten "Dracula" path and talk to common villagers will discover that Romania runs far deeper than Ceauşescu's effects. Here, the joy of travel comes in peeling the layers from the nation's recent history to find what lies beneath. Romanians go out of their way to make visitors feel at home, and travelers daring enough to explore will find a dynamic people eager to grow and hopeful in spite of their past.

For more coverage of Romania, brave *Let's Go: Eastern Europe 2001*.

FACTS AND FIGURES

Official Name: Romania.

Government: Republic.

Capital: Bucharest.

Land Area: 230,340 sq. km.

Geography: Mountains, plains.

Climate: Temperate; cold, foggy winters; sunny summers with thunderstorms.

Major Cities: Bucharest, Cluj-Napoca, Braşov.

Population: 22,411,120.

Languages: Romanian (official), Hungarian, German.

Religions: Romanian Orthodox (70%), Roman Catholic (6%), Protestant (6%).

Income per capita: US$3900.

Major Exports: Textiles and footwear, metals and metal products.

DISCOVER ROMANIA

Romania is blessed with sky-tickling snowy peaks, a superb chunk of Black Sea coast, and culturally rich cities—all at half the price of similar attractions in Western Europe. Vast and hectic **Bucharest,** the capital, surprises with good museums, expanses of green parks, myriad historical monuments, and an *über*-hip, *über*-Euro night scene (p. 777). For a hefty dose of Transylvanian vampire mythology, visit **Bran,** home to the legendary castle of Count Dracula (p. 782). Nearby **Braşov** provides access to the trails and slopes of the Transylvanian Alps (p. 782). Culture is centered in **Cluj-Napoca,** Romania's student capital and the most diverse city in the country (p. 781). For a holier take on Romania, visit the secluded **Bukovina Monasteries** near Gura Humorului (p. 784).

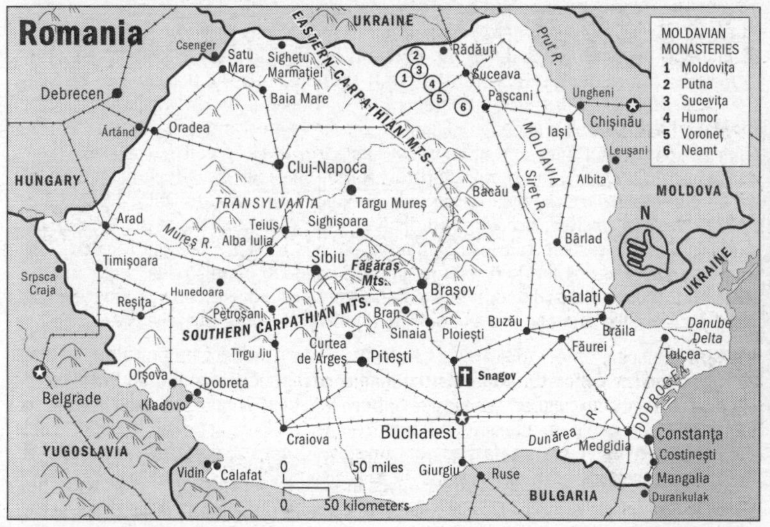

ESSENTIALS

WHEN TO GO

As Romania suffers fairly hot summers and cold winters, spring and fall are the best times to visit. Winters can be very cold and the mountains are always colder than the lowlands; there is often a lot of precipitation. The coasts are more moderate.

DOCUMENTS AND FORMALITIES

Americans do not need visas for stays of up to 30 days. Citizens of Australia, Canada, Ireland, New Zealand, South Africa, and the UK all need visas to enter Romania. Single-entry visas (US$35) are good for 30 days within three months of the date of issue, multiple-entry visas (US$70) for 180 days, and transit visas (US$35) for three days. Obtain a visa at a Romanian embassy; it is possible to obtain a visa at the border (consult your consulate), but if you fly into Romania your airline may require that you have a visa. Get a visa extension at a local police station.

EMBASSIES AND CONSULATES

Embassies and consulates of other countries in Romania are in **Bucharest** (p. 777).

Romanian Embassies at home: Canada, 655 Rideau St., Ottawa, ON K1N 6A3 (] (613) 789 53 45; fax 789 43 65; email romania@cyberus.ca); **South Africa,** 117 Charles St., P.O. Box 11295, Brooklyn, 0011 (] (012) 46 69 41; fax 46 69 47); **UK,** 4 Palace Green, Kensington, London W8 4QD (] (020) 79 37 96 66; fax 79 37 80 69); **US,** 1607 23rd St. NW, Washington, D.C. 20008 (] (202) 332 48 48; fax 232 47 48; email consular®roembus.org; www.roembus.org).

GETTING AROUND

BY PLANE. Numerous airlines fly into Bucharest. **TAROM** (Romanian Airlines) is in the process of updating its aging fleet; it flies direct from Bucharest to New York, Chicago, and major European cities. The renovation of Bucharest's Otopeni International Airport has improved it, but the airport is still far from ideal.

BY TRAIN. To buy **international tickets** in Romania, go to the **CFR** (Che-Fe-Re) office in larger towns. While students discounts are technically for Romanians only, an ISIC might get you a 50% discount. **CFR** sells domestic **train** tickets up to 24hr. before the train's departure. After that, only train stations sell tickets. The English timetable *Mersul Trenurilor* is useful (L12,000). Schedule info is available at ☎221 in most cities. **Interrail** is accepted; **Eurail** is not. There are four types of trains: *InterCity* ("IC" on timetables and at train stations), *rapid* (in green), *accelerat* (red), and *personal* (black). International trains (often blue) are usually indicated by "i" on timetables. *InterCity* trains stop only at major cities. *Rapid* trains (also 3 digits) are the next fastest; *accelerat* trains have four digits starting with "1" and are slower. Take the fastest train you can, most often *accelerat*. Also opt for **first class** (*clasa-întîi;* wagons marked with a "1" on the side; 6 people per compartment) instead of **second class** (8 people per compartment); it's well worth it. On **overnight train,** shell out for first class in a *vagon de dormit* (sleeping carriage).

BY BUS. Buses connect major cities in Romania to Athens, Istanbul, Prague, and various cities in Western Europe. Since plane and train tickets to Romania are often expensive, buses are a good—if slow—option. It is best to take a domestic train to the border and catch an international bus from there. Buying tickets straight from the carrier saves you from paying commission. Domestically only take buses if there is no other option; look for signs for the *autogară* (bus station) in each town.

BY CAR. While far from perfect, Romania's road conditions are passable. An **International Driving Permit** and **Green Card** insurance are required. The **speed limit** is 60kph in residential areas, 90kph on expressways. The **Automobil Clubul Român (ACR),** Soseaua Colentina nr. 1, Bucharest (☎ (01) 252 41 40; www.acr.ro), provides roadside assistance. In Bucharest, dial ☎927 for **emergency** help.

BY BIKE AND BY THUMB. **Biking** is neither common nor very safe. *Let's Go* does not recommend **hitchhiking.** If you do go, know that drivers expect a payment similar to the price of a train ticket for the distance traveled, although some kind souls will take you for free or accept what you can afford. No nighttime hitchhiking.

TOURIST SERVICES AND MONEY

TOURIST OFFICES. **ONT** (National Tourist Office) used to be one of the most corrupt government agencies in Romania. Times have changed, but while you won't have to bribe anyone, the information will not necessarily be correct. ONT also moonlights as a **private tourist agency,** selling travel packages for a commission.

MONEY. The Romanian unit of currency is the *leu*, plural **lei** (abbreviated L). The banknotes are L500, L1000, L5000, L10,000, L50,000, and L100,000. While many establishments accept US dollars or DM, you should pay for everything in *lei* to avoid rip-offs and to save your hard currency for bribes and emergencies. **Private exchange bureaus** litter the country; not many take **credit cards** or **traveler's checks.** Shop around for good rates. Dollars and Deutchmarks are preferred, although other Western currencies can usually be exchanged somewhere. Always keep receipts for money exchanges. **ATMs,** which generally accept Cirrus, Plus, MC, and Visa and give *lei* at reasonable rates, are rare outside major cities. **Hostel** beds average US$10-12; budget **hotels** can range wildly from US$10-35. **Meals** are incredibly cheap at US$2-5. It is customary to give (and receive) inexact change for purchases, generally rounding to the nearest L500; this suffices as a **tip** in restaurants.

ACCOMMODATIONS AND CAMPING

While some **hotels** charge foreigners 50-100% more than locals, lodging is still relatively cheap. One-star hotels are on par with mediocre European youth hostels, two-star places are decent, and those with three are good but expensive. In some places, going to ONT (in resorts, the *Dispecerat de Cazare*) and asking for a room may get a price at least 50% lower than that quoted by the hotel. **Private accommoda-**

tions are generally the way to go; be aware that renting a room "together" means sharing a bed. Rooms run US$6-10 per person, sometimes with breakfast and other amenities. See the room and fix a price before accepting. Many towns allow foreign students to stay in **university dorms** at low prices. Ask at the university rectorate; ONT *might* help. **Campgrounds** are crowded and often have frightening bathrooms.

FOOD AND DRINK

Romanian food is fairly typical of Central Europe, with a bit of Balkan and French influence thrown in. Bucharest is the only place to find non-Romanian cuisine. Lunch usually starts with a soup, called *supă* or *ciorbă* followed by a main dish (typically grilled meat) and dessert. Soups can be very tasty; try *ciorbă de perişoare* (with vegetables and ground meatballs) or *supă cu găluşte* (with fluffy dumplings). Pork comes in several varieties, of which *muşchi* and *cotlet* are the best quality. For dessert, *clătite* (crepes), *papanaşi* (doughnuts with jam and sour cream), and *tort* (creamy cakes) can all be fantastic if they're fresh. Some restaurants charge by weight (usually 100g) rather than by portion. *Garnituri*, the extras that come standard with a meal, are usually charged separately, down to that dollop of mustard. As a rule, you're paying for everything the waiters put in front of you. "Fast food" in Romania means pre-cooked and microwaved.

COMMUNICATION

MAIL. Request *par avion* for **airmail,** which takes 10-19 days to reach international destinations. Mail can be received general delivery through *Poste Restante.*

TELEPHONES. Almost all public phones are orange and accept **phone cards,** although a few archaic blue phones take L500 coins. Buy L50,000 phone cards at telephone offices, major Bucharest Metro stops, and some post offices. Rates run L10,000 per min. to neighboring countries, L18,000 per min. to most of Europe, and L30,000 per min. to the US. **International direct dial numbers** include: **AT&T Direct,** ☎01 800 42 88; **BT Direct,** ☎01 800 44 44; **Canada Direct,** ☎01 800 50 00; **MCI WorldPhone,** ☎01 800 18 00; and **Sprint,** ☎01 800 08 77. Make calls from major cities. **Local calls** cost L500-1500 and can be made from any phone; a busy signal may just indicate a connection problem. To make a phone call *prin commandă* (with the help of the operator at the telephone office), write down the destination, duration, and phone number for your call. Pay up front, and ask for the rate per minute.

LANGUAGES. **Romanian** is a Romance language; those familiar with French, Italian, Spanish, or Portuguese should be able to read signs. **German** and **Hungarian** are widely spoken in Transylvania. **French** is a second language for the older generation, **English** for the younger. Get cuddly with Romanian on p. 981.

HOLIDAYS

Holidays: New Year's Day (Jan. 1-3); Epiphany (Jan. 6); Orthodox Christmas (Jan. 7); Orthodox Easter (Apr. 30-May 1); National Day (Dec. 1); and Christmas (Dec. 25-26).

BUCHAREST ☎01

Once the fabled beauty at the end of the Orient Express, Bucharest (boo-koo-RESHT; pop. 2 million) is famed today for its infamous Communist makeover under Romanian dictator Nicolae Ceauşescu, who in his 25 years in power managed to undo most of the city's splendor. After escaping war-time destruction, Neoclassical architecture, old neighborhoods, and Ottoman remnants were replaced with concrete blocks and Communist monuments. Today, the metropolis is a somber ghost of its former self. Luckily, Romania's current government is slowly beginning to give Bucharest a desperately needed face-lift.

GETTING THERE AND GETTING AROUND

Airplanes: Otopeni Airport (☎230 00 22), 18km from the city. Buses from the airport go to "Centru" near Hotel Intercontinental Piața Universității (M2: Piața Universității). Bus #783 to Otopeni leaves from Piața Unirii every 20min. Buy **international tickets** at the **CFR/TAROM office,** Str. Brezoianu 10 (☎313 42 95). M2: Piața Universității; with the National Theater on your left, take a right onto B-dul Regina Elisabeta, a left after McDonald's, and a left after 1 block onto Brezoianu.

Trains: Gara de Nord (☎228 08 80. M3: Gara de Nord) is the principal station. L4000 to enter the station if you're not catching a train. To: **Sofia** (10-12hr., 3 per day, L431,000); **Budapest** (14-17hr., 6 per day, L606,000); **İstanbul** (20-24hr., 1 per day, L498,000); and **Kiev** (30hr., 1 per day, L772,000).

Buses: Filaret, Cuțitul de Argint 2 (☎335 11 40). M2: Tineretului. South of the city center. **Fotopoulos Express** (☎335 82 49) goes to **Athens. Toros,** B-dul. Dinicu Golescu kiosk (☎223 18 98), and **Murat,** B-dul Dinicu Golescu 31 (☎638 39 92), go to **İstanbul.** It is better to take buses than trains. **Double T** (☎313 36 42), affiliated with Eurail, goes to Western Europe. International bus companies are near Piața Dorobanților.

Public Transportation: Buses, trolleys, and **trams** cost L2500. Buy tickets from a kiosk; you can't get them on board. Validate on board or face a fine. Beware pickpockets during peak hours, especially on bus #133. The **Metro** offers reliable, less crowded service to major points in Bucharest and runs 5am-11:30pm. L7000 cards are good for 2 trips.

Taxis: Getax, ☎95 31. **Colbăcescu,** ☎94 51. **Cristaxi,** ☎94 61. Expect to pay at least L2000 per km, and arrange the price *(prețul)* beforehand; L30-60,000 is probably the best you'll get. Bargain harshly, and *never* pay more than US$10.

ORIENTATION AND PRACTICAL INFORMATION

Bucharest's six sectors circle clockwise around the city. In the northern portion are **Piața Victoriei** and **Piața Romană,** as well as the train station, **Gara de Nord.** In the southeast corner are what remains of Bucharest's **Old Town** and **Piața Unirii, Piața Universității,** and **Piața Revolutiei.** Gara de Nord lies along the M3 metro line just west of the Centru. Take a train (dir. Dristor II) one stop to Piața Victoriei, change to the M2 line to Depoul; take this train one stop to Piața Romana, two stops to Piața Universității, or three stops to Piața Unirii. For a great guide to the city, get *Bucharest in Your Pocket* (L20,000) at many museums, bookstores, and some hotels.

Tourist Information: Best found at major hotels.

Embassies: Australia, B-dul. Unirii 74, Ef. 5 (☎320 98 02). M2: Piața Unirii. Open M-W 9:30am-12:30pm. **Canada,** Str. Nicolae Iorga 36 (☎222 98 45). M2: Piața Romană. Open M-F 8:30am-noon. **Ireland** (consulate), Str. V. Lascăr 42 (☎211 39 67). M2: Piața Romană. Open M-F 10am-noon and 2-4pm. **UK,** Str. Jules Michelet 24 (☎312 03 03). M2: Piața Romană. Open M-Th 9am-noon and F 9am-11am. **US,** Str. Tudor Arghezi 7/9 (☎210 40 42; after hours ☎210 01 49). M2: Piața Universității. Consulate at Str. Nicolae Filipescu 26. Open M-Th 8-5pm. Citizens of **New Zealand** should contact UK embassy. Citizens of **South Africa** should contact embassy in Budapest (see p. 514).

Currency Exchange: Exchange houses are everywhere; **ATMs,** located at major banks, always give the best rates. Don't change money on the street; scams are prevalent.

American Express: Marshall Tourism, Bd. Magheru 43, 1st fl., #1 (☎223 12 04). M2: Piața Romană. Cannot cash traveler's checks. Open M-F 9am-5:30pm, Sa 10am-1pm.

Luggage Storage: At Gara de Nord. Foreigners pay L7100 or L14,200. Open 24hr.

Police: ☎955. **Ambulance:** ☎961. **Fire:** ☎981.

Pharmacies: Farmadex, Calea Moșilor 280 (☎211 95 60).

Internet Access: Internet-PCNet, Calea Victoriei 25 (☎311 26 82). M2: Piața Universității; just south of Bd. Regina Elisabeta. L15,000 per 30min. Open M-Sa 10am-10pm.

Telephones: Telephone office, Calea Victoriei 37. Open M-F 8am-8pm, Sa 8am-2pm. Orange phone cards L20,000, L50,000, or L100,000.

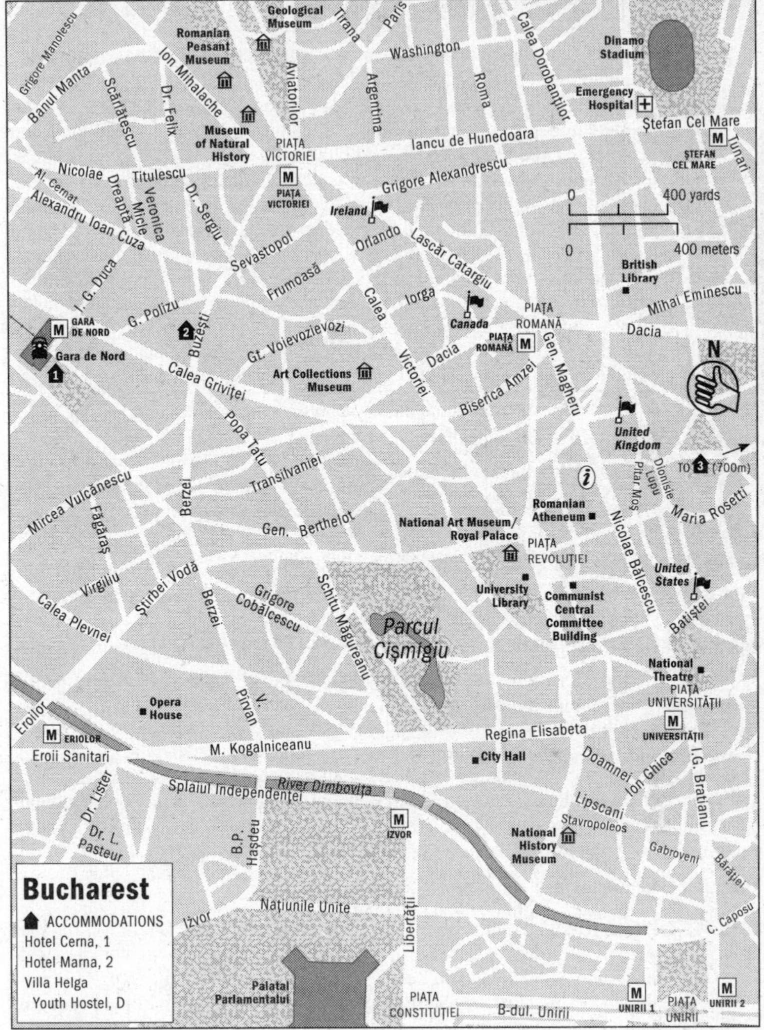

Post Office: Str. Matei Millo 10 (☎315 90 30). M2: Piața Universității. Open M-F 7:30am-7:30pm, Sa 7:30am-2pm. *Poste Restante* nearby, next to Hotel Carpati. Address mail to be held: First name SURNAME, *Poste Restante,* Str. Matei Millo 10, Bucharest **70154.**

ACCOMMODATIONS AND FOOD

It's difficult to find good rooms for less than L300-400,000 per person.

Villa Helga Youth Hostel, Str. Salcâmilor 2 (☎610 22 14). M2: Piața Romană; take bus #86, 79, or 133 two stops; or take M3: Gara de Nord; and take any of same buses 6 stops. This brings you to Piața Gemeni, east along Bd. Dacia from Piața Romană. Take a right on Str. Gemini Lascăr, a left at the triangular green, another left onto Str. Viitorului, and a final right on Str. Salcâmilor. Don't trust the "staffers" at Gara de Nord; they're scam artists. The real staff, however, is friendly and funny. Breakfast included. Kitchen. Laundry free. US$12.

Hotel Cerna, Str. Golescu 29 (☎311 05 35). M3: Gara de Nord. One-star hotel next to the train station. Singles L225-415,000; doubles L310-640,000; triples L875,000.

Hotel Marna, Str. Buzeşti 3 (☎659 67 33; fax 312 94 55). M3: Gara de Nord. One-star hotel with decent rooms. Close to the train station and central Bucharest. Breakfast included. Singles L250,000; doubles L420-690,000.

For the best Romanian food in town, head east from M2: Piaţa Romană on Bd. Dacia to Piaţa Gemeni, then walk two more blocks and take a right on Toamnei; after an intersection on the right, you'll find **Nicoreşti,** Str. Maria Rosetti 40. (Open M-Sa 9am-11pm, Su 1-11pm.) **Caru' cu Bere** (The Cart o' Beer), Str. Stavropoleos 5 (M2: Piaţa Universităţi), was founded in 1879. It's one of the few remaining famous facades of Bucharest's past, and the food isn't bad either. (Entrees L30-60,000. Open daily 10am-midnight.) Enjoy a light meal at artsy **Mes Amis,** Str. Lipscani 82 (M2: Piaţa Unirii or Piaţa Universităţi), in a tiny alley between Lipscani and Gabroveni. (Meals L25-35,000. Open M-Sa noon-2am and Su 5pm-2am; food served until 12:30am.) **Paradis 2,** Str. Hristo Botev 10 (M2: Piaţa Universităţi), serves Middle Eastern entrees. (Entrees L20-40,000. Open daily 9am-10:30pm.) **Open-air markets** offering all manner of veggies and more abound in Bucharest—good ones are at Piaţa Amzei, Piaţa Matache, and Piaţa Gemeni.

SIGHTS

Bucharest is on the brink of something, although nobody seems to know what it is. Wide streets with classical villas, communist apartments, fledgling businesses, and green parks leave a confusing impression of the past, while Bucharest remains uncertain about its future.

CIVIC CENTER. In order to create the long dreamed-of Socialist capital, Ceauşescu destroyed 5 sq. km of Bucharest's historic center, demolishing over 9000 19th-century houses and displacing more than 40,000 Romanians. The unfinished **Civic Center** is united by B-dul Unirii, intentionally built slightly larger than the Champs-Elysées, after which it was modeled. Its centerpiece, the **Parliamentary Palace** (Palatul Parlamentului), is the world's second-largest building (after the Pentagon in Washington, DC) and was built by 70,000 workers using raw materials exclusively from Romania. Begun (appropriately) in 1984, the building's interior is still under construction. *(M2: Unirii. For tours, use the entrance to the left of the building as you approach. Open daily 10am-4pm. Tours L40,000.)*

SIGHTS OF THE REVOLUTION. Bucharest is slowly putting the memory of the revolution behind it. White crosses and plaques remind visitors of those who died during the revolution of 1989; locals no longer slow down as they go by to pay homage to the events of the past. **Piata Universităţii** houses memorials to victims of both the 1989 and June 1990 revolutions. Demonstrators perished fighting Ceauşescu's forces here December 21, 1989, the day before his fall. Students had been protesting the neo-Communist government in the small Piaţa 22 Decembrie 1989, opposite Hotel Intercontinental, since April; displeased, the government bused in over 10,000 Romanian miners in June to squash the protestors, killing 21 students. *(M2: Piaţa Universităţii; behind the fountain.)* With Hotel Intercontinental on your left, make a right onto Bd. Regina Elisabeta and then a right onto Calea Victoriei to reach **Piaţa Revoluţiei,** where the first shots of the revolution were fired December 21, 1989.

PARKS. Bucharest's extensive park system is a lovely respite from the urban grime. Sprawling, beautiful **Herăstrău Park** is just north of downtown. Within the park lies Bucharest's largest lake, wandering peacocks, and the small Island of Roses. *(M2: Aviatorilor.)* One of Bucharest's oldest parks, the **Cişmigiu Gardens,** is filled with elegant paths and a little lake where you can rent paddle boats. *(M2: Piaţa Universităţii. With Hotel Intercontinental on your left, make a right on Bd. Regina Elisabeta and walk for a few minutes. Open daily 8am-8pm. Paddle boats L25,000 per hr.)*

MUSEUMS. Bucharest's museums vary in quality, but can often provide a nice break from the hectic pace on the city's streets. The **Museum of the Romanian Peasant** (Muzeul Tăranului Român), Şos. Kiseleff 3, is the colorful star of the bunch. *(M2,3: Piata Victoriei. Open Tu-Su 10am-6pm, last admission 5pm. L20,000.)*

OTHER SIGHTS. If you're in the mood for something truly Romanian, visit the huge **market** at the "Obor" Metro stop. Among other things, you're likely to find eggs, raw wool, rusty nails, Bulgarian cigarettes, Turkish Levis, shower heads, ceramic plates, and ducks. *(M3: Obor.)* Several of modern Bucharest's most fashionable streets are sights in and of themselves; be sure to stroll along **Calea Victoriei, Şos. Kiseleff, B-dul. Aviatorilor,** and **B-dul. Magheru.** The sidestreets just off Piaţa Victoriei and Calea Dorobanţilor, with names like Paris, Washington, and Londra, brim with villas and houses typical of beautiful 19th-century Bucharest.

ENTERTAINMENT

THEATER AND OPERA. Theater and **opera** are cheap diversions in Bucharest, but there are no shows June through September. Tickets are sold at each theater's box office and go on sale the Saturday before the performance. Try the **Teatrul Naţional,** Bd. N. Bălcescu 2 (☎613 91 75; M2: Piaţa Universităţii), also home to **Teatrul de Operetă** (☎313 63 48). **Atheneul Român** (☎315 68 75; M2: Piaţa Universităţi) holds excellent classical music concerts. **Opera Română,** Bd. M.L. Kogălniceanu 70 (☎313 18 57; M1,3: Eroilor), stages top-notch opera for ridiculously cheap prices.

NIGHTLIFE. For nighttime debauchery, pack a map (streets are poorly lit) and cab fare. **Underground,** Calea Victoria 26, is a new trendy bar playing "underground" music. Its motto is: "Be different, feel different." (Open midnight-3am.) Walk down Bd. Brătianu and take the third right to find **Club A,** Str. Blanari 14 (M2: Piaţa Universitătii), run by the University of Bucharest's School of Architecture and always packed by 11pm. (Cover Tu-Th men L25,000, women free; F-Sa L30,000. Open M-Th 11pm-5am, F 11pm-7am, Sa 9pm-7am, Su 9pm-5am.) Hyper **Swing House,** Str. Gabroveni 20, draws an enthusiastic crowd. Live music nightly, with weekly swing performances. (Drink min. L30,000. M2: Piaţa Unirii. Open daily 3pm-6am.) **The Dubliner Irish Pub,** Bd. N. Titulescu 18, has the best Guinness south of the Carpathians. (M2, 3: Piaţa Victoriei. Open daily noon-2am.) To get to the hottest discos during the school year (Oct. to late June), take the last metro (11:30pm) to Semănătoarea and let the noisy crowd lead you through the maze of dorms. **Maxxx** is one well-known club, but the turnover is high. (Cover for men L15,000 M-Th, F L25,000, women free M-F; Sa L20,000 until 11:30pm, L40,000 after.)

TRANSYLVANIA

Though the name evokes images of a dark, evil land of black magic and vampires, Transylvania *(Ardeal)* is a region of green hills and mountains descending gently from the Carpathians to the Hungarian Plain, dotted with towns. The vampire legends, however, have their roots in the architecture: Transylvanian buildings are tilted, jagged, and more sternly Gothic than anywhere else in Eastern Europe.

CLUJ-NAPOCA ☎064

Cluj-Napoca (CLOOZH na-PO-ka) is Transylvania's unofficial capital and student center, but loses much of its vitality with the student exodus in June. Colorful, relaxed, and relatively Western (with a sizable Hungarian minority), Cluj is a good starting point for a journey farther into Transylvania or north to Maramureş. The 80m Gothic steeple of the Catholic **Church of St. Michael** (Biserica Sf. Mihail) pierces the skyline in **Piaţa Unirii.** With your back to the church, head left down Bd. Eroilor to the Byzantine-Romanian **Orthodox Cathedral** (Catedrala Arhiepiscopală). Walk back in the direction of Piaţa Unirii and make a right onto Bd. Ferdinand, then a left after the bridge to the steps leading up Cetătuie Hill for a full view of the city. To visit the serene **Botanical Gardens** (Grădină Botanica), go back to Piața Unirii, take a right (with your back to the statue) on Str. Napoca, and take a left on Str. Coh. Bilașcu. (Open daily 9am-6pm. L5000. Useful map L3000.)

Trains (☎19 24 75) run from Piața Mihai Viteazul to Brașov (5hr., 8 per day, L80,000); Bucharest (7hr., 7 per day, L45,600); and Budapest (9-12hr., 4 per day, round-trip L400,000). **Buses** (☎43 52 78) go from Str. Giordano Bruno 3 to Budapest (9hr., 4 per week, L180,000). From the train station, the bus station is a quick walk to the right and another right across a bridge. Cross the street and head down Str. Horea, which becomes to Bd. Regele Ferdinand (previously Str. Gh. Doja) after crossing the river and ends in the main square, **Piața Unirii. ATMs** are along Bd. Ferdinand and surround Piața Unirii. Check **email** at the **Kiro Internet Cafe,** Bd. Ferdinand 6, third floor. (L7000 per hr. Open 24hr.) On the corner of Piața Unirii and Str. Napoca, right in the center of things, is **Hotel Continental.** (☎19 14 41. Breakfast included. Singles US$9; doubles US$18.) **Postal code:** 3400.

BRAȘOV ☎068

Brașov (BRA-shohv) is an ideal starting point for excursions into the mountains. Its exquisite city center is also a worthwhile stop in itself. Beyond the square along Str. Gh. Barițiu looms the Lutheran **Black Church** (Biserica Neagră), Romania's most celebrated Gothic church, so named because it was charred by fire in 1689. (Open M-Sa 10am-5pm. L8100, students L4000.) **Piața Sfatului** and **Str. Republicii** are perfect for a stroll. To see the mountains without breaking a sweat, ride a **cable car** *(telecabina)* up Muntele Tâmpa from Aleea T. Brediceanu. Look for steep, stone steps off the main road. (Open M noon-6pm, Tu 9:30am-6pm, W-F 9:30am-7pm, Sa-Su 9:30am-8pm. L15,000, round-trip L20,000.) To climb a road less traveled, trails on Aleea T. Brediceanu lead to the majestic **Weaver's Bastion** and other **medieval ruins.**

Trains go to Bucharest (3-4hr., up to 25 per day, L31,000) and Cluj-Napoca (5-6hr., 6 per day, L70,000). Get train info at **CFR** on Str. Republicii. (Open M-F 8am-7pm, Sa 9am-1pm.) To get from the station to town, take bus #4 (dir. Piața Unirii; 2 rides L4700) to the main **Piața Sfatului** (10min.); descend in front of Black Church. Good **maps** (under US$1) are at kiosks on Str. Republicii. **ATMs** line the streets of Brașov. Check **email** at the **Internet Club,** Republicii 49 (Open daily 8am-10pm. L15,000 per hr.) **Private rooms** in Brașov are the virtually exclusive domain of a short woman with dark brown hair and blue eyes named Maria Bolea, though she is often imitated. (☎31 19 62; cellular ☎ (094) 81 69 70. Rooms about US$10 per night.) Or try **Hotel Aro Sport,** Sfautul Ioan 4. Take a left off Str. Mureșenilor going to Piața Sfatului. (Reception 24hr. Single L224,000; doubles L228,000.) For Romanian and Mexican food and free shots of *palinka* head to **Bella Musica,** Str. G. Baritu nr. 2. (Entrees L50,000-70,000. Open daily 1pm-midnight.) **Postal code:** 2200.

EXCURSIONS FROM BRAȘOV: BRAN AND SIGHIȘOARA. It's a dark and stormy night—the perfect setting for **Bran,** once the home of **Vlad Țepeș Dracula** (literally Vlad the Impaler, son of Dracul), the supposed villain-hero of Bram Stoker's famed novel *Dracula.* As Prince of Wallachia, Vlad Țepeș was charged with protecting the Bran pass, and had to impale some Turks as part of his job. The tale is more fiction than fact—Țepeș never even lived in the **castle** at Bran. Despite its lack of vampiric significance, the castle is worth a visit. (Open Tu-Su 9am-5pm. L50,000, students L35,000.) To get to Bran from Brașov, take a **trolleybus** to "Autogară 2" (officially "Gară Bartolomeu"), where **buses** go to Bran (45min., every hr., L8000). To reach the castle, get off at the main stop by the "Cabana Bran Castle—500m" sign. Then take the main road back toward Brașov and take the first right. For **tourist info,** call ☎23 68 84. (Open daily 8am-6pm.) ☎**068.**

Sighișoara (see-ghee-SHWAH-rah) is perhaps Transylvania's most pristine and enchanting medieval town. Surrounded by mountains and crowning a green hill, the citadel's gilded steeples and old clock tower have survived centuries of attacks, fires, and dozens of floods. The **Citadel** (Cetate), built by the Saxons in

DRACULA, UNCENSORED While Bran castle may be underwhelming, the gruesome exploits of its temporary tenant make the hack horror novel pale in comparison. Born in Sighişoara in 1431, Vlad Ţepeş' father (also Vlad) was a member of the Order of the Dragon, a society charged with defending Catholicism from infidels. Hence the name by which he ruled: Vlad Dracul ("Dragon"), and his son's moniker Dracula, "son of the dragon," which was corrupted to "son of the devil" as word of his atrocities spread. In 1444, Vlad's father shipped his two sons off to a Turkish prison to placate an Ottoman ruler. There Vlad learned the tortures for which he would become infamous. Of these, his personal favorite of was impalement: a victim was pulled down a stake driven up his anus by two horses tied to his spread legs. When the Turks invaded Wallachia in 1462, they were met by some 20,000 of their kinsmen impaled in this manner outside Dracula's territory. Horrified, the Turks retreated. Dracula also practiced such terror tactics on his own people. In order to combat poverty in his realm, for example, the benevolent ruler invited the destitute and disabled to his palace for a banquet...and then had them burned to death. By the height of his rule, his subjects were so terrified into obedience that Dracula placed a gold cup in Tirgovişte Square, which remained undisturbed for the length of his reign.

1191, is now a tiny medieval city-within-a-city. For a walking tour of the Citadel, follow the white and red arrows that start next to Vlad Dracul's house. (Open Tu-F 9am-6pm, Sa-M 9am-4pm.) Once a year, in July or August, the town hosts a huge free **medieval festival.** To reach the center from the train station, take a right on **Str. Libertătii,** and your first left onto **Str. Gării,** veer left at the Russian cemetery, turn right, cross the footbridge over river **Târnava Mare,** and walk down Str. Morii. **Bobby's Hostel,** Str. Tache Ionescu 18, is one of Romania's few real youth hostels. (☎77 22 32. Dorms US$5; doubles US$12.) **Hotel Non-Stop** is across from the train station. (☎77 59 01. Doubles L160,000-180,000.) Across from Bobby's is the **Joker Restaurant.** (Entrees L25,000-30,000. Open M-Sa noon-11pm, Su 2pm-11pm.) **Trains** run to Bucharest (5hr., 10 per day, L70,000) and Brasov (2hr., L80,000). ☎**065.**

SINAIA ☎044

The Romanian royal family chose to live in Sinaia when they were away from Cotroceni in Bucharest. Though the construction of **Peleş Castle** (Castelul Peleş) began in 1873, it nonetheless has central heating, electric lights, and an elevator. (Open W noon-5pm, Th-Su 9:15am-5pm; last entry 4:15pm. L75,000, students L45,000.) While Peleş was built by King Carol I, the equally striking **Pelişor Castle,** built in the early 20th century, was designed by his wife Queen Maria, who wanted it to fit progressive modern tastes. (Open W noon-5pm, Th-Su 9:15am-5pm. L60,000, students L30,000.) The **cable car** *(telecabina)* to **Cota 1400** (L20,000, round-trip L35,000) leads to alpine hikes. Along the Bucegi range, the yellow stripe trail leads intense hikers on a strenuous four-hour climb from **Cota 2000,** past **Babele** (2200m, accessible by cable car from the nearby town of Buşteni) to **Omu** (2500m), the highest peak of Bucegi. (Cable cars run 8:30am-6pm W-Su.)

Trains go to Bucharest (2hr., every hr., L40,000) and Braşov (1hr., every hr., L31,000). From the station, cross the street, climb two flights of stairs, take a left onto a cobblestone ramp at the first landing, climb the first steps, and take two left turns onto **Bd. Carol I,** the main street. Large hotels sell bad **maps** of the trails (L4000). From the main street, head left with your back to the train station, go left of the large digital clock, and left at the small bridge to **Vila Retezatu,** Str. Kogalniceanu 64. (☎31 47 47. L200,000). For more comfortable rooms and an equally central location, try **Vila Camelia,** Str. Spatar 2. At the clock, bear right. (☎31 45 55. Doubles L300,000.) If you're hungry from hiking, head to **Cabana Furnica,** Str. Furnica 50, for savory local cuisine. (Open 9:30am-9:30pm. Entrees L20,000-L50,000.) Or, descend to the main street and head over to **Pizza Caparţi,** B-dul Carol I 39 (L40,000-60,000). **Postal code:** 2180.

NORTHERN ROMANIA

Nestled against Ukraine and Hungary, the Maramureş region of northern Romania is known for its stunning woodcarving and reverence for sacred traditions. These days, few visitors find reason to venture into the area's rolling hills, but those who do are rewarded with the peaceful, seldom-seen traditions of village life.

SIGHETU-MARMAŢIEI ☎062

The northern town of Sighetu-Marmaţiei (see-GHEH-too mar-MAH-tsee-ay, or just Sighet) shows the clash between rural past and industrial present like few other places in the world. Sighet's dirty streets are unlikely to be called charming, but they do offer access to the unique surrounding countryside and a fascinating glimpse into a kind of living Romanian history. On Corneliu Coposu, the **Memorial to the Victims of Communism and the Resistance** has earned worldwide acclaim and UNESCO patronage. Take a right off the main street after the map. (Open W-Su 10am-5pm. L4000.) The **Outdoor Folk Architecture Museum,** on the Dobăieş hill, is reachable from the town center by bus (every hr., L5000), or by a 30-minute walk down Ştefan cel Mare away from the yellow church; follow the signs to the left away from the road. (Open Tu-Su 10am-6pm. L5000, students L2000.) Fabulously scenic, the **train** ride from Cluj-Napoca is an experience in itself (7hr., 1 per day, L45,000); trains also go to Bucharest (13½hr., 1 per day, L100,000). To reach the town center, walk four long blocks down Str. Iuliu Maniu away from the train tracks to the yellow church. The best map of town is posted on a large board several blocks to your left, at the other end of the town center. **Mini-Hotel Măgură,** Str. Iuliu Maniu 44, has very cheap rooms. (Reception noon-midnight. L75-100,000 per person.) In the town center, tons of little markets offer variety at low prices.

MOLDAVIA AND BUKOVINA

Eastern Romania, which once included the neighboring Republic of Moldova, extends from the Carpathians to the Prut River. Starker than Transylvania and more developed than Maramureş, Moldavia (as the region is called) is home to the achingly beautiful and strangely painted monasteries of Bukovina.

GURA HUMORULUI ☎033

Within walking distance of the Humor and Voroneţ and on the road to other monasterial wonders, the tiny town of Gura Humorului is ideal for exploring the monasteries of Bukovina by day and relax into mountain scenery at night. Excellent car tours of the region's **monasteries** and an underground salt mine featuring two chapels and a tennis court are available at the **Dispecerat de Cazare,** Str. Câmpului 30 (☎23 88 63); take a left off Ştefan cel Mare from the train station. (Open 24hr. Check adjoining Vila Fabian if the office is closed. Tours US$20-30.)

Trains come from: Suceava (1hr., 5 per day, L25,000), Bucharest (8hr., 1 per day, L131,100), and Cluj-Napoca (6hr., 5 per day, L82,900).To reach the town center from the train station, make a right onto Ştefan cel Mare and continue over the bridge. **Email** divine revelations from **Internet Cafe,** Bd. Bucovinii. (L15,000 per hr. Open daily 9am-11pm.) The **Dispecerat de Cazare** (see above) provides rooms in villas in the hills. (Doubles US$8-10. 20% discount in fall, 30% in winter except Christmas, New Year's, and Easter.) Get **groceries** from the markets lining Ştefan cel Mare, including **Supermagazin** across from Internet Cafe. (Open 24hr.)

EXCURSION FROM GURA HUMORULUI: BUKOVINA MONASTERIES. Bukovina's otherworldly painted monasteries hide among green hills and rustic farming villages. Built 500 years ago by Ştefan cel Mare and his successors, the exquisite structures serenely mix Moldavian architecture, Romanian soul, and Christian dogma. Reaching them on public transport can be a trial of faith; instead, go on a tour organized by the tourist office in Gura Humorului. Dress modestly.

Voroneţ Blue (Albastru de Voroneţ), a brilliantly colored 15th-century paint, haunts Romanian art conservationists looking for a modern version. The beautiful frescoes on the monastery's porch are a panorama representing the Eastern Orthodox ecclesiastical calendar. *Jesse's Tree*, on the south wall, displays the genealogy of Jesus, while the north wall depicts scenes from Genesis and Adam's pact with the Devil. To reach Voroneţ from Gura Humorului, catch a bus from the bus station (10min., M-F 3 per day, L10,000) or, on foot, take a left from the train station and another left onto Cartierul Voroneţ; the monastery is at the end of a scenic 5km walk. (Open daily 8am-8pm. L10,000; students L5000.)

Humor, displaying the oldest frescoes in Bukovina, is known for the depiction of the Virgin Mary's life on the south wall. Based on a poem by the patriarch of Constantinople, it shows her saving Constantinople from a Persian attack in 626. The Siege is part of a larger Hymn and Prayer to the Saints. The Final Judgement is on the porch. To get to Humor from Gura Humorului, walk right on Ştefan cel Mare from the train or bus station and walk to the center of town. At the fork near a park on the right, follow Str. M. Humorulu to the left and continue 6km to the monastery. (Open daily 8am-8pm. L10,000, students L5000. Cameras L20,000.)

Moldoviţa, known for its yellow, is the largest of the painted monasteries, and its frescoes are among the best preserved. Painted in 1537, it has a Last Judgement, Jesse's Tree, and a monumental Siege of Constantinople. The *Siege of 626*, painted on the exterior wall to the right of the entrance, depicts the ancient fortress in an uncanny 16th-century light. (Open daily 7am-8pm.) **Buses** run from the bus station in Gura Humorului to Vatra Dornei (45min., 3 per day, L30,000).

Immaculately white and beautifully simple, the **Putna** complex encompasses the marble-canopied **tomb of Ştefan cel Mare** and a **museum.** (Monastery open daily 8am-8pm; free. Museum open daily 9am-5pm. L5000, students L1500. Church open daily 9am-5pm; free.) Built between 1466 and 1469, Putna was the first of 38 monasteries founded by Ştefan cel Mare, who built one church after each battle he won. He left Putna's location up to God: climbing a nearby hill to the left of the monastery (marked by a cross), he shot an arrow into the air. A piece of the oak it struck is on display at the museum, along with a number of manuscripts and religious garb. For the scenic ride to Putna, catch direct **trains** from Suceava, 75km southeast (2½hr., 5 per day, L22,000). Exiting the platform, take a right, then a left at the first intersection and keep walking.

RUSSIA (РОССИЯ)

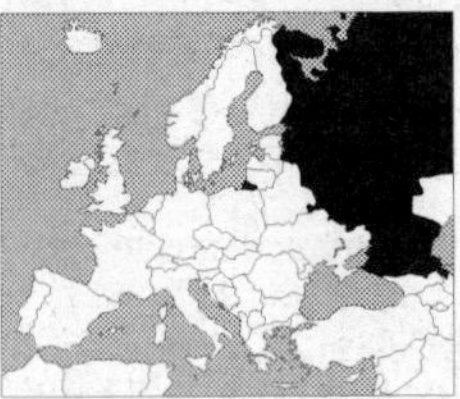

RUBLES

US$1 = 28R	10R = US$0.36
CDN$1 = 19R	10R = CDN$0.53
UK£1 = 41R	10R = UK£0.25
IR£1 = 32R	10R = IR£0.32
AUS$1 = 16R	10R = AUS$0.62
NZ$1 = 12R	10R = NZ$0.84
SAR1 = 4R	10R = SAR2.50
DM1 = 13R	10R = DM0.78
EUR€1 = 25R	10R = EUR€0.40

Country code: 7. **International dialing prefix:** 810. From outside Russia, dial int'l dialing prefix (see inside back cover) + 7 + city code + local number.

Ten years after the fall of the Evil Empire, we still don't understand Russia, and it still doesn't understand us. The current paradoxes in which it exists go beyond any of the clichés visited upon it by Western journalists. Vaguely repentant former communists man the ship of state under the standard of the market,

FACTS AND FIGURES

Official Name: Russian Federation.
Government: Federation.
Capital: Moscow.
Land Area: 17,075,200 sq. km.
Geography: Western plains, Ural Mountains, Siberian plateau.
Climate: Humid continental to sub-arctic.
Population: 146,390,000.
Languages: Russian.
Religions: Nonreligious (74%), Russian Orthodox (16%), Muslim (10%).
Income Per Capita: US$4000.
Major Exports: Petroleum, natural gas, wood products, metals, and chemicals.

while impoverished pensioners long for a rosy-tinted Soviet past. Heedless of the failing provinces, cosmopolitan Moscow indiscriminately gobbles down hyper-capitalism, while St. Petersburg struggles not to resemble a ghost capital. No one has much affection left for the West, by whom most Russians feel profoundly betrayed. Russia can be a bureaucratic nightmare that would have made Trotsky blush, but it is many ways the ideal destination for a budget traveler—inexpensive and well-served by public transportation, with hundreds of neglected monasteries, kremlins, and churches.
How much longer can you sit there without *Let's Go: Eastern Europe 2001?*

DISCOVER RUSSIA

Moscow is more than memories of revolution: the spires of St. Basil's are brilliant in real life than in photos, and the collections of the Kremlin—including the Fabergé eggs—are mind-boggling (see p. 791). Rivaling other cultural capitals, **St. Petersburg** flaunts Europe's largest art collection at the Hermitage, the opulence of the Summer and Winter Palaces, and one of the world's best ballet companies (see p. 802).

ESSENTIALS

WHEN TO GO

The best time to visit is May-September. Spring and fall can be unpredictable with periodic snow flurries; it will also be very slushy. Winter in Moscow and St. Petersburg can be very picturesque, uncrowded, and romantic. Dress warmly.

DOCUMENTS AND FORMALITIES

Citizens of Australia, Canada, Ireland, New Zealand, South Africa, the UK, and the US all require a **visa** to enter Russia; you need an **invitation** stating your itinerary and dates of travel to get a visa. Travel agencies that advertise discounted tickets to Russia often can provide visas. **Info Travel,** 387 Harvard St., Brookline, MA 02146 (☎ (617) 566 21 97; email infostudy@aol.com), and **Academic Travel,** 1302 Commonwealth Ave., Boston, MA 02134 (☎ (617) 566 52 72; email actravel@myway.com), both provide invitations and visas to Russia starting at US$150.

Visa assistance is also available at **www.visatorussia.com.** A larger but more expensive operation (US$225) is **Russia House.** In the **US,** they are at 1800 Connecticut Ave. NW, Washington, D.C. 20009 (☎ (202) 986 60 10; email lozansky@aol.com). In Russia, contact them at 44 Bolshaya Nikitskaya, Moscow 125040 (☎ (095) 290 34 59; email aum@glasnet.ru). The following can also give invitations and/or visas for tourists: **Host Families Association (HOFA),** 5-25 Tavricheskaya, 193015 St. Petersburg, Russia (☎/fax (812) 275 19 92; e-mail hofa@usa.net); **Red Bear Tours/Russian Passport,** Suite 11, 401 St. Kilda Rd., Melbourne 3004, Australia (☎ (613) 98 67 38 88;

ww.travelcentre.com.au); **Traveler's Guest House,** Bolshaya Pereyaslavskaya 50, 10th Fl., Moscow, Russia 129401 (☎ (095) 971 40 59; tgh@startravel.ru).

Many hotels will **register your visa** for you on arrival, as should the organizations listed above. Some travel agencies in Moscow and St. Petersburg will also register your visa for approximately US$30. As a last resort, you'll have to climb into the seventh circle of bureaucratic hell known is the central **OVIR** (ОВИР) office (in Moscow called UVIR—УВИР) to register.

EMBASSIES AND CONSULATES

All embassies of other countries in Russia are in **Moscow** (see p. 791); many consulates are also in **St. Petersburg** (see p. 802).

Russian Embassies at Home: Australia, 78 Canberra Ave., Griffith ACT 2603 Canberra (☎ (06) 295 90 33, visa info ☎295 18 47; fax 295 94 74); **Canada,** 285 Charlotte St., Ottawa, ON K1N 8L5 (☎ (613) 235 43 41, visa info 236 09 20; fax 236 63 42); **Ireland,** 186 Orwell Rd., Rathgar, Dublin 14 (☎/fax (01) 492 35 25, visa info ☎492 34 92); **New Zealand,** 57 Messines Rd., Karori, Wellington (☎ (04) 476 61 13, visa info ☎476 67 42; fax 476 38 43; email eor@netlink.co.nz); **South Africa,** Butano Building, 316 Brooks St., Menlo Park 0081, Pretoria; P.O. Box 6743, Pretoria 0001 (☎ (012) 362 13 37, visa info ☎344 48 12; fax 362 01 16); **UK,** 13 Kensington Palace Gardens, London W8 4QX (☎ (020) 72 29 36 28, visa info 72 29 8 027; fax 77 27 86 25; email harhouse1@harhouse1.demon.co.uk); **US,** 2650 Wisconsin Ave., N.W., Washington, D.C. 20007 (☎ (202) 298 57 00; fax 298 57 35).

GETTING THERE AND GETTING AROUND

Upon entrance to the country, you'll be given a **Customs Declaration Form** to declare all your valuables and foreign currency; don't lose it. Everything listed on the customs form must be on you when you leave the country. Anything that might be regarded by the customs officials as a work of art or any "old" books—that is, those published before 1975—must be assessed by the Ministry of Culture (located at 17 Malaya Morskaya in St. Petersburg and at Neglinnaya 8/10, office 29 in Moscow). These kind folks will look over your find and usually assess a 100% tax; be sure to have your receipt to establish the value of your item. You will not be permitted to take these items out of the country without a receipt proving you have paid the tax. Keep receipts for any expensive or antique-looking souvenirs. You cannot legally bring rubles into or out of the country. In August 1999, the US State Department issued a travel advisory regarding bringing Global Positioning Systems (G.P.S.), cellular phones, and other radio transmission devices into Russia. Failure to register such devices can (and does) result in search, seizure, and arrest.

BY PLANE. Flying into Moscow or St. Petersburg is the easiest way to enter Russia, which boasts a not-so-reliable air system almost monopolized by **Aeroflot.** Nascent alternative **Transair** services only select cities.

BY TRAIN. If you find yourself passing through Belarus by train you will need a US$20-30 **transit visa.** Trains are generally the best way to move about the country; buy your ticket well ahead of time if you have an important connection to make or your visa is about to expire. If you plan ahead, you'll have your choice of four **classes.** The best is *lyuks* (люкс), or *2-myagky* (2-person soft; мягкий)—a place in a two-bunk cabin in the same car as second-class *kupeyny* (купейний), which has four bunks. On hot nights, air conditioned *lyuks*, available on major lines, may be worth the cost. The next class is *platskartny* (плацкартный), a car with 52 shorter, harder bunks. Aim for places 1-33; places 34-37 are next to the foul bathrooms, and places 38-52 get horribly hot in the summer. Women traveling alone can try to buy out a *lyuks* compartment for security, or can travel *platskartny* with the regular folk and depend on the crowds to shame would-be harassers. *Platskartny* is also a good idea on the theft-ridden St. Petersburg-Moscow line, as you are less likely to be targeted. *Elektrichka* (commuter rail; marked on signs as пригородные поезда; *prigorodnye poezda*) has its own platforms; buy tickets at the *kassa*.

BY BUS. Buses, cheaper than trains, are your best bet for shorter distances. They are often crowded and overbooked, however; don't be shy about ejecting people who try to sit in your seat. On the Hungarian **Ikarus** buses, you'll get seated in a fairly comfy reclining chair, and should be able to store luggage for free. Travel between Finland and St. Petersburg is cheaper by bus than by train.

BY TAXI AND BY THUMB. Hailing a **taxi** is indistinguishable from **hitchhiking,** and should be treated with equal caution. Most drivers who stop will be private citizens trying to make a little extra cash (despite the recent restriction on this technically illegal activity). Those seeking a ride should stand off the curb and hold out a hand into the street, palm down; when a car stops, riders tell the driver the destination before getting in; he will either refuse the destination altogether or ask *Skolko?* (How much?), leading to protracted negotiations. Non-Russian speakers will get ripped off unless they manage a firm agreement on the price—if the driver agrees without asking for a price, you must ask *skolko?* yourself (sign language works too). Never get into a car that has more than one person in it.

TOURIST SERVICES AND MONEY

EMERGENCY. Fire: ☎01. **Police:** ☎02. **Emergency:** ☎03.

TOURIST OFFICES. There are two types of Russian tourist office—those that only arrange tours and those that offer general travel services. Offices of the former type are often unhelpful or even rude, but those of the latter are often eager to assist, particularly with visa registration. Big hotels are often a better bet for maps.

MONEY. The **ruble** was revalued in 1998, losing three zeros; the old currency is gradually being phased out. You must show your passport when you exchange money. Find an *Obmen Valyuty* (Обмен Валюты; currency exchange), hand over your currency—most will exchange US dollars and Deutschmarks, and some also accept French francs and British pounds—and receive your rubles. **Do not exchange money on the street.** Banks offer the best combination of good rates and security. You'll have no problem changing rubles back at the end of your trip (just keep exchange receipts), but don't exchange large sums at once, as the rate is unstable. **ATMs** (*bankomat;* банкомат) linked to all major networks and credit cards can be found all over most cities. Major **credit cards,** especially **Visa,** are often accepted. Main branches of banks will usually accept **traveler's checks** and give cash advances on credit cards, most often Visa. Although you'll have to pay in rubles, it's wise to keep US$20 on hand. Be aware that most establishments do not accept crumpled, torn, or written-on bills. A **budget day** will run you between US$30-40. In St. Petersburg and Moscow (but nowhere else) a 5-10% **tip** is becoming customary.

BUSINESS HOURS. Most establishments, even train ticket offices and "24-hour stores", close for a **lunch break** sometime between noon and 3pm. Places tend to close at least 30 minutes earlier than they should, if they choose to open at all.

ACCOMMODATIONS AND CAMPING

The only **hostels** in Russia are in St. Petersburg and Moscow, and even those average US$18 per night. Reserve well in advance, especially in summer. **Hotels** offer several classes of rooms. "Lux," usually two-room doubles with TV, phone, fridge, and bath, are the most expensive. "Polu-lux" rooms are singles or doubles with TV, phone, and bath. The lowest priced rooms are *bez udobstv* (без удобств), which means one room with a sink. Expect to pay 300-450R for a single in a budget hotel. Usually only cash is accepted as payment. In many hotels, hot water (and sometimes all water) is only on a few hours per day. Reservations may help you get on the good side of management, which is often inexplicably suspicious of backpackers. **University dorms** offer cheap rooms; some accept foreign students for about US$5-10 per night. Don't expect sparkling bathrooms or reliable hot water. Make arrangements with an institute from home. **Homestays,** arranged through a tourist office, are often the cheapest (50-100R per night) and best option in the country.

HEALTH AND SAFETY

Russian bottled water is often mineral water; water in much of Russia is drinkable in small doses, but not in Moscow and St. Petersburg; boil it to be safe. A gamma globulin shot will lower your risk of hepatitis A. For **medical emergencies,** either leave the country or go to the American Medical Centers at St. Petersburg or Moscow; these clinics have American-born and trained doctors and speak English.

Reports of **crime** against foreigners are on the rise, particularly in Moscow and St. Petersburg. Although it is hard to look Russian (especially with a huge pack on your back), try not to flaunt your true nationality. Your trip will be that much more pleasant if you never have to file a crime report with the local *militsia,* who will not speak English and will probably not help you. Reports of mafia warfare are scaring off tourists, but unless you bring a shop for them to blow up, you are unlikely to be a target. After the recent eruption of violence in the Northern Caucasus, the Dagestan and Chechnyan regions of Russia are to be avoided.

FOOD AND DRINK

Cuisine is a medley of dishes both delectable and disgusting; tasty borscht can come in the same meal as *salo* (pig fat). Food is generally better in the south. The largest meal of the day, *obed* (lunch; обед), includes: *salat* (salad; салат), usually cucumbers and tomatoes or beets and potatoes with mayonnaise or sour cream; *sup* (soup; суп); and *kuritsa* (chicken; курица) or *myaso* (meat; мясо), often called *kotlyety* (cutlets; котлеты) or *beefshteaks* (beefsteaks; бифштекс). Ordering a few *zakuski* (small appetizers; закуски) instead of a main dish can save money. A cafe (кафе) or *stolovaya* (cafeteria; столовая) is cheaper than a restaurant, but the latter may be unsanitary. The market (rynok; рынок) sells fruits and vegetables, meat, fresh milk, butter, honey, and cheese. Wash and dry everything before you eat it. On the streets, you'll see *blini* (stuffed crepes), *shashlyki* (barbecued meat on a stick; шашлыки) and *kvas* (квас), an alcoholic dark-brown drink.

COMMUNICATION

MAIL. Mail service is much more reliable leaving the country than coming in. Letters to the US will arrive as soon as a week after mailing, although letters to other destinations take 2-3 weeks. Airmail, if you want to risk it, is *avia* (авиа). Send your mail certified (заказное; 16R) to reduce the chance of it being lost. If you're sending anything other than paper goods into the abyss that is the Russian mail system, you'll need to fill out a customs form at the post office. Regular letters to the US cost 7R; postcards cost 5R. **DHL** operates in most large cities. **Poste Restante** is "Писмо До Востребования" (Pismo Do Vostrebovania).

TELEPHONES. New phones take **phone cards,** are good for both local and intercity calls, and often have instructions in English. Phone cards are sold at central telephone offices, Metro stations and newspaper kiosks. For five-digit numbers, insert a "2" between the dialing code and the phone number. For intercity calls dial 8, wait for the tone, then dial the city code. Direct **international** calls can be made from telephone offices and hotel rooms: dial 8, wait for the tone, then dial 10 and the country code. Calls to Europe run US$1-1.50 per min.; to the US and Australia about US$1.50-2.00. You cannot call collect, unless using AT&T service, which will cost your party dearly (US$8 first min.; US$2.78 each additional min. to the US). Prices for calls to the US are 9-25R per min. To call from a telephone office, you can buy tokens or phone cards, or simply prepay your calls and use the *mezhdugorodnye* telephones; be sure to press the *otvet* (reply; ответ) button when your party answers. **International direct dial** numbers include: **AT&T Direct,** ☎ 755 50 42 in Moscow, ☎325 50 42 in St. Petersburg; **BT Direct,** ☎810 80 01 10 10 44; **Canada Direct,** ☎755 50 45 in Moscow, ☎747 33 25 in St. Petersburg, from other cities ☎8 10 800 110 1012; **MCI WorldPhone,** ☎747 33 22 in Moscow, ☎960 22 22 in St. Petersburg; and **Sprint,** ☎747 33 24 in Moscow, ☎8 10 800 110 20 11 in St. Petersburg. When calling from another city, dial 8-095 or 8-812 before these codes; you pay for the call to Moscow or St. Petersburg and the international connection.

LANGUAGE. Take some time with the **Cyrillic** alphabet; it will make getting around and getting by immeasurably easier. For more info on Cyrillic and some Russian phrases, see p. 981.

HOLIDAYS AND FESTIVALS

Holidays: New Year's (Jan. 1-2), Orthodox Christmas (Jan. 7), Defenders of the Motherland Day (Feb. 23), Orthodox Easter (Apr. 15), Labor Day (May 1-2), Victory Day (May 9), Independence Day (June 12), Day of Accord and Reconciliation (Nov. 7), Constitution Day (Dec. 12).

Festivals: In June, when the sun barely touches the horizon, St. Petersburg holds a series of evening concerts as part of the **White Nights Festival;** in the 3rd week of June it moves outside for music under the stars.

MOSCOW (МОСКВА) ☎095

Moscow has an audacity of place—a persistent sense of itself on the cusp of world history. Riding the crest of the recent bubble economy has returned the city to its 19th-century magnificence—Stalin's massive edifices now stand out like monsterland anachronisms amidst the restored pink-and-green of the new old city. If one keeps to the 16th-century sidestreets, it is possible to glimpse what Napoleon saw with the city at his feet: golden domes sparkling over the great mass of Asia. But Moscow's circles, emanating from the Kremlin like the early Muscovite conquests and spiraling into a crumbling wasteland on the peripheries, mirror the condition of its residents: living on the margins of a system they don't understand and never authorized, flinging themselves into the city center only to return wasted to their concrete blocks. Post-ideological, post-apocalyptic, post-whatever-the-hell-you-want, Moscow is in your face. Brutal, tiring, and not as unsafe as it is maddening, Moscow at the beginning of the millennium is most definitely the end of the world.

GETTING THERE AND GETTING AROUND

Flights: International flights arrive at **Sheremetyevo-2** (Шереметьево-2; ☎956 46 66). Vans (look for the "автолайн" sign in front) run to M2: Rechnoy Vokzal (20min., every 10min. 7am-10pm, 10R). Or, take bus #851 or 551 to M2: Rechnoy Vokzal (Речной Вокзал) or bus #517 to M7: Planyornaya (Планёрная, 10R). Most flights within the former USSR fly out of **Vnukovo** (Внуково; ☎234 86 56), **Bikovo** (Биково; ☎558 47 38), **Domodedovo** (Домодедово; ☎234 86 55), or **Sheremetyevo-1** (☎578 23 72). Buy tickets at the *kassa* (касса) at the **Central Airport Station** (Tsentralny Aerovokzal; Центральный Аэровокзал; ☎155 09 22) Leningradsky pr. 37a, 2 stops on tram #23 or trolley #12 or 70 from M2: Aeroport. Express bus schedules are posted outside the station. Taxis to the center will try to rip you off—try bargaining the price down.

Trains: Buying tickets in Russia can be enormously frustrating. If you don't speak Russian, you may want to buy through **Intourist** or your hotel; you'll pay more, but you'll be spared the hassle of the *vokzal* (вокзал; station) experience. Buy tickets for the *elektrichka* (local trains) at the *prigorodniye kassa* (local ticket booths; пригородная касса) in each station. Tickets for longer trips can be purchased at the **Central Train Agency** (Tsentralnoe Zheleznodorozhnoe Agenstvo; Центральное Железнодорожное Агенство), to the right of Yaroslavsky Vokzal (see below). Use window #10 or 11 for Russia and Commonwealth of Independent States destinations; windows #5, 6, or 7 for international. Schedules are posted to the left. *Kassa* open daily 8am-1:30pm and

2:30-10pm. There is 24hr. service at the stations themselves. Tickets to Helsinki are sold on the 2nd floor of Leningradsky Vokzal, at windows #27 and 28. Open daily 8am-10:30pm. Moscow's 9 train stations are on the metro's circle line (M4).

Leningradsky Vokzal (Ленинградский), Komsomolskaya pl. 3. M1,4: Komsomolskaya. To: Helsinki (15hr. 1 per day, 2800R); St. Petersburg (9hr., 15 per day, 84R); and Tallinn (14hr., 1 per day, 1297R).

Kazansky Vokzal (Казанский), Komsomolskaya pl. 2, opposite Leningradsky Vokzal, serves the east and southeast.

Yaroslavsky Vokzal (Ярославский), Komsomolskaya pl. 5, is the starting point for the Trans-Siberian Railroad. To Vladivostok (160hr., 3-4 per week, 610R).

Paveletsky Vokzal (Павлецкий), Pavletskaya pl. 1, serves the Crimea and eastern Ukraine.

Kursky Vokzal (Курский), ul. Zemlyanoi Val 29/1 serves Sevastopol (30hr., 1 per day, 573R); and the Caucasus.

Rizhsky Vokzal (Рижский) Rizhkaya pl. 79/3. To Rīga (16hr., 2 per day, 947R) and Estonia.

Belorussky Vokzal (Белорусский), pl. Tverskaya Zastavy 7. To: Berlin (27hr., 1 per day); Minsk (9-13hr., 6 per day, 377R); Prague (33hr., 1 per day); Vilnius (15hr., 1-2 per day, 1021R); and Warsaw (20hr., 3 per day).

Kievsky Vokzal (Киевский), pl. Kievskovo Vokzala, sends trains to Kiev (17hr., 4 per day, 374R).

Public Transportation: The **Metro** is large and efficient—a masterpiece of Stalinist urban planning. There are 9 Metro lines; in *Let's Go,* "M1" indicates a stop on line 1, "M1,6" indicates a stop served by lines 1 and 6, etc. Runs daily 6am-1am. Passages between lines or stations are indicated by signs of a man walking up stairs; individual exit signs indicate street names. A station serving more than 1 line may have more than 1 name. Buy token-cards (4R) from the *kassa* inside stations. Consult the **metro maps** at the end of this book. Buy **bus** and **trolley** tickets from gray kiosks labeled "проездные билеты" or the driver (4R). Punch your ticket when you get on, or risk a 10R fine.

Taxis: Taxi stands have a round sign with a green T. If you don't speak Russian, you'll get ripped off, particularly if you don't know Moscow. Ask around for the going rate and agree on a price before you get in. Be sure the meter is turned on.

ORIENTATION AND PRACTICAL INFORMATION

A series of concentric rings radiates outward from the **Kremlin** (Kreml; Кремль) and **Red Square** (Krasnaya ploshchad; Красная Площадь). The outermost **Moscow Ring Road** marks the city limits, but most sights lie within the **Garden Ring** (Sadovoe Koltso; Садовое Кольцо). Main shopping streets include **Novy Arbat** (Новый Арбат), which runs west parallel to the Metro's blue lines, and **Ul. Tverskaya** (Тверская), which extends north along the green line. Familiarize yourself with the Cyrillic alphabet and orient yourself by the Metro (which stops within 15min. of anywhere in the city). **Anglyskaya Kniga,** Ul. Kuznetsky, sells extensive city maps (30R) in English. Cyrillic maps are at kiosks all over the city. Also refer to the **color maps** at the front of this book, in both English and Cyrillic. Be careful when crossing streets—drivers are notoriously oblivious to pedestrians.

TOURIST, FINANCIAL, AND LOCAL SERVICES

Tourist Offices: TransTours Voyages, Nikitsky per. 4a (Никитский; ☎203 32 24, 203 32 24, or 203 19 54; fax 203 31 59). M1: Okhotny Ryad. Offers visa registration.

Budget Travel: Student Travel Agency Russia (STAR), ul. Baltyskaya 9, 3rd fl. (чл. Ьелтийская; ☎797 95 55). M2: Sokol. Open M-F 10am-6pm, Sa 11am-4pm.

Embassies: All embassies open M-F unless otherwise noted. **Australia,** Kropotkinsky per. 13 (Кропоткинский; ☎956 60 70). M3: Smolenskaya. Open M-Tu and Th-F 9am-12:30pm and 1:30-5pm. **Belarus,** ul. Maroseyka 17/6 (Маросейка; ☎924 70 31). **Canada,** Starokonyushenny per. 23 (Староконюшенный; ☎956 66 66). M1: Kropotkinskaya. Open 8:30am-1pm and 2-5pm. **China,** ul. Druzhby 6 (Дружбы; ☎147 42 83). **Estonia,** Kalzhny per. 8 (Калжний; ☎290 50 13). M3: Arbatskaya. Open M-Th 10am-noon. **Ireland,** Grokholsky per. 5 (Грохольсций; ☎742 09 07). M4,5: Prospekt Mira. Open 9:30am-1pm and 2:30pm-5:30pm. **Lithuania,** Borisoglebsky per. 10

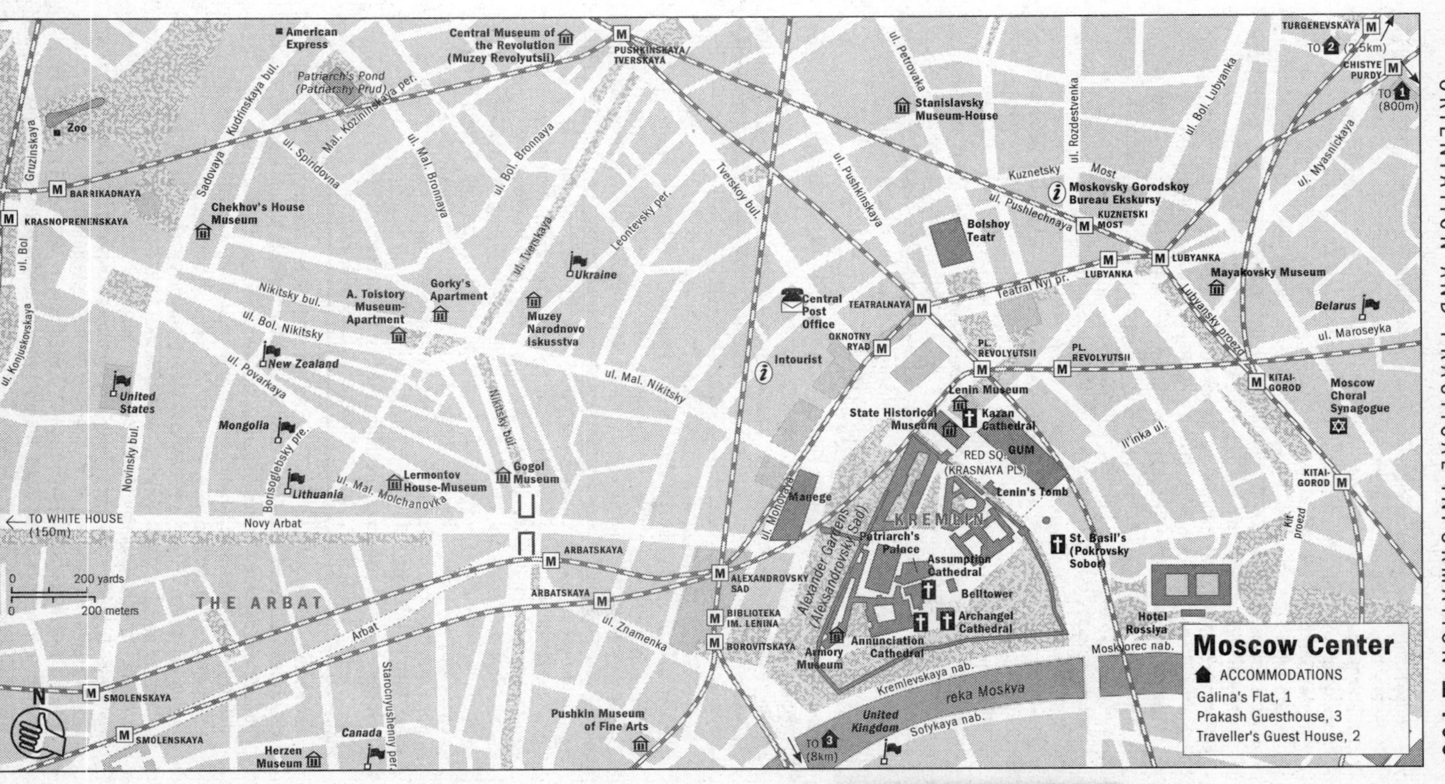
American Express
Central Museum of the Revolution (Muzey Revolyutsii)
PUSHKINSKAYA/ TVERSKAYA
ul. Petrovaka
TURGENEVSKAYA
TO 2 (2.5km)
CHISTYE PURDY
TO 1 (800m)
Patriarch's Pond (Patriarshy Prud)
Mal. Kozinhinskaya per.
Zoo
Gruzinskaya
Sadovaya Kudrinskaya bul.
ul. Spiridovna
ul. Mal. Bronnaya
ul. Bol. Bronnaya
Stanislavsky Museum-House
ul. Rozdestvenka
ul. Bol. Lubyanka
ul. Myasnickaya
BARRIKADNAYA
KRASNOPRENENSKAYA
Chekhov's House Museum
Leontevsky per.
ul. Tverskaya
Tverskoy bul.
ul. Pushkinskaya
Kuznetsky Most
Moskovsky Gorodskoy Bureau Ekskursy
ul. Pushlechnaya
KUZNETSKI MOST
Bolshoy Teatr
ul. Bol
Ukraine
LUBYANKA
Mayakovsky Museum
Nikitsky bul.
A. Tolstory Museum-Apartment
Gorky's Apartment
Muzey Narodnovo Iskusstva
Central Post Office
TEATRALNAYA
Teatral Nyj pr.
Lubyansky proezd
Belarus
ul. Konjuskovskaya
ul. Bol. Nikitsky
OKNOTNY RYAD
ul. Maroseyka
New Zealand
Intourist
PL. REVOLYUTSII
ul. Povarkaya
ul. Mal. Nikitsky
KITAI-GOROD
Moscow Choral Synagogue
United States
Lenin Museum
Mongolia
State Historical Museum
Kazan Cathedral
Il'inka ul.
Novinsky bul.
Borisoglebsky pre.
Nikitsky bul.
RED SQ. (KRASNAYA PL.)
GUM
Lithuania
ul. Mal. Molchanovka
Lermontov House-Museum
Gogol Museum
ul. Mohovaya
Manege
Lenin's Tomb
KREMLIN
TO WHITE HOUSE (150m)
Novy Arbat
Alexander Gardens (Alexandrovsky Sad)
Patriarch's Palace
St. Basil's (Pokrovsky Sobor)
Kit proezd
ARBATSKAYA
ALEXANDROVSKY SAD
Assumption Cathedral
0 200 yards
0 200 meters
THE ARBAT
Belltower
BIBLIOTEKA IM. LENINA
Archangel Cathedral
Hotel Rossiya
Arbat
ul. Znamenka
BOROVITSKAYA
Annunciation Cathedral
Armory Museum
Moskvorec nab.
Kremlevskaya nab.
reka Moskva
N
SMOLENSKAYA
Starocnyushenny per.
Pushkin Museum of Fine Arts
United Kingdom
Sofykaya nab.
Canada
Herzen Museum
TO 3 (8km)
Moscow Center
ACCOMMODATIONS
Galina's Flat, 1
Prakash Guesthouse, 3
Traveller's Guest House, 2

RUSSIA

(Борисоглебский; ☎291 26 43). M3: Arbatskaya. Open 9-11:30am. **New Zealand,** ul. Povarskaya 44 (Поварская; ☎956 35 79). M4,6: Krasnopresnenskaya. Open M-F 9am-5:30pm. **South Africa,** Bolshoy Strochinovsky per. 22/25 (Большой Строченовский; ☎230 68 69). **UK,** Sofiyskaya nab. 14 (Софийская; ☎956 72 00). M1,3,8: Borovitskaya. **Ukraine,** Leontyevsky per. 18 (Леонтьевский; visa ☎229 10 79), off ul. Tverskaya. M3: Tverskaya. **US,** Novinsky 19/23 (Новинский; ☎252 24 51 through 252 24 58; consular section ☎956 42 42 and 255 95 55; fax 956 42 61). M6: Krasnopresnenskaya. A US passport will let you cut the long lines. Open M-F 9am-6pm.

Currency Exchange: *Moscow Express Directory,* free in most luxury hotels, lists places to buy and cash traveler's checks. Usually only main branches of large banks will change traveler's checks or issue cash advances. Nearly every bank and hotel has an **ATM;** particularly reliable is the one in the lobby of the **Gostinitsa Intourist Hotel.** There is an AmEx ATM in the lobby of the AmEx office (see below).

American Express: ul. Sadovaya-Kudrinskaya 21a, Moscow 103001 (Садовая-Кудринская; ☎755 90 00; fax 755 90 04). M2: Mayakovskaya; cross the street/parking lot ahead and turn left on Bolshaya Sadovaya (Большая Садовая), which becomes Sadovaya-Kudrinskaya. Cashes traveler's checks. Open M-F 9am-5pm, Sa 10am-2pm. **AmEx ATM** in lobby (24hr.).

English Bookstores: Angliyskaya Kniga (Английская Книга), ul. Kuznetsky most 18. M6: Kuznetsky most. Open M-F 10am-2pm and 3-7pm, Sa 10am-2pm and 3-6pm.

Laundromat: California Cleaners, Pokhodny 24 (Походный; ☎493 53 11). 20 locations around Moscow. Free pick-up and delivery. 90R per kg. Open 9am-9pm.

RUSSIA

EMERGENCY AND COMMUNICATIONS

Emergencies: Ambulance: ☎03. **Fire:** ☎01. **Police:** ☎02. ☎284 47 13 for lost credit cards. ☎299 11 80 to report offenses *by* the police.

24hr. Pharmacies: Leningradsky pr. 74 (Ленинградский; ☎151 45 70). M2: Sokol. **Ul. Tverskaya 25/9** (Тверская; ☎299 24 59 and 299 79 69). M2: Tverskaya. **Ul. Zemlyanoi Val 25** (Земляной Вал; ☎917 12 85). M4: Kurskaya.

Medical Assistance: American Medical Center, Grokholsky per. 1 (Грохольский; ☎933 77 00). M4: Prospekt Mira. US$175 per visit. Open M-F 8am-8pm, Sa 9am-5pm; 24hr. for emergencies, although you will pay more. Vtoroy Tverskoy-Yamskoy per. 10 (2-ой Тверской-Ямской;]956 33 66). M2: Mayakovskaya. US$215 per visit. Open M-F 8am-8pm, Sa 9am-5pm; 24hr. for emergencies; again, they cost more.

Internet Access: Image.ru (Имидж.ру), ul. Novoslobodskaya 16 (Новослободская). M8: Mendeleevskaya; next to the Metro. 40R per hr. **Internet Chevignon Cafe,** Stoleshnikov per. 14, 2nd fl. (Столзшнiков пзр). M2: Tverskaya; walk downhill on Tverskaya, turn left onto Stoleshnikov, and enter through the Chevignon shop. One drink (35-100R per drink, 50R min.) buys 30min. of access. Open daily 11am-11pm. **Partiya Internet Cafe** (Партия), Volgogradsky pr. 1 (Волгоградский). M6: Proletarskaya. US$3 per hr. Open daily 10am-8pm. See below for access at **Traveler's Guest House** (3R per min.) and **G&R Hostel Asia** (US$1 per 15min.).

Telephones: Moscow Central Telegraph (see **Post Offices** below). To **call abroad,** go to the 2nd hall with phones. No collect or calling card calls. Prepay at counter. Use the *mezhdunarodnye telefony* (international telephone cabinets; международные телефоны). To Europe US$1-1.50 per min.; to the US and Australia US$1.50-2 per min. Open 24hr. **Local calls** need new phone cards; buy from Metro stops and kiosks.

Post Offices: Moscow Central Telegraph, ul. Tverskaya 7, uphill from the Kremlin. M1: Okhotny Ryad. **International mail** service at window #32; **faxes** at windows #11-12; **telegrams** at window #13. Open M-F 8am-2pm and 3-9pm, Sa 8am-2pm and 3-7pm, Su 9am-2pm and 3-7pm. For **Poste Restante,** address mail: Москва **103009,** До востребования (POSTE RESTANTE), SURNAME, First name. Poste Restante at windows #38 and 39, although they might send you to Myasnitskaya 26 (Мясницкая) if they don't have it. Poste Restante is also at the **Gostinitsa Intourist Hotel post office,** ul. Tverskaya 3/5. Address mail to be held: SURNAME, First name, До востребования, K-600, Гостиница Интурист, ул7 Тверская 3/5, Москва. Open M-F 9am-noon and 1-6pm. Bring unwrapped **packages** you want to send to the Intourist post office or to Myasnitskaya 26 (Мясницкая). **Intourist** post office open M-F 9am-noon and 1-8pm.

ACCOMMODATIONS

The lack of a hard-core backpacking culture on the Moscow accommodations scene results in slim pickings and overpriced rooms. Women standing outside major rail stations rent **private rooms** (*sdayu komnatu;* сдаю комнату) or **apartments** (*sdayu kvartiru;* сдаю квартиру). The places below are as cheap as it gets.

G&R Hostel Asia, ul. Zelenodolskaya 3/2, 14th fl. (Зеленодольская; ☎378 00 01; www.hostels.ru). M6: Ryazansky Prospekt; in the tall gray building with "Гостиница" in large letters on top, visible from either metro exit. Clean rooms and helpful staff. TV, fridge in each room. Far from the center, but close to the Metro. Transport to and from the airport US$20. Visa invitations US$25. Reception open 9am-9pm. Dorms US$13; singles US$18-22; doubles US$15-21.50. 10% off with HI, RYHA, or ISIC.

Traveller's Guest House, ul. Bolshaya Pereyaslavskaya 50, 10th fl. (Большая Переяслаская; ☎971 40 59; email tgh@glas.apc.org). M4,5: Prospekt Mira (Проспект Мира); walk 10min. north along pr. Mira, take the 3rd right on Banny per. (Банный), and turn left at the end of the street. It's the white, 12-story building across the street. TGH's greatest virtue is its clientele; almost every budget traveler stays there, and the bulletin board serves as an open forum for travel advice. Clean rooms and kitchen facilities. Laundry US$2. Check-out 11am. Airport pick-up and drop-off US$40. Russian **visa invitations** US$40. Dorms US$18; singles US$36; doubles US$48-54.

Galina's Flat, ul. Chaplygina 8, #35, 5th fl. (Чаплыгина; ☎921 60 38; email galinas.flat@mtu-net.ru). M1: Chistye Prudy; take bul. Chistoprudny (Чистопрудный), then the 1st left on Kharitonevsky per. (Харитоньевский), the 2nd right on Chaplygina, go through the courtyard, turn right, enter by the "Уникум" sign, and it's upstairs on the right. Homey Russian apartment with easygoing atmosphere. Hot showers. Kitchen facilities. Call ahead. Dorm US$8; doubles US$20, US$15 when used as singles.

Gostinitsa Kievskaya, ul. Kievskaya 2 (☎240 14 44). M3,4: Kievskaya; just outside the train station. Spacious old rooms and soft beds in a great location. Singles with bath 345R; doubles with bath 455R.

Prakash Guesthouse, ul. Profsoyuznaya 83, kor. 1 (2nd entrance), 3rd fl. (Профсоюзная; ☎334 82 01; email prakash@matrix.ru). M5: Belyaevo (Беляево); take the exit nearest the last car, follow *perekhod* to the end, exit from the last stairway on the left, and it's the 4th building on your right, at the 1st intersection. Go through the gate and around the back; enter from the last entrance to the right of the main one. Office on 2nd fl. Call ahead to be met at the Metro. Friendly if remote lodgings catering (not exclusively) to Indian guests. Rooms with shower, toilet, and phone. Free email. Breakfast US$6. Reception 7am-11pm. Dorm US$15; singles US$30; doubles US$40.

FOOD

Eating out ranges from expensive to insanely expensive. Many restaurants list prices in US dollars to avoid changing their menus to keep up with inflation. The ubiquitous and varied kiosk fare are a cheap alternative. Still, the comfort and convenience of a restaurant can also be affordable, if you look for local cuisine, and many of the higher-priced places have begun to offer lunch (бизнес ланч) specials (typically available noon-4pm; US$4-6). Moscow's first **McDonald's** (Макдоналдс—not that you need the Cyrillic, ye seeker of the Golden Arches) continues the steady homogenization of world culture at many locations; the biggest is at ul. Bolshaya Bronnaya 29 (Большая Бронная; M6: Pushkinskaya) and ul. Arbat 50/52 (Арбат; M3: Smolenskaya). **Russkoe Bistro** (Русское Бистро) is like a Russian McDonald's—traditional food, fast—with locations all over town. (Open daily 9am-11pm.)

RUSSIAN

Vremya Est (Время Есть), ul. Lesnaya 1/2 (Лесная). M4: Belorusskaya; in the complex across the street from the station. Tavern-like restaurant serving Russian food with a European twist. Friendly service and one of Moscow's largest selections of beer. Main dishes 145-195R. Happy hour M-F 3-7pm. Open daily noon-5am.

RUSSIA

Cafe-Bar Rioni (Риони), Arbat 43. M3: Smolenskaya. Sit inside to hide from the crowds or outside for fabulous people-watching. Full meals 250R. Open daily 11am-11pm.

Praga (Прада), Arbat 2. M3: Arbatskaya; near the corner of Novy Arbat. Home of the famous "Praga" torte sold all over Moscow. The restaurant is *very* pricey, but the bakery around back sells delectable pastries and mini-cakes (8R). Open daily 10am-9pm.

ETHNIC

Moscow Bombay (Бомбей), Glinishchevsky per. 3 (Глинищевский; ☎292 97 31). M6: Pushkinskaya; walk downhill on Tverskaya and turn left on Glinishchevsky. A relaxing atmosphere in which to enjoy Indian specialties. Vegetarian options. Entrees 100-375R. 10% student discount. Reservations recommended, especially on weekends. Open daily noon-midnight.

Mama Zoya's, Sechenovsky per. 18 (Сеченовский). M1: Kropotkinskaya; walk 4 blocks down ul. Ostozhenka (Остоженка) and take a right on Sechenovsky. Turn right at the Mama Zoya's sign and head to the basement in the back of the building. Family-style Georgian feasts, live Georgian music. Entrees 50-80R. Open daily noon-midnight.

Guria's, Komsomolsky pr. 7/3 (Комсомольский). M1, 4: Park Kultury; on the corner of ul. Frunze opposite St. Nicholas of the Weavers. Tasty Georgian fare. Most main dishes 40-90R. Open daily 11am-10pm.

Patio Pizza, ul. Tverskaya 3 (Тверская; ☎292 08 91). M1: Okhotny Ryad. Also at ul. Volkhonka 13a (Волхонка; ☎298 25 30). M1: Kropotkinskaya. Four additional locations around the city. This place rocks, and everyone in Moscow knows it. Thin-crust pizzas US$2.50-12.50. All-you-can-eat salad bar US$6. Open daily noon-midnight.

Kishmish (Кишмиш), ul. Novy Arbat 28 (Новый Арбат). M3: Arbatskaya. Also at ul. Barrikadnaya 8/9. M6: Barrikadnaya. Popular restaurant serving Central Asian cuisine. English menu. Lamb and chicken shashliks (45-55R) and a great salad bar (105R). Arbat location open 11am-3am; Barrikadnaya location open 11am-midnight.

MARKETS AND SUPERMARKETS

Vendors bring everything from a handful of cherries to an entire produce section to sell at Moscow's many markets. A visit is worthwhile just for the sights: sides of beef, piles of tomatoes, peaches, grapes, jars of glowing honey, and huge pots of flowers crowd together in a visual bouquet. The biggest are **Central Market** (M8: Tsvetnoy Bulvar), next to the Old Circus; **Rizhsky Market** (M5: Rizhskaya); and **Veshchevoy Market** (M3, 4: Kievskaya). Impromptu markets (usually 10am-8pm), where produce is sold by the kilogram (bring your own bag), spring up around metro stations; try Turgenevskaya, Kuznetsky Most, Aeroport, Baumanskaya, and between Novoslobodskaya and Mendeleevskaya. **Eliseevsky Gastronom** (Елисеевский), ul. Tverskaya 14 (M2: Tverskaya), is Moscow's most famous grocery and is as much a feast for your eyes as it is a place to buy food. It has higher prices than most other groceries (if you dare demean it by calling it a grocery. (Open M-F 8am-9pm, Sa 10am-7pm.) Or, try **Gastronom Tsentralny,** a.k.a. Sedmoi Kontinent (Седмой Континент), ul. Bolshaya Lbuyanka 1½ (Большая Лобянка). M1, 7: Lubyanka. (Open 24hr.) **Wash fruit and vegetables with bottled water.**

SIGHTS

Moscow's sights reflect the city's strange history: visitors can choose between 16th-century churches and Soviet-era museums, but there's little in between. Moscow also suffers from the 200 years when St. Petersburg was the tsar's seat—there are no grand palaces, and the city's art museums, lacking the Hermitage's financial resources for purchases of foreign art, only contain the very best Russian works. Despite the fact that the Soviet regime destroyed 80% of the city's pre-revolutionary splendor, the capital still packs in enough sights to occupy visitors for over a week.

RED SQUARE (KRASNAYA PL.)

There is nothing red about Red Square (Krasnaya ploshchad; Красная площадь); *krasnaya* meant "beautiful" long before the Communists co-opted it. Red Square, a

700m-long lesson in history and culture, has been the site of everything from a giant farmer's market to public hangings. On one side, the **Kremlin,** the seat of the Communist Party for 70-odd years, is the historical and religious heart of Russia; on the other, **GUM,** once a market and the world's largest purveyor of Soviet "consumer goods," is now an upscale shopping mall. Also flanking the square are **St. Basil's Cathedral,** the **State Historical Museum,** and **Lenin's Tomb.**

ST. BASIL'S CATHEDRAL. There is perhaps no more familiar symbol of Moscow than St. Basil's Cathedral (Pokrovsky Sobor or Sobor Vasiliya Blazhennovo; Собор Василия Блаженного), with its crazy-quilted onion domes. Completed in 1561, it was commissioned by Ivan the Terrible to celebrate his 1552 victory over the Tatars in Kazan. The cathedral bears the moniker of a holy fool, Vasily (Basil in English), who correctly predicted that Ivan would murder his own son. The labyrinthine interior—unusual for Orthodox churches—is filled with both religious and purely decorative frescoes. *(M3: Ploshchad Revolutsy;* Площадь Революции. *Open M, W-Su 11am-6pm;* kassa *closes at 5:30pm. 90R, students 45R. Buy tickets from the* kassa *to the left of the entrance, then proceed upstairs.)*

LENIN'S TOMB. You've seen his likeness in bronze all over the city; now see him in the eerily-luminescent flesh. The Party is finally over and Lenin's historical legacy has come into question—while his name and face are coming down all over Moscow, his mausoleum still stands in front of the Kremlin. In the glory days, this squat red structure (Mavzoley V.I. Lenina; Мавзолей В.И. Ленина) was guarded by fierce goose-stepping guards, and the line to get in was three hours long. The line is still long, and the guards are still stone-faced, but on the whole, amused curiosity characterizes the atmosphere. Entrance to the mausoleum also gives access to the **Kremlin wall,** where Stalin, Brezhnev, Andropov, Gagarin, and John Reed (author of *Ten Days That Shook the World*) are buried. *(Open Tu-Th and Sa-Su 10am-1pm.)*

THE KREMLIN

Complex open F-W 10am-5pm. Armory and Diamond Fund open F-W 10-11:30am, noon-1:30, 2:30-4, and 4:30-6pm. Armory 290R, students 145R. Diamond Fund 250R. Entrance to all cathedrals 200R, students 110R; after 4pm 90R, students 45R. Cameras 30R. Buy tickets at the kassa *in Alexander Gardens, on the west side of the Kremlin, and enter through Borovitskaya gate in the southwest corner if you're going to the Armory; enter between the* kassa *if you're skipping it. English-speaking guides offer tours at outrageous prices; haggle.*

The Kremlin (Kreml; Кремль) sits geographically and historically in the center of Moscow: it's where Ivan the Terrible reigned with his iron fist; Napoleon simmered while Moscow burned; Stalin ruled from behind the Iron Curtain; and where the USSR was dissolved in 1991. But despite this tremendous political history, the Kremlin's magnificent churches are the real attraction. Besides the sights listed below, the only other place in the complex you can actually enter is the **Kremlin Palace of Congresses,** the square white monster built by Khrushchev in 1961 for Communist Party Congresses; today it's a summer theater.

CATHEDRAL SQUARE. Follow the eager masses to Cathedral Square, home to the most famous gold domes in Russia. As you enter through Borovitskaya gate, the first church to the left is the **Annunciation Cathedral** (Blagoveshchensky Sobor; Благовещеиский Собор), which guards luminous icons by Andrei Rublev and Theophanes the Greek. The square **Archangel Cathedral** (Arkhangelsky Sobor; Архангельский Собор), gleaming with vivid icons and frescoes, is the final resting place for many of the tsars who ruled before Peter the Great, including Ivans III (the Great) and IV (the Terrible) and Mikhail Romanov. **Assumption Cathedral** (Uspensky Sobor; Успенский Собор) at the center of the square, is the oldest cathedral in the Russian state. Behind it, the **Patriarch's Palace** (Patriarshy Dvorets; Патриарший Дворец) houses the **Museum of 17th-Century Russian Applied Art and Life.** To the right of the Assumption Cathedral is **Ivan the Great's Belltower** (Kolokolnya Ivana Velikovo; Колокольня Ивана Великого). Directly behind the belltower is the **Tsar Bell** (Tsar-kolokol; Царь-колокол), the world's largest. It has never rung and probably never will—a 1737 fire caused a piece weighing 11½ tons to crack off.

ARMORY MUSEUM AND DIAMOND FUND. The nine rooms of the Armory Museum and Diamond Fund (Oruzheynaya i Vystavka Almaznovo Fonda; Оружейная и Вьставка Алмазного Фонда), to the left as you enter the Kremlin complex, contain all of the riches of the Russian Church and state not currently in St. Petersburg's Hermitage; marvel at the opulence of the Russian court. Room 3, on the second floor, holds the legendary **Fabergé eggs,** each revealing an impossibly intricate jewelled miniature; room 6 holds thrones, crowns, and other royal necessities; and room 9 contains royal coaches and sleds. The Diamond Fund, in an annex of the Armory, has still more glitter, including a 190-carat diamond given to Catherine the Great by Gregory Orlov, a "special friend."

CHURCHES, MONASTERIES, AND SYNAGOGUES

NOVODEVICHY CONVENT AND CEMETERY. You can't miss this most famous of Moscow's monasteries (Новодевичий Монастырь), thanks to its high brick walls, golden domes, and (on Su) tourist buses. Tsars and nobles kept the coffers filled by exiling their well-dowried wives and daughters here when they grew tired of them. The **Smolensk Cathedral** (Smolensky Sobor; Смоленский Собор), in the center of the convent, shows off Russian icons and frescoes. As you exit the convent gates, turn right and follow the exterior wall back around to the **cemetery** (kladbishche; кладбище)—a massive pilgrimage site that cradles the graves of famous artists, politicians, and military men, including Gogol, Chekhov, Stanislavsky, Bulgakov, Shostakovich, Mayakovsky, and other luminaries. *(M1: Sportivnaya. Take the exit out of the Metro that doesn't go to the stadium, take a right, and it's several blocks down on the left. Open W-M 10am-5:30pm; cathedrals close at 4:45pm. Closed first M of each month. Admission to grounds 30R, students 15R. Smolensk Cathedral 68R, students 38R; special exhibits 68R, students 38R. Cemetery open daily in summer 9am-7pm; in winter 9am-6pm; 20R. Cyrillic maps of cemetery 5R. Buy tickets at the small kiosk across the street from the entrance.)*

CATHEDRAL OF CHRIST THE SAVIOR. The city's most controversial landmark is the enormous, gold-domed Cathedral of Christ the Savior (Khram Khrista Spositelya; Храм Христа Спасителя), which replaced a public pool in the early 90s when it was discovered that water vapor from the pool was damaging paintings at the nearby Pushkin Museum. After winning the battle for the site, the Orthodox Church and mayor Yury Luzhkov constructed the cathedral in a mere two years. *(M1: Kropotkinskaya; between ul. Volkhonka (*Волхонка*) and the Moscow River. Free, but donations welcome. Service schedule varies.)*

MOSCOW CHORAL SYNAGOGUE. First constructed in the 1870s, the Moscow Choral Synagogue is a break from the city's ubiquitous onion domes. Though it functioned during Soviet rule, all but the bravest Jews were deterred by KGB agents who photographed anyone who entered. Today more than 200,000 Jews officially live in Moscow, and services are increasingly well-attended. The graffiti occasionally sprayed on the building serves as a sad reminder that anti-Semitism in Russia is not dead. *(Bolshoy Spasoglinishchevsky per. 10 (*Большой Спасогинищевский*). M5,6: Kitai-Gorod. Go north on Solyansky Proezd (*Солянский Проезд*) and take the 1st left. Open daily 9:30am-8pm; Sabbath services Sa 9am.)*

PEDESTRIAN AREAS AND PARKS

THE ARBAT. A pedestrian shopping arcade, the Arbat was once a showpiece of *glasnost* and a haven for political radicals, Hare Krishnas, street poets, and *metallisty* (heavy metal rockers). Today, the flavor of political rebellion has been replaced by the more universal taste of capitalism, including McDonald's, Baskin Robbins, and Benetton. A quick bite or a leisurely meal in one of many outdoor cafes provides the ideal venue for extensive people-watching. *(M3: Arbatskaya.)*

PUSHKIN SQUARE AND PATRIARCH'S POND. **Pushkin Square** (Pushkinskaya Pl.) is the center of free speech in Moscow—the site of evangelizing missionary groups, amateur politicians handing out petitions, and all major Russian news organizations. Follow ul. Bolshaya Bronnaya, next to Mickey D's, down to the bottom of the hill, turn right, and follow ul. Malaya Bronnaya to **Patriarch's Pond** (Patriarshy Prud;

Патриаршие Пруды), where Mikhail Bulgakov's *The Master and Margarita* begins. This region, known as the Margarita, is popular with artsy students and old men playing dominoes. *(M6: Pushkinskaya; halfway up ul. Tverskaya from Red Square.)*

GORKY PARK. In summer, droves of out-of-towners and young Muscovites promenade, relax, and ride the roller coaster at Moscow's **amusement park;** in winter the entire park becomes an **ice rink.** It's a fun spot to mingle with delighted kids and feel nostalgic about childhood. *(M1,4: Park Kultury or M4,5: Oktyabrskaya. From the Park Kultury stop, cross Krimsky most. From Oktyabrskaya, walk downhill on Krimsky val. and enter through the main gate. Open daily 10am-midnight. General admission 15-25R. Most rides 15-75R.)*

KOLOMENSKOE SUMMER RESIDENCE. Another respite from Moscow's chaos is the tsars' summer residence on a wooded slope above the Moskva River. Stroll through the grounds to the main gate, which overlooks the river. Red-coated guards with handy axes and fur-lined hats patrol the entrance, an authentic if kitschy throwback. Directly in front stands the 16th-century **Assumption Cathedral** (Uspenskaya Sobor). *(M2: Kolomenskaya; follow the exit signs to "к музею Коломенское." Turn right out of the Metro and walk about 400m to the main entrance gate. Grounds open daily 7am-10pm. Free. Museums open Tu-Su 11am-6pm. 60-70R, students 30-35R.)*

IZMAYLOVSKY PARK. Rather far out, the park (Измайловский Парк) is best known for its colossal weekend **market,** Vernisazh (Вернисаж). Arrive late Sunday afternoon, when people want to go home and are willing to make a deal. *Everything* is sold here, from carpets and samovars to military uniforms and old Soviet money. *(M3: Izmaylovsky Park. Go left and follow the hordes. Open Sa-Su 9am-midnight, although many vendors begin packing up at 5pm. 10R entrance fee.)*

RUSSIA

MUSEUMS

Many museums in Moscow, especially the less famous ones, will have signs only in Russian. It is often possible to call ahead for a tour in English. The **Moscow Metro,** one of the most beautiful metros in the world, is worth a tour of its own. All stations are unique, and those inside the Circle Line are elaborate, with mosaics, sculptures, and chandeliers. It's only 4R, and you can stay on as long you as like. **Kievskaya, Mayakovskaya,** and **Ploshchad Revolutsii** stations are particularly good, as are **Komsomolskaya, Novoslobodskaya, Rimskaya,** and **Mendeleevksaya.**

Tretyakov Gallery (Tretyakovskaya Galereya; Третьяковская Галерея), Lavrushinsky per. 10 (Лаврушинский; ☎203 77 88, 951 13 62, and 238 13 78), in Zamoskvareche. M7: Tretyakovskaya; turn left and then left again, take an immediate right onto Tolmachevsky per. (Толмачевский пер.), and turn right after two blocks on Lavrushensky per. A veritable treasure chest of Russian national art, mostly from the 18th and 19th centuries, but also works by several early 20th century artists. The heart of the gallery is the collection of icons; its crown jewel is the 12th-century Vladimir *Virgin Mary* icon from Constantinople. 210R, students 120R. Open Tu-Su 10am-8:30pm.

State Tretyakov Gallery (Gosudarstvennaya Tretyakovskaya Galereya; Государственная Третьяковская Галерея), ul. Krymsky Val 10 (Крымский Вал; ☎238 13 78). M1,4: Park Kultury. Opposite the Gorky Park entrance on the right side. Picks up chronologically where the Tretyakov leaves off. The greatest Russian art of the 20th century. Open Tu-Su 10am-7:30pm; *kassa* closes at 6:30pm. 210R, students 120R.

Museum of Contemporary Russian History (Централный Музей Современной Истории России; Tsentralny Muzei Sovremennoi Istorii Rossii), ul. Tverskaya 21. M6: Pushkinskaya; walk a block uphill on Tverskaya, and turn left. Covers Russian history from the Revolution of 1905 to the present day in exhausting if somewhat disorganized detail. All signs in Russian. Open Tu-Sa 10am-6pm, Su 10am-5pm. 10R.

Pushkin Museum of Fine Arts (Muzey Izobrazitelnykh Iskusstv im. A.S. Pushkina; Музей Изобразительных Искусств им. А.С. Пушкина), ul. Volkhonka 12 (☎203 95 78). M1: Kropotkinskaya. The most famous art museum in Russia after the Hermitage, with collections of Impressionist, Renaissance, Egyptian, and Classical art. To the left of the main entrance is the **Museum of Private Collections,** with foreign and Russian art from the 19th and 20th centuries. Pushkin open Tu-Su 10am-7pm; *kassa* closes at 6pm. The Private

Collections open W-Su noon-7pm; *kassa* closes at 6pm. Pushkin 210R, students 120R. Private Collections 40R, students 20R.

Central Museum of the Armed Forces of the USSR (Tsentralny Muzey Vooruzhennykh Sil SSSR; Центральный Музей Вооруженных Сил СССР), ul. Sovetskoy Armii 2 (Советской Армии; ☎281 48 77). M4: Novoslobodskaya; walk down ul. Seleznevskaya (Селезневская) to the square/rotary (10min.), pass a huge theater, and bear right at the fork. One of the more interesting and better organized military museums. Open W-Su 10am-5pm. Closed second Tu and last week of each month. 15R, students 10R.

AUTHORS' HOUSES

Russians take immense pride in their formidable literary history, preserving authors' houses in their original state, down to half-empty teacups on the mantlepiece. Each is guarded by a team of fiercely loyal *babushki*

RUSSIA

Lev Tolstoy Estate, ul. Lva Tolstovo 21 (Льва Толстого; ☎246 94 44). M1,4: Park Kultury; walk down Komsomolsky pr., turn right at the corner on ul. Lva Tolstovo, and it's three blocks up on the left. The author lived here in the winters of 1882-1901. One of the most perfectly preserved house-museums in Moscow. Open in summer Tu-Su 10am-6pm; off season 10am-3:30pm. Closed last F of each month. 100R, students 50R.

Gorky's Museum-House, ul. Malaya Nikitskaya 6/2 (Малая Никитская; ☎290 51 30). M3: Arbatskaya; cross Novy Arbat, turn right on Merelyakovsky per. (Мерзляковский пер.), cross the small park, and it's directly across from you. Entrance is on ul. Spiridonova to the left. A pilgrimage site more for its architectural interest (art nouveau) than for its collection of Maxim Gorky's possessions. Open W and F noon-7pm, Th and Sa-Su 10am-5pm. Closed last Th of each month. Free; 5-10R donation requested.

Pushkin Museum (Музей Пушкина; Muzey Pushkina), nab. Reki Moyki 12 (Реки Мойки; ☎311 38 01). M2: Nevsky; walk right on Nevsky, turn right onto nab. Reki Moyki, and follow the canal; it's the yellow building on the right. The former residence of Russia's adored poet displays his personal effects, while the adjacent literary exposition exhibits his drafts and sketches. Open M and W-Su 10:30am-5pm; closed last F of each month. Tour 25R, students 10R; English-language residence tour 60R.

Mayakovsky Museum (Музей им. В. В. Маяковского; Muzey im B.B. Mayakovskovo), Lubyansky pr. 3/6 (Лубянский; ☎928 25 69). M1,8: Lubyanka; the museum hides behind a bust of Mayakovsky. More a walk-through work of futurist art than a museum, with the avant-garde poet and artist's papers and art work arranged in a four-story assemblage of bizarrely oriented chairs, spilled paint, and chicken wire. Open M-Tu and F-Su 10am-6pm, Th 1-9pm. 50R. Call ahead for an English tour (600R).

ENTERTAINMENT

Moscow is a large, fast-paced city with the entertainment options to prove it. From September to June, it boasts some of the world's best theater, ballet, and opera, along with excellent orchestras. Advance tickets can be very cheap (US$2-5).

Bolshoy Teatr (Big Theater; Большой Театр), Teatralnaya pl. 1 (☎292 00 50). M2: Teatralnaya Pl. Home to both the opera and the world-renowned ballet companies, with consistently excellent performances. Champagne and caviar at intermission. Daily performances Sept.-June 7pm. Tickets 30-1000R. *Kassa* open noon-7pm.

Maly Teatr, Teatralnaya pl. 1/6 (Малый Театр; ☎923 26 21). M2: Teatralnaya. Just right of the Bolshoy. Affiliate at Bolshaya Ordynka 69 (☎237 31 81 and 237 44 72). The "Small Theater" shows different productions nightly, mostly Russian classics of the 19th and 20th centuries, like Tolstoy or Chekhov. Daily performances at 7pm. All performances in Russian. Tickets from 20-35R. *Kassa* open Tu-Su noon-3pm and 4-6:30pm.

Musical Operetta Theater, ul. Bolshaya Dmitrovka 6 (☎292 04 05), around the left side of the Bolshoy. M2: Teatralnaya. Year-round. Shows at 7pm. Tickets 25-150R.

Tchaikovsky Conservatory's Big and Small Halls, Triumfalnaya pl. 4/31 (☎299 36 81). M2: Mayakovskaya. During intermission, locals sneak into the Big Hall (Bolshoy Zal; Большой Зал) to admire its pipe organ and chandeliers. Tickets from 100R. Back-row tickets for the Maly Zal (Small Hall; Малый Зал) just 5R. Concerts almost daily 7pm plus Su 2pm. *Kassa* in Big Hall open daily noon-7pm. Closed in summer.

Great Moscow Circus, pr. Vernadskovo 7 (Вернадского; ☎930 28 15 and 930 02 72). M1: Universitet. It was the greatest show on earth, but all the big stars defected or died; now it's the greatest show in Moscow. Performances W, F 7pm; Sa-Su 3 and 7pm. Tickets 35-70R. *Kassa* open daily 10:30am-1pm and 2-7:30pm.

NIGHTCLUBS AND BARS

Moscow's nightlife is the most kickin' action this side of the Volga, and certainly the most varied, expensive, and dangerous in Eastern Europe. Many of the more interesting clubs enjoy flaunting their high cover charges and strict face control policies. Check the weekend editions of *The Moscow Times* or *The Moscow Tribune* for club reviews and music festival listings. *The Moscow Times's* Friday pull-out section, *The Beat,* provides an excellent synopsis of each week's events, as well as up-to-date restaurant, bar, and club reviews.

RUSSIA

Propaganda, Bolshoy Zlatoustinsky per. 7 (Большой Златоустинский). M6,7: Kitai-Gorod; walk down ul. Maroseika and take a left on Bolshoy Zlatoustinksy per. Hip, unpretentious student crowd with a hefty percentage of backpackers bounces to top American and European DJs. Hopping, even on Sunday, but gets extraordinarily hot. Beer 50-65R. Cover F-Sa 70R. Open M-W and Su noon-12:30am, Th noon-3am, F 10pm-6am, Sa 3pm-6am.

Hungry Duck, Pushechnaya ul. 9 (Пушечная). M1: Kuznetsky Most. Enter the courtyard beyond the iron gate and follow the red neon arrows in. There's no sign, which is just as well, since no one can agree whether it's called "Fiesta" or "Hungry Duck." Lively crowd dances on the table, the bar, and everywhere in between (until they fall over drunk, that is). A bizarre variety of theme nights. Beers 60-90R. Cover for men 100-200R, women free-50R. Open daily 8pm-6am.

Chance (Шанс), ul. Volochayevskaya 11/5 (Волочаевская; www.gay.ru/chance), in Dom Kultury Serp i Molot (Дом Культуры Серп и Молот). M8: Ploshchad Ilicha; walk down ul. Sergia Radonezhskovo all the way through the third open driveway on the right, walk up the stairs when you see tram tracks, and it's straight ahead on top of the hill. The oldest gay club in Moscow is popular with a mixed crowd of ravers, punks, students, and New Russians—more "gay-friendly" than strictly gay. Euro-black attire. Beers 40-60R. Cover up to 200R depending on time, day, and gender. Open daily 11pm-6am.

Doug and Marty's Boar House, Zemlyanoi val 26. M3: Kurskaya, opposite the train station. About as American as you can get in Moscow, prices included. Packed on weekends. Beer 50-110R. Cover for men 100R, women 60R. Open 24hr.

TaxMan, Krymsky Val. 10 (Крымский Вал). M6: Oktyabrskaya; walk downhill on Krymsky val. Inexpensive drinks and musical variety attract a mixed but low-key crowd. Bar and dancing downstairs, bar and billiards upstairs. Beer 40R. Cover (after 7pm) varies, usually 70-90R. Open daily noon-6am.

Krizis Zhanra, Prechistensky per. 22/4 (Пречистенский). M1: Kropotkinskaya; walk away from Church of Christ the Savior on ul. Prechistenka (Пречистенка), take the 3rd right onto Prechistensky per., enter the courtyard on the right at #18, and turn left. Great place to grab a beer. Extremely popular with local and foreign students. Czech beers 50R. Live concerts daily 8:30-11pm—arrive early. Open daily 11am-11pm.

EXCURSION FROM MOSCOW: SERGIEV POSAD

Possibly Russia's most famous pilgrimage point, Sergiev Posad (Сергиев Посад) attracts wandering Orthodox believers with a mass of churches huddled at its main sight—**St. Sergius's Trinity Monastery** (Troitsko-Sergieva Lavra; Троицко-Сергиева Лавра). After decades of state-propagated atheism, the stunning monastery, founded around 1340, is again a religious center; the paths between the churches are dotted with monks in flowing robes. (Open daily 8am-6pm.) Although each church is exquisite, the opulence of Russian Orthodoxy is best visible inside the **Trinity Cathedral** (Troitsky Sabor; Троицкий Собор), where the numerous covered heads and quickly crossing hands captivate visitors as much as the gilded Andrei Rublyov icons. *Elektrichki* (commuter trains) run to Sergiev Posad from Moscow's Yaroslavsky Vokzal (1½hr., every 30-40min., round-trip 32R).

ST. PETERSBURG (САНКТ-ПЕТЕРБУРГ) ☎812

In St. Petersburg, Russia suddenly becomes wide boulevards, brightly colored façades, glorious palaces, and artistic revelry. This splendor is exactly what Peter the Great intended when he founded the city in 1703 atop a drained swamp on the Gulf of Finland; the land was strategically chosen to drag Russia away from Byzantium and toward the West. But St. Petersburg was also the birthplace of the 1917 revolution, which would turn Russia decisively away from the western world. St. Petersburg's name changes reflected the currents of its history; German-sounding *Sankt Peterburg* was changed to Petrograd during WWI, which the Bolsheviks traded in for the more proletarian Leningrad in 1924, only to reclaim St. Petersburg when Lenin fell out of favor. Yet it was Leningrad that suffered the brutal 900-day siege in WWII by the Nazis, during which close to a million people died. Despite—or because of—its turbulent past, the city has proved a muse; the splendid palaces have inspired the masterpieces of Dostoevsky, Gogol, Tchaikovsky, and Stravinsky, while the seedy cafes and dark courtyards of the city's underbelly fostered the revolutionary dreams of Lenin and Trotsky. Moscow may be the embodiment of Mother Russia's bold, post-apocalyptic youth, but St. Petersburg remains the majestic and mysterious symbol of Peter's great Russian dream.

RUSSIA

GETTING THERE AND GETTING AROUND

Flights: The main airport, **Pulkovo** (Пулково), has two terminals: Pulkovo-1 for domestic and Pulkovo-2 for international flights. M2: Moskovskaya. From the Metro, take bus #39 for Pulkovo-1 (30-40min.), or bus #13 for Pulkovo-2 (25-30min.). Hostels can usually arrange for a taxi (usually US$30-40).

Trains: Tsentralnye Zheleznodorozhnye Kassy (Центральные Железнодорожные Кассы; Central Ticket Offices), Canal Griboedova 24. Foreigners must purchase international tickets at windows #2-4. Expect long lines and few English-speaking tellers. Prices vary slightly by train; go to the individual stations to purchase tickets on the day of departure. Check your ticket to see which station your train leaves from. Open M-Sa 8am-8pm, Su 8am-6pm.

Varshavsky Vokzal (Варшавский Вокзал). M1: Baltiskaya (Балтийская). To: **Rīga** (12hr., 1 per day, 825-1400R); **Tallinn** (8hr., 1 per day, 325-560R); **Vilnius** (13hr., 1 per day, 640-980R); and **Warsaw** (27hr., 1 per day, 1090-1340R).

Vitebsky Vokzal (Витебский Вокзал). M1: Pushkinskaya (Пушкинская). To **Kiev** (28hr., 2 per day, 506-803R) and **Odessa** (36hr., 1 per day, 650-1100R).

Moskovsky Vokzal (Московский Вокзал). M1: Pl. Vosstaniya. To: **Moscow** (6-9hr., 15 per day, 305R); **Novgorod** (4½hrs., 1 per day, 306R); and **Sevastopol** (36hr., 1 per day, 770-1200R).

Finlyandsky Vokzal (Финляндский Вокзал). M1: Pl. Lenina (Ленина). To **Helsinki** (6hr., 2 per day, 1330-23004R).

Buses: nab. Obvodnovo Kanala 36 (Обводного Канала; ☎166 57 77). M4: Ligovsky pr. Take tram #19, 25, 44, or 49 or trolley #42 from the M1 stop across the canal. Facing the canal, turn right and walk two long blocks. The station is on your right; enter through the back. For the Baltic States, the **Eurolines Agency** (Agenstro Eurolains, Агенство Евролайнс; ☎168 27 40), ul. Shkapina 10 (Щкапина), M1: Baltiiskaya (Балтийская), sends buses to Tallinn, Riga, and Vilnius.

Local Transportation: The efficient, safe **Metro** (Метро) runs daily 5:30am-12:30am. 4 lines run through the center from the outskirts. A Metro **token** (жетон; *zheton*) costs 3R. **Buses, trams,** and **trolleys** run 6am-midnight; buy tickets (2R) from the driver.

Taxis: Marked cabs are 5R per km. Haggle over flat fares for unofficial cabs. They are generally safe, but never get into a car with more than one person already in it.

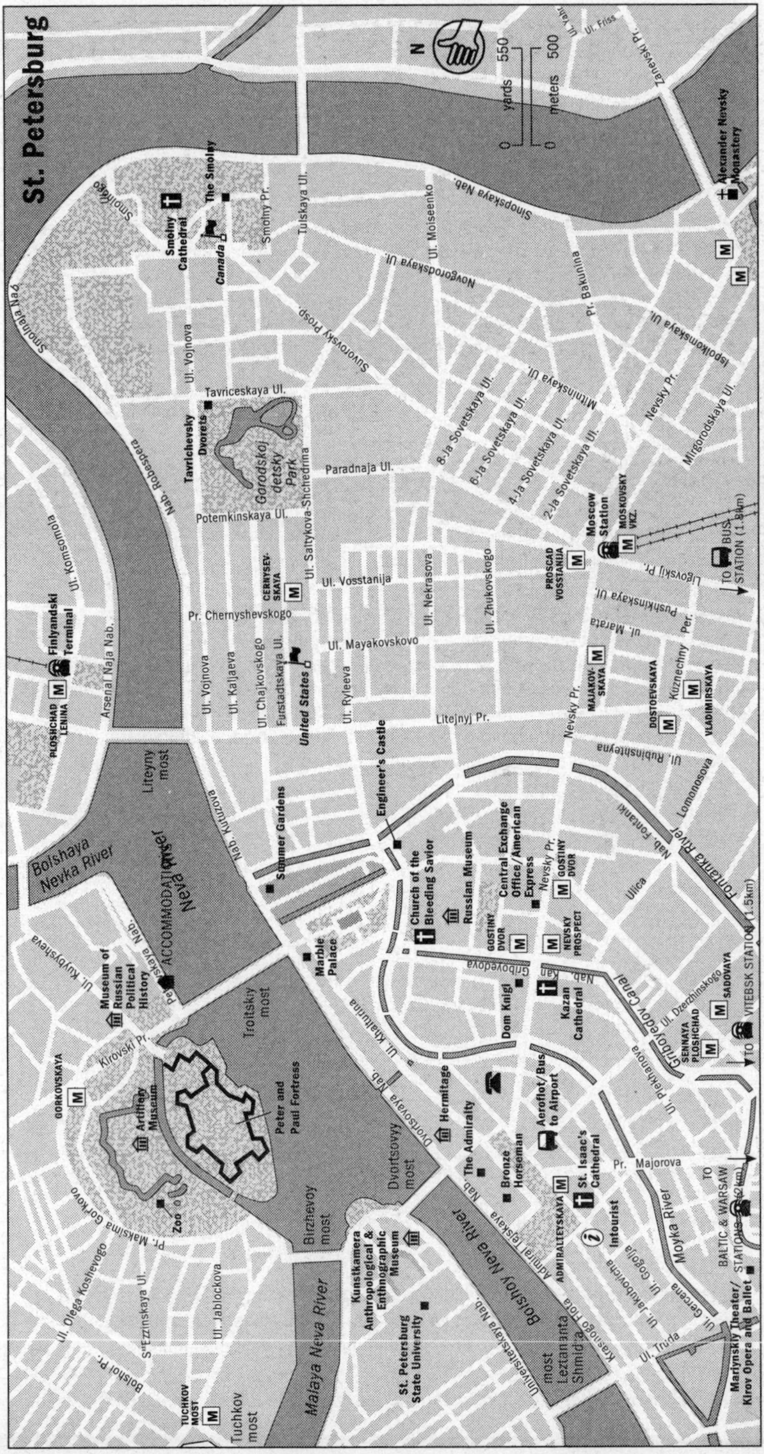
St. Petersburg
N
0 yards 550
0 meters 500
Smolny Cathedral
The Smolny
Canada
Smolny Pr.
Tulskaya Ul.
Ul. Moiseenko
Sinopskaya Nab.
Alexander Nevsky Monastery
Novgorodskaya Ul.
Suvorovsky Prosp.
Pr. Bakunina
Ispolkomskaya Ul.
Mitninskaya Ul.
Nevsky Pr.
Mirgorodskaya Ul.
Ul. Vojnova
Tavriceskaya Ul.
Tavrichevsky Dvorets
Gorodskoj detsky Park
Paradnaja Ul.
8-Ja Sovetskaya Ul.
6-Ja Sovetskaya Ul.
4-Ja Sovetskaya Ul.
2-Ja Sovetskaya Ul.
Moscow Station
MOSKOVSKY VKZ.
PROSCAD VOSSTANIJA
Nab. Robespera
Potemkinskaya Ul.
Ul. Saltykova-Shchedrina
Ul. Vosstanija
Ul. Nekrasova
Ul. Zhukovskogo
Ligovskij Pr.
Pushkinskaya Ul.
TO BUS STATION (1.8km)
Ul. Komsomola
Finlyandski Terminal
PLOSHCHAD LENINA
Arsenal Naja Nab.
Pr. Chernyshevskogo
CERNYSEV-SKAYA
Ul. Mayakovskovo
United States
Ul. Vojnova
Ul. Kaljaeva
Ul. Chajkovskogo
Furstadtskaya Ul.
Ul. Ryleeva
Litejnyj Pr.
Ul. Marata
MAJAKOV-SKAYA
Kuznechny Per.
DOSTOEVSKAYA
VLADIMIRSKAYA
Ul. Rubinshteyna
Liteyny most
Engineer's Castle
Summer Gardens
Nab. Kutuzova
Bolshaya Nevka River
Neva River
ACCOMMODATIONS
Church of the Bleeding Savior
Russian Museum
Central Exchange Office/American Express
Nevsky Pr.
GOSTINY DVOR
Nab. Fontanki
Lomonosova
Fontanka River
Ulica
TO VITEBSK STATION (1.5km)
Marble Palace
Griboyedova
Nab. Kan
NEVSKY PROSPECT
Kazan Cathedral
Dom Knigi
Griboyedov Canal
Ul. Dzerzhinskogo
SADOVAYA
SENNAYA PLOSHCHAD
Ul. Plekhanova
Ul. Kuybysheva
Museum of Russian Political History
Petrovskaya Nab.
Troitsky most
Kirovski Pr.
Ul. Khalturina
GORKOVSKAYA
Artillery Museum
Peter and Paul Fortress
Hermitage
Dvortsovaya Nab.
Aeroflot/Bus to Airport
The Admiralty
Bronze Horseman
St. Isaac's Cathedral
Pr. Majorova
TO BALTIC & WARSAW STATIONS (2km)
Dvortsovyy most
ADMIRALTEYSKAYA
Intourist
Moyka River
Zoo
Pr. Maksima Gorkovo
Birzhevoy most
Kunstkamera Anthropological & Ethnographic Museum
Bolshoy Neva River
Admiral Teiskaya Nab.
Ul. Gogolja
Ul. Jakubovicha
Ul. Gercena
Ul. Olega Koshevogo
Sezzinskaya Ul.
Ul. Jablockova
Malaya Neva River
St. Petersburg State University
Universitetskaya Nab.
most Leytenanta Shmidta
Krasnogo Flota
Ul. Truda
Mariinsky Theater/ Kirov Opera and Ballet
Bolshoi Pr.
TUCHKOV MOST
Tuchkov most

RUSSIA

ORIENTATION AND PRACTICAL INFORMATION

The city center lies on mainland St. Petersburg between the south bank of the **Neva River** and the north bank of the **Fontanka River. Nevsky prospekt** (Невский Проспект) runs through this downtown area; housing most of St. Petersburg's major sights, including the Winter and Summer Palaces, the Hermitage, and main cathedrals. **Moscow Train Station** (Moskovsky Vokzal; Московский Вокзал), the city's main train station, is near the midway point of Nevsky pr. East of downtown and across the Neva sprawls **Vasilevsky Island,** the city's largest island; most of its sights congregate on the eastern edge in the **Strelka** neighborhood. On the north side of the Neva and across from the Winter Palace is a small archipelago housing the Peter and Paul Fortress, the **Petrograd Side** residential neighborhood, and the wealthy **Kirov Island** trio; this is the historic heart of the city. The easiest means of navigation is the **Metro.** In the center, **trolleys** #1, 5, and 22 go up and down Nevsky pr.

TOURIST AND FINANCIAL SERVICES

Tourist Office: Ost-West Contact Service, ul. Mayakovskovo 7 (Маяковского; ☎327 34 16; email sales@ostwest.com). Visa support. Open M-F 10am-6pm, Sa noon-6pm.

Budget Travel: Sindbad Travel (FIYTO), 3-ya Sovetskaya ul. 28 (3-я Советская; ☎327 83 84; email sindbad@sindbad.ru). In the International Hostel. Arranges tickets, tours, and adventure trips. 10-80% discounts on plane tickets. English spoken. Open M-F 9:30am-8pm, Sa-Su 10am-5pm.

Adventure Travel: Wild Russia, ul. Mokhovaya 28-10 (Моховая; ☎273 65 14; email yegor@wildrussia.spb.ru). Outdoor trips around St. Petersburg (weekends US$40-100).

Consulates: Canada, Malodetskoselsky pr. 32 (Малодетскосельский; ☎325 84 48). M1: Tekhnologichesky Institut. Open M-F 9:30am-1pm and 2-5pm. **UK,** pl. Proletarskoi Diktatury 5 (Пролетарской Диктатуры; ☎320 32 00). M1: Chernyshevskaya. Open M-F 9:30am-1pm and 2-5:30pm. **US,** ul. Furshtatskaya 15 (Фурштатская; ☎275 17 01; 24-hour emergency ☎274 86 92; e-mail acs_stpete@state.gov). M1: Chernyshevskaya. Open M-F 9:30am-5:30pm. American citizen services 9:30am-1:30pm. Citizens of **Australia** and **New Zealand** should contact their embassies in Moscow (see p. 792), or the UK consulate in emergencies.

Currency Exchange: Look for "Обмен валюты" (*obmen valyuty*) signs everywhere. **Central Exchange Office,** ul. Mikhailovskaya 4 (Михайловская; ☎110 55 48). Off Nevsky pr. across from Grand Hotel Europe. M3: Gostiny Dvor. Keep receipts to change rubles back into hard currency, but it still might not be possible. Open M-Sa 9am-1:30pm and 2:30-8pm, Su 9:30am-1:30pm and 2:30-7pm.

LOCAL SERVICES

English-Language Bookstore: Anglia British Bookshop (Англия), nab. Reki Fontanki (Реки Фонтанки; ☎279 82 84). Open M-F 10am-7pm, Sa-Su 11am-6pm.

EMERGENCY AND COMMUNICATIONS

Emergency: Police, ☎02. Multilingual police office specifically for crimes against foreigners at ul. Zakharevskaya 19 (Захаревская; ☎278 30 14).

Pharmacies: Nevsky pr. 22. Open M-F 8am-10pm, Sa 9am-9pm, Su 11am-7pm. At night enter in back.

Medical Assistance: American Medical Center, ul. Serpukhovskaya 10 (Серпуховская; ☎326 17 30). M1: Tekhnologichesky Institut (Технологический Институт).

Internet Access: Tetris Internet Cafe (Тетрис), Chernyakhovskovo 33 (Черняховского; ☎164 48 77; www.dux.ru). M4: Ligovsky Prospekt. Exit the metro, turn left onto Ligovsky pr., go straight for 5min., turn left at the sign, and follow the street to the end, then turn left on Chernyakhovo. 70R per hr. **Cityline Internet,** Nevsky pr. 88. 15R per 10min.; 70R per hr. Both **Hostel Holiday** and **International Youth Hostel (HI)** (see **Accommodations,** below) have free email at their web addresses.

Telephones: Central Telephone and Telegraph, Bolshaya Morskaya ul. 3/5 (Большая Морская). Facing the Admiralty, it's right off Nevsky pr. near Dvortsovaya pl. Prepay phone calls in the *kassa* in the 2nd (intercity) or 3rd (international) hall. For long-distance calls, push 8 and wait for the tone before dialing. Open 24hr. To make intercity calls on the street, use any pay phone that takes phone cards. 25 units cost 60R, 400 units 360R. 1 unit per min. for local calls; 48 units per min. to the US. Cards can be purchased from the Central Telephone Office, metro stations, or new street kiosks.

Post Office: ul. Pochtamtskaya 9 (Почтамтская). From Nevsky pr., go west on ul. Malaya Morskaya (Малая Морская), which becomes ul. Pochtamtskaya. It's about two blocks past Isaakievsky Sobor on the right. Open M-Sa 9am-8pm, Su 10am-6pm. Address mail to be held: SURNAME, First name, До Востребования, **190 000** Санкт-Петербург, Главпочтамт, Russia.

ACCOMMODATIONS

International Youth Hostel (HI), 3-ya Sovetskaya ul. 28 (3-я Советская; ☎329 80 18; fax 329 80 19; email ryh@ryh.ru). M1: Pl. Vosstaniya. Walk along Suvorovsky pr. (Суворовский) for three blocks, then turn right on 3-ya Sovetskaya ul. A cheery, tidy hostel in a pleasant neighborhood. Breakfast included. Minimal kitchen. Laundry US$4 for 4kg. Internet. Check-out 11am. Curfew 1am. Dorms US$17; with ISIC US$18; non-members US$19.

Hostel "Holiday" (HI), Nab. Arsenalnaya 9 (Арсенальная; ☎327 10 70; email info@hostel.spb.ru). M1: Pl. Lenina. Exit at Finlyandsky Vokzal, turn left on ul. Komsomola (Комсомола), right on ul. Mikhailova. At the end of the street turn left on Arsenalnay; it's on the left. Visa support (single-entry US$30). Breakfast. Internet. Call ahead. Dorms US$14; doubles US$76. US$1 discount for HI/ISIC; US$2 after five days.

Petrovsky Hostel, ul. Baltyskaya 26 (Балтийская; ☎252 75 63). M1: Narvskaya. From the Metro, turn left on pr. Stachek (Стачек). Don't cross the street into the park with the statue; turn left on ul. Baltyskaya. Although far from the center, it's clean, comfortable, and cheap. Call 2-3 months ahead for summer housing. Kitchen. Check-in by midnight. Dorms 150-170R; a few luxury rooms 300-500R.

FOOD

St. Petersburg's menus vary little, but many places harbor top-secret methods of preparing tasty old Russian classics. Unfortunately, menus are often only in Cyrillic—good luck. Fast food venues dot the city. Cafes have long been pivotal to St. Petersburg culture, inspiring Dostoevsky's frightening tales of Russian urban life and Lenin's dreams of revolution; today's cafes are mostly mainstream, with only vague echoes of former glory. **Markets** stock tons of stuff; bargain and play hard to get. The **covered market,** at Kuznechny per. 3 (Кузнечьный), just around the corner from M1: Vladimirskaya, and the **Maltsevsky Rynok** (Мальцевский Рынок), ul. Nekrasova 52 (Некрасова), at the top of Ligovsky pr. (Лиговский; M1: Pl. Vosstaniya), are the biggest and most exciting. For **groceries,** head to **Magazin #11** (Магасин; M1, 3: Pl. Vosstaniya), Nevsky pr. 105. (Open daily 10am-10pm.)

Note that there is no effective water purification system in St. Petersburg, making exposure to **giardia** very likely. Always boil tap water at least 10 minutes, dry veggies, and drink bottled water.

The Idiot (Идиоть), nab. Moyky 82 (Мойки). M4: Sadovaya; 5min. down the Moyka from Isaakievskaya pl. Expat hangout with vegetarian cuisine. Homemade meals 75-125R. Happy hour 6:30-7:30pm. Open daily noon-11pm.

Tbilisi (Тбилиси), ul. Sytninskaya 10 (Сытнинская). M2: Gorkovskaya. Follow the wrought-iron fence around Park Lenina away from the fortress until the Sytny (Сытный) market; Tbilisi is behind it. Georgian cuisine is the best in Russia; good food for a good atmosphere. Entrees 50-75R. Open daily noon-11pm.

Kafe Hutorok (Хуторок), 3-ya Sovetskaya ul. 24. M1: Pl. Vosstaniya. Very Russian: good food and lots of alcohol. Entrees 75-125R. Alcohol 8-90R. Open daily 10am-11pm.

Tandoor (Тандур), Voznesensky pr. 2. M2: Nevsky Prospekt; on the corner of Admiralteysky pr., two blocks to the left after the end of Nevsky pr. Quality Indian food worth the price. Dinner US$15-25; lunch special noon-4pm US$10. Open daily noon-11pm.

Kolobok (Колобок), ul. Tchaikovskovo 40 (Чайковского). M1: Chernyshevskaya; turn right on pr. Chernyshevskovo for one block. Cheap, greasy, and fast. Sweet and savory rolls 4-10R; main dishes 25-50R; 15% discount with ISIC. Open daily 7:30am-9pm.

Koshkin Dom (Cat's House; Кошкин Дом), Liteyny pr. 23 (Литейний) and ul. Vosstaniya 2 (Восстания). M1: Pl. Vosstaniya. Soups and carnivorous entrees 30-75R. Open 24hr.

Skazka (Сказка; Fairy Tale), 1-ya Sovetskaya 12 (1-я Советская). M1: Pl. Vosstaniya. *Bliny* (Russian crepes) stuffed in several different ways (10-40R). Open 24hr.

RUSSIA

SIGHTS

THE HERMITAGE. Originally a collection of 225 paintings bought by Catherine the Great in 1764, the State Hermitage Museum (Эрмитаж), the world's largest art collection, rivals the Louvre and the Prado in architectural, historical, and artistic significance. The **Winter Palace** (Zimny Dvorets; Зимний Дворец), commissioned in 1762, reflects the extravagant tastes of the Empress Elizabeth, Peter the Great's daughter. By the end of the 1760s, the collection had become too large for the **Summer Palace,** and Catherine appointed Vallin de la Mothe to build the **Small Hermitage** (Maly Hermitage; Малый Эрмитаж), where she could retreat by herself or with one of her lovers. The **Great Hermitage** (Veliky Hermitage; Великий Эрмитаж) and the **Hermitage Theater** (Hermitazhny Teatr; Эрмитажный Театр) were completed in the 1780s. Stasov, a famous imperial Russian architect, built the fifth building, the **New Hermitage** (Novy Hermitage; Новый Эрмитаж), in 1851. The tsars lived with their collection here until 1917, after which the museum complex was nationalized. It is impossible to absorb the whole museum in a day or even a week—indeed, only 5% of the three million-piece collection is on display at any one time. Ask for an indispensable English guide at the information desk near the *kassa*.

The **Palace Square** (Dvortsovaya Ploshchad; Дворцовая Площадь), the huge windswept expanse in front of the Winter Palace, has witnessed many turning points in Russia's history. Here, Catherine took the crown after overthrowing her husband, Tsar Peter III; Nicholas II's guards fired into a crowd of peaceful demonstrators on "Bloody Sunday" in 1905, leading to the 1905 revolution; and Lenin's Bolsheviks seized power from the provisional government during the storming of the Winter Palace in October 1917. *(Dvortsovaya nab. 34 (Дворцовая). M2: Nevsky Prospekt. Exiting the Metro, turn left and walk down Nevsky pr. to its end at the Admiralty. Head right, onto and across Palace Square. ☎ 110 96 25. Open Tu-Su 10:30am-6pm; cashier and upper floors close 1hr. earlier.* Kassa *located on the river side of the building. 250R, students free. Cameras 75R. Lines can be long; come early. Students get tickets at* kassa *5.)*

AROUND ST. ISAAC'S CATHEDRAL. Glittering, intricately-carved masterpieces of iconography await beneath the dome of **St. Isaac's Cathedral** (Isaakievsky Sobor; Исаакиевский Собор), a massive example of 19th-century architecture. On a sunny day, the 100kg of pure gold that coat the dome shine for miles. Some of Russia's greatest artists have worked on the murals and mosaics in the ornate interior. *(M2: Nevsky Prospekt. Exiting the Metro, turn left and walk to the end of Nevsky pr. Turn left onto Admiraltevsky pr.; the cathedral is at the corner of Admiraltevsky and Voznesensky pr. Open Tu-Su 11am-6pm. 200R, students 100R. Colonnade open M-Tu and Th-Su 11am-5pm; 80R, students 40R. The* kassa *is to the right of the cathedral. Foreigners buy tickets inside the church.)*

FORTRESS OF PETER AND PAUL. Across the river from the Hermitage, the walls and golden spire of the **Fortress of Peter and Paul** (Petropavlovskaya Krepost; Петропавловская Крепость) beckon. Construction of the fortress began on May 27, 1703, a date now considered the birthday of St. Petersburg. Originally intended as a defense against the Swedes, it never saw battle; Peter I defeated the northern

A MUSEUM-GOER IN A STRANGE LAND Like many museums in Eastern Europe, those in Russia charge foreigners much higher rates than natives. In desperation, some travelers don a fluffy fur hat, snarl a little, push the exact number of rubles for a Russian ticket toward the *babushka* at the *kassa*, and remain stoically mute. Go ahead and try; it might work. Once inside, don't worry about forgetting to see anything–the *babushki* in each room won't let you. Many museums, with floors made of precious inlaid wood, will ask visitors to don *tapochki*, giant slippers that go over your shoes and transform the polished gallery floor into a veritable ice rink. There are no guardrails–only irreplaceable imperial china–to slow your stride. Hang onto handrails on the way up and down, or after navigating dozens of slippery wooden exhibition rooms you will meet an unfortunate end on the marble stairs.

invaders before the bulwarks were finished. Inside, the **Peter and Paul Cathedral** (Petropavlovsky Sobor; Петропавловский Собор) glows with rosy marble walls and a breathtaking Baroque iconostasis—a partition with intricate iconography. Before entering the main vault you will pass through the recently-restored **Chapel of St. Catherine the Martyr.** The bodies of the Romanovs—Tsar Nicholas II and his family, along with their faithful servants—were entombed here on July 17, 1998, the 80th anniversary of their murders at the hands of the Bolsheviks. After the fortress ceased to function as a defense against the Swedes, Peter turned it into a prison for dissidents; the condemned were held at **Trubetskoy Bastion** (Трубецкой Бастион). The fortress's southwest corner is a reconstruction of the prison where Peter the Great held and tortured his first son, Aleksei. Dostoevsky, Gorky, Trotsky, and Lenin's older brother also spent time here. *(M2: Gorkovskaya. Exiting the Metro, turn right on Kamennoostrovsky pr.* (Каменноостровский)*, the street in front of you (there is no sign). Follow the street to the river and cross the bridge to the island fortress. Open M and Th-Su 11am-6pm, Tu 11am-5pm; closed last Tu of each month. US$3, students US$1.50; additional sites 10-40R. Purchase a single ticket for most sites at the* kassa *in the middle of the island or in the smaller* kassa *to the right just inside the main entrance.)*

ALEKSANDR NEVSKY MONASTERY. A major pilgrimage spot and peaceful strolling place, **Aleksandr Nevsky Monastery** (Aleksandro-Nevskaya Lavra; Александро-невская Лавра) became one of four Orthodox monasteries to have received the highest monastic title of *"lavra"* in 1797. The 1716 **18th-Century Necropolis,** or **Lazarus Cemetery** (Lazarevskoye Kladbishche; Лазаревское Кладбище) is the city's oldest burial ground. The nearby **Artists' Necropolis** (Nekropol Masterov Uskusstv; Некраполь Мастеров Искусств), also known as the **Tikhvin Cemetery** (Tikhvinskoye Kladbishche; Тихвинское Кладбище), is the permanent resting place of **Fyodor Dostoevsky, Pyotr Tchaikovsky,** and **Nikolai Rimsky-Korsakov.** The **Church of the Annunciation** (Blagoveshchenskaya Tserkov; Благовещенская Церковь), farther along the central stone path on the left, is the original burial place of the Romanovs, who were moved to Peter and Paul Cathedral in 1998. The **Trinity Cathedral** (Svyato-Troitsky Sobor; Свято-Троицкий Собор) is at the end of the path, teeming with *babushki* energetically crossing themselves. (*M3, 4: Pl. Aleksandra Nevska. The 18th-Century Necropolis lies to the left of the entrance; the Artists's Necropolis is to the right. Cemeteries open M-W and F-Su 10am-5pm. Cemeteries 30R, students 15R. Modest dress.)*

ALONG NEVSKY PROSPEKT. Most of St. Petersburg's biggest sites cluster around the western end of Nevsky pr., the city's 4.5km main thoroughfare. The Prospekt begins at the **Admiralty** (Admiralteystvo; Адмиралтий), whose golden spire—painted black during WWII to disguise it from German artillery bombers—towers over the surrounding gardens and nearby Palace Square. *(M2: Nevsky. Exit the Metro, turn left, and walk to the end of Nevsky pr.)* To the left of the Admiralty as you face it from the Nevsky side, the **Bronze Horseman** (Peter the Great) is as one of the most widely-recognized symbols of the city; copies are all over Russia. *(M2: Nevsky. Exiting the Metro, turn left and walk to the end of Nevsky pr.)* Walking back east on Nevsky pr., the Roman-style **Kazan Cathedral** (Kazansky Sobor; Казанский Собор) looms to the right. Less commercialized than some of the other cathedrals, incense hangs heavily in the air and the icons are illuminated by candles lit by the faithful. *(M2: Nevsky. Open daily 8am-6pm. Free.)* Half a block down, looking up Canal Griboedov to the left, you can see the brilliantly colored **Church of the Bleeding Savior** (Spas Na Krovi; Спас На Крови), which sits on the site of the 1881 assassination of Tsar Aleksandr II. *(Open M-Tu and Th-Su 11am-7pm;* kassa *closes at 6pm. 250R, students 100R.)* Much farther down Nevsky, some of the bloodiest confrontations of the February Revolution of 1917 took place in **Uprising Square** (Ploshchad Vosstaniya; Площадь Восстания). *(Take M1 to Ploshchad Vosstaniya.)*

PISKARYOV MEMORIAL CEMETERY. (Piskaryovskoye Memorialnoye Kladbishche; Пискарёвское Мемориальное Кладбище). To understand St. Petersburg's obsession with WWII, come to the remote and hauntingly tranquil Piskaryov Memorial Cemetery. Close to a million people died during the 900-day German army siege of the city; this cemetery is their grave. An eternal flame and grassy mounds with the year are all that mark the dead. The monument says: "No one is forgotten; nothing is forgotten." *(M2: Ozerki (Озерки). Go right out of the exit to the stop on the same side of the street as the Metro for bus #123. Ride about 16 stops (30min.); the cemetery's on the left.)*

OTHER MUSEUMS. The collection at the **Russian Museum** (Russky Muzey; Русский Музей) ranges from medieval icons to the avant-garde, arranged chronologically. *(M3: Gostiny Dvor; down ul. Mikhailovsky past the Grand Hotel Europe. Open M 10am-5pm, W-Su 10am-6pm;* kassa *closes M 4pm, W-Su 5pm. 240R, students 120R, children up to 7 free.)* Next to the Russian Museum, **Kunstkamera Anthropological and Ethnographic Museum** (Muzey Antropologii i Etnografii—Kunstkamera; Музей Антропологии и Этнографии—Кунсткамера) exhibits the arts and crafts, traditions, and cultures of the former Russian empire, Soviet Union, and modern Russia. *(Open Tu-Su 11am-6pm;* kassa *closes at 5pm. 40R, students 20R.)* **Dostoevsky House** (Dom Dostoevskovo; Дом Достоевского), Kuznechny per. 5/2 (Кузнечный) is where Dostoevsky wrote *The Brothers Karamazov*. *(M1: Vladimirskaya; go around the corner to the right. Open Tu-Su 11am-6pm;* kassa *closes 5:30pm; closed last W of each month. 60R, students 30R.)* Find Soviet propaganda and artifacts from the "Great Patriotic War" at the **Museum of Russian Political History** (Muzey Politicheskoy Istorii Rossii; Музей Политической Истории России), ul. Kuybysheva 2/4. *(M2: Gorkovskaya. Go down Kamen noostrosky toward the mosque and turn left on Kuybysheva. Open F-W 10am-6pm. 60R, students 30R.)*

ENTERTAINMENT

St. Petersburg's famed White Nights lend the night sky a pale glow from mid-June to early July. In summer, lone misanthropes stroll under the illuminated night sky and watch the bridges over the Neva go up at 1:30am. Walk on the same side of the river as your hotel—the bridges don't go back down until 4-5am, though some close briefly between 3 and 3:20am. In the third week of June, when the sun barely touches the horizon, the city holds a series of outdoor evening concerts as part of the **White Nights Festival**, which lasts from the end of May to the end of June. Check kiosks, posters, and the monthly *Pulse* for more info. It is fairly easy to get tickets to world-class performances for as little as 20-30R, although many of the renowned theaters are known to grossly overcharge foreigners; buying Russian tickets from scalpers will save you money but you'll have to dress up and play Russian at the show. A monthly program in Russian is usually posted throughout the city.

THEATER, MUSIC, AND CIRCUS. The **Mariinsky Teatr** (Марийнский), a.k.a. the "Kirov," Teatralnaya pl. 1 (Театральная), M4: Sadovaya, where Tchaikovsky's *Nutcracker* and *Sleeping Beauty* premiered, is one of the most famous ballet halls in the world. Pavlova, Nureyev, Nizhinsky, and Baryshnikov all started here. For two weeks in June, the theater hosts the **White Nights Festival.** Tickets go on sale ten days in advance. (☎114 43 44. 20-300R for foreigners. *Kassa* open W-Su 11am-3pm and 4-7pm.) **Maly Teatr** (Small Theater; Малый Театр), a.k.a. "Mussorgsky," pl. Iskusstv 1 (Искусств), is open July through August, when Mariinsky is closed. (☎219 19 49.

Shows at noon, 7pm. Tickets 5-30R for Russians, up to 200R for foreigners. *Kassa* open daily 11am-3pm and 4-7:15pm. Bring your passport.) **Shostakovich Philharmonic Hall,** Mikhailovskaya ul. 2, M3: Gostiny Dvor, opposite the Grand Hotel Europe, has both classical and modern concerts. (☎110 42 57. Performances at 4pm and 7pm. Tickets from 20R.) **Aleksandrinsky Teatr** (Александринский Театр), pl. Ostrovskovo 2, M3: Gostiny Dvor, attracts famous Russian actors and companies. (☎110 41 03. Tickets 10-80R. *Kassa* open M-F 11am-3pm and 4-7:15pm, Sa-Su 11am-3pm and 4-6:15pm.) The Russian circus, while justly famous, is not for animal rights activists; **Tsirk** (Circus; Цирк), nab. Fontanki 3, near the Russky Muzey, M3: Gostiny Dvor, is Russia's oldest traditional circus. (☎314 84 78. Closed from mid-June until Sept. Shows at 11:30am, 3pm, and 7pm. Tickets from 20R. *Kassa* open daily 11am-7pm.)

NIGHTLIFE. During the pre-Gorbachev era, St. Petersburg was the heart of the Russian underground music scene; today, the city still hosts a large number of interesting clubs. Be careful when going home; cabs are usually a safe bet, but make sure your bridge isn't up. Check the Friday issue of *St. Petersburg Times* and *Pulse* for current events, special promotions, and up-to-the-minute club reviews. **Mama,** (Мама), ul. Malaya Monetnaya 3b (Малая Монетная), M2: Gorkovskaya, is very hip, very young, very techno, and rages very late. (Drinks 15-30R. Cover 60-100R. Open F-Sa 11:50pm-6am.) **Griboyedov,** ul. Voronezhskaya 2A (Воронежная), M4: Ligovsky Prospekt, once a bomb shelter, is now one of the hottest clubs in the city. (Cover 40-70R. Open W-M 6pm-6am.) **Moloko** (Молоко; Milk), Perekupnoy per. 12 (Перекупной), M3, 4: Pl. Aleksandra Nevskovo, has separate spaces for conversation and gyration. (Cover 20-40R.) **JFC Jazz Club** is at Shpalernaya ul. 33 (Шпалерная), M1: Chernyshevskaya. (☎272 98 50. Cover 60-100R. Open daily 7-11pm.) You wouldn't be reading *Let's Go: Europe* if we didn't tell you where to get your Guinness (US$3)—**The Shamrock,** ul. Dekabristov 27 (Декабристов), M4: Sadovaya, is the place, across from the Mariinsky in Teatralnaya pl. (Open daily noon-2am.) **69 Club,** 2-aya Krasnoarmeiskaya 6 (2-ая Красноармеиская), attracts both gay and straight clubbers, although recent management crackdowns have aimed at limiting the number of heterosexuals. (M1: Technologichesky Institut. Cover around 100R. Open Tu-Su 11pm-4am.)

EXCURSIONS FROM ST. PETERSBURG

Ride the suburban *elektrichka* trains out of St. Petersburg to join in the Russian love affair with the countryside. The palaces at Peterhof, Tsarskoye Selo, and Pavlovsk stand on what was German territory during the siege of Leningrad from 1942 to 1944. All were burned to the ground during the Nazi retreat, but Soviet authorities provided the staggering sums of money necessary to rebuild these symbols of rich cultural heritage during the postwar reconstruction.

PETERHOF (Петергоф). Formerly known as Petrodvorets (Петродворец), Peterhof is the largest and most thoroughly restored of the palaces. The entire complex is 300 years old, although many tsars added their own touches in the intervening years. To get through the gates you must pay an admission fee that grants access to the **Lower Gardens,** a perfect place for a picnic along the shores of the Gulf of Finland. (Open daily 9am-9pm. 120R, students 60R.) To work up an appetite, tour through the **Grand Palace** (Bolshoy Dvorets; Большой Дворец). Wanting to create his own Versailles, Peter started building the first residence here in 1714, but his daughter Empress Elizabeth (and later, Catherine the Great) greatly expanded and remodeled it. (☎427 95 27. Open Tu-Su 10:30am-6pm; *kassa* closes at 5pm; closed last Tu of the month. English tours 120R. Cameras 80R; video 200R. 230R, students 115R.) The **Hermitage Pavilion** served as a setting for the amusement of the palace residents; its 17th- and 18th-century European art is well worth seeing. (Open Tu-Su 10:30am-5pm. 86R, students 43R.) On the other side of the path facing the quay stands **Monplaisir,** where Peter actually lived; the big palace was only for special occasions. (Open M-Tu and Th-Su 10:30am-6pm. 170R, students 85R.) Next door is

BABUSHKA BOYCOTT They push harder than anyone on the buses and metro. They bundle up to the ears on even the hottest days in scarves and winter coats, then strip down to teeny-weeny bikinis and sunbathe on the banks of the Neva. They are *babushki,* and they mean business. Technically, *babushka* means grandma, but under the Soviet system, once it became all right to be rude, Russians began using it as a generic term for elderly women. In any case, be warned: if a *babushka* gets on the bus or metro, no matter how hardy she looks, and how weak and tired you feel, surrender your seat, or prepare for the verbal pummeling of a lifetime.

the **Catherine Building** (Ekaterininsky Korpus; Екатерининский Корпус), where Catherine the Great lay low while her husband was being overthrown on her orders. (Open M-W and F-Su 10:30am-6pm. Cameras 60R; video 150R. 86R, students 43R.) In the same complex, you can follow the sound of children's happy shrieks to the **joke fountains,** which, with one misstep, splash their giggling victims. Near the end of the center path to the right, a **Wax Museum** contains likenesses of historical figures ranging chronologically from Ivan the Terrible to the equally sinister Rasputin. (Open daily 9am-5pm. 50R, students 25R.) Take the **elektrichka** from the Baltyskaya Vokzal (Балтийская; M1: Baltiyskaya; 40min., every 15min., 8R). Buy tickets from the office (*prigorodnye kassa;* Пригородные касса) in the courtyard—ask for "NO-viy Peter-GOFF, too-DAH ee oh-BRAHT-nah." Get off at Novy Peterhof (sit in the 1st car or you might not see the station sign until it's too late).

TSARSKOYE SELO/PUSHKIN (Царское Село)/(Пушкин). South of the city, **Tsarskoye Selo** (Tsar's Village) surrounds Catherine the Great's summer residence, a gorgeous azure, white, and gold Baroque palace overlooking sprawling, English-style parks. The area was renamed "Pushkin" during the Soviet era, although the train station—Detskoe Selo (Детсоз Село)—retained part of the old name. Most Russians use "Pushkin" to refer to the town. The opulent residence, named **Catherine's Palace** (Ekaterininsky Dvorets) after Empress Elizabeth's mom Catherine I, was largely destroyed by the Nazis; each room exhibits a photograph of it in war-torn condition. Many of the salons, especially the huge, glittering **Grand Hall** ballroom, have been magnificently restored. (☎465 53 08. Open W-M 10am-5pm; closed last M of the month. Photos 100R; video 230R. 220R, students 110R.) Bring a picnic and wander through the lovely 1400 acres of **Catherine Park,** a melange of English, French, and Italian styles. (Open daily 10am-11pm. 50R, students 25R; free after 6pm.) Take any **elektrichka** from Vitebsky vokzal (M1: Pushkinskaya). To buy your ticket, go to the bunker-like building behind the station to the right and ask for "Pushkin" (tickets 6R). All trains leaving from platforms #1-3 stop in Pushkin (30min.). From the station, it's a 10-minute ride on bus #371 or 382 (2R) to the end.

PAVLOVSK (Павловск). Catherine the Great gave the park and gardens at Pavlovsk to her son Paul in 1777, perhaps to keep her eye on him. The largest **park** of all the outlying palaces, Pavlovsk's lush, shady paths wind among wild foliage, bridges, and pavilions. (Small garden open daily 9am-8pm. Park open 24hr. 20R, students 12R.) Paul's **Great Palace** is not as spectacular as his mother's at Tsarskoye Selo, but is worth a visit nonetheless. (Open M-Th and Sa-Su 10am-6pm. 180R, students 90R.) Although visits to Pushkin and Pavlovsk can be combined in one day, a leisurely visit is more enjoyable. To reach Pavlovsk, get off at the **elektrichka** stop after Tsarskoye Selo/Pushkin on trains leaving from platforms #1-3 at Vitebsky vokzal. To get to the palace from the train station, take bus #370, 383, or 383A. To get to Pushkin from Pavlovsk, take bus #370 or 383 from the Great Palace, or bus #473 from Pavlovsk Station (3R).

SLOVAKIA (SLOVENSKO)

SLOVAK KORUNY

US$1 = 48SK	10SK = US$0.21
CDN$1 = 32SK	10SK = CDN$0.31
UK£1 = 67SK	10SK = UK£0.14
IR£1 = 54SK	10SK = IR£0.18
AUS$1 = 27SK	10SK = AUS$0.36
NZ$1 = 20SK	10SK = NZ$0.49
SAR1 = 6.80SK	10SK = SAR1.46
DM1 = 22SK	10SK = DM0.46
EUR€1 = 43SK	10SK = EUR€0.24

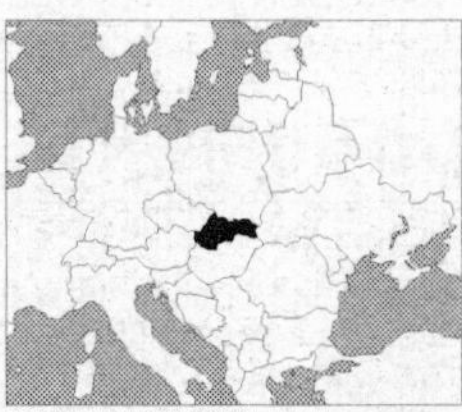

Country code: 421. **International dialing prefix:** 00. From outside Slovakia, dial int'l dialing prefix (see inside back cover) + 421 + city code + local number.

After centuries of nomadic invasions, Hungarian domination, and Soviet industrialization, Slovakia has finally emerged as an independent country. Freedom has introduced new challenges, however, as the older generation reluctantly gives way to their chic, English-speaking offspring. The nation remains in a state of generational flux between industry and agriculture, unable to muster the resources necessary for an easy Westernization and unwilling to return to its past. A strange mixture of fairy-tale traditionalism and easy-going youth has resulted, which combines with low prices to create a haven for budget travelers. From tiny villages to the busy streets of its capital, Slovakia is coming to grips with progress, as the good old days retreat to castle ruins, pastures, and the stunning Tatras above.

For more on Slovakia's wacky adventures, try *Let's Go: Eastern Europe 2001*.

FACTS AND FIGURES

Official Name: Slovak Republic.

Government: Parliamentary democracy.

Capital: Bratislava.

Land Area: 48,800 sq. km.

Geography: Mountainous, with lowlands in the southwest and east.

Climate: Temperate; cool summers and cold, cloudy, humid winters.

Major Cities: Bratislava, Košice, Lučenec, Banská Bystrica.

Population: 5,400,000.

Languages: Slovak, Hungarian.

Religions: Roman Catholic (60%), atheist (10%), Protestant (8%).

Average Income Per Capita: US$8,300.

Major Exports: Machinery and transport equipment, manufactured goods.

DISCOVER SLOVAKIA

Slovakia is an outdoor-lover's paradise. In the west, the **Low Tatras** near **Liptovský Mikuláš** are a relatively deserted mountain range with everything from day hikes in the wooded foothills to overnight treks above the tree line (p. 818). You'll have to battle with German and Slovak tourists to tackle the trails and slopes of the **High Tatras** near **Starý Smokovec,** but it'll be worth it to witness the snow-capped peaks of this range, one of the best—and cheapest—mountain playlands in Europe (p. 818). Farther south, **Slovenský Raj National Park** offers miles of ravine-crossing, cliff-climbing, heart-stopping treks and ice caves ripe for spelunking (p. 819).

ESSENTIALS

WHEN TO GO

The weather is best May-September. Rain is not uncommon any time of the year—winters are very cold, damp, and snowy. No matter what time of year, take warm clothing if you plan to travel into the mountains. November-February is the best time for skiing, and August is the best time for hiking.

DOCUMENTS AND FORMALITIES

Citizens of South Africa and the US can visit Slovakia without a **visa** for up to 30 days; Australia, Canada, Ireland, New Zealand, and the UK 90 days. To apply for a visa, contact an embassy or consulate in person or by mail; processing takes two business days (single-entry US$20; double-entry US$22; 90-day multiple-entry US$40; 180-day multiple-entry US$62; transit—good for 30 days—US$20). Visa prices vary with exchange rate. Travelers must also register their visa within three days of entering Slovakia; hotels will do this automatically. If you intend to stay longer or get a visa extension, notify the Office of Border and Alien Police.

EMBASSIES AND CONSULATES

All foreign embassies are in **Bratislava** (see p. 816).

Slovakian Embassies at Home: Australia, 47 Culgoa Circuit, O'Malley, Canberra ACT 2606 (☎ (6) 290 15 16; fax 290 17 55; slovak@cyberone.com.au); **Canada,** 50 Rideau Terrace, Ottawa, ON K1M 2A1 (☎ (613) 749 44 42; fax 749 49 89; email slovakemb@sprint.ca); **South Africa,** 930 Arcadia St., Arcadia, Pretoria; P.O. Box 12736, Hatfield, 0028 (☎ (012) 342 20 51; fax 342 36 88); **UK,** 25 Kensington Palace Gardens, London W8 4QY (☎ (020) 7243 08 03; fax 77 27 58 24; www.slovakembassy.co.uk); **US,** 2201 Wisconsin Ave. NW, Suite 250, Washington, D.C. 20007 (☎ (202) 965 51 60; fax 965 51 66; www.slovakemb.com).

GETTING THERE AND GETTING AROUND

BY PLANE. Bratislava does have an international airport, but entering the country by air may be inconvenient and expensive. Flying to nearby Vienna, Austria, and taking a bus or train from there is much cheaper and takes about the same time.

BY TRAIN. International rail links connect Slovakia to its neighbors. **EastRail** is valid in Slovakia; **Eurail** is not. You'll pay extra for an *InterCity* or *EuroCity* fast train, and if there's a boxed R on the timetable, a *miestenka* (reservation; 7Sk) is required. If you board the train without a reservation, expect to pay an extra 150Sk fine. Larger towns on the **railway** have many *stanice* (train stations); the *hlavná stanica* is the main one. Tickets must be bought before boarding the train, except in the tiniest towns. **ŽSR** is the national train company. **Cestovný poriadok** (58Sk), the master schedule, is also printed on a large, round board in stations. In western Slovakia, *odchody* (departures) and *príchody* (arrivals) are posted on yellow and white signs, respectively—double check the display board for the *nástupište* (gate). In eastern Slovakia, ask *"Je to správne nástupište do...?"* ("Is this the right platform for...?") Reservations are recommended for *expresný* trains and first-class seats, but are not necessary for *rychlík* (fast), *spešný* (semi-fast), or *osobný* (local) trains. First and second class are relatively comfortable.

BY BUS. In many hilly regions, **ČSAD** or **SAD buses** are the best and sometimes the only option. Except for long trips, buy tickets on the bus. Schedule symbols include: **X,** weekdays only; **a,** Saturdays and Sundays only; **r** and **k,** excluding holi-

days. **Numbers** refer to the days of the week on which the bus runs—1 is Monday, 2 is Tuesday, and so forth. *"Premava"* means including and *"nepremava"* is except; following those words are often lists of dates (day, then month).

BY CAR, BIKE, AND THUMB. Taxis are fairly safe and convenient, but expensive; be sure to check the price of the trip before getting in. However, gas is expensive, at US$2.50 per gallon. On highways the **speed limit** is 130kph/80mph; on other roads it is 90kph/55mph. For **Alfa** (the Slovak Road Rescue System), dial ☎154. The Slovaks love to ride **bikes,** especially in the Tatras, the foothills of West Slovakia, and Šariš. **VKÚ** publishes color maps of most regions (70-80Sk). Road conditions in Slovakia are generally good. **Hitchhiking** is not very successful nor common; if you do, use a sign. *Let's Go* does not recommend hitchhiking.

TOURIST SERVICES AND MONEY

EMERGENCY. Ambulance: ☎155. **Fire:** ☎150. **Police:** ☎158.

TOURIST OFFICES. The main tourist information offices form a loose conglomeration called **Asociácia Informačných Centier Slovenska (AICS);** look for the green logo. The offices are invariably on or near the town's main square; the nearest one can often be found by dialing ☎186. English is often spoken here. **SATUR,** the Slovak branch of the old Czechoslovakian Čedok, seems more interested in flying Slovaks abroad on package tours, but may be of some help.

MONEY. One hundred **halér** make up one **Slovak koruna (Sk).** The currency rates above are those for September, 2000; with inflation around 14%, expect both rates and prices quoted in *koruny* to change significantly over the next year. Post offices tend to have better exchange rates than banks. **Všeobecná Úverová Banka (VÚB)** has offices in even the smallest towns and cashes AmEx/Eurocheque **traveler's checks** for a 1% commission; most offices give MC cash advances. Many Slovenská Sporiteľňa bureaus handle Visa **cash advances.** Cirrus/MC/Visa/Plus **ATMs** can be found in all but the smallest towns. Leave your **AmEx** at home—it's useless in Slovakia. **Tipping** is common in restaurants. Most people round up—an 8-10% tip is generous and marks you as a tourist. A very basic day in Slovakia (staying in campgrounds and shopping at grocery stores) averages US$15; a more extravagant day (hostels and restaurants) averages US$20-25.

ACCOMMODATIONS AND CAMPING

Foreigners will often pay up to twice as much as Slovaks for the same room. Finding cheap accommodations in Bratislava before the student dorms open in July is impossible, and without reservations, the outlook in Slovenský Raj and the Tatras can be bleak. Otherwise, it's not difficult to find a bed as long as you call ahead. The tourist office, **SATUR,** or **Slovakotourist** can usually help. **Juniorhotels (HI),** though uncommon, are a step above the usual hostel. In the mountains, **chaty** (mountain huts/cottages) range from plush quarters for 400Sk per night to a friendly bunk and outhouse for 150Sk. **Hotel** prices fall dramatically outside Bratislava and the High Tatras, and hotels are rarely full. **Pensions** *(penzióny)* are less expensive than hotels and often more fun. Two forms of *ubytovanie* (lodging) cater mainly to Slovaks: **stadiums** and sport centers often run hotels on their lots, and **workers' hostels** generally offer hospital-like rooms. **Campgrounds** lurk on the outskirts of most towns, and many offer bungalows. Camping in national parks is illegal.

FOOD AND DRINK

Slovakia emerged from its 1000-year Hungarian captivity with a taste for paprika, spicy *guláš*, and fine wines. The national dish, *bryndžové halušky*, is a plate of dumpling-esque pasta smothered in a thick sauce of sheep or goat cheese that sometimes comes flecked with bacon. Slovakia's second-favorite dish is *pirogy*, a pasta-pocket filled with potato or *bryndža* cheese, topped with bacon bits. *Pstruh* (trout), often served whole, is also popular. *Kolačky* (pastry) is baked with cheese, jam or poppy seeds, and honey. Enjoy flavorful wines at a *vináreň* (wine hall). *Pivo* (beer) is served at a *pivnica* or *piváreň* (tavern). The favorite Slovak beer is *Zlatý Bažant*, a light, slightly bitter Tatran brew. Slovakia produces several brandies: *slivovica* (plum), *marhulovica* (apricot), and *borovička* (juniper-berry).

COMMUNICATION

MAIL. Slovakia has an efficient **mail** service, taking two to three weeks depending on the destination. Almost every post office (*pošta*) provides **Express Mail Services,** but to send a package abroad, a trip to a *colnice* (customs office) is in order. *Poste Restante* mail with a "1" after the city name will arrive at the main post office.

TELEPHONES. Card phones are common, and although they sometimes refuse your card (150Sk), they're much better than the coin-operated variety. Purchase cards at kiosks and telecommunications offices near some post offices. **International direct dial numbers** include: **AT&T Direct,** ☎00 42 70 01 01; **BT Direct,** ☎0800 044 01; **Canada Direct,** ☎0800 00 01 51; **MCI WorldPhone,** ☎08000 001 12; **Sprint,** ☎0042 18 71 87.

LANGUAGES. Slovak, closely related to **Czech,** is a tricky Slavic language, but any attempt to speak it will be appreciated. **English** is not uncommon among Bratislava youth, but people outside the capital are more likely to speak **German,** and those near the border, **Polish.** You can find English-speakers in tourist offices and cities. **Russian** is understood, but not always welcome.

HOLIDAYS AND FESTIVALS

Holidays: Independence Day (Jan. 1); Epiphany (Jan. 6); Good Friday (Apr. 21); Easter (Apr. 24); Labor Day (May 1); Sts. Cyril and Methodius Day (July 5); Anniversary of Slovak National Uprising (Aug. 29); Constitution Day (Sept. 1); Our Lady of the Seven Sorrows (Sept. 15); All Saint's Day (Nov. 1); Christmas (Dec. 24-26).

BRATISLAVA ☎7

Directly between Vienna and Budapest, Bratislava is experienced most often as a pit stop on the way to bigger cities. It has for hundreds of years been abused by foreign rulers, but in the last five years major renovations have improved the city's outlook. Polluted roadways and crumbling buildings are being cleared away. The streets are full of cafes, street performers, and stunning Baroque architecture. Bratislava Castle looms above the city as a Slovak symbol of national pride. Resist the temptation to pass over Bratislava for Prague, and it will surprise you.

GETTING THERE AND GETTING AROUND

Trains: Bratislava Hlavná stanica (☎50 58 44 84), north of the city center. International tickets at counters #5-13. **Wasteels** (☎52 49 93 57), with an office in front, sells discounted tickets to those under 26. Open M-F 8:30am-4:30pm. To: **Vienna** (1½hr., 3 per day, 248Sk); **Budapest** (2½-3hr., 7 per day, 660Sk, Wasteels 654Sk); **Prague** (5hr., 7 per day, 300Sk); **Warsaw** (8hr., 1 per day, 1400Sk, 811Sk); **Kraków** (8hr., 1 per day, 1080Sk, 865Sk); and **Berlin** (10hr., 2 per day, 3600Sk, 2534Sk).

Buses: Mlynské nivy 31 (☎09 84 22 22 22), east of the city center. More reliable and frequent than trains for domestic transport. Check ticket for bus number (č. aut.) since several different buses may depart from the same stand. To: **Vienna** (1½hr., 7 per day, 400Sk); **Budapest** (4hr., 2 per day, 400Sk); and **Prague** (5hr., 8 per day, 247Sk).

Public Transportation: Daytime **trams** and **buses** (4am-11pm) cost 6-18Sk per ride, depending on time; buy tickets for specific times at kiosks or the orange *automats* in most bus stations. **Night buses** marked with black and orange numbers in the 500s require 2 tickets; they run at midnight and at 3am. Most trams pass by Nám. SNP, while most buses stop at the north base of Nový Most. 1000Sk fine for no ticket. **Tourist passes** are sold at some kiosks: 1-day 70Sk, 2-day 130Sk, 3-day 160Sk, 7-day 240Sk.

Hitchhiking: Those hitching to **Vienna** cross most SNP and walk down Viedenská cesta; though this road also goes to **Hungary** via Győr, fewer cars head in that direction. Hitchers to **Prague** take bus #121 or 122 from the city center to the Patronka stop. *Let's Go* does not recommend hitchhiking.

ORIENTATION AND PRACTICAL INFORMATION

Bratislava is a proverbial stone's throw from the borders of Austria and Hungary. Avoid getting off at the **Nové Mesto** train station; it's much farther from the center than **Hlavná stanica** (Main Station). To get downtown from Hlavná stanica, head straight past the waiting buses, turn right on Šancová and left on Štefánikova; or take tram #1 to "Poštová" at Nám. SNP (the city center lies between Nám. SNP and the river). From there, Uršulínska leads to the tourist office. Take trolleybus #215 from the bus station to the center; or turn right on Mlynské nivy, walk 10 minutes to Dunajska, then follow it to Kamenné nám. (a block from the tourist office).

SLOVAKIA

Tourist Offices: Bratislavská Informačná Služba (BIS), Klobučnicka 2 (☎54 43 37 15 and 54 43 43 70; email bis@bratislava.sk). Sells **maps** (28Sk), gives tours, and books rooms (singles 900-2500Sk) for a 50Sk fee. Open M-F 8am-7pm, Sa-Su 9am-2pm.

Embassies: Canada (honorary consulate), Mišíkova 28 (☎52 44 21 75). Open M-F 8:30am-noon and 1:30pm-4pm. **UK,** Panská 16 (☎54 41 96 32). Open M-F 8:30am-12:30pm and 1:30-5pm. **US,** Hviezdoslavovo nám. 4 (☎54 43 08 61; emergency ☎ (0903) 70 36 66; fax 54 41 51 48). Open M-F 8am-4:30pm. Citizens of **South Africa, Australia, New Zealand,** and **Ireland** should contact the British embassy.

Currency Exchange: VÚB, Gorkého 9 (☎59 55 79 76). 1% commission on traveler's checks. **Cash advances** on V, MC. Open M-W and F 8am-5pm, Th 8am-noon. A **24hr. currency exchange** machine is outside Československá Obchodná Banka. Changes US$, DM, and UK£ into Sk for no commission. **ATMs** are all over the center.

Emergency: Fire: ☎150. **Medical:** ☎155. **Police:** ☎158.

Pharmacy: Nám. SNP 20 (☎54 43 29 52), at Gorkého and Laurinská. Open M-F 7:30am-7pm, Sa 8am-5pm, Su 9am-5pm.

Internet Access: Internet Club, Jesenského 7 (☎09 03 96 71 21). Five fast PCs. 2Sk per min. Open M-Sa 9am-6:30pm.

Post Office: Nám. SNP 35 (☎54 43 51 80). *Poste Restante* at counter #5. Open M-F 7am-8pm, Sa 7am-2pm. Address mail to be held: First name SURNAME, Poste Restante, Nám. SNP 35, **81000** Bratislava 1, Slovakia.

ACCOMMODATIONS

In July and August, several dorms open as hostels. Good off-season deals are hard to find. Most cheap beds are near the station on the northeast side of town, a 20-minute walk (5-min. tram ride) from the city center.

Pension Gremium, Gorkého 11 (☎54 13 10 26). Central location just off Hviezdoslavovo nám. Sparkling private showers, huge fans, and a popular cafe downstairs. Some street noise. English spoken. Breakfast included. Check-out noon. Only five rooms, so call ahead. Singles 890Sk; doubles 1290-1600Sk.

Youth Hostel Bernolak, Bernolákova 1 (☎52 49 77 24). From the train station, take bus #23, 74, or 218 or tram #3 to "Račianské Mýto." From the bus station, take bus #121 or 122. A friendly hostel. All rooms have baths. Check-out 9am. Open July-Sept. 15. Doubles 600Sk, 540Sk with Euro26, HI, or ISIC.

FOOD

West Slovakia produces a celebrated, strong-flavored *Modra* wine. A few restaurants serve the region's spicy meat mixtures. If all else fails, you can chow at one of the city's ever-present burger stands. For **groceries,** try **Tesco Potraviny,** Kamenné nám. 1. (Open M-W 8am-7pm, Th 8am-8pm, F 8am-9pm, Sa 8am-6pm, Su 9am-6pm.)

Prašná Bašta, Zámočnícka 11 (☎54 43 49 57). Tasty traditional Slovak dishes 88-185Sk. Open daily 11am-11pm.

Crepa, Michalská 22, near Františkánske nám. Excellent crepes 25-140Sk. Open M-Th 8am-11pm, F 8am-midnight, Sa 10am-midnight, Su 10am-11pm.

Vegetarian Jedáleň, Laurinská 8. Cafeteria-style lunch spot popular with local businessfolk and young Slovak herbivores. Entrees 50-100Sk. Open M-F 11am-3pm.

YOU WANT FRIES WITH THAT? Just when you thought the hardest challenge in ordering food was comprehending Slovak, you come to a Bratislava burger stand. A *syrový burger* (cheeseburger) costs less than a *hamburger so syrom* (hamburger with cheese) because, as the stand owner will explain with humiliatingly clear logic, a cheeseburger is made of cheese—*only* cheese. A *pressburger,* named after Bratislava's former moniker Pressburg, consists of bologna on a bun, and hamburgers are actually ham. Everything comes boiled except, of course, the cheese.

SIGHTS

NÁM. SNP AND ENVIRONS. With the exception of Devín Castle, almost all of the sights worth seeing are in **Old Bratislava** (Stará Bratislava), centered around Nám. SNP. From Nám. SNP, which commemorates the bloody Slovak National Uprising (SNP) against fascism, walk down Uršulínska to Primaciálné nám. and the Neoclassical **Primate's Palace** (Primaciálný Palác), Primaciálné nám. 1, which dates from 1781. Napoleon and Austrian Emperor Franz I signed the Peace of Pressburg here in 1805. *(Open Tu-Su 10am-5pm. 20Sk.)* A walk to the left as you exit the palace down Klobučnícka leads to **Hlavné nám.** On your left as you enter the square is the **Town History Museum** (Muzeum Histórie Mesta) with a wonderful 1:500 model of 1945-55 Bratislava. *(Open Tu-F 10am-5pm, Sa-Su 11am-6pm. Model free. 25Sk, students 10Sk.)* Take a right up Zámočnicka, a left onto Michalská, left on Sedláska—which travels through Hlavné nám. and becomes Rybárska Brána—to the eastern side of **Hviezdoslavovo nám.** Continue straight down Mostová (the continuation of Rybárska Brána on the other side of the square) and turn left at the Danube to reach the **Slovak National Gallery,** Rázusovo nábr., which displays artwork from the Gothic and Baroque periods as well as some modern works. *(Open Tu-Su 10am-6pm. 35Sk, students 10Sk.)* Continue with the Danube on your left to the **New Bridge** (Nový Most) and turn right on Staromestská. Cross the highway on the far side of St. Martin's using the pedestrian overpass to view articles of a vanished population at the **Museum of Jewish Culture** (Múzeum Židovskej Kultúry), Židovská 17. *(Open M-F and Su 11am-5pm. Last entry 4:30pm. 60Sk, 40Sk.)*

BRATISLAVA CASTLE. Visible from much of the city, the four-towered Bratislava Castle (Bratislavský hrad) is the city's defining landmark. Take Ventúrska from Hviezdoslavovo nám., then turn left on Panská, turn right on Kapitulská, left in front of St. Martin's Cathedral, and cross the Starometská freeway via the overpass. Follow Zámocké schody to the castle. The castle burned in 1811 and was bombed during WWII; what's left today is a communist-era restoration. Its towers provide fantastic views of the Danube. The ruins of **Devín Castle** sit above the Danube and Morava rivers. Take bus #29 from below Nový Most to 9km west of Bratislava (Štrbská stop). The site has been one of strategic importance since 5000 BC, and recovered artifacts from its history are displayed inside.

THE TATRA MOUNTAINS (TATRY)

The mesmerizing High Tatras span the border between Slovakia and Poland and are home to hundreds of hiking and skiing trails along the Carpathians' highest peaks (2650m). They are one of the most compact ranges in the world, featuring sky-scraping hikes, glacial lakes, and super-deep snows. Cheap mountain railways and accommodations add to the allure for the budget hiker.

The Tatras are a great place for a hike, but in winter a guide is almost always necessary; even in summer many of the hikes are extremely demanding and require experience. For current conditions and weather info, check www.tanap.sk.

STARÝ SMOKOVEC. Starý Smokovec (STAH-ree SMO-ko-vets) is the High Tatras's most central resort and, founded in the 17th century, one of the oldest. Cheap beds down the road in **Horný Smokovec** make it accessible to the budget traveler. The town itself was developed with tourists in mind, but the trails from town are spectacular. The funicular to **Hrebienok** (1285m) leads to hiking country; to hike it, start at the funicular station behind Hotel Grand (behind the train station) and head 35 minutes up the green trail. Another 20 minutes from Hrebienok, the green trail leads north to the foaming **Cold Waterfall** (Studeného Potoka). The eastward blue trail descends from the waterfall to **Tatranská Lomnica** (1¾hr.). The hike to **Malá Studená Dolina** (Little Cold Valley) is also fairly relaxed; take the red trail from Hrebienok to the hut **Zamkovského chata** (1475m; ☎442 26 36; 260Sk per person) and onto the green trail which climbs above the tree-line to a high lake and **Téryho chata** (2015m; 4hr.; ☎442 52 45; breakfast included; 270Sk per person).

SLOVAKIA

TEŽ **trains** arrive from Poprad (30min., every hr., 14Sk) at the town's lowest point, below the central road. **Buses** to many Tatra resorts stop in a parking lot to the right, facing uphill, of the train station. Facing uphill, head up the road that runs just left of the train station, then cross the main road veering left. The **Tatranská Informačná Kancelária,** in Dom Služieb, has weather info and sells hiking maps, including the crucial **VKÚ sheet 113.** (☎44 23 34 40; fax 442 31 27. Open M-F 8am-5:30pm, Sa 8am-1pm.) Turn right on the main road from the stations and walk 10 minutes to **Hotel Šport,** which offers a cafe, sauna, pool, and massage parlor. (☎442 23 61; fax 442 27 19. Breakfast 70Sk. Singles 405Sk; doubles 710Sk; triples 1005Sk.) **Grocers** dot Starý Smokovec; five are on the main road. ☎**0969.**

EXCURSION FROM STARÝ SMOKOVEC: ŠTRBSKÉ PLESO. Placid Štrbské Pleso (Lake Štrbské; SHTERB-skay PLAY-so) is the Tatras's most-beloved ski resort. Several beautiful **hikes** begin from the town, but just one lift runs in summer, hoisting visitors to **Chata pod Soliskom** (1840m), overlooking the lake and the expansive plains behind Štrbské Pleso. (Runs June 25-Sept. 9 8am-4pm. July-Aug. 100Sk, round-trip 150Sk; June and Sept. 70Sk, 100Sk.) The yellow route heads from the east side of the lake (follow the signs to Hotel Patria) out along **Mlynická dolina** to mountain lakes and **Vodopády Skok** (waterfall). It then crosses **Bystré Sedlo** (saddle; 2314m) and circles **Štrbské Solisko** (2302m) before returning to Štrbské Pleso (8-9hr.). TEŽ **trains** arrive hourly from **Starý Smokovec** (30min., 18Sk).

LIPTOVSKÝ MIKULÁŠ. Liptovský Mikuláš (LIP-tov-skee MEE-koo-lash) is fairly drab, but it is a good springboard for hiking in the **Low Tatras** (Nízke Tatry). To scale **Mt. Ďumbier,** the region's tallest peak (2043m), catch an early bus (25min., every hr., 12Sk) from platform #11 at the bus station to Liptovský Ján and follow the blue trail up the Štiavnica River to the **Ďumbierske sedlo** (saddle) by Chata (hut) generála M.R. Štefanika (5hr.). Then take the red trail to the ridge, which leads to the summit (1½hr.). Descend the ridge and follow the red sign to neighboring peak **Chopok** (2024m), the second-highest in the range. Stay overnight at the hut there, **Kammená chata** (80Sk), or just have a beer (30Sk). From Chopok, it's a pleasant and winding walk down the blue trail to the **bus** stop behind the Hotel Grand at Orupné (1¾hr.). **Trains** from Bratislava to Liptovský Mikuláš (4hr., 9 per day, 252Sk) are cheaper and more frequent than buses. Get to the town center by following Štefánikova toward the gas station at the far end of the bus station, then turn right onto Hodžu. The **tourist office,** Nám. Mieru 1, in the Dom Služieb complex on the north side of town, books private rooms (20% deposit) and sells local hiking maps; ask for VKÚ sheets #122 and 123 for 79Sk and 68Sk. (☎552 24 18; email infolm@trynet.sk. Open mid-June to mid-Sept. and mid-Dec. to Mar. M-F 8am-7pm, Sa 8am-2pm, Su noon-6pm; reduced hours off season.) **Hotel Kriváň,** Štúrova 5, is across the square from the tourist office. (☎552 24 14. Singles 300-420Sk; doubles 470-620Sk.) ☎**0849.**

SLOVENSKÝ RAJ. The Slovenský Raj (Slovak Paradise) National Park lies south-east of the Nizke Tatry. Instead of heavily touristed peaks, there are forested hills and deep ravines with terrific waterfalls. Life moves at a slightly slower pace in the tiny villages and grassy meadows, and hikers and skiers have left a legacy in the beautiful trails connecting them. **Dedinsky** (pop. 400) is the largest town on Slovenský Raj's southern border. Get a copy of **VKÚ sheet 124** (79-85Sk) before entering the region. The **Dobšinská Ice Caves** (Dobšinská ľadová jaskyňa), a 23km stretch of ice, holds 110,000 cubic meters of water still frozen from the last Ice Age. The 30-minute tour covers 475m of the cave, with hall after hall of frozen columns, gigantic ice wells, and hardened waterfalls. To get here from Dedinky, take the 7:20am, 10:56am, or 2:39pm **train** for two stops (9Sk, 15min.). The one road from the cave train station leads 100m out to the main road. Turn left, and the cave parking lot is 250m ahead. From the parking lot, the blue trail leads up a steep incline to the cave. (Open Tu-Su May 15-June and Sept. 9:30am-2pm; July-Aug. 9am-4pm. Hourly Slovak tours 90Sk, students 70Sk; in English 140Sk, 110Sk. 20-person minimum for English tours.) No one said getting to paradise was easy, but the best way is to catch the **bus** from **Poprad** (dir. Rožňava; 1hr., 6 per day, 38Sk), which stops at a junction 2km south of Dedinky. Watch for the huge blue road sign at the intersection, just before the bus stop. From the intersection, walk down the road that the bus didn't take, turn right at the intersection after the basin, cross the dam after the train station, turn left, and walk 10 minutes to Dedinky. **Hotel Priehrada** rents comfortable rooms. (☎798 12 12. Reduced rates Sept. to mid-Dec. and Apr.-June. 250Sk per person. **Camping** tents 25Sk, plus 25Sk per person.) ☎**0942.**

SLOVENIA (SLOVENIJA)

SLOVENIAN TOLARS

US$1 = 233SIT	100SIT = US$0.43
CDN$1 = 158SIT	100SIT = CDN$0.63
UK£1 = 341SIT	100SIT = UK£0.29
IR£1 = 266SIT	100SIT = IR£0.38
AUS$1 = 134SIT	100SIT = AUS$0.74
NZ$1 = 100SIT	100SIT = NZ$1.00
SAR1 = 33.50SIT	100SIT = SAR2.98
DM1 = 107SIT	100SIT = DM0.93
EUR€1 = 209SIT	100SK = EUR€0.48

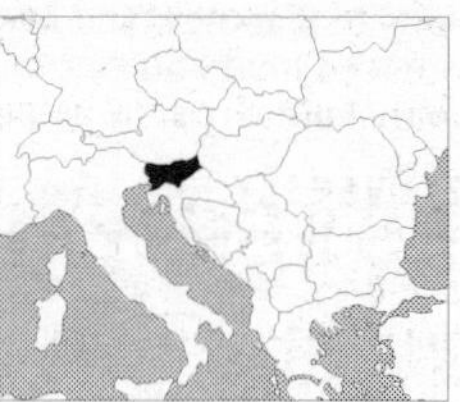

Country code: 386. **International dialing prefix:** 00. From outside Slovenia, dial int'l dialing prefix (see inside back cover) + 386 + city code + local number

Slovenia, the most prosperous of Yugoslavia's breakaway republics, revels in its newfound independence, modernizing rapidly while turning a hungry eye toward the West. It has quickly separated itself from its neighbors, using liberal politics and a high GDP to gain entrance into highly sought-after trade and security alliances. For a country half Switzerland's size, Slovenia, on the "sunny side of the Alps," is also extraordinarily diverse: in a day, you can breakfast on an Alpine peak, lunch under the Mediterranean sun, and dine in a vineyard on the Pannonian plains.

For more coverage of Slovenia, check out *Let's Go: Eastern Europe 2001*.

FACTS AND FIGURES

Official Name: Republic of Slovenia.
Government: Parliamentary democratic republic.
Capital: Ljubljana.
Geography: Mountains, valleys, and plateaus.
Land Area: 20,256 sq. km.
Population: 1,950,000.
Languages: Slovenian.
Religions: Roman Catholic (71%), atheist (4%), other (25%).
Income per capita: US$10,300.

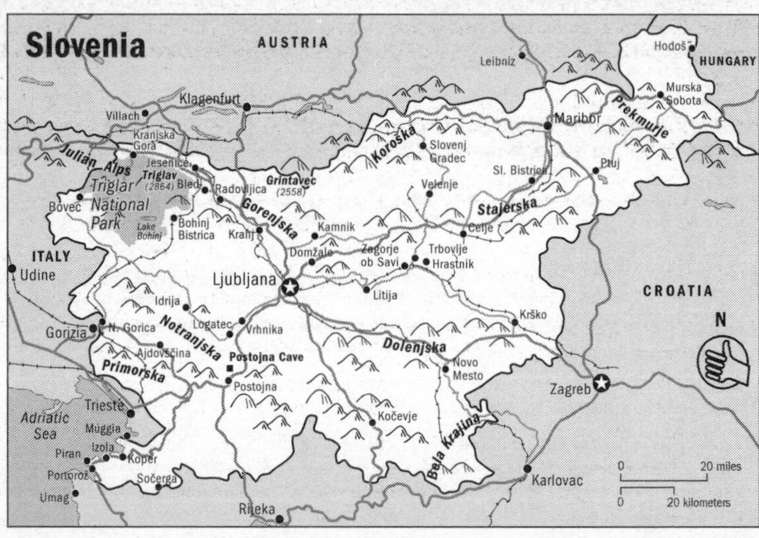

DISCOVER SLOVENIA

Any visit to this Balkan oddball must start in youthful **Ljubljana** (p. 823), which has the splendid majesty of the Habsburg cities and a cafe scene on par with Paris or Vienna. Most visitors venture to Slovenia for its Alpine delights. In the **Julian Alps, Lake Bled** (p. 825) and **Lake Bohinj** (p. 826) are traversed by miles of hikes—ranging from relaxed to treacherous—in summer. In winter, they host very snowy, steep, and relatively cheap skiing.

ESSENTIALS

WHEN TO GO

April through October is a a great time to visit; it's warm and dry, perfect beach weather. It can be chilly in the mountains, even in summer. Tourists show up in July and August, so earlier or later is best. Winter is cold, snowy, and for skiing.

DOCUMENTS AND FORMALITIES

Australian, Canadian, Irish, New Zealand, UK, and US citizens can visit without **visas** for up to 90 days. South Africans need visas (3-month single-entry or 5-day transit US$26; 3-month multiple entry US$52). Apply in your home country.

EMBASSIES AND CONSULATES

All foreign embassies and consulates are located in **Ljubljana** (p. 823).

Slovenian Embassies at Home: Australia, Level 6, St. George's Bldg., 60 Marcus Clarke St., Canberra ACT 2601 (☎ (02) 62 43 48 30; http://slovenia.webone.com.au); **Canada,** 150 Metcalfe St., #2101, Ottawa, ON K2P 1P1 (☎ (613) 565 57 81; fax 565 57 83); **UK,** Cavendish Ct. 11-15, Wigmore St., London W1H 9LA (☎ (020) 74 95 77 75; www.embassy-slovenia.org.uk); **US,** 1525 New Hampshire Ave. NW, Washington, D.C. 20036 (☎ (202) 667 53 63; fax 667 45 63; www.embassy.org/slovenia).

GETTING THERE AND GETTING AROUND

BY PLANE. Commercial flights arrive at the **Ljubljana Airport,** which has regular bus service to the city 23km away. The national carrier **Adria Airways** (☎ (386) 61 136 24 99; fax 61 323 356) flies to European capitals. A regular **hydrofoil** service also runs between Venice and Portorož. Flying into the country is the best option if you are traveling a long distance; otherwise, trains are better. Flying to Vienna and taking the train from there to Ljubljana is most cost-efficient.

BY TRAIN. Trains are cheap, clean, and reliable. It's best to avoid peak commuting hours near Ljubljana. Round-trip tickets are 20% cheaper than two one-way tickets. For most international destinations, travelers under 26 can get a 20% discount; check at the Ljubljana station (look for the **BIJ-Wasteels** logo). First and second class do not differ much; save your money and opt for the latter. Domestic tickets are 30% off for ISIC holders. Ask for a *"popust"* (discount). *"Vlak"* means train, *"prihodi vlakov"* means arrivals, and *"odhodi vlakov"* means departures. Schedules usually list trains by direction; look for trains that run *dnevno* (daily).

BY BUS. Buses are roughly 25% more expensive than trains, but run to some otherwise inaccessible places in the mountains. Tickets are sold at the station or on board; put your luggage in the passenger compartment if it's not too crowded.

BY CAR, BY THUMB, OR BY BIKE. For those traveling by **car,** the **Automobile Association of Slovenia**'s emergency telephone number is ☎987. *Let's Go* does not recommend **hitchhiking,** which is uncommon in Slovenia. If not traveling by bus or train, most Slovenes transport themselves by **bike;** most towns have a bike rental office.

TOURIST SERVICES AND MONEY

TOURIST OFFICES. **Tourist offices** (www.ntz-nta.si/tourism/index.htm) are located in most major cities and tourist spots. The staff are helpful, speak English and German, provide basic information, and assist in finding accommodations. The main tourist organization in Slovenia is **Kompas.**

MONEY. The national **currency** is the **Slovenian tolar** (Sit). Currency prices tend to be stable and are measured in Deutschmarks (DM) rather than dollars (US$). Rates vary, but tend to be better in major cities; post offices have the worst of all. Most **exchange offices** are quicker, easier, and offer fair rates. Major **credit cards** are widely accepted. **AmEx traveler's checks** and **Eurocheques** are often accepted. **ATMs** are common. **Hostels** average US$10-12; restaurant **meals** run US$4-7. **Tipping** is not expected, although rounding up will be appreciated; 10% is sufficient for good service. There's a 20% **value-added tax,** but for purchases over 9000Sit, it is refundable at the border (ask in the store for a tax-free check).

ACCOMMODATIONS AND CAMPING

At the height of tourist season prices are steep, services slow, and rooms scarce. The seaside, packed as early as June, is claustrophobic in July and August. Tourists also tend to swarm to the mountains during these months, and student rooms are generally available late June to early September. **Youth hostels** and **student dormitories** are cheap, but are generally open only in summer (June 25-Aug. 30). While hostels are often the cheapest (2500-3000Sit) and most fun option, **private rooms** are the only cheap option on the coast and at Lake Bohinj; prices rarely exceed US$30. Inquire at the tourist office or look for *Zimmer frei* or *Sobe* signs on the street. **Pensions** are pricey. **Campgrounds** can be crowded, but are in excellent condition.

SLOVENIA

FOOD AND DRINK

For homestyle cooking, try a *gostilna* or *gostišče* (interchangeable words for a restaurant with a country flavor). Start with *jota*, a soup with potatoes, beans and sauerkraut. *Svinjska pečenka* (roast pork) is tasty, but vegetarians should look for *štruklji*—large, slightly sweet dumplings eaten as a main dish. A favorite dessert is *potica*, a sheet of pastry spread with a rich filling (usually walnut) and rolled up. The country's wine making tradition dates from antiquity. *Renski Rizling* and *Šipon* are popular whites. while *Cviček* and *Teran* are well-known reds. Good beers include *Laško* and *Union.* For something stronger, try *žganje*, a strong fruit brandy. The most enchanting alcoholic concoction is *Viljamovka*, distilled by monks who get a full pear inside the bottle. Tap water is drinkable everywhere.

COMMUNICATION

EMERGENCY. **Ambulance:** ☎112. **Fire:** ☎112. **Police:** ☎113.

MAIL. Mail is cheap and reliable. To send letters via airmail, ask for *letalsko.* Air mail takes 1-2 weeks to reach North America, Australia, New Zealand, and South Africa. To the US, **letters** cost 105Sit and **postcards** cost 95Sit; to the UK, 100Sit for letters, 90Sit for postcards; to Australia and New Zealand, 110Sit and 100Sit. Mail can be received general delivery through *Poste Restante.*

TELEPHONES. While at the post office, purchase a **magnetic phone card** (750Sit per 50 impulses, which yields 90 seconds to the US). Cards are also available at kiosks and gas stations. Call ☎901 for English-speaking operator-assisted collect calls. If you want to call collect from a post office, say "*P.O. pogovor.*" Calling the US is over US$6 per minute. If you must, try the phones at the post office and pay when you're finished. Slovenia is changing all of its numbers; many will change through 2001, and therefore some of the numbers we list will be wrong.

LANGUAGES. Slovene, a Slavic language, employs the Latin alphabet. Most young people speak at least some **English,** but the older generation (especially in the Alps) is more likely to understand **German** (in the north) or **Italian** (along the Adriatic). You also might find some **Hungarian** in the East.

HOLIDAYS AND FESTIVALS

Holidays: New Year's Day (Jan. 1-2); Culture Day (Prešeren Day; Feb. 8); Easter (Apr. 23-24); National Resistance Day (WWII; Apr. 27); Labor Day (May 1-2); National Day (June 25); Assumption (Aug. 15); Reformation Day (Oct. 31); Remembrance Day (Nov. 1); Christmas (Dec. 25); Independence Day (Dec. 26).

Festivals: The **International Jazz Festival** in Ljubljana hosts the world's best jazz musicians every June. The **International Summer Festival** in Ljubljana is a two-month (July-Aug.) extravaganza of opera, theater, and classical music.

LJUBLJANA ☎061

With a fair share of the cosmopolitan atmosphere befitting a capital city, Ljubljana (pop. 275,000) can still be traversed in half an hour by foot. The city's architecture is relatively new for Europe, having been rebuilt since an 1895 earthquake. A massive student population ensures that bars and clubs can be found on virtually every corner, but the scene thrives more on cafes and arts festivals. If you are arriving after some time in Central Europe, the prices will stop you in your monetary tracks.

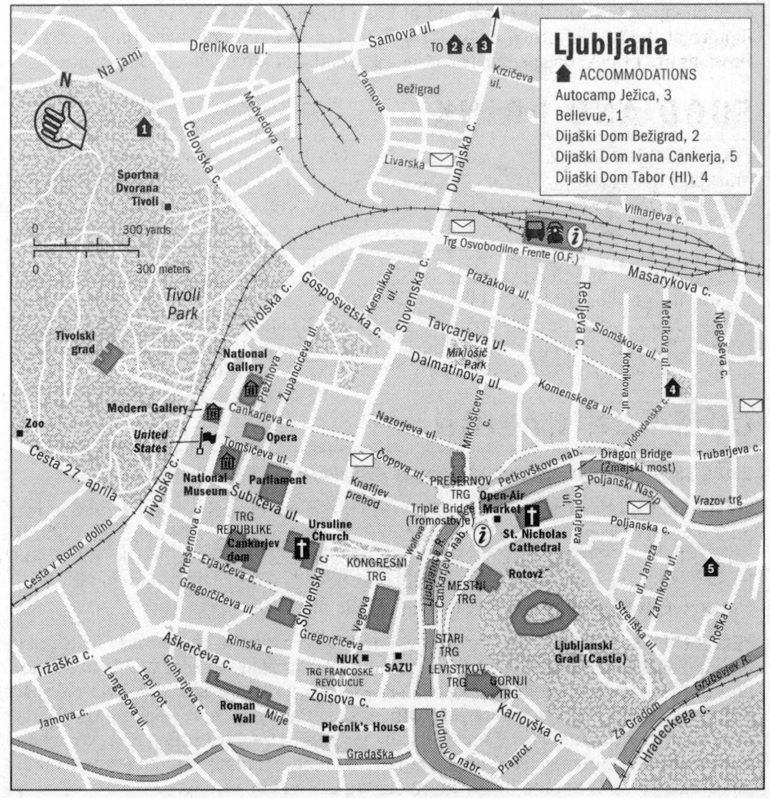

GETTING THERE AND GETTING AROUND

Trains: Trg. O.F. 6 (☎291 33 32). To: **Zagreb** (2½hr., 7 per day, 2400Sit); **Trieste** (3hr., 3 per day, 4000Sit); **Vienna** (5-6hr., 2 per day, 10,500Sit); **Venice** (6hr., 3 per day, 6000Sit); and **Budapest** (9¼hr., 2 per day, 9000Sit).

Buses: Trg. O.F. 4 (☎234 46 06), by train station. **Zagreb** (3hr., 3 per day, 2570Sit).

Public Transportation: Buses run until midnight. Drop 140Sit in change in the box beside the driver or buy 100Sit tokens at post offices and kiosks. **Ljubljanski potniški promet,** Trdinova 3, sells 1-day (350Sit) and weekly (1650Sit) passes.

ORIENTATION AND PRACTICAL INFORMATION

The **train** and **bus stations** are on **Trg. Osvobodilne Fronte** (**Trg. O.F.** or **O.F. Square**). Turn right as you exit the train station, left onto **Miklošiceva cesta,** and follow it to **Prešernov trg.,** the main square. After crossing the **Tromostovje** (Triple Bridge), **Stari Miasto** (Old Town) emerges at the castle hill's base.

Tourist Office: Tourist Information Center (TIC), Stritarjeva 1 (☎306 12 35 and 306 12 15), off Adamič-Lundrovo nabr. English brochures. Open June-Sept. M-F 8am-8pm, Sa-Su 10am-6pm; Oct.-May M-F 8am-6pm, Sa-Su 10am-6pm.

Embassies and Consulates: Australia, Trg. Republike 3 (☎125 42 52). Open M-F 9am-1pm. **UK,** Trg. Republike 3 (☎200 39 10; fax 125 01 74). Open M-F 9am-noon. **US,** Prešernov cesta (☎200 55 99; fax 200 55 55). Open M-F 9am-noon and 2-4pm.

Currency Exchange: Finicky **ATMs** are all over the city, but accepted cards vary widely.

Luggage storage: At train station; look for the *garderoba.* 220Sit per day. Open 24hr.

24hr. Pharmacy: Miklošičeva 24 (☎31 45 58).

Internet Access: Cybercafe Podhod, Plečnikov Podhod, between Maximarket and Kongresni trg. 2. 7Sit per min. Open daily July-Aug. 7am-10pm, Sept.-June 7am-2pm.

Post Office: Slovenska 32. Poste Restante (poštno ležeče pošiljke) received at Slovenska 32. Open M-F 7am-8pm, Sa 7am-1pm. Address mail to be held: First name SURNAME, *Poste Restante,* Slovenska 32, **1101** Ljubljana, Slovenia.

ACCOMMODATIONS AND FOOD

Ljubljana is not heavily touristed by backpackers and, therefore, lacks true budget accommodations. There is a nightly **tourist tax** (187Sit). The tourist office (see above) finds private singles (2200-3500Sit) and doubles (4000-5500Sit).

Dijaški Dom Tabor (HI), Vidovdanska 7 (☎31 60 69; fax 32 10 60). Go left from the train station, right on Resljeva, left on Komenskega, and left on Vidovdanska. Clean; popular with backpackers. Free Internet access 6am-10pm. Laundry 1000Sit. Breakfast included. Open June 25-Aug. 28. 2263Sit per person with student ID.

Dijaški Dom Bežigrad, Kardeljeva pl. 28 (☎34 28 67). From the train station, turn right and walk to the intersection with Slovenska. Take bus #6 (dir. Črnuče) or 8 (dir. Ježica) to "Stadion" (5min.) and walk one block to the crossroads. Open mid-June to Aug. daily; Sept.-May Sa-Su. Singles 2813-3313Sit; doubles and triples 1813-2813Sit.

Autocamp Ježica, Dunajska 270 (☎568 39 13; email acjezica@siol.net). Follow directions to Dijaški dom Bežigrad (see above), but take bus #8 and get off at "Ježica." Reception 24hr. 627Sit per adult with tent; single bungalows 5500Sit.

The cheapest eateries are **cafeterias.** In the basement of **Maximarket** on Trg. Republike is a **grocery store** (open M-F 9am-8pm, Sa 8am-5pm). **Pizzeria Foculus,** Gregorčičeva 3, between Slovenka and the river, serves huge pizzas with tons of toppings. (Open M-F 10am-midnight, Sa-Su noon-midnight.)

SIGHTS AND ENTERTAINMENT

The best way to see the city is to meet in front of the *rotovž* (city hall), Mestni trg. 1, for the two-hour **walking tour** in English and Slovene. (June-Sept. daily 5pm; Oct.-May Su 11am. 700Sit, students 500Sit.) A short walk from the *rotovž* down Stritarjeva across the **Triple Bridge** (Tromostovje), which majestically guards the **Old Town,** leads to the main square, **Prešernov trg.,** with its 17th-century Neoclassical **Franciscan Church** (Frančiškanska cerkev). Cross the bridge back to the Old Town and take a left along the water. Continuing along the river, you'll see a massive **outdoor market** on your right (open M-Sa 9am-6pm, Su 9am-2pm) on Vodnikov Trg. At the market's end, the **Dragon Bridge** (Zmajski most) stretches back across the Ljubljanica. On the opposite side of Vodnikov trg., the narrow path Studentovska leads uphill to **Ljubljana Castle** (Ljubljanski Grad), which dates from at least 1144, although what you see is 400-500 years younger. (Open June-Sept. 10am-dark, Oct.-May 10am-5pm. Tower 300Sit, students 150Sit.) Back across the river at Prešernov trg., a left onto Wolfova, which becomes Gosposka, take a right onto Zoisova cesta, and a left onto Emonska ul. Across the bridge and behind the church is the **Plečnik Collection** (Plečnikova zbrika), Karunova 4, which chronicles the life and personality of Ljubljana's most famous architect. (Open Tu and Th 10am-2pm. 600Sit, students 300Sit.) Walking back, take a left onto Zoistova and a right onto Slovenska. After the **Ursuline Church,** take a left to find **Trg. Republike,** home to the national Parliament, the colossal Maximarket, and Cankarjev *Domj*, the city's cultural center.

The **Ljubljana International Summer Festival** (July-Aug.) is a conglomeration of opera, theater, and music performances. **Casa del Papa,** Celovška 54a, takes its name in reference to Hemingway, who would have enjoyed the dark-wood, cabana-style decor and Latin beats from the club downstairs. (Open daily 8pm-5am.) **Le Petit Café,** Trg. Francoske revolucije 4, is a francophile cafe and *the* student hang-out in Ljubljana, placed strategically next to the university library. (Open M-F 7:30am-11pm, Sa 9am-11pm, Su noon-11pm.)

EXCURSION FROM LJUBLJANA: ŠKOCJANSKE CAVES

Škocjanske jama is an amazing system of **caverns,** said to have inspired literary greats like Dante Alighieri, with limestone formations and a 120m gorge created by the Reca River. (☎ (067) 63 28 40. June-Sept. 10am-5pm Tours every hr.; Oct.-May 10am, 1, and 3pm. 1500Sit, students 700Sit.) **Trains** run from Ljubljana to Divača (1½hr., 19 per day, 1300Sit). Follow signs out of town for the cave (45min.).

BLED ☎064

Alpine hills, snow-covered peaks, an opaque lake, and a stately castle make Bled one of Slovenia's most striking destinations. On the island in the middle of the lake, the **Church of the Assumption,** largely rebuilt in the 17th century, retains a unique pre-Romanesque apse. Get there by renting a **boat** for 1000Sit per hr., hopping on a **gondola-style boat** (round-trip 1500Sit), or even swimming. High above the water perches the picture-perfect 16th-century **Bled Castle** (Blejski grad), which houses a **museum** detailing the history of the Bled region; the path to the castle is on Grajska cesta. (Open daily 8am-8pm. 600Sit, students 500Sit, children 300Sit.)

Trains arrive in Lesce (☎74 11 13), 5km from Bled on the Ljubljana-Salzburg-Munich line (from Ljubljana 1hr., 500 Sit); frequent **buses** (10min., 210Sit) shuttle to **Ljubljanska** (the main street) and then the **bus station,** cesta Svobode 4 (closer to the hostel and castle). **Buses** also run directly from Ljubljana (1½hr., 1 per hr., 980Sit). **Turističko društvo,** cesta Svobode 15, has maps and the *Bled Tourist News*. (☎574 11 22; fax 574 15 55. Open July and Aug. M-Sa 8am-10pm, Su 10am-10pm; off-season hours vary.) To find **private rooms** yourself, look for *sobe* signs on Prešernova and Ljubljanska. The newly-renovated **Bledec Youth**

Hostel, Grajska cesta 17, is a find. From the bus station, turn left and follow the street all the way up. (☎74 52 50. Reserve ahead. Reception in summer 7am-8pm; in winter 7am-7pm. 2400Sit; members and students 2000Sit.) To get to **Camping Zaka-Bled,** Kidričeva 10c, from the bus station, walk downhill on cesta Svobode, turn left, and walk along the lake for 25 minutes with the water to the right. (☎575 20 00. Reception 24hr. Check-out 3pm. Open Apr.-Oct. 1400Sit.) Grab **groceries** at **Zivila Kranj,** in the shopping complex on Ljubljanska cesta 13. (Open daily 6am-midnight.) **Postal code:** 4260.

LAKE BOHINJ (BOHINJSKO JEZERO) ☎064

Although only 30km southwest of Bled, Bohinjsko (BOH-heen-sko) Jezero is worlds away. Surrounded by the **Triglav National Park,** the glacial lake is Slovenia's center for alpine tourism. **Hikes** from the lake's shores range from casual to nearly impossible. Trails throughout Slovenia are marked with a white circle inside a red circle; look for the blaze on trees and rocks. Pick up maps (1300Sit) at the tourist office. **Triglav,** the highest point in Slovenia, is a challenging two-day journey from town. The most popular and accessible destination is **Savica Waterfall** (Slap Savica). Take a bus from Ribčev Laz to "Bohinj-Zlatorog," get off at Hotel Zlatorog, and follow signs uphill (1hr. to trailhead at Koča pri Savici, then 20min. to waterfall).

Trains from Ljubljana (via Jesenice; 2½hr., 8 per day, 1200Sit) arrive in **Bohinjska Bistrica,** 6km from Lake Bohinj. **Buses** from Ljubljana (2hr., every hr., 1400Sit) pass through Bled (35min., 510Sit) and Bohinjska Bistrica (10min., 250Sit), on their way to the lake; they stop at Hotel Jezero in Ribčev Laz before continuing on to Hotel Zlatorog in Ukanc, on the other side of the lake. The **tourist office,** Ribčev Laz 48, arranges accommodations (1300-1600Sit per person, plus tourist tax) and changes money. (☎572 33 70; fax 572 33 30. Open July-Aug. M-Sa 8am-8pm, Su 8am-6pm; Sept.-June M-Sa 8am-6pm, Su 9am-3pm.) To get to **AvtoCamp Zlatorog,** Ukanc 2, take the bus to Hotel Zlatorog and backtrack a bit. (☎572 34 82; fax 572 34 46. Check-out noon. July-Aug. 1600Sit; May-June and Sept. 1000Sit.) The **Mercator supermarket** is next to the tourist office. (Open M-F 7am-8pm, Sa 7am-5pm.) **Postal code:** 4265.

SPAIN (ESPAÑA)

PESETAS

US$1 = 193.52	100PTAS = US$0.52
CDN$1 = 130.66PTAS	= CDN$0.77
UK£1 = 271.27PTAS	= UK£0.37
IR£1 = 211.27PTAS	= IR£0.47
AUS$1 = 108.22PTAS	= AUS$0.92
NZ$1 = 82.62PTAS	= NZ$1.21
SAR1 = 27.13PTAS	= SAR3.69
EUR€1 = 166.37PTAS	= EUR€0.60

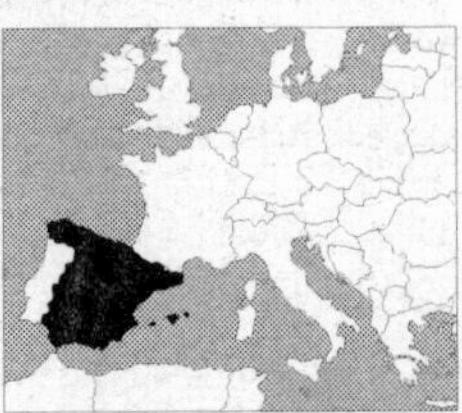

Country Code: 34. **International dialing prefix:** 00. Spain has no city codes. From outside Spain, dial int'l dialing prefix (see inside back cover) + 34 + local number.

Spain is a budget traveler's dream. The landscape is a microcosm of all that Europe has to offer, with lush wilderness reserves, long sunny coastlines, snowy mountain peaks and the dry, golden plains wandered by Don Quijote. Art lovers flock to the northeast, home of the likes of Chagall, Dalí and Gaudí. Adventure-seekers trek through the northern Pyrenees, and architecture buffs are drawn to the country's stunning Baroque, Mudejar and Mozarabic cathedrals and palaces. From the south come flamenco, bullfighting and *tapas*, the passionate cultural expressions that set Spain apart from the rest of Europe. The raging nightlife of Madrid, Barcelona and the Balearic Islands continues well after sunrise. You can do Spain in one week, one month, or one year. But you must do it at least once.

For more detailed coverage of the glories of Spain, grab the scintillating and delicious *Let's Go: Spain, Portugal, and Morocco 2001*.

FACTS AND FIGURES

Official Name: Kingdom of Spain.

Government: Constitutional Monarchy.

Capital: Madrid.

Land Area: 504,784 sq. km.

Geography: Varied, from mountain ranges to green countryside to sandy coastline.

Climate: Hot and relatively dry during summer months (Apr.-Oct.) and wetter during winter months.

Major Cities: Madrid, Barcelona, Valencia, Sevilla, Granada.

Population: 39,371,000; urban 78%, rural 22%.

Languages: Spanish (Castilian); Catalan, Valencian, Basque, Galician dialects.

Religions: Roman Catholicism (though no longer the official religion).

Average Income Per Capita: US$23,408.

Major Exports: Agriculture, machinery.

DISCOVER SPAIN

Begin in **Madrid** (p. 832), soaking in its unique blend of art, architecture, and cosmopolitan life; after days of ogling at art and nights of the dance 'til dawn regime; take your bleary-eyed self to the austere palace of **El Escorial** (p. 842) outside the city and the twisting streets of **Toledo** (p. 843), once home to El Greco and a thriving Jewish community. Head off into Central Spain, Don Quixote territory, to the famed university town of **Salamanca** (p. 845) and then down to beautiful and intriguing **Sevilla** (p. 853), the center of Andalucía, Spain's southernmost region. Delve deeper into Arab-influenced Andalucía at the stunning mosque in **Córdoba** (p. 849) and the world-famous Alhambra in **Granada** (p. 861). The tanning fields of the **Costa del Sol** stretch along the Mediterranean; join in at posh **Marbella** (p. 860). Move up along the east coast to **Valencia** to indulge in native paella and oranges (p. 866). The northeast's gem is **Barcelona** (see p. 867) one of Europe's most vibrant cities. After a tour of bizarre Modernista architecture and raging nightlife, discover the beaches of the **Costa Brava** and enchanting seaside resort of **Tossa de Mar** (p. 879). The nearby town of **Figueres** (p. 879) is home to Salvador Dalí's engaging museum/monument to himself, while **Girona** boasts a perfectly preserved medieval center (p. 878). Farther north is the natural haven of the **Pyrenees** (p. 880), where adventure tourism reigns. Moving westward, in the heart of the Basque Country, **San Sebastián** (p. 883) entertains with beaches and fabulous tapas bars; **Bilbao** (p. 886), home of the incredible Guggenheim museum, is only a daytrip away. The **Camino de Santiago** pilgrimage (p. 891) winds along the northern coast to the **Santiago de Compostela** cathedral (p. 890), the unrivaled monarch of Spanish religious monuments. Spain also offers some of the world's craziest nightlife, the most famous being the 24-hour party that is **Ibiza** (p. 888) on the Balearic Islands.

ESSENTIALS

WHEN TO GO

Summer is **high season** (*temporada alta*) for the coastal and interior regions; winter is high season for ski resorts. In many parts of the country, high season includes **Semana Santa** (Holy Week; mid-April) and festival days. Tourism reaches its height in August; the coastal regions overflow while inland cities empty out, leaving behind closed offices, restaurants and lodgings. Traveling in the **off season** (*temporada baja*) has the advantage of noticeably lighter crowds and lower prices, but smaller towns virtually shut down, and tourist offices and sights cut their hours nearly everywhere.

DOCUMENTS AND FORMALITIES

A **passport** allows Canadian, British, New Zealand, and US citizens to remain for 90 days. South African and Australian citizens need a **visa** to enter. Foreign embassies are in Madrid (see p. 836); all countries have consulates in Barcelona (see p. 868). Australia, UK, and US also have consulates in Sevilla (see p. 853). Another Canadian consulate is in Málaga; a South African consulate is in Bilbao; UK consulates are also in Bilbao, Palma de Mallorca, Ibiza, Alicante, and Málaga; more US consulates are in Málaga, Valencia, La Coruña, and Palma de Mallorca.

EMBASSIES AND CONSULATES

Spanish Embassies at Home: Australia, 15 Arkana St., Yarralumla, ACT 2600; mailing address: P.O. Box 9076, Deakin, ACT 2600. (☎ (02) 62 73 35 55); **Canada,** 74 Stanley Ave., Ottawa, ON K1M 1P4 (☎ (613) 747 22 52); **Ireland,** 17A Merlyn Park, Ballsbridge, Dublin 4 (☎ (01) 269 16 40); **New Zealand,** refer to embassy in Australia; **South Africa,** 169 Pine St., Arcadia, P.O. Box 1633, Pretoria 0083 (☎ (012) 344 38 75); **UK,** 39 Chesham Pl., London SW1X 8SB (☎ (020) 72 35 55 55); **US,** 2375 Pennsylvania Ave. NW, Washington, D.C. 20037 (☎ (202) 728 23 30; www.spainemb.org).

GETTING AROUND

BY PLANE. Airports in Madrid and Barcelona handle most international flights. **Iberia** (in US and Canada ☎ (800) 772 46 42; in UK ☎ (020) 78 30 00 11; in Spain ☎ 902 40 05 00; in South Africa ☎ (11) 884 92 55; in Ireland ☎ (1) 407 30 17; www.iberia.com) serves all domestic locations and all major international cities. **Air Europa** (US ☎ (888) 238 76 72 or (718) 244 60 16; Spain ☎ 902 30 06 00; www.aireuropa.com) flies out of New York City and most European cities to Spain. Discounts available. **SpanAir** (in US ☎ (888) 545 57 57; in Spain ☎ 902 13 14 15; fax 971 49 25 53; www.spanair.com) also offers international and domestic flights.

BY TRAIN. **Eurailpasses** and **Europasses** are good options if Spain is only a pit stop on your Euro-tour as Spanish rail service tends to be cheaper on its own. **RENFE** (www.renfe.es), the national rail system, has clean, punctual, reasonably priced trains with various levels of service. Its network radiates from Madrid; many small towns are not served. *Alta Velocidad Española* (AVE) trains are the fastest between Madrid-Córdoba-Sevilla. *Talgos* are almost as quick; *Talgo 200s* run on *AVE* rails—lines head from Madrid to Málaga, Algeciras, Cádiz, and Huelva. *Intercity* is cheaper and a bit dowdier, but still fairly speedy. *Estrellas* are slow night trains with bunks. *Cercanías* (commuter trains) go from cities to suburbs and nearby towns. *Tranvía*, *semidirecto*, and *correo* trains are slug-slow.

There are several **RailEurope** passes that cover travel within Spain. You must purchase railpasses at least 15 days before departure. Call 1-800-4EURAIL in the US or go to www.raileurope.com. **Spain Flexipass** offers three days of unlimited travel in a two-month period (1st-class US$200, 2nd-class US$155; up to 7 additional rail-days US$35, US$30 each). **Iberic Flexipass** offers three days of unlimited first-class travel in Spain and Portugal (US$205); up to seven additional rail-days cost US$45 each. **Spain Rail 'n' Drive Pass** is good for three days of unlimited first-class train travel and two days of unlimited mileage in a rental car within a two-month period. Prices from US$255-365, depending on how many people are traveling and the type of car.

BY BUS. In Spain, ignore romanticized versions of European train travel—**buses** are cheaper, run more frequently, and are sometimes even faster than trains. Additionally, buses are the only public transportation to and within isolated areas. Spain has many private companies instead of one national bus line, making trip planning something of an ordeal; fortunately, most cities now have centralized bus stations.

BY FERRY. The main company, **Transmediterranea** (☎902 45 46 45; www.transmediterranea.com), links the mainland to the **Balearic Islands** (daily from Barcelona and Valencia).

BY CAR. Spain has an extensive road grid covering close to 340,000km; 7000km are highways, making it easy to drive from the Pyrenees all the way down to Andalucía. Gas prices average 130-140ptas per liter. **Speed limits** are as follows: 50kph (30 mph) in cities; 90 or 100kph (56 or 62 mph) outside cities; and 120kph (74 mph) on expressways. In residential areas the speed limit is 20kph (12 mph); roads marked **A** for *autopista* are toll roads. **Renting a car** in Spain is considerably cheaper than in many other European countries. International rental companies offer services throughout the country, but you may want to check with **Atesa** (www.atesa.es), Spain's largest national rental agency. The Spanish automobile association is **Real Automóbil Club de España (RACE),** C. Jose Abascal, 10, Madrid (☎914 47 32 00). **Taxis** are readily available in almost every city, and they are much wiser form of transportation than a personal car in Madrid and Barcelona.

BY BIKE AND BY THUMB. With hilly terrain and extremely hot summer weather, **biking** is difficult but can be done. Renting a bike should be easy, especially in the flatter southern region. **Hitchers** report that Castilla, Andalucía, and Madrid offer little more than a long, hot wait. The Mediterranean Coast and the islands are much more promising. *Let's Go* does not recommend hitchhiking.

TOURIST SERVICES AND MONEY

EMERGENCY. Local Police: ☎091. **National Police:** ☎092. **Ambulance:** ☎124.

TOURIST OFFICES. The Spanish Tourist Office operates an extensive official website (www.tourspain.es) and has 29 offices abroad. Municipal tourist offices, called *oficinas de turismo*, are a good stop to make upon arrival in a town; they usually have free maps and region-specific advice for travelers.

Tourist Boards at Home: Canada, Tourist Office of Spain, 2 Bloor St. West, Suite 3402, Toronto, ON M4W 3E2 (☎ (416) 961 31 31; fax 961 19 92). **UK:** Spanish National Tourist Office, 22-23 Manchester Sq., London W1M 5AP (☎ (171) 486 80 77; fax 486 8034; info.londres@tourspain.es). **US:** Tourist Office of Spain, 666 Fifth Ave., 35th Fl., New York, NY 10103 (☎ (212) 265 88 22; fax 265 88 64). **Additional offices** in Chicago, IL (☎ (312) 642 19 92), Beverly Hills, CA (☎ (323) 658 71 88) and Miami, FL (☎ (305) 358 19 92).

SPAIN

MONEY. The currency is the **peseta** (pta), available in coins of 1, 5, 10, 25, 50, 100, 200 and 500ptas and notes of 1000, 2000, 50000, and 10,0000ptas. **Banco Central Hispano** often provides good rates for travelers' checks. A "bare-bones day" (**camping** or sleeping in cheap **hostels,** buying food at supermarkets) runs about 5000ptas (US$30-35). A more comfortable day (sleeping in nicer hostels, eating at restaurants, and going out at night) can cost 7500ptas (US$50).

Tipping is not very common. In restaurants, all prices include service charge. Satisfied customers occasionally toss in some spare change—usually no more than 5%—but this is purely optional. Many people give train, airport and hotel porters 100ptas per bag, while taxi drivers sometimes get 5-10%. Bargaining is common at flea markets and with street vendors. Travelers can try bargaining for hostel prices in the off-season, especially in less-touristed areas. Spain has a 7% **Value Added Tax,** known as IVA, on all restaurant and accommodations. The prices listed in *Let's Go* include IVA unless otherwise mentioned. Retail goods bear a much higher 16% IVA, although listed prices are usually inclusive. Non-EU citizens who have stayed in the EU fewer than 180 days can claim back the tax paid on purchases at the airport. Ask the shop for a tax return form.

ACCOMMODATIONS AND CAMPING

TYPES OF ACCOMMODATIONS. The cheapest and barest options are **casas de huéspedes** and **hospedajes,** while **pensiones** and **fondas** tend to be a bit nicer. All are basically just boarding houses. Higher up the ladder, **hostales** generally have sinks in bedrooms and provide sheets and lockers, while **hostal-residencias** are similar to hotels in overall quality. The government rates *hostales* on a two-star system; even establishments receiving one star are typically quite comfortable. The system also fixes each *hostal*'s prices, posted in the lounge or main entrance. If you have any trouble (with rates or service), ask for the **libro de reclamaciones** (complaint book), which by law must be produced on demand. The argument will usually end immediately, since all complaints must be forwarded to the authorities within 48 hours.

HOSTELS. Red Española de Albergues Juveniles (REAJ), C. José Ortega y Gasset, 71, Madrid 28006 (☎91 347 77 00; fax 91 401 81 60), the Spanish Hostelling International (HI) affiliate, runs 165 youth hostels year-round. Prices generally run between 1500-2500ptas for guests under 26 and higher for older ones. Breakfast is usually included. Hostels usually lockout around 11:30am, and have curfews between midnight and 3am. Don't expect much privacy—rooms typically have from 4 to 20 beds in them. To reserve a bed in high season (July-Aug. and during *fiestas*), call well in advance. A **Youth Hostel Card (HI)** is usually required, but occasionally, guests can stay in a hostel without one and pay extra.

CAMPING. Campgrounds are generally the cheapest choice for two or more people. Most charge separate fees per person, per tent, and per car; others charge for a *parcela*—a small plot of land—plus per-person fees. Tourist offices provide info, including the *Guía de campings*. Reservations are necessary in the summer.

FOOD AND DRINK

Breakfast consists of coffee or hot chocolate and *bollos* (rolls) or *churros* (lightly fried fritters). Lunch, served between 2 and 3pm, is several courses. Supper, a light meal, begins at around 10pm. Some restaurants are "open" from 8am until 1 or 2am, but most only serve meals from 1 to 4pm and from 8pm until midnight. Prices for a full meal start at about 800ptas in the cheapest *bare-restaurantes*. Many places offer a *plato combinado* (main course, side dishes, bread, and sometimes a beverage) for about 500-1200ptas or a *menú del día* (two or three set dishes, bread, beverage, and dessert) for roughly 800-1500ptas. If you ask for a *menu*, this is what you may receive; the word for menu is *carta*. Tapas (small nibbles of savory meats and vegetables cooked according to local recipes) are truly tasty. *Raciones* are large tapas served as entrees. Bocadillos are sandwiches on hunks of bread. Specialties include *tortilla de patata* (potato omelette), *jamón serrano* (smoked ham), *calamares fritos* (fried squid), *arroz* (rice), *chorizo* (spicy sausage), *gambas* (shrimp), *lomo* (pork), paella (steamed saffron rice with seafood, chicken, and vegetables), and *gazpacho* (cold tomato-based soup). Vegetarians should learn the phrase *"yo soy vegetariano"* (I am a vegetarian) and specify that means no *jamón* (ham) or *atún* (tuna). *Vino blanco* is white wine and *tinto* is red. Beer is *cerveza;* Mahou and Cruzcampo are the most common brands. *Sangría* is red wine, sugar, brandy, and fruit. *Tinto de verano* is red wine with flavored seltzer.

COMMUNICATION

MAIL. Air mail *(por avión)* takes around six days to reach North America (115ptas), approximately three days to the UK and Ireland, and up to 10 days to Australia and New Zealand. **Surface mail** *(por barco)*, while considerably less expensive than air mail, can take over a month, and packages will take two to three months. **Registered** or **express mail** *(registrado* or *certificado)*, is the most reliable way to send a letter or parcel home, and takes four to seven business days (letter postage 237ptas). **Stamps** are sold at post offices and tobacconists (*estancos* or *tabacos*). To send mail *Poste Restante*, address the letter as follows: SURNAME, First name; Lista de Correos; City Name; Postal code; SPAIN; AIR MAIL.

TELEPHONE. The central phone company is **Telefónica.** Local calls cost 20ptas. Make local calls with a phone card, issued in denominations of 1000 and 2000ptas and available at tobacconists (*estancos* or *tabacos*) and most post offices. International calls can be made with phone cards, but are very expensive; call home with an international calling card issued by your phone company. Contact the operator for your service provider by dialing the appropriate **international toll-free access number: AT&T,** ☎900 99 00 11; **Australia Direct,** ☎900 99 00 61; **BT Direct,** ☎900 99 00 44; **Canada Direct,** ☎900 99 00 15; **Eircom,** ☎900 99 03 53; **MCI WorldPhone Direct,** ☎900 99 00 14; **Sprint,** ☎900 99 00 13; **Telecom New Zealand Direct,** ☎900 99 00 64; **Telkom South Africa Direct;** ☎900 99 00 27.

INTERNET ACCESS. An increasing number of bars offer Internet access for 600-1000ptas per hour. Sometimes libraries or tourist offices offer access for a small fee. The website www.tangaworld.com also lists 200 cybercafes across Spain.

LANGUAGE. Catalán is spoken in Catalunya, Valencian in Valencia. The Basque (Euskera) language is common in north-central Spain, and Galician (Gallego, related to Portuguese) is in the once-Celtic northwest. Spanish (Castilian, or *castellano*) is spoken everywhere.

HOLIDAYS AND FESTIVALS

Holidays: New Year's Day (Jan. 1-2); Epiphany (Jan. 6); Maundy Thursday (Apr. 12); Good Friday (Apr. 13); Easter (Apr. 15); Labor Day (May 1); Corpus Christi (June 22); Feast of St. James the Apostle (July 25); La Asunción (Aug. 25); National Day (Oct. 12); All Saints' Day (Nov. 1); Constitution Day (Dec. 6); Feast of the Immaculate Conception (Dec. 8); Christmas (Dec. 25).

Festivals: Just about everything closes down during festivals. Almost every town has several, and in total there are more than 3000. All of Spain will celebrate **Carnaval** from Feb. 15 to 25; the biggest parties are in Catalunya and Cádiz. Valencia will host the annual **Las Fallas** in mid-Mar. From Apr. 9 to 15, the entire country will honor the Holy Week, or **Semana Santa.** Sevilla's **Feria de Abril** takes place in late Apr. Pamplona's infamous **San Fermines** (Running of the Bulls) will break out from July 6 to 14. For more fiesta info, see www.tourspain.es, www.SiSpain.org, or www.cyberspain.es.

MADRID

After decades of Franco's totalitarian repression, Madrid's youth burst out during the 1980s, an era known as *la Movida* (the "Movement"). The newest generation, too young to recall the Franco years, seems neither cognizant of the city's historic landmarks nor preoccupied with the future—youths have taken over the streets, shed their parents' decorous reserve, and captured the present. Bright lights and a perpetual stream of cars and people blur the distinction between 4pm and 4am, and infinitely energized *madrileños* crowd bars and discos until dawn. Madrid's sights and culture equal its rival European capitals, and have twice the intensity.

GETTING THERE AND GETTING AROUND

Flights: ☎902 40 05 00. **Aeropuerto Internacional de Barajas,** 15km northeast of Madrid. The new **Barajas metro line** connects the airport to Madrid. Follow metro signs to line #8 to Mar de Cristal, switch to line #4, and at Goya change to line #2 to get to Sol, smack in the city center. Another option is the **Bus-Aeropuerto** (look for "EMT" signs outside), which goes to Pl. de Colón (every 15-25min. 4:45am-10pm, every hr. 10pm-1:45am; 385ptas). From the plaza (M: Colón; brown line, L4), the metro runs all over town. **Iberia,** Santa Cruz de Marcenado, 2 (☎91 587 81 56). M: San Bernardo. Open M-F 9:30am-2pm and 4-7pm.

Trains: ☎91 328 90 20. Two stations have long-distance service. The **RENFE Main Office,** C. Alcalá, 44, is at Gran Vía (☎91 534 05 05). M: Banco de España. Sells tickets for Chamartín as well as AVE and Talgo tickets. Open M-F 9:30am-8pm.

Estación Chamartín, on Agustín de Foxá. (24hr. ☎93 49 01 122 for international destinations, ☎90 224 02 02 for domestic destinations.) M: Chamartín. Bus #5 departs beyond the lockers for Sol (45min.). To: **Barcelona** (7hr., 10 per day, 6585ptas); **Lisbon** (10hr., 1 per day, 6700ptas); **Paris** (13hr., 1 per day, 19,300ptas); and **Nice** (22hr., 1 per day, 21,000ptas).

Estación Atocha (☎91 328 90 20). M: Atocha. Serves Andalucía, Castilla-La Mancha, Extremadura, Valencia, Castilla y León, Sierra de Guadarrama, and El Escorial. To: **Sevilla** (2½hr., 19 per day, 8400-9900ptas) and **Córdoba** (1¾hr., 16 per day, 5100-7200ptas).

Buses: Private companies have stations, but most buses pass through Estación Sur.

Estación Sur de Autobuses (☎91 468 42 00 or 91 468 45 11), on C. Méndez Álvaro, s/n. M: Méndez Álvaro.

Estación Auto Res, Pl. Conde de Casal, 6 (☎91 551 72 00). M: Conde de Casal. To: **Salamanca** (2½-3¼hr., 21-22 per day, 1480-2250ptas) and **Valencia** (4hr., 13 per day, 2875-3175ptas).

Estación La Sepulvedana, Po. Florida 11 (☎91 530 48 00). M: Príncipe Pío (via extension from M: Ópera). To: **Segovia** (1½hr., 2 per hr., 825ptas) and **Ávila** (1½hr., 3-8 per day, 930ptas).

Public Transportation: Empresa Municipal de Transportes (**EMT;** ☎91 406 88 10). The clean, efficient **metro** (☎91 580 19 80) runs 6am-1:30am. Single ride 135ptas; **bonotransporte** (10-ride pass) 705ptas. Keep your ticket until you leave the metro. **Buses** run daily 6am-11:30pm and cost 135ptas per ride (10-ride pass 705ptas). The *Plano de los Transportes* is free at the tourist office. *Madrid en Autobús* is free from bus kiosks. Night buses (N1-N20), or *buho* (owls), run from Pl. Cibeles to the outskirts every 30min. 11:30pm-3am, every hr. 3-6am.

Taxis: ☎91 445 90 08 or 91 447 32 32. Base fare 190ptas, plus 50-75ptas per km and supplements. A taxi between the city center and the airport costs about 3000ptas.

Hitchhiking: Hitchhiking, neither popular nor safe, is rarely legal; the Guardia Civil de Tráfico deposits highway hitchers at nearby towns or on a bus. Hitchers try message boards at HI hostels for ride-share offers. *Let's Go* does not recommend hitchhiking.

ORIENTATION AND PRACTICAL INFORMATION

Marking the epicenter of both Madrid and Spain, **"Kilometro 0"** in **Puerta del Sol** ("Sol" for short) is within walking distance of most sights. To the west is the **Plaza Mayor,** the **Palacio Real,** and the **Ópera** district. East of Sol lies **Huertas**—centered around Pl. Santa Ana, bordered by C. Alcalá to the north, Po. Prado to the east and C. Atocha to the south—the pulse of cafe, theater, and museum life. The area north of Sol is bordered by the **Gran Vía,** which runs northwest to **Plaza de España.** North of Gran Vía are three club and bar-hopping districts, linked by **Calle de Fuencarral: Malasaña, Bilbao,** and **Chueca.** Modern Madrid is beyond Gran Vía and east of Malasaña and Chueca. East of Sol, the tree-lined thoroughfare **Paseo de la Castellana-Paseo de Recoletos-Paseo de Prado** splits Madrid in two, running from **Atocha** in the south to **Plaza Castilla** in the north, passing the Prado, the fountains of **Plaza Cibeles,** and **Plaza Colon.** Northwest of Sol lies **Argüelles,** an energetic neighborhood of families and students from **Moncloa,** the student district centered on C. Isaac Peral. Get a map from the tourist office and use this book's **color map** of Madrid's metro. Madrid is safer than its European counterparts, but Gran Vía, Pl. Dos de Mayo in Malasaña, Pl. de Chueca, and Pl. de España are intimidating late at night.

TOURIST AND FINANCIAL SERVICES

Tourist Offices: Municipal, Pl. Mayor, 3 (☎91 366 54 77 or 91 588 16 36; fax 91 366 54 77). M: Sol. Open M-F 10am-8pm, Sa 10am-2pm and 3-8pm. **Regional/Provincial Office of the Comunidad de Madrid,** main office: Duque de Medinacelia, 2 (☎91 429 49). **Branch** at the **airport** (☎91 305 86 56), in the international arrivals area. (Open M-F 8am-8pm, Sa 8am-1pm.)

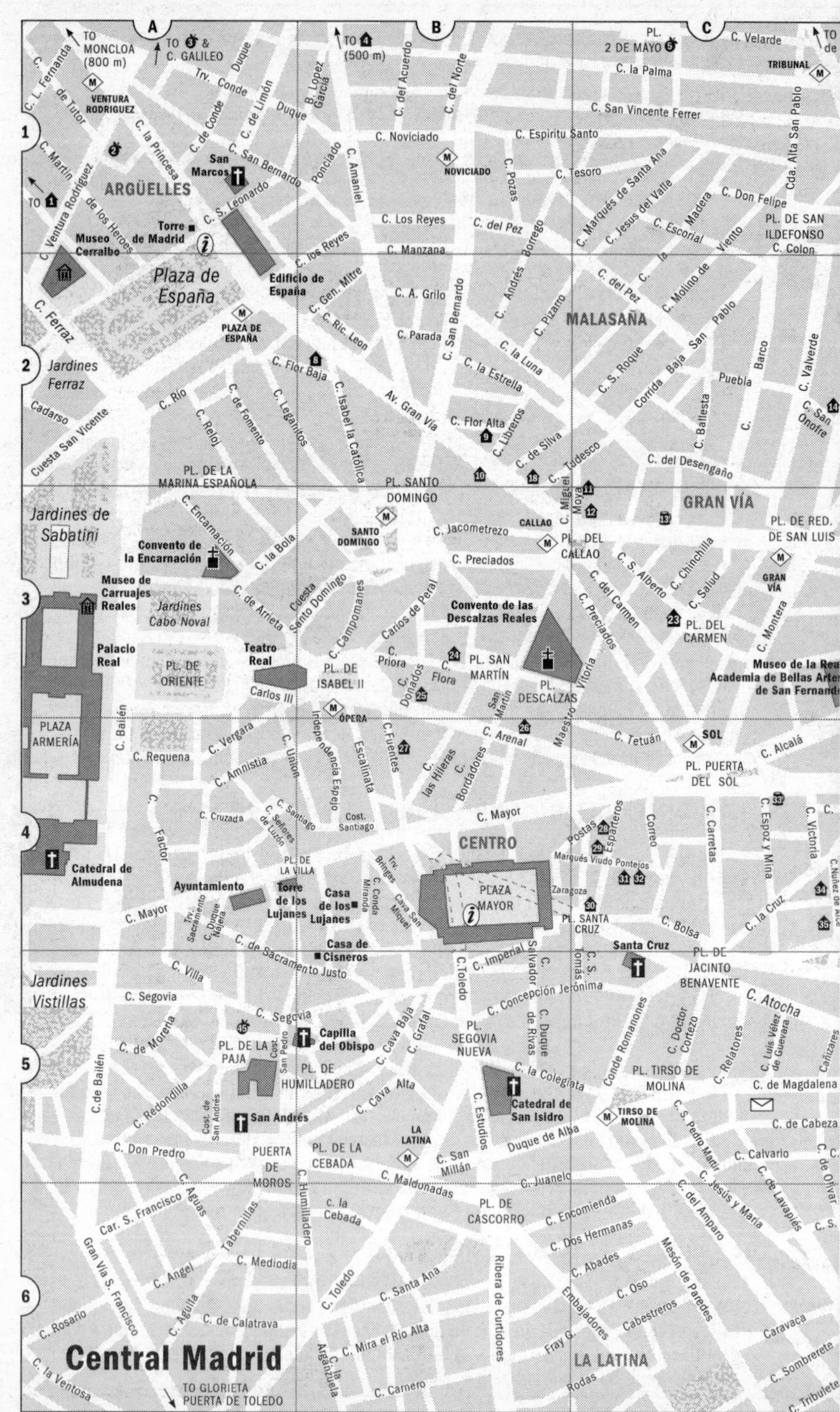
Central Madrid
ARGÜELLES
MALASAÑA
GRAN VÍA
CENTRO
LA LATINA
Plaza de España
Jardines Ferraz
Jardines de Sabatini
Jardines Cabo Noval
Jardines Vistillas
Museo Cerralbo
Torre de Madrid
Edificio de España
San Marcos
Convento de la Encarnación
Museo de Carruajes Reales
Palacio Real
PLAZA ARMERÍA
PL. DE ORIENTE
Teatro Real
Catedral de Almudena
Convento de las Descalzas Reales
Museo de la Real Academia de Bellas Artes de San Fernando
PLAZA MAYOR
Ayuntamiento
Torre de los Lujanes
Casa de los Lujanes
Casa de Cisneros
Santa Cruz
Capilla del Obispo
San Andrés
Catedral de San Isidro
TO MONCLOA (800 m)
TO GLORIETA PUERTA DE TOLEDO
VENTURA RODRIGUEZ
NOVICIADO
TRIBUNAL
PLAZA DE ESPAÑA
SANTO DOMINGO
CALLAO
GRAN VÍA
ÓPERA
SOL
LA LATINA
TIRSO DE MOLINA
PL. 2 DE MAYO
PL. DE SAN ILDEFONSO
PL. SANTO DOMINGO
PL. DE LA MARINA ESPAÑOLA
PL. DEL CALLAO
PL. DE RED. DE SAN LUIS
PL. DEL CARMEN
PL. SAN MARTÍN
PL. DESCALZAS
PL. DE ISABEL II
PL. PUERTA DEL SOL
PL. DE LA VILLA
PL. SANTA CRUZ
PL. DE JACINTO BENAVENTE
PL. SEGOVIA NUEVA
PL. DE LA PAJA
PL. DE HUMILLADERO
PL. TIRSO DE MOLINA
PL. DE LA CEBADA
PUERTA DE MOROS
PL. DE CASCORRO
Av. Gran Vía
C. Mayor
C. Arenal
C. Preciados
C. Atocha
C. Toledo
C. de Segovia
C. de Bailén
C. Ferraz
C. la Princesa
C. San Bernardo
C. Fuencarral
C. Alcalá
Ribera de Curtidores
Gran Vía S. Francisco

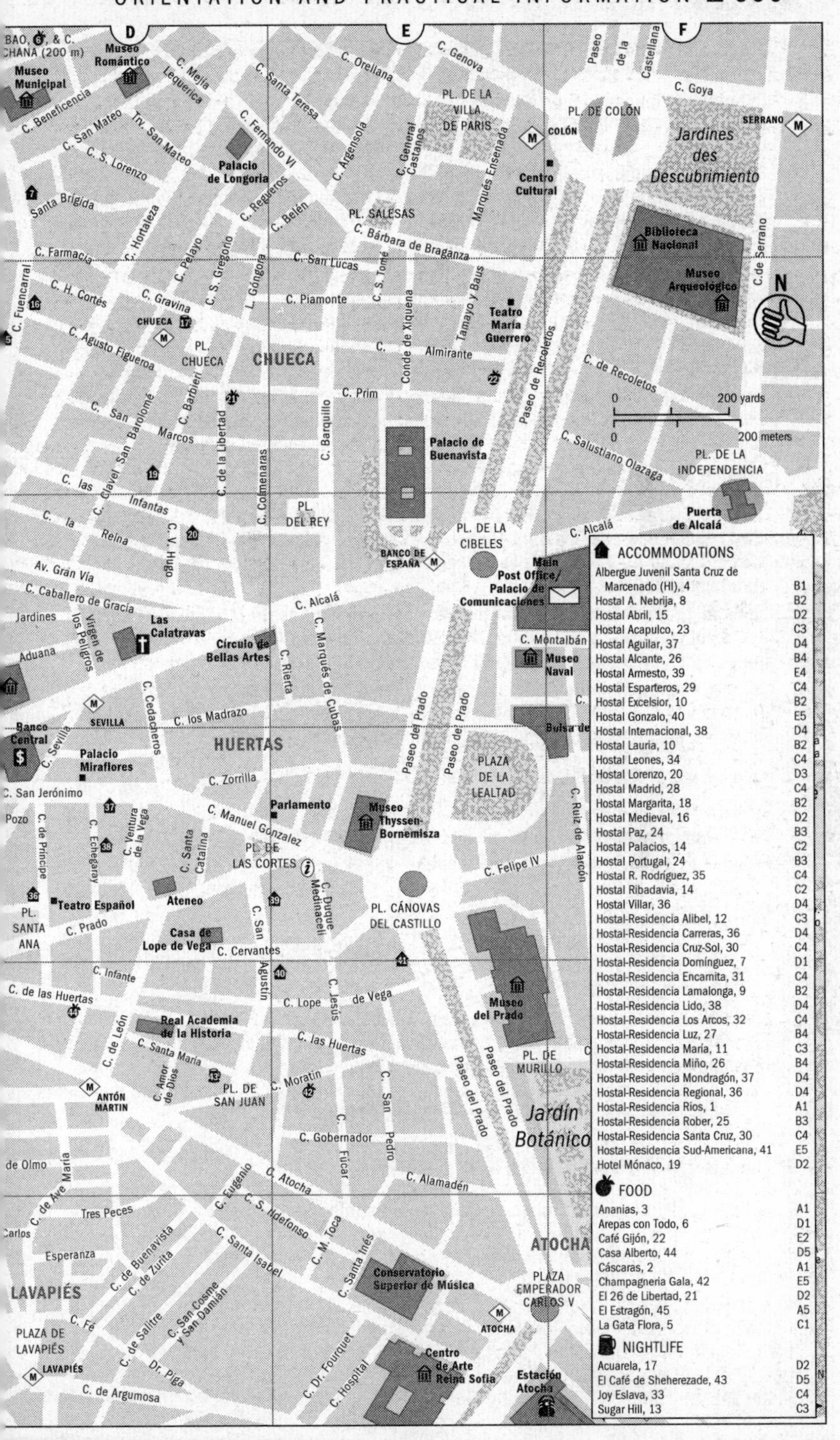
D
E
F
Museo Romántico
Museo Municipal
C. Beneficencia
C. Mejía Lequerica
C. Santa Teresa
C. Orellana
C. Genova
Paseo de la Castellana
C. Goya
PL. DE LA VILLA DE PARIS
PL. DE COLÓN
COLÓN
SERRANO
Jardines des Descubrimiento
C. San Mateo
Trv. San Mateo
C. S. Lorenzo
C. Fernando VI
Palacio de Longoria
C. Argensola
C. General Castaños
Marqués Ensenada
Centro Cultural
Santa Brígida
C. Regueros
C. Belén
PL. SALESAS
C. Bárbara de Braganza
Biblioteca Nacional
Museo Arqueológico
C. de Serrano
C. Hortaleza
C. Farmacia
C. Pelayo
C. S. Gregorio
L. Góngora
C. San Lucas
C. S. Tomé
C. Fuencarral
C. H. Cortés
C. Gravina
C. Piamonte
C. Conde de Xiquena
Tamayo y Baus
Teatro María Guerrero
Paseo de Recoletos
CHUECA
C. Agusto Figueroa
PL. CHUECA
CHUECA
C. Almirante
C. de Recoletos
0
200 yards
200 meters
C. Barbieri
C. de la Libertad
C. Prim
C. San Marcos
C. Barquillo
Palacio de Buenavista
C. Clavel
San Bartolomé
C. Colmenaras
C. Salustiano Olazaga
PL. DE LA INDEPENDENCIA
C. las Infantas
C. la Reina
C. V. Hugo
PL. DEL REY
PL. DE LA CIBELES
Puerta de Alcalá
C. Alcalá
BANCO DE ESPAÑA
Av. Gran Vía
C. Caballero de Gracia
Main Post Office/ Palacio de Comunicaciones
Jardines
Virgen de los Peligros
Las Calatravas
C. Alcalá
C. Marqués de Cubas
C. Montalbán
Museo Naval
Aduana
Círculo de Bellas Artes
C. Rierta
C. Cedaceros
SEVILLA
C. los Madrazo
Paseo del Prado
Paseo del Prado
Bolsa de
Banco Central
C. Sevilla
Palacio Miraflores
HUERTAS
PLAZA DE LA LEALTAD
C. Zorrilla
C. San Jerónimo
Pozo
C. de Principe
C. Echegaray
C. Ventura de la Vega
C. Santa Catalina
Parlamento
Museo Thyssen-Bornemisza
C. Manuel Gonzalez
PL. DE LAS CORTES
C. Ruiz de Alarcón
C. Felipe IV
C. Duque Medinaceli
PL. SANTA ANA
Teatro Español
Ateneo
C. San Agustín
PL. CÁNOVAS DEL CASTILLO
C. Prado
Casa de Lope de Vega
C. Cervantes
C. Infante
C. de las Huertas
C. Lope de Vega
C. Jesús
Museo del Prado
Real Academia de la Historia
C. de León
C. Santa María
C. las Huertas
Paseo del Prado
Paseo del Prado
PL. DE MURILLO
ANTÓN MARTIN
C. Amor de Dios
PL. DE SAN JUAN
C. Moratín
C. San Pedro
C. Fúcar
Jardín Botánico
C. Gobernador
de Olmo
C. de Ave María
C. Atocha
C. Alamadén
Tres Peces
C. Eugenio
C. S. Ildefonso
Carlos
C. Santa Isabel
C. M. Toca
ATOCHA
Esperanza
C. de Buenavista
C. de Zurita
C. Santa Inés
Conservatorio Superior de Música
PLAZA EMPERADOR CARLOS V
LAVAPIÉS
C. San Cosme y San Damián
C. Fe
ATOCHA
PLAZA DE LAVAPIÉS
C. de Saltre
Dr. Piga
C. Dr. Fourquet
C. Hospital
Centro de Arte Reina Sofía
Estación Atocha
LAVAPIÉS
C. de Argumosa
ACCOMMODATIONS
Albergue Juvenil Santa Cruz de Marcenado (HI), 4 B1
Hostal A. Nebrija, 8 B2
Hostal Abril, 15 D2
Hostal Acapulco, 23 C3
Hostal Aguilar, 37 D4
Hostal Alcante, 26 B4
Hostal Armesto, 39 E4
Hostal Esparteros, 29 C4
Hostal Excelsior, 10 B2
Hostal Gonzalo, 40 E5
Hostal Internacional, 38 D4
Hostal Lauria, 10 B2
Hostal Leones, 34 C4
Hostal Lorenzo, 20 D3
Hostal Madrid, 28 C4
Hostal Margarita, 18 B2
Hostal Medieval, 16 D2
Hostal Paz, 24 B3
Hostal Palacios, 14 C2
Hostal Portugal, 24 B3
Hostal R. Rodríguez, 35 C4
Hostal Ribadavia, 14 C2
Hostal Villar, 36 D4
Hostal-Residencia Alibel, 12 C3
Hostal-Residencia Carreras, 36 D4
Hostal-Residencia Cruz-Sol, 30 C4
Hostal-Residencia Domínguez, 7 D1
Hostal-Residencia Encarnita, 31 C4
Hostal-Residencia Lamalonga, 9 B2
Hostal-Residencia Lido, 38 D4
Hostal-Residencia Los Arcos, 32 C4
Hostal-Residencia Luz, 27 B4
Hostal-Residencia María, 11 C3
Hostal-Residencia Miño, 26 B4
Hostal-Residencia Mondragón, 37 D4
Hostal-Residencia Regional, 36 D4
Hostal-Residencia Rios, 1 A1
Hostal-Residencia Rober, 25 B3
Hostal-Residencia Santa Cruz, 30 C4
Hostal-Residencia Sud-Americana, 41 E5
Hotel Mónaco, 19 D2
FOOD
Ananias, 3 A1
Arepas con Todo, 6 D1
Café Gijón, 22 E2
Casa Alberto, 44 D5
Cáscaras, 2 A1
Champagneria Gala, 42 E5
El 26 de Libertad, 21 D2
El Estragón, 45 A5
La Gata Flora, 5 C1
NIGHTLIFE
Acuarela, 17 D2
El Café de Sheherezade, 43 D5
Joy Eslava, 33 C4
Sugar Hill, 13 C3

General Info Line: ☎010. 20ptas per min. Ask for *inglés* and they'll transfer you to an English speaking operator. From outside Madrid ☎91 901 300 600.

Embassies: Embassies open M-F; call for hours. **Australia,** Pza. Descubridor Diego de Ordás, 3 (☎91 441 93 00; fax 442 53 62; www.embaustralia.es). **Canada,** C. Núñez de Balboa, 35 (☎91 423 32 50; fax 423 32 51; www.canada-es.org). M: Velázquez. **Ireland,** Claudio Coello, 73, (☎91 576 35 00; fax 435 16 77). **New Zealand,** Pl. de la Lealtad, 2 (☎91 523 02 26; fax 91 523 01 71). M: Banco de España. **South Africa,** Claudio Coello, 91, 6th fl. (☎91 435 66 88; fax 91 577 74 14). **UK,** C. Fernando El Santo, 19 (☎91 319 02 00; fax 91 319 04 23). M: Colón. **US,** C. Serrano, 75 (☎91 577 40 00; fax 91 577 57 35; www.embusa.es). M: Rubén Darío.

Currency Exchange: Banco Central Hispano, Pl. Canalejas, 1 (☎91 558 11 11) M: Sol. No commission on exchange; the best rates on AmEx checks. From Sol follow C. San Jeronimo to Pl. Canalejas. Open Apr.-Sept. M-F 8:30am-2:30pm, Sa 8:30am-1pm; Oct.-Mar. M-Th 8:30am-4:30pm, F 8:30am-2:30pm, Sa 8:30am-1pm.

American Express: Pl. Cortés, 2 (☎91 322 54 52; info ☎91 322 54 00). M: Sevilla. No commission on cash or AmEx traveler's checks; 750ptas fee for non-AmEx traveler's checks. Holds mail for 30 days and helps send and receive wired money.

LOCAL SERVICES

Luggage Storage: Barajas Airport, in *consigna*. One day 425ptas, 2-15 days 530-740ptas per day, after 15 days 105-210ptas per day. At **Estacion Chamartín** and **Estación Atocha** 400-600ptas per day. Open daily 6:30am-12:30am. **Estación Sur de Autobuses,** 800ptas per day.

Gay and Lesbian Services: Colectivo de Gais y Lesbianas de Madrid (COGAM), C. Fuencarral 37 (☎/fax 91 523 00 70). M: Gran Vía. Open M-Sa 5-9pm. **GAI-INFORM** (☎91 523 00 70) has info about gay associations and activities. Open daily 5-9pm.

Laundromat: Lavandería, C. Cervantes 1. M: Puerta del Sol or Banco de España. From Pl. Santa Ana follow C. Prado, turn right on C. Leon, and left onto C. Cervantes. Wash 400ptas, dry 100ptas per 9min. Open M-Sa 9am-8pm.

EMERGENCY AND COMMUNICATIONS

Emergency: ☎112. **Local Police:** ☎092. **National Police:** ☎091.

Crisis Lines: Rape Hotline: ☎91 574 01 10. Open M-F 10am-2pm and 4-7pm.

Medical Assistance: ☎061. **Anglo-American Medical Unit,** Conde de Aranda 1, 1st fl. (☎91 435 18 23). M: Serrano or Retiro. Open 9am-8pm. **Late-night pharmacy,** ☎098.

Internet Access: Euronet, C. Mayor, 1, 4th floor, office 11 (☎91 655 021 793). M: Sol. Unbeatable 250ptas per hr. Open 10am-11pm. **Interpublic,** C. San Jeronimo, 18. M: Sol. 299ptas per hr. Open 9:30am-midnight. **Internet Silico,** C. Fernando el Catolico, 80. M: Moncloa. 500ptas per hr.

Post Office: Palacio de Comunicaciones, C. Alcala, 51, in Pl. Cibeles (☎902 19 71 97). M: Banco de España. Open M-Sa 8:30am-9:30pm, Su 9am-2pm. Receive *Poste Restante* at windows 80-82; passport required. Send packages at door N (enter from C. Montlaban). Postal Express is at door K (enter from Paseo del Prado). Address mail to be held: First Name SURNAME, *Lista de Correos,* **28080** Madrid, Spain.

ACCOMMODATIONS AND CAMPING

Make reservations for summer visits. Expect to pay 2600ptas in a basic hostel, less for a *pensión*, and more in a two-star *hostal*. **Viajes Brújula,** estación Atocha at the AVE terminal, books rooms (but no HI hostels) for 400ptas and a deposit; go in person. (☎91 539 11 73. Open M-F 8am-10pm.) Tourist offices provide info about the 13 or so **campsites** within 50km of Madrid. **Centro,** the triangle between Puerta del Sol, Opera, and Plaza Mayor, is full of *hostales*. You'll pay for the prime location. The cultural hotbed of **Huertas,** framed by C. San Jeronimo, C. las Huertas and C. Atocha, is almost as central and more fun. Festive **Malasaña** and **Chueca,** bisected by C. Fuencarral, host cheap rooms in the heart of the action, but the party won't stop for sleep. *Hostales*, like temptations, are everywhere among **Gran Vía's** neon sex shops and scam artists, but accommodations tend to be grimy and overpriced.

EL CENTRO: SOL, ÓPERA, AND PLAZA MAYOR

Hostal Paz, C. Flora, 4, 1st and 4th fl. (☎91 547 30 47). M: Ópera. Don't be deterred by the dark street, parallel to C. Arenal, off C. Donados or C. Hileras. Comfortably sheltered from street noise. Satellite TV, A/C, and spotless, spacious bathrooms. Laundry 1200ptas. Singles 2500ptas; doubles 3800-4300ptas; triples 5700ptas.

Hostal-Residencia Luz, C. Fuentes, 10, 3rd fl. (☎91 542 07 59), off C. Arenal. M: Ópera. Redecorated rooms with hardwood floors and elegant furniture. Satellite TV, fax, and public phone. Don't pay extra for a private bath; the common ones are gorgeous. Laundry 1000ptas. Singles 2500ptas; doubles 3700ptas; triples 5500ptas.

Hostal Esparteros, C. Esparteros, 12, 4th fl. (☎/fax 91 521 09 03). Cheap, sparkling rooms with either balcony or large windows. Incredible owner ensures a fantastic stay. Laundry. Singles 2000-2700ptas; doubles 3200-3700ptas; triples 4400-5500ptas.

Hostal-Residencia Rober, C. Arenal, 26, 5th fl. (☎91 541 91 75). M: Ópera. Vying for cleanest in the capital. Brilliant balcony views down Arenal. TVs, A/C, and no smoking. Singles 3600-4500ptas; doubles 5700ptas; triples 7000ptas.

HUERTAS

Hostal Aguilar, C. San Jerónimo, 32, 2nd fl. (☎91 429 59 26 or 429 36 61; fax 91 429 26 61). M: Sol. Clean, modern rooms with phone, A/C, TV, and vast bathroom. Singles 4000ptas; doubles 6000ptas; triples 8000ptas; 2000ptas per extra person.

Hostal-Residencia Mondragón, C. San Jerónimo, 32, 4th fl. (☎91 429 68 16). M: Sol. Great value. Hot water only in communal bathrooms. Singles 2000ptas; doubles 3000ptas; triples 3900ptas.

Hostal-Residencia Sud-Americana, Po. Prado, 12, 6th fl. (☎91 429 25 64). M: Antón Martín or Atocha. Across from the Prado. All with faux-leather armchairs, some with balconies. Airy doubles facing the Prado have incredible views of the Paseo. Singles 2600ptas; doubles 5000ptas; triple 7000ptas.

GRAN VÍA

Hostal A. Nebrija, Gran Vía, 67, 8th fl., elevator A (☎91 547 73 19). M: Pl. España. Pleasant and spacious rooms in a very tidy building. Four rooms with huge windows reveal the best hostel views in Madrid; call ahead to reserve one. Singles 3300ptas; doubles 4500ptas; triples 6300ptas.

Hostal Margarita, Gran Vía, 50, 5th fl. (☎/fax 91 547 3549). M: Callao. Airy and tastefully sparse rooms, with big windows, pretty bathrooms, TVs, and telephones. Laundry 1200ptas. Singles 3400ptas; doubles 5100ptas; triples 6900ptas.

MALASAÑA AND CHUECA

Hostal Palacios and **Hostal Ribadavia,** C. Fuencarral 25, 1st-3rd fl. (☎91 531 10 58 or 91 531 48 47). M: Gran Vía. Both run by cheery family. Palacios (1st and 2nd fl.) has larger rooms. Ribadavia (3rd fl.) is older but comfortable. TVs. Singles 2500-3500ptas; doubles 4000ptas-5000ptas; triples 6000-7000ptas; quads 9000ptas.

Hostal Abril, C. Fuencarral, 39, 4th fl. (☎91 531 53 38). M: Tribunal or Gran Vía. Brand-new doors and granite floors; some fluorescent lighting. Singles 2000-2500ptas; doubles 3500-3800ptas; triples 4500-5200ptas.

ELSEWHERE IN MADRID

Albergue Juvenil Santa Cruz de Marcenado (HI), C. Santa Cruz de Marcenado, 28 (☎91 547 45 32; fax 91 548 11 96). M: Argüelles; follow C. Alberto Aguilera away from C. Princesa, turn right on C. Serrano Jóve, and turn left on C. Santa Cruz de Marcenado. Modern, renovated facilities. Members only; HI (YHA) cards 1800ptas. Breakfast included. Lockers 200ptas. 3-day max. stay. Reception 9am-1:30pm. Strict curfew 1:30am. Reserve ahead. 1820ptas; under 26 1200ptas.

Camping Osuna (☎91 741 05 10; fax 91 320 63 65), on Av. Logroño. M: Canillejas. Cross the pedestrian overpass, walk through the parking lot, turn right along the freeway, pass under a freeway and arch, and look for signs to the right. Or grab the #101 bus from the metro toward Barajas; ask for the campsite. Showers, laundry, and restaurant. Electricity 625ptas. 690ptas per person, per tent, and per car; add 7% IVA.

FOOD

In Madrid, it's not hard to fork it down without forking over too much. **Pl. Santa Ana** in **Huertas** is a favorite snack spot, and you might sit next to a real Spanish person. **Calles Echegaray, Ventura de la Vega,** and **Manuel Fernández González** are also good places for budget eats. Start your search in the **Lavapiés-La Latina-Atocha** area, south of Sol between C. Atocha and C. Toledo, at the La Latina metro stop. Cafes and hip restaurants stretch to **Pl. de la Paja.** Outdoor eateries cluster by Calle Agurrosa at Lavapiés and creep uphill to Huertas. **Malasaña** and **Chueca,** both above Gran Vía, are divided along C. Hortaleza. Malasaña's restaurants often feature adventurous menus filled with veggie options. Chueca's flamboyantly gay district has an assortment of colorful places to start a night of debauchery. Overflowing with bars, clubs, and restaurants, the area north of **Glorieta de Bilbao**, in the "V" formed by C. Fuencarral and C. Luchana and including Pl. Olavide, is Madrid's ethnic food buffet. In middle-class **Argüelles,** the quiet *terrazas* on C. Pintor Rosales overlook the park. Madrid bartenders used to cover *(tapar)* drinks with saucers to keep out flies. So servers put snacks on the saucers, and there you have it: *tapas*. Most *tapas* bars (a.k.a. *tascas* or *tabernas*) are open noon to 4pm and 8pm to midnight or later. Some double as restaurants, and many cluster around **Plaza Mayor** and **Plaza Santa Ana.** The *Guia del Ocio* lists vegetarian havens under the section *"Otras Cocinas."* Also try www.mundovegetariano.com. Grab **groceries** at **%Dia, Simago, El Corte Inglés,** or the **Mercado de San Miguel,** on Pl. San Miguel, off the northwest corner of Pl. Mayor. (Most open M-F 9:30am-2:30pm and 5:15-8:15pm, Sa 9am-2:30pm.)

El Estragón, Pl. de la Paja, 10 (☎91 365 89 82). M: **La Latina.** Follow C. Duque de Alba, turn right to Pl. Puerta de Moros, and leave the church on your right; it's on the far side of Pl. de la Paja. Vegetarian food makes diehard carnivores reconsider. Creative *menú* (M-F 1200ptas; Sa-Su and night 2475ptas). Open daily 1-4pm and 8pm-1am.

Museo del Jamón, C. San Jerónimo, 6 (☎91 521 03 46), in **Centro.** M: Sol. Don't miss this or one of five other much-loved locations. Succulent Iberian ham served in every form your piggish little heart could desire. *Menú* 1000ptas, combo plates 650-950ptas. Open M-Th 9am-12:30am, F-Sa 9am-1am, Su 10am-12:30am.

La Gata Flora, C. 2 de Mayo, 1 and C. San Vicente Ferrer, 33 (☎91 523 10 26), in **Chueca.** M: Noviciado or Tribunal. Pink exterior and huge servings. *Menú* 1075ptas. Pizza 850-1000ptas. Open Su-Th noon-1am, F-Sa noon-3am.

El 26 de Libertad, C. Libertad, 26, off C. las Infantas (☎91 522 25 22). M: **Chueca.** Innovative and exotic Spanish cuisine. Fantastic lunch *menú* 1300ptas. Open M-Th 1-4pm and 8pm-midnight, F-Sa 1-4pm and 9pm-12:30am, Su 1-4pm.

Arepas con Todo, C. Hartzenbusch, 19 (☎91 448 75 45), off C. Cardenal Cisernos, which is off C. Luchana. Classic Columbian restaurant with a different menu (1600-2000ptas) every night of the month and 60 fixed dishes (1800-2400ptas). For dinner, make reservations. Open M-W 2pm-1am.

Cáscaras, C. Ventura Rodríguez, 7 (☎91 542 83 36), in **Argüelles.** M: Ventura Rodríguez. Lounge in the sleek interior to enjoy tapas, pinchos, and ice-cold Mahou beer. Vegetarian entrees 800-985ptas. Open M-F 7am-1am, Sa-Su 10am-2am.

Ananias, C. Galileo, 9 (☎91 448 68 01), in **Argüelles.** Castillian food lovingly prepared in this friendly down-home spot. Particularly busy on Sundays. The *rabo de toro* (1300ptas) is not to be missed. Starters 500ptas, entrees 1000-2500ptas.

Champagneria Gala, C. Moratin, 22 (☎91 429 25 62), down the hill on Moratin from C. Atocha. Decor as colorful and varied as its pan-cooked, rice-based dishes. *Menú* (1750ptas) includes choice of paella, salad, bread, wine, and dessert. Make reservations on weekends. Open daily 1:30-5pm and 9pm-12:30am.

SIGHTS

Madrid, as large as it may seem, is a walker's city. The word *paseo* refers to a major avenue, but literally means "a stroll." From Sol to Cibeles and from the Plaza Mayor to the Palacio Real, sights will kindly introduce themselves. The shade of the **Retiro** or a sidewalk cafe allows a break from Madrid heat and a chance to take in the best sight—its people. The municipal tourist office's *Plano de Transportes* map, which marks monuments as well as bus and metro lines, is indispensable.

EL CENTRO: SOL, ÓPERA, AND PLAZA MAYOR

PUERTA DEL SOL. **Kilómetro 0**—the origin of six national highways—marks the center of the city (and of the country) in the most chaotic of Madrid's plazas. Puerta del Sol (Gate of Sun) blazes with taxis, bars, and street performers. The statue **El Oso y el Madroño,** a bear and strawberry tree, is a popular meeting place. *(M: Sol.)*

PLAZA MAYOR. Juan de Herrera, architect of El Escorial, also designed this plaza. Its elegant arcades, spindly towers, and verandas, erected for Felipe III in 1620, came to define "Madrid-style" architecture and inspired every peering *balcón* thereafter. The bullfights once held here are now but ghosts haunting the plaza's lively cafes with live flamenco performances. Pl. Mayor awakens at night as *madrileños* surface and tourists multiply. *(M: Sol; from Puerta del Sol, walk down C. Mayor.)*

CATEDRAL DE SAN ISIDRO. This 17th-century church reigned as Madrid's cathedral from the late 19th century until the Catedral de la Almudena was consecrated in 1993. *(At the intersection of C. Toledo and C. Sacramento. M: Latina; from Pta. del Sol, go down C. Mayor through Pl. Mayor, and exit onto C. Toledo. Open for mass only.)*

PLAZA DE LA VILLA. This small, quiet plaza marks the heart of what was old Madrid. The stunning courtyard features exquisite tiling and architecture. The **Torre de los Lujanes,** a 15th-century building on the eastern side of the plaza, is the sole remnant of the once-lavish residence of the Lujanes family. The characteristically Hapsburg 17th-century **Ayuntamiento** (Town Hall) was both the mayor's home and the city jail. *(M: Sol; head down C. Mayor past the Pl. Mayor and it's on your left.)*

THE PALACIO REAL. This amazingly luxurious palace was built for the first Bourbon King, Felipe V, to replace the Alcázar after it burned down. It took 40 years to build, and the decoration of its 2000 rooms with 20km of tapestry dragged on for a century. *(M: Sol; go down C. Mayor past Pl. de la Villa and turn right on C. de Bailén. Open Apr.-Sept. M-Sa 9am-6pm, Su 9am-3pm; Oct.-Mar. M-Sa 9:30am-5pm, Su 9am-2pm. 900ptas, with tour 1000ptas; students 400ptas, 100ptas. W free for EU citizens.)* The view from the center of the **Campo del Moro,** which runs from the palace down to the river, is out of a fairy tale. *(Enter down the hill and opposite the palace. Free.)* The palace faces **Plaza de Oriente,** a sculpture garden. *(From Pta. Sol, take C. Arenal to the plaza. Free.)*

CATEDRAL DE LA ALMUDENA. Begun in 1879 and finished a century later, the cathedral's interior is a modern contrast to the gilded Palacio Real. Controversy surrounded its recent face-lift: the stained-glass windows and frescoes are an almost psychedelic mix of the traditional and the abstract. *(M: Sol. From Pta. Sol, go down C. Mayor and it's just across C. Bailén. Open M-Sa 1-7pm. Closed during mass. Free.)*

HUERTAS, GRAN VÍA, MALASAÑA, CHUECA, AND ARGÜELLES

East of Pta. del Sol, the **Huertas** reflects its literary ilk, from famed authors' houses to legendary cafes. Home to Cervantes, Góngora, Calderón, and Moratín, the neighborhood enjoyed a fleeting return to literary prominence when Hemingway hung out here. *(M: Sol.)* **Gran Vía,** which stretches from Pl. de Callao to Pl. de España and is lined with massive skyscrapers, fast-food joints, and bustling stores, is the busiest street in Madrid. *(M: Callao and Pl. España.)* **Malasaña** and **Chueca** represent Madrid's alternative scene; the area between C. de Fuencarral and C. de San Bernardo, north of Gran Vía, boasts avant-garde architecture, chic eateries, and the city's hippest fashion. Out of the way in **Argüelles,** Goya's frescoed dome in the beautiful **Ermita de San Antonio de la Florida** arches above his own buried corpse. *(M:*

Príncipe Pío; turn left on C. de Buen Altamirano, go through the park, turn left on Po. Florida, and it's at the end of the street. Open Tu-F 10am-2pm and 4-8pm, Sa-Su 10am-2pm. Free.) **Temple de Debod,** Spain's only Egyptian temple, was built by Pharaoh Zakheramon in the 4th century BC. *(M: Argüelles; walk down C. Princesa and turn right on C. Ventura Rodriguez into the Parque de la Montaña; it's on the left. Open in summer Tu-Su 10am-1:45pm and 6-7:45pm; Tu-F 10am-2pm and 6-8pm, Sa-Su 10am-2pm; off season Tu-F 10am-2pm and 4-6pm, Sa-Su 10am-2pm. 300ptas, students 150ptas. W and Su free.)* Stop and smell the **Rosaleda** (rose garden) at the bottom of **Parque del Oeste.** *(M: Moncloa. From the metro, take C. Princesa. Open daily 10am-8pm.)* The **Faro de Moncloa,** a 92m metal tower near the **Museo de América,** offers spectacular views of the city. *(Open M-F. 200ptas.)*

THE RETIRO AND ENVIRONS

Parque del Retiro, a great picnic and tanning zone, was intended as a *buen retiro* (nice retreat) for Felipe IV. The **Estanque Grande,** a lake in the middle of the park, is popular among rowers. *(From M: Retiro, enter on Av. Mejico, which leads to the lake. Boat rentals daily 9:30am-8:30pm.)* South of the lake, the exquisite steel-and-glass **Palacio de Cristal** hosts art shows. *(Open Tu-Sa 11am-2pm and 5-8pm, Su 10am-2pm. Admission price varies.)* The **Palacio de Velázquez** exhibits works in conjunction with the Museo de Arte Reina Sofía. *(Turn right on C. Alcalá, walk through Pta. Alcalá, pass the Estanque, and turn left on Paseo del Venezuela. Open M-Sa 11am-8pm, Su 11am-6pm. Free.)*

EL PARDO

Built as a hunting lodge for Carlos I in 1547, **El Pardo** was subsequently enlarged by generations of Hapsburg and Bourbon royalty into the magnificent country palace it is today. The palace is renowned for its collection of tapestries, several of which were designed by Goya. Franco resided here from 1940-1975. Admission to the palace's **chapel** and the nearby **Casita del Príncipe** is free. *(Catch bus #601, 15min., 150ptas, in front of the Ejército del Aire building above M: Moncloa. Open Apr.-Sept. M-F 9:30am-6pm, Su 9:25am-1:40pm; Oct.-Mar. M-F 10:30am-5pm, Su 9:55am-1:40pm. Compulsory 45min. Spanish tour. 650ptas, students 250ptas; W free for EU citizens.)*

MUSEUMS

The worthwhile **Paseo del Arte** ticket grants admission to the Museo del Prado, Colección Thyssen-Bornemisza, and Centro de Arte Reina Sofía (1275ptas).

Museo Thyssen-Bornemisza (☎91 369 01 51; www.museothyssen.org), on the corner of Po. Prado and C. San Jerónimo. M: Banco de España. Bus #6, 14, 27, 37, or 45. This 18th-century palace houses a fabulous art collection accumulated by generations of the Austro-Hungarian magnates. The museum surveys it all, parading canvases and sculptures by many of the greats, including El Greco, Titian, Caravaggio, Picasso, Rothko, Hopper, Mondrian, Klee, Chagall, and Dalí. To view the collection in chronological order, observing the evolution of styles and themes, begin on the top floor and work your way down. Open Tu-Su 10am-7pm. 700ptas, students 400ptas, under 12 free.

Museo Nacional Centro de Arte Reina Sofía, C. Santa Isabel, 52 (☎91 467 50 62), opposite Estación Atocha at the southern end of Po. Prado. M: Atocha. The centerpiece of the 20th-century collection is Picasso's masterwork *Guernica,* displaying the agony of the Nazi bombing of the Basque town of Guernica for the Fascists during the Spanish Civil War. Works by Miró, Julio González, Juan Gris, Picasso, and Dalí also illustrate the essential role of Spanish artists in Cubism and Surrealism. Open M and W-F 10am-9pm, Su 10am-2:30pm. 500ptas, students 250ptas; Sa after 2:30pm and Su free.

Museo del Prado (☎91 420 37 68), on Po. Prado at Pl. Cánovas del Castillo. M: Banco de España. One of Europe's finest museums, its walls are graced by Goya's "black paintings," Velázquez's *Las Meninas,* a strong Flemish collection with works by Van Dyck, van der Weyden, Albrecht Dürer, Pieter Brueghel the Elder, and Rubens (a result of the Spanish Hapsburgs' long reign over the Netherlands), and other works by Titian, Raphael, Tintoretto, Botticelli, Bosch, and El Greco. Open Tu-Sa 9am-7pm, Su 9am-2pm. 500ptas, students 250ptas; Sa 2:30-7pm and Su free.

Museo de América, Av. Reyes Católicos, 6 (☎91 549 26 41), next to the Faro de Moncloa. M: Moncloa. This under-appreciated museum documents the cultures of America's pre-Columbian civilizations and the effects of the Spanish conquest. Open Tu-Sa 10am-3pm, Su 10am-2:30pm. 500ptas, students 250ptas; Su free.

Museo de la Real Academia de Bellas Artes de San Fernando, C. Alcalá, 13 (☎91 522 14 91). M: Sol or Sevilla. An excellent collection of the Old Masters, surpassed only by the Prado. In the same building, the **Calcografía Real** (Royal Print and Drawing Collection) housed Goya's studio. Both open Tu-F 9am-7pm, Sa-M 9am-2:30pm. 400ptas, students 200ptas; W and Oct. 12, May 18, and Dec. 16 free.

Monasterio de las Descalzas Reales (☎91 559 74 04), on Pl. Descalzas, between Pl. Callao and Pta. de Sol. M: Callao or Sol. Home to 26 Franciscan nuns and an impressive collection of religious art. Open Tu-Th and Sa 10:30am-12:45pm and 4-5:45pm, F 10:30am-12:45pm, Su 11am-1:45pm. 700ptas, students 300ptas. EU citizens free W.

ENTERTAINMENT

CLASSIC CAFES. Spend an afternoon lingering over a *café con leche* and soak up Madrid's culture in these historic cafes. **Café Gijón,** Po. Recoletos, 21 (M: Colón), a 113-year-old literati hangout, hopes its historical significance will divert attention from its high prices. (Open daily 9am-1:30am.) Sink into leather couches at **Café Círculo de Bellas Artes,** C. Alcalá, 42. (M: Banco de España. Cover 100ptas. Open M-F 9am-1am, Sa-Su 9am-3am.) Or, gaze at the Palacio Real from the ritzy **Café de Oriente,** Pl. Oriente, 2. (M: Ópera. Open Su-Th 8:30am-1:30am, F-Sa 8:30am-1:30am.)

EL RASTRO (FLEA MARKET). For hundreds of years, El Rastro has been a Sunday morning tradition in Madrid. From Pl. Mayor and its Sunday stamp and coin market, walk down C. Toledo to Pl. Cascorro (M: La Latina), where the market begins, and follow the crowds to the end, at the bottom of C. Ribera de Curtidores.

FILM, THEATER, AND MUSIC. Anyone interested in live entertainment should stop by the **Circulo de Bellas Artes,** C. Marquez de Casa Riera, 2 (☎91 360 54 00; e-mail presa@c-bellasartes.es) at C. Alcala, 47; their monthly magazine *Minerva*, is fantastic. (M: Sevilla or Banco de España.) Check in the *Guía del Ocio* (125ptas) and the entertainment supplements of Friday's newspapers for info on the city-sponsored movies, plays, and concerts. Look out for July's **Fescinal,** a film festival at the Parque de la Florida. Subtitled films are shown in many theaters, including **Alphaville** and **Renoir**—check for *v.o. (versión original)* listings. For live theater, head to Huertas. In July and August, **Pl. Mayor, Lavapiés,** and **Villa de París** frequently host plays. **Teatro Español,** C. Principe, 25 (☎91 429 62 97; M: Sol), **Teatro de la Comedia,** C. Principe, 14 (☎91 521 49 31; M: Sevilla), and the superb **Teatro María Guerrero,** C. Tamayo y Baus, 4 (☎91 319 47 69; M: Colon) have fantastic reputations. The **Auditorio Nacional,** C. Príncipe de Vergara, 146 (☎91 337 01 00; M: Cruz del Rayo), home to the National Orchestra, features Madrid's best classical music performances (800-4200ptas). **Flamenco** tends to be tourist-oriented and expensive. If you must, try **Casa Patas,** Casa Canizares, 10. (☎91 369 04 96. Shows Th-Sa midnight.)

SPORTS. Spanish sports fans go ballistic for **fútbol** (soccer to North Americans). Every Sunday and some Saturdays from September and June, one of two local teams plays at home. **Real Madrid** plays at Estadio Santiago Bernabeu, Po. Castellana, 104. (☎91 457 11 12; M: Lima). **Atlético de Madrid** plays at Estadio Vicente Calderón, C. Virgen del Puerto 67 (☎366 47 07; M: Pirámides or Marqués de Vadillos). Tickets cost 3000-7000ptas. **Corridas** (bullfights) are held during the Festival of San Isidro and every Sunday from March to October; they are less frequent the rest of the year. **Plaza de las Ventas,** C. Alcalá, 237, east of central Madrid, is the biggest ring in Spain. (☎91 356 22 00. M: Ventas. Tickets 450-15,200ptas.)

NIGHTLIFE

Spaniards average one hour less sleep each night than other Europeans, and *madrileños* claim to need even less than that. Proud of their nocturnal offerings (they'll say with a straight face that Paris or New York bored them), they don't retire until they've "killed the night"—and a good part of the next morning. As the sun sets, *terrazas* and *chiringuitos* (outdoor cafes/bars) spill across sidewalks. *Madrileños* start in the *tapas* bars of **Huertas,** move to the youthful scene in **Malasaña,** and end at the crazed parties of the **Chueca** or late-night clubs of Gran Vía. **Bilbao** and **Moncloa** are student-filled. Madrid's gay scene, centered on **Pl. Chueca,** is fantastic. Most clubs don't heat up until around 2am; don't be surprised by a line still waiting outside at 5:30am. The *entrada* (cover) can be as high as 2000ptas, but usually includes a drink. Bouncers on power trips love to make examples; try to dress well and avoid being overcharged or denied. Women may not be charged at all, so bat those eyelashes, ladies.

Joy Eslava, C. Arenal, 11. M: **Sol** or Ópera. Three-tiered theater-turned-disco. Young crowd grooves to disco, techno, R&B, and salsa. Cover 2000-2500ptas; includes 1 drink. Open M-Th 11:30pm-5:30am, F-Sa 7pm-6am.

El Café de Sheherezade, C. Santa María, 18, a block from C. Huertas. M: Antón Martín. Recline on opulent pillows while sipping libations. Middle Eastern decor. Personal *pipas* (pipes; 800-1200ptas) that filter smoke through whisky or water. Open daily 7pm-5am.

Acuarela, C. Gravina, 8, off C. Hortaleza. M: **Chueca.** Buddhas, candles, and antique furniture perfect for chilling. Liquor 500ptas. Open Su-Th 3pm-2am, F-Sa 3pm-4am.

Sugar Hill, Mesonero Romanos, 13. M: **Gran Vía** or Callao. The only hip-hop club in town. Cover 1500ptas includes 1 drink. Open Sa 12:45-5:30am. **Goa After Club** blasts techno in the same building. Cover 1000ptas, includes 1 drink. Open Sa-Su 6-10am.

Café Jazz Populart, C. Huertas, 22. Extensive bar hosts local and foreign talent. Live jazz, blues, reggae, and flamenco. Slightly older crowd. Shows Su-W 11pm, F-Sa 11pm and 12:30am. Open Su-Th 6pm-12:30am, F-Sa 6pm-3am.

Cafe del Toro, C. San Andres, 38. M: Tribunal. An outdoor cafe indoors. Hosts live entertainment nightly from acoustic music to stand-up comedy (200ptas). Beer 300ptas, drinks 600-800ptas. Open Su-Th 7pm-3am, F-Sa 7pm-3:30am.

Trocha, C. Huertas, 55. M: Anton Martin or **Sol.** Jazz tunes and cushioned wicker couches. Brazilian *capirinhas* (lime, ice, rum and sugar drinks) 725ptas at the bar, 750ptas seated). Open Su-Th 8pm-3am, F-Sa 8pm-4am.

Kapital, C. Atocha, 125, 1 block off Po. Prado. M: **Atocha.** This macro-*discoteca* impresses with 7 floors of overstimulation packed with glittery 20-year-olds. Cover 2000ptas (includes 1 drink). Open Th 12:30-6am, F-Su 6-11pm and 12:30-6am.

EXCURSIONS FROM MADRID

EL ESCORIAL. The **Monasterio de San Lorenzo del Escorial** was a gift from Felipe II to God, the people, and himself, commemorating his victory over the French at the battle of San Quintín in 1557. By the town of **San Lorenzo,** it is filled with artistic treasures, two palaces, a church, two pantheons, and a magnificent library. *Don't* come on Monday, when the complex shuts down. Enter by the gate on the west side, on C. Floridablanca, into a collection of Flemish tapestries and paintings. The adjacent **Museos de Arquitectura** and **Pintura** chronicle El Escorial's construction and include masterpieces by Bosch, El Greco, Titian, Tintoretto, Velázquez, Zurbarán, Van Dyck, and others. The **Palacio Real,** lined with 16th-century *azulejos* (tiles), includes the **Salón del Trono** (Throne Room), Felipe II's spartan 16th-century apartments, and the luxurious 18th-century rooms of Carlos III and Carlos IV. The macabre **Panteón Real** is filled with monarchs' tombs and glitters with gold and marble designs from 1654. (Open Tu-Su Apr.-Sept. 10am-7pm; Oct.-Mar. 10am-6pm. 900ptas, students 400ptas; W free for EU citizens. Tour 1000ptas. Autocares Herranz **buses** leave Madrid's "Moncloa" metro station for El Escorial's **Plaza Virgen de Gracia,** the center of town (50min., every 15min., round-trip 805ptas). Autocares

Herranz, C. Rey, 27, sells tickets to Madrid. From C. Rey, with your back to the bus station, turn right, follow the street, and turn right up C. Floridablanca to get to the **tourist office,** C. Floridablanca, 10. (☎918 90 15 54. Open M-F 10am-2pm and 3-5pm, Sa 9:55am-1:55pm.) **Trains** (☎918 90 07 14) also chug to Ctra. Estación, 2km from El Escorial, from Madrid's Atocha and Chamartín stations (1hr., every 20min., 810ptas); from the station, take a shuttle bus to the Pl. Virgen de Gracia.

EL VALLE DE LOS CAÍDOS. In a valley of the Sierra de Guadarrama, 8km north of El Escorial, Franco built the overpowering **Santa Cruz del Valle de los Caídos** (Valley of the Fallen) as a memorial to those who died in the Civil War. The massive granite cross was meant to honor only those who died "serving *Dios* and *España*," i.e., the fascist Nationalists. Thousands of non-fascists forced to build the monument died during its construction. Franco is buried beneath the high altar, but there is no mention of his tomb in tourist literature—testimony to the dictator's legacy. It is accessible only via El Escorial. (Open daily June-Aug. 9:30am-7pm; Sept.-May 10am-6pm. Mass daily 11am. 800ptas, students 350ptas; W free EU citizens. Funicular 350ptas.) Autocares Herranz runs a **bus** to the monument (15min.; leaves El Escorial Tu-Su 3:15pm, returns 5:30pm; round-trip 1030ptas includes admission).

CENTRAL SPAIN

Castilla La Mancha, surrounding Madrid to the west and south, is one of Spain's least-developed regions; medieval cities and olive groves sprinkle the land. On the other sides of Madrid are **Castilla y León's** dramatic cathedrals. Despite glorious historical architecture and history, the region has not been as economically successful as its more high-tech neighbors. Farther west, bordering Portugal, stark **Extremadura's** arid plains bake under intense summer sun, relieved by scattered patches of glowing sunflowers and refreshingly few tourists.

CASTILLA LA MANCHA

SPAIN

Cervantes chose to set Don Quixote's adventures in La Mancha (*manxa* is Arabic for parched earth) in an effort to evoke a cultural and material backwater. No fantasy of the Knight of the Sad Countenance is needed to transform the austere beauty of this battered, windswept plateau. Its tumultuous history, gloomy medieval fortresses, and awesome crags provide enough food for the imagination.

TOLEDO

Modern-day Toledo (pop. 65,000) may be marred by armies of tourists and caravans of kitsch, but this former capital of the Holy Roman, Visigoth, and Muslim empires remains a treasure trove of Spanish culture. The city's churches, synagogues, and mosques reflect a time when Spain's three religions peacefully coexisted.

PRACTICAL INFO, ACCOMMODATIONS, AND FOOD. **Trains** (☎925 22 30 99) arrive from Madrid's Estación Atocha (1½hr., 10-20 per day, 775ptas) at Po. Rosa, 2, opposite the Puente de Azarquiel. Take bus #5 or 6 from the right of the station to Pl. Zocodóver (120ptas), follow C. Armas downhill as it changes names and leads through the gates (Puerta Nueva de Bisagra), and cross the intersection to reach the **tourist office.** (☎925 22 08 43. Open M-Sa 9am-7pm, Su 9am-3pm.) Surf the **Internet** at **Scorpions,** on C. Pintor Matías Moreno. (100ptas per 5min. Open daily noon-midnight.) To get from the station to the **Residencia Juvenil San Servando (HI),** on Castillo San Servando (10min.), cross the street, then turn left and immediately right up Callejón del Hospital; when the steps reach a road, turn right and right again, and follow signs to the Hospital Provincial. (☎925 22 45 54. Laundry. Reception 7am-11:50pm. Curfew 12:30am. Sometimes closed—call ahead.

1400ptas, under 27 1200ptas.) From Pl. Zocodóver, head up C. Sillería, go diagonally left through Pl. San Agustín, and turn right to get to **Pensión Castilla,** C. Recoletos, 6. (☎925 25 63 18. Singles 2200ptas; doubles with bath 3900ptas.) At the edge of the old city and downhill from Po. San Cristobal you'll find the high-class **Pensión Descalzos,** C. Descalzos, 30. (☎925 22 28 88. Singles 3500ptas; doubles 5600ptas. Add IVA.) To **camp** at **Circo Romano,** Av. Carlos III, 19, go through Puerta de Bisagra, take a left, then walk to the large rotary; it's the second "spoke" on the right. (☎925 22 04 42. 550ptas per person; 570ptas per tent; 550ptas per car.) Try Toledo's marzipan delights at the ubiquitous *pastelerías*, or have a square meal at **Restaurante El Zoco,** C. Barrio Rey, 7, off Pl. Zocodóver. (*Menús* 950-1500ptas. Open daily 1:30-4pm and 8-10:30pm.) **Postal code:** 45070.

SIGHTS AND ENTERTAINMENT. The vast collection of museums, churches, synagogues, and mosques (many closed on Mondays) lie within the city walls; despite well-marked streets, you'll probably get lost. Southwest of Pl. Zocodóver, Toledo's grandiose **cathedral** at the Arco de Palacioz boasts five naves, delicate stained glass, and unapologetic ostentation. (Open July-Aug. M-Sa 10:30am-7pm, Su 2-6pm; Sept.-June M-Sa 10:30am-6pm, Su 2-6pm. 700ptas; tickets sold at the store opposite the entrance. Dress modestly.) Toledo's most formidable landmark, the **Alcázar,** Cuesta Carlos V, 2, a block from Pl. Zocodóver, has been a stronghold of Romans, Visigoths, Moors, and Fascists. Today, it houses a military museum. (Open Tu-Su 9:30am-2pm. 200ptas; EU citizens free W.) Greek painter Doménikos Theotokópoulos, or **El Greco,** spent most of his life in Toledo. His works are displayed throughout town; on the west side, the **Iglesia de Santo Tomé,** on Pl. Conde, houses his *El entierro del Conde de Orgaz (Burial of Count Orgaz)*. (Open daily June-Aug. 10am-7pm; Sept.-May 10am-6pm. 200ptas.) Downhill and to the left lies the **Casa Museo de El Greco,** C. Samuel Levi 3, with 19 of his works. (Open Tu-Sa 10am-2pm and 4-6pm, Su 10am-2pm. 200ptas, students free; Sa and Su afternoons free.) The impressive **Museo de Santa Cruz,** C. Cervantes, 3, off Pl. Zocodóver, also exhibits some El Grecos in its eclectic collection. (Open M 10am-2pm and 4-6:30pm, Tu-Sa 10am-6:30pm, Su 10am-2pm. 200ptas, students 100ptas.) The 14th-century **Sinagoga del Tránsito,** on C. Samuel Levi, hides an ornate interior and houses the **Museo Sefardí.** (Open Tu-Sa 10am-2pm and 4-6pm, Su 10am-2pm. 400ptas, students 200ptas; free Sa 4-6pm and Su.) The 12th-century **Sinagoga de Santa María la Blanca,** down the street to the right, was built as a mosque, used as the city's main synagogue, and was converted to a church in 1492. (Open daily June-Aug. 10am-2pm and 3:30-7pm; Sept.-May 10am-2pm and 3:30-6pm. 200ptas.) At the western edge of the city, the Franciscan **Monasterio de San Juan de los Reyes** has great views. (Open daily June-Aug. 10am-2pm and 3:30-6pm; Sept.-May 10am-2pm and 3:30-5pm. 200ptas.) For nightlife, try **C. Santa Fe,** east of the arch from Pl. Zocodóver, which brims with local youths. **Enebro,** on Pl. Santiago Caballeros off C. Cervantes, lures customers with free tapas. (Beer 300ptas. Open until 3am.) The town goes crazy for **Corpus Christi,** the eighth Sunday after Easter.

CUENCA

Cuenca (pop. 47,000) is a hilltop city surrounded by rivers and stunning rock formations. The enchanting old city safeguards most of its charm, including the famed *casas colgadas* (hanging houses) that dangle above the Río Huécar, on C. Obispo Vaero off Pl. Mayor. Carefully cross the San Pablo bridge to **Hoz del Huécar** for a spectacular view of the *casas* and cliffs. Many of the *casas* now house museums; on Pl. Ciudad de Ronda is the excellent **Museo de Arte Abstracto Español.** (Open Tu-F and holidays 11am-2pm and 4-6pm, Sa 11am-2pm and 4-8pm, Su 11am-2:30pm. 500ptas, students 250ptas.) A perfectly square **cathedral** sits in Pl. Mayor. (Open June-Aug. 11am-2pm and 4-6pm; Sept.-May 10:30am-2pm and 4-6pm. Free.)

Trains arrive on Po. Ferrocarril, in the new city, from Madrid's Estación Atocha (2½-3hr., 5 per day, 1390ptas) and Valencia (3½hr.). **Buses** roll into C. Fermín Caballero, by the train station, from Madrid (2½hr.). From either station, go left to the first bus shelter and take bus #1 or 2 (every 20min., 85ptas) to the **tourist office,** Pl. Mayor. (☎969 23 21 19. Open daily July-Aug. 10:30am-2pm and 4:30-7:30pm; Sept.-June 10am-2pm and 4-6:30pm.) **Hostal-Residencia Posada de San José,** C. Julián Romero, 4, is by the cathedral. (☎969 21 13 00. Singles 2600-4400ptas; doubles 4400-8600ptas; triples 5900-11,600ptas. Add 7% IVA.) Head up C. San Pedro from the cathedral past Pl. Trabuco; **Pensión Tabanqueta** is at C. Trabuco, 13. (☎969 21 12 90. Singles 2000ptas; doubles 4000ptas; triples 6000ptas.) Grab **groceries** at **%Día,** on Av. Castilla La Mancha at Av. República Argentina. (Open M-Th 9:30am-2pm and 5:30-8:30pm, F-Sa 9am-2:30pm and 5:30-9pm.) **Postal code:** 16004.

CASTILLA Y LEÓN

Castilla y León's cities emerge like islands from a sea of burnt sienna. The majestic Gothic cathedrals, slender Romanesque belfries along the Camino de Santiago, and Salamanca's intricate sandstone have emblazoned themselves as national images.

SALAMANCA

For centuries, the gates of Salamanca have welcomed scholars, saints, rogues, and royals. The bustling city is famed for its golden sandstone architecture as well as for its university—the oldest in Spain, and once one of the "four leading lights of the world," along with the universities of Bologna, Paris, and Oxford.

PRACTICAL INFO, ACCOMMODATIONS, AND FOOD. **Trains** chug from Po. Estación Ferrocarril (☎923 12 02 02) to: Ávila (1¾hr., 2 per day, 865-1095ptas); Madrid (2½hr., 4 per day, 2130ptas); and Lisbon (6hr., 1 per day, 4800ptas). **Buses** run from Av. Filiberto Villalobos 71-85 (☎923 23 67 17) to: Madrid (2½-3hr., 21 per day, 1460-1480ptas); León (2½hr., 1-3 per day, 1160ptas); and Segovia (3hr., 1-2 per day, 1280ptas). Bus #1 (100ptas) from the train station and bus #4 from the bus station head to Gran Vía, a block from Pl. Mercado (next to the town center at Pl. Mayor). The **tourist office** is at Pl. Mayor 14. (☎923 21 83 42. Open M-Sa 9am-2pm and 4:30-6:30pm, Su 10am-2pm and 4:30-6:30pm.) Access the **Internet** at **Informática Abaco Bar,** C. Zamora 7. (150ptas per 30min. Open M-F 9:30am-2am.)

Reasonably priced *hostales* and *pensiones* cater to the floods of students, especially off **Pl. Mayor** and **C. Meléndez.** **Pensión Estefanía,** C. Jesús 3-5 off Pl. Mayor, has a prime location and clean rooms. (☎923 21 73 72. Showers 150ptas. Singles 2000ptas; doubles with shower 3500ptas; triples 4800ptas.) Ideal for groups, **Pensión Bárez,** C. Meléndez 19, 1st fl., has several large, simple rooms. (☎923 21 74 95. Showers 150ptas. Singles 1500ptas; doubles 3500ptas; triples 4500ptas.) Albetur buses shuttle **campers** from Gran Vía (every 30min.) to the classy **Regio,** 4km toward Madrid on the Ctra. Salamanca. (☎923 13 88 88. 450ptas per person; 850ptas per tent; 450ptas extra per car.) **Champion,** C. Toro 64, has a downstairs **supermarket.** (Open M-Sa 9:30am-8:30pm.) Cafes and restaurants surround Pl. Mayor; full meals in cheaper back alley spots run around 1000ptas. **Restaurante El Bardo,** C. Compañía 8, between the Casa de las Conchas and the Clerecía, is a traditional Spanish restaurant with veggie options and a lively bar downstairs. (Entrees 1100-1900ptas. Open daily 1:30-4:30pm and 9:30-11:30pm., bar until 1am.) **Postal code:** 37001.

SIGHTS AND ENTERTAINMENT. The **Plaza Mayor,** designed by Alberto Churriguera, exemplifies the best of the city's famed architecture and has been called one of the most beautiful squares in Spain. Between its nearly 100 sandstone arches hang medallions with bas-reliefs of famous Spaniards, from El Cid to Franco. Walk down C. Rua Mayor to Pl. San Isidro to reach the 15th-century **Casa de las Conchas** (House of Shells), one of Salamanca's most famous landmarks, adorned by over 300 rows of scallop shells chiseled in sandstone. Go down Patio de las Escuelas, off C. Libreros (which leads south from Pl. San Isidro), to enter the **Universidad,** founded in 1218. The university's 16th-century **entry facade** is one of the best examples of Spanish Plateresque, named for the delicate filigree work of *plateros* (silversmiths). Hidden in the sculptural work lies a tiny hidden frog; according to legend, those who can spot the frog without assistance will be blessed with good luck and even marriage. Inside the Patio de Escuelas Menores, the University Museum contains the **Cielo de Salamanca,** a 15th-century fresco of the zodiac. (Open M-F 9:30am-1:30pm and 4-7:30pm, Sa 9:30am-1:30pm and 4-7pm, Su 10am-1:30pm. 300ptas, students 150ptas.) Continue down Rua Mayor to Pl. Anaya to reach the *vieja* (old) and *nueva* (new) cathedrals. Begun in 1513 to accommodate the growing tide of Catholics, the spindly-spired late-Gothic **Catedral Nueva** wasn't finished until 1733. The smaller Romanesque **Catedral Vieja** (1140) has a striking cupola with depictions of apocalyptic angels separating the sinners from the saved. The **museum** in the latter houses a Mudéjar Salinas organ, one of the oldest organs in Europe. (*Nueva* open daily Apr.-Sept. 9am-2pm and 4-8pm; Oct.-Mar. 9am-1pm and 4-6pm. Free. *Vieja*, cloister, and museum have the same hours. 300ptas.) If religious zeal intrigues you, inquire at the tourist office about Salamanca's impressive **convents.** Resembling a Tiffany jewelry box, **Casa Lis Museo Art Nouveau Y Art Deco,** C. Gibraltar, 14, behind the cathedrals, houses the oddities of Miguel de Lis's art nouveau and art deco collection. (Open Apr. 1-Oct. 15 Tu-F 11am-2pm and 5pm-9pm, Sa-Su 11am-9pm; Oct. 16-Mar. 31 Tu-F 11am-2pm and 4-7pm, Sa-Su 11am-8pm. 300ptas.)

Nightlife centers on **Pl. Mayor, C. Bordadores,** and **Gran Vía. Camelot,** C. Bordadores 3, a monastery-turned-club on the Gatsby and Cum Laude (C. Prior) club-hopping routes. Top 40 songs pop at the popular **Café Moderno,** Gran Vía 75. **Birdland,** C. Azafranal 57 by Pl. España, features jazz. A mixed gay and straight clientele grooves under black lights at **Submarino,** C. San Justo 27, built to resemble an old submarine.

EXCURSION FROM SALAMANCA: CIUDAD RODRIGO. A medieval town of fabulous masonry and honey-colored stone, Ciudad Rodrigo rises from the plains near the Portuguese border. The **cathedral** is the town's masterpiece; with biblical and mythological scenes illustrated in intricate stonework, the **cloister** alone is worth the trip. Fascinating figures festoon the columns, making love, playing peek-a-boo, or nibbling body parts. The cathedral's **museum** includes an ancient clavichord and Velázquez's *Llanto de Adam y Eva por Ariel muerto.* (Cathedral open daily 10am-1pm and 4-7pm. Free. Cloister and museum open daily 10am-1pm and 4-7pm. 200ptas.) **Buses** arrive from Salamanca (1¼hr., 5-12 per day, 735ptas).

LEÓN

Formerly the center of Christian Spain, today León is best known for its 13th-century Gothic **cathedral** on La Pulchra Leonina, arguably the most beautiful cathedral in Spain. Its spectacular blue stained-glass windows have earned the city the nickname *La Ciudad Azul* (The Blue City) and alone warrant a trip to León. The cathedral's **museum** displays gruesome wonders, including a sculpture depicting the skinning of a saint. (Cathedral open daily in summer 8:30am-1:30pm and 4-8pm; off-season closes at 7pm. Free. Museum open M-F 9:30am-2pm and 4-7pm, Sa 9:30am-12:30pm and 4pm-6:30pm. 500ptas. Claustro 100ptas.) The **Basílica de San Isidoro,** dedicated in the 11th century to San Isidoro de Sevilla, houses the bodies of countless royals in the impressive *Panteón Real.* From Pl. Santo Domingo, walk down C. Ramón y Cajal. (Open July-Aug. M-Sa 9am-8pm, Su 9am-2pm; Sept.-June M-Su 9am-1:30pm and 4-7pm, Su 9am-2pm. 400ptas.) In the "early" evening, the area around **Pl. San Martín** sweats with bars, discos, and techno-pop. After 2am, the crowds stagger to the discos and bars of **C. Lancia** and **C. Conde de Guillén. Fiestas** commemorating St. John and St. Peter take place June 21-30, as does a *corrida de toros* (bullfight).

Trains (☎987 27 02 02) run from Av. Astorga 2 to Madrid (4½hr., 8 per day, 3380ptas) and La Coruña (4½-7hr., 3 per day, 3900ptas). **Buses** (☎987 21 10 00) leave from Po. Ingeniero Saenz de Miera for Madrid (4½hr., 8-12 per day, 2665ptas). Go right from the train station (or left from the bus station) and follow Av. de Palencia, which crosses the river to Pl. Guzmán el Bueno, becomes Av. de Ordoño II, and leads to the cathedral and the adjacent **tourist office,** Pl. Regla 3. (☎987 23 70 82; fax 987 27 33 91. Open M-F 9am-2pm and 5-7:30pm, Sa-Su 10am-2pm and 4:30-8:30pm.) The friendly proprietors at **Hostal Oviedo,** Av. Roma 26, 2nd fl., off Pl. Guzmán el Bueno, offer huge rooms. (☎987 22 22 36. Singles 2000ptas; doubles 3500ptas; triples 5500ptas.) Nearby is **Hostel Orejas,** Av. Roma, 26, 2nd fl. This hostel is pricey, but has cable TV and free Internet access. (☎987 25 29 09. Breakfast included. 5500ptas; doubles 6500ptas.) Pick up **groceries** at **Día Auto Servicion,** in Pl. Picara Justina (open M-Sa 9:30am-2:15pm and 5-8:15pm), or eat a meal for 900-950ptas at **Calle Ancha,** on C. Ancha, 11, between C. General Mola and C. Conde Luna (open daily noon-4pm and 9:15pm-midnight, F-Sa 9:15pm-3:30am). **Postal code:** 24071.

EXCURSION FROM LEÓN: ASTORGA. Astorga's fanciful **Palacio Episcopal,** designed by Antoni Gaudí in the late 19th century, now houses the **Museo de los Caminos.** (Open daily June-Sept. 10am-2pm and 4-8pm; Oct.-May 11am-2pm and 3:30-6:30pm. 500ptas.) Opposite the *palacio* is Astorga's cathedral and museum with a detailed 18th-century facade. (Open daily June-Sept. 9:30-10:30am and 5-6:30pm; Oct.-May 9:30am-10:30am and 4:30-6pm. Free.) **Trains** run from León (45min., 8 per day, 400ptas). **Buses** are more frequent (40min., 16 per day, 405ptas).

SPAIN

EXTREMADURA

In a land of harsh beauty and cruel extremes, arid plains bake under an intense summer sun, relieved only by scattered patches of glowing sunflowers. These lands hardened New World conquistadors such as Hernán Cortés and Francisco Pizarro.

TRUJILLO

Trujillo (pop. 10,000) is an unspoiled joy dotted with medieval palaces, Roman ruins, Arabic fortresses, and churches of all eras (open daily 9am-2pm and 4:30-7pm; 200ptas each or 800ptas for all). Its most impressive monument is its highest: the **10th-century Moorish castle** provides a panoramic view of Extremadura from its hilltop position. Twentieth-century residents take pride in the well-preserved beauty of their churches, palace, and castle, adorning them with lovely gardens and flowering vines. Cheese-makers and connoisseurs fill the Pl. Mayor each May to celebrate the **Feria Nacional del Queso**. A short bus ride away, **Mérida** ("little Rome"; pop. 60,000) has the most Roman ruins in Spain and hosts some of Europe's finest classical and modern theater and dance during the **Festival de Teatro Clásico.**

Buses run from Madrid (2½hrs., 10 per day, round-trip 3665ptas) and Cáceres (45min., 6-10 per day, 485ptas). To get to the Pl. Mayor (15min.), turn left as you exit the station (up C. de las Cruces), right on C. de la Encarnación, following signs to the tourist office, then left on C. Chica; turn left on C. Guia and right on C. Burgos, continuing onto the Plaza. The **tourist office,** across the Plaza, posts info in its windows when closed. (☎927 32 26 77. Open daily 10am-2pm and 4-8pm. English spoken.) The **Pensión Boni,** C. Mingo de Ramos, 11, off Pl. Mayor to the right of the church, offers airy patio rooms, floor-to-ceiling windows, and a comfy TV lounge. (☎927 32 16 04. Singles 2000ptas; doubles 3000ptas, with bath 4500ptas; luxury triple with full bath and A/C 7500ptas.) Grab a shaded table in the interior garden of **Meson Alberca,** C. Victoria, 8. Enjoy the three-course menu (1650ptas), featuring dishes like *migas* and gazpacho, in this tourist-free sanctum of the old city. (☎927 32 22 32. Open Su-Tu and Th-Sa 11am-midnight.) **Postal code:** 10200.

SPAIN

SOUTHERN SPAIN (ANDALUCÍA)

Andalucía is all that you expect Spain to be—white-washed villages and streets lined with orange trees, olive groves, flamenco shows, bullfighting, and tall pitchers of *sangria.* The Moors arrived in AD 711 and bequeathed the region with far more than the flamenco music and gypsy ballads proverbially associated with southern Spain by sparking the European Renaissance and reintroducing the wisdom of Classical Greece and the Near East. Under their rule, Sevilla and Granada reached the pinnacle of Islamic arts, and Córdoba matured into the most culturally influential Islamic city. The dark legacy of Andalucía is its failure to progress economically; stagnant industrialization and severe drought have mired the region in indefinite recession. Still, warm-hearted residents retain an unshakable faith in the good life—good food, good drink, and spirited company.

FERRIES TO MOROCCO

Ferries hop the Straits of Gibraltar from **Gibraltar** and **Algeciras.** From Gibraltar, **Tourafrica Int. Ltd.,** 2a Main St. (☎776 66; fax 767 54), sails to **Tangier** (3 per week; UK£20, round-trip UK£30). From Algeciras, boats go in summer to **Ceuta** (1½hr., 24-28 per day, 2890-3095ptas) and **Tangier** (2½hr.; 12 per day; 3500ptas per person, 20% off with Eurail). Service is limited in winter and is not offered during bad weather.

AT&T Direct® Service

The easy way to call home from anywhere.

AT&T Access Numbers

Austria ● 0800-200-288	France........0800-99-00-11
Belarus × ....8◆800-101	Gambia ● 00111
Belgium ● 0-800-100-10	Germany 0800-2255-288
Bosnia ▲ 00-800-0010	Ghana 0191
Bulgaria ▲ 00-800-0010	Gibraltar 8800
Cyprus ● 080-900-10	Greece ● 00-800-1311
Czech Rep. ▲00-42-000-101	Hungary ● 06-800-01111
Denmark 8001-0010	Iceland ● 800-9001
Egypt ● (Cairo) ‡....510-0200	Ireland ✓......1-800-550-000
Finland ● 0800-110-015	Israel 1-800-94-94-949

Italy●	**172-1011**	**Russia (Moscow)▸▲●**	**755-5042**
Luxembourg✚	**800-2-0111**	**(St. Petersbg.)▸▲●**	**325-5042**
Macedonia●	**99-800-4288**	**Slovakia▲**	**00-42-100-101**
Malta	0800-890-110	**South Africa**	**0800-99-0123**
Monaco●	**800-90-288**	**Spain**	**900-99-00-11**
Morocco	002-11-0011	**Sweden**	**020-799-111**
Netherlands●	**0800-022-9111**	**Switzerland●**	**0800-89-0011**
Norway	**800-190-11**	**Turkey●**	**00-800-12277**
Poland▲●	**00-800-111-1111**	**Ukraine▲**	**8◆100-11**
Portugal▲	**800-800-128**	U.A. Emirates●	800-121
Romania●	**01-800-4288**	**U.K.**	**0800-89-0011**

FOR EASY CALLING WORLDWIDE

1. Just dial the AT&T Access Number for the country you are calling from. *2.* Dial the phone number you're calling. *3.* Dial your card number.

For access numbers not listed ask any operator for **AT&T Direct®** Service.
In the U.S. call 1-800-331-1140 for a wallet guide listing all worldwide AT&T Access Numbers.
Visit our Web site at: **www.att.com/traveler**
Bold-faced countries permit country-to-country calling outside the U.S.

- ● Public phones require coin or card deposit to place call.
- ▲ May not be available from every phone/payphone.
- ✚ Public phones and select hotels.
- ◆ Await second dial tone.
- ▸ Additional charges apply when calling from outside the city.
- † Outside of Cairo, dial "02" first.
- ✖ Not available from public phones or all areas.
- ✔ Use U.K. access number in N. Ireland.

When placing an international call ***from*** the U.S., dial 1 800 CALL ATT.

EMEA ©8/00 AT&T

CÓRDOBA

Nowhere else do the remnants of Spain's ancient Islamic, Jewish, and Catholic heritage so visibly intermingle, a legacy reflected in Córdoba's unique art and architecture. Today, springtime festivals, flower-filled patios, and a busy nightlife still make Córdoba (pop. 315,000) one of Spain's most beloved cities.

GETTING THERE AND GETTING AROUND

Trains: (☎957 40 02 02), on Av. de América. To: **Sevilla** (45min., 18 per day, 2300ptas); **Madrid** (2-6hr., 32 per day, 3700-6100ptas); **Málaga** (2¼-3hr., 18 per day, 1650-3000ptas); **Cádiz** (2¾-4hr., 7 per day, 2370-3700ptas); **Granada** (4½hr., 3 per day, 2130-2785ptas); **Algeciras** (4-5½hr., 3 per day, 2800-3400ptas); and **Barcelona** (10-11hr., 7 per day, 6100-8400ptas). Student discounts for all fares. For international tickets, contact **RENFE,** Ronda de los Tejares 10 (☎957 49 02 02).

Buses: Estación de Autobuses, Glorieta de las Tres Culturas, s/n, across from the train station (☎957 40 40 40; fax 957 40 44 15). **Alsina Graells Sur** (☎957 40 40 40; tickets 957 27 81 00) covers most of Andalucía. To: **Sevilla** (2hr., 10-13 per day, 1200ptas); **Granada** (3hr., 8 per day, 1635-1810ptas); **Málaga** (3-3½hr., 5 per day, 1540ptas); and **Algeciras** (5hr., 2 per day, 2805ptas). **Bacoma** (☎957 45 65 14) runs daily to **Barcelona** (10hr., 1 per day, 8475ptas). **Socibus** (☎902 22 92 92) sends exceptionally cheap buses to **Madrid** (4½hr., 7 per day, 1600ptas) and departs from C. de los Sastres in front of Hotel Melía. **Empresa Rafael Ramírez** (☎957 42 21 77) runs buses to nearby towns and camping sites.

ORIENTATION AND PRACTICAL INFORMATION

The modern and commercial northern half of Córdoba extends from the train station on **Avenida de América** southeast to **Plaza de las Tendillas,** the city center. From the train station, walk down Av. de America, turn right on Av. Cervantes, left on C. Concepción, and continue straight into the plaza. From the bus station on C. Diego Serrano, exit left, make an immediate left, head right on Av. Medina Azahara, go through the park, go into Pl. A Grilo, and continue down C. Concepción; or take bus #3 from the front of the bus station to Pl. Tendillas. The medieval, more touristed part of Córdoba is the disorienting **Judería** (old Jewish quarter), extending from Pl. Tendillas past the **Mezquita** and **Alcázar** to the banks of the Río Guadalquivir.

Tourist Offices: Tourist Office of Andalucía, C. Torrijos 10 (☎957 47 12 35), in the Junta de Andalucía, on the west side of the Mezquita. From the train station, take bus #3 along the river until the stone arch on the right, then head a block up C. Torrijos. English-speaking staff with good, free maps of the monument section and info on all of Andalucía. Open May-Sept. M-F 9:30am-8pm, Sa 10am-7pm, Su 10am-2pm; Oct.-Apr. M-Sa 9:30am-6pm, Su 10am-2pm. **Oficina Municipal de Turismo y Congresos** (☎957 20 05 22), on Pl. Judá Leví, next to the youth hostel, has Córdoba-specific info. Open June-Sept. M-Sa 8:30am-2:30pm.

Currency Exchange: Banco Central Hispano (☎957 47 42 67), Pl. Tendillas, charges no commission. Open June-Aug. M-F 8:30am-2:30pm; Sept.-May M-F 8:30am-2:30pm, Sa 9am-1pm. Banks and ATMs dot Pl. Tendillas.

Luggage Storage: Lockers at the train and bus stations (300-600ptas). Open 24hr.

Emergency: ☎091 or 092. **Police:** ☎957 47 75 00, on Av. de Medina Azaharah, by the main bus station. **Ambulance:** ☎29 55 70. **Fire:** ☎080.

Medical Assistance: Red Cross Hospital (☎957 42 06 66; emergencies 22 22 22), on Pl. Victoria. English spoken. The Pl. Tendillas **pharmacy** has a list of night pharmacies.

Internet Access: El Navegante Café Internet, C. Llanos del Pretorio 1, at the intersection of Av. América and Paso del Brillante. 300ptas per 30min. 500ptas per hr. Open daily 8am-4pm and 5pm-3am.

Post Office: C. Cruz Conde 15 (☎902 19 71 97), just north of Pl. Tendillas. Open M-F 8:30am-8:30pm, Sa 9:30am-2pm. Address mail to be held: First Name SURNAME, *Lista de Correos*, C. Cruz Conde 15, **14070** Córdoba, Spain.

ACCOMMODATIONS AND CAMPING

Most accommodations cluster near the train station, around the Judería, and off Pl. Tendillas. Call up to several months ahead during *Semana Santa* and summer.

Residencia Juvenil Córdoba (HI), (☎957 29 01 66; fax 29 05 00), on Pl. Juda Levi, 2min. west of the Mezquita, in the Judería. The best place to stay in Córdoba. Breakfast included. Reception 24hr. Check-in 1pm. Check-out 10am. Reservations recommended. 2140ptas; under 26 1605ptas; nonmembers add 300ptas.

Hostal La Fuente, C. San Fernando 51 (☎957 48 78 27). From the Mezquita, follow C. Corregidor Luis de la Cerda east to C. San Fernando. Relax in the traditional bar or courtyard. All rooms with bath. Singles 3000ptas; doubles 4000-5000ptas.

Hostal Deanes, C. Deanes 6 (☎957 29 37 44). From the northeast corner of the Mezquita, take C. Cardenal Herrero and turn right onto C. Romero (which becomes C. Deanes). Perfectly situated. No reservations. Doubles 4000ptas, with bath 5000ptas.

Hostal-Residencia Séneca, C. Conde y Luque, 7 (☎/fax 957 47 32 34), 2 blocks from the Mezquita; follow C. Céspedes. Impeccably maintained by energetic owners. Reserve 1-2 months ahead. Breakfast included. 1200ptas extra for A/C, all other rooms have fans. Singles 2300-4750ptas; doubles 4300-5900ptas; triples 6150-6600ptas.

Hostal Maestre, C. Romero Barros, 4-5 (☎957 47 53 95), off C. de San Fernando. All rooms have private bathrooms. A/C 500ptas. Singles 2500-2850ptas; doubles 4000-5000ptas; triples 5000-6500ptas. 10% discount for *Let's Go* readers and groups.

Hostal La Calleja, Calleja de Rufino Blanco y Sanchez, 6 (☎/fax 957 48 66 06), at the intersection of C. Calereros and C. Cardenal Gonzalez. Spacious rooms, bathrooms and private patios. All rooms have TVs; some have A/C. Reception 24hr. Single 2700ptas; double 4200ptas, with bath 4800ptas; triple with bath 6000ptas.

Camping Municipal, Av. Brillante, 50 (☎957 28 21 65). From the train station, turn left on Av. América, left on Av. Brillante, and walk uphill for 20min. Alternatively, take bus #10 or 11 from Av. Cervantes near the station. Pool, currency exchange, supermarket, restaurant, free showers, and laundry service. Camping equipment for rent. Wheelchair accessible. Individual tent 400 ptas, family tent 560ptas.

FOOD

Walk five minutes from the Mezquita area in any direction to find reasonably priced specialties—like gazpacho, *salmorejo* (a gazpacho-like cream soup topped with hard-boiled eggs and ham), and *rabo de toro* (bull's tail simmered in tomato sauce). Try the small restaurants on **C. Doctor Fleming,** or the cheaper eateries in **Barrio Cruz Conde,** around **Av. Menéndez Pidal** and **Pl. Tendillas.** Stock up at **Supermarket Champion,** on C. Jesús María, just south of Pl. Tendillas. (Open M-Sa 9:15am-9:15pm.)

El Pincantón, C. Fernández Ruano 19. From the northwest corner of the Mezquita, walk up Romero and turn left on Fernández. Take ordinary tapas, pour on *salsa picante*, and stick it in a roll for lunch (150-300ptas). Open daily 10am-3pm and 8pm-midnight.

Taberna Santa Clara, C. Osio, 2. From the east side of the Mezquita, take C. Martinez Rucker and turn left. Spacious patio dining and exquisite meals. Entrees 800-1800ptas, salads 650ptas. Open Th-Tu 12am-4pm and 7-11pm.

Sociedad de Plateros, C. San Francisco, 6, between C. San Fernando and Pl. Potro. A Córdoba mainstay since 1872. Tapas 200ptas, *raciones*, and *media raciones* 400-1000ptas. Open summer M-Sa; winter Tu-Su. Meals served 1-4pm and 8pm-midnight.

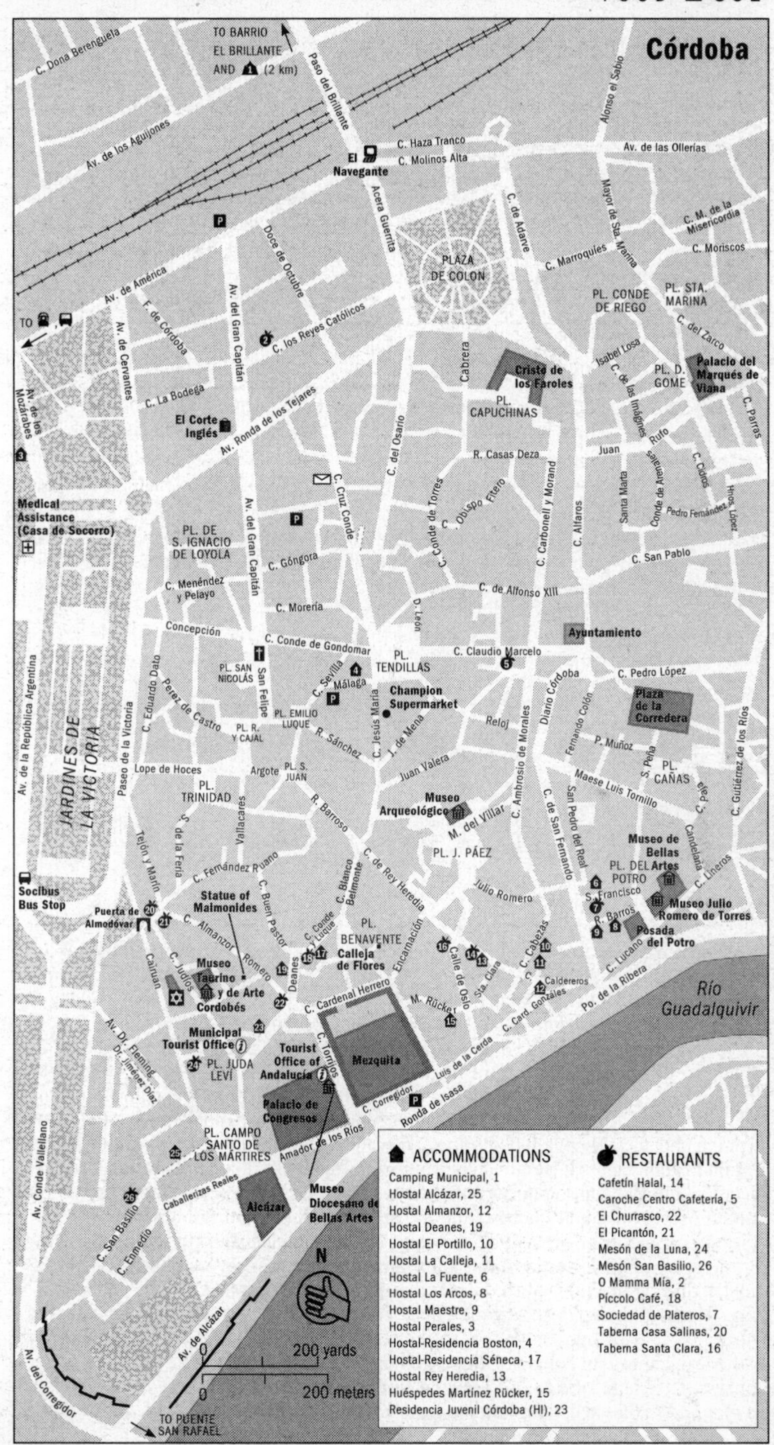

Córdoba
TO BARRIO EL BRILLANTE AND (2 km)
C. Dona Berenguela
Av. de los Aguijones
Paso del Brillante
El Navegante
C. Haza Tranco
C. Molinos Alta
Av. de las Ollerías
Alonso el Sabio
Acera Guerrita
C. de Adarve
Mayor de Sta. Marina
C. M. de la Misericordia
C. Moriscos
C. Marroquíes
PLAZA DE COLON
Doce de Octubre
Av. de América
TO
F. de Córdoba
Av. de Cervantes
Av. del Gran Capitán
C. los Reyes Católicos
PL. CONDE DE RIEGO
PL. STA. MARINA
C. del Zarco
Isabel Losa
Palacio del Marqués de Viana
PL. D. GOME
C. de las Imágenes
Cristo de los Faroles
Cabrera
PL. CAPUCHINAS
C. Parras
C. La Bodega
El Corte Inglés
Av. Ronda de los Tejares
Av. de los Mozárabes
C. del Osario
R. Casas Deza
Juan Rufo
C. Cidros
Conde de Arenales
Santa Marta
Medical Assistance (Casa de Socorro)
C. Cruz Conde
C. Conde de Torres
C. Obispo Fitero
C. Carbonell y Morand
C. Alfaros
Pedro Fernández
Hnos. López
PL. DE S. IGNACIO DE LOYOLA
C. Góngora
C. San Pablo
C. Menéndez y Pelayo
C. de Alfonso XIII
C. Morería
D. León
Concepción
C. Conde de Gondomar
Ayuntamiento
PL. TENDILLAS
C. Claudio Marcelo
Av. de la República Argentina
PL. SAN NICOLÁS
San Felipe
C. Sevilla
Málaga
Champion Supermarket
C. Pedro López
C. Eduardo Dato
Perez de Castro
Paseo de la Victoria
PL. EMILIO LUQUE
C. Jesús María
Diario Córdoba
Plaza de la Corredera
JARDINES DE LA VICTORIA
PL. R. Y CAJAL
R. Sánchez
J. de Mena
Reloj
Fernando Colón
P. Muñoz
C. Gutiérrez de los Ríos
Lope de Hoces
Argote
PL. S. JUAN
Juan Valera
S. Pedro
PL. CAÑAS
PL. TRINIDAD
R. Barroso
Museo Arqueológico
C. Ambrosio de Morales
Maese Luis Tornillo
C. Peña
Vallacares
S. de la Feria
M. del Villar
C. de San Fernando
San Pedro del Real
Tejón y Marín
PL. J. PÁEZ
Museo de Bellas Artes
Candelaria
C. Fernández Ruano
C. Blanco Belmonte
C. de Rey Heredia
PL. DEL POTRO
C. Lineros
Socibus Bus Stop
Statue of Maimonides
C. Buen Pastor
Julio Romero
S. Francisco
Museo Julio Romero de Torres
Puerta de Almodóvar
C. Almanzor
C. Conde y Luque
PL. BENAVENTE
Encarnación
R. Barros
Posada del Potro
Calleja de Flores
Calle de Oslo
C. Cabezas
C. Lucano
C. Judíos
Romero
Deanes
Sta. Clara
Caldereros
Río Guadalquivir
Cairuan
Museo Taurino y de Arte Cordobés
C. Cardenal Herrero
M. Rücker
C. Card. Gonzáles
Po. de la Ribera
Av. Dr. Fleming
Dr. Jiménez Díaz
Municipal Tourist Office
Tourist Office of Andalucía
C. Torrijos
Mezquita
Luis de la Cerda
PL. JUDA LEVÍ
Palacio de Congresos
C. Corregidor
Ronda de Isasa
PL. CAMPO SANTO DE LOS MÁRTIRES
Amador de los Ríos
Av. Conde Vallellano
Caballerizas Reales
Alcázar
Museo Diocesano de Bellas Artes
C. San Basilio
C. Enmedio
N
Av. de Alcázar
Av. del Corregidor
0
200 yards
0
200 meters
TO PUENTE SAN RAFAEL
ACCOMMODATIONS
Camping Municipal, 1
Hostal Alcázar, 25
Hostal Almanzor, 12
Hostal Deanes, 19
Hostal El Portillo, 10
Hostal La Calleja, 11
Hostal La Fuente, 6
Hostal Los Arcos, 8
Hostal Maestre, 9
Hostal Perales, 3
Hostal-Residencia Boston, 4
Hostal-Residencia Séneca, 17
Hostal Rey Heredia, 13
Huéspedes Martínez Rücker, 15
Residencia Juvenil Córdoba (HI), 23
RESTAURANTS
Cafetín Halal, 14
Caroche Centro Cafetería, 5
El Churrasco, 22
El Picantón, 21
Mesón de la Luna, 24
Mesón San Basilio, 26
O Mamma Mía, 2
Píccolo Café, 18
Sociedad de Plateros, 7
Taberna Casa Salinas, 20
Taberna Santa Clara, 16

SIGHTS

Considered the most important Islamic monument in the Western world, Córdoba's famous **Mezquita** was built in AD 784 to surpass all other mosques in grandeur. Visitors enter through the **Patio de los Naranjos,** an arcaded courtyard featuring carefully spaced orange trees and fountains; inside, 850 pink and blue marble, alabaster, and stone columns support hundreds of two-tiered, red-and-white striped arches. At the far end of the Mezquita lies the **Capilla Villaviciosa,** which had a strong influence on Spanish architecture. In the center, intricate marble Byzantine mosaics—a gift from Emperor Constantine VII—shimmer across the arches of the **Mihrab,** the dome where the Muslims guarded the Quran. Although the town rallied violently against the proposed erection of a **cathedral** in the center of the mosque after the Christians conquered Córdoba in 1236, the towering **Crucero** (transept) and **Coro** (choir dome) were soon built. (Open daily Apr.-June 10am-7:30pm; July-Oct. 10am-7pm; Nov.-Mar. 10am-6pm. 900ptas, ages 8-13 450ptas. Same ticket valid for **Museo Diocesano de Bellas Artes.** (Open June-Sept. M-F 9:30am-3pm, Sa 9:30am-1:30pm; Oct.-Mar. M-F 9:30am-1:30pm and 3:30-5:30pm, Sa 9:30am-1:30pm. 150ptas)

The **Judería** (Jewish quarter) is the historic area northwest of the Mezquita. Downhill from the Moorish arch, the small **Sinagoga,** on C. Judíos, is one of Spain's few remaining synagogues, a solemn reminder of the 1492 expulsion of the Jews. (Open Tu-Sa 10am-2pm and 3:30-5:30pm, Su 10am-1:30pm. Free.) Just to the south along the river is the **Alcázar,** constructed for Catholic monarchs in 1328 during the conquest of Granada. Ferdinand and Isabella bade Columbus adios here, and the building served as Inquisition headquarters (1490-1821). (Open May-Sept. Tu-Sa 10am-2pm and 6-8pm, Su 9:30am-3pm; Oct.-Apr. Tu-Sa 10am-2pm and 4:30-6:30pm, Su 9:30am-3pm. Gardens open July-Aug. 8pm-midnight. 300ptas, students 150ptas; F free.) The **Museo Taurino y de Arte Cordobés,** on Pl. Maimonides, highlights the history and lore of the bullfight. (Open May-Sept. Tu-Sa 10am-2pm and 6-8pm, Su 9:30am-3pm; Oct.-Apr. Tu-Sa 10am-2pm and 5-7pm, Su 9:30am-3pm. 450ptas, students 225ptas; F free.) There is a **combined ticket** for the Alcázar, Museo Taurino y de Arte Cordobés, and the **Museo Julio Romero,** which displays Romero's sensual portraits of Córdoban women. (1075ptas, students 550ptas.)

ENTERTAINMENT

Hordes of tourists flock to see the flamenco dancers at the **Tablao Cardenal,** C. Torrijos 10, facing the Mezquita. (☎957 48 33 20. 2800ptas includes 1 drink. Shows Tu-Sa 10:30pm.) The price is high, but a bargain compared to Sevilla and Madrid standards. Or check out **La Bolería,** C. Pedro López 3. (☎957 48 38 39. 1500ptas includes 1 drink. Shows daily at 10:30pm.) Starting the first weekend in June, the **Barrio Brillante,** uphill from Av. de América, is the place to be. Well-dressed young Córdobeses walk the streets, hopping from one packed outdoor bar to another until reaching a dance club. Take bus #10 from RENFE until 11pm; a cab should cost 500-900ptas. Or walk up Av. Brillante to where C. Poeta Emilia Prados meets C. Poeta Juan Ramon Jiménez. Go through **Cafetería Terra** to discover a massive open-air patio where myriad **bars** converge. From there, pubs and clubs, including **El Cachao,** line **Av. Brillante.** There is a **taxi stand** by the gas station at the corner of Av. Brillante and C. Las Acacias. During the cooler winter months, nightlife shifts to the pubs surrounding the Universidad de Córdoba, mostly on C. Antonio Maura and C. Camino de los Sastres. Of Córdoba's festivals, floats, and parades, **Semana Santa,** in early April, is the most extravagant. During the **Festival de los Patios,** in the first two weeks of May, the city erupts with classical music concerts, flamenco dances, and a city-wide decorated patio contest. Late May brings the **Feria de Nuestra Señora de la Salud** *(La Feria),* a week of colorful garb, live dancing, and nonstop drinking.

EXCURSION FROM CÓRDOBA: MADINAT AL-ZAHRA

Built in the **Sierra Morena** mountain range by Abderramán III for his favorite wife, Azahara, this 10th-century medina was considered one of the greatest palaces of its time. The site, long thought to be mythical, was discovered in the mid-19th century, excavated in the early 20th century, and today is one of Spain's most impressive archaeological finds. (☎957 32 91 30. Open May-Sept. Tu-Sa 10am-2pm and 6-8:30pm, Su 10am-2pm; Oct.-Apr. Tu-Sa 10am-2pm and 4-6:30pm, Su 10am-2pm. 250ptas, EU citizens free.) **Córdoba Vision** offers a 2½-hour guided visit to the site in English. (☎957 23 17 34. 2500ptas.) Reaching Madinat Al-Zahra takes some effort if you don't go with an organized tour. The **0-1 bus** leaves every hour from Av. República Argentina in Córdoba for Cruce Medina Azahara; from there walk 45min. to the palace. (☎957 25 57 00, or ask at the tourist office. 115ptas.)

SEVILLA ☎954

Site of a Roman acropolis, capital of the Moorish empire, focal point of the Spanish Renaissance, and guardian angel of traditional Andalusian culture, Sevilla has yet to disappoint visitors. Jean Cocteau included it with Venice and Peking in his trio of magical cities, and the city has inspired operas by Bizet, Mozart, and Rossini. The 16th-century maxim *"Qui non ha visto Sevilla non ha visto maravilla"*—one who has not seen Sevilla has not seen a marvel—remains true today.

GETTING THERE AND GETTING AROUND

Flights: Aeropuerto San Pablo (☎44 90 00), 12km from town on Ctra. Madrid. A taxi from the center of town costs about 2000ptas. **Los Amarillos** (☎98 91 84) runs a bus there from the Hotel Alfonso XIII in the Pta. Jerez (every 30-40min., 350ptas).

Trains: Estación Santa Justa, on Av. Kansas City (☎41 41 11). Buses C1 and C2 run from just left of the station as you exit. **RENFE,** C. Zaragoza 29 (☎54 02 02), is near Pl. Nueva. Open M-F 9am-1:15pm and 4-7pm. To: **Córdoba** (45min.-1½hr., 23 per day, 1090-2800ptas); **Madrid** (2½hr., 20 per day, 8400-9900ptas); **Málaga** (2½hr., 5 per day, 2130ptas); **Granada** (3hr., 5 per day, 2660ptas); **Valencia** (8½hr., 4 per day, 5300ptas); and **Barcelona** (12hr., 6 per day, 6400ptas).

Buses: There are two bus stations; many companies run out of each one.

Prado de San Sebastián (☎41 71 11), on C. Manuel Vazquez Sagastizabal, serve mainly Andalucía. **Transportes Alsina Graells** (☎41 88 11) goes to: **Córdoba** (2hr., 10-13 per day, 1225ptas); **Málaga** (2½hr., 10-12 per day, 1850ptas); and **Granada** (3hr., 9 per day, 2400ptas). **Transportes Comes** (☎41 68 58) runs to **Cádiz** (1½hr., 12 per day, 1385ptas). **Los Amarillos** (☎98 91 84) serves **Marbella** (3hr., 1-2 per day, 975ptas). **Enatcar-Barcelona** (☎(902) 42 22 42) heads to **Valencia** (10hr., 2 per day, 6485ptas) and **Barcelona** (16hr., 1 per day, 9755ptas).

The newer **Plaza de Armas** (☎90 77 37), on the river bank at Puente del Cachorro, serves destinations beyond Spain. Buses C1, C2, C3, and C4 stop nearby. **Socibus** (☎90 11 60) runs to **Madrid** (6hr., 15 per day, 2745ptas) and **Lagos** (6hr., 1 per day, 2590ptas). **Damas** (☎90 80 40) serves **Lisbon** (9hr., 1 per day, 4800ptas).

Public Transportation: Buses run every 10min. 6am-11:15pm and converge on Pl. Nueva, Pl. Encarnación, and in front of the cathedral on Av. Constitución. Limited **night service** departs from Pl. Nueva (every hr. midnight-2am). **Single-ride** 125ptas, **bonobús** (10 rides with transfers) 650ptas. Buses C3 and C4 circle the center; #34 hits the youth hostel, university, cathedral, and Pl. Nueva.

ORIENTATION AND PRACTICAL INFORMATION

Most of the city, including the old **Barrio de Santa Cruz,** lies on the east bank of the **Río Guadalquivir.** The historic **Barrio de Triana,** the **Barrio de Santa Cecilia,** and the **fairgrounds** occupy the west bank. The **cathedral,** next to Barrio de Santa Cruz, is Sevilla's centerpiece; **Av. de la Constitución** runs alongside it. **El Centro** (downtown), a busy commercial pedestrian zone, lies north of the cathedral starting where Av.

Constitución hits **Plaza Nueva.** To reach El Centro from the **train station,** catch bus #32 to Plaza de la Encarnacíon, north of the cathedral. Walk from the **Prado de San Sebastián bus station;** cross the main road, and head to the right one block past the Jardines de Murillo. C. Santa María La Blanca will be on the left. From Barrio Santa Cruz it is a 10-minute walk along C. Ximénez de Enciso and C. Rodrigo Caro to the cathedral. Bus C4 connects Plaza de Armas to Pr. San Sebastián. To walk to El Centro from the **Pl. Armas bus station** (10min.), walk along the river on the left three blocks and make a right onto C. Alfonso XII.

Tourist Offices: Centro de Información de Sevilla, C. Arjona, 28 (☎50 56 00), huge info source at the Puente Isabel II. Open M-F 9am-9pm, Sa-Su 8:30am-2:30pm. **Junta de Andalucía,** Av. Constitución, 21B (☎22 14 04; fax 22 97 53), near the cathedral.

Consulates: Australia, Federico Rubio, 14 (☎95 422 09 71; fax 95 421 11 45); **UK,** Pl. Nueva, 87 (☎22 88 74; fax 95 421 03 23); **US,** Po. Delicias, 7 (☎23 18 85; fax 23 20 40).

American Express: Pl. Nueva, 7 (☎21 16 17). Holds mail, changes money, yadda yadda yadda. Open M-F 9:30am-1:30pm and 4:30-7:30pm, Sa 10am-1pm.

Luggage Storage: At both **bus stations** and the **train station** (250-500ptas per day).

Laundromat: Lavandería Auto-servicio, C. Castelar, 2. From the cathedral, walk 2 blocks on G. Vinuesa and turn left. 1000ptas. Open M-F 9:30am-1:30pm and 3-8:30pm, Sa-Su 9am-2pm.

Emergency: ☎091 or 092. **Police:** Av. Paseo de las Delicias, 15 (☎61 54 50).

Medical Assistance: Ambulatorio Esperanza Macarena (☎42 01 05). **Hospital Universitario Virgen Macarena** (☎24 81 81), Av. Dr. Fedriani. English spoken.

Internet Access: WORKcenter, C. San Fernando, 1, at the Puerta de Jerez. 100ptas per 10min. Open 24hr.

Post Office: Av. Constitución 32 (☎21 64 76), opposite the cathedral. Open M-F 10am-8:30pm, Sa 9:30am-2pm. Address mail to be held: First Name SURNAME, *Lista de Correos,* Av. Constitución 32, **41080** Sevilla, Spain.

SPAIN

ACCOMMODATIONS AND CAMPING

Rooms vanish and prices soar during *Semana Santa* and the *Feria de Abril;* reserve ahead. The narrow streets east of the cathedral around **C. Santa María la Blanca** are full of cheap, central hostels. Hostels by the **Pl. de Armas** bus station, mostly on C. Gravina, are most convenient to **El Centro** and the lively C. Betis on the west bank of the river. The disorienting array of narrow streets by Pl. de la Encarnación in El Centro hosts fewer hostels.

Hostal Sierpes, C. Corral del Rey, 22 (☎22 49 48), in **Santa Cruz.** Singles 3000-4000ptas, with bath 4000-5000ptas; doubles 4000-6000ptas, 5500-10,000ptas; triples 5500-8000ptas, 7000-14,000ptas.

Hostal Rio Sol, C. Marquéz de Parada, 25 (☎22 90 38), 1 block from **Pl. de Armas** bus station. Newly renovated bathrooms. Single with sink 2000ptas, with bath 3000-4000ptas; doubles with bath 6500ptas; triples with bath 9000ptas.

Pensión Vergara, C. Ximénez de Enciso, 11, 2nd fl. (☎21 56 68), at C. Mesón del Moro in **Santa Cruz.** Impeccably clean 15th-century house. 2500ptas per person.

Hostal Sánchez Sabariego, C. Corral del Rey, 23 (☎21 44 70), in **Santa Cruz.** Follow C. Argote de Molina from the right of the cathedral; next to Hostal Sierpes. Friendly atmosphere and antique furniture. Singles 4000ptas; doubles 8000ptas; triples 9000ptas.

Hostal Lis, C. Escarpín 10 (☎21 30 88), on an alley near Pl. Encarnación in **El Centro.** Sevillian tile motif. Singles 3000ptas; doubles 6000-7000ptas; triples 9000ptas.

Hostal Paris, C. San Pedro Mártir, 14 (☎22 98 61 or 21 96 45), off C. Gravina near **Pl. de Armas.** Classy. Singles 3500ptas; doubles 6000ptas. Student discounts.

Hostal Residencia Gala, C. Gravina, 52 (☎21 45 03), by **Pl. de Armas.** Friendly owner. Some windowless rooms; no A/C. Laundry. Singles 3000ptas, with bath 4000ptas; doubles 4500ptas, 6000ptas; triples with bath 7500ptas.

Sevilla Youth Hostel (HI), C. Isaac Peral 2 (☎61 31 50; fax 61 31 58). Bus #34 from Pr. San Sebastián stops behind it after Po. Delicias. Out of the way, but clean. 2140ptas, under 27 1605ptas. Members only; sells HI cards.

Hostal-Residencia Córdoba, C. Farnesio 12 (☎22 74 98), off C. Fabiola in **Santa Cruz.** From the cathedral, head all the way up C. Mateos Gago. Immaculate and spacious, with a beautiful patio. Singles 3500-5000ptas, with shower 4500-7000ptas; doubles 5500-8000ptas, 7000-9500ptas.

Camping Sevilla, Ctra. Madrid-Cádiz, 534 (☎51 43 79), 12km from the city. From Pr. San Sebastián, take bus #70 to "Parque Alcosa" and walk 800m. Showers, market, and pool. 475ptas per person, per car, and per tent; children 375ptas.

FOOD

Sevilla, which claims to be the birthplace of tapas, keeps its cuisine light. Popular venues for *el tapeo* (tapas-barhopping) are **Triana, Barrio Santa Cruz,** and **El Arenal.** Locals imbibe Sevilla's own Cruzcampo beer, a light, smooth pilsner. **Mercado del Arenal,** between C. Almansa and C. Arenal, has meat, produce, and screaming vendors. (Open M-Sa 9am-2pm.) **Grocery** shop at **%Día supermarket,** on C. San Juan de Ávila, near El Corte Inglés. (Open M-F 9:30am-2pm and 6:30-9pm, Sa 9am-1pm.)

Pizzeros Orsini & Angelo, C. Luchana, 2, 2 blocks from Pl. del Salvador in **El Centro.** The aroma of their fresh-baked creations filters out of this tiny pizza joint. Pizzas 400-950ptas, salads 400-700ptas. Open daily 1-4pm and 8pm-1am.

La Vega de Triana, C. Asturias at Pl. San Martín de Porres. Wine barrel tables, friendly service, and top-rate tapas make for a lively meal. Tapas 200-300ptas, raciones 1100-1300ptas. Open daily 11am-midnight.

Restaurante-Bar El Baratillo/Casa Chari, C. Pavia 12, on a tiny street off C. Dos de Mayo in Santa Cruz. Ask in advance for the *tour-de-force:* paella (2500ptas for 2). *Menú* 500ptas. Open M-F 9am-11pm, Sa noon-5pm.

Freiduría Santa Ana, C. Pureza, 61, parallel to C. Betis, 1 block from the river. Both the fresh fried fish and the restaurant itself are local institutions. Free samples ease the wait. Seafood served by the kg. Open Tu-Su 7pm-midnight. Closed Aug.

Café-Bar Campanario, C. Mateos Gago, 8, 1/2 block from the cathedral, on the right. Packed day and night, this place mixes the best jugs of sangría around (1200-1500ptas). Tapas 175-325ptas, raciones 650-1000. Open daily noon-midnight.

Café Cáceres, C. San José, 24. Buffet breakfast Sevilla style. Choose from an impressive spread of cheeses and jams. *Desayuno de la casa* (orange juice, coffee, ham, eggs, toast) 650ptas. Entrees 600-1100ptas. Open daily 7:30am-8pm.

SPAIN

SIGHTS

THE CATHEDRAL. To clear space for Sevilla's most impressive sight, Christians razed an Almohad mosque in 1401, leaving only the **Patio de Los Naranjos** (orange trees) and the famed **La Giralda** minaret. That tower and its siblings in Marrakesh and Rabat are the oldest and largest surviving Almohad minarets. The **cathedral**—the third-largest in the world—took over 100 years to complete and is the largest Gothic edifice ever constructed. The **retablo mayor** (altarpiece) is a golden wall of intricately wrought figurines depicting 36 biblical scenes. Circle the choir to view the **Sepulcro de Cristóbol Colón** (allegedly Columbus' tomb). His coffin-bearers represent the grateful kings of Castilla, León, Aragón, and Navarra. The cathedral's **Sacristía Mayor** museum holds Riberas, Murillos, and a glittering Corpus Christi icon. The neighboring **Sacristía de los Cálices** (or **de los Pintores**) displays minor canvases by Zurbarán and Goya. In the corner of the cathedral are the perfectly oval **cabildo** (chapter house) and the **Sala de Las Columnas.** *(Cathedral complex and Giralda open M-Sa 10:30am-5pm, Su 2-6pm. 700ptas, students 200ptas, under 12 free; Su free.)*

ALCÁZAR. The imposing 9th-century walls of the Alcázar, which faces the cathedral next to Pl. Triunfo, date from the Moorish era—as do several interior spaces, including the exquisitely carved **Patio de las Muñecas** (Patio of the Dolls). Of the later Christian additions to the palace, the most exceptional is the **Patio de las Doncellas** (Maid's Court), with ornate archways and complex tilework. The astonishing golden-domed **Salón de los Embajadores** is where Fernando and Isabel supposedly welcomed Columbus back from America. *(Open Tu-Sa 9:30am-7pm, Su 9:30am-6pm. 700ptas; students, disabled, under 16, and 65+ free. English audio guide 400ptas.)*

PLAZA DE TOROS DE LA REAL MAESTRANZA. The tiled boardwalk leads to Pl. de Toros de la Real Maestranza, a temple of bullfighting. Home to one of the two great bullfighting schools (the other is in Ronda), the plaza fills to capacity for the 13 *corridas* of the *Feria de Abril* as well as weekly fights. The museum inside has costumes, paintings, and antique posters. *(Open on non-bullfight days 9:30am-2pm and 3-7pm, on bullfight days 9:30am-3pm. Tours every 30min., 500ptas.)*

BARRIO DE SANTA CRUZ. King Fernando III forced Jews fleeing Toledo to live in the Barrio de Santa Cruz, now a neighborhood of weaving alleys and courtyards. Beyond C. Lope de Rueda, off C. Ximénez de Enciso, is the **Plaza de Santa Cruz.** South of the plaza are the **Jardines de Murillo,** a shady expanse of shrubbery. Pl. Santa Cruz's church houses the grave of the artist Murillo, who died after falling from a scaffold while painting ceiling frescoes in a Cádiz church. Nearby, **Iglesia de Santa María la Blanca,** built in 1391, features Murillo's *Last Supper*. *(On C. Santa María la Blanca. Open M-Sa 10-11am and 6:30-8pm, Su 9:30am-2pm and 6:30-8pm.)*

LA MACARENA. This area northwest of El Centro is named for the Virgin of Sevilla, not the popular mid-90s dance. A stretch of 12th-century **murallas** (walls) runs between the Pta. Macarena and the Pta. Córdoba on the Ronda de Capuchinos road. At the west end is the **Basílica Macarena,** whose venerated image of *La Virgen de la Macarena* is paraded through town during *Semana Santa*. A **treasury** within glitters with the virgin's jewels and other finery. *(On Pl. San Gil. Open daily 9:30am-1pm and 5-8pm. Basilica free. Treasury 400ptas.)* On the *ruta de los conventos*, **Convento de Santa Paula** includes a church with Gothic, Mudéjar, and Renaissance elements. *(On Pl. Sta. Paula. Open Tu-Su 10:30am-12:30pm and 4:30-6:30pm.)* The **museum** next door has Ribera's *St. Jerome*. *(Open Tu-Su 11am-noon and 4:30-6:30pm.)*

OTHER SIGHTS. Lovely tropical gardens and innumerable courtyards abound in the monstrous **Parque de María Luisa,** southeast of the city center. *(Open daily 8am-10pm.)* Bordering the park, the expansive neighboring **Plaza de España** showcases mosaics. In the Aristocratic Quarter, the 15th-century **Casa de Pilatos** displays Medieval and Renaissance influences. *(Pl. Pilatos. Open 9am-7pm. 1000ptas.)* The **Iglesia de El Salvador** shines with cathedral-like splendor. *(Pl. Salvador, 1 block from C. Sierpes. Open daily 6:30-9pm.)* The **Museo Provincial de Bellas Artes** in El Arenal boasts Spain's finest collection of Sevilla School painters (especially Murillo and Zurbarán), as well as works by foreign masters El Greco and Jan Breughel. *(Pl. Museo 9. Open Tu 3-8pm, W-Sa 9am-8pm, Su 9am-3pm. 250ptas, students and EU citizens free.)* The 12-sided **Torre del Oro** (Gold Tower) houses engravings and drawings of Sevilla's port. *(Open Sept.-July Tu-F 10am-2pm, Sa-Su 11am-2pm. 100ptas. Tu free.)*

ENTERTAINMENT AND NIGHTLIFE

FLAMENCO, BULLFIGHTS, AND FESTIVALS. Get your flamenco fix at **Los Gallos,** Pl. Santa Cruz 11, on the west edge of Barrio Santa Cruz. (Cover and 1 drink 3500ptas. Shows nightly at 9pm and 11:30pm.) The cheapest place to buy **bullfight** tickets is at the ring on Po. Marqués de Contadero; or try the booths on C. Sierpes, C. Velázquez, or Pl. Toros (3000-13,000ptas). Sevilla's world-famous **Semana Santa** (Holy Week) festival, during which penitents in hoods guide candle-lit floats, lasts from Palm Sunday to Good Friday. The last week of April, the city explodes with the **Feria de Abril** (April Fair), which began as a 19th-century popular revolt against foreign influence and continues today as a popular revolt against sobriety, raging through the night with circuses, bullfights, and flamenco shows.

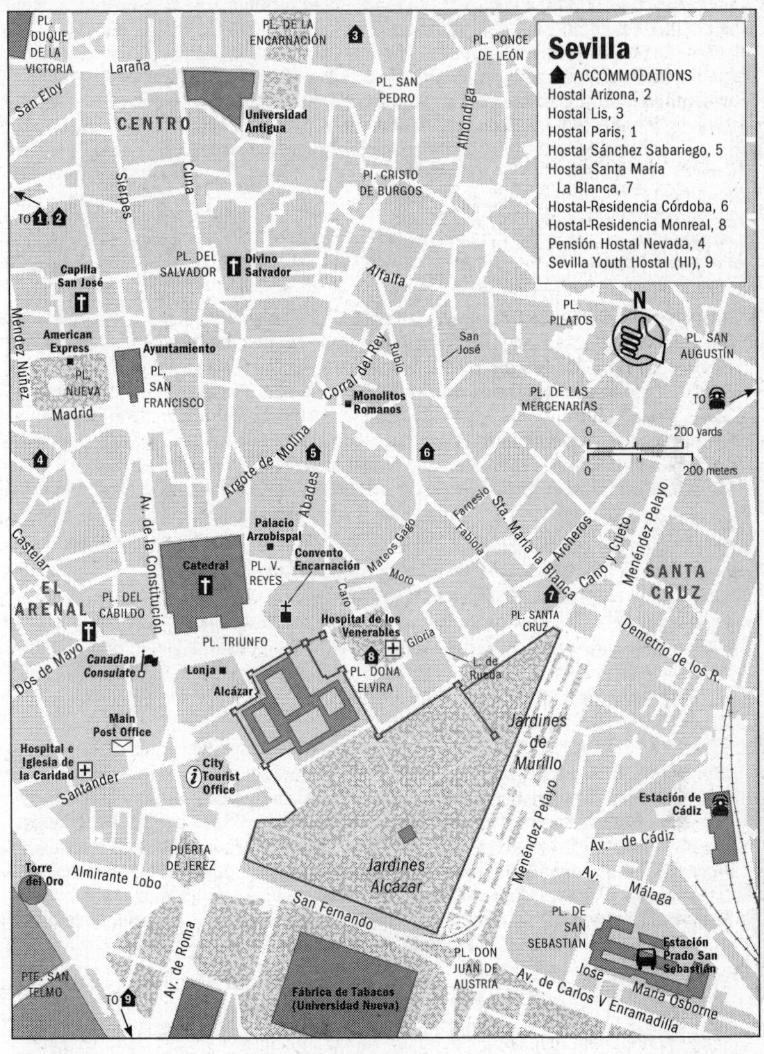

NIGHTLIFE. Sevilla's reputation for gaiety is tried and true—most clubs don't get going until well after midnight, and the real fun often starts after 3am. Popular bars cluster around **Pl. Alfalfa** in El Centro, **C. Mateos Gago** near the cathedral, **C. Adriano** in El Arenal, and **C. Betis** in Triana. **La Carbonería,** C. Levies 18, off C. Santa María La Blanca, in Santa Cruz, has a huge patio and free nightly flamenco. (Open M-Sa 8pm-3:30am, Su 8pm-2:30am.) Throngs of young people start the night at **Capote Bar,** at the Pte. Isabel II, in El Centro. Live music, from pop-rock to Latin, plays all summer. (Open daily 11pm-3am.) Every midnight at **El Tamboril,** Pl. Santa Cruz, the lights go out and an altar to the *Virgen del Rocio* is gloriously lit as the patron saint is serenaded in flamenco style. (Open daily 10pm-dawn.) **La Antigua Bodeguita,** Pl. del Salvador, 6, in El Centro, specializes in beer. (Open daily 12:30-4pm and 8pm-midnight). In Santa Cruz, across from the cathedral, the Irish bartenders at **Flaherty,** C. Alemanes, 7, serve pints for 600ptas. (Open Su-Th 11am-2am, F-Sa until 3am.)

EXCURSIONS FROM SEVILLA

CÁDIZ. Cádiz (pop. 155,000), considered Europe's oldest inhabited city, has a powerful ocean on one side, a placid bay on the other, and a bunch of history in between. The city is legendary for its **Carnaval** festivities (Feb. 22-Mar. 4, 2001), but attracts visitors year-round with golden, pebble-strewn **beaches. Playa de la Caleta** is the most convenient, but better sand awaits in the new city; take bus #1 from Pl. España (115ptas) and get off at Pl. Glorieta Ingeniero (in front of McDonald's) to roast at the squeaky clean **Playa Victoria.** Back in town, the gold-domed, 18th-century **cathedral** is considered the last great cathedral built by colonial riches. From Pl. San Juan de Dios, follow C. Pelota. (Museum open Tu-F 10am-1pm and 4-7pm, Sa 10am-1pm. Cathedral open M-F 5:30-8pm. 500ptas.) RENFE **trains** (☎956 25 43 01) arrive at Pl. Sevilla, off Av. Puerto, from Sevilla (2hr., 12 per day, 1290ptas) and Córdoba (5hr., 10-12 per day, 3900ptas). From the train station, walk past the fountain with the port on your right and look left for **Pl. San Juan de Dios** (the old town center). Transportes Generales Comes **buses** (☎956 22 78 11) arrive at Pl. Hispanidad, 1, from Sevilla (2hr., 11 per day, 1385ptas). From the bus station, walk five minutes down Av. Puerto with the port on your left and Pl. de San Juan de Dios will be after the park on your right, with the **tourist office** at #11. (☎956 24 10 01. Open M-F 9am-2pm and 5-8pm.) Most *hostales* huddle by the harbor, in Pl. San Juan de Dios, and just behind it on C. Marqués de Cádiz. **Hostal Colón** is at C. Marqués de Cádiz, 6. (☎956 28 53 51. Singles 2300ptas; doubles 4000ptas; triples 5000ptas.)

ARCOS DE LA FRONTERA. The most touristed *pueblo blanco* (white village) on *la ruta de los pueblos blancos*, Arcos (pop. 33,000) is a romantic treasure with Roman ruins at every turn. Wander among winding alleys and hanging flowers in the **old quarter,** and marvel at the stunning view from **Pl. Cabildo.** The square houses the **Iglesia de Santa María,** a mix of Baroque, Renaissance, and Gothic styles. From C. Corregidores, Transportes Generales Comes **buses** (☎956 70 20 15) go to: Cádiz (1½hr., 6 per day, 675ptas); Ronda (1¾hr., 4 per day, 950ptas); and Costa del Sol (3-4hr., 1 per day, 1535-2060ptas). Los Amarillos buses (☎956 70 02 57) go to Jerez (15min., 8-18 per day, 300ptas) and Sevilla (2hr., 2 per day, 905ptas). To reach the old quarter from the bus station, exit left, turn left, and continue 20 minutes uphill on C. Muñoz Vásquez as it changes names. A block to the right is the **tourist office,** on Pl. Cabildo. (☎956 70 22 64. Open June-Aug. M-F 10am-2pm and 5:30-7:30pm, Sa 9am-2pm and 5-6:30pm, Su 10:30am-12:30pm; Sept.-May M-F 9am-2pm and 5-7pm, Sa 10am-2pm and 5-6:30pm, Su 10:30am-12:30pm.) The upstairs rooms in **Pensión El Patio,** C. Dean Espinosa, 4, behind Iglesia de Santa María, have their own terraces. (☎956 70 23 02. Doubles 4000ptas, with bath 6000ptas.)

RONDA. The stomach-churning ascent is most people's first impression of Ronda (pop. 38,000), the birthplace of bullfighting; it's the effect on their hearts that's not soon forgotten. Divided by a 100m gorge, the city has long attracted artistic types—German poet Rainer Maria Rilke wrote his *Spanish Elegies* here and Orson Welles had his ashes buried on a bull farm outside of town. Bullfighting aficionados charge over to Ronda's **Plaza de Toros,** Spain's oldest bullring (est. 1785) and cradle of the modern *corrida*. The **Museo Taurino** inside is filled with interesting factoids. (Open daily June-Sept. 10am-8pm; Oct.-May 10am-6pm. 500ptas.) The precipitous gorge, carved by the Río Guadalevín, dips below the **Puente Nuevo,** opposite Pl. España. **Trains** (☎95 287 16 73), Av. Alférez Provisional, near Av. Andalucía, run to Algeciras (2hr., 6 per day, 910ptas). Change at Bobadilla for: Málaga (2hr., 6 per day, 1225ptas); Granada (3hr., 3 per day, 1800ptas); and Sevilla (3hr., 2 per day, 2955ptas). **Buses** (☎95 218 70 61) go from Pl. Concepción García Redondo, 2, near Av. Andalucía, to: Marbella (1½hr., 8 per day, 605ptas); Málaga (2½hr., 8 per day, 1120ptas); Sevilla (2½hr., 5 per day, 1335ptas); and Cádiz (4hr., 5 per day, 1610ptas). To reach the town center from the **train station,** turn right on Av. Andalucía and follow it through Pl. Merced past the **bus station** (it becomes C. San José) until it ends.

Take a left on C. Jerez and follow it past the lush park and Pl. Toros to **Plaza de España** and the new bridge. The **tourist office** is at Pl. España, 1. (☎95 287 12 72. Open M-F 9am-2pm and 4-7pm, Sa-Su 10am-3pm.) **Hostal Ronda Sol,** C. Almendra, 11, is a brown house with brown bed covers and a brown chihuahua. (☎95 287 44 97. Singles 1700ptas; doubles 2800ptas; triples 4000ptas.) Excellent restaurants line the area around **Pl. España** and the streets heading to **Cra. Espinel. Postal code:** 29400.

GIBRALTAR

PHONE CODE	☎350 from the UK; ☎350 from the US; and ☎9567 from Spain. For **USA Direct,** dial ☎88 00; for **BT Direct,** ☎84 00.

Anglophiles and homesick Brits will get jolly well excited over Gibraltar's fish 'n' chips, while everyone else goes batty over the tax-free cigarettes (about UK£0.90). Britain and Spain have long contested the enclave, considered the end of the world by the ancients; now it's one of the last outposts of the British empire. Despite the Rock's history and refreshingly diverse population, it's basically a tourist trap. Admire the view of Iberia and the Straits from the imposing Rock, speak some English, then scurry back to the Spanish coast. Cable cars run from the southern end of Main St. to the northern tip of the massif known as **Top of the Rock,** stopping halfway up at **Apes' Den,** home to a colony of monkeys that has inhabited the Rock since before the Moorish invasion. The ruins of a Moorish wall crumble down the road from the cable car station to the south, near the spooky chambers of **St. Michael's Cave.** (Cable car runs every 10min. M-Sa 9:30am-6pm. UK£3.65, round-trip UK£4.90. Includes Apes' Den and cave.)

Buses arrive in the bordering Spanish town of **La Línea** from: Algeciras (40min., 2 per hr., 235ptas); Marbella (1¾hr., 4 per day, 695ptas); Cádiz (3hr., 5 per day, 1500ptas); Málaga (3¼hr., 4 per day, 1270ptas); Granada (5-6hr., 2 per day, 2475ptas); Sevilla (6hr., 3 per day, 2640ptas); and Madrid (7hr., 2 per day, 3280ptas). From the bus station, walk toward the Rock; the border is five minutes away. After passing Spanish customs and Gibraltar's passport control, cross the airport tarmac and head along the highway into town (20min.), or catch bus #9 or 10 (UK£0.40 or 100ptas). The **tourist office,** in Duke of Kent House, Cathedral Sq., is across the park from the Gibraltar Museum. (☎450 00; fax 749 43. Open M-F 9am-5:30pm.) **Emile Youth Hostel Gibraltar,** Montague Boston, off Line Wall Rd., across from the square at the beginning of Main St., offers cramped bunkbeds but clean communal bathrooms. (☎511 06. Breakfast included. Flexible lock-out 10:30am-4:30pm. Dorms UK£12; singles UK£15; doubles UK£26.) **Toc H Hostel,** Line Wall Rd., is stuffed with plants, cats, and travelers. Walk toward the Rock on Main St., turn right just before the arch at Southport Gate, then left in front of Hambros Bank. (☎734 31. Singles UK£6; doubles UK£10.) For fish (sticks) and (potato) chips head to the **Safeway** in the Europort commercial complex. (Open M-Sa 8am-8pm.)

ALGECIRAS

Algeciras' attractive **old neighborhood** often hides from the tourists stuck in the dingy port, which offers access to Gibraltar and Morocco; Moroccan migrant workers, Spanish army recruits, and tourists traffic the area day and night. RENFE **trains** (☎902 24 02 02) run from Ctra. Cádiz, way down C. Juan de la Cierva, to: Granada (4hr., 4 per day, 2415-2665ptas); Córdoba (5hr., 5 per day, 2575-4500ptas); Málaga (3½hr., 2 per day, 2100ptas); and Madrid (6hr., 5 per day, 5200-9100ptas). Empresa Portillo **buses** (☎956 65 10 55) leave from Av. Virgen del Carmen, 15, for Granada (5hr., 2 per day, 2595ptas) and the Costa del Sol; Linesur (☎956 66 76 49) runs from Av. Virgen del Carmen, 31, to Sevilla (3hr., 8 per day, 1985ptas); and Transportes Generales Comes (☎956 65 34 56) goes from C. San Bernardo, 1 to La Línea/Gibraltar (45min., 2 per hr., 235ptas). To get from the train or bus stations to the **tourist office,** on C. Juan de la Cierva, follow C. San Bernardo/C. Juan de la Cierva along the tracks toward the port, past a parking lot on the left. (☎956 57 26 36; fax 956 57 04 75. Open M-F 9am-2pm.) To get to the **ferry** port from the tourist office, continue down C. Juan de la Cierva and turn left on Av. Virgen del Carmen. Hostels cluster around **C. José Santacana,** parallel to Av. Marina a block inland. To get to **Hostal Rif,** C. Rafael de Muro 11, follow C. Santacana into the market square, bear left around the kiosk, and continue a block up C. Rafael del Muro. (☎956 65 49 53. Singles 1200-1500ptas; doubles 2400ptas; quads 4800ptas.) **Postal code:** 11203.

COSTA DEL SOL

The coast sold its soul to the Devil, and now he's collecting; artifice covers once-natural charms, as chic promenades and swank hotels line its shore. The Costa del Sol extends from Tarifa in the southwest to Cabo de Gata, east of Almería; post-industrial Málaga is in the middle. To the northeast, rocky beaches have preserved some natural beauty. Summer brings swarms of tourists (reserve ahead), but nothing detracts from the coast's eight months of spring and four months of summer.

MÁLAGA. In the hundred years since the Romantics discovered Málaga (pop. 531,140) high-rises have replaced its 19th-century villas and the beach is better known for its bars than untouched sand. Yet Málaga, a transport hub, brims with historic monuments. Guarding the east end of Po. Parque, the 11th-century **Alcazaba** structure, originally built as a Moorish palace, contains Roman ruins and a Moroccan art museum. (Open W-M 9:30am-7pm.) Picasso's birthplace now houses the **Picasso Foundation,** Pl. Merced. (Open M-Sa 11am-2pm and 5-8pm, Su 11am-2pm. Free.)

From **Estación de Málaga** (☎95 236 02 02), Esplanada de la Estación, **trains** go to: Córdoba (2hr., 12 per day, 2000-2800ptas); Sevilla (3hr., 5 per day, 2130ptas); Madrid (7hr., 1 per day, 8000ptas); and Barcelona (13hr., 3 per day, 6400-8400ptas). One block from the RENFE station along C. Roger de Flor, **buses,** Po. Tilos (☎95 235 00 61), go to: Marbella (1½hr., every hr., 615ptas); Granada (2hr., 17 per day, 1205ptas); Algeciras (3hr., 17 per day, 1390ptas); Córdoba (3hr., 5 per day, 1500ptas); Sevilla (3hr., 6-10 per day, 1900ptas); and Madrid (7hr., 10 per day, 2650ptas). To reach the town center from the bus station, take bus #4 or 21; from the train station, take bus #3 (115ptas). The **tourist office,** Av. Cervantes, 1, is in a little gray house on Po. Parque. (☎95 260 44 10. Open M-F 8:15am-2:45pm and 4:30-7pm, Sa 9:30am-1:30pm.) Most budget establishments are in the old town, between Pl. Marina and Pl. Constitución. **Hostal La Palma,** C. Martínez, 7, is off C. Marqués de Larios. (☎95 222 67 72. Singles 2000-3000ptas; doubles 3500-5000ptas; triples 3300-4500ptas; quads 4400-6000ptas.) **Hostal Aurora,** Muro de Puerta Nueva, 1, is five minutes from Pl. Constitución. (☎95 222 40 04. Singles 2000-3000ptas; doubles 3200-4500ptas.) Seaside Po. Marítimo stretches toward the lively beachfront district **El Pedregalejo** (bus #11 or 40min. on foot), where restaurants specialize in fresh seafood. A **supermarket** is in **El Corte Inglés,** Av. Andalucía, 4-6, opposite the post office. (Open June-Aug. M-Sa 10am-10pm; Sept.-May 10am-9:30pm.) In summer, folks crowd the bars in **El Pedregalejo** and between **C. Comedias** and **C. Granada,** which leads out of Pl. Constitución. **Postal code:** 29080.

SPAIN

The *casco antiguo* gets crowded on weekends, but the Euro-elite scene at **Puerto Banús** is hopping all week long. Bars and clubs lining the yacht port and the parallel C. Ribera are hard to miss. Buses run there on the hour all night along Av. Ricardo Soriano (dir. San Pedro, 125ptas). Taxis from Marbella (1300ptas) will also stop near the port's most popular people-watching, celebrity-sighting hangout, **Sinatra Bar.** (Mixed drinks 700-1200ptas. Opens daily at 11pm.) For a more down-to-earth experience, the terrace-level **Terra Blues,** C. Ribera, keeps it cool with top-40 music and less frenzied patrons. Around 4am, the action shifts to the clubs, where **Comedia,** (terrace-level, C. Ribera) draws in the younger crowds and **Flicks Bar,** farther down C. Ribera, rocks until dawn. (Cover for men 2000ptas.)

MARBELLA. International jet-setters choose five-star Marbella (pop. 100,000) to dock their yachts in and to live the glitzy, glam life, but it's possible to have a budgeted good time. The controversial mayor has "cleaned up" the "marginal" elements (drug dealers, prostitutes, fellow politicians, etc.); so come before he turns on backpackers. The beaches beckon with 320 days of sunshine per year, but no visit would be complete without a stroll through the **casco antiguo** (old town), a maze of streets and whitewashed facades. The **Museo del Grabado Español Contemporáneo,** on C. Hospital Bazán, is a treasure trove of engravings by Miró, Picasso, Dalí, Goya, and contemporary artists. (Open M-F 10:15am-2pm and 5:30-8:30pm. 300ptas.) With 22km of **beach,** Marbella offers a variety of sizzling settings, from below its chic promenade to **Playa de las Chapas,** 10km east via the Fuengirola bus. City buses ride along Av. Richard Soriano (dir. San Pedro; 135ptas) to the trendy, sparkling sands of **Puerto Banús.** After dark, the rowdiest corner of the *casco antiguo* is at C. Mesoncillo and C. Peral. Between the beach and the old town, **C. Puerta del Mar** has several gay bars. **Puerto Banús** (p. 860) is always lively. Buses run on the hour all night along **Av. Ricardo Soriano** (dir. San Pedro, 125ptas) to the clubs lining the yacht port and the parallel **C. Ribera.**

Accessible only by bus, the new **station** (☎95 276 44 00) atop Av. Trapiche sends **buses** to: Málaga (1½hr., every 30min., 610ptas); Algeciras (1½hr., 9 per day, 770ptas); Granada (4hr., 4 per day, 1820ptas); Sevilla (4hr., 3 per day, 1975ptas); Madrid (7½hr., 10 per day, 3085ptas); and Barcelona (16hr., 3 per day, 9365ptas). To reach the main strip, exit and walk left, make the first right on Av. Trapiche, and follow any downhill route to the perpendicular Av. Ramón y Cajal, which becomes Av. Ricardo Soriano on the way to Puerto Banús. C. Peral curves up from Av. Ramón y Cajal around the *casco antiguo.* The **tourist office** (☎95 282 35 50) is on Pl. Naranjos. in the old town. A **branch** (☎95 282 35 50) is on C. Glorieta de la Fontanilla. (Both open June-Aug. M-F 9:30am-9pm; Sept.-May M-F 9:30am-8pm, Sa 10am-2pm.) The area in the *casco antiguo* around Pl. Naranjos is packed with quick-filling hostels. **Hostal del Pilar,** C. Mesoncillo, 4, is off C. Peral, an extension of C. Huerta Chica; from the bus station, it is off C. San Francisco. (☎95 282 99 36. 1500-2500ptas; roof 1000-1500ptas.) The excellent **Albergue Juvenil (HI),** C. Trapiche, 2, downhill from the bus station, is just like a proper hotel, but affordable. (☎95 277 14 91. 1100-1800ptas; under 27 800-1300ptas. **Tents** outside 700ptas per person.) On the Marbella-Fuengirola bus line, ask the bus driver to stop at **Camping Marbella Playa.** (☎95 277 83 91. 325-585ptas per person; 530-980ptas per tent.) A **24-hour minimarket** beckons from the corner of C. Pablo Casals and Av. Fontanilla, which intersects with Av. Ricardo Soriano. **Postal code:** 29600.

GRANADA

"Give him alms, woman! For there is nothing crueler in life than to be blind in Granada," proclaims an inscription in the spectacular red-clay Alhambra, the palace-fortress complex in the hills of Granada. The last Muslim stronghold in Spain, Granada was lost by the ruler Boabdil to Catholic monarchs Fernando and Isabel in 1492. Although the Christians torched all the mosques and the lower city, embers of Granada's Arab essence still linger; the Albaicín, an enchanting maze of Moorish houses and twisting alleys, is Spain's best-preserved Arab quarter.

GETTING THERE AND GETTING AROUND

Trains: RENFE Station (☎902 24 02 02), Av. Andaluces. To: **Sevilla** (4-5hr., 5 per day, 2665ptas); **Madrid** (5-6hr., 2 per day, 3800ptas); **Algeciras** (5-7hr., 3 per day, 2675ptas); and **Barcelona** (12-13hr., 2 per day, 6500ptas).

Buses: Ctra. Madrid, near C. Arzobispo Pedro de Castro. **Alsina Graells** (☎958 18 54 80) runs to: **Córdoba** (3hr., 9 per day, 1540ptas); **Sevilla** (3hr., 9 per day, 2380ptas); **La Línea/Gibraltar** (4½hr., 2 per day, 2475ptas); **Algeciras** (5hr., 6 per day, 2595ptas); and **Madrid** (5hr., 14 per day, 1980ptas). **Bacoma** (☎958 15 75 57) goes to: **Alicante** (6hr., 5 per day, 3410ptas) and **Valencia** (8hr., 4 per day, 4995ptas).

Public Transportation: Take bus #10 from the bus station to the youth hostel, C. de Ronda, C. Recogidas, or C. Acera de Darro; or take bus #3 to Av. Constitución, Gran Vía, or Pl. Isabel la Católica. "Bus Alhambra" leaves from Pl. Nueva. All buses 120ptas, *bonobus* (15 tickets) 1000ptas. Handy free map at the tourist office.

ORIENTATION AND PRACTICAL INFORMATION

The geographic center is the small **Plaza de Isabel la Católica,** the intersection of the city's two main arteries, **Calle de los Reyes Católicos** and **Gran Vía de Colón.** To reach Gran Vía and the **cathedral** from the train station, walk three blocks up Av. Andaluces to take bus #3-6, 9, or 11 from Av. Constitución; from the bus station, take bus #3. Two blocks uphill on C. Reyes Católicos sits **Plaza Nueva.** Downhill on C. Reyes Católicos lies Pl. Carmen, site of the **Ayuntamiento** and Puerta Real. The **Alhambra** commands the steep hill up from Pl. Nueva.

Tourist Office: Oficina Provincial, Pl. Mariana Pineda, 10 (☎/fax 958 22 66 88; www.dipgra.es). From Pta. Real, turn right onto C. Angel Ganivet, then take a right 2 blocks later to reach the plaza. Open M-F 9:30am-7pm, Sa 10am-2pm.

American Express: C. Reyes Católicos, 31 (☎958 22 45 12), between Pl. Isabel la Católica and Pta. Real. Open M-F 9am-1:30pm and 2-9pm, Sa 10am-2pm and 3-7pm.

Luggage Storage: At the train and bus stations. 400ptas. Open daily 4-9pm.

Laundromat: C. La Paz 19. From Pl. Trinidad, take C. Alhóndiga and turn right. Wash 400ptas; dry 200ptas. Open M-F 9:30am-2pm and 4:30-8:30pm, Sa 9am-2pm.

Emergency: ☎091 or ☎092. **Police:** C. Duquesa 21 (☎958 24 81 00).

Medical Assistance: Clínica de San Cecilio, C. Dr. Oloriz, 16 (☎958 28 02 00 or ☎958 27 20 00), on the road to Jaén. **Ambulance:** ☎958 28 44 50.

Internet Access: Net, C. Buensuesco, 22, a block from Pl. Trinidad, and 2 other locations. 100ptas per hr. All open M-Sa 9am-1am, Su 3pm-1am.

Post Office: On Pta. Real, at C. Acera de Darro and C. Angel Ganinet. Wires money; fax service available. Open M-F 8am-9pm, Sa 9:30am-2pm. Address mail to be held: First name SURNAME, *Lista de Correos,* Pta. Real, **18009** Granada, Spain.

ACCOMMODATIONS

Near **Pl. Nueva,** hostels line Cuesta de Gomérez, the street leading uphill to the Alhambra. The area around C. Mesones and C. Alhóndiga is close to the cathedral; hostels cluster around **Pl. Trinidad,** at the end of C. Mesones as you approach from Pta. Real. Hostels are sprinkled along **Gran Vía.** Call ahead during *Semana Santa.*

SPAIN

Hostal Venecia, Cuesta de Gomérez, 2, 3rd fl. (☎958 22 39 87). Exceptionally clean, cozy abode. Singles 1800ptas; doubles 3500ptas; triples 5100ptas; quads 6800ptas.

Hostal Residencia Britz, Cuesta de Gomérez, 1 (☎/fax 958 22 36 52), on the corner of Pl. Nueva. Luxurious beds and green-tiled bathrooms. Laundry. Reception 24hr. Singles 2500ptas, with bath 4000ptas; doubles 4100ptas, 5700ptas. *Let's Go* discount 6%.

Hostal Antares, C. Cetti Meriém, 10 (☎958 22 83 13), at C. Elvira, 1 block from Gran Vía and the cathedral. Spotless, cheap, and in a great location. All rooms with balconies and sinks. Singles 2500ptas; doubles 3500ptas; triples 5250ptas.

Albergue Juvenil Granada (HI), Av. Ramón y Cajal, 2 (☎958 00 29 00; fax 958 00 29 01). From the bus station, take bus #10 (from the train station, #11) to "El Estadio de la Juventud." Reception 24hr. 2300ptas; under 27 1800ptas; nonmembers add 300ptas.

Hostal-Residencia Lisboa, Pl. Carmen, 29 (☎958 22 14 13), near the cathedral. Take C. Reyes Católicos from Pl. Isabel la Católica; Pl. Carmen is on the left. Singles 2700-4000ptas; doubles 4000-5800ptas; triples 5400-7800ptas.

Hospedaje Almohada, C. Postigo de Zarate, 4 (☎958 20 74 46), near the cathedral. From Pl. Trinidad, walk 1 block down C. Duquesa; it's to the right down C. Málaga (no sign; big red door). Social courtyard. Laundry. Singles 2000ptas; doubles 3700ptas.

Hostal Zurita, Pl. Trinidad, 7 (☎958 27 50 20), near the cathedral. Beautiful rooms. Singles 2000ptas; doubles 4000-5000ptas; triples 5000-7000ptas.

Hostal Gran Vía, Gran Vía, 17 (☎958 27 92 12), 4 blocks from Pl. Isabel la Católica. Clean, bright rooms. Singles 2500ptas; doubles 3000-4500ptas; triples 5500ptas.

Sierra Nevada, Av. Madrid, 107 (☎958 15 00 62). Take bus #3 or 10. Lots of trees and hot showers. Open Mar.-Oct. 560ptas per person, per tent, and per car.

Central Granada Overview

ACCOMMODATIONS

- Albergue Juvenile Granada (HI), 1
- Hostal Antares, 10
- Hostal Sevilla, 2
- Hostal Zurita, 3
- Hospedaje Almohada, 4
- Pensión Olympia, 6
- Hostal-Residencia Londres, 5
- Hostal-Residencia Zacatín, 8
- Hostal Gran Vía, 7
- Hostal-Residencia Lisboa, 9
- Hostal Residencia Britz, 11
- Hostal Venecia, 12
- Hostal Gomérez, 13
- Hostal Navarro-Ramos, 14

FOOD

Cheap North African cuisine abounds near the **Albaicín,** while teahouses and cafes crowd **C. Caldereria Nueva,** off C. Elvira, which leads out of the plaza. Nibble on *tapas* around **Pl. Nueva.** When ordering drinks, tapas are **free** in Granada. **La Nueva Bodega,** C. Cetti Meriém, 9, off C. Elvira, serves *menús* for 1000-1100ptas. (Open daily noon-midnight.) Students hang out at **Botánico Cafe,** C. Málaga, 3, two blocks from Pl. Trinidad. (Entrees 800-1500ptas. Open M-Th 10am-1am, F-Sa 10am-3am, Su noon-1am.) Veggie delights await at **Naturi Albaicín,** C. Caldereria Nueva, 10; try the *berenjenas rellenas* (stuffed eggplant). *Menús* are 950-1150ptas. (Open Sa-Th 1-4pm and 7-11pm, F 7-11pm.) Feast on immense portions of fresh seafood high on the Albaicín at **El Ladrillo II,** on C. Panaderos, off Cuesta del Chapiz. (Open daily 12:30pm-1:30am.) Granada's most famous ice cream shop is **La Veneziana,** Gran Vía, 4. (Open daily 11am-1am.) Stock up at the **market** on C. San Augustín, or at **Supermercado T. Mariscal,** on C. Genil, next to El Corte Inglés. (Open M-F 9:30am-2pm and 5-9pm, Sa 9:30am-2pm.)

SIGHTS

THE ALHAMBRA. The age-old saying holds true: "If you have died without seeing the Alhambra, you have not lived." From the streets of Granada, the Alhambra appears simple, blocky, faded—but up close the fortress-palace reveals its astoundingly elaborate detail. The first Nazarite King Alhamar built the fortress **Alcazaba,** the section of the complex with the oldest recorded history. A dark, spiraling staircase leads up to a 360° view of Granada and the mountains. Follow signs to the *Palacio Nazaries* to see the stunningly ornate **Alcázar,** a royal palace built for the Moorish rulers Yusuf I (1333-1354) and Mohammed V (1354-1391), where tourists gape at dripping stalactite archways, multicolored tiles, and sculpted fountains. Fernando and Isabel respectfully restored the Alcázar after they drove the Moors from Spain, but two generations later, Emperor Carlos V demolished part of it to make way for his **Palacio de Carlos V;** although glaringly incongruous when juxtaposed with such Moorish splendor, many consider it one of the most beautiful Renaissance buildings in Spain. Over a bridge are the vibrant blossoms, towering cypresses, and streaming waterways of **El Generalife,** the sultan's vacation retreat. *(Follow C. Cuesta de Gomérez from Pl. Nueva, and be prepared to pant (20min.). Or, take the Alhambra-Neptuno microbus (every 5min., 120ptas) from Pl. Nueva. ☎958 22 15 03. Open Apr.-Sept. daily 8:30am-8pm; Oct.-Mar. M-Sa 9am-5:45pm. Nighttime visits June-Sept. Tu, Th, and Sa 10-11:30pm; Oct.-May Sa 8-10pm. 1000ptas. Limited visitors per day, so arrive early.)*

SPAIN

THE CATHEDRAL QUARTER. Downhill from the Alhambra, the **Capilla Real** (Royal Chapel), Fernando and Isabel's private chapel, exemplifies Christian Granada. The **crypt** houses their lead caskets. The **sacristy** houses Isabel's private art collection, which favors 15th-century Flemish and German artists, as well as the glittering **royal jewels.** *(Both open Apr.-Sept. M-Sa 10:30am-1pm and 4-7pm, Su 11am-1pm; Oct.-Mar. M-Sa 10:30am-1pm and 3:30-6:30pm, Su 11am-1pm. 350ptas.)* The adjacent **cathedral,** Spain's first of pure Renaissance style, was built from 1523-1704 on the foundation of a major Arab mosque. *(Open daily Apr.-Sept. 10:30am-1:30pm and 4-7pm; Oct.-Mar. 10:30am-1:30pm and 3:30-6:30pm. Closed Su morning. 350ptas.)*

THE ALBAICÍN. The Moors built their first fortress in this fascinating and gorgeous old Arab quarter. After the Reconquest, a small Arab population clung to the neighborhood on the hill until their expulsion in the 17th century. A labyrinth of steep slopes and dark narrow alleys, the Albaicín warrants caution at night. Take C. Acera de Darro from Pl. Nueva, climb the Cuesta del Chapiz on the left, then wander through Muslim ramparts past whitewashed walls dripping with bright flowers. The terrace adjacent to **Iglesia de San Nicolás** affords the city's best view of the Alhambra, especially in winter, when snow adorns the Sierra Nevada. *(Bus #12 runs from beside the cathedral to C. Pagés, at the top of the Albaicín. Another Alhambra bus goes from Pl. Nueva to the top; from there, walk down C. Agua through Pta. Arabe.)*

ENTERTAINMENT AND NIGHTLIFE

The *Guía del Ocio*, sold at newsstands (100ptas), lists clubs, pubs, and cafes. The tourist office also distributes the monthly *Cultura en Granada*. A smoky, intimate setting awaits at **Eshavira** (☎958 29 08 29), on C. Postigo de la Cuna, in an alley off C. Azacayes, between C. Elvira and Gran Vía. This joint is *the* place to go for flamenco or jazz (1-drink min.; call for schedule). The most boisterous nightspots crowd **C. Pedro Antonio de Alarcón,** from Pl. Albert Einstein to Ancha de Gracia, while hip new bars and clubs line **C. Elvira** from C. Cárcel to C. Cedrán. Gay bars cluster around **C. del Darro, Parque del Triunfo,** and the **Paseo del Salón. Sur,** C. Reyes Católicos, 55, two blocks from Pl. Nueva, is Granada's trendiest *bare-musicale.* (Open daily 10pm-6am.) Decked out bar hoppers stop at **Temple,** C. Elvira, 98. (Open daily from 10pm.) The uphill trek to **Vaticano,** Camino del Sacromonte, 33, is rewarded with a spectacular view of the Alhambra at dawn. (Open daily from 11pm.)

HIKING AND SKIING NEAR GRANADA: SIERRA NEVADA

The peaks of **Mulhacén** (3481m) and **Veleta** (3470m), Spain's highest, sparkle with snow and buzz with tourists for most of the year. **Ski** season runs from December to April. The rest of the year, tourists **hike, parasail,** and take **jeep tours.** Before you go, check road and snow conditions (☎958 24 91 19) and hotel vacancies.

EASTERN SPAIN (VALENCIA)

Valencia's rich soil and famous orange groves, nourished by Moor-designed irrigation systems, have earned its nickname, *Huerta de España* (Spain's Orchard). Dunes, sandbars, jagged promontories, and lagoons mark the grand coastline, and lovely fountains and pools grace carefully landscaped public gardens in Valencian cities. The famed Spanish rice dish *paella* was created somewhere in Valencia.

ALICANTE (ALACANT)

Sun-drenched Alicante (pop. 285,000) is dutifully entertaining, yet quietly charming. While nightlife energizes the city, Alicante's mosaic-lined waterside Explanada relaxes it at sunset. High above the rows of bronzed bodies, the ancient *castillo*, spared by Franco, guards the tangle of streets in the cobblestone *casco antiguo.*

PRACTICAL INFO, ACCOMMODATIONS, AND FOOD. RENFE **trains** (☎902 24 02 02) run from **Estación Término** on Av. Salamanca, at the end of Av. Estación, to: Valencia (1½-2hr., 12 per day, 2900-4700ptas); Madrid (4hr., 8 per day, 4700-6900ptas); and Barcelona (4½-6hr., 9 per day, 6000-9900ptas). Trains from **Estació Marina,** Av. Villajoyosa, 2 (☎96 526 27 31), on Explanada d'Espanya, serve the Costa Blanca. **Buses,** C. Portugal, 17 (☎96 513 07 00), run to: Valencia (1980ptas); Granada (6hr., 5 per day, 3375ptas); Madrid (6½hr., 7 per day, 3000ptas); and Barcelona (8hr., 6 per day, 4700ptas). From the bus station, turn left on C. d'Italia, take the third right on Av. Dr. Gadea, and turn left at the waterfront to reach the Explanada d' Espanya. The **tourist office** is by the bus station. (☎592 98 02. Open June-Aug. M-Sa 9am-2:30pm and 5-8pm, Sept.-May 9am-2:30pm.) Log on the **Internet** at **Yazzgo,** Explanada, 3. (250ptas per 30min. Open daily 8am-11:30pm.) For lodgings, opt for the newer section of town. The **Pensión Les Monges Palace,** C. Monjas, 2, is behind the Ayuntamiento, in the center of the historic district. (☎96 521 50 46. Singles 2100-3200ptas; doubles 3900-5000ptas; triples 5000-6000ptas.) The nicest hostel owner ever (ever.) is at **Habitaciones México,** C. General Primo de Rivera, 10, off the end of Av. Alfonso X El Sabio. (☎96 520 93 07. Singles 1900-2200ptas; doubles 3600-4200ptas; triples 6000ptas.) Take bus #21 to **camp** at **Playa Mutxavista.** (☎96 565 45 26. 520ptas per person and per tent.) Try the *bare-restaurantes* in the *casco antiguo*, between the cathedral and the castle steps. The **market** is near Av. Alfonso X El

Sabio. (Open M-Sa 8am-2pm.) Buy basics at **Supermarket Mercadona,** C. Alvarez Sereix, 5, off Av. Federico Soto. (Open M-Sa 9am-9pm.) **Postal code:** 03070.

SIGHTS AND ENTERTAINMENT. Complete with drawbridges, dark passageways, and hidden tunnels, the Carthaginian **Castell de Santa Bárbara** keeps silent guard over Alicante's beach. A paved road from the old section of Alicante leads to the top, but most people take the **elevator** from an entrance on Av. Jovellanos, across the street from Playa Postiguet. (Castle open Apr.-Sept. 10am-7:30pm; Oct.-Mar. 9am-6:30pm; free. Elevator 400ptas.) A crowd of Valencian modernist art pieces roosts along with a few Mirós, Picassos, Kandinskys, and Calders in the **Museu de Arte del Siglo XX La Asegurada,** Pl. Santa Maria, 3, at the east end of C. Mayor. (Open May-Sept. Tu-Sa 10:30am-1:30pm and 6-9pm, Su 10:30am-1pm; Oct.-Apr. Tu-Sa 10am-1pm and 5-8pm, Su 10am-1pm. Free.) Alicante's own **Playa de El Postiguet** attracts sun worshipers, as do nearby **Playa de San Juan** (take TAM bus #21, 22, or 31) and **Playa del Mutxavista** (take TAM bus #21). Warm-weather nightlife also centers on the **Playa de San Juan;** the **Trensnochador** night train (July-Aug. F-Sa and every other Su-Th every hr. 10:30pm-6am; round-trip 150-700ptas) runs from Estació Marina to stops along the beach, where clubs are packed until dawn. Try **Penélope, Pachá, KU, KM,** and **Insomnia** (cover from 1500ptas; open nightly until 9am) at the "Disco Benidorm" stop (round-trip 650ptas). In Alicante itself, most start their evening in the pubs and tapas bars of the *casco antiguo.* The **new port** and the old section of town, **El Barne,** overflow with *bare-musicales.*

COSTA BLANCA

This "white coast" that extends from Denía through Calpe, Alicante, and Elche derives its name from its fine, white sands. UBESA **buses** (Valencia ☎96 340 08 55) run to Gandía (1½hr., 12 per day) and Calpe (3-3½hr., 10 per day). From Alicante, buses run to Calpe (1½hr., 18 per day). **Trains** also run hourly from Valencia to Alicante. Going to **Calpe** (Calp) is like stepping into a Dalí landscape. The town cowers beneath the **Peñó d'Ifach** (327m), a giant rock protrusion dropping straight to the sea. The energetic seaside town of **Gandía** thrives off its beautiful coastline. The **tourist office,** Marqués de Campo, is opposite the train station. (☎96 287 77 88. Open June-Aug. M-F 10am-2pm and 4:30-7:30pm, Sa 10am-1pm; Sept.-May M-F 9:30am-1:30pm and 4-7pm, Sa 10am-1pm.) La Amistad **buses** (8 per day, 125ptas) go from outside the train station in Gandía to **Platja de Piles,** 10km south, where you'll find beach, beach, and more beach. To sleep (and play) at the fantastic **Alberg Mar i Vent (HI)** in Platja, follow the signs down C. Dr. Fleming. The beach is literally out the back door. (☎96 283 17 48. Sheets 300ptas. Flexible 3-day max. stay. Curfew Su-Th 2am, F-Sa 4am. Open Feb. 15-Dec. 15. Call in advance. Dorms 800ptas, with breakfast 900ptas, with full board 1900ptas; 26+ 300-500ptas extra.)

SPAIN

NORTHEAST SPAIN

The Northeast encompasses the country's most avidly regionalistic areas, as well as some of its best cuisine. **Catalunyans** are justly proud of their treasures, from mountains to beaches to hip Barcelona. The glorious **Pyrenees** line the French border. Little-known **Navarra** gets its 15 minutes of fame once a year when bulls run through Pamplona's streets. Industrious **Aragón** packs in busy cities and the most dramatic parts of the Pyrenees. The **Basques** are fiercely regionalistic, but share their beautiful coasts and rich history. The **Balearic Islands** are always ready for the next party.

CATALUNYA

From rocky Costa Brava to the lush Pyrenees and chic Barcelona, Catalunya is a vacation in itself. Graced with the nation's richest resources, it is one of the most prosperous regions. Catalán is the region's official language (though most everyone is bilingual), and local cuisine is lauded throughout Spain.

BARCELONA

Barcelona's frenetic energy radiates from its cafes, parks, and discos. Refereeing two tugs of war—Spanish culture pushing against Catalán individualism and old-world simplicity pulling against contemporary style—Barcelona is animated by its inner struggles. Amid graceful Gothic churches, a serpentine old town, wrought-iron balconies, and grand, tree-lined avenues, Antoni Gaudí's technicolor flights of fancy battle for attention with the city's latest architectural triumphs—carefully angled and glassy-white museums and malls. This passionate existence has made Barcelona Spain's trendsetter and Europe's fastest growing tourist center.

GETTING THERE AND GETTING AROUND

Flights: El Prat de Llobregat airport (☎93 298 38 38), 12km southwest of Barcelona. To get to the central Pl. Catalunya, take the **Aerobus** (40min., every 15min., 500ptas) or a RENFE **train** (20min., every 30min., 305-350ptas). City **bus** EN goes to Pl. Espanya (every hr. until 2:40am, 145ptas). A **taxi** to the city costs 3000-4500ptas.

Trains: Estació Barcelona-Sants (☎902 24 02 02), on Pl. Països Catalans. M: Sants-Estació. Main domestic and international terminal. **RENFE** train line has service almost anywhere in Spain and Europe (☎902 24 02 02; www.renfe.es). To: **Valencia** (3hr., 15 per day, 5000-7200ptas); **Montpellier, France,** with connections to Geneva and Paris (4½hr., 3 per day, 12,608-43,800ptas); **Madrid** (7-8hr., 6 per day, 6500-8400ptas); **Sevilla** (12hr., 3 per day, 10,000-27,700ptas); and **Milan** (13hr., 1 per day, 12,608-43,800ptas). **Estació França** (☎902 24 02 02), on Av. Marqués de L'Argentera. M: Barceloneta. Serves a few domestic and international routes.

Buses: Estació del Nord, C. Ali-bei 80 (☎93 265 65 08). M: Arc de Triomf ("Nàpols" exit). **Enatcar** (☎93 245 25 28) buses go to **Valencia** (4hr., 16 per day, 2690ptas) and **Madrid** (8hr., 18 per day, 2690ptas). **Sarfa** (☎93 265 65 08) buses serve the **Costa Brava. Linebús** (☎93 265 07 00) goes to **Paris** (15hr., 6 per week, 11,200-22,900ptas).

Ferries: Trasmediterránea (☎902 45 46 45), Estació Marítima-Moll Barcelona, Moll de Sant Bertran. M: Drassanes; follow Las Ramblas to the Columbus monument, which points the way. In summer, boats go almost daily to the Balearic Islands (see p. 887).

Hitchhiking: *Let's Go* does not recommend hitchhiking. Those hitching to France often take Av. Meridiana from M: Fabra i Puig to reach highway A7. Those en route to Valencia take bus #7 from Rambla Catalunya on the Gran Vía side to the *autopista* ("A"). Hitchhiking on *autopistas* is illegal, but is permitted on national highways ("N").

Public Transportation: ☎010. Pick up a *Guia d'Autobusos Urbans de Barcelona* for metro and bus routes. **Buses** run 5am-10pm and cost 150ptas per ride. The **metro** runs M-Th 5am-11pm, F-Sa 5am-2am, Su 6am-midnight; buy tickets from vending machines or stations (150ptas). A **T1 Pass** (825ptas) is valid for 10 rides on bus, metro, and commuter rail and can be shared; a **T-DIA Card** (625ptas or 1600ptas) lasts one or three days of unlimited bus or metro travel. **Nitbus** (160ptas) runs 10:30pm-4:30am.

Taxis: ☎93 330 03 00. First 6min. or 1.9km 300ptas; each additional km 110ptas.

Car Rental: Docar, C. Montnegre 18 (☎93 439 81 19). From 4700ptas per day, plus 23ptas per km including insurance. Open M-F 8:30am-2pm and 3:30-8pm, Sa 9am-2pm.

ORIENTATION AND PRACTICAL INFORMATION

Barcelona slopes gently upward from the harbor to the mountains. **Passeig de Colón** runs parallel to the shore; from Pg. Colón, **Las Ramblas,** the city's main thoroughfare, runs from the harbor to **Plaça de Catalunya,** the city's center. Las Ramblas is divided into five parts: **Rambla de Santa Mónica, Rambla de Caputxins, Rambla de Sant Josep, Rambla de Estudis,** and **Rambla de Canaletas.** The **Barri Gòtic** area is enclosed by Las Ramblas to the west and **Vía Laietana** to the east, and is bisected by east-west **Carrer de Ferran.** East of Vía Laietana lies the maze-like neighborhood of **La Ribera,** which borders the **Parc de la Ciutadella** and the **Estació de França** train station. Farther east is the **Vila Olímpica,** along with a shiny array of malls, discos, and hotels. West of Las Ramblas is **El Ravel,** including the shrinking red-light district. Farther west rises **Montjuïc,** a picturesque hill crammed with sights. South of Pg. Colón, a bridge leads from the **Port Vell** (Old Port) to the ultramodern malls **Moll d'Espanya** and **Maremagnum.** The gridded **L'Eixample** district, a product of urban expansion, fans toward the hills from Pl. Catalunya and is split by the main shopping street **Passeig de Gràcia. Avinguda Diagonal** separates L'Eixample from **Gràcia,** a residential area farther north. The peak of **Tibidabo** to the northwest is the highest point in Barcelona. For more detail, refer to this book's **color maps** of the city and metro.

Barcelona is fairly safe, even at night, but secure your valuables while in outdoor cafes, in the Pl. Reial and Barri Gòtic, and on Las Ramblas, and be careful deep in El Ravel. Most areas with nightlife are well-policed, lit, and generally safe.

TOURIST AND FINANCIAL SERVICES

Tourist Offices: ☎010, 906 30 12 82, or 93 304 34 21; www.barcelonaturisme.com. **Informacio Turistica at Plaça Catalunya,** Pl. Catalunya 17-S. M: Catalunya. The biggest, best, and busiest tourist office. Open daily 9am-9pm. **Branches** at Pl. Sant Jaume I (M: Jaume I), in the Barcelona-Sants train station (M: Sants-Estació), and at the airport. **Mobile info offices** dot the city in the summer.

Budget Travel: Unlimited Student Travel (USIT), Rda. Universidad 16 (☎902 32 52 75; www.unlimited.es), 1½ blocks from Pl. Catalunya. M: Catalunya. Also at C. Rocafort 116-118, 2 blocks from M: Rocafort. Open M-F 10am-8pm, Sa 10am-1:30pm. Bring your ISIC card.

Consulates: Australia, Gran Vía Carlos III 98, 9th fl. (☎933 30 94 96; fax 934 11 09 04). **Canada,** Elisen da de Pinos, 8. (☎932 04 27 00; fax 932 04 27 01). **Ireland,** Grand Vía Carlos III 94 (☎93 451 90 21; fax 934 11 29 21). **New Zealand,** Traversa de Gracia 64, 4th fl. (☎932 09 03 99; fax 932 02 08 90). **South Africa,** Teodora Lamadrid 7-11 (☎934 18 64 45; fax 934 18 05 38). **UK,** Av. Diagonal, 477, 13th fl. (☎933 66 62 00; fax 933 66 62 21). **US,** Pg. Reina Elisenda de Moncada, 23 (☎932 80 22 27; fax 932 05 52 06).

Currency Exchange: ATMs give the best rates (at no commission); the next best are at **banks.** Banks open M-F 8:30am-2pm.

American Express: Pg. Gràcia 101 (24hr. ☎900 99 44 26; fax 93 415 37 00). M: Diagonal. Entrance on C. Rosselló. Mail held. Open M-F 9:30am-6pm, Sa 10am-noon. Another AmEx on Las Ramblas 74. Open daily 9am-midnight.

LOCAL SERVICES

SPAIN

Luggage Storage: Lockers (300-600ptas) at **Estació del Nord** (24hr.); **Estació França** also has lockers. (400-600ptas. Open daily 6am-11pm.)

El Corte Inglés: Pl. Catalunya 14, Av. Diagonal 471-473, and Av. Diagonal 617. Great map and everything else you've ever wanted. Open M-Sa 10am-9:30pm.

English Bookstores: LAIE, Av. Pau Claris 85 (☎93 318 17 39), 1 block from the Gran Vía. M: Urquinaona or Pl. Catalunya. Open M-F 10am-9pm, Sa 10:30am-9pm. **The Bookstore,** C. La Granja 13 (☎93 237 95 19), in Gràcia off Travesera del Dalt. M: Lesseps. Book trade. Open M-Sa 11am-1:30pm and 2:30-7pm.

Laundromat: Tintoreria Ferran, C. Ferran, 11. M: Liceu. Ferran is off Las Ramblas, just below Liceu. 1500ptas for full service. Open daily 8:30am-2pm and 4:30-7:30pm.

EMERGENCY AND COMMUNICATIONS

Emergency: Medical, ☎061. **National police,** ☎091. **Local police,** ☎092.

Police: Las Ramblas 43 (☎93 344 13 00), opposite Pl. Reial and next to C. Nou de La Rambla. M: Liceu. English spoken. Open 7am-midnight.

Pharmacies: Late-night pharmacies rotate; check pharmacy windows for listings.

Hospitals: Barcelona Centro Médico (BCM), Av. Diagonal 612, 2nd fl., #14 (☎93 414 06 43). Coordinates referrals, especially for foreigners.

Telephones: Pick up a phone card at tobacco stores, tourist offices, post offices, or some newspaper stands on Las Ramblas. Directory assistance ☎1003.

Barcelona Overview

ACCOMMODATIONS

Albergue de Juventud Kabul, 14
Albergue Juvenil Palau, 17
Casa de Huéspedes Mari-Luz, 16
El Toro Bravo, 20
H.-R. Capitol & Hotel Toledano, 4
H.-R. Europa, 11
H.-R. Lausanne, 6
H.-R. Oliva, 2
H.-R. Rembrandt, 7
Hostal Aviñyó, 18
Hostal Fernando, 12
Hostal Fontanella, 5
Hostal Girona, 3
Hostal La Terrassa, 10
Hostal Levante, 15
Hostal Malda, 8
Hostal Marítima, 19
Hostal Paris, 9
Hostal Rey Don Jaume I, 13
Pensión L'Isard, 1

Internet Access: Net Movil, Las Ramblas, 130 (☎93 342 42 04). M: Liceu. Equipped with 50 high-speed computers. 300ptas per 15min., 10ptas per additional minute.

Post Office: On Pl. Antoni López (☎93 318 38 31), at the end of Vía Laietana, portside. M: Jaume I or Barceloneta. Fax. Open M-F 8:30am-9:30pm. Address mail to be held: First name SURNAME, *Lista de Correos*, Pl. Antoni López, Barcelona 08003, Spain.

ACCOMMODATIONS AND CAMPING

Although *albergues* (hostels) and *pensiones* abound, visitors without reservations will scramble for a room in summer. The **Ciutat Vella,** between Pl. Catalunya and the shore, includes the **Barri Gòtic, Las Ramblas, El Ravel,** and **La Ribera** and offers a wealth of budget accommodations, but in July and August you *must* call ahead. **Lower Barri Gòtic** hostels are the hippest, but be careful at night; **Upper Barri Gòtic,** north of C. Portaferrisa, is pricier with a more serene ambiance. **L'Eixample** offers the safest, most beautiful hostels. Hostels are marked by signs with a big "P" or "H."

LOWER BARRI GÒTIC

Hostal Fernando, C. Ferrán 31 (☎93 301 79 93). M: Liceu. Renovated and sparkling, the hostel charms with its sociability and multilingual staff. Internet. Dorms 2100ptas; singles 2800ptas; doubles with bath 6500ptas; triples with bath 7500ptas.

Hostal Residencia Rembrandt, C. Portaferrissa 23 (☎/fax 93 318 10 11). M: Liceu. From the port, walk north on Las Ramblas and turn right on C. Portaferrissa. Themed rooms ranging from "little kid" to "regal." Breakfast 400ptas. Singles 3200ptas; doubles 5000ptas, with bath 6700ptas; triples 7000ptas.

Hostal Levante, Baixada de San Miguel 2 (☎93 317 95 65). M: Liceu; walk down C. Ferrán, turn right on C. Avinyó, and take your 1st left. TV lounge and knowledgeable owner. Reception 24hr. Singles 3500ptas; doubles 5500-6500ptas.

Hostal Avinyo, C. Avinyó 42 (☎93 318 79 45; fax 318 68 93). M: Drassanes. Annually renovated. 1700-1900ptas per person, with bath 2300-2600ptas.

Hostal Malda, C. Pí 5 (☎93 317 30 02). M: Liceu. From Las Ramblas, head east on C. Portaferrissa, take the 4th right, and look for the green "Galleries Maldo" sign. Singles 1500ptas; doubles 3000ptas, with bath 3500ptas; triples 4000ptas, 4500ptas.

Hotel Call, Arco San Ramón del Call 4 (☎93 302 11 23). M: Liceu. From Las Ramblas, take C. Boqueria and veer left onto C. Call. Private phones. Ask for a balcony. Singles 4500ptas; doubles 6000ptas; triples 8000ptas; quads 7500ptas. Add 7% IVA.

Hostal Layetana, Pl. Ramón Berenguer el Gran 2 (☎/fax 93 319 20 12). M: Jaume I; it's on your left one block from the sea. Sink into the leather chairs. Singles 2700ptas; doubles 4700ptas, with bath 5900ptas; triples 6400ptas, 8000ptas. Add 7% IVA. V, MC.

Hotel Rey Don Jaume I, C. Jaume I 11 (☎93 310 62 08). M: Jaume I. Rooms with bath and phone. Singles 5000ptas; doubles 7400ptas; triples 10,500ptas.

Albergue de Juventud Kabul, Pl. Reial 17 (☎93 318 51 90). M: Liceu. Head to the port on Las Ramblas and turn left after C. Ferrán; it's on the near right corner of the *plaça.* Legendary for its reputation as a 24hr. party. If you're looking for sobriety and worry about the safety of your stuff, go elsewhere. TV, Internet, and pool table. Sheets 200ptas. Laundry. Flexible 5-night max. stay. Reception 24hr. Dorms 2200ptas.

Hostal Paris, Cardenal Casañas 4 (☎93 301 37 85; fax 93 412 70 96), on Las Ramblas opposite M: Liceu. Central location. Singles 3000ptas, with bath 6500ptas; doubles 4800ptas, 7500ptas; triples with bath 7500ptas.

Casa de Huéspedes Mari-Luz, C. Palau 4 (☎93 317 34 63), 1 block from Pl. Sant Jaume. M: Jaume I or Liceu. Take C. Ciutat to C. Templaris, then take the 2nd left. Ultra-clean rooms. Kitchen. Laundry 800ptas. Dorms 1900ptas; doubles 4800ptas.

Albergue Juvenil Palau (HI), C. Palau 6 (☎93 412 50 80). M: Liceu. From Las Ramblas, take C. Ferrán to C. Enseyança, which becomes C. Palau. A small, tranquil refuge in the heart of the Barri Gòtic. Common room with TV. Breakfast included. Kitchen. Reception 7am-3am. Curfew 3am. Sheets 200ptas. Dorms 1900ptas.

UPPER BARRI GÒTIC

Hostal Fontanella, Vía Laietana 71 (☎/fax 317 59 43). M: Urquinaona; head down Vía Laietana. A life-size doll-house with flowing curtains and embroidered towels. Reservations with deposit. Singles 3000-4000ptas; doubles 5000-6900ptas.

Hotel Toledano/Hostal Residencia Capitol, Las Ramblas 138 (☎93 301 08 72). M: Pl. Catalunya. Almost luxury. Hostel singles 3600ptas; doubles 5100ptas; triples 6500-7200ptas. Hotel 3900-4400ptas; 7600ptas; 9500ptas; quads 10,600ptas. Add IVA.

Hostal Residencia Lausanne, Av. Portal de L'Angel 24 (☎93 302 11 39). M: Pl. Catalunya. On one of Barcelona's most happening streets, the hostel is almost as grand as its imperial facade. Doubles 5500-6000ptas.

EL RAVEL

Pensión L'Isard, C. Tallers 82 (☎93 302 51 83), near MACBA, the contemporary art museum. M: Universitat; exit at "Pelai," go left after one block, and turn left at the pharmacy. Simple elegance. Singles 2400ptas; doubles 4400-5000ptas; triples 6000ptas.

Residencia Australia, Ronda Universitat, 11 (☎93 317 41 77). M: Universitat. Family feel; rooms with embroidered sheets, curtains, and balconies. Quiet time at 10pm. Curfew 4am. Singles 3000ptas; doubles 4800ptas-6000ptas. V, MC.

L'EIXAMPLE

Hostal Residencia Oliva, Pg. Gràcia 32, 4th fl. (☎93 488 01 62 or 93 488 17 89), at C. Diputació. M: Pg. Gràcia. Classy wood-worked bureaus, bed frames, mirrors, and TVs. Reservations essential. Singles 3200ptas; doubles 6200ptas, with bath 7200ptas.

Hostal Residencia Windsor, Rambla Catalunya 84 (☎93 215 11 98), near the intersection of C. Mallorca. M: Pg. Gràcia. Lives up to its royal name. Singles 3900ptas, with bath 4900ptas; doubles 6500ptas, 7900ptas. Add 7% IVA.

GRÁCIA

Hostal Bonavista, C. Bonavista 21 (☎93 237 37 57). M: Diagonal. Head toward the fountain at the end of Pg. Gràcia and take the first right. Cute, clean, cared-for rooms. Showers 300ptas. Singles 2500ptas; doubles 3800ptas, with bath 4800ptas.

CAMPING

El Toro Bravo (☎936 37 34 62), 11km south of Barcelona. Take intercity bus L95 (20-45min., 200ptas) from Pl. Catalunya or Pl. Espanya. **Filipinas** (☎936 58 28 95) is 1km down the road from El Toro Bravo. Both 1300ptas per person; 775ptas per tent.

SPAIN

FOOD

Barcelona's restaurants draw on both the Spanish and Catalán culinary traditions. For the cheapest meals, 1000-1300ptas *menús* are posted in the restaurants on Barcelona's side streets. The crowded eateries on **Las Ramblas** and near the **port** are often great for ambiance but also higher in price and lower in quality than places in less-touristed areas like **El Ravel, La Ribera,** and **Gràcia.** Many of the best restaurants serve *cuisina del mercado*, menus created daily from fresh market offerings. Look out for *colmados* (traditional food shops)—they typically have hidden back room tables for feasting. Foodstands-cum-restaurants in Barcelona's 40 marketplaces may look grimy but are often delicious. The weekly *Guía del Ocio* (available at newsstands, 125ptas) lists additional dining options. Be aware that many restauranteurs close up shop and take vacations in August. Most un-touristed places are closed Sundays. Catalán favorites include *pa amb tomaquet* (bread with tomato and olive oil), *botufarra amb monjetes* (sausage and beans), *espinacs a la catalana* (spinach with pinenuts and raisins, and *cap i pota* (head and hoof). Make your own meal at awe-inspiring **La Boqueria,** officially Mercat de Sant Josep, off Las Ramblas outside of the Liceu metro station. (Open M-Sa 7am-8pm.) Or try the daily **Mercat de Sant Antoni,** (M: Sant Antoni), Barcelona's biggest flea market. **Champion Supermarket** is at Las Ramblas, 113. (Open M-Sa 9am-9pm.)

BARRI GÒTIC

La Fonda, C. Escudellers, 10. M: Drassanes or Liceu. Off Las Ramblas. The classiest atmosphere for the cheapest prices in Barcelona. Starters 275-700ptas, entrees 500-1000ptas. Open daily 1-3:30pm and 8:30-11:30pm.

Irati, C. Cardenal Casañas, 17. Excellent Basque tapas bar. Bartenders pour *sidra* (cider) from 3 ft. above the glass. Tapas 140ptas. Entrees average 2000ptas. Open Tu-Sa noon-midnight, Su noon-5pm; tapas served M-Sa noon-3pm and 7-11pm.

Il Mercante Di Venezia, C. Jose Anselmo Clave, 11. M: Drassanes. Romantic ambiance, especially if you love your tummy. Appetizers 375-800ptas, pasta under 1000ptas, meat 1175-1800ptas. Open Tu-Su 1:30-3:30pm and 8:30-midnight.

Juicy Jones, Cardenal Casañas, 7. M: Liceu; go down Las Ramblas and take the 1st left. Fabulous veggie cuisine in a psychedelic setting. *Menú* 1100ptas (available after 1pm). Juice of the day 375ptas. Open daily 10am-11:15pm.

Peimong, C. Templaris, 6-10. M: Liceu; take C. Ferrán off Las Ramblas to Pl. Sant Jaume, turn right on C. Ciutat, and take the 2nd right. Meat-lovers rejoice! Peruvian-style meals under 900ptas. Open Tu-Su 1-5pm and 8pm-midnight.

Els Quatre Gats, C. Montsió, 3. M: Catalunya; go down Av. Portal de L'Angel and take your 2nd left. Picasso loved it *and* designed the menu. Delicious tapas 150-650ptas. Live music 9pm-1am. Open M-Sa 9am-2am, Su 5pm-2am. Closed Aug.

El Cervol Roig, C. Comtal, 19. M: Urquinaona. Patrons stuff huge platters of fish and meat into their mouths while rattling off stock quotes. Lunch menu 1195ptas, starters 700ptas, entrees 1300-2500ptas. Open daily 9am-9pm.

Terrablava, Via Laietana, 55. All-you-can-eat from an endless line of fresh salads, veggies, pastas, pizza, meat dishes, and fruit; 1095ptas. Open daily 1pm-1am.

The Bagel Shop, C. Canuda, 25. M: Catalunya; take the first left off Las Ramblas. Real breakfast joint with a huge selection. Open M-Sa 9:30am-11:30pm.

Gelateria Italiana, C. Cucurull, 2. Better than Candyland. 175-250ptas. Open daily.

ELSEWHERE IN BARCELONA

Colibri, Riera Alta, in **El Ravel.** Take C.I. Carme and take the 6th right onto Riera Alta; Colibri is 2 blocks up on the left. Market cuisine brings freshness, flair, and service to Barcelona. Impeccable wine selection. Dishes 1200-2500ptas. Open nightly.

Restaurante Can Lluís, C. Cera, 49, in **El Ravel.** M: San Antoni; go down Ronda S. Pau and take the 2nd left. For over 100 years, Can Lluís has defined Catalán cuisine. Try the *cabrit* (goat), *conill* (rabbit), or *vedella* (veal). The 3-course midday *menú* is an excellent value at 950ptas. Open M-Sa 1:30-4pm and 8:30-11:30pm.

LLuna Plena, C. Montcada 2, in **La Ribera.** M: Jaume I; take C. Princesa and turn left onto C. Montcada. Classy decor. The afternoon *menú* is a steal at 1000ptas. Open Tu-Sa 1-4pm and 8-11pm, Su 1-4pm. Closed Aug.

Restaurante Chino, C. Tallers, 70. M: **Catalunya** or Universitat. Take C. Tallers from Pl. Universitat or Las Ramblas. Filling, inexpensive pan-Asian cuisine. Dishes 595-900ptas. Open daily noon-4:30pm and 8pm-midnight.

Restaurante Riera, C. Joaquín Costa, 30, in **El Ravel.** M: Liceu or Universitat. Off C. Carme from Liceu, or off Ronda de Sant Antoni from Universitat. 3-course gorge-fest (750ptas). Open daily 1-4pm and 8-11:30pm.

La Habana Vieja, Carrer dels Banys Vells, 2, in **La Ribera.** Cuban drumbeats tempt you to dance while the delicious food convinces you to stay put. Meat dishes 1600-2000ptas. Open M-Th 8pm-1am, F-Sa 1-4pm and 8pm-1am.

Txirimira, C. Princesa, 11, in **La Ribera.** Enough tapas to feed a village; over 40 varieties for 140ptas each. Open Tu-Su noon-midnight.

La Provenca, C. Provenca, 242 (☎93 323 23 67), in **L'Eixample.** Mediterranean-influenced dishes. Serves *carpaccio* (thinly sliced raw meat with parmesan cheese) and fresh fish. 1290-1700ptas. Dress well. Open daily 1:30-5:30pm, 9-11:30pm.

Saler, Consejo de Ciento, 316, in **L'Eixample.** Serves Galician specialties, seafood, and fish. Entrees 950-2300ptas, *menú* 1075ptas. Open M-Sa 1-4pm and 8:30-11:30pm.

ba-ba-reeba, Pg. Gràcia, 28. M: **Pg. Gràcia.** So many tapas. Open daily 9am-2am.

Comme-Bio, Gran Vía de les Corts Catalanes, 603. M: **Catalunya.** Creative all-veggie selection. Open M-Sa 9am-midnight, Su noon-midnight.

SIGHTS

Barcelona's *Modernista* treasures define the city. Long, bustling **Las Ramblas** and the lovely **Barri Gòtic,** Barcelona's "old city," are traditional tourist areas, but don't neglect the vibrant **La Ribera** and **El Ravel,** the upscale avenues of **L'Eixample,** the panoramic city views from **Montjuïc** and **Tibidabo,** Gaudí's **Palau Güell,** and harborside **Port Olímpic**. The **Ruta del Modernisme** pass (600ptas, students 400ptas) grants a 50% discount on *Modernista* masterpieces: Casa Lleó Morera, Palau Güell, La Sagrada Familia, Casa Milà (La Pedrera), Palau de la Música, Casa-Museu Gaudí, Fundació Antoni Tápies, and the Museu d'Art Modern. Buy passes at the **Casa Lleó Morera,** on the corner of Pg. Grácia and C. Consedel (☎93 488 01 39). In summer, the air-conditioned, hop-on, hop-off **Bus Turístic** stops at 25 sights; hop on at Pl. Catalunya, in front of El Corte Inglés. (Buses run daily Apr.-Dec. every 10-30min. 9am-9:30pm. Day pass 1800ptas, 2-day 2300ptas.) Many museums offer **free admission** the first Sunday of each month; almost all close on Mondays.

LAS RAMBLAS

This pedestrian-only median strip is a veritable urban carnival, where street performers dance, fortune-tellers survey palms, human statues shift poses, vendors hawk birds and flowers, and artists sell their work. Comprised of five distinct segments (Canaletes, Estudis, Sant Josep, Capuxtins, and Santa Monica), the boulevard buzzes with activity from Pl. Catalunya in the north to the port in the south.

UPPER LAS RAMBLAS. Visitors who wish to return to Barcelona are supposed to sample the water at the **Font de Canaletes** (more a pump than a fountain). Halfway down Las Ramblas, **Joan Miró's** pavement mosaic brightens the street.

PALAU GÜELL. The Palau Güell has the most spectacular Gaudí interior in Barcelona. The rooftop displays his first use of *trencadis*, the covering of surfaces with shards of ceramic or glass. *(C. Nou de la Rambla, 3-5, 2 blocks from Teatre Liceu. Open M-Sa 10am-1pm and 4-7pm. 400ptas, students 200ptas. Arrive early.)*

THE PORT. Farther down Las Ramblas, Barcelona has refurbished its waterfront with the Vila Olímpica and the expansion of Port Vell. The picturesque port clamors with seaside eateries, loud discotecas, overpriced shops, the **Museu de la Historia de Catalunya,** and the **Maremagnum** mall. The mall's **L'aquàrium de Barcelona** features an 80m glass tunnel and a moving walkway through a tank of sharks. *(M: Barceloneta. Open July-Aug. 9:30am-11pm; Sept.-June 9:30am-9pm. 1450ptas, students 10% off.)*

MUSEU D'ART CONTEMPORANI (MACBA). Designed by American architect Richard Meier, this sparse building allows art to speak for itself. The museum focuses on avant-garde work from the interwar period, surrealism, and contemporary art. *(Pl. dels Angels, 1. M: Universitat or Catalunya. Open M and W-F 11am-8pm, Sa 10am-8pm, Su 10am-3pm. 775ptas, students 550ptas, children free; W 375ptas.)*

OTHER SIGHTS. The disaster-prone opera house, **Gran Teatre del Liceu,** Las Ramblas, 61, is on the corner of C. Sant Pau. At the port end of Las Ramblas, the **Monument a Colom** towers above the city, with a confused Christopher Columbus pointing proudly toward Libya. *(Elevator open June-Sept. daily 9am-8:30pm; Oct.-Mar. M-F 10am-1:30pm and 3:30-7:30pm, Sa-Su 10am-6:30pm; Apr.-May M-F 10am-1:30pm and 3:30-7:30pm, Sa-Su 10am-7:30pm. 250ptas, children 150ptas.)*

BARRI GÒTIC

While the weathered streets of the Barri Gòtic have retained a medieval air, the growing tourist boom has infused liveliness into the area, once a Catalán ghetto.

SPAIN

PLAÇA DE SANT JAUME. The handsome Pl. de Sant Jaume has been Barcelona's political center since Roman times. The square is dominated by the **Palau de la Generalitat,** seat of Catalunya's autonomous government, and the **Ajuntament,** the Spanish government's seat. *(Palau open 2nd and 3rd Su of each month 10am-2pm. 30min. English tours. Ajuntament open Sa-Su 10am-2pm. Free.)*

ESGLÉSIA CATEDRAL DE LA SANTA CREU. Above Pl. Seu rise the jagged spires of the 14th-century Gothic Església Catedral de la Santa Creu. Barcelona's patron saint and Christian martyr Santa Euália lies in the church **crypt.** Geese waddle around the periphery of the lovely **cloister.** *(Cathedral open daily 8am-1:30pm and 4-7pm. Coro (choral chamber) 125ptas. Cloister open daily 9am-1:15pm and 4-7pm. Free. Elevator to the roof runs M-F 9:30am-12:30pm and 4-6:30pm, Sa-Su 9:30am-12:30pm. 200ptas.)*

LA RIBERA

Formerly home to Barcelona's fishermen, gritty La Ribera has developed an artistic flair. **Galleries,** trendy eateries, and little crafts shops pack the narrow streets. Most of the action begins on **C. Montcada.**

PALAU DE LA MÚSICA CATALANA. *Modernista* architect Lluís Domènech i Montaner designed the amazing, must-see, adjective-defying Palau de la Música Catalana. *(C. Sant Francesc de Paula, 2, off Vía Laietana near the Pl. Urquinaona. ☎93 268 10 00. For performance info,* *see* p. 876. *Open M-F 10am-9pm. Mandatory tours every 30min., 10:30am-3pm; 700ptas, students 500ptas; 350ptas with Ruta del Modernisme pass. Box office open M-Sa 10am-9pm, Su from 1hr. before concert. Tickets 1000-26,000ptas.)*

MUSEU PICASSO. The museum boasts the world's best collection from Picasso's formative years (the beginning of his Blue Period), as well as prints, ceramics, and pencil sketches by 11-year-old Pablo. The collection includes an excellent display of his Cubist interpretations of Velázquez's *Las Meninas*. *(C. Montcad, 15-19. M: Jaume I; walk down C. Princesa, and C. Montcada is on the right. Open Tu-Sa 10am-8pm, Su 10am-3pm. 750ptas, students 400ptas, under 16 free.)*

SANTA MARIA DEL MAR. Ribera's streets converge at the 14th-century Gothic **Església Santa María del Mar's** octagonal towers. The church would collapse if they were two feet higher. *(Open M-Sa 9am-1:30pm and 4:30-8pm, Su 9am-2pm and 5-8:30pm.)*

PARC DE LA CIUTADELLA AND VILA OLÍMPICA

The peaceful **Parc de la Ciutadella** once housed the fortress where Barcelona's influential citizens were imprisoned by Felipe V in the early 18th century. Host of the 1888 Universal Exposition, the park now harbors the wacky **Cascada** fountains, a zoo, a pond, and several museums, including the eclectic **Museu d'Art Modern,** in the center of the park on Pl. Armes. *(M: Barceloneta or Arc de Triomf. Open Tu-Sa 10am-7pm, Su 10am-2:30pm. 500ptas, students 350ptas.)* The **Vila Olímpica,** beyond the east side of the zoo, was built to house 15,000 athletes and entertain millions of tourists for the 1992 Olympics; today it's home to public parks, a shopping center, and offices. In **Barceloneta,** average **beaches** stretch out from the port. *(M: Ciutadella/Vila Olímpica; walk along the waterfront on Ronda Litoral toward the 2 towers.)*

MARVELOUS MODERNISME In the late 19th and early 20th centuries, Barcelona's flourishing bourgeoisie commissioned a new class of architects to build their houses, reshaping the face of L'Eixample with *Modernista* architecture that employed revolutionary shapes, materials, and spaces to reflect the signs and symbols of Catalunya. **Antoni Gaudí's** serpentine rooftops, warrior-like chimneys, and skeletal facades are perhaps the most famous examples of this style. A staunch regionalist, Gaudí incorporated an array of Catalán symbols and myths in his organic architecture and designed every feature of his boisterous buildings, down to the furniture, colorful ceramic mosaics, and elaborate light fixtures. Gaudí's creations are architectural breakthroughs that have since been imitated only with the aid of advanced computer technology and mathematics.

L'EIXAMPLE

The Catalán Renaissance and the growth of Barcelona during the 19th century pushed the city past its medieval walls and into ordered modernity. The carefully designed **Eixample** (uh-SHOMP-luh) neighborhood gave rise to *passeigs* (streets) lined with high-brow shopping and stunning *Modernista* spectacles.

SAGRADA FAMILIA. Only Gaudí's genius could draw thousands of tourists to a half-finished church; the architect himself guessed that the **Temple Expiadori de la Sagrada Familia** would take 200 years to complete. Gaudí lived in the complex for 11 years, until he was run over by a trolley in 1926. A **museum** displays a model of the structure as it was meant to be completed. *(On C. Marinara, between C. Mallorca and C. Provença. M: Sagrada Familia. Open daily Apr.-Aug. 9am-8pm; Sept.-Oct. and Mar. 9am-7pm; Nov.-Feb. 9am-6pm. Tours Apr.-Oct. 11:30am, 1, 4, and 6:30pm; Nov.-May 11:30am and 1pm. Church and museum 800ptas, students 600ptas. Elevator 200ptas.)*

MANZANA DE LA DISCORDIA. A short walk from Pl. Catalunya, the odd-numbered side of Pg. Gràcia, between Aragó and Consell de Cent, is popularly known as *la manzana de la discordia* (block of discord), referring to the aesthetic competition of three buildings on the block. At the **Casa Lleó i Morera,** by Domènech i Montaner, you can buy the **Ruta del Modernisme** pass and tour the interior of sprouting flowers, stained glass, and doorway sculptures. Puig i Cadafalch went for a geometric, Moorish-influenced pattern on the facade of **Casa Amatller** at #41. Gaudí's balconies ripple and blue-purple tiles sparkle on **Casa Batlló** at #43. Experts and tourists alike debate the meaning of the facade; many claim that it represents Catalunya's patron Sant Jordi (Saint George) slaying his dragon (with the chimney as the lance).

CASA MILÀ (LA PEDRERA). *Modernisme* buffs consider the spectacular Casa Milà apartment building, popularly known as *La Pedrera* (Stone Quarry), Gaudí's most refined work. The winding attic houses the **Espai Gaudí,** a multimedia presentation of Gaudí's life and works. Chimneys resembling soldiers and curved mounds decorated with broken champagne bottles sit on the **rooftop.** One floor below, a **restored apartment** exhibits the interior of a Gaudí home during the industrial revolution. *(Pg. Gràcia, 92. Enter around the corner on C. Provença. Open daily 10am-8pm. Tours M-F at noon and 6pm, Sa-Su 11am. 600ptas, students 350ptas.)*

MONTJUÏC

Whoever controlled Montjuïc (Hill of the Jews) ruled Barcelona. Dozens of despots have modified the **Castell de Monjuïc,** built atop an ancient Jewish cemetery; Franco made it one of his "interrogation" headquarters. *(Take the funicular from Pl. Raquel Meller (M: Parallel) to Av. Miramar, then take the teleferic cable car to the top. Cable car runs every 10min., 225ptas, round-trip 375ptas.)* The **Fonts Luminoses** (Illuminated Fountains), dominated by the **Font Mágica** (Magic Fountain), are visible from Pl. Espanya up Av. Reina María Cristina. From May to October, lasers light up the fountains. *(From M: Espanya, catch bus #50 at Av. Reina María Cristina. Displays every 10min. 9:30-11:30pm.)* The **Palau Nacional,** behind the fountains up the stairs, houses the Romanesque and Gothic art of the **Museu Nacional d'Art de Catalunya.** *(Open Tu-W and F-Sa 10am-7pm, Th 10am-9pm, Su 10am-2:30pm. 800ptas, with temporary exhibits 900ptas; with youth card 50% off.)* Up the hill and past some gardens lies **Estadi Olímpic de Montjuïc.** *(Open daily 10am-8pm. Free.)* About 100m down Av. Miramar from the stadium is the **Fundació Joan Miró,** housing a variety of his works. *(Miramar 71-75, on Pl. Neptú. M: Espanya. Open July-Sept. Tu-W and F-Sa 10am-8pm, Th 10am-9:30pm, Su 10am-2:30pm; Oct.-June Tu-W and F-Sa 10am-7pm, Th 10am-9:30pm, Su 10am-2:30pm. 800ptas, students 450ptas.)*

PARC GÜELL

On a hill just north of Gràcia lies one of Barcelona's greatest treasures and perhaps the world's most enchanting public park. Gaudí intended Parc Güell to be a garden city, designing the dwarfish multicolored houses and sparkling ceramic-mosaic stairways for the city's elite. When only two aristocrats signed on, it became a park instead. Inside, an elegant white staircase adorned with patterned tiles and a giant, gaping salamander leads to a pavilion supported by 86 pillars and decked out by the longest park bench in the world, a tile-shard, serpentine wonder. In the midst of the park awaits the **Casa-Museu Gaudí,** the architect's former home. *(Take bus #24 from Pg. Gràcia, or take the metro to "Vallarca," walk straight down Av. L'Hospítal Militar, take a left onto Baixada de la Gloria, and take the outdoor escalators uphill. Park open daily May-Aug. 10am-9pm; Apr. and Sept. 10am-8pm; Mar. and Oct. 10am-7pm; Nov.-Feb. 10am-6pm. Free. Museum open daily May-Sept. 10am-8pm; Oct. and Mar.-Apr. 10am-7pm; Nov.-Feb. 10am-6pm. 300ptas.)*

TIBIDABO

This area's name comes from its smashing view of Barcelona, the Pyrenees, the Mediterranean, and even (on clear days) Mallorca; in St. Matthew's Gospel, the devil tempts Jesus with spell-binding scenery, saying "All this I will give to you *(tibi dabo)* if you fall prostrate and worship me." For thrills, ride the elevator up the nearby **Torre de Collserola** communications tower (500ptas), or try the adjacent **Parc d'Atraccions,** a favorite of Barcelona's youngsters. *(Open June W-F 10am-6pm, Sa-Su noon-8pm; July-Aug. M-F noon-10pm, Sa-Su noon-1am. Unlimited use of 12 rides 1900ptas, no rides 700ptas.)* The **Tibibús** (270ptas) runs from Pl. Catalunya to the Torre de Collserola (every 30min.-1hr., 270ptas); commuter **trains** (round-trip including funicular and attraction park entrance 1900ptas) go from Pl. Catalunya to Av. Tibidabo. To reach the mountaintop, take the city bus on weekdays and the **Tramvia Blau** (Blue Train) on weekends. At the top of the street, take the funicular (200ptas).

ENTERTAINMENT

For entertainment tips, pick up the *Guía del Ocio* (www.guiadelociobcn.es) at any newsstand (125ptas). The **Gran Teatre del Liceu,** Ramblas, 51-59 (☎93 485 99 00; www.liceubarcelona.com), one of the world's leading opera stages until the interior was destroyed by fire in 1994, has reopened. **Palau de la Música Catalana,** C. San Francesc de Paula, 2, off Vía Laietana near Pl. Urquinaona, stages a variety of concerts. (See p. 874. ☎93 268 10 00. Tickets 1000-26,000ptas. Box office open M-Sa 10am-9pm, Su 1hr. prior to concert.) The **Grec-Barcelona** summer festival (www.grecbcn.com) turns the city into an international theater, music, and dance extravaganza from late June to mid-August. For festival info, ask at the tourist office or contact **Institut de Cultura de Barcelona (ICUB),** Palau de la Virreina, Ramblas 99. (☎93 301 77 75. Open M-F 10am-2pm and 4-8pm.) Buy tickets through **TelEntrada** (☎902 10 12 12; www.telentrada.com) or the Pl. Catalunya tourist office.

Grab face paint to join **F.C. Barcelona** at the **Nou Camp** stadium for **fútbol.** (☎93 496 36 00. Box office C. Aristedes Maillol 12/18.) The **sardana,** Catalunya's regional dance, is a popular Barcelona amusement; join the dance circle in front of the cathedral, on Pl. Sagrada Familia, or at Parc de la Ciutadella on Sundays at noon. Bullfights are held at the **Plaça de Toros Monumental,** on C. Castillejos, 248. (☎913 56 22 00. June-Oct. Su at 7pm; doors open at 5:30pm. Tickets 2600-15,000ptas.) The **Festa de Sant Jordi** (St. George; Apr. 23) celebrates Catalunya's patron saint with a feast. Men give women roses, and women give men books (how progressive).

NIGHTLIFE

The Barcelona evening begins at *bares-restaurantes* or *cervecerías*, moves to the *bares-musicales*, and ends after sunrise in discotecas. *Cerveceriás* on **Las Ramblas** and in surrounding neighborhoods **Barri Gòtic** and **El Raval** range from the *fútbol*-obsessed pub to the elegant lounge. The farther from Las Ramblas and the narrower the street, the less touristy the bar. The trendiest *bares-musicales* are scattered around **Gracia.** Smaller and far less crazy than the raging discotecas, the DJs still know how to rev up the well-dressed crowds. Consult the *Guía del Ocio* for information on movies, live concerts, bars and discos, and cultural events.

BARS

Les Bosq des Fades, just off Las Ramblas near the wax museum. M: Drassanes. A fairytale world with gnarled trees and a bridge. Open Su-Th until 1:30am, F-Sa until 2:30am.

La Oveja Negra, C. Sitges, 5. M: Catalunya; go down Las Ramblas, turn right on C. Tallers, and take the 1st left. The most popular tavern in town. Large *sangría* 1700ptas. Open M-Th 9am-2:30am, F 9am-3:30am, Sa-Su 5pm-3am.

Margarita Blue, C. J. A. Clavé, 6, off Las Ramblas. M: Drassanes. Mexican-themed bar serves blue margaritas and retro 80s pop. Margaritas 350ptas before 10:30pm, 450ptas after. Open Su-W 11:30pm-2am, Th-F 11:30pm-3am, Sa-Su 7pm-3am.

LOUNGES

El Cafe Que Pone Muebles Navarro, Riera Alta 4-6. Hordes drink themselves silly and sink into comfy couches. Beer 250ptas. Open Tu-Th 5pm-1am, F-Sa 5pm-2:30am.

Harlem Jazz Club, C. Comtesa de Sobradiel, 8. M: Liceu. Live jazz, folk, or acoustic rock every night. Su-Th free, Sa 500ptas with drink. Open daily 10pm-4am.

BARES-MUSICALES

Lizard, Platon 15. Rap, hip-hop, and funk in devil-red decor. Open Th-Sa 11:30pm-3am.

Universal, Maria Cubi, 182. *Bare-musicale* for social climbers. Open 11pm-3am.

Mas i Mas, Maria Cubi, 199. Packed and intimate. Open Th-Sa 11pm-3am.

I COULD HAVE DANCED ALL NIGHT

Club bouncers can be finicky, and what's hip varies daily. Dress well; guys should beware ridiculously high covers. Expect to pay 600ptas for a beer and at least 900ptas for drinks, more still at Maremagnum and Port Olímpic. Lower Montjuïc houses the "disco theme park" **Poble Espanyol,** Av. Marqués de Comillas, Barcelona's craziest disco experience. Clubs include the outdoor **La Terrazza, Torres de Avila,** and **Sixty Nine.** (M: Pl. Espanya. Open nightly July-Aug., Sept.-June Th-Sa.) Clubs get going after 1:30am; dancing lasts until 9am. *Discotecas* blare music all over **Olympic Village.** From M: Ciutadella-Vila Olímpica (L4); walk down C. Marina toward the twin towers; there's **no cover** anywhere. Walk down Las Ramblas and cross the wavy bridge to **Maremagnum** for a three-level maze of clubs. Some of the biggest and best *discotecas* are outside the touristed Ramblas area. Try **Otto Zutz,** C. Lincoln, 15, (M: FFCC Muntaner; open W-Sa midnight-5am) or **KGB,** C. Alegre de Dalt, 55 (M: Joanic; walk along Pi i Maragall and take the 1st left; open F-Su 1-8am).

EXCURSIONS FROM BARCELONA

SPAIN

MONTSERRAT. On the mountain of Montserrat, a wandering 9th-century mountaineer had a blinding vision of the Virgin Mary. In the 11th century, a **monastery** was founded to worship the Virgin; the site, with its interplay of limestone, quartz, and slate stone, has evolved into a major pilgrimage center. The monastery's ornate **basilica** is above Pl. Creu. Right of the main chapel is a route through the **side chapels** that leads to the 12th-century Romanesque **La Moreneta** (the black Virgin Mary), Montserrat's venerated icon. (Open daily in summer 8-10:30am, noon-6:30pm, and 7:30-8:30pm.) In Pl. Santa María, the **Museo de Montserrat** exhibits a range of art, from an Egyptian mummy to several Picassos. (Open daily in summer 9am-6pm; off season 9:30am-6:30pm. 500ptas, students 300ptas.) The **Santa Cova funicular** descends from Pl. Creu to paths that wind along to ancient hermitages. (Every 20min. In summer daily 10am-1pm and 2-6pm; off season Sa-Su only. Round-trip 360ptas.) Take the **St. Joan funicular** for more inspirational views. (Mar.-Oct. every 20min. 10am-5:30pm. Round-trip 895ptas.) The dilapidated **St. Joan monastery** and **shrine** are 20 minutes from the highest station. The real prize is **Sant Jerónim** (1235m) with mystical views of the celebrated rock formations, about two hours from Pl. Creu (1hr. from the terminus of the St. Joan funicular); after 45 minutes, take a sharp left at the little old chapel. FFCC **trains** (☎93 205 15 15) to Montserrat leave Barcelona's M: Espanya (1hr., every hr., round-trip including cable car pass 1905ptas); get off at Aeri de Montserrat, *not* Olesa de Montserrat. From the base of the mountain at the other end, the **Aeri cable car** runs to the monastery. (Every 15min. M-F 9:25am-1:45pm and 2:20-6:35pm, Sa-Su 2:20-6:35pm; round-trip 950ptas, included in train fare.) From the upper cable car station, turn left and walk to the **Pl. Creu info booth.** (☎93 877 72 01. Open July-Sept. daily 10am-7pm; Oct.-June M-F 9am-6pm, Sa-Su 10am-7pm.)

SITGES. The resort town of Sitges is a trendy playground of prime tanning, lively cultural festivals, an international gay community, and wired nightlife, just 40km south of Barcelona. Mainland Spain's Ibiza equivalent, Sitges has better **beaches** than the Balearic hotspot, 10 minutes from the train station via any street. In town, **C. Parellades** is the main tourist drag. Late-night foolhardiness clusters around **C. Primer de Maig,** which runs directly from the beach, and its continuation, **C. Marques Montroig.** The wild things are at the "disco-beach" **Atlántida,** in Sector Terramar. Grind at the legendary **Pachá,** on Pg. Sant Didac, in nearby Vallpineda. Buses run from midnight to 4am to the two discos from C. Primer de Maig. During **Carnaval** (Feb. 15-25, 2001), Sitges bursts into a frenzy of dancing, costumes, and alcohol. **Cercanías Trains** link Sitges to Barcelona's Sants Station and M: Gràcia (40min., every 15min., 310-355ptas). The **tourist office** is on Pg. Vilafranca. From the train station, turn right on C. Artur Carbonell and go downhill. (☎93 894 42 51. Open in summer daily 9am-9pm; in winter W-M 9am-2pm and 4-6:30pm.) If you plan to sleep in Sitges, reserve early. **Hostal Parelladas,** C. Parellades, 11, is a block from the beach. (☎93 894 08 01. Singles 2800ptas; doubles 5800ptas.)

GIRONA (GERONA)

A Roman settlement and important medieval port, Girona (pop. 73,500) was one of the few Spanish cities where Christians, Arabs, and Jews peacefully coexisted. It was also the founding place of the Jewish tradition of Kabbala, mystical and numerological readings of the Torah. The Riu Onyar separates the medieval alleys and Romanesque buildings of the old city from the Spanish dwellings of the new.

PRACTICAL INFO, ACCOMMODATIONS, AND FOOD. Girona is Costa Brava's transport center: all trains between Barcelona and southern France stop here, and scores of buses travel daily to the Costa Brava. **Trains** (☎972 24 02 02) depart from off C. Barcelona in the new town to: Figueres (45min., 22 per day, 325ptas); Barcelona (1¼hr., 21 per day, 1265ptas); Madrid (9-10½hr., 1 per day, 6000-7500ptas); and Paris (11hr., 1 per day, 16,900ptas). **Buses** (☎972 21 23 19) depart from around the corner. To get to the old city, head straight through the parking lot, turn left on C. Barcelona, bear right via C. Santa Eugenia to the Gran Vía de Jaume I, continue straight across to C. Nou, and cross the Pont de Pedra. The **tourist office,** Rambla Llibertat 1, is directly on the other side. (☎972 22 65 75; fax 972 22 66 12. Open M-F 9am-8pm, Sa 8am-2pm and 4-8pm, Su 9am-2pm.) The 14th-century **Hostal Residencia Bellmirall,** C. Bellmirall, 3, by the cathedral, features delightful stone rooms. (☎972 20 40 09. Breakfast included. Open Mar.-Dec. 15. Singles 4990-5280ptas; doubles 7920-8580ptas.) The ultra-modern **Alberg-Residència Cerverí de Girona (HI),** C. Ciutadans, 9, is on the street to the left of the Pont de Pedra. (☎972 21 81 21. Breakfast included. Sheets 350ptas. Laundry. Reserve through the Barcelona office (☎93 483 83 63). Members only; sells HI cards. 2500ptas, under 25 1900ptas.) The **Pensió Viladomat,** C. Ciutadans, 5, is next to the hostel. (☎972 20 31 76. Singles 2300ptas; doubles 4500-6500ptas; triples 6500ptas.) Girona abounds with innovative Catalán cuisine; for excellent, inexpensive food, try restaurants along **C. Cort Reial** or **Pl. Independència. Café Le Bistrot,** Pujada Sant Domènec, 4, packs in locals. (Lunch *menú* 1400ptas. Open M-Th 1-5pm and 7pm-1:30am, F-Sa 1-5pm and 7pm-1am.) Pick up cheap grub at the **market** in Parc de la Devesa (open Tu and Sa 8am-3pm), or at **Caprabo,** C. Sequia, 10, a block from C. Nou off the Gran Vía. (Open M-Sa 9am-1:30pm and 5-8:30pm.) **Postal code:** 17070.

SIGHTS AND ENTERTAINMENT. Wander through the old city, across the river from the train station. Crossing Pont de Pedra, turn left down Rambla de la Llibertat, continue on C. Argenteria, bear right across C. Cort Reial, climb the stairs, and head left to reach C. Força. **El Call,** the medieval Jewish neighborhood, begins at C. Sant Llorenç; take a right off C. Força into a narrow alley. The once-thriving community was virtually wiped out by the 1492 Inquisition. Enter **Centre Bonastruc Ça Porta,** a museum on the site of Girona's last synagogue, on C. Sant Llorenç about halfway up the hill. (Open June-Oct. M-Sa 10am-8pm, Su 10am-2pm; Nov.-May M-Sa

10am-6pm, Su 10am-2pm. Free.) Uphill on C. Força and around the corner to the right, the Gothic **cathedral** rises up 90 Rococo steps from the plaza. Its **Tesoro Capitular** contains some of Girona's most precious possessions, including the **Tapis de la Creació,** a 15th-century tapestry of the creation story. (Open July-Aug. Tu-Su 10am-2pm and 4-7pm; Sept.-June Tu-Sa 10am-2pm and 4-7pm, Su 10am-2pm. 500ptas.) Check out the New City's **Museu del Cinema,** Sèquia, 1. (Open June-Sept. Tu-Su 10am-8pm; Oct.-May Tu-F 10am-6pm, Sa 10am-8pm, Su 11am-3pm. 500ptas, students 250ptas.) The **Rambla** and **Pl. de Independencia** are the places to see and be seen. In the summer, witness *sardanas*, traditional Catalán dances involving 10-12 musicians serenading a ring of dancers. Bars near **Pl. Ferrán Catòlic** draw big crowds, but in summer, head to **Parc de la Devesa,** across the river from the old town and several blocks to the left. The old quarter bars host an artsier scene.

EXCURSIONS FROM GIRONA: THE COSTA BRAVA

TOSSA DE MAR. Falling in love in (and with) Tossa is easy. The pretty town (pop. 3800), 40km north of Barcelona, is packed with tourists every summer. But Tossa draws on its legacy as a 12th-century village, its cliff-studded landscape, its **calas** (small coves), and its small-town charm to resist becoming the average resort. Inside the walled **Vila Vella** (Old Town), spiraling alleys lead to a tiny plaza, where the **Museu Municipal** displays 20s and 30s art as well as antiquities from the nearby **Vila Romana.** (Open June-Sept. Tu-Su 10am-7pm; Oct.-May Tu-Su 10am-1pm and 3-6pm. 1000ptas.) After sunning and splashing at **La Platja Gran,** try hiking, biking, boating, or scuba diving. Sarfa **buses** run to Pl. de les Nacions Sense Estat, at the corner of Av. Pelegrí and Av. Ferrán Agulló, from Girona (1hr., 1-2 per day, 615ptas) and Barcelona (1½hr., 8-9 per day, 1070ptas). The **tourist office** shares the building. (☎972 34 01 08. Open mid-June to mid-Sept. M-Sa 9am-9pm, Su 10am-1pm; May to mid-June and mid-Sept. to Oct. M-Sa 10am-1pm and 4-8pm; Nov.-Apr. M-F 10am-1pm and 4-7pm, Sa 10am-1pm.) Surf the **Internet** at **Cyber-Cafe Bar La Playa,** C. Socors, 6. (300-400ptas per 15min. Open May-Oct. M-Sa 10am-midnight.) **Pensión Pepi,** C. Sant Miguel, 10, has cozy rooms with baths. Turn left off Av. de Pelegrí onto Maria Auxiliadora, and veer right onto C. Sant Miguel. (☎972 34 05 26. Singles 2000-3000ptas; doubles 4000-5000ptas. V, MC.) To get to **Fonda/Can Lluna,** C. Roqueta, 20, turn right off Pg. Mar onto C. Peixeteras, walk through C. Estalt, turn left at the end, and head straight for a breathtaking view. (☎972 34 03 65. 1750-2000ptas per person.) **Camp** at **Can Martí** (☎972 34 08 51), at the end of Rambla Pau Casals, off Av. Ferrán Agulló. People-watch at **Restaurant Marina,** C. Tarull, 6. (*Menú* 1400ptas. Open *Semana Santa*-Oct. daily 11am-11pm.) **Postal code:** 17320.

FIGUERES. In 1974, Salvador Dalí chose his native, beachless **Figueres** (pop. 35,000), 36km north of Girona, as the site to build a museum to house his works, catapulting the city to instant fame. Despite his reputation as a self-promoting fascist, his self-monument is undeniably a masterpiece—and Spain's second most popular museum. The **Teatre-Museu Dalí,** in Pl. Gala i S. Dalí, parades the artist's erotically nightmarish drawings, extraterrestrial landscapes, and bizarre installations. From the Rambla, take C. Girona, which becomes C. Jonquera, and climb the steps. (Open daily July-Sept. 9am-7:45pm; Oct.-June Tu-Su 10:30am-5:45pm. 1000ptas, students and seniors 800ptas.) **Trains** (☎972 20 70 93) run to: Girona (30min., 21 per day, 375ptas) and Barcelona (1½hr., 21 per day, 1300ptas). **Buses** (☎972 67 33 54) go to Girona (1hr., 4-6 per day, 475ptas); Cadaqués (1¼hr., 2-5 per day, 490ptas); and Barcelona (2¼hr., 4-6 per day, 1750ptas). The **tourist office** is on Pl. Sol. (☎972 50 31 55. Open July-Aug. M-Sa 9am-9pm, Su 9am-3pm; Apr.-June and Oct. M-F 8:30am-3pm and 4:30-8pm, Sa 9:30am-1:30pm and 3:30-6:30pm; Sept. and Nov.-Apr. M-F 8:30am-3pm.) Get on the **Internet** at **Bar-Arcadia,** C. Sant Antoni, 7. (500ptas per 30min. Open M-Sa 9am-10pm.) Finding a room can be a surreal experience, but **Alberg Tramuntana (HI),** C. Anciet de Pagès, 2, by the tourist office, is full of amenities. (☎972 50 12 13. Breakfast included. Reception daily 8:30am-1pm and 4-11pm. Lockout M-F 2-4pm, Sa-Su 1-7pm. Curfew midnight; in summer open for 10min. at 1, 2, 3, and 4am. Reserve in advance through the Barcelona office (☎93 483 83 63) or call the hostel 2-3 days ahead. Members only; sells HI cards. 2500ptas, under 26 1900ptas.) The luxurious **Hostal La Barrentina,** is at C. Lasauca, 13. (☎972 67 64 12. Singles 3500ptas; doubles 6000ptas.) Buy **groceries** at **MAXOR,** Pl. Sol, 5. (Open July-Sept. M-F 8am-9pm, Sa 9am-9pm; Oct.-June M-Sa 8am-8:30pm.) **Postal code:** 17600.

CADAQUÉS. The rocky beaches of Cadaqués (pop. 2000) have attracted artists, writers, and musicians—not to mention tourists—ever since Dalí built his summer home here in the 30s. The **Centre d'Art Perrot-Moore,** C. Vigilant, 1, near the town center, houses a Dalí erotic fantasy room and a number of Picassos. (Open daily July-Aug. 10:30am-1:30pm and 4:30-8:30pm; Apr.-June and Sept.-Oct. M-Sa 10:30am-1:30pm and 4-8pm, Su 10:30am-1:30pm. 800ptas, students 500ptas.) **Casa-Museu Salvador Dalí,** Port Lligat, Dalí's home until 1982, is complete with a lip-shaped sofa. Follow signs to Port Lligat (bear right with your back to the statue of liberty) and then to the Casa de Dalí. (Open daily mid-June to mid-Sept. 10:30am-9pm; mid-Mar. to mid-June and mid-Sept. to Nov. Tu-Su 10:30am-6pm. 1200ptas, students 700ptas.) **Buses** arrive from Figueres (1hr., 3-5 per day, 500ptas); Girona (2hr., 1-2 per day, 940ptas); and Barcelona (2½hr., 2-5 per day, 2045ptas). With your back to the Sarfa office at the bus stop, walk right along Av. Caritat Serinyana; the **tourist office,** C. Cotxe, 2, is off Pl. Frederic Rahola opposite the *passeig*. (☎972 25 83 15. Open July-Aug. M-Sa 10am-2pm and 4-9pm, Su 10:30am-1pm; Sept.-June M-Sa 10:30am-2pm and 4-8pm.) **Hostal Cristina,** C. Riera, has waterfront rooms. (☎972 25 81 38. Singles 3000ptas; doubles 4000-6000ptas.) **Camping Cadaqués,** Ctra. Portlligat, 17, is on the left on the way to Dalí's house. (☎972 25 81 26. Open late Mar.-Sept. 15. 565ptas per person; 710ptas per tent; 565ptas per car; add 7% IVA.) Pack a **picnic** from **Super Auvi,** C. Riera. (Open mid-July to Aug. M-Sa 8:30am-1:30pm and 4:30-8:30pm, Su 8:30am-1pm; Sept. to mid-July M-Sa 8am-2pm and 4-9pm.) **Postal code:** 17488.

THE PYRENEES

The jagged green mountains, Romanesque churches, and tranquil towns of the Pyrenees draw hikers and high-brow skiers in search of outdoor adventures. Mist and fog obscure visibility at high altitudes, creating either a dreamy atmosphere or slightly nerve-racking driving conditions. *Ski España* lists vital statistics of all ski stations in Spain. Without a car, transport is tricky, but feasible.

VAL D'ARAN. Some of the Catalán Pyrenees' most dazzling peaks cluster around Val d'Aran, in the northwest corner of Catalunya. The Val d'Aran is best known for its chic ski resorts—the Spanish royal family's favorite slopes are those of **Baquiera-Beret.** The **Albergue Era Garona (HI),** in the town of **Salardú,** is accessible by shuttle **bus** in high season from Vielha. (☎973 64 52 71; reservations ☎934 83 83 63. Breakfast included. 1900-2250ptas.) For skiing info, contact the **Oficeria de Baquiera-Beret** (☎973 64 44 55; fax 973 64 44 88) or the tourist office in Vielha (☎973 64 01 10).

The biggest town in the valley, **Vielha** (pop. 3500) welcomes hikers and skiers to its lively streets with every service outdoorsy types might desire. Only 12km from Baquiera-Beret, shuttle **buses** connect the two in July and August (schedules at the tourist office). Alsina Graells **buses** (☎639 38 03 73) run to Barcelona (5½hr., 4 per day, 3325ptas). The **tourist office,** C. Sarriulèra, 6, is a block upstream from the *plaça*.(☎973 64 01 10; fax 973 64 05 37. Open July to mid-Sept. daily 10am-1pm and 4:30-7:30pm; mid-Sept. to June M-Sa 10am-1pm and 4:30-7:30pm.) Check **email** at **CCV Informatica,** Edif. Val D'Aran. (500ptas per 30min. Open M-Sa 9:30am-1:30pm and 4:30-8pm.) **Camins,** Av. Pas d'Arro, 5 (☎973 64 24 44), can help plan outdoor adventures. Several inexpensive *pensiones* cluster at the end of C. Reiau, off Pg. Libertat (which intersects Av. Casteiro at Pl. Sant Antoni); try **Casa Vicenta** at #3. (☎973 64 08 19. Singles 2500-3000ptas; doubles 4000-4500ptas.) **Postal code:** 25530.

PARQUE NACIONAL DE ORDESA. Ordesa's Aragonese Pyrenees will reduce even the most seasoned travelers to stupefaction. Well-maintained trails cut across idyllic forests, jagged rock faces, snow-covered peaks, rushing rivers, and magnificent waterfalls. The **visitor center "El Parador"** is beyond the Ordesa park entrance. (Open daily June 9am-1:30pm and 4-7pm; July-Aug. 9am-1pm and 3:30-7pm; Apr.-May 9am-2pm and 3:30-6pm.) The **Soaso Circle** is the most practical hike; frequent signposts mark the five-hour journey, which can be cut to a two-hour loop. Enter the park through the village of **Torla,** where you can buy the indispensable *Editorial Alpina* guide (2000ptas). Reach Torla by Compañía Hudebus **bus** (☎974 21 32 77) from **Sabiñánigo** (55min., 1-2 per day, 355ptas), in turn accessible by La Oscense **bus** (☎974 35 50 60) from **Jaca** (July only; 30min., 1-2 per day, 110ptas) or any **train** on the Zaragoza-Huesca-Jaca line. A **bus** shuttles between Torla and **Ordesa** (July-Aug. only; every 15min., round-trip 200ptas). Off season, you'll have to **hike** the 8km to the entrance or cab it (☎974 48 61 53; 1500-2000ptas). Within the park, many **refugios** (mountain huts, usually without facilities) allow overnight stays. The 120-bed **Refugio Góriz** is a four-hour hike from the parking lot where the bus drops you off. (☎974 34 12 01. 1000ptas.) In Torla, ascend C. Francia a block to **Refugio L'Atalaya,** C. Francia, 45 (☎974 48 60 22), and **Refugio Briet** (☎974 48 62 21), across the street. (Both 1000ptas.) Opposite Refugio L'Atalaya, **Compañia de Ordesa** (☎974 48 64 17) rents bikes and organizes excursions. Outside Torla are **Camping Río Ara** (☎974 48 62 48) and **Camping San Anton** (☎974 48 60 63). (Open Apr.-Oct. Both 550ptas per person, per tent, and per car.) Stock up at **Supermercado Torla,** on C. Francia. (Open daily Feb.-Nov. 8am-2pm and 4-8pm; Dec.-Jan. 10am-2pm and 4-8pm.)

JACA. For centuries, Santiago-bound pilgrims would cross the Pyrenees, nest in Jaca (pop. 14,000) for the night, and be off by dawn. They had the right idea; use it as launching pad for nearby skiing and hiking. RENFE **trains** (☎974 36 13 32) run from C. Estación to Zaragoza (3hr., 2 per day, 1325ptas) and Madrid (7hr., 1 per day, 4200ptas); **buses** shuttle from the station to the Ayuntamiento on the central C. Mayor. Alosa **buses** (☎974 35 50 60) run to Zaragoza (2hr., 1 per day, 1460ptas) and Pamplona (2hr., 1 per day, 860ptas). The **tourist office,** Av. Regimiento de Galicia, 2, is off C. Mayor. (☎974 36 00 98. Open July-Aug. M-F 9am-2pm and 4:30-8pm, Sa 10am-1:30pm and 5-8pm, Su 10am-1:30pm; Sept.-June M-F 9am-1:30pm and 4:30-7pm, Sa 10am-1pm and 5-7pm.) To get to the **Albergue Juvenil de Escuelas Pias (HI),** Av. Perimetral, 6, from C. Mayor, turn left on C. Regimiento de Galicia, left on Av. Perimetral, and right after the bend on the dirt driveway before the skating rink. (☎974 36 05 36. Breakfast included. Curfew midnight. 3100ptas; under 28 2500ptas; nonmembers add 500ptas.)

SWM SEEKING... Tall, dark, handsome, rich, famous, respected, powerful, and searching for life partner. Enjoys water sports (competed on the Olympic sailing team). Educated at Georgetown. Looking for that special someone–attractive, charismatic, and preferably of noble lineage–to share interests and raise a family.

His name is Felipe, the Prince of Asturias and heir to the Spanish throne. All eyes have turned to Felipe–past 30, with two recently married older sisters–to choose the next set of genes that will contribute to the Bourbon dynasty. Whom will he choose for his queen when he takes over one of Europe's last remaining powerful monarchies? The competition is fierce. Lovely ladies from wealthy families are stalking the streets of Madrid and the slopes of the Val d'Aran, but so far there are no frontrunners. Cross your fingers and pack something nice–you could be the next Queen of Spain.

NAVARRA

The spirit of the Navarrese emanates from the rustic Pyrenean *pueblos* on the French border to bustling Pamplona to the dusty villages in the south. Bordered by Basque Country to the west and Aragón to the east, tiny villages welcome tourists.

PAMPLONA (IRUÑA)

Long, long ago, Pamplona's fiesta in honor of its patron saint, San Fermín, was just another religious holiday. But ever since Ernest Hemingway wrote *The Sun Also Rises*, hordes of visitors from around the world have come the week of July 6-14 to witness and experience *San Fermines*, the legendary "Running of the Bulls."

PRACTICAL INFO, ACCOMMODATIONS, AND FOOD. RENFE **trains** (☎948 13 02 02) run from off Av. San Jorge to: Zaragoza (2hr., 6 per day, 1565-1900ptas); San Sebastián (2hr., 2 per day, 1195-1500ptas); Madrid (5hr., 8 per day, 4200ptas); and Barcelona (6-8hr., 3 per day, 4100-5300ptas). **Buses** (☎948 22 38 54) go from C. Conde Oliveto, at C. Yanguas y Miranda, to: San Sebastián (1hr., 9 per day, 790ptas); Bilbao (2hr., 6-7 per day, 1520-1600ptas); Zaragoza (2-3hr., 6-7 per day, 1655ptas); Madrid (5hr., 4-7 per day, 3215ptas); and Barcelona (5½hr., 3-4 per day, 2820ptas). From the bus station, turn left on Av. Conde Oliveto, take the second left at the Pl. Príncipe de Viana rotary on Av. San Ignacio, continue to the end of Po. Sarasate, bear right to Pl. Castillo, take C. San Nicolas, turn right on C. San Miguel, and walk through Pl. San Francisco to reach the **tourist office,** C. Eslava, 1; from the train station, take bus #9 (95ptas) to the end, cut across Po. Sarasate, walk diagonally left to Pl. Castillo, and follow the directions above. (☎948 20 65 40; fax 948 20 70 34. Open during *San Fermines* daily 10am-5pm; July-Aug. M-Sa 10am-2pm and 4-7pm, Su 10am-2pm; Sept.-June M-F 10am-2pm and 4-7pm, Sa 10am-2pm.) During *San Fermines*, **store luggage** at the Escuelas de San Francisco, the big stone building at one end of Pl. San Francisco. (300ptas. Open 24hr.) **Email** from the **iturNet cibercafé,** C. Iturrama, 1, at C. Abejeras. (500ptas per hr. Open M-Sa 10am-2pm and 4:30-10pm; during *San Fermines* daily 9am-2pm.)

SPAIN

And now, kids, a lesson in supply and demand: smart *sanferministas* book their rooms up to a year (at least two months) in advance, often paying rates up to four times higher than those listed here. Beware hawkers at the train and bus stations—quality and prices vary tremendously. Check the newspaper *Diario de Navarra* for **casas particulares.** Many roomless folks are forced to sleep on the lawns of the Ciudadela or on Pl. Fueros, Pl. Castillo, or the banks of the river. Be careful—if you can't store your backpack (storage fills fast), sleep on top of it. To reach the impressive **Pensión Santa Cecilia,** C. Navarrería, 17, follow C. Chapitela, take the first right on C. Mercaderes, and make a sharp left. (☎948 22 22 30. Laundry. *San Fermines* dorms 6000ptas; rest of year singles 2500ptas, doubles 4000-5000ptas, triples 6000ptas.) Clean doubles await at **Fonda La Aragonesa,** at C. San Nicolás, 22. (☎948 22 34 28. *San Fermines* 9000ptas; rest of year 3000-3500ptas.) Show up early during the fiesta (no reservations) to get a room at **Fonda La Montañesa,** C. San Gregorio, 2. (☎948 22 43 80. *San Fermines* singles 6000ptas, doubles 12,000ptas; rest of year 1800ptas, 3500ptas.) To get to **Camping Ezcaba,** 7km away in Eusa, take the La Montañesa **bus** from Pl. Toros to Eusa (4 per day) to the end. (☎948 33 03 15. Open June-Oct. *San Fermines* 1100ptas per person, per tent, and per car; rest of year 540ptas.) Look for food near Pensión Santa Cecilia, above **Pl. San Francisco,** and around **Po. Ronda. Calles Navarrería** and **Po. Sarasate** host *bocadillo* bars. **Vendi,** at C. Hilarión Eslava and C. Mayor, has **groceries.** (Open during *San Fermines* M-Sa 9am-2pm; otherwise M-F 9am-2pm and 5:30-7:30pm, Sa 9am-2pm.) **Postal code:** 31001.

SIGHTS AND ENTERTAINMENT. Pamplona's rich architectural legacy is reason enough to visit during the 51 other weeks of the year. The restored late 14th-century **Gothic cathedral** is at the end of C. Navarrería. (Open M-F 10am-1:30pm and 4-7pm, Sa 10am-1:30pm. Tours at 10:30, 11:30am, 12:30, and 5pm. 500ptas.) The impressive walls of the pentagonal **Ciudadela** once humbled even Napoleon; today the Ciudadela hosts free exhibits and concerts in summer. From the old quarter, pick up C. Redín at the far end of the cathedral plaza, head left along the walls past the **Portal de Zumalacárregui** and along the Río Arga, and bear left through the **Parque de la Taconera.** (Open daily 7:30am-10pm; closed for *San Fermines.* Free.) Throughout the year, **Pl. de Castillo** is the social heart of the city. Hemingway's favorite haunt was the **Café-Bar Iruña,** immortalized in *The Sun Also Rises.* (Open during *San Fermines* daily 8am-4am; rest of year 5pm-2am.) The young and the restless booze up at bars in the *casco antiguo,* around **Calles de Jarauta, San Nicolás,** and **San Gregorio.**

Although Pamplona is usually very safe, crime skyrockets during *San Fermines,* when some folks come to take advantage of tourists. Beware of assaults and muggings, do not roam alone at night, and take care in the *casco antiguo.*

LOS SAN FERMINES (JULY 6-14). Visitors overcrowd Pamplona for one week in search of Europe's greatest party. Pamplona delivers an eight-day frenzy of parades, bullfights, parties, dancing, fireworks, concerts, and wine. Pamplonese, clad in white with red sashes and bandanas, literally throw themselves into the merry-making, displaying obscene levels of both physical stamina and alcohol tolerance. The "Running of the Bulls," called the *encierro,* is the focal point of *San Fermines;* the first *encierro* of the festival takes place on July 7 at 8am and is repeated at 8am every day for the next seven days. Hundreds of bleary-eyed, hungover, hyper-adrenalized runners flee from large bulls as bystanders cheer from barricades, windows, balconies, and doorways. Both the bulls and the mob are dangerous; terrified runners flee for dear life, and react without concern for those around them. Hemingway had the right idea: don't run. Watch the *encierro* from the bullring; arrive around 6:45am. Tickets for the Grada section of the ring are available before 7am. (M-F 450ptas, Sa-Su 600ptas.) You can watch for free, but the free section is overcrowded, making it hard to see and breathe. If you want to participate in the bullring excitement, line up by the Pl. Toros well before 7:30am and run in *before* the bulls are in sight. **Be very careful; follow the tourist office's guidelines for running.** To watch a bullfight, wait in the line that forms at the bullring around 8pm (from 2000ptas). As one fight ends, tickets go on sale for the next day. Once the running ends, insanity spills into the streets and gathers steam until nightfall, when it explodes with singing in bars, dancing in alleyways, spontaneous parades, and a no-holds-barred party in Pl. Castillo, Europe's biggest open-air dance floor.

BASQUE COUNTRY (PAÍS VASCO)

Basque Country's varied landscape resembles a nation complete unto itself, combining cosmopolitan cities, verdant hills, industrial wastelands, and quaint fishing villages. Many believe that the strongly nationalistic Basques are the native people of Iberia, as their culture and language date back several millennia.

SAN SEBASTIÁN (DONOSTIA)

Glittering on the shores of the Cantabrian Sea, coolly elegant San Sebastián (pop. 180,000) welcomes visitors. Locals and tourists down *pintxos* (tapas) and drinks in the *parte vieja* (old city), which claims the world's most bars per square meter.

GETTING THERE AND GETTING AROUND

Trains: RENFE, Estación del Norte (☎943 28 30 89), on Po. Francia, on the east side of Puente María Cristina. To: **Pamplona** (2hr., 2-12 per day, 1500ptas); **Zaragoza** (4hr., 4 per day, 2700-3900ptas); **Madrid** (8hr., 4 per day, 4600-4800ptas); **Paris** (8-11hr., 3-4 per day, 11,000ptas); and **Barcelona** (9hr., 2-3 per day, 4700-4900ptas).

Buses: Most buses pass through the central station on Pl. Pío XII, about 13 blocks south of Av. Libertad on Av. Sancho el Sabio. Several private companies operate out of the tiny station around the corner. Bus #28 goes to the city center from the bus station.

PESA, Av. Sancho el Sabio, 33 (☎943 46 29 52), goes to **Bilbao** (1¼hr., every 30min., 1120ptas). **Continental Auto,** Av. Sancho el Sabio, 31 (☎943 46 90 74), serves **Madrid** (6hr., 9-12 per day, 3800ptas). From Po. Vizcaya, 16, **La Roncalesa** (☎943 46 10 64) runs to **Pamplona** (1hr., 9 per day, 790ptas); **Vibarsa** (☎902 10 13 63) serves **Barcelona** (7hr., 3-5 per day, 2450-3350ptas). **Turytrans** (☎943 46 23 60) serves **Paris** (11 hr., 1 per day, 9400ptas).

ORIENTATION AND PRACTICAL INFORMATION

The city center and most monuments and beaches lie on a peninsula on the west side of the **Río Urumea;** at the tip, the **Monte Urgulla** juts out into the bay. Inland, nightlife rages and budget accommodations and restaurants cluster in the **parte vieja.** At the south end of the peninsula is the commercial area. From the bus station, head right (north) up Av. Sancho el Sabio toward the cathedral, ocean, and *parte vieja.* East of the river are the **RENFE station, Barrio de Gros,** and the **Playa de la Zurriola.** Head straight from the train station, cross the Puente María Cristina (bridge), head right at the fountain for four blocks, then left on Av. Libertad to the port; the *parte vieja* will lie to your right and the **Playa de la Concha** to your left.

Tourist Office: Centro de Atracción y Turismo (☎943 48 11 66; fax 943 48 11 72), on C. Reina Regente, on the corner of the plaza by the river. From the train station, turn right immediately after crossing the Puente María Cristina and turn left on C. Reina Regente at the Puerte de Zurriola. From the bus station, go down Av. Sancho el Sabio, bear right at Pl. Centenario onto C. Prim, and follow the river. At the 3rd bridge, Puente Zurriola, turn left into the plaza. Open June-Sept. M-Sa 8am-8pm, Su 10am-1pm; Oct.-May M-Sa 9am-2pm and 3:30-7pm, Su 10am-1pm.

Luggage Storage: At **RENFE station.** 400ptas per day. Open daily 7am-11pm.

Laundromat: Lavomatique, C. Iñigo, 13, off C. San Juan. Wash 575ptas; dry 400ptas. Open M-F 10am-1pm and 4-7pm, Sa-Su 10am-2pm.

Emergency: ☎091. **Police: Municipal** (☎943 45 00 00), on C. Easo.

Medical Assistance: Casa de Socorro, C. Bengoetxea, 4 (☎943 44 06 33).

Internet Access: Donosti-Net, C. Embletran, 2, at the corner of C. Narrica (☎943 42 58 70). 50ptas per 15min. Open daily 9am-9pm.

Post Office: C. Urdaneta, by the cathedral. *Poste Restante* at window #11. Open M-F 8:30am-8:30pm, Sa 9:30am-2pm. Address mail to be held: First name SURNAME, *Lista de Correos*, C. Urdaneta, 2080 San Sebastián, Spain **20006.**

ACCOMMODATIONS AND CAMPING

Desperate backpackers will scrounge for rooms in July and August, particularly during *San Fermines* (July 6-14) and *Semana Grande* (starts Su of the week of Aug. 15); September's film festival is not much better. Budget options center in the *parte vieja* and by the cathedral. The tourist office has lists of accommodations and most hostel owners know of **casas particulares**—feel free to ask for help.

PARTE VIEJA

Pensión Amaiur, C. 31 de Agosto, 44, 2nd fl. (☎943 42 96 54). From Alameda del Boulevard, go up C. San Jerónimo to the end and turn left. Rooms have distinctive charm and gorgeous bathrooms. English and French spoken. Semana Santa-Oct. 3000-3800ptas per person; Nov.-Semana Santa 1900-2500ptas.

Pensión San Lorenzo, C. San Lorenzo, 2 (☎943 42 55 16), off C. San Juan. Recently refurbished. Internet. Kitchen. July-Sept. doubles 7000-8000ptas; Oct.-June doubles 4000ptas; singles sometimes available.

Pensión Larrea, C. Narrica, 21, 1st fl. (☎943 42 26 94). Adorable owner has a reputation as the "best mom in town." July-Aug. singles 3000ptas, doubles 5000ptas, triples 6000ptas; Sept.-June 2500ptas, 4000ptas, 5000ptas.

Pensión Loinaz, C. San Lorenzo, 17 (☎943 42 67 14), off C. San Juan. Laundry. July-Aug. doubles 5500-6000ptas, triples 8500ptas; Apr.-June 4000ptas, 6000ptas; Sept.-Mar. 3500ptas, 5000ptas; singles sometimes available (3000-3500ptas).

Pension Urgull, Esterlines, 10, 3rd fl. (☎943 43 00 47). Attractive old rooms with tall windows, small balconies, and sinks. July-Aug. singles 3000ptas, doubles 5000-6000ptas; Sept.-June 3500ptas, 2500ptas.

OUTSIDE THE PARTE VIEJA

Albergue Juvenil la Sirena (HI), Po. Igueldo, 25 (☎943 31 02 68), to the far west. Take bus #24 from the train or bus station to Av. Zumalacárregui (in front of the San Sebastián Hotel); then take Av. Brunet toward the mountain and turn left at the end. HI and ISIC members only. Breakfast included. Sheets 395ptas. Laundry. Lockout 11am-3pm. Curfew June-Aug. daily 2am; Sept.-May Su-Th midnight, F-Sa 2am. June-Oct. 15 and *Semana Santa* 2555ptas, under 27 2100ptas; Oct. 15-May 2000ptas, 1600ptas.

Pensión La Perla, C. Loiola, 10, 2nd fl. (☎943 42 81 23), on the street directly ahead of the cathedral. Attractive rooms with polished floors, bath, and TV. July-Sept. singles 4000ptas, doubles 6000ptas; Oct.-June 3500ptas, 4500ptas.

Pensión Urkia, C. Urbieta, 12, 3rd fl. (☎943 42 44 36). C. Urbieta runs west of the cathedral; it's a block north at C. Arrasate. Hotel feel. July-Sept. doubles 6000ptas, triples 9000ptas; Oct.-June singles 3000ptas, doubles 4000ptas, triples 6000ptas.

Camping: Camping Igueldo (☎943 21 45 02), 5km west. Take bus #16 (dir. Barrio de Igueldo-Camping; every 30min., 110ptas) from Alameda del Boulevard. Reception June-Aug. 8am-midnight; Sept.-May 9am-1pm and 5-9pm. June-Aug. 2889ptas for tent and 2 people, 425ptas per additional person; Sept.-May 1386ptas, 357ptas.

FOOD

Pintxos (tapas; rarely more than 175ptas each), chased down with the fizzy regional white wine *txacoli*, are a religion here; bars in the old city spread an array of enticing tidbits on toothpicks or bread. The entire *parte vieja* seems to exist for no other purpose than to feed. Sample the to-die-for delicacies at **Bar La Cepa,** C. 31 de Agosto, 7-9. (*Pintxos* 160-325ptas. *Bocadillos* 450-475ptas. Open daily 1pm-midnight.) The **Caravanseri Café,** C. San Bartolomé, 1, by the cathedral, has fabulous veggie options. (Open M-Th 8am-midnight, F-Sa 8am-1am, and Su 10:30am-midnight.) **Mercado de la Bretxa,** on Alameda del Boulevard at C. San Juan, sells fresh produce. (Open M-Sa 9am-9pm.) **Super Todo Todo,** on Alameda del Boulevard around the corner from the tourist office, also sells **groceries.** (Open M-Sa 8:30am-9pm.)

SPAIN

SIGHTS AND ENTERTAINMENT

San Sebastián's most attractive sight is the city itself—green walks, grandiose buildings, and the placid bay. The views from **Monte Igueldo,** west of the center, are the best in town: by day, the countryside meets the ocean in a line of white and blue, and by night the flood-lit **Isla Santa Clara** (island) seems to float on a ring of light. The walk up the mountain is not too strenuous, but the weary can take a funicular. A mini amusement park also awaits those who scale the peak (170ptas). Across the bay from Monte Igueldo, **Monte Urgull,** at the northern tip of the *parte vieja* jutting out into the bay, is crowned by the overgrown **Castillo de Santa Cruz de la Mota,** in turn topped by the statue of the **Sagrado Corazón de Jesús.** (Open daily June-Aug. 8am-8pm; Sept.-May 8am-6pm.) Directly below the hill, on Po. Nuevo in the *parte vieja*, the serene **Museo de San Telmo** resides in a Dominican monastery strewn with Basque funerary relics, a montage of artifacts, El Grecos, and dinosaur skeletons. (Open Tu-Sa 10:30am-1:30pm and 4-8pm, Su 10:30am-2pm. Free.) To the west, the **Plaza Constitución** features the ornate portal of **Iglesia Santa María** and numbered balconies dating from the plaza's days as a bull ring. The gorgeous **Playa de la Concha** curves along the city's western shore, which turns into the smaller and steeper **Playa de Ondarreta** beyond the **Palacio de Miramar.**

Tickets sell out for the five-day **Festival de Jazz** (☎943 48 11 79; www.jazzaldia.com), in mid- to late July. **Semana Grande** (Big Week; week of Aug. 15) explodes with concerts, a fireworks festival, and more. All year, the *parte vieja* lets loose after dark. **C. Fermín Calbetón,** three blocks in from Alameda del Boulevard, sweats

WHAT THE DEVIL ARE THEY TXPEAKING?

Linguists cannot pinpoint the origin of the Basque language *euskera*, though its commonalities with Caucasian and African dialects suggest that prehistoric Basques may have migrated from the Caucasus via Africa. Called *la lengua del diablo* (the devil's tongue) by other Spaniards, *euskera* symbolizes cultural self-determination. Franco banned *euskera* and forbade giving children Basque names (like Iñaki or Estibaliz), but since his death there has been a resurgence of everything from *euskera* TV shows to *ikastolas* (Basque schools). Still, only half a million natives, mainly in País Vasco and northern Navarra, speak *euskera*.

bars. Along the beach, music starts thumping at midnight. A fave among expats and young travelers, **The World's End,** Po. de Salamanca, 14, is a block from the *parte vieja* toward the beach. (Open Su-Th 2pm-2:30am, F-Sa 2pm-3:30am.) **Bar Tas-Tas,** C. Fermín Calbetón, 35, attracts backpackers. (Open daily 3pm-3am.) **Zibbibo,** Plaza Sarriegi, 8, is a hip little club with a dance floor and a blend of hits and techno. (*Grande sangrias* 650ptas. Open Su-Th 6pm-2am, F-Sa until 3:30am.) **Molly Malone,** C. San Martin, 55, off the Paseo de la Concha, outside the *parte vieja*, is an Irish pub popular with locals. (Beer 400-600ptas. Open 3pm-3am.)

BILBAO (BILBO)

Graced with the marvelous new Guggenheim Museum, Bilbao (pop. 1,200,000) is finally overcoming its reputation as a bourgeois, business-minded industrial center. Its medieval *casco viejo*, wide 19th-century boulevards lined by grand buildings, and stunning new subway and riverwalk make Bilbao well worth a stop.

PRACTICAL INFO, ACCOMMODATIONS, AND FOOD. RENFE **trains** (☎94 423 86 23) arrive at the **Estación de Abando,** Pl. Circular 2, from: Salamanca (5½-6½hr., 2 per day, 3500ptas); Madrid (5¾-9hr., 3 per day, 4200-4400ptas); and Barcelona (9½-11hr., 2 per day, 5100ptas). From Pl. Circular, head right around the station and cross the Puente del Arenal (bridge) to reach Pl. Arriaga, the entrance to the *casco viejo*. Most **bus companies** leave from the **Termibús terminal,** C. Gurtubay, 1 (☎94 439 52 05; M: San Mamés), on the west side of town, for: San Sebastián (1¼hr.; M-Sa every 30min., Su every hr.; 1120ptas); Pamplona (2hr., 5-6 per day, 1580ptas); Zaragoza (4hr., 9-10 per day, 2430ptas); and Salamanca (5hr.; 1-2 per day, 3200ptas). To get to the *casco viejo* from the bus station, exit the terminal and turn left, where you'll see three red Metro rings at the bottom of the stairs. Take the metro (140ptas, keep your ticket) to "Casco Viejo." **ANSA (GETSA, VIACAR)** buses leave from C. Autonomía, 17 (☎94 444 31 00) for: Burgos (2hr., 4-5 per day, 1435ptas); Madrid (4-5hr., 10-17 per day, 3270ptas); and Barcelona (7hr., 3-4 per day, 4900ptas.) To get to the ANSA terminal from the Termibús station, go left as you exit down C. Hurtado de Amézaga and bear right at Pl. Zabálburu onto C. Autonomía. To reach the **tourist office,** on Pl. Arenal, turn left across the bridge from the train station. (☎94 479 57 60; www.bilbao.net. Open M-F 9am-2pm and 4-7:30pm, Sa 9am-2pm, Su 10am-2pm.) Take Gran Vía from the *casco viejo*, turn left on C. Maria Diaz de Haro, and take the first right to **El Señor de la Red,** C. Rodriguez Arias, 69, to check **email.** (200ptas per 30min. Free coffee. Open daily 10am-10pm.)

After crossing the Puente del Arenal toward the *casco viejo*, turn right on C. Ribera, left on C. Santa María, and left on C. Jardines to reach **Hostal Mardones,** #4, 3rd fl. The lovely rooms have marble sinks. (Singles 4000-5000ptas; doubles 5600-6600; triples 8500-10,500ptas.) **Pensión Méndez,** C. Santa María, 13, 4th fl., is insulated from the raging nightlife below. (Singles 3000-6000ptas; doubles 5000-8000ptas; triples 7500-10,000ptas.) Run by a cool young couple, **Hostal Gurea,** C. Bidebarrieta, 14, offers good beds and polished floors. (Singles 3600-3900ptas; doubles 4000-4800ptas.) **Mercado de la Ribera,** on the bank of the river heading left from the tourist office, is Spain's biggest indoor market. (Open daily 7am-noon.) Get **groceries** at the huge **Champión,** Pl. Santos Juanes. (Open M-Sa 9am-9pm.) **Postal code:** 48005.

SIGHTS AND ENTERTAINMENT. Frank O. Gehry's **Guggenheim Museum Bilbao,** Av. Abandoibarra 2, can only be described as breathtaking. Lauded by the international press, it has catapulted Bilbao into cultural stardom. The US$100 million building's undulating curves of glistening titanium, limestone, and glass resemble an iridescent scaly fish. The museum currently hosts rotating exhibits culled from the Guggenheim Foundation's collection. From Pl. Circular, head down Gran Vía, right across Pl. de Frederico Moyúo, and down Alameda de Recalde. (☎94 435 90 00; www.guggenheim.bilbao.es. Open Tu-Su 10am-8pm. 1200ptas, students 600ptas. Joint admission with Museo de Bellas Artes 900ptas.) From the Guggenheim, follow the Alameda de Mazarredo to the often overshadowed **Museo de Bellas Artes,** Pl. Museo, 2, which hordes an impressive collection of 12th- to 20th-century art. (Open Tu-Sa 10am-8pm, Su 10am-2pm. 600ptas, students 200ptas; W free.) Revelers in the *casco viejo* spill into the streets, especially on **C. Barrencalle** (Barrenkale). A young crowd jams at **C. Licenciado Poza** on the west side of town. For a mellower scene, people-watch at the elegant 19th-century **Café Boulevard,** C. Arenal, 3. (Open M-Th 7:30am-midnight, F-Sa 8am-2am, Su 11am-midnight.)

EXCURSION FROM BILBAO: GUERNICA (GERNIKA). On April 26, 1937, the Nazi "Condor Legion" released an estimated 29,000kg of explosives on Guernica, obliterating 70% of a city in three hours. The nearly 2000 people who were killed in the bombings were immortalized in Pablo Picasso's stark masterpiece *Guernica*, now in Madrid's Reina Sofía gallery (see p. 840). The rebuilt city offers little aside from the **Gernika Museoa,** Foru Plaza 1, which features an exhibition chronicling the bombardment (open July-Aug. daily 10am-7pm; Sept.-June M-Sa 10am-2pm and 4-7pm, Su 10am-2pm), but it's a good daytrip for those interested in learning about this infamous event. **Trains** (☎94 625 11 82) roll in from Bilbao (45min., 315ptas).

BALEARIC ISLANDS

Perhaps dreaming of the fortunes to be made in the 20th-century tourist industry, nearly every culture with boats tried to conquer the *Islas Baleares*. The foreign invasion continues as two million tourists flood the islands' discos and beaches each year. Culture-philiacs and shopaholics will fall for **Mallorca**'s high-class act and stunning natural beauty. **Ibiza,** a counterculture haven since the 1960s, offers some of the best nightlife in all of Europe. The smaller islands, **Formentera** and **Menorca,** rest upon unspoiled sands, hidden coves, and mysterious Bronze Age megaliths.

GETTING THERE AND GETTING AROUND

Fast, cheap **flights** to the islands are the easiest way to get there. Those under 26 often get discounts from **Iberia/Aviaco Airlines** (☎902 40 05 00; www.iberia.com), which flies to Palma de Mallorca and Ibiza from: Madrid (1hr., students round-trip 25-30,000ptas); Barcelona (40min., students round-trip 10-20,000ptas); and Valencia. **Air Europa** (☎902 24 00 42) and **SpanAir** (☎902 13 14 15; www.spanair.com) offer budget flights to and between the islands. Most cheap round-trip **charters** include a week's stay in a hotel; some companies called *mayoristas* sell leftover spots as "seat-only" deals. **Ferries** to the islands are a less popular mode of transport. **Trasmediterránea** (☎902 45 46 45; www.trasmediterranea.com) departs from Barcelona's Estació Marítima Moll and Valencia's Estació Marítima for Mallorca and Ibiza. **Buquebus** (☎902 41 42 42 or 934 81 73 60; email reservas@buquebus.es) goes from Barcelona to Palma (4hr., 2 per day, 8150ptas). Book airplane or ferry tickets through a travel agency in Barcelona, Valencia, or on the islands.

Within the islands, **ferries** are the most cost-efficient; they run from Palma to Mahón (6½hr., Su, 3045ptas) and Ibiza (2½-4½hr., 6 per week, 3330-5210ptas). **Iberia** flies from Palma to Ibiza (35min., 4 per day, 8900ptas) and Mahón, Menorca (35min., 4 per day, 8900ptas). All three major islands have good **bus** systems, although Ibiza's is the only one that makes sense. A day's **car** rental costs around 4500ptas, **mopeds** 2700ptas per day, and **bikes** 1000ptas per day.

MALLORCA

Since Roman times, Mallorca has been a popular member of the in-crowd. Yet amid the tourism, lemon groves and olive trees adorn the jagged cliffs of the north coast, and lazy bays and caves scoop into the rest of the coast. The capital of the Balearics, **Palma** (pop. 323,000) embraces conspicuous consumption, but still manages to please with its well-preserved old quarter, colonial architecture, and local flavor. The tourist office distributes a list of over 40 nearby **beaches,** many a mere bus ride from Palma; one popular choice is **El Arenal** (Platja de Palma; bus #15), 11km southeast (toward the airport). After sunning, head to the streets around **Pl. Reina** and **La Llotja** to imbibe. **ABACO,** C. Sant Joan, 1, in the Barri Gòtic near the waterfront, is perfect for a cocktail. (Drinks 1100-2200ptas. Open daily 9pm-12:30am.) Every Friday, *El Día de Mundo* (125ptas) lists bars and discos. The area by **Plaça Reina** and **La Llotja** flows with bar-hoppers. Palma's clubbers start nights in the *bares-musicales* along the **Paseo Maritimo** strip, including **Mira Blau, Cafe Thalassa, Made in Brazil,** and **Aqua** (drinks around 1000ptas). Others boogie near **El Terreno**—clubs are center on **Pl. Gomilia** and along **C. Joan Miró.** Word is that **Pachá,** Av. Gabriel Roca, will found an island. For now it has to make do with a large club. (Cover 2000-3000ptas, try for free tickets at bars in town. Open midnight-6am.)

To get from the airport to the center, take bus #17 to **Pl. d'Espanya** (15min., every 20min., 295ptas). To continue to the **tourist office,** C. Sant Dominic, 11, take Pg. Marítim (a.k.a. Av. Juan Roca) to Av. Antoni Maura, follow C. Conquistador out of Pl. de la Reina, and continue on C. Sant Dominic. (☎971 71 15 27. Open M-F 9am-8pm, Sa 9am-1:30pm.) **Branches** are in Pl. Espanya, Pl. Reina, and the airport. **Hostal Bonany,** C. Almirante Cervera, 5, has a pool and patio. Take bus #3, 20, 21, or 22 from Pl. Espanya to Av. Joan Miró and walk up C. Camilio José Cela. Take the first right, then the first left. (☎971 73 79 24. Breakfast included. Singles 3600ptas; doubles 5800ptas.) From the port, go left on Av. Gabriel Roca and turn right on C. Argentina to reach the lovely **Hostal Cuba,** C. San Magí, 1. (☎971 73 81 59. Singles 2000ptas; doubles 4000ptas; triples 5500ptas.) Take bus #15 from Pl. Espanya (every 8min., 175ptas) and ask to get off at Hotel Acapulco to reach the palatial **Alberg Platja de Palma (HI),** C. Costa Brava, 13. (☎971 26 08 92. Breakfast included. Laundry. Reception 8am-3am. Curfew Su-Th midnight, F-Sa 3am. 1500ptas; members only.) **Camp** at **Platja Blava,** at km 8 on the highway between Alcúdia and C'an Picafort. Take Autocares Mallorca (2 per day, 575ptas) from Pl. Espanya. (☎971 53 78 63. 600ptas per person; 1300-3000ptas per site.) **Servicio y Precios,** on C. Felip Bauzà, near Pl. Reina, has **groceries.** (Open M-F 8:30am-8:30pm, Sa 9am-2pm.)

IBIZA

A 1960s hippie enclave, Ibiza (pop. 84,000) has long forgotten its roots in favor of new-age decadence, as style warriors arrive in droves to debauch themselves in a sex- and substance-driven summer culture. Ibiza's thriving gay community lends credence to its image as a center of tolerance, but the island's high price tags preclude true diversity. Oh, and Ibiza has **beaches,** too. **Eivissa** (Ibiza City) is the world's biggest 24-hour party; the show begins at sunset. Wrapped in 16th-century walls, **Dalt Vila** (High Town) hosts 20th-century urban bustle in the city's oldest buildings. Its twisting, sloping streets lead to the 14th-century **cathedral** and superb views of the city and ocean. No beach is within quick walking distance, but **Platja de Talamanca, Platja des Duros, Platja d'en Bossa,** and **Platja Figueredes** are at most 20 minutes away by bike; buses also leave from Av. Isidor Macabich 20 for Platja d'en Bossa (every 30min., 125ptas). The most beautiful beach near Eivissa is **Playa de Las Salinas,** where the nude sunbathers are almost as perfect as the crystal-blue water and silk-like sand. The crowds return from the beaches by nightfall, when even the clothing stores (open until 1am) dazzle with throbbing techno and flashing lights. The bar scene centers around **Calle Barcelona;** the real fun begins when the sun goes down. **Calle Virgen** is the center of gay nightlife. The island's **discos** (virtually all of which have a mixed gay/straight crowd) are world-famous and ever-changing. Refer to *Ministry in*

Ibiza or *Party Sun*, free at many hostels, bars, and restaurants. The **Discobus** runs to and from all the major hotspots (runs midnight-6:30am, 250ptas). Wild, wild **Privilege** is best known for Monday night's kinky "manumission" parties. (Cover from 4000ptas. Open June-Sept. M and W-Sa midnight-7am.) Playful **Pachá,** on Pg. Perimitral, is 20 minutes from the port. (Cover 5000ptas; includes 1 drink. Open daily 11:15pm-7:30am.) Forget everything in the crazed lights of **Amnesia,** a mock-British club on the road to San Antonio. (Cover 4000-7000ptas. Open daily midnight-6am.) Cap off your night with a dancing morning in **Space,** Platja de Bossa (open daily 8am-6am), then cruise to **Bora Bora,** on Platja de Bossa, which catches the crowd around 4pm.

The local paper *Diario de Ibiza* (www.diariodeibiza.es; 125ptas) features an *Agenda* page with everything you need to know about Ibiza. The **tourist office,** C. Antoni Riquer, 2, is on the water. (☎971 30 19 00; www.ibizaonline.com. Open M-F 9:30am-1:30pm and 5-7pm, Sa 10:30am-1pm.) Cheap accommodations in town are rare. The letters "CH" *(casa de huespedes)* mark many doorways; call the owners at the phone number on the door. If you are willing to splurge an extra US$15-$20 per night, a small hotel may be the way to go, especially in Platja D'en Bossa and San Antonio. **Hostal Residencia Ripoll,** at C. Vicente Cuervo, 14, has fans in all interior rooms. (☎971 31 42 75. July-Sept. singles 3500ptas; doubles 5500ptas.) **Hostal Residencia Sol y Brisa** is at Av. B. V. Ramón, 15, parallel to Pg. Vara de Rey. (☎971 31 08 18; fax 971 30 30 32. Singles 3500ptas; doubles 6000ptas.) For a **supermarket,** try **Comestibles Tony,** Carrer d'Enmig, 1. (Open daily 9am-2pm and 5-8pm.)

FORMENTERA

Formentera is a true island paradise. A 35-minute ferry ride from **Eivissa** (call **Trasmapi-Febesa** ☎971 31 07 11; 1285ptas) brings you to deserted beaches and stunning bays. Rent a **moped** (2500ptas per day) at one of the dozens of places along the port **La Savina.** Shaped like an upside-down "u," Formentera's two southernmost tips are shrines to the island's fantastic beauty; each is flanked by a **lighthouse** situated on 200 ft. cliffs jutting out of the sea. Cool air and the scent of pine trees mark the windy ascent to either of these breathtaking look-out points. Drive through the mountainous regions of La Mola to Punta de Sa Ruda or by the olive groves and wispy grass to Cap de Barbaria. Splash in the turquoise Mediterranean waters off **Platja de Llevant** and the **Platja de Ses Salines** (for both head from the port and follow signs to Verede de Ses Salines). Learn how to **windsurf** or test your **sailing** skills with **Wet 4 Fun** on **Es Pujols** beach. (Sailboat 4900ptas per hr.; windsurfing 2200ptas per hr.; parasailing 5900ptas). **Hostal Maysi,** Playa Arenal, km 11, is on some of the finest white sand on the island. (☎971 328 547. Singles 6000ptas; doubles 8000ptas.) The serene rooms in **Hostal Costa Azul,** Playa de Migjorn, km 7, are complemented by a quiet beach. (☎971 32 80 24. 3755ptas per person.)

NORTHWESTERN SPAIN

Northwestern Spain is the country's best-kept secret; its seclusion is half its charm. Rainy **Galicia** hides mysterious Celtic ruins, left when the Celts made a pit stop on its quiet beaches along the west coast. Tiny **Asturias** is tucked on the northern coast, allowing access to its dramatic Picos de Europa.

GALICIA (GALIZA)

If, as the Galician saying goes, "rain is art," then there is no gallery more beautiful than the northwest's misty skies. Often veiled in silvery drizzle, it is a province of fern-laden eucalyptus woods, slate-roofed fishing villages, and endless white beaches. Locals speak *gallego*, a linguistic link between Castilian and Portuguese.

SANTIAGO DE COMPOSTELA

Santiago has drawn pilgrims eager to gaze at one of Christianity's holiest cities. The cathedral marks the end of the *Camino del Santiago*, a pilgrimage believed to halve one's time in purgatory. Today, sunburnt pilgrims, street musicians, and hordes of tourists fill the streets.

PRACTICAL INFO, ACCOMMODATIONS, AND FOOD. **Trains** (☎981 52 02 02) go from C. De Hórreo, in the southern end of the city, to León (6½hr., 1 per day, 3600ptas) and Madrid (8hr., 3 per day, 5900ptas). From the station, cross the street, bear right at the top of the stairs, take C. Hórreo to Pr. Galicia (*not* Av. Lugo), and go a block to C. Bautizatos, from which Rúa do Franco (C. Franco), Rúa do Vilar (C. Vilar), and Rúa Nova (C. Nueva) lead to the cathedral at the city center. **Buses** (☎981 58 77 00) run from C. San Cayetano (20min. from downtown) to: Madrid (8-9hr., 4 per day, 5135ptas); San Sebastián (13½hr., 2 per day, 7150ptas); and Bilbao (11¼hr., 1-2 per day, 6345ptas). From the station, take bus #10 or bus C Circular to Pr. Galicia (100ptas). The **tourist office** is at Rúa Vilar, 43. (☎981 58 40 81. Open M-F 10am-2pm and 4-7pm, Sa 11am-2pm and 5-7pm, Su 11am-2pm.) Check **email** at **Nova 50,** R. Nova, 50. (200ptas per hr. Open daily 9am-1am.)

Hostels, *pensiones*, and restaurants cluster around **C. Vilar, C. Franco,** and **C. Raíña.** **Hospedaje Ramos,** C. Raíña, 18, 2nd fl., above O Papa Una restaurant, is super-cozy. (☎981 58 18 59. Singles 1800-2000ptas; doubles 3350-3650ptas.) From Pr. Galicia, turn right on C. Fonte San Antonio and left up the granite street to reach **Hospedaje Itatti,** Pr. Mazarelos, 1. (☎981 58 06 29. Singles 2000-3000ptas, doubles 3500-5000ptas.) **Hospedaje Santa Cruz** is at C. Vilar 42, 2nd fl. (☎981 56 01 11. Singles 2000-3000ptas; doubles 3500-5000ptas.) Take bus #6 or 9 to get to **Camping As Cancelas,** C. 25 de Xullo, 35, 2km from the cathedral on the northern edge of town. (☎981 58 02 66. 575ptas per person; 615ptas per car and per tent.) Bars and cafeterias line the old town streets, offering a variety of remarkably inexpensive *menús*. **Supermercados Lorenzo Froiz,** Pr. Toural, is one block into the old city from Pr. Galicia. (Open M-Sa 9am-3pm and 5-9pm.) **Postal code:** 15701.

SPAIN

SIGHTS AND ENTERTAINMENT. Offering a cool, quiet sanctuary to priest, pilgrim, and tourist alike, Santiago's **cathedral** rises above the lively old city center. Each of its four facades is a masterpiece from a different era, and entrances open up onto four plazas: Platerías, Quintana, Obradoiro, and Azabaxería. The southern **Praza de Platerías** is the oldest of the facades; the Baroque **Obradoiro** facade encases the Maestro Mateo's **Pórtico de la Gloria,** considered the crowning achievement of Spanish Romanesque sculpture. The remains of **St. James** lie beneath the high altar in a silver coffer. Inside the **museum** are gorgeous 16th-century tapestries and two poignant statues of the pregnant Virgin Mary. (Cathedral open daily 7am-9pm. Museum open June-Sept. M-Sa 10am-1:30pm and 4-7:30pm, Su and holidays 10am-1:30pm and 4-7pm; Oct.-May M-Sa 11am-1pm and 4-6pm, Su and holidays 10am-1:30pm and 4-7pm. 500ptas.) Those curious about the Camino de Santiago can head to the **Museo das Peregrinacións,** Pl. San Miguel. (Open Tu-F 10am-8pm, Sa 10:30am-1:30pm and 5-8pm, Su 10:30am-1:30pm. 400ptas, students 200ptas.) At night, crowds look for post-pilgrimage fun. Students hit the bars and clubs off **Pl. Roxa** (take C. Montevo Ríos). Stop at **Casa das Crechas,** Vía Sacra, 3, just off Pl. Quintana, for Guinness and other magical brews. A traditional Irish pub, **Moore's and Co,** Av. Figueroa, 1, on the corner of Rodrigo de Padrón, has theme nights. (Bar open M-F 8pm-3am, Sa-Su 8pm-4am.)

EXCURSION FROM SANTIAGO: O CASTRO DE BAROÑA. Nineteen kilometers south of the town of **Noya** is a little-known treasure of historical intrigue and mesmerizing natural beauty: the seaside remains of the 5th-century Celtic fortress **O Castro de Baroña.** Its foundations dot the isthmus, ascending to a rocky promontory above the sea and then descending to a crescent beach. Castromil **buses** from Santiago to Muros stop in Noya (50min., every hr., 400ptas) and Hefsel **buses** from Noya to Riveira stop at O Castro—tell the driver your destination (30min., 205ptas).

THESE BOOTS WERE MADE FOR WALKING

One night in AD 813, a hermit trudged through the hills on the way to his hermitage. Suddenly, bright visions revealed the long-forgotten tomb of the Apostle James ("Santiago" in Spanish). Around this *campus stellae* (field of stars) the cathedral of Santiago de Compostela was built, and around this cathedral a world-famous pilgrimage was born. Since the 12th century, thousands of pilgrims have traveled the 750-870km of the **Camino de Santiago.** Clever Benedictine monks built monasteries to host *peregrinos* (pilgrims) along the *camino,* helping to make Santiago's cathedral the world's most frequented Christian shrine. The scalloped conch shell, used for dipping in streams along the way, has become a symbol of the Camino de Santiago; the shells, tied onto weathered backpacks, make pilgrims easy to spot, as do crook-necked walking sticks and sunburned faces. Pilgrims must cover 100km on foot or horse or 200km on bike to receive *La Compostela,* the cathedral's certificate of completion. Shelters along the way offer free lodging to pilgrims and stamp "pilgrims' passports." At 30km per day, walking the entire *camino* takes about a month. For inspiration along the way, keep in mind that you are joining the ranks of such illustrious pilgrims as Fernando and Isabel, Francis of Assisi, Pope John Paul II, and Shirley MacLaine. For more info, contact the **Officinal de Acogida del Peregrino,** C. Vilar 1 (☎981 56 24 19).

RÍAS ALTAS

The small *rías* of the Costa Muerte are the forgotten corner of Galicia, but the beaches here are arguably the country's cleanest, loveliest, and least crowded.

LA CORUÑA (A CORUÑA). Nearly blinded by the reflection of the sun on La Coruña's harborside wall of windows, sailors nicknamed it the Crystal City. The effect is just as mesmerizing today. Countless cafes and restaurants line the new *paseo*, Europe's longest seaside promenade (8km). Large gardens, bustling plazas crowned by gorgeous fountains, a sprawling historic sector, gargantuan shopping malls, three renowned **beaches,** and nonstop nightlife also await. Hercules allegedly erected the 2nd-century **Torre de Hércules,** now the world's oldest working lighthouse, upon the remains of an unfortunate enemy; you can climb a 239-step tunnel to the pinnacle. Take bus #9 or 13 (115ptas), or walk the path from the Orzán and Riazor beaches. (Open daily Apr.-Sept. 10am-7pm; Oct.-Mar. 10am-6pm. 250ptas.) **Trains** (☎981 15 02 02) go from Pr. San Cristóbal to Santiago de Compostela (1hr., 20-23 per day, 545-645ptas) and Madrid (8½-11hr., 1-3 per day, 6200-17,400ptas). **Buses** (☎981 23 96 44) go from C. Caballeros, across Av. Alcalde Molina from the train station, to: Santiago (50min.-1½hr., 17 per day, 825ptas); Oviedo (5hr., 4 per day, 3175ptas); and Madrid (8½hr., 5-6 per day, 4955-6975ptas). From the bus station, take bus #1 or 1A (115ptas) to the **tourist office,** on Dársena de la Marina. (☎/fax 981 22 18 22. Open Sept. 16-July 14 M-F 9am-2pm and 4:30-6:30pm, Sa 10:30am-1:30pm; Sept. 15-July 15 M-F 9am-2pm and 4:30-6:30pm, Sa 10:30am-1pm and 5-7pm, Su 10am-2pm, 5-7pm.) **Hospedaje María Pita,** C. Riego de Agua, 38, 3rd fl., has a homey feel. (☎981 22 11 87. Doubles 2900-3500ptas.) For **groceries,** go to **Supermercados Claudio.** (Open daily 9am-3pm and 5-9pm.)

RIBADEO AND CEDEIRA. Fern-covered rainforests give way to Ribadeo's soft, empty beaches lacing the coast. Even the influx of summer residents can't spoil the stunning Galician scenery of the ghostly town (pop. 9300). Just past the dock, the *paséo maritimo* harbors spectacular views of **Praia os Bloques.** Incredible rock archways plunge into the sea at **Praia as Catedrais,** a 9km hike or short bike ride away. The **tourist office** is in Pl. de España within El Parque de San Francisco. (☎982 12 86 89. Open in summer M-F 8am-3pm and 4-7pm, Sa 10am-2pm and 4-8pm; off season M-F 8am-3pm and 4-7pm.) The FEVE train station (☎982 13 07 39) is 15 minutes from Pl. España on R. Villafranco del Bierzo. **Trains** go to El Ferrol (3hr., 4 per day, 1160ptas) and Oviedo (3½hr., 2 per day, 1280ptas). IASA **buses** run to Vivero

SPAIN

(1½hr., M-F 3 per day, 625ptas) and La Caruña (2½-3½hr., M-Sa 4 per day, 1550-1980ptas). ALSA, off Pr. de España, serves Oviedo (3-3¾hr., 6 per day, 1700ptas).

Small **Cedeira** (pop. 8500) offers pretty beaches and wild countryside. The **Santuario de San Andrés de Teixido** (a steep 12km hike from town) still hosts pagan cults with thriving rituals. **Bus** service is sparse; RIALSA runs from Cedeira to El Ferrol (1hr., 7 per day, 420ptas), where buses connect to La Coruña. To get to Vivero, take an IASA bus from C. Ezequiel Lopez, 28 to Campo do Hospital (15min., 4 per day, 120ptas), then change to the Campo do Hospital-Vivero IASA bus line. The **tourist office** is at C. Ezequiel Lopez, 22. (☎981 48 21 87. Open Apr.-Sept. M-F 10:30am-1:30pm and 5-8pm, Sa 10am-2pm, Su and holidays noon-2pm.) **Hostal Chelsea,** Pr. Sagrado Corazón, 9, is by the bus stop. (☎981 48 23 40. Doubles 4000-4500ptas.)

ASTURIAS

Sky-scraping cliffs and hell-reaching ravines lend an epic scope to the tiny land of Asturias, tucked between the Basque Country and Galicia.

PICOS DE EUROPA

God bless plate tectonics—300 million years ago, 'twas a mere flapping of Mother Nature's limestone bedsheet that erected the Picos de Europa, a mountain range of curious variation and chaotic beauty. Most of the area has environmental protection as the **Picos de Europa National Park.** Near the **Cares Gorge** (Garganta del Cares) lie the most popular trails and peaks. For a list of mountain **refugios** (cabins with bunks but not blankets) and general park info, contact the **Picos de Europa National Park Visitors Center** (☎985 84 86 14).

OVIEDO. Oviedo (pop. 200,000), the area's capital and transport hub, provides an excellent base for exploring the mountains. ALSA **buses** (☎985 28 12 00) arrive in Pl. Primo de Rivera from: León (2hr., 8 per day, 1030ptas); Burgos (4¼hr., 2 per day, 1540ptas); Madrid (5hr., 10-14 per day, 3825-6000ptas); and Santiago de Compostela (5½-7hr., 3-4 per day, 3740ptas). C. Fray Ceferino leads from the other side of the plaza to C. Uría, where RENFE **trains** (☎985 24 33 64) arrive from León (2-2½hr., 7 per day, 945-2300ptas) and Madrid (6-9hr., 3 per day, 5900ptas). Walking down C. Uría with the station behind you, the old city is to the left; its two main plazas are **Pl. Mayor** and **Pl. de Alfonso II,** known to locals as Pl. de la Catedral and to tourists as Pl. de la **Tourist Office.** (☎985 21 33 85. Open M-F 9:30am-1:30pm and 4:30-6:30pm, Sa 9am-2pm.) To get to **Residencia Juvenil Ramón Menéndez Pidal,** C. Julián Clavería, 14, just off Pl. Toros, take bus #2 from C. Uría. (☎985 23 20 54. 1066ptas, with breakfast 1325ptas; under 27 780ptas, 941ptas.) Near the cathedral are **Pensión Pomar,** C. Jovellanos 7 (☎985 22 27 91; singles 3000-4000ptas; doubles 4000-5000ptas; triples 4500-6000ptas), and **Pensión Martinez,** C. Jovellanos 5 (☎985 21 53 44; singles 1600ptas; doubles and triples 3000ptas). Grab **groceries** at **El Corte Inglés,** on C. General Elorza, opposite the bus station. (Open M-Sa 10am-9:30pm.)

HIKING. Before scaling the mountains, load up on **maps** and other info in Oviedo. **TIVE,** C. Calvo Sotelo, 5, is a budget travel agency with info on hiking and excursions. (☎985 23 60 58. Open M-F 8am-3pm.) **ICONA,** C. Arquitecto Reguera, 13, 2nd fl. (☎985 24 14 12), has trail and camping info. ALSA **buses** run from Oviedo to several other good bases from which to explore the mountains, including **Cangas de Onís** (1½-1¾hr., 700ptas) and **Covadonga** (1¾hr., 785ptas).

SWEDEN (SVERIGE)

SWEDISH KRONOR

US$1 = 9.75KR	1KR = US$0.10
CDN$1 = 6.59KR	1KR = CDN$0.15
UK£1= 13.71KR	1KR = UK£0.07
IR£1 = 10.63KR	1KR = IR£0.09
AUS$1 = 5.48KR	1KR = AUS$0.18
NZ$1 = 4.20KR	1KR = NZ$0.24
SAR1 = 1.37KR	1KR = SAR0.73
EUR€1 = 8.38KR	1KR = EUR€0.12

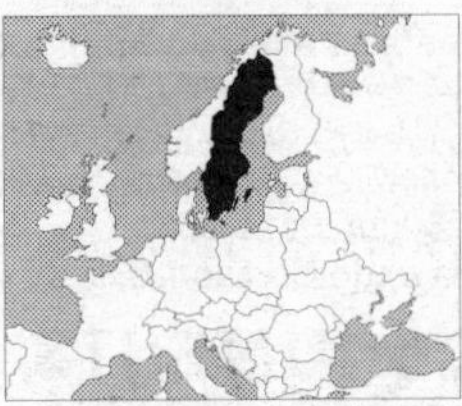

Country code: 46. **International dialing prefix:** 009. From outside Sweden, dial int'l dialing prefix (see inside back cover) + city code + local number.

The Swedish concept of *lagom* (moderation) implies that life should be lived somewhere between wealth and poverty, ecstasy and depression. Yet Sweden defies the *lagom* stereotype with definite extremes, stretching from the mountainous Arctic reaches of northern Kiruna to the flat, temperate farmland and white sand beaches of Skåne and Småland in the south. Dalarna, Värmland, and Norrland evoke images of quiet woods, folk music, and rustic country Midsummer celebrations, while the capital city of Stockholm shines as a thoroughly cosmopolitan center. Sweden's mythic early history of violent Viking conflict and conquest has given way to a successful experiment with egalitarian socialism and a role as an international peacekeeper. Culturally, Sweden is often thought of as the land of fiddlers and hurdy-gurdy accordions, but film director Ingmar Berman and playwright August Strindberg gained fame for their dark sophistication. Lasse Hallström's films, like *My Life as a Dog*, reveal the wide range of Swedish humor.

FACTS AND FIGURES

Official Name: Kingdom of Sweden.
Government: Constitutional Monarchy.
Capital: Stockholm.
Land Area: 43,075 sq. km.
Geography: Mostly flat lowlands, with some hills; low mountains in west.
Climate: Cold winter, cool summers.
Major Cities: Göteborg, Malmö, Jönköping, Örebro.
Population: 8,912,000. Urban 83%, Rural 17%.
Language: Swedish.
Religions: Evangelical Lutheran (94%), Roman Catholic (1.5%).
Average Income Per Capita: US$19,700.
Major Exports: Machinery, motor vehicles, paper products, wood.

DISCOVER SWEDEN

The natural starting point for any tour of Sweden is vibrant **Stockholm,** arguably one of the most attractive capitals in Europe. **Gamla Stan,** the city's medieval core, features the stunning Royal Palace (p. 897). Daytrip to the similarly awe-inspiring **Drottningholm Palace,** home to the Swedish royal family (p. 904), and **Uppsala,** the alleged site of early pagan activity, today just home to 20,000 students (p. 905). If you want to go North, consider a student flight or a night train to **Kiruna,** where you can explore Sami culture, underground mines, and vast stretches of true Arctic wilderness (p. 912.) On the western coast, Sweden's second-largest city, **Gothenburg,** counterbalances Stockholm's frenetic atmosphere with a laid-back attitude and elegant cafe culture (p. 909). Off the eastern coast in the Baltic Sea, the island of **Gotland,** rife with medieval churches, white-sand beaches, and prehistoric sites, invites travelers to bike, camp, and enjoy many of its attractions for free (p. 906).

ESSENTIALS

WHEN TO GO

The best time to visit Sweden is in the summer, when daytime temperatures average 20°C (68°F) in the south and 16°C (61°F) in the north; nights can get chilly. Bring an umbrella for frequent light rains. If you go in winter, bring heavy cold-weather gear; temperatures are frequently below -5°C (23°F). The midnight sun is best seen early June to mid-July.

DOCUMENTS AND FORMALITIES

South Africans need a **visa** for stays of any length. Citizens of Australia, New Zealand, Canada, the UK, Ireland, and the US can visit for up to 90 days without one, but this three-month period begins upon entry into any Scandinavian country; for more than 90 days in any combination of Finland, Iceland, Norway, and/or Sweden, you will need a visa.

EMBASSIES AND CONSULATES

Embassies and consulates of other countries in Sweden are in **Stockholm** (p. 778).

Swedish Embassies at Home: Australia, 5 Turrana St., Yarralumla, Canberra, ACT 2600 (☎62 73 30 33; fax 62 73 32 98); **Canada,** 377 Dalhousie St., Ottawa ON K1N 9N8 (☎ (613) 241 85 53; fax 241 22 77); **South Africa,** P.O. Box 3982, Cape Town 8000 (☎ (021) 25 39 88; fax 25 10 16); **UK,** 11 Montagu Pl., London W1H 2AL (☎ (020) 79 17 64 00; fax (020) 79 17 64 75); **US,** 1501 M St. NW, Washington, DC 20005 (☎ (202) 467 26 00; fax 467 26 56).

GETTING AROUND

BY PLANE. Most international flights land in Stockholm, although domestic flights also connect to northern Sweden. **Transwede** (☎ (020) 22 52 25) and **SAS,** in Australia (☎ (02) 92 99 98 00); South Africa (☎ (021) 419 86 86 or ☎ (011) 884 56 00); Sweden (☎ (020) 72 77 27); UK (☎ (0845) 60 72 77 27); US (☎ (800) 221 23 50); www.scandinavian.net/travel/start/se/index.asp), offer youth fares on flights within Scandinavia. SAS also offers domestic and international "Air Passes"; see p. 64.

BY TRAIN. **Statens Järnvägar (SJ),** the state railway company, runs reliable and frequent trains throughout the southern half of Sweden. Seat **reservations** (15-40kr) are required on some trains (indicated by a R, IN, or IC on the schedule), and are recommended on all other routes. Reservations are also mandatory on the new high-speed **X2000** trains (to Stockholm, Gothenburg, Malmö, and Mora); they are included in the normal ticket price, but are additional for railpass holders (reservations ☎ (020) 75 75 75; toll-free in Sweden). In southern Skåne, private **pågatågen** trains service Helsingborg, Lund, Malmö, and Ystad; **InterRail** and **Scanrail** passes are valid. Northern Sweden is served by two main rail routes: the coastal **Malmbanan** runs north from Stockholm through Boden, Umeå, and Kiruna to Narvik, Norway; from Midsummer (June 22-23, 2001) to early August, the privately run **Inlandsbanan** also travels farther inland from Mora to Gällivare.

Eurail is valid in Sweden. The buy-in-Scandinavia **Scanrail Pass** allows five days within 15 (1575kr, under 26 1190kr) or 21 consecutive days (2510kr, 1815kr) of unlimited rail travel through Scandinavia, and free or discounted ferry rides. This differs from the buy-outside-Scandinavia **Scanrail Pass** (see p. 59). A rail link over the new **Øresund bridge** connects Copenhagen, Denmark to Malmö in a breezy 35 minutes, certainly the fastest way to enter Sweden from Continental Europe.

BY BUS. In the north, buses may be a better option than trains. **Swebus** (☎ (08) 655 90 00) is the main company, offering service all over Sweden, Norway, and Denmark. **Swebus Express** (☎ (020) 64 06 40; toll-free in Sweden) serves southern Sweden only. **Bus Stop** (☎ (08) 440 85 70) reserves tickets for buses from Stockholm. Bus tickets are treated as an extension of the rail network, and can be bought from state railways. You can also buy tickets on the bus. Express buses offer discounts for children, seniors, students, and youth. Bicycles are not allowed on buses.

BY FERRY. If you don't want to take the new **Øresund bridge,** you can ferry from **Copenhagen** to **Malmö** (see p. 907). **Ystad** (see p. 908) sends boats to **Bornholm** and **Poland.** Ferries from **Gothenburg** (see p. 909) serve **Frederikshavn, Denmark; Kiel, Germany;** and **Newcastle** and **Harwich, England.** From **Stockholm** (see p. 897), ferries run to the **Åland Islands, Gotland, Turku,** and **Helsinki.** North of Stockholm, **Silja Line ferries** (☎ (090) 71 44 00) connect **Umeå** and **Vaasa, Finland.**

BY CAR. Swedish roads are good, and remarkably uncrowded. Unleaded **gas** costs an average of US$1 per liter. When gas stations are closed, look for pumps marked "*sedel automat*," which operate after hours. To get on the *strak* (highway), ask for the *entre* (entrance); getting off, look for an *aufart* (exit), and then probably for *parkering* (parking). **Renting** a car within Sweden averages US$40-115 per day, including VAT. Special discounts abound, particularly if you opt for a fly/drive package or if you rent for an extended period.

BY BIKE. Sweden is a biker's heaven; paths cover most of the country, particularly in the south, and you can complete a trip of Sweden on the hostel-spotted **Sverigeleden bike route.** Contact STF (see below) for info.

TOURIST SERVICES AND MONEY

EMERGENCY. Police, ambulance, and **fire:** ☎ 112.

TOURIST OFFICES. Every town and nearly every village has a tourist office. For more info before arriving in Sweden, contact the **Swedish Tourist Board: UK,** 11 Montagu Pl., London W1H 2AL (☎ (020) 77 24 58 68; fax 77 24 58 72); **US,** 655 Third Ave., New York, NY 10017 (☎ (212) 885 97 00; fax 885 97 10; www.gosweden.org).

MONEY. The unit of Swedish **currency** is the **krona,** divided into 100 *öre.* Bills come in denominations of 20, 50, 100, and 500kr; coins come in 1 and 5kr, and 10 and 50 *öre.* Many post offices are also banks. **Tipping** is not expected, as gratuities are usually added to the bill; however, in cities, tipping 10-15% at restaurants is becoming common. Add 10% for taxis. The **VAT** in Sweden is a shocking 25%. Luckily, for purchases of more than $13 in a single store during a single visit, you can receive a VAT refund of 20%.

BUSINESS HOURS. Banks are usually open M-F 9:30am-3pm (6pm in some large cities). **Stores** stay open M-F 9am-6pm, Sa 10am-1pm. **Museums** are usually open Tu-Su 10am-4pm.

ACCOMMODATIONS AND CAMPING

Youth hostels *(vandrarhem)* in Sweden cost about 100-150kr per night. The 300 HI-affiliated hostels run by the **Svenska Turistföreningen (STF)** are invariably top-notch (nonmembers pay 40kr extra per night). Most hostels have kitchens, laundry, and common areas. To reserve ahead, call the hostel directly or contact the STF headquarters in Stockholm (☎ (08) 463 22 70); all sell **Hostelling International (HI)** membership cards (250kr) or offer guest cards. Tourist offices often book beds in hostels for no fee, and can help find **private rooms** (100-250kr). **Private hotels** are very good as well. More economical hotels are beginning to offer reduced-service rooms at prices competitive with hostels, especially for groups of three or more. STF also manages **mountain huts** in the northern wilds with 10-80 beds that cost 155-195kr in high season (nonmembers 195-245kr). Huts are popular; plan ahead.

Many **campgrounds** (80-110kr per site) also offer *stugor* (cottages) for around 85-175kr per person. **International Camping Cards** are not valid in Sweden; **Swedish**

MIDSUMMER MADNESS For Midsummer (June 22-23, 2001), Swedes emerge to celebrate the sun after a long, dark winter. Families, villagers, and amorous youngsters dance around the **Midsommarstång,** a cross-shaped pole with two rings dangling from the ends always erected on the Friday of the festival. Its phallic construction symbolizes the fertilization of the soil it is staked in, and thoughts of other fertilization abound as girls place flowers under their pillows to induce dreams of their future spouses. The largest celebrations are in Dalarna, where alcohol and pickled herring flow freely and people flood the city for a two-day party. Note that during Midsummer most transportation lines and establishments are closed.

Camping Cards are virtually mandatory. Year-long memberships (60kr per family) are available through **Sveriges Campingvärdars Riksförbund (SCR),** Box 255, 451 17 Uddevalla (email ck@camping.se), or at any SCR campground. You may camp for **free** for one or two nights anywhere (except gardens and farmland), as long as you respect the flora, fauna, and the owner's privacy, and pick up all garbage. Pick up the *Right (and Wrongs) of Public Access in Sweden* brochure from STF or from tourist offices, or call the **Swedish Environmental Protection Agency** (☎ (08) 698 10 00).

FOOD AND DRINK

Food is very expensive in restaurants and not much cheaper in grocery stores. Rely on supermarkets and outdoor fruit and vegetable markets. Ubiquitous stands provide the most kebabs for your kronor (25-35kr for meat, rice, and veggies). Potatoes are the national staple; these and other dishes are invariably smothered with dill. Try tasty milk products like *messmör* (spreadable cheese) and *filmjölk*, a fluid yogurt. When you tire of groceries, seek out restaurants offering an affordable *dagens rätt* (40-60kr), a daily special including an entree, salad, bread, and drink, often all-you-can-eat and usually available only at lunch. A real beer *(starköl)* costs 10-15kr in stores and 30-50kr per pint in city pubs. The cheaper, weaker *lättöl* (alcohol up to 3.5%) can be purchased at supermarkets and convenience stores for 8-12kr per 0.5L. Although the drinking age is 18, bars and many nightclubs have age restrictions as high as 25.

COMMUNICATION

MAIL. Mailing a postcard or letter from Sweden to Australia, Canada, New Zealand, the US, and South Africa costs 8kr.

TELEPHONES. Most payphones only accept **phone cards** *(Telefonkort);* buy them at newsstands and post offices in 30, 60, or 120 units (35kr, 60kr, and 100kr). **International direct dial** numbers include: **AT&T,** ☎ 020 79 56 11; **Sprint,** ☎ 020 79 90 11; **MCI WorldPhone Direct,** ☎ 020 79 59 22; **Australia Direct,** ☎ 020 79 90 61, **Canada Direct,** ☎ 020 79 90 15; **BT Direct,** ☎ 020 79 91 44; **Ireland Direct,** ☎ 020 79 93 53; **Telecom New Zealand Direct,** ☎ 020 79 84 31; and **Telkom South Africa Direct,** ☎ 020 79 90 27.

LANGUAGE. Swedish. Almost all Swedes speak some English; most under 50 are fluent. Impress that special Swedish someone with a few phrases from p. 981.

HOLIDAYS AND FESTIVALS

Holidays: New Year's Day (Jan. 1); Epiphany (Jan. 5-6); Easter Sunday and Monday (Apr. 23-24); Valborg's Eve (Apr. 30); May Day (May 1); Ascension Day (June 1); National Day (June 6); Whit Sunday and Monday (June 11-12); Midsummer's Eve and Midsummer (June 22-23); All Saints' Eve and Day (Nov. 3-4); Christmas Eve and Day (Dec. 24-25); Boxing Day (Dec. 26); New Year's Eve (Dec. 31).

Festivals: Midsummer incites family frolicking and bacchanalian dancing around Midsummer poles. July and Aug. bring two special festivals, the *surströmming* (rotten herring) and crayfish parties.

STOCKHOLM ☎ 08

Stockholm may well be the best-kept secret in Europe. The city's identity is largely shaped by its omnipresent waters—in the canals and channels of the Baltic Sea and Lake Mälaren and deep in the city's salty history. Neutrality in the past century's wars has preserved Stockholm's history in the cobblestone streets of the Old Town and the Continental elegance of the North Island, but the city pushes ahead on the cutting edge of Internet technology, interior and industrial design, architecture, and pop music. Stockholm's cosmopolitan streets teem with world-class museums, chic nightspots, and famously friendly locals who make any stay a pleasant experience.

GETTING THERE AND GETTING AROUND

Flights: Arlanda Airport (☎797 60 00), 45km north of the city. **Flygbussar** buses (☎686 37 87) run between the airport and Cityterminalen (40min., every 10min. 4:25am-10pm, 60kr, public transport passes not valid). **Bus** #583 runs from the airport to "J" railway stop "Märsta" (10min., 35kr or 5 coupons, SL pass valid); Centralen is 40min. farther by train (120kr). Without a Stockholm card or SL pass, buses are better deals. Cards available at the Pressbyrån (see below).

Trains: Centralstation (info and reservations ☎ (020) 75 75 75). T-bana: T-Centralen. To: **Oslo** (6hr., 2 per day, 505kr, under 25 353kr); **Copenhagen** (7-8hr., 5-6 per day, 527kr, 371kr); and **Berlin** (18hr., 2 per day, 1100kr, 900kr). See p. 894 for info on **reservations.** **Lockers** 15-35kr per 24hr. **Showers** 25kr.

Buses: Cityterminalen, above Centralstation. **Terminal Service** (☎762 59 97) to the airport (60kr) and to Gotland ferries (50kr). **Bus Stop** (☎440 85 70) handles longer routes. To: **Gothenburg** (7hr., 7 per day, 220-315kr, under 25 175-250kr); **Malmö** (10hr., 2 per day, 280-395kr, 225-315kr); and **Copenhagen** (10hr., 1 per day, 390kr).

Ferries: Most ferries discounted 50% with Scanrail and free with Eurail. **Silja Line,** Kungsg. 2 (☎22 21 40), sails overnight to: **Mariehamn** (5hr., 1 per day, 99kr); **Turku (Åbo), Finland** (10-11hr., 2 per day, 275-385kr); and **Helsinki** (16hr., 1 per day, 585kr; book ahead). To get to the terminal, take T-bana to "Gärdet" and follow "Värtahamnen" signs, or take the Silja bus (14kr) from Cityterminalen. **Viking Line** sails to: **Mariehamn** (5½hr., 1 per day, round-trip 99kr); **Turku (Åbo)** (12hr., 2 per day, 222-321kr, with Scanrail 111kr); and **Helsinki** (15hr., 1 per day, 321kr). Viking Line terminal is at Stadsgården on Södermalm. T-bana: Slussen. **Destination Gotland** (☎20 10 20) sails to **Visby, Gotland** from Nynäshamn, 1hr. south of the city (see p. 906).

Public Transportation: SL office (☎600 10 00), Sergels Torg. T-bana: T-Centralen. Open M-F 7am-9pm, Sa-Su 8am-9pm. **Walk-in office** in Centralstation basement open M-Sa 6:30am-11:15pm, Su 7am-11:15pm. Most destinations cost 2 coupons (14kr, 1hr. unlimited bus/subway transfer). **Rabattkuponger** (95kr), books of 20 coupons, are at Pressbyrån news agents. The **SL Turistkort** (Tourist Card) is valid on buses, subways, commuter trains, and trams and ferries to Djurgården (24hr. 70kr, 72hr. 135kr). The **Stockholm Card** is valid. **Tunnelbana** (subway) runs 5am-12:30am. From 12:30-5:30am, it's replaced by night buses. Check schedules at bus stops.

Taxis: High fares. Many cabs have fixed prices; try to agree on a price beforehand. 435kr from airport to Centralstation. **Taxi Stockholm** (☎15 00 00); **Taxicard** (☎97 00 00).

Bike Rental: Skepp & Hoj (☎660 57 57), on Djurgårdsbron. Bikes and rollerblades 150kr per day, 500kr per week. Open daily 9am-9pm.

Hitchhiking: Waiting on highways is illegal in Sweden, and hitching is uncommon among travelers. Hitchers going south take the T-bana to the gas station on Kungens Kurva in Skärholmen; those going north take bus #52 to Sveaplan and stand on Sveav. at Nortull. *Let's Go* does not recommend hitchhiking.

ORIENTATION

The compact, almost entirely walkable city spans seven small islands (linked by the T-bana) at the junction of **Lake Mälaren** to the west and the **Baltic Sea** to the east. The northern island is divided into two sections: **Norrmalm**—home to Centralstation and the shopping district on Drottningg.—and **Östermalm,** which boasts the elegant waterfront **Strandvägen** and much of the nightlife fanning out from **Stureplan Square.** The mainly residential western island, **Kungsholmen,** has the Stadshuset (City Hall) and grassy beaches. The southern island of **Södermalm,** formerly a slum, is known as Stockholm SoHo and hosts cafes, artists, and an extensive gay scene. Södermalm's little sister, **Långholmen,** is a nature preserve, while **Djurgården** is a veritable nature playground and site of the Nordiska and Vasa Museums. At the center of these five islands is **Gamla Stan** (Old Town) island, which surrounds the main street, Västerlånggatan. Gamla Stan's neighbor **Skeppsholmen** (best reached via Norrmalm) harbors mostly museums. The city's streets are easy to navigate for even the hapless tourist: each one begins with the number one at the end closest to the city palace (in Gamla Stan)—the lower the numbers, the closer you are to Gamla Stan.

Stockholm

ACCOMMODATIONS

- Brygghuset, 1
- City Backpackers' Vandrarhem, 2
- Columbus Hotell-Vandrarhem, 8
- Gustaf af Klint, 7
- Hostel af Chapman/Skeppsholmens Vandrarhem, 9
- Långholmens Vandrarhem, 3
- M/S Rygerfjord, 5
- Mälarens, 6
- Zinkensdamm Vandrarhem, 4

T METRO STATIONS

PRACTICAL INFORMATION

Tourist Offices: Sweden House, Hamng. 27 (☎789 24 90; fax 789 24 91; email info@stoinfo.se; www.stoinfo.se), in the northeast corner of Kungsträdgården. From Centralstation, walk up Klarabergsg. to Sergels Torg (the plaza with the 50-foot glass tower) and bear right on Hamng. A vital resource for travelers staffed by friendly, multilingual agents. Sells the **Stockholm Card** and the **Touristcard.** Arranges and sells tickets for excursions, theater, opera, and concerts. Open June-Aug. M-F 8am-7pm, Sa-Su 9am-5pm; Sept.-May M-F 9am-6pm, Sa-Su 10am-3pm. The **Hotel Centralen,** at the train station (☎789 24 25; fax 791 86 66; email hotels@stoinfo.se), books rooms (20-50kr). Color map 15kr. Open daily May-Sept. 7am-9pm; Oct.-Apr. 9am-6pm.

Embassies: Australia, Sergels Torg 12, 11th fl. (☎613 29 00, emergencies 020 79 84 80; fax 24 74 14); **Canada,** Tegelbacken 4 (☎453 30 00; fax 24 24 91); **Ireland,** Ostermalmsg. 97 (☎661 80 05; fax 660 13 53); **South Africa,** Linnég. 76 (☎24 39 50, emergencies 07 08 56 75 35; fax 660 71 36). **UK,** Skarpög. 6-8 (☎671 90 00, emergencies 07 04 28 49 97; fax 662 99 89). **US,** Strandvagen 101 (☎783 53 00; fax 661 19 64).

Currency Exchange: Forex in Centralstation (☎411 67 34; open daily 7am-9pm), in Cityterminalen (☎21 42 80; open M-F 8am-8pm, Sa 8am-5pm), and at Sweden House (☎20 03 89). 15kr commission per traveler's check, 20kr for cash.

American Express: Norrlandsg. 21 (☎411 05 40). T-bana: Östermalmstorg. No fee to cash AmEx traveler's checks, 20kr for cash. Open M-F 9am-5pm, Sa 9am-1pm.

Gay and Lesbian Services: RFSL, (Swedish Federation for Sexual Equality), Sveav. 57 (☎736 02 13; www.rfsl.se). T-bana: Rådmansg. Distributes *Queer Xtra (QX),* with bar, club, and events listings. Open M-Th noon-8pm, F noon-6pm, Sa-Su 1-4pm. **Sweden House** distributes *QX* as well as the **QueerMap,** which maps Stockholm's gay hotspots.

Emergencies: Ambulance, Fire, and **Police:** ☎112.

Pharmacy: Look for the green and white "Apotek" signs. **Apotek C. W. Scheele,** Klarabergsg. 64, at the overpass over Vasag. T-bana: T-Centralen. Open 24hr.

Medical Assistance: ☎463 91 00.

Internet Access: Stadsbibliotek, Odeng. 59, in the annex. T-bana: Odenplan. 20min. free. Open M-Th 11am-7pm. **Café Access** (☎50 83 14 89), in the basement of the Kulturhuset on Sergels Torg. Short-time use 1kr per min.; for 20kr 30min. Open in summer M-F 10am-6pm, Sa-Su 11am-4pm; in winter Tu-F 10am-7pm, Sa-Su 11am-5pm.

Telephones: Buy phone cards at **Pressbyrån** stores for 35 (30kr), 65 (60kr), or 120 (100kr) units. **National directory assistance:** ☎079 75. 15kr per min.

Post Office: Drottningg. 53 (☎781 46 82). Open M-F 8am-7pm, Sa 10am-3pm. Address mail to be held: First Name SURNAME, *Poste Restante,* Drottningg. 53, **10110** Stockholm 1, Sweden. Also in Centralstation (☎781 22 98). Open daily 10am-7pm.

ACCOMMODATIONS AND CAMPING

Summer demands reservations, and many HI hostels limit stays to five nights. If you haven't booked ahead, arrive around 7am. Stockholm's several **boat-hostels (botels)** are a novel solution to space issues, but they can be cramped and noisy—request a room on the water side of the boat. Note that many independent (non-HI) hostels are hotel/hostels; specify if you want to stay in a dorm-style hostel, or risk paying hotel rates. **Campers** should bring insect repellent to ward off the infamous Swedish mosquitoes. If you don't have a (mandatory) **Swedish Camping Card,** either site below will sell you one for 49kr. Using an SL bus pass (or Stockholm Card) is the cheapest way to get to the more remote campsites.

Hostel af Chapman/Skeppsholmens Vandrarhem (HI/STF) (☎463 22 66; www.meravsverige.nu), on Skeppsholmen. From T-Centralen, take bus #65; or, walk 20min. along the waterfront. A majestic 19th-century sailing ship moored in an ideal location. Nothing beats the view from the boat, but landlubbers may opt for the modern on-shore hostel. Some non-reservable beds available daily at 7:15am. Breakfast 55kr. Kitchen.

Laundry 35kr. Reception 24hr. Lockout 11am-3pm. Boat curfew 3am. Accepts email reservations. Dorms 100-130kr; doubles 300kr; non-members add 40kr.

City Backpackers' Vandrarhem, Upplandsgatan 2A (☎20 69 20; www.svif.se), in Normalm. From Centralstation, go left on Vasag. and bear right on Upplandsgaten (10min.). Airy hostel close to the station. Kitchen. Laundry. Reception June-Sept. 8am-noon and 2-7pm; Oct.-May 9am-noon and 2-7pm. Dorms 150-180kr; doubles 450kr.

Columbus Hotell-Vandrarhem, Tjärhovsg. 11 (☎644 17 17; email columbus@columbus.se), in Södermalm. 3 blocks east of T-bana: Medborgarplatsen. This former brewery, prison, and plague hospital is clean, bright, and spacious. Breakfast 50kr. Kitchen and bar. Reception 24hr. Accepts email reservations. Dorms 145kr; singles 370kr.

Mälarens, Södermalarstrand, Kajplats 6 (☎644 43 85; www.rodabatan.nu). T-bana: Slussen (lower exit); then walk 300m west, on the lake side of the shore. Small rooms with plenty of red-velvet and nautical charm. Breakfast 45kr. Reception in cafe 8-10am, in office 8-11pm. Check-out 10am. Accepts email reservations. Dorms 160kr; singles 290kr; doubles 350kr; quads 740kr.

Brygghuset, Norrtullsg. 12N (☎31 24 24; fax 31 02 06). From T-bana: Odenplan ("Odenplan" exit), walk 2 blocks north on Norrtullsg.; or, walk 25min. from city center. Bright, clean rooms. Reception 8am-noon and 3-10pm. Lockout noon-3pm. Curfew 2am; you can get a key for 20kr. Open June to mid-Sept. Dorms 130kr; doubles 320kr.

Zinkensdamm Vandrarhem (HI), Zinkens Väg 20 (☎616 81 00; email info@zinkensdamm.swedenhotels.se), in Södermalm. From T-bana: Zinkensdamm, head south on Ringv. 3 blocks, then turn right on Zinkens Väg. Kitchen, TV, laundry, bike rental, and pub. Reception 24hr. Accepts email reservations. 135kr, non-members 175kr.

Långholmens Vandrarhem (HI), Kronohäktet (☎668 05 10; email vandrarhem@langholmen.com), on Långholmen. T-bana: Hornstull; then walk north on Långholmsg., turn left onto Högalidsg., hang a right on Långholmsbron over the bridge, then turn left and walk 300m. Clean converted prison cells in a quiet, lakeside hostel—prison life never looked so good. Breakfast 60kr. Sheets 40kr. Kitchen, cafe/pub, and laundry. Reception 24hr. Check-out 10am. Accepts email reservations. 155kr, nonmembers 195kr.

M/S Rygerfjord, Söder Mälarstrand Kajplats 12 (☎84 08 30; www.rygerfjord.se). T-bana: Mariatorget; exit towards Mariatorget, follow Torkel Knutssonsg. down to the water, and look for the sign. Tight rooms and an on-deck bar in summer. Breakfast 35kr. Reception 7am-1am. Check-out 11am. Dorms 145kr; doubles 330kr.

Gustaf af Klint, Stadsgårdskajen 153 (☎640 40 77; www.gustafafklint.com), in Södermalm. A former Navy ship moored 200m east of T-bana: Slussen (lower exit). Breakfast 45kr. Laundry. Reception in summer 24hr. Dorms 120kr; cabins 140kr; doubles 320kr.

Ängby Camping, Blackebergsv. 24 (☎37 04 20; fax 37 82 26; email reservation@angbycamping.se), on Lake Mälaren. T-bana: Ängbyplan; go downstairs, turn left on Färjestadsvägen, bear left at the fork, and it's at the bottom of the road. Reception 7am-11pm in summer; reduced off season. Open year-round. 110kr for 2 people with tent.

FOOD

Your best budget bet is to gorge on all-you-can-eat breakfasts offered by most hostels, then track down lunch specials (*dagens rätt*, 45-80kr, usually 11:30am-3pm). Cafes line **Götgatan,** in Södermalm (T-bana: Slussen or Medborgarplatsen), and many cheap eateries are on **Odengatan** (T-bana: Odengatan or Tekniska Hogskolan). Get **groceries** at **Hempköp City,** on Sergels Torg (walk left out of the train station and turn right on Klarabergsg.; open M-F 8am-9pm, Sa-Su 10am-9pm), **Wasahalla,** Upplandsg. 28 (T-bana: Centralen, then turn left on Vasag. and bear right on Upplandsg.; open daily 9am-8pm), or the **open-air fruit market,** at Hötorget Sq. (M-Sa 7am-6pm).

Herman's, Fjällg. 23A, in Södermalm. T-bana: Slussen, then take the steps or the lift up to Katarinavägen, walk away from Gamla Stan (8min.), and bear left on Fjällg. Superlative vegetarian buffet and one of Stockholm's best views. Lunch 60kr; dinner 85kr. Open M-F 11am-9pm, Sa-Su noon-9pm; in summer daily until 11pm.

Café Birger, Birger Jarlsg. 11. T-bana: Östermalmstorg, then walk down Birger Jarlsg. toward the water (5min.). The only thing that beats the king-sized sandwiches at this low-key cafe is the fabulous people-watching on chic Birger Jarlsg. Sandwiches 30-50kr. Open Su-Th 11am-11pm, F-Sa noon-midnight.

Sandy's, Kungsg. 57 and Klarabergsg. 31. Coffee, fresh-squeezed OJ, yogurt with muesli, and a sandwich for 33kr. Open M-F 7:30am-7pm, Sa 11am-5pm.

Café Sten Sture, Trångsund 10; entrance on Ankargränd. This medieval-prison-turned-cafe once housed King Gustav III's assassin. Open daily 10am-9pm.

Pauli's Café, Dramaten 2 trappen, 2nd fl., in Nybroplan. T-bana: Östermalmstorg; then walk down Birger Jarlsg. toward the water. Upstairs in the National Theater. Summer lunch buffet of Swedish delicacies 70kr. Buffet daily 11:30am-2pm.

SIGHTS

Founded in the 13th century, Stockholm's long history has contributed to the development of a rich cultural tradition that even trickles down to the subway—the decorated stops are called the longest art exhibit in the world. The **Stockholmskortet** (Stockholm Card; 24hr. 199kr, 48hr. 398kr, 72hr. 498kr), available at tourist offices in Sweden House and Central Station, covers admission to most museums and allows unlimited transportation on the subways and buses.

KUNGSHOLMEN AND STADSHUSET (CITY HALL). On the tip of Kungsholmen closest to Gamla Stan towers the regal **Stadshuset.** Jutting 106m into the skyline, the **Stadshustornet** (city hall tower) offers a stunning aerial view of downtown, while the building itself is emblematic of the quirky National Romantic architectural style. The interior boasts municipal chambers in the shape of Viking Ships; the **Blå Hallen** (Blue Hall, although it is *not* blue), where the Nobel Prize dinner is held; and the mosaic-tiled **Gyllene Hallen** (Gold Hall), where Nobels, nobles, and other notables dance the rest of the night away. *(Hantverkarg. 1. T-bana: Rådhuset, then walk east on Hantverkarg. ☎508 290 58 59. Compulsory tours daily June-Aug. 10, 11am, noon, and 2pm; Sept.-May 10am and noon. 40kr. Tower open daily May-Sept. 10am-4:30pm. 15kr.)*

GAMLA STAN (OLD TOWN). Across the water from Stadshuset and at the center of Stockholm's islands is the city's medieval core. The main pedestrian street, **Västerlångg.,** is packed with cafes, shops, and cheesy tourist paraphernalia. *(T-bana: Gamla Stan. Or take bus #46 or 55.)* On nearby **Stora Nyg.** and **Österlångg.,** the commercial onslaught is a little less severe, especially at night. *(Tours of the Old Town depart June-Aug. M, W, and F at 7pm. Meet at the Obelisk in Slottsbacken outside the palace. 50kr.)* At the top of Gamla Stan's winding streets is **Stortorget** (town square), where the annual **Julmarknad** (Christmas Fair) serves hot *glögg* (spiced wine) and sells handicrafts. Behind the square is the impressive **Storkyrkar** (Royal Chapel), site of royal weddings and the dramatic medieval sculpture of Stockholm's patron Saint Göran (George) slaying the dragon. *(Open daily May-Aug. 9am-6pm; Sept.-Apr. 9am-4pm. Free.)* The crown of Gamla Stan is the stunning **Kungliga Slottet** (Royal Palace), winter home of the Swedish royal family and site of the daily Changing of the Guard. The **State Apartments** are the most worthwhile attraction, although you can also swing by the **Skattkammaren** (Royal Treasury) to drool over royal regalia and the crown jewels or visit the **armory** and **Gustav III's Antikmuseum** (Museum of Antiquities). *(☎402 61 30; www.royalcourt.se. All four open daily May-Aug. 10am-4pm; Sept.-Apr. Tu-Su noon-3pm. State apartments 50kr; treasury 50kr; armory 60kr; Museum of Antiquities 50kr; ticket for all four 100kr, students 70kr. English-language tours included in admission. Changing of the Guard (30 min.) in summer M-Sa noon, Su 1pm; rest of year W and Sa at noon and Su at 1pm.)*

SKEPPSHOLMEN AND BLASIEHOLMEN. On Skeppsholmen, the island east of Gamla Stan, the **Moderna Museet** (Modern Museum) and **Arkitekturmuseet** (Architecture Museum) are housed in adjacent buildings recently designed by Rafael Moneo. Although the buildings have received mixed reviews, the Moderna's pop art collection is nonetheless regarded as one of Europe's finest. *(Moderna Museet ☎519 552 79; Arkitekturmuseet ☎587 21 000. T-bana: Kungsträdgården; then walk toward the water on Södra Blasieholmshamner, cross the bridge to Skeppsholmen, and follow the signs. Both open in summer Tu-F 11am-10pm; reduced hours in winter. Moderna Museet 60kr, students 40kr; Arkitektur-*

museet 45kr, 30kr; joint ticket 80kr, 65kr.) On Södra Blasieholmshamnen before the bridge to Skeppsholmen, the **National Museet** (National Museum) has works by Rembrandt, Renoir, and Rodin, but also honors national artists such as Carl Larsson, Anders Zorn, and Eugen Jansson. *(☎51 95 44 28; www.nationalmuseum.se. T-bana: Kungsträdgården. Open Mar.-Dec. Tu 11am-8pm, W-Su 11am-5pm; Jan.-Feb. Tu and Th 11am-8pm, W and F-Su 11am-5pm. 60kr, under 16 free.)*

DJURGÅRDEN. The extraordinary **Vasa Museet** houses a mammoth wooden warship that sank on her maiden voyage in 1628, before even leaving the harbor; it was discovered, raised, and salvaged in the 1960s and 70s. *(Galärvarvsv. 14. Take bus #44, 47, or 69. Open June 10-Aug. 20 daily 9:30am-7pm; Aug. 21-June 9 M-Tu and Th-Su 10am-5pm, W 10am-8pm. 60kr.)* Next door, the **Nordiska Museet** (Nordic Museum) presents an innovative exhibit on Swedish history and culture from the Viking age to the modern era of Volvo, ABBA, and Electrolux. *(Djurgårdsvägen 6-16. Bus #44 or 47. Open daily 10am-9pm. 60kr.)* On the far side of the island, **Prins Eugens Waldemarsudde,** home of the full-time prince and part-time painter, contains his major works and personal collection. The seaside grounds also boast a spectacular sculpture garden. *(Prins Eugen Väg 6. Bus #47. Open Tu-Su May-Aug. 11am-5pm, Sept.-Apr. 11am-4pm. 50kr.)* A national park in the heart of the city occupies most of Djurgården. **Skansen** is an open-air museum featuring 150 historical buildings, handicrafts, and a zoo. The homes—extracted from different periods of Swedish history—are inhabited by costumed actors. *(Bus #44 or 47 from Drottningg. and Klarabergsg. in Sergels Torg, opposite T-Centralen. Park and zoo open daily May 10am-8pm; June-Aug. 10am-10pm; Sept.-Apr. 10am-4pm. Historical buildings open daily May-Aug. 11am-5pm; Sept.-Apr. 11am-3pm. 60kr.)*

ENTERTAINMENT

The three stages of the national theater, **Dramaten,** Nybroplan (☎667 06 80), feature Swedish- and English-language performances of August Strindberg and other playwrights (80-350kr). The **Operan** (☎24 82 40) offers opera and ballet (70-350kr). Cheaper student, obstructed view, or rush tickets are often available. The **Konserthuset** at Hötorget (☎10 21 10) features classical music by the Stockholm Philharmonic; concerts are also held at the **Globen** arena (☎600 34 00; 50-300kr). Pop music venues include **Skansen** (☎57 89 00 05) and the stage at **Gröna Lund** (☎670 76 00), Djurgården's huge outdoor Tivoli amusement park. (Open late Apr. to early Sept. M-Th noon-11pm, F-Sa noon-midnight, Su noon-9pm. Tickets 125-300kr.) Check theater and concert listings in *Stockholm this Week*, then visit Sweden House or call BiljettDirekt (☎077 170 70 70) for tickets. In summer, **Kungsträdgården** (a large park bordered by Kungsträdgårdsg. and Vastra Trädgårdsg) hosts several free outdoor concerts. For events info, check out *What's On*, at the tourist office.

Stockholm's festivals include the world-class **Jazz and Blues Festival** in July at Skansen (☎747 92 36; www.stockholmjazz.com); **Strindberg Festival** (late Aug. or early Sept.; ☎34 14 01; www.strindberg.stockholm.se/festivalen); and **Stockholm Pride** (late July; ☎33 59 55; www.stockholmpride.org).

NIGHTLIFE

Stockholm's beautiful people and their admirers party until 5am at the many nightclubs and bars around Stureplan in **Östermalm** (T-bana: Östermalmtorg); be prepared for steep cover and long lines. **Södermalm** ("Söder"), across the river, is the core of Stockholm's gay scene; pick up *QX (Queer Extra)* or the QueerMap for entertainment and nightlife info. Most establishments close between 1 and 3am. The bars and cafes line **Götgatan** (T-bana: Slussen, Medborgplatsen, or Skanstull); new cafes and bars are also blossoming in **Vasastaden** (T-bana: Sankt Eriksplan) and **Kungsholmen** (T-bana: Rådhuset). Stockholm's size and the excellent **night bus** service allow revelers to partake of any or all of these scenes in a single night. Alcohol is expensive at bars (35-55kr) but cheap (10-15kr per 0.5L) at **Systembolaget** state liquor stores. (Open M-F 9am-5pm.)

Daily News Cafe, Kungsträgården, next to Sweden House. T-bana: T-Centralen, then walk down Klarabergsgatan as it turns into Hamngatan and turn right at Sweden House. The "Daily," as regulars call it, delivers great live and house music to a slick but friendly clientele. Different music and cover each night; call for a schedule. Cover around 60kr; occasionally includes drinks. Open Su-Th 9pm-3am, F-Sa 9pm-5am.

La Cucaracha, Bondeg., in Söder. T-bana: Skanstull; walk up Götg. away from the Globe Arena (giant golf ball) and turn right on Bondeg. Latin rhythms heat the dance floor after 11pm. Beer 30kr, mixed drinks 60-70kr. 23+. Open M-Sa 5pm-1am, Su 3pm-1am.

Bröderna Olssons Garlic and Shots, Folkungag. 84 in Söder, across from the Columbus Hostel. T-bana: Medborgarplatsen. Funky vodka bar with an electric atmosphere. Try the trademark garlic-flavored beer. 100 unique shots (33kr each). Open daily 5pm-1am.

Snaps, Medborgarplatsen, in the free-standing yellow house. Popular bar and bistro with a basement dance floor (jungle, reggae, and dance music). Beer 38kr, mixed drinks 58-78kr. Women 23+, men 25+. Open M-Tu 5pm-1am, W-Sa 5pm-3am.

Pelikan, Blekingeg. 40, in Söder. T-bana: Skanstull; walk up Götg. away from the Globe Arena and right on Blekingeg. Unpretentious crowds fill this smoky, well-lit beer hall adjoining the darker and artsier **Kristaller.** Beer 37kr, mixed drinks 40-50kr. 23+.

Tranan, Karlbergsv. 14, in Vastaden across from T-bana: Odenplan. A young, hip-but-not-too-hip crowd gathers at this trendy sit-down bar to hear sweet beats and sip pricey drinks. The Chemical Brothers have been known to play here as "secret guests" when in town. Beer 44kr, mixed drinks 62kr. 23+. No cover. Open daily 5pm-1am.

Fasching, Kungsg. 63. T-bana: T-Centralen. Sweden's best spot for live jazz, latin, blues, funk, fusion, and world music in a funky loft-like space. Cover 70-250kr. Open 8pm-midnight. Used as a regular disco F-Sa midnight-3am.

EXCURSIONS FROM STOCKHOLM

Stockholm is situated in the center of an archipelago, where the mainland gradually crumbles into the Baltic. The islands in either direction—east toward the Baltic or west toward Lake Mälaren—are well worth exploration. Visit the **Excursion Shop** in Sweden House (see p. 900). **Ferries** to the archipelago leave from the **Stromkajen** docks between Gamla Stan and Skeppsholmen in front of the Grand Hotel (T-Bana: Jakobskyrka) or the **Nybrohamnen** docks (T-Bana: Ostermalmstorg., then walk down Birger Jarlsgatan toward the water).

LAKE MÄLAREN. The island of **Björkö** on Lake Mälaren is home to **Birka,** where the Vikings established the country's first city. It was also the site of Sweden's first encounter with Christianity in AD 829. Today you can visit the fabulously interesting excavation sites, burial mounds, and Viking museum. A **ferry** departs Stockholm from the **Stadshusbron** docks next to the Stadshuset at 10am (1¾hr.). Go to "T-Centralen," then walk toward the water. The boat leaves Björkö at 3:45pm. (1hr. guided tour, museum admission, and round-trip ferry 200kr; available May-Sept.)

The Swedish royal family's home, **Drottningholm Palace,** is only 45 minutes away by ferry. The ghost of elegant Drottning (Queen) Larisa Ulrika, for whom the palace was a wedding gift, presides over lush Baroque gardens and extravagant Rococo interiors. Catch the English tour of the palace's **theater.** (2 per hr.; 40kr, students 10kr). **Kina Slott,** Drottningholm's Chinese pavilion, was an 18th-century royal summer cottage. (Palace open daily May-Aug. 10am-4:30pm; Sept. noon-3:30pm. 50kr, students 25kr. Pavilion open daily May-Aug. 11am-4:30pm; Sept. noon-3:30pm; Apr. and Oct. 1-3:30pm. 50kr, 25kr.) Strömma Kanalbolaget **ferries** depart from Stadshusbron mid-June to mid-August. (Every 30min. 9:30am-4pm; return every hr. 10:30am-5:30pm. 85kr.) Or, take the **subway** to T-bana: Brommaplan, then take bus #301-323.)

If you have the urge to brush shoulders with more royalty, **Gripsholm Castle** looms over the bucolic hamlet of **Mariefred.** Built in 1380 on Lake Mälaren by Lord High Chancellor Bo Jonsson Grip, the castle is adorned with portraits and its original Renaissance wall paintings and furniture. (Open May-Aug. daily 10am-4pm; Sept. Tu-Su 10am-3pm; Oct.-Dec. Sa-Su 10am-3pm; Jan.-Apr. Sa-Su noon-3pm. 50kr, students 25kr.) A short walk from the castle is **Grafikens Hus,** once the royal barn and now a print-making workshop. (Open May-Aug. daily 11am-5pm; Sept.-Apr. Sa-Su

11am-5pm. 40kr.) To get to Mariefred, take the **train** to Läggesta, then catch **bus** #303 (15kr) and ask the driver to drop you off at the castle (1hr. total).

THE ARCHIPELAGO (SKÄRGÅRD). The lovely islands of the Stockholm archipelago are lush and wooded close to the city, and grow increasingly rocky and dramatic toward the Baltic. The archipelago is perfect for picnicking, hiking, and swimming; if you plan to take a dip, though, remember the words of one Stockholmer: "It's the Baltic: how cold it is depends on how brave you are." The **Waxholmsbolaget ferry company** (☎679 58 30) serves even the tiniest islands and offers the 16-day **Båtluffarkortet card** (275kr), good for unlimited boat travel. The excursions shop at Sweden House in Stockholm (see p. 900) sells the ferry pass and has information on hostels and camping, as well as kayak and canoe rentals. Overnight stays in the area's 20 **hostels** must be booked months ahead, but the odd night may be available on short notice. There are hostels on **Möja** in the outer archipelago (☎571 647 20) and **Vaxholm,** near Stockholm (☎541 322 40). Consult Sweden House for complete listings. Or, enjoy **free camping** courtesy of the law of public access (see p. 896) on almost any island except Sandhamn. (Some islands are also in military protection zones and are not open to foreigners.)

To try your hand at fishing or investigate the waterways by canoe or kayak, rent **boats** on Vaxholm (☎541 377 90) or on Üto (☎501 576 68). **Vaxholm** is a fortress town founded in 1647, small enough to explore by foot and accessible by boat. (A **ferry** departs from Nybroplar in Stockholm at noon and returns 4:30pm.) **Utö** has great bike paths; **bike rental** and ferry packages are available from Sweden House. **Sandhamn,** three hours from Stockholm, is ideal for swimming and **sailing.** On the island of **Öja,** puzzle your way through the labyrinth north of Landsort, reputed to bring luck to fishermen. Take the *pendeltag* from Stockholm to Nynashamn, take bus #852 from there to Ankarudden, and hop the ferry to Landsort (2½hr.).

UPPSALA. Once a hotbed of pagan spirituality and the cradle of Swedish civilization, Uppsala is now a Nordic Oxbridge, sheltering the 20,000 students of Sweden's oldest university. Scandinavia's largest cathedral, the magnificent Gothic **Domkyrka,** where Swedish monarchs were once crowned, looms just over the river. (Open daily 8am-6pm. Tours in English June-Aug. M-Sa 1pm.) The university museum, **Gustavianum,** across from the Domkyrka, houses scientific curiosities and the **Anatomical Theater,** the site of 18th-century public human dissections. (Open May-Sept. daily 11am-4pm; Sept.-May W and F-Su 11am-4pm, Th 11am-9pm.) Some claim that **Gamla Uppsala** (Old Uppsala), 4km north of the town center, was the site of a pagan temple. Today, little remains save huge burial mounds of monarchs and the **Gamla Uppsala Kyrka**, one of Sweden's oldest churches. (Open daily May-Aug. 9am-6pm; Sept.-Apr. 9am-4pm. Free.) Near the mounds, a new museum, the **Gamla Uppsala Historiskt Centrum,** outlines the history of the mounds and the archaeological excavations there. (Open daily May 20-Aug. 20 10am-5pm; Aug. 21-Sept. 30 10am-4pm. 50kr, students 40kr, under 16 free.) Take bus #2, 20, 24, or 54 (16kr) north from Dragarbrunnsg. After exhausting Uppsala, you can hop the boat to **Skokloster,** a dazzling Baroque palace built between 1654 and 1676. (Open daily May-Aug. 11am-4pm. 60kr, students 40kr. Boat departs in summer Tu-Su 11:30am from Islandsbron on Östra Åg. and Munkg.; returns 5:15pm. Round-trip 110kr.)

Trains pull in from **Stockholm** (40min., every hr., 70kr, under 25 50kr). To get from the station to the **tourist office,** Fyristorg 8, walk right on Kungsg., left on St. Persg., and cross the bridge. (☎27 48 00. Open in summer M-F 10am-6pm, Sa 10am-3pm, Su noon-2pm; in winter closed Su.) For renovated rooms in a lovely pastoral setting, try **Sunnersta Herrgård (HI),** Sunnerstav. 24, 6km south of town. Take bus #20 or 50 (16kr) from Dragarbrunnsg. to Herrgårdsv., cross the street, walk two blocks down the path behind the kiosk, and walk 50m left. (☎32 42 20. Breakfast 60kr. Reception 8-11am and 5-9pm. Open May-Aug. Dorms 170kr, non-members 210kr; singles 320kr, 360kr.) **Fyrishov Camping,** Idrottsg. 2, off Svartbäcksg., is 2km from the city center. Take bus #4 or 6 (bus #50 or 54 at night; 10min.) to "Fyrishov." (☎27 49 60. Reception 7am-10pm. Tents 85kr; 4- to 5-bed huts June-Aug. 8 545kr. Swedish Camping Card required; 60kr.) **Postal code:** 75101. ☎**018.**

GOTLAND

Gotland, 300km south of Stockholm, is Sweden's biggest island, famed for its green meadows, white sand beaches, and its capital, **Visby,** whose wall is the oldest medieval monument in Scandinavia. A long history of seafaring and prosperous merchant trade has allowed many distant and ancient cultures to leave their imprint on Gotland's culture.

GETTING THERE AND GETTING AROUND. Destination Gotland ferries (☎ (0498) 20 10 20) sail to Visby from **Nynäshamn,** south of Stockholm (3-5hr.), and **Oskarshamn,** north of Kalmar (2½-4hr.). Fares are highest on weekends (215-430kr) and cheapest for early-morning and late-night departures (June-Aug. 2-5 per day, Oct.-May 1 per day; 130-205kr, students 80-130kr; with Scanrail 50% off). To get to Nynäshamn from **Stockholm,** take the *Flygbussar* bus from Cityterminalen (1hr., 65kr) or the *pendeltag* (commuter train) from Centralstation (45min., 35kr; *rabattkuponger* and SL passes valid). To get to Oskarshamn, hop on a bus (2hr., 75kr) or train from **Kalmar.** If you're planning your trip from Stockholm, **Gotland City,** Kungsg. 57A, books ferries and has tourist info. (☎ (08) 406 15 00. Open June-Aug. M-F 9:30am-6pm, Sa 10am-2pm; Sept.-May M-F 9:30am-5pm.)

To explore the island, pick up a bus timetable at the ferry terminal or at the Visby **bus station,** outside the wall north of the city at Kung Magnusväg 1 (☎ (0498) 21 41 12). Bus rides cost 11-42kr (bikes 20kr extra). **Cycling** along Gotland's extensive paths and bike-friendly motorways is the best way to explore its flat terrain.

VISBY. Once you reach Gotland, walk 10 minutes to the left as you exit the ferry terminal to get to the **tourist office,** Hamng. 4. (☎20 17 00. Open mid-June to mid-Aug. M-F 7am-7pm, Sa-Su 8am-6pm; May to mid-June and late Aug. M-F 8am-5pm, Sa-Su 10am-4pm; Sept. M-F 8am-5pm, Sa-Su 11am-2pm; Oct.-Apr. M-F 10am-noon and 1-3pm.) Dozens of **bike rental** shops surround the ferry terminal. Stay at **Visby Fängelse Vandrarhem,** Skeppsbron 1, 300m to the left as you exit the ferry terminal. You'll recognize it by the friendly barbed wire atop the walls—the yellow building housed a 19th-century prison. (☎20 60 50. Reception M-F 11am-2pm, Sa-Su 11am-noon; call ahead to arrive at another time. Reserve ahead. Dorms 200kr; bed in a double cell 300kr.) Otherwise, **Gotlandsresor,** Färjeleden 3, 200m right of the ferry terminal, will help you book ferries and find a room. (☎20 12 60. Open daily June-Aug. 6am-10pm, 11:30pm when a late ferry comes in; Sept.-May 8am-6pm.) **Private rooms** cost 285kr for singles and 425kr for doubles (outside the city walls 240kr and 380kr). Catch a local to teach you how to play **Kubb,** a Viking game that today is only played in Gotland. Oh, and don't mind the concrete sheep—they're herding traffic in the right direction. **Postal code:** 62101. ☎**0498.**

ELSEWHERE ON GOTLAND. Great daytrips from Visby include visits to the mystical monoliths on **Fårö,** off the northern tip of the island (bus #23, 2hr.); the blazing beaches of **Tofta,** 15km south (bus #31, 30min.); and the calcified cliffs of **Hoburgen,** at the island's southernmost tip (bus #11, 3hr.). **Gotlandsresor** (see above) can get you info on the more than 30 hostels, campgrounds, and bike rentals elsewhere on the island. You can also take advantage of the right of public access (see p. 896).

SOUTHERN SWEDEN

Swedes love their summer houses in this mild region, graced with wide fields of waving grasses and flat beaches. The **Halland** coast and southwest **Småland** coastline, between Västervik and Kalmar, are especially popular.

KALMAR ☎0480

In downtown Kalmar, the elegant Renaissance castle **Kalmar Slott** is the site of the inception of the 1397 Kalmar Union, which attempted to unite Denmark, Norway, Sweden, and Finland. (Open daily June-Aug. 10am-6pm; Apr.-May and Sept. 10am-

4pm; Oct.-Mar. 2nd weekend of each month 11am-3:30pm. 60kr, students 30kr.) The castle hosts an annual **Renaissance Festival** in late June and early July (☎45 14 92 for info and tickets). The Baroque **Kalmar Domkyrka,** on Stortorget, has the splendor of a major cathedral. (Open M-F 8am-7pm, Sa-Su 9am-7pm.) The **Kalmar Läns Museum,** Skeppsbrog. 51, has relics from the wreckage of the 17th-century warship, **Kronan,** which sank in a 1676 battle against the Danes. (Open daily mid-June to mid-Aug. 10am-6pm; mid-Aug. to mid-June 10am-4pm. 50kr, students 20kr.) In nearby towns, collectively dubbed **Glasriket** (Kingdom of Crystal), artisans craft exquisite hand-blown crystal. To visit workshops at **Orrefors** (☎ (0481) 34 19) and **Kosta Boda** (☎ (0478) 345 00), take bus #138 (1hr., 60kr) from the train station. (Both open M-F 9am-6pm, Sa 10am-4pm, Su noon-4pm.)

Trains and **buses** arrive south of town, across the bay from the castle. To get from the train station to the **tourist office,** Larmg. 6, go right on Stationsg., turn left on Ölandsg., and look left. (☎153 50. Open June and Aug. M-F 9am-7pm, Sa 10am-3pm, Su 1-6pm; July M-F 9am-8pm, Sa 10am-5pm; Oct.-Apr. M-F 9am-5pm; May and Sept. M-F 9am-5pm, Sa 10am-1pm.) To get from the tourist office to the **Kalmar Vandrarhem (HI),** Rappeg. 1, on the island of Ängö, go north on Larmg., turn right on Södra Kanalg., cross the bridge, and turn left on Angöleden; it will be on the right. (☎129 28. Breakfast 49kr. Reception June-Aug. 8-10am and 4:30-10pm; Sept.-May 8-10am and 4:30-9pm. 145kr, nonmembers 185kr.) **Stensö Camping** is 2km south of Kalmar. (☎888 03. Call ahead. June-Aug. 125kr; Apr. and Sept.-Oct. 100kr.) Restaurants cluster around **Larmtorget. Postal code:** 39101.

EXCURSION FROM KALMAR: ÖLAND. Visible from Kalmar's coast, the island of **Öland** stretches over 100km of green fields and white sand beaches. The royal family roosts here on holiday, and Crown Princess Victoria's birthday, Victoriadagen (July 14), is celebrated island-wide. Commoners flock to the **beaches** of Löttorp and Böda in the north and Grönhögen and Ottenby in the south. **Buses** #101 and 106 go from Kalmar's train station to Öland (30-40kr). Öland's **tourist office** (☎56 06 00) is in Färjestaden. Sleep at **Vandrarhem Borgholm,** Rosenfors (☎107 56), or **Vandrarhem Böda** (☎220 38), on Melböda in Löttorp. ☎**0485.**

MALMÖ ☎040

As the Swedish endpoint of the new bridge to Copenhagen, Malmö is a town to watch. To reach the beautiful **Stortorget** square from the train station, walk straight out onto Malarbron Hamng. Continue through the square and look left for another square, **Lilla Torg.** The **Form Design Center,** Lilla Torg 9, presents the cutting edge of Swedish design. (☎664 51 50. Open Tu-F 11am-5pm, Th 11am-6pm, Sa 10am-4pm, Su noon-4pm. Free.) In the west end, the reconstructed **Malmöhus Castle** houses the **Malmös Museer,** which documents the city's history. (☎34 44 00. Open daily June-Aug. 10am-4pm; Sept.-May noon-4pm. 40kr, students 20kr.) The **Malmö Konsthall,** St. Johannesg. 7, exhibits modern art. (Open daily 11am-5pm, W 11am-11pm. Free.)

The **train station** and **harbor** lie north of the Old Town. Pilen **ferries** (☎23 44 11) run to Copenhagen (45min., 59kr). **Trains** arrive from Copenhagen (35min., 200kr, under 25 145), Gothenburg (3½hr., 415kr, 295kr) and Stockholm (4½-6hr., 585kr, 415kr). The **tourist office** is in the train station. (Open June-Aug. M-F 9am-7pm, Sa-Su 10am-2pm and 5-7pm; Sept.-May M-F 9am-5pm, Sa 10am-2pm.) Log on at the stylish **Cyberspace C@fé,** Engelbrektsg. 13, off Lilla Torg. (22kr per 30min. Open daily 10am-10pm.) From the train station or harbor, cross the canal and Norra Vallg. and take bus #21 to Vandrarhemmet and the **Vandrarhem Malmö (HI),** Backav. 18. (☎822 20. Breakfast 38kr. Reception 8-10am and 4-8pm. 125kr, nonmembers 165kr.) Or, **camp** in the giant Malmöhus Park for free. **Postal code:** 20110.

LUND ☎046

What Oxford and Cambridge are to England, Uppsala and Lund are to Sweden. Lund University's antagonism with its scholarly northern neighbors in Uppsala has inspired countless pranks, drag shows, and drinkfests in Lund's bright streets. The town's ancient Romanesque **cathedral,** St. Laurentius, is an impressive 900-year-old

THE MISSING LINK Easily spotted from Copenhagen, the southern coast of Sweden is surprisingly close across the strait of Øresund. Sweden and Denmark have always been connected by innumerable ferry links and a long history of cultural (and, in ancient times, military) exchange; last summer that relationship was cemented with the dedication of the 17km bridge-tunnel complex known as the "fixed link," the first bridge to connect continental Europe and Scandinavia. From Malmö it is only a 35-minute train ride to the Copenhagen city center, while the old route via Helsingør/Helsingborg took over an hour. Since the opening of the bridge, "Øresund" is the buzzword on everyone's lips. Municipal and national leaders and citizens alike hold high hopes that the new bridge and recent investments will make the region the centerpiece of Scandinavia and Northern Europe.

reminder of the time when Lund was the religious center of Scandinavia; note the 14th-century astronomical clock. To find the cathedral from the train station, walk straight across Bang. and Knut den Storestorg, then turn left on Kyrkog. (Open M-Sa 8am-6pm, Su 9-6.) Head through the park behind the cathedral to the University campus, where you'll find events information at **Student Info,** at the student union. (☎280 45 45; www.lu.se/intsek/international/whatsup.html. Open Sept.-May M-F 10am-4pm.) **Kulturen,** at the end of Sankt Anneg. on Tegnerplastén, is an engrossing open-air museum with 17th- and 18th-century homes, churches, and history displays. (Open May-Sept. daily 11am-5pm; Oct.-Apr. Tu-Su noon-4pm. 40kr.)

Lund is easily accessible from Malmö on most **SJ trains** and by local **pågatågen** (10min., 6-7 per day, 30kr; railpasses valid). The **tourist office,** Kyrkog. 11, opposite the cathedral, books 175kr rooms for a 50kr fee. (☎35 50 40. Open June-Aug. M-F 10am-6pm, Sa-Su 10am-2pm; Sept. and May M-F 10am-5pm, Sa 10am-2pm; Oct.-Apr. M-F 10am-5pm.) Rest your tired limbs at the delightful but cramped **HI Hostel Tåget** (The Train), Vävareg. 22, housed in authentic 1940s sleeping cars. Take the overpass to the park side of the station. (☎14 28 20. Reception daily Apr.-Oct. 8-10am and 5-8pm, Nov.-Mar. 5-7pm. Call ahead. 110kr, nonmembers 140kr.) To get to **Källby Camping,** take bus #1 (dir. Klostergården) and ask to be let off at the campground. (☎35 51 88. Open mid-June to Aug. 30kr per tent.) Mårtenstorget features a fresh fruit and vegetable **market.** (Open M-Sa 7am-2:30pm.) **Mejeriet,** Stora Söderg. 64, packs a bar, movie theater, and lots of summer events into a former dairy. Hours vary with shows; call ☎12 38 11 for info. **Postal code:** 22101.

YSTAD ☎0411

Travelers passing through Ystad en route to Bornholm, Denmark (p. 281) often miss out on this quiet town's charms. The pedestrian **Stora Östergatan** leads to **Stortorget,** the market square; south of the square lies the ancient monastery **Gråbrödraklostret.** (Open M-F noon-5pm, Sa-Su noon-4pm. Free.) **Ales Stenar** (Ale's Stones), a mysterious circular stone formation outside the city dating from the late Iron Age, is accessible in summer via bus #322 (30min., 20-30kr; bus rarely runs Sa-Su). Trafikken (☎180 65) and Scandlines (☎ (042) 18 63 00) **ferries** leave from behind the train station for Bornholm (2½ hr., 3 per day in summer, 140kr; with Scanrail 50% off) and **Świnoujście,** Poland. **Trains** pull in from Malmö (1hr., 5-6 per day, 60kr). The **tourist office** is across from the station. (☎57 76 81. Open mid-June to mid-Aug. M-F 9am-7pm, Sa 10am-7pm, Su 11am-6pm; mid-Aug. to mid-June M-F 9am-5pm.) The train station houses the new hostel **Vandrarhemmet Stationer.** (☎ (070) 857 79 95. Breakfast 45kr. Reception June-Aug. 5-7pm and 9-10pm; Oct.-May 5-6pm. 160kr.) To get to the beachfront **Vandrarhem Kantarellen** or **Sandskogens Camping,** turn right from the station and walk about 2km on Österleden, then turn right on Fritidsvägen (30min.). Or, take bus #572 (5min., 8kr) from the station. (Hostel ☎665 66. Reception 9-10am and 4-6pm. Kitchen. Call ahead. 120kr, nonmembers 160kr. Camping ☎192 70. 105kr.) Get **groceries** at **Saluhallen,** off the main square at the corner of Theatergrand and St. Västerg. (Open daily 8am-9pm.) **Postal code:** 27101.

GOTHENBURG (GÖTEBORG) ☎031

The hub of Swedish industry and home to a once-bustling industrial port, Göteborg (YUH-ta-boy) now moves at a slow, leisurely pace. Passenger ferries line up under the mostly silent harbor side cranes, and locals and travelers alike find themselves with plenty of time to enjoy the thriving cafe culture of this luxurious, tasteful city.

PRACTICAL INFO, ACCOMMODATIONS, AND FOOD. **Trains** go from Nordstaden to: Malmö (3½hr.; 9 per day; 395kr, under 25 275kr); Stockholm (3½-6hr.; 10 per day; 520kr, 355kr); and Oslo (4½hr.; 3 per day; 407kr, 282kr). Stena Line **ferries** (☎704 00 00) sail to Frederikshavn, Denmark (3hr., 15 per day, 80kr) and Kiel, Germany (14hr., 820kr). SeaCat **hydrofoils** (☎775 08 00) go to Frederikshavn (1¾hr., 4 per day, 100-120kr); Scandinavian Seaways (☎65 06 50) steams to Newcastle, England (22hr., 1125kr). The **tourist office,** Kungsportsplatsen 2, sells **Göteborg Cards,** which grant public transit and admission to various attractions (95kr). From the station, cross Drottningtorget and follow Östra Larmag. from the right of the Radisson (☎61 25 00. Open May daily M-F 9am-6pm; late June to early Aug. daily 9am-8pm; early June and late Aug. M-F 9am-6pm, Sa-Su 10am-2pm; Sept.-Apr. M-F 9am-5pm, Sa 10am-2pm.) The stylish **stadsbibliotek** (city library), on Götaplatsen, has free **Internet.** (Open M-Th 10am-8pm, F 10am-6pm, Sa 11am-4pm.)

To reach the modern, well-appointed **Slottskogens Hostel (STF/HI),** Vegag. 21, take tram #1 or 2 (dir. Frölunda) to "Olivedalsg." and walk uphill on Olivedalsg. to Vegag. (☎42 65 20; fax 14 21 02. Kitchen, sauna, and **bike rental.** Reception 8am-noon and 3-10pm. Check-in 3-6pm. Dorms 95-110kr; singles 205kr; non-members add 40kr.) The quiet **Masthuggsterrassen (SVIF),** Masthuggsterrassen 8, is perched on the harbor. Take tram #3, 4, or 9 to "Masthuggstorget," cross the square diagonally, go down Angra Långg away from the center, walk up the stairs, and follow the signs along the terrace. (☎42 48 20; fax 42 48 21. Reception 8-10am and 5-8pm. Dorms 130kr; doubles 350kr; quads 480kr.) To reach the **Stigbergsliden Hostel (STF/HI),** Stigbergsliden 10, take tram #3 or 4 to "Stigbergstorget" and walk east down the hill. (☎24 16 20; fax 24 65 20; email vandrarhem.stigbergsliden@swipnet.se. Reception 8-10am and 4-10pm. Check-in 4-6pm. Dorms 110kr; singles 205kr; doubles 260kr; non-members add 40kr.) Pitch your tent at **Kärralund Camping,** Olbersg. Catch tram #5 to "Welanderg.," then go east on Olbersg. (☎84 02 00; fax 84 05 00. Reception 7am-11pm. 130kr per tent; rooms 110-150kr.) **Matilda,** on Saluhallen, is a farm-style kitchen that whips up top-notch sandwiches and pastries (20-37kr). From the tourist office, cross Kungsportsplatsen and walk straight ahead onto Saluhallen, a side street off Kungstorget. (Open May 31-July 3 M-F 10am-6pm, Sa 10am-4pm; July 5-30 M-F 11am-5pm.) **Pasta, etc.,** at the corner of Nordhamsg. and Plantageg. in Linnéstan, serves pasta so good you'll forget about the "etc." **Postal code:** 40401.

SIGHTS AND ENTERTAINMENT. To the south of Nordstaden, just across Drottningtorget (main square) and the Hamn canal, is the bustling shopping district of **Inom Vallgraven. Kungsport Avenyn,** the city's main drag, stretches from Kungsportsplatsen next to the tourist office all the way to **Götaplatsen,** site of Carl Milles' famous **sculpture fountain** of Poseidon. The size of Poseidon's manhood caused an uproar when the design was unveiled; it was later modified. On the same square, the regal **Konstmuseet** houses a thoroughly engrossing collection of Nordic art as well as the **Hasselblad Center,** an excellent photo exhibition. (Open May-Aug. M-F 11am-4pm, Sa-Su 11am-5pm; Sept.-Apr. Tu and Th-F 11am-4pm, W 11am-9pm, Sa-Su 11am-5pm. 35kr.) The **Göteborgs Operan,** Lilla Bommen (☎13 13 00), an architectural marvel that mimics a ship at full mast, is en route to the **Göteborg Maritime Centrum,** which features a large number of docked ships and sailing vessels that you can board and tour. (Opera in session during winter; inquire about tickets at the tourist office. Maritime center open daily May-June and Aug. 10am-6pm; July 10am-9pm; Sept.-Nov. and Mar.-Apr. 10am-4pm. 35kr.) The **Stadsmuseet,** Norra Hamng. 12, houses exhibits on city history, from Vikings to the city's post-industrial rebirth. (Open daily June-Aug. 11am-4pm; Sept.-Apr. Tu and Th-Su 11am-4pm, W 11am-8pm.

40kr, students 10kr.) One canal farther to the west lies **Linnéstan,** easily the most charming neighborhood in the city. This picturesque and relatively untouristed quarter branches off in winding streets from Linnég and Järntorget. **Göteborgs Skärgård** (archipelago) is a summer paradise for beach-goers and sailors. The islands range from seven minutes to one hour away from the mainland. The secluded beach on **Vrångö** island in the archipelago makes a good daytrip; take tram #4 to "Saltholmen," then catch a **ferry** (☎69 64 00).

Göteborg has a thriving theater and classical music scene—pick up *What's on in Göteborg* at the tourist office. At night, a chic crowd struts down **Kungportsavenyn.** Get warmed up at the pub **Bryggeriet,** Kungportsavenyn 19 (open F-Sa until 3am, Su-Th until 2am) before you hit the jumping dance floor at **Havanna,** Kungportsavenyn 15. (Occasional live music. No cover; women 20+, men 22+.) A hip and more relaxed bar culture can be found in **Linnéstan. Happy Bar** is centrally located on Linné., at the intersection of Prinsg., and makes a good spot for a drink. (Open M-Th 11am-midnight, F-Sa noon-1am, Su noon-10pm.)

EXCURSION FROM GOTHENBURG: VARBERG. Between Gothenburg and Malmö, coastal Varberg beckons with expansive beaches and the spectacular **Varberg Fortress** overlooking the waters of the Kattegatt. (Tours mid-June to mid-Aug. every hr. 11am-4pm. 30kr.) South of town, the shallow bay of **Apelviken** offers some of the best windsurfing and surfing in northern Europe. Follow the *Strandpromenaden* along the beach 2km south of town. **Surfer's Paradise,** Söderg. 22, rents gear and gives tips. From the tourist office, walk away from the train station on Västra Vallg., then turn left on Söderg. (☎67 70 55. Call ahead.) To explore the gorgeous beaches (some nude), **rent bikes** at **BF Cykel,** Östra Langg. 47. From the tourist office, walk away from the water on Kyrkog. until you reach Östra Langg. (70kr per day. Open M-F 9:30am-6pm, Sa 9:30am-2pm.) **Trains** arrive from Gothenborg (1hr., 100kr, under 25 70kr) and Malmö (2½hr., 290kr, 205kr). To get from the station to the **tourist office,** in Brunnsparken, walk four blocks right on Västra Vallg. (☎887 70. Open mid-June to mid-Aug. M-Sa 9am-7pm, Su 3-7pm; mid-Aug. to mid-June M-F 9am-5pm.) Sleep at **Varbergs Fästning Vandrarhem,** inside the fortress, which was used as the Crown Jail from 1852 to 1931. Being locked up was never this popular; book ahead. (☎887 88. Reception June-Aug. 8-10am and 5-9pm; Sept.-May call ahead. Dorms 135kr; singles 130kr.) **Apelvikens Camping** is on the beach. (☎141 78. Open late Mar. to Oct. 120-160kr.) **Postal code:** 43201. ☎**0340.**

THE GULF OF BOTHNIA

Sweden's Gulf of Bothnia can be gentle and dramatic, rural and sophisticated, lively and peacefully remote. The beautiful, unblemished stretch of coastline south of Örnsköldsvik contrasts with the lively university town of Umeå.

ÖRNSKÖLDSVIK. Off the beaten track and main train route is Örnsköldsvik (Urn-SHULDS-vik; Ö-vik to locals), surrounded by ski-jump-draped hills and a harbor of tiny islands waiting to be explored. Most visitors use the town as a base for superb **hiking.** The 130km **Höga Kusten Leden (High Coast Trail)** links Ö-vik with Veda in the south and winds along the most beautiful, dramatic section of Sweden's Baltic coast. Pick up a trail guide (75kr) at the tourist office for info on transport links and huts along the way. Several **day hikes** are also conveniently near—the **Yellow Trail** loops an easy 6km. You'll find the trail head on Hantverkareg; from the tourist office, walk uphill on Nyg. and turn right on Hantverkareg. Throughout the island of **North Ulvön** are scenic hiking trails, the most rewarding of which leads to the peak of **Lotsberget Mountain.** The **M/S Otilia** sails from Örnsköldsvik at 9:30am, arrives at Ulvön at noon, and departs for Ö-vik at 3pm (100kr round-trip), stopping en route at the island of **Trysunda,** which also has beautiful hiking trails and a beach (arrives 11am, departs for Ö-vik 4pm; 70kr round-trip). **Gene Fornby,** a 2000-year-old settlement 6km from Ö-vik, has been rebuilt to look as it did in AD 500. (Open daily late June to early Aug. 11am-5pm; tours every hr. 1-4pm. 50kr, children 20kr.)

Buses run to Örnsköldsvik from Umeå (2hr., 95kr) and Östersund (4½hr., 210kr) in the north, and Sundsvall in the south (2hr., 6-7 per day, 120kr). To get from the train to the bus station in Sundsvall, take a left out of the train station, walk through the tunnel, turn right into another tunnel, and when you emerge, look for Kyrkog. and turn left. You will run into the main esplanade; turn right and the bus terminal is at the end. The **tourist office,** Nyg. 18, books rooms and cottages. (☎125 37; fax 881 23. Open mid-June to mid-Aug. M-F 9am-7pm, Sa 9am-3pm, Su 10am-3pm; Apr. to mid-June and mid-Aug. to Sept. M-F 10am-5pm, Sa 10am-2pm; Oct.-May M-F 10am-5pm.) To get there, walk up the steps behind the bus station, follow Fabriksg., and turn left on Nyg. **Strand City Hotel,** Nyg. 2, is downhill from the tourist office and offers no-frills rooms. (☎106 10. 140kr.) **STF Vandrarhem Örnsköldsvik (HI),** Högsnäsgården pl. 1980, is a 15-minute ride on bus #42 (19kr; M-F last bus 9pm) into the cow-pie-scented countryside. (☎702 44. Reception in summer 9-10am and 5-7pm; off season 9-10am. 110kr, non-members 150kr.) **Postal code:** 89101. ☎**0660.**

UMEÅ. Umeå (OOM-eh-oh; pop. 104,000), the largest city in northern Sweden, is a lively and fast-growing university town. Adventurous souls head for the 30km **Umeleden bike and car trail,** which snakes past old hydropower stations, gardens, restaurants, and **Baggböle Herrgård,** a delightful cafe in a 19th-century mansion. (Open Tu-Su noon-8pm.) A bridge upriver allows for a more manageable 15km loop. **Oves Cykelservice,** Storg. 87, rents **bikes.** (☎12 61 91. 40kr per day. Open M-F 8am-5pm, Sa 10am-2pm.) Regular trains do not run out of Umeå, but the private **Sweden Train Company** goes from Umeå north to Kiruna and Narvik, Norway. They honor some Sweden Rail passes; for info, call the **Avanda travel office** in Umeå (☎14 28 90). **Trains** run from Umeå to Luleå (5½hr.). **Buses** operated by Norrlands Kusten (toll-free ☎ (020) 511 513) and Ybuss (toll-free ☎ (020) 51 15 13) run down the coast to Stockholm (11hr.) and north to Luleå and on to Kiruna and Narvik. The train station is across from the bus terminal. To get to the **tourist office,** Renmarkstorget 15, which lists private rooms from 150kr, walk straight down Rådhusesplanaden from the train station and turn right on Skolg. (☎16 16 16; www.umea.se. Open mid-June to late Aug. M-F 8am-7pm, Sa 10am-5pm, Su 11am-5pm; late Aug. to Sept. M-F 10am-6pm, Sa 10am-2pm; Oct.-Apr. M-F 10am-5pm; May to mid-June M-F 10am-6pm, Sa 10am-2pm.) To get to the **Youth Hostel (HI),** V. Esplanaden 10, from the train station, go straight up Rådhusesplanaden, turn right on Skolg., and left on V. Esplanaden. (☎77 16 50. Laundry 10kr. Reception 8-10am and 5-9pm. 110-130kr, nonmembers 150-170kr.) Take Holmsund bus #124 from Vasaplan to **Ljumvikens Camping;** tell the bus driver your destination. (☎417 10. 75kr per tent.) **Postal code:** 90101. ☎**090.**

LULEÅ. At the mouth of the **Lule Älv** lies Luleå (LOOL-eh-oh), a perky town with lively cafes and nightlife along **Storgatan,** the main drag. The nearby 15th-century church town **Gammelstad** is a UNESCO World Heritage site. Going to church used to require a day's travel in winter, so local farmers built hundreds of tiny cottages near the church to house their families on Sunday night. Take bus #8, 9, or 32 for 20kr. (Church open in summer M-F 8am-5pm, Sa 8am-2pm, Su 8am-5pm; off season call ☎43 51 12 to arrange a visit.) The mostly uninhabited **Luleå archipelago** awaits exploration by ferry, canoe, or kayak; the **M/S Favourite** (book through the tourist office) and the **M/S Laponia** (☎29 35 00) both run daily ferries to different islands. The **tourist office,** Storg. 43b, books rooms (120-450kr) for free. From the train station, cross Prästg. and follow it to the right, walk diagonally across the park, cross Hermalingsg., and tromp up Storg. (☎29 35 00. Open in summer M-F 9am-7pm, Sa-Su 10am-4pm; off season M-F 10am-6pm, Sa 10am-2pm.) The **Örnviks Youth Hostel (HI),** Örnviksv. 87, is in a nature reserve 6km away. Take bus #6 (13kr) and ask the driver to drop you off after the bridge; cross the road, walk back toward the bridge, and follow the path into the field on your right. At night, buses go to the front door. (☎25 23 25. Kitchen. Reception 7am-11pm. 100-120kr, non-members 140-160kr.) **EFS Sundet** is the closest **campground;** take bus #6. (☎25 20 74. Reception 8am-9pm. Open June-Aug. 75kr per tent; 2-bed cabins 300kr.) **Postal code:** 97101. ☎**0920.**

LAPLAND (SÁPMI)

The "Southerners" living south of the Arctic Circle imagine that Lapland consists of reindeer herds roaming through dense forest, thick snow, unrelenting darkness, and bitter cold for half the year, while perpetual light rules the other half. They're right. The lure here is nature, from swampy forests in the vast lowlands to the spectacular rounded mountains rising up to meet the Norwegian border. Swedish Lapland is home to 20,000 reindeer-tending **Sami** ("Lapps" is derogatory), descendants of prehistoric Scandinavians modern Sami use helicopters and snowmobiles to herd their reindeer.

GETTING THERE AND GETTING AROUND

There are two **rail** routes to Lapland. The **coastal route** runs from Stockholm through Boden, Umeå, and Kiruna to Narvik, Norway, along the **Malmbanan.** From Midsummer (June 22-23 in 2001) to early August, the privately-run **Inlandsbanan** travels from Mora to Gällivare. A train leaves daily at 7:35am from the "Morastrand" train station in **Mora** and arrives at **Östersund** at 1:55pm (160kr); another train leaves Östersund daily at 7:05am and arrives at **Gällivare** at 10pm (320kr, from Mora 480kr). Another private company, **Tågkompaniet,** often provides the only train link between towns; unfortunately, their schedules are not observed very strictly. For information, contact any Avanda travel agency in Umeå (☎ (090) 14 28 90). **Buses,** most of which do not accept railpasses, are the only way to smaller towns and are generally the best way to travel in the north. Call ☎ (020) 47 00 47 for schedules.

TRAINS AND BUSES TO NORWAY AND FINLAND

Two **trains** go daily from **Luleå** to **Narvik, Norway** (6½hr.), stopping in **Gällivare, Kiruna,** and **Abisko.** The route from Kiruna to Narvik is stunning. **Buses** link Kiruna to **Karesuando** on the Finnish border (2½hr., 1-2 per day, 125kr), then continue to **Skibotn, Norway,** or **Kilpisjärvi** and **Muonio.** Finland is also accessible by bus from **Boden.** Railpasses are valid on all **buses** from Boden to **Haparanda,** on the Finnish border.

KIRUNA. The only large town in Swedish Lapland, Kiruna (pop. 90,000) is a wilderness oasis. The world's largest underground **mine** put Kiruna on the map and is still the main draw. (Mandatory tours depart from the tourist office June-Aug. every hr. 10am-4pm. 140kr.) Nearby **Jukkasjärvi** is home to the spectacular **Ice Hotel.** For obvious reasons, the hotel exists only in the winter and is rebuilt every fall, although part of it is preserved in a warehouse year-round. (Tours depart from the tourist office 4-5 times per day. 140kr.) **ESRANGE,** a space center with a mapping control center and rocket/balloon launch facility, lies 40km outside Kiruna. Astronomers come here to study the *aurora borealis* and the ozone layer. (Tours depart from the tourist office June-Aug. M-F noon. 140kr.) **Buses** run regularly to Kiruna from Luleå (200kr) and Jokkmokk (100kr). Tågkompaniet **trains** run from Luleå and north to Abisko, Riksgränsen, Sweden, and Narvik, Norway. Regular **flights** (☎680 00) go to and from Stockholm for the **Kiruna Flygplats.** (2-3 per day; 500kr, students 300kr, standby 250kr.) The **Kiruna-Lappland tourist office** is in the **Folkshuset** in the town center. Walk straight from the train station and follow the footpath through the tunnel, then walk uphill to the top. The agents book rooms, schedule tours, and arrange dog-sled adventures in winter. (☎188 80; www.lappland.se. Open June-Aug. M-F 9am-9pm, Sa-Su 9am-7pm; Sept.-May M-F 9am-5pm.) Uphill from the tourist office is the **STF youth hostel,** Bergmästareg. 7. (☎171 95. Dorms 120kr; singles 240kr; doubles 300kr.) **Postal code:** 98135. **☎0980.**

SWEDEN

ÖSTERSUND ☎063

Östersund is a natural stopover from Trondheim for travelers heading to or from Norway and a required one for those riding the length of the **Inlandsbanan.** The festive lakeside town welcomes visitors with boating and swimming in summer and skiing in winter. **Lake Storsjön** is home to a cousin of the Loch Ness monster, which King Oscar II and a crew of Norwegian whalers tried unsuccessfully to capture in 1894. See their harpoons at the **Jamtli museum,** north of the city center on Kyrkg., which also features Sami photography, crafts, Viking paintings, and costumed actors in an open-air museum. Take bus #2 from the city center. (Open mid-June to Aug. daily 11am-5pm; Sept. to mid-June Tu-Su 11am-5pm.) The **Storsjö monster** mania persists today—there is a 10,000kr prize for the best summer sighting and the city is sponsoring a name contest. Rent a **bike** at **Cykelogen,** Kyrkg. 45. (☎12 20 80; open M-F 10am-1pm and 2-6pm, Sa 10am-2pm; 100kr per day), and pedal over the footbridge to **Frösön Island,** once thought to be the home of Viking gods.

Trains run to Trondheim (5½hr., 300kr) and Stockholm (6hr., 500kr), and into Lapland (1 per day to Gällivare, 320kr). The **tourist office,** Rådhusg. 44, books rooms for free. From the train station, walk up the hill on your left and continue down Prästg.; hang a right up Postgränd one block. (☎14 40 01. Open June-Aug. M-Sa 9am-9pm, Su 10am-7pm; Sept.-May M-F 9am-5pm.) Östersund's splendid **Youth Hostel (HI)** is 600m from the station on Södra Gröng., and has kitchenettes and TVs in all rooms. Walk left out of the train station, and turn right on Gränzg. Trudge uphill to the church, turn right on Rådhusg.; and look for the gas station at the corner of Stuguvagen. The hostel is behind the gas station. (☎13 91 00. Reception 8am-noon and 4-8pm; also open for Inlandsbanan arrivals. 100kr.) Wild strawberries grow on the thatched roof of **Frösötornets Härbärge hostel,** overlooking the city. Take bus #5 from the city center (last bus 10:20pm) to avoid the hellish climb. (☎51 57 67. Reception 9am-9pm. Open May-Oct. 125kr.) Take bus #2, 6, or 9 to **Östersunds Camping** at Fritidsbyn. (☎14 46 15. Tents 90kr.) Stock up at the **supermarket Hemköp** at Kyrkg. 56. (Open M-F 9am-7pm, Sa 9am-4pm, Su noon-5pm.) **Postal code:** 83101.

DALARNA

Three hours west of Stockholm, Dalarna is the seat of Sweden's national folk culture, the place to be for Midsummer, and Sweden's *Smultronstället*—a secret place where people go to commune with nature, themselves, and their significant others. Scores of Swedes spend their summer holidays here in the woods.

MORA. An excellent base from which to explore Dalarna, bright, compact Mora skirts the western shore of Lake Siljan and inspired Swedish painter Anders Zorn (1860-1920), whose collection and house are at the **Zornmuseet,** Vasag. 36. (Open May-Sept. M-Sa 9am-5pm, Su 11am-5pm; Oct.-Apr. M-Sa noon-5pm, Su 1-4pm. 30kr, students 25kr. Guided tours 35kr, 30kr.) The legendary red wooden **dalahäst** (Dalecarlian) horses are hand-made in **Nusnäs,** 10km east of Mora (bus #108, 15min., 15kr), but their celebrity has come at a price: brothers Nils and Grannas Olsson now run competing factories. (Open mid-June to mid-Aug. M-F 9am-6pm, Sa-Su 9am-5pm; mid-Aug. to mid-June M-F 8am-5pm, Sa 10am-2pm. Free.) The **Inlandsbanan** train route begins in Mora (see p. 912) and runs to Östersund and Gällivare. The **tourist office,** which books rooms in private homes (135-155kr) for a 25kr fee, is in Mora's "Central" train station. (☎265 50. Open mid-June to mid-Aug. M-F 9am-8pm, Sa-Su 11am-7pm; mid-Aug. to mid-June M-F 9am-5pm, Sa 10am-1pm.) The stop "Morastrand" is closer to the sites in town. The **Youth Hostel (HI),** Fredsg. 6, is 500m from "Morastrand"; turn right on the main road and cross the street when you see Målkull Ann's Cafe, which is the hostel office after hours. (☎381 96. Reception 8-10am and 5-7pm. 140kr, nonmembers 180kr.) Browse the bakeries on **Kyrkog. Cafe Helmers,** on Kyrkog. near the corner of Koppmanag., serves to-die-for Swedish pastries. (Open 8am-8pm.) Load up at the **ICA supermarket,** also on Kyrkog. (Open M-Sa 9am-8pm, Su 11am-8pm.) **Postal code:** 79201. ☎**0250.**

LEKSAND. Over 20,000 people flock to this town above Lake Siljan for Midsummer festivities, featuring a maypole, folk music, and the **Siljansrodden,** a series of churchboat competitions that revives the tradition of rowing to church. The annual **Musik vid Siljan** festival in Leksand and Rättvik (the first few weeks of July) has classical and folk music from around the world. (☎ (0248) 102 90; www.siljan.se. Tickets 50-375kr.) The **tourist office,** inside the Leksand train station, has more details. (☎ 803 00; www.siljan-dalarna.com. Open mid-June to mid-Aug. M-F 9am-8pm, Sa-Su 10am-7pm; mid-Aug. to mid-June M-F 9am-5pm, Sa 10am-1pm.) From Leksand's quay you can take breezy summer **cruises** on the *M/S Gustaf Wasa* a few times a day to Rättvik and Mora (☎ (010) 252 32 92 or (010) 252 32 92; 2-4hr., 80-120kr).

Accommodations are often hard to come by (packed during Midsummer), but the tourist office can find you a private room for a 25kr fee (doubles from 275kr). Try the **Solvi SMU-gård,** Rättviksv. 60, near the station, a combination **campground,** lodge, and country kitchen whose main building is a red farmhouse. From the station, turn left on Stationsg., right on Leksandsvägen, left on Tällbergsvagen, and left again on Rättviksvagen. (☎ 100 90. Reception 8am-9pm. Triples 300kr; quads 400kr; tents 100kr.) Otherwise, call the **STF hostel (HI),** 2.5km from the train station, and ask for directions. (☎ 152 50. Reception 8am-noon and 4-6pm. 120kr.) A 20-minute walk along the road toward Tällberg brings you to swimming and camping at **Camping Stugby.** (☎/fax 803 13. 100kr per tent.) Pick up the essentials at **ICA Supermarket,** Leksandsv. 5. (Open M-Sa 9am-8pm, Su 10am-8pm.) **Postal code:** 79301. ☎ **0247.**

FALUN. Like other towns in Dalarna, Falun has a relaxed atmosphere and a pleasant city center, and is surrounded by lakes, forests, and rolling meadows. At heart it is an industrial town, best known for its **copper mines.** The mines are well worth a visit; from the tourist office, walk back toward the train station, and turn left on Gruvg., passing three traffic circles. (Open daily June-Aug. 10am-5pm. Mandatory tour 50min.) Falun is a fairly major transportation hub, but if you are coming from Lake Siljan, you will likely have to change trains in **Borlänge** (20min., once every 2hr., 40kr). Falun's **tourist office** is at Trotzg. 10-12. From the train station, bear left on the pedestrian path until you clear the bike racks, then bear right on the path, turn left under the first tunnel, and you'll come out of the park on Trotzg. (☎ 830 50; www.welcome.falun.se. Open June-Aug. M-F 9am-7pm, Sa 9am-6pm, Su 10am-5pm; Sept.-May M-F 9am-6pm, Sa 9am-2pm.) A sparkling **STF youth hostel** is 3km from the center of town at Hälsinggårdsvägen 7. Take bus #701, 704, or 712 (10min., 13kr) from Trotzg., near the tourist office. (☎ 105 60. Breakfast 65kr. Laundry. Reception 8am-noon and 4-8pm. 115kr.) **Postal code:** 79183. ☎ **023.**

SWITZERLAND

(SCHWEIZ, SVIZZERA, SUISSE)

SWISS FRANCS

US$1 = 1.77SFR	1SFR = US$0.56
CDN$1 = 1.20SFR	1SFR = CDN$0.84
UK£1 = 2.49SFR	1SFR = UK£0.40
IR£1 = 1.93SFR	1SFR = IR£0.52
AUS$1 = 1.00SFR	1SFR = AUS$1.00
NZ$1 = 0.76SFR	1SFR = NZ$1.31
SAR1 = 0.25SFR	1SFR = SAR04.02
EURO€1 = 1.52SF	1SFR = EURO€0.6

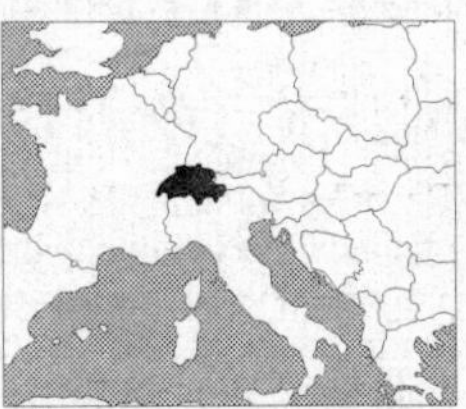

Country code: 41. **International dialing prefix:** 00. From outside Switzerland, dial int'l dialing prefix (see inside back cover) + 41 + city code + local number.

The unparalleled natural beauty of Switzerland entices hikers, skiers, bikers, paragliders, and scenery gazers from all over the globe to romp about its Alpine playground. Three-fifths of the country is dominated by mountains: the Jura cover the northwest region, bordering France, while the Alps stretch gracefully across the entire lower half of Switzerland, flirting with Italy in the southern Lepontine chain and colliding with Austria in the eastern Rhaetian Alps. The cities that lie around blue lakes fed by the mountain glaciers make their own claim to fame as international centers of commerce and diplomacy. While the stereotypes of Switzerland as a "Big Money" banking and watch-making mecca are to some extent true (nearly 4% of the Swiss are employed in the banking industry), its energetic youth culture belies its staid reputation. Although the country is not known for being cheap, the best things—warm Swiss hospitality and sublime vistas—are priceless.

For the real skinny, check out *Let's Go: Austria and Switzerland 2001*.

FACTS AND FIGURES

Official Name: Confederation Helvetica.

Government: Federal Republic.

Capital: Bern.

Land Area: 41,290 sq. km.

Geography: Flat, rolling plains spotted with glacial lakes in the north, Alpine mountains in the south.

Climate: Varies with altitude; cold, rainy or snowy winters, cool to warm summers.

Major Cities: Geneva, Bern, Basel, Zurich, Lucerne, Lugano.

Population: 7,500,000.

Languages: Swiss German, French, Italian, Romansch.

Religions: Roman Catholic (46%), Protestant (40%).

Average Income Per Capita: US$26,400

Major Exports: Machinery, chemicals, watches.

DISCOVER SWITZERLAND

Follow the Swiss to the mountains. Head directly for **Interlaken** (p. 935), a backpacker town brimming with paragliding, bungee jumping, canyoning, river rafting, kayaking, and other adventure opportunities. Most importantly, Interlaken provides easy access to the waterfall hikes in the **Lauterbrunnen Valley** (p. 937) and the other wonders of the **Jungfrau Region.** Continue on to the **Valais,** with hiking and year-round skiing in **Zermatt** (p. 938). While many come to Switzerland to commune with nature, others come to commune with other backpackers: popular hotspots include **Montreux** (especially during the Jazz Festival; p. 925), cosmopolitan **Geneva** (p. 919), and cutting-edge, consumer-culture **Zurich** (p. 928). Backpacker getaway hostels hidden away in the hills are an up-and-coming phenomenon: explore the Swiss countryside from **Leysin** and **Gryon** (p. 925). Finally, taste the *dolce vita* in Italian Switzerland, with stops at **Lugano** (p. 940), and **Locarno** (p. 939).

ESSENTIALS

WHEN TO GO

November to March is ski season; prices in eastern Switzerland double and travelers need reservations months in advance. The situation is reversed in the summer, when the flatter, western half of Switzerland fills up. Sights and accommodations are cheaper and less crowded in the shoulder season (May-June, Sept.-Oct.); call ahead to check that the Alpine resort areas will be open then.

DOCUMENTS AND FORMALITIES

EMBASSIES AND CONSULATES

Embassies and consulates of other countries in Switzerland are all in **Bern** (p. 934).

Swiss Embassies at Home: Australia, 7 Melbourne Ave., Forrest, **Canberra,** ACT 2603 (☎ (02) 62 73 39 77; fax 62 73 34 28); **Canada,** 5 Marlborough Ave., Ottawa, ON KIN 8E6 (☎ (613) 235 18 37); **Ireland,** 6 Ailesbury Rd., Ballsbridge, Dublin 4 (☎ (01) 218 63 82); **New Zealand,** 22 Panama St., Wellington (☎ (04) 472 15 93); **South Africa,** 818 George Ave., Arcadia 0083, P.O. Box 2289, 0001 Pretoria (☎ (012) 43 67 07); during the sessions of Parliament (Jan.-June), the embassy is based in Capetown, P.O. Box 1546, Capetown 8000 (☎ (021) 426 12 01/02); **UK,** 16-18 Montague Place, London W1H 2BQ (☎ (020) 76 16 60 00); **US,** 2900 Cathedral Ave. NW, Washington D.C. 20008-3499 (☎ (202) 745 79 00; www.swissemb.org).

GETTING THERE AND GETTING AROUND

BY PLANE. Airfares to Switzerland peak between July and August, and during the holidays. During ski season, it may be cheaper to fly to a non-skiing destination, like Paris or Frankfurt, then take the train. **Swiss Air** flies to all cities in Switzerland. **EasyJet** (☎ (0870) 600 00 00; www.easyjet.com) flies from London to Geneva and Zurich (UK£47-136). From Ireland, **Aer Lingus** (☎ (01) 886 88 88; www.aerlingus.ie) goes from Dublin, Cork, Galway, Kerry, and Shannon to Zürich for IR£102-240.

BY TRAIN. Federal **(SBB, CFF)** and private railways connect most towns and villages. **Schnellzüge** (express trains) speed between cities, while **Regionalzüge** chug into small towns. **Eurail, Europass,** and **Interrail** passes are all valid. The **Swiss Transfer Ticket** is good for a one-day trip from any entry point (airport or border crossing) to any Swiss destination and the return trip within a period of one month (US$71). The **Swiss Card** offers the same deal as the Transfer Ticket, plus 50% off unlimited rail and bus tickets (US$104). The **SwissPass** offers unlimited rail travel for four, eight, 15, 21, or 31 days. It also grants unlimited urban transportation in 36 cities and on certain private railways and lake steamers, and 25% discounts on excursions to most mountaintops. (Adult 2nd-class 4-day pass US$160, 8-day $220, 15-day $265, 21-day $305, and 1-month $345.) The **Swiss Flexipass** entitles you to any three to nine days of unlimited rail travel in a one-month period with the same benefits as the SwissPass. (Adult 2nd-class 3-day pass US$156, 4-day US$184, 5-day US$212, 6-day US$240, 7-day US$261, 8-day US$282, 9-day US$303.) For national **rail info,** dial ☎ (090) 030 03 00.

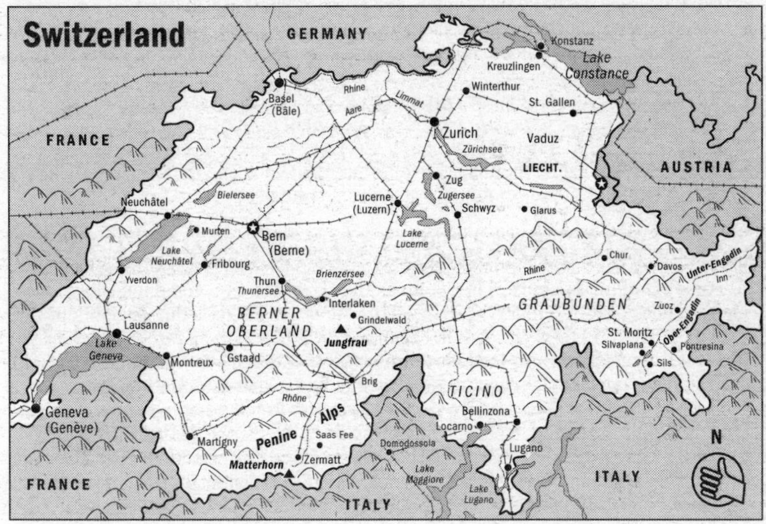

BY BUS AND FERRY. PTT **postal buses,** a barrage of banana-colored coaches, connect villages and towns. SwissPasses are valid on many buses, but Eurailpasses are not. Even with the SwissPass, you might have to pay a bit extra (5-10SFr) if you're riding one of the faster buses. In cities, public buses run to outlying areas. Buy tickets at the automatic machines at most bus stops, and expect a 30-50SFr fine for riding without a ticket. *Tageskarten*, valid for 24 hours of travel, run 2-7.50SFr, but most Swiss cities are small enough to cover on foot. On most lakes, notably Lake Geneva, Lake Neuchâtel, and Lake Lucerne, **ferries** run between towns. SwissPasses generally grant free passage; Eurail may get you a discount.

BY CAR. Swiss highways are excellent, and roads at altitudes of up to 1500m generally remain open throughout winter. The speed limits are 50kph in cities, 80kph on open roads, and 120kph on highways.

BY BIKE AND BY THUMB. May, June, and September are prime biking months in Switzerland. Most ferries let you take your bike for free or for a nominal fee, and you can always ship your bike on trains. Nearly every train station in Switzerland has bike rental for 27SFr per day. The **Touring Club Suisse,** Cyclo Tourisme, chemin Riantbosson 11-13, CH-1217 Meyrin (☎ (022) 785 12 22), will send you information. In Switzerland, **hitching** (called "autostop") is only legal at rest stops or at the entrance ramps to highways. Some large cities in Switzerland offer a ride service *(Mitfahrzentrale)*, a cross between hitchhiking and the ride boards common at many universities, which pairs drivers with riders; the fee varies according to destination. *Let's Go* does not recommend hitchhiking.

TOURIST SERVICES AND MONEY

EMERGENCY. Police: ☎ 117. **Ambulance:** ☎ 144. **Fire:** ☎ 118.

TOURIST OFFICES. The **Swiss National Tourist Office,** marked by a standard blue **"i"** sign, is represented in nearly every town in Switzerland; most speak English. The English language website for Swiss tourism is www.myswitzerland.com.

Tourist Boards at Home: UK and **Ireland,** Swiss Court, London W1V 8EE (☎ (02) 78 51 17 10); **US** and **Canada,** 6608 Fifth Ave., New York, NY 10020 (US ☎ (212) 757 59 44; email info.usa@switzerlandtourism.ch; Canada ☎ (800) 100 200 30).

MONEY. The Swiss monetary unit is the **Swiss Franc (SFr),** divided into 100 *centimes* (called *Rappen* in German Switzerland). Coins come in 5, 10, 20, and 50 *centimes* and 1, 2, and 5SFr; bills come in 10, 20, 50, 100, 500, and 1000SFr. Currency exchange is easiest at ATMs, train stations, and post offices, where rates are comparable to bank rates but commissions are smaller. Switzerland is not the cheapest destination; expect to pay US$20 per night for a **hostel** and $12 for a basic sit-down **meal.** There is no **VAT,** although there are frequently tourist taxes of a few SFr for a night at hostel. **Gratuities** are automatically factored into prices. However, it is considered polite to round up your bill as a nod of approval for good service.

ACCOMMODATIONS AND CAMPING

Accommodations in Switzerland are usually clean, orderly, and expensive. **Hotels** and **pensions** tend to charge at least US$35-40 for a single, while **hostel** beds are usually US$18 and up. The local **HI** organization is the *Schweizer Jugendherbergen* (SJH or Swiss Youth Hostels; www.youthhostel.ch). Non-HI members can stay in all of these hostels, but are usually charged a US$5 surcharge. The smaller, more informal **Swiss Backpackers (SB)** organization tends to appeal to young, foreign travelers interested in socializing. **Camping** in Switzerland is less about getting out into nature and more about having a cheap place to sleep. Most sites are open only in summer, but some sites are specifically set aside for winter camping. Prices average US$6 per person, US$6 per site.

FOOD AND DRINK

Switzerland's hearty cooking will keep you warm through those frigid alpine winters but will skyrocket your cholesterol. Bernese *Rösti*, a plateful of hash brown potatoes skilleted and sometimes flavored with bacon or cheese is prevalent in the German regions, as is *fondue* in the French. Try Valaisian *raclette*, made by melting cheese over a fire, then scraping it onto a baked potato and garnishing with meat or vegetables. Self-serve cafeterias and supermarkets Migros and Co-op supply the most essential Swiss culinary invention, milk chocolate (*Lindt*, *Toblerone*, and *Nestlé* are native favorites), on the cheap. Each canton has its own local **beer.** Beer is relatively cheap, often less expensive than soda. Order *ein helles* for a light beer, *ein dunkles* for a dark one.

COMMUNICATION

MAIL. Airmail from Switzerland averages 7-20 days to North America, although times are more unpredictable from smaller towns. Domestic letters take 1-3 days.

TELEPHONES. The simplest way to call within the country is to use a pay phone, which usually only accept **phone cards.** Wherever possible, use a calling card for international phone calls, as the long-distance rates for national phone services are often exorbitant. **Prepaid phone cards** and **major credit cards** can be used for direct international calls, but are still less cost-efficient. Phone cards are available at kiosks, post offices, or train stations. **International direct dial** numbers include: **AT&T** (☎ (022) 90 30 11); **BT Direct** (☎ (0800) 20 02 09); **Canada Direct** (☎ (0800) 20 02 17); **MCI WorldPhone Direct** (☎ (022) 90 30 12); **Sprint** (☎ (0800) 20 02 36); and **Telkom South Africa Direct** (☎ (022) 90 30 27).

LANGUAGES. German, French, Italian, and Romansch. English is the most common second language in Switzerland, and most urban Swiss speak it fluently. Leap right in with our language charts (p. 981), you multilingual fool, you.

SKIING AND HIKING

Switzerland's 9000km of **hiking paths** range from simple foothill excursions to ice-axe-wielding glacier expeditions. Bands of white-red-white mark trails; if there are no markings, you're on an "unofficial" trail (most are well maintained). Blue-white-blue markings indicate that a trail requires special equipment, either for difficult rock climbs or glacier climbing. **Swiss Alpine Club (SAC) huts** are modest and practical for those interested in trekking in higher, more remote areas of the Alps. Bunk rooms sleep 10 to 20 side by side, with blankets but no electricity or running water provided. One night's stay without food averages 30SFr (members 20-25SFr). Membership costs 126SFr. Contact the SAC, Sektion Zermatt, Haus Dolomite, CH-3920 Zermatt, Switzerland (☎ (028) 67 26 10). The best maps to bring are the **Freytag-Berndt** and **Kümmerly-Frey** maps (around US$10), available in Swiss bookstores.

Skiing in Switzerland is often less expensive than in North America if you avoid the pricey resorts. **Passes** (valid for transportation to, from, and on lifts) run 30-50SFr per day and 100-300SFr per week. A week of lift tickets, equipment rental, lessons, lodging, and *demi-pension* (half-pension—breakfast plus one other meal, usually dinner) averages 475SFr. **Summer skiing** is no longer as prevalent as it once was, but is still available in Zermatt.

HOLIDAYS AND FESTIVALS

Holidays: New Year's Day (Jan. 1-2); Good Friday (Apr. 5); Easter Monday (Apr. 5); Labor Day (May 1); Ascension Day (June 1); Whitmonday (June 11); Swiss National Day (Aug. 1); and Christmas (Dec. 25-26).

Festivals: Check out Basel's **Fasnacht** (Carnival; Mar.); Geneva's **Escalade**; summer **Open-Air** music festivals all over the country; the Montreux **JazzFest** (July); Bern's **Gurtenfestival** (mid-July); **Paléo Festival Nyon** near Geneva (late July); and the **Open-Air St. Gallen** (late June). Try heiwww.unige.ch/switzerland/culture/events.htm or www.music.ch for more info.

FRENCH SWITZERLAND

GENEVA (GENÈVE, GENF) ☎022

Step onto one of Geneva's lakeside quays, and you'll see bankers barking into cellular phones, students strolling hand-in-hand, and families just enjoying the shore. There is no typical resident of this small city (pop. 178,000). In 1536 Geneva welcomed a young, unknown John Calvin to its cathedral; later, aesthetes and free thinkers, including Voltaire, Madame de Staël, and Rousseau, lived here. Today, multinational organizations like the Red Cross and the United Nations continue to lend the city an international feel that contrasts strongly with the homogeneity of most Swiss towns. Indeed, many say that the only thing Geneva shares with the rest of Switzerland is its neutral foreign policy and the state religion, banking.

GETTING THERE AND GETTING AROUND

Flights: Cointrin Airport (☎717 71 11, flight info ☎799 31 11) is a **Swissair** (☎ (0848) 800 700) hub. **Air France** (☎827 87 87) and **British Airways** (☎ (0848) 801 010) also service Geneva. **Bus** #10 connects to the city center (15min., every 6min., 2.20SFr), while the **train** (6min., every 10 min., 4.80SFr) runs to Gare Cornavin.

Trains: Gare Cornavin, on pl. Cornavin (www.sbb.ch). To: **Bern** (2hr., every hr., 40SFr); **Lyon** (2hr.; every hr.); **Basel** (3hr., every hr., 72SFr); **Interlaken** (3hr., every hr., 65SFr); 58SFr, under 26 48SFr); **Paris** (3¾hr.; every hr.; 196SFr, under 26 166SFr); **Milan** (4-5hr.; 10 per day; 164SFr, under 26 132SFr); and **Zurich** (3½hr., every hr., 77SFr). Office open M-F 8:30am-7pm, Sa 9am-5pm. **Gare des Eaux-Vives** (☎736 16 20), on the eastern edge of the city, connects to France via tram #12 (dir. Amandoliers SNCF). To **Annecy** (1½hr., 6 per day, 14SFr) and **Chamonix** (2½hr., 4 per day, 24SFr).

Ferries: CGN (☎741 52 31) runs hugely popular routes to **Lausanne** and **Montreux,** departing from quai du Mont-Blanc. Round-trip 47-57SFr.

Public Transportation: Transport Publics Genevois (☎308 34 34), next to the tourist office in Gare Cornavin. Open daily 6:15am-8pm. 1hr. of bus travel 2.20SFr; 3 stops or fewer 1.50SFr. Day passes 5SFr for 1 zone, 8.50SFr for 4. Buses run roughly 5:30am-midnight. **Noctambuses** (3SFr) run 1:30-4:30am. Buy multi-fare and day tickets at the train station, others at automatic vendors at every stop. Stamp multi-use tickets before boarding or risk a 60SFr fine. SwissPass valid on all buses; Eurail not valid.

Taxis: Taxi-Phone (☎331 41 33). 6.30SFr base fare, 2.70SFr per km. Taxi from airport to city 25-30SFr (15-20min.; 4 passengers max.).

Bike Rental: Genève Roule, pl. Montbrillant 17 (☎740 13 43), behind the station. 5 free bikes (50SFr deposit). Nicer ones from 5SFr per day. Open daily 7:30am-9:30pm.

Hitchhiking: *Let's Go* does not recommend hitchhiking. Those headed to Germany or northern Switzerland reportedly take bus #4 to "Jardin Botanique." Those headed to France take bus #4 to "Palettes," then line D to St. Julien.

ORIENTATION AND PRACTICAL INFORMATION

On the southwestern shore of **Lac Léman** (Lake Geneva), the labyrinthine streets of the *vieille ville* surround the **Cathédrale de St-Pierre** and the **university.** Banks, bistros, and boutiques line the **Rhône River** to the north. Farther north, the United Nations, Red Cross, and World Trade Organization overlook the city. Carry your **passport** with you at all times; the French border is close by, and regional buses and local trams (#12 and 16) often cross it.

TOURIST, FINANCIAL, AND LOCAL SERVICES

Tourist Offices: The **main office,** r. du Mont-Blanc 18 (☎909 70 00; www.geneve-tourisme.ch), 5min. from Cornavin toward the pont du Mont-Blanc in the Central Post Office Building. English-speaking staff books hotel rooms (5SFr fee), offers walking tours, and maintains a board listing budget accommodations. Open July-Aug. 9am-6pm; Sept.-June M-Sa 9am-6pm. In summer, head for the magic bus, Geneva's **Centre d'Accueil et de Renseignements** (CAR; ☎731 46 47), parked by the Metro Shopping entrance to Cornavin Station. Open daily June 15-Sept. 15 9am-11pm.

Consulates: Australia, chemin des Fins 2 (☎799 91 00); **Canada,** av. de l'Ariana 5 (☎919 92 00); **New Zealand,** chemin des Fins 2 (☎929 03 50); **South Africa,** r. de Rhône 65 (☎849 54 54); **UK,** r. de Vermont 37 (☎918 24 26); **US,** World Trade Center Bldg. #2 (☎798 16 05; recorded info ☎798 16 15).

Currency Exchange: ATMs have the best rates. **Gare Cornavin** offers good rates, no commission on traveler's checks, and credit card advances (200SFr min.); also arranges Western Union transfers. Open daily Nov.-Mar. 6:45am-8pm, Apr.-Oct. 6:45am-9:30pm. Western Union desk open daily 7am-7pm.

Gay and Lesbian Services: Dialogai, r. de la Navigation 11-13 (☎738 02 00). Publishes *Dialogai,* a guide to French-speaking Switzerland's gay scene. Open M-Th 2-7pm.

Laundromat: Lavseul, r. de-Monthoux 29 (☎735 90 51 or 732 61 46). Wash 5SFr. Dry 1SFr per 10 min. Open 7am-midnight.

EMERGENCIES AND COMMUNICATIONS

Emergencies: Police: r. de Berne 6, next to the post office (☎117 or ☎715 38 50). **Fire:** ☎118. **Ambulance:** ☎144.

Medical Assistance: Hôpital Cantonal, r. Micheli-du-Crest 24 (☎372 33 11). Bus #1 or 5 or tram #12. Call the **Association des Médecins** (☎320 84 20) for walk-in clinic.

Pharmacy: Four pharmacies stay open until 9 or 11pm nightly; consult *Genève Agenda* for contact information. The pharmacy at the train station has the longest regular hours.

Internet Cafes: Open Vidéo Club, r. Chantepoulet. 5SFr per hr. Open M-Th 9:30am-3am, F 9:30am-5am, Sa 11am-5am, Su 3pm-1am. **Point 6,** r. de Vieux-Billard 7a, off r. des Bains (☎800 26 00). 6SFr per hr., 4SFr per 30min. Open M-Tu and Th noon-midnight, W 10am-midnight, F noon-2am, Sa 10am-2am, Su 10am-10pm.

Poste Centrale, r. de Mont-Blanc 18, a block from Gare Cornavin in the Hôtel des Postes. Open M-F 7:30am-6pm, Sa 8:30am-noon. Address mail to be held: First name SURNAME, *Poste Restante,* Genève 1 Mont-Blanc, **CH-1211,** Geneva.

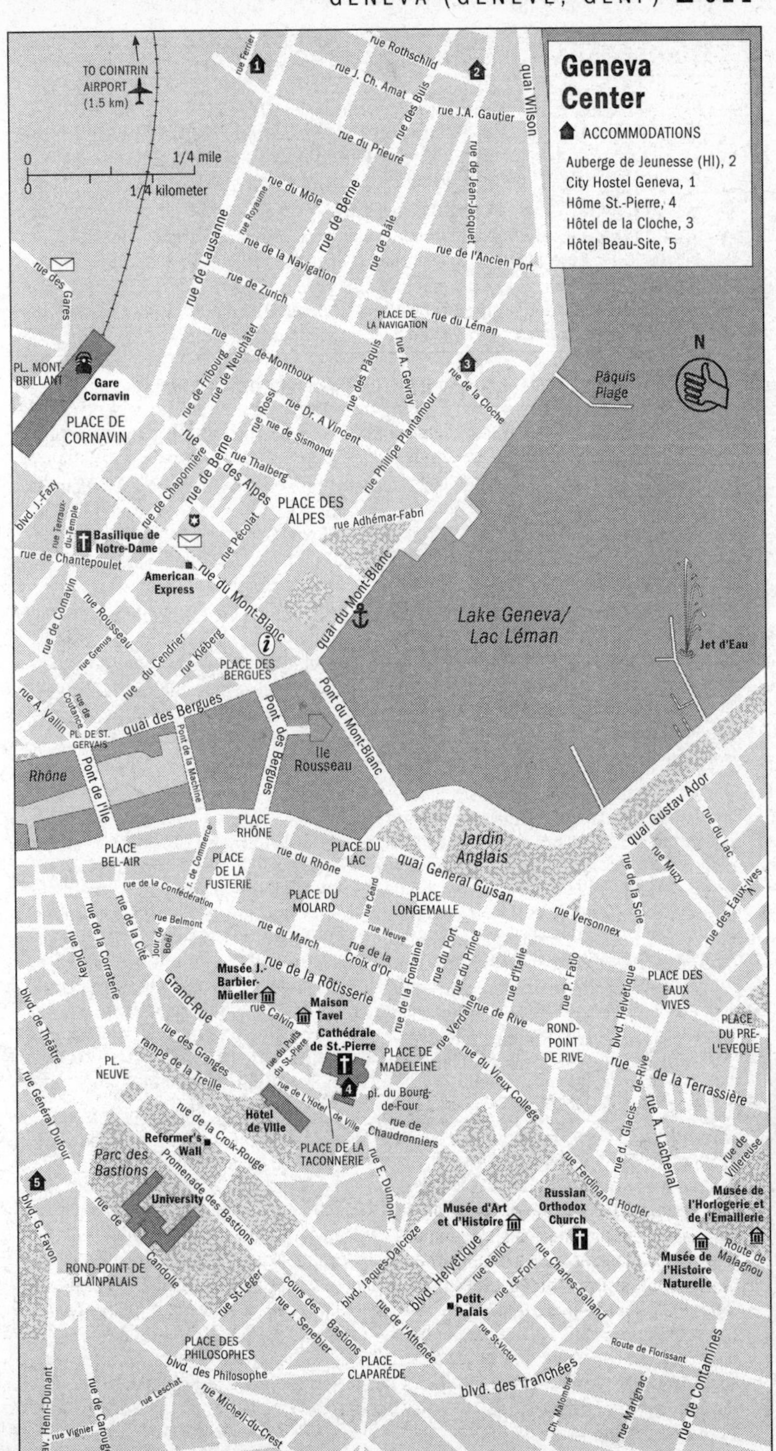
Geneva Center
ACCOMMODATIONS
Auberge de Jeunesse (HI), 2
City Hostel Geneva, 1
Hôme St.-Pierre, 4
Hôtel de la Cloche, 3
Hôtel Beau-Site, 5
TO COINTRIN AIRPORT (1.5 km)
0 1/4 mile
0 1/4 kilometer
Gare Cornavin
PLACE DE CORNAVIN
Basilique de Notre-Dame
American Express
PLACE DES ALPES
PLACE DES BERGUES
Lake Geneva/ Lac Léman
Jet d'Eau
Pâquis Plage
Île Rousseau
Rhône
Jardin Anglais
PLACE BEL-AIR
PLACE DE LA FUSTERIE
PLACE DU MOLARD
PLACE LONGEMALLE
Musée J.-Barbier-Mueller
Maison Tavel
Cathédrale de St.-Pierre
Hôtel de Ville
Reformer's Wall
Parc des Bastions
University
Musée d'Art et d'Histoire
Russian Orthodox Church
Petit-Palais
Musée de l'Horlogerie et de l'Emaillerie
Musée de l'Histoire Naturelle
PLACE DES EAUX VIVES
ROND-POINT DE RIVE
ROND-POINT DE PLAINPALAIS
PLACE DES PHILOSOPHES
PLACE CLAPARÈDE

ACCOMMODATIONS AND CAMPING

You can usually find dorm beds and hostel rooms in Geneva, but hotels fill quickly, so reserve in advance. If the places listed below are booked, try one of the 50 others listed in *Info Jeunes* (free at the tourist office); the tourist office also maintains a board in Gare Cornavin with free direct phone connections to Geneva hotels.

City Hostel Geneva, r. Ferrier 2 (☎901 15 00; www.cityhostel.ch). From the station, turn left on r. de Lausanne, turn left on r. de Prieuré, and right on r. Ferrier. Internet 7SFr per hr. Linens 3SFr. Reception 8-11:30am and 3-10pm. Single-sex dorms 24SFr; singles 50SFr; doubles 70SFr.

Auberge de Jeunesse (HI), r. Rothschild 28-30 (☎732 62 60). Walk left from the station down r. de Lausanne, turn right on r. Rothschild, and take bus #1 (dir. Wilson) to the end. Breakfast included. Laundry. 5-night max. stay. Reception in summer 6:30-10am and 4pm-midnight, in winter 6:30-10am and 5pm-midnight. Lockout in summer 10am-4pm, in winter 10am-5pm. Dorms 24SFr; doubles 65-75SFr; quads 99SFr.

Cité Universitaire, av. Miremont 46 (☎839 22 11). Take bus #3 (dir. Crêts-de-Champel) from the Le Popeye restaurant on pl. de 22 Cantons, on the far right as you exit the station, to the end. Institutional housing with TV rooms, disco (open Th and Sa, free for guests), ping-pong, and small grocery. Reception M-F 8am-noon and 2-10pm, Sa 8am-noon and 6-10pm, Su 9-11am and 6-10pm. For dorms only: lockout 11am-6pm, curfew 11pm. Dorms (July-Sept. only) 17SFr; singles 38SFr; doubles 55SFr; studios with kitchenette and bathroom 68SFr.

Hôme St-Pierre, cours St-Pierre 4 (☎310 37 07), meters from the cathedral. Cross pont du Mont-Blanc from the station, head up rampe de la Treille, and take the 3rd right (15min.). Spectacular rooftop views and a convivial atmosphere. **Women only.** Breakfast M-Sa 5SFr. Laundry 7SFr. Reception M-Sa 9am-noon and 4-8pm, Su 9am-noon. Reserve ahead. Dorms 23SFr; singles 36-45SFr; doubles 50-60SFr.

Camping Pointe-à-la-Bise (☎752 12 96), on chemin de la Bise. Take bus #9 to Rive, then bus E (north) to Bise (about 7km). Reception 8am-noon and 4-8pm. Open Apr.-Oct. No tents provided. 6SFr per person, 18SFr per bed.

FOOD

You can find anything from sushi to paella in Geneva, but you may need a banker's salary to foot the bill. *Boulangeries* and *pâtisseries* offer gourmet food at budget prices. In the **Les Paquîs** area, almost any sort of ethnic food is available. Around **pl. du Cirque** and **plaine de Plainpalais** are a number of cheap, student-oriented "tea rooms," offering bakery and traditional fare at reasonable prices. Many supermarkets also have cafeterias with some of the best deals available, and *Info Jeunes* lists university cafeterias that won't tax your wallet. Pick up **groceries** at **Co-op,** on the corner of r. du Commerce and r. du Rhône, in the Centre Rhône Fusterie. (Open M 9am-6:45pm, Tu-W and F 8:30am-6:45pm, Th 8:30am-8pm, Sa 8:30am-5pm.)

Le Rozzel, Grand-Rue 18. Take bus #5 to pl. Neuve and walk up the hill past the cathedral on r. Jean-Calvin to Grand-Rue. Sit outside and enjoy Breton-style crepes (dinner 7-17SFr, dessert 5-12SFr). Open M-F 8am-10pm, Sa 10am-10pm.

Restaurant Manora, r. de Cornavin 4, 3min. to the right of the station in the Placette department store. Self-serve restaurant with salads (from 4.20SFr), fruit tarts (3.20SFr), and main dishes (from 11SFr). Open M-Sa 7am-9pm, Su 9am-9pm.

La Crise, r. de Chantepoulet 13. From the station, turn right on r. de Cornavin and left on r. de Chantepoulet. Healthy veggie portions with slender prices. Quiche and veggies 8.50SFr, soup 3.50SFr. Open M-F 6am-8pm, Sa 6am-3pm.

Auberge de Saviese, r. des Pâquis 20. From Gare Cornavin, turn left onto r. de Lausanne and right on r. de Zurich, which brings you to r. des Pâquis. Load up on traditional Swiss specialties. Excellent *fondue au cognac* (19.50SFr), and *raclette* with all the trimmings (30SFr). Open M-F 9am-10:30pm, Sa-Su 6-11pm.

SIGHTS AND ENTERTAINMENT

VIEILLE VILLE AND WATERFRONT. Begin exploring the city in the *vielle ville*, where the **Cathédrale de St-Pierre** stands as austere testimony to Calvin's Reformation of Geneva. Its 157-step **north tower** offers a spectacular view, and the ruins of a Roman sanctuary, a 4th-century basilica, and a 6th-century church rest in an **archaeological site** below the cathedral. *(Cathedral open June-Sept. M-Sa 9am-7pm, Su 11:30am-1pm; Oct.-May M-Sa 10am-noon and 2-5pm, Su 11am-12:30pm and 1:30-5pm. Tower open July-Aug., closes 30min. before the cathedral. 3SFr. Archaeological site open June-Sept. Tu-Sa 11am-5pm, Su 10am-5pm; Oct.-May Tu-Sa 2-5pm, Su 10am-noon and 2-5pm. 5SFr, students 3SFr.)* Near the west end of the cathedral sits the 14th-century **Maison Tavel,** Geneva's oldest civilian medieval building—a posh, fortified urban palace that today houses a historical municipal **museum.** *(Open Tu-Su 10am-5pm. Free.)* A few steps away is the 15th- to 17th-century **Hôtel de Ville** (Town Hall), where world leaders met on August 22, 1864 to sign the **Geneva Convention** that still governs conduct during war. The **Grand-Rue** leading away from the Hôtel de Ville is crammed with art galleries, medieval workshops, and 18th-century mansions; plaques along the street commemorate famous residents, including philosopher Jean-Jacques Rousseau, born at #40. Below the cathedral on r. de la Croix-Rouge, the lovely **Parc des Bastions** includes the **Mur des Réformateurs** (Reformers' Wall), a sprawling collection of bas-relief narrative panels and the towering figures of the Reformers themselves, including Knox, Calvin, and Cromwell. A stroll down its center walkway, the Promenade des Bastions, will lead you to the world-class **Petit-Palais,** where you will find works by Picasso, Renoir, Gauguin, Cezanne, and Chagall. *(Terrasse St-Victor 2, off bd. Helvétique. Take bus #17 to Petit Palais or #1, 3, or 5 to Claparède. Open M-F 10am-6pm, Sa-Su 10am-5pm. 10SFr, students 5SFr.)* A couple of blocks east of the Petit-Palais rise the glittering domes of the **Russian Orthodox Church,** whose interior is filled with hauntingly beautiful icons, stained glass, and a heavy aroma of incense. *(R. Toepffer. Take r. des Chaudronniers from the* vieille ville.*)*

As you descend toward the lake from the cathedral, medieval lanes give way to wide, flower-lined quays, chic boutiques and watch shops, and cosmopolitan Geneva is revealed. The largest fountain in the world, the **Jet d'Eau,** down quai Gustave-Ardor on the waterfront, spews a spectacular plume of water 140m into the air (about seven tons at once). The waterfront's quays and beaches (like **Paquis Plage,** on the left bank) offer stunning views of the lake and surrounding mountains.

INTERNATIONAL HILL. Spectacular views of Lac Léman with Mont-Blanc in the background await in a series of garden-parks on the northern side of Geneva, up the hill behind the train station. Climb higher to Geneva's international city, home to myriad embassies and multilateral organizations. The highlight is the **International Red Cross Museum,** which details the organization's history and addresses its humanitarian efforts in an emotional tour-de-force. *(Av. de la Paix 17. Take bus #8, F, V, or Z to Appia or Ariana. Open W-M 10am-5pm. 10SFr, students 5SFr. Audio tours 5SFr.)* In the Red Cross's shadow stands the European headquarters of the **United Nations,** housed in the building that once sheltered the League of Nations. The guided tour of the UN proves less interesting than the constant traffic of international diplomats often wearing handsome non-Western dress. *(Open July-Aug. daily 9am-6pm; Apr.-June and Sept.-Oct. daily 10am-noon and 2-4pm; Nov.-Mar. M-F 10am-noon and 2-4pm. 8.50SFr, students 6.50SFr.)*

ENTERTAINMENT AND NIGHTLIFE

Genève Agenda, available at the tourist office, is your guide to fun, with listings ranging from major festivals to movies (movies run about 16SFr; "v.o." indicates original language, with French and sometimes German subtitles, and "st. ang." indicates English subtitles). In July and August, the **Cinelac** turns Genève Plage into an open-air cinema screening mostly American films. There's also the biggest celebration of **American Independence Day** outside the US (July 4), and the **Fêtes de Genève** in early August, filled with international music and fireworks. **Free jazz concerts** take place in July and August at the **Théâtre de Verdure** in Parc de la Grange.

Geneva's internationalism has brought an incredible diversity to its nightlife. Summer nightlife centers around the **Pl. du Bourg-de-Four,** below Cathédrale de St-Pierre, and the village of **Carouge** (take tram #12 to pl. du Marché), home to **Au Chat Noir,** r. Vautier 13, a popular venue for live jazz, funk, rock, salsa, and sax-moaning blues concerts every night. (Open M-Th 6pm-4am, F 6pm-5am, Sa 9pm-5am, Su 9pm-4am. Concerts 9:30pm; 15SFr.) Back in the *vieille ville,* consort with the artsy patrons of the famous, chic bar **La Clémence,** pl. du Bourg-de-Four 20 (open M-Th 7am-12:30am, F-Sa 7am-1:30am), or chat merrily in the friendly Irish cellar bar **Flanagan's,** r. du Cheval-Blanc 4, off Grand-Rue. (Guinness 8SFr. Live music Th-Sa 10pm-2am. Open daily 4pm-2am.) A single strand of red lights traverse the sophisticated, gay friendly **Sunset Cafe,** R. de la Navigation. (Open W-Su 5pm-midnight.)

LAUSANNE ☎021

The story of Lausanne is a tale of two cities: the *vieille ville* is cosmopolitan and businesslike, while the Ouchy lakefront is lazy and fairly decadent. In the *vielle ville* (M: Lausanne-Flan), take the medieval covered stairs to the hilltop to reach the Gothic **Cathedral,** consecrated in 1275 under Holy Roman Emperor Rudolph and Pope Gregory X. Climb the 200-step **tower** for a spectacular view of the city, lake, and mountains. (Cathedral open daily July to mid-Sept. 7am-7pm; mid-Sept. to June 7am-5pm.) While in the neighborhood, check out the brand-new **Museum of Design and Contemporary Applied Arts.** (☎315 25 30. Open Tu 11am-9pm, W-Su 11am-6pm. 6SFr, students and seniors 4SFr.) Stretch your legs on Ouchy's main promenades, the **quai de Belgique** and **pl. de la Navigation.** The **Musée Olympique,** quai d'Ouchy 1, is a high-tech temple to modern Olympians with a smaller exhibit on the ancient games. (Open May-Sept. M-W and F-Su 9am-6pm, Th 9am-8pm; Oct.-Apr. Tu-W and F-Su 9am-6pm, Th 9am-8pm. 14SFr, students 9SFr. Idyllic grounds free.) Lausanne's most enthralling cultural repository may be the **Collection de l'Art Brut,** av. des Bergières 11, filled with disturbing and beautiful artwork by atypical artists—institutionalized schizophrenics, peasants, and convicted criminals—whose biographies are nearly as fascinating as the art. Take bus #2 or 3 to "Jomini." (☎647 54 35. Open Tu-Su 11am-1pm and 2-5pm. 6SFr, students 4SFr.)

Frequent **trains** (☎157 22 22) arrive at pl. de la Gare 9, halfway between the *vieille ville* and the lakefront, from: Geneva (50min., every 30min., 20SFr); Basel (2½hr., 2 per hr., 62SFr); Montreux (20min., every 30min., 9.40SFr); and Zurich (2½hr., 3 per hr., 67SFr). From the train station, take **Métro Ouchy** or **bus** #1, 3, or 5 to downtown. The **tourist office,** in the train station, reserves rooms for 3% of the rate. (☎613 73 73; www.lausanne.tourisme.ch. Open daily 9am-7pm.) To reach the large, gleaming **Jeunotel (HI),** chemin du Bois-de-Vaux 36, take bus #2 (dir. Bourdonette) to "Bois-de-Vaux," cross the street, and follow the signs. (☎626 02 22; fax 626 02 26. Dorms 25-32SFr; singles 58-82SFr; doubles 88-104SFr; triples 105SFr; quads 140SFr.) Conveniently located near the waterfront and *vielle ville,* **La Croisée,** av. Marc Dufour 15, is a 15-minute walk from the train station. Take av. du Ruchonnet and continue as it turns into av. Marc Dufour. (☎321 09 09. Dorms 30-40 SFr; singles 90SFr; doubles 130SFr; triples 165-195SFr; quads 220-260SFr.) To get to the lakeside **Camping de Vidy,** chemin du Camping 3, take bus #2 from M: Ouchy (dir. Bourdonnette) to "Bois-de-Vaux," then cross the street and go down chemin du Boix-de-Vaux past Jeunotel. The office is straight ahead across rte. de Vidy. (☎622 50 00; fax 622 50 01. Shower included. Reception 8am-12:30pm and 5-8pm. 6.50SFr, students 6SFr; tents 7-11SFr; 1- to 2-person bungalows 54SFr; 3- to 4- person bungalows 86SFr. City tax 1.20SFr per person, 1.30SFr per car.) Restaurants, cafes, and bars cluster around **pl. St-François** and the *vieille ville.* **Migros supermarket,** av. de Rhodanie 2, is near M: Ouchy. (Open M 9am-9:45pm, Tu-Sa 8am-9:45pm.) **Postal code:** CH-1001.

MONTREUX ☎021

Montreux is postcard Switzerland at its swanky, genteel best. The gloomy medieval **Chateau de Chillon,** on a nearby island, is one of Switzerland's most visited attractions. It features all the comforts of home—prison cells, a torture chamber, and a weapons room. The priest François de Bonivard spent four years manacled in the dungeon for preaching Reformation doctrine and inspired Lord Byron's *The Prisoner of Chillon,* as well as works by Rousseau, Hugo, and Dumas. (☎966 89 10. Open daily Apr.-Sept. 9am-6pm; Mar. and Oct. 9:30am-5pm; Nov.-Feb. 10am-4pm. 7SFr, students 5.50SFr.) Take the CGN **ferry** (13SFr, under 26 5.50SFr) or bus #1 to "Chillon" (2.60SFr). The **Montreux Jazz Festival,** famous for exceptional music and one of Europe's biggest parties, pushes everything aside for 15 days starting the first Friday in July. Write to the tourist office well in advance, call the **Jazz Boutique** ticket sellers (☎963 82 82; open mid-Mar. to summer), or check out www.montreuxjazz.com for info and tickets (39-69SFr). The **Jazz Off** is a budget alternative—500 hours of free, open-air concerts by both new and established musicians.

Trains (☎963 45 15) arrive on av. des Alpes from: Geneva (1hr., every 30min., 29SFr); Lausanne (20min., every 5-25min., 9.40SFr); and Bern (1½hr., every hr., 40SFr). Descend the stairs opposite the station, head left on Grand-Rue, and look to the right for the **tourist office,** on pl. du Débarcadère. (☎962 84 84; fax 963 78 95. Open mid-June to mid-Sept. daily 8:30am-7pm; late Sept. to early June M-F 8:30am-5pm, Sa-Su 10am-3pm.) Cheap rooms are scarce during the jazz festival; book ahead. To get to the modern and social **Auberge de Jeunesse Montreux (HI),** passage de l'Auberge 8, walk 20 minutes along the lake past the Montreux Tennis Club. (☎963 49 34. Laundry 8SFr. Reception daily Apr.-Sept. 7-10am and 4-11pm; Oct.-Mar. 7:30-9:30am and 5-10pm. Lockout 10am-4pm. Curfew midnight; key available with passport deposit. Dorms 29SFr; doubles 38-42SFr. Nonmembers add 5SFr.) To reach the **Hôtel Pension Wilhelm,** r. du Marché 13-15, from the station, take a left on av. des Alpes, walk three minutes, and take a left on r. du Marché. (☎963 14 31. Breakfast included. Reception daily 7am-midnight. Closed Oct.-Feb. unless you call ahead. Singles (off season only) 65SFr; doubles 50-120SFr.) To **camp** at **Les Horizons Bleus,** take bus #1 to Villeneuve and follow the lake to the left for five minutes. (☎960 15 47. Reception 9am-12:30pm and 4-9pm. 7SFr per person; 6-12SFr per tent.) The **Co-op,** Grand-Rue 80, offers **groceries.** (Open M-F 8am-12:15pm and 2-6:30pm, Sa 8am-5pm.) **Postal code:** CH-1820.

EXCURSIONS FROM MONTREUX: LEYSIN AND GRYON. From small (Leysin) to diminutive (Gryon), these towns are unlikely stops on a grand European tour. However, both boast idyllic locations between breathtaking mountains and fantastic hostels that are ideal places to recharge. Anglophone-friendly **Leysin** is full of once-mobile backpackers who came, saw, and stayed, bolstering a local industry catering to skiers, snowboarders, climbers, mountain bikers, paragliders, and hikers. The **tourist office** (☎494 22 44), in the Centre Sportif, up the road to the left from the pl. du Marché, provides **hiking maps,** while the **Swiss Climbing School** (☎494 18 46) organizes **trekking** and all alpine activities. Fifty meters from skiing and biking trails, the **Hiking Sheep Guesthouse,** in Villa La Joux, features shining facilities, breathtaking balconies, and a super-friendly manager. (☎494 35 35. June 15-Dec. 15 dorms 26SFr, doubles 33SFr; Dec. 16-June 14 30SFr, 35SFr.) To reach Leysin, take the **cog rail** from **Aigle** (30min., every hr., 8-10SFr), accessible by **train** from Montreux (10min., 2 per hr.) and Lausanne (30min., 2 per hr.). **☎024.**

Tiny **Gryon** has experienced a relative population explosion in recent years (now pop. 1000), but this doesn't seem to have marred its untouched, tranquil setting. Its main draw is the **Swiss Alp Retreat,** housed in the **Chalet Martin,** a pocket of Australian and Swiss enthusiasm high in the Alps. To reach the hostel from the Gryon stop, take a right, head uphill, and follow the signs. The English-speaking staff maintains a cooperative-style establishment where bohemian backpackers taking a "vacation from their vacation" have been known to stay... and stay. The hostel rents skis and videos, and has daily sign-ups for **cheese farm tours, paragliding, thermal baths,** and other daily excursions. (Internet. Reception 9am-9pm. 25SFr 1st night, 40SFr for 2-night stay, 100SFr per week; 3SFr more in winter.) To reach Gryon, take the **cog rail** from **Bex** (30min., every hr., 5.60SFr, Swisspass and Eurail valid), one stop down from Aigle on the rail line.

NEUCHÂTEL ☎032

Neuchâtel's glorious, butter-colored edifices look like they could melt into the turquoise waters of its eponymous lake; the city's mouth-watering bakeries and cafes please visitors just as much. The city's sights cluster in a walkable but steep area. From pl. des Halles, next to pl. Pury, take r. du Château to the **Collégiale** church and the chateau for which the city is named. (Church open Oct.-Mar. 9am-6:30pm, Apr.-Sept. 9am-8pm. Free concerts last F of each month. Chateau tours Apr.-Sept. M-F every hr. 10am-noon and 2-4pm, Sa 10-11am and 2-4pm, Su 2-4pm.) Downhill from the chateau on r. Jehanne-de-Hochberg, climb the **Tour des Prisons** (Prison Tower) for a 360° view of the city. (Open Apr.-Sept. 8am-6pm. 1SFr.) Neuchâtel has a number of museums; among them is the **Musée d'Art et d'Histoire,** Esplanade Léopold-Robert 1, in a magnificent building on the waterfront. The museum covers the city's history and a range of art; most explanations are not offered in English. (Open Tu-Su 10am-5pm. 7SFr, students 4SFr, under 17 and Th free.)

Trains run frequently to: Bern (45min., 17.20SFr); Geneva (1½hr., 42SFr); Basel (1¾hr., 37-52SFr); and Interlaken (2hr., 42SFr). From the station, take bus #6 to pl. Pury and the center of town. From pl. Pury, face the lake and walk to the left to reach the **tourist office,** Hôtel des Postes. (☎889 68 90; www.ne.ch/tourism. Open mid-June to mid-Sept. M-F 9am-6:30pm, Sa 9am-5pm, Su 2-5pm; late Sept. to early June M-F 9am-noon and 1:30-5:30pm, Sa 9am-noon.) The quirky **Oasis Neuchâtel,** r. du Suchiez 35, overlooks the lake. From pl. Pury, take bus #1 (dir. Cormondrèche) to "Vauseyon"; walk back toward town, then take the stairs marked "Escaliers de Suchiez." The hostel is marked by yellow happy faces. (☎731 31 90. Breakfast included. Reception daily 8-10am and 5-9pm.) If it's full, ask for the *Hôtel Restaurant* guide. The laid-back **Crêperie Bach et Buck,** av. du Premier-Mars 22, sells crepes under 10SFr. (Served M-Th 11:30am-2pm and 5:30-10pm, F-Sa 11:30am-2pm and 5:30-11:30pm, Su 6-10pm.) Opposite the *crêperie* is the Casino de la Rotonde; the **Bar Au 21,** behind the casino, has a younger, more relaxed crowd. (Open M-Th 7am-1am, F 7am-2am, Sa 5pm-2am, Su 5pm-1am.) **Postal code:** CH-2001.

GERMAN SWITZERLAND

BASEL (BÂLE) ☎061

Perched on the Rhine a stone's throw from France and Germany, Switzerland's third-largest city (rhymes with "nozzle"; pop. 193,000) blends the two cultures into a distinct character of its own. Basel harbors a large medieval quarter and one of the oldest universities in Switzerland—graduates include Erasmus, Bernoulli, and Nietzsche—as well as an amazing assemblage of museums.

PRACTICAL INFO, ACCOMMODATIONS, AND FOOD. Basel has three **train stations:** the French SNCF and Swiss SBB stations (☎157 22 22; 1.19SFr per min.) are on Centralbahnpl., near the Altstadt. The German DB station (☎690 11 11) is across the Rhine down Greifeng. Trains chug to: Zurich (1hr., every 15-30min., 31SFr); Bern (1¼hr., every hr., 37SFr); Geneva (3hr., every hr., 72SFr); Paris (5-6hr.; 12 per day; 138SFr, under 26 25% off); and Munich via Zurich (5¼hr.; every hr.; 204SFr, under 26 25% off). To reach the **tourist office,** Schifflände 5, from the SBB station, take tram #1 to Schifflände; the office is on the river, near the Mittlere Rheinbrücke. (☎268 68 68; www.baseltourismus.ch. Open M-F 8:30am-6pm.) Find **Inter-**

net access at **Domino,** Steinenvorstadt 54. (10-12SFr per hr. Must be 18. Open M-Th 9am-midnight, F-Sa 9am-1am, Su 1pm-midnight.) Take tram #1 or 8 to Marktpl. and walk one block from the river to find the **post office.** (Open M-W and F 7:30am-6:30pm, Th 7:30am-8pm, Sa 8am-noon.)

Basel's biggest shortcoming is its lack of cheap lodgings; call ahead to ensure a spot in the only hostel in town. Walk from the SBB station down Aeschengraben to St. Alban Anlage, then follow the signs downhill from the tower to the **Jugendherberge (HI),** St. Alban-Kirchrain 10. (☎272 05 72. Breakfast included. Laundry. Reception 7-10am and 2pm-midnight. Check out 7-10am. Dorms 29-31SFr; singles 79SFr; doubles 49SFr. Jan.-Feb. 19 and Nov.-Dec. 2.50SFr less.) The **Hotel-Pension Steinenschanze,** Steinengraben 69, is a three-star hotel with phones and TVs in every room. From the SBB station, turn left on Centralbahnstr., follow the signs for Heuwaage, go up the ramp under the bridge, and turn left on Steinengraben. (☎272 53 53. Breakfast included. Students 3-night max. stay. Singles 110-180SFr, under 25 with ISIC 60SFr; doubles 160-250SFr, 100SFr.) For **Camp Waldhort,** Heideweg 16, in Reinach, take tram #11 to Landhof, backtrack 200m, cross the main street, and follow the signs. (☎711 64 29. Reception 7am-12:30pm and 2-10pm. Open Mar.-Oct. 7SFr per person, 10SFr per tent.) **Barfüsserpl., Marktpl.,** and the streets connecting them are full of restaurants. For **groceries,** migrate to **Migros** at Steinenvorstadt, Clarapl. 17 (both open M-W and F 8am-6:30pm, Th 8am-9pm, Sa 7:30am-5pm), or at Bahnhof SBB (open M-F 6am-10pm, Sa-Su 7:30am-10pm). **Postal codes:** CH-4000 to CH-4059.

SIGHTS AND ENTERTAINMENT. Most sights lie on the **Groß-Basel** (Greater Basel) side of the Rhine, on the same side as the train station, including the **Münster** (cathedral), on the site of an ancient Celtic settlement and a Roman fort. Visit the tombs of Erasmus and Bernoulli, or climb the tower for a view extending to the Black Forest. (Open Easter-Oct. 15 M-F 10am-5pm, Sa 10am-4pm, Su 1-5pm; Oct. 16-Easter M-Sa 11am-4pm, Su 2-4pm. Free; tower 3SFr.) From the *Münster*, walk away from the river up Münsterberg and turn right on Freiestr. to reach the Marktpl. and the blinding red, green, and gold **Rathaus** (town hall). Basel has an astounding 30 museums; the most interesting is the **Kunstmuseum** (Fine Arts Museum), St. Alban-Graben 16, which dates from 1661 and houses an outstanding collection of works by old and new masters, including Picasso, Klee, and Giacametti. (Tram #2 to "Kunstmuseum." Open Tu and Th-Su 10am-5pm, W 10am-7pm. 7SFr, students 5SFr; first Su of the month free.) Included with admission to the Kunstmuseum is the nearby **Museum für Gegenwartskunst** (Museum of Contemporary Art), St. Alban-Rheinweg 60, which houses important pieces by Calder, Johns, Warhol, Lichtenstein, and Pollock. (Open Tu-Su 11am-5pm.) Perhaps the true star of Basel's museum cast is the **Fondation Beyeler,** Baselstr. 107, in the suburb of Riehen. Take tram #6 (dir. Riehen Grenze) to "Riehen Dorf," then walk straight for five minutes. The museum is full of works of masters, and the sublime landscaping complements the art fabulously. (Open daily 10am-6pm, W 10am-8pm. 12SFr, students 9SFr.) Check out the **Museum Jean Tinguely** for the artist's fascinating fountains and other creations. (Tram #2 or 15 to Wettsteinpl., then bus #31 to "Museum Tinguely." Open W-Su 11am-7pm. 7SFr, students 5SFr.)

Head to **Barfüsserpl.** for evening bar-hopping. **Atlantis,** Klosterburg 10, is a multi-level, sophisticated bar that sways to reggae, jazz, and funk. (Concerts 10-23SFr. Open M-Th 11am-2am, F 11am-4am, Sa 5pm-4am.) **Brauerei Fischerstube,** Rheing. 45, is an old-school *Biergarten* adjacent to Basel's only brewery. (Beer 2.50-5.90SFr. Open M-Th 10am-midnight, F-Sa 10am-1am, Su 5pm-midnight.) In a year-round party town, Basel's carnival, or **Fasnacht,** distinguishes itself. The festivities commence the Monday before Lent with the *Morgenstraich*, a not-to-be-missed 4am parade over 600 years old, and end precisely 72 hours later (Mar. 5-7, 2001).

ZURICH (ZÜRICH) ☎01

Switzerland has a bank for every 1200 people, and about half of those are in Zurich, where battalions of executives charge daily to the world's premier gold exchange and fourth-largest stock exchange. But there's more to Zurich than money. Over the centuries, Ulrich Zwingli, James Joyce, and a group of raucous young artists calling themselves Dadaists bred a tradition of countercultural thinking in Zurich—a phenomenon that still runs through the veins of the Altstadt and the student quarter, steps away from the rabid capitalism of the Bahnhofstraße shopping district.

GETTING THERE AND GETTING AROUND

Flights: Kloten Airport (☎816 25 00), the main hub for **Swissair** (☎ (0848) 80 07 00). **Trains** go to the Hauptbahnhof (every 10-20min., 5.40SFr; Eurail and Swisspass valid).

Trains: Hauptbahnhof, on Bahnhofpl. To: **Basel** (1hr., 2-4 per hr., 31SFr); **Bern** (1¼hr., 1-2 per hr., 48SFr); **Geneva** (3hr., every hr., 77SFr); **Munich** (4hr., 4 per day, 91SFr); **Milan** (4½hr., every hr., 76SFr); **Salzburg** (6hr., 3 per day, 102SFr); **Venice** (7½hr., every hr., 99SFr); **Paris** (8hr., every hr., 137SFr); and **Vienna** (9hr., 5 per day, 131SFr).

Public Transportation: All public buses, trams, and trolleys run 5:30am-midnight. **Short rides** (fewer than 5 stops) 2.10SFr; **long rides** 3.60SFr. Buy a ticket before boarding and validate it in the machine or face a fine (from 50SFr). A **Tageskarte** is good for 1 day of unlimited public transport (7.20SFr). **Nightbuses** run F-Sa 1, 1:30, 2, and 3am.

Taxis: ☎444 44 44 or ☎222 22 22. 6SFr base fare and 3SFr per km.

Bike Rental: At the baggage counter *(Gepäckexpedition Fly-Gepäck)* in the station. 27SFr per day; add 7SFr if you leave it at another station. Open daily 6:45am-7:45pm.

Hitchhiking: *Let's Go* does not recommend hitchhiking. Hitchers to **Basel, Geneva, Paris,** or **Bonn** often take tram #4 to Werdhölzli or bus #33 to Pfingstweidstr.; to **Lucerne, Italy,** and **Austria,** they take tram #9 or 14 to Bahnhof Wiedikon and walk down Schimmelstr. to Silhölzli; to **Munich,** they take streetcar #14 or 7 to Milchbuck and walk to Schaffhauserstr. toward St. Gallen and St. Margarethen.

ORIENTATION AND PRACTICAL INFORMATION

The **Hauptbahnhof,** on the western bank of the **Limmat River,** sits at the top of Bahnhofstr., which overflows with bankers and well-coiffed shoppers by day. The university district on the hillside of the eastern bank pulses nightly with crowded bars and hip restaurants. Sprawling along the Limmat, the **Altstadt** is a giant pedestrian zone. The Altstadt's **Limmatquai,** which becomes Uto-Quai and Seefeldquai across the bridge from the Hauptbahnhof, is a favorite stroll.

Tourist Offices: Main office (☎214 40 00; fax 215 40 44; www.zurichtourism.ch; hotel reservation service ☎215 40 40), in the Hauptbahnhof. Open Apr.-Oct. M-F 8:30am-8:30pm, Sa-Su 8:30am-6:30pm; Nov.-Mar. M-F 8:30am-7pm, Sa-Su 8:30am-6:30pm.

Consulates: UK, Minervastr. 117 (☎383 65 60). Open M-F 9am-noon. **US,** Dufourstr. 101 (☎422 25 66). Open M-F 10am-1pm. **Australian, Canadian, Irish,** and **South African** citizens should contact embassies in Bern. **New Zealand**'s consulate is in Geneva.

Currency Exchange: At the Hauptbahnhof. Cash advances on V, MC, DC. Open daily 6:30am-10pm. **Credit Suisse,** Bahnhofstr. 53. 2.50SFr commission. Open M-F 9am-6pm, Th 9am-7pm, Sa 9am-4pm. **ATMs** are all over (most only take MC).

American Express: Uraniastr. 14, CH-8023 (☎228 77 77). Open M-F 8:30am-6pm.

Luggage Storage: At the Hauptbahnhof. Lockers 4-8SFr per day. Luggage storage 5SFr at the *Gepäck* counter. Open daily 6am-10:50pm.

Laundromat: Wäscherei, at the Haldenegg tram stop (tram #6 or 10). Wash and dry 10.20SFr per 5kg. Open M-Sa 7am-10pm, Su 10:30am-10pm.

Emergencies: Police: ☎117. **Fire:** ☎118. **Ambulance:** ☎144; English spoken.

Medical Assistance: ☎269 69 69.

24-Hour Pharmacy: Theaterstr. 14 (☎252 56 00), on Bellevuepl.

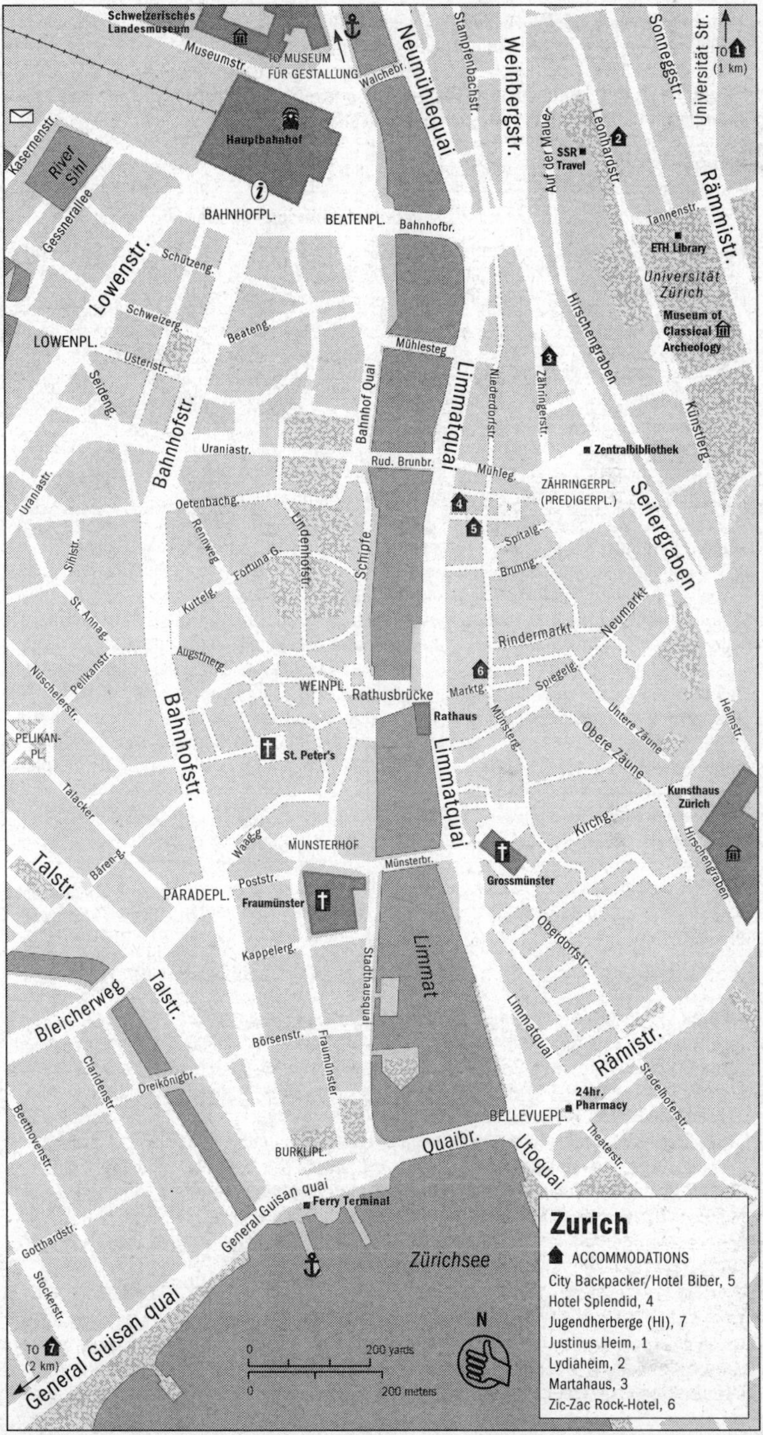

Zurich

ACCOMMODATIONS

- City Backpacker/Hotel Biber, 5
- Hotel Splendid, 4
- Jugendherberge (HI), 7
- Justinus Heim, 1
- Lydiaheim, 2
- Martahaus, 3
- Zic-Zac Rock-Hotel, 6

Schweizerisches Landesmuseum
Museumstr.
TO MUSEUM FÜR GESTALLUNG
Walchebr.
Neumühlequai
Stampfenbachstr.
Weinbergstr.
Sonneggstr.
Universität Str.
TO 1 (1 km)
Kasernenstr.
River Sihl
Hauptbahnhof
Auf der Mauer
SSR Travel
Leonhardstr.
Rämmistr.
Tannenstr.
ETH Library
Universität Zürich
Museum of Classical Archeology
Gessnerallee
BAHNHOFPL.
BEATENPL.
Bahnhofbr.
Schützeng.
Lowenstr.
Schweizerg.
Beateng.
LOWENPL.
Usteristr.
Mühlesteg
Limmatquai
Niederdorfstr.
Zähringerstr.
Hirschengraben
Seideng.
Bahnhofstr.
Bahnhof Quai
Künstlerg.
Uraniastr.
Zentralbibliothek
Rud. Brunbr.
Mühleg.
ZÄHRINGERPL. (PREDIGERPL.)
Oetenbachg.
Seilergraben
Rennweg
Lindenhofstr.
Schipfe
Spitalg.
Sihlstr.
Fortuna G.
Brunng.
Kuttelg.
St. Annag.
Rindermarkt
Neumarkt
Augstinerg.
Pelikanstr.
Nüschelerstr.
WEINPL.
Rathusbrücke
Marktg.
Spiegelg.
Rathaus
Münsterg.
Untere Zäune
Heimstr.
PELIKANPL.
St. Peter's
Obere Zäune
Kunsthaus Zürich
Talacker
Kirchg.
Waagg.
MÜNSTERHOF
Münsterbr.
Grossmünster
Talstr.
Bären-g.
Poststr.
PARADEPL.
Fraumünster
Oberdorfstr.
Kappelerg.
Stadthausquai
Limmat
Bleicherweg
Börsenstr.
Fraumünster
Claridenstr.
Dreikönigbr.
Rämistr.
Stadelhoferstr.
24hr. Pharmacy
BELLEVUEPL.
Beethovenstr.
BURKLIPL.
Quaibr.
Utoquai
Theaterstr.
General Guisan quai
Ferry Terminal
Gotthardstr.
Zürichsee
Stockerstr.
N
0 200 yards
0 200 meters
TO 7 (2 km)

SWITZERLAND

Internet Access: Telefon Corner, downstairs in the train station. 5SFr per hr. with 10SFr deposit. Open M-F 7am-10:30pm, Sa-Su 9am-9pm.

Post Office: Main Office, Sihlpost, Kasernestr. 97, behind the station. Open M-F 7:30am-8pm, Sa 8am-4pm. Address mail to be held: Sihlpost, *Postlagernde Briefe* für First name SURNAME, **CH-8021** Zürich, Switzerland. **Branches** throughout the city.

ACCOMMODATIONS AND CAMPING

Reserve at least a day in advance, especially during the summer.

Justinus Heim Zürich, Freudenbergstr. 146 (☎361 38 06). Take tram #9 or 10 to Seilbahn Rigiblick, then take the hillside tram (by the Migros) uphill to the end. Quiet rooms overlooking Zurich. Breakfast included. Reception 8am-noon and 5-9pm. Singles 35-60SFr; doubles 80-100SFr; triples 120-140SFr.

Martahaus, Zähringerstr. 36 (☎251 45 50). Turn left from the station, cross Bahnhofbrücke, and take the 2nd (sharp) right after Limmatquai at the Seilgraben sign. The most comfortable budget accommodations in the Altstadt. Breakfast included. Reception 24hr. Dorms 35SFr; singles 70SFr; doubles 98-108SFR; triples 120SFr.

Foyer Hottingen, Hottingenstr. 31 (☎256 19 19). Take tram #3 (dir. Kluspl.) to Hottingerpl. to reach this impeccably clean and newly renovated house with a multilingual staff. Breakfast included. Reception 6am-midnight. Dorms 30SFr; singles 65-95SFr; doubles 100-140SFr; triples 130SFr; quads 160SFr; quints 200SFr.

Jugendherberge Zürich (HI), Mutschellenstr. 114 (☎482 35 44). Take tram #7 (dir. Wollishofen) to Morgental and backtrack 5min. along Mutschellenstr. Breakfast included. Laundry. Dorms 31SFr; doubles 90SFr; nonmembers add 5SFr.

The City Backpacker-Hotel Biber, Niederdorfstr. 5 (☎251 90 15). Cross Bahnhofbrücke in front of the station and turn right on Niederdorfstr. A party-happy deck and a prime location for bar-hopping. Sheets 3SFr. Laundry 9SFr. Internet 10SFr per hr. Reception 8-11am and 3-10pm. Dorms 27-29SFr; singles 65SFr; doubles 88SFr.

Camping Seebucht, Seestr. 559 (☎482 16 12). Take tram #11 to Bürklipl., then catch bus #161 or 165 to Stadtgrenze. Market and cafe. Tents and caravans available. Showers 2SFr. Reception 7:30am-noon and 3-10pm. Open May to late Sept. 8SFr per person, 12SFr per tent; 1.50SFr tax.

FOOD

The cheapest meals in Zurich are at *Würstli* stands (sausage and bread 5SFr). The city prides itself on its *Geschnetzeltes mit Rösti*, slivered veal in cream sauce with hash-brown potatoes. For **groceries,** try the **Co-op Super Center,** next to the train station. (Open M-F 7am-8pm, Sa 7am-4pm.) The **Manor** department store, Bahnhofstr. 75, has a self-serve restaurant on the fifth floor. (Open M-F 9am-8pm, Sa 9am-4pm.)

Bodega Española, Münsterg. 15. Delicious Catalán delights. Egg and potato tortilla dishes 15.50SFr. Enormous salads 9.50SFr. Open daily 10am-12:30am.

Gran-Café, Limmatquai 66. Outdoor seating and some of the cheapest meals around. Daily *Menüs* (11.80SFr) are guaranteed in 7min. or they're free. Open M-F 6am-midnight, Sa-Su 7:30am-midnight.

Hiltl, Sihlstr. 28. Trade carrots with the swank vegetarian elite. Salad buffet 4.60SFr per 100g. Indian dinner buffet 4.60SFr per 100g. Open M-Sa 7am-11pm, Su 11am-11pm.

Raclette Stube, Zähringerstr. 16. Family-oriented restaurant serving high-quality Swiss fare. Fondue 23.50SFr per person. Open daily from 6pm.

SIGHTS

ALTSTADT. The stately causeway of capitalism known as **Bahnhofstraße** dominates Zurich's left bank and hosts Cartier, Rolex, Chanel, and Armani. Halfway down Bahnhofstr. lies **Paradeplatz,** the town center, under which Zurich's banks reputedly keep their gold reserves. Off Paradepl., the 13th-century Gothic **Fraumünster** stands tall. Marc Chagall designed its stunning stained-glass windows in the late 1960s, fusing the Old and New Testaments in the five panels. *(Open May-Sept. M-Sa 9am-noon and 2-6pm, Su 2-6pm; Oct. M-Sa 10am-noon and 2-5pm; Mar.-Apr. 10am-noon and 2-4pm.)* Next to the Fraumünster, **St. Peter's Church** has the largest clock face in Europe, with a second hand nearly 4m long. Across the Münsterbrücke, the **Grossmünster's** twin spires piece the skyline; here Ulrich Zwingli spearheaded the Reformation in German-speaking Switzerland (one of his Bibles lies in a protected case near the pulpit from which he preached). Head up to the top of one of the spires for a panoramic view. *(Church open daily Mar. 15-Oct. 9am-6pm, Nov.-Mar. 14 10am-4pm; free. Tower open Mar.-Oct. daily 1:30-5pm, Nov.-Feb. Sa-Su 1:30-4:30pm; 2SFr.)* Follow Münsterg. to **Spiegelgasse** for a slice of the city's history: Lenin lived at #14, while Dadaism got its start at #3 (now Castel DADA, a bar; see **Nightlife** p. 931).

MUSEUMS. The incredible **Kunsthaus Zürich** covers Western art from the 15th century to the present with an undeniable bias toward the 20th century. Local artists, including Giacometti and Hodler, mix with the international set. *(Heimpl. 1. Take tram #3, 5, 8, or 9 to Kunsthaus. Open Tu-Th 10am-9pm, F-Su 10am-5pm. 4SFr, students and disabled 3SFr; Su free.)* The **Museum Rietberg,** in two villas in Rieter Park, focus on non-European art. The Park-Villa Rieter holds Chinese, Japanese, and Indian drawings, while Villa Wesendonck focuses on sculpture. *(Gablerstr. 15. Tram #7 to Museum Rietberg. Rietberg open Tu-Sa 1-5pm, Su 10am-5pm; Wesendonck open Tu and Th-Su 10am-5pm, W 10am-8pm. 5SFr, students 3SFr.)* The **Museum of Classical Archaeology** astounds with replicas of nearly every great statue in the ancient world from 800 BC on, as well as Greco-Roman art on the first floor. *(Rämistr. 73. Take tram #6, 9, or 19 to ETH. Open Tu-F 1-6pm, Sa-Su 11am-5pm. Free.)* Near the train station, the **Museum für Gestaltung** (Design Museum) ruminates on the relationship of design to man. *(Ausstellungstr. 60. Take tram #4 or 13 to Museum für Gestaltung. Open Tu and Th-F 10am-6pm, W 10am-9pm, Sa-Su 11am-6pm. 10SFr, students 6SFr.)*

OTHER SIGHTS. The grave of **James Joyce** rests in the **Fluntern Cemetery,** accessible by tram #6, 9, or 10 to "Zoo." Nearby, the **Zurich Zoo** exhibits over 2000 animal species. *(Zürichbergstr. 221. Open Mar.-Oct. 8am-6pm; Nov.-Feb. 8am-5pm.)* Visitors who trek to the **Lindt and Sprüngli Chocolate Factory** are rewarded with a free souvenir box of chocolate. *(Seestr. 204. Take S1 or S8 or bus #165 to Kilchberg; turn right out of the station, turn left down the 1st street, take an immediate right, and continue for 3min. ☎ 716 22 33. Open W-F 10am-noon and 1-4pm. All exhibits in German. Free.)*

NIGHTLIFE

Niederdorfstr. rocks as the epicenter of Zurich's nightlife (although women may not want to walk alone in this area at night), while Münsterg. and Limmatquai are lined with cafes and bars. Pick up *ZüriTip* for hotspots. On summer Friday and Saturday nights, **Hirschenpl.** hosts sword-swallowers and other daredevil street performers. Locals and students crowd the terrace at **Double-U (W) Bar,** Niederdorfstr. 21, on the first floor of Hotel Schafli. (Open M-Th 2pm-late, F-Su 4pm-later.) The **Casa Bar,** Münsterg. 30, is a tiny, crowded pub with first-rate live jazz. (Open daily 7pm-2am.) **Castel DADA,** next to Casa Bar, is a lively bar and disco on the former site of the "Cabaret Voltaire." (Open Su-Th 6pm-2am, F-Sa 8pm-2am. Disco open until 4am.) Each August, the **Street Parade** draws international ravers for a giant techno party.

ST. GALLEN ☎071

Book lovers gasp at St. Gallen's astounding main attraction, the **Stiftsbibliotek** (Abbey Library), a Baroque library designated a World Heritage Treasure by UNESCO. Perfectly preserved golden spines, lavishly carved and polished exotic wood bookcases, and shiny parquet enhance its lending collection of 140,000 volumes and illuminated manuscripts. Umberto Eco was seen sniffing around here to get inspiration for *The Name of the Rose.* (Open Apr.-Oct. M-Sa 9am-noon and 1:30-5pm, Su 10am-noon and 1:30-4pm; Nov.-Mar. M-Sa 9am-noon and 1:30-4pm. 7SFr, students 5SFr.) The enormous windows of the Abbey's 8th-century **Kathedrale St.**

Gallen light up the gilded gate spanning the interior of the church. (Open daily 7am-6pm except during Mass.) The city's four museums are all on **Museumstraße,** on the other side of Marktpl. from the train station. The larger **History** and **Ethnology Museums** are at #50, while the small but well-curated **Art** and **Natural History Museums** reside at #32. (All open Tu-Sa 10am-noon and 2-5pm, Su 10am-5pm. Ticket for all four 10SFr, students 4SFr.) In late June, the **Open Air St. Gallen Music Festival** features over 20 live bands; past performers include the Beastie Boys, Garbage, and James Brown. (☎222 21 21; www.openairsg.ch. 3-day tickets 144SFr.)

Trains roll to: Zurich (1hr., 29SFr); Bern (2½hr., 65SFr); Munich (3hr., 4 per day, 63SFr, under 26 49SFr); and Geneva (4½hr., 95SFr). To get to the **tourist office,** Bahnhofpl. 1a, head through the bus stop and past the fountain on the left; it's on the right. (☎227 37 37. Tours June 12-Sept. M, W, and F 2pm; 15SFr. Open M-F 9am-noon and 1-6pm, Sa 9am-noon.) Get on the **Internet** at **Quanta,** Bohl 9, across from the Marktpl. bus stop. (3.50SFr per 15min., 10SFr per hr. Open M-Sa 10am-11pm, Su noon-11pm.) The **Jugendherberge St. Gallen (HI),** Jüchstr. 25, perches on a hill above town. Take the orange train (dir. Trogener) from the Appenzeller/Trogener station next to the main station to Schülerhaus; walk uphill, turn left across the train tracks, and head downhill. (☎245 47 77. Breakfast included. Reception daily 7-10am and 5-10:30pm. Check-out 10am. Closed Dec. 17-first week in Mar. Dorms 24-33SFr; singles 58SFr; doubles 66SFr; nonmembers add 5SFr.) **Hotel Elite,** Metzgerg. 9-11, is simple and central. (☎222 12 36. Breakfast included. Singles 60-70SFr; doubles 110SFr.) St. Gallen's cheapest sit-down meals are in the **Migros restaurant,** St. Leonhardstr. one block behind the train station. (Restaurant open M-W and F 6:30am-6:30pm, Th 6:30am-9pm, Sa 6:30am-5pm. **Supermarket** open M-W and F 8am-6:30pm, Th 8am-9pm, Sa 8am-5pm.) **Postal code:** CH-9000.

EXCURSION FROM ST. GALLEN: APPENZELL. St. Gallen is an ideal urban base from which to hike the pastoral hills of **Appenzell,** which offers great **hiking** without the temperature extremes of Zermatt or the Ticino region. Ask at the **tourist office,** Hauptg. 4 (☎788 96 41; www.myappenzellerland.ch), next to the *Rathaus*, for a detailed trail map and hiking suggestions. The office also makes hotel reservations, books cable car excursions, and arranges **cheesemaking** tours. The ever-present aroma of *Appenzeller* cheese lingers around **Gasthaus Hof,** on Landsgemeindepl. in the center of town, a family-run restaurant that provides guest rooms in a separate house. (☎787 22 10. Breakfast included. Check-in 11am-midnight. Restaurant open 8am-11pm. Dorms 28SFr; singles 65SFr-95SFr; doubles 130SFr.) Many hiking trails are dotted with *Gasthöfe* (guesthouses), splendid old farmhouses and restaurants for the road-weary. The rattling but prompt **Appenzellerbahn** chugs between Appenzell and **St. Gallen** (1hr., 2 per hr., 10SFr). ☎**071.**

LUCERNE (LUZERN) ☎041

Lucerne just may be the fondue pot at the end of the rainbow—the Swiss traveler's dream come true. The city is small but cosmopolitan, satisfying sophisticated culture lovers while providing a plethora of adventurous outdoor opportunities. Sunrise over the city's most acclaimed peak, **Mount Pilatus,** has hypnotized hikers and artists, including Twain, Wagner, and Goethe, for centuries.

PRACTICAL INFO, ACCOMMODATIONS, AND FOOD. Trains pull into the Bahnhofpl. (☎157 22 22) at least hourly from: Basel (1¼hr., 31SFr); Bern (1½hr., 32SFr); Geneva (3hr., 70SFr); Interlaken (2hr., 26SFr); Lausanne (2½hr., 58SFr); Lugano (2¾hr., 58SFr); Zurich (1hr., 22SFr); and Zurich airport (1¼hr., 26SFr). The train station is the cheapest place to rent a **bike** (26SFr per day). Local **VBL buses** depart in front of the station. (1 zone 1.70SFr, 2 zones 2.20SFr; Swiss Pass valid.) The **tourist office,** in the station, has a free reservation service. Ask about the **Visitor's Card,** which, in conjunction with a hotel or hostel stamp, gives discounts for museums, bars, car rental, and more. (☎227 17 17. Open May-Oct. M-F 8:30am-7:30pm, Sa-Su 9am-7:30pm; Nov.-May M-F 8:30am-6pm, Sa 9am-6pm, Su 9am-1pm.)

C+A Clothing, on Hertensteinstr. at the top of the Altstadt, satisfies your **Internet** cravings. (Free. Open M-W 9am-6:30pm, Th-F 9am-9pm, Sa 8:30am-4pm.) The main branch of the **post office** is near the station on the corner of Bahnhosfstr. and Bahnhorpl. (Open M-F 7:30am-6:30pm, Sa 8am-noon.) Address mail to be held: First name SURNAME, Postlagernde Briefe, Hauptpost; **CH-6000** Luzerne 1.

Inexpensive beds are limited in Lucerne, so call ahead. To reach **Backpackers,** Alpenquai 42, turn right from the station onto Inseliquai, which becomes Alpenquai. (☎360 04 20. Sheets 3SFr. Kitchen. Reception 7:30-10am and 4-11pm. 22-28SFr.) From the station, walk on Bahnhofstr. along the river at Speurbrucke, and turn left onto St. Karliquai to get to **Tourist Hotel Luzerne,** St. Karliquai 12, which offers cheap, clean rooms near the Alstadt. (☎410 24 74. Breakfast included. Internet. Laundry 10SFr. Dorms 30-33SFr; doubles 108SFr, students 98SFr; quads 172SFr, 156SFr; in winter rooms 10-15SFr less per person.) Take bus #18 to "Jugendherberge" for the **Jugendherberge (HI),** Sedelstr. 12. After 7:30pm, take bus #19 to "Rosenberg," continue in the direction of the bus, and bear right at the fork. (☎420 88 00. Breakfast included. Laundry 12SFr. Reception Apr.-Oct. 7-10am and 2pm-midnight; Nov.-Mar. 7-9:30am and 4pm-midnight. Dorms May-Oct. 31SFr, Nov.-Apr. 28SFr; doubles 38-44SFr.) Take bus #2 (dir. Würzenbach) to "Verkehrshaus" to reach **Camping Lido,** Lidostr. 8, on the beach. (☎370 21 46. Showers 0.50SFr per 3min. Reception 8am-6pm. Open Mar. 15-Oct. 6.50SFr per person, 3SFr per tent, 5SFr per car.) Pick up **groceries** at **Migros,** in the station. (Open M-W and Sa 6:30am-8pm, Th-F 6:30am-9pm, Su 8am-8pm.) The location at Hertensteinstr. 44 also has a **restaurant.** (Grocery and restaurant open M-W 8:30am-6:30pm, Th-F 8:30am-9pm, Sa 8am-4pm.)

SIGHTS AND ENTERTAINMENT. The Altstadt, across Spreuerbrücke from the station, is famous for its frescoed houses, especially those on Hirschenpl. For a taste of the middle ages, traipse along the 660-year-old **Kapellbrücke,** a wooden-roofed bridge running from left of the train station to the Altstadt and ornately decorated with Swiss historical scenes. Farther down the river from the Kapellbrücke lies the quieter, more interesting **Spreuerbrücke,** decorated by Kaspar Meglinger's eerie *Totentanz* (Dance of Death) paintings. For a magnificent view of Lucerne, climb the ramparts of the medieval city *(Musegg Mauern)*. Take the trail on the far side of the wall to reach stairs up to the path along the wall; several towers have stairs to the top. East of the wall, join the hordes to view the city mascot, the dying **Lion of Lucerne,** carved into a cliff on Denkmalstr. Mark Twain called the monument, honoring the Swiss Guard who died defending Marie Antoinette in Revolutionary Paris, "the most mournful and moving piece of stone in the world."

The **Picasso Museum,** Furreng. 21, in Am Rhyn Haus, is one of Lucerne's best offerings, graced by 200 photographs of the artist and his family taken by close friend David Duncan. Head down Rathausquai from Schwanenpl. and bear right on Furreng. (Open daily Apr.-Oct. 10am-6pm; Nov.-Mar. 11am-1pm and 2-4pm. 6SFr, students 3SFr.) Walk 15 minutes along the lake to reach the **Verkehrshaus der Schweiz** (Transport Museum), Lidostr. 5, which features a planetarium, IMAX shows, and a virtual reality exhibit. (Open daily Apr.-Oct. 9am-6pm; Nov.-Mar. 10am-5pm. 18SFr, students 16SFr. IMAX 14SFr. 33% discount with Eurail.) The **Richard Wagner Museum,** Wagnerweg 27, in the composer's former lakeside home, displays his letters, scores, and instruments. Turn right from the station and walk 25 minutes along the lake. (Open Mar. 15-Nov. 30 Tu-Su 10am-noon and 2-5pm. 5SFr, students 4SFr.) After 7pm, the action moves from the Altstadt to Haldenstr. and the streets near the station. **Hexenkessel,** Haldenstr. 21, going for that mock-pagan look, is a two-story cauldron of loud music and spinning DJs. (Obligatory beer 7SFr. Open daily 9pm-2:30am.) **Open Air Kino Luzerne** shows nightly movies from mid-July to mid-Aug. at the outdoor theater in the **Seepark** near Backpackers Luzern (14SFr); check at the tourist office for listings. Lucerne attracts big names for its **Blue Balls Festival** (July 21-29, 2001) and fall **Blues Festival** (Nov. 8-11, 2001).

EXCURSIONS FROM LUCERNE: MT. PILATUS AND RIGI KULM. From **Mt. Pilatus** (2132m), the view of the Alps is phenomenal. For a memorable trip, catch a boat from Lucerne to Alpnachstad (90min.), ascend by the **world's steepest cogwheel train** (48° gradient), descend by cable car to Krienz, and take the bus back to Lucerne (entire trip 77.60SFr; with Eurail or Swisspass 41SFr). Lower the price and up the exercise by taking a train or boat to Hegiswil and hiking to Fräkmüntegg (3hr.), a halfway point on the cable car (22SFr; 25% off with Eurail or Swisspass).

Across the sea from Pilatus soars the **Rigi Kulm,** which has a view of the lake and its magnificent neighbor. Sunrise on the summit is a must-see for any Lucerne visitor. **Ferries** run from Lucerne to Vitznau, where you can catch a cogwheel train to the summit. You can also conquer Rigi on foot; it's five hours from Vitznau to the top, and anyone who tires can pick the train up at Rigi Kaltbad (3hr. up the hill) to drag them the rest of the way. For sunrise viewing, stay at **Massenlager Rigi Kulm,** on the summit. (☎855 03 03. Reception 8am-10pm. 25SFr.) Take the train back, take the cable car from Rigi Kaltbad to Weggis, and return to Lucerne by boat (round-trip 86SFr; with Eurail or Swisspass 42SFr). ☎**041.**

BERN ☎031

Although Bern has been Switzerland's capital since 1848, don't expect a slick political machine—Bern prefers to focus on the lighter things in life. Indeed, you'll probably see more suitors than suits in Bern: the city is known for chocolate-maker Toblerone, flowers, bears, and a decidedly romantic design.

PRACTICAL INFO, ACCOMMODATIONS, AND FOOD. Trains (☎157 22 22; or ☎0900 300 300, 24hr., 1.19SFr per min.) run to Bahnhofpl. from Interlaken (50min., every hr., 25SFr); Zurich (1¼hr., 2 per hr., 48SFr); Basel (1¼hr., 2 per hr., 37SFr); Lucerne (1½hr., every hr., 32SFr); Geneva (2hr., 2 per hr., 50SFr); Milan (3½hr., 13 per day, 73SFr); Paris (4½hr., 4 per day, 109SFr); Munich (5½hr., 4 per day, 123SFr); Berlin (8hr., 3 per day, 254SFr); and Vienna (10½hr., 4 per day, 162SFr.) Those under 26 get 25% off international fares. **Bern Tourismus,** on the street level of the station, makes free reservations. (☎328 12 12. Open June-Sept. daily 9am-8:30pm; Oct.-May M-Sa 9am-6:30pm, Su 10am-5pm. Tours daily in summer; 6-23SFr.) There is an excellent **branch** at the bear pits. (Open June-Sept. daily 9am-5pm; Oct. and Mar.-May daily 10am-4pm; Nov.-Feb. F-Su 10am-4pm.) Check **email** at the **Soundwerk Café,** Wasserwerkg. 5, on the river near the bottom of Nydeggbr. (Free. Open M-F 11am-7pm, Sa 11am-4pm.)

To get from the station to the **Jugendherberge (HI),** Weiherg. 4, cross the tram lines, go down Christoffelg., take the road through the gates left of the Park Café, and follow the signs down to Weiherg. (☎311 63 16; fax 312 52 40. Breakfast 6SFr. Laundry 6SFr. 3-night max. stay. Reception June-Sept. 7-9:30am and 3pm-midnight; Oct.-May 7-9:30am and 5pm-midnight. Check-out 10am. Reserve by fax. Closed two weeks in Jan. Dorms 28SFr; overflow mattresses on the floor 14SFr; tax 1.25SFr; nonmembers add 5SFr.) **Pension Marthahaus,** Wyttenbachstr. 22a, is in a quiet suburb. From the station, turn left on Bollwerk, cross Lorrainebr., bear right onto Victoriastr., and take the first left on Wyttenbachstr. Or, take bus #20 (dir. Wyler) to "Gewerbeschule," then the first right. (☎332 41 35; email martahaus@bluewin.ch. Breakfast included. Laundry 8SFr. Reception 7:30am-9pm. Reserve ahead. Singles 60-90SFr; doubles 95-120SFr; triples 120-150SFr. 5-10SFr less in winter.) To reach the **Landhaus Hotel,** Altenbergstr. 4/6, take bus #12 (dir. Schlosshalde) to "Bärengraben" and walk down to the Aare on the left. (☎331 41 66; email landhaus@spectravels.ch. Breakfast included with doubles, with dorms 7SFr. Kitchen. Laundry 4-6SFr. Internet. Dorms 30SFr; doubles 110-140SFr.) To get to **Camping Eichholz,** Strandweg 49, take tram #9 to "Wabern," backtrack 50m, and take the first right. (☎961 26 02. Showers 1SFr. Laundry 5SFr. Open May-Sept. Reserve ahead. 6.90SFr per person, students 5.50SFr; tents 5-8.50SFr; rooms 15-22SFr.)

Manora, Bubenbergpl. 5a, has tasty salads, fruit, and entrees. (Open M-Sa 6:30am-11pm, Su 8:30am-11:15pm.) Popular with quirky types, the bustling **Café des Pyrénées,**

Kornhauspl. 17, offers inventive sandwiches. (Open M-F 9am-12:30am, Sa 8am-5pm.) Produce **markets** sprawl daily over Bärenpl. (May-Oct. 8am-6pm) and Tu and Sa over Bundespl. (year-round). **Migros,** on Marktg., has **groceries** and a restaurant. (Open M-W and F 8am-6:30pm, Th 8am-9pm, Sa 7am-4pm.) **Postal code:** CH-3000.

SIGHTS AND ENTERTAINMENT. Dominating the Aare is the **Bundeshaus** (Parliament), which should be the starting point for a city tour. (When Parliament is not in session, 45min. tours every hr. M-Sa 9-11am and 2-4pm, Su 10-11am and 2-3pm.) Take Kockerg. or Herreng. to the 15th-century **Münster** (cathedral); for a prime view, climb the 100m tower. (Open Easter-Oct. Tu-Sa 10am-5pm, Su 11:30am-5pm; Nov.-Easter Tu-F 10am-noon and 2-4pm, Sa 10am-noon and 2-5pm, Su 11am-2pm. Tower closes 30min. earlier. 3SFr.) From Münsterpl., take Münsterg. to Hotelg., take a right, then a left on Kramg. to the 13th-century **Zytglogge** (clock tower). More entertaining than the figures who come to life four minutes before every hour are the gasping crowds of tourists. (Interior tours daily June-Sept. 11:30am and 6:30pm, May and Oct. 4:30pm.) Follow Kramg., which becomes Gerechtigkeitsg., and cross the Nydeggbrücke to reach the **Bärengraben** (bear pits). Though the bear is a historical symbol in Bern, the creatures today exist mainly to be photographed. (Open daily June-Sept. 8am-6pm, Oct.-May 8am-dusk.)

The **Kunstmuseum** (Fine Arts Museum), Hodlerstr. 8-12, offers an array of world-class art, including the world's largest **Paul Klee** collection (2500 works). Take a left on Bollwerk from the station, walk toward Lorrainebr., then turn right on Hodlerstr. (Open Tu 10am-9pm, W-Su 10am-5pm. 7SFr, students and seniors 5SFr, under 16 free.) Cross the Aare at Kirchenfeldebr. to get to **Helvetiapl.,** where several more museums cluster. The most interesting is the **Bernisches Historisches Museum,** Helvetiapl. 5, filled with paintings and artifacts spanning hundreds of years. Much smaller is **Albert Einstein's House,** Kramg. 49 in the *Altstadt,* between the clock tower and the cathedral, the scientist's residence from 1903-1905. It was here that he conceived the theory of relativity; now it houses some of his papers. (Open Feb.-Nov. Tu-F 10am-5pm, Sa 10am-4pm. 3SFr, students and children 2SFr.)

Berner Altstadtsommer features free dance and music concerts in the squares of the Altstadt. July's **Gurten Festival** attracts big names like Bob Dylan and Björk (www.gurtenfestival.ch). From mid-July to mid-August, **OrangeCinema** screens recent films (including many American ones; www.orangecinema.ch). At night, the fashionable folk linger in the *Altstadt,* while a seedier scene gathers under the Lorrainebrücke, behind and to the left of the station down Bollwerk. The popular **Le Pery Bar,** Schmiedenpl. 3, off Kornhauspl., is a bar with dancing on the first floor. (Open M-W 5pm-1:30am, Th 5pm-2:30am, F-Sa 5pm-3:30am.) The **Klötzlikeller Weine Stube,** Gerechtigkeitsg. 62, is the city's oldest wine cellar. (3.40-5.20SFr per glass. Open Tu-Th 4pm-12:30am, F-Sa 4pm-1:30am.)

INTERLAKEN ☎033

Located between the crystal-blue Thunersee and Brienzersee lakes at the base of the largest mountains in Switzerland, Interlaken has earned its place as one of Switzerland's prime tourist attractions. Nearby adventure playgrounds and the natural beauty of its surroundings make the town a favorite backpacker haunt.

PRACTICAL INFORMATION, ACCOMMODATIONS, AND FOOD. The **Westbahnhof** (☎826 47 50) borders the Thunersee in the town center; the **Ostbahnhof** (☎828 73 19) is on the Brienzersee, 10 minutes from the center. **Trains** arrive at both from Bern (25SFr); Lucerne (27SFr); Zurich (62SFr); Geneva (65SFr); and Lugano (72SFr). Trains to the **mountains** leave Ostbahnhof (June-Sept. every 30min.; Sept.-May every hr.) to Grindelwald (9.40SFr) and Lauterbrunnen (6.20SFr). To get from the Westbahnhof to the **tourist office,** Höheweg 37, in the Hotel Metropole, turn left on Bahnhofpl. and right on Bahnhofstr., which becomes Höheweg. (☎822 21 21. Open July-Aug. M-F 8am-6pm, Sa 9am-noon; Sept.-June M-F 8am-noon and 2-6pm, Sa 9am-noon.) Rent **bikes** at either station (21SFr per half day).

Don't let hustlers at the station pressure you into letting them take you to an accommodation. The **Backpackers Villa Sonnenhof,** Alpenstr. 16, diagonally across Höhenmatte from the tourist office, offers spacious, airy rooms with priceless mountain views. (☎826 71 71; fax 826 71 72; email backpackers@villa.ch. Breakfast included. Kitchen. Internet. Bike rental. Reception 7:45-11am and 4-9pm. Reserve ahead. Dorms 29-33SFr; doubles 74SFr. Add 3SFr for Jungfrau view, balcony, and bathroom. V, MC, AmEx.) Reminiscent of an American college fraternity house, **Balmer's Herberge,** Hauptstr. 23-25, is in the nearby village of Matten. Head left from Westbahnhof, bear right onto Bahnhofstr., turn right on Centralstr., and follow the signs. Reservations are not accepted; sign in and return at 5pm, when beds are assigned. (☎822 19 61; fax 823 32 61. Small breakfast included. Showers 1SFr per 5min. Kitchen. Laundry. Bike rental. Reception in summer 6:30am-11pm; off season 6:30-9am and 4:30-11pm. Internet. 2- to 8-bed dorms 19-28SFr; doubles 56SFr. Overflow mattresses 13SFr.) **The Funny Farm,** down Hauptstr. past Balmer's, is more like a commune than a youth hostel, offering volleyball, a pool, and an outdoor bar. (☎ (079) 652 61 27. Breakfast included. Internet. 25SFr.) **Hotel Alpina,** Hauptstr. 44, has spacious rooms equipped with sinks, TVs, towels, and fluffy, warm comforters. Reserve ahead by email. (☎822 80 31; email alpina_interlaken@bluewin.ch. Reception 7am-midnight. No curfew. Closed in Nov. Singles and doubles 42SFr.) **Camping Sackgut** is just across the river from the Ostbahnhof. (☎ (079) 656 89 58. Open May-Oct. Reception 9-11am and 4-7pm. 14.10-22.10SFr per person with tent.)

Many hostels serve cheap food, but you can eat for even less at **Migros market,** across from Westbahnhof, or at their restaurant upstairs. (Open M-Th 8am-6:30pm, F 8am-9pm, Sa 7:30am-4pm.) Revelers head to **Buddy's,** Höheweg 33, a small, crowded English pub. (Open Su-Th 10am-1am, F-Sa 10am-1:30am.) Drunken herds then migrate to Interlaken's oldest disco, **Johnny's Dancing Club,** Höheweg 92, downstairs in the Hotel Carlton. (Open Tu-Su 9:30pm-3am.) **Postal code:** CH-3800.

OUTDOORS AND HIKING. Interlaken's steep precipices, raging rivers, and open spaces are prime spots for such adrenaline-pumping activities as paragliding, whitewater rafting, bungee-jumping, and canyoning (putting on a wetsuit and harness and rappeling and swimming down a waterfall). Competition has driven prices down, and most companies charge similar rates. **Alpin Raft** (AR; ☎823 41 00), the original adventure company, has wild Australian guides. **Alpine Center** (AC; ☎823 55 23), the newest and smallest company, provides the most personal service. Both companies offer **paragliding** (AR/AC 140SFr); **canyoning** (AR 95SFr, AC 115SFr); **river rafting** (AR 95SFr, AC 90SFr); and **skydiving** (AR/AC 380SFr). Alpin Raft also offers **bungee-jumping** (155SFr) and **hang gliding** (155SFr). Horse and hiking tours, as well as rock-climbing lessons, are available upon request. On the Brienzersee, Alpin Raft's **sea kayaking** provides a challenging day in the sun and on the water.

Swiss Alpine Guides (☎822 60 00; fax 822 61 51) leads full-day ice-climbing clinics (May-Oct., 145SFr, warm clothing rental included), as well as full-day glacier treks (daily in summer; 120SFr). Interlaken's winter activities include skiing, snowboarding, ice canyoning, snow rafting, and glacier skiing. Contact the **tourist office,** Höheweg 37 (☎826 53 00), or any of the adventure companies for info. There are three **skiing** areas in the Jungfrau region. (Info ☎828 71 11; www.jungfraubahn.ch. Day passes 52SFr, 2-day 105SFr.)

Interlaken's adventure sports industry is thrilling and usually death-defying, but accidents do happen. Be aware that on July 27, 1999, 19 adventure-seeking tourists were killed by a sudden flash flood while canyoning on the Saxeten river.

The towns closer to the mountains offer more serious **hiking,** but Interlaken has a few good hikes of its own. The most worthwhile hike ascends to the **Harder Kulm.** The half-day hike reveals a striking mountainscape, including the Eiger, Mönch, and Jungfrau (only the last is visible from Interlaken). From the Ostbahnhof, head toward town and take the first road bridge across the river; follow the yellow signs and then the white-red-white *Bergweg* flashes on the rocks. From the top, signs lead back to the Westbahnhof. A **funicular** runs from the trailhead near the Ostbahnhof to the top. (May-Oct. 2hr. up, 1½hr. down. 12.80SFr, round-trip 20SFr; 25% off with Eurailpass or SwissPass.) More horizontal trails lead along the lakes.

JUNGFRAU REGION

The most famous and visited region of the Bernese Oberland, the Jungfrau area has attracted tourists for hundreds of years with glorious hiking trails and permanently snow-capped peaks. The three most famous mountains are **Jungfrau** (Maiden), **Eiger** (Ogre), and **Mönch** (Monk). Locals say that the monk protects the maiden by standing between her and the ogre, but at 4158m she could probably beat the puny Eiger (3970m) up. From Interlaken, the valley splits at the foot of the Jungfrau: the eastern valley contains Grindelwald, with easy access to two glaciers, while the western valley (the Lauterbrunnen) hosts many smaller towns including Wengen, Gimmelwald, Murren, and Lauterbrunnen. The two valleys are divided by an easily hikeable ridge. Pick up the *Lauterbrunnen/Jungfrau Region Wanderkarte* (15SFr at any tourist office) for an overview of the hikes.

GRINDELWALD. Beneath the Eiger's north face and within walking distance of the only glaciers accessible by foot in the Bernese Oberland, Grindelwald is a cold-weather paradise for hikers, climbers, and skiers. To reach the trail leading up the side of the **Obere Grindelwaldgletscher** (Upper Glacier), take the postal bus from Grindelwald (dir. Grosse Scheidegg) to "Oberslaubkule," walk uphill, and follow the "Glecksteinhütte" signs to the right. Access to the **Untere Grindelwaldgletscher** (Lower Glacier), a moderately steep hike, is closer to town: walk up the main street away from the station, follow signs downhill to "Pfingstegg," and follow signs up the valley to "Stieregg," a hut that offers food to the weary (4hr. round-trip). The **Männlichen** can be reached by the Männlichen Gondalbahn. From the station, a quick hike scales the Männlichen peak before continuing as a flat, one-hour hike to Kleine Scheidegg and its intimate views of the three peaks.

Jungfraubahn **trains** run from Interlaken's Ostbahnhof (9.40SFr). There is also a bus from Balmers (round-trip 15SFr). To reach the **tourist office,** in the Sport-Zentrum, turn right from the station. (☎854 12 12; fax 854 12 10. Open July-Aug. M-F 8am-7pm, Sa 8am-5pm, Su 9-11am and 3-5pm; Sept.-June M-F 8am-noon and 2-6pm, Sa 8am-noon and 2-5pm.) The **Jugendherberge (HI)** sits in a beautiful wooden chalet above town. Exit the train station, turn left, go straight (5-7min.), cut uphill to the right (8min.) just before "Chalet Alpenblume," and follow the steep trail all the way up the hill. (☎853 10 09; fax 853 50 29. Breakfast included. Bikes 15SFr per day. Dorms 26.30-29.80SFr; doubles 48.80-51.30SFr.) The bright blue **Mountain Hostel,** at the Grund station next to the river, is equally far, but worth it. Turn right out of the station, then right on the small trail toward "Grund"; go to the bottom of the valley, bearing right at the Glacier Hotel. (☎853 39 00; fax 853 47 30. Breakfast included. Dorms 32SFr; doubles 84SFr.) To **camp** at **Gletscherdorf,** turn right out of the station, take the first right after the tourist office, and then the third left. (☎853 14 29. 9.10SFr per person; 9SFr per tent.) Frugal gourmets shop at the **Co-op** across from the tourist office. (Open M-F 8am-6:30pm, Sa 8am-4pm.) A **Migros supermarket** lies farther down the main street, away from the station. (Open M-F 8am-noon and 1:30-6:30pm, Sa 8am-4pm.) **Postal code:** CH-3818. ☎ **036.**

LAUTERBRUNNEN. The "loud springs" that give the Lauterbrunnen Valley its name are 72 waterfalls that plummet down the walls of the narrow, glacier-cut valley. **Lauterbrunnen Town,** in the middle of the valley, is an ideal base for hiking and skiing. It also lies near the **Staubbach Falls** (280m). To reach the main trail, follow the right branch of the main road as it leaves town and eventually dwindles to a dirt trail. The first segment of the trail leads past the Staubbach, Spissbach, Agertenbach, and Mümenbach Falls (40min.). The greatest of them all, the **Trümmelbach Falls,** comprising 10 glacier-bed chutes that gush up to 20,000L of water per second. Explore tunnels, footbridges, and an underground elevator en route. (Elevator open daily July-Aug. 8am-6pm; Apr.-June and Sept.-Nov. 9am-5pm. 10SFr.) The trail continues on to **Stechelberg** (1½hr.), where **cable cars** leave for Gimmelwald (7.40SFr), Mürren (14.40SFr), Birg (34SFr), and Schilthorn (49.60SFr). The first two are free with the Swisspass, and Eurailers get 25% off all four.

Trains connect to Lauterbrunnen Town from Interlaken's Ostbahnhof (20min., 6am-11pm, 6.20SFr). The **tourist office** is 200m left of the station on the main street. (☎855 85 68; fax 855 85 69. Open M-F 8am-noon and 2-6pm; July-Aug. also Sa 9am-noon and 1-5pm.) The clean, comfortable **Valley Hostel** is left off the main street, down a driveway, and past the Co-op on the right. (☎855 20 08. Reception 8am-10pm. Dorms 20SFr; doubles 50SFr.) To reach **Hotel Staubbach** from the station, go left on the main street toward the waterfall (400m); the hotel is on the left. The rooms, most with private bath, have unobstructed views of the Staubbach Falls. (☎855 54 54. Breakfast included. Dorms 35-40SFr; singles 50SFr, with shower 60SFr; doubles 70-120SFr. 5SFr more per person in high season.) **Camping Jungfrau,** up the main street from the station toward the large waterfall, has cheap beds, kitchens, showers, lounges, and a store. (☎856 20 10; fax 856 20 20. Reception in summer 8am-9pm; off season 8am-noon and 2:30-6:30pm. 8-10SFr per person, 6-15SFr per tent. Dorms 20-22SFr.) Pick up **groceries** at the **Co-op,** near the post office on the main road. (Open M-F 8am-noon and 2-6:30pm, Sa 8am-noon and 1:30-4pm.) **Postal code:** CH-3822. ☎**033.**

ZERMATT AND THE MATTERHORN ☎027

A trick of the valley blocks out the great Alpine summits surrounding **Zermatt,** allowing the **Matterhorn** (4478m) to rise alone above the town. The Matterhorn is the Holy Grail for serious climbers—that is those with loads of money (around 800SFr), experience, equipment, and time to train in the area. Fortunately, miles of spectacular, well-marked paths are accessible to all visitors. No visit to Zermatt is complete without struggling up to the **Hörnlihütte,** the base camp for climbs up to the Matterhorn and a strenuous four- to five-hour hike past the tiny **Schwarzsee.** A **cable car** also runs to the Schwarzsee (20.50SFr, 33SFr round-trip). Zermatt is one of the world's best-equipped ski centers, with 245km of challenging **ski runs** in winter and more summer ski trails than any other Alpine resort. **Ski and boot rental** prices are fairly standard (50SFr per day). A one-day **ski pass** in any of the individual regions runs between 62SFr and 77SFr.

Cars and buses are illegal in Zermatt to preserve the Alpine air—the only way in is the hourly BVZ (Brig-Visp-Zermatt) **rail line.** Connect via Visp (from Lausanne; 35SFr) or Stalden-Saas (from Saas Fee; 1hr., 31SFr). The **tourist office,** on Bahnhofpl. in the station complex, sells hiking maps for 25SFr. (☎967 01 81; fax 967 01 85. Open mid-June to mid-Oct. M-F 8:30am-6pm, Sa 8:30am-7pm, Su 9:30am-noon and 4-7pm; mid-Oct. to mid-June M-Sa 8:30am-noon and 1:30-7pm.) The **Alpine Center,** on Bahnhofstr., to the right from the station past the post office, houses the **Bergführerbüro** (Guides Office; ☎966 24 60; fax 966 24 69) and **Skischulbüro** (Ski School Office; ☎967 24 66). **Hotel Bahnhof,** one minute from the station (turn left down Bahnhofstr. as you exit), offers hotel housing at hostel rates. (☎967 24 06; email Hotel_Bahnhof@hotmail.com. Laundry. Reception 8am-8pm. Open mid-Dec. to mid-Oct. Dorms 30SFr; singles 52-56SFr; doubles 82-88SFr.) The **Matterhorn Hostel** is a 12-minute walk from the station; turn right along Bahnhofstr., left at the church, and right after the river on Schluhmattstr. (☎968 19 19; email info@matterhornhostel.com. Laundry. Internet. Reception 7:30-11am and 4-10pm. Dorms 24-29SFr.) **Camping Matterhorn Zermatt,** on Bahnhofstr., is five minutes to the left of the station. (☎967 39 21. Reception May-Sept. 8:30-9:30am and 5:30-7pm. 8.50-9SFr.) **Café-Konditorei Hörnli,** also on Bahnhofstr., is a relaxed little place. (Breakfast 6-14SFr, salads 8.50SFr. Open daily mid-July to mid-Aug. 7:30am-10pm; mid-Aug. to mid-July 7:30am-7pm.) Pick up **groceries** at **Co-op Center** opposite the station. (Open M-Sa 8:30am-12:15pm and 1:45-6:30pm.) **Postal code:** CH-3920.

YODELING FOREVER Yodeling is usually part of the picture-book image of Switzerland, alongside holey cheese and numbered bank accounts. For the 100,000-plus people who gather every three years at the Federal Yodeling Festival, the traditional Alpine song with alternating high falsetto and low chest notes is more than just a cherished tradition; it is a matter of national pride at a time when neutral Switzerland feels increasingly isolated and unloved, its reputation tarnished by allegations of wartime collusion with the Nazis. "We Swiss have had to take a little bit of criticism in the last few years," Swiss Vice President Adolf Ogi said in 1999, "but no one has ever criticized us for our yodelers, alphorn blowers and flag swingers." Yodeling's often piercing tones carry long distances and can help lone mountaineers locate each other. In its basic form, "natural yodeling," it has no words and is based on a melody, revolving around six syllables. It has been suggested that yodeling may have started as an imitation of the haunting, echoing sound of the 13-ft. alphorn, another traditional means of communication in the high Alps. In 2002, the Yodeling Festival will head to the western city of Fribourg, straddling the language divide between French and German speakers, as wordless yodeling does, according to its enthusiasts. The tradition lives on even among Swiss who have moved away from their home, with participants from as far afield as Canada, New Zealand, and South Africa.

ITALIAN SWITZERLAND (TICINO)

Ever since Switzerland won the Italian-speaking canton of Ticino (*Tessin* in German and French) from Italy in 1512, the region has been renowned for its mix of Swiss efficiency and Italian *dolce vita*—no wonder the rest of Switzerland vacations here among jasmine-laced villas painted the bright colors of Italian *gelato*. Lush vegetation, emerald lakes, and shaded castles render Ticino's hilly countryside as romantic as its famed resorts, Locarno and Lugano.

LOCARNO ☎091

On the shores of Lake Maggiore, Locarno basks in warm, near-Mediterranean breezes and bright sun, with luxuriant palm trees replacing the rugged Alps. During its **international film festival** each August (www.pardo.ch), 150,000 people descend on one of the most important movie premiere events in the world. For centuries, visitors journeyed to Locarno solely to see the **Madonna del Sasso** (Madonna of the Rock) church, accessible by foot or **funicular** (next to the McDonald's by the station; 6SFr round-trip, 4.50SFr with SwissPass). The orange-yellow complex includes a densely ornate sanctuary and a museum next door. (Grounds open daily 7am-7pm. Museum open Apr.-Oct. M-F 2-5pm, Su 10am-noon and 2-5pm; 2.50SFr, students 1.50SFr.) Heed the call of Locarno's lake by renting a **paddle-** or **motorboat** along the shore or catching a **ferry** (1¼hr., 9 per day, 20SFr) to the botanical gardens on the nearby island of **Brissago.** (Gardens open 9am-6pm. 6SFr.)

Trains (☎743 65 64) run from P. Stazione to: Lugano (45min., 2 per hr., 16.40SFr); Milan (2½hr., several per day, 63SFr); Zurich (2¾hr., every hr., 60SFr); and Lucerne (3hr., 2 per hr., 56SFr). Change in Domodossola, Italy (1¾hr., 2 per hr., 41SFr) for: Geneva (5¾hr., 91SFr); Montreux (4¾hr., 74SFr); or Zermatt (4hr., 88SFr). From the station, walk diagonally to the right, cross V. della Stazione, continue through pedestrian V. alla Ramogna, and cross Largo Zorzi to the left to reach the **tourist office** on P. Grande, in the same building as the *Kursaal* (casino). (☎751 00 91; www.maggiore.com. Open mid-Mar. to mid-Oct. M-F 9am-6pm, Sa 10am-4pm, Su 10am-noon and 1-3pm; mid-Oct. to mid-Mar. M-F 9am-6pm.) The **Pensione Città Vecchia,** 13 Via Toretta, has the best prices and location in town. From P. Grande, turn right on Via Toretta (*not* vigola Toretta; look for a brown sign with the *alberghi* on it) and continue to the top. (☎751 45 54; email cittavecchia@datacomm.ch. Check-in 1-6pm; call ahead to arrive later. Open Mar.-Oct. Dorms 22-24SFr; singles 33-35SFr; doubles 64-76SFr.) From the station, turn left, follow V. alla Romogna to P. Grande, turn right on V. della Motta, bear left on V. B. Rusca past P.S. Francesco, take V. Varenna, and follow the signs to reach the **Palagiovani Youth Hostel (HI),** 18 V. Varenna. (☎756 15 00. Laundry 6SFr. Reception in summer 8-10am and 3-11:30pm; in winter 8-10am and 3-10:30pm. Dorms 31-38SFr; doubles 33-43SFr; off season 2.50SFr less.) Dining and revelry center on P. Grande and the lake, both excellent areas to seek out your favorite variety of *gelato*. On Largo Zorzi by the ferry dock, join a young crowd at **Ristorante Debarcadero.** (Pizza from 10.50SFr. Open 8:30am-midnight.) For **groceries,** try **Aperto,** at the station (open daily 6am-10pm) or **Migros,** on P. Grande (open M-Sa 9am-7pm). **Postal code:** CH-6600.

EXCURSION FROM LOCARNO: ASCONA. In addition to enjoying Ascona's tropical sunshine and sparkling water, history buffs can trace the steps of the 19th-century leftist thinkers and bohemian artists who tried to establish Utopia on the mountain above, known as **Monte Verità.** The **tourist office** (☎791 00 90; email buongiorno@maggiore.ch; www.maggiore.ch) is in the Casa Serodine, behind the **Chiesa SS Pietro e Paolo.** Reach Ascona by **bus** #31 from Locarno (15min., every 15min., 2.40SFr), or by **ferry** (1hr., 6 per day, day-pass 11SFr).

LUGANO ☎091

Lugano, Switzerland's third-largest banking center, lies in the crevassed bay between San Salvatore and Monte Brè. Warmed by a Mediterranean climate, Lugano's shady streets are lined with tiles, climbing vines, and blood-red wildflowers. The leafy frescoes of the 16th-century **Cattedrale San Lorenzo,** just below the train station, are still magnificently vivid. The national monument **Basilica Sacro Cuore,** on C. Elevezia, has frescoes featuring Swiss hikers alongside the disciples. The most spectacular fresco in town, however, is the gargantuan *Crucifixion* which adorns the **Chiesa Santa Maria degli Angiuli,** on the waterfront to the right of the tourist office. Armed with topographic **maps** and **trail guides** (sold at the tourist office, lent at the hostel), hikers can tackle **Monte Brè** (933m) or **Monte San Salvatore** (912m). The **ASBEST Adventure Company,** V. Basilea 28 (☎966 11 14), offers **snowshoeing, skiing** (full-day 90SFr), **paragliding** (165SFr), and **canyoning** (from 90SFr).

Trains (☎0900 30 03 00) run to: Locarno via Bellinzona (1hr., 2 per hr., 16.40SFr); Zurich (3½hr., every hr., 62SFr); Bern via Lucerne (5hr., every hr., 77SFr); and Milan (1½hr., every hr., 14SFr). From the station, cross the Centro footbridge, take V. Cattedrale onto V. Pessina, go left on V. dei Pesci, and left again on Riva via Vela for the **tourist office.** (☎913 32 32. Open Apr.-Oct. M-F 9am-6:30pm, Sa 9am-12:30pm and 1:30-5pm, Su 10am-2pm; Nov.-Mar. M-F 9am-12:30pm and 1:30-5pm.) To reach the luxury-villa-turned-independent-hostel **Hotel Montarina,** 1 V. Montarina, walk 200m to the right from the station and cross the tracks. (☎966 72 72; info@montarina.ch. Sheets 4SFr. Reception 8am-10pm. Open Mar.-Oct. Dorms 25SFr; singles 50-65SFr; doubles 100-120SFr.) To reach the posh **Ostello della Gioventù (HI)** 13 V. Cantonale, in Lugano-Savosa, exit left from the station, go down the second ramp, cross the street, go 100m uphill, catch bus #5 to Crocifisso (6th stop), then backtrack and turn left up V. Cantonale. (☎966 27 28. Breakfast 7SFr. Reception daily 7am-12:30pm and 3-10pm. Curfew 10pm. Open mid-Mar. to Oct. Dorms 23SFr; singles 35SFr; doubles 56-70SFr.) To **camp** at **La Palma** (☎605 25 61) or **Eurocampo** (☎605 21 14), two of the five sites in Agno, take the Ferrovia-Lugano-Ponte-Tresa (FLP) train to Agno (4.40SFr), turn left from the stop, and left on V. Molinazzo. (Open Apr.-Oct. 7-7.50SFr per person, 6-10SFr per tent.) **La Tinèra,** 2 V. dei Gorini, behind Credit Suisse in P. della Riforma, is a low-lit underground restaurant with great specials. (Open M-Sa 8:30am-3pm and 5:30-11pm.) Get **groceries** at **Migros supermarket,** 15 V. Pretoria, two blocks left of the post office. (Open M-F 8am-6:30pm, Sa 7:30am-5pm.) The **Pave Pub,** riva Albertolli 1, is a self-proclaimed beer museum, with 50 brands. (Open daily 11am-1am.) **Postal code:** CH-6900.

TURKEY (TÜRKİYE)

TURKISH LIRA

US$1 = 666,667TL	100,000TL = US$0.15
CDN$1 = 450,116TL	= CDN$0.22
UK£1 = 934,492TL	= UK£0.11
IR£1 = 727,790TL	= IR£0.14
AUS$1 = 372,800TL	= AUS$0.27
NZ$1 = 284,600TL	= NZ$0.35
SAR1 = 93,467TL	= SAR1.07

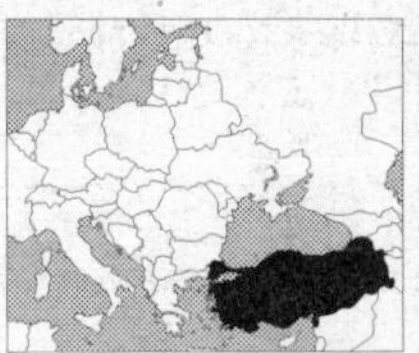

Country code: 90. **International dialing prefix:** 00. From outside Turkey, dial int'l dialing prefix (see inside back cover) + 90 + city code + local number.

Merely 77 years old, Turkey has inherited the combined riches of Ancient Greeks and Romans, the Byzantines, and the Ottomans. Asia Minor has seen more than 10,000 years of cultural traffic, and each civilization has left a layer of debris for the intrepid traveler to unearth. Pristine meadows, sun-soaked beaches, cliffside monasteries, medieval churches, archaeological treasures, and countless cups of *çay* (tea) await the explorer. Following the creation of the East Roman Empire, Constantinople (İstanbul) became the center of Greek Orthodox culture. The Selçuk Turks encroached upon the Byzantine Empire from the 11th to the 14th centuries, and the Ottomans conquered İstanbul in 1453. The Ottoman Empire lasted from the early 1400s to the end of WWI. Early 20th-century leader Mustafa Kemal (Atatürk), equating modernization with Westernization, abolished the Ottoman Caliphate, romanized the alphabet, and set up a democratic government. Recent history is dominated by the military, which occupied Northern Cyprus in 1974, organized three coups, and spearheaded conflicts with Kurdish rebels in the southeast. In December 1999, after a long struggle, partially due to a questionable human rights record, Turkey was nominated for EU membership. In May 2000, Ahmet Necdet Sezer, who has stated his intent to establish higher standards for democracy and rule of law, was elected Turkey's 10th president.

For true Turkish delight, consult the fun and informative *Let's Go: Turkey 2001*.

FACTS AND FIGURES

Official Name: Turkey.

Government: Republican Parliamentary Democracy.

Capital: Ankara.

Land Area: 770,760 sq. km.

Geography: Mostly mountains. Narrow coastal plain; high central plateau.

Climate: Temperate; hot, dry summers with mild, wet winters; harsher in interior.

Major Cities: İstanbul, Ankara, İzmir.

Population: 65,000,000.

Languages: Turkish (official), Kurdish, Arabic.

Religions: Sunni Muslim (98.8%), Shiite Muslim (1%), Christian and Jewish (0.2%).

Income Per Capita: US$2900.

Major Exports: Textiles 30%, foodstuffs 15%, iron and steel products 13%.

DISCOVER TURKEY

Bargain at bazaars and marvel at Ottoman palaces in **İstanbul** (p. 945). Swing northeast to **Edirne,** the former Ottoman capital and home to the finest mosque in all of Turkey (p. 956), before trekking down the sparkling **Aegean Coast.** From **Çanakkale,** make daytrips to the famed battlefield of **Gallipoli** and the ruins of **Troy,** former home of that babe whose face launched a thousand ships (p. 958). Head south to the beaches of **Kuşadası** (p. 960) and the unparalleled ruins of **Ephesus** (p.

961). Partake in after-hours hijinks in **Bodrum** (p. 962), where folks boogie down all night, every night in the "Bedroom of the Mediterranean," then head inland to **Aphrodisias,** near **Pamukkale,** to visit some of antiquity's best temples (p. 962). From there it's just a bit farther south to the **Mediterranean Coast** and the **Turkish Riviera,** where **Ölüdeniz,** near **Fethiye,** tempts with a secluded blue lagoon and the waterfalls of the **Butterfly Valley** (p. 964). Pass through **Kaş** to reach the eternal flame of **Olimpos** (p. 965). Then hit the central **Cappadocia** region, where **Göreme,** a surreal world of underground cities (p. 968), awaits.

ESSENTIALS

WHEN TO GO

Summer (especially July-Aug.) is high tourist season. Late spring and early fall temperatures are far milder and prices may be at least 10% lower, but some facilities and sights close in the off season. During Ramadan, the Islamic holy month, public eating, drinking, and smoking are generally taboo during daylight hours.

DOCUMENTS AND FORMALITIES

Canadians and New Zealanders can stay for up to three months without a visa; South Africans are permitted to stay visa-free for one month. Citizens of Australia, Ireland, the UK, and the US require visas; it is most convenient to get them upon arrival in Turkey. A three-month visa costs AUS$30 for Australians, UK£10 for British citizens, IR£13 for Irish citizens, and US$45 for US citizens.

EMBASSIES AND CONSULATES

Foreign embassies are all in **Ankara** (p. 966); consulates are in **İstanbul** (p. 946).

Turkish Embassies at Home: Australia, 60 Muggaway, Red Hill, Canberra ACT 2603 (☎ (02) 62 95 02 27; fax 62 39 65 92); **Canada,** 197 Wurtemburg St., Ottawa, ON K1N 8L9 (☎ (613) 789 40 44; fax 789 34 42); **Ireland,** 11 Clyde Rd., Ballsbridge, Dublin 4 (☎ (01) 668 52 40; fax 668 50 14); **New Zealand,** 15-17 Murphy St., Level 8, Wellington (☎ (4) 472 12 90; fax 472 12 77); **South Africa,** 1067 Church St., Hatfield, Pretoria 0181 (☎ (12) 342 60 53; fax 342 60 52); **UK,** 43 Belgrave Sq., London SWIX 8PA (☎ (020) 73 93 02 02; fax 73 93 00 66); **US,** 1714 Massachusetts Ave. NW, Washington, DC 20008 (☎ (202) 612 67 06; fax 612 67 44); consular section open M-F 10am-1pm; phones staffed 2:30-4:30pm.

GETTING AROUND

BY PLANE. Turkish Airlines (THY), Delta, and major European airlines fly into **İstanbul,** with some flights to **Ankara** and **Antalya.** THY (www.thy.com), with offices in **New York** (☎ (212) 339 96 50), **Sydney** (☎ (02) 92 99 84 00), and **London** (☎ (020) 77 66 93 00), connects over 30 Turkish cities. Domestic flights average US$80 one-way; student discounts are available.

BY TRAIN. Trains link Turkey to Athens and Bucharest, but some lines may be suspended due to political crises in the Balkans. Trains are cheap, but they follow circuitous routes painfully slowly. **Eurail** is not valid; **InterRail** passes are. With a Eurail pass, take the train to Alexandroupolis, Greece, and ride the bus from there.

BY BUS. Frequent, modern, and cheap, buses connect all Turkish cities and are the best way to get around. In large cities, bus companies run free shuttles called *servis* from their town offices to the *otogar* (bus station), which is often located quite a distance away. Buy tickets from local offices or purchase them directly at the station. Many lines grant students a 10% discount. **Fez Travel,** 15 Akbıyık Cad., Sultanahmet, İstanbul (☎ (212) 516 90 24; www.feztravel.com) offers a hop-on, hop-off "backpacker bus" loop (June-Oct. US$175, under 26 US$165).

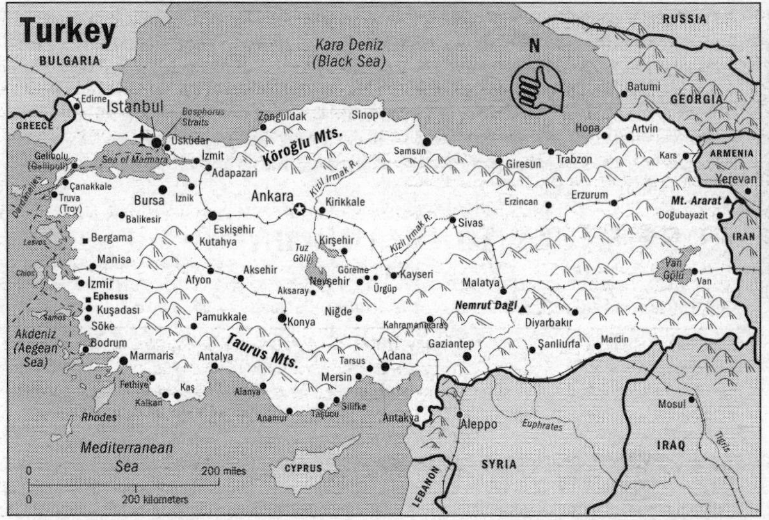

BY FERRY. Multiple ferry routes connect **Greece** and Turkey's **Aegean Coast:** boats run from **Lesvos** and **Hios** to **Çeşme; Samos** to **Kuşadası; Kos** to **Bodrum;** and **Rhodes** to **Bodrum.** Boats also arrive from **Italy:** ferries go from **Venice** to **İzmir** and **Antalya,** and from **Brindisi** to **Çeşme.** For more info on ferries connecting to and from the Aegean Coast, see p. 957. Boats also connect Greece to Turkey's **Mediterranean Coast,** for example, from **Rhodes** to **Marmaris;** see p. 964. Domestic **Turkish Maritime Lines** (TML) ferries sail from **İstanbul** to **İzmir** and to destinations on the Black Sea Coast. Most ferries are comfortable and well equipped. Fares jump sharply in July and August, but student discounts are often available. Reserve ahead, and check in at least two hours in advance. If you arrive in Turkey by boat, expect to pay a US$11 Turkish port tax. Most countries also charge a port tax for exit (US$17 in Greece).

BY DOLMUŞ AND BY CAR. Expensive shared taxis known as **dolmuş** (usually minibuses) let passengers off at any point along a fixed route; they leave whenever they fill up. The **speed limit** is 50kph. (31mph) in cities, 90kph. (55mph) on highways, and 130kph. (80mph) on *oto yolu* (toll roads). You must have an International Driving Permit (IDP) to drive; *Let's Go* does not encourage driving. If you get in an accident, file a report with the **traffic police** (☎118). Contact the **Turkish Touring and Automobile Association** (TTOK; ☎ (242) 282 81 40) for more info.

BY MOPED AND BY THUMB. Mopeds are an easy, cheap way to tour coastal areas and the countryside. Expect to pay US$20-35 per day; remember to bargain. Be sure to ask if the quoted price includes tax and insurance. *Let's Go* does not recommend **hitchhiking** in Turkey. Lone women should **never** hitchhike. However, those who choose to accept the risks of hitchhiking generally pay half what the trip would cost by bus. The hitching signal is a waving hand or the standard thumb.

TOURIST SERVICES AND MONEY

EMERGENCY. Ambulance: ☎112. **Police:** ☎155.

TOURIST OFFICES. Virtually every town has a **tourist office.** The website for Turkish tourism is www.turkey.org.

MONEY. Turkey's **currency,** the *lira* (TL), comes in denominations of 10,000,000; 5,000,000; 1,000,000; 500,000; 250,000; and 100,000TL. Coins are in values of 100,000; 50,000; 25,000; 10,000; and 5000 TL. Because the *lira* suffers from sky-high inflation, *Let's Go* quotes prices in US dollars. **Tip** taxi drivers, hotel porters, and waiters (leave it on the table) about US$1 for good service. 15-20% tips are required only in ritzy restaurants, where service may be included *(servis dahil)*. **Bargaining** is common at markets, bazaars, and carpet shops. Allow the seller to name a price, counter with a lower price (less than what you intend to pay, but not less than half the seller's price), and let the fun begin! A 10-20% **value-added tax** (*katma değer vergisi;* KDV) is included in the prices of most goods. Theoretically, it can be reclaimed upon departure.

ACCOMMODATIONS AND CAMPING

Clean, cheap accommodations are available nearly everywhere. Basic rooms cost US$6-10 for a single and US$14-20 for a double. **Pensions** *(pansiyon)*, by far the most common accommodations, are often private homes with rooms for travelers; don't expect toilet paper or towels. Most towns have a **hamam,** or bathhouse, where you can get a steam bath for US$4; they schedule different times for men and women. **Camping** is popular, and cheap campgrounds abound (around US$2 per person). Official government campsites are open from April or May to October.

HEALTH AND SAFETY

The most significant **health** concerns are parasites and other gastrointestinal ailments. Never drink unbottled or unpurified water, and be wary of food from street vendors. Eat fruits with thick peels that can be removed. Always carry toilet paper; expect to encounter pit toilets. Signs in pharmacy windows indicate night-duty pharmacies *(nöbetçi)*. If you're caught doing **drugs** in Turkey (or are caught in the company of someone who is), you're screwed. Stories of lengthy prison sentences and dealer-informers are true; embassies are utterly helpless in all cases. Exporting **antiques** is punishable by imprisonment. Foreign **women,** especially those traveling alone, attract significant attention. Catcalls and other forms of verbal harassment are common; physical harassment is rare. One way of deflecting unwanted attention is showing displeasure by making a scene; try the expressions "*ayıp!*" ("shame!") or "*haydi git*" ("go away"). Holler "eem-DAHT" ("help") if the situation gets out of hand. Touristed areas may be more comfortable for women. Dress modestly, especially farther east. **Travel to the southeast should be undertaken only after careful consideration of the risks involved.** Some provinces are effectively in a state of civil war and under martial law as Kurdish guerillas fight for separation.

FOOD AND DRINK

Staples like *çorban salatası* (shepherd's salad), *mercimek çorbası* (lentil soup), rice pilaf, and *yoğurt* are not listed on *lokanta* (restaurant) menus; their availability is understood. *Et* is the word for meat: lamb is *kuzu*, veal is *dana eti*. Chicken, usually called *tavuk*, becomes *piliç* when roasted. *Kebap*, the most famous Turkish meat dish, ranges from skewer *(şiş)* or spit *(döner)* broiling to oven roasting. *Köfte* are medallion-sized, spiced meatballs. Turks eat a lot of seafood; *kalamar* (squid), *midye* (mussels), and *balık* (fish). **Vegetarians** often enjoy *meze* (appetizers). *Dolma* are peppers, grape leaves, or eggplant stuffed with rice and served with or without meat. Turks drink **tea** *(çay)* hot, with sugar. **Coffee** (*kahve)* comes unsweetened *(sade)*, medium-sweet *(orta)* and sweet *(şekerli)*. Ice-cold *rakı*, an anise seed liquor, is the **national drink.** *Baklava*, a flaky pastry with nuts and soaked in honey, and Turkish Delight *(lokum)* are the most famous Turkish sweets.

COMMUNICATION

MAIL. PTTs (Post, Telegraph, and Telephone offices) are well marked by yellow signs. Some PTTs may charge a small sum for *Poste Restante.* **Airmail** from Turkey takes 1-2 weeks; mark cards and envelopes "uçak ile" and tell the vendor the letter's destination: *Avustralya*, *Kanada*, *Büyük Bretanya* (Great Britain), *İrlanda*, *Yeni Zelanda* (New Zealand), *Güney Afrika* (South Africa), or *Amerika*.

TELEPHONES. Make international calls at post offices. New phones accept **phone cards** *(telekart)*, available at the PTT, while old ones require tokens *(jeton)*. Card phones have English directions. For **directory assistance,** dial ☎118; for an **international operator,** dial ☎115. **International direct dial** numbers include: **AT&T,** ☎00 800 122 77; **Sprint,** ☎00 800 144 77; **MCI WorldPhone Direct,** ☎00 800 111 77; **Canada Direct,** ☎00 800 166 77; **BT Direct,** ☎00 800 44 11 77; **Ireland Direct,** ☎00 800 353 11 77; **Australia Direct,** ☎00 800 61 11 77; and **Telkom South Africa Direct,** ☎00 800 27 11 77.

LANGUAGE AND CUSTOMS. When a Turk raises his chin and clicks his tongue, he means *hayır* (no); this gesture is sometimes accompanied by a shutting of the eyes or the raising of eyebrows. *Evet* (yes) may be signalled by a sharp downward nod. It is considered rude to point your finger or the sole of your shoe toward someone. Although public displays of affection are considered inappropriate, Turks often greet one another with a kiss on both cheeks.

HOLIDAYS AND FESTIVALS

Holidays: New Year's Day (Jan. 1); National Sovereignty and Children's Day (Apr. 23); Ataturk Commemoration and Youth and Sports Day (May 1); Victory Day (Aug. 30); and Republic Day (Oct. 29). During **Ramadan** (Nov. 17-Dec. 15), pious Muslims abstain from eating, drinking, smoking, and sex between dawn and dusk; businesses may have shorter hours, and public eating is inappropriate. During the 3-day **Şeker Bayramı** (Sugar Holiday), which marks the end of Ramadan, bus and train tickets and hotel rooms may be scarce. **Kurban Bayramı** (Sacrifice Holiday), when animals are slaughtered and distributed to the poor, occurs a few months after Ramadan.

İSTANBUL

Straddling two continents and three millennia of history, İstanbul exists on an incomprehensible scale, set against a densely historic landscape of Ottoman mosques, Byzantine mosaics, and Roman masonry. The Bosphorus Straits have proven both the city's lifeline and its curse, providing a strategic location between two seas and two continents that has attracted countless sieges from covetous neighbors. Having withstood innumerable demographic shifts, wars, natural disasters, and foreign occupations, İstanbul naturally comprises a unique mix of civilizations, a composition evident not only in architecture and religious practices, but also in everyday customs. Conservative black-veiled women merge in the swelling crowds with younger women in Western dress, and major religious and historic sights double as the backdrops for love scenes in Turkish pop videos. Explore the İstanbul beyond carpet salesmen and backpacker bars, and venture out into neighborhood produce markets, back-alley tea shops, and Byzantine fortifications. **☎212 (European side) and ☎216 (Asian side)**

GETTING THERE AND GETTING AROUND

Flights: Atatürk Havaalanı, 30km from the city. The domestic and international terminals are connected by **bus** (every 20min. 6am-11pm). To reach **Sultanahmet,** take a Havaş **shuttle bus** from either terminal to Aksaray (every 30min., US$7), then walk 1 block south to Millet Cad. and take an Eminönü-bound **tram** to the Sultanahmet stop. Or take a **taxi** (US$4) to the Yeşilköy train station and take the commuter rail *(tren)* to the end of the line in Sirkeci. A direct taxi to Sultanahmet costs US$17-20. To reach **Taksim,** take the Havaş shuttle to the end of the line (45min., every 30min., US$7). To reach the airport, have a private service such as **Karasu** (☎638 66 01) or **Zorlu** (☎638 04 35) pick you up from your hostel (US$5.50) or take the Havaş shuttle from the McDonald's in Taksim (45min., every 30min., US$6.75).

Buses: Esenler Otobüs Terminal (☎658 00 36), in Esenler, 3km from central İstanbul. Serves intercity buses. To get there, take the tram to Yusufpaşa (1 stop past Aksaray; US$0.50), walk 1min. to the Aksaray Metro station on broad Adnan Menderes Bul., and take the Metro to the *otogar* (15min., US$0.40). Most companies have **courtesy buses** *(servis)* that run to the *otogar* from Eminönü, Taksim, and elsewhere in the city (free with bus ticket purchase). Various companies serve additional international destinations. The following have good reputations; be careful when choosing a company.

Ulusoy (☎658 30 00; fax 658 30 10). To: **Athens** (21hr.; Th and Sa 1 per day; US$60, students US$51); **Bodrum** (13hr.; 3per day; US$31, students US$27); and **İzmir** (9hr.; 4 per day; US$28, students US$24).

Varan (☎658 02 74). To **Ankara** (6hr.; 7 per day; US$25, students US$23) and **Bodrum** (14hr.; 2 per day; US$31, students US$28.50).

Kamil Koç (☎658 20 00). To **Ankara** (6hr.; every hr.; US$22, students US$20) and **Bursa** (4hr.; every 30min.; US$9, students US$8.25).

Pamukkale (☎/fax 658 22 22). To **Pamukkale** (10hr.; 7 per day; US$21, students US$19).

Parlak Tur (☎658 17 55). To **Prague** (2 days; departs Sa 4pm; US$100, students US$95).

Trains: In virtually every case, it's faster and cheaper to take intercity buses.

Haydarpaşa Garı (☎ (216) 336 04 75), on the Asian side. Sends trains to Anatolia. Take the ferry (every 20min., US$0.65) from Karaköy pier #7, halfway between Galata Bridge and the Karaköy tourist office. Rail tickets for Anatolia can be bought in advance at the **TCDD** office upstairs. To **Ankara** (6½-9hr., 6-7 per day, US$6-12).

Sirkeci Garı (☎ (212) 527 00 50), in Eminönü, downhill from Sultanahmet toward the Golden Horn. Connect to most European cities through Athens or Bucharest. Some lines may be suspended due to political crises in the Balkans. Call ahead for info and student fares. To: **Athens** (24hr., 1 per day, US$60); **Bucharest** (17hr., 1 per day, US$30); and **Budapest** (40hr., 1 per day, US$90).

Ferries: Turkish Maritime Lines (☎249 92 22), near Karaköy pier #7, just left of the **Haydarpaşa** ferry terminal. Look for the building with the blue awning marked *Denizcilik İşletmeleri*. Ferries leave for **Bandırma,** with train connections to **İzmir** (combination ticket US$10-25). Points on the Bosphorus are served by less frequent and more expensive day cruises. Local ferries run between Europe and Asia. Pick up a timetable (*feribot tarifesi;* US$0.60) at any pier. Fast **seabus** catamarans also run along the ferry routes. Address any questions to **Seabus Information** (☎ (216) 362 04 44).

Public Transportation: Buses serve most stops every 10min. 5am-10:30pm, less frequently 10:30pm-midnight. Signs on the front indicate destination; on the right side, major stops. **Dolmuş** run during daylight hours and early evening and are found near most major bus hubs, including Aksaray and Eminönü. In neighborhoods far from the bustle of Taksim and Sultanahmet they serve as local group taxis, and it is best to hail them down as they crawl along streets picking up passengers on their way back into the center of İstanbul. A **tramvay** (tram) runs from Eminönü to Zeytinburnu (US$0.50); follow the tracks back to Sultanahmet even if you don't actually take it. **AKBİL** is an **electronic ticket system** that works on municipal ferries, buses, trams, seabuses, and the subway (but not *dolmuş*). A deposit of US$5 will get you a plastic tab to which you can add money in 1,000,000TL increments and which will save you 15-50% on fares. Add credit at any white IETT public bus booth with the "AKBİL *satılır*" sign (at bigger bus and tram stops); press your tab into the reader, remove it, insert a 1,000,000TL note, and press again. **Regular tickets** are not interchangeable. Tickets for trams and buses without ticket sellers are available from little white booths, while ferries and seabuses take *jeton* (tokens), available at ferry stops.

Taxis: Little yellow speed-demons. Taxi drivers are even more reckless than other İstanbul drivers. Scams are widespread. Be alert when catching a cab in Sultanahmet or Taksim. One light on the meter means day rate while 2 mean night rate. Check change carefully. Rides within the city center shouldn't be more than US$5.

ORIENTATION AND PRACTICAL INFORMATION

The **Bosphorus Strait** (Boğaz) separates Asia from Europe. Turks call the western, European side of İstanbul **Avrupa** and the eastern, Asian side **Asya.** The **Golden Horn,** a river originating outside the city, splits Avrupa into northern and southern parts. Directions are usually specified by district (i.e. Kadıköy, Taksim, or Fatih). Most of the sights and tourist facilities are in **Sultanahmet,** south of the Golden Horn, toward the eastern end of the peninsula. The other half of "Europe" is focused on **Taksim Square,** the commercial and social center of the northern European bank. Two main arteries radiate from the square: **İstiklâl Caddesi,** the main downtown shopping street, and the hotel-lined **Cumhuriyet Caddesi.** The Asian side of İstanbul is primarily residential but offers rewarding wandering at a relaxed pace. Sultanahmet, Taksim, and Kadıköy (on the Asian side) are the districts that will be the most relevant for the majority of visitors to the city.

TOURIST, FINANCIAL, AND LOCAL SERVICES

Tourist Office: 3 Divan Yolu (☎/fax 518 87 54), in Sultanahmet, in the white metal kiosk, at the north end of the Hippodrome. Open daily 9am-5pm. **Branches** in the Sirkeci train station, in the Atatürk Airport, and the Karaköy Maritime Station.

Travel Agencies: Indigo Tourism and Travel Agency, 24 Akbıyık Cad. (☎517 72 66; fax 518 53 33), in the heart of the hotel cluster in Sultanahmet. Sells ISICs with valid student ID (US$15) and GO 25 cards (US$10). Also sells bus, plane, and ferry tickets, arranges airport shuttle service, and holds mail. Internet service upstairs (US$1.50 per hr.). Open in summer daily 8:30am-7:30pm; in winter M-Sa 9:30am-6pm.

Consulates: All open M-F. Area code ☎212. **Australia,** 58 Tepecik Yolu, Etiler (☎257 70 50; fax 257 70 54). **Canada,** 107/3 Büyükdere Cad., Bengün Han, Gayrettepe (☎272 51 74; fax 272 34 27). **Ireland** (honorary), 25/A Cumhuriyet Cad., Mobil Altı, Elmadağ (☎246 60 25). **New Zealand,** Level 24, 100-102 Maya Akar Center, Büyükdere Cad., Esentepe (☎275 28 89; fax 275 50 08). **South Africa,** Serbetci ış Merkezi, 106/15 Büyükdere Cad., Esentepe (☎288 04 28; fax 275 76 42). **UK,** 34 Meşrutiyet Cad., PK33, Beyoğlu/Tepebaşı (☎293 75 40; fax 245 49 89). **US,** 104-108 Meşrutiyet Cad., Tepebaşı (☎251 36 02; fax 251 32 18).

Currency Exchange: *Bureaux de change* open M-F 8:30am-noon and 1:30-5pm; most charge no commission. Banks exchange traveler's checks.

American Express: Türk Express, 47/1 Cumhuriyet Cad., 3rd fl. (☎235 95 00), uphill from Taksim Sq. Open M-F 9am-6pm. Their office in the **Hilton Hotel lobby** (☎230 15 15), Cumhuriyet Cad., helps when Türk Express is closed. Neither grants cash advances or accepts wired money. Open daily 8:30am-8:30pm.

Laundromats: Star Laundry, 18 Akbıyık Cad. (☎638 23 02), below Star Pension in Sultanahmet. Wash and dry US$1.50 per kg (2kg min.). Open daily 8am-8pm.

EMERGENCY AND COMMUNICATIONS

Emergency: ☎155. **Tourist Police:** at the beginning of Yerebatan Cad. in Sultanahmet (24hr. ☎527 45 03 or ☎528 53 69; fax 512 76 76).

Medical Assistance: American Hospital, Admiral Bristol Hastanesi, 20 Güzelbahçe Sok., Nişantaşı (☎231 40 50). The **German Hospital,** 119 Sıraselviler Cad., Taksim (☎251 71 00) is more conveniently located for Sultanahmet hostelers.

Internet Access: The **Antique Internet Café,** 51 Kutlungun Sok., offers a fast connection–despite its name. US$1.50 per hr. Open daily 24hr.

Post Office: The **PTT** (Post, Telegraph, and Telephone) office nearest Sultanahmet is the yellow booth opposite the entrance to Hagia Sophia. **Main branch,** 25 Büyük Postane Sok, in Sirkeci. Stamp and **currency exchange** services open 8:30am-midnight. Phones open 24hr. Address mail to be held: First name SURNAME, *Poste Restante,* Merkez 3 Postane, PTT, Sirkeci, 25 Büyük Postane Sok., **5270050** İstanbul.

ACCOMMODATIONS

Budget accommodations are mainly in **Sultanahmet,** a.k.a. Tourist Central, bounded by Hagia Sophia, the Blue Mosque, and Topkapı Palace. The sidestreets around **Sirkeci** train station and **Aksaray** offer tons of dirt-cheap hotels, but are not the most pleasant places to stay. Rates can rise by 20% in July and August.

İstanbul Hostel, 35 Kutlugün Sok. (☎516 93 80). From the path between the Hagia Sophia and the Blue Mosque, walk south down Tevfikhane Sok. to Kutlugün Sok; it's on the right. If you had to choose a hostel floor off of which to eat, this would be it. Internet. Happy Hour 6:30-9:30pm (beer US$2). Dorms US$7; doubles US$16.

Orient International Hostel, 13 Akbıyık Cad. (☎517 94 93; www.hostels.com/orienthostel), 2 blocks south of Hagia Sophia. Happy hour daily until 10pm, but music and drinks keep the party going. Free belly dancing M, W, F 10pm, and *nargile* (water pipe) use Th and Su 9pm. Internet. Dorms US$7; doubles US$17-$35; quads US$28.

Moonlight Pension, 87 Akbıyık Cad. (☎517 54 29; email moonlight@superonline.com). Clean rooms, a kind staff, and clear rooftop views away from the noisy backpacker scene. Laundry. Kitchen. Internet. Dorms US$5; doubles US$16; triples US$21.

Nayla Palace Pansion, 22 Kutlugün Sok. (☎516 35 67). A homey atmosphere, quiet garden courtyard, and rooftop lounge make a good backpacker hideaway. Breakfast included. Internet. Dorms US$5; singles US$15; doubles US$25-30; triples US$35.

Side Pension/Hotel Side, 20 Utangaç Sok. (☎517 65 90; www.sidehotel.com), near the entrance of the Four Seasons Hotel. This hotel/pension combination occupies the 2 handsome wooden buildings by the corner of Tevfikhane Sok. and Utangaç Sok. Breakfast included on rooftop terrace. *Pension* singles US$20; doubles US$25; triples US$35. Add US$10 for bath. Hotel singles US$40; doubles US$50; triples US$60.

Alp Guesthouse, Akbıyık Cad., 4 Adliye Sok. (☎517 95 70). Head down Tevfikhane Sok., turn left after the Four Seasons, and take the 1st right. Family-run guesthouse with Mediterranean ambiance. Spacious, spotless rooms. Beautiful terrace. Free airport transport with 3-day stay. Internet free. Singles US$30; doubles US$50; triples US$60.

Poem Hotel, Akbıyık Cad., 12 Terbıyık Sok. (☎/fax 517 68 36). The place to go to splurge. Luxurious rooms are marked with titles of Turkish poems instead of room numbers; all have Bosphorus views. Turkish breakfast (included) served in garden. Internet free. Singles US$55; doubles US$70-95; triples US$90-115. Subtract 25% in winter.

Bahaus Guesthouse, Akbıyık Cad., 11 Bayram Fırını Sok. (☎517 66 97). From the front of the Blue Mosque, strut down Mimar Mehmet Ağa Cad. 2 blocks, and turn left on Akbıyık Cad. Spare, standard rooms. Terrace has various musical instruments available. Breakfast included. Singles US$20; doubles US$30-35; triples US$40.

Sultan Hostel, 3 Terbıyık Sok. (☎516 92 60; email sultan@feztravel.com), off Akbıyık Cad., around the corner from Orient Hostel. Gaze at the Sea of Marmara from the rooftop restaurant. Happy hour 5-8pm. Internet. Belly dancing Tu and Sa; water pipe nights M and Th. Dorms US$6.50; singles US$13; doubles US$18; quads US$28.

Yücelt Hostel/Interyouth Hostel, 6/1 Caferiye Cad. (☎513 61 50; www.yucelthostel.com). Massive 3-building complex has billiards, table tennis, computer service, travel library, book exchange, safes, luggage storage, and videos in the rooftop lounge. Laundry. Dorms US$7-9; singles US$18; doubles US$18; triples US$27.

FOOD

Sultanahmet's heavily advertised "Turkish" restaurants are easy to find, but much better meals can be found on **İstiklâl Cad.** and around **Taksim.** Small Bosphorus towns such as **Arnavutköy** and **Sariyer** (on the European side) and **Çengelköy** (on the Asian side) are the best places for fresh fish. **Kanlıca,** on the Asian side, reputedly has the best **yogurt.** Covered boats in **Eminönü** and **Karaköy** fry up **fish sandwiches** on board (US$1.50). Good kebap shops are everywhere, but quality tends to be better in more residential areas. **Ortaköy** is the place for baked potatoes stuffed with all kinds of fillings. Because of space considerations and cultural differences, there are very few supermarkets. Luckily, **markets** all over the city sell cheese, bread, produce, and more—all at rock-bottom prices. Browse the fresh selection of produce in the city's **open-air markets;** the best is the daily one in **Beşiktaş,** near Barbaros Cad.

SULTANAHMET AND DİVAN YOLU

Doy-Doy, 13 Şifa Hamamı Sok. From the south end of the Hippodrome, walk down the hill around the Blue Mosque and look for the blue and yellow sign. Easily the best and cheapest of Sultanahmet's cheap eats, 3-story Doy-Doy keeps locals and backpackers coming back. Tasty *kebap* and salads (US$3.50 and under). Open 8:30am-late.

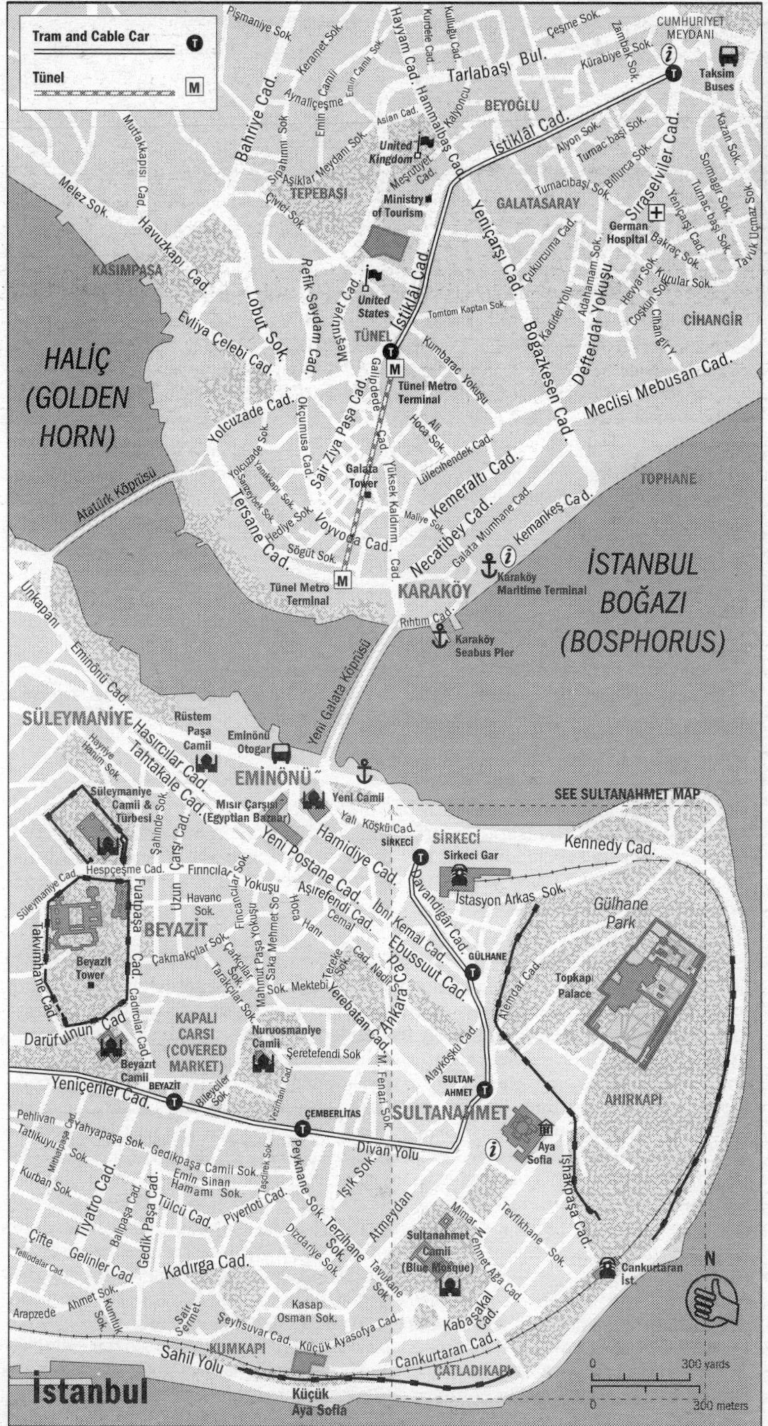

Tram and Cable Car
Tünel
İstanbul
HALİÇ (GOLDEN HORN)
İSTANBUL BOĞAZI (BOSPHORUS)
BEYOĞLU
TEPEBAŞI
GALATASARAY
KASIMPAŞA
TÜNEL
CİHANGİR
TOPHANE
KARAKÖY
SÜLEYMANİYE
EMİNÖNÜ
SİRKECİ
BEYAZIT
KAPALI CARSI (COVERED MARKET)
SULTANAHMET
AHIRKAPI
KUMKAPI
ÇATLADIKAPI
CUMHURIYET MEYDANI
Taksim Buses
United Kingdom
Ministry of Tourism
United States
German Hospital
Tünel Metro Terminal
Galata Tower
Karaköy Maritime Terminal
Karaköy Seabus Pier
Rüstem Paşa Camii
Eminönü Otogar
Yeni Camii
Mısır Çarşısı (Egyptian Bazaar)
Süleymaniye Camii & Türbesi
Sirkeci Gar
Gülhane Park
Topkapı Palace
Beyazıt Tower
Beyazıt Camii
Nuruosmaniye Camii
Aya Sofia
Sultanahmet Camii (Blue Mosque)
Cankurtaran İst.
Küçük Aya Sofia
SEE SULTANAHMET MAP
İstiklâl Cad.
Tarlabaşı Bul.
Kennedy Cad.
Meclisi Mebusan Cad.
Divan Yolu
Yeniçeriler Cad.
Sahil Yolu
Kadırga Cad.
Hamidiye Cad.
Yeni Galata Köprüsü
Atatürk Köprüsü
0 300 yards
0 300 meters
N

Dârüzziyâfe, 6 Şifahane Cad., is perfect after a visit to the Süleymaniye Mosque or a walk around Beyazit. The lamb cutlet in olive oil with onions, rosemary and basil (US$7) is notable, as is their *çilek keşkül* (strawberry pudding; US$2). Many vegetarian options. No alcohol–they serve rosehip nectar instead. Open daily 9am-11pm.

Can Restaurant, 10 Divan Yolu (☎527 70 30). Across the street from the tourist information office at the north end of the Hippodrome. This no-nonsense, dirt-cheap cafeteria offers inexpensive line fare out front and dining tables in the rear. Veggie combination plates from US$1.75; meat dishes US$2.50-5. Open 8am-9pm.

Cennet, 90 Divan Yolu (☎513 14 16), on the right side of the road as you walk from Sultanahmet toward Aksaray, 3min. from the Sultanahmet tram. Watch women make *gözleme* (Anatolian pancakes) in the center of the restaurant. Divine cheese pancake US$1.75. Live Turkish music and dancing nightly. Open daily 10am-midnight.

Pudding Shop, 6 Divan Yolu. A pitstop on the Hippie Trail to the Far and Middle East during the 70s, it was the setting for the drug deal scene in *Midnight Express*. It is now a self-serve restaurant (dishes US$1.50-2.50) and super dessert stop whose walls are lined with newspaper clippings and notes about its storied past. Continental breakfast US$2.

İSTİKLÂL CADDESİ AND TAKSİM

Haci Baba, 49 İstiklâl Cad., has perfected a wide range of Turkish standards in its 78 years. The menu is big; pick something from the deli case in front or try the immense, vegetarian *meze* selection. Entrees around US$7. Open daily 10am-10pm.

Naregatsi Cafe, Upstairs at the mouth of Sakizağacı Cad., across from the Ağa Camii. Gourmet cafe fare in the midst of a galactic, high-speed collision of kitsch and concept art. Inflatable superheroes, a collection of board games, and the occasional live accordion complement the cappuccino (4 flavors, US$3.50). Open noon-11:30pm.

İnci Pastahanesi, 126 İstiklâl Cad., has served the neighborhood for 53 years under the same owner. The specialty is the scandalously cheap *profiterol*, a creme-filled cake smothered in chocolate sauce (US$1.40). Open daily 7am-9pm.

Great Hong Kong Restaurant, 12B İnönü Cad., off Taksim Square. Chinese favorites, from wonton soup to Huajiao prawns. Open daily noon-3pm and 6-11:30pm.

SIGHTS

İstanbul hosts an incomparable array of world-famous churches, mosques, palaces, and museums. Most budget travelers spend a lot of time in **Sultanahmet,** the area around the **Hagia Sophia,** south of and uphill from Sirkeci. Merchants crowd the district between the **Grand Bazaar,** east of the university, and the **Egyptian Bazaar,** just southeast of Eminönü.

HAGIA SOPHIA (AYA SOFİA)

Hagia Sophia opened in December of AD 537. Covering 7570 square meters and rising 55.6m, it was then the grandest building in the world. Upon entering the church and marvelling at its girth, which was even larger than King Solomon's temple in Jerusalem, Emperor Justinian I reportedly exclaimed, "Solomon, I have outdone you!" Twenty years later, an earthquake brought the dome crashing to the ground. The new dome went up in AD 563. After falling to the Ottomans in 1453, Hagia Sophia was converted into a mosque and remained one until Atatürk established it as a museum in 1932. Hagia Sophia's austere interior amplifies its awesome size. The nave is overshadowed by the massive, gold-leaf mosaic dome. The **mihrab,** the calligraphy-adorned portal pointing toward Mecca, stands in the **apse,** which housed the altar during the mosque's Orthodox incarnation. The elaborate marble square in the floor marks the spot where Byzantine emperors were once crowned. The **minber,** the platform used to address the crowd at Muslim prayer, is atop the stairway to the right of the *mihrab*. At the back end of the **narthex,** a quiet hallway with lace-like column capitals at the north side of the building, is the famed **sweating pillar,** sheathed in bronze. The pillar has a hole where you can insert your finger to collect the odd drop of water, believed to possess healing powers. Be prepared to wait—the perspiration is slow in coming. The **gallery** contains Byzantine mosaics uncovered from beneath a thick layer of Ottoman plaster. *(Museum open Tu-Su 9:30am-4:30pm. Gallery open Tu-Su 9:30-4pm. US$6.50.)*

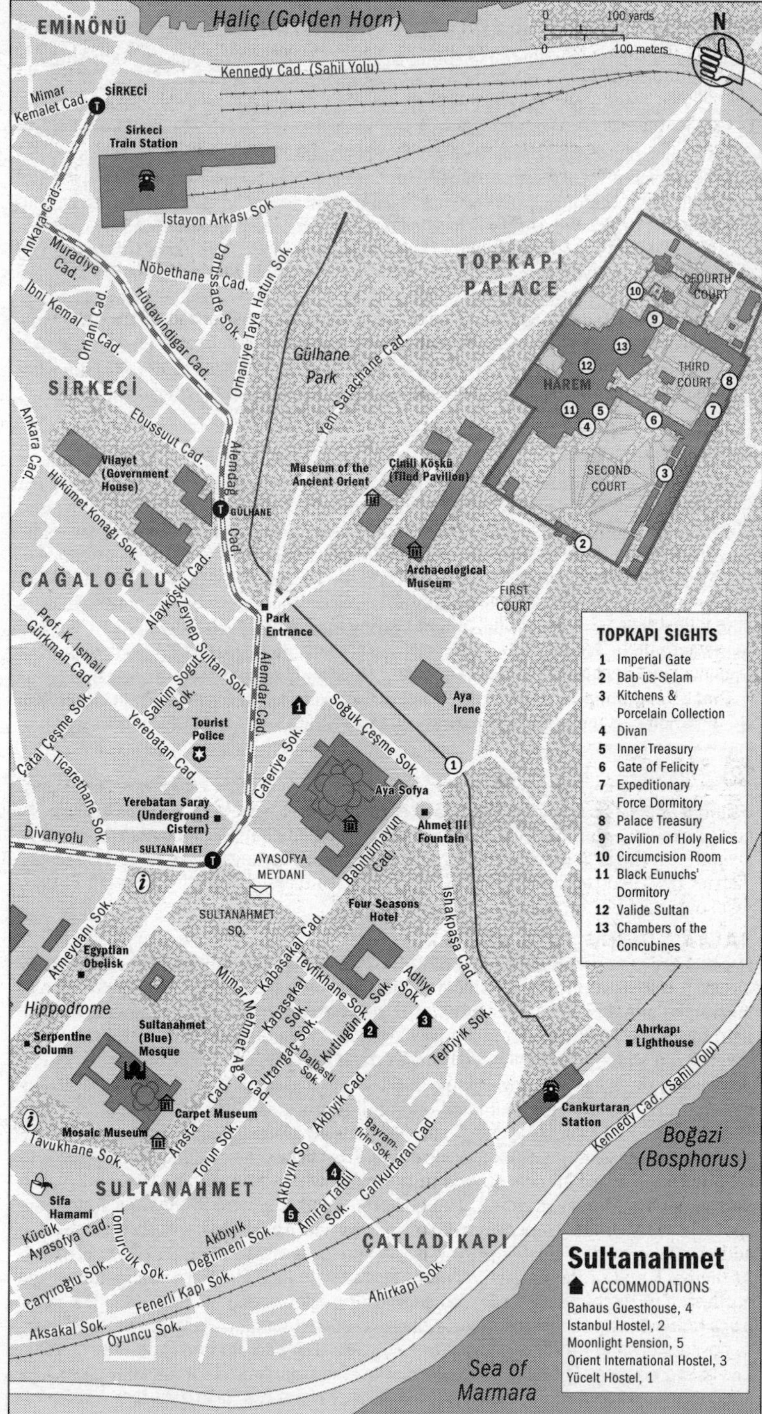
EMİNÖNÜ
Haliç (Golden Horn)
0 100 yards
0 100 meters
N
Kennedy Cad. (Sahil Yolu)
Mimar Kemalet Cad.
SİRKECİ
Sirkeci Train Station
Istayon Arkası Sok.
Ankara Cad.
Muradiye Cad.
Nöbethane Cad.
Darüssade Sok.
Orhaniye Taya Hatun Sok.
İbni Kemal Cad.
Orhani Cad.
Hüdavendigar Cad.
TOPKAPI PALACE
FOURTH COURT
Gülhane Park
Yeni Saraçhane Cad.
THIRD COURT
HAREM
SİRKECİ
Ebussuut Cad.
Alemdağ Cad.
Vilayet (Government House)
Museum of the Ancient Orient
Çinili Köşkü (Tiled Pavilion)
SECOND COURT
GÜLHANE
Hükümet Konağı Sok.
Archaeological Museum
CAĞALOĞLU
Alayköşkü Cad.
FIRST COURT
Park Entrance
Prof. K. Ismail Gürkman Cad.
Zeynep Sultan Sok.
Salkım Soğut Sok.
Alemdar Cad.
Aya Irene
Çatal Çeşme Sok.
Yerebatan Cad.
Tourist Police
Soğuk Çeşme Sok.
Ticarethane Sok.
Caferiye Sok.
Aya Sofya
Yerebatan Saray (Underground Cistern)
Ahmet III Fountain
Divanyolu
SULTANAHMET
Babıhümayun Cad.
AYASOFYA MEYDANI
SULTANAHMET SQ.
Four Seasons Hotel
Ishakpaşa Cad.
Atmeydanı Sok.
Egyptian Obelisk
Kabasakal Cad.
Tevfikhane Sok.
Adliye Sok.
Mimar Mehmet Ağa Cad.
Kabasakal Sok.
Kutlugün Sok.
Hippodrome
Serpentine Column
Sultanahmet (Blue) Mosque
Utangaç Sok.
Dalbastı Sok.
Terbiyik Sok.
Ahırkapı Lighthouse
Akbıyık Cad.
Carpet Museum
Arasta Cad.
Mosaic Museum
Cankurtaran Station
Kennedy Cad. (Sahil Yolu)
Tavukhane Sok.
Torun Sok.
Bayram-fırın Sok.
Cankurtaran Cad.
Boğazi (Bosphorus)
Akbıyık So
Sifa Hamami
SULTANAHMET
Amiral Tafdil Sok.
Küçük Ayasofya Cad.
Tomurcuk Sok.
Akbıyık Değirmeni Sok.
ÇATLADIKAPI
Caryıroğlu Sok.
Fenerli Kapı Sok.
Ahırkapı Sok.
Aksakal Sok.
Oyuncu Sok.
Sea of Marmara
TOPKAPI SIGHTS
1 Imperial Gate
2 Bab üs-Selam
3 Kitchens & Porcelain Collection
4 Divan
5 Inner Treasury
6 Gate of Felicity
7 Expeditionary Force Dormitory
8 Palace Treasury
9 Pavilion of Holy Relics
10 Circumcision Room
11 Black Eunuchs' Dormitory
12 Valide Sultan
13 Chambers of the Concubines
Sultanahmet
ACCOMMODATIONS
Bahaus Guesthouse, 4
Istanbul Hostel, 2
Moonlight Pension, 5
Orient International Hostel, 3
Yücelt Hostel, 1

BLUE MOSQUE (SULTANAHMET CAMİİ)

Between the Hippodrome and Hagia Sophia, the Blue Mosque, Sultan Ahmet's response to Hagia Sophia in 1617, is named for its beautiful blue İznik tiles. Not as large as Hagia Sophia, but still massive, the mosque's internal framework of iron bars enables the entire structure to bend in earthquakes (so far, it has withstood 20). Enter from the east side through the **courtyard.** The mosque's **six minarets** are the primary source of its fame; at the time, only the mosque at Mecca had six minarets, and the thought of equaling that sacred edifice was considered heretical. Sultan Ahmet circumvented this difficulty by financing the construction of a seventh minaret at Mecca. A small stone from the **Ka'aba** at Mecca is almost invisible from the tourists' area. *(Open Tu-Sa 8:30am-12:30pm, 1:45-3:45pm, and 5:30-6:30pm. Donation requested. Dress modestly—no shorts or tank tops, and women must wear head coverings. Speak quietly.)* The small, square, single-domed structure in front of the Blue Mosque, **Sultan Ahmet's Tomb** (Sultanahmet'in Türbesi), contains the sultan's remains as well as those of his wife and sons, Osman II and Murat IV. The holy relics include strands of Muhammed's beard. *(Open Tu-Su 9:30am-4:30pm. US$1, students free.)*

THE HIPPODROME (AT MEYDANI)

Behind the Blue Mosque, the remains of this ancient Roman circus form a pleasant park whose tranquility defies its turbulent history. Built by the Roman Emperor Septimus Severus in AD 200, the Hippodrome was the site of chariot races and public executions. Constantine, the first Byzantine Emperor, enlarged the racetrack to 500m on each side. The tall, northernmost column with hieroglyphics is the **Egyptian Obelisk** (Dikili Taş), erected by the Pharaoh Thutmosis III in 1500 BC and brought from Egypt to Constantinople in the 4th century by Emperor Theodosius I. Farther south, the subterranean bronze stump is all that remains of the **Serpentine Column,** originally placed at the Oracle of Delphi. The southernmost column is the **Column of Constantine,** whose original gold-plated bronze tiling was looted by members of the Fourth Crusade during the sack of Constantinople. On the east side of the Hippodrome along Atmeydanı Sok. is the superb **Museum of Turkish and Islamic Art** (İbrahim Paşa Sarayı). The Ottoman calligraphy is particularly impressive. *(Museum open Tu-Su 9:30am-4:30pm. US$2, students US$1.20.)*

TOPKAPI PALACE (TOPKAPI SARAYI)

The main entrance is on Babıhümayun Cad., the cobblestone street off Hagia Sophia square. Open Tu-Su 9am-4:30pm. US$6.50. Harem open Tu-Su 9am-4pm; mandatory tours every 30min. 9:30am-3:30pm. US$4.

Towering from the high ground at the tip of the old city, hidden behind walls up to 12m high, Topkapı Palace was the nerve center of the Ottoman Empire from the 15th to the 19th centuries. Topkapı offers unparalleled insight into the wealth, excess, cruelty, and artistic vitality that characterized the Ottoman Empire at its peak. Built by Mehmet the Conqueror between AD 1458 and 1465, the palace became an imperial residence under Süleyman the Magnificent. The palace is divided into a series of courts surrounded by palace walls.

FIRST AND SECOND COURTYARDS. The general public was permitted entrance via the **Imperial Gate** to the first courtyard, where they watched executions, traded, and viewed the nexus of the Empire's glory. At the end of the first courtyard, the capped conical towers of the **Gate of Greeting** (Bab-üs-Selam) mark the entrance to the second courtyard. To the right beyond the colonnade, the **Imperial kitchens,** feature distinctive vaulted chimneys and house three collections of porcelain and silver. The last set of doors on the left of the narrow alley leads to the palace's world-famous **Chinese and Japanese porcelain collections.** Across the courtyard, where ostriches and eunuchs once roamed, lie the **Privy Chambers** *(Kubbealtı)*, whose window grilles, awnings, walls, and ceilings are bathed in gold leaf. The **Council Chamber,** the room closest to the Harem, retains its original classical Ottoman calligraphic decor. Abutting the Council Chamber is the plush Rococo-style room in which the **Grand Vizier** received foreign dignitaries. Next door and to the right is the **Inner Treasury,** which holds various cutting and bludgeoning instruments.

THIRD COURTYARD. The third courtyard, officially known as **Enderun** (inside), is accessible through the **Gate of Felicity.** The **School of Expeditionary Pages** holds a costume collection that traces the evolution of imperial costumes. Move along down the colonnade to the incredible **Palace Treasury,** where ornate gold objects, the legendary **Topkapı dagger** (essentially three giant emeralds with a knife sprouting out of them), the 86-carat **Spoonmaker's Diamond,** and much more await your ogling. Just on the other side of the courtyard is the **Pavilion of Holy Relics,** which houses the booty taken by Selim the Grim after the Ottoman capture of Egypt as well as gifts sent by the governor of Mecca and Medina upon Selim's victory.

FOURTH COURTYARD. Three passages lead into the fourth courtyard. If Topkapı can be thought of as the brain of the Ottoman Empire, then the fourth courtyard certainly qualifies as the pleasure center, as it was amongst these pavilions, gardens, and fountains that the infamous merriments and sordid garden parties occurred. From the broad marble terrace at the west end, you can take in the uninterrupted vistas of the Sea of Marmara and the Bosphorus. The **Revan Pavilion,** the building farthest from the edge of the terrace, was built in 1635 to commemorate Sultan Murat IV's Revan campaign; at the other end of the portico is the **Circumcision Room,** an octagonal chamber that overhangs the edge of the pavilion, built by Ibrahim the Mad. At the other end of the terrace stands the **Bağdat Köşku,** Murat I's monument to his capture of Baghdad in 1638. An octagonal/cruciform base supports the dome; the interior sports an amazing radial symmetry.

HAREM. The Harem's 400-plus rooms housed the sultan, his immediate family, and a small army of servants, eunuchs, and general assistants. Because it was forbidden for men other than the sultan and his sons to live here, the Harem became a source of intrigue and the subject of endless gossip. The mandatory tour proceeds to the **Black Eunuchs' Dormitory** on the left, then into the women's section of the harem, beginning with the chambers of the **Valide Sultan,** the sultan's mother. If a concubine attracted the sultan's affections or if the sultan spent a night with her, she would be promoted to nicer quarters with the chance for further advancement; if she bore the sultan a son, she could become his wife (one of eight).

OTHER SIGHTS

THE ARCHAEOLOGICAL MUSEUM COMPLEX. Mehmet the Conqueror built the **tiled pavilion** to view athletic competitions below; the display covers the spectrum of Ottoman tile-making, including some rare early İznik tiles. The smaller building adjacent to the tiled pavilion, the **Museum of the Ancient Orient,** is rarely open; hidden inside is an excellent collection of stone artifacts from Anatolia, Mesopotamia, and Egypt dating from the first and 2nd millennia BC. The **Archaeology Museum** contains one of the world's great collections of Classical and Hellenistic art. *(About 100m downhill from the 1st courtyard of Topkapı Palace. When the palace is closed, enter the museums through Gülhane Park; a separate road next to the park ticket booths leads to the complex. Complex open Tu-Su 9:30am-5pm. US$5.)*

GRAND BAZAAR (KAPALI ÇARŞISI). Consisting of over 4000 shops, several banks, mosques, police stations, and restaurants, this enormous "covered bazaar" could be a city in itself. It began in 1461 as a modest affair during the reign of Mehmet the Conqueror, but today forms the entrance to the massive mercantile sprawl that starts at Çemberlitaş and covers the hill down to Eminönü, ending at the **Egyptian Spice Bazaar** (Mısır Çarşısı) and the Golden Horn waterfront. This colorful, chaotic, labyrinthine world combines all the best and worst of shopping in Turkey. Although the bazaar is loosely organized according to specific themes, much of it is a jumble of shops selling carpets, hookah pipes, bright baubles, copper filigree shovels, Byzantine-style icons on red velvet, Turkish daggers, embroidered pillows, amber jewelry, silver flintlock guns, musical instruments, chess sets, hand puppets, and, of course, evil-eye keychains. Through banter and barter, haggle and hassle, a day spent at the

Kapalı Çarşısı is bound to tempt, titillate, and tantalize even the most experienced traveler. You'll surely get lost, so enjoy the ride. *(From Sultanahmet, follow the tram tracks toward Aksaray for 5min. until you see the Nuruosmanıye Camii on the right. Walk down Vezirhanı Cad. for a block, keeping the mosque on your left. Follow the crowds left into the bazaar. Open M-Sa 9am-7pm.)*

YEREBATAN SARAYI (UNDERGROUND CISTERN). This subterranean "palace" is actually a vast underground cavern whose shallow water eerily reflects the images of its 336 supporting columns, all illuminated by colored ambient lighting. Echoing sounds of dripping water and muted classical tunes accompany strolls across the elevated wooden walkways. Underground walkways linking it to Topkapı Palace were blocked to curb rampant trafficking in stolen goods and abducted women. *(With your back to Hagia Sophia, the entrance is 175m away on the left side of Yerebatan Cad. Open daily 9:30am-5:30pm. US$4, students US$3.25.)*

SÜLEYMANİYE COMPLEX (SÜLEYMANİYE KÜLLİYESİ). To the north of İstanbul University sits the massive and elegant Süleymaniye Camii, one of architect Sinan's great masterpieces, part of a larger complex that includes **tombs,** an **imaret** (soup kitchen), and several **medreses** (Islamic schools). Walk along the Süleymaniye Camii's southwest side to the large arch just below the dome and enter the mosque's central courtyard through the smaller tourist entrance to the left of the main door. After removing your shoes (women should also put on a headscarf), proceed inside the vast and perfectly proportioned mosque. The stained-glass windows are the work of the master Sarhoş İbrahim (İbrahim the Drunkard). *(From the university, head out the northwest gate to Süleymaniye Cad. From Sultanahmet, either walk along the tramvay (15min.) or take it to the "Üniversite" stop, walk across the square, and take Besim Ömer Paşa Cad. past the walls of the university to Süleymaniye Cad. Mosque open Tu-Su 9:30am-4:30pm, except during prayers.)* Prof. Sıddık Sami Onar Sok. runs between the university and the mosque. Passing through the graveyard brings you to the superbly decorated **royal tombs** of Süleyman I and his wife, Haseki Hürrem. (*Open Tu-Su 9:30am-4:30pm. Donation requested.)*

PRINCE'S ISLANDS (ADALAR). The craggy Prince's Islands are known simply as the *Adalar* (islands). **Büyükada** is the largest and most enjoyable island, with pine forests, swimming spots, and peaceful walks. **Yöruk Ali** is the main **beach** and picnicking spot; you can also take the buggy to **Luna Park** (no more than US$7.50; 10-15min.), the local amusement park on the far side of the island. The main forms of transportation on the islands are **walking, biking,** and **horse-and-buggy rides.** The lovely **Ideal Aile Pansiyon,** 14 Kadıyoran Cad. is a haunted house masterpiece with huge rooms. *(☎ 382 68 57. US$13 per person.)* **Ferries** depart from the north side of Eminönü or Kabataş; look for "Sirkeci Adalar" signs. *(3-4 per day, round-trip US$2.)*

HAMAMS (TURKISH BATHS)

Women should request female washers. Self service is always an option; signal your preference by showing the attendants your bar of soap and wash cloth.

Mihrimah Hamamı, (☎523 04 87), right next to Mihrimah Mosque on Fevzi Paşa Cad., about 50m from Edirnekapı. One of the better local baths: large, quiet, clean, and cheap. The heat is usually turned all the way up for maximum dilation. Bath US$4; massage US$3.50. Men's section open 7am-midnight; women's section 8am-7pm.

Çinli Hamamı, in Fatih, near the butcher shops at the end of Itfaiye Cad. Built for the pirate Barbarossa, this bath is excellent and authentic. It retains a few of its original İznik and Kütahya tiles. Bath US$5; massage US$6. Both sections open 8am-8pm.

Galatasaray Hamamı (for men ☎244 14 12; for women ☎249 43 42), at the end of Turanacıbaşı Sok., off İstiklâl Cad. just uphill from Galatasaray. Pricey, a bit touristy, and the place to go if you want a scrub down in opulence. Bath and massage US$22. Men's section open daily 7am-11pm; women's section 8am-8pm.

THE *HAMAM* EXPERIENCE Pay the entrance fee plus additional charges for massage, *kese* (abrasive mitt), and soap and towel *(peştemal).* Men generally strip and wrap the *peştemal* around their waists. Turkish women frequently strip in the bath, but wear underwear under the *peştemal* until you gauge the sensibilities of a given *hamam.* Some have a hot, sauna-like room where you can warm yourself to the point of near-lightheadedness. After you've worked up a sweat, proceed to the warm main room, which has a large, heated stone *(göbek taşı).* Bathe yourself at the basins (one per person), pouring a mixture of hot and cold water over yourself using the bowl provided. Keep soap suds clear of the basin water, and take care not to douse others. Men should never drop their *peştemal;* cleaning your lower half is tricky, but not impossible. Don't be shocked if your masseur or masseuse is only wearing underwear. The massage is sometimes harder than what visitors expect; say *"lütfen daha yumuşak"* ("gentler please") if you are in pain. After the massage and *kese,* used to strip excess skin cells beyond all imagination, you will usually be sponged gently and shampooed. Once you feel you have reached optimum cleanliness, return to your cubicle, order a drink to rehydrate, and relax before returning to the dusty world outside.

NIGHTLIFE

İstanbul's best clubs and bars are poorly advertised, so unplanned club hopping usually proves fruitless, but options abound. Small, relaxed **cafe-bars** serve tea in the afternoon and alcohol in the evening, often with a jazz soundtrack. Cavernous **rock bars** range from dark, heavy metal halls to mellow classic rock hangouts. Convenient and cheap **backpacker bars** are concentrated in the **Sultanahmet** area. The hippest **clubs and discos** often move from unlisted locations in Taksim in the winter to unlisted summer locations throughout the city. The Beşiktaş end of **Ortaköy** is a maze of upscale hangouts; along the coastal road toward **Arnavutköy** are a string of open-air clubs (cover US$18-45). Bouncers are highly selective, but wander between Ortaköy and **Bebek** and try your luck. Men heading out without female companions will have a tough time getting into some of the more upscale clubs and bars, which require every man to be accompanied by at least one woman in order to keep the dance floors co-ed. İstanbul night action is centered around **Taksim** and **İstiklâl Cad.** Sultanahmet's bars all lie within 100m of one another; beer is standardized at US$1-1.25. Male-only *çay* houses, backgammon parlors, and dancing shows tend to be dingy and dangerous. *Let's Go* does not recommend these establishments. Team up with others and take cabs when out late, even in nicer areas. Cafe-bars and backpacker bars tend to be less threatening than rock bars or clubs.

Jazz Stop, at the end of Büyük Parmakkapı Sok in Taksim. A mixed group of music lovers mostly sit while live bands lay the blues on thick. Live music daily 11pm. Beer US$3. Liquor from US$6. No cover June-Aug.; Sept.-May F-Sa US$10. Open 11am-4am.

Riddim, 6 Büyük Parmakkapı Sok. Dedicated to spinning reggae all night long. The crowd won't stop dancing to Jamaican, African, and island music. Unaccompanied men turned away on weekends. Beer US$2.50. Open F-Sa 8pm-4am, Su-Th 8pm-2am.

Mordi Cafe Bar, 47 Akbıyık Cad., down the street from the Orient Hostel. Dark wood and candles enhance the mood of this clean backpacker bar. Nice place to relax with a beer, quiet conversation, and some good jazz, rock, or folk. Happy hour until 10pm.

Peyote, İmam Adnan Sok., next to Leman Kültür. This humble spot is one of Taksim's cheapest venues for live music. Beer US$1.25. Live music Tu-Sa at 11:30pm. Cover F-Sa US$7.50; includes 1 drink. Open M-Sa 6pm-4am.

Madrid Bar, İpek Sok., off Küçük Parmakkapı Sok., which is off İstiklâl Cad. Surrealist Spanish paintings decorate this small, mellow spot, popular with Turkish students and young foreigners looking for the cheapest pints in Taksim (US$1.25). Open 2pm-2am.

Kemancı, 150m down Siraselviler Cad. on the right, up the stairs in a big archway. The immense downstairs venue hosts local bands tearing through sped-up U2 and Judas Priest covers. Upstairs, a slightly older crowd cheers as bands pound out loud covers of American tunes. Beer US$2.50. Cover F-Sa US$12.50, Su-Th US$3. Open noon-4am.

EDİRNE ☎284

In almost 2000 years of historical prominence, Edirne has experienced a mixed and fickle fate, ranging from imperial splendor to hostile occupation. It has been a Roman outpost, an Ottoman capital, and a modern Greek military possession. An easy *dolmuş* ride from the Greek (7km away) or Bulgarian (20km) border, Edirne once nourished the genius of Sinan, the quintessential Ottoman architect. His masterpiece, the **Selimiye Camii,** considered by many to be Turkey's finest mosque, presides over the city with 71m-tall minarets, a 32m-wide dome, and 999 windows. Its vast, ornately-decorated interior is even more impressive. Another Edirne must-see is the **Beyazıt Complex,** built in the late 1480s by the court architect of Beyazıt II. The centerpiece is the **Beyazıt Camii,** a beautiful, single-domed mosque surrounded by multi-domed buildings designed to be schools, storehouses, and asylums. For a long but pleasant walk to the complex, follow Horozlu Bayir Cad. from its origin near the Sokollu Hamamı across two bends of the river. Unfortunately, only the wing once used for medical purposes is open; it now houses Trakya University's Museum of Health. (Open Tu-Su 8:30am-5:30pm. US$1.50.) Back in town, Sinan's 16th-century **Sokollu Hamamı,** beside the Üç Şerefeli Camii, has superior service and inspiring architecture. (☎225 21 93. US$2.50, with massage US$6.25. Open daily 7am-11pm for men; 9am-6pm for women.) Those less interested in cleanliness can get down and dirty with the competitors who don giant leather breeches, slather themselves in oil, and hit the mats for the **Kırkpınar Grease Wrestling Festival,** which comes to town in early July; call the tourist office for details.

Numerous companies send **buses** from the *otogar*, 2km from the city center, to: İstanbul (2-3½hr., US$5-8.25), Bursa (7hr., US$16.50), Ankara (9hr., US$20), and İzmir (9hr., US$15.50). Before you buy a ticket, especially to İstanbul, be sure to shop around. Upon arrival, walk across the four-lane road opposite the *otogar* and hail one of the frequent *dolmuş* heading to town. The **tourist office,** 17 Talat Paşa Cad., 300m from the town center, has free maps. (☎213 92 08. Open June-Aug. M-F 8:30am-5:30pm and occasional weekend hours; Sept.-May M-F 8:30am-5:30pm.) The wonderful **Hotel Kervansaray,** along Hürriyet Meydanı on Eski Camii Altı, was built in the 16th century for tired camel caravans. Exquisite gardens, a cloistered courtyard, and stone hallways recall early Ottoman days. (☎225 21 95; fax 212 04 62. Turkish bath. Internet. Singles US$30; doubles US$60; triples US$90. V, MC.) The basic **Hotel Aksaray** is at the intersection of Maarif Cad. and Ali Paşa Ortakapı Cad. (☎225 39 01. Singles US$8.25; doubles US$15-16.50; triples US$20-21.50.) Don't leave town without sipping *çay* (US$0.25-0.40) at **Şera Park Café,** on Selimiye Meydanı, in the park between Selimiye Camii and Eski Camii. **Postal code:** 22100.

BURSA ☎224

In the shadow of the slopes of Mt. Uludağ, Bursa is both one of Turkey's holiest cities and a major industrial center. Surrounded by fertile plains and filled with vast gardens and parks, the city has been dubbed "Green Bursa." Its fantastic early Islamic architecture is also some of the most stunning in all of Turkey. Most of Bursa's sights lie roughly in a long row along Atatürk Cad. and its continuations. The immense **Ulu Cami** stands in the center of town on Atatürk Cad. The domes, arranged in four rows of five with a glass center, hover above a large fountain, one of the more unique features of the mosque. From the statue of Atatürk, head east along Atatürk Cad., bear right, and continue along Yeşil Cad. following the "Yeşil" signs to reach the blue-green hilltop **Yeşil Türbe** (Green Tomb; open daily 8:30am-noon and 1-5:30pm) and the onion-shaped minaret caps of the 15th-century **Yeşil Camii** across the street. *Şehade* (royal sons) are buried in tombs surrounding the **Muradiye Camii,** a testament to the early Ottoman practice of fratricide (the eldest son made a practice of killing his younger brothers to ensure a smooth succession). To reach the complex, catch a "Muradiye" *dolmuş* or bus from the Atatürk Cad./Heykel area. (Open daily 8:30am-noon and 1-5:30pm. US$0.60.) Bursa's fabled **mineral baths** are in the **Çekirge** ("Grasshopper") area west of the city. On Çekirge Cad. is the shiny **Eski Kaplıca** ("old bath"), one of the finest baths in the country, with a hot pool, a hotter pool, and a great massage room. Take bus #40 or a Çekirge *dolmuş* and ask for Eski Kaplıca. (☎233 93 00. Men US$7.50; women US$6; scrub or massage US$5.50.) On the road to Çekirge is the **Karagöz Sanat Evi** with exhibitions on shadow theater from around the world. (☎232 87 27. Open M-Sa 11am-4pm. US$1.50, students US$0.80.) The master **puppeteer** R. Sinasi Çelikkol gives performances every Wednesday and Saturday at 11am. A short trip away, **Mt. Uludağ** is a popular ski area during the winter and a picturesque picnic area, with bright flowers and carpets of evergreen trees, in summer. From Bursa, take bus 3-C, 3-İ, or any with a "Teleferik" sign from Peron 1 on Atatürk Cad. (every 5-10min., US$0.40). Alternately, catch the *dolmuş* from behind Adliye and Heykel (US$0.60).

In Bursa, Kamil Koç **buses** go from the terminal, 20km outside the city center, to İstanbul (3½hr., US$8.25); İzmir (5hr., every hr., US$8.25); Ankara (5½hr., every hr., US$9.25); Çeşme (8hr., 2 per day, US$11); and Kuşadası (7½hr, 4 per day, US$11). Local bus #90/A goes downtown (US$0.45). **Seabuses** (☎ (226) 812 04 99) go between İstanbul and Yalova (35min.-1hr., 14 per day, US$4-7.50), from which buses connect to Bursa (1hr., every 30min., US$2.50). To get to the **tourist office,** head to the Ulu Cami side of Atatürk Cad., walk past the fountain toward the Atatürk statue, and go down the stairs on the left. (☎220 18 48. Open daily May-Sept. 8:30am-6pm; Oct.-Apr. 8am-5pm.) **Elite Internet Cafe** is at 37 Yeşil Cad. before the overpass leading to the Emir Sultan Cami. (US$1.30 per hr. Open daily 10am-1am.) Find the basic but friendly **Otel Güneş** at 75 İnebey Cad. (☎222 14 04. Singles US$10; doubles US$16.50; triples US$21.50; quads US$24.) Walk along Atatürk Cad. toward Ulu Cami with the mosque on your right and turn left after the PTT to get to **Lâl Otel,** 79 Maksem Cad. (☎221 17 10. Shower US$1.75. Same prices as Otel Güneş.) Follow Atatürk Cad. 1.5km west, pass the Tophane Parki, and bear left onto Sakarya Cad. to the Arap Şükrü district, which features fish restaurants, bars, and pubs and is as close to a nightlife as Bursa gets. **Kebapçı İskender** claims to have invented the unbeatable dish *İskender kebap* (lamb with tomato sauce, bread, and yogurt; US$2.50) in 1867; one branch is at 7 Ünlü Cad. and another by the Cultural Center on Atatürk Bul. (Open daily 11am-9pm.) **Postal code:** 16300.

BORDER CROSSINGS: BULGARIA AND GREECE

By far the easiest way to cross into **Bulgaria** from Turkey is to take a direct bus from İstanbul. Or, for a more adventurous route, take a local bus (US$1) to **Kapıkale,** the Turkish border town, 18km west of Edirne, where two options await. A direct train runs to **Sofia** (8hr., departs daily 3:30am, US$19) and a *dolmuş* (US$1) goes to the Turkish border, just several (hot) kilometers away from **Andreevo, Bulgaria.** Would-be crossers have to walk (if the guards will allow it) or hitch a ride on a bus crossing the border directly from İstanbul. On the other side, you have to catch a taxi from Andreevo to **Plovdiv,** the closest town with direct transport to Sofia.

The easiest way to cross into **Greece** is also a direct bus from İstanbul; the border crossing between **Pazarkule** and the Greek border (open 9am-noon) is inconvenient, but feasible. From Edirne, you can either take a taxi all the way to Pazarkule (15min., US$6.25), or catch the local bus to **Karaağiç** (US$0.50) and then walk the remaining 2km to Pazarkule. Though the 1km between the Turkish and Greek border posts is a no-man's land (no one may walk through without a military escort), Greek taxis usually wait at the border to ferry travelers across the stretch to **Kastanies,** from which you can make bus and train connections to elsewhere in Greece.

AEGEAN COAST

Classical ruins and a serpentine coastline conceal beaches on Turkey's once-tranquil Aegean coast, an increasingly popular destination for tourists. Framed by 5000-year-old mythology and history, the region's intensely rich culture offers an eyeful for photographers, archaeologists, nature lovers, and hedonistic nomads.

 FERRIES TO GREECE AND ITALY

From **Çeşme,** ferries run to **Hios, Greece** (1hr.; July 1-Sept. 10 Tu and Th-Sa; June and Sept. 11-30 Tu, Th, and Sa-Su; May and Oct. Tu and Th; Nov.-Apr. Th; US$30, round-trip US$40; US$10 Greek port tax for stays longer than a day). From June to September, **Turkish Maritime Lines** (☎ (232) 712 10 91) runs ferries from **Çeşme** to **Brindisi, Italy** (36hr.; Th-F 11am, M and F 11pm; deck passage US$95). From **Kuşadası,** ferries head to **Samos, Greece** (1½hr.; in summer daily 8:30am and 4:30pm, in winter 2 per week; US$30 including US$10 port tax). From Bodrum, **Bodrum Express Lines** (☎ (252) 316 40 67) runs ferries to **Kos** (1½hr., May-Sept. 1 per day) as well as hydrofoils to **Kos** (15min.; 1 per day; US$21, round-trip US$24) and **Rhodes** (2¼hr.; 1 per week; US$43, round-trip US$48-63).

GALLIPOLI (GELİBOLU) ☎286

The strategic position of the Gallipoli Peninsula on the Dardanelles made it the backdrop of a major WWI Allied offensive which sought to take Constantinople and create a Balkan front. Eighty thousand Ottomans and more than 200,000 soldiers of the British Empire—Englishmen, Australians, New Zealanders, and Indians—lost their lives in the blood-soaked stalemate. This battle launched its hero **Atatürk** into his status as Turkey's founding father. It's best to visit the battlefields from nearby **Eceabat** or **Çanakkale. Hassle Free Travel Agency,** 61 Cumhuriyet Meydani (☎213 59 69; email hasslefree@anzachouse.com), in Çanakkale, and the **Down Under Travel Agency** (see Down Under Hostel, below; agency ☎814 29 40; fax 814 29 41; email d.under@mailexcite.com and TJs_Tours@excite.com; tours US$14), in Eceabat, both offer **tours.** To visit on your own, take a **dolmuş** to the **Kabatep Müzesi** from Eceabat. (☎814 12 97. Museum open daily 8:30am-noon and 1-5:30pm. US$1.20.)

Gallipoli town is a more expensive and less convenient base for touring the battlefields, but is also a relaxing destination of its own. **Çanakkale Truva** (☎566 11 83 or 566 26 26) operates **buses** from Gallipoli to: Çanakkale (US$2); Edirne (2 per day, US$5); İstanbul (16 per day, US$7.50); and İzmir (9 per day, US$9). A **minibus** runs every hour to Eceabat (30min., US$1). From the bus station, walk 1km with the sea to your right to reach the center of town. To reach the **Yılmaz Hotel,** 8 Liman Mevkii, walk from the **Liman Meydanı** (the main square) across the bridge next to the old watchtower. (☎566 12 56. Breakfast included. Tours US$25. Singles US$10. 10% *Let's Go* reader discount.) In **Eceabat,** the **Down Under Hostel,** 39 Topçular Sok., has spotless doubles and triples with bath and a helpful, English-speaking staff. (☎814 10 65; fax. 814 29 41. **Internet** US$2 per hr. US$5 per person.)

ÇANAKKALE ☎286

With cheap accommodations and good bus connections, Çanakkale (pop. 60,000) is a great base for exploring Gallipoli and Troy. The **Çimenlik Kalesi** (Grassy Castle), 200m from the harbor, combines a park and naval museum. (Open Tu-W and F-Su 9am-noon and 1:30-5pm. US$0.75, students US$0.30.) **Buses** arrive frequently from: İstanbul (5hr., US$10); İzmir (5hr., US$8); and Bursa (4½hr., US$6.50). To get to the **tourist office,** 67 İskele Meydanı, go left from the station, take a right on Demircioğlu Cad, and follow the signs marked *Feribot* to the docks; it's on the left. (☎/fax 217 11 87. Open M-F 8am-7pm, Sa-Su 10am-6pm.) **Anzac House,** 61 Cumhuriyet Meydanı, arranges tours of Gallipoli and Troy through the Hassle Free Tour Agency. Facing Cumhuriyet Meydani with your back to the ferry docks, it is immediately on your right. (☎213 59 69. Dorms US$5; singles US$10; doubles US$14.50; triples US$18.)

TROY (TRUVA) ☎286

Troy, made famous by Homer, remained under a blanket of mythology until Heinrich Schliemann, millionaire-cum-archaeologist, uncovered the ancient city 32km south of Çanakkale—proving that the stories are more than fiction and that lovely Helen and the wooden horse are worthy of their place in history books. Nine distinct strata of Bronze Age fortifications are explained in the **Excavation House.** (Site and house open daily in summer 8:30am-7:30pm; off season 8am-5pm. US$2.50, students US$1.25.) **Down Under Travel Agency** (☎814 24 31; email d.under@mailexcite.com), based in Eceabat (see above), has excellent tours conducted by İlhami ("T.J.") Gezici (US$8) when there are sufficient tourists. **Anzac House** (☎213 59 69) leads tours from Çanakkale at 9am (US$8); arrive by 8:30am and bring water. Or, visit the site by taking a **dolmuş** from the lot in Çanakkale (every 30min., US$0.80).

BERGAMA (PERGAMON) ☎232

Ancient **Pergamon,** once capital of the Roman province of Asia, boasted the second-largest library in the world. Ruins of this great Hellenistic and Roman city dominate the city's hilltop. From the river (near the Pension Athena), cross the bridge, head diagonally to the right and uphill through the old town, follow the paved road until you come to a gate, and follow the path to the right up to the temples and marble ruins of the **Acropolis.** On your way up, the Hellenistic **theater,** which once seated 10,000, comes into spectacular view. Farther up, you can try to land three coins on top of the column inside the **wishing well** for good luck. Follow the yellow signs from Atatürk Meydanı on the west side of town to reach the famed **Asclepion,** an ancient healing center where the foremost doctor of the ancient world, native-born Galen, once worked. A marble colonnade, theater, and healing rooms remain today. (Open daily 8:30am-5:30pm. US$3.50, ISIC-toting students free.) Near the river and the old part of Pergamon stand the remnants of **Kızıl Avlu,** a pagan temple that became one of the Seven Churches of the Apocalypse mentioned in the Book of Revelations (Rev. 2:3: "This is where Satan has his altar"). Pergamon is across the river from the pleasant, modern town of **Bergama,** which sends **buses** to: İzmir (2hr., 2 per hr., US$3.25); Ankara (10hr., departs 9:30am and 8:45pm, US$18); and İstanbul (10hr., departs 9:30am and 9:25pm, US$19.50). From the bus station, walk 1km right on İzmir Cad. and turn left on Cumhuriyet Meydanı to reach the **tourist office.** (☎633 18 62. Open daily Apr.-Sept. 8:30am-noon and 1-7pm; Oct.-Mar. M-F 8:30am-noon and 1-5:30pm.) **Pension Athena,** on the road beyond İstiklâl Meydanı, boasts, "Not the best, but we're trying to get there." Chalk one up for honest advertising. (☎633 34 20. Laundry US$6. US$5-7; 10% off with *Let's Go.*) **Postal code:** 35700.

İZMİR ☎232

İzmir (pop. 3 million), formerly **Smyrna** (reputed to be the birthplace of Homer), rose from the rubble of the 1922 Turkish War of Independence to become Turkey's third-largest city. Along the waterfront, İzmir is a cosmopolitan city with wide boulevards, plazas, and plenty of greenery; but in many places, İzmir is a bleak, factory-laden wasteland. *Çay salonular* (teahouses), the cries of children and street vendors, and a full-fledged **bazaar** (open M-Sa 9am-8pm) line the streets of Anafartalar Cad. İzmir's **Archaeological Museum,** near Konak Square, houses finds from Ephesus and other local sites. (Open Tu-Su 9am-5pm. US$2.50.) Uphill from the archaeological museum, the **Ethnographical Museum** displays traditional folk art in a lovely old Ottoman house. (Open Tu-Su 9am-noon and 1-5pm. US$1.25.) From mid-June to early August, the **International İzmir Festival** brings Turkish and international acts to İzmir, Çeşme, and Ephesus. (For tickets and info, call the numbers listed in the İzmir Festival brochure distributed at the tourist office, or visit www.izmirfestival.org. Tickets US$5-16.) Budget hotels, cheap restaurants, bus company offices, and the **Basmane train station** are around **9 Eylül Meydanı,** a rotary at the center of the Basmane district. **Buses** run from **Yeni Garaj,** İzmir's new intercity bus station, to: Kuşadası (1hr., every 1½hr., US$3.25); Bodrum (4hr., every hr., US$10); Marmaris (5hr., every hr., US$10); Bursa (5hr., every hr., US$8); Ankara (8hr., every hr., US$13.75); and İstanbul (9hr., every hr., US$18). Take city bus #50, 51, 53, 54, 60, 601, or 605 from the station (US$0.50; buy tickets from the kiosk before boarding) and tell the driver you want **"Basmane Meydanı,"** which is the same as **9 Eylül Meydanı.** From there, walk down Gazi Bul. to the first main intersection, then turn right onto Gazi Osmanpaşa Bul. The **tourist office** is on the right at 1/1D Gazi Osman Paşa Bul., 30m northwest of the İzmir Hilton Hotel. (☎445 73 90. Open in summer M-F 8:30am-6:30pm, Sa-Su 9am-5pm; in winter M-F 8:30am-5:30pm, Sa

9am-5pm.) **Hotel Oba,** 1369 Sok. #27, four blocks down 1369 Sok from 9 Eylül Meydanı, combines cheap prices, clean lodgings, and great amenities. (☎441 96 05. Breakfast included. Singles US$12; doubles US$16.) Walk south from 9 Eylül Meydanı on Anafartalar Cad., pass the train station on your left, and turn right onto 1294 Sok. Quiet, cool, and clean **Hotel Akpınar** is at #13. Every room has a window and a TV. (☎446 38 96 or 484 16 34. Self-service laundry free, full service US$3.25. Singles US$5, with bath US$8; doubles US$8, with bath US$11.50.) **Postal code:** 35000.

EXCURSION FROM IZMIR: SART (SARDIS). While small, Sardis stands out as Turkey's best restored archaeological site. The **old city** boasts a magnificent two-story **gymnasium,** a long-deserted **swimming pool,** a ruined **Palaestra,** and a gorgeous **synagogue.** The patterns of the synagogue's 3rd-century mosaic floors are strangely juxtaposed with Corinthian and Doric columns. (Open daily 8am-5pm. US$1.60, students US$1.) The amazing 4th-century BC **Temple of Artemis** was one of the largest temples of the ancient world. (Open daily 8am-8pm; in winter 8am-5pm. US$1.60, students US$1.) Take a **bus** bound for Salihli from the upper floor of İzmir's Yeni Garaj (1½hr., every 30min., US$2.50) and ask to be let off at Sart; you will be dropped near a yellow "Temple of Artemis" sign, by the shops scattered along the highway. The gymnasium, synagogue, and baths are about 50m ahead on the left. Catch return buses back to İzmir from across the road from where you were dropped off (every 30min., around US$3).

ÇEŞME ☎223

A breezy seaside village an hour west of İzmir, Çeşme has gained popularity for its cool climate, crystal-clear waters, and proximity to the Greek island of Chios. With a long ribbon of clean, powder-white sand flanked by rolling dunes, **Altınkum Beach** is one of Turkey's finest. *Dolmuş* run to Altınkum from the lot in Çeşme, by the tourist office (15min., June-Sept. every 20min., US$0.75). Çeşme's most impressive site is the **castle,** which houses a sparse **Archaeological Museum.** (Open Tu-Su 8:30am-noon and 1-5:30pm. US$1.60.) **Buses** (☎712 64 99) run from the *otogar*, at the corner of A. Menderes Cad. and Çevre Yolu Cad., to: İzmir (1½hr., every 30min., US$3.25); Ankara (10hr., 2 per day, US$17.50); and İstanbul (11hr., 2 per day, US$20). Buy **ferry** tickets from **Ertürk Tourism and Travel Agency,** 6/7 Beyazıt Cad., next to the *kervansaray*. (☎712 67 68. Open daily in summer 8am-9:30pm; in winter 8am-6:30pm.) From the main gate of the *otogar*, follow Turgutozal Cad. down to the sea, turn right, and walk 300m to the main square in front of the castle. The **tourist office,** 8 İskele Meydanı, is across from the castle and *kervansaray*, by numerous budget accommodations. (☎/fax 712 66 53. Open in summer M-F 8:30am-7pm, Sa-Su 9am-5pm; in winter M-F 8am-5pm.) **Tarhan Pension,** 9 Çarşı Sok., Musalla Mah., near the *kervansaray* (turn left after the "No Problem" cafe), is clean and cozy. (☎712 65 99. Breakfast included. Kitchen. Laundry. Singles US$8; doubles US$16; triples US$24.) Walking away from the sea, turn onto Mektep Sok a block beyond İnkılap Cad. and then right again onto Dellal Sok.; the refreshingly clean **Filiz Pension** is at #16. (☎712 67 94. US$8 per person.) **Postal code:** 35930.

KUŞADASI ☎256

Kuşadası's picturesque setting on sea-sloping hills, its excellent sand beaches, and its proximity to archaeological wonders have ensured the town's place as a grand resort. While Kuşadası is swamped with tourists of all kinds, it has managed to retain its charm. The goodies for sale at the **Grand Bazaar** and **Barbaros Hayrettin Paşa Bul.** are, contrary to the claims of shop owners, expensive, but it's free to browse. Crowded but clean **beaches,** including Ladies Beach (Kadınlar Plajı), are just a *dolmuş* ride away. **Dilek National Park,** a nature reserve 26km away, is fantastic for swimming, walking, and picnicking. (Open daily in high season 8am-8pm; off season 8am-5pm. US$1.20 per person; US$8 per car.) No trip would be complete without seeing **Pigeon Island** (Güvercinada), the peninsula covered with Kuşadası's namesake bird. (10min. walk from the tourist office with the sea on your right.)

Buses leave from Kahramanlar Sok., about 2km from the town center. Pamukkale buses (☎612 09 38) go to: İzmir (1½hr., every 20min., US$4); Bodrum (2½hr., 2 per day, US$9); Pamukkale (3½hr., 1 per day, US$9); Marmaris (4hr., 1 per day, US$11.50); Fethiye (5½hr., 1 per day, US$13); Ankara (9hr., 3 per day, US$21); and İstanbul (9hr., 6 per day, US$22.75). City **dolmuş** run from the lot next to the bus station to Selçuk (30min., every 20min., US$1.20) via Ephesus (ask to be let off). The **tourist office,** 13 Liman Cad., is at Güvercin Ada Sok., in the port area. (☎614 11 03. Open May-Oct. daily 8am-5:30pm; Nov.-Apr. M-F 8am-5:30pm.) **Ekol Travel** with **WorldSpan,** Kıbrıs Cad., 9/1 Buyral Sok, sells ferry tickets; you get 15% off with *Let's Go*. (☎614 92 55. Open daily May-Nov. 8:30am-10pm; Dec.-Apr. 8:30am-5:30pm.) From the harbor, turn right onto Urğulu Sokak to get to the lovely **Golden Bed Pansiyon,** 4 Arslanlar Cad, off Yıldırım Cad. (☎/fax 614 87 08. Free transport to and from the station and Ephesus. Breakfast included. Laundry. US$5-6.) The fabulous **Hotel Sammy's Palace,** 14 Kıbrıs Cad., will pay for your cab fare from the bus station and transport to and from Ephesus. It's ideal for social backpackers. (☎612 25 88; cell ☎ (532) 274 21 29. Laundry. Internet. Roof US$2.50; dorms US$5; singles US$11.50; doubles US$16. 10% off with *Let's Go*.) **Camp** at **Önder,** 2km north of town on Atatürk Bul. (☎618 15 90. US$5 per person; US$1 per tent.) Walking away from the sea, turn left at Yapı Kredi and take the first right to **Yuvam Ev Yemekleri ve Mantı Evi,** Camikebir Mah., 7 Kaleiçi, behind the post office. (Homemade *mantı* available Th US$2. Open daily 8am-10pm.) The nighttime havoc of the aptly-named **Barlar Sokak** (Bars Street) spills out onto the roads. **Postal code:** 09400.

SELÇUK ☎232

Selçuk is the most convenient base for exploring Ephesus, and also offers several notable archaeological sites of its own. The colossal **Basilica of Saint John** lies off Atatürk Cad. on the supposed site of St. John's grave. (Open daily 8am-6:30pm. US$2.50.) A few hundred meters down Dr. Sabri Yayla Bulvarı, walking away from town with the tourist office on your right, are the sad remains of the **Temple of Artemis,** one of the **seven wonders of the ancient world.** (Open 8:30am-5:30pm. Free.) The stunning 14th-century **İsa Bey Camii** is at the foot of the hill on which the Basilica of St. John and the Ayasoluk castle stand. (Open 10min. before and after prayer times.) The **Ephesus Museum** (Efes Müzesi), directly across from the tourist office, houses a world-class collection of recent finds from Ephesus. (Open daily 8:30am-noon and 1-5:30pm. US$5.) **Trains** go to İzmir (1½hr., 7 per day, US$1.20). **Buses** run from the *otogar*, at the corner of Şabahattın Dede Cad. and Atatürk Cad., to: İzmir (1hr., every 20min., US$3.25); Bodrum (3hr., every hr., US$9); Marmaris (4hr., every 2hr., US$8); Fethiye (6hr., every 2hr., US$12); Ankara (9hr., 1 per day, US$18); and İstanbul (10hr., 3-7 per day, US$19.50). **Minibuses** run to Kuşadası (20min., every 20min., US$1.20). Beware the infamous bus station hawkers. The **tourist office,** 35 Agora Çarşısı, Atatürk Mah., is on the southwest corner of Sabahattındede and Atatürk Cad. (☎892 63 28. Open Apr.-Dec. M-F 8:30am-noon and 1-5:30pm, Sa-Su 9am-5pm; Jan.-Mar. M-F 8:30am-noon and 1-5:30pm.) Guests at the **Artemis Guest House,** Atatürk Mah., 1012 Sok. 2, are greeted with a refreshing drink and shown to their carpeted rooms. (☎892 61 91; email jimmy@egenet.com.tr. Internet. Laundry. US$5.) The **All Blacks Hotel and Pension,** offers free transport to Ephesus. (☎892 36 57; email abnomads@egenet.com.tr. Internet. Singles US$6; doubles US$12; triples US$18. Room prices negotiable.) **Australian New Zealand Pension,** 7 Prof. Miltner Sok., behind the museum, offers free rides to Ephesus, the beach, and other sites. (☎892 60 50. Laundry. Dorms US$3; rooms US$5-6.50. With *Let's Go* 15% off.)

EXCURSION FROM SELÇUK: EPHESUS (EFES). Ephesus has a concentration of Classical art and architecture surpassed only by Rome and Athens; the ruins rank first among Turkey's ancient sites in terms of sheer size and state of preservation. Guided tours are not necessary. On the left of the road to the lower entrance is the **Vedius Gymnasium,** built in AD 150; beyond the vegetation are the horseshoe-shaped remains of the city's **stadium.** Just inside the lower entrance, a dirt path leads to the right to the ruins of the **Church of the Seven Councils.** After the Ecumenical Council met here in AD 431 to iron out the Nestorian Heresy, which called the Virgin Mary's divinity into question, the church became known as the **Church of the Virgin Mary.** A tree-lined path leads from the main entrance to the **Arcadiane,** Ephesus's main drag. **The Grand Theater** is a stunning, restored beast carved into the side of Mt. Pion. From the theater, walk along **Marble Way,** which has a metal inscription thought to be the world's first advertisement—it's for a brothel. The slight incline signals the beginning of the **Street of Curetes,** which leads to the **Library of Celsus,** the brothel, the 5th-century **Baths of Scholastica,** and the ruins of the **Temple of Hadrian.** Further up the hill on the left are the ruins of the exquisite **Fountain of Trajan.** The building on the left as you walk up the ramp is the **Prytaneion,** which was dedicated to the worship of **Vesta** and contained an eternal flame tended by the **Vestal Virgins.** The road that runs by the top entrance leads to the **House of the Virgin Mary** (8km, 1-1½hr. on foot), where Mary lived after leaving Jerusalem. (☎892 64 02. Site open 8am-6pm. US$6.50.) The easiest way to get to Ephesus from **Kuşadası** or **Selçuk** is to take hotels' free shuttle service. Or, from the Kuşadası *otogar*, take a **dolmuş** to Selçuk and ask to stop at Ephesus (30min., US$1). From the Selçuk *otogar*, take a Pamucak-bound *dolmuş* (5min., every 30min.-1hr., US$0.50). **Taxis** run from Selçuk to the site (US$4). It's also an easy **walk** from Selçuk (25min.).

PAMUKKALE ☎258

Pamukkale ("Cotton Castle"), formerly ancient Hierapolis (Holy City), has been drawing the weary and the curious to its thermal springs for more than 23 centuries. A favorite getaway spot for vacationing Romans almost two millennia ago, the warm **baths** at Pamukkale still bubble away. (Open 24hr. US$5.50.) Don't leave town without a dip in the warm fizzy waters of the **sacred fountain** at the Pamukkale Motel. (☎272 20 24. Pool open daily 8am-8pm. US$5 per 2hr.) Behind the Pamukkale Motel, the enormous and well-preserved **Grand Theater** dominates the **ruins of Hierapolis.** The former city bath has been converted into a spectacular **Archaeological Museum** housing finds unearthed by Italian archaeologists. (Open Tu-Su 8am-5pm. US$1.60.) **Buses** to Pamukkale stop in the center of Pamukkale Köyü; some direct buses arrive from Kuşadası and pass through Selçuk (3½hr., 3 per day, US$5), but the usual route is through Denizli, where buses arrive from: İzmir (4hr., 30 per day, US$6.50); Marmaris (4hr., 9 per day, US$6.50); Bodrum (5hr., 5 per day, US$8); Kuşadası (4hr., direct 11am and 5pm; or, take a bus to Selçuk, US$3.25, then take a *dolmuş*); and İstanbul (10hr., 7 per day, US$16). *Dolmuş* go between Denizli and Pamukkale (30min., every 30min.-1hr., US$0.75). Many accommodations, including those listed here, offer free **pick-up** from Denizli. The **tourist office** is at the top of the hill, within the site gates. (☎272 20 77; fax 272 28 82. Open May 15-Sept. 15 daily 8am-noon and 1:30-6:45pm; in winter M-F 8am-noon and 1-5pm.) The **Koray Hotel,** 27 Fevzi Çakmak Cad., has a beautiful courtyard adorned with grapevines. (☎272 23 00; fax 272 20 95. Singles US$12; doubles US$18. Cheaper in winter.) Just outside Cumhuriyet Meydanı, the backpacker-friendly **Meltem Motel** is at 9 Kuzey Sok. (☎272 24 13; email meltenmotel@superonline.com.tr. US$5 per person. Dorms US$4.) Both hotels have swimming pools with local thermal water.

EXCURSION FROM PAMUKKALE: APHRODISIAS. Still under excavation, the **ruins of Aphrodisias** are expected to eclipse Ephesus in grandeur. The highlights include the soaring Ionic columns of the **Temple of Aphrodite,** an ancient 30,000-seat **stadium**, one of the best-preserved stadiums ever excavated, and a new and well-funded **museum** near the site entrance that features a fabulous collection of Roman-era sculpture. (In summer, site and museum open daily 9am-6:30pm; in winter 8am-5:30pm. Site US$4, museum US$4.) Make the ruins a daytrip from Pamukkale; **buses** leave daily at 9:30am and depart Aphrodisias at 2:30pm (2hr., round-trip US$10). Many hotels make additional trips if they have enough interested guests.

BODRUM ☎252

Bodrum's nightlife is notorious, its beaches divine, and its ruins impressive. Before it became the "Bedroom of the Mediterranean," the ancient city of **Halicarnassus** was known for **Herodotus,** the "father of history," and for the 4th-century BC funerary monument to King Mausolus, so magnificent that its **mausoleum** (where we get the word) was declared one of the **seven wonders of the ancient world.** Unfortunately, most of the remains were destroyed, buried beneath modern Bodrum, or shipped to London's British Museum. To reach the mausoleum, turn onto Kirkateyn Sok. from Neyzen Tevfik Cad. (Open in summer Tu-Su 8am-noon and 1-5:30pm; off season Tu-Su 8am-noon and 1-5pm. US$2, students US$1.) Bodrum's formidable **castle,** built over the ruins of an ancient acropolis by crusaders from the Knights of St. John, now features a flock of peacocks, exhibits, the remains of a 4th-century BC Carian Princess, and the **Museum of Underwater Archaeology,** home of the oldest shipwreck ever discovered. (Open Tu-Su 8am-noon and 1-5pm. US$5, students US$2.50.) Visit **Ali Güven's shop,** Çarşı Mah., Kosophan Sok., off Cumhuriyet Cad., about two blocks from the harbor; Ali's famous sandals may be out of your league (US$150-200), but you can watch him craft shoes for the likes of Bette Midler and Mick Jagger. The opulent **Halikarnas Disco,** on Z. Müren Cad., at the end of Cumhuriyet Cad., flashes strobes 1km from the center of town. (Cover US$18. Beer US$3.) The club **Hadi Gari,** Cumhuriyet Cad., by the castle, fuses elegance and funk. (Open midnight-4am.) Nightlife abounds on **Cumhuriyet Cad.;** start shaking that tush.

From the *otogar* on Cevat Şakir Cad., Pamukkale **buses** (☎316 13 69 or 316 30 76) go to: Kuşadası (2½hr., every hr., US$6); Marmaris (3hr., every hr., US$5); İzmir (4hr., every hr., US$7); Pamukkale (5hr., 3 per day, US$7); Fethiye (5hr., 4 per day, US$7); Bursa (10hr., 3 per day, US$13); Ankara (11hr., 2 per day, US$14.50); and İstanbul (12hr., 3 per day, US$19). **Dolmuş** go from the *otogar* to Marmaris (3hr., every hr., US$6). **Turkish Airlines** (☎313 31 72) flies to İstanbul and Ankara (1hr., 4 per day, US$90). **Bodrum Express Lines** (☎316 40 67; fax 313 00 77) has offices in the *otogar* and past the castle on the right toward the sea. For info on **ferries** to Greece, see p. 958. The **tourist office,** 48 Barış Meydanı, at the foot of the castle, has room listings. (☎316 10 91; fax 316 76 94. Open Apr.-Oct. daily 8:30am-5:30pm; Nov.-Mar. M-F 8am-noon and 1-5pm.) To get from the *otogar* to the peaceful **Emiko Pansiyon,** Atatürk Cad., 11 Uslu Sok., follow Cevat Şakir Cad. toward the castle, turn left on Atatürk Cad., and turn right after 50m down the sign-covered alley, including one for Emiko Pansiyon. (☎/fax 316 55 60. Breakfast US$2. Kitchen. Laundry. Singles US$15; doubles US$20.) **Otel Kilavuz,** 50 Atatürk Cad., boasts a pool and bar. (☎316 38 92; fax 316 2852. Singles US$12; doubles US$16.) Turn onto Atatürk Cad. from Cevat Şakir Cad. and turn left into the second alleyway for **Tarçin's** tasty home-made meals. (Meals US$4-9. Open M-F 8am-6pm.) **Postal code:** 48400.

EXCURSIONS FROM BODRUM: BODRUM PENINSULA. Bodrum's popularity among Turks stems largely from its location at the head of the **Bodrum Peninsula,** where traditional villages mingle with coastal vistas and dramatic crags. Explore the peninsula's greener northern coast or its drier, sandier southern coastline. Tour **boats** bound for **beaches** on the peninsula's southern coast skirt the front of the castle (depart daily 9-11am, return 5-6pm; US$12 including lunch). Check the tour schedule at the dock. Popular destinations include **Kara Ada** (Black Island), where orange clay from deep within a cave reputedly restores youthful beauty (US$0.60), and **Deveplajı** (Camel Beach), where the beach's namesakes offer rides (US$4 per 10min.). The peninsula's northern end, calmer than the southern coast, has rocky beaches and deep water. **Dolmuş** depart frequently from Bodrum's *otogar* for the quiet shores, swimming docks, and clear water of **Gölköy** and **Türkbükü** (30min., US$1); the sand paradise of **Yahşi,** Bodrum's longest beach (30min., every 15min., US$1); the peaceful shore of **Bağla** (40min., every 30min., US$1); and the sunken ruins of **Mindos,** near **Gümüşlük's** beach (40min., US$1.40).

MEDITERRANEAN COAST

At turns chic, garish, and remote, the Mediterranean coast stretches along lush national parks, sun-soaked beaches, and shady pine forests. By day, travelers take tranquil boat trips, hike among waterfalls, and explore submerged ruins; by night, they visit Ephesus, dance under the stars, and sleep in treehouses.

 FERRIES TO GREECE

From **Marmaris, catamarans** (1hr.; May-Oct. 1 per day, Nov.-Apr. 2 per week; round-trip US$35); **hydrofoils** (1hr., May-Oct. 2 per day, US$40-60); and **ferries** (1½hr.; when there are enough cars, round-trip US$25 plus taxes) all go to **Rhodes.** Make reservations the day before at a travel agency; try **Yeşil Marmaris** (☎ (252) 412 64 86).

MARMARİS ☎252

Marmaris contains all the beach town necessities: eclectic tourist shops, seaside restaurants, beautiful wooden yachts, a boisterous beachfront, and decadent night-time festivities. Boats set off from the natural harbor for spectacular nearby coves, where pine-blanketed cliffs reach down into the clear water and toward the Greek island of Rhodes (ask at the Interyouth Hostel about excursions). To get from the tourist office to the 16th-century **castle,** take the street to the right, turn left into the bazaar, go right down the alley after the Sultan Restaurant, and climb to the top of the stairs. A lush garden complete with peacocks and turtles fills the inner courtyard, while the paths along the ramparts offer panoramic views of the Marmaris harbor. (Open Tu-Su 8:30am-noon and 2-5:30pm. US$1.20, students US$0.60.) It's hard to tell which is hotter in Marmaris: the burning sun or the blazing nightlife. Head to bars behind the tourist office on **Barlar Sok.** (a.k.a. **Bar St.**). **Buses** (☎412 30 37) go from Mustafa Münir Elgin Bul. to: Bodrum (3¾hr., every hr., US$4); İzmir (4½hr., every hr., US$9); Pamukkale (4½hr, every hr., US$6); Kuşadası (5hr., June 15-Sept. 15 1 per day, US$9); Ankara (11hr., 3 per day, US$25); İstanbul (12½hr., 3 per day, US$20-23); and Göreme (14hr., 1 per day, US$16). From the bus station, out of town on Mustafa Münir Elgin Bul., take a *dolmuş* (US$0.40) or taxi (US$3) to the central Ulusal Egemenlik Bul., which hosts the Tansaş Shopping Center and the *dolmuş* hub. The **tourist office** is 250m along Kordon Cad. (☎412 72 77. Open in summer daily 9am-6pm; in winter M-F 8am-5:30pm.) The **Interyouth Hostel,** Tepe Mah., 42 Sok. No. 45, is deep in the bazaar; from the Atatürk statue, take the first left. Turn right inside the bazaar and the youth hostel is on the right. (☎412 36 87; email interyouth@turk.net. Breakfast and dinner included. Laundry. Internet. Dorms US$5; rooms US$13; with ISIC, HI, or IYTC card US$1 off.) **Postal code:** 48700.

DALYAN AND KAUNOS (CAUNOS) ☎252

The placid village of Dalyan seems to have grown out of the nearby breezy river. Carian **rock tombs** built into cliffs are visible from the harbor, and thick reed beds teem with wildlife just a few minutes away. Dalyan's sites are best seen on **boat tours** that visit the ruins of ancient **Kaunos** (☎284 28 45; open in summer 8am-7pm; in winter 9am-5pm; US$1.80, students free); **İztuzu Beach,** where endangered loggerhead turtles lay their eggs by night (open 8am-8pm; beach chair rental US$4); and local **mud baths** and **thermal springs** (open 7am-7:30pm; US$0.80). **Boat tour** offices are behind the **turtle statue** in town (tours US$12 including lunch). The *dolmuş* from Ortaca stops in front of the mosque. Facing the PTT, turn left, follow the road right, and go straight. The area with the turtle statue and mosque is directly ahead. Facing the river, walk left along Maraş Sok. to find plenty of *pansiyons*, restaurants, and a few bars. City **buses** go to Ortaca (20min., every 15min., US$0.40), where you can get a bus headed to Fethiye (1¼hr., US$2.40) and Marmaris (1½hr., US$2.40). A new *dolmus* line runs directly to Marmaris and Fethiye (3 per day, US$1.80). With your back to the turtle statue, head into the passageway across Maraş Sok. to reach the **tourist office.** (☎284 42 35. Open daily in summer 8:30am-noon and 1-6pm; in winter 8:30am-noon and 1-5:30pm.) From the turtle statue, walk 75m down Maraş Sok., make the second left on 10 Sok., and walk a block to find **Gül Motel Pension.** (☎284 24 67. Singles US$6; doubles US$12.) **Postal code:** 48840.

FETHIYE ☎252

Fethiye, on a harbor ringed by pine forests and mountains, is a peaceful base on the backpacker circuit. The marvelous pebble **beach** and **Blue Lagoon** in **Ölüdeniz**—a peninsula of beach cradled in wooded hills and lapped by clear water—are an easy trip. Enter from Tabiat Park, on the right of the road. From the *dolmuş* station, it's a 20-minute walk or a US$6 taxi ride to the tip. (Park and lagoon open 6:30am-9pm. US$1.20.) Take a **boat** from the beach in Ölüdeniz (45min., 3 per day, US$3) to reach the tiny, beautiful bay of **Butterfly Valley,** home to waterfalls and the nocturnal orange-and-black Jersey Tiger butterfly. Paths marked by blue dots wind their way up to two waterfalls (US$1, students US$0.50). To reach Ölüdeniz from Fethiye, take a **dolmuş** from the stop near the intersection of Hastane and Atatürk Cad. (20-25min., every 10min., round-trip US$3). In Fethiye, **Fetur,** 50m past the tourist office on Fevzi Çakmak Cad., arranges daily tours. (☎614 20 34. Open daily 9am-5:30pm.) But come back to enjoy Fethiye's colorful bazaar, and nightlife.

Buses run frequently from Fethiye's *otogar* on Ölüdeniz Cad. Coastal road buses can drop off passengers anywhere, so there's no need to wait for a specific bus. If there are no *servis* shuttles to the center, take a *dolmuş* to the PTT in town (every 5min., US $0.40). From there, walk down Atatürk Cad. to the **tourist office,** 1/A İskele Meydanı. (☎/fax 614 15 27. Open daily 8:30am-5pm; in winter M-F 8am-5pm.) Call for free pickup from the *otogar* to the utterly fantastic **Ferah Pansiyon 2,** Karagözler Ordu Cad. No. 21. (☎/fax 614 28 16. Breakfast included. Delicious dinner US$5. Laundry. Dorms US$3.60; US$10 per room.) **Postal code:** 48300.

KAŞ ☎242

Sandwiched between sea and mountains, cosmopolitan Kaş is refreshingly hassle-free. Its pleasant streets are lined with cheap, hospitable lodgings, excellent restaurants, and laid-back bars. A peninsula curving around one side of the town's harbor creates a calm, rock-lined lagoon ideal for swimming in the cool turquoise water. The city also serves as a gateway to the backpacker haven of Olimpos (see below). The *otogar*, uphill on Atatürk Cad., sends buses to Fethiye (2hr., 6 per day, US$3.60); Antalya (3hr., every 30min., US$5.40); İzmir (9hr., 4 per day, US$16); Ankara (11hr., 2 per day, US$19); and İstanbul (15hr., 4 per day, US$24). The **tourist office,** 5 Cumhuriyet Meydanı, is to the left as you face the back of the Atatürk statue. (☎836 12 38; fax 836 16 95. Open daily in summer 8am-noon and 1-7pm; in winter M-F 8am-5pm.) Budget **pansiyons** line the sidestreets to the right of Atatürk Bul. (as you head from the *otogar* to the waterfront). Airy rooms, all with large bath, tile floors, and balcony await at **Hermes Pension,** 2 Imdi Cad. (☎836 32 22. Breakfast US$2.50. Singles US$9; doubles US$12; triples US$16.) **Postal code:** 07580.

OLIMPOS ☎242

Olimpos awes visitors with its scenery. Tall cliffs streaked mauve, red, and gray tower above acres of pine forest and orange orchards. **Roman and Byzantine ruins** lie hidden among the vines of a marshy jungle. Wander through to discover ancient temples and the crumbling walls of medieval castles. A pebble beach awaits at the end of the road. (Ruins and beach US$2.80, students US$1.85. Hold on to your ticket stub.) The town's other main attraction is **Chimæra,** the perpetual flame springing from the mountainside 7km away. Mythology explains the flame as the breath of the Chimæra, a mythical beast; geologists suggest natural methane gas. **Bus tours** leave Olimpos at 9:30pm (2½hr., US$2.80); ask at any hostel for details. To get to Olimpos from Kaş, take an Antalya-bound **bus.** Buses stop at a rest station on the main road. From there, *dolmuş* run to the tree-house-*pansiyons* (15min., every hr., US$1.15), dropping passengers off at the place of their choice. As Olimpos is classified as an archaeological site, the use of concrete is banned, so resourceful locals have constructed **treehouse pansiyons,** which line the dirt road to the beach and ruins. **Şaban Pansiyon** is relaxed and welcoming, with 21 treehouses. (☎892 12 65. Breakfast and excellent dinner included. Treehouses US$7 per person; bungalows US$10 per person; rooms US$13 per person.) **Postal code:** 07350.

ANTALYA ☎242

Capital of the so-called Turquoise Riviera, Antalya has a dual persona. Concrete block buildings of contemporary Antalya encircle *Kaleiçi* ("inside the fortress"), the crescent-shaped old city that brims with Ottoman houses, pensions, and restaurants. **The Antalya Museum,** 2 Konyaatı Bul., 2.5km from town, won the 1988 European Museum of the Year Award for its exhibits ranging from prehistoric times to the founding of the Turkish Republic. *Dolmuş* labeled "Konyaaltı/Liman" head along Cumhuriyet Bul., which changes its name to Konyaaltı Bul., stopping at the large "D" signs (US$0.30). Get off at the yellow museum signs before heading downhill to the beach. The tram (US$0.25) also runs from Kaleiçi to the museum. (Open Tu-Su in summer 9am-6pm; in winter 8am-5pm. US$6, students US$4.50.) **Lara** and **Konyaaltı** beach are both accessible by *dolmuş* (to Lara from the Doğu Garaj, to Konyaaltı from Konyaaltı Bul.; US$0.30). Every fall, the huge **Antalya Altın Portakal** ("Golden Orange") Film Festival features international and Turkish cinema.

Planes fly from Antalya International Airport (domestic flights ☎330 30 30, international flights ☎330 36 00), 15km outside of town, to İstanbul (US$61, students US$51) and various foreign cities. Buses run between the Turkish Airlines THY office, next to the tourist office, and Antalya Airport in summer (10 per day, US$3). **Buses** leave from the orange *otogar*, 4km out of town at Anadolu Kavşağı, for: Olimpos (1¼hr., every 20min., US$1.50); Kaş (3hr., every 30min., US$4); Bodrum (8hr., US$15); Göreme (10hr., 2 per day, US$16); and İstanbul (12hr., US$17). Gray buses (US$0.40) run from outside the *otogar* to the city center, near Kaleiçi. The **tourist office,** on Cumhuriyet Cad., is to the left of the red fluted minaret and past the military complex. (☎241 17 47. Open M-F 8am-7pm, Sa-Su 9am-7pm; in winter M-F 8am-5pm, Sa-Su 10am-5pm.) Virtually all of the 200 pensions and hotels within the ancient walls of Kaleiçi include private shower and breakfast in their prices. **La Paloma Pansiyon,** Kılıçarslan Mah., 60 Hesapçı Sok., offers gorgeous rooms. (☎244 79 24. Singles US$20; doubles US$35.) Backpackers hang out at **Sabah Pansiyon,** Kaleiçi Kılıçarslan Mah., 60 Hesapçı Sok. (☎247 53 45. Singles US$6; doubles US$8-18; roof, couch, or floor US$3; camping US$2.50-3.) **Postal code:** 07000.

CENTRAL TURKEY

While the Aegean and Mediterranean coasts suffer from rampant tourism, Central Turkey hosts some of the country's most authentic and hospitable towns—from sophisticated Ankara to the surreal underground cities of Cappadocia.

ANKARA ☎312

Rising from the Anatolian plains, Ankara is unquestionably the seat of the Turkish Republic. In 1923, after the Turkish War of Independence, Atatürk planned and built this city overnight. Today, Ankara is an administrative metropolis as well as the nation's premier college town, which contributes to a vibrant nightlife.

PRACTICAL INFO, ACCOMMODATIONS, AND FOOD. Trains arrive from the *otogar*, 1.5km southwest of Ulus Square on the end of Cumhuriyet Bul., from İstanbul (6½-9½hr., 7 per day, US$4-35) and İzmir (15hr., 3 per day, US$9). To get to the city center, follow the covered tunnel past the last platform into the "Maltepe" station of the east-west **Ankaray subway,** which stops in Kızılay and Ulus (5-ride pass US$2.50, students US$1.50). The Ankaray also connects to the **bus terminal** (AŞTİ or *otogar*), 5km west in Söğütözü, from which buses depart frequently for: İstanbul (5½hr., 150 per day, US$15); İzmir (8hr., 65 per day, US$13); Marmaris (10hr., 6 per day, US$15); and Bodrum (12hr., 11 per day, US$16.50). The English-speaking **tourist office,** 121 Gazi Mustafa Kemal Bul., is directly outside the "Maltepe" Ankaray station. (☎231 55 72. Open daily 9am-5pm.) **Embassies** in Ankara include: **Australia,** 83 Nenehatun Cad., Gaziomanpaşa (☎446 11 80); **Canada,** 75 Nenehatun Cad. (☎436 12 75); **New Zealand,** 13/4 İran Cad., Kavaklıdere (☎467 90 56); **Northern Cyprus,** 20 Rabat Sok., Gaziosmanpaşa (☎446 29 20); **South Africa,** 27 Filistin Sok., Gaziomanpaşa (☎446 40 56); **UK,** 46A Şehit Ersan Cad., Çankaya (☎468 62 30); and **US,** 110 Atatürk Bul. (☎468 61 10). Check **email** at the **Internet Center Café,** 107 Atatürk Bul. (US$1.25 per hr. Open daily 9am-11pm.)

Of the two main accommodations centers, **Ulus** is cheaper, but student-oriented **Kızılay** is safer and cleaner. Head south on Atatürk Bul., take the fourth left after the McDonald's on Meşrutiyet Cad., and take the third right on Selânik Cad. to reach the peaceful **Otel Ertan,** 70 Selânik Cad, in Kızılay. (☎418 40 84. Singles US$15.50; doubles US$24.50.) To get to the **M.E.B. Özel Çağdaş Erkek Öğrenci Yurdu,** 15 Neyzen Tevfik Sok., Maltepe, from the Demirtepe Ankaray stop, walk 100m along Gazi Mustafa Kemal Bul. with the mosque to your right, take the stairs down just past the mosque, and walk up on Neyzen Tevfik Sok.; it's on the left. (☎232 29 54. July-Aug. co-ed; rest of year male students only. Singles US$10; doubles US$20.) In Ulus, no one beats the quality and prices at **Otel Zümrüt,** Şehit Teğmen Kalmaz Cad., No. 16. From the equestrian statue, go south on Atatürk Bul. and take the second left. (☎309 15 54. Singles US$7-10.50; doubles US$12-17; triples US$17-21.) **Otel Hisar,** Hisarparkı Cad., No. 6, is east of the statue, toward the citadel. (☎311 98 89. Singles US$6.50; doubles US$11.) The main culinary neighborhoods are **Kızılay, Ulus' Gençlik Park,** and the more posh **Hisar** and **Kavaklıdere.** In Kızılay, **Göksu Restaurant,** 22A Bayındur Sok., has classy Turkish and European food at the right price. (Open noon-midnight.) In Ulus, **Uludağ Et Lokantası,** Denizciler Cad., No. 54, is possibly the tastiest restaurant in Ankara. (Özel Uludağ kebab US$3.50.) Gima **supermarkets** are on Anafartalar Cad. in Ulus and Atatürk Bul. in Kızılay. **Postal code:** 06443.

SIGHTS AND ENTERTAINMENT. The fantastic **Museum of Anatolian Civilizations** (Anadolu Medeniyetleri Müzesi) lies at the foot of the citadel looming over the old town. The museum is in a restored 15th-century Ottoman *han* (inn) and *bedesten* (covered bazaar) and features a world-class collection of artifacts. From the equestrian statue in Ulus, walk east to the top of Hisarparkı Cad., turn right at the bottom of the Citadel steps, and follow the Citadel boundaries. (Open Tu-Su 8:30am-5:30pm. US$3, students US$2.) Don't miss **Atatürk's mausoleum, Anıt Kabir;** nearly 1km long, it houses Atatürk's sarcophagus and personal effects. Take the subway to "Tandoğan" and follow the signs; when you reach the unmarked entrance guarded by two soldiers, head 10 minutes uphill. (Open M 1:30-5pm, Tu-Su 9am-5pm. Free.) The immense **Kocatepe Mosque** looms east of Kızılay on Mithat Paşa Cad. Take the subway to "Kızılay" then walk along Ziya Gökalp Cad. until you hit Mithat Paşa Cad (10min.). Completed in 1987, it's billed as a 16th-century mosque utilizing 20th-century technology, like glowing digital clocks that indicate prayer times. At night, dig the live music in the bars of **Kızılay;** pub life centers on **İnkilâp Sok.** and the livelier **Bayındır Sok.,** to the left of Kızılay. The **S.S.K. İşhanı,** on the corner of Ziya Gökalp Cad. and Selânik Cad., is packed with live music bars.

CAPPADOCIA

Cappadocia's unique landscape began to take shape 10 million years ago, when volcanic lava and ash hardened into a layer of soft rock called tufa. Rain, wind, and flooding from the Kızılırmak River shaped the tufa into striking, cone-shaped monoliths called *peribaca* ("fairy chimneys"), grouped in cave-riddled valleys and along gorge ridges. Throughout Cappadocia, otherworldly moonscapes, stairs, windows, and sentry holes have been carved into the already eerily-eroded rock.

NEVŞEHIR ☎384

Nevşehir is the region's transport hub and not much else. Even when tickets appear to be direct to Göreme or Ürgüp, you are probably getting a *servis* shuttle to Nevşehir and then a regular bus from there. **Dolmuş** leave frequently from outside the tourist office for Göreme and Ürgüp (US$0.75). They stop at the *otogar* (bus station) on their way out of town. **Buses** run to: Ankara (4hr., 11 per day, US$7.50); Bursa (9hr., 1 per day, US$13.75); İstanbul (10hr., 5 per day, US$15); İzmir (12hr., 2 per day, US$15); and Bodrum (14hr., 1 per day, US$18.75). From the main bus station, Lale Cad. runs uphill on your right toward the city center. From Lale Cad., outside the Göreme and Nevşehir ticket agencies, turn left at the intersection and you will see the multilingual **tourist office,** 14 Yeni Kayseri Cad. (☎213 36 59. Open Apr.-

Nov. M-F 8am-5:30pm, Sa-Su 9:30am-5pm; Nov.-Mar. M-F 8am-5pm.) If you have to spend the night, **Otel Nisa,** 35 Yeni Kayseri Cad, has sweet balcony views. (☎213 58 43. Breakfast included. Singles US$8; doubles US$15; triples US$18.)

GÖREME ☎384

Göreme brims with fairy chimneys, cave-houses, friendly locals, and happy backpackers. The city goes all out with its cave theme—most bars and discos are subterranean, and *pansiyons* often have "cave" rooms.

PRACTICAL INFO, ACCOMMODATIONS, AND FOOD. **Buses** go via Nevşehir to: Ankara (4hr., 14 per day, US$8); Bursa (10hr., 2 per day, US$16); Pamukkale (10hr., 4 per day, US$14); İstanbul (11hr., 8 per day, US$16); İzmir (11hr., 3 per day, US$16); Olimpos (12hr., 4 per day, US$19); Marmaris (14hr., 5 per day, US$20); and Bodrum (14hr., 3 per day, US$20). The **bus station,** in the center of town, contains the town's only official **tourist office** (☎271 25 58), which just has lodgings info. As you exit the station, the main road is directly in front of you. The city government has set prices for non-dorm rooms in the town's **hostels:** US$5 per person, US$7 with bathroom; singles run up to US$10. However, starred **hotels** can charge higher rates. The friendly **Köse Pansiyon**, a renowned backpacker haven, is behind the PTT, on the main road just past the turn-off for the Open-Air Museum. (☎271 22 94. Dorms US$4.) Lounge in one of the cave rooms in **Peri Pansiyon,** on the right side walking east on the road to the Open-Air Museum. Get some sunlight during breakfast in the floral courtyard. (☎271 21 36. Singles US$7-10; doubles US$20; cave singles US$10; luxury caves US$25.) The view from the **Kookaburra Pansiyon** (☎271 25 49), behind the bus terminal, is fantastic. Drop your pack at the trendy, new **Panoramic Pension** (☎271 20 40), past the mosque and up the hill in front of the *otogar*. The excellent **Paradise Pansiyon** is on the road to the Open-Air Museum. (☎/fax 271 22 48. Laundry. US$6.) **Göreme Dilek Camping,** across from Peri Pansiyon, is a vast campsite and pool snuggled among phallic rocks. (☎271 23 96. US$3 per person in tent; US$10 per caravan; US$8 tent rental; US$4.50 per site.) **Cafe Doci@,** to the left as you exit the *otogar*, has mammoth burgers (US$3) and Internet. Across the street, **Orient** charms its clientele with *sac tava* (US$4). **Postal code:** 50180.

SIGHTS AND HIKING. One of Cappadocia's biggest draws is its **Open-Air Museum,** 2km out of Göreme on the Ürgüp road, which contains seven Byzantine churches, a convent, and a kitchen/refectory. In the 4th century, St. Basil founded one of the first Christian monasteries here, setting down religious tenets that influenced the entire Western monastic movement. The churches are laden with frescoes; spectacular scenes from Jesus' life lie within the **Karanlık Kilise** (Dark Church). Walk 100m from the bus station in Göreme and take a right at the first major intersection. (Open 8am-5pm. Museum US$5.25; Dark Church US$10.)

Cappadocia's breathtaking landscape is a **hiking** heaven. From Göreme's Museum Way, you can descend into **Kirmizi Vadi** (Rose Valley), where bizarre, multi-colored rock formations make for one of the area's better hikes. Although rewarding, the 10km valley can be confusing. There are exits at 3km and 7km, for those who wish to arrange return transportation. You'll end up in Çavuşin, where you can take the Avanos-Nevşehir **bus** or the Avanos-Zelve-Göreme-Ürgüp **minibus** back to Göreme (M-F every 30min. until 6pm, Sa-Su every hr.) or take a **taxi** (US$5). Other notable hikes include the more challenging **Pigeon Valley** or amusing **Love Valley (a.k.a "Penis Valley")** named after its massive, phallic rock formations. Although most area hikes are moderate and safe, hiking with partners, tour groups, or guides are your best bets to hit all sights, stay safe, and navigate trickier areas. Women traveling alone might especially want to consider this option. Competing **guided tour** companies peddle similar products (US$30). Try **Zemi Tours** (☎271 25 76), with an office on the road leading from the *otogar* to the museum.

EXCURSIONS FROM GÖREME: UNDERGROUND CITIES AND ÇAVUŞIN. Cappadocia contains almost 200 **underground cities; Kaymaklı** and **Derinkuyu** are the largest. Carved from tufa, the cities were designed with mind-boggling ingenuity;

low, narrow passages were easily blocked by massive boulders, hindering prospective invaders who fell to their deaths over sudden, concealed drops. Beware uncharted tunnels. All explorable areas are lit (but flashlights are handy) and marked—red arrows lead down, blue arrows lead up. (Cities open daily in summer 8am-5pm. US$3.75 each) From Göreme, **dolmuş** run to Nevşehir (US$0.50) and then go on to Kaymaklı (30min. total, US$0.60) and Derinkuyu (45min. total, US$0.80).

Escape to the nearby provincial village of **Çavuşin** (2km from Göreme) to visit Cappadocia's oldest church, the 5th-century **St. John the Baptist.** Or head over to Zelve's **Open Air Museum** (open daily 8am-5:30pm; US$4), where ruins of tufa villages make for hours of exploring, climbing, and burrowing (but mind gaps and holes underfoot). Both the Ürgüp-Avanos **minibus** and the Göreme-Avanos **bus** pass through Çavuşin. On foot, follow the main road past Çavuşin, take a right up the dirt road behind the pottery shop, and continue to climb for a magnificent ridge walk.

ÜRGÜP ☎384

Ürgüp emerges from a collage of bizarre rock formations, early Christian dwellings, and old Greek mansions. The city offers fewer *pansiyons* and neo-hippies than Göreme, but tourists will appreciate Ürgüp's organized information network, central *otogar*, and proximity to points of interest. **Kayseri Cad,** the main road, and **Güllüce Cad.,** which leads the 20m from the *otogar*, intersect at the town square, marked by an Atatürk statue. Bring a special friend to the co-ed **Tarihi Şehir Hamamı,** in the main square; complete bath with massage, scrub, and sauna runs US$8 per person. (Open daily 7am-11pm.) Cappadocia is one of Turkey's major viticultural regions, with its center in Ürgüp. Uphill to the right behind the Atatürk statue is the renowned **Turasan Winery,** supplier of 60% of Cappadocia's wines, which offers free tours and tastings in its rock-carved wine cellar. (Open 8am-8pm; tours available until 5pm.) Several wine shops around the main square also offer free tastings. **Han Çırağan,** by the *hamam*, serves a special of cheese, mushrooms, carrots and peppers (US$4). Its adjoining bar specializes in all-you-can-drink "Turkish nights" (US$12). At night, the dance floor is packed at **Prokopi Pub Bar,** in the town square.

Buses head to a range of cities, but schedules are highly spontaneous. English-speaking **Aydın Altan** of **Nevtur** (☎341 43 02) will answer bus-related questions. The **tourist office** is in the garden on Kayseri Cad.; follow the signs from anywhere in the city. (☎341 40 59. Open daily Apr.-Oct. 8am-7pm; Nov.-Mar. 8am-5pm.) Fork right at the *hamam* and go uphill to the classy **Hotel Suburban.** (☎341 46 45. US$10 per person.) **Bahçe Hostel,** opposite the *hamam*, has spacious, if unspectacular, rooms. (☎341 33 14. Single US$7; doubles US$10; triples US$15.) **Postal code:** 50400.

UKRAINE (УКРАЇНА)

UKRAINE

HRYVNY

US$1 = 5.56HV	1HV = US$0.18
CDN$1 = 3.71HV	1HV = CDN$0.27
UK£1 = 8.00HV	1HV = UK£0.13
IR£1 = 6.24HV	1HV = IR£0.16
AUS$1 = 3.15HV	1HV = AUS$0.32
NZ$1 = 2.35HV	1HV = NZ$0.43
SARI = 0.79HV	1HV = SAR1.27
DM1 = 2.51HV	1HV = DM0.40
EUR€1 = 4.91HV	1HV = EUR€0.20

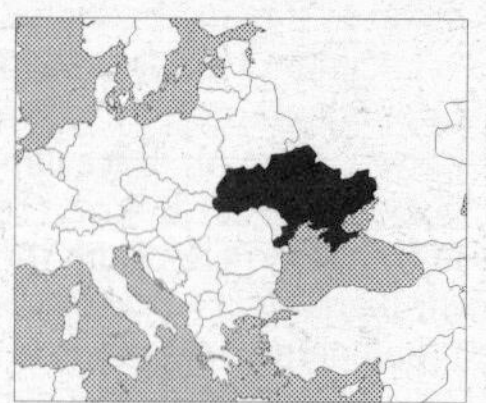

Country code: 380. **International dialing prefix:** 00. From outside Ukraine, dial int'l dialing prefix (see inside back cover) + 380 + city code + local number.

Vast, fertile, and perpetually tempting to invaders, newly independent Ukraine oscillates between nostalgic, overbearing Russia on one side and a bloc of *nouveau riche* on the other. Ukraine's citizens—from the old *babushki* to the cell-phone-sporting *biznesmeni*, from the village boys to the urban-high-heeled women—live in a world of past splendor and current corruption. As if in a time warp, Ukraine offers fascinating museums and theater, wonderful castles, and the magnificent Black Sea coast, spirited and lively even after years of Soviet order and post-Soviet chaos. With no beaten path from which to stray, the challenges of exploring Ukraine reward with a genuine and intriguing look into Ukrainian life. This country offers many treasures, but you'll have to find them yourself. Ukraine, with its own troubles, isn't inclined to play host.

For more detailed coverage of Ukraine, refer to *Let's Go: Eastern Europe 2001*.

FACTS AND FIGURES

Official Name: Ukraine.
Government: Republic.
Capital: Kiev.
Land Area: 603,700 sq. km.
Geography: Plains.
Climate: Temperate continental.
Major cities: Kiev, Lviv, Odessa.

Population: 49,811,174.
Languages: Ukrainian, Russian.
Religions: Ukrainian Orthodox (29%), Uniate (7%), Protestant (4%).
Average Income Per Capita: US$2200.
Major Exports: Metals, petroleum products, machinery, transport equipment.

DISCOVER UKRAINE

Getting to Ukraine is worth the hassle: the country has impressive cities, miles of Black Sea beaches, and expanses of country sprawling in between. Start any trip to Ukraine in **Kiev;** once the seat of the Kievan Rus dynasty, the modern city's park-covered environs and riverside vistas are a breathtaking backdrop to an incomparable mix of urban rush and provincial charm (p. 974). **Lviv,** in Western Ukraine, is an undiscovered jewel (p. 977). Khrushchev gave **Crimea** to Ukraine, and the Russians didn't object—maybe they were too drunk to realize how much sun and fun they were losing (p. 979). Farther west, **Odessa,** the former-USSR party town, has an international air and a feisty population (p. 979).

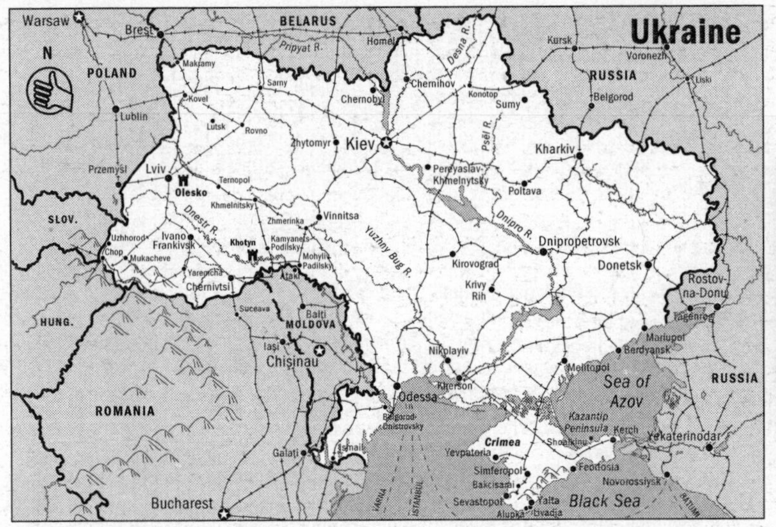

ESSENTIALS

WHEN TO GO

The best time to visit is May-September, when it's warmer. Spring and early fall can be unpredictable; snow flurries are almost always possible. Winter is bitter cold. Along the Black Sea, summers are hot and winters are mild.

DOCUMENTS AND FORMALITIES

Travelers from Australia, Canada, Ireland, New Zealand, the UK and the US arriving in Ukraine must have a **visa,** which requires an **invitation** from a citizen or official organization, or a tourist voucher from a travel agency. Regular single-entry visa processing for Americans at a Ukrainian embassy or consulate—with invitation in hand—ordinarily takes up to nine days. Single-entry visas cost US$30, double-entry US$60, multiple-entry US$120, and transit US$15, not including the $US45 processing fee. For transit visas no invitation is required. See **Russia** (p. 787) for organizations that arrange **invitations** and visas. Diane Sadovnikov also arranges invitations; fax her a month in advance (US ☎ (757) 463 69 06, fax (757) 463 55 26, Ukraine ☎/fax 044 516 24 33; travel-ims@attglobal.net). When proceeding through **customs** you will be required to declare all valuables and foreign currency above US$1000 (including traveler's checks). It is forbidden to bring Ukrainian currency to Ukraine. Foreigners arriving at Kiev's Borispol airport must purchase a $23 health insurance policy; it is essentially an entry tax and doesn't provide health care.

Upon arrival, check into a hotel, where the staff will register your visa for you, or register with the hall of nightmares that is the **Office of Visas and Registration** (UVIR; ОВИР), in Kiev at blv. Tarasa Shevchenka 34 (Тараса Шевченка), or at police stations in smaller cities, within your first three days in the country. Visas may also be extended here. If you do not get your visa registered, you may get hassled or fined when trying to leave. **Do not lose the paper given to you when entering the country to supplement your visa;** it is required to leave the country. If you have a double-entry visa, you'll be given a re-entry slip (*vyezd;* въезд) when you arrive.

EMBASSIES AND CONSULATES

All foreign embassies are in **Kiev** (see p. 975).

Ukrainian Embassies at Home: Canada, 310 Somerset W., Ottawa, ON K2P 0J9 (☎ (613) 230 29 61; fax 230 24 00); **South Africa,** 398 Marais Brooklyn, Pretoria; P.O. Box 57291 Arcadia, 0007 (☎ (012) 46 19 46; fax 46 19 44); **UK,** 78 Kensington Park Rd., London W11 2 PL (☎ (171) 727 63 12; 792 17 08); **US,** 3350 M St. NW, Washington, DC 20007 (☎ (202) 333 75 07; fax 333 75 10; www.ukremb.com).

GETTING THERE AND GETTING AROUND

BY PLANE. Air International Ukraine (US ☎ (800) 876 01 14; in Kiev ☎ (44) 221 83 80 or 234 45 28; www.ukraine-international.com/eng) flies to Kiev, Lviv, and Odessa from a number of European capitals. Air France, ČSA, Lufthansa, LOT, Malév, SAS, and Swissair also fly to Kiev, generally once or twice a week.

BY TRAIN. Trains run frequently from all of Ukraine's neighbors, and are the most popular way of entering the country and traveling long distances. When coming from a non-ex-Soviet country, expect a two-hour stop at the border. On most trains within Ukraine there are two classes: *platzkart*, where you'll be crammed in with *babushki* and their baskets of strawberries, and *coupé*, a more private four-person compartment, but still with disgusting bathrooms. Unless you are determined to live local, pay the extra two dollars for *coupé;* it can make the trip tolerable. You'll have a few minutes to show your ticket to cashiers or fellow passengers, look helpless, and say "платформа?" (plaht-FORM-ah?)

BY BUS. Buses are cheaper and more frequent than trains and provide the best means to travel around the country. Bus schedules are generally reliable, but low demand can cause cancellations. Buy tickets at the *kassa* (box office); if they're sold out, go directly to the driver, who will magically find a seat.

BY MARSHRUTKE, BY TAXI, AND BY THUMB. In cities, private minibuses called *marshrutke* run along the same routes as public transport; they are slightly more expensive but faster. **Taxi** drivers love to rip off foreigners, so set the price before the ride. **Hitchhikers** are common on Ukrainian roads, holding signs with the desired destination. *Let's Go* does not recommend hitchhiking.

TOURIST SERVICES AND MONEY

EMERGENCY. Fire: ☎ 01. **Police:** ☎ 02. **Emergency:** ☎ 03.

TOURIST OFFICES. There is no state-run tourist office. Remnants of Soviet **Intourist** have offices in hotels and provide tourist-related information, although usually not in English. They're used to dealing with groups, to whom they sell "excursion" packages to nearby sights.

MONEY. In September 1996, Ukraine decided to wipe the extraneous zeros off most prices by replacing the **karbovanets** (Krb; a.k.a. kupon) with a new currency, the **hryvnia** (гривна; hv; plural hryvny); each hryvnia is worth 100,000 karbovantsi. **Exchanging** US dollars and Deutschmarks is simple, but other currencies pose difficulties; *Obmin Valyut* (Обмін Валют) kiosks in the center of most cities offer the best rates. **Traveler's checks** can be changed into dollars for small commissions. **Western Union** is everywhere. Most banks will give Visa and Mastercard cash advances for a high commission. The lobbies of fancier hotels usually exchange US dollars at poor rates. **Private money changers** lurk near legitimate kiosks, ready with brilliant schemes for ripping you off. **Do not** exchange money with them; it's illegal. **ATMs** abound in cities. Although locals don't usually leave **tips,** most expats give 10%. Accommodations in Ukraine average US$10-12; meals run US$5-7.

ACCOMMODATIONS AND CAMPING

Not all **hotels** accept foreigners, and those that do often charge them many times more than what a Ukrainian would pay. Although room prices in Kiev are astronomical, singles run anywhere from 5hv to 90hv in the rest of the country. The phrase *samoe deshovoe miesto* (самое дешёвое место) means "the cheapest place." More expensive hotels aren't necessarily nicer, and in some hotels, women lodging alone may be mistaken for prostitutes. Most cities have cheap hotels above the train stations—these are usually seedy and unsafe. Standard hotel rooms include a TV, phone, and a refrigerator. You will be given a *vizitka* (визитка; hotel card) to show to the hall monitor (дежурная; dezhurnaya) to get a key; surrender it on leaving the building. Valuables should never be left unattended; ask at the desk if there's a **safe. Hot water** is a rarity—ask before checking in. **Private rooms** can be arranged through overseas agencies or bargained for at the train station. Most cities have a **campground,** which is a remote hotel with trailers for buildings. The old Soviet complexes can be quite posh (and quite expensive), with saunas and restaurants. Free camping is illegal, and enforcement is merciless.

FOOD AND DRINK

There are few choices between new, fancy restaurants catering to tourists and the *stolovayas* (cafeterias), dying bastions of cheap, hot food. Non-fresh *stolovaya* food can knock you out of commission for hours, while a good *stolovaya* meal is a triumph of the human spirit. **Vegetarians** will have to create their own meals from potatoes, mushrooms, and cabbage. Produce is sold at **markets;** bring your own bag. **State food stores** are classified by content: *hastronom* (гастроном) sell packaged goods; *moloko* (молоко) milk products; *ovochi-frukty* (овочі-фрукты) fruits and vegetables; *myaso* (мясо) meat; *hlib* (хліб) bread; *kolbasy* (колбаси) sausage; and *ryba* (риба) fish. Drinking **tea** is a national ritual.

HEALTH AND SAFETY

While Ukraine is neither violent nor politically volatile, it is poor and its people desperate. Keep your foreign profile low, watch your belongings, and don't make easy acquaintances, especially on the street. Don't be afraid to initiate contact; people who don't go out of their way to approach you can generally be trusted. The risk of **crime,** although made much of, isn't much greater than in the rest of Eastern Europe. It's a wise idea to **register** with your embassy once you get to Ukraine.

Water is bad and hard to find in the bottled version; it's best to boil it or learn to love brushing your teeth with soda. Fruits and vegetables from open **markets** are generally safe, although storage conditions and pesticides make thorough washing imperative. Meat purchased at public markets should be checked very carefully and cooked thoroughly. Embassy officials say that Chernobyl-related **radiation** poses minimal risk to short-term travelers, but the region should be given a wide berth.

COMMUNICATION

MAIL. Mail is cheap and quite reliable (about 10 days to the US). The easiest way to mail letters is to buy pre-stamped envelopes at the post office. **Poste Restante** (До Вострeбования in Russian, До Запитание in Ukrainian) is available.

TELEPHONES. Telephones are stumbling toward modernity. The easiest way to make international calls with a calling card or collect is with **Utel** (Ukraine telephone). Buy a Utel **phonecard** (sold at most Utel phone locations) and dial the **international direct dial** number (counted as a local call): **AT&T,** ☎ (8) 100 11—wait for another tone after the 8; **BT Direct,** ☎ (8) 10 04 41; **Canada Direct,** ☎ (8)100 17; **MCI,** ☎ (8) 100 13; and **Sprint,** ☎ (8) 100 15. Or, call at the central telephone office—guess how long your call will take, pay at the counter, and they'll direct you to a booth.

JUST FOR THE TASTE When the sun is high and the steppe is hotter than a Saharan parking lot, Aussies thirst for a *Fosters,* Czechs a *Pilsner,* and Yankees a *Bud,* but a true Ukrainian won't have anything other than a ladle of **kvas** (квас). In Kiev you'll see it served from siphons, in the provinces from rusty cisterns. The taste—kind of like beer without the hops—varies depending on the container, but it all comes down to acidic bread bubbles; the drink is based on a sourdough solution that rushes tingling into your bloodstream. It's so addictive that Kiev drinks *kvas* all summer, even in the rain, when groups of young tots, middle-aged shoppers, and love-struck teenagers huddle around toothless tap-masters, all under one leaky umbrella.

Dial 810, followed by country code, city code, and number. Calling is expensive: per minute charges are, to Eastern Europe, US$0.06; Western Europe, US$1.50; and North America, US$2.50 per minute. There's no need to dial a country code when calling Moldova. For **intercity calls** inside Ukraine, dial 8, then the city code and number. Local calls from gray pay phones generally cost 10-30hv. For an English-language operator, dial ☎8 192.

LANGUAGES. It's extremely difficult to travel without knowing some **Ukrainian** or **Russian.** In Kiev, Odessa, and Crimea, Russian is more common than Ukrainian (although all official signs are in Ukrainian). In Transcarpathia, Ukrainian is preferred—people will speak Russian with you only if they know you are not Russian. *Let's Go* uses Ukrainian names in Kiev and Western Ukraine, and Russian in Crimea and Odeshchina. For basic phrases, see p. 981.

HOLIDAYS AND FESTIVALS

Holidays: New Year's (Jan. 1); Orthodox Christmas (Jan. 7); International Women's Day (Mar. 8); Good Friday (Apr. 13); Orthodox Easter (Apr. 15); Labor Day (May 1-2); Victory Day (1945; May 9); Holy Trinity (June 18-19); Constitution Day (June 28); Independence Day (1991; Aug. 24).

Festivals: Every Mar., Kiev hosts international drama troupes for a 2-week multilingual **theater festival.** The wildest party in Eastern Europe is in **Kazantip,** near Yalta (Aug.), when the entire town morphs into a **radioactive rave.**

KIEV (KYIV; КИЇВ) ☎044

Once the USSR's third-largest city, Kiev doesn't seem to have quite figured out how to become a thriving capital(ist) metropolis. Locals still prefer to store their money in dollars under their pillows, hesitant foreign investment and stagnant political reform are daily headlines, and visiting Americans are more likely to shop for wives than tourist kitsch. This lull, however, provides an untouristed environment to enjoy Kiev's rich (albeit crumbling) medieval cathedrals and 17th-century facades.

GETTING THERE AND GETTING AROUND

Flights: The international **Kiev-Borospil Airport** (Київ-Бориспіль; ☎296 75 29) is 30min. southeast of the city. The city **bus** or a *marshrutne taksi* (маршрутне таксі) runs to MR: Livoberezhna (Лівобережна) every 20min. or when they fill up. (10-20hv).

Trains: Kiev-Passazhyrsky (Київ-Пассажирський), Vokzalna pl. (☎005). MR: Vokzalna. In the main ticketing room on the 1st fl., arrivals are listed on the left, departures on the right. **Tickets** can be purchased on the 1st fl. in hall 4 or at **Intourist,** 2nd fl. Open daily 8am-1pm, 2-7pm, and 8pm-7am. **Passports** are required to buy international tickets. If Intourist or the *kasa* claims not to have tickets, try again 6hr. and 2hr. before departure. Scalpers add 4-6hv to the price, but may have unavailable tickets. To: **Bratislava** (18hr., 1 per day, 500hv); **Budapest** (25hr., 1 per day, 440hv); **Lviv** (12hr., 6 per day, 24hv); **Minsk** (12-13hr., 1 per day, 70hv); **Moscow** (15-17hr., 15 per day, 60-95hv); **Prague** (34hr., 1 per day, 650hv); and **Warsaw** (15hr., 2 per day, 190hv). **Luggage storage** 2hv.

Buses: Tsentralny Avtovokzal (Центральний Автовокзал), Moskovska pl. 3 (Московьска; ☎265 04 30), is 10min. past Libidska, the last stop on the MG line. Go right and then left out of the Metro; take bus #4 or walk 100m down the big highway and follow it to the right for 300m. To: **Moscow** (21hr., 2 per day, 42hv); **Odessa** (10hr., 6 per day, 55hv); and **Prague** (30hr., 2 per day, 330hv). **Pivdenna** (Південна), pr. Akademyka Hlushkova 3 (Академика Глушкова; ☎263 40 04), and **Podil** (Поділ), vul. Nyzhny Val 15a (Нижній Вал), serve nearby cities.

Public Transportation: The three intersecting lines of the **Metropoliten** are efficient but limited: blue (MB), green (MG), and red (MR). Buy blue tokens, which are good on all public transport, at the "Каса" *(Kasa)* for 0.50hv. "Перехід" *(perekhid)* indicates a walkway to another station, "вихід у місто" *(vykhid u misto)* an exit onto the street, and "вхід" *(vkhid)* an entrance to the metro. **Trolleys, buses,** and **marshrutne taksi** go where the Metro doesn't. Marshrutne taksi are private vans numbered with bus routes. Bus tickets cost 0.50hv and are sold at kiosks; buy taksi tickets (0.75hv) on board.

UKRAINE

ORIENTATION AND PRACTICAL INFORMATION

Almost all attractions and services lie in western Kiev, on the right bank of the Dnipro. Two Metro stops away from the train station, the busy boulevard **Khreshchatik** (Хрещатик) satisfies most tourist needs, except housing. The center of Kiev is vul. Khreshchatik's fountained **Maydan Nezalezhnosti** (Майдан Незалежності).

Tourist Office: Kiev still lacks decent tourist offices. **Ukraine Hotel,** Tarassa Shevchaka bd. 5, is your best bet for guidance. MB: Ploshcha Iva Tolstovo. **Tourist Office** (Туристичне бюро; Turistichne byuro), vul. Khmelnytskoho 13 (Хмельницького; ☎226 21 96 or 224 85 42). Open M-F 9am-5pm. **Yana** (Яна), vul. Saksahanskoho 42 (Саксаганського; ☎443 84 39). Open M-F 9am-5pm.

Embassies: Australia, vul. Kominternu 18/137 (Комінтерну; ☎235 75 86). Open 10am-1pm. **Belarus,** vul. Yanvarskogo Vossttanaya 6 (Январского Восстанія; ☎290 02 01). Open M-F 10am-5pm. **Canada,** vul. Yaroslaviv Val 31 (Ярославів Вал; ☎464 11 44). Open M-Tu and Th-F 8:30am-noon. **Latvia,** vul. Desyatynna, 4/6 (Десятинна; ☎462 07 08). Open M-F 10am-5pm. **Moldova,** vul. Sichnevoho Postannya 6 (Січневого Постання; ☎290 06 10). Open M-F 9am-1pm and 3-6pm. MR: Arsenalna. **Russia,** pr. Kutuzova 8 (Кутузова; ☎244 09 63). Open M-Th 9am-6pm, F 9am-5pm. **UK,** vul. Desyatynna 9 (☎462 00 11). Open M-F 9am-5:30pm. **US,** vul. Pimonenko 6 (Пімоненко; ☎246 80 48; after-hours emergency ☎216 38 05; www.usemb.kiev.ua). Services for Americans citizens 9-11:30am and 2:30-4pm.

Medical Assistance: Check with the **US Embassy** (see above) for a list of safe hospitals. **Emergency Care Center,** vul. Mechnikova 1 (☎227 92 30). The **American Medical Center,** vul. Berdicherska 1 (☎211 65 55) is expensive.

Internet Access: Kiber Cafe (Кібер Кафе), Proriznaya 21 (☎228 05 48). 10hv per hr. Open daily 10am-2am.

Telephones: Myzhmisky Perehovorny Punkt (Мижміський Переговорний Пункт), at the post office, or **Telefon-Telefaks** (Телефон-Телефакс), around the corner (enter on Khreshchatyk). Both open 24hr. Dial AT&T or MCI operators from **Utel** phones. Calls within Kiev require phone cards. Buy Utel **phone cards** (10hv, 20hv, and 40hv) at the post office or a hotel. For more info, see p. 973.

Post Office: vul. Khreshchatyk 22, next to Maydan Nezalezhnosti. *Poste Restante* at counters #29-30. Address mail to be held: First Name SURNAME, *Poste Restante,* **252 001** Київ-1, Почтамт до Воетребоваиия, UKRAINE. Open M-Sa 8am-9pm, Su 9am-7pm. **Postal code:** 252 001.

ACCOMMODATIONS AND FOOD

Accommodations in Kiev suffer from an unfortunate combination of capitalist prices and socialist quality. **Grazhdanski Aviatski Institut Student Hotel,** vul. Nyzhinska 29E (Ніжіньска), is the best deal if you don't mind the trek (50min. total). From behind MR: Vokzalna, turn right into the passageway leading to the trams.

Ride six or seven stops on tram #1K or 7 to Hramatna (Граматна), "Industrailna" (Індустраільна). Backtrack one-and-a-half blocks, go right onto vul. Nizhinska, cross at the first intersection with a trolleybus, then follow the path into the complex. Keep the first building on your right as you walk diagonally to block "Д." After passing Д on the right, look for the "Гостиница Фпк" sign above the entrance. (☎484 90 59. Luxury singles 45.50hv; doubles 55.44hv; spartan rooms 10hv.) Or, try **Akademichniy Hotel** (Академічний), vul. Perovskoyi Sofiy 6/11 (Перовської Софії) MR: Shuliavska (Шулявська). Turn right out of the Metro and head down Prospekt Peremohy (Перемоги). Take the second right to vul. Perovskoyi; the hotel is the stately building on the right. Comforts and price of a hotel for middle-aged guests. (☎/fax 446 90 31. Singles with bath and phone US$30; doubles US$45.)

For those on a tight budget, the best food option is a trip to one of Kiev's *rynki* (markets); **Bessarabsky Rynok** (Бессарабский Ринок), vul. Khreshchatyk and bul. Shevchenka (Шевченка), has the best meat and produce. **Supermarket 7/24,** vul. Baseyna 1/2 (Басеїна), behind Bessarabsky Rynok, is open, well, 24/7. **Café Panorama** (Кафе Панорама), down Andryivsky uzviz from St. Andrew's Church, past the statue and up the wooden steps to the right, serves simple beef or chicken *shashlik* for 15hv with fabulous views. (Open in summer daily 11am-11pm.) **Pantagruel** (Пантагрюель), vul. Lysenko 1 (Лисенко), next to MG: Zoloty Vorota, serves mouth-watering, authentic Italian food. (Entrees 25-40hv. Live music F-Sa 8-10pm. Open M-Th and Su 11am-11pm, F-Sa 11am-2am.)

SIGHTS AND ENTERTAINMENT

VULITSYA KHRESHCHATYK AND ENVIRONS. Broad and commercial **vul. Khreshchatyk** (Хрещатик) begins at the intersection with Boulevard Taras Shevchenko and goes up to **Independence Plaza** (Maydan Nezalezhnosti), a fountain-filled fun stop filled with street performers. *(Just off vul. Khreshchatyk; turn left when you reach MG: Maidan Nezalezhnosti.)* Historical monuments celebrating Prince Volodymyr (who converted Kievan Rus to Christianity) and the brave soccer players who resisted the Nazis are found in **Khreshchaty Park,** under the silver **Arch of the Brotherhood.**

VOLODYMYRSKA VULITSYA: ST. SOPHIA TO GOLDEN GATE. The **St. Sophia Monastery** complex, with its splendid icons, was the religious center of Kievan Rus and is currently a focal point of Ukrainian nationalism. Its golden domes, separated from those of the St. Mikhail monastery by the austere statue of Bohdan Khmelnytsky, are what tourists come to Kiev to see. *(Volodymyrska vul. 24. From Independence Plaza, just northwest of MG: Maidan Nezalezhnosti, head west up Sofiyska vul.; or, take tram #16 from Maydan Nezalezhnosti. Open F-Tu 10am-5:30pm, W 10am-4:30pm. 6hv; 1hr. tour 10hv; architectural museum and exhibits each 2hv extra. Cameras 10hv.)* Next to the **Golden Gate** (Zoloty Vorota; Золоти Ворота), once the entrance to the city, is a statue of Yaroslav the Wise by the Metro station. *(MR, MG: Zoloty Vorota.)* Several other small churches are scattered throughout the area.

ANDRIVSKY UZVIZ AND THE PODIL DISTRICT. Andrivsky Uzviz (path) can be reached by funicular from the subway. *(Funicular departs from just south of MB: Poshtova. From St. Sophia, walk north on Volodymyrska vul., bear right on Mikhailivska pl., and turn left on vul. Mikhailivska. Runs daily every 5min. 6:30am-11pm. 0.30hv.)* Or, walk down the winding cobblestone path from Mikhailivska Sq. Ascend the gray steps at the corner of Desatynia and Volodymyrska to see the ruins of the oldest stone church of Kievan Rus and the **National History Museum.** *(Open M-Sa 9am-5pm.)* Nearby is the impressive **St. Andrew's Cathedral.** Down twisting streets are a collection of local art displays, an array of souvenirs, and writer Mikhail Bulgakov's home. The path spills out into the **Podil** district, the church-filled center of Kiev in the 10th and 11th centuries. Just east of the *ploscha*, the **Chernobyl Museum,** Provulok Zhorevii 1, uses powerful imagery to convey the magnitude of the nuclear disaster; ask to see the video of the explosion. *(Open M-Sa 10am-6pm; closed last M of each month. Free.)*

THE ARTIFICIAL FAMINE In 1930, the first of the USSR's 5-year plans collectivized agriculture and set state quotas for agricultural production. In Ukraine the policies were met with fierce opposition and farmers destroyed their livestock in protest. Stalin, in order to break the resistance, raised grain quotas for the Crimea, the Caucasus, the lower Volga, and part of Belarus to impossible levels. Exit visas for the region were prohibited and taking from the harvest before the state had had its "share" was punishable by death. The effects were devastating: the most conservative estimates put the death toll from starvation from winter 1932 to summer 1933 at 4.8 million, not including the atrocities committed by the thousands of troops sent to enforce collectivization. Stalin himself confessed to "ten of millions" of deaths in a conversation with Winston Churchill in August 1942. Historians, pouring over what Soviet records they could find, put the official number at 6-8 million.

BABYN YAR AND ST. CYRIL'S. The **monument at Babyn Yar** is a moving tribute to the first victims of the Nazis in Ukraine. The statue, a group of interlocking figures falling to their deaths from an incline above the grass that now covers the pit, is accompanied by a plaque stating that 100,000 Kievans died there, though current estimates count the victims' numbers—mostly Jews—at twice that figure. *(From Maydan Nezalezhnosti, 10 stops on trolley #16.)* **St. Cyril's Church,** the multi-domed shelter of Kiev's frescoes, is nearby. *(From Babyn Yar, 6 stops on trolley #27 towards MB: Petrivka.)*

KIEV-PECHERY MONASTERY. Kiev's oldest and holiest religious site, the mysterious **Kiev-Pechery Monastery** (Kievo-Pecherska Lavra; Києво-Печерська Лавра) deserves a full day of exploration. Apart from the many museums, the complex houses the **Holy Trinity Church,** the **Refractory Church,** and the fascinating **caves** where saints and the monastery's monks lie mummified and entombed. Buy a candle (0.50hv) before you enter to help you navigate the caves. Turning left from the monastery exit and continuing down the street brings you to a series of patriotic monuments, culminating with the huge silver **motherland statue** overlooking the eternal flame with gorgeous views of the river. *(MR: Arsenalna; left as you exit; walk 20min. down vul. Sichnevoho Povstanyiya. Monastery open daily 9:30am-7pm. Ticket for churches and exhibitions 8hv, students 4hv. Caves open W-M 9-11:30am and 1-4pm. Dress modestly.)*

NIGHTLIFE. Check out *Kyiv Post* and *What's On* (www.whatson-kyiv.com) for listings. **Rock Cafe** (Рок Кафе), vul. Horodetskoho 10 (MG: Maydan Nezalezhnosti), is an easygoing coffee shop that becomes an expat bar at night. Walk 300m to the right of the steps; the cafe is on your right. (Drinks 5hv. Open daily 11am-3am.) **Al Capone,** Kostyantynivska 26, in a converted cinema, is the boss of late boogying.

LVIV (ЛЬВІВ) ☎0322

Dear Abby,

Divorced from Poland in 1945 after 600 years of ups and down, I recently went through a breakup with the USSR, for whom I had cooked and slaved for over 45 years. In spite of my age, I feel ready to show myself to the world. I just want to be loved, admired, and remembered. My steeple-filled city center teems with energy that can't be found anywhere else in Ukraine, and, if I do say so myself, I'm fun!

Worthy and waiting, Lviv

PRACTICAL INFO, ACCOMMODATIONS, AND FOOD. Trains (☎748 20 68) go from pl. Vokzalna (Вокзальна) to: Kraków (8hr., 1 per day, 95hv); Kiev (12-16hr., 8 per day, 28-50hv); Odessa (14hr., 3 per day, 35-50hv); Bratislava (18hr., 1 per day, 320hv); Budapest (14hr., 1 per day, 217hv); Prague (21hr., 1 per day, 350hv); and Moscow (29hr., 4 per day, 135hv). **Tickets** are available at Intourist windows #23-25. Tram #1 runs from the train station to the Old Town; tram #6 to the north end of pr. Svobody. The main **bus station,** on vul. Stryska (Стрийська; ☎63 24 73), on the outskirts of town, sends buses to Kraków (8hr., 1 per day, 74hv) and Warsaw (10hr., 4 per day, 83hv). From the bus station, bus #18 goes to the train station, from which trams go into town. **Lviv Intourist,** in the Hotel George, plans guided **tours**. (☎72 67 40; fax 97 12 87. Open M-F 9am-5pm. Tours for 1-3 people US$10-30.) Check **email** at **Internet Cafe,** vul. Zelena 14, behind the busy pizzeria San Remo. (1hv per 15min.) To find **Hotel Lviv,** vul. 700-Richna Lvova (700-Річчя Львова), a few blocks north of pr. Svobody, take tram #6 from the train station to the Opera House; the hotel is seven blocks behind it on the left. (☎79 22 70. Singles 37-67hv; doubles 23-52hv.) **Hotel George,** pl. Mitskevycha 1, is pretty but pricey; take tram #1. (☎72 59 52. Breakfast included. Singles 80-330hv; doubles 95-380hv.) Pl. Rynok is the restaurant and cafe center of Lviv; the most convenient **market** is **Halytsky Rynok** (Галицький Ринок), behind the flower stands across from St. Andrew's Church. **U Pani Stefi** (У Пані Стефи), pr. Svobody 8, has traditional Ukrainian food. (Main dishes 10-15hv. Open daily 10am-10pm.) **Postal code:** 79000.

UKRAINE

SIGHTS AND ENTERTAINMENT. Before you venture into the heart of the city, a great way to introduce yourself to Lviv is to climb up to **High Castle Hill** (Vysoky Zamok; Высокий Замок), the former site of the Galician King's Palace. Now a Ukrainian flag and the television tower hover above the panoramic view. Follow vul. Krivonoca (Кривоноса) from its intersection with Hotny and Halytskono and go until you pass #39, then take a left down the long shaded dirt road to wind your way up around the hill counter-clockwise. Begin a tour of the city on Pr. Svobody, dominated by the dazzlingly complex exterior of the **Theater of Opera and Ballet** (Teatr Opery ta Baletu; Театра Опери та Балету). You don't have to love opera, and you don't even need a tux; you just have to marvel at the great space, great voices, and great sets. (☎72 88 60. Front row seats 6-10hv.) **Museum of National Architecture** (Muzey Narodnoi Architektury ta Pobutu u Lvovi; Музей Народноі Архітектури та Побуту у Львові) at Shevchenkivsky Hay (Шевченківський Гай), can be reached on tram #2 or 7 to Mechnikova; head all the way up the hill, bearing right at the top to reach the outdoor museum. (Open Tu-Su 11am-7pm. 1hv.) The heart of the city is **pl. Rynok,** the historic market square, surrounded by countless churches and richly decorated merchant homes dating from the 16th to 18th centuries. Just beyond the gaze of the trident-armed Neptune statue atop the 19th-century **town hall** is pl. Katedralna (Катедральна), where the grand Polish **Catholic Cathedral** (Katolitsky Sobor; Католицкий собор) stands.

Opera, experimental drama, cheap tickets, and an artistic population make Lviv's performance halls the city's second most frequented institution after cafes. Buy tickets at each theater's *kasa* or at the *teatralny kasy* (ticket windows; театральни каси), pr. Svobody 37. (Open M-Sa 10am-1pm and 2:30-6pm.) Before the show, stop at a club-cafe; try **Italiisky Dvoryk** (Італійський Дворик), pl. Rynok 6, Lviv's hippest, with Renaissance decor. (Coffee 1.20hv. Open daily 10am-8pm.) At **Club-Cafe Lyalka** (Клуб-Кафе Лялька), vul. Halytskoho 1 (Галицького), below the Teatr Lyalok (Puppet Theater), artsy-types do shots while arguing with the sophisticated wine-sippers. (Wine 2.50hv. Jazz on W. Cover 5hv disco nights. Open M-F 1-11pm, Sa-Su 11am-1am.)

SIMFEROPOL (СІМФЕРОПОЛЬ) ☎0652

God made the Crimea, and all Simferopol (sim-fer-ROH-pul) got was a lousy but unavoidable train station. **Trains** run from ul. Gagarina (Гагарина; ☎005) to: Odessa (14hr., 1 per day, 36hv); Kiev (19hr., 5 per day, 72hv); Moscow (28hr., 4 per day, 96.50hv); Lviv (32hr., 2 per day, 71hv); and Minsk (35hr., 1 per day, 86hv). **Buses** for Yalta leave from the train station (2hr., 3 per hr., 5hv), but most other buses leave from the bus station, ul. Kievskaya 4, accessible from the train station by bus #2 and 6 and by bus #4 from the city center. The best place to sleep is on the train out of town, but if you have a layover, you can stay at the central **Gostinitsa Ukraina** (Украина), ul. Rozy Lyuksemburg 7-9. Ride bus #5 three stops to the hotel. (☎51 01 65. Singles 37.50-90hv; doubles 57-127hv; triples 78hv.)

YALTA (ЯЛТА) ☎0654

The gaudy Yalta waterfront, with its hot dog vendors and computerized astrology stands, dashes any illusion that this is still the city of Chekhov, Rachmaninov, and Tolstoy. Enjoy Yalta for what it is: a lovely, historic city weathering the storm of capitalism as best it can. If you're an **Anton Chekhov** fan, head to ul. Kirova 112, where you can explore **White Dacha,** the house he built, the garden he planted, and the museum about him. Take trolleybus #1 to Pionerskaya (Пионерская), cross the street, and walk up the hill. (Open Tu-Su 10am-5:15pm. 10hv, students 5hv.)

Buses (☎34 20 92) leave from Moskovskaya ul. 57 for Simferopol (2hr., every 30min., 5.60hv). Across the way, the **trolleybus station** sends more comfortable trolleys to the Simferopol train station (2½hr., every 20min., 4.80hv). From either station, take trolleybus #1 uphill to Sovetskaya pl. (Советская), then walk two blocks toward the sea. **Intourist,** ul. Drazhinskovo 50, is in Hotel Yalta. (Maps 5hv. Open daily 9am-5pm.) **Eugenia Travel,** Ul. Roosvelta 5, is at the Sea Terminal. (☎21 85 83.) **Internet** access is available at **Internet Club Yalta,** ul. Marshaka 9, on the corner of ul. Pushinskaya. (4hv per hr. Open 10am-11pm.) Bus station *babushki* often offer great deals on private rooms (20-30hv is good; more as you approach the waterfront). **Hostinitsa Krym** (Крым), Moskovskaya ul. 1/6, is a central hotel. (☎32 60 01. Call ahead. Singles 30hv; doubles 50hv; triples 65hv.) To get to **Motel-Camping Polyana Skazok** (Поляна Сказок), ul. Kirova 167 (Кірова), take bus #11, 26, or 27 from the bus station or bus #8 from city center to "Поляна Сказок," then walk 20 minutes uphill. (☎39 74 39. No tents. 2-person bungalows US$5; motel doubles US$10.) **Yalos** (Ялос), nab. Lenina, serves Ukrainian, American, and Italian cuisine. (Live music nightly. Entrees 5-19hv. Open noon-late.)

EXCURSIONS FROM YALTA. Only an hour **hike** or a 15-minute **boat** ride from Yalta, **Livadia** hosted the imprecisely named **Yalta Conference,** when Churchill, Roosevelt, and Stalin met in February 1945 at Tsar Nicholas II's summer palace to hash out postwar territorial claims. The **Great Palace** (Veliky Dvorets; Великий Дворец) is worth the visit regardless of its historical significance. (Open in summer daily 10am-6pm; off season Th-Tu 10am-4pm. 8hv, students 6hv.) **Buses** #26 and 27 run to Livadia from Yalta (10min., every 30-40min., 0.65hv).

ODESSA (ОДЕССА) ☎0482

Long ago, Odessa became an important port, populated by merchants and vagabonds from across Europe and Central Asia; its geography and luck helped it prosper and allowed it to grow gloriously corrupt. Today, the splendor endures, but Odessites are wistful for the city's once-upon-a-time greatness. A haven for intellectuals as well as thieves and *mafiosi*, Odessa has taken to post-Soviet crime like a fish to water, becoming one of the parent cities of the Russian mafia. The party town of the former USSR still hums, just at a lower frequency.

PRACTICAL INFO, ACCOMMODATIONS, AND FOOD. Trains go from pl. Privokzalnaya (Привокзальная), at the north end of ul. Pushkinskaya, to: Kiev (12hr., 2 per day, 38hv); Lviv (16hr., every day, 45hv); Moscow (26hr., 3 per day, 121hv); and St. Petersburg (35hr., every day, 112hv). Trams #2, 3, and 12 run along ul. Preobrazhenskaya to ul. Deribasovskaya. **Buses** go from ul. Dzerzhinskovo 58 (Дзержинского) to Kiev (12hr., 4 per day, 39hv) and Simferopol (8hr., 2 per day, 26hv); take tram #5 from the train station or #15 from downtown. Both stop four blocks from the station. Buy tickets at least the night before. **Morskoy Vokzal** (Морской Вокзал; Sea Terminal), ul. Suvorov 12 (Суворов) sends **ferries** to Istanbul (1-2 days, 4 per week, 150hv). **Eugenia Travel** in Morskoy Vokzal arranges tours, sells ferry tickets, and the staff speaks English. Ask for the director, Janna Belovsova. (☎22 05 54, office ☎21 85 81.) Get **Internet** access at **Komputer-Klub,** ul. Preobrazhenskaya 38. (Преобаженская; 4.50hv per hr., 4hv after 11pm. Open 24hr.) **Private rooms** are cheap (from US$5 per person), but you'll be lucky to get anything near the city center. Take tram #3 or 12 from the train station to the downtown hotels, all near noisy pl. Grecheskaya (Греческая) and ul. Deribasovskaya (Дерибасовская). Charming **Passazh** (Пассаж), ul. Preobrazhenskaya 34, is next to the real Passazh. (☎20 48 49. Singles 59-107hv; doubles 56-135hv.) **Tsentralny** (Центральный), ul. Preobrazhenskaya 40, has big rooms. (☎26 84 06. Singles 50hv-94hv; doubles 60-132hv; triples 90-160hv.) The **Privoz mega-market** (Привоз), Privoznaya ul., is near the train station. **Postal code:** 65 000.

SIGHTS AND ENTERTAINMENT. Street culture centers on **ul. Deribasovskaya,** inhabited by jazz musicians, mimes, and young hipsters. Take a left on ul. Rishelevskaya from the end of the street to find the **Museum of the Black Sea Fleet** (Muzey morskovo flota; Музей морского флота), ul. Lanzheronovskaya 6 (Ланжероновская), and its collection of model ships. (Open M-W and F-Su 11am-5pm. 2hv. Russian tour 8hv.) Left off ul. Deribasovskaya onto ul. Yekaterinskaya, the statue of the **Duc de Richelieu,** the city's first governor, stares down the **Potemkin Stairs** (Potomkinski skhody; Потемкинскап сходп) toward the shiny port, **Morskoy Vokzal.** Director Sergei Eisenstein used the stairs in his 1925 silent epic *Battleship Potemkin*, and the name stuck. The **Literature Museum** (Literaturny muzey; Литературный Музей), Lanzheronovskaya 2, takes a fascinating look at the city's intellectual and cultural heritage. (☎22 32 13. Open Tu-Su 10am-5pm. 6hv.) Odessa's main quarry lies directly underneath the city and over time became the world's longest series of **catacombs.** During the Nazi occupation, the resistance was based here, and the city has set up a superb subterranean **museum** in its honor. Eugenia Travel (see above) organizes tours in English (US$45 per group; times and prices negotiable). The farther from the center you go, the cleaner the **beaches;** most are reachable either by public transport or walking. Trolley #5 goes to **Arkadiya** (Аркадия); **Lanzheron** (Ланжерон), the beach closest to central Odessa, and **Otrada** (Отрада). Trams #17 and 18 go to **Golden Shore** (Zolotoy Bereg; Золотой Берег), **Chayka** (Чайка), and **Kurortny** (Курортный) beaches. **Vidrada** (Видрада) is a pleasant walk from Odessa through Park Shevchenko.

The **Opera and Ballet Theater** (Teatr Opery i Baleta; Театр Оперы и Балета), at the end of ul. Rishelevskaya, has Sunday shows at noon. Buy tickets in advance from the ticket office to the right of the theater. (Open M-F 10:30am-5pm, Sa-Su 10:30am-4pm. 15-25hv, US$3-35 when a major act comes to town.) Odessa truly never sleeps. The restaurants, cafes, and bars on **ul. Deribasovskaya** hop all night with beer, vodka, and music ranging from Euro-techno to Slavic folk. **Gambrinus** (Гамбринус), at #31, at the intersection with ul. Zhukova (Жукова), is a historic landmark. (Open daily 10am-11pm.) The concentration of discos in **Arkadiya** (trolley #7 from the train station, #5 from pl. Grechskaya) attracts Odessa's hippest crowds.

APPENDIX

GLOSSARY

B=British, **C**=Czech, **F**=French, **Fi**=Finnish, **G**=German, **Gr**=Greek, **I**=Italian, **Ir**=Irish, **S**=Spanish, **T**=Turkish

addition (F): check
aérogare (F): air terminal
agora (Gr): a level city square; marketplace
Autobahn, autoroute (G, F): motorway
ayuntamiento (S): city hall
Bahnhof (G): train station
billet (F): ticket
boulangerie (F): bakery
Brauhaus (G): brewhouse
Brücke (G): bridge
bureau d'échange (F): money exchange desk
caff (B): diner-style restaurant
calle (S): street
cambio (I): change
campo (I): market
carnet (F): packet
carrer (S): street
casco antiguo/viejo (S): old city
cave (F): wine cellar
çay (T): tea
centre commercial (F): shopping plaza
cerveza (S): beer
chambres d'hôtes (F): bed and breakfasts
charcuterie (F): shop selling cooked meats
ciudad nueva (S): new city
ciudad vieja (S): old city
ciudad vella (S): old city
con bagno (I): (room) with private bath
confiserie (F): candy store
corso (I): principal street or avenue
craic (Ir): fun, good times, etc.
domatia (Gr): room in private home
douche (F): shower
doccia (I): shower
Dusche (G): shower
entrée (F): appetizer
essence (F): gasoline
est (F): east
ferrovia (I): railways
Flohmarkt (G): flea market
Flughafen (G): airport
Flugzeug (G): airplane
foyer (F): student dorm
Fremdenverkehrsamt (G): tourist office
gabinetto (I): toilet, WC
gare (F): train station
gare routière (F): bus station
Gasse (G): alley, street
gîte d'étape (F): hostel
grilli (Fi): fast-food stand
hamam (T): bathhouse
hauptbahnhof (G): main train station
hebdomadaire (F): weekly
Hlavní nádraží (C): main station
hospedajes (S): cheap lodging
Innenstadt (G): city center
kaamos (Fi): polar night
kahuila (Fi): café
Kauppatori (Fi): market square
kesähotelli (Fi): summer hotels
Lager (G): dorm-style accommodations
laverie (F): laundromat
leoforeo (Gr): bus
Mahlzeit (G): meal; Enjoy your meal!
marché (F): outdoor market
marché aux puces (F): flea market
midi (F): noon
minuit (F): midnight
Mittag (G): noon
Mitternacht (G): midnight
monnaie (F): change
nádraží (C): station
Neustadt (G): new city
nord (F, G): north
ouest (F): west
olut (Fi): beer
ost (G): east
otogar (T): bus station
panini (I): sandwiches
paleochora (Gr): old town
pansiyon (T): typical accommodation
paseo (S): promenade (abbreviated *po.*)
passeig (S): promenade (abbreviated *pg.*)
pâtisserie (F): pastry shop
pensione (S): room in private home
piazza (I): city square
piazzale (I): large open square
plaça, place, plateia, Platz, (S, F, Gr, G): square
plage (F): beach
plat (F): main course
playa (S): beach
pleio (Gr): ferry
pont (F): bridge
préservatif (F): condom
primi (I): first course (usually pasta)
Privatzimmer (G): room in a private home
ravintola (Fi): restaurant
Rechnung (G): bill, check
retkeilymaja (Fi): youth hostel
S-Bahn (G): short-distance commuter rail
secondi (I): second course (usually meat or fish)
spiaggia (I): beach
Strand (G): beach
Straße (G): street
sud (F, G): south
télécarte (F): phone card
télépherique (F): cable car lift
torvet (D): main square
trad (B): traditional Irish jazz
via (I): street
viale (I): street
vicolo (I): alley, lane

GREEK	ENG.	GREEK	ENG.	GREEK	ENG.	GREEK	ENG.
Α, α	A, a	Η, η	I, i; E,e	Ν, ν	N, n	Τ, τ	T, t
Β, β	V, v	Θ, θ	Th, th	Ξ, ξ	X, x	Υ, υ	Y, y; I, i
Γ, γ	G, g; Y, y	Ι, ι	I, i	Ο, ο	O, o	Φ, φ	F, f
Δ, δ	D, d	Κ, κ	K, k	Π, π	P, p	Χ, χ	Ch, ch; H, h
Ε, ε	E, e	Λ, λ	L, l	Ρ, ρ	R, r	Ψ, ψ	Ps, ps
Ζ, ζ	Z, z	Μ, μ	M, m	Σ, σ, ς	S, s	Ω, ω	O, o

CYR.	ENG.	CYR.	ENG.	CYR.	ENG.	CYR.	ENG.
А, а	a ("ah")	И, и	i ("ee")	Р, р	r	Ш, ш	sh
Б, б	b	Й, й	y	С, с	s	Щ, щ	shch
В, в	v	К, к	k	Т, т	t	Ъ, ъ	(hard–no sound)
Г, г	g	Л, л	l	У, у	u ("oo")	Ы, ы	y ("pit")
Д, д	d	М, м	m	Ф, ф	f	Ь, ь	(soft–no sound)
Е, е	ye or e	Н, н	n	Х, х	kh ("ch")	Э, э	eh
Ё, ё	yo ("aw")	О, о	o ("aw")	Ц, ц	ts	Ю, ю	yoo
Ж, ж	zh ("j")	П, п	p	Ч, ч	ch	Я, я	yah
З, з	z						

ENGLISH	FRENCH	PRONOUNCED	SPANISH	PRONOUNCED
THE BASICS	**Pronunciation:** "ay" rhymes with "bay"; "ai" rhymes with "eye"; in French, *n* is nasal, not consonantal.			
hello	bonjour	bo*n*-ZHOOR	hola	OH-la
goodbye	au revoir	oh-VWAH	adios/hasta luego	a-dee-OS/a-sta LWAY-go
please	s'il vous plaît	see-voo-PLAY	por favor	por fa-VOR
thank you/you're wel-come	merci/je vous en pris (*f.*) de rien (*inf.*)	mer-SEE/zhe vooz o*n* PREE/de ree-E*N*	gracias/de nada	GRA-see-as/day NA-da
yes/no	oui/non	wee/no*n*	sí/no	see/no
excuse me/sorry	Excusez-moi/Désolé/Pardon	eks-kyou-zay MWA/day-zo-lay/par-DO*N*	perdón	per-DONE
How are you?	(Comment) ça va?	(ko-mo*n*) sa VA?	¿Como está?	koh-moh es-TA?
Fine/well.	(Ça va) bien.	(sa va) BYE*N*.	Así así./Bien.	a-SEE a-SEE/byen
Do you speak English?	Parlez-vous anglais?	par-lay voo o*n*-GLAY?	¿Habla inglés?	a-bla ing-GLEHS?
What's your name? My name is...	Comment vous appelez-vous? Je m'appelle...	ko-mo*n* vooz AH-pe-lay voo? zhe ma-PEL...	¿Cómo se llama? Me llamo...	KO-mo say YA-ma?/may YA-mo...
Sorry?/Please repeat	Pardon?/Répétez, s'il vous plaît.	par-DO*N*?/ray-pay-TAY, see-voo-PLAY.	¿Perdón?	pair-DON?
I don't understand	Je ne comprends pas.	zhe ne kom-PRO*N*-pa.	No entiendo.	no en-TYEN-do.
How do you say...?	Comment dit-on...en français?	ko-mo*n* dee-to*n*...o*n* fro*n*-SAY?	¿Cómo se dice...en español?	ko-mo say DEE-say...en es-pan-YOL?
How much...?	Ça coûte combien?	sa koot kom-BYE*N*?	¿Cuánto cuesta...?	kwan-to KWEST-a?
Help!/Stop!	Au secours!/Arrêtez!	o-se-KOOR!/a-re-TAY!	¡Socorro!/¡Déjame!	so-KO-ro/DAY-ha-may
DIRECTIONS				
Where is...?	Où est...?	oo ay...?	¿Dónde está...?	don-day es-TA..?
straight ahead	toute droite	toot dwat	derecho	deh-REH-cho
(to the) right/left	(à) droite/gauche	a DWAT/GOHSH	(a la) derecha/izquierda	(a la) deh-REH-cha/es-KYAIR-da
near/far	loin/proche	lwa*n*/prohsh	cerca/lejos	SAIR-ka/lay-hos
I'm lost.	Je me suis égaré (m.)/égarée (f.).	zhe me sweez ay-ga-RAY/ay-ga-RAY	Estoy perdido (m.)/perdida (f.).	eh-stoy pair-DEE-do/pair-DEE-da
town center	centre ville	so*n*-truh VEE-yuh	el centro	el SEN-tro
post office	la poste	la POST	correos	ko-RAY-os
the police	la police	la poh-LEES	la policia	la po-lee-SEE-ya
the hospital	l'hôpital	loh-pee-TAL	el hospital	el os-pee-TAL
a doctor	un médecin	*un* mayd-SA*N*	un doctór	oon dok-TOR
telephone	téléphone	tay-lay-FON	teléfono	teh-LEH-fo-no
bathroom	les toilettes/la salle de bain	lay twah-LET/la sal de BE*N*	el baño	el BA-nyo
TRANSPORTATION				
bus station	la gare routière	la gar roo-tee-AIR	estación de autobús	eh-sta-SYON day ow-to-BOOS
train station	la gare	la GAR	estación de tren	eh-sta-SYON day TRAYN
arrival/departure	arrivée/départ	a-ree-VAY/day-PAR	llegada/salida	yay-GA-da/sa-LEE-da
ticket/supplement	billet/supplément	bee-YAY/soo-play-MO*N*	billete/suplemento	bee-YAY-tay/soo-pluh-MEN-to
platform/track	voie	vwah	anden/vía	AN-dehn/VEE-ya
entrance/exit	entrée/sortie	o*n*-TRAY/sor-TEE	entradas/salida	ayn-TRA-das/sa-LEE-da
seat reservation	réservation de place	ray-zer-va-SYO*N* de plas	reserva	ray-SAIR-va
timetable	horaire	or-AIR	horario	oh-RAR-ee-o
berth/couchette	place couchée/couchette	plas koo-SHAY/koo-SHET	cama/cabina de literas	KA-ma/ka-BEE-na day lee-TEH-ras
I would like a one-way (round-trip) ticket to...	Je voudrais un billet (aller-retour) pour...	zhe voo-DRAY *un* bee-YAY (a-lay re-TOOR) poor...	Quisiera un billete ida (de ida y vuelta) a...	kee-SYAIR-a oon bee-YAY-tay EE-da (day EE-da ee VWAIL-ta) a...
first/second class	première/deuxième class	pre-MYAIR/DEU-zyem klas	primera/segunda clase	pree-MAIR-a/say-GOON-da KLA-say
left luggage	consigne	ko*n*-SEEN-yuh	consigna	kon-SEEG-na

GERMAN	PRONOUNCED	ITALIAN	PROUNOUNCED
THE BASICS			
hallo	HA-lo	buon giorno/buona sera/ buona notte	bwon JOR-no/bwo-nah SAYR-uh/bwo-nah NO-tay
Auf Wiedersehen (*f.*)/ Tschüs (*inf.*)	owf VEE-der-zayn/choos	arrivederci (*f.*) ciao (*inf.*)	a-ree-vuh-DAYR-chee/chow
bitte	BI-tuh	per favore	payr fa-VOR-ay
danke/bitte	DAHNG-kuh/BI-tuh	grazie/prego	GRA-tsee/PRAY-go
ja/nein	yah/nain	sì/no	see/no
Entschuldigung/Verzeihung	ent-SHOOL-di-gung/fer-TSAI-ung	scusi/mi dispiace	SKOO-zee/mee
Wie geht es Ihnen?/ Wie geht es dir?	vee GAYT es ee-nen?/vee GAYT es deer?	Come sta (*f.*)/stai (*inf.*)?	koh-may-STA/STAI
Mir geht es gut.	meer gayt es GOOT.	Sto bene.	sto BAY-nay
Sprechen Sie Englisch?	shpre-khen zee ENG-glish?	Parla inglese?	par-la ing-GLAY-zay?
Wie heißen Sie? Ich heiße...	vee HAI-sen zee? ikh HAI-se...	Come si chiama? Mi chi-amo...	ko-may see kee-AH-ma? mee kee-AH-mo...
Bitte/Können Sie das wieder-holen?	BI-tuh/kun-nen zee das vee-der-HO-len?	Prego/Potrebbe ripetere?	PRAY-go/po-TRAY-bay ree-pay-TAYR-ay?
Ich verstehe nicht.	ikh fer-SHTAY-uh neekht.	Non capisco.	non ka-PEE-sho
Wie sagt man...auf Deutsch?	vee ZAHGT mahn...owf doitsh?	Come si dice...?	ko-may see DEE-chay...?
Wieviel kostet...?	vee-feel KOS-tet?	Quanto costa...?	kwan-to KOHS-sta...?
Hilfe!/Hör auf!	HIL-fuh!/her OWF!	Aiuto!/Ferma!	ai-OO-toh!/FAYR-ma!
DIRECTIONS			
Wo ist...?	vo ist...?	Dov'è...?	DOH-vay...?
gerade aus	ge-RAH-duh ows	sempre diritto	sem-pray deer-EE-toh?
(nach) rechts/links	(nahkh) rekhts/links	(a) destra/sinistra	(a) DES-tra/see-NEES-tra
nahe/weit	nah/vait	lontano/vicino	lon-TAH-noh/vee-CHEE-noh
Ich habe mich verirrt.	ikh hah-buh meekh fer-EERT.	Mi sono perso (m.)/persa (f.)	mee soh-noh PAYR-soh/ PAYR-sa
das Zentrum	das TSEN-trum	il centro	eel CHEN-troh
die Post	dee POST	posta	POHS-ta
die Polizei	dee po-li-TSAI	la polizia	la poh-LEE-tsee-a
das Krankenhaus	das KRANK-en-hows	l'ospedale	lohs-pe-DAH-lay
der Arzt	dare ARTST	dottore	doh-TOR-ay
das Telefon	das teh-leh-FUN	telefono	tay-LAY-foh-noh
die Toilette	dee twah-LET	il bagno	eel BAH-nyoh
TRANSPORTATION			
Zentraler Omnibusbahnhof (ZOB)	tsen-TRAH-ler ohm-nee-boos-BAHN-hohf	autostazione	sta-tsee-OH-nay dee OW-toh-boos
der Bahnhof	dare BAHN-hohf	stazione	sta-tsee-OH-nay
die Ankunft/die Abfahrt	dee AHN-koonft/dee AHB-fart	l'arrivo/la partenza	la-REE-voh/la par-TEN-za
die Fahrkarte/ die Zuschlag	dee FAHR-kar-tuh/dee TSOO-shlag	biglietto/supplemento	bee-LYEH-toh/soo-play-MEN-toh
der Bahnstein/ das Gleis	dare BAHN-shtain/das GLAIS	binario	bee-NAR-ee-oh
der Eingang/ der Ausgang	dare AIN-gahng/dare OWS-gahng	l'ingresso/l'uscita	lin-GRES-OH/LOO-shee-tah
die Sitzplatzreservierung	dee zits-plahts-re-zer-VEER-ung	prenotazione posti	pray-noh-ta-tsee-OH-nay POS-tee
der Fahrplan	dare FAHR-plahn	orario	o-RAH-ree-oh
Bettplatz/Liegeplatz	BET-plahts/LEE-guh-plahts	letto/cuccetta	LEH-toh/koo-CHE-ta
Ich möchte eine einfache Fahrkarte (Rückfahrkarte) nach...	ikh MEUKH-tuh ai-nuh AIN-fahkh-uh FAR-kar-tuh (REUKH-far-kar-tuh) nahkh...	Vorrei un biglietto solo andata (andata e ritorna) per...	vo-RAY oon bee-LYEH-toh SO-lo an-DAH-ta (an-DAH-ta ay ree-TOR-na) payr...
erste/zweite Klasse	ayr-stuh/tsvai-tuh klah-suh	prima/seconda classe	PREE-ma/se-KON-da KLA-suh
Schliessfächer (lockers)	SHLEES-fekh-er	deposito bagagli	day-PO-zee-toh ba-GA-lyee

APPENDIX

ENGLISH	FRENCH	PRONOUNCED	SPANISH	PRONOUNCED
What time does the train/bus/ferry leave?	A quelle heure part le train/autobus/bac?	ah kel er par le TRE*N*/OW-toh-boos/bahk?	¿Cuándo sale el tren/autobús/barca de pasaje?	KWAN-do SA-lay el TRAYN/ow-to-BOOS/BAR-ka day pa-SA-khe
Do you stop at...?	Vous arrêtez à...?	vooz A-re-tay ah...?	¿Para en/a...?	PA-ra ayn/a...?
bus stop (tram stop)	arrêt d'autobus (arrêt de tramway)	a-reh DOW-toh-boos (a-reh de TRAHM-way)	parada de autobus	pa-RA-da day OW-to-boos
car	voiture	vwah-TOOR	coche	KOH-chay
taxi	taxi	TAHK-see	taxi	TAK-see

ACCOMMODATIONS

ENGLISH	FRENCH	PRONOUNCED	SPANISH	PRONOUNCED
hotel	l'hôtel	loh-TEL	el hotel	el oh-TEL
hostel	auberge de jeunesse	oh-BAYRZH de zheu-NES	hostal/albergue	oh-STAHL/al-BAYR-gway
guesthouse	(no equivalent)		pensión	pen-SYON
I'd like a single/double.	Je voudrais une chambre simple/pour deux.	zheu voo-DRAY oon shahm-bre SAM-ple/poor DEU	Quisiera un cuarto simple/un doble.	kee-see-AY-ra oon KWAR-to SEEM-play/oon DOH-blay.
camping	camping	kahm-PING	camping	KAHM-ping
I'd like to make a reservation.	Je voudrais faire une réservation.	zhe voo-DRAY FAYR oon RAY-sayr-va-syo*n*	Quisiera hacer una reserva.	kee-see-AY-ra ah-SAYR oo-na ray-SAYR-va

TIME AND NUMBERS

ENGLISH	FRENCH	PRONOUNCED	SPANISH	PRONOUNCED
yesterday	hier	ee-AIR	ayer	a-YAYR
today	aujourd'hui	oh-zhoor-DWEE	hoy	oy
tomorrow	demain	de-ME*N*	mañana	mah-NYAH-nah
day after tomorrow	l'après-demain	l'ah-PREH-duh-MA*N*	(no equivalent)	
morning	matin	mah-TE*N*	mañana	mah-NYAH-nah
afternoon	après-midi	ah-pray-mee-DEE	tarde	TAR-day
What time do you open/close?	A quelle heure êtes-vous ouvert/fermé?	a kel er et-vooz oo-VERT/fayr-MAY?	¿A que hora abre/cierra?	a kay O-ra AH-bray/see-AYR-ra?
Monday, Tuesday, Wednesday, Thursday, Friday, Saturday, Sunday	lundi, mardi, mercredi, jeudi, vendredi, samedi, dimanche	LEU*N*-dee, MAR-dee, MAYR-cre-dee, ZHEU-dee, VO*N*-dre-dee, SAHM-dee, DEE-mo*n*sh	lunes, martes, miércoles, jueves, viernes, sábado, domingo	LOO-nays, MAR-tays, MYAYR-koh-lays, HWAY-vays, VYAYR-nays, SA-ba-do, do-MING-go
one	un	*un*	uno	OO-no
two	deux	deu	dos	dos
three	trois	twah	tres	trays
four	quatre	kaht	cuatro	KWAH-tro
five	cinq	sangk	cinco	SEENG-ko
six	six	sees	seis	says
seven	sept	set	siete	SYAY-tay
eight	huit	weet	ocho	OH-cho
nine	neuf	neuf	nueve	NWAY-vay
ten	dix	dees	diez	dyays
eleven	onze	*onz*	once	OHN-say
twelve	douze	dooz	doce	DOH-say
twenty	vingt	va*n*	veinte	VAYN-tay
thirty	trente	tro*n*	treinta	TRAYN-ta
forty	quarante	KAH-ro*n*	cuarenta	kwa-REN-ta
fifty	cinquante	SANG-ko*n*	cinquenta	seen-KWEN-ta
sixty	soixante	SWAH-so*n*	seseta	say-SAY-ta
seventy	soixante-dix	swah-so*n*-DEES	setenta	say-TAYN-ta
eighty	quatre-vingt	KAH-truh-va*n*	ochenta	oh-CHAYN-ta
ninety	quatre-vingt-dix	kah-truh-va*n*-DEES	noventa	noh-VAYN-ta
one hundred	cent	so*n*	cien	syayn
one thousand	mille	meel	mil	meel

GERMAN	PRONOUNCED	ITALIAN	PROUNOUNCED
Um wieviel Uhr fährt der Zug/der Autobus/die Fähre ab?	oom VEE-feel oor FAYRT dare TSOOG/dare OW-toh-boos/dee FAY-ruh AHB?	A che ora parte il treno/l'autobus/il traghetto?	a kay O-ra PAR-tay eel TRAY-noh/LOW-toh-boos/eel tra-GE-toh?
Halten Sie an...?	HAL-ten zee ahn...?	Ferma a...?	FAYR-ma a...?
Bushaltestelle (Straßebahn-haltestelle)	BOOS-hal-tuh-shte-luh (SHTRAH-suh-bahn-hal-tuh-shte-luh)	fermata dell'autobus	fayr-MAH-ta del-OW-toh-boos
Auto/Wagen	OW-toh/VAH-gen	macchina/automobile	MA-chee-na/ow-toh-MOH-bee-lay
Taxi	TAHK-see	tassí	TAH-see
Hotel	ho-TEL	albergo	al-BAYR-go
Jugendherberge	YOO-gent-hayr-bayr-guh	ostello	oh-STEL-oh
Gasthof/Gästehaus	GAST-hof/GAY-stuh-hows	pensione	pen-SYOHN
Ich möchte ein Einzelzimmer/Doppelzimmer	ikh MEUKH-tuh ain AIN-tsel-tsi-muh/DOH-pel-tsi-muh	Vorrei una càmera síngola/doppia.	vor-AY oo-na KAH-may-rah SING-go-la/DOH-pyah
Campingplatz	KAHM-ping-plahts	campeggio	kahm-PAY-jyoh
Ich möchte eine Reservierung machen.	ikh MEUKH-tuh ai-nuh re-zayr-VEER-ung mah-khen.	Vorrei fare una prenotazione.	vor-AY FA-ray oo-na pray-noh-tah-tsee-OH-nay
gestern	GES-tern	ieri	ee-AYR-ee
heute	HOY-tuh	oggi	OH-jee
morgen	MOR-gen	domani	doh-MAH-nee
übermorgen	OO-buh-mor-gen	dopodomani	doh-poh-doh-MAH-nee
Morgen	MOR-gen	mattina	mah-TEE-nah
Nachmittag/Abend	NAHKH-mi-tak/AH-bent	pomeriggio	poh-may-REE-jyoh
Um wieviel Uhr öffnen/schließen sie?	oom VEE-feel oor UHF-nen/SHLEE-sen zee?	A che ora si apre/chiude...?	a kay O-ra see AH-pray/kee-OO-day
Montag, Dienstag, Mittwoch, Donnerstag, Frei-tag, Samstag/Sonnabend, Sonntag	MOHN-tak, DEEN-shtak, MIT-vohkh, DOH-ner-shtak, FRAI-tak, ZAM-stak/ZOHN-a-bent, ZOHN-tak	lunedí, martedí, mercoledí, giovedí, venerdí, sabato, domenica	loo-NAY-dee, mar-TAY-dee, mayr-koh-LAY-dee, jyoh-VAY-dee, vay-NAYR-dee, SAH-bah-toh, doh-MEH-nee-kah
eins	ains	uno	OO-no
zwei	tsvai	due	DOO-ay
drei	drai	tre	tray
vier	feer	quattro	KWAH-troh
fünf	feunf	cinque	CHING-kway
sechs	zeks	sei	say
sieben	ZEE-ben	sette	SEH-tay
acht	akht	otto	OH-toh
neun	noin	nove	NOH-vay
zehn	tsayn	dieci	DYAY-chee
elf	elf	undici	oon-DEE-chee
zwölf	tsveulf	dodici	doh-DEE-chee
zwanzig	TSVAN-tsik	venti	VEHN-tee
dreißig	DRAI-sik	trenta	TREHN-ta
vierzig	FEER-tsik	quaranta	kwa-RAHN-ta
fünfzig	FEUNF-tsik	cinquanta	chIng-KWAHN-ta
sechzig	ZEKH-tsik	sessanta	se-SAHN-ta
siebzig	ZEEP-tsik	settanta	se-TAHN-ta
achtzig	AKH-tsik	ottanta	oh-TAHN-ta
neunzig	NOYN-tsik	novanta	no-VAHN-ta
hundert	HOON-dert	cento	CHEN-toh
tausend	TOW-sent	mille	MEE-lay

APPENDIX

ENGLISH	BULGARIAN	PRONOUNCED	CZECH	PRONOUNCED
hello	Добър ден	DOH-bur den	Dobrý den	DO-bree den
goodbye	Довиждане	doh-VEEZH-dan-eh	Na shledanou	nah SLEH-dah-noh-oo
please	Извинете	eez-vi-NEH-teh	Prosím	PROH-seem
thank you	Благодаря	blahg-oh-dahr-YAH	Děkuji	DYEH-koo-yih
yes/no	Да/Не	dah/neh	Ano/ne	AH-no/neh
sorry/excuse me	съжалявам	suhj-ha-LYA-vahm	Promiňte	PROH-mihn-teh
Do you speak English?	Говорите ли Английски?	go-VO-rih-te li an-GLEES-keeh	Mluvíte anglicky?	MLOO-vit-eh ahng-GLIT-ski
I don't understand.	Не разбирам.	neh rahz-BIH-rahm	Nerozumím.	neh-rohz-oo-MEEM
Help!	Помощ!	PO-mosht	Pomoc!	poh-MOTS
Where is...?	Къде е?	kuh-DEH eh	Kde?	k-DEH
left/right/straight ahead	отляво/отдясно/направо	ot-LYAH-vo/ot-DYAHS-no/na-PRA-vo	vlevo/vpravo/rovně	VLE-voh/FPRA-voh/ROV-nyeh
What time does [the train/bus/boat] (depart/arrive)?	В колко часа (заминава/пристига) [влакът/автобус/ферибот]?	V kol-ko cha-sah (za-mee-NAH-va/prih-STEE-ga) [VLA-kat/af-toe-BUS/feh-ree-bot]	Kdy (odjíždí/přijíždí) [vlak/autobus/lod']?	k-DEE (ot-yeezh-dee/pree-yeezh) [vlahk/OUT-oh-boos/loadge]
today/tomorrow/yesterday	Днес/утре/вчера	dness/oo-treh/VCHEH-rah	dnes/zítra/včera	dness/ZEE-tra/FCHE-ra
I'd like a (one-way/round-trip) ticket.	Искам един билет (отиване/отиване и връщане).	EES-kahm eh-DEEN bee-LEHT (oh-TEE-va-neh/oh-TEE va-neh ee VRIH-shta-neh)	Prosím (jen tam/zpáteční) jízdenku do...	PROH-seem (yen tam/SPAH-tech-nyee) YEEZ-denkoo DOH...
How much is it?	Колко Струва?	KOHL-ko STROO-va	Kolik stojí?	KOH-lihk STOH-yee
hostel	общежитие	ob-shteh-jeet-yeh	mládežnická noclehárna	mla-dezh-nit-ska nots-le-haar-na
hotel	хотел	hotel	hotel	ho-TELL
camping	лагеруване	lageruvane	kemping	KEM-ping
I'd like a (single/double) room.	Искам (самостоятелна/за двама) стая.	EES-kahm (sa-mo-sto-YA-tel-na/za DVA-ma) STA-ya	Prosím (jednolůžkový/dvoulůžkový) pokoj.	PROH-seem (YED-no-loosh-ko-vee/DVOH-loosh-ko-vee) PO-koy

ENGLISH	FINNISH	PRONOUNCED	GREEK	PRONOUNCED
hello	hei	hey	Γεια σας	YAH-sas
goodbye	näkemiin	NA-kay-meen	αντιο	an-DEE-oh
please	pyydän	BU-dan	Παρακαλω	pah-rah-kah-LO
thank you	kiitos	KEE-tohss	Ευχαριστω	ef-hah-ree-STO
yes/no	kyllä/ei	EW-la/AY	Ναι / Οχι	NEH/OH-hee
sorry/excuse me	anteeksi	ON-take-see	Συγνομη	seeg-NO-mee
Do you speak English?	Puhutteko englantia?	POO-hoot-teh-kaw ENG-lan-ti-ah?	Μιλας αγγλικα?	mee-LAHS ahn-glee-KAH?
I don't understand.	En ymmärrä.	ehn OOM-ma-ruh.	Δεν καταλαβαινω.	dhen kah-tah-lah-VEH-no.
Help!	Apua!	AH-poo-ah	βοηθεια!	vo-EETH-ee-ah!
Where is...?	Missä on...?	MEESS-ah OWN	Που ειναι...?	pou EE-neh...?
left/right/straight ahead	vasen/oikea/suoraan	VAHSS-en/OY-kay-ah/SOOA-rahn	αριστερα / δεξια / ευθεια	a-ree-stair-AH/dek-see-AH/ef-THEE-a
What time does [the train/bus/boat] (depart/arrive)?	Mihin aikaan [juna/bussi/laiva] (lähtee/saapuu)	ME-hin EYE-ka-ahn [yoo-na/BOOSE-ee/LIVE-a] (leh-tee/SAA-poo-oo)?	Τι ωρα (φευγει/φτα νει) [το τρενο / το λεωφορειο / το καραβι]?	tee OR-ah (feev-yee/ftah-nee) [toe TRAY-no/toe lee-oh-for-EE-oh/toe kah-RAH-vee]
today/tomorrow/yesterday	tänään/huomenna/eilen	YEH-nehhn/HOOA-main-na/EYE-lane	σημερα/αυριο/χθες	SEE-mer-a/AV-ree-o/k-THES
I'd like a (one-way/round-trip) ticket.	Saisinko (menolipun/menopaluulipun).	SAY-sing-koah (MAY-no-LIP-poon/MAY-no-PAH-looo-LIP-poon)	Θα ηθελα (μονο εισιτηριο / εισιτηριο με επιστροφη).	tha ETH-eh-la (mo-NO ee-see-TEE-ree-o/ee-see-TEE-ree-o me eh-pee-stro-FEE)
How much does it cost?	Paljonko tämä maksaa?	PA-lee-onk-o teh-meh MOCK-sah	ποσο κανει?	PO-so KAH-nee
hostel	retkeilymaja	rett-keh-eel-oo-my-ah	ξενωναζ νεοτητοζ	zee-NO-naz nee-OH-tee-toes
hotel	hotelli	ho-TELL-ee	ξενοδοχειο	zee-no-do-HEE-oh
camping	leirintäalue	lay-rin-teh-ah-loo-eh	καμπιγκ	KAHM-ping
I'd like a (single/double) room?	Haluaisin (yhden/kahden) hengen huoneen.	HAH-loo-eye-seen (oo-den/kah-den) hen-gen hoo-oh-neen	Θελω ενα (μονο / διπλο) δωματιο	THEL-oh EH-na (mon-OH/dee-PLO) doh-MA-tee-oh

APPENDIX

DANISH	PRONOUNCED	DUTCH	PRONOUNCED	ESTONIAN	PRONOUNCED
goddag/hej	go-DAY/HI	hallo	hallo	tere	TEH-re
farvel/hejhej	fah-VEL/HI-hi	tot ziens	toht-zeens	head aega	hed AEH-gah
vær så venlig	VAIR soh VEN-li	alstublieft	ALST-ew-bleeft	palun	PA-lun
tak	TACK	dank u wel	dahnk ew vel	tänan	TEH-nan
ja/nej	ya/nye	ja/nee	ya/nay	jaa/ei	yah/ay
undskyld	UN-scoold	excuseert u mij	ex-kew-ZAYRT ew my	Vabandage	vah-pan-TAGE-euh
Taler du engelsk?	TAY'-luh dou ENG'-elsk	Spreekt u engels?	spraykt ew ENG-els	Kas te räägite inglise keelt?	Kas te RA-A-gite INGlise keelt
Jeg forstår ikke.	yai for-STOR IG-guh	Ik begrijp u niet.	ik beh-GHRIPE ew neet	Ma ei saa aru.	ma ee sa AH-roo
Hjælp!	yelp	help!	help	Appi!	APP-pi
Hvor er?	voa' air	Waar iz...?	var iss	Kus on...?	kuhs on
til venstre/til højre/lige ud	till VEN-struh/till HOY-ruh/lee oothe	links/rechts/rechtdoor	links/hrechts/hrecht-door	vasakul/paremal/otse edasi	VA-sa-cul/PA-ray-mal/AWT-seh AY-duh-see
Hvornår (går/ankommer) [toget/bussen/båden]?	vor-NOR (gore/AN-kom-ma) [TOE'-et/BOOSE-en/BOTHE-en]?	Hoe laat (vertrecht/komt) de [trein/bus/kom] ?	HOO laht (ver-TRE-CHT/komt) de [trine/buhs/kom]	Mis kell (lähels/saabub) [rong/buss/paat]?	meese kell (LA-helss/SAH-boob) [hrong/bus/paht]?
i dag/i morgen/i går	ee-DAY/ee-MORN/ee-GORE	vandaag/morgen/gisteren	fon-DAHG/MOR-ghun/GHIST-er-un	täna/eile/homme	TEN-ah/EYHL/OH-may
Jeg vil gerne ha en (enkelbillet/tur-retur billet) til ...	YAI vil' GAIR-nuh ha een (EHN-kul-bill-ETT/TOOR-re-TOOR bill-ETT) till...	Ik wil graag (een enkele reis/retour).	ik vil khrahk ayn (ENG-kuh-luhrice/ruh-toor)	Palun, (üheotsa/edasi-tagasi) piletit	PA-loon (EW-heh-awt-sah/Eh-da-see-TA-ga-see) PEE-let-it
Hvad koster det?	va KOS'-tor dey	Wat kost dit?	vaht kost dit	Kui palju?	kwee PAL-you
vandrerhjem	VAN-drar-yem	jeugdherberg	yuh-ahghd-hair-bearght	ühiselamu	ew-hee-sel-a-moo
hotel	ho-TELL	hotel	ho-TELL	hotell	ho-TELL
campingplads	CAM-ping-plass	kamperen	kahm-PAHR-en	laagriplats	LAH-gree-plats
Jeg ønsker et (enkeltværelse/dobbeltværelse).	YAI URN-ska it (EHN-kult-vair-ELL-sih/DOP-ult-vair-ELL-sih)	Ik wil graag een (een-/twee-) persoonskamer.	ik vil ghrahgh ayn (AYN/TVAY) per-sones-kah-mer	Ma sooviksin(ühelist/kahelist).	ma SOO-vik-sin (EW-hel-ist/KA-hel-ist)

HUNGARIAN	PRONOUNCED	LATVIAN	PRONOUNCED	LITHUANIAN	PRONOUNCED
jó napot	YOH naw-pot	labdien	LAHB-dyen	Labądien	Lah-bah-DEE-yen
szia	SEE-ya	Uz redzēšanos	ooz red-zee-shun-wass	viso gero	VYEE-so GYEH-ro
kérem	KAY-rem	lūdzu	LOOD-zuh	Prašau	prah-SHAU
köszönöm	KUR-sur-num	paldies	PAHL-dee-yes	Ačiu	AH-chyoo
igen/nem	EE-gen/nem	jā/nē	yah/ney	Taip/Ne	TAY-p/neh
sajnálom	shoy-na-lawm	atvainojos	AHT-vine-wa-ywoss	Atsiprašau	ahts-yi-prah-SHAoo
Beszél angolul?	BES–el AWN-gohlul	Vai Jūs runājat angliski	vie yoose ROO-na-yaht AHN-glee-skee	Ar Jūs kalbate angliškai?	ahr yoose KAHL-bah-te AHNG-lish-kigh
Nem értem	NEM AYR-tem	Es nesaprotu	ehs NEH-sa-proh-too	Aš nesuprantu.	ahsh ne-soo-pran-too
Segítség!	SHEH-gheet-shayg	Palidzājiet!	PAH-leedz-ayee-et	Gelbėkite!	GYEL-beh-kyi-te
Hol van...?	hole von	Kur ir...?	kuhr ihr	Kur yra...?	koor ee-RAH
bal/jobb/elöre	ball/yobe/eh-LEW-ray	kreisi/labi/pa taisno	kray-sih/lah-bih/puh-TICE-nwah	į kairę/į dešinę/važiuokite pirmyn	EE kigh-reh/EE deh-shi-neh/vazh-yo-kee-tay PEER-meen
Mikor (indul/érkesik) [vonat/busz-komp].	MEE-kawr (EEN-dool/AIR-keh-zik) [VO-nawt/boose/komp]	Kad (atiet/pienâkt) [vilciens/autobuss/prâmis].	cud (uh-tyat/pyah-nahkt) [VILLT-see-anss/OW-to-boose/prah-miss]	Kada (atvyksta/išvyksta) [traukinys/autobusas/laivas]?	ka-DAH (aht-vyook-sta/EESH-vooksta) [trav-KEEN-oose/OW-toe-bus/LIVE-us]
ma/holnap/tegnap	ma/OLE-nap/teg-nap	šodien/rīt/vakar	SHWA-dee-ahn/reet/VAH-kahr	šiandien/vakar/rytoj	SHYEN-dien/VAA-car/ree-TOY
Szeretnék egy (jegyet csak oda/returjegyet).	SEH-rett-nake edge (YED-jet chok AW-daw/rih-toor-YED-jet).	Es vēlos (vienā virzienāĽturp un atpakal) bileti.	ess VAIH-lywoss (VYA-na VIR-zeea-na/toorp oon AHT-pa-kal) bee-let-ee	Aš norėčiau bilieta į vienąĽabi puses.	ahsh no-RYEH-chi-aoo
Mennyibe kerül?	menyeebeh keh rewl	Cik maksā?	sikh MAHK-sah	Kiek kainuoja?	KEE-yek KYE-new-oh-yah
szálló	SA-lo	jaunieđu viesnīca	yow-nya-duh vyess-nee-tsah	jaunimo viešbutis	YAWN-ee-mo VYESH-boo-teese
szálloda	SA-lo-da	viesnīca	vyess-nee-tsah	viešbutis	VYESH-boo-teese
kemping	KEM-ping	kempings	kem-ping	kemping	kem-ping
Szeretnék egy (egyágyas/kétágyas) szobát	SEH-rett-nake edge (EDGE-ah-dyosh/KAY-tah-dyosh) SAW-baat.	Es vēlos istabu (vienai/divām) personām.	ess VAIH-lywoss IH-stah-boo (VYA-nye/DIH-vahm) PAIR-swa-nahm	Aš norėčiau kambario (vienviečio/dviviečio).	ahsh no-RYEH-chi-aoo KAHM-bah-rio (vyen-VYEEA-chyo/dvyee-VYEEA-chyo)

APPENDIX

ENGLISH	NORWEGIAN	PRONOUNCED	POLISH	PRONOUNCED
hello	hallo	hah-LOH	cześć	tcheshch
goodbye	ha det	HAA-deh	do widzenia	doh vee-DZHEN-ya
please	vær så god	VAIR-seh go	proszę	PROH-sheh
thank you	takk	TAHK	dziękuję	jeng-KOO-yeh
yes/no	Ja/Ikke or Ne	yah/IK-eh, nay	tak/nie	tak/nyeh
sorry/excuse me	unnskyld	OON-shool	Przepraszam	psheh-PRAH-sham
Do you speak English?	Snakker du engelsk?	SNA-kuh doo ENG-elsk	Czy Pan(i) mówi po anglicki?	tcheh PAHN (-ee) MOO-vee poh an-GLITS-kee
I don't understand.	Jeg forstår ikke.	yai four-STOR IK-eh	Nie rozumiem	nyeh roh-ZOO-myem
Help!	Hjelpe!	YELP-eh	Na pomoc!	nah POH-motz
Where is...?	Hvor er...?	VOR air...?	Gdzie jest...?	gdzheh yest
left/right/straight ahead	til venstre/til høyre/rett frem.	till VEN-struh/till HOY-ruh/reht frem	lewo/prawo/prosto	leh-vo/prah-vo/pross-toh
What time does [the train/bus/boat] (depart/arrive)?	Når (går/kommer) [toget/bussen/båten]?	nor (gore/COMB-air) TOE-geh/BOOSE-en/BOAT-en	O której godzinie (przychodzi/odchodzi) [pociąg/autobus]?	POHT-shawng/OW-toh-boos
today/tomorrow/yesterday	i dag/morgen/i går	ee DAHG/ee MORN/ee GORE	dzis/jutro/wczoraj	dzeess/yeeoo-tro/VCHORE-eye
I'd like a (one-way/round-trip) ticket.	Jeg vil gjerne ha (enkelt-billet/tur-retur)	YAI vill YAR-na ha (ENG-kult-bill-LET/TOOR rih-TOOR)	Poproszę bilet (w jedną stronęľtam i z powrotem)	poh-PROH-sheh BEE-leht (VYEHD-nawng STROH-neh/tahm ee spoh-VROH-tehm)
How much does it cost?	Hvor mye koster det?	VOR MEW-eh KOST-er deh?	Ile to kosztuje?	EE-leh toh kosh-TOO-yeh
hostel	vandrerhjem	VON-druh-yem	schronisko młodzieżowe	schrhon-isk-oh mwod-zyeh-zhoh-veh
hotel	hotell	ho-TELL	hotel	ho-tell
camping	camping	CAM-ping	kemping	kem-ping
I'd like a (single/double) room?	Jeg vil gjerne ha et (enkeltrom/dobbeltrom)	YAI vill YAIR-na ha ett (ENG-kult-room/DUB-elt-room)	Chciał(a) bym pokój (jednoosbowy/dwuosobowy)	KHTS-HAHW(a) bihm POH-kooy (yehd-noo-soh-BOH-vih/dvohoo-soh-BOH-vih)

ENGLISH	SERBO-CROATIAN	PRONOUNCED	SLOVAK	PRONOUNCED
hello	zdravo	ZDRAH-vo	dobrý deň	DOH-bree dyeny
goodbye	doviđenja	do-vee-JEHN-ya	do videnia	doh vee-DEN-yah
please	molim	MO-leem	prosím	PROH-seem
thank you	hvala vam	HVAH-la vahm	dakujem	dyak-uh-yem
yes/no	da/ne	da/neh	áno/nie	AH-no/nyieh
sorry/excuse me	oprostite	aw-PROSS-tee-tay	prepáčte	preh-padch-tyeh
Do you speak English?	Govorite li engleski?	GO-vor-i-teh lee eng-LEH-ski	Hovoríte po anglicky?	HO-voh-ree-tyeh poh ahn-glits-kih
I don't understand.	Ne razumijem.	neh ra-ZOO-mi-yem	Nerozumiem.	nyeh-RO-zuh-meem
Help!	U pomoć!	OO pomoch	Pomoc!	poh-mots
Where is...?	Gdje je?	g-DYEH YEH	Kde je?	gDYEH yeh
left/right/straight ahead	lijevo/desno/pravo	LYEH-vo/DESS-no/PRAH-vo	vlavo/vpravo/rovno	VLYAH-vo/VPRAH-vo/ROHV-no
What time does [the train/bus/boat] (depart/arrive)?	Kada [vlak/autobus/brod] (polazil/dolazil)?	KAH-da [vlok/ow-TOE-boose/brod] (poh-la-zil/doh-la-zil)	Kedy (odchádza/prichádza) [vlak/autobus/loč]?	keh-dee (wode-chahdz-ah/pree-chahdz-ah) [vlahk/ow-toe-bus/loatch]
today/tomorrow/yesterday	danas/sutra/jučer	DA-nass/SOO-tra/YOO-chay	dnes/zajtra/včera	dnyes/zai-tra/fcheh-rah
I'd like a (one-way/round-trip) ticket to...	Htio bih (u jednom smjerna/povratna karta) za...	HTEE-o beeh (oo YEH-dnom smee-YEH-roo/POV-rat-na KAR-ta) zah...	Prosím si... (jednosmerny/spiatočný) lístok.	PROH-SEEM sih (yed-no-smair-nee/spee-ya-toch-nee) lease-tok
What does it cost?	Koliko to košta?	KO-li-koh toh KOH-shta	Coto stojí?	KOH-to STOH-yee
hostel	omladinsko prenoćište	om-la-din-skoh preh-no-chish-teh	turistická ubytovňa mládeže	TOO-rist-ih-kah OO-bit-ov-nya MLAH-deh-zhe
hotel	hotel	hotel	hotel	HO-tell
camping	camping	cam-ping	kemping	KEM-ping
I'd like a (single/double) room?	Želio bih (jednokrevetnu/dvokrevetnu) sobu.	ZHEL-i-o bih (yed-no-KREH-vet-noo/dvoh-KREH-vet-noo) SO-bu	Potrebujem (jednoložkovú izbu/izbu pre dve osoby)	PO-tre-bu-yem (YED-no-loozh-ko-voo iz-buh) (IZ-buh preh DVEH oh-so-bih)

PORTUGUESE	PRONOUNCED	ROMANIAN	PRONOUNCED	RUSSIAN	PRONOUNCED
olá	oh-LAH	bună ziua	BOO-nuh zee-wah	добрый день	DOH-brih DYEN
adeus	ah-DAY-oosh	la revedere	la reh-veh-deh-reh	До свидания	dah svee-DA-nya
por favor	pur fah-VOR	Vă rog	vuh rohg	пожалуйсто	pa-ZHA-loo-sta
obrigado(-a) *(m./f.)*	oh-bree-GAH-doo/da	Mulţumesc	mool-tsoo-MESK	спасибо	spa-SEE-bah
sim/não	seeng/now	da/nu	dah/noo	да/нет	dah/nyet
desculpe	dish-KOOL-peh	Scuzaţi-mă	skoo-ZAH-tzee muh	извините	eez-vee-NEET-yeh
Fala inglês?	FAH-lah een-GLAYSH?	Vorbiţi englezeşţe?	vor-BEETZ ehng-leh-ZESH-teh	Вы говорите по английски?	vih go-vo-REE-tyeh po ahn-GLEE-ske?
não compreendo	now kompreeAYNdoo	Nu înţeleg	noo ihn-TZEH-lehg	Я не понимаю	ya nee pa-nee-MA-yoo
Socorro!	so-ko-RO!	Ajutor!	AH-zhoot-or	Помогите!	pah-mah-GHEE-tyeh
Onde é que é ...?	OHN-deh eh keh eh	Unde...?	OON-deh	Где...?	g-dye
esquerda/direita/em frente	ish-CARE-da/dee-RAY-ta/ayn FRAIN-teh	stânga/dreapta/drept înainte	stoong-gah/DRAY-ahp-ta/DREPT oon-EYE-een-tay	налево/направо/прямо	na-LYEV-ah/na-PRA-va/PRYA-moh
A que horas (parte/chega) o [combóio/camioneta/barco]?	ah keh AW-rahsh (PAR-teh/cheh-gah) oh kohn-BOY-oo/kam-yoo-NET-ah/bar-koh	La ce oră (pleacăĽ soseşte) [trenul/autobuzul/vaporul]?	la-CHAY orr-uh (PLAYUH-ker/so-SESH-teh) [tray-nool/OW-toe-booze-ool/va-poe-rool]	В котором часу [поезд/автобус/корабль] (приезжает/уезжает)?	V kah-tor-um cha-soo [poy-yezd/af-toe-boose/kah-rah-bil] (pree-yeh-zhy-yet/oo-yeh-zhy-yet)
hoje/amanhã/ontem	OH-zheh/ah-ming-YAH/ohn-tane	astăzi/mâine/ieri	AHSS-teuh-zi/MUH-ee-neh/YAIR-ee	сегодня/завтра/вчера	see-VOD-nya/ZAHF-tra/fchee-RAH
Queria um bilhete (simples/de ida e volta)	kay-ree-ah um bee-YEH-teh (seem-plays/deh EE-da ee VOL-ta)	Aş dori un bilet (dus/dus întors)	AHSH doe-ree oon bee-LET (doose/doose uhn-torse)	Можно билет (в один конец/туда и обратно)	MWOZH-nuh beel-yet (v ah-DEEN kah-NYETS/too-DAH ee ah-BRAHT-na)
Quanto custa?	KWAHN-too KOOSH-tah?	Cât costă?	kiht KOH-stuh	Сколько стоит?	SKOHL-ka STOH-yet?
pousada de juventude	poh-ZA-da deh zhoo-vain-TOO-deh	pensiune	pen-SYOO-neh	общежитие	ahb-SHAZH-eet-tyeh
Hotel	ot-TEL	hotel/motel	hotel/motel	гостиница	gah-STEE-nyit-sa
campismo	cahm-peez-mo	camping	CAM-ping	жить в палатках	ZHEET v PA-lat-kach
Tem um quarto individual / duple?	tem om-KWAR-toe een-DE-vee-DU-ahl/DOO-play?	Aş dori o cameră cu (un loc/două locuri).	AHSH doe-ree oh cah-meh-ruh koo (oon lok/DOE-uh LOK-oor-ee).	Я бы хотел номер на (одного/двоих)	yah kah-TYEL bee NAW-meer na (AHD-na-vo/dvah-EEK)

SLOVENE	PRONOUNCED	SWEDISH	PRONOUNCED	TURKISH	PRONOUNCED
idravo	ee-drah-voh	goddag/hej	go-DOG/HEY	merhaba	MEHR-hah-bah
na svidenje	nah SVEE-den-yeh	adjö/hej då	a-DYEUH/HEY-daw	alahsmaladžk	eee-YEE goon-lehr
prosim	PROH-seem	var så snålla	VARR so SNELL-uh	lütfen	LEWT-fen
hvala	HVAA-lah	tack	talk	teşekkur ederim	tesh-ekur edeh-rim
ja/ne	yah/neh	ja/nej	yah/ney	evet/hayır	EH-vet/HI-yuhr
oprostite	oh-proh-stee-teh	förlåt	fer-LOTT	affedersiniz	ahf-feh-DER-see-neez
Govorite angleško?	go-vo-REE-te ang-LEH-shko	pratar du engelska?	PROH-ter doo ENG-ell-skuh?	İngilizce biliyor musunuz?	EEN-gee-leez-jeh bee-lee-YOR-moo-su-nooz
Ne razumem	neh rah-ZOO-mehm	Jag förstår inte.	YAW fir-SHTOOR IN-tuh	Anlamadım.	ahn-luh-mah-dim
Na pomoč!	na poh-MOTCH!	Hjälp!	yelp!	Imdat!	EEEm-Daht!
Kje je...?	kyeh yeh...?	Var är... ?	varr air...	...nerede?	NEHR-eh-deh
na levi/na desni/naravnost	na leh-wee/na des-nee/nar-ow-nost	vänster/höger/rakt fram	VENN-ster/HEUR-ger/rakt FRAHM	sol/sağ/doğru	sohl/sa-a/doh-roo
Ob kateri uri [vlak/avtobus/ladja] (odpelje/pripelge)	op ka-teh-ree oo-ree [wlahk/AW-toe-bus/lad-ya](ot-PEL-yeh/prip-el-geh)	När (avgår/kommer) [tåget/bussen/båten]?	NAIR (AHV-gore/KOM-mar) [TOE-get/BOOSE-en/BO-ten]	[Otobüs/Tren/Vapur] ne zaman (kalkar/gelir)	[oh-toe-boose/tren/va-POOR] neh za-mahn (kal-kar/geh-leer)
danes/jutri/včeraj	DAH-ness/YOU-tree/WCHEH-ray	idag/imorgon/igår	ee-DOG/ee-MOR-on/ee-GOR	bugün/yarın/dün	boo-goon/yahr-un/doon
Rad bi (enosmerno/povratno) vozovnico.	rat bih za (EH-no-smer-no/po-VRUT-no) voh-ZOW-nih-tso	Jag vil gärna ha en (enkelbiljett/returbiljett)	YAW vil-YAIR-nuh-ha en (EN-kul-bill-yet/re-TOOR-bill-yet)	(sırf gidiş/gidiş-dönüş) bir bilet istiyorum	(serf gi-DEESH/gi-DEESH der-NYOOSH) beer be-LET i-STEE-yo-rum
Koliko to stane?	koh-lee-koh toh stah-neh	Hur mycket kostar det?	hoor-MOOK-eh KOST-ar day?	...ne kadar?	neh kah-dar?
mladinski dom	mla-dinsk-ih dom	vandrarhem	VON-dra-hem	gençlik yurdu	gench-LIK YOOR-du
hotel	hoh-tel	hotell	ho-TELL	otel	oh-tell
autokamp	ow-toe-kamp	campingplats	CAM-ping-plots	kamp yeri	camp yair-ee
Rad/Rada *(m/f)* bi (enoposteljno/dvoposteljo) sobo	raht/RA-da bee (en-o-POST-el-nyo/dvoh-POST-el-nyo) so-bo.	Jag vil gårna ha ett (enkelrum/dubbelrum)?	YAW vil-YAIR-nuh-ha et (EHN-kel-room/DOO-bel-room)	(Tek/çif) kişilik bir oda istiyorum.	(Tehk/cheeft) keesh-ee-leek beer aw-dah ee-STEE-yo-rum.

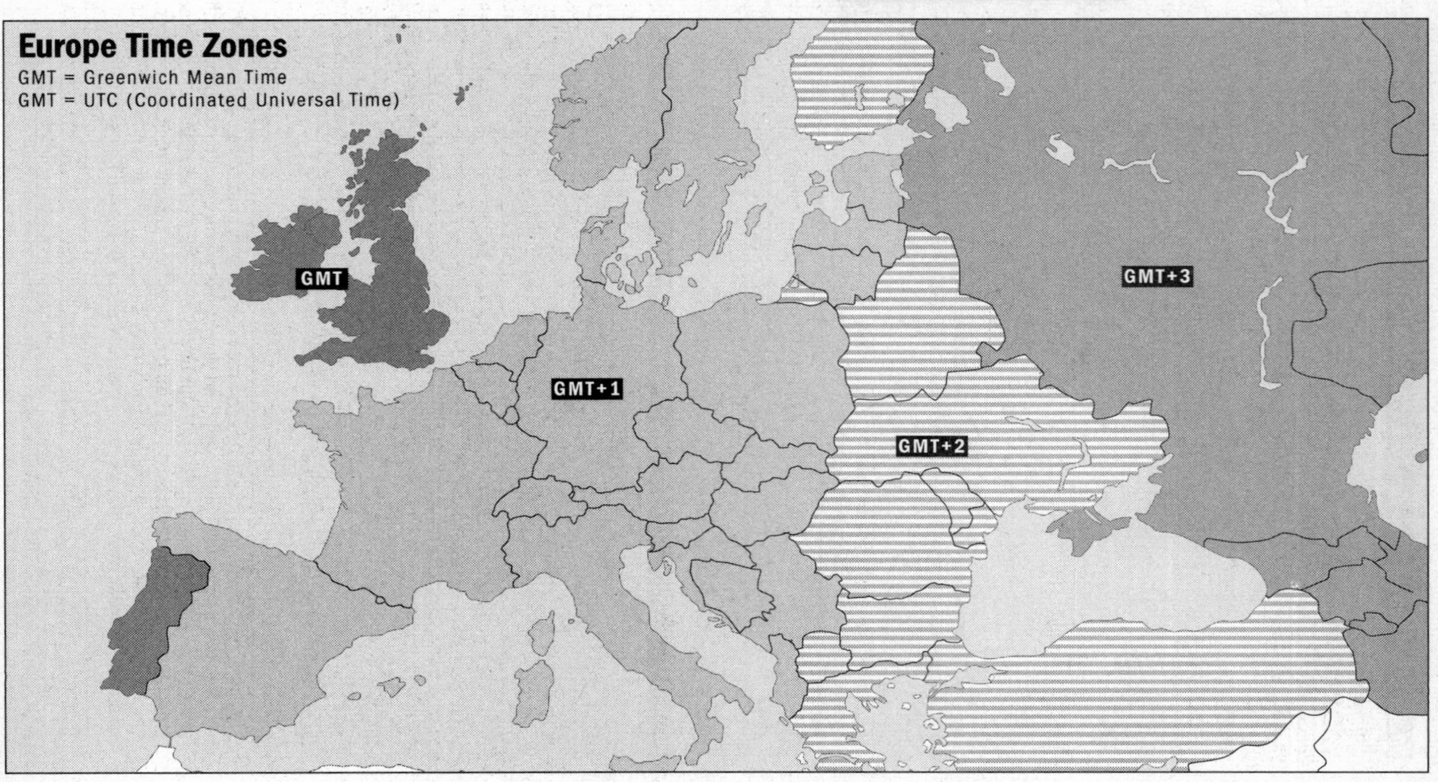
Europe Time Zones
GMT = Greenwich Mean Time
GMT = UTC (Coordinated Universal Time)
GMT
GMT+1
GMT+2
GMT+3

ABOUT LET'S GO

FORTY-ONE YEARS OF WISDOM

As a new millennium arrives, *Let's Go: Europe*, now in its 41st edition and translated into seven languages, reigns as the world's bestselling international travel guide. For over four decades, travelers criss-crossing the Continent have relied on *Let's Go* for inside information on the hippest backstreet cafes, the most pristine secluded beaches, and the best routes from border to border. In the last 20 years, our rugged researchers have stretched the frontiers of backpacking and expanded our coverage into Asia, Africa, Australia, and the Americas. This year, we've introduced a new city guide series with books on San Francisco and our hometown, Boston. Now, our seven city guides feature sharp photos, more maps, and an overall more user-friendly design. We've also returned to our roots with the inaugural edition of *Let's Go: Western Europe.*

It all started in 1960 when a handful of well-traveled students at Harvard University handed out a 20-page mimeographed pamphlet offering a collection of their tips on budget travel to passengers on student charter flights to Europe. The following year, in response to the instant popularity of the first volume, students traveling to Europe researched the first full-fledged edition of *Let's Go: Europe*, a pocket-sized book featuring honest, practical advice, witty writing, and a decidedly youthful slant on the world. Throughout the 60s and 70s, our guides reflected the times. In 1969 we taught travelers how to get from Paris to Prague on "no dollars a day" by singing in the street. In the 80s and 90s, we looked beyond Europe and North America and set off to all corners of the earth. Meanwhile, we focused in on the world's most exciting urban areas to produce in-depth, fold-out map guides. Our new guides bring the total number of titles to 51, each infused with the spirit of adventure and voice of opinion that travelers around the world have come to count on. But some things never change: our guides are still researched, written, and produced entirely by students who know first-hand how to see the world on the cheap.

HOW WE DO IT

Each guide is completely revised and thoroughly updated every year by a well-traveled set of nearly 300 students. Every spring, we recruit over 200 researchers and 90 editors to overhaul every book. After several months of training, researcher-writers hit the road for seven weeks of exploration, from Anchorage to Adelaide, Estonia to El Salvador, Iceland to Indonesia. Hired for their rare combination of budget travel sense, writing ability, stamina, and courage, these adventurous travelers know that train strikes, stolen luggage, food poisoning, and marriage proposals are all part of a day's work. Back at our offices, editors work from spring to fall, massaging copy written on Himalayan bus rides into witty, informative prose. A student staff of typesetters, cartographers, publicists, and managers keeps our lively team together. In September, the collected efforts of the summer are delivered to our printer, who turns them into books in record time, so that you have the most up-to-date information available for your vacation. Even as you read this, work on next year's editions is well underway.

WHY WE DO IT

We don't think of budget travel as the last recourse of the destitute; we believe that it's the only way to travel. Living cheaply and simply brings you closer to the people and places you've been saving up to visit. Our books will ease your anxieties and answer your questions about the basics—so you can get off the beaten track and explore. Once you learn the ropes, we encourage you to put *Let's Go* down now and then to strike out on your own. You know as well as we that the best discoveries are often those you make yourself. When you find something worth sharing, please drop us a line. We're Let's Go Publications, 67 Mount Auburn St., Cambridge, MA 02138, USA (email: feedback@letsgo.com). For more info, visit our website, www.letsgo.com.

INDEX

C

D

INDEX

G

H

INDEX

O

P

R

T

MAP INDEX

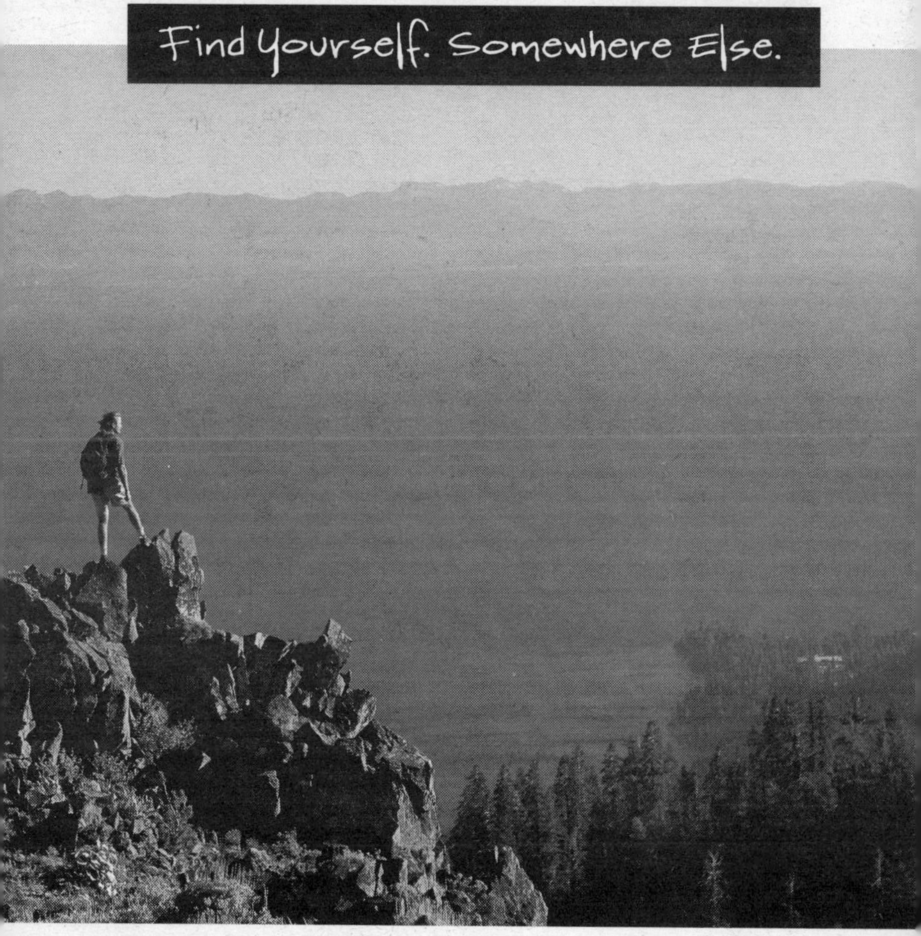
Find Yourself. Somewhere Else.

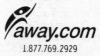

Will you have enough stories to tell your grandchildren?
Yahoo! Travel
Do You Yahoo!?

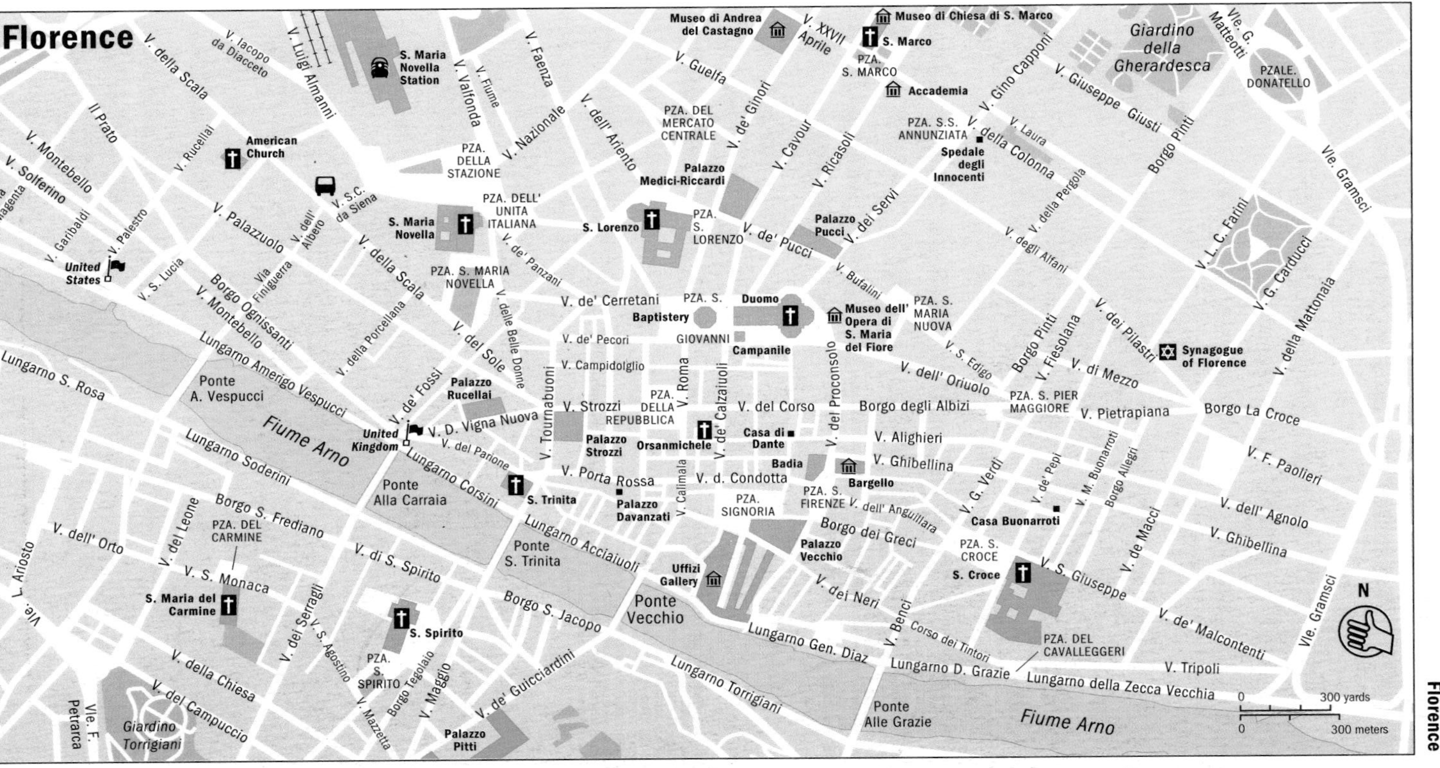

Florence
V. della Scala
V. Iacopo da Diacceto
V. Luigi Almanni
S. Maria Novella Station
V. Valfonda
V. Fiume
V. Faenza
V. Nazionale
V. dell' Ariento
Museo di Andrea del Castagno
V. XXVII Aprile
S. Marco
Museo di Chiesa di S. Marco
PZA. S. MARCO
Accademia
V. Guelfa
V. de' Ginori
V. Cavour
V. Ricasoli
V. Gino Capponi
V. Giuseppe Giusti
Giardino della Gherardesca
Vle. G. Matteotti
PZALE. DONATELLO
Il Prato
V. Rucellai
American Church
V. Montebello
V. Solferino
Via Magenta
V. Garibaldi
V. Palestro
United States
V. S. Lucia
V. Palazzuolo
V. dell' Albero
V. S.C. da Siena
Via Finiguerra
Borgo Ognissanti
V. Montebello
V. della Porcellana
PZA. DELLA STAZIONE
PZA. DELL' UNITA ITALIANA
S. Maria Novella
PZA. S. MARIA NOVELLA
V. della Scala
V. de' Panzani
V. delle Belle Donne
V. del Sole
PZA. DEL MERCATO CENTRALE
Palazzo Medici-Riccardi
S. Lorenzo
PZA. S. LORENZO
V. de' Pucci
Palazzo Pucci
V. dei Servi
PZA. S.S. ANNUNZIATA
Spedale degli Innocenti
V. della Colonna
V. Laura
V. della Pergola
V. degli Alfani
Borgo Pinti
Vle. Gramsci
V. L. C. Farini
V. G. Carducci
V. della Mattonaia
Lungarno S. Rosa
Ponte A. Vespucci
Lungarno Amerigo Vespucci
Fiume Arno
V. de' Fossi
United Kingdom
V. D. Vigna Nuova
Palazzo Rucellai
V. del Parione
V. Tornabuoni
V. de' Cerretani
V. de' Pecori
V. Campidolglio
V. Strozzi
Palazzo Strozzi
PZA. S. GIOVANNI
Baptistery
Duomo
Campanile
PZA. DELLA REPUBBLICA
V. Roma
V. de' Calzaiuoli
Orsanmichele
V. del Corso
Casa di Dante
Badia
Museo dell' Opera di S. Maria del Fiore
V. Bufalini
PZA. S. MARIA NUOVA
V. del Proconsolo
V. S. Egidio
V. dell' Oriuolo
Borgo Pinti
V. Fiesolana
V. dei Pilastri
V. di Mezzo
Synagogue of Florence
PZA. S. PIER MAGGIORE
Borgo degli Albizi
V. Pietrapiana
Borgo La Croce
V. F. Paolieri
Lungarno Soderini
Ponte Alla Carraia
Lungarno Corsini
S. Trinita
V. Porta Rossa
Palazzo Davanzati
V. Calimala
V. d. Condotta
PZA. SIGNORIA
PZA. S. FIRENZE
Bargello
V. Alighieri
V. Ghibellina
V. dell' Anguillara
Borgo dei Greci
V. G. Verdi
V. de' Pepi
V. M. Buonarroti
Borgo Allegri
Casa Buonarroti
V. de Macci
V. dell' Agnolo
V. Ghibellina
Vle. L. Ariosto
V. dell' Orto
V. del Leone
Borgo S. Frediano
PZA. DEL CARMINE
V. S. Monaca
S. Maria del Carmine
V. di S. Spirito
Ponte S. Trinita
Lungarno Acciaiuoli
Uffizi Gallery
Palazzo Vecchio
Ponte Vecchio
V. dei Neri
PZA. S. CROCE
S. Croce
V. S. Giuseppe
V. de' Malcontenti
Vle. Gramsci
N
V. dei Serragli
V. S. Agostino
S. Spirito
PZA. S. SPIRITO
Borgo Tegolaio
V. Maggio
V. Mazzetta
Borgo S. Jacopo
V. de' Guicciardini
Palazzo Pitti
Lungarno Gen. Diaz
V. Benci
Corso dei Tintori
Lungarno D. Grazie
PZA. DEL CAVALLEGGERI
V. Tripoli
Lungarno della Zecca Vecchia
Lungarno Torrigiani
Ponte Alle Grazie
Fiume Arno
0 300 yards
0 300 meters
V. della Chiesa
V. del Campuccio
Giardino Torrigiani
Vle. F. Petrarca

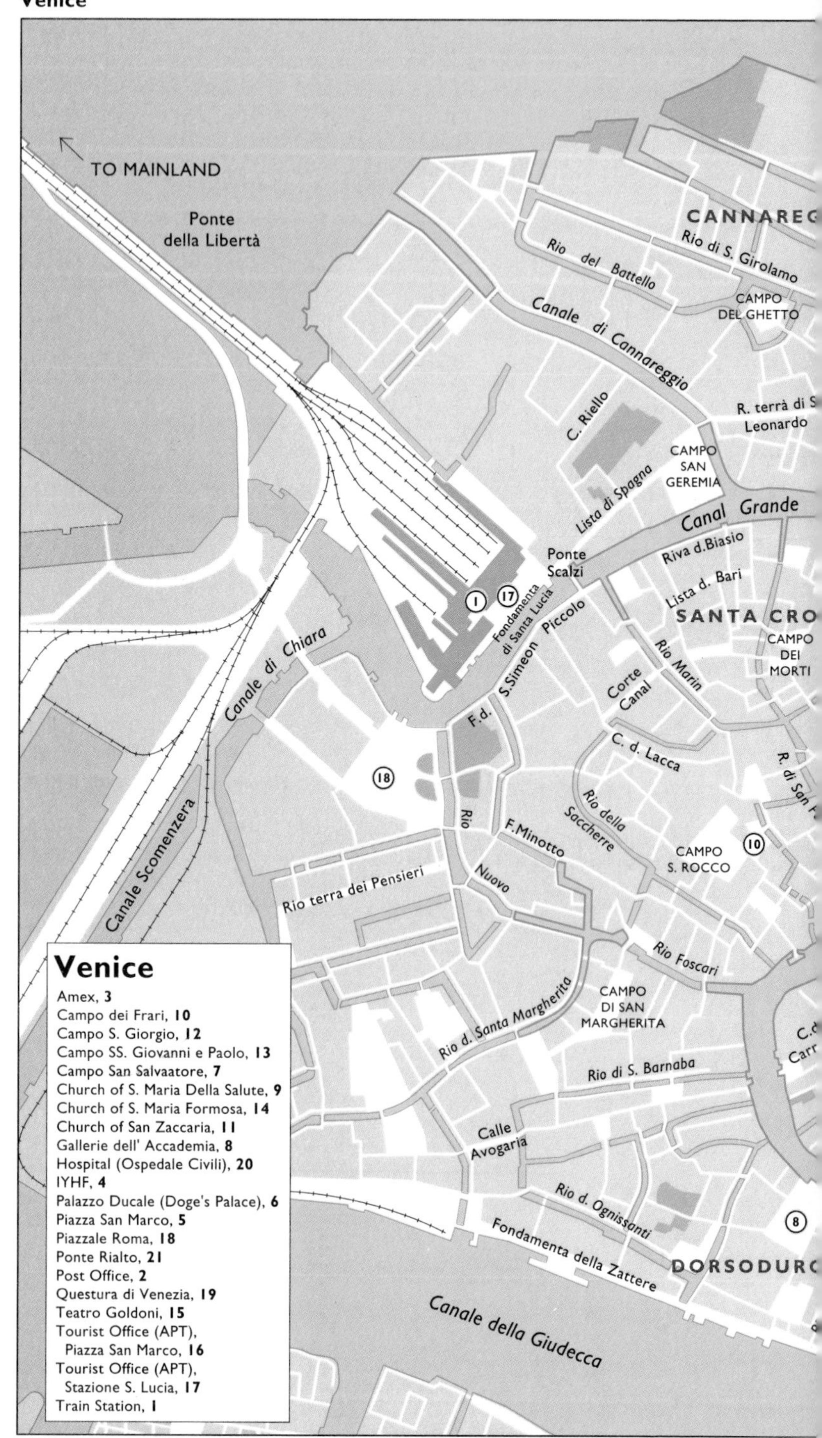
TO MAINLAND
Ponte della Libertà
CANNAREG
Rio di S. Girolamo
Rio del Battello
CAMPO DEL GHETTO
Canale di Cannareggio
C. Riello
R. terrà di S Leonardo
CAMPO SAN GEREMIA
Lista di Spagna
Canal Grande
Ponte Scalzi
Riva d.Biasio
Lista d. Bari
Fondamenta di Santa Lucia
SANTA CRO
CAMPO DEI MORTI
F.d. S.Simeon Piccolo
Canale di Chiara
Rio Marin
Corte Canal
C. d. Lacca
R. di San
Rio della Saccherre
Rio
F.Minotto
Nuovo
CAMPO S. ROCCO
Canale Scomenzera
Rio terra dei Pensieri
Rio Foscari
CAMPO DI SAN MARGHERITA
Rio d. Santa Margherita
Rio di S. Barnaba
Calle Avogaria
Rio d. Ognissanti
Fondamenta della Zattere
DORSODURO
Canale della Giudecca
Venice
Amex, 3
Campo dei Frari, 10
Campo S. Giorgio, 12
Campo SS. Giovanni e Paolo, 13
Campo San Salvaatore, 7
Church of S. Maria Della Salute, 9
Church of S. Maria Formosa, 14
Church of San Zaccaria, 11
Gallerie dell' Accademia, 8
Hospital (Ospedale Civili), 20
IYHF, 4
Palazzo Ducale (Doge's Palace), 6
Piazza San Marco, 5
Piazzale Roma, 18
Ponte Rialto, 21
Post Office, 2
Questura di Venezia, 19
Teatro Goldoni, 15
Tourist Office (APT), Piazza San Marco, 16
Tourist Office (APT), Stazione S. Lucia, 17
Train Station, 1

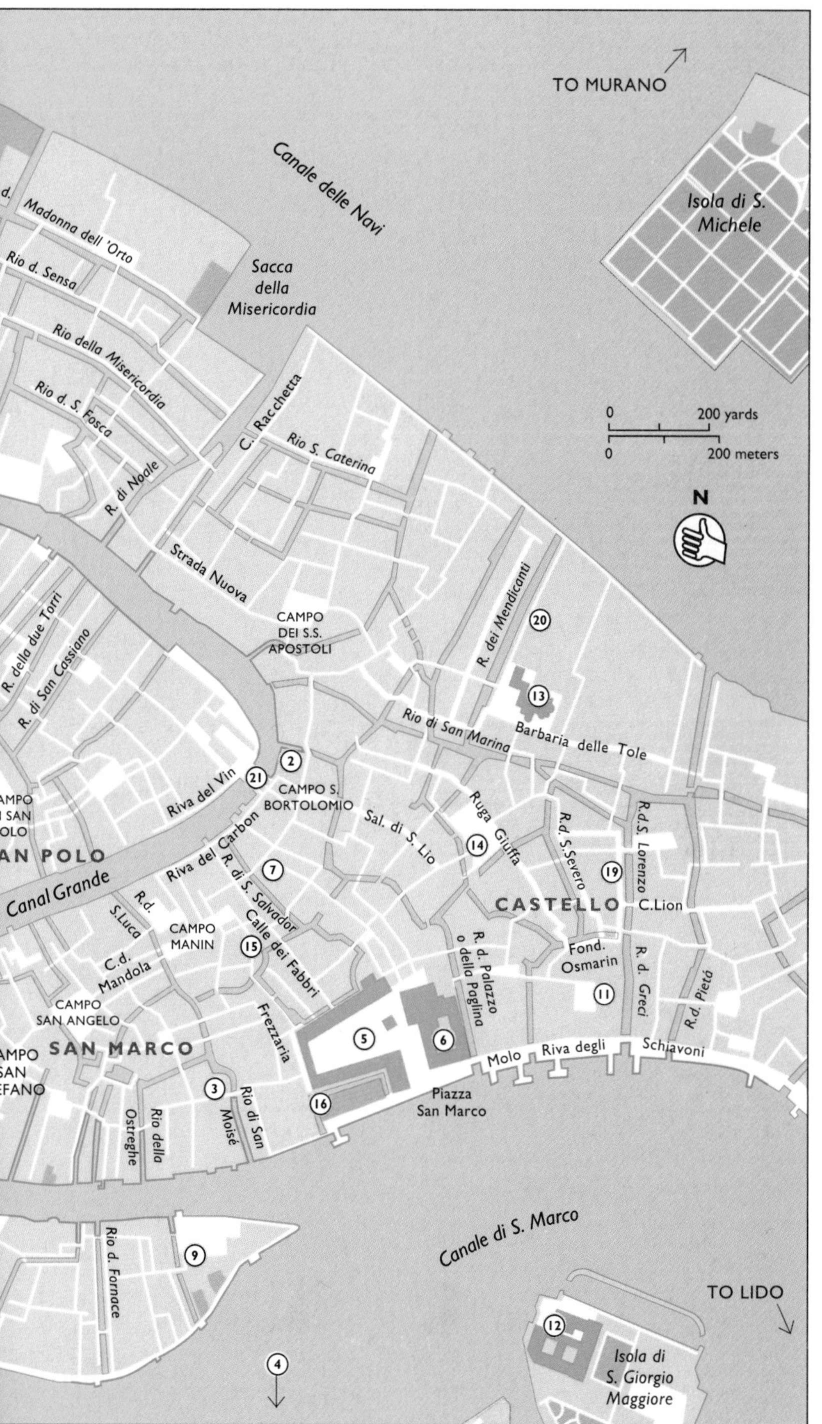
TO MURANO
Canale delle Navi
Isola di S. Michele
Madonna dell 'Orto
Rio d. Sensa
Sacca della Misericordia
Rio della Misericordia
Rio d. S. Fosca
C. Racchetta
Rio S. Caterina
R. di Noale
0 200 yards
0 200 meters
N
Strada Nuova
R. dei Mendicanti
CAMPO DEI S.S. APOSTOLI
R. della due Torri
R. di San Cassiano
Rio di San Marina
Barbaria delle Tole
CAMPO S. BORTOLOMIO
Riva del Vin
Sal. di S. Lio
Ruga Giuffa
R.d. S.Severo
R.d.S. Lorenzo
AN POLO
Riva del Carbon
R. di S. Salvador
Canal Grande
CASTELLO
C.Lion
R.d. S.Luca
CAMPO MANIN
Calle dei Fabbri
Fond. Osmarin
C.d. Mandola
R. d. Palazzo o della Paglina
R. d. Greci
R.d. Pietà
CAMPO SAN ANGELO
Frezzaria
SAN MARCO
Molo
Riva degli
Schiavoni
Piazza San Marco
Rio di San Moisé
Rio della Ostreghe
Rio d. Fornace
Canale di S. Marco
TO LIDO
Isola di S. Giorgio Maggiore

Milan

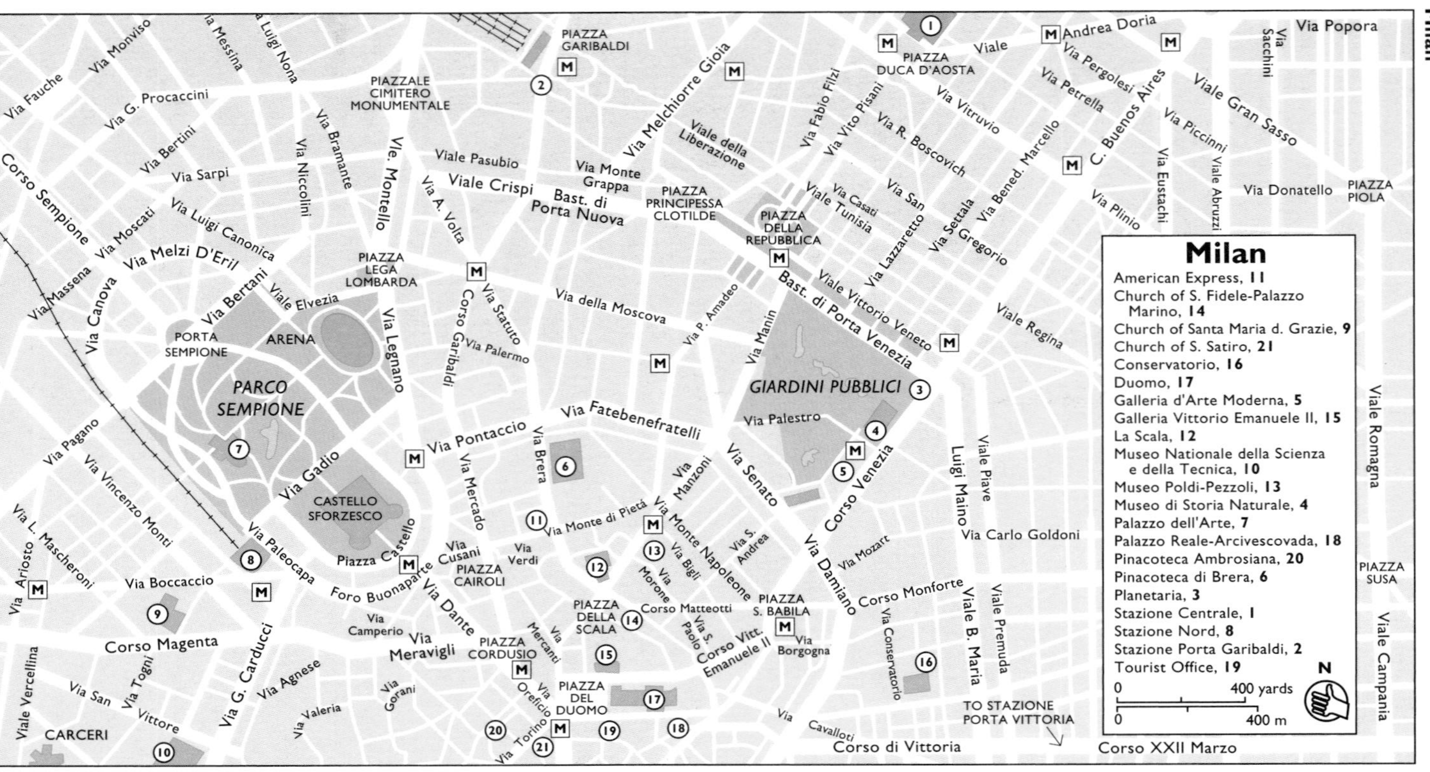

Milan
American Express, 11
Church of S. Fidele-Palazzo Marino, 14
Church of Santa Maria d. Grazie, 9
Church of S. Satiro, 21
Conservatorio, 16
Duomo, 17
Galleria d'Arte Moderna, 5
Galleria Vittorio Emanuele II, 15
La Scala, 12
Museo Nationale della Scienza e della Tecnica, 10
Museo Poldi-Pezzoli, 13
Museo di Storia Naturale, 4
Palazzo dell'Arte, 7
Palazzo Reale-Arcivescovada, 18
Pinacoteca Ambrosiana, 20
Pinacoteca di Brera, 6
Planetaria, 3
Stazione Centrale, 1
Stazione Nord, 8
Stazione Porta Garibaldi, 2
Tourist Office, 19
0
400 yards
0
400 m
N
Viale Romagna
Viale Campania
PIAZZA SUSA
PIAZZA PIOLA
Via Popora
Via Sacchini
Viale Gran Sasso
Via Donatello
Viale Abruzzi
Via Piccinni
Via Eustachi
C. Buenos Aires
Via Plinio
Andrea Doria
Via Pergolesi
Via Petrella
Via Bened. Marcello
Viale Regina
PIAZZA DUCA D'AOSTA
Via Vitruvio
Via Settala
Gregorio
Via R. Boscovich
Via San
Via Lazzaretto
Viale Vittorio Veneto
Bast. di Porta Venezia
GIARDINI PUBBLICI
Corso Venezia
Viale Piave
Luigi Maino
Via Carlo Goldoni
Viale Premuda
Viale B. Maria
TO STAZIONE PORTA VITTORIA
Corso XXII Marzo
Corso Monforte
Via Conservatorio
Via Mozart
Via Damiano
Corso di Vittoria
Via Cavalloti
Via Vito Pisani
Via Fabio Filzi
Via Casati
Viale Tunisia
PIAZZA DELLA REPUBBLICA
Via Manin
Via Palestro
Via Senato
PIAZZA S. BABILA
Via Borgogna
Via S. Andrea
Via Monte Napoleone
Corso Vitt. Emanuele II
Via S. Paolo
Corso Matteotti
Via Bigli
Via Morone
Via Manzoni
Via P. Amadeo
Via Melchiorre Gioia
Viale della Liberazione
PIAZZA PRINCIPESSA CLOTILDE
Via Fatebenefratelli
Via della Moscova
PIAZZA GARIBALDI
Via Monte Grappa
Bast. di Porta Nuova
Via Monte di Pietá
PIAZZA DELLA SCALA
PIAZZA DEL DUOMO
Via Mercanti
Via Orefici
Via Torino
Via Brera
Via Verdi
Viale Pasubio
Viale Crispi
Via Statuto
Via Palermo
Corso Garibaldi
Via Pontaccio
Via Mercado
Via Cusani
PIAZZA CAIROLI
PIAZZA CORDUSIO
Via Dante
Via Meravigli
Via A. Volta
PIAZZALE CIMITERO MONUMENTALE
Vle. Montello
PIAZZA LEGA LOMBARDA
Via Legnano
Piazza Castello
Foro Buonaparte
CASTELLO SFORZESCO
Via Camperio
Via Gorani
Via Bramante
Via Niccolini
ARENA
Viale Elvezia
Via Gadio
PARCO SEMPIONE
Via Paleocapa
Via Agnese
Via Valeria
Via G. Carducci
Via Luigi Nona
Via Messina
Via Bertani
PORTA SEMPIONE
Via Sarpi
Via Luigi Canonica
Via Melzi D'Eril
Via Bertini
Via G. Procaccini
Via Moscati
Via Monviso
Via Canova
Via Boccaccio
Corso Magenta
Via Togni
Via San Vittore
Via Vincenzo Monti
Via Pagano
Via Massena
Corso Sempione
Via Fauche
Via L. Mascheroni
Via Ariosto
CARCERI
Viale Vercellina

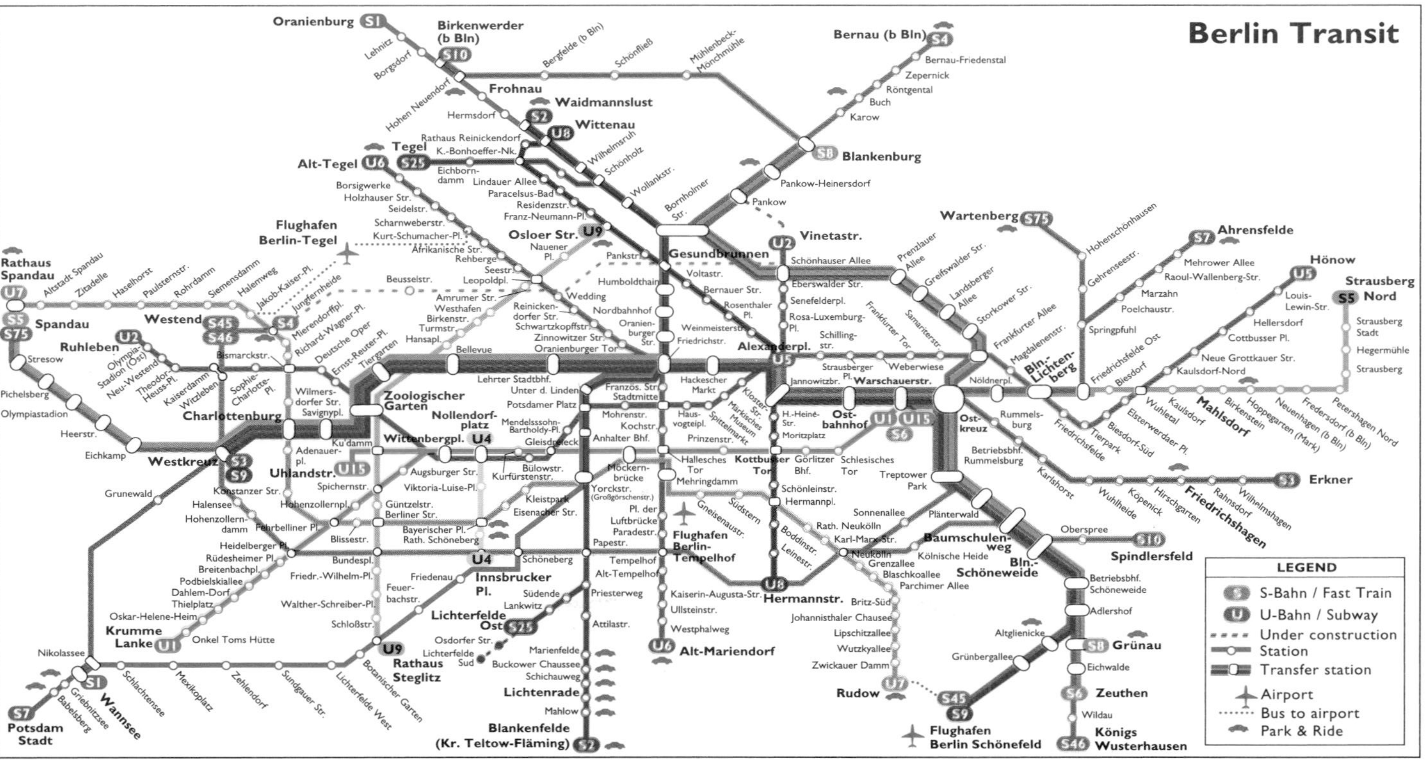

Berlin Transit
LEGEND
S-Bahn / Fast Train
U-Bahn / Subway
Under construction
Station
Transfer station
Airport
Bus to airport
Park & Ride
Oranienburg
Lehnitz
Borgsdorf
Birkenwerder (b Bln)
Hohen Neuendorf
Frohnau
Hermsdorf
Waidmannslust
Wittenau
Bergfelde (b Bln)
Schönfließ
Mühlenbeck-Mönchmühle
Bernau (b Bln)
Bernau-Friedenstal
Zepernick
Röntgental
Buch
Karow
Blankenburg
Pankow-Heinersdorf
Pankow
Vinetastr.
Wartenberg
Ahrensfelde
Mehrower Allee
Raoul-Wallenberg-Str.
Marzahn
Poelchaustr.
Springpfuhl
Hohenschönhausen
Gehrenseestr.
Hönow
Louis-Lewin-Str.
Hellersdorf
Cottbusser Pl.
Neue Grottkauer Str.
Kaulsdorf-Nord
Strausberg Nord
Strausberg Stadt
Hegermühle
Strausberg
Petershagen Nord
Fredersdorf (b Bln)
Neuenhagen (b Bln)
Hoppegarten (Mark)
Birkenstein
Mahlsdorf
Kaulsdorf
Wuhletal
Elsterwerdaer Pl.
Biesdorf-Süd
Biesdorf
Friedrichsfelde Ost
Tierpark
Friedrichsfelde
Bln.-Lichtenberg
Magdalenenstr.
Frankfurter Allee
Storkower Str.
Landsberger Allee
Greifswalder Str.
Prenzlauer Allee
Schönhauser Allee
Gesundbrunnen
Bornholmer Str.
Wollankstr.
Schönholz
Wilhelmsruh
Rathaus Reinickendorf
K.-Bonhoeffer-Nk.
Lindauer Allee
Paracelsus-Bad
Residenzstr.
Franz-Neumann-Pl.
Osloer Str.
Pankstr.
Voltastr.
Bernauer Str.
Rosenthaler Pl.
Weinmeisterstr.
Eberswalder Str.
Senefelderpl.
Rosa-Luxemburg-Pl.
Alexanderpl.
Schillingstr.
Strausberger Pl.
Weberwiese
Frankfurter Tor
Samariterstr.
Nöldnerpl.
Rummelsburg
Betriebsbhf. Rummelsburg
Karlshorst
Ostkreuz
Warschauerstr.
Ostbahnhof
Jannowitzbr.
Erkner
Wilhelmshagen
Rahnsdorf
Friedrichshagen
Hirschgarten
Köpenick
Wuhlheide
Spindlersfeld
Oberspree
Bln.-Schöneweide
Baumschulenweg
Plänterwald
Treptower Park
Schlesisches Tor
Görlitzer Bhf.
Kottbusser Tor
Moritzplatz
H.-Heine-Str.
Klosterstr.
Märkisches Museum
Spittelmarkt
Hausvogteipl.
Hackescher Markt
Friedrichstr.
Oranienburger Str.
Oranienburger Tor
Nordbahnhof
Humboldthain
Wedding
Reinickendorfer Str.
Schwartzkopffstr.
Zinnowitzer Str.
Leopoldpl.
Amrumer Str.
Westhafen
Birkenstr.
Turmstr.
Hansapl.
Seestr.
Rehberge
Afrikanische Str.
Kurt-Schumacher-Pl.
Scharnweberstr.
Seidelstr.
Holzhauser Str.
Borsigwerke
Alt-Tegel
Tegel
Eichborndamm
Nauener Pl.
Beusselstr.
Flughafen Berlin-Tegel
Jungfernheide
Jakob-Kaiser-Pl.
Halemweg
Siemensdamm
Rohrdamm
Paulsternstr.
Haselhorst
Zitadelle
Altstadt Spandau
Rathaus Spandau
Spandau
Stresow
Pichelsberg
Olympiastadion
Heerstr.
Eichkamp
Ruhleben
Olympia-Stadion (Ost)
Neu-Westend
Theodor-Heuss-Pl.
Kaiserdamm
Witzleben
Westend
Sophie-Charlotte-Pl.
Bismarckstr.
Richard-Wagner-Pl.
Mierendorffpl.
Deutsche Oper
Ernst-Reuter-Pl.
Tiergarten
Bellevue
Lehrter Stadtbhf.
Unter d. Linden
Französ. Str.
Stadtmitte
Mohrenstr.
Potsdamer Platz
Mendelssohn-Bartholdy-Pl.
Gleisdreieck
Kochstr.
Anhalter Bhf.
Möckernbrücke
Hallesches Tor
Prinzenstr.
Mehringdamm
Gneisenaustr.
Südstern
Hermannpl.
Schönleinstr.
Rath. Neukölln
Boddinstr.
Leinestr.
Hermannstr.
Karl-Marx-Str.
Neukölln
Sonnenallee
Köllnische Heide
Grenzallee
Blaschkoallee
Parchimer Allee
Britz-Süd
Johannisthaler Chaussee
Lipschitzallee
Wutzkyallee
Zwickauer Damm
Rudow
Flughafen Berlin-Tempelhof
Pl. der Luftbrücke
Paradestr.
Tempelhof
Alt-Tempelhof
Kaiserin-Augusta-Str.
Ullsteinstr.
Westphalweg
Alt-Mariendorf
Yorckstr. (Großgörschenstr.)
Papestr.
Priesterweg
Attilastr.
Marienfelde
Buckower Chaussee
Schichauweg
Lichtenrade
Mahlow
Blankenfelde (Kr. Teltow-Fläming)
Südende
Lankwitz
Lichterfelde Ost
Osdorfer Str.
Lichterfelde Süd
Schöneberg
Innsbrucker Pl.
Friedenau
Feuerbachstr.
Rathaus Steglitz
Botanischer Garten
Lichterfelde West
Sundgauer Str.
Zehlendorf
Mexikoplatz
Schlachtensee
Nikolassee
Wannsee
Griebnitzsee
Babelsberg
Potsdam Stadt
Kleistpark
Eisenacher Str.
Bayerischer Pl.
Rath. Schöneberg
Bülowstr.
Kurfürstenstr.
Nollendorfplatz
Wittenbergpl.
Augsburger Str.
Viktoria-Luise-Pl.
Güntzelstr.
Berliner Str.
Blissestr.
Bundespl.
Friedr.-Wilhelm-Pl.
Walther-Schreiber-Pl.
Schloßstr.
Spichernstr.
Hohenzollernpl.
Fehrbelliner Pl.
Heidelberger Pl.
Rüdesheimer Pl.
Breitenbachpl.
Podbielskiallee
Dahlem-Dorf
Thielplatz
Oskar-Helene-Heim
Onkel Toms Hütte
Krumme Lanke
Zoologischer Garten
Ku'damm
Uhlandstr.
Adenauerpl.
Wilmersdorfer Str.
Savignypl.
Charlottenburg
Westkreuz
Halensee
Hohenzollerndamm
Konstanzer Str.
Grunewald
Altglienicke
Grünbergallee
Flughafen Berlin Schönefeld
Betriebsbhf. Schöneweide
Adlershof
Grünau
Eichwalde
Zeuthen
Wildau
Königs Wusterhausen

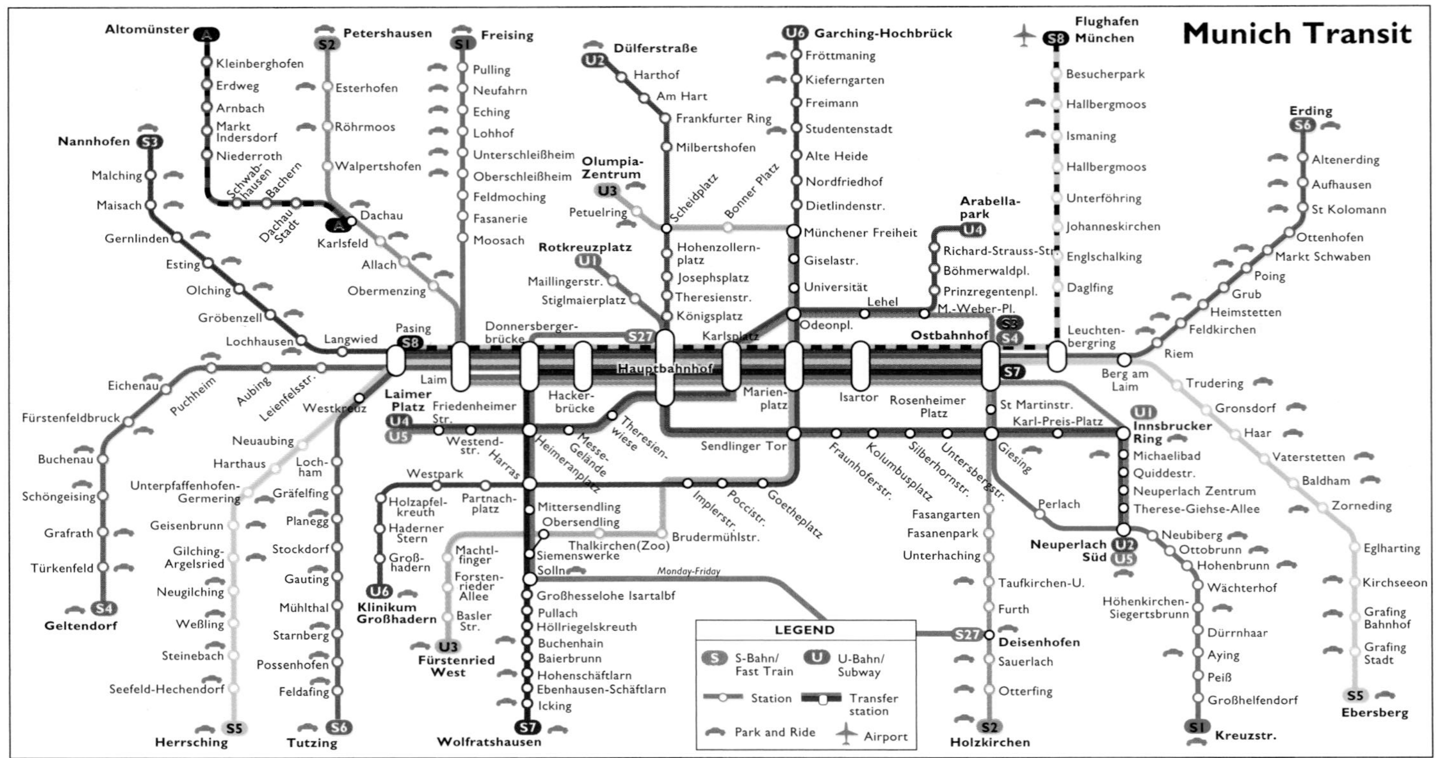
Munich Transit
Altomünster
Kleinberghofen
Erdweg
Arnbach
Markt Indersdorf
Niederroth
Schwabhausen
Bachern
Dachau Stadt
Petershausen
Esterhofen
Röhrmoos
Walpertshofen
Dachau
Karlsfeld
Allach
Obermenzing
Freising
Pulling
Neufahrn
Eching
Lohhof
Unterschleißheim
Oberschleißheim
Feldmoching
Fasanerie
Moosach
Nannhofen
Malching
Maisach
Gernlinden
Esting
Olching
Gröbenzell
Lochhausen
Langwied
Pasing
Dülferstraße
Harthof
Am Hart
Frankfurter Ring
Milbertshofen
Olympia-Zentrum
Petuelring
Scheidplatz
Bonner Platz
Rotkreuzplatz
Maillingerstr.
Stiglmaierplatz
Hohenzollernplatz
Josephsplatz
Theresienstr.
Königsplatz
Garching-Hochbrück
Fröttmaning
Kieferngarten
Freimann
Studentenstadt
Alte Heide
Nordfriedhof
Dietlindenstr.
Münchener Freiheit
Giselastr.
Universität
Odeonpl.
Lehel
Arabellapark
Richard-Strauss-Str.
Böhmerwaldpl.
Prinzregentenpl.
M.-Weber-Pl.
Ostbahnhof
Flughafen München
Besucherpark
Hallbergmoos
Ismaning
Unterföhring
Johanneskirchen
Englschalking
Daglfing
Leuchtenbergring
Erding
Altenerding
Aufhausen
St Kolomann
Ottenhofen
Markt Schwaben
Poing
Grub
Heimstetten
Feldkirchen
Riem
Berg am Laim
Trudering
Gronsdorf
Haar
Vaterstetten
Baldham
Zorneding
Eglharting
Kirchseeon
Grafing Bahnhof
Grafing Stadt
Ebersberg
Donnersbergerbrücke
Karlsplatz
Hauptbahnhof
Marienplatz
Isartor
Rosenheimer Platz
Laim
Eichenau
Puchheim
Aubing
Leienfelsstr.
Westkreuz
Fürstenfeldbruck
Buchenau
Schöngeising
Grafrath
Türkenfeld
Geltendorf
Neuaubing
Harthaus
Unterpfaffenhofen-Germering
Geisenbrunn
Gilching-Argelsried
Neugilching
Weßling
Steinebach
Seefeld-Hechendorf
Herrsching
Lochham
Gräfelfing
Planegg
Stockdorf
Gauting
Mühlthal
Starnberg
Possenhofen
Feldafing
Tutzing
Laimer Platz
Friedenheimer Str.
Westendstr.
Hackerbrücke
Theresienwiese
Messe-Gelände
Heimeranplatz
Harras
Westpark
Partnachplatz
Holzapfelkreuth
Haderner Stern
Großhadern
Klinikum Großhadern
Machtlfinger
Forstenrieder Allee
Basler Str.
Fürstenried West
Mittersendling
Obersendling
Thalkirchen (Zoo)
Siemenswerke
Solln
Brudermühlstr.
Implerstr.
Poccistr.
Goetheplatz
Sendlinger Tor
Monday-Friday
Großhesselohe Isartalbf
Pullach
Höllriegelskreuth
Buchenhain
Baierbrunn
Hohenschäftlarn
Ebenhausen-Schäftlarn
Icking
Wolfratshausen
Fraunhoferstr.
Kolumbusplatz
Silberhornstr.
Untersbergstr.
Giesing
St Martinstr.
Karl-Preis-Platz
Innsbrucker Ring
Michaelibad
Quiddestr.
Neuperlach Zentrum
Therese-Giehse-Allee
Perlach
Neuperlach Süd
Neubiberg
Ottobrunn
Hohenbrunn
Wächterhof
Höhenkirchen-Siegertsbrunn
Dürrnhaar
Aying
Peiß
Großhelfendorf
Kreuzstr.
Fasangarten
Fasanenpark
Unterhaching
Taufkirchen-U.
Furth
Deisenhofen
Sauerlach
Otterfing
Holzkirchen
LEGEND
S-Bahn/ Fast Train
U-Bahn/ Subway
Station
Transfer station
Park and Ride
Airport

Hamburg Transit
LEGEND
U-Bahn Subway
S-Bahn/ Fast Train
Station
Park and Ride
Limited Service
Long-Distance Trains
Transfer station
Airport
Tarif-Großbereich Hamburg
Barmstedt
Barmstedt Brunnenstr.
Voßloch
Bokholt
Sparrieshoop
Langenmoor
Elmshorn
Tornesch
Prisdorf
Pinneberg
Thesdorf
Halstenbek
Krupunder
Elbgaustr.
Eidelstedt
Eidelstedt Ost
Schnelsen
Burgwedel
Bönningstedt
Hasloh
Quickborn Süd
Quickborn
Ellerau
Tanneneck
Meeschensee
Ulzburg Süd
Ulzburg
Kaltenkirchen Süd
Kaltenkirchen
Kaltenkirchen Holstentherme
Haslohfurth
Quickborner Str.
Friedrichsgabe
Moorbek-Halle
Norderstedt Mitte
Richtweg
Garstedt
Ochsenzoll
Kiwittsmoor
Langenhorn-Nord
Langenhorn-Markt
Fuhlsbüttel-Nord
Fuhlsbüttel
Klein Borstel
EXPRESS BUS
Ohlsdorf
Poppenbüttel
Wellingsbüttel
Hoheneichen
Kornweg
Ohlstedt
Hoisbüttel
Buckhorn
Volksdorf
Ahrensburg
Ahrensburg-West
Buchenkamp
Meiendorfer Weg
Berne
Farmsen
Trabrennbahn
Wandsbek-Gartenstadt
Alter Teichweg
Straßburger Str.
Wandsbek-Markt
Wandsbeker Chaussee
Wandsbek
Wandsbek Ost
Rahlstedt
Ahrensburg-Ost
Schmalenbeck
Kiekut
Großhansdorf
Niendorf-Nord
Schippelsweg
Joachim-Mähl-Str.
Niendorf-Markt
Hagendeel
Hagenbecks Tierpark
Lutterothstr.
Osterstr.
Emilienstr.
Christuskirche
Schlump
Stellingen
Langenfelde
Diebsteich
Sengelmannstr.
Alsterdorf
Lattenkamp
Hudtwalckerstr.
Kellinghusenstr.
Eppendorfer Baum
Hoheluftbrücke
Sierichstr.
Borgweg
Saarlandstr.
Alte Wöhr
Rübenkamp
Habichtstr.
Barmbek
Friedrichsberg
Dehnhaide
Hamburger Str.
Mundsburg
Uhlandstr.
Lübecker Str.
Lohmühlenstr.
Ritterstr.
Wartenau
Berliner Tor
Hasselbrook
Landwehr
Burgstr.
Hammer Kirche
Rauhes Haus
Horner Rennbahn
Legienstr.
Billstedt
Merkenstr.
Steinfurther Allee
Mümmelmannsberg
Klosterstern
Hallerstr.
Alster
Dammtor
Stephansplatz
Jungfernstieg
Hauptbahnhof
Nord
Süd
Mönckebergstr.
Meßberg
Steinstr.
Rathaus
Rödingsmarkt
Baumwall
Stadthausbrücke
Landungsbrücken
St. Pauli
Feldstr.
Sternschanze
Messehallen
Gänsemarkt
Holstenstr.
Altona
Königstr.
Reeperbahn
Wedel
Rissen
Sülldorf
Iserbrook
Blankenese
Hochkamp
Klein Flottbek
Othmarschen
Bahrenfeld
Rothenburgsort
Tiefstack
Billwerder-Moorfleet
Mittlerer Landweg
Nettelnburg
Bergedorf
Reinbek
Wohltorf
Aumühle
Friedrichsruh
Hammerbrook
Veddel
Wilhelmsburg
Elbe
Harburg
Meckelfeld
Maschen
Hittfeld
Harburg Rathaus
Heimfeld
Neuwiedenthal
Neugraben

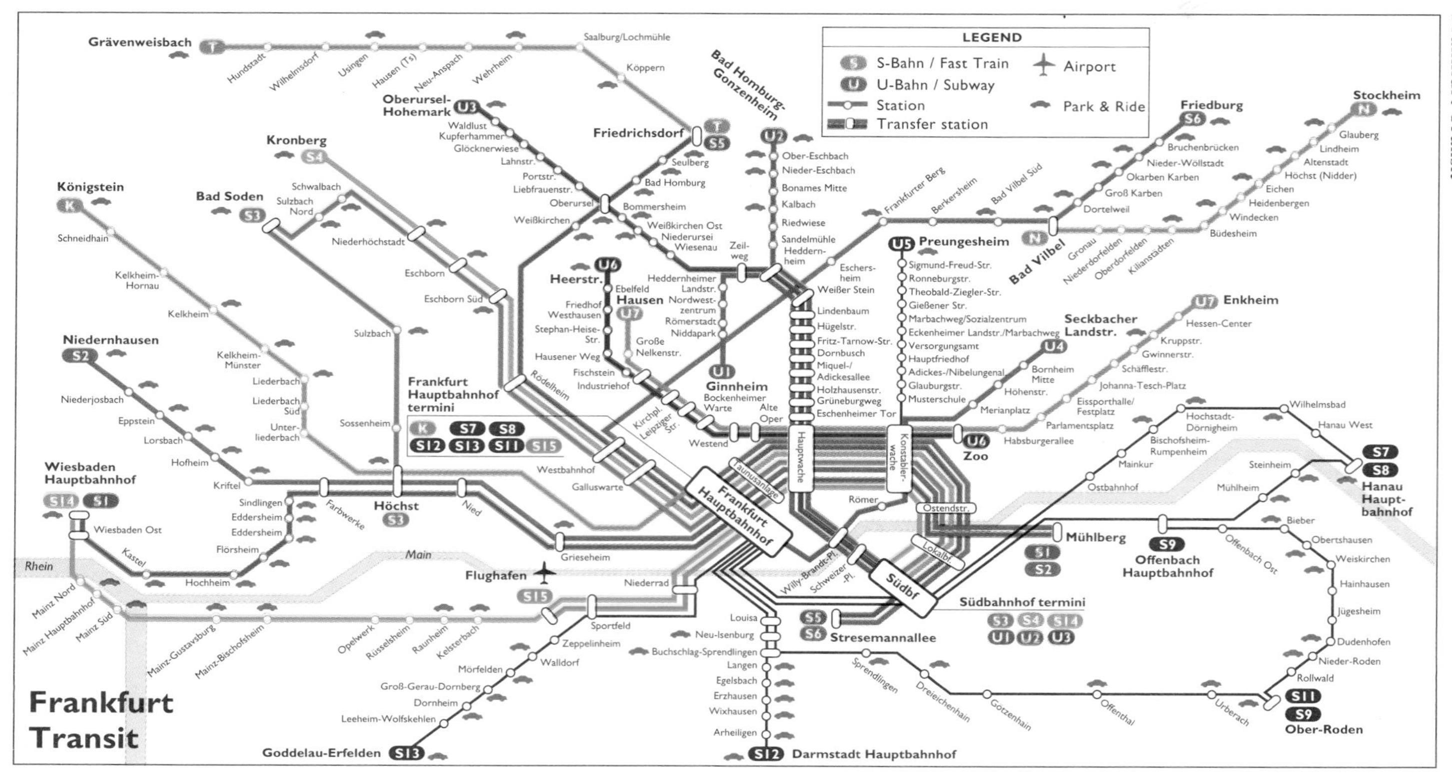
LEGEND
S-Bahn / Fast Train
U-Bahn / Subway
Station
Transfer station
Airport
Park & Ride
Frankfurt Transit
Grävenweisbach
Hundstadt
Wilhelmsdorf
Usingen
Hausen (Ts)
Neu-Anspach
Wehrheim
Saalburg/Lochmühle
Köppern
Friedrichsdorf
Bad Homburg-Gonzenheim
Ober-Eschbach
Nieder-Eschbach
Bonames Mitte
Kalbach
Riedwiese
Sandelmühle
Heddernheim
Zeilweg
Oberursel-Hohemark
Waldlust
Kupferhammer
Glöcknerwiese
Lahnstr.
Portstr.
Liebfrauenstr.
Oberursel
Weißkirchen
Seulberg
Bad Homburg
Bommersheim
Weißkirchen Ost
Niederursei
Wiesenau
Kronberg
Königstein
Schneidhain
Kelkheim-Hornau
Kelkheim
Kelkheim-Münster
Liederbach
Liederbach Süd
Unterliederbach
Bad Soden
Sulzbach Nord
Schwalbach
Niederhöchstadt
Eschborn
Eschborn Süd
Sulzbach
Sossenheim
Niedernhausen
Niederjosbach
Eppstein
Lorsbach
Hofheim
Kriftel
Wiesbaden Hauptbahnhof
Wiesbaden Ost
Kastel
Hochheim
Flörsheim
Eddersheim
Sindlingen
Farbwerke
Höchst
Nied
Griesheim
Rhein
Main
Flughafen
Mainz Nord
Mainz Hauptbahnhof
Mainz Süd
Mainz-Gustavsburg
Mainz-Bischofsheim
Opelwerk
Rüsselsheim
Raunheim
Kelsterbach
Sportfeld
Zeppelinheim
Walldorf
Mörfelden
Groß-Gerau-Dornberg
Dornheim
Leeheim-Wolfskehlen
Goddelau-Erfelden
Frankfurt Hauptbahnhof termini
Heerstr.
Friedhof Westhausen
Stephan-Heise-Str.
Hausener Weg
Fischstein
Industriehof
Ebelfeld
Hausen
Große Nelkenstr.
Heddernheimer Landstr.
Nordwestzentrum
Römerstadt
Niddapark
Ginnheim
Bockenheimer Warte
Alte Oper
Westend
Kirchpl.
Leipziger Str.
Rödelheim
Westbahnhof
Galluswarte
Taunusanlage
Frankfurt Hauptbahnhof
Niederrad
Louisa
Neu-Isenburg
Buchschlag-Sprendlingen
Langen
Egelsbach
Erzhausen
Wixhausen
Arheiligen
Darmstadt Hauptbahnhof
Eschersheim
Weißer Stein
Lindenbaum
Hügelstr.
Fritz-Tarnow-Str.
Dornbusch
Miquel-/Adickesallee
Holzhausenstr.
Grüneburgweg
Eschenheimer Tor
Hauptwache
Konstablerwache
Römer
Willy-Brandt-Pl.
Schweizer-Pl.
Südbf
Südbahnhof termini
Stresemannallee
Ostendstr.
Lokalbf.
Mühlberg
Preungesheim
Sigmund-Freud-Str.
Ronneburgstr.
Theobald-Ziegler-Str.
Gießener Str.
Marbachweg/Sozialzentrum
Eckenheimer Landstr./Marbachweg
Versorgungsamt
Hauptfriedhof
Adickes-/Nibelungenal.
Glauburgstr.
Musterschule
Frankfurter Berg
Berkersheim
Bad Vilbel Süd
Bad Vilbel
Gronau
Niederdorfelden
Oberdorfelden
Kilianstädten
Friedburg
Bruchenbrücken
Nieder-Wöllstadt
Okarben Karben
Groß Karben
Dortelweil
Stockheim
Glauberg
Lindheim
Altenstadt
Höchst (Nidder)
Eichen
Heidenbergen
Windecken
Büdesheim
Enkheim
Hessen-Center
Kruppstr.
Gwinnerstr.
Schäfflestr.
Johanna-Tesch-Platz
Eissporthalle/Festplatz
Parlamentsplatz
Habsburgerallee
Zoo
Seckbacher Landstr.
Bornheim Mitte
Höhenstr.
Merianplatz
Wilhelmsbad
Hanau West
Hochstadt-Dörnigheim
Bischofsheim-Rumpenheim
Mainkur
Ostbahnhof
Hanau Hauptbahnhof
Steinheim
Mühlheim
Offenbach Hauptbahnhof
Offenbach Ost
Bieber
Obertshausen
Weiskirchen
Hainhausen
Jügesheim
Dudenhofen
Nieder-Roden
Rollwald
Ober-Roden
Urberach
Offenthal
Götzenhain
Dreieichenhain
Sprendlingen

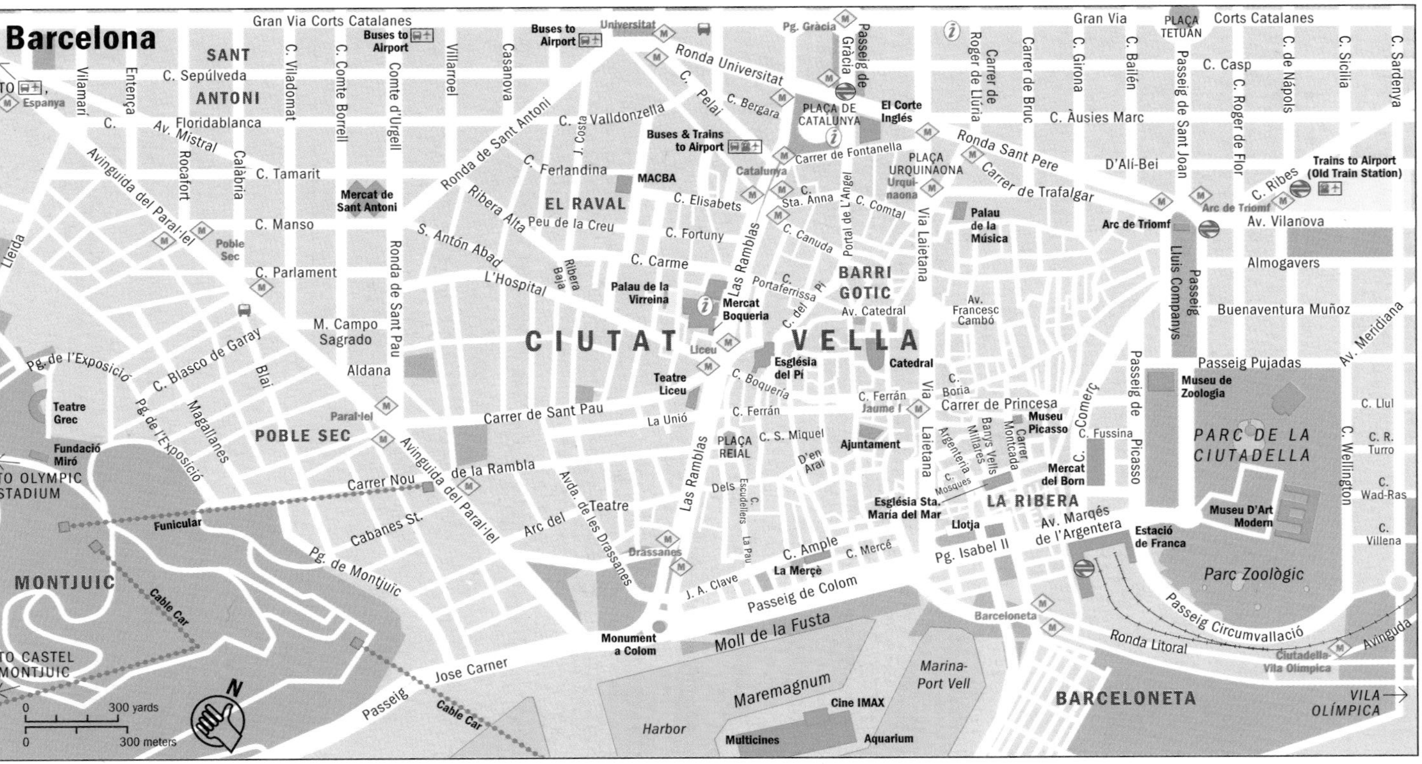

Barcelona
Gran Via Corts Catalanes
Buses to Airport
Buses to Airport
Universitat
Pg. Gràcia
Passeig de Gràcia
Gran Via
Plaça Tetuán
Corts Catalanes
To Espanya
Vilamarí
Entença
C. Sepúlveda
Sant Antoni
C. Viladomat
C. Comte Borrell
Comte d'Urgell
Villarroel
Casanova
Ronda Universitat
C. Pelai
C. Bergara
Plaça de Catalunya
El Corte Inglés
Carrer de Roger de Llúria
Carrer de Bruc
C. Girona
C. Bailén
Passeig de Sant Joan
C. Casp
C. Roger de Flor
C. de Nápols
C. Sicilia
C. Sardenya
C. Àusies Marc
C. Floridablanca
Av. Mistral
Rocafort
Calàbria
C. Tamarit
Ronda de Sant Antoni
J. Costa
C. Valldonzella
Buses & Trains to Airport
Carrer de Fontanella
Plaça Urquinaona
Ronda Sant Pere
Carrer de Trafalgar
D'Alí-Bei
Trains to Airport (Old Train Station)
C. Ribes
Arc de Triomf
Av. Vilanova
Avinguda del Paral·lel
C. Ferlandina
MACBA
Catalunya
Mercat de Sant Antoni
El Raval
C. Elisabets
C. Sta. Anna
Portal de l'Angel
C. Comtal
Urquinaona
Via Laietana
Palau de la Música
Almogavers
Poble Sec
C. Manso
Ribera Alta
Peu de la Creu
C. Fortuny
C. Canuda
Lleida
S. Antón Abad
C. Carme
Las Ramblas
C. Parlament
Ronda de Sant Pau
L'Hospital
Ribera Baja
Palau de la Virreina
Mercat Boqueria
C. Portaferrissa
C. del Pi
Barri Gotic
Av. Catedral
Av. Francesc Cambó
Passeig Lluis Companys
Buenaventura Muñoz
Av. Meridiana
M. Campo Sagrado
Ciutat Vella
Liceu
Pg. de l'Exposició
C. Blasco de Garay
Blai
Aldana
Teatre Liceu
Església del Pi
Catedral
Passeig Pujadas
Museu de Zoologia
C. Boqueria
C. Ferrán
Jaume I
C. Boria
Carrer de Princesa
Passeig de Picasso
C. Comerç
Teatre Grec
Pg. de l'Exposició
Magallanes
Paral·lel
Carrer de Sant Pau
La Unió
C. Ferrán
C. Llul
Poble Sec
Plaça Reial
C. S. Miquel
D'en Arai
Ajuntament
Argenteria
Banys Vells
Millares
Carrer Montcada
Museu Picasso
C. Fussina
Parc de la Ciutadella
C. Wellington
C. R. Turro
Fundació Miró
To Olympic Stadium
Avinguda del Paral·lel
de la Rambla
Carrer Nou
Avda. de les Drassanes
Dels
C. Escudellers
C. Mosques
Mercat del Born
C. Wad-Ras
Teatre
Església Sta. Maria del Mar
La Ribera
Museu D'Art Modern
Funicular
Cabanes St.
Arc del
Llotja
Av. Marqués de l'Argentera
Estació de França
C. Villena
Drassanes
La Pau
C. Ample
C. Mercé
Pg. Isabel II
Montjuïc
Pg. de Montjuïc
J. A. Clave
La Mercè
Parc Zoològic
Cable Car
Passeig de Colom
Barceloneta
Passeig Circumvallació
Monument a Colom
Moll de la Fusta
Ronda Litoral
Avinguda
To Castel Montjuïc
Ciutadella-Vila Olímpica
Jose Carner
Marina-Port Vell
Maremagnum
Cine IMAX
Barceloneta
Vila Olímpica
N
0
300 yards
0
300 meters
Passeig
Cable Car
Harbor
Multicines
Aquarium

Madrid Metro

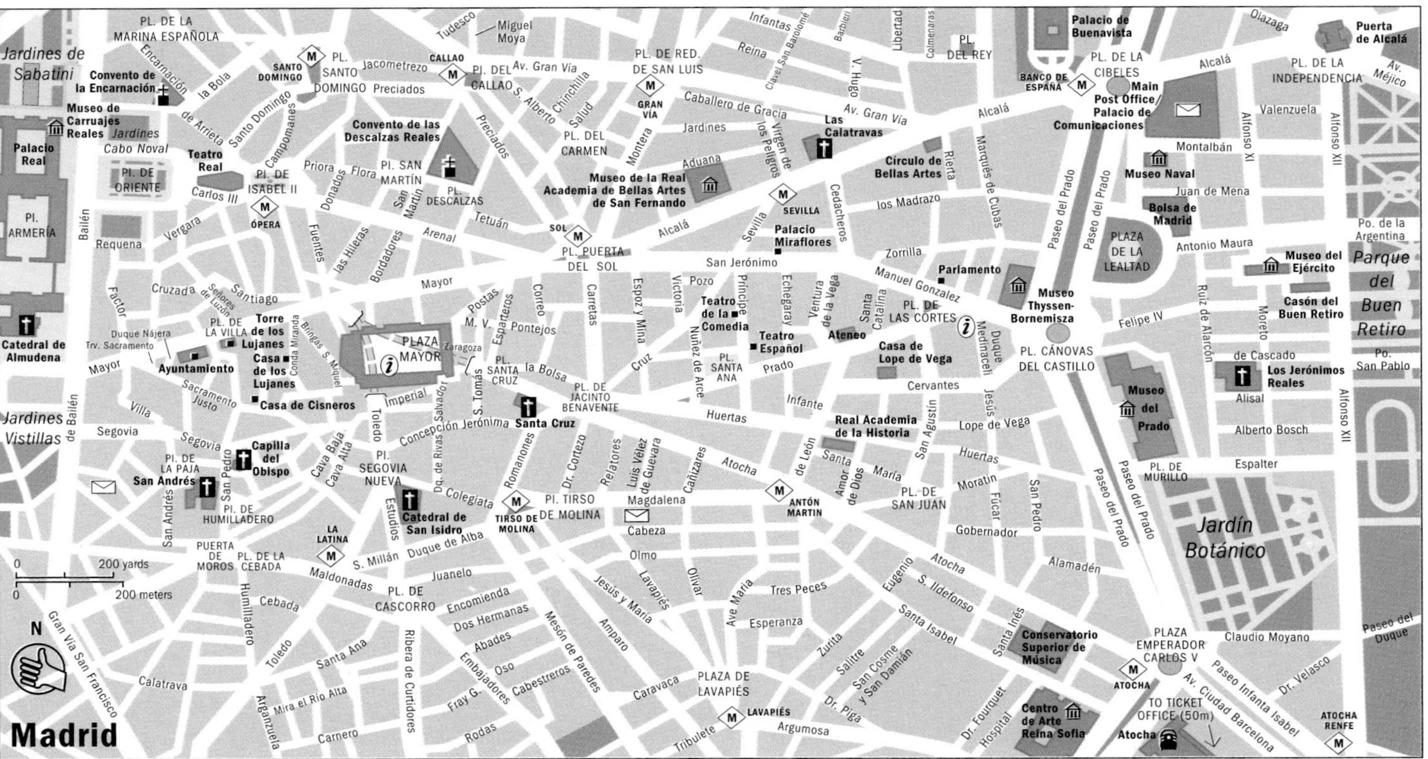
Madrid
Jardines de Sabatini
Convento de la Encarnación
Museo de Carruajes Reales
Palacio Real
PL. DE ORIENTE
Teatro Real
PL. DE ISABEL II
ÓPERA
PL. ARMERÍA
Catedral de Almudena
Jardines Vistillas
PL. DE LA MARINA ESPAÑOLA
SANTO DOMINGO
PL. SANTO DOMINGO
CALLAO
PL. DEL CALLAO
Convento de las Descalzas Reales
PL. SAN MARTÍN
PL. DESCALZAS
PL. DE RED. DE SAN LUIS
GRAN VÍA
PL. DEL CARMEN
Museo de la Real Academia de Bellas Artes de San Fernando
SOL
PL. PUERTA DEL SOL
SEVILLA
Palacio Miraflores
Las Calatravas
Círculo de Bellas Artes
PL. DEL REY
Palacio de Buenavista
BANCO DE ESPAÑA
PL. DE LA CIBELES
Main Post Office/Palacio de Comunicaciones
PL. DE LA INDEPENDENCIA
Puerta de Alcalá
Museo Naval
Bolsa de Madrid
PLAZA DE LA LEALTAD
Museo del Ejército
Parque del Buen Retiro
Casón del Buen Retiro
Los Jerónimos Reales
Parlamento
Museo Thyssen-Bornemisza
PL. DE LAS CORTES
PL. CÁNOVAS DEL CASTILLO
Museo del Prado
Casa de Lope de Vega
Ateneo
Teatro de la Comedia
Teatro Español
PL. SANTA ANA
Real Academia de la Historia
PLAZA MAYOR
Torre de los Lujanes
Casa de los Lujanes
PL. DE LA VILLA
Ayuntamiento
Casa de Cisneros
PL. SANTA CRUZ
Santa Cruz
PL. DE JACINTO BENAVENTE
Capilla del Obispo
PL. DE LA PAJA
San Andrés
PL. DE HUMILLADERO
PL. SEGOVIA NUEVA
Catedral de San Isidro
TIRSO DE MOLINA
Pl. TIRSO DE MOLINA
ANTÓN MARTÍN
PL. DE SAN JUAN
PL. DE MURILLO
Jardín Botánico
LA LATINA
PUERTA DE MOROS
PL. DE LA CEBADA
PL. DE CASCORRO
PLAZA DE LAVAPIÉS
LAVAPIÉS
Conservatorio Superior de Música
Centro de Arte Reina Sofía
PLAZA EMPERADOR CARLOS V
ATOCHA
TO TICKET OFFICE (50m)
Atocha
ATOCHA RENFE
Paseo del Prado
Alcalá
Av. Gran Vía
Mayor
Arenal
San Jerónimo
Atocha
Huertas
Alfonso XII
Alfonso XI
Bailén
Ribera de Curtidores
Gran Via San Francisco
0 200 yards
0 200 meters
N

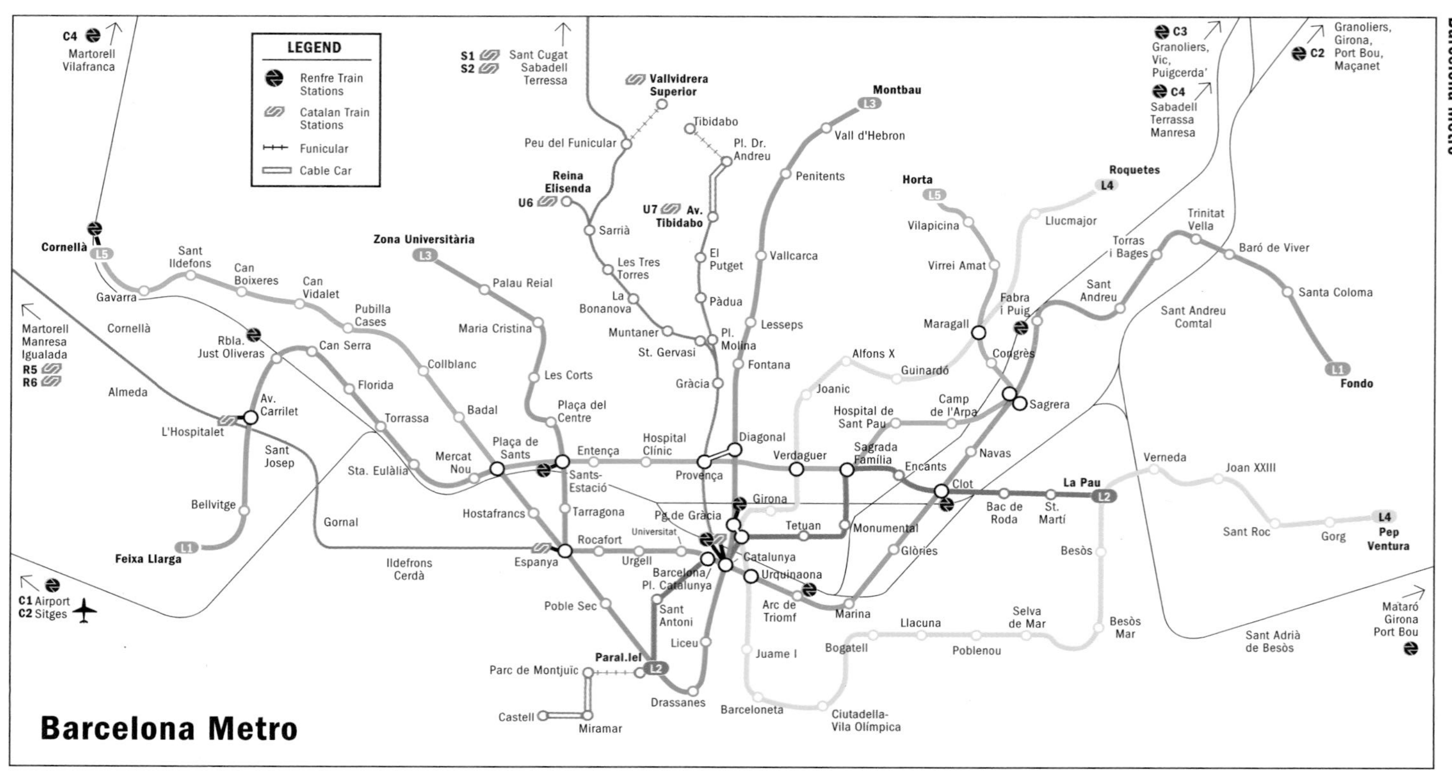
LEGEND
Renfe Train Stations
Catalan Train Stations
Funicular
Cable Car
C4 Martorell Vilafranca
S1 S2 Sant Cugat Sabadell Terressa
Vallvidrera Superior
Montbau
C3 Granoliers, Vic, Puigcerda'
C4 Sabadell Terrassa Manresa
C2 Granoliers, Girona, Port Bou, Maçanet
Peu del Funicular
Tibidabo
Pl. Dr. Andreu
Vall d'Hebron
Penitents
Reina Elisenda U6
U7 Av. Tibidabo
Horta
Roquetes
Sarrià
Vilapicina
Llucmajor
Trinitat Vella
Torras i Bages
Baró de Viver
Cornellà
Zona Universitària
Sant Ildefons
Can Boixeres
Can Vidalet
Palau Reial
Les Tres Torres
El Putget
Vallcarca
Virrei Amat
Santa Coloma
Sant Andreu
Sant Andreu Comtal
Gavarra
Pubilla Cases
La Bonanova
Pàdua
Fabra i Puig
Martorell Manresa Igualada R5 R6
Cornellà
Maria Cristina
Lesseps
Maragall
Rbla. Just Oliveras
Can Serra
Muntaner
Pl. Molina
St. Gervasi
Alfons X
Congrès
Fontana
Collblanc
Guinardó
L1 Fondo
Almeda
Florida
Les Corts
Gràcia
Joanic
Av. Carrilet
Camp de l'Arpa
Sagrera
Hospital de Sant Pau
Badal
Torrassa
Plaça del Centre
L'Hospitalet
Diagonal
Navas
Sant Josep
Hospital Clínic
Plaça de Sants
Sagrada Família
Verneda
Mercat Nou
Entença
Verdaguer
Encants
Joan XXIII
Sta. Eulàlia
Sants-Estació
Provença
La Pau
Clot
Girona
Bac de Roda
St. Martí
Bellvitge
Tarragona
Hostafrancs
Pg de Gràcia
Tetuan
Monumental
Sant Roc
Gorg
L4 Pep Ventura
Gornal
Universitat
Rocafort
Feixa Llarga
Catalunya
Besòs
Glòries
Ildefons Cerdà
Espanya
Urgell
Barcelona/ Pl. Catalunya
Urquinaona
C1 Airport C2 Sitges
Poble Sec
Sant Antoni
Arc de Triomf
Marina
Llacuna
Selva de Mar
Besòs Mar
Mataró Girona Port Bou
Liceu
Juame I
Bogatell
Poblenou
Sant Adrià de Besòs
Paral.lel
Parc de Montjuïc
Drassanes
Barceloneta
Castell
Miramar
Ciutadella-Vila Olímpica
Barcelona Metro

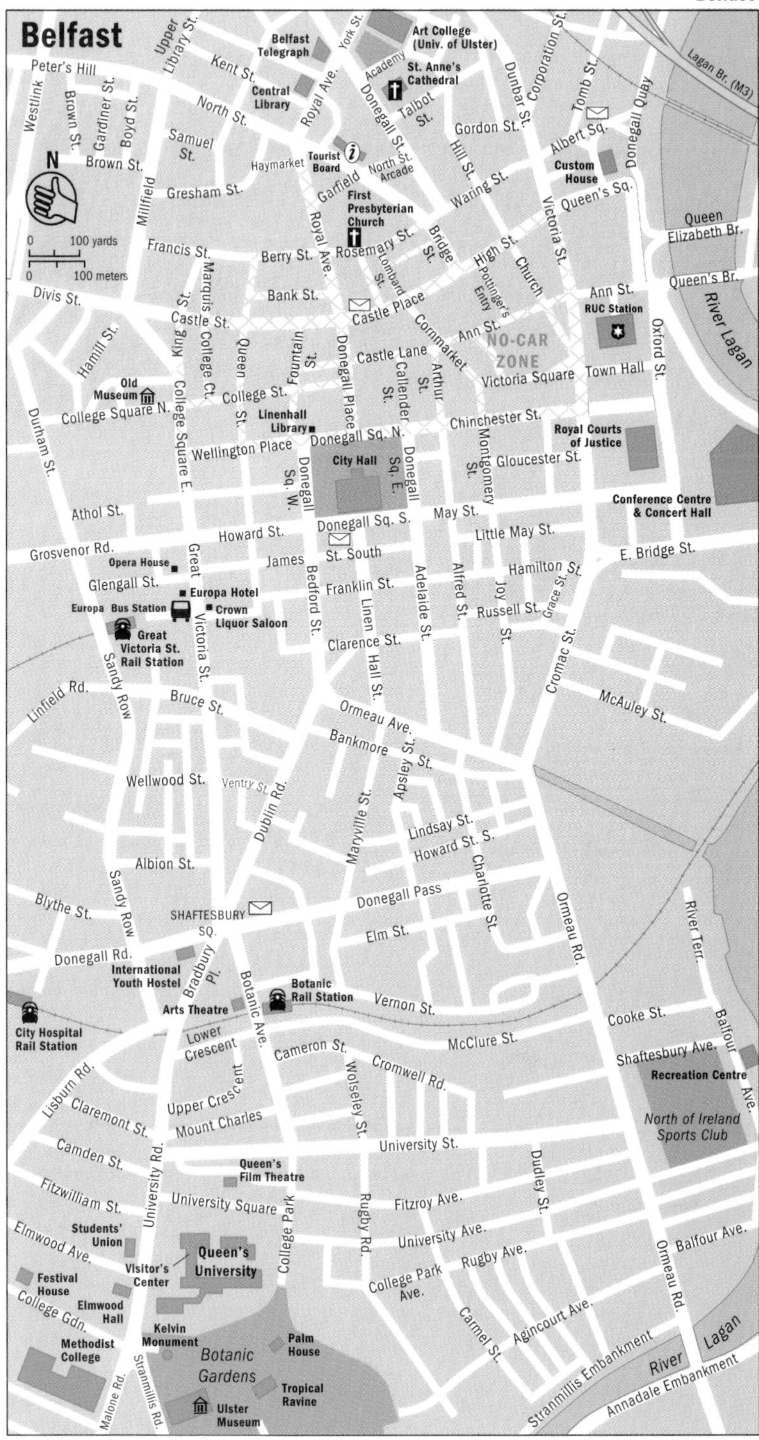
Belfast
N
0 100 yards
0 100 meters
Peter's Hill
Westlink
Brown St.
Gardiner St.
Boyd St.
Upper Library St.
Kent St.
North St.
Samuel St.
Brown St.
Millfield
Gresham St.
Francis St.
Divis St.
Belfast Telegraph
Central Library
York St.
Royal Ave.
Art College (Univ. of Ulster)
Academy
St. Anne's Cathedral
Donegall St.
Talbot St.
Dunbar St.
Corporation St.
Tomb St.
Lagan Br. (M3)
Donegall Quay
Gordon St.
Albert Sq.
Custom House
Hill St.
Haymarket
Tourist Board
North St. Arcade
Garfield
First Presbyterian Church
Waring St.
Queen's Sq.
Victoria St.
Queen Elizabeth Br.
Berry St.
Royal Ave.
Rosemary St.
Lombard St.
Bridge St.
High St.
Pottinger's Entry
Church
Queen's Br.
Bank St.
Castle Place
Ann St.
RUC Station
River Lagan
Oxford St.
Hamill St.
King St.
Castle St.
College Ct.
Marquis
Queen St.
Fountain St.
Donegall Place
Castle Lane
Cornmarket
Ann St.
NO-CAR ZONE
Callender St.
Arthur St.
Victoria Square
Town Hall
Old Museum
College St.
College Square N.
College Square E.
Durham St.
Linenhall Library
Donegall Sq. N.
Chinchester St.
Montgomery St.
Royal Courts of Justice
Wellington Place
City Hall
Donegall Sq. W.
Donegall Sq. E.
Gloucester St.
Athol St.
Conference Centre & Concert Hall
May St.
Donegall Sq. S.
Howard St.
Grosvenor Rd.
Little May St.
James
St. South
E. Bridge St.
Opera House
Great Victoria St.
Bedford St.
Adelaide St.
Alfred St.
Joy St.
Hamilton St.
Glengall St.
Europa Hotel
Franklin St.
Grace St.
Europa Bus Station
Crown Liquor Saloon
Russell St.
Great Victoria St. Rail Station
Linen Hall St.
Clarence St.
Cromac St.
Sandy Row
Linfield Rd.
Bruce St.
Ormeau Ave.
McAuley St.
Bankmore St.
Apsley St.
Wellwood St.
Ventry St.
Dublin Rd.
Maryville St.
Lindsay St.
Howard St. S.
Charlotte St.
Albion St.
Sandy Row
Ormeau Rd.
Blythe St.
SHAFTESBURY SQ.
Donegall Pass
River Terr.
Elm St.
Donegall Rd.
International Youth Hostel
Bradbury Pl.
Botanic Ave.
Botanic Rail Station
Vernon St.
City Hospital Rail Station
Arts Theatre
Lower Crescent
Cameron St.
McClure St.
Cooke St.
Balfour Ave.
Cromwell Rd.
Shaftesbury Ave.
Recreation Centre
Lisburn Rd.
Claremont St.
Upper Crescent
Mount Charles
Wolseley St.
North of Ireland Sports Club
Camden St.
University Rd.
University St.
Queen's Film Theatre
Dudley St.
Fitzwilliam St.
University Square
College Park
Rugby Rd.
Fitzroy Ave.
Students' Union
University Ave.
Ormeau Rd.
Balfour Ave.
Elmwood Ave.
Queen's University
Visitor's Center
College Park Ave.
Rugby Ave.
Festival House
College Gdn.
Elmwood Hall
Carmel St.
Agincourt Ave.
Methodist College
Kelvin Monument
Palm House
Botanic Gardens
Stranmillis Embankment
River Lagan
Tropical Ravine
Malone Rd.
Stranmillis Rd.
Ulster Museum
Annadale Embankment

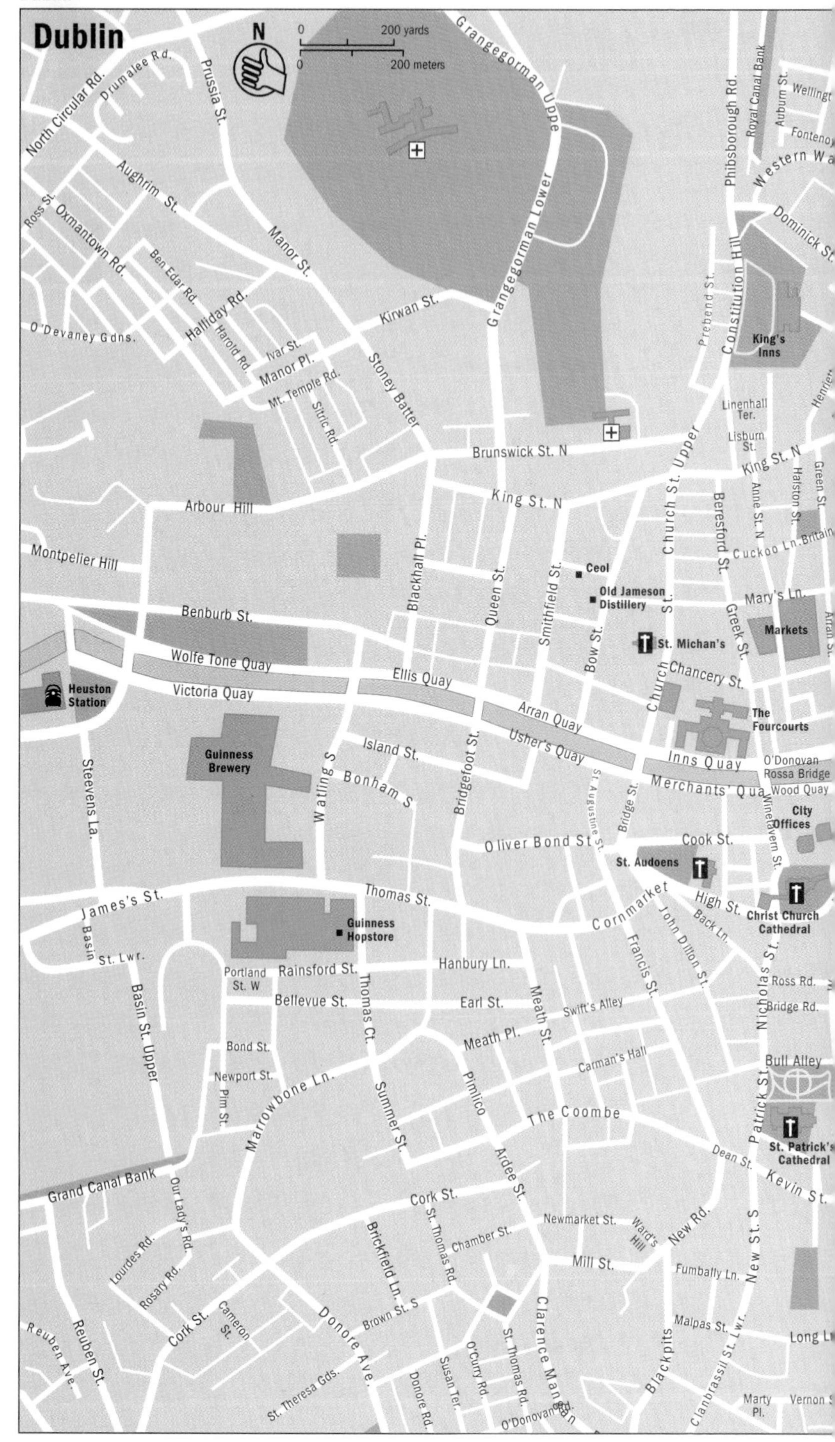
Dublin
N
0
200 yards
0
200 meters
Grangegorman Upper
Grangegorman Lower
North Circular Rd.
Drumalee Rd.
Prussia St.
Aughrim St.
Ross St.
Oxmantown Rd.
Ben Edar Rd.
Manor St.
Halliday Rd.
Harold Rd.
Kirwan St.
O'Devaney Gdns.
Ivar St.
Manor Pl.
Mt. Temple Rd.
Sitric Rd.
Stoney Batter
Brunswick St. N
King St. N
Arbour Hill
Montpelier Hill
Blackhall Pl.
Queen St.
Smithfield St.
Ceol
Old Jameson Distillery
Bow St.
Benburb St.
Wolfe Tone Quay
Victoria Quay
Ellis Quay
Arran Quay
Usher's Quay
Heuston Station
Guinness Brewery
Island St.
Bonham S
Watling S
Bridgefoot St.
Steevens La.
Oliver Bond St
St. Augustine St.
Bridge St.
St. Audoens
Cook St.
James's St.
Thomas St.
Cornmarket
Guinness Hopstore
Basin St. Lwr.
Basin St. Upper
Portland St. W
Rainsford St.
Thomas Ct.
Hanbury Ln.
Bellevue St.
Earl St.
Meath St.
Swift's Alley
Francis St.
John Dillon St.
Back Ln.
High St.
Bond St.
Newport St.
Pim St.
Marrowbone Ln.
Summer St.
Meath Pl.
Pimlico
Carman's Hall
The Coombe
Grand Canal Bank
Our Lady's Rd.
Lourdes Rd.
Rosary Rd.
Cork St.
St. Thomas Rd.
Chamber St.
Brickfield Ln.
Ardee St.
Newmarket St.
Ward's Hill
New Rd.
Mill St.
Cork St.
Cameron St.
Donore Ave.
Brown St. S
Reuben Ave.
Reuben St.
St. Theresa Gds.
Donore Rd.
Susan Ter.
O'Curry Rd.
St. Thomas Rd.
Clarence Mangan
O'Donovan Rd.
Blackpits
Fumbally Ln.
Malpas St.
Clanbrassil St. Lwr.
Marty Pl.
Vernon S
Long L
New St. S
Dean St.
Kevin St.
St. Patrick's Cathedral
Patrick St.
Bull Alley
Nicholas St.
Ross Rd.
Bridge Rd.
Christ Church Cathedral
Winetavern St.
City Offices
Wood Quay
O'Donovan Rossa Bridge
Merchants' Qua
Inns Quay
The Fourcourts
Chancery St.
Church St.
St. Michan's
Church St. Upper
Markets
Greek St.
Mary's Ln.
Beresford St.
Cuckoo Ln.
Britain
Anne St. N
Halston St.
Green St.
Arran St.
King St. N
Lisburn St.
Linenhall Ter.
Prebend St.
Constitution Hill
King's Inns
Henrie
Dominick St.
Western Wa
Phibsborough Rd.
Royal Canal Bank
Auburn St.
Wellingt
Fonteno

St. George's
Mountjoy Sq.
Dublin Writers Museum
Hugh Lane Gallery
Abbey Presbyterian
Nat'l Wax Museum
Garden of Remembrance
Parnell Sq.
Gate Theatre
James Joyce Center
Rotunda Hospital
Connolly Station
Tyrone House
Moore St. Market
Inner Dock
Busarus
Financial Services Center
George's Dock
General Post Office
Custom House
Liberty Hall
St. Mary's Church
Global Internet Cafe
Hot Press
River Liffey
O'Connell Bridge
Ha'Penny Footbridge
Tara St. Station
Stock Exchange
Bank of Ireland
Town Hall
Dublin Castle
Pearse Station
Trinity College
American Express
Central Cybercafé
Planet Cyber Cafe
National Gallery
National Library
Mansion House
Leinster House
St. Adelaide Hospital
National Museums
Government Buildings
Merrion Sq.
St. Stephen's Green
Number 29
Bank of Ireland
University College Dublin
National Concert Hall
Fitzwilliam Sq.

Cork and Galway

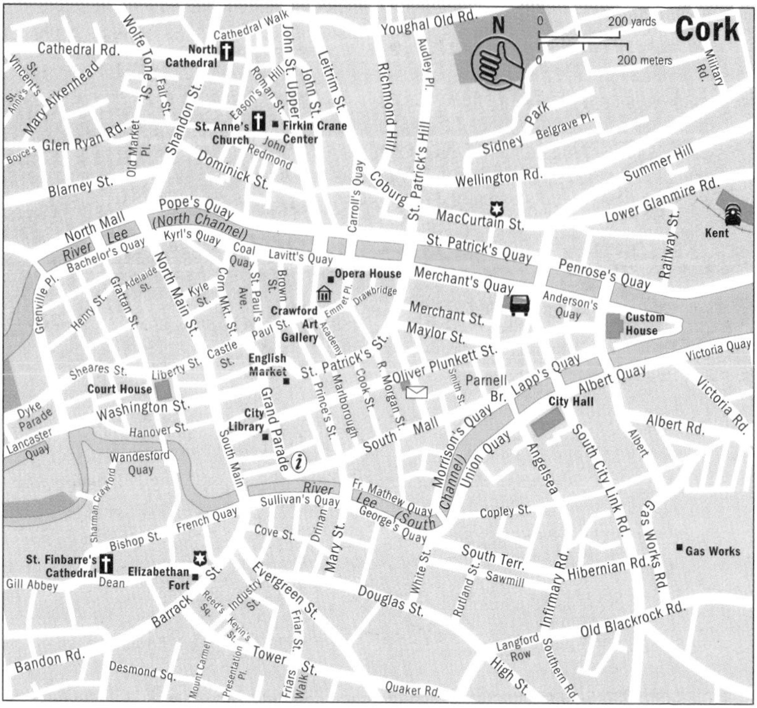

Cork

N
0 200 yards
0 200 meters
Cathedral Walk
Youghal Old Rd.
Military Rd.
Cathedral Rd.
Wolfe Tone St.
North Cathedral
John St. Upper
John St.
Leitrim St.
Richmond Hill
Audley Pl.
St. Vincent's
St. Anne's Pk.
Mary Aikenhead
Fair St.
Shandon St.
Eason's Hill
Roman St.
St. Anne's Church
Firkin Crane Center
John Redmond
Sidney Park
Belgrave Pl.
Boyce's
Glen Ryan Rd.
Old Market Pl.
Dominick St.
Carroll's Quay
Coburg
St. Patrick's Hill
Wellington Rd.
Summer Hill
Blarney St.
Pope's Quay
(North Channel)
MacCurtain St.
Lower Glanmire Rd.
Railway St.
Kent
North Mall
River Lee
Kyrl's Quay
Coal Quay
Lavitt's Quay
St. Patrick's Quay
Penrose's Quay
Bachelor's Quay
Grenville Pl.
Opera House
Merchant's Quay
Henry St.
Grattan St.
Adelaide St.
North Main St.
Kyle St.
Corn Mkt. St.
St. Paul's Ave.
Brown St.
Emmet Pl.
Drawbridge
Anderson's Quay
Custom House
Crawford Art Gallery
Academy
Merchant St.
Paul St.
Maylor St.
Castle St.
Oliver Plunkett St.
Victoria Quay
Sheares St.
Liberty St.
English Market
St. Patrick's St.
R. Morgan St.
Smith St.
Parnell Br.
Lapp's Quay
Albert Quay
Court House
Cook St.
Marlborough
Prince's St.
Grand Parade
City Hall
Victoria Rd.
Dyke Parade
Washington St.
City Library
South Mall
Morrison's Quay
Albert Rd.
Lancaster Quay
Hanover St.
South Main
Union Quay
Albert
South City Link Rd.
Wandesford Quay
Angelsea
River Lee (South Channel)
Fr. Mathew Quay
Sullivan's Quay
George's Quay
Copley St.
Gas Works Rd.
Sharman Crawford
French Quay
Cove St.
Drinan
Mary St.
Gas Works
Bishop St.
White St.
South Terr.
Hibernian Rd.
St. Finbarre's Cathedral
Elizabethan Fort
Dean
Gill Abbey
Barrack St.
Reed's Sq.
Industry St.
Evergreen St.
Rutland St.
Sawmill
Infirmary Rd.
Douglas St.
Friar St.
Kevin's St.
Old Blackrock Rd.
Bandon Rd.
Mount Carmel
Presentation Pl.
Tower St.
Langford Row
Desmond Sq.
Friars Walk
High St.
Southern Rd.
Quaker Rd.

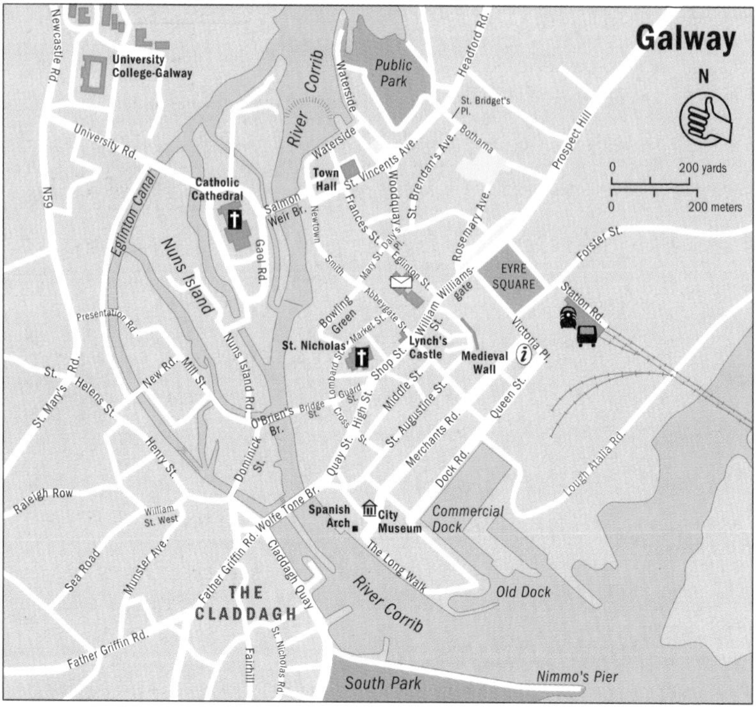

Galway

N
0 200 yards
0 200 meters
Newcastle Rd.
University College-Galway
Headford Rd.
Public Park
River Corrib
Waterside
St. Bridget's Pl.
University Rd.
Bothar na
Prospect Hill
Catholic Cathedral
Town Hall
St. Vincents Ave.
Woodquay
St. Brendan's Ave.
N59
Eglinton Canal
Salmon Weir Br.
Newtown
Frances St.
Daly's Pl.
Rosemary Ave.
Nuns Island
Gaol Rd.
Smith
Mary St.
Eglinton St.
Forster St.
EYRE SQUARE
Williams-gate
William St.
Abbeygate St.
Bowling Green
Station Rd.
Presentation Rd.
Market St.
Lynch's Castle
St. Nicholas'
Nuns Island Rd.
Medieval Wall
Victoria Pl.
St. Helens St.
St. Mary's Rd.
New Rd.
Mill St.
Shop St.
Middle St.
Lombard St.
Guard St.
Bridge St.
Cross St.
High St.
St. Augustine St.
Queen St.
O'Brien's Br.
Henry St.
Merchants Rd.
Lough Atalia Rd.
Dominick St.
Quay St.
Dock Rd.
Raleigh Row
Wolfe Tone Br.
William St. West
Spanish Arch
City Museum
Commercial Dock
Sea Road
Munster Ave.
Father Griffin Rd.
Claddagh Quay
The Long Walk
River Corrib
Old Dock
THE CLADDAGH
Father Griffin Rd.
Fairhill
St. Nicholas Rd.
Nimmo's Pier
South Park

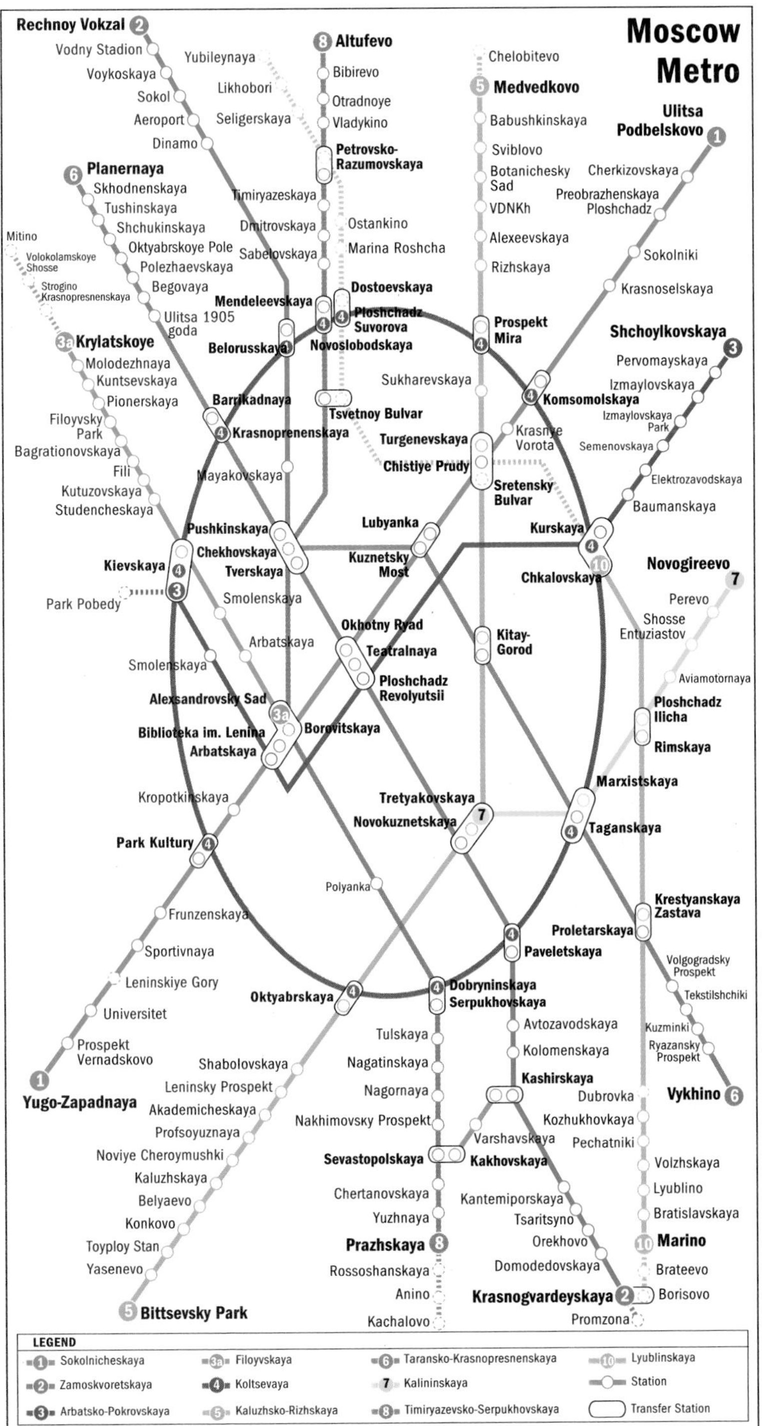

Moscow Metro
Rechnoy Vokzal
Vodny Stadion
Voykoskaya
Sokol
Aeroport
Dinamo
Yubileynaya
Likhobori
Seligerskaya
Altufevo
Bibirevo
Otradnoye
Vladykino
Petrovsko-Razumovskaya
Chelobitevo
Medvedkovo
Babushkinskaya
Sviblovo
Botanichesky Sad
VDNKh
Alexeevskaya
Rizhskaya
Ulitsa Podbelskovo
Cherkizovskaya
Preobrazhenskaya Ploshchadz
Sokolniki
Krasnoselskaya
Planernaya
Skhodnenskaya
Tushinskaya
Shchukinskaya
Oktyabrskoye Pole
Polezhaevskaya
Begovaya
Ulitsa 1905 goda
Timiryazeskaya
Dmitrovskaya
Sabelovskaya
Ostankino
Marina Roshcha
Mitino
Volokolamskoye Shosse
Strogino
Krasnopresnenskaya
Mendeleevskaya
Dostoevskaya
Ploshchadz Suvorova
Novoslobodskaya
Belorusskaya
Prospekt Mira
Shchoylkovskaya
Pervomayskaya
Izmaylovskaya
Izmaylovskaya Park
Semenovskaya
Elektrozavodskaya
Baumanskaya
Krylatskoye
Molodezhnaya
Kuntsevskaya
Pionerskaya
Filoyvsky Park
Bagrationovskaya
Fili
Kutuzovskaya
Studencheskaya
Sukharevskaya
Komsomolskaya
Krasnye Vorota
Barrikadnaya
Krasnoprenenskaya
Tsvetnoy Bulvar
Turgenevskaya
Chistiye Prudy
Sretensky Bulvar
Mayakovskaya
Pushkinskaya
Chekhovskaya
Tverskaya
Lubyanka
Kuznetsky Most
Kurskaya
Chkalovskaya
Novogireevo
Perevo
Shosse Entuziastov
Kievskaya
Park Pobedy
Smolenskaya
Arbatskaya
Okhotny Ryad
Teatralnaya
Ploshchadz Revolyutsii
Kitay-Gorod
Aviamotornaya
Ploshchadz Ilicha
Rimskaya
Smolenskaya
Alexsandrovsky Sad
Biblioteka im. Lenina
Arbatskaya
Borovitskaya
Marxistskaya
Kropotkinskaya
Tretyakovskaya
Novokuznetskaya
Taganskaya
Park Kultury
Polyanka
Krestyanskaya Zastava
Proletarskaya
Frunzenskaya
Paveletskaya
Sportivnaya
Volgogradsky Prospekt
Leninskiye Gory
Tekstilshchiki
Oktyabrskaya
Dobryninskaya
Serpukhovskaya
Universitet
Kuzminki
Ryazansky Prospekt
Avtozavodskaya
Kolomenskaya
Tulskaya
Prospekt Vernadskovo
Yugo-Zapadnaya
Shabolovskaya
Nagatinskaya
Kashirskaya
Vykhino
Leninsky Prospekt
Nagornaya
Dubrovka
Akademicheskaya
Nakhimovsky Prospekt
Kozhukhovkaya
Profsoyuznaya
Varshavskaya
Pechatniki
Noviye Cheroymushki
Sevastopolskaya
Kakhovskaya
Volzhskaya
Kaluzhskaya
Lyublino
Belyaevo
Chertanovskaya
Kantemiporskaya
Bratislavskaya
Konkovo
Yuzhnaya
Tsaritsyno
Toyploy Stan
Prazhskaya
Orekhovo
Marino
Yasenevo
Rossoshanskaya
Domodedovskaya
Brateevo
Anino
Krasnogvardeyskaya
Borisovo
Bittsevsky Park
Kachalovo
Promzona
LEGEND
Sokolnicheskaya
Zamoskvoretskaya
Arbatsko-Pokrovskaya
Filoyvskaya
Koltsevaya
Kaluzhsko-Rizhskaya
Taransko-Krasnopresnenskaya
Kalininskaya
Timiryazevsko-Serpukhovskaya
Lyublinskaya
Station
Transfer Station

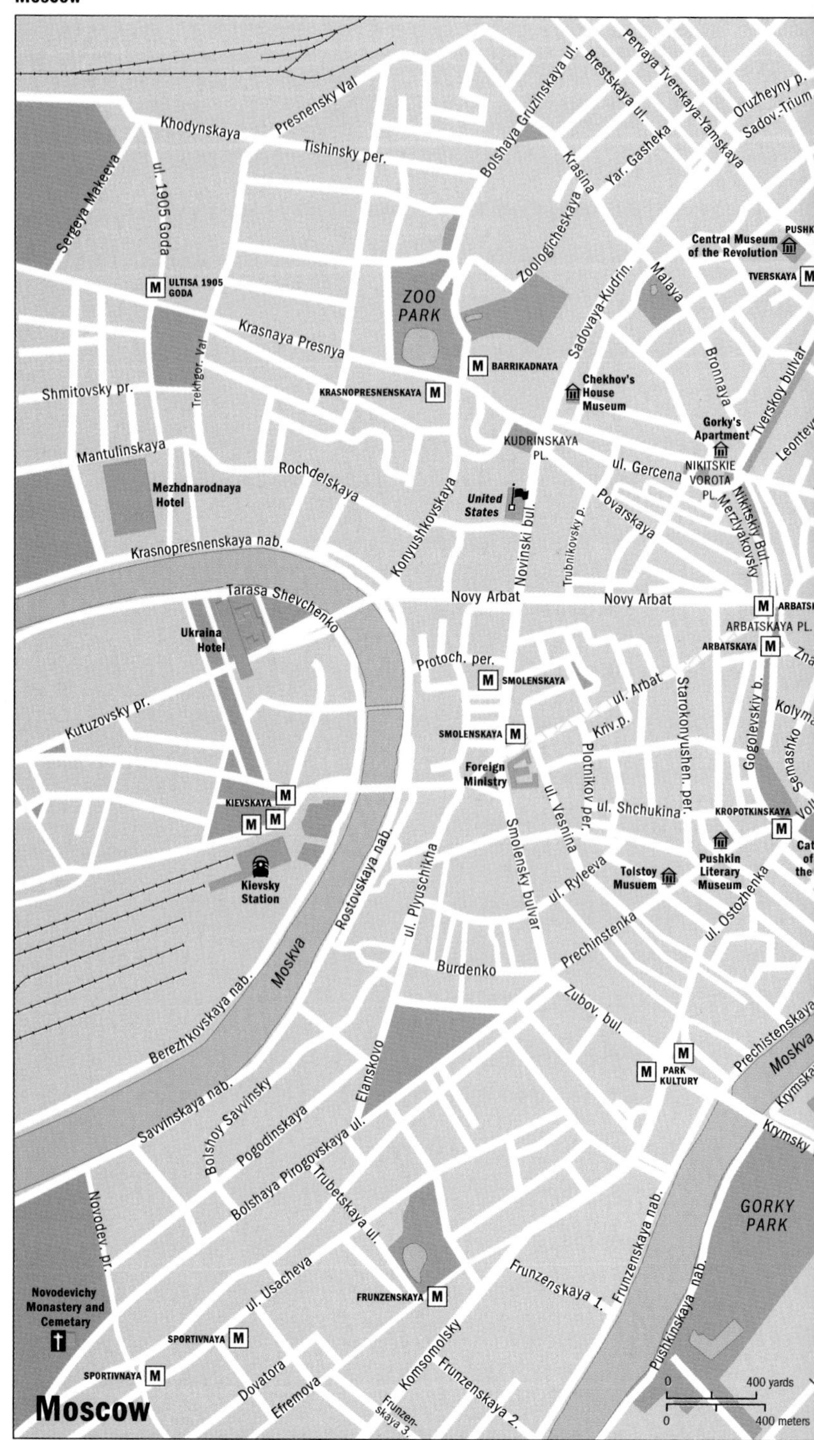
Moscow
Khodynskaya
Presnensky Val
Tishinsky per.
Sergeya Makeeva
ul. 1905 Goda
ULTISA 1905 GODA
Bolshaya Gruzinskaya ul.
Brestskaya ul.
Pervaya Tverskaya-Yamskaya
Oruzheyny p.
Sadov.-Trium
Krasina
Yar. Gasheka
Zoologicheskaya
Central Museum of the Revolution
TVERSKAYA
ZOO PARK
Sadovaya-Kudrin.
Malaya
Krasnaya Presnya
BARRIKADNAYA
Bronnaya
Tverskoy bulvar
Shmitovsky pr.
Trekhgor. Val
KRASNOPRESNENSKAYA
Chekhov's House Museum
Gorky's Apartment
Mantulinskaya
KUDRINSKAYA PL.
NIKITSKIE VOROTA PL.
ul. Gercena
Rochdelskaya
Mezhdnarodnaya Hotel
United States
Povarskaya
Konyushkovskaya
Novinski bul.
Trubnikovsky p.
Nikitskiy Bul.
Merzlyakovsky
Krasnopresnenskaya nab.
Tarasa Shevchenko
Novy Arbat
ARBATSKAYA PL.
ARBATSKAYA
Ukraina Hotel
Protoch. per.
SMOLENSKAYA
ul. Arbat
Starokonyushen. per.
Kutuzovsky pr.
Kriv.p.
Gogolevskiy b.
SMOLENSKAYA
Plotnikov per.
Semashko
Foreign Ministry
KIEVSKAYA
ul. Vesnina
ul. Shchukina
KROPOTKINSKAYA
Smolensky bulvar
Rostovskaya nab.
ul. Plyuschikha
Kievsky Station
ul. Ryleeva
Tolstoy Museum
Pushkin Literary Museum
ul. Ostozhenka
Prechinstenka
Moskva
Burdenko
Zubov. bul.
Berezhkovskaya nab.
Prechistenskaya
PARK KULTURY
Elanskovo
Savvinskaya nab.
Bolshoy Savvinsky
Pogodinskaya
Bolshaya Pirogovskaya ul.
Trubetskaya ul.
Krymsky
Novodev. pr.
Frunzenskaya nab.
GORKY PARK
Novodevichy Monastery and Cemetary
ul. Usacheva
FRUNZENSKAYA
Frunzenskaya 1.
SPORTIVNAYA
Pushkinskaya nab.
Komsomolsky
SPORTIVNAYA
Dovatora
Efremova
Frunzenskaya 2.
Frunzen-skaya 3.
0
400 yards
0
400 meters

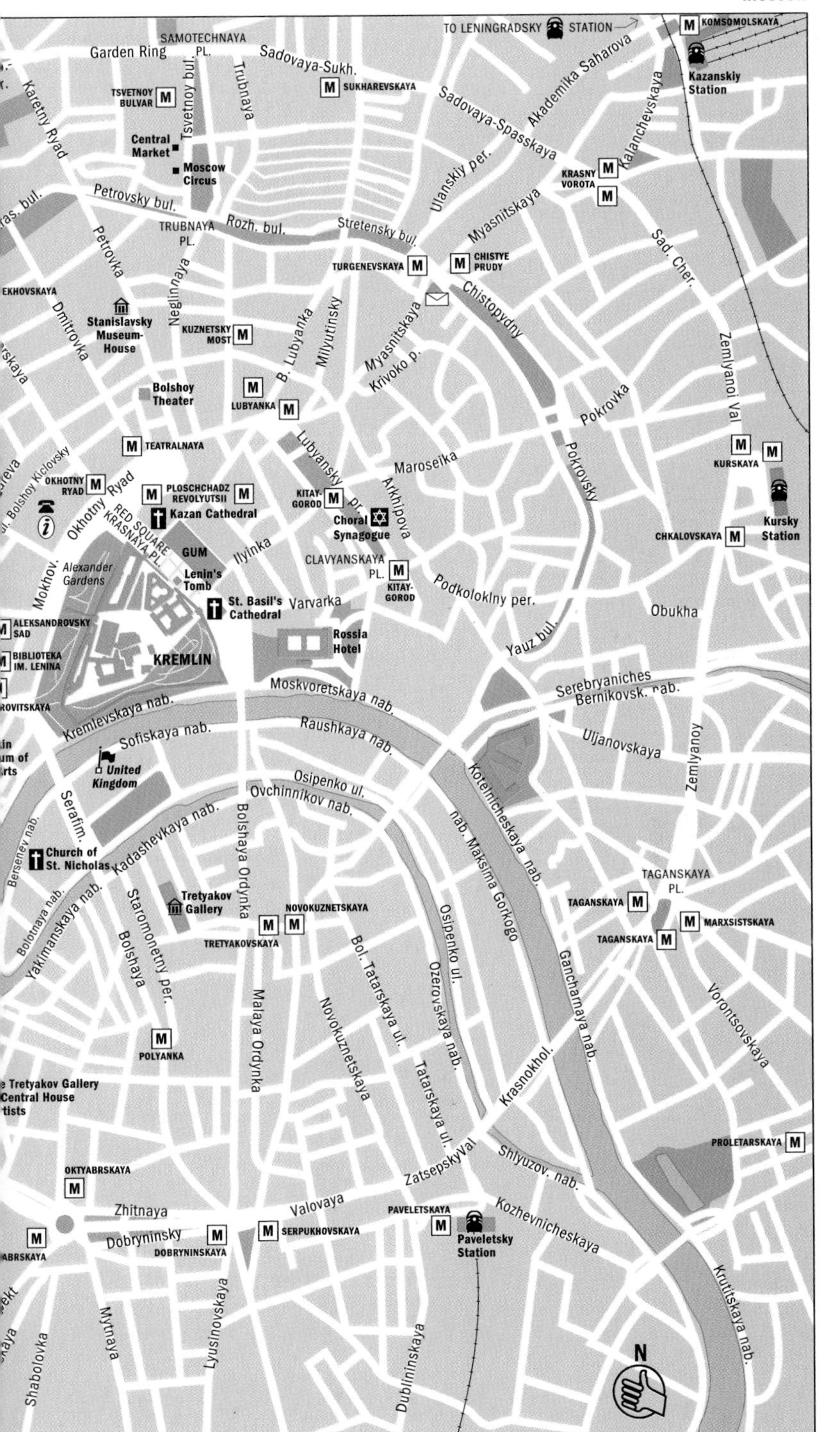
TO LENINGRADSKY STATION
KOMSOMOLSKAYA
Kazanskiy Station
SAMOTECHNAYA PL.
Garden Ring
Sadovaya-Sukh.
SUKHAREVSKAYA
Sadovaya-Spasskaya
Akademika Saharova
Kalanchevskaya
Karetny Ryad
TSVETNOY BULVAR
Tsvetnoy bul.
Trubnaya
Central Market
Moscow Circus
Ulanskiy per.
KRASNY VOROTA
Petrovsky bul.
TRUBNAYA PL.
Rozh. bul.
Stretensky bul.
Myasnitskaya
Sad. Cher.
TURGENEVSKAYA
CHISTYE PRUDY
Chistopydny
Petrovka
Neglinnaya
Dmitrovka
Stanislavsky Museum-House
KUZNETSKY MOST
B. Lubyanka
Milyutinsky
Myasnitskaya
Krivoko p.
Zemlyanoi Val
Bolshoy Theater
LUBYANKA
Pokrovka
TEATRALNAYA
Lubyansky pr.
Maroseika
Arkhipova
Pokrovsky
KURSKAYA
OKHOTNY RYAD
Okhotny Ryad
PLOSCHCHADZ REVOLYUTSII
KITAY-GOROD
Kursky Station
Kazan Cathedral
Choral Synagogue
RED SQUARE KRASNAYA PL.
CHKALOVSKAYA
GUM
Ilyinka
CLAVYANSKAYA PL.
KITAY-GOROD
Mokhov.
Alexander Gardens
Lenin's Tomb
Podkoloklny per.
St. Basil's Cathedral
Varvarka
Obukha
ALEKSANDROVSKY SAD
Rossia Hotel
BIBLIOTEKA IM. LENINA
KREMLIN
Yauz bul.
Moskvoretskaya nab.
Serebryaniches
Bernikovsk. nab.
Kremlevskaya nab.
Sofiskaya nab.
Raushkaya nab.
Uljanovskaya
United Kingdom
Zemlyanoy
Osipenko ul.
Ovchinnikov nab.
Kotelnicheskaya nab.
Serafim.
Kadashevkaya nab.
Bolshaya Ordynka
nab. Maksima Gorkogo
Bersenev nab.
Church of St. Nicholas
TAGANSKAYA PL.
Tretyakov Gallery
Staromonetny per.
TAGANSKAYA
MARXSISTSKAYA
Bolotnaya nab.
NOVOKUZNETSKAYA
TAGANSKAYA
Yakimanskaya nab.
TRETYAKOVSKAYA
Bol. Tatarskaya ul.
Osipenko ul.
Bolshaya
Gancharnaya nab.
Novokuznetskaya
Ozerovskaya nab.
Vorontsovskaya
POLYANKA
Malaya Ordynka
Krasnokhol.
Tatarskaya ul.
PROLETARSKAYA
ZatsepskyVal
Shlyuzov. nab.
OKTYABRSKAYA
PAVELETSKAYA
Zhitnaya
Valovaya
Kozhevnicheskaya
Dobryninsky
SERPUKHOVSKAYA
Paveletsky Station
DOBRYNINSKAYA
Krutitskaya nab.
Lysinovskaya
Mytnaya
Shabolovka
Dubininskaya
N

Московское Метро

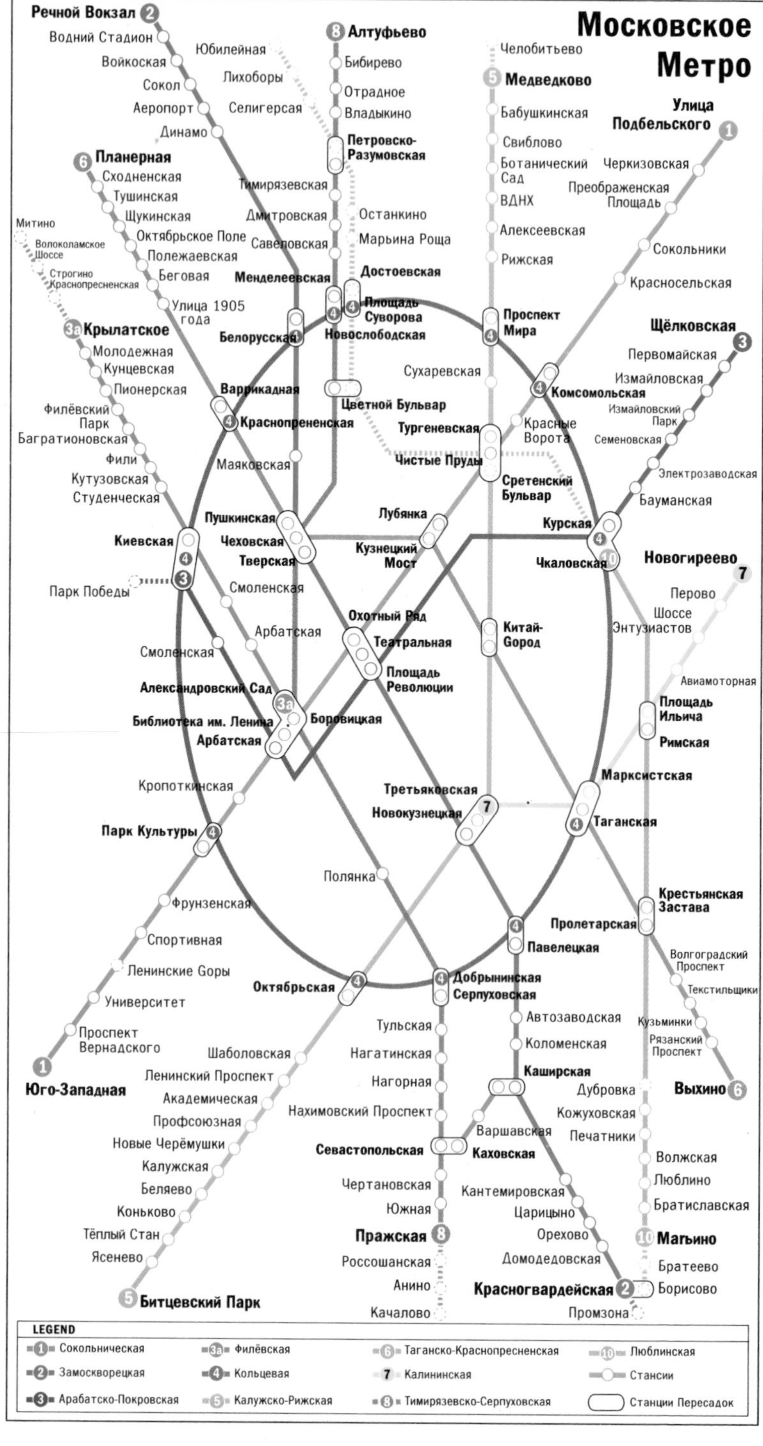
Московское Метро
Речной Вокзал
Водний Стадион
Войкоская
Сокол
Аэропорт
Динамо
Юбилейная
Лихоборы
Селигерсая
Алтуфьево
Бибирево
Отрадное
Владыкино
Петровско-Разумовская
Тимирязевская
Дмитровская
Савеловская
Менделеевская
Челобитьево
Медведково
Бабушкинская
Свиблово
Ботанический Сад
ВДНХ
Алексеевская
Рижская
Улица Подбельского
Черкизовская
Преображенская Площадь
Сокольники
Красносельская
Планерная
Сходненская
Тушинская
Щукинская
Октябрьское Поле
Полежаевская
Беговая
Улица 1905 года
Митино
Волоколамское Шоссе
Строгино
Краснопресненская
Крылатское
Молодежная
Кунцевская
Пионерская
Филёвский Парк
Багратионовская
Фили
Кутузовская
Студенческая
Останкино
Марьина Роща
Достоевская
Площадь Суворова
Новослободская
Белорусская
Проспект Мира
Сухаревская
Щёлковская
Первомайская
Измайловская
Измайловский Парк
Семеновская
Электрозаводская
Бауманская
Комсомольская
Красные Ворота
Варрикадная
Краснопрененская
Цветной Бульвар
Тургеневская
Чистые Пруды
Сретенский Бульвар
Маяковская
Пушкинская
Чеховская
Тверская
Лубянка
Кузнецкий Мост
Курская
Чкаловская
Новогиреево
Перово
Шоссе Энтузиастов
Авиамоторная
Киевская
Парк Победы
Смоленская
Арбатская
Охотный Ряд
Театральная
Площадь Революции
Китай-Город
Смоленская
Александровский Сад
Библиотека им. Ленина
Арбатская
Боровицкая
Площадь Ильича
Римская
Марксистская
Таганская
Кропоткинская
Третьяковская
Новокузнецкая
Парк Культуры
Полянка
Крестьянская Застава
Пролетарская
Фрунзенская
Спортивная
Ленинские Горы
Университет
Проспект Вернадского
Юго-Западная
Октябрьская
Добрынинская
Серпуховская
Павелецкая
Автозаводская
Коломенская
Волгоградский Проспект
Текстильщики
Кузьминки
Рязанский Проспект
Выхино
Тульская
Нагатинская
Нагорная
Нахимовский Проспект
Севастопольская
Каховская
Варшавская
Каширская
Шаболовская
Ленинский Проспект
Академическая
Профсоюзная
Новые Черёмушки
Калужская
Беляево
Коньково
Тёплый Стан
Ясенево
Битцевский Парк
Чертановская
Южная
Пражская
Россошанская
Анино
Качалово
Кантемировская
Царицыно
Орехово
Домодедовская
Красногвардейская
Промзона
Дубровка
Кожуховская
Печатники
Волжская
Люблино
Братиславская
Марьино
Братеево
Борисово
LEGEND
Сокольническая
Замоскворецкая
Арабатско-Покровская
Филёвская
Кольцевая
Калужско-Рижская
Таганско-Краснопресненская
Калининская
Тимирязевско-Серпуховская
Люблинская
Стансии
Станции Пересадок

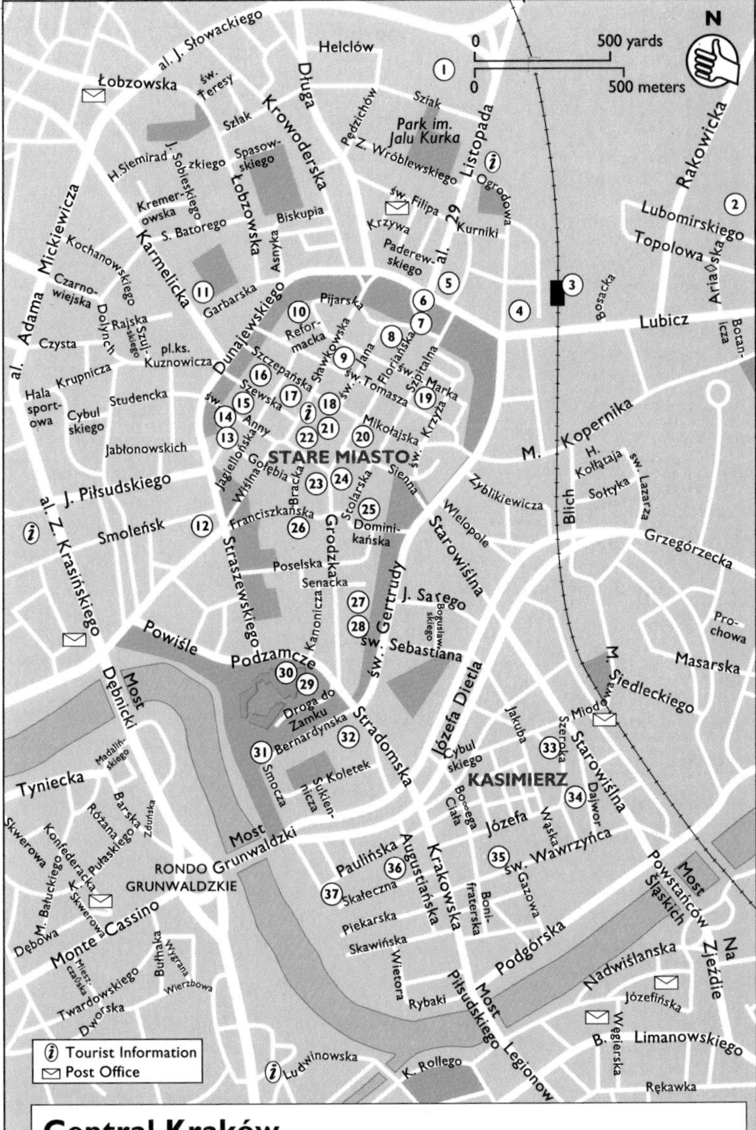

Central Kraków

Akademia Ekonomiczna, **2**
Almatur Office, **24**
Barbican, **6**
Bernardine Church, **32**
Bus Station, **4**
Carmelite Church, **11**
Cartoon Gallery, **9**
City Historical Museum, **17**
Collegium Maius, **14**
Corpus Christi Church, **35**
Czartoryski Art Museum, **8**
Dominican Church, **25**
Dragon Statue, **31**
Filharmonia, **12**
Franciscan Church, **26**
Grunwald Memorial, **5**
Jewish Cemetery, **33**
Jewish Museum, **34**
Kraków Głowny Station, **3**
Monastery of the Reformed Franciscans, **10**
Muzeum Historii Fotografii, **23**
Orbis Office, **19**
Pauline Church, **37**
Police Station, **18**
Politechnika Krakowska, **1**
St. Andrew's Church, **28**
St. Anne's Church, **15**
St. Catherine's Church, **36**
St. Florian's Gate, **7**
St. Mary's Church, **20**
St. Peter and Paul Church, **27**
Stary Teatr (Old Theater), **16**
Sukiennice (Cloth Hall), **21**
Town Hall, **22**
University Museum, **13**
Wawel Castle, **29**
Wawel Cathedral, **30**

Prague

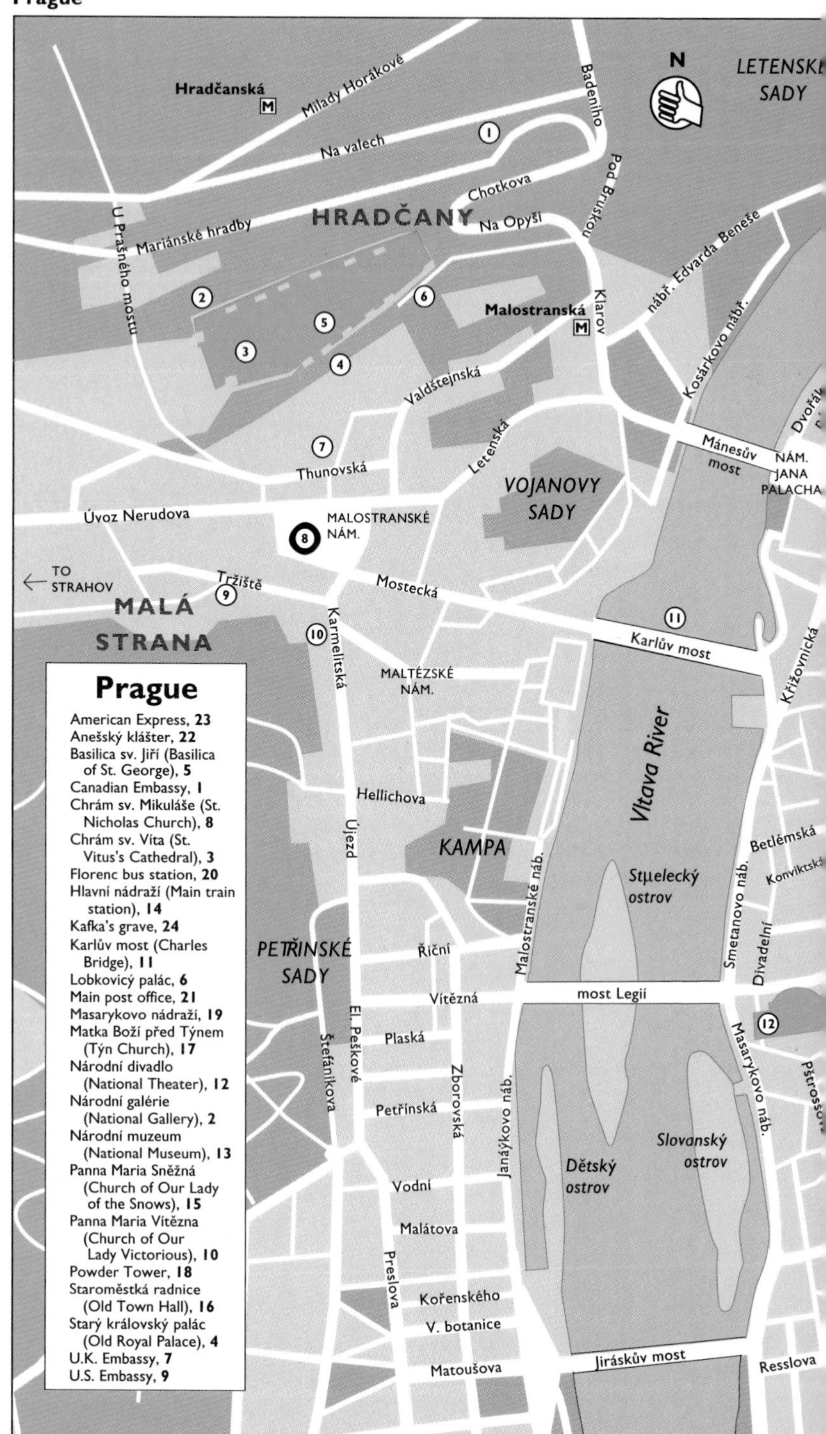

Prague

American Express, **23**
Anešský klášter, **22**
Basilica sv. Jiří (Basilica of St. George), **5**
Canadian Embassy, **1**
Chrám sv. Mikuláše (St. Nicholas Church), **8**
Chrám sv. Víta (St. Vitus's Cathedral), **3**
Florenc bus station, **20**
Hlavní nádraží (Main train station), **14**
Kafka's grave, **24**
Karlův most (Charles Bridge), **11**
Lobkovicý palác, **6**
Main post office, **21**
Masarykovo nádraží, **19**
Matka Boží před Týnem (Týn Church), **17**
Národní divadlo (National Theater), **12**
Národní galérie (National Gallery), **2**
Národní muzeum (National Museum), **13**
Panna Maria Sněžná (Church of Our Lady of the Snows), **15**
Panna Maria Vítězna (Church of Our Lady Victorious), **10**
Powder Tower, **18**
Staroměstká radnice (Old Town Hall), **16**
Starý královský palác (Old Royal Palace), **4**
U.K. Embassy, **7**
U.S. Embassy, **9**

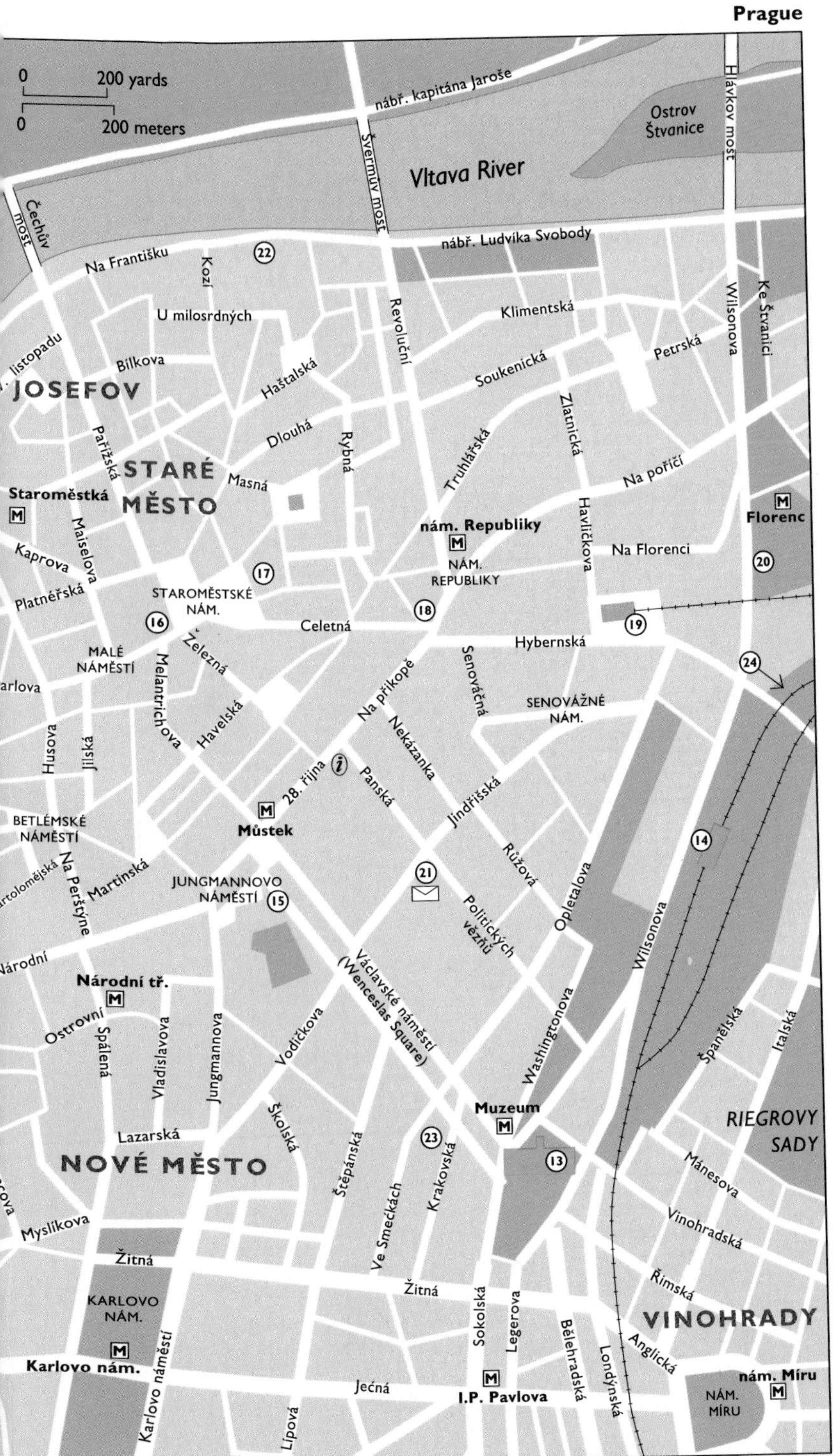
0 200 yards
0 200 meters
Vltava River
Ostrov Štvanice
nábř. kapitána Jaroše
Švermův most
Hlávkov most
Čechův most
nábř. Ludvíka Svobody
Na Františku
Kozí
U milosrdných
Revoluční
Klimentská
Wilsonova
Ke Štvanici
listopadu
Bílkova
Haštalská
Soukenická
Petrská
JOSEFOV
Pařížská
Dlouhá
Rybná
Zlatnická
Truhlářská
STARÉ MĚSTO
Masná
Na poříčí
Staroměstská
Maiselova
nám. Republiky
Havlíčkova
Florenc
Na Florenci
Kaprova
NÁM. REPUBLIKY
Platnéřská
STAROMĚSTSKÉ NÁM.
Celetná
Hybernská
MALÉ NÁMĚSTÍ
Železná
Melantrichova
Senovážná
arlova
Na příkopě
SENOVÁŽNÉ NÁM.
Nekázanka
Husova
Jilská
Havelská
Panská
28. října
Jindřišská
BETLÉMSKÉ NÁMĚSTÍ
Můstek
Růžová
Na Perštýně
artolomějská
Martinská
JUNGMANNOVO NÁMĚSTÍ
Politických vězňů
Opletalova
Wilsonova
Národní
Václavské náměstí (Wenceslas Square)
Národní tř.
Washingtonova
Španělská
Italská
Ostrovní
Spálená
Vladislavova
Jungmannova
Vodičkova
Muzeum
RIEGROVY SADY
Lazarská
Školská
Štěpánská
Krakovská
Mánesova
NOVÉ MĚSTO
Vinohradská
Myslíkova
Ve Smečkách
Žitná
Římská
KARLOVO NÁM.
Sokolská
Legerova
Bělehradská
Londýnská
VINOHRADY
Karlovo nám.
Karlovo náměstí
Ječná
I.P. Pavlova
Anglická
nám. Míru
NÁM. MÍRU
Lípová
13
14
15
16
17
18
19
20
21
22
23
24

Central Budapest

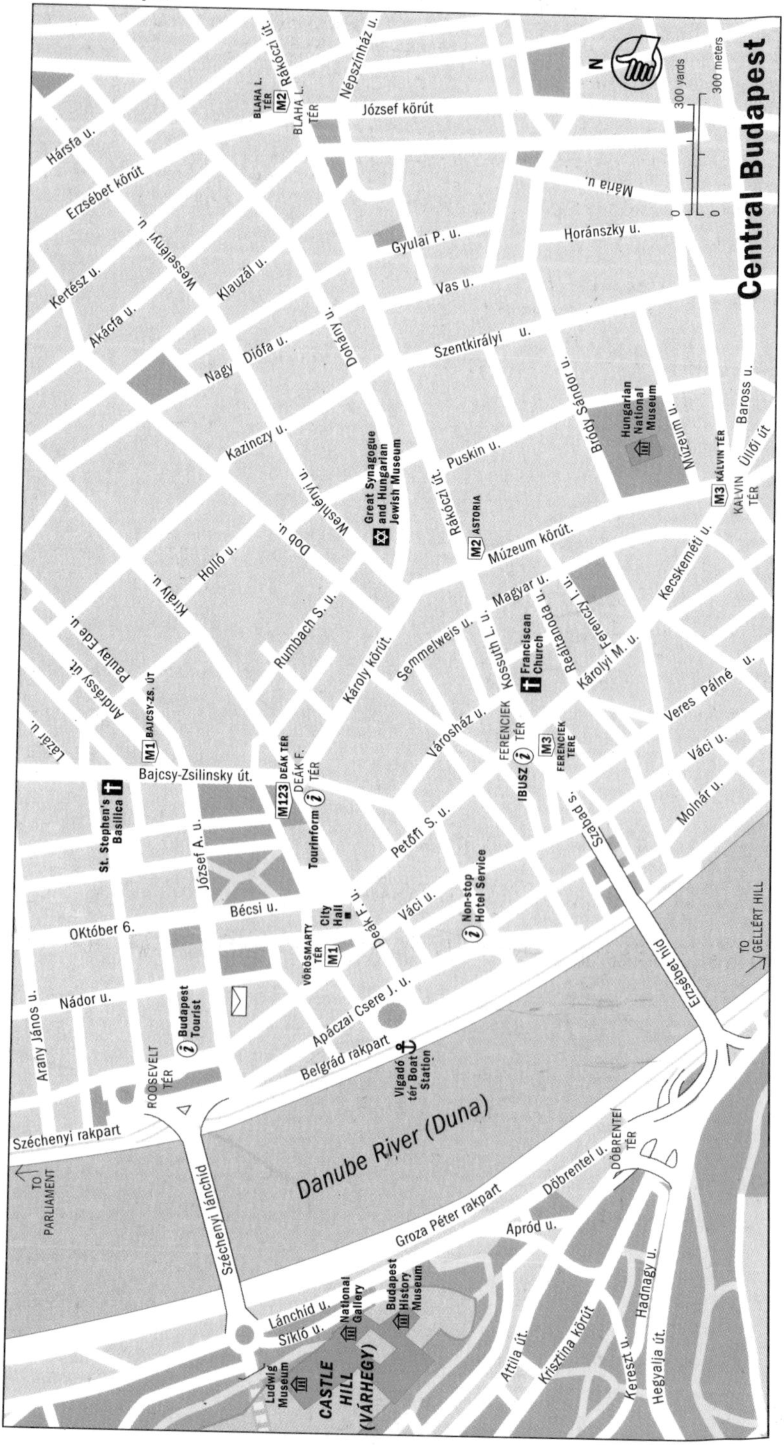

Central Budapest

N

0 300 yards
0 300 meters

Rákóczi út
BLAHA L. TÉR
M2
Népszínház u.
József körút
Hársfa u.
Erzsébet körút
Mária u.
Wesselényi u.
Klauzál u.
Gyulai P. u.
Horánszky u.
Kertész u.
Vas u.
Akácfa u.
Dohány u.
Szentkirályi u.
Nagy Diófa u.
Bródy Sándor u.
Hungarian National Museum
Kazinczy u.
Great Synagogue and Hungarian Jewish Museum
Puskin u.
Múzeum u.
Baross u.
Wesselényi u.
Rákóczi út
M2 ASTORIA
M3 KÁLVIN TÉR
KÁLVIN TÉR
Üllői út
Dob u.
Múzeum körút
Holló u.
Király u.
Kecskeméti u.
Magyar u.
Rumbach S. u.
Károly körút
Semmelweis u.
Kossuth L. u.
Franciscan Church
Reáltanoda u.
Ferenczy I. u.
Károlyi M. u.
Paulay Ede u.
Andrássy út
Lázár u.
M1 BAJCSY-ZS. ÚT
Városház u.
FERENCIEK TÉR
M3 FERENCIEK TERE
Veres Pálné u.
Váci u.
Bajcsy-Zsilinszky út
M123 DEÁK TÉR
DEÁK F. TÉR
St. Stephen's Basilica
IBUSZ
Molnár u.
József A. u.
Tourinform
Petőfi S. u.
Szabad s.
Non-stop Hotel Service
Bécsi u.
City Hall
Deák F. u.
Váci u.
OKtóber 6.
VÖRÖSMARTY TÉR
M1
Arany János u.
Nádor u.
Budapest Tourist
Apáczai Csere J. u.
Erzsébet híd
TO GELLÉRT HILL
Belgrád rakpart
Vigadó tér Boat Station
ROOSEVELT TÉR
Széchenyi rakpart
Danube River (Duna)
TO PARLIAMENT
DÖBRENTEI TÉR
Döbrentei u.
Groza Péter rakpart
Apród u.
Széchenyi lánchíd
Lánchíd u.
Sikló u.
National Gallery
Budapest History Museum
Hadnagy u.
Ludwig Museum
CASTLE HILL (VÁRHEGY)
Attila út
Krisztina körút
Kereszt u.
Hegyalja út